Law Relating to
Trusts and Trustees

Publishing History

First edition (1878)	Arthur Underhill
Second edition (1884)	Arthur Underhill
Third edition (1889)	Arthur Underhill
Fourth edition (1894)	Arthur Underhill
Fifth edition (1901)	Arthur Underhill
Sixth edition (1904)	Arthur Underhill
Seventh edition (1912)	Arthur Underhill
Eighth edition (1926)	Arthur Underhill
Ninth edition (1939)	Sir Arthur Underhill and Edward Bagshaw
Tenth edition (1950)	C Montgomery White QC and MM Wells
Eleventh edition (1959)	C Montgomery White QC and MM Wells
Twelfth edition (1970)	RT Oerton
Thirteenth edition (1979)	DJ Hayton
Fourteenth edition (1987)	DJ Hayton
Fifteenth edition (1995)	DJ Hayton
Sixteenth edition (2003)	DJ Hayton

Underhill and Hayton

Law Relating to
Trusts and Trustees

Sixteenth Edition

David J Hayton   MA, LLB, LLD
of the Inner Temple and Lincoln's Inn, Barrister;
Professor of Law, King's College, London University;
sometime Recorder and Acting Justice of The Bahamas' Supreme Court

Butterworths
LexisNexis™

Members of the LexisNexis Group worldwide

United Kingdom	LexisNexis Butterworths Tolley, a Division of Reed Elsevier (UK) Ltd, Halsbury House, 35 Chancery Lane, London, WC2A 1EL, and 4 Hill Street, Edinburgh EH2 3JZ
Argentina	LexisNexis Argentina, BUENOS AIRES
Australia	LexisNexis Butterworths, CHATSWOOD, New South Wales
Austria	LexisNexis Verlag ARD Orac GmbH & Co KG, VIENNA
Canada	LexisNexis Butterworths, MARKHAM, Ontario
Chile	LexisNexis Chile Ltda, SANTIAGO DE CHILE
Czech Republic	Nakladatelství Orac sro, PRAGUE
France	Editions du Juris-Classeur SA, PARIS
Hong Kong	LexisNexis Butterworths, HONG KONG
Hungary	HVG-Orac, BUDAPEST
India	LexisNexis Butterworths, NEW DELHI
Ireland	Butterworths (Ireland) Ltd, DUBLIN
Italy	Giuffrè Editore, MILAN
Malaysia	Malayan Law Journal Sdn Bhd, KUALA LUMPUR
New Zealand	LexisNexis Butterworths, WELLINGTON
Poland	Wydawnictwo Prawnicze LexisNexis, WARSAW
Singapore	LexisNexis Butterworths, SINGAPORE
South Africa	LexisNexis Butterworths, Durban
Switzerland	Stämpfli Verlag AG, BERNE
USA	LexisNexis, DAYTON, Ohio

© Reed Elsevier (UK) Ltd 2003

A CIP Catalogue record for this book is available from the British Library.

ISBN 0 406 938 849

ISBN 0-406-93884-9

9 780406 938848

Typeset by YHT Ltd, London
Printed and bound in Great Britain by Clays Ltd, St Ives Plc

Visit Butterworths LexisNexis *direct* at www.butterworths.com

Preface

Since the last edition in 1995 there have been very significant developments indeed in English legislation and case-law, and some interesting developments in foreign legislation and case-law. Such foreign developments may not only provide guidance for similar English trust situations but they may provoke conflict of laws issues (of increasing relevance for trusts with assets and beneficiaries in several jurisdictions) which raise reflections upon the potential for use of foreign trusts of English assets and for further development of English law. If English courts are prepared to recognise foreign trusts of English assets where the characteristics of such trusts extend beyond those permitted by English law, one needs to take a hard look at the scope for developing English trust law. On the other hand, there must be some limits to the recognition of features of alleged foreign trusts which require close scrutiny of the irreducible core content of the trust concept and rules of English public policy.

It seems that with globalisation will come greater harmonisation, although some key differences will exist between ring-fenced fund structures in Europe ('Euro-trusts'), English trusts ('Anglo-trusts'), and flexible trusts in offshore jurisdictions that market their trust law with financial services as a key alternative to tourism ('Caribbo-trusts')*. The export of the fundamental principles of English trust law has been a great success story (instanced by many page proofs of this edition being marked up while I was abroad in October, speaking at conferences in Miami, Nassau and Cayman).

As in previous editions, the principles of the law of private trusts are extracted and formulated after the fashion of Articles of a Code. This enables the busy practitioner to see at a glance the general principles governing a particular topic. To resolve a particular problem the practitioner can then turn to the appropriate parts of the subsequent commentary which, in its detailed discussion of case law and of construction of statutes, illustrates and explains the application of the principles. The Code-like approach, revealing the structure of relevant principles and their relationships, should also help to provide a good overall 'picture' of the subject. As a developing, mainly judge-made picture, the picture will always be unfinished, but an attempt is made to indicate how the outer parts of the picture are likely to be developed and how even some of the inner parts may be touched up. The aim is to meet the needs of the reflective practitioner.

In this edition I have not hesitated to re-write Articles wholly or substantially in view of major legislation, cases and academic publications which have led to this edition having 106 more pages than the last edition. This should be no surprise, taking account of the following legislation directly or indirectly affecting trusts and trustees: Trusts of Land and Appointment of Trustees Act 1996, Human Rights Act 1998, Trustee Delegation Act 1999, Contracts (Rights of Third Parties) Act 1999, Financial Services and Markets Act 2000, Trustee Act 2000, Land Registration Act 2002 and Proceeds of Crime Act 2002.

As well as an enlarged wholly re-written Chapter 23 dealing with the increasingly important conflict of law issues, the following Articles have been substantially revised

---

* Further see D J Hayton, S C Kortmann & H L Verhagen (eds) *Principles of European Trust Law* (Kluwer, 1999); D J Hayton (ed) *Modern International Developments in Trust Law* (Kluwer, 1999); D J Hayton (ed) *Extending the Boundaries of Trusts and Similar Ring-Fenced Funds* (Kluwer, 2002).

or wholly re-written: Arts 1 (nature of the trust concept), 28 (nature of resulting and constructive trusts), 29 (automatic resulting trusts), 44 and 45 (Settled Land Act settlements and trusts of land), 52 (duty of reasonable care), 53 (investment powers and duties), 55 (delegation powers and duties), 60 (core accounting duties), 61 (general duties of trustees in exercising powers), 69 (rights of absolutely entitled beneficiaries, cross-referring to Variation of Trusts Act 1958 difficulties), 83 (trustees' rights to reimbursement and indemnity), 87 (right to court's assistance), 89 (measure of trustee's liability), 92 (tracing against trustee or other fiduciary), 96 (limitation of actions) and 100 (personal liability of third parties involved in a breach of trust).

Three developing trends appear: towards greater autonomy being permitted in settlor's trust instruments; towards restricting strict liability on a 'but for' causation test to trustees who do what they are not entitled to do, with an approach akin to common law negligence for trustees who do badly what is within their powers; towards pension trust principles diverging from ordinary or private trust principles, taking account of sections 50 and 67 of the Pensions Act 1995 and of the beneficiaries also being settlors who have earned rights and expectations as deferred pay. It is thus justifiable for the *Hastings-Bass* principle to treat pension trustees' decisions as void if they might have been different if a relevant consideration had not been overlooked, but this ought not to be the case for ordinary trusts. In the case of pension trusts it is easy to slip into the language of judicial review concerned with legitimate expectations of beneficiaries and *Wednesbury* unreasonableness, but for ordinary trusts the acts of trustees should stand if not contrary to the expectations and purposes of the settlor and it is not shown that they would have acted differently but for overlooking a relevant factor, so long probably as any mistake relates to the act in question and not the consequences or advantages thereof.

The massive burden of producing a new edition within a time-frame acceptable to the publishers led me to seek very valuable and much-appreciated assistance with Articles 86, 87, 88, 92, 94, 100 and 101 and Chapter 23. I am most grateful to Leon Sartin BA, LLM, Barrister of 5 Stone Buildings, Lincoln's Inn, for updating Articles 86, 87 and 88 (court assistance), taking account of the new Civil Procedure Rules including the recent Rule 64, and to my wife, Linda Hayton LLB, Barrister of Arden Chambers, 2 John Street, London WC1N 2ES for updating Article 94 (Criminal breaches of trust). I am particularly grateful to Charles Mitchell BA, Dip Law, LLM, PhD, Reader, King's College London Law School, for updating Articles 92, 100 and 101 (on proprietary claims via the tracing process against trustees and third parties, and on personal claims against third parties involved in a breach of trust or other fiduciary obligation) with substantial revision of Article 100.

I am also particularly grateful to Professor Jonathan Harris of Birmingham University Law School for preparing the draft of a lengthy new Chapter 23 'Conflict of Laws and the Hague Trusts Convention', replacing the old chapter on that topic. His recent book, *The Hague Trust Convention*, impressed me — and I was Head of the UK Delegation to the XVth Session of The Hague Conference that was responsible for the Convention. His draft, with some fine tuning, is the new Chapter 23.

Needless to say, I am most grateful to the publishers for preparing the index and the tables of cases and statutes. Please note that instead of 'ibid' identical footnotes appear.

It is hoped that the law is accurately stated as at 1 November 2002.

Finally, in these increasingly litigious days, please note that the views herein are for the purpose of further consideration only and are not to be acted upon without independent professional advice: no responsibility can be accepted for any loss occasioned to any person, no matter howsoever caused or arising as a result of, or in consequence of, action taken or refrained from in reliance on the contents hereof.

David Hayton
of King's College
and 5 Stone Buildings,
Lincoln's Inn WC2A 3XT

All Saint's Day 2002

Contents

Preface   *v*
Table of Statutes   *xiii*
Table of Statutory Instruments   *xxix*
Table of Cases   *xxxi*

DIVISION ONE   PRELIMINARY DEFINITIONS

1 Definitions of trust, trustee, trust property, beneficiary, settlor and breach of trust   3
2 Definitions of legal and equitable estates and interests   48
3 Definitions of express, implied, resulting and constructive trusts   53
4 Definitions of simple and special trusts or bare and active trusts   57
5 Definitions of fixed and discretionary trusts   63
6 Definitions of executed and executory trusts   66

DIVISION TWO   EXPRESS OR DECLARED TRUSTS

Chapter 1   Introduction
7 Analysis of an express or declared trust   71

Chapter 2   Matters essential to the prima facie validity of an express trust
8 Analysis of an express or declared trust   74
9 The constitution of trusts   144
10 What property is capable of being made the subject of a trust   182
11 The legality of the expressed object of the trust   189
12 Necessity or otherwise of writing and signature   232

Chapter 3   Validity of declared trusts in relation to latent matters
13 Who may be a settlor or trustee   268
14 Who may be beneficiaries   272
15 When a trust is voidable for failure of consideration or purpose or for mistake, or fraud   273
16 Effect of the bankruptcy of the settlor on the validity of a settlement   287
17 Effect of settlements intended to prejudice creditors apart from bankruptcy   291
18 When a trust designed to defeat dependants may be set aside pro tanto under a court order   295

19 Miscellaneous instances where a trust may be set aside to thwart criminals 297

Chapter 4 The interpretation of executory trusts
20 Executory trusts not construed as strictly as executed trusts 299
21 Distinction between executory trusts arising under marriage articles and wills respectively 302
22 How far the wife is bound by covenants to settle property 305
23 Property which is prima facie excluded from a covenant to settle other or after-acquired property 306
24 What property is comprised in a general covenant to settle property to which the wife is presently entitled 310
25 What is comprised in a covenant to settle after-acquired property of the wife 310
26 Covenants to settle a definite interest in property 314
27 Covenants to settle property exceeding a certain value 315

DIVISION THREE   TRUSTS IMPLIED BY LAW

Chapter 5   Introduction
28 Analysis of trusts of property implied by law 321

Chapter 6   Resulting trusts
29 Automatic resulting trusts where equitable interest not wholly disposed of, so there is some failure of the trusts 329
30 Resulting trusts arising where trusts declared illegal 343
31 Resulting trusts where purchase made in another's name or property voluntarily transferred to another 349
32 To whom property results 369

Chapter 7   Constructive trusts
33 Constructive trusts of traceable products owned by persons in fiduciary positions 379
34 Constructive trusts of trust property or its traceable product owned by strangers to the trust 406
35 Constructive trusts of property to prevent fraudulent or unconscionable conduct 409
36 Constructive trusts imposed upon a vendor under a specifically enforceable contract 438

DIVISION FOUR   THE ADMINISTRATION OF A TRUST

Chapter 8   Disclaimer and acceptance of trusts
37 The number of trustees permissible 447
38 Disclaimer of a trust 449
39 Acceptance of a trust 451

Chapter 9   The estate of the trustee and its incidents
40 Estate taken by the trustee 454
41 The incidents of the trustee's estate 456

42 The effect of the Limitation Act 1980 on the trustee's estate   458
43 The effect of the trustee's bankruptcy   460

Chapter 10   Trusts of land
44 Pre-1997 'old' Settled Land Act Settlements   464
45 Post-1996 Trusts of Land   465

Chapter 11   The trustee's duties
46 Duty of trustee concerning acceptance of trust or additional trust property   485
47 Duty of trustee to obey the directions of the settlement unless deviation sanctioned by the court   493
48 Duty of trustee to act impartially in the sense of fairly and disinterestedly, between the beneficiaries   529
49 Duty of trustee to sell improper property   548
50 Duty of trustee, as between tenant for life and remainderman, in relation to property pending conversion   552
51 Duty of trustee in relation to the payment of outgoings out of corpus and income respectively   563
52 Duty of trustee to exercise reasonable care and skill   575
53 Powers and duties of trustee in relation to the investment of trust funds   597
54 Duty of trustee to see that he transfers trust property only to beneficiaries or to objects of a power of appointment or only to persons authorised under the trust instrument or the general law to receive such property (eg as custodian or portfolio manager)   623
55 Duty of trustees not to delegate their duties or powers unless authorised   631
56 Duty of trustees to act jointly where more than one   644
57 Duty of trustee not to set up jus tertii   648
58 Duty of trustee to act gratuitously unless otherwise authorised, as is usual nowadays   651
59 Duty of trustee not to traffic with or otherwise profit by trust property nor to cause loss from a conflict between his fiduciary duty and his self-interest   659
60 Duty of trustee to be ready with his accounts   671

Chapter 12   The powers of the trustees
61 General principles applicable to powers of trustees   688
62 Managerial powers of trustees with particular reference to sales   703
63 Power of trustees to give receipts   705
64 Powers with regard to reversionary interests   706
65 General administrative powers of trustees   707
66 Power to allow maintenance to infants   709
67 Power of advancement   717
68 Suspension of the trustee's powers by administration action   726

Chapter 13   Powers of the beneficiaries
69 Power of a sole beneficiary or of the beneficiaries collectively to extinguish the trust   729
70 Power of one of several beneficiaries partially interested in a special trust   737

Chapter 14 The death, retirement, or removal of trustees and the appointment of new trustees
71 Devolution of the office and estate on death of trustees 740
72 Retirement or removal of a trustee 743
73 Appointment of new trustees 751
74 Appointment of trustees for sale of land 775
75 Vesting of trust property in new trustees 776

Chapter 15 Appointment of a judicial trustee
76 Statutory power of the court to appoint a judicial trustee 785

Chapter 16 The Public Trustee
77 The nature and functions of the Public Trustee, and the guarantee of the State to be answerable for his breaches of trust 789
78 The appointment of the Public Trustee as an ordinary trustee 794
79 The appointment and removal of the Public Trustee or certain corporate bodies as mere 'custodian trustee' 796
80 The respective duties, rights, and liabilities of the custodian trustee and managing trustees 799
81 Special rules relating to the Public Trustee 801

Chapter 17 Administration of new trusts created under limited powers in the original settlement
82 By whom new trusts created under powers of appointment are to be carried out 803

Chapter 18 The rights of the trustee
83 Right to reimbursement and indemnity 810
84 Right to discharge on completion of trusteeship 827
85 Right to pay trust funds into court in certain circumstances 829

Chapter 19 The right of trustees and beneficiaries to seek the assistance of the Public Trustee or the court in auditing or in administrating the trust
86 Right of trustee or beneficiary to official audit of the trust through the Public Trustee 831
87 Right of trustee or beneficiary to take the direction of the court in relation to specific questions 832
88 Right under certain circumstances to have the trust administered under the direction of the court 847

DIVISION FIVE THE CONSEQUENCES OF A BREACH OF TRUST

Chapter 20 The liability of the trustees
89 The measure of the trustee's liability for breach of trust 851
90 Joint and several liability of trustees 877
91 Set-off of gain on one breach against loss on another not allowed 878
92 Property acquired by trustee or fiduciary can be traced and claimed by the beneficiaries or principal 880
93 Application for interim remedy to safeguard the trust property if endangered 903
94 Dishonest breach of trust may be a crime 907

Chapter 21   Protection accorded to trustees in case of breach of trust
95 General protection of trustees who have acted reasonably and
   honestly   913
96 Limitation of actions by beneficiaries against trustees   920
97 Concurrence of or waiver or release by the beneficiaries   931
98 Protection against the acts of co-trustee   938
99 Trustees generally entitled to contribution inter se, but may be entitled
   to be indemnified by co-trustee or beneficiary who instigated
   breach   940

Chapter 22   Liability of third parties and beneficiaries
100 Personal liability of third parties or beneficiaries who are involved in a
    breach of trust   950
101 Tracing and following trust property and its proceeds into the hands of
    third parties, and claiming assets in their hands   983

DIVISION SIX   THE HAGUE TRUSTS CONVENTION

Chapter 23   Conflicts of Laws and The Hague Trusts Convention
102 The Hague Convention on the Law Applicable to Trusts and on their
    Recognition, implemented by the Recognition of Trusts Act 1987   1007

Index

Table of Statutes

References in this table to *Statutes* are to Halsbury's Statutes of England (Fourth Edition) showing the volume and page at which the annotated text of the Act will be found. Page references printed in **bold** type indicate where the Act is set out in part or in full.

PAGE

Accessories and Abettors Act 1861 (12 *Statutes* 86)
s 8 291
Administration of Estates Act 1925 (17 *Statutes* 419) 211, 212, 652
s 1 . . . . 740, 759
2 759
(2) 18
3 740
(1) 18
5 158
7 . . . . 19, 742, 743
9 . . . . 781, 791
21A 158
28 382
33 . . . . 53, 469, 1020
(1) 1042
(4) 377
(5) 554, 561
36 778
(1) 455
(4) 455, 470, 664
41 . . . . .19, 543, 544, 545, 611, 829
(2) 611
42 . . . . 714, 760, 829
45 . . . . 370, 377
46 409
(1)(i)–(v) 378
(vi) 377, 378
47 434
(1)(iii) 546, 547, 719
49(1)(a) 264, 546, 547
51(3) 65, 716
55(1)(xix) 455
Administration of Estates Act 1971 (17 *Statutes* 494)
s 10(2) 708
Administration of Justice Act 1920 (22 *Statutes* 476) 1061
Administration of Justice Act 1965 (11 *Statutes* 876)
s 2 658
6(1) 868

PAGE

Administration of Justice Act 1982 (50 *Statutes* 614)
s 19 263
20 280
21 . . . . .83, 133, 136, 280, 330
22 . . . . 67, 80, 136
Administration of Justice Act 1985 (41 *Statutes* 127)
s 9 620
48 . . . . 830, 915
(1), (2) 627, 834
50 . . . . . .19, 750, 768, 785, 788
(4) 788
Adoption Act 1976 (6 *Statutes* 211)
s 42(5) 735
45 . . . . 623, 914
(3) 626
Agricultural Holdings Act 1986 (1 *Statutes* 779) 572
s 86(1) 567
87 567
89(1) 573
Sch 7 573
Anti–terrorism, Crime and Security Act 2001 . . . . 298, 344, 489
Apportionment Act 1870 (23 *Statutes* 48) 214, 555, 558, 716
Arbitration Act 1996 (2 *Statutes* 566) . . 215
s 82(2) 216
Army Act 1955 (3 *Statutes* 49)
s 141 187
190, 203 187
Bankruptcy Act 1914
s 42 . . . . 57, 289
(1) 312
Bills of Sale Act 148
Bodies Corporate (Joint Tenancy) Act 1899 (37 *Statutes* 111) 774
British Nationality Act 1948 (31 *Statutes* 19)
s 34 273
Sch 4 273

PAGE

British Nationality Act 1981 (31 Statutes
          157)
   s 50 273
Capital Gains Tax Act 1979
   s 52(1), (2) 696
      54 808
      72(4) 91
Charitable Trusts (Validation) Act 1954
          (5 *Statutes* 888) 105, 110
   s 1(1). 107, 108
      (2), (3) 109
      2(1)–(3) 109
      3. 110
Charities Act 1960 (5 *Statutes* 898)
   s 14 . . . . 341, 342
      (5) 342
      18 83
      28 645
      34 645
      38 774
      48 774
   Sch 7
      Pt II 774
Charities Act 1993 (5 *Statutes* 942)
   s 14(7) 342
      33 115
      35 448
   Pt VII(ss 50–62). 798
Children Act 1975
   Sch 3
      para 43 196
Children Act 1989 (6 *Statutes* 370) . . . 474
   s 2. 364
Civil Jurisdiction and Judgments Act 1982
          (22 *Statutes* 545)
   s 7(2). 1059
      18, 19 1061
      32(1) 1061
      33 1061
      41(2) 1057
      45(3) 1059
   Sch 3c (Lugano Convention) . . . 1057
   Sch 4 1057
   Sch 6 1061
   Sch 7 1061
Civil Jurisdiction and Judgments Act 1991
   Sch 1 1057
Civil Liability (Contribution) Act 1978 (13
          Statutes 604) 947, 1041
   s 1. 943
      (1), (6) 942
      2(1), (2) 943
      6(1). 942
      7(1)–(3) 942
      10(2) 942
Coal Industry Act 1994 (29 *Statutes* 813)
   Sch 5
      para 2 799
Coal Industry Nationalisation Act 1946
          (29 *Statutes* 95)
   s 37 799

PAGE

Commonhold and Leasehold Reform Act
          2002 457
   s 109 458
   Sch 3
      para 8 458
   Sch 5
      para 8 472
   Sch 6
      para 3(7) 458
   Sch 8
      para 33 458
Companies Act 1867
   s 25 536
Companies Act 1900 536
Companies Act 1948
   s 78 155
      320 14
Companies Act 1985(8 *Statutes* 88) . 41, 256,
                                        411
   s 35 271
      35A, 35B 271
      130 537
      182 19
      183 . . . . 19, 151, 155
      192 40
      (1), (2) 595
      310 393
      313 53
      314 53
      320 392
      322A 392
      360 . . . . 645, 647, 1056
      395 . . . . 15, 43, 148
      399 15
      425 537
      615 14
      654 370
      690A (2) 1059
      725 1059
      727 . . . . 857, 917
Companies Act 1989 (8 *Statutes* 872)
   s 95 15
      108 271
      207 619
Compensation (Defence) Act 1939 (9
          Statutes 74) 443
Compulsory Purchase Act 1965 (9 *Statutes*
          212) 567
Consumer Credit Act 1974 (11 *Statutes*
          17) 968
Contracts (Applicable Law) Act 1990 (11
          Statutes 245)
   s 2(2). 1050
Contracts (Rights of Third Parties) Act
          1999 (11 *Statutes* 308). 9, 10, 113, 169,
                                    170, 172, 173,
                                    179, 181, 182, 185,
                                    245, 327
   s 1. 168
Conveyancing Act 1881(37 *Statutes* 104)
   s 34 776
      38 741

PAGE

Conveyancing Act 1911
s 8 742
County Courts Act 1959
s 52 751
County Courts Act 1984 (11 *Statutes* 701)
s 23 . . . . 521, 763, 829
24(3) 521
Sch 2
para 1 776
Court of Probate Act 1857 158
Court of Probate Act 1858 158
Courts and Legal Services Act 1990(11 *Statutes* 1293)
s 71(2) 834
Sch 10
para 63 834
Criminal Justice Act 1987 (12 *Statutes* 986)
s 12 911
Criminal Justice Act 1988 (12 *Statutes* 1014)
Pt IV(ss 35, 36) 298
s 39c (2) 966
93A 966
Criminal Justice Act 1993
Pt III(ss 27–35) 298, 344
Pt V(ss 52–64) 907
Criminal Law Act 1967(12 *Statutes* 316) 763
s 1 753
10 753
(2) 751
Sch 3
Pt III 751, 753
Criminal Law Act 1977 (12 *Statutes* 668) 291
s 1–5 911
Criminal Procedure (Insanity) Act 1964 (12 *Statutes* 302)
s 1 435
Data Protection Act 1998 (7 *Statutes* 389) 682
Deeds of Arrangement Act 1914 (4 *Statutes* 680)
s 2, 3 141
Domicile and Matrimonial Proceedings Act 1973 (27 *Statutes* 715)
s 1 , 3 231
Drug Trafficking Act 1994 (12 *Statutes* 1492)
s 50 966
Educational (Miscellaneous Provisions) Act 1953
s 14 495
Emergency Laws (Miscellaneous Provisions) Act 1953 571
s 9 . . . . 494, 528
Enduring Powers of Attorney Act 1985 (1 *Statutes* 97) 25, 639, 644
Environmental Protection Act 1990 (35 *Statutes* 712)
Pt IIA(ss 78A–78YC) 814

PAGE

Exchange Control Act 1947
s 18(2) 223
29 190
(3) 223
Factors Act 1889(1 *Statutes* 45) . . . 16, 407, 968
Family Law Act 1996 (27 *Statutes* 1136) 274
s 15 1044
Sch 2 1044
Family Law Reform Act 1969 (6 *Statutes* 121) 206, 225, 305, 377, 754
s 1 . . . . 268, 498
(1), (2) 205
(4) 205
(7) 205, 597, 711
12 268
14 . . . . 212, 626
15 . . . . 210, 212, 626
(3) 211
(7) 217, 218
16 626
17 626
Sch 3
para 7 205
Family Law Reform Act 1987 (6 *Statutes* 353) 377
s 1, 19 218
20 626
Finance Act 1973
s 16, 17 64
Finance Act 1978
s 54 214
Finance Act 1985 (41 *Statutes* 300)
s 82 239
Finance Act 1986 (42 *Statutes* 932)
s 100 710
Finance Act 1989 (42 *Statutes* 1065)
s 67–93 47
Sch 5 47
Finance Act 1995 (43 *Statutes* 1134)
s 68 711
Sch 17 711
Financial Services Act 1986 (30 *Statutes* 162) 272, 526
s 192(1) (a)–(c) 600
Financial Services and Markets Act 2000 . . . 271, 448, 489, 497, 966
s 19 272
22 272
Pt VIII(ss 118–131 907
s 236 45
242 46
243(4), (5) 46
244–248 46
253 . . . . 46, 596
Sch 2 272
Fines and Recoveries Act 1833(37 *Statutes* 37)
s 36 34
Fire Prevention (Metropolis) Act 1774
s 83 443

PAGE

Foreign Judgments (Reciprocal Enforce-
    ment) Act 1933 (22 *Statutes*
    482) 1061
Forfeiture Act 1982 (12 *Statutes* 754)
    s 1(2). 435
    2(1), (3), (4) 435
    (7). 435
    5 435
Friendly Societies Act 1829 340
Friendly Societies Act 1896
    s 79(4) 340
Gas Act 1986 (19 *Statutes* 468)
    Pt II(ss 49–61) 798
Highways Act 1980 (20 *Statutes* 64)
    s 212, 213 . . . . 567, 568
Hire Purchase Act 1964 (11 *Statutes*
    4) 407
Historic Buildings and Ancient Monu-
    ments Act 1953 (32 Statutes 527)
    s 8(5). 201
    8A(5) 201
    8B(5) 201
Housing Act 1996 457
Human Rights Act 1998 (7 *Statutes*
    497) 190, 224, 685
    s 3(1). 506
    6(1). 219
    (3)(a) 219
    Sch 1
    Pt I
        art 8 . . . . **219**
            (1), (2) 582
        9 . . . . **219**
        14. . . . . **219**
    Protocol 1
        art 1 . . . . **219**
Income and Corporation Taxes Act 1988
    (44 *Statutes* 1)
    s 3 534
    18(3) 533
    348 533
    660A(2) 1040
    660B 711
    672 499
    673 98
    675 499
    686 . . . . 64, 716, 818
    687 . . . . 64, 716
Income Tax Act 1952
    s 415(1)(d) 332
    (2). 332
Infants Relief Act 1874
    s 2 269
Inheritance (Provision for Family and
    Dependants) Act 1975 (17 *Statutes*
    505) 72, 78, 81
    s 10 295
    (2)(a) 297
    (b) 297
    (7) 297
    11 296
    (2)(c) 297

PAGE

Inheritance (Provision for Family and
    Dependants) Act 1975—*contd*
    s 12(1) 297
    (2) 296
    13 1048
    (1), (2) 297
    25(1) 232, 296
Inheritance Tax Act 1984 (formerly
    Capital Transfer Tax Act 1984) (42
    Statutes 671)
    s 49–50 64
    51, 52 . . . . 64, 710
    53–64 64
    65 . . . . 64, 609
    66–70 64
    71 . . . . 64, 303, 499, 610
    72 . . . . 64, 271
    73, 74 271
    75 . . . . 64, 271
    76–82 64
    83 . . . . 64, 68
    84 64
    91 68
    142 . . . . 80, 279
    204(2) 813
    272 308
Insolvency Act 1986 (4 *Statutes* 721) . . . 349
    s 110 607
    238 287
    239 . . . . 287, 290
    253 141
    283(3) 461
    306 214
    335A 480, 481
    (3) 468, 482
    339 . . . . . 57, 72, 289, 294, 354
    (1). 288
    (2). 288
    (3). 287
    340 . . . . 72, 291, 354
    (2)–(5) 288
    341 . . . . 289, 291, 294
    (1)(b), (c). 288
    (2). 288, 290
    (3). 288
    (4). 288
    342 . . . . 289, 291, 294
    (1)(a), (b). 290
    (d), (g). 290
    (2). 289
    352 291
    357 291
    423 293
    (1). 291
    (2). 292
    (3). 291, 292, 294
    424(1)(a)–(c) 292
    425(1)(a), (b). 293
    (1)(d) 293
    (2). 292, 293
    435 288
    (5). 290

PAGE

Insolvency Act 2000 141
Insolvency (No 2) Act 1994 (4 *Statutes*
1130) 291
International Convention Implementa-
tion Act 1990
s 1(4). 1050
Interpretation Act 1978 (41 *Statutes*
576) 774
Sch 1 . . . . 608, 653
Intestates Estates Act 1952 (17 *Statutes*
477)
Sch 1 . . . . 377, 378
Ireland Act 1949 (7 *Statutes* 775)
s 3(1) (a) (i). 273
Judicature Act 1873 . . . . . . 36, 49, 179
s 25(2) 255
(6) 152
Judicature Act 1875 179
Judicial Trustees Act 1896 (48 *Statutes*
227) 788, 857
s 1(1), (2) 785
(3) 786, 787
(4) 787
(5) 658, 786
(6) 786, 787
(7) 788
2 785
3 914
4 788
(1) 786
Land Charges Act 1925. . . . . 35, 51, 988
Land Charges Act 1972 (37 *Statutes*
569) 35, 51, 256, 411, 988
s 7 141
Land Registration Act 1925 (37 *Statutes*
423) 35, 51, 256, 411
s 3(xvi) 50
5, 9 . . . . 150, 407, 408
20 . . . . 150, 408, 706
(1) 407, 1003
23 . . . . 150, 407, 706
(1) 407, 1003
41 456
44(2) 605
47 778
59(1) 141
(6) 141, 407
69 150
70 408
(1)(g) 50, 991
86(2) 1003
Land Registration Act 1997 (37 *Statutes*
724)
s 1 . . . . 455, 470
Land Registration Act 2002 . . 51, 150, 605
s 4 470
(1)(a) 455
11, 12 . . . . 407, 408
24 456
26 . . . . 469, 470, 483, 706
27 778
27(5)(a) 456

PAGE

Land Registration Act 2002—*contd*
s 28 . . . . 407, 408
29 . . . . .407, 408, 706, 1003
30 . . . . .407, 408, 706, 1003
33(a) 1003
96, 97 . . . . 459, 460
114 57
116 . . . . . 254, 287, 354, 426, 991
Sch 1 408
Sch 3 . . . . 50, 51, 408
Sch 6 925
para 1–7. 460
11, 12. 460
Land Transfer Act 1897(37 Statutes
60). 742
Landlord and Tenant Act 1954 (23 *Statutes* 139). 581
s 41(1), (2) 383
Landlord and Tenant Act 1987 (23 *Statutes* 394)
s 42 114
Law of Property Act 1922
s 110(9). 745
(10) 746
Law of Property Act 1925 (37 *Statutes*
120) . . . 50, 51, 205, 248, 257, 477
s 1 454
(1). 49, 608, 609
(3). 49
(4). 598, 608, 609
(6). 157, 269
(7). 26
2 . . . . 468, 483, 633, **987**
3 988
4 . . . . 49, 454
(2). 183
9(1). 776, **779**
15 481
19 . . . . 53, 268
20 . . . . 269, 754, 764
24 . . . . 470, 986
25 986
(1) 469
26(3) 472, 475
27 . 468, 483, 633, 641, 646, 741, 884
(2) 19, 448, 705, 706, 745,
746, 765, 795
28 . . . . 479, 527, 552
(1) 25, 571, 571
(2) **571**
29 . . . . 479, 736
30 . . . . . . .33, 356, 479, 480, 481
34 . . . . 53, 385, 469
(1) 351
35 . . . . 53, 385
36 . . . . 53, 385, 469
40 . . . . 233, 236, 247
(1) 237
44(2) 605
(5) 991
47 443
53 . . . . 129, 409

PAGE

Law of Property Act 1925—*contd*
s 53(1) 255
    (a) 236, 237
    (b) 53, 54, 76, 233, **236**,
       237, 238, 239, 244, 247, 254,
       255, 256, 262, 422, 433,
       1016, 1019
    (c) 79, 145, 151, 233, 235,
       236, 237, 238, 239, 240, 241,
       242, 243, 244, 245, 246, 247,
       273, **520**, 619, 777
   (2) . .53, 234, 235, 255, 257, 354, 520
55(d) 234, 236, 423
56 169
60 . . . . 66, 300
  (3) 255, 350, **368**
72(4) 663
101 604
107 986
111, 113 986
130 . . . . 66, 300
131 . . . . 66, 300, 301
136 152
  (1) 183
137 . . . . 236, 672
  (3) 492
  (4)–(6) 1002
  (8) 492, 685, 1002
  (9) 1002
138 1002
155 518
162(1) **201**
163 . . . . 194, 196
  (2) 199
164 . . . . . .204, 206, 207, 715, 1042
  (1) 209, 230
165 . . . . 204, 206
166 208
167–170 449
172 293
175 . . . . **712, 713**
198 . . . . 986, 989, 991
199 . . . . 408, **986**
  (1) **990**
205(1) 49, 795
    (ii) 245, 368, 470
    (ix) 640
    (x) 608
    (xx) 368
    (xxi) 470
    (xxvi) 447, 689
    (xxviii) 448, 705
Law of Property Act 1969 (37 *Statutes* 547)
s 25(9), (10) 991
Law of Property (Amendment) Act
    1859(17 Statutes 408)
s 31 . . . . 634, 939
Law of Property (Amendment) Act 1924
    (37 *Statutes* 117)
Sch 5
  Pt II
    para 5(4) **745**

PAGE

Law of Property (Amendment) Act 1926
    (37 *Statutes* 536) 987
s 3 448
7 627
Schedule 627
Law of Property (Miscellaneous Provi-
    sions) Act 1989 (37 *Statutes* 658)
s 1 827
2 . . . . **234**, 422, 520
  (1) 233, 234, 429, 430, 432
  (2),(3) 233
  (5) 234, 430, 520
Law of Property (Miscellaneous Provi-
    sions) Act 1994 (17 *Statutes* 568)
s 14 . . . . 781, 791
16 19
88 25
101 25
104 25
Law Reform (Married Women and Tort-
    feasors) Act 1935 (27 *Statutes*
    738) 215, 303, 317, 940
s 6 942
Law Reform (Miscellaneous Provisions)
    Act 1970 (27 *Statutes* 703)
s 2(1) 365
Law Reform (Succession) Act 1995 (17
    Statutes 575) 546
Leasehold Reform Act 1967 . . . . 383, 457
Leasehold Reform, Housing and Urban
    Development Act 1992 (23 *Statutes*
    495) 457
s 93A 458
Legitimacy Act 1976 (6 *Statutes* 202)
s 7 . . . . 623, 914
  (3) 626
Limitation Act 1939 . . . . . 53, 924, 929
s 7(5) 459
19 . . . . 922, 923
  (2) 6
20 922
26 923
Limitation Act 1980 (24 *Statutes* 698) . .974,
    934, 981
s 10 . . . . 942, 943
15 925
  (2) 460
  (5) 926
18 459
21 . . . . 922, 929, 933
  (1) 19, 920, 922, 923,
    924, 925, 926, 928, 930
    (a) 922
    (b) 924
  (2) 920, 925
  (3) 6, 19, 921, 922, 923,
    924, 925, 927, 928
  (4) 921
22 . . . . 19, 922, 925, 929
  (a) 921, 922
  (b) 921
23 . . . . 921, 923, 928

PAGE

Limitation Act 1980—*contd*
s 28 921
29 926
30, 31 926
32(1)(a) 923
(b) 923, 931
(2) 931
(3), (4) 930
36(2) 930
38 920
(1) 53, 922
Sch 1
para 9 . . . . 458, 459
Limitation Amendment Act 1980 (17 *Statutes* 533)
s 10 158
Limitation (Enemies and War Prisoners) Act 1945 (24 *Statutes* 695) 921
s 1 929
2(1), (3) 929
Literary and Scientific Institutions Act 1854 (24 *Statutes* 152)
s 30 127
Local Government Act 1985 (25 *Statutes* 674)
Pt II(ss 2 –17) 798
London Building Act 1930 (26 *Statutes* 51) 568
London Government Act 1963 (26 *Statutes* 412)
s 40 568
London Regional Transport Act 1984 (26 *Statutes* 860) 798
Lunacy Act 1890
s 128, 129 755
148(3) 212
Married Women (Restraint upon Anticipation) Act 1949 (27 *Statutes* 741) 215
Married Women's Property Act 1882(27 *Statutes* 732) 309, 312, 317
s 11 170
Married Women's Property Act 1870 . . 364
Matrimonial and Family Proceedings Act 1984 (37 *Statutes* 1083)
s 17, 24 1044
Matrimonial Causes Act 1973 (27 *Statutes* 928) 72, 187, 1017, 1045
Pt II(ss 21–40) 274
s 22, 23 295
24 . . . . 210, 212, 295, 317, 427
(1) (c) 1044
27 295
31 295
37 . . . . . 246, 295, 347, 415, 582
(4) 295
(5), (6) 296
Matrimonial Homes Act 1973 482
Matrimonial Homes Act 1983 480
Matrimonial Proceedings and Property Act 1970 (27 *Statutes* 866)
s 37 . . . . 352, 421

PAGE

Mental Health Act 1959 (28 *Statutes* 813)
s 103(4) 522, 717
149(1) 522
Sch 7
Pt I 522
Mental Health Act 1983 (28 *Statutes* 829) . . . 212, 545, 763, 766, 1022
s 1(2) 269, 751
Pt VII(ss 93–113) . 521, 522, 751, 761, 769
s 93 769
94 755
(2) 269
95 522
96 . . . . 269, 270, 751
(1), (2) 755
(3) 522, 717
97 269
99 474
148 522
(1) 751
Sch 4 751
para 14 522
Mercantile Law Amendment Act 1856(11 *Statutes* 222)
s 5 940
Misrepresentation Act 1967 (29 *Statutes* 978)
s 2(1) 685
Mortmain and Charitable Uses Act 1888 774
National Health Service Act 1946 (30 *Statutes* 714)
s 7(2) 495
National Heritage Act 1983 (32 *Statutes* 628)
s 33 201
Sch 4
para 10 201
Naval and Marine Pay and Pensions Act 1865(3 *Statutes* 980)
s 4, 5 187
Nullity of Marriage Act 1971
s 11, 12 270
Parish Councils and Burial Authorities (Miscellaneous Provisions) Act 1970 (5 *Statutes* 846) 120
s 1 203
Partnership Act 1890(32 *Statutes* 895)
s 10 965
Patents Act 1977 (33 *Statutes* 137)
s 39 399
Pension Schemes Act 1993 (33 *Statutes* 581)
s 119, 121 668
151(2) 867
163 201
Pensions Act 1995 (33 *Statutes* 799) . 46, 577
s 7 751
20 651
22 462
23 . . . . 462, 751
24 462

PAGE

Pensions Act 1995—*contd*
s 25 462
32 . . . . 644, 645
33 596
34 . . . . 596, 597, 622
(1)–(3) 600
(5) 600
35 . . . . 597, 622
(1) 601
(2) 601
(3) 601
(4) 601
(5) 601
(7) 600
36 . . . . 601, 622
(1), (3), (4). 601
39 . . . . 660, 668
40 601
50 . . . . 692, 696
56 601
67 692
68 493
69 493
71 499
95 752
124(1). 600
Perpetuities and Accumulations Act 1964
(33 *Statutes* 1078) . 86, 115, 120, 124,
125, 129, 191, 194,
206, 225, 301, 1042, 1051
s 1 195
(1), (2) 193
2 . . . . 205, 731
(1) (a), (b) 195
(2)–(4) 195
3 . . . . 188, 376
(1) 126, 196
(2) 196, 198, 200
(3) . . 112, 113, 126, 196, 198, 200, 208
(4) 121, 196
(5) 121, 192, 196
4 192
(1), (2) 197
(3) 197, 228
(4) 113, 126, 197, 228
(5) 196, 228
(6) 196
(7) 196
5 . . . . 192, 197
6 . . . . **227**, 333
7 . . . . 26, 200
8 . . . . 196, 200
(2) 201
12 . . . . 118, 203, 369, 376
(1) 121, 229
(2) 229
13(1) 204
(2) 204
14 . . . . 205, 731
15(2) 204
(4) 203
(5) 200, 520, 724

PAGE

Powers of Attorney Act 1971 (1 *Statutes*
55) 25, 633
s 5 . . . . **628**
9(2). 622
Powers of Criminal Courts Act 1973
s 35 912
(1) 907
36–38 912
Proceeds of Crime Act 1995 (12 *Statutes*
1574) 298, 344
Proceeds of Crime Act 2002 . . . . 298, 344
s 11 298
322 488
(2) (a) 488
(3) 487
323 . . . . 487, 488
(2) (a) 488
324 . . . . 487, 488
(2) (a) 488
(3) 488
325 . . . . 488, 489
(2) 490
(6)–(8) 489
(10), (11) 489
328(1), (3), (4) 489
329 . . . . 488, 489
330(1)–(6) 488
330(8) 966
331 488
335 490
(2) 488
(3) 487
(11) 487
Sch 6
Pt I. 489
Protection of Trading Act 1980 (47 *Sta-*
tutes 391)
s 5 1062
Public Health (London) Act 1936 . . . 568
Public Trustee Act 1906 (48 *Statutes*
230) 791
s 2(1). 789
(2) 790, 795, 802
(3) 790
(4) 790, 794, 796
(5) 790
3(4) 802
4 . . . . 448, 658
(1) 796
(2) (a)–(c) 799
(d)–(h). 800
(i) 796
(3) 796, 797
5 795
(1) 789, 794
(2)–(4) 794
7 651
(1) 790
9 . . . . 658, 790
(5) 793
10 . . . . 801, 802, 832

PAGE

Public Trustee Act 1906—*contd*
s 11(1) 789
  (2), (5) 801
  13 832
  (1) 831
  (5) 832
Public Trustee (Fees) Act 1957 (48 *Statutes* 558). 658, 790
s 1 792
  (2), (3) 793
Race Relations Act 1965
s 5 224
Race Relations Act 1968 224
s 1–6 223
  9 223
Real Property Act 1845
s 6 183
Recognition of Trusts Act 1987 (48 *Statutes* 599). 908, 1007, 1014, 1017, 1042, 1050, 1055
s 1(1). 1012
  (2). . . . **1020**, 1021, 1022, 1033, 1053
  (3). 1046
  (5). 1013
  2 1012
Sch 1 (Hague Convention on the Law Applicable to Trusts and on their Recognition) . . 114, 188, 772, 1007, 1011, 1023
Ch I–IV **1007**
art 1 1010
  2 . . . . .6, 1010, 1053, 1055
  (1) 1015
  (2) (a), (b). 1015
  (c). 1016
  3 . 1010, 1016, 1018, 1020, 1021, 1053
  4 . . . .1010, 1022, 1047, 1048, 1051
  5 1010
  6 . . . . .1010, 1031, 1035
  (2) 1032
  7 . . . . . 1010, 1032, 1035, 1036
  (2)(a) 1035
  8 . . . . 521, 1010
  (1) 1040
  (2)(a) 1024, 1041, 1046
  (b), (c) 1041
  (d), (e) 1042
  (f) 1042, 1051
  (g). 1026, 1042, 1043
  (h). 1043, 1044, 1045
  (i),(j). 1045
  9 . . . . 1010, 1041
  10 . . . . 1010, 1039
  11 . . 6, 189, 1010, 1041, 1053, 1055
  (2) 1053
  (3) 1053
  (d) 1054
  12 1010
  (2) 1029
  13 . . . . 7, 1031, 1055
  14 . . . . 1010, 1053
  15 . . . 189, 1010, 1050, 1051, 1054

PAGE

Recognition of Trusts Act 1987—*contd*
art 15(1)(a) 1046
  (b) 1045, 1047
  (c) 1030, 1047
  (d) 1042, 1048, 1053
  (e), (f). 1049
  (2) 1049
  16 . . . . . 189, 1010, 1045, 1046, 1049, 1051, 1053
  (2), (3). 1050
  17. . . . . 1010, 1037
  18 . . 114, 189, 1010, 1045, 1046, 1048, 1049, 1050, 1051
  20 1053
  (1) 1020
  22 . . . . 1010, 1013
  23 1032
Regulatory Reform Act 2001. 675
Road Traffic Act 1972
s 148(4) 170
Sale of Goods Act 1979 (39 *Statutes* 68) 16, 407, 968
Settled Land Act 1890 573
Settled Land Act 1925 (48 *Statutes* 247) . .7, 49, 51, 410, 457, 479, 572, 598, 607, 619, 688, 704, 705, 718, 742, 771, 1002
s 1(1). 463
  (v) 35
  (7). 463
  4 . . . . 463, 737
  5 463
  6 . . . . 463, 737
  7 463
  8 463
  9 463
  (2). 454
  10 . . . . 463, 611
  17 483
  18 448
  (1) (c). 463
  19 463
  20 463
  (1) 639
  21 463
  23, 24 463
  36(4) 351
  38, 39 463
  41–48 463
  64 . . . . 187, 494, 500, 501, 522, 525, 527, 528, 529, 571
  68 660
  73 610
  (1)(ii) 567, 568
  (iii). 573
  (xi). 611
  (2) 611
  75(2) 463, 464, 610, 611
  (4) 610, 637
  (4в), (4c) 637
  83 . . . . 573, 574
  94 . . . . 448, 741
  102 571

PAGE

Settled Land Act 1925—*contd*
s 104, 106 . . . . 463, 465
108 . . . . 463, 465
117(1) (iv) 716
(xxiv) 447, 689
(xxvi) 463
(xxx) 448
Sch 3 573
Settled Land and Trustee Acts (Court's
General Powers) Act 1943 (48 *Statutes* 556). 529
s 1 . . . . 494, 571
(2)–(5) **528**
Sex Discrimination Act 1975 (7 *Statutes*
36) 224
Social Security Act 1973 (40 *Statutes* 71)
s 69 201
Social Security Act 1986 (40 *Statutes* 193)
s 86(1) 201
Sch 10
Pt I. 201
Social Security Pensions Act 1975 (33
Statutes 541)
s 65(1) 201
Sch 4 201
Solicitors Act 1974 (41 *Statutes* 20)
s 32 870
37 . . . . 7, 170, 387
66(a) 818
71(3) 814
75 50
Status of Aliens Act 1914 (31 *Statutes* 15)
s 17 273
Statute Law (Repeals) Act 1969 (41 *Sta-
tutes* 559)
Schedule
Pt III 449
Statute of Frauds 1677 (11 *Statutes*
220) 257
Statute of Limitations 1623 . . . . 255, 459
Stock Transfer Act 1963 (30 *Statutes* 76)
s 1 151
Stock Transfer Act 1982 (30 *Statutes* 138)
s 1(2) 245
Superannuation Act 1972 (33 *Statutes*
470)
s 1 187
5(1) 187
Supplementary Benefits Act 1976 (40
Statutes 101)
s 17 364
Supreme Court Act 1981 (11 *Statutes*
1043)
s 37 903
39 750
51(3), (4) 840
Supreme Court of Judicature (Consolidation) Act 1925
s 192 210
Taxation of Chargeable Gains Act 1992
(43 *Statutes* 348)
s 60(2) 60

PAGE

Taxation of Chargeable Gains Act 1992—
contd
s 62(6) 80, 279
69 808
(2) 696
(3) 915
70 60
71 . . . . 64, 726, 806, 808, 1040
72 64
80–84 517
86 499
87 517
227, 228 271
229 . . . . 47, 271
230, 231 271
Taxes Management Act 1970 (42 *Statutes*
126)
s 106(2). 533
Terrorism Act 2000
s 14 489
15–17 490
18 . . . . 489, 490
19, 20 490
21 490
21A 489, 490, 966
(6) 966
Theft Act 1968 (12 *Statutes* 488)
s 1 907
2 907
(1) 911
3 907
(1), (2) 907
4 907
(1) 907
(2) (a) 907
5 907
(1) 907, 909, 910
(2) 908, 911
(3) 908
6 . . . . 907, 911
15–17 911
19, 20 911
25 910
Thellusson Act (39 & 40 Geo 3, c 98) . .204,
208
Town and Country Planning Act 1990 (46
Statutes 500)
Pt V (ss 119–136) 457
s 135 457
Trading with the Enemy Act 1939 (50
Statutes 342) 212, 273, 929
Trustee Act 1888 . . . . 923, 933
s 6 947
Trustee Act 1893
s 10(1) 756
(2) (c). 745
(5) 745
11(1), (3) 746
12 776
22 741
24 634
(1) 939

PAGE

Trustee Act 1893—*contd*

s 25 753
43 947

Trustee Act 1925 (48 *Statutes* 453) 548,
644, 799

s 4 . . . . **579**
8 . . . . 605, 606, 917
(1) 605
(2) 605
(3) 571
9 605
10 605
(1) 605
(2) 605
(3) 606, 607, 612
(5) 606
11(1) 607
(2) 568, 607
12 581
(1), (2) 704
13 . . . . 581, 705
14 . . . . 705, 741, 884
(1) 705
(2) 705, 745, 795
(3) 705
15 . . . 576, 578, 579, 590, 708, 820
(f) 787
16 723
(1), (2) 704
18 741
(1) 740, **741**
(2) 19, 740, 742, 743
19 . . . . . 565, 569, 576, 588, 890
(1), (2) 577
(5) 564, 569
20 . . . . **588**, 750
(1) 589
22 576
(1), (2) 707
(3) 543, 544, 706
(4) 565, 574, 575, 832
23 634
(1) 635, 646
(2) 634, 635
(3) 646
24 . . . . 581, 705
25 . . . . . 622, 633, 642, 644, 759
(2) 643
(3) 643
(4) 643
(5) 643, 669
(7) 634, 642
(8) 643
27 . . . . 623, 626, **627**, 628,
830, 914
28 990
29 628
30 . . . . 634, 938, 940
(1) 635, **939**
31 . . . . . . 26, 711, 712, 715, 716,
725, 733, 807, 1038, 1042
(1)(i) 709

PAGE

Trustee Act 1925—*contd*

s 31(1)(ii) 710, 713, 714
(2) 586, 709
(i) 710, 715
(b) 504
(ii) 65, 710, 715
(3) 710, 713, 714
(4) 65, 711, 716
(5) 711
32 . . . . . . 26, 509, 704, 718,
1038, 1042
(1)(c) 503
(2) 718
33 . . . . 213, 214
(1) 210
(i), (ii) 501, 511
34 . . . . **447**
(2)(a) 448
(3) 752
35 470
(1), (3), (4) 775
36 . . . . . 26, 461, 473, 743, 745,
751, **756**, 760, 774
(1) 643, 750, 764, 771, 772
(a) 756, 761
(b) 756, 761
(6) 760, 762, 765
(b) 761
(6A) 757, 761
(6B)–(6D) 757
(8) 753, 761
(9) 750, 761
37 . . . . . . 743, 745, **758**, 761, 807
(1)(b) 762
(c) 706, 745, 746, 773
(d) 776
(2) 745
38 . . . . **758**
39 . . . . .19, 448, 486, **746**, 748, 760
40 . . . . 756, 760, 761, **776**
(1) 777
(b) 778
(2) 605, 746, 748, 750, 777
(3) 750
(4) 776
41 . . 743, 751, 753, **763**, 766, 767, 773
(4) 768
42 . . . . 658, **763**
43 . . . . **763**
44 . . . . 778, **779**, 782
(vi) 780
45 . . . . 779, **780**
49 . . . . 779, **781**
50 . . . . 779, **781**
51 . . . . 155, 779, **781**, 782
(1)(ii) 780
52 . . . . 779, **782**
53 . . . . 779, **783**
54 . . . . . 751, 755, 769, 779, **783**
55 . . . . 779, **784**
56 . . . . 779, **785**

PAGE

Trustee Act 1925—*contd*
s 57 . . . . .8, 33, 37, 212, 472, 499, 500,
509, 510, 522, 524, 525, 526,
527, 528, 571, 600, 611,
622, 667, 668, 691
(1) 494
(2), (3) 525
58 . . . . 751, **768**, 779, **784**
59 . . . . **769**
60 . . . . 751, **769**
61 . . . 8, 405, 494, 580, 584, 585, 625,
626, 629, 631, 665, 728, 775,
853, 857, 865, 913, 914, 916,
917, 920, 941
62 . . . . 941, 947
63 829
(1) 830
63A 776
68 . . . . 779, 920
(1) 18, 447, 689
(9) 742
(14) 781
(15) 447, 689
(17) 18, 53
(18) 448, 764, 795
69(1) 18, 742
(2) 704, 711, 712, 715,
718, **745**, 746, 812
Sch 3
para 2, 3 605
Trustee Act 2000 (48 *Statutes* 619) . . . 58,
527, 548, 584, 590, 655, 813, 938
s 1 . . . . 466, 467, 549, 575, 576,
602, 613, 615, 700, 706,
708, 919, 940
(1)(a) 577
(b) 577
2 . . . . 549, 575, 602, 613
3 . . . . 25, 549, 597, 601, 602,
604, 689, 703
(1) 509, 600, 604, 605
(2) 604
(3) 597, 605
(4) 605
4 . . . . . . 25, 472, 550, 576, 601,
602, 604, 605, 613, 614, 689
(1) 592, 604
(2) 579, 598, 603, 614, 700
(3) 598, 603, 615, 700
5 . . . . . . 25, 472, 497, 576, 601,
602, 604, 605, 613, 615,
621, 689, 700
(1) 598, 601, 604
(2) 598, 603
(3) 550, 598, 602, 603
(4) 598, 602
6 . . . . 25, 601, 604
(1) 496, 591, 599, 604
(b) 592
(2) 597
7 . . . . .25, 496, 597, 601, 604
(2) 599, 604

PAGE

Trustee Act 2000—*contd*
s 7(3) 600
8 . . . . 471, 552, 597, 601, 612, 703
(1) 509, 549, 583, 598, 607
(b) 609
(c) 610
(2) 583
(a) 598
(3) . . 472, 544, 569, 581, 588, 598, 608
9 496
Pt IV(ss 11–27) 593
s 11 . . . . . . 599, 622, 635, 636, 638,
641, 643, 646, 648, 678, 703, 832
(2) 632, 635
(a) 543, 625, 635
(3) 632, 636
(4) 636
(5) 636
12 . . . . 599, 703
(1) 632, 636
(2) 636
(3) 632, 636
(4) 636
13 . . . . 599, 704
(1), (2) 636
(4), (5) 637
14 . . . . 599, 703
(1) 637
(2) 632, 636, 637
(3) 636, 637
15 . . . . . 599, 622, 700, 703, 704
(1) 632, 638
(2) 632, 637
(a), (b) 638
(3) 637, 638
(4) 638
(5) 638
16 . . . 577, 599, 619, 620, 632, 703
17 . . . . . 599, 619, 620, 632, 703
18 . . . 586, 599, 619, 620, 632, 703
(2) 599
19 . . . . 599, 619, 632, 703
(1), (2) 620
(3) 58
(4) 620
(5) 569, 620
(6), (7) 620
20 . . . . 599, 619, 632, 703
(1), (2) 620
21 . . . . 599, 703
(3) 591, 593, 621, 633, 642
22 . . . . . 576, 590, 599, 621, 633,
637, 641, 700, 703
(1) 621, 642
(2) 642
(4) 621
23 . . . . 599, 621, 703
(1) . . . 543, 590, 633, 641, 642
24 . . . . 621, 622, 638
25(2) 599, 620
(5) 622
26 591

Trustee Act 2000—*contd*

s 26(a)	620, 621, 622, 637, 638
(b)	621, 622, 637, 638
28	653
(1), (3)	652
(4)	652
(5)	653
(6)	652
29	659
(1)	651, 653, 658
(2)	651, 653, 659
(b)	654
(3), (4)	653
31	644
(1)	564, 565, 812
(2)	812
32	632
(2)	620, 637
(3)	620
34	564, 569, 588
35	550
(2) (c)	609
36	577, 597, 599, 619
37	577, 597, 599, 619, 635
(4)	635
38	577, 597, 599, 619, 635
39	564
Sch 1	549, 575, 576, 615, 700
para 1	577, 603, 613
2	577, 613
3	577, 635, 641
(1)	621, 642
(a)–(d)	633
(e)	633, 642
(2)	621, 642
4, 5	569, 577
6	577
7	577, 591, 592, 594,
	601, 604, 621, 633, 641
10(1) (a), (b)	464
(2)	464
Sch 2	
para 7–9	572, 598, 610
10	50, 572, 598, 610
(1), (2)	610
11–17	572, 598, 610
19	705
20	578, 708
22(a)	707
45(1)	466, 471
(3)	472
47	467, 569, 641
Sch 3	
para 7(1)	608

Trustee Delegation Act 1999 (48 *Statutes* 610)

s 1	633, 644
(1)	644
(8)	644
2	633
(2), (3)	644
3	633

Trustee Delegation Act 1999—*contd*

s 5	633, 642, 669
6	644
7	643, 644
8	644, 757, 761

Trustee Investments Act 1961 (48 *Statutes* 567) 25, 192, 548, 597, 600

s 4(4), (6)	603
6	614
Sch 1	
Pt II	
para 14	608

Trusts of Land and Appointment of Trustees Act 1996 (37 *Statutes* 689) . . . 53, 248, 481, 987, 1020

s 1	464, 544
(1)	448, 1025
(a)	447, 469, 480
(b)	627
(2) (a)	464, 465, 469
(b)	464
(3)	465
2	67, 300, 447, 689
(1)	463
(2)	464
(3)	464, 610
(4)	464
(5)	464
(6)	716
3	188, 377, 464, 466
(1)	372, 471
(2), (3)	471
4	552
(1)	466, 469, 470
(2)	470
(3)	466, 470
6	457, 703, 704
(1) 465, 466, 471, 571, 608
(2)	58, 466, 473
(3) . . . 466, 471, 598, 607, 608
(5)	483
(6) 465, 466, 472, 483
(8)	465, 483
(9)	466, 472
7	466
(1)	472
(2)	473
(3)	472
(5)	472, 473
8(1)	466, 472, 473
(2)	465, 466
(3)	464
9 . . . 466, 633, 640, 669, 703, 737
(1)	465, 639
(3)	640, 641
(4)	640
(5)	640
(6)	639
(7)	465, 640
9A	467, 569
(3), (5), (6)	633, 641
10	472

PAGE

Trusts of Land and Appointment of Trustees Act 1996—*contd*

s 10(1) 465, 467, 474
(2) 474
(3) 467
(a), (b) 474
11 . . . . 187, 464, 582
(1) . . . 465, 467, 472, 475, 483, 637
(b) 640
(2) 467, 472, 475
(c) 473, 475
(3) 467, 475
(4) 475
12 . . . . 351, 640
(1) 467, 476, 478, 737
(a), (b) 477
(2) 467, 476, 477, 737
13 . . . . 351, 356
(1) 467, 476, 737
(2) 467, 478, 737
(3) 467, 476, 477, 737
(4) 468, 478
(5) 478
(6) 477, 478
(7) 737
(8) 478
14 . . . . . . 33, 356, 425, 471, 473,
476, **479**, 613, 691
(1) 468, 472
(2) 468
(3) 468
15 . . . . 33, 425, 613
(1) 468
(4) 468
16(1) 468, 483
(2), (3) 469, 483
(5) 483
(6) 464
17(2) 480
(3) 448, 480
(5) 480
18(1) 479, 480
19 . . . . . . 58, 300, 473, 498, 503,
504, 729, 733, 736,
743, 747, 750, 759
(1) 748
(2) 748, 749
(b) 750
(3) (b) 819
(c) 749
(4) 749
20(1), (2) 750
21 . . . . 743, 750
(1) 749
(5)–(7) 748
22 503
(1) 473, 639, 748
(2) 639
(3) 480, 639, 748
23(1) 447, 474, 689
(2) 470, 598, 639, 640
25(2) 640

PAGE

Trusts of Land and Appointment of Trustees Act 1996—*contd*

Sch 1 1025
para 4 474
5 . . . . .66, 188, 464
Sch 2
para 3–5. 469
Sch 3
para 3(3) 705
(8) 528
(9) 447, 752
(10) 775
(11) 757
(12) 758
(13) 746
(14) 777
4 . . . . 468, 483
(8) (b) 706
23 482
Sch 4 . . . . 477, 640
Unfair Contracts Terms Act 1977 (11 *Statutes* 229) 596
s 10 933
Universities and College Estates Act 1925 (15 *Statutes* 107) 465, 469, 598
Variation of Trusts Act 1958 (48 *Statutes* 561) 28, 133, 214, 246, 505,
510, 515, 516, 523, 525, 526,
544, 631, 655, 729, 734, 735,
773, 1017, 1044
s 1 . . . . 493, 733
(1) 501, 521
(a) 521
(2) 511
(3) 503
(5) 501
(6) 522
War Damage Act 1943 563
Welfare Reforms and Pensions Act 1999 187
Wills Act 1837 (50 *Statutes* 575) . . 3, 60, 129,
150, 247, 248, 257,
258, 359, 409, 487, 652
s 9 233
15 . . . . 264, 265
33 . . . . 263, 264
Wills Act 1963 (50 *Statutes* 609)
s 6(1) 1028
Wills (Soldiers and Sailors) Act 1918 (50 *Statutes* 604) 269

Australia

Trusts (Hague Convention) Act 1991 1012

Bahamas

Trustee Act 1998
s 3(2) (c) 60
Trusts (Choice of Governing Law) Act 1989

	PAGE
s 8(b)	1045

Cayman

Special Trusts Alternative Regime Law 676, 1051

Holland

Dutch Civil Code
  art 84(3) of Book 3 1054
Wet Conflichtenrecht Trusts 1995
  art 4 1054

Jersey

Trusts (Amendment No 2) (Jersey) Law
  1991 1012
Trusts (Jersey) Law 1983 . . . . 772, 1012

	PAGE

United States of America

Uniform Prudent Investor Act 615
Uniform Trust Code
  s 409 . . . . 114, 123
  603, 604, 608 60
  1010(b) 814

European Legislation

Regulations
Regulation (EC) No 44/2001 (Brussels
    Regulation)
  art 1, 2 1057
  5(6) 1058
  6 1058
  22(1) 1057
  23(4) 1058
  27, 28 1058
  60(1) 1057

Table of Statutory Instruments

Page references printed in **bold** type indicate where the Statutory Instrument is set out in part or in full.

PAGE

British Gas Corporation Dissolution Order 1990, SI 1990/147 798
Civil Jurisdiction and Judgements (Amendment) Order 2001. . . 1057
Civil Jurisdiction and Judgements Order 2001
  Sch 1
    para 9 1057
        12 1059
Civil Procedure Rules 1998, SI 1998/3132 682
  Pt 2
    r 2 (3) 835
    PD 2
      para 5.1(d), (e). 839
  Pt 5
    r 5.4 (2). 838
  Pt 6
    r 6.20(10) 292, 1060
      (11)–(15) **1060**
    6.21(1)(b) 1060
  Pt 7 . . . . 768, 834, 835, 836
  Pt 8 . . . . 747, 768, 836, 846
    r 8.1 (2). 836
      (3). 837
      (6). 836
    8.2 (b). 839
      (d), (e). 834
    8.2A. 834, 836
    PD 8
      section A
        table 1 834
        para A.1(1) 627, 836
          (2), (3). 836
          A.2(1) 627, 836
  Pt 12
    PD 12
      section A 627
  Pt 16
    r 16.2(5) 955
    16.5(2)(a) 913
  Pt 19
    r 19.7. . . . . 522, 836, 903
    19.7A(1) 836
    19.7A(2) 836

PAGE

Civil Procedure Rules 1998—*contd*
    19.8A(2) 836
  Pt 21
    r 21.2, 21.10 522
  Pt 25 903
    r 25.1(1) 904
    25.4. 904
  Pt 31
    r 31.16 679
    PD 31. 679
  Pt 39
    r 39.2(3)(f) 838
    PD 39
      para 1.5. 838
  Pt 44 . . . . 846, 847
    r 44.3(2) 841
    44.4(1) 840, 846
      (2) 815, 840
      (3) 815, 840
    44.5(1)(b) 840
  Pt 48
    r 48.3. 834
    48.4. 815
      (2) 834
      (3) 840
  Pt 50 726
    r 50.1. . . . . 710, 832
  Pt 64
    r 64 . . .508, 522, 726, 747, 819, 832,
      833, 834, 835, 836, 837, 838, 839,
          840, 843, 845, 846
  Sch 1 . . . . 726, 832
Rules of the Supreme Court
  Ord 5
    r 2(b). 837
    3 747
    4(2)(a), (b). 837
  Ord 15
    r 14 836
  Ord 50
    r 11–14 707
  Ord 65
    r 1 847
  Ord 85 . . . . . . 522, 819, 853
    r 1 832
    2 (formerly Ord 55 r 3) 649, 846, 906

PAGE

Civil Procedure Rules 1998—*contd*
  Rules of the Supreme Court—*contd*
    r 2 (2) 833, 845
      (3) 833
    r 2(3)(d) 667
      (e) 95
      (5) 180
    3 726
      (1), (2). 836
    5 (formerly Ord 55 r 10) . 846, 847
      (1) 833
    8 836
    9 834
    RSC PD 85. 522
    para 2 839
      4.1 836
      5.1 838
      6.1 838
      7.1–7.4 837
      7.6 . . . . 837, 838
      7.7 838
      7.9 845
      7.10 838
      7.11 839
      9 840
  Ord 93
    r 2 . . . . 801, 832, 834
Companies (Tables A to F) Regulations
    1985, SI 1985/805
  Schedule
    Table A
      art 5 647
      29–31 19
      106 647
Court Funds Rules 1987, SI 1987/821 . . 868
Financial Services and Markets Act 2000
    (Carrying on of Regulated Activi-
    ities by Way of Business) Order
    2001, SI 2001/1177
  art 4 600
Financial Services and Markets Act 2000
    (Regulated Activities) Order 2001,
    SI 2001/544
  art 66 272
Gas Act 1986 (Nominated Company)
    Order 1986, SI 1986/1317. . . . 798
Judicial Trustees Rules 1897, SI 1897
  r 5 (1) 785, 786
Judicial Trustees Rules 1972, SI 1972/
    1096 . . . . 785, 786
Judicial Trustees Rules 1983, SI 1983/370
  r 3 . . . . 785, 786
    6 786
    8 787
    9 786
    11 788
    12–13 786
  r 14 . . . . 786, 787
    15, 16 787

PAGE

Land Registration Rules 1925, SR & O
    1925/1093
  r 83 (3) 150
Land Registration Rules 1978, SI 1978/1601
  r 8 150
Land Registration Rules 1990, SI 1990/314
  r 9 150
Money Laundering Regulations 1993, SI
    1993/1933 966
National Assistance (Assessment of
    Resources) Regulations 1992, SI
    1992/2977 615
Personal and Occupational Pension
    Schemes (Perpetuities) Regula-
    tions 1990, SI 1990/1143 201
Public Trustee (Custodian Trustee) Rules
    1975, SI 1975/1189 . . 448, 796, 797
Public Trustee (Custodian Trustee) Rules
    1976, SI 1976/836 796
Public Trustee (Custodian Trustee)
    (Amendment) Rules 1985, SI
    1985/132 796
Public Trustee (Custodian Trustee) Rules
    1987, SI 1987/1891 . . 448, 796, 799
Public Trustee (Custodian Trustee) Rules
    1994, SI 1994/2519 . . . . 448, 799
Public Trustee (Fees) Order 1999, SI
    1999/855 . . . . . . 790, 792, 832
Public Trustee Rules 1912, SI 1912/348
  r 6 . . . . 790, 794
    (d) 796
    7 796
    8 . . . . 790, 795
    (2) 794
    (3) 795
    12 831
    25–28 801
    30 . . . . 448, 796, **797**
    31, 32 831
    33 832
    34 831
Public Trustee Rules 1916, SI 1916/489
  r 3 795
Occupational Pension Schemes (Invest-
    ment) Regulations 1996, SI1996/
    3127 601
Recognition of Trusts Act 1987 (Com-
    mencement) Order 1987, SI 1987/
    1177 . . . . 1010, 1013
Rules of the Supreme Court (Amendment
    No 2) 1983, SI 1983/1181
  Ord 44
    r 10 713
Uncertified Securities Regulations 1995,
    SI 1995/3272
  reg 32 (5) 151, 245, 619
    33 (1) (c) 619
  Sch 1
    para 13 619

Table of Cases

A

A v C [1981] QB 956n, [1980] 2 All ER 347, [1981] 2 WLR 629, [1980] 2 Lloyd's Rep 200, [1982] RPC 509; affd [1982] 1 Lloyd's Rep 166 903

AEG Unit Trust (Managers) Ltd's Deed, Re, Midland Bank Executor and Trustee Co Ltd v AEG Unit Trust (Managers) Ltd [1957] Ch 415, [1957] 2 All ER 506, [1957] 3 WLR 95, 101 Sol Jo 517 . . . . 207, 208, 732

AG Securities v Vaughan [1990] 1 AC 417, [1988] 2 All ER 173, [1988] 2 WLR 689, 56 P & CR 168, 20 HLR 212, 132 Sol Jo 301, [1988] 1 EGLR 36, [1988] 7 LS Gaz R 39, [1988] NLJR 23, [1988] 06 EG 112, CA; revsd [1990] 1 AC 417, [1988] 3 All ER 1058, [1988] 3 WLR 1205, 57 P & CR 17, 21 HLR 79, [1988] 2 EGLR 78, [1989] 1 LS Gaz R 39, [1988] 47 EG 193, HL 59

AMP (UK) plc v Barker [2001] Pens LR 77, [2001] WTLR 1237, 3 ITELR 414 . . . 277, 279, 696, 697

Aas v Benham [1891] 2 Ch 244, 65 LT 25, CA 23, 398, 404

Abacus (CI) Ltd v Al Sabah (2001) 3 ITELR 467 . . . . 32, 63

Abacus Trust Co (Isle of Man) Ltd v National Society for the Prevention of Cruelty to Children [2001] WTLR 953 . . . . 696, 699

Abbatt v Treasury Solicitor. See Conveyances dated June 13, 1933, August 17, 1933 and September 2, 1950, Re, Abbatt v Treasury Solicitor

Abbey Glen Property Corpn v Stumborg (1976) 65 DLR (3d) 235, [1976] 2 WWR 1; on appeal (1978) 85 DLR (3d) 35, [1978] 4 WWR 28 390

Abbey National Building Society v Cann (1989) 57 P & CR 381, [1989] 2 FLR 265, [1989] Fam Law 314, CA; affd [1991] 1 AC 56, [1990] 1 All ER 1085, [1990] 2 WLR 832, 60 P & CR 278, [1990] 2 FLR 122, [1990] Fam Law 397, 22 HLR 360, [1990] 17 LS Gaz R 32, [1990] NLJR 477, HL. .351, 584, 608, 891

Abbey National plc v Moss [1994] 2 FCR 587, [1994] 1 FLR 307, [1994] Fam Law 255, 26 HLR 249, CA 477

Abbey National plc v Solicitors' Indemnity Fund Ltd [1997] PNLR 306. 962

Abbott, Re, Peacock v Frigout [1893] 1 Ch 54, 62 LJ Ch 46, 3 R 72, 41 WR 154, 67 LT 794. . . . . 198, 225, 229

Abbott Fund Trusts, Re, Smith v Abbott [1900] 2 Ch 326, 69 LJ Ch 539, 48 WR 451 113, 336

Abdulla v Shah [1959] AC 124, [1959] 2 WLR 12, 103 Sol Jo 15, PC. 442

Aberconway's Settlement Trusts, Re, McLaren v Aberconway [1953] Ch 647, [1953] 2 All ER 350, 97 Sol Jo 454, CA 114, 118

Aberdeen Town Council v Aberdeen University (1877) 2 App Cas 544, HL . . . 385, 659, 669

Abergavenny's (Marquess) Estate Act Trusts, Re, Marquess of Abergavenny v Ram [1981] 2 All ER 643, [1981] 1 WLR 843, 125 Sol Jo 291 719

Abigail v Lapin [1934] AC 491, 51 WN 149, 103 LJCP 105, [1934] All ER Rep 720, 51 CLR 58, 151 LT 429, 24 SRNSW 395, 8 ALJ 198, HL. 1000

Aboriginal Development Commission v Treka Aboriginal Arts and Crafts Ltd [1984] 3 NSWLR 502 143

Abrahams, Re, Abrahams v Abrahams [1908] 2 Ch 69, 77 LJ Ch 578, 99 LT 240 981

Abrahams, Re, Abrahams v Bendon [1911] 1 Ch 108, 80 LJ Ch 83, 55 Sol Jo 46, 103 LT 532 714

Abrahams v Abrahams' Trustee in Bankruptcy [1999] 31 LS Gaz R 38, [2000] WTLR 593, [1999] BPIR 637 . . . . 353, 363, 365

Abrahams' Will Trusts, Re, Caplan v Abrahams [1969] 1 Ch 463, [1967] 2 All ER 1175, [1967] 3 WLR 1198, 111 Sol Jo 794 . . . . .100, 103, 694, 699, 724
Acton v Woodgate (1833) 2 My & K 492, 3 LJ Ch 83, 39 RR 251, [1824-34] All ER Rep 115. . . . . 141, 142
Adam & Co International Trustees Ltd v Theodore Goddard [2000] 13 LS Gaz R 44, 144 Sol Jo LB 150, [2000] WTLR 349 . . . . .744, 746, 752, 775
Adams, Re, Adams v Adams [1893] 1 Ch 329, 62 LJ Ch 266, 3 R 222, 41 WR 329, 37 Sol Jo 131, 68 LT 376 712
Adams, Re, Verrier v Haskins [1906] WN 220, 51 Sol Jo 113 714
Adams v Adams [1892] 1 Ch 369, 61 LJ Ch 237, 40 WR 261, 36 Sol Jo 215, 66 LT 98, 8 TLR 236, CA 217
Adams v Bank of New South Wales [1984] 1 NSWLR 285, NSWCA 959, 970
Adams v Cape Industries plc [1990] Ch 433, [1991] 1 All ER 929, [1990] 2 WLR 657, [1990] BCLC 479, [1990] BCC 786, [1990] 11 LS Gaz R 36, CA 1061
Adams v Clifton (1826) 1 Russ 297, 25 RR 53 631
Adams v Clutterbuck (1883) 10 QBD 403, 52 LJQB 607, 31 WR 723, 48 LT 614 1027
Adams v Taunton (1820) 5 Madd 435 450
Adams and Kensington Vestry, Re (1884) 27 Ch D 394, 54 LJ Ch 87, 32 WR 883, 51 LT 382, CA 74, 133, 135, 441
Adams' Trust, Re (1879) 12 Ch D 634, 48 LJ Ch 613, 28 WR 163, 41 LT 667 . 744, 753, 766
Adams' Trustees' and Frost's Contract, Re [1907] 1 Ch 695, 76 LJ Ch 408, 51 Sol Jo 427, 96 LT 833 805
Adlard, Re, Taylor v Adlard [1954] Ch 29, [1953] 3 WLR 914, 97 Sol Jo 814, sub nom Re Adlard's Settlement Trust, Re Campbell's Settlement Trust, Re Fulton's Settlement Trust, Taylor v Adlard [1953] 2 All ER 1437 . . . . 164, 165
Adlington v Cann (1744) 3 Atk 141 233
Aequitas Ltd v Sparad No 100 Ltd [2001] NSWSC 14 959
Affréteurs Réunis SA v Leopold Walford (London) Ltd [1919] AC 801, 88 LJKB 861, 14 Asp MLC 451, 24 Com Cas 268, 121 LT 393, 35 TLR 542, HL 170
Agar v George (1876) 2 Ch D 706, 24 WR 696, 34 LT 487. 310
Agip (Africa) Ltd v Jackson [1990] Ch 265, [1992] 4 All ER 385, [1989] 3 WLR 1367, [1990] BCC 899, 134 Sol Jo 198, [1990] 2 LS Gaz R 34; affd [1991] Ch 547, [1992] 4 All ER 451, [1991] 3 WLR 116, 135 Sol Jo 117, CA 253, 895, 901, 959, 960, 964, 965, 968, 969, 970, 972, 973, 974
Agricultural Credit Corpn of Saskatchewan v Pettyjohn [1991] 3 WWR 689, 79 DLR (4th) 22, 90 Sask R 206, CA 902
Agricultural Mortgage Corpn plc v Woodward (1994) 70 P & CR 53, [1996] 2 FCR 796, [1996] 1 FLR 226, [1996] Fam Law 149, [1995] 1 BCLC 1, [1994] BCC 688, [1995] 1 EGLR 1, [1995] 04 EG 143, CA. 289, 295
Ahmed v Kendrick (1987) 56 P & CR 120, [1988] 2 FLR 22, [1988] Fam Law 201, CA. . 480
Aikin (Surveyor of Taxes) v Macdonald's Trustees (1894) 3 TC 306, 32 SLR 85 818
Ainsbury v Millington [1987] 1 All ER 929, [1987] 1 WLR 379n, 131 Sol Jo 361, [1987] LS Gaz R 1241, HL. 839
Ainsworth, Re, Finch v Smith [1915] 2 Ch 96, 84 LJ Ch 701, 113 LT 368, 31 TLR 392 . . 948
Ainsworth, Re, Yates v Wormald [1921] 2 Ch 179, 91 LJ Ch 15, 49 Sol Jo 403, 125 LT 755. 805
Air Canada v M & C Travel Ltd [1993] 3 SCR 787, 108 DLR (4th) 592, 15 OR (3d) 804n 16, 42, 961
Air Jamaica Ltd v Charlton [1999] 1 WLR 1399, 143 Sol Jo LB 158, PC . . 4, 201, 321, 332, 333, 338, 693, 732
Airey, Re, Airey v Stapleton [1897] 1 Ch 164, 66 LJ Ch 152, 45 WR 286, 41 Sol Jo 128, 76 LT 151. 632
Aitken v Christy Hunt plc [1991] PLR 1 499
Akerman, Re, Akerman v Akerman [1891] 3 Ch 212, 61 LJ Ch 34, 40 WR 12, [1891-4] All ER Rep 196, 65 LT 194 . . . . 980, 981
Akeroid v Smithson (1780) 2 Dick 566, 3 P Wms 22n, sub nom Ackroyd v Smithson 1 Bro CC 503, [1775-1802] All ER Rep 227, 1 Wh & T 68 . . . . .330, 332, 369, 371
Akeroyd's Settlement, Re, Roberts v Akeroyd [1893] 3 Ch 363, 63 LJ Ch 32, 7 R 405, 69 LT 474, CA 334
Akron Tyre Co Pty Ltd v Kittson (1951) 82 CLR 477 826
Al Wahab, The. See Amin Rasheed Shipping Corpn v Kuwait Insurance Co, The Al Wahab
Alati v Kruger (1955) 94 CLR 216, ALR 1047, [1956] QSR 306, 29 ALJ 512 286
Albacruz (Cargo Owners) v Albazero (Owners), The Albazero [1977] AC 774, [1976] 3 All

ER 129, [1976] 3 WLR 419, [1976] 2 Lloyd's Rep 467, 120 Sol Jo 570, 126 NLJ 953,
HL 10, 170
Albert Road (Nos 56 and 58), Norwood, Re [1916] 1 Ch 289, 85 LJ Ch 187, 114 LT 357 . 774,
779
Alcock v Sloper (1833) 2 My & K 699, 39 RR 334 551
Aldhous, Re, Noble v Treasury Solicitor [1955] 2 All ER 80, [1955] 1 WLR 459, 99 Sol Jo 276 627
Alers-Hankey v Teixeira (9 April 2002, unreported), BC CA 957, 958
Alexander's Settlement, Re, Jennings v Alexander [1910] 2 Ch 225, 79 LJ Ch 656, 45 Sol Jo
602, 102 LT 909 279
Alford, Re (1886) 32 Ch D 383 500
Ali v Khan [2002] EWCA Civ 974 368
Allan v Rea Bros Trustees Ltd [2002] WTLR 625 408
Allan's Will Trusts, Re, Curtis v Nalder [1958] 1 All ER 401, [1958] 1 WLR 220, 102 Sol Jo
140 . . . . 226, 334
Allcard v Skinner (1887) 36 Ch D 145, 56 LJ Ch 1052, 36 WR 251, [1886-90] All ER Rep 90,
57 LT 61, 3 TLR 751, CA 274, 276, 281, 282, 285
Allcard v Walker [1896] 2 Ch 369, 65 LJ Ch 660, 44 WR 661, 40 Sol Jo 499, 74 LT 487 . 982
Allen, Re, Faith v Allen [1953] Ch 810, [1953] 2 All ER 898, [1953] 3 WLR 637, 97 Sol Jo
606, CA 85, 99, 100, 103
Allen v Coster (1839) 1 Beav 202, 9 LJ Ch 131 709
Allen v Jackson (1875) 1 Ch D 399, 40 JP 262, 45 LJ Ch 310, 24 WR 306, 33 LT 713, CA . 190,
220, 221
Allen v Rea Bros Trustees Ltd (2002) 4 ITELR 627 . . . . 974, 975
Allen v Roughley (1955) 94 CLR 98, [1955] ALR 1017, 29 ALJ 603 648
Allen v Seckham (1879) 11 Ch D 790, 43 JP 685, 48 LJ Ch 611, 28 WR 26, 41 LT 260,
CA 992
Allen v Snyder [1977] 2 NSWLR 685, CA 56, 423
Allen-Meyrick's Will Trusts, Re, Mangnall v Allen-Meyrick [1966] 1 All ER 740, [1966] 1
WLR 499, 109 Sol Jo 957 . . . . 28, 213, 496, 690, 833
Allhusen v Whittell (1867) LR 4 Eq 295, 36 LJ Ch 929, [1861-73] All ER Rep 149, 16 LT
695 . . . . 561, 565
Allied Carpets Group plc v Nethercott [2001] BCC 81 969
Allott, Re, Hanmer v Allott [1924] 2 Ch 498, 94 LJ Ch 91, [1911-13] All ER Rep 810, 132 LT
141, CA 200
Allsop, Re, Whittaker v Bamford [1914] 1 Ch 1, 83 LJ Ch 42, [1911-13] All ER Rep 834, 58
Sol Jo 9, 109 LT 641, 30 TLR 18, CA 626, 629, 631, 914, 915, 918
Allsopp's Marriage Settlement Trusts, Re, Public Trustee v Cherry [1959] Ch 81, [1958] 2
All ER 393, [1958] 3 WLR 78, 102 Sol Jo 489 210
Alsop Wilkinson (a firm) v Neary [1995] 1 All ER 431, [1996] 1 WLR 1220, [1995] NLJR
52n 292, 648, 816, 818, 819, 833, 837, 838, 841, 842, 845
Alston, Re, Alston v Houston [1901] 2 Ch 584, 70 LJ Ch 869 . . . . 563, 982
Aluminium Industrie Vaassen BV v Romalpa Aluminium Ltd [1976] 2 All ER 552, [1976] 1
WLR 676, 119 Sol Jo 318; affd [1976] 2 All ER 552, [1976] 1 WLR 676, [1976] 1 Lloyd's
Rep 443, 120 Sol Jo 95, CA 8, 15, 17, 22
Amalgamated Investment and Property Co Ltd v John Walker & Sons Ltd [1976] 3 All ER
509, [1977] 1 WLR 164, 120 Sol Jo 252, 239 Estates Gazette 277, CA 442
Amalgamated Investment and Property Co Ltd (in liquidation) v Texas Commerce Inter-
national Bank Ltd [1982] QB 84, [1981] 1 All ER 923, [1981] 2 WLR 554, 125 Sol Jo
133; affd [1982] QB 84, [1981] 3 All ER 577, [1981] 3 WLR 565, [1982] 1 Lloyd's Rep
27, 125 Sol Jo 623, CA 242, 250
American Cyanamid Co v Ethicon Ltd [1975] AC 396, [1975] 1 All ER 504, [1975] 2 WLR
316, [1975] FSR 101, [1975] RPC 513, 119 Sol Jo 136, HL 904
Ames, Re, Ames v Taylor (1883) 25 Ch D 72, 32 WR 287 652
Ames' Settlement, Re, Dinwiddy v Ames [1946] Ch 217, [1946] 1 All ER 689, 115 LJ Ch 344,
90 Sol Jo 188, 175 LT 222, 62 TLR 300 274
Amin Rasheed Shipping Corpn v Kuwait Insurance Co, The Al Wahab [1984] AC 50, [1983]
2 All ER 884, [1983] 3 WLR 241, [1983] 2 Lloyd's Rep 365, 127 Sol Jo 492, HL . . 1037
Anderson v Elsworth (1861) 3 Giff 154, 30 LJ Ch 922, 7 Jur NS 1047, 139 RR 60, 9 WR 888, 4
LT 822 273
Anderson v Patton [1948] 2 DLR 202 . . . . 60, 247
Andrabell Ltd (in liquidation), Re, Airborne Accessories Ltd v Goodman [1984] 3 All ER
407, [1984] BCLC 522 17
Andrew's Trust, Re, Carter v Andrew [1905] 2 Ch 48, 74 LJ Ch 462, 53 WR 585, 49 Sol Jo

565, 92 LT 766, 21 TLR 512, [1904-7] All ER Rep Ext 1595 . . . . 83, 113, 336
Andrews, Re, Edwards v Dewar (1885) 30 Ch D 159, 54 LJ Ch 1049, 34 WR 62, 53 LT 422   818
Andrews v Partington (1791) 3 Bro CC 401, [1775-1802] All ER Rep 209 194
Androma Pty Ltd, Re [1987] 2 Qd R 134 185
Angora Trust, Re [2001] WTLR 1081. . . . . 624, 673, 674, 675, 702, 734
Anisminic Ltd v Foreign Compensation Commission [1969] 2 AC 147, [1969] 1 All ER 208,
    [1969] 2 WLR 163, 113 Sol Jo 55, HL 699
Anker-Petersen v Anker-Petersen [2000] WTLR 581 . . . . . . 509, 522, 525, 526, 532, 622
Anker-Petersen v Christensen [2002] WTLR 313 . . . . 277, 697
Annesley, Re, Davidson v Annesley [1926] Ch 692, 95 LJ Ch 404, 135 LT 508, 42 TLR
    584. 190, 231, 270, 1027, 1028, 1031
Anning v Anning (1907) 4 CLR 1049, 13 ALR 709, 3 QCLLR 136. 154
Anon (1596) Co Litt 3b, sub nom Blodwell v Edwards Cro Eliz 509, Moore KB 430, sub nom
    Bladwell v Edwards Noy 35. 190
Anon (1697) 2 Eq Cas Abr 85, 1 Com 43 983
Anon (1821) 6 Madd 10. 581
Ansell Rubber Co Pty Ltd v Allied Rubber Industries Pty Ltd [1972] RPC 811, [1967] VR 37   874
Anslow, Re, ex p Barber (1880) 28 WR 522, 42 LT 411 880
Anson v Potter (1879) 13 Ch D 141, 41 LT 582. 402
Anstis, Re, Chetwynd v Morgan (1886) 31 Ch D 596, 34 WR 483, 54 LT 742, 2 TLR 335,
    CA 139, 167, 186
Anstis, Re, Morgan v Chetwynd (1886) 31 Ch D 596, 34 WR 483, 54 LT 742, 2 TLR 335,
    CA 139, 167, 186
Anthony v Donges [1998] 2 FLR 775, [1998] Fam Law 666 81
Antoniades v Villiers [1990] 1 AC 417, [1988] 3 All ER 1058, [1988] 3 WLR 1205, 57 P & CR
    17, 21 HLR 79, [1988] 2 EGLR 78, [1989] 1 LS Gaz R 39, [1988] 47 EG 193, HL . 61
Applebee, Re, Leveson v Beales [1891] 3 Ch 422, 60 LJ Ch 793, 40 WR 90, 65 LT 406 . . 158,
                                                                                  162
Appleby, Re, Walker v Lever, Walker v Nisbet [1903] 1 Ch 565, 72 LJ Ch 332, 51 WR 455, 47
    Sol Jo 334, 88 LT 219, CA 200, 229, 553, 563
Appleby v Cowley (1982) Times, 14 April 22, 250, 388
Arab Monetary Fund v Hashim (No 9) (1994) Times, 11 October. . . 942, 943, 1021, 1041,
                                                                              1043, 1049
Aratra Potato Co Ltd v Egyptian Navigation Co, The El Amria [1981] 2 Lloyd's Rep 119,
    [1981] Com LR 136, CA. .1059
Arbib and Class's Contract, Re [1891] 1 Ch 601, 60 LJ Ch 263, 39 WR 305, 64 LT 217,
    CA. 449, 451, 452
Archer v Kelly (1860) 1 Drew & Sm 300, 29 LJ Ch 911, 6 Jur NS 814, 127 RR 115, 8 WR 684, 2
    LT 796 313
Archer-Shee v Garland (Inspector of Taxes) [1931] AC 212, 100 LJKB 170, 144 LT 508, 47
    TLR 171, sub nom Garland (Inspector of Taxes) v Archer-Shee 15 TC 693, HL . . 52
Ardagh's Estate, Re [1914] 1 IR 5, 48 ILT 45. . . . . 789, 1041
Arden, Re, Short v Camm [1935] Ch 326, 104 LJ Ch 141, 79 Sol Jo 68, 152 LT 453 . . 66, 300
Areso v Coutts & Co [2001] WTLR 797 360
Arklow Investments Ltd v Ian Duart Maclean [2000] 1 WLR 594, 144 Sol Jo LB 81, PC . 405
Armitage, Re, Armitage v Garnett [1893] 3 Ch 337, 63 LJ Ch 110, 7 R 290, 69 LT 619, 9 TLR
    630, CA 542
Armitage, Re, Ellam v Norwich Corpn [1972] Ch 438, [1972] 2 WLR 503, 70 LGR 305, 116
    Sol Jo 62, sub nom Re Armitage's Will Trusts, Ellam v City and County of Norwich
    [1972] 1 All ER 708 35
Armitage v Nurse [1998] Ch 241, [1997] 2 All ER 705, [1997] 3 WLR 1046, [1997] PLR 51,
    74 P & CR D13, CA 28, 31, 37, 59, 494, 529, 592, 593, 594, 595, 616, 621,
                                        624, 672, 675, 681, 683, 700, 702,
                                        812, 863, 921, 923, 926, 930, 939,
                                        940, 955, 956, 1052
Armory v Delamirie (1721) 1 Stra 505, 93 ER 664, [1558-1774] All ER Rep 121 885
Armour v Thyssen Edelstahlwerke AG [1991] 2 AC 339, [1990] 3 All ER 481, [1990] 3 WLR
    810, [1991] 1 Lloyd's Rep 95, [1991] BCLC 28, [1990] BCC 925, 134 Sol Jo 1337, 1990
    SLT 891, HL 14, 41
Armstrong, Re, ex p Gilchrist (1886) 17 QBD 521, 51 JP 292, 55 LJQB 578, 34 WR 709, 55 LT
    538, 2 TLR 745, CA 504, 733
Armstrong v Jackson [1917] 2 KB 822, 86 LJKB 1375, [1916-17] All ER Rep 1117, 61 Sol Jo
    631, 117 LT 479, 33 TLR 444. 23

Arning v James [1936] Ch 158, 105 LJ Ch 27, 154 LT 252 . . . . 658, 797

Arno, Re, Healey v Arno [1947] Ch 198, [1947] 1 All ER 64, [1947] LJR 435, 91 Sol Jo 27, 176 LT 152, 63 TLR 58, CA 534

Arnott, Re [1899] IR 201 . . . . 30, 34, 613, 645

Ashburn Anstalt v Arnold [1989] Ch 1, [1988] 2 All ER 147, [1988] 2 WLR 706, 55 P & CR 137, 132 Sol Jo 416, [1987] 2 EGLR 71, [1988] 16 LS Gaz R 43, 284 Estates Gazette 1375, CA 51, 253, 255, 325, 327, 411, 1003

Ashburnham's Trust, Re (1885) 54 LT 84, DC 728

Ashby, Re, ex p Wreford [1892] 1 QB 872, 9 Morr 77, 40 WR 430, 66 LT 353 . 142, 209, 213

Ashby v Blackwell and Million Bank Co (1765) Amb 503, 2 Eden 299 . . . . 245, 623, 624

Ashe v Mumford (2000) 33 HLR 756, [2000] 43 LS Gaz R 38, [2000] All ER (D) 1452, [2001] BPIR 1, CA 351

Ashton, Re, Ballard v Ashton [1920] 2 Ch 481, 89 LJ Ch 583, 65 Sol Jo 44, 124 LT 374 . 209

Ashurst v Pollard [2001] Ch 595, [2001] 2 All ER 75, [2001] 2 WLR 722, sub nom Pollard v Ashurst [2001] 03 LS Gaz R 42, CA 51, 188, 189

Aslan v Murphy [1989] 3 All ER 130, [1990] 1 WLR 766, 59 P & CR 407, 21 HLR 532, [1989] 2 EGLR 57, [1989] NLJR 936, [1989] 38 EG 109, CA 62

Assets Co Ltd v Mere Roihi [1905] AC 176, PC 974

Assets Realisation Co v Trustees, Executors and Securities Insurance Corpn (1895) 65 LJ Ch 74, 44 WR 126 744

Associated Alloys Pty Ltd v ACN 001 452 106 Pty Ltd (2001) 74 ALJR 862 . . . 16, 42, 44, 76, 139, 168, 185, 438

Associated Provincial Picture Houses Ltd v Wednesbury Corpn [1948] 1 KB 223, [1947] 2 All ER 680, 45 LGR 635, 112 JP 55, [1948] LJR 190, 92 Sol Jo 26, 177 LT 641, 63 TLR 623, CA 692

Astbury v Beasley (1869) 17 WR 638 586

Aste, Re, Mossop v Macdonald (1918) 87 LJ Ch 660, 118 LT 433 554

Aston, Re (1883) 23 Ch D 217, 31 WR 801, 48 LT 195, CA 747

Astor's Settlement Trusts, Re, Astor v Scholfield [1952] Ch 534, [1952] 1 All ER 1067, 96 Sol Jo 246, [1952] 1 TLR 1003 . . . . .38, 82, 88, 99, 110, 111, 113, 114, 119, 120, 122, 123, 129, 203

Atkin's Will Trusts, Re, National Westminster Bank Ltd v Atkins [1974] 2 All ER 1, [1974] 1 WLR 761, 118 Sol Jo 391 193

Atkinson, Re, Barbers' Co v Grose-Smith [1904] 2 Ch 160, 73 LJ Ch 585, 53 WR 7, 90 LT 825, CA 537, 553, 562

Atkinson's Will Trust, Re, Prescott v Child [1957] Ch 117, [1956] 3 All ER 738, [1956] 3 WLR 900, 100 Sol Jo 859 375

Atkinson's Will Trusts, Re, Atkinson v Hall [1978] 1 All ER 1275, [1978] 1 WLR 586, 122 Sol Jo 148 . . . . .82, 332

Atlantic Baron, The. See North Ocean Shipping Co Ltd v Hyundai Construction Co Ltd, The Atlantic Baron

Atlas Cabinets v National Trust Co (1990) 68 DLR (4th) 161 57

Atlas Maritime Co SA v Avalon Maritime Ltd, The Coral Rose [1991] 4 All ER 769, [1991] 1 Lloyd's Rep 563, CA 61

Attenborough (George) & Son v Solomon [1913] AC 76, 82 LJ Ch 178, [1911-13] All ER Rep 155, 57 Sol Jo 76, 107 LT 833, 29 TLR 79, HL 18

A-G v Alford (1855) 4 De GM & G 843, 3 Eq Rep 952, 1 Jur NS 361, 102 RR 406, 3 WR 200, 24 LTOS 265 . . . . 867, 869

A-G v Campbell (1872) LR 5 HL 524, 41 LJ Ch 611 . . . . 1033, 1034

A-G v Clack (1839) 1 Beav 467, 3 Jur 215 727

A-G v Cocke [1988] Ch 414, [1988] 2 All ER 391, [1988] 2 WLR 542, 132 Sol Jo 418 676, 920, 922, 928

A-G v Cordwainers' Co (1833) 3 My & K 534 35

A-G v Daugars (1864) 28 JP 726, 33 Beav 621, 10 Jur NS 966, 12 WR 363 940

A-G v De Winton [1906] 2 Ch 106, 4 LGR 549, 70 JP 368, 75 LJ Ch 612, 54 WR 499, 50 Sol Jo 405, 22 TLR 446. 22

A-G v Goddard (1929) 98 LJKB 743, 73 Sol Jo 514, 45 TLR 609 22

A-G v Gower (1736) 2 Eq Cas Abr 685 983

A-G v Guardian Newspapers Ltd (No 2) [1990] 1 AC 109, [1988] 3 All ER 545, [1988] 2 WLR 805; on appeal [1990] 1 AC 109, [1988] 3 All ER 545, [1988] 2 WLR 805, 132 Sol Jo 566, [1988] NLJR 47, CA; affd [1990] 1 AC 109, [1988] 3 All ER 545, [1988] 3 WLR 776, [1988] NLJR 296, [1990] LRC (Const) 938, HL 379, 386, 399

A-G v Hardy (1851) 1 Sim NS 338, 20 LJ Ch 450, 15 Jur 441 666

A-G v Herrick (1772) Amb 712 106
A-G v Jacobs-Smith [1895] 2 QB 341, 59 JP 468, 64 LJQB 605, 14 R 531, 43 WR 657, 39 Sol Jo
   538, 72 LT 714, 11 TLR 411, CA 167
A-G v Jewish Colonization Association [1901] 1 KB 123, 65 JP 21, 70 LJQB 101, 49 WR 230,
   83 LT 561, 17 TLR 106, CA 1033, 1034, 1036
A-G v Johnson [1907] 2 KB 885, 76 LJKB 1150, 97 LT 720 1029
A-G v Jonathan Cape Ltd [1976] QB 752, [1975] 3 All ER 484, [1975] 3 WLR 606, 119 Sol Jo
   696 403
A-G v Lady Downing (1769) Amb 550, 2 Dick 414 77
A-G v Leicester Corpn (1844) 7 Beav 176 957
A-G v Lloyds Bank Ltd [1935] AC 382, 104 LJKB 523, [1935] All ER Rep 518, 152 LT 577,
   HL 369, 374
A-G v Lord Dudley (1815) Coop G 146, 14 RR 226 665
A-G v Lord Gore (1740) Barn Ch 145, sub nom A-G v Lord Gower 9 Mod Rep 224 . . . 730
A-G v National Provincial and Union Bank of England. See Tetley, Re, National Provincial
   and Union Bank of England Ltd v Tetley
A-G v Plowden. See Grove-Grady, Re, Plowden v Lawrence
A-G v Sands (1669-1670) Freem Ch 129, Hard 488, Nels 130, 3 Rep Ch 33 189
A-G v Schonfeld [1980] 3 All ER 1, [1980] 1 WLR 1182, 124 Sol Jo 542 905
A-G v Scott. See Wilson v Dennison
A-G v Stephens (1834) 3 My & K 347 77
A-G v Wax Chandlers' Co (1873) LR 6 HL 1, 37 JP 532, 42 LJ Ch 425, 21 WR 361, 28 LT 681 137
A-G v Webster (1875) LR 20 Eq 483, 44 LJ Ch 766 203
A-G v Wilson (1840) Cr & Ph 1, 10 LJ Ch 53, 4 Jur 1174, 47 RR 173 . . . . . . 877, 940
A-G for Hong Kong v Reid [1994] 1 AC 324, [1994] 1 All ER 1, [1993] 3 WLR 1143, [1993]
   NLJR 1569, 137 Sol Jo LB 251, PC 9, 24, 37, 56, 379, 380, 387, 392, 396,
                  399, 407, 659, 880, 883, 889, 890, 903, 909
A-G of Hong Kong v Humphreys Estate (Queen's Gardens) Ltd [1987] AC 114, [1987] 2 All
   ER 387, [1987] 2 WLR 343, 54 P & CR 96, 131 Sol Jo 194, [1987] LS Gaz R 574, PC 250
A-G of Ontario v Stavro (1994) 119 DLR (4th) 750 . . . . 624, 673
A-G of the Bahamas v Royal Trust Co [1986] 3 All ER 423, [1986] 1 WLR 1001, 130 Sol Jo
   526, [1986] LS Gaz R 2487, PC 105
A-G's Reference (No 1 of 1985) [1986] QB 491, [1986] 2 All ER 219, [1986] 2 WLR 733, 83
   Cr App Rep 70, 150 JP 242, [1986] Crim LR 476, 130 Sol Jo 299, [1986] LS Gaz R 1226,
   [1986] BSMD 75, CA 387, 908, 909
A-G's Reference (No 2 of 1999) [2000] QB 796, [2000] 3 All ER 182, [2000] 3 WLR 195,
   [2000] 2 Cr App Rep 207, [2000] IRLR 417, [2000] Crim LR 475, [2000] 2 BCLC 257,
   [2000] 09 LS Gaz R 39, CA 963
Attwater v Attwater (1853) 18 Beav 330, 23 LJ Ch 692, 18 Jur 50, 2 WR 81, 22 LTOS 150 . 738
Atwood v Maude (1868) 3 Ch App 369, 16 WR 665 275
Augustus v Permanent Trustee Co (Canberra) Ltd (1971) 124 CLR 245, [1971] ALR
   661 . . . . 1034, 1036
Austen v Taylor (1759) Amb 376, 1 Eden 361 299
Austen's Settlement, Re (1878) 38 LT 601 772
Austin v Keele (1987) 72 ALR 579, 10 NSWLR 283, 61 ALJR 605, PC . 354, 412, 413, 415, 425
Australia and New Zealand Banking Group Ltd v Westpac Banking Corpn (1988) 164 CLR
   662, 78 ALR 157, 62 ALJR 292, HC of A 971
Australian Postal Corpn v Lutak (1991) 21 NSWLR 584 891
Aveline v Melhuish (1864) 2 De GJ & Sm 288, 10 Jur NS 788, 139 RR 108, 12 WR 1020, 10 LT
   830 931
Aveling v Knipe (1815) 13 RR 240, 19 Ves 441 . . . . 12, 357
Avoso v Coutts & Co [2001] WTLR 797 247
Ayerst (Inspector of Taxes) v C & K (Construction) Ltd [1976] AC 167, [1975] 2 All ER 537,
   [1975] 3 WLR 16, [1975] STC 345, 50 TC 651, 54 ATC 141, [1975] TR 117, 119 Sol Jo
   424, HL 21, 52
Ayerst v Jenkins (1873) LR 16 Eq 275, 38 JP 37, 42 LJ Ch 690, 21 WR 878, 29 LT 126 . . 344,
                        345, 348, 349
Ayles v Cox, ex p Attwood (1853) 17 Beav 584, sub nom Ayles v Cox, ex p Cox 22 LTOS 232 768
Aylwin's Trusts, Re (1873) LR 16 Eq 585, 42 LJ Ch 745, 21 WR 864, 28 LT 865 210

B

B, Re [1987] 2 All ER 475, [1987] 1 WLR 552, [1987] 2 FLR 155, [1987] Fam Law 242, 131
   Sol Jo 658, [1987] LS Gaz R 1573 694

B (child: property transfer), Re [1999] 3 FCR 266, [1999] 2 FLR 418, [1999] Fam Law 535, CA 74

Bacharach's Will Trusts, Re, Minden v Bacharach [1959] Ch 245, [1958] 3 All ER 618, [1959] 2 WLR 1, 103 Sol Jo 16 . . . . 279, 280

Backhouse, Re, Findlay v Backhouse [1921] 2 Ch 51, 90 LJ Ch 443, 65 Sol Jo 580, 125 LT 218 226

Backhouse v Backhouse [1978] 1 All ER 1158, [1978] 1 WLR 243, 121 Sol Jo 710 . . . 276

Bacon, Re, Grissel v Leathes (1893) 62 LJ Ch 445, 3 R 459, 41 WR 478, 37 Sol Jo 340, 68 LT 522 566

Bacon, Re, Toovey v Turner [1907] 1 Ch 475, 76 LJ Ch 213, 96 LT 690 741

Bacon v Clark (1836) 3 My & Cr 294, 45 RR 261 873

Bacon v Pianta (1966) 114 CLR 634, [1966] ALR 1044, HC of A 114, 129

Bacon (MC) Ltd, Re [1991] Ch 127, [1990] 3 WLR 646, [1990] BCLC 607, [1990] BCC 430 . . . . 288, 291, 294

Baden v Société Générale pour Favoriser le Développement du Commerce et de l'Industrie en France SA [1992] 4 All ER 161, [1983] BCLC 325, [1993] 1 WLR 509n; affd [1992] 4 All ER 279n, [1985] BCLC 258n, CA 890, 915, 952, 956, 958, 959, 968, 973, 974, 983, 989

Baden's Deed Trusts, Re, Baden v Smith [1969] 2 Ch 388, [1969] 1 All ER 1016, [1969] 3 WLR 12, 113 Sol Jo 149, CA; revsd sub nom McPhail v Doulton [1971] AC 424, [1970] 2 All ER 228, [1970] 2 WLR 1110, 114 Sol Jo 375, HL 26, 27, 64, 81, 84, 85, 86, 88, 90, 92, 93, 94, 95, 98, 99, 100, 101, 112, 130, 132, 146, 191, 689, 690, 692, 728

Baden's Deed Trusts (No 2), Re [1972] Ch 607, [1971] 3 All ER 985, [1971] 3 WLR 475, 115 Sol Jo 488; affd [1973] Ch 9, [1972] 2 All ER 1304, [1972] 3 WLR 250, 116 Sol Jo 356, CA 27, 84, 86, 87, 88, 92, 95, 98, 100, 101

Badfinger Music v Evans [2002] EMLR 35, [2001] WTLR 1 . . . . .401, 402, 405, 658

Badger, Re, Badger v Woolley [1915] WN 166, 84 LJ Ch 567, 113 LT 150 765

Bagnall's Trusts, Re, Flynn v Dalgleish [1901] 1 IR 255 386

Bahin v Hughes (1886) 31 Ch D 390, 55 LJ Ch 472, 34 WR 311, 54 LT 188, 2 TLR 276, CA 941, 944, 945, 946

Bahr v Nicolay (No 2) (1988) 164 CLR 604, 78 ALR 1, 62 ALJR 268 411

Bailey v Barnes [1894] 1 Ch 25, 63 LJ Ch 73, 7 R 9, 42 WR 66, 38 Sol Jo 9, 69 LT 542, CA 50

Baillie, Re, Fitzgerald v Noad (1886) 2 TLR 660 . . . . 257, 262

Bain, Re, Public Trustee v Ross [1930] 1 Ch 224, 99 LJ Ch 171, [1929] All ER Rep 387, 142 LT 344, 45 TLR 617, CA 106

Bainbrigge v Browne (1881) 18 Ch D 188, 50 LJ Ch 522, 29 WR 782, 44 LT 705 . 50, 281, 284

Baird v Baird [1990] 2 AC 548, [1990] 2 All ER 300, [1990] 2 WLR 1412, [1990] ICR 525, [1991] Fam Law 96, 134 Sol Jo 725, [1990] 23 LS Gaz R 28, PC 60, 246, 593

Baird v Lord Advocate [1979] AC 666, [1979] 2 All ER 28, [1979] 2 WLR 369, [1979] STC 229, [1979] TR 29, 123 Sol Jo 186, HL 204

Bairstow v Queens Moat Houses plc [2001] EWCA Civ 712, [2001] 2 BCLC 531, [2001] All ER (D) 211. . . . . 857, 865

Baker, Re, Baker v Public Trustee [1924] 2 Ch 271, 93 LJ Ch 599, 68 Sol Jo 645, 131 LT 763 559

Baker v Archer-Shee [1927] AC 844, 96 LJKB 803, 71 Sol Jo 727, 137 LT 762, 43 TLR 758, [1927] All ER Rep Ext 755, sub nom Archer-Shee v Baker 11 TC 749, HL . . . 52, 64

Baker v Baker [1993] 2 FLR 247, [1993] Fam Law 475, 25 HLR 408, [1993] 14 LS Gaz R 43, CA 248, 249

Baker v Carter (1835) 1 Y & C Ex 250, 4 LJ Ex Eq 12, 41 RR 267 670

Baker v Monk (1864) 28 JP 407, 33 Beav 419, 10 Jur NS 624, 12 WR 521, 10 LT 86; affd (1864) 4 De GJ & Sm 388 277

Baker v Peck (1861) 129 RR 920, 9 WR 472, 4 LT 3 665

Baker v Sutton (1836) 1 Keen 224, 5 LJ Ch 264, 44 RR 65, [1835-42] All ER Rep 431 . . 106

Baker (GL) Ltd v Medway Building and Supplies Ltd [1958] 3 All ER 540, [1958] 1 WLR 1216, 102 Sol Jo 877, CA 922, 923, 925

Baker's Settlement Trusts, Re [1964] 1 All ER 482n, [1964] 1 WLR 336n, 108 Sol Jo 157 . 511

Balfour's Settlement, Re, Public Trustee v Official Receiver [1938] Ch 928, [1938] 3 All ER 259, 107 LJ Ch 429, 82 Sol Jo 493, 159 LT 83, 54 TLR 895 212

Balfron Trustees Ltd v Peterson [2001] IRLR 758, [2001] NLJR 1180 959

Balkin v Peck (1997) 43 NSWLR 766, 1 ITELR 717 . . . . 811, 822

Ball's Settlement, Re [1968] 2 All ER 438, [1968] 1 WLR 899, 112 Sol Jo 445 . 504, 509, 519

Ballman, Re, ex p Garland (1804) 1 Smith KB 220, 10 Ves 110, [1803-13] All ER Rep 750. . . . . .457, 811, 824, 825

Balsh v Hyham (1728) 2 Eq Cas Abr 741, 2 P Wms 453 823

Baltic Flame, The. See Petroleo Brasiliero SA v Mellitus Shipping Inc, The Baltic Flame [2001] EWCA Civ 418

Banca Carige SpA Cassa di Risparmio di Genova e Imperia v Banco Nacional de Cuba [2001] 3 All ER 923, [2001] 2 Lloyd's Rep 147, [2001] 2 BCLC 407, [2001] All ER (D) 120 (Apr), sub nom Banco Nacional de Cuba, Re [2001] 1 WLR 2039, 145 Sol Jo LB 124. 292

Banfield, Re, Lloyds Bank Ltd v Smith [1968] 2 All ER 276, [1968] 1 WLR 846, 112 Sol Jo 396. . . . . 106, 129

Bank of America v Arnell [1999] Lloyd's Rep Bank 399. 974

Bank of Credit & Commerce International (Overseas) v Jan (17 November 1999, unreported) 924

Bank of Credit and Commerce International (Overseas) Ltd v Akindele [1999] BCC 669; on appeal [2001] Ch 437, [2000] 4 All ER 221, [2000] 3 WLR 1423, [2000] BCC 968, [2000] 26 LS Gaz R 36, [2000] NLJR 950, [2000] All ER (D) 798, CA . . 951, 967, 974, 975, 976

Bank of Credit and Commerce International SA (No 8), Re [1998] AC 214, [1997] 4 All ER 568, [1997] 3 WLR 909, [1998] 1 BCLC 68, [1997] NLJR 1653, sub nom Morris v Agrichemicals [1997] BCC 965, 141 Sol Jo LB 229, HL 153

Bank of Ireland Home Mortgages Ltd v Bell [2001] 3 FCR 134, [2001] 2 FLR 809, [2001] Fam Law 805, [2001] All ER (D) 2105, [2001] 2 All ER (Comm) 920, CA. . . 480, 481

Bank of New South Wales v Vale Corpn (Management) Ltd (21 October 1981, unreported) 973

Bank of New Zealand v New Zealand Guardian Trust Co [1999] 1 NZLR 664, [2000] 2 LRC 357, NZCA 661, 701, 857, 858, 866, 876

Bank of Nova Scotia Trust (Bahamas) Ltd v Borletta (11 March 1985, unreported) . . . 62

Bank of Scotland v A Ltd [2001] EWCA Civ 52, [2001] 3 All ER 58, [2001] 1 WLR 751, [2001] 09 LS Gaz R 41, [2001] NLJR 102, 145 Sol Jo LB 21, [2001] All ER (D) 81, [2001] 1 All ER (Comm) 1023 . . . . 489, 959, 967

Bank Tejarat v Hong Kong and Shanghai Banking Corpn (CI) Ltd and Hong Kong and Shanghai Bank Trustee (Jersey) Ltd [1995] 1 Lloyd's Rep 239 . . . . 957, 960

Bankers Trust Co v Shapira [1980] 3 All ER 353, [1980] 1 WLR 1274, 124 Sol Jo 480, CA 904

Bankes, Re, Reynolds v Ellis [1902] 2 Ch 333, 71 LJ Ch 708, 50 WR 663, 46 Sol Jo 601, 87 LT 432. 1023

Bankes v Salisbury Diocesan Council of Education Inc [1960] Ch 631, [1960] 2 All ER 372, [1960] 2 WLR 916, 104 Sol Jo 449. 774

Bankgesellschaft Berlin AG v Makris (22 January 1998, unreported) 957, 983

Bankhead's Trusts, Re (1856) 2 K & J 560, 4 WR 589 999

Banks v Goodfellow (1870) LR 5 QB 549, 39 LJQB 237, [1861-73] All ER Rep 47, 22 LT 813 269

Banks v Ripley [1940] Ch 719, [1940] 3 All ER 49, 109 LJ Ch 345, 84 Sol Jo 358, 163 LT 419, 56 TLR 731 . . . . 279, 300

Bankway Properties Ltd v Dunsford [2001] EWCA Civ 528, [2001] 1 WLR 1369, [2001] 2 EGLR 36, [2001] 26 EG 164, [2001] EGCS 53 62

Banner Homes Group plc v Luff Developments Ltd [2000] Ch 372, [2000] 2 All ER 117, [2000] 2 WLR 772, [2000] 2 BCLC 269, [2000] 06 LS Gaz R 35, [2000] EGCS 15, 144 Sol Jo LB 83, 79 P & CR D29, CA 80, 254, 326, 354, 412, 423, 426

Bannister, Re, Heys-Jones v Bannister (1921) 90 LJ Ch 415, 125 LT 54 304

Bannister v Bannister [1948] 2 All ER 133, [1948] WN 261, 92 Sol Jo 377, CA . . . 255, 410

Banque Belge pour L'Etranger v Hambrouck [1921] 1 KB 321, 90 LJKB 322, 26 Com Cas 72, 65 Sol Jo 74, 37 TLR 76, CA 895, 992

Banque Financière de la Cité v Parc (Battersea) Ltd [1999] 1 AC 221, [1998] 1 All ER 737, [1998] 2 WLR 475, [1998] 15 LS Gaz R 31, [1998] NLJR 365, [1998] EGCS 36, 142 Sol Jo LB 102, HL 902, 977

Banque Nationale de Paris v Hew [2001] 1 SLR 300 . . . . 961, 964

Barber, Re, Burgess v Vinicome (1886) 34 Ch D 77, 56 LJ Ch 216, 35 WR 326, 55 LT 882 653

Barbour's Settlement, Re, National Westminster Bank Ltd v Barbour [1974] 1 All ER 1188, [1974] 1 WLR 1198, 118 Sol Jo 681 655

Barclay, Re, Barclay v Andrew [1899] 1 Ch 674, 68 LJ Ch 383, 80 LT 702 868

Barclay v Barclay [1970] 2 QB 677, [1970] 2 All ER 676, [1970] 3 WLR 82, 21 P & CR 908, 114 Sol Jo 456, 215 Estates Gazette 439, CA 477

Barclay v Owen (1889) 60 LT 220 . . . . 541, 543, 667

Barclays Bank Ltd v Abbas (7 May 1985, unreported) 352

Barclays Bank Ltd v Quistclose Investments Ltd [1970] AC 567, [1968] 3 All ER 651, [1968] 3 WLR 1097, 112 Sol Jo 903, HL 12, 44, 116, 330, 342, 357, 461

Barclays Bank Ltd v WJ Simms, Son and Cooke (Southern) Ltd [1980] QB 677, [1979] 3 All

ER 522, [1980] 2 WLR 218, [1980] 1 Lloyd's Rep 225, 123 Sol Jo 785 971
Barclays Bank plc v Boulter [1999] 4 All ER 513, [1999] 1 WLR 1919, [1999] 3 FCR 529,
   [1999] 2 FLR 986, [2000] Fam Law 25, 32 HLR 170, [1999] 42 LS Gaz R 41, [1999]
   NLJR 1645, [1999] 49 EG 97, [1999] EGCS 121, 143 Sol Jo LB 250, 79 P & CR D1, HL 983
Barclays Bank plc v Eustice [1995] 4 All ER 511, [1995] 1 WLR 1238, [1995] 2 BCLC 630,
   [1995] BCC 978, [1995] NLJR 1503, [1996] BPIR 1, CA 295
Barclays Bank plc v O'Brien [1994] 1 AC 180, [1993] 4 All ER 417, [1993] 3 WLR 786,
   [1994] 1 FCR 357, [1994] 1 FLR 1, [1994] Fam Law 78, 26 HLR 75, [1993] 46 LS Gaz R
   37, [1993] NLJR 1511, 137 Sol Jo LB 240, HL 281, 282, 596
Barclays Bank plc v Quincecare Ltd [1992] 4 All ER 363, 1988 FLR 166, [1988] 1 FTLR 507 974
Barclays Bank plc v Weeks Legg & Dean (a firm) [1999] QB 309, [1998] 3 All ER 213, [1998]
   3 WLR 656, 77 P & CR 320, [1998] 21 LS Gaz R 38, [1998] 25 LS Gaz R 33, [1998] 40
   EG 182, 142 Sol Jo LB 180, 76 P & CR D27, [1998] PNLR 729, CA 13
Barclays Bank plc v Willowbrook International Ltd [1987] BCLC 717n, [1987] 1 FTLR 386,
   CA 16
Bardissy v D'Souza [1999] HKCFI 85 961
Bardswell v Bardswell (1838) 9 Sim 319, 7 LJ Ch 268, 47 RR 252 80
Baring, Re, Jeune v Baring [1893] 1 Ch 61, 62 LJ Ch 50, 3 R 37, 41 WR 87, 67 LT 702, 9 TLR
   7. 564
Baring's Settlement Trusts, Re, Baring Bros & Co Ltd v Liddell [1940] Ch 737, [1940] 3 All
   ER 20, 109 LJ Ch 337, 84 Sol Jo 382, 163 LT 403, 56 TLR 777 212
Barker, Re, Ravenshaw v Barker (1898) 46 WR 296, 77 LT 712 . . . . 879, 913, 914
Barker v Peile (1865) 2 Drew & Sm 340, 34 LJ Ch 497, 11 Jur NS 436, 5 New Rep 425, 143 RR
   150, 13 WR 573, 12 LT 50 847
Barker's Trusts, Re (1875) 1 Ch D 43, 45 LJ Ch 52, 24 WR 264. . . . . . . 461, 744, 753
Barkworth v Young (1856) 4 Drew 1, 26 LJ Ch 153, 3 Jur NS 34, 113 RR 97, 5 WR 156, 28
   LTOS 199 237
Barlow Clowes International Ltd (in liquidation) v Vaughan [1992] 4 All ER 22, [1992]
   BCLC 910, CA 881, 892, 893, 998
Barlow's Will Trusts, Re [1979] 1 All ER 296, [1979] 1 WLR 278, 122 Sol Jo 646 . .84, 85, 90,
   99, 100
Barnardo's Homes v Special Income Tax Comrs [1921] 2 AC 1, 90 LJKB 545, 65 Sol Jo 433,
   125 LT 250, 37 TLR 540, sub nom R v Income Tax Acts Special Purposes Comr, ex p Dr
   Barnardo's Homes National Incorporated Association 7 TC 646, HL. 1029
Barnes v Addy (1874) 9 Ch App 244, 43 LJ Ch 513, 22 WR 505, 30 LT 4 . . . 388, 585, 953,
   957, 970
Barnes v Ross [1896] AC 625, HL 524
Barnett v Sheffield (1852) 1 De GM & G 371, 21 LJ Ch 692, 16 Jur 942, 91 RR 122 . . . 980
Barratt, Re, National Provincial Bank Ltd v Barratt [1925] Ch 550, 94 LJ Ch 345, [1925] All
   ER Rep 193, 133 LT 133 553
Barratt v Wyatt (1862) 30 Beav 442, 31 LJ Ch 652, 8 Jur NS 1045, 32 RR 349, 10 WR 454, 6 LT
   801. 626
Barret v McCormack (1999) 4 ITELR 1 964
Barrett, Re, Whitaker v Barrett (1889) 43 Ch D 70, 59 LJ Ch 218, 38 WR 59. 727
Barrett v Hartley (1866) LR 2 Eq 789, 12 Jur NS 426, 14 WR 684, 14 LT 474 651
Barron v Willis [1900] 2 Ch 121, CA; on appeal sub nom Willis v Barron [1902] AC 271, 71
   LJ Ch 609, 86 LT 806, 18 TLR 602, HL 283, 666
Barry's Trusts, Re, Barry v Smart [1906] 2 Ch 358, 75 LJ Ch 676, 54 WR 621, 50 Sol Jo 615, 95
   LT 165, CA. 817
Barsht v Tagg [1900] 1 Ch 231, 69 LJ Ch 91, 48 WR 220, 44 Sol Jo 133, 81 LT 777, 16 TLR
   100. 441
Bartlett v Barclays Bank Trust Co Ltd [1980] Ch 515, [1980] 1 All ER 139, [1980] 2 WLR
   430, 124 Sol Jo 85 . . . . . . 560, 575, 577, 585, 587, 591, 612, 618, 855, 918, 919
Bartlett v Barclays Bank Trust Co Ltd (No 2) [1980] Ch 515, [1980] 2 All ER 92, [1980] 2
   WLR 430, 124 Sol Jo 221 . . . . 854, 856, 858, 859, 868, 879
Barton v Barton (1857) 3 K & J 512, 3 Jur NS 808. 209
Barton v London and North Western Rly Co (1889) 24 QBD 77, 59 LJQB 33, 38 WR 197, 62
   LT 164, 6 TLR 70, CA 19
Barton v North Staffordshire Rly Co (1888) 38 Ch D 458, 57 LJ Ch 800, 36 WR 754, [1886-
   90] All ER Rep 288, 58 LT 549, 4 TLR 403 19
Barton's Trust, Re (1868) LR 5 Eq 238, 37 LJ Ch 194, 16 WR 392, 17 LT 594 530
Basden's Settlement Trusts, Re, Basden v Basden [1943] 2 All ER 11 526
Basham, Re [1987] 1 All ER 405, [1986] 1 WLR 1498, [1987] 2 FLR 264, [1987] Fam Law

310, 130 Sol Jo 986, [1987] LS Gaz R 112 . . . . .161, 234, 248, 250, 815

Basham, Re, Hannay v Basham (1883) 23 Ch D 195, 52 LJ Ch 408, 31 WR 743, 48 LT 476 824

Baskerville v Thurgood (1992) 100 Sask LR 214, [1992] 5 WWR 193, 46 ETR 28, 18 WAC 214, CA 20, 282, 596

Bassett v Nosworthy (1673) Cas temp Finch 102, 2 White & Tud LC 163 983

Bassil v Lister (1851) 9 Hare 177, 20 LJ Ch 641, 15 Jur 964, 17 LTOS 263 . . 204, 206, 208

Bastard v Proby (1788) 2 Cox Eq Cas 6 304

Bate v Hooper (1855) 5 De GM & G 338, 104 RR 146, 3 WR 639 . . . . 934, 982

Bate v Scales (1806) 8 RR 345, 12 Ves 402. 870

Bateman v Davis (1818) 3 Madd 98, 18 RR 200 . . . . 497, 861

Bateman's Will Trusts, Re, Brierley v Perry [1970] 3 All ER 817, [1970] 1 WLR 1463, 114 Sol Jo 707. . . . . 258, 261

Bater v Bater [1999] 4 All ER 944, [1999] EGCS 111, sub nom Bater v Greenwich London Borough Council [1999] 3 FCR 254, [1999] 2 FLR 993, [1999] Fam Law 694, 32 HLR 127, [1999] 33 LS Gaz R 30, CA. 296

Bates, Re, Hodgson v Bates [1907] 1 Ch 22, [1906] WN 191, 76 LJ Ch 29, [1904-7] All ER Rep 450, 51 Sol Jo 27, 95 LT 753, 23 TLR 15 555

Bates, Re, Mountain v Bates [1928] Ch 682, 97 LJ Ch 240, [1928] All ER Rep 126, 72 Sol Jo 468, 139 LT 162 536

Bates (Thomas) & Son Ltd v Wyndham's (Lingerie) Ltd [1981] 1 All ER 1077, [1981] 1 WLR 505, 41 P & CR 345, 125 Sol Jo 32, 257 Estates Gazette 381, CA 278

Bates' Will Trusts, Re, Jenks v Bates [1946] Ch 83, [1945] 2 All ER 688, 115 LJ Ch 142, 89 Sol Jo 531, 174 LT 305, 62 TLR 52 534

Bathe, Re, Bathe v Public Trustee [1925] Ch 377, 133 LT 132, sub nom Re Bathe, Public Trustee v Bathe 95 LJ Ch 37 220

Batstone v Salter (1875) 10 Ch App 431, 44 LJ Ch 760, 23 WR 816, 33 LT 4. 361

Battle Abbey Settled Estate, Re, Webster v Troubridge [1933] WN 215, sub nom Re Webster, Webster v Troubridge 176 LT Jo 143 573

Batty, Re, Public Trustee v Bell [1952] Ch 280, [1952] 1 All ER 425, 96 Sol Jo 120, [1952] 1 TLR 412. 718

Baughesellschaft Berlin AG v Makris (22 January 1999, unreported) 983

Baumgartner v Baumgartner (1987) 11 Fam LR 915, 164 CLR 137, 76 ALR 75, 62 ALJR 29, HC of A 326

Bawden's Settlement, Re, Besant v London Hospital Board of Governors [1953] 2 All ER 1235, [1954] 1 WLR 33n, 98 Sol Jo 11 105

Bayley v Boulcott (1828) 4 Russ 345 149

Baynard v Woolley (1855) 20 Beav 583 . . . . 903, 982

Baynes, Re, Public Trustee v Leven Corpn [1944] 2 All ER 597, 89 Sol Jo 34 106

Beachway Management Ltd v Wisewell [1971] Ch 610, [1971] 1 All ER 1, [1970] 3 WLR 1118, 22 P & CR 40, 114 Sol Jo 885, 216 Estates Gazette 1404 200

Beal v South Devon Rly Co (1864) 3 H & C 337, 12 WR 1115, [1861-73] All ER Rep 972, 11 LT 184, Ex Ch 594

Beale's Settlement Trusts, Re, Huggins v Beale [1932] 2 Ch 15, 101 LJ Ch 320, [1931] All ER Rep 637 . . . . 33, 472, 475, 526, 613

Beaman v ARTS Ltd [1949] 1 KB 550, [1949] 1 All ER 465, 93 Sol Jo 236, 65 TLR 389, CA 923, 930

Beaney, Re [1978] 2 All ER 595, [1978] 1 WLR 770, 121 Sol Jo 832 . . . . . . 269, 270

Beard, Re, Beard v Hall [1908] 1 Ch 383, 77 LJ Ch 265, 98 LT 315, 24 TLR 225 . . 189, 230

Beard, Re, Reversionary and General Securities Co Ltd v Hall [1908] 1 Ch 383, 77 LJ Ch 265, 98 LT 315, 24 TLR 225 230

Beardmore Trusts, Re [1952] 1 DLR 41 80

Beater, Re, ex p Edmonds (1862) 4 De GF & J 488, sub nom Beater, Re, Dennant and Russ, ex p Coster's Executors 31 LJ Bcy 15, 8 Jur NS 629, sub nom Coster, Re, Beater & Co, ex p Coster's Executors 10 WR 372, 6 LT 199 823

Beatty v Vance. See Butler, Re, Beatty v Vance

Beatty's Will Trusts, Re, Hinves v Brooke [1990] 3 All ER 844, sub nom Re Beatty, Hinves v Brooke [1990] 1 WLR 1503 . . . . 26, 97, 98, 105, 667, 692, 804

Beatty's Will Trusts (No 2), Re (1991) 11 Tru LI 77 . . . . 516, 773, 1041

Beaty v Curson (1868) LR 7 Eq 194, 38 LJ Ch 161, 17 WR 132, 20 LT 61 846

Beauclerk, Re (1862) 11 WR 203 829

Beauclerk v Ashburnham (1845) 8 Beav 322, 14 LJ Ch 241, 9 Jur 146, 4 LTOS 431 . 531, 592, 610, 613

Beaufort (Duke) v Patrick (1853) 17 Beav 60 253

Beaumont, Re, Woods v Beaumont [1910] WN 181, 79 LJ Ch 744, 103 LT 124. 212

Beckett's Settlement, Re, Re Beckett, Eden v Von Stutterheim [1940] Ch 279, 109 LJ Ch 81,
    84 Sol Jo 133, 163 LT 78, 56 TLR 342 . . . . 503, 725

Beckford v Beckford (1774) Lofft 490 . . . . 350, 366

Beckley v Newland (1723) 2 P Wms 182. 184

Bective (Countess) v Federal Comr of Taxation (1932) 47 CLR 417, 38 ALR 362, 6 ALJ 110,
    2 ATD 80 . . . . 34, 35

Bective v Hodgson (1864) 10 HL Cas 656, 33 LJ Ch 601, 10 Jur NS 373, 3 New Rep 654, 138
    RR 350, 12 WR 625, 10 LT 202 372

Beddington, Re, Micholls v Samuel [1900] 1 Ch 771, 69 LJ Ch 374, 48 WR 552, 82 LT 557, 16
    TLR 291. 546

Beddoe, Re, Downes v Cottam [1893] 1 Ch 547, 62 LJ Ch 233, 2 R 223, 41 WR 177, 37 Sol Jo
    99, 68 LT 595, CA 37, 180, 815, 834, 837, 841, 847

Beddoes v Pugh (1859) 26 Beav 407, 122 RR 161 649

Beddy, Re (1953) unreported, cited in [1956] Ch 105 at 120 106

Beech, Re, Saint v Beech [1920] 1 Ch 40, 89 LJ Ch 9, 122 LT 117 559

Beecher v Major (1865) 2 Drew & Sm 431, 6 New Rep 370, 143 RR 219, 13 WR 1054, 62 ER
    684, 13 LT 54. 149

Beeny, Re, Ffrench v Sproston [1894] 1 Ch 499, 63 LJ Ch 312, 42 WR 577, 38 Sol Jo 235, 70
    LT 160 903

Beesty's Will Trusts, Re, Farrar v Royal Alfred Merchant Seamen's Society [1966] Ch 223,
    [1964] 3 All ER 82, [1964] 3 WLR 689, 108 Sol Jo 481 149

Begbie v Crook (1835) 2 Bing NC 70, 44 LJCP 264, 2 Scott 128 449

Begg-MacBrearty (Inspector of Taxes) v Stilwell [1996] 4 All ER 205, [1996] 1 WLR 951,
    [1996] STC 413, 68 TC 426, [1996] 15 LS Gaz R 31, 140 Sol Jo LB 110 711

Behrers v Heilbut (1956) 222 L Jo 290 278

Belar Pty Ltd v Mahaffery [2000] 1 Qd R 477 822

Belk v Slack (1836) 1 Keen 238, 44 RR 71. 374

Bell v Barnett (1872) 21 WR 119 385

Bell v Lever Bros Ltd [1932] AC 161, 101 LJKB 129, 37 Com Cas 98, [1931] All ER Rep 1, 76
    Sol Jo 50, 146 LT 258, 48 TLR 133, HL. 24, 402

Bell Houses Ltd v City Wall Properties Ltd [1966] 2 QB 656, [1966] 2 All ER 674, [1966] 2
    WLR 1323, 110 Sol Jo 268, CA 270

Bell's Indenture, Re, Bell v Hickley [1980] 3 All ER 425, [1980] 1 WLR 1217, 123 Sol Jo
    322. . . . . .859, 872, 873, 875, 965

Bellamy and Metropolitan Board of Works, Re (1883) 24 Ch D 387, 47 JP 550, 52 LJ Ch 870,
    31 WR 900, 48 LT 801 631

Belmont Finance Corpn Ltd v Williams Furniture Ltd [1979] Ch 250, [1979] 1 All ER 118,
    [1978] 3 WLR 712, 122 Sol Jo 743, CA 955, 956, 957

Belmont Finance Corpn Ltd v Williams Furniture Ltd (No 2) [1980] 1 All ER 393, CA . 951,
    957, 968, 974

Benarty (No 2), The. See Lister (R A) & Co Ltd v E G Thomson (Shipping) Ltd, The
    Benarty (No 2)

Benbow v Davies (1848) 11 Beav 369, 83 RR 198 450

Benbow v Townsend (1833) 1 My & K 506, 2 LJ Ch 215, 36 RR 359 343

Bence, Re, Smith v Bence [1891] 3 Ch 242, 60 LJ Ch 636, 65 LT 530, 7 TLR 593, CA . . 190,
    229

Bence v Gilpin (1868) LR 3 Exch 76, 37 LJ Ex 36, 16 WR 705, 17 LT 655 451

Bendy, Re, Wallis v Bendy [1895] 1 Ch 109, 64 LJ Ch 170, 13 R 95, 43 WR 345, 71 LT 750 307

Bendyshe, Re (1857) 26 LJ Ch 814, 3 Jur NS 727, 5 WR 816, 29 LTOS 341 829

Benett, Re, Ward v Benett [1906] 1 Ch 216, 75 LJ Ch 122, 54 WR 237, 50 Sol Jo 125, 94 LT
    72, CA 741

Benett v Wyndham. See Bennett v Wyndham

Benett-Stanford Settlement Trusts, Re, Atwood v Benett-Stanford [1947] 1 All ER 888,
    [1947] LJR 1073, 177 LT 301. 301

Benham's Will Trusts, Re [1995] STC 210. 83

Beningfield v Baxter (1886) 12 App Cas 167, 56 LJPC 13, 56 LT 127, PC 661

Benjamin, Re, Neville v Benjamin [1902] 1 Ch 723, 71 LJ Ch 319, 46 Sol Jo 266, 86 LT 387,
    18 TLR 283 . . . . 508, 869, 916

Benn v Hardinge (1992) 66 P & CR 246, CA. 50

Bennet v Bennet (1879) 10 Ch D 474, 27 WR 573, 40 LT 378 . . . . 364, 367

Bennett, Re, Midland Bank Executor and Trustee Co Ltd v Fletcher [1943] 1 All ER 467, 87
    Sol Jo 102 813

Bennett, Re, Sucker v A-G [1960] Ch 18, [1959] 3 All ER 295, [1959] 3 WLR 427, 103 Sol Jo
    618.   82
Bennett, ex p (1805) 8 RR 1, 10 Ves 381   . . . .   665, 668
Bennett v Burgis (1846) 5 Hare 295, 15 LJ Ch 231, 10 Jur 153   492
Bennett v Colley (1832) 5 Sim 182, 35 RR 135   903
Bennett v Wyndham (1857) 23 Beav 521, 3 Jur NS 1143, 113 RR 247, 5 WR 410, 29 LTOS
    138; on appeal sub nom Benett v Wyndham (1862) 4 De GF & J 259   . . . .   524, 813
Bennison, Re, Cutler v Boyd (1889) 60 LT 859 . . . .   497, 623, 873
Benson, Re, Elletson v Pillers [1899] 1 Ch 39, 68 LJ Ch 5, 47 WR 264, 79 LT 590   .   903, 906
Benson v Whittam (1831) 5 Sim 22, 1 LJ Ch 94, 35 RR 113   138
Bentham, Re, Pearce v Bentham (1906) 94 LT 307   554
Bentley, Re, Public Trustee v Bentley [1914] 2 Ch 456, 84 LJ Ch 54, [1914-15] All ER Rep
    164, 111 LT 1097   793
Bentley v Craven (1853) 18 Beav 75   . . . .   23, 666
Benyon v Nettlefold (1850) 20 LJ Ch 186, 15 Jur 209, 3 Mac & G 94, 87 RR 25, 17 LTOS 149   345
Berchtold, Re, Berchtold v Capron [1923] 1 Ch 192, 92 LJ Ch 185, 67 Sol Jo 212, 128 LT
    591. . . . .   188, 1026, 1029, 1031
Berens, Re, Berens v Berens [1888] WN 95   . . . .   833, 839
Beresford v Beresford (1857) 23 Beav 292, 113 RR 147   524
Beresford v Royal Insurance Co Ltd [1938] AC 586, [1938] 2 All ER 602, 107 LJKB 464, 82
    Sol Jo 431, 158 LT 459, 54 TLR 789, HL   434
Beresford-Hope, Re, Aldenham v Beresford-Hope [1917] 1 Ch 287, 86 LJ Ch 182, 116 LT
    79   . . . .   300, 304
Berkeley (Earl), Re, Inglis v Countess of Berkeley [1968] Ch 744, [1968] 3 All ER 364,
    [1968] 3 WLR 253, 112 Sol Jo 601, CA 204, 207, 533, 566, 572
Berkeley v Berkeley [1946] AC 555, [1946] 2 All ER 154, 25 ATC 209, 115 LJ Ch 281, 90 Sol
    Jo 345, 175 LT 153, 62 TLR 478, HL   597
Berkeley Applegate (Investment Consultants) Ltd, Re, Harris v Conway [1989] Ch 32,
    [1988] 3 All ER 71, [1988] 3 WLR 95, [1989] BCLC 28, 4 BCC 274, 132 Sol Jo 896,
    [1988] 26 LS Gaz R 41 . . . .   462, 657
Berkeley's (Earl) Will, Re, Re Gloucester and Berkeley Canal Act 1870 (1874) 10 Ch App 56,
    44 LJ Ch 3, 23 WR 195, 31 LT 531.   574
Berkley v Poulett (1976) 120 Sol Jo 836, [1977] 1 EGLR 86, 242 Estates Gazette 39, 241
    Estates Gazette 911, CA   439
Bermuda International Securities Ltd v KPMG (a firm) [2001] EWCA Civ 269, (2001) 145
    Sol Jo LB 70, [2001] All ER (D) 337 (Feb), [2001] 3 CPLR 252   679
Bernard v Josephs [1982] Ch 391, [1982] 3 All ER 162, [1982] 2 WLR 1052, 4 FLR 178, 126
    Sol Jo 361, CA 351, 355, 413, 415, 416, 421, 422, 424
Bernard's Settlement, Re, Bernard v Jones [1916] 1 Ch 552, 85 LJ Ch 414, 60 Sol Jo 458, 114
    LT 654   372
Bernhardt v Galsworthy [1929] 1 Ch 549, 98 LJ Ch 284, 140 LT 685.   726
Berry, Re, Lloyds Bank Ltd v Berry [1962] Ch 97, [1961] 1 All ER 529, [1961] 1 WLR 329,
    105 Sol Jo 256   . . . .   549, 553, 554, 555, 560
Berry v Geen [1938] AC 575, 159 LT 122, sub nom Re Blake, Berry v Geen [1938] 2 All ER
    362, 107 LJ Ch 173, 82 Sol Jo 491, 54 TLR 703, HL 205, 502, 730, 732
Berry v Gibbons (1873) 8 Ch App 747, 38 JP 4, 42 LJ Ch 89, 21 WR 754, 29 LT 88   .   726, 727
Berry v Usher (1805) 11 Ves 87.   158
Berry's Settlement, Re, Birkenhead v Smith [1966] 3 All ER 431n, [1966] 1 WLR 1515, 110
    Sol Jo 772   508
Berton, Re, Vandyk v Berton [1939] Ch 200, [1938] 4 All ER 286, 108 LJ Ch 139, 82 Sol Jo
    890, 159 LT 566, 55 TLR 40   552
Berwick-on-Tweed Corpn v Murray (1857) 7 De GM & G 497, 26 LJ Ch 201, 109 RR 218, 5
    WR 208, sub nom Berwick Corpn v Murray, Berwick Corpn v Dobie 3 Jur NS 1, 847, 28
    LTOS 277   870
Bester v Perpetual Trustee Co Ltd [1970] 3 NSWLR 30. . . . .   282, 285, 286
Beswick v Beswick [1968] AC 58, [1967] 2 All ER 1197, [1967] 3 WLR 932, 111 Sol Jo 540,
    HL 10, 38, 168, 169, 170, 171, 172, 178
Bethel, Re (1971) 17 DLR (3d) 652, [1971] 2 OR 316; affd sub nom Jones v Executive
    Officers of T Eaton Co Ltd (1973) 35 DLR (3d) 97   84
Bethell v Abraham (1873) LR 17 Eq 24, 43 LJ Ch 180, 22 WR 179, [1861-73] All ER Rep 811,
    29 LT 715; affd (1874) 3 Ch D 590n, 22 WR 745, 31 LT 112.   727
Betts, Re, Maclean v Betts (1897) 41 Sol Jo 209; affd (1899) 48 WR 73, CA   461
Betty, Re, Betty v A-G [1899] 1 Ch 821, 68 LJ Ch 435, 80 LT 675 . . . . .   564, 568, 569, 572

Beulah Park Estate, Re, Sargood's Claim (1872) LR 15 Eq 43 . . . . 810, 818

Bevan v Webb [1905] 1 Ch 620, 74 LJ Ch 300, 53 WR 651, 93 LT 298 . . . . 383, 384, 385

Beverly, Re, Watson v Watson [1901] 1 Ch 681, 70 LJ Ch 295, 49 WR 343, 45 Sol Jo 259, 84 LT 296, 17 TLR 228 544

Beyleveld & Patterson (2002) 118 LQR 623 219

Bickerton's Settlement, Re, Shaw v Bickerton [1942] Ch 84, [1942] 1 All ER 217, 111 LJ Ch 132, 85 Sol Jo 481, 166 LT 38 376

Biddencare Ltd, Re [1994] 2 BCLC 160, [1993] BCC 757 843

Biddulph, Re, ex p Norris (1869) 4 Ch App 280, 38 LJ Bcy 5, 17 WR 452, 19 LT 755 . . 877

Biddulph v Williams (1875) 1 Ch D 203. 330

Bigg v Queensland Trustees Ltd [1990] 2 Qd R 11 428

Bigger, Re [1977] Fam 203, [1977] 2 All ER 644, [1977] 2 WLR 773, 121 Sol Jo 172 . . 797

Bignold's Settlement Trusts, Re (1872) 7 Ch App 223, 41 LJ Ch 235, 20 WR 345, 26 LT 176. . . . . .744, 753, 754, 766

Bill v Cureton (1835) 2 My & K 503, 4 LJ Ch 98, 39 RR 258, [1835-42] All ER Rep 317 . 141

Billson v Crofts (1873) LR 15 Eq 314, 37 JP 565, 42 LJ Ch 531, 21 WR 504 210

Bindley v Mulloney (1869) LR 7 Eq 343, 17 WR 510, 20 LT 263 218

Bingham v Lord Clanmorris (1828) 2 Mol 253 449

Binions v Evans [1972] Ch 359, [1972] 2 All ER 70, [1972] 2 WLR 729, 23 P & CR 192, 116 Sol Jo 122, 222 Estates Gazette 2147, CA 410

Binney v Ince Hall Coal and Cannel Co (1866) 35 LJ Ch 363, 14 LT 392 645

Birch v Blagrave (1755) Amb 264 . . . . 343, 361

Birch v Curtis [2002] WTLR 965 429

Birch v Treasury Solicitor [1951] Ch 298, [1950] 2 All ER 1198, 94 Sol Jo 838, [1951] 1 TLR 225, CA 150

Birchall, Re, Birchall v Ashton (1889) 40 Ch D 436, 37 WR 387, 60 LT 369, CA . . 245, 449, 453, 758, 761

Bird, Re, Re Evans, Dodd v Evans [1901] 1 Ch 916, 70 LJ Ch 514, 49 WR 599, 45 Sol Jo 327, 84 LT 294 . . . . 563, 982

Bird v Harris (1870) LR 9 Eq 204, 39 LJ Ch 226, 18 WR 374, 23 LT 213 137

Bird v Maybury (1864) 33 Beav 351, 140 RR 166 138

Birks v Micklethwaite (1864) 33 Beav 409, 33 LJ Ch 510, 10 Jur NS 302, 140 RR 196, 12 WR 505, 10 LT 85; on appeal (1864) 34 LJ Ch 362, 13 LT 31 940

Birmingham, Re, Savage v Stannard [1959] Ch 523, [1958] 2 All ER 397, [1958] 3 WLR 10, 102 Sol Jo 454 . . . . 439, 441

Birmingham v Renfrew (1937) 57 CLR 666, 43 ALR 520, [1937] VLR 327, 11 ALJ 188, HC of A 82, 266, 427, 428, 431

Birmingham Midshires Mortgage Services Ltd v Sabherwal (1999) 80 P & CR 256, CA . . 254, 326, 354, 413, 423, 426, 977

Biron v Mount (1857) 24 Beav 642, 27 LJ Ch 191, 4 Jur NS 43, 30 LTOS 344 142

Birse Construction Ltd v Haiste Ltd [1996] 2 All ER 1, [1996] 1 WLR 675, 47 Con LR 162, [1996] 02 LS Gaz R 29, 76 BLR 26, 140 Sol Jo LB 25, CA. 942

Birt v Burt (1877) 11 Ch D 773n, 36 LT 943 . . . . '. . 883

Biscoe, Re, Biscoe v Biscoe [1914] WN 302, 111 LT 902 307

Bishop, Re, National Provincial Bank Ltd v Bishop [1965] Ch 450, [1965] 1 All ER 249, [1965] 2 WLR 188, 109 Sol Jo 107 . . . . 360, 361

Bishop v Bonham [1988] 1 WLR 742, [1988] BCLC 656, 4 BCC 347, 132 Sol Jo 933, CA . 702

Bishopsgate Investment Management Ltd (in liquidation) v Homan [1995] Ch 211, [1995] 1 All ER 347, [1994] 3 WLR 1270, [1994] BCC 868, [1994] 36 LS Gaz R 37, 138 Sol Jo LB 176, CA. 885, 886, 899, 902

Bishopsgate Investment Management Ltd (in provisional liquidation) v Maxwell [1993] Ch 1, [1992] 2 All ER 856, [1992] 2 WLR 991, [1992] BCLC 475, [1992] BCC 222, [1992] 18 LS Gaz R 35, 136 Sol Jo LB 69, CA 685, 881, 897

Biss, Re, Biss v Biss [1903] 2 Ch 40, 72 LJ Ch 473, 51 WR 504, [1900-3] All ER Rep 406, 47 Sol Jo 383, 88 LT 403, CA 22, 382, 385

Black v Black's Trustees 1950 SLT (Notes) 32, OH 1024

Black v S Freeman & Co (1910) 12 CLR 105, 17 ALR 541, HC of A 897

Blackburn v Stables (1814) 13 RR 120, 2 Ves & B 367 304

Blacklocks v JB Developments (Godalming) Ltd [1982] Ch 183, [1981] 3 All ER 392, [1981] 3 WLR 554, 43 P & CR 27, 125 Sol Jo 356 . . . . 50, 991, 1003

Blackwell v Blackwell [1929] AC 318, sub nom Blackwell, Re, Blackwell v Blackwell 98 LJ Ch 251, [1929] All ER Rep 71, 73 Sol Jo 92, 140 LT 444, 45 TLR 208, HL . . 258, 259, 262, 263, 265

Blackwell's Settlement Trust, Re, Blackwell v Blackwell [1953] Ch 218, [1953] 1 All ER 103,
    [1953] 2 WLR 94, 46 R & IT 64, 97 Sol Jo 29, CA 500, 524
Blackwood v Borrowes (1843) 65 RR 729, 4 I Eq R 609, 2 Con & Law 459, 4 Dr & War 441 878
Blagrave's Settled Estates, Re [1903] 1 Ch 560, 72 LJ Ch 317, 51 WR 437, [1900-3] All ER
    Rep 319, 47 Sol Jo 334, 88 LT 253, 19 TLR 280, CA 573
Blaiberg, Re, Blaiberg and Public Trustee v De Andia Yrarrazaval and Blaiberg [1940] Ch
    385, [1940] 1 All ER 632, 109 LJ Ch 166, 84 Sol Jo 287, 162 LT 418, 56 TLR 487. . 102
Blair v Duncan [1902] AC 37, 71 LJPC 22, 50 WR 369, 86 LT 157, 18 TLR 194, HL . . . 105
Blair v Vallely & Blair [2000] WTLR 615 667
Blake, Re [1887] WN 173, CA 269, 754, 755
Blake, Re [1955] IR 89 231
Blake, Re, Blake v Power (1889) 37 WR 441, 60 LT 663. . . . . 277, 343
Blake, Re, Gawthorne v Blake [1917] 1 Ch 18, 86 LJ Ch 160, 61 Sol Jo 71, 115 LT 663 . 440,
                                                                                            441
Blake, Re, Jones v Blake (1885) 29 Ch D 913, 54 LJ Ch 880, 33 WR 886, 53 LT 302, CA . 846
Blake v Blake (1786) 3 P Wms 10n, 1 RR 35, 1 Cox Eq Cas 266 383
Blakely Ordnance Co, Re, ex p New Zealand Banking Corpn (1867) 3 Ch App 154, 37 LJ Ch
    418, 16 WR 533, 18 LT 132 983
Bland's Settlement, Re, Bland v Perkin [1905] 1 Ch 4, 74 LJ Ch 28, 91 LT 681 313
Blandy Jenkins' Estate, Re, Jenkins v Walker [1917] 1 Ch 46, 86 LJ Ch 76, 115 LT 483. . 58
Blathwayt v Baron Cawley [1976] AC 397, [1975] 3 All ER 625, [1975] 3 WLR 684, 119 Sol Jo
    795, HL. 100, 101, 103, 220, 222, 224
Blausten v IRC [1972] Ch 256, [1972] 1 All ER 41, [1972] 2 WLR 376, 47 TC 542, [1971] TR
    363, 115 Sol Jo 871, CA. 91, 94, 132
Bleckly, Re, Bleckly v Bleckly [1951] Ch 740, [1951] 1 All ER 1064, 95 Sol Jo 335, [1951] 1
    TLR 902, CA. 194
Blodwell v Edwards. See Anon
Bloye's Trust, Re (1849) 19 LJ Ch 89, 2 H & Tw 140, 14 Jur 49, 1 Mac & G 488, [1843-60] All
    ER Rep 1092, 15 LTOS 157; affd sub nom Lewis v Hillman (1852) 3 HL Cas 607, 19
    LTOS 329 665
Blue Resoucres Ltd v Law Society of Upper Canada (1995) 120 DLR (4th) 751 59
Blundell, Re, Blundell v Blundell (1888) 40 Ch D 370, 57 LJ Ch 730, 36 WR 779, [1886-90]
    All ER Rep 837, 58 LT 933, 4 TLR 506 . . . . 877, 986
Blundell, Re, Blundell v Blundell (1890) 44 Ch D 1, 59 LJ Ch 269, 38 WR 707, 62 LT 620, CA 824
Blyth v Fladgate [1891] 1 Ch 337, 60 LJ Ch 66, 39 WR 422, 63 LT 546, 7 TLR 29. . 381, 877,
                                                                              941, 948, 952, 953
Blythe v Granville (1842) 13 Sim 190, 12 LJ Ch 82, 6 Jur 961, 60 RR 319 311
Boardman v Phipps. See Phipps v Boardman
Boddington v Lawton [1994] ICR 478 127
Bodmin (Lady) v Vandenbendy (1683) 1 Vern 179 983
Boe v Alexander (1987) 41 DLR (4th) 520 590
Bogg v Raper (1998) 1 ITELR 267. . . . . .282, 593, 594, 596
Boldero, Re, ex p Pease (1812) 1 Rose 232, 19 Ves 25 461
Boles and British Land Co's Contract, Re [1902] 1 Ch 244, 71 LJ Ch 130, 50 WR 185, 46 Sol
    Jo 123, 85 LT 607 . . . . 660, 662, 668
Bolkiah v KPMG (a firm) [1999] 2 AC 222, [1999] 1 All ER 517, [1999] 2 WLR 215, [1999] 1
    BCLC 1, [1999] NLJR 16, 143 Sol Jo LB 35, [1999] PNLR 220, HL 403, 406
Bolling v Hobday (1882) 31 WR 9 460
Bolton v Curre [1895] 1 Ch 544, 64 LJ Ch 164, 13 R 174, 43 WR 521, 71 LT 752 . . 948, 980
Bomore Road (No 9), Re [1906] 1 Ch 359, 75 LJ Ch 157, 13 Mans 69, 54 WR 312, 94 LT 403 774
Bond (Inspector of Taxes) v Pickford [1983] STC 517, 57 TC 301, CA 726, 803, 806,
                                                                              807, 808, 1040
Bond v Walford (1886) 32 Ch D 238, 55 LJ Ch 667, 54 LT 672, 2 TLR 469 274
Bond Worth Ltd, Re [1980] Ch 228, [1979] 3 All ER 919, [1979] 3 WLR 629, 123 Sol Jo 216   15
Bone v Cook (1824) M'Cle 168, 13 Price 332, 28 RR 697 938
Bone v Pollard (1857) 24 Beav 283, 116 RR 121 350
Bone v Stamp Duties Comr for State of New South Wales (1974) 132 CLR 38, 3 ALR 561, 48
    ALJR 310, 4 ATR 553 . . . . .157, 158, 159, 162
Booth, Re, Booth v Booth [1894] 2 Ch 282, 63 LJ Ch 560, 8 R 256, 42 WR 613 137
Booth, Re, Hattersley v Cowgill (1917) 86 LJ Ch 270, 116 LT 465 80
Booth v Booth (1838) 1 Beav 125, 8 LJ Ch 39, 2 Jur 938, 49 RR 304. . . . . 452, 645, 948
Booth v Ellard (Inspector of Taxes) [1980] 3 All ER 569, [1980] 1 WLR 1443, [1980] STC
    555, 53 TC 393, [1980] TR 203, 124 Sol Jo 465, CA 48, 59, 734

Borden (UK) Ltd v Scottish Timber Products Ltd [1981] Ch 25, [1979] 3 All ER 961, [1979] 3 WLR 672, [1980] 1 Lloyd's Rep 160, 123 Sol Jo 688, CA. 900
Borell v Dann (1843) 2 Hare 440 166
Borland's Trustee v Steel Bros & Co Ltd [1901] 1 Ch 279, 70 LJ Ch 51, 49 WR 120, 17 TLR 45 . . . . 401, 402
Borough Court Estate, Re [1932] 2 Ch 39, 101 LJ Ch 316, [1931] All ER Rep 56, 75 Sol Jo 830, 147 LT 476 572
Borwick, Re, Borwick v Borwick [1933] Ch 657, 102 LJ Ch 199, [1933] All ER Rep 737, 77 Sol Jo 197, 149 LT 116, 49 TLR 288 222
Boscawen v Bajwa [1995] 4 All ER 769, [1996] 1 WLR 328, 70 P & CR 391, [1995] 21 LS Gaz R 37, CA. 55, 327, 331, 408, 881, 895, 902, 968, 977, 983, 993, 996
Bostock v Floyer (1865) LR 1 Eq 26, 35 Beav 603, 35 LJ Ch 23, 11 Jur NS 962, 147 RR 316, 14 WR 120, 13 LT 489 625
Bostock's Settlement, Re, Norrish v Bostock [1921] 2 Ch 469, 91 LJ Ch 17, [1921] All ER Rep 125, 126 LT 145, 66 Sol Jo (WR) 7, CA 66, 300
Boston's (Lord) Will Trusts, Re, Inglis v Lord Boston [1956] Ch 395, [1956] 1 All ER 593, [1956] 2 WLR 700, 100 Sol Jo 209 . . . . 465, 573
Bosworth, Re, Martin v Lamb (1889) 58 LJ Ch 432 . . . . 672, 687
Bouch, Re, Sproule v Bouch (1885) 29 Ch D 635, CA; revsd sub nom Bouch v Sproule (1887) 12 App Cas 385, 56 LJ Ch 1037, 36 WR 193, [1886-90] All ER Rep 319, 57 LT 345, HL 530, 535
Boucherett, Re, Barne v Erskine [1908] 1 Ch 180, 77 LJ Ch 205, 52 Sol Jo 77, 98 LT 32 . 756
Boughton v Knight (1873) LR 3 P & D 64, 37 JP 598, 647, 42 LJP & M 25, 41, [1861-73] All ER Rep 40, 28 LT 562 269
Boulter, Re, Capital and Counties Bank v Boulter [1922] 1 Ch 75, 91 LJ Ch 250, [1921] All ER Rep 167, 126 LT 653, 66 Sol Jo (WR) 14 221
Boulting v Association of Cinematograph, Television and Allied Technicians [1963] 2 QB 606, [1963] 1 All ER 716, [1963] 2 WLR 529, 107 Sol Jo 133, CA 401, 404
Boulton's Settlement Trust, Re, Stewart v Boulton [1928] Ch 703, [1928] WN 157, 97 LJ Ch 243, 139 LT 288 211
Bourne, Re, Davey v Bourne [1906] 1 Ch 697, 75 LJ Ch 474, 94 LT 750, 22 TLR 417, CA 158
Bourne v Buckton (1851) 2 Sim NS 91, 21 LJ Ch 193, 19 LTOS 372 206
Bourne v Keane [1919] AC 815, 89 LJ Ch 17, [1918-19] All ER Rep 167, 63 Sol Jo 606, 121 LT 426, 35 TLR 560, HL 123
Bourne v Mole (1845) 8 Beav 177, 68 RR 59 906
Bourne's Settlement Trusts, Re, Bourne v Mackay [1946] 1 All ER 411, 115 LJ Ch 152, 90 Sol Jo 200, 174 LT 281, 62 TLR 269, CA 206
Boursot v Savage (1866) LR 2 Eq 134, 30 JP 484, 35 LJ Ch 627, 14 WR 565, 14 LT 299 . 983, 984, 990
Bouverie, Re, Bouverie v Marshall [1952] Ch 400, [1952] 1 All ER 408, 96 Sol Jo 90, [1952] 1 TLR 355 104
Bouygues Offshore SA v Caspain Shipping Co [1998] 2 Lloyd's Rep 461, CA 1059
Bowden, Re, Andrew v Cooper (1890) 45 Ch D 444, 59 LJ Ch 815, 39 WR 219 922
Bowden, Re, Hulbert v Bowden [1936] Ch 71, 105 LJ Ch 23, [1935] All ER Rep 933, 79 Sol Jo 625, 154 LT 157 . . . . .153, 164, 165, 730
Bowen v Phillips [1897] 1 Ch 174, 66 LJ Ch 165, 4 Mans 370, 45 WR 286, 41 Sol Jo 188, 75 LT 628 904
Bowen-Jones v Bowen-Jones [1986] 3 All ER 163, [1986] NLJ Rep 894 . . . . . . 788, 815
Bower v Smith (1871) LR 11 Eq 279, 40 LJ Ch 194, 19 WR 399, 24 LT 118 . . . . 308, 316
Bower Williams, Re, ex p Trustee [1927] 1 Ch 441, 96 LJ Ch 136, [1927] B & CR 21, [1927] All ER Rep 275, 71 Sol Jo 122, 136 LT 752, 43 TLR 225, CA. 312
Bowes, Re, Earl Strathmore v Vane [1896] 1 Ch 507, 65 LJ Ch 298, 44 WR 441, 74 LT 16 113, 118, 731
Bowlby, Re, Bowlby v Bowlby [1904] 2 Ch 685, 73 LJ Ch 810, 53 WR 270, 48 Sol Jo 698, 91 LT 573, CA 714
Bowles v Stewart (1803) 1 Sch & Lef 209 932
Box v Barclays Bank plc [1998] 18 LS Gaz R 33, [1998] Lloyd's Rep Bank 185 . . . 897, 968
Boyce v Boyce (1849) 16 Sim 476, 80 RR 123 81
Boyes, Re, Boyes v Carritt (1884) 26 Ch D 531, 53 LJ Ch 654, 32 WR 630, 50 LT 581 . . . . .233, 257, 260, 261, 332
Brace, Re, Gurton v Clements [1954] 2 All ER 354, [1954] 1 WLR 955, 98 Sol Jo 456 .36, 101, 137, 138
Brackenbury v Brackenbury (1820) 2 Jac & W 391, 22 RR 180 344

Bradley, Re, ex p Walton (1910) 54 Sol Jo 377 580
Bradley v Fox Ill App 2d 106, 129 NE 2d 699 (1955) 434
Bradley v Riches (1878) 9 Ch D 189, 47 LJ Ch 811, 26 WR 910, 38 LT 810 990
Bradshaw v University College of Wales, Aberystwyth [1987] 3 All ER 200, [1988] 1 WLR 190,
    132 Sol Jo 51, [1988] LS Gaz R 34 38
Bradstock Pension Scheme Trustees Ltd v Bradstock Group plc [2002] EWHC 1461 (Ch),
    [2002] PLR 327, [2002] All ER (D) 109 (Jun), Times, 10 July 579, 708
Bradwell, Re, Goode v Board of Trustees for Methodist Church Purposes [1952] Ch 575,
    [1952] 2 All ER 286, 96 Sol Jo 462, [1952] 2 TLR 96 . . . . 209, 230
Bradwell v Catchpole (1700) 19 RR 180, 3 Swan 78n 938
Brady v Brady [1920] 1 IR 170, CA 383
Braithwaite v A-G [1909] 1 Ch 510, 79 JP 209, 78 LJ Ch 314, 100 LT 599, 25 TLR 333 . . 209
Branco v Veira (1995) 9 ETR (2d) 49 1038
Brandlyn v Ord (1738) 1 Atk 571, 1 West 512 1000
Brandon, Re, Samuels v Brandon (1932) 49 TLR 48 567
Brandon v Robinson (1811) 11 RR 226, 1 Rose 197, 18 Ves 429, [1803-13] All ER Rep
    290 . . . . .190, 210, 214, 738
Brandt's (William) Sons & Co v Dunlop Rubber Co Ltd [1905] AC 454, 74 LJKB 898, 11
    Com Cas 1, [1904-7] All ER Rep 345, 93 LT 495, 21 TLR 710, HL 151, 152
Bransbury's Will Trusts, Re, Grece v Bransbury [1954] 1 All ER 605, [1954] 1 WLR 496, 98
    Sol Jo 179 718
Brassard v Smith [1925] AC 371, 94 LJPC 81, 132 LT 647, 41 TLR 203 1029
Brassey's Settlement, Re, Barclays Bank Ltd v Brassey [1955] 1 All ER 577, [1955] 1 WLR
    192, 99 Sol Jo 149 526
Bray v Hammersley (1830) 3 Sim 513; affd sub nom Bray v Bree (1834) 8 Bli NS 568, 2 Cl &
    Fin 453, HL 198
Bray v West (1838) 9 Sim 429, 47 RR 278 . . . . 449, 450
Brazier v Hudson (1836) 8 Sim 67, sub nom Brasier v Hudson 5 LJ Ch 296 159
Breadner v Granville-Grossman [2001] Ch 523, [2000] 4 All ER 705, [2001] 2 WLR 593,
    [2000] WTLR 829 . . . . 690, 698, 875
Breadner v Granville-Grossman (Costs) [2001] WTLR 377 . . . . .837, 838, 841, 845
Brennan v Morphett (1908) 6 CLR 22 264
Brewer v Swirles (1854) 23 LJ Ch 542, 2 Eq Rep 493, 18 Jur 1069, 97 RR 180, 2 Sm & G 219, 2
    WR 339, 24 LTOS 57 931
Brewer v Westminster Bank Ltd [1952] 2 All ER 650, 96 Sol Jo 531, [1952] 2 TLR 568; on
    appeal (1953) Times, 5 February, CA 648
Brice v Stokes (1805) 8 RR 164, 11 Ves 319, 2 White & Tud LC 631, [1803-19] All ER Rep
    401 . . . . .576, 647, 931, 940
Brickenden v London Loan & Savings Co [1934] 3 DLR 465, PC 660
Bridgen, Re, Chaytor v Edwin [1938] Ch 205, [1937] 4 All ER 342, 107 LJ Ch 124, 81 Sol Jo
    922, 158 LT 238, 54 TLR 100 212
Bridges v Mees [1957] Ch 475, [1957] 2 All ER 577, [1957] 3 WLR 215, 101 Sol Jo 555, 169
    Estates Gazette 817 . . . . 438, 459
Brier, Re, Brier v Evison (1884) 26 Ch D 238, 33 WR 20, 51 LT 133, CA . . . 634, 939, 940
Brierley, Re, Brierley v Brierley (1894) 12 R 55, 43 WR 36, 38 Sol Jo 647, CA 131
Briggs v Hartley (1850) 19 LJ Ch 416, 14 Jur 683, 87 RR 514, 15 LTOS 273 82
Briggs v IRC (1932) 17 TC 11 539
Briggs v Massey (1882) 51 LJ Ch 447, 30 WR 325, 46 LT 354, CA 864
Briggs v Parsloe [1937] 3 All ER 831, 81 Sol Jo 702 771
Briggs v Penny (1851) 16 Jur 93, 3 Mac & G 546, 87 RR 192, 18 LTOS 101 233
Bright v Legerton (1861) 2 De GF & J 606, 30 LJ Ch 338, 7 Jur NS 559, 9 WR 239, 3 LT 713,
    CA 930
Brinks Ltd v Abu-Saleh (No 3) [1996] CLC 133 . . . . 957, 964
Brinnand v Ewens (1987) 19 HLR 415, [1987] 2 EGLR 67, 284 Estates Gazette 1052, CA . 250
Brisbane City Council v A-G for Queensland [1979] AC 411, [1978] 3 All ER 30, [1978] 3
    WLR 299, 122 Sol Jo 506, PC 930
Bristol and West Building Society v Mothew (t/a Stapley & Co) [1998] Ch 1, [1996] 4 All ER
    698, [1997] 2 WLR 436, [1996] NLJR 1273, 140 Sol Jo LB 206, [1997] PNLR 11, sub
    nom Mothew v Bristol & West Building Society 75 P & CR 241, CA 5, 22, 37, 387,
                                    436, 618, 659, 701, 852, 857, 858, 863, 866
Bristol Athenæum, Re (1889) 43 Ch D 236, 59 LJ Ch 116, 1 Meg 452, 38 WR 396, 61 LT 795,
    6 TLR 83 127

Bristol's Settled Estates, Re, Bristol v Jermyn [1964] 3 All ER 939, [1965] 1 WLR 469, 109 Sol Jo 236. . . . . 501, 503, 511, 783
British & Commonwealth Holdings plc (No 3), Re [1992] 1 WLR 672, [1992] BCLC 322, [1992] BCC 58 43
British Airways Pension Schemes [2000] Pens LR 311 . . . . 843, 844
British America Elevator Co v Bank of British North America [1919] AC 658, 88 LJPC 118, 121 LT 100, PC 970, 972, 973
British Coal Corpn v British Coal Staff Superannuation Scheme Trustees Ltd [1995] 1 All ER 912, [1994] ICR 537. 499
British Power Traction and Lighting Co Ltd, Re, Halifax Joint Stock Banking Co Ltd v British Power Traction and Lighting Co Ltd [1910] 2 Ch 470, 79 LJ Ch 666, 54 Sol Jo 749, 103 LT 451. 824
British Red Cross Balkan Fund, Re, British Red Cross Society v Johnson [1914] 2 Ch 419, 84 LJ Ch 79, [1914-15] All ER Rep 459, 58 Sol Jo 755, 111 LT 1069, 30 TLR 662 . 336, 370
British School of Egyptian Archaeology, Re, Murray v Public Trustee [1954] 1 All ER 887, [1954] 1 WLR 546, 98 Sol Jo 216 341
British South Africa Co v Companhia de Moçambique [1893] AC 602, 63 LJQB 70, 6 R 1, [1891-4] All ER Rep 640, 37 Sol Jo 756, 69 LT 604, 10 TLR 7, HL 1059
British Transport Commission v Gourley [1956] AC 185, [1955] 3 All ER 796, [1956] 2 WLR 41, [1955] 2 Lloyd's Rep 475, 34 ATC 305, 49 R & IT 11, [1955] TR 303, 100 Sol Jo 12, HL. 860
Brittlebank v Goodwin (1868) LR 5 Eq 545, 37 LJ Ch 377, 16 WR 696 674
Broadhurst v Balguy (1841) 1 Y & C Ch Cas 16, 57 RR 212 . . . . 931, 934
Broadwood's Settlements, Re, Broadwood v Broadwood [1908] 1 Ch 115, 77 LJ Ch 18, 98 LT 217. 562
Brockbank, Re, Ward v Bates [1948] Ch 206, [1948] 1 All ER 287, [1948] LJR 952, 92 Sol Jo 141. . . . . 59, 498, 686, 734, 736, 746, 759
Brocklehurst's Estate, Re [1978] Ch 14, [1977] 3 WLR 696, 121 Sol Jo 633, sub nom Re Brocklehurst, Hall v Roberts [1978] 1 All ER 767, CA 282
Brogden, Re, Billing v Brogden (1888) 38 Ch D 546, 37 WR 84, [1886-90] All ER Rep 927, 59 LT 650, 4 TLR 521, CA. 578
Bromley v Tryon. See Wilson's Will Trusts, Re, Tyron v Bromley Wilson
Bromson, Re (1958) 14 DLR (2d) 51, [1958] OR 367, [1958] OWN 220 . . . . . 530, 590
Brook's Settlement, Re, Brook v Brook [1968] 3 All ER 416, [1968] 1 WLR 1661, 112 Sol Jo 845. . . . . 518, 520
Brooke, Re, Brooke v Brooke [1894] 2 Ch 600, 64 LJ Ch 21, 8 R 444, 71 LT 398, [1891-4] All ER Rep Ext 1294 814
Brooke v Pearson (1859) 27 Beav 181, 5 Jur NS 781, 122 RR 364, 7 WR 638, 34 LTOS 20 209
Brooke Bond & Co Ltd's Trust Deed, Re, Brooke v Brooke Bond & Co Ltd [1963] Ch 357, [1963] 1 All ER 454, [1963] 2 WLR 320, 107 Sol Jo 94 . . . . 665, 668, 799
Brooks, Re, Coles v Davis (1897) 76 LT 771 544
Brooks v Brooks [1996] AC 375, [1995] 3 All ER 257, [1995] 3 WLR 141, [1995] 3 FCR 214, [1995] 2 FLR 13, [1995] Fam Law 545, [1995] 31 LS Gaz R 34, [1995] NLJR 995, 139 Sol Jo LB 165, HL 317
Brooks v Keith (1861) 1 Drew & Sm 462, 7 Jur NS 482, 127 RR 189, 9 WR 565, 4 LT 541. 313
Brooks' Settlement Trusts, Re, Lloyds Bank Ltd v Tillard [1939] Ch 993, [1939] 3 All ER 920, 109 LJ Ch 28, 83 Sol Jo 545, 161 LT 158, 55 TLR 914 . . . . 132, 153, 164, 166, 175, 180, 183, 185, 308, 502, 610
Broome v Monck (1805) 10 Ves 597, [1803-13] All ER Rep 631 440
Broomhead (J W) (Vic) Pty Ltd (in liquidation) v J W Broomhead Pty Ltd [1985] VR 891. . . . . 450, 452, 811, 821, 823
Brophy v Bellamy (1873) 8 Ch App 798, 43 LJ Ch 183, 29 LT 380 727
Brotherton v IRC [1978] 2 All ER 267, [1978] 1 WLR 610, [1978] STC 201, 52 TC 137, [1977] TR 317, 122 Sol Jo 164, L(TC) 2667, CA 715
Brougham (Lord) v Lord Poulett (1855) 19 Beav 119, 24 LJ Ch 233, 1 Jur NS 151, 105 RR 85, 24 LTOS 248 564
Brougham and Vaux's (Lord) Settled Estates, Re [1954] Ch 24, [1953] 2 All ER 655, [1953] 3 WLR 465, 97 Sol Jo 540 573
Browell v Reed (1842) 1 Hare 434, 11 LJ Ch 272, 6 Jur 530, 58 RR 130 450
Brown, Re, District Bank Ltd v Brown [1954] Ch 39, [1953] 2 All ER 1342, [1953] 3 WLR 877, 97 Sol Jo 796 . . . . 193, 209, 214, 215, 738
Brown, Re, Ingall v Brown [1904] 1 Ch 120, 73 LJ Ch 130, 52 WR 173, 90 LT 220 . . . 221
Brown, Re, Wace v Smith [1918] WN 118, 62 Sol Jo 487 . . . . 597, 652

Brown v Bennett [1998] 2 BCLC 97, [1999] BCC 91; affd [1999] 1 BCLC 649, [1999] BCC
    525, CA 957, 959, 968, 969, 970
Brown v Bennett (No 2) (18 October 2000, unreported) 958
Brown v Bennett [2002] 2 All ER 273, [2002] 1 WLR 713, [2002] 02 LS Gaz R 27, [2001]
    NLJR 1733, 145 Sol Jo LB 267, [2001] All ER (D) 247 (Nov) 955
Brown v Brown (1868) LR 7 Eq 185, 38 LJ Ch 153, 17 WR 98, 19 LT 594 281
Brown v Brown (1993) 31 NSWLR 582 . . . . 350, 362, 365
Brown v Burdett (1882) 21 Ch D 667, 52 LJ Ch 52, 47 LT 94 . . . . 123, 218
Brown v Casamajor (1799) 4 Ves 498 138
Brown v GIO Insurance Ltd [1998] 09 LS Gaz R 29, [1998] Lloyd's Rep IR 201, CA   89, 215
Brown v Gellatly (1867) 2 Ch App 751, 15 WR 1188, 17 LT 131, [1861-73] All ER Rep Ext
    2080 . . . . .550, 552, 554, 557, 611
Brown v Gould [1972] Ch 53, [1971] 2 All ER 1505, [1971] 3 WLR 334, 22 P & CR 871, 115
    Sol Jo 406 . . . . 80, 84, 90, 96
Brown v Higgs (1799) 4 RR 323, 4 Ves 708; re-heard (1800) 5 Ves 495; affd (1803) 8 Ves 561;
    on appeal (1813) 18 Ves 192, HL 74
Brown v How (1740) Barn Ch 354 730
Brown v IRC [1965] AC 244, [1964] 3 All ER 119, [1964] 3 WLR 511, 42 TC 42, 43 ATC 244,
    [1964] TR 269, 108 Sol Jo 636, 192 Estates Gazette 457, 1964 SC (HL) 180, 1964 SLT
    302 . . . . 22, 386, 401, 659
Brown v Sansome (1825) M'Cle & Yo 427, 29 RR 813 870
Brown and Sibly's Contract, Re (1876) 3 Ch D 156, 24 WR 782, 35 LT 305 . . . . 198, 229
Browne, Re, Ward v Lawler [1944] IR 90 259
Browne v Browne [1989] 1 FLR 291, [1989] Fam Law 147, CA 32, 63
Browne v Cross (1851) 14 Beav 105, 92 RR 48 934
Browne v Lord Kenyon (1818) 3 Madd 410, 18 RR 261 374
Browne's Will, Re (1859) 27 Beav 324, 122 RR 142 732
Brumridge v Brumridge (1858) 27 Beav 5, 122 RR 297 938
Brunker v Perpetual Trustee Co (1937) 57 CLR 555 . . . . 151, 155
Brunning, Re, Gammon v Dale [1909] 1 Ch 276, 78 LJ Ch 75, 99 LT 918 566
Bruty v Edmundson (1915) 85 LJ Ch 568, 113 LT 1197 284
Bryant, Re, Bryant v Hickley [1894] 1 Ch 324, 63 LJ Ch 197, 8 R 32, 42 WR 183, 38 Sol Jo 79,
    70 LT 301 711
Bryant, Isard & Co, Re [1925] 4 DLR 157, 57 OLR 471, 5 CBR 799 22
Brydges v Brydges (1796) 3 Ves 120, [1775-1802] All ER Rep 530 299
Buchanan v Hamilton (1801) 5 Ves 722 . . . . 743, 744
Buchanan-Wollaston's Conveyance, Re, Curtis v Buchanan-Wollaston [1939] Ch 738, [1939]
    2 All ER 302, 108 LJ Ch 281, 83 Sol Jo 376, 160 LT 399, 55 TLR 604, CA   469, 477, 479
Buckeridge v Glasse (1841) Cr & Ph 126, 10 LJ Ch 134, 5 Jur 163, 54 RR 241 . . . 451, 931
Buckingham v Francis [1986] 2 All ER 738, [1986] BCLC 353, 2 BCC 98, 984, [1986] PCC
    347 871
Buckinghamshire Constabulary Widows' and Orphans' Fund Friendly Society, Re,
    Thompson v Holdsworth [1978] 2 All ER 571, [1978] 1 WLR 641, 122 Sol Jo 317. . 340
Buckinghamshire Constabulary Widows' and Orphans' Fund Friendly Society, Re,
    Thompson v Holdsworth (No 2) [1979] 1 All ER 623, [1979] 1 WLR 936, 122 Sol Jo
    557 . . . . 118, 124, 127, 332, 337, 338, 339, 340, 370
Buckinghamshire's (Earl) Settlements Trusts, Re, Cole v Hope-Morley (1977) Times, 29
    March 721
Buckton, Re, Buckton v Buckton [1907] 2 Ch 406, 76 LJ Ch 584, 97 LT 332, 23 TLR 692   834,
    840, 841
Buckton's Settlement Trusts, Re, Public Trustee v Midland Bank Executor and Trustee Co
    Ltd [1964] Ch 497, [1964] 2 All ER 487, [1964] 2 WLR 1318, 108 Sol Jo 378 . . . 226
Bulkeley v Stephens [1896] 2 Ch 241, 65 LJ Ch 597, 44 WR 490, [1895-9] All ER Rep 196, 40
    Sol Jo 458, 74 LT 409, 12 TLR 350 . . . . 540, 541
Bulkley v Wilford (1834) 8 Bli NS 111, 2 Cl & Fin 102, HL 410, 858
Bull v Bull [1955] 1 QB 234, [1955] 1 All ER 253, [1955] 2 WLR 78, 99 Sol Jo 60, CA . . 351,
    737
Bullas v Public Trustee [1981] 1 NSWLR 641 735
Bullen v Wisconsin 240 US 625 (1916) .1031
Bullock, Re, Good v Lickorish (1891) 60 LJ Ch 341, 39 WR 472, 64 LT 736, 7 TLR 402 . 213,
    738
Bullock v Bullock (1886) 56 LJ Ch 221, 55 LT 703, 3 TLR 131 576
Bullock v Downes. See Downes v Bullock

Bullock v Lloyds Bank Ltd [1955] Ch 317, [1954] 3 All ER 726, [1955] 2 WLR 1, 99 Sol Jo
28 . . . . 274, 277, 282, 283, 284, 285, 286, 819, 937
Bullock's Will Trusts, Re, Bullock v Bullock [1915] 1 Ch 493, 84 LJ Ch 463, 59 Sol Jo 441,
112 LT 1119 229
Bulmer, Re, ex p Greaves [1937] Ch 499, [1937] 1 All ER 323, 106 LJ Ch 268, [1936-1937] B
& CR 196, 81 Sol Jo 117, 156 LT 178, 53 TLR 303, CA 22
Bulwer v Astley (1844) 1 Ph 422, 13 LJ Ch 329, 8 Jur 523, 65 RR 416 565
Burden v Burden (1813) 12 RR 210, 1 Ves & B 170, [1803-13] All ER Rep 573 653
Burdick v Garrick (1870) 5 Ch App 233, 39 LJ Ch 369, 18 WR 387 . . . . . . 8, 393, 870
Burger King Corpn v Hungry Jack's Pty Ltd (21 June 2001, unreported), NSWCA . . . 961
Burgess v Rawnsley [1975] Ch 429, [1975] 3 All ER 142, [1975] 3 WLR 99, 30 P & CR 221,
119 Sol Jo 406, 235 Estates Gazette 371, CA 274, 333
Burgess v Wheate (1759) 1 Eden 177, 1 Wm Bl 123 189
Burke, Re, Burke v Burke [1908] 2 Ch 248, 77 LJ Ch 597, 99 LT 86 600
Burke v Burke [1974] 2 All ER 944, [1974] 1 WLR 1063, 118 Sol Jo 98, CA 481
Burland v Earle [1902] AC 83, 71 LJPC 1, 9 Mans 17, 50 WR 241, 85 LT 553, 18 TLR 41,
PC 23
Burley, Re, Alexander v Burley [1910] 1 Ch 215, 79 LJ Ch 182, 101 LT 805, 26 TLR 127 . 134,
136
Burney v Macdonald (1845) 15 Sim 6, 9 Jur 588, 6 LTOS 1 263
Burney's Settlement Trusts, Re [1961] 1 All ER 856, [1961] 1 WLR 545, 105 Sol Jo 207 . 510
Burns v Burns [1984] Ch 317, [1984] 1 All ER 244, [1984] 2 WLR 582, [1984] FLR 216,
[1984] Fam Law 24, 128 Sol Jo 173, [1984] LS Gaz R 893, CA . . 56, 412, 413, 414, 415,
417, 421, 422, 424
Burns v Turnbull 294 NY 889 (1945) 59
Burrell v Burrell's Trustees 1915 52 SLR 312, 1915 SC 333 . . . . 283, 664
Burrough v Philcox (1840) 5 My & Cr 72, 5 Jur 453, 48 RR 236 . . . . 26, 74, 130
Burroughes v Abbott [1922] 1 Ch 86, 91 LJ Ch 157, [1921] All ER Rep 709, 66 Sol Jo 141,
126 LT 354, 38 TLR 167 533
Burroughs-Fowler, Re, Trustee of the Property of Burroughs-Fowler (a bankrupt) v Bur-
roughs-Fowler [1916] 2 Ch 251, 85 LJ Ch 550, [1916] HBR 108, 60 Sol Jo 538, 114 LT
1204, 32 TLR 493 209
Burrowes v Lock (1805) 8 RR 33, 856, 10 Ves 470, 1 White & Tud LC 446, [1803-13] All ER
Rep 477 629
Burrows v Walls (1855) 5 De GM & G 233, 3 Eq Rep 960, 104 RR 95, 3 WR 327, 25 LTOS
18 . . . . 671, 931, 935
Burrows and Burrows v Sharpe [1991] Fam Law 67, 23 HLR 82, CA 248, 249
Burton, Re (1994) 126 ALR 557 32
Burton's Settlement Trusts, Re, Public Trustee v Montefiore [1955] Ch 60, [1954] 3 All ER
231, [1954] 3 WLR 574, 98 Sol Jo 734; revsd [1955] Ch 348, [1955] 1 All ER 433, [1955]
2 WLR 452, 99 Sol Jo 148, CA 374, 375
Burton's Settlements, Re, Scott v National Provincial Bank Ltd [1955] Ch 82, [1954] 3 All
ER 193, [1954] 3 WLR 581, 98 Sol Jo 734 . . . . 89, 101, 153, 175, 185, 631
Busfield, Re (20 February 1999, unreported) 559
Busk v Aldam (1874) LR 19 Eq 16, 44 LJ Ch 119, 23 WR 21, 31 LT 370 . . . . . 803, 805
Butler, Re, Beatty v Vance [1916] 1 IR 66 307
Butler v Butler (1877) 7 Ch D 116, 47 LJ Ch 77, 26 WR 85, 37 LT 518, CA . . 906, 941, 947
Butler v Carter (1868) LR 5 Eq 276, 37 LJ Ch 270, 16 WR 388, 18 TLR 11 944
Butler v Gray (1869) 5 Ch App 26, 39 LJ Ch 291, 18 WR 193, 25 LT 227 130
Butlin-Sanders v Butlin [1985] FLR 204, [1985] Fam Law 126 276
Butlin's Settlement Trusts, Re, Butlin v Butlin [1976] Ch 251, [1976] 2 All ER 483, [1976] 2
WLR 547, 119 Sol Jo 794 . . . . 166, 278, 644, 645, 697, 698
Butt v Kelson [1952] Ch 197, [1952] 1 TLR 214, sub nom Butt, Re, Butt v Kelson [1952] 1
All ER 167, CA 686, 736
Butterworth, Re, ex p Russell (1882) 19 Ch D 588, 51 LJ Ch 521, 30 WR 584, 46 LT 113, CA 293
Buttle v Saunders [1950] 2 All ER 193, [1950] WN 255, 94 Sol Jo 369, 66 (pt 1) TLR
1026 . . . . 580, 582, 614, 905
Buxton v Buxton (1835) 1 My & Cr 80 . . . . 578, 584
Buxton v Public Trustee (1962) 41 TC 235 107
Byrchall v Bradford (1822) 6 Madd 235 . . . . 861, 863
Byrne Austraia Pty Ltd (No 2), Re [1981] 2 NSWLR 364 462

C

C (a patient), Re [1991] 3 All ER 866, [1992] 1 FLR 51, [1991] Fam Law 521, 8 BMLR 1,
    [1991] NLJR 671 269
C v S [1999] 2 All ER 343, [1999] 1 WLR 1551, [1998] NLJR 1723, [1999] Lloyd's Rep Bank,
    CA 967
CA Pacific Finance Ltd, Re [2000] 1 BCLC 494 78
CCSD v ISPT Pty Ltd (1999) 2 ITELR 1 36
CIBC Mortgages plc v Pitt [1994] 1 AC 200, [1993] 4 All ER 433, [1993] 3 WLR 802, [1994] 1
    FCR 374, [1994] 1 FLR 17, [1994] Fam Law 79, 26 HLR 90, [1993] 46 LS Gaz R 37,
    [1993] NLJR 1514, HL 287
CL, Re [1969] 1 Ch 587, [1968] 1 All ER 1104, [1968] 2 WLR 1275, 112 Sol Jo 254 . 503, 512,
                                                                        513, 521
CMG, Re [1970] Ch 574, [1970] 2 All ER 740n, [1970] 3 WLR 80, 114 Sol Jo 399 . . . 282
CMS Dolphin Ltd v Simonet [2001] 2 BCLC 704 968
CWHT, Re [1978] Ch 67, [1978] 1 All ER 210, [1977] 3 WLR 880, 121 Sol Jo 776 . 522, 717
Cabburn, Re, Gage v Rutland (1882) 46 LT 848 846
Cable (Lord), Re, Garratt v Waters [1976] 3 All ER 417, [1977] 1 WLR 7, 120 Sol Jo 317. 1033
Caborne, Re, Hodge and Nabarro v Smith [1943] Ch 224, [1943] 2 All ER 7, 112 LJ Ch 210,
    87 Sol Jo 201, 169 LT 109, 59 TLR 309 . . . . 190, 219, 230
Cadell v Palmer (1833) 10 Bing 140, 7 Bli NS 202, 1 Cl & Fin 372, 3 Moo & S 571, HL . 189,
                                                                             192
Cadogan v Cadogan [1977] 1 All ER 200, [1977] 1 WLR 1041, 32 P & CR 388; revsd [1977] 3
    All ER 831, [1977] 1 WLR 1041, 35 P & CR 92, 121 Sol Jo 443, CA 293
Cafe v Bent (1843) 3 Hare 245, 13 LJ Ch 169, 8 Jur 141 727
Cafe v Bent (1845) 5 Hare 24, 9 Jur 653 552
Caffrey v Darby (1801) 6 Ves 488 . . . . 855, 856
Cain's Settlement, Re, Cain v Cain [1919] 2 Ch 364, 88 LJ Ch 513, 121 LT 496 568
Caldy Manor Estate Ltd v Farrell [1974] 3 All ER 753, [1974] 1 WLR 1303, 29 P & CR 238,
    118 Sol Jo 681, 232 Estates Gazette 709, CA 214
Calverley v Green (1984) 9 Fam LR 940, 155 CLR 242, 56 ALR 483, 59 ALJR 111, HC of
    A 350, 352, 362
Cambridge v Rous (1802) 6 RR 199, 8 Ves 12 225
Cameron, Re [1999] Ch 386, [1999] 2 All ER 924, [1999] 3 WLR 394, [1999] 16 LS Gaz R
    35 . . . . 546, 722
Cameron v M & W Mack (ESOP) Trustee Ltd [2002] WTLR 647 499
Cammell, Re, Public Trustee v A-G [1925] WN 36, 69 Sol Jo 345 130
Cammell v Cammell [1965] P 467, [1964] 3 All ER 255, [1964] 3 WLR 791, 108 Sol Jo 200 1044
Cammell v Sewell (1858) 3 H & N 617, 27 LJ Ex 447, 4 Jur NS 978, 32 LTOS 196; affd (1860)
    5 H & N 728, 29 LJ Ex 350, 6 Jur NS 918, 8 WR 639, 2 LT 799, Ex Ch 1028
Camoys (Lord) v Best (1854) 19 Beav 414 753
Campbell v Griffin [2001] EWCA Civ 990, [2001] NPC 102, 82 P & CR D43, [2001] WTLR
    981 . . . . 248, 249
Campbell v Walker (1800) 5 RR 135, 5 Ves 678 . . . . 581, 662, 667
Canada Safeway Ltd v Thompson [1952] 2 DLR 591 940
Canadian Aero Service Ltd v O'Malley [1974] SCR 592, 40 DLR (3d) 371, Can SC . . . 390
Cann v Cann (1884) 33 WR 40, 51 LT 770 586
Canning's Will Trusts, Re, Skues v Lyon [1936] Ch 309, 105 LJ Ch 241, 154 LT 693. 226, 229
Cannon v Hartley [1949] Ch 213, [1949] 1 All ER 50, [1949] LJR 370, 92 Sol Jo 719, 65 TLR
    63 . . . . 9, 167, 168, 169, 175, 182, 306, 312, 316
Canson Enterprises Ltd v Broughton & Co [1991] SCR 534, 131 NR 321, [1992] 1 WWR 245,
    9 CCLT (2d) 1, 85 DLR (4th) 129, 39 CPR (3d) 449 . . . . . . 405, 659, 856, 864, 865
Cantor v Cox (1975) 239 Estates Gazette 121 346
Cape Breton Co, Re (1885) 29 Ch D 795, 54 LJ Ch 822, 33 WR 788, 53 LT 181, 1 TLR 450,
    CA; affd sub nom Cavendish-Bentinck v Fenn (1887) 12 App Cas 652, 57 LJ Ch 552, 36
    WR 641, [1886-90] All ER Rep 333, 57 LT 773, HL 23, 24, 666
Capell v Winter [1907] 2 Ch 376, 76 LJ Ch 496, 51 Sol Jo 570, 97 LT 207, 23 TLR 618 . 50,
                                                                        984, 1001
Caplin's Will, Re (1865) 2 Drew & Sm 527, 34 LJ Ch 578, 11 Jur NS 383, 6 New Rep 17, 143
    RR 273, 13 WR 646, 12 LT 526 130
Carapiet's Trusts [2002] WTLR 989 . . . . 105, 1036
Carberry v M'Carthy (1881) 7 LR Ir 328 131
Carl-Zeiss-Stiftung v Herbert Smith & Co (a firm) (No 2) [1969] 2 Ch 276, [1969] 2 All ER

367, [1969] 2 WLR 427, [1969] FSR 40, [1969] RPC 338, 112 Sol Jo 1021, CA . 650, 877, 951, 953, 954, 964, 968, 985, 989

Carlton v Goodman [2002] EWCA Civ 545, [2002] 2 FLR 259, [2002] Fam Law 595, sub nom Goodman v Carlton [2002] 22 LS Gaz R 36 . . . . 352, 353, 355

Carne v Long (1860) 24 JP 676, 2 De GF & J 75, 29 LJ Ch 503, 6 Jur NS 639, 8 WR 570, 2 LT 552 . . . . 114, 124

Carnell v Harrison [1916] 1 Ch 328, 85 LJ Ch 155, 60 Sol Jo 121, 114 LT 478; on appeal [1916] 1 Ch 328, 85 LJ Ch 321, [1916-17] All ER Rep 827, 60 Sol Jo 290, 114 LT 478, CA 269

Carpenter, Re (1854) Kay 418, 101 RR 687 768

Carr v Living (1860) 28 Beav 644, 126 RR 276 209

Carr's Trusts, Re, Carr v Carr [1904] 1 Ch 792, 73 LJ Ch 459, 52 WR 595, 48 Sol Jo 395, 90 LT 502, CA. 829

Carreras Rothmans Ltd v Freeman Mathews Treasure Ltd [1985] Ch 207, [1985] 1 All ER 155, [1984] 3 WLR 1016, [1984] BCLC 420, [1985] PCC 222, 128 Sol Jo 614, [1984] LS Gaz R 2375. . . . . 13, 116

Carrick v Errington (1726) Mos 9, 2 P Wms 361; affd sub nom Errington v Carrick (1728) 5 Bro Parl Cas 390. 349

Carrington, Re, Ralphs v Swithenbank [1932] 1 Ch 1, 100 LJ Ch 299, [1931] All ER Rep 658, 145 LT 284, CA 440

Carroll, Re, Brice v Carroll [1902] 2 Ch 175, 71 LJ Ch 596, 50 WR 650, 86 LT 862 . . . 986

Carroll v Graham [1905] 1 Ch 478, 74 LJ Ch 398, 53 WR 549, 92 LT 66, CA 817

Carruthers v Carruthers [1896] AC 659, HL 647

Carson v Sloane (1884) 13 LR Ir 139 980

Carter, Re (1892) 41 WR 140 554

Carter v Carter (1857) 3 K & J 617, 27 LJ Ch 74, 4 Jur NS 63, 112 RR 308, 30 LTOS 349 . 1002

Carter v Hungerford [1917] 1 Ch 260, 86 LJ Ch 162, 115 LT 857 . . . . 154, 165

Carter (Inspector of Taxes) v Sharon [1936] 1 All ER 720, 20 TC 229, 80 Sol Jo 511 . . 151

Cartwright v Cartwright (1853) 3 De GM & G 982, 22 LJ Ch 841, 1 Eq Rep 138, 17 Jur 584, 98 RR 405, 1 WR 245, 43 ER 385, 31 LTOS 214 190

Carver v Duncan (Inspector of Taxes) [1985] AC 1082, [1984] 3 WLR 1209, [1984] STC 556, 59 TC 125, 128 Sol Jo 704, [1984] LS Gaz R 2624, CA; affd [1985] AC 1082, [1985] 2 All ER 645, [1985] 2 WLR 1010, [1985] STC 356, 59 TC 125, 129 Sol Jo 381, HL . .65, 206, 208, 563, 564, 568, 569, 574

Carville, Re, Shone v Walthamstow Borough Council [1937] 4 All ER 464. 106

Case v James (1861) 3 De GF & J 256, 30 LJ Ch 749, 7 Jur NS 869, 131 RR 688, 9 WR 771, 4 LT 664 999

Casio Computer Co Ltd v Sayo [2001] EWCA Civ 661, [2001] 06 LS Gaz R 45, [2001] IL Pr 694 . . . . 959, 1043

Cason v Odell (1986) 75 Revue Critique de Droit International Prive 66 1048

Cassel, Re, Public Trustee v Mountbatten [1926] Ch 358, 95 LJ Ch 281, [1927] All ER Rep 739, 70 Sol Jo 504, 134 LT 724, 42 TLR 338 . . . . 123, 200

Cassidy, Re [1979] VR 369 735

Castell and Brown Ltd, Re, Roper v Castell and Brown Ltd [1898] 1 Ch 315, 67 LJ Ch 169, sub nom Re Castell and Brown Ltd, ex p Union Bank of London 46 WR 248, 42 Sol Jo 213, 78 LT 109, 14 TLR 194 1001

Castellain v Preston (1883) 11 QBD 380, 52 LJQB 366, 31 WR 557, [1881-5] All ER Rep 493, 49 LT 29, CA 443

Castle v Castle (1857) 1 De G & J 352, 3 Jur NS 723, 118 RR 127, 5 WR 643, 29 LTOS 243 138

Cater's Trusts (No 2), Re (1858) 25 Beav 366, 119 RR 453 828

Catherall, Re, Lloyds Bank Ltd v Griffiths (3 June 1959, unreported) 119

Cattell, Re, Cattell v Cattell [1907] 1 Ch 567, 76 LJ Ch 242, 96 LT 612, 23 TLR 331; affd [1914] 1 Ch 177, 83 LJ Ch 322, 58 Sol Jo 67, 110 LT 137, CA 204

Catterson v Clark (1906) 95 LT 42, CA 817

Caus, Re, Lindeboom v Camille [1934] Ch 162, 103 LJ Ch 49, [1933] All ER Rep 818, 77 Sol Jo 816, 150 LT 131, 50 TLR 80 122

Cave v Cave (1880) 15 Ch D 639, 28 WR 798, sub nom Chaplin v Cave, Cave v Cave 49 LJ Ch 505, 42 LT 730 . . . . 597, 984, 990, 1001

Cave v Mackenzie (1877) 46 LJ Ch 564, 37 LT 218 397

Cave v Robinson Jarvis and Rolf (a firm) [2002] UKHL 18, [2002] 2 All ER 641, [2002] 2 WLR 1107, [2002] 20 LS Gaz R 32, [2002] NLJR 671, [2002] 19 EG 146 (CS) . . . 931

Cavendish v Strutt (1903) 19 TLR 483 276

Cavendish Browne's Settlement Trusts, Re, Horner v Rawle [1916] WN 341, 61 Sol Jo 27 . 177,
179, 306

Cavendish-Bentinck v Fenn. See Cape Breton Co, Re

Cawthorne, Re (1848) 12 Beav 56, sub nom Re Cawthorne's Trusts, Re Harwood 18 LJ Ch
116, sub nom Re Harewood 12 LTOS 529 829

Cazenove, Re, Perkin v Bland (1919) 122 LT 181 735

Cecil v Langdon (1884) 28 Ch D 1, 54 LJ Ch 313, 33 WR 1, 51 LT 618, CA 755

Cedar Transport Group Ltd v First Wyvern Property Trustees Co Ltd (1980) 258 Estates
Gazette 1077 442

Chadwick v Heatley (1845) 2 Coll 137, 9 Jur 504, 5 LTOS 303 827

Chaine-Nickson v Bank of Ireland [1976] IR 393 673

Chalinder and Herington, Re [1907] 1 Ch 58, 76 LJ Ch 71, 51 Sol Jo 69, 96 LT 196, 23 TLR
71 652

Chalmers v Pardoe [1963] 3 All ER 552, [1963] 1 WLR 677, 107 Sol Jo 435, PC 358

Chamberlayne v Brockett (1872) 8 Ch App 206, 37 JP 261, 42 LJ Ch 368, 21 WR 299, [1861-
73] All ER Rep 271, 28 LT 248 . . . . .121, 129, 201, 203

Chambers, Re [2001] WTLR 1375 280

Chambers v Goldwin (1804) 1 Smith KB 252, 7 RR 181, 9 Ves 254, [1803-13] All ER Rep 255,
cited in 13 Ves 377, 378 651

Chambers v Minchin (1802) 6 RR 111, 7 Ves 186, [1775-1802] All ER Rep 511 631

Chambers' Will Trusts, Re, Official Trustees of Charitable Funds v British Union for Abolition of Vivisection [1950] Ch 267, 66 (pt 1) TLR 595 . . . . 120, 203

Chan v Cresdon Pty Ltd (1989) 168 CLR 242, 89 ALR 522 49

Chan v Zacharia (1983) 154 CLR 178, 53 ALR 417, 58 ALJR 353, HC of A . . . 23, 380, 405

Chance, Re, Westminster Bank Ltd v Chance [1962] Ch 593, [1962] 1 All ER 942, [1962] 1
WLR 409, 106 Sol Jo 285 . . . . 532, 560

Chance's Settlement Trusts, Re, Chance v Billing [1918] WN 34, 62 Sol Jo 349 211

Chancellor, Re, Chancellor v Brown (1884) 26 Ch D 42, 53 LJ Ch 443, 32 WR 465, 51 LT 33,
CA 551, 555

Chaplin v Leslie Frewin (Publishers) Ltd [1966] Ch 71, [1966] 2 WLR 40, 109 Sol Jo 776; on
appeal [1966] Ch 71, [1965] 3 All ER 764, [1966] 2 WLR 40, 109 Sol Jo 871, CA . . 269

Chapman, Re, Cocks v Chapman [1896] 2 Ch 763, 65 LJ Ch 892, 45 WR 67, [1895-9] All ER
Rep 1104, 40 Sol Jo 715, 75 LT 196, 12 TLR 625, CA 575, 584, 590, 634, 939

Chapman, Re, Hales v A-G [1922] 1 Ch 287; on appeal [1922] 2 Ch 479, 91 LJ Ch 527, 66 Sol
Jo 522, 127 LT 616, CA 106, 332

Chapman v Bradley (1863) 4 De GJ & Sm 71, 10 Jur NS 5, 3 New Rep 182, 12 WR 140, 9 LT
495 274

Chapman v Browne [1902] 1 Ch 785, 71 LJ Ch 465, 86 LT 744, 18 TLR 482, CA 917

Chapman v Chapman. See Chapman's Settlement Trusts, Re, Chapman v Chapman

Chapman's Settlement Trusts, Re, Chapman v Chapman [1953] Ch 218, [1953] 1 All ER
103, [1953] 2 WLR 94, 46 R & IT 64, 97 Sol Jo 29, CA; affd sub nom Chapman v
Chapman [1954] AC 429, [1954] 1 All ER 798, [1954] 2 WLR 723, 33 ATC 84, 47 R &
IT 310, [1954] TR 93, 98 Sol Jo 246, HL 500, 515, 523, 524, 525, 527

Chapman's Settlement Trusts (No 2), Re Chapman v Chapman [1959] 2 All ER 47n, [1959]
1 WLR 372, 103 Sol Jo 273 515

Chapman's Settlement Trusts, Re, Jones v Chapman [1978] 1 All ER 1122, [1977] 1 WLR
1163, 121 Sol Jo 619, CA 194

Chapple, Re, Newton v Chapman (1884) 27 Ch D 584, 33 WR 336, 51 LT 748 652

Chardon, Re, Johnston v Davies [1928] Ch 464, 97 LJ Ch 289, [1927] All ER Rep 483, 139
LT 261 . . . . .110, 118, 120, 203

Charleton, Re, Bracey v Sherwin [1911] WN 54, 55 Sol Jo 330 218

Charterbridge Corpn Ltd v Lloyds Bank Ltd [1970] Ch 62, [1969] 2 All ER 1185, [1969] 3
WLR 122, [1969] 2 Lloyd's Rep 24, 113 Sol Jo 465, 208 Estates Gazette 1203 . . . 271

Charteris, Re, Charteris v Biddulph [1917] 2 Ch 379, 86 LJ Ch 658, 61 Sol Jo 591, 117 LT
391, CA 17, 545

Chase Manhattan Bank NA v Israel-British Bank (London) Ltd [1981] Ch 105, [1979] 3 All
ER 1025, [1980] 2 WLR 202, 124 Sol Jo 99 . . . . . . 324, 336, 436, 898, 971, 1049

Chase Manhattan Equities Ltd v Goodman [1991] BCLC 897, [1991] BCC 308 . . 61, 62, 681

Chattock v Muller (1878) 8 Ch D 177 423

Chaytor, Re, Chaytor v Horn [1905] 1 Ch 233, 74 LJ Ch 106, 53 WR 251, [1904-7] All ER Rep
230, 92 LT 290 556

Cheese v Thomas [1994] 1 All ER 35, [1994] 1 WLR 129, 69 P & CR 316, [1995] 1 FCR 162,
[1994] 1 FLR 118, [1994] Fam Law 80, 26 HLR 426, [1993] NLJR 1368, CA 657

Chellaram v Chellaram [1985] Ch 409, [1985] 1 All ER 1043, [1985] 2 WLR 510, 128 Sol Jo
877. . . . . 189, 773, 1033, 1034, 1036, 1037, 1038, 1042
Chellaram v Chellaram (No 2) [2002] EWHC 632 (Ch), [2002] 3 All ER 17, [2002] NLJR
639. . . . . 10.13, 1033, 1034, 1035, 1036, 1038, 1039, 1058, 1059, 1060
Chelsea Cloisters Ltd (in liquidation), Re (1980) 41 P & CR 98, 131 NLJ 482, CA . . . 14
Cherry's Trusts, Re, Robinson v Wesleyan Methodist Chapel Purposes Trustees [1914] 1 Ch
83, 83 LJ Ch 142, [1911-13] All ER Rep 900, 58 Sol Jo 48, 110 LT 16, 30 TLR 30 . . 796
Chessels v British Telecommunications plc [2002] WTLR 735 . . . . 840, 843
Chesterfield's (Earl) Trusts, Re (1883) 24 Ch D 643, 52 LJ Ch 958, 32 WR 361, [1881-5] All
ER Rep 737, 49 LT 261 . . . . 552, 559, 560
Chettiar (Palaniappa) v Arunasalam Chettiar [1962] AC 294, [1962] 1 All ER 494, [1962] 2
WLR 548, 106 Sol Jo 110, PC. 344, 345
Chetwynd's Settlement, Re, Scarisbrick v Nevinson [1902] 1 Ch 692, 71 LJ Ch 352, 50 WR
361, 46 Sol Jo 296, 86 LT 216, 18 TLR 348 . . . . 743, 747, 767
Chichester Diocesan Fund and Board of Finance Inc v Simpson [1944] AC 341, [1944] 2 All
ER 60, 113 LJ Ch 225, 88 Sol Jo 246, 171 LT 141, 60 TLR 492, HL 105, 788
Chief Constable of Leicestershire v M [1988] 3 All ER 1015, [1989] 1 WLR 20, 133 Sol Jo 47,
[1989] 4 LS Gaz R 43, [1988] NLJR 295 25
Childers v Childers (1857) 1 De G & J 482, 26 LJ Ch 743, 3 Jur NS 1277, 11 RR 185, 5 WR
859, 30 LTOS 3, CA 237, 343, 344
Chillingworth v Chambers [1896] 1 Ch 685, 65 LJ Ch 343, 44 WR 388, 40 Sol Jo 294, 74 LT
34, 12 TLR 217, CA 660, 936, 941, 944, 945, 947, 951
Chinn v Collins (Inspector of Taxes) [1981] AC 533, [1981] 1 All ER 189, [1981] 2 WLR 14,
[1981] STC 1, 54 TC 311, [1980] TR 467, 125 Sol Jo 49, L(TC) 2817, HL 236
Chirnside, Re [1974] VR 160 . . . . 431, 543
Chisholm, Re, Legal Reversionary Society v Knight (1898) 43 Sol Jo 43 788
Chisholm (Ian) Textiles Ltd v Griffiths [1994] 2 BCLC 291, [1994] BCC 96 15
Chitty's Will Trust, Re, Thomas's Will Trusts, Ransford (or Ransferd) v Lloyds Bank Ltd
[1970] Ch 254, [1969] 3 WLR 643, 113 Sol Jo 798, sub nom Re Thomas's Will Trust
[1969] 3 All ER 1492 . . . . 108, 109
Chohan v Saggar [1992] BCC 306, [1991] NPC 111 294
Chohan v Saggar [1993] BCLC 661, [1992] BCC 750; on appeal [1994] 1 BCLC 706, [1994]
BCC 134, CA 293
Choithram (T) International SA v Pagarani [2001] 2 All ER 492, [2001] 1 WLR 1, 145 Sol Jo
LB 8, [2001] 1 LRC 694, [2000] WTLR 277, PC 36, 147, 150, 166
Cholmondeley v IRC [1986] STC 384, [1986] LS Gaz R 2243 . . . . 52, 210
Christ's Hospital v Grainger (1849) 13 JP 778, 19 LJ Ch 33, 1 H & Tw 533, 14 Jur 339, 1 Mac
& G 460, 84 RR 128, [1843-60] All ER Rep 204, 15 LTOS 497 . . . . 118, 201
Christie v Gosling (1866) LR 1 HL 279, 35 LJ Ch 667, 15 LT 40 304
Christie v Ovington (1875) 1 Ch D 279, 24 WR 204 58
Christie-Miller's Settlement Trusts, Re, Westminster Bank Ltd v Christie-Miller [1961] 1 All
ER 855n, [1961] 1 WLR 462, 105 Sol Jo 256 . . . . 132, 504, 518
Churchill, Re, Hiscock v Lodder [1909] 2 Ch 431, 79 LJ Ch 10, 53 Sol Jo 697, 101 LT 380 713
Churchill v Denny (1875) LR 20 Eq 534, 44 LJ Ch 578, 23 WR 825 307
Churston Settled Estates, Re [1954] Ch 334, [1954] 2 WLR 386, 98 Sol Jo 178, sub nom Re
Churston Settled Estates, Freemantle v Baron Churston [1954] 1 All ER 725 . . . 198
Cia de Seguros Imperio (a body corporate) v Heath (REBX) Ltd (formerly CE Heath & Co
(North America) Ltd) [2001] 1 WLR 112, [2000] 2 All ER (Comm) 787, [2001]
Lloyd's Rep IR 109, [2000] PNLR 795, CA. 922
Cigala's Settlement Trusts, Re (1878) 7 Ch D 351, 47 LJ Ch 166, 26 WR 257, 38 LT 439 . 1029
Citadel General Assurance Co Ltd v Lloyds Bank Canada [1997] 3 SCR 805, 152 DLR (4th)
411 . . . . .954, 961, 973, 976
Citro (a bankrupt), Re [1991] Ch 142, [1990] 3 All ER 952, [1990] 3 WLR 880, [1991] 1 FLR
71, [1990] Fam Law 428, 134 Sol Jo 806, [1990] 28 LS Gaz R 43, [1990] NLJR 1073,
CA 481, 482
City of London Building Society v Flegg [1988] AC 54, [1987] 3 All ER 435, [1987] 2 WLR
1266, 54 P & CR 337, [1988] 1 FLR 98, [1988] Fam Law 17, 19 HLR 484, 131 Sol Jo 806,
[1987] LS Gaz R 1966, [1987] NLJ Rep 475, HL 50, 355, 737, 1003
Clack v Holland (1854) 19 Beav 262, 24 LJ Ch 13, 18 Jur 1007, 105 RR 134, 2 WR 402, 24
LTOS 49 . . . . 579, 819
Clare v Clare (1882) 21 Ch D 865, 51 LJ Ch 553, 30 WR 789, 46 LT 851 824
Clark, Re, Clark v Clark [1926] Ch 833, 95 LJ Ch 325, [1926] B & CR 77, [1925] All ER Rep
219, 70 Sol Jo 344, 135 LT 666 211

Clark v Girdwood (1877) 7 Ch D 9, 47 LJ Ch 116, 26 WR 90, 37 LT 614, CA 274
Clark v Hoskins (1868) 37 LJ Ch 561, 16 WR 1159, 19 LT 331, CA 589
Clark v Malpas (1862) 31 Beav 80; on appeal (1862) 26 JP 451, 4 De GF & J 401, 31 LJ Ch
   696, 135 RR 212, 10 WR 677, 6 LT 596 277
Clark Boyce v Mouat [1994] 1 AC 428, [1993] 4 All ER 268, [1993] 3 WLR 1021, [1993] 40
   LS Gaz R 42, [1993] 3 NZLR 641, 137 Sol Jo LB 231, PC 22, 400, 404, 659
Clark's Estate, Re 21 NY 2d 478, 236 NE 2d 152, 288 NYS 2d 993 (1968) 1031
Clarke, Re, Bracey v Royal National Lifeboat Institution [1923] 2 Ch 407, 92 LJ Ch 629,
   [1923] All ER Rep 607, 67 Sol Jo 680, 129 LT 310, 39 TLR 433 106
Clarke, Re, Clarke v Clarke [1901] 2 Ch 110, 70 LJ Ch 631, 49 WR 628, 45 Sol Jo 484, 84 LT
   811, 17 TLR 479. 125
Clarke, Re, Coombe v Carter (1887) 36 Ch D 348, 56 LJ Ch 981, 36 WR 293, 31 Sol Jo 676, 57
   LT 823, 3 TLR 818, CA 184
Clarke v Earl of Dunraven and Mount-Earl, The Satanita [1897] AC 59, 66 LJP 1, 8 Asp MLC
   190, 75 LT 337, 13 TLR 58, HL 245
Clarke v Earl of Ormonde (1821) Jac 108, [1814-23] All ER Rep 329 677
Clarke v Franklin (1858) 4 K & J 257, 27 LJ Ch 567, 116 RR 325, 6 WR 836, 31 LTOS
   381 . . . . 369, 377
Clarke v Heathfield [1985] ICR 203, [1985] LS Gaz R 599, CA 767, 905
Clarke v Heathfield (No 2) [1985] ICR 606 . . . . 743, 767
Clarke v Ramuz [1891] 2 QB 456, 56 JP 5, 60 LJQB 679, [1891-4] All ER Rep 502, 65 LT 657,
   7 TLR 626, CA 441, 442
Clarke v Swaile (1762) 2 Eden 134. 671
Clarke's Settlement, Re [1902] 2 Ch 327, 71 LJ Ch 593, 50 WR 585, 46 Sol Jo 499, 86 LT 653,
   18 TLR 610 573
Clarke's Will Trusts, Re [1961] 3 All ER 1133, [1961] 1 WLR 1471, 105 Sol Jo 1085 . . . 520
Clarkson v Clarkson (26 April 1994, unreported) 289
Clarkson v Davies [1923] AC 100, 92 LJPC 27, [1923] B & CR 42, 128 LT 452, [1922] All ER
   Rep Ext 809, [1923] 1 DLR 113, [1922] 3 WWR 913, PC 924
Clarkson v Robinson [1900] 2 Ch 722, 69 LJ Ch 859, 48 WR 698, 83 LT 164 652
Clavering v Ellison (1859) 7 HL Cas 707, 29 LJ Ch 761 . . . . 101, 104
Clay v Clay [1999] WASCA 8 952
Clayton v Clayton [1930] 2 Ch 12, 99 LJ Ch 498, [1930] All ER Rep 735, 143 LT 696 . . . 828
Clayton v Ramsden [1943] AC 320, [1943] 1 All ER 16, 112 LJ Ch 22, 86 Sol Jo 384, 168 LT
   113, 59 TLR 75, HL 102, 220
Clayton's Case. See Devaynes v Noble, Clayton's Case
Cleaver, Re, Cleaver v Insley [1981] 2 All ER 1018, [1981] 1 WLR 939, 125 Sol Jo 445 . . 82,
   259, 266, 427, 428, 429, 431, 432
Cleaver v Mutual Reserve Fund Life Association [1892] 1 QB 147, 56 JP 180, 61 LJQB 128, 40
   WR 230, [1891-4] All ER Rep 335, 36 Sol Jo 106, 66 LT 220, 8 TLR 139, CA. . . . 434
Clegg v Edmondson (1857) 8 De GM & G 787, 26 LJ Ch 673, 3 Jur NS 299, 114 RR 336, 29
   LTOS 131 . . . . 22, 385, 935
Clegg v Fishwick (1849) 19 LJ Ch 49, 1 H & Tw 390, 13 Jur 993, 1 Mac & G 294, 84 RR 61, 15
   LTOS 472 385
Cleveland's (Duke) Estate, Re, Hay v Wolmer [1895] 2 Ch 542, 65 LJ Ch 29, 13 R 715, 73 LT
   313 . . . . 552, 559, 560
Clinton's Trust, Re, Holloway's Fund (1871) LR 13 Eq 295, 41 LJ Ch 191, 20 WR 326, 26 LT
   159 313
Clinton's Trust, Re, Weare's Fund (1871) LR 13 Eq 295, 41 LJ Ch 191, 20 WR 326, 26 LT 159 313
Clinton's Will, Re (1910) 27 WN 125, 10 SRNSW 465 906
Clitheroe's Settlement Trusts, Re [1959] 3 All ER 789, [1959] 1 WLR 1159, 103 Sol Jo
   961. . . . . .503, 507, 511, 514, 515
Clore's Settlement Trusts, Re, Sainer v Clore [1966] 2 All ER 272, [1966] 1 WLR 955, 110 Sol
   Jo 252. 720
Clough v Bond (1838) 3 My & Cr 490, 8 LJ Ch 51, 2 Jur 958, 45 RR 314, 40 ER 1159 . . 495,
   625, 631, 646, 648, 855, 856, 862, 873
Clough v Dixon (1841) 10 Sim 564, sub nom Clough v Bond 11 LJ Ch 52, 6 Jur 49 . . . 742
Clough v Killey [1996] NPC 38, 72 P & CR D22, CA 423
Clough v Lambert (1839) 10 Sim 174, 3 Jur 672, 59 ER 579 174
Clough v Samuel. See Reis, Re, ex p Clough
Clough Mill Ltd v Martin [1984] 3 All ER 982, [1985] 1 WLR 111, [1985] BCLC 64, 128 Sol
   Jo 850, [1985] LS Gaz R 116, CA 8, 14, 15, 17, 22, 41, 77

Clout and Frewer's Contract, Re [1924] 2 Ch 230, 93 LJ Ch 624, [1924] All ER Rep 798, 68
  Sol Jo 738, 132 LT 483 . . . . 449, 452
Cloutte v Storey [1911] 1 Ch 18, 80 LJ Ch 193, 103 LT 617, [1908-10] All ER Rep Ext 1073,
  CA 631, 692, 698, 770, 820, 999
Clutterbuck's Settlement, Re, Bloxam v Clutterbuck [1905] 1 Ch 200, 73 LJ Ch 698, 53 WR
  10, 48 Sol Jo 621 307
Coaks, Re, Coaks v Bayley [1911] 1 Ch 171, 80 LJ Ch 136, 103 LT 799 . . . . . . 562, 983
Coates, Re, Ramsden v Coates [1955] Ch 495, [1955] 1 All ER 26, [1954] 3 WLR 959, 98 Sol
  Jo 871. . . . . 90, 93, 216
Coates to Parsons, Re (1886) 34 Ch D 370, 56 LJ Ch 242, 35 WR 375, 56 LT 16, 3 TLR
  173. . . . . 753, 756
Cochrane, Re, Shaw v Cochrane [1955] Ch 309, [1955] 1 All ER 222, [1955] 2 WLR 267, 99
  Sol Jo 96. 334
Cochrane v Cochrane [1922] 2 Ch 230, 91 LJ Ch 605, [1922] All ER Rep 614, 66 Sol Jo 522,
  127 LT 737, 38 TLR 607 631
Cochrane v IRC [1974] STC 335, 49 TC 299, 53 ATC 109, [1974] TR 111, 1974 SC 158 . 18
Cochrane v Moore (1890) 25 QBD 57, 54 JP 804, 59 LJQB 377, 38 WR 588, [1886-90] All ER
  Rep 731, 63 LT 153, 6 TLR 296, CA 151
Cockburn v Edwards (1881) 18 Ch D 449, 51 LJ Ch 46, 30 WR 446, 45 LT 500, CA . . . 666
Cockburn's Will Trusts, Re, Cockburn v Lewis [1957] Ch 438, [1957] 2 All ER 522, [1957] 3
  WLR 212, 101 Sol Jo 534 . . . . 20, 455, 624, 760, 768
Cocker v Quayle (1830) 1 Russ & M 535 . . . . 631, 948
Cockerell v Cholmeley (1830) 1 Russ & M 418 . . . . 931, 935
Cockerell's Settlement Trusts, Re, Cockerell v National Provincial Bank Ltd [1956] Ch 372,
  [1956] 2 All ER 172, [1956] 2 WLR 1050, 49 R & IT 399, 100 Sol Jo 342 . . . 472, 526
Cockerill, Re, Mackaness v Percival [1929] 2 Ch 131, 98 LJ Ch 281, 141 LT 198 214
Cocks v Manners (1871) LR 12 Eq 574, 36 JP 244, 40 LJ Ch 640, 19 WR 1055, 24 LT 869 125
Cocksedge v Cocksedge (1844) 14 Sim 244, 13 LJ Ch 384, 8 Jur 659, 65 RR 574, 60 ER 351, 3
  LTOS 374 190
Coco v AN Clark (Engineers) Ltd [1968] FSR 415, [1969] RPC 41 403
Codd, Re [1975] 2 All ER 1051n, [1975] 1 WLR 1139, 119 Sol Jo 530 655
Cogan v Duffield (1876) 2 Ch D 44, 45 LJ Ch 307, 24 WR 905, 34 LT 593, CA. 300
Cogan v Stephens (1835) 1 Beav 482n, 5 LJ Ch 17 . . . . 369, 372
Coggs v Bernard (or Barnard) (1703) 1 Com 133, 2 Ld Raym 909, 1 Salk 26, 2 Salk 522, 3
  Salk 11, 268, Holt KB 13, 131, 528, 569, 91 ER 25, 92 ER 107, [1558-1774] All ER Rep 1 858
Cohen, Re, Cohen v Cohen [1915] WN 361, 60 Sol Jo 239 369
Cohen, Re, Cohen v Cohen [1918] WN 252, 62 Sol Jo 682 785
Cohen, Re, National Provincial Bank Ltd v Katz [1953] Ch 88, [1953] 1 All ER 378, [1953] 1
  WLR 303, 97 Sol Jo 96 360
Cohen's Executors and LCC, Re [1902] 1 Ch 187, 71 LJ Ch 164, 50 WR 117, 86 LT 73 . 742
Cohen's Settlement Trusts, Re, Eliot-Cohen v Cohen [1965] 3 All ER 139, [1965] 1 WLR
  1229, 109 Sol Jo 680 514
Cohen's Will Trusts, Re, Re Cohen's Settlement Trusts [1959] 3 All ER 523, [1959] 1 WLR
  865, 103 Sol Jo 600. 514
Cohen's Will Trusts, Re, Cullen v Westminster Bank Ltd [1936] 1 All ER 103 . . . 374, 376
Colbeam Palmer Ltd v Stock Affiliates Pty Ltd [1972] RPC 303, 122 CLR 25. 874
Cole, Re, ex p Trustee of Property of Bankrupt v Cole [1964] Ch 175, [1963] 3 All ER 433,
  [1963] 3 WLR 621, 107 Sol Jo 664, CA 151
Cole v Muddle (1852) 10 Hare 186, 22 LJ Ch 401, 16 Jur 853, 90 RR 332, 20 LTOS 107 . 980
Coleman, Re, Henry v Strong (1888) 39 Ch D 443, 58 LJ Ch 226, 60 LT 127, CA. . 213, 629
Coleman, Re, Public Trustee v Coleman [1936] Ch 528, [1936] 2 All ER 225, 105 LJ Ch 244,
  155 LT 402. . . . . 226, 229, 334
Coleman v Bucks and Oxon Union Bank [1897] 2 Ch 243, 66 LJ Ch 564, 45 WR 616, 41 Sol
  Jo 491, 76 LT 684 . . . . 973, 986
Coleman v Harvey [1989] 1 NZLR 723 900
Coleman v Myers [1977] 2 NZLR 225, NZCA. 21
Coles v Coles [1901] 1 Ch 711, 70 LJ Ch 324, 84 LT 142 308
Coles v Trecothick (1804) 1 Smith KB 233, 7 RR 167, 9 Ves 234, [1803-13] All ER Rep 14 23,
  660, 671
Collard's Will Trusts, Re, Lloyds Bank Ltd v Rees [1961] Ch 293, [1961] 1 All ER 821, [1961]
  2 WLR 415, [1961] TR 325, 105 Sol Jo 208 . . . . 718, 719
Collens, Re, Royal Bank of Canada (London) Ltd v Krogh [1986] Ch 505, [1986] 1 All ER
  611, [1986] 2 WLR 919, 130 Sol Jo 373, [1986] LS Gaz R 1901 231

Coller's Deed Trusts, Re, Coller v Coller [1939] Ch 277, [1937] 3 All ER 292, 106 LJ Ch 326, 81 Sol Jo 550, 157 LT 84, 53 TLR 859, CA. 533, 566

Collie v Merlow Nominees Pty Ltd [2001] Victoria SC 39 826

Collier (Official Assignee) v Creighton [1993] 2 NZLR 534 . . . . 405, 930, 934

Collier v Collier [2002] EWCA Civ 1095. 346

Collier v McBean (1865) 34 Beav 426, 34 LJ Ch 155, 11 Jur NS 592, 6 New Rep 192, 145 RR 593, 13 WR 766, 12 LT 790; affd (1865) 1 Ch App 81, 30 JP 99, 35 LJ Ch 144, 12 Jur NS 1, 145 RR 593, 14 WR 156, 13 LT 484 1002

Collings v Lee [2001] 2 All ER 332, 82 P & CR 27, [2000] 43 LS Gaz R 37, 81 P & CR D26, CA 397, 991

Collings v Wade [1903] 1 IR 89 942

Collins, Re, Collins v Collins (1886) 32 Ch D 229, 50 JP 821, 55 LJ Ch 672, 34 WR 650, [1886-90] All ER Rep 683, 55 LT 21, 2 TLR 423 524

Collins, Re. See Robinson v Collins

Collins v Brebner [2000] Lloyds Rep PN 587. . . . . 661, 856

Collins v Collins (1833) 2 My & K 703, 39 RR 337. 551

Collins v Elstone [1893] P 1, 62 LJP 26, 1 R 458, 41 WR 287, 67 LT 624, 9 TLR 16 . . . 280

Collins (Philip) Ltd v Davis [2000] 3 All ER 808, [2000] EMLR 815 978

Collyer v Isaacs (1881) 19 Ch D 342, 51 LJ Ch 14, 30 WR 70, [1881-5] All ER Rep 828, 45 LT 567, CA 183, 184

Colyear v Countess of Mulgrave (1836) 2 Keen 81, 5 LJ Ch 335, 4 RR 191 173

Colyer, Re (1880) 50 LJ Ch 79, 43 LT 454. 747

Colyer v Finch (1856) 5 HL Cas 905, 26 LJ Ch 65, 3 Jur NS 25, 10 ER 1159, [1843-60] All ER Rep 1020, 28 LTOS 27 594

Colyton Investments Pty Ltd v McSorley (1962) 107 CLR 177 19

Comax Secure Business Services Ltd v Wilson (21 June 2001, unreported) 957

Combe, Re, Combe v Combe [1925] Ch 210, 94 LJ Ch 267, [1925] All ER Rep 159, sub nom Re Coombe, Coombe v Coombe 69 Sol Jo 397, 133 LT 473 131

Comberbach, Re, Saunders v Jackson (1929) 73 Sol Jo 403 160

Comiskey v Bowring-Hanbury [1905] AC 84, 74 LJ Ch 263, 53 WR 402, 92 LT 241, 21 TLR 252, HL. 133, 134, 135

Commission for the New Towns v Cooper (Great Britain) Ltd [1995] Ch 259, [1995] 2 All ER 929, [1995] 2 WLR 677, 72 P & CR 270, [1995] NPC 34, [1995] 2 EGLR 113, [1995] 26 EG 129, 139 Sol Jo LB 87, CA 278

Commonwealth and Central Wool Committee v Colonial Combing Spinning and Weaving Co Ltd (1922) 31 CLR 421, 29 ALR 138 (Aust HC) 34

Commonwealth of Australia v Verwayen (1990) 170 CLR 394, 95 ALR 321, 64 ALJR 540 . 248

Commonwealth Reserves I v Chodar [2001] 2 NZLR 374 . . . . 326, 327

Compagnie Commerciale Andre SA v Artibell Shipping Co Ltd 2001 SC 563, OH . . . 972

Compagnie Financière et Commerciale du Pacifique v Peruvian Guano Co (1882) 11 QBD 55, 52 LJQB 181, 31 WR 395, 48 LT 22, CA 679

Compaq Computer Ltd v Abercorn Group Ltd (t/a Osiris) [1993] BCLC 602, [1991] BCC 484. . . . . 15, 17, 41

Competitive Insurance Co Ltd v Davies Investments Ltd [1975] 3 All ER 254, [1975] 1 WLR 1240, 119 Sol Jo 559 . . . . 953, 968

Compton, Re, Powell v Compton [1946] 1 All ER 117 122

Compton (Marquis of Northampton) v Compton (Marchioness of Northampton) and Hussey [1960] P 201, [1960] 2 All ER 70, [1960] 3 WLR 476, 104 Sol Jo 705 . . . 750

Comr of Taxes v Pratt Estate Co Ltd [1934] NZLR 347 535

Condrin, Re, Coloham v Condrin [1914] 1 IR 89 350

Connell's Settlement, Re, Re Benett's Trusts, Fair v Connell [1915] 1 Ch 867, 84 LJ Ch 601, 113 LT 234. . . . . 193, 375

Connor's Estate, Re (1970) 10 DLR (3d) 5, 72 WWR 388 84

Conolly, Re, Conolly v Conolly [1910] 1 Ch 219, 79 LJ Ch 148, 101 LT 783, 26 TLR 189 . 133

Conquest, Re, Royal Exchange Assurance v Conquest [1929] 2 Ch 353, 98 LJ Ch 441, [1929] All ER Rep 608, 141 LT 685 572

Conservative and Unionist Central Office v Burrell (Inspector of Taxes) [1982] 2 All ER 1, [1982] 1 WLR 522, [1982] STC 317, 55 TC 671, [1981] TR 543, 126 Sol Jo 50, CA . 118, 123, 127

Consiglio Trusts, Re (1973) 36 DLR (3d) 658, [1973] 3 OR 326 767

Constantinidi v Ralli [1935] Ch 427, 104 LJ Ch 249, 79 Sol Jo 195, 152 LT 489 277

Consterdine v Consterdine (1862) 31 Beav 330, 31 LJ Ch 807, 8 Jur NS 906, 135 RR 451, 10 WR 727, 7 LT 122 647

Consul Development Pty Ltd v DPC Estates Pty Ltd (1975) 132 CLR 373, 5 ALR 231, 49 ALJ
   74, HC of A 396, 961
Continental Caoutchouc and Gutta Percha Co v Kleinwort Sons & Co (1904) 9 Com Cas
   240, 52 WR 489, 48 Sol Jo 383, 90 LT 474, 20 TLR 403, CA 971, 972
Control Centre Pty Ltd v Ty (24 July 1995, unreported) 958
Conveyances dated June 13, 1933, August 17, 1933 and September 2, 1950, Re, Abbatt v
   Treasury Solicitor [1969] 3 All ER 1175, [1969] 1 WLR 1575, 113 Sol Jo 739, CA . . 127
Conway v Fenton (1888) 40 Ch D 512, 58 LJ Ch 282, 37 WR 156, 59 LT 928 810
Conybeare's Settlement, ex p (1853) 94 RR 887, 1 WR 458 771
Conyngham, Re, Conyngham v Conyngham [1921] 1 Ch 491, 90 LJ Ch 364, 65 Sol Jo 342,
   125 LT 300, 37 TLR 420, CA 333
Conyngham v Conyngham (1750) 1 Ves Sen 522 452
Cook, Re, Beck v Grant [1948] Ch 212, [1948] 1 All ER 231, [1948] LJR 902, 92 Sol Jo 125,
   64 TLR 97 . . . . 6, 273
Cook v Addison (1869) LR 7 Eq 466, 38 LJ Ch 322, 17 WR 480, 20 LT 212 880
Cook v Deeks [1916] 1 AC 554, 85 LJPC 161, [1916-17] All ER Rep 285, 114 LT 636, PC . 23,
                                               390, 398, 402
Cook v Fountain (1676) 3 Swan 585 54
Cook v Hutchinson (1836) 1 Keen 42, 44 RR 11 330
Cook (Inspector of Taxes) v Medway Housing Society Ltd [1997] STC 90, 69 TC 319 . . 601
Cook Industries Inc v Galliher [1979] Ch 439, [1978] 3 All ER 945, [1978] 3 WLR 637, 122
   Sol Jo 367 . . . . 188, 900
Cook's Settlement Trusts, Re, Royal Exchange Assurance v Cook [1965] Ch 902, [1964] 3 All
   ER 898, [1965] 2 WLR 179, 109 Sol Jo 77 . . . . 9, 167, 169, 175, 176, 177, 181
Cooke, Re, Randall v Cooke [1916] 1 Ch 480, 85 LJ Ch 452, 60 Sol Jo 403, 114 LT 555 . 530,
                                            547
Cooke v Lamotte (1851) 15 Beav 234, 21 LJ Ch 371 274
Cooke v Turner (1846) 14 Sim 493, 17 LJ Ex 106, 15 M & W 727 217
Cooke's Settlement, Re, Tarry v Cooke [1913] 2 Ch 661, 83 LJ Ch 76, 58 Sol Jo 67, 109 LT
   705 544
Cooke's Trusts, Re (1887) 56 LJ Ch 637, 35 WR 608, 56 LT 737, 3 TLR 558 1023
Cookes' Contract, Re (1877) 4 Ch D 454 . . . . 740, 741
Cookson v Lee (1853) 23 LJ Ch 473, 21 LTOS 258, CA 669
Coomber, Re, Coomber v Coomber [1911] 1 Ch 723, 80 LJ Ch 399, 104 LT 517, CA 284, 285
Coombes v Brookes (1871) LR 12 Eq 61, 41 LJ Ch 114, 19 WR 1002, 25 LT 198 766
Coombes v Smith [1986] 1 WLR 808, [1987] 1 FLR 352, [1987] Fam Law 123, 130 Sol Jo 482,
   [1986] LS Gaz R 2238 . . . . 140, 251
Cooper (No 2), Re (1978) 90 DLR (3d) 715, 21 OR (2d) 579 919
Cooper, Re, Cooper v Cooper [1913] 1 Ch 350, 82 LJ Ch 222, 57 Sol Jo 389, 108 LT 293 715
Cooper, Re, Cooper v Vesey (1882) 20 Ch D 611, [1882] WN 96, 51 LJ Ch 862, 30 WR 648,
   47 LT 89, CA 368
Cooper (Colin), Re, Le Neve-Foster v National Provincial Bank Ltd [1939] Ch 811, [1939] 3
   All ER 586, 108 LJ Ch 388, 83 Sol Jo 671, 161 LT 127, CA 261, 653
Cooper v Cooper (1888) 13 App Cas 88, 59 LT 1, HL 1023
Cooper v Luxor (Eastbourne) Ltd [1939] 4 All ER 411, CA; on appeal sub nom Luxor
   (Eastbourne) Ltd v Cooper [1941] AC 108, [1941] 1 All ER 33, 110 LJKB 131, 46 Com
   Cas 120, 85 Sol Jo 105, 164 LT 313, 57 TLR 213, HL 391
Cooper and Allen's Contract for Sale to Harlech, Re (1876) 4 Ch D 802, 46 LJ Ch 133, 25
   WR 301, 35 LT 890 . . . . 580, 581, 705
Cooper's Conveyance Trusts, Re, Crewdson v Bagot [1956] 3 All ER 28, [1956] 1 WLR 1096,
   100 Sol Jo 620 . . . . 341, 376
Cooper's Settlement, Re, Cooper v Cooper [1962] Ch 826, [1961] 3 All ER 636, [1961] 3
   WLR 1029, 105 Sol Jo 887 509
Cope v Keene (1968) 118 CLR 1 . . . . 161, 162
Cope's Estate, Re [1954] 1 All ER 698, [1954] 1 WLR 608, 98 Sol Jo 253 750
Copland's Settlement, Re, Johns v Carden [1900] 1 Ch 326, 69 LJ Ch 240, 82 LT 194 . . 564,
                                                 568
Copp v Wood [1962] 2 DLR (2d) 224 149
Coral Rose, The. See Atlas Maritime Co SA v Avalon Maritime Ltd, The Coral Rose
Corbett v Bond Pearce (a firm) [2001] EWCA Civ 531, [2001] 3 All ER 769, [2001] NLJR
   609, [2001] Lloyd's Rep PN 501, [2001] PNLR 31, [2001] WTLR 419 281
Corbett v IRC [1938] 1 KB 567, [1937] 4 All ER 700, 21 TC 449, 107 LJKB 276, 82 Sol Jo 34,
   158 LT 98, 54 TLR 279, CA 64

Corbishley's Trusts, Re (1880) 14 Ch D 846, 49 LJ Ch 266, 28 WR 536 264
Cordwell v Mackrill (1766) Amb 515, 2 Eden 344 985
Corin v Patton (1990) 169 CLR 540, 92 ALR 1 . . . . 154, 155
Comr of Stamp Duties v ISPT (1992) 2 ITELR 1 813
Cornmell v Keith (1876) 3 Ch D 767, 45 LJ Ch 689, 24 WR 633, 35 LT 29 310
Cornthwaite v Frith (1851) 4 De G & Sm 552, 87 RR 471 142
Cornwallis's (Lord) Case (1704) 2 Eq Cas Abr 250, 466, Freem Ch 279, sub nom Lassells v
    Lord Cornwallis 1 Eq Cas Abr 242, Prec Ch 232, 2 Vern 465 804
Cornwell v Barry (Inspector of Taxes) (1955) 36 TC 268, 34 ATC 257, 48 R & IT 763, [1955]
    TR 255 65
Corporacion Nacional del Cobre de Chile v Sogemin Metals Ltd [1997] 2 All ER 917, [1997]
    1 WLR 1396, [1996] 46 LS Gaz R 29, [1997] NLJR 161, [1997] CLC 435 866
Corsellis, Re, Lawton v Elwes (1887) 34 Ch D 675, 51 JP 597, 56 LJ Ch 294, 35 WR 309, 56 LT
    411, 3 TLR 355, CA 653
Cory, Re, Cory v Morel [1955] 2 All ER 630, [1955] 1 WLR 725, 99 Sol Jo 435 334
Cory v Gertcken (1816) 2 Madd 40, 17 RR 180 935
Cotgrave v Cotgrave [1992] Fam 33, [1991] 4 All ER 537, [1991] 3 WLR 567, [1991] FCR
    838, [1992] 1 FLR 10, [1991] Fam Law 378, CA 187
Cothay v Sydenham (1788) 2 Bro CC 391 . . . . 623, 629
Cotter, Re, Jennings v Nye [1915] 1 Ch 307, 84 LJ Ch 337, 59 Sol Jo 177, 112 LT 340 . . 754,
                                                                                        771
Cotton's Trustees and London School Board, Re (1882) 19 Ch D 624, 51 LJ Ch 514, 30 WR
    610, [1881-5] All ER Rep 926, 46 LT 813 730
Coulls v Bagot's Executor and Trustee Co Ltd (1967) 119 CLR 460, [1967] ALR 385, 40
    ALJR 471, HC of A 10, 170
Coulson's Trust, Re (1857) 4 Jur NS 6 829
Coulthard v Disco Mix Club Ltd [1999] 2 All ER 457, [2000] 1 WLR 707, [1999] EMLR 434 854
Countryside (No 3) Pty Ltd v Bayside Brunswick Pty Ltd (20 April 1994, unreported) . . 822
County NatWest Ltd v Barton [2002] 4 All ER 494, CA 661
Courage Group's Pension Schemes, Re, Ryan v Imperial Brewing and Leisure Ltd [1987] 1
    All ER 528, [1987] 1 WLR 495, 131 Sol Jo 507, [1987] LS Gaz R 1573 499
Courtauld's Settlement, Re, Courtauld v Farrer [1965] 2 All ER 544n, [1965] 1 WLR 1385,
    109 Sol Jo 739 . . . . .132, 133, 504, 518
Courtier, Re, Coles v Courtier (1886) 34 Ch D 136, 51 JP 117, 56 LJ Ch 350, 35 WR 85, 55 LT
    574, CA 564, 572, 589
Courtier, Re, Courtier v Coles (1886) 34 Ch D 136, 51 JP 117, 56 LJ Ch 350, 35 WR 85, 55 LT
    574, CA 564, 572
Coutts v Acworth (1869) LR 8 Eq 558, 38 LJ Ch 694, 17 WR 1121, 21 LT 224 276
Couturier, Re, Couturier v Shea [1907] 1 Ch 470, 76 LJ Ch 296, 51 Sol Jo 342, 96 LT 560,
    [1904-7] All ER Rep Ext 1191 714
Coventry's (Earl) Indentures, Re, Smith v Earl of Coventry [1974] Ch 77, [1973] 3 All ER 1,
    [1973] 3 WLR 122, 117 Sol Jo 547 . . . . 198, 807
Coverdale v Eastwood (1872) LR 15 Eq 121, 37 JP 212, 42 LJ Ch 118, 21 WR 216, 27 LT 646 140
Cowan v Scargill [1985] Ch 270, [1984] 2 All ER 750, [1984] 3 WLR 501, [1984] ICR 646,
    [1984] IRLR 260, 128 Sol Jo 550 . . . . .532, 570, 576, 582, 591, 592, 601,
                                                                    613, 614, 615, 617, 853
Cowan de Groot Properties Ltd v Eagle Trust plc [1992] 4 All ER 700, [1991] BCLC
    1045 .884, 957, 960, 968, 974
Cowcher v Cowcher [1972] 1 All ER 943, [1972] 1 WLR 425, 116 Sol Jo 142 54
Cowell v Gatcombe (1859) 27 Beav 568, 122 RR 531 631
Cowin, Re, Cowin v Gravett (1886) 33 Ch D 179, 56 LJ Ch 78, 34 WR 735 672
Cowley, Re, Souch v Cowley (1885) 53 LT 494 . . . . 35, 137
Cowley (Earl) v Wellesley (1866) LR 1 Eq 656, 35 Beav 635, 147 RR 334, 14 WR 528, 14 LT
    245 . . . . 574, 575
Cowman v Harrison (1852) 10 Hare 234, 22 LJ Ch 993, 17 Jur 313, 90 RR 334, 1 WR 96, 21
    LTOS 148 80
Cowper v Stoneham (1893) 3 R 242, 68 LT 18 877
Cowper-Smith v Anstey [1877] WN 28 312
Cowx v Foster (1860) 1 John & H 30, 29 LJ Ch 886, 6 Jur NS 1051, 70 ER 649, sub nom Cox v
    Forster 2 LT 797 805
Cox v Barnard (1850) 8 Hare 310 . . . . .173, 174, 175, 179
Coxen, Re, McCallum v Coxen [1948] Ch 747, [1948] 2 All ER 492, [1948] LJR 1590, 92 Sol
    Jo 442 . . . . .81, 89, 101, 102, 215, 832

Cozens, Re, Green v Brisley [1913] 2 Ch 478, 82 LJ Ch 421, 57 Sol Jo 687, 109 LT 306 . 145, 149

Crabb v Arun District Council [1976] Ch 179, [1975] 3 All ER 865, [1975] 3 WLR 847, 119 Sol Jo 711, CA 248, 249, 328

Crabb v Crabb (1834) 1 My & K 511, 3 LJ Ch 181, 36 RR 362 361

Crabtree, Re, Thomas v Crabtree [1912] WN 24, 106 LT 49, CA 535, 555

Cradock v Piper (1850) 19 LJ Ch 107, 1 H & Tw 617, 14 Jur 97, 1 Mac & G 664, 84 RR 223, 15 LTOS 61 653

Crago v McIntyre [1976] 1 NSWLR 729 270

Craig, Re, Meneces v Middleton [1971] Ch 95, [1970] 2 All ER 390, [1970] 2 WLR 1219, 114 Sol Jo 171 282

Craig v Lamoureux [1920] AC 349, 89 LJPC 22, 122 LT 208, 36 TLR 26, PC . . . 282, 283

Crane v Davis (1981) Times, 13 May 367

Cranleigh Precision Engineering Ltd v Bryant [1964] 3 All ER 289, [1965] 1 WLR 1293, [1966] RPC 81, 109 Sol Jo 830 399

Craven, Re, Watson v Craven [1914] 1 Ch 358, 83 LJ Ch 403, 58 Sol Jo 138, 109 LT 846 . . . . 544, 566

Craven v Brady (1869) 4 Ch App 296, 38 LJ Ch 345, 17 WR 505, 23 LT 57 190

Craven v Craddock [1868] WN 229; revsd [1869] WN 48, 20 LT 638. 496

Craven's Estate, Re, Lloyds Bank Ltd v Cockburn (No 2) [1937] Ch 431, [1937] 3 All ER 33, 106 LJ Ch 311, 81 Sol Jo 436 . . . . 526, 720

Crawford v Forshaw (1890) 43 Ch D 643, 59 LJ Ch 348, 38 WR 412, 62 LT 63; on appeal [1891] 2 Ch 261, 60 LJ Ch 683, 39 WR 484, 65 LT 32, CA 450, 741

Crawley Borough Council v Ure [1996] QB 13, [1996] 1 All ER 724, [1995] 3 WLR 95, 71 P & CR 12, [1996] 1 FCR 6, [1995] 1 FLR 806, [1995] Fam Law 411, 27 HLR 524, CA 582

Crawshay, Re, Dennis v Crawshay (1888) 60 LT 357, 5 TLR 144 522

Crawshay, Re, Hore-Ruthven v Public Trustee [1948] Ch 123, [1948] 1 All ER 107, [1948] LJR 586, 92 Sol Jo 95, 64 TLR 67, CA 631

Crédit Lyonnais Bank Nederland NV v Burch [1997] 1 All ER 144, 74 P & CR 384, [1997] 2 FCR 1, [1997] 1 FLR 11, [1997] Fam Law 168, 29 HLR 513, [1996] 5 Bank LR 233, [1996] 32 LS Gaz R 33, [1996] NLJR 1421, 140 Sol Jo LB 158, CA 276, 282

Cresswell v Dewell (1863) 4 Giff 460, 10 Jur NS 354, 3 New Rep 148, 141 RR 28, 12 WR 123, 10 LT 22 931

Cresswell v Potter [1978] 1 WLR 255n 276

Crichton v Crichton [1896] 1 Ch 870, 65 LJ Ch 491, 74 LT 357, CA 937

Cricklewood Property and Investment Trust Ltd v Leighton's Investment Trust Ltd [1945] AC 221, [1945] 1 All ER 252, 114 LJKB 110, 89 Sol Jo 93, 172 LT 140, 61 TLR 202, HL 442

Crippen's Estate, Re [1911] P 108, 80 LJP 47, [1911-13] All ER Rep 207, 55 Sol Jo 273, 104 LT 224, 27 TLR 258 434

Crisp v Mullings (1974) 233 Estates Gazette 511; on appeal (1975) 239 Estates Gazette 119, CA 350, 352, 362

Criterion Properties plc v Stratford UK Properties LLC [2002] EWHC 496 (Ch), [2002] 2 BCLC 151 . . . . 962, 975, 989

Crocker, Re, Crocker v Crocker [1916] 1 Ch 25, 85 LJ Ch 179, 114 LT 61, [1914-15] All ER Rep Ext 1211 546

Crockett v Crockett (1848) 2 Ph 553, 17 LJ Ch 230, 12 Jur 234, 78 RR 183, 10 LTOS 409 138

Croft v Adam (1842) 12 Sim 639, 11 LJ Ch 386, 6 Jur 522, 56 RR 126 130

Crompton and Evans' Union Bank v Burton [1895] 2 Ch 711, 64 LJ Ch 811, 13 R 792, 44 WR 60, 73 LT 181 906

Crook's Settlement, Re, Re Glasier's Settlement, Crook v Preston [1923] 2 Ch 339, 92 LJ Ch 495, [1923] All ER Rep 697, 129 LT 284 313

Croome v Croome (1889) 61 LT 814, HL 334, 335

Cross, Re, Harston v Tenison (1882) 20 Ch D 109, 51 LJ Ch 645, 30 WR 376, 45 LT 777, CA 906, 934

Crouch v Crédit Foncier of England (1873) LR 8 QB 374, 42 LJQB 183, 21 WR 946, 29 LT 259 983

Crowden v Aldridge [1993] 3 All ER 603, [1993] 1 WLR 433, [1993] 11 LS Gaz R 45 . . 18

Crowe v Appleby (Inspector of Taxes) [1975] 3 All ER 529, [1975] 1 WLR 1539, [1975] STC 502, 51 TC 457, 54 ATC 177, [1975] TR 151, 119 Sol Jo 776, L(TC) 2561; affd [1976] 2 All ER 914, [1976] 1 WLR 885, [1976] STC 301, 51 TC 457, [1976] TR 105, L(TC) 2584, CA 735, 739

Crowhurst Park, Re, Sims-Hilditch v Simmons [1974] 1 All ER 991, [1974] 1 WLR 583, 28 P & CR 14, 118 Sol Jo 331 . . . . 19, 756

Crowther, Re, Midgley v Crowther [1895] 2 Ch 56, 64 LJ Ch 537, 13 R 496, 43 WR 571, [1895-9] All ER Rep 1208, 72 LT 762, 11 TLR 380 . . . . 551, 554, 555

Croxon, Re, Ferrers v Croxton [1915] 2 Ch 290, 84 LJ Ch 845, [1914-15] All ER Rep 816, 59 Sol Jo 693, 113 LT 1103 533

Croxton v May (1878) 9 Ch D 388, 27 WR 325, 39 LT 461, CA 735

Cuckmere Brick Co Ltd v Mutual Finance Ltd [1971] Ch 949, [1971] 2 All ER 633, [1971] 2 WLR 1207, 22 P & CR 624, 115 Sol Jo 288, [1971] RVR 126, CA 581

Cuddon v Tite (1858) 1 Giff 395, 4 Jur NS 579, 6 WR 606, 31 LTOS 340 441

Cukurooa Celik Enduustrisi AS v Hill Taylor Dickinson (a firm) (1 June 1996, unreported) 954, 970

Cull's Trusts, Re (1875) LR 20 Eq 561, 44 LJ Ch 664, 23 WR 850, 32 LT 853 . . . 628, 629, 829, 830

Cullen v A-G for Ireland (1866) LR 1 HL 190, 12 Jur NS 531, 14 WR 869, 14 LT 644 . . 259

Cumberland Consolidated Holdings Ltd v Ireland [1946] KB 264, [1946] 1 All ER 284, 115 LJKB 301, 174 LT 257, 62 TLR 215, CA 442

Cummins v Cummins (1845) 72 RR 29, 8 I Eq R 723, 3 Jo & Lat 64 451

Cunard's Trusts, Re (1878) 48 LJ Ch 192, 27 WR 52 772

Cunnack v Edwards [1896] 2 Ch 679, 61 JP 36, 65 LJ Ch 801, 45 WR 99, 75 LT 122, 12 TLR 614, CA 339

Cunningham v Foot (1878) 3 App Cas 974, 26 WR 858, 38 LT 889, HL 34, 137, 330

Cunningham and Bradley and Wilson, Re [1877] WN 258, 12 LJNC 214 762

Cunningham and Frayling, Re [1891] 2 Ch 567, 60 LJ Ch 591, 39 WR 469, 64 LT 558 . . 58

Curnick v Tucker (1874) LR 17 Eq 320 . . . . 134, 135

Currant v Jago (1844) 1 Coll 261, 8 Jur 610, 6 RR 63, 3 LTOS 240 . . . . 350, 366

Currie, Re (1878) 10 Ch D 93, 27 WR 369, 40 LT 110 780

Currie v Hamilton [1984] 1 NSWLR 687 . . . . 352, 422

Curryer's Will Trusts, Re, Wyly v Curryer [1938] Ch 952, [1938] 3 All ER 574, 107 LJ Ch 417, 82 Sol Jo 625, 159 LT 599, 54 TLR 1055 229

Curteis v Wormald (1878) 10 Ch D 172, 27 WR 419, 40 LT 108 . . . . . . 369, 371, 376

Curteis' Trusts, Re (1872) LR 14 Eq 217, 41 LJ Ch 631, 26 LT 863 . . . . . 350, 362, 364

Curtis v Hutton (1808) 14 Ves 537 188

Curtis v Lukin (1842) 5 Beav 147, 11 LJ Ch 380, 6 Jur 721 208

Curtis v Rippon (1820) 5 Madd 434, 21 RR 327 80

Curtis v Sheffield (1882) 21 Ch D 1, 51 LJ Ch 535, 30 WR 581, 46 LT 177, CA 839

Cussons Ltd, Re (1904) 73 LJ Ch 296, 11 Mans 192 460

Custance's Settlements, Re, Keppel v Douglas [1946] Ch 42, [1945] 2 All ER 441, 114 LJ Ch 293, 89 Sol Jo 381, 173 LT 195, 61 TLR 541 212

Custom Credit Corpn Ltd v Rari Nominees Pty Ltd (1982) 8 WAR 42 813

Customs and Excise Comrs v Richmond Theatre Management Ltd [1995] STC 257 . . 16, 25, 76, 900, 901

Customs and Excise Officers' Mutual Guarantee Fund, Re, Robson v A-G [1917] 2 Ch 18, 86 LJ Ch 457, 117 LT 86, 33 TLR 311 . . . . 336, 848

D

DEG-Deutsche Investitions- und Entwicklungsgesellschaft mbh v Koshy (No 2) [2002] 1 BCLC 478 . . . . 924, 928

DG Finance Ltd v Scott & Eagle Star Insurance Ltd unreported 10

DHN Food Distributors Ltd v Tower Hamlets London Borough Council [1976] 3 All ER 462, [1976] 1 WLR 852, 74 LGR 506, 32 P & CR 240, 120 Sol Jo 215, 239 Estates Gazette 719, CA 439, 520

DHN Food Transport Ltd v London Borough of Tower Hamlets [1976] 3 All ER 462, [1976] 1 WLR 852, 74 LGR 506, 32 P & CR 240, 120 Sol Jo 215, 239 Estates Gazette 719, CA 235

DKLR Holding Co (No 2) Pty v CSD (NSLU) (1982) 40 ALR 1 273

DKLR Holding Co (No 2) Pty Ltd v Stamp Duties Comr (NSW) (1982) 149 CLR 431 . 15, 243

DWS, Re [2001] Ch 568, [2001] 1 All ER 97, [2000] 3 WLR 1910, [2001] 1 FCR 339, [2000] NLJR 1788, CA 434

D'Abo v Paget (No 2) [2000] WTLR 863 . . . . 840, 841

Dacre, Re, Whitaker v Dacre [1915] 2 Ch 480, 60 Sol Jo 44; affd [1916] 1 Ch 344, 85 LJ Ch 274, 60 Sol Jo 306, 114 LT 387, CA 824, 980

D'Adhemar (Viscountess) v Bertrand (1865) 35 Beav 19 764

Daily Telegraph Newspaper Co Ltd v McLaughlin [1904] AC 776, 73 LJPC 95, 1 CLR 243, 91 LT 233, 20 TLR 674, PC 270

Dale, Re, Proctor v Dale [1994] Ch 31, [1993] 4 All ER 129, [1993] 3 WLR 652, [1994] Fam

Law 77, [1993] 14 LS Gaz R 43, [1993] NLJR 544, 137 Sol Jo LB 83 . . . 262, 265, 427, 428, 430, 433

Dale v IRC [1954] AC 11, [1953] 2 All ER 671, [1953] 3 WLR 448, 34 TC 468, 32 ATC 294, 46 R & IT 513, [1953] TR 269, 97 Sol Jo 538, HL 652

Dallas, Re [1904] 2 Ch 385, 73 LJ Ch 365, 52 WR 567, 48 Sol Jo 260, 90 LT 177, CA . . 1002

Daly v Sydney Stock Exchange Ltd (1986) 160 CLR 371 . . . . 25, 435

Dalziel, Re, Midland Bank Executor and Trustee Co Ltd v St Bartholomew's Hospital [1943] Ch 277, [1943] 2 All ER 656, 112 LJ Ch 353, 87 Sol Jo 281, 169 LT 168, 59 TLR 408 . . . . 118, 120, 121, 189, 202

Damberg v Damberg (2001) 4 ITELR 65, NSWCA 363

Dance v Goldingham (1873) 8 Ch App 902, 38 JP 164, 42 LJ Ch 777, 21 WR 761, 29 LT 166 . . . . 903, 905

D'Angibau, Re, Andrews v Andrews (1879) 15 Ch D 228, 49 LJ Ch 182, 28 WR 311, 41 LT 645; affd (1880) 15 Ch D 236, 49 LJ Ch 756, 28 WR 930, [1874-80] All ER Rep 1184, 43 LT 135, CA. 167, 170, 174, 181

Daniel v Warren (1843) 2 Y & C Ch Cas 290, 7 Jur 462, 60 RR 148 551

Daniel's Settlement Trusts, Re (1875) 1 Ch D 375, 45 LJ Ch 105, 24 WR 227, 34 LT 308, CA 274

Daniele Muritano v Agencia del Territorio, Ufficio Provinciale di Pisa (22 December 2001, unreported) 1056

Danish Bacon Co Ltd Staff Pension Fund, Re, Christensen v Arnett [1971] 1 All ER 486, [1971] 1 WLR 248, 115 Sol Jo 95 . . . . 246, 247

Danson, Re (1899) 48 WR 73, 43 Sol Jo 706 . . . . 743, 766, 768

Darby, Re, Farrell v Fargus (1943) 87 Sol Jo 381, 59 TLR 418 718

Darby, Re, Russell v MacGregor [1939] Ch 905, [1939] 3 All ER 6, 108 LJ Ch 347, 83 Sol Jo 436, 160 LT 602, 55 TLR 792, CA 565

Dargie, Re, Miller v Thornton-Jones [1954] Ch 16, [1953] 2 All ER 577, [1953] 1 WLR 991, 97 Sol Jo 506 812

Darlington Borough Council v Wiltshier Northern Ltd [1995] 3 All ER 895, [1995] 1 WLR 68, [1994] 37 LS Gaz R 49, 69 BLR 1, 11 Const LJ 36, 138 Sol Jo LB 161, CA . 170, 171

Darnley (Earl) Re, Clifton v Darnley [1907] 1 Ch 159, 76 LJ Ch 58, 51 Sol Jo 82, 95 LT 706, 23 TLR 93 552

Dartnall, Re, Sawyer v Goddard [1895] 1 Ch 474, 64 LJ Ch 341, 12 R 237, 43 WR 644, [1895-9] All ER Rep 890, 72 LT 404, CA 677

Davenport v Bishopp (1843) 2 Y & C Ch Cas 451, 12 LJ Ch 492, 7 Jur 1077, 60 RR 234, 9 LTOS 33; affd (1846) 1 Ph 698, 65 RR 483 . . . . 167, 169, 173, 176, 182

Davenport v Marshall [1902] 1 Ch 82, 71 LJ Ch 29, 50 WR 39, 46 Sol Jo 30, 85 LT 340 . 311

Daveron, Re, Bowen v Churchill [1893] 3 Ch 421, 63 LJ Ch 54, 3 R 685, 42 WR 24, 37 Sol Jo 631, 69 LT 752, 9 TLR 570 200

Davey, Re, Prisk v Mitchell [1915] 1 Ch 837, 84 LJ Ch 505, 113 LT 60, CA 229

Davidson v Kimpton (1881) 18 Ch D 213, 29 WR 912, 45 LT 132 735

Davies, ex p (1852) 16 Jur 882, 93 RR 880 574

Davies, Re, Davies v Mackintosh [1957] 3 All ER 52, [1957] 1 WLR 922, 101 Sol Jo 611 . 333

Davies, Re, Lloyd v Cardigan County Council [1915] 1 Ch 543, 13 LGR 437, 79 JP 291, 84 LJ Ch 493, 59 Sol Jo 413, 112 LT 1110 121

Davies, Re, Lloyds Bank Ltd v Mostyn (1932) 49 TLR 5, CA 106

Davies v Davies (1841) 4 Beav 54, 55 RR 16 302

Davies v Davies (1869) LR 9 Eq 468, 39 LJ Ch 343, 18 WR 634, 22 LT 505 . . . . 274, 285

Davies v Hodgson (1858) 25 Beav 177, 27 LJ Ch 449, 4 Jur NS 252, 119 RR 379, 6 WR 355, 31 LTOS 49 . . . . 626, 934

Davies v Otty (No 2) (1865) 35 Beav 208, 34 LJ Ch 252, 5 New Rep 391, 147 RR 113, 13 WR 484, 12 LT 789 . . . . 343, 346, 369

Davies (Paul A) (Australia) Pty Ltd (in liquidation) v Davies [1983] 1 NSWLR 440 . . . 880, 886, 891

Davies' Trusts, Re (1914) 59 Sol Jo 234 830

Davis, Re, Davis v Davis [1902] 2 Ch 314, 71 LJ Ch 539, 51 WR 8, 86 LT 523 . . . 869, 870

Davis, Re, Muckalt v Davis [1887] WN 186, 57 LJ Ch 3, 57 LT 755 814

Davis, Re, Thomas v Davis [1923] 1 Ch 225, 92 LJ Ch 322, 67 Sol Jo 297, 128 LT 735, 39 TLR 201 106

Davis, Re, ex p James (1832) 1 Deac & Ch 272 810

Davis v Duke of Marlborough (1818) 2 Wils Ch 130, 1 Swan 74 . . . . 186, 187

Davis v Hutchings [1907] 1 Ch 356, 76 LJ Ch 272, 96 LT 293 629

Davis v Richards and Wallington Industries Ltd [1991] 2 All ER 563, [1990] 1 WLR 1511 66, 67, 300, 337, 370, 743, 751

Davis v Vale [1971] 2 All ER 1021, [1971] 1 WLR 1022, 115 Sol Jo 347, CA . .   352, 358, 415

Davis' Trusts, Re (1871) LR 12 Eq 214, 40 LJ Ch 566, 19 WR 944 764

Davison's Settlement, Re, Cattermole Davison v Munby [1913] 2 Ch 498, 83 LJ Ch 148, 58 Sol Jo 50, 109 LT 666. 301

Davitt v Titcumb [1990] Ch 110, [1989] 3 All ER 417, [1990] 2 WLR 168, 134 Sol Jo 21, [1990] 1 LS Gaz R 30. 434

Davron Estates Ltd v Turnshire Ltd (1982) 133 NLJ 937, CA. 442

Davy v Garrett (1878) 7 Ch D 473, sub nom Davy Bros Ltd v Garrett 47 LJ Ch 218, 26 WR 225, 38 LT 77, CA 955

Dawes v Tredwell (1881) 18 Ch D 354, 29 WR 793, 45 LT 118, CA 306

Dawkins, Re, Dawkins v Judd [1986] 2 FLR 360, [1986] Fam Law 295 297

Dawson, Re, Arathoon v Dawson [1906] 2 Ch 211, 75 LJ Ch 604, 54 WR 556, 94 LT 817   566

Dawson, Re, Union Fidelity Trustee Co Ltd v Perpetual Trustees Co Ltd (1966) 84 WN 399, [1966] 2 NSWLR 211 . . . . 855, 856, 875

Dawson v Clarke (1811) 18 Ves 247 938

Dawson v Prince (1857) 2 De G & J 41, 27 LJ Ch 169, 4 Jur NS 497, 6 WR 171, 30 LTOS 237   999

Dean, Re, Cooper-Dean v Stevens (1889) 41 Ch D 552, 58 LJ Ch 693, 60 LT 813, 5 TLR 404. . . . . .120, 122, 202, 203

Dean v MacDowell (1878) 8 Ch D 345, 42 JP 580, 47 LJ Ch 537, 26 WR 486, 38 LT 862, CA   385

Dean v Prince [1954] Ch 409, [1954] 1 All ER 749, [1954] 2 WLR 538, 47 R & IT 494, 98 Sol Jo 215, CA 495

Deans, Re, Westminster Bank Ltd v Official Solicitor [1954] 1 All ER 496, [1954] 1 WLR 332, 98 Sol Jo 110 781

Dearle v Hall (1823) 3 Russ 1, [1824-34] All ER Rep 28 . . . . 236, 1002

Debtor, A, Re, ex p Official Receiver, Trustee of the Property of Debtor v Morrison [1965] 3 All ER 453, [1965] 1 WLR 1498, 109 Sol Jo 701. 289

De Bussche v Alt (1878) 8 Ch D 286, 47 LJ Ch 381, 3 Asp MLC 584, [1874-80] All ER Rep 1247, 38 LT 370, CA 8, 665

De Clifford's (Lord) Estate, Re, Lord De Clifford v Quilter [1900] 2 Ch 707, 69 LJ Ch 828, 44 Sol Jo 689, 83 LT 160, 16 TLR 547 . . . . 917, 918

De Francesco v Barnum (1890) 45 Ch D 430, 60 LJ Ch 63, 39 WR 5, [1886-90] All ER Rep 414, 63 LT 438, 6 TLR 463. 268

Delamere's Settlement Trusts, Re, Kenny v Cunningham-Reid [1984] 1 All ER 584, [1984] 1 WLR 813, 128 Sol Jo 318, [1984] LS Gaz R 1597, CA. 715, 716

De La Warr's (Earl) Estates, Re (1881) 16 Ch D 587, 50 LJ Ch 383, 29 WR 350, 44 LT 56 . . . . 564, 574

Delehunt v Carmody (1986) 161 CLR 464 350

Deloitte, Re, Griffiths v Deloitte [1926] Ch 56, 95 LJ Ch 154, [1925] All ER Rep 118, 70 Sol Jo 161, 135 LT 150. . . . . 193, 205

De Lusignan v Johnson (1973) 117 Sol Jo 854, 230 Estates Gazette 499. . . . . . 256, 411

Delves v Gray [1902] 2 Ch 606, 71 LJ Ch 808, 51 WR 56, 87 LT 425 665

De Maudsley v Palumbo [1996] FSR 447, [1996] EMLR 460, Times, 19 December . 395, 403

Demerara Bauxite Co v Hubbard [1923] AC 673, 92 LJPC 148, 129 LT 517 283

De Mestre v West [1891] AC 264, 55 JP 613, 60 LJPC 66, 64 LT 375, PC 166, 167

Den Haag Trust, Re (1998) 1 OFLR 495 677

Denby (William) & Sons Ltd Sick and Benevolent Fund, Re, Rowling v Wilks [1971] 2 All ER 1196, [1971] 1 WLR 973, 115 Sol Jo 290 . . . . 127, 339

De Nicols, Re, De Nicols v Curlier [1900] 2 Ch 410, 69 LJ Ch 680, 48 WR 602, 44 Sol Jo 573, 82 LT 840, 16 TLR 461 1047

Denley's Trust Deed, Re, Holman v HH Martyn & Co Ltd [1969] 1 Ch 373, [1968] 3 All ER 65, [1968] 3 WLR 457, 112 Sol Jo 673 . . . 92, 95, 98, 99, 101, 110, 111, 112, 118, 124

Dennis v McDonald [1982] Fam 63, [1982] 1 All ER 590, [1982] 2 WLR 275, 3 FLR 409, 12 Fam Law 84, 126 Sol Jo 16, CA 356

Dennis's Settlement Trusts, Re, Dennis v Dennis [1942] Ch 283, [1942] 1 All ER 520, 111 LJ Ch 166, 86 Sol Jo 119, 166 LT 243, 58 TLR 405. 212

Denny v Yeldon [1995] 3 All ER 624, [1995] PLR 37, [1995] 1 BCLC 560 462

Densham (a bankrupt), Re, ex p trustee of bankrupt v Densham [1975] 3 All ER 726, [1975] 1 WLR 1519, 119 Sol Jo 774 . . . . 57, 289, 350, 354

Dent v Bennett (1839) 4 My & Cr 269, 8 LJ Ch 125, 3 Jur 99, 48 RR 94 274

Dent v Dent [1996] 1 All ER 659, [1996] 1 WLR 683, [1996] 3 FCR 753, [1996] 1 FLR 815, [1996] Fam Law 355 277

Denton v Donner (1856) 23 Beav 285 668

De Quetteville v De Quetteville, Re De Quetteville (1903) 19 TLR 383, CA 846

Derby v Scottish Equitable plc [2001] EWCA Civ 369, [2001] 3 All ER 818, [2001] NLJR 418,
    sub nom Scottish Equitable plc v Derby [2001] 2 All ER (Comm) 274 978
Derby & Co Ltd v Weldon (Nos 3 and 4) [1990] Ch 65, [1989] 2 WLR 412, 133 Sol Jo 83, sub
    nom Derby & Co Ltd v Weldon (No 2) [1989] 1 All ER 1002, CA. 905
Derby & Co Ltd v Weldon (No 6) [1990] 3 All ER 263, [1990] 1 WLR 1139, 134 Sol Jo 1041,
    [1990] 28 LS Gaz R 45, [1990] NLJR 1001, CA 900, 904
De Ros' Trust, Re, Hardwicke v Wilmot (1885) 31 Ch D 81, 55 LJ Ch 73, 34 WR 36, 53 LT
    524 306
De Sommery, Re, Coelenbier v De Sommery [1912] 2 Ch 622, 82 LJ Ch 17, 57 Sol Jo 78, 107
    LT 253, 823 . . . . .741, 742, 760, 770
Despard, Re, Hancock v Despard (1901) 17 TLR 478 536
De Tabley (Lord), Re, Leighton v Leighton (1896) 75 LT 328 . . . . 572, 573
De Teissier's Settled Estates, Re, Re De Teissier's Trusts, De Teissier v De Teissier [1893] 1
    Ch 153, 62 LJ Ch 552, 3 R 103, 111, 41 WR 184, 186, 37 Sol Jo 46, 47, 68 LT 275, 9 TLR
    62, [1891-4] All ER Rep Ext 1186 573
Detmold, Re, Detmold v Detmold (1889) 40 Ch D 585, 58 LJ Ch 495, 37 WR 442, 61 LT
    21 . . . . 209, 212, 215
Devaynes v Noble, Clayton's Case (1816) 1 Mer 572, [1814-23] All ER Rep 1 891
Devaynes v Noble, Clayton's Case (1816) 8 LJ Ch 256, 1 Mer 529, 572, 35 ER 767, [1814-23]
    All ER Rep 1 994
Devereux, Re, Toovey v Public Trustee [1911] 2 Ch 545, 80 LJ Ch 705, [1911-13] All ER Rep
    641, 55 Sol Jo 715, 105 LT 407, 27 TLR 574 789
Devey v Thornton (1851) 9 Hare 222, 22 LJ Ch 163, 89 RR 404 . . . . 623, 630, 648
De Vigier v IRC [1964] 2 All ER 907, [1964] 1 WLR 1073, 42 TC 24, 43 ATC 223, [1964] TR
    239, 108 Sol Jo 617, HL. 604, 700, 813, 815, 819
De Visme, Re (1863) 2 De GJ & Sm 17, 33 LJ Ch 332, 139 RR 7, 12 WR 140, 9 LT 668 . 364
Devos v Devos (1970) 10 DLR (3d) 603, [1970] 2 OR 323, CA 1037
Dewar v Dewar [1975] 2 All ER 728, [1975] 1 WLR 1532, 119 Sol Jo 681 . . . 149, 245, 368
Dexter Ltd (in administrative receivership) v Harley (2001) Times, 2 April 1043
Dextra Bank and Trust Co Ltd v Bank of Jamaica [2002] 1 All ER (Comm) 193,
    PC 978, 979
Dhingra v Dhingra (1999-2000) 2 ITELR 262, CA 75
Dibbs v Goren (1849) 11 Beav 483. 982
Dick, Re, Knight v Dick [1953] Ch 343, [1953] 1 All ER 559, 97 Sol Jo 149, CA 29
Dickins v Harris [1866] WN 93, 14 LT 98 903
Dickinson v Dillwyn (1869) LR 8 Eq 546, 39 LJ Ch 266, 17 WR 1122, 22 LT 647 . . 308, 312
Dickinson's Settlements, Re, Bickersteth v Dickinson [1939] Ch 27, 108 LJ Ch 40, 82 Sol Jo
    744, 159 LT 614 711
Diggles, Re, Gregory v Edmondson (1888) 39 Ch D 253, 59 LT 884, CA 74, 133
Dillwyn v Llewelyn (1862) 4 De GF & J 517, 31 LJ Ch 658, 8 Jur NS 1068, 10 WR 742, [1861-
    73] All ER Rep 384, 6 LT 878 . . . . 157, 234, 248
Dimes v Scott (1828) 4 Russ 195, 28 RR 46, [1824-34] All ER Rep 653 . . . . 557, 878, 879
Dimos (t/a Leo Dimos & Associates) v Dikeakos Nominees Pty Ltd (1997) 149 ALR 113, 68
    FCR 39 . . . . 811, 820, 826
Dingle v Turner [1972] AC 601, [1972] 1 All ER 878, [1972] 2 WLR 523, 116 Sol Jo 195, HL 108
Diplock, Re, Diplock v Wintle [1948] Ch 465, [1948] 2 All ER 318, [1948] LJR 1670, 92 Sol
    Jo 409, 484, CA; affd sub nom Ministry of Health v Simpson [1951] AC 251, [1950] 2
    All ER 1137, 94 Sol Jo 777, 66 (pt 2) TLR 1015, HL . . .17, 21, 154, 165, 280, 407, 408,
                        698, 788, 880, 881, 884, 885, 886, 890, 891,
                        892, 893, 895, 901, 922, 925, 928, 968,
                        975, 977, 982, 989, 993, 994, 995, 997
Dipple v Corles (1853) 11 Hare 183, 90 RR 633. 73
Director, Real Estate and Business Broker v NRS Mississauga Inc (2000) 194 DLR (4th) 527 971
Dive, Re, Dive v Roebuck [1909] 1 Ch 328, 78 LJ Ch 248, 100 LT 190 606
Diwell v Farnes [1959] 2 All ER 379, [1959] 1 WLR 624, 103 Sol Jo 431, 173 Estates Gazette
    823, CA 351
Dix v Burford (1854) 19 Beav 409 938
Dixon, Re, Dixon v Charlesworth [1903] 2 Ch 458, 72 LJ Ch 642, 51 WR 652, 88 LT
    862 . . . . 189, 190, 209
Dixon, Re, ex p Griffin (1826) 2 Gl & J 114, 2 Gl & J 114. 644
D'Jan of London Ltd, Re [1994] 1 BCLC 561, [1993] BCC 646, [1993] 31 LS Gaz R 38 . 917
Docker v Somes (1834) 2 My & K 655, 3 LJ Ch 200, [1824-34] All ER Rep 402 . . . 870, 875
Docksey v Docksey (1708) 2 Eq Cas Abr 506 330

Dodds v Hills (1865) 2 Hem & M 424, 71 ER 528, 12 LT 139 . . . . 256, 1002
Dodds v Tuke (1884) 25 Ch D 617, 53 LJ Ch 598, 32 WR 424, 50 LT 320. . . . . . 811, 818
Dodkin v Brunt (1868) LR 6 Eq 580 . . . . .77, 764
Dodsworth v Dodsworth (1973) 228 Estates Gazette 1115, [1973] EGD 233, CA 248
Dodwell & Co Ltd's Trust, Re, Baker v Timmins [1979] Ch 301, [1979] 2 WLR 169, 123 Sol
    Jo 98, sub nom Re Dodwell & Co Ltd's Trust Deed [1978] 3 All ER 738 . . . 204, 208
Doe d Read v Godwin (1822) 1 Dow & Ry KB 259. 741
Doe d Chidgey v Harris (1847) 16 M & W 517 . . . . 449, 451, 452
Doe d Hayter v Joinville (1802) 3 East 172, 6 RR 585 82
Doering v Doering (1889) 42 Ch D 203, 58 LJ Ch 553, 37 WR 796 . . . .824, 951, 980, 983
Doland's Will Trusts, Re, Westminster Bank Ltd v Phillips [1970] Ch 267, [1969] 3 All ER
    713, [1969] 3 WLR 614, 113 Sol Jo 798 280
Donaldson v Donaldson (1854) Kay 711, 23 LJ Ch 788, 1 Jur NS 10, 2 WR 691, [1843-60] All
    ER Rep 200, 23 LTOS 306 268
Donn, Re, Donn v Moses [1944] Ch 8, [1943] 2 All ER 564, 113 LJ Ch 61, 87 Sol Jo 406, 169
    LT 335, 60 TLR 30. 102
Dougan v Macpherson [1902] AC 197, 71 LJPC 62, 50 WR 689, 86 LT 361, HL . . 671, 935
Doughty, Re, Burridge v Doughty [1947] Ch 263, [1947] 1 All ER 207, 176 LT 173, 63 TLR
    257, CA 536, 538, 539
Douglas, Re, Obert v Barrow (1886) 35 Ch D 472; affd (1887) 35 Ch D 472, 56 LJ Ch 913, 35
    WR 740, [1886-90] All ER Rep 228, 56 LT 786, 3 TLR 589, CA. 28
Douglas v Archbutt (1858) 2 De G & J 148, 27 LJ Ch 271, 4 Jur NS 315, 6 WR 306, 31 LTOS 4 659
Douglas v Bolam [1900] 2 Ch 749, 70 LJ Ch 1, 49 WR 163, 45 Sol Jo 29, 83 LT 448, 17 TLR 1,
    CA 751, 786
Douglas's Will Trusts, Re, Lloyds Bank Ltd v Nelson [1959] 2 All ER 620, [1959] 1 WLR 744,
    103 Sol Jo 657; affd [1959] 3 All ER 785, [1959] 1 WLR 1212, 104 Sol Jo 126, CA . 612
Dove v Everard (1830) 1 Russ & M 231, Taml 376, 32 RR 200 . . . . 452, 453
Dover v Buck (1865) 5 Giff 57, 11 Jur NS 580, 5 New Rep 444, 12 LT 136 665
Dover Coalfield Extension Ltd, Re [1908] 1 Ch 65, 77 LJ Ch 94, 15 Mans 51, [1904-7] All ER
    Rep 161, 52 Sol Jo 43, 98 LT 31, 24 TLR 52, CA 389
Dowding's Settlement Trusts, Re, Gregory v Dowding [1904] 1 Ch 441, 73 LJ Ch 194, 52 WR
    293, 48 Sol Jo 191, 90 LT 82 307
Downes v Bullock (1858) 25 Beav 54; affd sub nom Bullock v Downes (1860) 9 HL Cas 1,
    [1843-60] All ER Rep 706, 3 LT 194 982
Downshire Settled Estates, Re, Marquess of Downshire v Royal Bank of Scotland [1953] Ch
    218, [1953] 1 All ER 103, [1953] 2 WLR 94, 46 R & IT 64, 97 Sol Jo 29, CA. . 500, 524,
                                                                                    527
Downsview Nominees Ltd v First City Corpn Ltd [1993] AC 295, [1993] 3 All ER 626, [1993]
    2 WLR 86, [1994] 1 BCLC 49, [1993] BCC 46, [1992] 45 LS Gaz R 26, 136 Sol Jo LB
    324, PC 49, 581
Dowse v Gorton [1891] AC 190, 60 LJ Ch 745, 40 WR 17, [1891-4] All ER Rep 1230, 64 LT
    809, HL. 814
Doyle v Blake (1804) 9 RR 76, 2 Sch & Lef 231 . . . . 449, 451, 632
Doyle v Crean [1905] 1 IR 252 375
Drake v Whipp [1996] 2 FCR 296, [1996] 1 FLR 826, [1996] Fam Law 472, 28 HLR 531, CA 417
Drake's Settlement, Re [1926] WN 132, 70 Sol Jo 621, 42 TLR 467 . . . . . 793, 794, 795
Dreger, Re (1976) 69 DLR (3d) 47 434
Drew v Martin (1864) 2 Hem & M 130, 33 LJ Ch 367, 10 Jur NS 356, 3 New Rep 637, 144 RR
    78, 12 WR 547, 71 ER 411, 10 LT 291 350
Drewe's Settlement, Re, Drewe v Westminster Bank Ltd [1966] 2 All ER 844n, [1966] 1 WLR
    1518, 110 Sol Jo 689 515
Drexel Burnham Lambert UK Pension Plan, Re [1995] 1 WLR 32 . . . . . 401, 655, 656,
                                                                        667, 668, 771
Druce's Settlement Trusts, Re [1962] 1 All ER 563, [1962] 1 WLR 363, 106 Sol Jo
    112. . . . . 510, 521
Drummond, Re, Ashworth v Drummond [1914] 2 Ch 90, 83 LJ Ch 817, [1914-15] All ER
    Rep 223, 58 Sol Jo 472, 111 LT 156, 30 TLR 429 125
Drummond v Collins (Surveyor of Taxes) [1915] AC 1011, 6 TC 525, 84 LJKB 1690, 59 Sol Jo
    577, 113 LT 665, 31 TLR 482, HL. 711
Drummond's Settlement, Re, Foster v Foster [1986] 3 All ER 45, [1986] 1 WLR 1096, 130
    Sol Jo 635; revsd [1988] 1 All ER 449, [1988] 1 WLR 234, 132 Sol Jo 192, [1988] 9 LS
    Gaz R 46, CA 194, 333

Dubai Aluminium Co Ltd v Salaam [1999] 1 Lloyd's Rep 415; on appeal [2001] QB 113, [2000] 3 WLR 910, CA .943, 965, 966, 974

Dubois, ex p (1787) 1 Cox Eq Cas 310 456

Duckwari plc, Re [1999] Ch 253, [1998] 3 WLR 913, 142 Sol Jo LB 163, sub nom Duckwari v Offerventure Ltd (No 2) [1998] 2 BCLC 315, [1998] 20 LS Gaz R 36, [1998] 22 LS Gaz R 28, CA. 851, 852, 853, 856

Duff's Settlement, Re, National Provincial Bank Ltd v Gregson [1951] Ch 923, [1951] 2 All ER 534, 95 Sol Jo 595, [1951] 2 TLR 474, CA 537

Dufour v Pereira (1769) 1 Dick 419, sub nom Durour v Perraro 2 Hargrave Juridical Arguments 304 .140, 427, 428, 430

Dugdale, Re, Dugdale v Dugdale (1888) 38 Ch D 176, 57 LJ Ch 634, 36 WR 462, 58 LT 581, [1886-90] All ER Rep Ext 1505 . . . . 190, 209, 214

Dullow v Dullow [1985] 3 NSWLR 531, [1985] 3 NSWLR 531 350

Dumbell, Re, ex p Hughes, ex p Lyon (1802) 6 RR 1, 6 Ves 617 666

Dunbar v Dunbar [1909] 2 Ch 639, 79 LJ Ch 70, [1908-10] All ER Rep 136, 101 LT 553, 26 TLR 21 362

Dunbar v Plant [1998] Ch 412, [1997] 4 All ER 289, [1997] 3 WLR 1261, [1998] 1 FLR 157, [1998] Fam Law 139, [1997] 36 LS Gaz R 44, CA 435

Dunbar Bank plc v Nadeem [1998] 3 All ER 876, [1998] 3 FCR 629, [1998] 2 FLR 457, [1998] Fam Law 595, 31 HLR 402, 77 P & CR D8, CA 287

Duncan v Dixon (1890) 44 Ch D 211, 59 LJ Ch 437, 38 WR 700, 62 LT 319, 6 TLR 222 . 269

Duncan v Lawson (1889) 41 Ch D 394, 53 JP 532, 58 LJ Ch 502, 37 WR 524, 60 LT 732 . . . . 188, 1027

Dundee General Hospitals Board of Management v Walker [1952] 1 All ER 896, sub nom Dundee General Hospitals v Bell's Trustees 1952 SC (HL) 78, 1952 SLT 270 . .89, 215, 915

Dunford and Elliott Ltd v Johnson and Firth Brown Ltd [1977] 1 Lloyd's Rep 505, [1978] FSR 143, 121 Sol Jo 53, [1976] LS Gaz R 1060, CA 403

Dungannon (Lord) v Smith (1846) 12 Cl & Fin 546, 10 Jur 721, 61 RR 137, HL 193

Dunlop Pneumatic Tyre Co Ltd v Selfridge & Co Ltd [1915] AC 847, 84 LJKB 1680, [1914-15] All ER Rep 333, 59 Sol Jo 439, 113 LT 386, 31 TLR 399, HL 170

Dunn, Re, Brinklow v Singleton [1904] 1 Ch 648, 73 LJ Ch 425, 52 WR 345, 48 Sol Jo 261, 91 LT 135 818

Dunn v Campbell (1879) 27 Ch D 254n 903

Dunn v Flood (1885) 28 Ch D 586, 54 LJ Ch 370, 33 WR 315, 52 LT 699, 1 TLR 206, CA 705

Dunne v Byrne [1912] AC 407, 81 LJPC 202, [1911-13] All ER Rep 1105, 56 Sol Jo 324, 106 LT 394, 28 TLR 257, PC. 106

Dunne v English (1874) LR 18 Eq 524, 31 LT 75, [1874-80] All ER Rep Ext 1916 . . . 23

Dunsany's Settlement, Re, Nott v Dunsany [1906] 1 Ch 578, 75 LJ Ch 356, 94 LT 361, CA 308

Dunstan, Re, Dunstan v Dunstan [1918] 2 Ch 304, 87 LJ Ch 597, [1918-19] All ER Rep 694, 63 Sol Jo 10, 119 LT 561 79

Dutton v Thompson (1883) 23 Ch D 278, 52 LJ Ch 661, 31 WR 596, 49 LT 109, CA . . 276

Duxbury's Settlement Trusts, Re [1995] 3 All ER 145, [1995] 1 WLR 425, [1994] 46 LS Gaz R 30, CA. 278, 698, 795

Duyvewaardt v Barber (1992) 71 BCLR 2d 396, 43 RFL (3d) 139, 19 BCAC 13, 34 WAC 13, BC CA 1039

Dyer v Dyer (1788) 2 RR 14, 2 Cox Eq Cas 92, [1775-1802] All ER Rep 205 . . . . . .12, 349

Dynamite Act v Rio Tinto Co [1918] AC 260, 87 LJKB 531, [1918-19] All ER Rep 127, 118 LT 181, 34 TLR 208, HL 1051

Dyson and Fowke, Re [1896] 2 Ch 720, 65 LJ Ch 791, 45 WR 28, 74 LT 759. 200

E

E v E [1989] FCR 591, [1990] 2 FLR 233, [1990] Fam Law 297. 1044

EMI Records Ltd v Ian Cameron Wallace Ltd [1983] Ch 59, [1982] 2 All ER 980, [1982] 3 WLR 245, 126 Sol Jo 465 815

EMM Capricorn Trustees Ltd v Compass Trustees Ltd (2002) 4 ITELR 34 1059

EVTR, Re, Gilbert v Barber [1987] BCLC 646, 3 BCC 389, CA 56, 116, 380

Eades, Re, Eades v Eades [1920] 2 Ch 353, 89 LJ Ch 604, 123 LT 777 . . . . . . 106, 741

Eady v Watson (1864) 33 Beav 481, 10 Jur NS 982, 140 RR 225, 12 WR 682, 10 LT 285 . 574

Eagle Star Insurance v Karasiewicz [2002] EWCA Civ 940, [2002] All ER (D) 240 (Apr) . 897, 902

Eagle Trust plc v SBC Securities Ltd [1992] 4 All ER 488, [1993] 1 WLR 484, [1991] BCLC 438 . . . . 960, 974, 989

Earl of Chesterfield v Jansen (1751) 2 Ves Sen 125 932
East, Re, Re Bellwood's Will Trusts (1873) 8 Ch App 735, 42 LJ Ch 480 . . . 269, 753, 754
East India Co v Atkyns (1720) 1 Com 346, 1 Stra 168 685
Eastern Counties Rly Co v Hawkes (1855) 5 HL Cas 331, 24 LJ Ch 601, 101 RR 183, 3 WR
    609, 25 LTOS 318 583
Eastes, Re, Pain v Paxon [1948] Ch 257, [1948] 1 All ER 536, [1948] LJR 917, 92 Sol Jo 206,
    64 TLR 216 106
Eaton, Re, Shaw v Midland Bank Executor and Trustee Co Ltd [1964] 3 All ER 229n, [1964]
    1 WLR 1269, 108 Sol Jo 656 . . . . 816, 837, 838
Eaton v Daines [1894] WN 32 . . . . 20, 760, 768
Eaves v Hickson (1861) 30 Beav 136, 7 Jur NS 1297, 132 RR 213, 10 WR 29, 5 LT
    598. . . . . 623, 625, 631
Ebrand v Dancer (1680) 2 Cas in Ch 26 . . . . 349, 366
Eddis v Chichester Constable [1969] 2 Ch 345, [1969] 2 All ER 912, [1969] 3 WLR 48, 113
    Sol Jo 386, CA 930, 931
Edell v Sitzer (2001) 4 ITELR 149 . . . . 82, 266, 431
Eden, Re, Ellis v Crampton [1957] 2 All ER 430, [1957] 1 WLR 788, 101 Sol Jo 481. . 84, 508
Edgar, Re, Cohen v Edgar [1939] 1 All ER 635, 83 Sol Jo 154 102
Edge v Pensions Ombudsman [1998] Ch 512, [1998] 2 All ER 547, [1998] 3 WLR 466,
    [1998] PLR 15; affd [2000] Ch 602, [1999] 4 All ER 546, [2000] 3 WLR 79, [2000] ICR
    748, [1999] PLR 215, [1999] 35 LS Gaz R 39, [1999] NLJR 1442, CA . . 486, 529, 530,
                                    549, 603, 610, 614, 654, 660, 667,
                                    668, 680, 692, 693, 701
Edinburgh Corpn v Lord Advocate (1879) 4 App Cas 823, HL 891
Edmonds v Edmonds [1965] 1 All ER 379n, [1965] 1 WLR 58, 108 Sol Jo 1047 211
Edward's Will Trusts, Re, Dalgleish v Leighton [1947] 2 All ER 521, [1948] LJR 60, 91 Sol Jo
    572; revsd sub nom Edwards' Will Trusts, Re, Dalgleish v Leighton [1948] Ch 440,
    [1948] 1 All ER 821, [1948] LJR 1364, 92 Sol Jo 297, CA 94
Edwards, Re (1873) 9 Ch App 97, 43 LJ Ch 265, 22 WR 144, [1861-73] All ER Rep 958, 29 LT
    712. . . . . 309, 311, 312
Edwards, Re, Newbery v Edwards [1918] 1 Ch 142, 87 LJ Ch 248, [1916-17] All ER Rep 258,
    62 Sol Jo 191, 118 LT 17, 34 TLR 135 555
Edwards v Carter [1893] AC 360, 58 JP 4, 63 LJ Ch 100, 1 R 218, [1891-4] All ER Rep 1259,
    69 LT 153, HL 269
Edwards v Edwards [1909] AC 275, 78 LJ Ch 504, 100 LT 84, HL. 192
Edwards v Fashion (1712) Prec Ch 332 350
Edwards v Hood-Barrs [1905] 1 Ch 20, 74 LJ Ch 167, [1904-7] All ER Rep 483, 91 LT 766, 21
    TLR 89 . . . . 580, 878
Edwards v Meyrick (1842) 2 Hare 60, 12 LJ Ch 49, 6 Jur 924 666
Edwards v West (1878) 7 Ch D 858, 47 LJ Ch 463, 26 WR 507, 38 LT 481 441
Edwards' Will Trusts, Re, Dalgleish v Leighton. See Edward's Will Trusts, Re, Dalgleish v
    Leighton
Edwards' Will Trusts, Re, Edwards v Edwards [1982] Ch 30, [1981] 2 All ER 941, [1981] 3
    WLR 15, 125 Sol Jo 258, CA 20, 24, 379, 455
Egbert v Butter (1856) 21 Beav 560 647
Egerton v Earl Brownlow (1853) 4 HL Cas 1, 8 State Tr NS 193, 23 LJ Ch 348, 18 Jur 71,
    [1843-60] All ER Rep 970, 21 LTOS 306 66
Egerton v Egerton [1949] 2 All ER 238, [1949] LJR 1683, 93 Sol Jo 551, 65 TLR 615, CA   218
Egg v Devey (1847) 10 Beav 444, 16 LJ Ch 509, 11 Jur 1023, 76 RR 170, 10 LTOS 243. . 933
Eglin v Sanderson (1862) 3 Giff 434, 8 Jur NS 329, 133 RR 156, 6 LT 151 677
Egmont (Earl) v Smith (1877) 6 Ch D 469, 46 LJ Ch 356 442
Eighmie, Re, Colbourne v Wilks [1935] Ch 524, 104 LJ Ch 254, 153 LT 295, 51 TLR 404. 119
Eiser's Will Trusts, Re, Fogg v Eastwood [1937] 1 All ER 244 . . . . 162, 213
El Ajou v Dollar Land Holdings plc [1993] 3 All ER 717, [1993] BCLC 735, [1993] BCC 698;
    revsd [1994] 2 All ER 685, [1994] 1 BCLC 464, [1994] BCC 143, CA . . . 25, 331, 405,
                                    408, 436, 880, 886, 900, 901, 960, 968,
                                    974, 992, 998, 999, 1021, 1043, 1049
El Ajou v Dollar Land Holdings plc (No 2) [1995] 2 All ER 213 . . . . 871, 998
El Amria, The. See Aratra Potato Co Ltd v Egyptian Navigation Co, The El Amria
Eldan Services Ltd v Chandag Motors Ltd [1990] 3 All ER 459 903
Elders Trustee & Executor Co Ltd v Higgins (1965) 113 CLR 426. 864
Electrolux Ltd v Hudson [1977] FSR 312 399

Eleftheria, The. See Owners of Cargo lately laden on board ship or vessel Eleftheria v The
   Eleftheria (Owners), The Eleftheria
Elford, Re, Elford v Elford [1910] 1 Ch 814, 79 LJ Ch 385, 54 Sol Jo 542, 102 LT 488 . . 551,
   555
Elford v Elford (1922) 64 SCR 125, 69 DLR 284, [1922] 3 WWR 339 346
Elias v George Sahely & Co (Barbados) Ltd [1983] 1 AC 646, [1982] 3 All ER 801, [1982] 3
   WLR 956, 126 Sol Jo 708, PC 234
Ellenborough, Re, Towry Law v Burne [1903] 1 Ch 697, 72 LJ Ch 218, 51 WR 315, 47 Sol Jo
   255, 87 LT 714 . . . . 153, 173, 175, 183, 184, 185, 264, 502
Ellerman Lines Ltd v Lancaster Maritime Co Ltd, The Lancaster [1980] 2 Lloyd's Rep 497 890
Ellerman's Settlement Trusts, Re, Hitch v Ruegg [1984] LS Gaz R 430 541
Elliot, Re, Kelly v Elliot [1896] 2 Ch 353, 65 LJ Ch 753, 44 WR 632, 40 Sol Jo 600, 75 LT 138,
   12 TLR 497 214
Elliot v Ince (1857) 7 De GM & G 475, 26 LJ Ch 821, 3 Jur NS 597, 5 WR 465, 30 LTOS 92 270
Elliot's Trusts, Re (1873) LR 15 Eq 194, 42 LJ Ch 289, 21 WR 455 . . . . . 829, 830, 846
Elliott, Re, Lloyds Bank Ltd v Burton-on-Trent Hospital Management Committee [1952] Ch
   217, [1952] 1 All ER 145, 96 Sol Jo 73, [1952] 1 TLR 298 . . . . 189, 202, 231
Elliott, Re, Montgomery v Potterton [1918] 1 IR 41 221
Elliott, Re, Public Trustee v Pinder [1918] 2 Ch 150, 87 LJ Ch 449, [1918-19] All ER Rep
   1151, 62 Sol Jo 383, 118 LT 675 206
Ellis, Re, Nettleton v Crimmins [1935] Ch 193, 104 LJ Ch 53, [1934] All ER Rep 58, 152 LT
   370 559
Ellis v Barker (1871) 7 Ch App 104, 41 LJ Ch 64, 20 WR 160, 25 LT 688 532
Ellis v Chief Adjudication Officer [1998] 2 FCR 51, [1998] 1 FLR 184, CA . . . 35, 80, 102,
   136, 137
Ellis v Kerr [1910] 1 Ch 529, 79 LJ Ch 291, 54 Sol Jo 307, 102 LT 417 663
Ellis v Maxwell (1841) 3 Beav 587, 10 LJ Ch 266, 52 RR 235 204
Ellis v Selby (1836) 1 My & Cr 286, 5 LJ Ch 214, 43 RR 188 105
Ellis's Settlement, Re, Ellis v Ellis [1909] 1 Ch 618, 78 LJ Ch 375, 100 LT 511, 26 TLR 166 309
Ellison v Ellison (1802) 6 RR 19, 6 Ves 656, [1775-1802] All ER Rep 119, 2 White & Tud LC
   8th ed 853 77
Elmore's Will Trusts, Re (1860) 6 Jur NS 1325, 119 RR 1113, 9 WR 66, 3 LT 359 574
Emery's Investments' Trusts, Re, Emery v Emery [1959] Ch 410, [1959] 1 All ER 577, [1959]
   2 WLR 461, 103 Sol Jo 257 346
Emmet's Estate, Re, Emmet v Emmet (1881) 17 Ch D 142, 50 LJ Ch 341, 29 WR 464, 44 LT
   172 . . . . 868, 869
Empress Engineering Co, Re (1880) 16 Ch D 125, 29 WR 342, 43 LT 742, [1874-80] All ER
   Rep Ext 1333, CA 170
Emuss v Smith (1848) 2 De G & Sm 722 441
Endacott, Re, Corpe v Endacott [1960] Ch 232, [1959] 3 All ER 562, [1959] 3 WLR 799, 58
   LGR 25, 103 Sol Jo 918, CA 28, 75, 82, 83, 106, 110, 111, 113, 118, 119, 123
Engels, Re, National Provincial Bank Ltd v Mayer [1943] 1 All ER 506, 87 Sol Jo 148, 168 LT
   311 193
England, Re (1830) 1 Russ & M 488 720
England v Public Trustee (1967) 112 Sol Jo 70, 205 Estates Gazette 651, CA 465
England's Settlement Trusts, Re, Dobb v England [1918] 1 Ch 24, 87 LJ Ch 73, 117 LT
   466 . . . . 578, 646, 815
English v Dedham Vale Properties Ltd [1978] 1 All ER 382, [1978] 1 WLR 93, 35 P & CR
   148, 121 Sol Jo 320, 245 Estates Gazette 747, 839, [1978] JPL 315 . . . . . 22, 397, 398
English & American Insurance Co Ltd, Re [1994] 1 BCLC 649 76
Equitable Reversionary Interest Society v Fuller (1861) 1 John & H 379, 30 LJ Ch 497, 7 Jur
   NS 307, 128 RR 429, 9 WR 400, 4 LT 50; affd (1861) 30 LJ Ch 848 574
Equiticorp Industries Group Ltd v R [1996] 3 NZLR 586 976
Equiticorp Industries Group Ltd (in Statutory Management) v R (Judgment No 47) [1998]
   2 NZLR 481 . . . . 956, 958, 961, 963, 976
Equity and Law Home Loans Ltd v Prestidge [1992] 1 All ER 909, [1992] 1 WLR 137, 63 P &
   CR 403, [1992] 1 FCR 353, [1992] 1 FLR 485, [1992] Fam Law 288, 24 HLR 76, [1992]
   2 LS Gaz R 31, CA 891
Erie Beach Co Ltd v A-G for Ontario [1930] AC 161, 99 LJPC 38, 142 LT 156, 46 TLR 33,
   PC 1029
Ernest v Croysdill (1860) 2 De GF & J 175, 29 LJ Ch 580, 6 Jur NS 740, 129 RR 51, 8 WR 736,
   2 LT 616 880
Ernest v Vivian (1863) 33 LJ Ch 513, 12 WR 295, 9 LT 785, [1861-73] All ER Rep Ext 1531 50

Errington v Carrick. See Carrick v Errington
Erskine's Settlement Trusts, Re, Hollis v Pigott [1971] 1 All ER 572, [1971] 1 WLR 162, 115
    Sol Jo 113 715
Essery v Cowlard (1884) 26 Ch D 191, 53 LJ Ch 661, 32 WR 518, 51 LT 60 . . . . . 274, 333
Estate Realties Ltd v Wignall [1992] 2 NZLR 615 965
Esteem Settlement, Re [2002] Jersey LR 53 894
Euroactividade AG v Mason Investment [1994] NPC 55. 901
Evan's Will Trusts, Re, Pickering v Evans [1921] 2 Ch 309, 91 LJ Ch 29, 65 Sol Jo 753, 125 LT
    822 552
Evans, Re, Evans v Evans (1887) 34 Ch D 597, 35 WR 586, 56 LT 768, CA . . 811, 814, 823
Evans, Re, Evans v Westcombe [1999] 2 All ER 777, 143 Sol Jo LB 72 . . . . 869, 915, 916
Evans, Re, Hewitt v Edwards [1940] Ch 629, 109 LJ Ch 216, 84 Sol Jo 319, 162 LT 420, 56
    TLR 630. 102
Evans, Re, Jones v Evans [1913] 1 Ch 23, 82 LJ Ch 12, 19 Mans 397, 57 Sol Jo 60, 107 LT
    604 535
Evans v Benyon (1887) 37 Ch D 329, 58 LT 700 . . . . .931, 936, 941, 944, 949
Evans v Bicknell (1801) 1 Coop temp Cott 480, 5 RR 245, 6 Ves 174. . . . . . . 457, 1001
Evans v Brunner, Mond & Co [1921] 1 Ch 359, 90 LJ Ch 294, 65 Sol Jo 134, 124 LT 469. 271
Evans v Carrington (1860) 25 JP 195, 2 De GF & J 481, 30 LJ Ch 364, 7 Jur NS 197, 45 ER
    707, 4 LT 65 281
Evans v Coventry (1854) 19 JP 37, 5 De GM & G 911, 3 Eq Rep 545, 104 RR 343, 3 WR 149, 5
    WR 187, 24 LTOS 186 904
Evans v Edmonds (1853) 13 CB 777, 22 LJCP 211, 17 Jur 883, 93 RR 732, 1 WR 412, 138 ER
    1407, 1 CLR 653, 21 LTOS 155 281
Evans v Evans [1985] 3 All ER 289, [1986] 1 WLR 101, [1986] 1 FLR 319, [1986] Fam Law
    103, 129 Sol Jo 833, [1985] LS Gaz R 3530, [1985] NLJ Rep 1008, CA 816, 843,
                                           844, 845
Evans v John (1841) 4 Beav 35, 55 RR 7 452
Evans v Walker (1876) 3 Ch D 211, 25 WR 7 197
Evans' Settlement, Re, Watkins v Whitworth-Jones [1967] 3 All ER 343, [1967] 1 WLR 1294,
    111 Sol Jo 811 718
Evans' Trusts, Re (1872) 7 Ch App 609, 41 LJ Ch 512, 20 WR 695, 26 LT 815 . . . 564, 574
Evans' Will Trusts, Re, Public Trustee v Gausby [1948] Ch 185, [1948] 1 All ER 381, [1949]
    LJR 555, 92 Sol Jo 72 793
Evanturel v Evanturel (1874) LR 6 PC 1, 43 LJPC 58, 23 WR 32, 31 LT 105 217
Evered, Re, Molineux v Evered [1910] 2 Ch 147, 79 LJ Ch 465, 54 Sol Jo 540, 102 LT 694, CA 133
Everett v Prythergch (1841) 12 Sim 363, 11 LJ Ch 6, 54, 6 Jur 3, 56 RR 68 905
Everitt v Everitt (1870) LR 10 Eq 405, 39 LJ Ch 777, 18 WR 1020, 23 LT 136 . . . . 276, 282
Evers v Challis (1859) 7 HL Cas 531, 29 LJQB 121, 5 Jur NS 825, 115 RR 257, 7 WR 622, 33
    LTOS 373 . . . . 190, 229
Evers's Trust, Re, Papps v Evers [1980] 3 All ER 399, [1980] 1 WLR 1327, 10 Fam Law 245,
    124 Sol Jo 562, CA 481
Eves, Re, Midland Bank Executor and Trustee Co Ltd v Eves [1939] Ch 969, 108 LJ Ch 374,
    83 Sol Jo 623, 161 LT 270, 55 TLR 961 534
Eves v Eves [1975] 3 All ER 768, [1975] 1 WLR 1338, 119 Sol Jo 394, CA. . . 413, 415, 416,
                                   420, 421, 423, 424
Ewart v Ewart (1853) 11 Hare 276, 1 Eq Rep 536, 17 Jur 1022, 90 RR 690, 1 WR 466 . . 308
Ewart v Taylor (Inspector of Taxes) [1983] STC 721, 57 TC 401 807
Exhall Coal Co Ltd, Re, Re Bleckley (1866) 35 Beav 449, 12 Jur NS 757, 14 WR 599, 14 LT
    280. 812
Exham v Beamish [1939] IR 336 231
Eykyn's Trusts, Re (1877) 6 Ch D 115, 37 LT 261 350
Eyre v Burmester (1862) 10 HL Cas 90, 6 LT 838 436
Eyre v Countess of Shaftesbury (1722) 2 Eq Cas Abr 710, 755, 2 P Wms 103, [1558-1774] All
    ER Rep 129, sub nom Earl Shaftsbury v Shaftsbury Gilb Ch 172, 24 ER 659 . . 740, 741
Eyre v Dolphin (1813) 12 RR 94, 2 Ball & B 290 383
Eyton, Re, Bartlett v Charles (1890) 45 Ch D 458, 59 LJ Ch 733, 39 WR 135, 63 LT 336,
    [1886-90] All ER Rep Ext 1187 999
Ezekiel's Settlement Trusts, Re, National Provincial Bank Ltd v Hyam [1942] Ch 230, [1942]
    2 All ER 224, 111 LJ Ch 155, 86 Sol Jo 76, 166 LT 137, CA 708

F

Faccenda Chicken Ltd v Fowler [1987] Ch 117, [1986] 1 All ER 617, [1986] 3 WLR 288, [1986] FSR 291, [1986] ICR 297, [1986] IRLR 69, 130 Sol Jo 573, CA 395

Falcke v Scottish Imperial Insurance Co (1886) 34 Ch D 234, 56 LJ Ch 707, 35 WR 143, 56 LT 220, 3 TLR 141, CA 250, 352

Falconer v Falconer [1970] 3 All ER 449, [1970] 1 WLR 1333, 114 Sol Jo 720, CA . . . 366

Falconer's Trusts, Re, Property and Estates Co Ltd v Frost [1908] 1 Ch 410, 77 LJ Ch 303 805

Fales v Canada Permanent Trustee Co (1976) 70 DLR (3d) 257 872

Falkiner, Re, Mead v Smith [1924] 1 Ch 88, 93 LJ Ch 76, [1923] All ER Rep 681, 68 Sol Jo 101, 130 LT 405 259

Fane v Fane (1879) 13 Ch D 228, 49 LJ Ch 200, 28 WR 348, 41 LT 551 848

Farhall v Farhall (1871) 7 Ch App 123, 41 LJ Ch 146, 20 WR 157, 25 LT 685 457

Farley v Westminster Bank [1939] AC 430, [1939] 3 All ER 491, 108 LJ Ch 307, 161 LT 103, 55 TLR 943, HL 106

Farmer v Dean (1863) 32 Beav 327, 138 RR 755 . . . . 401, 667

Farnham's Settlement, Re, Law Union and Crown Insurance Co v Hartopp [1904] 2 Ch 561, 2 LGR 1050, 73 LJ Ch 667, 48 Sol Jo 604, 91 LT 780, CA 568, 571

Farrant v Blanchford (1863) 1 De GJ & Sm 107, 32 LJ Ch 237, 9 Jur NS 423, 137 RR 164, 11 WR 294, 7 LT 770 .933, 934, 935, 944

Farrar v Barraclough (1854) 97 RR 184, 2 Sm & G 231, 2 WR 244 934

Farrar v Farrars Ltd (1888) 40 Ch D 395, 58 LJ Ch 185, 37 WR 196, 60 LT 121, 5 TLR 164, CA 664

Farrington v Row McBride & Partners [1985] 1 NZLR 83 . . . . 22, 24, 660

Favorke v Steinkopff [1922] 1 Ch 174, sub nom Re Steinkopff, Favorke v Steinkopff 91 LJ Ch 165, 126 LT 597 1029

Fawcett, Re, Public Trustee v Dugdale [1940] Ch 402, 109 LJ Ch 124, 84 Sol Jo 186, 162 LT 250, 56 TLR 468 558

Fawcett v Whitehouse (1829) 1 Russ & M 132, 8 LJOS Ch 50, 39 ER 51 386

Featherstonhaugh v Fenwick (1810) 17 Ves 298, 31 WR 318, [1803-13] All ER Rep 89 . . 385

Feistel v King's College, Cambridge (1847) 10 Beav 491, 16 LJ Ch 339, 11 Jur 506, 7 LTOS 222 187

Fellows v Owen (1705) Freem Ch 283, 286, 2 Vern 504, 515, sub nom Fellows v Mitchell 1 P Wms 81 647

Fellows' Settlement, Re (1856) 2 Jur NS 62, 106 RR 921 574

Fentem, Re, Cockerton v Fentem [1950] 2 All ER 1073, 94 Sol Jo 779 220

Fenwick v Clarke (1862) 4 De GF & J 240, 31 LJ Ch 728, 10 WR 636, 6 LT 593 . . 543, 982

Fenwick v Greenwell (1847) 10 Beav 412, 11 Jur 620, 76 RR 154 578

Ferguson v IRC [1970] AC 442, [1969] 1 All ER 1025, [1969] 2 WLR 1116, 46 TC 1, 48 ATC 50, [1969] TR 63, 113 Sol Jo 286, 1969 SC (HL) 103, 1969 SLT 201 533

Ferraby v Hobson (1847) 2 Ph 255, 16 LJ Ch 499, 78 RR 86 583

Festing v Taylor (1862) 27 JP 281, 3 B & S 217, 235, 32 LJQB 41, 9 Jur NS 44, 1 New Rep 32, 11 WR 70, 122 ER 89, 7 LT 429, Ex Ch 533

Fetherstone v West (1871) IR 6 Eq 86 . . . . 941, 945

Feuer Leather Corpn v Frank Johnstone & Sons [1981] Com LR 251 989

Ffennell's Settlement, Re, Re Ffennell's Estate, Wright v Holton [1918] 1 Ch 91, 87 LJ Ch 54, 62 Sol Jo 103, 118 LT 171, 34 TLR 86 . . . . 369, 497

Fickus, Re, Farina v Fickus [1900] 1 Ch 331, 69 LJ Ch 161, 48 WR 250, 44 Sol Jo 157, 81 LT 749 140

Field v Lord Donoughmore (1841) 58 RR 253, 1 Dr & War 227 142

Field's Will Trusts, Re, Parry-Jones v Hillman [1950] Ch 520, [1950] 2 All ER 188, 66 (pt 1) TLR 1221 102

Fielding v Fielding [1978] 1 All ER 267, [1977] 1 WLR 1146n, 121 Sol Jo 729, CA . . . 427

Figg v Clarke (Inspector of Taxes) [1997] 1 WLR 603, [1997] STC 247, 68 TC 645, [1996] 10 LS Gaz R 21, 140 Sol Jo LB 66 735

Figgis, Re, Roberts v MacLaren [1969] 1 Ch 123, [1968] 1 All ER 999, [1968] 2 WLR 1173, 112 Sol Jo 156 . . . . 359, 360, 361

Finch v Finch (1975) 119 Sol Jo 793, CA 351, 366

Finch v Pescott (1874) LR 17 Eq 554, 43 LJ Ch 728, 22 WR 437, 30 LT 156 . . . . 810, 818

Finden v Stephens (1846) 2 Ph 142, 16 LJ Ch 63, 1 Coop temp Cott 318, 10 Jur 1019, 8 LTOS 249; on appeal (1848) 17 LJ Ch 342, 11 LTOS 325 142

Fine Industrial Commodities Ltd v Powling (1954) 71 RPC 253 399

Finers (a firm) v Miro [1991] 1 All ER 182, [1991] 1 WLR 35, 134 Sol Jo 1039, [1990] NLJR 1387, CA 613, 648, 649, 967

Finger's Will Trusts, Re, Turner v Ministry of Health [1972] Ch 286, [1971] 3 All ER 1050, [1971] 3 WLR 775, 115 Sol Jo 790 129
Finlay v Darling [1897] 1 Ch 719, 66 LJ Ch 348, 45 WR 445, 41 Sol Jo 405, 76 LT 461 . . 307
Finlay v Howard (1842) 59 RR 793, 2 Dr & War 490 764
Finnemore, Re [1992] 1 All ER 800, [1991] 1 WLR 793 261
Firth, Re, Sykes v Ball [1938] Ch 517, [1938] 2 All ER 217, 107 LJ Ch 251, 82 Sol Jo 332, 158 LT 489, 54 TLR 633 541
Fish, Re, Bennett v Bennett [1893] 2 Ch 413, 62 LJ Ch 977, 2 R 467, 69 LT 233, CA . . . 655, 659
Fisher, Re, Harris v Fisher [1943] Ch 377, [1943] 2 All ER 615, 113 LJ Ch 17, 87 Sol Jo 372, 169 LT 289, 59 TLR 446 . . . . 549, 551, 555
Fisher v Mansfield [1997] 2 NZLR 230 431
Fisher v Shirley (1889) 43 Ch D 290, 59 LJ Ch 29, 38 WR 70, 61 LT 668 . . . . . . 311, 313
Fisk v A-G (1867) LR 4 Eq 521, 32 JP 52, 15 WR 1200, 17 LT 27 225
Fitch v Weber (1848) 6 Hare 145, 17 LJ Ch 361, 12 Jur 645, 77 RR 56, 11 LTOS 83 . . . 371
Fitzgerald, Re, Surman v Fitzgerald [1904] 1 Ch 573, 73 LJ Ch 436, 52 WR 432, 48 Sol Jo 349, 90 LT 266, 20 TLR 332, CA . . . 52, 213, 215, 569, 738, 1030, 1031, 1050, 1051, 1052
Fitzgerald v Masters (1956) 95 CLR 420 279
Fitzgerald's Settlement, Re, Fitzgerald v White (1887) 37 Ch D 18, 57 LJ Ch 594, 36 WR 385, 57 LT 706, CA 141, 142
Fitzgibbon v Scanlan (1813) 1 Dow 261, 14 RR 62 382
Fitzwilliam (Countess) v IRC [1990] STC 65; on appeal [1992] STC 185, CA; affd sub nom Fitzwilliam v IRC [1993] 3 All ER 184, [1993] 1 WLR 1189, [1993] STC 502, [1993] 45 LS Gaz R 46, 137 Sol Jo LB 184, sub nom Fitzwilliam (Countess) v IRC 67 TC 614, HL 62, 183, 184
Flamank, Re, Wood v Cock (1889) 40 Ch D 461, 58 LJ Ch 518, 37 WR 502, 60 LT 376 . . 277
Flavel's Will Trusts, Re, Coleman v Flavel [1969] 2 All ER 232, [1969] 1 WLR 444, 113 Sol Jo 189 . . . . .66, 83, 105, 109, 302
Flavell, Re, Murray v Flavell (1883) 25 Ch D 89, 53 LJ Ch 185, 32 WR 102, [1881-5] All ER Rep 267, 49 LT 690, CA 170, 172, 173
Fleet Disposal Services Ltd, Re [1995] 1 BCLC 345, [1995] BCC 605 . . . . . . 25, 76, 147
Fleetwood, Re, Sidgreaves v Brewer (1880) 15 Ch D 594, 49 LJ Ch 514, 29 WR 45 . . . 264
Fletcher v Collis [1905] 2 Ch 24, 74 LJ Ch 502, 53 WR 516, 49 Sol Jo 499, 92 LT 749, CA 933, 948
Fletcher v Fletcher (1844) 4 Hare 67, 14 LJ Ch 66, 8 Jur 1040, 67 RR 6 . 145, 162, 173, 174, 176, 177, 179, 180, 903
Fletcher v Green (1864) 33 Beav 426, 3 New Rep 626, 140 RR 199 . . . . . 877, 879, 942
Flower (C) and Metropolitan Board of Works, Re, Re M Flower and Metropolitan Board of Works (1884) 27 Ch D 592, 53 LJ Ch 955, 32 WR 1011, 51 LT 257 . .619, 631, 644, 646
Flower's Settlement Trusts, Re, Flower v IRC [1957] 1 All ER 462, [1957] 1 WLR 401, 36 ATC 22, 50 R & IT 150, [1957] TR 29, 101 Sol Jo 189, CA 333
Floyer v Bankes (1869) LR 8 Eq 115 . . . . 190, 214
Foley v Burnell (1783) 1 Bro CC 274; affd (1785) 4 Bro Parl Cas 319, Rom 1, [1558-1774] All ER Rep 123, HL 903
Foley v Hill (1848) 2 HL Cas 28, 9 ER 1002, [1843-60] All ER Rep 16 8
Foligno's Mortgage, Re (1863) 32 Beav 131, 138 RR 674 . . . . 830, 846
Follett, Re, Barclays Bank Ltd v Dovell [1955] 2 All ER 22, [1955] 1 WLR 429, 99 Sol Jo 275, CA 334
Foord, Re, Foord v Conder [1922] 2 Ch 519, 92 LJ Ch 46, [1922] All ER Rep 166, 128 LT 501 . . . . 137, 260, 335
Forbes v Cochrane (1824) 2 B & C 448, 2 State Tr NS 147, 2 LJOSKB 67, 3 Dow & Ry KB 679, [1824-34] All ER Rep 48 1051
Ford v Earl of Chesterfield (1853) 16 Beav 516, 22 LJ Ch 630, 96 RR 249, 1 WR 217, 20 LTOS 288 450
Forder, Re, Forder v Forder [1927] 2 Ch 291, 96 LJ Ch 314, [1927] B & CR 84, [1927] All ER Rep 324, 137 LT 538, CA 211, 212
Forest of Dean Coal Mining Co, Re (1878) 10 Ch D 450, 27 WR 594, 40 LT 287 . . 491, 903
Forrest v Forrest (1865) 34 LJ Ch 428, 11 Jur NS 317, 5 New Rep 299, 148 RR 611, 13 WR 380, 11 LT 763 350
Forshaw v Higginson (1855) 20 Beav 485, 26 LJ Ch 170, 109 RR 510 846
Forshaw v Welsby (1860) 30 Beav 243, 30 LJ Ch 331, 7 Jur NS 299, 132 RR 256, 9 WR 225, 4 LT 170 . . . . 274, 277
Forster v Abraham (1874) LR 17 Eq 351, 43 LJ Ch 199, 22 WR 386 771

Forster v Hale (1798) 4 RR 128, 3 Ves 696; affd (1800) 5 Ves 308 . . . .   236, 237
Forster v Williams Deacon's Bank Ltd [1935] Ch 359, 104 LJ Ch 132, [1935] All ER Rep 374,
    79 Sol Jo 145, 152 LT 433, 51 TLR 254, CA 658, 797
Forster-Brown, Re, Barry v Forster-Brown [1914] 2 Ch 584, 84 LJ Ch 361, 112 LT 681 . .   530,
    544, 547
Forster's Settlement, Re, Forster v Custodian of Enemy Property for England [1942] Ch 199,
    [1942] 1 All ER 180, 111 LJ Ch 149, 86 Sol Jo 49, 166 LT 297, 58 TLR 99   211, 691, 726
Forster's Settlement, Re, Michelmore v Byatt [1954] 3 All ER 714, [1954] 1 WLR 1450, 98
    Sol Jo 852 . . . .   524, 526
Fortex Group Ltd v MacIntosh (in receivership and liquidation) [1998] 3 NZLR 171, NZCA   325
Foskett v McKeown [1998] Ch 265, [1997] 3 All ER 392, [1998] 2 WLR 298, CA; revsd [2001]
    1 AC 102, [2000] 3 All ER 97, [2000] 2 WLR 1299, 144 Sol Jo LB 231, [2000] Lloyd's
    Rep IR 627, HL 4, 391, 880, 881, 885, 886, 887, 889, 890, 894,
    896, 897, 900, 902, 968, 993, 994, 995, 997, 998
Foster, Re, Hunt v Foster [1920] 1 Ch 391, 89 LJ Ch 206, 122 LT 585   547
Foster, Re, Lloyd v Carr (1890) 45 Ch D 629, 60 LJ Ch 175, 39 WR 31, 63 LT 443 . . .   553
Foster v Dawber (1860) 1 Drew & Sm 172, 127 RR 63, 8 WR 646   449
Foster v Driscoll [1929] 1 KB 470, 98 LJKB 282, [1928] All ER Rep 130, 140 LT 479, 45 TLR
    185, CA   1051
Foster v Elsley (1881) 19 Ch D 518, 51 LJ Ch 275, 30 WR 596   142
Foster v Spencer [1996] 2 All ER 672 . . . .   657, 810
Foster's Policy, Re, Menneer v Foster [1966] 1 All ER 432, [1966] 1 WLR 222, 110 Sol Jo
    151 . . . .   171, 172
Foster's Trusts, Re (1886) 55 LT 479, 2 TLR 803   766
Foundling Hospital (Governors and Guardians) v Crane [1911] 2 KB 367, 80 LJKB 853, 105
    LT 187, CA   247
Fountain Forestry Ltd v Edwards [1975] Ch 1, [1974] 2 All ER 280, [1974] 2 WLR 767, 118
    Sol Jo 367   19
Fountaine, Re, Fountaine v Lord Amherst [1909] 2 Ch 382, 78 LJ Ch 648, [1908-10] All ER
    Rep 969, 101 LT 83, 25 TLR 689, CA. 923, 926, 947
Fountaine v Pellet (1791) 1 Ves 337 . . . .   563, 568
Foveaux, Re, Cross v London Anti-Vivisection Society [1895] 2 Ch 501, 64 LJ Ch 856, 13 R
    730, 43 WR 661, 39 Sol Jo 671, 73 LT 202, 11 TLR 540   122
Fowkes v Pascoe (1875) 10 Ch App 343, 44 LJ Ch 367, 23 WR 538, [1874-80] All ER Rep 521,
    32 LT 545, CA 343, 350, 358, 359, 367, 368
Fowler, Re, Fowler v Odell (1881) 16 Ch D 723, 29 WR 891, 44 LT 99 . . . . . .   572, 589
Fowler v Cohn (1856) 21 Beav 360, 2 Jur NS 315, 111 RR 124, 4 WR 412, 27 LTOS 25. .   805
Fox, Re [1951] 3 DLR 337, [1951] OR 378, OWN 375   427
Fox, Re, ex p Barry (1873) LR 17 Eq 113, 43 LJ Bcy 18, 22 WR 205, 29 LT 620   461
Fox, Re, Wodehouse v Fox [1904] 1 Ch 480, 73 LJ Ch 314, 52 WR 229, 48 Sol Jo 223, 90 LT
    477.   719
Foxton v Manchester and Liverpool District Banking Co (1881) 44 LT 406   973
Frame, Re, Edwards v Taylor [1939] Ch 700, [1939] 2 All ER 865, 108 LJ Ch 217, 83 Sol Jo
    438, 160 LT 620, 55 TLR 746.   138
Framlington Group plc v Anderson [1995] 1 BCLC 475, [1995] BCC 611   23
Francis v Francis (1854) 5 De GM & G 108, 104 RR 47   883
Fraser v Evans [1969] 1 QB 349, [1969] 1 All ER 8, [1968] 3 WLR 1172, 112 Sol Jo 805, CA   403
Fraser v Imperial Bank of Canada (1912) 23 WLR 445, 47 SCR 313, 10 DLR 232   1002
Fraser v Murdoch (1881) 6 App Cas 855, sub nom Robinson v Murdock 30 WR 162, 45 LT
    417, HL.   543, 811, 813, 821, 823, 825
Fraser v Thames Television Ltd [1984] QB 44, [1983] 2 All ER 101, [1983] 2 WLR 917, 127
    Sol Jo 379   395
Frawley v Neill (1999) 143 Sol Jo LB 98, [2000] CP Rep 20, Times, 5 April, CA   930
Freeguard v Royal Bank of Scotland plc (1998) 79 P & CR 81, CA   1000
Freeland, Re, Jackson v Rodgers [1952] Ch 110, 95 Sol Jo 802, sub nom Jackson v Rodger
    [1952] 1 All ER 16, [1951] 2 TLR 1076 . . . .   .160, 161, 162, 163
Freeman, Re, Shilton v Freeman [1908] 1 Ch 720, 77 LJ Ch 401, 52 Sol Jo 262, 98 LT 429, 24
    TLR 300, CA   105
Freeman v Cox (1878) 8 Ch D 148, 47 LJ Ch 560, 26 WR 689 . . . .   903, 906
Freeman's Settlement Trusts, Re (1887) 37 Ch D 148, 57 LJ Ch 160, 36 WR 71, 57 LT
    798. . . . .   655, 772
Freer v Unwins Ltd [1976] Ch 288, [1976] 1 All ER 634, [1976] 2 WLR 609, 31 P & CR 335,
    120 Sol Jo 267   256

Freeston's Charity, Re, Sylvester v University College, Oxford [1979] 1 All ER 51, [1978] 1
    WLR 741, 122 Sol Jo 294, CA 250, 544, 932, 936
Freke v Lord Carbery (1873) LR 16 Eq 461, 21 WR 835 . . . . 188, 1026, 1027
Freman, Re, Dimond v Newburn [1898] 1 Ch 28, 77 LT 460, sub nom Re Freeman, Dimond
    v Newburn 67 LJ Ch 14 572
Freman v Whitbread (1865) LR 1 Eq 266, sub nom Freeman v Whitbread 35 LJ Ch 137, 148
    RR 107, 14 WR 188, 13 LT 550 540
Freme's Contract, Re [1895] 2 Ch 256; affd [1895] 2 Ch 778, 64 LJ Ch 862, 44 WR 164, 73
    LT 366, CA. 833, 839
French v Hobson (1803) 9 Ves 103 931
Frewen v Law Life Assurance Society [1896] 2 Ch 511, 65 LJ Ch 787, 44 WR 682, 40 Sol Jo
    621, 75 LT 17. . . . . 563, 565
Frey v Royal Bank of Scotland (Nassau) Ltd (2001) 3 ITELR 775 . . . . 277, 278
Fribance v Fribance [1957] 1 All ER 357, [1957] 1 WLR 384, 101 Sol Jo 188, CA 366
Friends' Provident Life Office v Hillier Parker May & Rowden (a firm) (Estates and General
    plc, third parties)) [1997] QB 85, [1995] 4 All ER 260, [1996] 2 WLR 123, 71 P & CR
    286, CA 943
Frish Ltd v Barclays Bank Ltd [1955] 2 QB 541, [1955] 3 All ER 185, [1955] 3 WLR 439, 99
    Sol Jo 561, 161 Estates Gazette 101, CA 383
Frith, Re, Newton v Rolfe [1902] 1 Ch 342, 71 LJ Ch 199, 86 LT 212 . . . . . . 823, 824
Frith v Cartland (1865) 2 Hem & M 417, 34 LJ Ch 301, 11 Jur NS 238, 144 RR 206, 13 WR
    493, [1861-73] All ER Rep 608, 12 LT 175 . . . . 461, 880, 883, 1000
Froese v Montreal Trust Co of Canada (1996) 137 DLR (4th) 725 858
Frost, Re, Frost v Frost (1889) 43 Ch D 246, 59 LJ Ch 118, 38 WR 264, 62 LT 25 . . 192, 225
Fry, Re, Chase National Executors and Trustees Corpn Ltd v Fry [1946] Ch 312, [1946] 2 All
    ER 106, 115 LJ Ch 225, 90 Sol Jo 346, 175 LT 392, 62 TLR 414 . . . . . . 151, 155
Fry, Re, Reynolds v Denne [1945] Ch 348, [1945] 2 All ER 205, 115 LJ Ch 3, 89 Sol Jo 349,
    173 LT 282, 61 TLR 449 . . . . 104, 193, 220
Fry v Fry (1859) 27 Beav 144, 28 LJ Ch 591, 5 Jur NS 1047, 122 RR 354, 34 LTOS 51 496, 872
Fry v Lane (1888) 40 Ch D 312, 58 LJ Ch 113, 37 WR 135, [1886-90] All ER Rep 1084, 60 LT
    12, 5 TLR 45 . . . . 276, 277
Fry v Tapson (1884) 28 Ch D 268, 54 LJ Ch 224, 33 WR 113, 51 LT 326 . . .583, 606, 634, 861
Fryer, Re, Martindale v Picquot (1857) 3 K & J 317, 26 LJ Ch 398, 3 Jur NS 485, 5 WR 522, 29
    LTOS 86 . . . . 647, 938
Fulford, Re, Fulford v Hyslop [1930] 1 Ch 71, 8 ATC 588, 99 LJ Ch 80, 142 LT 185. . . 710
Fulham, Re (1850) 15 Jur 69 574
Fuller, Re [1900] 2 Ch 551, 69 LJ Ch 738, 49 WR 90, 83 LT 208 755
Fuller v Knight (1843) 6 Beav 205, 12 LJ Ch 182, 63 RR 51 . . . . 951, 980
Furness (Viscount) Re, Wilson v Kenmare [1943] Ch 415, [1944] 1 All ER 66, 112 LJ Ch 317,
    87 Sol Jo 390, 169 LT 314, 59 TLR 418 . . . . 726, 727
Fyfe v Garden [1946] 1 All ER 366, HL 184
Fyfe v Irwin [1939] 2 All ER 271, 83 Sol Jo 454 . . . . 373, 374
Fyffes Group Ltd v Templeman [2000] 2 Lloyd's Rep 643, [2000] 25 LS Gaz R 40 . 399, 405,
                                                                                957, 958
Fyler v Fyler (1841) 3 Beav 550, 5 Jur 187 957
Fysh v Page (1956) 96 CLR 233, HC of A 930

G

G (infants), Re [1899] 1 Ch 719, 68 LJ Ch 374, 47 WR 491, 80 LT 470. 137
GKN Bolts and Nuts Ltd Sports and Social Club, Re, Leek v Donkersley [1982] 2 All ER 855,
    [1982] 1 WLR 774, 126 Sol Jo 327 339
Gadd, Re, Eastwood v Clark (1883) 23 Ch D 134, 52 LJ Ch 396, 31 WR 417, 48 LT 395,
    CA 726, 754, 759
Gage, Re, Hill v Gage [1898] 1 Ch 498, 67 LJ Ch 200, 46 WR 569, 78 LT 347 120
Gage v King [1961] 1 QB 188, [1960] 3 All ER 62, [1960] 3 WLR 460, 104 Sol Jo 644 . . 360
Gaite's Will Trusts, Re, Banks v Gaite [1949] 1 All ER 459, 93 Sol Jo 148, 65 TLR 194 . . 193
Galbraith's Goods, Re [1951] P 422, [1951] 2 All ER 470n, 95 Sol Jo 548, [1951] 2 TLR 412 750
Gallagher (NT) & Son Ltd (in liquidation), Re, Shierson v Tomlinson [2002] EWCA Civ
    404, [2002] 3 All ER 474, [2002] 1 WLR 2380, [2002] 2 BCLC 133 . . . . . 141, 340
Galmerrow Securities Ltd v National Westminster Bank (20 December 1990, unreported) 1032
Galmerrow Securities Ltd v National Westminster Bank plc [2002] WTLR 125 . . . 406, 596,
                                                                                617, 651, 963
Galzier v Australian Men's Health (No 2) [2001] NSWSC 6 854

Gandy v Gandy (1885) 30 Ch D 57, 54 LJ Ch 1154, 33 WR 803, [1881-5] All ER Rep 376, 53
  LT 306, 1 TLR 520, CA 113, 170
Gape, Re, Verey v Gape [1952] Ch 418, [1952] 1 All ER 827, 96 Sol Jo 595, [1952] 1 TLR
  971; affd [1952] Ch 743, 96 Sol Jo 595, [1952] TLR 477, sub nom Gape's Will Trusts,
  Re, Verey v Gape [1952] 2 All ER 579, CA 101, 102, 839
Gardiner, Re [1942] NZLR 199 . . . . 431, 543
Gardiner, Re, Gardiner v Gardiner [1971] 2 NSWLR 494 36
Gardiner, Re, Gardiner v Smith [1901] 1 Ch 697, 70 LJ Ch 407 206
Gardiner's Trusts, Re (1886) 33 Ch D 590, 55 LJ Ch 714, 35 WR 28, 55 LT 261 762
Gardner, Re, Huey v Cunningham [1923] 2 Ch 230, 92 LJ Ch 569, 67 Sol Jo 517, 129 LT
  206 . . . . 263, 264, 265
Gardner v Lachlan (1836) 8 Sim 123, Donnelly 119, 5 LJ Ch 332, [1835-42] All ER Rep 615;
  affd (1838) 4 My & Cr 129, 8 LJ Ch 82, 2 Jur 1056, [1835-42] All ER Rep 615 . . . 169
Gardner v Rowe (1828) 5 Russ 258, 7 LJOS Ch 2 . . . . 236, 237, 255
Gardom, Re, Le Page v A-G [1914] 1 Ch 662, 83 LJ Ch 681, 108 LT 955, CA; revsd sub nom
  Le Page v Gardom [1915] WN 216, 84 LJ Ch 749, 59 Sol Jo 599, 113 LT 475, HL . 105
Gare, Re, Filmer v Carter [1952] Ch 80, [1951] 2 All ER 863, 95 Sol Jo 744, [1951] 2 TLR
  1003 106
Garland, ex p. See Ballman, ReGarner v Moore (1855) 3 Drew 277, 24 LJ Ch 687, 3 Eq Rep
  1017, 106 RR 345, 3 WR 497, 26 LTOS 11 . . . . 726, 727
Garnett, Re, Gandy v Macaulay (1884) 32 WR 474, 50 LT 172; on appeal (1885) 31 Ch D 1,
  CA 931, 935, 936
Garnett, Re, Richardson v Greenep (1905) 74 LJ Ch 570, [1904-7] All ER Rep 479, 93 LT 117 274
Garnett's Goods, Re [1894] P 90, 63 LJP 82, 6 R 579, 70 LT 37 258
Garrard v Frankel (1862) 26 JP 727, 30 Beav 445, 31 LJ Ch 604, 8 Jur NS 985 50
Garrard v Lord Lauderdale (1830) 3 Sim 1, 30 RR 105; affd (1831) 2 Russ & M 451, [1824-
  34] All ER Rep 109 141
Garrett, Re, Croft v Ruck [1934] Ch 477, 103 LJ Ch 244, [1934] All ER Rep 128, 151 LT 194 717
Garrett v Wilkinson (1848) 2 De G & Sm 244, 79 RR 197 364
Garside, Re, Wragg v Garside [1919] 1 Ch 132, 88 LJ Ch 116, [1918-19] All ER Rep 1139, 63
  Sol Jo 156, 120 LT 339, 35 TLR 129 . . . . 209, 229
Gartside v IRC [1968] AC 553, [1967] 2 All ER 173, [1967] 3 WLR 671, 46 ATC 25, [1967]
  TR 31, 111 Sol Jo 521, CA; revsd [1968] AC 553, [1968] 1 All ER 121, [1968] 2 WLR
  277, 46 ATC 323, [1967] TR 309, 111 Sol Jo 982, HL 64, 480, 503, 733, 749
Gascoigne v Gascoigne [1918] 1 KB 223, 87 LJKB 333, 118 LT 347, 34 TLR 168 346
Gascoigne v Thwing (1685) 1 Vern 366 330
Gaskell's Settled Estates, Re [1894] 1 Ch 485, 63 LJ Ch 243, 8 R 67, 42 WR 219, 38 Sol Jo 200,
  70 LT 554 573
Gassiot, Re, Fladgate v Vintners' Co (1901) 70 LJ Ch 242, 17 TLR 216 120
Gatenby v Morgan (1876) 1 QBD 685, 45 LJQB 597, 35 LT 245 373
Gatti's Voluntary Settlement Trusts, Re, De Ville v Gatti [1936] 2 All ER 1489, 80 Sol Jo 704,
  52 TLR 674 373
Gaussen v Whatman (1905) 93 LT 101 589
Geaves, ex p. See Strahan, Re, ex p Geaves
Gee, Re, Wood v Staples [1948] Ch 284, [1948] 1 All ER 498, [1948] LJR 1400, 92 Sol Jo
  232 . . . . 389, 652
Gee v Liddell (1866) 35 Beav 621, 147 RR 332 147
Geering, Re, Gulliver v Geering [1964] Ch 136, [1962] 3 All ER 1043, [1962] 3 WLR 1541,
  106 Sol Jo 919 . . . . 712, 713, 715
Gencor ACP Ltd v Dalby [2000] 2 BCLC 734, [2001] WTLR 825 . . . . .380, 956, 957, 961
General Accident Fire and Life Assurance Corpn Ltd v IRC [1963] 3 All ER 259, [1963] 1
  WLR 1207, 42 ATC 313, 107 Sol Jo 870, sub nom Lacy's Settlement Trustee (General
  Accident, Fire and Life Assurance Corpn Ltd) v IRC [1963] TR 321, CA . . . 210, 212
General Estates Co, Re, ex p City Bank (1868) 3 Ch App 758, 16 WR 919, 18 LT 894 . . 983
George, Re (1877) 5 Ch D 837, 47 LJ Ch 118, 26 WR 65, 37 LT 204, CA 714
George Newnes Group Pension Fund, Re (1969) 98 J Inst of Actuaries 251 . . . . 495, 497
Gerard (Lord), Re, Oliphant v Gerard (1888) 58 LT 800 308
German v Yates (1915) 32 TLR 52 151
German Mining Co, Re, ex p Chippendale (1853) 4 De GM & G 19, 22 LJ Ch 926, 2 Eq Rep
  983, 17 Jur 745, 21 LTOS 221 . . . . .810, 811, 812, 825
Gess, Re, Gess v Royal Exchange Assurance [1942] Ch 37, 111 LJ Ch 117 628
Gestetner Settlement, Re, Barnett v Blumka [1953] Ch 672, [1953] 1 All ER 1150, [1953] 2
  WLR 1033, 32 ATC 102, 46 R & IT 467, [1953] TR 113, 97 Sol Jo 332 . . . . 92, 95, 98

Ghost v Waller (1846) 9 Beav 497, 73 RR 411 933
Gibbard, Re, Public Trustee v Davis [1966] 1 All ER 273, [1967] 1 WLR 42, 110 Sol Jo
    871. . . . . 90, 93, 216
Gibbins v Taylor (1856) 22 Beav 344, 111 RR 394, 4 WR 432. 942
Gibbon v Mitchell [1990] 3 All ER 338, [1990] 1 WLR 1304 . . . 59, 214, 274, 277, 510, 697
Gibbons v Wright (1954) 91 CLR 423, 28 ALJ 111. 270
Gibbs v Gerberich 1 Ohio App 2d 93 (1964) 892
Gibbs v Glamis (1841) 11 Sim 584, 5 Jur 378. 141
Gibbs v Rumsey (1813) 13 RR 88, 2 Ves & B 294, [1803-13] All ER Rep 701 349
Giblin v McMullen (1868) LR 2 PC 317, 5 Moo PCCNS 434, 38 LJPC 25, 17 WR 445, 16 ER
    578, 21 LT 214 594
Gibson's Settlement Trusts, Re, Mellors v Gibson [1981] Ch 179, [1981] 1 All ER 233,
    [1981] 2 WLR 1, 125 Sol Jo 48 690
Gilbert v Overton (1864) 2 Hem & M 110, 33 LJ Ch 683, 10 Jur NS 721, 4 New Rep 420, 144
    RR 64, 12 WR 1141, 10 LT 900 . . . . 151, 183, 268
Giles, Re (1886) 55 LJ Ch 695, 34 WR 712, 55 LT 51 . . . . 829, 846
Giles, Re, Giles v Giles [1972] Ch 544, [1971] 3 All ER 1141, [1971] 3 WLR 640, 115 Sol Jo
    428. . . . . 434, 435
Gillan v Morrison (1847) 1 De G & Sm 421, 11 Jur 861, 9 LTOS 352 822
Gillespie, Re (1969) 3 DLR (3d) 317, [1969] 1 OR 585. 429
Gillett v Holt [2001] Ch 210, [2000] 2 All ER 289, [2000] 3 WLR 815, [2000] 1 FCR 705,
    [2000] 2 FLR 266, [2000] Fam Law 714, [2000] 12 LS Gaz R 40, 144 Sol Jo LB 141, 80 P
    & CR D3, CA 161, 234, 248, 249, 251, 252, 413
Gillett's Will Trusts, Re, Barclays Bank Ltd v Gillett [1950] Ch 102, [1949] 2 All ER 893, 93
    Sol Jo 742, 65 TLR 727 712
Gillies v Keogh [1989] 2 NZLR 327 326
Gillingham Bus Disaster Fund, Re, Bowman v Official Solicitor [1958] Ch 300, [1958] 1 All
    ER 37, [1957] 3 WLR 1069, 101 Sol Jo 974; affd [1959] Ch 62, [1958] 2 All ER 749,
    [1958] 3 WLR 325, 102 Sol Jo 581, CA 106, 108, 109, 113, 336, 337
Gillott's Settlement, Re, Chattock v Reid [1934] Ch 97, 102 LJ Ch 332, [1933] All ER Rep
    334, 77 Sol Jo 447, 149 LT 419 . . . . 9, 76, 212, 437
Gilmour v Coats [1949] AC 426, [1949] 1 All ER 848, [1949] LJR 1034, 93 Sol Jo 355, 65 TLR
    234, HL 105, 122
Gilroy v Stephens (1882) 51 LJ Ch 834, 30 WR 745, 46 LT 761. . . . . 586, 868
Gisborne v Gisborne (1877) 2 App Cas 300, 46 LJ Ch 556, 25 WR 516, 36 LT 564, [1874-80]
    All ER Rep Ext 1698, HL 551, 680, 702, 726
Gissing v Gissing [1971] AC 886, [1970] 2 All ER 780, [1970] 3 WLR 255, 21 P & CR 702, 114
    Sol Jo 550, 216 Estates Gazette 1257, HL 351, 352, 412, 413, 414, 417,
                                          418, 419, 420, 421, 422, 423, 424, 426
Giumelli v Giumelli (1999) 73 ALJR 547 326
Gjers, Re, Cooper v Gjers [1899] 2 Ch 54, 68 LJ Ch 442, 47 WR 535, 43 Sol Jo 497, 80 LT
    689. . . . . 564, 568, 572
Glacier Bay, The. See West of England Shipowners Mutual Insurance Association (Lux-
    embourg) v Cristal Ltd, The Glacier Bay
Gladdon v Stoneman (1808) 1 Madd 143n 904
Glegg v Bromley [1912] 3 KB 474, 81 LJKB 1081, [1911-13] All ER Rep 1138, 106 LT 825, CA 151
Glencore International AG v Metro Trading Inc [2001] 1 Lloyd's Rep 284, [2001] 1 All ER
    (Comm) 103 882
Glenko Enterprises Ltd v Keller [2001] 1 WWR 229 961
Glennie v McDougall & Cowans Holdings Ltd [1934] 3 DLR 360; revsd [1935] 2 DLR
    561. . . . . 22, 659
Glenny and Hartley, Re (1884) 25 Ch D 611, 53 LJ Ch 417, 32 WR 457, 50 LT 79 . . . 753
Glenorchy (Lord) v Bosville (1733) 2 Eq Cas Abr 743, Cas temp Talb 3, For 3, [1558-1774]
    All ER Rep 328 . . . . 66, 301
Global Custodians Ltd v Mesh (2000) 2 ITELR 327 685
Glubb, Re, Bamfield v Rogers [1900] 1 Ch 354, 69 LJ Ch 278, 82 LT 412, CA 274
Gluckstein v Barnes [1900] AC 240, 69 LJ Ch 385, 7 Mans 321, 82 LT 393, 16 TLR 321,
    HL. 22, 23, 402
Goddard v DFC New Zealand Ltd [1991] 3 NZLR 580 952
Godden, Re, Teague v Fox [1893] 1 Ch 292, 62 LJ Ch 469, 3 R 67, 41 WR 282, 68 LT 116 559
Godfree, Re, Godfree v Godfree [1914] 2 Ch 110, 83 LJ Ch 734 556
Godfrey's Trusts, Re (1883) 23 Ch D 205 780

Godwin, Re, Coutts & Co v Godwin [1938] Ch 341, [1938] 1 All ER 287, 107 LJ Ch 166, 82
    Sol Jo 113, 158 LT 166, 54 TLR 339 793
Godwin's Settlement, Re, Godwin v Godwin (1918) 87 LJ Ch 645, 62 Sol Jo 729, 119 LT
    643 . . . . 580, 586
Goff, Re, Featherstonehaugh v Murphy (1914) 58 Sol Jo 535, 111 LT 34 161
Goff v Goff [1934] P 107, 103 LJP 57, 78 Sol Jo 299, 151 LT 36, 50 TLR 318 1044
Golay, Re, Morris v Bridgewater [1965] 2 All ER 660, [1965] 1 WLR 969, 109 Sol Jo 517 . 80
Gold v Hill [1999] 1 FLR 54, [1998] Fam Law 664, 142 Sol Jo LB 226 247
Gold v Rosenberg [1997] 3 SCR 767 . . . . 961, 976
Goldcorp Exchange Ltd (in receivership), Re [1995] 1 AC 74, [1994] 2 All ER 806, [1994] 3
    WLR 199, [1994] 2 BCLC 578, [1994] NLJR 792, sub nom Kensington v Unrepre-
    sented Non-allocated Claimants [1994] 24 LS Gaz R 46, 138 Sol Jo LB 127, PC . 9, 20,
                                   21, 25, 42, 67, 76, 78, 79, 145,
                               148, 168, 325, 400, 900
Goldsworthy v Brickell [1987] Ch 378, [1987] 1 All ER 853, [1987] 2 WLR 133, 131 Sol Jo
    102, [1987] LS Gaz R 654, CA 282, 285, 936
Gollin's Declaration of Trust, Re, Turner v Williams [1969] 3 All ER 1591, [1969] 1 WLR
    1858, 113 Sol Jo 904 . . . . .543, 544, 545, 719
Gompertz v Gompertz (1846) 2 Ph 107, 16 LJ Ch 23, 10 Jur 937, 78 RR 43 376
Gompertz v Kensit (1872) LR 13 Eq 369, 36 JP 548, 41 LJ Ch 382, 20 WR 313, 26 LT 95 844
Gonin, Re [1979] Ch 16, [1977] 3 WLR 379, 121 Sol Jo 558, sub nom Re Gonin, Gonin v
    Garmeson [1977] 2 All ER 720 . . . . 158, 160, 161, 234
Gooch, Re, Gooch v Gooch (1890) 62 LT 384, 6 TLR 224. 364
Goodchild, Re, Goodchild v Goodchild [1997] 3 All ER 63, [1997] 1 WLR 1216, [1997] 2
    FLR 644, sub nom Goodchild v Goodchild [1997] 3 FCR 601, [1997] NLJR 758,
    CA 266, 428, 431
Goode, Re, Spiller v Kennedy [1960] VR 117. 201
Goode Durrant Administration v Biddulph [1995] 1 FCR 196, [1994] 2 FLR 551, 26 HLR
    625 286
Goodenough, Re, Marland v Williams [1895] 2 Ch 537, 65 LJ Ch 71, 13 R 454, 44 WR 44, 39
    Sol Jo 656, 73 LT 152. . . . . 552, 559
Goodenough v Tremamondo (1840) 2 Beav 512, 50 RR 262 552
Goodier v Edmunds [1893] 3 Ch 455, 62 LJ Ch 649, 37 Sol Jo 526 200
Goodman v Gallant [1986] Fam 106, [1986] 1 All ER 311, [1986] 2 WLR 236, 52 P & CR 180,
    [1986] 1 FLR 513, [1986] Fam Law 159, 129 Sol Jo 891, CA 351, 355, 421
Goodson, Re [1971] VR 801 . . . . 125, 127, 128
Goodson v Ellisson (1827) 3 Russ 583 846
Goodson's Settlement, Re, Goodson v Goodson [1943] Ch 101, [1943] 1 All ER 201, 112 LJ
    Ch 158, 87 Sol Jo 57, 168 LT 167, 59 TLR 144 533
Goold's Will Trusts, Re, Lloyd's Bank Ltd v Goold [1967] 3 All ER 652, 111 Sol Jo
    812. . . . . 373, 374, 375
Goose v Wilson Sandford & Co (No 2) [2000] EWCA Civ 73, [2001] Lloyd's Rep PN 189 957
Gordon, Re, Public Trustee v Bland [1942] Ch 131, [1942] 1 All ER 59, 111 LJ Ch 114, 86
    Sol Jo 21, 166 LT 102, 58 TLR 112 547
Gordon, Re, Roberts v Gordon (1877) 6 Ch D 531, 46 LJ Ch 794, 37 LT 627 . . . 449, 453
Gordon v Douce [1983] 2 All ER 228, [1983] 1 WLR 563, 4 FLR 508, 13 Fam Law 149, 127
    Sol Jo 324, CA 425
Gordon v Gonda [1955] 2 All ER 762, [1955] 1 WLR 885, 99 Sol Jo 525, CA . 385, 398, 854,
                                             870, 871
Gordon v Gordon (1821) 3 Swan 400 281
Gordon v Holland (1913) 82 LJPC 81, 108 LT 385, PC 1000
Gordon v Trail (1820) 8 Price 416 . . . . 810, 818
Gordon's Settlement, Re, Hunt v Mortimer [1924] 1 Ch 146, 93 LJ Ch 187, 68 Sol Jo 323,
    130 LT 502. 948
Gordon's Will Trusts, Re, National Westminster Bank Ltd v Gordon [1977] Ch 27, [1976] 2
    All ER 577, [1976] 3 WLR 387, 120 Sol Jo 541; revsd [1978] Ch 145, [1978] 2 All ER
    969, [1978] 2 WLR 754, 122 Sol Jo 148, CA 214
Gore-Grimes v Grimes [1937] IR 470 364
Gorman (a bankrupt), Re, ex p Trustee of the Bankrupt v Bankrupt [1990] 1 All ER 717,
    [1990] 1 WLR 616, [1990] 2 FLR 284, [1990] Fam Law 430, [1990] 19 LS Gaz R
    41 . . . . 352, 355, 356, 421, 422, 425
Gorog v Kiss (1977) 78 DLR (3d) 690, 78 DLR (3d) 690, 16 OR (2d) 569, Ont CA . 343, 348
Gosling v Gosling (1859) John 265, 5 Jur NS 910, 123 RR 107 731

Gott, Re, Glazebrook v Leeds University [1944] Ch 193, [1944] 1 All ER 293, 113 LJ Ch 124, 88 Sol Jo 103, 170 LT 210, 60 TLR 214 . . . . 82, 102

Gough v Bult (1847) 16 Sim 45, 17 LJ Ch 10, 80 RR 19; affd (1848) 16 Sim 50, 17 LJ Ch 401, 12 Jur 859, 80 RR 80, 13 LTOS 86 130

Gough v Smith [1872] WN 18 . . . . 645, 647

Gould v Robertson (1851) 4 De G & Sm 509, 87 RR 457 142

Goulding v James [1997] 2 All ER 239, CA 502, 508, 510, 731, 733

Gouldsworth v Knights (1843) 8 JP 8, 12 LJ Ex 282, 11 M & W 337, 63 RR 619 645

Gourju's Will Trusts, Re, Starling v Custodian of Enemy Property [1943] Ch 24, [1942] 2 All ER 605, 112 LJ Ch 75, 86 Sol Jo 367, 168 LT 1, 59 TLR 47 . . . . 211, 212, 214

Gow v Forster (1884) 26 Ch D 672, 32 WR 1019, 51 LT 394 571

Gowan, Re, Gowan v Gowan (1880) 17 Ch D 778, 50 LJ Ch 248 . . . . 303, 305

Gower's Settlement, Re [1934] Ch 365, 103 LJ Ch 164, [1934] All ER Rep 796, 150 LT 449 783

Grabowski v Grangemore Investments [2002] EWHC 851 (Ch) 886

Grace, ex p (1799) 1 Bos & P 376, 90 RR 917 382

Graham Australia Pty Ltd v Perpetual Trustees Ltd [1992] PLR 193 . . . . 498, 499

Grainge v Wilberforce (1889) 5 TLR 436 . . . . 235, 238

Grant v Edwards [1986] Ch 638, [1986] 2 All ER 426, [1986] 3 WLR 114, [1987] 1 FLR 87, [1986] Fam Law 300, 130 Sol Jo 408, [1986] LS Gaz R 1996, [1986] NLJ Rep 439, CA 56, 157, 250, 251, 347, 352, 354, 412, 413, 415, 416, 417, 419, 420, 422, 423, 424, 425, 426

Grant v Grant (1865) 34 Beav 623, 34 LJ Ch 641, 11 Jur NS 787, 6 New Rep 347, 13 WR 1057, 55 ER 776, 12 LT 721 149

Grant's Will Trusts, Re, Harris v Anderson [1979] 3 All ER 359, [1980] 1 WLR 360, 124 Sol Jo 84 . . . . 111, 113, 114, 127, 128, 129, 340

Graves v Dolphin (1826) 1 Sim 66, 5 LJOS Ch 45, 27 RR 166 . . . . 190, 209, 214

Gray, Re, ex p Gray (1835) 4 Deac & Ch 778, 2 Mont & A 283, 4 LJ Bcy 70 456

Gray v Gray (1852) 2 Sim NS 273, 21 LJ Ch 745, 89 RR 297, 20 LTOS 23 147

Gray v Haig (1855) 20 Beav 219 887

Gray v New Augarita Porcupine Mines Ltd [1952] 3 DLR 1, PC. 23

Gray v Perpetual Trustee Co Ltd [1928] AC 391, 97 LJPC 85, [1928] All ER Rep 758, 139 LT 469, 44 TLR 654 . . . . 427, 429

Gray v Siggers (1880) 15 Ch D 74, 49 LJ Ch 819, 29 WR 13 . . . . 551, 554, 555

Grayburn v Clarkson (1868) 3 Ch App 605, 37 LJ Ch 550, 16 WR 716, 18 LT 494 584

Greasley v Cooke [1980] 3 All ER 710, [1980] 1 WLR 1306, 124 Sol Jo 629, CA . . 248, 250, 251

Great Berlin Steamboat Co, Re (1884) 26 Ch D 616, 54 LJ Ch 68, 51 LT 445, CA 218

Greaves' Settled Estates, Re, Jones v Greaves [1900] 2 Ch 683, 69 LJ Ch 596, 49 WR 236, 44 Sol Jo 610, 82 LT 799 714

Greaves' Will Trusts, Re, Public Trustee v Ash [1954] Ch 434, [1954] 1 All ER 771, [1954] 2 WLR 557, 98 Sol Jo 214 631

Green, ex p (1832) 2 Deac & Ch 113, 2 LJ Bcy 2 456

Green, Re, Lindner v Green [1951] Ch 148, [1950] 2 All ER 913, 94 Sol Jo 742, 66 (pt 2) TLR 819 . . . . 140, 429, 431

Green, Re, Shears v Lloyds Bank Ltd [1935] WN 151, 180 LT Jo 114, 80 L Jo 176 . . . 133

Green (a bankrupt), Re, ex p Official Receiver v Cutting [1979] 1 All ER 832, [1979] 1 WLR 1211, 122 Sol Jo 572 184

Green v Cobham [2000] WTLR 1101 . . . . .278, 456, 696, 699

Green v Green (Barclays Bank, third party) [1981] 1 All ER 97, [1981] 1 WLR 391 . . . 296

Green v Marsden (1853) 1 Drew 646, 22 LJ Ch 1092, 1 Eq Rep 437, 54 RR 789, 1 WR 511, 22 LTOS 17 80

Green v Paterson (1886) 32 Ch D 95, 56 LJ Ch 181, 34 WR 724, 54 LT 738, CA 174

Green v Russell [1959] 2 QB 226, [1959] 2 All ER 525, [1959] 3 WLR 17, 103 Sol Jo 489, CA 3, 5, 10, 171

Green v Spicer (1830) 1 Russ & M 395, Taml 396, 8 LJOS Ch 105, 32 RR 232 . 209, 214, 738

Green v Wynn (1869) 4 Ch App 204, 38 LJ Ch 220, 17 WR 385, 20 LT 131 335

Green's Will Trusts, Re, Fitzgerald-Hart v A-G [1985] 3 All ER 455 . . . . . 193, 195, 508

Greenhill v North British and Mercantile Insurance Co [1893] 3 Ch 474, 62 LJ Ch 918, 3 R 674, 42 WR 91, 37 Sol Jo 632, 69 LT 526 306

Greenwell v Greenwell (1800) 5 Ves 194 524

Greenwood, Re, Greenwood v Firth (1911) 105 LT 509 . . . . 578, 708

Greer, Re, Greer v Greer [1907] 1 IR 57 1001

Gregory v Gregory (1815) Coop G 201; affd (1821) Jac 631 934
Gregory v Williams (1817) 3 Mer 582, 17 RR 136, 36 ER 224. 170
Gregson's Trusts, Re (1886) 34 Ch D 209, 56 LJ Ch 286, 35 WR 286. 743
Grenfell v Dean and Canons of Windsor (1840) 2 Beav 544, 50 RR 279 186
Grenville-Murray v Earl of Clarendon (1869) LR 9 Eq 11, 39 LJ Ch 221, 18 WR 124, 21 LT
    448 143
Gresley v Mousley (1859) 4 De G & J 78, 28 LJ Ch 620, 5 Jur NS 583, 124 RR 164, 7 WR 427,
    33 LTOS 154 . . . . 436, 934
Grey v IRC [1958] Ch 375, [1958] 1 All ER 246, [1958] 2 WLR 168, 36 ATC 296, [1957] TR
    293, 102 Sol Jo 84; revsd [1958] Ch 690, [1958] 2 All ER 428, [1958] 3 WLR 45, 37 ATC
    136, [1958] TR 165, 102 Sol Jo 469, CA; affd [1960] AC 1, [1959] 3 All ER 603, [1959] 3
    WLR 759, 38 ATC 313, [1959] TR 311, 103 Sol Jo 896, HL 145, 233, 235, 237,
                                                          238, 239, 240, 244, 246, 730
Grey (Lord) v Lady Grey (1677) Cas temp Finch 338, 1 Cas in Ch 296, 2 Swan 594 . . . 364
Grieveson v Kirsopp (1838) 2 Keen 653, 6 LJ Ch 261, 44 RR 305 74
Griffin v Brady (1869) 39 LJ Ch 136, 18 WR 130 630
Griffith, Re, Carr v Griffith (1879) 12 Ch D 655, 28 WR 28, 41 LT 540 542
Griffith, Re, Jones v Owen [1904] 1 Ch 807, 73 LJ Ch 464, 90 LT 639 . . . . . . 811, 818
Griffith v Hughes [1892] 3 Ch 105, 62 LJ Ch 135, 40 WR 524, 36 Sol Jo 504, 66 LT 760 . 941
Griffith v Owen [1907] 1 Ch 195, 76 LJ Ch 92, 96 LT 5, 23 TLR 91 385
Griffith v Ricketts (1849) 7 Hare 299, 19 LJ Ch 100, 399, 14 Jur 166, 325, 82 RR 11, 15 LTOS
    43 142
Griffiths v Porter (1858) 25 Beav 236, 119 RR 403 . . . . .626, 934, 982, 983
Griffiths v Vere (1803) 148 RR 317, Tudor LC Real Prop 618, 9 Ves 127 . . . . . 189, 230
Griffiths v Williams (1977) 248 Estates Gazette 947, CA 248
Griggs v Gibson, ex p Maynard (No 2) (1866) 35 LJ Ch 458, 14 WR 538 524
Grimond v Grimond [1905] AC 124, 74 LJPC 35, 92 LT 477, 21 TLR 323, HL 105
Grimthorpe, Re [1958] Ch 615, [1958] 1 All ER 765, [1958] 1 WLR 381, 102 Sol Jo
    231 . . . . 810, 812, 818
Grimthorpe (Lord), Re, Beckett v Lord Grimthorpe [1908] 2 Ch 675, 78 LJ Ch 20, 99 LT
    679, 25 TLR 15, CA 6, 369, 377
Grindey, Re, Clews v Grindey [1898] 2 Ch 593, 67 LJ Ch 624, 47 WR 53, 79 LT 105, 14 TLR
    555, [1895-9] All ER Rep Ext 1628, CA 914, 918
Groos, Re, Groos v Groos [1915] 1 Ch 572, 84 LJ Ch 422, 59 Sol Jo 477, 112 LT 984 . .1028
Gross, Re, ex p Kingston (1871) 6 Ch App 632, 40 LJ Bcy 91, 19 WR 910, 25 LT 250 . . 607
Gross v French (1975) 238 Estates Gazette 39, CA 365
Grotian, Re, Cox v Grotian [1955] Ch 501, [1955] 1 All ER 788, [1955] 2 WLR 695, 99 Sol
    Jo 220 194
Grove v Price (1858) 26 Beav 103, 122 RR 46 578
Grove v Search (1906) 22 TLR 290 581
Grove-Grady, Re, Plowden v Lawrence [1929] 1 Ch 557, 98 LJ Ch 261, [1929] All ER Rep
    158, 73 Sol Jo 158, 140 LT 659, 45 TLR 261, CA; on appeal sub nom A-G v Plowden
    [1931] WN 89, 171 LT Jo 308, 71 L Jo 329, HL 122
Grover's Will Trusts, Re, National Provincial Bank Ltd v Clarke [1971] Ch 168, [1970] 1 All
    ER 1185, [1970] 2 WLR 574, 114 Sol Jo 207 548
Grundy, Re, Grundy v Holme (1917) 117 LT 470 . . . . 542, 553
Grupo Torras SA v Al Sabah (No 5) (24 June 1999, unreported); affd [2001] 1 CL 75, [2001]
    Lloyd's Rep Bank 36 . . . 951, 956, 959, 961, 962, 964, 965, 967, 976, 1021, 1043, 1049
Grupo Torras SA and Torras Hostench London Ltd v Sheikh Fahad Mohammed Al-Sabah
    [1995] 1 Lloyd's Rep 374; affd [1996] 1 Lloyd's Rep 7, CA 63
Guardian Ocean Cargoes Ltd, Transorient Ship Cargoes Ltd, Middle East Agents SAL and
    Med Lines SA v Banco do Brasil SA [1991] 2 Lloyd's Rep 68; affd [1994] 2 Lloyd's Rep
    152, CA 76, 116
Guardian Ocean Cargoes Ltd, Transorient Ship Cargoes Ltd, Middle East Agents SAL and
    Med Lines SA v Banco do Brasil SA (No 3) [1992] 2 Lloyd's Rep 193; affd sub nom
    Guardian Ocean Cargoes Ltd, Transorient Ship Cargoes Ltd, Middle East Agents SAL
    and Med Line SA v Banco do Brasil SA (Nos 1 and 3) [1994] 2 Lloyd's Rep 152,
    CA 12, 859, 867, 871
Guardian Trust and Executors Co of New Zealand Ltd v Public Trustee of New Zealand
    [1942] AC 115, [1942] 1 All ER 598, 111 LJPC 119, 167 LT 162, 58 TLR 132, [1942]
    NZLR 294, sub nom Public Trustee of New Zealand v Guardian Trust and Executors
    Co of New Zealand Ltd [1942] 2 WWR 289 . . . . 650, 919
Guest v Webb [1965] VR 427 261

Guinness plc v Saunders [1990] 2 AC 663, [1990] 1 All ER 652, [1990] 2 WLR 324, [1990]
    BCLC 402, 134 Sol Jo 457, [1990] 9 LS Gaz R 42, HL 393, 401, 407, 658
Guinness's Settlement, Re, Guinness v SG Warburg (Executor and Trustee) Ltd [1966] 2 All
    ER 497, [1966] 1 WLR 1355, 110 Sol Jo 636 . . . . . . .334, 471, 550, 556, 561, 691
Gulbenkian's Settlements, Re, Hacobian v Maun [1968] Ch 126, [1967] 3 All ER 15, [1967]
    3 WLR 1112, 111 Sol Jo 686, CA; affd sub nom Whishaw v Stephens [1970] AC 508,
    [1968] 3 WLR 1127, 112 Sol Jo 882, sub nom Re Gulbenkian's Settlement Trusts,
    Whishaw v Stephens [1968] 3 All ER 785, HL 29, 83, 84, 85, 88, 90, 92, 93,
                             94, 95, 96, 100, 146, 690, 691, 702
Gulbenkian's Settlement Trusts (No 2), Re, Stevens v Maun [1970] Ch 408, [1969] 2 All ER
    1173, [1969] 3 WLR 450, 113 Sol Jo 758 . . . .   28, 52, 496, 690
Gulliver v Vaux (1746) 8 De GM & G 167n, 114 RR 83 209
Gully v Cregoe (1857) 24 Beav 185, 116 RR 88 134
Gunnell v Whitear (1870) LR 10 Eq 664, 39 LJ Ch 869, 18 WR 883, 22 LT 645 830
Gunther's Will Trusts, Re, Alexander v Gunther [1939] Ch 985, [1939] 3 All ER 291, 108 LJ
    Ch 395, 83 Sol Jo 545, 161 LT 156, 55 TLR 890. . . . .   530, 547
Gwembe Valley Development Co Ltd v Koshy [1998] 2 BCLC 613. 928
Gwyon, Re, Public Trustee v A-G [1930] 1 Ch 255, 99 LJ Ch 104, 73 Sol Jo 833, 46 TLR 96,
    sub nom Public Trustee v A-G 142 LT 321. 202
Gyhon, Re, Allen v Taylor (1885) 29 Ch D 834, 54 LJ Ch 945, 33 WR 620, 53 LT 539, CA 846

H

H (minors) (sexual abuse: standard of proof), Re [1996] AC 563, [1996] 1 All ER 1, [1996]
    2 WLR 8, [1996] 1 FCR 509, [1996] 1 FLR 80, [1996] Fam Law 74, 140 Sol Jo LB 24, HL 956
H, Re [1990] 1 FLR 441, [1990] Fam Law 175 435
H v W (1857) 3 K & J 382, 112 RR 196, 69 ER 1157 190
H's Estate, Re, H v H (1875) 1 Ch D 276, 45 LJ Ch 749, 2 Char Pr Cas 80, 24 WR 317. . 905
HMF, Re [1976] Ch 33, [1975] 2 All ER 795, [1975] 3 WLR 395, 119 Sol Jo 661 269
Habergham v Vincent (1793) 2 Ves 204, 4 Bro CC 353 233
Habib Bank Ltd v Habib Bank AG Zurich [1981] 2 All ER 650, [1981] 1 WLR 1265, [1982]
    RPC 1, 125 Sol Jo 512, CA. 242, 250
Haden, Re, Coling v Haden [1898] 2 Ch 220, 67 LJ Ch 428 306
Hadley, Re, ex p Hadley (1851) 5 De G & Sm 67, 21 LJ Ch 109, 16 Jur 98, 18 LTOS 118. 761
Hagan v Waterhouse (1991) 34 NSWLR 308 998
Hagger, Re, Freeman v Arscott [1930] 2 Ch 190, 99 LJ Ch 492, [1930] All ER Rep 620, 143
    LT 610 . . . .   427, 431
Hahesy v Guiry [1917] 1 IR 371; affd [1918] 1 IR 135, 52 ILT 101, Ir CA 383
Hain's Settlement, Re, Tooth v Hain [1961] 1 All ER 848, [1961] 1 WLR 440, 105 Sol Jo 154,
    CA 99, 132
Haines, Re, Johnson v Haines (1952) Times, 7 November 122
Hale v Hale (1876) 3 Ch D 643, 24 WR 1065, 35 LT 933 225
Hale v Sheldrake (1889) 60 LT 292, 5 TLR 276. 870
Halewood International Ltd v Addleshaw Booth & Co [2000] Lloyd's Rep PN 298, [2000]
    PNLR 788 406
Haley v Bannister (1820) 4 Madd 275, 20 RR 299, 56 ER 707, [1814-23] All ER Rep 700 . 204
Halifax plc v Omar [2002] EWCA Civ 121, [2002] 2 P & CR 377, [2002] 16 EG 180 (CS) 902
Halifax Building Society v Brown [1995] 3 FCR 110, [1996] 1 FLR 103, [1996] Fam Law 85,
    27 HLR 511, CA. 417
Halifax Building Society v Thomas [1996] Ch 217, [1995] 4 All ER 673, [1996] 2 WLR 63,
    CA 387, 435, 895
Halifax Mortgage Service Ltd v Muirhead (1997) 76 P & CR 418, [1997] NPC 171, CA . 902
Halifax Mortgage Services Ltd v Stepsky [1996] Ch 207, [1996] 2 All ER 277, [1996] 2 WLR
    230, [1996] 2 FCR 97, [1996] 1 FLR 620, [1996] Fam Law 279, 28 HLR 522, [1996] 01
    LS Gaz R 21, 140 Sol Jo LB 9, CA 990
Hall, Re [1994-95] Cayman ILR 456 841
Hall, Re, Barclays Bank Ltd v Hall [1951] 1 All ER 1073, 95 Sol Jo 300, [1951] 1 TLR 850 713
Hall, Re, Foster v Metcalfe [1903] 2 Ch 226, 72 LJ Ch 554, 51 WR 529, [1900-3] All ER Rep
    371, 42 Sol Jo 514, 88 LT 619, CA. 543
Hall, Re, Hall v Hall (1885) 54 LJ Ch 527, 33 WR 508, 51 LT 901. 754
Hall, Re, Public Trustee v Montgomery [1944] Ch 46, [1943] 2 All ER 753, 113 LJ Ch 67, 87
    Sol Jo 423, 169 LT 387, 60 TLR 84 . . . .   210, 212
Hall v Hall (1868) LR 1 P & D 481, 32 JP 503, 37 LJP & M 40, 16 WR 544, 18 LT 152 . . 283
Hall v Hall (1873) 8 Ch App 430, 42 LJ Ch 444, 21 WR 373, 28 LT 383 276

Hall v Hallet (1784) 1 RR 3, 1 Cox Eq Cas 134 662

Hall's Estate, Re, Hall v Knight and Baxter [1914] P 1, 83 LJP 1, [1911-13] All ER Rep 381, 58 Sol Jo 30, 109 LT 587, 30 TLR 1, CA. 434

Hallett & Co, Re, ex p Blane [1894] 2 QB 237, 63 LJQB 573, 1 Mans 25, 9 R 278, 42 WR 305, 70 LT 361, 10 TLR 287, CA 885

Hallett's Estate, Re, Cotterell v Hallett (1880) 13 Ch D 696, 49 LJ Ch 415, 28 WR 732, [1874-80] All ER Rep 793, 42 LT 421, CA 8, 17, 22, 37, 880, 881, 882, 883, 886, 891, 895, 901

Hallett's Estate, Re, Knatchbull v Hallett (1880) 13 Ch D 696, 49 LJ Ch 415, 28 WR 732, [1874-80] All ER Rep 793, 42 LT 421, CA 8, 17, 22, 37, 393, 461, 880, 881, 882, 883, 886, 891, 895, 901

Hallows v Lloyd (1888) 39 Ch D 686, 58 LJ Ch 105, 37 WR 12, 59 LT 603 . . . . 491, 492, 629, 1003

Halsted's Will Trusts, Re, Halsted v Halsted [1937] 2 All ER 570 722

Hambleden's (Viscount) Will Trusts, Re [1960] 1 All ER 353n, [1960] 1 WLR 82, 104 Sol Jo 127. 519

Hambro v Duke of Marlborough [1994] Ch 158, [1994] 3 All ER 332, [1994] 3 WLR 341, [1994] 24 LS Gaz R 47 . . . . 187, 527

Hamilton, Re, FitzGeorge v FitzGeorge (1921) 124 LT 737, CA 213, 738

Hamilton, Re, Trench v Hamilton [1895] 1 Ch 373; on appeal [1895] 2 Ch 370, 64 LJ Ch 799, 12 R 355, 43 WR 577, 39 Sol Jo 524, sub nom Re Hamilton, Re Ashtown, Trench v Hamilton 72 LT 748, CA 74, 133, 134

Hamilton v Hamilton [1892] 1 Ch 396, 61 LJ Ch 220, 40 WR 312, 36 Sol Jo 216, 66 LT 112 269

Hamilton v Tighe [1898] 1 IR 123 574

Hamilton-Russell Executors v IRC [1943] 1 All ER 166, 25 TC 200; revsd sub nom IRC v Hamilton-Russell Executors [1943] 1 All ER 474, 25 TC 200, 87 Sol Jo 255, CA 52, 64, 730

Hamilton-Snowball's Conveyance, Re [1959] Ch 308, [1958] 2 All ER 319, [1958] 2 WLR 951, 122 JP 305, 102 Sol Jo 401 443

Hamlin v Hamlin [1986] Fam 11, [1985] 2 All ER 1037, [1985] 3 WLR 629, [1986] 1 FLR 61, [1985] Fam Law 323, 129 Sol Jo 700, CA 296

Hamlyn v John Houston & Co [1903] 1 KB 81, 72 LJKB 72, 51 WR 99, 47 Sol Jo 90, 87 LT 500, 19 TLR 66, CA 966

Hammersley v Baron de Biel (1845) 12 Cl & Fin 45, 69 RR 18, HL 140

Hammersmith and Fulham London Borough Council v Monk [1992] 1 AC 478, [1992] 1 All ER 1, [1991] 3 WLR 1144, 90 LGR 38, 63 P & CR 373, [1992] 2 FCR 129, [1992] 1 FLR 465, [1992] Fam Law 292, 24 HLR 206, [1992] 1 EGLR 65, [1992] 3 LS Gaz R 32, [1992] 09 EG 135, 136 Sol Jo LB 10, HL 582, 604, 646, 813

Hammond v Mitchell [1992] 2 All ER 109, [1991] 1 WLR 1127, sub nom H v M [1991] FCR 938, [1992] 1 FLR 229, [1991] Fam Law 473 . . . . 414, 415, 418

Hammond v Osbourn [2002] WTLR 1125, CA 281, 282

Hampden v Wallis (1884) 27 Ch D 251, 54 LJ Ch 1175, 32 WR 977, 51 LT 357 903

Hampden Settlement Trusts, Re [1977] TR 177, [2001] WTLR 195 . . . . . . 720, 809

Hampton, Re, Public Trustee v Hampton (1918) 88 LJ Ch 103, 63 Sol Jo 68 790

Hanbey's Will Trusts, Re, Cutlers' Co v President and Governors of Christ's Hospital, London (or London Corpn) [1956] Ch 264, [1955] 3 All ER 874, [1956] 2 WLR 23, 100 Sol Jo 15 201

Hanbury v Kirkland (1829) 3 Sim 265 647

Hanchett v Briscoe (1856) 22 Beav 496 948

Hancock v Smith (1889) 41 Ch D 456, 58 LJ Ch 725, [1886-90] All ER Rep 306, 61 LT 341, 5 TLR 459, CA 881, 891

Hancock v Watson [1902] AC 14, 71 LJ Ch 149, 50 WR 321, [1900-3] All ER Rep 87, 85 LT 729, HL 83, 369, 372, 374

Handcock's Trusts, Re (1889) 23 LR Ir 34, 42 193

Hanley v Pearson (1879) 13 Ch D 545, 41 LT 673 277

Hanlon, Re, Heads v Hanlon [1933] Ch 254, 102 LJ Ch 62, [1932] All ER Rep 851, 76 Sol Jo 868, 148 LT 448 . . . . 190, 220

Hannah v Hodgson (1861) 30 Beav 19, 30 LJ Ch 738, 7 Jur NS 1092, 132 RR 159, 9 WR 729, 5 LT 42 631

Hanson v Lorenz [1987] 1 FTLR 23, [1986] NLJ Rep 1088, CA 388, 400

Happé v Happé [1991] 4 All ER 527, [1990] 1 WLR 1282, [1991] FCR 23, [1990] 2 FLR 212, [1990] Fam Law 400, [1990] 24 LS Gaz R 43, CA 187

Harari's Settlement Trusts, Re, Wordsworth v Fanshawe [1949] 1 All ER 430, [1949] WN 79,
   [1949] LJR 675, 93 Sol Jo 102 . . . . 599, 612
Harbin v Masterman [1896] 1 Ch 351, 65 LJ Ch 195, 44 WR 421, [1895-9] All ER Rep 695, 40
   Sol Jo 129, 73 LT 591, 12 TLR 105, CA 566
Harcourt, Re, White v Harcourt [1911] WN 214, 56 Sol Jo 72, 105 LT 747 315
Hardaker v Moorhouse (1884) 26 Ch D 417, 53 LJ Ch 713, 32 WR 638, 50 LT 554 . . . 754
Harding, Re, Harding v Paterson [1923] 1 Ch 182, 92 LJ Ch 251, [1922] All ER Rep 557, 67
   Sol Jo 298, 128 LT 562 740
Hardman v Johnson (1815) 3 Mer 347 383
Hardoon v Belilios [1901] AC 118, 70 LJPC 9, 49 WR 209, 83 LT 573, 17 TLR 126, PC . 811,
                                                                                 821, 822
Hardwick v Johnson [1978] 2 All ER 935, [1978] 1 WLR 683, 122 Sol Jo 162, CA 413
Hardwicke (Lord) v Vernon (1799) 4 Ves 411 670
Hardy v Fothergill (1888) 13 App Cas 351, 53 JP 36, 58 LJQB 44, 37 WR 177, [1886-90] All
   ER Rep 597, 59 LT 273, 4 TLR 603, HL 184
Hardy v Reeves (1800) 5 Ves 426 985
Hardy v Shaw [1976] Ch 82, [1975] 2 All ER 1052, [1975] 2 WLR 1002, 119 Sol Jo 408 . 720
Hare Trust, Re (2001) 4 ITELR 288 . . . . 31, 116, 835
Harford's Trusts, Re (1879) 13 Ch D 135, 28 WR 239, 41 LT 382 747
Hargraves' Trusts, Re, Leach v Leach [1937] 2 All ER 545. 274
Hargreaves, Re, Hargreaves v Hargreaves [1900-3] All ER Rep 80, 88 LT 100, CA 547
Hargreaves, Re, Midgley v Tatley (1889) 43 Ch D 401, 59 LJ Ch 384, 38 WR 470, 62 LT 473,
   CA 197
Harker's Will Trusts, Re, Kean v Harker [1969] 3 All ER 1, [1969] 1 WLR 1124, 113 Sol Jo
   588 333
Harle v Jarman [1895] 2 Ch 419, 64 LJ Ch 779, 13 R 610, 43 WR 618, 73 LT 20 269
Harmer v Armstrong [1934] Ch 65, 103 LJ Ch 1, [1933] All ER Rep 778, 149 LT 579, CA   9
Harmony and Montague Tin and Copper Mining Co, Re, Spargo's Case (1873) 8 Ch App
   407, 42 LJ Ch 488, 21 WR 306, [1861-73] All ER Rep 261, 28 LT 153 901
Harpur's Will Trusts, Re, Haller v A-G [1962] Ch 78, [1961] 3 All ER 588, [1961] 3 WLR 924,
   105 Sol Jo 609, CA 107, 108, 110
Harries v Church Comrs for England [1993] 2 All ER 300, [1992] 1 WLR 1241, [1992] 41 LS
   Gaz R 36, 135 Sol Jo LB 180 . . . . 601, 613, 616
Harris, Re, Cope v Evans [1945] Ch 316, [1945] 1 All ER 702, 114 LJ Ch 302, 89 Sol Jo 282,
   173 LT 284, 61 TLR 364 212
Harris v Black (1983) 46 P & CR 366, 127 Sol Jo 224, CA 476, 582
Harris v Harris (No 2) (1861) 29 Beav 110, 131 RR 477 982
Harris v Newton (1877) 46 LJ Ch 268, 25 WR 228, 36 LT 173 376
Harris v Sharp (21 March 1989, unreported) 77, 450
Harris v Shuttleworth [1994] ICR 991, [1994] IRLR 547, [1995] OPLR 79, CA . 691, 692, 693
Harris Investments Ltd v Smith [1934] 1 DLR 748. . . . . 1034, 1036
Harris' Settlement, Re, Dent v Harris (1940) 84 Sol Jo 205, 162 LT 358, 56 TLR 429 . . 725
Harrison, Re, Day v Harrison (1920) 90 LJ Ch 186 359
Harrison, Re, Hunter v Bush [1918] 2 Ch 59, 87 LJ Ch 433, [1918-19] All ER Rep 785, 62 Sol
   Jo 568, 118 LT 756. 373
Harrison, Re, Townson v Harrison (1889) 43 Ch D 55, 59 LJ Ch 169, 38 WR 265, 61 LT 762 567
Harrison v Forth (1695) Prec Ch 51 983
Harrison v Graham unreported 451
Harrison v Randall (1851) 9 Hare 397, 21 LJ Ch 294, 16 Jur 72 . . . . 494, 529
Harrison v Tew (1988) Times, 30 November 183
Harrison (Properties) Ltd v Harrison [2001] EWCA Civ 1467, [2002] 1 BCLC 162, [2001]
   WTLR 1327 . . . . 924, 928
Harrison's Settlement Trusts, Re, Morris v Harrison-Sleap [1965] 3 All ER 795, [1965] 1
   WLR 1492, 109 Sol Jo 997 . . . . 743, 767, 782
Harrison's Share under Settlement, Re, Harrison v Harrison [1955] Ch 260, [1954] 2 All ER
   453, [1954] 3 WLR 156; affd [1955] Ch 260, [1955] 1 All ER 185, [1955] 2 WLR 256, 99
   Sol Jo 74, CA. 501
Harrison's Trusts, Re (1852) 22 LJ Ch 69, 94 RR 794, 1 WR 58, 20 LTOS 123 . . . 744, 753
Harrods Ltd v Lemon [1931] 2 KB 157, 100 LJKB 219, [1931] All ER Rep 285, 75 Sol Jo 119,
   144 LT 657, 47 TLR 248, CA 405
Harrow London Borough Council v Johnstone [1997] 1 All ER 929, [1997] 1 WLR 459,
   [1997] 2 FCR 225, [1997] 1 FLR 887, [1997] Fam Law 478, 29 HLR 475, [1997] 15 LS
   Gaz R 26, [1997] NLJR 413, HL. 582

Hart (Inspector of Taxes) v Briscoe [1979] Ch 1, [1978] 1 All ER 791, [1978] 2 WLR 832, [1978] STC 89, 52 TC 53, [1977] TR 285, 293, 121 Sol Jo 852, L(TC) 2663 . . 199, 807, 1040

Hart v O'Connor [1985] AC 1000, [1985] 2 All ER 880, [1985] 3 WLR 214, 129 Sol Jo 484, [1985] LS Gaz R 2658, PC 270

Hart v Tribe (1854) 18 Beav 215, 23 LJ Ch 462, 2 WR 289, 23 LTOS 124 134

Hart & Co v Michael. See Michael v Hart & Co

Hart's Will Trusts, Re, Hart v Hart [1943] 2 All ER 557 613

Hartigan Nominees Pty Ltd v Rydge (1992) 29 NSWLR 405 . . . . 61, 677, 682, 684

Harvard Securities Ltd (in liquidation), Re, Holland v Newbury [1997] 2 BCLC 369, [1998] BCC 567 78

Harvell v Foster [1954] 2 QB 367, [1954] 2 All ER 736, [1954] 3 WLR 351, 98 Sol Jo 540, CA 19, 20, 760

Harvey, Re, Peek v Savory (1888) 39 Ch D 289, 60 LT 79, CA 190, 229

Harvey, Re, Toronto General Trusts v Harvey (1932) 41 OWN 420 162

Harvey, Re, Westminster Bank Ltd v Askwith [1941] 3 All ER 284, 85 Sol Jo 481 526

Harvey v Olliver [1887] WN 149, 57 LT 239 . . . . 492, 815

Harwood v Harwood [1992] 1 FCR 1, [1991] 2 FLR 274, [1991] Fam Law 418, CA . 355, 421

Harwood v Tooke (1812) 2 Sim 192, 29 RR 81 184

Hastings Corpn v Letton [1908] 1 KB 378, 77 LJKB 149, 15 Mans 58, 97 LT 582, 23 TLR 456, DC 774

Hastings-Bass, Re, Hastings-Bass v IRC [1975] Ch 25, [1974] 2 All ER 193, [1974] 2 WLR 904, [1974] STC 211, 53 ATC 87, [1974] TR 87, 118 Sol Jo 422, CA . . . 94, 95, 456, 694, 697, 699, 724

Hatch, Re, Hatch v Hatch [1919] 1 Ch 351, 88 LJ Ch 147, [1918-19] All ER Rep 357, 63 Sol Jo 389, 120 LT 694 982

Hatch, Re, Public Trustee v Hatch [1948] Ch 592, [1948] 2 All ER 288, [1948] LJR 1393, 92 Sol Jo 456 . . . . 101, 369, 373

Hatch v Hatch (1804) 1 Smith KB 226, 9 Ves 292, [1803-13] All ER Rep 74 . . . . . 22, 281

Hatfeild's Will Trusts, Re, Hatfeild v Hatfeild [1958] Ch 469, [1957] 2 All ER 261, [1957] 3 WLR 28, 101 Sol Jo 480 333

Hatton, Re, Hockin v Hatton [1917] 1 Ch 357, 86 LJ Ch 375, 61 Sol Jo 253, 116 LT 281 . 538

Havelock v Havelock, Re Allan (1881) 17 Ch D 807, 50 LJ Ch 778, 29 WR 859, 44 LT 168 524

Hawker's Settled Estates, Re (1897) 66 LJ Ch 341, 45 WR 440, 41 Sol Jo 333, 76 LT 287 . 572

Hawkesley v May [1956] 1 QB 304, [1955] 3 All ER 353, [1955] 3 WLR 569, 99 Sol Jo 781 . . . . 28, 496, 624, 672, 674

Hawkins, Re, White v White [1916] 2 Ch 570, 86 LJ Ch 25, 61 Sol Jo 29, 115 LT 543 . . 209, 229

Hawkins v Hawkins (1920) SRNSW 550 539

Hay, Re, Leech v Hay [1932] NI 215 229

Hay's Settlement Trusts, Re [1981] 3 All ER 786, [1982] 1 WLR 202, 125 Sol Jo 866 . . . . 26, 27, 29, 31, 62, 90, 91, 92, 93, 94, 96, 97, 674, 680, 689, 690, 692, 723, 803, 809

Hayes v Oatley (1872) LR 14 Eq 1, 41 LJ Ch 510, 26 LT 816 803

Hayes's Will Trusts, Re, Pattinson v Hayes [1971] 2 All ER 341, [1971] 1 WLR 758, 115 Sol Jo 310, 219 Estates Gazette 1181 . . . . 17, 18

Haygarth, Re, Wickham v Holmes [1912] 1 Ch 510, 81 LJ Ch 255, 56 Sol Jo 239, 106 LT 93 201

Hayim v Citibank NA [1987] AC 730, [1987] 3 WLR 83, 131 Sol Jo 660, [1987] LS Gaz R 1573, PC 591, 692

Hayman v Nicoll [1944] 3 DLR 551 259

Haynes' Will Trusts, Re, Pitt v Haynes [1949] Ch 5, [1948] 2 All ER 423, [1948] LJR 1745, 92 Sol Jo 456 212

Haywood v Haywood (13 July 2000, unreported) 418

Hazeldine, Re, Public Trustee v Hazeldine [1918] 1 Ch 433, 87 LJ Ch 303, 62 Sol Jo 350, 118 LT 437 557

Head v Gould [1898] 2 Ch 250, 67 LJ Ch 480, 46 WR 597, 42 Sol Jo 553, 78 LT 739, 14 TLR 444 . . . . 590, 918, 946

Headington's Trust, Re (1857) 27 LJ Ch 175, 114 RR 516, 6 WR 7 830

Healey v Brown [2000] WTLR 780 234

Healey v Brown [2002] 19 EG 147 (CS) 428, 429, 431, 432

Healey v Brown [2002] WTLR 789 266

Hearn (Inspector of Taxes) v Morgan [1945] 2 All ER 480, 26 TC 478, 173 LT 361, 61 TLR 552 658

Hearn v Younger [2002] EWHC 963 (Ch) 694, 696, 697
Heartley v Nicholson (1875) LR 19 Eq 233, 44 LJ Ch 277, 23 WR 374, 31 LT 822. . . .   147
Heasman v Pearse (1871) 7 Ch App 275, 41 LJ Ch 705, 20 WR 271, 26 LT 299.   201
Heath v Lewis (1853) 3 De GM & G 954, 22 LJ Ch 721, 1 Eq Rep 55, 17 Jur 443, 98 RR 386, 1
    WR 314, 21 LTOS 135   221
Heath's Will Trusts, Re, Hamilton v Lloyds Bank Ltd [1949] Ch 170, [1949] 1 All ER 199,
    [1949] LJR 641, 93 Sol Jo 59   215
Heathcote v Hulme (1819) 1 Jac & W 122, 20 RR 245 . . . .   870, 871, 874
Heberley, Re [1971] NZLR 325   273
Hedderwick's Trustees v Hedderwick's Executors (1910) 47 SLR 238, 1910 SC 333, 1910 1
    SLT 36   332
Hedley Byrne & Co Ltd v Heller & Partners Ltd [1964] AC 465, [1963] 2 All ER 575, [1963]
    3 WLR 101, [1963] 1 Lloyd's Rep 485, 107 Sol Jo 454, HL 24, 493, 685
Heinl v Jyske Bank (Gibraltar) Ltd [1999] 34 LS Gaz R 33, [1999] Lloyd's Rep Bank 511,
    CA 957, 959, 968
Heming's Trust, Re (1856) 3 K & J 40, 26 LJ Ch 106, 2 Jur NS 1186, 5 WR 33, 28 LTOS
    99 . . . .   829, 846
Hemmens v Wilson Browne (a firm) [1995] Ch 223, [1993] 4 All ER 826, [1994] 2 WLR 323,
    [1994] 2 FLR 101, [1993] 45 LS Gaz R 45   281
Henderson, Re, Henderson v Henderson [1940] Ch 764, [1940] 3 All ER 295, 109 LJ Ch
    363, 84 Sol Jo 441, 56 TLR 871 . . . .   743, 744, 765, 766, 767, 795
Henderson, Re, Public Trustee v Reddie [1940] Ch 368, [1940] 1 All ER 623, 109 LJ Ch 169,
    84 Sol Jo 255, 162 LT 376, 56 TLR 423 . . . .   540, 541
Henderson v Merrett Syndicates Ltd [1995] 2 AC 145, [1994] 3 All ER 506, [1994] 3 WLR
    761, [1994] NLJR 1204, HL 24, 857
Henderson v Rothschild & Sons (1886) 33 Ch D 459, 55 LJ Ch 939, 34 WR 769, 55 LT 165;
    affd (1887) 56 LJ Ch 471, 35 WR 485, 56 LT 98, 3 TLR 364, CA   141
Henderson's Trusts, Re, Schreiber v Baring [1969] 3 All ER 769, [1969] 1 WLR 651, 113 Sol
    Jo 328, CA   718
Hendy Lennox (Industrial Engines) Ltd v Grahame Puttick Ltd [1984] 2 All ER 152, [1984]
    1 WLR 485, [1984] 2 Lloyd's Rep 422, [1984] BCLC 285, 128 Sol Jo 220, [1984] LS Gaz
    R 585   17
Hengler, Re, Frowde v Hengler [1893] 1 Ch 586, 62 LJ Ch 383, 3 R 207, 41 WR 491, 68 LT 84   570
Henley v Wardell (1988) Times, 29 January   718
Henriques v Bensusan, Bank of England Claim (1872) 20 WR 350   141
Henry, Re, Gordon v Gordon [1907] 1 Ch 30, 76 LJ Ch 74, 95 LT 776   566
Henry v Armstrong (1881) 18 Ch D 668, 30 WR 472, 44 LT 918   276
Henry v Hammond [1913] 2 KB 515, 82 LJKB 575, 12 Asp MLC 332, 57 Sol Jo 358, 108 LT
    729, 29 TLR 340, [1911-13] All ER Rep Ext 1478 . . . .   37, 76
Hepplewhite's Will Trusts, Re (1977) Times 21 January 218, 225
Hepworth v Hepworth (1870) LR 11 Eq 10, 40 LJ Ch 111, 19 WR 46, 23 LT 388 . .   363, 367
Herdegen v Federal Comr of Taxation (1988) 84 ALR 271 . . . .   59, 79
Hernando, Re, Hernando v Sawtell (1884) 27 Ch D 284, 53 LJ Ch 865, 33 WR 252, 51 LT
    117. . . . .   231, 1031, 1047
Heseltine v Heseltine [1971] 1 All ER 952, [1971] 1 WLR 342, 135 JP 214, 114 Sol Jo 972,
    CA. 57, 347, 361
Hetherington, Re [1990] Ch 1, [1989] 2 WLR 1094, sub nom Re Hetherington, Gibbs v
    McDonnell [1989] 2 All ER 129, 133 Sol Jo 457.   123
Hetherington's Trusts, Re (1886) 34 Ch D 211, 56 LJ Ch 174, 35 WR 285, 55 LT 806 . .   762
Hewett, Re, Eldridge v Iles [1918] 1 Ch 458, [1918-19] All ER Rep 530, 118 LT 524, sub nom
    Re Hewitt, Eldridge v Iles 87 LJ Ch 209   220
Hewitt v Loosemore (1851) 9 Hare 449, 21 LJ Ch 69, 15 Jur 1097, 89 RR 526, 18 LTOS
    133.   1001
Hewitt's Estate, Re, Gateshead Corpn v Hudspeth (1883) 53 LJ Ch 132, 49 LT 587 . . .   106
Hewitt's Settlement, Re, Hewitt v Hewitt [1915] 1 Ch 228, 84 LJ Ch 358, 59 Sol Jo 177, 112
    LT 287, 31 TLR 81 . . . .   789, 1038, 1047
Hey's Estate, Re, Walker v Gaskill [1914] P 192, 83 LJP 152, 59 Sol Jo 45, 111 LT 941, 30 TLR
    637.   429
Heyworth's Contingent Reversionary Interest, Re [1956] Ch 364, [1956] 2 WLR 1044, 100
    Sol Jo 342, sub nom Re Heyworth's Settlements [1956] 2 All ER 21 . . .   526, 709, 783
Hicklin, Re, Public Trustee v Hoare [1917] 2 Ch 278, 86 LJ Ch 740, [1916-17] All ER Rep
    658, 61 Sol Jo 630, 117 LT 403, 33 TLR 478   574

Higginbottom, Re [1892] 3 Ch 132, 62 LJ Ch 74, 3 R 23, [1891-4] All ER Rep 1070, 67 LT
190 . . . . 736, 751, 759
Higgins v Hill (1887) 56 LT 426, 3 TLR 403 184
Highett and Bird's Contract, Re [1902] 2 Ch 214, 71 LJ Ch 508, 50 WR 424, 46 Sol Jo 380, 87
LT 159; on appeal [1903] 1 Ch 287, 72 LJ Ch 220, 51 WR 227, 87 LT 697, CA . . . 441
Highway v Banner (1785) 1 Bro CC 584 302
Highway Foods International Ltd (in administrative receivership), Re [1995] 1 BCLC 209,
[1995] BCC 271 14
Higinbotham v Holme (1811-12) (1803) 19 Ves 88, [1803-13] All ER Rep 504, sub nom
Higginbotham v Holme Mont 479n 209
Hilbers v Parkinson (1883) 25 Ch D 200, 53 LJ Ch 194, 32 WR 315, 49 LT 502 308
Hill, Re, Hill v Hill (1881) 50 LJ Ch 551, 45 LT 126 . . . . 553, 562, 563
Hill v Bishop of London (1738) 1 Atk 618 329
Hill (Viscount) v Dowager Viscountess Hill [1897] 1 QB 483, 66 LJQB 329, 45 WR 371, 41
Sol Jo 292, 76 LT 103, 13 TLR 227, CA 133
Hill v Gomme (1839) 5 My & Cr 250, 9 LJ Ch 54, 4 Jur 165, [1835-42] All ER Rep 118 . 166
Hill v Hill (1904) 8 OLR 710, 5 OWR 2, 25 CLT 41 359
Hill v Langley (1988) Times, 28 January 671
Hill v Permanent Trustee Co of New South Wales Ltd [1930] AC 720, [1930] All ER Rep 87,
144 LT 65, sub nom Re Hill, Hill v Permanent Trustee Co of NSW 99 LJPC 191, PC 536
Hill v Trenery (1856) 23 Beav 16, 113 RR 9 524
Hill v Wilson (1873) 8 Ch App 888, 42 LJ Ch 817, 21 WR 757, 29 LT 238, [1861-73] All ER
Rep Ext 1146 149
Hill's Trusts, Re [1874] WN 228 772
Hillas-Drake, Re, National Provincial Bank Ltd v Liddell [1944] Ch 235, [1944] 1 All ER 375,
113 LJ Ch 137, 88 Sol Jo 103, 170 LT 240, 60 TLR 261 . . . . 530, 547
Hilliard v Fulford (1876) 4 Ch D 389, 46 LJ Ch 43, 25 WR 161, [1874-80] All ER Rep 247, 35
LT 750 . . . . 626, 982
Hillier, Re, Hillier v A-G [1954] 2 All ER 59, [1954] 1 WLR 700, 98 Sol Jo 319, CA . . . 341
Hillingdon Estates Co v Stonefield Estates Ltd [1952] Ch 627, [1952] 1 All ER 853, 50 LGR
587, 2 P & CR 415, [1952] 1 TLR 1099 442
Hillsdown Holdings plc v Pensions Ombudsman [1997] 1 All ER 862, [1996] PLR 427,
[1996] OPLR 291 662
Hilton, Re, Gibbes v Hale-Hinton [1909] 2 Ch 548, 79 LJ Ch 7, 17 Mans 19, 101 LT 229 . 645
Hinckley Singapore Trading Pte Ltd v Sogo Department Stores (S) Pte Ltd (2001) 4 ITELR
301 76
Hine v Hine [1962] 3 All ER 345, [1962] 1 WLR 1124, 106 Sol Jo 589, CA 413
Hinves v Hinves (1844) 3 Hare 609, 64 RR 446 548
Hirachand Punamchand v Temple [1911] 2 KB 330, 80 LJKB 1155, 55 Sol Jo 519, 105 LT
277, 27 TLR 430, [1911-13] All ER Rep Ext 1597, CA 180
Hitch v Stone (Inspector of Taxes) [2001] EWCA Civ 63, [2001] STC 214, 73 TC 600, [2001]
09 LS Gaz R 40 . . . . 59, 62
Hivac Ltd v Park Royal Scientific Instruments Ltd [1946] Ch 169, [1946] 1 All ER 350, 115
LJ Ch 241, 90 Sol Jo 175, 174 LT 422, 62 TLR 231, CA 402
Hoare Trustees v Gardner (Inspector of Taxes) [1979] Ch 10, [1978] 1 All ER 791, [1978] 2
WLR 839, [1978] STC 89, 52 TC 53, [1977] TR 293, 121 Sol Jo 852, L(TC)
2663 . . . . 245, 726
Hobbs v Wayet (1887) 36 Ch D 256, 56 LJ Ch 819, 36 WR 73, 57 LT 225 . . . 811, 813, 823
Hobday v Peters (No 3) (1860) 28 Beav 603, 126 RR 262 585
Hobley, Re (1997) Times, 16 June 429
Hobourn Aero Components Ltd's Air Raid Distress Fund, Re, Ryan v Forrest [1946] Ch 86,
[1945] 2 All ER 711, 115 LJ Ch 50, 89 Sol Jo 590, 174 LT 91, 62 TLR 69; on appeal
[1946] Ch 194, [1946] 1 All ER 501, 115 LJ Ch 158, 90 Sol Jo 260, 174 LT 428, 62 TLR
313, CA 336
Hobson, Re, Walter v Appach (1885) 55 LJ Ch 422, 34 WR 70, 53 LT 627 . . . . 552, 560
Hockey v Western [1898] 1 Ch 350, 67 LJ Ch 166, 46 WR 312, 42 Sol Jo 232, 78 LT 1, 14 TLR
201, CA 629
Hoddinott v Hoddinott [1949] 2 KB 406, 93 Sol Jo 296, 65 TLR 266, CA 361
Hodge, Re, Hodge v Griffiths [1940] Ch 260, 109 LJ Ch 185, 84 Sol Jo 113, 162 LT 155, 56
TLR 327 35
Hodge, Re, Midland Bank Executor and Trustee Co Ltd v Morrison [1943] Ch 300, [1943] 2
All ER 304, 112 LJ Ch 241, 87 Sol Jo 274, 169 LT 155, 59 TLR 373 333
Hodges, Re, Hodges v Hodges [1899] 1 IR 480 814

Hodgkinson, Re, Hodgkinson v Hodgkinson [1895] 2 Ch 190, 64 LJ Ch 663, 12 R 297, 43 WR 594, 39 Sol Jo 468, 72 LT 617, [1895-9] All ER Rep Ext 2136, CA 846
Hodgkinson v Simms [1994] 3 SCR 377, [1994] 9 WWR 609, 22 CCLT (2d) 1, 117 DLR (4th) 151. . . . . 20, 22
Hodgson, ex p (1812) 12 RR 171, 19 Ves 206 209
Hodgson, Re, Weston v Hodgson [1913] 1 Ch 34, 82 LJ Ch 31, 57 Sol Jo 112, 107 LT 607. . . . . 211, 724
Hodgson v Marks [1971] Ch 892, [1970] 3 All ER 513, [1970] 3 WLR 956, 21 P & CR 737, 114 Sol Jo 770, 215 Estates Gazette 441; revsd [1971] Ch 892, [1971] 2 All ER 684, [1971] 2 WLR 1263, 22 P & CR 586, 115 Sol Jo 224, CA 50, 54, 234, 255, 256, 257, 333, 368, 410
Hodgson v Smithson (1856) 8 De GM & G 604, 26 LJ Ch 110, 2 Jur NS 1199, 111 RR 120, 5 WR 3, 28 LTOS 73 373
Hodson, Re, Williams v Knight [1894] 2 Ch 421, 63 LJ Ch 609, 8 R 346, 42 WR 531, 38 Sol Jo 457, 71 LT 77, 10 TLR 471. . . . . 269, 306
Hodson's Settlement, Re (1851) 9 Hare 118, sub nom Re Hodgson's Settlement 20 LJ Ch 551, 15 Jur 552, 17 LTOS 241 764
Hogg, Re [1983] LS Gaz R 2838 565
Hoghton v Hoghton (1852) 15 Beav 278, 21 LJ Ch 482, 17 Jur 99, 92 RR 421 274
Holden, Re, ex p Official Receiver (1887) 20 QBD 43, 57 LJQB 47, 36 WR 189, 58 LT 118, DC 818, 842
Holden, Re, Isaacson v Holden [1935] WN 52, 179 LT Jo 235 628
Holder, Re, National Provincial Bank Ltd v Holder [1953] Ch 468, [1953] 2 All ER 1, [1953] 2 WLR 1079, 97 Sol Jo 353. 561
Holder v Holder [1968] Ch 353, [1966] 2 All ER 116, [1966] 3 WLR 229, 110 Sol Jo 569; on appeal [1968] Ch 353, [1968] 1 All ER 665, [1968] 2 WLR 237, 112 Sol Jo 17, 205 Estates Gazette 211, CA 23, 451, 660, 661, 662, 669, 670, 932, 936
Holding and Management Ltd v Property Holding and Investment Trust plc [1988] 2 All ER 702, [1988] 1 WLR 644, 132 Sol Jo 626, [1988] 11 LS Gaz R 43; affd [1990] 1 All ER 938, [1989] 1 WLR 1313, 21 HLR 596, 134 Sol Jo 262, [1990] 1 EGLR 65, [1990] 05 EG 75, CA 736, 810, 840, 842
Holford's Settlement, Re, Lloyds Bank Ltd v Holford [1945] Ch 21, [1944] 2 All ER 462, 114 LJ Ch 71, 171 LT 379, 61 TLR 47 199
Holland, Re, Gregg v Holland [1902] 2 Ch 360, 71 LJ Ch 518, 9 Mans 259, 50 WR 575, 46 Sol Jo 483, 86 LT 542, 18 TLR 563, CA 166, 209, 236
Holland, Re, Howarth's Trusts (1881) 16 Ch D 672, 50 LJ Ch 271, 20 WR 499, 144 LT 561. . . . . 780, 782
Holliday (a bankrupt), Re, ex p Trustee of the Property of the Bankrupt v Bankrupt [1981] Ch 405, [1980] 3 All ER 385, [1981] 2 WLR 996, 125 Sol Jo 411, CA 481, 482
Holliday, Re, Houghton v Adlard [1947] Ch 402, [1947] 1 All ER 695, [1947] LJR 1086, 91 Sol Jo 278, 76 LT 478, 63 TLR 255 560
Hollington Bros Ltd v Rhodes [1951] 2 All ER 578n, [1951] WN 437, [1951] 2 TLR 691. . . . . 256, 411
Hollingworth v Tooke. See Tooke v Hollingworth
Holmes, Re (1885) 29 Ch D 786, 55 LJ Ch 33, CA. 1002
Holmes v Coghill (1802) 6 RR 166, 7 Ves 499; affd (1806) 8 RR 323, 12 Ves 206 804
Holmes v Godson (1856) 8 De GM & G 152, 25 LJ Ch 317, 2 Jur NS 383, 114 RR 73, 4 WR 415, 27 LTOS 8 209
Holmes v Williams [1895] WN 116. . . . . 383, 385
Holmes (W & R) and Cosmopolitan Press Ltd's Contract, Re [1944] Ch 53, [1943] 2 All ER 716, 113 LJ Ch 14, 87 Sol Jo 414, 169 LT 367, 60 TLR 56 200
Holroyd v Marshall (1862) 10 HL Cas 191, 33 LJ Ch 193, 9 Jur NS 213, 138 RR 108, 11 WR 171, 11 ER 999, [1861-73] All ER Rep 414, 7 LT 172, HL 175, 184, 502, 826
Holt, Re, Re Rollason, Holt v Holt [1897] 2 Ch 525, 66 LJ Ch 734, 45 WR 650, 41 Sol Jo 642, 76 LT 776 . . . . 941, 947
Holt v Heatherfield Trust Ltd [1942] 2 KB 1, [1942] 1 All ER 404, 111 LJKB 465, 86 Sol Jo 174, 166 LT 251, 58 TLR 274 152
Holt's Settlement, Re, Wilson v Holt [1969] 1 Ch 100, [1968] 1 All ER 470, [1968] 2 WLR 653, 112 Sol Jo 195, [1968] BTR 122 . . . . 235, 246, 439, 509, 511, 519
Holton's Settlement Trusts, Re, Holton v Holton [1918] WN 78, 88 LJ Ch 444, 62 Sol Jo 403, 119 LT 304. 678
Holzberg v Sasson (1986) 75 Revue Critique de Droit International Prive 685 1048
Hong Kong Bank Trustee Co v Farrer Tan [1988] 1 MLJ 485 123

Honywood v Honywood [1902] 1 Ch 347, 71 LJ Ch 174, 86 LT 214 . . . . 563, 565
Hood, Re, Public Trustee v Hood [1931] 1 Ch 240, 100 LJ Ch 115, [1930] All ER Rep 215, 74
   Sol Jo 549, 143 LT 691, 46 TLR 571, CA 106
Hood v Clapham (1854) 19 Beav 90, 24 LJ Ch 193, 1 Jur NS 78, 105 RR 67, 3 WR 78, 24
   LTOS 206 982
Hood v Franklin (1873) LR 16 Eq 496, 21 WR 724 . . . . 316, 317
Hood v Oglander (1865) 34 Beav 513, 34 LJ Ch 528, 11 Jur NS 498, 6 New Rep 57, 145 RR
   639, 13 WR 705, 12 LT 626 . . . . 214, 738
Hood of Avalon (Lady) v Mackinnon [1909] 1 Ch 476, 78 LJ Ch 300, 53 Sol Jo 269, 100 LT
   330, 25 TLR 290 274
Hooper, Re, Parker v Ward [1932] 1 Ch 38, 101 LJ Ch 61, [1931] All ER Rep 129, 146 LT
   208 . . . . 120, 129
Hooper v Smart (1875) 1 Ch D 90, 45 LJ Ch 99, 24 WR 152, 33 LT 499 980
Hooper's Settlement Trusts, Re, Bosman v Hooper [1948] Ch 586, [1948] 2 All ER 261,
   [1948] LJR 1455, 92 Sol Jo 362 228
Hooper's Trusts, Re (1865) 11 Jur NS 479, 5 New Rep 463, 147 RR 827, 13 WR 710, 12 LT
   137 316
Hope Johnstone, Re, Hope Johnstone v Hope Johnstone [1904] 1 Ch 470, 73 LJ Ch 321, 90
   LT 253, 20 TLR 282 218
Hope's Will Trust, Re, Hope v Thorp [1929] 2 Ch 136, 98 LJ Ch 249, [1929] All ER Rep 561,
   141 LT 509 526
Hopkins v Myall (1830) 2 Russ & M 86, 34 RR 25 631
Hopkinson, Re, Dyson v Hopkinson [1922] 1 Ch 65, 91 LJ Ch 128, 126 LT 649, 66 Sol Jo
   (WR) 18 377
Hopper v Conyers (1866) LR 2 Eq 549, 12 Jur NS 328, 14 WR 628 880
Hora v Hora (1863) 33 Beav 88, 140 RR 25 138
Horn, Re, Westminster Bank Ltd v Horn [1946] Ch 254, [1946] 2 All ER 118, 115 LJ Ch 271,
   90 Sol Jo 307, 175 LT 194, 62 TLR 408, CA 546
Horne, Re, Wilson v Cox Sinclair [1905] 1 Ch 76, 74 LJ Ch 25, 53 WR 317, 92 LT
   263 . . . . 948, 981, 982
Horsfall v Haywards (a firm) [1999] 1 FLR 1182, [1999] Fam Law 383, 143 Sol Jo LB 66,
   [1999] PNLR 583, CA 281
Horsnaill, Re, Womersley v Horsnaill [1909] 1 Ch 631, 78 LJ Ch 331, 100 LT 603 . . . 735
Hosegood v Pedler (1896) 66 LJQB 18, 13 TLR 6 811
Hoskin's Trusts, Re (1877) 5 Ch D 229, 46 LJ Ch 274, 35 LT 935; on appeal (1877) 6 Ch D
   281, 46 LJ Ch 817, 25 WR 779, CA. 803, 828, 846
Hospital Products Ltd v United States Surgical Corpn (1984) 156 CLR 41, 55 ALR 417, 58
   ALJR 587, 4 IPR 291, [1985] LRC (Comm) 411, HC of A 20, 400, 404
Hotchkys, Re, Freke v Calmady (1886) 32 Ch D 408, 55 LJ Ch 546, 34 WR 569, [1886-90] All
   ER Rep 1104, 55 LT 110, CA 564, 565, 571, 572, 589
Houghton, Re, Hawley v Blake [1904] 1 Ch 622, 73 LJ Ch 317, 52 WR 505, [1904-7] All ER
   Rep 486, 48 Sol Jo 312, 90 LT 252, 20 TLR 276 . . . . 18, 708
Houghton, Re, Houghton v Houghton [1915] 2 Ch 173, 84 LJ Ch 726, 59 Sol Jo 562, 113 LT
   422, 31 TLR 427 435
Houghton v Fayers [2000] 1 BCLC 511, [2000] Lloyd's Rep Bank 145, CA 956, 974
Hourigan v Trustees Executors and Agency Co Ltd (1934) 51 CLR 619, [1934] ALR 283,
   [1934] VLR 279, 8 ALJ 146 934
Houston v Burns [1918] AC 337, 87 LJPC 99, 118 LT 462, 34 TLR 219, HL 105
Hovenden v Lord Annesley (1806) 9 RR 119, 2 Sch & Lef 607 460
How v Earl Winterton (1902) 51 WR 262, 47 Sol Jo 146 817
Howard's Will Trusts, Re, Levin v Bradley [1961] Ch 507, [1961] 2 All ER 413, [1961] 2 WLR
   821, 105 Sol Jo 347 104
Howarth, Re, Macqueen v Kirby [1916] WN 50, 60 Sol Jo 307 . . . . 303, 304
Howe v Earl of Dartmouth (1802) 6 RR 96, 7 Ves 137, 1 White & Tud LC 68, [1775-1802] All
   ER Rep 24 . . . . 548, 558
Howell, Re, Re Buckingham, Liggins v Buckingham [1915] 1 Ch 241, 84 LJ Ch 209, [1914-
   15] All ER Rep 211, 112 LT 188, CA 80
Howes, Re, Howes v Platt (1905) 21 TLR 501 . . . . 366, 367
Howlett, Re, Howlett v Howlett [1949] Ch 767, [1949] 2 All ER 490, [1949] LJR 1632, 93 Sol
   Jo 632, 65 TLR 569 . . . . 925, 931
Hoy v Master (1834) 6 Sim 568, 3 LJ Ch 134, 38 RR 176 80
Hoyle, Re, Hoyle v Hoyle [1893] 1 Ch 84, 62 LJ Ch 182, 2 R 145, 41 WR 81, 37 Sol Jo 46, 67
   LT 674, CA 237

Hoyles, Re, Row v Jagg [1911] 1 Ch 179, 80 LJ Ch 274, 55 Sol Jo 169, 103 LT 817, 27 TLR
   131, CA 1026
Hoyles, Re, Row v Jagg (No 2) [1912] 1 Ch 67, 81 LJ Ch 163, 56 Sol Jo 11, 105 LT
   663 . . . . 553, 563
Hubbard's Will Trusts, Re, Marston v Angier [1963] Ch 275, [1962] 2 All ER 917, [1962] 3
   WLR 682, 106 Sol Jo 705 . . . . 226, 334
Hubbuck, Re, Hart v Stone [1896] 1 Ch 754, 65 LJ Ch 271, 44 WR 289, 40 Sol Jo 257, 73 LT
   738, CA 560, 562
Hughes v Empson (1856) 22 Beav 181, 111 RR 321 584
Hughes v Kelly (1843) 61 RR 109, 5 I Eq R 286, 2 Con & Law 223, 3 Dr & War 482 . . . 137
Hughes v Key (1855) 20 Beav 395 844
Hughes v Wells (1852) 9 Hare 749, 16 Jur 927, 89 RR 651, 68 ER 717, 20 LTOS 136 . . 931
Hughes v Young (1862) 32 LJ Ch 137, 9 Jur NS 376, 1 New Rep 166, 39 RR 310 312
Hughes-Hallett v Indian Mammoth Gold Mines Co (1882) 22 Ch D 561, 52 LJ Ch 418, 31
   WR 285, 48 LT 107 813
Hughes' Settlement, Re, Hughes v Schooling [1924] 2 Ch 356, 94 LJ Ch 57, [1924] 2 All ER
   Rep 373, 68 Sol Jo 791, 133 LT 470 316
Huguenin v Baseley (1807) 9 RR 276, 14 Ves 273, 1 White & Tud LC 259, [1803-13] All ER
   Rep 1 . . . . 274, 276, 282
Hulkes, Re, Powell v Hulkes (1886) 33 Ch D 552, 55 LJ Ch 846, 34 WR 733, 35 WR 194,
   [1886-90] All ER Rep 659, 55 LT 209 . . . . 623, 626, 864
Hulton, Re, Midland Bank Executor and Trustee Co Ltd v Thompson [1936] Ch 536,
   [1936] 2 All ER 207, 105 LJ Ch 273, 80 Sol Jo 386, 155 LT 226, 52 TLR 507 . . . 793
Hume v Richardson (1862) 4 De GF & J 29, 31 LJ Ch 713, 8 Jur NS 686, 135 RR 18, 10 WR
   528, 6 LT 624 557
Hume Nisbet's Settlement, Re (1911) 55 Sol Jo 536, 27 TLR 461 536
Humerston v Humerston (1716) Gilb Ch 128, Prec Ch 455, 1 Eq Cas Abr 207 pl 8, sub nom
   Humberston v Humberston 1 P Wms 332, 2 Vern 737 . . . . 299, 301
Humphry's Estate, Re (1855) 1 Jur NS 921 747
Hunt v Luck [1902] 1 Ch 428, 71 LJ Ch 239, 50 WR 291, [1900-3] All ER Rep 295, 46 Sol Jo
   229, 86 LT 68, 18 TLR 265, CA 991
Hunt v Severs [1994] 2 AC 350, [1994] 2 All ER 385, [1994] 2 WLR 602, [1994] 2 Lloyd's
   Rep 129, [1994] 32 LS Gaz R 41, [1994] NLJR 603, 138 Sol Jo LB 104, HL . . 143, 180
Hunter, Re [1958] 77 NZLR 654 535
Hunter v Allen [1907] 1 IR 212 385
Hunter v Atkins (1834) 3 My & K 113, Coop temp Brough 464, 41 RR 30 276
Hunter v A-G [1899] AC 309, 68 LJ Ch 449, 47 WR 673, [1895-9] All ER Rep 558, 43 Sol Jo
   530, 80 LT 732, 15 TLR 384, HL 106
Hunter v Moss [1993] 1 WLR 934; affd [1994] 3 All ER 215, [1994] 1 WLR 452, [1994] 8 LS
   Gaz R 38, 138 Sol Jo LB 25, CA 15, 67, 78, 79
Hunter's Trustees v Mitchell 1930 SC 978 534
Hunter's Will Trusts, Re, Gilks v Harris [1963] Ch 372, [1962] 3 All ER 1050, [1962] 3 WLR
   1442, 113 JP 25, 106 Sol Jo 938 . . . . .211, 723, 803, 809
Huntingford v Hobbs [1993] 1 FCR 45, [1993] 1 FLR 736, [1992] Fam Law 437, 24 HLR
   652, [1992] NPC 39, [1992] EGCS 38, CA 351, 352, 353, 355, 422
Hurst, Re, Addison v Topp (1892) 67 LT 96, 8 TLR 528, CA 396, 492, 543, 575,
   576, 579, 590
Hussey v Palmer [1972] 3 All ER 744, [1972] 1 WLR 1286, 116 Sol Jo 567, CA . . 12, 57, 248,
   357, 413
Hussien v Chong Fook Kam [1970] AC 942, [1969] 3 All ER 1626, [1970] 2 WLR 441, 114
   Sol Jo 55, PC 488
Hutchinson v Stephens (1834) 5 Sim 498, 3 LJ Ch 239 766
Hutchinson and Tenant, Re (1878) 8 Ch D 540, 26 WR 904, 39 LT 86 135
Hyde v Pearce [1982] 1 All ER 1029, [1982] 1 WLR 560, 126 Sol Jo 119, CA 459
Hylton v Hylton (1754) 2 Ves Sen 547 276
Hypo-Mortgage Services Ltd v Robinson [1997] 2 FCR 422, [1997] 2 FLR 71, [1997] Fam
   Law 544, CA 1003
Hyslop, Re, Hyslop v Chamberlain [1894] 3 Ch 522, 64 LJ Ch 168, 8 R 680, 43 WR 6, 38 Sol
   Jo 663, 71 LT 373 161

I

ILG Travel Ltd (in administration), Re [1995] 2 BCLC 128, [1996] BCC 21 16
ISC Technologies Ltd v Guerin [1992] 2 Lloyd's Rep 430 1060

IVS Enterprises Ltd v Chelsea Cloisters Management Ltd (1999) 13 Tru LR 111 982
Imperial Food Ltd's Pension Scheme, Re [1986] 2 All ER 802, [1986] 1 WLR 717, 130 Sol Jo
447, [1986] LS Gaz R 1641. . . . . 495, 497
Imperial Group Pension Trust Ltd v Imperial Tobacco Ltd [1991] 2 All ER 597, [1991] 1
WLR 589, [1991] ICR 524, [1991] IRLR 66 499
Imperial Land Co of Marseilles, Re, ex p Larking (1877) 4 Ch D 566, 46 LJ Ch 235, CA . 659
Imperial Mercantile Credit Association v Coleman (1873) LR 6 HL 189, 42 LJ Ch 644, 21
WR 696, 29 LT 1 23
Inche Noriah v Shaik Allie Bin Omar [1929] AC 127, 98 LJPC 1, [1928] All ER Rep 189, 140
LT 121, 45 TLR 1 284
Inchiquin (Lord) v French (1744) Amb 33, 1 Cox Eq Cas 1, sub nom O'Brien v Lord
Inchiquin Ridg temp H 230 265
Independemt Trustee Services Ltd v Rowe [1998] OPLR 77 821
Indian Oil Corpn Ltd v Greenstone Shipping SA (Panama), The Ypatianna [1988] QB 345,
[1987] 3 All ER 893, [1987] 3 WLR 869, [1987] 2 Lloyd's Rep 286, 131 Sol Jo 1121,
[1987] LS Gaz R 2768 885
Industrial Concrete Products Bhd v Concrete Engineering Products Ltd [2001] 2 MLJ 332 961
Industrial Development Consultants Ltd v Cooley [1972] 2 All ER 162, [1972] 1 WLR 443,
116 Sol Jo 255 . . . . 23, 390, 405
Infabrics Ltd v Jaytex [1985] FSR 75; affd [1987] FSR 529, CA 885
Ingle v Partridge (No 2) (1865) 34 Beav 411 583
Ingram, Re [1951] VLR 424 107
Ingram v IRC [1995] 4 All ER 334, [1995] STC 564, [1995] NPC 92, [1995] 23 LS Gaz R 33,
139 Sol Jo LB 128; revsd [1997] 4 All ER 395, [1997] STC 1234, [1997] NPC 129,
[1997] 34 LS Gaz R 29, 141 Sol Jo LB 204, CA; on appeal [2000] 1 AC 293, [1999] 1 All
ER 297, [1999] 2 WLR 90, [1999] STC 37, [1999] 03 LS Gaz R 32, [1998] EGCS 181,
143 Sol Jo LB 52, HL 58, 180, 664, 927
IRC v Baddeley [1955] AC 572, [1955] 1 All ER 525, [1955] 2 WLR 552, 35 TC 661, 34 ATC
22, 48 R & IT 157, 99 Sol Jo 166, HL. 106
IRC v Bernstein [1960] Ch 444, [1960] 1 All ER 697, [1960] 2 WLR 554, 39 TC 391, 39 ATC
117, 53 R & IT 301, [1960] TR 21, 104 Sol Jo 250; affd [1961] Ch 399, [1961] 1 All ER
320, [1961] 2 WLR 143, 39 TC 391, 39 ATC 415, [1960] TR 369, 105 Sol Jo 128,
CA 205, 709, 715, 718, 725
IRC v Berrill [1982] 1 All ER 867, [1981] 1 WLR 1449, [1981] STC 784, 58 TC 429, [1981]
TR 347, 125 Sol Jo 625 . . . . 52, 64
IRC v Blott [1921] 2 AC 171, 8 TC 101, 90 LJKB 1028, 65 Sol Jo 642, 125 LT 497, 37 TLR 762,
HL 535
IRC v Botnar [1999] STC 711, 72 TC 205, CA 1040
IRC v Brandenburg [1982] STC 555, 126 Sol Jo 229 . . . . 210, 214
IRC v Brebner (1966) 43 TC 705, 45 ATC 228, [1966] TR 203; on appeal [1967] 2 AC 18,
[1967] 1 All ER 779, [1967] 2 WLR 1001, 43 TC 705, 46 ATC 17, [1967] TR 21, 111 Sol
Jo 216, 1967 SC (HL) 31, 1967 SLT 113 294
IRC v Broadway Cottages Trust [1955] Ch 20, [1954] 3 All ER 120, [1954] 3 WLR 438, 35 TC
577, 98 Sol Jo 588, L(TC) 1703, sub nom Broadway Cottages Trust v IRC 33 ATC 305,
47 R & IT 574, [1954] TR 295, CA. 84, 98, 110
IRC v Buchanan [1958] Ch 289, [1957] 2 All ER 400, [1957] 3 WLR 68, 37 TC 365, 36 ATC
36, 50 R & IT 223, [1957] TR 43, 100 Sol Jo 502, L(TC) 1823, CA 246
IRC v Cook [1946] AC 1, [1945] 2 All ER 377, 26 TC 489, 114 LJPC 69, 173 LT 211, HL. 534
IRC v Cookson [1977] 2 All ER 331, [1977] 1 WLR 962, [1977] STC 140, 50 TC 705, 715,
[1977] TR 17, 121 Sol Jo 544, L(TC) 2629, CA 519
IRC v Crawley [1987] STC 147, 59 TC 728, [1987] LS Gaz R 742 578
IRC v Dick (2001) 4 ITELR 317 4
IRC v Eversden (Greenstock's Executors) [2002] EWHC 1360 (Ch), [2002] STC
1109 . . . . 478, 737
IRC v Ezra [1935] AC 96, 104 LJ Ch 24, [1934] All ER Rep 749, 152 LT 217, 51 TLR 152, HL 304
IRC v Hamilton-Russell Executors. See Hamilton-Russell Executors v IRC
IRC v Hashmi [2002] WTLR 19 . . . . 291, 295
IRC v Hawley [1928] 1 KB 578, 13 TC 327, 6 ATC 1021, 97 LJKB 191, 138 LT 710 . . . 18
IRC v Holmden [1968] AC 685, [1968] 1 All ER 148, [1968] 2 WLR 300, 46 ATC 337, [1967]
TR 323, 112 Sol Jo 31, HL 519
IRC v Lloyds Private Banking Ltd [1998] STC 559, [1998] 2 FCR 41, [1999] 1 FLR 147,
[1999] Fam Law 309, [1998] 19 LS Gaz R 23, 142 Sol Jo LB 164 65
IRC v Lord Rennell. See Rennell v IRC

IRC v McMullen [1981] AC 1, [1980] 1 All ER 884, [1980] 2 WLR 416, 54 TC 413, [1980] TR
        85, 124 Sol Jo 206, L(TC) 2795, 130 NLJ 260, HL 74, 90, 110, 146
IRC v Miller [1930] AC 222, 15 TC 25, 99 LJPC 87, [1930] All ER Rep 713, 74 Sol Jo 138, 142
        LT 497, 46 TLR 207, HL   64
IRC v Mills. See Mills v IRC
IRC v Raphael [1935] AC 96, 104 LJ Ch 24, [1934] All ER Rep 749, 152 LT 217, 51 TLR 152,
        HL 304
IRC v Schroder [1983] STC 480, 57 TC 94   .   .   .   .   30, 32, 97, 754
IRC v Silverts Ltd [1951] Ch 521, [1951] 1 All ER 703, 29 TC 491, 30 ATC 26, 44 R & IT 220,
        95 Sol Jo 298, [1951] 1 TLR 593, CA 58, 800
IRC v Wright [1927] 1 KB 333, 11 TC 181, 95 LJKB 982, 135 LT 718, CA. 535
Inman, Re, Inman v Inman [1915] 1 Ch 187, 84 LJ Ch 309, 59 Sol Jo 161, 112 LT 240   . 555
Innes, Re, Barclay v Innes (1908) 125 LT Jo 60 546
Innes, Re, Innes v Innes [1910] 1 Ch 188, 79 LJ Ch 174, 101 LT 633   .   .   .   79, 161, 162, 163
Innes (Inspector of Taxes) v Harrison [1954] 1 All ER 884, [1954] 1 WLR 668, 35 TC 594, 33
        ATC 77, 47 R & IT 223, [1954] TR 81, 98 Sol Jo 269. 770
International Factors Ltd v Rodriguez [1979] QB 351, [1979] 1 All ER 17, [1978] 3 WLR
        877, 122 Sol Jo 680, CA. 907
International Sales and Agencies Ltd v Marcus [1982] 3 All ER 551, [1982] 2 CMLR
        46   .   .   .   .   271, 974
Investors Compensation Scheme Ltd v West Bromwich Building Society [1998] 1 All ER 98,
        [1998] 1 WLR 896, [1998] 1 BCLC 531, [1997] NLJR 989, [1997] PNLR 541, [1997]
        CLC 1243, HL   499
Inwards v Baker [1965] 2 QB 29, [1965] 1 All ER 446, [1965] 2 WLR 212, 109 Sol Jo 75,
        CA 157, 234, 248, 358
Irby, Re (1853) 17 Beav 334 829
Irby v Irby (No 3) (1858) 25 Beav 632, 4 Jur NS 989, 119 RR 577, 6 WR 853, 32 LTOS 141 980
Irvine v Sullivan (1869) LR 8 Eq 673, 38 LJ Ch 635, 17 WR 1083 . . . . . . 260, 330, 342
Irving, Re, ex p Brett (1877) 7 Ch D 419, 26 WR 376, 37 LT 507, [1874-80] All ER Rep Ext
        817, sub nom Re Irving, ex p Bushby 47 LJ Bcy 38 . . . . 42, 76
Isaac, Re, Cronbach v Isaac [1897] 1 Ch 251, 66 LJ Ch 160, 45 WR 262, 41 Sol Jo 244, 75 LT
        638, CA 844
Iveagh v IRC [1954] Ch 364, [1954] 1 All ER 609, [1954] 2 WLR 494, 33 ATC 47, 47 R & IT
        157, 159, [1954] TR 47, 98 Sol Jo 194   .   .   .   .   1031, 1033, 1034, 1037
Ives (ER) Investment Ltd v High [1967] 2 QB 379, [1967] 1 All ER 504, [1967] 2 WLR 789,
        110 Sol Jo 963, 201 Estates Gazette 199, CA 248, 253
Ivin v Blake (1993) 67 P & CR 263, [1994] 2 FCR 504, [1995] 1 FLR 70, [1995] Fam Law 72,
        CA 56, 352, 412, 416, 418, 421, 422

J

JW v Morgan Trust Co of the Bahamas Ltd (2002) 4 ITELR 541 . . . . 532, 603
Jackson, Re, Jackson v Talbot (1882) 21 Ch D 786. 572
Jackson v Dickinson [1903] 1 Ch 947, 72 LJ Ch 761, 88 LT 507, 19 TLR 350 940
Jackson v Horizon Holidays Ltd [1975] 3 All ER 92, [1975] 1 WLR 1468, 119 Sol Jo 759,
        CA 10, 170
Jackson v Nerman (1933) unreported   769
Jackson's Will, Re (1879) 13 Ch D 189, 49 LJ Ch 82, 28 WR 209, 41 LT 499. . . . 310, 314
Jacques Settled Estates, Re [1930] 2 Ch 418, 99 LJ Ch 534, [1930] All ER Rep 407, 144 LT
        103. 572
Jacubs v Rylance (1874) LR 17 Eq 341, 43 LJ Ch 280   951
Jaffray v Marshall [1994] 1 All ER 143, [1993] 1 WLR 1285, [1993] 15 LS Gaz R 39 . 560, 862,
                                                                           868, 872, 887, 948
Jagger v Jagger (1883) 25 Ch D 729, 53 LJ Ch 201, 32 WR 284, 49 LT 667 204
Jago v Jago (1893) 68 LT 654, 9 TLR 351 452
James, ex p (1803) 8 Ves 337, [1803-13] All ER Rep 78. . . . . 660, 661
James, Re, James v James [1935] Ch 449, 104 LJ Ch 247, [1935] All ER Rep 235, 153 LT
        277. . . . . 160, 161, 162
James v Allen (1817) 3 Mer 17, 17 RR 4   105
James v Couchman (1885) 29 Ch D 212, 54 LJ Ch 838, 33 WR 452, 52 LT 344,1 TLR 305   276
James v Dean (1808) 8 RR 178, 15 Ves 236   .   .   .   . 382, 383
James v Frearson (1842) 1 Y & C Ch Cas 370, 57 RR 384 . . . . 449, 451
James v May (1873) LR 6 HL 328, 42 LJ Ch 802, 29 LT 217 813

James v Williams [2000] Ch 1, [1999] 3 All ER 309, [1999] 3 WLR 451, 79 P & CR 421, [1999] 2 FCR 498, [1999] 15 LS Gaz R 30, 78 P & CR D17, CA. 382, 924, 952

Japan Leasing (Europe) plc, Re [1999] BPIR 911, [2000] WTLR 301 . . . . 56, 437

Jared v Clements [1903] 1 Ch 428, 72 LJ Ch 291, 51 WR 401, 47 Sol Jo 435, 88 LT 97, 19 TLR 219, CA 984

Jarman's Estate, Re, Leavers v Clayton (1878) 8 Ch D 584, 42 JP 662, 47 LJ Ch 675, 26 WR 907, 39 LT 89 105

Jarratt v Aldam (1870) LR 9 Eq 463, 18 WR 511, 22 LT 192, sub nom Jarratt v Oldham 39 LJ Ch 349 285

Jarvis, Re, Edge v Jarvis [1958] 2 All ER 336, [1958] 1 WLR 815, 102 Sol Jo 546 . . 383, 385, 931, 935

Jebb, Re, Ward-Smith v Jebb. See Ward-Smith v Jebb

Jee v Audley (1787) 1 Cox Eq Cas 324 193

Jefferies, Re, Finch v Martin [1936] 2 All ER 626 732

Jefferys v Jefferys (1841) Cr & Ph 138 165

Jenkins, Re, Williams v Jenkins [1915] 1 Ch 46, 84 LJ Ch 349 210

Jenkins (Inspector of Taxes) v Brown [1989] 1 WLR 1163, [1989] STC 577, 62 TC 226 . 734

Jenkins v Jenkins [1928] 2 KB 501, 97 LJKB 400, [1928] All ER Rep 546, 72 Sol Jo 319, 139 LT 119, 44 TLR 483 158

Jenkins and H E Randall & Co's Contract, Re [1903] 2 Ch 362, 72 LJ Ch 693, 88 LT 628 . . . . 875, 884

Jenner v Turner (1880) 16 Ch D 188, 45 JP 124, 50 LJ Ch 161, 29 WR 99, 43 LT 468 . . 220

Jennings v Rice [2002] EWCA Civ 159, [2002] All ER (D) 324 (Feb) 248, 249

Jervis, Re (1919) 146 LT Jo 215 572

Jervis v Wolferstan (1874) LR 18 Eq 18, 43 LJ Ch 809, 30 LT 452, [1874-80] All ER Rep Ext 1933 . . . . 811, 821

Jervoise, Re (1848) 12 Beav 209, 85 RR 76 999

Jervoise v Duke of Northumberland (1820) 1 Jac & W 559, 21 RR 229, [1814] All ER Rep 222 . . . . 299, 302

Jewell's Settlement, Re, Watts v Public Trustee [1919] 2 Ch 161, 88 LJ Ch 357, [1918-19] All ER Rep 1161, 121 LT 207 980

Jewish National Fund Inc v Royal Trust Co [1965] SCR 784, 53 DLR (2d) 577, 52 WWR 410, Can SC 1036, 1037

Jirna Ltd v Mister Donut of Canada Ltd (1971) 22 DLR (3d) 639, Ont CA; affd (1973) 40 DLR (3d) 303, Can SC 400

Job v Job (1877) 6 Ch D 562, 26 WR 206 585

Jobson v Palmer [1893] 1 Ch 71, 62 LJ Ch 180, 3 R 173, 41 WR 264, 67 LT 797, 9 TLR 106 585

Jodrell v Jodrell (1845) 9 Beav 45, 15 LJ Ch 17, 9 Jur 1022, 73 RR 274, 50 ER 259, 6 LTOS 186 218

Jodrell v Jodrell (1851) 14 Beav 397, 92 RR 157, 51 ER 339 218

Joel, Re, Johnson v Joel [1936] 2 All ER 962 535

Joel's Will Trusts, Re, Rogerson v Brudenell-Bruce [1967] Ch 14, [1966] 2 All ER 482, [1966] 3 WLR 209, 110 Sol Jo 570 . . . . 716, 717

John v James [1986] STC 352 . . . . 655, 657, 860, 871

John's Assignment Trusts, Re, Niven v Niven [1970] 2 All ER 210n, [1970] 1 WLR 955, 114 Sol Jo 396 666

Johns v James (1878) 8 Ch D 744, 47 LJ Ch 853, 26 WR 821, sub nom Jones v James 26 WR 821, 39 LT 54, CA 141

Johnson, Re, Cowley v Public Trustee [1915] 1 Ch 435, 84 LJ Ch 393, 59 Sol Jo 333, 112 LT 935 556

Johnson, Re, Pitt v Johnson (1914) 111 LT 130, 30 TLR 505, CA 193

Johnson, Re, Shearman v Robinson (1880) 15 Ch D 548, 49 LJ Ch 745, 29 WR 168, 43 LT 372 . . . . 812, 814, 823, 824

Johnson v Ball (1851) 5 De G & Sm 85, 16 Jur 538, 18 LTOS 182 . . . . 258, 262

Johnson v Fesemeyer (1858) 3 De G & J 13 666

Johnson Johnson, Re, ex p Matthews and Wilkinson [1904] 1 KB 134, 73 LJKB 220, 11 Mans 14, 52 WR 304, 90 LT 61, DC 209, 212

Johnson's Settlement Trusts, Re, McClure v Johnson [1943] Ch 341, [1943] 2 All ER 499, 112 LJ Ch 297, 87 Sol Jo 291, 169 LT 220, 59 TLR 434 . . . . 199, 374

Johnson's Trusts, Re (1866) LR 2 Eq 716, 12 Jur NS 616 201

Johnson's Will Trusts, Re, National Provincial Bank Ltd v Jeffrey [1967] Ch 387, [1967] 1 All ER 553, [1967] 2 WLR 152, 110 Sol Jo 811 219

Johnston, Re, Mills v Johnston [1894] 3 Ch 204, 63 LJ Ch 753, 8 R 563, 42 WR 616, 38 Sol Jo
   564, 71 LT 392 730
Johnston, Re, Mills v Johnston [1911] WN 234, 105 LT 701 795
Johnston v Johnston (1884) 33 WR 239, 52 LT 76 . . . . 274, 281, 286
Joicey, Re, Joicey v Elliot [1915] 2 Ch 115, 84 LJ Ch 613, 113 LT 437, CA 211
Jonathan v Tilley (1988) 12 Tru Ll 36 974
Jones, Re, Farrington v Forrester [1893] 2 Ch 461, 62 LJ Ch 966, 3 R 496, 69 LT 45, [1891]
   All ER Rep Ext 1564 269
Jones, Re, Jones v Jones [1933] Ch 842, 102 LJ Ch 303, [1933] All ER Rep 830, 77 Sol Jo 467,
   149 LT 417, 49 TLR 516 534
Jones, Re, Jones v Searle (1883) 49 LT 91 . . . . 586, 869
Jones, Re, Meacock v Jones [1932] 1 Ch 642, 101 LJ Ch 307, [1932] All ER Rep 804, 147 LT
   137 713
Jones, Re, Midland Bank Executor and Trustee Co Ltd v Jones [1953] Ch 125, [1953] 1 All
   ER 357, [1953] 2 WLR 283, 97 Sol Jo 96 . . . . 89, 101, 215
Jones, Re, Public Trustee v Jones [1945] Ch 105, 115 LJ Ch 33, 89 Sol Jo 22, 173 LT 357, 61
   TLR 120 . . . . 93, 807
Jones, Re, Richards v Jones [1898] 1 Ch 438, 67 LJ Ch 211, 46 WR 313, 42 Sol Jo 269, 78 LT
   74 . . . . 80, 135
Jones v AMP Perpetual Trustee Co NZ Ltd [1994] 1 NZLR 690 . . . . . 388, 405, 613, 665
Jones v Badley (1868) 3 Ch App 362, 16 WR 713, 19 LT 106, CA 257, 262
Jones v Challenger [1961] 1 QB 176, [1960] 1 All ER 785, [1960] 2 WLR 695, 104 Sol Jo 328,
   175 Estates Gazette 695, CA 469, 477, 479, 481, 645
Jones v Executive Officers of T Eaton Co Ltd. See Bethel, Re
Jones v Foxall (1852) 15 Beav 388, 21 LJ Ch 725, 92 RR 473 . . . . . . .867, 869, 870, 871
Jones v Higgins (1866) LR 2 Eq 538, 35 LJ Ch 403, 14 WR 448, 14 LT 126 . . . . 451, 934
Jones v Jones (1876) 1 QBD 279, 45 LJQB 166, 24 WR 274, 34 LT 243 . . . . . . 220, 221
Jones v Jones [1977] 2 All ER 231, [1977] 1 WLR 438, 33 P & CR 147, 120 Sol Jo 802,
   CA 250, 351
Jones v Lewis (1751) 2 Ves Sen 240 585
Jones v Lipman [1962] 1 All ER 442, [1962] 1 WLR 832, 106 Sol Jo 531 . . . 256, 411, 706
Jones v Lock (1865) 1 Ch App 25, 35 LJ Ch 117, 11 Jur NS 913, 14 WR 149, 13 LT 514 . 146
Jones v Maynard [1951] Ch 572, [1951] 1 All ER 802, 95 Sol Jo 269, [1951] 1 TLR 700 . 360
Jones v Powell (1841) 4 Beav 96 727
Jones v Roberts [1995] 2 FLR 422, [1995] Fam Law 673 435
Jones v Shipping Federation of British Columbia (1963) 37 DLR (2d) 273, 41 WWR
   636 . . . . 60, 215
Jones v Smith (1841) 1 Hare 43, 11 LJ Ch 83, 6 Jur 8, 58 RR 22; on appeal (1843) 1 Ph 244,
   66 ER 943 991
Jones v Thomas (1733) 3 P Wms 243 983
Jones & Sons (a firm) (Trustee) v Jones [1997] Ch 159, [1996] 4 All ER 721, [1996] 3 WLR
   703, [1996] 19 LS Gaz R 29, 140 Sol Jo LB 123, CA 882, 895
Jones' Will, Re (1876) 2 Ch D 362, 45 LJ Ch 428, 24 WR 697, sub nom Re Jones' Settlement
   Trusts 35 LT 25 313
Jones' Will Trusts, Re, Soames v A-G [1947] Ch 48, [1946] 2 All ER 281, 115 LJ Ch 307, 90
   Sol Jo 405, 175 LT 403 710
Jonton Pty Ltd [1992] 1 Qd R 105 324
Jopling v IRC [1940] 2 KB 282, [1940] 3 All ER 279, 109 LJKB 734, 84 Sol Jo 525, 163 LT
   361, 56 TLR 877 544
Jordan, Re, Hayward v Hamilton [1904] 1 Ch 260, 73 LJ Ch 128, 52 WR 150, 48 Sol Jo 142,
   90 LT 223 877
Jordan's Trusts, Re [1903] 1 IR 119 . . . . 731, 735
Jorden v Money (1854) 5 HL Cas 185, 23 LJ Ch 865, 101 RR 116, 10 ER 868, [1843-60] All
   ER Rep 350, 24 LTOS 160 140
Joscelyne v Nissen [1970] 2 QB 86, [1970] 1 All ER 1213, [1970] 2 WLR 509, 114 Sol Jo 55,
   CA 278
Joseph v Lyons (1884) 15 QBD 280, 54 LJQB 1, 33 WR 145, 51 LT 740, 1 TLR 16,
   CA 183, 989
Joseph's Will Trusts, Re [1959] 3 All ER 474n, [1959] 1 WLR 1019, 103 Sol Jo 833 . . . 519
Josselyn v Josselyn (1837) 9 Sim 63 730
Jothann v Irving Trust Co 270 NYS 721, 277 NYS 955 (1934) 596
Jowitt, Re, Jowitt v Keeling [1922] 2 Ch 442, 91 LJ Ch 449, [1922] All ER Rep 330, 66 Sol Jo
   577, 127 LT 466, 38 TLR 688 530

Joyce v De Moleyns (1845) 69 RR 318, 2 Jo & Lat 374, 8 IR Eq 215 1000
Joyce v Joyce [1979] 1 All ER 175, [1978] 1 WLR 1170, 122 Sol Jo 745 930
Jubb, Re (1941) 20 ATC 297 534
Jubilee Cotton Mills Ltd (Official Receiver and Liquidator) v Lewis [1924] AC 958, 93 LJ Ch
    414, [1925] B & CR 16, 68 Sol Jo 663, 40 TLR 621, sub nom Re Jubilee Cotton Mills Ltd
    131 LT 579, HL 22
Judd v Brown (bankrupts) (Nos 9587 and 9588 of 1994) [1998] 2 FLR 360, [1998] Fam Law
    514, [1997] BPIR 470; revsd (1999) 79 P & CR 491, [1999] 1 FLR 1191, [1999] Fam
    Law 523, [1999] BPIR 517, CA 482
Judd and Poland and Skelcher's Contract, Re [1906] 1 Ch 684, 75 LJ Ch 403, 54 WR 513, 50
    Sol Jo 389, 94 LT 595, CA 704
Jullian, Re, ex p Dumas (1754) 1 Atk 232, 2 Ves Sen 582 . . . . 883, 885
Jump, Re, Galloway v Hope [1903] 1 Ch 129, 72 LJ Ch 16, 51 WR 266, 87 LT 502 . . . 200
Justice v Wynne (1860) 12 I Ch R 289, CA. 1002

K

K, Re [1985] Ch 85, [1985] 1 All ER 403, [1985] 2 WLR 262, [1985] FLR 558, [1985] Fam
    Law 129, 129 Sol Jo 132, [1985] LS Gaz R 1335; affd [1986] Ch 180, [1985] 2 All ER
    833, [1985] 3 WLR 234, [1986] 1 FLR 79, [1985] Fam Law 19, 129 Sol Jo 364, [1985]
    LS Gaz R 2242, [1985] NLJ Rep 655, CA 18, 434
K, Re [1988] Ch 310, [1988] 1 All ER 358, [1988] 2 WLR 781, [1988] 2 FLR 15, [1988] Fam
    Law 203, 131 Sol Jo 1488, [1987] NLJ Rep 1039 270
KH Enterprise v Pioneer Container, The Pioneer Container [1994] 2 AC 324, [1994] 2 All
    ER 250, [1994] 3 WLR 1, [1994] 1 Lloyd's Rep 593, [1994] 18 LS Gaz R 37, PC . .1059
Kalfelis v Bankhaus Schröder, Münchmeyer, Hengst & Co: 189/87 [1988] ECR 5565, ECJ 1057
Kali Bakhsh Singh v Ram Gopal Singh (1913) 30 TLR 138 284
Kane v Radley-Kane [1999] Ch 274, [1998] 3 All ER 753, [1998] 3 WLR 617, [1998] 3 FCR
    502, [1998] 24 LS Gaz R 33, 142 Sol Jo LB 189, sub nom Radley-Kane, Re [1998] 2 FLR
    585, [1998] Fam Law 525 667
Kapetan Georgis, The. See Virgo Steamship Co SA v Skaarup Shipping Corpn, The Kapetan
    Georgis
Karak Rubber Co Ltd v Burden (No 2) [1972] 1 All ER 1210, [1972] 1 WLR 602, [1972] 1
    Lloyd's Rep 73, 115 Sol Jo 888 . . . . 954, 960
Karger v Paul [1984] VR 161 . . . . 617, 694, 703
Kasperbauer v Griffith [2000] 1 WTLR 333, CA 247, 257
Katz, Re (1981) 112 DLR (3d) 529. 535
Kauter v Hilton (1953) 90 CLR 86 . . . . 60, 149, 247
Kavanagh v Best [1971] NI 89 18
Kay, Re, Mosley v Kay [1897] 2 Ch 518, 46 WR 74, 13 TLR 582, sub nom Re Kay, Mosley v
    Keyworth 66 LJ Ch 759 . . . . 918, 919
Kay's Settlement, Re, Broadbent v Macnab [1939] Ch 329, [1939] 1 All ER 245, 108 LJ Ch
    156, 83 Sol Jo 55, 160 LT 172, 55 TLR 332 . . . . . . 9, 169, 176, 177, 179, 181, 182
Kaye v Powel (1791) 1 Ves 408 730
Kaye and Hoyle's Contract, Re (1909) 53 Sol Jo 520 200
Kayford Ltd, Re [1975] 1 All ER 604, [1975] 1 WLR 279, 118 Sol Jo 752 . . . . . . 14, 461
Kearns v Hill (1990) 21 NSWLR 107, CA 499
Keech v Sandford (1726) 2 Eq Cas Abr 741, Sel Cas Ch 61, Cas temp King 61, 25 ER 223,
    [1558-1774] All ER Rep 230 . . . . 22, 382, 887
Keefe v Law Society of New South Wales (1998) 44 NSWLR 451 894
Keeler's Settlement Trusts, Re, Keeler v Gledhill [1981] Ch 156, [1981] 1 All ER 888, [1981]
    2 WLR 499, 125 Sol Jo 170. 656
Kemp v Burn (1863) 4 Giff 348, 9 Jur NS 375, 1 New Rep 257, 11 WR 278, 7 LT 666 . . 672,
                                                                                    687
Keen, Re, Evershed v Griffiths [1937] Ch 236, [1937] 1 All ER 452, 106 LJ Ch 177, 81 Sol Jo
    97, 156 LT 207, 53 TLR 320, CA 258, 261, 262, 263
Kehr, Re, Martin v Foges [1952] Ch 26, [1951] 2 All ER 812, 95 Sol Jo 711, [1951] 2 TLR
    788. . . . . 714, 1042
Keily v Monck (1795) 3 Ridg Parl Rep 205. 220
Kekewich v Manning (1851) 1 De GM & G 176, 21 LJ Ch 577, 16 Jur 625, 91 RR 53, 18 LTOS
    263. . . . . 151, 268
Kellett v Kellett (1868) LR 3 HL 160 373
Kelly, Re, Cleary v Dillon [1932] IR 255. 122

Kelly v Cooper [1993] AC 205, [1992] 3 WLR 936, [1994] 1 BCLC 395, [1992] 43 LS Gaz R
   30, PC 20, 400, 403, 404
Kelly v Nichols (1891) 17 RI 306, 21 Atl Rep 906 123
Kelly v Walsh (1878) 1 LR Ir 275 149
Kemmis v Kemmis (Welland intervening) [1988] 1 WLR 1307, [1988] 2 FLR 223, [1989] 3
   LS Gaz R 43, CA. 296
Kemp's Settled Estates, Re (1883) 24 Ch D 485, 52 LJ Ch 950, 31 WR 930, 49 LT 231, CA 771
Kempson v Ashbee (1874) 10 Ch App 15, 39 JP 164, 44 LJ Ch 195, 23 WR 38, 31 LT 525 284
Kemtron Industries Pty Ltd v Comr of Stamp Duties [1984] 1 Qd R 576 . . . . . 820, 826
Kendall v Granger (1842) 5 Beav 300, 11 LJ Ch 405, 6 Jur 919, 59 RR 509 106
Kennedy, Re, Kennedy v Official Solicitor to the Supreme Court [1980] CLY 2820 . . . 296
Kennedy v De Trafford [1897] AC 180, 66 LJ Ch 413, 45 WR 671, [1895-9] All ER Rep 408,
   76 LT 427, HL 385
Kennedy v Kennedy [1914] AC 215, 83 LJPC 63, 51 SLR 581, 109 LT 833, PC 200
Kensit, Re [1908] WN 235 795
Kenworthy v Bate (1802) 6 Ves 793 805
Ker's Settlement Trusts, Re [1963] Ch 553, [1963] 1 All ER 801, [1963] 2 WLR 1210, 107 Sol
   Jo 415. . . . . 521, 1042, 1044
Kerr v British Leyland (Staff) Trustees Ltd [2001] WTLR 1071 695
Kersey, Re, Alington v Alington [1952] WN 541, 96 Sol Jo 851 104
Kershaw's Trusts, Re (1868) LR 6 Eq 322, 37 LJ Ch 751, 16 WR 963, 18 LT 899 720
Khoo, Re (1933) 2 MLJ 119 123
Khoo Cheng Teow, Re [1932] Straits Settlement Reports 226 203
Khoo Tek Keong v Ch'ng Joo Tuan Neoh [1934] AC 529, 103 LJPC 161, 152 LT
   53 . . . . 612, 917
Kidd, Re, Kidd v Kidd (1894) 8 R 261, 42 WR 571, 70 LT 648 811
Kieran, Re, Matthews v Kieran [1916] 1 IR 289, 50 ILT 175 130
Kiernan v M'Cann [1920] 1 IR 99, 54 IRLT 34 383
Kilbee v Sneyd (1828) 2 Moll 186 632
Killick v Pountney (1999) Times, 30 April, [2000] WTLR 41 283
Kilpin v Kilpin (1834) 1 My & K 520, 36 RR 367 366
King, Re, Henderson v Cranmer [1931] WN 232, 75 Sol Jo 781 106
King, Re, Kerr v Bradley [1923] 1 Ch 243, 92 LJ Ch 292, 67 Sol Jo 313, 128 LT 790 . . . 119
King v Denison (1813) 12 RR 227, 1 Ves & B 260 . . . . 329, 334, 335
King v King (1857) 1 De G & J 663, 27 LJ Ch 29, 4 Jur NS 721, 6 WR 85, 30 LTOS
   177. . . . . 631, 829, 830
King v Mullins (1852) 1 Drew 308, 20 LTOS 178 827
King (Don) Productions Inc v Warren [2000] Ch 291, [1999] 2 All ER 218, [1999] 3 WLR
   276, [1999] 1 Lloyd's Rep 588, [2000] 1 BCLC 607, [1999] EMLR 402, CA . . .10, 183,
                                                   379, 380, 384, 398, 733
King-Ansell v Police [1979] 2 NZLR 531, NZCA. 223
King's Motors (Oxford) Ltd v Lax [1969] 3 All ER 665, [1970] 1 WLR 426, 21 P & CR 507,
   114 Sol Jo 168 80
King's Settlement, Re, King v King [1931] 2 Ch 294, 100 LJ Ch 359, [1931] All ER Rep 692,
   145 LT 517. 1000
King's Will Trusts, Re, Assheton v Boyne [1964] Ch 542, [1964] 1 All ER 833, [1964] 2 WLR
   913, 108 Sol Jo 335, 189 Estates Gazette 879 . . . . 20, 455, 470, 760, 776, 778
King's Will Trusts, Re, Newman v Andrews (1959) 173 Estates Gazette 627 664
Kingan v Matier [1905] 1 IR 272 308
Kingcome, Re, Hickley v Kingcome [1936] Ch 566, [1936] 1 All ER 173, 105 LJ Ch 209, 80
   Sol Jo 112, 154 LT 462, 52 TLR 268 534
Kingdon v Castleman (1877) 46 LJ Ch 448, 25 WR 345, 36 LT 141 . . . . 580, 585
Kingham, Re, Kingham v Kingham [1897] 1 IR 170 . . . . 569, 572
Kingsnorth Trust Ltd v Tizard [1986] 2 All ER 54, 51 P & CR 296, sub nom Kingsnorth
   Finance Co Ltd v Tizard [1986] 1 WLR 783, 130 Sol Jo 244, [1986] LS Gaz R
   1231 . . . . 706, 987, 991
Kingston (Earl) v Lady Elizabeth Pierepont (1681) 1 Vern 5 218
Kinloch v Secretary of State for India in Council (1880) 15 Ch D 1, 49 LJ Ch 571, 28 WR 619,
   42 LT 667; on appeal (1882) 7 App Cas 619, 51 LJ Ch 885, 30 WR 845, 47 LT 133,
   HL. 7, 143
Kinsels v Caldwell [1975] ALR 337. 84
Kipping, Re, Kipping v Kipping [1914] 1 Ch 62, 83 LJ Ch 218, 109 LT 919, CA . . 735, 739
Kirkham v Peel (1880) 43 LT 171; on appeal (1881) 44 LT 195 . . . . 21, 386

Kirkman v Booth (1848) 11 Beav 273, 18 LJ Ch 25, 13 Jur 525, 83 RR 158, 13 LTOS 482 . . 485
Kirpalani v Hathiramani (1992) 46 ETR 256 367
Kirwan v Daniel (1847) 5 Hare 493, 16 LJ Ch 191, 11 Jur 235, 71 RR 202, 8 LTOS 554 . 142
Kitney v MEPC Ltd [1978] 1 All ER 595, [1977] 1 WLR 981, 35 P & CR 132, 121 Sol Jo 355,
    243 Estates Gazette 131, CA 256, 411
Kleinwort Benson Ltd v Lincoln City Council [1999] 2 AC 349, [1998] 4 All ER 513, [1998] 3
    WLR 1095, [1998] NLJR 1674, [1998] RVR 315, 142 Sol Jo LB 279, HL 982
Kleinwort Benson Ltd v Vaughan and Vaughan [1994] NPC 31; on appeal [1995] NPC 195,
    [1996] CLC 620, CA 984
Kleinwort's Settlements, Re, Westminster Bank Ltd v Bennett [1951] Ch 860, [1951] 2 All
    ER 328, 95 Sol Jo 415, [1951] 2 TLR 91 . . . . 538, 539
Kling v Keston Properties Ltd (1983) 49 P & CR 212, [1984] LS Gaz R 1683 1003
Klug v Klug [1918] 2 Ch 67, 87 LJ Ch 569, 62 Sol Jo 471, 118 LT 696 . . . .94, 95, 97, 690,
                                                                          691, 720, 728
Knapman, Re, Knapman v Wreford (1881) 18 Ch D 300, 50 LJ Ch 629, 30 WR 395, 45 LT
    102, [1881-5] All ER Rep Ext 1758, CA 818, 980
Knapp, Re, Spreckley v A-G [1929] 1 Ch 341, 98 LJ Ch 95, 140 LT 533 208
Knight v Boughton. See Knight v Knight
Knight v Bowyer (1857) 23 Beav 609, 26 LJ Ch 769, 3 Jur NS 968, 6 WR 28, 30 LTOS 95; on
    appeal (1858) 2 De G & J 421, 27 LJ Ch 520, 4 Jur NS 569, 6 WR 565, 31 LTOS
    287 183
Knight v Browne (1861) 30 LJ Ch 649, 7 Jur NS 894, 126 RR 832, 9 WR 515, 4 LT 206 . 209
Knight v Frost [1999] 1 BCLC 364 936
Knight v Knight (1840) 3 Beav 148, 9 LJ Ch 354, 4 Jur 839, 52 RR 74; affd sub nom Knight v
    Boughton (1844) 11 Cl & Fin 513, 8 Jur 923, HL 73, 80, 134
Knight v Marjoribanks (1849) 2 H & Tw 308, 2 Mac & G 10 662
Knight's Trusts, Re (1859) 27 Beav 45, 28 LJ Ch 625, 5 Jur NS 326, 33 LTOS 54 . . 830, 846
Knight's Will, Re (1883) 26 Ch D 82; on appeal (1884) 26 Ch D 82, 63 LJ Ch 223, 32 WR 417,
    50 LT 550, CA 763
Knocker v Youle [1986] 2 All ER 914, [1986] 1 WLR 934, 130 Sol Jo 542, [1986] LS Gaz R
    2568 . . . . 503, 506, 508, 610, 733, 749
Knott, Re, Bax v Palmer (1887) 56 LJ Ch 318, 35 WR 302, 56 LT 161 . . . . . . 811, 824
Knott v Cottee (1852) 16 Beav 77, 16 Jur 752 . . . . 853, 857, 861
Knowles' Will Trusts, Re, Nelson v Knowles [1948] 1 All ER 866, 92 Sol Jo 322, CA . . 382
Knox's Trusts, Re [1895] 1 Ch 538, 64 LJ Ch 402, 13 R 392, 43 WR 442; affd [1895] 2 Ch 483,
    64 LJ Ch 860, 72 LT 761, CA 630, 780, 840
Koch Shipping Inc v Richards Butler [2002] Lloyd's Rep PN 201 406
Kolb's Will Trusts, Re, Lloyd's Bank Ltd v Ullman [1962] Ch 531, [1961] 3 All ER 811,
    [1961] 3 WLR 1034, 105 Sol Jo 888; on appeal (1962) 106 Sol Jo 669, CA 83
Koorootang Nominees Pty Ltd v Australia and New Zealand Banking Group Ltd [1998] 3 VR
    16 976
Korkontzilas v Soulos (1997) 146 DLR (4th) 214 . . . . 323, 326
Krasner v Dennison [2001] Ch 76, [2000] 3 All ER 234, [2000] 3 WLR 720, 144 Sol Jo LB
    205, sub nom Dennison v Krasner [2000] NLJR 543, [2000] BPIR 410, CA . . 187, 190,
                                                                          209
Krawitz's Will Trusts, Re, Krawitz v Crawford [1959] 3 All ER 793, [1959] 1 WLR 1192, 103
    Sol Jo 1004 102
Kronheim v Johnson (1877) 7 Ch D 60, 47 LJ Ch 132, 26 WR 142, 37 LT 751 . . . 58, 233,
                                                                          237, 352
Kumar (a bankrupt), Re, ex p Lewis v Kumar [1993] 2 All ER 700, [1993] 1 WLR 224, [1994]
    2 FCR 373, [1993] 2 FLR 382, [1993] Fam Law 470, [1993] BCLC 548 291
Kuwait Airways Corpn v Iraqi Airways Co (No 3) [2002] UKHL 19, [2002] 3 All ER 209,
    [2002] 2 WLR 1353, [2002] 1 All ER (Comm) 843 . . . . 976, 1050
Kuwait Oil Tanker Co SAK v Al Bader [2000] 2 All ER (Comm) 271, CA . . 1021, 1043, 1049
Kwok Chi Leung Karl v Comr of Estate Duty [1988] 1 WLR 1035, [1988] STC 728, 132 Sol Jo
    1118, PC 170, 176, 1029

                                              L

LAC Minerals Ltd v International Corona Resources Ltd [1990] FSR 441, 44 BLR 1, [1989] 2
    SCR 574, 101 NR 239, 69 OR (2d) 287, 35 ETR 1, 61 DLR (4th) 14, 26 CPR (3d) 97, 36
    OAC 57, 6 RPR (2d) 1, Can SC 20, 326, 398, 400, 405
Labouchere v Tupper (1857) 11 Moo PCC 198, 5 WR 797, 29 LTOS 357 825
Lacey, ex p (1802) 6 Ves 625 659

Laing's Settlement, Re, Laing v Radcliffe [1899] 1 Ch 593, 68 LJ Ch 230, 47 WR 311, 43 Sol
    Jo 315, 80 LT 228 612
Lake, Re, ex p Howe Trustees [1903] 1 KB 439, 72 LJKB 213, 51 WR 496, 47 Sol Jo 205, 88
    LT 31 . . . . 852, 861, 875
Lake Bathurst Australasian Gold Mining Co, Re, Barnard v Bagshaw (1862) 3 De GJ & Sm
    355, 9 Jur NS 220, 7 LT 544 648
Lake v Bayliss [1974] 2 All ER 1114, [1974] 1 WLR 1073, 28 P & CR 209, 118 Sol Jo
    532 . . . . 442, 444, 883
Lake v Gibson (1729) 1 Eq Cas Abr 290; affd sub nom Lake v Craddock (1732) 3 P Wms 158,
    [1558-1774] All ER Rep 419 350
Lake v Lake [1989] STC 865 278
Laker Airways Inc v FLS Aerospace Ltd [2000] 1 WLR 113, [1999] 2 Lloyd's Rep 45, [1999]
    CILL 1508 406
Lambe v Eames (1871) 6 Ch App 597, 40 LJ Ch 447, 19 WR 659, 25 LT 174   . 36, 133, 135
Lambert v Peyton (1860) 8 HL Cas 1, 125 RR 1 302
Lambert v Thwaites (1866) LR 2 Eq 151, 35 LJ Ch 406, 14 WR 532, 14 LT 159 132
Lampitt v Poole Borough Council (Taylor, third parties) [1991] 2 QB 545, [1990] 2 All ER
    887, [1990] 3 WLR 179, 49 BLR 82, CA 942
Lancashire v Lancashire (1848) 2 Ph 657, 17 LJ Ch 270, 12 Jur 363, 75 RR 106, 12 LTOS 21 449
Lancashire Loans Ltd v Black [1934] 1 KB 380, 103 LJKB 129, [1933] All ER Rep 201, 150
    LT 304, CA. 281, 283, 284
Lancaster, The. See Ellerman Lines Ltd v Lancaster Maritime Co Ltd, The Lancaster
Landau (a bankrupt) Re, Pointer v Landau [1998] Ch 223, [1997] 3 All ER 322, [1997] 3
    WLR 225, [1997] PLR 25, [1997] 2 BCLC 515, 141 Sol Jo LB 28, [1997] BPIR 229, sub
    nom Re L (a bankrupt) [1997] 2 FLR 660, [1998] Fam Law 68. . . . . 153, 170, 176
Lander v Weston (1855) 3 Drew 389, 25 LJ Ch 235, 2 Jur NS 58, 4 WR 158, 26 LTOS
    254 873
Lane v Debenham (1853) 11 Hare 188, 17 Jur 1005, 90 RR 637, 1 WR 465, 22 LTOS
    143 . . . . 740, 741
Lane v Dighton (1762) Amb 409 . . . . 343, 880
Lane's Trust, Re (1854) 3 WR 134, 24 LTOS 181 829
Langford v Gascoyne (1805) 11 Ves 333 631
Langham v Sanford (1811) 17 Ves 435; affd (1816) 2 Mer 6, 19 Ves 641 330
Langton v Langton [1995] 3 FCR 521, [1995] 2 FLR 890, [1996] Fam Law 86 276
Lansdowne's Will Trusts, Re, Marquis of Lansdowne v Earl of Shelburne [1967] Ch 603,
    [1967] 1 All ER 888, [1967] 2 WLR 992, 111 Sol Jo 258 . . . . 520, 783
Lanyon, Re, Lanyon v Lanyon [1927] 2 Ch 264, 96 LJ Ch 487, [1927] All ER Rep 61, 71 Sol
    Jo 865, 137 LT 806, 43 TLR 714 . . . . 101, 220
Lapin v Abigail. See Abigail v Lapin
Larkin, Re (1913) 13 SRNSW 691 143
Lashmar, Re, Moody v Penfold [1891] 1 Ch 258, 60 LJ Ch 143, 64 LT 333, CA   . . 145, 235,
                                                                                      238
Lassence v Tierney (1849) 2 H & Tw 115, 14 Jur 182, 1 Mac & G 551, 84 RR 158, [1843-60]
    All ER Rep 47, 15 LTOS 557 . . . . 369, 372, 373, 374, 375, 376
Last, Re [1958] P 137, [1958] 1 All ER 316, [1958] 2 WLR 186, 102 Sol Jo 89 . . . . 79, 81
Latec Investments Ltd v Hotel Terrigal Pty Ltd (1965) 113 CLR 265, [1966] ALR 775, 39
    ALJR 110, HC of A. 50
La Touche v Earl of Lucan (1840) 7 Cl & Fin 772, West 477, 2 Dru & Wal 432, HL . . . 141
Lauer and Stekl, Re (1974) 47 DLR (3d) 286, [1974] 6 WWR 490, BCCA; affd sub nom
    Lauer v Stekl [1976] 1 SCR 781, [1976] 2 WWR 382, 54 DLR (3d) 159n 559
Law v Law (1735) Cas temp Talb 140, 3 P Wms 391 344
Law Society v Southall [2001] BPIR 303; revsd sub nom Law Society v Southall [2001] EWCA
    Civ 2001, [2002] BPIR 336, [2001] WTLR 719 . . . . 293, 294
Law Society of Upper Canada v Toronto-Dominion Bank (1998) 169 DLR (4th) 353 . . 886
Lawes v Bennett (1785) 1 Cox Eq Cas 167 440
Lawrie v Bankes (1858) 4 K & J 142, 27 LJ Ch 265, 4 Jur NS 299, 6 WR 244, 70 ER 59, 32
    LTOS 18 . . . . 631, 720
Lawson v Lawson [1999] Ch 373, CA 346
Laye, Re, Turnbull v Laye [1913] 1 Ch 298, 82 LJ Ch 218, 20 Mans 124, 57 Sol Jo 284, 108 LT
    324 . . . . 213, 738
Layton v Martin [1986] 2 FLR 227, [1986] Fam Law 212 421
Leahy v A-G for New South Wales [1959] AC 457, [1959] 2 All ER 300, [1959] 2 WLR 722,
    103 Sol Jo 391, 33 ALJR 105, PC 107, 110, 111, 113, 114, 124, 125, 129, 202

Leake v Robinson (1817) 2 Mer 363 194
Leake's Trusts, Re (1863) 32 Beav 135, 9 Jur NS 453, 1 New Rep 417, 11 WR 352, 7 LT
   816 . . . . 829, 846
Learoyd v Whiteley. See Whiteley, Re, Whiteley v Learoyd
Leask, Re, Richardson v Leask (1891) 65 LT 199 833
Lee v Lee (1876) 4 Ch D 175, 46 LJ Ch 81, 25 WR 225, 36 LT 138 306
Lee v Sankey (1873) LR 15 Eq 204, 21 WR 286, 27 LT 809 . . . . .646, 924, 950, 955
Lee v Showmen's Guild of Great Britain [1952] 2 QB 329, [1952] 1 All ER 1175, 96 Sol Jo
   296, [1952] 1 TLR 1115, CA 693
Lee, Behrens & Co Ltd, Re [1932] 2 Ch 46, 101 LJ Ch 183, [1931] B & C R 160, [1932] All ER
   Rep 889, 147 LT 348, 48 TLR 248 271
Lee-Parker v Izzet (No 2) [1972] 2 All ER 800, [1972] 1 WLR 775, 23 P & CR 301, 116 Sol Jo
   446 248
Leedham v Chawner (1858) 4 K & J 458, 116 RR 760, 32 LTOS 221 . . . . 810, 815
Leeds (Duke) and the Coal Acts 1938 to 1943, Re, Duke of Leeds v Davenport [1947] Ch
   525, [1947] 2 All ER 200, [1947] LJR 1141, 91 Sol Jo 467, 177 LT 503, 63 TLR 547 . 500
Leek, Re, Darwen v Leek [1967] Ch 1061, [1967] 2 All ER 1160, [1967] 3 WLR 576, 47 ATC
   28, 111 Sol Jo 500; on appeal [1969] 1 Ch 563, [1968] 1 All ER 793, [1968] 2 WLR
   1385, 47 ATC 28, [1967] TR 375, 112 Sol Jo 444, CA. 27, 88, 89, 130, 131, 146
Lees' Settlement Trusts, Re [1896] 2 Ch 508, 65 LJ Ch 770, 44 WR 680, 75 LT 178 . . . 782
Le Foe v Le Foe and Woolwich plc [2002] 1 FCR 107, [2001] 2 FLR 970, [2001] Fam Law
   739 . . . . 417, 418, 425
Legerwood v Perpetual Trustee Co Ltd (1997) 41 NSWLR 532 259
Legg v Mackrell (1860) 2 De GF & J 551, 4 LT 568 450
Legh's Settled Estate, Re [1902] 2 Ch 274, 66 JP 600, 71 LJ Ch 668, 50 WR 570, 46 Sol Jo 569,
   86 LT 884 . . . . 567, 573
Legh's Settlement Trusts, Re, Public Trustee v Legh [1938] Ch 39, [1937] 3 All ER 823, 107
   LJ Ch 6, 81 Sol Jo 701, 157 LT 270, 53 TLR 1036, CA 199, 201
Leigh v Burnett (1885) 29 Ch D 231, 54 LJ Ch 757, 33 WR 578, 52 LT 458 385
Leigh v Pantin [1914] 2 Ch 701, 84 LJ Ch 345, 112 LT 26 740
Leigh-White v Ruttledge [1914] 1 IR 135 309
Leigh's Settlement Trusts, Re [1981] CLY 2453 . . . . 543, 545
Leigh's Will Trusts, Re, Handyside v Durbridge [1970] Ch 277, [1969] 3 All ER 432, [1969]
   3 WLR 649, 113 Sol Jo 758. 18
Leinster (Duke), Re (1889) 23 LR Ir 152 570
Lemann's Trusts, Re (1883) 22 Ch D 633, 52 LJ Ch 560, 31 WR 520, 48 LT 389 . . 743, 764
Le Marchant v Le Marchant (1874) LR 18 Eq 414, 22 WR 839 . . . . 134, 135
Lemenda Trading Co Ltd v African Middle East Petroleum Co Ltd [1988] QB 448, [1988] 1
   All ER 513, [1988] 2 WLR 735, [1988] 1 Lloyd's Rep 361, 132 Sol Jo 538 1051
Lemos Trust, Re [1992] CILR 26 685
Lemos v Coutts & Co (Cayman) Ltd [1992-93] CILR 460 . . . . 217, 678
Lench v Lench (1805) 10 Ves 511 349
Leon, Re [1892] 1 Ch 348, 66 LT 390, sub nom Re L 36 Sol Jo 198, CA 782
Leonard, Re, ex p Lewis (1819) 1 Gl & J 69 878
Leong v Lim Beng Chye [1955] AC 648, [1955] 2 All ER 903, [1955] 3 WLR 303, 99 Sol Jo
   524, PC 217, 220, 231
Le Page v Gardom. See Gardom, Re, Le Page v A-G
Lepine, Re, Dowsett v Culver [1892] 1 Ch 210, 61 LJ Ch 153, [1891-4] All ER Rep 945, 66 LT
   360, CA 543
Leslie v Baillie (1843) 2 Y & C Ch Cas 91, 12 LJ Ch 153, 7 Jur 77 . . . . 623, 628
Leslie (J) Engineers Co Ltd, Re [1976] 2 All ER 85, [1976] 1 WLR 292, 120 Sol Jo 146 . 997
Leslie's Hassop Estates, Re [1911] 1 Ch 611, 80 LJ Ch 486, 55 Sol Jo 384, 104 LT 563, 27 TLR
   352 . . . . 794, 795
Leslie's Settlement Trusts, Re (1876) 2 Ch D 185, 45 LJ Ch 668, 24 WR 546, 34 LT 239 . 574
Lesser, Re [1947] VLR 366 720
Lester, Re, Lester v Lester [1942] Ch 324, [1942] 1 All ER 646, 111 LJ Ch 197, 86 Sol Jo 168,
   58 TLR 250 . . . . 35, 136, 137, 138
Letherbrow, Re, Hopp v Dean [1935] WN 34, 179 LT Jo 161 628
Letterstedt v Broers (1884) 9 App Cas 371, 53 LJPC 44, [1881-85] All ER Rep 882, 51 LT
   169 . . . . .744, 765, 767, 853
Letts v IRC [1956] 3 All ER 588, [1957] 1 WLR 201, 35 ATC 367, 49 R & IT 782, [1956] TR
   337, 101 Sol Jo 130. 152

Leven and Melville (Earl), Re, IRC v Williams Deacon's Bank Ltd [1954] 3 All ER 81, [1954] 1 WLR 1228, 47 R & IT 666, [1954] TR 325, 98 Sol Jo 591 246
Lever, Re, Cordwell v Lever [1897] 1 Ch 32, 66 LJ Ch 66, 45 WR 172, 41 Sol Jo 98, 75 LT 383; on appeal (1897) 76 LT 71, CA 568
Leverhulme, Re, Cooper v Leverhulme (No 2) [1943] 2 All ER 274, 169 LT 294 84
Leveson-Gower's Settled Estate, Re [1905] 2 Ch 95, 74 LJ Ch 540, 53 WR 524, 49 Sol Jo 482, 92 LT 836 . . . . 568, 573
Levick's Will Trusts, Re, ffennell v IRC [1963] 1 All ER 95, [1963] 1 WLR 311, 41 ATC 313, [1962] TR 333, 107 Sol Jo 235 1040
Levy, Re, Barclays Bank Ltd v Board of Guardians and Trustees for the Relief of the Jewish Poor [1960] Ch 346, [1960] 1 All ER 42, [1960] 2 WLR 278, 104 Sol Jo 86, CA 114, 126, 681, 732
Lewellin v Mackworth (1740) 2 Eq Cas Abr 579, sub nom Llevellyn v Mackworth Barn Ch 445 460
Lewis, Re, Davies v Harrison [1907] 2 Ch 296, 76 LJ Ch 539, 51 Sol Jo 531, 97 LT 636 . . . . 561, 562
Lewis, Re, Jennings v Hemsley [1939] Ch 232, [1939] 3 All ER 269, 108 LJ Ch 177, 82 Sol Jo 931, 159 LT 600, 55 TLR 53 813
Lewis v Cotton [2001] WTLR 1117 . . . . 428, 429
Lewis v Hillman. See Bloye's Trust, Re
Lewis v Madocks (1810) 7 RR 10, 17 Ves 48 . . . . 184, 307
Lewis v Nobbs (1878) 8 Ch D 591, 47 LJ Ch 662, 26 WR 631 . . . . .493, 586, 619, 647, 940
Lewis v Trask (1882) 21 Ch D 862 824
Lewis' Will Trust, Re, Whitelaw v Beaumont [1951] WN 591, 95 Sol Jo 789, [1951] 2 TLR 1032 104
Lewis's of Leicester Ltd, Re [1995] 1 BCLC 428, [1995] BCC 514 . . . . 16, 77
Ley v Ley (1868) LR 6 Eq 174, 37 LJ Ch 328, 16 WR 509, 18 LT 126 565
Libby v Kennedy (1998) OPLR 213 . . . . 644, 654
Liddiard, Re (1880) 14 Ch D 310, 49 LJ Ch 373, 28 WR 574, 42 LT 621 . . . . . 772, 1041
Life Association of Scotland v Siddal (1861) 3 De GF & J 58, 7 Jur NS 785, 9 WR 541, [1861-73] All ER Rep 892, 4 LT 311 . . . . 381, 931, 934, 952
Liles v Terry [1895] 2 QB 679, 65 LJQB 34, 44 WR 116, [1895-99] All ER Rep 1018, 40 Sol Jo 53, 73 LT 428, 12 TLR 26, CA 282, 283
Lillingston, Re, Pembery v Pembery [1952] 2 All ER 184, [1952] WN 358, 96 Sol Jo 462, [1952] 1 TLR 1622 150
Lim Teng Huan v Ang Swee Chuan [1992] 1 WLR 113, 64 P & CR 233, [1992] 1 LS Gaz R 33, 135 Sol Jo LB 212, PC .234, 242, 248, 250
Lind, Re, Industrials Finance Syndicate Ltd v Lind [1915] 2 Ch 345, 84 LJ Ch 884, [1915] HBR 204, [1914-15] All ER Rep 527, 59 Sol Jo 651, 113 LT 956, CA . . 16, 42, 139, 168, 175, 184, 185, 437
Linden Gardens Trust Ltd v Lenesta Sludge Disposals Ltd [1994] 1 AC 85, [1993] 3 All ER 417, [1993] 3 WLR 408, 36 Con LR 1, [1993] 45 LS Gaz R 39, [1993] NLJR 1152, 137 Sol Jo LB 183, HL 170
Lindo v Lindo (1839) 1 Beav 496, 8 LJ Ch 284 936
Lindsay v Miller [1949] VLR 13 . . . . 1033, 1034, 1039
Lindsay Petroleum Co v Hurd (1874) LR 5 PC 221, 22 WR 492 930
Lindsay's Settlement (No 2), Re [1941] Ch 119, [1941] 1 All ER 143, 110 LJ Ch 42, 85 Sol Jo 21, 164 LT 331, 57 TLR 235 573
Lindus and Hortin v IRC (1933) 17 TC 442, 12 ATC 140 211
Lingard v Bromley (1812) 1 Ves & B 114 . . . . 940, 944
Linsley, Re, Cattley v West [1904] 2 Ch 785, 73 LJ Ch 841, 53 WR 173, 43 Sol Jo 606 . . . . 677, 945
Lipinski's Will Trusts, Re, Gosschalk v Levy [1976] Ch 235, [1977] 1 All ER 33, [1976] 3 WLR 522, 120 Sol Jo 473 . . . . .36, 90, 112, 118, 124, 125, 127, 128, 129, 137, 138, 202, 339, 731
Lipkin Gorman v Karpnale Ltd [1992] 4 All ER 331, [1987] 1 WLR 987, [1986] FLR 271, [1987] BCLC 159, 131 Sol Jo 940, [1987] LS Gaz R 2272, [1986] NLJ Rep 659; on appeal [1992] 4 All ER 409, [1989] 1 WLR 1340, [1989] FLR 137, [1989] BCLC 756n, 134 Sol Jo 234, [1990] 4 LS Gaz R 40, [1989] NLJR 76, CA; varied sub nom Lipkin Gorman (a firm) v Karpnale Ltd [1991] 2 AC 548, [1992] 4 All ER 512, [1991] 3 WLR 10, [1991] NLJR 815, 135 Sol Jo LB 36, HL . 856, 866, 881, 897, 960, 974, 977, 979, 996
Lister, Re, ex p Bradford Overseers and Bradford Corpn [1926] Ch 149, sub nom Re Lister,

Bradford Corpn v Durrance 24 LGR 67, 90 JP 33, 95 LJ Ch 145, [1926] B & CR 5, [1925] All ER Rep 467, 134 LT 178, 42 TLR 143, CA 449, 453

Lister v Hodgson (1867) LR 4 Eq 30, 15 WR 547 285

Lister & Co v Stubbs (1890) 45 Ch D 1, 59 LJ Ch 570, 38 WR 548, [1886-90] All ER Rep 797, 63 LT 75, 6 TLR 317, CA 24, 387, 393, 909

Lister (R A) & Co Ltd v E G Thomson (Shipping) Ltd, The Benarty (No 2) [1987] 3 All ER 1032, [1987] 1 WLR 1614, 131 Sol Jo 1286, [1987] LS Gaz R 2536 942

Lister's Will Trusts, Re [1962] 3 All ER 737, [1962] 1 WLR 1441, 106 Sol Jo 1011 . . . 507, 509, 514

Litt's Will Trusts, Re, Parry v Cooper [1946] Ch 154, [1946] 1 All ER 314, 115 LJ Ch 114, 90 Sol Jo 116, 174 LT 184, 62 TLR 303, CA 375

Littauer Glove Corpn v F W Millington (1920) Ltd (1928) 44 TLR 746 1061

Little v Neil (1862) 31 LJ Ch 627, 10 WR 592 130

Livesey v Livesey (1827) 3 Russ 287, 6 LJOS Ch 13 982

Llanover Settled Estates, Re [1926] Ch 626, 95 LJ Ch 419, [1926] All ER Rep 631, 135 LT 363 54

Llewellin's Will Trusts, Re, Griffiths v Wilcox [1949] Ch 225, [1949] 1 All ER 487, [1949] LJR 724, 93 Sol Jo 148 . . . . 389, 656

Llewellyn's Settlement, Re, Official Solicitor v Evans [1921] 2 Ch 281, 90 LJ Ch 493, 126 LT 285 . . . . 74, 131

Lloyd v Attwood (1859) 3 De G & J 614, 29 LJ Ch 97, 5 Jur NS 1322, 33 LTOS 209 . . . 937

Lloyd v Banks (1868) 3 Ch App 488, 37 LJ Ch 881, 16 WR 988 989

Lloyd v Grace, Smith & Co [1912] AC 716, 81 LJKB 1140, [1911-13] All ER Rep 51, 56 Sol Jo 723, 107 LT 531, 28 TLR 547, HL 966

Lloyd v Lloyd (1852) 2 Sim NS 255, 21 LJ Ch 596, 16 Jur 306, 19 LTOS 84 . . . . 190, 220

Lloyd-Jones v Clark-Lloyd [1919] 1 Ch 424, 88 LJ Ch 278, 63 Sol Jo 317, 120 LT 578, 35 TLR 273, CA 383

Lloyd's v Harper (1880) 16 Ch D 290, 50 LJ Ch 140, 29 WR 452, 43 LT 481, CA . . . 9, 10, 170, 176

Lloyd's Settlement, Re, Lloyd v Leeper [1967] 2 All ER 314n, [1967] 2 WLR 1078, 111 Sol Jo 258 515

Lloyds and Scottish Finance Ltd v Cyril Lord Carpets Sales Ltd [1992] BCLC 609, 129 NLJ 366, HL 15

Lloyds Bank Ltd, Re, Bomze and Lederman v Bomze [1931] 1 Ch 289, 100 LJ Ch 45, [1930] All ER Rep 479, 144 LT 276, 47 TLR 38 282

Lloyds Bank Ltd v Bullock [1896] 2 Ch 192, 65 LJ Ch 680, 44 WR 633, 40 Sol Jo 545, 74 LT 687, 12 TLR 435 990

Lloyds Bank Ltd v Bundy [1975] QB 326, [1974] 3 All ER 757, [1974] 3 WLR 501, [1974] 2 Lloyd's Rep 366, 118 Sol Jo 714, CA 282

Lloyds Bank Ltd v E B Savory and Co [1933] AC 201, 102 LJKB 224, 38 Com Cas 115, [1932] All ER Rep 106, 49 TLR 116, 44 Ll L Rep 231, sub nom Savory & Co v Lloyds Bank Ltd 148 LT 291, HL 405

Lloyds Bank Ltd v Marcan [1973] 2 All ER 359, [1973] 1 WLR 339, 25 P & CR 65, 117 Sol Jo 187; affd [1973] 3 All ER 754, [1973] 1 WLR 1387, 117 Sol Jo 761, 228 Estates Gazette 1919, CA 293, 294, 295

Lloyds Bank plc v Byrne [1993] 2 FCR 41, [1993] 1 FLR 369, [1993] Fam Law 183, 23 HLR 472, CA 480, 481

Lloyds Bank plc v Carrick [1996] 4 All ER 630, 73 P & CR 314, [1996] 2 FCR 771, [1996] 2 FLR 600, [1997] Fam Law 94, [1996] 14 LS Gaz R 30, [1996] NLJR 405, 140 Sol Jo LB 101, CA 253, 411, 426

Lloyds Bank plc v Duker [1987] 3 All ER 193, [1987] 1 WLR 1324, 131 Sol Jo 1358, [1987] LS Gaz R 3254 . . . . 529, 532, 667, 739

Lloyds Bank plc v Independent Insurance Co Ltd [2000] QB 110, [1999] 2 WLR 986, [1999] 03 LS Gaz R 31, [1999] 1 All ER (Comm) 8, CA 971

Lloyds Bank plc v Rosset [1989] Ch 350, [1988] 3 All ER 915, [1988] 3 WLR 1301, 57 P & CR 62, [1989] 1 FLR 51, [1988] Fam Law 472, [1989] 1 LS Gaz R 39, [1988] NLJR 149, CA; revsd [1991] 1 AC 107, [1990] 1 All ER 1111, [1990] 2 WLR 867, 60 P & CR 311, [1990] 2 FLR 155, [1990] Fam Law 395, 22 HLR 349, [1990] 16 LS Gaz R 41, [1990] NLJR 478, HL 56, 76, 157, 325, 326, 347, 352, 355, 412, 413, 415, 416, 418, 419, 420, 421, 422, 424, 425, 426

Local Registration of Title (Ireland) Act 1891 and Smith, Re (1918) 52 ILT 113 383

Loch v Bagley (1867) LR 4 Eq 122, 15 WR 1103 . . . . 303, 305, 731

Locker's Settlement Trusts, Re, Meachem v Sachs [1978] 1 All ER 216, [1977] 1 WLR 1323, 121 Sol Jo 796 . . . . 28, 86, 496, 689
Lockhart v Reilly (1856) 25 LJ Ch 697, 4 WR 438, 27 LTOS 49 . . . . 941, 945
Lodwig, Re, Lodwig v Evans [1916] 2 Ch 26, 85 LJ Ch 585, 60 Sol Jo 494, 114 LT 881, 32 TLR 491, CA 197
Lofthouse, Re (1885) 29 Ch D 921, 54 LJ Ch 1087, 33 WR 668, 53 LT 174, CA . 94, 690, 711
Logan v Uttlesford District Council and Hammond [1984] CA Transcipt 263 942
Logan v Uttlesford District Council and Hammond [1986] NLJ Rep 541, CA 942
Logicrose Ltd v Southend United Football Club Ltd [1988] 1 WLR 1256, 132 Sol Jo 1591 387
Lohia v Lohia [2000] 34 LS Gaz R 41, [2001] WTLR 101; on appeal sub nom Lohia v Lohia [2001] EWCA Civ 1691, [2001] All ER (D) 375 (Oct) 368
London and Canadian Loan and Agency Co Ltd v Duggan [1893] AC 506, 63 LJPC 14, 1 R 413, 9 TLR 600, PC 983, 989
London and Cheshire Insurance Co Ltd v Laplagrene Property Co Ltd [1971] Ch 499, [1971] 1 All ER 766, [1971] 2 WLR 257, 22 P & CR 108, 114 Sol Jo 912, 217 Estates Gazette 531 439
London and County Banking Co v Goddard [1897] 1 Ch 642, 66 LJ Ch 261, 45 WR 310, 41 Sol Jo 295, 76 LT 277, 13 TLR 233 748
London and County Banking Co Ltd v London and River Plate Bank Ltd (1888) 21 QBD 535, 57 LJQB 601, 37 WR 89, 61 LT 37, 4 TLR 774, CA. 343
London and Mashonaland Exploration Co Ltd v New Mashonaland Exploration Co Ltd [1891] WN 165 . . . . 24, 402
London and South Western Rly Co v Gomm (1882) 20 Ch D 562, 51 LJ Ch 530, 30 WR 620, [1881-5] All ER Rep 1190, 46 LT 449, CA 192
London Joint Stock Bank v Simmons [1892] AC 201, 56 JP 644, 61 LJ Ch 723, 41 WR 108, [1891-4] All ER Rep 415, 36 Sol Jo 394, 66 LT 625, 8 TLR 478, HL 1002
London Regional Transport Pension Fund Trustee Co Ltd v Hatt [1993] PLR 227 . 706, 745, 746
London Syndicate v Lord (1878) 8 Ch D 84, 48 LJ Ch 57, 26 WR 427, 38 LT 329, CA . . 903
London Underground Ltd v National Union of Rail, Maritime and Transport Workers [2001] ICR 647, sub nom National Union of Rail, Maritime and Transport Workers v London Underground Ltd [2001] IRLR 228, CA 963, 992
London Wine Co (Shippers) Ltd, Re [1986] PCC 121 . . . . 78, 148
Londonderry's Settlement, Re, Peat v Walsh [1965] Ch 918, [1964] 3 All ER 855, [1965] 2 WLR 229, 108 Sol Jo 896, CA 672, 677, 678, 680, 681, 683, 684, 702, 817, 842
Long, Re, Lovegrove v Long [1901] WN 166 213
Longfield Parish Council v Robson (1913) 29 TLR 357 . . . . 8, 23, 397
Longman, Re, Westminster Bank Ltd v Hatton [1955] 1 All ER 455, [1955] 1 WLR 197, 99 Sol Jo 169 210
Longmate v Ledger (1860) 2 Giff 157, 6 Jur NS 481, 128 RR 72, 8 WR 386, 2 LT 256; affd (1860) 4 De GF & J 402 277
Longton v Wilsby (1897) 76 LT 770 383
Longuet v Hockley (1870) 22 LT 198 574
Lonrho plc v Fayed [1992] 1 AC 448, [1991] 3 All ER 303, [1991] 3 WLR 188, [1991] BCLC 779, [1991] BCC 641, 135 Sol Jo LB 68, HL 325
Lonrho plc v Fayed (No 2) [1991] 4 All ER 961, [1992] 1 WLR 1 . . . . . . 325, 326, 407
Lonsdale (Earl) v Beckett (1850) 4 De G & Sm 73, 19 LJ Ch 342, 87 RR 292, 16 LTOS 229 . . . . 758, 762
Lonsdale & Thompson Ltd v Black Arrow Group plc [1993] Ch 361, [1993] 3 All ER 648, [1993] 2 WLR 815, 65 P & CR 392, [1993] 2 Lloyd's Rep 428, [1993] 1 EGLR 87, [1993] 11 LS Gaz R 46, [1993] 25 EG 145 443
Lord v Australian Elizabethan Theatre Trust (1991) 30 FCR 491, 102 ALR 681, 5 ACSR 587 . . . . 117, 172
Lord v Bunn (1843) 2 Y & C Ch Cas 98, 60 RR 56 . . . . 213, 629, 738
Lord and Fullerton's Contract, Re [1896] 1 Ch 228, 65 LJ Ch 184, 44 WR 195, 40 Sol Jo 113, 73 LT 689, CA 449, 453
Lord's Settlement, Re, Martins Bank Ltd v Lord [1947] 2 All ER 685, [1948] LJR 207, 91 Sol Jo 654 228
Love, Re, Hill v Spurgeon (1885) 29 Ch D 348, 54 LJ Ch 816, 33 WR 449, 52 LT 398, CA 844
Lovell, Re, Sparks v Southall [1920] 1 Ch 122, 88 LJ Ch 540, 64 Sol Jo 35, 122 LT 26, 35 TLR 715 . . . . 218, 221
Lovett v Lovett [1898] 1 Ch 82, 67 LJ Ch 20, 46 WR 105, [1895-9] All ER Rep 474, 42 Sol Jo 81, 77 LT 650 502

Low v Bouverie [1891] 3 Ch 82, 60 LJ Ch 594, 40 WR 50, [1891-4] All ER Rep 348, 65 LT
   533, 7 TLR 582, CA 492, 672, 1002
Low v Peers (1770) Wilm 375. 190
Lowndes, Re, ex p Trustee (1887) 18 QBD 677, 56 LJQB 425, 4 Morr 139, 35 WR 549, 56 LT
   575, DC 289
Lowrie, Re, ex p Trustee of the Bankrupt v Bankrupt [1981] 3 All ER 353 482
Lowry v Fulton (1839) 9 Sim 104, 47 RR 188 . . . . 452, 453
Lowson v Coombes [1999] Ch 373, [1999] 2 WLR 720, [1999] 2 FCR 731, [1999] 1 FLR 799,
   [1999] Fam Law 91, [1999] 01 LS Gaz R 23, 77 P & CR D25, CA 343, 347
Lowson v Copeland (1787) 2 Bro CC 156 . . . . 579, 846
Lowther v Bentinck (1874) LR 19 Eq 166, 44 LJ Ch 197, 23 WR 156, [1874-80] All ER Rep
   362, 31 LT 719 720
Lowther v Carlton (1741) 2 Atk 242, Barn Ch 358, Cas temp Talb 187 1000
Lubbock v British Bank of South America [1892] 2 Ch 198, 61 LJ Ch 498, 41 WR 103, 67 LT
   74, 8 TLR 472, [1891-4] All ER Rep Ext 1753 536
Lucie-Smith v Gorman [1981] CLY 2866 442
Lucking's Will Trusts, Re, Renwick v Lucking [1967] 3 All ER 726, [1968] 1 WLR 866, 112
   Sol Jo 444 . . . . .585, 586, 645, 648, 939
Luddy's Trustee v Peard (1886) 33 Ch D 500, 55 LJ Ch 884, 35 WR 44, [1886-90] All ER Rep
   968, 55 LT 137, 2 TLR 841. 666
Luders v Anstey (1799) 4 Ves 501 140
Luders v Anstey (1800) 5 Ves 213 140
Luke v South Kensington Hotel Co (1879) 11 Ch D 121, 48 LJ Ch 361, 27 WR 514, [1874-80]
   All ER Rep 1293, 40 LT 638, CA 644, 645, 708
Lulham, Re, Brinton v Lulham (1885) 33 WR 788, 53 LT 9, CA 382
Lupton v White (1808) 15 Ves 432, [1803-13] All ER Rep 336 . . . . 880, 885
Lutea Trustees Ltd v Orbis Trustees Guernsey Ltd 1998 SLT 471 594
Luxor (Eastbourne) Ltd v Cooper. See Cooper v Luxor (Eastbourne) Ltd
Lyell v Kennedy (1889) 14 App Cas 437, 59 LJQB 268, 38 WR 353, 62 LT 77, HL. . . 8, 381,
   950, 952
Lynch v Burke [1995] 2 IR 159 359
Lynch Blosse, Re, Richards v Lynch Blosse [1899] WN 27, 43 Sol Jo 297 557
Lyne-Stephens and Scott-Miller's Contract, Re [1920] 1 Ch 472, 64 Sol Jo 341, 123 LT 8, 36
   TLR 307, sub nom Re Stephens and Scott-Miller's Contract 89 LJ Ch 287, CA . . . 443
Lyne's Settlement Trusts, Re, Re Gibbs, Lyne v Gibbs [1919] 1 Ch 80, 88 LJ Ch 1, [1918-19]
   All ER Rep 419, 63 Sol Jo 53, 120 LT 81, 35 TLR 44, CA 369
Lynn v Beaver (1823) 23 RR 185, Turn & R 63 330
Lysaght, Re, Hill v Royal College of Surgeons [1966] Ch 191, [1965] 2 All ER 888, [1965] 3
   WLR 391, 109 Sol Jo 577 . . . . 38, 77, 450
Lyse v Kingdon (1844) 1 Coll 184, 8 Jur 418, 3 LTOS 72 877
Lyus v Prowsa Developments Ltd [1982] 2 All ER 953, [1982] 1 WLR 1044, 44 P & CR 213,
   126 Sol Jo 102 . . . . 255, 257, 328, 408, 411, 706, 1003

M

Mabbett, Re, Pitman v Holborrow [1891] 1 Ch 707, 60 LJ Ch 279, 39 WR 537, 64 LT
   447. . . . . 533, 566, 732
Maber, Re, Ward v Maber [1928] Ch 88, 97 LJ Ch 101, 138 LT 318 206
Maberly, Re, Maberly v Maberly (1886) 33 Ch D 455, 56 LJ Ch 54, 34 WR 771, 55 LT 164, 2
   TLR 832. 613
Mabo v Queensland (No 2) (1992) 175 CLR 1, 107 ALR 1, 66 ALJR 408, HC of A . . . 7
Macadam, Re, Dallow and Moscrop v Codd [1946] Ch 73, [1945] 2 All ER 664, 115 LJ Ch 14,
   89 Sol Jo 531, 173 LT 395, 62 TLR 48 . . . . 388, 389, 542
McArdle, Re [1951] Ch 669, [1951] 1 All ER 905, 95 Sol Jo 284, CA. 152
Macaulay's Estate, Re, Macaulay v O'Donnell [1943] Ch 435n, HL 114
McBlain v Cross (1871) 25 LT 804 237
McBride, Re (1980) 107 DLR (3d) 233 231
McBride v Hudson (1962) 107 CLR 604 535
M'Caig v University of Glasgow (1907) 44 SLR 198, 1907 SC 231, 14 SLT 600 123
M'Caig's Trustees v Kirk-Session of United Free Church of Lismore (1915) 52 SLR 347, 1915
   SC 426, 1915 1 SLT 152 123
McCarthy & Stone Ltd v Julian S Hodge & Co Ltd [1971] 2 All ER 973, [1971] 1 WLR 1547,
   22 P & CR 1040, 115 Sol Jo 607 . . . . 50, 1002
McCathie v McCathie [1971] NZLR 58 165

McCausland v Duncan Lawrie Ltd [1996] 4 All ER 995, [1997] 1 WLR 38, 74 P & CR 343, [1996] NPC 94, [1996] 26 LS Gaz R 19, [1996] NLJR 1387, [1996] EGCS 103, CA . 235
McCausland v Young [1949] NI 49. 222
McClure's Trusts, Re, Carr v Commercial Union Insurance Co [1906] WN 200, 76 LJ Ch 52, 51 Sol Jo 67, 95 LT 704, 23 TLR 42 . . . . 568, 574
McCormick v Grogan (1869) 4 App Cas 82, LR 4 HL 82, 17 WR 961 . . . . 134, 234, 254, 255, 257, 258
Macculloch v Anderson [1904] AC 55, HL. 544
McCullough v Elliott (1922) 62 DLR 257 977
McCullough v Marsden Estate (1919) 45 DLR 645, 17 Alta LR 553, [1919] 1 WWR 689, CA 902, 977
Macdonald v Hauer (1972) 72 DLR (3d) 110 944
McDonald v Horn (1993) Times, 12 October; affd [1995] 1 All ER 961, [1995] ICR 685, [1994] NLJR 1515, CA 788, 815, 816, 840, 842, 843, 844, 845
Macdonald v Irvine (1878) 8 Ch D 101, 47 LJ Ch 494, 26 WR 381, 38 LT 155, CA . . . 549, 550, 569
MacDonald v MacDonald [1957] 2 All ER 690 366
McDonald v Moran (1938) 12 MPR 424. 261
Macdonald v Myerson [2001] EWCA Civ 66, [2001] NPC 20, [2001] 06 LS Gaz R 47 . . 343
McDonic v Hetherington (1997) 142 DLR (4th) 648. 965
McDonnel v White (1865) 11 HL Cas 570, 145 RR 305 . . . . 933, 935
Macduff, Re, Macduff v Macduff [1896] 2 Ch 451, 65 LJ Ch 700, 45 WR 154, [1895-9] All ER Rep 154, 40 Sol Jo 651, 74 LT 706, 12 TLR 452, CA 105
McEachern, Re, Gambles v McEachern [1911] WN 23, 55 Sol Jo 204, 103 LT 900. . . . 569
McEacharn's Settlement Trusts, Re, Hobson v McEacharn [1939] Ch 858, 108 LJ Ch 326, 83 Sol Jo 622, 161 LT 263, 55 TLR 937 612
Macedo v Stroud [1922] 2 AC 330, 91 LJPC 222, 128 LT 45 150
McEwan v Crombie (1883) 25 Ch D 175, 53 LJ Ch 24, 32 WR 115, 49 LT 499 824
M'Fadden v Jenkyns (1842) 1 Ph 153, 12 LJ Ch 146, 7 Jur 27, 65 RR 354, [1835-42] All ER Rep 206 . . . . 79, 233
Macfarlane v IRC (1929) 14 TC 532, 8 ATC 227, 1929 SC 453, 1929 SLT 395 818
McFarlane v McFarlane [1972] NI 59, CA 418, 421
M'Gachen v Dew (1851) 15 Beav 84, 92 RR 315. 951
McGaw, Re, McIntyre v McGaw [1919] WN 288, 64 Sol Jo 209 586
McGeorge, Re, Ratcliff v McGeorge [1963] Ch 544, [1963] 1 All ER 519, [1963] 2 WLR 767, 107 Sol Jo 253 . . . . 712, 715
McGrath v Wallis [1995] 3 FCR 661, [1995] 2 FLR 114, [1995] Fam Law 551, [1995] 15 LS Gaz R 41, CA. 362, 363
McHardy and Sons (a firm) v Warren [1994] 2 FLR 338, [1994] Fam Law 567, CA . . . 417, 421, 422
Machin v National Power plc [1998] Pen LR 295, [2001] WTLR 741. . . . . 840, 842, 843
Machu, Re (1882) 21 Ch D 838, 30 WR 887, 47 LT 557 . . . . 190, 738
MacIver's Settlement, Re, MacIver v Rae [1936] Ch 198, 105 LJ Ch 21, [1935] All ER Rep 889, 154 LT 339, 52 TLR 25 562
McIlwraith v McIlwraith 24 July 2002, (2002) 152 NLJ 1414 814
Mac-Jordan Construction Ltd v Brookmount Erostin Ltd (in receivership) [1992] BCLC 350, 56 BLR 1, CA 9, 42, 79, 139, 148, 168
Mackay, Re, Griessemann v Carr [1911] 1 Ch 300, 80 LJ Ch 237, 103 LT 755, [1908-10] All ER Rep Ext 1112 919
Mackay, Re, Mackay v Gould [1906] 1 Ch 25, 75 LJ Ch 47, 54 WR 88, 50 Sol Jo 43, 93 LT 694 624
Mackay v Douglas (1872) LR 14 Eq 106, 41 LJ Ch 539, 20 WR 652, 26 LT 721 293
McKee v Paradise 575 Sup Ct 124, 299 US 122 (1936) 79
M'Kenny v Barnsley Corpn (1894) 10 TLR 533, CA 127
Mackenzie, Re, Bain v Mackenzie [1916] 1 Ch 125, 85 LJ Ch 197, 114 LT 283 805
McKenzie v McDonald (1927) 33 ALR 51, [1927] VLR 134, 48 ALT 138 874
Mackenzie's Settlement, Re (1867) 2 Ch App 345, 36 LJ Ch 320, 15 WR 662, 16 LT 138. . . . . 310, 315
Mackie v Herbertson (1884) 9 App Cas 303, HL 167
Mackinnon v Stewart (1850) 1 Sim NS 76, 20 LJ Ch 49, 89 RR 24 141
McKnight v Titus (1933) 6 MPR 282 359
Mackreth v Symmons (1808) 10 RR 85, 15 Ves 329, 2 White & Tud LC 946, [1803-13] All ER Rep 103 983

Maclaren's Settlement Trusts, Re, Royal Exchange Assurance v Maclaren [1951] 2 All ER
    414, 95 Sol Jo 624, [1951] 2 TLR 209 . . . . 538, 541
McLean v Burns Philp Trustee Co Pty Ltd (1985) 2 NSWLR 623 . . . . 822, 847
Maclean's Trusts, Re (1874) LR 19 Eq 274, 44 LJ Ch 145, 23 WR 206, 32 LT 632 830
Macleay, Re (1875) LR 20 Eq 186, 44 LJ Ch 441, 23 WR 718, 32 LT 682 . . . . . 215, 738
Maclennan, Re, Few v Byrne [1939] Ch 750, [1939] 3 All ER 81, 108 LJ Ch 364, 83 Sol Jo
    438, 160 LT 612, 55 TLR 830, CA 534
M'Mahon v Featherstonhaugh [1895] 1 IR 182 902
Macmillan Inc v Bishopsgate Investment Trust plc (10 December 1993, unreported) . . 58
Macmillan Inc v Bishopsgate Investment Trust plc (No 3) [1995] 3 All ER 747, [1995] 1
    WLR 978; on appeal [1996] 1 All ER 585, [1996] 1 WLR 387, [1995] 43 LS Gaz R 25,
    [1995] TLR 573, 139 Sol Jo LB 225, CA. 256, 1029, 1054
McNally, Re [1967] NZLR 521 664
Macnamara v Carey (1867) 15 WR 374, IR 1 Eq 9, 18 Ir Jur 293 580
Macnamara v Jones (1784) 2 Dick 587 814
McPhail v Doulton. See Baden's Deed Trusts, Re, Baden v Smith
Macquarie Bank Ltd v Sixty-Fourth Throne Pty Ltd [1998] 3 VR 133, CA 963
Maddison v Alderson (1883) 8 App Cas 467, 47 JP 821, 52 LJQB 737, 31 WR 820, [1881-5] All
    ER Rep 742, 49 LT 303, HL 140
Maddock, Re, Butt v Wright [1899] 2 Ch 588, 68 LJ Ch 655, 47 WR 684, 43 Sol Jo 676, 81 LT
    320 845
Maddock, Re, Llewelyn v Washington [1902] 2 Ch 220, 71 LJ Ch 567, 50 WR 598, 86 LT 644,
    CA 264, 265
Maddy's Estate, Re, Maddy v Maddy [1901] 2 Ch 820, 71 LJ Ch 18, 45 Sol Jo 673, 85 LT
    341 . . . . 303, 317
Magrath v Morehead (1871) LR 12 Eq 491, 41 LJ Ch 120, 24 LT 868 . . . . . 66, 304, 731
Maguire v Makaronis (1997) 188 CLR 449, 144 ALR 729 . . . . 287, 856
Maharaj v Chand [1986] AC 898, [1986] 3 All ER 107, [1986] 3 WLR 440, 130 Sol Jo 633,
    [1986] LS Gaz R 2568, PC 248, 412, 413, 419
Maharanee Serthadevi Gaekwar of Baroda v Wildenstein [1972] 2 QB 283, [1972] 2 All ER
    689, [1972] 2 WLR 1077, 116 Sol Jo 221, CA 1059
Mahoney v Purnell [1996] 3 All ER 61, [1997] 1 FLR 612, [1997] Fam Law 169 . 24, 286, 327
Mair, Re, Williamson v French [1909] 2 Ch 280, 78 LJ Ch 711, 101 LT 70 212
Makepeace v Rogers (1865) 4 De GJ & Sm 649, 34 LJ Ch 396, 11 Jur NS 314, 5 New Rep 499,
    13 WR 566, 12 LT 221, CA. 393
Makin (William) & Sons Ltd, Re [1992] PLR 177, [1993] BCC 453, [1993] OPLR 171 . . 462
Malam, Re, Malam v Hitchens [1894] 3 Ch 578, 63 LJ Ch 797, 13 R 38, 38 Sol Jo 708, 71 LT
    655 . . . . 536, 539
Malcolm v O'Callaghan (1837) 3 My & Cr 52 817
Malim v Keighley (1795) 2 Ves 333; affd (1795) 2 RR 229, 2 Ves 529 134
Mallalieu v Drummond (Inspector of Taxes) [1983] 2 AC 861, [1983] 2 All ER 1095, [1983]
    3 WLR 409, [1983] STC 665, 57 TC 330, 127 Sol Jo 538, HL. 294
Mallinson Consolidated Trusts, Re, Mallinson v Gooley [1974] 2 All ER 530, [1974] 1 WLR
    1120, 118 Sol Jo 549 225
Mallott v Wilson [1903] 2 Ch 494, 72 LJ Ch 664, [1900-3] All ER Rep 326, 89 LT 522 . 35, 77,
                                                                                150, 155, 450
Malmesbury v Malmesbury (1862) 31 Beav 407 698
Malpass, Re, Lloyds Bank plc v Malpass [1985] Ch 42, [1984] 2 All ER 313, [1984] 3 WLR
    372, 128 Sol Jo 334, [1984] LS Gaz R 1916 80
Maltby Marriage Settlement, Re, Aylen v Gaud [1953] 2 All ER 220, [1953] 1 WLR 765, 97
    Sol Jo 421 . . . . 311, 313
Manchester Trust Ltd v Furness, Withy & Co Ltd [1895] 2 QB 539, 8 Asp MLC 57, 1 Com Cas
    39, 14 R 739, 44 WR 178, 73 LT 110, sub nom Manchester Trust Ltd v Turner, Withy &
    Co Ltd 64 LJQB 766, 11 TLR 530, CA 989
Mandla v Dowell Lee [1983] 2 AC 548, [1983] 1 All ER 1062, [1983] 2 WLR 620, [1983] ICR
    385, [1983] IRLR 209, 127 Sol Jo 242, HL. 223
Mangles v Dixon (1852) 3 HL Cas 702, 88 RR 296, [1843-60] All ER Rep 770, 19 LTOS 260 983
Manifest Shipping Co Ltd v Uni-Polaris Shipping Co Ltd [2001] UKHL 1, [2001] 1 All ER
    743, [2001] 2 WLR 170, [2001] 1 Lloyd's Rep 389, [2001] 1 All ER (Comm) 193,
    [2001] Lloyd's Rep IR 247 974
Manisty's Settlement, Re, Manisty v Manisty [1974] Ch 17, [1973] 2 All ER 1203, [1973] 3
    WLR 341, 117 Sol Jo 665 . . . . . .27, 29, 62, 93, 95, 96, 97, 673, 674, 676, 690, 691

Manning v Gill (1872) LR 13 Eq 485, 36 JP 436, 41 LJ Ch 736, 12 Cox CC 274, 20 WR 357, 26
    LT 14 270
Mansel, Re, Smith v Mansel [1930] 1 Ch 352, 99 LJ Ch 128, [1929] All ER Rep 189, 142 LT
    281 547
Mansel v Norton (1883) 22 Ch D 769, 52 LJ Ch 357, 31 WR 325, 48 LT 654, CA 567
Mansell v Mansell (1732) 2 Eq Cas Abr 748, 2 Barn KB 187, Cas temp Talb 252, 2 P Wms 678,
    [1558-1774] All ER Rep 343 992
Mansfield v Shaw (1818) 3 Madd 100, 18 RR 201 904
Manufacturers Trust Co v Becker 338 US 304, 70 Sup Ct 127 (1949) 396
Mara v Browne [1895] 2 Ch 69, 64 LJ Ch 594, 72 LT 765, 11 TLR 352; on appeal [1896] 1 Ch
    199, 65 LJ Ch 225, 44 WR 330, 40 Sol Jo 131, 73 LT 638, 12 TLR 111, CA . . 381, 921,
                                                          926, 948, 950, 951, 952, 965
March v Russell (1837) 3 My & Cr 31, 6 LJ Ch 303, 1 Jur 588, 45 RR 196, [1835-42] All ER
    Rep 501 931
Marinari v Lloyds Bank plc (Zubadi Trading Co intervening): C-364/93 [1996] QB 217,
    [1996] 2 WLR 159, [1996] All ER (EC) 84, [1995] ECR I-2719, ECJ 1057
Marjoribanks, Re, Marjoribanks v Dansey [1923] 2 Ch 307, 92 LJ Ch 609, 67 Sol Jo 659, 129
    LT 669 . . . . 553, 562
Marker v Marker (1851) 9 Hare 1, 20 LJ Ch 246, 15 Jur 663, 89 RR 305, 17 LTOS 176. . 931
Marlborough (Duke), Re, Davis v Whitehead [1894] 2 Ch 133, 63 LJ Ch 471, 8 R 242, 42 WR
    456, 38 Sol Jo 289, 70 LT 314, 10 TLR 296 256
Marlborough (Duke) v A-G [1945] Ch 78, [1945] 1 All ER 165, 114 LJ Ch 83, 89 Sol Jo 82,
    172 LT 21, 61 TLR 159, CA 1034, 1037, 1039, 1047
Marley v Mutual Security Merchant Bank and Trust Co Ltd [1991] 3 All ER 198, PC . . 833,
                                                                        835, 837
Marlow v Pitfeild (1719) 2 Eq Cas Abr 516, 1 P Wms 558 895
Marner's Trusts, Re (1866) LR 3 Eq 432, 36 LJ Ch 58, 12 Jur NS 959, 15 WR 99, 15 LT
    237 . . . . 564, 574
Marples v Bainbridge (1816) 1 Madd 590, 16 RR 271 190
Marriott v Abell (1869) LR 7 Eq 478, 38 LJ Ch 451, 17 WR 569, 20 LT 690 374
Marriott v Kinnersley (1830) Taml 470, 31 RR 109 938
Marsden v Regan [1954] 1 All ER 475, [1954] 1 WLR 423, 98 Sol Jo 144, CA . . . 913, 914,
                                                                        915, 919
Marsh, ex p (1744) 1 Atk 158 461
Marsh v Keating (1834) 1 Bing NC 198, 8 Bli NS 651, 2 Cl & Fin 250, 1 Mont & A 592, 1 Scott
    5, [1824-34] All ER Rep 226, HL 895
Marsh v Von Sternberg [1986] 1 FLR 526, [1986] Fam Law 160 425
Marshal v Crutwell (1875) LR 20 Eq 328, 39 JP 775, 44 LJ Ch 504 . . . . . 359, 361, 363
Marshall, Re, Graham v Marshall [1928] Ch 661, 97 LJ Ch 415, [1928] All ER Rep 694, 139
    LT 189 . . . . 369, 373
Marshall, Re, Marshall v Marshall [1914] 1 Ch 192, 83 LJ Ch 307, [1911-13] All ER Rep 671,
    58 Sol Jo 118, 109 LT 835, CA 544, 735, 739
Marshall, Re, Marshall v Whateley [1920] 1 Ch 284, 89 LJ Ch 204, [1920] All ER Rep 190, 64
    Sol Jo 241, 122 LT 673 . . . . 212, 269
Marshall v Crowther (1874) 2 Ch D 199, 23 WR 210 . . . . 563, 565
Marshall v Holloway (1820) 19 RR 94, 2 Swan 432, [1814-23] All ER Rep 395 655
Marshall (Inspector of Taxes) v Kerr [1995] 1 AC 148, [1994] 3 All ER 106, [1994] 3 WLR
    299, [1994] STC 638, 67 TC 56, 138 Sol Jo LB 155, HL. 18, 52, 68
Marshall v Sladden (1849) 7 Hare 428, 19 LJ Ch 57, 14 Jur 106 770
Marshall (Thomas) (Exports) Ltd v Guinle [1979] Ch 227, [1978] 3 All ER 193, [1978] 3
    WLR 116, [1979] FSR 208, [1978] ICR 905, [1978] IRLR 174, 122 Sol Jo 295 . . . 402
Marshall Futures Ltd v Marshall [1992] 1 NZLR 316 975
Marshall's Will Trusts, Re [1945] Ch 217, [1945] 1 All ER 550, 114 LJ Ch 118, 89 Sol Jo 142,
    172 LT 267, 61 TLR 267 . . . . 5, 785
Marsland, Re, Lloyds Bank Ltd v Marsland [1939] Ch 820, [1939] 3 All ER 148, 108 LJ Ch
    344, 83 Sol Jo 564, 161 LT 1, 55 TLR 819, CA 428
Marston Thompson & Evershed plc v Benn [1998] CL 613 812
Martin, Re [1900] WN 129. 788
Martin v City of Edinburgh District Council [1989] 1 PLR 9, 1988 SLT 329, 1988 SCLR 90 613
Martin v Martin (1959) 110 CLR 297, 33 ALJR 362, HC of A. 345
Martin v Maugham (1844) 8 JP 532, 14 Sim 230, 13 LJ Ch 392, 8 Jur 609, [1843-60] All ER
    Rep 717, 3 LTOS 433. . . . . 208, 230

Martin's Trusts, Re, Land, Building, Investment and Cottage Improvement Co v Martin
    (1887) 34 Ch D 618, 56 LJ Ch 695, 34 WR 524, 56 LT 241 768
Martyn, Re, Re Toutt's Will (1884) 26 Ch D 745, 54 LJ Ch 1016, 32 WR 734, 50 LT 552 . 782
Mascall v Mascall (1984) 50 P & CR 119, 128 Sol Jo 663, [1984] LS Gaz R 2218, CA. .77, 151,
    155, 156
Mason, Re, Mason v Mason [1891] 3 Ch 467, 61 LJ Ch 25. 205
Mason v Farbrother [1983] 2 All ER 1078 . . . . 522, 525
Mason's Orphanage and London and North Western Rly Co, Re [1896] 1 Ch 54, 65 LJ Ch
    32, 44 WR 61, 40 Sol Jo 34, 73 LT 465, 12 TLR 18; on appeal [1896] 1 Ch 596, 65 LJ Ch
    439, 44 WR 339, 40 Sol Jo 352, 74 LT 161, 12 TLR 236, CA 666
Massey v Banner (1820) 1 Jac & W 241, 4 Madd 413, 21 RR 150 . . . . 576, 607
Massingberd's Settlement, Re, Clark v Trelawney (1890) 63 LT 296, CA . .497, 861, 869, 873
Massy v Gahan (1889) 23 LR Ir 518 560
Masterman-Lister v Jewell [2002] EWHC 417 (QB), [2002] All ER (D) 247 (Mar). . . . 269
Masters, Re, Coutts & Co v Masters [1953] 1 All ER 19, [1953] 1 WLR 81, 97 Sol Jo
    10 . . . . 655, 658
Matharu v Matharu (1994) 68 P & CR 93, [1994] 3 FCR 216, [1994] 2 FLR 597, [1994] Fam
    Law 624, 26 HLR 648, CA 248
Matheson, Re, ex p Worrell v Matheson (1994) 121 ALR 605 462
Mathew v Brise (1845) 15 LJ Ch 39, 10 Jur 105, 63 RR 69, 7 LTOS 1 634
Mathew v TM Sutton Ltd [1994] 4 All ER 793, [1994] 1 WLR 1455, [1994] NLJR 1278,
    [1994] CCLR 140 870
Mathias v Mathias (1858) 4 Jur NS 780, 107 RR 157, 3 Sm & G 552, 32 LTOS 25 811
Matthews v Ruggles-Brice [1911] 1 Ch 194, 80 LJ Ch 42, 103 LT 491 821
Maxwell Communications Corpn plc (No 2), Re [1994] 1 All ER 737, [1993] 1 WLR 1402,
    [1994] 1 BCLC 1, [1993] BCC 369. 43
May, Re, Eggar v May [1917] 2 Ch 126, 86 LJ Ch 698, 61 Sol Jo 577, 117 LT 401, 33 TLR
    419. 222
May, Re, Eggar v May [1932] 1 Ch 99, 101 LJ Ch 12, [1931] All ER Rep 558, 75 Sol Jo 741,
    146 LT 56, 48 TLR 3, CA 222
May v Taylor (1843) 7 JP 690, 12 LJCP 314, 7 Jur 515, 6 Man & G 261, 64 RR 778, 6 Scott NR
    974, 1 LTOS 256 456
May's Settlement, Re, Public Trustee v Meredith [1926] Ch 136, 95 LJ Ch 230, [1925] All ER
    Rep 444, 134 LT 696 722
May's Will Trusts, Re, May and Stanford v Burch [1941] Ch 109, 110 LJ Ch 96, 84 Sol Jo 561,
    57 TLR 22 . . . . 753, 766
Mayn v Mayn (1867) LR 5 Eq 150, 17 LT 439 67
Mayo, Re, Mayo v Mayo [1943] Ch 302, [1943] 2 All ER 440, 59 TLR 395, sub nom Re Mayo's
    Will Trusts 112 LJ Ch 257, 169 LT 205 479
Mead, Re, Public Trustee v Mead (1918) 88 LJ Ch 86, 119 LT 724, CA 720
Mead's Trust Deed, Re, Briginshaw v National Society of Operative Printers and Assistants
    [1961] 2 All ER 836, [1961] 1 WLR 1244, 105 Sol Jo 569 108
Medland, Re, Eland v Medland (1889) 41 Ch D 476, 58 LJ Ch 572, 37 WR 753, 60 LT 851, 5
    TLR 523, CA 579
Medlock, Re, Ruffle v Medlock (1886) 55 LJ Ch 738, 54 LT 828 714
Mégret, Re, Tweedie v Maunder [1901] 1 Ch 547, 70 LJ Ch 451, 84 LT 192 270
Meinertzhagen v Davis (1844) 13 LJ Ch 457, 1 Coll 335, 8 Jur 973, 66 RR 88, 3 LTOS
    452. . . . . 762, 772
Mellor, Re, Mellor v Mellor [1898] 1 Ch 290, 67 LJ Ch 151, 46 WR 328, 78 LT 72 . . . 805
Melton, Re, Milk v Towers [1918] 1 Ch 37, 87 LJ Ch 18, [1917] HBR 246, [1916-17] All ER
    Rep 672, 117 LT 679, 34 TLR 20, CA. 980
Melville v IRC [2001] EWCA Civ 1247, [2002] 1 WLR 407, [2001] STC 1271, [2001] 37 LS
    Gaz R 39, [2002] 1 WLR 407, CA 243, 308, 504, 733
Mendes v Guedalla (1862) 2 John & H 259, 31 LJ Ch 461, 8 Jur NS 878, 10 WR 482, 6 LT 746 940
Merchant Taylors' Co v A-G (1871) 6 Ch App 512, 35 JP 774, 40 LJ Ch 545, 19 WR 641, 25 LT
    109. 137
Mercier v Mercier [1903] 2 Ch 98, 72 LJ Ch 511, 51 WR 611, [1900-3] All ER Rep 375, 47 Sol
    Jo 492, 88 LT 516, CA 366
Mercury Communications Ltd v Director General of Telecommunications [1994] 36 LS Gaz
    R 36, 138 Sol Jo LB 183, CA; revsd [1996] 1 All ER 575, [1996] 1 WLR 48, HL . . 839
Meridian Global Funds Management Asia Ltd v Securities Commission [1995] 2 AC 500,
    [1995] 3 All ER 918, [1995] 3 WLR 413, [1995] 2 BCLC 116, [1995] BCC 942, [1995]
    28 LS Gaz R 39, PC 963, 992

Merlin v Blagrave (1858) 25 Beav 125, 119 RR 356 623
Merryweather v Jones (1864) 4 Giff 509, 10 Jur NS 290, 141 RR 305, 12 WR 524, 66 ER 807,
   10 LT 62 190
Mertins v Joliffe (1756) Amb 311 983
Mesnard v Welford (1853) 22 LJ Ch 1053, 1 Eq Rep 237, 17 Jur 815, 1 WR 443, 21 LTOS 164,
   sub nom Mennard v Welford 1 Sm & G 426 753
Messeena v Carr (1870) LR 9 Eq 260, 39 LJ Ch 216, 18 WR 415, 22 LT 3 . . . 533, 644, 645
Metall und Rohstoff AG v Donaldson Lufkin & Jenrette Inc [1990] 1 QB 391, [1988] 3 All
   ER 116, [1988] 3 WLR 548, 132 Sol Jo 1149; varied [1990] 1 QB 391, [1989] 3 All ER
   14, [1989] 3 WLR 563, CA 57, 325, 899
Metcalfe's Trusts, Re (1864) 28 JP 260, 2 De GJ & Sm 122, 33 LJ Ch 308, 10 Jur NS 287, 3
   New Rep 657, 12 WR 538, 10 LT 78 830
Metropolitan Bank v Heiron (1880) 5 Ex D 319, 29 WR 370, 43 LT 676, CA 24, 393
Mettoy Pension Trustees Ltd v Evans [1991] 2 All ER 513, [1990] 1 WLR 1587 . . .26, 27, 28,
                       29, 86, 94, 97, 132, 499, 680, 690,
                       695, 724, 728, 745, 848
Meux, Re, Gilmour v Gilmour [1958] Ch 154, [1957] 2 All ER 630, [1957] 3 WLR 377, 55
   LGR 456, 107 Sol Jo 611 . . . . 722, 783
Mewburn's Settlement, Re, Perks v Wood [1934] Ch 112, 103 LJ Ch 37, [1933] All ER Rep
   663, 77 Sol Jo 467, 150 LT 76 . . . . 722, 803, 809
Meyer v Montriou (1841) 4 Beav 343 906
Meyer v Simonsen (1852) 5 De G & Sm 723, 21 LJ Ch 678, 90 RR 204, 19 LTOS 337 . . 552,
                               557
Michaelv Calhil (1945) 72 CLR 509 559
Michael v Hart & Co [1901] 2 KB 867, 70 LJKB 1000, 50 WR 154, 85 LT 548, 17 TLR 761; on
   appeal [1902] 1 KB 482, 71 LJKB 265, 50 WR 308, 86 LT 474, 18 TLR 254, CA; affd sub
   nom Hart & Co v Michael (1903) 89 LT 422, HL 872
Michelham's Will Trusts, Re [1964] Ch 550, [1963] 2 All ER 188, [1963] 2 WLR 1238, 107
   Sol Jo 254 . . . . 220, 518
Michell's Trusts, Re (1878) 9 Ch D 5, 48 LJ Ch 50, 26 WR 762, 38 LT 462, CA 313
Middleton v Dodswell (1806) 13 Ves 266 903
Middleton v Pollock, ex p Elliott (1876) 2 Ch D 104, 45 LJ Ch 293 145
Middleton v Reay (1849) 7 Hare 106, 18 LJ Ch 153, 13 Jur 116 764
Midland Bank plc v Cooke [1995] 4 All ER 562, [1996] 1 FCR 442, [1995] 2 FLR 915, [1995]
   Fam Law 675, 27 HLR 733, [1995] 30 LS Gaz R 34, [1995] NLJR 1543, 139 Sol Jo LB
   194, CA 326, 418, 424, 425, 426
Midland Bank plc v Dobson and Dobson [1986] 1 FLR 171, [1986] Fam Law 55, 75, [1985]
   NLJ Rep 751, CA 250, 414
Midland Bank plc v Pike [1988] 2 All ER 434 480
Midland Bank plc v Watt [1994] EGCS 113 59
Midland Bank plc v Wyatt [1995] 3 FCR 11, [1995] 1 FLR 697, [1995] Fam Law 299, [1997] 1
   BCLC 242, [1996] BPIR 288 . . . . 30, 59, 145, 293, 294, 1034
Midland Bank Trust Co Ltd v Green [1981] AC 513, [1981] 1 All ER 153, [1981] 2 WLR 28,
   42 P & CR 201, 125 Sol Jo 33, HL 256, 411
Midland Bank Trustee (Jersey) Ltd v Federated Pension Services [1995] Jer LR 352, [1996]
   PLR 179 . . . . 586, 594, 864
Midleton's Will Trusts, Re, Whitehead v Earl of Midleton [1969] 1 Ch 600, [1967] 2 All ER
   834, [1967] 3 WLR 965, 111 Sol Jo 637 . . . . 502, 733
Miles, Re [1903] 2 Ch 518, 72 LJ Ch 704, 52 WR 47, 47 Sol Jo 655, 88 LT 863 814
Miles v Bull (No 2) [1969] 3 All ER 1585, 21 P & CR 23, 212 Estates Gazette 1255 . 256, 411
Mill v Hill (1852) 3 HL Cas 828, 88 RR 356 383
Mill's Declaration of Trust, Re, Midland Bank Executor and Trustee Co Ltd v Mill [1950] 1
   All ER 789, 66 (pt 1) TLR 87; affd [1950] 2 All ER 292, CA 225
Millar's Trustees v Polson (1897) 24 R 1038, 34 SLR 798, 5 SLT 94 . . . . . 492, 578, 938
Millard v Eyre (1793) 2 Ves 94 743
Miller v Cameron (1936) 54 CLR 572 767
Miller v Harrison (1871) IR 5 Eq 324 149
Miller v Huddlestone (1851) 21 LJ Ch 1, 15 Jur 1043, 3 Mac & G 513, 87 RR 171, 18 LTOS
   147 568
Miller v IRC [1987] STC 108, Ct of Sess 64, 65, 206
Miller v Miller (1872) LR 13 Eq 263, 41 LJ Ch 291, 20 WR 324 . . . . 551, 554
Miller v Priddon (1852) 1 De GM & G 335, 21 LJ Ch 421, 91 RR 108, 18 LTOS 323 . . . 762
Miller v Stapleton [1996] 2 All ER 449; on appeal (30 July 1996, unreported), CA . . . 867

Miller's Agreement, Re, Uniacke v A-G [1947] Ch 615, [1947] 2 All ER 78, [1948] LJR 567,
    177 LT 129. . . . . 171, 172
Miller's Deed Trusts, Re [1978] LS Gaz R 454 . . . . 587, 862
Milligan v Mitchell (1833) 1 My & K 446 905
Millner's Estate, Re (1872) LR 14 Eq 245, 42 LJ Ch 44, 20 WR 823, 26 LT 825. 735
Mills v Drewitt (1855) 20 Beav 632, 1 Jur NS 816, 3 WR 626, 25 LTOS 293 930
Mills v IRC [1973] Ch 225, [1972] 3 All ER 977, [1972] 3 WLR 980, [1973] STC 1, 49 TC
    367, 51 ATC 263, [1972] TR 245, 116 Sol Jo 802, CA; revsd sub nom IRC v Mills [1975]
    AC 38, [1974] 1 All ER 722, [1974] 2 WLR 325, [1974] STC 130, 49 TC 367, 53 ATC 34,
    [1974] TR 39, 118 Sol Jo 205, HL 268, 269
Mills' Trusts, Re (1888) 40 Ch D 14, 37 WR 81, 60 LT 442, CA. 780
Milroy v Lord (1862) 4 De GF & J 264, 31 LJ Ch 798, 8 Jur NS 806, 135 RR 135, [1861-73] All
    ER Rep 783, 7 LT 178 . . . . . 146, 147, 149, 154, 166, 169, 173, 179, 180, 182, 233
Minchell's Will Trusts, Re [1964] 2 All ER 47 79
Ministry of Health v Simpson. See Diplock, Re, Diplock v Wintle
Minors v Battison (1876) 1 App Cas 428, 46 LJ Ch 2, 25 WR 27, 35 LT 1, HL 726
Mitchell v Homfray (1881) 8 QBD 587, 50 LJQB 460, 29 WR 558, 45 LT 694, CA. . . 283, 285
Mitchell v O'Brien [2002] All ER (D) 125 (Feb) 887
Mitchelson v Piper (1836) 8 Sim 64, Donnelly 89, 5 LJ Ch 294, 42 RR 104 . . . . 726, 727
Mitford v Reynolds (1842) 1 Ph 185, 12 LJ Ch 40, 7 Jur 3, [1835-42] All ER Rep 331 . . 225
Mitford v Reynolds (1848) 16 Sim 105, 17 LJ Ch 238, 12 Jur 197, 80 RR 27, [1843-60] All ER
    Rep 118, 10 LTOS 499 122
Moate v Moate [1948] 2 All ER 486, 92 Sol Jo 484. . . . . 362, 365
Modelboard Ltd v Outer Box Ltd [1993] BCLC 623, [1992] BCC 945 15
Moggridge v Thackwell (1792) 1 Ves 464, 3 Bro CC 517, [1775-1802] All ER Rep 218; on
    appeal (1803) 7 Ves 36; affd (1807) 13 Ves 416, [1803-13] All ER Rep 754, HL . . 77
Mohan v Roche [1991] 1 IR 560 . . . . 455, 778
Mollo v Mollo [1999] EGCS 117, [2000] WTLR 227 . . . . .415, 417, 418, 423, 425
Molton v Camroux (1848) 18 LJ Ex 68, 2 Exch 487, 12 Jur 800, 76 RR 669; affd (1849) 18 LJ
    Ex 356, 4 Exch 17, 80 RR 461, 13 LTOS 305 270
Molyneux v Fletcher [1898] 1 QB 648, 67 LJQB 392, 46 WR 576, 42 Sol Jo 254, 78 LT 111, 14
    TLR 211 . . . . 721, 947
Monck's (Lady) Will, Re, Monck v Croker [1900] 1 IR 56, Ir CA 374
Moncrieff's Settlement Trusts, Re [1962] 3 All ER 838n, [1962] 1 WLR 1344, 106 Sol Jo 878 506
Mond v Hyde [1999] QB 1097, [1998] 3 All ER 833, [1999] 2 WLR 499, [1998] 2 BCLC 340,
    [1998] 31 LS Gaz R 35, 142 Sol Jo LB 242, CA 491
Monolithic Building Co, Re, Tacon v Monolithic Building Co [1915] 1 Ch 643, 84 LJ Ch 441,
    21 Mans 380, [1914-15] All ER Rep 249, 59 Sol Jo 332, 112 LT 619, CA . . . 256, 411
Montagu's Settlement Trusts, Re, Duke of Manchester v National Westminster Bank Ltd
    [1987] Ch 264, [1992] 4 All ER 308, [1987] 2 WLR 1192, 131 Sol Jo 411, [1987] LS Gaz
    R 1057 . . . . 4, 407, 408, 873, 890, 933, 951, 960, 974, 975, 983, 989, 994
Montefiore v Browne (1858) 7 HL Cas 241, 4 Jur NS 1201 141
Montefiore v Guedalla [1903] 2 Ch 723, 73 LJ Ch 13, 52 WR 151, [1900-3] All ER Rep 384,
    47 Sol Jo 877, 89 LT 472 771
Montfort (Lord) v Lord Cadogan (1810) 13 RR 270, 17 Ves 485, [1803-13] All ER Rep 482;
    varied (1816) 2 Mer 3, 19 Ves 635, [1803-13] All ER Rep 482 . . . . 451, 931
Montreal Trust Co of Canada v Hickman [2001] NFCA 42 . . . . 951, 955
Monty Financial Services Ltd v Delmo [1996] 1 VR 65 767
Monypenny v Dering (1852) 2 De GM & G 145, 22 LJ Ch 313, 17 Jur 467, [1843-60] All ER
    Rep 1098, 19 LTOS 320 225
Moore, Re, McAlpine v Moore (1882) 21 Ch D 778, 30 WR 839 . . . . . 760, 764, 768
Moore, Re, Moore v Pope Benedict XV [1919] 1 IR 316, 53 ILT 217 105
Moore, Re, Prior v Moore [1901] 1 Ch 936, 70 LJ Ch 358, 49 WR 484, [1900-3] All ER Rep
    140, 84 LT 501, 17 TLR 356 . . . . 84, 120, 203
Moore, Re, Trafford v Maconochie (1888) 39 Ch D 116, 52 JP 596, 57 LJ Ch 936, 37 WR 83,
    [1886-90] All ER Rep 187, 59 LT 681, 4 TLR 591, CA 218
Moore v Darton (1851) 4 De G & Sm 517, 20 LJ Ch 626, 87 RR 464, [1843-60] All ER Rep
    814, 18 LTOS 24 73
Moore v M'Glynn [1894] 1 IR 74 24
Moore v M'Glynn [1904] 1 IR 334 824
Moore v Ulster Bank (1909) 43 ILTR 136 524
Moravian Society, Re (1858) 22 JP 527, 26 Beav 101, 4 Jur NS 703, 122 RR 45, 6 WR 851, 31
    LTOS 377 . . . . 744, 753

More v Mayhow (1663) 1 Cas in Ch 34, Freem Ch 175 983
More v More (1889) 37 WR 414, 60 LT 626 574
Morgan, Re, Brown v Jones [1927] WN 180, 71 Sol Jo 650 844
Morgan, Re, Pillgrem v Pillgrem (1881) 18 Ch D 93, 50 LJ Ch 834, 30 WR 223, 45 LT 183,
   CA 22, 382, 1000
Morgan v Gronow (1873) LR 16 Eq 1, 42 LJ Ch 410, 28 LT 434 198
Morgan v Swansea Urban Sanitary Authority (1878) 9 Ch D 582, 27 WR 283 58
Morice v Bishop of Durham (1804) 7 RR 232, 9 Ves 399, [1803-13] All ER Rep 451; on
   appeal (1805) 10 Ves 522 . . . . 82, 91, 105, 110, 122, 332
Moritz, Re, Midland Bank Executor and Trustee Co Ltd v Forbes [1960] Ch 251, [1959] 3
   All ER 767, [1959] 3 WLR 939, 103 Sol Jo 962 . . . . 816, 837, 838
Morland v Cook (1868) LR 6 Eq 252, 37 LJ Ch 825, 16 WR 777, 18 LT 496 991
Morley, Re, Morley v Haig [1895] 2 Ch 738, 64 LJ Ch 727, 13 R 680, 44 WR 140, 73 LT
   151 . . . . 552, 560, 569
Morley v Loughnan [1893] 1 Ch 736, 62 LJ Ch 515, 3 R 592, 68 LT 619, 9 TLR 214   273, 276
Morley v Rennoldson (1843) 2 Hare 570, 12 LJ Ch 372, 7 Jur 938, 62 RR 236, 1 LTOS
   12 . . . . 190, 221
Morris, Re (1889) 23 LR Ir 333 825
Morris, Re [2001] WTLR 1137 270
Morris v Livie (1842) 1 Y & C Ch Cas 380, 11 LJ Ch 172, 57 RR 391, [1835-42] All ER Rep 77   980
Morris v Morris (1858) 4 Jur NS 802, 111 RR 909 584
Morris v Morris [1982] 1 NSWLR 61 248
Morris v Morris (1993) 9 WAR 150 . . . . 677, 686
Morris v Whiting (1913) 26 WLR 494, 15 DLR 254, 2 Man R 56, 5 WWR 936 238
Morris' Settlement Trusts, Re, Adams v Napier [1951] 2 All ER 528, 95 Sol Jo 609,
   CA 211, 723, 803, 809
Morris's Will Trusts, Re, Public Trustee v Morris [1960] 3 All ER 548, [1960] 1 WLR 1210,
   104 Sol Jo 934 . . . . 537, 553, 562
Morrison, Re, Morrison v Morrison [1901] 1 Ch 701, 70 LJ Ch 399, 8 Mans 210, 49 WR 441,
   45 Sol Jo 344, 84 LT 383, 17 TLR 330 522
Mortgage Corpn Ltd v Shaire [2001] Ch 743, [2001] 4 All ER 364, [2001] 3 WLR 639, 80 P &
   CR 280, [2000] 2 FCR 222, [2000] 1 FLR 973, [2000] Fam Law 402, [2000] 3 EGLR
   131, [2000] 11 LS Gaz R 37, [2000] EGCS 35, [2000] BPIR 483 .421, 423, 480, 481, 482
Morton v Brighouse [1927] SCR 118, [1927] 1 DLR 1009 . . . . 161, 162
Morton v Tewart (1842) 2 Y & C Ch Cas 67, 60 RR 35 237
Moryoseph v Moryoseph [1920] 2 Ch 33, 89 LJ Ch 376, [1920] All ER Rep 216, 64 Sol Jo 497,
   123 LT 569 369
Mosley v Ward (1805) 8 RR 249, 11 Ves 581 869
Moss, Re, Hobrough v Harvey [1949] 1 All ER 495, 93 Sol Jo 164, 65 TLR 299 122
Moss v Cooper (1861) 1 John & H 352, 128 RR 410, 4 LT 790 . . . . 260, 263
Moss v Integro Trust (BVI) Ltd (1998) 1 OFLR 427 630
Moss's Trusts, Re (1888) 37 Ch D 513, 57 LJ Ch 423, 36 WR 316, 58 LT 468 762
Moss's Trusts, Re, Moss v Allen [1945] 1 All ER 207, 114 LJ Ch 152, 89 Sol Jo 69, 172 LT 196,
   61 TLR 147 102
Mossop v Mossop [1989] Fam 77, [1988] 2 All ER 202, [1988] 2 WLR 1255, [1988] 2 FLR
   173, [1988] Fam Law 334, 132 Sol Jo 1033, [1988] NLJR 86, CA 350, 362, 365
Motz v Moreau (1860) 13 Moo PCC 376, 8 WR 395, PC 285
Mount Edgcumbe (Earl), Re [1950] Ch 615, [1950] 2 All ER 242, 94 Sol Jo 369, 66 (pt 1)
   TLR 1174 527
Mountain v Styak [1922] NZLR 131 . . . . 237, 255
Mountford v Scott [1975] Ch 258, [1974] 1 All ER 248, [1973] 3 WLR 884, 26 P & CR 497,
   117 Sol Jo 584, 230 Estates Gazette 974; affd [1975] Ch 258, [1975] 1 All ER 198,
   [1975] 2 WLR 114, 29 P & CR 401, 118 Sol Jo 755, 234 Estates Gazette 819, CA . . 166
Mountgarret, Re, Mountgarret v Ingilby [1919] 2 Ch 294, 88 LJ Ch 405, 68 Sol Jo 626, 121
   LT 414, 35 TLR 585 301
Mousley v Carr (1841) 4 Beav 49, 10 LJ Ch 260, 55 RR 13 557
Movitex Ltd v Bulfield [1988] BCLC 104, 2 BCC 99, 403 . . . . 393, 661
Moxham v Grant [1900] 1 QB 88, 69 LJQB 97, 7 Mans 65, 48 WR 130, 44 Sol Jo 58, 81 LT
   431, 16 TLR 34, CA 944
Moxon, Re [1916] 2 Ch 595, 86 LJ Ch 33, [1916-17] All ER Rep 438, 61 Sol Jo 42, 115 LT 673   795
Moxon's Will Trusts, Re, Downey v Moxon [1958] 1 All ER 386, [1958] 1 WLR 165, 102 Sol
   Jo 124. . . . . 719, 720
Moyle v Moyle (1831) 2 Russ & M 710, 34 RR 186 . . . . 493, 586

Muckleston v Brown (1801) 6 Ves 52. 348
Mucklow v Fuller (1821) Jac 198, 23 RR 186 . . . . 452, 938
Muffett, Re, Jones v Mason (1888) 39 Ch D 534, 57 LJ Ch 1017, 37 WR 9, 59 LT 499, 4 TLR
    738. 565
Muggeridge v Stanton (1859) 1 De GF & J 107 350
Muir v City of Glasgow Bank (1879) 4 App Cas 337, 27 WR 603, [1874-80] All ER Rep 1017,
    40 LT 339, HL 812
Muir v IRC [1966] 3 All ER 38, [1966] 1 WLR 1269, 43 TC 367, 45 ATC 185, [1966] TR 165,
    110 Sol Jo 448, CA 84, 98, 132
Muir (or Williams) v Muir [1943] AC 468, 112 LJPC 39, 1943 SC (HL) 47, 1944 SLT 67 . 807
Muirhead, Re, Muirhead v Hill [1916] 2 Ch 181, 85 LJ Ch 598, [1916-17] All ER Rep 771,
    115 LT 65 541
Mulholland's Will Trusts, Re, Bryan v Westminster Bank Ltd [1949] 1 All ER 460, [1949] LJR
    1078, 93 Sol Jo 148. . . . . 660, 668
Muller, Re, Cassin v Mutual Cash Order Co Ltd [1953] NZLR 879 367
Mulligan, Re, Hampton v PGG Trust Ltd and Corbett [1998] 1 NZLR 481 . . 531, 599, 613,
                                                              618, 692, 864, 916, 946
Munch v Cockerell (1840) 5 My & Cr 178, 9 LJ Ch 153, 4 Jur 140, 48 RR 270 645
Munton, Re, Munton v West [1927] 1 Ch 262, 96 LJ Ch 151, 136 LT 661, CA . 647, 877, 939
Murphy's Settlements, Re, Murphy v Murphy [1998] 3 All ER 1, [1999] 1 WLR 282 . .28, 116,
                                                              593, 624, 673, 674
Murphy's Trusts, Re [1900] 1 IR 145. 688
Murray, Re, Martins Bank Ltd v Dill [1955] Ch 69, [1954] 3 All ER 129, [1954] 3 WLR 521,
    98 Sol Jo 716, CA 104
Murray v IRC (1926) 11 TC 133, 5 ATC 607, 1926 SLT 714 818
Muschinski v Dodds (1985) 160 CLR 583, 62 ALR 429, 60 ALJR 52, HC of A . . .34, 35, 56,
                                                              57, 275, 326
Musgrave, Re, Machell v Parry [1916] 2 Ch 417, 85 LJ Ch 639, 60 Sol Jo 694, 115 LT
    149. . . . . 948, 981, 982
Mussoorie Bank Ltd v Raynor (1882) 7 App Cas 321, 51 LJPC 72, 31 WR 17, 46 LT
    632. . . . . 74, 77, 79, 133
Mutton v Peat [1900] 2 Ch 79, 69 LJ Ch 484, 48 WR 486, 44 Sol Jo 427, 82 LT 440, CA . 986
Mutual Life and Citizens' Assurance Co Ltd v Evatt [1971] AC 793, [1971] 1 All ER 150,
    [1971] 2 WLR 23, [1970] 2 Lloyd's Rep 441, 114 Sol Jo 932, [1971] ALR 235, PC . 493
Mutual Life Assurance Society v Langley (1886) 32 Ch D 460, 54 LT 326, CA 1002

N

N's (Mr & Mrs) 1989 Settlement (1998/99) 1 ITELR 803 512
Naas v Westminster Bank Ltd. See Westminster Bank Ltd v Wilson
Nail v Punter (1832) 5 Sim 555, 35 RR 188, 58 ER 447 . . . . 931, 932
Nanney v Williams (1856) 22 Beav 452, 111 RR 435 283
Nant-y-glo and Blaina Ironworks Co v Grave (1878) 12 Ch D 738, 26 WR 504, 38 LT
    345. . . . . .854, 862, 872, 874
Nanus Asia Inc v Standard Chartered Bank [1990] HKLR 396 . . . . .24, 399
Napier v Light (1974) 119 Sol Jo 166, 236 Estates Gazette 273, CA 736
Napier and Ettrick (Lord) v RF Kershaw Ltd [1993] AC 713, [1993] 1 All ER 385, [1993] 2
    WLR 42, [1993] 1 Lloyd's Rep 197, [1993] 9 LS Gaz R 43, 137 Sol Jo LB 44,
    HL 443, 899
Nash, Re (1881) 16 Ch D 503, 29 WR 294, 44 LT 40. 782
Nash, Re, Miller v Allen [1965] 1 All ER 51, [1965] 1 WLR 221, 109 Sol Jo 94 . . . 207, 713
Nash v Allen (1889) 42 Ch D 54, 58 LJ Ch 754, 37 WR 646, 61 LT 193. 305
Nash's Settlement, Re (1882) 51 LJ Ch 511, 30 WR 406, 46 LT 97 193
Nathan, Re [2002] WTLR 1061 217
National Anti-Vivisection Society v IRC [1948] AC 31, [1947] 2 All ER 217, 26 ATC 309, 41 R
    & IT 99, [1947] LJR 1112, 177 LT 226, 63 TLR 424, 311, L(TC) 1432, sub nom IRC v
    National Anti-Vivisection Society 28 TC 311, HL 122, 908
National Anti-Vivisection Society Ltd v Duddington (1989) Times, 23 November 844
National Carriers Ltd v Panalpina (Northern) Ltd [1981] AC 675, [1981] 1 All ER 161,
    [1981] 2 WLR 45, 43 P & CR 72, 125 Sol Jo 46, HL 442
National Financial Co, Re, ex p Oriental Commercial Bank (1868) 3 Ch App 791, 16 WR
    994, 18 LT 895 813
National Grid Co plc v Mayes [2001] UKHL 20, [2001] 2 All ER 417, [2001] 1 WLR 864,
    [2001] ICR 544, [2001] IRLR 394, [2001] NLJR 572, 145 Sol Jo LB 98 499

National Provincial Bank Ltd v Ainsworth [1965] AC 1175, [1965] 2 All ER 472, [1965] 3
WLR 1, 109 Sol Jo 415, HL 50, 253
National Shawmut Bank v Cumming 325 Mass 457, 91 NE 2d 337 (1950) 1036
National Trust Co Ltd v Osadchuk [1943] SCR 89. 666
National Trustees Co of Australasia v General Finance Co of Australasia [1905] AC 373, 74
LJPC 73, 54 WR 1, 92 LT 736, 21 TLR 522 . . . 577, 626, 913, 914, 915, 919, 920, 935
National Trustees Executors & Agency Co v Tuck [1967] VR 847 735
National Westminster Bank Ltd v Barclays Bank International Ltd [1975] QB 654, [1974] 3
All ER 834, [1975] 2 WLR 12, [1974] 2 Lloyd's Rep 506, 118 Sol Jo 627 971
National Westminster Bank plc v Morgan [1985] AC 686, [1985] 1 All ER 821, [1985] 2 WLR
588, [1985] FLR 266, 17 HLR 360, 129 Sol Jo 205, [1985] LS Gaz R 1485, [1985] NLJ
Rep 254, HL 281
Nationwide Building Society v Various Solicitors (No 3) [1999] EGCS 15, [1999] PNLR 606,
Times, 1 March 856, 866
Neale v Davies (1854) 5 De GM & G 258, 23 LJ Ch 744, 2 Eq Rep 530, 2 WR 358 . . . 649
Neazor v Hoyle (1962) 32 DLR (2d) 131, 37 WWR 104 368
Needham, Re (1844) 6 I Eq R 537, 1 Jo & Lat 34 . . . . 452, 453
Neeld, Re, Carpenter v Inigo-Jones [1962] Ch 643, [1962] 2 All ER 335, [1962] 2 WLR 1097,
106 Sol Jo 449, CA. 18, 103, 104, 220
Neeld, Re, Inigo-Jones v Inigo-Jones (No 3) [1969] 2 All ER 1025, [1969] 1 WLR 988, 113
Sol Jo 527 104
Neil, Re, Hemming v Neil (1890) 62 LT 649 . . . . 213, 629
Neill v Neill [1904] 1 IR 513 524
Nelson, Re, Nelson v Nelson (1947) 91 Sol Jo 533. 160
Nelson, Re, Norris v Nelson [1928] Ch 920n, 97 LJ Ch 443n, 140 LT 371n, CA 730
Nelson (Earl) v Lord Bridport (1846) 8 Beav 547, 10 Jur 1043, 68 RR 174, 9 LTOS
471. . . . . 183, 188, 1027
Nelson v Nelson (1995) 184 CLR 538, 132 ALR 133, 70 ALJR 47 . . . . . . 350, 362, 365
Nelson v Rye [1996] 2 All ER 186, [1996] 1 WLR 1378, [1996] FSR 313, [1996] EMLR
37 . . . . 928, 930, 935
Neo v Neo (1875) LR 6 PC 382 . . . . 94, 121
Nesbitt, Re (1887) 19 LR Ir 509. 762
Neste Oy v Lloyds Bank plc, The Tiiskeri, Nestegas and Ensken [1983] 2 Lloyd's Rep 658,
[1983] Com LR 185, 133 NLJ 597 437
Nestle v National Westminster Bank plc [2000] WTLR 795; affd [1994] 1 All ER 118, [1993]
1 WLR 1260, CA. 396, 491, 529, 531, 549, 576, 579, 590, 595
599, 603, 610, 611, 613, 614, 615, 616, 617,
618, 689, 692, 703, 862, 863, 864, 867
Nettlefold's Trusts, Re (1888) 59 LT 315 . . . . 688, 728
Neville v Fortescue (1848) 16 Sim 333, 12 Jur 908. 552
Neville v Matthewman [1894] 3 Ch 345, 63 LJ Ch 734, 7 R 511, 42 WR 675, 38 Sol Jo 694, 71
LT 282, CA. 903, 906
Neville v Wilson [1997] Ch 144, [1996] 3 All ER 171, [1996] 3 WLR 460, [1996] 2 BCLC 310,
CA 235, 520
Neville Estates Ltd v Madden [1962] Ch 832, [1961] 3 All ER 769, [1961] 3 WLR 999, 105
Sol Jo 806 128
Neale v Davies (1854) 5 De GM & G 258, 23 LJ Ch 744, 2 Eq Rep 530, 2 WR 358 . . . 648
New, Re, Re Leavers, Re Morley [1901] 2 Ch 534, [1900-03] All ER Rep 763, sub nom Re
New's Settlement, Langham v Langham, Re Leavers, Leavers v Hall, Re Morley, Fraser v
Leavers 70 LJ Ch 710, 50 WR 17, 45 Sol Jo 706, 85 LT 174, CA. . . . 37, 523, 524, 529
New, Prance and Garrard's Trustee v Hunting [1897] 2 QB 19, 66 LJQB 554, 4 Mans 103, 45
WR 577, 41 Sol Jo 511, 76 LT 742, 13 TLR 397, CA; affd sub nom Sharp v Jackson
[1899] AC 419, 68 LJQB 866, 6 Mans 264, [1895-9] All ER Rep 755, 80 LT 841, 15 TLR
418, HL. 142, 147
New York Life Insurance Co v Public Trustee [1924] 2 Ch 101, 93 LJ Ch 449, 68 Sol Jo 477,
131 LT 438, 40 TLR 430, CA 1029
New Zealand Insurance Co Ltd v Probate Duties Comr [1973] VR 659 52
New Zealand Netherlands Society Oranje Inc v Kuys [1973] 2 All ER 1222, [1973] 1 WLR
1126, [1974] RPC 272, 117 Sol Jo 565, [1973] 2 NZLR 163, PC. . 21, 393, 399, 401, 405
Newbould, Re, Carter v Newbould (1913) 110 LT 6, CA 377
Newen, Re, Newen v Barnes [1894] 2 Ch 297, 58 JP 767, 63 LJ Ch 863, 8 R 309, 43 WR 58, 70
LT 653 . . . . 762, 771
Newey, Re [1994] 2 NZLR 590 . . . . 428, 429

Newham v Newham (1822) 1 LJOS 23, 25 RR 272 934
Newlon Housing Trust v Alsulaimen [1999] 1 AC 313, [1998] 4 All ER 1, [1998] 3 WLR 451,
    [1998] 3 FCR 183, [1998] 2 FLR 690, [1998] Fam Law 589, 30 HLR 1132, [1998] NLJR
    1303, 142 Sol Jo LB 247, HL 246, 296, 582
Newman v Newman (1885) 28 Ch D 674, 54 LJ Ch 598, 33 WR 505, 52 LT 422, 1 TLR
    211 . . . . 660, 671
Newman v Real Estate Debenture Corpn Ltd and Flower Decorations Ltd [1940] 1 All ER
    131, 162 LT 183 990
News International plc v Clinger (17 November 1998, unreported) 958
Newsome v Flowers (1861) 26 JP 100, 30 Beav 461, 31 LJ Ch 29, 7 Jur NS 1268, 10 WR 26, 5
    LT 570 . . . . 648, 649
Newton v Askew (1848) 11 Beav 145, 12 Jur 531, 12 LTOS 2 . . . . 149, 671, 677
Newton v Newton (1868) 4 Ch App 143, 38 LJ Ch 145, 17 WR 238 . . . . . . 1000, 1001
Ng (a bankrupt), Re, Ng v Ng (trustee) [1998] 2 FLR 386, [1998] Fam Law 515, [1997] BCC
    507, [1997] BPIR 267 480
Nicholson, Re, Eade v Nicholson [1909] 2 Ch 111, 78 LJ Ch 516, [1908-10] All ER Rep 669,
    100 LT 877 . . . . 550, 555
Nicholson, Re, Nicholson v Perks [1974] 2 All ER 386, [1974] 1 WLR 476, 118 Sol Jo
    133 352
Nicholson v Field [1893] 2 Ch 511, 62 LJ Ch 1015, 3 R 528, 42 WR 48, 69 LT 299 . 756, 759
Nicholson v Tutin (1855) 2 K & J 18, 1 Jur NS 1201, 110 RR 84 142
Nicholson's Will Trusts, Re, Ortmans v Burke [1936] 3 All ER 832 543
Nickels, Re, Nickels v Nickels [1898] 1 Ch 630, 67 LJ Ch 406, 46 WR 422, [1895-9] All ER
    Rep 783, 42 Sol Jo 414, 78 LT 379 544
Nicloson v Wordsworth (1818) 19 RR 86, 2 Swan 365 450
Niell v Morley (1804) 9 Ves 478 270
Nightingale v Lawson (1785) 1 Cox Eq Cas 181, 1 Bro CC 440 564
Nightingale Mayfair Ltd v Mehta [2000] WTLR 901, [1999] All ER (D) 1501 353
Nikko Hotels (UK) Ltd v MEPC plc [1991] 2 EGLR 103, [1991] 28 EG 86 89
Nimmo v Westpac Banking Corpn [1993] 3 NZLR 218 253
Niru Battery Manufacturing Co v Milestone Trading Ltd [2002] EWHC 1425 (Comm),
    [2002] 2 All ER (Comm) 705 979
Nisbet v Shepherd [1994] 1 BCLC 300, [1994] BCC 91, CA 151
Nisbet and Potts' Contract, Re [1905] 1 Ch 391, 74 LJ Ch 310, 53 WR 297, 92 LT 448, 21
    TLR 261; affd [1906] 1 Ch 386, 75 LJ Ch 238, [1904-07] All ER Rep 865, 50 Sol Jo 191,
    22 TLR 233, sub nom Re Nesbitt and Potts' Contract 54 WR 286, 94 LT 297, CA . . 983
Nissen v Grunden (1912) 14 CLR 297, 18 ALR 254 (Aust HC) 766
Nives v Nives (1880) 15 Ch D 649, 49 LJ Ch 674, 29 WR 302, 42 LT 832, [1874-80] All ER Rep
    Ext 1438 439
Nixon, Re, Gray v Bell [1904] 1 Ch 638, 73 LJ Ch 446, 48 Sol Jo 396 813
Noad v Backhouse (1843) 2 Y & C Ch Cas 529, sub nom Node v Backhouse 12 LJ Ch 446, 7
    Jur 808 903
Nocton v Lord Ashburton [1914] AC 932, 83 LJ Ch 784, [1914-15] All ER Rep 45, 111 LT
    641, HL 22, 24, 659, 858, 866, 934
Norberg v Wynrib (1992) 92 DLR (4th) 449, Can SC 897
Norfolk's (Duke) Case (1678) 1 Vern 164, 3 Ch Cas 1 189
Norfolk's (Duke) Settlement Trusts, Re, Earl of Perth v Fitzalan-Howard [1982] Ch 61,
    [1981] 3 All ER 220, [1981] 3 WLR 455, 125 Sol Jo 554, CA 597, 659
Norman v Federal Comr of Taxation (1963) 109 CLR 9, [1964] ALR 131, HC of
    A 151, 155, 184
Norman v Kynaston (1861) 3 De GF & J 29, 30 LJ Ch 189, 7 Jur NS 129, 9 WR 259, 3 LT
    826 375
Norris, Re, Allen v Norris (1884) 27 Ch D 333, 53 LJ Ch 913, 32 WR 955, 51 LT 593 . . 753,
    771
Norris v Wright (1851) 14 Beav 291 581
North, Re, Garton v Cumberland [1909] 1 Ch 625, 78 LJ Ch 344 . . . . 551, 553
North, Re, North v Cusden [1952] Ch 397, [1952] 1 All ER 609, 96 Sol Jo 181, [1952] 1 TLR
    674 35
North v Crompton (1671) 1 Cas in Ch 196 330
North and South Trust Co v Berkeley [1971] 1 All ER 980, [1971] 1 WLR 470, [1970] 2
    Lloyd's Rep 467, 115 Sol Jo 244 . . . . 23, 403
North Devon and West Somerset Relief Fund Trusts, Re, Baron Hylton v Wright [1953] 2 All
    ER 1032, [1953] 1 WLR 1260, 97 Sol Jo 728 341

North Ocean Shipping Co Ltd v Hyundai Construction Co Ltd, The Atlantic Baron [1979]
  QB 705, [1978] 3 All ER 1170, [1979] 3 WLR 419, [1979] 1 Lloyd's Rep 89, 123 Sol Jo
  352. 274
North-West Transportation Co Ltd and Beatty v Beatty (1887) 12 App Cas 589, 56 LJPC 102,
  36 WR 647, 57 LT 426, 3 TLR 789, PC 21
Northage, Re, Ellis v Barfield [1891] WN 84, 60 LJ Ch 488, 64 LT 625, 7 TLR 464 . 535, 536
Northcliffe, Re, Arnholz v Hudson [1925] Ch 651, 95 LJ Ch 41, 133 LT 466. 264
Northcliffe's Settlements, Re [1937] 3 All ER 804, 81 Sol Jo 716, CA. 772
Northcote's Will Trusts, Re, Northcote v Northcote [1949] 1 All ER 442, [1949] WN
  69 . . . . 386, 651
Northern Counties of England Fire Insurance Co v Whipp (1884) 26 Ch D 482, 53 LJ Ch
  629, 32 WR 626, [1881-5] All ER Rep 51, 51 LT 806, CA 1001
Northern Developments (Holdings) Ltd, Re (6 October 1978, unreported) . . 112, 113, 116
Northland Bank v Wilson (1999) 249 AR 201. 958
Northumberland (Duke), Re, Halifax v Northumberland [1951] Ch 202, [1950] 2 All ER
  1181, 94 Sol Jo 805, 66 (pt 2) TLR 1045 573
Norton, Re, Wyatt v Bain [1949] WN 23, CA 374
Norton v Johnstone (1885) 30 Ch D 649, 55 LJ Ch 222, 34 WR 13 . . . . 563, 567
Norton v Pritchard (1845) 5 LTOS 2 589
Norton's Will Trusts, Re, Lightfoot v Goldson [1948] 2 All ER 842, 92 Sol Jo 634, sub nom
  Re Norton, Lightfoot v Blo Norton Parochial Church Council [1949] LJR 53, 64 TLR
  582. 106
Norway v Norway (1834) 2 My & K 278, 3 LJ Ch 111, 39 RR 211 . . . . 449, 450
Norwich Pharmacal Co v Customs and Excise Comrs [1974] AC 133, [1973] 2 All ER 943,
  [1973] 3 WLR 164, [1973] FSR 365, [1974] RPC 101, 117 Sol Jo 567, HL. 904
Norwich Union Fire Insurance Society Ltd v Central Auto Salvage (London) Ltd (30 July
  1993, unreported), CA 957
Nottage, Re, Jones v Palmer [1895] 2 Ch 649, 64 LJ Ch 695, 12 R 571, 44 WR 22, [1895-9] All
  ER Rep 1203, 39 Sol Jo 655, 73 LT 269, 11 TLR 519, CA 114, 202
Notting Hill Housing Trust v Brackley [2001] EWCA Civ 601, [2002] HLR 10, [2001] 35 EG
  106, [2001] 18 EG 175 (CS), 82 P & CR D48, [2001] L & TR 34 . . . . . . 476, 582
Nugent v Nugent [1908] 1 Ch 546, 77 LJ Ch 271, 52 Sol Jo 262, 98 LT 354, 24 TLR 296, CA 22
Nunburnholme (Lord), Re, Wilson v Nunburnholme [1911] 2 Ch 510, 81 LJ Ch 85, 56 Sol
  Jo 34, 105 LT 666; revsd [1912] 1 Ch 489, 81 LJ Ch 347, 56 Sol Jo 343, 106 LT 361,
  CA 730, 732
Nunneley v Nunneley and Marrian (1890) 15 PD 186, 39 WR 190, 63 LT 113 1044
Nutter v Holland [1894] 3 Ch 408, 63 LJ Ch 932, 7 R 491, 43 WR 18, 38 Sol Jo 707, 71 LT
  508, CA 833, 906

O

O-D Bank v Bankrupt Estate of WKR (1999) ZR 98 No 52 pp 225 et seq discussed [2000]
  JTCP 141-148 59
Oatway, Re, Hertslet v Oatway [1903] 2 Ch 356, 72 LJ Ch 575, 88 LT 622. . . . . 880, 886,
  887, 889
O'Connell, Re, Mawle v Jagoe [1903] 2 Ch 574, 72 LJ Ch 709, 52 WR 102, 89 LT 166 . . 308
O'Connor v Tanner [1917] AC 25, [1917] 1 IR 56, 51 ILT 25, HL 369
Octans Investments Pty Ltd v Knight (1979) 144 CLR 360. . . . . 811, 820, 826
Oddy, Re [1911] 1 Ch 532, 80 LJ Ch 404, [1911-13] All ER Rep 744, 55 Sol Jo 348, 104 LT
  338, 27 TLR 312. . . . . 802, 832
Official Receiver in Bankruptcy v Schultz (1990) 170 CLR 306 18
Ogden, Re, Brydon v Samuel [1933] Ch 678, 102 LJ Ch 226, [1933] All ER Rep 720, 77 Sol
  Jo 216, 149 LT 162, 49 TLR 341. . . . . 125, 132
Ogilvie, Re, Ogilvie v Ogilvie [1919] WN 32, 88 LJ Ch 159, 63 Sol Jo 246, 120 LT 436, 35 TLR
  218. 535
Ogilvie v Ryan [1976] 2 NSWLR 504 419
Ojjeh Trust, Re (1992-3) CILR 348 686
O'Keefe, Re, Poingdestre v Sherman [1940] Ch 124, [1940] 1 All ER 216, 109 LJ Ch 86, 84
  Sol Jo 44, 162 LT 62, 56 TLR 204 1028
Oldfield, Re, Oldfield v Oldfield [1904] 1 Ch 549, 73 LJ Ch 433, 48 Sol Jo 298, 90 LT 392,
  CA 73, 134
Oldham, Re, Hadwen v Myles [1925] Ch 75, 95 LJ Ch 148, [1924] All ER Rep 288, 69 Sol Jo
  193, 132 LT 658. . . . . 427, 429
Oldham, Re, Oldham v Myles [1927] WN 113, 71 Sol Jo 491. 565

Oliver, Re, Newbald v Beckitt (1890) 62 LT 533 . . . . 34, 35, 137
Oliver, Re, Theobald v Oliver [1927] 2 Ch 323, 96 LJ Ch 496, 71 Sol Jo 710, 137 LT 788   928
Oliver, Re, Watkins v Fitton [1947] 2 All ER 162, [1947] LJR 1400, 91 Sol Jo 421, 177 LT 308   712
Oliver, Re, Wilson v Oliver [1908] 2 Ch 74, 77 LJ Ch 547, 99 LT 241 552
Oliver v Court (1820) Dan 301, 8 Price 127, [1814-23] All ER Rep 645 581
Oliver v Hinton [1899] 2 Ch 264, 68 LJ Ch 583, 48 WR 3, 43 Sol Jo 622, 81 LT 212, 15 TLR
    450, CA 1001
Oliver v Hunting (1890) 44 Ch D 205, 59 LJ Ch 255, 38 WR 618, 62 LT 108 237
Olsson v Dyson (1969) 120 CLR 365, 43 ALJR 77 152
Omar Family Trust [2000] WTLR 713 . . . . 31, 116, 835, 844
Onslow v Wallis (1849) 9 LJ Ch 27, 1 H & Tw 513, 13 Jur 1085, 1 Mac & G 506, 16 LTOS 1   238
Ontario Securities Commission and Greymac Credit Corpn, Re (1986) 55 OR (2d) 673, 30
    DLR (4th) 1; affd (1988) 52 DLR (4th) 767n, Ont CA 881, 892, 894
Ontario Treasurer v Blonde [1947] AC 24, [1947] LJR 410, 62 TLR 637, PC 1029
Oppenheim's Will Trusts, Re, Westminster Bank Ltd v Oppenheim [1950] Ch 633, [1950] 2
    All ER 86, 66 (pt 1) TLR 1040 212
Oppenheimer, Re, Oppenheimer v Boatman [1907] 1 Ch 399, 76 LJ Ch 287, 14 Mans 139,
    96 LT 631, [1904-7] All ER Rep Ext 1172 541
Oppenheimer v Cattermole [1976] AC 249, [1975] 1 All ER 538, [1975] 2 WLR 347, [1975]
    STC 91, [1975] TR 13, HL 1050
Orakpo v Manson Investments Ltd [1978] AC 95, [1977] 3 All ER 1, [1977] 3 WLR 229, 35 P
    & CR 1, 121 Sol Jo 632, HL 895
Oram, Re, Oram v Oram [1940] Ch 1001, [1940] 4 All ER 161, 109 LJ Ch 427, 84 Sol Jo 549,
    164 LT 264 . . . . 530, 547
Ord v Noel (1820) 5 Madd 438 581
Ord v White (1840) 3 Beav 357 983
O'Reilly v Alderson (1849) 8 Hare 101, 85 RR 233 770
Orme, Re, Evans v Maxwell (1883) 50 LT 51 364
O'Rorke v Bolingbroke (1877) 2 App Cas 814, 26 WR 239, HL 277
O'Rourke (Inspector of Taxes) v Binks [1992] STC 703, 65 TC 165, [1992] 32 LS Gaz R 38,
    CA 91
O'Rourke v Darbishire [1920] AC 581, 89 LJ Ch 162, [1920] All ER Rep 1, 64 Sol Jo 322, 123
    LT 68, 36 TLR 350, HL 677
Orr v Ford (1989) 167 CLR 316, 84 ALR 146, 63 ALJR 198, HC of A 934
Orr v Newton (1791) 2 Cox Eq Cas 274, PC 584
Orrett v Corser (1855) 21 Beav 52, 1 Jur NS 882, 3 WR 604, 25 LTOS 278 . . 580, 949, 981
Orwell's Will Trusts, Re, Dixon v Blair [1982] 3 All ER 177, [1982] 1 WLR 1337, 126 Sol Jo
    593 652
Orwin v A-G [1998] FSR 415, [1998] 2 BCLC 693, CA 782
Osiris Trustees Ltd, Re [2000] WTLR 933, 2 ITELR 404 . . . . 30, 32, 754
Osmond v Fitzroy (1731) 3 P Wms 129 274
Osmund, Re, Midland Bank Executor and Trustee Co Ltd v Mason [1944] Ch 66, [1944] 1
    All ER 12, 87 Sol Jo 447, 60 TLR 95; revsd sub nom Osmund, Re, Midland Bank
    Executor and Trustee Co Ltd v A-G [1944] Ch 206, [1944] 1 All ER 262, 113 LJ Ch 141,
    88 Sol Jo 111, 170 LT 156, 60 TLR 222, CA 332
Osoba, Re, Osoba v Osoba [1979] 2 All ER 393, [1979] 1 WLR 247, 123 Sol Jo 35,
    CA 83, 113, 133, 335, 336
O'Sullivan v Management Agency and Music Ltd [1985] QB 428, [1985] 3 All ER 351,
    [1984] 3 WLR 448, 128 Sol Jo 548, CA . 24, 286, 402, 405, 436, 657, 859, 860, 869, 871
Ottaway v Norman [1972] Ch 698, [1971] 3 All ER 1325, [1972] 2 WLR 50, 116 Sol Jo 38,
    220 Estates Gazette 1434 . . . . 81, 259, 260, 262, 266
Ottley v Gilby (1845) 8 Beav 602, 14 LJ Ch 177, 68 RR 218, 4 LTOS 411 . . . 672, 678, 687
Otway v Gibbs [2001] WTLR 467 . . . . 76, 146
Oughtred v IRC [1958] Ch 383, [1958] 1 All ER 252, [1958] 2 WLR 174, 36 ATC 291, [1957]
    TR 289, 102 Sol Jo 85; revsd [1958] Ch 678, [1958] 2 All ER 443, [1958] 3 WLR 64, 102
    Sol Jo 468, sub nom IRC v Oughtred 37 ATC 148, [1958] TR 177, CA; on appeal sub
    nom Oughtred v IRC [1960] AC 206, [1959] 3 All ER 623, [1959] 3 WLR 898, 38 ATC
    317, [1959] TR 319, 103 Sol Jo 896, HL 235, 240, 439, 520
Outen's Will Trusts, Re, Starling v Outen [1963] Ch 291, [1962] 3 All ER 478, [1962] 3 WLR
    1084, 106 Sol Jo 630 536
Overton v Banister (1844) 3 Hare 503, 8 Jur 906, 64 RR 386 . . . . 931, 935
Ovey v Ovey [1900] 2 Ch 524, sub nom Re Ovey, Ovey v Ovey 69 LJ Ch 804, 49 WR 45, 83 LT
    311 600

Owen, Re, Owen v IRC [1949] 1 All ER 901, [1949] TR 189, [1949] LJR 1128, 93 Sol Jo 287 151
Owen, Re, Slater v Owen [1912] 1 Ch 519, 81 LJ Ch 337, 56 Sol Jo 381, 106 LT
   671. . . . . .554, 559, 564, 568, 570
Owen v Delamere (1872) LR 15 Eq 134, 42 LJ Ch 232, 21 WR 218, 27 LT 647 . . . 457, 825
Owen v Williams (1773) Amb 734, 1 Bro CC 199n. 386
Owens v Greene [1932] IR 225 359
Owens Corning Fiberglas (UK) Pension Plan Ltd, Re [2002] PLR 323, [2002] All ER (D)
   191 (Jun), Times, 8 July 579, 708
Owers, Re, Public Trustee v Death [1941] Ch 389, [1941] 2 All ER 589, 110 LJ Ch 157, 85 Sol
   Jo 341, 165 LT 94 813
Owners of Cargo lately laden on board ship or vessel Eleftheria v The Eleftheria (Owners),
   The Eleftheria [1970] P 94, [1969] 2 All ER 641, [1969] 2 WLR 1073, [1969] 1 Lloyd's
   Rep 237, 113 Sol Jo 407 1059
Oxley, Re, John Hornby & Sons v Oxley [1914] 1 Ch 604, 83 LJ Ch 442, 58 Sol Jo 319, 110
   LT 626, 30 TLR 327, CA 814

P

P v P [1978] 3 All ER 70, [1978] 1 WLR 483, 122 Sol Jo 230, CA 427
Paddon v Richardson (1855) 7 De GM & G 563, 3 Eq Rep 933, 1 Jur NS 1192, 109 RR 230, 26
   LTOS 33 . . . . 449, 584
Pagarani, Re (1998/99) 2 OFLR 1. 161
Page, Re, Jones v Morgan [1893] 1 Ch 304, 62 LJ Ch 592, 3 R 171, 41 WR 357. . . 672, 677
Page v Cox (1852) 10 Hare 163, 90 RR 314 73
Pagels v MacDonald (1936) 54 CLR 519 18
Paget, Re, Mellor v Mellor [1898] 1 Ch 290, 67 LJ Ch 151, 46 WR 328, 78 LT 72 . . . 805
Paget's Settlement, Re, Baillie v De Brossard [1965] 1 All ER 58, [1965] 1 WLR 1046, 109 Sol
   Jo 577. . . . . 521, 1044
Pain, Re, Gustavson v Haviland [1919] 1 Ch 38, 87 LJ Ch 550, 63 Sol Jo 178, 119 LT 647   980
Paine v Countess of Warwick [1914] 2 KB 486, sub nom White v Paine 83 LJKB 895, 58 Sol Jo
   381, 30 TLR 347. 182
Paine v Meller (1801) 6 Ves 349, [1775-1802] All ER Rep 155 443
Paine's Trusts, Re (1885) 28 Ch D 725, 54 LJ Ch 735, 33 WR 564, 52 LT 323 771
Palairet v Carew (1863) 32 Beav 564, 32 LJ Ch 508, 9 Jur NS 426, 11 WR 449, 8 LT
   139. . . . . 589, 743
Palette Shoes Pty Ltd v Krohn (1937) 58 CLR 1. . . . . 42, 76, 139, 168, 184, 185, 438
Palk, Re, Re Drake, Chamberlain v Drake (1892) 41 WR 28, 36 Sol Jo 626 942
Pallant v Morgan [1953] Ch 43, [1952] 2 All ER 951, [1952] 2 TLR 813 . . . .80, 255, 412,
                                                                                423, 924
Palmer, Re, Lancashire and Yorkshire Reversionary Interest Co v Burke [1907] 1 Ch 486, 76
   LJ Ch 406, 96 LT 816. . . . . 629, 630, 828
Palmer v Bank of New South Wales (1975) 113 CLR 150, ALJR 320 . . . . .82, 140
Palmer v Locke (1880) 15 Ch D 294, 50 LJ Ch 113, 28 WR 926, 43 LT 454, CA . . . 29, 32
Palmer v Simmonds (1854) 2 Drew 221, 100 RR 98, 2 WR 313 . . . . 79, 134
Palmer v Young (1684) 1 Eq Cas Abr 380, 1 Vern 276 385
Papillon v Voice (1728) 1 Eq Cas Abr 185, Kel W 27, 2 P Wms 471, Fitz-G 38; affd (1728) Kel
   W 34, 2 P Wms 478 . . . . 66, 301
Paradise Motor Co Ltd, Re [1968] 2 All ER 625, [1968] 1 WLR 1125, 112 Sol Jo 271,
   CA 151, 245, 350, 367, 450
Paragon Finance plc v Staunton [2001] EWCA Civ 1466, [2002] 2 All ER 248, [2002] 1 WLR
   685, [2001] 44 LS Gaz R 36, 145 Sol Jo LB 244, [2001] 2 All ER (Comm) 1025, sub nom
   Staunton v Paragon Finance plc [2002] 2 P & CR 279, [2002] 1 P & CR D22 . . . 693
Paragon Finance plc v Thakerar & Co [1999] 1 All ER 400, 142 Sol Jo LB 243, CA . . 12, 53,
                                                            76, 255, 257, 322, 324, 382, 920,
                                                            922, 923, 924, 928, 930, 952
Paramasivam v Flynn (1998) 160 ALR 203 1043
Paramount Airways Ltd (in administration), Re [1993] Ch 223, [1992] 3 All ER 1, [1992] 3
   WLR 690, [1992] BCLC 710, [1992] BCC 416, 136 Sol Jo LB 97, CA. 288, 292
Pardo v Bingham (1868) LR 6 Eq 485 804
Pares, Re, Re Scott Chad, Scott Chad v Pares [1901] 1 Ch 708, 70 LJ Ch 426, 81 LT
   385. . . . . 315, 316
Parfitt v Lawless (1872) LR 2 P & D 462, 36 JP 822, 41 LJP & M 68, 21 WR 200, 27 LT 215 282
Park, Re, Public Trustee v Armstrong [1932] 1 Ch 580, 101 LJ Ch 295, [1931] All ER Rep
   633, 147 LT 118 . . . . 90, 91, 93

Parker v Bolton (1835) 5 LJ Ch 98, 42 RR 285 301
Parker v Clark [1960] 1 All ER 93, [1960] 1 WLR 286, 104 Sol Jo 251 140
Parker v Judkin [1931] 1 Ch 475, 100 LJ Ch 159, [1931] All ER Rep 222, 144 LT 662, CA 35
Parker v McKenna (1874) 10 Ch App 96, 44 LJ Ch 425, 23 WR 271, 31 LT 739 . . 393, 665
Parker and Beech's Contract, Re [1887] WN 27, 56 LJ Ch 358, 35 WR 353, 56 LT 96 . . 580,
    581, 986
Parker-Tweedale v Dunbar Bank plc [1991] Ch 12, [1990] 2 All ER 577, [1990] 3 WLR 767,
    60 P & CR 83, [1990] Fam Law 433, 134 Sol Jo 886, [1990] 29 LS Gaz R 34, [1990]
    NLJR 169, CA. 49, 676
Parker's Trusts, Re [1894] 1 Ch 707, 63 LJ Ch 316, 70 LT 165 . . . . 742, 756, 761
Parker's Will, Re, Kilroy and Callan v Parker and McGauran [1966] IR 309 130
Parkin, Re, Hill v Schwarz [1892] 3 Ch 510, 62 LJ Ch 55, 3 R 9, 41 WR 120, 36 Sol Jo 647, 67
    LT 77. . . . . 175, 179
Parkinson (Sir Lindsay) & Co Ltd's Trusts Deed (or Settlement Trusts), Re Bishop v Smith
    [1965] 1 All ER 609n, [1965] 1 WLR 372, 109 Sol Jo 176 837
Parnall v Parnall (1878) 9 Ch D 96, 26 WR 851 80
Parrott, Re, Walter v Parrott (1886) 33 Ch D 274, 34 WR 553, 55 LT 132, CA . 303, 304, 305
Parry, Re, Brown v Parry [1947] Ch 23, [1946] 2 All ER 412, [1947] LJR 81, 90 Sol Jo 478,
    175 LT 395, 62 TLR 543 . . . . 558, 559
Parry v Warrington (1820) 6 Madd 155 555
Parsons, Re, ex p Belchier, ex p Parsons (1754) Amb 218, sub nom Belchier v Parsons 1
    Keny 38 . . . . 607, 634
Parsons, Re [1927] 2 DLR 1001 135
Parsons, Re, Barnsdale and Smallman v Parsons [1940] Ch 973, [1940] 4 All ER 65, 109 LJ
    Ch 458, 84 Sol Jo 550, 163 LT 323, 57 TLR 23 . . . . 755, 764, 771
Partington, Re, Partington v Allen (1887) 57 LT 654, 3 TLR 828 . . . . 916, 918
Partington, Re, Reigh v Kane [1902] 1 Ch 711, 71 LJ Ch 472, 50 WR 388, 46 Sol Jo 337, 86
    LT 194, 18 TLR 387 572
Partridge v Equity Trustees Executors & Agency Co Ltd (1947) 75 CLR 149, [1947] ALR 552,
    21 ALJ 321, HC of A 708
Pascoe v Turner [1979] 2 All ER 945, [1979] 1 WLR 431, 123 Sol Jo 164, CA . 157, 248, 249
Pass v Dundas (1880) 29 WR 332, 43 LT 665 938
Passant v Jackson [1986] STC 164, 59 TC 230, [1986] LS Gaz R 876, CA 18
Passee v Passee [1988] 1 FLR 263, [1988] Fam Law 132, CA 412, 421, 422, 424
Patman v Harland (1881) 17 Ch D 353, 50 LJ Ch 642, 29 WR 707, [1881-5] All ER Rep 637,
    44 LT 728 991
Patrick, Re, Bills v Tatham [1891] 1 Ch 82, 60 LJ Ch 111, 39 WR 113, 32 Sol Jo 798, 63 LT
    752, 7 TLR 124, CA 9
Patten and Edmonton Union Poor Guardians, Re (1883) 52 LJ Ch 787, 31 WR 785, 48 LT
    870 . . . . 875, 880, 884
Paul, Re, Public Trustee v Pearce [1921] 2 Ch 1, 90 LJ Ch 446, 125 LT 566 198
Paul v Constance [1977] 1 All ER 195, [1977] 1 WLR 527, 7 Fam Law 18, 121 Sol Jo 320,
    CA 73, 75, 76, 146, 147, 233, 238
Paul v Paul (1882) 20 Ch D 742, 51 LJ Ch 839, 30 WR 801, 47 LT 210, CA 166
Pauling's Settlement Trusts, Re, Younghusband v Coutts & Co [1961] 3 All ER 713, [1962] 1
    WLR 86, 106 Sol Jo 135; on appeal [1964] Ch 303, [1963] 3 All ER 1, [1963] 3 WLR
    742, 107 Sol Jo 492, CA 250, 284, 285, 286, 691, 719, 721, 919,
    921, 930, 931, 932, 934, 936, 937
Pauling's Settlement Trusts (No 2), Re, Younghusband v Coutts & Co [1963] Ch 576, [1963]
    1 All ER 857, [1963] 2 WLR 838, 42 ATC 97, [1963] TR 157, 107 Sol Jo 395 . 531, 767,
    941, 947, 948
Pavlou (a bankrupt), Re [1993] 3 All ER 955, [1993] 1 WLR 1046, [1993] 2 FLR 751, [1993]
    Fam Law 629, [1993] 11 LS Gaz R 43 . . . . .355, 356, 425, 473
Pawlett v A-G (1667) Hard 465 189
Pawson's Settlement, Re, Higgins v Pawson [1917] 1 Ch 541, 86 LJ Ch 380, 116 LT 559, 33
    TLR 233. 913
Payne, Re, Taylor v Payne [1927] 2 Ch 1, 96 LJ Ch 291, [1927] All ER Rep 223, 137 LT
    117. . . . . 374, 376
Payne v Evens (1874) LR 18 Eq 356 677
Payne's Settlement, Re, Kibble v Payne (1886) 54 LT 840 . . . . 383, 386
Peachdart Ltd, Re [1984] Ch 131, [1983] 3 All ER 204, [1983] 3 WLR 878, [1983] BCLC
    225, 127 Sol Jo 839, [1984] LS Gaz R 204 15
Peacock, Re (1880) 14 Ch D 212, 49 LJ Ch 228, 28 WR 801, 43 LT 99 . . . . . . 769, 784

Peacock v Burt (1834) 4 LJ Ch 33, 41 RR 199 1000
Peacock v Colling (1885) 54 LJ Ch 743, 33 WR 528, 53 LT 620, CA 763
Peacock's Settlement, Re, Kelcey v Harrison [1902] 1 Ch 552, 71 LJ Ch 325, 50 WR 473, 46
    Sol Jo 297, 86 LT 414. 803
Pearce v Gardner (1852) 10 Hare 287, 90 RR 377, 1 WR 98 497
Pearce v Pearce (1856) 22 Beav 248, 25 LJ Ch 893, 2 Jur NS 843, 28 LTOS 34 . 752, 775, 952
Pearce v Wright (1926) 39 CLR 16. 35
Pearks v Moseley (1880) 5 App Cas 714, 50 LJ Ch 57, 21 WR 1, 43 LT 449, HL . . 192, 194,
                                                                                    228
Pearse v Green (1819) 1 Jac & W 135, 20 RR 25, [1814-23] All ER Rep 405 . . 671, 677
Pearse's Settlement, Re, Pearse v Pearse [1909] 1 Ch 304, 78 LJ Ch 73, 53 Sol Jo 82, 100 LT
    48 . . . . 188, 307
Pearson, Re, ex p Stephens (1876) 3 Ch D 807, 25 WR 126, 35 LT 68 209
Pearson v IRC [1980] Ch 1, [1979] 1 All ER 273, [1979] 2 WLR 353, [1978] STC 627, [1978]
    TR 349, 123 Sol Jo 185; on appeal [1980] Ch 1, [1979] 3 All ER 7, [1979] 3 WLR 112,
    [1979] STC 516, [1979] TR 195, 123 Sol Jo 490, CA; affd [1981] AC 753, [1980] 2 All
    ER 479, [1980] 2 WLR 872, [1980] STC 318, [1980] TR 177, 124 Sol Jo 377, HL . 64, 65,
                                                                                    639
Peatfield v Benn (1853) 17 Beav 522, 23 LJ Ch 497, 2 WR 68 768
Pechar, Re [1969] NZLR 574. 434
Pechel v Fowler (1795) 2 Anst 549 581
Peco Arts Inc v Hazlitt Gallery Ltd [1983] 3 All ER 193, [1983] 1 WLR 1315, 127 Sol Jo 806 930
Peczenik's Settlement (or Settlement Trusts), Re, Cole v Ingram [1964] 2 All ER 339, [1964]
    1 WLR 720, 108 Sol Jo 462. . . . . 599, 612
Pedder's Settlement Trusts, Re (1870) LR 10 Eq 585, 40 LJ Ch 77 313
Peel's (Sir Robert) Settled Estates, Re [1910] 1 Ch 389, 79 LJ Ch 233, 54 Sol Jo 214, 102 LT
    67, 26 TLR 227 . . . . 540, 541
Peel's Settlement, Re, Biddulph v Peel [1911] 2 Ch 165, 80 LJ Ch 574, 55 Sol Jo 580, 105 LT
    330. 547
Peel's Settlement Trusts, Re, Millard v Peel [1964] 3 All ER 567, [1964] 1 WLR 1232, 108 Sol
    Jo 858. . . . . 311, 312, 313
Peffer v Rigg [1978] 3 All ER 745, [1977] 1 WLR 285, 33 P & CR 60, 120 Sol Jo 332, 242
    Estates Gazette 123. . . . . 411, 983
Pehrsson (Trustee of the Property of) v Greyerz (16 June 1999, unreported) 156
Peillon v Brooking (1858) 25 Beav 218, 53 ER 620 1033
Pelly, Re, Ransome v Pelly [1957] Ch 1, [1956] 2 All ER 326, 100 Sol Jo 379, CA 386
Pennell v Deffell (1853) 4 De GM & G 372, 23 LJ Ch 115, 1 Eq Rep 579, 18 Jur 273, 1 WR
    499, 22 LTOS 126 880
Pennington, Re, Penninton v Pennington [1914] 1 Ch 203, 83 LJ Ch 54, 20 Mans 411, 109
    LT 814, 30 TLR 106, CA 537
Pennington, Re, Stevens v Pennington [1915] WN 333 537
Pennington v Waine [2002] EWCA Civ 227, [2002] 4 All ER 215, [2002] 1 WLR 2075 . . 155,
                                                                                    166
Penrose, Re, Penrose v Penrose [1933] Ch 793, 102 LJ Ch 321, 149 LT 325, 49 TLR
    285. . . . . 26, 32
Pentland v Stokes (1812) 2 Ball & B 68 460
Pepin v Bruyère [1902] 1 Ch 24, 71 LJ Ch 39, 50 WR 34, 46 Sol Jo 29, 85 LT 461, CA . . 1026
Pepper (Inspector of Taxes) v Hart [1993] AC 593, [1993] 1 All ER 42, [1992] 3 WLR 1032,
    [1992] STC 898, 65 TC 421, [1993] ICR 291, [1993] IRLR 33, [1993] NLJR 17, [1993]
    RVR 127, [1993] 2 LRC 153, HL 474
Pepper v Tuckey (1844) 69 RR 250, 2 Jo & Lat 95, 7 IR Eq 572 768
Peppercorn v Wayman (1852) 5 De G & Sm 230, 21 LJ Ch 827, 16 Jur 794 450
Peppiatt v Nichol (21 August 1998, unreported) 973
Percival v Wright [1902] 2 Ch 421, 71 LJ Ch 846, 9 Mans 443, 51 WR 31, 46 Sol Jo 616, 18
    TLR 697. 21
Percy's Goods, Re, Fairland v Percy (1875) LR 3 P & D 217, 44 LJP & M 11, 39 LJP 632, 23
    WR 597, 32 LT 405 825
Perkins, Re, Brown v Perkins [1907] 2 Ch 596, 77 LJ Ch 16, [1904-7] All ER Rep 273, 97 LT
    706. 566
Perkins' Settlement Trusts, Re, Leicester-Warren v Perkins [1912] WN 99, 56 Sol Jo 412 . 212
Perowne, Re, Perowne v Moss [1951] Ch 785, [1951] 2 All ER 201, [1951] 1 TLR
    1135 . . . . 130, 131
Perpetual Executors and Trustees Association of Australia Ltd v Roberts [1970] VR 732 . 1040

Perpetual Executors and Trustees Association of Australia Ltd v Wright (1917) 23 CLR 185, 23 ALR 177, [1917] VLR 372 (Aust HC) 345
Perpetual Trustee Co Ltd v Tindal (1940) 63 CLR 232, 14 ALJ 130 (Aust HC) 132
Perrin v Lyon (1807) 9 East 170. 220
Perring v Draper [1997] EGCS 109 812
Perrins v Bellamy [1898] 2 Ch 521, 67 LJ Ch 649, 46 WR 682, 79 LT 109; on appeal [1899] 1 Ch 797, 68 LJ Ch 397, 47 WR 417, 43 Sol Jo 437, 80 LT 478, CA 914, 918
Perrott and King's Contract, Re (1904) 90 LT 156. 741
Perry v Perry (1870) 18 WR 482. 720
Peso-Silver Mines Ltd v Cropper [1966] SCR 673, 58 DLR (2d) 1, 56 WWR 641, Can SC 392, 396
Peter v Beblow (1993) 77 BCLR 2d 1, [1993] 1 SCR 980, [1993] 3 WWR 337, 44 RFL (3d) 329, 48 ETR 1, 101 DLR (4th) 621, Can SC 323, 326, 597
Peterson v Peterson (1866) LR 3 Eq 111, 36 LJ Ch 101, 15 WR 164 982
Petroleo Brasiliero SA v Mellitus Shipping Inc, The Baltic Flame [2001] EWCA Civ 418, [2001] 2 Lloyd's Rep 203, [2001] 1 All ER (Comm) 993 . . . . 942, 1041
Petrotrade Inc v Smith [2000] 1 Lloyd's Rep 486 957
Pettifor's Will Trusts, Re, Roberts v Roberts [1966] Ch 257, [1966] 1 All ER 913, [1966] 2 WLR 778, 110 Sol Jo 191 . . . . 517, 735
Pettingall v Pettingall (1842) 11 LJ Ch 176 . . . . 119, 122
Pettit, Re, Le Fevre v Pettit [1922] 2 Ch 765, 91 LJ Ch 732, [1922] All ER Rep 163, 66 Sol Jo 667, 127 LT 491, 38 TLR 787. 534
Pettitt v Pettitt [1970] AC 777, [1969] 2 All ER 385, [1969] 2 WLR 966, 20 P & CR 991, 113 Sol Jo 344, 211 Estates Gazette 829, HL. 350, 352, 358, 361, 366, 413, 415, 421
Pettkus v Becker [1980] 2 SCR 834, 117 DLR (3d) 257, 34 NR 384, 19 RFL (2d) 165, 8 ETR 143, Can SC 323
Pexton (Inspector of Taxes) v Bell [1976] 2 All ER 914, [1976] 1 WLR 885, [1976] STC 301, 120 Sol Jo 368, L(TC) 2584, CA. 544
Peyton v Robinson (1823) 1 LJOS Ch 191, 25 RR 278 485
Pfeiffer (E) Weinkellerei-Weineinkauf GmbH & Co v Arbuthnot Factors Ltd [1988] 1 WLR 150, [1987] BCLC 522, 3 BCC 608, [1987] BTLC 207, 132 Sol Jo 89, [1988] 6 LS Gaz R 38 . . . . 15, 17
Pfrimmer Estate, Re [1936] 2 DLR 123 593
Phan v Phan (1940) 9 MLJ 44 123
Phelps' Settlement Trusts, Re (1885) 31 Ch D 351, 55 LJ Ch 465, 54 LT 480 . . . 743, 764
Philbrick's Settlement, Re (1865) 34 LJ Ch 368, 11 Jur NS 558, 5 New Rep 502, 13 WR 570, 12 LT 261 803
Philippi v IRC [1971] 3 All ER 61, [1971] 1 WLR 1272, 47 TC 75, 50 ATC 37, [1971] TR 167, 115 Sol Jo 427, L(TC) 2404, CA. 294
Philipson-Stow v IRC [1961] AC 727, [1960] 3 All ER 814, [1960] 3 WLR 1008, 39 ATC 394, [1960] TR 333, 104 Sol Jo 1055, HL. 1026, 1029, 1040
Phillimore, Re, Phillimore v Herbert [1903] 1 Ch 942, 72 LJ Ch 591, 88 LT 765 553
Phillips, Re, Lawrence v Huxtable [1931] 1 Ch 347, 100 LJ Ch 65, [1930] All ER Rep 165, 144 LT 178. 804
Phillips v Lamdin [1949] 2 KB 33, [1949] 1 All ER 770, [1949] LJR 1293, 93 Sol Jo 320 . 441
Phillips v Manufacturers' Securities Ltd (1917) 86 LJ Ch 305, 116 LT 290, CA 401
Phillips v Mullings (1871) 7 Ch App 244, 41 LJ Ch 211, 20 WR 129 . . . . 274, 276
Phillips v Phillips (1862) 4 De GF & J 208, 31 LJ Ch 321, 8 Jur NS 145, 135 RR 97, 10 WR 236, 5 LT 655 . . . . 50, 436, 983
Phillips v Phillips (1885) 29 Ch D 673, 54 LJ Ch 943, 33 WR 863, 53 LT 403, CA 384
Phillips v Phillips [1993] 3 NZLR 159 . . . . 326, 425
Phillips v Probyn [1899] 1 Ch 811, 68 LJ Ch 401, 43 Sol Jo 456, 80 LT 513, 15 TLR 324 . 345
Phillips v Silvester (1872) 8 Ch App 173, 42 LJ Ch 225, 21 WR 179, 27 LT 840. 441
Phillips Bros Ltd v Sierra Leone (1995) 3 CLR 316 . . . . 7, 143
Phillips-Higgins v Harper [1954] 1 QB 411, [1954] 1 All ER 116, [1954] 2 WLR 117, 98 Sol Jo 45; affd [1954] 1 QB 411, [1954] 2 All ER 51n, [1954] 2 WLR 782, 98 Sol Jo 250, CA 930
Phillipson v Gatty (1848) 7 Hare 516, 13 Jur 318, 12 LTOS 445; on appeal (1850) 2 H & Tw 459, 82 RR 228 934
Phipps v Ackers (1842) 9 Cl & Fin 583, 6 Jur 745, 4 Man & G 1107, 5 Scott NR 955, HL . 225
Phipps v Boardman [1964] 2 All ER 187, [1964] 1 WLR 993, 108 Sol Jo 619; on appeal [1965] Ch 992, [1965] 1 All ER 849, [1965] 2 WLR 839, 109 Sol Jo 197, CA; affd sub nom Boardman v Phipps [1967] 2 AC 46, [1966] 3 All ER 721, [1966] 3 WLR 1009, 110

Sol Jo 853, HL 23, 24, 384, 387, 393, 398, 401, 402, 404,
405, 611, 655, 657, 852, 854, 875, 889, 936
Phipps v Lovegrove (1873) LR 16 Eq 80, 42 LJ Ch 892, 21 WR 590, 28 LT 584 . . . 492, 660
Pickering v Earl of Stamford (1793) 2 Ves 272, 4 Bro CC 214 935
Pickering v Pickering (1839) 4 My & Cr 289, 8 LJ Ch 336, 3 Jur 743, [1835-42] All ER Rep
534 548
Piddocke v Burt [1894] 1 Ch 343, 63 LJ Ch 246, 8 R 104, 42 WR 248, 38 Sol Jo 141, 70 LT 553   385
Piercy, Re, Whitwham v Piercy [1895] 1 Ch 83, 64 LJ Ch 249, 13 R 106, 43 WR 134, 39 Sol Jo
43, 71 LT 745, 11 TLR 21 . . . . 188, 1026, 1031
Piercy v Roberts (1832) 1 My & K 4, 2 LJ Ch 17, 36 RR 239 209
Pilcher v Rawlins (1872) 7 Ch App 259, 41 LJ Ch 485, 20 WR 281, 25 LT 291 . . 50, 983, 984
Pilkington v IRC. See Pilkington's Will Trusts, Re, Pilkington v Pilkington
Pilkington's Will Trusts, Re, Pilkington v Harrison [1937] Ch 574, [1937] 3 All ER 213, 106
LJ Ch 360, 81 Sol Jo 459, 157 LT 132, 53 TLR 745 1040
Pilkington's Will Trusts, Re, Pilkington v Pilkington [1959] Ch 699, [1959] 2 All ER 623,
[1959] 3 WLR 116, 40 TC 416, 103 Sol Jo 528; on appeal [1961] Ch 466, [1961] 2 All
ER 330, [1961] 2 WLR 776, 40 TC 416, 105 Sol Jo 422, CA; on appeal sub nom
Pilkington v IRC [1964] AC 612, [1962] 3 All ER 622, [1962] 3 WLR 1051, 40 TC 416,
41 ATC 285, [1962] TR 265, 106 Sol Jo 834, HL 199, 711, 719, 720, 721,
723, 724, 803, 808, 809
Pilling, Re, ex p Ogle, ex p Smith (1873) 8 Ch App 711, 42 LJ Bcy 99, 21 WR 938 . . . 870
Pilling's Trusts, Re (1884) 26 Ch D 432, 53 LJ Ch 1052, 32 WR 853 780
Pilmer v Duke Group Ltd (in liquidation) [2001] 2 BCLC 773, {2001] HCA 31, HC of A . 961
Pine Pass Oil and Gas Ltd v Pac Petroleum Ltd (1968) 70 DLR (2d) 196 396
Pinewood Joinery (a firm) v Starelm Properties Ltd [1994] 2 BCLC 412, [1994] BCC 569   295
Pinion, Re, Westminster Bank Ltd v Pinion [1965] Ch 85, [1964] 1 All ER 890, [1964] 2
WLR 919, 108 Sol Jo 296, CA 218
Pink, Re, Pink v Pink [1912] 2 Ch 528, 81 LJ Ch 753, [1911-13] All ER Rep 1037, 56 Sol Jo
668, 107 LT 338, 28 TLR 528, CA 161
Pioneer Container, The. See KH Enterprise v Pioneer Container, The Pioneer Container
Piper, Re, Dodd v Piper [1946] 2 All ER 503, 90 Sol Jo 528, 175 LT 426, 62 TLR 618 . . 189,
222, 231
Piper v Moulton (1881) 72 Me 155 (1881) 121
Pirbright v Salwey [1896] WN 86 120
Pirelli General Cable Works Ltd v Oscar Faber & Partners [1983] 2 AC 1, [1983] 1 All ER 65,
[1983] 2 WLR 6, 127 Sol Jo 16, 21 BLR 99, 265 Estates Gazette 979, HL 493
Pit v Cholmondeley (1754) 2 Ves Sen 565 853
Pitcairn, Re, Brandreth v Colvin [1896] 2 Ch 199, 65 LJ Ch 120, 44 WR 200, [1895-9] All ER
Rep 1244, 73 LT 430 . . . . .550, 551, 560, 611
Pitt, Re, Pitt v Mann (1928) 44 TLR 371 . . . . 20, 760
Pitt v PHH Asset Management Ltd [1993] 4 All ER 961, [1994] 1 WLR 327, 68 P & CR 269,
[1993] 2 EGLR 217, [1993] NLJR 1187, [1993] 40 EG 149, [1994] Conv 58, CA . . 235
Pitt Rivers, Re, Scott v Pitt Rivers [1902] 1 Ch 403, 66 JP 275, 71 LJ Ch 225, 50 WR 342, 46
Sol Jo 246, 86 LT 6, 18 TLR 272, CA 259
Pitts, Re, Cox v Kilsby [1931] 1 Ch 546, 100 LJ Ch 284, 145 LT 116, 47 TLR 293 435
Platamone v Staple (1815) Coop G 250 343
Platt, Re (1969) unreported 214
Platt, Re, Sykes v Dawson [1916] 2 Ch 563, 86 LJ Ch 114, [1916-17] All ER Rep 570, 61 Sol Jo
10, 115 LT 524 532
Platt v Platt [1999] 2 BCLC 745; affd on other grounds [2001] 1 BCLC 698, CA . . . 21, 24
Playfair, Re, Palmer v Playfair [1951] Ch 4, 66 (pt 1) TLR 1203, sub nom Re Hickman's Will
Trusts, Re Playfair, Palmer v Playfair [1950] 2 All ER 285 263
Playfair v Cooper (1853) 17 Beav 187, 23 LJ Ch 341, 343, 1 Eq Rep 137, 1 WR 216, 376, 21
LTOS 40, 177 . . . . 565, 567, 568
Plews v Samuel [1904] 1 Ch 464, 73 LJ Ch 279, 52 WR 410, 48 Sol Jo 276, 90 LT 533 . . 440
Plowright v Lambert (1885) 52 LT 646 662
Plumptre's Marriage Settlement, Re, Underhill v Plumptre [1910] 1 Ch 609, 79 LJ Ch 340,
54 Sol Jo 326, 102 LT 315, 26 TLR 321 . . . . . . 166, 167, 173, 176, 179, 186, 309
Pocock's Policy, Re (1871) 6 Ch App 445, 40 LJ Ch 681, 19 WR 801, 25 LT 233 809
Poland v Beal 192 Mass 559 (1906) 822
Pole v Pole (1748) 1 Ves Sen 76 363
Pole v Pole [1924] 1 Ch 156, 93 LJ Ch 145, 68 Sol Jo 184, 130 LT 333, CA 371

Policy No 6402 of Scottish Equitable Life Assurance Society, Re [1902] 1 Ch 282, 71 LJ Ch
189, 50 WR 327, 85 LT 720, 18 TLR 210 350
Pollard v Jackson (1993) 67 P & CR 327, CA 382
Pollock, Re, Pugsley v Pollock [1943] Ch 338, [1943] 2 All ER 443, 112 LJ Ch 345, 87 Sol Jo
373, 169 LT 282, 59 TLR 456 714
Pollock v Ennis [1921] 1 IR 181 77
Polly Peck International plc (in administration) (No 2), Re [1998] 3 All ER 812, CA . . 57,
327, 1022
Polly Peck International plc (in administration) v Henry [1999] 1 BCLC 407 . . . 462, 655
Polly Peck International plc v Nadir (No 2) [1993] BCLC 187; revsd [1992] 4 All ER 769,
[1992] 2 Lloyd's Rep 238, [1992] NLJR 671, CA 253, 408, 650, 904, 960,
968, 971, 974, 983, 989
Ponder, Re, Ponder v Ponder [1921] 2 Ch 59, 90 LJ Ch 426, [1921] All ER Rep 164, 65 Sol Jo
455, 125 LT 568 . . . . 19, 20, 760, 768
Ponsford v HMS Aerosols Ltd [1979] AC 63, [1978] 2 All ER 837, [1978] 3 WLR 241, 38 P &
CR 270, 122 Sol Jo 487, 247 Estates Gazette 1171, HL 80
Poole v Pass (1839) 1 Beav 600, 8 LJ Ch 305 574
Poole Bathurst's Estate, Re, South Wales Rly Act 1845 and South Wales Amendment Act
1846, ex p Bathurst (1854) 18 Jur 568, 23 LTOS 218, sub nom Poole Bathurst's Estate,
Re 2 Sm & G 169 762
Poole's Settlements' Trusts, Re, Poole v Poole [1959] 2 All ER 340, [1959] 1 WLR 651, 103
Sol Jo 432 510
Pooley, Re (1888) 40 Ch D 1, 58 LJ Ch 1, 37 WR 17, [1886-90] All ER Rep 157, 60 LT 73, 5
TLR 21, CA 597, 652
Pooley v Quilter (1858) 4 Drew 184 668
Popat v Shonchhatra [1997] 3 All ER 800, [1997] 1 WLR 1367, 94 LS Gaz R 22, 141 Sol Jo LB
163, CA 384
Pope, Re, Sharp v Marshall [1901] 1 Ch 64, 70 LJ Ch 26, 49 WR 122, 45 Sol Jo 45 . . . 229
Pope v Pope (1839) 10 Sim 1, 51 RR 202 . . . . 79, 80
Popham, Re, Butler v Popham [1914] WN 257, 58 Sol Jo 673, 111 LT 524 565
Porrett v White (1885) 31 Ch D 52, 55 LJ Ch 79, 34 WR 65, 53 LT 514, CA 903
Porter, Re, Porter v Porter [1925] Ch 746, 95 LJ Ch 46, [1925] All ER Rep 179, 133 LT
812 . . . . 83, 121
Porter v Moore [1904] 2 Ch 367, 73 LJ Ch 729, 52 WR 619, 48 Sol Jo 573, 91 LT 484 . . 492
Portington v Rogers (1613) 2 Brownl 65, 138, sub nom Portington's Case 10 Co Rep 35b 209
Portland (Duke of) v Lady Topham (1864) 11 HL Cas 32, 34 LJ Ch 113, 10 Jur NS 501, 12
WR 697, [1861-73] All ER Rep 980, 10 LT 355 631
Portman Building Society v Dusangh [2000] 2 All ER (Comm) 221, [2000] Lloyd's Rep Bank
197, 80 P & CR D20, [2001] WTLR 117, CA 276
Portman Building Society v Hamlyn Taylor Neck [1998] 4 All ER 202, 77 P & CR 66, [1998]
31 EG 102, 76 P & CR D16, CA 971
Portsmouth (Earl) v Fellows (1820) 5 Madd 450, 21 RR 335 . . . . 744, 765
Postlethwaite, Re, Postlethwaite v Rickman (1888) 53 JP 357, 37 WR 200, 60 LT 514, 5 TLR
76, CA 665
Potter's Will Trusts, Re [1944] Ch 70, [1943] 2 All ER 805, 113 LJ Ch 173, 170 LT 26, 60 TLR
155, CA 67, 304
Potts, Re, ex p Taylor [1893] 1 QB 648, 62 LJQB 392, 10 Morr 52, 4 R 305, 41 WR 337, 37 Sol
Jo 306, 69 LT 74, 9 TLR 308, [1891-4] All ER Rep Ext 1544, CA 212
Pouey v Hordern [1900] 1 Ch 492, 69 LJ Ch 231, 82 LT 51, 16 TLR 191 . . . . 270, 1048
Powell, Re, Bodvell-Roberts v Poole (No 2) (1918) 144 LT Jo 459 497
Powell v London and Provincial Bank [1893] 2 Ch 555, 62 LJ Ch 795, 2 R 482, 41 WR 545, 37
Sol Jo 476, 69 LT 421, 9 TLR 446, CA 984, 1000
Powell v Powell [1900] 1 Ch 243, 69 LJ Ch 164, 44 Sol Jo 134, 82 LT 84 . . . 281, 284, 285
Powell v Thompson [1991] 1 NZLR 597 . . . . 326, 976
Power, Re, Public Trustee v Hastings [1947] Ch 572, [1947] 2 All ER 282, 91 Sol Jo 409, 177
LT 245 609
Power v Banks [1901] 2 Ch 487, 66 JP 21, 70 LJ Ch 700, 49 WR 679, 85 LT 376, 17 TLR 621 884
Power Curber International Ltd v National Bank of Kuwait SAK [1981] 3 All ER 607, [1981]
1 WLR 1233, [1981] 2 Lloyd's Rep 394, [1981] Com LR 224, 125 Sol Jo 585 . . . 1029
Power's Settlement Trusts, Re, Power v Power [1951] Ch 1074, [1951] 2 All ER 513, 95 Sol Jo
467, [1951] 2 TLR 355, CA 757, 771
Poyser, Re, Landon v Poyser [1908] 1 Ch 828, 77 LJ Ch 482, 99 LT 50 547

Poyser, Re, Landon v Poyser [1910] 2 Ch 444, 79 LJ Ch 748, [1908-10] All ER Rep 374, 103
    LT 134 566
Pozot's Settlement Trusts, Re, Westminster Bank Ltd v Guerbois [1952] Ch 427, [1952] 1 All
    ER 1107, [1952] 1 TLR 1042, CA 210, 212
Practice Direction [1945] WN 80 784
Practice Direction [1985] 1 All ER 884, 129 Sol Jo 208 784
Practice Direction [1987] 1 All ER 403, [1987] 1 WLR 63, 131 Sol Jo 20 269
Practice Note (citation of authorities) [2001] 2 All ER 510, [2001] 1 Lloyd's Rep 725, [2001]
    1 FCR 764, sub nom Practice Direction [2001] 1 WLR 1001 78
Practice Note (trust proceedings: prospective costs orders) [2001] 3 All ER 574, [2001] 1
    WLR 1082 . . . . .834, 837, 838, 843
Pratt v Johnson [1959] SCR 102, 16 DLR (2d) 385 140
Pratt's Settlement Trusts, Re, McCullum v Phipps-Hornby [1943] Ch 356, [1943] 2 All ER
    458, 112 LJ Ch 251, 87 Sol Jo 265, 169 LT 181, 59 TLR 352 . . . . 198, 229
Pratt's Will Trusts, Re, Barrow v McCarthy [1943] Ch 326, [1943] 2 All ER 375, 112 LJ Ch
    269, 87 Sol Jo 319, 169 LT 263, 59 TLR 371 526
Pre-Cam Exploration and Development Ltd v McTavish (1966) 57 DLR (2d) 57 390
Precision Dippings Ltd v Precision Dippings Marketing Ltd [1986] Ch 447, [1985] 3 WLR
    812, [1985] BCLC 385, 129 Sol Jo 683, CA 968
Prevost, Re, Lloyds Bank Ltd v Barclays Bank Ltd [1930] 2 Ch 383, 99 LJ Ch 425, 74 Sol Jo
    488, 143 LT 743, 46 TLR 557. 125
Price v Berrington (1851) 15 Jur 999, 3 Mac & G 486, 87 RR 157, 18 LTOS 56. 270
Price v Loaden (1856) 21 Beav 508 . . . . 828, 905
Price Waterhouse v MacCulloch (1986) 25 DLR (4th) 126. 670
Pride v Fooks (1840) 2 Beav 430, 9 LJ Ch 234, 4 Jur 213, 50 RR 227. 864
Priestley v Ellis [1897] 1 Ch 489, 66 LJ Ch 240, 45 WR 442, 41 Sol Jo 296, 76 LT 187 . . 141,
                                                                                       142
Priestman v Tindall (1857) 24 Beav 244. 941
Princess Ann of Hesse v Field [1963] NSWR 998, 89 WNNSW 66 766
Pritt v Clay (1843) 6 Beav 503, 63 RR 160, 1 LTOS 409. 936
Private Trusts Corpn v Grupo Torras SA (1997/98) 1 OFLR 443 . . . . 32, 63
Protheroe v Protheroe [1968] 1 All ER 1111, [1968] 1 WLR 519, 19 P & CR 396, 112 Sol Jo
    151, 205 Estates Gazette 889, CA 383, 384
Prudential Assurance Co Ltd v Newman Industries Ltd (No 2) [1981] Ch 257, [1980] 2 All
    ER 841, [1980] 3 WLR 543, 124 Sol Jo 756; revsd [1982] Ch 204, [1982] 1 All ER 354,
    [1982] 2 WLR 31, 126 Sol Jo 32, CA 392, 864
Pryce, Re, Nevill v Pryce [1917] 1 Ch 234, 86 LJ Ch 383, [1916-17] All ER Rep 573, 61 Sol Jo
    183, 116 LT 149. . . . . 9, 169, 176, 181
Public Trustee v Cooper [2001] WTLR 901 . . . . 579, 603, 663, 701, 835, 853
Pugh, Re, Banting v Pugh [1887] WN 143. 611
Pugh v Heath (1882) 7 App Cas 235, 51 LJQB 367, 30 WR 553, 46 LT 321, HL 49
Pugh's Will Trusts, Re, Marten v Pugh [1967] 3 All ER 337, [1967] 1 WLR 1262, 111 Sol Jo
    480. . . . . .91, 94, 260, 332, 342
Pullan v Koe [1913] 1 Ch 9, 82 LJ Ch 37, [1911-13] All ER Rep 334, 57 Sol Jo 97, 107 LT
    811. . . . . 9, 16, 42, 76, 139, 166, 167, 168, 181, 437
Pumfrey, Re, Worcester City and County Banking Co Ltd v Blick (1882) 22 Ch D 255, 52 LJ
    Ch 228, 31 WR 195, 48 LT 516 . . . . 815, 819
Pye (JA) (Oxford) Ltd v Graham [2002] UKHL 30, [2002] 3 All ER 865, [2002] 3 WLR 221 460
Pyle, Re, Pyle v Pyle [1895] 1 Ch 724, 64 LJ Ch 477, 13 R 396, 43 WR 420, 39 Sol Jo 346, 72
    LT 327 441

Q

Quazi v Harrow London Borough Council [2001] EWCA Civ 601, [2001] HLR 14 . 476, 582
Queensland Mines Ltd v Hudson (1978) 18 ALR 1, 52 ALJR 399, PC 392, 405
Queenstown Dry Docks Shipbuilding and Engineering Co [1918] 1 IR 356 . . . . 774, 779
Quicke's Trusts, Re, Poltimore v Quicke [1908] 1 Ch 887, 77 LJ Ch 523, 98 LT 610, 24 TLR
    23 589

R

R v Charity Comr for Engalnd and Wales, ex p Baldwin (2001) 33 HLR 48, [2001] WTLR
    137. . . . . 27, 693, 694
R v Chief Metropolitan Stipendiary Magistrate, ex p Secretary of State for the Home
    Department [1989] 1 All ER 151, [1988] 1 WLR 1204, 132 Sol Jo 1430, [1988] 39 LS
    Gaz R 42 490

R v Clowes (No 2) [1994] 2 All ER 316, CA 37, 76, 599, 611, 908, 910
R v Commission for the New Towns, ex p Tomkins [1988] RVR 106, [1989] JPL 763; affd
   (1988) 87 LGR 207, 58 P & CR 57, sub nom Tomkins v Commission for the New Towns
   [1989] 1 EGLR 24, [1988] RVR 219, [1989] 12 EG 59, CA 582
R v Common Professional Examination Board, ex p Mealing-McCleod (2000) Times, 2 May,
   CA 13
R v Cooke [1986] AC 909, [1986] 2 All ER 985, [1986] 3 WLR 327, 83 Cr App Rep 339, 150
   JP 498, [1987] Crim LR 114, 130 Sol Jo 572, [1986] NLJ Rep 730, HL 910, 911
R v Criminal Injuries Compensation Board, ex p A [1999] 2 AC 330, [1999] 2 WLR 974,
   [1999] COD 244, 143 Sol Jo LB 120, HL 699
R v Daly [1974] 1 All ER 290, [1974] 1 WLR 133, 58 Cr App Rep 333, 138 JP 245, [1974]
   Crim LR 263, 118 Sol Jo 66, CA. 912
R v Dimsey [2000] QB 744, [2000] 3 WLR 273, [2000] 1 Cr App Rep 203, [1999] STC 846,
   [1999] 30 LS Gaz R 28, CA; affd sub nom R v Dimsey [2001] UKHL 46, [2002] 1 AC
   509, [2001] 4 All ER 786, [2001] 3 WLR 843, [2002] 1 Cr App Rep 167, [2001] STC
   1520 59
R v District Auditor No 3 Audit District of West Yorkshire Metropolitan County Council, ex p
   West Yorkshire Metropolitan County Council [1986] RVR 24 . . . . . 82, 89, 93, 112
R v Dubar [1995] 1 All ER 781, [1994] 1 WLR 1484, [1995] 1 Cr App Rep 280, [1994] 21 LS
   Gaz R 41, 138 Sol Jo LB 104, C-MAC 908
R v Feely [1973] QB 530, [1973] 1 All ER 341, [1973] 2 WLR 201, 57 Cr App Rep 312, 137 JP
   157, [1973] Crim LR 193, 117 Sol Jo 54, CA 910, 911
R v Ghosh [1982] QB 1053, [1982] 2 All ER 689, [1982] 3 WLR 110, 75 Cr App Rep 154, 146
   JP 376, [1982] Crim LR 608, 126 Sol Jo 429, CA 910, 962
R v Governor of Brixton Prison, ex p Levin [1997] QB 65, [1996] 4 All ER 350, [1996] 3
   WLR 657, [1997] 1 Cr App Rep 335, 140 Sol Jo LB 94; affd [1997] AC 741, [1997] 3 All
   ER 289, [1997] 3 WLR 117, [1998] 1 Cr App Rep 22, [1997] Crim LR 891, [1997] 30 LS
   Gaz R 28, [1997] NLJR 990, 141 Sol Jo LB 148, HL 908
R v HM Coroner for East Kent, ex p Spooner, Spooner, Reynolds and Reynolds (1987) 88 Cr
   App Rep 10, 152 JP 115, 3 BCC 636 963
R v Inwood (1974) 60 Cr App Rep 70, CA 912
R v Klineberg [1999] 1 Cr App Rep 427, [1999] Crim LR 417, [1998] 46 LS Gaz R 34,
   CA 908
R v Kneeshaw [1975] QB 57, [1974] 1 All ER 896, [1974] 2 WLR 432, 58 Cr App Rep 439,
   138 JP 291, [1974] Crim LR 263, 118 Sol Jo 218, CA. 912
R (on the application of Heather) v Leonard Cheshire Foundation [2002] EWCA Civ 366,
   [2002] 2 All ER 936 219
R v Mainwaring (1981) 74 Cr App Rep 99, CA 908
R v Secretary of State for Transport, ex p Factortame Ltd (No 3): C-221/89 [1992] QB 680,
   [1991] 3 All ER 769, [1992] 3 WLR 288, [1991] ECR I-3905, [1991] 3 CMLR 589,
   [1991] 2 Lloyd's Rep 648, [1991] NLJR 1107, ECJ 273
R v Shadrokh-Cigari [1988] Crim LR 465, CA 908
R v Stapleton (1863) 4 B & S 629, 10 Jur NS 44, 129 RR 867, 19 WR 49, 9 LT 322 . . . 456
R v Sterry (1840) 4 PD 122, 12 Ad & El 84, 9 LJMC 105, 54 RR 546 456
R v Wain [1995] 2 Cr App Rep 660, CA. 908
R v Williams [1942] AC 541, [1942] 2 All ER 95, 111 LJPC 86 1029
R v Williams [1953] 1 QB 660, [1953] 1 All ER 1068, [1953] 2 WLR 937, 37 Cr App Rep 71,
   117 JP 251, 97 Sol Jo 318, CCA 911
R v Wills (1990) 92 Cr App Rep 297, CA 908
RBC Dominion Securities Inc v Dawson (1994) 111 DLR (4th) 230 979
RWG Management Ltd v Corporate Affairs Comr [1985] VR 385 . . . . . . 811, 812, 822
Rabaiotti Settlements, Re [2001] Fam Law 808, [2000] WTLR 953, 2 ITELR 763 . 28, 61, 672,
                                     677, 682, 684, 685, 1044
Rabin v Gerson Berger Association Ltd [1986] 1 All ER 374, [1986] 1 WLR 526, 130 Sol Jo
   15, [1986] NLJ Rep 17, CA 83
Raby v Ridehalgh (1855) 7 De GM & G 104, 24 LJ Ch 528, 1 Jur NS 363, 109 RR 46, 3 WR
   344, 3 Eq R 901 . . . . 531, 945, 948
Racal Group Services Ltd v Ashmore [1994] STC 416; affd [1995] STC 1151, 68 TC 86,
   CA 166, 279
Race v Race (5 July 2002, unreported) 546
Rackstraw's Trusts, Re (1885) 33 WR 559, 52 LT 612, 1 TLR 388 780
Radcliffe, Re, European Assurance Society v Radcliffe (1878) 7 Ch D 733, 26 WR 417 . . 727

Radcliffe, Re, Radcliffe v Bewes, [1892] 1 Ch 227, 61 LJ Ch 186, 40 WR 323, 36 Sol Jo 151, 66
    LT 363, CA. 133
Radnor's (Earl) Will Trusts, Re (1890) 45 Ch D 402, 59 LJ Ch 782, 6 TLR 480, CA . 817, 842,
                                                                                    846
Rae (Inspector of Taxes) v Lazard Investment Co Ltd [1963] 1 WLR 555, 41 TC 1, 42 ATC
    84, [1963] TR 149, 107 Sol Jo 474, HL 537
Raffaele v Raffaele [1962] WAR 29. 248
Rafidian Bank v Saipem (2 March 1994, unreported) 37, 524
Rahman v Chase Bank (CI) Trust Co Ltd [1991] JLR 103 . . . . 30, 59
Raikes v Lygon [1988] 1 All ER 884, [1988] 1 WLR 281, 132 Sol Jo 126, [1988] 3 LS Gaz R
    34 . . . . 114, 118, 527
Raine, Re, Tyerman v Stansfield [1929] 1 Ch 716, 98 LJ Ch 244, 141 LT 25 713
Ralli's Will Trust, Re, Calvocoressi v Rodocanachi [1964] Ch 288, [1963] 3 All ER 940,
    [1964] 2 WLR 144, 108 Sol Jo 74 . . . . . . 160, 162, 163, 164, 173, 181, 183, 268
Ralli's Will Trusts, Re, Ralli's Marriage Settlement [1964] Ch 288, [1963] 3 All ER 940,
    [1964] 2 WLR 144, 108 Sol Jo 74 . . . . . . 160, 162, 163, 164, 173, 181, 183, 268
Rampal v Rampal (No 2) [2001] EWCA Civ 989, [2002] Fam 85, [2001] 3 WLR 795, [2001] 2
    FCR 552, [2001] 2 FLR 1179, [2001] Fam Law 731, [2001] 29 LS Gaz R 37, [2001]
    NLJR 1006, 145 Sol Jo LB 165 434
Ramsden v Dyson and Thornton (1866) LR 1 HL 129, 12 Jur NS 506, 14 WR 926 . . . 157
Ramsden v Hylton (1751) 2 Ves Sen 304, [1558-1774] All ER Rep 439 936
Randall v Errington (1805) 10 Ves 423 660
Randall v Russell (1817) 3 Mer 190, 17 RR 56 383
Randell, Re, Randell v Dixon (1888) 38 Ch D 213, 57 LJ Ch 899, 36 WR 543, [1886-90] All
    ER Rep 159, 58 LT 626, 4 TLR 307 120
Ranelagh's (Lord) Will, Re (1884) 26 Ch D 590, 53 LJ Ch 689, sub nom Re Ranelagh's
    (Viscount) Will, Beeton v London School Board 32 WR 714, 51 LT 87 383
Rank's Settlement Trusts, Re, Newton v Rollo [1979] 1 WLR 1242, 123 Sol Jo 720 . . . 806
Ransome, Re, Moberley v Ransome [1957] Ch 348, [1957] 2 WLR 556, 101 Sol Jo 302, sub
    nom Re Ransome's Will Trusts [1957] 1 All ER 690 . . . . 194, 209, 715
Ranson v Ranson [1988] 1 WLR 183, [1988] 1 FLR 292, [1988] Fam Law 128, 132 Sol Jo 90,
    [1988] 3 LS Gaz R 35, CA 187
Raphael v Boehm (1805) 8 RR 95, 11 Ves 92, [1903-13] All ER Rep 669; affd (1807) 13 Ves
    407. 868
Rasmanis v Jurewitsch [1968] 2 NSWR 166; on appeal [1970] 1 NSWR 650, 70 SRNSW
    407. . . . . 411, 434
Ratcliff, Re [1898] 2 Ch 352, 67 LJ Ch 562, 42 Sol Jo 654, 78 LT 834 788
Ratcliffe v Barnard (1871) 6 Ch App 652, 40 LJ Ch 777, 19 WR 764, CA 1001
Rattenberry, Re, Ray v Grant [1906] 1 Ch 667, 75 LJ Ch 304, 54 WR 311, 50 Sol Jo 240, 94 LT
    475, 22 TLR 249. 713
Raulin v Fischer [1911] 2 KB 93, 80 LJKB 811, 104 LT 849, 27 TLR 220 1062
Raval (a bankrupt), Re [1998] 2 FLR 718, [1998] Fam Law 590, [1998] BPIR 389 . . . 482
Raven, Re, Spencer v National Association for the Prevention of Consumption and Other
    Forms of Tuberculosis [1915] 1 Ch 673, 84 LJ Ch 489, [1914-15] All ER Rep 353, 113
    LT 131 . . . . .215, 530, 590, 832
Rawlings v Rawlings [1964] P 398, [1964] 2 All ER 804, [1964] 3 WLR 294, 108 Sol Jo 424,
    CA 477
Rawluk v Rawluk (1990) 65 DLR (4th) 161 324
Rawson Trust v Perlman Butts OCM, Vol II, p 35-54, Bahamas Sup Ct 754
Rawson Trust v Perlman 1 BOCM 135 (Bahamas Supreme Court Eq No 194 of 1984) . 29, 31
Rawsthorne v Rowley [1909] 1 Ch 409n, 78 LJ Ch 235n, 100 LT 154n, 24 TLR 51, CA . . 492
Raybould, Re, Raybould v Turner [1900] 1 Ch 199, 69 LJ Ch 249, 48 WR 301, 82 LT
    46 . . . . 813, 824, 825
Rayner v Preston (1881) 18 Ch D 1, 45 JP 829, 50 LJ Ch 472, 29 WR 547, 44 LT 787,
    CA 443, 890
Reader v Fried [2001] Victoria SC 459 934
Reading, Re, Edmonds v Reading [1916] WN 262, 60 Sol Jo 655 . . . . 948, 981
Reading v A-G [1951] AC 507, [1951] 1 All ER 617, 95 Sol Jo 155, [1951] 1 TLR 480, HL 22
Recher's Will Trusts, Re, National Westminster Bank Ltd v National Anti-Vivisection Society
    Ltd [1972] Ch 526, [1971] 3 All ER 401, [1971] 3 WLR 321, 115 Sol Jo 448 . . 118, 124,
                                                                    125, 126, 127, 339, 340
Record v Bell [1991] 4 All ER 471, [1991] 1 WLR 853, 62 P & CR 192 235

Redding, Re, Thompson v Redding [1897] 1 Ch 876, 66 LJ Ch 460, 45 WR 457, 41 Sol Jo
405, 76 LT 339 572
Rede v Oakes (1864) 4 De GJ & Sm 505, 34 LJ Ch 145, 10 Jur NS 1246, 5 New Rep 209, 13
WR 303, 11 LT 549 . . . . 580, 581
Redgate, Re, Marsh v Redgate [1903] 1 Ch 356, 72 LJ Ch 204, 51 WR 216 805
Redington v Redington (1794) 3 Ridg Parl Rep 106 363
Redman v Rymer (1889) 60 LT 385; on appeal (1891) 65 LT 270, 7 TLR 425, CA . 824, 989
Redrow v Pedley [2002] Pens LR 339. 867
Rees, Re, Lloyds Bank Ltd v Rees [1954] Ch 202, [1954] 2 WLR 59, 98 Sol Jo 28, sub nom Re
Rees' Will Trusts, Lloyds Bank Ltd v Rees [1954] 1 All ER 7 . . . . . . 211, 715, 724
Rees, Re, Williams v Hopkins [1949] Ch 541, [1949] 1 All ER 609, [1949] LJR 898, 93 Sol Jo
182; affd [1950] Ch 204, [1949] 2 All ER 1003, 66 (pt 1) TLR 23, CA . . . 3, 137, 260,
330, 342
Reeve, Re, Reeve v Reeve [1935] Ch 110, 104 LJ Ch 101, [1934] All ER Rep 21, 152 LT 254 547
Regal (Hastings) Ltd v Gulliver (1942) [1967] 2 AC 134n, [1942] 1 All ER 378, HL . . 21, 22,
23, 390, 391, 392, 402, 861
Regier v Campbell-Stuart [1939] Ch 766, [1939] 3 All ER 235, 108 LJ Ch 321, 83 Sol Jo 497,
161 LT 30, 55 TLR 798 23
Regional Municipality of Peel v Canada (1993) 98 DLR (4th) 140. 597
Registered Securities Ltd, Re [1991] 1 NZLR 545 . . . . 881, 893, 894
Registrar of the Accident Compensaton Tribunal v Comr of Taxation (1993) 178 CLR 145 143
Rehden v Wesley (1861) 29 Beav 213, 131 RR 530. 634
Reich, Re, Public Trustee v Guthrie (1924) 40 TLR 398 102
Reichert v Dresdner Bank: 115/88 [1990] ECR I-27, ECJ 1057
Reid, Re (1921) 64 DLR 598, 50 OLR 595. 359
Reid v Thompson and M'Namara (1851) 2 I Ch R 26 . . . . , . 631
Reid-Newfoundland Co v Anglo-American Telegraph Ltd [1912] AC 555, 81 LJPC 224, 106
LT 691, 28 TLR 385, PC. 386, 909
Reis, Re, ex p Clough [1904] 2 KB 769, 73 LJKB 929, 11 Mans 229, 53 WR 122, 48 Sol Jo 506,
91 LT 592, 20 TLR 547, CA; on appeal sub nom Clough v Samuel [1905] AC 442, 74
LJKB 918, 12 Mans 347, 54 WR 114, 93 LT 491, 21 TLR 702, HL 186
Reiss Engineering Co Ltd v Harris [1985] IRLR 232, EAT. 399
Reliance Permanent Building Society v Harwood-Stamper [1944] Ch 362, [1944] 2 All ER
75, 113 LJ Ch 290, 88 Sol Jo 273, 171 LT 132, 60 TLR 480 581
Remnant's Settlement Trusts, Re, Hooper v Wenhaston [1970] Ch 560, [1970] 2 All ER 554,
[1970] 2 WLR 1103, 114 Sol Jo 398 . . . . 512, 513
Renard's Estate, Re 56 NY 2d 973, 453 NYS 3d 625 1031
Rendell's Trusts, Re (1915) 139 LT Jo 249. 765
Rennell v IRC [1962] Ch 329, [1961] 3 All ER 1028, [1963] 2 WLR 745, 42 ATC 55, [1963]
TR 73, 107 Sol Jo 232; affd sub nom IRC v Lord Rennell [1964] AC 173, [1963] 1 All
ER 803, [1963] 2 WLR 745, 42 ATC 55, [1963] TR 73, 107 Sol Jo 232, HL 167
Representation Blampied, Re (28 January 1994, unreported) 31
Representation of I (2001) 4 ITELR 446 579
Revel v Watkinson (1748) 1 Ves Sen 93, [1558-1774] All ER Rep 284 . . . . . . 524, 567
Revenue Comrs v Pelly [1940] IR 122 . . . . 1033, 1034
Reynell v Sprye (1852) 1 De GM & G 660, 21 LJ Ch 633, 91 RR 228 344
Reynette-James, Re, Wightman v Reynette-James [1975] 3 All ER 1037, [1976] 1 WLR 161,
119 Sol Jo 682 280
Ricarde-Seaver's Will Trusts, Re, Midland Bank Executor and Trustee Co Ltd v Sandbrook
[1936] 1 All ER 580, 80 Sol Jo 385, 154 LT 599, 52 TLR 508. 715
Rice v Rice (1854) 2 Drew 73, 23 LJ Ch 289, 2 Eq Rep 341, 2 WR 139, 22 LTOS 208 . . 50
Richard v Mackay (1987) 11 Tru LI 23 . . . . 770, 773, 1041
Richards, Re, Williams v Gorvin (1883) 50 LT 22 376
Richards v Delbridge (1874) LR 18 Eq 11, 43 LJ Ch 459, 22 WR 584 . . .145, 146, 147, 149
Richards v Mackay (1990) 1 Offshore Tax Planning Review 1 516
Richardson, Re, ex p St Thomas's Hospital (Governors) [1911] 2 KB 705, 80 LJKB 1232, 18
Mans 327, 105 LT 226, CA. 826
Richardson, Re, Morgan v Richardson [1896] 1 Ch 512, 65 LJ Ch 512, 44 WR 279, 40 Sol Jo
225, 74 LT 12. . . . . 544, 667
Richardson's Will Trusts, Re, Public Trustee v Llewellyn-Evans' Trustee [1958] Ch 504,
[1958] 1 All ER 538, [1958] 2 WLR 414, 102 Sol Jo 176 . . . . 211, 212
Richerson, Re, Scales v Heyhoe [1892] 1 Ch 379, 61 LJ Ch 202, 40 WR 233, 36 Sol Jo 200, 66
LT 174 . . . . 180, 369, 377

Rickard, Re, Rickard v Robson (1862) 26 JP 709, 31 Beav 244, 31 LJ Ch 897, 8 Jur NS 665, 135 RR 422, 10 WR 657, 7 LT 87 202
Ricketts v Ricketts (1891) 64 LT 263 949
Riddell, Re, Public Trustee v Riddell [1936] Ch 747, [1936] 2 All ER 1600, 105 LJ Ch 378, 80 Sol Jo 595, 155 LT 247, 52 TLR 675 793
Rider v Kidder (1805) 53 RR 269, 10 Ves 360, 32 ER 884, [1803-13] All ER Rep 366 . . 343, 349, 362
Ridley, Re, Ridley v Ridley [1904] 2 Ch 774, 48 Sol Jo 641, 91 LT 189, sub nom Ridley's Trusts, Re 73 LJ Ch 696 741
Ridsdel, Re, Ridsdel v Rawlinson [1947] Ch 597, [1947] 2 All ER 312, [1947] LJR 1486, 91 Sol Jo 483 . . . . 708, 786, 787
Rigby v Den Decorating Systems Ltd (15 March 1999, unreported), CA 955, 956
Rigden v Vallier (1751) 3 Atk 731, 2 Ves Sen 252, [1558-1774] All ER Rep 510 350
Rimmer v Rimmer [1953] 1 QB 63, [1952] 2 All ER 863, 96 Sol Jo 801, [1952] 2 TLR 767, CA 360, 366
Rimmer v Webster [1902] 2 Ch 163, 71 LJ Ch 561, 50 WR 517, 86 LT 491, 18 TLR 548 . 983
Risch v McFee (1990) 61 P & CR 42, [1991] FCR 168, [1991] 1 FLR 105, [1991] Fam Law 176, [1990] 29 LS Gaz R 33, CA 358
Robb, Re, Marshall v Marshall [1953] Ch 459, [1953] 2 WLR 819, 97 Sol Jo 263, sub nom Re Robb's Will Trusts, Marshall v Marshall [1953] 1 All ER 920 . . . . 204, 207
Robbins, Re, Robbins v Legge [1907] 2 Ch 8, 76 LJ Ch 531, 51 Sol Jo 445, 96 LT 755, CA 533, 566
Roberts, Re (1983) 70 FLR 158 767
Roberts, Re, Knight v Roberts (1897) 41 Sol Jo 468, 76 LT 479, CA 918
Roberts, Re, Repington v Roberts-Gawen (1881) 19 Ch D 520, 45 LT 450, CA . . . 197, 201
Roberts v Roberts [1986] 2 All ER 483, [1986] 1 WLR 437, [1986] 2 FLR 152, 130 Sol Jo 315, [1986] LS Gaz R 1554 187
Roberts Settlement Trusts, Re (1959) Times, 8 April 507
Roberts' Will Trusts, Re, Younger v Lewins [1937] Ch 274, [1937] 1 All ER 518, 106 LJ Ch 232, 81 Sol Jo 199, 156 LT 213, 53 TLR 358 793
Roberts' Trusts, Re (1869) 38 LJ Ch 708, 17 WR 639 829
Robertson v Morrice (1845) 9 Jur 122, 72 RR 766, 4 LTOS 430 147
Robertson's Will Trusts, Re [1960] 3 All ER 146n, [1960] 1 WLR 1050, 104 Sol Jo 726 . . 518
Robinson, Re, McLaren v Public Trustee [1911] 1 Ch 502, 80 LJ Ch 381, [1911-13] All ER Rep 296, 55 Sol Jo 271, 104 LT 331 . . . . 948, 982
Robinson, Re, Pickard v Wheater (1885) 31 Ch D 247, 55 LJ Ch 307, 53 LT 865 833
Robinson v Collins [1975] 1 All ER 321, sub nom Re Collins, Robinson v Collins [1975] 1 WLR 309, 119 Sol Jo 66 545
Robinson v Harkin [1896] 2 Ch 415, 65 LJ Ch 773, 44 WR 702, 40 Sol Jo 600, 74 LT 777, 12 TLR 475 . . . . 942, 945
Robinson v Macdonnell (1816) Holt NP 612n, 5 M & S 228 175
Robinson v Pett (1734) 2 Eq Cas Abr 454, 3 P Wms 249, 2 White & Tud LC 605 sub nom Robinson v Lorkin 2 Barn KB 435 . . . . 449, 651
Robinson v Preston (1858) 4 K & J 505, 27 LJ Ch 395, 4 Jur NS 186, 116 RR 432, 31 LTOS 366 350
Robinson v Randfontein Estates [1921] App D 168 23
Robinson v Robinson (1851) 1 De GM & G 247, 21 LJ Ch 111, 16 Jur 255, 91 RR 73, 18 LTOS 293 . . . . 584, 863
Robinson's Settlement Trusts, Re, Heard v Heard [1976] 3 All ER 61, [1976] 1 WLR 806, 120 Sol Jo 525 514
Robinson's Will Trusts, Re, Public Trustee v Gotto [1963] 1 All ER 777, [1963] 1 WLR 628, 107 Sol Jo 476 226
Robson v Flight (1865) 4 De GJ & Sm 608, 34 LJ Ch 226, 11 Jur NS 147, 5 New Rep 344, 146 RR 478, 13 WR 393, 11 LT 725 77
Rochefoucauld v Boustead [1897] 1 Ch 196, 66 LJ Ch 74, sub nom De la Rochefoucauld v Boustead 45 WR 272, 41 Sol Jo 156, 75 LT 502, 13 TLR 118, CA . . . 54, 234, 236, 255, 257, 349, 659, 924
Rochford v Hackman (1852) 9 Hare 475, 21 LJ Ch 511, 16 Jur 212, 19 LTOS 5 210
Rochford's Settlement Trusts, Re, Rochford v Rochford [1965] Ch 111, [1964] 2 All ER 177, [1964] 2 WLR 1339, 108 Sol Jo 279 . . . . 206, 207
Rodbard v Cooke (1877) 25 WR 555, 36 LT 504 647
Rodway v Landy [2001] EWCA Civ 471, [2001] Ch 703, [2001] 2 WLR 1775, [2001] 44 EG 151, 145 Sol Jo LB 116, [2001] All ER (D) 30 (Apr) 473, 478, 481

Roe v Nix [1893] P 55, 62 LJP 36, 1 R 472, 68 LT 26, 9 TLR 128 269
Rogers, Re, Public Trustee v Rogers [1915] 2 Ch 437, 84 LJ Ch 837, 60 Sol Jo 27, 113 LT
   916. . . . . 551, 555
Rogers' Question, Re [1948] 1 All ER 328, CA 366
Rogers' Settlement, Re, Arnott v Rogers [1951] Ch 450, [1951] 1 All ER 236 . . . 307, 310
Rolled Steel Products (Holdings) Ltd v British Steel Corpn [1982] Ch 478, [1982] 3 All ER
   1057, [1982] 3 WLR 715, 126 Sol Jo 495, [1982] LS Gaz R 1291; on appeal [1986] Ch
   246, [1985] 3 All ER 52, [1985] 2 WLR 908, [1984] BCLC 466, 128 Sol Jo 629, [1984]
   LS Gaz R 2357, CA. 271, 392, 402, 494, 604, 700, 813, 968, 975
Roome v Edwards (Inspector of Taxes) [1982] AC 279, [1981] 1 All ER 736, [1981] 2 WLR
   268, [1981] STC 96, 54 TC 359, [1981] TR 1, 125 Sol Jo 150, HL . . . 456, 696, 726,
                        803, 806, 807, 915
Roper-Curzon v Roper-Curzon (1871) LR 11 Eq 452, 19 WR 519, 24 LT 406. 722
Ropner's Settlement Trusts, Re, Ropner v Ropner [1955] Ch 260, [1954] 2 All ER 453,
   [1954] 3 WLR 156; affd [1955] Ch 260, [1955] 1 All ER 185, [1955] 2 WLR 256, 99 Sol
   Jo 74, CA 501
Ropner's Settlements Trusts, Re, Ropner v Ropner [1956] 3 All ER 332n, [1956] 1 WLR 902,
   100 Sol Jo 530 . . . . 722, 783
Roscoe (James) (Bolton) Ltd v Winder [1915] 1 Ch 62, 84 LJ Ch 286, [1915] HBR 61, 112
   LT 121, [1914-15] All ER Rep Ext 1375 . . . . 42, 886, 892
Rose, Re, Midland Bank Executor and Trustee Co Ltd v Rose [1949] Ch 78, [1948] 2 All ER
   971, [1949] LJR 208, 92 Sol Jo 661 . . . . 150, 151
Rose, Re, Rose v IRC [1952] Ch 499, [1952] 1 All ER 1217, 31 ATC 138, [1952] TR 175,
   [1952] 1 TLR 1577, CA. 56, 154, 155, 450
Rose v Bartlett (1633) Cro Car 292 742
Rose v Rose (1986) 7 NSWLR 679 145
Rose (Frederick E) (London) Ltd v William H Pim Jnr & Co Ltd [1953] 2 QB 450, [1953] 2
   All ER 739, [1953] 3 WLR 497, [1953] 2 Lloyd's Rep 238, 97 Sol Jo 556, CA . . . 278
Rosenthal, Re, Schwarz v Bernstein [1972] 3 All ER 552, [1972] 1 WLR 1273, 51 ATC 371,
   [1972] TR 329, 116 Sol Jo 666 914
Rosewood Trust Ltd v Schmidt [2001] WTLR 1081 . . . . 28, 116, 504, 593
Rosher, Re, Rosher v Rosher (1884) 26 Ch D 801, 53 LJ Ch 722, 32 WR 821, 51 LT 785 . 738
Ross, Re, Ross v Waterfield [1930] 1 Ch 377, 99 LJ Ch 67, [1929] All ER Rep 456, 142 LT
   189, 46 TLR 61 . . . . 188, 1027, 1028
Ross v Caunters [1980] Ch 297, [1979] 3 All ER 580, [1979] 3 WLR 605, 123 Sol Jo 605 . 280
Rossiter v Rossiter (1863) 14 I Ch R 247 . . . . 67, 302
Roth, Re, Goldberger v Roth [1895-9] All ER Rep 455, 74 LT 50 645
Rothmore Farms Pty Ltd v Belgravia Pty Ltd [1999] FCA 745 . . . . 811, 820
Rouse v 100F Autralia Trustees Ltd [2000] WTLR 111, (1999-2000) 2 ITELR 289 . 28, 672, 685
Routledge's Trusts, Re, Routledge v Saul [1909] 1 Ch 280, 99 LT 919, sub nom Re Rou-
   tledge, Saul v Routledge 78 LJ Ch 136 . . . . 741, 763
Rowan v Dann [1991] EGCS 19; affd (1991) 64 P & CR 202, [1991] EGCS 138,
   CA 116, 275, 346, 369
Rowe, Re, Merchant Taylors' Co v London Corpn (1914) 30 TLR 528 105
Rowe v Chichester (1773) Amb 715 22
Rowe v Prance [1999] 2 FLR 787, [1999] Fam Law 623, [1999] 21 LS Gaz R 41, [1999] EGCS
   75, [2000] WTLR 249. . . . . 73, 76, 238
Rowe v Sanders [2002] EWCA Civ 242, [2002] 2 All ER 800n 187, 190
Rowland v Divall [1923] 2 KB 500, 92 LJKB 1041, [1923] All ER Rep 270, 67 Sol Jo 703, 129
   LT 757, CA. 14
Rowland v Morgan (1848) 2 Ph 764, 18 LJ Ch 78, 13 Jur 23, 78 RR 282 846
Rowlandson v National Westminster Bank Ltd [1978] 3 All ER 370, [1978] 1 WLR 798,
   [1978] 1 Lloyd's Rep 523, 122 Sol Jo 347 960
Rowley v Adams (1849) 2 HL Cas 725, 81 RR 363 579
Rowlls, Re, Walters v Treasury Solicitor [1900] 2 Ch 107, 69 LJ Ch 562, 48 WR 562, [1900-3]
   All ER Rep 756, 44 Sol Jo 448, 82 LT 633, CA 550
Rowlls v Bebb [1900] 2 Ch 107, 69 LJ Ch 562, 48 WR 562, [1900-3] All ER Rep 756, 44 Sol Jo
   448, 82 LT 633, CA 471, 552, 560
Roy v Roy [1996] 1 FLR 541, CA 355
Royal Bank of Scotland v Skinner 1931 SLT 382 972
Royal Bank of Scotland plc v Etridge (No 2) [1998] 4 All ER 705, [1998] 3 FCR 675, [1998] 2
   FLR 843, [1998] Fam Law 665, 31 HLR 575, [1998] 32 LS Gaz R 31, [1998] NLJR 1390,
   76 P & CR D39, CA; on appeal sub nom Royal Bank of Scotland v Etridge (No 2)

[2001] UKHL 44, [2001] 4 All ER 449, [2001] 3 WLR 1021, [2002] 1 Lloyd's Rep 343, [2001] 3 FCR 481, [2001] 2 FLR 1364, [2001] Fam Law 880, [2001] NLJR 1538, [2001] 43 EG 184 (CS), [2001] 2 All ER (Comm) 1061, [2002] 1 P & Cr D25 . . . . 281, 282, 283, 284, 287, 596
Royal Boskalis Westminster NV v Mountain [1999] QB 674, [1997] 2 All ER 929, [1998] 2 WLR 538, [1997] LRLR 523, CA 1051
Royal Bristol Permanent Building Society v Bomash (1887) 35 Ch D 390, 56 LJ Ch 840, [1886-90] All ER Rep 283, 57 LT 179. 441
Royal Brompton Hospital NHS Trust v Hammond [2001] EWCA Civ 550, [2001] BLR 297, 145 Sol Jo LB 118, [2001] All ER (D) 130, [2001] Lloyd's Rep PN 526; affd sub nom Royal Brompton Hospital NHS Trust v Hammond (Taylor Woodrow Construction (Holdings) Ltd, Part 20 defendant) [2002] UKHL 14, [2002] 2 All ER 801, [2002] 1 WLR 1397, [2002] 1 All ER (Comm) 897 . . . . 942, 943, 947
Royal Brunei Airlines Sdn Bhd v Tan [1995] 2 AC 378, [1995] 3 All ER 97, [1995] 3 WLR 64, [1995] BCC 899, [1995] 27 LS Gaz R 33, [1995] NLJR 888, PC. 594, 800, 950, 953, 954, 956, 957, 959, 961, 962, 970, 973, 975, 976
Royal Exchange Assurance v Hope [1928] Ch 179, 97 LJ Ch 153, [1927] All ER Rep 67, 72 Sol Jo 68, 138 LT 446, 44 TLR 160, CA 176
Royal Trust Bank v National Westminster Bank plc [1996] 2 BCLC 682, [1995] BCC 128; on appeal [1996] 2 BCLC 699, [1996] BCC 613, CA 16, 77
Royce's Will Trusts, Re, Tildesley v Tildesley [1959] Ch 626, [1959] 3 All ER 278, [1959] 3 WLR 254, 103 Sol Jo 675, CA 652
Royscott Spa Leasing Ltd v Lovett [1995] BCC 502, [1994] NPC 146, CA 295
Rücker v Scholefield (1862) 1 Hem & M 36, 32 LJ Ch 46, 9 Jur NS 17, 1 New Rep 48, 136 RR 18, 11 WR 137 . . . . 374, 376
Rudd's Will Trusts, Re, Wort v Rudd [1952] 1 All ER 254, [1952] WN 49, [1952] 1 TLR 44 538
Ruddock, Re, Newberry v Mansfield [1908-10] All ER Rep 725, 102 LT 89, CA 544, 840
Rudkin v Dolman (1876) 35 LT 791 . . . . 233, 256, 332
Rumball, Re, Sherlock v Allan [1956] Ch 105, [1955] 3 All ER 71, [1955] 1 WLR 1037, 48 R & IT 672, 99 Sol Jo 579, CA 106
Rushworth's Case (1676) Freem Ch 13 385
Russell v Jackson (1852) 10 Hare 204, 90 RR 336 . . . . 256, 262
Russell v Scott (1936) 53 WN 178, 55 CLR 440, 42 ALR 375, 36 SRNSW 454, 10 ALJ 211 . . . . 247, 359
Russell-Cooke Trust Co v Prentis [2002] EWHC 2227 (Ch) 891, 894
Rutanen v Ballard 424 Mass 723 (1997) 20, 596
Ryall v Ryall (1739) 1 Atk 59 349
Ryder v Bickerton (1743) 1 Eden 149n, 3 Swan 80n 672
Rye v Ashfield Nominees Ltd NLJ, 2 August 2001 826
Rye v Rye [1962] AC 496, [1962] 1 All ER 146, [1962] 2 WLR 361, 106 Sol Jo 94, 181 Estates Gazette 69, HL 6, 273, 663

S

S (gifts by mental patient), Re [1997] 2 FCR 320, [1997] 1 FLR 96, [1997] Fam Law 92 . 269
SEC v Chenery Corpn 318 US 80 (1943) 21
STG Valmet Trustees Ltd v Brennan [2002] WTLR 273. . . . . . . .837, 838, 841, 843, 844
Sackville-West v Viscount Holmesdale (1870) LR 4 HL 543, 39 LJ Ch 505 . . . . 66, 299, 304
Saco Gold Pty Ltd, Re (1983) 33 SASR 99 462
Saffron Walden Second Benefit Building Society v Rayner (1880) 14 Ch D 406, 49 LJ Ch 465, 28 WR 681, 43 LT 3, CA 990
Sainsbury v IRC [1970] Ch 712, [1969] 3 All ER 919, [1969] 3 WLR 760, 48 ATC 306, [1969] TR 305, 113 Sol Jo 855 . . . . 27, 64
Sainsbury's Settlement, Re, Sainsbury v First CB Trustee Ltd [1967] 1 All ER 878, [1967] 1 WLR 476, 111 Sol Jo 177 515
St Andrew's Allotment Association's Trusts, Re, Sargeant v Probert [1969] 1 All ER 147, [1969] 1 WLR 229, 20 P & CR 404, 112 Sol Jo 927 339
St Aubyn v Humphreys (1856) 22 Beav 175 307
St John (Lord) v Lady St John (1803) 11 Ves 526, 32 ER 1192 344
St Thomas's Hospital (Governors) v Richardson [1910] 1 KB 271, 79 LJKB 488, 17 Mans 129, 101 LT 771, CA 461, 826

Sale, Re, Nisbet v Philp [1913] 2 Ch 697, 83 LJ Ch 180, 58 Sol Jo 220, 109 LT 707 . . . 542, 553, 562

Sale v Moore (1827) 1 Sim 534, 27 RR 239 80

Sales, Re, Sales v Sales [1911] WN 194, 55 Sol Jo 386 754

Saliba v Falzon [1998] NSWSC 302 . . . . 1013, 1030, 1033

Salomons, Re, Public Trustee v Wortley [1920] 1 Ch 290, 89 LJ Ch 222, [1920] All ER Rep 768, 64 Sol Jo 241, 122 LT 670, 36 TLR 212 829

Salt v Cooper (1880) 16 Ch D 544, 50 LJ Ch 529, 29 WR 553, [1874-80] All ER Rep 1204, 43 LT 682, CA. 49

Salters Trusts, Re (1866) 17 I Ch R 176 720

Salusbury v Denton (1857) 21 JP 726, 3 K & J 529, 26 LJ Ch 851, 3 Jur NS 740, 5 WR 865, 30 LTOS 63 . . . . 81, 130

Sampson, Re, Sampson v Sampson [1906] 1 Ch 435, 75 LJ Ch 302, 54 WR 342, 50 Sol Jo 239, 94 LT 241 . . . . 757, 771

Sanchez v Sanchez 547 So 2d 945 (1989) 1047

Sandbach, Re, Royds v Douglas [1933] Ch 505, 102 LJ Ch 173, 149 LT 44 537

Sandbrook, Re, Noel v Sandbrook [1912] 2 Ch 471, 81 LJ Ch 800, [1911-13] All ER Rep 559, 56 Sol Jo 721, 107 LT 148 221

Sanders v Deligne and Barns (1692) Freem Ch 123, sub nom Saunders v Dehew 2 Vern 271 1002

Sanders v Miller (1858) 25 Beav 154, 6 WR 454 564

Sanders' Trusts, Re (1866) LR 1 Eq 675, 12 Jur NS 351, 14 WR 576 374

Sanderson's Settlement Trusts, Re [1961] 1 All ER 25n, [1961] 1 WLR 36, 105 Sol Jo 17 . 521

Sanderson's Trust, Re (1857) 3 K & J 497, 26 LJ Ch 804, 3 Jur NS 658, 112 RR 357, 5 WR 864, 30 LTOS 140 . . . . 113, 209, 336

Sanford, Re, Sanford v Sanford [1901] 1 Ch 939, 70 LJ Ch 591, 84 LT 456 . . . . . 80, 135

Sargeant v National Westminster Bank plc (1990) 61 P & CR 518, CA 486, 656, 660, 667

Satanita, The. See Clarke v Earl of Dunraven and Mount-Earl, The Satanita

Satnam Investments Ltd v Dunlop Heywood & Co Ltd [1999] 3 All ER 652, [1999] FSR 722, [1999] 1 BCLC 385, [1998] NPC 169, [1999] 02 LS Gaz R 30, [1998] EGCS 190, [1999] Lloyd's Rep PN 201, CA 24, 395, 399, 401, 957

Saunders (Executrix of Will of Gallie) v Anglia Building Society [1971] AC 1004, [1970] 3 All ER 961, [1970] 3 WLR 1078, 22 P & CR 300, 114 Sol Jo 885, HL. 699

Saunders v Vautier (1841) 4 Beav 115; affd (1841) Cr & Ph 240, 10 LJ Ch 354, 54 RR 286, [1835-42] All ER Rep 58 . . . . . . 9, 27, 59, 180, 205, 238, 433, 486, 730, 822, 1045

Saunders and Halom, Re (1986) 32 DLR (4th) 503, BCCA 617, 703

Sawyer v Sawyer (1885) 28 Ch D 595, 54 LJ Ch 444, 33 WR 403, 52 LT 292, 1 TLR 265, CA 935

Saxone Shoe Co Ltd's Trust Deed, Re, Re Abbott's Will Trusts, Abbott v Pearson [1962] 2 All ER 904, [1962] 1 WLR 943, 106 Sol Jo 687 . . . . . . 84, 107, 108, 109, 112, 132

Sayer Trust, Re, MacGregor v Sayer [1957] Ch 423, [1956] 3 All ER 600, [1957] 2 WLR 261, 101 Sol Jo 130 . . . . 84, 114, 130, 131, 132, 330

Sayre v Hughes (1868) LR 5 Eq 376, 37 LJ Ch 401, 16 WR 662, 18 LT 347 364

Scales v Baker (1859) 28 Beav 91, 6 Jur NS 1134, 8 WR 287, 54 ER 300, 3 LT 73 880

Scally v Southern Health and Social Services Board [1992] 1 AC 294, [1991] 4 All ER 563, [1991] 3 WLR 778, [1991] ICR 771, [1991] IRLR 522, 135 Sol Jo LB 172, HL . . .28, 593, 624, 673, 681

Scandinavian Trading Tanker Co AB v Flota Petrolera Ecuatoriana, The Scaptrade [1983] QB 529, [1983] 1 All ER 301, [1983] 2 WLR 248, [1983] 1 Lloyd's Rep 146, 126 Sol Jo 853, 133 NLJ 133, CA; affd [1983] 2 AC 694, [1983] 2 All ER 763, [1983] 3 WLR 203, [1983] 2 Lloyd's Rep 253, 127 Sol Jo 476, HL 400

Scaptrade, The. See Scandinavian Trading Tanker Co AB v Flota Petrolera Ecuatoriana, The Scaptrade

Scarisbrick Re-settlement Estates, Re [1944] Ch 229, [1944] 1 All ER 404, 113 LJ Ch 148, 88 Sol Jo 127, 170 LT 245, 60 TLR 263 528

Schaefer v Schuhmann [1972] AC 572, [1972] 1 All ER 621, [1972] 2 WLR 481, 116 Sol Jo 121, [1972-73] ALR 501, PC 140

Schalit v Joseph Nadler Ltd [1933] 2 KB 79, 102 LJKB 334, [1933] All ER Rep 708, 149 LT 191, 49 TLR 375, DC 49, 51, 456

Schar, Re, Midland Bank Executor and Trustee Co Ltd v Damer [1951] Ch 280, [1950] 2 All ER 1069, 94 Sol Jo 804, 66 (pt 2) TLR 1131 449

Schebsman, Re, ex p Official Receiver, Trustee v Cargo Superintendents (London) Ltd and Schebsman [1943] Ch 366, [1943] 2 All ER 387, 112 LJ Ch 338, 87 Sol Jo 282, 169 LT 215, 59 TLR 443; affd [1944] Ch 83, [1943] 2 All ER 768, 113 LJ Ch 33, 88 Sol Jo 17, 170 LT 9, 60 TLR 128, CA 10, 170, 171, 172

Scheuerman v Sheuerman (1916) 52 SCR 625, 28 DLR 223, 10 WWR 379 256
Schintz's Will Trusts, Re, Lloyds Bank Ltd v Moreton [1951] Ch 870, [1951] 1 All ER 1095, 95 Sol Jo 369 258
Schneider, Re, Kirby v Schneider (1906) 22 TLR 223 . . . . 584, 645
Schnieder v Mills [1993] 3 All ER 377, [1993] STC 430 279
Schobelt v Barber (1966) 60 DLR (2d) 519, [1967] 1 OR 349 434
Scholefield v Redfern (1863) 2 Drew & Sm 173, 32 LJ Ch 627, 9 Jur NS 485, 1 New Rep 465, 143 RR 74, 11 WR 453, 8 LT 487 540
Scholfield v Spooner (1884) 26 Ch D 94, 53 LJ Ch 777, 32 WR 910, 51 LT 138, CA . . . 307
Schuppan (a bankrupt) (No 2), Re [1997] 1 BCLC 256, [1997] BPIR 271 413
Scoones v Galvin and the Public Trustee [1934] NZLR 1004 . . . . 151, 155
Scotney v Lomer (1886) 31 Ch D 380, 55 LJ Ch 443, 34 WR 407, 54 LT 194, CA . . 803, 805
Scott, Re, Scott v Scott [1911] 2 Ch 374, 80 LJ Ch 750, 105 LT 577 333
Scott, Re, Widdows v Friends of the Clergy Corpn [1975] 2 All ER 1033, [1975] 1 WLR 1260, 119 Sol Jo 508 . . . . 333, 334
Scott v Becher (1817) 18 RR 722, 4 PR 346 906
Scott v Metropolitan Police Comr [1975] AC 819, [1974] 3 All ER 1032, [1974] 3 WLR 741, 60 Cr App Rep 124, 139 JP 121, 118 Sol Jo 863, HL 911
Scott v National Trust for Places of Historic Interest or Natural Beauty [1998] 2 All ER 705, sub nom Ex p Scott [1998] 1 WLR 226, sub nom R v National Trust for Places of Historic Interest or National Beauty, ex p Scott [1998] JPL 465 . . . . . 680, 694, 702
Scott v Scott (1963) 109 CLR 649, HC of A 875, 880, 886
Scott v Surman (1742) Willes 400 . . . . 883, 885
Scottish Co-operative Wholesale Society Ltd v Meyer [1959] AC 324, [1958] 3 All ER 66, [1958] 3 WLR 404, 102 Sol Jo 617, 1958 SC (HL) 40 24
Scowcroft, Re, Ormrod v Wilkinson [1898] 2 Ch 638, 67 LJ Ch 697, [1895-9] All ER Rep 274, 43 Sol Jo 11, 79 LT 342, 15 TLR 4 106
Scrivener v Smith (1869) LR 8 Eq 310 574
Scruttons Ltd v Midland Silicones Ltd [1962] AC 446, [1962] 1 All ER 1, [1962] 2 WLR 186, 106 Sol Jo 34, sub nom Midland Silicones Ltd v Scruttons Ltd [1961] 2 Lloyd's Rep 365, HL 170
Sculthorpe v Tipper (1871) LR 13 Eq 232, 41 LJ Ch 266, 20 WR 276, 26 LT 119 584
Seaconsar Far East Ltd v Bank Markazi Jomhouri Islami Iran [1994] 1 AC 438, [1993] 4 All ER 456, [1993] 3 WLR 756, [1994] 1 Lloyd's Rep 1, [1993] 42 LS Gaz R 42, [1993] NLJR 1479n, 137 Sol Jo LB 239, HL 1060
Seager v Copydex Ltd [1967] 2 All ER 415, [1967] 1 WLR 923, [1967] RPC 349, [1967] RPC 349, 111 Sol Jo 335, CA 403
Seagram v Knight (1867) 2 Ch App 628, 36 LJ Ch 918, 15 WR 1152, 17 LT 47, [1861-73] All ER Rep Ext 2101, CA 158
Seale's Marriage Settlement, Re [1961] Ch 574, [1961] 3 All ER 136, [1961] 3 WLR 262, 105 Sol Jo 257 . . . . 508, 516, 772
Sechiari, Re, Argenti v Sechiari [1950] 1 All ER 417, 94 Sol Jo 194, 66 (pt 1) TLR 531 . . . . 538, 539
Second East Dulwich 745th Starr-Bowkett Building Society, Re (1899) 68 LJ Ch 196, 47 WR 408, 43 Sol Jo 206, 79 LT 726 917
Secretary of State for Education and Science v Tameside Metropolitan Borough Council [1977] AC 1014, [1976] 3 All ER 665, [1976] 3 WLR 641, 120 Sol Jo 539, CA; on appeal [1977] AC 1014, [1976] 3 All ER 665, [1976] 3 WLR 641, 75 LGR 190, 120 Sol Jo 735, HL 699
Secretary of State for Trade and Industry v Deverell [2001] Ch 340, [2000] 2 All ER 365, [2000] 2 WLR 907, [2000] 2 BCLC 133, [2000] BCC 1057, [2000] 03 LS Gaz R 35, 144 Sol Jo LB 49, CA 63
Segbedzi v Segbedzi [2002] WTLR 83 916
Segelman, Re [1996] Ch 171, [1995] 3 All ER 676, [1996] 2 WLR 173 280
Sekhon v Alissa [1989] 2 FLR 94, [1989] Fam Law 355 . . . . 346, 351, 365
Selangor United Rubber Estates Ltd v Cradock (a bankrupt) (No 3) [1968] 2 All ER 1073, [1968] 1 WLR 1555, [1968] 2 Lloyd's Rep 289, 112 Sol Jo 744 . . . . . 381, 952, 957, 960, 974, 986, 990
Selangor United Rubber Estates Ltd v Cradock (a bankrupt) (No 4) [1969] 3 All ER 965, [1969] 1 WLR 1773, 113 Sol Jo 894 979
Selby, Re, Church v Tancred [1903] 1 Ch 715, 72 LJ Ch 324, 51 WR 510, 47 Sol Jo 319, 88 LT 164 212
Selby v Bowie (1863) 9 Jur NS 425, 2 New Rep 2, 11 WR 606, 8 LT 372 582

Selby-Walker, Re, Public Trustee v Selby-Walker [1949] 2 All ER 178. 713
Selby's Will Trusts, Re, Donn v Selby [1965] 3 All ER 386, [1966] 1 WLR 43, 110 Sol Jo 74 103
Seldon v Davidson [1968] 2 All ER 755, [1968] 1 WLR 1083, 112 Sol Jo 463, CA . . 349, 361, 368
Sembaliuk v Sembaliuk (1985) 15 DLR (4th) 303 245
Sen v Headley [1991] Ch 425, [1991] 2 All ER 636, [1991] 2 WLR 1308, 62 P & CR 277, [1996] 1 FCR 692, [1991] 2 FLR 449, [1991] Fam Law 373, 135 Sol Jo 384, [1991] NLJR 384, CA 150, 253, 434
Senior, Re, Senior v Wood [1936] 3 All ER 196, 80 Sol Jo 952 711
Sewell, Re, White v Sewell [1909] 1 Ch 806, 78 LJ Ch 432, 16 Mans 113, 100 LT 883 . . 981
Sewell's Estate, Re (1870) LR 11 Eq 80, 40 LJ Ch 135, sub nom Re London and North Western Rly (New Works and Additional Powers) Act 1869, Re Sewell's Trusts 19 WR 220, 23 LT 835 551
Shafto v Adams (1864) 4 Giff 492, 33 LJ Ch 287, 10 Jur NS 121, 3 New Rep 363, 141 RR 292, 9 LT 676 184
Shafto's Trusts, Re (1885) 29 Ch D 247, 54 LJ Ch 885, 33 WR 728, 53 LT 261 756
Shah v Shah [2001] EWCA Civ 527, [2002] QB 35, [2001] 4 All ER 138, [2001] 3 WLR 31 150
Shaker v Al Bedrawi [2002] EWCA Civ 1452 864
Shallcross v Oldham (1862) 2 John & H 609, 10 WR 291, 5 LT 824 909
Shallcross v Wright (1850) 12 Beav 505, 85 RR 155 371
Sharman's Will Trusts, Re, Public Trustee v Sharman [1942] Ch 311, [1942] 2 All ER 74, 111 LJ Ch 257, 86 Sol Jo 174, 167 LT 285 . . . . 449, 451, 452
Sharp, Re, Rickett v Rickett [1906] 1 Ch 793, 75 LJ Ch 458, 50 Sol Jo 390, 95 LT 522, 22 TLR 368. 982
Sharp v Jackson. See New, Prance and Garrard's Trustee v Hunting
Sharp's Settlement Trusts, Re, Ibbotson v Bliss [1973] Ch 331, [1972] 3 All ER 151, [1972] 3 WLR 765, 116 Sol Jo 666 . . . . .504, 716, 717, 733
Sharpe (a bankrupt), Re, Trustee of the Bankrupt v Sharpe [1980] 1 All ER 198, [1980] 1 WLR 219, 39 P & CR 459, 124 Sol Jo 147 . . . . 12, 248, 253, 324, 357, 407
Sharples v Adams (1863) 32 Beav 213, 1 New Rep 460, 11 WR 450, 8 LT 138 1002
Shaw, Re, Public Trustee v Day [1957] 1 All ER 745, [1957] 1 WLR 729, 101 Sol Jo 408; on appeal [1958] 1 All ER 245n, CA 28, 82, 110, 113, 120, 122, 791
Shaw, Re, Public Trustee v Little [1914] WN 141, 58 Sol Jo 414, 110 LT 924, 30 TLR 418, CA 792, 794, 795
Shaw v Applegate [1978] 1 All ER 123, [1977] 1 WLR 970, 35 P & CR 181, 120 Sol Jo 424, CA 936
Shaw v Cates [1909] 1 Ch 389, 78 LJ Ch 226, 100 LT 146. 606
Shaw v Ford (1877) 7 Ch D 669, 47 LJ Ch 531, 26 WR 235, 37 LT 749 209
Shaw v Foster (1872) LR 5 HL 321, 42 LJ Ch 49, 20 WR 907, 27 LT 281 . . . . . 438, 441
Shaw v Lawless (1838) 5 Cl & Fin 129, 47 RR 41, 1 Dr & Wal 512, HL 113, 142
Shaw's Settlement, Re, Shaw v Shaw [1951] Ch 833, [1951] 1 All ER 656, [1951] 1 TLR 470 724
Shearson Lehman Hutton Inc v Maclaine Watson & Co Ltd (No 2) [1990] 3 All ER 723, [1990] 1 Lloyd's Rep 441, [1990] NLJR 247 871
Shee, Re, Taylor v Stoger [1934] Ch 345, 103 LJ Ch 183, [1934] All ER Rep 623, 150 LT 451 564
Sheffield (Earl) v London Joint Stock Bank (1888) 13 App Cas 333, 57 LJ Ch 986, 37 WR 33, 58 LT 735, 4 TLR 389, HL. .1002
Sheldon, Re, Nixon v Sheldon (1888) 39 Ch D 50, 58 LJ Ch 25, 37 WR 26, 59 LT 133. . . . . 550, 552, 555
Sheldon v RHM Outhwaite (Underwriting Agencies) Ltd [1996] AC 102, [1995] 2 All ER 558, [1995] 2 WLR 570, [1995] 2 Lloyd's Rep 197, [1995] 22 LS Gaz R 41, [1995] NLJR 687, HL 931
Shelley v Shelley (1868) LR 6 Eq 540, 37 LJ Ch 357, 16 WR 1036 . . . . 67, 74, 135
Shelton's Settled Estate (or Estates), Re, Shelton v Shelton [1945] Ch 158, [1945] 1 All ER 283, 114 LJ Ch 198, 89 Sol Jo 152, 172 LT 237, 61 TLR 220 . . . . 299, 301
Shenton, Re [1935] Ch 651, 104 LJ Ch 311, [1934-1935] B & CR 201, [1935] All ER Rep 920, 153 LT 343. 708
Shephard v Cartwright [1955] AC 431, [1954] 3 All ER 649, [1954] 3 WLR 967, 98 Sol Jo 868, HL 12, 361, 362, 363, 367
Shepherd v Federal Comr of Taxation (1965) 113 CLR 385, [1966] ALR 969, 39 ALJR 351, 14 ATD 127, HC of A. 152, 184
Shepherd v Mouls (1845) 4 Hare 500, 14 LJ Ch 366, 9 Jur 506 . . . . . .861, 863, 872, 875
Sheppard v Thompson [2001] All ER (D) 07 (Dec) 892
Sheppard's Settlement Trusts, Re [1888] WN 234 763

Sheppard's Trusts, Re (1862) 4 De GF & J 423, 32 LJ Ch 23, 9 Jur NS 711, 1 New Rep 76, 11
    WR 60, 7 LT 377 . . . . 768, 784
Sherborne's (Lord) Settled Estate, Re [1929] 1 Ch 345, 98 LJ Ch 273, 141 LT 87 . . . 572
Sherdley v Sherdley [1986] 2 All ER 202, [1986] 1 WLR 732, [1986] STC 266, [1986] 2 FLR
    326, [1986] Fam Law 272, 150 JP 305, 130 Sol Jo 356, [1986] LS Gaz R 1636, [1986]
    NLJ Rep 464, CA; revsd [1988] AC 213, [1987] 2 All ER 54, [1987] 2 WLR 1071, [1987]
    STC 217, [1987] FCR 149, [1987] 2 FLR 242, [1987] Fam Law 385, 151 JP 715, 131 Sol
    Jo 504, [1987] LS Gaz R 1492, [1987] NLJ Rep 363, HL 278
Sherman, Re, Re Walters, Trevenen v Pearce [1954] Ch 653, sub nom Re Sherman, Tre-
    venen v Pearce [1954] 1 All ER 893, [1954] 2 WLR 903, 98 Sol Jo 302 662
Sherry v Sherry [1991] 1 FLR 307, [1991] Fam Law 180, CA. 296
Sherwood, Re (1840) 3 Beav 338, 10 LJ Ch 2, 4 Jur 982, 52 RR 146 . . . . 651, 659
Shewen v Vanderhorst (1830) 2 Russ & M 75; on appeal (1831) 1 Russ & M 347, 1 LJ Ch 107 726
Shierson v Tomlinson. See Gallagher (NT) & Son Ltd (in liquidation), Re, Shierson v
    Tomlinson
Shipman v Shipman [1991] FCR 628, [1991] 1 FLR 250, [1991] Fam Law 145 296
Shipwrecked Fishermen and Mariners' Royal Benevolent Society, Re [1959] Ch 220, [1958]
    3 All ER 465, [1958] 3 WLR 701, 102 Sol Jo 878 525
Shirt v Westby (1808) 16 Ves 393 713
Shore v Shore (1859) 4 Drew 501, 28 LJ Ch 940, 113 RR 436, 7 WR 390 . . . 563, 568, 575
Shortill v Grannen (1920) 55 DLR 416, 47 NBR 463 359
Shortridge, Re [1895] 1 Ch 278, 60 JP 38, 64 LJ Ch 191, 12 R 81, 43 WR 257, 39 Sol Jo 134,
    71 LT 799, 11 TLR 135, CA 755, 771
Shovelton v Shovelton (1863) 32 Beav 143, 1 New Rep 226, 138 RR 683 134
Sichel's Settlements, Re, Sichel v Sichel [1916] 1 Ch 358, 85 LJ Ch 285, 114 LT 546 755, 756
Sick and Funeral Society of St John's Sunday School, Golcar, Re [1973] Ch 51, [1972] 2 All
    ER 439, [1972] 2 WLR 962, 116 Sol Jo 355 . . . . 336, 339, 340
Sidmouth v Sidmouth (1840) 2 Beav 447, 9 LJ Ch 282, 50 RR 235, [1835-42] All ER Rep 339 363
Siew Soon Wah v Yong Tong Hong [1973] AC 836, [1973] 2 WLR 713, 117 Sol Jo 341, PC 248
Sifton v Sifton [1938] AC 656, [1938] 3 All ER 435, 107 LJPC 97, 82 Sol Jo 680, 159 LT 289,
    54 TLR 969 . . . . .101, 102, 104, 839
Siggers v Evans (1855) 5 E & B 367, 24 LJQB 305, 1 Jur NS 851, 103 RR 521, 3 CLR 1209, 25
    LTOS 213 142
Sigsworth, Re, Bedford v Bedford [1935] Ch 89, 104 LJ Ch 46, 78 Sol Jo 735, 152 LT 329, 51
    TLR 9. . . . . 261, 262, 434
Silkstone and Haigh Moor Coal Co v Edey [1900] 1 Ch 167, 69 LJ Ch 73, 48 WR 137, 44 Sol
    Jo 41 664
Sillibourne v Newport (1855) 1 K & J 602, 1 Jur NS 608, 3 WR 653 727
Silver v Silver [1958] 1 All ER 523, [1958] 1 WLR 259, 102 Sol Jo 174, CA 365
Silverwood v Silverwood and Whiteley (1997) 74 P & CR 453, CA 343
Simmons' Trusts, Re, Simmons v Public Trustee [1956] Ch 125, [1955] 3 All ER 818, [1956]
    2 WLR 16, 220 LT 355 . . . . 527, 571
Simpson, Re, Chadderton v Simpson [1952] Ch 412, [1952] 1 All ER 963, 96 Sol Jo 262,
    [1952] 1 TLR 868 631
Simpson, Re, Simpson v Simpson [1904] 1 Ch 1, 73 LJ Ch 53, 52 WR 310, 48 Sol Jo 83, 89 LT
    542, CA 311
Simpson v Brown (1864) 13 WR 312, 11 LT 593 720
Simpson v Earles (1847) 11 Jur 921, 81 RR 928 551
Simpson v Simpson [1992] 1 FLR 601, [1989] Fam Law 20 . . . . 270, 276
Simson, Re, Fowler v Tinley [1946] Ch 299, [1946] 2 All ER 220, [1947] LJR 183, 90 Sol Jo
    418, 175 LT 314, 62 TLR 498 . . . . 105, 106
Sinclair, Re, ex p Chaplin (1884) 26 Ch D 319, 53 LJ Ch 732, 51 LT 345, CA 295
Sinclair v Brougham [1914] AC 398, 83 LJ Ch 465, [1914-15] All ER Rep 622, 58 Sol Jo 302,
    111 LT 1, 30 TLR 315, HL. 22, 393, 881, 891, 895, 899, 993
Sinclair v Fell [1913] 1 Ch 155, 82 LJ Ch 105, 57 Sol Jo 145, 108 LT 152, 29 TLR 103 . . 311
Sinclair v Lee [1993] Ch 497, [1993] 3 WLR 498, [1994] 1 BCLC 286, sub nom Re Lee,
    Sinclair v Lee [1993] 3 All ER 926 . . . . 538, 539
Sinclair-Hill v Sothcott (1973) 26 P & CR 490, 226 Estates Gazette 1399 442
Sinclair's Life Policy, Re [1938] Ch 799, [1938] 3 All ER 124, 107 LJ Ch 405, 82 Sol Jo 545,
    159 LT 189, 54 TLR 918 . . . . .10, 172
Singh v Bhasin (1998) Times, 21 August, [2000] WTLR 275 . . . . 815, 845
Singlehurst v Tapscott Steamship Co Ltd [1899] WN 133, 43 Sol Jo 717, CA. 913
Sitwell v Bernard (1801) 5 RR 374, 6 Ves 520, [1775-1802] All ER Rep 308 555

Skeats' Settlement, Re, Skeats v Evans (1889) 42 Ch D 522, 58 LJ Ch 656, 37 WR 778, 61 LT
  500 . . . . 29, 691, 762, 771
Skinner, Re, Cooper v Skinner [1904] 1 Ch 289, 73 LJ Ch 94, 52 WR 346, 89 LT 663 . . 678
Skinner's Trusts, Re (1860) 1 John & H 102, 8 WR 605, 3 LT 177. 113
Slade v Chaine [1908] 1 Ch 522, 77 LJ Ch 377, 52 Sol Jo 240, 98 LT 352, CA . 553, 563, 861
Slater, Re, Slater v Jonas (1915) 85 LJ Ch 432, 113 LT 691 . . . . 551, 555
Sledmore v Dalby (1996) 72 P & CR 196, CA. 248
Slee, Re, Midland Bank Executor and Trustee Co Ltd v Slee [1962] 1 All ER 542, [1962] 1
  WLR 496, 106 Sol Jo 352 . . . . 530, 546, 547
Sleeman v Wilson (1871) LR 13 Eq 36, 20 WR 109, 25 LT 408 934
Slocock's Will Trusts, Re [1979] 1 All ER 358 278
Smallwood v Rutter (1851) 9 Hare 24, 20 LJ Ch 332, 15 Jur 370, 17 LTOS 118. 846
Smart's Goods, Re [1902] P 238, 71 LJP 123, 46 Sol Jo 587, 87 LT 142, 18 TLR 663. . . 258
Smirthwaite's Trusts, Re (1871) LR 11 Eq 251, 40 LJ Ch 176, 19 WR 381, 23 LT 726 . 77, 764
Smith, Re (1971) 16 DLR (3d) 130; affd (1971) 18 DLR (3d) 405. . . . . 531, 618
Smith, Re, Arnold v Smith [1896] 1 Ch 171, 65 LJ Ch 269, [1895-9] All ER Rep 1175, 74 LT
  14 551
Smith, Re, Champ v Marshallsay (1890) 64 LT 13 149
Smith, Re, Eastick v Smith [1904] 1 Ch 139, 73 LJ Ch 74, 52 WR 104, 89 LT 604, 20 TLR
  66 . . . . 741, 742, 752
Smith, Re, Franklin v Smith [1928] Ch 10, 97 LJ Ch 1, 71 Sol Jo 744, 138 LT 81 307
Smith, Re, Henderson-Roe v Hitchins (1889) 42 Ch D 302, 58 LJ Ch 860, 37 WR 705, 61 LT
  363 . . . . 714, 760
Smith, Re, Johnson v Bright-Smith [1914] 1 Ch 937, 83 LJ Ch 687, 58 Sol Jo 494, 110 LT 898,
  30 TLR 411 . . . . 125, 201
Smith, Re, Lawrence v Kitson [1916] 2 Ch 206, 85 LJ Ch 802, 60 Sol Jo 555, 115 LT 68, 32
  TLR 546 1027
Smith, Re, Public Trustee v Aspinall [1928] Ch 915, 97 LJ Ch 441, 140 LT 369 . 27, 183, 503,
                                                                      610, 730, 732, 735
Smith, Re, Public Trustee v Smith [1932] 1 Ch 153, 100 LJ Ch 409, [1931] All ER Rep 617,
  75 Sol Jo 780, 146 LT 145, 48 TLR 44, CA. 106
Smith, Re, Robson v Tidy [1900] WN 75 306
Smith, Re. See Local Registration of Title (Ireland) Act 1891 and Smith, Re
Smith, Re, Smith v Smith (1902) 71 LJ Ch 411, 46 Sol Jo 358, 86 LT 401, 18 TLR
  432 . . . . 585, 624, 914
Smith, Re, Smith v Smith [1916] 1 Ch 369, 85 LJ Ch 473, [1916] HBR 66, 60 Sol Jo 368, 114
  LT 680 212
Smith, Re, Smith v Smith [2001] 3 All ER 552, [2001] 1 WLR 1937, [2001] 28 LS Gaz R 43,
  [2001] NLJR 784 245
Smith, Re, Smith v Thompson (1902) 71 LJ Ch 411, 46 Sol Jo 358, 86 LT 401, 18 TLR
  432 . . . . 631, 914
Smith, Re, Vincent v Smith [1930] 1 Ch 88, 99 LJ Ch 27, 142 LT 178 572
Smith v Anderson (1880) 15 Ch D 247, 50 LJ Ch 39, 29 WR 21, [1874-80] All ER Rep 1121,
  43 LT 329, CA 5, 36, 45
Smith v Cock [1911] AC 317, 80 LJPC 98, 104 LT 1 709
Smith v Cooke, Storey v Cooke [1891] AC 297, 60 LJ Ch 607, 40 WR 67, 65 LT 1,
  HL 141, 335
Smith v Cremer (1875) 24 WR 51 678
Smith v Croft [1986] 2 All ER 551, [1986] 1 WLR 580, [1986] BCLC 207, 2 BCC 99, 010, 130
  Sol Jo 314, [1986] LS Gaz R 3672 816
Smith v Deshaw (1951) 116 V 441 (1951) 149
Smith v Houblon (1859) 26 Beav 482 133
Smith v Hurst (1852) 10 Hare 30, 22 LJ Ch 289, 17 Jur 30, 90 RR 263, 20 LTOS 303 . . 141
Smith v Jones [1954] 2 All ER 823, [1954] 1 WLR 1089, 98 Sol Jo 540 . . . . 50, 991
Smith v Law Guarantee and Trust Society Ltd [1904] 2 Ch 569, 73 LJ Ch 733, 12 Mans 66, 91
  LT 545, 20 TLR 789, CA 537
Smith v Matthews, Re Matthews's Settlement (1861) 3 De GF & J 139, 30 LJ Ch 445, 7 Jur NS
  378, 130 RR 63, 9 WR 644, 4 LT 266 . . . . 237, 255
Smith v Morgan [1971] 2 All ER 1500, [1971] 1 WLR 803, 22 P & CR 618, 115 Sol Jo 288 80
Smith v Nelson (1905) 92 LT 313 870
Smith v Osborne (1857) 6 HL Cas 375, 3 Jur NS 1181, 6 WR 21, 30 LTOS 57 314
Smith v Patrick [1901] AC 282, 70 LJPC 19, 38 SLR 613, 84 LT 740, 17 TLR 477, 3 F (HL) 14,
  HL 612

Smith v Smith (1870) 5 Ch App 342, 18 WR 742 193
Smith v Smith and Smith (1975) 120 Sol Jo 100 475
Smith v Wheeler (1669) 1 Mod Rep 16 730
Smith's Estate, Re (or Re Smith), Bilham v Smith [1937] Ch 636, [1937] 3 All ER 472, 106 LJ
   Ch 377, 81 Sol Jo 611, 157 LT 511, 53 TLR 910. 810
Smith's Trusts, Re (1870) LR 9 Eq 374, 18 WR 513, 22 LT 220 . . . . 564, 574
Smith's Will Trusts, Re, Smith v Melville [1936] 2 All ER 1210, 80 Sol Jo 612, 155 LT 248 537
Smither v Willock (1804) 9 Ves 233 373
Smyth, Re [1970] ALR 919. 152
Smyth, Re, Leach v Leach [1898] 1 Ch 89, 67 LJ Ch 10, 46 WR 104, 42 Sol Jo 81, 77 LT 514,
   14 TLR 77 1029
Smyth v Byrne [1914] 1 IR 53 383
Snook v London and West Riding Investments Ltd [1967] 2 QB 786, [1967] 1 All ER 518,
   [1967] 2 WLR 1020, 111 Sol Jo 71, CA 61
Snowden, Re, Smith v Spowage [1979] Ch 528, [1979] 2 All ER 172, [1979] 2 WLR 654, 123
   Sol Jo 323 . . . . 259, 265
Snowdon v Dales (1834) 6 Sim 524, 3 LJ Ch 188, 3 RR 173, [1824-34] All ER Rep
   425 . . . . .190, 209, 214, 738
Soar v Ashwell [1893] 2 QB 390, 4 R 602, 42 WR 165, [1891-4] All ER Rep 991, 69 LT 585,
   CA 54, 382, 924, 950
Soar v Foster (1858) 4 K & J 152, 4 Jur NS 406, 6 WR 265, 70 ER 64, 31 LTOS 381 . 350, 366
Sociedad Financiera Sofimeca v Kleinwort Benson (Jersey) Trustees Ltd (13 July 1993,
   unreported) 30
Society of Lloyd's v Robinson [1999] 1 WLR 756, [1999] 22 LS Gaz R 34, 143 Sol Jo LB 150,
   [1999] 1 All ER (Comm) 545, HL 499
Solicitor (1951 M 234), Re [1952] Ch 328, [1952] 1 All ER 133, 96 Sol Jo 59 . . . 461, 766
Solicitors (in the matter of a firm of) [2000] 1 Lloyd's Rep 31 406
Solomon (a bankrupt), Re, ex p Trustee of Property of Bankrupt v Solomon [1967] Ch 573,
   [1967] 2 WLR 172, 110 Sol Jo 978, sub nom Re Debtor, ex p Trustee v Solomon [1966]
   3 All ER 255 480
Solomon, Re, Nore v Meyer [1912] 1 Ch 261, 81 LJ Ch 169, 56 Sol Jo 109, 105 LT 951, 28
   TLR 28; on appeal [1913] 1 Ch 200, 82 LJ Ch 160, 108 LT 87, CA 606
Somerset, Re [1887] WN 122. . . . . 747, 765
Somerset, Re, Somerset v Earl Poulett [1894] 1 Ch 231, 63 LJ Ch 41, 7 R 34, 42 WR 145, 38
   Sol Jo 39, 69 LT 744, 10 TLR 46, CA 601, 606, 926, 936, 941, 948
Somes, Re, Smith v Somes [1896] 1 Ch 250, 65 LJ Ch 262, 44 WR 236, 40 Sol Jo 210, 74 LT
   49, 12 TLR 152 29
Sonley v Clock-makers' Co (1780) 1 Bro CC 81 . . . . .77, 774
Sorochan v Sorochan (1986) 29 DLR (4th) 1, [1986] 2 RFL (3d) 225 (Can SC) 323
Sottomayor v De Barros (1877) 3 PD 1, 47 LJP 23, 26 WR 455, [1874-80] All ER Rep 94, 37
   LT 415, CA. 1023
Southampton (Lord) v Brown (1827) 6 B & C 718, 5 LJOSKB 253 169
Southampton's (Lord) Estate, Re, Allen v Lord Southampton, Banfather's Claim (1880) 16
   Ch D 178, 50 LJ Ch 218, 29 WR 231, 43 LT 687 . . . . 623, 629
Space Investments Ltd v Canadian Imperial Bank of Commerce Trust Co (Bahamas) Ltd
   [1986] 3 All ER 75, [1986] 1 WLR 1072, [1986] BCLC 485, 2 BCC 99, 302, 130 Sol Jo
   612, [1986] LS Gaz R 2567, PC 25, 461, 664, 885, 900, 901, 903
Spafax (1965) Ltd v Dommett (1972) 116 Sol Jo 711, CA 84
Speight, Re, Speight v Gaunt (1883) 22 Ch D 727, CA; affd sub nom Speight v Gaunt (1883)
   9 App Cas 1, 48 JP 84, 53 LJ Ch 419, 32 WR 435, 50 LT 330, HL 576, 634
Spellson v George (1987) 11 NSWLR 300 . . . . 28, 116, 624, 673
Spence, Re, Quick v Ackner [1949] WN 237 . . . . .259, 261, 262, 263
Spence v Brown [1988] Fam Law 291, CA 357
Spencer, Re, Lloyds Bank Ltd v Spencer [1935] Ch 533, 104 LJ Ch 127, 153 LT
   121. . . . . 709, 715, 725
Spencer, Re, Spencer v Hart (1881) 51 LJ Ch 271, 30 WR 296, 45 LT 645 986
Spencer v Topham (1856) 22 Beav 573, 2 Jur NS 865, 111 RR 488, 28 LTOS 56 666
Spencer's Settled Estates, Re [1903] 1 Ch 75, 51 WR 262, 88 LT 159, sub nom Re Hammond
   Spencer's Settled Estates 72 LJ Ch 59. 771
Spencer's Will, Re (1887) 57 LT 519, 3 TLR 822, CA 259
Spens v IRC [1970] 3 All ER 295, [1970] 1 WLR 1173, 46 TC 276, 49 ATC 89, [1970] TR 85,
   114 Sol Jo 668 . . . . 52, 519, 724
Spicer, Re, Spicer v Spicer (1901) 84 LT 195 . . . . .67, 304

Spiliada Maritime Corpn v Cansulex Ltd, The Spiliada [1987] AC 460, [1986] 3 All ER 843,
  [1986] 3 WLR 972, [1987] 1 Lloyd's Rep 1, 130 Sol Jo 925, [1987] LS Gaz R 113, [1986]
  NLJ Rep 1137, HL 1059, 1060
Spiro v Glencrown Properties Ltd [1991] Ch 537, [1991] 1 All ER 600, [1991] 2 WLR 931, 62
  P & CR 402, [1990] NPC 90, 134 Sol Jo 1479, [1991] 1 EGLR 185, [1990] NLJR 1754,
  [1991] 02 EG 167 235
Spitzel's Will Trusts, Re, Spitzel v Spitzel [1939] 2 All ER 266, 83 Sol Jo 378 194
Sporle v Barnaby (1864) 10 Jur NS 1142, 13 WR 151, 11 LT 412 623
Sprague, Re, Miley v Cape (1880) 43 LT 236 131
Sprange v Barnard (1789) 2 Bro CC 585 . . . . 80, 81
Springett v Dashwood (1860) 2 Giff 521, 7 Jur NS 93, 3 LT 542 . . . . 671, 677
Springette v Defoe (1992) 65 P & CR 1, [1992] 2 FCR 561, [1992] 2 FLR 388, [1992] Fam
  Law 489, 24 HLR 552, [1992] NPC 34, CA 351, 352, 353, 415, 418, 421, 422
Spurgeon v Collier (1758) 1 Eden 55 992
Spurling's Will Trusts, Re, Philpot v Philpot [1966] 1 All ER 745, [1966] 1 WLR 920, 110 Sol
  Jo 408 . . . . .810, 818, 840, 844
Squire's Settlement, Re [1946] WN 11, 115 LJ Ch 90, 90 Sol Jo 19, 174 LT 150, 62 TLR 133 796
Stacey v Elph (1833) 1 My & K 195, 2 LJ Ch 50, 36 RR 306 . . . . . .449, 452, 453, 668
Stackhouse v Barnston (1805) 10 Ves 453 933
Stafford v Fiddon (1857) 23 Beav 386, 113 RR 191 . . . . 586, 867, 869
Stafford v Stafford (1857) 1 De G & J 193, 4 Jur NS 149, 29 LTOS 368 . . . . . . 931, 932
Stamford (Earl), Re, Payne v Stamford [1896] 1 Ch 288, 65 LJ Ch 134, 44 WR 249, 40 Sol Jo
  114, 73 LT 559, 12 TLR 78 . . . . .753, 760, 768, 771, 827
Stamford (Earl) v Hobart (1710) 3 Bro Parl Cas 31, HL 299, 300, 301
Stamford and Warrington (Earl), Re, Payne v Grey [1916] 1 Ch 404, 85 LJ Ch 241, 114 LT
  551 . . . . 571, 573
Stamford and Warrington (Earl), Re, Payne v Grey [1925] Ch 162, 94 LJ Ch 294, 69 Sol Jo
  194, 133 LT 337; on appeal [1925] Ch 589, 94 LJ Ch 294, 69 Sol Jo 589, 133 LT 337, CA 639
Stamp Duties Comr v Bone [1977] AC 511, [1976] 2 All ER 354, [1976] 2 WLR 968, [1976]
  STC 145, [1976] TR 117, 120 Sol Jo 421, PC 157, 162
Stamp Duties Comr v ISPT Pty Ltd (1999) 2 ITELR 1 5
Stamp Duties Comr (Queensland) v Livingston [1965] AC 694, [1964] 3 All ER 692, [1964]
  3 WLR 963, 43 ATC 325, [1964] TR 351, 108 Sol Jo 820, PC 17, 18, 21, 52, 68,
                                                            116, 154, 165, 1029
Stamp Duties Comrs v Byrnes [1911] AC 386, 80 LJPC 114, 104 LT 515, 27 TLR 408 . . 364
Stamps Comptroller (Victoria) v Howard-Smith (1936) 54 CLR 614, 42 ALR 198, [1936]
  VLR 15, 10 ALJ 39, HC of A 152
Standard Bank London Ltd v Canara Bank [2002] EWHC 1032 (Comm), [2002] All ER (D)
  340 (May) 971
Standard Chartered Bank Ltd v IRC [1978] 3 All ER 644, [1978] 1 WLR 1160, [1978] STC
  272, [1978] TR 45, 122 Sol Jo 698 1029
Standing v Bowring (1885) 31 Ch D 282, 55 LJ Ch 218, 34 WR 204, [1881-5] All ER Rep 702,
  54 LT 191, 2 TLR 202, CA 145, 349, 350, 358, 367, 450
Standing v Gray [1903] 1 IR 49 573
Stanford v Roberts [1901] 1 Ch 440, 83 LT 756, sub nom Re Stanford, Stanford v Roberts 70
  LJ Ch 203, 49 WR 315, 45 Sol Jo 219 573
Staniar v Evans (1886) 34 Ch D 470, 56 LJ Ch 581, 35 WR 286, 56 LT 87, 3 TLR 215 . . 142
Stanley v IRC [1944] KB 255, [1944] 1 All ER 230, 26 TC 12, 113 LJKB 292, 170 LT 140, 60
  TLR 209, CA 65, 710, 716
Stanley v Lennard (1758) Amb 355, 1 Eden 87 66
Stannard v Fisons Pension Trust Ltd [1992] IRLR 27, [1991] PLR 225, CA . . . 496, 694, 695
Stannard v IRC [1991] Pens LR 225 694
Stapleford Colliery Co, Re, Barrow's Case (1879) 14 Ch D 432, 49 LJ Ch 498, 28 WR 270, 41
  LT 755; on appeal (1880) 14 Ch D 432, 49 LJ Ch 498, 42 LT 891, CA 1000
Stapleton, Re, Stapleton v Stapleton [1946] 1 All ER 323, 90 Sol Jo 139, 174 LT 188 . . 712
Stapleton-Bretherton, Re, Weld-Blundell v Stapleton-Bretherton [1941] Ch 482, [1941] 3 All
  ER 5, 110 LJ Ch 197, 85 Sol Jo 447, 166 LT 45 171
Stapylton Fletcher Ltd, Re [1995] 1 All ER 192, [1994] 1 WLR 1181, [1994] 2 BCLC 681 . 78
State Bank of India v Sood [1997] Ch 276, [1997] 1 All ER 169, [1997] 2 WLR 421, 76 P &
  CR 47, [1996] 42 LS Gaz R 28, 140 Sol Jo LB 255, CA 898, 987
Stead, Re, Witham v Andrew [1900] 1 Ch 237, 69 LJ Ch 49, 48 WR 221, 44 Sol Jo 146, 81 LT
  751 262
Stead v Mellor (1877) 5 Ch D 225, 46 LJ Ch 880, 25 WR 508, 36 LT 498 80

Steadman v Steadman [1976] AC 536, [1974] 2 All ER 977, [1974] 3 WLR 56, 29 P & CR 46,
    118 Sol Jo 480, HL. 234, 423
Steed's Will Trusts, Re, Sandford v Stevenson [1960] Ch 407, [1960] 1 All ER 487, [1960] 2
    WLR 474, 104 Sol Jo 207, CA. 503, 507, 508, 510
Steel, Re, Public Trustee v Christian Aid Society [1979] Ch 218, [1978] 2 All ER 1026, [1978]
    2 WLR 950, 122 Sol Jo 148. 91
Steel v Wellcome Custodian Trustees Ltd [1988] 1 WLR 167, 131 Sol Jo 1589, [1987] LS Gaz
    R 3335 509
Steel Wing Co Ltd, Re [1921] 1 Ch 349, 90 LJ Ch 116, [1920] B & CR 160, [1920] All ER Rep
    292, 65 Sol Jo 240, 124 LT 664 152
Steele v Paz Ltd [1993-95] Manx LR 426, CA. 29, 30, 32, 754
Steele v Paz Ltd [1993-95] Manx LR 102 . . . . 691, 835
Steele's Will Trusts, Re, National Provincial Bank Ltd v Steele [1948] Ch 603, [1948] 2 All
    ER 193, [1948] LJR 1888, 92 Sol Jo 392. . . . . 74, 133, 134, 135, 300
Stenning, Re, Wood v Stenning [1895] 2 Ch 433, 13 R 807, 73 LT 207, [1895-9] All ER Rep
    Ext 2045. . . . . 881, 891
Stephens v Avery [1988] Ch 449, [1988] 2 All ER 477, [1988] 2 WLR 1280, [1988] FSR 510,
    132 Sol Jo 822, [1988] NLJR 69 218
Stephens v Cuckfield RDC [1960] 2 QB 373, [1960] 2 All ER 716, [1960] 3 WLR 248, 58
    LGR 213, 11 P & CR 248, 124 JP 420, 104 Sol Jo 565, CA 372
Stephens Travel Service International Pty Ltd v Qantas Airways Ltd (1988) 13 NSWLR 331
    (NSW CA) 16
Stephenson (Inspector of Taxes) v Barclays Bank Trust Co Ltd [1975] 1 All ER 625, [1975] 1
    WLR 882, [1975] STC 151, 50 TC 374, 53 ATC 357, [1974] TR 343, 119 Sol Jo
    169 . . . . .9, 734, 736, 737, 739
Stevens v Hutchinson [1953] Ch 299, [1953] 2 WLR 545, 97 Sol Jo 171, sub nom Re No 39
    Carr Lane, Acomb, Stevens v Hutchinson [1953] 1 All ER 699 480
Stevens v Robertson (1868) 37 LJ Ch 499, 16 WR 724, 18 LT 427 . . . . 497, 932
Steward v Poppleton [1877] WN 29 . . . . 308, 316
Stewart, Re, Stewart v McLaughlin [1908] 2 Ch 251, 77 LJ Ch 525, [1908-10] All ER Rep 133,
    99 LT 106, 24 TLR 679 .159, 161, 162, 163
Stewart's Trustees v Stewart 1927 SC 350, 126 SLT 400 204
Stiles v Guy (1849) 19 LJ Ch 185, 1 H & Tw 523, 84 RR 111, 14 LTOS 305, sub nom Styles v
    Guy 14 Jur 355, 1 Mac & G 422 . . . . 452, 647
Stimpson's Trusts, Re, Stimpson v Stimpson [1931] 2 Ch 77, 100 LJ Ch 312, [1931] All ER
    Rep 809, 145 LT 249 . . . . 718, 724
Stirling, Re, Union Bank of Scotland Ltd v Stirling [1954] 2 All ER 113, [1954] 1 WLR 763,
    98 Sol Jo 337 259
Stock v McAvoy (1872) LR 15 Eq 55, 42 LJ Ch 230, 21 WR 521, 27 LT 441 . . . . 363, 364
Stokes, Re, Bowen v Davidson [1928] Ch 716, 97 LJ Ch 273, [1928] All ER Rep 406, 72 Sol Jo
    384, 139 LT 331. 713
Stokes v Anderson [1991] FCR 539, [1991] 1 FLR 391, [1991] Fam Law 310, CA . . 326, 352,
                                         354, 412, 421, 422, 423, 424, 425
Stokes v Cheek (1860) 28 Beav 620, 29 LJ Ch 922. . . . . 533, 566, 732
Stokes v Prance [1898] 1 Ch 212, 67 LJ Ch 69, 46 WR 183, 42 Sol Jo 68, 77 LT 595 . 497, 873
Stokes' Trusts, Re (1872) LR 13 Eq 333, 41 LJ Ch 290, 20 WR 396, 26 LT 181 . . . 747, 846
Stone, Re [1989] 1 Qd R 351. 411
Stone v Hoskins [1905] P 194, 74 LJP 110, 54 WR 64, 93 LT 441, 21 TLR 528 . 140, 428, 430
Stone v Stone (1869) 5 Ch App 74, 39 LJ Ch 196, 18 WR 225, 22 LT 182 168
Stoneham, Re, Stoneham v Stoneham [1919] 1 Ch 149, 88 LJ Ch 77, [1918-19] All ER Rep
    1051, 63 Sol Jo 192, 120 LT 341. 162
Stoneham's Settlement Trusts, Re, Popkiss v Stoneham [1953] Ch 59, [1952] 2 All ER 694,
    [1952] 2 TLR 614 . . . . 758, 759
Stonor v Curwen (1832) 5 Sim 264 302
Story v Gape (1856) 2 Jur NS 706, 106 RR 974 934
Stott v Milne (1884) 25 Ch D 710, 50 LT 742, CA 564, 574, 810
Stott v Ratcliffe (1982) 126 Sol Jo 310, CA. 480
Strachan, Re, ex p Cooke (1876) 4 Ch D 123, 41 JP 180, 46 LJ Bcy 52, 25 WR 171, 35 LT 649,
    CA 882, 992
Strafford (Earl), Re, Royal Bank of Scotland Ltd v Byng [1978] 3 All ER 18, [1978] 3 WLR
    223, 122 Sol Jo 472; affd [1980] Ch 28, [1979] 1 All ER 513, [1979] 2 WLR 459, 123 Sol
    Jo 50, CA 708

Strahan, Re, ex p Geaves (1856) 8 De GM & G 291, 25 LJ Bcy 53, 2 Jur NS 65, 4 WR 536, 27
    LTOS 129 . . . . 485, 491, 492
Strakosch, Re, Temperley v A-G [1948] Ch 37, [1947] 2 All ER 607, [1948] LJR 369, 91 Sol Jo
    625, 63 TLR 577; affd [1949] Ch 529, [1949] 2 All ER 6, [1949] LJR 1477, 93 Sol Jo 372,
    65 TLR 383, CA 106
Strange v Fooks (1863) 4 Giff 408, 9 Jur NS 943, 2 New Rep 507, 11 WR 983, 8 LT 789 . 931
Stratford v Shayle-George [2001] NZCA 299 858
Strathcona (Lord) Steamship Co Ltd v Dominion Coal Co Ltd [1926] AC 108, 95 LJPC 71,
    16 Asp MLC 585, 31 Com Cas 80, [1925] All ER Rep 87, 134 LT 227, 42 TLR 86, PC 183
Stratheden and Campbell (Lord), Re, Alt v Lord Stratheden and Campbell [1894] 3 Ch 265,
    63 LJ Ch 872, 8 R 515, 42 WR 647, 38 Sol Jo 602, 71 LT 225, 10 TLR 574 201
Stratton, Re, Knapman v A-G [1931] 1 Ch 197, 100 LJ Ch 62, [1930] All ER Rep 255, 74 Sol
    Jo 787, 144 LT 169, 47 TLR 32, CA 106
Stratton's Disclaimer, Re, Stratton v IRC [1958] Ch 42, [1957] 2 All ER 594, [1957] 3 WLR
    199, 36 ATC 145, [1957] TR 161, 101 Sol Jo 533, CA. 246
Stratulatos v Stratulatos [1988] 2 NZLR 424 248
Stretton, Re, Stretton v Clegg [1942] WN 95 747
Strickland v Symons (1884) 26 Ch D 245, 53 LJ Ch 582, 32 WR 889, 51 LT 406, CA. 142, 824,
                                                                                         825
Strong v Bird (1874) LR 18 Eq 315, 43 LJ Ch 814, 22 R 788, [1874-80] All ER Rep 230, 30 LT
    745 . . . . 157, 159, 165
Stroud v Gwyer (1860) 28 Beav 130, 6 Jur NS 719, 126 RR 57, 2 LT 400 . . . . . 553, 563
Stroud Architectural Systems Ltd v John Laing Construction Ltd (1993) 35 Con LR 135,
    [1994] 2 BCLC 276, [1994] BCC 18, [1993] BLM (April) 3 15
Stuart, Re, Johnson v Williams [1940] 4 All ER 80, 84 Sol Jo 524, CA 843
Stuart, Re, Smith v Stuart [1897] 2 Ch 583, 66 LJ Ch 780, 46 WR 41, 77 LT 128 . . 913, 914,
                                                                                         917
Stuart v Norton (1860) 14 Moo PCC 17, 9 WR 320, 3 LT 602 635
Stuart v Stuart (1841) 3 Beav 430, 10 LJ Ch 148, 5 Jur 3 531
Stuart-Hutcheson v Spread Trustee Co Ltd [2002] WTLR 1213 . . . . 674, 677
Stubbs v Sargon (1838) 3 My & Cr 507, 7 LJ Ch 95, 2 Jur 150, 44 RR 241 330
Sturgess v Pearson (1819) 4 Madd 411, 20 RR 316. 374
Styles v Guy. See Stiles v Guy
Sudbrook Trading Estate Ltd v Eggleton [1983] 1 AC 444, [1982] 3 All ER 1, [1982] 3 WLR
    315, 44 P & CR 153, 126 Sol Jo 512, 265 Estates Gazette 215, HL 80
Sudeley (Lord) v A-G [1897] AC 11, 61 JP 420, 66 LJQB 21, 45 WR 305, 75 LT 398, 13 TLR
    38, [1895-9] All ER Rep Ext 1904, HL 1029
Sudeley (Lord) and Baines & Co, Re [1894] 1 Ch 334, 63 LJ Ch 194, 8 R 79, 42 WR 231, 70
    LT 549 200
Suenson-Taylor's Settlement, Re, Moores v Moores [1974] 3 All ER 397, [1974] 1 WLR 1280,
    118 Sol Jo 757 . . . . 584, 602, 704
Suffert's Settlement, Re, Suffert v Martyn-Linnington [1961] Ch 1, [1960] 3 All ER 561,
    [1960] 3 WLR 796, 104 Sol Jo 892 . . . . 505, 506, 507
Suffolk v Lawrence (1884) 32 WR 899 833
Sullivan, Re, Dunkley v Sullivan [1930] 1 Ch 84, 99 LJ Ch 42, [1929] All ER Rep 564, 142 LT
    187, 45 TLR 590. 554
Surtees v Surtees (1871) LR 12 Eq 400, 19 WR 1043, 25 LT 288 300
Susanni's Trusts, Re (1877) 47 LJ Ch 65, 26 WR 93 130
Sutherland Settlement Trusts, Re [1953] Ch 792, [1953] 2 All ER 27, [1953] 2 WLR 1163, 97
    Sol Jo 387 . . . . 573, 613
Suttill v Graham [1977] 3 All ER 1117, [1977] 1 WLR 819, 7 Fam Law 211, 121 Sol Jo 408,
    CA 356
Sutton, Re, Stone v A-G (1885) 28 Ch D 464, 54 LJ Ch 613, 33 WR 519 106
Sutton v Jones (1809) 15 Ves 584 668
Sutton v Wilders (1871) LR 12 Eq 373, 41 LJ Ch 30, 19 WR 1021, 25 LT 292 625
Swain v Law Society [1981] 3 All ER 797, [1982] 1 WLR 17, 125 Sol Jo 542, CA; revsd [1983]
    1 AC 598, [1982] 2 All ER 827, [1982] 3 WLR 261, 126 Sol Jo 464, HL. . .7, 23, 37, 56,
                                                                380, 386, 387, 388, 389,
                                                                596, 934, 936
Swale v Swale (1856) 22 Beav 584, 111 RR 495 . . . . 645, 646, 905
Swaledale Cleaners Ltd, Re [1968] 3 All ER 619, [1968] 1 WLR 1710, 112 Sol Jo 781, CA 155
Swales v IRC [1984] 3 All ER 16, [1984] STC 413, [1984] LS Gaz R 2300 . . . . . 690, 710
Swan, Re (1864) 2 Hem & M 34, 4 New Rep 53, 144 RR 21, 12 WR 738, 10 LT 334 . 543, 829

Swannell, Re, Morice v Swannell (1909) 101 LT 76 212
Swanwick House, Prestbury, Re [1939] 3 All ER 531 573
Swasey v American Bible Society 57 Me 527 (1869) 121
Sweetapple v Bindon (1705) 2 Vern 536 303
Sweetapple v Horlock (1879) 11 Ch D 745, 48 LJ Ch 660, 27 WR 865, 41 LT 272 . . 310, 314
Sweeting, Re, Sweeting v Sweeting [1988] 1 All ER 1016 441
Swift v Dairywise Farms Ltd [2000] 1 All ER 320, [2000] 1 WLR 1177, [2000] 1 BCLC 632,
    [2000] BCC 642, [1999] EGCS 137; revsd in part sub nom Swift v Dairywise Farms Ltd
    [2001] EWCA Civ 145, [2001] 1 BCLC 672 182
Swinburne, Re, Sutton v Featherley [1926] Ch 38, 95 LJ Ch 104, [1925] All ER Rep 313, 70
    Sol Jo 64, 134 LT 121, CA 151
Swindle v Harrison [1997] 4 All ER 705, [1997] PNLR 641, CA. . . 22, 23, 24, 327, 659, 661,
                                                          701, 852, 865, 866, 876
Swinnock v Crisp (1681) Freem Ch 78, sub nom Anon 2 Vent 353 720
Swires (Inspector of Taxes) v Renton [1991] STC 490, 64 TC 315 . . . . 726, 807
Swiss Bank Corpn v Lloyds Bank Ltd [1982] AC 584, [1980] 2 All ER 419, [1980] 3 WLR 457,
    124 Sol Jo 741, CA; affd [1982] AC 584, [1981] 2 All ER 449, [1981] 2 WLR 893, 125 Sol
    Jo 495, HL 77
Sykes v Land [1984] 2 EGLR 8, 271 Estates Gazette 1264, CA 476
Sykes v Sykes (1871) LR 13 Eq 56, 41 LJ Ch 25, 20 WR 90, 25 LT 560 . . . . . 190, 214
Symes v Hughes (1870) LR 9 Eq 475, 39 LJ Ch 304, 22 LT 462 . . . . . . 343, 345, 369
Symm's Will Trusts, Re, Public Trustee v Shaw [1936] 3 All ER 236, 80 Sol Jo 994 . 741, 742
Synge v Synge [1894] 1 QB 466, 58 JP 396, 63 LJQB 202, 9 R 265, 42 WR 309, [1891-4] All ER
    Rep 1164, 70 LT 221, 10 TLR 194, CA 140
Synnot v Simpson (1854) 5 HL Cas 121, 23 LTOS 263 142

T

T v T (joinder of third parties) [1997] 1 FCR 98, [1996] 2 FLR 357, [1996] Fam Law 669 1044
T's Settlement Trusts, Re [1964] Ch 158, [1963] 3 WLR 987, 107 Sol Jo 981, sub nom Re
    Towler's Settlement Trusts [1963] 3 All ER 759 . . . . 509, 511
TB, Re [1967] Ch 247, [1966] 3 All ER 509, [1967] 2 WLR 15, 110 Sol Jo 977 149
TR Technology Investment Trust plc, Re [1988] BCLC 256, 4 BCC 244, [1988] FTLR 483   4
TSB Bank plc v Camfield [1995] 1 All ER 951, [1995] 1 WLR 430, [1995] 2 FCR 254, [1995]
    1 FLR 751, [1995] Fam Law 298, 27 HLR 205, [1995] 03 LS Gaz R 37, [1995] NLJR 215,
    CA 286
TTS International v Cantrade Private Bank (1995) 4 JITCP 60n 967
Tabor v Brooks (1878) 10 Ch D 273, 48 LJ Ch 130, 39 LT 528 551
Tailby v Official Receiver (1888) 13 App Cas 523, 58 LJQB 75, 37 WR 513, [1886-90] All ER
    Rep 486, 60 LT 162, 4 TLR 726, HL 153, 184, 185, 826
Talbot v Earl Radnor (1834) 3 My & K 252, 41 RR 64 . . . . 623, 846
Talbot (Earl) v Hope Scott (1858) 4 K & J 139, 116 RR 271 . . . . 903, 905
Talbot v Jevers (1875) LR 20 Eq 255, 44 LJ Ch 646, 23 WR 741 730
Talbot v Marshfield (1867) LR 4 Eq 661 727
Talbot v Marshfield (1865) 2 Drew & Sm 549, 6 New Rep 288, 13 WR 885, 12 LT 761 . . 679
Talbot v Marshfield (1868) 3 Ch App 622, 32 JP 725, 19 LT 223 672
Talbot v O'Sullivan (1880) LR 6 Ir 302 138
Talbot v Talbot [1968] Ch 1, [1967] 2 All ER 920, [1967] 3 WLR 438, 111 Sol Jo 278, CA   80
Tallack v Tallack and Broekema [1927] P 211, 96 LJKB 117, [1927] All ER Rep 676, 71 Sol Jo
    521, 137 LT 487, 43 TLR 467 1044
Tallatire, Re [1885] WN 191 . . . . 754, 759
Tan v Tan (1946) 12 MLJ 159 123
Tancred's Settlement, Re, Somerville v Tancred [1903] 1 Ch 715, 72 LJ Ch 324, 51 WR 510,
    [1900-3] All ER Rep 251, 47 Sol Jo 319, 88 LT 164 . . . . 212, 246
Tang Man Sit (Personal Representatives) v Capacious Investments Ltd [1996] AC 514,
    [1996] 1 All ER 193, [1996] 2 WLR 192, [1996] 05 LS Gaz R 32, 140 Sol Jo LB 29,
    PC 871, 874
Tankel v Tankel [1999] 1 FLR 676, [1999] Fam Law 93 278
Tankel v Tankel [2002] EWCA Civ 227 166
Tanner v Tanner [1975] 3 All ER 776, [1975] 1 WLR 1346, 119 Sol Jo 391, CA . . 225, 345
Target Holdings Ltd v Redferns (a firm) [1994] 2 All ER 337, [1994] 1 WLR 1089, CA; revsd
    [1996] AC 421, [1995] 3 All ER 785, [1995] 3 WLR 352, [1995] 31 LS Gaz R 36, [1995]
    NLJR 1164, 139 Sol Jo LB 195, HL 495, 625, 661, 851, 852, 854, 855, 856,
                                            857, 861, 862, 864, 868, 872, 877, 948

Tarleton v Hornby (1835) 1 Y & C Ex 333 940
Tarnpolsk, Re, Barclays Bank Ltd v Hyer [1958] 3 All ER 479, [1958] 1 WLR 1157, 102 Sol Jo
    857 103
Tatam v Williams (1844) 3 Hare 347, 64 RR 325 935
Tate v Williamson (1866) 2 Ch App 55, LR 1 Eq 528, 15 WR 321, 15 LT 549; on appeal
    (1866) 2 Ch App 55, CA 276, 284, 666
Tatham, Re, National Bank Ltd and Matthews v Mackenzie [1945] Ch 34, [1945] 1 All ER
    29, 114 LJ Ch 9, 88 Sol Jo 407, 172 LT 14, 61 TLR 76 534
Taylor, Re, Lloyds Bank Ltd v Jones [1957] 3 All ER 56, [1957] 1 WLR 1043, 101 Sol Jo 816 333
Taylor, Re, Taylor v Wade [1894] 1 Ch 671, 63 LJ Ch 424, 8 R 186, 42 WR 373, 38 Sol Jo 288,
    70 LT 556 . . . . 951, 981
Taylor, Re, Waters v Taylor [1926] Ch 923, 96 LJ Ch 17, 137 LT 17 . . . . 535, 536
Taylor v Clark (1841) 1 Hare 161, 11 LJ Ch 189, 6 Jur 76 557
Taylor v Davies [1920] AC 636, 89 LJPC 65, 123 LT 121, PC 922, 924
Taylor v Dickens [1998] 3 FCR 455, [1998] 1 FLR 806, [1998] Fam Law 191 252
Taylor v Lewis (1891) 12 LRNSW Eq 258 143
Taylor v London and County Banking Co [1901] 2 Ch 231, 70 LJ Ch 477, 49 WR 451, 45 Sol
    Jo 394, 84 LT 397, 17 TLR 413, CA 1001
Taylor v Plumer (1815) 3 M & S 562, 2 Rose 457, [1814-23] All ER Rep 167 . . . . 880, 882,
    883, 895
Taylor v Russell [1892] AC 244, 61 LJ Ch 657, 41 WR 43, 36 Sol Jo 379, 66 LT 565, 8 TLR
    463, HL 1001
Taylor v Taylor (1853) 3 De GM & G 190, 22 LJ Ch 742, 1 Eq Rep 239, 17 Jur 583, 98 RR 104,
    1 WR 398, 21 LTOS 213 371
Taylor v Taylor [1956] NZLR 99 248
Taylor's Trusts, Re, Matheson v Taylor [1905] 1 Ch 734, 74 LJ Ch 419, 53 WR 441, 49 Sol Jo
    418, 92 LT 558 . . . . 542, 553, 562
Taylors Fashions Ltd v Liverpool Victoria Trustees Co Ltd [1981] 2 WLR 576n, [1981] Com
    LR 34, 251 Estates Gazette 159, [1982] QB 133n, [1981] 1 All ER 897 . . 242, 248, 250,
    328, 411
Tebbs, Re, Redfern v Tebbs [1976] 2 All ER 858, [1976] 1 WLR 924, 120 Sol Jo 525 . . 854
Tebbs v Carpenter (1816) 1 Madd 290, 16 RR 224 579
Tee v Ferris (1856) 20 JP 563, 2 K & J 357, 25 LJ Ch 437, 2 Jur NS 807, 110 RR 262, 4 WR
    352 . . . . 260, 262
Tee v Tee [1999] 2 FLR 613, CA 427, 482
Tegg, Re, Public Trustee v Bryant [1936] 2 All ER 878, 80 Sol Jo 552 222
Tempest, Re (1866) 1 Ch App 485, 35 LJ Ch 632, 12 Jur NS 539, 14 WR 850, 14 LT 688, CA 770
Tempest v Lord Camoys (1866) 35 Beav 201, 14 WR 326, 14 LT 8 77
Tempest v Lord Camoys (1882) 21 Ch D 571, 51 LJ Ch 785, 31 WR 326, 48 LT 13,
    CA 702, 726, 736, 848
Tempest v Lord Camoys (1888) 52 JP 532, 58 LT 221 771
Temple v Thring (1887) 56 LJ Ch 767, 56 LT 283 586
Tennant v Trenchard (1869) 4 Ch App 537, 38 LJ Ch 169, 20 LT 856 670
Tepper's Will Trusts, Re, Kramer v Ruda [1987] Ch 358, [1987] 1 All ER 970, [1987] 2 WLR
    729, [1987] 2 FLR 439, [1987] Fam Law 379, 131 Sol Jo 327, [1987] LS Gaz R
    1057 . . . . 83, 84, 89, 101, 103, 220
Tetley, Re, National Provincial and Union Bank of England Ltd v Tetley [1923] 1 Ch 258,
    CA; affd sub nom A-G v National Provincial and Union Bank of England [1924] AC
    262, [1923] All ER Rep 123, 68 Sol Jo 235, 40 TLR 191, sub nom Re Tetley, A-G v
    National Provincial and Union Bank of England 93 LJ Ch 231, 131 LT 34, HL . . . 106
Tett v Phoenix Property and Investment Co Ltd [1984] BCLC 599; revsd [1986] BCLC 149,
    2 BCC 99, 140, 129 Sol Jo 869, [1986] LS Gaz R 116, CA 77, 151, 154, 155
Texas Co v Bombay Banking Co (1919) LR 46 Ind App 250 986
Thatcher's Trusts, Re (1859) 26 Beav 365 225
Thatcher's Trusts, Re (1884) 26 Ch D 426, 53 LJ Ch 1050, 32 WR 679 715
Thellusson v Woodford (1805) 1 Bos & PNR 357, 8 RR 104, 11 Ves 112, 32 ER 1030, [1803-
    13] All ER Rep 30, HL 203, 204
Thirty-Eight Building Ltd, Re [1999] 1 BCLC 416, [1999] BCC 260, [1999] BPIR 620 . . 290
Thomas, Re, Andrew v Thomas [1916] 2 Ch 331, 85 LJ Ch 519, 60 Sol Jo 537, 114 LT 885, 32
    TLR 530, CA 537
Thomas, Re, Thomas v Thompson [1930] 1 Ch 194, 99 LJ Ch 140, [1929] All ER Rep 129,
    142 LT 310 526
Thomas, Re, Weatherall v Thomas [1900] 1 Ch 319, 69 LJ Ch 198, 48 WR 409 568

Thomas, Re, Wood v Thomas [1891] 3 Ch 482, 60 LJ Ch 781, 40 WR 75, 65 LT 142 . . 552,
556
Thomas v IRC [1981] STC 382, [1981] TR 83 511
Thomas v Kelly (1888) 13 App Cas 506, 58 LJQB 66, 37 WR 353, [1886-90] All ER Rep 431,
60 LT 114, 4 TLR 683, HL. 184
Thomas v Thomas [1956] NZLR 785 248
Thomas v Thomas [1996] 2 FCR 544, [1995] 2 FLR 668, [1995] Fam Law 672, CA . . 32, 63
Thomas v Times Book Co Ltd [1966] 2 All ER 241, [1966] 1 WLR 911, 110 Sol Jo 252 . 151
Thomas v Williams (1883) 24 Ch D 558, 52 LJ Ch 603, 31 WR 943, 49 LT 111 727
Thomas d Evans v Thomas (1796) 3 RR 306, 6 Term Rep 671 82
Thomas's Will Trusts, Re, Powell v Thomas [1930] 2 Ch 67, 99 LJ Ch 286, 74 Sol Jo 201, 144
LT 64 231
Thomason v Moses (1842) 5 Beav 77, 6 Jur 403, 59 RR 421 83
Thompson, Re, Public Trustee v Lloyd [1934] Ch 342, 103 LJ Ch 162, [1933] All ER Rep
805, 150 LT 451 . . . . 119, 122
Thompson, Re, Thompson v Thompson [1906] 2 Ch 199, 75 LJ Ch 599, 54 WR 613, 95 LT
97 . . . . 198, 199
Thompson, Re, Thompson v Watkins [1908] WN 195 566
Thompson v Clive (1848) 11 Beav 475, 83 RR 224 678
Thompson v Finch (1856) 22 Beav 316, 8 De GM & G 560, 25 LJ Ch 681, 114 RR 247, 27
LTOS 330 . . . . .647, 940, 941, 945
Thompson v Fisher (1870) LR 10 Eq 207, 18 WR 860 . . . . 301, 304
Thompson v Simpson (1841) 58 RR 298, 1 Dr & War 459 985
Thompson v Thompson (1970) 114 Sol Jo 455, CA 361
Thompson's Settlement, Re, Thompson v Thompson [1986] Ch 99, [1985] 2 All ER 720,
[1985] 3 WLR 486, 129 Sol Jo 575 . . . . .384, 387, 661, 664, 666
Thompson's Settlement Trusts, Re, Thompson v Alexander [1905] 1 Ch 229, 74 LJ Ch 133,
91 LT 835, 21 TLR 86 . . . . 752, 774
Thompson's Trustee in Bankruptcy v Heaton [1974] 1 All ER 1239, [1974] 1 WLR 605, 118
Sol Jo 295 . . . . 22, 384, 385
Thomson, Re, Thomson v Allen [1930] 1 Ch 203, 99 LJ Ch 156, 142 LT 253 . . . . 17, 24
Thomson v Clydesdale Bank Ltd [1893] AC 282, 62 LJPC 91, 1 R 255, [1891-4] All ER Rep
1169, 69 LT 156, HL 986
Thomson v Eastwood (1877) 2 App Cas 215, HL 671, 933, 935
Thomson's Settlement Trusts, Re [1944] Ch 70, [1943] 2 All ER 805, 113 LJ Ch 173, 170 LT
26, 60 TLR 155, CA 304
Thorley, Re, Thorley v Massam [1891] 2 Ch 613, 60 LJ Ch 537, 39 WR 565, 64 LT 515, 7 TLR
479, [1891-4] All ER Rep Ext 2074 652
Thorn v IRC [1976] 2 All ER 622, [1976] 1 WLR 915, [1976] STC 208, [1976] TR 63, 120 Sol
Jo 216 . . . . 519, 730
Thorndike v Hunt (1859) 3 De G & J 563, 28 LJ Ch 417, 5 Jur NS 879, 32 LTOS 346, sub
nom Re Hunt, Thorndike v Hunt 121 RR 232, 7 WR 246, 33 LTOS 99 999
Thorne, Re, Thorne v Campbell-Preston [1917] 1 Ch 360, 86 LJ Ch 261, 61 Sol Jo 268, 116
LT 540 . . . . 307, 315
Thorne v Heard and Marsh [1895] AC 495, 64 LJ Ch 652, 11 R 254, 44 WR 155, 73 LT 291,
11 TLR 464, HL 923
Thornhill's Settlement, Re [1941] Ch 24, [1940] 4 All ER 83, 84 Sol Jo 537, 163 LT 297, 57
TLR 28; affd [1941] Ch 24, [1940] 4 All ER 249, 111 LJ Ch 5, 84 Sol Jo 633, 164 LT 190,
57 TLR 76, CA 465
Thornton v Stokill (1855) 1 Jur NS 751, 26 LTOS 26 . . . . 861, 875
Thorpe, Re, Vipont v Radcliffe [1891] 2 Ch 360, 60 LJ Ch 529, 64 LT 554 386
Three Rivers District Council v Bank of England (No 3) [2000] 2 WLR 15, [1999] 4 All ER
800n, CA; on appeal [2000] 3 All ER 1, [2000] 2 WLR 1220, [2000] 3 CMLR 205,
[2000] NLJR 769, [2000] All ER (D) 690, HL 595, 959
Thrells Ltd (in liquidation) v Lomas [1993] 2 All ER 546, [1993] 1 WLR 456, [1992] PLR
233, [1993] BCC 441 . . . . 94, 97, 690
Thrupp v Collett (1858) 26 Beav 125, 5 Jur NS 111, 32 LTOS 365 218
Thureau, Re, Mitchell v Holland [1948] ALR 487 107
Thursby v Thursby (1875) LR 19 Eq 395, 44 LJ Ch 289, 23 WR 500, 32 LT 189 . . 551, 554
Tibbits v Tibbits (1816) Jac 317, 2 Mer 96n, 23 RR 79, 19 Ves 657 80
Tierney v Wood (1854) 19 Beav 330, 23 LJ Ch 895, 105 RR 164, 2 WR 577, 23 LTOS
266 . . . . 233, 237

Tiger v Barclays Bank Ltd [1951] 2 KB 556, [1951] 2 All ER 262, 95 Sol Jo 400, [1951] 2 TLR
102; affd [1952] 1 All ER 85, CA 491, 747, 827

Tilley's Will Trusts, Re, Burgin v Croad [1967] Ch 1179, [1967] 2 All ER 303, [1967] 2 WLR
1533, 111 Sol Jo 237 . . . . 880, 886, 887, 888, 889, 890, 994, 995

Tillott, Re, Lee v Wilson [1892] 1 Ch 86, 61 LJ Ch 38, 40 WR 204, 65 LT 781 . . . 624, 672,
673, 677, 678

Tilt, Re, Lampet v Kennedy (1896) 40 Sol Jo 224, 74 LT 163, 12 TLR 162 . . 175, 264

Timber Engineering Co Pty Ltd v Anderson [1980] 2 NSWLR 488 958

Timmins v Moreland Street Property Co Ltd [1958] Ch 110, [1957] 3 All ER 265, [1957] 3
WLR 678, 101 Sol Jo 815, CA. 234

Timmis, Re, Nixon v Smith [1902] 1 Ch 176, 71 LJ Ch 118, 50 WR 164, 46 Sol Jo 122, 85 LT
672 . . . . 742, 760

Timpson's Executors v Yerbury (Inspector of Taxes) [1936] 1 KB 645, [1936] 1 All ER 186,
20 TC 155, 105 LJKB 749, 80 Sol Jo 184, 154 LT 283, CA 151, 152

Timson v Ramsbottom (1837) 2 Heen 35 1003

Tindal, Re (1892) 9 TLR 24 536

Tinker v Tinker [1970] P 136, [1970] 1 All ER 540, [1970] 2 WLR 331, 21 P & CR 102, 114
Sol Jo 32, 213 Estates Gazette 635, CA 346, 347

Tinker's Settlement, Re [1960] 3 All ER 85n, [1960] 1 WLR 1011, 104 Sol Jo 805 . 512, 513

Tinsley v Milligan [1994] 1 AC 340, [1993] 3 All ER 65, [1993] 3 WLR 126, [1994] 2 FCR 65,
[1993] 2 FLR 963, HL 343, 345, 347, 354, 355, 362, 366, 368

Tito v Waddell (No 2) [1977] Ch 106, [1977] 3 All ER 129, [1977] 2 WLR 496, 121 Sol Jo
10 . . . . 5, 7, 21, 22, 23, 143, 387, 661, 664, 671, 874, 927, 930

Titterton v Oates [2001] WTLR 319 . . . . 765, 767

Tod, Re, Bradshaw v Turner [1916] 1 Ch 567, 85 LJ Ch 668, [1916-17] All ER Rep 1054, 60
Sol Jo 403, 114 LT 839, 32 TLR 344 . . . . 547, 566

Tod v Barton [2002] EWHC 264 (Ch), (2002) 4 ITELR 715 . . . . . 1013, 1023, 1033, 1036

Todd v Moorhouse (1874) LR 19 Eq 69, 23 WR 155, 32 LT 8 568

Tollemache, Re [1903] 1 Ch 457, sub nom Re T 72 LJ Ch 225, 51 WR 568, 47 Sol Jo 254, 88
LT 13; affd sub nom Tollemache, Re [1903] 1 Ch 955, 72 LJ Ch 539, 51 WR 597, 88 LT
670, CA 524

Tollemache, Re, Forbes v Public Trustee [1930] WN 138, 169 LT Jo 519, 69 L Jo 423 . . 546

Tom's Settlement, Re, Rose v Evans [1987] 1 All ER 1081, [1987] 1 WLR 1021, 131 Sol Jo
916, [1987] LS Gaz R 2045. 194

Tomlinson, Re, Tomlinson v Andrew [1898] 1 Ch 232, 67 LJ Ch 97, 46 WR 299, 42 Sol Jo
114, 78 LT 12 . . . . 568, 572

Tooke v Hollingworth (1793) 5 Term Rep 215; affd sub nom Hollingworth v Tooke (1795) 2
Hy Bl 510 883

Tootal Clothing Ltd v Guinea Properties Management Ltd (1992) 64 P & CR 452, [1992] 2
EGLR 80, [1992] 41 EG 117, [1993] Conv 89, CA 235

Torre v Browne (1855) 5 HL Cas 555, 24 LJ Ch 757, 26 LTOS 129 533

Total Oil Great Britain Ltd v Thompson Garages (Biggin Hill) Ltd [1972] 1 QB 318, [1971]
3 All ER 1226, [1971] 3 WLR 979, 115 Sol Jo 848, 220 Estates Gazette 1591, CA . . 442

Town Investments Ltd v Department of the Environment [1978] AC 359, [1977] 1 All ER
813, [1977] 2 WLR 450, 34 P & CR 48, 121 Sol Jo 203, [1977] RVR 76, HL . . . 143

Towndrow, Re, Gratton v Machen [1911] 1 Ch 662, 80 LJ Ch 378, 104 LT 534. 980

Townend v Townend (1859) 1 Giff 201, 5 Jur NS 506, 114 RR 405, 7 WR 529, 33 LTOS 143 870

Townley v Bedwell (1808) 14 Ves 591 440

Townley v Sherborn (1634) Cro Car 312, Toth 151, J Bridg 35, 2 White & Tud LC
627 . . . . 645, 647

Townsend's Estate, Re, Townsend v Townsend (1886) 34 Ch D 357, 56 LJ Ch 227, 35 WR
153, 55 LT 674, 3 TLR 204. . . . . 228, 333

Townshend v Harrowby (1858) 27 LJ Ch 553, 4 Jur NS 353, 114 RR 545, 6 WR 413, 31 LTOS
33 . . . . .243, 306, 307, 308

Townson v Tickell (1819) 3 B & Ald 31, 22 RR 291, [1814-23] All ER Rep 164 . . . 449, 451

Tracy v Mandalay Pty Ltd (1952) 88 CLR 215 23

Trafford's Settlement, Re, Moore v IRC [1985] Ch 32, [1984] 1 All ER 1108, [1984] 3 WLR
341, 128 Sol Jo 333, [1984] LS Gaz R 900, sub nom Moore and Osborne v IRC [1984]
STC 236 64

Train v Clapperton [1908] AC 342, 77 LJPC 124, HL 213, 738

Trautwein v Richardson [1946] ALR 129, HC of A 349

Travis, Re, Frost v Greatorex [1900] 2 Ch 541, 69 LJ Ch 663, 49 WR 38, 44 Sol Jo 625, 83 LT
241, CA 349, 730

Treaty Group Inc v Simpson (2001) 103 ACWS (3d) 1072 978
Tregonwell v Sydenham (1815) 3 Dow 194, 15 RR 40 . . . . 333, 335, 349
Trendtex Trading Corpn v Crédit Suisse [1980] QB 629, [1980] 3 All ER 721, [1980] 3 WLR
    367, 124 Sol Jo 396, CA; affd [1982] AC 679, [1981] 3 All ER 520, [1981] 3 WLR 766,
    [1981] Com LR 262, 125 Sol Jo 761, HL 1029
Trevor v Trevor (1847) 1 HL Cas 239, 73 RR 58 301
Tribe v Tribe [1996] Ch 107, [1995] 4 All ER 236, [1995] 3 WLR 913, 71 P & CR 503, [1996]
    1 FCR 338, [1995] 2 FLR 966, [1996] Fam Law 29, [1995] 32 LS Gaz R 30, [1995] NLJR
    1445, 139 Sol Jo LB 203, CA 343, 346, 348
Trident General Insurance Co Ltd v McNiece Bros Pty Ltd (1988) 165 CLR 107, 80 ALR 574,
    62 ALJR 508, HC of A 10, 172
Trident Holdings Ltd v Danand Investments Ltd (1988) 49 DLR (4th) 1 823
Triffit Nurseries v Salads Etcetera Ltd [2000] 2 Lloyd's Rep 74, [2000] 1 BCLC 761, [2000] 1
    All ER (Comm) 737, CA. 883
Triffitt's Settlement, Re, Hall v Hyde [1958] Ch 852, [1958] 2 All ER 299, [1958] 2 WLR 927,
    102 Sol Jo 282 . . . . 32, 90, 804, 807
Tringham's Trusts, Re, Tringham v Greenhill [1904] 2 Ch 487, 73 LJ Ch 693, 91 LT 370, 20
    TLR 657. 300
Triplex Safety Glass Co Ltd v Scorah [1938] Ch 211, [1937] 4 All ER 693, 107 LJ Ch 91, 55
    RPC 21, 81 Sol Jo 982, 157 LT 576, 54 TLR 90 399
Trollope's Will Trusts, Re, Public Trustee v Trollope [1927] 1 Ch 596, 96 LJ Ch 340, [1927]
    All ER Rep 365, 71 Sol Jo 310, 137 LT 375 . . . . 554, 557
Tropical Capital Investments Ltd v Stanlake Holdings Ltd (1992) unreported, CA . . . 116
Trustees Executors and Agency Co Ltd v Margottini [1960] VR 417 . . . . 215, 1031, 1040
Trustees of the British Museum v A-G [1984] 1 All ER 337, [1984] 1 WLR 418, 128 Sol Jo
    190, [1984] LS Gaz R 585 509
Trustor AB v Smallbone (9 May 2000, unreported), CA. 1021, 1043, 1049
Trustor AB v Smallbone (No 2) [2001] 3 All ER 987, [2001] 1 WLR 1177, [2001] 2 BCLC
    436, [2001] 20 LS Gaz R 40, [2001] NLJR 457, 145 Sol Jo LB 99 . . . . . 63, 968, 970
Trutch v Lamprell (1855) 20 Beav 116 648
Tryon, Re (1844) 8 JP 408, 7 Beav 496, 64 RR 132, 2 LTOS 516 450
Tse Kwong Lam v Wong Chit Sen [1983] 3 All ER 54, [1983] 1 WLR 1349, [1983] BCLC 88,
    127 Sol Jo 632, PC 664
Tubbs, Re, Dykes v Tubbs [1915] 2 Ch 137, 84 LJ Ch 539, 59 Sol Jo 508, 113 LT 395, CA   574
Tuck's Settlement Trusts, Re, Public Trustee v Tuck [1978] Ch 49, [1978] 1 All ER 1047,
    [1978] 2 WLR 411, 121 Sol Jo 796, CA 84, 89, 90, 100, 101, 103, 216, 832
Tucker, Re [1918] VLR 460 648
Tucker, Re, Tucker v Tucker [1894] 1 Ch 724, 63 LJ Ch 223, 8 R 113, 42 WR 266, 38 Sol Jo
    218, 70 LT 127; affd [1894] 3 Ch 429, 63 LJ Ch 737, 12 R 141, 71 LT 453, CA. . . 612
Tucker v Bennett (1887) 38 Ch D 1, 57 LJ Ch 507, 58 LT 650, CA 284
Tucker v Burrow (1865) 2 Hem & M 515, 34 LJ Ch 478, 11 Jur NS 525, 6 New Rep 139, 144
    RR 245, 13 WR 771, 12 LT 485 . . . . 350, 367
Tucker v Hernaman (1853) 4 De GM & G 395, 22 LJ Ch 791, 1 Eq Rep 360, 17 Jur 723, 102
    RR 186, 1 WR 498, 21 LTOS 251 846
Tudor Grange Holdings Ltd v Citibank NA [1992] Ch 53, [1991] 4 All ER 1, [1991] 3 WLR
    750, [1991] BCLC 1009 933
Tufnell, Re, Byng v Turnell (1902) 18 TLR 705 923
Tumbridge v Care (1871) 19 WR 1047, 25 LT 150 350
Turkington, Re, Owen v Benson [1937] 4 All ER 501, 81 Sol Jo 1041 125
Turner, Re, Barker v Ivimey [1897] 1 Ch 536, 66 LJ Ch 282, 45 WR 495, 41 Sol Jo 313, 76 LT
    116, 13 TLR 249. . . . . .913, 914, 917, 918, 945
Turner, Re, Wood v Turner [1907] 2 Ch 126, 76 LJ Ch 492, 96 LT 798, 23 TLR 524, CA. 818
Turner v Collins (1871) 7 Ch App 329, 41 LJ Ch 558, 20 WR 305, 25 LT 779 285
Turner v Hancock (1882) 20 Ch D 303, 51 LJ Ch 517, 30 WR 480, 46 LT 750, CA . . . 818
Turner v Maule (1850) 15 Jur 761, 16 LTOS 455 . . . . 753, 754
Turner v Turner [1984] Ch 100, [1983] 2 All ER 745, [1983] 3 WLR 896, 127 Sol Jo
    842. . . . . 680, 691, 698
Turner's Will Trusts, Re, Bridgman v Turner [1960] Ch 122, [1959] 2 All ER 689, [1959] 3
    WLR 498, 103 Sol Jo 545 508
Turner's Will Trusts, Re, District Bank Ltd v Turner [1937] Ch 15, [1936] 2 All ER 1435, 106
    LJ Ch 58, 80 Sol Jo 791, 155 LT 266, 52 TLR 713, CA 709, 711, 715, 725
Turner's Will Trusts, Re, Westminster Bank Ltd v Turner [1968] 1 All ER 321, [1968] 1 WLR
    227, 111 Sol Jo 913. . . . . 511, 546

Turnley, Re (1866) 1 Ch App 152, 35 LJ Ch 313, 12 Jur NS 305, 14 WR 322, 13 LT 662 . 574
Turton v Benson (1719) 10 Mod Rep 445, 1 P Wms 496, Prec Ch 522, 1 Stra 240, 2 Vern 764,
    1 Eq Cas Abr 88 pl 2 . . . . 983, 1001
Turton v Turton [1988] Ch 542, [1987] 2 All ER 641, [1987] 3 WLR 622, 55 P & CR 88,
    [1988] 1 FLR 23, [1987] Fam Law 383, 131 Sol Jo 540, [1987] LS Gaz R 1492,
    CA 351, 354, 355, 425, 426
Tweddle v Atkinson (1861) 25 JP 517, 1 B & S 393, 30 LJQB 265, 8 Jur NS 332, 9 WR 781,
    [1861-73] All ER Rep 369, 4 LT 468 170
Tweedale v Tweedale (1878) 7 Ch D 633, 47 LJ Ch 530, 26 WR 457, 38 LT 137 . . . 74, 131
Twinsectra Ltd v Yardley [2000] WTLR 527, [1999] Lloyd's Rep Bank 438, [2000] Lloyd's
    Rep PN 239, CA; revsd sub nom Twinsectra Ltd v Yardley [2002] UKHL 12, [2002] 2
    AC 164, [2002] 2 All ER 377, [2002] 2 WLR 802, [2002] 19 LS Gaz R 32, [2002] NLJR
    469, [2002] 38 EG 204 (CS), HL 12, 13, 25, 44, 116, 117, 262, 330, 331, 342,
                                                908, 950, 951, 953, 955, 956, 958, 959,
                                                961, 962, 967, 970, 974, 976
Twyne's Case (1602) 3 Co Rep 80b, [1558-1774] All ER Rep 302, sub nom Chamberlain v
    Twyne Moore KB 638 295
Tyars v Alsop (1889) 53 JP 212, 37 WR 339, 61 LT 8, 5 TLR 242, CA 273, 283
Tyler, Re, Tyler v Tyler [1891] 3 Ch 252, 60 LJ Ch 686, 40 WR 7, 65 LT 367, 7 TLR 654,
    CA 121, 201
Tyler's Fund Trusts, Re, Graves v King [1967] 3 All ER 389, [1967] 1 WLR 1269, 111 Sol Jo
    794 . . . . 247, 260, 342
Tyssen, Re, Knight-Bruce v Butterworth [1894] 1 Ch 56, 63 LJ Ch 114, 8 R 22, 42 WR 172, 38
    Sol Jo 58, 69 LT 689 . . . . 803, 805

                                            U

US v Fontana 528 F Supp 137 (1981). 324
US International Marketing Ltd v National Bank of New Zealand Ltd (20 June 2002,
    unreported) 967
Ullswater, Re, Barclays Bank Ltd v Lowther [1952] Ch 105, [1951] 2 All ER 989, [1951] 2
    TLR 1024 . . . . 561, 565
Ulrich v Ulrich and Felton [1968] 1 All ER 67, [1968] 1 WLR 180, 19 P & CR 669, 111 Sol Jo
    889, CA 362
Ulverston and District New Hospital Building Trusts, Re, Birkett v Barrow and Furness
    Hospital Management Committee [1956] Ch 622, [1956] 3 All ER 164, [1956] 3 WLR
    559, 100 Sol Jo 603, CA 341
Underhill v Roden (1876) 2 Ch D 494, 45 LJ Ch 266, 24 WR 574, 34 LT 227 334
Underwood v Stevens (1816) 1 Mer 712. . . . . 493, 634, 939
Ungurian v Lesnoff [1990] Ch 206, [1989] 3 WLR 840, [1990] FCR 719, [1990] 2 FLR 299,
    [1990] Fam Law 93 . . . . 248, 410
Uniacke, Re (1844) 68 RR 220, 1 Jo & Lat 1 . . . . 452, 453
Union Bank of Australia Ltd v Murray-Aynsley [1898] AC 693, 67 LJPC 123 986
United Bank of Kuwait plc v Sahib [1997] Ch 107, [1995] 2 All ER 973, [1995] 2 WLR 94,
    [1996] 1 FLR 379, [1996] Fam Law 87; affd [1997] Ch 107, [1996] 3 All ER 215, [1996]
    3 WLR 372, 73 P & CR 177, [1996] 2 FLR 666, [1997] Fam Law 17, [1996] NPC 12,
    CA 253, 426, 1000
United Mizrahi Bank Ltd v Doherty [1998] 2 All ER 230, [1998] 1 WLR 435 . . . 650, 985
United Overseas Bank Ltd v Iwuanyanwa (20 March 2001, unreported) 353
Unity Joint-Stock Mutual Banking Association v King (1858) 25 Beav 72, 27 LJ Ch 585, 4 Jur
    NS 470, 6 WR 264, 31 LTOS 128 248
Universe Tankships Inc of Monrovia v International Transport Workers Federation, The
    Universe Sentinel [1980] 2 Lloyd's Rep 523, [1981] ICR 129, [1980] IRLR 363, CA; on
    appeal [1983] 1 AC 366, [1982] 2 All ER 67, [1982] 2 WLR 803, [1982] 1 Lloyd's Rep
    537, [1982] ICR 262, [1982] IRLR 200, 126 Sol Jo 275, HL . 74, 90, 110, 118, 127, 339
University of London Medical Sciences Institute Fund, Re, Fowler v A-G [1909] 2 Ch 1, 78 LJ
    Ch 562, 53 Sol Jo 302, 100 LT 423, 25 TLR 358, CA 341
University of Manitoba v Sanderson Estate (1998) 155 DLR (4th) 40 428
University of Nottingham v Fishel [2000] ICR 1462 658
Upfull's Trust, Re (1851) 21 LJ Ch 119, 3 Mac & G 281 829
Upton v Brown (1879) 12 Ch D 872, 48 LJ Ch 756, 28 WR 38, 41 LT 340. 334
Upton v Brown (1884) 26 Ch D 588, 54 LJ Ch 614, 32 WR 679, 51 LT 591 570
Urch v Walker (1838) 3 My & Cr 702, 7 LJ Ch 292, 2 Jur 487, 45 RR 360 451
Utley, Re, Russell v Cubitt [1912] WN 147, 56 Sol Jo 518, 106 LT 858 . . . . . . 802, 832

V

VGM Holdings Ltd, Re [1942] Ch 235, [1942] 1 All ER 224, 111 LJ Ch 145, 86 Sol Jo 63, 58
    TLR 131, CA 979
Vachell v Roberts (1863) 32 Beav 140 552
Vacuum Oil Co Pty Ltd v Wiltshire (1945) 72 CLR 319 814
Vadasz v Pioneer Concrete (SA) Pty Ltd (1995) 184 CLR 102, 130 ALR 570, HC of A . . 287
Valletort Sanitary Steam Laundry Co Ltd, Re, Ward v Valletort Sanitary Steam Laundry Co
    Ltd [1903] 2 Ch 654, 72 LJ Ch 674, 89 LT 60, 19 TLR 593 1001
Vandepitte v Preferred Accident Insurance Corpn of New York [1933] AC 70, 102 LJPC 21,
    [1932] All ER Rep 527, 76 Sol Jo 798, 148 LT 169, 49 TLR 90, PC 10, 170, 171
Vandervell v IRC [1967] 2 AC 291, [1967] 1 All ER 1, [1967] 2 WLR 87, 43 TC 519, 45 ATC
    394, [1966] TR 315, 110 Sol Jo 910, L(TC) 2214, HL 54, 55, 115, 154, 233,
                     240, 241, 243, 244, 246, 273, 329, 330, 331,
                    332, 350, 367, 503, 593, 733, 820, 1052
Vandervell Trustees Ltd v White [1971] AC 912, [1970] 3 All ER 16, [1970] 3 WLR 452, 46
    TC 341, 49 ATC 142, [1970] TR 129, 114 Sol Jo 652, HL 241
Vandervell's Trusts (No 2), Re, White v Vandervell Trustees Ltd [1974] Ch 269, [1974] 1 All
    ER 47, [1973] 3 WLR 744, 117 Sol Jo 856; revsd [1974] Ch 269, [1974] 3 All ER 205,
    [1974] 3 WLR 256, 118 Sol Jo 566, CA 54, 55, 76, 129, 233, 238, 240,
                    241, 250, 330, 332, 362, 367
Van Gruisen's Will Trusts, Re, Bagger v Dean [1964] 1 All ER 843n, [1964] 1 WLR 449, 108
    Sol Jo 237 513
Vanneck v Benham [1917] 1 Ch 60, 86 LJ Ch 7, [1916-17] All ER Rep 741, 115 LT
    588 . . . . 307, 315
Vansittart v Vansittart (1858) 22 JP 704, 2 De G & J 249, 27 LJ Ch 289, 4 Jur NS 519, 119 RR
    109, 6 WR 386, 44 ER 984, 31 LTOS 4 218
Van Straubenzee, Re, Boustead v Cooper [1901] 2 Ch 779, 70 LJ Ch 825, 45 Sol Jo 738, 85
    LT 541, 17 TLR 755 550
Vatcher v Paull [1915] AC 372, 84 LJPC 86, [1914-15] All ER Rep 609, 112 LT 737,
    PC 29, 93, 631
Vaughan, Re, Halford v Close [1883] WN 89 208
Vaughan, Re, Vaughan v Thomas (1886) 33 Ch D 187, 51 JP 70, 35 WR 104, 55 LT 547, 2
    TLR 725 . . . . 119, 120
Vaughton v Noble (1861) 30 Beav 34, 132 RR 166 951
Venture, The [1908] P 218, 77 LJP 105, 11 Asp MLC 93, 99 LT 385, CA 12, 351
Verney's Settled Estates, Re [1898] 1 Ch 508, 67 LJ Ch 243, 46 WR 348, 42 Sol Jo 308, 78 LT
    191 574
Vernon (Trustees of Employees Fund of William Vernon & Sons Ltd) v IRC [1956] 3 All ER
    14, [1956] 1 WLR 1169, 36 TC 484, 35 ATC 176, 49 R & IT 396, [1956] TR 119, 100 Sol
    Jo 632, L(TC) 1773 . . . . 107, 109
Vestey's (Lord) Executors v IRC [1949] 1 All ER 1108, 31 TC 1, 28 ATC 89, 42 R & IT 314,
    325, [1949] TR 149, L(TC) 1490, HL 32, 613
Vestey's (Baron) Settlement, Re, Lloyds Bank Ltd v O'Meara [1951] Ch 209, [1950] 2 All ER
    891, CA 711, 712, 724, 783
Vickery, Re, Vickery v Stephens [1931] 1 Ch 572, 100 LJ Ch 138, [1931] All ER Rep 562, 144
    LT 562, 47 TLR 242 939
Viditz v O'Hagan [1900] 2 Ch 87, 69 LJ Ch 507, 48 WR 516, 44 Sol Jo 427, 82 LT 480, 16 TLR
    357, CA 269, 1023
Villar, Re, Public Trustee v Villar [1929] 1 Ch 243, 98 LJ Ch 223, [1928] All ER Rep 535, 72
    Sol Jo 761, 140 LT 90, 45 TLR 13, CA 84
Vine v Raleigh [1891] 2 Ch 13, 60 LJ Ch 675, 63 LT 573; on appeal [1891] 2 Ch 22, 60 LJ Ch
    675, CA 205
Vinogradoff, Re, Allen v Jackson [1935] WN 68, 179 LT Jo 274 . . . . . . 53, 359, 367, 754
Virgo Steamship Co SA v Skaarup Shipping Corpn, The Kapetan Georgis [1988] 1 Lloyd's
    Rep 352, [1988] FTLR 180 1041
Vita Food Products Inc v Unus Shipping Co Ltd [1939] AC 277, [1939] 1 All ER 513, 108
    LJPC 40, 19 Asp MLC 257, 44 Com Cas 123, 83 Sol Jo 295, 160 LT 579, 55 TLR 402, PC1031
Von Brockdorff v Malcolm (1885) 30 Ch D 172, 55 LJ Ch 121, 33 WR 934, [1881-5] All ER
    Rep 1068, 53 LT 263 803
Von Knierem v Bermuda Trust Co Ltd and Grosvenor Trust Co Ltd (13 July 1994, unre-
    ported, Supreme Court of Bermuda 1 BOCM 116) 30, 31, 33, 60, 116, 754
Voyce v Voyce (1991) 62 P & CR 290, CA 248, 253, 426

Vyse v Foster (1872) 8 Ch App 309, 42 LJ Ch 245, 21 WR 207, 27 LT 774; affd (1874) LR 7
     HL 318, 44 LJ Ch 37, 23 WR 355, 31 LT 177 . . . . 17, 21, 668, 810, 867, 870, 871, 878

W

Wace v Mallard (1851) 21 LJ Ch 355, sub nom Ware v Mallard 16 Jur 492, 18 LTOS 194 . 134
Wade v Cox (1835) 4 LJ Ch 105 937
Wagstaff, Marriage of, Re (Gruber, intervener) (1990) 14 Fam LR 78, [1990] FLC 77, 976, 99
     FLR 390 891
Wait, Re [1927] 1 Ch 606, 96 LJ Ch 179, [1927] B & CR 140, [1926] All ER Rep 433, 71 Sol
     Jo 56, 136 LT 552, 43 TLR 150, CA 78
Wakeham v Mackenzie [1968] 2 All ER 783, [1968] 1 WLR 1175, 19 P & CR 565, 112 Sol Jo
     504 423
Wakley, Re, Wakley v Vachell [1920] 2 Ch 205, 89 LJ Ch 321, [1920] All ER Rep 749, 64 Sol
     Jo 357, 123 LT 150, 36 TLR 325, CA 542, 553, 562
Wale, Re, Wale v Harris [1956] 3 All ER 280, [1956] 1 WLR 1346, 100 Sol Jo 800 . 152, 162,
                                                                                        165
Walker, Re [1905] 1 Ch 160, 74 LJ Ch 86, 91 LT 713, CA 269
Walker, Re, Macintosh-Walker v Walker [1908] 2 Ch 705, 77 LJ Ch 755, 99 LT 469 . . . 190
Walker, Re, Public Trustee v Walker [1939] Ch 974, [1939] 3 All ER 902, 109 LJ Ch 1, 83 Sol
     Jo 731, 161 LT 223, 55 TLR 1092 . . . . 210, 211
Walker, Re, Summers v Barrow [1901] 1 Ch 259, 70 LJ Ch 229, 49 WR 167, 45 Sol Jo 119 759
Walker, Re, Walker v Duncombe [1901] 1 Ch 879, 70 LJ Ch 417, 49 WR 394, 84 LT
     193 . . . . 500, 524, 817
Walker, Re, Walker v Walker (1890) 59 LJ Ch 386, 62 LT 449 . . . . 543, 606
Walker v Linom [1907] 2 Ch 104, 76 LJ Ch 500, 51 Sol Jo 483, 97 LT 92 . . . . . 983, 1001
Walker v Smalwood (1768) Amb 676 727
Walker v Standard Chartered Bank (27 February 1998, unreported) 968
Walker v Stones [2001] QB 902, [2000] 4 All ER 412, [2001] 2 WLR 623, [2000] 35 LS Gaz R
     36, [2000] Lloyd's Rep PN 864, [2000] WTLR 975, CA . . 494, 529, 593, 594, 595, 618,
                                                                 700, 852, 864, 939, 961
Walker v Symonds (1818) 19 RR 155, 3 Swan 1, [1814-23] All ER Rep 71 . . . 646, 647, 931,
                                                                              936, 938, 944
Walker v Walker [1983] Fam 68, [1983] 2 All ER 909, [1983] 3 WLR 421, 4 FLR 779, 13 Fam
     Law 181, 127 Sol Jo 442, CA 187
Walker's Settled Estate, Re [1894] 1 Ch 189, 63 LJ Ch 314, 8 R 370, 38 Sol Jo 80, 70 LT 259,
     10 TLR 77 573
Walker's Settlement Trusts, Re, Watson v Walker [1936] Ch 280, 105 LJ Ch 49, [1934-1935]
     B & CR 279, 154 LT 564, 52 TLR 118 . . . . 553, 562
Wall v Bright (1820) 1 Jac & W 494, 37 ER 456 438
Wallace's Settlements, Re [1968] 2 All ER 209, [1968] 1 WLR 711, 112 Sol Jo 381 . 501, 511,
                                                                                        518
Waller v Waller [1967] 1 All ER 305, [1967] 1 WLR 451, 111 Sol Jo 94 906
Wallersteiner v Moir (No 2) [1975] QB 373, 508n, [1975] 1 All ER 849, [1975] 2 WLR 389,
     119 Sol Jo 97, CA 853, 857, 862, 868, 870, 871
Wallgrave v Tebbs (1855) 20 JP 84, 2 K & J 313, 25 LJ Ch 241, 2 Jur NS 83, 4 WR 194, 26
     LTOS 147 . . . . 257, 260
Wallwyn v Coutts (1815) 3 Sim 14, 3 Mer 707, 30 RR 117 141
Walsh v Loughman [1991] 2 VR 351 488
Walsh v Wallinger (1830) 2 Russ & M 78, Taml 425, 9 LJOS Ch 7 130
Walter and Sullivan Ltd v J Murphy & Sons Ltd [1955] 2 QB 584, [1955] 1 All ER 843,
     [1955] 2 WLR 919, 99 Sol Jo 290, CA 152
Walters, Re, See Sherman, Re, Re Walters, Trevenen v Pearce
Walters v Woodbridge (1878) 7 Ch D 504, 47 LJ Ch 516, 26 WR 469, 38 LT 83, CA . 810, 818
Walton v Walton (1807) 14 Ves 318 . . . . 329, 330
Walton's Settlement, Re, Walton v Peirson [1922] 2 Ch 509, 92 LJ Ch 32, [1922] All ER Rep
     439, 66 Sol Jo 666, 127 LT 626, CA 278
Waltons Stores (Interstate) Ltd v Maher (1988) 164 CLR 387, 76 ALR 513, 62 ALJR 110, HC
     of A 248
Wangford v Wangford (1704) Freem KB 520, 11 Mod Rep 38, sub nom Wankford v
     Wankford 1 Salk 299, 3 Salk 162, Holt KB 311 . . . . 158, 159, 162
Wanklyn v Wilson (1887) 35 Ch D 180, 56 LJ Ch 209, 35 WR 332, 56 LT 52, 3 TLR 277 . 903
Warburton v Sandys (1845) 14 Sim 622, 14 LJ Ch 431, 9 Jur 503, 65 RR 652, 5 LTOS
     262 . . . . 740, 741

Ward, Re, Bemment v Balls (1878) 47 LJ Ch 781 626
Ward, Re, Gillett v Ward [1968] WAR 33, 42 ALJ 227 . . . . 151, 155
Ward, Re, Public Trustee v Ward [1941] Ch 308, 165 LT 115, sub nom Re Ward Public
    Trustee v Berry [1941] 2 All ER 125, 110 LJ Ch 171, 85 Sol Jo 255, 57 TLR 473, CA   105
Ward v Audland (1845) 8 Beav 201, 14 LJ Ch 145, 9 Jur 384, 68 RR 65. . . . . . 179, 182
Ward v Brunt [2000] WTLR 731 . . . . 384, 388
Ward v Butler (1824) 2 Mol 533. 452
Ward v Duncombe [1893] AC 369, 62 LJ Ch 881, 1 R 224, 42 WR 59, 69 LT 121, HL . . 263
Ward v Kirkland [1967] Ch 194, [1966] 1 All ER 609, [1966] 1 WLR 601, 110 Sol Jo 289. 248
Ward v Ward (1843) 2 HL Cas 777n, 9 ER 1287 579
Ward, Lock & Co Ltd v Long [1906] 2 Ch 550, 75 LJ Ch 732, 95 LT 345, 22 TLR 798. . 185
Ward-Smith v Jebb (1964) 108 Sol Jo 919; on appeal sub nom Jebb, Re, Ward-Smith v Jebb
    [1966] Ch 666, [1965] 3 All ER 358, [1965] 3 WLR 810, 109 Sol Jo 613, CA. . 918, 946
Ward's Will Trusts, Re, Ringland v Ward [1936] Ch 704, [1936] 2 All ER 773, 105 LJ Ch 315,
    80 Sol Jo 486, 155 LT 346, 52 TLR 605 536
Ware v Cann (1830) 10 B & C 433, 8 LJOSKB 164, 5 Man & Ry KB 341, 34 RR 469 . . . 214
Wareham, Re, Wareham v Brewin [1912] 2 Ch 312, 81 LJ Ch 578, 56 Sol Jo 613, 107 LT 80,
    CA 549, 552, 555
Waring v Waring (1852) 3 I Ch R 331 583
Warman International Ltd v Dwyer (1995) 182 CLR 544, 128 ALR 201 . . . . 402, 405, 958
Warman International Ltd v Dwyer (1995) 69 ALJR 362 . . . . 23, 391, 657, 874
Warner v Sampson [1958] 1 QB 404, [1958] 1 All ER 44, [1958] 2 WLR 212, 102 Sol Jo 107,
    170 Estates Gazette 740; revsd [1959] 1 QB 297, [1959] 1 All ER 120, [1959] 2 WLR
    109, 103 Sol Jo 91, 173 Estates Gazette 43, CA 18
Warren, Re, Public Trustee v Fletcher [1939] Ch 684, [1939] 2 All ER 599, 108 LJ Ch 311, 83
    Sol Jo 455, 161 LT 32, 55 TLR 796 746
Warren v Gurney [1944] 2 All ER 472, CA. 362, 363, 364
Warrick v Warrick and Kniveton (1745) 3 Atk 291. 985
Warter v Anderson (1853) 11 Hare 301, 1 Eq Rep 266, 1 WR 493, 21 LTOS 219 . . 817, 828
Warwick v Richardson (1842) 11 LJ Ex 351, 10 M & W 284, 62 RR 608. 945
Wasserberg, Re, Union of London and Smiths Bank Ltd v Wasserberg [1915] 1 Ch 195, 84
    LJ Ch 214, [1914-15] All ER Rep 217, 59 Sol Jo 176, 112 LT 242 150
Waterman's Will Trusts, Re, Lloyds Bank Ltd v Sutton [1952] 2 All ER 1054, 96 Sol Jo 850,
    [1952] 2 TLR 877 . . . . 577, 586, 919
Waters, Re, Preston v Waters [1889] WN 39 544
Waters v Waters (1857) 26 LJ Ch 624, 3 Jur NS 654, 112 RR 434, 29 LTOS 310 376
Wates Construction (London) Ltd v Franthom Property Ltd (1991) 53 BLR 23, CA. . . . 21
Watford Corpn's and Ware's Contract, Re [1943] Ch 82, [1943] 1 All ER 54, 112 LJ Ch 94,
    87 Sol Jo 30, 168 LT 153, 59 TLR 98 442
Watkin v Watson-Smith [1986] CLY 424, Times, 3 July 276
Watling v Lewis [1911] 1 Ch 414, 80 LJ Ch 242, 104 LT 132 812
Watson, Re (1881) 19 Ch D 384, 30 WR 554, 45 LT 513 782
Watson, Re (1904) 49 Sol Jo 54 687
Watson, Re, Brand v Culme-Seymour [1928] WN 309, 166 LT Jo 439 568
Watson v Hayes (1839) 5 My & Cr 125, 9 LJ Ch 49, 4 Jur 186, 48 RR 249 . . . . 330, 334
Watson v Holland (Inspector of Taxes) [1985] 1 All ER 290, [1984] STC 372 . . . 369, 374
Watson v Parker (1843) 6 Beav 283, 12 LJ Ch 221, 7 Jur 143. 173
Watson v Watson (1864) 33 Beav 574. 546
Watson v Young (1885) 28 Ch D 436, 54 LJ Ch 502, 33 WR 637 . . . . . . 190, 225, 229
Watt v Wood (1862) 2 Drew & Sm 56, 31 LJ Ch 338, 10 WR 335 206
Watt's Settlement, Re (1851) 9 Hare 106, 20 LJ Ch 337, 15 Jur 459, 17 LTOS 139 . 753, 754
Watt's Will Trusts, Re, Watt v Watt [1936] 2 All ER 1555 . . . . 204, 209, 715
Watts, Re, Coffey v Watts [1931] 2 Ch 302, 100 LJ Ch 353, 145 LT 520. 198
Watts v Girdlestone (1843) 6 Beav 188, 12 LJ Ch 363, 7 Jur 501, 63 RR 49 861
Watts and Ready v Storey (1983) 134 NLJ 631, [1983] CA Transcript 319, CA 250
Wavefront Trading Ltd v Po Sang Bank Ltd [1999] HKFCI 5 967
Way's Trusts, Re (1864) 2 De GJ & Sm 365, 34 LJ Ch 49, 10 Jur NS 1166, 5 New Rep 67, 13
    WR 149, 11 LT 495 . . . . 152, 183
Wayling v Jones (1993) 69 P & CR 170, [1996] 2 FCR 41, [1995] 2 FLR 1029, [1996] Fam
    Law 88, [1995] Conv 409, CA. 252
Weall, Re, Andrews v Weall (1889) 42 Ch D 674, 58 LJ Ch 713, 37 WR 779, 61 LT 238, 5 TLR
    681 . . . . 564, 634

Webb, Re, Barclays Bank Ltd v Webb [1941] Ch 225, [1941] 1 All ER 321, 110 LJ Ch 89, 85
    Sol Jo 129, 164 LT 307, 57 TLR 355 . . . . 171, 172
Webb, Re, Leedham v Patchett (1890) 63 LT 545 . . . . 814, 824
Webb v Earl of Shaftesbury (1802) 6 RR 154, 7 Ves 480, [1775-1802] All ER Rep 201   651, 659,
    727, 905
Webb v Sadler (1873) 8 Ch App 419, 42 LJ Ch 498, 21 WR 394, 28 LT 388 805
Webb v Webb [1992] 1 All ER 17, [1991] 1 WLR 1410; on appeal (1992) Financial Times, 11
    March, CA; refd sub nom Webb v Webb: C-294/92 [1994] QB 696, [1994] 3 All ER 911,
    [1994] 3 WLR 801, [1994] ECR I-1717, ECJ . .51, 188, 189, 900, 1018, 1031, 1036, 1058
Webb's Estate, Re (1992) 57 SASR 193 .1038
Webster v Le Hunt (1861) 8 Jur NS 345, 9 WR 918, 4 LT 72. 589
Wedderburn v Wedderburn (1838) 4 My & Cr 41, 8 LJ Ch 177, 3 Jur 596. 887
Weeding v Weeding (1861) 1 John & H 424, 30 LJ Ch 680, 7 Jur NS 908, 9 WR 431, 4 LT
    616. . . . . 440, 441
Weeding's Estate, Re (1858) 4 Jur NS 707, 111 RR 894 768
Weekes' Settlement, Re [1897] 1 Ch 289, 66 LJ Ch 179, 45 WR 265, 41 Sol Jo 225, 76 LT
    112. . . . . .74, 131
Weiner's Will Trusts, Re, Wyner v Braithwaite [1956] 2 All ER 482, [1956] 1 WLR 579, 100
    Sol Jo 400 . . . . 735, 739
Weir v Bell (1878) 3 Ex D 238, 47 LJQB 704, 26 WR 746, 38 LT 929, CA 585
Welch, Re (1854) 23 LJ Ch 344, 2 WR 310 720
Welch v Bank of England [1955] Ch 508, [1955] 1 All ER 811, 99 Sol Jo 236 . . . 648, 938
Weldtech Equipment Ltd, Re [1991] BCLC 393, [1991] BCC 16 . . . . 15, 41
Wellesley (Lord) v Withers (1855) 4 E & B 750, 24 LJQB 134, 1 Jur NS 706, 99 RR 727, 3 CLR
    1187, 25 LTOS 79 449
Wellington (Duke), Re, Glentanar v Wellington [1947] Ch 506, [1947] 2 All ER 854, [1947]
    LJR 1451, 91 Sol Jo 369, 63 TLR 295; affd [1948] Ch 118, [1947] 2 All ER 854, [1949]
    LJR 612, 92 Sol Jo 11, 64 TLR 54, CA 188, 1027
Wellington's (Duke) Parliamentary Estates, Re, King v Wellesley [1972] Ch 374, [1971] 2 All
    ER 1140, [1971] 3 WLR 184, 22 P & CR 867, 115 Sol Jo 549. . . . . 568, 573
Wells, Re, Boyer v Maclean [1903] 1 Ch 848, 72 LJ Ch 513, 51 WR 521, 88 LT 355, [1900-3]
    All ER Rep Ext 1066 524
Wells, Re, Loggie v Wells [1967] 3 All ER 908, [1968] 1 WLR 44, 111 Sol Jo 969 785
Wells, Re, Wells v Wells [1962] 1 All ER 812, [1962] 1 WLR 397, 106 Sol Jo 176; affd [1962] 2
    All ER 826, [1962] 1 WLR 874, 106 Sol Jo 410, CA 655, 659
Wells v Malbon (1862) 31 Beav 48, 31 LJ Ch 344, 8 Jur NS 249, 135 RR 344, 10 WR 364, 6 LT
    39 . . . . 846, 847
Welsh Development Agency v Export Finance Co Ltd [1992] BCLC 148, [1992] BCC 270,
    CA 15
Welsh Hospital (Netley) Fund, Re, Thomas v A-G [1921] 1 Ch 655, 90 LJ Ch 276, [1921] All
    ER Rep 170, 65 Sol Jo 417, 124 LT 787 . . . . 336, 341, 370
Wenger's Settlement, Re, Wenger v Baldwin (1963) 107 Sol Jo 981 193
Wenlock (Baroness) v River Dee Co (1887) 19 QBD 155, 56 LJQB 589, 35 WR 822, 57 LT
    320, CA 824, 895
Wentworth v Wentworth [1900] AC 163, 69 LJPC 13, 81 LT 682, 16 TLR 81, PC . . 496, 552,
    559
West, Re, Denton v West [1921] 1 Ch 533, 90 LJ Ch 342, 65 Sol Jo 379, 125 LT 117, 37 TLR
    433 547
West, Re, George v Grose [1900] 1 Ch 84, 69 LJ Ch 71, 48 WR 138, 44 Sol Jo 89, 81 LT
    720. . . . . 34, 330, 335
West, Re, Westhead v Aspland [1913] 2 Ch 345, 82 LJ Ch 488, [1911-13] All ER Rep 692, 109
    LT 39. 713
West v Houghton (1879) 4 CPD 197, 43 JP 607, 27 WR 678, 40 LT 364 . . . . 10, 170, 171
West v Lazard [1993] Jersey LR 165 4
West v Williams [1898] 1 Ch 488, 67 LJ Ch 213, 46 WR 362, 78 LT 147 210
West London Commercial Bank v Reliance Permanent Building Society (1885) 29 Ch D 954,
    54 LJ Ch 1081, 33 WR 916, 53 LT 442, 1 TLR 609, CA 1000
West of England and South Wales District Bank v Murch (1883) 23 Ch D 138, 31 WR 467,
    sub nom West of England Bank v Murch, Re Booker & Co 52 LJ Ch 784, 48 LT
    417. . . . . 522, 762
West of England Shipowners Mutual Insurance Association (Luxembourg) v Cristal Ltd,
    The Glacier Bay [1996] 1 Lloyd's Rep 370, CA 216

West Sussex Constabulary's Widows, Children and Benevolent (1930) Fund Trusts, Re, Barnett v Ketteringham [1971] Ch 1, [1970] 1 All ER 544, [1970] 2 WLR 848, 114 Sol Jo 92, 134 JP Jo 119, 120 NLJ 225 . . . . 332, 337, 338, 339, 341, 370

Westby's Settlement, Re, Westby v Ashley [1950] Ch 296, [1950] 1 All ER 479, 66 (pt 1) TLR 515, CA 212

Westdeutsche Landesbank Girozentrale v Islington London Borough Council [1994] 4 All ER 890, 91 LGR 323; varied [1994] 4 All ER 890, [1994] 1 WLR 938, [1994] 8 LS Gaz R 38, 138 Sol Jo LB 26, CA; revsd [1996] AC 669, [1996] 2 All ER 961, [1996] 2 WLR 802, 95 LGR 1, [1996] NLJR 877, 140 Sol Jo LB 136, HL 4, 15, 54, 56, 57, 243, 273, 274, 323, 324, 325, 327, 329, 332, 335, 350, 354, 357, 407, 435, 436, 578, 870, 881, 885, 886, 897, 898, 899, 975, 994, 1021, 1022

Westdock Realisations Ltd, Re [1988] BCLC 354, 4 BCC 192. 843

Westmeath (Marquis) v Marchioness of Westmeath (1831) 1 Dow & CI 519, HL 218

Westminster Bank Ltd v Wilson [1938] 3 All ER 652, 82 Sol Jo 695, CA; revsd sub nom Naas v Westminster Bank Ltd [1940] AC 366, [1940] 1 All ER 485, 109 LJ Ch 138, 84 Sol Jo 333, 162 LT 277, 56 TLR 381, HL 4, 139

Westminster Bank Ltd's Declaration of Trust, Re [1963] 2 All ER 400n, [1963] 1 WLR 820, sub nom Abbott v Service 107 Sol Jo 681 517

Westminster City Council v Croyalgrange Ltd [1986] 2 All ER 353, [1986] 1 WLR 674, 84 LGR 801, 83 Cr App Rep 155, 150 JP 449, [1986] Crim LR 693, 130 Sol Jo 409, [1986] LS Gaz R 2089, [1986] NLJ Rep 491, HL 488

Westminster City Council v Haywood [1998] Ch 377, [1997] 2 All ER 84, [1997] 3 WLR 641, [1998] ICR 920, CA 867

Weston, Re, Davies v Tagart [1900] 2 Ch 164, 69 LJ Ch 555, 48 WR 467, 82 LT 591 . 951, 981

Weston's Settlements, Re, Weston v Weston [1969] 1 Ch 223, [1968] 1 All ER 720, [1968] 2 WLR 1154, 47 ATC 237, [1968] TR 215, 112 Sol Jo 137; affd [1969] 1 Ch 223, [1968] 3 All ER 338, [1968] 3 WLR 786, 47 ATC 324, [1968] TR 295, 112 Sol Jo 641, CA . . 513, 515, 772

Westpac Banking Corpn v Savin [1985] 2 NZLR 41, NZCA 970

Westpac Building Corpn v M M Kembla New Zealand Ltd [2001] 2 NZLR 298 973

Westphal, Re [1972] NZLR 792 . . . . 114, 126, 732

Weth v Attorney General (No 1) [2001] WTLR 155 843

Wethered v Wethered (1828) 2 Sim 183, 29 RR 77 184

Wetherell v Langston (1847) 17 LJ Ex 338, 1 Exch 634, 74 RR 794, Ex Ch 450

Wharton v Masterman [1895] AC 186, 64 LJ Ch 369, 11 R 169, 43 WR 449, [1895-9] All ER Rep 687, 72 LT 431, 11 TLR 301, HL 205, 730, 731

Wheatley v Purr (1837) 1 Keen 551, 6 LJ Ch 195, 1 Jur 133 147

Wheeler, Re, Hankinson v Hayter [1904] 2 Ch 66, 73 LJ Ch 576, 52 WR 586, 48 Sol Jo 493, 91 LT 227 981

Wheeler v Smith (1859) 1 Giff 300, 29 LJ Ch 194, 6 Jur NS 62, 114 RR 456, 8 WR 173, 1 LT 430 . . . . 349, 358

Wheeler v Warner (1823) 1 Sim & St 304, 24 RR 176 74

Wheeler and De Rochow, Re [1896] 1 Ch 315, 65 LJ Ch 219, 44 WR 270, 73 LT 661. . . . . 755, 756

Wheelwright v Walker (1883) 31 WR 912, 48 LT 867. 905

Whichelow, Re, Bradshaw v Orpen [1953] 2 All ER 1558, [1954] 1 WLR 5, 98 Sol Jo 12 . . . . 686, 735, 736

Whishaw v Stephens. See Gulbenkian's Settlements, Re, Hacobian v Maun

Whiston's Settlement, Re, Lovat v Williamson [1894] 1 Ch 661, 63 LJ Ch 273, 8 R 175, 42 WR 327, 38 Sol Jo 253, 70 LT 681 . . . . 299, 300

Whitaker, Re, Rooke v Whitaker [1929] 1 Ch 662, 98 LJ Ch 312, 141 LT 28 572

Whitbread v Smith (1854) 3 De GM & G 727, 23 LJ Ch 611, 2 Eq Rep 377, 18 Jur 475, 98 RR 285, 2 WR 177, 23 LTOS 2. . . . . 563, 565

Whitby v Von Luedecke [1906] 1 Ch 783, 75 LJ Ch 359, 54 WR 415, 94 LT 432 199

White, Re, Pennell v Franklin [1898] 2 Ch 217, 67 LJ Ch 502, 46 WR 676, 42 Sol Jo 635, 78 LT 770, 14 TLR 503, CA 597, 652

White, Re, White v Edmond [1901] 1 Ch 570, 70 LJ Ch 300, 49 WR 429, 45 Sol Jo 294, 84 LT 199 735

White, Re, White v White [1893] 2 Ch 41, 62 LJ Ch 342, 2 R 380, 41 WR 683, [1891-4] All ER Rep 242, 37 Sol Jo 249, 68 LT 187, CA 105

White v Bijou Mansions Ltd [1937] Ch 610, [1937] 3 All ER 269, 81 Sol Jo 498, 157 LT 105,

53 TLR 818; affd [1938] Ch 351, [1938] 1 All ER 546, 107 LJ Ch 212, 82 Sol Jo 135, 158
LT 338, 54 TLR 458, CA 991
White v Briggs (1848) 2 Ph 583, 15 Sim 300, 17 LJ Ch 196, 78 RR 203 75
White v Grane (1854) 18 Beav 571, 23 LJ Ch 863, 2 WR 328, 2 WR 320 . . . . . . .94, 690
White v Jones [1995] 2 AC 207, [1993] 3 All ER 481, [1993] 3 WLR 730, [1993] 23 LS Gaz R
43, [1993] NLJR 473, CA; affd [1995] 2 AC 207, [1995] 1 All ER 691, [1995] 2 WLR
187, [1995] 3 FCR 51, [1995] NLJR 251, 139 Sol Jo LB 83, HL 280, 281
White v Paine. See Paine v Countess of Warwick
White v White (1804) 4 RR 161, 9 Ves 554. 564
White-Popham Settled Estates, Re [1936] Ch 725, [1936] 2 All ER 1486, 105 LJ Ch 368, 80
Sol Jo 816, 155 LT 553, CA 527
White's Settlement, Re, Pitman v White [1930] 1 Ch 179, 99 LJ Ch 49, 142 LT 279, 46 TLR
30 556
Whitehead's Will Trusts, Re, Burke v Burke [1971] 2 All ER 1334, [1971] 1 WLR 833, 115 Sol
Jo 389. . . . . 770, 772, 773, 1041
Whitehead's Will Trusts, Re, Public Trustee v White [1959] Ch 579, [1959] 2 All ER 497, 103
Sol Jo 491 542
Whiteley, Re, London (Bishop) v Whiteley [1910] 1 Ch 600, 79 LJ Ch 405, 55 Sol Jo 291, 102
LT 313, 26 TLR 309 644
Whiteley, Re, Whiteley v Learoyd (1886) 33 Ch D 347, 51 JP 100, 55 LJ Ch 864, 55 LT 564, 2
TLR 864, CA; affd sub nom Learoyd v Whiteley (1887) 12 App Cas 727, 57 LJ Ch 390,
36 WR 721, 58 LT 93, 3 TLR 813, HL 576, 861, 906
Whiteside v Whiteside [1950] Ch 65, [1949] 2 All ER 913, 66 (pt 1) TLR 126, CA 278
Whitfield, Re [1920] WN 256, [1920] All ER Rep 668, 125 LT 61 . . . . 535, 611
Whitfield v Brand (1847) 16 LJ Ex 103, 16 M & W 282, 73 RR 502 461
Whiting's Settlement, Re, Whiting v De Rutzen [1905] 1 Ch 96, 74 LJ Ch 207, 53 WR 293, 49
Sol Jo 83, 91 LT 821, 21 TLR 83, CA 217, 220, 221
Whitney v Smith (1869) 4 Ch App 513, 17 WR 579, 20 LT 468 947
Whitrick, Re, Sutcliffe v Sutcliffe [1957] 2 All ER 467, [1957] 1 WLR 884, 101 Sol Jo 574, CA 279
Whittaker v Kershaw (1890) 45 Ch D 320, sub nom Re Kershaw, Whittaker v Kershaw 60 LJ
Ch 9, 39 WR 22, 63 LT 203, CA 813
Whittingham v Whittingham [1979] Fam 9, [1978] 3 All ER 805, [1978] 2 WLR 936, 36 P &
CR 164, 8 Fam Law 171, 122 Sol Jo 247; affd [1979] Fam 9, [1978] 3 All ER 805, [1978]
2 WLR 936, 36 P & CR 164, 8 Fam Law 171, 122 Sol Jo 247, CA 296
Whitton's Trusts, Re (1869) LR 8 Eq 352 574
Wicks v Firth (Inspector of Taxes) [1983] 2 AC 214, [1983] 1 All ER 151, [1983] 2 WLR 34,
[1983] STC 25, 56 TC 318, [1983] IRLR 80, 127 Sol Jo 37, 133 NLJ 61, HL . . 112, 114
Widdow's Trusts, Re (1871) LR 11 Eq 408, 40 LJ Ch 380, 19 WR 468, 24 LT 87 735
Wight v Olswang (1999) 1 ITELR 783, Times, 18 May, CA. 593
Wight v Olswang (No 2) [2000] 18 LS Gaz R 37, [2000] Lloyd's Rep PN 662, [2000] WTLR
783; revsd [2001] Lloyd's Rep PN 269, [2001] WTLR 291, CA 618
Wightman v Cousins [1932] NI 61 835
Wightman v Townroe (1813) 1 M & S 412, 14 RR 475 457
Wightwick's Will Trusts, Re, Official Trustees of Charitable Funds v Fielding-Ould [1950] Ch
260, [1950] 1 All ER 689, 94 Sol Jo 239, 66 (pt 1) TLR 592 . 118, 120, 122, 189, 203, 918
Wiglesworth v Wiglesworth (1852) 16 Beav 269, 96 RR 126 . . . . 647, 906
Wilcock, Re, Kay v Dewhirst [1898] 1 Ch 95, 67 LJ Ch 154, 46 WR 153, 42 Sol Jo 115, 77 LT
679. 374
Wilcocks' Settlement, Re (1875) 1 Ch D 229, 45 LJ Ch 163, 24 WR 290, 33 LT 719 . . . 209
Wild v Banning (1866) LR 2 Eq 577, 35 LJ Ch 594, 12 Jur NS 464, 14 LT 845 335
Wild v Pensions Ombudsman [1997] 1 FCR 248, [1996] 2 FLR 680, [1996] Fam Law 667,
140 Sol Jo LB 108 693
Wilder v Pigott (1882) 22 Ch D 263, 52 LJ Ch 141, 31 WR 377, 48 LT 112 306
Wildes v Davies (1853) 22 LJ Ch 495, 1 Sm & G 475, 1 WR 253, 21 LTOS 206 206
Wilding v Bolder (1855) 21 Beav 222, 111 RR 69 772
Wiles v Gresham (1854) 2 Drew 258, 23 LJ Ch 667, 2 Eq Rep 560, 2 WR 355; affd (1854) 5 De
GM & G 770, 24 LJ Ch 264, 3 Eq Rep 116, 100 RR 21, 3 WR 87 . . . . 579, 878, 879
Wilkes v Allington [1931] 2 Ch 104, 100 LJ Ch 262, 75 Sol Jo 221, 144 LT 745, 47 TLR 307 150
Wilkes v Spooner [1911] 2 KB 473, 80 LJKB 1107, 55 Sol Jo 479, 104 LT 911, 27 TLR 426, CA 50
Wilkes' (Beloved) Charity, Re (1851) 20 LJ Ch 588, 3 Mac & G 440, 17 LTOS 101 . . . 702
Wilkins v Hogg (1861) 31 LJ Ch 41, 8 Jur NS 25, 133 RR 47, 10 WR 47, 5 LT 467, CA. . 938
Wilkinson, Re, Neale v Newell [1978] Fam 22, [1978] 1 All ER 221, [1977] 3 WLR 514, 7
Fam Law 176, 121 Sol Jo 375 296

Wilkinson v Duncan (1857) 23 Beav 469, 26 LJ Ch 495, 3 Jur NS 530, 113 RR 228, 5 WR 398,
   29 LTOS 35 560
Wilkinson v Parry (1828) 4 Russ 272, 28 RR 84 . . . . 743, 931
Wilkinson v Wilkinson (1871) LR 12 Eq 604, 40 LJ Ch 242, 19 WR 558, 24 LT 314 . . . 219
Wilks, Re, Keefer v Wilks [1935] Ch 645, 104 LJ Ch 297, [1935] All ER Rep 787, 153 LT 255,
   51 TLR 489 1042
Willey, Re [1890] WN 1, CA 760, 768
Williams, Re, Williams v All Souls, Hastings (Parochial Church Council) [1933] Ch 244, 102
   LJ Ch 58, [1932] All ER Rep 724, 148 LT 310 133
Williams, Re, Williams v Williams [1897] 2 Ch 12, 66 LJ Ch 485, 45 WR 519, 41 Sol Jo 452, 76
   LT 600, CA. 133, 134
Williams, Re, Williams v Williams [1912] 1 Ch 399, 81 LJ Ch 296, 56 Sol Jo 325, 106 LT 584 212
Williams v Allen (No 2) (1863) 32 Beav 650 . . . . 948, 982
Williams v Barton [1927] 2 Ch 9, 96 LJ Ch 355, [1927] All ER Rep 751, 71 Sol Jo 370, 137 LT
   294, 43 TLR 446. . . . . 379, 389, 906
Williams v Byron (1901) 18 TLR 172 918
Williams v Holland [1965] 2 All ER 157, [1965] 1 WLR 739, 109 Sol Jo 237, 193 Estates
   Gazette 1033, CA 18
Williams v IRC [1965] NZLR 395 . . . . .173, 175, 264, 502
Williams v Scott [1900] AC 499, 49 LJPC 77, 49 WR 33, 82 LT 727, 16 TLR 459 . . 663, 665,
                                                                                    671
Williams v Staite [1979] Ch 291, [1978] 2 All ER 928, [1978] 2 WLR 825, 36 P & CR 103, 122
   Sol Jo 333, CA 248, 249
Williams v Teale (1847) 6 Hare 239, 77 RR 100 301
Williams v Williams (1863) 32 Beav 370, 138 RR 766 . . . . 350, 362
Williams v Williams (1881) 17 Ch D 437, 44 LT 573 . . . . 953, 954
Williams v Williams [1976] Ch 278, [1977] 1 All ER 28, [1976] 3 WLR 494, 120 Sol Jo 434,
   CA 427, 481, 482
Williams & Glyn's Bank Ltd v Boland [1979] Ch 312, [1979] 2 All ER 697, [1979] 2 WLR
   550, 38 P & CR 622, 123 Sol Jo 183, CA; affd [1981] AC 487, [1980] 2 All ER 408,
   [1980] 3 WLR 138, 40 P & CR 451, 124 Sol Jo 443, [1980] RVR 204, HL . . 50, 51, 256,
                                                                         351, 411, 706, 1003
Williams and Glyns Bank plc v Astro Dinamico Cia Naviera SA and Georgian Shipping
   Enterprises SA [1984] 1 All ER 760, [1984] 1 WLR 438, [1984] 1 Lloyd's Rep 453, 128
   Sol Jo 189, HL 1059
Williams-Ashman v Price and Williams [1942] Ch 219, [1942] 1 All ER 310, 86 Sol Jo 49, 166
   LT 359, sub nom Ashman v Price and Williams 111 LJ Ch 157 . . . . 953, 954
Williams' Settlement, Re (1858) 4 K & J 87, 116 RR 266, 6 WR 218, 32 LTOS 9 829
Williams' Settlement, Re, Williams v Williams [1911] 1 Ch 441, 80 LJ Ch 249, 55 Sol Jo 236,
   104 LT 310. 313
Williams' Trustees v IRC [1947] AC 447, [1947] 1 All ER 513, 27 TC 409, [1948] LJR 644,
   176 LT 462, 63 TLR 352, HL. 106, 107
Williams' Trusts, Re (1887) 36 Ch D 231, 56 LJ Ch 1088, 36 WR 100, 56 LT 884 . . 759, 764,
                                                                                    780
Williams' Trusts, Re (2000) 2 ITELR 313 594
Williams' Will Trusts, Re, Chartered Bank of India, Australia and China v Williams [1953]
   Ch 138, [1953] 1 All ER 536, [1953] 2 WLR 418, 97 Sol Jo 133. 720
Williams' Will Trusts, Re, Williams v Richardson [1955] Ch 260, [1954] 2 All ER 453, [1954]
   3 WLR 156. 501
Williamson v Codrington (1750) Belt's Supp 215, 1 Ves Sen 511 . . . . . . 173, 174, 177
Willis, Re, Shaw v Willis [1920] 2 Ch 358, 64 Sol Jo 601; revsd [1921] 1 Ch 44, 90 LJ Ch 94, 65
   Sol Jo 43, 124 LT 290, 37 TLR 43, CA 741
Willis v Barron. See Barron v Willis
Willis v Kibble (1839) 1 Beav 559, 49 RR 452. 651
Willis v Willis (1740) 2 Atk 71 330
Willis (J) & Son v Willis [1986] 1 EGLR 62, 277 Estates Gazette 1133, [1986] Conv 406, CA 249
Willmott v Barber (1880) 15 Ch D 96, 49 LJ Ch 792, 28 WR 911, 43 LT 95; on appeal (1881)
   17 Ch D 772, 45 LT 229, CA 249, 250, 935
Wills, Re, Dulverton v Macleod [1939] Ch 705, [1939] 2 All ER 775, 108 LJ Ch 286, 83 Sol Jo
   438, 160 LT 635, 55 TLR 822. 547
Wills, Re, Wills v Hamilton [1915] 1 Ch 769, 84 LJ Ch 580, [1914-15] All ER Rep 289, 59 Sol
   Jo 477, 113 LT 138. 565

Wills' Trust Deeds, Re, Wills v Godfrey [1964] Ch 219, [1963] 1 All ER 390, [1963] 2 WLR 1318, 107 Sol Jo 475 . . . . 28, 29, 90, 132, 504, 690, 741, 742

Wills' Will Trusts, Re, Wills v Wills [1959] Ch 1, [1958] 2 All ER 472, [1958] 3 WLR 101, 102 Sol Jo 490 . . . . .193, 197, 200, 722, 724

Wilmington Trust Co v Mutual Life Insurance Co of New York 26 Del Ch 397 1039

Wilson, Re [1964] 1 All ER 196, [1964] 1 WLR 214, 108 Sol Jo 155 801

Wilson, Re, Alexander v Calder (1885) 28 Ch D 457, 54 LJ Ch 487, 33 WR 579 846

Wilson, Re, Moore v Wilson [1907] 1 Ch 394, 76 LJ Ch 210, 96 LT 453 555

Wilson, Re, Wilson v Wilson (1916) 142 LT Jo 41 79

Wilson v Dennison (1750) Amb 82, sub nom A-G v Scott 1 Ves Sen 413 644

Wilson v Dent (1830) 3 Sim 385 237

Wilson v Duguid (1883) 24 Ch D 244, 53 LJ Ch 52, 31 WR 945, 49 LT 124 130

Wilson v Law Debenture Trust Corpn plc [1995] 2 All ER 337, [1994] PLR 141 . . 672, 680. 702

Wilson v Moore (1833) 1 My & K 126; affd (1834) 1 My & K 337, 36 RR 272, [1824-34] All ER Rep 508 877

Wilson v Turner (1883) 22 Ch D 521, 53 LJ Ch 270, 31 WR 438, 48 LT 370, CA . . 691, 709, 711

Wilson v Wilson (1848) 1 HL Cas 538, 12 Jur 467, 73 RR 158, 1 White & Tud LC 604, 9 ER 870; on appeal (1854) 5 HL Cas 40, 23 LJ Ch 697 218

Wilson-Barkworth, Re, Burstall v Deck (1933) 50 TLR 82 77

Wilson's Will Trusts, Re, Tyron v Bromley Wilson [1950] 2 All ER 955, CA; affd sub nom Bromley v Tryon [1952] AC 265, [1951] 2 All ER 1058, [1951] 2 TLR 1119, HL . 79, 101

Wimbush, Re, Richards v Wimbush [1940] Ch 92, [1940] 1 All ER 229, 109 LJ Ch 71, 84 Sol Jo 13, 162 LT 133, 56 TLR 151 542

Winchilsea's (Earl) Policy Trusts, Re (1888) 39 Ch D 168, 58 LJ Ch 20, 37 WR 77, 59 LT 167 810

Windeatt's Will Trusts, Re [1969] 2 All ER 324, [1969] 1 WLR 692, 113 Sol Jo 450 . 516, 772

Winder's Will Trust, Re, Westminster Bank Ltd v Fausset [1951] Ch 916, [1951] 2 All ER 362, 95 Sol Jo 467, [1951] 2 TLR 93 538

Windsor Steam Coal Co (1901) Ltd, Re [1929] 1 Ch 151, 98 LJ Ch 147, 140 LT 80, CA 913, 919, 939

Winkworth v Christie, Manson and Woods Ltd [1980] Ch 496, [1980] 1 All ER 1121, [1980] 2 WLR 937 . . . . 999, 1028

Winkworth v Edward Baron Development Co Ltd [1987] 1 All ER 114, [1986] 1 WLR 1512, 53 P & CR 378, [1987] 1 FLR 525, [1987] Fam Law 166, [1987] BCLC 193, 3 BCC 4, 130 Sol Jo 954, [1987] LS Gaz R 340, HL 352, 421

Winslow, Re, Frere v Winslow (1890) 45 Ch D 249, 60 LJ Ch 20, 39 WR 120, 63 LT 485 . . . . 543, 982

Winterstoke's Will Trusts, Re, Gunn v Richardson [1938] Ch 158, [1937] 4 All ER 63, 107 LJ Ch 122, 81 Sol Jo 882, 158 LT 404, 54 TLR 20 541

Wintle v Nye [1959] 1 All ER 552, [1959] 1 WLR 284, 103 Sol Jo 220, HL 282

Wise v Perpetual Trustee Co [1903] AC 139, 72 LJPC 31, 51 WR 241, 87 LT 569, 19 TLR 125 . . . . 124, 823

Wise v Piper (1880) 13 Ch D 848, 49 LJ Ch 611, 28 WR 442, 41 LT 794 731

Wise v Wise (1845) 69 RR 329, 2 Jo & Lat 403 452

Withington v Withington (1848) 16 Sim 104, 80 RR 27 753

Wittke, Re, Reynolds and Gorst v King Edward's Hospital Fund for London and Custodian of Enemy Property [1944] Ch 166, [1944] 1 All ER 383, 113 LJ Ch 161, 88 Sol Jo 86, 171 LT 8, 60 TLR 205 . . . . 212, 214

Wohlleben v Canada Permanent Trust Co [1977] 2 SCR 302, 70 DLR (3d) 257, 11 NR 487 (Can SC), [1976] 6 WWR 10 . . . . 916, 941

Wokingham Fire Brigade Trusts, Re, Martin v Hawkins [1951] Ch 373, [1951] 1 All ER 454, 49 LGR 335, 115 JP 159, 95 Sol Jo 137, [1951] 1 TLR 446 341

Wolffe's Will Trusts, Re, Shapley v Wolffe [1953] 2 All ER 697, [1953] 1 WLR 1211, 97 Sol Jo 539 . . . . 189, 231

Wollaston v King (1869) LR 8 Eq 165, 38 LJ Ch 61, 392, 17 WR 641, 20 LT 1003 198

Wollaston v Tribe (1869) LR 9 Eq 44, 18 WR 83, 21 LT 449 276

Wolverhampton and Dudley Breweries plc v Trusthouse Forte Catering Ltd [1984] 2 EGLR 141, 272 Estates Gazette 1072 279

Wombwell, Re, ex p Trustee [1921] B & CR 17, sub nom Wombwell, Re [1921] All ER Rep 483, 125 LT 437, 37 TLR 625 209

Wombwell's Settlement, Re, Clerke v Menzies [1922] 2 Ch 298, 92 LJ Ch 18, [1922] All ER Rep 115, 127 LT 295 274

Wood, Re, Barton v Chilcott [1949] Ch 498, [1949] 1 All ER 1100, [1949] LJR 1509, 93 Sol
    Jo 357 . . . . 105, 111
Wood, Re, Tullett v Colville [1894] 3 Ch 381, 63 LJ Ch 790, 7 R 495, 71 LT 413, CA . . 193,
                                                                                        200
Wood v Cox (1837) 2 My & Cr 684, 6 LJ Ch 366, 1 Jur 720, 45 RR 156 . . . . 137, 330, 335
Wood v Weightman (1872) LR 13 Eq 434, 20 WR 459, 26 LT 385 631
Wood's (A M) Ships' Woodite Protection Co Ltd, Re (1890) 2 Meg 164, 62 LT 760, 6 TLR
    301 21
Wood's Will Trusts, Re, Wood v Donnelly [1952] Ch 406, [1952] 1 All ER 740, 96 Sol Jo 261,
    [1952] 1 TLR 670 104
Woodar Investment Development Ltd v Wimpey Construction UK Ltd [1980] 1 All ER 571,
    [1980] 1 WLR 277, 124 Sol Jo 184, HL 10, 170
Woodard v Woodard [1995] 3 All ER 980, [1992] RTR 35, [1997] 1 FCR 533, [1996] 1 FLR
    399, [1991] Fam Law 470, CA 150
Woodburn's Will, Re (1857) 1 De G & J 333, 26 LJ Ch 522, 3 Jur NS 799, 118 RR 121, 5 WR
    642, 29 LTOS 206, 222 . . . . 830, 846
Woodgate, Re (1886) 2 TLR 674 106
Woodgate's Settlement, Re (1856) 5 WR 448 765
Woodhouse, Re, Public Trustee v Woodhouse [1941] Ch 332, [1941] 2 All ER 265, 110 LJ
    Ch 214, 85 Sol Jo 367, 165 LT 368, 57 TLR 598 . . . . 550, 560
Woodin, Re, Woodin v Glass [1895] 2 Ch 309, 64 LJ Ch 501, 12 R 302, 43 WR 615, 39 Sol Jo
    558, 72 LT 740, CA 714
Woodmeston v Walker (1831) 2 Russ & M 197, 9 LJOS 257, 39 ER 370 566
Woods, Re, Gabellini v Woods [1904] 2 Ch 4, 73 LJ Ch 204, 48 Sol Jo 207, 90 LT 8 . . . 554
Woods v Woods (1836) 1 My & Cr 401, Donnelly 61, 43 RR 214 138
Woodyatt v Gresley (1836) 3 Mont & A 169n, 8 Sim 180, Donnelly 135, 42 RR 153 . . . 951
Wooldridge, Re, Wooldridge v Coe [1920] WN 78 981
Wong Lai-Ying v Chinachen Investments Co Ltd [1978] HKLR 1, PC 442
Wootton's Will Trusts, Re, Trotter v Duffin [1968] 2 All ER 618, [1968] 1 WLR 681, 112 Sol
    Jo 174 . . . . 83, 105, 110
Worcester Works Finance Ltd v Cooden Engineering Co Ltd [1972] 1 QB 210, [1971] 3 All
    ER 708, [1971] 3 WLR 661, 115 Sol Jo 605, CA 909
Wordingham v Royal Exchange Trust Co Ltd [1992] Ch 412, [1992] 3 All ER 204, [1992] 2
    WLR 496, [1992] 17 LS Gaz R 44 280
Worrall v Harford (1802) 8 Ves 4 . . . . 142, 810, 812
Worthington, Re, Leighton v MacLeod [1954] 1 All ER 677, [1954] 1 WLR 526, 98 Sol Jo
    196 655
Worthington Pumping Engine Co v Moore (1902) 20 RPC 41, 19 TLR 84 399
Wragg, Re, Wragg v Palmer [1919] 2 Ch 58, 88 LJ Ch 269, [1918-19] All ER Rep 233, 63 Sol
    Jo 535, 121 LT 78 . . . . 544, 601
Wratten v Hunter [1978] 2 NSWLR 367 238
Wray v Steele (1814) 13 RR 124, 2 Ves & B 388 349
Wright, Re, Hegan v Bloor [1920] 1 Ch 108, 88 LJ Ch 452, [1918-19] All ER Rep 825, 64 Sol
    Jo 21, 121 LT 549 29
Wright v British Railways Board [1983] 2 AC 773, [1983] 2 All ER 698, [1983] 3 WLR 211,
    127 Sol Jo 478, HL 560
Wright v Callender (1852) 2 De GM & G 652, 21 LJ Ch 787, 16 Jur 647, [1843-60] All ER Rep
    508, 19 LTOS 308 533
Wright v Carter [1903] 1 Ch 27, 72 LJ Ch 138, 51 WR 196, [1900-3] All ER Rep 706, 87 LT
    624, 19 TLR 29, CA 23, 282, 283, 284
Wright v Chard (1859) 4 Drew 673, 5 Jur NS 1334, 113 RR 501, 8 WR 35, 1 LT 138; affd
    (1860) 1 De GF & J 567, 29 LJ Ch 415, 6 Jur NS 476, 113 RR 501, 8 WR 334, 2 LT 104 649
Wright v Ginn [1994] OPLR 83 579
Wright v Morgan [1926] AC 788, 95 LJPC 171, [1926] All ER Rep 201, 135 LT 713 . 662, 875,
                                                                                        880
Wright v Pearson (1758) 1 Eden 119, 2 Keny 361, Ambl 356 299
Wright v Robert Leonard (Development) Ltd [1994] NPC 49, [1994] EGCS 69, CA . . . 235
Wright v Snowe (1848) 2 De G & Sm 321, 79 RR 220 935
Wright v Vanderplank (1856) 8 De GM & G 133, 25 LJ Ch 753, 2 Jur NS 599, 114 RR 6, 4 WR
    410, 27 LTOS 91 283
Wright's Settled Estates, Re (1900) 83 LT 159 573
Wright's Settlement Trusts, Re, Wright v Wright [1945] Ch 211, [1945] 1 All ER 587, 114 LJ
    Ch 196, 89 Sol Jo 306, 172 LT 345, 61 TLR 307 535

Wright's Trusts, Re (1857) 3 K & J 419, 112 RR 212 827
Wright's Will Trusts, Re [1981] LS Gaz R 841 . . . . 89, 101, 215
Wright's Will Trusts, Re (21 July 1982, unreported) 82, 88
Wrightson, Re, Wrightson v Cooke [1908] 1 Ch 789, 77 LJ Ch 422, 98 LT 799, [1908-10] All
    ER Rep Ext 1399 . . . . 766, 932
Wrightson Ltd v Fletcher Challenge Nominees Ltd [2001] UKPC 23 [2001] All ER (D) 89
    (May), [2001] OPLR 249 . . . . .475, 495, 691, 732
Wroe v Seed (1863) 4 Giff 425, 9 Jur NS 1122, 9 LT 254 678
Wu Koon Tai v Wu Yau Loi [1997] AC 179, [1996] 3 WLR 778, [1996] NPC 139, 140 Sol Jo
    LB 221, [1996] 3 HKC 559, PC 18
Wyatt, Re, Gowan v Wyatt (1889) 60 LT 920 . . . . 307, 334
Wykes, Re, Riddington v Spencer [1961] Ch 229, [1961] 2 WLR 115, 105 Sol Jo 109, sub
    nom Re Wykes' Will Trusts, Riddington v Spencer [1961] 1 All ER 470. 108
Wyld v Silver [1963] Ch 243, [1963] 1 QB 169, [1962] 3 All ER 309, [1962] 3 WLR 841, 60
    LGR 461, 106 Sol Jo 875, CA 50
Wylly's Trust, Re (1860) 25 JP 84, 28 Beav 458, 6 Jur NS 906, 126 RR 217, 8 WR 645, 2 LT 788 829
Wyman v Paterson [1900] AC 271, 69 LJPC 32, 82 LT 473, 16 TLR 270, HL 586
Wynn's Will Trusts, Re, Public Trustee v Newborough [1952] Ch 271, [1952] 1 All ER 341,
    96 Sol Jo 120, [1952] 1 TLR 278 . . . . .190, 215, 590, 832
Wynne v Humberston (1858) 27 Beav 421, 28 LJ Ch 281, 5 Jur NS 5, 122 RR 469, 32 LTOS
    268 457
Wynne v Tempest [1897] 1 Ch 110, 66 LJ Ch 81, 45 WR 183, 41 Sol Jo 127, 75 LT 624, 13
    TLR 128 941
Wynne v Tempest [1897] WN 43, 13 TLR 360 . . . . 917, 938, 940

                                    X

X v A [2000] 1 All ER 490, [2000] 1 EGLR 19, [1999] 39 LS Gaz R 38, [2000] 01 EG 94, 143
    Sol Jo LB 239 . . . . 526, 531, 578, 810, 811, 813, 814, 819, 820

                                    Y

Yaxley v Gotts [2000] Ch 162, [2000] 1 All ER 711, [1999] 3 WLR 1217, 79 P & CR 91, [1999]
    2 FLR 941, [1999] Fam Law 700, 32 HLR 547, [1999] NPC 76, [1999] 2 EGLR 181,
    [1999] EGCS 92, 143 Sol Jo LB 198, 78 P & CR D33, CA . . . 234, 249, 254, 326, 328,
                                                            354, 412, 413, 423, 426, 520
Yem v Edwards (1857) 22 JP 495, 1 De G & J 598, 3 K & J 564, 27 LJ Ch 23, 4 Jur NS 647, 6
    WR 20, 30 LTOS 110 383
Yerburgh, Re, Yerburgh v Yerburgh [1928] WN 208 . . . . 20, 760
York and North Midland Rly Co v Hudson (1853) 16 Beav 485, 22 LJ Ch 529, 96 RR 228, 1
    WR 187, 510, 22 LTOS 29 386
Yorke, Re, Barlow v Yorke [1911] 1 Ch 370, 80 LJ Ch 253, 104 LT 134 . . . . . . 180, 815
Youde v Cloud (1874) LR 18 Eq 634, 44 LJ Ch 93, 22 WR 764 492
Young, Re, Trye v Sullivan (1885) 28 Ch D 705, 54 LJ Ch 1065, 33 WR 729, 52 LT 754 . 360
Young, Re, Young v Young [1951] Ch 185, 94 Sol Jo 762, sub nom Re Young's Will Trusts,
    Young v Young [1950] 2 All ER 1040 548
Young, Re, Young v Young [1951] Ch 344, [1950] 2 All ER 1245, 94 Sol Jo 839, [1951] 1 TLR
    262 264
Young v Murphy [1996] 1 VR 279 . . . . 903, 906, 965
Young v Peachy (1742) 2 Atk 254 368
Young v Sealey [1949] Ch 278, [1949] 1 All ER 92, [1949] LJR 529, 93 Sol Jo 58 . . . 60, 149,
                                                                        247, 359, 367
Young's Estate, Re (1934) 103 LJP 75, 78 Sol Jo 431, 151 LT 221, 50 TLR 424 658
Younghusband v Gisborne (1844) 1 Coll 400; affd (1846) 15 LJ Ch 355, 10 Jur 419, 66 RR
    120, 7 LTOS 221 . . . . 209, 738
Ypatianna, The. See Indian Oil Corpn Ltd v Greenstone Shipping SA (Panama), The
    Ypatianna
Yunghanns v Cabdoora No 19 Pty Ltd (1999) 2 ITELR 589 903

                                    Z

Z Trust, Re [1997] Cayman ILR 248 . . . . 29, 31, 754
Zekelman, Re (1971) 19 DLR (3d) 652 512
Zive, Re (1977) 77 DLR (3d) 669 535

Preliminary definitions

DIVISION ONE

Preliminary definitions

Article
1   Definitions of trust, trustee, trust property, beneficiary, settlor
     and breach of trust   3
2   Definitions of legal and equitable estates and interests   48
3   Definitions of express, implied, resulting and constructive trusts   53
4   Definitions of simple and special trusts or bare and active trusts   57
5   Definitions of fixed and discretionary trusts   63
6   Definitions of executed and executory trusts   66

ARTICLE 1

**Definitions of trust, trustee, trust property, beneficiary, settlor and
breach of trust**

A trust is an equitable obligation, binding a person (called a trustee)
to deal with property owned by him (called trust property, being
distinguished from his private property) for the benefit of persons
(called beneficiaries or, in old cases, *cestuis que trust*), of whom he may
himself be one[1], and any one of whom may enforce the obligation[2].
Any act or neglect on the part of a trustee which is not authorised or
excused by the terms of the trust instrument, or by law, is called a
breach of trust[3]. The trustee's functions as to managing the trust

---

1 Unless he takes on the face of a will as trustee of a half-secret trust when evidence not
  complying with the Wills Act 1837 is inadmissible to contradict the apparently exclusive status
  of trustee: *Re Rees* [1950] Ch 204, [1949] 2 All ER 1003, CA.
2 Charitable purpose trusts enforceable by the Attorney-General or the Charity Commissioners
  (representing the Crown as *parens patriae*) are outside the scope of this work, while the
  anomalous valid testamentary 'trusts' for erection and maintenance of sepulchral monuments, for maintenance of pet animals of the deceased and for saying of masses in private for
  the soul of the deceased (see pp 118–123, post) are essentially powers to perform those
  activities, since no-one has positive rights to compel performance of such activities. It may be
  that the courts will develop the obligation characteristic of the trust so that a trust validly
  arises where a trustee owns property not just for the benefit of charitable purposes
  (enforceable by the Attorney-General or the Charity Commissioners) but also for the benefit
  of non-charitable purposes where the settlor has appointed an enforcer so that positive
  enforcement of the purposes is possible: see pp 114–116 post.
3 This sentence was expressly approved by Romer LJ in *Green v Russell* [1959] 2 QB 226 at 241.

property or distributing income or capital to beneficiaries may, under the terms of a trust, be subject to fiduciary or personal powers vested in another person[4], such as a person designated as protector or a beneficiary currently entitled to income or, even, the settlor or his widow. The settlor of property is the person who creates a trust of that particular property[5], whether, as normal, by transferring – or doing everything necessary to be done by him[6] to transfer – title to that property to the trustee and declaring trusts thereof or, exceptionally, by retaining certain property over which he declares trusts of which he is to be trustee.

When a settlor creates a trust he not only creates personal obligations of loyalty and care, binding the trustee of the trust property to produce accounts of the trusteeship available to be falsified or surcharged by the beneficiaries, but he also confers on a beneficiary an equitable proprietary interest in the trust property and its fruits, which enables the beneficiary to trace the product thereof[7] and claim there should be restored to the trust fund (or himself if an absolutely entitled beneficiary) all or a proportionate part thereof – or, if the product has depreciated in value, claim an equitable lien be imposed thereon for the amount due under the accounting process. A beneficiary's proprietary interest arises as soon as the settlor has transferred – or has done everything necessary to be done by him to transfer – title to the trust property to a trustee, but the personal obligations of trusteeship do not arise until the trustee has knowledge of the trust[8], yet does not disclaim the trusteeship[9]. A beneficiary's equitable proprietary interest in the trust property binds a third party to whom trust property is wrongfully transferred unless the latter proves that he was a bona fide purchaser of the legal title to such property without notice of the beneficiary's interest or was protected by a statutory provision (eg conferring good title on a purchaser of land if he pays the purchase money to two trustees or a trust corporation)[10].

---

4 See pp 29–34 post.

5 Sometimes a dummy settlor is used to create a trust of £100 before the real settlor transfers property of significant value to the trustee: *Re TR Technology Investment Trust plc* [1988] BCLC 256, 263–264; *West v Lazard* [1993] Jersey LR 165, 201–204. When X adds property to an existing trust fund such property is new trust property of which X is the settlor: *C I R v Dick* (2001) 4 ITELR 317 at para 40. Also see *Air Jamaica Ltd v Charlton* [1999] 1 WLR 1399 at 1409 for an employee's separate settlement within a pension trust fund.

6 See pp 154–157 post.

7 See Arts 92 and 101 post and *Foskett v McKeown* [2001] 1 AC 102, HL.

8 *Westdeutsche Landesbank Girozentrale v Islington London Borough Council* [1996] AC 669 at 689, 705, 707 and 709; *Re Montagu's Settlement Trust* [1987] 1 Ch 264 at 271–273, 278, and 285. See also *Naas v Westminster Bank* [1940] AC 366, HL. It is possible for a settlor, without the trustee's knowledge, to transfer title to land or shares or chattels to the trustee or to covenant with the trustee that the settlor's executor will transfer £1million to the trustee within one year of the settlor's death to the intent that the trustee holds the benefit of the covenant forthwith for specified beneficiaries. A testator's will may also create trusts without the knowledge of the intended trustee.

9 Equity will not allow a trust to fail for want of a trustee. If the trustee disclaims then the settlor (or his personal representative) holds the property as trustee: it is thus the unilateral act of the settlor that creates this trust as if he had declared himself trustee in the first place.

10 Further see Art 101 post.

In all previous editions the first sentence defined a trust as 'an equitable obligation, binding a person (who is called a trustee) to deal with property *over which he has control* (which is called the trust property for the benefit of persons... [continuing as in the above first sentence]', such sentence being expressly approved by Romer LJ in *Green v Russell*[11] and by Cohen J in *Re Marshall's Will Trusts*[12]. However, James LJ in *Smith v Anderson*[13] stated, 'A trustee is a man who is the *owner of the property* and deals with it as principal as owner and as master, subject only to an equitable obligation to account to some persons to whom he stands in the relation of trustee and who are his *cestuis que trust*', while Mason P recently stated[14] 'it is of the essence of a trust that property is vested in the trustee'.

Trusteeship is ownership-management, not agency-management or bailee-management: a person who deals with property owned by another but over which he has control as agent or as bailee or as attorney under a power of attorney for the benefit of another person is not a trustee of property, although in relation to particular property he may in certain circumstances be under fiduciary duties similar to those of a trustee. One can understand that, where a trustee is interested in 10,000 shares out of 5 million shares of XYZ plc owned by a custodian, a layman may regard the trustee as having control over 10,000 of those shares but a lawyer regards the trustee as owning a one five-hundredth equitable interest in the pool of 5 million shares as equitable tenant in common with all others interested in such pool of securities owned by the custodian. Thus, Article I(I) of *Principles of European Trust Law*[15] states, 'In a trust, a person called the trustee owns assets segregated from his private patrimony and must deal with those assets (the "trust fund") for the benefit of another person called "the beneficiary" or for the furtherance of a purpose.'

Believing that the term 'breach of trust' had not been defined in any case or textbook Megarry V-C in *Tito v Waddell (No 2)*[16] concerned himself with two American formulations: (1) 'every omission or violation by a trustee of a duty which equity lays on him is a breach of trust'; (2) 'a trustee commits a breach of trust if he violates any duty which he owes as trustee to the beneficiaries'. The first formulation is the wider since it would make a breach by a trustee of some duty imposed on him otherwise than under the law of trusts into a breach of trust. In any event defining a breach of trust in terms of a breach of duty raises the further question of what is meant by a breach of duty. Megarry V-C took the view that a trustee owed no 'duty' not to purchase the trust property or not to purchase a beneficiary's interest in the trust property without making proper disclosure, but was under a disability in respect of such matters, such disability being not a specific part of the law of trusts but part of a general rule of equity that certain persons (eg agents, solicitors, directors, trustees, personal representatives, liquidators) are subject to fiduciary obligations creating certain consequences if they carry through certain transactions without, where appropriate, complying with certain require-

11 [1959] 2 QB 226 at 241.
12 [1945] Ch 217 at 219.
13 (1880) 15 Ch D 247 at 275.
14 *Stamp Duties Comr v ISPT Pty Ltd* (1999) 2 ITELR 1 at 15 (New South Wales CA).
15 Published by Kluwer Law International and edited by D Hayton, S Kortmann and H Verhagen. The Principles, prepared by an international working group, are intended to guide non-trust jurisdictions desirous of implementing The Hague Trusts Convention.
16 [1977] Ch 106 at 246–250; *Bristol & West BS v Mothew* [1998] Ch 1 at 16–18.

ments. It thus followed that the six year limitation period in Limitation Act 1939, s 19(2) (now Limitation Act 1980, s 21(3)), for 'an action by a beneficiary in respect of any breach of trust' did not apply to a trustee's purchase of the trust property or of a beneficiary's interest without proper disclosure.

Other definitions[17] have been formulated to summarise the effect of all the various rules that are responsible for the concept of the trust which, unlike a corporation, is not a legal person, but it is not considered worthwhile to examine such definitions since it is the rules from which the definitions result that are of much greater practical concern. However, the distinctive features of a trust are well illuminated by Article 2 of The Hague Convention on the Law Applicable to Trusts and on their Recognition as follows.

'For the purposes of this Convention, the term "trust" refers to the legal relationships created—inter vivos or on death—by a person, the settlor, when assets have been placed under the control of a trustee for the benefit of a beneficiary or for a specified purpose.

A trust has the following characteristics—

a the assets constitute a separate fund and are not a part of the trustee's own estate;

b title to the trust assets stands in the name of the trustee or in the name of another person on behalf of the trustee;

c the trustee has the power and the duty, in respect of which he is accountable, to manage, employ or dispose of the assets in accordance with the terms of the trust and the special duties imposed upon him by law.

The reservation by the settlor of certain rights and powers, and the fact that the trustee may himself have rights as a beneficiary, are not necessarily inconsistent with the existence of a trust.'

This last sentence reflects the impossibility of A holding on trust for A alone[18], whilst recognising the possibility of A vesting property in A and B on trust for A for life, remainder to B and C equally, with express power for A as settlor to revoke the trust or to delete or add persons as beneficiaries and with express power in A's lifetime for whoever happen to be trustees from time to time to appoint trust capital to, or settle it upon, spouses or children of beneficiaries. Such a flexible trust is valid though it may be unsatisfactory from a tax point of view and may be liable to be set aside on A's bankruptcy.

Unfortunately Article 2 in it references to assets 'under the control of a trustee' and 'title to assets ... in the name of another person on behalf of a trustee' reflects the layman's viewpoint where a custodian owns a million shares in XYZ plc and the trustee is interested in 10,000 of them so that the layman believes the trust assets to be 10,000 shares in XYZ plc rather than a one hundredth equitable interest in the million shares. At first sight, the width of Article 2 allows agency-management of assets owned by another to qualify as a trust, but if this were intended then the Trusts Convention would have a provision dealing with its relationship to the earlier Agency Convention and it has no such provision. Furthermore as Article 11 indicates, at the core of the Convention is an owner of property, but that part of his property which is trust property constitutes a separate fund immune from claims of the owner-trustee's creditors, heirs and spouse. Thus the Trusts Convention

---

17 Keeton and Sheridan, *Law of Trusts* (13th edn) p 3; Lewin, *The Law of Trusts* (17th edn) paras 1–01 to 1–08; Pettit, *Equity and the Law of Trusts* (8th edn) pp 24–25; Scott, *Law of Trusts* (4th edn) para 2.

18 *Re Cook* [1948] Ch 212, [1948] 1 All ER 231 4th; *Re Lord Grimthorpe* [1908] 2 Ch 675, CA; cf *Rye v Rye* [1962] AC 496, [1962] 1 All ER 146, HL.

should not be construed as extending to agency and bailment arrangements: if it did there would be no scope for Article 13 to enable States that do not have the 'trust' to refuse to recognise trusts that are local except for the choice of a foreign governing law and a foreign trustee, because all states have 'agency'.

Article 1 of Principles of European Trust Law[19], designed to help countries efficiently implement The Hague Trust Convention (whether or not they want to restrict the trust concept to a special personal obligation not creating proprietary rights against third parties) is based upon the trust as 'ownership management'. Under Article 1(1) 'In a trust, a person called "the trustee" owns assets segregated from his private patrimony and must deal with those assets ("the trust fund") for the benefit of another person for the furtherance of a purpose.'

The nature of an English trust is probably best appreciated by contrasting other ways in which English law may provide for someone to deal with property for the benefit of others.

Trust and governmental or public obligation

The Crown will often be administering property for others in the exercise of the Crown's governmental functions. Such a relationship is not an equitable relationship enforceable in the courts[20]. The Crown will have the whole legal and equitable interest in the property and will be subject to no equitable obligations in administering the property. Similarly, the Law Society acting in a public capacity under s 37 of the Solicitors Act 1974 so as to obtain insurance cover for practising solicitors was entitled to retain the commission it received in arranging the 'master policy' for solicitors[1].

Trust and agency

Agency is a common law relationship arising where a person, known as the agent, has express or implied authority to act on behalf of another, known as the principal, and consents so to act. An agent, like a trustee, is thus acting to promote the interests of another but the agency relationship is based on agreement between principal and agent: this is not so in the case of trustee and beneficiary. During his agency the agent can act on behalf of the principal as a means whereby the principal and third parties are placed in contractual relations: a trustee cannot involve his beneficiaries in such relations but must act so as to be personally liable (though with a right of indemnity from the trust property for proper acts). An agent need never have any control over his principal's property and even where he is employed to deal with his principal's property he will not have title to it: a trustee always has the title to the trust property (except for settled land under the Settled Land Act 1925).

Agency is normally terminated on death of either principal or agent. A trust will not terminate merely because the trustees have died and a bene-

---

19 See *Principles of European Trust Law* (Edited by D Hayton, S Kortmann and H Verhagen) Kluwer Law International, 1999.
20 *Kinloch v Secretary of State of India* (1880) 15 Ch D 1; on appeal (1882) 7 App Cas 619; *Tito v Waddell (No 2)* [1977] 3 All ER 129 at 216–228. Cf *Mabo v Queensland (No 2)* (1992) 175 CLR 1 (Aust HC); *Phillips Bros Ltd v Sierra Leone* [1995] 3 CLR 316.
1 *Swain v Law Society* [1983] 1 AC 598, [1982] 2 All ER 827, HL.

ficiary's death will only terminate his particular interest. The settlor's death is immaterial after his gift has created the trust. Once a trust has been created the settlor cannot intervene at all, even with the agreement of the trustees, unless the trust deed reserved a power for him to intervene for a specified purpose: the contract of agency can be modified at any time by agreement between the principal and agent. If the beneficiaries are all ascertained adults of full capacity they can terminate the trust at will: a principal cannot terminate the agency at will unless he reserves such a specific right in the contract of agency.

The common law governing the agency relationship has been supplemented by intervention by the equitable jurisdiction, which is prepared to treat the relationship as a fiduciary relationship for the purpose of imposing a liability to account upon an agent who makes a personal profit out of his privileged position without his principal's informed consent. To this extent agents are under similar disabilities or obligations as trustees but with the further disadvantage that Trustee Act 1925, ss 57 and 61, are unavailable to them.

The common law relationship between principal and agent is that of creditor and debtor giving rise to a personal claim: thus if the debtor is insolvent the personal claim will abate with the claims of the other creditors. The equitable relationship of trustee and beneficiary, whereunder the nominal ownership is vested in the trustee so that the beneficiary has an equitable proprietary interest, is such that if the trustee is insolvent the trust property is unavailable for the trustee's creditors. The trust property is claimed as their own by the trust beneficiaries if it is identifiable and, for this purpose, the beneficiaries have an equitable right to trace the trust property into other property into which it has been converted after the trust property has been mixed with the trustee's own funds.

In certain circumstances equity intervenes to treat an agent as a constructive trustee or under fiduciary duties similar to those of a trustee. Thus if the principal instructs his agent to purchase Blackacre for the principal and the agent purports to purchase Blackacre for himself the agent will be held constructive trustee thereof for the principal[2]. If an agent has property given to him by his principal for sale, investment or safe custody the agent will be under fiduciary duties similar to those of a trustee[3]. The position is the same when an agent receives property on behalf of his principal, eg by way of collection of rents or debts, so long as he is required contractually or otherwise to keep such moneys separately identifiable from his own property: otherwise he is liable to account as debtor only[4]. Where the agent is a fiduciary, not liable as debtor only, then the equitable right to trace will be available and on the agent's insolvency the principal's direct or traced property will be claimed by the principal and not be available for the agent's creditors. This will also be the case where property is received by an agent on his own behalf as a bribe or by way of secret profit so that he ought to account

---

2 *Longfield Parish Council v Robson* (1913) 29 TLR 357.
3 *Re Hallett's Estate* (1880) 13 Ch D 696, CA; *De Bussche v Alt* (1878) 8 Ch D 286, CA; *Burdick v Garrick* (1870) 5 Ch App 233.
4 *Lyell v Kennedy* (1889) 14 App Cas 437, HL; *Foley v Hill* (1848) 2 HL Cas 28; *Aluminium Industrie Vaassen BV v Romalpa Aluminium Ltd* [1976] 2 All ER 552, [1976] 1 WLR 676; *Clough Mill Ltd v Martin* [1984] 3 All ER 982, [1985] 1 WLR 111, CA.

for it to his principal and 'Equity considers done that which ought to be done.'[5]

Trust and contract

A contract is a creature of the common law and creates a personal right against the other party to the contract. At common law, only the parties to the contract can sue on it, but under the Contracts (Rights of Third Parties) Act 1999 it is now possible for third parties to enforce contracts for their benefit where intended by the contracting parties. A contract is essentially a bargain: it is based upon agreement and it requires for its validity some valuable consideration or to be incorporated in a deed, the formalities for a deed importing the consideration.

A trust is an equitable obligation which creates a proprietary interest in the beneficiaries capable of binding third parties. No consideration[6] is required for its validity: it is, perhaps, best regarded as the equitable equivalent of a common law gift and so leaves no right in the creator of the trust, known as the settlor, to enforce, vary or revoke the terms of the trust, unless such rights be expressly reserved at the time of the creation of the trust. Thus, if S vests property in B on trust to pay the income to C for life and after C's death to divide the capital among X, Y and Z, then C, X, Y and Z being of full capacity can together (if unanimous) insist on B dividing the property between them at once, notwithstanding the protests of S[7]. It is the beneficiaries alone who can enforce the trust (or terminate the trust if unanimous and of full capacity).

A person may enter into a contract to create a trust and the contract will be enforceable, whether specifically or in damages, so ensuring that property ultimately becomes vested in trustees upon trust for the beneficiaries, unless the contract related to an unascertained part of a larger fund and no money was set aside before the insolvency of the obligee[8]. However, if the promise to create a trust is merely in a deed unsupported by valuable consideration it will be unenforceable by an equitable decree for specific performance since 'equity will not assist a volunteer'[9], although equity will not prevent a covenantee who is also a beneficiary from suing at common law for damages on his own account[10].

Contractual rights, like other choses in action, may be the subject matter of a trust[11]. Thus, if S is entitled to be repaid a loan of £1,000 at 10% pa he may assign this to trustees to hold on trust for certain beneficiaries. He may

---

5 *A-G for Hong Kong v Reid* [1994] 1 AC 324, [1994] 1 All ER 1, PC.

6 Consideration may be present, eg where a trust is created in consideration of the primary beneficiary's marriage or where in consideration of a £20,000 loan by F to G in 1978 G agrees to settle and does settle £60,000 on X, Y and Z in 1988.

7 *Saunders v Vautier* (1841) 4 Beav 115; *Stephenson v Barclays Bank Trust Co Ltd* [1975] 1 All ER 625.

8 *Mac-Jordan Construction Ltd v Brookmount Erostin Ltd* (1991) 56 BLR 1, [1992] BCLC 350, CA, endorsed in *Re Goldcorp Exchange Ltd* [1994] 2 All ER 806 at 823, PC. If the contract relates to specific property that becomes vested in the obligee then the trust will affect such property: *Pullan v Koe* [1913] 1 Ch 9; *Re Gillott's Settlement* [1934] Ch 97.

9 *Re Pryce* [1917] 1 Ch 234; *Re Kay's Settlement* [1939] Ch 329; *Re Cook's Settlement Trusts* [1965] Ch 902, [1964] 3 All ER 898. Further see pp 176–179, post.

10 *Cannon v Hartley* [1949] Ch 213, [1949] 1 All ER 50.

11 *Lloyd's v Harper* (1880) 16 Ch D 290, CA; *Harmer v Armstrong* [1934] Ch 65, CA; *Re Patrick* [1891] 1 Ch 82, CA.

similarly assign to trustees rights to royalties or competition prize rights entitling him or his assignees to £50 per week for ten years. Indeed contractual rights not assignable at law, because involving the benefit of agreements for personal services, may be the subject matter of a declaration of trust by the person having the benefit of the contract[12].

Since contractual rights may be trust property it is possible for X to obtain the benefit of a contract made between A and B for the benefit of X, although X is not a party to the contract, if X can show that A contracted expressly or impliedly as trustee of the benefit of the contract for X so that A is at once both settlor and trustee: as a beneficiary X can enforce his interest in the trust property against B[13]. Everything hinges upon whether or not A intended to create a trust of the benefit of the contract. The courts have become increasingly reluctant to find such an intention if only because this renders the contract between A and B incapable of being varied by them without X's consent, a result often not contemplated by A[14]. Usually, the courts rightly adjudge the claim to a trust relationship to be a transparent device to evade the privity of contract doctrine[15]. Nowadays, X can seek to have A and B confer enforceable rights upon him under the Contracts (Rights of Third Parties) Act 1999.

However, it is still very important to realise that a trust is very distinct from a contract.

(1) As a result of an intention to make a gratuitous transfer – or pursuant to a contract with some person to make a transfer – of title to property to a trustee for the benefit of beneficiaries (or for a charitable or other permitted purpose) the settlor is wholly divested of his interest in the property and has no rights in respect thereof against the trustee, except as reserved under whatever variety of structure he has created for the management of the property. A party to a contract inevitably has rights against the other party to the contractual transaction: settlors and trustees have no rights against each other, and the subsequent death or mental capacity of the settlor is an irrelevance.

(2) Transfer of title of the settlor's property to the trustee immediately confers property rights on the beneficiaries which will bind third parties other than bona fide purchasers from the trustee without notice of the

---

12 *Don King Productions Inc v Warren* [2000] Ch 291, [1999] 2 All ER 218, CA.

13 A can recover substantial damages from B to be held on trust for X where A holds the benefit of the contract on trust for X: *Lloyd's v Harper* (1880) 16 Ch D 290, CA. If no such trust can be imported then the general rule is that A can only claim for his own actual loss and so usually recover only nominal damages, *West v Houghton* (1879) 4 CPD 197; *The Albazero* [1977] AC 774, [1976] 3 All ER 129, HL. *Jackson v Horizon Holidays* [1975] 3 All ER 92, [1975] 1 WLR 1468, CA appears out of line in applying a dictum in *Lloyd's v Harper* (1880) 16 Ch D 290 at 321 out of context as pointed out by the House of Lords in *Woodar Investment Development Ltd v Wimpey Construction UK Ltd* [1980] 1 All ER 571 at 576; cf *Coulls v Bagot's Executor and Trustee Co Ltd* (1967) 119 CLR 460 at 501–502. In an appropriate case where A's damages will be inadequate he may be able to satisfy the requirements for a decree of specific performance: *Beswick v Beswick* [1968] AC 58, [1967] 2 All ER 1197, HL. Further see pp 170–171, post.

14 *Vandepitte v Preferred Accident Insurance Corpn of New York* [1933] AC 70, PC; *Re Sinclair's Life Policy* [1938] Ch 799, [1938] 3 All ER 124; *Re Schebsman* [1944] Ch 83, CA; *Green v Russell* [1959] 2 QB 226, [1959] 2 All ER 525, CA; *Beswick v Beswick* [1968] AC 58, [1967] 2 All ER 1197, HL; *Trident General Insurance Co Ltd v McNiece Bros* (1988) 165 CLR 107; *DG Finance Ltd v Scott & Eagle Star Insurance Ltd* (unreported), CA, discussed by NS Price in (1996) 59 MLR 738–741.

15 The intent to create a trust must be affirmatively proved: *West v Houghton* (1879) 4 CPD 197 at 203; *Vandepitte v Preferred Accident Insurance Corpn* [1933] AC 70 at 79–80.

trust (or protected by the overreaching process whereby the beneficiaries' interests are transposed from sold trust property to the proceeds of sale as replacement trust property). The trustee can thus be guilty of the crime of theft if appropriating trust property for the benefit of himself or other non-beneficiaries, and the trust property is not available to satisfy the creditors of the settlor or pass to the trustee's heirs.

(3) If the trustee was unaware of the transfer he must disclaim his interest as soon as practicable or, where necessary transfer the property at the beneficiaries' expense (unless the settlor is prepared to pay) to the settlor or the personal representative of the settlor to hold as trustee; otherwise, the trustee will be regarded as accepting the obligations attached automatically to the office of trustee (save as otherwise provided in the trust instrument) and which are owed exclusively to the beneficiaries.

(4) Trusteeship is not being party to a bilateral contract but is an office, so that the death or mental incapacity of a trustee simply leads to the appointment of a replacement trustee (as also is normal if the trustee becomes insolvent), whether by the other trustees or a person named for this purpose in the trust instrument or, in default, by the court. The right to remuneration out of the trust fund (and the benefit of exemption clauses) is an incident of the office, the beneficiaries (and, of course, the settlor) not being personally liable to pay the trustee.

(5) A major breach of trust unlike a major breach of contract confers no right to treat the trust as terminated but makes the wrongdoing trustee liable to be replaced by the court if not voluntarily resigning in favour of a new trustee.

(6) A breach of trust unlike a breach of contract confers no right to damages upon particular beneficiaries for their loss: the right of the beneficiary (whether the life tenant or the remainderman entitled to capital on his death, whether having a vested interest or a contingent interest and whether defeasible or indefeasible or merely an interest under a discretionary trust) is to make the trustee produce accounts of its trusteeship and to restore to the trust fund the amount found due after falsifying the accounts (a strict liability where the trustee did something it was not entitled to do) and surcharging the accounts (where the trustee negligently failed to do what it should have done). Any amount of extra income then produced after such accounting process must be paid to the life tenant or, in the case of a discretionary trust, paid to the discretionary beneficiaries interested in income in such amounts as the trustee sees fit in its discretion. Any amount of extra capital produced will be available for investment and for distribution on the life tenant's death or for the benefit of discretionary beneficiaries interested in capital.

(7) Most trusts, unlike contracts, endure for a long period of time, during which circumstances can change very much from those foreseen by the settlor. Thus, the court has a special jurisdiction to advise the trustee on the proper scope of its powers and on whether a proposed action would be a proper exercise of its powers, while also having power to enlarge the trustee's powers and, on behalf of infants and unborn or unascertained beneficiaries, agree a change of the beneficial provisions of a trust instrument if for their benefit and agreed to by all the existing beneficiaries of full capacity.

(8) A settlor can declare himself trustee of particular assets that he owns, but a person cannot contract with himself.

Trust and loans or charges concerning goods supplied on credit

Loans require special examination. First, a loan must be distinguished from the resulting trust that arises where A provides B with £15,000 towards the purchase of Blackacre (or other property) in B's name, when B will hold the property upon trust for A and himself in proportion to their contributions, so that A will have a beneficial interest in the property which will appreciate (or depreciate) with the value of the property[16]. In the event of B's bankruptcy A's interest will not be available for B's creditors. If A had merely lent B £15,000 at 10% pa repayable over 20 years then, when B had purchased Blackacre, A would merely have had a personal contractual claim against B for the principal and interest irrespective of how much the property might appreciate with inflation over the years[17]. If A had had the £15,000 debt and interest thereon secured on Blackacre by means of a mortgage A would still only have been entitled to the principal and interest, but he would have the right to sell the security, Blackacre, in order to ensure that he received his principal and interest (and legal costs) but no more. A would be a secured creditor in the event of B's bankruptcy if his £15,000 loan had been secured by means of a mortgage: if no such mortgage had been created then A would rank as an ordinary unsecured creditor with priority subsequent to secured creditors.

Quistclose or Twinsectra trusts

A loan arrangement may commence to enable the borrower only to carry out a particular purpose resulting, if the purpose is performed, in a pure loan relationship excluding any trust relationship, but in the event of non-performance of the purpose the lender can rely on the loaned money being held on trust for the lender. This was the situation in *Barclay's Bank Ltd v Quistclose Investments Ltd*[18].

Rolls Razor Ltd (with a large overdraft with Barclays Bank) had declared a dividend on its shares which it could not pay except under an arrangement with Quistclose whereby a loan of £209,719 8s 6d was made by Quistclose to Rolls Razor 'for the purpose of paying the final dividend on 24 July next'. The money was paid into a separate account at Barclays Bank with whom it was agreed by confirming letter of 15 July that the account would 'only be used to meet the dividend due on 24 July'. On 17 July Rolls Razor went into liquidation.

The Bank claimed that the money was owned beneficially by Rolls Razor subject to a personal debtor-creditor relationship to repay an equivalent sum of money to Quistclose: thus the Bank could set off the money against Rolls Razor's overdraft.

Quistclose claimed that the money had been given to Rolls Razor impressed with a primary trust to pay it out to the shareholders of Rolls Razor

---

16 *Dyer v Dyer* (1788) 2 Cox Eq Cas 92; *The Venture* [1908] P 218, CA; *Shephard v Cartwright* [1955] AC 431, [1954] 3 All ER 649, HL. In *Hussey v Palmer* [1972] 3 All ER 744, [1972] 1 WLR 1286, the dissenting judgment of Cairns LJ is to be preferred: (1973) 89 LQR 2; (1973) 37 Conv 65; (1973) 323 CLJ 41; *Re Sharpe (a bankrupt)* [1980] 1 All ER 198, [1980] 1 WLR 219.

17 *Aveling v Knipe* (1815) 19 Ves 441; *Guardian Ocean Cargoes Ltd v Banco de Brasil (Nos 1 & 3)* [1994] 2 Lloyd's Rep 152, CA (a trust requires money not to be usable as the recipient's own free money, as also emphasised in *Paragon Finance Ltd v Thakerar* [1999] 1 All ER 400 at 416 per Millett LJ) and in *Twinsectra Ltd v Yardley* [2002] UKHL 12 at para [74] per Lord Millett.

18 [1970] AC 567, [1968] 3 All ER 651, HL.

as a dividend (so long as such payment would still have been lawful if made out of the company's own money)[19] and a secondary trust to repay it to Quistclose if the primary trust failed: only if payment had been made to the shareholders in accordance with the primary trust would Rolls Razor's status have been converted from that of trustee into that of a contractual debtor.

The House of Lords unanimously accepted Quistclose's claim to the money. As Peter Gibson J subsequently explained it:

'The principle is that equity fastens on the conscience of the person who receives from another property transferred for a specific purpose only and not therefore for the recipient's own purposes, so that such person will not be permitted to treat the property as his own or to use it for other than the stated purpose ... if the common intention is that property is transferred for a specific purpose ... the transferee cannot keep the property if for any reason that purpose cannot be fulfilled.'[20]

In *Quistclose* the Bank, a purchaser, had notice of the arrangement of Rolls Razor with Quistclose. Subsequently in *R v Common Professional Examination Board, ex p Mealing-McCleod*[1] Lloyds Bank lent M-M £6,000 to be used as security for costs of an appeal by payment into court, but the money was to be returned to the Bank if her appeal was successful. The Court of Appeal held that the court was bound by a trust of the money, dischargeable only if the money had to be used to pay the other side's costs of the appeal, so that it could not order the money in court to be used to satisfy orders for costs made against M-M in different proceedings between the same parties.

In *Twinsectra Ltd v Yardley* Lord Millett[2] analysed the *Quistclose* trust:

'to be an entirely orthodox example of the kind of default trust known as a resulting trust. The lender pays the money to the borrower by way of a loan, but he does not part with the entire beneficial interest in the money, and insofar as he does not, it is held on a resulting trust for the lender from the outset ... it is the borrower who has a very limited use of the money, being obliged to apply for it for the stated purpose or to return it. He has no beneficial interest in the money , which remains throughout in the lender subject only to the borrower's power or duty to apply the money in accordance with the lender's instructions. When the purpose fails, the money is returnable to the lender, not under some new trust in his favour which only comes into being on the failure of the purpose, but because the resulting trust in his favour is no longer subject to any power on the part of the borrower to make use of the money. Whether the borrower is obliged to apply the money for the stated purpose or is merely at liberty to do so and whether the lender can countermand the borrower's mandate while it is still capable of being carried out, must depend on the circumstances of the particular case ... . Provided the power is stated with sufficient clarity for the court to be able to determine whether it is still capable of being carried out or whether the money has been misapplied , it is sufficiently certain to be enforced. If it is uncertain, then the borrower has no

---

19 This qualification seems required by necessary implication for otherwise the shareholder beneficiaries of the primary trust would have acquired an indefeasible interest at the time of payment of Quistclose's money to Rolls Razor. They were not even joined as parties. Further see F Oditah (1992) 108 LQR 459.

20 *Carreras Rothmans Ltd v Freeman Mathews Treasure Ltd* [1985] Ch 207 at 222, [1985] 1 All ER 155 at 165. Thus the receipt by a solicitor of loan funds from a third party under a solicitor's undertaking to apply them for a particular purpose renders the solicitor a trustee of such funds: *Barclays Bank v Weeks Legg & Dean* [1999] QB 309 at 324, CA, and *Twinsectra Ltd v Yardley* [2002] UKHL 12 at paras [13], [99] and [100].

1 (2000) Times, 2 May.

2 [2002] UKHL 12 at paras [100] and [101].

authority to make any use of the money at all and must return it to the lender under a resulting trust.'

Reservation of title, charges or trusts

Company liquidations create many situations where it is claimed that a company's obligations have been transformed from contract to property, from debt to trust, so that the claimant may claim property as his own in priority to mere creditors. The form of words used can be decisive in establishing whether the requisite intent to create a trust was present. The words may be part of a contract.

A customer may send money to a company for goods under a contract for the company to supply him with the goods. If the goods are not supplied (eg because of the liquidation of the company) the customer will merely be a general unsecured creditor of the company for the amount of the money he sent unless a trust has been created. He may create a trust of his money until he receives title to the goods by using appropriate words when he sends the money, or the company may similarly create a trust covering customers' moneys when received by the company[3]. The customer's equitable interest in the money or its traceable product will protect him until he is supplied with the goods unless the company wrongfully uses the money to pay off debts of creditors having no notice of the misapplication, so that the equitable right to a proprietary remedy via the tracing process (explained in Article 92) is of no avail. In such a way he may retain the beneficial ownership of his money until supplied with the goods.

If a vendor supplies goods to a company under a contract of sale, he may provide, by appropriate words in the contract, for title to such goods unsold by the company to remain in himself until he has received payment in full for the supplied goods[4] or until he has received payment in respect of all debts due to him from the company, including debts concerning other supplied goods[5]. In such a case he will be no mere debtor if the company goes into liquidation but will be fully entitled to his own property in the company's possession.

However, if the legal and beneficial title passes to the company or if legal title alone purports to pass to the company and the vendor is entitled to repossess the goods if the company does not make full payment for them,

---

3 *Re Kayford Ltd* [1975] 1 All ER 604, [1975] 1 WLR 279 cogently criticised by Goodhart and Jones (1980) 43 MLR 489, 496–498 for not holding that the company's unilateral declaration of trust was a voidable preference of the customers under Companies Act 1948, s 320 (now Companies Act 1985, s 615), though it has been applied by the Court of Appeal in *Re Chelsea Cloisters* (1980) 41 P & CR 98 to tenants' damage deposits paid into a separate account after a company was having financial problems that subsequently led to its liquidation.

4 *Clough Mill Ltd v Martin* [1984] 3 All ER 982, [1985] 1 WLR 111, CA. Indeed, in *Re Highway Foods International Ltd* [1995] 1 BCLC 209 it was held that if goods were sold subject to a retention of title clause and the buyer then sold the goods on to a sub-purchaser, that sale also being subject to a retention of title clause, and delivered the goods to the sub-purchaser, unless and until the sub-purchaser paid the buyer the price of the goods, the original seller could claim title to the goods in the hands of the sub-purchaser, irrespective of ss 2(1) and 9 of the Factors Act 1889.

5 *Armour v Thyssen Edelstahlwerke A-G* [1991] 2 AC 339, [1990] 3 All ER 481, HL though there were no outstanding debts for other goods: if the vendor recovers goods for which he has been paid then, to prevent unjust enrichment, it seems he should refund their price for total failure of consideration: *Rowland v Divall* [1923] 2 KB 500 CA; *Clough Mill Ltd v Martin* [1984] 3 All ER 982, example of Goff LJ at 987–988.

then the company will be treated as having created a charge[6] over the goods which will be void against a liquidator or administrator or a purchaser of the property subject to the charge if not registered under Companies Act 1985, s 395[7]. Equity looks to the substance and reality of the transaction which is the provision of security for a debt[8], the company having the right to the property once it has repaid the relevant debt.

Where the vendor supplies to the company material to use to manufacture new goods, the vendor's contract with the company may provide for the vendor to have legal and beneficial title to such goods or for the company to hold such goods on trust for the vendor until payment in full for the material or until the company sells the goods to its customers. Here the company will be treated as having created a charge over the goods which will be void against a liquidator or administrator or a purchaser of the property subject to the charge if not registered under Companies Act 1985, s 395[9].

If the vendor seeks to protect himself further by providing that the proceeds of sale of his materials or of new goods manufactured using his materials are to be paid into a separate bank account to be held by the company on trust for him until he receives payment, it seems that a fund is being set aside by the company as security for payment of a debt so that there is a charge which will be void if not registered under Companies Act 1985, s 395[10]. After all, the vendor is surely supposed only to be entitled to a sum equal to the undischarged balance due from the company and not to obtain as a windfall the remainder of the moneys in the account representing the company's profit.

However, there will be no charge within s 395 if the company purchaser expressly contracted that it will be trustee of a specified percentage or fractional part of re-sale proceeds received by it or such a percentage or fractional part[11] of such proceeds as is equivalent to the amount owing to the

6 *Re Bond Worth Ltd* [1980] Ch 228, [1979] 3 All ER 919. Where the vendor is legal beneficial owner he cannot acquire a separate equitable interest until he has passed full ownership to the purchaser: *Westdeutsche Landesbank v Islington London Borough Council* [1996] AC 669, 706, 714; *DKLR Holding Co (No 2) Pty Ltd v Stamp Duties Comr* (1982) 149 CLR 431.
7 See Companies Act 1985, s 399 substituted by Companies Act 1989, s 95 and *Stroud Architectural Systems Ltd v John Laing Construction Ltd* [1994] BCC 18.
8 A similar problem arises as to whether a transaction in a sale or a secured loan, ie a charge: see *Welsh Development Agency v Export Finance Co* [1992] BCLC 148, CA; *Lloyds and Scottish Finance Ltd v Cyril Lord Carpets Sales Ltd* [1992] BCLC 609, HL.
9 *Clough Mill Ltd v Martin* [1984] 3 All ER 982, [1985] 1 WLR 111, CA; *Re Peachdart Ltd* [1984] Ch 131, [1983] 3 All ER 204; *Modelboard Ltd v Outer Box Ltd* [1993] BCLC 623.
10 *Pfeiffer v Arbuthnot Factors* [1988] 1 WLR 150; *Re Weldtech Equipment Ltd* [1991] BCC 16; *Compaq Computer Ltd v Abercorn Group* [1993] BCLC 602; *Ian Chisholm Textiles Ltd v Griffiths* [1994] 2 BCLC 291. It seems that the Court of Appeal in *Aluminium Industrie Vaasen BV v Romalpa Aluminium Ltd* [1976] 2 All ER 552, [1976] 1 WLR 676, CA overlooked the underlying charge nature of the contract so that the decision has been distinguished to death.
11 Assuming £50,000 is owed by P to V in respect of goods made with V's materials and sold for £100,000, P will hold the £100,000 on the agreed trust (see footnote 13 post) for itself and V equally. Assuming P's bank account was not overdrawn by more than £50,000, an equitable lien or charge arises by operation of law to enable V to trace an amount of £50,000 into and out of such an account (see pp 884–887 post). If the agreement related not to a trust of a specific portion of the £100,000 proceeds but only to a trust of an amount corresponding to the amount of the debt (of £50,000) then owed by P to V, a problem arises as to the certainty of subject-matter because there is no £50,000 fund segregated from the remaining money unless reliance can be placed on the unsatisfactory *Hunter v Moss* [1994] 3 All ER 215, CA, discussed post p 78, so that no more than a contractual charge can arise requiring registration under s 395.

vendor by the purchaser at the time of receipt of such proceeds. On receipt of the proceeds Equity treats as done that which ought to be done[12] and because of this, 'even if the proceeds were paid into a general bank account there could be a tracing remedy where the recipient was obliged to hold a particular portion of the proceeds on trust'[13]. To reinforce the vendor's position the recipient purchaser should be expressly placed under an obligation to transfer the relevant amount of money into the vendor's own account within a short period of five to ten working days and under an obligation in that period not to permit the amount credited in its general account to fall below the relevant amount held on trust for the vendor[14].

Of course, the arrangement must not be a sham (disguising a debtor-creditor relationship) in form[15] or substance where from the outset the company purchaser, to take advantage of the cash flow, is permitted by the vendor to use all the general account money as if beneficially owned by the company purchaser. Even if there be a real trust arrangement one must be aware that the vendor's equitable right, to trace assets and impose a lien over them or claim proportionate ownership of them, will be worthless if the purchaser in breach of trust uses all the general account money to pay off creditors without notice of the vendor's rights.

Trust and bailment

Bailment is a common law institution which only applies to personal chattels, being a deposit of personal chattels for redelivery to the bailor or according to his direction after the purpose of the bailment (eg safe custody, cleaning, repair, hire etc) has been carried out. Trusts are equitable only and any property may be held on trust. It is the bailor who can enforce or vary the bailment whilst the settlor cannot enforce or vary the trust (unless he specially reserves such power). The general property or general ownership remains in the bailor, whilst the bailee is said to have only a special property or special ownership in the chattels bailed: thus an unauthorised sale by a bailee normally[16] does not pass title to the chattels. A transfer (eg of shares in a company) which simultaneously confers both possession and ownership upon the transferee cannot create a bailment because an owner of assets cannot constitute himself their bailee at common law. A trustee has full legal title (not merely possession) so an unauthorised sale by him will vest a good title in a bona fide purchaser of a legal interest for value without notice of the trust. In the event of the bankruptcy of the bailee or of the trustee the bailor and beneficiaries remain respectively entitled to the bailed chattels or the trust property. A bailee is in a similar position to a trustee in that both are subject to fiduciary obligations concerning the property in their control: in

---

12 Consideration having been fully given for acquisition of the after-acquired asset: *Pullan v Koe* [1913] 1 Ch 9; *Re Lind* [1915] 2 Ch 345; *Barclays Bank plc v Willowbrook International Ltd* [1987] BCLC 717n, CA; *Associated Alloys Pty Ltd v ACN 001 452 106 Pty Ltd* (2001) 74 ALJR 862.

13 Per Gaudron, McHugh, Gummow and Hayne JJ in *Associated Alloys Pty Ltd v ACN 001 452 106 Pty Ltd* (2001) 74 ALJR 862. Also see *Stephens Travel Service International Pty Ltd v Quantas Airways Ltd* (1988) 13 NSWLR 331, applied in *Re ILG Travel Ltd* [1995] 2 BCLC 128 and *Air Canada v M & C Travel Ltd* [1993] 3 SCR 787 at 804–805.

14 *Royal Trust Bank v National Westminster Bank* [1996] 2 BCLC 682, CA; *Re Lewis' of Leicester* [1995] 1 BCLC 428.

15 *Customs and Excise Comrs v Richmond Theatre Management Ltd* [1995] STC 257.

16 Exceptions exist under the Factors Act 1889, Sale of Goods Act 1979, estoppel. On bailment generally see N E Pulmer, *Bailment* (2nd ed).

the case of unauthorised sales by either the proceeds are subject to proprietary remedies via the tracing process[17]. In the special case where a vendor retains legal and equitable title to goods supplied to a purchaser who has authority to sell the goods but is bailee of them until sale one has to examine the facts carefully to discover whether or not the relationship of bailor and bailee is fiduciary[18]. One must ask whether the bailee was selling on his own account with an obligation merely to account as a debtor for the purchase price due to the vendor-bailor or whether the bailee had to pay proceeds of sale into a separate account for the vendor-bailor subject to some remuneration being paid for the bailee's services.

Trusts and the administration of a deceased's estate

Personal representatives like trustees are subject to fiduciary obligations preventing them from profiting from their administration of a deceased's estate[19]. However, the duty of personal representatives is owed to the estate as a whole and thus, unlike trustees, the personal representatives do not have to hold the balance evenly between those interested in income and those interested in capital[20]. Furthermore, if assets are wrongfully abstracted from the estate a pecuniary or residuary legatee (or a creditor) may follow and recover the assets on behalf of the estate for use in due course of administration: this remedy 'asserts the estate's right of property, not the property right of creditor or legatee'.[1] A trust beneficiary follows and recovers assets on his own behalf by virtue of his equitable proprietary right, although exercise of his right may also require restitution to the trust of assets for the benefit of other beneficiaries as well. An unpaid or underpaid legatee (or creditor) also has a well-established special personal claim against even innocent persons benefiting under a wrongful administration of a deceased's estate[2]. The claim is limited to the amount which cannot be recovered from the personal representatives and will not lie against a bona fide purchaser without notice or a person who can make out the defence of change of position. The orthodox view is that trust beneficiaries have no such personal claim against third parties and are restricted to tracing trust assets, if traceable, or seeking to make personally liable to account as constructive trustees persons involved in trustees' wrongful conduct[3]. However, it now seems likely that to prevent the unjust enrichment of the recipient of trust property a personal claim will lie against such recipient subject to the defence of bona fide purchaser without notice and of change of position.

Whilst the task of a trustee generally is the continuous administration of

---

17 *Re Hallett's Estate* (1880) 13 Ch D 696 at 710; *Aluminium Industrie Vaassen BV v Romalpa Aluminium Ltd* [1976] 2 All ER 552, [1976] 1 WLR 676.

18 *Re Andrabell Ltd (in liquidation)* [1984] 3 All ER 407; *Hendy Lennox (Industrial Engines) Ltd v Grahame Puttick Ltd* [1984] 2 All ER 152, [1984] 1 WLR 485; approved by the Court of Appeal in *Clough Mill Ltd v Martin* [1984] 3 All ER 982, [1985] 1 WLR 111, CA. The presumption is that the purchaser is selling on his own account and is not a fiduciary bailee: *Pfeiffer v Arbuthnot Factors* [1988] 1 WLR 150; and see *Compaq Computers Ltd v Abercorn Group* [1993] BCLC 602.

19 *Stamp Duties Comr v Livingston* [1965] AC 694, [1964] 3 All ER 692; *Re Thomson* [1930] 1 Ch 203; *Vyse v Foster* (1874) LR 7 HL 318.

20 *Re Charteris* [1917] 2 Ch 379, CA; *Re Hayes' Will Trusts* [1971] 2 All ER 341, [1971] 1 WLR 758.

1 *Stamp Duties Comr v Livingston* [1965] AC 694 at 713–714.

2 *Ministry of Health v Simpson* [1951] AC 251, [1950] 2 All ER 1137, HL.

3 See Articles 33, 92, 100 and 101.

trust property for the beneficiaries, the task of a personal representative is to collect the assets of the deceased, discharge taxes, debts and expenses and distribute the remaining assets amongst the persons entitled under the deceased's will or intestacy. For this purpose 'whatever property comes to the executor virtute officii comes to him in full ownership without distinction between legal and equitable interests: the whole property is his[4] subject to the fiduciary obligation to wind up the estate in the proper manner. Thus 'no legatee, devisee or next-of-kin has any beneficial interest in the assets being administered'.[5] During the period of administration those interested under a will or intestacy only have an equitable right or chose in action to have the deceased's estate properly administered, though this chose may be disposed of by will or inter vivos, whether expressly or by operation of law upon the bankruptcy of the residuary legatee[6]. Thus, while a devisee of land comprised in an unadministered estate cannot convey the land *in specie* until completion of the administration, he can validly contract to sell land before such completion[7]. By way of contrast beneficiaries under a trust (not being a charitable trust or a discretionary trust[8] where the beneficiaries are not all ascertained and of full capacity) have the equitable beneficial ownership, whilst the trustee only has the nominal ownership. It should be mentioned that though it is clear that a residuary devise or bequest does not confer a vested defeasible equitable interest in the subject matter thereof as from the testator's death, subject to the personal representatives' right to have resort thereto for payment of debts and expenses, some cases indicate that a *specific* devise or bequest does confer a vested defeasible equitable interest in the subject matter thereof from the testator's death, subject to the personal representatives' right of resort[9]: this appears very doubtful in view of the general statement of principles discussed above[10].

Whilst 'trustee' in the Trustee Act 1925 includes a personal representative where the context admits[11] many distinctions exist. The authority of trustees to deal with all types of property is joint only[12]. The general rule is that personal representatives have joint *and several* authority so that the act of any one of them in exercise of their power is binding on the others and the deceased's estate[13]. Exceptionally, a conveyance of freehold or leasehold land and contracts relating thereto made after 30 June 1995[14], must be made by

---

4 *Stamp Duties Comr v Livingston* [1965] AC 694 at 701. See also *Pagels v MacDonald* (1936) 54 CLR 519 at 526; *Passant v Jackson* [1986] STC 164, CA.

5 *Re Hayes' Will Trusts* [1971] 1 WLR 758 at 764; *Cochrane v IRC* [1974] STC 335.

6 *Re Leigh's Will Trusts* [1970] Ch 277, [1969] 3 All ER 432; *Official Receiver in Bankruptcy v Schultz* (1990) 170 CLR 306; *Crowden v Aldridge* [1993] 3 All ER 603, [1993] 1 WLR 433; *Marshall v Kerr* [1995] 1 AC 148, 157–158, HL.

7 *Wu Koon Tai v Wu Yau Loi* [1997] AC 179, PC.

8 See Article 5.

9 *IRC v Hawley* [1928] 1 KB 578 at 583; *Re Neeld* [1962] Ch 643 at 687–688; *Williams v Holland* [1965] 1 WLR 739 at 743–744; *Re K* [1986] Ch 180 at 188.

10 *Stamp Duties Comr v Livingston* [1965] AC 694 at 713–714; *Re Hayes' Will Trusts* [1971] 1 WLR 758 at 764; *Kavanagh v Best* [1971] NI 89 at 93–94; *Re K* [1986] Ch 180 at 197; Law Com No 188 (1989) para 2.16.

11 Trustee Act 1925, ss 68(1), (17), 69(1).

12 *Attenborough v Solomon* [1913] AC 76.

13 *Attenborough v Solomon* [1913] AC 76; *Re Houghton* [1904] 1 Ch 622 (executor compromising claim by co-executor against estate); *Warner v Sampson* [1958] 1 QB 404, [1958] 1 All ER 44, CA (denial of claimant landlord's title by one executor binds co-executors in forfeiture proceedings).

14 Law of Property (Miscellaneous Provisions) Act 1994, s 16.

all the personal representatives or under a court order[15], though one of several personal representatives could previously enter into a valid contract of sale of land binding the others and the estate, so long as he did not purport to act for the others without their authority[16]. The other exception is that all the personal representatives who are registered shareholders of a company must execute any transfer of the shares if it is to be valid[17].

A sole personal representative acting as such (unlike a sole trustee other than a trust corporation) can give a valid receipt for capital money arising on a trust for sale of land[18]. A personal representative (unlike a trustee) has the statutory power of appropriation under Administration of Estates Act 1925, s 41. A 12-year limitation period applies to claims to the estate of a deceased person[19] whilst a six year period applies to breach of trust actions[20], though no limit exists in the case of fraudulent trustees or property retained by a personal representative or trustee or converted to his own use[1]. Whilst a trustee is permitted to retire[2], a personal representative holds his office for life unless the grant of probate or letters of administration was for a limited period or he is released by the court appointing a substitute[3]. If the personal representative dies without having completed administration of the deceased's estate the court will appoint an *administrator de bonis non administratis* to continue the administration unless the personal representative is an executor who appoints an executor when such executor upon taking out a grant of probate becomes executor by representation of the estate being administered as well as the estate of the deceased executor[4]. The statutory power of appointing new trustees is available to trustees[5] or the personal representative of a last surviving trustee[6] but is not available to a personal representative qua personal representative[7].

Since the offices of personal representative and trustee are not mutually exclusive[8] it is often the case that the same persons are appointed executors and trustees or a personal representative becomes also a trustee of the deceased's property owing to the maxim that equity will not let a trust fail for want of a trustee. It is well established that once a personal representative has discharged all the debts and liabilities of the estate he becomes a trustee for

---

15 Administration of Estates Act 1925, ss 2(2), 3(1).
16 *Fountain Forestry Ltd v Edwards* [1975] Ch 1, [1974] 2 All ER 280, where since one personal representative had purported to contract for himself and the other representative (when the other had no knowledge of this and refused to ratify the contract) there was no contract to be enforced, the first personal representative being open to action for breach of warranty of authority; cf *Colyton Investments Pty Ltd v McSorley* (1962) 107 CLR 177.
17 *Barton v North Staffordshire Rly Co* (1888) 38 Ch D 458; *Barton v London and North Western Rly Co* (1889) 24 QBD 77; Companies Act 1985, ss 182, 183, Table A, Part I, arts 29–31.
18 Law of Property Act 1925, s 27(2).
19 Limitation Act 1980, s 22.
20 Limitation Act 1980, s 21(3).
1 Limitation Act 1980, s 21(1).
2 Trustee Act 1925, ss 36, 39.
3 *Harvell v Foster* [1954] 2 QB 367, [1954] 2 All ER 736, CA; Administration of Justice Act 1985, s 50.
4 Administration of Estates Act 1925, s 7.
5 Trustee Act 1925, s 36.
6 Trustee Act 1925, ss 36(1)(b), 18(2). An executor who has not obtained a grant of probate may appoint under s 36(1)(b) but his title to appoint can only be proved by production of a grant of probate or letters of administration with the will annexed: *Re Crowhurst Park* [1974] 1 WLR 583 at 593–594.
7 *Re Ponder* [1921] 2 Ch 59.
8 *Harvell v Foster* [1954] 2 QB 367, [1954] 2 All 736, CA.

the purposes of having the trustee's statutory power of appointing new trustees[9], though qua personal representative he remains liable as such until the estate has been properly distributed to the appropriate beneficiaries[10]. The statutory appointment of trustees by a personal representative who has discharged all the debts and liabilities is effective to confer on the newly appointed trustees the powers and discretions contained in the will[11]. However, they cannot deal with the legal estate in land until a written assent is executed in their favour owing to the much criticised decision of Pennycuick J in *Re King's Will Trusts*[12] where there was overlooked the line of cases concerned with establishing that a personal representative on completing administration of the estate becomes a trustee thereof[13]. Counsel accepted the correctness of *Re King's Will Trusts* in *Re Edwards' Will Trusts*[14] where the Court of Appeal held that an assent to the vesting of an equitable interest in land may be inferred from conduct of the personal representative in circumstances where he is also the person beneficially entitled to the land under the deceased's will or intestacy.

Trust and fiduciary relationship

A fiduciary relationship exists as Ford and Lee indicate[15] where

(a) one person, the fiduciary, has undertaken to act in the interests of another person, the principal, or in the interest of the fiduciary and another person;

(b) as part of the arrangement between the fiduciary and the principal the fiduciary has a power or discretion capable of being used to affect the interests of the principal in a legal or practical sense;

(c) the principal is vulnerable to abuse by the fiduciary of his or her position; and

(d) the principal has not agreed as a person of full capacity who is fully informed, to allow the fiduciary to use the power or discretion solely in his or her own interests.

---

9 *Eaton v Daines* [1894] WN 32; *Re Ponder* [1921] 2 Ch 59; *Re Pitt* (1928) 44 TLR 371; *Re Yerburgh* [1928] WN 208; *Re Cockburn's Will Trusts* [1957] Ch 438, [1957] 2 All ER 522.

10 *Harvell v Foster* [1954] 2 QB 367, [1954] 2 All ER 736, CA.

11 *Re Cockburn's Will Trusts* [1957] Ch 438, [1957] 2 All ER 522.

12 [1964] Ch 542, [1964] 1 All ER 833.

13 See note 10, above, and E C Ryder (1976) Current Legal Problems 60; R R A Walker (1964) 80 LQR 328; but contrast C Stebbings [1984] Conv 423.

14 [1982] Ch 30 at 40, CA.

15 *Principles of the Law of Trusts* (2nd edn) p 1002. Also see J C Shepherd in 'Towards a Unified Concept of Fiduciary Relationships' (1981) 97 LQR 51; Goff and Jones' *Law of Restitution*, Chapter 33; P D Finn, 'The Fiduciary Principle', being Chapter 1 in T G Youdan (ed) *Equity, Fiduciaries and Trusts* (1989, Carswell, Canada) concluding at p 54. 'A person will be a fiduciary in his relationship with another when and insofar as that other is entitled to expect that he will act in that other's or in their joint interest to the exclusion of his own several interest'; P D Finn, 'Fiduciary Law and the Modern Commercial World', being Chapter 1 in E McKendrick (ed) *Commercial Aspects of Trusts & Fiduciary Obligations* (1992, Clarendon Press). *Hospital Products Ltd v United States Surgical Corpn* (1984) 156 CLR 41, 55 ALR 417; *LAC Minerals Ltd v International Cocoa Resources Ltd* (1989) 61 DLR (4th) 14; *Hodgkinson v Simms* [1994] 3 SCR 377; *Re Goldcorp Exchange Ltd* [1995] 1 AC 74 at 98, [1994] 2 All ER 806 at 821, Lord Mustill emphasising that if a fiduciary relationship is alleged to exist where there is a contractual relationship, 'the essence of a fiduciary relationship is that it creates obligations of a different character from those deriving from the contract itself'. The extent of a fiduciary relationship may, of course, be restricted by a contract: *Kelly v Cooper* [1993] AC 205, PC. A fiduciary in breach of key obligations cannot rely on an exclusion clause: *Baskerville v Thurgood* (1992) 100 Sask LR 214, CA; *Rutanen v Ballard* (1997) Mass 723 at 733.

The key is that the fiduciary's conduct has reasonably led the principal to expect that the fiduciary will subordinate his own private interest to the interest of the principal[16]: thus a fiduciary relationship can exist not just where there has been an express or an implied undertaking by the fiduciary to the principal but also where the fiduciary's relationship with the principal is one in which subordination of the former's interest to the latter's interest is reasonably expected by the latter – fiduciary relationships with fiduciary duties are imposed by equity not by agreement of the parties.

The categories of cases in which fiduciary duties and obligations arise spring from factual circumstances so the types of relationship of the parties are no more closed than the categories of negligence at common law. A fiduciary often has property vested in him or under his control but this need not be the case. Where a fiduciary qua fiduciary does have vested in him – or under his control – property, such property has the essential characteristic of trust property in that it cannot be used or disposed of by the fiduciary for his own benefit but must be used or disposed of for the benefit of other persons[17].

Equity is seen at its flexible pragmatic best (or worst) in dealing with fiduciaries since even the extent and content of the duties or disabilities of a fiduciary varies according to the particular category of fiduciary in the context under consideration. As Lord Mustill has emphasised[18], to describe someone as a fiduciary without more, is meaningless for, as Frankfurter J said in *SEC v Chenery Corpn* 318 US 80,85–86 (1943):

'to say that a man is a fiduciary only begins an analysis; it gives direction to further inquiry. To whom is he a fiduciary? What obligation does he owe as a fiduciary? In what respect has he failed to discharge these obligations? And what are the consequences of his deviation from duty?'

Moreover, 'a person may be in a fiduciary position quoad a part of his activities and not quoad other parts'[19]. Whilst a trustee is always a fiduciary, in various contexts the following have also been held to be fiduciaries: personal representatives[20], agents[1], a prospective purchaser of land purporting to act

---

16 See chapters by L Hoyano, J Glover and D Hayton in P B H Birks (ed) *Privacy and Loyalty,* Oxford 1997.

17 *Tito v Waddell (No 2)* [1977] 3 All ER 129 at 230–231; *Ayerst v C & K (Construction) Ltd* [1976] AC 167 at 180; *Wates Construction (London) Ltd v Franthom Property Ltd* (1991) 53 BLR 23, CA.

18 *Re Goldcorp Exchange Ltd* [1995] 1 AC 74 at 98, [1994] 2 All ER 806 at 821.

19 *New Zealand Netherlands Society Oranje Inc v Kuys* [1973] 2 All ER 1222 at 1225. Thus a director qua director owes a fiduciary duty to his company (though not its shareholders or creditors) whilst qua shareholder he does not owe any fiduciary duty in respect of his voting power as shareholder except that it cannot be used to perpetrate a fraud on the minority shareholders: *Regal (Hastings) Ltd v Gulliver* [1967] 2 AC 134n, [1942] 1 All ER 378, HL; *Re AM Wood's Ships Woodite Protection Ltd* (1890) 62 LT 760; *Percival v Wright* [1902] 2 Ch 421; *North-West Transportation Co v Beatty* (1887) 12 App Cas 589; cf *Coleman v Myers* [1977] 2 NZLR 225; revsd [1977] 2 NZLR 225, (NZCA); see also (1977) 40 MLR 471 and (1978) 41 MLR 585. Exceptionally in *Platt v Platt* [1999] 2 BCLC 745 the active director-shareholder was held to owe fiduciary duties to his passive brother director-shareholders when he misrepresented the company's position to enable him to buy them out cheaply.

20 *Stamp Duties Comr v Livingston* [1965] AC 694, [1964] 3 All ER 692; *Re Diplock* [1948] Ch 465, [1948] 2 All ER 318, CA; *Vyse v Foster* (1874) LR 7 HL 318.

1 *Kirkham v Peel* (1880) 43 LT 171 at 172; *New Zealand Netherlands Society Oranje Inc v Kuys* [1973] 2 All ER 1222 at 1225.

as the vendor's agent in making a planning application[2], bailees[3], directors[4], solicitors and other professional advisers (eg accountants, stock-brokers)[5], company promoters[6], partners[7], receivers[8], liquidators[9], members of a committee of inspection in bankruptcy[10], borough treasurers[11], guardians[12], employees[13], tenants for life[14]. If certain fiduciaries, eg trustees, personal representatives, agents, tenants for life, renew a lease subject to the fiduciary relationship it must always be held automatically on a constructive trust for the beneficiaries[15]. Other fiduciaries may retain the lease for themselves if they show they have not in fact abused their position[16].

One must distinguish the proscriptive[17] fiduciary duties inherent in a fiduciary relationship from prescriptive duties (eg to use proper care and skill) arising at common law out of a contract or in equity out of a fiduciary relationship. As Millett LJ stated[18]:

'The expression "fiduciary duty" is properly confined to those duties which are peculiar to fiduciaries and the breach of which attracts legal consequences differing from those consequent upon the breach of other duties. Unless the expression is so limited it is lacking in practical utility. In this sense it is obvious that not every breach of duty by a fiduciary is a breach of fiduciary duty .... It is similarly inappropriate to apply the expression to the obligation of a trustee or other fiduciary to use proper skill and care in the discharge of his duties .... The distinguishing obligation of a fiduciary is the obligation of loyalty. The principal is entitled to the single-minded loyalty of his fiduciary .... Breach of fiduciary obligation connotes disloyalty or infidelity. Mere incompetence is not enough.'

All fiduciaries are subject to the rule 'that no person standing in a fiduciary position, when a demand is made upon him by the person to whom he stands in the fiduciary relationship to account for profits acquired by him by reason of the opportunity and the knowledge, or either, resulting from it, is entitled to defeat the claim upon any ground save that he made the profits with the

2 *English v Dedham Vale Properties Ltd* [1978] 1 All ER 382, [1978] 1 WLR 93.
3 *Aluminium Industrie Vaassen BV v Romalpa Aluminium Ltd* [1976] 2 All ER 552, [1976] 1 WLR 676; *Clough Mill Ltd v Martin* [1984] 3 All ER 982, [1985] 1 WLR 111, CA.
4 *Sinclair v Brougham* [1914] AC 398, HL; *Regal (Hastings) Ltd v Gulliver* [1967] 2 AC 134n, [1942] 1 All ER 378, HL.
5 *Re Hallett's Estate* (1880) 13 Ch D 696, CA; *Re Bryant* [1925] 4 DLR 157; *Brown v IRC* [1965] AC 244 at 265; *Nocton v Lord Ashburton* [1914] AC 932, HL; *Glennie v McDougall & Cowans Holdings Ltd* [1935] SCR 257; *Clark Boyce v Mount* [1994] 1 AC 428, [1993] 4 All ER 268, PC; *Farrington v Rowe McBride & Partners* [1985] 1 NZLR 83; *Hodgkinson v Simms* (1994) 117 DLR (4th) 151.
6 *Gluckstein v Barnes* [1900] AC 240, HL; *Jubilee Cotton Mills Ltd (official receiver and liquidator) v Lewis* [1924] AC 958; (1970) 86 LQR 493 (J H Gross).
7 *Clegg v Edmondson* (1857) 8 De GM & G 787; *Thompson's Trustee v Heaton* [1974] 1 All ER 1239, [1974] 1 WLR 605.
8 *Nugent v Nugent* [1908] 1 Ch 546.
9 *Tito v Waddell (No 2)* [1977] 3 All ER 129 at 229–230.
10 *Re Bulmer* [1937] Ch 499, [1937] 1 All ER 323.
11 *A-G v De Winston* [1906] 2 Ch 106. In *Appleby v Cowley* (1982) Times, 14 April a head of barristers' chambers was held to be a fiduciary.
12 *Hatch v Hatch* (1804) 9 Ves 292.
13 *Reading v A-G* [1951] AC 507, [1951] 1 All ER 617; *A-G v Goddard* (1929) 98 LJKB 743 at 745.
14 *Rowe v Chichester* (1773) Amb 715; *Re Biss* [1903] 2 Ch 40 at 56, 61.
15 *Keech v Sandford* (1726) Sel Cas Ch 61; *Re Morgan* (1881) 18 Ch D 93; *Re Biss* [1903] 2 Ch 40.
16 *Re Biss* [1903] 2 Ch 40; *Thompson's Trustee in Bankruptcy v Heaton* [1974] 1 All ER 1239 at 1250.
17 The 'no profit' and 'no conflict of interest' rules summarised by Millett LJ in *Bristol and West Building Society v Mothew* [1998] Ch 1 at 18, [1996] 4 All ER 698 at 711–712 endorsed by Hobhouse LJ in *Swindle v Harrison* [1997] 4 All ER 705 at 720.
18 *Bristol and West Building Society v Mothew* [1998] Ch 1 at 18.

knowledge and assent of the other person'.[19] It matters not that the fiduciary acted in good faith and that the profit made by the fiduciary could not have been made by the person to whom he stands in the fiduciary relationship[20]. The extent to which a fiduciary can ever use for his own benefit (or for strangers to the fiduciary relationship under consideration) information received by him in his fiduciary capacity is uncertain[1]. It seems that partners may take advantage of information received as a partner (unless received on terms that it will be kept confidential)[2] so long as the use made of the information is outside the scope of the partnership business[3].

A fiduciary cannot purchase property affected by the fiduciary relationship unless he can show that, in fact, he did not abuse his position, ie he gave the best price after making full disclosure of all material facts[4]. In the case of a trustee purchasing trust property the purchase is automatically voidable *ex debito justitae* except in very limited special circumstances[5]. A fiduciary cannot purchase any beneficial interest of his beneficiary in property affected by the fiduciary relationship unless he can show that, in fact, he did not abuse his position ie he gave the best price after making full disclosure of all material facts[6]. Unlike cases where undue influence is presumed there is nothing to stop the fiduciary purchasing from his beneficiary property not affected by the fiduciary relationship.

Any sale of a fiduciary's property to his beneficiary is voidable unless full and proper disclosure of his interest is made[7]. If the right to rescind is lost (eg owing to a disposition of the property by the beneficiary) or if the beneficiary does not wish to rescind but to recover the fiduciary's profits can such profits be recovered? They clearly can if the fiduciary sold to the beneficiary property acquired after he became a fiduciary because such property and therefore the profits therefrom are regarded as held on behalf of the beneficiary[8]. If the fiduciary, however, had acquired the property before he became a beneficiary the old orthodox view[9] is that the beneficiary cannot recover the profit because to allow him to do so would be to make a fresh

---

19 *Boardman v Phipps* [1967] 2 AC 46 at 105; *Chan v Zachariah* (1983) 154 CLR 178; *Swain v Law Society* [1982] 1 WLR 17 at 37 endorsed [1983] 1 AC 598, 619, though reversing the Court of Appeal; *Warman International Ltd v Dwyer* (1995) 69 ALJR 362.

20 *Boardman v Phipps* [1967] 2 AC 46, [1966] 3 All ER 721, HL; *Regal (Hastings) Ltd v Gulliver* [1967] 2 AC 134n, [1942] 1 All ER 378; *Industrial Development Consultants Ltd v Cooley* [1972] 2 All ER 162, [1972] 1 WLR 443; *Warman International Ltd v Dwyer* (1995) 69 ALJR 362.

1 *Boardman v Phipps* [1967] 2 AC 46 at 102–103, 126. See pp 390–398, post.

2 *North and South Trust Co Ltd v Berkeley* [1971] 1 All ER 980, [1971] 1 WLR 470.

3 *Aas v Benham* [1891] 2 Ch 244, CA. Also see *Framlington Group v Anderson* [1995] 1 BCLC 475.

4 *Dunne v English* (1874) LR 18 Eq 524 at 533.

5 *Holder v Holder* [1968] Ch 353, [1968] 1 All ER 665; *Tito v Waddell (No 2)* [1977] 3 All ER 129 at 241; see Article 61, post.

6 *Coles v Trecothick* (1804) 9 Ves 234 at 247; *Wright v Carter* [1903] 1 Ch 27, CA; *Tito v Waddell (No 2)* [1977] 3 All ER 129 at 241; see Article 59, post. In making a loan to his principal the fiduciary must prove the transaction was fair and that he had disclosed all material facts: *Swindle v Harrison* [1997] 4 All ER 705, CA.

7 *Imperial Mercantile Credit Association v Coleman* (1873) LR 6 HL 189; *Armstrong v Jackson* [1917] 2 KB 822.

8 *Cooke v Deeks* [1916] 1 AC 554 at 563; *Bentley v Craven* (1853) 18 Beav 75; *Regier v Campbell-Stuart* [1939] Ch 766, [1939] 3 All ER 235; *Re Cape Breton Co* (1885) 29 Ch D 795 at 803–804; *Longfield Parish Council v Robson* (1913) 29 TLR 357; *Gluckstein v Barnes* [1900] AC 240; *Gray v New Augarita Porcupine Mines* [1952] 3 DLR 1 at 12–14; *Robinson v Randfontein Estates* [1921] App D 168 (SA SC App Div).

9 *Re Cape Breton Co* (1885) 29 Ch D 795; *Tracey v Mandalay Pty Ltd* (1952) 88 CLR 215 at 241; *Burland v Earle* [1902] AC 83.

bargain between the parties. Today[10] there is much to be said for the strict prophylactic view that in both cases the crucial vitiating factor is the failure to disclose the self-dealing, so making the fiduciary in the latter of the two cases also personally liable to account for the profit (even in the absence of deceit, misrepresentation or undue influence).

It should be noted that if a fiduciary in a position of conflict between his self interest and his fiduciary duty provides advice tainted by such conflict then he may be personally liable to replace any loss caused thereby, with interest thereon[11]. Indeed, if a claimant shows that he suffered loss from any breach of the defendant's fiduciary duty (including such a duty arising from the defendant's undue influence over the claimant[12]) the court can order the defendant to compensate the claimant for that loss[13].

In some circumstances a fiduciary will not be allowed to carry on a business which competes with that carried on behalf of his beneficiary[14]. Oddly enough, it seems that a director may escape this rule, at least if he is a non-service director[15].

In certain circumstances equity intervenes further by treating a fiduciary as a constructive trustee of particular property. Thus, a fiduciary instructed to acquire Blackacre or to acquire the benefit of certain contracts will be a constructive trustee thereof despite any claim that his acquisition was for his personal benefit[16]. A fiduciary, who exploits property or confidential information the subject of a fiduciary relationship, is constructive trustee of any profits made out of such exploitation[17]. A fiduciary who exploits his fiduciary position so as to obtain a secret commission or a bribe is also a constructive trustee thereof (if it or its traceable product is still retained by the fiduciary)[18]. Where a fiduciary is a constructive trustee of property the equitable right to trace will be available and on the fiduciary's insolvency the beneficiary's property or its traceable product will be claimed by the beneficiary and will not be available for the fiduciary's general creditors.

---

10 Goff & Jones, *Law of Restitution* (5th edn) p 726; at the very least the fiduciary must be liable to the extent that he sold his property above market value: *Cavendish Bentinck v Fenn* (1887) 12 App Cas 652 at 659.

11 *Nocton v Lord Ashburton* [1914] AC 932, HL; *Farrington v Rowe McBride & Partners* [1985] 1 NZLR 83; Meagher Gummow & Lehane, *Equity, Doctrines & Remedies* (3rd edn) p 338; equitable compensation under *Nocton v Lord Ashburton* (supra) was accepted as a viable possibility in *O'Sullivan v Management Agency and Music Ltd* [1985] QB 428, [1985] 3 All ER 351, CA, though Lord Browne-Wilkinson obiter in *Henderson v Merrett Syndicates Ltd* [1995] 2 AC 145, [1994] 3 All ER 506, HL considered such to have been replaced by negligence liability under *Hedley Byrne* [1964] AC 465, HL: but see J D Heydon (1995) 111 LQR 1.

12 *Mahoney v Purnell* [1996] 3 All ER 61.

13 *Swindle v Harrison* [1997] 4 All ER 705, CA; *Platt v Platt* [1999] 2 BCLC 745.

14 *Re Thomson* [1930] 1 Ch 203; cf *Moore v McGlynn* [1894] 1 IR 74; Partnership Act 1890, s 30.

15 *London and Mashonaland Exploration Co Ltd v New Mashonaland Exploration Co Ltd* [1891] WN 165; *Bell v Lever Bros Ltd* [1932] AC 161 at 145; cf *Scottish Co-operative Wholesale Society v Meyer* [1959] AC 324 at 366–367.

16 See note 8, above, and *Re Edwards Will Trusts* [1982] Ch 30 at 41, CA.

17 *Boardman v Phipps* [1967] 2 AC 46, [1966] 3 All ER 721, CA; *Nanus Asia Co Inc v Standard Chartered Bank* [1990] HKLR 396 (dishonest 'tippee' liable); *Satnam Investments Ltd v Dunlop Heywood & Co Ltd* [1999] 3 All ER 652, CA (no liability of a stranger who took advantage of opportunity first discovered through breach of a fiduciary's duty to his principal).

18 *A-G for Hong Kong v Reid* [1994] 1 AC 324, [1994] 1 All ER 1, PC (holding *Lister & Co v Stubbs* (1890) 45 Ch D 1, CA and *Metropolitan Bank v Heiron* (1880) 5 Ex D 319, CA to be wrong).

Fiduciary relationship and debt

Beneficiaries' proprietary rights to property held on constructive trust for them must not be confused with their personal rights as mere creditors in equity or at law.

Thus, where a bank trustee lawfully deposits money with itself as banker pursuant to express authority in the trust instrument so that the beneficiaries' moneys, like other customers' moneys, belong absolutely and beneficially to the bank, there can only be an unsecured personal claim for a sum corresponding to the amount paid into the deposit account with interest thereon[19]. The new trustee appointed in place of the insolvent bank trustee can only rank in the liquidation of the bank as an unsecured creditor on behalf of the trust in respect of the chose in action that was acquired in place of the trust moneys, which ceased to be impressed with the trust on payment into the bank account.

Similarly, if an employee of a stockbroking firm advises D to leave his money on deposit with the firm till appropriate investments can be made when the market picture becomes clearer, when the firm has not told the employee or D that the firm's parlous financial situation makes such deposit precarious, the firm will be in breach of its duty of disclosure as a fiduciary. However, upon the insolvency of the firm D will only have a personal claim for the debt owed him[20]. If D had rescinded the transaction in time so as to revest the equitable title to the money in himself this may have enabled him to make an equitable proprietary tracing claim against any traceable product of such money[1].

Trusts and powers

A power is the authority to deal with or dispose of property which one does not own and which may or may not be vested in one. Some powers are legal such as the power of attorney[2] which enables the holder of the power to perform various functions like the conveyance of a legal estate in land, and the mortgagee's power of sale under Law of Property Act 1925, ss 88, 101 and 104. Trustees have statutory powers of investment[3], sale[4], leasing[5], main-

---

19 *Space Investments Ltd v Canadian Imperial Bank of Commerce Trust Co (Bahamas) Ltd* [1986] 3 All ER 75, [1986] 1 WLR 1072, PC.

20 *Daly v Sydney Stock Exchange* (1986) 160 CLR 371, 65 ALR 193 (Aust HC) where a claim against the Stock Exchange Compensation Fund failed because the firm had not received the money for or on behalf of D or as trustee and so there had been no defalcation of trust funds. D had an equitable right to avoid the voidable contract of loan but he had not elected to exercise this right before the firm failed: he could not at the same time treat the contract as on foot and yet deny the borrower's title to the money which the contract conferred. For other instances of debtor-creditor relationships see *Chief Constable of Leicestershire v M* [1988] 3 All ER 1015; *Customs and Excise Comrs v Richmond Theatre* [1995] STC 257; and *Re Goldcorp Exchange Ltd* [1995] 1 AC 74, [1994] 2 All ER 806, PC. Cf *Re Fleet Disposal Services Ltd* [1995] 1 BCLC 345.

1 *El Ajou v Dollar Land Holdings plc* [1993] 3 All ER 717 at 734; *Daly v Sydney Stock Exchange* (1986) 160 CLR 371 at 388–390; and *Twinsectra Ltd v Yardley* [2000] WTLR 527 at 568, CA; but see *Re Goldcorp Exchange Ltd* [1994] 2 All ER 806 at 825–826.

2 Powers of Attorney Act 1971, Enduring Powers of Attorney Act 1985.

3 Trustee Investments Act 1961 until replaced by the Trustee Act 2000, ss 3–7.

4 Law of Property Act 1925, s 28(1).

5 Law of Property Act 1925, s 28(1).

tenance[6], advancement[7], and a power of appointing new trustees[8]. A particularly significant distributive (as opposed to administrative) power is the power of appointment which enables the donee of the power (whether a trustee or a relative of the settlor or whoever) to determine who are to be the beneficial recipients of property whether of an income or capital nature. Such category of power is always equitable[9]. Essentially, a power will be *general* if the donee may appoint to anyone including himself, otherwise it will be a special power[10]. Where a special power is exercisable in favour of everyone but a small excepted class (eg the settlor, his spouse, and past and present trustees) it is often referred to as a hybrid or an intermediate power[11]. Whilst a power can exist independently of a trust, powers are usually to be found in instruments creating trusts, eg in wills or deeds.

The essential difference between a trust and a power is succinctly expressed in the statement 'A trust is imperative, a power discretionary'. A trustee *must* act in accordance with the terms of the trust: the donee of a power *may* act or not as he chooses in his discretion. If a discretionary trust is not being carried out the court can replace the obstructive trustees or authorise representative persons of classes of beneficiaries to prepare a scheme of distribution or, if a proper basis for distribution appears, itself direct a distribution[12]. In the case of fiduciary powers it has been held that the court has similar positive powers of intervention, but it seems that this should be restricted to very special circumstances such as powers to confer extra benefits on persons who are already beneficiaries and not merely objects of a power of appointment (eg to augment pensions under pension fund trusts where the beneficiaries have purchased their rights and expectations)[13].

An instrument by its terms may (1) make an absolute gift to a person subject only to a moral obligation to benefit members of a class of persons; (2) make someone a personal donee of a special power of appointment with no obligation even to consider exercising the power; (3) make someone (not a trustee) a fiduciary donee of a special power of appointment with an obligation to consider exercising the power, but no obligation actually to exercise the power; (4) confer upon trustees of the instrument a special power of appointment with an obligation to consider exercising the power, but no obligation actually to exercise the power, so that if such power be not exercised the property will either pass to those specified expressly or impliedly[14] as taking in default of appointment or result to the settlor's estate; or (5) impose an enforceable duty upon the trustees of the instrument to

---

6 Trustee Act 1925, s 31.
7 Trustee Act 1925, s 32.
8 Trustee Act 1925, s 36.
9 Law of Property Act 1925, s 1(7).
10 *Re Penrose* [1933] Ch 793; Perpetuities and Accumulations Act 1964, s 7.
11 *Re Hay's Settlement Trusts* [1981] 3 All ER 786, [1982] 1 WLR 202; *Re Beatty's Will Trusts* [1990] 3 All ER 844.
12 *McPhail v Doulton* [1971] AC 424 at 457.
13 *Mettoy Pension Trustees Ltd v Evans* [1991] 2 All ER 513, [1990] 1 WLR 1587.
14 For example, *Burrough v Philcox* (1840) 5 My & Cr 72; Article 8(2)(a), post. Where, after a special power, the court implies a trust in default of appointment in favour equally of the objects of the special power the terms 'trust power' or 'power in the nature of the trust' have sometimes been used to describe such a situation. Such a shorthand description is dangerously misleading especially since the same description has sometimes confusingly been used for situation (5), more properly regarded as a discretionary trust, and the test for certainty of objects for a fixed trust for a class of persons equally is stricter than the test for certainty of objects of a discretionary trust for a class of persons: Article 8(1)(b), post.

consider which beneficiaries within a specified class are to be the recipients of income or capital as the case may be *and* to distribute the income or capital to those beneficiaries considered in the trustees' discretion to be the proper recipients thereof in all the circumstances (to the extent that there is no valid exercise of a power to dispose of income or capital otherwise eg to charity or by way of accumulation). Situation (5) is sometimes referred to as a 'trust power' or 'power in the nature of a trust' owing to the discretionary power of selection the trustees are *obliged* to exercise but it is submitted that it is conceptually clearer to refer to it as a discretionary trust[15].

It is a question of construction[16] to determine which of these five situations was intended to be created by the words used by the person executing the instrument in question. Apart from the differences apparent in the above specification of the five situations, in (5) (where there is a discretionary trust) if the beneficiaries are adults under no disability and entitled between them to the whole beneficial interest they can terminate the trust and divide the trust property between them or they can jointly assign their interest so that their assignee becomes absolutely entitled under a bare trust[17]. In contrast all the beneficial objects of a *power* are helpless except to the extent they may individually compel the donee of the power to consider exercising the power; however, after such consideration, he may lawfully refuse to exercise the power. A fiduciary donee must consider periodically whether to exercise it, consider the range of objects, and the appropriateness of individual appointments[18]. The test for certainty of beneficiaries is the same for the discretionary trust in situation (5) as for the powers in situations (3) and (4), though a stricter test applies in situation (4) to the trust in default of appointment if it is for equal division amongst a fixed class[19]. The trustees' duty of inquiry and ascertainment of possible beneficiaries is higher where trustees have to carry out discretionary trusts than where they merely have to consider whether or not to exercise a power: a wider more systematic survey is required in the case of a discretionary trust[20]. It does not seem necessary to inform objects of a fiduciary power that they are objects until considering the appropriateness of any individual appointments and considering that, for the trustee's decision to be an adequately informed one[1] they need to obtain information from particular individuals: such individuals having become aware of the existence of the power can then require the trustees to consider exercising the power from time to time, especially in their favour[2].

In contrast, for there to be the necessary accountability of the trustees to

---

15 For example, per Stamp LJ in *Re Baden's Deed Trusts (No 2)* [1973] Ch 9 at 26; Megarry V-C in *Re Hay's Settlement Trusts* [1981] 3 All ER 786 at 793 and Warner J in *Mettoy Pension Trustees Ltd v Evans* [1991] 2 All ER 513 at 546. A discretionary trust is said to be 'exhaustive' if all its income has to be distributed among beneficiaries and 'non-exhaustive' if some of its income may be accumulated: *Sainsbury v IRC* [1970] Ch 712, [1969] 3 All ER 919.

16 See approach of Bentley J in *Re Leek* [1967] 1 Ch 1061.

17 *Re Smith* [1928] Ch 915; *Saunders v Vautier* (1841) Cr & Ph 240. Often beneficiaries will be unborn or minors. If the discretionary class is very wide there is the further practical difficulty that it will be impossible to ascertain every class member so making it impossible to take advantage of the *Re Smith* principle.

18 *Re Hay's Settlement Trusts* [1981] 3 All ER 786 at 793.

19 *McPhail v Doulton* [1971] AC 424, [1970] 2 All ER 228 and pp 66–71, post.

20 *McPhail v Doulton* [1971] AC 424, [1970] 2 All ER 228; *Re Baden's Deed Trust (No 2)* [1973] Ch 9, [1972] 2 All ER 1304; *Re Manisty's Settlement* [1974] Ch 17, [1973] 2 All ER 1203; *Re Hay's Settlement Trusts* [1982] 1 WLR 202.

1 *R v Charity Comr for England and Wales, ex p Baldwin* [2001] WTLR 137, 148–150.

2 *Re Manisty's Settlement* [1973] 2 All ER 1203 at 1209–1210.

the beneficiaries that is at the core of the trust obligation requiring correlative rights and duties regarding beneficiaries and trustees[3], beneficiaries of
full capacity[4] need to be informed so far as practicable that they are beneficiaries so that they have a meaningful efficacious right upon which to found
the trust obligation[5]. The fundamental right of any beneficiary[6] is the right to
see the trust documents, especially the trust accounts (with supporting documentation and explanations) with a view to falsifying or surcharging them, so
that the trustees are under an enforceable meaningful obligation. It may well
be that the settlor normally intends to confer a similar *locus standi* on the
objects of powers of appointment[7], but the settlor can expressly exclude this
if desired because it is only the trustee-beneficiary obligation that is the
foundation of the trust concept[8].

Where it is hoped that certain purposes (other than charitable purposes)
may be carried out, a power for these purposes has the advantage that its
validity does not depend upon the existence of someone capable of supervising its exercise[9]: the lack of someone to enforce a trust is fatal to its validity
save in special anomalous cases that are not to be extended[10]. If a trust were
intended to be created it cannot be saved by being treated as a power: a
finding of an intention to create an imperative obligation to act is inconsistent with a finding of an intention to confer only an opportunity to act[11].

In the absence of express authorisation to the contrary in the instrument
creating powers or trusts, neither powers nor trusts can be released by the
donees or trustees respectively except where the donee is a personal donee as
opposed to a fiduciary donee[12]. Potential beneficiaries under powers or discretionary trusts may validly release the donees or trustees from their duties
so that the potential beneficiaries cease to be such[13]. If trustees' discretionary
powers over income are not exercised within a reasonable time the discretion
is extinguished[14] whereas discretionary *trusts* over income remain exercisable
despite the passing of time, though only in favour of such persons as would
have been objects of the discretion had it been exercised within a reasonable
time[15].

---

3 *Armitage v Nurse* [1998] Ch 241 at 253 referring to 'an irreducible core of obligations owed by
   the trustees to the beneficiaries and enforceable by them which is fundamental to the concept of a trust. If the beneficiaries have no rights enforceable against the trustees there are no
   trusts.'
4 *Hawkesley v May* [1956] 1 QB 304.
5 *Re Murphy's Settlement* [1998] 3 All ER 1; and see *Scally v Southern Health and Social Services Board*
   [1992] 1 AC 294 at 306–307.
6 *Re Murphy's Settlement* [1998] 3 All ER 1; *Armitage v Nurse* [1998] Ch 241 at 261, but a particular
   beneficiary may temporarily have no rights (eg where the settlor-beneficiary is the Chancellor
   of the Exchequer) or may have a significant conflicting interest adverse to the trust that
   excludes his right: *Rouse v 100F Australia Trustees Ltd* [2000] WTLR 111; *Re Rabaiotti's 1989
   Settlement* [2000] WTLR 953.
7 *Spellson v George* (1987) 11 NSWLR 300.
8 *Re Angora Trust, Rosewood Trust Ltd v Schmidt* [2001] WTLR 1081.
9 *Re Douglas* (1887) 35 Ch D 472; *Re Shaw* [1957] 1 All ER 745, [1957] 1 WLR 729, CA.
10 *Re Endacott* [1960] Ch 232, [1959] 3 All ER 562, CA.
11 *Re Shaw* [1957] 1 WLR 729 at 746; *Re Endacott* [1960] Ch 232 at 246.
12 *Re Wills' Trust Deeds* [1964] Ch 219, [1963] 1 All ER 390; *Mettoy Pension Trustees Ltd v Evans*
   [1991] 2 All ER 513 at 545. Powers or trusts may, of course, be deleted on an application
   under the Variation of Trusts Act 1958.
13 *Re Gulbenkian's Settlement Trusts (No 2)* [1970] Ch 408, [1969] 2 All ER 1173.
14 *Re Allen-Meyrick's Will Trusts* [1966] 1 All ER 740, [1966] 1 WLR 499; *Re Gulbenkian's Settlement
   Trusts (No 2)* [1970] Ch 408, [1969] 2 All ER 1173.
15 *Re Locker's Settlement Trusts* [1978] 1 All ER 216, [1977] 1 WLR 1323.

Fiduciary powers, personal powers and protectors

A personal power may be one of three types. In a rare case a settlor may confer a power on a donee with intent to confer full dominion over the relevant property on the donee or full power to withhold consent to particular courses of action[16] so as to enable the donee to protect his own interests, so that the donee can act as selfishly as he wishes purely to benefit himself eg in discharging his legal or moral obligations to persons whom he would otherwise seek to benefit from his own resources[17]. More commonly, a settlor will confer a power on a donee (eg his widow) with intent that the donee is to be wholly unaccountable in the courts in respect of the power's exercise or non-exercise, so long as upon any exercise of the power only objects of the power are to benefit[18], it being a fraud upon the power (actionable by the beneficiaries entitled in default of a proper exercise of the power) if the donee exercises it to benefit persons (like herself) who are not objects of the power[19]. Otherwise, 'the donee is entitled to prefer one object to another from any motive he pleases, and however capriciously he exercises the power the court will uphold it'.[20] In a third scenario, the holder of the power will be under a fiduciary duty from time to time to consider whether or not it is appropriate to exercise a power (eg a trustee with power to add anyone in the world other than an Excepted Class to the class of beneficiaries or of objects of powers of appointment or to delete anyone from such a class), but the actual decision to exercise or not to exercise the power is to be an unchallengeable personal function[1] unless amounting to a fraud on the power.

In contrast, a fiduciary power is one conferred upon someone (usually holding an office like that of trustee or protector) for the benefit of the beneficiaries, so that he must independently consciously consider from time to time whether or not to exercise it and he must exercise it responsibly according to the purpose for which it was conferred on him and not perversely to any sensible expectation of the settlor, eg by exercising it capriciously or arbitrarily or in bad faith; moreover, a fiduciary power cannot be released unless the trust instrument specifically authorises it[2].

A trust instrument sometimes provides for someone to play the role of a 'protector'. Such role can be played by a 'committee' or 'board' or even by a company, which could be independent of, or be controlled by, the settlor. The nature of the role and the rights and powers of the protector will depend upon the terms of the trust instrument. The protector may hold negative powers, as where his consent is requisite before the trustees carry out certain transactions, or positive overriding powers enabling him to direct the trustees in certain matters or to appoint or remove trustees. Because the protector

---

16 *Rawson v Perlman* 1 BOCM 135 (Bahamas Supreme Court Eq No 194 of 1984); *Re Z Trust* [1997] CILR 248.

17 *Re Wills' Trust Deeds* [1964] Ch 219 at 228.

18 *Whishaw v Stephens* [1970] AC 508 at 518; *Re Hay's Settlement Trusts* [1982] 1 WLR 202; *Re Wills' Trust Deed* [1964] Ch 219; *Re Somes* [1896] 1 Ch 250; *Steele v Paz Ltd* [1993–95] Manx LR 426.

19 *Vatcher v Paull* [1915] AC 372; *Re Dick* [1953] Ch 343, CA, *Palmer v Locke* (1880) 15 Ch D 294; *Mettoy Pension Trustees Ltd v Evans* [1991] 2 All ER 513 at 545.

20 Per Lawrence J in *Re Wright* [1920] 1 Ch 108 at 118.

1 See p 97 post.

2 *Re Hay's Settlement Trusts* [1981] 3 All ER 786, [1982] 1 WLR 202; *Re Manisty's Settlement* [1974] Ch 17, [1973] 2 All ER 1203; *Re Skeats Settlement* (1889) 42 Ch D 522. Further see D J Hayton in (1999) 32 Vanderbilt J Transnat Law 555 at 579–589.

merely has powers vested in him and not trust property he is not a trustee. Exceptionally, if the trusteeship is a sham[3] so that the trustees are wholly nominees for the protector bound to do his bidding for the benefit of the beneficiaries (or, perhaps, of himself) then the protector will be regarded as a trustee[4] for the beneficiaries (or, in an extreme case, as where the settlor is the protector, as sole beneficial owner).

The role of a protector is usually a fiduciary role[5] (unless expressly or necessarily implied otherwise in the trust instrument or from the circumstances, as where the settlor or a beneficiary is a protector with power to protect his own selfish interests) to safeguard the trust from various hazards, whether relating to the trustee (eg exorbitant charges, inadequate investment performance, unsatisfactory exercise of distributive functions vis-à-vis discretionary beneficiaries) or to beneficiaries (eg disputing what the trustees might do on their own) or to the trust arrangements (eg tax or other problems relating to the trust jurisdiction or to a corporate trustee's change of residence or ownership or opening of offices in a jurisdiction where pressure could be exerted). Examples of powers expressly given to a protector are powers to:

(1)   monitor and agree the trustees' fees;
(2)   require an accounting or audit, with power to nominate the auditors;
(3)   conduct periodic reviews of the administration of the trust;
(4)   approve self-dealing by the trustees;
(5)   remove and appoint trustees;
(6)   initiate the migration of the trust or to be the judge of facts concerning whether the trust has automatically migrated upon the occurrence of certain events;
(7)   be consulted or have veto powers before the trustees make any discretionary payments to beneficiaries or objects of a power;
(8)   be consulted or have veto powers over sales of particular shareholdings or other trust property;
(9)   withhold consent where requisite before any beneficiary can institute legal proceedings against the trustee (for its conduct during the settlor's lifetime)[6];
(10) withhold consent to trustees' proposed exercise of a power to amend the administrative or managerial terms of the trust;
(11) direct generally or only in specific areas the exercise of trustees' investment or other managerial discretions;

---

3 *Rahman v Chase Bank (CI) Trust Co Ltd* [1991] JLR 103; *Midland Bank plc v Wyatt* [1995] 1 FLR 697; see pp 59–60, post.

4 Perhaps managing trustee: *Re Arnott* [1899] Ir R 201.

5 *Steel v Paz Ltd* [1993–95] Manx LR 426; *Re Osiris Trustees* (2000) 2 ITELR 404; *IRC v Schroder* [1983] STC 480; *Sociedad Financiera Sofimeca v Kleinwort Benson (Jersey) Trustees Ltd* (13 July 1993, unreported, Jersey Royal Court) discussed in Matthews & Sowden, *Jersey Law of Trusts* (3rd edn) (Keyhaven) p 130; *Von Knierem v Bermuda Trust Co Ltd and Grosvenor Trust Co Ltd* (13 July 1994, unreported, Supreme Court of Bermuda 1 BOCM 116) *Scott on Trusts* (4th edn) vol IIA Para 185. Statutory recognition of a protector is found in the Cook Islands, The Bahamas, Belize and British Virgin Islands. Further, see D W M Waters *The Protector: New Wine in Old Bottles* in *Trends in Contemporary Trust Law* (ed A J Oakley), Clarendon Oxford 1996 and A Duckworth, *Protectors-Fish or Fowl* in (1995) 4 JTCP 131 and (1996) 5 JTCP 18.

6 This can, however, negate the trust obligation if the protector is the settlor or the settlor's dummy, so that in the settlor's lifetime capital and income in substance are held to the order of the settlor, no beneficiary having any right to complain of this, because the power is a personal one.

(12) veto the settlor's exercise of a reserved power if believing him to be under duress in his home jurisdiction or to be suffering from a mental disorder;

(13) make or approve additions to, or deletions from, the class of beneficiaries or objects of powers.

Of course, the existence of some of these express powers will give rise to some necessarily implied rights eg to see trust accounts and to an indemnity out of the trust fund for properly incurred expenses, but an express power to charge fees will be needed[7]. So far, the courts[8] have assumed that protectors, who are office holders, have *locus standi* since recognition of their office and their powers requires this.

In determining the scope of a protector's duty a court will need to consider the settlor's purposes[9] in conferring particular powers on the protector (so that, ideally, the purposes should be properly documented at the time) as well as the terms of any exemption or other clause in the trust instrument that in any way relates to the protector's position. Indeed, a court may well take the view that if the protector is an unpaid friend or relative of the settlor then the extent of the fiduciary duty is to act in good faith, while if the protector is a paid professional then he is subject to the full fiduciary responsibilities applicable to trustees,[10] but, like trustees, he can be expressly exempted from liability for breach of fiduciary duty if a clause so provides, so long as the breach does not involve recklessness or dishonesty[11].

Exceptionally, where the first protector office-holder is the settlor with a selfish interest to promote in respect of a particular trust asset it will be possible to hold that a particular power is personal, as also is likely where the first protector is a beneficiary with selfish interests that the settlor must have taken into account[12]. Thus, the beneficiary's power is personal. Alternatively, if it be fiduciary, the court may hold that there is a necessarily implied authorisation of a conflict of interest which allows the beneficiary, after due consideration of other beneficiaries' interests, to exercise the power despite personal benefit accruing therefrom[13].

However, normally where the settlor or a beneficiary is a protector the powers of such protector will be presumed fiduciary so far as they relate to the removal and appointment of trustees and the investment role of the trustees, because those powers will be presumed to be exercisable to promote

---

7 *Re Representation Blampied* (28 January 1994, unreported), Jersey Royal Court (a fiduciary cannot profit from his position without authorisation).

8 *Re Representation Blampied* (28 January 1994, unreported), Jersey Royal Court; *Von Knierem v Bermuda Trust Co* Vol 1 BOCM pp 116–125; *Re Omar Family Trust* [2000] WTLR 713, 714; *Re Hare Trust* (2001) 4 ITELR 288.

9 *Re Hay's Settlement Trusts* [1981] 3 All ER 786 at 792. Exceptionally, the protector may be intended by the settlor to protect the settlor's interests rather than the beneficiaries' interests, which seems the real justification for the court's decision in the *Von Knierem* case (note 8).

10 Except to the extent that the circumstances of his appointment by the settlor may necessarily impliedly relieve him from a need to avoid a conflict of interest and duty as in *Re Z Trust* [1997] CILR 248.

11 *Armitage v Nurse* [1998] Ch 241, CA.

12 *Rawson Trust v Perlman* (Bahamas Sup Ct Eq No 194 of 1984) BOCM Vol 1 pp 35–54.

13 *Re Z Trust* [1997] CILR 248 where the judge held the beneficiary-protector's power was probably personal, but if it was fiduciary there was a necessarily implied authority to exercise the power and thereby benefit the beneficiary-protector, so upholding the consent of a protector committee to an amendment of the beneficial provisions of the trust fund so as to benefit beneficiary members of the protector committee at the expense of other beneficiaries.

the interests of the beneficiaries as a whole[14]. In respect of the trustees' role as discretionary distributors of income or capital to beneficiaries it seems that there is good scope for argument that the protector's power to withhold consent to proposed distributions or to direct distributions is a personal power, especially in the case of a settlor who is the protector[15].

Rather than rely on default law, a settlor should consider (with the benefit of professional advice) what mechanism should be employed for succession to the protectorship (even though it appears[16] that the court has inherent jurisdiction to appoint someone to be protector, where it is clear that such an office is crucial to the operation of the trust, and, presumably, has inherent jurisdiction to remove a protector in breach of protectorship duties or mentally incapacitated) and what particular powers, duties, rights and exemptions he wishes to confer on his protector. It is up to the settlor alone to decide how to deal with the settlor's property by transferring it to trustees for the benefit of beneficiaries, who will not look a gift-horse in the mouth and so must take the benefit with associated burdens arising from the existence of fiduciary or personal powers – unless they choose to disclaim their interest.

Where it is the settlor who has reserved to himself personal powers as protector which will enable him to act capriciously and irresponsibly without being accountable before any court, no doubt, he will not expect that he could ever be accused of acting capriciously, irresponsibly or recklessly; but to guard against such an irritating ungrateful accusation he can block any court action by expressly ensuring that his powers are exclusively merely personal. However, if he has an expressly personal power from time to time to replace the current trustee with a new one, there is a grave danger that the trustee will be regarded as in his thrall, so that the trust is in substance a bare trust for the settlor or, perhaps a true trust for several beneficiaries, including himself, but one where there is virtually no likelihood that the trustees will fail to comply with the settlor's request for trust funds to be distributed to him (so such funds can be regarded as available assets where claims of divorcing spouses[17] or other creditors[18] are concerned).

If the settlor can expressly confer personal powers on himself as concerns particular aspects of his trust, the question arises whether he can expressly authorise others as protector to have exclusively personal powers so as to block any court challenges to the exercise of the protector's discretion eg in adding or deleting persons as beneficiaries or objects of powers or removing Trustee A and appointing Trustee B, whether or not also exporting the trust through Trustee B being in a different jurisdiction, the law of which is chosen by the protector to govern the trust. Such challenges can obviously be detrimental to the smooth running of the trust and provoke lengthy and costly

---

14 *Vestey's Executors v IRC* [1949] 1 All ER 1108, HL; *IRC v Schroder* [1983] STC 480; *Re Burton* (1994) 126 ALR 557; *Re Osiris Trustees* (1999–2000) 2 ITELR 404.
15 Cf *Re Triffit's Settlement* [1958] Ch 852; *Re Penrose* [1933] Ch 793, *Palmer v Locke* (1880) 15 Ch D 294.
16 *Steel v Paz Ltd* [1993–95] Manx LR 426.
17 *Browne v Browne* [1989] 1 FLR 291; *Thomas v Thomas* [1995] 2 FLR 668 and Australian cases; *Re Marriage of Goodwin* (1990) 14 Fam LR 801; *Re Marriage of Davidson* (1990) 14 Fam LR 817.
18 *Private Trust Corpn v Grupo Torras SA* (1997/98) 1 OFLR 443, but see *Abacus (CI) Ltd v Al Sabah* (2001) 3 ITELR 467.

litigation[19]. The answer to the question hinges on whether or not there is an irreducible core minimum content of protectorship in the same way that there is for trusteeship and whether or not there should be less concern over protectors than over trustees, just as there is less concern over objects of powers of appointment than over beneficiaries.

In *Armitage v Nurse* Millett LJ stated[20]:

> 'There is an irreducible core of obligations owed by the trustees to the beneficiaries and enforceable by then which is fundamental to the concept of a trust. If the beneficiaries have no rights enforceable against the trustees there are no trusts. But I do not accept that these core obligations include the duties of care and skill, prudence and diligence. The duty of the trustees to perform the trusts honestly and in good faith for the benefit of the beneficiaries is the minimum necessary to give substance to the trusts.'

He then held that exemption clauses cannot exempt trustees from liability for dishonest or reckless breaches of trust but can exempt them from liability for negligence, whether gross or ordinary negligence.

One can therefore argue that particular powers of a protector (or of any designated person) expressly or by necessary implication in all the circumstances require the protector (or other person) to consider whether or not to exercise them from time to time, as appropriate in all the circumstances, and, if relating to investment or managerial matters, must be exercised with the standard of care applicable to trustees, while particular powers may only be required to be exercised honestly and in good faith for the benefit of the beneficiaries as a whole. Otherwise, however, if the settlor understands what he is doing and clearly intends that the powers of a protector, even a professional independent protector, are to be exclusively personal, so that their exercise is to be beyond challenge in the courts unless they are proved to have committed a fraud upon their powers, then the court should respect the settlor's intentions, as they should any exemptions from liability for negligence.

Where a trustee cannot act without the protector's consent and the giving or withholding of such consent is a fiduciary power, the trustee should not simply acquiesce in the refusal of consent if he reasonably believes such refusal is perverse. He should apply to the court under ss 14 and 15 of the Trusts of Land and Appointment of Trustees Act 1996 if English land be involved or s 57 of the Trustee Act 1925[1] if the administrative disposition of trust property is involved or otherwise ask the court for directions, as also ought to be done if the protector positively directs the trustee to take certain steps which the trustee reasonably believes would amount to a breach of fiduciary duty (as perverse to any sensible expectations of the settlor) or

---

19 For example, *Von Knierem v Bermuda Trust Co* (Bermuda Equity nos 154 and 162 of 1994 of 1994 BOCM Vol 1 pp 116–125). The problem can be avoided by employing a custodian trustee to hold the trust assets. A managing trustee sacked by the protector will not need to be informed of the identity of the new trustee and will have no cause to complain if the trust instrument provides that a replaced trustee cannot be liable for anything happening as a result of the appointment of the replacement trustee.

20 [1998] Ch 241, 253.

1 *Re Beale's Settlement Trusts* [1932] 2 Ch 15 which also indicates that it may be that the withholding of consent under a personal power can be overridden under the Trusts of Land and Appointment of Trustees Act 1996, ss 14 and 15 replacing Law of Property Act 1925, s 30, or Trustee Act 1925, s 57 where such withholding is clearly disproportionately detrimental to the interests of the beneficiaries as a whole in the proper administration of the trust property.

would otherwise involve the trustee in a breach of its equitable standards of care[2]. However, it should be open to the settlor to deal with the inter-relationship of trustees and protector by expressly providing that if the protector withholds his consent or gives a positive direction, then the trustees are under no liability whatsoever if they simply acquiesce in what the protector has decided, being always irrebuttably regarded as having no reasonable grounds for questioning the decisions of the protector. Any beneficiary's remedy for improper breach of fiduciary duty should then only lie against the protector if he were under such a duty.

After all, the settlor may be the protector with a personal power to direct the trustees' in their investment functions (so long as such directions do not personally benefit himself or his spouse). He may have successfully built up a £20 million portfolio of investments which he transferred to trustees on discretionary trusts for his descendants , their spouses and cohabitees under which he requires the trustees to speculate with the trust fund as if they were absolute beneficial owners thereof who could afford to lose the whole fund without it in any way whatsoever affecting their standard of living, and the trustees are not to be liable for any investment losses if they acted honestly. Indeed, to avoid delay in implementing his directions, it will be better if the settlor's trust instrument requires delegation of the trustees' investment duties to the settlor (or his dummy company) with the trustees having no power in the settlor's lifetime to revoke such delegation unless[3] they have actual knowledge of the settlor's mental incapacity or unless at the end of a relevant accounting year they discover the trust fund is worth one tenth of its value the preceding year.

Trusts and charges, personal obligations and conditional gifts

If T makes a testamentary or intervivos gift to B and requires B to make some payment to C or perform some obligation in C's favour there are five possible legal consequences[4]:

(1) T's words may be treated as creating B a trustee for C[5].

(2) T's words may be treated as creating an equitable charge in C's favour on the property given to B. The charge attaches to the property (whether taken by B or someone else upon B's disclaimer) so as to give C an equitable security interest though it imposes no personal fiduciary obligations upon B[6]. Thus, on the charge being satisfied B will hold the property beneficially[7] unlike a trustee who, on the termination of express trusts, holds the property on a resulting trust for the settlor[8]. During the subsistence of the charge B will not be accountable for rents and profits

---

2 *Re Arnott* [1899] Ir R 209; *Commonwealth and Central Wool Committee* (1922) 31 CLR 421 at 470; *Scott on Trusts* (4th edn) Vol IIA para 185, and cf express exclusion in s 36 of the Fines and Recoveries Act 1833 of court's power to control or interfere with exercise by the protector of a settlement of his power of consent.

3 Total absence of a power to revoke the delegation would mean that the trustees would simply be custodian trustees of the investments and the protector managing trustee thereof.

4 See (1952) 11 Camb LJ 240 (Thomas). See also *Countess of Bective v Federal Comr of Taxation* (1932) 47 CLR 417 and *Muschinski v Dodds* (1985) 160 CLR 583 at 605–607.

5 See Article 7(2)(c), post.

6 *Cunningham v Foot* (1878) 3 App Cas 974 at 992–993.

7 *Re Oliver* (1890) 62 LT 533.

8 *Re West* [1900] 1 Ch 84.

arising from the charged property[9]: a trustee is so accountable in respect of the trust property. B is in a similar position to a trustee only in that neither he nor a trustee is ordinarily personally responsible for any insufficiency of the property to produce the sum charged or the expected beneficial interest[10]. C is in a similar position to the beneficiary of a trust in that his rights are equitable and so may only be overridden if the property affected by those rights is purchased by a bona fide purchaser of a legal interest for value without notice[11] or, in the case of land, by a purchaser protected under the Land Charges Acts 1925 or 1972 or the Land Registration Act 1925 owing to absence of an entry protecting the equitable charge[12]. C is in a different position from a beneficiary under a trust in that C's remedy, if his charge is not met, is to apply for sale of the charged property and payment out of the proceeds thereof.

(3) T's words may be construed as making a gift to B if B undertakes a personal equitable obligation in C's favour signified by B's acceptance of the gift. C will then obtain a personal right against B but no right against the gifted property. Then B has the choice of taking the property and performing the obligation in C's favour *or* of declining both in which case C will receive nothing. If a trust had been created C would have been secure for a trust does not fail for want of a trustee, eg if the trustee predeceases the testator or disclaims[13]. On the other hand, B's obligation if he accepts the gift may be greater than those of a trustee for he is personally required to perform the obligation even if it costs him more than the value of the property received[14]. In an exceptional case the court may find that an equitable charge and a personal obligation were intended by the testator to co-exist[15].

(4) T's words may be construed as giving property to B subject to a condition subsequent so that if B does not, after receiving the property, go on to perform the condition he will forfeit his interest in the property. So long as B performs the condition the property is B's absolutely beneficially[16]. If B breaks the condition (eg where freehold land has been devised to him subject to a condition subsequent) then T's specific devisee or residuary devisee or next of kin, as the case may be, having the right of

---

9 *Re Oliver* (1890) 62 LT 533.

10 *Re Cowley* (1885) 53 LT 494.

11 *Parker v Judkin* [1931] 1 Ch 475, CA.

12 Settled Land Act 1925, s 1(1)(v), will apply if the charge is voluntary in which case no protection is possible under the Land Charges Act for the overreachable charge.

13 *Re Armitage* [1972] Ch 438, sub nom *Re Armitage's Will Trusts, Ellam v City and County of Norwich* [1972] 1 All ER 708; *Mallott v Wilson* [1903] 2 Ch 494.

14 *Re Hodge* [1940] Ch 260; *Re North* [1952] Ch 397, [1952] 1 All ER 609. The cases on conditional gifts concern testamentary gifts but inter vivos gifts should be subject to the same principles: *Countess of Bective v Federal Comr of Taxation* (1932) 47 CLR 417 at 418; *Muschinski v Dodds* (1985) 160 CLR 583 (Aust HC) per Brennan and Dawson JJ.

15 *Re Lester* [1942] Ch 324, [1942] 1 All ER 646. It will be important to distinguish between a charge and a condition where property is devised, say, to a son and two daughters in unequal shares subject to payment by the son and daughters of an annuity to their widowed mother for her life: as a charge the annuity will be borne rateably but as a personal obligation the annuity will be payable equally by the joint obligors: *Pearce v Wright* (1926) 39 CLR 16.

16 *A-G v Cordwainers' Co* (1883) 3 My & K 534, as will also be the case if the condition is void for uncertainty. In *Ellis v Chief Adjudication Officer* [1998] 1 FLR 184, CA, a mother's gift of her flat to her daughter on condition she cared for her mother in the flat was upheld, so that on evicting the mother and selling the flat, part of the proceeds had to be paid to the mother, after allowing for mortgage payments by the daughter.

entry for breach of condition, may enter and determine B's estate. The disadvantage of this is that C thereby loses all hope of obtaining his interest from B and so suffers unless he happens to have the right of entry[17]. For this reason the courts are more likely to protect C if they find this accords with T's intention by construing T's words as creating a trust or charge or personal obligation[18].

(5) Finally, T's words may be treated merely as indicating his motive[19] for leaving property to B so that B takes an absolute beneficial interest, eg 'to my wife, B, that she may support herself and the children according to their needs'.

Summary analysis of a trust

From the foregoing comparisons with other legal relationships it will be seen it is convenient to regard a trust as 'an obligation', that is to say, 'a tie of equity (*vinculum juris*), whereby one person is bound to perform or forbear some act for another'.[20] The obligation is an equitable one, and until the amalgamation of the courts of common law and equity, was enforceable only in courts of equity; and although, by the Judicature Act 1873, all courts take cognisance of trusts, yet they are treated as equitable rights giving rise to defences applicable only to equitable rights, and remediable only by equitable remedies. It is also an obligation relating exclusively to property. An obligation to do or forbear from doing some act not relating to property is not a trust, whatever else it may be. A trust is 'of property': the trustee is under obligations owed to beneficiaries in respect of specific property owned by the trustee.

An English trust has the following characteristics:

(i) Title to the trust property is vested in the trustee[1], who alone can sue or be sued, a trust not being a legal person. Thus, a purported transfer to 'The Smith Family Trust' should strictly rank as a nullity as a transfer to no-one: it should be to the legal persons (eg X and Y) who already own some property subject to the obligations set out in the instrument creating The Smith Family Trust. However, since it is easy to see what was intended, the courts[2] are prepared to construe the transfer as to the trustees of The Smith Family Trust.

(ii) The trust property is not part of the trustee's own estate but must be kept for the benefit of beneficiaries or for beneficial purposes as a separate protected fund immune from any claims of the trustee's

---

17 See (1952) 11 Camb LJ 240 at 242–245 (Thomas); Megarry and Wade, *The Law of Real Property* (6th edn) pp 65–71; *Re Gardiner* [1971] 2 NSWLR 494.

18 *Lambe v Eames* (1871) 6 Ch App 597; *Re Brace* [1954] 2 All ER 354, [1954] 1 WLR 955; Article 8(2)(b), post.

19 See for example, the presumption in the Administration of Justice Act 1982, s 22 for testamentary gifts to spouses and issue; *Re Lipinski's Will Trust* [1976] Ch 235.

20 The words quoted are an adaptation of the description of 'obligation', referring to the Roman *Obligatio*, in the Article on 'Obligation' in vol 16 of the Encyclopaedia Britannica (15th edn 1955), under the editorship in respect of law of Abraham Wolf.

1 *Smith v Anderson* (1880) 15 Ch D 247 at 275; *CCSD v ISPT Pty Ltd* (1999) 2 ITELR 1 at 15; Article 1(1) of *Principles of European Trust Law* (Kluwer Law International, 1999). At law the trustee appears to be the owner, having absolute rights in respect of the property and the benefit thereof, but in equity the benefit is vested in the beneficiaries and the rights of the trustee are restricted.

2 *Choithram International SA v Pagarani* [2001] 1 WLR, PC.

creifuls, heirs or spouse[3]: this fund extends beyond the original trust assets to accruals thereto (of a capital or income nature) and to assets representing the rightful or wrongful product of trust assets[4] eg assets rightfully purchased by trustees as new investments with the proceeds of sale of old investments and also assets wrongfully acquired by trustees purportedly for themselves as their private property with such proceeds of sale.

(iii) The trustee holds an office for the duration of the trust, such office being subject to onerous fiduciary proscriptive duties[5] and to equitable prescriptive duties in default of contrary provision in the terms of the trust. Enforceability of these duties by the beneficiaries (not the settlor) is at the core of the trust concept[6], although in the case of charitable purpose trusts the trustees' duties are enforceable in the public interest by the Attorney-General or the Charity Commissioners (as the representatives of the Crown as *parens patriae*).

(iv) Because many trusts are in operation for a lengthy period (which can be as long as 125 years[7]) so that many unforeseeable matters may arise in vastly changing social and economic circumstances during the life of the trust, the court has a supportive, supervisory jurisdiction[8] (in addition to its punitive enforcement role) that the trustees or the beneficiaries can invoke to help further the settlor's purposes in creating the trust, eg the court can advise the trustees whether they have power to act in particular circumstances and, if they do not, then the court can authorise them to act in an expedient manner; where the trustees fear that they might be held to have acted improperly in bringing or defending proceedings, so that they would not be able to recover their costs from the trust fund, the trustees can obtain the court's authority for them to act, so ensuring that they can so recover their costs even if losing the legal proceedings.

(v) The beneficiaries (or the Attorney-General or the Charity Commissioners in the case of charitable purpose trusts) not only have personal rights against a trustee to have the value of the trust fund restored to what it should have been but for a breach of trust (which rights may extend to a third party[9] who dishonestly interferes with the obligations

---

3 *Henry v Hammond* [1913] 2 KB 515 at 521 endorsed by *R v Clowes (No 2)* [1994] 2 All ER 316 at 325, CA.

4 'That which is the fruit of the trust property or the trusteeship is itself trust property', per Oliver LJ in *Swain v Law Society* [1982] 1 WLR 17 at 36; *A-G of Hong Kong v Reid* [1994] 1 AC 324 at 338; *Re Hallett's Estate* (1880) 13 Ch D 696, CA.

5 For the distinction between proscriptive fiduciary duties (the 'no profit' and 'no conflict of interest and duty' rules) and prescriptive equitable duties see *Bristol and West Building Society v Mothew* [1998] Ch 1, CA.

6 *Armitage v Nurse* [1998] Ch 241 at 253 where Millett LJ refers to 'an irreducible core of obligations owed by the trustees to the beneficiaries and enforceable by them which is fundamental to the concept of a trust. If the beneficiaries have no rights enforceable against the trustees there are no trusts'. However, it may well be that the court will come to uphold trusts for furthering non-charitable purpose trusts that are expressly made enforceable by a person designated by the trust instrument.

7 For example, where a perpetuity period is chosen of royal lives plus 21 years, so that the Law Commission in its Report *The Rules against Perpetuities and Excessive Accumulations* (Law Com no 251) recommends a fixed period of 125 years as the maximum perpetuity period.

8 For example, *Re New* [1901] 2 Ch 534; *Rafidian Bank v Saipem* (2 March 1994, unreported, CA), Trustee Act 1925, s 57; *Re Beddoe* [1893] 1 Ch 547; RSCO 85.

9 See Article 100 post.

owed to the beneficiaries – or to the Attorney General or Charity Commissioners) but have equitable proprietary rights[10] in the trust fund (as defined in (ii) above). These rights bind not just the trustees but also third parties unless such are bona fide purchasers of the legal title without notice of the equitable rights or are protected by statutory overreaching provisions (eg when purchasing land from two trustees or a trust corporation). The settlor has no right to enforce his trust unless he happens to be a beneficiary or takes exceptional steps to reserve such a right[11].

(vi) Where the settlor has effectively transferred legal title to trustees but has failed effectively to divest himself of all his beneficial interest in favour of beneficiaries or of charitable purposes, then the trustees hold the trust fund under a resulting trust for the settlor to the extent he failed so to divest himself[12] (unless in the case of charitable trusts the settlor had a paramount general charitable intention, in which event the trust fund is applied *cy-près* to a closely allied purpose[13]).

It is noteworthy that a trust is not a contract – like a contract for the benefit of a third party or a contract of agency – because the trustee's obligations are independent obligations owed to the beneficiaries who have correlative rights against the trustee entitled to charge for its services out of the trust fund as an incident of the office of trustee, while the dissolution, death or incapacity of the trustee does not affect the continuing existence of the trust in respect of which someone else will take over the office of trustee. Indeed, a trust ,conferring immediate equitable proprietary interests on beneficiaries, can arise without the knowledge and agreement of the trustee (eg in the case of a testamentary trust or the case of property, like land or shares, that can be transferred into the name of another without the need to tell such person) but if the trustee refuses to act and disclaims the trust property, the settlor or his executor, if he is dead, takes the property as trustee. A breach of trust confers no right to treat the trust as terminated: it merely entitles the beneficiaries to falsify or surcharge the trustee's accounts of its trusteeship to ascertain the amount the trustee needs to restore to the trust, and to apply to the court to replace the trustee.

---

10 Exceptionally, the trust structure may be so organised contractually as to exclude beneficiaries from having equitable interests in the property owned by the trustees eg in the case of most unit trusts. Here a unit only confers a right to a proportion of the net value of the trust fund, measured as the difference between its assets and liabilities, calculated and realisable under the terms contractually agreed in the trust instrument. The unit is a chose in action redeemable and transferable as provided in the trust instrument. Further, see K F Sin *The Legal Nature of the Unit Trust* (Clarendon, Oxford 1997) Chapter 5. A trust only arises when the trust is wound up so that assets held for the unit-holders are ascertained. The position of the trustee is similar to that of an executor with legal and beneficial ownership, although the unit holders have a legal chose in action while the legatees have an equitable chose in action.

11 Once the settlor has unilaterally transferred his entire interest in particular property to the trustee this amounts to complete fulfilment of his purposes, so that he drops out of the picture; *Re Astor's Settlement Trusts* [1952] Ch 534 at 542; *Bradshaw v University College of Wales* [1987] 3 All ER 200 at 203. Exceptionally, he could enter into a contract with the trustee whereby the trustee agrees to produce accounts to the settlor in his lifetime and to restore to the trust fund any amount due on the taking of accounts, to be enforceable under *Beswick v Beswick* [1968] AC 58, HL principles; or, under trust law, the settlor could perhaps reserve to himself *locus standi* as enforcer of the trustee's obligations in addition to the beneficiaries; see pp 114–116 post.

12 See Article 29 post.

13 For example, *Re Lysaght* [1966] Ch 191.

The attractive commercial qualities of the trust[14]

It has been seen that a trust is, essentially, a fiduciary relationship with respect to property, subjecting the trustee who owns the property to duties to deal with the property for the benefit of persons (including himself if so designated). Any one of these persons, known as beneficiaries, can enforce the obligations of the trustee, which arise as the result of a manifestation of an intention to create a trust by a person known as the settlor. The trustee is the legal person who acts on behalf of the trust because it has no legal personality of its own, unlike a company. However, the assets of the trust constitute a separate fund available only for the beneficiaries and not for the trustee's creditors if the trustee becomes insolvent. The beneficiaries are regarded as having equitable ownership of the assets in the legal ownership of the trustee. If the trustee in breach of trust wrongfully transfers the legal ownership in particular assets to a third party, then the beneficiaries can still assert their equitable ownership against those assets and so trace such assets (or, even, the product of such assets) into the hands of anyone who is not a bona fide purchaser of the assets without notice of the breach of trust or protected by special statutory provisions.

It can therefore be seen that strong security is provided for beneficiaries by virtue of their equitable ownership of trust assets. Furthermore, the settlor has freedom to lay down all the terms of the trust creating whatever rights and duties he wishes in the trustee, so long as they are not uncertain, illegal or contrary to public policy, and he does not have to comply with the formal rules for the incorporation and regulation of a company.

The trust is, therefore, a very flexible, useful device: its uses are as unlimited as the imagination of lawyers in taking account of the wishes of bankers and businessmen in the commercial context. Indeed, this has led to the enactment of legislation to prevent avoidance of tax and to protect the interests of investors and creditors.

The following trusts can be regarded as types of commercial trust as opposed to the family trust created by way of gift for a settlor's family to preserve the family wealth from extravagant behaviour of family members and from the demands of taxation for a perpetuity period which may be a certain period of up to 80 years or an uncertain period expiring 21 years from the death of the last survivor of specified persons alive when the trust was created.

Trusts as a commercial security device

The trust is particularly useful as a means of holding security over the same assets of the debtor (eg land and stocks and shares) for a large number of creditors. It is most convenient for the security to be vested in an independent trustee or one of the creditors to be held on trust for all the creditors, eg in the case of syndicated loans. Administration and realisation of the security are made much easier when there is one security holder rather than many.

---

14 Generally see chapters of D Hayton, J Langbein and D Waters in D Hayton (Ed) *Modern International Developments in Trust Law* (Kluwer Law International 1999); chapters of D Hayton and S Worthington in D Hayton (Ed) *Extending the Boundaries of Trusts and Similar Ring-Fenced Funds in the Twenty-First Century* (Kluwer Law International 2002) and D Hayton *The Association of Corporate Trustees: English Trusts and Their Commercial Counterparts in Continental Europe: A Report.*

The major advantage, however, is that it is very easy to replace one creditor with another (eg on sales of participations in the syndicated loan) without the need to assign interests in security and to comply with the relevant formalities to reflect the new ownership of the interest in security. The security remains vested in the trustee: there is simply a change in the identities of the beneficiaries for whom the trustee holds the security; and the new beneficiary's interest is the old equitable interest of the old beneficiary so that rights of priority are unaffected without the need for the co-operation of the other creditors, or of the debtor as required for the novation of debts.

The holding of security on trust also facilitates security structures where the same security is to benefit successive groups of creditors whose claims will come into existence at different times, eg where, in project financing, security is granted over the project assets to a trustee for the benefit not only of the bank participating in the initial grant of finance but also for banks who may at some future time provide additional finance. If the trust were not used, the banks participating in each successive grant of finance would have to take separate security over the same assets with the priority problems this would raise for them. Indeed, pari passu ranking in respect of the security would require complex contracts between all the creditors. However, the trust instrument will set out how the proceeds of realisation are to be applied and the order of application may be pari passu or howsoever set out.

Incidentally, it does not matter that the trustee is an independent trustee not in its personal capacity a creditor of the debtor or is a bank in a syndicate holding the security as trustee for all and so personally a creditor of the debtor for an amount less than the total amount secured. The full amount due and the security for such amount are respectively due to, and held by, the trustee qua trustee, who can claim for the benefit of the beneficiaries the full amount due and enforce the security for such amount.

While reserving certain exclusive powers to the trustee (eg on agreeing amendments to the trust instrument or on waiving defaults) it is, however, possible for the debtor to give parallel payment undertakings to the trustee and to the beneficiary bondholders as in the typical Eurobond issue: payment under one undertaking will pro tanto discharge liability under the other. Normally, as in the case of the trust for debenture holders where a company charges property to a trustee and confers rights over it as security to be held on trust for the debenture holders, who lend money to the company in return for debenture stock, the trustee exclusively has the right to sue on the covenant to repay and to enforce the security. The debenture stock trustee will normally be given power to appoint administrative receivers or managers to carry on the business of the company, though the trust deed will normally confer some powers upon the majority of the debenture stock holders in general meeting, eg the power to assent to modifications of the rights of the holders as a class. The Companies Act 1985, s 192 negatives any clause purporting to exclude a debenture trustee from liability for negligent breaches of trust, but allows the debenture holders at a meeting to give a subsequent release to a trustee relating to specific acts or omissions. Moreover, the London Stock Exchange imposes requirements on debenture trusts, eg as to who can be a trustee and the need to have at least one trustee independent of the company.

The trust is also crucial to efficiency in financial markets by the successful exploitation of other intermediate securities where an underlying security is issued (or agreed to be issued) in paper form to an intermediate depositary or custodian or nominee, who holds the paper security (or the issuer's obligation to issue it) for the investors. To avoid problems over the need for specific allocation of certain identified assets to be held on trust for the specific investors, the intermediary will hold its proprietary interest (or its personal chose in action) on trust for the investors as equitable tenants in common in fractional shares appropriate to the value of the relevant investments by the respective investors, of whom there may well be thousands rather than hundreds.

The trust is also used as a security device where a buyer raises finance on the security of imported goods (so that he can pay for, obtain and sell the goods so that he can then repay the loan) by pledging the bill of lading and other shipping documents to the lender. This requires delivery of the bill and the other documents to the lender, either indorsed to the lender or left blank. The problem is that the buyer needs these very documents to obtain the goods from the shipping company but if the lender parts with possession unconditionally the pledge will be extinguished since it requires the pledgee to have possession. The solution is to have the buyer provide the lender with a 'trust letter' or 'trust receipt' in which he undertakes that, in consideration of the release of the documents to him, he will hold them on trust for the lender and will hold the goods and the proceeds of sale on trust for the lender. This enables the lender to be deemed to continue in constructive possession so that the pledge remains valid.

There are limits to the use of the trust as a security device because it is not always possible to make something a trust simply by having documents that use the terminology of trusts nor is it possible to have a trust until assets have been specifically transferred or appropriated (ie set apart) to be held upon trust. A supplier of materials to a company can safeguard the supplier's interests, in the event of the company's insolvency without having paid for the materials, if it has reserved legal beneficial ownership of the materials until paid for them and such unpaid for materials remain unsold in the company's possession[15]. The supplier can repossess them. However, if legal title to the materials has passed to the company but the company is supposed, by virtue of the supplier's terms of contract, to hold the materials on trust for the supplier until payment, this is regarded not as a true trust but as an equitable charge over the materials to secure moneys due[16]. Such charge will be void against the company's creditors on liquidation of the company unless registered under the Companies Act 1985 which would then make frequent expeditious dealings with the company's property.

The position is the same if the so-called 'trust' for the supplier until payment purports to extend to goods manufactured using the supplier's materials and to the proceeds of sale of such goods, such proceeds being required to be paid into a separate 'trust account' to be held as security for payment of moneys due[17]. The position is different, however, and there is a true trust if the company contracts to pay into a separate trust account on trust for the supplier that proportion of the proceeds of sale which represents the amount due to the supplier in respect of the supplier's outstanding unpaid invoices

---

15 *Clough Mill v Martin* [1984] 3 All ER 982, [1985] 1 WLR 111, CA; *Armour v Thyssen Edelstahlwerke AG* [1991] 2 AC 339 [1990] 3 All ER 481, HL.
16 *Clough Mill v Martin* [1984] 3 All ER 982, [1985] 1 WLR 111, CA; *Re Weldtech Equipment Ltd* [1991] BCC 16.
17 *Compaq Computer Ltd v Abercorn Group Ltd* [1993] BCLC 602.

for materials supplied to the manufacturing company or that part of the proceeds of sale remaining after deduction of the commission due to the company upon selling the supplier's airline tickets[18].

Where a settlor declares itself trustee of a specific part of its property then if it is not creating an equitable tenancy in common it should actually set apart that specific part as emphasised in a Court of Appeal decision concerned with the retention money trust fund in building construction contracts[19]. Take a contract between an employer and a building contractor containing a clause entitling the employer to retain, say, 5% of money certified by the architect as due to the contractor: half becomes payable when the architect provides the certificate of practical completion and the other half becomes payable when the architect provides the certificate of making good defects. The clause requires the 5% to be paid into a separate retention trust fund to be held by the employer without any obligation to invest it but with a right to any interest produced by the money and a right to use the money to remedy defects in the construction of the contracted for building. If it so happens that the employer does not actually pay the money into a separate account but pays the money into its own account for its general purposes and then becomes insolvent, the contractor is simply an ordinary unsecured creditor even if, say, £200,000 is due to the contractor under the retention trust clause and there happens to be £250,000 in the employer's own account.

By way of contrast, if the employer had contracted or covenanted that it would hold upon trust for the contractor any money received from a specific third party (like the company funding the project releasing an amount equivalent to the retention moneys due) and did so receive, say, £200,000 then, on receipt, that specific £200,000 would become impressed with the trust for the contractor[20]. Equity looks on that as done which ought to be done. The contractor will be able to trace this £200,000 into the company's own account, assuming that there had never been less than £200,000 in such account[1]. If £200,000 had, instead, been spent on acquiring an asset now worth £220,000 then the contractor would instead be able to claim equitable ownership of this traceable product of the £200,000.

The principle that Equity looks on that as done which ought to be done underlies subordination trusts, a common modern use of trusts as a means of segregating and preserving assets for another person.

Trusts as a commercial device to segregate assets for other persons

Subordination trusts well exemplify the use of trusts as a means of segregating assets for the benefit of other persons. Subordination is a transaction whereby one creditor, the 'subordinated' or 'junior' creditor, agrees not to be paid by a borrower or other debtor until another creditor, the 'senior' creditor, of the common debtor has been paid. Like the taking of security, subordination is relevant only if the debtor is insolvent because until then

18 *Associated Alloys Pty Ltd v ACN 001 452 806 Pty Ltd* (2001) 74 ALJR 862; *Air Canada – M & L Travel Ltd* (1994) 108 DLR (4th) 592; *Palette Shoes Pty Ltd v Krohn* (1937) 58 CLR 1. Further see p 15 ante.
19 *Mac-Jordan Construction Ltd v Brookmount Erostin Ltd* [1992] BCLC 350, approved in *Re Goldcorp Exchange Ltd* [1994] 2 All ER 806, 823, PC; but see pp 78–79 post.
20 *Pullan v Koe* [1913] 1 Ch 9; *Re Irving* (1877) 7 Ch D 419; *Re Lind* [1915] 2 Ch 345, CA.
1 *Roscoe v Winder* [1915] 1 Ch 62.

both junior and senior creditor can be paid in full. The fundamental object of a subordination is that it should be successful on the debtor's insolvency but, for full efficiency, it needs also to be successful if the junior creditor becomes insolvent. For these purposes, under a 'turnover' agreement the junior creditor can agree to hold whatever he might recover in respect of the junior debt up to the amount of the senior debt upon trust for the senior creditor.

However, to avoid practical problems (over the registrability of such agreements under the Companies Act 1985, s 395) raised by any doubts[2] as to whether such agreement might constitute a security interest (as in substance a charge over the proceeds of the junior debt to secure the senior debt), it is common to use a trust deed[3] under which the junior debt is payable by the debtor to a trustee who holds what is recovered in respect of the debt on trust first for the benefit of the senior creditor by paying it the amount of the senior debt and, then, anything remaining is held for the benefit of the junior creditors. The debtor's covenant in favour of the trustee can be a covenant parallel to the obligation of the debtor to pay the junior creditors, eg by virtue of their holding of subordinated bonds, and the debtor can be authorised to pay the bondholders direct until an event of default occurs whereupon the debtor must pay the trustee. In these circumstances, there is no charge because the trustee has no property of its own which it can charge, while the junior creditors are simply taking a limited interest under a trust. Payments in respect of the junior debt after the junior creditor's insolvency will not fall into the junior creditor's insolvent estate. The subordination trust will bite on the proceeds as soon as they come into existence even if this is after the insolvency.

Subordination trusts fulfil many purposes. A senior creditor, like a bank, may wish to subordinate insiders of the debtor, such as a parent company or a major shareholder, eg in the case of project financing. Alternatively, insiders or major suppliers may be persuaded to subordinate their claims to induce bank creditors not to enforce their loans in the hope that the borrower will survive and prosper. A debtor may wish to increase its capital base and have subordinated debt ranking as new primary capital for the purpose of supervision of capital adequacy of banks or insurance companies. Where loans are to finance a take-over or a management buy out on highly leveraged terms, lenders may be prepared to lend on a subordinated basis, encouraging senior lenders to lend more because of the cushion of the junior debt. Because this type of financing is located midway between debt and equity it is referred to as mezzanine debt by professionals, though, because such financing is risky newspapers refer to such bond issues as junk bonds.

Another common example of segregating and safeguarding assets through the trust device is found in a securitisation transaction involving the transfer by a creditor to a special purpose vehicle ('SPV') of claims for payment against debtors but in circumstances where payment will actually be made to the creditor. During the period between receiving such payments and transferring them as agreed to the SPV the creditor will be required to place

---

2 See P R Wood, *The Law of Subordinated Debt* (Sweet & Maxwell Ltd, 1990) p 40.
3 A trust deed will always be used if there is a large class of junior creditors. Neither subordination trusts nor contractual subordination contravene the application of the fundamental pari passu rule for treatment of creditors in insolvency: *Re British & Commonwealth Holdings plc (No 3)* [1992] 1 WLR 672; *Re Maxwell Communications Corpn plc (No 2)* [1994] 1 All ER 737, [1993] 1 WLR 1402.

them to the credit of a dedicated trust account[4] at its bank separate from all its other bank accounts, it being a trustee of the amount standing to its credit in the trust account for the SPV. If the creditor-trustee becomes insolvent the SPV will be entitled to claim the money in the trust account as the equitable owner thereof. It follows that the creditor's contract claims will be kept off its balance sheet, which can be advantageous[5], while early receipt of the payment for a future income stream will strengthen the creditor's trading position.

Quistclose[6] trusts are also common. On the basis of the House of Lords' decision in that case, Q Ltd can lend £1 million to R Ltd on trust for a specified purpose (like paying a dividend in 14 days' time) but if the specified purpose cannot be carried out, then the money is held on trust by R Ltd for Q Ltd, though if the purpose is achieved then R Ltd is simply to be a debtor of Q Ltd in respect of the loan. Thus, if R Ltd went into liquidation within the 14-day period so that it could not pay out the dividend, Q Ltd will be treated as equitable owner of the money, which will therefore be unavailable for R Ltd's creditors.

Sinking fund trusts are also common. Money is regularly paid to trustees so that an adequate amount of money will be available in due course to carry out a particular purpose benefiting persons, eg major repairs or renewals for blocks of flats or for old heritage property, or replacement of oil drilling rigs or land reclamation after working-out of a mine[7].

Trading trusts

Instead of forming a limited company, a trading trust can be created to enable the trustees to carry on a trade for the benefit of beneficiaries under the trust. It is possible for the trust to be simply for A for life, remainder to B, or a discretionary trust for A,B,C and D, their spouses and their descendants and their spouses but, as a business proposition, a trading trust will be for the benefit of such persons as may be or may become the holders of transferable certificates evidencing beneficial fractional interests in the trust fund. In some States in America it seems such persons can have the same limitation of liability as is extended to shareholders of private companies but in England this is not normally the case, so that an indemnity can be claimed from such

---

4 Temporarily lodging the money in the creditor's general account will suffice (*Associated Alloys Pty Ltd v ACN 001 452 106 Pty Ltd* (2001) 74 AJLR 862; *Re ILG Travel* [1995] 2 BCLC 128) but there is then more of a danger that the creditor could squander the money on paying off its own creditor so that the money becomes untraceable.

5 The purpose of such securitisation transactions will be to take the creditor's contract claims off the balance sheet of the creditor company, so it is important for the SPV not to be a subsidiary of the company so as to avoid consolidation of the accounts of the SPV and the company. This will be achieved by the company holding the SPV shares on charitable trusts (though expecting little value to be ultimately available for the charitable purposes). The SPV will fund the purchase of the creditor's claims by borrowing the money or by issuing debt securities. Getting assets off the creditor company's balance sheet makes its gearing look better, whilst its financial covenants will not be breached if the SPV gets into difficulties; and in the cases of banks it makes it easier to comply with capital ratio requirements.

6 *Barclays Bank Ltd v Quistclose Investments Ltd* [1970] AC 567, [1968] 3 All ER 651, HL, well considered by C E F Rickett (1991) 107 LQR 608 and pp 325–355 Waters (ed) *Equity, Fiduciaries and Trusts* (1993, Carswell, Canada), and explained by Lord Millett in *Twinsectra v Yardley* [2002] UKHL 12, paras [68]–[103] on which see pp 12–13 ante.

7 See 'The Role of the Trust in Environmental Law' by D W M Waters, in Waters (ed) *Equity, Fiduciaries and Trusts* (1993, Carswell, Canada).

persons by creditors if the trustee, which is usually a limited liability company, does not satisfy their claims.

Except for tax considerations, there are very few cases where it is sensible to use a trust rather than a company for the conduct of a business because of the risks to creditors that makes them wary of dealing with a trustee[8], eg if the trustee may not be wealthy enough to pay the debt or if the trustee acted beyond its or his or her powers or exercised its or his or her powers improperly or if there may be special circumstances preventing any indemnity being obtained from beneficiaries. In England tax considerations do not favour the creation of a trading trust.

Unit trusts (or Collective Investment Schemes)

A unit trust[9] is an investment trust, as opposed to a trading trust, and is sometimes known as a collective investment scheme or a mutual fund. However, in the UK one must distinguish between 'unit trust' and 'investment trust' because the latter expression is used as shorthand for an investment trust *company*, a *company* quoted on the London Stock Exchange with the sole activity of making investments, generally in the shares of other companies. A shareholder in an investment trust company has no legal or equitable interest in the investments owned by the company, and the share price will stand at a discount to the net asset value because the current value of the shareholder's shares will depend not just on the underlying current value of the company's investments but also on the dividend policy of the company's board of directors, who generally are subject to fewer controls than the manager of a unit trust. In contrast[10], any unitholder can sell his units to the manager at a price directly corresponding to the underlying current value of the investments in the unit trust, while the manager can issue new units all the time (a unit trust being open-ended, unlike an investment trust company). However open-ended investment companies[11] ('OEIC's) as open-ended as unit trusts can now be created with share prices directly reflecting the value of underlying assets.

It is the manager who sets up the arrangement embodied in the trust deed with the trustee and then finds investors to provide the money to be forwarded by the manager to the trustee, who then issues unit certificates to the investors. The trustee acts as a type of custodian trustee to hold the investors'

---

8 See DJ Hayton in J Glasson, *International Trust Laws* (Jordan Publishing, looseleaf) Section B chapter 5 'Trading Trusts' paras B5.14–B5.20. Further see Trust Law Consultation Paper and the Report *Rights of Creditors Against Trustees and Trust Funds* (www.kcl.ac.uk/depsta/law/tlc).

9 Generally, see KFS in *The Legal Nature of the Unit Trust*, Oxford University Press, 1997, bringing out the point at pp 284–292 that, normally, unit holders have no proprietary interest in the underlying assets until termination of the trust, beforehand only having a personal right to a sum of money representing a proportion of the net value calculated and realisable as provided in the Trust Agreement. It follows that when units are first issued to an investor he should not be regarded as a settlor of the monies paid over to purchase the units, which make him owner of the chose in action but not the owner of any proportion of the underlying trust assets until the termination of the trust.

10 Another contrast is that shareholders have a right to attend an Annual General Meeting and vote on various matters so as to bind the company, whilst beneficiaries have no right to such a meeting where they can exercise voting rights to bind the trustees unless the trust instrument expressly confers such a right upon them, eg debenture trusts. Unit trust holders are not members of any company or partnership: *Smith v Anderson* (1880) 15 Ch D 247, CA.

11 See Financial Services and Markets Act 2000, s 236.

money and investments purchased with the money on trust for the investor unit holders. It must follow all instructions properly given by the manager who manages the portfolio of investments but, where the unit trust is an authorised unit trust open to public subscription, it must take reasonable care to ensure that the manager acts within its powers, keeps adequate records and manages the scheme in accordance with the Regulations for Collective Investment Schemes. Section 253 of the Financial Services and Markets Act 2000 prevents the trustee or manager being exempted from liability for 'any failure to exercise due care and diligence in the discharge of' their functions, while s 243(4) and (5) require the manager and the trustee to be companies incorporated in the UK or another European Economic Area State and to be independent of each other.

Unit trusts not authorised by the Financial Services Authority under the Financial Services and Markets Act 2000, ss 242–248 cannot be sold to the public and have such tax disadvantages that, in practice, unit holders are confined to bodies exempt from charge to tax on capital gains, eg pension funds and charities. In recent years the types of investments that can be held by a unit trust if it is to be an authorised unit trust have been much extended so that there can be futures and options funds, geared futures and options funds, property funds and warrant funds.

Pension fund trusts

Occupational pension schemes are the main form of private pension arrangement in the UK, their main purpose being to provide income after retirement from work but they usually also provide a lump sum on retirement and death during employment and make provision for early retirement on grounds of ill-health or disability. Over 11 million employees are members of occupational pension schemes while 7 million receive occupational pensions. Most occupational pension schemes were set up as irrevocable trusts, though nowadays (to avoid onerous financial and accounting responsibilities of companies not wishing to have to provide a trust fund providing for percentages of final salary to be paid to retirees) most involve payment of contributions over to an assurance company which contracts to provide the agreed benefits in due course. Employees then carry their pension kit-bag on their backs from one employment to the next. Regulation of such companies makes it highly unlikely that insolvency will occur so as to thwart the expectations of those contracting with such companies. However trust funds are entirely separate from the funds of the employer in relation to whom it is set up, so that if the employer becomes insolvent the pension funds are not available to the company's creditors but are security for payment of benefits to pensioners. This is the theory: in practice, there was a danger that a domineering managing director could act dishonestly and pressurise compliant trustees in various ways so as to dissipate much of the trust fund in attempts to save the skin of the managing director and his companies. Trustees and auditors are now alerted to these problems and the Pensions Law Review Committee produced a report which the Pensions Act 1995 has implemented in order to tighten up the position. There is very strong public interest in occupational pensions because of the importance of enabling people to look after themselves properly after they retire and because of tax exemptions allowed in respect of pension trusts. Because of the potential difficulties beneficiaries face if seeking to contest trustees' decisions, a Pensions

Ombudsman has very wide powers to intervene against trustees and require payments to be made.

Employee trusts

It is in the public interest to encourage employees of companies to work hard so as to improve the profitability of their company-employer and thereby increase the value of shares in the company. Accordingly, favourable tax exemptions exist to enable the company to transfer shares to trustees to set them aside for particular employees, who will only be liable to income tax on dividends and who, on sale of their shares after three years, will only be liable to capital gains tax[12]. Usually an employee share plan involves two trusts. First, a general employee trust which buys shares in the company, using company funds or borrowed money guaranteed by the company, and, second, a profit sharing trust which buys company shares with moneys provided by the company and appropriates shares to particular employees. This structure has tax advantages while the employee trust provides a ready market for the sale of shares in a private company and provides a possible defence mechanism against a hostile take-over bid.

Miscellaneous commercial uses of trusts

Businessmen can use trusts for any purpose benefiting persons if such purpose be a sensible business purpose and the use of the trust involves no practical or tax disadvantages. Some miscellaneous examples are as follows:

(1) to deal with the death of a partner there may be a partnership buy-sell agreement funded by insurance held by a trustee for the partners. The insurance money will provide funds to enable the surviving partners to buy the interest of the deceased partner, thereby avoiding sale of the partnership assets which might jeopardise the business;

(2) to reduce or eliminate tax relating to intellectual property royalties the owner may assign the right to receive royalties to a trust situated in a low tax or no-tax jurisdiction (or to a company so situated). It is important that the jurisdiction is party to various international conventions enabling the mutual recognition of each other's intellectual property rights so that rights to royalties can be enforced;

(3) to further the best interests of a family in a family company, the elderly founder of the company may rely much on his second son, B, who is managing director and who has a 26% shareholding. By his will the founder might leave his 54% shareholding to B on trust for the founder's three other children, A, C and D, if alive at B's death or earlier attainment of the age of 65 years (with a substitutionary clause for the issue of A, C and D if A, C or D die before the contingency[13] is satisfied). This allows the business-minded B to control matters in the best interests of the family.

At B's death aged 64 it may be that his children, E and F, have a 13%

---

12 For the tax advantages of Employee Share Ownership Plans (ESOPs) see Finance Act 1989, ss 67–73, Sch 5, Taxation of Chargeable Gains Act 1992, s 229, as amended.

13 If the interests are not contingent but absolute then the beneficiaries will be able to call for the trust property to be transferred to themselves and so frustrate the settlor's purposes: see Article 70, post.

shareholding each, while the deceased A's only child has an 18% share-holding, the deceased C's two children each have a 9% shareholding, while D has an 18% shareholding. They can contract with each other for their shares to be held by a trustee to vote the rights on the shares as the parties direct in respect of the shares to which they are respectively entitled but, in the event of an offer being made to acquire all or any part of the shares, if a specified majority of the parties wish to dispose of their shares then the trustee is to take such action as in his opinion is likely to result in all the trust shares being disposed of to the best advantage. There can be further provisions preventing any party from disposing of his equitable interest in his shares under the trust unless first offering it to the other parties at a fair value to be fixed by an independent valuer if not agreed[14].

Another example of a voting trust is to cater for a joint venture of A and B carried on via a company the shares in which are mainly owned by A but B is to enjoy a higher percentage of voting rights than his minority shareholding warrants. A could contractually bind himself to vote certain of his shares as B directs but if A broke the agreement and voted against B's instructions the votes would be validly cast and bind the company. To avoid this, the shares and voting rights can be vested in an independent trustee to hold dividends, etc for A but to vote as directed by B who will know that the trustee will vote as directed.

Conclusion

The lack of rigid formal requirements for the creation and operation of trusts, unlike companies, and the tremendous flexibility allowed in inserting clauses in trust instruments make the trust a very useful device for achieving any commercial purpose if there are no tax disadvantages in its use and no practical disadvantages flowing from its lack of legal personality. Maitland, a great legal historian and trusts lawyer, has written[15],

'If we were asked what is the greatest and most distinctive achievement performed by Englishmen in the field of jurisprudence I cannot think that we should have any better answer to give than this, namely the development from century to century of the trust idea.'

ARTICLE 2

Definitions of legal and equitable estates and interests

The interest of a beneficiary in trust property is called an equitable estate or interest or right because it was originally only recognised in courts of equity. A legal estate or interest, on the other hand, is that proprietary interest which has been acquired with all the formalities which are required by the common or statute law for conferring perfect ownership, though it may have subsequently devolved upon the death of one or more holders. A trustee usually, but not neces-

14 See, eg *Booth v Ellard* [1980] 3 All ER 569, [1980] 1 WLR 1443, CA.
15 *Selected Essays* (1936) p 129.

sarily or always, has the legal ownership of trust property: it is possible for a trustee to hold an equitable interest upon trust for beneficiaries.

Distinction still important

The fundamental and ineradicable distinctions which exist between legal and equitable estates remain despite the so-called 'fusion' of law and equity[16]. As Lord Selborne said, in introducing the Judicature Act 1873 into the House of Lords:

> 'if trusts are to continue, there must be a distinction between what we call a legal and equitable estate. The legal estate is in the person who holds the property for another; the equitable estate is in the person beneficially interested. The distinction between law and equity is, within certain limits, real and natural, and it would be a mistake to suppose that what is real and natural ought to be disregarded, although under our present system it is often pushed beyond these limits.'[17]

The old legal estate, therefore, still subsists; and although equitable interests (a term which is now preferred to the old 'equitable estates')[18] are now recognised by all branches of the Supreme Court, and may therefore in a sense be called legal, it has been found more convenient to retain the old nomenclature, 'legal' and 'equitable', signifying, as it does, a real and substantial difference, which would still exist, even although the terms had themselves been abolished. In the case of land this is recognised by the Law of Property Act 1925[19].

Estate of trustees not necessarily legal

It must not, however, be assumed that the estate of a trustee is always legal. The beneficial interest of the beneficiary is always equitable, so long as the trust subsists; but so also may be the estate of the trustee. For instance, the trust property may consist of the beneficial interest of a tenant in common or a beneficial interest under another settlement. Exceptionally, under the Settled Land Act 1925, the trustees of settled land, unless they are statutory owners, have no interest or estate therein at all. Instead, the beneficiary who is life tenant holds the legal estate on trust for himself and the other beneficiaries. This enables him to manage the trust though capital moneys (eg arising upon a sale) must be paid to the Settled Land Act trustees, who then need to invest or apply the monies in their discretion after consulting the

---

16 For exposure of the fusion fallacy see Jill Martin [1994] Conv 13, Meagher, Gummow & Lehane *Equity: Doctrines and Remedies* (3rd edn) pp 44–70; *Schalit v Joseph Nadler Ltd* [1933] 2 KB 79; *Chan v Cresdon Pty Ltd* (1989) 168 CLR 242 at 252–256; *Parker-Tweedale v Dunbar Bank plc* [1991] Ch 12, [1990] 2 All ER 577, CA; *Downsview Nominees Ltd v First City Corpn Ltd* [1993] AC 295, [1993] 3 All ER 626, PC. The Act was intended only to be procedural as recognised by Jessel MR in *Salt v Cooper* (1880) 16 Ch D 544 at 549 though 'there is no reason why the courts in shaping principles, whether their origins lie in the common law or in Equity, should not have regard to both common law and equitable concept and doctrines, borrowing from either as may be appropriate' as Sir Anthony Mason stated in Waters (ed) *Equity, Fiduciaries and Trusts* (1993, Carswell) pp 7–8.

17 Hansard (NS), Vol 214, p 333, and see Lord Cairns' views in *Pugh v Heath* (1882) 7 App Cas 235 at 237.

18 See Law of Property Act 1925, s 1(3).

19 See s 1(1), (3), s 4 and s 205(1) which defines 'legal estates' and 'equitable interests'.

tenant for life, so as to give effect to his wishes so far as consistent with the general interest of the settlement[20].

Importance of difference between legal and equitable estates

The difference between legal and equitable estates is not merely of theoretical interest. A legal title prevails against the whole world unless statute-barred[1] whilst an equitable title does not prevail against a bona fide purchaser of a legal estate for value without notice of the equitable interest affecting the legal estate[2] or against a purchaser of the legal estate who complies with the overreaching provisions of the Law of Property Act 1925 or the Settled Land Act 1925 or the Land Registration Act 1925 or 2002. Where a question of priority arises between two claimants with equitable interests then the equitable interest that arose first in time will prevail over the second unless the first claimant was fraudulent or grossly negligent or is otherwise estopped from claiming priority[3]. Thus a purchaser of an equitable interest without notice will not normally take free of prior equitable interests.

Distinction between equitable interests and mere equities

An equity which is ancillary to or dependent upon an interest in land[4] (eg a right to recover property by having a conveyance set aside for fraud or undue influence or rectified)[5] must be distinguished from an equitable interest, though some old cases refer indiscriminately to equitable interests as equities. A purchaser of an equitable (or legal) interest without notice of the equity will take free of the equity[6]. It would seem that such a purchaser should also be immune from an equitable claim via the tracing process, where the claim relates to a mere equity, eg to rescind for undue influence.

Registered land: overriding and minor interests

If a person in actual occupation of land happens to have either an equitable interest[7] or a mere equity[8], that is not protected by entry on the register as a minor interest, this ranks as an overriding interest[9], unless inquiry was made

---

20 Settled Land Act 1925, s 75 as substituted by Trustee Act 2000, Sch 2, para 10.
1 *Wyld v Silver* [1963] Ch 243, [1962] 3 All ER 309, CA; *Benn v Hardinge* (1992) 66 P & CR 246, CA.
2 *Pilcher v Rawlins* (1872) 7 Ch App 259; *Wilkes v Spooner* [1911] 2 KB 473, CA.
3 *Rice v Rice* (1854) 2 Drew 73; *Capell v Winter* [1907] 2 Ch 376. If the second claimant was a purchaser of his equitable interest without notice he could obtain priority over the prior equitable interest if he subsequently acquired the legal estate without being a party to a breach of trust: *Bailey v Barnes* [1894] 1 Ch 25 at 36; *McCarthy & Stone Ltd v J S Hodge & Co Ltd* [1971] 1 WLR 1547 at 1556.
4 *National Provincial Bank Ltd v Ainsworth* [1965] AC 1175 at 1238, HL per Lord Upjohn.
5 *Ernest v Vivian* (1863) 33 LJ Ch 513; *Latec Investments Ltd v Hotel Terrigal Pty Ltd* (1965) 113 CLR 265; *Bainbrigge v Browne* (1881) 18 ChD 188; *Garrard v Frankel* (1862) 30 Beav 445; *Smith v Jones* [1954] 2 All ER 823, [1954] 1 WLR 1089.
6 *Phillips v Phillips* (1862) 4 De GF & J 208 at 218.
7 *Hodgson v Marks* [1971] Ch 892, [1971] 2 All ER 684, CA; *Williams & Glyn's Bank v Boland* [1981] AC 487, [1980] 2 All ER 408, HL.
8 *Blacklocks v J B Developments (Godalming) Ltd* [1982] Ch 183, [1981] 3 All ER 392.
9 Land Registration Act 1925, ss 70(1)(g), 3(xvi) or Land Registration Act 2002, Sch 3. If the inherent nature of the interest, however, is overreachable then it will be overreached on payment of capital moneys to two trustees or a trust corporation: *City of London Building Society*

of him and he failed to disclose his interest. An overriding interest binds the whole world irrespective of notice[10]. Exceptionally, equitable interests under Settled Land Act settlements and mortgages can only be minor interests and so will be void against subsequent purchasers unless protected by entry on the register of title[11].

Rights in rem and in personam

There has been some controversy over the nature of an equitable interest under a trust[12]. To what extent is the beneficiary's interest in rem and to what extent a right *in personam?*

It has often been said that legal interests are rights *in rem* whilst equitable interests are rights in personam. Since rights are given only against persons not things what is meant is that legal rights prevail against persons generally whilst equitable rights prevail against a limited group of persons. This limited group formerly comprised persons who were not bona fide purchasers of a legal estate for value without notice and now includes persons who are not able to take advantage of special protective provisions in the 1925 property legislation, eg the overreaching provisions of the Law of Property Act 1925, the registration provisions of the Land Charges Acts 1925 and 1972 and of the Land Registration Act 1925 or 2002.

At other times it is said that equitable rights under trusts are rights in personam in the sense that each trust beneficiary has a personal right against the trustees to ensure due performance of the trusts and to ensure that the trustees properly discharge their duties. This well reflects the practical working of the trust. Thus where D holds a French immovable on trust for C but refuses to transfer it to C when C demands this, C's legal proceedings in England are not 'proceedings which have as their object rights *in rem* in immovable property'[13], when the court of the French *lex situs* would have had extensive jurisdiction. C's action is only *in personam,* seeking only to assert rights against D. The immovable nature of the property and its location are irrelevant to the issues (whether D held the property on trust for C under a resulting trust and so could be compelled to transfer it to C), which would have been the same if the dispute had concerned a London flat or a yacht. However a beneficiary under a trust of land cannot himself distrain at law for rent due from a tenant granted a lease by the trustees[14]. Any necessary action against the tenant is the trustees' responsibility as legal owners and they will be personally responsible to the beneficiary if in breach of their duties.

On the other hand, a beneficiary does have a right in rem in the sense of a 'real' or 'proprietary' right where he can exercise equitable proprietary remedies via the tracing process against strangers in possession of the trust property, or its traceable product[15]. If, however, the trustee sold the trust

v Flegg [1988] AC 54, [1987] 3 All ER 435, HL. In an exceptional case, irrespective of the position according to principles of property law, equity may act in personam against the conscience of the purchaser or mortgagee to prevent him getting away with unconscionable behaviour: *Ashburn Austalt v Arnold* [1989] Ch 1, [1988] 2 All ER 147, CA.

10 *Williams & Glyn's Bank v Boland* [1981] AC 487, [1980] 2 All ER 408, HL.
11 Land Registration Act 1925, ss 86(2), (3), 106(2); Land Registration Act 2002, Sch 3.
12 (1899) 15 LQR 294 (Hart); (1917) 17 Col LR 269 (A W Scott); (1917) 17 Col LR 467 (H Stone); (1954) 32 Can BR 510 (V Latham); (1967) 45 Can BR 219 (D Waters).
13 *Webb v Webb* [1994] QB 696. Also see *Ashurst v Pollard* [2001] Ch 595, [2001] 2 All ER 75, CA.
14 *Schalit v Joseph Nadler Ltd* [1933] 2 KB 79.
15 See Article 101, post.

property to a bona fide purchaser and then dissipated the proceeds of sale, the beneficiary is left merely with his equitable chose in action against the trustee which will be worthless if the trustee is bankrupt. A beneficiary may similarly be regarded as interested in the res, the subject of the trust, where he is a sane adult absolutely indefeasibly entitled as against the trustees to the trust property within the *Saunders v Vautier* principle[16]. Where a beneficiary (eg an adult life tenant) is currently entitled to income produced by the trust property he is taxable on his income from the stocks, shares etc comprising the trust property as soon as it is received by the trustees[17] rather than when it is received by him from the trustees pursuant to their personal duty to account to him for it[18]. He is regarded as having part of the equitable ownership of the assets themselves[19] so if they are foreign he is treated as interested in foreign assets. Thus, if property is held in trust for A for life, remainder to B absolutely, A is regarded as having an equitable life interest in the property and B an equitable interest in remainder: indeed, between them, A and B, if they agree, can call for the property to be vested in them or otherwise dealt with as they direct.

A beneficiary under a discretionary trust (eg to trustees on trust to distribute the income in their absolute discretion between such of B, C and D their spouses and issue as they see fit) is in a specially weak position. His hope of receiving income is not a full equitable proprietary interest capable of assignment by way of gift, though he can release his equitable right to be considered for receipt of income[20]. It seems that the discretionary trustees (like personal representatives of an unadministered estate[1] and a company subject to a winding up order)[2] have ownership subject to onerous fiduciary duties in circumstances where the beneficiaries have no full equitable proprietary interest though they may exercise proprietary remedies via the tracing process to restore property or its traceable product to the trust.

Because there is a proprietary response via the tracing process to the event of a settlor's earlier creation of a fixed or a discretionary trust, it is proper to regard beneficiaries under either type of trust as having proprietary *in rem* rights. However, a discretionary beneficiary only has the right to have the recovered traced property added back to the trust fund in the hope that some thereof may, perhaps, be distributed to him pursuant to an exercise of the trustee's discretion. In contrast, L, a life tenant, is himself absolutely entitled to obtain traceable income, while the lost traceable capital has to be restored to the trust fund, to which R will become absolutely entitled on L's death where the trust was for L for life, remainder to R. Thus, in concerning oneself with external aspects of the trust in trying to trace and recover trust

16 See Article 69, post.
17 *Baker v Archer-Shee* [1927] AC 844, HL; *Hamilton-Russell's Executors v IRC* (1943) 25 TC 200 at 207–208; *Spens v IRC* [1970] 3 All ER 295 at 299; *IRC v Berrill* [1982] 1 All ER 867 at 880; *New Zealand Insurance Co Ltd v Probate Duties Comr (Victoria)* [1973] VR 659.
18 Some foreign jurisdictions take this view or used to take this view: *Archer-Shee v Garland* [1931] AC 212, HL, also making it clear that English law will recognise the nature of rights under a foreign settlement as governed by the foreign proper law; see also *Re Fitzgerald* [1904] 1 Ch 573.
19 *New Zealand Insurance Co Ltd v Probate Duties Comr* [1973] VR 659; *Cholmondeley v IRC* [1986] STC 384.
20 *Re Gulbenkian's Settlement (No 2)* [1970] Ch 408, [1969] 2 All ER 1173.
 1 *Stamp Duties Comr (Queensland) v Livingston* [1965] AC 694, [1964] 3 All ER 692; *Marshall v Kerr* [1995] 1 AC 148, HL.
 2 *Ayerst v C & K (Construction) Ltd* [1976] AC 167, [1975] 2 All ER 537, HL.

property and its traceable product, beneficiaries have *in rem* rights, but so far as concerns the internal operation of a trust the beneficiaries have *in personam* rights against the trustees for the proper performance of the trusts. The *situs* of a discretionary beneficiary's equitable chose in action has to be where the trustee resides and administers the trust (in the absence of contrary statutory provision), although in the case of a beneficiary absolutely entitled to income or to both capital and income, the Revenue can claim that such beneficiary has an *in rem* interest located where the trust assets are located.

ARTICLE 3

Definitions of express, implied, resulting and constructive trusts

Trusts either arise under statute[3] or are created:
(1) intentionally by the act of the settlor, in which case they are called express trusts; or
(2) by implication of a court of equity so that the legal title to property is in one person and the equitable right to the beneficial enjoyment thereof is in another, in which case they are called implied trusts which may further be subdivided into resulting trusts and constructive trusts. A resulting trust of property arises as a long-stop (to locate beneficial ownership) in favour of a transferor where there is (a) an absence of any enforceable[4] express or inferred declaration of trust affecting property gratuitously transferred to the transferee (not being the transferor's spouse or child) or purchased from a third party in the name of such a transferee or (b) an enforceable express or inferred declaration of a trust affecting property transferred to a trustee but the transferor failed to divest himself wholly of his beneficial interest. A constructive trust of property arises on proof of recognised categories of special circumstances where a court of equity considers it unconscionable for the owner of the property to hold it for his own benefit to the exclusion of the claimant.

The distinction between (1) express trusts and (2) implied, resulting or constructive trusts is vital as far as the formalities for the creation of trusts are concerned[5]. Furthermore, a person incapable of being an express trustee may be a trustee of implied, resulting or constructive trusts[6]. A trust is an

---

3 For example, the trusts declared by ss 313 and 314 of the Companies Act 1985 of certain sums improperly received by directors as compensation for loss of office, the trusts arising in respect of legal estates conveyed to minors or co-owned under Law of Property Act 1925, ss 19, 34–36 (as amended by Trusts of Land and Appointment of Trustees Act 1996), the trusts arising on intestacy under Administration of Estates Act 1925, s 33.

4 See Law of Property Act 1925, s 53 (1)(b).

5 Law of Property Act 1925, s 53(1), (2). Old cases concerned with pre-Limitation Act 1939 distinctions between express trustees and constructive trustees remain of assistance according to *Paragon Finance plc v Thakerar* [1999] 1 All ER 400, CA, although the 1939 Act and its replacement, the Limitation Act 1980 apply to all trusts express, implied, resulting and constructive: Limitation Act 1980, s 38(1), incorporating the Trustee Act 1925, s 68(17), definition of 'trustee'.

6 *Re Vinogradoff* [1935] WN 68.

express trust whether expressed in certain unambiguous language or whether inferred from uncertain ambiguous words and conduct of the settlor, eg where the settlor uses precatory words of entreaty, prayer or expectation intending them exceptionally to be imperative and binding in the circumstances[7]. An express trust which fails to observe the requisite statutory formalities may be vindicated by the imposition of a resulting trust or a constructive trust or an estoppel.

The phrase 'implied trust' is nowadays normally[8] used to cover both resulting and constructive trusts since both are not express trusts, though it has sometimes been used to cover only resulting trusts[9]. But for the fact that the phrase 'implied trust' is still used in statutes on the *ex abundante* cautela principle, it would be better to ignore 'implied' trusts and classify trusts as 'express' 'resulting' or 'constructive'.

Resulting trusts

As Lord Upjohn stated[10], 'In reality, the so-called presumption of a resulting trust is no more than a long-stop to provide the answer when the relevant facts and circumstances fail to yield a solution.' Thus, if a bank, under what it believes to be a valid loan contract, transfers legal beneficial ownership in £2 million to a local authority to use freely as its own money there can be no resulting trust[11] (eg to prevent the unjust enrichment of the local authority) when it subsequently turns out that the contract was void because the authority lacked capacity to enter into the contract. Similarly, if the evidence reveals the transferor made an enforceable[12] express or inferred declaration of trust of property gratuitously transferred into the name of, or bought by the transferor in the name of, the transferee (or also of the transferor), then no question arises of a resulting trust being imposed to locate beneficial ownership in the transferor – unless it then turns out that the trusts declared by the transferor failed for some reason to divest himself wholly of his beneficial interest and had not revealed any actual intention that he was to be excluded from any benefit from the trust fund in any circumstances whatsoever[13].

---

7 (1927) LQR 15; *Re Llanover Settled Estates* [1926] Ch 626.

8 *Cook v Fountain* (1676) 3 Swan 585 at 591: *Cowcher v Cowcher* [1972] 1 All ER 943 at 949.

9 Trustee Act 1925, s 68(17); Sometimes it has been used to cover only presumed resulting trusts (*Soar v Ashwell* [1893] 2 QB 390, CA; *Re Llanover Estates* [1926] Ch 626) and sometimes to cover presumed resulting trusts and constructive trusts arising out of informally expressed common intentions: Slade LJ giving the Childe & Co Oxford Lecture 1984 on *The Informal Creation of Interests in Land*, p 4.

10 *Vandervell v IRC* [1967] 2 AC 291 at 313.

11 *Westdeutsche Landesbank v Islington London Borough Council* [1996] AC 669, 689, 708, 716, 718, 720, 738. Contrast R Chambers *Resulting Trusts* Oxford University Press 1997.

12 In *Hodgson v Marks* [1971] Ch 892, CA, where A transferred her house to B on oral trust (not satisfying Law of Property Act 1925, s 53(1)(b)) for A, such express trust was enforceable under *Rochefoucauld v Boustead* [1897] 1 Ch 196, CA, to prevent statute being used as an instrument of fraud: see W J Swadling in Chapter 4 of P Birks & F Rose (eds) *Restitution and Equity Vol 1: Resulting Trusts and Equitable Compensation* LLP London 2000.

13 *Westdeutsche Landesbank v Islington London Borough Council* [1996] AC 669, 708. In *Re Vandervell's Trusts (No 2)* [1974] Ch 269 Vandervell wanted an option to be retained to buy back the very valuable shareholding transferred at his direction by his trustee to the Royal College of Surgeons for sufficient dividend income to be paid to endow a professorship, and wanted the option to be held on trusts to be decided later: hence a resulting trust arose, he not having declared trusts of the option nor having abandoned any interest of himself for *bona vacantia* issues then to arise.

However, if there is no evidence revealing the transferor's real intentions eg to make a loan or outright gift or an enforceable declaration of trust of property gratuitously transferred into the name of, or bought by the transferor in the name of, the transferee (or also of the transferor), then a resulting trust will arise by operation of law[14] in favour of the transferor unless rebutted by the presumption of advancement[15] where the transferee was the transferor's spouse or child.

Incidentally, the transferor for resulting trust purposes is the legal beneficial owner or the beneficial owner who directs the trustee of the legal title to transfer it to another[16]. Where the trustee in breach of trust transfers the trust property to a transferee, the latter as a matter of property law will take title free from the beneficiaries' interests only if he is a bona fide purchaser of a legal interest for value without notice of those equitable proprietary interests. If not such a purchaser, he will forthwith hold the property on constructive trust for the beneficiaries, although no personal liability to account in respect of the property can arise until he becomes aware of the trust. He will need to produce accounts for the period of his ownership showing what he has done with the property and the income therefrom and the traceable product thereof. The court will treat the defendant as holding such property on constructive trust[17] for the claimant beneficiaries and will order the defendant to transfer it to the claimants or to trustees for the claimants if not themselves absolutely beneficially entitled. This is a direct vindication of the beneficiaries' proprietary rights. Indeed, if, while unaware of the trust the defendant used the traceable trust property (eg the proceeds of sale of a trust asset improperly transferred to the defendant) to discharge a pre-existing debt[18] of the defendant, the claimants will stand in the shoes of such creditor and have a subrogation claim for the amount of their money used to discharge the defendant's debt and unjustly enriching him at their expense. Once aware of the trust the defendant will be personally liable for dealing with the beneficiaries' property in any way other than returning it to them or to trustees for them[19].

Constructive trusts

A constructive trust of property is a trust imposed by equity in respect of property on proof of a variety of special circumstances (discussed in Articles 33 to 35) where equity considers it unconscionable for the owner of particular property to hold it purely for his own benefit. It confers a *proprietary* right on the claimant and so must be distinguished from the *personal* right afforded by Equity to a claimant against a defendant who no longer has, or who never had, any trust property in his hands, but whose conscience is affected by his dishonest involvement in a breach of trust (or other fiduciary

---

14 Equity automatically imputes a presumed intention in the absence of ousting evidence of the transferor's real intention: see E Simpson in Chapter 1 of P Birks & E Rose (supra) rightly criticising the view of Megarry V-C in *Re Vandervell's Trusts (No 2)* [1974] Ch 269. One first looks for real intentions.

15 See pp 361–367 post.

16 See Lord Upjohn in *Vandervell v IRC* [1967] 2 AC 291, 312, *pace* Lord Millett (1998) 114 LQR 399, 401.

17 Millett LJ in *Boscawen v Bajwa* [1996] 1 WLR 328, 334–335.

18 If a new debt was incurred, then the defence of change of position may well be available: see p 995 post.

19 See Art 100 post.

duty), so that Equity historically made him personally liable to account as if he had been an express trustee acting in breach of trust, so he was said to be accountable as a constructive trustee[20].

To impose a constructive trust in respect of specific property it is necessary to prove facts which fit the accepted special circumstances directly or by analogy, for the court cannot impose a constructive trust whenever justice and good conscience require it and thereby indulge idiosyncratic notions of fairness and justice[1]. Often the constructive trust is imposed to vindicate equitable proprietary rights under an express or resulting trust and to give effect to the settlor's intentions, binding the trustee as an incident of his office, that the original trust property and subsequent additions to it and the fruits thereof and property subsequently replacing such property (in the rightful or even wrongful operation of the trust) are to be held as the trust fund for the beneficiaries[2]. Sometimes, the special circumstances require parties' actual, apparent or presumed intentions to be taken into account, where it has become unconscionable for the defendant to repudiate such intentions which would be possible but for the intervention of equity[3].

Express, resulting and constructive trusts tend to be mentioned in one breath as if they are similar substantive institutions, so enhancing the legitimacy of constructive trusts which play a vital role in supporting express and resulting trusts and which developed as such vital adjunct[4]. In the case of express and resulting trusts the court compels the trustees to give effect to the beneficiaries' rights because they are express or resulting trustees. It is now apparent that a constructive trust is a vindicatory institution which equity imposes to preclude the retention or assertion of beneficial ownership of property (by persons who are express or resulting trustees or who, for special reasons, are to be treated as if they were express trustees) to the extent that such retention or assertion would be contrary to some principle of equity[5]. It is because some principle of equity compels the defendant to hold the whole or part of particular property in equity for the plaintiff that the defendant is constructive trustee thereof: it is not because the defendant is a constructive trustee that he is compelled to hold his property in equity for the plaintiff[6].

The constructive trust traditionally arises when a particular principle of equity makes it the defendant's duty to hold property or a part thereof in equity for the plaintiff so that the court when imposing the constructive trust is retrospectively vindicating a pre-existing proprietary right[7]. There is,

---

20 See Art 100 post.

1 Lord Denning's attempts to do this (condemned in 13 and 14th editions hereof) have been rejected in England and in Australia: *Grant v Edwards* [1986] Ch 638, [1986] 2 All ER 426, CA; *Burns v Burns* [1984] Ch 317, CA; *Muschinski v Dodds* (1985) 62 ALR 429; *Lloyds Bank v Rosset* [1991] 1 AC 107, [1990] 1 All ER 1111, HL; *Ivin v Blake* (1993) 67 P & CR 263, CA.

2 *Re EVTR* [1987] BCLC 646 at 651, CA; *Swain v Law Society* [1981] 3 All ER 797 at 813, CA; *A-G of Hong Kong v Reid* [1994] 1 AC 324.

3 For example, mutual wills, secret trusts, common intention constructive trusts and see *Allen v Snyder* [1977] 2 NSWLR 685 at 699 per Samuel JA and *Re Rose* [1952] Ch 499, CA and *Re Japan Leasing (Europe) plc* [2000] WTLR 301.

4 For example, transferees of trust property taking as constructive trustees unless bona fide purchasers for value without notice, trustees holding a lease renewed to themselves or profits made from their trust on constructive trust for the express trust beneficiaries.

5 See per Deane J in High Court of Australia in *Muschinski v Dodds* (1985) 62 ALR 429 at 451–453.

6 Cf *Scott on Trusts* (4th edn) para 462.

7 *Westdeutsche Landesbank v Islington London Borough Council* [1996] AC 669, 714.

however, scope for the court to impose a remedial constructive trust with prospective effect only[8], particularly to protect innocent third parties and especially where the circumstances are similar to those generating a claim on flexible equitable proprietary estoppel principles[9].

As Lord Browne-Wilkinson states[10] of an institutional constructive trust:

'[It] arises by operation of law as from the date of the circumstances which give rise to it: the function of the court is merely to declare that such trust has arisen in the past. The consequences that flow from such trust having arisen (including the possibly unfair consequences to third parties who in the interim have received trust property) are also determined by rules of law, not under a discretion. A remedial constructive trust is different. It is a judicial remedy giving rise to an enforceable equitable obligation: the extent to which it operates retrospectively to the prejudice of third parties is in the discretion of the court. Whether English law should follow the United States and Canada by adopting the remedial constructive trust will have to be decided in some future case when the point is directly in issue.'

Subsequently the Court of Appeal[11] has held that there is no scope for any remedial constructive trust to be imposed when the defendant is insolvent because such imposition is not available to enable the court to oust the statutory insolvency rules.

Constructive and resulting trusts have often been insufficiently distinguished by judges[12] dealing with family homes since both are exempt from written formalities. There is a danger that confusion of the requirements for the two types of trust may follow from a confusion of the two[13]. A significant practical distinction where the legal owner is insolvent is that a purchaser's resulting trust share proportionate to her contribution is safe from being upset under s 339 of the Insolvency Act 1986 unlike the gift element under a constructive trust[14].

ARTICLE 4

Definitions of simple and special trusts or bare and active trusts

Trusts are divided into simple and special trusts according to the nature of the duty imposed on the trustee:
(1) a simple trust is a trust in which the trustee is a mere repository of the trust property, with no active management duties to perform. Such a trustee is called a passive or, more frequently, a bare trustee;

---

8 *Westdeutsche Landesbank v Islington London Borough Council* [1996] AC 669, 714; *Metall und Ruhstoff AG v Donaldson Lufkin & Jenrette Inc* [1990] 1 QB 391 at 479; *Muschinsti v Dodds* (1985) 160 CLR 583 (Aus HC); *Atlas Cabinets v National Trust Co* (1990) 68 DLR (4th) 161 at 173–174; P. Ferguson (1993) 109 LQR 114; D J Hayton (1993) 109 LQR 485.

9 See pp 248–254, post. However under the Land Registration Act 2002, s 116, proprietary estoppel interests (and mere equities) are to take effect from the time the equity arose as an interest capable of binding successors in title.

10 *Westdeutsche Landesbank v Islington London Borough Council* [1996] AC 669 at 714.

11 *Re Polly Peck International plc (No 2)* [1998] 3 All ER 812, 827, 831.

12 For example, Lord Denning in *Hussey v Palmer* [1972] 1 WLR 1286 at 1289, CA: 'This [question of resulting or constructive trust] is more a matter of words than anything else. The two run together.'

13 For example, *Heseltine v Heseltine* [1971] 1 All ER 952, [1971] 1 WLR 342, CA.

14 *Re Densham (a bankrupt)* [1975] 3 All ER 726, [1975] 1 WLR 1519 dealing with its predecessor, Bankruptcy Act 1914, s 42.

(2) a special trust is a trust in which a trustee is appointed to carry out some scheme particularly pointed out by the settlor, and is called upon to exert himself actively in the execution of the settlor's intention. The trustee of a special trust is called an active trustee.

Example of a simple trust

A devised property to B in trust for C, a person who is of full age and capacity. Here the trust is a simple trust, as the only duty which B has to perform is to convey the legal estate to C, or C's nominee if so requested; and B is a passive or bare trustee[15]. His function is to hold the property to convey it to C or to whom C might direct. If X a transferee of such property from B knows (or suspects but deliberately abstains from inquiry lest the truth be discovered) that B is a bare trustee he will not acquire a good title unless C authorised the transfer[16]. B is not independent of C but neither is he a mere cypher[17] so that B cannot be compelled by C to grant a lease or create other obligations binding B. Indeed in the case of a trust of land, B has power to convey the land to C (if of full age and capacity) even if C had not required this[18], although C would prevent this by directing B to convey the land to X for C.

Where the term 'bare trust' is used in a statutory context its meaning will depend on such context and any statutory definition, eg under the Trustee Act 2000 where all the beneficiaries together (taking account not just of concurrent interests but also successive interests) are of full age and capacity[19]. A custodian trustee is not a bare trustee[20].

Example of a special trust

But, if the trust had been during C's life to collect the rents and profits, and to pay thereout the cost of repairs and insurance, and to pay the residue of such rents and profits to C during his life, and after C's death to hold the property in trust for D, the trust would have been a special trust during the life of C, and B would have been an active trustee, since during that period he would have had active duties to perform. Upon C's death, however, the trust would have become a simple trust, and B a bare trustee, inasmuch as the active duties originally attached to the trustee's office would have lapsed on the death of C, and the only duty remaining would have been to convey the legal estate to D or at his direction and to account to D for B's stewardship of the property. It should perhaps be noted here that the distinction sometimes made by the layman whereby one of a body of trustees is regarded as the active or managing trustee, while the others take no part in the management

15 *Christie v Ovington* (1875) 1 Ch D 279; *Re Cunningham and Frayling* [1891] 2 Ch 567. Cf *Morgan v Swansea Urban Sanitary Authority* (1878) 9 Ch D 582; *Re Blandy Jenkins Estate* [1917] 1 Ch 46.
16 *MacMillan Inc v Bishopsgate Investment Trust* (unreported decision of Millett J delivered in redacted form, 10 December 1993); also see *Kronheim v Johnson* (1877) 7 Ch D 60. If D holds on trust for E a lease by D to E is a nullity: *Ingram v IRC* [1995] STC 564.
17 *Ingram v IRC* [1997] 4 All ER 395 at 424, approved by the House of Lords in [2000] 1 AC 293, 305, 310.
18 Trusts of Land and Appointment of Trustees Act 1996, s 6(2).
19 Trustee Act 2000, s 19(3). In a similar situation where all the beneficiaries have *Saunders v Vautier* rights (see Art 70 post) the Trusts of Land and Appointment of Trustees Act 1996, s 19 enables them to direct the trustees to retire and convey the trust fund to a new trustee or trustees as if only a bare trust existed.
20 *IRC v Silverts* [1951] Ch 521, CA.

of the trust, has no foundation in law, so far at any rate as the question of liability is concerned.

Where a trustee holds property for a beneficiary or beneficiaries absolutely entitled to call for the property to be transferred to them or at their direction under the rule in *Saunders v Vautier*[1], but until such call has powers and discretions to exercise[2], then he will be an active trustee[3] and not an agent or nominee or bare trustee. However, usage of the term 'bare trustee' may extend in context to trusts where beneficiaries are absolutely entitled under the rule in *Saunders v Vautier*[4], so the property is held to their order.

Sham trusts

One must note that a trust which appears on its face to be an active trust with sundry beneficiaries may be held to be a sham[5], so that, despite the appearance of creating equitable rights in others, the equitable beneficial ownership is intended to remain with the settlor and the agreed[6] real duty of the trustee is only to manage and distribute the property as the settlor directs. The subsequent conduct of the parties is admissible evidence that they were parties to the sham[7].

The key to the sham is that the persons appearing to be beneficiaries on the face of the trust instrument are not intended to have any rights enforceable against the trustees[8] even though on the face of it they appear to have such rights. The substance of the matter is that the settlor has all the rights, even if it appears that it is the beneficiaries who have all the rights. However, to keep a nervous settlor happy and to protect nervous trustees where beneficiaries appear to have been given significant interests, there may be inserted a term in the trust instrument which is inconsistent with the specified beneficiaries having any rights (eg a clause stating that during the

---

1 (1841) 4 Beav 115.
2 *Re Brockbank* [1948] Ch 206, [1948] 1 All ER 287.
3 *Booth v Ellard* [1980] 3 All ER 569, [1980] 1 WLR 1443, CA. A, B and C will be regarded as 'absolutely entitled against the trustees' for Capital Gains Tax purposes if they are concurrently entitled but not if they are together successively entitled with *Saunders v Vautier* rights.
4 Further see *Herdegen v Federal Comr of Taxation* (1988) 84 ALR 271 at 282; *Blue Resources Ltd v Law Society of Upper Canada* (1995) 120 DLR (4th) 751 and Trustee Act 2000, s 19(3).
5 *Rahman v Chase Bank (CI) Trust Co Ltd Jersey Royal Court* [1991] JLR 103; *Midland Bank plc v Wyatt* [1994] EGCS 113; *Burns v Turnbull* 294 NY 889 (1945); *R v Dimsey* [2000] QB 744, 772–773, [1999] STC 846, 870–871, CA. On sham documents generally see *Stone v Hitch* [2001] EWCA Civ 63, [2001] STC 214. For a Zurich court holding a Guernsey trust to be a sham see, *O-D Bank v Bankrupt Estate of WKR* (1999) ZR 98 No 52 pp 225 et seq discussed [2000] JTCP 141–158.
6 Where the settlor declares himself trustee his intention is crucial, but trustees who knowingly become trustees receiving trust assets from the settlor need to agree to receiving trust assets and acting as trustee of a true trust or a sham trust. If a settlor's poor English led him to believe that in executing the trustee's discretionary trust instrument the trust fund was held to his order like a glorified bank account, but the trustee intended to operate a proper trust for beneficiaries, then the settlor's intention should be honoured, although if regarded as creating a proper trust by mistake he could, anyhow, set it aside for mistake: *Gibbon v Mitchell* [1990] 3 All ER 338.
7 *AG Securities v Vaughan* [1990] 1 AC 417; *Midland Bank plc v Wyatt* [1995] 1 FLR 697 (declaration of trust of their house by H and W in favour of W and their children held a sham, W being a party to the sham when she 'merely went along with the "shammer" neither knowing or caring about what she was signing'.
8 As Millett LJ stated in *Armitage v Nurse* [1998] Ch 241 at 253, 'If the beneficiaries have no rights enforceable against the trustees there are no trusts'.

settlor's[9] lifetime, the trustees in no circumstances are under any duty to account to the 'beneficiaries' and are always to be exempt from any liabilities howsoever arising to such 'beneficiaries'). The intentional insertion of such a specific clause should lead the court to give effect to the clause by holding that the whole equitable interest remains in the settlor, although in exceptional circumstances, it would be open to the court to disregard such a clause as repugnant to, or inconsistent with, a true trust intended by the settlor[10].

Close attention must be paid to the terms of a trust. Thus, where S transfers property to trustees on trust in S's lifetime to pay the income or capital to him or at his direction and, after his death, to hold the capital equally for his children or for such persons in such shares as S may designate in signed writing, the trustees will be holding the property to S's order, the full equitable interest remaining in him, with the purported disposition after his death being testamentary[11] and void if not complying with the Wills Act 1837, while if complying with the Wills Act it might be accidentally revoked by a subsequent will. By way of contrast, S would have formally divested himself of his equitable ownership if he had settled his property on trusts for others but had reserved a general power of appointment or a power of revocation[12]: the trustees would not hold such property to the order of S until he ordered it in the exercise of his reserved powers. The presence of such powers, however, will normally have very adverse tax consequences and may expose the trust assets to claims of a deceased settlor's dependants or forced heirs.

Furthermore, the critical distinction[13] between a trustee holding to the order of the settlor and a trustee holding to the order of the settlor only if the settlor orders it is a fine one, which a trustee can easily overlook by treating itself as bound to do what the settlor directs, even though he has not exercised his power of appointment or revocation to recover full equitable ownership of the settled property. Where the settlor does wish to exercise much significant influence over the conduct of the trustee, an informal arrangement with the trustee may leave the trust wide open to allegations of being a sham. It is better for the settlor to reserve specific powers of direction or veto so that the trustee can explain its actions by reference to these powers

---

9 If the beneficiaries are only intended to have rights arising on the settlor's death then the disposition on death of such rights is testamentary, requiring compliance with the Wills Act formalities: cf *Re Pfrimmer's Estate* [1936] 2 DLR 400; *Kauter v Hilton* (1953) 90 CLR 86 at 100; *Anderson v Patton* [1948] 2 DLR 202; *Baird v Baird* [1990] 2 AC 548, PC; *Tampson v Browne* (1835) My & K 32 at 35–36.

10 Indeed, such term could be void as an attempt to oust the jurisdiction of the courts, *Jones v Shipping Federation of British Columbia* (1963) 37 DLR (2d) 273.

11 Under the American Uniform Trust Code, ss 603, 604 and 608 such a trust, if revocable, is characterised as a lifetime, not a testamentary disposition, as is the case under the Bahamian Trustee Act 1998, s 3(2)(i) even if the trust is irrevocable, but the English forum will use its own characterisation rules to treat such trusts as testamentary, so as to create a resulting trust of English assets as part of the settlor's estate at death which will need to have been disposed of in a formally valid will.

12 *Young v Sealey* [1949] Ch 278 at 284, 294; *Kauter v Hilton* (1953) 90 CLR 86, 98–99, 100–101; *Scott on Trusts* (4th edn) Vol 1A pp 125–129, 141–142. In form this is a proper trust but in substance it might be run as a sham: one indicator may be nominal fees paid to the trustee of a very valuable trust fund; another indicator might be if the trustee were removable at the whim of someone holding a personal power to replace the trustee, particularly if that someone were the settlor, but there may be good reason for an independent protector to have such a personal power in order to avoid the problems that a disgruntled removed trustee could raise if the power were fiduciary as in *Von Knierem v Bermuda Trust Co* (1994) 1 Butts OCM 116.

13 Accepted by IRC in interpreting Taxation of Chargeable Gains Act 1992, ss 60(2), 70.

in a true trust. In case trusts that are true trusts in form are subsequently attacked as sham trusts in substance it will be necessary to have plenty of written evidence documenting either the exercise by the settlor or a protector of specific powers reserved in the trust instrument or independent conscious discretions exercised by the trustee: unless such written evidence of the trustee's discretion is established by oral cross-examination to be a sham (perhaps amounting to conspiracy to defraud the Revenue) the trust will then be proved a true trust. It is purely a question of fact whether or not a trust is in substance a sham.

The sham doctrine is a general one capable of applying to all transactions[14], eg not just the creation of a trust but an appointment under a special power sub-settling trust assets (as where property is settled on accumulation trusts for 21 years for the settlor's five children equally if alive at the end of the 21 years but with power to appoint income or capital revocably or irrevocably to the settlor's children or grandchildren and after 20 years 363 days the trust assets are revocably re-settled in five stirpital shares on the settlor's grandchildren, but with power to appoint all or part of the one fifth shares to a relevant child, in circumstances where a child alleges the substance was that the trustees were to hold to the order of the children, so that he is entitled to one fifth of the trust assets when the trustees break the alleged agreement to let him have his fifth share whenever he wants it).

Letters of wishes

Where the settlor has provided a letter of wishes or let the trustees make a memorandum of his wishes (a factual distinction which should make no legal difference when both are utilised to indicate the settlor's intention), the trustees must be careful to provide documentation revealing that they consciously exercised an independent discretion when making decisions, naturally taking serious account of the settlor's wishes but appreciating that the ultimate decision was theirs. For the trustees to give effect exactly to the settlor's wishes is very dangerous because it lays them wide open to the charge that either the trust deed on its own is a sham, because the real trust terms incorporate the legally binding letter of wishes, not just a legally *significant* document, or the trustees have committed a breach of trust in automatically following the settlor's *legally significant* (but not legally binding) wishes without consciously exercising an independent discretion. To prevent them from being legally binding, letters of wishes should be written at a distinctly different date from that of creation of the trust or a transfer of substantial assets to the trustees, should be expressed to have no legally binding force and the wishes should not be expressed in too precise or forceful a manner. If the letter is expressed to be confidential and not to be revealed to the beneficiaries then, on current authority, a beneficiary has no absolute right to see the letter[15]. However, if somehow (eg by discovering a copy of a draft letter of wishes in the deceased settlor's safe and comparing its terms with what the trustees have done) the beneficiary establishes a prima

---

14 *Chase Manhattan Equities Ltd v Goodman* [1991] BCLC 897; *Snook v London and West Riding Investments Ltd* [1967] 2 QB 786, [1967] 1 All ER 518, CA; *Antoniades v Villiers* [1990] 1 AC 417, [1988] 3 All ER 1058, HL; *Atlas Maritime Co SA v Avalon Maritime Ltd* [1991] 4 All ER 769 at 779, CA.

15 *Hartigan Nominees Pty Ltd v Rydge* (1992) 29 NSWLR 405, CA; *Re Rabbaiotti's Settlement* [2000] WTLR 953; see p 680 post.

facie case either that the trust terms should include the letter as incorporated into the trust instrument[16] or that the trustees have not exercised a dispositive power 'in a responsible manner according to its purpose'[17] but have acted 'for reasons which are irrational perverse or irrelevant to any sensible expectation of the settlor'[18] then he may bring a legal action against the trustees and thereby take advantage of rules of civil procedure to obtain disclosure of the letter of wishes. However, so long as the trustees do take into account the legally significant letter of wishes the decision is theirs, so that they can properly decide to act contrary to the settlor's wishes taking account of all the relevant circumstances[19].

Of course, if the trustees act contrary to such letter of wishes it will place them on the defensive if they are attacked by a beneficiary who has a copy of the letter. As a result, it seems, in principle, that a settlor should be able to create a letter of wishes intended only to be of *moral* significance and not legal significance. Thus, the following letter should be taken at its face value (unless the court is prepared to find that it should be treated as a mere pretence[20]):

> 'This letter is not to be regarded as indicating in a legally significant way the purposes for which the powers in my trust deed have been conferred on my trustees because I do not want them to have any extra legal obligations placed upon them by this letter so as to have to go out of their way to defend their conduct. I believe the imposition of such extra legal obligations would cause more difficulties than benefits to accrue, creating greater cost burdens and proving likely to upset relationships between my beneficiaries. Thus, my trustees are only to be under a moral obligation to take into account the following wishes of mine and shall not be accountable before the courts in relation to taking into account or failing to take into account such wishes. Indeed, they are not legally obliged to pass this letter on to successor trustees although I would hope they would consider themselves morally bound to do so.'

Available assets of settlor scenario

Where there is not a trust for the settlor absolutely as a matter of form or substance, but the settlor is the primary beneficiary to whom trust funds can be distributed, perhaps without the need to consider the interests of other beneficiaries, so that in practice there is no real likelihood of the independent trustee turning down a request for funds from the settlor, then the trust funds can be regarded as available assets of the settlor where claims of divorcing spouses or creditors are concerned. Thus, a spouse may have a substantial financial order made against her in the belief the trustees will put

---

16 It may be that pleading the letter of wishes is a legally binding part of the settlor's trust instrument will suffice on its own, a beneficiary being entitled to see the trust instrument (even if expressed to be confidential): see *Chase Manhattan Equities Ltd v Goodman* [1991] BCLC 897 at 923.

17 *Re Hay's Settlement Trust* [1981] 3 All ER 786 at 792.

18 *Re Manisty's Settlements* [1973] 2 All ER 1203 at 1210.

19 *Bank of Nova Scotia Trust (Bahamas) Ltd v Borletta* (11 March 1985, Bahamas Supreme Court unreported) discussed [1994] 1 JIP 35–38.

20 *Aslan v Murphy* [1989] 3 All ER 130, 133; *Fitzwilliam v IRC* [1990] STC 65, 118; *Bankway Properties v Dunsford* [2001] EWCA Civ 528, [2001] 1 WLR 1369; *Hitch v Stone* [2001] EWCA Civ 63, [2001] STC 214.

her in funds to relieve her of financial embarrassment[1], while a freezing order[2] may be made against the trustees so that the trust fund remains available in the jurisdiction to enable the trustees to put the settlor in funds to prevent him from being bankrupted or otherwise put in financial difficulties by a creditor's judgment debt.

Furthermore, in a case where the trust structure cannot be entirely disregarded as a sham where the whole beneficial interest remains in the settlor, but where the settlor is a beneficiary or object of a power under the trust or another trust to whom assets can be transferred, and, in reality, the trustee is not an independent trustee but will do the settlor's bidding when directed by the settlor so as to distribute the trust fund for the benefit of the settlor, rather than any other beneficiary or object of a power, a disclosure or freezing order in relation to the trust assets can be made in proceedings against the settlor personally, with a view to making such assets available to satisfy the claimant's claim[3]. The position is similar to that where the settlor has reserved a power of revocation or of appointment in his own favour.

ARTICLE 5

Definitions of fixed and discretionary trusts

Trusts are divided into fixed and discretionary trusts according to the nature of the beneficial interests under the trusts:

(1) a fixed trust is a trust in which a beneficiary has a current fixed entitlement to an ascertainable part of the net income, if any, of the trust fund after deduction of sums paid by the trustees in the exercise of their *administrative* powers of management: the beneficiary has an interest in possession under the trust;

(2) a discretionary trust is a trust in which a beneficiary has no such absolute current right to direct the trustees to pay him an ascertainable part of the net income. Typically, this is the case where a beneficiary will receive income only if the trustees positively decide to carry out their duty to distribute income by favouring him rather than another member of the class of potential beneficiaries. There is also the 'atypical' case where a beneficiary must receive the income unless the trustees exercise *distributive* powers to divert

---

1 *Browne v Browne* [1989] 1 FLR 291, CA; and also see *Thomas v Thomas* [1996] 2 FCR 544, CA and pair of Australian cases *Re Marriage of Goodwin* (1990) 14 Fam LR 801; *Re Marriage of Davidson* (1990) 14 Fam LR 817.

2 *Private Trust Corpn v Grupo Torras SA* (1997/98) 1 OFLR 443 (CA, Bahamas), but if it appears that the trust fund represented the settlor's own assets (rather than fraudulently obtained assets) and that payment out of the whole fund to the settlor would only satisfy a tiny percentage of his huge debts, so that the payment would be of no assistance in avoiding bankruptcy and would deprive the other beneficiaries of all hope of benefiting, then the trustees are entitled to refuse to make any payment to the settlor (*Abacus (CI) Ltd v Al Sabah* (2001) 3 ITELR 467), so that no freezing order should be made.

3 *Grupo Torras v Fahad* [1995] 1 Lloyd's Rep 374. The court may look through a company or a trust or an *anstalt*: *Trustor AB v Smallbone (No 2)* [2001] 1 WLR 1177 (interposed *anstalt* ignored). For comparable evidence to show directors subject to a shadow director's control, like trustees subject to the settlor's control, see *Secretary of State for Trade and Industry v Deverell* [2001] Ch 340, CA.

the income elsewhere (eg under a power to appoint income, within six months of receiving it, to charity) or to withhold it (eg a power to accumulate income where there is no certainty that accumulations will ultimately pass to the beneficiary or his personal representatives): the discretion-conferring distributive or re-distributive powers prevent an interest in possession arising (eg where B is a life tenant subject to distributive powers)[4]. A discretionary trust will be exhaustive where all income *must* be distributed in the trustees' discretion amongst the class of beneficiaries: it will be non-exhaustive where all income must be distributed in the trustees' discretion amongst the class of beneficiaries *except* to the extent that income may be otherwise dealt with pursuant to a power in that behalf, eg a power of accumulation or a power to pay income to charity[5].

Significance

The inheritance tax treatment of discretionary trusts is radically different from the treatment of fixed trusts[6]. Significant capital gains tax[7] and income tax[8] differences also exist. The test for certainty of beneficiaries for the validity of a trust differs according to whether the trust is a fixed trust or an 'atypical' discretionary trust on the one hand or a 'typical' discretionary trust on the other hand[9].

Illustrations of fixed and discretionary trusts

A trust is a fixed trust where property (whether or not income-producing) has been settled on an adult, A, for life or for an entailed interest or on A until he attains the age of 50. It matters not that the trust is revocable or the trustees have power to appoint capital elsewhere so that thenceforth A's interest in possession will have ceased wholly or partly. However, a discretion or a power which can be exercised after income arises so as to withhold it from A prevents A having an interest in possession at all. A power to accumulate income is treated as a power to withhold unless any accumulations must be held for the otherwise entitled beneficiary or his personal representatives[10].

A trust is a discretionary trust in the obvious case where property is given to

---

4 *Gartside v IRC* [1968] AC 553, [1968] 1 All ER 121, HL; *Pearson v IRC* [1981] AC 753, [1980] 2 All ER 479, HL: *Re Trafford's Settlement* [1985] Ch 32, [1984] 1 All ER 1108 (present sole object of class of beneficiaries that was open and not closed has no interest in possession since another class member might come into existence before a reasonable time for the distribution of accrued income had elapsed); *Miller v IRC* [1987] STC 108.
5 *Sainsbury v IRC* [1970] Ch 712, [1969] 3 All ER 919.
6 Inheritance Tax Act 1984, ss 49–84.
7 Taxation of Chargeable Gains Act 1992, ss 71, 72; where a life interest in possession is a narrower concept than an interest in possession.
8 Finance Act 1973, ss 16, 17 replaced by Income and Corporation Taxes Act 1988, ss 686, 687 as amended; *Corbett v IRC* [1938] 1 KB 567 at 577; *Baker v Archer-Shee* [1927] AC 844; *IRC v Miller* [1930] AC 222; *Hamilton Russell's Executors v IRC* (1943) 25 TC 200; *IRC v Berrill* [1982] 1 All ER 867, [1981] 1 WLR 1449.
9 *McPhail v Doulton* [1971] AC 424, HL.
10 Revenue Press Notice [1976] BTR 418, Foster's Inheritance Tax Division W.

trustees to distribute the income therefrom amongst such of A's children, grandchildren, nephews, nieces, great-nephews and great-nieces as the trustees see fit. Less obviously there is a discretionary trust where property is settled on a minor, M, for life or on M for an entailed interest where Trustee Act 1925, s 31, is not ousted: the effect of s 31 is to convert M's apparently vested interest into a contingent interest for it imposes a trust to accumulate income during M's minority, but with power to apply income for M's maintenance, education or benefit, and it provides that if M does not attain 18 years or marry thereunder the accumulations are not to pass to M's personal representatives but, instead, are to pass as an accretion to the capital to the person entitled to capital[11].

Administrative powers and dispositive or distributive powers

An administrative power is, but a dispositive or distributive power is not, compatible with a beneficiary having an interest in possession under a fixed trust. 'The line between [them] may be difficult to draw but that does not mean that there is not a valid distinction ... A life tenant has an interest in possession but his interest only extends to the net income of the property after deduction from the gross income of expenses etc properly incurred in the management of the trust by the trustees in the exercise of their powers. A dispositive power is a power to dispose of the net income.'[12] There is a distinction 'properly to be drawn between powers directed to the preservation of the trust estate for the benefit of life tenant and remaindermen alike, and a discretionary power the exercise of which is intended to have an effect on the actual benefits which the beneficiaries as such become entitled to receive[13].

A power which might affect the destination of net income after it has arisen (eg a power to accumulate income or to divert it for the benefit of other beneficiaries) is a dispositive power. What then is the status of the common power enabling the trustees 'to apply any income of the Trust Fund in or towards the payment or discharge of any duties, taxes, costs, charges, fees or other outgoings which but for the provisions of this clause would be payable out of or charged upon the capital of the Trust Fund'? It empowers 'taking income away from the income beneficiaries and bestowing it on the capital beneficiaries, so that capital is augmented'[14], so that prima facie it seems a dispositive power, though in obiter dicta Viscount Dilhorne has asserted that it was an administrative power in context[15]. This may be justified on the basis that the clause is merely an ancillary power intended to

---

11 Trustee Act 1925, s 31(2)(ii); *Stanley v IRC* [1944] KB 255, [1944] 1 All ER 230; *Cornwell v Barry* (1955) 36 TC 268. Exceptionally, s 31(4) provides that in the case of a vested annuity accumulations made during the annuitant's minority are, in any event, to be held upon trust for the annuitant or his personal representatives absolutely. Freehold land settled on a minor absolutely is treated as entailed if the minor dies without attaining 18 years or marrying thereunder: Administration of Estates Act 1925, s 51(3).

12 *Pearson v IRC* [1981] AC 753 at 774–775 per Viscount Dilhorne, HL.

13 *Pearson v IRC* [1981] AC 753 at 785 per Lord Keith. In *Miller v IRC* [1987] STC 108 the Court of Session held that a power to make a payment out of income in order to meet the depreciation of capital value was an administrative power.

14 *Carver v Duncan (Inspector of Taxes)* [1985] AC 1082 at 1122, [1985] 2 All ER 645 at 654, HL, per Lord Templeman.

15 *Pearson v IRC* [1981] AC 753 at 775. See also *IRC v Lloyd's Private Banking* [1998] STC 559. Further see J Kessler *Drafting Trusts and Will Trusts* (6th edn, 2002), Chapter 18.

emphasise the flexibility of trustees' powers to utilise income or capital (especially if mixed in one bank account) as is most convenient for dealing with pressing liabilities from time to time without affecting the trustees' duty overall to maintain a fair balance between life tenant and remaindermen in apportioning or allocating expenditure[16].

ARTICLE 6

Definitions of executed and executory trusts

Express trusts when created are either executed or executory:
(1) an executed trust is one where the trust property is vested in trustees or personal representatives and the particular interests taken by the beneficiaries are exactly delimited[17]. The settlor has done everything within his inter vivos or testamentary powers to give effect to specific trusts;
(2) an executory trust is one where the trust property is vested in trustees or personal representatives but the interests to be taken by the beneficiaries remain to be delimited in some subsequent instrument pursuant to the settlor's clear general intention or where the property intended to be subjected to trusts is the subject of an enforceable agreement to create a trust whether for delimited beneficiaries or beneficiaries that remain to be delimited[18].

Significance

The language of executed trusts is interpreted in a strict technical fashion whilst the language of executory trusts is interpreted in a liberal untechnical fashion[19]. A trust will be executed where the settlor has been his own conveyancer or draftsman and executory where he has contemplated, expressly or by necessary implication, the execution of some further instrument providing detailed clauses to implement his general intentions[20]. However, even an executory trust will fail if its language is insufficiently clear to indicate generally the trusts intended by the settlor, eg where a testator left a share of residue to trustees 'for the formation of a superannuation bonus fund for the employees' of a named company[1].

The abolition or simplification of technicalities involving words of limitation has made the difference between executed and executory trusts much less significant since the Law of Property Act 1925, ss 60, 130, 131 and since the abolition of entails in 1996[2].

---

16 Further see Foster's Inheritance Tax E1.43.
17 *Stanley v Lennard* (1758) 1 Eden 87; *Egerton v Earl Brownlow* (1853) 4 HL Cas 1 at 210.
18 *Sackville-West v Viscount Holmesdale* (1870) LR 4 HL 543; *Papillon v Voice* (1728) 2 P Wms 471. This definition was applied in *Davis v Richards and Wallington Industries Ltd* [1991] 2 All ER 563 at 588.
19 *Re Bostock's Settlement* [1921] 2 Ch 469 but cf *Re Arden* [1935] Ch 326; *Lord Glenorchy v Bosville* (1733) Cas temp Talb 3.
20 *Egerton v Earl Brownlow* (1853) 4 HL Cas 1.
1 *Re Flavel's Will Trusts* [1969] 2 All ER 232, [1969] 1 WLR 444; *Magrath v Morehead* (1871) LR 12 Eq 491.
2 Trusts of Land and Appointment of Trustees Act 1996, Sch 1, para 5.

The ramifications of tax law are now such that executory trusts are rare for it is normally better to specify executed trusts at the outset, having then fully considered all the tax implications.

Marriage articles, wills and interim pension trusts

Executory trusts are always found in marriage articles[3], otherwise they are sometimes found in wills (usually home-made), though it is possible to find them in inter vivos dispositions other than marriage articles[4], such as in company's interim pension deeds[5], or in trustees transferring assets to non-resident trustees to declare trusts thereof to substantially the same effect as the original trusts. Most trusts created in professionally drafted wills are executed trusts where the beneficial interests are exactly specified, though the personal representatives of the testator may subsequently have to vest the trust property in themselves qua trustees or in other trustees. However, will trusts are executory, for example, where a testator directs that on B's marriage a strict settlement of Blackacre shall be made in B's favour as counsel shall advise[6] (so taking effect after 1996 as a trust of land[7]) or where a testator in his home-made will gives 'All my property in trust for my wife and children' when it is up to the court to decide whether the wife was meant to have a life interest or an absolute interest, whether as joint tenant or tenant in common. However under s 22 of the Administration of Justice Act 1982, 'Except where a contrary intention is shown it shall be presumed that if a testator devises or bequeaths property to his spouse in terms which in themselves would give an absolute interest to the spouse but by the same instrument purports to give his issue an interest in the same property, the gift to the spouse is absolute notwithstanding the purported gift to the issue.'

Relationship to completely and incompletely constituted trusts

All inter vivos executed trusts are completely constituted trusts where the trust property has been effectively vested in trustees by the settlor. However, if the settlor gratuitously declares himself a trustee of 1,000 specific shares in a private company, part of a larger shareholding held by him, in which he is to retain the remaining beneficial interest, or of £10,000 in a building society account containing a larger sum, in which he is also to retain the remaining beneficial interest, then no trust, capable of being an executed trust, should exist until the relevant property intended to be subject to trusts has been separated from the settlor's property and so set aside on the relevant trusts[8]. In contrast, testamentary trusts to similar effect will be executed trusts, the deceased inevitably having divested himself of all beneficial interest so that

---

3 There is a strong presumption to favour children and so restrict a wife's interest to a life interest if a remainder is given for the 'wife and children' *Rossiter v Rossiter* (1863) 14 I Ch R 247.

4 *Mayn v Mayn* (1867) LR 5 Eq 150. A settlor's executory trusts may be contained in correspondence with a trustee in an off-shore trust jurisdiction which is to execute a trust deed on the face of which it appears as settlor.

5 *Davis v Richards and Wallington Industries Ltd* [1991] 2 All ER 563, [1990] 1 WLR 1511.

6 Cf *Re Spicer* (1901) 84 LT 195; *Re Potter's Will Trusts* [1944] Ch 70, [1943] 2 All ER 805; *Shelley v Shelley* (1868) LR 6 Eq 540 at 549.

7 Trusts of Land and Appointment of Trustees Act 1996, s 2.

8 *Re Goldcorp Exchange Ltd* [1995] 1 AC 74, [1994] 2 All ER 806; p 78, post indicating that *Hunter v Moss* [1994] 3 All ER 215, [1994] 1 WLR 452, CA was incorrectly decided.

the part not passing to the specific beneficiary will pass to the residuary legatee (or, if none, to the next of kin).

Testamentary trusts, whether executed or executory, are not completely constituted until the personal representatives vest the intended trust property in trustees in due course of administration, the beneficiaries having originally an equitable chose in action which only matures into a full equitable interest under a trust when the personal representatives assent to the property vesting in trustees or themselves qua trustees[9].

An executory inter vivos trust requires a completely constituted trust of the relevant property or the property in question (though not yet vested in trustees) to be the subject of an enforceable agreement.

---

9 *Stamp Duties Comr (Queensland) v Livingston* [1965] AC 694, [1964] 3 All ER 692; *Marshall v Kerr* [1995] 1 AC 148, [1994] 3 All ER 106, HL; Inheritance Tax Act 1984, ss 83, 91.

DIVISION TWO

Express or declared trusts

Chapter
1 Introduction   71
2 Matters essential to the prima facie validity of an express trust   73
3 Validity of declared trusts in relation to latent matters   268
4 The interpretation of executory trusts   299

CHAPTER 1

Introduction

ARTICLE 7

Analysis of an express or declared trust

(1) In order that an express trust may be prima facie binding on the
settlor the following conditions are essential.

(a) The settlor must have used language from which the court finds,
as a fact, an intention to create a trust of ascertainable property in
favour of ascertainable persons whose ability to enforce the trust
underpins the binding obligation inherent in the trust concept[1].
The test for ascertaining such persons is stricter for fixed trusts
than for discretionary trusts[2]. If either the property or the beneficiaries cannot be ascertained with certainty, there can be no trust
for the beneficiaries, the settlor remaining beneficial owner of the
property[3]. If the trust is for abstract, impersonal purposes rather
than for persons, whether individual or corporate, it will be void[4]
unless the purposes are exclusively charitable[5] (or perhaps[6], there
is an expressly designated enforcer of certain workable non-
charitable purposes) except for certain anomalous cases relating
to the maintenance of animals, tombs etc[7]. Even a trust for persons
will be void if it is administratively unworkable or capricious[8].

(b) If the trust be voluntary the intention to create the trust must have
been implemented by way of completely constituting the trust[9] (ie
the settlor's interest in the property must have been transferred to
a trustee or the settlor must have declared himself trustee of
property specifically appropriated for the beneficiaries) or the
settlor must have died leaving a will or codicil creating trusts of his
property. Otherwise, the intended trust is binding only where the

1 Article 8, post.
2 See pp 84–85, post.
3 See pp 82–83, post.
4 See pp 110–114, post.
5 See pp 82, 105 and 107, post.
6 See pp 114–116, post.
7 See pp 118–123, post.
8 See pp 91 and 123, post.
9 See Article 9, post.

settlor has agreed to create it by a contract based on valuable consideration (which includes marriage), in which case the court acts on the maxim that equity considers that to be done which ought to be done.

(c) The trust property must be of such a nature as to be capable of being settled[10].

(d) The object of the trust must be lawful[11] so that the trust must satisfy the rules against remoteness, accumulations and inalienability as well as not be illegal, immoral etc.

(e) The settlor must have complied with any requisite formalities for completely constituting the trust[12].

These essentials for prima facie validity are examined at length in Chapter 2.

(2) But a trust, prima facie valid, may yet be impeachable:

(a) by the settlor or his successors in title, by reason of his incapacity[13]; or the incapacity of the beneficiaries[14]; or by reason of some mistake made by, or fraud practised on, the settlor, as its creation[15]; or

(b) by the settlor's creditors, by reason of it having been made with an intention to put assets beyond their reach[16]; or because it infringes sections 339 and 340 of the Insolvency Act 1986[17]; or

(c) by future purchasers of the property from the settlor without notice of the trust, where the trust property is land, and the trust was intended by the settlor to defeat the claims of future purchasers[18];

(d) by a settlor's dependants if the trust were designed to defeat their claims under the Matrimonial Causes Act 1973 or the Inheritance (Provision for Family and Dependants) Act 1975[19].

(e) under specific ad hoc legislation preventing criminals from profiting from their crimes[20].

These latent flaws are considered in Chapter 3.

(3) Lastly, where the trust is executory[1] a very liberal construction is given to the language, so as to give effect to the manifest intentions of the settlor[2].

These questions of construction are dealt with in Chapter 4.

---

10 See Article 10, post.
11 Article 11, post.
12 Article 12, post.
13 Article 13, post.
14 Article 14, post.
15 Article 15, post.
16 Article 16, post.
17 Article 17, post.
18 Article 18, post.
19 Article 19, post.
20 See pp 297–298, post.
 1 See Article 6, ante.
 2 Articles 20–27, post.

CHAPTER 2

Matters essential to the prima facie validity of an express trust

Article
8   Language sufficient to create a trust for persons   74
9   The constitution of trusts   144
10 What property is capable of being made the subject of a trust   182
11 The legality of the expressed object of the trust   189
12 Necessity or otherwise of writing and signature   232

ARTICLE 8

Language sufficient to create a trust for persons

(1) No technical expressions are necessary for the creation of an express trust[1]. It is sufficient if the settlor evinces with reasonable certainty:

(a) an intent to create a trust;

(b) the trust property[2];

(c) the persons (individual or corporate) intended to be beneficiaries; and

(d) the purpose of the trust so that the trust is administratively workable and not capricious;

providing always that for there to be a valid, and therefore enforceable, trust the trust must be intended to be directly or indirectly for the benefit of persons (individual or corporate) so that some person has locus standi to enforce the trust unless the trust is for charitable purposes, when enforceable by the Attorney General, or for a limited anomalous number of non-charitable purposes relating to the maintenance of animals, tombs etc[3], although there is scope[4] for the courts to uphold non-charitable purpose trusts if the settlor's trust instru-

---

1 *Paul v Constance* [1977] 1 WLR 527, CA; *Rowe v Prance* [2000] WTLR 249; *Dipple v Corles* (1853) 11 Hare 183; *Page v Cox* (1852) 10 Hare 163; *Moore v Darton* (1851) 4 De G & Sm 517.
2 *Knight v Knight* (1840) 3 Beav 148; affd sub nom *Knight v Boughton* (1844) 11 Cl & Fin 513 at 548, HL; and explained by CA in *Re Oldfield* [1904] 1 Ch 549, CA.
3 See pp 118–123, post.
4 See pp 114–116 post.

ment provides for a person with locus standi to enforce the purpose trust, assuming it to be workable and restricted to a valid perpetuity period.

(2) Whether an intention to create a trust is sufficiently evinced is in each case a question of interpretation. There is a well-established rule of construction that where an instrument is capable of two inter-pretations, one of which would give effect to the purpose of the per-son who drew it up, and the other of which would frustrate such purpose, to prefer the former interpretation to the latter[5]. An inten-tion to create a trust or no such intention[6] may even be inferred from the context. In particular:

(a) an apparent power of appointment among such of a class as the donee of the power may select[7], unaccompanied by a gift over in default of appointment[8], may raise an inference that a fixed trust was intended in favour of the class in default of appointment if there appears to be a general intention to benefit the objects of the power[9], and they are sufficiently indicated; alternatively, the apparent power may be treated as in the nature of a discretionary trust for the class members[10];

(b) a gift by will to a person, followed by precatory words expressive of the testator's request, recommendation, desire, hope or con-fidence, that the property will be applied in favour of others, may exceptionally create a trust, if, on the will as a whole, it appears that the testator intended the words to be imperative[11], but the court will not presume the imposition of a precatory trust merely from the presence of particular precatory words[12];

(c) a devise or bequest 'upon condition' or 'to the intent' that a benefit may be conferred on a third party, may create a trust for the third party if, on construing the whole will, the court comes to the conclusion that a trust, and not a charge merely, or a personal obligation, or a condition entailing forfeiture, was intended[13];

(d) a contract to create a trust of which specific performance would be

---

5 *Universe Tankships Inc of Monrovia v International Transport Workers' Federation* [1983] 1 AC 366 at 406, [1982] 2 All ER 67 at 93; *IRC v McMullen* [1981] AC 1 at 14, [1980] 1 All ER 884 at 890, CA.

6 *Re B (Child:Property Transfer)* [1999] 3 FCR 266, CA. (Divorce consent order transferring house to mother as to 70 per cent 'for the benefit of the child, J', and 30 per cent for the father, held by the Court of Appeal not to create a trust for J, so the mother could retain such percentage of proceeds of sale).

7 This principle has been extended to a power of appointment in favour of a single individual, sed quaere, *Tweedale v Tweedale* (1878) 7 Ch D 633 (see p 131, post; *Wheeler v Warner* (1823) 1 Sim & St 304).

8 *Burrough v Philcox* (1840) 5 My & Cr 72; *Grieveson v Kirsopp* (1838) 2 Keen 653; *Brown v Higgs* (1799) 4 Ves 708.

9 *Re Weekes' Settlement* [1897] 1 Ch 289; *Re Llewellyn's Settlement* [1921] 2 Ch 281.

10 See p 130–132, post.

11 *Shelley v Shelley* (1868) LR 6 Eq 540; *Re Steele's Will Trusts* [1948] Ch 603, [1948] 2 All ER 193.

12 *Re Adams and Kensington Vestry* (1884) 27 Ch D 394; *Re Diggles* (1888) 39 Ch D 253; *Re Hamilton* [1895] 1 Ch 373; on appeal [1895] 2 Ch 370, and cases there cited; *Re Steele's Will Trusts* [1948] Ch 603, [1948] 2 All ER 193; and *Mussoorie Bank v Raynor* (1882) 7 App Cas 321.

13 See pp 136–138, post.

ordered is considered to be an executory trust, conferring on parties who could sue for specific performance the same rights and imposing the same liabilities as if the contract had been actually performed.

(3) On the other hand, persons to whom payments are directed to be made by trustees are not necessarily beneficiaries, and cannot enforce such directions if the object of the payments, as gathered from the whole instrument, was not to confer benefits on the payees, but to facilitate the administration of an estate or to relieve the owner of trouble or inconvenience. In many cases the so-called trustee is regarded as an agent.

PARAGRAPH 1

Reasons for the rule that technical language is unnecessary

The latitude of expression allowed to the creator of a trust is an instance of the maxim that 'Equity regards the intention rather than the form'. Wherever the intent to create a trust is apparent, it will (other matters being in order) be carried into effect, however crudely or elliptically it may have been expressed.

Express direction or declaration

Of course, the words 'in trust for', or 'upon trust to', are the most proper for expressing a fiduciary purpose; but wherever a person vests property in another and shows an intention that it is to be applied for the benefit of third parties who are sufficiently pointed out, an express trust will be created, whatever form of words may have been used. Thus where A devised or granted freehold lands unto and to the use of B, and 'directed' him to sell it and pay the proceeds to C, or directed him to apply the property for the benefit of C a trust was created in favour of C[14], although the word 'trust' was not used.

Similarly, if a person states that particular property he owns is to be regarded as much his cohabitee's as his own, this will reveal an intention to create a trust for both of them, a person being able to create a trust without knowing it, just as he may speak prose without knowing it. Thus, as in *Paul v Constance*[15], a man might open a bank deposit account in his name alone, having ensured that his female co-habitant could be authorised to draw on the account using a note with his signature, and pay in a capital sum. Bingo winnings treated as their winnings might subsequently be paid in and £150 might be withdrawn for their Christmas presents and their Christmas food. At various times the man might say to the female, 'The money is as much yours as mine'. These words will be interpreted in context as amounting to an

---

14 *White v Briggs* (1848) 2 Ph 583. See also *Re Endacott* [1960] Ch 232, [1959] 3 All ER 562, CA, where a testator gave his residuary estate to a parish council 'for the purpose of providing some useful memorial to myself'. The Court of Appeal held that the words quoted were not merely expository but intended to impose an obligation in the nature of a trust which was void as a pure purpose trust.

15 [1977] 1 All ER 195, [1977] 1 WLR 527. Also see *Dhingra v Dhingra* (1999) 2 ITELR 262.

express declaration of trust of the bank account moneys in equal shares, the court 'dealing with simple people, unaware of the subtleties of equity, but understanding very well indeed their own situation'[16].

However the use of 'our house', 'our flat' or 'our home' in ordinary social contexts will not be regarded as indicative of ownership, only of joint occupation or residence[17], but the use of 'our boat' in a serious discussion between the owner and his cohabitee may indicate shared beneficial ownership under a trust[18].

Trust property to be separate from other property

An intent to create a trust of specific property will involve an intent that such property be kept separate from other trust or private property of the trustee, so that a property relationship is intended and not a personal debtor-creditor relationship[19]. Thus if a recipient of money:

'is not bound to keep the money separate, but is entitled to mix it with his own money and deal with it as he pleases, and when called upon to hand over an equivalent sum of money, then he is not a trustee of the money but merely a debtor.'[20]

A requirement to keep moneys separate is an indicator that they are impressed with a trust: the absence of such a requirement, if there are no other indicators of a trust, normally negatives it. The fact that a transaction contemplates the mingling of funds is, therefore, not necessarily fatal to a trust, eg where investors' moneys are to be pooled for the purposes of buying a particular type of investment to be held on trust for them as equitable tenants in common[1]. Similarly, a valid trust exists where B contracts with C that after receiving full consideration from C, if he receives proceeds of sale materialising from some specified future property he will hold it (or a specified percentage or fractional part thereof[2]) on trust for C, though he can hold such money briefly in his own bank account before transmitting it on to C: such money belongs in Equity to C from the moment received by B so that C has the benefit of the tracing rules[3]. The contract should spell out that the relevant amount of money is to be transferred into C's account or a trust

16 [1977] 1 All ER 195 at 197, [1977] 1 WLR 527 at 530. Also see the benevolent decision in *Re Vandervell's Trusts (No 2)* [1974] Ch 269, [1974] 3 All ER 205, CA.

17 *Lloyds Bank v Rosset* [1991] 1 AC 107 at 130 and *Otway v Gibbs* [2001] WTLR 467 at 472. Declarations of trusts of land are unenforceable in any event unless evidenced in signed writing within LPA 1925, s 53(1)(b) or there is a resulting trust or detrimental reliance sufficient to create a constructive trust or an equitable proprietary estoppel.

18 *Rowe v Prance* [2000] WTLR 249.

19 See pp 10–12, ante and *Paragon Finance plc v Thakerar* [1999] 1 All ER 400 at 416, per Millett LJ; *Hinckley Singapore Trading Pte Ltd v Sogo Department Stores Pte Ltd* (2001) 4 ITELR 301 (Singapore CA); *Re English & American Insurance Co Ltd* [1994] 1 BCLC 649; *Re Fleet Disposal Services Ltd* [1995] 1 BCLC 345; *Guardian Ocean Cargoes Ltd v Banco da Brasil* [1994] 2 Lloyd's Rep 152, CA.

20 *Henry v Hammond* [1913] 2 KB 515 at 521, endorsed by CA in *R v Clowes (No 2)* [1994] 2 All ER 316 at 325 and applied in *Customs and Excise Comrs v Richmond Theatre Management* [1995] STC 257.

1 *Re Goldcorp Exchange Ltd* [1995] 1 AC 74, [1994] 2 All ER 806, PC; *R v Clowes (No 2)* [1994] 2 All ER 316, CA.

2 *Associated Alloys Pty Ltd v ACN 001 452 106 Pty Ltd* (2001) 74 ALJR 862, p 15–16 ante.

3 *Associated Alloys Pty Ltd v ACN 001 452 106 Pty Ltd* (2001) 74 ALJR 862 and *Re Irving* (1877) 7 Ch D 419; *Pullant v Koe* [1913] 1 Ch 9; *Re Gillott's Settlements* [1934] Ch 97; *Palette Shoes Pty Ltd v Krohn* (1937) 58 CLR 1 at 27.

account for C within a short period of receipt (eg five working days) and that B should not let the amount credited in its general account receiving the proceeds of sale fall below the relevant amount to be held on trust for C[4].

Trusts do not fail for want of a trustee

In the case of a will trust it matters not that the testator fails to appoint trustees[5] or that the appointed trustees predecease the testator[6] or disclaim the trust[7] or are not capable of taking the trust property[8]. The personal representatives will hold the property with power to appoint trustees who can then exercise all the power vested in the trustees[9]. In the case of inter vivos trusts the settlor must do all that he can to vest the trust property in specific existing persons of full capacity but disclaimer by them[10] or refusal of registration of them as shareholders by the board of directors in the case of shares[11] will not invalidate the trust since the settlor will hold the property subject to the trusts. Exceptionally, 'If it is of the essence of a trust that the trustees selected by the settlor and no-one else shall act as the trustees of it and those trustees cannot or will not undertake the office, the trust must fail.'[12]

Trusts intended may amount to charges

As already explained at pp 14–16, if contracting parties enter into a transaction using the terminology of 'trust', but the legal effect of the transaction is to give rise to an equitable charge because the intended 'trust' fund is simply to provide security for an obligation then no trust arises, the parties being taken to intend the legal consequences of their acts[13].

Trusts intended may yet be void for uncertainty

However, intention to create a trust is not of itself sufficient (even where the most direct and imperative words are used)[14], if either the property, or the persons to be benefited, or the way in which they are to be benefited be not indicated with reasonable certainty.

4 *Royal Trust Bank v National Westminster Bank* [1996] 2 BCLC 682, CA; *Re Lewis' of Leicester* [1995] 1 BCLC 428. If, despite such terms, C ignores B's breach of them and, in practice allows B to use the money as B's own, then the trust will have been replaced with a debtor-creditor relationship.
5 *Ellison v Ellison* (1802) 6 Ves 656; *Dodkin v Brunt* (1868) LR 6 Eq 580; *Pollock v Ennis* [1921] 1 IR 181.
6 *A-G v Stephens* (1834) 3 My & K 347; *Moggridge v Thackwell* (1792) 3 Bro CC 517; *A-G v Lady Downing* (1766) Amb 550; *Tempest v Lord Camoys* (1866) 35 Beav 201; *Re Smirthwaite's Trusts* (1871) LR 11 Eq 251.
7 *Robson v Flight* (1865) 4 De GJ & Sm 608; *Re Wilson-Barksworth* (1933) 50 TLR 82.
8 *Sonley v Clock-makers Co* (1780) 1 Bro CC 81.
9 See cases in note 6, supra.
10 *Mallott v Wilson* [1903] 2 Ch 494 criticised by P Matthews [1981] Conv 141, but accepted as good law by the Court of Appeal in *Harris v Sharp* (21 March 1989, unreported).
11 *Tett v Phoenix Property and Investment Co Ltd* [1984] BCLC 599; *Mascall v Mascall* (1984) 50 P & CR 119, CA.
12 *Re Lysaght* [1966] Ch 191 at 207, [1965] 2 All ER 888 at 896.
13 *Clough Mill Ltd v Martin* [1985] 1 WLR 111, CA; *Swiss Bank Corpn v Lloyds Bank* [1980] 2 All ER 419 at 426.
14 See *Mussoorie Bank v Raynor* (1882) 7 App Cas 321 at 331.

Illustrations of uncertainty as to the property or shares therein

If a settlor intends to create a trust by transferring property to trustees then, of necessity, he must transfer specific property to those trustees and declare trusts relating to such specific property. One would logically expect that if he is to declare himself trustee of his own property for particular beneficiaries, his declaration must relate to specific property identified as trust property separate from his private property that remains subject to claims of his private creditors, divorcing spouse and persons with claims on his death under the Inheritance (Provision for Family and Dependants) Act 1975. If he intends to hold all of the £20,000 in his building society account or all his 200 shares in Smith Co Ltd, a private company, or all his 20 cases of Chateau Lafite 1961 on trust for himself and another as equitable tenants in common as to four fifths and one fifth respectively, there is certainty as to the money, the shares and the wine. There is an uncertainty problem, however, if instead, he intends to create a trust of £4,000 out of the £20,000 or of 40 of the shares or 4 of the cases of wine. An intention to create a trust of a specific quantity of assets cannot be construed as an intention to create an equitable tenancy in common in a larger quantity of assets[15]: an intention to hold 40 shares on trust for X is very different from an intention to hold for X a one fifth undivided share in each of 200 shares or in a composite holding of 200 shares.

As Lord Mustill stated of the former type of intention in *Re Goldcorp Exchange Ltd*[16], 'It makes no difference what the parties intended if what they intend is impossible as is the case with an immediate transfer of [legal or equitable] title to goods whose identity is not yet known ... It is impossible to have [legal or equitable] title to goods when nobody knows to which goods the title relates.' Thus, it has been very clearly held[17] that the immediate transfer of legal or equitable title to goods whose identity is not yet known is impossible, eg 20 out of 80 cases of Chateau Lafite 1961. Surprisingly, in *Hunter v Moss*[18] the Court of Appeal held that a gratuitous declaration of trust by S of 50 of his 950 shares in a particular private company was valid. The extempore judgment has two major weaknesses. It distinguished *Re London Wine Shippers Ltd*[19] on the false basis that the case had no relevance for declarations of trust and then held[20], 'just as a person can give by will a specified number of his shares in a certain company, so equally he can declare himself a trustee of 50 of his shares in MEL and that is effective to give a beneficial proprietary interest to the beneficiary under the trust'. This overlooks the crucial difference between inter vivos and testamentary dispositions. On death a testator is totally divested of all his legal and beneficial title in all his assets in favour of his executor[1] who becomes subject to equitable obligations to effect the testator's wishes so far as practicable after

---

15 *Re London Wine Co Shippers Ltd* [1986] PCC 121; *Re Wait* [1927] 1 Ch 606, CA.

16 *Re Goldcorp Exchange Ltd* [1995] 1 AC 74 at 90 and 92.

17 *Re Goldcorp Exchange Ltd* [1995] 1 AC 74, [1994] 2 All ER 806, PC; *Re Stapylton Fletcher Ltd* [1995] 1 All ER 192: now see Sale of Goods (Amendment) Act 1995.

18 [1994] 3 All ER 215, [1994] 1 WLR 452, criticised in detail (1994) 110 LQR 335, but applied in two cases not to be cited in court by *Practice Note* [2001] 2 All ER 510 (*Re Harvard Securities* [1997] 2 BCLC 369 and *Re CA Pacific Finance* [2000] 1 BCLC 494).

19 [1986] PCC 121.

20 [1994] 3 All ER 215 at 222, [1994] 1 WLR 452 at 459.

1 Thus the true lifetime analogy is with the situation where S declares he holds 50 of his 950 shares for B and 900 for C, so that B and C between them have full beneficial ownership entitling them under the *Saunders v Vautier* principle to demand the shares from S.

payment of debts, expenses and taxes. In his lifetime a settlor is only divested of his beneficial entitlement to his assets where one knows to which assets such divestment relates.

In view of the erroneous analogy in *Hunter v Moss* and of the ringing endorsement of *Re London Wine Shippers Ltd* by the Privy Council in *Re Goldcorp Exchange Ltd* [2] (argued before the Court of Appeal decision in *Hunter v Moss*) it is respectfully submitted that *Hunter v Moss* should not be followed where a registered shareholder declares himself trustee of a specific number of his shares rather than a specific fraction or percentage of his whole shareholding: there is no sound reason for distinguishing trusts of goods from trusts of intangibles[3].

However, where the intangibles are shares in a public company whose shares are held by a nominee under the CREST system with, say, 1 million shares recorded as held, say, for Cazenove & Co, whose records state that 20,000 shares are held for S, S does not actually own 20,000 shares: he owns a one fiftieth equitable interest in Cazenove's pool of 1 million shares which may amount to a one fifth equitable interest in the public company's shares held by the nominee. Thus, if S declares himself trustee of his 20,000 shares in the company, the court will need to construe this otherwise nonsensical, impossible declaration as a declaration of trust of his one fiftieth interest in Cazenove's interest. It would seem to follow that if S happened to declare himself trustee of 10,000 of his 20,000 shares then, because he does not own any shares, his declaration should be construed as a trust of half of the fiftieth interest he does own in Cazenove's interest. Thus certainty of subject matter of the trust is present[4]. While a testator may validly leave his residuary estate (after payment of debts, expenses, taxes and legacies) on trusts, any purported trusts of the bulk of his residuary estate for X and the remaining minor part for Y will be void since it is impossible to determine what is the trust property[5]. Where a testator gives property to, or in trust for, his wife, and directs that *such part of it as may not be required by her* shall, after her death, be held in trust for his children, the latter trust is void for uncertainty, for no one can say how much the wife may or may not require[6]. Thus the wife takes

---

2 [1995] 1 AC 74, [1994] 2 All ER 806, PC. Also see *MacJordan Construction Ltd v Brookmount Erostin Ltd* [1992] BCLC 350, (1991) 56 BLR 1, CA; a specifically enforceable contractual right of a contractor to have his employer set aside a retention fund trust of money for the contract does not relate to specific money, so the contractor has no equitable proprietary interest till the retention fund is actually set up; similarly see *McKee v Paradise* 575 Sup Ct 124, 299 US 122 (1936).

3 The Court of Appeal in *Hunter v Moss* (supra) did not attempt to do this (mass-produced tangibles being as identical as intangible fungibles), though this had been done at first instance: [1993] 1 WLR 934 at 946. Where A is owed £5,000 by B, A can declare himself trustee of his chose in action for C, but B cannot be trustee of £5,000 for C till he segregates it: *M'Fadden v Jenkyns* (1842) 1 Ph 153, cf *Re Innes* [1910] 1 Ch 188 at 193 and Australian High Court in *Herdegen v Federal Comr of Taxation* (1988) 84 ALR 271.

4 The applicability of Law of Property Act, s 53 (1)(c) needs to be considered where S declares himself trustee for B absolutely or B and C absolutely where they are of full age and capacity: see pp 238–239 post.

5 *Palmer v Simmonds* (1854) 2 Drew 221; cf *Bromley v Tyron* [1952] AC 265, [1951] 2 All ER 1058, HL.

6 Per Sir A Hobhouse in *Mussoorie Bank v Raynor* (1882) 7 App Cas 321 at 331; and see *Pope v Pope* (1839) 10 Sim 1; and *Re Minchell's Will Trust* [1964] 2 All ER 47 (wife taking absolutely where estate bequeathed to her 'for her life', with precatory words for disposing of whatever was left at her death). See also *Re Dunstan* [1918] 2 Ch 304; but cf *Re Wilson* (1916) 142 LT Jo 41 and *Re Last* [1958] P 137, [1958] 1 All ER 316 where on the construction of the wills it was held that the first taker was limited to a life interest only.

the property absolutely. Administration of Justice Act 1982, s 22 now states, 'Except where a contrary intention is shown it shall be presumed that if a testator devises or bequeaths property to his spouse in terms which in themselves would give an absolute interest to the spouse but by the same instrument purports to give his issue an interest in the same property the gift to the spouse is absolute notwithstanding the purported gift to the issue.'

On similar uncertainty grounds, directions to a legatee 'to remember' certain persons[7], or 'to give what should remain at her death'[8], or 'to reward very old servants and tenants according to their deserts'[9], or (after an absolute gift to a wife) a direction that at her death 'such parts of my estate as she shall not have sold or disposed of' should be held in trust for certain other persons[10], have all been held void for uncertainty as to the property. The trust property has to be certain when the trust is created not just when the trust terms are to begin to operate. Thus in Canada an inter vivos trust set up on the separation of the settlor from his wife to take effect upon the settlor's death when the trustee was to hold three fifths of the settlor's net estate for the wife for life or until re-marriage, remainder for their two children, was held void for uncertainty as to the property[11].

On the other hand, a trust to pay a 'reasonable income' to a beneficiary has been held to refer to an objective standard, which could if necessary be quantified by the court, and therefore not to fail for uncertainty[12]. Similarly, a trust will be valid if it is to purchase an annuity of £10,000 pa for X for life or to purchase a school fees annuity policy to enable X to attend public school for five years by providing no less than is considered sufficient to cover the fees of a boarder at the Leys School, Cambridge. It suffices that there is a formula or method for identifying the subject matter of a trust, eg where a testator wishes to ensure that he takes advantage[13] of the whole of the 0%

---

7 *Bardswell v Bardswell* (1838) 9 Sim 319.

8 *Parnall v Parnall* (1878) 9 Ch D 96; *Sprange v Barnard* (1789) 2 Bro CC 585; *Tibbits v Tibbits* (1816) 19 Ves 657; *Pope v Pope* (1839) 10 Sim 1.

9 *Knight v Knight* (1840) 3 Beav 148; affd sub nom *Knight v Boughton* (1844) 11 Cl & Fin 513, HL; and see *Stead v Mellor* (1877) 5 Ch D 225.

10 *Re Jones* [1898] 1 Ch 438; distinguished in *Re Sanford* [1901] 1 Ch 939. For other examples of trusts void for uncertainty as to the property, see *Sale v Moore* (1827) 1 Sim 534; *Hoy v Master* (1934) 6 Sim 568; *Curtis v Rippon* (1820) 5 Madd 434; *Cowman v Harrison* (1852) 10 Hare 234; and *Green v Marsden* (1853) 1 Drew 646. See also *Re Booth* (1917) 86 LJ Ch 270; and *Re Howell* [1915] 1 Ch 241.

11 *Re Beardmore Trusts* [1952] 1 DLR 41 (the inter vivos equivalent of *Sprange v Barnard* (1789) 2 Bro CC 585).

12 *Re Golay* [1965] 2 All ER 660, [1965] 1 WLR 969; *Ellis v Chief Adjudication Officer* [1998] 1 FLR 184, CA (valid condition requiring donee-daughter to allow donor-mother to live in donated flat so long as was reasonably practicable and to provide the donor with an acceptable standard of living); cf 'reasonable price' or 'reasonable rent' in *Talbot v Talbot* [1968] Ch 1, [1967] 2 All ER 920, CA; *Smith v Morgan* [1971] 2 All ER 1500, [1971] 1 WLR 803; *Brown v Gould* [1972] Ch 53, [1971] 2 All ER 1505; *King's Motors (Oxford) Ltd v Lax* [1969] 3 All ER 665, [1970] 1 WLR 426; *Ponsford v HMS Aerosols Ltd* [1979] AC 63, [1978] 2 All ER 837, HL; *Sudbrook Trading Estate Ltd v Eggleton* [1983] 1 AC 444, [1982] 3 All ER 1, HL. A court will overcome all technical difficulties to defeat a defendant fraudulently relying on uncertainty: *Banner Homes Group plc v Luff Developments Ltd* [2000] Ch 372, CA; *Pallant v Morgan* [1953] Ch 43 at 49–50 and constructive trusts of fair shares: p 412, post; *Re Malpass* [1985] Ch 42, [1984] 2 All ER 313 (testamentary option to purchase at value 'as agreed with the District Valuer' upheld and inquiry directed as to price where the valuer refused to value since there was no official need to value).

13 If a testator's will is not tax-efficient the legatees within two years of his death may re-write the will with effect from death for capital gains tax and inheritance tax purposes: Inheritance Act 1984, s 142, and Taxation of Chargeable Gains Act 1992, s 62(6).

band for inheritance tax applicable on his death so as to leave on trust or otherwise a cash legacy (or a legacy of such number of shares in a private company as shall ultimately be agreed with the Revenue to be of the value) of such an amount as may be bequeathed before inheritance tax becomes payable thereon at a rate above 0%.

However a bequest of 'such minimal part of my estate as [my wife] might be entitled to under English law for maintenance purposes' was held void for uncertainty in the absence of adequate criteria for ascertaining the wife's entitlement[14], so the wife's course of action was to apply for reasonable financial provision under the Inheritance (Provision for Family and Dependants) Act 1975.

A curious example of uncertainty in regard to the beneficial shares in property is afforded by the case of *Boyce v Boyce*[15]. Here a testator devised his four houses in Southwold to trustees in trust for his wife for life, and after her death in trust to convey one of them, whichever she might choose, to his daughter Maria in fee, and to convey the others to his daughter Charlotte in fee. Maria died in the testator's lifetime and therefore could not choose any particular house, and it was held that in consequence the trust in favour of Charlotte was void for uncertainty, so that on the widow's death the four houses were held on resulting trust. If the trustees had been given a discretion to determine the quantum of the beneficiaries' interest, then there would have been a valid discretionary trust, but any failure to exercise the discretion would enable the court to intervene and appoint new trustees or, if a basis for distribution appears, order distribution, whether on an equal or unequal basis[16].

Floating (or suspended) trusts

It used to be thought that if property were bequeathed essentially to X to pass on whatever was left at his death to Y, then this would normally be treated as an absolute gift to X[17] but, in an exceptional case, the court in context might be able to find that the property had to be held on trust for X for life, remainder to Y absolutely[18].

There is now a third possibility where the testator and X have reached an express or implied agreement, since Brightman J in *Ottaway v Norman* stated[19]:

'I am content to assume for present purposes, but without so deciding, that if property is given to [X] on the understanding that [X] will dispose by his will of such assets, if any, as he may have at his command at his death in favour of [Y], a valid trust is created in favour of [Y] which is in suspense during the lifetime of [X] but attaches to the estate of [X] at the moment of [X's] death.'

14 *Anthony v Donges* [1998] 2 FLR 775.
15 (1849) 16 Sim 476. Nowadays, a court might be more ready to construe the trust as of four houses for Charlotte subject to the right of Maria to choose one of them for herself.
16 *McPhail v Doulton* [1971] AC 424 at 457, HL. *Salusbury v Denton* (1857) 3 K & J 529; *Re Coxen* [1948] Ch 747, [1948] 2 All ER 492.
17 *Sprange v Barnard* (1789) 2 Bro CC 585.
18 *Re Last* [1958] P 137, [1958] 1 All ER 316.
19 [1972] Ch 698 at 713.

Further elucidation is present in an earlier Australian case, *Birmingham v Renfrew*[20], where Dixon J (as he then was) stated[1]:

'The purpose must often be to enable the survivor during his life to deal as absolute owner with the property passing under the will of the party first dying. The object is to put the survivor in a position to enjoy for his own benefit the full ownership so that he may convert it and expend the proceeds if he choose. But when he dies he is to bequeath what is left in the manner agreed upon. It is only by the special doctrines of equity that such a floating obligation, suspended, so to speak, during the lifetime of the survivor can descend upon the assets at his death and crystallise into a trust. No doubt, gifts and settlements inter vivos, if calculated to defeat the intention of the compact, could not be made by the survivor and his right of disposition inter vivos is therefore not unqualified.'

Where this third possibility arises it thus seems that X has an absolute interest subject to an equitable fiduciary obligation during his lifetime neither to transfer the property nor to contract to transfer the property with destructive intent to prevent the property passing to Y[2]. The obligation is rather nebulous so that a well-advised testator would leave the property to trustees for X for life, remainder to Y but give X and the trustees a joint power to appoint capital to X.

Uncertainty as to the beneficiaries or as to the way in which the property is to be applied

Where the uncertainty arises[3] in relation either to the persons intended to be benefited[4], or to the way in which[5], or the period for which, the property is to be applied, then unless the trust is for charitable purposes, in which event if a general charitable intention is present the court[6] or the Charity Commis-

---

20 (1937) 57 CLR 666.
 1 (1937) 57 CLR 666 at 689, endorsed by Nourse J in *Re Cleaver* [1981] 2 All ER 1018, [1981] 1 WLR 939. The survivor must not give away considerable portions of the capital or do anything else with it that would be inconsistent with the spirit and the obvious intention and purpose of the agreement: *Edell v Sitzer* (2001) 4 ITELR 149 at 169–170.
 2 It would seem that Y should have a proprietary base to justify a proprietary remedy via the tracing process. Quaere whether Y should have a right to ensure that X kept a separate account of the property received by him subject to the fiduciary obligation? Presumably, if Y predeceased X then X's fiduciary obligation would cease. Further see *Palmer v Bank of New South Wales* (1975) 113 CLR 150.
 3 *Doe d Hayter v Joinville* (1802) 3 East 172; *Thomas d Evans v Thomas* (1796) 6 Term Rep 671.
 4 *Re Astor's Settlement Trusts* [1952] Ch 534, [1952] 1 All ER 1067, where Roxburgh J said this derived from the principle that the court will not recognise as valid a trust which it cannot both enforce and control, as to which see *Morice v Bishop of Durham* (1805) 10 Ves 522; see also *Re Shaw* [1957] 1 All ER 745, [1957] 1 WLR 729; compromised on appeal [1958] 1 All ER 245n, CA (trusts for alphabet reform). The whole trust for a class of beneficiaries fails if although part of the class is certain, part is uncertain: *Re Wright's Will Trusts* (21 July 1982, unreported), CA, (1999) 13 Trust L I 48.
 5 *Briggs v Hartley* (1850) 19 LJ Ch 416. *Re Endacott* [1960] Ch 232, [1959] 3 All ER 562, CA (for 'providing some useful memorial to myself'); *Re Atkinson's Will Trusts* [1978] 1 All ER 1275, [1978] 1 WLR 586 ('worthy causes'); *R v District Auditor No 3 Audit District of West Yorkshire Metropolitan County Council, ex p West Yorkshire Metropolitan County Council* [1986] RVR 24.
 6 *Re Gott* [1944] Ch 193, [1944] 1 All ER 293; *Re Shaw* [1957] 1 All ER 745, [1957] 1 WLR 729, CA; compromised on appeal [1958] 1 All ER 245n, CA. Note, however, that the court's powers to order a scheme arises only when the gift concerned is made by way of trust: when it is a direct gift (eg a testamentary gift to a non- existent beneficiary, from which a general charitable intention can be deduced) the court cannot order a scheme and the subject matter of the gift must be administered as directed by Her Majesty the Queen: *Re Bennett* [1960] Ch 18, [1959] 3 All ER 295.

sioners[7] can always settle a scheme, the trust is void[8].

There is, however, an important difference to be noted between trusts void for uncertainty as to the property, and those void for uncertainty as to beneficiaries, or as to the way in which the property is intended to be applied. Where it is held that there is uncertainty as to the property intended to be settled, it is obvious that no further question can arise; for if there is no property capable of identification there is nothing to litigate about. But where the property is described with sufficient certainty, and the words actually used, or the surrounding circumstances, make it clear that, although the donor has not sufficiently specified the objects of his bounty or the way in which the property was intended to be dealt with, yet he never meant the trustee to take the entire beneficial interest, it is different; and in such cases (which are treated of in Division Three, post) the law implies a resulting trust in favour of the donor or persons claiming under him.

Where a trust for beneficiaries is intended to benefit them absolutely but in specified ways which are uncertain or exhaustively carried out then the specified purposes are regarded as the motive of the trust which is thus valid for the beneficiaries[9].

Where it is the way in which a valid trust fund is to be invested that is void for uncertainty (eg a direction to trustees to invest in shares in the 'blue chip' category) then one falls back on the statutory powers of investment applicable in the absence of express powers of investment[10]. Although the concept of 'blue chip' shares is objectively conceptually uncertain it may be that the test of certainty for administrative powers is less than the test of certainty for powers of appointment affecting beneficial interests, so that a power to invest in 'such shares as my trustees consider to be within the "blue chip" category' may be sufficiently certain[11]. Uncertainty may sometimes be avoided if it arises from a provision which does not properly express the settlor's intention and which the court can construe so as to express this intention correctly and thus to eliminate the uncertainty[12].

Uncertainty as to period of duration of trust

Trusts of income limited to a period which is impossible of ascertainment are void for uncertainty.

---

7 See the Charities Act 1960, s 18.
8 *Thomason v Moses* (1842) 5 Beav 77; *Re Porter* [1925] Ch 746; *Re Endacott* [1960] Ch 232, [1959] 3 All ER 562, CA; *Re Flavel's Will Trusts* [1969] 2 All ER 232, [1969] 1 WLR 444.
9 *Re Andrew's Trust* [1905] 2 Ch 48; *Re Osoba* [1979] 2 All ER 393, [1979] 1 WLR 247, CA; *Hancock v Watson* [1902] AC 14, HL.
10 *Re Kolb's Will Trusts* [1962] Ch 531, [1961] 3 All ER 811.
11 *Re Kolb's Will Trusts* [1962] Ch 531 at 539 per Cross J and contrast p 89, post.
12 As, eg in *Re Wootton's Will Trusts* [1968] 2 All ER 618 and *Whishaw v Stephens* [1970] AC 508, sub nom *Re Gulbenkian's Settlement Trusts, Whishaw v Stephens* [1968] 3 All ER 785, HL. By Administration of Justice Act 1982, s 21, discussed by R Kerridge and J Rivers in *The Construction of Wills* (2000) 116 LQR 311, extrinsic evidence, including evidence of the testator's intention, may be admitted to assist in the interpretation of a will in so far as it is meaningless or the language used is ambiguous on the face of it or in so far as evidence, other than evidence of the testator's intention, shows that the language used is ambiguous in the light of the surrounding circumstances. Evidence of counsel's opinion given at or prior to the execution of an inter vivos trust deed is not admissible to explain the meaning of the deed since this will be a breach of the parol evidence rule: *Rabin v Gerson Berger Association Ltd* [1986] 1 All ER 374, [1986] 1 WLR 526, CA. See also *Re Tepper's Will Trusts* [1987] 1 All ER 970; *Re Benham's Will Trusts* [1995] STC 210.

Thus, where a testatrix bequeathed £500 to trustees to be applied in keeping up a tomb until the expiration of the period of twenty-one years from the death of the last survivor of all persons living at her death, it was held that, quite apart from any question whether the rule against perpetuities was infringed, the trust was void for uncertainty, as it would be impossible to ascertain when the last life would be extinguished[13].

On the other hand a trust limited by reference to the life of the survivor of a large class, eg the descendants of Queen Victoria, is not void, it is merely difficult and expensive, but not actually impossible, to discover when such survivor dies[14]. For a royal lives perpetuity clause it is nowadays safer to use the descendants of King George VI.

Uncertainty as to beneficiaries under fixed trusts

A fixed trust is void unless at the outset it can be seen clearly that *all* the beneficiaries thereunder are then ascertainable or will be ascertainable when the time comes under the trust to distribute capital or income[15]. Just as a trust for A for life remainder to B absolutely is valid, so is a trust for A (a bachelor) for life remainder to his children equally and a trust to divide a fund equally between such persons as shall on X's death be his statutory next of kin or his dependants. However, a trust to divide a fund equally between next of kin and dependants of persons currently or formerly employed by ICI Ltd or by any company on the board of which an ICI Ltd director currently sits will be void unless a comprehensive list of such beneficiaries can be drawn up so as to enable an equal division to be made[16]. Except where the potential number of beneficiaries is very high and the value of the trust fund relatively low[17] it will usually be possible to draw up a comprehensive list of the persons ranking as beneficiaries at the time for distribution of the trust fund. However, a small class may be void for conceptual uncertainty, eg a trust for 'my old friends' or 'my business associates' where no criteria can be ascertained from the trust instrument or other admissible evidence for determining exactly who can be old friends or business associates[18]. Thus a trust for equal division among 'my friends' would be void[19].

---

13 *Re Moore* [1901] 1 Ch 936. This case was considered and distinguished in *Muir v IRC* [1966] 3 All ER 38, [1966] 1 WLR 1269, CA, where it was said that if there was no present uncertainty, the mere possibility of uncertainty arising in the future did not invalidate the trust.

14 *Re Villar* [1929] 1 Ch 243, CA; and see *Re Leverhulme (No 2)* [1943] 2 All ER 274.

15 *Whishaw v Stephens* [1970] AC 508 at 524, sub nom *Re Gulbenkian's Settlement Trusts, Whishaw v Stephens* [1968] 3 All ER 785 at 793B; *Kinsels v Caldwell* [1975] ALR 337.

16 *IRC v Broadway Cottages Trusts* [1955] Ch 20, [1954] 3 All ER 120; *McPhail v Doulton* [1971] AC 424 at 450, [1970] 2 All ER 228 at 244f; *Re Sayer* [1957] Ch 423, [1956] 3 All ER 600.

17 *Whishaw v Stephens* [1970] AC 508 at 519, sub nom *Re Gulbenkian's Settlement Trusts, Whishaw v Stephens* [1968] 3 All ER 785 at 788, HL. The court requires substantial probability that all the beneficiaries can be ascertained even if much difficulty and much expense is likely: *Re Saxone Shoe Co Ltd's Trusts Deed* [1962] 2 All ER 904, [1962] 1 WLR 943 not following *Re Eden* [1957] 2 All ER 430, [1957] 1 WLR 788.

18 *Re Baden's Deed Trusts (No 2)* [1973] Ch 9, [1972] 2 All ER 1304; *Brown v Gould* [1972] Ch 53, [1971] 2 All ER 1505; *Re Connor Estate* (1970) 10 DLR (3d) 5; *Re Bethel* (1971) 17 DLR (3d) 652; affd sub nom *Jones v Executive Officers of the T Eaton Co Ltd* (1973) 35 DLR (3d) 97; *Re Tuck's Settlement Trusts* [1978] Ch 49, [1978] 1 All ER 1047, CA; *Re Tepper's Will Trusts* [1987] 1 All ER 970.

19 As opined by Browne-Wilkinson J in *Re Barlow's Will Trusts* [1979] 1 All ER 296 at 299, [1979] 1 WLR 278 at 281, 282. A fixed or discretionary trust for 'customers' would also seem void for uncertainty due to difficulties of distinguishing 'ex-customers': *Sparfax (1965) Ltd v Dommett* (1972) 116 Sol Jo 711, Times, 14 July, CA.

Uncertainty as to beneficiaries under discretionary trusts

The old test

Until the House of Lords' three to two majority decision in *McPhail v Doulton*[20] it was taken for granted that a trust, whether fixed or discretionary, was void for uncertainty if a comprehensive list of beneficiaries could not be drawn up[1]. After all, trusts are imperative: they must be carried out by trustees, though, in default, it must be possible for the court to enforce and carry out the trusts. If trustees failed to carry out discretionary trusts then, since it would be invidious and injudicious for the court to discriminate between the possible discretionary beneficiaries, the court would have to act on the maxim 'Equality is equity' and so distribute the trust fund equally between the beneficiaries, so making it vital that a comprehensive list be capable of being drawn up to know into what number of shares to divide the fund equally.

The new test: as for objects of powers of appointment

However, in *McPhail v Doulton* the House of Lords assimilated the test for uncertainty of beneficiaries under discretionary trusts to the test for certainty of objects under a mere power. Earlier in *Whishaw v Stephens*[2] the House of Lords had laid down that a mere power is valid, even though a comprehensive list of its objects cannot be drawn up, so long as it is possible to say with certainty of any given postulant that he definitely is an object of the power or that he definitely is not an object of the power: a mere power will be void if, although one or a few persons can definitely be said to be within the power, there are persons of whom it cannot be said 'with certainty who is within and who is without the power'[3]. The underlying reasoning was that trustees with a mere power do not *have* to exercise it, so that the court cannot compel the trustees to exercise it: the objects of the power have a mere spes and the persons entitled in default of exercise of the power have full equitable interests which entitle them to restrain the trustees from exercising the power in favour of persons outside the power. Thus, 'the trustees or the court must be able to say with certainty who is within and who is without the power'[4]. In obiter dicta the House of Lords (Lord Reid reserving his position) clearly affirmed the comprehensive list test of certainty for beneficiaries under discretionary trusts, since such trusts have to be executed by the court in the event of default by the trustees, execution being impossible unless there can be equal division.

In *McPhail v Doulton* Lords Hodson and Guest reaffirmed their view in *Re Gulbenkian's Settlement Trusts* but Lord Wilberforce (with whom Lord Reid and

---

20 [1971] AC 424, [1970] 2 All ER 228, HL; (1971) 87 LQR 31 (JW Harris); [1971] CLJ 68 (JA Hopkins); (1974) 37 MLR 643 (Y Grbich).

1 *Whishaw v Stephens* [1970] AC 508, sub nom *Re Gulbenkian's Settlement Trusts, Whishaw v Stephens* [1968] 3 All ER 785.

2 [1970] AC 508, sub nom *Re Gulbenkian's Settlement Trusts, Whishaw v Stephens* [1968] 3 All ER 785.

3 [1970] AC 508 at 525, sub nom *Re Gulbenkian's Settlement Trusts, Whishaw v Stephens* [1968] 3 All ER 785 at 794A. It seems the possibility of the power being exercised to confer equal interests on all the objects is ignored in ascertaining the validity of the power. Any such exercise would presumably be void for capriciousness.

4 [1970] AC 508 at 525. The authority of *Re Allen* [1953] Ch 810, [1953] 2 All ER 898, CA, for the view that conceptual uncertainty does not vitiate conditions precedent is most doubtful in view of the favoured 'is or is not' approach of the House of Lords in *Gulbenkian and McPhail* despite the views of Browne-Wilkinson J in *Re Barlow's Will Trusts* [1979] 1 All ER 296, p 99, post.

Viscount Dilhorne concurred) held that the test for certainty of beneficiaries under discretionary trusts should be assimilated to the 'is or is not' test for certainty of objects under a mere power: after all, in practical substance there is very little difference between the position of objects of a discretionary power and beneficiaries under a discretionary trust. Lord Wilberforce relied on certain eighteenth century cases for the proposition that execution by the court does not require equal division, especially where equal division is surely the last thing the settlor ever intended[5]. Referring to the discretionary trust in question as a 'trust power' (as opposed to a mere power) he laid down:

> 'In the case of a trust power, if the trustees do not exercise it, the court will do so in the manner best calculated to give effect to the settlor's or testator's intentions. It may do so by appointing new trustees, or by authorising or directing representative persons of the classes of beneficiaries to prepare a scheme for distribution, or even, should the proper basis for distribution appear, by itself directing the trustees so to distribute.'[6]

Having stated the law, Lord Wilberforce then remitted the case to the High Court[7], whence an appeal was made to the Court of Appeal[8], for a determination whether the discretionary trust in question was valid or void for uncertainty. Certain problems then emerged as to the proper scope of what, at first sight, seems a simple clear test.

Scope of the new test

The discretionary trust in question was for the trustees to make 'at their absolute discretion grants to or for the benefit of any of the officers and employees or ex-officers or ex-employees of the Company or to any relatives or dependants of any such persons in such amounts at such times and on such conditions (if any) as they think fit'. When the trust was created the company had about 1,300 officers and employees, the company having been incorporated 14 years previously in 1927. It became clear that the trustees could not trace numbers of short-term ex-employees (who had moved on since 1927) or, therefore, their relatives and dependants[9].

In the Court of Appeal, Stamp LJ took the view that the 'is or is not' test, for certainty of beneficiaries under discretionary trusts and of objects under powers, required that the court must be able to say of any given postulant that he definitely *is* a member of the class of beneficiaries or he definitely is *not* such a member, ie the name of any given person must be capable of being put either in a 'Yes' box or a 'No' box. Thus, a discretionary trust would be void if it was impossible to say of a given postulant either that he was or that he was not a member of the beneficial class, ie if his name had to be put into

---

5 The comprehensive list test will only apply at the end of the trust period if the discretionary trust instrument reveals that the settlor requires equal division at the end of the trust period.

6 [1971] AC 424 at 457, [1970] 2 All ER 228 at 247b; *Re Locker's Settlement Trusts* [1978] 1 All ER 216 at 219. In *Mettoy Pension Trustees Ltd v Evans* [1991] 2 All ER 513, [1990] 1 WLR 1587 Warner J held that the court's power of intervention to enforce discretionary trusts extended to discretionary powers but it is likely that this will be restricted to the context of pension fund trusts where the beneficiaries have earned their right to be considered for being further benefited under discretionary powers.

7 [1972] Ch 607, [1971] 3 All ER 985.

8 [1973] Ch 9, [1972] 2 All ER 1304, CA.

9 [1972] Ch 607. Where the discretionary trust is for future as well as existing persons it must be restricted to the perpetuity period or reliance must be placed on Perpetuities and Accumulations Act 1964: see pp 195–200, post.

a 'Don't know' box. Accordingly, if 'relative' meant descendant of a common ancestor, so that A was a relative of B if at some time over hundreds or thousands of years they both traced their descent from a common ancestor, the discretionary trust would be void. Whilst many persons definitely would be relatives within the 'Yes' box there would be an infinitely greater number of persons, neither known to be relatives nor known to be non-relatives, needing to be placed within the 'Don't know' box. The apparently clear concept thus turned out, in effect, to be an uncertain 'grey' concept. However, Stamp LJ was prepared to treat relatives as meaning statutory next of kin in which case any given postulant would be bound to fall within the 'Yes' box or the 'No' box. 'Dependants' created no problems of conceptual certainty, only of evidential certainty, which of itself does not invalidate a trust since the court can always resolve the matter on the evidence presented to it on an application for directions.

Sachs and Megaw LJJ disagreed with Stamp LJ on the issue of 'relatives'. Sachs LJ took the robust practical view that the expression 'relatives' in its broadest sense would not cause the slightest difficulty in practice since the trustees would not distribute to a person who failed to prove he was a relative: if a person is not proved to be within the class of relatives then he is not in it.

Megaw LJ endorsed this. He also pointed out, first, that, since *McPhail v Doulton*, a discretionary trust does not fail simply because it is impossible to ascertain every member of the class of beneficiaries and to draw up a comprehensive list thereof. Second, the view of Stamp LJ that the 'is or is not' test means that a discretionary trust will fail if it cannot be shown of any individual that he definitely is *or definitely is not* a member of the class, is to contend 'in substance and reality that it does fail simply because it is impossible to ascertain every member of the class'[10]. With respect, this second point seems fallacious since in ascertaining whether *any* (as opposed to every) individual is or is not a member of the class it is not necessary to ascertain *every* member of the class and draw up a comprehensive list, eg if there are roughly 5,000 potential class members the trustees need only survey each of say 2,000 individuals placing each of them definitely inside or definitely outside the discretionary class according to clear conceptual criteria.

Be that as it may, Megaw LJ went on to say[11]:

> 'In my judgment, much too great emphasis is placed on the words "or is not". To my mind, the test is satisfied if, as regards at least a substantial number of objects, it can be said with certainty that they fall within the trust, even though as regards a substantial number of other persons, if that ever for some fanciful reason felt to be considered, the answer would have to be, not "they are outside the trust", but "it is not proven whether they are in or out". What is a "substantial number" may well be a question of common sense and of some degree in relation to the particular trust; particularly where, as here, it would be fantasy, to use a mild word, to suggest that any practical difficulty would arise in the fair, proper and sensible administration of this trust in respect of relatives and dependants.'

Two comments may be made on the above remarks. First, is it wrong to emphasise the need to ascertain those who are not class members when a person alleging a breach of trust will need to show that the trustees distributed to an individual who was not a class member? Second, the rule that a discretionary trust is valid if a 'substantial' number of persons can be placed in the

---

10 [1973] Ch 9 at 23, [1972] 2 All ER 1304 at 1313.
11 [1973] Ch 9 at 24, [1972] 2 All ER 1304 at 1313.

'Yes' box of clear beneficiaries, even though a substantial number have to be placed in the 'Don't know' box of persons of whom it cannot be said they *are* beneficiaries or they are *not* beneficiaries, introduces uncertainty into the test of certainty of beneficiaries. Apart from the obvious uncertainty in the word 'substantial' does the rule operate to validate a discretionary trust as in *McPhail v Doulton* but to which there was added a conceptually uncertain clause such as 'any other person to whom I may be under a moral obligation and any of my old friends'?[12] Moreover, it is not so far removed from the view rejected by the House of Lords in *Whishaw v Stephens*[13] in relation to powers (and so in relation to discretionary trusts by *McPhail v Doulton*)[14] namely the view[15] that a power (or discretionary trust) is valid if the trustees can say with certainty of any one person or any few persons[16] that he or they are within the scope of the power (or discretionary trust), though uncertainty exists as to whether other persons are within or without the power (or discretionary trust).

Ultimately, everything must hinge upon how the court will deal with B's allegation that the trustees wrongfully paid income to X, whom B alleges is not a relative of S, where there is no evidence capable of proving whether or not X is a relative. If the evidential burden of proof rests on B as well as the legal burden of proof[17] so that the trustees are free to pay income to X or, indeed, to any Tom, Dick or Harry since it is impossible to prove that they are not relatives of S through some possible ancient common ancestor, then the 'trust' should be void for uncertainty and administrative unworkability. However, if the evidential burden of proof rests on the trustees once B has provided prima facie evidence that X is not a relative, then the trust will be valid, since the trustees will be under an enforceable duty to pay only those who can produce the relevant birth and marriage certificates. This justifies the majority view of Sachs and Megaw LJJ who endorsed the views of Brightman J at first instance when he had pointed out[18]. 'A supposed relative to whom a grant is contemplated would, in strictness, be bound to produce the relevant birth and marriage certificates or other sufficient evidence to prove his or her relationship. If the relationship is sufficiently proved the

---

12 Alternatively, may the court have power to strike out the offending concept and sever it from the valid concepts within the class or classes of beneficiaries? Cf *Re Leek* [1969] 1 Ch 563 at 586; *Re Gulbenkian's Settlement Trusts* [1968] Ch 126 at 138. The orthodox view is that there is no authority in the trustees or the court to make any distribution among a smaller class than that pointed out by the donor: *Whishaw v Stephens* [1970] AC 508 at 524, sub nom *Re Gulbenkian's Settlement Trusts* [1968] 3 All ER 785 at 792, HL per Lord Upjohn; *McPhail v Doulton* [1971] AC 424 at 456, [1970] 2 All ER 228 at 246, HL per Lord Wilberforce. Consider also the implications of the views of Megaw LJ for cases like *Re Astor's Settlement Trusts* [1952] Ch 534, [1952] 1 All ER 1067, where a substantial number of persons came within clause 7(b) for the relief or benefit of persons, or families or dependants thereof, actually or formerly engaged in journalism or in the newspaper business or any branch thereof, applied by the Court of Appeal in *Re Wright's Will Trusts* (21 July 1982, unreported) reported in (1999) 13 Trust L I 48.
13 [1970] AC 508, sub nom *Re Gulbenkian's Settlement Trusts, Whishaw v Stephens* [1968] 3 All ER 785.
14 [1971] AC 424, [1970] 2 All ER 228, HL.
15 *Re Gulbenkian's Settlement Trusts* [1968] Ch 126, [1967] 3 All ER 15, CA.
16 Megaw LJ in *Re Baden's Deed Trusts (No 2)* [1973] Ch 9 at 24, [1972] 2 All ER 1304 at 1313, treats the rejected view as concerning one single person being within the power or the trust but Lord Upjohn in *Whishaw v Stephens* [1970] AC 508 at 524, sub nom *Re Gulbenkian's Settlement Trusts, Whishaw v Stephens* [1968] 3 All ER 785 at 792, in his example of two or three individuals being clearly 'old friends' treats the rejected view as concerning one or a few persons clearly within a power or trust.
17 On legal and evidential burdens see *Cross on Evidence* (9th edn) Ch 4.
18 [1972] Ch 607 at 626, [1971] 3 All ER 985 at 995.

trustees will be entitled to make the grant. If no sufficient evidence can be produced the trustees would have no option but to decline to make a grant.'

The ease with which common ancestry can be traced back many thousands of years by DNA testing makes it necessary for a settlor or testator not to create a discretionary trust or power for his relatives generally, which could extend to an unworkable[19] 100 million Europeans, but to restrict them in some way to descendants of a designated ancestor alive 100 years ago or so.

Resolution of uncertainty

Questions of evidential uncertainty will be resolved by the court if need be, though it is possible[20] to make express provision for the trustees or the Chief Rabbi or the testator's widow conclusively to resolve any evidential uncertainty, so obviating any need to apply to the court.

Since conceptual uncertainty cannot be resolved by the court it would seem that a fortiori it cannot be resolved by a provision purporting to make the opinion of the trustees conclusive in cases of such uncertainty. If ex hypothesi the court cannot decide who are persons with whom B 'has had a social or other relationship', or persons who 'have moral claims' on a testator, or persons who are 'old friends' of the testator, it is difficult to see how the trustees can[1]. In exercising their fiduciary role or defending it against a challenge in the courts there are surely no clear conceptual criteria to guide them or justify their actions so that the matter is not justiciable, not capable of resolution by any reasoning process.

As Jenkins J said in *Re Coxen*[2]:

'If the testator had insufficiently defined the state of affairs on which the trustees were to form their opinion he would not have saved the condition from invalidity on the ground of uncertainty merely by making their opinion the criterion, although the declaration by the trustees of this or that opinion would be an event about which in itself there could be no uncertainty.'

This view was followed in *Re Jones*[3]; *Re Burton's Settlement*[4], and in *Re Wright's Will Trusts*[5] where a bequest to trustees 'to use the same at their absolute

---

19 Two and a half million members of a class made a discretionary trust for such class void for administrative unworkability in *R v District Auditor No 3 Audit District of West Yorkshire Metropolitan County Council, ex p West Yorkshire Metropolitan County Council* [1986] 26 RVR 24.
20 *Re Tuck's Settlement Trusts* [1978] Ch 49, [1978] 1 All ER 1047, CA; *Dundee General Hospitals Board of Management v Walker* [1952] 1 All ER 896, HL.
 1 *Re Coxen* [1948] Ch 747, [1948] 2 All ER 492; *Re Jones* [1953] Ch 125; *Re Burton's Settlement* [1955] Ch 82 at 95; *Re Wright's Will Trusts* [1981] LS Gaz R 841.
 2 [1948] Ch 747 at 761–762.
 3 [1953] Ch 125, [1953] 1 All ER 357.
 4 [1955] Ch 82 at 95.
 5 [1981] LS Gaz R 841 (and on appeal reported in (1999) 13 Trust L I 48) despite the unorthodox dicta of Lord Denning in *Re Tuck's Settlement Trusts* [1978] Ch 49 at 60 and 62, [1978] 1 All ER 1047 at 1052–1054, CA favouring allowing the Chief Rabbi to resolve conceptual uncertainty and the unorthodox dicta of Harman LJ in *Re Leek* [1969] 1 Ch 563 at 579, [1968] 1 All ER 793 at 797, CA favouring the validity of a trust for such persons as the trustees considered have a moral claim on the settlor. It may well be that resolution by the Chief Rabbi can be justified in *Re Tuck's Settlement Trusts* either because it related to a condition precedent where a 'core meaning' will suffice (see p 99, post) or because the matter of Jewish faith can be resolved as an evidential matter (cf *Re Tepper's Will Trusts* [1987] Ch 358, post, p 103), or because the Chief Rabbi can be regarded as an expert acting as such, rather than an arbitrator, so as to be able to resolve related questions of law and fact: *Brown v GIO Insurance Ltd* [1998] Lloyd's Rep IR 201; *Nikko Hotels (UK) Ltd v MEPC* [1991] 2 EGLR 103 at 108.

discretion for such people and institutions as they think have helped me or my late husband' failed for conceptual uncertainty. Any apparent distinction between (i) a trust for 'such persons as have helped me or otherwise have moral claims upon me' with a subsequent clause empowering the opinion of the trustees to be decisive in cases of doubt and (ii) a trust for 'such persons as my trustees consider to have helped me or otherwise have moral claims upon me' is surely a 'distinction without a difference' as Sir George Jessel MR would have said[6].

If the arbiter were not the trustees but the testator's widow the position is very likely different. An individual, like a widow, having a personal power, as opposed to a trustee having a fiduciary power, is unhampered by fiduciary duties and cannot have the power taken away from her[7]. She can release the power[8], or decide never to bother to consider exercising it, or exercise the power initially by an appointment to trustees of a discretionary trust who then can exercise the discretion that formerly she had despite the *Delegatus non potest delegare* principle[9], or exercise it capriciously without bothering to consider the range of objects[10], though she cannot go outside the range of objects or commit a fraud on the power (eg by exercising the power in B's favour subject to obtaining a pre-arranged benefit from B). In *Re Coates*[11] a testator provided, 'If my wife feels that I have forgotten any friend I direct my executors to pay to such friend or friends as are nominated by my wife a sum not exceeding £25 per friend with a maximum aggregate payment of £250 so that such friends may buy a small memento of our friendship' and this was upheld[12]. It is clear from *Re Hay's Settlement Trusts*[13] that one can validly confer on the widow power, for example, to add to the class of beneficiaries anyone else (other than herself or the trustees) so that one may certainly qualify that by adding 'particularly anyone she considers a friend of the testator'.

Apparent conceptual uncertainty may be saved from actual uncertainty by benignant construction. As Lord Hailsham has emphasised[14]:

6 See the approach of Eveleigh LJ in *Re Tuck's Settlement Trusts* [1978] Ch 49 at 66, [1978] 1 All ER 1047 at 1057.
7 *Re Park* [1932] 1 Ch 580 at 582. Query whether it would be repugnant to the core trust obligation to confer upon the trustees an effective expressly personal, non-fiduciary, non-challengeable power to determine conclusively those who fall within the class of discretionary beneficiaries designated by the settlor. Can trustees be allowed to define the limits of their own obligations?
8 *Re Wills' Trust Deeds* [1964] Ch 219 at 237.
9 *Re Triffitt's Settlement* [1958] Ch 852 at 864.
10 *Re Hay's Settlement Trusts* [1981] 3 All ER 786 at 792, [1982] 1 WLR 202 at 209. It may well be that a personal power need not satisfy the test for conceptual certainty of fiduciary powers: it should be enough that one or more persons are within the 'core' meaning of the concept. See CT Emery (1982) 98 LQR 551 at 582: this could now justify *Re Gibbard* [1966] 1 All ER 273, [1967] 1 WLR 42 where T left his residuary estate to his niece for life with power for her to appoint by her will among 'any of my old friends' and she did so, and Plowman J upheld this.
11 [1955] Ch 495, [1955] 1 All ER 26. Also see p 216, post.
12 Roxburgh J seemed to regard the concept in context as certain enough but the decision pre-dated *Whishaw v Stephens* [1970] AC 508, sub nom *Re Gulbenkian's Settlement Trusts, Whishaw v Stephens* [1968] 3 All ER 785, HL and *McPhail v Doulton* [1971] AC 424, [1970] 2 All ER 228, HL. On 'friends' see *Re Barlow's Will Trusts* [1979] 1 All ER 296 and *Brown v Gould* [1972] Ch 53, [1971] 2 All ER 1505.
13 [1981] 3 All ER 786, [1982] 1 WLR 202.
14 *IRC v McMullen* [1981] AC 1 at 11, [1980] 1 All ER 884 at 890, HL. Also see *Re Lloyd's Trust Instrument* cited in *Brown v Gould* [1972] Ch 53, [1971] 2 All ER 1505 and *Universe Tankships Inc of Monrovia v International Transport Worker's Federation* [1983] 1 AC 366 at 406, [1982] 2 All ER 67 at 93, HL. See the benevolent *Re Lipinski's Will Trusts* [1976] Ch 235.

'Where it is claimed that there is an ambiguity, a benignant construction should be given if possible. This was the maxim of the civil law: *semper in dubiis benigniora praeferenda sunt.* There is a similar maxim in English law: *ut res magis valeat quam pereat.* It applies where a gift is capable of two constructions one of which would make it void and the other effectual.'

Thus, a residuary bequest 'to those beneficiaries who have only received small amounts' may be validated in context by being restricted to those who had received legacies of £25, £50 and £100 where other legatees had received £200 or £250[15]. Similarly, a private discretionary trust for 'Cambridge students' might be validated by restricting it to students from time to time studying as junior members of the University of Cambridge, so excluding students at Cambridge language schools and students elsewhere whose homes are in Cambridge, while a will trust for 'my relatives' might be restricted to relatives 'known by me to be relatives'.

A trust must be administratively workable

As long ago as 1805 Lord Eldon stated[16]:

'As it is a maxim that the execution of a trust shall be under the control of the court it must be of such a nature that it can be under that control; so that the administration of it can be reviewed by the court, or the court itself can execute the trust: a trust, therefore, which in case of maladministration could be reformed and a due administration directed.'

Thus he held void a purported trust for 'objects of benevolence and liberality' since no clear criteria existed to enable the court to control or execute the trust. Here the administrative unworkability arises, as it always must, in the case of conceptual uncertainty. However, a discretionary trust may be conceptually certain but, nevertheless, may be administratively unworkable. Thus, a trust of funds to be applied in such manner as the trustee sees fit (otherwise than for his own benefit) or for such persons (other than himself) as the trustee sees fit will be void since no clear criteria exist to enable the court to control or execute the trust[17], though it is clear that anything can be done otherwise than for the trustee's benefit and everyone in the world is a beneficiary except the trustee. How would the trustee begin to try to decide what to do? As Clauson J stated in *Re Park*:

'It is clearly settled that if a testator creates a trust he must mark out the metes and bounds which are to fetter the trustee, or as has been said, the trust must not be too vague for the court to enforce, and that is why a gift to trustees for such purposes as they in their discretion think fit is an invalid trust: there are no metes and bounds within which the trust can be defined, and unless the trust can be defined the court cannot enforce it[18].'

Essentially, the terms of the trust must be justiciable: a court must act

---

15 *Re Steel* [1978] 2 All ER 1026 at 1032. See also *O'Rourke v Binks* [1992] STC 703, CA for 'small' in s 72(4), Capital Gains Tax Act 1979.
16 *Morice v Bishop of Durham* (1805) 10 Ves 522 at 539–540.
17 *Re Pugh's Will Trusts* [1967] 3 All ER 337, [1967] 1 WLR 1262; *Blausten v IRC* [1972] Ch 256 at 266, 271, 272, 273, per Buckley LJ]; *Re Hay's Settlement Trusts* [1981] 3 All ER 786, [1982] 1 WLR 202 where Megarry V-C, if necessary, would have been prepared to hold a discretionary trust for everyone, but the settlor her spouse and the trustees, void for administrative unworkability.
18 [1932] 1 Ch 580 at 583, approved in *Blausten v IRC* [1972] Ch 256 at 271.

judicially according to some clear criteria expressly or impliedly provided by the trust instrument or by extrinsic admissible evidence. If such criteria do not exist then obviously the court will not be in a position to have the information required to carry out or control the trust: it cannot resort to pure guesswork for this is to fulfil a non-justiciable function.

In the case of discretionary trusts, as Lord Wilberforce made clear in *McPhail v Doulton*[19], the court may execute the trust by appointing appropriate persons to be new trustees to carry out the trusts, or by directing representative persons of different classes of beneficiaries to prepare a scheme of distribution distributing the funds amongst the different classes, or, even, should the proper basis for distribution appear, by itself directing distribution of the trust fund. However, as Lord Wilberforce went on to say[20], the trust will be void 'where the meaning of the words used is clear but the definition of beneficiaries is so hopelessly wide as not to form anything like a class so that the trust is administratively unworkable or in Lord Eldon's words one that cannot be executed. I hesitate to give examples for they may prejudice future cases, but perhaps "all the residents of Greater London" will serve. I do not think that a discretionary trust for "relatives" even of a living person falls within this category'.

Lord Wilberforce's example of a discretionary trust for all the residents of Greater London being void is perhaps borderline[1] since it can be envisaged that a former Chairman of the Greater London Council[2] could create a trust to provide benefits for Greater London residents, perhaps with the motive of alleviating the strain, stress and squalor of living in and travelling within Greater London[3]. However, in the absence of admissible evidence of any intent of the settlor it seems the trustees (and the court) could not begin to ascertain criteria for determining which residents are to benefit and in what degree. It seems necessary for there to be criteria expressly or impliedly provided by the trust instrument or by extrinsic admissible evidence sufficient to enable the court to 'police' matters after deciding upon persons appropriate to be appointed trustees in place of recalcitrant trustees or after appointing representatives of appropriate classes of beneficiaries to draw up a scheme of distribution for approval by the court.

In practice it seems from *McPhail v Doulton*[4]; *Re Denley's Trust Deed*[5] and *Re Gestetner*[6] that the court will be loath to inhibit the flexibility of widely drafted

---

19 [1971] AC 424 at 457, [1970] 2 All ER 228 at 247.

20 [1971] AC 424, [1970] 2 All ER 228. In *Whishaw v Stephens* [1970] AC 508, sub nom *Re Gulbenkian's Settlement Trusts, Whishaw v Stephens* [1968] 3 All ER 785 at 788. Lord Reid had stated, 'There may be a class of case where, although the description of a class of beneficiaries is clear enough, any attempt to apply it to the facts would lead to such administrative difficulties that it would for that reason be held to be invalid'.

1 (1974) 38 Conv 269 (L McKay): (1974) 37 MLR 643.

2 An example suggested by Megarry V-C in *Re Hay's Settlement Trusts* [1981] 3 All ER 786 at 795, [1982] 1 WLR 202 at 212.

3 If the trust were exclusively charitable it could be valid, a cy près scheme making the trust administratively workable if a paramount charitable intention existed.

4 [1971] AC 424, [1970] 2 All ER 228; *Re Baden's Deed Trusts (No 2)* [1973] Ch 9, [1972] 2 All ER 1304, where the trust was valid for the trustees to make 'at their absolute discretion grants to or for the benefit of any of the officers and employees or ex-officers or ex-employees of the Company or to any relatives or dependants of any such persons in such amounts at such times and on such conditions (if any) as they think fit'.

5 [1969] 1 Ch 373, [1968] 3 All ER 65.

6 [1953] Ch 672, [1953] 1 All ER 1150, where a special power was valid though exercisable in favour of four named individuals, any descendant (or spouse thereof) of the settlor's father

discretionary trusts by holding them void for administrative unworkability. However, in *R v District Auditor No 3 Audit District of West Yorkshire Metropolitan County Council, ex p West Yorkshire Metropolitan County Council*[7] the Divisional Court held that a discretionary trust for the purpose of benefiting as many as two and a half million inhabitants of West Yorkshire would be administratively unworkable, even assuming the presence of conceptual certainty. The inhabitants had to be benefited within eleven months in any of four specified ways: (1) to assist economic development in the county in order to relieve unemployment and poverty, (2) to assist bodies concerned with youth and community problems, (3) to assist and encourage ethnic and other minority groups, and (4) to inform all interested and influential persons of the consequences of the proposed abolition of the Council (and other metropolitan county councils) and of other proposals concerning local government in the county. The trust was thus also void as a pure purpose trust since administrative unworkability prevented anyone having locus standi to enforce the trust. To be on the safe side, it will be as well for draftsmen of discretionary trusts for the 'benefit' of large classes of persons to provide guiding criteria for the trustees to consider in exercising their discretion.

Must powers be administratively workable ?

Re Gestetner, in fact, concerned a special power of very wide ambit[8] rather than a discretionary trust, and the question arises whether a power needs to be administratively workable at all or to the same degree as a discretionary trust. It seems that a power vested in someone not as trustee but as a private individual need not be administratively workable since the private individual is under no fiduciary obligation subject to the control of the court[9] (though an appointment cannot be a fraud on the power, ie for a purpose beyond the scope of the power)[10]. Thus, a personal power conferred on a widow to appoint amongst a conceptually uncertain class such as the testator's old friends should be validly exercised if confined to those within the 'core' meaning of the concept and might even be effective unless in favour of some person clearly outside the uncertain 'penumbra' of meaning[11].

---

and uncle, five named charities, any former employee of the settlor or his wife, any director or employee (or spouse thereof) or ex-director or ex-employee (or spouse thereof) of Gestetner Ltd or of any company of which the directors for the time being included any director of Gestetner Ltd. If a Gestetner director became a director of Woolworth or ICI or Unilever the expansion in numbers would be dramatic. *McPhail v Doulton* [1971] AC 424, [1970] 2 All ER 228, and *Whishaw v Stephens* [1970] AC 508, sub nom *Re Gulbenkian's Settlement Trusts, Whishaw v Stephens* [1968] 3 All ER 785, HL seem to treat *Re Gestetner* as a good decision though the administrative unworkability point seems never to have been raised in respect of the decision. This has encouraged Templeman J and Megarry V-C to treat special powers as not subject to the test of administrative workability: *Re Manisty's Settlement* [1974] Ch 17, [1973] 2 All ER 1203; *Re Hay's Settlement Trusts* [1981] 3 All ER 786, [1982] 1 WLR 202: see pp 95–96 post.

7 [1986] RVR 24.

8 See preceding note 6.

9 *Re Park* [1932] 1 Ch 580; *Re Jones* [1945] Ch 105; *Whishaw v Stephens* [1970] AC 508 at 518, sub nom *Re Gulbenkian's Settlement Trusts, Whishaw v Stephens* [1968] 3 All ER 785 at 787; *Re Hay's Settlement Trusts* [1981] 3 All ER 786 at 792, [1982] 1 WLR 202 at 209, so justifying *Re Coates* [1955] Ch 495 and *Re Gibbard* [1967] 1 WLR 42 if needing a post-*Whishaw v Stephens* [1970] AC 508 justification.

10 *Vatcher v Paull* [1915] AC 372 and see pp 518, 692, post.

11 See C T Emery (1982) 98 LQR 551 at 582; Hayton and Marshall: *Commentary and Cases on Law of Trusts* (11th edn) para 3–114.

Trustees with special powers are under a fiduciary obligation to consider whether or in what way they shall exercise their powers and they must not exceed their powers[12], whether by going outside the class of objects or using their powers capriciously or mala fide or for reasons that are irrational, perverse or irrelevant to any sensible expectation of the settlor or for a purpose other than one for which the powers were given to them. Indeed, in an extreme case an improper refusal to consider exercising a power may lead the court to intervene positively to correct the situation even by directing an exercise of the power[13]. Admittedly, except in pension fund cases, where the power is to benefit beneficiaries, not to appoint to objects of a power, it is exceptionally difficult to find instances where the court has exercised positive control, but the negative control exercised by the court is significant, for those entitled in default of a valid exercise of the power must clearly be entitled to restrain the trustees from exercising it save among those within the power[14] and taking into account factors within the scope or purpose of the power[15].

Accordingly, Buckley LJ (with whom Orr and Salmon LJJ agreed) in *Blausten v IRC*[16] took the view that a power would be void if 'of so wide an extent that it would be impossible for the court to say whether or not the trustees were properly exercising it and so wide that it would be impossible for the trustees to consider in any sensible manner how they should exercise it, if at all, from time to time'. He went on to hold valid a power for trustees during the settlor's lifetime to add to a specified class of beneficiaries anyone in the world (other than the settlor or the trustees) *if approved in writing by the settlor*: this meant the settlor had set metes and bounds to the beneficial interests which he intended to permit to be created under the settlement. Buckley LJ clearly would have regarded such power void but for the requirement of the settlor's written approval[17]. One might consider that a power to add anyone in the world to the class of beneficiaries (other than the settlor or the trustees) is so wide that, in the absence of admissible evidence of restrictive criteria, it would be impossible for the court to invalidate an appointment of everyone in the world (except the settlor and the trustees) to the class of beneficiaries, made to simplify matters by obviating the need for innumerable ad hoc appointments of particular individuals from time to time in order to benefit them. A trust for everyone in the world (except the settlor and the trustees) has long been treated as void for administrative unworkability[18].

---

12 *Whishaw v Stephens* [1970] AC 508 at 518, sub nom *Re Gulbenkian's Settlement Trusts, Whishaw v Stephens* [1968] 3 All ER 785 at 787; *McPhail v Doulton* [1971] AC 424 at 449, 456, [1970] 2 All ER 228 at 240, 247; *Re Hay's Settlement Trusts* [1981] 3 All ER 786, [1982] 1 WLR 202.

13 *Klug v Klug* [1918] 2 Ch 67; *White v Grane* (1854) 18 Beav 571; *Re Lofthouse* (1885) 29 Ch D 921; *Mettoy Pension Trustees Ltd v Evans* [1991] 2 All ER 513, [1990] 1 WLR 1587; *Thrells Ltd v Lomas* [1993] 2 All ER 546, [1993] 1 WLR 456.

14 This is the rationale for the 'is or is not' test in *Whishaw v Stephens* [1970] AC 508, sub nom *Re Gulbenkian's Settlement Trusts, Whishaw v Stephens* [1968] 3 All ER 785.

15 *Re Hastings-Bass* [1975] Ch 25 at 41, [1974] 2 All ER 193 at 203.

16 [1972] Ch 256 at 273, [1972] 1 All ER 41 at 50. However, see *Re Edwards Will Trusts* [1947] 2 All ER 521, where a testamentary power for trustees to appoint to such persons and for such purposes as they might see fit was held void for uncertainty by Jenkins J though the validity of such a power in an inter vivos trust seems to have been assumed. In [1948] Ch 440 the Court of Appeal made the same assumption though reversing Jenkins J on another ground.

17 [1972] Ch 256 at 271, 272, [1972] 1 All ER 41 at 49, 50.

18 *Re Pugh's Will Trusts* [1967] 3 All ER 337, [1967] 1 WLR 1262; *Neo v Neo* (1875) LR 6 PC 382; *Re Hay's Settlement Trusts* [1981] 3 All ER 786 at 796. If the trustees exercised the power by adding a conceptually uncertain or administratively unworkable class of beneficiaries this would not invalidate the whole trust but would be an invalid exercise of the power.

However, in *Re Manisty's Settlement*[19] Templeman J held valid a power to add anyone in the world (other than members of a defined small 'Excepted Class') to the class of beneficiaries under a discretionary trust. After all, there were instances like *Re Gestetner*[20] where special powers had been upheld despite being in favour of a very wide class of objects and where, in practice, it would be virtually impossible for the courts to control or impeach the exercise of such powers; so why draw a line between such powers and powers to add anyone (except a tiny excepted class) to the class of beneficiaries, the latter advantageously arming the trustees against all developments and contingencies. A response to this argument is that in the case of discretionary trusts the administrative workability test determines as a matter of degree when a wide class of beneficiaries has become too wide to be acceptable and this test should apply to powers, the House of Lords having indicated that the rules on discretionary trusts and discretionary powers should be assimilated. However, Templeman J boldly treated the obiter dicta of Buckley LJ as having been made without the benefit of counsel having fully explored the implications of *Re Gestetner*[1] *Whishaw v Stephens*[2]; *McPhail v Doulton*[3] and *Re Baden's Deed Trusts (No 2)*[4]. He treated the test of administrative workability as formulated in *McPhail v Doulton* as applying only to trusts which may have to be executed and administered by the court and not to powers where the court has a more limited function[5]: thus 'a power cannot be uncertain merely because it is wide in ambit'[6]. However, he accepted the court could intervene if the trustees exercised a power 'capriciously, that is to say, act for reasons which could be said to be irrational, perverse or irrelevant to any sensible expectation of the settlor'[7]. He continued[8]:

> 'The objection to the capricious exercise of a power may well extend to the creation of a capricious power. A power to benefit residents of Greater London is capricious because the terms of the power negative any sensible intention on the part of the settlor. If the settlor intended and expected the trustees would have regard to persons with some claims on his bounty or some interest in an institution favoured by the settlor, or if the settlor had any other sensible intention or expectation, he would not have required the trustees to consider only an accidental conglomeration of persons who have no discernible link[9] with the settlor or with any institution. A capricious power negatives a sensible consideration by the trustees of the exercise of the power. But a wide power, be it special or intermediate, does not negative or prohibit a sensible approach by the trustees to the consideration and exercise of their powers.'

19 [1974] Ch 17, [1973] 2 All ER 1203.
20 See preceding note 6.
 1 [1953] Ch 672, [1953] 1 All ER 1150.
 2 [1970] AC 508, sub nom *Re Gulbenkian's Settlement Trusts, Whishaw v Stephens* [1968] 3 All ER 785.
 3 [1971] AC 424, [1970] 2 All ER 228.
 4 [1972] Ch 607, [1971] 3 All ER 985; affd [1973] Ch 9, [1972] 2 All ER 1304. He might also have mentioned *Re Denley's Trust Deed* [1969] 1 Ch 373, [1968] 3 All ER 65, where Goff J held valid a power to allow a sports ground to be used for the benefit of such other persons in the world as the trustees might see fit.
 5 [1974] Ch 17 at 29, [1973] 2 All ER 1203 at 1213. He played down the court's function in respect of powers: see *Klug v Klug* [1918] 2 Ch 67; *Re Hastings-Bass* [1975] Ch 25, [1974] 2 All ER 193, CA and RSC Ord 85, r 2(3)(e).
 6 [1974] Ch 17 at 24, [1973] 2 All ER 1203 at 1213.
 7 [1974] Ch 17 at 26, [1973] 2 All ER 1203 at 1208.
 8 [1974] Ch 17 at 27, [1973] 2 All ER 1203 at 1211.
 9 Would it make a difference if the settlor were a proud Cockney whose relatives and friends were all Cockneys resident in London?

However, it seems a wide power must be capable of being exercised sensibly and the court must be able to intervene if it is exercised for reasons which are irrational, perverse or irrelevant to any sensible expectation of the settlor. Thus, the settlor's expectations must somehow be discerned and so some degree of administrative workability is required for trustees' fiduciary powers. It is noteworthy that Templeman J remarked[10]:

'In *Gestetner* it was impossible to derive any assistance from the terms of the power, save that the trustees, it could be assumed, were expected to have regard to the considerations which might move the settlor to confer bounty on the beneficiaries. A similar expectation may be implied from an intermediate power, and in the present case *if the settlement is read as a whole the expectations of the settlor are not difficult to discern.*'

In *Re Hay's Settlement Trusts*, however, Megarry V-C endorsed the views of Templeman J on a power to add persons to the existing beneficiaries (when one may, perhaps, discern that such persons ought to relate in some way to such beneficiaries) and upheld a power to appoint to anyone in the world (except X, Y and Z), considering that 'dispositions ought, if possible, to be upheld and the court ought not to be astute to find grounds on which a power can be invalidated'[11]. He rejected the submission 'that the power is so wide that it would be impossible for the trustees to consider in any sensible manner how to exercise it and also impossible for the court to say whether or not they were properly exercising it', stating, 'If I have correctly stated the extent of the duties of trustees in whom a mere power is vested, I do not see what there is to prevent the trustees from performing these duties.'[12]
Earlier he had stated[13]:

'A trustee to whom, as such, a power is given is bound by the duties of his office in exercising that power to do so in a responsible manner according to its purpose. It is not enough for him to refrain from acting capriciously; he must do more ...

Apart from the obvious duty of obeying the trust instrument, and in particular of making no appointment that is not authorised by it, the trustee must, first, consider periodically whether or not he should exercise the power; second, consider the range of objects of the power; and third, consider the appropriateness of individual appointments.'

Superficially, there seems nothing to *prevent* trustees from exercising a power to appoint amongst 'old friends' of the settlor, until one considers the justiciability of issues raised if a beneficiary entitled in default of appointment challenges the appropriateness of an appointment, whereupon it becomes apparent that the power is void for administrative unworkability and conceptual uncertainty[14]. Should the position be any different if the power is 'to appoint to anyone in the world (except X, Y and Z) so that my old friends may be benefited' or, worse, just a power 'to appoint to anyone in the world except X, Y and Z' without any guidance at all?

---

10 [1974] Ch 17 at 24–25, [1973] 2 All ER 1203 at 1209.
11 [1981] 3 All ER 786 at 795.
12 [1981] 3 All ER 786 at 794.
13 [1981] 3 All ER 786 at 793.
14 *Re Lloyd's Trust Investments* unreported but cited in *Brown v Gould* [1972] Ch 53 at 57, [1971] 2 All ER 1505 at 1507; *Re Gulbenkian's Settlement Trusts* [1968] 3 All ER 785 at 792–793.

Currently, first instance decisions[15] establish that administrative workability is essential for discretionary trusts because they are positively justiciable, a beneficiary having the right to obtain the intervention of the court positively to ensure the trusts are carried out, while administrative workability is not essential for discretionary powers because they are only negatively justiciable, an object of the power having only the right to obtain the intervention of the court negatively to restrain or invalidate wrongful actions by the trustees. Logically, one would have thought that the need for justiciability, whether positive or negative, underlies the requirement of administrative workability. Furthermore, as *Mettoy Pension Trustees Ltd v Evans*[16] emphasises, there are some extreme cases where discretionary powers are positively carried out by the courts: thus, it is not correct to distinguish discretionary trusts from discretionary powers by saying that the former are positively and negatively justiciable while the latter are only negatively justiciable.

Therefore, on the safety first principle a power of appointment should be restricted to a sensible class of persons and then there should be a power for trustees to add persons to the specified class which should provide some express guidance for the trustees (eg to add persons proposed in writing by existing class members taking account of the proposer's written reasons why such addition would have been likely to meet with the settlor's approval) unless a letter of wishes provides such guidance.

Indeed the best course to take to provide the greatest flexibility will be expressly to provide that the trustee's power to appoint to anyone in the World (other than say the trustee and its employees, their spouses, descendants and dependants, and the settlor and his spouse) is a *fiduciary* one, in the sense that the trustee, must periodically consider whether or not to exercise it, but that any exercise or non-exercise of the power is to be a *personal* decision unchallengeable in the courts unless amounting to a fraud on the power[17]. The *ex officio* duties of trustees in exercising discretionary *trusts* must be fiduciary to underpin the core trustee – beneficiaries obligation, but the optional discretionary *powers* of appointment need not be fiduciary so far as concerns the actual conscious exercise or non-exercise of such powers and the settlor can make this expressly clear or this may arise by necessary implication. One sympathises with the view of Megarry V-C that[18]

---

15 *Re Manisty's Settlement* [1974] Ch 17, [1973] 2 All ER 1203 and *Re Hay's Settlement Trusts* [1981] 3 All ER 786, [1982] 1 WLR 202 were followed in *IRC v Schroder* [1983] STC 480 and in *Re Beatty's Will Trusts* [1990] 3 All ER 844, sub nom *Re Beatty, Hinves v Brooke* [1990] 1 WLR 1503 where counsel conceded that a power in an inter vivos deed for trustees to appoint to anyone in the world would be valid, and Hoffmann J held that such a power in a will was valid because there was no so-called rule against the delegation of a testator's will-making function to invalidate it.

16 [1991] 2 All ER 513, [1990] 1 WLR 1587 and *Thrells Ltd v Lomas* [1993] 2 All ER 546, [1993] 1 WLR 456, both being pension fund cases where the beneficiaries had earned their rights and where the company employer and sole trustee had become insolvent so its liquidator could not exercise powers relating to the surplus that could favour either creditors or beneficiaries because of an irreconcilable conflict of interest. Also see *Klug v Klug* [1918] 2 Ch 67 (court will intervene to direct positive exercise of power if a trustee's attitude is that he is not going to bother considering using his powers to benefit B because B is not worthy of consideration and a situation arises where no trustee could refuse to exercise the power in favour of B unless acting capriciously, ie for reasons irrational perverse or irrelevant to any sensible expectation of the settlor).

17 For detailed discussion of the distinction between fiduciary powers and personal powers see pp 29–33 ante.

18 *Re Hay's Settlement Trust* [1981] 3 All ER 786 at 795.

'dispositions ought, if possible to be upheld and the court ought not to be astute to find grounds on which a power can be invalidated', but, to uphold this view it is neither necessary nor logical to draw a distinction between the exercise of fiduciary discretionary trusts and fiduciary discretionary powers: to uphold his view he could have held that by necessary implication the exercise of the power to appoint anyone in the world was a personal and not a fiduciary function, such benignant construction saving the settlor's intentions from being ineffective.

In the case of testamentary trusts there is no so-called rule against the delegation of a testator's will-making function to invalidate the broadest powers of appointment[19].

Initial and supervening administrative unworkability

The question of administrative workability or not has to be determined as of the date property is effectively subjected to trusts[20]. Are the trusts then valid thereafter or are they inherently voidable in that they may subsequently become void for administrative unworkability, eg where there are initially 1,000 members of a discretionary trust class consisting of (1) issue of X and of X's spouse and (2) employees or ex-employees or directors or ex-directors of X Ltd or of any company of which the directors for the time being included any director of X Ltd and (3) issue of persons within class (2), and after 70 years (when the trust fund with many X Ltd shares is worth £12 billion) the class consists of about 80 million members with X Ltd's directors being on the boards of various multi-national companies as well as of taken-over companies? Harman and Goff JJ in *Gestetner*[1] and *Re Denley*[2] seem to have assumed that a trust must be certain or administratively workable at any given time. On this basis subsequent supervening unworkability could invalidate a trust, the ever-present possibility of a resulting trust in the settlor's favour causing him tax problems in respect of any undistributed income[3]. However, in *Muir v IRC*[4] the Court of Appeal endorsed the view of Pennycuick J that the possibility of future uncertainty did not make a presently certain trust invalid so the settlor was not liable for tax on undistributed income.

One may expect that the courts will be reluctant to be driven to find a trust administratively unworkable when, on its creation, it was possible to find it workable owing to the settlor's clear express or implied criteria for the carrying out of the trusts and when DNA testing was unavailable to reveal the millions of relatives a person has. Perhaps the solution lies in permitting the trustees to make a valid sub-settlement or re-settlement on a smaller certain workable class of beneficiaries pursuant to a power in that behalf or the solution could lie in Lord Wilberforce's dicta in *McPhail v Doulton*[5] laying down that the court, if called on to execute a discretionary trust, will do so in the manner best calculated to give effect to the settlor's intentions as by authorising or directing representative persons of the classes of beneficiaries

19 *Re Beatty's Will Trusts* [1990] 3 All ER 844, sub nom *Re Beatty, Hinves v Brooke* [1990] 1 WLR 1503.
20 *Re Baden's Deed Trusts (No 2)* [1972] Ch 607; affd [1973] Ch 9.
1 [1953] Ch 672 at 684.
2 [1969] 1 Ch 373 at 386, [1968] 3 All ER 65 at 71; *IRC v Broadway Cottages Trust* [1955] Ch 20 at 29.
3 Income and Corporation Taxes Act 1988, s 673.
4 [1966] 3 All ER 38 at 44, 45 per Harman LJ.
5 [1971] AC 424 at 457, [1970] 2 All ER 228 at 247.

to prepare a scheme of distribution or, should the proper basis for distribution appear, by itself directing the trustees so to distribute. This heralds a jurisdiction similar to the cy prés jurisdiction for charitable trusts despite the denials of such jurisdiction by the High Court in *Re Astor's Settlement Trusts*[6] and *Re Denley's Trust Deed*[7]. So far as concerns persons originally within a certain administratively workable settlement, *Re Hain's Settlement Trusts*[8] indicates that the settlement cannot subsequently be invalidated because some of the class of beneficiaries may have disappeared or become impossible to find or it has been forgotten who they were.

Uncertain conditions for benefiting: conditions precedent

In the case of a fixed trust for division equally between my tall friends the trust will fail since a comprehensive list of beneficiaries cannot be drawn up. If there is a discretionary trust or a fiduciary power for the benefit of such of my tall friends as my trustees may see fit, then the trust will also fail due to the lack of conceptually clear criteria for determining whether any given postulant is or is not a member of the class of possible beneficiaries[9].

If, however, there is a testamentary gift of £1,000 or of a painting to each of my tall friends, this is valid according to Browne-Wilkinson J in *Re Barlow's Will Trusts*[10]. He considered it sufficient in such a case that it is possible to say of one or more persons that he or they undoubtedly qualify, even though it may be impossible to say of others whether or not they qualify[11]. Query whether his benevolent decision should be restricted to testamentary trusts like the decisions in the anomalous purpose trust cases that are regarded as concessions to human sentiment[12].

It seems anomalous and illogical to have a less strict approach for gifts to individuals than for class gifts under a discretionary trust or fiduciary power. An executor or trustee directed to make payments or transfer paintings to qualifying beneficiaries owes an enforceable obligation to such beneficiaries, who are in a stronger position than objects of discretionary trusts or powers. The default beneficiary, entitled to the balance after proper payments or transfers, has a right to sue the executor or trustee for benefiting persons who are not qualifying beneficiaries. To protect himself the executor or trustee must have a right to obtain the court's directions as to precisely whom he may or may not benefit, so that a comprehensive list needs to be capable of being drawn up. The uncertain penumbra of meaning attached to 'tall friends' makes the concept uncertain so that in many instances the court will find it impossible to decide whether or not a person is a tall friend. If the court, like Browne-Wilkinson J, allows just persons within the restricted 'core'

---

6 [1952] Ch 534, [1952] 1 All ER 1067.
7 [1969] 1 Ch 373 at 388, [1968] 3 All ER 65 at 72.
8 [1961] 1 All ER 848, [1961] 1 WLR 440, CA.
9 *McPhail v Doulton* [1971] AC 424, [1970] 2 All ER 228, HL pp 85–86, ante.
10 [1979] 1 All ER 296, [1979] 1 WLR 278 applying *Re Allen* [1953] Ch 810, CA decided before the new post-1970 approach.
11 The testatrix by will directed her executor 'to allow any member of my family and any friends of mine who may wish to do so to purchase' various of her paintings at a low 1970 valuation. If one painting was the best bargain by far, how could the offeree be found except by putting all names of potential offerees into a hat and drawing out one name? How could all such names be ascertained? Can they really be restricted just to persons within the 'core' meaning of family and friends?
12 See pp 118–123, post.

meaning of friends to qualify in the case of a trust to make individual gifts to qualifying persons, then, consistently, discretionary trusts and powers for members of a qualifying class ought to be valid and be capable of being exercised in favour of persons within the 'core' meaning of the class description. However House of Lords authority[13] is to the contrary, so that Brown-Wilkinson J accepted[14] that a discretionary trust or power for 'my friends' would be void for uncertainty.

Where the individual gifts are not to each person who comes within a qualifying class description (eg £5,000 to each of my friends' children who marry persons of the Jewish faith and of Jewish parentage) but to specific ascertained individuals if they satisfy the qualifying conditions (eg Shalom House to my elder son, Abraham, if he marries a woman of Jewish faith and of Jewish parentage, but if he does not, then for my younger son, Gideon, if he marries such a woman) there seems more scope, as a concession to human sentiment, to accept the individual's entitlement if he satisfies the 'core' meaning of the requisite concept. Thus, a gift to the eldest son of A if he is a member of the Church of England and an adherent to the doctrine of that Church is valid[15].

As a matter of logic, where conceptually uncertain words are used, conditions precedent should not be treated more liberally than conditions subsequent which are strictly treated as the following paragraphs show: just as B forfeits his interest if the requisites of a condition subsequent affecting his interest are satisfied, so, if A statisfies a condition precedent, B loses his interest in default of A satisfying the requisites of the condition precedent. Surely, in both instances B ought to be able to ascertain precisely and distinctly upon what requisites being satisfied his claim is to be overridden by A's claim.

Uncertain conditions for forfeiture: conditions subsequent

Uncertainty frequently arises in the case of conditions for forfeiture and particularly in conditions for forfeiture on non-residence, engaging in professional or public activities, marrying outside a particular religion or race or failing to comply with a name and arms clause. Such conditions subsequent where a vested interest is subsequently, upon a certain condition, to be divested must be distinguished from conditions precedent where an interest is only to be taken in the first place if the qualifying condition is satisfied[16]. The former type of condition is negative and destructive: it operates to take away someone's existing interest. The latter type is positive and constructive: it operates to give someone an interest. This is the justification for the test of certainty for a condition subsequent being strict, even stricter than the test of certainty of beneficiaries under a discretionary trust[17]. Whether a condition is

---

13 *Whishaw v Stephens* [1970] AC 508, sub nom *Re Gulbenkian's Settlement Trusts, Whishaw v Stephens* [1968] 3 All ER 785, HL; *McPhail v Doulton* [1971] AC 424, [1970] 2 All ER 228, HL.

14 *Re Barlow's Will Trusts* [1979] 1 WLR 278 at 281.

15 *Re Allen* [1953] Ch 810 at 817; L Mackay [1980] Conv 263 at 277; C T Emery (1982) 98 LQR 551 at 564.

16 *Re Allen* [1953] Ch 810, [1953] 2 All ER 898; *Blathwayt v Baron Cawley* [1976] AC 397, [1975] 3 All ER 625; *Re Tuck's Settlement Trusts* [1978] Ch 49, [1978] 1 All ER 1047, CA; *Re Abrahams' Will Trusts* [1969] 1 Ch 463, [1967] 2 All ER 1175.

17 *Whishaw v Stephens* [1970] AC 508 at 523, sub nom *Re Gulbenkian's Settlement Trusts, Whishaw v Stephens* [1968] 3 All ER 785 at 791; *Re Baden's Deed Trusts (No 2)* [1973] Ch 9 at 30, [1972] 2 All ER 1304 at 1318.

precedent or subsequent can be a very nice point and where a condition precedent is satisfied this operates, in fact, to divest the default beneficiaries of their interest so the distinction between the two sorts of condition is difficult to justify, though only the House of Lords can now abolish the distinction[18].

In order that a condition subsequent may be valid it must at all times be possible to predicate with absolute certainty what event will cause forfeiture. The rule was expressed by Lord Cranworth in *Clavering v Ellison*[19] as follows:

'Where a vested estate is to be divested by a condition on a contingency that is to happen afterwards that contingency must be such that the court can see from the beginning precisely and distinctly upon the happening of what event it was that the preceding estate was to determine.'

This language must, however, be closely analysed[20], for there is a distinction between uncertainty in expression and uncertainty in operation, and a provision will not be void for uncertainty merely because it is difficult to construe[1]. Where the language employed embodies a concept of sufficient certainty a condition will not be void although there may be difficulty in ascertaining whether it has occurred[2], but it is otherwise where the concept is itself uncertain[3]. A condition can thus be void for conceptual uncertainty but if the condition is conceptually certain it will not be vitiated by any evidential uncertainty.

A condition subsequent, otherwise void for conceptual uncertainty, will not be saved by the fact that the opinion of the trustees or some third party is the deciding factor. The concept on which the trustees or third party are to found their opinion must, itself, be certain[4]. The opinion of the trustees or third party may, however, be used to resolve matters where there would otherwise be evidential uncertainty.

Conditions as to residence

When a testator directed that certain payments should be made to his daughter 'only so long as she shall continue to reside in Canada', it was held by the Privy Council that, inasmuch as a categorical answer could not be given to the question upon what event the daughter's interest would determine so

---

18 *Re Tuck's Settlements Trusts* [1978] Ch 49, [1978] 1 All ER 1047, CA.
19 (1859) 7 HL Cas 707 at 725; but see *Re Coxen* [1948] Ch 747, [1948] 2 All ER 492.
20 See *Re Lanyon* [1927] 2 Ch 264.
  1 *Re Wilson's Will Trusts* [1950] 2 All ER 955 at 963, CA, per Sir Raymond Evershed MR; affd sub nom *Bromley v Tyron* [1952] AC 265, [1951] 2 All ER 1058, HL; *Re Denley* [1969] 1 Ch 373.
  2 *Blathwayt v Baron Cawley* [1976] AC 397, [1975] 3 All ER 625, HL ('be or become a Roman Catholic'); *Re Gape* [1952] Ch 743, sub nom *Gape's Will Trusts, Re Vercy v Gape* [1952] 2 All ER 579, ('permanent residence') CA; *Re Burton's Settlements* [1955] Ch 82, [1954] 3 All ER 193; and see *Re Hatch* [1948] Ch 592, [1948] 2 All ER 288. See also *McPhail v Doulton* [1971] AC 424 at 457; *Re Baden's Deed Trusts (No 2)* [1973] Ch 9, [1972] 2 All ER 1034, CA; *Re Tepper's Will Trusts* [1987] Ch 358, [1987] 1 All ER 970.
  3 *Sifton v Sifton* [1938] AC 656, [1938] 3 All ER 435, PC; *Re Brace* [1954] 2 All ER 354, [1954] 1 WLR 955 ('provide a home' held to be uncertain).
  4 *Re Coxen* [1948] Ch 747, [1948] 2 All ER 492; *Re Jones* [1953] Ch 125, [1953] 1 All ER 357; *Re Wright's Will Trusts* [1981] LS Gaz R 841. Lord Denning's remarks in *Re Tuck's Settlement Trusts* [1978] Ch 49, [1978] 1 All ER 1047, CA appear unorthodox and, perhaps should be restricted to conditions precedent with which the case was concerned or Jewish faith may, perhaps, be regarded as a matter of evidence as in *Re Tepper's Will Trusts* [1987] Ch 358, [1987] 1 All ER 970 or the Chief Rabbi may now be regarded as having acted as expert and not as arbitrator; see p 89, ante.

that she would know at all times if she was committing a breach of the condition, that condition as a condition subsequent was void for uncertainty[5].

This decision appears to have met with the approval of the House of Lords[6], but in subsequent cases the court has been able to escape its results by finding sufficient distinctions in the language to be construed. Thus a condition for forfeiture if in the opinion of trustees a beneficiary should have ceased 'permanently to reside' in a certain house has been upheld on the grounds that in the context of the particular will 'residence' meant personal residence, that permanent cesser of personal residence connoted removal with no animus revertendi and that it would not be impossible to decide whether this event had or had not happened[7]. Likewise a condition for forfeiture on failing to 'take up permanent residence in England' has been upheld as embodying a concept of sufficient certainty known to English law in ascertaining the issue of domicile. Here again 'permanent' was regarded as the decisive word[8].

On the other hand, a condition that a beneficiary should occupy certain freehold property has been held to be void for uncertainty since it was impossible to ascertain the degree of occupation necessary to fulfil it[9].

Conditions as to professions or offices

Where a testator gave life interests to two ladies and provided that they should forfeit such interests if they should 'willingly adopt and carry on any profession or professional calling, whether for gain or otherwise', the condition was held void for uncertainty[10], and where a testator stipulated that his sons should not 'become candidates for or enter Parliament or undertake any other public office', the court, though not expressing any view as to whether or not the condition was void for uncertainty, thought there were good grounds for suggesting that it might be[11].

Conditions as to religion and parentage

A strict approach was heralded by the House of Lords in *Clayton v Ramsden*[12] which concerned a condition subsequent providing for forfeiture on marriage with a person 'not of Jewish parentage and of the Jewish faith'[13]. It was unanimously held that the first limb (and therefore the whole condition) was void for uncertainty and in obiter dicta a four to one majority concluded that the second limb was also void. Recently, a more liberal approach prevailed in

---

5 *Sifton v Sifton* [1938] AC 656, [1938] 3 All ER 435. However in *Ellis v Chief Adjudication Officer* [1998] 1 FLR 184 the Court of Appeal upheld a deed of gift of a flat by a mother to her daughter, D, on condition D repaid the mortgage and allowed her mother to reside in the flat under D's care, so on eviction the mother was entitled to part of the proceeds of sale.
6 See *Clayton v Ramsden* [1943] AC 320, [1943] 1 All ER 16, HL.
7 *Re Coxen* [1948] Ch 747, [1948] 2 All ER 492.
8 *Re Gape* [1952] Ch 418, [1952] 1 All ER 827; affd [1952] Ch 743, sub nom *Gapes Will Trusts, Re Vercy v Gape* [1952] 2 All ER 579, CA.
9 *Re Field's Will Trusts* [1950] Ch 520, [1950] 2 All ER 188.
10 *Re Reich* (1924) 40 TLR 398.
11 *Re Edgar* [1939] 1 All ER 635, actually decided on grounds of public policy.
12 [1943] AC 320, [1943] 1 All ER 16.
13 See also *Re Gott* [1944] Ch 193, [1944] 1 All ER 293; *Re Evans* [1940] Ch 629; *Re Krawitz's Will Trusts* [1959] 3 All ER 793, [1959] 1 WLR 1192; *Re Blaiberg* [1940] Ch 385, [1940] 1 All ER 632; *Re Donn* [1944] Ch 8, [1943] 2 All ER 564; *Re Moss' Trusts* [1945] 1 All ER 207.

the House of Lords in *Blathwayt v Baron Cawley*[14] where a condition for forfeiture upon someone being or becoming a Roman Catholic was upheld as a less vague conception than someone being or not being of the Jewish faith. However, even Jewish faith may validly be the subject matter of a condition precedent qualifying someone to take a particular interest[15] for the test of certainty for a condition precedent is less than that for a condition subsequent[16]. The Court of Appeal has continued the liberal approach in dealing with a condition precedent concerned with marriage to an 'approved wife' being 'a wife of Jewish blood by one or both of her parents and who has been brought up in and has never departed from and at the date of her marriage continues to worship according to the Jewish faith'[17]. It was held that this meant that the wife should have some Jewish blood so that there were not the problems met in a case[18] where it was required simply that X should be 'of Jewish blood' or 'of Jewish parentage' and it was uncertain whether 100 or 75 or 50% blood or parentage would suffice. Subsequently[19], a condition subsequent providing for forfeiture on marriage outside the Jewish faith was not automatically struck down. Scott J rather benevolently gave leave for evidence to be adduced as to the settlor's concept of Jewish faith on the basis that if this was sufficiently certain the clause would be upheld.

Draftsmen, of course, should err as much as possible on the side of particularising forfeiting events (eg by referring to particular religious rites upon marriage or conversion under the religion in question) or, if more flexibility is required, should provide for the settlor's concept of someone being of the Jewish faith or the Roman Catholic faith to be the concept of a particular Chief Rabbi or Bishop for the time being when the matter arises for resolution, the decision of such Chief Rabbi or Bishop to be conclusive as the opinion of an expert, not merely that of an arbitrator[20].

Names and arms clauses

The former tendency of the courts to hold that provisions for forfeiture in the traditional form of name and arms clauses are void for uncertainty has been reversed by the decision of the Court of Appeal in *Re Neeld*[1]. The clause in that case required each of several beneficiaries within the space of one year to

' ... take upon himself and use upon all occasions the surname of "Neeld" only and quarter the arms of "Neeld" with his or her own family arms ... '

and it extended to the husband of a female beneficiary. The clause went on to provide that if a beneficiary

14 [1976] AC 397, [1975] 3 All ER 625, HL.
15 *Re Abrahams' Will Trusts* [1969] 1 Ch 463, [1967] 2 All ER 1175; *Re Selby's Will Trusts* [1965] 3 All ER 386, [1966] 1 WLR 43; *Re Tuck's Settlement Trusts* [1978] Ch 49, [1978] 1 All ER 1047, CA; *Re Tepper's Will Trusts* [1987] Ch 358, [1987] 1 All ER 970.
16 *Re Allen* [1953] Ch 810, [1953] 2 All ER 898, CA; *Blathwayt v Baron Cawley* [1976] AC 397, [1975] 3 All ER 625; *Re Tuck's Settlement Trusts* [1978] Ch 49, [1978] 1 All ER 1047, CA.
17 *Re Tuck's Settlement Trusts* [1978] Ch 49, [1978] 1 All ER 1047, CA.
18 *Re Tarnpolsk* [1958] 3 All ER 479, [1958] 1 WLR 1157.
19 *Re Tepper's Will Trusts* [1987] Ch 358, [1987] 1 All ER 970.
20 *Re Tuck's Settlement Trusts* [1978] Ch 49, [1978] 1 All ER 1047 explained at p 89, ante.
 1 [1962] Ch 643, [1962] 2 All ER 335, CA.

'. . . shall refuse or neglect or discontinue to take or use such surname and arms . . . then after the expiration of the said space of one year . . . '

his interest should cease. The court, in upholding the clause, held that in general a name and arms clause following the language of established precedent is not void for uncertainty merely because it imposes an obligation to 'take and use' or to 'assume' or to 'use on all occasions' a surname, or because it provides for defeasance if the beneficiary in question 'disuses' or 'ceases to use' the surname, for these expressions are not so uncertain as to make the provision invalid and they satisfy the test laid down in *Clavering v Ellison*[2] as restated in *Sifton v Sifton*[3] – that is to say, can the court and the parties concerned see from the beginning precisely and distinctly upon the happening of what events it is that the previous vested estate is to determine? Earlier cases in a contrary sense[4] were disapproved.

Questions may clearly arise as to what acts or events amount to a disuse of, or to a discontinuance of use of, or to ceasing to use, a surname. In *Re Howard's Will Trusts*[5], Wilberforce J held that one single instance of failure to use a surname on an occasion when a surname could appropriately be used would be sufficient of itself to bring about a forfeiture. But this dictum was disapproved in *Re Neeld*[6] by Upjohn and Diplock LJJ, who took the view that the inadvertent use by a beneficiary of his former surname on one or more occasions after he had assumed the new one should be treated as de minimis and would not therefore result in defeasance.

The Court of Appeal also held in *Re Neeld*[7] that a clause such as that with which they were concerned is not void as being contrary to public policy merely because it imposes an obligation of change of name on a man to whom a female beneficiary is married or whom she may subsequently marry[8].

As has already been noted, the clause with which this case was concerned required each beneficiary not only to change his surname but also to 'quarter the arms of 'Neeld' with his or her own family arms'. The case had a sequel in *Re Neeld (No 3)*[9], in which Megarry J considered the practical effect of this requirement. During the time which had elapsed since the decision of the Court of Appeal in the first case the plaintiff beneficiary had (as appears from the title of the second case) changed his surname, but he had not quartered the arms of Neeld with his family arms, because he had no family arms with which to quarter them. Megarry J held, however, that the effect of the clause was to require the plaintiff to obtain some family arms for himself and then to quarter the arms of Neeld with those arms (and that he must do both these things within the time limit specified by the clause).

---

2 (1859) 7 HL Cas 707.
3 [1938] AC 656, [1938] 3 All ER 435, PC.
4 On the question of uncertainty, the following cases were expressly disapproved: *Re Lewis' Will Trusts* [1951] WN 591; *Re Bouverie* [1952] Ch 400, [1952] 1 All ER 408; *Re Wood's Will Trusts* [1952] Ch 406, [1952] 1 All ER 740; and *Re Kersey* [1952] WN 541. The case of *Re Murray* [1955] Ch 69, [1954] 3 All ER 129 was not disapproved because the decision in that case rested upon the use of particular language in the provision in question.
5 [1961] Ch 507, [1961] 2 All ER 413.
6 [1962] Ch 643, [1962] 2 All ER 335, CA.
7 [1962] Ch 643, [1962] 2 All ER 335, CA.
8 On this question of public policy, the following cases were expressly disapproved: *Re Fry* [1945] Ch 348, [1945] 2 All ER 205; and *Re Kersey* (see note 4, above). It may also be assumed that the case of *Re Howard's Will Trusts* [1961] Ch 507, [1961] 2 All ER 413 has been overruled on this question.
9 [1969] 2 All ER 1025, [1969] 1 WLR 988.

Discretionary trusts for benevolent purposes

Cases in which the question of uncertainty has arisen have frequently come before the courts in relation, first, to attempts on the part of testators to create discretionary trusts in favour of vague objects of benevolence not falling within the legal definition of charity and, second, to trusts where the objects are so described that the property could be used exclusively for charitable purposes but could, nevertheless, be devoted in whole or in part to non-charitable purposes. Only if every purpose to which trust property can lawfully be devoted is charitable are trusts charitable in law[10] and thus exempt from failure through uncertainty (unless they were in existence before 16 December 1952, and were validated by the Charitable Trusts (Validation) Act 1954)[11]. Vague purpose trusts may be void not just because they are too uncertain but because there is no-one with locus standi to enforce them, or because they infringe the rule against inalienability which prevents income being tied up for longer than the perpetuity period. It seems that they cannot be attacked for contravening the so-called principle against delegation of the will-making power[12].

An example of the first class is afforded by *Grimond v Grimond*[13]: where the testator had directed his trustees to divide a part of his residuary estate among 'such charitable or religious institutions and societies as they think fit'. If, however, the trust had been for charitable or religious *purposes*, instead of for charitable or religious *institutions* it would have been good[14], but being partly for charitable objects and partly for objects not charitable (since the purposes of a religious institution may lack the element of public benefit, and thus, not be charitable)[15], the beneficiaries were not pointed out with sufficient certainty.

Trusts for purposes vaguely described as 'benevolent'[16], 'charitable *or* benevolent'[17], 'philanthropic'[18], 'hospitable'[19], 'patriotic'[20], or for 'religious,

10 *Chichester Diocesan Fund and Board of Finance Inc v Simpson* [1944] AC 341, [1944] 2 All ER 60, HL; *A-G of the Bahamas v Royal Trust Co* [1986] 3 All ER 423, [1986] 1 WLR 1001, PC.

11 See p 107, post.

12 *Re Beatty's Will Trusts* [1990] 3 All ER 844, sub nom *Re Beatty, Hinves v Brooke* [1990] 1 WLR 1503.

13 [1905] AC 124. See also *Blair v Duncan* [1902] AC 37 ('charitable or public'); *Ellis v Selby* (1836) 1 My & Cr 286 ('charitable or other'); *Re Jarman's Estate* (1878) 8 Ch D 584; and *Re Macduff* [1896] 2 Ch 451 ('charitable or benevolent'); see also *Houston v Burns* [1918] AC 337, HL; *Re Gardom* [1914] 1 Ch 662, CA; revsd sub nom *Le Page v Gardom* [1915] WN 216, HL; *Re Rowe* (1914) 30 TLR 528; *Re Moore* [1919] 1 IR 316; *Re Wood* [1949] Ch 498, [1949] 1 All ER 1100; *Re Flavel's Will Trusts* [1969] 2 All ER 232, [1969] 1 WLR 444.

14 *Re White* [1893] 2 Ch 41, CA; *Re Ward* [1941] Ch 308, sub nom *Re Ward Public Trustee v Berry* [1941] 2 All ER 125, CA; a trust simply 'for religious purposes' or 'for educational purposes' is valid in the absence of a context subverting it eg restriction to a contemplative order of nuns or to employees of a particular company.

15 *Gilmour v Coats* [1949] AC 426, [1949] 1 All ER 848, HL..

16 *Morice v Bishop of Durham* (1804) 9 Ves 399; *James v Allen* (1817) 3 Mer 17; *Re Freeman* [1908] 1 Ch 720, CA; *Houston v Burns* [1918] AC 337; and see *Re Simson* [1946] Ch 299, [1946] 2 All ER 220, where a gift to an individual for his 'benevolent work' was held to fail.

17 *Chichester Diocesan Fund and Board of Finance Inc v Simpson* [1944] AC 341, [1944] 2 All ER 60, HL, and see *Re Bawden's Settlement* [1953] 2 All ER 1235 ('objects or purposes of charity or benevolence or amelioration of human suffering'). See also *Re Wootton's Will Trusts* [1968] 2 All ER 618, [1968] 1 WLR 681 where the objects of a trust included any 'organisation or body not being registered as a charity but in the opinion of my trustees as having charitable objects', and it was held that this definition was not limited to objects which were charitable in law, and *A-G of Bahamas v Royal Trust Co* [1986] 3 All ER 423, [1986] 1 WLR 1001, PC and *Re Carapiet's Trusts* [2002] WTLR 989.

18 *Re Macduff* [1896] 2 Ch 451, CA.

social and physical well-being'[1], or 'for parochial purposes' or 'for parish work'[2] (not necessarily equivalent to 'church purposes' by which are meant purposes connected with the services of the church)[3] or 'generally useful'[4] or 'worthy causes'[5] are void for uncertainty because these purposes might be satisfied without applying any part of the fund for charity, and the court will not intervene to direct the fund into charitable channels[6]. Thus the Attorney-General cannot interfere on behalf of charity, and no other person can interfere because no one can predicate of himself that he is a beneficiary[7]. But a bequest to 'my country England' or to a defined area is a good charitable bequest and enforceable by the Attorney-General[8], possibly on the ground that, where no purpose is defined, a charitable purpose is implicit in the context[9]. Again, trusts for purposes 'charitable *and* pious'[10], 'charitable *and* deserving'[11], 'religious *and* charitable'[12] have been upheld, for in such cases the purposes are not alternatively charitable *or* not charitable as the trustee may decide, but are confined to charities of a particular class.

In this connection the case of *Re Clarke*[13] is instructive as showing that where there is a trust to divide a residue among four objects, three of which are charitable and the fourth is not and is too uncertain, the property will be divided into fourths, three of which will go to the charities and the fourth to the next of kin of the testator as on a partial intestacy.

19 *Re Hewitt's Estate* (1883) 53 LJ Ch 132.
20 *Re Tetley* [1923] 1 Ch 258, CA; affd sub nom *A-G v National Provincial and Union Bank of England* [1924] AC 262, HL.
 1 *IRC v Baddeley* [1955] AC 572, [1955] 1 All ER 525, HL (distinguished in *Re Banfield* [1968] 2 All ER 276, [1968] 1 WLR 846), but see now the Recreational Charities Act 1958.
 2 *Farley v Westminster Bank* [1939] AC 430, [1939] 3 All ER 491, HL; *Re Bain* [1930] 1 Ch 224, CA; *Re Stratton* [1931] 1 Ch 197, CA; *Dunne v Byrne* [1912] AC 407, but a gift to the holder of an office of a charitable character virtute officii, which is prima facie a gift on charitable trusts, will not be avoided by the addition of words confining the use of the fund to the area in which the office is exercised, see *Re Rumball* [1956] Ch 105, [1955] 3 All ER 71, CA (gift to bishop for time being of named diocese to be used as he thinks fit in his diocese upheld—but this case was distinguished in *Re Endacott* [1960] Ch 232, [1959] 3 All ER 562, CA, where it was held the mere fact that a gift was made to a parish council did not render it charitable), and see *Re Simson* [1946] Ch 299, [1946] 2 All ER 220 (gift to a vicar for his work in the parish upheld), and *Re Eastes* [1948] Ch 257, [1948] 1 All ER 536, distinguishing *Re Davies* (1932) 49 TLR 5, CA. In *Re Rumball* [1956] Ch 105, [1955] 3 All ER 71, the Court of Appeal expressly reserved the question whether *Re Beddy* (1953) unreported (gift to bishop for such purposes in his diocese as he might choose held void for uncertainty) was rightly decided.
 3 *Re Gare* [1952] Ch 80, [1951] 2 All ER 863.
 4 *Kendall v Granger* (1842) 5 Beav 300; *Re Woodgate* (1886) 2 TLR 674; and see *Re Endacott* [1960] Ch 232, [1959] 3 All ER 562, CA.
 5 *Re Gillingham Bus Disaster Fund* [1959] Ch 62, [1958] 2 All ER 749, CA.
 6 *Re Strakosch* [1948] Ch 37, [1947] 2 All ER 607; affd [1949] Ch 529, [1949] 2 All ER 6, CA.
 7 See *Hunter v A-G* [1899] AC 309, HL; *Re Davis* [1923] 1 Ch 225; *Re Chapman* [1922] 2 Ch 479, where the words were 'to be retained by my executor for such objects and such purposes as he may at his discretion select and to be at his own disposal'; and *Re Carville* [1937] 4 All ER 464.
 8 *Re Smith* [1932] 1 Ch 153, CA; *Re Baynes* [1944] 2 All ER 597; *Re Norton's Will Trusts* [1948] 2 All ER 842 upholding a gift for the benefit of a parish as distinct from a gift 'for parish work', as to which, see *Farley v Westminster Bank* [1939] AC 430, HL.
 9 *Williams' Trustees v IRC* [1947] AC 447, [1947] 1 All ER 513, HL; *Re Strakosch* [1949] Ch 529, [1949] 2 All ER 6, CA.
10 *A-G v Herrick* (1772) Amb 712. But cf *Re Eades* [1920] 2 Ch 353, where 'and' was read 'or'.
11 *Re Sutton* (1885) 28 Ch D 464.
12 *Baker v Sutton* (1836) 1 Keen 224; *Re Scowcroft* [1898] 2 Ch 638. See also *Re Hood* [1931] 1 Ch 240, CA, where the dominant provision was religious.
13 [1923] 2 Ch 407. Followed in *Re King* [1931] WN 232.

Statutory validation of certain trusts

Certain trusts which would otherwise have failed for the reasons just discussed may be validated by the Charitable Trusts (Validation) Act 1954. This Act validates what it calls 'imperfect trust provisions' contained in instruments taking effect *before* 16 December 1952 eg where a testator died before then, leaving his estate to his widow for life, remainder on imperfect trust provisions. An imperfect trust provision means

> ' . . . any provision declaring the objects for which property is to be held or applied, and so describing those objects that, consistently with the terms of the provision, the property could be used exclusively for charitable purposes, but could nevertheless be used for purposes which are not charitable.'[14]

It should be noted that a trust provision falls within this definition only if it enables the property to be used 'exclusively for charitable purposes'. Thus a trust primarily for the benefit of non-charitable purposes will not be an imperfect trust provision within the Act merely because the trustees have power to administer it so that charitable objects can benefit in addition to, but not to the exclusion of, the non-charitable objects[15].

Again, if a trust provision is to fall within the terms of the Act, it must (1) declare the objects of the trust and (2) describe them in such a way that the property could be used exclusively for charitable purposes but could nevertheless be used for non-charitable *purposes*[16]. This condition is not fulfilled by a provision which simply requires property to be transferred to one or more institutions, since this does not amount to a declaration of the objects of the trust, still less are those objects described so as to indicate the purposes for which the property can be used[17]. The condition is similarly not fulfilled where trust property can be paid or applied for the direct benefit of individuals with no purposes prevailing[18].

Another question arising out of s 1(1) is whether the Act applies to all trust provisions which would in fact allow property to be used exclusively for charitable purposes but would nonetheless allow it to be used for noncharitable purposes, or whether the trust provision must itself differentiate in some way between these two purposes and include both an express reference to a charitable purpose and an express reference to a non-charitable pur-

---

14 See s 1(1) of the Act.
15 *Vernon v IRC* [1956] 3 All ER 14, [1956] 1 WLR 1169; *Buxton v Public Trustee* (1962) 41 TC 235; *Sir Howell Jones Williams Trust* Annual Report of the Charity Commissioners 1977, paras 71–80, applying the 1954 Act to the London Welsh trust held non-charitable in *Williams Trustees v IRC* [1947] AC 447, the social and recreational element being excluded.
16 Thus in *Buxton v Public Trustee* (1962) 41 TC 235 Plowman J held the Act did not apply to trusts 'to promote and aid the improvement of international relations and intercourse' since such trusts did not allow the property to be used exclusively for charitable purposes.
17 *Re Harpur's Will Trusts* [1962] Ch 78, [1961] 3 All ER 588, CA criticised by Picarda's *Law Relating to Charities* (1st edn) pp 161–162. The trust in this case was to divide a fund 'between such institutions and associations having for their main object the assistance and care of soldiers, sailors, airmen, and other members of H M Forces who have been wounded or incapacitated during recent world wars' in such manner and proportions as the trustees thought fit. It was conceded that these words were not apt to confine the institutions to those devoted exclusively to charitable objects. The trust was held not to be a trust to apply property for certain purposes but to distribute it among certain institutions.
18 *Re Saxone Shoe Co Ltd's Trust Deed* [1962] 2 All ER 904, [1962] 1 WLR 943 (essentially a private discretionary trust). Contrast the more liberal approach in Australia and New Zealand where legislation goes further: *Re Thureau* [1948] ALR 487; *Re Ingram* [1951] VLR 424; *Leahy v A-G for New South Wales* [1959] AC 457, [1959] 2 All ER 300.

pose. In other words, would the Act apply to a trust simply 'for public purposes', which could include both charitable and non-charitable objects, or is its operation confined to trusts which provide for the property to be used 'for charitable or benevolent purposes' or adopt some wording of that kind? In *Re Gillingham Bus Disaster Fund*[19], Harman J at first instance adopted the latter (narrower) interpretation, but his comments were obiter[20]. When this case went to appeal, his decision was affirmed by the majority of the Court of Appeal who expressed some sympathy with his view on this point, but did not decide it or express an opinion of their own. On the other hand, Ormerod LJ, who dissented and to whose decision alone the point was relevant, decided in favour of the former (wider) interpretation, and considered the subsection unambiguous. In these circumstances, Buckley LJ felt free to adopt the wider interpretation in a later case, that of *Re Wykes*[1], where he was concerned with a trust of property to be used:

' ... as a benevolent or welfare fund or for welfare purposes for the sole benefit of the past, present and future employees ... '

of a company. This decision was subsequently considered in two cases which came before Cross J. In the first[2] he impliedly supported it, saying:

'A benevolent or welfare fund is closely akin to a trust for the relief of poverty. If Mr Wykes had been told that the form of words he had chosen was open to objection, and had been advised expressly to confine the potential beneficiaries to poor persons, he would very likely have agreed without hesitation.'

In the second case[3], he assumed that it was correct and added:

'In such a phrase as "welfare purposes" there is at least some flavour of charity which may justify ... saying that the testator was seeking to benefit the public through the relief of a limited class.'

Although there is clearly a conflict of opinion on this point, the cases at present decided do indicate that the wider interpretation is the correct one, subject perhaps to the qualification that the trust provision must at some point and in some way include a hint of specifically charitable intent.

This leads naturally to another point. The Act does not operate to validate what are essentially private trusts. It is true that it may validate a trust for the benefit of a particular group of people who do not amount to a section of the community for the purposes of the law relating to charitable trusts[4], but this will be so only if the trust is to promote purposes rather than to benefit these people as individuals, and, of course the trust will be confined to those charitable purposes. Thus it was held that the words used in the trust pro-

---

19 [1958] Ch 300, [1958] 1 All ER 37; affd [1959] Ch 62, [1958] 2 All ER 749, CA.
20 It would appear, however, from his remarks in *Re Harpur's Will Trusts* [1962] Ch 78, [1961] 3 All ER 588, that Harman LJ may have intended these comments to amount to an alternative ground for his decision.
1 [1961] Ch 229, sub nom *Re Wykes Will Trusts, Riddington v Spencer* [1961] 1 All ER 470.
2 *Re Mead's Trust Deed* [1961] 2 All ER 836, [1961] 1 WLR 1244. In this case Cross J held that a trust to provide a convalescent home for members of a trade union and a home for aged members no longer able to support themselves and for the wives of such members was validated by the Act and restricted to those members of the union only who were poor persons and, in the case of the home for the aged, retired members and their wives.
3 *Re Saxone Shoe Co Ltd's Trust Deed* [1962] 2 All ER 904, [1962] 1 WLR 943. As to this case, see the text, below. The broader approach was conceded to be correct in *Re Chitty's Will Trust* [1970] Ch 254, sub nom *Re Thomas's Will Trusts* [1969] 3 All ER 1492.
4 See *Dingle v Turner* [1972] AC 601, [1972] 1 All ER 878, HL.

vision with which Buckley J was concerned in *Re Wykes* (quoted above) did create a trust for purposes and that the provision was therefore validated by the Act. The effect of the Act, in that case, was to confine the purposes of the trust to the sole, charitable purpose for which, having regard to the class of its beneficiaries, it could be used—that is, the relief of poverty. But in *Re Saxone Shoe Co Ltd's Trust Deed*[5] Cross J distinguished this type of provision from the one then before him, which he held to amount essentially to a trust for the application of capital and income for the benefit of a class of persons in any way the trustees might think fit and was more in the nature of a private discretionary trust than of a trust for purposes.

The Act goes on to provide that if the trust in question does amount to an imperfect trust provision contained in an instrument taking effect before 16 December 1952[6], then it is to be treated:

(a) as respects the period before the commencement of the Act (30 July 1954) as if the whole of its declared objects were charitable; and

(b) as respects the period after the commencement of the Act as if it had required the property in question to be held or applied for its declared objects in so far, and only in so far, as they authorised use for charitable purposes[7].

The Act applies to dispositions of all kinds, and to covenants to make dispositions, which would otherwise be invalid but which would have been valid if their objects had been exclusively charitable[8], except to the extent that the capital or income of the property to which they relate has, before 16 December 1952, been paid or conveyed to or for the benefit of the persons who were entitled on the footing that the trust was invalid[9]. For the purposes of the Act a disposition which creates more than one interest in the same property, whether by way of settlement or otherwise, is to be treated as a separate disposition in relation to each interest created[10]. This provision was considered in *Re Gillingham Bus Disaster Fund*[11] where an appeal had been made for funds for three purposes, two of which were not charitable and the third (worthy causes) included both charitable and non-charitable objects. Section 1(1) could not apply to the fund as a whole since it could not be used in its entirety for charitable purposes and it was held (Ormerod LJ dissenting) that there was no separate disposition for the third purpose.

The Act provides for limitation periods and contains limited savings for the

---

5 [1962] 2 All ER 904, [1962] 1 WLR 943. Compare *Re Flavel's Will Trusts* [1969] 2 All ER 232, [1969] 1 WLR 444.

6 A document inviting gifts of property for objects declared by the document is to be treated as an instrument taking effect when it is first issued; s 1(3) of the 1954 Act.

7 Section 1(2).

8 Section 2(1). In regard to this subsection, Upjohn J said in *Vernon v IRC* [1956] 3 All ER 14, [1956] 1 WLR 1169 that it was 'plainly pointing to invalidity under the rule against perpetuities, or on the ground of uncertainty or in some similar ground'. The trust provision before him (see note 15 on p 107, ante) was intended to give effect to a scheme sanctioned by the court. Even if it had amounted to an imperfect trust provision, his Lordship held that it would not have fallen within the terms of s 2(1) because '[the] scheme is not invalid at all'. In such circumstances the imperfection of the trusts declared by the scheme having been indicated, the trustees and the Attorney-General had the right, or the duty, to bring the matter before the court with a view to the trusts being amended.

9 Section 2(2).

10 Section 2(3); *Re Chitty's Will Trust* [1970] Ch 254, sub nom *Re Thomas's Will Trust* [1969] 3 All ER 1492.

11 [1958] Ch 300, [1958] 1 All ER 37; affd [1959] Ch 62, [1958] 2 All ER 749.

rights of persons who had become entitled, on the footing that the trust in question was invalid, to property comprised in it[12].

The Act does not apply to trusts contained in instruments which take effect on or after 16 December 1952. In respect of these the law stated in the immediately preceding section of this book remains unaffected.

The beneficiary principle

There are plenty of judicial statements that for there to be a valid trust there must be a beneficiary or cestui que trust (corporate or human) in whose favour performance of the trust may be decreed[13] unless the trust falls within a group of exceptional anomalous cases relating to the maintenance of animals, tombs etc, when it is valid but unenforceable so that it is regarded as a power that the trustees may exercise if they wish[14]. However charitable trusts for purposes are valid since they are enforceable by the Attorney-General[15]. Mere powers for abstract, impersonal but certain, workable purposes are valid[16] but they merely enable trustees to exercise them and, of course, do not compel the trustees. It has been suggested that all pure purpose 'trusts' should be treated as not being in the nature of trusts since unenforceable but in the nature of powers so as to be valid, but this approach seems only to be open to the House of Lords[17].

The beneficiary principle first became apparent in *Morice v Bishop of Durham* where Sir William Grant MR stated[18]:

'There can be no trust over the exercise of which this court will not assume control; for an uncontrollable power of disposition would be ownership and not trust. If there be a clear trust but for uncertain objects the property, that is the subject of the trust, is undisposed of ... But this doctrine does not hold good with regard to trusts for charity. *Every other trust must have a definite object. There must be somebody in whose favour the court can decree performance.*'

This quotation usefully reveals how inter-related are the three principles that a trust will be void if (1) administratively unworkable so as not to be capable of being controlled or executed by the court or (2) if uncertain as to its objects or (3) if there is no beneficiary able to enforce the trust in his favour in the courts. A fourth principle is also interrelated, namely the *Saunders v Vautier*[19] principle whereby the beneficiaries, if unanimous, can

---

12 Section 3. As to this section, see *Re Harpur's Will Trusts* [1962] Ch 78, [1961] 3 All ER 588, CA.

13 *Morice v Bishop of Durham* (1804) 9 Ves 399 at 404–405; *Re Chardon* [1928] Ch 464; *Re Astor's Settlement Trusts* [1952] Ch 534, [1952] 1 All ER 1067; *Leahy v A-G for New South Wales* [1959] AC 457 at 478, PC; *Re Denley's Trust Deed* [1969] 1 Ch 373, [1968] 3 All ER 65.

14 *Re Endacott* [1960] Ch 232, [1959] 3 All ER 562; pp 118–123, post.

15 *Leahy v A-G for New South Wales* [1959] AC 457 at 479. On charitable trusts see generally *Tudor on Charities* and Picarda's *Law Relating to Charities*. Nowadays, enforcement is also possible by the Charity Commissioners or an 'interested person' within Charities Act 1993, s 33.

16 *Re Wooton's Will Trusts* [1968] 2 All ER 618 at 623.

17 *IRC v Broadway Cottages Trust* [1955] Ch 20 at 36, CA; *Re Shaw* [1957] 1 WLR 729 at 731; *Re Endacott* [1960] Ch 232 at 246, CA. Further see Morris & Leach *Rule against Perpetuities* (2nd edn) pp 319 et seq; (1945) 58 Harvard LR 548 (Scott). If it is unclear whether a trust or power was intended then the court should find in favour of a power on the basis, 'Verba ita sunt intelligenda ut res magis valeat quam pereat': *IRC v McMullen* [1981] AC 1 at 11, HL; *Universe Tankships Inc of Monrovia v International Transport Workers Federation* [1983] 1 AC 366 at 406, HL.

18 *Morice v Bishop of Durham* (1804) 9 Ves 399 at 404–405.

19 See Article 70, post.

terminate their trust and obtain the trust property for themselves if they are all ascertained and between themselves absolutely entitled to the trust property, each being of full age and capacity. If the beneficiaries between them can obtain the trust property then clearly the beneficiary principle is satisfied.

This century the beneficiary principle has come into prominence as a ground on its own for invalidating purported trusts. In *Re Wood*[20] Harman J held, 'A gift on trust must have a cestui que trust and there being here no cestui que trust the gift must fail.' In *Re Astor*[1] Roxburgh J held trusts void on the ground that they were not trusts for individuals but for purposes. In *Re Endacott*[2] the Court of Appeal endorsed this, treating the anomalous cases of valid pure purpose trusts as concessions to human sentiment that were not to be extended. In *Leahy v A-G for New South Wales*[3] a gift upon trust for a contemplative, and therefore non-charitable, Order of Nuns was held by the Privy Council to be void for perpetuity as a gift intended to be by way of endowment for the religious purposes of the Order for the benefit of future nuns as much as (if not more than) existing nuns. However, Viscount Simonds, dealing with an extra ground for invalidating the gift as a purpose trust, said[4]:

> 'A gift can be made to persons (including a corporation) but it cannot be made to a purpose or to an object: so also a trust may be created for the benefit of persons as cestuis que trust but not for a purpose or object unless the purpose or object be charitable. For a purpose or object cannot sue, but, if it be charitable, the Attorney General can sue and enforce it.'

The beneficiary principle and purpose trusts for beneficiaries with standing to sue

Since then the position in respect of purpose trusts has been developed by Goff J in *Re Denley* who, after quoting Viscount Simonds' words, above, stated[5]:

> 'Where, then, the trust though expressed as a purpose is directly or indirectly for the benefit of an individual or individuals, it seems to me that it is in general outside the mischief of the beneficiary principle.'

Earlier he had said[6]:

> 'I think there may be a purpose or object trust, the carrying out of which would benefit an individual or individuals, where that benefit is so indirect or intangible or which is otherwise framed so as not to give those persons any locus standi to apply to the court to enforce the trust, in which case the beneficiary principle would apply to invalidate the trust, quite apart from any question of uncertainty or perpetuity. Such cases can be considered if and when they arise. The present is not of that character and it will be seen that clause 2(d) of the trust deed expressly states that, subject to any rules and regulations made by the trustees, the employees of the company shall be entitled to the use and enjoyment of the land. Apart from this

20 [1949] Ch 498 at 501.
  1 [1952] Ch 534, [1952] 1 All ER 1067. Also *Re Grant's Will Trusts* [1979] 3 All ER 359, [1980] 1 WLR 360.
  2 [1960] Ch 232, [1959] 3 All ER 562.
  3 [1959] AC 457, [1959] 2 All ER 300.
  4 [1959] AC 457 at 478, [1959] 2 All ER 300 at 307.
  5 [1969] 1 Ch 373 at 383–384, [1968] 3 All ER 65 at 69.
  6 [1969] 1 Ch 373 at 382–383, [1968] 3 All ER 65 at 69.

possible exception the beneficiary principle is confined to purpose or object trusts which are abstract or impersonal. The objection is not that the trust is for a purpose or object per se, but that there is no beneficiary or cestui que trust.'

In *Re Lipinski's Will Trusts*[7] Oliver J (as he then was) expressly adopted these remarks in upholding a residuary bequest upon trust 'as to one half thereof for the Hull Judeans (Maccabi) Association to be used solely in the work of constructing the new buildings for the Association and/or improvements to the said buildings' since the prescribed purpose was clearly intended for the benefit of the members of the Association. In *Re Denley's Trust Deed* Goff J had upheld inter vivos trusts for a specified perpetuity period of land to be maintained and used for the purpose of a recreation or sports ground for the benefit of the employees of Martyn & Co Ltd. In both cases the Association members[8] and the employees respectively had a right to have the court enforce the trusts in their favour.

The employees in *Re Denley* had locus standi as beneficiaries intended to obtain personal enjoyment out of the recreation ground and who could indeed be regarded as licensees under clause 2(d) of the Settlement Deed (analogous to irrevocable contractual licensees). The court could execute the trust positively by ordering the trustees to allow the employees to use the land for recreational purposes and negatively by restraining any improper use or disposition of the land[9]. In view of the later *McPhail v Doulton*[10] presumably the court could, as in the case of discretionary trusts, appoint new trustees to carry out the trusts in place of defaulting trustees or even, perhaps, authorise or direct representative persons to prepare a scheme, eg of regulations respecting use of the land. It would seem also from *McPhail v Doulton* that the beneficiaries, not being intended to take equal fixed interests, need not be capable of ascertainment in a comprehensive list so long as any given postulant can be ascertained as being a beneficiary or not being a beneficiary. Thus a trust as in *Re Saxone Shoe Co Ltd's Trust Deed*[11] for 'the provision of pensions for and donations to present and past employees and the education and benefit of their dependants' might now be held valid as a purpose trust directly or indirectly for the benefit of beneficiaries, if limited to the perpetuity period or, otherwise, saved by s 3(3) of the Perpetuities and Accumulations Act 1964. Indeed, in *Wicks v Firth*[12] it was assumed that a trust to provide educational scholarships for the settlor employer's employees' children and restricted to a specified perpetuity period was valid.

The beneficiary principle requires a beneficiary with locus standi to have the trust positively enforced. It will not be satisfied merely by the presence of a person who will be benefited by the carrying out of the trust, eg the owner of a school where a trust provides for the education of the settlor's son at that school[13] or a

---

7 [1976] Ch 235, [1977] 1 All ER 33. In *Re Northern Development (Holdings)* (6 October 1978, unreported) Megarry V-C accepted purpose trusts 'of the type recognised in *Re Denley*' (see (1985) 101 LQR 280) as did the Divisional Court in *R v District Auditor No 3 Audit District of West Yorkshire Metropolitan County Council, ex p West Yorkshire Metropolitan County Council* [1986] RVR 24 discussed p 93, ante.

8 Oliver J regarded the members as beneficially entitled with the expressed purpose only being morally binding: see p 127, post.

9 [1969] 1 Ch 373 at 388, [1968] 3 All ER 65 at 72.

10 [1971] AC 424, [1970] 2 All ER 228; p 86, ante.

11 [1962] 2 All ER 904, [1962] 1 WLR 943.

12 [1983] 2 AC 214, [1983] 1 All ER 151, HL.

13 *Shaw v Lawless* (1838) 5 Cl & Fin 129 at 155; *Gandy v Gandy* (1885) 30 Ch D 57; p 142, post.

settlor who would feel benefited and fulfilled if his desires were carried out[14]. A person cannot enforce a trust merely because he may incidentally benefit from the performance of the trust just as a person who incidentally may benefit by the performance of a contract cannot enforce that contract (assuming after the Contracts (Rights of Third Parties) Act 1999, the parties did not intend the benefiting term to be enforceable by him).

The beneficiary principle will not be satisfied by the fact that there is some person in the background (eg a residuary legatee of the settlor or next of kin under a resulting trust) with an interest in applying to the court if the primary purpose trust is not effectively carried out, for there will virtually always be such a person[15] so validating virtually all purpose trusts, which is not the position[16]. Such a person, after all, is not interested in having the purpose trust enforced in his favour: his interest is only in the failure, or the declaring to be invalid, of the purpose trust.

The question arises whether purpose trusts of the valid *Re Denley* type should be categorised as an intermediate category between trusts for individuals and trusts for pure abstract purposes rather than as trusts for individuals. It seems better to regard them as trusts for individuals[17]. After all under the rule in *Saunders v Vautier* if S creates a trust to spend £10,000 on planting trees on land held for A for life remainder to B, A and B can claim the £10,000[18]. If S creates a trust for the maintenance and care of B for B's life it is a question of construction whether B has absolute entitlement to the income for whatever purpose he wants[19] or whether B is only entitled to claim what is necessary for the specified purpose[20]. As trusts for individuals the trusts will benefit from the application of the 'wait and see' and other provisions of the Perpetuities and Accumulations Act 1964[1].

In the case of apparent purpose trusts it is submitted that it is a question of construction in every case whether the trust is primarily for the benefit of a class of individuals, with the specified way in which they are to enjoy the

---

14 *Re Astor's Settlement Trusts* [1952] Ch 534 at 542.

15 In a rare case he might not currently be ascertainable (eg be unborn or the person who is Warden of All Souls College at the expiry of the perpetuity period).

16 *Re Shaw* [1957] 1 All ER 745, [1957] 1 WLR 729, CA; *Re Endacott* [1960] Ch 232, [1959] 3 All ER 562, CA; *Leahy v A-G for New South Wales* [1959] AC 457, [1959] 2 All ER 300.

17 *Re Grant's Will Trusts* [1979] 3 All ER 359 at 368, [1980] 1 WLR 360; P J Millett (now Lord Millett) (1985) 101 LQR 268 at 281–282.

18 *Re Bowes* [1896] 1 Ch 507 from which Goff J in *Re Denley's Trust Deed* claimed assistance; also *Re Skinner's Trusts* (1860) 1 John & H 102 (bequest of £1,000 to provide for publishing testator's manuscript books to the best advantage of the testator's grandson, G, to provide a fund for his university education, was construed as being for G's benefit so he could claim the £1,000 when publication was not a paying proposition).

19 *Re Andrew's Trust* [1905] 2 Ch 48; *Re Osoba* [1979] 2 All ER 393, [1979] 1 WLR 247, CA.

20 *Re Sanderson's Trusts* (1857) 3 K & J 497; *Re Abbott Fund Trust* [1900] 2 Ch 326; *Re Gillingham Bus Disaster Fund* [1958] Ch 300, [1958] 1 All ER 37.

1 See pp 191–202, post. Purpose trusts for people validated by *Re Denley* should not be regarded as purpose trusts, subject at the outset to the rule against inalienability, but as people trusts, subject to the benevolent provisions of the Perpetuities and Accumulations Act 1964, despite the apparent view of Megarry V-C to the contrary based on *Re Denley* trusts being an intermediate category of purpose trust: *Re Northern Development (Holdings) Ltd* (6 October 1978, unreported) discussed by C E F Rickett (1991) 107 LQR 608 at 611 fn 13. A trust created today in the terms of the *Re Denley* trusts should be saved by s 3(3) of the 1964 Act covering discretionary trusts, though a resulting trust should arise at the end of the statutory perpetuity period: a *Re Denley* endowment trust for present and future members of a club should on expiry of the statutory period (without any earlier dissolution of the club) be saved by s 4(4): see p 126, post.

benefit being secondary, or whether the specified purpose in which they will be involved to a greater or lesser extent is of the essence of the gift, with the indirect benefit to individuals being secondary. In the former category there will be scope for application of the rule in *Saunders v Vautier* so long as a fluctuating class is not involved[2], while in the latter category there will be no such scope and the purpose trust will be void for infringing the beneficiary principle unless it is a charitable trust. Within the former category will be trusts providing a maintenance fund for historic buildings and gardens owned by trustees for the benefit of beneficiaries[3] or providing a sinking fund for repairs to a block of flats for the benefit of the lessees[4] or providing for the education of employees' children[5]. Within the latter category will be trusts for furthering the overriding purposes of a political party[6] or of a non-charitable religious order[7] or of an unincorporated society[8].

Incidentally, if property is transferred inter vivos on void pure purpose trusts it seems that the transferee trustee will hold the property on resulting trust for the transferor but will be regarded as authorised by the transferor to have power to apply the property for the stated purpose until the transferor decides otherwise[9] (eg by demanding a re-transfer of the property to himself) or the transferor dies: in the case of similar void testamentary trusts there can be no such deemed authority on the part of the deceased testator or bene-ficiary entitled on failure of such trusts.

Scope to develop enforcer principle

Where lack of a beneficiary to enforce a trust has been a ground for holding a non-charitable purpose trust to be void, there have also been other grounds such as the absence of an express valid perpetuity period rendering the trust void for infringing the rule against inalienability[10] or the absence of workable certain purposes[11]. Moreover, in none of the cases rejecting non-charitable purpose trusts did the settlor in his trust instrument expressly arrange for there to be an enforcer positively interested in performance of the purposes.

Nowadays, many trusts governed by foreign trust laws, such as the laws of Jersey, Isle of Man, Bermuda, Cayman Islands or s 409 of the American Uniform Trust code, have an enforcer expressly appointed as such in the trust instrument that creates valid non-charitable purpose trusts according to the relevant governing law. Under the Recognition of Trusts Act 1987, incorporating The Hague Trusts Convention, those trusts[12] need to be recognised as such[13], unless the English court is prepared to apply Article 18 so as to disregard the Convention if its application would be manifestly

---

2 *Re Levy* [1960] Ch 346 at 363, CA; *Re Westphal* [1972] NZLR 792 at 794–795.
3 *Re Aberconway's Settlement Trusts* [1953] Ch 647, [1953] 2 All ER 350, CA; *Raikes v Lygon* [1988] 1 All ER 884, [1988] 1 WLR 281; Inheritance Tax Act 1984, Sch 4.
4 Landlord and Tenant Act 1987, s 42.
5 *Wicks v Firth* [1983] 2 AC 214, [1983] 1 All ER 151, HL.
6 *Re Grant's Will Trusts* [1979] 3 All ER 359, [1980] 1 WLR 360; *Bacon v Pianta* (1966) 114 CLR 634 (Aust HC).
7 *Leahy v A-G for New South Wales* [1959] AC 457, [1959] 2 All ER 300, PC.
8 *Carne v Long* (1860) 2 De GF & J 75; *Re Macaulay's Estate* [1943] Ch 435n, HL.
9 *Re Sayer Trust* [1957] Ch 423 at 437.
10 *Re Nottage* [1895] 2 Ch 649; *Leahy v A-G for New South Wales* [1959] AC 457.
11 *Re Astor's Settlement Trusts* [1952] Ch 534.
12 Article 2.
13 Article 11.

incompatible with public policy. Is it really manifestly incompatible with English public policy to permit a non-charitable purpose trust to be enforceable where an expressly appointed enforcer has locus standi positively to apply to the court for enforcement of the trust against the trustees, just as a charitable purpose trust is enforceable against the trustees by the Attorney-General or the Charity Commissioners or 'an interested person'[14], and a trust for beneficiaries is enforceable against the trustees by the beneficiaries?

In each case the trustees are under enforceable obligations as required at the core of the trust concept. Just as a car needs an engine so a trust needs an enforcer. If this be correct[15], then non-charitable purposes of a trust governed not just by a relevant foreign law but also by English law should be valid if the trust instrument has expressly provided for an enforcer and the purposes are certain and workable[16] and limited to a valid perpetuity period[17]. Thus, trusts (restricted to a royal lives plus twenty-one years perpetuity period) to further the purposes of the Labour Party to be enforceable by the Leader of such Party from time to time or to further the purposes of a particular self-interested group (the profession of barrister, solicitor or doctor or a contemplative order of nuns) to be enforceable by the head of such group from time to time, should be valid.

Of course, if instead of the trust fund having to be used up for suchlike purposes, the purpose was merely holding and maintaining particular assets (eg an art collection as an undivided private collection) or developing the value of the trust fund, then the alleged purpose would be regarded as an investment power, with the settlor not having disposed of the underlying beneficial interest in the assets transferred to trustees.

Furthermore, as Article 60 shows, it is fundamental to an English trust for beneficiaries that the beneficiaries have rights to enforce the trust. Thus, if a settlor used the most extreme type of Cayman Special Trusts Alternative Regime (STAR) trust to create a discretionary trust for the purpose of benefiting his descendants, none of whom had any right under STAR to enforce the trust, such right of enforcement being expressly vested in another person, then it seems that the English court should characterise the descendants as only objects of a power of appointment under a resulting trust for the settlor, who as beneficial owner could at any time revoke the trustee's authority to distribute assets to such objects[18].

A final issue is whether a settlor or a protector can have locus standi conferred on him by the trust instrument so as to become an enforcer where the trust is a trust for beneficiaries. Here, there is in England the core *Saunders v Vautier* principle whereby, if unanimous and all of full age and capacity and between them absolutely entitled to the whole beneficial interest, the beneficiaries can terminate the trust, regardless of the settlor's intentions, and obtain the property for themselves, so frustrating any other

---

14 With the consent of the Commissioners or the court: Charities Act 1993, s 33.

15 For favourable and unfavourable views respectively, see D J Hayton, *Overview and Comment* and *Developing the Obligation Characteristic of the Trust*, reprinted from (2001) 117 LQR 97, and P B Matthews *From Obligation to Property and Back Again?* in D J Hayton (ed) *Extending the Boundaries of Trusts and Similar Ring-Fenced Funds* (Kluwer Law International, 2002).

16 No cy-près jurisdiction exists for non-charitable, as opposed to charitable, trusts unless created by statute, as in the case of most foreign non-charitable trusts.

17 No 'wait and see' is possible since the Perpetuities and Accumulations Act 1964 does not apply to non-charitable purpose trusts which, by the rule against inalienability, are void from the outset if not restricted to a valid common law perpetuity period.

18 *Vandervell v IRC* [1967] 2 AC 291 at 317, per Lord Upjohn.

purposes of the settlor[19]. Clearly, any rights of enforcement of an English trust that would encroach upon such principle must be ineffective so as not to encroach upon the core of the English trust concept, although the English court would surely accept as fully valid trusts governed by foreign trust laws (such as those of all but one of the States in the USA) which have no *Saunders v Vautier* principle and insist on the carrying out of material purposes of the settlor regardless of all the beneficiaries' wishes.

However, in principle, there seems no reason why a person other than the beneficiaries should not be capable of having locus standi conferred upon him by the settlor's trust instrument (eg to safeguard the interests of a beneficiary as yet unborn or unascertained) so long as he does not interfere with beneficiaries' *Saunders v Vautier* rights. Objects of a power of appointment can have locus standi conferred upon them to make the trustee account for its conduct even though the trust fund belongs beneficially to those beneficiaries entitled in default of appointment[20]. Why should the court not facilitate the wish of the settlor on his trust deed that he or a protector[1] should have the right to make the trustee account so long as there is a beneficiary unborn, unascertained or not of full age and capacity?

Loan purpose trusts

The beneficiary principle has been considered in connection with the *Barclays Bank Ltd v Quistclose Investments Ltd*[2] type of trust where A lends money to B under a primary temporary trust to use the money only for the purpose of paying B's creditors, resulting if the purpose is performed in a pure loan relationship between A and B (excluding any trust relationship), but with a trust arising in A's favour if the purpose is not performed. Where is the beneficial interest in the money pending its application by B? Must it remain in A or may it be in B's creditor, C, or may it be in suspense, with C merely having a right to compel B to apply the property in accordance with A's directions, analogous to the right of a residuary legatee under a will[3] to compel the executor to administer the estate according to the testator's directions? In special circumstances Megarry V-C[4] took the last view which Peter Gibson J regarded as a general rule in *Carreras Rothmans Ltd v Freeman Matthews Treasure Ltd*[5].

---

19 See Art 70 post.
20 *Spellson v George* (1987) 11 NSWLR 300; *Re Murphy's Settlement* [1999] 1 WLR 282; but they need not – *Re Angora Trusts, Rosewood Trust Ltd v Schmidt* [2001] WTLR 1081.
1 *Re Hare Trust* (2001) 4 ITELR 288. In *Von Knierem v Bermuda Trust* (1994) 1 BOCM 116 and *Re Omar Family Trust (No 565 of 1997)* [2000] WTLR 713 at 714 the protector had locus standi.
2 [1970] AC 567, ante p 12; applied in *Re EVTR Ltd* [1987] BCLC 646, CA; *Rowan v Dann* (1991) 64 P & CR 202, CA; *Guardian Ocean Cargoes Ltd v Banco de Brasil* [1991] 2 Lloyd's Rep 68, 87 but rejected by CA in [1994] CLC 243; *Tropical Capital Investment Ltd v Stanlake Holdings Ltd* (unreported, CA, noted [1992] LMCLQ 3).
3 *Stamp Duties Comr (Queensland) v Livington* [1965] AC 694, [1964] 3 All ER 692, p 17, ante.
4 *Re Northern Developments (Holdings) Ltd* (6 October 1978, unreported) cited in *Carreras Rothmans Ltd v Freeman Matthews Treasure Ltd* [1985] 1 All ER 155 at 166. In *Twinsectra Ltd v Yardley* [2002] UKHL 12 Lord Millett at para [87] considered there was a powerful argument for the result of the arrangements in *Northern Developments* being to vest a beneficial interest in the company's subsidiary from the start, so that there was no *Quistclose* trust.
5 [1985] Ch 207, [1985] 1 All ER 155.

However, Peter Millett QC has emphasised[6] that the matter turns on A's intention and that no new enforceable purpose trust arises enforceable by the settlor qua settlor or where the beneficial interest is in suspense. He considered guidelines for ascertaining A's intentions to be as follows[7]:

'1. If A's intention was to benefit C, or his object would be frustrated if he were to retain a power of revocation, the transaction will create an irrevocable trust in favour of C, enforceable by C but not by A. The beneficial interest in the trust property will be in C.

2. If A's intention was to benefit B (though without vesting a beneficial interest in him), or to benefit himself by furthering some private or commercial interest of his own, and not (except incidentally) to benefit C, then the transaction will create a trust in favour of A alone and B will hold the trust property in trust to comply with A's directions. The trust will be enforceable by A but not by C. The beneficial interest will remain in A.

3. Where A's object was to save B from bankruptcy by enabling him to pay his creditors, the prima facie inference is that set out in paragraph 2 above. Wherever that is the correct inference:

(i)   Where A has an interest of his own, separate and distinct from any interest of B, in seeing that the money is applied for the stated purpose, B will be under a positive obligation, enforceable by A, to apply it for that purpose. Where A has no such interest, B will be regarded as having a power, but no duty, to apply it for the stated purpose, and A's remedy will be confined to preventing the misapplication of the money.

(ii) Prima facie, A's directions will be regarded as revocable by him; but he may contract with B not to revoke them without B's consent.

(iii) Communication to C of the arrangements prior to A's revocation will effect an assignment of A's equitable interest to C, and convert A's revocable mandate into an irrevocable trust for C.'

Since then, as Lord Millett in *Twinsectra v Yardley*[8], he has rejected any question of the beneficial ownership being in suspense, holding that where the loaned monies are not freely at the disposal of the borrower but must be kept separate to be used only for a particular purpose, whether benefiting people or for an abstract purpose, then there is a resulting trust for the lender with the transferee having a power (or a duty) to apply the money for the stated purpose. Whether the borrower is obliged to apply the money for the stated purpose or is merely at liberty to do so, and whether the lender can countermand the borrower's mandate while it is still capable of being carried out, must depend on the circumstances of the particular case, taking account of the above guidelines in his LQR article. So long as the power is stated with sufficient clarity for the court to be able to determine whether it is still capable of being carried out or whether the money has been misapplied, it is sufficiently certain to be enforced. Otherwise, the borrower cannot make any use of the money and must return it to the lender under the resulting trust.

Points for draftsmen

Of course, a draftsman should ensure that no problems arise. If a settlor or testator wishes pure purposes to be carried out, powers in that behalf may be

---

6 (1985) 101 LQR 269.

7 (1985) 101 LQR 290. For valuable discussion on the nature of *Quistclose* trusts see *Lord v Australian Elizabethan Theatre Trust* (1991) 102 ALR 681; C E F Rickett in (1991) 107 LQR 608 and in Waters (ed) *Equity, Fiduciaries and Trusts* (1993, Carswell, Canada) pp 325–355.

8 [2002] UKHL 12 at paras [77]–[102] and Lord Hoffmann at para [13].

created if trustees can be relied upon to exercise the powers within an expressly restricted perpetuity period (eg royal lives plus 21 years) and the purposes are certain and workable with, perhaps an internal *cy-près* mechanism[9]. Otherwise, a company can be created with the pure purposes (eg anti-vivisection) as its objects and the requisite funds can be given outright to the company. Alternatively, it seems that funds may be given as an accretion to the funds of an unincorporated association subject to the contractual rights and liabilities of the members inter se but subject to no trusts[10]. Otherwise, funds can be given to trustees to pay the income therefrom to the A Charity Co for such company to dispose of as it wishes for so long as the following purposes ... shall happen to be carried out but as soon as such purposes shall not be carried out then to pay such income to the B Charity Co for such company to dispose of as it wishes for so long as the said purpose shall happen to be carried out and so on to the Z Charity Co if need be, ensuring that the balance of income is sufficient to interest a charity[11].

In the earlier cases of *Re Bowes*[12] and *Re Aberconway's Settlement Trusts*[13] it had been assumed that trusts were valid respectively for planting trees on the estate and for the upkeep and development of gardens within an estate since indirectly for the benefit of the individuals interested in the estate. Nowadays, when the beneficiary principle is more prominent it will be as well if draftsmen specifically express in the trust instrument the persons intended to be benefited making it clear that they are to have the right to have the trusts positively enforced[14], eg when drafting trusts of maintenance funds for historic buildings to obtain advantageous inheritance tax and capital gains tax treatment or when drafting sinking fund trusts for the upkeep of blocks of flats.

The exceptional cases

In what follows, consideration is given to the exceptional, or anomalous, group of cases in which a testamentary trust, though it is not charitable nor for the benefit of any beneficiary, is still valid (if unenforceable, so operating as if a power). They were reviewed by the Court of Appeal in the case of *Re Endacott*[15]. The court accepted the classification put forward by Dr Morris and Professor Barton Leach in the following passage from their book, *The Rule against Perpetuities*:

---

9 Of course, a trustee could be given a substantial beneficial interest liable to forfeiture if he failed to spend £x a year in exercising his power to carry out pure abstract purposes.

10 *Re Recher's Will Trusts* [1972] Ch 526, [1971] 3 All ER 401; *Re Lipinski's Will Trusts* [1976] Ch 235, [1977] 1 All ER 33; *Universe Tankships Inc of Monrovia v International Transport Workers Federation* [1983] 1 AC 366, [1982] 2 All ER 67, HL; *Re Bucks Constabulary Widows' and Orphans' Fund Friendly Society (No 2)* [1979] 1 All ER 623, [1979] 1 WLR 936; *Conservative and Unionist Central Office v Burrell (Inspector of Taxes)* [1982] 2 All ER 1 at 7, CA.

11 *Re Chardon* [1928] Ch 464; *Christ's Hospital v Grainger* (1849) 1 Mac & G 460, ousting the Perpetuities and Accumulations Act 1964, s 12. The income must be freely alienable and so not subject to trusts preventing this: *Re Dalziel* [1943] Ch 277, [1943] 2 All ER 656; *Re Wightwick's Will Trusts* [1950] Ch 260, [1950] 1 All ER 689.

12 [1896] 1 Ch 507.

13 [1953] Ch 647, [1953] 2 All ER 350, CA.

14 Under *Re Denley's Trusts Deed* [1969] 1 Ch 373, [1968] 3 All ER 65, principles endorsed in *Re Lipinski's Will Trusts* [1976] Ch 235, [1977] 1 All ER 33. Also see *Raikes v Lygon* [1988] 1 All ER 884, [1988] 1 WLR 281.

15 [1960] Ch 232, [1959] 3 All ER 562, CA.

'We proceed to examine these "anomalous" exceptions. It will be found that they fall into the following groups: (1) trusts for the erection or maintenance of monuments or graves; (2) trusts for the saying of masses, in jurisdictions where such trusts are not regarded as charitable; (3) trusts for the maintenance of particular animals; (4) trusts for the benefit of unincorporated associations (though this group is more doubtful); (5) miscellaneous cases.'

Of the miscellaneous cases in group (5), only one was specifically referred to in *Re Endacott*, above, and that was *Re Catherall*[16], where a gift to a vicar and churchwardens for a suitable memorial to the testator's parents and sisters was upheld by Roxburgh J, who said: 'Such a trust as this is valid whether charitable or not'; but the Court of Appeal held that in any event the decision could be justified on the ground 'that in its context the purposes were limited to religious (ie charitable) purposes'. A number of the other miscellaneous cases had been reviewed in *Re Astor's Settlement Trusts*[17], where Roxburgh J had shown that in many instances they must have been decided per incuriam and held that they did not justify the conclusion that a Court of Equity will recognise a direction to apply funds for non-charitable purposes in a manner which no court could control or enforce. In *Re Endacott*, above, this view was impliedly affirmed by Lord Evershed, MR while Harman LJ said:

'I applaud the orthodox sentiments expressed by Roxburgh J in *Re Astor's Settlement Trusts*, and I think, as I think he did, that though one knows that there have been decisions at times which are not satisfactorily classified, but are perhaps merely occasions when Homer had nodded, at any rate these cases stand by themselves and ought not to be increased in number, nor indeed followed, except where the one is exactly like another. Whether it would be better that some authority should now say that those cases were wrongly decided, this perhaps is not the moment to consider. At any rate, I cannot think that a case of [the present] kind, the case of providing outside a church an unspecified and unidentified memorial is the kind of instance which should be allowed to add to those troublesome, anomalous and aberrant cases.'

On a strict view it would be possible to restrict the exceptional cases to trusts contained in a will and so drafted that trust property not applied for the prescribed purpose should fall into residue[18]. The traditional form of order can then be made, the trustees undertaking to apply the trust property for the prescribed purpose but the residuary beneficiary being given liberty to apply to the court on the trustees failing to do so[19]. However, it would seem the principle should extend to a will trust of residue for prescribed purposes, the next of kin being given liberty to apply[20].

Trusts to raise and keep in repair graves and sepulchral monuments

Although it would seem that the court could not *enforce* a trust for applying money in the erection of a tomb or monument or the repair of a grave or tomb not forming part of the fabric of a church[1] (insomuch as there would

---

16 (3 June 1959, unreported).
17 [1952] Ch 534, [1952] 1 All ER 1067.
18 *Re Thompson* [1934] Ch 342 at 344; *Re Astor's Settlement Trusts* [1952] Ch 534 at 546.
19 *Pettingall v Pettingall* (1842) 11 LJ Ch 176.
20 *Re Endacott* [1960] Ch 232 at 240.
 1 It would be a valid charitable trust if the tomb could be regarded as part of the fabric of the church or if the trust were for the maintenance of the churchyard generally: *Re King* [1923] 1 Ch 243; *Re Vaughan* (1886) 33 Ch D 187; *Re Eighmie* [1935] Ch 524.

be no beneficiary interested in applying to the court to enforce the trust)² it was said in *Re Dean* that such trusts are not *void*, but merely duties of imperfect obligation, and that the trustees may safely spend the moneys on the prescribed object if they please³. North J added that he knew of nothing to prevent a gift of a sum of money to trustees upon trust to apply it for the repair of such a monument, if the donor took care to limit the time for which the trust was to last, so as to provide for its cesser within the perpetuity period applicable under the rule against inalienability⁴. If the time is not so limited the trust will fail ab initio.

In *Re Chardon*⁵, Romer J, in a considered judgment, held that a legacy in trust to pay the income therefrom to a cemetery company, so long as the company kept a grave in order, was a good trust, as the rule against remoteness was directed against interests which vested outside the perpetuity period, not against interests which, having vested, continued beyond it; and the interests both of the company and of the residuary legatees were vested interests, subject to no trusts, and they could combine to dispose of the whole legacy. The rule against inalienability could not be infringed since the company's determinable interest in income could be freely disposed of since no trusts were imposed on the use of the income. In *Re Chardon* the learned judge did not decide what would happen in the case of a gift over in the event of a condition being broken. It appears, however, that at common law a gift over to commence on the breach of the condition would be bad and that on such breach the property would fall into residue⁶. A simple direction that on breach of the condition the fund should fall into residue would, it seemed, be unobjectionable⁷. However, where the disposition taking advantage of *Re Chardon* is made after 15 July 1964 the position is altered by the Perpetuities and Accumulations Act 1964. After creating the trust to pay income to the cemetery company so long as the grave is kept in good order, the disposition might continue in any one of three basic ways⁸.

---

2 *Re Astor's Settlement Trusts* [1952] Ch 534, [1952] 1 All ER 1067; *Re Shaw* [1957] 1 All ER 745 at 758, per Harman J.

3 (1889) 41 Ch D 552 at 557, per North J.

4 *Pirbright v Salwey* [1896] WN 86; *Re Hooper* [1932] 1 Ch 38, cases where the trust was for upkeep so long as the law allows, and see *Re Astor's Settlements Trusts* [1952] Ch 534, [1952] 1 All ER 1067. See pp 202–203, post.

5 [1928] Ch 464. The case has been criticised mainly in relation to the gift over not to the determinable interest (see eg *Tudor on Charities* (5th edn) p 701, and articles by W O Hart in 53 LQR 24, and M J Albery in 54 LQR 258), but, counsel having admitted it to be indistinguishable, it was followed in *Re Chambers' Will Trusts* [1950] Ch 267, though distinguished in *Re Wightwick's Will Trusts* [1950] Ch 260, [1950] 1 All ER 689, where income was subjected to trusts so as not to be freely alienable: cf *Re Dalziel* [1943] Ch 277, [1943] 2 All ER 656.

6 *Re Chambers' Will Trusts* [1950] Ch 267; *Re Gage* [1898] 1 Ch 498; *Re Hooper* [1932] 1 Ch 38; *Re Vaughan* (1886) 33 Ch D 187. See also *Re Moore* [1901] 1 Ch 936, where an unsuccessful attempt was made to extend the period to twenty-one years after the death of the survivor of all persons living at the testator's death, which made it void for uncertainty. A bequest to a club of a portrait in trust to hang it up and retain it in a conspicuous part of the Hall of a City company was upheld; but a further gift, conditional upon the acceptance of the gift aforesaid, of £4,000 upon trust out of the income to keep the picture in repair and to apply the surplus income to persons of a particular description without reference to age or poverty was held not charitable and therefore void on grounds of perpetuity: *Re Gassiot* (1901) 70 LJ Ch 242.

7 *Re Randell* (1888) 38 Ch D 213, and see *Re Wightwick's Will Trusts* [1950] Ch 260, [1950] 1 All ER 689.

8 Although it has nothing to do with the subject matter of this work and therefore does not deserve to be considered in detail, attention may perhaps be drawn to the Parish Councils and Burial Authorities (Miscellaneous Provisions) Act 1970, which provides one solution to

(1) It could go on to make an express gift over to designated beneficiaries upon the grave not being kept in good order. The gift over may be void for remoteness but the 'wait and see' provisions of the Act (see p 195, post) mean that the voidness of the gift over cannot be taken for granted until it is known that the corporation had not in fact broken the condition within the perpetuity period. Once the remoteness has rendered the gift over invalid, the only consequence of the happening of the determining event would be a resulting trust, and this would seem to attract the application of s 12(1) of the Act. The end result would seem to be that once the perpetuity period is past (ie the perpetuity period notionally supplied by s 3(4) and (5) of the Act) without the happening of the determining event, so that the gift over must fail, the corporation's interest becomes an absolute interest under s 12(1).

(2) Alternatively, the disposition might not go on at all—that is, it might stop after making the initial gift. In this event a resulting trust would arise as soon as the determining event occurred, and so the disposition would fall squarely and from the outset within the terms of s 12(1). The resulting trust would be subject to the rule against perpetuities and if the perpetuity period passed without the happening of the determining event, so that the resulting trust became void for remoteness, the corporation would again acquire an absolute interest.

(3) Or again, the disposition might go on (as the disposition in *Re Chardon* itself actually did) in a way which fell in a sense between the two possibilities already mentioned, by spelling out the resulting trust which would have arisen in any case—that is, by stating specifically the trusts which would have arisen automatically if nothing had been stated. For example, if the disposition was contained in a will it might simply say that on the happening of the determining event the gift was to fall into residue. Whether this would also attract the operation of s 12(1) is not quite so clear, but it certainly seems illogical that a disposition of this kind should escape. On this basis, the position would be as in (2) above, rather than the residuary gift taking effect as before 1964.

A testator may make a gift to a charity conditionally upon his tomb being kept in repair, with a gift over to another charity in the event of the tomb being allowed to fall into disrepair[9]. In *Re Dalziel*[10], Cohen J pointed out that such a gift will only be upheld where there is no more than an inducement to the first charity to repair the tomb and the testator has not imposed any legal obligation to apply part of the income for that purpose. The American courts have held that a trust to keep in repair for ever the tombs *of a class* (eg the testator's family) is a charitable trust and valid, although a similar trust to keep up the tomb of an individual is not; but the distinction seems somewhat unreal[11], and it is believed that it would not be made in English law.

---

the problem posed by the desire to have a grave or tomb maintained. Section 1 of the Act permits local authorities or burial authorities to make an agreement to maintain (inter alia) certain graves, vaults, tombstones or other memorials for a period not exceeding 99 years.

9 *Re Tyler* [1891] 3 Ch 252; *Chamberlayne v Brockett* (1872) 8 Ch App 206 at 211; *Re Davies* [1915] 1 Ch 543. But dist. *Re Porter* [1925] Ch 746.

10 [1943] Ch 277, [1943] 2 All ER 656.

11 *Swasey v American Bible Society* 57 Me 527 (1869); *Piper v Moulton* 72 Me 155 (1881). Contrast *Neo v Neo* (1875) LR 6 PC 382.

Trusts for the benefit of dogs, horses, etc

On similar principles, a trust, limited in point of time within the rule against perpetuities, to apply money for keeping specified pet animals in comfort during their lives, is perfectly legal, although no person could enforce it[12]. Testamentary expressions like 'so far as the law allows' will validly restrict the period to 21 years but the court will not treat such an expression as implicit in order to save the gift[13]. Moreover, a trust of undefined continuance for the benefit of animals will be upheld as a valid charitable trust if, in its execution there is 'necessarily involved benefit to the public'[14], as in the case of a gift for 'the welfare of cats and kittens needing care and attention' which has been held to develop the finer side of human nature of which care for old and sick animals is a manifestation[15]. Applying this test the House of Lords has held that an anti-vivisection society is not a charity[16] since the material benefits of vivisection to man outweigh the moral benefit alleged to flow from the success of the society's project and since the need to change the law in order to prohibit vivisection gave the trust a disqualifying political complexion.

A trust to promote fox-hunting has been upheld[17], though fox-hunting may be promoted otherwise than by maintaining and exercising horses and hounds, the judge, perhaps being over-influenced by the fact that the executors and trustees could hold the property subject to an undertaking to apply it to the named object, with the residuary beneficiary being given leave to apply to the court upon the trustees failing in their duty. It may well be that the residuary beneficiary, Trinity Hall, only objected pro forma in respect of this gift from an alumnus. This anomalous case should not be extended to other sports (like angling) and if any of these anomalous cases is to be overruled this seems a prime candidate.

Gifts for masses

In *Re Caus*[18] it was held that a gift for the saying of masses is charitable, on the grounds that it enables a ritual act, recognised by a large proportion of Christians as the central act of their religion, to be performed and assists in the endowment of priests to perform that act, and accordingly the rule

---

12 *Pettingall v Pettingall* (1842) 11 LJ Ch 176; *Re Dean* (1889) 41 Ch D 552 though wrong in suggesting lives other than human lives may be used in ascertaining the perpetuity period: *Re Haines* (1952) Times, 7 November and *Mitford v Reynolds* (1848) 16 Sim 105; and see *Re Kelly* [1932] IR 255. These cases must be regarded as anomalous and exceptional and in no way destructive of the principle laid down in *Morice v Bishop of Durham* (1805) 10 Ves 522, that there must be someone in whose favour the court could decree specific performance (*Re Astor's Settlement Trusts* [1952] Ch 534, [1952] 1 All ER 1067, and see *Re Shaw* [1957] 1 All ER 745, [1957] 1 WLR 729, compromised on appeal [1958] 1 All ER 245n, CA).

13 *Re Compton* [1946] 1 All ER 117; *Re Kelly* [1932] IR 255.

14 *Re Grove-Grady* [1929] 1 Ch 557 at 882, CA, per Romer LJ; on appeal sub nom *A-G v Plowden* [1931] WN 89, HL.

15 *Re Moss* [1949] 1 All ER 495.

16 *National Anti-Vivisection Society v IRC* [1948] AC 31, [1947] 2 All ER 217, overruling *Re Foveaux* [1895] 2 Ch 501. Trustees who had acted on the basis that the latter case was good law were relieved against breach of trust in *Re Wightwick's Will Trusts* [1950] Ch 260, [1950] 1 All ER 689.

17 *Re Thompson* [1934] Ch 342.

18 [1934] Ch 162, but some doubt was cast on this decision in *Gilmour v Coats* [1949] AC 426 at 451–452, 454, [1949] 1 All ER 848 at 858, 859, HL.

against perpetuities does not apply to it. *Re Hetherington*[19] has accepted *Re Caus* as good law in respect of the saying of masses in public though not in private. However even if a gift for the saying of private masses be non-charitable it seems it could still be valid if restricted to the perpetuity period[20].

Capricious trusts relating to the management of inanimate objects

Where directions are given to trustees to manage property in a manner absolutely capricious, and without either human interest or benefit to any living being, it would seem that the trust is absolutely void, and that the person entitled to the property by law can claim it at once as if the trust had never been declared. Thus, where a house was devised to trustees in trust to block up windows and doors for 20 years, and at the end of that period to convey it to A in fee, it was held that the first trust was void, and that the heir-at-law took the house during the 20 years[1]. So in America it has been held that a trust to keep a favourite clock of the testator in repair was void[2]. It is, however, difficult in principle to distinguish these cases from those relating to the keeping up of tombs, unless the latter are allowed as a concession to human weakness or sentiment[3]. The whole of the cases relating to this question require to be reviewed by the House of Lords before any intelligible principle can be extracted from them.

Unincorporated associations

An unincorporated association has the following features[4]: (1) it is composed of two or more persons bound together for a common purpose; (2) those persons have mutual rights and duties arising from a contract between them; (3) the association has rules to determine (a) who controls the association and its funds and (b) the terms on which such control is exercisable; (4) the association can be joined or left at will. This fourth feature was not at issue in *Conservative and Unionist Central Office v Burrell (Inspector of Taxes)* and it seems too restrictive since there may well be rules restricting new membership or the freedom to leave at will and why should such rules negative the existence of an unincorporated association?

Gifts to or in trust for unincorporated associations raise technical problems that will amaze or confound laymen wishing to benefit such an association.

---

19 [1990] Ch 1, sub nom *Re Hetherington, Gibbs v McDonnell* [1989] 2 All ER 129 (*sed quaere* when the justification of assisting in the endowment of the priesthood applies equally to masses said in public or in private).

20 *Bourne v Keane* [1919] AC 815 at 874–75, per Lord Buckmaster; in Malaysia and Singapore trusts for ancestor worship (Sin Chew or Chin Shong ceremonies) have been held valid anomalous non-charitable purpose trusts if restricted to the perpetuity period: *Re Khoo* (1933) 2 MLJ 119; *Phan v Phan* (1940) 9 MLJ 44; *Tan v Tan* (1946) 12 MLJ 159; *Hong Kong Bank Trustee Co v Farrer Tan* [1988] 1 MLJ 485.

 1 *Brown v Burdett* (1882) 21 Ch D 667. But cf *Re Cassel* [1926] Ch 358, where a trust to keep in repair and pay rent, rates, and taxes of a dwelling house was held good until it vested absolutely in possession.

 2 *Kelly v Nichols* (1891) 17 RI 306, but now see Uniform Trust Code 2000, s 409. For antagonistic Scots cases see, eg *M'Caig v University of Glasgow* 1907 SC 231; *M'Caig's Trustees v Kirk Session of United Free Church of Lismore* 1915 SC 426.

 3 As explained in *Re Astor's Settlement Trusts* [1952] Ch 534, [1952] 1 All ER 1067 and *Re Endacott* [1960] Ch 232, CA.

 4 *Conservative and Unionist Central Office v Burrell (Inspector of Taxes)* [1982] 2 All ER 1, [1982] 1 WLR 522, CA.

The technical problems flow from the fact that an unincorporated association is not a legal person capable of owning property and of being the subject of legal rights and duties. Association property thus has to be vested in a few leading members as trustees for all the members of the association, though moneys will be dealt with by a treasurer operating an association bank account separate from his personal account. The trust will be a bare trust for the members (except to the extent that some specific statute might prevent members of certain societies from winding up the society and dividing up its property between themselves). The trustees or other organ under the club's constitution may enter into contracts or, exceptionally, may be authorised to create trusts binding the club's property. To the extent such valid trusts have not been created, the club's property belongs to the members subject to their contract inter se under the club's constitution and subject to creditors' claims resulting from contracts made by the trustees or other organ[5].

The technical problems in the way of gifts to or in trust for such clubs relate to the need for trusts to satisfy the beneficiary principle[6], the test for certainty of objects[7], the rule against remoteness of vesting ensuring that beneficiaries' interests must vest in interest within the perpetuity period[8], and the rule against inalienability ensuring that income, subject to non-charitable trusts or powers is not rendered inalienable for longer than the perpetuity period[9]. Whether or not such principles, tests or rules are satisfied hinges upon the construction placed upon the settlor's or testator's intentions[10], taking into account the terms of his gift, the rules and nature[11] of the association to which he is giving (he being presumed to know such)[12] and the nature of the gifted property[13].

The first question is whether or not the donor intended to create a bare trust of his property in the hands of the treasurer or other officer so that it can be freely spent on everyday expenses (without the need to distinguish capital from income and to spend only the income) or an endowment trust requiring the capital to be set apart from the club's general assets and only the income to be used in the specified manner. Until the Perpetuities and Accumulation Act 1964 endowment trusts were void unless restricted to the perpetuity period: after that Act they will be valid for the statutory perpetuity period if not restricted to the common law perpetuity period, unless they are pure abstract purpose trusts that are non-charitable, in which event they will be void for infringing the rule against inalienability (unaffected by the 1964 Act) as well as void for infringing the beneficiary principle. The critical question in the case of an endowment trust is, therefore, whether it satisfies

---

5 *Re Bucks Constabulary Widows' and Orphans' Fund Friendly Society (No 2)* [1979] 1 All ER 623, [1979] 1 WLR 936. However, exceptionally, the beneficiaries of the bare trust are not liable to indemnify the trustees in respect of any liabilities incurred beyond the extent of the assets of the club: *Wise v Perpetual Trustee Co* [1903] AC 139.
6 *Re Denley's Trust Deed* [1969] 1 Ch 373, [1968] 3 All ER 65; *Re Lipinski's Will Trusts* [1976] Ch 235, [1977] 1 All ER 33; *Leahy v A-G for New South Wales* [1959] AC 457, [1959] 2 All ER 300.
7 See pp 84–85 ante.
8 See p 192, post.
9 See p 202, post.
10 *Leahy v A-G for New South Wales* [1959] AC 457, [1959] 2 All ER 300.
11 *Re Recher's Will Trusts* [1972] Ch 526, [1971] 3 All ER 401; cf *Re Lipinski's Will Trusts* [1977] 1 All ER 33 at 43.
12 *Carne v Long* (1860) 2 De GF & J 75 at 79.
13 *Leahy v A-G for New South Wales* [1959] AC 457, [1959] 2 All ER 300.

the beneficiary principle as clarified by *Re Denley's Trust Deed*[14] or contravenes it as a non-charitable purpose trust (assuming that the law does not develop so as to allow such a trust to be valid if enforceable by an expressly designated enforcer having locus standi to sue).

The following constructions are possible, though the modern trend is to adopt the fourth construction (post) in the absence of a clear intention on the part of the donor or testator to create an endowment trust of his property. Thus, a gift or legacy to an unincorporated society will be valid under the fourth construction as accruing to society funds generally under a bare trust, in the absence of a clear intention that the property is to be held as an endowment on trust, as would be the case if one million pounds were bequeathed to the Lawn Tennis Association on trust to use the income for furthering the tennis playing standards of English people of all ages, such trust being void for infringing the beneficiary principle and the rule against inalienability, whether the LTA be an unincorporated body or a company limited by guarantee. Where the trust is for present and future members of the unincorporated body it would now seem to be valid under the third construction (post).

(1) No trust exists for the gift is a valid absolute out-and-out gift to the present[15] aggregate of persons described by the group name under which they associate[16], eg the X Club, the Y Society, the Z Association. Any member of the association may claim his aliquot share under a joint tenancy or tenancy in common.

This construction is possible even if the gift is to the association with the motive of being used for its general purposes[17] though nowadays the recently developed fourth construction, below, will be more likely since the settlor/testator would probably not intend that the individual members could forthwith divide up his gift among themselves[18]. However, the old approach was benevolent in preventing the gift being for the future members and so necessarily upon an endowment trust and so void under the common law rule against remoteness before the 1964 Perpetuities and Accumulations Act.

(2) A trust exists for the present members (ie those at the date of the gift) of the association jointly or equally[19]. Where there is a clear trust this has

---

14 See pp 111–113, ante.

15 A trust would necessarily be involved if the organisation or trustees were intended to be legally bound to benefit future members, so that the property would still be held for them when they materialised.

16 *Cocks v Manners* (1871) LR 12 Eq 574 (share of residue 'to the Dominican Convent at Carisbrooke payable to the superior for the time being'); *Re Smith* [1914] 1 Ch 937 (bequest to 'the society or institution known as the Franciscan Friars of Clevedon in the County of Somerset'); *Re Ogden* [1933] Ch 678; *Leahy v A-G for New South Wales* [1959] AC 457, [1959] 2 All ER 300, PC.

17 *Re Ogden* [1933] Ch 678 at 681; *Re Clarke* [1901] 2 Ch 110 (bequest to the committee for the time being of the Corps of Commissionaires in London to aid in the purchase of their barracks or in any other way beneficial to the Corps).

18 *Re Recher's Will Trusts* [1972] Ch 526, [1971] 3 All ER 401; *Re Lipinski's Will Trusts* [1976] Ch 235, [1977] 1 All ER 33; *Re Goodson* [1971] VR 801.

19 *Re Drummond* [1914] 2 Ch 90, though the Privy Council in *Leahy v A-G for New South Wales* [1959] AC 457, [1959] 2 All ER 300, PC had reservations as to whether it would have come to the same conclusion on the facts since an intention to benefit future members seemed present. The same objection applies to *Re Prevost* [1930] 2 Ch 383 and *Re Turkington* [1937] 4 All ER 501. Nowadays, it seems these cases would be validated under the fourth construction, below. The cases decided before Brightman J first fully explained in *Re Recher's Will Trusts*

the merit of validating the gift, though since a bare trust for present members is equivalent in effect to an absolute out-and-out gift it is perhaps a little unusual to create a trust if only present members are intended to be benefited rather than future members as well.

(3) A trust exists for present and future members of the association, including instances where the trust is for purposes primarily for the personal benefit of present and future members thereby satisfying the beneficiary principle[20], so the gift is in the nature of an endowment, the capital having to be set aside and kept intact so that the income may be used for the benefit of the members of the club from time to time. Such trust would have been void under the old common law rule against remoteness since persons could become members and obtain a beneficial interest outside the perpetuity period[1]. To be valid the trust would have needed to be restricted to members from time to time until 21 years after the death of the last survivor of all the descendants of, eg King George VI, living at the date of creation of the trust or the earlier dissolution of the club. Without such restriction the trust would now seem to be valid if created after the 1964 Perpetuities and Accumulations Act. Under s 3(1) of the Act the trust is treated as valid until it becomes established that a vesting of beneficial interests must occur (if at all) after the statutory period of 21 years from the death of the last survivor of the statutory lives in being. Thus, one waits and sees if the club is dissolved before expiry of this period, because in such event the then members will take absolute vested interests in the trust property to the exclusion of all others. If it becomes apparent at the expiry of the statutory period that, since the club has not been dissolved, persons can still become members and obtain a beneficial interest outside the statutory period, then it seems that s 4(4) of the 1964 Act may apply to exclude such future persons from the class of beneficiaries, so the then class members take absolute vested interests in the trust property to the exclusion of all others[2].

(4) No endowment trust exists because the gift is a valid absolute out-and-out gift to the present members of the association beneficially as an accretion

---

[1972] Ch 526 at 538–539 how unincorporated bodies held their property are most unsatisfactory, since they failed to recognise that the imagined problems arising in respect of legacies to unincorporated bodies arose equally in respect of property already held by such bodies and yet such bodies could validly hold and use such property for the benefit of purposes and of future members.

20 See p 110, ante. Where the members have joined together for a social and recreational purpose or to secure some personal advantage the beneficiary principle will be satisfied: where they combined in pursuit of some altruistic non-charitable purpose the beneficiary principle should still be satisfied if the members under the constitution can wind up the association and divide the property between themselves and the settlor's trust terms are not construed as overriding the members' rights under the constitution and creating an enduring non-charitable purpose trust within the fifth construction below.

1 The gift cannot be saved by the principle that a gift of income indefinitely for A and his successors in title is a gift of the capital to A for such principle cannot be applied where the beneficiary is a fluctuating group of successive generations of members: *Re Levy* [1960] Ch 346 at 363, CA; *Re Westphal* [1972] NZLR 792 at 794–795.

2 Exceptionally, if the trust were construed as a discretionary endowment trust for the members until dissolution of the club, then on such dissolution or the later expiry of the statutory perpetuity period there should be a resulting trust to the settlor or his estate under s 3(3) of the 1964 Act. Trusts for persons (as opposed to trusts for purposes) are not invalidated by the rule against inalienability: see p 191, post. On the 1964 Act see pp 195–197.

to the body's property to be dealt with according to the rules of the body by which the members are contractually bound[3]. Moneys will thus be paid over to the treasurer to go into the account he maintains separately from his own personal account, whilst other property will be vested in trustees under a bare trust for the members in accordance with the body's rules[4].

Usually, the members will be able by a contractually specified majority (or, otherwise, unanimously)[5] to divide the subject-matter of the gift between themselves so that there is a valid bare trust. In the very rare case where beneficiaries cannot obtain beneficial interests by dividing the property up between themselves because statute prohibits this[6] or because on dissolution the assets must pass on to another body to carry on the purposes of the dissolved club, then the trust cannot be a bare trust for members: it would seem to be a purpose trust with the gifted assets often being regarded as an endowment, so that one will need to consider the fifth and subsequent constructions that follow. However, a legacy not by way of endowment but intended to augment the general funds of a body available for discharging any liabilities, should be valid as directly or indirectly benefiting the members with locus standi to ensure their body's funds are properly spent.

In *Re Lipinski's Will Trusts*[7] Oliver J upheld a residuary bequest 'upon trust as to one half thereof for the Hull Judeans (Maccabi) Association in memory of my late wife to be used solely in the work of constructing the new buildings for the Association and/or improvements to the said buildings'. Benevolently, he treated the reference to the wife as a tribute, a motive, throwing no light on the question whether or not a permanent endowment was intended, and he treated the 'used solely' reference as a superadded direction of no legal force, though a strong moral intimation of which of the Association's purposes the testator would most like carried out. He held that the testator's moneys could be spent on capital or income expenses or could even be divided between the members if they took the necessary measures under the Association's constitution. The testator's moneys accrued to the general funds of the Association for the benefit of the members.

In *Re Grant's Will Trusts*[8] Vinelott J did not uphold the gift of a testator's estate 'to the Labour Party Property Committee for the benefit of [which he construed as "in trust for"] the Chertsey HQ of the Chertsey & Walton Constituency Labour Property' ('CLP'), providing that if the headquarters ceased to be in the Chertsey UDC Area (1972) his estate should pass to the

---

3 *Re Lipinski's Will Trusts* [1976] Ch 235, [1977] 1 All ER 33; *Re Recher's Will Trusts* [1972] Ch 526; *Re Bucks Constabulary Widows' and Orphans' Fund Friendly Society (No 2)* [1979] 1 All ER 623, *Universe Tankship Inc of Monrovia v International Transport Workers Federation, The Universe Sentinel* [1980] 2 Lloyd's Rep 523, CA; on appeal [1983] 1 AC 366, [1982] 2 All ER 67, HL; *Conservative and Unionist Central Office v Burrell (Inspector of Taxes)* [1982] 2 All ER 1 at 7; *Re Goodson* [1971] VR 801; *Boddington v Lawton* [1994] ICR 478.

4 *Re Bucks Constabulary Widows' and Orphans' Fund Friendly Society (No 2)* [1979] 1 All ER 623, [1979] 1 WLR 936; Friendly Societies Act 1974, s 53.

5 *Re Grant's Will Trusts* [1979] 3 All ER 359 at 366; *Re Recher's Will Trusts* [1972] Ch 526 at 539; *Re William Denby & Sons Ltd Sick and Benevolent Fund* [1971] 1 WLR 973 at 978–979 but of *M'Kenny v Barnsley Corpn* (1894) 10 TLR 533, CA; *Abbatt v Treasury Solicitor* [1969] 1 WLR 1575 at 1583.

6 For example, Literary and Scientific Institutions Act 1854, s 30, *Re Bristol Athenaeum* (1889) 43 Ch D 236. But see *Re Grant's Will Trusts* [1979] 3 All ER 359 at 366 discussed below.

7 [1976] Ch 235, [1977] 1 All ER 33.

8 [1979] 3 All ER 359, [1980] 1 WLR 360 where the impact of Perpetuities and Accumulations Act 1964, ss 3 and 4 was not considered.

National Labour Party ('NLP'). He held the estate was intended to be kept intact to provide a permanent endowment to pass to the NLP if the pre-scribed event occurred, so that the gift was void for perpetuity (whether under the rule against remoteness if construed as a gift for present and future members of the CLP, or the rule against inalienability if construed as a purpose trust, quite apart from infringing the beneficiary principle if con-strued as an abstract political purpose trust).

He could not accept that the bequest should be construed as a gift to the CLP members at the testator's death with the superadded direction of no legal force that they would use it for HQ purposes, though accruing to the general funds of the CLP. He said[9], 'The fact that it is a gift to trustees and not in terms to an unincorporated association militates against construing it as a gift to the members at the date the gift takes effect and against con-struing the words indicating the purposes for which the property is to be used as expressing the testator's motive and not as imposing any trust'. Further-more, the CLP members were not under the CLP rules entitled to divide the CLP funds amongst themselves but were subordinated to the NLP who could demand the funds, and the CLP rules were unalterable except with the NLP's consent. He might have added that any finding of a gift to the CLP members, whether directly or as an accrual to the CLP general funds, was already precluded by his prior holding that the bequest was meant as a permanent endowment, the Committee having to keep the capital intact to use the income for ever for HQ purposes, unless the HQ ceased to be in Chertsey when the capital was to be handed over to the NLP.

But for this crucial prior holding there seems no reason, where ex hypo-thesi the gifted property is available for payment of general expenses (whe-ther of a capital or income nature) and so accrues to the general funds of the association, why it should be necessary for members to be able to divide such funds amongst themselves so long as the members have locus standi to ensure that the funds are used to pay for general expenses benefiting them as members. It is also worth noting that what one strict judge may construe as an apparent endowment trust might be construed by a liberal judge as a bare trust obligation obliging the trustees to transfer the property to the treasurer or other officer(s) of the unincorporated association as an accretion to the funds or other property of the association[10].

In *Neville Estates Ltd v Madden*[11] Cross J appears to treat this fourth con-struction as creating a new limited form of proprietary interest. He stated that the gift is construed as 'a gift to the existing members not as joint tenants but subject to their respective contractual rights and liabilities towards one another as members. In such a case a member cannot sever his share. It will accrue to the other members on his death or resignation, even though such members include persons who became members after the gift took effect. It will not be open to objection on the score of perpetuity or uncertainty unless there is something in its terms or circumstances or in the rules of the asso-ciation which preclude the members at any given time from dividing the subject of the gift between them.' These views have not yet been subject to thorough judicial scrutiny, though often cited.

9 [1979] 3 All ER 359, [1980] 1 WLR 360 at 372.
10 For example, *Re Lipinski's Will Trusts* [1976] Ch 235, [1977] 1 All ER 33; *Re Goodson* [1971] VR 801.
11 [1962] Ch 832 at 849.

One may object that the members' interests must as a matter of property law be severable even if contractual remedies like injunctions or damages may be available in respect of severances. Perhaps, the proper analysis is that the ordinary form of co-proprietary interest subsists in each member but that each member has contracted not to sever his joint interest and not to exercise his right to claim an aliquot share on resignation or death or, even, whilst a member unless, under the appropriate rules, the members between them decide to divide up the assets. As a matter of contract or of estoppel when a member resigns (or dies) he (or his executor) cannot claim his aliquot share or claim that his equitable interest could not have passed on resignation (or death) to the other members without signed writing as required by Law of Property Act 1925, s 53 (or the Wills Act 1837)[12].

The final sentence of Cross J requires qualification. If the fourth construction is ousted by the terms or circumstances of the gift or the rules of the association, an endowment trust for present and future members within the third construction will not be open to objection on the score of uncertainty or perpetuity after the Perpetuities and Accumulations Act 1964: an endowment trust for non-charitable purposes will, however, be open to objection on the score of uncertainty or perpetuity (ie the rule against inalienability) or of infringing the beneficiary principle.

(5) An endowment trust exists for abstract or impersonal non-charitable purposes. Here the trust will be void for infringing the beneficiary principle, unless it falls within the anomalous group of exceptional cases earlier discussed[13], though even then the rule against inalienability will need to be satisfied by restriction to the common law perpetuity period if the trust is to be valid[14]. Thus, a trust to provide a Jewish community centre in Hull would be void[15], just as an endowment trust for a contemplative order of nuns[16] or for the Communist Party[17] or for the Socialist Party[18] is void unless the courts are prepared to develop an enforcer principle validating such trusts if the settlor's trust instrument expressly arranges for there to be an enforcer[19] (eg, the leader from time to time of the Socialist Party to be enforcer of a trust to further the purposes of the Socialist Party).

(6) A trust exists for charitable purposes, so there is no need to satisfy the beneficiary principle or the rule against inalienability or, indeed, the certainty principle as long as the charitable intent is sufficiently certain[20].

---

12 See also Ford *Unincorporated Non-Profit Associations*, pp 5–7, 21–23; Morris and Leach, *The Rule against Perpetuities* (2nd edn) pp 313 et seq, *Re Vandervell's Trusts (No 2)* [1974] Ch 269, [1974] 1 All ER 47, B. Green (1980) 43 MLR 628.
13 See pp 118–123, ante.
14 *Re Hooper* [1932] 1 Ch 38; *Re Astor's Settlement Trusts* [1952] Ch 534, [1952] 1 All ER 1067.
15 *Re Lipinski's Will Trusts* [1976] Ch 235 at 248, [1977] 1 All ER 33 at 44.
16 *Leahy v A-G for New South Wales* [1959] AC 457, [1959] 2 All ER 300, PC.
17 *Bacon v Pianta* (1966) 114 CLR 634.
18 *Re Grant's Will Trusts* [1979] 3 All ER 359, [1980] 1 WLR 360.
19 See p 114 ante.
20 *Re Banfield* [1968] 2 All ER 276, [1968] 1 WLR 846; *Re Finger's Will Trusts* [1972] Ch 286, [1971] 3 All ER 1050; *Chamberlayne v Brockett* (1872) 8 Ch App 206.

PARAGRAPH 2(A)

Powers in the nature of trusts

When faced with an apparent special power of appointment amongst a defined class where there is no gift over in default of appointment the court may treat the apparent power as being in the nature of a discretionary trust for the class members[1] or as a mere power followed by an implied fixed trust in default of appointment in favour of the class members equally[2]. In reading the cases care must be taken in ascertaining which of these alternatives prevailed in the light of the ambiguous language often used by the courts to describe either alternative, eg 'trust power', 'power in the nature of a trust'. For large classes the former alternative is likely and for small classes the latter alternative: the test for certainty of objects of a trust is less strict for discretionary trusts than for fixed trusts[3].

If the power is just a power and no trust can be implied in default of appointment then there will be a resulting trust in favour of the settlor/ testator if the power is not exercised[4]. The crucial question is whether the court can ascertain a general intention to benefit the objects of the power. The leading authority is *Burrough v Philcox*[5]. There, a testator directed that certain property should be held in trust for his two children for life, with remainder to their issue. He declared that if they should both die without issue, the survivor of them should have power to dispose of the property by will amongst such of the testator's nephews and nieces or their children as such survivor should select. No appointment was made. It was held that the class members took the property equally. Lord Cottenham said:

'Where there appears *a general intention in favour of a class*, and a particular intention in favour of individuals of a class to be selected by another person, and the particular intention fails, from that selection not being made, the court will carry into effect the general intention in favour of the class.'

So, where a testator gave personalty to his widow for life, and to be at her disposal by her will, 'therewith to apply part for charity, the remainder to be at her disposal among my relations, in such proportions as she may be pleased to direct', and the widow died without appointing the property, it was held that half was to be held in trust for charitable purposes, and the residue for the testator's relatives according to the Statutes of Distribution[6].

Gift over in default of appointment destroys implied trust

The fact of there being a gift over in default of selection of any member of the class is, of course, fatal to any such trust for such class, even although the

---

1 *Re Parker's Will* [1966] IR 309; *McPhail v Doulton* [1971] AC 424, [1970] 2 All ER 228, HL; *Re Leek* [1967] Ch 1061, [1967] 2 All ER 1160; affd [1969] 1 Ch 563, [1968] 1 All ER 793, CA.
2 *Wilson v Duguid* (1883) 24 Ch D 244; *Walsh v Wallinger* (1830) 2 Russ & M 78; *Re Kieran* [1916] 1 IR 289.
3 See p 84–85, ante.
4 *Re Sayer* [1957] Ch 423, [1956] 3 All ER 600; *Re Perowne* [1951] Ch 785, [1951] 2 All ER 201.
5 (1840) 5 My & Cr 72; *Wilson v Duguid* (1883) 24 Ch D 244.
6 *Salusbury v Denton* (1857) 3 K & J 529; *Re Caplin* (1865) 2 Drew & Sm 527; *Little v Neil* (1862) 10 WR 592; *Gough v Bult* (1847) 16 Sim 45; affd (1848) 17 LJ Ch 401; and see also *Re Susanni* (1877) 47 LJ Ch 65; *Butler v Gray* (1869) 5 Ch App 26; *Croft v Adam* (1842) 12 Sim 639; and *Re Cammell* [1925] WN 36.

gift is void[7]. But a residuary gift is not 'a gift over' for this purpose[8].

No implied trust unless general intention to benefit apparent

On the other hand, the question is always one of construction of the particular instrument, the lack of a gift over being no more than an argument as to what the settlor's intention really was; for a resulting trust may be implied[9].

The tendency of the court has for many years been against inferring trusts from powers unless there are some other expressions indicating a general intention to benefit the class. Thus, in *Re Weekes' Settlement*[10] there was a gift to the testatrix's husband for life, with power by deed or will to dispose of the property amongst their children.

Romer J, after elaborately examining all the decisions, pointed out that there was no *gift to such of the class* as the husband might appoint, but merely a bare power to appoint among a class, and that the mere giving of a power did not itself show that general intention to benefit the class which was apparent in cases where the selection only was confided to the donee of the power.

Similarly in *Re Combe*[11], Tomlin J refused to infer a trust in default of appointment in favour of the testator's 'relations of the whole blood', a vague phrase which of itself raised no inference of any intention to benefit them.

In *Re Perowne*[12] Harman J refused to imply a gift over in favour of the objects of the power where the power of appointment was in favour of persons described by the testatrix as her 'family', saying:

> 'Where, in a marriage settlement, there is a gift to such of the children as A shall appoint, or in trust for such class as he shall be writing indicate, it is very easy to assume a gift over in default, because that is the natural thing to suppose; but where the class is large and indefinite it seems to me much more difficult to imply a gift over.

The case visualised by Harman J, at the beginning of the passage quoted had occurred in *Re Llewellyn's Settlement*[13], where Russell J inferred the existence of an implied trust in a marriage settlement containing a trust to convey to such children as the wife should appoint with no gift over in default of appointment. An additional ground for making the necessary inference was in that case afforded by the fact that there was an *express trust to convey* to such of the children as the wife should appoint.

More recently the cases have concerned broader classes of beneficiaries where the question was not whether there could be implied a trust in default of exercise of the power of appointment but whether the power was not itself really a discretionary trust. The judgment of Buckley J in *Re Leek*[14] is most helpful though every case must depend on its own circumstances the question being whether there is a fiduciary duty to distribute amongst members of a specified class of objects, the only discretion given to the donee of the power being to decide which particular objects shall benefit and when and

---

7 *Re Sprague* (1880) 43 LT 236.
8 *Re Brierley* (1894) 43 WR 36, CA.
9 *Re Sayer* [1957] Ch 423 at 437, [1956] 3 All ER 600 at 607.
10 [1897] 1 Ch 289; and see also *Carberry v M'Carthy* (1881) 7 LR Ir 328.
11 [1925] Ch 210. It is conceived that the decision of Malins V-C, in *Tweedale v Tweedale* (1878) 7 Ch D 633, cannot be supported.
12 [1951] Ch 785, [1951] 2 All ER 201.
13 [1921] 2 Ch 281.
14 [1967] Ch 1061, [1967] 2 All ER 1160; affd [1969] 1 Ch 563, [1968] 1 All ER 793, CA.

how[15], or whether there is no duty to distribute so that whether any object at all is to benefit is left entirely to the discretion of the donee[16].

Distinction between express and implied gifts in default

Where there is an express gift in default of appointment the takers in default take a vested defeasible interest from the date the trust took effect[17]. However, where there is an implied gift in default of appointment the court implies an intention to give the property in default of appointment equally to those only to whom the donee of the power might have given it. Thus, if the power be exercisable only by will the takers in default are those objects living at the death of the holder of the power[18].

The release of powers

For various reasons (eg tax) it may be advisable for powers to be released and a well drafted trust instrument will normally contain an express authorisation enabling the donees of powers to release them, in which case there is no problem in releasing a power[19]. Otherwise, the position seems to be as follows[20]:

(a) If a 'power' of appointment is one in the nature of a trust, it can never be released.

(b) If a power is not in the nature of a trust, then:

    (i)   It cannot be released if it was conferred upon the trustees of the property to which it relates in virtue of their office.

    (ii) It cannot be released if it was conferred upon persons who were in fact the trustees of the property to which it relates and, although it was conferred upon them by name and not by reference to their office, they were selected as donees of the power because they were the trustees.

    (iii) Otherwise the power can be released (eg a personal power of a widow) but if held by persons as office holders (eg as trustees of some other trust) the release cannot exclude their successors in office from being capable of exercising the power (though a complete exercise of the power could have such de facto effect)[1].

---

15 *Re Ogden* [1933] Ch 678; *Re Saxone Shoe Co Ltd's Trust Deed* [1962] 2 All ER 904, [1962] 1 WLR 943; *Re Hain's Settlement Trust* [1961] 1 All ER 848, [1961] 1 WLR 440; *McPhail v Doulton* [1971] AC 424, [1970] 2 All ER 228; reversing sub nom *Re Baden's Deed Trust* [1969] 2 Ch 388, [1969] 1 All ER 1016.

16 *Re Sayer* [1957] Ch 423, [1956] 3 All ER 600.

17 *Re Books' Settlement Trusts* [1939] Ch 993, [1939] 3 All ER 920.

18 *Lambert v Thwaites* (1866) LR 2 Eq 151; *Perpetual Trustee Co Ltd v Tindal* (1940) 63 CLR 232 at 247.

19 Powers may be similarly affected if a power is completely exercised exhausting it, or if the property is so dealt with that the power is implicitly extinguished: *Re Christie-Miller's Settlement* [1961] 1 All ER 855n, [1961] 1 WLR 462; *Re Courtauld's Settlement* [1965] 2 All ER 544n, [1965] 1 WLR 1385; *Muir v IRC* [1966] 3 All ER 38, [1966] 1 WLR 1269, CA; *Blausten v IRC* [1972] Ch 256, [1972] 1 All ER 41.

20 *Re Wills' Trust Deeds* [1964] Ch 219, [1963] 1 All ER 390; (1968) 84 LQR 77 (A J Hawkins); *Muir v IRC* [1966] 3 All ER 38, [1966] 1 WLR 1269. The actual decision in *Re Wills' Trust Deeds* probably cannot stand with the CA decision in *Muir v IRC*: see *Mettoy Pension Trustees Ltd v Evans* [1991] 2 All ER 513 at 546.

1 *Re Wills' Trust Deeds* [1964] Ch 219, [1963] 1 All ER 390. Buckley J suggested that where in default of exercise of the power of appointment there is a trust express or implied in favour of

(c) Whether the 'power' is a power or really a trust, an arrangement under the Variation of Trusts Act 1958 may effectively release or extinguish the 'power' expressly or impliedly[2].

PARAGRAPH 2(B)

Precatory trusts depend wholly on interpretation

The subject of precatory trusts, ie transfers or bequests of property to another, coupled with words of prayer, entreaty, recommendation, expectation, or the like (which according to ordinary usage would not bear an imperative connotation), is not free from difficulty, owing to the conflict between the modern decisions and those of an earlier age. If, however, it be borne in mind that this question is not one of *law*, but merely one of the true interpretation of the document which contains the precatory words, much confusion will be avoided. Regarded in that light, and applying the dictum of Lord Lindley[3], that

> 'when I see an intention clearly expressed in a will, and find no rule of law opposed to giving effect to it, I disregard previous cases',

the conflict of authorities to a large extent becomes immaterial.

The expression 'precatory trusts' is a little misleading in that where precatory words are construed as creating a trust then such trust is a perfectly ordinary trust with no unusual characteristics as pointed out by Rigby LJ in *Re Williams*[4].

The modern rule as to precatory words stated and contrasted with the former rule

The modern way of judging whether precatory expressions are intended to impose enforceable trusts might be stated thus:

> If a gift in terms absolute is accompanied by a desire, wish, recommendation, hope, or expression of confidence that the donee will use it in a certain way, no trust to that effect will attach to it, unless, on the will as a whole, the court comes to the conclusion that a trust was intended[5].

In other words, it is a question of construction of the particular instrument, and not a question of any supposed rule of courts of equity[6].

This is almost the precise opposite of the rule laid down in the older cases which might have been stated as follows:

---

the objects of the power then the power cannot be released but this seems erroneous in view of *Smith v Houblon* (1859) 26 Beav 482; *Re Radcliffe* [1892] 1 Ch 227, CA; *Re Evered* [1910] 2 Ch 147, CA.

2 *Re Courtauld's Settlement* [1965] 2 All ER 544n, [1965] 1 WLR 1385.

3 Also see Goff LJ in *Re Osoba* [1979] 2 All ER 393 at 396, CA.

4 [1897] 2 Ch 12 at 27.

5 *Comiskey v Bowring-Hanbury* [1905] AC 84, HL; *Hill v Hill* [1897] 1 QB 483 at 487; *Re Hamilton* [1895] 2 Ch 370; *Re Williams* [1897] 2 Ch 12; *Lambe v Eames* (1871) 6 Ch App 597; *Re Adams and the Kensington Vestry* (1884) 27 Ch D 394; *Re Diggles* (1888) 39 Ch D 253; *Mussoorie Bank v Raynor* (1882) 7 App Cas 321; *Re Conolly* [1910] 1 Ch 219; *Re Williams* [1933] Ch 244; *Re Green* [1935] WN 151. Extrinsic evidence may be allowable: Administration of Justice Act 1982, s 21.

6 *Re Steele's Will Trusts* [1948] Ch 603, [1948] 2 All ER 193.

If a gift in terms absolute is accompanied by a desire, wish, recommendation, hope, or expression of confidence that the donee will use it in a certain way, a trust to that effect will attach to it[7].

But even when the older rule stood unimpeached there was a clear consensus of judicial opinion that precatory expressions are only prima facie imperative and that the inference is capable of being rebutted by the context[8], while, even now that the modern rule has become firmly established, the court will not hesitate to infer the existence of a trust where the testator has made apparently conscious use of a formula held in a case decided before the emergence of the modern rule, but never since questioned, to create a trust[9].

Authorities for modern rule

As Lindley LJ observed in *Re Hamilton*[10]:

'We are bound to see that the beneficiaries are not made trustees unless intended to be made so by their testator. ... You must take the will which you have to construe and see what it means, and if you come to the conclusion that no trust was intended, you say so, although previous judges have said the contrary on some wills more or less similar to the one which you have to construe.'

The same view was expressed later by Romer J in *Re Williams*[11]:

'The rule you have to observe is simply this. In considering whether a precatory trust is attached to any legacy, the court will be guided by the intention of the testator apparent in the will, and not by any particular words in which the wishes of the testator are expressed.'

And in *Comiskey v Bowring-Hanbury*[12] Lord Davey said:

'The words "in full confidence", are, in my opinion, neutral. I think it would be impossible to regard them as technical words in any sense. They are words which may or may not create a trust, and whether they do so or not must be determined by the context.'

While in *Re Steele's Will Trusts*[13] Wynn-Parry J summarised the matter thus:

'The manner in which the modern view has evolved is, I think, simply that the courts have indicated that there is established in the older authorities no binding or overriding rule of construction which would disentitle one to look at each will and to extract from that will what was the true intention of the particular testator or testatrix.'

7 *Malim v Keighley* (1795) 2 Ves 333 at 529; *Knight v Knight* (1840) 3 Beav 148; affd sub nom *Knight v Boughton* (1844) 11 Cl & Fin 513 ('I trust to the liberality of my successors ... '); *Palmer v Simmonds* (1854) 2 Drew 221 ('having full confidence'); *Curnick v Tucker* (1874) LR 17 Eq 320; *Le Marchant v Le Marchant* (1874) LR 18 Eq 414 ('in full confidence'); *Hart v Tribe* (1854) 18 Beav 215 ('being convinced'); *Gully v Cregoe* (1857) 24 Beav 185 ('feeling assured and having every confidence'). See also *Wace v Mallard* (1851) 21 LJ Ch 355; *Shovelton v Shovelton* (1863) 32 Beav 143.
8 See for example *McCormick v Grogan* (1869) LR 4 HL 82.
9 *Re Steele's Will Trusts* [1948] Ch 603, [1948] 2 All ER 193; see the text at p 135, post.
10 [1895] 2 Ch 370 at 373, approved in *Re Oldfield* [1904] 1 Ch 549, CA.
11 [1897] 2 Ch 12 at 14; and see also *Re Burley* [1910] 1 Ch 215.
12 [1905] AC 84 at 89.
13 [1948] Ch 603, [1948] 2 All ER 193.

Illustrations of the application of the modern rule

It may be useful to look at the relevant words in certain wills which the court has construed in accordance with the modern rule. The case which, perhaps, marks the turn of the tide is *Lambe v Eames*[14], where a testator had given his estate to his widow 'to be at her disposal in any way she may think best *for the benefit of herself and family*'. It was held that the latter words imposed no trust on the widow in favour of the family, and Lord Justice James commented severely on former decisions which had imposed trusts where none were intended.

A similar decision was given in *Re Adams and the Kensington Vestry*[15], where a testator gave all his estate unto and to the absolute use of his wife, her heirs, executors, administrators and assigns, in full confidence that she would do what was right as to the disposal thereof between his children, either in her lifetime or by will after her decease. It was held that, under these words, the widow took an absolute interest in the property, unfettered by any trust in favour of the children.

On the other hand, in *Comiskey v Bowring- Hanbury*[16], the House of Lords held that the words 'in full confidence' were, on the construction of the whole will, intended to create a trust. There the testator gave all his property to his wife 'absolutely, in full confidence that she will make such use of it as I should have made myself, and that at her death she will devise it to such one or more of my nieces as she may think fit. *And in default of any disposition by her thereof by her will or testament, I here direct* that all my estate and property acquired by her under this my will shall at her death be divided among the surviving said nieces.'

Besides being of the highest authority this case forms an excellent example of the application of the present rule that intention must be gathered from the will as a whole. Although the testator's language was ambiguous it is difficult to resist the inference, collected from the whole of the passage quoted, that his intention was to restrict his widow to a life estate with a power of appointment among the nieces[17]. This interpretation appears to ignore the word 'absolutely', but to place too unbending and strict an interpretation on any single word in a will irrespective of other expressions of an inconsistent character therein would in many cases lead to the disappointment of the testator's intentions.

In *Re Steele's Will Trusts*[18], it was again held that a binding precatory trust had been created. There the testatrix had, in a will prepared with professional aid, used with regard to certain jewellery, the identical formula which, in a case[19] which had stood for 80 years without any doubt being cast on the correctness of the decision, had been held to create a valid trust and it was held that the testatrix here intended the jewellery to devolve in the same

---

14 (1871) 6 Ch App 597, followed in *Re Hutchinson and Tenant* (1878) 8 Ch D 540.
15 (1884) 27 Ch D 394. This case appears to overrule *Curnick v Tucker* (1874) LR 17 Eq 320; *Le Marchant v Le Marchant* (1874) LR 18 Eq 414, where the precatory words were practically identical, since any argument to the contrary based on difference in meaning between 'absolute use' and 'sole use and benefit' seems too refined to be acceptable.
16 [1905] AC 84, HL.
17 *Re Jones* [1898] 1 Ch 438 and *Re Parsons* [1927] 2 DLR 1001; but cf *Re Sanford* [1901] 1 Ch 939.
18 [1948] Ch 603, [1948] 2 All ER 193; (1968) 32 Conv (NS) 361 (P St J Langan).
19 *Shelley v Shelley* (1868) LR 6 Eq 540.

manner as the jewellery in the earlier case was directed to devolve by the order made therein.

Gift in will and precatory words in codicil

If the gift is contained in a will and the precatory expressions in a codicil, there is more chance of an inference in favour of a trust than where the gift and the precatory words are contained in the same instrument. Thus where a testatrix by her will gave a legacy of £2,300 to R and by a first codicil said 'I wish R to use £1,000 part of the legacy for the endowment in his own name of a cot' at a named hospital, and by a second codicil said 'I wish R after endowing the cot to use the balance of the legacy for charitable purposes', it was held that R was merely a trustee[20].

Spouse and issue under wills

By the Administration of Justice Act 1982, s 22, 'Except where a contrary intent is shown, it shall be presumed that if a testator devises or bequeaths property to his spouse in terms which in themselves would give an absolute interest to the spouse but by the same instrument purports to give his issue an interest in the same property, the gift to the spouse is absolute notwithstanding the purported gift to the issue.'

Interpretation of wills

Extensive evidence, including evidence of the testator's intention, may be admitted to assist in the interpretation of a will (a) insofar as any part of it is meaningless, or (b) insofar as the language used in any part of it is ambiguous on the face of it, or (c) insofar as evidence, other than evidence of the testator's intention, shows that the language used in any part of it is ambiguous in the light of the surrounding circumstances[1].

PARAGRAPH 2(C)

How far apparent testamentary[2] conditions are construed as charges, trusts or personal obligations

Whether a devise or bequest to A in terms *upon condition* or *to the intent* that some benefit may be conferred on B creates a trust or merely a charge or a personal liability on A if he accepts the devise or bequest is often a most difficult question. As in the case of precatory words, however, it is entirely a question of interpretation of the will[3]. If the true interpretation is that the property was beneficially given to A subject to a definite sum being paid to B,

---

20 *Re Burley* [1910] 1 Ch 215.

1 Administration of Justice Act 1982, s 21, discussed by R Kerridge and J Rivers (2000) 116 LQR 287 at 311–316.

2 For inter vivos contractual conditions creating trusts or charges in the context of commercial contracts for the supply of goods and for the protection of the vendor see pp 12–16, 39, ante, and for an inter vivos gift of a flat subject to a valid condition requiring the donee to allow the donor to live in the flat as long as was reasonably practicable and to provide the donor with a reasonable standard of living, see *Ellis v Chief Adjudication Officer* [1998] 1 FLR 184, CA.

3 *Re Lester* [1942] Ch 324, [1942] 1 All ER 646. Further see pp 133–135, ante.

then the gift to A will not be construed as conditional; for failure to perform such a condition, whether due to A's refusal to perform it or to his death in the lifetime of the testator, would result not merely in forfeiting A's interest, but also in depriving B of the benefits which were intended to be conferred on him[4]. Nor will it be construed as a trust, if a charge or equitable lien for the sum payable to B would meet the case[5], though such a charge may be coupled with a personal obligation[6]. If on the other hand the true interpretation is that the testator intended that A should hold the property for the benefit of himself and B or a fortiori if he did not intend A to take beneficially at all, a trust and not a mere charge will be created[7]. It should be added that words which on their face appear to impose a condition may be construed as merely precatory and explanatory of the testator's motive in making the gift[8].

Illustrations

As is always the case in questions depending on the interpretation of particular documents and not on rules of positive law the authorities are unsatisfactory, but the following illustrations will, at least, serve to show the effect attributed by the courts to different forms of words which have been variously construed as imposing trusts, charges and personal obligations.

In *Cunningham v Foot*[9] property was devised to A on condition of his well and truly paying legacies.

Lord Cairns LC said:

'Well and truly pay must mean simply on condition of well and truly paying; and therefore, it being established in law that a devise to A "paying" a sum of money to B is not a trust, but is a charge, it must also be the law that a devise to A "to well and truly pay" to B is not a trust but is a charge; and a devise to A, "on the condition of well and truly paying", must be a charge and not a trust.'[10]

On the other hand, in *Merchant Taylors' Co v A-G*[11] a testator had devised houses to the company 'to this intent and upon this condition', viz, to provide garments for 24 poor persons each year and to 'gather the whole residue of the rents into a stock and therewith repair and if need be rebuild the houses', with a gift over to another City company for the same purposes if the Merchant Taylors failed to carry out his behests. The income in course of time greatly exceeded what was required for the purposes expressed in the will, and the question then arose whether the will created a charitable trust (in which case the balance would have to be applied for charity cy-près), or

---

4 *Re Oliver* (1890) 62 LT 533, where the principles of the court are very lucidly stated by Chitty J.
5 *Cunningham v Foot* (1878) 3 App Cas 974, per Lord Cairns; *Hughes v Kelly* (1843) 3 Dr & War 482, ii; *Wood v Cox* (1837) 2 My & Cr 684; *Re Foord* [1922] 2 Ch 519.
6 *Re Lester* [1942] Ch 324, [1942] 1 All ER 646.
7 *Cunningham v Foot* (1878) 3 App Cas 974; *Merchant Taylors' Co v A-G* (1871) 6 Ch App 512; *A-G v Wax Chandlers' Co* (1873) LR 6 HL 1; *Bird v Harris* (1870) LR 9 Eq 204; *Re Cowley* (1885) 53 LT 494; *Re Oliver* (1890) 62 LT 533; *Re G* [1899] 1 Ch 719; *Re Booth* [1894] 2 Ch 282; *Re Rees' Will Trusts* [1950] Ch 204, CA.
8 *Re Brace* [1954] 2 All ER 354, [1954] 1 WLR 955 (condition that A 'will always provide a home for B' precatory only); *Re Lipinski's Will Trusts* [1976] Ch 235, p 127, ante; but binding inter vivos condition in *Ellis v Chief Adjudication Officer* [1998] 1 FLR 184, CA for donor-mother to be cared for in donated flat by donee-daughter.
9 (1878) 3 App Cas 974.
10 (1878) 3 App Cas 974 at 990; and see also *Re Oliver* (1890) 62 LT 533.
11 (1871) 6 Ch App 512.

whether it was a beneficial devise to the company merely charged with the charitable dole.

It was ultimately held that it was a trust and not a mere charge on the ground, apparently, that there was no indication that any beneficial interest whatever was intended to be given to the company, the testator having expressly provided what was to be done with the whole of the rents and having merely not foreseen that there would in course of time be more than was needed for the purposes expressed.

In *Re Frame*[12] property was bequeathed to A on condition that she adopted one of the testator's daughters and made certain payments to two other daughters.

Simonds J said:

'A devise or bequest, on condition that the devisee or legatee makes certain payments does not import a condition in the strict sense of the word, but imports a trust, so that though the devisee or legatee dies before the testator, and the gift does not take effect, yet the payments must be made for it is a trust, and no trust fails for want of trustees. ... Much argument has been directed as to what is involved in the condition that she adopts my daughter. It seems clear that ... what is intended is not any single formal act but a series of acts to establish the relationship of parent and child. ... So far as adoption involves the giving of care, advice and affection, this court cannot compel that such things be given. However, seeing that it involves the duty of maintenance that is a trust which the court can enforce. ... It will not allow the whole to fail because a part cannot be enforced.'

In *Re Lester*[13], where a testator had bequeathed certain shares to his son 'subject ... to the payment by him' of an annuity to another son and, after the latter's death, of certain deferred annuities, it was held that a personal obligation was imposed on the legatee but that the words used were not apt to create a charge on the shares.

Words of expectation or explanatory of motive

It is well settled that mere words of expectation, or words explanatory of the donor's motive, never impose trusts on the donee. Thus, if a legacy be given to a father 'the better to enable him to bring up his children', no trust is thereby created; for such words are only explanatory of the donor's motive[14]. But where, on the other hand, there was a bequest of income to A, '*that he may use it* for the benefit of himself, and the maintenance and education of his children', it was held that a trust was intended to be imposed upon A to maintain and educate his children[15].

---

12 [1939] Ch 700, [1939] 2 All ER 865.

13 [1942] Ch 324, [1942] 1 All ER 646.

14 *Brown v Casamajor* (1799) 4 Ves 498; *Benson v Whittam* (1831) 5 Sim 22; and cf *Re Brace* [1954] 2 All ER 354, [1954] 1 WLR 955.

15 *Woods v Woods* (1836) 1 My & Cr 401; *Crockett v Crockett* (1848) 2 Ph 553; and *Talbot v O'Sullivan* (1880) LR 6 Ir 302; and see *Bird v Maybury* (1864) 33 Beav 351; *Hora v Hora* (1863) 33 Beav 88; *Castle v Castle* (1857) 1 De G & J 352. On motive also see *Re Lipinski's Will Trusts* [1976] Ch 235, [1977] 1 All ER 33, p 127, ante.

PARAGRAPH 2(D)

Agreement to create trusts

The rule that a valid agreement to create a trust in futuro, is sufficient to create a trust in praesenti, so as to bind the property in the hands of the parties, or those having notice of the agreement, depends on the maxim that 'Equity regards that as done which ought to be done.' As Lindley LJ stated[16], 'Where the obligation to do what ought to be done is not an absolute duty, but only an obligation arising from contract, that which ought to be done is only treated as done in favour of some person entitled to enforce the contract or against the person liable to perform it.'

It follows, therefore, that where a trust is alleged to have been created by an *agreement* to do something, its validity depends on the question whether the agreement is one of which courts of equity would decree specific performance[17]. If it was merely a voluntary promise (or even a covenant under seal, not supported by valuable consideration), no trust will be created; for equity gives no assistance to volunteers, and consequently there is nothing which can, under the foregoing maxim, be regarded by the court as done. This distinction between trusts depending on contracts, and trusts actually declared, will be emphasised in Article 9, post.

It is worth noting that one can declare a trust of property one presently owns, including choses in action like existing book debts, but there is also a doctrine of Equity that when a person contracts to hold on trust for X or to assign to X property of a certain description which is either not then in existence (like future book debts) or is not then owned by the contractor, who has received the consideration for the contract, then when property satisfying the contractual description is acquired by the contractor he is regarded as trustee of the property for X whose claims therefore prevail over his creditors[18].

Marriage articles

An instance of trusts arising out of contract is afforded by marriage articles though these are very much less common than they used to be. Where it is desired to settle property on a marriage which is arranged to take place upon such short notice that there is no time to draw up a formal settlement, articles of agreement are signed, by which, in consideration of the marriage, the parties agree to execute a formal settlement, vesting certain property upon trusts indicated more or less roughly. Thereupon equity, regarding that as done which ought to be done, fastens a trust on the property, and treats any dealings with it inconsistent with the agreement, not only as a breach of contract, but also as a breach of trust.

So, also, where a father, in contemplation of his daughter's marriage, *contracts* to leave her a specified sum, or an aliquot part of his estate, and dies without fulfilling his promise, his estate will be bound to make good the

---

16 *Re Anstis* (1886) 31 Ch D 596 at 605, CA.
17 See *Westminster Bank v Wilson* [1938] 3 All ER 652; *Mac-jordan Construction Ltd v Brookmount Erostin Ltd* [1992] BCLC 350, CA; *Pullan v Koe* [1913] 1 Ch 9 (after-acquired property within marriage settlement covenant automatically subject to settlement trusts).
18 *Re Lind* [1915] 2 Ch 345 at 360; *Palette Shoes Pty Ltd v Krohn* (1937) 58 CLR 1 at 26–27; *Associated Alloys Pty Ltd v ACN 001452106 Pty Ltd* (2000) 74 ALJR 862.

contract[19]. There must, however, have been a binding contract; a mere representation of intention will not suffice, even although the marriage took place on the faith of it[20].

Mutual wills and joint wills

Mutual wills and joint wills were dealt with under this head in previous editions.

Where two persons (usually, but not necessarily, husband and wife) make an arrangement as to the disposal of their property after their respective deaths and agree not to alter such arrangement and make mutual wills in pursuance of that arrangement, then if one dies, and the survivor subsequently revokes[1] or alters his own will, then although probate will be granted of the last-mentioned will the survivor's personal representatives will hold his estate on trust to give effect to the provisions of his mutual will[2].

As Lord Camden LJ said in *Dufour v Pereira*[3]:

'The parties by the mutual will do each of them devise, upon the engagement of the other, that he will likewise devise in manner therein mentioned. The instrument is the evidence of agreement; and he that dies first, does by his death carry the agreement on his part into execution. If the other then refuses, he is guilty of fraud, can never unbind himself and becomes a trustee of course.'

However, the agreement at the date of making the wills to create a trust in futuro does not then create a trust in praesenti. Not only is mutual revocation possible during their joint lives but individual revocation is possible provided notice is given to the other, such notice even being supplied by the death of the first to die with a revoked or altered will[4]. The trust is only operative at the death of the first to die and is really in the nature of a constructive trust so it is dealt with at pp 427–432, post.

PARAGRAPH 3

Illusory trusts

Sometimes a disposition which at first sight appears to be a trust in favour of another or others may prove to be illusory, if the document or the surrounding circumstances lead to the conclusion that no trust for the benefit

---

19 *Luders v Anstey* (1799) 4 Ves 501; (1800) 5 Ves 213; *Hammersley v de Biel* (1845) 12 Cl & Fin 45 at 61n; *Coverdale v Eastwood* (1872) LR 15 Eq 121; *Synge v Synge* [1894] 1 QB 466, CA. See also *Parker v Clark* [1960] 1 All ER 93, [1960] 1 WLR 286, especially at 100; *Palmer v Bank of New South Wales* (1975) ALJR 320, and *Schaefer v Schuhmann* [1972] AC 572, [1972] 1 All ER 621, PC for the problems relating to testamentary contracts generally.

20 *Hammersley v de Biel* (1845) 12 Cl & Fin 45 at 61n; *Jorden v Money* (1854) 5 HL Cas 185; *Maddison v Alderson* (1883) 8 App Cas 467 at 473; *Re Fickus* [1900] 1 Ch 331. It will be difficult to use marriage as a detriment for the purposes of establishing a proprietary estoppel claim: cf. *Coombes v Smith* [1986] 1 WLR 808. Further see pp 250–252, post.

1 This includes revocation on subsequent marriage; see *Re Green* [1951] Ch 148, [1950] 2 All ER 913.

2 *Stone v Hoskins* [1905] P 194.

3 (1769) 1 Dick 419; and see *Stone v Hoskins* [1905] P 194.

4 *Dufour v Pereira* (1796) 1 Dick 419; *Stone v Hoskins* [1905] P 194; *Pratt v Johnson* (1959) 16 DLR (2d) 385.

of such person or persons was intended[5].

Thus, where a man who is in debt makes provision for payment of his debts generally, by vesting property in trustees upon trust to pay them, but does so without the knowledge of his creditors, the trustees do not necessarily become trustees *for the creditors.*

> 'The motive of the party executing the deed may have been either to benefit his creditors or to promote his own convenience; and the court there has to examine into the circumstances, for the purpose of ascertaining what was the true purpose of the deed; and this examination does not stop with the deed itself, but must be carried on to what has subsequently occurred, because the party who has created the trust may, by his own conduct, or by the obligations which he has permitted his trustee to contract, have created an equity against himself.'[6]

Inferences arising with regard to creditors' deeds[7]

Prima facie a trust deed for payment of the settlor's creditors *generally*, is deemed to have been made for the debtor's convenience. The transaction is regarded as being the same as if he had put a sum of money into the hands of an agent with directions to apply it in paying certain debts, and such a trust is revocable, the debtor being, in fact, the sole beneficiary[8]. On the other hand, where the creditors are parties to the arrangement, the inference then is that the deed was intended to create a trust in *their* favour, which they are entitled to call on the trustee to execute[9]. However, even though they are not made parties, yet if the debtor has given them notice of the existence of the deed,

---

5 Where A lends money to B for the specific purpose of enabling B to pay creditors or particular creditors see pp 116–118, ante. For sham trusts see p 59, ante.

6 Per Turner V-C in *Smith v Hurst* (1852) 10 Hare 30.

7 The general law as to such deeds is outside the scope of this work. Under the Deeds of Arrangement Act 1914, s 2 a deed of arrangement for the benefit of creditors generally, or if the debtor was insolvent at the date of execution thereof, for the benefit of any three or more of them is void if not registered within seven days of its execution. If it is for the benefit of creditors generally it will be void unless it has received the written assent of a majority in number and value of the creditors within 21 days of registration: s 3 of the 1914 Act. If the deed affects unregistered land it should be registered under Land Charges Act 1972, s 7 whilst if it affects registered land it should be protected by a caution against dealing: Land Registration Act 1925, s 59(1) and (6). Use of deeds of arrangement can be frustrated by a dissenting creditor petitioning for bankruptcy. To avoid this the Insolvency Act 1986 (as amended by the Insolvency Act 2000) introduced 'voluntary arrangements,' which provide a moratorium on other insolvency proceedings. A qualified insolvency petitioner must be the 'nominee' to act in relation to the voluntary arrangement either as trustee or otherwise for the purpose of supervising its implementation: Insolvency Act 1986, s 253. There is a public register of voluntary arrangements, the Deeds of Arrangement Act 1914 not applying to such arrangements. The trusts created by a voluntary arrangement take effect according to the terms of the arrangement, and in default of such terms providing for what is to happen on liquidation or bankruptcy, the trusts continue thereafter: *Shierson v Tomlinson* [2002] EWCA Civ 404, [2002] 3 All ER 474.

8 *Wallwyn v Coutts* (1815) 3 Sim 14; *Garrard v Lauderdale* (1830) 3 Sim 1; affd (1831) 2 Russ & M 451; *Acton v Woodgate* (1833) 2 My & K 492; *Bill v Cureton* (1835) 2 My & K 503 at 511; *Gibbs v Glamis* (1841) 11 Sim 584; *Henriques v Bensusan* (1872) 20 WR 350; *Johns v James* (1878) 8 Ch D 744, CA; *Henderson v Rothschild* (1886) 33 Ch D 459. But see *Re Fitzgerald's Settlement* (1877) 37 Ch D 18; and *Priestley v Ellis* [1897] 1 Ch 489, deciding otherwise as to trusts for creditors after settlor's death.

9 *Mackinnon v Stewart* (1850) 1 Sim NS 76; *La Touche v Earl of Lucan* (1840) 7 Cl & Fin 772; *Montefiore v Browne* (1858) 7 HL Cas 241; and see *Smith v Cooke* [1891] AC 297, HL.

and has expressly or impliedly told them that they may look to the trust property for payment, they may become beneficiaries[10]:

(1) if they have been thereby induced to exercise forbearance in respect of their claims[11], or

(2) if they have assented to the deed and actively (and not merely passively) acquiesced in it, or

(3) if they have acted under its provisions and complied with its terms, and the other side has expressed no dissatisfaction;

but not otherwise[12].

Moreover, where the trust is for particular named creditors (at all events where the facts show that the object of the settlor was to give them a preference over the general body of his creditors)[13], the inference is that they were intended to be benefited; and a similar inference arises where the deed provides for payment of the settlor's debts *at his death* with remainders over[14]. And where it provides for such payment *either* in the settlor's lifetime *or* after his death, it can (it would seem) be enforced by the creditors unless he revokes it in his lifetime[15].

Direction to trustees to pay costs, etc

Where the trustees are, by the settlement, directed to pay all costs, charges, and expenses of the deed, and other incidental charges and expenses of the trust, and to reimburse themselves, and then to pay over the residue to third parties, the solicitor who prepared the deed, and acted as solicitor to the trustees, is not a beneficiary. The trust might, of course, be enforced, but not by him[16].

Direction to employ and pay a named person

Even a positive direction to the trustees of a will to employ a particular person and to allow him a salary, does not create a trust in his favour[17]. Thus, a direction in a will appointing a particular person solicitor to the trust estate, imposes no trust or duty on the trustees of the will to employ and pay him[18]. Whilst there is a very strong presumption against construing such directions as constituting trusts, in principle, it would appear that a sufficiently strong

---

10 Lord Cranworth in *Synnot v Simpson* (1854) 5 HL Cas 121; *Biron v Mount* (1857) 24 Beav 642.

11 Per Sir John Leach in *Acton v Woodgate* (1833) 2 My & K 492.

12 Per Lord St Leonards in *Field v Donoughmore* (1841) 1 Dr & War 227; see also *Nicholson v Tutin* (1855) 2 K & J 18; *Kirwan v Daniel* (1847) 5 Hare 493; *Griffith v Ricketts* (1849) 7 Hare 299; *Cornthwaite v Frith* (1851) 4 De G & Sm 552; *Siggers v Evans* (1855) 5 E & B 367; *Gould v Robertson* (1851) 4 De G & Sm 509; *Re Ashby, ex p Wretford* [1892] 1 QB 872. In essence, it seems the debtor needs to be estopped in all the circumstances from alleging he had no intention to create the trust.

13 *New, Prance and Garrard's Trustee v Hunting* [1897] 2 QB 19.

14 See per Lord Cranworth in *Synnot v Simpson* (1854) 5 HL Cas 121; *Re Fitzgerald's Settlement* (1887) 37 Ch D 18.

15 *Priestley v Ellis* [1897] 1 Ch 489.

16 *Worrall v Harford* (1802) 8 Ves 4; *Foster v Elsley* (1881) 19 Ch D 518. See also *Strickland v Symons* (1884) 26 Ch D 245; and *Staniar v Evans* (1886) 34 Ch D 470, negating the right of a creditor of trustees to proceed against the *estate*.

17 *Shaw v Lawless* (1838) 5 Cl & Fin 129.

18 *Foster v Elsley* (1881) 19 Ch D 518; *Finden v Stephens* (1846) 2 Ph 142.

expression by a settlor/testator of his intention to create a trust could be effective as held in Australia[19].

Funds confined to state officials for distribution

The funds voted by Parliament for the public service are not trust funds in the hands of the Secretaries of State (who receive them from the Treasury) in favour of private persons[20]. And on similar grounds, where Queen Victoria, by royal warrant, granted booty of war to the Secretary of State to India, *in trust* to distribute amongst the persons found entitled to share in it by the Court of Admiralty, it was held that the warrant did not operate as a declaration of trust in favour of such persons, but merely made the Secretary of State the *agent of the Sovereign* for the purpose of distributing the fund[1]. Similarly in *Tito v Waddell (No 2)*[2] the Crown was held to be merely under a governmental obligation to the Banabans in respect of the phosphate-rich Ocean Island so that no fiduciary obligations existed. The position is exhaustively analysed by Megarry V-C[3].

Injured claimant's claims for voluntary carers' services

The law with respect to the services of a third party who provides voluntary care for a tortiously injured claimant and who has no cause of action of his or her own against the tortfeasor is that the claimant may recover the value of the services, past and anticipated, so that he may recompense the voluntary carer, eg his spouse or daughter. The House of Lords has held[4] that the claimant recovers such damages on trust for the carer. This will lead to a bare trust of the amount due to the carer for past services, but what is the position concerning the sum received in respect of future services, especially if the claimant dies prematurely or recovers more speedily than anticipated so that a surplus is available? Surely, it will not be held on resulting trust for the tortfeasor but will be retained by the claimant or his estate. Moreover, the current carer is surely not intended to have any right to insist on being the 'beneficiary-carer', eg if the claimant prefers to replace his wife by his daughter or by some paid third party. Thus, it seems that the amount representing cover for future services is held by the claimant on discretionary trust for paying for such care as he wants but otherwise for himself absolutely: this is an illusory trust because in reality he is in the position of absolute beneficial owner of such money.

---

19 *Taylor v Lewis* (1891) 12 LRNSW Eq 258; *Re Larkin* (1913) 13 SRNSW 691.
20 *Grenville-Murray v Earl of Clarendon* (1869) LR 9 Eq 11.
 1 *Kinloch v Secretary of State for India* (1880) 15 Ch D 1; on appeal (1882) 7 App Cas 619, HL, reaffirmed by the House of Lords in *Town Investments Ltd v Department of the Environment* [1978] AC 359.
 2 [1977] Ch 106, [1977] 3 All ER 129.
 3 [1977] 3 All ER 129 at 219–228; cf *Phillip Bros v Sierra Leone* (1995) 3 CLR 316 and Australian cases, *Aboriginal Development Corpn v Treka Aboriginal Arts and Crafts Pty Ltd* [1984] 3 NSWLR 502, CA and *Registrar of the Accident Compensation Tribunal v Comr of Taxation* (1993) 178 CLR 145, HC.
 4 *Hunt v Severs* [1994] 2 AC 350, [1994] 2 All ER 385, HL well criticised by P Matthews [1994] CJQ 302.

ARTICLE 9

The constitution of trusts

(1) A trust is completely constituted either:

(a) by the settlor declaring that certain property vested in him is to be held henceforth by him on certain trusts; or

(b) by the settlor effectively transferring certain property to trustees and declaring the trusts upon which the trustees are to hold such property.

Thus, if the settlor voluntarily intends to constitute a trust by the second method (or to make a gift directly to an intended donee) but fails because the property has not been effectively transferred to the intended trustees (or to the intended donee) then the settlor cannot be treated as retaining the property qua trustee thereof for the intended beneficiaries (or donee) except if statute so provides specifically or if he has done everything necessary to be done by him in order to make it possible for another to transfer the property (eg in the case of shares or land not yet transferred by entry on the appropriate register). Exceptionally, a settlor may be estopped from denying that he holds certain property on trust; and the appointment by the settlor of one or more of his trustees to the executorship of his will may on his death completely constitute a trust of specific property not effectively transferred to trustees in his lifetime so long as his intention to create a trust still existed at his death.

(2) A completely constituted trust is binding upon the settlor (and his personal representatives), though voluntary, just as a gift is binding upon the donor (and his personal representatives): it is irrevocable unless an express power of revocation was reserved at the time of constituting the trust.

(3) An incompletely constituted trust is unenforceable by a volunteer since equity will not assist a volunteer but is enforceable (even if volunteers are thereby benefited) by someone who gave consideration for the settlor's promise or covenant or, where the settlement was made in consideration of marriage, by someone (eg children) within the marriage consideration. Equity will not frustrate a volunteer suing at common law (unless special circumstances involving fraud, undue influence, etc are present) so a volunteer who is a covenanting party to the deed can sue the settlor on the covenant at common law and obtain full damages. Just as the benefit of a contract may be the subject matter of a completely constituted trust if this is intended by the settlor, so may the benefit of a voluntary covenant (whether relating to existing property or future property) be the subject matter of a completely constituted trust if this is intended by the settlor, in which case the trustees and the volunteer beneficiaries can enforce the trusts in the usual way. If the settlor intended not to create a trust of the benefit of the covenant itself, but only to create a trust of the property within the covenant when or if he transferred it to the trus-

tees, the covenant is unenforceable by volunteers. If the trustees seek the court's directions whether or not they should sue the settlor for common law damages for breach of covenant they will be directed not to sue: it will not be a breach of trust if, in view of this, they decide not to sue without first seeking the court's directions. Indeed, since ex hypothesi the trustees are not holding the benefit of the covenant itself on trust for the beneficiaries they must hold it on a resulting trust for the settlor, so that the action on the covenant against the settlor is groundless.

PARAGRAPH 1

Declaration of self as trustee

Here the property is already vested in the settlor/trustee so the problems can only relate to whether the settlor intended not merely to benefit someone, but to make himself a trustee for that person, and to which of his property the settlor intended his trusteeship obligation to relate. The court has to ascertain that the settlor manifested an intention[5] to become a trustee of certain of his property set aside[6] for certain beneficiaries, though there is no need for such intention to be communicated to the beneficiaries[7]. However, if no communication of an informal declaration is made to any beneficiary it will be presumed that no final unequivocal intention had been formed to create a binding declaration of trust[8]. Even a formal declaration of trust will be open to the allegation of a sham trust if put in the settlor's safe and not communicated to any beneficiary[9].

Informal expressions of intent to declare himself a trustee will suffice, though the layman will have to select his informal words carefully for the courts insist on the nice distinction between the expression 'I give and make over this property to you' and 'I undertake to hold this property for you'[10]. The first is a purported out-and-out transfer whilst the second is a declaration of trust of retained property, though in both cases a layman might well broadly think of himself as making a gift.

However, if the layman attempted to transfer property to another out-and-out, but failed to effect it in accordance with legal requirements as far as he could[11], then equity will not assist the volunteer donee by construing the attempted transfer as a declaration of trust; otherwise, all attempted and

---

5 The intention must be manifested in writing if the trust property is land but may be oral or even inferred from conduct otherwise; though where a beneficiary directs his trustees to hold the trust property for A this amounts to a disposition of the beneficiary's equitable interest to A and so must be in writing within the Law of Property Act 1925, s 53(1)(c), and a beneficiary, B, declaring that he holds his interest on trust absolutely for X will, as a bare trustee, drop out of the picture so that the trustees hold for X instead of for B so that B has essentially assigned his interest, which again requires writing within s 53(1)(c): *Grey v IRC* [1960] AC 1, [1959] 3 All ER 603, HL; *Re Lashmar* [1891] 1 Ch 258; p 238, post.
6 *Re Goldcorp Exchange Ltd* [1995] 1 AC 74, [1994] 2 All ER 806, PC, p 78, ante.
7 *Middleton v Pollock, ex p Elliott* (1876) 2 Ch D 104; *Standing v Bowring* (1885) 31 Ch D 282, CA; *Rose v Rose* (1986) 7 NSWLR 679 at 686; *Fletcher v Fletcher* (1844) 4 Hare 67.
8 *Re Cozens* [1913] 2 Ch 478.
9 *Midland Bank plc v Wyatt* [1995] 1 FLR 697.
10 *Richards v Delbridge* (1874) LR 18 Eq 11.
11 See p 150, post.

imperfect transfers would take effect as declarations of trust when, after all, the attempted out-and out *transfer* is the clearest evidence that the donor did not intend to *retain* the property and create a trust thereof with himself as trustee[12]. Where the donor's intentions are unclear then the court, in order to give effect to the general intention of the donor to benefit the donee, may be prepared to apply the maxim 'Verba ita sunt intelligenda ut res magis valeat quam pereat'[13] particularly where the court is 'dealing with simple people unaware of the subtleties of equity but understanding well their own domestic situation' as remarked by Scarman LJ in *Paul v Constance*[14].

This case concerned an effective oral express declaration of trust in informal terms.

C and P lived together as man and wife. C received £950 damages for personal injuries. C and P saw a bank manager to open a deposit account telling him they were not married. They accepted his suggestion that the account should be in C's name, though P could draw on it with C's signed authority. On many occasions C told P, 'The money is as much yours as mine'. Some joint bingo winnings were paid into the account and there was one withdrawal only of money from the account which was for the shared purposes of C and P. It was held that in context C's words were equivalent to C declaring himself a trustee of the moneys in the account for P and himself equally, so P was entitled on his death to half the moneys.

Scarman LJ usefully summarised the two leading cases on the subject of declarations of trust as follows[15]:

'The first of the two cases is *Jones v Lock*[16]. In that case Mr Jones, returning home from a business trip to Birmingham, was scolded for not having brought back anything for his baby son. He went upstairs and came down with a cheque made out in his own name for £900 and said, in the presence of his wife and nurse: "Look you here, I give this to baby", and he then placed the cheque in the baby's hand. It was obvious that he was intending to make a gift of the cheque to his baby son but it was clear, as Lord Cranworth LC held, that there was no effective gift then and there made of the cheque; it was in his name and had not been endorsed over to the baby. Other evidence showed that he had in mind to go and see his solicitor, Mr Lock, to make proper provision for the baby boy, but unfortunately he died before he could do so. *Jones v Lock* was a classic case where the intention to make a gift failed because the gift was imperfect. So an attempt was made to say: "Well, since the gift was imperfect, nevertheless, one can infer the existence of a trust." But Lord Cranworth LC would have none of it.

In the other case *Richards v Delbridge*[17] the facts were that a Mr Richards, who employed a member of his family in his business, was minded to give the business to the young man. He evidenced his intention to make this gift by endorsing on the lease of the business premises a short memorandum to the effect that[18]:
"This deed [ie the deed of leasehold] and all thereto belonging I give to *Edward* … [ie the boy] from this time forth with all the stock in trade"
Jessel MR, who decided the case, said that there was in that case the intention to

---

12 *Milroy v Lord* (1862) 4 De GF & J 264; *Richards v Delbridge* (1874) LR 18 Eq 11.
13 *Re Gulbenkian's Settlement Trusts* [1968] Ch 126, [1967] 3 All ER 15; *Re Leek* [1969] 1 Ch 563, [1968] 1 All ER 793, CA; *Re Baden's Deed Trusts* [1969] 2 Ch 388, [1969] 1 All ER 1016; *IRC v McMullen* [1981] AC 1 at 11, [1980] 1 All ER 884 at 890, HL per Lord Hailsham.
14 [1977] 1 All ER 195 at 197. Contrast the lack of an immediate donative intent in *Otway v Gibbs* [2001] WTLR 467, PC.
15 [1977] 1 All ER 195 at 198.
16 (1865) 1 Ch App 25.
17 (1874) LR 18 Eq 11.
18 (1874) LR 18 Eq 11.

make a gift, but the gift failed because it was imperfect; and he refused from the circumstances of the imperfect gift to draw the inference of the existence of a declaration of trust or the intention to create one. The ratio decidendi appears clearly from the report[19]. It is a short passage, and because of its importance I quote it:

"In *Milroy v Lord*[20] Lord Justice Turner, after referring to the two modes of making a voluntary settlement valid and effectual, adds these words: 'The cases, I think, go further, to this extent, that if the settlement is intended to be effectuated by one of the modes to which I have referred, the court will not give effect to it by applying another of those modes. If it is intended to take effect by transfer, the court will not hold the intended transfer to operate as a declaration of trust, for then every imperfect instrument would be made effectual by being converted into a perfect trust.' It appears to me that that sentence contains the whole law on the subject".'

In exceptional cases it may be possible for a court to find that though there has been no actual express declaration of trust it is possible to infer a declaration of trust from acts showing that a person has constituted himself a trustee, ie from conduct evincing an intent to deal with his property so that somebody else to his own exclusion acquires the beneficial interest in his property[1]. Thus G, an executor and residuary legatee, directed by the testator to pay 8% interest on £2,000 to W for life might, if satisfied that the testator really meant the sum to be £3,000, actually so tell W and himself till his death pay interest on £3,000 to W. This will make G trustee of the additional £1,000 for W's life[2]. Similarly, where a residuary legatee, R, purchases £2,000 of X stock in his own name to give effect to the testator's wishes, expressed but not effected before death to add such stock to trusts of which R was trustee and R gives the beneficiary a power of attorney to receive the dividends from the stock, there will be held to be a trust of the £2,000 X stock[3].

An exceptional case is *Choithram International SA v Pagarani*[4] where, a month before he died of cancer, P organised an elaborate ceremony one afternoon at his London bedside to establish a philanthropic Foundation in the form of a Jersey trust of which he was settlor and one of the Trustees. He executed the trust deed in the presence of three other Trustees, being his son, his accountant and the First Secretary of the Indian High Commission. Their evidence was that he orally made an immediate gift of all his wealth in his four British Virgin Islands companies 'to the Foundation'. Indeed, the minutes of those companies' meetings held in the evening of that day recorded that the directors (including P, who signed the minutes) acknowledged P's gift of such wealth to the Foundation and that the Trustees of the Foundation were henceforth the holders of the shares and credit balances with the companies. Before P died the gifted shares and balances were not legally transferred to the other Trustees, so it was alleged that the gift to the Foundation was imperfect.

---

19 (1874) LR 18 Eq 11.
20 (1862) 4 De GF & J 264 at 274–275.
1 *Paul v Constance* [1977] 1 All ER 195 at 198; *Richards v Delbridge* (1874) LR 18 Eq 11 at 14; *Heartley v Nicholson* (1875) LR 19 Eq 233 at 242; *Re Fleet Disposal Services Ltd* [1995] 1 BCLC 345 agency account under agency agreement held in surrounding circumstances to be trust account.
2 *Gee v Liddell* (1866) 35 Beav 621; *New, Prance and Garrard's Trustee v Hunting* [1897] 2 QB 19.
3 *Gray v Gray* (1852) 2 Sim NS 273; *Robertson v Morrice* (1845) 9 Jur 122; *Wheatley v Purr* (1837) 1 Keen 551.
4 [2001] 1 WLR 1, PC

Lord Browne-Wilkinson for the Privy Council held, in context, that:

> 'The words "I give to the Foundation"[a non-existent legal entity] can only mean "I give to the Trustees of the Foundation trust deed to be held by them on the trusts of the Foundation trust deed". Although the words are apparently words of outright gift they are essentially words of gift on trusts.'

Did it matter that P had not transferred the shares and credit balances to all the Trustees? As Lord Browne-Wilkinson stated:

> 'What then is the position where the trust property is vested in one of the body of Trustees viz TCP? TCP has, in the most solemn circumstances, declared that he is giving (and later that he has given) property to a trust which he himself has established and of which he has appointed himself to be a Trustee. All this occurs in one composite transaction taking place on February 17. There can be no distinction between the case where the donor declares himself to be sole Trustee for a donee or a purpose and the case where he declares himself to be one of the Trustees... in the absence of special factors[5], where one out of a larger body of trustees has the trust property vested in him he is bound by the trust and must give effect to it by transferring the trust property into the name of all the Trustees.'

It is difficult to see how P's afternoon words of gift on trust could be construed as a declaration that P was not giving away the relevant assets to the Trustees of the Foundation but was himself retaining them as trustee thereof. It may be that the Privy Council has created an exception to the *Milroy v Lord* principle where the donor is already a trustee and intends particular property owned by him to be subjected to the terms of the trust of which he is one of the trustees. Alternatively, it may be that if P's afternoon words on their own did not perfect his gift, then at the evening meeting he must be taken to have declared himself trustee of the relevant property and so to have perfected his gift.

No problems arise as to certainty of subject matter of a declaration of trust where the settlor's declaration relates to specific property, eg 'my one and only Picasso painting, all my shares in ICI plc, all my money currently in my Woolwich Building Society account'. However, if it relates to part of his unascertained property in which he retains an interest[6] and he has not declared himself trustee for himself and another as equitable co-owners with specified fractions or percentages, no trust can arise till there has been a segregation or appropriation of specific property out of the larger mass of property, eg where it is intended to create a trust of 20 cases out of 80 cases of Chateau Latour 1982 in the settlor's cellar[7] or of £1,000 out of £5,000 in the settlor's Woolwich Building Society account[8].

---

5 A special factor would exist if no trust was intended to arise till the intended trust property had been vested in all the intended trustees.

6 If he divests himself of all his equitable interest, eg I hold 20 of my 80 cases of Chateaux Lafite 1961 for X and 60 for Y this should be effective in favour of X and Y as to one quarter and three quarters of the whole 80 cases due to their *Saunders v Vautier* rights to the 80.

7 *London Wine Co (Shippers) Ltd* [1986] PCC 121 endorsed in *Re Goldcorp Exchange Ltd* [1995] 1 AC 74, [1994] 2 All ER 806, PC.

8 *Mac-Jordan Construction Ltd v Brookmount Erostin Ltd* [1992] BCLC 350, CA endorsed in *Re Goldcorp Exchange Ltd* (supra) but for 50 of 950 shares see p 78, ante. A person for value, may create an immediate charge for say £1,000 on property but a company chargor will need to register the charge under Companies Act 1985, s 395 and an individual chargor will need to comply with the Bills of Sale Acts in respect of movable property.

A present irrevocable declaration of trust

Superficially, there appear to be some dicta of Romilly MR[9] and Neville J[10] indicating that a declaration of trust to be valid needs not only to be a present declaration but also to be 'irrevocable'. Of course, a declaration of trust must be 'present' in the sense that 'I declare I hold my ICI Ltd shareholding in trust for myself for life, remainder to X for life, remainder to Y absolutely' is a valid trust[11] whilst 'I declare that on my death I will declare a trust of my ICI shareholding for X for life, remainder to Y absolutely' is a mere promise to constitute a trust in the future[12]. However, there is no reason in principle why S should not declare 'I hold my shareholding in ICI Ltd on trust for A for life, remainder to B absolutely, providing that I reserve a power to revoke the settlement without prejudice to any prior distribution of income or capital'[13]. The use of the word 'irrevocable' in the dicta is surely meant to indicate merely that the settlor must have made a final binding unequivocal decision to take upon himself forthwith the role of trustee, rather than that the incorporation of a power of revocation prevents the constitution of any valid trust. A transfer or declaration of trust of property will be presumed irrevocable[14]. The reservation to the settlor of power to revoke an inter vivos trust does not make the trust testamentary[15]. In exercising its powers to settle the property of a mental patient the court will normally make the settlement revocable just in case the patient recovers his capacity[16].

The effective transfer of the trust property to trustees

Gifts to trustees for the benefit of beneficiaries have to satisfy the same rules as gifts directly to donees[17]: otherwise the transfer is incomplete and the intended beneficiary cannot sue to enforce completion of the transfer since he is a volunteer[18] nor can he claim that the donor should be treated as having declared a trust of the property for him, since the donor's attempted incomplete transfer of the property is absolutely inconsistent with an intention to retain the property on trust for him[19]. In an exceptional case, how-

---

9 *Grant v Grant* (1865) 34 Beav 623 at 625.
10 *Re Cozens* [1913] 2 Ch 478 at 486 'Where a declaration of trust is relied on the court must be satisfied that a present irrevocable declaration of trust has been made'.
11 *Kelly v Walsh* (1878) 1 LR Ir 275; *Re Smith* (1890) 64 LT 13.
12 *Bayley v Boulcott* (1828) 4 Russ 345.
13 *Beecher v Major* (1865) 2 Drew & Sm 431 at 437; *Smith v Deshaw* 116 V 441 (1951) (Supreme Court of Vermont); *Copp v Wood* [1962] 2 DLR (2d) 224.
14 *Newton v Askew* (1848) 11 Beav 145; *Miller v Harrison* (1871) IR 5 Eq 324; *Re Beesty's Will Trusts* [1966] Ch 223 at 233 pointing out that while the exercise of powers of appointment construed in a deed or will and exercisable by deed is irrevocable unless the contrary is stated, there is flexibility for powers that are exercisable informally to be regarded as exercised revocably in context.
15 *Young v Sealey* [1949] Ch 278 at 284 and 294; *Kauter v Hilton* (1953) 90 CLR 86 at 98–101.
16 *Re TB* [1967] Ch 247, [1966] 3 All ER 509.
17 Quaere whether a trustee/donee is free to accept cash offered as a gift not as a gift but as a loan, eg in the case of family trusts holding shares in the family company where the 'donor' may perhaps need the money later to support the company; cf *Dewar v Dewar* [1975] 2 All ER 728, [1975] 1 WLR 1532, decided in ignorance of *Hill v Wilson* (1873) 8 Ch App 888 where Mellish J at 896 stated, 'In order to make out a gift it must be shown not only that the cheque was sent as a gift. It requires the assent of both minds to make the gift as it does to make a contract.'
18 'Equity will not assist a volunteer', p 166, post.
19 *Milroy v Lord* (1862) 4 De GF & J 264; *Richards v Delbridge* (1874) LR 18 Eq 11.

ever, where the donor has done all in his power that it is necessary for him to do, but some further act is necessary to perfect the gift (eg registration of a share transfer or of a transfer of registered land) the court will artificially treat the donor as himself trustee of the property until the gift is perfected by the requisite further act[20]. Furthermore, if a trustee, T, declares that henceforth particular property of his is to be held on the trusts of which he is a trustee or is to be held on trust for a named Trust or Foundation, construed as on trust for the trustees of such Trust or Foundation, then he is bound to transfer such property into the names of all the trustees[1].

The gift may be inter vivos or by way of donatio mortis causa or by will. Assuming the will satisfies the requisite formalities and the debts, expenses and liabilities do not exhaust the intended subject matter of the gift, then the personal representatives must in the appropriate manner vest the subject matter in the trustees for the beneficiaries[2].

The donatio mortis causa requires the donor's intention in contemplation of death to make a gift immediately, but conditional on death, so as to be subject to a right of revocation until the donor's death[3]. There must be delivery of the subject matter of the gift or of something representing it which provides the donee with some effective means of obtaining it[4]. It is most unusual for a gift to a trustee to be by means of a donatio mortis causa and a nice distinction has to be drawn between a donatio mortis causa and an attempt to make a testamentary gift which must satisfy the Wills Act formalities[5].

Inter vivos gifts have to be completed according to the nature of the property involved.

A legal estate in unregistered land requires delivery[6] of a duly executed[7] deed to the intended trustee (except for grants of leases not exceeding three years). If he disclaims the donor takes over as trustee of the trusts[8].

Registered land requires the transferee to be registered on the Land Register as proprietor of the land: he is taken to become registered proprietor as of the day on which the appropriate documents are delivered to the Land Registry[9]. If this final step has not yet taken place, but otherwise the donor has done all that is necessary for him to do (eg executing the transfer form and delivering it to the transferee together with the land certificate if in

---

20 *Re Rose* [1949] Ch 78, [1948] 2 All ER 971; p 154, post.

1 *Choithram International SA v Pagarani* [2001] 1 WLR 1.

2 Until then the beneficiaries have a chose in action and not an equitable interest under a trust: see p 17, ante.

3 *Wilkes v Allington* [1931] 2 Ch 104; *Re Lillingston* [1952] 2 All ER 184.

4 *Re Wasserberg* [1915] 1 Ch 195; *Birch v Treasury Solicitor* [1951] Ch 298, [1950] 2 All ER 1198; *Sen v Headley* [1991] Ch 425, [1991] 2 All ER 636, CA (delivery of title deeds to land suffices); *Woodard v Woodard* [1991] Fam Law 470, [1995] 3 All ER 980, CA (car keys).

5 See p 247, post.

6 While physical delivery is common, technical delivery is simply the intention that the deed is to be binding forthwith so that the grantor may be bound before his deed comes into the custody of the grantee or even before the grantee knows of it, although the grantee can disclaim once he knows of it: *Macedo v Stroud* [1922] 2 AC 330 at 337, PC.

7 A signature needs to be made in the presence of a witness attesting the signature, but a signatory is estopped from claiming the witnesses' attestation was made in the signatory's absence where the other party had been led to rely on the deed being valid: *Shah v Shah* [2001] EWCA Civ 527, [2002] QB 35.

8 *Mallot v Wilson* [1903] 2 Ch 494.

9 Land Registration Act 1925, ss 5, 9, 20, 23, 69; LR Rule 83(3) see Land Registration Rules 1978, r 8 as amended by Land Registration Rules 1990, r 9. Under the Land Registration Act 2002 instantaneous electronic transfers will become the norm in some years' time.

his control) it seems the donor will be treated exceptionally as himself holding the property on a trust enforceable at the suit of the beneficiaries[10].

Traditionally company shares (other than bearer securities transferable merely by delivery) require delivery of a duly executed form of transfer to the intended trustee, coupled with delivery of the share certificates relating thereto, and finally registration of the intended trustee as registered owner of the shares[11]. If this final step has not yet taken place the donor will be treated exceptionally as himself holding the shares on a trust enforceable at the suit of the beneficiaries[12], assuming he has done everything else required of him, eg obtaining Exchange Control consent[13]. However shares in public limited companies within the CREST system for transfer of shares are transferred electronically with electronic recording of the names of transferees, who receive no share certificates and who have no legal title to the relevant shares because they are equitable tenants in common with proportionate equitable interests in the pool of relevant shares. Assignments of such equitable interests in the CREST system do not need to comply with s 53(1)(c) of the Law of Property Act 1925[14].

Chattels require the donor to deliver them actually or constructively[15] with the intention to give or to deliver a duly executed deed of gift.

Negotiable instruments are transferable by delivery. However, a gift of money by cheque drawn on the donor is not complete until the cheque is cleared, for until then the cheque is merely a revocable authority or mandate[16]. Where the donor endorses and hands over to trustees a cheque drawn by a third party for full consideration it seems this should effectively constitute the trust. Similarly, an irrevocable banker's draft given to trustees should constitute the trust[17].

Where the donor only has an equitable interest, whether an interest under a trust or an interest in land, like an equitable lease[18] or an estate contract or an equitable chose in action, it must be disposed of in writing signed by the person disposing of the same or by his agent lawfully authorised in writing[19].

10 *Re Ward* [1968] WAR 33; *Scoones v Galvin and Public Trustee* [1934] NZLR 1004; *Brunker v Perpetual Trustee Co* (1937) 57 CLR 555; *Mascall v Mascall* (1984) 50 P & CR 119, CA.

11 Companies Act 1985, s 183; Stock Transfer Act 1963, s 1. Inessential irregularities, eg the transferee's signature or the addresses of the transferor and transferee or even the failure to state the amount of consideration may be ignored: *Re Paradise Motor Co Ltd* [1968] 2 All ER 625, [1968] 1 WLR 1125, CA; *Nisbet v Shepherd* [1994] 1 BCLC 300, CA.

12 *Re Rose* [1949] Ch 78, [1948] 2 All ER 971; *Tett v Phoenix Property and Investment Co Ltd* [1984] BCLC 599 at 619.

13 *Re Fry* [1946] Ch 312, [1946] 2 All ER 106.

14 Regulation 32(5) of the Uncertificated Securities Regulations 1995, SI 1995/3272.

15 *Cochrane v Moore* (1890) 25 QBD 57, CA; *Re Cole* [1964] Ch 175, [1963] 3 All ER 433, CA; *Thomas v Times Book Co Ltd* [1966] 2 All ER 241, [1966] 1 WLR 911.

16 *Re Swinburne* [1926] Ch 38, CA; *Re Owen* [1949] 1 All ER 901.

17 *Carter v Sharon* [1936] 1 All ER 720.

18 *Gilbert v Overton* (1864) 2 Hem & M 110; *Kekewich v Manning* (1851) 1 De GM & G 176.

19 Law of Property Act 1925, s 53(1)(c). This principle of gifts of equitable choses being complete in equity without any valuable consideration is not affected by the Law of Property Act, s 136, which enables such gifts to be made in a further manner; *Re Pain* [1919] 1 Ch 38 at 44–45; *William Brandt's Sons & Co v Dunlop Rubber Co Ltd* [1905] AC 454 at 461, 'The statute does not forbid or destroy equitable assignments or impair their efficacy in the slightest degree'; *Norman v Federal Comr of Taxation* (1963) 109 CLR 9 at 30; *Timpson's Executors v Yerbury* [1936] 1 KB 645, [1936] 1 All ER 186. The dictum of Parker J in *Glegg v Bromley* [1912] 3 KB 474 at 491, 'If there be no consideration there can be no equitable assignment' must be confined to the assignment of a *future* debt taking effect as an agreement to assign it when it is an existing debt: see per Lush J in *German v Yates* (1915) 32 TLR 52.

The assignment will take effect immediately if so intended even if the assignee is unaware of it, although the assignee can disclaim once aware of it[20].

Certain legal choses in action, like patents, copyrights, life assurance policies, bills of lading and shares, require to be transferred according to the appropriate statutory formalities or require the donor to have done everything required of him to enable the transfer to become effective. Otherwise (eg for debts) the Judicature Act 1873, s 25(6), and the Law of Property Act 1925, s 136, created a statutory form of assignment enabling legal choses in action to be assigned at law where previously only an equitable assignment had been possible. In equity legal choses in action could be assigned by written or oral acts revealing an intention to assign[1] and by communication thereof to the assignee – or perhaps even without such communication[2]. Nowadays, a donor seeking to make a gift of a legal chose in action, like a debt, should ideally satisfy Law of Property Act 1925, s 136, which requires and authorises an absolute assignment (not purporting to be by way of charge only) (1) to be in writing signed by the assignor and (2) to be notified in writing by the assignor or assignee or whoever to the debtor before proceedings are commenced. However, by satisfying requirement (1) the donor has done all that is necessary by *him* to be done in order to make the gift at law so the gift will be complete in equity[3]. If the absolute assignment were made orally then requirement (1) would not be satisfied and so the gift would be incomplete, taking effect merely as a promise to make a complete gift which would be unenforceable unless valuable consideration had been provided[4]. Where s 136 is unavailable as where part of a debt is assigned[5] then it seems the gift of part of the debt will be complete in equity if the donor orally or in writing revealed an intention to assign which he communicated to the trustee/donee[6].

Only existing property, and not future property, is capable of being assigned, so that a purported assignment of future property can only take

---

20 *Re Way's Trust* (1864) 2 De GJ & Sm 365.

1 *William Brandt's Sons & Co v Dunlop Rubber Co Ltd* [1905] AC 454 at 462; *Re Wale* [1956] 3 All ER 280 at 283; *Letts v IRC* [1956] 3 All ER 588, [1957] 1 WLR 201. An intention to assign is an intent of A to divest himself of certain rights and vest them in B: this must be distinguished from a mere revocable mandate or authority: *Stamps Comptroller (Victoria) v Howard-Smith* (1936) 54 CLR 614.

2 *Stamps Comptroller (Victoria) v Howard-Smith* (1936) 54 CLR 614 at 622; cf declarations of trust not requiring communication to the beneficiary. But see *Timpson's Executors v Yerbury* [1936] 1 KB 645 at 658, CA.

3 *Holt v Heatherfield Trust Ltd* [1942] 2 KB 1, [1942] 1 All ER 404: the absence of consideration is immaterial since the gift is treated as a completed gift: *Re McArdle* [1951] Ch 669, [1951] 1 All ER 905, CA.

4 *Olsson v Dyson* (1969) 120 CLR 365. It is, however, open to the English court to give effect to a gratuitous oral or unsigned equitable assignment of an existing legal chose in action made in accordance with equitable rules continuing to exist independently of s 136, with the court imposing a trust on the assignor to protect the interest of the assignee and requiring the assignor as a matter of procedure to be joined as a party to the assignee's action against the obligor to ensure that the assignor was bound by the decision: see G J Tolhurst (2002) 118 LQR 98 at 101 and *Lewin on Trusts* (17 edn), para 3–31.

5 *Re Steel Wing Co Ltd* [1921] 1 Ch 349; *Walter and Sullivan Ltd v J Murphy & Sons Ltd* [1955] 2 QB 584, [1955] 1 All ER 843, CA.

6 *Re Smyth* [1970] ALR 919; *Shepherd v Federal Taxation Comr* (1965) 113 CLR 385 (Aust HC).

effect if it is for valuable consideration and so regarded as a contract[7]. A trust may be validly created of an existing debt (eg due from a bank to the settlor) even, it seems, if the debtor (eg the bank) is the trustee of the trust , in which event the debtor has an equitable obligation to the beneficiaries on the same terms as the debt to make payment into the trust fund[8]. The settlor must be responsible for the trust property becoming vested in the trustees, whether he or his duly authorised agent is directly responsible. If Trust 'A' property settled by A is appointed by the trustees in favour of S then S can actually receive the property and subsequently settle it under the 'S' trust, an existing trust already created by him, or under a fresh trust. Alternatively, S may authorise or mandate the 'S' trustees to receive the property and so inform the 'A' trustees: on receipt by the 'S' trustees, without having received any revocation of their authority or mandate, the property will be fully subject to the 'S' trust[9]. If S wishes he can create a trust and make as its trustees the Trust 'A' trustees, directing them in the trust deed to hold any property held by them qua Trust 'A' trustees, but which is subsequently appointed to him absolutely to be held by them qua his trustees[10] though, in principle, this direction, if voluntary[11] and therefore unenforceable, should be capable of being effectively revoked before any such appointment is made[12].

If S voluntarily covenants to transfer to the 'S' trustees any property appointed to S under a special power in that behalf, contained in the 'A' trust set up by A, and property is appointed to S absolutely at a time when a third party has fortuitously appointed the 'S' trustees to be trustees of the 'A' trust (not so unlikely if the 'S' trustees are a major trust corporation) then S is entitled to obtain the appointed property for himself free from any trusts since his voluntary obligation is unenforceable and he is in no way responsible for vesting title to the appointed property in the trustees[13]. However, if S authorises the trustees holding the appointed property qua trustees of the 'A' trust to hold the property qua S's trustees, then the 'S' trust of the property will be completely constituted.

As will be seen later in dealing with the rule in *Strong v Bird*[14] a settlor who has not effectively transferred property to trustees in his lifetime may regularise the position if he appoints one or more of the trustees to be his executors, thereby obtaining the property on his death, so long as the intention to transfer the property for the benefit of the trust beneficiaries continued unchanged till the settlor's death.

If the settlor dies without having effectively transferred property to his

---

7 *Tailby v Official Receiver* (1888) 13 App Cas 523 at 543; *Re Ellenborough* [1903] 1 Ch 697. Expectancies under wills or under the exercise of a power of appointment are classic future property, but a chose in action relating to future property is no less an existing chose in action because it is not immediately recoverable by action: *Re Landau* [1997] 3 All ER 322 at 328.

8 *Re Bank of Credit and Commerce International SA (No 8)* [1998] AC 214 at 226–228 on analagous charge of bank over customer's deposit account. The value of the trust of the debt or contractual promise will depend on the solvency of the debtor-promisor.

9 *Re Bowden* [1936] Ch 71.

10 *Re Burton's Settlements* [1955] Ch 82, [1954] 3 All ER 193.

11 Or not otherwise binding as being to give effect to a condition contained in a will as in *Re Burton's Settlements* [1955] Ch 82, [1954] 3 All ER 193, or being an irrevocable power of attorney.

12 *Re Bowden* [1936] Ch 71, though cf *Re Burton's Settlements* [1955] Ch 82 at 104.

13 *Re Brooks' Settlement Trusts* [1939] Ch 993, [1939] 3 All ER 920.

14 See p 157, post.

trustees in his lifetime and his executor, mistakenly believing himself legally bound to effect the transfer, then effects the transfer to trustees, Astbury J[15] has opined that this would be effective as against those interested under the deceased's will. Even then it would seem that the personal representative should be personally liable to the will beneficiaries, and can the executor really be allowed to perfect the transfer so as to prevent the will beneficiaries claiming the property from the transferees, since the executor does not have as much freedom as the deceased settlor had to perfect the transfer, for the executor holds the property subject to fiduciary obligations owed to the will beneficiaries and not as absolute owner like the settlor?[16]

Exceptional cases

Settlor (or his agent) does everything necessary for him, as opposed to others, to do to transfer the property to trustees

Milroy v Lord[17] laid down that the transferor/settlor must 'have done everything which according to the nature of the property was necessary to be done in order to transfer the property'[18]. The question then arose whether for the transfer to be perfect or complete in equity the transferor (1) must ensure that all necessary acts are done to transfer title irrespective of the fact that the participation of a third party is necessary (eg in transferring shares or registered land), (2) must do all acts which he *can* do even though it may be equally possible for the transferee to do them[19] (eg forwarding the appropriate documents to a company or to the Land Registry) or (3) must do only those acts which it is obligatory *upon him* to do[20] (eg giving the transfer form and certificate of title to the transferee who can himself forward them to the appropriate registering authority).

The third approach has prevailed[1]. In *Re Rose*[2] the donor on 30 March 1943 had executed valid transfers of certain shares in a private company and handed them to the donee together with the relevant certificates by 5 April 1943. The donee forwarded the documents to the company which registered the transfer on 30 June 1943. The Court of Appeal held that the gift was perfected by 5 April, it being crucial to the estate duty position on the donor's death in 1947 that the gift was perfected by 10 April 1943. In respect of the interregnum period the donor held the legal title to the shares upon trust for the donee so that any dividends in that period would be held for the donee. If the company directors had exercised their right under the company's articles to refuse to register the transfer the indications are that the court would still have treated the gift as perfect by 5 April and the legal

---

15 *Carter v Hungerford* [1917] 1 Ch 260.
16 *Re Diplock* [1948] Ch 465, [1948] 2 All ER 318; *Stamp Duties Comr (Queensland) v Livingston* [1965] AC 694, [1964] 3 All ER 692, PC.
17 (1862) 4 De GF & J 264.
18 *Milroy v Lord* (1862) 4 De GF & J 264 at 274.
19 *Anning v Anning* (1907) 4 CLR 1049 at 1079–1082, per Higgins J.
20 *Anning v Anning* (1907) 4 CLR 1049 at 1079–1082, per Griffith CJ.
1 In Australia as well as in England: *Corin v Patton* (1990) 169 CLR 540.
2 [1952] Ch 499, [1952] 1 All ER 1217, followed in *Tett v Phoenix Property and Investment Co Ltd* [1984] BCLC 599. See also *Vanderell v IRC* [1967] 2 AC 291 at 330; (1967) 30 MLR 461 (N Strauss).

interest thereafter vested in the donor as trustee[3]. An analogy may be drawn with the position after disclaimer by a trustee[4].

The Court of Appeal distinguished the earlier decision of Romer J in *Re Fry*[5] whilst accepting it as correct, on the basis that there the American donor had not done everything required of him since his transfer of shares in an English company could not be registered without Treasury consent. The donor completed the necessary forms and submitted them to the Treasury but died before consent was obtained. Romer J held the gift was not perfected by the time of the donor's death so that the donor's executors could not go on to complete the gift. If the gift in *Re Fry* was imperfect because Treasury consent, necessary for the share transfer to proceed, had not been obtained by the relevant time, why was the gift in *Re Rose* not imperfect because the directors' consent necessary for the share transfer to proceed had not been obtained by the relevant time?[6] The Court of Appeal did not face up to this but its views may be supported on the basis that the directors' consent is the ultimate consent and is a negative requirement, rather than a positive requirement, in that the transfer must automatically be registered within two months unless the directors' discretion to refuse to register is exercised within the two months[7].

For types of property other than shares where third party acts are required for legal title to pass (eg registered land) a similar principle applies, namely, that the transferor must do all according to the nature of the property that it is obligatory upon him alone to do (eg deliver an executed transfer and the land certificate)[8].

It would seem that if the transferee lost the transfer form or it was destroyed in a fire then the equitable interest he had acquired should justify the court requiring the transferor to execute a fresh transfer[9].

In *Re Rose*[10] sufficient emphasis was put on the early April delivery of the share certificates together with the transfer forms executed on 30 March for the probable *ratio* to be that equitable title did not pass on 30 March but only passed once the share certificates were delivered together with the transfer forms. Minds did not focus clearly on this issue since it sufficed if equitable title passed by 10 April and delivery had occurred before then.

However, in *Pennington v Waine*[11] Clarke LJ (but not Arden or Schiemann

---

3 [1952] Ch 499 at 510. The trust would determine when, the directors having chosen not to object to a proposed transferee, the legal interest passed on registration of the transferee as owner. Meanwhile, voting rights and dividends would be held to the transferee's order. The trust seems constructive rather than express since the transferor did not intend to hold upon trust but to have the transferee hold the property beneficially or on trust for others; see p 433, post.

4 *Mallott v Wilson* [1903] 2 Ch 494, p 450, post.

5 [1946] Ch 312, [1946] 2 All ER 106.

6 (1976) 40 Conv (NS) 139 (L McKay); (1955) 33 Canadian BR 284 (LA Sheridan).

7 Companies Act 1948, s 78 (now Companies Act 1985, s 183); *Re Swaledale Cleaners Ltd* [1968] 3 All ER 619, [1968] 1 WLR 1710, CA; *Tett v Phoenix Property and Investment Co Ltd* [1984] BCLC 599.

8 See Australian and New Zealand cases on Torrens title land: *Re Ward* [1968] WAR 33, 42 ALJ 227; *Norman v Federal Taxation Comr* (1963) 109 CLR 9 at 24–34 (Aust HC) per Windeyer J; *Brunker v Perpetual Trustee Co* (1937) 57 CLR 555; *Scoones v Galvin and the Public Trustee* [1934] NZLR 1004. Also *Mascall v Mascall* (1984) 50 P & CR 119, CA; *Corin v Patton* (1990) 169 CLR 540.

9 *Mascall v Mascall* (1984) 50 P & CR 119, CA; *Corin v Patton* (1990) 169 CLR 540 at 559–560; Trustee Act 1925, s 51.

10 [1952] Ch 499, CA.

11 [2002] EWCA Civ 227, [2002] 4 All ER 215.

LJJ) held that execution of a stock transfer form forthwith took effect as an equitable assignment in favour of the transferee without the necessity of delivering the form and the relevant certificate either to the transferee or the relevant company – unless the transferor intended the assignment not to have effect until a later date. He regarded this as following from basic principle and some unguarded dicta of Evershed MR and Jenkins LJ in *Re Rose* which indicated 30 March as the date from which legal title was held on trust for the transferee (despite earlier emphasis on the importance of delivery of certificates and forms).

It follows from this view of Clarke LJ that there is no difference between O, the owner, of 1,000 shares in XY Co Ltd writing a letter to D stating 'I hold my 1,000 shares in XY Co Ltd on trust for you', or 'I hereby assign my beneficial interest in my 1,000 shares in XY Co Ltd to you', or executing a stock transfer form 'I hereby transfer 1,000 shares in XY Co Ltd out of my name to D of such and such an address. I request that such entry is made in the register as is necessary to give effect to this transfer.' However, in the last case, unlike the first two, O is not intending to create an equitable interest in favour of D. He is intending to transfer to D legal title which, when transferred, will carry with it the beneficial interest. His intention to transfer ownership is premised upon an effective transfer of the legal title.

Thus, when O has put it out of O's power to prevent D becoming registered with legal title, then O cannot deny D's equitable entitlement, but not before then. So long as O or O's agent has the transfer form or the relevant certificate without which D cannot become registered, O retains beneficial ownership[12] unless there are special circumstances which make it unconscionable for O to deny D equitable entitlement, as held by Arden and Schiemann LJJ in *Pennington v Waine* (and also by Clarke LJ as an alternative *ratio*).

Here, Ada owned 1,500 shares in a private family company with 2,000 issued shares, and her share certificate was in the company's custody. She told her nephew Harold she was giving him 400 shares and wanted him to become a director. She instructed a partner in the company's firm of auditors to prepare a transfer form, which she executed and returned to the partner, who happened to put it in the company's file (not Ada's file) in his office, told Harold of Ada's gift saying Harold (who was company secretary) need take no action, and asked Harry to sign a prescribed form of consent to act as a director, which Harold did and which Ada countersigned. Shortly afterwards, Ada made a will leaving Harold 620 shares so that with the 400 shares he would have a 51% shareholding. Within a month Ada was dead, the above events occurring in the preceding three months.

Despite delivery of the transfer form to the partner as Ada's agent, and not the agent of Harold or the company, so that, prima facie, Ada had a right to change her mind and destroy the transfer form so as to prevent Harold becoming registered shareholder, Arden and Schiemann LJJ held it had become unconscionable for Ada to change her mind and refuse to hand over the transfer form once Harold signed the consent to act as director. It followed it also was unconscionable for her executors to refuse to hand over the share transfer form to Harold.

---

12 Hence the emphasis in *Mascall v Mascall* (1984) 50 P & CR 119, CA and *Trustee of the Property of Pehrsson v Greyerz* (16 June 1999, unreported) PC, on the necessity for the donee to have under his control everything necessary to constitute his title completely, so the donor has no power to prevent this.

Alternatively, when Ada's agent, the partner, had informed Harold of Ada's gift of 400 shares to him and assured Harold that this required no action on his part, this should be construed as meaning that Ada and the partner became agents for Harold for the purpose of submitting the share transfer form to the company, and Harold 'must be taken to have proceeded on the basis that [this assurance] would be honoured'[13]. The implication is that Harold altered his position to his detriment by acting as director despite the apparent absence of qualification shares for a directorship which would have led to vacation of the directorship before Ada's death if equity did not treat him as owner of the requisite shares.

Conveyance to a minor

A minor cannot hold a legal estate in land[14] so a conveyance attempting to vest a legal estate in a minor operates as a declaration that the land is held in trust for the minor, the grantor being the trustee; although if the legal estate is purportedly conveyed to persons of full age as well, then those persons hold in trust for the minor.

Equitable proprietary estoppel

If a settlor tells his son that the son can take possession of a plot of land, Blackacre, which is to be held for the son for life, remainder to his widow, remainder to his children equally, and the son to the settlor's knowledge builds a house thereon, then the son can compel the settlor or the settlor's personal representatives to perfect the gift on principles of equitable proprietary estoppel epitomised in cases such as *Dillwyn v Llewelyn*[15]; *Ramsden v Dyson*[16]; *Inwards v Baker*[17]; and *Pascoe v Turner*[18], discussed pp 248–252, post. Similarly, if A tells B that his house is now hers absolutely so that she acts to her detriment in reliance thereon the court may find that A holds the house on a bare trust for B so that he can be compelled to vest the legal title in B beneficially[19]. If he had told her that the house was half hers so that she acted to her detriment in reliance thereon the court might find that he held the house on trust for himself and her in equal shares[20].

The rule in Strong v Bird

To appreciate *Strong v Bird*[1] it is necessary to consider the position at law and in equity where a deceased creditor had appointed his debtor as his executor. As pointed out by Mason J in *Bone v Stamp Duties Comr*[2] the common law treated the appointment as extinguishing or releasing the debt on the basis:

'that a debt was no more than the right to sue for the money owing by the debtor and that a personal action was discharged when it was suspended by the voluntary

---

13 See Arden LJ at para 68.
14 Law of Property Act 1925, s 1(6).
15 (1862) 4 De GF & J 517.
16 (1866) LR 1 HL 129.
17 [1965] 2 QB 29, [1965] 1 All ER 446, CA.
18 [1979] 2 All ER 945, [1979] 1 WLR 431, CA.
19 *Pascoe v Turner* [1979] 2 All ER 945, [1979] 1 WLR 431, CA.
20 *Lloyds Bank v Rosset* [1991] 1 AC 107; *Grant v Edwards* [1986] 2 All ER 426 at 439, CA.
 1 (1874) LR 18 Eq 315.
 2 (1974) 132 CLR 38 at 53, appeal allowed on other grounds by Privy Council in *Stamp Duties Comr v Bone* [1977] AC 511, [1976] 2 All ER 354, PC.

act of the person entitled to bring it. An executor could not maintain an action against himself; the action to recover the debt was suspended by his appointment which came about by the voluntary act on the part of the testator ... [the true basis of the common law rule] lay in the significance attributed to a voluntary act on the part of the testator, the person entitled to bring the action. Once this is recognised, the true character of the rule is perceived. It reflected the presumed intention of the party having the right to bring the action and was not absolute in its operation.'

Since the administrators are not selected by the voluntary act of the testator the common law did not treat the appointment by the court of the administrator as the release of any debt due to the deceased from the administrator[3]. The procedural obstacle prevented the administrator from suing himself in his life-time but after his death an action could be brought against his estate for the debt if still outstanding.

In equity the debtor (whether the creditor's executor or administrator) was treated as having paid the debt to the estate and hence having assets in his hands which were distributable amongst creditors and persons beneficially interested in the estate[4].

Strong v Bird decided that equity should allow the common law position to prevail and thus not require the executor to account for the debt if the testator had manifested an intention to forgive the debt in his lifetime and this intention had continued till his death.

The common law position thus takes on special significance and so should be elaborated further. The cases[5] seem to establish the debt was released if the debtor appointed executor took out a grant of probate or if he intermeddled but died before taking out a grant of probate or, it seems, if he died before intermeddling or taking out a grant since the executor's title to sue commences as from the testator's death[6]. The release operated to extinguish the debt against beneficiaries but not against creditors. However, there was no release if the debtor renounced probate (or upon being cited to take out probate did not appear to the citation) since he was then treated as if he had never been appointed executor. The Administration of Estates Act 1925, s 5 (replacing the provisions in the Court of Probate Acts 1857 and 1858) now provides that where a person appointed executor survives the testator but dies without having taken out probate the representation to the testator and the administration of his estate are to devolve and be committed as if such person had not been appointed executor. However, it seems unlikely that this has affected the common law release of such person's debt[7] since such person's death cannot be said to be a wilful voluntary act (eg renunciation)

---

3 *Wankford v Wankford* (1704) 1 Salk 299; *Seagram v Knight* (1867) 2 Ch App 628, CA; *Re Gonin* [1977] 2 All ER 720 at 734. Presumably there would be no release if the debtor as executor of the deceased creditor's executor became executor by representation of the deceased creditor. Now Administration of Estates Act 1925, s 21A, added by Limitation Amendment Act 1980, s 10, extinguishes a debt due to the deceased from his administrator or executor by representation though such person remains accountable for the debt where he would be so accountable if he had been appointed an executor by the deceased's will.

4 *Berry v Usher* (1805) 11 Ves 87; *Jenkins v Jenkins* [1928] 2 KB 501.

5 *Wankford v Wankford* (1704) 1 Salk 299; *Re Bourne* [1906] 1 Ch 697; *Jenkins v Jenkins* [1928] 2 KB 501; *Bone v Stamp Duties Comr* (1974) 132 CLR 38; *Re Applebee* [1891] 3 Ch 422.

6 Where the debtor was jointly or jointly and severally liable with others there was a release if he was appointed executor, and, where as sole debtor he was appointed one of several executors there was also a release even, it seems, if only the others took out probate so long as he did not renounce or refuse to appear to a citation.

7 *Re Applebee* [1891] 3 Ch 422.

rejecting the testator's intention to release the debt manifested in the appointment of the debtor as executor.

In *Strong v Bird* B borrowed £1,100 from his stepmother living with him and paying £212.10s each quarter for her board. The loan was to be repaid by £100 deductions from the stepmother's next 11 quarterly payments. She did this for two quarters but then she expressly forgave B the debt and insisted on paying the full £212.10s each quarter. She continued to make these full quarterly payments till her death. She had appointed B executor in her will and he proved the will. The residuary legatees sought to make B account to them for the debt due to the estate since the oral release of the debt was ineffective.

Jessel MR held, however, that the debt had been released at common law by B's appointment as executor and although in equity B would be liable to account for the amount of the debt this had been displaced in equity by B proving that his stepmother up to her death had an unchanged intention to forgive him the outstanding £900. This intention was perfected at law by B becoming his stepmother's executor and there was 'no equity against him to take the property away from him.'[8] In his judgment Jessel MR vacillates between treating the appointment of B as executor as releasing the debt at law and treating the grant of probate in B's favour as releasing the debt at law. On balance it would seem he treated the grant of probate as perfecting the gift of the £900 by causing 'a change of the property at law'[9] to take place. Strictly speaking, though immaterial to the facts of *Strong v Bird*, it would seem at law that it is the intention of the testator manifested in appointing his debtor as his executor and leaving this part of his will unchanged till his death that is itself the making of a gift of the debt so causing a change of the property at law[10].

Extension from forgiveness of debts to perfecting gifts

Where a donor intends to make a gift of specific property but fails to comply with the legal formalities for transferring the legal title to the intended donee and goes on to appoint the donee his executor and then dies, the appointment itself is no perfect gift at law of the specific property unlike the case of a debt due from a previously imperfectly released debtor. Nevertheless, in *Re Stewart*[11] Neville J extended the principle of *Strong v Bird* to an imperfect gift of specific bonds made by the testator in his lifetime to his wife, by handing to her his brokers' letter that they had purchased specified bonds for him, after she had proved his will alongside his other appointed executors. He said[12]:

'Where a testator has expressed the intention of making a gift of personal estate belonging to him to one who upon his death becomes his executor, the intention continuing unchanged, the executor is entitled to hold the property for his own benefit. The reasoning by which the conclusion is reached is of a double character—first, that the vesting of the property in the executor at the testator's death completes the imperfect gift made in the lifetime and secondly, that the intention

8 (1874) LR 18 Eq 315 at 318.
9 (1874) LR 18 Eq 315 at 318.
10 *Wankford v Wankford* (1704) 1 Salk 299; *Bone v Stamp Duties Comr* (1974) 132 CLR 38; *Brazier v Hudson* (1836) 8 Sim 67.
11 [1908] 2 Ch 251.
12 [1908] 2 Ch 251 at 254.

of the testator to give the beneficial interest to the executor is sufficient to countervail the equity of beneficiaries under the will, the testator having vested the legal estate in the executor. The whole of the property in the eye of the law vesting in each executor, it seems to me immaterial whether the donee is the only executor or one of them; nor do I think the rule is confined to cases of the release of a debt owing by the donee.'

Whilst *Strong v Bird* negatively left the situation as it was at law *Re Stewart* went a bold step further by positively treating a gift as effective even though the law did not. However, it has been followed at first instance[13] and treated as good law in the Court of Appeal[14].

A problematic question is what suffices as an imperfect gift. Must there be delivery of some indicia of title? Take X with £15,000 in a building society deposit account where 90 days' notice of withdrawal is required. He signs the withdrawal form but, on being informed of the interest penalty if 90 days' notice is not given, he then gives the requisite notice and takes away the withdrawal form. He tells Y that his intention is to open an account in the joint names of X and Y and pay the £15,000 into this. Upon expiry of the 90 days X feels unwell and in the evening hands the withdrawal form to Y, together with a note authorising the building society to pay Y if opening a new account in the names of X and Y. The following morning X dies and the building society therefore correctly refuses to pay the £15,000 out when Y presents the document in the afternoon, stating that X is dead so that he should have the whole £15,000. Y then takes out a grant of probate as X's executor. By virtue of *Re Stewart* Y should be entitled to the £15,000 but would this be the case if X had not delivered the signed withdrawal form to Y? Presumably, there could be no requisite[15] intention to make an immediate gift before expiry of the 90 days period and, once such period expired, would an intent to make an immediate gift require handing over the withdrawal form with accompanying authorisation or writing a cheque out for £15,000 and handing it to Y to open a joint account with it? Indeed should the perfection of imperfect gifts under *Re Stewart* principles require the same sort of delivery of indicia as is required for donationes mortis causa?

Strong v Bird itself was based not on delivery of anything but simply on evidence of an express intention to forgive the debt, supported by full quarterly payments. This would justify mere evidence of intention without delivery of any indicia as sufficient for the *Re Stewart* extension to imperfect gifts, but it is arguable that, in extending the negative release of debts principle of *Strong v Bird* to the perfection of positive gifts, positive delivery of some indicia should be required. However, in most cases of imperfect gifts if there is no delivery of some indicia relating to the subject of the purported immediate gift it is unlikely that there will be found an intent to make an immediate gift as opposed to an intent to make a gift in the future.

13 *Re Comberbach* (1929) 73 Sol Jo 403; *Re James* [1935] Ch 449; *Re Nelson* (1947) 91 Sol Jo 533; see also *Re Ralli's Will Trusts* [1964] Ch 288, [1963] 3 All ER 940; *Re Gonin* [1979] Ch 16, sub nom *Re Gonin, Gonin v Gameson* [1977] 2 All ER 720.

14 *Re Freeland* [1952] Ch 110, sub nom *Jackson v Rodger* [1952] 1 All ER 16, counsel unreservedly accepting *Re Stewart* as correct.

15 See following footnote and text to which it relates.

This adds significance to the requirement[16] for an intent to make a present gift. However, once the pass has been sold by Equity assisting a volunteer and perfecting an imperfect immediate gift, it is, arguably, illogical for Equity to refrain from assisting a volunteer under an imperfect gift of specific property to be made at a future time (other than the donor's death when testamentary requirements must be satisfied) once that time has arrived, assuming that the donor has not changed his intention by then. After all, equitable proprietary estoppel principles extend to present and future gifts as *Re Basham*[17] and *Gillett v Holt*[18] show.

Erroneous extension to administrators

In *Re James*[19] Farwell J further extended *Re Stewart* to perfect an imperfect gift of real property made by a donor by merely handing the title deeds to his housekeeper who, on the donor's intestacy, had herself appointed by the court one of two *administratrices* of the donor's estate, thereby obtaining the legal estate to the house. This is difficult to justify and it has been doubted by Walton J in *Re Gonin*[20] and rejected by the British Virgin Islands' Court of Appeal[1]. After all, it is the voluntary act of the testator in appointing his debtor as his executor that at law released or extinguished the debt while the appointment of an administrator is an act of the law and, even then, it is often pure chance that determines which of many persons entitled to a grant of letters of administration finally takes them out. For this reason at law the appointment by the court of an administrator, who happened to be a debtor of the deceased, did not release the debt so that *Strong v Bird* itself would have been differently decided if the defendant had been an administrator and not an executor.

The need for intent to make an immediate gift

The rule in *Strong v Bird* has so developed that an imperfect *immediate* gift of specific[2] existing[3] real[4] or personal property will be perfected if the intended donee is appointed the donor's executor alone or with others[5] (whether or

---

16 *Re Innes* [1910] 1 Ch 188; *Re Freeland* [1952] Ch 110, sub nom *Jackson v Rodger* [1952] 1 All ER 16; *Cope v Keene* (1968) 118 CLR 1, and a fortiori when the donor's death is the future occasion so the gift is testamentary in nature; *Re Hyslop* [1894] 3 Ch 522; *Re Pink* [1912] 2 Ch 528 at 536 and 538–539. It follows that *Re Goff* (1914) 111 LT 34 is of doubtful authority (donor intended to forgive debt only if donor predeceased donee yet Sargant J applied *Strong v Bird*).

17 [1987] 1 All ER 405, [1986] 1 WLR 1498.

18 [2001] Ch 210.

19 [1935] Ch 449.

20 [1977] 2 All ER 720 at 734.

1 *Re Pagarani* (1998/99) 2 OFLR 1.

2 The subject matter of the intended gift must be specific so that a sum of money must be 'sufficiently identified to enable it to be separated from the rest of the estate of the testator': *Re Innes* [1910] 1 Ch 188 at 193.

3 *Morton v Brighouse* [1927] 1 DLR 1009; a present intention to make an immediate gift of after-acquired property does not suffice to attract the *Strong v Bird* principle. However, once the pass is sold and equity assists a volunteer and perfects an imperfect gift as in *Re Stewart* [1908] 2 Ch 251, is it not inconsistent for equity to draw back and refrain from assisting a volunteer who is not a volunteer under an immediate gift of existing property but a volunteer under an immediate gift of future property or a volunteer under a promise to make a gift in the future of specific property?

4 *Re James* [1935] Ch 449.

5 *Re Stewart* [1908] 2 Ch 251. Each joint tenant is treated as having the whole property.

not he proves the will or intermeddles)[6] or becomes one of the donor's administrators[7] or executors by representation, so long as the intention to make an immediate gift continues unchanged till the donor's death[8]. Whether the donee's title derived from the donor can then be relied on against creditors (as opposed to the beneficiaries' will or intestacy) is doubtful: in principle it should not avail against creditors since a common law release of a debt by appointment of the debtor as executor did not avail against creditors[9].

Where the intended donee of the title to the subject matter of the intended gift is a trustee or one of several trustees it seems that the rule in *Strong v Bird* can apply to perfect the trust, for the equity of the beneficiaries under the intended trust of the property should be sufficient to countervail the equity of the testamentary beneficiaries[10]. Thus, if S makes an imperfect immediate gift of specific existing property to the trustees of his settlement then if one (or more) of the trustees is appointed S's executor or one of his executors this should completely constitute the trusts relating to the property so long as S's intention to make the gift continues unchanged till his death[11].

If S voluntarily covenants to pay £20,000 to his trustees or to transfer stocks and shares or lands to the value of £80,000 to his trustees then *Strong v Bird* cannot apply if a trustee becomes S's executor because separate specific identifiable property is not concerned[12].

There is a further problem with voluntary covenants in that the very fact that the subject matter thereof is not immediately transferred to trustees[13] indicates that the settlor, S, did not have 'a present intention to make an

---

6 *Re Applebee* [1891] 3 Ch 422; *Re Harvey* (1932) 41 OWN 420 (donor a minor appointed as a joint executor though only permitted by the will to take out probate on attaining his majority); *Wankford v Wankford* (1704) 1 Salk 299.

7 *Re James* [1935] Ch 449.

8 *Re Stoneham* [1919] 1 Ch 149 at 158, P O Lawrence J indicates that if the imperfect gift is confirmed by the will this suffices to satisfy the requirement of continuing intention up to death even if there were contrary expressions of the testator between the date of his will and his death: also see *Cope v Keene* (1968) 118 CLR 1 at 8. A contrary intention ousting *Strong v Bird* will be present if the testator lends to X a car which she had previously intended to give to B, or if a testator later takes security for a debt which she had previously forgiven, or if a testatrix forgets that investments had been settled by her ineffectually and for the rest of her life treats them as still her own or, it seems, if a testator specifically devises or bequeaths property to a third party or otherwise demonstrates that he has forgotten or is overriding his original intent to give the property to B: *Re Freeland* [1952] Ch 110, sub nom *Jackson v Rodger* [1952] 1 All ER 16; *Re Eiser's Will Trusts* [1937] 1 All ER 244; *Re Wale* [1956] 3 All ER 280, [1956] 1 WLR 1346; *Morton v Brighouse* [1927] 1 DLR 1009.

9 *Bone v Stamp Duties Comr* (1974) 132 CLR 38; *Stamp Duties Comr v Bone* [1976] 2 All ER 354 at 359, 360, PC.

10 This adopts the reasoning of Neville J in *Re Stewart* [1908] 2 Ch 251 at 254 cited at p 159, ante.

11 *Re Ralli's Will Trusts* [1964] Ch 288, [1963] 3 All ER 940, where counsel submitted that the rule in *Strong v Bird* could only apply 'where the plaintiff was claiming on his own behalf and not on behalf of volunteers' at 294 but Buckley J rejected this at 301: 'In my judgment the circumstance that the plaintiff holds the fund because he was appointed a trustee of the will is irrelevant. He is at law the owner of the fund and the means by which he became so have no effect upon the quality of his legal ownership. The question is: For whom if anyone does he hold the fund in equity?' Also see *Re Wale* [1956] 3 All ER 280, [1956] 1 WLR 1346 where the executors would have taken as trustees.

12 *Re Innes* [1910] 1 Ch 188 at 193. If S had intended forthwith to create a binding trust of the covenant then the beneficiaries would have an interest under the trust: *Fletcher v Fletcher* (1844) 4 Hare 67.

13 And the settlor does not expressly declare that the *covenant* itself is to be held on trust: see p 173, post.

immediate gift'[14] of the subject matter if, indeed, the covenant does not expressly state that the property is to be transferred upon some future date or future event, eg the falling into possession of a reversionary interest owned by S. The covenant is thus 'an announcement of what a man intends to do in the future and is not intended by him as a gift in the present'[15] so as to fall outside the *Strong v Bird* requirement of a present intention to make an immediate gift as laid down in *Re Freeland*[16] and in *Re Innes*[17].

However, it is arguable that once the pass has been sold and equity assists a volunteer and perfects an imperfect gift as in *Re Stewart*[18] it is inconsistent for equity to draw back and refrain from assisting a volunteer under an imperfect gift of specific property to be made at a future time (other than the donor's death when testamentary formalities must be observed) once that time has arrived, when the donor's intention continued till death and the donee became his executor. In *Re Innes*[19] Parker J considered it would be 'exceedingly dangerous' if this were the case but his underlying reasoning is that a promise to give in the future is unenforceable, unless given for value, and equity will not assist a volunteer: however, an imperfect immediate gift is unenforceable unless made for value and equity will not assist a volunteer *except* where the donor's intention continued till death and the donee became his executor[20]. Logically the *Strong v Bird* exception should exist in both cases, though in *Re Freeland*[1] the Court of Appeal assumed that the views of Parker J in *Re Innes* represented the law since counsel apparently accepted this. In principle, a voluntary covenant to transfer specific property in the future to trustees should thus fall within *Strong v Bird* (as dramatically extended by *Re Stewart*) if a trustee is appointed an executor of the settlor[2].

Doubtful extension to lifetime acquisition of legal title by trustee without impropriety perfecting gifts

Indeed, in *Re Ralli's Will Trusts*[3], taking his cue from the extension of *Strong v Bird* principles to acquisition of legal title to imperfectly gifted property by an administrator-donee, Buckley J upheld the fortuitous vesting in T, the sole surviving trustee of S's voluntary settlement, of property that was the subject of S's covenant to transfer certain existing and after-acquired property and that was owned by T in his capacity as sole surviving trustee[4] of S's father's will

---

14 *Re Freeland* [1952] Ch 110 at 118, per Jenkins LJ.
15 *Re Innes* [1910] 1 Ch 188 at 193, per Parker J.
16 [1952] Ch 110.
17 [1910] 1 Ch 188.
18 [1908] 2 Ch 251.
19 [1910] 1 Ch 188.
20 *Re Stewart* [1908] 2 Ch 251.
 1 [1952] Ch 110.
 2 Alternative grounds for supporting this view would be to treat the covenant as manifesting an ever-continuing intent so that when the future time arrived there could then be said to be an intent to make an immediate gift. As an unsatisfactory last resort it might be possible to treat the covenant as an exception to the general rule for though the covenant technically is not a present gift most lay settlors would treat a covenant as a gift of sorts that worsens their material position.
 3 [1964] Ch 288, with clause 7 fully set out in [1963] 3 All ER 940.
 4 If there had been another trustee, Y, of the will trusts, Y might need to obtain the directions of the court, trustees holding property jointly and having to act unanimously. Because Y is not a trustee-covenantee of S's voluntary settlement does he not hold the will trust fund on trust for S and her personal representatives, so that he will be liable for breach of trust if he co-operates with T to transfer the assets to T to be held as part of the voluntary settlement? If Y

trusts for S's mother for life, remainder to S and her sister equally – T had been appointed trustee of the latter trusts by a third party some years after appointment as trustee of S's voluntary settlement.

Buckley J first held that, pending transfer to S's voluntary settlement trustees of property within clause 7 thereof, the effect of clause 8 was that S's existing equitable interest in remainder should in the hands of S (or her personal representatives) be held on the trusts of S's settlement. That was decisive in entitling the beneficiaries thereunder to equitable interests in half of the actual assets happening to comprise the will trust fund on S's mother's death.

However, as an alternative ratio, under clause 7 S had covenanted to transfer to the trustees all existing and after-acquired property she owned or would come to own (with specified exceptions) and, because T, her covenantee, had legal title to the actual assets within that covenant which comprised half the trust fund held by T fortuitously as sole surviving trustee of S's father's will trusts, such property automatically became held on the trusts of S's voluntary settlement at her mother's death. Thus, if S were still alive (rather than dying before her mother died in 1961) it was 'indisputable'[5] that she could not claim that T was disentitled from insisting he held on the trusts of her settlement half the assets in the father's fund at the death of her mother because S had 'solemnly covenanted under seal to assign [half] the fund to'[6] T, and her personal representatives could be no better off than she.

With respect, *Re Brooks' Settlement Trusts*[7] not cited to Buckley J, makes it clear that S could have claimed that the assets became hers on her mother's death despite her solemn but voluntary covenant. Only the settlor or her duly authorised agent can completely constitute a trust, just as at common law only the donor or his duly authorised agent can make a gift. Thus, in *Re Brooks' Settlement Trusts*, S solemnly covenanted with T in his 1929 voluntary settlement that he would transfer to T anything appointed to him under his father's will trusts. T then fortuitously happened to be trustee of the will trusts when S's mother in 1939 exercised her power of appointment thereunder to appoint £3,517 to S. Although T owned this money as trustee of the will trusts, Farwell J held T was not entitled to hold this money as trustee of S's voluntary settlement, so that S was personally entitled to the £3,517.

It follows that the alternative ratio in *Re Ralli's Will Trusts* is based on an erroneous premise, although the decision is fully justifiable on the basis of its first ratio, that clause 8 was an effective valid declaration of S's existing property, which included her half interest in remainder under her father's will trusts. Only if S had expressly or by necessary implication authorised T, holding assets *qua* trustee of another trust for S, to hold those assets qua trustee of S's trust should there be a completely constituted trust of such assets as part of S's trust[8].

Mistaken perfection of gifts by executors

If S makes an imperfect gift of property to trustees of his settlement and dies,

---

will not co-operate with T, then T cannot be liable to the voluntary settlement beneficiaries. Indeed, if T does not co-operate as co-trustee with Y of the will trusts to transfer the assets to S or her personal representatives will T not be acting in breach of trust?

5 [1964] Ch 288 at 301.
6 [1964] Ch 288 at 301.
7 [1939] Ch 993.
8 As in *Re Bowden* [1936] Ch 71 and *Re Adlard* [1954] Ch 29.

his intention to make the gift continuing unchanged till his death, and his executor, mistakenly believing himself legally bound to perfect the gift, perfects the gift, Astbury J opined[9] that this would be effective against the beneficiaries entitled under S's will. This seems an extremely doubtful extension of *Strong v Bird*[10] which itself would surely have been decided differently if the debtor had not been appointed executor but had had his debt released by the executor. After all, an executor does not have as much freedom as the deceased had to release debts and perfect gifts since the executor holds the property under fiduciary obligations owed to the beneficiaries under the deceased's will and not as absolute owner like the deceased[11]. Thus, the position is different from that where the donor makes an incomplete gift of property and afterwards *himself*, unintentionally, includes it in a conveyance to the donee when the later conveyance is held to perfect the gift.

PARAGRAPH 2

Many cases establish the elementary proposition that just as a gift is binding upon a donor and his personal representatives so a completely constituted trust is binding upon a settlor and his personal representatives, unless at the time of the gift or of constituting the trust a power of revocation was expressly reserved to the donor/settlor.

Thus in *Re Wale*[12] a settlor executed a voluntary settlement containing a recital that the settlor had transferred certain investments into the names of the trustees (the settlor's two sons) to be held on the trusts thereof. In fact none of the investments were so transferred but at the date of the settlement some of them, the 'A' investments, were registered in the settlor's name, whilst the 'B' investments were registered in the names of the settlor and the two sons, though held for the settlor absolutely beneficially. The settlement was clearly ineffective as regards the 'A' investments since the settlor had neither declared herself trustee of them nor transferred them to the trustees. However, it was effective as regards the 'B' investments since the settlement amounted to an effective assignment of the settlor's equitable interest in the 'B' investments. Thus, whilst the 'A' investments formed part of the settlor's estate on her death the 'B' investments could not be claimed by her personal representatives but were fully subject to the trusts of her voluntary settlement.

Similarly, if a settlor voluntarily covenants with trustees to settle any property to which she might become entitled on her father's death and then knowingly allows this property after her father's death to be transferred to the trustees she will not be able to reclaim this property nor to obtain rectification of the deed so as to contain a power of revocation[13].

---

9 *Carter v Hungerford* [1917] 1 Ch 260 at 273. Also see *McCathie v McCathie* [1971] NZLR 58 at 63.

10 (1874) LR 18 Eq 315.

11 *Stamp Duties Comr (Queensland) v Livingston* [1965] AC 694, [1964] 3 All ER 692; *Re Diplock* [1948] Ch 465, [1948] 2 All ER 318.

12 [1956] 3 All ER 280, [1956] 1 WLR 1346; *Jefferys v Jefferys* (1841) Cr & Ph 138.

13 *Re Bowden* [1936] Ch 71; *Re Adlard* [1954] Ch 29, sub nom *Re Adlard's Settlement Trusts, Re Campbell's Settlement Trust, Re Fulton's Settlement Trust, Taylor v Adlard* [1955] 2 All ER 1437; *Paul v Paul* (1882) 20 Ch D 742. Rectification would only be possible if there were clear evidence that a power of revocation had originally been intended to be inserted in the voluntary settlement: *Re Butlin's Settlements Trusts* [1976] Ch 251, [1976] 2 All ER 483. Further see *Racal*

Once a trust has been completely constituted it matters not that the beneficiaries are volunteers[14] (ie persons not providing consideration in money or money's worth or within marriage consideration). However, where equity's assistance is necessary to constitute a trust as yet incompletely constituted then it is crucial whether or not beneficiaries are volunteers in view of the general maxim, 'Equity will not assist volunteers'[15].

PARAGRAPH 3

Equity will not assist a volunteer

As Lord Browne-Wilkinson stated in *Choitham International SA v Pagarani*[16]: 'Although equity will not aid a volunteer, it will not strive officiously to defeat a gift'. A court of equity will not assist a volunteer by requiring a would-be donor to perfect an inchoate intention to confer a bounty. For this reason the maxim is often referred to as 'Equity will not perfect an imperfect gift'[17]. Thus the would-be donor must make a perfect gift to the intended beneficiary (whether inter vivos or by testamentary disposition) or create a completely constituted trust by making a perfect gift to the intended trustees for the intended beneficiaries or by declaring himself trustee of property appropriated for the intended beneficiaries[18].

However, the would-be donor/settlor can be specifically compelled to perfect his gift if the intended beneficiary provided valuable consideration[19] (whether in money or money's worth or by marriage) or comes within the scope of marriage consideration: the fact that the promise to make the gift is contained in a deed and so a covenant avails the intended beneficiary nought so far as equity is concerned[20].

A settlement is in consideration of marriage if made before and in consideration of marriage or if agreed to be made before and in consideration of marriage and actually executed after the marriage[1]. Within the scope of marriage consideration are the parties, their children, and more remote

---

Group Services Ltd v Ashmore [1994] STC 416 at 425; affd [1995] STC 1151, CA; *Tankel v Tankel* [2002] EWCA Civ 227.

14 *Paul v Paul* (1882) 20 Ch D 742.

15 Contrast *Pullan v Koe* [1913] 1 Ch 9 (consideration) with *Re Plumptre's Marriage Settlement* [1910] 1 Ch 609 (volunteers).

16 [2001] 2 All ER 492 at 501 applied in *Pennington v Waine* [2002] EWCA Civ 227, [2002] 4 All ER 215.

17 Certain exceptions exist as seen pp 154–164, ante.

18 *Milroy v Lord* (1862) 4 De GF & J 264 at 274–275.

19 Chitty, *Law of Contracts* (28th edn) chapter 3, Treitel, *Law of Contract* (9th edn) chapter 3. In *Milroy v Lord* a settlement was considered as not for value where expressed to be in consideration of one dollar though in *Mountford v Scott* [1975] Ch 258, [1975] 1 All ER 198, the Court of Appeal treated £1 as value to enable specific performance to be ordered. It is insufficient to show 'good consideration' viz natural affection for family or friends or moral obligation. Inadequacy of consideration is no ground for resisting specific performance unless it is 'so gross as of itself to prove fraud or imposition on the part of the purchaser': *Burell v Dann* (1843) 2 Hare 440 at 450.

20 *Re Plumptre's Marriage Settlement* [1910] 1 Ch 609; *Re Brooks' Settlement Trusts* [1939] Ch 993. In circumstances where the settlor intended a trust of the benefit of the covenant (a chose in action) a volunteer may enforce the trust of that property like trusts of other types of property: see p 173, post.

1 *Re Holland* [1902] 2 Ch 360; *Hill v Gomme* (1839) 5 My & Cr 250 at 254; *De Mestre v West* [1891] AC 264.

issue[2]. Early cases allowing children of a former marriage or a possible later marriage or illegitimate children to be within the scope of marriage consideration can now, it seems, only be supported on the basis that such children's interests were so closely interwoven with the interests of the children of the marriage that the latter could benefit only on terms allowing the former to benefit[3].

Where an intended beneficiary who has provided consideration or is within a marriage consideration does enforce a contract or covenant to create a trust of certain property this may enure for the benefit of volunteers. Thus, if someone within a marriage consideration and having a life interest sues to have covenanted property brought into the settlement, the court will order this and will not exclude volunteers taking under the settlement when the life interest determines[4]. But for this the volunteers would have been unable to claim any of the covenanted property as *Re Plumptre's Marriage Settlement* shows[5], because 'that which ought to be done is only treated as done in favour of some person entitled to enforce the contract as against the person liable to perform it'.

Here, a settlement in consideration of marriage contained the usual covenant by husband and wife with the trustees for the settlement of after-acquired property of the wife. The husband subsequently gave some stocks to the wife and, after her death without issue, the question arose whether the next of kin of the wife (who took the settled fund in default of issue) could call upon the trustees to enforce the covenant against the wife's personal representative, who happened to be the husband. Eve J held that since the next of kin were volunteers and since there was neither a completely constituted trust of the stocks that were the subject matter of the covenant, nor of the benefit of the covenant itself the next of kin's claim failed.

By way of contrast, in a similar situation, but where a wife did not settle £285 pursuant to an after-acquired property covenant in her marriage settlement but died leaving nine children, Swinfen-Eady J held[6] that, since the children were within the marriage consideration, the moment the wife received £285 it was specifically bound by the covenant enforceable in the children's favour[7]. Thus, part of the £285 paid by the wife to the husband and invested by him in bearer bonds deposited with his bank could be traced and would have to be transferred to the settlement trustees, whose claim at law for damages for breach of the covenant had long since been statute-barred, more than 30 years having elapsed since the breach of covenant.

---

2 *A-G v Jacobs-Smith* [1895] 2 QB 341, CA; *Re Cook's Settlement Trusts* [1965] Ch 902, [1964] 3 All ER 898.

3 *Mackie v Herbertson* (1884) 9 App Cas 303 at 337; *De Mestre v West* [1891] AC 264 at 270; *A-G v Jacobs-Smith* [1895] 2 QB 341, CA; *Rennell v IRC* [1962] Ch 329 at 341; affd sub nom *IRC v Rennell* [1964] AC 173, [1963] 1 All ER 803, HL; *Re Cook's Settlement Trusts* [1965] Ch 902 at 914. If of full capacity, such children should be made parties and covenantees so as to be able to enforce their rights at common law on *Cannon v Hartley* principles [1949] Ch 213, [1949] 1 All ER 50, p 169, post.

4 *Davenport v Bishopp* (1843) 2 Y & C Ch Cas 451; affd (1846) 1 Ph 698; *Re D'Angibau* (1880) 15 Ch D 228 at 242, CA.

5 [1910] 1 Ch 609 at 619; *Re Cook's Settlement Trusts* [1965] Ch 902, [1964] 3 All ER 898.

6 *Pullan v Koe* [1913] 1 Ch 9.

7 Where a covenant is specifically enforceable in B's favour then at B's behest (but not volunteers of an incompletely constituted trust) 'equity looks on as done that which ought to be done': *Re Anstis* (1886) 31 Ch D 596 at 605, per Lindley LJ, though if B does have the trust completely constituted then volunteers will benefit: *Davenport v Bishopp* (1843) 2 Y & C Ch Cas 451.

It should be noted that a covenant merely to pay a capital sum of money not specifically earmarked (such as in a safety deposit box or a bank deposit account or received under someone's will) does not attract the equitable remedy of specific performance for equity to look on that as done which ought to be done and treat the money as subject to trusts. Thus in *Stone v Stone*[8] the beneficiaries, though purchasers and not volunteers, were without remedy when the action at law on a covenant to settle £1,000 had become barred under the Statute of Limitations. Similarly, in *Mac-Jordan Construction Ltd v Brookmount Erostin Ltd*[9] the beneficiary-contractor under a contract requiring the employer to set up a retention trust fund was without a proprietary remedy when the employer became insolvent without having set aside out of money in its bank account the requisite amount required for the retention trust fund. The contractor would, however, have had an equitable proprietary interest if the employer's obligation had related to specified funds payable and paid to it by a third party financier[10].

Possible impact of Contracts (Rights of Third Parties) Act 1999 on post-10 May 2000 contracts or covenants to settle property

Section 1 of the Act which 'does not affect any right or remedy of a third party that exists apart from this Act' provides that 'a person who is not a party to a contract ("a third party") may in his own right enforce a term of the contract if (a) the contract expressly provides that he may, or (b) the term purports to confer a benefit on him' unless 'on a proper construction of the contract it appears that the parties did not intend the term to be enforceable by the third party.' By s 1(5) 'there shall be available to the third party any remedy that would have been available to him in an action for breach of contract if he had been a party to the contract (and the rules relating to damages, injunctions, specific performance and other relief shall apply accordingly).' It follows that, since a volunteer-beneficiary who is actually a party to a deed can only recover damages for his own loss[11] and not obtain specific performance for the benefit of the trust fund, a volunteer-beneficiary-third-party cannot obtain specific performance; but if the parties to the deed were not volunteers, as in the case of settlements in consideration of marriage, so that they could obtain specific performance, then the third parties will similarly be able to obtain specific performance, unless on a proper construction it appears that the parties did not intend the relevant term to be enforceable by the third parties.

It seems likely that the courts will hold that, in properly construing marriage settlements, the traditional intention of the parties is for the covenant to settle after-acquired property of the spouses to be enforceable by the spouses and their issue, but not by the next-of-kin beneficiaries entitled in default of issue and who are intended only to benefit to the extent of

---

8 (1869) 5 Ch App 74; cf *Beswick v Beswick* [1968] AC 58, [1967] 2 All ER 1197, HL.

9 [1992] BCLC 350, CA endorsed by PC in *Re Goldcorp Exchange Ltd* [1995] 1 AC 74, [1994] 2 All ER 806.

10 *Pullan v Koe* [1913] 1 Ch 9; *Re Lind* [1915] 2 Ch 345, CA; *Palette Shoes Pty Ltd v Krohn* (1937) 58 CLR 1 at 26–27; *Associated Alloys Pty Ltd v ACN 001 452 106 Pty Ltd* (2000) 74 ALJR 862.

11 *Cannon v Hartley* [1949] Ch 213. Query whether gratuitous covenants in deeds no longer requiring seals should be treated as governed by the law of contract, anchored upon the doctrine of consideration, when a covenant is a formal method to enable the common law to regard a promise as legally binding and remediable in damages irrespective of consideration.

property actually transferred to the trustees. Thus the 1999 Act is probably of no assistance to such default beneficiaries but, in drafting modern settlements, it should be made clear that such beneficiaries are not to have enforcement rights if this position is desired.

Equity will not frustrate a volunteer suing at law

Assuming that fraud, mistake, undue influence or oppressive unconscionable conduct[12] is not involved, equity will not intervene to injunct a volunteer from suing at common law for damages for breach of covenant. Thus in *Cannon v Hartley*[13] a volunteer, who was a party to a settlement deed and covenantee thereunder, was held entitled to recover full damages at common law for breach of the covenant with her, Romer J stating[14]:

'The plaintiff, although a volunteer, is not only a party to the deed but is also a direct covenantee under the very covenant upon which she is suing. She does not require the assistance of the court to enforce the covenant for she has a legal right to enforce it. She is not asking for equitable relief but for damages at common law for breach of covenant.'

To succeed at common law and obtain damages for his own loss, the volunteer, if not being a covenantee under a deed poll, had to be a party to the inter partes deed[15] as well as a covenantee since Law of Property Act 1925, s 56, allowing non-parties to sue if covenantees, had been treated as covering only land or other real property[16]. It follows that B cannot sue at common law where S in a deed with T promised T that S would transfer to T non-land to be held on trust for B. However, for deeds after 10 May 2000, B will have the same remedies as if he had been a party to the deed unless, on a proper construction, it appears that the parties did not intend the relevant term (eg relating to the settlor's after-acquired property from specified sources) to be enforceable by B[17]. Traditionally, in creating a voluntary settlement with an after-acquired property covenant in favour of the trustee, the settlor did not intend any beneficiary to be able to enforce the covenant[18], and it seems likely that the courts will follow such traditional approach and not assist beneficiaries. Clearly, nowadays the draftsman should expressly state that the beneficiaries are not to have enforcement rights if this is the desired position.

Completely constituted trusts of the benefit of contracts or covenants

Just as money, shares or land may be the subject matter of a trust so may choses in action like a debt or the benefit of a contract or covenant to

---

12 See Meagher, Gummow and Lehane *Equity: Doctrines and Remedies*, (3rd edn) Part IV.

13 [1949] Ch 213, [1949] 1 All ER 50. See also *Milroy v Lord* (1862) 4 De GF & J 264 at 278, per Turner LJ and *Davenport v Bishopp* (1843) 2 Y & C Ch Cas 451 at 460, per Knight-Bruce VC.

14 [1949] Ch 213 at 223.

15 *Lord Southampton v Brown* (1827) 6 B & C 718; *Gardner v Lachlan* (1836) 8 Sim 123.

16 *Beswick v Beswick* [1968] AC 58, [1967] 2 All ER 1197, HL a 3 to 2 majority view (see pp 76, 81, 87, 94, 105).

17 See Contracts (Rights of Third Parties) Act 1999 outlined at p 168 ante.

18 See *Re Pryce* [1917] 1 Ch 234; *Re Kay's Settlement Trusts* [1939] Ch 329; *Re Cook's Settlement Trusts* [1965] Ch 902; and p 176 post.

transfer specific shares or land[19] or property materialising under a will or under the exercise of a power of appointment[20].

Contracts

The common law position before the Contracts (Rights of Third Parties) Act 1999 was that, where contracts are concerned, if A promises B for value that A will pay money or transfer property to C there is a perfectly valid contract between A and B but C cannot sue on the contract since he is not a party to the contract and has not provided the consideration therefor[1]. However, if B at the time of making the contract was acting as trustee for C or intended to hold the benefit of the contract as trustee for C, or later declares himself trustee thereof for C, then from the time of the contract or the subsequent declaration of trust, C, with equity's assistance though a volunteer[2], will be able to enforce the contract, joining B as co-defendant, if B is not prepared to be plaintiff, and C will obtain specific performance or full damages as appropriate to the subject matter of the contract[3]. If a trust exists then C is much better off than under the common law contractual position.

At common law where the contract between A and B was expressed to be for C's benefit C has no rights and, if B sues for damages for breach, the general rule[4] is that B can only secure nominal damages, for a plaintiff can only receive substantial damages (as in tort) to the extent that he suffers damage[5]. However, in an appropriate case B may be able to obtain a decree

---

19 *Gregory v Williams* (1817) 3 Mer 582; *Les Affréteurs Réunis SA v Leopold Walford (London) Ltd* [1919] AC 801, HL; *Re D'Angibau* (1880) 15 Ch D 228; *Re Empress Engineering Co* (1880) 16 Ch D 125, CA; *Lloyd's v Harper* (1880) 16 Ch D 290, CA; *Re Flavel* (1883) 25 Ch D 89, CA; *Gandy v Gandy* (1885) 30 Ch D 57, CA; *Re Schebsman* [1944] Ch 83, CA.

20 'A chose in action is no less a chose in action because it is not immediately recoverable by action', per Lord Oliver in *Kwok Chi Leung Karl v Comr of Estate Duty* [1988] 1 WLR 1035 at 1040, applied in *Re Landau* [1997] 3 All ER 322 at 328.

1 *Tweddle v Atkinson* (1861) 1 B & S 393; *Dunlop Pneumatic Tyre Co Ltd v Selfridge & Co Ltd* [1915] AC 847, HL; *Scruttons Ltd v Midland Silicones Ltd* [1962] AC 446, [1962] 1 All ER 1, HL.

2 Since there is a completely constituted trust it is immaterial that he is a volunteer.

3 *Les Affréteurs Réunis SA v Leopold Walford (London) Ltd* [1919] AC 801, HL; *Lloyd's v Harper* (1880) 16 Ch D 290, CA; *Vandepitte v Preferred Accident Insurance Corpn of New York* [1933] AC 70 at 79, PC.

4 Certain statutory exceptions exist (eg Married Women's Property Act 1882, s 11; Road Traffic Act 1972, s 148(4); Solicitors Act 1974, s 37) and there is a general common law exception: 'In a commercial contract concerning goods where it is in the contemplation of the parties that the proprietary interests in the goods may be transferred from one owner to another after the contract has been entered into and before the breach which causes loss or damage to the goods, an original party to the contract, if such be the intention of the parties, is to be treated in law as having entered into the contract for the benefit of all persons who have or may acquire an interest in the goods before they are lost or damaged and is entitled to recover by way of damages for breach of contract the actual loss sustained by those for whose benefit the contract is entered into': *The Albazero* [1976] 3 All ER 129 at 137, per Lord Diplock. For an extension of this to building contracts see *Linden Gardens Trust Ltd v Lenesta Sludge Disposals Ltd* [1994] 1 AC 85 at 114–115, HL and *Darlington Borough Council v Wiltshier Northern Ltd* [1995] 1 WLR 68, CA. There may also be an exception where B may claim full damages where A contracted with B to discharge a debt owed to C by B and, perhaps, where B has actually performed in C's favour that (or part of that) which A failed to perform *Coulls v Bagot's Executor Co Ltd* (1967) 119 CLR 460 at 501–502, per Windeyer J; (1948) 21 Aust LJ 424 (Dr J G Starke); *Beswick v Beswick* [1968] AC 58 at 88, per Lord Pearce.

5 *West v Houghton* (1879) 4 CPD 197; *Beswick v Beswick* [1968] AC 58, [1967] 2 All ER 1197, HL; *The Albazero* [1977] AC 774, [1976] 3 All ER 129, HL; *Woodar Investment Developments Ltd v Wimpey Construction UK Ltd* [1980] 1 All ER 571, [1980] 1 WLR 277, HL disapproving the reasoning of Lord Denning MR in *Jackson v Horizon Holidays Ltd* [1975] 3 All ER 92, [1975] 1

of specific performance, so obtaining full benefits for C as in *Beswick v Beswick*[6], all the more so where damages would be inadequate. Of course, if A carries out the contract and benefits C then B cannot complain and C is absolutely entitled to do as he wishes with the money or property transferred to him by A so long as not intended to be a nominee for B[7].

To circumvent the circumscribed common law contractual position many attempts have been made on C's behalf to claim that B holds the benefit of the contract on trust for C. Originally, the courts were quite sympathetic to such claims, sometimes being prepared to find that an intention to benefit C sufficed to show an intention to create a trust, just as originally the courts were quite willing to find that precatory words sufficed to show an intention to create a trust.

The position then developed that C has a heavy onus to discharge in proving that B intended to make himself a trustee of the benefit of the contract for C for it is became crystal clear that 'An intention to provide benefits for someone else and to pay for them does not in itself give rise to a trusteeship'[8]. As du Parcq LJ said in *Re Schebsman*[9], 'It is true that by the use possibly of unguarded language a person may create a trust ... but unless an intention to create a trust is clearly to be collected from the language used and the circumstances of the case I think the court ought not to be astute to discover indications of such an intention.' In *Re Webb Farwell* J said[10], 'It is for a person to make clear by the language used that he is constituting himself a trustee and the absence of any clear words to that effect makes it difficult to establish a trust.' 'The intention to constitute the trust must be affirmatively proved.'[11]

The crux of the matter is that one must not 'disregard the dividing line between the case of a trust and the simple case of a contract made between two persons for the benefit of a third party'[12]. If an express or implied intention on B's behalf to constitute himself a trustee cannot be found then the court cannot impose a constructive trusteeship in order to do 'justice' and benefit C: a constructive trust[13] cannot be used as a means of conferring rights on C where B has merely failed to declare a trust for C in proper fashion, otherwise all imperfect express trusts would take effect as constructive trusts!

Most of the cases concern policies of assurance[14] or other arrangements

WLR 1468, CA; where Lord Denning MR based himself on a dictum of Lush LJ in *Lloyd's v Harper* ignoring the fact that Lush LJ was concerned with a completely constituted trust of a contract held by A on trust for B when he said, 'I consider it to be an established rule of law that where a contract is made with A for the benefit of B, A can sue on the contract for the benefit of B and recover all that B could have recovered if the contract had been made with B himself'. Similarly see Dillon LJ in *Darlington Borough Council v Wiltshier Northern Ltd* [1995] 1 WLR 68, CA.

6 [1968] AC 58, [1967] 2 All ER 1197.
7 *Re Schebsman* [1943] Ch 366, [1943] 2 All ER 387; affd [1944] Ch 83, [1943] 2 All ER 768; *Re Stapleton-Bretherton* [1941] Ch 482; *Re Miller's Agreement* [1947] Ch 615, [1947] 2 All ER 78; *Beswick v Beswick* [1968] AC 58 at 71, per Lord Reid.
8 *Green v Russell* [1959] 2 QB 226 at 231, per Romer LJ.
9 [1944] Ch 83 at 104; (1944) 7 MLR 123 (GL Williams).
10 [1941] Ch 225, [1941] 1 All ER 321.
11 *West v Houghton* (1879) 4 CPD 197 at 203; *Vandepitte v Preferred Accident Insurance Corpn of New York* [1933] AC 70 at 79–80, PC per Lord Wright.
12 *Re Schebsman* [1944] Ch 83 at 84, per Lord Greene MR.
13 See Article 35, post. A constructive test would only be imposed to prevent a person taking an advantage for himself where to do so would be inequitable or unconscionable.
14 *Re Webb* [1941] Ch 225, [1941] 1 All ER 321 (reviewing earlier cases); *Re Foster's Policy* [1966] 1 All ER 432, [1966] 1 WLR 222.

taking effect on death, eg under partnership deeds or company schemes[15]. In respect of policies two points emerge as stated by Plowman J[16]: 'First that the mere fact that [B] takes out a policy which is expressed to be for the benefit of [C] or on behalf of [C] does not constitute a trust for [C]; second that the mere fact that the policy provides that policy moneys are to be payable to [C] does not create a trust in favour of [C].' As Farwell J stated in *Re Webb*[17]:

> 'The whole matter rests entirely upon the true construction of the policy in question. I think that one must take it that unless there is in the policy something which does establish reasonably clearly that the assured was in fact constituting, and intending to constitute, himself a trustee for the third party of the assurance moneys, the third party is not and the personal representatives of the assured are, entitled to the money payable.'

The fact that rights under the policy can be varied without the consent of the third party does not mean that no trust can exist[18]: after all, a beneficiary can have an interest that is defeasible upon revocation of the trust or upon the exercise of a power of appointment in someone else's favour. Indeed the subject-matter of a trust may be a contract inherently variable by B if in his absolute unfettered discretion a variation is in the best interests of C. A trust can still exist where powers of surrender or agreeing to modification are vested in the alleged trustee so as to be exercisable only in the third party's best interests[19]. However, if surrender moneys can be held by the alleged trustee for his own benefit[20] and not for the third party this will negative any trust, at least until a time arises when the alleged trustee ceases to be entitled to hold surrender moneys or other benefits for himself alone[1].

Where B is deceased and no trust of the benefit of his contract with A exists his personal representative (who may happen to be the third party, C, in question) may be able to obtain an order qua B's representative against A compelling A to perform the obligation in favour of C as happened in *Beswick v Beswick*[2], so a finding of no trust need not necessarily be fatal to C.

Voluntary covenants

If A voluntarily covenants (ie promises in a deed) with B to pay money or transfer property to B for the benefit of C then C cannot have any rights[3] (other than any conferred by the Contracts (Rights of Third Parties) Act 1999[4]) unless he can show that A intended B to hold property on trust for C and that this property is vested in B on trust for C. Assuming there is shown

---

15 *Re Flavell* (1883) 25 Ch D 89, CA; *Re Schebsman* [1944] Ch 83, [1943] 2 All ER 768, CA; *Re Miller's Agreement* [1947] Ch 615, [1947] 2 All ER 78.
16 *Re Foster's Policy* [1966] 1 All ER 432 at 436.
17 [1941] Ch 225 at 234. However, for varying reasons the majority of the Australian High Court in *Trident General Insurance Co Ltd v McNeice Bros Pty Ltd* (1988) 165 CLR 107, 80 ALR 574 (Aust HC) held that third party beneficiaries under contracts of insurance could, even apart from special statutory provision, sue the promisor directly. Further see *Re Australian Elizabethan Theatre Trust* (1991) 30 FCR 491 at 503.
18 *Re Flavell* (1883) 25 Ch D 89; *Re Webb* [1941] Ch 225, [1941] 1 All ER 321.
19 *Re Webb* [1941] Ch 225, [1941] 1 All ER 321.
20 *Re Sinclair's Life Policy* [1938] Ch 799, [1938] 3 All ER 124; *Re Schebsman* [1944] Ch 83, [1943] 2 All ER 768, CA.
1 *Re Foster's Policy* [1966] 1 All ER 432, [1966] 1 WLR 222; *Re Webb* [1941] Ch 225, [1941] 1 All ER 321.
2 [1968] AC 58, [1967] 2 All ER 1197, HL.
3 He is neither a party nor a covenantee nor has he provided any consideration.
4 See p 168 ante.

to be an intent to create a trust for C, there is no problem when the subject matter of the covenant is actually transferred to B[5]. If it has not yet been transferred, and if as existing property it is not subject to an express declaration of trust until it or its subject matter is actually transferred[6], then C has no rights (other than any conferred by the above 1999 Act) unless the covenant itself is the subject matter of the trust, so the question arises whether A intended to create a trust *of the covenant* for C or intended only to create a trust *of the subject matter of the covenant* if or when transferred to B.

The crux of the matter for C's claims is thus *intention to create a trust* of the benefit of the voluntary covenant just as in the cases of alleged trusts of the benefit of contracts. Originally, the courts were quite sympathetic to such claims[7] just as originally they were quite ready to find an intention to create a trust in precatory words or situations[8]. Alternatively, the courts were prepared to assume that, even if no completely constituted trusts of the covenant existed, B could be left to pursue his common law remedy for damages for breach of covenant[9] without considering whether such damages should be, nominal or otherwise, held for C or for A under a resulting trust[10]. Indeed, in *Milroy v Lord*[11] the Court of Appeal, if B were not willing to pursue his common law remedy, was prepared to insert in its decree a direction that C be at liberty to use B's name in the common law action overlooking that this would be equity assisting a volunteer where the court had already held that no completely constituted trust existed. The possibility of B obtaining common law damages and thus *himself* constituting A's trusts will be examined after the question of completely constituted trusts of the benefit of covenants has been investigated.

If A merely covenants with X that he will transfer £20,000 to B on trust for C it is clear that A does not intend X to be trustee of the covenant so that A is liable at law only to X or X's personal representative if he fails to transfer the money[12].

In *Fletcher v Fletcher*[13], essentially, A covenanted in a voluntary deed with B that if his illegitimate sons C1 and C2 or either of them should survive him his personal representatives should within 12 months of his death pay £60,000 to B upon trust for C1 and C2 or such of them as should attain 21. A retained possession of the deed and the first B heard of the deed was after A's death. B then refused to act as trustee or sue A's executors or hold any money on trust for C1, the survivor of C1 and C2. Wigram VC held the voluntary

---

5 A may do this voluntarily or someone within a marriage consideration may enforce it, so indirectly benefiting the volunteer.

6 *Re Ralli's Will Trusts* [1964] Ch 288, [1963] 3 All ER 940. If the subject matter is a spes it may not be the subject matter of an effective declaration of trust (or assignment): *Re Ellenborough* [1903] 1 Ch 697; *Williams v IRC* [1965] NZLR 395; see p 175, post.

7 *Williamson v Codrington* (1750) 1 Ves Sen 511. *Cox v Barnard* (1850) 8 Hare 310; *Watson v Parker* (1843) 6 Beav 283; *Fletcher v Fletcher* (1844) 4 Hare 67.

8 See p 133, ante.

9 *Davenport v Bishopp* (1843) 2 Y & C Ch Cas 451 at 460, per Knight-Bruce V-C; *Milroy v Lord* (1862) 4 De GF & J 264 at 278, per Turner LJ; *Re Flavell* (1883) 25 Ch D 89 at 99, per North J; *Re Plumptre's Marriage Settlement* [1910] 1 Ch 609, where, though holding that no completely constituted trust existed to assist volunteer next of kin, Eve J investigated without demur the trustees' claim for common law damages, though finding it statute-barred.

10 See p 179, post.

11 (1862) 4 De GF & J 264.

12 *Colyear v Countess of Mulgrave* (1836) 2 Keen 81.

13 (1844) 4 Hare 67.

deed was effective and that the executors should pay the £60,000 to C1[14] on the footing that A intended to create a completely constituted trust of the covenant, a debt being a perfect chose in action. In the circumstances involving secrecy and the fact that the whole deed would be futile unless it was really intended to confer equitable rights on the only possible beneficiaries C1 and C2, it is quite understandable that Wigram VC treated the deed as if it had had expressly inserted therein some clause such as 'to the intent that the benefit of this covenant shall be held by B upon trust'.

Wigram VC stated[15]:

'I cannot, I admit, do anything to perfect the liability of the author of the trust if it is not already perfect. The covenant, however, is already perfect. The covenantor is liable at law, and the court is not called upon to do any action to perfect it. One question made in argument has been whether there can be a trust of a covenant the benefit of which shall belong to a third party but I cannot think there is any difficulty in that ... [citing *Clough v Lambert*[16]]. Where the transaction is of such a nature that there is no doubt of the intention of A, while dealing with his own property to constitute B a trustee for C and B has accepted the trust may not C be in a position to compel B to enforce the legal right which the trust deed confers upon him? If the trustees have in this case accepted the trust I think the decision in *Clough v Lambert*[17] applies [allowing C to succeed]; and if they have not accepted the trust I scarcely think that fact can make a difference. It is an extraordinary proposition that nothing being wanted to perfect the liability of the estate to pay the debt, the plaintiff has no right in equity to obtain the benefit of the trust. ... The testator has bound himself absolutely. There is a debt created and existing. I give no assistance against the testator. I only deal with him as he has dealt by himself and, if in such a case the trustee will not sue without the sanction of the court I think it is right to allow the cestui que trust to sue for himself, in the name of the trustee, either at law, or in this court, as the case may require. The rights of the parties cannot depend on mere accident or caprice.'

The case may be invoked as authority for the broad proposition that a covenant to create a money debt of a sum certain, even though payable on a future uncertain date, will always be the subject of a completely constituted trust or with the narrow proviso that this is only if the settlor/covenantor intended to create a trust of the covenant rather than a trust of the moneys if or when transferred. This narrower proposition is clearly to be preferred in principle with its emphasis on intention rather than the nature of the subject matter of the covenant.

Indeed, covenants to transfer other property such as specific shares or land create choses in action similar to debts (though requiring straightforward quantification) and, whilst some cases concerning such covenants have been held to be instances of completely constituted trusts of the covenant[18], other cases concerning such covenants have been held not to be instances of completely constituted trusts of the covenant[19]. Even a covenant for further assurance has been held to create a debt so that there was a completely

---

14 This avoided circuity of actions.
15 (1844) 4 Hare 67 at 74.
16 (1839) 10 Sim 174.
17 (1839) 10 Sim 174.
18 *Williamson v Codrington* (1750) 1 Ves Sen 511; *Cox v Barnard* (1850) 8 Hare 310.
19 *Green v Paterson* (1886) 32 Ch D 95; *Re D'Angibau* (1880) 15 Ch D 228.

constituted trust of such covenant[20]. However, it has been suggested[1] that a covenant to settle after-acquired property is not a chose in action capable of being the subject matter of a trust just as future property or a spes cannot be the subject of a trust or of an assignment.

At law, an assignment of future property (ie an expectancy or hope of receiving property in the future[2] such as under someone's will or intestacy or future book-debts to arise in a business or future royalties or future income from a particular source) is void since a man cannot assign what he does not have and he only has existing property[3]. Equity, however, where the assignment was for value will treat the assignment as a contract to assign the property when received, if received, and will compel the assignor to transfer the property received[4]: if no value was given the assignment is wholly inoperative[5]. A trust must be of existing property and not future property, so, just as an assignment of future property to trustees is void at law and inoperative in equity unless for value, a declaration of trust by A that he holds future property on trust for C is inoperative unless for value[6]. If A contracts for value to assign future property when received, if received, equity will enforce such obligation and common law damages can be claimed for breach of contract[7]. If A covenants to assign future property when received, if received, then equity will not enforce such obligation in favour of volunteers, but only in favour of someone who provided value or is within marriage consideration provided for the marriage settlement containing such covenant to transfer after-acquired property[8]. However, a volunteer who is a covenantee can obtain full damages at common law under a deed poll or, if also a party, under a deed inter partes, so if A covenants to assign to a volunteer, B, any property A may acquire on A's father's death under the will or intestacy of such father, B may obtain full damages if the covenant is broken[9].

Since there is a presently existing covenant in favour of B, vesting rights in B, it seems B may himself subsequently declare a trust of the after-acquired property covenant in favour of C. Thus, there seems no reason in principle why A, when entering into the after-acquired property covenant with B, cannot intentionally create a completely constituted trust of the benefit of the covenant with B in favour of C, eg 'I, A, hereby covenant to assign to B any property that I may subsequently acquire under the will or intestacy of my father, F, now aged 70 years, to the intent that B shall immediately hold the benefit of this present covenant on trust for C absolutely'. It will then be immaterial that C is a volunteer since the trust is completely constituted.

---

20 *Cox v Barnard* (1850) 8 Hare 310 at 312, per Knight-Bruce VC.
1 WA Lee (1969) 85 LQR 213 based on *Re Cook's Settlement Trusts* [1965] Ch 902, [1964] 3 All ER 898.
2 Distinguish a present existing property right, eg a contingent equitable interest in remainder under a trust.
3 *Robinson v Macdonnell* (1816) 5 M & S 228 at 236; *Holroyd v Marshall* (1862) 10 HL Cas 191 at 220; *Re Tilt* (1896) 74 LT 163.
4 The assignee's equitable interest under a specifically enforceable contract attaches to the property on the assignor acquiring it: *Holroyd v Marshall* (1862) 10 HL Cas 191, HL.
5 *Re Tilt* (1896) 74 LT 163; *Re Ellenborough* [1903] 1 Ch 697.
6 *Williams v IRC* [1965] NZLR 395.
7 *Re Parkin* [1892] 3 Ch 510; *Re Burton's Settlements* [1955] Ch 82, [1954] 3 All ER 193; *Re Ellenborough* [1903] 1 Ch 697; *Re Lind* [1915] 2 Ch 345, CA.
8 *Re Brooks' Settlement Trusts* [1939] Ch 993; *Re Ellenborough* [1903] 1 Ch 697.
9 *Cannon v Hartley* [1949] Ch 213, [1949] 1 All ER 50.

Indeed, in *Davenport v Bishopp*[10] Knight-Bruce VC indicated there could be a completely constituted trust of a covenant to settle after-acquired property. Moreover, in *Lloyd's v Harper*[11] the Court of Appeal held there was a trust of the benefit of a promise to pay an uncertain amount on an uncertain future date, which is hardly different from a promise to assign an expectancy, and in *Royal Exchange Assurance v Hope*[12] Tomlin J recognised a trust of a promise to pay a sum of money arising only on a person's death before a certain date which might or might not occur. Thus, it would seem that a covenant to settle after-acquired property or an analogous covenant can itself be the subject matter of a completely constituted trust[13]. After all, 'a chose in action is no less a chose in action because it is not immediately recoverable by action'[14]. In the case of such covenants concerning future property it seems sensible to presume rebuttably that the settlor intended not to create a trust of the covenant but only a trust of the property after it had materialised and had been transferred to the trustees.

In *Re Plumptre's Marriage Settlement*[15]; *Re Pryce*[16]; *Re Kay's Settlement*[17] and *Re Cook's Settlement Trusts*[18] particular covenants to settle after-acquired property or analogous covenants were treated as not themselves the subject matter of a completely constituted trust, so that volunteers had no rights to enforce the covenants against the settlors once the settlors had acquired the property, the subject matter of the covenants.

The first two cases concerned marriage settlements where there were no issue so that in default the next of kin, who were volunteers, were entitled to the settled property, and where the settlor had not carried out his obligations under the usual after-acquired property covenant to settle such property on the trusts of the settlement. In both cases[19] Eve J treated the volunteer next of kin as interested only in a voluntary executory contract to create a trust as distinct from being interested under a complete voluntary trust such as existed in *Fletcher v Fletcher*[20]. It would seem this was because the settlor did not intend to create a trust of the covenant so as to confer immediate rights on the next of kin (as well as the issue) but only intended to create a trust of the property, the subject matter of the covenant, if or when, having acquired it, he actually transferred it to the trustees, so that only at that future time would the next of kin have equitable rights, though in the interval the issue, if any, would be able to enforce the covenant as being within the marriage consideration, but not the next of kin since they were mere volunteers.

In *Re Kay's Settlement*[1] a voluntary settlement executed by a spinster contained a covenant in the usual form to settle after-acquired property. Six years later she married: she then had three children. Having become entitled to

10 (1843) 2 Y & C Ch Cas 451 at 460.
11 (1880) 16 Ch D 290, CA.
12 [1928] Ch 179, CA.
13 Further see (1976) 92 LQR 427 (Meagher and Lehane) though not dealing with the resulting trust difficulty where the covenantee sues the settlor; (1975) 91 LQR 236 (Barton).
14 Per Lord Oliver in *Kwok Chi Leung Karl v Comr of Estate Duty* [1988] 1 WLR 1035 at 1040 applied in *Re Landau* [1997] 3 All ER 322 at 328.
15 [1910] 1 Ch 609.
16 [1917] 1 Ch 234.
17 [1939] Ch 329, [1939] 1 All ER 245.
18 [1965] Ch 902, [1964] 3 All ER 898.
19 Particularly see [1910] 1 Ch 609 at 618 and [1917] 1 Ch 234 at 241.
20 (1844) 4 Hare 67.
 1 [1939] Ch 329, [1939] 1 All ER 245.

property within the scope of the covenant she refused to settle it. The trustees applied to the court for directions. Counsel for the volunteer children began by submitting that the children were not interested only in a voluntary executory agreement to settle the after-acquired property but under a completely constituted trust, but then conceded despite this[2] that the trustees could not obtain an order in equity for specific performance of the covenant and so concentrated on submitting that they could be left to their remedy of damages at common law for breach of the after-acquired property covenant and the settlor's implied covenant for further assurance. Not surprisingly, Simonds J treated the volunteer children as interested only in a voluntary executory agreement to settle the after-acquired property: the settlor's obligation lay in an unenforceable voluntary covenant and not under any trust[3].

Finally, in *Re Cook's Settlement Trusts*[4] Sir Herbert, as life tenant, and his son Sir Francis, as remainderman, for value agreed that certain settled property (including a Rembrandt) should become Sir Francis' absolutely subject to Sir Francis resettling some of the property (not the Rembrandt) and covenanting with the trustees of the resettlement that, in case any of certain pictures (including the Rembrandt) should be sold in Sir Francis' lifetime, the net proceeds of sale should be paid over to the resettlement trustees on the resettlement trusts in favour of Sir Francis' children, who were volunteers. The resettlement was executed. Later Sir Francis gave the Rembrandt to his third wife who desired to sell it. The trustees took out a summons to determine their obligations upon any such sale.

In a somewhat elliptical judgment Buckley J stated[5]:

'Counsel [for Sir Francis] submits that the covenant was a voluntary and executory contract to make a settlement in a future event. ... Counsel for the second and third defendants have contended that on the true view of the facts there was an immediate settlement of the obligations created by the covenant and not merely a covenant to settle something in the future. It was said that by the agreement Sir Herbert bought the rights arising under the covenant for the benefit of the cestuis que trust under the settlement and that, the covenant being made in favour of the trustees, these rights became assets of the trust. He relied on *Fletcher v Fletcher; Williamson v Codrington* and *Re Cavendish Browne's Settlement Trusts*. I am not able to accept this argument. The covenant with which I am concerned did not, in my opinion, create a debt enforceable at law, that is to say, a property right, which although to bear fruit only in the future and on a contingency was capable of being the subject of an immediate trust, as was held to be the case in *Fletcher v Fletcher*[6]. Nor is this covenant associated with property which was the subject of an immediate trust as in *Williamson v Codrington*[7]. Nor did the covenant relate to property which then belonged to the covenantor as in *Re Cavendish Browne's Settlement Trusts*[8]. In contrast to all these cases, this covenant on its true construction is, in my opinion, an executory contract to settle a particular fund or particular funds of money which

---

2 [1939] Ch 329 and 339. An intent to confer immediate equitable rights when they are born on children, who are volunteers and have no other rights, is more likely than an intent to confer immediate equitable rights on next of kin, who are volunteers as in *Re Pryce* when the issue, if any, had rights as being within the marriage consideration.

3 [1939] Ch 329 at 342. In context it would seem the settlor did not intend her children to have enforceable rights to after-acquired property.

4 [1965] Ch 902, [1964] 3 All ER 898.

5 [1965] Ch 902 at 913.

6 (1844) 4 Hare 67; see p 173, ante.

7 (1750) 1 Ves Sen 511 (an American plantation including slaves!).

8 [1916] WN 341 (realty and personalty to which covenantor was already entitled under the wills of persons already deceased).

at the date of the covenant did not exist and which might never come into existence. It is analogous to a covenant to settle an expectation or to settle after-acquired property. The case, in my judgment, involves the law of contract not the law of trusts.'

In any event, Buckley J went on to hold that the covenant operated only upon a sale by Sir Francis and not by his wife-donee. However, it is submitted that Buckley J's approach is erroneous if it is concerned merely with the type of property that happens to be the subject of the covenant in question for, as already seen, it seems that any covenant is an existing chose in action that may be the subject of a trust, regardless of the type of property that happens to be within the scope of the covenant. Surely it is the intention of the settlor/covenantor that is the crucial factor. It is very difficult to believe that Buckley J would have held that no trust of the covenant could exist if the settlor/covenantor had ended his covenant with the clause, 'to the intent that the benefit of this covenant shall immediately be held by my Trustees upon the Trusts hereof'. In the circumstances Buckley J's judgment is best interpreted as finding that there was no intention to create a trust of property in the form of the covenant so as to be immediately enforceable by the children volunteers, but only an intention to create a trust of the subject matter of the covenant if or when it materialised and was transferred to the trustees for the children, so that only at that future time would the children have equitable rights, though in the interval Sir Herbert (or, it seems, his executors)[9] would be able to enforce the covenant, having provided consideration therefor.

It is thus considered that nothing displaces the fundamental requirement of intention in the law of trusts so that if the settlor/covenantor intended to create immediate equitable rights in the beneficiaries to enforce the covenant (whether relating to existing or future property) there will be a completely constituted trust of the covenant. On the other hand, if he only intended the beneficiaries to have equitable rights in the property within the scope of the covenant within the scope of the covenant if or when he transferred the property to the trustees, then there will be no completed constituted trust of the covenant as will normally be the intention in respect of next of kin under marriage settlements, issue within the marriage consideration having their interests safeguarded by their contractual rights and the equitable maxim 'Equity looks on as done that which ought to be done'. Whilst this test of intention is a clear one, like the test of intention to create a trust of the benefit of a contract[10], there is plenty of scope for controversy over the application of the test in particular circumstances.

It would seem that if the deed containing the voluntary covenant also contains a covenant for further assurance then the court will be more likely to find that there was an intention to create a completely constituted trust of

---

9 *Beswick v Beswick* [1968] AC 58, [1967] 2 All ER 1197, HL. Such action by Sir Herbert or his personal representatives would completely constitute the trust for the children, but the trustees could not compel Sir Herbert or his personal representatives to take such action nor could they join them as co-defendants in an attempt to take advantage of their contractual rights. Sir Herbert and his personal representatives owe no duty to the children or the trustees to exercise their contractual rights and so they cannot be forced to become parties to an action concerning such rights.

10 See p 170, ante.

either or both covenants[11] and should so find if, otherwise, there is no real scope for the operation of the covenant for further assurance. It would further seem that if the deed does not contain an express covenant to assign future or after-acquired property but contains a purported assignment of future property (taking effect in equity, if consideration is provided, as a covenant to assign it when acquired) the court should not find that there was any intention to create a trust of the covenant but only of the property when acquired and transferred to trustees[12]. Indeed, where the covenant relates to future property there should be a rebuttable presumption that the settlor/covenantor intended not to create a trust of the covenant but only a trust of the property when acquired and transferred to trustees[13]. Finally, in the straightforward case of A, in a deed only consisting of one covenant, covenanting with B on trust wholly for C it seems there should, perhaps, be a presumption that A intended to create immediate equitable rights in C's favour by creating a trust of the covenant where the whole transaction would be futile except on the basis that this is the case[14]. However, for post-10 May 2000 covenants it would seem such covenant would be enforceable under the Contracts (Rights of Third Parties) Act 1999 without the need to find a trust of the covenant.

For the draftsman the moral is to insert a clause expressly stating the intention of the settlor/covenantor, whether to create a trust of a covenant or to confer enforcement rights on a third party beneficiary under the 1999 Act.

Trustees' common law action for damages for breach of voluntary covenant

If there is a completely constituted trust of the benefit of the voluntary covenant then not only can the volunteer beneficiaries enforce it specifically but the trustees themselves as the covenantees can obtain full damages for breach of covenant and they will, of course, hold such damages (as the fruit or product of the covenant) on trust for the volunteer beneficiaries[15].

If there is no completely constituted trust of the benefit of the voluntary covenant the trustees as covenantees can prima facie still claim full damages[16] for breach of the voluntary covenant. However, ex hypothesi they are not holding the covenant itself on a completely constituted trust for the volunteer beneficiaries and since ex hypothesi they hold the covenant qua trustees they surely must, therefore, hold the covenant on a resulting trust for the covenantor/settlor[17]. If the covenant, and the right to damages for breach of

---

11 *Cox v Barnard* (1850) 8 Hare 310 at 312 and 313; *Milroy v Lord* (1862) 4 De GF & J 264 at 278; *Re Cavendish-Browne's Settlement Trust* [1916] WN 341.

12 As in *Re Kay's Settlement* [1939] Ch 329, [1939] 1 All ER 245, in respect of property appointed under a special power. Cf *Cox v Barnard* (1850) 8 Hare 310.

13 *Re Plumptre's Marriage Settlement* [1910] 1 Ch 609.

14 *Fletcher v Fletcher* (1844) 4 Hare 67.

15 *Cox v Barnard* (1850) 8 Hare 310; *Ward v Audland* (1845) 8 Beav 201; (1847) 16 M & W 862; *Re Cavendish-Browne's Settlement Trust* [1916] WN 341. If no trust of the covenant exists but consideration has been provided therefor (eg by issue under a marriage settlement) then damages may also be claimed: *Re Parkin* [1892] 3 Ch 510.

16 At common law if property valued at £x was not transferred to the covenantee then clearly the covenantee's loss was £x, the position in equity of the beneficiaries being immaterial to the common law position before the Judicature Acts. Thus, full damages and not nominal damages will be awarded: cf *Re Cavendish-Browne's Settlement Trust* [1916] WN 341 and DW Elliott (1980) 76 LQR 100 at 112; JL Barton (1975) 91 LQR 236 at 238.

17 The prospective beneficiaries only have a spes that the subject matter of the covenant will be transferred to the trustees by the settlor. See also (1969) 85 LQR 213 (WA Lee).

covenant, is held on resulting trust for the covenantor/settlor then surely so must any damages obtained for breach of covenant. It follows that since the settlor is, under the resulting trust, an absolutely entitled beneficiary of full capacity he must under the *Saunders v Vautier*[18] principle be able to terminate such trust and prevent the trustees from launching upon such a pointless exercise as a suit against himself for damages. It should thus be an end of the matter as soon as the settlor (or his personal representative) makes it clear to the trustees that he does not want to be sued[19].

After all, whilst prospective volunteer beneficiaries with a spes that the settlor will carry out his voluntary promise to transfer property to trustees for them are dependent upon the whim of the settlor, it is surely wrong that they should be dependent upon the whim of the trustees suing or not suing[20]. Indeed, if the settlor has chosen not to constitute a trust of certain property surely the trustees cannot themselves have a right to constitute the trust[1]. The essence of the matter seems that since the settlor has not created a completely constituted trust of the voluntary covenant he must ex hypothesi have reserved to himself the right if he chooses to constitute a trust of the property, the subject of the covenant, at a later date, having lined up the trustees as his agents to receive the trust property[2] but, meanwhile, they are to hold the covenant on a resulting trust for him.

In practice, if trustees are considering taking action on behalf of the trust they will need to obtain the leave of the court for otherwise they will be at personal risk as to the costs unless they can establish the costs were properly incurred[3]. If their position is doubtful they may also, at the cost of the trust fund, obtain directions from the court as to the position[4]. It is clear that if the court is involved it will direct the trustees that they ought not to sue for

---

18 (1841) 4 Beav 115; see Article 70, post.

19 See *Ingram v IRC* [1997] 4 All ER 395 at 424 where Millett LJ also endorses *Hirachand Punamchand v Temple* [1911] 2 KB 330, CA, where plaintiff money-lenders accepted a lesser sum from the defendant's father in satisfaction, of a debt and then sued the defendant for the balance. It is noteworthy that Vaughan-Williams LJ held that any money recovered would be held in trust for the defendant's father and 'there might have been a defence in a court of law on the ground that any money recoverable by the plaintiffs was recoverable by them merely as trustees for the father and that, under the circumstances disclosed by the correspondence the relations between father and son were such that it was impossible to suppose that the father wished to insist on payment by the son' (p 337), and Fletcher-Moulton LJ said, 'If there be any difficulty in formulating a defence at common law I have no hesitation in saying that a court of equity would have regarded the plaintiffs as disentitled to sue except as trustees for the father and would have restrained them from suing' (p 342). Also see *Hunt v Severs* [1994] 2 All ER 385 at 394, HL where it was held that a plaintiff claiming damages for personal injury can recover damages in respect of the care voluntarily provided by X and will hold them on trust for X (see p 143, ante) except where X is also the defendant tortfeasor because it would he pointless and circular if the plaintiff were to recover £y from X which was then to be held on trust for X.

20 The acts, neglects or default of trustees cannot be allowed to affect the rights of their beneficiaries: *Fletcher v Fletcher* (1844) 4 Hare 67 at 78; *Re Richerson* [1892] 1 Ch 379.

1 Only the settlor (or his agent) can constitute his trust: see p 164 ante and *Re Brook's Settlement Trusts* [1939] Ch 993 where the trustees' obtaining title to the intended trust property without the settlor's consent did not completely constitute the trust.

2 *Milroy v Lord* (1862) 4 De GF & J 264 at 277 where Turner LJ in discussing the fact that the settlor's imperfect gift of shares to the intended trustee could have been carried out under a power of attorney held by the trustee stated, 'A court of Equity could not I think, decree the agent of the settlor to make the transfer, unless it could decree the settlor himself to do so and it is plain that no such decree could have been made against the settlor.'

3 *Re Beddoe* [1893] 1 Ch 547, CA; *Re Yorke* [1911] 1 Ch 370.

4 Rules of Supreme Court Order 85, r 2(5).

common law damages for breach of covenant where the settlor did not create a completely constituted trust of the benefit of the covenant[5]. Since this is well established there is no need for the trustees to bother the court and the trustees have a complete defence if any beneficiary seeks to make them liable for breach of trust for not suing the covenantor for damages[6].

Three cases of first instance establish that the trustees will be directed not to sue for damages for breach of a voluntary covenant where the settlor/covenantor did not create a completely constituted trust of the covenant. *Re Pryce*[7] established the proposition in 1917 and it has simply been followed in *Re Kay's Settlement*[8] and, despite academic criticism[9], by *Re Cook's Settlement Trusts*[10].

In *Re Pryce* trustees took out a summons asking whether they needed to take proceedings in respect of a breach of the wife's covenant in her marriage settlement to transfer after-acquired property to trustees. Eve J in a reserved judgment held there was no completely constituted trust of the covenant and directed the trustees that they ought not to take proceedings, stating[11]:

'[Her next of kin] are volunteers and although the court would probably compel fulfilment of the contract to settle at the instance of any persons within the marriage consideration[12] and in their favour will treat the outstanding property as subjected to an enforceable trust[13] "volunteers have no right whatever to obtain specific performance of a mere covenant which has remained as a covenant and has not been performed": see per James LJ in *Re D'Angibau*. Nor could damages be awarded either in this court, or, I apprehend, at law where since the Judicature Act 1873, the same defences would be available to the defendant as would be raised in an action brought in this court for specific performance or damages. In these circumstances, seeing that the next of kin could neither maintain an action to enforce the covenant nor for damages for breach of it, and that the settlement is not a declaration of trust constituting the relationship of trustee and cestui que trust between the defendant and the next of kin, in which case effect could be given to the trusts even in favour of volunteers, but is a mere voluntary contract to create a trust, ought the court now for the sole benefit of volunteers to direct the trustees to take proceedings to enforce the defendant's covenant? I think it ought not; to do so would be to give the next of kin by indirect means relief they cannot obtain by any direct procedure and would in effect be enforcing the settlement.'

Whilst the result in *Re Pryce* is correct Eve J's reasoning is insupportable. It is a fallacy that the Judicature Act 'fusion' made defences available to a defendant in Chancery also available to a defendant at law so that the

---

5 *Re Pryce* [1917] 1 Ch 234; *Re Kay's Settlement* [1939] Ch 329, [1939] 1 All ER 245; *Re Cook's Settlement Trusts* [1965] Ch 902, [1964] 3 All ER 898.
6 *Re Ralli's Will Trusts* [1964] Ch 288 at 301–302. For consideration of the Contracts (Rights of Third Parties) Act 1999 where the beneficiary might have tried to sue under the Act but failed or have been advised that he would fail see p 182 post.
7 [1917] 1 Ch 234.
8 [1939] Ch 329, [1939] 1 All ER 245.
9 (1960) 76 LQR 100 (DW Elliot); (1962) 78 LQR 228 (JA Hornby).
10 [1965] Ch 902, [1964] 3 All ER 898; [1965] CLJ 46 (GH Jones).
11 [1917] 1 Ch 234 at 241.
12 *Re D'Angibau* (1880) 15 Ch D 228 at 242, 246.
13 *Pullan v Koe* [1913] 1 Ch 9.

Chancery defence of 'volunteer' is available to a defendant at law[14]. Moreover, except in specially limited cases of fraud, undue influence etc equity never actively intervened to prevent a volunteer pursuing his rights at law, equity's maxim being 'equity will not assist a volunteer' and not 'equity will frustrate a volunteer in equity and at law'[15].

Since the result in *Re Pryce* has been followed in *Re Kay's Settlement*[16] (or, indeed, extended from 'the trustees ought not to sue' to 'the trustee must not sue') and *Re Cook's Settlement Trusts*, and since it also accords with the resulting trust reasoning already propounded, it is submitted that it is now beyond doubt that where there is no completely constituted trust of a voluntary covenant the trustees will be directed not to sue the covenantor for common law damages. If a bold trustee did sue (eg because also a beneficiary or married to a beneficiary or indemnified fully as to costs by a beneficiary) it is submitted that it is likely that such action would fail on the basis that the covenant, the right to damages for breach of the covenant and any actual damages, must in principle be held on a resulting trust for the settlor/covenantor, making the action groundless.

This is reinforced if one considers that the beneficiaries should have no rights to damages under the Contracts (Rights of Third Parties) Act 1999 because in the absence of creating a completely constituted trust of the benefit of the covenant, it seems that the settlor did not intend the covenant to be enforceable by the beneficiaries already benefiting sufficiently in the trust property already vested in the trustee for them. Nowadays, a well-drafted settlement should make clear that beneficiaries are not to have enforcement rights in respect of the settlor's covenants with his trustee if this be the desired position as often will be the case.

ARTICLE 10

What property is capable of being made the subject of a trust

All property real or personal[17], legal or equitable, at home or abroad and whether in possession or action, remainder or reversion, and whether vested or contingent, may be made the subject of a trust, unless:

(1) the policy of the law or some statutory enactment has made it inalienable; or

14 After all, hardship maybe a defence to an action in equity for specific performance but not to a common law action for damages. Moreover, the Judicature Acts did not alter the substantive law by making promises under seal unenforceable at common law without valuable consideration: *Cannon v Hartley* [1949] Ch 213, [1949] 1 All ER 50; (1960) 76 LQR 100,109,111 (DW Elliot); Meagher, Gummow and Lehane, *Equity Doctrine and Remedies*, para 234.
15 *Davenport v Bishopp* (1843) 2 Y & C Ch Cas 451 at 260; *Ward v Audland* (1845) 8 Beav 201 at 211; *Milroy v Lord* (1862) 4 De GF & J 264 at 273 and 278; *Cannon v Hartley* [1949] Ch 213, [1949] 1 All ER 50.
16 Where Simonds J emphasised [1939] Ch 329 at 339, 'The question before me is not whether if she [the settlor] were sued such an action would succeed (as to which she might have a defence, I know not what) but whether in the circumstances the trustees ought to be directed to take proceedings against her. '
17 Even a herd of deer may be the subject of a trust: (*White v Paine* (1914) 83 LJKB 895) or a milk quota (*Swift v Dairywise Farms Ltd* [2000] 1 All ER 320).

(2) where the property is land abroad, the trusts sought to be created are inconsistent with the lex loci situs[18].

Equitable interests

A person, holding an agreement for a lease, assigned all his interest under it to trustees upon certain trusts. Here, although the legal term was not in the settlor, it was held to be a good settlement, because he had conveyed his equitable interest in the property[19]. In *Re Ralli's Will Trusts*[20] there was held to be an effective declaration of trust by the settlor under which she held her equitable remainder interest on trust for certain beneficiaries until she actually transferred to the trustees the property that would become hers absolutely upon her remainder falling into possession. The interest of a beneficiary in default of appointment is an existing equitable interest but the interest or, rather, spes of the object of a power is a mere expectancy[1], as, in essence, is the interest of one of a number of beneficiaries under a discretionary trust, except that if all the discretionary beneficiaries (as opposed to mere objects of a power of appointment) who between them are absolutely beneficially entitled to the whole equitable interest in income or capital or both, are of full capacity and of one mind, then they can dispose of the equitable interest as they see fit[2].

Choses in action

A owes £1,000 to B. B assigns this debt to trustees upon certain trusts. This transaction is perfectly good. Equity, almost always, enforced contracts for the sale of choses in action though, subject to certain exceptions the common law did not; but the common law rule is abrogated as regards absolute assignments of debts or other legal choses in action by s 136(1) of the Law of Property Act 1925. By s 4(2) of the same Act, replacing part of s 6 of the Real Property Act 1845, contingent and future interests and possibilities, *coupled with an interest in real estate*, may be granted or assigned at law. But it is otherwise in the case of possibilities in personal estate which still remain assignable only in equity if for value[3].

Lord Shaw has emphasised[4], 'The scope of the trusts recognised in equity is unlimited. There can be a trust of a chattel or of a chose in action or of a right or obligation under an ordinary legal contract; just as much as a trust of land.' Thus, it has been held[5] that a plaintiff can even assign his interest in litigation to trustees on protective trusts for himself and his son. Moreover, even though a contract is not assignable at law, a trust may be declared of it unless the terms of the contract prohibit this[6].

---

18 *Earl Nelson v Lord Bridport* (1846) 8 Beav 547.
19 *Gilbert v Overton* (1864) 2 Hem & M 110; and see also *Re Way's Trust* (1864) 2 De GJ & Sm 365 and *Knight v Bowyer* (1857) 23 Beav 609; affd (1858) 2 De G & J 421.
20 [1964] Ch 288, [1963] 3 All ER 940. Also see *Fitzwilliam v IRC* [1993] 1 WLR 1189, HL.
1 *Re Brooks' Settlement Trusts* [1939] Ch 993, [1939] 3 All ER 920.
2 *Re Smith* [1928] Ch 915.
3 *Joseph v Lyons* (1884) 15 QBD 280; *Collyer v Isaacs* (1881) 19 Ch D 342, CA; and *Re Ellenborough* [1903] 1 Ch 697.
4 *Lord Strathcona Steamship Co Ltd v Dominion Coal Co Ltd* [1926] AC 108 at 124, PC.
5 *Harrison v Tew* (1988) Times, 30 November.
6 *Don King Productions Inc v Warren* [2000] Ch 291 at 321, affd at 335–336, CA.

Reversionary interests

A reversion, whether vested or contingent, is assignable both at law and in equity, and may therefore be made the subject of a trust[7].

Expectancies or future property

At law, assignments of property to be acquired in the future pass nothing. Thus, a gratuitous assignment of all X's 'right title and interest in and to all the dividends' which might be declared in respect of certain shows is an ineffective transfer of a mere expectancy[8]. However, a gratuitous assignment of all X's 'right title and interest in and to an amount equal to 90% of the income which may accrue during a period of three years from the date hereof under a' specified licence agreement providing for royalties to be paid by the licensee to the assignor was held an effective transfer of presently existing property, namely 90% of that portion of the assignor's existing contractual rights entitling him to royalties at a fixed rate during the period (rather than the mere expectancy of 90% of such payments, as might accrue due to the assignor during the period)[9].

Equity, however, may be able to regard assignments of expectancies, *if for value*, as contracts to assign the property when it comes into existence[10]; and although they are uncertain in their inception (inasmuch as the property is incapable of ascertainment at the date of the assignment) the property is nevertheless capable of identification when the subject has come into existence and the assignment becomes enforceable[11]. Such assignments, which do not require any particular form of words so long as the intention to assign is reasonably clear[12], are therefore not void for uncertainty. Thus, an assignment of all moneys to which the assignor was or might become entitled under any settlement, will, or other document, was held to be good in equity[13], and a similar conclusion was arrived at by the House of Lords where the property assigned was all book debts due and owing or which during a named period *might become due* and owing to the assignor[14]. In the early case of *Lewis v Madocks*[15], specific performance was ordered of a covenant by the husband in a marriage settlement that he would:

---

7 *Shafto v Adams* (1864) 4 Giff 492; *Fitzwilliam v IRC* [1993] 3 All ER 184, [1993] 1 WLR 1189, HL.

8 *Norman v Federal Comr of Taxation* (1963) 109 CLR 9 (Aust HC). An assignment of property to which one might become entitled on the death of a specified living person is clearly ineffective: *Re Ellenborough* [1903] 1 Ch 697.

9 *Shepherd v Federal Comr of Taxation* (1965) 113 CLR 385 (Aust HC). Further see Meagher, Gummow & Lehane (3rd edn) paras 639–646 on these fine distinctions.

10 *Wethered v Wethered* (1828) 2 Sim 183, and see also *Beckley v Newland* (1723) 2 P Wms 182; *Harwood v Tooke* (1812) 2 Sim 192; *Higgins v Hill* (1887) 56 LT 426; *Collyer v Isaacs* (1881) 19 Ch D 342; *Re Clarke* (1887) 36 Ch D 342, CA; *Tailby v Official Receiver* (1888) 13 App Cas 523, HL; *Hardy v Fothergill* (1888) 13 App Cas 351, HL; *Thomas v Kelly* (1888) 13 App Cas 506, HL; *Re Ellenborough* [1903] 1 Ch 697 at 700.

11 See per Lord Herschell in *Tailby v Official Receiver* (1888) 13 App Cas 523 at 530, HL; and *Holyroyd v Marshall* (1862) 10 HL Cas 191 at 210, per Lord Westbury.

12 *Fyfe v Garden* [1946] 1 All ER 366 at 372, HL, per Viscount Maugham.

13 *Re Clarke* (1887) 36 Ch D 348, CA.

14 *Tailby v Official Receiver* (1888) 13 App Cas 523, HL. Also see *Re Lind* [1915] 2 Ch 345, CA; *Palette Shoes Pty Ltd v Krohn* (1937) 58 CLR 1, at 27–28; and *Re Green* [1979] 1 All ER 832 at 843 (assignment of future earnings from assignor's own skill and knowledge).

15 (1810) 17 Ves 48, stated to be good law in *Re Reis* [1904] 2 KB 769 at 783, per Stirling LJ.

'by deed or will convey give devise and assure all and singular his ready money goods chattels and personal estate and effects to and for the use and behoof of the spouses and the survivor of them'

upon certain trusts. An assignment of the copyright of an unwritten book has also been held to be good[16]. Another example is the covenant to settle after-acquired property of the wife commonly found in marriage settlements. As, however, such assignments are really only regarded as contracts, it follows that equity will not enforce them unless the conscience of the assignor is bound by valuable consideration having been given[17] or for some other reason[18].

Effect of bankruptcy on assignments of future or after-acquired property or covenants relating thereto

Tailby v Official Receiver[19] establishes that where X for consideration agrees to assign, or purports presently to assign an expectancy to Y, and the consideration has been paid or executed, then any property acquired by X within his obligation forthwith automatically vests the equitable interest therein in Y, because Equity regards as done that which ought to be done. As Dixon J said in *Palette Shoes Pty Ltd v Krohn*[20]:

'because value has been given on the one side, the conscience of the other party is bound when the subject matter comes into existence. Because his conscience is bound, equity fastens upon the property itself and makes him a trustee of the legal rights of ownership for the assignee ... [the assignee's right] may survive the assignor's bankruptcy because it attaches without more eo instanti when the property arises and gives the assignee an equitable interest therein.'

He endorsed *Re Lind*[1] to similar effect where L had assigned his expectancy (in what he hoped to inherit on the death of his mother, who was alive but not of sound mind) as security for loans by A and then B. L then became bankrupt but, later, after being discharged, assigned his expectancy to C. The Court of Appeal held that A and B had priority over C.

Commercial advantage of the principle enshrined in the above remarks of Dixon J can be taken in reservation of title clauses where a supplier of raw materials has a manufacturer contract that it will be trustee of proceeds of sale of manufactured goods (incorporating the raw materials) as to one fifth for the supplier and four fifths for itself or holding on trust for the supplier such fractional part of such proceeds then received as is equivalent to the amount then owing by it to the supplier and the rest on trust for itself[2]. In non-commercial cases, as where there are covenants in marriage settlements relating to after-acquired property, it seems that there should be no auto-

16 *Ward, Lock & Co v Long* [1906] 2 Ch 550.
17 *Re Ellenborough* [1903] 1 Ch 697; *Re Brooks' Settlement Trusts* [1939] Ch 993, [1939] 3 All ER 920. And see Article 9, ante.
18 *Re Burton's Settlement Trusts* [1955] Ch 82, [1954] 3 All ER 193, where the assignor's conscience was bound because the assignment was made in compliance with a condition in a will and to enable her to take benefits thereunder. On possible impact of Contracts (Rights of Third Parties) Act 1999, see pp 168, 179 ante.
19 (1888) 13 App Cas 523, HL.
20 (1937) 58 CLR 1 at 26–27; and *Re Androma Pty Ltd* [1987] 2 Qd R 134 at 152–154.
 1 [1915] 2 Ch 345.
 2 *Associated Alloys Pty Ltd v ACN 001 452 106 Pty Ltd* (2000) 74 ALJR 862 (High Court of Australia); pp 15–16 ante.

matic arising of an equitable interest in favour of volunteers as well as those providing (or being within) the marriage consideration[3]. The equitable interest ought only to attach to the property if there is then some beneficiary who gave value with an interest to enforce the covenant: there may be no such beneficiary by reason of the previous death of that beneficiary or from the property in question having become vested in him or her so that the property is 'at home'[4]. Thus, if in consideration of marriage, property was settled on A for life then B for life with remainder to their children, but in default of children for their statutory next of kin and A and B entered into the usual after- acquired property covenants, then if B inherited property within the scope of such covenant after A had died childless, no equitable interest in favour of the volunteer next of kin would arise.

PARAGRAPH (A)

Property inalienable by reason of public policy

Salaries or pensions are inalienable only if given to enable persons to perform duties connected with the public service, or so that they may be in a fit state of preparation to perform those duties. In *Grenfell v Dean and Canons of Windsor*[5] a canon of Windsor had assigned the canonry and the profits to the plaintiff to secure a sum of money. There was no cure of souls, and the only duties were residence within the castle and attendance in the chapel for twenty-one days a year.

In giving judgment for the plaintiff and upholding the assignment the Master of the Rolls said:

> 'If he (the canon) had made out that the duty to be performed by him was a public duty, or in any way connected with the public service, I should have thought it right to attend very seriously to that argument, because there are various cases in which public duties are concerned, in which it may be against public policy, that the income arising from the performance of those duties should be assigned; and for this simple reason, because the public is interested, not only in the performance from time to time of the duties, but also in the fit state of preparation of the party having to perform them. Such is the reason in the cases of half-pay where there is a sort of retainer, and where the payments which are made to officers, from time to time, are the means by which they, being liable to be called into public service, are enabled to keep themselves in a state of preparation for performing their duties.'

So, in *Davis v Duke of Marlborough*[6], the Lord Chancellor said:

> 'A pension for past services may be aliened, but a pension for supporting the grantee in the performance of future duties is inalienable.'

Alimony or maintenance granted to a spouse by the Family Division or the magistrates is similarly not assignable.

---

3 *Re Reis* [1904] 2 KB 769, CA: the availability of specific performance is crucial, unlike the position in commercial cases mentioned in the three preceding footnotes.
4 *Re Anstis* (1886) 31 Ch D 596, CA; *Re Plumptre's Marriage Settlement* [1910] 1 Ch 609.
5 (1840) 2 Beav 544.
6 (1818) 1 Swan 74.

Property inalienable by statute

Some classes of property are expressly made inalienable by statute. Thus, in *Davis v Duke of Marlborough*[7], it was held that a pension granted by statute to the first duke and his successors in the title 'for the more honourable support of the dignities' was not alienable, since it was held that, the object of Parliament in granting it was that 'it should be kept in mind that it was for a memento and a perpetual memorial of national gratitude for public services'.

Deferred pay or military reward payable to any officer, soldier or airman of the Army, Air Force or Royal Marines, or any pension, allowance or relief payable to any such officer, soldier or airman, or to his wife, or to his widow, child or other dependant, or to any person in respect of military or air force service, are also made unassignable by statute[8]. It has been held[9] that, while such legislation inhibits the court from making any order which would prevent the receipt by the pensioner in due course of any pension or gratuity, etc to which he is entitled in the future, it does not inhibit the court in making any other kind of order (like a lump sum order on divorce) once the pensioner has safely received the sum of money to which he is due. While statute[10] makes unassignable naval pensions payable to an officer, seaman or a marine, or to an officer's widow, allowances from the compassionate fund, marine half pay, and payments, rewards etc, in respect of services in the navy and marines to a subordinate officer, marine or seaman, the Court of Appeal has held[11] that such statute does not restrict the court's powers to make orders eg under the Matrimonial Causes Act 1973. In general, salaries or pensions, not given in respect of public services, are freely assignable[12].

By s 5(1) of the Superannuation Act 1972 any assignment or agreement to assign any benefit payable under a scheme made under s 1 of the Act is void.

To qualify for favoured tax treatment as approved pension arrangements, the benefits of such arrangements have to be made non-assignable expressly in their terms, but this did not prevent them falling into the ownership of the pensioner's trustee on bankruptcy[13] until so provided by the Welfare Reform and Pensions Act 1999[14]. This Act[15] also contains overriding provisions for the sharing of rights under pensions arrangements upon divorce.

PARAGRAPH (B)

Trusts of foreign immovables

The distinction between immovables and movables is not the same as that between real and personal property. Leasehold land ranks as personalty but

---

7 (1818) 1 Swan 74. However, the land granted to the Duke is subject to the court's powers under Settled Land Act 1925, s 64: *Hambro v Duke of Marlborough* [1994] Ch 158, [1994] 3 All ER 332.
8 Army Act 1955, ss 141, 190, 203; *Walker v Walker* [1983] Fam 68, [1983] 2 All ER 909, CA; *Roberts v Roberts* [1986] 2 All ER 483, [1986] 1 WLR 437, Air Force Act 1955, ss 141, 190; *Ranson v Ranson* [1988] 1 WLR 183, CA.
9 *Happe v Happe* [1991] 4 All ER 527, [1990] 1 WLR 1282, CA.
10 Naval and Marine Pay and Pensions Act 1865, ss 4, 5.
11 *Cotgrave v Cotgrave* [1992] Fam 33, [1991] 4 All ER 537, CA.
12 *Feistel v King's College, Cambridge* (1847) 10 Beav 491.
13 *Rowe v Sanders* [2002] EWCA Civ 242, [2002] All ER 800n; *Krasner v Dennison* [2001] Ch 76, CA.
14 Welfare Reform and Pensions Act 1999, s 11.
15 Welfare Reform and Pensions Act 1999, Pt IV.

is an immovable, while a trust for sale of land, until s 3 of the Trusts of Land and Appointment of Trustees Act 1996 came into force, was personalty, but also an immovable[16]. Naturally and practically the lex situs has crucial significance for immovables, especially where it has particular policy interests, eg prohibiting unbarrable entails altogether[17], or future interests which might vest at too remote a time[18], or testamentary gifts for charitable purposes made within one year of death[19], or testamentary dispositions contrary to forced indefeasible shares in favour of the widow and children[20]. The lex situs may even lead to a restrictive interpretation of an after-acquired property covenant, eg so that it did not extend to after-acquired Jersey land when Jersey law prohibited married women from conveying such land except for adequate pecuniary compensation[1].

If the lex situs does not sanction trusts of land inter vivos 'trusts', necessarily of specific land transferred to 'trustees', subject to an express choice[2] of English law will be ineffective to create equitable or other proprietary interests under the lex situs in favour of the beneficiaries[3], though the rights or powers of the trustees may be recognised to some extent if the lex situs has adopted The Hague Convention on the Recognition of Trusts[4]. If the matter be litigated in the courts of the lex situs it seems the transfer will either be void so that the land still is the settlor's or the 'trustees' will hold the land as nominee of or agent for the settlor. This leaves it open to the settlor to sell the land and settle the proceeds or to take advantage of some analogous institution of the lex situs to enable the land to be held for the benefit of others. However, if exceptionally, the English courts have jurisdiction[5] to determine an equitable in personam matter between A and B resident in England concerning foreign land then the court may find that B holds the foreign land on trust for A and order B to execute such documents as the foreign law requires to vest ownership in the land in A[6] or order B to sell the land and remit the proceeds to a in England[7].

In the case of English testamentary trusts, where necessarily the English settlor-testator is dead, it seems that a trust of foreign land comprised within the testator's residuary estate held on the usual trusts for sale will be given effect, as will a specific devise of foreign land on trust for sale[8] except to the

---

16 *Freke v Lord Carbery* (1873) LR 16 Eq 461 (leaseholds); *Re Berchtold* [1923] 1 Ch 192 (trust for sale).

17 *Earl Nelson v Bridport* (1846) 8 Beav 547. Nowadays entails can no longer be created: Trusts of Land and Appointment of Trustees Act 1996, Sch 1, para 5.

18 *Freke v Lord Carbery* (1873) LR 16 Eq 461. Nowadays one can wait and see so that trusts are not void from the outset: Perpetuities and Accumulations Act 1964, s 3.

19 *Curtis v Hutton* (1808) 14 Ves 537; *Duncan v Lawson* (1889) 41 Ch D 394: since then the Mortmain and Charitable Uses Acts 1736 and 1888 have been repealed.

20 *Re Ross* [1930] 1 Ch 377 (legitima portio). A foreign state concerned only with its own nationals may let an English national domiciled in England devise land in the foreign state free from any legitima or legitim: cf *Re Duke of Wellington* [1948] Ch 118, [1947] 2 All ER 854, CA, and the current position in Spain, Netherlands, Greece, Finland and Denmark: see D J Hayton (ed) *European Succession Laws* (2 edn 2002, Jordans).

1 *Re Pearse's Settlement* [1909] 1 Ch 304.

2 On choice of law see Division 6, post.

3 See Rule 117 of Dicey & Morris, *Conflict of Laws* (13th edn).

4 See Division 6, post.

5 See Rule 116 of Dicey & Morris, *Conflict of Laws* (13th edn).

6 *Webb v Webb* [1991] 1 WLR 1410 accepted on appeal to European Court [1994] QB 696, [1994] 3 All ER 911; *Cook Industries Inc v Galliher* [1979] Ch 439, [1978] 3 All ER 945.

7 *Ashurst v Pollard* [2001] 2 All ER 75, CA.

8 *Re Piercy* [1895] 1 Ch 83.

extent that the foreign lex situs gives effect to heirs' indefeasible shares[9]. The English trustees will be under valid in personam obligations enforceable by the beneficiaries in the English courts to sell the land and hold the proceeds on trust for the beneficiaries. In the exceptionally rare case where the draftsman does not employ a trust for sale it seems the intended trust will fail where the trust concept is unknown to the lex situs, except to the extent that The Hague Convention on the Recognition of Trusts[10] may have been implemented so as to enable some effect to be given to the intended trust, so that a resulting trust does not arise.

English inter vivos or testamentary trusts of foreign movables will be valid except to the extent they conflict with any mandatory rules (relating to matter like insolvency, transfer of title to property, heirs indefeasible rights) of the law applicable under the choice of law rules of the forum or any strong principle of public policy of the lex situs[11]. The English trustees will often owe beneficiaries valid in personam obligations enforceable in the English courts[12] even if in the lex situs the concept of the trust is unknown, but it is possible that there may be a resulting trust for the settlor in some circumstances.

ARTICLE 11

The legality of the expressed object of the trust[13]

(1) A trust created for a purpose illegal by English law is void[14]. Private trusts of this character mostly fall under one of the following classes: (a) trusts for the tying-up of property for an unlawful period[15] whether

---

9 Most European countries (except, eg Italy, Spain, Netherlands, Finland and Denmark) accept the English renvoi to the lex situs as being the lex successionis: see Hayton (ed), *European Succession Laws* (2 edn 2002, Jordans).

10 See Division 6, post.

11 Hague Convention on the Law Applicable to Trusts and on their Recognition Articles 11, 15, 16, 18, pp 1046–1052, post.

12 *Chellaram v Chellaram* [1985] Ch 409, [1985] 1 All ER 1043; *Webb v Webb* [1994] QB 696; *Ashurst v Pollard* [2001] 2 All ER 75, CA.

13 In addition to trusts that are void for illegality, trusts may become void for breach of conditions so long as those conditions are lawful. Such conditions may be either precedent (so that the trust never comes into force at all unless and until the condition is performed), or subsequent so as to cause a forfeiture after the trust has arisen. If a condition is subsequent and is impossible, uncertain, contrary to public policy or illegal the condition is void and the interest becomes absolute: *Re Beard* [1908] 1 Ch 383. If a condition is precedent and attached to realty then failure to perform the condition defeats the gift. In respect of personalty 'where a condition precedent is originally impossible or is made so by the act or default of the testator or is illegal as involving malum prohibitum, the bequest is absolute just as if the condition had been subsequent. But where the performance of the condition is the sole motive of the bequest or its impossibility was unknown to the testator or the condition which was possible in its creation has since become impossible by act of God or where it is illegal as involving malum in se ... both gift and condition are void': per Harman J in *Re Elliott* [1952] Ch 217 at 221; *Re Wolffe* [1953] 1 WLR 1211 at 1216; *Re Piper* [1946] 2 All ER 503.

14 *A-G v Sands* (1668) Hard 488; *Pawlett v A-G* (1667) Hard 465; *Burgess v Wheate* (1759) 1 Eden 177; *Duke of Norfolk's Case* (1678) 3 Ch Cas 1. As to trusts void for attempting to alter the law of devolution of an absolute equitable gift, see *Re Dixon* [1903] 2 Ch 458.

15 *Cadell v Palmer* (1833) 1 Cl & Fin 372; Tud Lead Cas Conv (ed 4) 578; *Griffiths v Vere* (1803) 9 Ves 127; Tud Lead Cas Conv (ed 4) 618; *Re Dalziel* [1943] Ch 277, [1943] 2 All ER 656; *Re Wightwick's Will Trusts* [1950] Ch 260, [1950] 1 All ER 689.

the tying-up is achieved by the trusts creating contingent interests for persons which might not vest till too remote a time or ensuring the immediate application of income for purposes which will continue for too long a period during which the trust income will be inalienable;

(b) trusts for accumulation of income beyond the period allowed by law;

(c) trusts by which it is sought to alter the devolution of property as prescribed by law, eg in the event of intestacy[16], bankruptcy or seizure of property in execution of a judgment[17];

(d) trusts restricting the power of alienation of the beneficiaries' interest[18];

(e) trusts ousting the jurisdiction of the courts[19] or operating in terrorem to induce the beneficiary not to apply to the courts[20];

(f) trusts promoting or encouraging immorality[1], the separation of spouses, fraud, dishonesty, or other matters contrary to public policy;

(g) trusts tending to the general restraint of marriage[2] (unless of a second marriage)[3], or encouraging breach of the sanctity of marriage[4] or interfering drastically with parental duties or otherwise infringing the Human Rights Act 1998;

(h) trusts made illegal by statute[5].

(2) An illegal or impossible trust will not normally vitiate other provisions in the settlement unconnected with the illegal purpose[6].

(3) Testamentary trusts of English movables (but not English immovables) created by a testator domiciled abroad are only valid to the extent that the testator's *lex domicilii*, as his *lex successionis* according to the English forum, allows such to be disposed of free from mandatory rules protecting the interests of the testator's children or other relatives or dependants[7]; inter vivos trusts of English movables and

---

16 *Re Walker* [1908] 2 Ch 705; *Re Dixon* [1903] 2 Ch 458.

17 *Graves v Dolphin* (1826) 1 Sim 66; *Snowdon v Dales* (1834) 6 Sim 524; *Brandon v Robinson* (1811) 18 Ves 429; *Re Machu* (1882) 21 Ch D 838; *Re Dugdale* (1888) 38 Ch D 176 at 182; *Rowe v Sanders* [2002] EWCA Civ 242, [2002] 2 All ER 800n; *Krasner v Dennison* [2001] Ch 76, CA.

18 *Floyer v Bankes* (1869) LR 8 Eq 115; *Sykes v Sykes* (1871) LR 13 Eq 56.

19 *Re Wynn's Will Trusts* [1952] Ch 271.

20 *Re Hanlon* [1933] Ch 254.

1 *Blodwell v Edwards* (1596) Cro Eliz 509.

2 See per Wilmot LCJ in *Low v Peers* (1770) Wilm 375; *Morley v Rennoldson* (1843) 2 Hare 570; *Lloyd v Lloyd* (1852) 2 Sim NS 255.

3 *Marples v Bainbridge* (1816) 1 Madd 590; *Lloyd v Lloyd* (1852) 2 Sim NS 255; *Craven v Brady* (1869) 4 Ch App 296; and as to second marriage of a man, *Allen v Jackson* (1875) 1 Ch D 399.

4 *Re Caborne* [1943] Ch 224, [1943] 2 All ER 7. This was a decision upon a condition; but it is thought that the same principles would be applied in the case of a trust.

5 For example, by the Exchange Control Act 1947, s 29 (settlement of property, otherwise than by will, so as to confer an interest on a person resident outside 'the scheduled territories'). These controls terminated on 23 October 1979. See further p 223, post.

6 *H v W* (1857) 3 K & J 382; *Cartwright v Cartwright* (1853) 3 De GM & G 982; *Merryweather v Jones* (1864) 4 Giff 509; *Cocksedge v Cocksedge* (1844) 14 Sim 244; *Evers v Challis* (1859) 7 HL Cas 531; *Watson v Young* (1885) 28 Ch D 436; *Re Harvey* (1888) 39 Ch D 289, CA; and *Re Bence* [1891] 3 Ch 242, CA.

7 *Re Annesley* [1926] Ch 692.

immovables transferred validly under the *lex situs* to trustees of an English (or other trust jurisdiction) trust by a settlor of foreign domicile, habitual residence or nationality are valid and unimpeachable except, perhaps, to the extent that the settlor reserves a general power of appointment or revocation and his *lex successionis* has mandatory rules protecting the interests after his death of his children or other relatives or dependants[8].

PARAGRAPH 1(A)

Distinguish rule against remoteness from rule against inalienability

Where trust property cannot be applied for people or purposes without distinguishing between capital and income, so that the capital has to be kept intact as endowment capital for the income therefrom to be applied for people or purposes for some time, two mutually exclusive rules prevent the endowment trust from lasting too long a time. The two rules appeared relatively similar before the Perpetuities and Accumulations Act 1964 so that in the case law trusts are often said to be void for perpetuity without it being made clear whether the perpetuity arises from the prospect of a contingent interest not becoming vested in persons till too remote a time or from the prospect of income having to be used forthwith for particular purposes for too long a period. In the former case it is clearer to refer to the rule against remoteness of vesting as making the trusts void. In the latter case it is proposed to refer to the rule against inalienability as making the trusts void though it can also be referred to as the rule against purpose trusts of excessive duration. After the 1964 Act came into operation it has become crucial to distinguish between a trust for people (or other legal persons) and a trust for purposes: it will be seen that there is a 'wait and see' validity for people trusts while purpose trusts (if non-charitable) remain void from the outset if not restricted to a valid perpetuity period.

The rule against remoteness applies to trusts where some persons are intended to obtain beneficial interests and ensures that some person or persons will ultimately become absolutely entitled to the trust property on or before expiry of the perpetuity period (it sufficing that at the end of the period the property is held for Y for life, remainder to Z, Y having a vested interest in possession and Z a vested interest in remainder). It thus covers trusts where persons have contingent equitable interests and even discretionary trusts for a huge unlistable class of beneficiaries where at the end of the perpetuity period the trust property will have to be distributed by the trustees between the beneficiaries on a discretionary *McPhail v Doulton*[9] basis.

The above rule has no scope where persons are not intended to obtain beneficial interests ie where from the outset the trust capital has to be held on abstract purpose trusts of a non-charitable nature, which will normally fall foul of the beneficiary principle unless within the small anomalous class of testamentary purpose trusts that are concessions to human sentiment[10] or unless such purpose trusts come to be enforceable if an enforcer has been

8 See p 232, post.
9 [1971] AC 424, [1970] 2 All ER 228, HL, p 86, ante.
10 See p 118, ante.

expressly appointed so as to impose workable obligations upon the trustee(s)[11]. Here, it is the rule against inalienability which fulfils the function of ensuring that some person or persons will become absolutely entitled to the trust property on or before expiry of the perpetuity period.

The rule against remoteness

A detailed examination of this rule is beyond the scope of this work but may be found in Morris and Leach, *The Rule against Perpetuities*, or Megarry and Wade, *The Law of Real Property*. The rule developed in the seventeenth century, though trusts void under the common law rule may now be saved by the Perpetuities and Accumulations Act 1964 if created in an instrument taking effect after 15 July 1964. Since the 1925 property legislation and the Trustee Investments Act 1961 enable trust capital to be freely transposed, the modern rationale of the rule is probably to prevent the dead from ruling the actions of the living for too long (by imposing requirements for entitlement to benefits) and to strike a balance between trust capital (which is safe capital, except where very broad powers of investment are conferred on trustees who are given full protection in exercising these powers) and 'risk' capital by converting trust capital into risk capital at the end of the perpetuity period. Indeed, economic and fiscal circumstances are such that trusts normally do not run for the full perpetuity period: instead, the trustees terminate the trust period at an earlier time pursuant to express powers in that behalf or exercise powers to distribute capital such that no trust property remains before expiry of the trust period.

The rule against remoteness is that a future interest in real or personal property is void unless at the outset it can be seen that the future interest is absolutely certain to vest in interest (as opposed to vest in possession[12]) if at all, not later than 21 years after the death of the last surviving causally relevant life in being at the creation of the interest[13]. The most fantastic outlandish possibilities of interests vesting outside the perpetuity period can thus destroy those interests.

Under the Perpetuities and Accumulations Act 1964, effective as of 16 July 1964 for instruments taking effect on or after that date (not being the exercise of a special power contained in a pre-16 July 1964 trust), it is possible to wait and see what actually happens until it becomes absolutely clear that a future interest is certain to vest outside the perpetuity period and only then is the interest void[14] unless it can be saved by application of the statutory class-closing rules in s 4 of the Act or by s 5 dealing with the unborn widow problem[15]. The Act also replaces causally relevant lives by a list of statutory lives in being[16] and allows a specific number of years not exceeding 80 to be

---

11 See p 114 ante.
12 For an interest to vest in interest the person(s) entitled must be ascertained (eg by having been born) and the interest must be ready to take effect in possession forthwith upon cesser of prior interests (eg by the beneficiary having satisfied the contingency such as attaining 25 years) while if the gift is a gift to a class the size of the benefit must also be known (so the exact number within the class must be known).
13 *Cadell v Palmer* (1833) 1 Cl & Fin 372; Tud Lead Cas Conv (ed 4) 578; *London and South Western Rly Co v Gomm* (1882) 20 Ch D 562, CA; *Edwards v Edwards* [1909] AC 275, HL; *Pearks v Moseley* (1880) 5 App Cas 714, HL. A period of gestation may be added to the 21 years where it exists.
14 Perpetuities and Accumulations Act 1964, s 3.
15 *Re Frost* (1889) 43 Ch D 246, and p 197, post.
16 Perpetuities and Accumulations Act 1964, s 3(5).

chosen as the perpetuity period so long as expressly specified in that behalf[17]. However, an instrument exercising a special power of appointment can only use a specific period of years if the trust deed creating the power used a specific period of years[18].

Only where a future interest is void under the common law rule against remoteness is there to be applied the 'wait and see' provisions and the statutory lives provisions of the 1964 Act. Thus, reliance is still often to be placed upon validity at common law with a royal lives perpetuity clause ensuring that all vesting in interest takes place 'within 21 years of the death of the last survivor of all the descendants of King George VI now living'.

The rule against remoteness cannot be evaded by imposing a condition that the person who receives the capital absolutely at the end of the perpetuity period must resettle the property upon certain trusts for his issue or forfeit the capital: such a condition is void as being repugnant to the absolute nature of the interest in capital[19]. However out of a sense of responsibility, the person ultimately receiving the capital (perhaps under the exercise of a power of appointment by the trustees) may well re-settle it on family discretionary trusts to preserve the wealth and influence of his family.

Whether a trust is void for remoteness depends on possible, not actual, events

In considering whether limitations or trusts offend against the rule against remoteness *possible* events are to be considered[20]. If the trust contingency *might* in some event be too remote, it will be void, notwithstanding that in the events which have actually happened it would have occurred so that someone obtained an interest that vested within the prescribed period. To be good the limitation must be one of which, at its creation, it could be predicated that it *must* necessarily vest within the prescribed period[1]. For this purpose, physical impossibility was ignored so that female octogenarians were assumed capable of child bearing[2]. However, it had to be assumed that trustees would observe legal proprieties and not commit a breach of trust[3] and that legitimate children would not be born to persons under the age of marriage. Thus, a gift by will to such of G's grandchildren living at the testatrix's death or born within five years therefrom and attaining 21 was upheld[4], since it would be impossible for a child of G born after the death of the testatrix to have a child within the five-year period. On the other hand, with regard to marriage

17 Perpetuities and Accumulations Act 1964, s 1(1) on which see *Re Green's Will Trusts* [1985] 3 All ER 455.

18 Perpetuities and Accumulations Act 1964, s 1(2).

19 *Re Wenger's Settlement* (1963) 107 Sol Jo 981; *Re Brown* [1954] Ch 39, [1953] 2 All ER 1342.

20 For a restatement of this principle see *Re Wills' Will Trusts* [1959] Ch 1, [1958] 2 All ER 472, where a power of advancement was possibly too remote in relation to some trusts but was held not to be too remote in relation to others under the same will.

1 *Re Atkins' Will Trusts* [1974] 2 All ER 1, [1974] 1 WLR 761; *Re Wood* [1894] 3 Ch 381; *Lord Dungannon v Smith* (1846) 12 Cl & Fin 546; *Smith v Smith* (1870) 5 Ch App 342; *Re Handcock's Trusts* (1889) 23 LR Ir 34; *Re Johnson* (1914) 111 LT 130; *Re Nash's Settlement* (1882) 51 LJ Ch 511; *Re Connell's Settlement, Re Benett's Trust* [1915] 1 Ch 867; *Re Engels* [1943] 1 All ER 506; and *Re Fry* [1945] Ch 348, [1945] 2 All ER 205. As to trusts to take effect in remainder upon the failure of such trusts, see pp 225 et seq, post.

2 *Jee v Audley* (1787) 1 Cox Eq Cas 324; *Re Deloitte* [1926] Ch 56.

3 *Re Atkins' Will Trusts* [1974] 2 All ER 1, [1974] 1 WLR 761.

4 *Re Gaite's Will Trusts* [1949] 1 All ER 459.

settlements coming into operation before 1926, a trust for such of the children of the marriage as should attain the age of 22 years, or any greater age, was necessarily void for remoteness because both husband and wife *might* die leaving the child under one year of age who could not attain a vested interest within 21 years. For class gifts to vest in interest not only must (1) the person or persons entitled be ascertained and (2) the interest be ready to take effect in possession forthwith, subject only to prior interests, but (3) the size of the benefit must be known[5]. Thus, if a single member of the class might possibly not satisfy requirements (1) and (2) till after expiry of the perpetuity period the whole gift failed since the other class members could not satisfy requirement (3) till after expiry of the perpetuity period.

Fortuitously, in some cases the rule in *Andrews v Partington*[6] might apply to close the class when the first member became entitled to claim his share in possession[7]. This closing of the class against those born later will fix the maximum number of shares and so may often save the gift[8]. The primary purpose of the *Andrews v Partington* rule is to enable beneficiaries within the class to know their shares so that the property can be distributed to them by executors or trustees as soon as possible but the rule is only a rule of presumptive construction so that it can be ousted expressly or impliedly[9].

For trusts in instruments coming into operation after 1925 but before the application of the 1964 Act, s 163 of the Law of Property Act 1925 ensured that where a gift would be void for remoteness by reason of its being expressed to vest at an age exceeding 21 years, the latter age is to be substituted for the age stated if it would then make the gift valid. This provision, however, was without prejudice to any provision whereby absolute vesting is made dependent on marriage or any other event before the age stated in the instrument creating the trust.

The rule against remoteness will not be transgressed when, although the specified event might not happen within the perpetuity period the gift is only to take effect if it does happen within the period[10], but it will be transgressed by a provision for defeasance on the notification to trustees of the happening of an event which, if it happens at all, *must* happen within the perpetuity period if the notification may not be received by the trustees until after the end of the period[11].

---

5 *Leake v Robinson* (1817) 2 Mer 363; *Pearks v Moseley* (1880) 5 App Cas 714 at 723.
6 (1791) 3 Bro CC 401; *Re Bleckley* [1951] Ch 740, [1951] 1 All ER 1064, CA; *Re Chapman's Settlement Trusts* [1978] 1 All ER 1122, [1977] 1 WLR 1163; (1954) 70 LQR 61 (JHC Morris).
7 If, however, the beneficiaries qualify simply by being born then if no child has been born when the will or deed takes effect the first child born does not scoop the pool, the class remaining open for all after-born children to be included: *Re Ransome* [1957] Ch 348 at 359.
8 It will not assist if it could not be invoked at the time of the disposition creating the class gift (certainty being required at the outset) or if it closed a class of beneficiaries taking at 25 years of age since the closed class might comprise a person under four years of age who would not attain 25 within 21 years of the death of the last life in being.
9 *Re Drummond's Settlement* [1988] 1 All ER 449, [1988] 1 WLR 234, CA; *Re Tom's Settlement* [1987] 1 All ER 1081, [1987] 1 WLR 1021.
10 *Re Grotrian* [1955] Ch 501, [1955] 1 All ER 788.
11 *Re Spitzel's Will Trusts* [1939] 2 All ER 266.

The 1964 Act improvements to the common law rule where otherwise the rule would make dispositions void

In relation to instruments to which it[12] applies the Act of 1964 makes substantial changes in the previous law stated above so as to save a gift that would be void at common law.

New provisions are made with regard to the possibility of parenthood[13]:

(a) Where in any proceedings a question arising on the rule against perpetuities turns on the ability of a person to have a child, it is to be presumed that a male can have a child at the age of 14 or over but not under that age, and that a female can have a child at the age of 12 or over, but not under that age[14]. A female is to be presumed incapable of childbearing over the age of 55, but there is no corresponding presumption as to males[15]. These presumptions apply also to the possibility that a person may have a child by adoption, legitimation 'or other means'[16]. In the case of a living person the presumptions may be rebutted by evidence showing that he or she will or will not be able to have a child at the time in question[17], but this provision for rebuttal does not apply to the possibility of having children by adoption, legitimation or other means[18].

(b) If such a question is decided by treating a person as unable to have a child at a particular time, and he or she does in fact have a child at that time, the court may make such order as it thinks fit for placing the persons interested in the property, so far as may be just, in the position in which they would have been if the question had not been decided in that way[19].

(c) Subject to the point just mentioned, where such a question is decided by making a presumption that a person is able or unable to have a child at a particular time, the same presumption shall be made if any question arises on the rule against perpetuities in any subsequent proceedings in connection with the same disposition[20].

The Act also enables a draftsman, instead of using common law lives in being for ascertaining the perpetuity period, to use a fixed period of years not exceeding 80 specified in that behalf[1].

The 1964 Act 'wait and see' principle saving trusts otherwise void

The Act introduces the principle of 'wait and see' by providing that where,

---

12 See p 191, ante and pp 199–200, post.
13 Perpetuities and Accumulations Act 1964, s 2.
14 Perpetuities and Accumulations Act 1964, s 2(1)(a).
15 Perpetuities and Accumulations Act 1964, s 2(1)(a).
16 Perpetuities and Accumulations Act 1964, s 2(4).
17 Perpetuities and Accumulations Act 1964, s 2(1)(b). Thus evidence of incurable incapacity may be given or that a woman over 55 recently had a child by the insertion of an embryo or could have a child in such fashion, she being the mother and her husband the father under the Human Fertilisation and Embryology Act 1990, ss 27 and 28.
18 Perpetuities and Accumulations Act 1964, s 2(4).
19 Perpetuities and Accumulations Act 1964, s 2(2).
20 Perpetuities and Accumulations Act 1964, s 2(3).
1 Perpetuities and Accumulations Act 1964, s 1. In *Re Green's Will Trusts* [1985] 3 All ER 455 Nourse J held it was unnecessary to specify a number of years and upheld a period specified as follows in a codicil: 'The period from the date of my death to 1 January 2020 is hereby specified as the Perpetuity Period for the trusts of the residue of my estate contained in my will.'

apart from this newly introduced principle[2] and the provisions of ss 4 and 5 (considered at pp 196–197, post):

(a) a disposition would otherwise be void on the ground that the interest disposed of might not become vested until too remote a time, the disposition is to be treated (unless and until it becomes established that the vesting must in fact occur too late) as if it was not subject to the rule against remoteness at all; and its becoming so established is not to affect the validity of anything previously done by way of advancement, application of intermediate income or otherwise[3];

(b) a disposition which consists of the conferring of a general power of appointment would be void on the ground that the power might not become exercisable until too remote a time, the disposition is to be treated (unless and until it becomes established that the power will not in fact be exercisable within the perpetuity period) as if the disposition were not subject to the rule against remoteness[4];

(c) a disposition (eg in the case of discretionary trusts) which consists of the conferring of any power, option or other right would be void on the ground that the right might be exercised at too remote a time, the disposition is to be treated as regards any exercise of the right which is in fact made within the perpetuity period as if it were not subject to the rule against remoteness, and is to be treated as void for remoteness only if, and so far as, the right is not fully exercised within that period[5].

In cases where the 'wait and see' principle comes into play, it is of course necessary to wait and see whether the event concerned does take place within the perpetuity period. The question then arises as to how the perpetuity period is to be determined for this purpose. Here, the Act contains special provisions[6] to the effect that where any one or more of certain persons listed and described in the Act[7] are individuals in being and ascertainable at the start of the perpetuity period, the duration of the period is in general to be the time during which they (or any of them) remain alive and 21 years thereafter. In other cases, the period is to be simply 21 years.

Section 163 of the Law of Property Act 1925, which deals with the reduction of a beneficiary's age to 21 to avoid the failure of his gift for remoteness and is summarised above, is repealed by the Act of 1964 and replaced by new provisions[8].

(a) The first of these applies where a disposition is limited by reference to the attainment by any person or persons of a specified age greater than 21, and it is apparent when the disposition is made (or it becomes

---

2 The 'wait and see' principle in s 3 always applies in priority to ss 4 and 5.
3 Perpetuities and Accumulations Act 1964, s 3(1).
4 Perpetuities and Accumulations Act 1964, s 3(2).
5 Perpetuities and Accumulations Act 1964, s 3(3). As to the *administrative* powers of trustees, see also s 8, summarised at p 201, post.
6 Perpetuities and Accumulations Act 1964, s 3(4) and (5). As to the desirability of this, see 80 LQR 486, 81 LQR 106, 86 LQR 357, 97 LQR 593 and (1986) 102 LQR 250.
7 See Perpetuities and Accumulations Act 1964, s 3(5).
8 Perpetuities and Accumulations Act 1964, s 4. It is provided by sub-s (5) that where this section has effect in relation to a disposition to which s 3 (summarised above) applies, the operation of s 4 is not to affect the validity of anything previously done in relation to the interest disposed of by way of advancement, application of intermediate income or otherwise. The defect arising from the fact that the repeal of s 163 was contained in s 4(6) will probably be held to have been remedied by the Children Act 1975. Sch 3, para 43, treating s 4(6) as a separate section despite the fact that para 43 does this as s 4(7) of the 1964 Act.

apparent later) that the disposition would (but for the Act) fail for remoteness, but that it would be saved if the specified age were to be reduced to the age of 21. In such a case, the disposition is to be treated for all purposes as if the age specified had been the nearest age to 21 which would have saved it[9].

(b) Where different ages exceeding 21 are specified in a disposition in regard to different persons, the provisions summarised in paragraph (a) above are to apply as if the reference to the disposition being saved if the specified age were to be reduced to the age of 21 were read as a reference to it being saved by the similar reduction of all the specified ages. Each one of the several ages specified is then to be notionally reduced so far as is necessary to save the disposition from failure through remoteness[10].

In the case of class gifts, if not valid at common law or under the effect of the class-closing rule in *Andrews v Partington*[11] or under the statutory 'wait and see' principle, s 4(4) of the 1964 Act operates to exclude from the class any potential members whose inclusion would cause the disposition to fail for remoteness. Section 4(3) makes special provision for combining this class reduction with the age reduction provisions already discussed where needed to save a disposition.

It may also be noted here that the Act[12] contains provisions designed to deal with a draftsman's trap sometimes called the trap of the 'unborn widow'. These apply where a disposition is limited by reference to the time of death of the survivor of two people, one of them a person in being at the start of the perpetuity period and the other any spouse of that person. If that time has not arrived when the perpetuity period ends, then the disposition is to be treated for all purposes (if this would save it from being void for remoteness) as being limited by reference to the time immediately before the end of the period so that a beneficiary's interest vests in interest at that time.

Property need not vest in possession within the prescribed period so long as it vests in interest

The rule against perpetuities does not require that the trust property shall vest absolutely *in possession* within the prescribed period. It suffices that it must necessarily vest absolutely *in interest*[13] in some person or persons, so that one can say with certainty at some time within that period that A as life tenant and B as absolute owner in remainder can collectively deal with the property. Thus, a trust for A for life, with remainder for any woman who may become his widow for life, with remainder for his children who shall attain 21, is good as a whole[14]. For although it is possible that the woman who may become A's widow has not been born at the date when the settlement comes into operation, yet at the end of 21 years after the death of A it will be possible to

---

9 Perpetuities and Accumulations Act 1964, s 4(1). Where there are several beneficiaries it is unclear whether there must be a once-for-all reduction to an age which will save all beneficiaries for certain or whether age reduction can be by stages as one waits and sees what happens: [1969] CLJ 286 (MJ Prichard). The former is more probable.
10 Perpetuities and Accumulations Act 1964, s 4(2).
11 See p 194, ante.
12 Perpetuities and Accumulations Act 1964, s 5.
13 This is the prima facie meaning of 'vested,' see *Re Wills' Will Trusts* [1959] Ch 1, [1958] 2 All ER 472, per Upjohn J. Also see p 192 n12, ante.
14 *Re Hargreaves* (1889) 43 Ch D 401 at 405; *Re Roberts* (1881) 19 Ch D 520, CA; *Evans v Walker* (1876) 3 Ch D 211; *Re Lodwig* [1916] 2 Ch 26, CA.

say that his widow (if any) and his children who have attained twenty-one are together the absolute owners of the property.

How far related trusts are invalidated

The question how far a trust which is void for remoteness invalidates other trusts connected with it is discussed on pp 225 et seq, post.

Validity of powers

At common law a general power was void if it might be acquired outside the perpetuity period[15], though the 1964 Act allows a 'wait and see' period so that the power only becomes void if it becomes established that it cannot be acquired, and so become exercisable, within the perpetuity period[16]. A general power exercisable only by will ranks as a special power for determining its validity for perpetuity purposes[17]. At common law a special power was void if it might be exercised outside the perpetuity period[18], though the 1964 Act allows a 'wait and see' period so that the power only becomes void in so far as it is not exercised within the perpetuity period[19]. This applies to the powers of selection between the beneficiaries under a discretionary trust.

Validity of trusts created under exercise of powers of appointment

The law apart from the 1964 Act

Where a person has a general power to appoint a trust fund to such persons as he may think fit, the rule against perpetuities applies to an appointment made thereunder in the same way as it would to a disposition by an absolute owner, the reason being that the property is treated as vesting in the donee of the power[20]. But where, under a settlement or will, a person has a limited or special power (such as the power to appoint among issue commonly found in marriage settlements) or a power to appoint with the consent of another[1] or a joint power[2] a person taking under the power is deemed to take directly under the instrument creating it[3], and for the purposes of the rule, the effect of the appointment at the date when it comes into operation, and not what the possibilities might have been if the actual wording of the appointment had been in force from the outset of the trust are considered[4]. If, judged on

---

15 *Bray v Hammersley* (1830) 3 Sim 513, HL.
16 Perpetuities and Accumulations Act 1964, s 3(2).
17 *Wollaston v King* (1869) LR 8 Eq 165; *Morgan v Gronow* (1873) LR 16 Eq 1.
18 *Re Abbott* [1893] 1 Ch 54.
19 Perpetuities and Accumulations Act 1964, s 3(3).
20 Per Roxburgh J in *Re Churston Settled Estates* [1954] Ch 334 at 346. In the report in [1954] 1 All ER 725 at 733, the more picturesque phrase 'being at home' in the donee of the power is used.
 1 *Re Watts* [1931] 2 Ch 302; *Re Churston's Settled Estates* [1954] Ch 334, sub nom *Re Churston Settled Estates, Freemantle v Baron Churston* [1954] 1 All ER 725.
 2 *Re Churston's Settled Estates* [1954] Ch 334, sub nom *Re Churston Settled Estates, Freemantle v Baron Churston* [1954] 1 All ER 725. This decision ran counter to the practice of many conveyancers (see Mr FE Farrer's note in Key and Elphinstone, *Precedents in Conveyancing*, (14th edn) Vol 2, at p 1049), but stands as an authority, especially since it has been applied in *Re Earl of Coventry's Indentures* [1974] Ch 77, [1973] 3 All ER 1.
 3 *Re Brown and Sibly's Contract* (1876) 3 Ch D 156; *Re Pratt's Settlement Trusts* [1943] Ch 356, [1943] 2 All ER 458.
 4 *Re Thompson* [1906] 2 Ch 199; *Re Paul* [1921] 2 Ch 1.

the facts at the date the appointment took effect, it would have been void for remoteness as an original trust, it will equally be void for remoteness as an appointment[5]. An example is afforded by the case of *Re Thompson*[6] which emphasises the fact that it is the factual situation at the date of the power's exercise that is crucial in ascertaining whether or not the perpetuity period, running from the date of the creation of the power, can be exceeded. There the original will gave a life interest to the testator's widow, with remainder upon such trusts for the testator's brother CT and his issue as the widow should appoint. The widow by her will appointed in favour of CT for life with remainder to his children who being born in her lifetime should attain 25, or being born after her death should attain 21. At her death (when the appointment first came into operation) all of CT's then existing children were 25.

It was contended that if the *words of appointment* had been written into the husband's will the trusts in favour of the children of CT who should attain twenty-five would have been void for remoteness. But Joyce J said:

> 'When it is stated that the test by which the validity of such a gift must be tried is to read it as inserted in the deed or will creating the power in the place of the power, it is not meant that the precise language of the instrument exercising the power is to be read into the instrument creating it. ... Inasmuch, therefore, as the will of the widow was so made that the persons who, according to the true construction of such will, were to take under it, and the shares they were to take would necessarily be ascertained and their interests vest not later than the expiration of twenty-one years from the death of CT, who was alive at the death of the testator, the appointment was perfectly valid.'

On the other hand, in *Re Legh's Settlement Trusts*[7], where in exercise of a special power in a settlement the donee of the power appointed to two objects of the power for their joint lives, with remainder to the survivor for life, it was held that the appointment to the survivor for life was void as it was a contingent interest and neither of the appointees was a life in existence at the date of the settlement creating the power.

Where the appointor has both a general and a special power of appointment over the same fund and makes a single testamentary appointment it may be material to know which power was in fact exercised. In general a special power will not be held to have been exercised in the absence of some expression of intention to exercise it[8].

Powers of advancement are subject to the rule against remoteness in the same way as special powers of appointment[9].

Changes made by the 1964 Act

In relation to instruments taking effect after its commencement, the Act of 1964 contains provisions of two different kinds.

First, the 'wait and see' provisions of the Act are applied by a special

---

5 Law of Property Act 1925, s 163 (2) applies to appointments where the *appointment* (not necessarily the power) comes into operation after 1925.
6 [1906] 2 Ch 199.
7 [1938] Ch 39, [1937] 3 All ER 823, following *Whitby v Von Leudecke* [1906] 1 Ch 783; and see *Re Johnson's Settlement Trusts* [1943] Ch 341, [1943] 2 All ER 499.
8 *Re Holford's Settlement* [1945] Ch 21, [1944] 2 All ER 462, reviewing many of the earlier cases.
9 *Pilkington v IRC* [1964] AC 612, [1962] 3 All ER 622; cf *Hart (Inspector of Taxes) v Briscoe* [1979] Ch 1, [1978] 1 All ER 791.

provision to powers of appointment, including powers of selecting between beneficiaries under a discretionary trust[10]. However, the Act only applies when both the creation and the exercise of the special power were under instruments taking effect after 15 July 1964[11].

Second, the Act contains a statement of rules, designed to clarify rather than to change the law, for ascertaining whether, for the purposes of the rule against perpetuities, a power of appointment is to be treated as a general or a special one[12]. If the power was expressed in the instrument creating it to be exercisable by one person only and is such that, at all times during its currency when that person is of full age and capacity, he could exercise it so as immediately to transfer to himself the whole of the interest governed by the power (and could do so without the consent of anyone else and without having to comply with any other condition except a purely formal one relating only to the mode of exercising the power), then the power is to be treated as a general one. Otherwise it is to be treated as special. But a power which is exercisable by will only is to be treated as a general power where it would be treated in that way if exercisable by deed.

Power of or trust for sale not limited in duration

Prior to the commencement of the Act of 1964, a trust of real estate forbidding a sale until the happening of an event (eg when the settlor's gravel pits were worked out) which might not happen within the allowed period was void[13]. A power of or trust for sale not expressly limited in point of duration was not, however, necessarily void; for there was a presumption that it was intended to be exercisable only before all beneficial interest should have vested absolutely in persons of full capacity, or, possibly, within a reasonable time after such interests were ascertained[14]. Even where it could be gathered that the settlor intended it to be exercised after that for purposes of division, it could still be exercised within the period allowed by the rule[15]. But where no successive interests were given and the property vested absolutely in persons of full capacity directly the settlement took effect, and no intention could be gathered that a power of a sale was merely given for facility of division, it was void for remoteness[16]. However, although the trust for, or power of, sale might be void, it was looked upon as mere machinery and would not avoid the trusts in favour of the beneficiaries if they took vested interests within the prescribed period[17].

The law has however been changed by s 8 of the Perpetuities and Accu-

---

10 See the Perpetuities and Accumulations Act 1964, s 3(2), (3).

11 Perpetuities and Accumulations Act 1964, s 15(5).

12 See the Perpetuities and Accumulations Act 1964, s 7.

13 *Re Wood* [1894] 3 Ch 381, CA; *Goodier v Edmunds* [1893] 3 Ch 455; *Re Daveron* [1893] 3 Ch 421.

14 *Re W & R Holmes and Cosmopolitan Press Ltd's Contract* [1944] Ch 53, [1943] 2 All ER 716. In some of the cases reference has been made to vesting *in possession* (eg *Re Lord Sudeley and Baines & Co* [1894] 1 Ch 334; but vesting in possession might occur after the expiry of the perpetuity period; see *Re Allott* [1924] 2 Ch 498, CA (power of leasing held invalid), and cf *Re Wills' Will Trusts* [1959] Ch 1, [1958] 2 All ER 472 (power of advancement).

15 *Re Lord Sudeley and Baines & Co* [1894] 1 Ch 334.

16 *Re Dyson and Fowke* [1896] 2 Ch 720; *Re Jump* [1903] 1 Ch 129; and see *Re Kaye and Hoyle's Contract* (1909) 53 Sol Jo 520; and *Kennedy v Kennedy* [1914] AC 215, distinguished, however, in *Re Cassel* [1926] Ch 358 which was followed in *Beachway Management Ltd v Wisewell* [1971] Ch 610, [1971] 1 All ER 1.

17 *Re Appleby* [1903] 1 Ch 565; *Goodier v Edmunds* [1893] 3 Ch 455; *Re Daveron* [1893] 3 Ch 421.

mulations Act 1964, which is almost unique among the provisions of the Act in applying to instruments taking effect before, as well as after, its commencement[18]. This section provides that the rule against perpetuities is not to apply at all to a power conferred upon trustees or other persons to sell, lease, exchange or otherwise dispose for full consideration, or to do any other act in the administration (as opposed to the distribution) of any property. Nor is the rule to prevent the payment to trustees or other persons of reasonable remuneration for their services. It is to be noted that the administrative powers which fall within this provision are strictly defined: they would not, for instance, include a power to dispose of property for less than full consideration, though they may well include a power to mortgage or charge. It is clear, however, that although administrative powers which did not fall within this definition would still be subject to the rule against perpetuities, they would have the benefit of the 'wait and see' provisions of the Act which have already been discussed[19].

Exceptions from rule against remoteness

The rule does not apply to trusts following estates tail since they can be barred[20], nor to a joint tenant's right of survivorship[1], nor to a contingent gift over from one charity to another[2]. However, if a gift to a private person is followed by a gift over to charity the gift over is subject to the rule[3] as is any trust for charity conditional upon a future uncertain event[4]. Pension trusts (otherwise subject to the rule[5]) will normally be exempt due to statutory exemption[6].

Furthermore, to put doubts at rest s 162 of the Law of Property Act 1925 is as follows:

> 162.—(1) For removing doubts, it is hereby declared that the rule of law relating to perpetuities does not apply and shall be deemed never to have applied—
> (a) To any power to distrain on or to take possession of land or the income thereof given by way of indemnity against a rent, whether charged upon or payable in respect of any part of that land or not; or
> (b) To any rentcharge created only as an indemnity against another rentcharge, although the indemnity rentcharge may only arise or become payable on

---

18 This is so at least 'for the purpose of enabling a power to be exercised at any time after the commencement of [the] Act notwithstanding that the power is conferred by an instrument which took effect before that commencement'; Perpetuities and Accumulations Act 1964, s 8(2).

19 See p 195, ante.

20 *Heasman v Pearse* (1871) 7 Ch App 275; *Re Haygarth* [1912] 1 Ch 510.

1 *Re Roberts* (1881) 19 Ch D 520; *Re Smith* [1914] 1 Ch 937 at 948; *Re Goode* [1960] VR 117 at 124; but for a gift to a survivor of two persons see *Re Legh's Settlement Trusts* [1938] Ch 39, CA.

2 *Christ's Hospital v Grainger* (1849) 1 Mac & G 460; *Re Tyler* [1891] 3 Ch 252; *Re Hanbey's Will Trusts* [1956] Ch 264, [1955] 3 All ER 874. There is a similar statutory exception for gifts over to charitable trusts from gifts for the endowment of a historic building or garden: Historic Buildings and Ancient Monuments Act 1953, ss 8(5), 8A(5), 8B(5) as amended by National Heritage Act 1983, s 33, Sch 4, para 10.

3 *Re Johnson's Trusts* (1866) LR 2 Eq 716.

4 *Chamberlayne v Brockett* (1872) 8 Ch App 206 at 211; *Re Lord Stratheden and Campbell* [1894] 3 Ch 265.

5 *Air Jamaica Ltd v Charlton* [1999] 1 WLR 1399, PC.

6 Social Security Act 1973, s 69 as amended by Social Security Pensions Act 1975, s 65(1), Sch 4 and Social Security Act 1986, s 86(1), Sch 10, Pt I; Personal and Occupational Pension Schemes (Perpetuities) Regs 1990; Pension Schemes Act 1993, s 163.

breach of a condition of stipulation; or

(c) To any power, whether exercisable on breach of a condition or stipulation or not, to retain or withhold payment of any instalment of a rentcharge as an indemnity against another rentcharge; or

(d) To any grant, exception, or reservation of any right of entry on, or user of, the surface of land or of any easements, rights, or privileges over or under land for the purpose of—

  (i)   winning, working, inspecting, measuring, converting, manufacturing, carrying away, and disposing of mines and minerals;

  (ii) inspecting, grubbing up, felling and carrying away timber and other trees, and the tops and lops thereof;

  (iii) executing repairs, alterations, or additions to any adjoining land, or the buildings and erections thereon;

  (iv) constructing, laying down, altering, repairing, renewing, cleansing, and maintaining sewers, watercourses, cesspools, gutters, drains, water-pipes, gas-pipes, electric wires or cables or other like works.

(2) This section applies to instruments coming into operation before or after the commencement of this Act.

Further reform of rule against remoteness

The Law Commission in a Report[7] (with a draft bill annexed) accepted by the Government has recommended a fixed period of 125 years within which an equitable interest must vest in instruments made after the reform is enacted (including appointments under a special power of appointment created beforehand).

The rule against inalienability or purpose trusts of excessive duration

This rule, makes void endowment[8] trusts for purposes of a non-charitable nature where one cannot be sure by the end of the perpetuity period the trust fund will be available to be spent freely on non-trust purposes because beneficially owned by persons who can spend the capital on themselves. The fact that the income has to be spent on trust purposes means that the income is inalienable and this has the effect of rendering the trust fund inalienable in that the trust fund must always be retained in one form or another to give effect to the income trusts[9].

The following are examples of trusts void for inalienability: a devise of 'Elmslea' to trustees upon trust for the purposes of a contemplative (and therefore non-charitable) order of nuns[10]; a bequest to trustees for the provision of an annual cup for the most successful yacht in a sailing club[11]; a bequest to trustees for the maintenance of a tomb that is not part of the fabric of a church[12].

---

7 Report on the Rules against Perpetuities and Excessive Accumulations (Law Com No 251, 1998).

8 If the trust fund can be freely disposed of without distinction between capital and income there are no perpetuity problems, eg *Re Lipinski's Will Trusts* [1976] Ch 235, [1977] 1 All ER 33.

9 It is immaterial that the investments within the capital fund can be freely transposed into other investments.

10 *Leahy v A-G for New South Wales* [1959] AC 457, [1959] 2 All ER 300.

11 *Re Nottage* [1895] 2 Ch 649; *Re Gwyon* [1930] 1 Ch 255.

12 *Re Rickard* (1862) 31 Beav 244; *Re Dean* (1889) 41 Ch D 552 at 557; *Re Elliott* [1952] 1 All ER 145; *Re Dalziel* [1943] Ch 277, [1943] 2 All ER 656.

As already discussed, gifts for unincorporated associations raise special problems in connection with the rule against inalienability and the rule against remoteness.

The rule against inalienability may be avoided by creating alienable determinable interests in income[13]. Thus a fund can be left to T1 and T2 upon trust to pay the income therefrom to the A Charity Co for such company to dispose of as it wishes for so long as the following purpose ... shall be carried out but as soon as such purpose shall not be carried out then on trust to pay the income to the B Charity Co for such company to dispose of as it wishes for so long as the purpose aforesaid shall be carried out [and so on to the Z Charity Co][14].

The perpetuity period beyond which an interest may not be inalienable is the same as for the common law rule against remoteness[15], ie causally relevant lives (if applicable) and 21 years because the operation of the rule against inalienability (or perpetual purpose trusts) is expressly excluded from the 1964 Act. The curiously worded s 15(4) of the Perpetuities and Accumulations Act 1964 expressly provides that nothing in the Act is to affect the operation of the rule rendering void[16] certain dispositions under which property is limited to be applied for purposes other than the benefit of any person or class of persons where the property may be so applied after the end of the perpetuity period applicable to the relevant disposition under such rule. Thus the perpetuity period, so far as the rule against inalienability is concerned, cannot be a period of years not exceeding 80 as allowed by s 1 of the Act for the rule against remoteness.

The rule against inalienability does not apply to charitable trusts[17].

PARAGRAPH 1(B)

Excessive Accumulations of income

No accumulation beyond one of six periods

At common law, the period for which money could be tied up so as to accumulate at compound interest was co-extensive with the period for which property might be tied up under the rule against remoteness, and the Law

---

13 *Re Chardon* [1928] Ch 464; *Re Chambers' Will Trusts* [1950] Ch 267; contrast *Re Wightwick's Will Trusts* [1950] Ch 260, [1950] 1 All ER 689.

14 The gifts over from one charity to another are exempt from the rule against remoteness and unaffected by Perpetuities and Accumulations Act 1964, s 12. Maintenance of private graves is possible for 99 years under the Parish Council and Burial Authorities (Miscellaneous Provisions) Act 1970, s 1.

15 *Thellusson v Woodford* (1805) 11 Ves 112 at 135, 146; *Re Dean* (1889) 41 Ch D 552 at 557 (though wrong in allowing animal lives to count as lives in being); *Re Moore* [1901] 1 Ch 936; *Re Astor's Settlement Trusts* [1952] Ch 534, [1952] 1 All ER 1067; *Re Khoo Cheng Teow* [1932] Straits Settlement Reports 226.

16 The draftsman actually states 'void for remoteness', considering the rule against inalienability or perpetual purpose trusts to make trusts for purposes void if they can continue till too remote a time, while using in s 1 'the rule against perpetuities' when referring to what we have earlier referred to, strictly, as the rule against remoteness concerned with trusts for people as opposed to trust for purposes.

17 *Chamberlayne v Brockett* (1872) 8 Ch App 206 at 211. Thus a 1585 charitable trust was upheld in *A-G v Webster* (1875) LR 20 Eq 483.

Commission in a Report[18] accepted by the Government has recommended that the accumulation period should be co-extensive with the recommended 125-year period for the rule against remoteness. However, when a testator directed his property to be accumulated during the lives of all his descendants living at his death[19], the common law power was seen to be unreasonably wide, especially by Members of Parliament who were sons of wealthy men and did not want themselves or their descendants kept out of income for too long. Accordingly, by the statute 39 & 40 Geo 3, c 98 (commonly known as the Thellusson Act after the testator of that name whose will provoked the Act)[20], now repealed and re-enacted by ss 164 and 165 of the Law of Property Act 1925, the period allowed for accumulations was restricted to one (and one only) of the following:

(a) the life of the grantor or settlor[1];
(b) 21 years from the death of the grantor, settlor, devisor or testator;
(c) the duration of the minorities of any persons who should be living, or en ventre sa mère, at the death of the grantor, settlor, devisor or testator; or
(d) the duration of the minority or respective minorities of any persons who, under the instrument directing the accumulation, would for the time being, if of full age, be entitled to the income directed to be accumulated. This period is not restricted to the minority of persons in existence at the time when the settlement came into force[2], although the statute does not permit the accumulations in that case to be made during the period before their birth[3].

In respect of instruments which take effect after the commencement, on 16 July 1964, of the Perpetuities and Accumulations Act 1964, however, it is provided[4] that the periods for which accumulation is permitted by s 164 of the Law of Property Act 1925 shall include two other periods, namely:

(e) a term of 21 years from the date of the making of the disposition (a disposition contained in a will being deemed to be made at the testator's death)[5]; or
(f) the duration of the minority or respective minorities of any person or persons in being at that date.

The Act also contains a declaration[6] that the restrictions imposed by s 164 apply in relation to a power to accumulate income whether or not there is a duty to exercise it, and whether or not it extends to income produced by the investment of income previously accumulated (viz whether compound or simple interest is involved). Companies, however, that are settlors are wholly exempt[7].

---

18 'Rules against Perpetuities and Excessive Accumulations' (Law Com No 251, 1998). Abolition of the Rule against Excessive Accumulations by a Regulatory Reform Order is proposed by Lord Chancellor's Consultation Paper CP 10/02.
19 *Thellusson v Woodford* (1805) 11 Ves 112, HL.
20 *Bassil v Lister* (1851) 9 Hare 177.
1 *Stewart's Trustees v Stewart* 1927 SC 350.
2 *Re Cattell* [1907] 1 Ch 567; affd [1914] 1 Ch 177; *Jagger v Jagger* (1883) 25 Ch D 729, and *Re Watts' Will Trusts* [1936] 2 All ER 1555.
3 *Ellis v Maxwell* (1841) 3 Beav 587 at 596.
4 See the Perpetuities and Accumulations Act 1964, s 13(1).
5 Perpetuities and Accumulations Act 1964, s 15(2).
6 Perpetuities and Accumulations Act 1964, s 13(2). This confirms the view in *Re Robb's Will Trusts* [1953] Ch 459, sub nom *Re Robb's Will Trusts, Marshall v Marshall* [1953] 1 All ER 920 (overruled on another point in *Re Berkley* [1968] Ch 744) endorsed by HL in *Baird v Lord Advocate* [1979] AC 666, [1979] 2 All ER 28, HL.
7 *Re Dodwell & Co Ltd's Trust Deed* [1979] Ch 301, sub nom *Re Dodwell & Co Ltd's Trust Deed* [1978] 3 All ER 738.

The statutory provisions set out above must now be construed in the light of the Family Law Reform Act 1969, the relevant parts of which came into force on 1 January 1970. By virtue of s 1(1) of the Act, a person attains full age at 18, instead of 21 and by virtue of the general provision in s 1(2) the references in the Acts of 1925 and 1964 to 'minority' or 'minorities' are to be construed accordingly. This does not, of course, affect the specific references in those Acts to periods of 21 years, which are not affected by the 1969 Act. Furthermore, it is provided by s 1(4) and Sch 3, para 7, that these changes are not to invalidate any direction for accumulation in a settlement or other disposition made by a deed, will or other instrument which was made before 1 January 1970 (and a will or codicil executed before that date is not to be treated for this purpose as having been made on or after that date merely because it has been confirmed by a codicil executed on or after that date: s 1(7)).

Right to terminate accumulations

The principle sometimes known as the rule in *Saunders v Vautier*[8] permits a beneficiary who is of full capacity to put an end to an accumulation which is entirely for his benefit. Thus a beneficiary (or beneficiaries acting together) may sometimes be able to prevent accumulation from continuing by bringing it to an end. In determining whether an existing beneficiary (or existing beneficiaries) were entitled to exercise this right, however, the law as it stood before the Act of 1964 did not permit a woman's incapacity to bear children to be taken into account[9]. But with respect to instruments taking effect after its commencement, the 1964 Act provides[10] that the new provisions relating to the possibility of future parenthood[11], which are contained in the Act and have already been mentioned[12], are to apply where any question arises as to the right of beneficiaries to put an end to accumulations of income, in the same way as they apply to questions arising on the rule against perpetuities.

Exclusions from accumulation rules

The statutory restriction of accumulations does not extend to any provision for payment of debts, or for raising portions for the legitimate children of the settlor, grantor, or devisor, or of any person taking any interest under the instrument directing such accumulations; nor to any direction as to the produce of timber upon any lands; nor to a trust or direction for keeping property in repair[13]; nor to the accumulation of surplus income under any statutory power or under the general law (powers of maintenance of infants

---

8 (1841) 4 Beav 115; *Wharton v Masterman* [1895] AC 186. See also Article 70, post.
9 *Re Deloitte* [1926] Ch 56. This case was doubted by the House of Lords in *Berry v Green* [1938] AC 575, sub nom *Re Blake, Berry v Green* [1938] 2 All ER 362, but in *IRC v Bernstein* [1960] Ch 444, [1960] 1 All ER 697, Danckwerts J said that despite the doubts cast upon it the former case was plainly binding on him as regards the principle which it laid down. It would now be saved by the operation of ss 14 and 2 of the 1964 Act.
10 Perpetuities and Accumulations Act 1964, s 14.
11 See the Perpetuities and Accumulations Act 1964, s 2.
12 See p 195, ante.
13 *Vine v Raleigh* [1891] 2 Ch 13; *Re Mason* [1891] 3 Ch 467. Maintaining property at its present value is not a true accumulation since the capital of the property is not augmented.

etc) made during a minority[14], nor to a direction to apply income for keeping up an insurance policy to mature on expiry of a lease, so preserving capital value[15].

The case of *Re Rochford's Settlement Trusts*[16] bears on the principles just stated. In that case the settlor had provided that estate duty payable in certain events should in effect be borne by the income of a trust fund. Some time after the settlement was made, events occurred which gave rise to estate duty liability, and if this liability was to be discharged out of the income of the fund the income would have to be accumulated for this purpose for a number of years.

Cross J held that these provisions fell within the terms of s 164 of the Law of Property Act 1925 and, since they made use of none of the accumulation periods permitted by that section, they were void with the consequence that the estate duty liability should be met out of capital. The provisions were not within the exception to s 164 whereby that section does not apply to accumulations for the payment of debts, because for this purpose the debt in question must be in existence as a legal liability (if only a contingent one) when the instrument providing for the accumulation takes effect. Had the settlement in this case been made after the commencement of the Perpetuities and Accumulations Act 1964, the provision would no doubt have been valid to the extent that it fell within the first of the two new accumulation periods permitted by that Act and mentioned above (ie accumulation for a term of 21 years from the date of the making of the disposition).

The exception for provisions for raising portions[17] was considered by the Court of Appeal in *Re Bourne's Settlement Trusts*[18]:

'The phrase "raising portions" is a technical phrase of conveyancing. A more accurate way to express the intention of the legislature might possibly have been to use the phrase "for creating portions". ... It has been settled quite clearly that the phrase "raising portions" does not cover the case where all that is done is to treat the accumulations as, and deal with them as, an addition to capital. Indeed, if that were what the phrase meant, any accumulation for the benefit of children would have fallen within the exception. The authorities come to this: that accumulations do not fall within this language unless they are themselves, as separate items, used for the purpose of portions. This must not be merely by way of addition to a capital gift. ... Where the settlement ... merely gives a power to deal with the accumulations so that the result could be described as a portion, it does not, in my opinion, satisfy the section. You cannot predicate of the provision in the settlement that it is

---

14 Law of Property Act 1925, s 165. An express trust for accumulation for any other permitted period is not invalidated by reason of accumulations also having been made under such statutory power or the general law. See *Re Maber* [1928] Ch 88. As to 'minority', see the provisions of the Family Law Reform Act 1969, discussed above.

15 *Re Gardiner* [1901] 1 Ch 697; and see *Miller v IRC* [1987] STC 108. Income applied for life policy premiums to increase capital may be an accumulation, *Carver v Duncan* [1985] AC 1082 at 1099–1100 querying *Bassil v Lister* (1851) 9 Hare 177. Lord Templeman at 1122–1124 seems to suggest that the test to be applied is whether the income is directed to be applied on a capital, as opposed to an income, expense; if so, there is an accumulation. The modern approach is to consider payment of premiums as a purchase of a commercial investment that falls outside the Acts: see Law Commission Consultation Paper No 133, paras 3–34 to 3–36 and Law Commission Report No 251, paras 9.33 to 9.35 and p 208 post.

16 [1965] Ch 111, [1964] 2 All ER 177.

17 As to the meaning of 'portions', see *Re Elliott* [1918] 2 Ch 150; *Watt v Wood* (1862) 2 Drew & Sm 56 at 60.

18 [1946] 1 All ER 411. See also *Wildes v Davies* (1853) 1 Sm & G 475; *Bourne v Buckton* (1851) 2 Sim NS 91.

a provision for "raising portions" when whether it is so used depends entirely on the discretion of some third person, who may use it that way, or who may not.'

There is little doubt that the statutory restrictions on accumulation apply to an implied trust to accumulate as well as to an express one, but it is sometimes difficult in such cases to determine whether there really is an implied trust to accumulate or not. Thus two cases[19] previously relied upon in support of the proposition just stated were disapproved by the Court of Appeal in *Re Berkeley*[20], not because the proposition was held to be wrong but because the court considered that those two cases (in common with the case they were themselves considering) did not involve any trust to accumulate, implied or otherwise, within the ambit of s 164. The facts were that the surplus income of a trust fund had been accumulated by trustees of a will in fulfilment of their obligation to protect an annuitant by securing the payment of an annuity which, under the will, was a continuing charge on the income of the trust fund. The court held that this retention of income to meet a possible future income need did not amount to an '[accumulation] for [a] ... period' within s 164. The court's reasons for reaching this conclusion may shed some light on the meaning of accumulation itself. Harman LJ said:

'Is this an accumulation? I think not. Accumulation to my mind involves the addition of income to capital, thus increasing the estate in favour of those entitled to capital and against the interests of those entitled to income.'

This seems a narrow definition of accumulation which would render its meaning more restricted than has hitherto been supplied[1]. Widgery LJ, at least, preferred a wider definition. He said:

'I doubt if the word "accumulation" signifies more than a simple aggregation of instalments of income to create a single fund ... '

But he added, referring to the words used in s 164:

' ... but the reference to accumulation for a *period* clearly implies in my judgment, a mounting fund which reaches a climax at the end of the period.'

Russell LJ did not venture a definition of accumulation, but rested his judgment on the ground that the case involved only a de facto accumulation made necessary by the trustees' uncertainty as to the availability of assets of the estate, and this at any rate was not an accumulation for a period within the meaning of s 164.

The statutory restrictions have no application to provisions for the accumulation of sums available for distribution, but not in fact distributed, under a deed constituting a unit trust[2], whether because all the unit holders could end the trust (or even ask in any year for all the income to be distributed and not added to capital) or because the legislation did not have any application to commercial situations. This latter reason followed the reasoning in *Bassil v*

19 *Re Robb's Will Trusts* [1953] Ch 459, sub nom *Re Robb's Will Trusts, Marshall v Marshall* [1953] 1 All ER 920; *Re Nash* [1965] 1 All ER 51.
20 [1968] Ch 744, [1968] 3 All ER 364, CA.
1 It seems, for instance, that the 'accumulation' involved in *Re Rochford's Settlement Trusts* [1965] Ch 111, [1964] 2 All ER 177, might not fall within this definition.
2 *Re AEG Unit Trust (Manager) Ltd's Deed* [1957] Ch 415, [1957] 2 All ER 506.

Lister[3] where a testator's direction to his trustees to pay the premiums on a policy of life assurance he had taken out on the life of his son out of the income of his residuary estate was held not to be an accumulation. Statute provides that no person (which has been held to mean individuals and not corporations) may 'settle or dispose' of property in breach of the restrictions against accumulations and there are many commercial transactions or commercial investments which are not properly within those terms, eg partnership agreements involving accumulation of profits for long periods, life insurance policies on the lives of debtors, a settlement of insurance policies with shares transferred to pay the premiums out of the dividends, unit trusts that capitalise part of their income, investment trusts split into capital and income shares. Such transactions and provisions for making payments in respect of them should therefore fall outside the rule[4]. This should also be the case for pension scheme trusts[5] though normally they will be created by a company settlor so as to fall outside the legislation anyway[6].

Accumulations for the purpose of purchasing land

By an Act passed in 1892, and now repealed, and re-enacted in altered form in s 166 of the Law of Property Act 1925[7], the period allowed by the Thellusson Act is further restricted, where the accumulation is directed by an instrument coming into operation after the 27 June 1892 and is to be made either wholly or partially for the purchase of land only, to the minority or respective minorities[8] of any person or persons who, under the instrument directing the accumulations, 'would for the time being (if of full age) be entitled to receive the rents, issues, profits, or income so directed to be accumulated'.

Excessive accumulation

If an express or implied trust for accumulation infringes the perpetuity period allowed under the rule against remoteness it is wholly void[9]. If within the perpetuity period but exceeding the authorised accumulation periods, the trust is restricted to the nearest period of the six authorised periods and

---

3 (1851) 9 Hare 177 followed in *Re Vaughan* [1883] WN 89; *Re AEG Unit Trust (Managers) Ltd's Deed* [1957] Ch 415, [1957] 2 All ER 506, though cf comments in *Carver v Duncan* [1985] AC 1082 at 1100, 1122–1124.

4 Megarry & Wade, *Law of Real Property* (6th edn) para 7–177, Law Com Consultation Paper No 133 para 3.35. Similarly on expiry of the accumulation period the trustees, if authorised by the trust deed, could transfer investments to a company wholly owned by them which could retain the income from such investments and effectively accumulate it.

5 Hansard (HC) 1 July 1964 vol 697, cols, 1503–1504.

6 *Re Dodwell & Co Ltd's Trust* [1979] Ch 301, sub nom *Re Dodwell & Co Ltd's Trust Deed* [1978] 3 All ER 738, assuming the company is not acting merely as nominee for an individual.

7 But not where the accumulations are directed for the purchase of land and other purposes (*Re Knapp* [1929] 1 Ch 341).

8 As to 'minority', see the provisions of the Family Law Reform Act 1969, discussed on p 205, ante.

9 *Curtis v Lukin* (1842) 5 Beav 147; *Martin v Maugham* (1844) 14 Sim 230. The Perpetuities and Accumulations Act 1964 does not seem to provide for the wait and see rules to apply, which seems unsatisfactory, unless one can strain the language of s 3(3) to treat 'any power option or other right' as extending to powers and duties to accumulate: see Megarry and Wade, *Law of Real Property* (6th edn) para 7–162 and Law Com Consultation Paper No 133 para 3.23 and Law Com Report No 251, para 9.24.

only the excess is void[10]. The income for the excess period goes to the person or persons who would have been entitled to such income if accumulation had not been directed[11] eg the settlor of a lifetime trust or the person entitled to residue or undisposed of property in the case of a testamentary trust[12].

Paragraph 1(c)

Attempts to alter the rules of devolution prescribed by law

If there is a trust of real or personal property for A absolutely, but if he dies intestate then for B, the divesting gift over to B is void as an attempt to alter the ordinary law of devolution[13]. In short, any trust creating an *absolute* equitable interest in A, but attempting to negative the statutory devolution on intestacy or the power of testamentary disposition, or the right of committing waste, or of alienating or charging the estate (even where there is a condition subsequently purporting to create a forfeiture) is, qua such attempt, void[14].

Settlements against the policy of bankruptcy law

A trust, with a condition or proviso that the interest of the beneficiary shall not be liable to the claims of creditors, is void so far as the condition or proviso is concerned[15]. The beneficiary's conditional interest (whether absolute or for life) will vest in his trustee in bankruptcy for the benefit of his creditors regardless of the condition. Similarly a man cannot make a settlement of his own property[16] upon *himself* until bankruptcy, and then over[17], and this is so even in the case of an ante-nuptial settlement, where it might fairly be urged to be part of *the wife's* terms of the marriage bargain[18]. It is submitted, however, that a man might on marriage settle his own property on an immediate discretionary trust for himself, etc, during his life, as there would then be no alteration of the trust to take effect on bankruptcy.

On the other hand, a trust created by a third party, to pay the income to A

10 *Re Watt's Will Trusts* [1936] 2 All ER 1555 at 1562; *Re Ransome* [1957] Ch 348 at 361.
11 Law of Property Act 1925, s 164(1). However, where there is a general charitable intention expressed with regard to the income it will be devoted to charity cy-près: *Re Bradwell* [1952] Ch 575, [1952] 2 All ER 286.
12 If the residue is held on trust for A for life, remainder to B it seems the excess income should be paid to A: *Re Hawkins* [1916] 2 Ch 570; *Re Garside* [1919] 1 Ch 132.
13 *Gulliver v Vaux* (1746) 8 De GM & G 167n; *Holmes v Godson* (1856) 8 De GM & G 152; *Barton v Barton* (1857) 3 K & J 512; *Re Wilcock's Settlement* (1875) 1 Ch D 229; *Re Dixon* [1903] 2 Ch 458; *Krasner v Dennison* [2001] Ch 76, CA. See also *Re Ashton* [1920] 2 Ch 481 (gift over if donee should die non compos held void).
14 Co Litt 222 b; *Portington's Case* (1613) 10 Co Rep 35b, 39 a; *Shaw v Ford* (1877) 7 Ch D 669; *Re Dugdale* (1888) 38 Ch D 176; *Braithwaite v A-G* [1909] 1 Ch 510; and see also *Carr v Living* (1860) 28 Beav 644; *Re Brown* [1954] Ch 39 and *Re Dixon* [1903] 2 Ch 458.
15 For example, see *Younghusband v Gisborne* (1844) 1 Coll 400; affd (1846) 15 LJ Ch 355; *Green v Spicer* (1830) 1 Russ & M 395; *Graves v Dolphin* (1826) 1 Sim 66; *Piercy v Roberts* (1832) 1 My & K 4; *Snowdon v Dales* (1834) 6 Sim 524; *Re Sanderson's Trust* (1857) 3 K & J 497.
16 *Re Holland* [1902] 2 Ch 360, overruling *Re Pearson* (1876) 3 Ch D 807; *Re Ashby* [1892] 1 QB 872.
17 *Knight v Browne* (1861) 7 Jur NS 894; *Brooke v Pearson* (1859) 27 Beav 181; *Re Burroughs-Fowler* [1916] 2 Ch 251; *Re Wombwell* (1921) 125 LT 437.
18 *Higinbotham v Holme* (1812) 19 Ves 88; *Ex p Hodgson* (1812) 19 Ves 206; *Re Pearson* (1876) 3 Ch D 807; but consider *Re Detmold* (1889) 40 Ch D 585, and *Re Johnson* [1904] 1 KB 134.

until he dies or becomes bankrupt or alienates or charges his life interest, and then over to B, is perfectly good[19], and may even take effect in respect of bankruptcy or alienation preceding the settlement[20]. The distinction between this valid determinable interest and the void conditional interest is that the determinable limitation is allowed since the limitation merely sets a natural limit to the interest whilst a condition or proviso cuts down the interest before it reaches its natural limit[1].

A trust creating a determinable life interest determining naturally upon bankruptcy or alienation (giving what is known as 'a protected life interest') is equally good where the trustee is, upon bankruptcy of or alienation by the beneficiary, given a discretion to apply the income for the benefit or maintenance of the bankrupt or his wife or issue[2], or any other indicated persons, *or any of them.* Such trusts are now so common that the Trustee Act 1925, in s 33, contains the following provisions intended to shorten wills and settlements by substituting a reference to 'protective trusts' for the rather lengthy clause formerly employed[3].

> (1) Where any income, including an annuity or other periodical income payment, is directed to be held on protective trusts for the benefit of any person[4] (in this section called 'the principal beneficiary') for the period of his life or for any less period, then, during that period[5] (in this section called the 'trust period') the said income shall, without prejudice to any prior interest, be held on the following trusts, namely:
> (i) Upon trust for the principal beneficiary during the trust period or until he, whether before or after the termination of any prior interest, does or attempts to do[6] or suffers any act or thing, or until any event happens, other than an

---

19 *Billson v Crofts* (1873) LR 15 Eq 314; *Re Aylwin's Trusts* (1873) LR 16 Eq 585, and cases there cited; and as to income accrued before forfeiture but not paid over, see *Re Jenkins* [1915] 1 Ch 46. Such a clause will be strictly construed; see *Re Longman* [1955] 1 All ER 455, [1955] 1 WLR 197 (gift over on an act whereby income vested in another; authority to pay dividends to creditors held not to cause a forfeiture because no dividend declared).

20 *West v Williams* [1898] 1 Ch 488; *Re Walker* [1939] Ch 974, [1939] 3 All ER 902.

1 *Brandon v Robinson* (1811) 18 Ves 429; *Rochford v Hackman* (1852) 9 Hare 475; Megarry and Wade, *Law of Real Property* (6th edn) pp 64–70

2 Note that by virtue of s 15 of the Family Law Reform Act, references in disposition made on or after 1 January 1970, to the child or children of any person, or to a person or persons related in some other manner to any person, are in certain circumstances to be construed as including references to illegitimate children and persons related through illegitimacy.

3 The effect is to engraft trusts on the life interest so that if the life interest is extinguished (eg by order of the divorce court) the engrafted trusts are extinguished also (*Re Allsopp's Marriage Settlement Trusts* [1959] Ch 81, [1958] 2 All ER 393). In *General Accident Fire and Life Assurance Corpn Ltd v IRC* [1963] 3 All ER 259, the Court of Appeal held that an order of the court under s 192 of the Supreme Court of Judicature (Consolidation) Act 1925 (now s 24 of the Matrimonial Causes Act 1973) to pay an annual sum of money during the wife's life did not bring about a forfeiture of the husband's protected life interest under s 33 of the Trustee Act 1925, and accordingly the discretionary trusts under s 33(1) did not arise. This was because the court order overrode the settlement trusts, was an event to which both life tenant and trustee had to bow, and was not such an event as was contemplated by s 33(1), this being intended as a protection to spendthrift or improvident or weak-minded life tenants.

4 Natural persons, not companies: *IRC v Brandenburg* [1982] STC 555.

5 *Cholmondeley v IRC* [1986] STC 384.

6 He need have no responsibility for this event unlike the position on a proper construction of some express trusts: *Re Hall* [1944] Ch 46, [1943] 2 All ER 753; *Re Pozot's Settlement Trust* [1952] Ch 427, [1952] 1 All ER 1107, CA.

advance under any statutory or express powers[7], whereby, if the said income were payable during the trust period to the principal beneficiary absolutely during that period, he would be deprived of the right to receive the same or any part thereof, in any of which cases, as well as on the termination of the trust period, whichever first happens, this trust of the said income shall fail or determine[8],

(ii) If the trust aforesaid fails or determines during the subsistence of the trust period, then, during the residue of that period, the said income shall be held upon trust for the application[9] thereof for the maintenance or support, or otherwise for the benefit, of all or any one or more exclusively[10] of the other or others of the following persons (that is to say)

(a) the principal beneficiary and his or her wife or husband, if any, and his or her children or more remote issue[11], if any; or

(b) if there is no wife or husband or issue of the principal beneficiary[12] in existence, the principal beneficiary and the persons who would, if he were actually dead, be entitled to the trust property or the income thereof or to the annuity fund, if any, or arrears of the annuity, as the case may be[13], as the trustees in their absolute discretion, without being

---

7 *Re Hodgson* [1913] 1 Ch 34; *Re Rees* [1954] Ch 202, sub nom *Re Rees' Will Trusts, Lloyds Bank Ltd v Rees* [1954] 1 All ER 7. A court order that the principal beneficiary shall charge his interest will create an equitable charge, and thus work a forfeiture, even though no deed of charge is executed (*Re Richardson's Will Trusts* [1958] Ch 504, [1958] 1 All ER 538). See also *Edmonds v Edmonds* [1965] 1 All ER 379n (attachment of earnings order to secure former wife's maintenance held to cause forfeiture).

8 Where the corpus becomes vested in the same person who has a protected life estate there is no merger: *Re Chance's Settlement Trusts* [1918] WN 34. Whether on the true construction of this sub-clause the principal beneficiary would on bankruptcy forfeit his interest absolutely so as to bring the discretionary trust into force, or whether if the bankruptcy was annulled or suspended under a compromise his interest would be restored does not seem very clear (see *Re Clark* [1926] Ch 833, and *Re Forder* [1927] 2 Ch 291). It is settled, however, that an order to discharge has no effect on the previous forfeiture: *Re Walker* [1939] Ch 974, [1939] 3 All ER 902.

9 The trustees must apply all income for the benefit of the persons mentioned under (a) and (b): *Re Gourju's Will Trusts* [1943] Ch 24, [1942] 2 All ER 605. If any income remains in the trustees' hands at the death of the first beneficiary it must be so applied thereafter: *Re Forster's Settlement* [1942] Ch 199, [1942] 1 All ER 180. All sums paid out of income in exercise of the trustees' discretion form part of the total income of the recipient for tax purposes (*Lindus and Hortin v IRC* (1933) 17 TC 442).

10 The donee of a power of appointment may sometimes wish to exercise it by giving a protected life interest to a beneficiary, but, with the possibility of a discretionary trust arising thereunder, this will only be effective if the power is construed as wide enough to permit the creation of new dispositive discretionary powers. Nineteenth-century powers of appointment in their context were construed narrowly but in more modern contexts the courts have too unquestioningly followed old case law (like *Re Joicey* [1915] 2 Ch 115, CA): see *Re Boulton's Settlement Trust* [1928] Ch 703; *Re Morris' Settlement Trusts* [1951] 2 All ER 528, CA. The latter case was followed, but reluctantly, in *Re Hunter's Will Trusts* [1963] Ch 372, [1962] 3 All ER 1050. Further see p 723 and Art 82, post.

11 The Family Law Reform Act 1969, s 15(3), provides that in relation to any disposition made after the coming into force of the section (on 1 January 1970) this reference to 'children or more remote issue' is to be construed as including a reference to any illegitimate child of the principal beneficiary and to anyone who would rank as such issue if he, or some other person through whom he is descended from the principal beneficiary, had been born legitimate.

12 See preceding note.

13 This sub-clause is not very lucid as it might very well happen that it would be impossible to determine who would be entitled at the death of the principal beneficiary. It has, therefore, been suggested that in using the statutory words 'on protective trusts' it might be wise to add the following words, viz: 'In the event of its being impossible to ascertain with certainty who would be entitled to the trust property or the income thereof or to the annuity fund, if any, or arrears of the annuity as the case may be, the income shall be held in trust for any relations of the principal beneficiary who would be entitled to his personal estate if he were then dead intestate under the provisions of the Administration of Estates Act 1925.' See 'relations' thus

liable to account for the exercise of such direction, think fit.

(2) This section does not apply to trusts coming into operation before the commencement of this Act, and has effect subject to any variation of the implied trusts aforesaid contained in the instrument creating the trust.

(3) Nothing in this section operates to validate any trust which would, if contained in the instrument creating the trust, be liable to be set aside.

A danger signal, however, appears in sub-s (3), from which it will be perceived that the pre-existing law is preserved as to the invalidity of such trusts; so that *where the settlor himself* is to take the income until some of the events mentioned in sub-s (1)(i) happen, then if the event which actually happens is bankruptcy, the income during the rest of his life will go to his creditors.

So far as the authorities go, however, such trusts are not invalid where the event which works a forfeiture is alienation or charge, whether it be voluntary by assignment, either legal or equitable[14], or mortgage of the settlor's defeasible life interest, or involuntary as by reason of a judicial charge created by a judgment or an order for the appointment of a receiver by way of equitable execution[15]. And, moreover, in such cases the *subsequent* bank-

---

defined in *Re Bridgen* [1938] Ch 205, [1937] 4 All ER 342. But note that in regard to deaths intestate on or after 1 January 1970, the Administration of Estates Act 1925 is amended so as to confer certain rights upon illegitimate persons: Family Law Reform Act 1969, s 14. See also s 15.

14 *Re Gillott's Settlement* [1934] Ch 97; *Re Haynes Will Trusts* [1949] Ch 5, [1948] 2 All ER 423.

15 *Re Detmold* (1889) 40 Ch D 585; *Re Johnson* [1904] 1 KB 134; *Re Perkin's Settlement Trusts* [1912] WN 99; and *Re Balfour's Settlement* [1938] Ch 928, [1938] 3 All ER 259. As to what constitutes a forfeiture under such trusts, see *Re Potts* [1893] 1 QB 648 at 661; *Re Beaumont* (1910) 79 LJ Ch 744; *Re Mair* [1909] 2 Ch 280 (no forfeiture where under the Trustee Act 1925, s 57, the court authorised capital moneys to be raised to enable the principal beneficiary to pay certain pressing liabilities since all settlements are subject to the overriding s 57); *General Accident Fire and Life Assurance Corpn Ltd v IRC* [1963] 3 All ER 259, [1963] 1 WLR 1207 (no forfeiture where under, what is now, the Matrimonial Causes Act 1973, s 24, the court orders income to be diverted from the husband to the wife, all settlements being subject to such overriding powers); *Re Swannell* (1909) 101 LT 76; *Re Williams* [1912] 1 Ch 399; and *Re Smith* [1916] 1 Ch 369, distinguished in *Re Forder* [1927] 2 Ch 291, CA; *Re Baring's Settlement Trusts* [1940] Ch 737, [1940] 3 All ER 20; *Re Dennis's Settlement Trusts* [1942] Ch 283, [1942] 1 All ER 520; *Re Haynes Will Trusts* [1949] Ch 5, [1948] 2 All ER 423; and *Re Richardson's Will Trusts* [1958] Ch 504, [1958] 1 All ER 538.

A forfeiture has also been held to take place if the principal beneficiary becomes an enemy for the purposes of the Trading with the Enemy Act 1939 (*Re Gourju's Will Trusts* [1943] Ch 24, [1942] 2 All ER 605; *Re Wittke* [1944] Ch 166, [1944] 1 All ER 383); but contrast *Re Hall* [1944] Ch 46, [1943] 2 All ER 753, and *Re Harris* [1945] Ch 316, [1945] 1 All ER 702, where the protective trusts were not in the statutory form, and it was held that no forfeiture was incurred by becoming an alien enemy; and *Re Pozot's Settlement Trusts* [1952] Ch 427, [1952] 1 All ER 1107, CA, where, again the trusts were not in the statutory form and it was held that there was no forfeiture because although the income was payable to the Custodian of Enemy Property the beneficiary's proprietary right to a life interest had not vested in the Custodian.

The appointment of a receiver in lunacy is not, of itself, sufficient to bring discretionary trusts into operation (*Re Marshall* [1920] 1 Ch 284; nor does charge of a lunacy percentage under the Lunacy Act 1890, s 148(3)). (NB The Lunacy Act 1890 has been repealed. Currently the Mental Health Act 1983, is applicable.) In any event such a charge is not such an incumbrance as is contemplated by the normal forfeiture clause (*Re Westby's Settlement* [1950] Ch 296, [1950] 1 All ER 479, CA, overruling *Re Custance's Settlements* [1946] Ch 42, [1945] 2 All ER 441). The fees payable to the percentage account are, analogous to the remuneration payable to an agent (*Re Westby's Settlements*, above) an arrangement for payment whereof will not lead to a forfeiture (*Re Tancred's Settlement; Re Selby* [1903] 1 Ch 715). Where trustees were directed to pay income to the principal beneficiary 'so long as he shall be able to give a personal discharge therefore' it was held that the appointment of a receiver in lunacy did not work a forfeiture, since the beneficiary could give a personal discharge through the receiver who was his statutory agent (*Re Oppenheim's Will Trust* [1950] Ch 633, [1950] 2 All ER 86).

ruptcy of the settlor will not invalidate the gift over which has already happened.

Another point that not infrequently arises is whether, under a discretionary trust (such as the statutory trust above set forth) *where the settlor is a third party*, and the defeasible life interest has been forfeited either by bankruptcy or alienation (voluntary or involuntary), the trustees can, *under the discretion* vested in them, continue to pay the income to the person whose life interest has determined. Obviously the object of such trusts is to enable this to be done if it can be. The authorities are, however, against the right of the trustees to do this[16], on the ground apparently that the life tenant, being bound to hand over to his creditor or assignee whatever his interest in the income may be, is none the less bound with regard to such part of the income as may be paid to him by the trustees in the exercise of their discretion; and that they, having notice of this equity, are equally bound not to pay him. This may seem to be a reductio and absurdum, since the trustees could not under any circumstances pay any part of the income to the creditor or assignee[17], so that it is difficult to see how the latter could suffer by the payment being made to the life tenant himself, or what claim he could have upon the trustees. Nevertheless, trustees under such circumstances have been made liable to the creditor or assignee[18], although, curiously enough, it is well settled that they are at liberty to *expend* the income for his benefit[19]. In one case it was held that the trustees might apply such part as they thought fit of the income for the benefit of the person whose life interest had determined without reference to any debt which such person might owe to the trust estate[20]. This case is distinct from that which has been more frequently before the courts where the contest is between the tenant of a protected life interest and his own assignee. The law is, therefore, in an anomalous and unsatisfactory state; and it is not considered that it has been in any way altered by the introduction by s 33 of the Trustee Act 1925 of the statutory 'protective trusts'. However, it seems that trustees can properly pay directly to a bankrupt discretionary beneficiary the basic amount necessary for supporting himself, his wife and his family. Indeed, if he has a wife she can be paid money as a discretionary beneficiary and she is free to use it for benefiting her husband and family, while expenses (eg of schooling children) can be paid directly to the creditor.

It need scarcely be said that, until they have notice of an act amounting to forfeiture, the trustees are justified in paying the income to the principal beneficiary[1]. Indeed, where forfeiture occurs on bankruptcy, now that the bankrupt's property does not vest retrospectively in the trustee in bankruptcy

---

16 *Re Coleman* (1888) 39 Ch D 443; *Re Neil* (1890) 62 LT 649, explained by Stirling LJ in *Re Fitzgerald* [1904] 1 Ch 573 at 593.

17 *Re Bullock* (1891) 64 LT 736; *Train v Clapperton* [1908] AC 342, HL; *Re Laye* [1913] 1 Ch 298; *Re Hamilton* (1921) 124 LT 737, CA. But cf *Lord v Bunn* (1843) 2 Y & C Ch Cas 98; which seems contra at first sight, but really turned on a question of construction.

18 *Re Coleman* (1888) 39 Ch D 443; *Re Neil* (1890) 62 LT 649, explained by Stirling LJ in *Re Fitzgerald* [1904] 1 Ch 573 at 593.

19 *Re Bullock* (1891) 64 LT 736; and cf *Re Coleman* (1888) 39 Ch D 443; and *Re Neil* (1890) 62 LT 649. But see *Re Ashby* [1892] 1 QB 872, where Vaughan Williams J thought that the bankrupt might be liable to account for sums paid to him, though, perhaps, just for the surplus above that needed for his mere support. See also *Re Allen-Meyrick's Will Trusts* [1966] 1 All ER 740 at 743.

20 *Re Eiser's Will Trusts* [1937] 1 All ER 244.

1 *Re Long* [1901] WN 166.

on the first available act of bankruptcy, it seems the trustees can pay the principal beneficiary until the bankruptcy order is made[2].

Upon forfeiture no apportionment of income occurs under the Apportionment Act 1870[3].

If a protected life tenant overlooks the forfeiture of his interest when surrendering his life interest in favour of the remaindermen, so that he believes that he has thereby vested the entire beneficial interest in both capital and income in the remaindermen to the exclusion of everyone else, he may have the court set aside the surrender by reason of his mistake[4].

Express and implied protective trusts

Protective trusts in the statutory form may be created by any words evincing a clear enough intention, eg 'upon protective trusts for the benefit of my sister'[5] or to B 'for a protective life interest'[6]. However, s 33 applies only where there is a human being and not a company as the principal beneficiary[7].

The statutory form may be expressly varied. The trustees may be given power to waive and determine the protective trust so that the beneficiary takes a full life interest[8]. Express provision may be made to enable the protected life tenant if he obtains the written approval of the trustees to enter into arrangements with the other settlement beneficiaries for dividing up the trust funds or otherwise re-arranging the beneficial interests as if he had an absolute life interest[9]. In the case of youthful indiscretions it may be advantageous to have a settlement contain a series of protective trusts, eg one set till B is 25, another from 25 to 35, another from 35 to 50 and another for the rest of B's life[10].

PARAGRAPH 1(D)

Restraint on alienation

Trusts designed to prevent the barring of entails, or imposing restrictions on the alienation of property *which has once been given absolutely* to the beneficiary are contrary to the policy of the law, and are therefore void[11], and the former

---

2 See Insolvency Act 1986, s 306.
3 *Re Gourju's Will Trust* [1943] Ch 24, [1942] 2 All ER 605.
4 *Gibbon v Mitchell* [1990] 3 All ER 338, [1990] 1 WLR 1304.
5 *Re Wittke* [1944] Ch 166, [1944] 1 All ER 383.
6 *Re Platt* (1969) unreported Current Law consolidation 10917.
7 *IRC v Brandenburg* [1982] STC 555 at 565, 569.
8 *Re Gordon's Will Trusts* [1977] Ch 27, [1976] 2 All ER 577.
9 This can avoid the need for an application under Variation of Trusts Act 1958.
10 (1958) 74 LQR 184 (RE Megarry).
11 *Floyer v Bankes* (1869) LR 8 Eq 115; *Sykes v Sykes* (1871) LR 13 Eq 56; and as to alienation *Snowdon v Dales* (1834) 6 Sim 524; *Green v Spicer* (1830) 1 Russ & M 395; *Graves v Dolphin* (1826) 1 Sim 66; *Brandon v Robinson* (1811) 18 Ves 429; *Ware v Cann* (1830) 10 B & C 433; *Hood v Oglander* (1865) 34 Beav 513; *Re Dugdale* (1888) 38 Ch D 176; *Re Cockerill* [1929] 2 Ch 131; *Re Elliot* [1896] 2 Ch 353; *Re Brown* [1954] Ch 39, [1953] 2 All ER 1342. A contract or covenant against alienation is valid since breach gives rise to a claim for damages and not to forfeiture of the property interest: *Caldy Manor Estate Ltd v Farrell* [1974] 3 All ER 753, [1974] 1 WLR 1303, CA. Since an absolute equitable interest cannot be inalienable, the Finance Act 1978, s 54, concerned with trustees holding company shares on trust absolutely for company employees, had to resort to the contract device to give effect to the government's scheme to benefit employees.

exception to this rule in the case of trusts limiting the power of married women to alienate their separate property *during coverture* has been abolished by statute[12]. It has, however, been held by the Court of Appeal that a restraint on alienation may be good even in the case of a man, if under the proper law of the trust such restraints are allowed[13]. And, of course, a trust creating a determinable interest for a person *until* he attempts to alienate, and then a gift over in favour of someone else, is good[14]. Even in the case of conditional interests, however, some partial restraint on alienation is possible[15].

PARAGRAPH 1(E)

Trust terms ousting the jurisdiction of the courts

Except as provided by statute (eg under the Arbitration Act 1996) no-one can exclude the jurisdiction of the courts upon questions of law as opposed to questions of fact. It is contrary to public policy to attempt to oust the court's jurisdiction to construe and control the construction and administration of a trust or a deceased's estate, while it is also repugnant to the actual rights conferred by a deed or a will (as would be determined by the court) to permit some third party to determine that the rights are such different rights as he or she considers them to be[16].

Trustees may be allowed to be the final arbiter on questions of fact, but the court has a residual part to play if the decision on fact is open to challenge on the ground of fraud or of being a perverse decision that no reasonable trustees would have reached unless ignoring a relevant factor or factors or taking account of an irrelevant factor or factors[17]. However, if the factual circumstances involve conceptual uncertainty that the court itself cannot resolve (eg the meaning of 'friend' or 'persons who have helped me' or 'persons who have a moral claim to share in my estate'), then the trustees cannot be allowed to exercise their fiduciary function to resolve the issue, because if such resolution is challenged the court has no justiciable criteria to enable it to adjudicate upon the matter[18]. Exceptionally, it seems, some third party, like the settlor-testator's widow or eldest child, may be given a personal, as opposed to a fiduciary, power to determine whether or not any particular

---

12 Married Women (Restraint upon Anticipation) Act 1949, whereby every restraint upon anticipation, whenever imposed, has ceased to have effect. Previously by the Law Reform (Married Women and Tortfeasors) Act 1935 restraints upon anticipation imposed by a statute or instrument passed or executed on or after 1 January 1936, had been declared void. On the construction of the 1935 Act, see *Re Heath's Will Trusts* [1949] Ch 170, [1949] 1 All ER 199.

13 *Re Fitzgerald* [1904] 1 Ch 573 (Scots law); *Trustees Executors and Agency Co Ltd v Margottini* [1960] VR 417. If the trust consists of immovables the lex situs will govern the matter.

14 *Re Detmold* (1889) 40 Ch D 585.

15 *Re Macleay* (1875) LR 20 Eq 186, distinguished in *Re Brown* [1954] Ch 39, [1953] 2 All ER 1342.

16 *Re Wynn's Will Trusts* [1952] Ch 271 (trustees cannot conclusively determine what moneys are to be capital and what are to be income, although they can have power to pay moneys to X whether the moneys happen to be income or capital); *Re Raven* [1915] 1 Ch 673; *Jones v Shipping Federation of British Columbia* (1963) 37 DLR (2d) 273.

17 *Dundee General Hospitals Board v Bell's Trustees* [1952] 1 All ER 896, HL (valid legacy to an Infirmary if my trustees [one of whom was Treasurer of the Infirmary] shall be satisfied that the Infirmary has not been taken over or otherwise placed under the control of the State); *The Glacier Bay* [1996] 1 Lloyd's Rep IR 201, CA; *Brown v GIO Insurance Ltd* [1998] Lloyd's Rep IR 201, CA.

18 *Re Wright's Will Trusts* [1981] LS Gaz R 841; *Re Coxen* [1948] Ch 747; *Re Jones* [1953] Ch 125.

individual was a 'friend' of the testator, such determination to be unchallengeable unless such individual could not possibly fall within the black core meaning of 'friend' nor the grey surrounding penumbra of meaning[19]. It would seem to follow that if a widow can resolve such issues by virtue of a personal power, then it should be open to a settlor-testator expressly to make this particular aspect of the functions of a trustee or executor subject only to a personal, as opposed to a fiduciary, obligation, so that a valid adjudication can be made.

Furthermore, if the trust instrument refers to the final and conclusive judgment of an independent expert an issue of fact which necessarily involves a solution of a question of construction, the expert's decision will be final and conclusive, so long as he did not address himself to the wrong question[20]. This explains why the Chief Rabbi can validly determine whether or not beneficiaries are of the Jewish faith[1].

If a settlement simply contains a clause that no breaches of trust actions are to be taken against the trustees without first resorting to arbitration under the Arbitration Act 1996, there is the problem that this does not amount to an arbitration agreement or contract within the Arbitration Act 1996[2]. A trust is not a contract but a unilateral transfer of assets to a person prepared to accept the office of trustee with the benefits and burdens attached to such office, one benefit being that the trustee can debit the trust fund with the expenses and costs of properly acting as trustee: it is not a contract between the settlor and the trustee that enables the trustee (or a successor-trustee) to debit the trust for the cost of trusteeship services.

However, it would seem that if a settlor, on behalf of himself and the beneficiaries deriving their interests through him, expressly contracts in the trust instrument with the trustee, on behalf of itself and its successors in title, that in consideration of undertaking the office of trustee (for the benefit of the settlor, the beneficiaries and itself) any breach of trust claim against the trustees shall be referred to arbitration by an arbitrator appointed by the Chair of the Chancery Bar Association or, failing such, by the Chair of the Bar Council, then this should amount to an arbitration agreement or contract. By taking the benefit of the trust deed the beneficiaries and trustee all become parties to the arbitration agreement and bound by it[3].

Trust terms operating to prevent beneficiaries applying to the courts

An *in terrorem* condition in a will or a trust to induce a legatee or beneficiary not to contest the will or trust on pain of forfeiting his interest in pure personalty will be ineffective, but a similar condition which expressly provides for the interest to pass or accrue to another person if the will or trust is contested is valid where the contest is unsuccessful and the will or trust is

---

19 *Re Coates* [1955] Ch 495; *Re Gibbard* [1966] 1 All ER 273; and p 90 ante. There should be no difference between a trust 'for my friends, providing that my widow's opinion as to who is such a friend shall be final and conclusive' and a trust 'for such persons as my widow considers to be my friends'.

20 *The Glacier Bay* [1996] 1 Lloyd's Rep 370 at 377–378.

1 *Re Tuck's Settlement Trusts* [1978] Ch 49 where Lord Denning's reasoning is unorthodox.

2 Although see L Cohen and M Staff in [1999] JTCP 203, 217–220.

3 Arbitration Act 1996, s 82(2).

upheld[4]. An essential attribute of property is the right to go to court to vindicate and protect such property so that such right cannot be ousted directly or indirectly[5]. A gift on trust for B until he brings court proceedings concerning the trust other than for the bona fide vindication and protection of his rights under the trust, and then over to others, should clearly be valid by analogy with determinable interests under protective trusts. Thus, where it is feared that a settlor's children may dispute his settlement once he dies, so that they can claim more under forced heirship rules or his will, their interests as discretionary beneficiaries can be made to determine, so as to improve the position of the remaining beneficiaries, if they bring any court proceedings in respect of the trust other than bona fide to assert their rights as beneficiaries thereunder to have the trust fund duly administered and distributed. If a disputant beneficiary subsequently repents before his case is heard or there is a subsequent family reconciliation, it will be helpful if the trust instrument confers a power on the trustees or another person (eg a protector) to add such automatically excluded person back into the class of beneficiaries.

It is, of course, possible for the trustee or a third party to have power to delete beneficiaries from the class of beneficiaries, so that such exclusion is not automatic upon certain events occurring but left to the discretion of the holder of the exclusionary power. However, a court may take the view that if trustees exercise this power against a beneficiary who has instituted legal proceedings, then this power has been exercised in breach of fiduciary duty so as to benefit and protect the trustees or the exercise amounts to a contempt of court as punishing the beneficiary for applying to the court[6]. On the other hand, if the settlor's letter of wishes clearly indicates that upon a son seeking to prefer his own interest via a forced heirship or other claim in preference to the settlor's broader family interests for successive generations, the settlor wants the trustees to exclude such son from being a beneficiary under the trustees' power in that behalf, then an experienced Chancery judge should uphold the trustees' actions and not consider them as any possible contempt of court, the son's defeasible interest only continuing until being properly defeated at the time anticipated and intended by the settlor.

PARAGRAPH 1(F)

Trusts for future illegitimate children

Since the Family Law Reform Act 1969 came into force on 1 January 1970 not only are dispositions in favour of existing 'en ventre sa mere' illegitimate children valid but also dispositions in favour of future illegitimate children.

---

4 *Re Nathan* [2002] WTLR 1061; *Evanturel v Evanturel* (1874) LR 6 PC 1, 29, PC, endorsing *Cooke v Turner* (1846) 15 M & W 727; and for related conditions against marriage see *Leong v Lim Beng Chye* [1955] AC 648, PC; *Re Whiting's Settlement* [1905] 1 Ch 96.

5 *Adams v Adams* [1892] 1 Ch 369, CA (properties left on trust to pay annuities thereout but if annuitant intermeddled or interfered with the trustees' management of the properties the annuity was to cease, so that a groundless frivolous action for appointing receiver in place of trustees caused loss of annuity, although seeking the protection of the court to vindicate and enforce rights would not cause such loss).

6 As in the *Lemos v Coutts & Co (Cayman) Ltd* litigation, some reported [1992–93] CILR 460.

Section 15(7) in fact provides that as respects such dispositions[7] 'any rule of law that a disposition in favour of illegitimate children not in being when the disposition takes effect is void as contrary to public policy' is abolished. Not only is the rule abolished but, broadly, whenever there is a reference in such dispositions to beneficiaries who are described by their relationship to another person, the reference (in the absence of contrary intention) is deemed to include a reference to beneficiaries who are so related through illegitimacy[8]. Section 15(7) has now been repealed and replaced by s 19 of the Family Law Reform Act 1987 which replaces the concept of the illegitimate child with that of the child of unmarried parents.

Trusts on separation of spouses

A trust to take effect upon the future separation of a husband and wife is void, as being contrary to public morals[9]; but a trust in reference to an immediate separation, *already agreed upon*, is good and enforceable[10]. If, however, the separation does not in fact take place, the trust becomes wholly void[11].

On the other hand, a trust in favour of a wife so long only as she shall cohabit with her husband, and on the cesser of such cohabitation a gift over to the husband, has been held valid[12]. Similarly a trust in favour of a deserted wife so long only as she shall be separated from her husband is good[13]. It has been pointed out[14] that 'only in a case where there is still a generally accepted moral code can the court refuse to enforce rights in such a way as to offend that generally accepted code'.

Miscellaneous trusts contrary to public policy

Case law indicates that the following trusts are void as against public policy (quite apart from problems concerning the beneficiary principle): trusts to provide for payment of fines of convicted poachers[15], to procure a peerage[16], to block up a house for 20 years[17], to provide a school for pickpockets or prostitutes[18], to place money to the credit of a company to create a false picture in case of enquiries of the bankers by persons about to do business with the company[19], to provide B with property only if he becomes destitute, so encouraging irresponsibility with money[20].

---

7 A disposition made by will is made on the date of execution of the will even though it cannot, of course, take effect till death: see s 15(8) of the 1969 Act.
8 Also see Family Law Reform Act 1987, s 1.
9 *Westmeath v Westmeath* (1831) 1 Dow & Cl 519, HL; *Re Moore* (1888) 39 Ch D 116, CA.
10 *Wilson v Wilson* (1848) 1 HL Cas 538; on appeal (1854) 5 HL Cas 40; *Vansittart v Vansittart* (1858) 2 De G & J 249; *Jodrell v Jodrell* (1845) 9 Beav 45; and see *Jodrell v Jodrell* (1851) 14 Beav 397, and *Egerton v Egerton* [1949] 2 All ER 238 at 242.
11 *Bindley v Mulloney* (1869) LR 7 Eq 343.
12 *Re Hope-Johnstone* [1904] 1 Ch 470, where the earlier cases are elaborately reviewed.
13 *Re Charleton* [1911] WN 54; *Re Lovell* [1920] 1 Ch 122 (will leaving annuity to deceased testator's mistress, W, living apart from H 'so long as she shall not return to live with H or remarry' upheld).
14 *Stephens v Avery* [1988] 2 All ER 477 at 481 per Browne-Wilkinson V-C.
15 *Thrupp v Collett* (1858) 26 Beav 125.
16 *Earl of Kingston v Lady Elizabeth Pierepont* (1681) 1 Vern 5.
17 *Brown v Burdett* (1882) 21 Ch D 667.
18 *Re Pinion* [1965] Ch 85, [1964] 1 All ER 890, CA.
19 *Re Great Berlin Steamboat Co* (1884) 26 Ch D 616, CA.
20 *Re Hepplewhite's Will Trusts* (1977) Times, 21 January.

However, if a trust term is designed to induce a separation of husband and wife it will be void, eg if providing a large amount of income for W upon separation, divorce or H's death but only a tiny amount whilst W lives with H[1]. The effect of finding the term void will depend upon whether the term is treated as a condition precedent or condition subsequent[2].

<small>PARAGRAPH 1(G)</small>

Human Rights Act 1998

By virtue of Article 8 of the Convention for the Protection of Human Rights and Fundamental Freedoms:

'1. Everyone has the right to respect for his private life and family life, his home and his correspondence.
2. There shall be no interference by a public authority with the exercise of this right except such as is in accordance with the law and is necessary in a democratic society in the interests of national security, public safety or the economic well-being of the country, for the prevention of disorder or crime, for the protection of health or morals, or for the protection of the rights and freedoms of others.'

By Article 9:

'1. Everyone has the right to freedom of thought, conscience and religion; this right includes freedom to change his religion or belief and freedom ... to manifest his religion or belief in worship, teaching, practice and observance.
2. Freedom to manifest one's religion or beliefs shall be subject only to such limitations as are prescribed by law and are necessary in a democratic society in the interests of public safety, for the protection of public order, health or morals, or for the protection of the rights and freedoms of others.'

Article 14, then incidentally provides:

'The enjoyment of the rights [as in Article 8] and freedoms as set forth in this Convention shall be secured without discrimination on any ground such as sex, race, colour, language, religion, political or other opinion, national or social origin, association with a national minority, property, birth or other status.'

Article 1 of Protocol No 1 (20 March 1952) provides:

'Every natural or legal person is entitled to the peaceful enjoyment of his possessions. No one shall be deprived of his possessions except in the public interest and subject to the conditions provided for by law and the general principles of international law.'

The Human Rights Act 1998 came into force on 22 October 2000 making it[3] 'unlawful for a public authority to act in a way which is incompatible with a Convention right', but trustees of private trusts[4] (including the Public Trustee) are not public authorities, although a court is a public authority[5] so that in interpreting trust terminology it will favour an interpretation that

---

1 *Re Johnson's Will Trusts* [1967] Ch 387, [1967] 1 All ER 553; *Re Caborne* [1943] Ch 224, [1943] 2 All ER 7; *Wilkinson v Wilkinson* (1871) LR 12 Eq 604.
2 See note 13, p 189, ante and p 230, post.
3 Human Rights Act 1998, s 6(1).
4 Trustees of charitable trusts are also not to be regarded as public authorities unless carrying out public duties delegated to them by a public authority: *R v Leonard Cheshire Foundation* [2002] EWCA Civ 366, [2002] 2 All ER 936.
5 Human Rights Act 1998, s 6(3)(a). See *Beyleveld & Pattinson* (2002) 118 LQR 623.

does not interfere with rights and freedoms protected in the Convention[6]. Thus the impact upon lawful or unlawful conditions is likely to be limited.

Trusts in restraint of marriage

Where property is settled in trust for a woman *for life*, with an executory gift over if she marry a man with an income from freeholds in 1795 of less than £500 a year, or if she marry any person of a particular trade, or if she marry a blood relation[7], (but not apparently if she cease to bear a particular surname)[8], the divesting gift over is prima facie bad, where its object, as gathered from its probable result[9], is to restrain marriage altogether. If, however, the trust over is to take effect only upon the first beneficiary marrying a particular person, it will be good, as not being in *general* restraint of marriage[10]. Partial restraints, if sufficiently certain in their terms[11], are prima facie valid except that where personalty is concerned a partial restraint will be void if intended merely in terrorem as where there is no clear gift over or no clear revocation of the gift upon the restraint being infringed[12].

Exception in case of ulterior motive

Where it appears that the intention of the testator or settlor was not to restrain the beneficiary from marrying but to ensure some other object a gift over on marriage may be upheld. Thus in *Re Hewett*[13], a testator gave an annuity of £1,200 to a woman with whom he was living and declared that if she should marry it should be reduced to £800 and that an annuity of £400 should then be applied to the benefit of his son by her. It was held that the testator's intention was not to restrain the woman from marrying but to provide for the son if she did, and that the declaration was valid.

Exception in cases of second marriage

The rule does not apply to second marriages. Thus Mellish LJ in *Allen v Jackson*[14] in delivering this judgment, after stating the general rule, said:

> 'It has never been decided that it (the rule) applies to second marriages. ... It appears to me very obvious that if it is regarded as a matter of policy, there may be very essential distinctions between a first and second marriage. At any rate, there is this, that in the case of a second marriage, whether of a man or a woman, the

---

6 See Lord Lester and David Pannick (2000) 116 LQR 380 and N Bamforth (2001) 117 LQR 34.
7 *Re Lanyon* [1927] 2 Ch 264; *Keily v Monck* (1795) 3 Ridg Parl Rep 205.
8 *Re Fry* [1945] Ch 348, [1945] 2 All ER 205, which suggested that a divesting gift over was bad in these circumstances, was disproved in *Re Neeld* [1962] Ch 643, [1962] 2 All ER 335, CA.
9 *Lloyd v Lloyd* (1852) 2 Sim NS 255; and see also *Re Bathe* [1925] Ch 377; and *Re Hanlon* [1933] Ch 254.
10 *Re Hanlon* [1933] Ch 254.
11 *Perrin v Lyon* (1807) 9 East 170; *Jenner v Turner* (1880) 16 Ch D 188. See cases on religious conditions such as persons 'not of Jewish parentage and of the Jewish faith': *Clayton v Ramsden* [1943] AC 320, [1943] 1 All ER 16, HL; *Blathwayt v Baron Cawley* [1976] AC 397, [1975] 3 All ER 625, HL; *Re Tepper's Will Trust* [1987] 1 All ER 970, discussed p 102, ante.
12 *Re Whiting's Settlement* [1905] 1 Ch 96, CA; *Leong v Lim Beng Chye* [1955] AC 648 at 660; *Re Hanlon* [1933] Ch 254.
13 [1918] 1 Ch 458; see also *Re Fentem* [1950] 2 All ER 1073 and *Jones v Jones* (1876) 1 QBD 279. Cf *Re Michelham's Will Trusts* [1964] Ch 550, [1963] 2 All ER 188.
14 (1875) 1 Ch D 399, CA.

person who makes the gift to the man or the woman may have been influenced by their friendship towards the wife in the one case, and towards the husband in the other.'

Gifts until marriage are good

But although conditional or executory gifts over *divesting* an estate on marriage are void if the probable effect would be to discourage marriage altogether, yet it is well established that a trust in favour of a person *until* marriage and then over is unobjectionable.

As was said by Wigram V-C in *Morley v Rennoldson*[15]:

'Until I heard the argument of this case, I had certainly understood that, without doubt, where property was limited to a person *until* she married, and when she married then over, the limitation was good. It is difficult to understand how this could be otherwise, for in such a case there is nothing to give an interest beyond the marriage. If you suppose the case of a gift of a certain interest, and that interest *sought to be abridged by a condition*, you may strike out the condition, and leave the original gift in operation; but if the gift is *until* marriage and no longer, there is nothing to carry the gift beyond the marriage.'

This distinction between executory gifts over on marriage and gifts *until* marriage is a fine one. But the distinction between a trust temporary in character and one unlimited but liable to be forfeited on the happening of an event is well established[16]. The law leans strongly against forfeiture, and therefore refuses to enforce it where it would tend to discourage acts which public policy regards as desirable. But it is quite a different matter to forbid temporary trusts which are to end on the happening of the same desirable event.

Condition requiring consent to marriage

Although a provision for *forfeiture* on marriage is prima facie invalid, the same invalidity does not attach to a condition subsequent requiring some person's consent to a marriage[17]. The reasons for this are obscure and not very satisfactory[18]; but it seems to be well settled. A consent once given, however, cannot be revoked[19].

Trusts tending to separate parent and child

Analogous to trusts in restraint of marriage are those tending to separate parent from child which are also void as being contrary to public policy. Thus, a condition was held void where it provided for the forfeiture of two grandchildren's interests if one or both of them should 'live with or be or continue under the custody, guardianship or control of their father'[20]. It is

15 (1843) 2 Hare 570. See also *Re Lovell* [1920] 1 Ch 122.
16 Formerly there was some tendency to construe gifts over on marriage as gifts until marriage; see *Allen v Jackson* (1875) 1 Ch D 399 at 404, per James LJ; *Jones v Jones* (1876) 1 QBD 279; and see also the judgment of Knight-Bruce LJ in *Heath v Lewis* (1853) 3 De GM & G 954; *Re Elliott* [1918] 1 IR 41. But it is thought unlikely that such a construction would be adopted now.
17 *Re Whiting's Settlement* [1905] 1 Ch 96, CA.
18 Per Vaughan Williams LJ in *Re Whiting's Settlement* [1905] 1 Ch 96, CA.
19 *Re Brown* [1904] 1 Ch 120.
20 *Re Boulter* [1922] 1 Ch 75; *Re Sandbrook* [1912] 2 Ch 471.

immaterial that the parent from whom the trust seeks to separate the child has been divorced by the other[1].

Trusts interfering with parental duty

Similarly, in *Re Borwick*[2], a condition subsequent providing that an interest which would otherwise vest at twenty-one should be forfeited if, before attaining that age, the beneficiary should 'be or become a Roman Catholic or not be openly or avowedly Protestant', was held void on the ground that it interfered with a parent in the exercise of his parental duty, which ought to be discharged solely with a view to the moral and spiritual welfare of the child and without being influenced by mercenary considerations affecting the child's worldly welfare. This was followed in *Re Tegg*[3] where a condition requiring that 'at no time may any child of hers go to or be sent to any Roman Catholic school for education' was held void as a fetter on the parent doing what she might think best for the welfare and education of her children.

However, these two decisions must now be treated as of very doubtful authority in view of *Blathwayt v Baron Cawley*[4] where the House of Lords upheld a forfeiture clause concerned with any tenant for life who 'shall be or become a Roman Catholic'. Such a clause may obviously influence the decision of an infant's parents as to what, if any, religious education he is to receive. However, where an infant is involved, the time for choice as to compliance or non-compliance with a condition must be postponed until majority and a reasonable time thereafter[5] when the beneficiary should be regarded as free from parental influence and able to choose a religion for *himself*. Thus, on one view such conditions do not interfere with parental duty[6]. On another – and preferable – view[7] such conditions may influence or interfere with parental duty since the religious teaching provided for the child by the parents must have a strong influence on the child's choice when adult, but such conditions ought not to be outlawed on ground of public policy. As Lord Fraser said[8];

> 'If a parent has strong convictions he may well regard the religious upbringing of his child as of overriding importance not to be set against purely material considerations; if, on the other hand, his religious convictions are weak or non-existent, he can weigh a testamentary benefit with a religious condition attached as one among the many factors affecting the welfare of his child. In neither case does the existence of the religious condition offend against public policy merely because it might affect the parent's action. One must remember also the public policy that a testator should be free ... to dispose of his property as he pleases. It would surely be going too far to say that a bequest for the benefit of a child to help with paying his school fees, payable on condition of his going to a particular school, would be contrary to public policy. Conversely, a condition of his not going to a particular type of school – say a fee- paying public school – ought not to be contrary to public

1 *Re Piper* [1946] 2 All ER 503.
2 [1933] Ch 657.
3 [1936] 2 All ER 878.
4 [1976] AC 397, [1975] 3 All ER 625, HL.
5 *Re May* [1917] 2 Ch 126; *Re May* [1932] 1 Ch 99, CA.
6 *McCausland v Young* [1949] NI 49; *Blaythwayt v Baron Cawley* [1976] AC 397 at 426, per Lord Wilberforce, and at 427 per Lord Simon.
7 [1976] AC 397 at 435, per Lord Cross, and at 442 per Lord Fraser.
8 [1976] AC 397 at 442.

policy either. In my opinion the same rules should apply to conditions about the religious upbringing of a child.'

PARAGRAPH 1(G)

Trusts made illegal by statute

Exchange Control restrictions were abolished in their entirety as from 23 October 1979. In case a future Government reintroduces them it seems worth noting that by s 29 of the Exchange Control Act 1947[9], a resident in the United Kingdom had to obtain Treasury consent to any settlement inter vivos (including the exercise of a power of appointment) which conferred an interest in trust property on a person who was resident outside the scheduled territories (ie the UK, including the Isle of Man and the Channel Islands, Gibraltar and the Republic of Ireland), but the settlement was only invalid so far as it purported to confer an interest on such person.

The Race Relations Act 1968 may also have a limited application in this context. Taking effect on 25 November 1968, the Act is directed against certain acts of racial discrimination. For the purposes of the Act a person discriminates against another if on the ground of colour, race or ethnic[10] or national origins he treats that other, in any situation to which the Act applies, less favourably than he treats or would treat other persons (and it is expressly declared that if a person is segregated from other persons he is treated less favourably than they are treated)[11]. The situations in which the Act operates to forbid acts of discrimination are those relating to the provisions of goods, facilities and services[12], to employment[13], to trade unions, and employers' and trade organisations[14], and to the provisions of housing accommodation, and business and other premises[15]. There are also provisions relating to advertisements and notices[16]. The Act refers expressly to charities and to acts which are done for charitable purposes[17]. As regards charitable trusts in existence when the Act took effect, the Act does not render unlawful any act done to comply with their provisions; but as regards charitable trusts created after this date the Act merely states that it is not to be construed as affecting any provision which confers benefits on persons of a particular race, particular descent or particular ethnic or national origins, or as rendering unlawful any acts done to comply with such a provision. Although it is not entirely clear, the intention apparently is to draw a distinction between discriminating in favour of persons for whom one feels particular sympathy, particular goodwill, or a particular affinity, and discriminating *against* persons for whom one

---

9 A transaction which was invalid under this section might be validated by Treasury certificate given subsequently, see sub-s (3) and s 18(2). The Treasury had delegated to the Bank of England the power to grant permission and certificates. Validation by certificate was unlikely if the trustees were, or had become, resident outside the jurisdiction.

10 Jews were held to be an ethnic group in *King-Ansell v Police* [1979] 2 NZLR 531 approved by HL in *Mandla v Dowell Lee* [1983] 2 AC 548, [1983] 1 All ER 1062, HL where Sikhs were held to be a racial group.

11 Race Relations Act 1968, s 1.

12 Race Relations Act 1968, s 2.

13 Race Relations Act 1968, s 3

14 Race Relations Act 1968, s 4.

15 Race Relations Act 1968, s 5.

16 Race Relations Act 1968, s 6.

17 Race Relations Act 1968, s 9.

has negative feelings. In relation to charities, discrimination of the former kind is not attacked by the Act, so that, for instance, it would not be unlawful for trustees to carry out a trust for the benefit of poor persons of a particular race. But discrimination of the latter kind is attacked; so that, for instance, it would seem to be unlawful for trustees to carry out a trust in favour of poor persons *except* those of a particular race—at least in so far as, in doing so, they committed acts of discrimination in any of the situations with which the Act is concerned (see above). As already mentioned, however, this applies only to trusts established after the coming into effect of the Act.

So far as private trusts are concerned, the Act contains no provisions which affect them expressly, but it does of course affect the actions of both trustees and beneficiaries in the same way as it affects those of other people. Thus trustees must not practice racial discrimination in their capacity as employers or in disposing of trust property; and the Race Relations Act 1965, s 5 is directed against landlords and others (whether trustees or not) who refuse consent to the assignment of a tenancy because of the colour, race or ethnic or national origins of the proposed assignee. But none of these matters is peculiar to trusts. It is just possible that the courts will become more ready to hold that provisions in private trusts which savour of racial discrimination (for example, one designed to discourage the marriage of a beneficiary to any person of a particular race or colour) are void as contrary to public policy, but the act contains no express provisions in this respect and the House of Lords in *Blathwayt v Baron Cawley*[18] exhibited no enthusiasm for moving in this direction to reduce the fundamental freedom of testamentary disposition.

The Sex Discrimination Act 1975, like the Race Relations Act, does not invalidate provisions in private trusts.

In the context of the Human Rights Act 1998[19] it remains to be seen how extensive will be the impact of a court ranking as a public authority in deciding cases where no public authority is involved as claimant or as defendant when it is unlawful only for a public authority to act in a way which is incompatible with a Convention right. Why should a settlor not have freedom to choose to confer beneficial interests upon descendants who satisfy clauses related to religion, race or colour and arrange for terminated or forfeited interests to accrue to qualifying descendants or to pass to a charity concerned with persons of a particular religion, race or colour[20]? The descendants will still have a right to pursue whatever religion they wish and to marry whomsoever they choose.

PARAGRAPH 2

Illegal trusts do not necessarily avoid other trusts in same settlement

Assuming that a trust is void for illegality, it is sometimes difficult to determine whether, and, if so, to what extent, the illegality affects other trusts in

---

18 [1976] AC 397, [1975] 3 All ER 625.
19 See p 219 ante.
20 As Lord Wilberforce stated in *Blathwayt v Lord Cawley* [1976] AC 397 at 426, 'Discrimination is not the same thing as choice; it operates over a larger and less personal area and neither by express provision nor by implication has private selection yet become a matter of public policy.'

the same instrument. Where the illegality is the consideration for the trust, then, of course, the whole instrument is tainted, as used to be the case in trusts in favour of a mistress and her future illegitimate children which were wholly void as tending to promote continued immorality[1]. Where an ascertainable part of the property is to be denoted to lawful trusts then those trusts of that part may be carried out[2]. If some conditions are valid and some void as contrary to public policy the valid conditions are severable and effective[3].

Cases arising under rule against perpetuities and accumulations

Cases, in which it is not so easy to follow the reasoning of the court, occur with regard to the rules against remoteness and accumulations. The underlying principle is, however, that a trust is illegal so far as it tends to infringe the object of the rule which forbids it, but no farther.

Trusts in remainder after trusts void under rule against perpetuities

The law apart from the 1964 Act

The objects of the rule against remoteness (more fully explained on pp 191 et seq, ante) are to prevent the dead from ruling the living from the grave and to prevent a trust fund (as opposed to the investments comprised therein) from being made entrepeneurially unavailable (as not in the hands of an absolute beneficial owner) for too long a period through having to be kept intact to await the outcome of contingencies. Consequently, not only trusts which may take effect beyond the prescribed limit but also trusts in remainder to take effect upon their failure – even though they be trusts in favour of living persons – are void in some circumstances[4].

Such trusts in remainder are, however, void only if they are dependent upon the previous void trust, that is to say, if upon the terms of the trust instrument, construed without regard to the rule against remoteness, it cannot from the beginning be affirmed that the ulterior trust must best indefeasibly, if it ever vests at all, before the expiration of the perpetuity period[5]. If at the expiration of that period the ulterior trust may still be accelerated or postponed or defeated by some event operating under the offending previous trust, the ulterior trust is dependent upon the previous void trust, and is itself void[6].

In *Re Abbott*[7], Stirling J said:

---

1 But see now the Family Law Reform Act 1969, p 217, ante and *Tanner v Tanner* [1975] 1 WLR 1346.
2 *Mitford v Reynolds* (1842) 1 Ph 185; and cf *Fisk v A-G* (1867) LR 4 Eq 521.
3 *Re Hepplewhite's Will Trusts* (1977) Times, 21 January.
4 *Cambridge v Rous* (1802) 8 Ves 12; *Re Thatcher's Trusts* (1859) 26 Beav 365; *Hale v Hale* (1876) 3 Ch D 643; and see *Watson v Young* (1885) 28 Ch D 436; and *Re Frost* (1889) 43 Ch D 246; *Re Abbott* [1893] 1 Ch 54.
5 An independent limitation is one intended to take effect whether or not the prior gift takes effect.
6 To be valid the ulterior trust must 'dovetail in and accord with previous limitations which are valid'; per Lord St Leonards LC in *Monypenny v Dering* (1852) 2 De GM & G 145 at 182; and see *Re Mill's Declaration of Trust* [1950] 1 All ER 789; affd [1950] 2 All ER 292, CA.
7 [1893] 1 Ch 54 at 57. It is odd that the courts do not apply the presumption in favour of early vesting illustrated by *Phipps v Ackers* (1842) 9 Cl & Fin 583; *Re Mallinson's Consolidated Trusts* [1974] 2 All ER 530, [1974] 1 WLR 1120.

'It is settled that any limitation depending or expectant upon a prior limitation which is void for remoteness is invalid. The reason appears to be that the persons entitled under the subsequent limitation are not intended to take *unless and until the prior limitation is exhausted*; and as the prior limitation which is void for remoteness can never come into operation, much less be exhausted, it is impossible to give effect to the intentions of the settlor in favour of the beneficiaries under the subsequent limitation.'

This passage was cited with approval by Farwell J in *Re Canning's Will Trusts*[8], and again by Clauson J in *Re Coleman*[9], where the learned judge said:

'Where, as in the present case, ... the limitation which it is sought to impeach creates a future interest which becomes vested in interest (though not in possession) within the limits of the rule against perpetuities and cannot in any event be subsequently divested by the operation of the earlier trust, it would be entirely inconsistent with the principle on which the decision in *Re Canning's Will Trusts* proceeds to hold such a future interest to be adversely affected by the invalidity of the trusts which it follows, but of which it is wholly independent.'

Difficulties of interpretation may arise where the settlor had expressly provided (perhaps by way of an accruer clause or a substitutional gift) for what is to happen to the trust property in the event of the 'failure' or the 'failure or determination' of the previous trust. As the decided cases stand at present, it seems that two questions arise in regard to such provisions: (a) is the failure of the previous trust *for remoteness* an event which, on the true construction of the trust instrument, was intended to bring them into operation? and (b) are they sufficiently independent of the previous trust as to remain effective notwithstanding its failure? Clearly these two questions are to some extent interrelated.

In *Re Robinson's Will Trusts*[10], an accruer provision was to take effect 'in the event of the failure or determination of' the previous trusts, which were admitted to be void for remoteness. Plowman J held that the words 'failure or determination' were wide enough to cover the event of total or partial failure for remoteness (and thus were not confined to failure arising simply from lack of beneficiaries) and that the accruer provision took effect. The decision was therefore based upon an affirmative answer being given to question (a), but it is thought that an affirmative answer to question (b) must be taken as having been impliedly given. Another case, *Re Hubbard's Will Trusts*[11], was decided soon afterwards and at a time when the former case had not been reported. There, Buckley J was faced with a very similar accruer provision which was to take effect 'on the failure or determination of' the previous trust. He held the previous trust void for remoteness and decided that the accruer provision was dependent upon the previous trust and expectant on its failure and that it did *not* take effect in these circumstances. His judgment (which contains a valuable review of the law governing the topic) was thus based upon the second of the two questions being answered in the negative. The first question was not raised or considered. Subsequently, in *Re Buckton's*

---

8 [1936] Ch 309.
9 [1936] Ch 528 at 535, [1936] 2 All ER 225 at 230; followed in *Re Allan's Will Trusts* [1958] 1 All ER 401, [1958] 1 WLR 220; *Re Backhouse* [1921] 2 Ch 51 is of doubtful authority; see Megarry and Wade, *Law of Real Property* (6th edn) para 7–083 and Buckley J in *Re Hubbard's Will Trusts* [1963] Ch 275, [1962] 2 All ER 917.
10 [1963] 1 All ER 777, [1963] 1 WLR 628.
11 [1963] Ch 275, [1962] 2 All ER 917.

Settlement Trusts[12], Pennycuick J was presented with a similar situation. In that case the trust instrument contained a substitutional gift which was to take effect 'in the event of there being a failure of' the previous trust. Both of the two cases just referred to were cited in this case, and the learned judge chose to follow *Re Hubbard's Will Trusts*, and not to follow *Re Robinson's Will Trusts*. He held that the failure for remoteness of the previous trust did not bring the substitutional gift into operation because the word 'failure' was not wide enough to cover a failure through remoteness (though the settlor could have provided for this if he had wished), and that the substitutional gift was dependent on the previous trust. He thus answered both question (a) and question (b) in the negative.

The weight of authority therefore is that an accruer provision, or substitutional gift, is not normally brought into effect by the failure of the previous trust for remoteness. It was suggested above that the two questions there posed were interrelated. It is plain from the decided cases that a negative answer to question (b) is fatal to the effectiveness of provisions of this kind: the answer to this question must be affirmative if these provisions are to be effective at all. The position in regard to question (a) seems not to be so simple. Clearly, if the provisions concerned were not, on the true construction of the instrument, intended to take effect in the event of the failure of the previous trusts for remoteness, they will not take effect in that event – but this seems to be subject to one qualification, namely that they will take effect if the previous trust has failed for want of beneficiaries *as well as* for remoteness. In *Re Buckton's Settlement Trusts*, above, the previous trust had admittedly failed for remoteness, but in fact there were no beneficiaries entitled to take under it, so that it could not have taken effect in any case. In these circumstances, it is clear from the judgment that the substitutional gift would have been effective if question (b) could have been answered in the affirmative – not because question (a) could be answered affirmatively, but because in the circumstances it would not have mattered whether the answer to question (a) was affirmative or not. The failure of the previous trust for remoteness was not an event which, on its construction, brought the substitutional gift into operation, but the failure of the previous trust for want of beneficiaries was clearly an event apt to do so.

Changes made by the 1964 Act

The Perpetuities and Accumulations Act 1964, s 6 states:

> 'A disposition shall not be treated as void for remoteness by reason only that the interest disposed of is ulterior to and dependent upon an interest under a disposition which is so void, and the vesting of an interest shall not be prevented from being accelerated[13] on the failure of the prior interest by reason only that the failure arises because of remoteness.'

The effect of this section is, in relation to instruments taking effect on or after 16 July 1964, to reverse the rule which formerly applied. Thus in those (now rarer) cases where a prior limitation is void for remoteness, a subsequent limitation will not be tainted with this fault and will remain effective even if it is dependent on the prior one. Each limitation must stand or fall by itself.

---

12 [1964] Ch 497, [1964] 2 All ER 487; (1964) 80 LQR 323 (RE Megarry).
13 As to acceleration, see p 333, post.

The application of the latter part of s 6 to accruer provisions and sub-stitutional gifts, such as those described above, now needs considering. Of the two questions, (a) and (b), previously posed, it seems clear that (b) will not arise and that such provisions will not fail merely because they are dependent on a previous trust which is void for remoteness. It also seems possible that question (a) is now immaterial since it seems that the fact that the prior interest failed for remoteness is not to prevent subsequent interests from being accelerated just as failure for want of beneficiaries did not pre-vent subsequent interests from being accelerated (assuming no other obstacle to acceleration existed such as a contingent interest intervening between the failed interest and the dependent interest)[14].

Trusts in favour of a class, some of which infringe rule against perpetuities

Under the law as it existed before the Perpetuities and Accumulations Act 1964 (and as it still applies to instruments which took effect before the commencement of the Act), in the case of a trust for A for life, and after her death for her children who may attain 21, and the issue *who shall attain 21* of such of them as shall die under that age, per stirpes, the whole of the lim-itations after the life estate of A were void. For although the *children* must attain 21 within the prescribed period, the issue of deceased children may not; and the gift being to a class as a whole, the one could not be separated from the other[15].

In regard to instruments to which it applies, the Act of 1964 has made extensive changes in the position. It will be remembered that s 4 of the Act introduced new provisions to validate a disposition which would otherwise fail for remoteness because it was limited by reference to the attainment of an age greater than 21, and that further provision was made for a case where different ages were specified for different persons. These provisions have already been discussed[16]. So far as the subject matter of the present part of the text is concerned, the same section of the Act goes on to make two further provisions. The first[17] excludes from the class of beneficiaries all those persons whose inclusion (as potential members of it, or as unborn persons who would at birth become actual or potential members of it) pre-vents the foregoing provisions of the section from saving the disposition. Such persons having been thus excluded from the class, the foregoing pro-visions of the section are then to operate to save the disposition. The second of the two provisions[18] applies to class dispositions to which the first does not apply (ie to those where the exclusion of class members would not allow the age reduction provisions to save the disposition). It excludes from the class of beneficiaries all those persons whose inclusion (as potential members of it, or as unborn persons who would at birth become actual or potential members of it) makes it apparent (at the time when the disposition is made or at some later time) that the disposition would be void for remoteness. This exclusion is not to be made, however, if it would exhaust the class altogether. It is also provided[19] that the operation of these provisions is not to affect the validity of

---

14 For example, *Re Townsend's Estate* (1886) 34 Ch D 357; see also (1964) 80 LQR 486 at 517–518.
15 *Pearks v Moseley* (1880) 5 App Cas 714; *Re Lord's Settlement* [1947] 2 All ER 685; *Re Hooper's Settlement Trusts* [1948] Ch 586, [1948] 2 All ER 261.
16 See p 196, ante.
17 Perpetuities and Accumulations Act 1964, s 4(3).
18 Perpetuities and Accumulations Act 1964, s 4(4).
19 Perpetuities and Accumulations Act 1964, s 4(5).

anything previously done in relation to the interest disposed of by way of advancement, application of intermediate income or otherwise.

Alternative trusts, one legal and the other illegal

But when there are alternative trusts (A and B), A being illegal and B legal, then if the contingency happens on which B was to take effect it will not be affected by the illegality of A[20]. For by giving effect to trust B the courts would in no way aid the illegality intended by Trust A, nor (the contingency having happened on which B was to come into force) would the intentions of the settlor be disregarded. If, however, the contingency on which B was to come into operation should never occur, then, of course, the whole instrument would be void, because the contingency contemplated by the settlor had not happened.

So again, where a trust for sale is void for remoteness but the beneficial interests in the proceeds are vested absolutely within the period limited by the rule, the latter will be good although the former may be bad[1].

Appointment of absolute interest with provision for defeasance which infringes the rule

Where under a special power of appointment an absolute interest is appointed subject to a provision for defeasance on the happening of a stated event, and the gift over fails for remoteness, the absolute appointment is unimpaired and remains in full force and effect[2].

In regard to instruments taking effect on or after 16 July 1964, the Perpetuities and Accumulations Act 1964[3] provides that in the case of a possibility of reverter on the determination of a determinable fee simple, or a possibility of a resulting trust on the determination of any other determinable interest in property, the rule against perpetuities shall apply to the provision which makes the interest determinable in the same way as it would apply if that provision were a condition subsequent giving rise on its breach to a right of re-entry (or to an equivalent right in the case of property other than land). Where the provision falls to be treated as void for remoteness, the determinable interest is to become an absolute one. However, if a determining event occurs or a condition is broken and the right of entry exercised during the valid wait and see period then the interest fails. The Act also provides[4] that where a disposition is subject to any such provision, or to any such condition subsequent, or to any exception or reservation, the disposition is to be treated for the purposes of the Act as including a separate

---

20 *Evers v Challis* (1859) 7 HL Cas 531; *Watson v Young* (1885) 28 Ch D 436; *Re Harvey* (1888) 39 Ch D 289; *Re Bence* [1891] 3 Ch 242; and see also *Re Abbott* [1893] 1 Ch 54. See *Re Bullock's Will Trusts* [1915] 1 Ch 493; and *Re Davey* [1915] 1 Ch 837; *Curryer's Will Trusts* [1938] Ch 952, [1938] 3 All ER 574; *Re Hay* [1932] NI 215; *Re Canning's Will Trusts* [1936] Ch 309; *Re Coleman* [1936] Ch 528, [1936] 2 All ER 225. As to the effect of adding *surplus* income (under a discretionary trust) to corpus after the expiration of 21 years, see *Re Hawkins* [1916] 2 Ch 570, and cases there cited; following *Re Garside* [1919] 1 Ch 132; dissenting from *Re Pope* [1901] 1 Ch 64.

1 *Re Appleby* [1903] 1 Ch 565.

2 *Re Pratt's Settlement Trusts* [1943] Ch 356, [1943] 2 All ER 458, following *Re Brown and Sibly's Contract* (1876) 3 Ch D 156.

3 Perpetuities and Accumulations Act 1964, s 12(1).

4 Perpetuities and Accumulations Act 1964, s 12(2).

disposition of any rights which arise by virtue of the provision, condition subsequent, exception or reservation.

Trusts infringing the law restricting accumulations

It might perhaps be thought that, by analogy to the action of the courts with regard to trusts which transgress the rule against remoteness, a trust which endeavoured to go beyond the period allowed for accumulations (see p 204, ante) would be wholly void; but this is not so. The statute merely prohibits accumulations going beyond the period prescribed by it, and, being in derogation of a common law right it is construed strictly. Consequently, since accumulations which exceed the most appropriate statutory period of accumulation, but are within the perpetuity period prescribed under the rule against remoteness, are not contrary to public policy as defined by common law, a trust for accumulation is good pro tanto, unless, of course, it exceeds the perpetuity in which case it is void in toto[5].

Trusts in remainder after illegal trust to accumulate

On similar principles, remainders to take effect after the period prescribed by the settlement for the accumulation of income are not rendered void on the ground that the prescribed period exceeds the statutory period. All that the statute does is to prohibit *accumulations* beyond a certain period. When that period comes to an end the accumulations stop, and the fact of the subsequent remainder being allowed in no way tends to a breach of the statutory rule. On the other hand, such remainders are not accelerated (for that would be contrary to the settlor's intentions); but there is a resulting trust in favour of the persons who, if no accumulation had been directed, would have been entitled to the income during the time which elapses between the expiration of the statutory period and the period prescribed by the settlement[6]. In the case of an illegal trust to accumulate declared by will, however, a resulting trust for the testator's next-of-kin may be excluded by the evidence of a general charitable intention and the court will carry this intention into effect by means of a scheme[7].

Trusts subject to impossible or illegal condition

If a term of a trust is a condition subsequent and is impossible, uncertain, contrary to public policy or illegal then the term is void and the interest becomes absolute[8].

If the term is a condition precedent and attached to realty then failure to perform the condition for whatever reason defeats the gift. In respect of personalty.

'where a condition precedent is originally impossible or is made so by the act or default of the testator or is illegal as involving malum prohibitum, the bequest is absolute just as if the condition had been subsequent. But where the performance of the condition is the sole motive of the bequest or its impossibility was unknown

---

5 See *Griffiths v Vere* (1803) 9 Ves 127; see p 208, ante.
6 Law of Property Act 1925, s 164(1).
7 *Martin v Maugham* (1844) 14 Sim 230; *Re Bradwell* [1952] Ch 575, [1952] 2 All ER 286.
8 *Re Beard* [1908] 1 Ch 383; *Re Caborne* [1943] Ch 224.

to the testator or the condition which was possible in its creation has since become impossible by Act of God or where it is illegal as involving *malum in se* ... both gift and condition are void.'[9]

It is high time these archaic, illogical[10] and anomalous rules were reformed.

PARAGRAPH 3

Testamentary trusts unknown to the law of settlor's domicile

English law distinguishes between immovables and movables for succession purposes, so that the *lex situs* governs immovables while the *lex domicilii* of the deceased at his death is his *lex successionis* for movables[11]. Thus English law governs succession to English immovables[12], and so gives effect to trusts thereof, though a deceased's foreign *lex successionis* applicable to his other property may allow countervailing compensation to be payable thereout in the foreign forum in satisfaction of the claims of forced heirs entitled indefeasibly to a fraction of the deceased's estate (including the value of his immovables). Succession to English movables of a foreign domiciliary is governed by the foreign *lex domicilii* so that forced heirship rights to English movables owned at his death by the foreign deceased will be recognised and implemented[13], and so pro tanto diminish the subject matter of trusts thereof.

Before 1974 a woman took, on marriage, the domicile of her husband and her domicile was dependent upon his, changing with his whilst the marriage lasted. On 1 January 1974, s 1 of the Domicile and Matrimonial Proceedings Act 1973 has the domicile of a wife ascertained by reference to the same factors as in the case of any other individual capable of having an independent domicile. However, where immediately before 1 January 1974 she was married, so having her husband's domicile by dependence, she is to be treated as retaining that domicile (as a domicile of choice if it is not also her domicile of origin) unless and until it is changed by acquisition or revival of another domicile either on or after that date.

Section 3 of the 1973 Act ensures that the time at which a person first becomes capable of having an independent domicile is when he attains sixteen years of age or marries thereunder.

Inter vivos trusts unknown to law of settlor's domicile

It is clear that questions of capacity, form and essential validity affecting

---

9 *Re Elliott* [1952] Ch 217 at 221; *Re Wolffe* [1953] 1 WLR 1211 at 1216; *Re Piper* [1946] 2 All ER 503; cf *Re Thomas' Will Trusts* [1930] 2 Ch 67. In *Re McBride* (1980) 107 DLR (3d) 233 testamentary condition precedent designed to promote the divorce of the testator's son was held not to be malum in se but only malum prohibitum so the gift was good, passing to the son free from the condition.

10 *Leong v Lim Beng Chye* [1955] AC 648 at 662; *Exham v Beamish* [1939] IR 336; *Re Blake* [1955] IR 89. See Law Commission Consultation Paper No 154 (1999).

11 See generally Hayton (ed), *European Succession Laws* (2nd edn, 2002) Jordans, Dicey & Morris, *Conflict of Laws* (13th edn) chap 27.

12 Dicey & Morris (supra) rules 135 and 140; *Re Collens* [1986] Ch 505; *Re Hernando* (1884) 27 Ch D 284.

13 Dicey & Morris (supra) rules 134 and 139; *Re Annesley* [1926] Ch 692.

English land are governed by the English *lex situs* irrespective of the settlor's domicile, habitual residence or nationality[14]. Thus, a foreign settlor can create valid inter vivos trusts of English land if complying with English domestic requirements, especially if he reinforces the significance of English law by express (or implied) choice of English law to govern his trust. The position seems to be the same for gratuitous transfers to trustees by foreign settlors of English movables as discussed below at pp 1047–1048.

Thus, if a foreign domiciliary has validly transferred by the *lex situs* English assets to English trustees of a trust governed by English law, such assets will not form part of the deceased settlor's estate governed by his foreign *lex successionis*, just as any inter vivos joint tenancy of English assets would require such assets to vest in the survivor and not to pass as part of the deceased's estate. Care should be taken, however, to ensure that no part of the trust fund is invested in the jurisdiction of the foreign heirs or a sympathetic jurisdiction or it could be appropriated in satisfaction of the heirs' claims.

Danger of general power of appointment or revocation

Reservation to the settlor of a general power of appointment or revocation is likely to lead to problems if claims are subsequently brought by the foreign settlor's forced heirs, because property settled inter vivos in respect of which such powers are reserved is automatically treated as part of the deceased's 'net estate' for claims under the Inheritance (Provision for Family and Dependants) Act 1975[15] if the deceased died domiciled in England. Because such property is automatically available for satisfying the provisions of the English *lex successionis* mandatory rules for the protection of heirs, why should it not be automatically available for satisfying forced heirship claims under the mandatory rules of the foreign *lex successionis*? What of the position if the settlement were made within six years of death with the intention of defeating a claim under the 1975 Act, so that there is a judicial discretion to set aside the settlement to the extent necessary to make reasonable provision for the applicant, taking account of various discretionary factors, if the deceased died domiciled in England? It is considered unlikely that the English court would be prepared to take on such a hypothetical discretionary exercise if the deceased died domiciled abroad, so as to ascertain an amount available for satisfying forced heirship claims. It may well be that the matter will not arise for decision because most foreign settlors who set up English trusts will make reasonable provision for their forced heirs (though not such extravagant provision as is provided by the law on forced heirship).

ARTICLE 12

Necessity or otherwise of writing and signature

(1) (a) A contract for the sale or other disposition of an interest in land (so covering a contract to create a trust of an interest in land or to dispose of a subsisting equitable interest in land) is void unless

---

14 Dicey & Morris (supra) rule 117.
15 See Inheritance (Provision for Family and Dependants) Act 1975, s 25(1). Some off-shore trust jurisdictions, like Bermuda, have similar provisions.

made in writing incorporating all the terms which the parties have expressly agreed in one document or, where contracts are exchanged, in each[16]. The document incorporating the terms (whether set out in itself or by reference to some other document) or, where contracts are exchanged, one of the documents incorporating the terms (but not necessarily the same one) must also be signed by or on behalf of each party to the contract[17].

(b) An express trust of any interest in land is unenforceable unless evidenced by writing signed by the person able to declare such trust or by his will[18].

(c) An oral declaration is sufficient to create a trust of pure personalty by a person both legally and beneficially entitled[19], or by a person authorised by a trust instrument orally to declare or appoint new trusts unless his declaration or appointment amounts to a disposition by him of his own subsisting equitable interest[20]. A disposition inter vivos of a subsisting equitable interest must be in writing signed by the disposor or his agent lawfully authorised in writing[1], and for this purpose a direction given by a person entitled in equity to trustees directing them to hold the trust property on trust for donees is a disposition of his equitable interest[2] as, it seems, is a declaration by such person that he holds his equitable interest on a simple bare trust for another person of full capacity[3].

(d) An express trust of any kind of property, if intended to be testamentary, must be created by a duly executed and attested will or codicil[4]. Even where property is devised or bequeathed to a person *as trustee* the trust cannot be declared by a subsequent instrument other than a codicil[5]. Failure to comply with the testamentary formalities leads to a resulting trust in favour of the testator's residuary legatee or devisee or, if there is no residuary legatee or devisee, or if residue were the subject of the intended trust, in favour of the persons entitled on his intestacy.

(2) Absence of the requisite formalities will not matter if a person otherwise prejudiced by such absence can invoke the principle that

16 Law of Property (Miscellaneous Provisions) Act 1989, s 2(1).

17 Law of Property (Miscellaneous Provisions) Act 1989, s 2(2),(3).

18 Law of Property Act 1925, ss 53(1)(b), 40; *Kronheim v Johnson* (1877) 7 Ch D 60; *Tierney v Wood* (1854) 19 Beav 330; *Rudkin v Dolman* (1876) 35 LT 791.

19 *M'Fadden v Jenkyns* (1842) 1 Ph 153; *Milroy v Lord* (1862) 4 De GF & J 264; *Grey v IRC* [1960] AC 1, [1959] 3 All ER 603, HL: *Paul v Constance* [1977] 1 All ER 195, [1977] 1 WLR 527, CA.

20 *Re Vandervell's Trusts (No 2)* [1974] Ch 269, [1974] 3 All ER 205, CA, *Grey v IRC* [1960] AC 1.

1 Law of Property Act 1925, s 53(1)(c). But see *Vandervell v IRC* [1967] 2 AC 291, [1967] 1 All ER 1, HL, p 243, post (if T holds on trust for B and, at B's request, transfers the property to X, this is effective to dispose of B's interest without writing signed by B).

2 *Grey v IRC* [1960] AC 1, [1959] 3 All ER 603, HL.

3 *Grey v IRC* [1958] Ch 375 at 382; revsd [1958] Ch 690 at 715, CA p 239, post.

4 Wills Acts 1837, s 9. In regard to attestation, the Wills Act 1837 is slightly amended by the Wills Act 1968. A disposition of a subsisting equitable interest or trust may be made by will: Law of Property Act 1925, s 53(1)(c).

5 *Adlington v Cann* (1744) 3 Atk 141; *Briggs v Penny* (1851) 3 Mac & G 546; *Re Boyes* (1884) 26 Ch D 531; *Habergham v Vincent* (1793) 2 Ves 204.

equity will not allow a statute to be used as an instrument of fraud[6] or the principle of equitable proprietary estoppel[7] or the doctrine of part performance[8] (available for unenforceable trusts but not void contractual arrangements) or can rely on the operation of resulting or constructive trusts[9]. The principle that equity will not allow a statute to be used as an instrument of fraud has taken on special refinements, in the case of secret or half secret testamentary trusts: see pp 257–266, post.

Contracts to create trusts

By the Law of Property (Miscellaneous Provisions) Act 1989, s 2:

> '(1) A contract for the sale or other disposition of an interest in land can only be made in writing and only by incorporating all the terms which the parties have expressly agreed in one document or, where contracts are exchanged in each.
>
> (2) The terms may be incorporated in a document either by being set out in it or by reference to some other document.
>
> (3) The document incorporating the terms or, where contracts are exchanged, one of the documents incorporating them (but not necessarily the same one) must be signed by or on behalf of each party to the contract.'

It follows that if, after 26 September 1989, the above requirements are not satisfied when S purports to contract to create a trust of an interest in land (which expressly extends to interests in the proceeds of sale of land, eg co-ownership interests behind a trust for sale) there is no contract at all. Thus, there is no scope[10] for the doctrine of part performance[11], available for unenforceable but otherwise valid arrangements, though nothing in s 2 affects the creation or operation of resulting or constructive trusts[12], which may arise independently or as a result of equitable proprietary estoppel principles[13]. The requisite writing may comprise several documents read together if they refer to the relevant transaction commencing with the document bearing the signature of the defendant or his agent and working back from there[14]. If the writing be defective because of the omission of a term expressly agreed by the parties in circumstances enabling the court to

---

6 *Rochefoucauld v Boustead* [1897] 1 Ch 196; *McCormick v Grogan* (1869) LR 4 HL 82.

7 *Inwards v Baker* [1965] 1 All ER 446; *Dillwyn v Llewelyn* (1862) 4 De GF & J 517; *Re Basham* [1987] 1 All ER 405; *Gillett v Holt* [2001] Ch 210, CA.

8 *Re Gonin* [1979] Ch 16 sub nom *Re Gonin, Gonin v Garmeson*, [1977] 2 All ER 720; *Steadman v Steadman* [1976] AC 536, [1974] 2 All ER 977, HL; Law of Property Act 1925, s 55(d).

9 Law of Property Act 1925, s 53(2); *Hodgson v Mark* [1971] Ch 892, [1971] 2 All ER 684.

10 *Yaxley v Gotts* [2000] Ch 162 at 172, CA.

11 *Steadman v Steadman* [1976] AC 536, [1974] 2 All ER 977, HL, as narrowly interpreted in *Re Gonin* [1979] Ch 16, sub nom *Re Gonin, Gonin v Garmeson* [1977] 2 All ER 720; Jones & Goodhart, *Specific Performance*, pp 96–106.

12 Law of Property (Miscellaneous Provisions) Act 1989, s 2(5).

13 *Yaxley v Gotts* [2000] Ch 162, CA; *Re Basham* [1986] 1 WLR 1498 at 1504, [1987] 1 All ER 405 at 410; *Lim Teng Huan v Ang Swee Chuan* [1992] 1 WLR 113.

14 *Timmins v Moreland Street Property Co Ltd* [1958] Ch 110, [1957] 3 All ER 265, CA; *Elias v George Sahely & Co (Barbados) Ltd* [1983] 1 AC 646, [1982] 3 All ER 801. These cases concerned with Law of Property Act 1925, s 40, replaced by the 1989 Act, are still relevant here. Note that mutual wills expressed to be irrevocable amount to contracts so that, to the extent they devise land they need to satisfy s 2(1) but a constructive trust is exempted by s 2(5) from s 2(1): *Healey v Brown* [2000] WTLR 780 (where the constructive trust ought to have extended beyond half the flat to the whole: pp 429–430, post).

rectify the document, then the rectified document can satisfy the requirements of s 2[15]. A liberal purposive interpretation has been given to the section by the courts in holding that it does not apply to the exercise of an option to purchase land[16], a collateral contract[17] (contained in a side letter signed only by one party) and an agreement supplemental to a contract which was no longer executory, having been duly carried out[18]. It does, however, apply to the subsequent variation of a contract within s 2[19], eg if the completion date is postponed.

A contract to create a trust of property other than land or an interest in land need satisfy no special formalities.

Contracts to dispose of existing equitable interests

If A has an equitable interest in pure personalty held by T prima facie no formalities need to be observed if he contracts to sell his interest. However, it can be argued that the constructive trusteeship imposed upon A when he enters into a specifically enforceable contract[20] to sell his equitable interest to B means that T holds on trust for A who holds on trust for B so that if A is a simple bare trustee with no active duties to perform he disappears from the picture leaving T holding on trust for B[1]. Since T formerly held on trust for A it can be said that A by his contract with B has made a disposition in B's favour of his equitable interest which must actually be in writing signed by A (or A's agent authorised in writing) or be void: Law of Property Act 1925, s $53(1)(c)$[2]. To this it may be riposted that s $53(2)$ itself states that s $53(1)$ is not to affect the creation or operation of resulting or constructive trusts so that without the need for any s $53(1)(c)$ writing B becomes equitable owner due to the constructive trust in his favour: this view has been taken by Upjohn J[3], Lord Radcliffe[4], Megarry J[5] and by Goff and Shaw LJJ[6] and has been held to be correct by the Court of Appeal in *Neville v Wilson*[7]. Furthermore, once the purchase price had been paid by B to A, A would not in any case be able to put forward successfully any claim to the equitable interest as Lord Cohen has indicated[8]. Indeed, the best riposte may be that where A contracts to sell his equitable interest to B the nature of his 'interested' constructive

---

15 *Wright v Robert Leonard (Developments) Ltd* [1994] EGCS 69; s 2(4), 1989 Act.
16 *Spiro v Glencrown Properties Ltd* [1991] Ch 537.
17 *Record v Bell* [1991] 1 WLR 853; *Pitt v PHH Asset Management Ltd* [1993] 4 All ER 961, [1994] 1 WLR 327.
18 *Tootal Clothing v Guinea Properties Management Ltd* (1992) 64 P & CR 452.
19 *McCausland v Duncan Lawrie Ltd* [1997] 1 WLR 38, CA.
20 See Article 36.
 1 Per Upjohn J in *Grey v IRC* [1958] Ch 375 at 382 and per Evershed MR [1958] Ch 690 at 715, CA; *Grainge v Wilberforce* (1889) 5 TLR 436; *Re Lashmar* [1891] 1 Ch 258.
 2 Lord Denning in *Oughtred v IRC* [1960] AC 206 at 233.
 3 *Oughtred v IRC* [1958] Ch 383, [1958] 1 All ER 252.
 4 *Oughtred v IRC* [1960] AC 206 at 227–228.
 5 *Re Holt's Settlement* [1969] 1 Ch 100, [1968] 1 All ER 470.
 6 *DHN Food Distributors Ltd v London Borough of Tower Hamlets* [1976] 3 All ER 462 at 472, 473, [1976] 1 WLR 852 at 865, 867.
 7 [1997] Ch 144.
 8 *Oughtred v IRC* [1960] AC 206 at 230. The case concerned a remainderman, R, who orally agreed to transfer his interest under the settlement in certain shares to the life tenant, L, in return for other shares owned absolutely by L. After L had transferred her shares to R the trustees transferred the trust shares to L. The House of Lords majority held, whatever the effect of s 53 on the oral agreement, the transfer by the trustees was stampable ad valorem as a transfer on sale giving full effect to the agreement.

trusteeship, vitally dependent upon the contractual obligations being carried out (particularly payment of the purchase price) means that A is not at the outset a simple bare trustee, so there is a true sub-trust and not a full assignment of A's equitable interest to B so that s 53(1)(c) is inapplicable. The position is analogous to the case where A declares a sub-trust of his equitable interest in property other than land for X for one year, remainder to Y absolutely (outside s 53) and after a year X's interest automatically ceases and Y becomes full beneficial owner (outside s 53).

In *Chinn v Collins*[9] the House of Lords held that no formalities were required for contractual dealings related to an equitable interest in shares in an English public company: 'As soon as there was an agreement for their sale accompanied or followed by payment of the price, the equitable title passed at once to the purchaser and all that was needed to perfect his title was notice to the trustee'. Since the contract related to shares in a public company specific performance was not available as a remedy, so that no constructive trust could arise: thus the availability or otherwise of specific performance and the creation of a constructive trust is immaterial. A contract to make a disposition of an equitable interest is thus not in itself a disposition within s 53(1)(c).

Declarations (or creations) of trusts

Assuming that the appropriate formalities have been observed in property becoming vested in S or in S vesting property in his trustees for his beneficiaries, problems may arise as to the formalities to be observed in S declaring the trusts upon which he himself is to hold specific property henceforth or upon which his trustees are to hold specific property henceforth.

By the Law of Property Act 1925, s 53(1)(b),

'A declaration of trust respecting any land or any interest therein must be manifested and proved by some writing signed by some person who is able to declare such trust or by his will.'

As for s 40 of the 1925 Act before replaced by the 1989 Act, the trust is not required to be created by signed writing but only evidenced, so that the writing may come into existence at any time after the declaration of the trusts[10]. Absence of the written evidence makes the trust unenforceable but not void[11] so that the doctrine of part-performance[12] may enable the trust to

9 [1981] AC 533 at 548, Lord Wilberforce mentioning that the assignee should give notice to the trustee because if the trustee were to pay dividends to the vendor and did not have notice of the purchaser's interest he would be discharged from any liability to the purchaser who would have to trace against the vendor holding the dividends as constructive trustee. Moreover, a further reason for giving notice to the trustee is that if the assignor were to make several assignments for value of his one equitable interest priority under the rule in *Dearle v Hall* (1828) 3 Russ 1, as affected by Law of Property Act 1925, s 137 depends not on the order of making the assignments but on the order in which assignees gave notice to the trustee: further see J De Lacy, *The Priority Rule of Dearle v Hall Restated* [1999] Conv 311.

10 *Forster v Hale* (1798) 3 Ves 696; *Gardner v Rowe* (1828) 5 Russ 258; *Rochefoucauld v Boustead* [1897] 1 Ch 196 at 206; *Re Holland* [1902] 2 Ch 360. The failure to comply with s 53(1)(b) must be expressly pleaded.

11 See the cases in preceding note. It seems that s 53(1)(b) requires s 53(1)(a) to be construed as not extending to a declaration of trust, so as to leave scope for s 53(1)(b) under the maxim 'generalia specialibus non derogant'.

12 Preserved by LPA 1925, s 55(d).

be enforced. The writing need not be in any special form[13] but it must comprehensively set out the terms of the trust and recognise that there was a clear intention to create a trust[14]. The written evidence may comprise several linked documents read together, working back from the document bearing the appropriate signature[15].

The requisite signature is of 'some person who is able to declare such trust'. It has been assumed that the absence of an express reference to an agent found in ss 40(1), 53(1)(a) and 53(1)(c) precludes a settlor's agent lawfully authorised in writing from providing the requisite written evidence to satisfy s 53(1)(b), but it may yet prove to be the case that such authorised agent will be regarded as 'some person who is able to declare' a trust on the settlor's behalf. The necessary signatory will be A where A declares himself trustee of Blackacre for B and will then be B if B subsequently declares himself trustee of his equitable interest therein for C for life, remainder to D absolutely[16]. If B had declared himself to be a simple bare trustee for E absolutely this really means that A holds for E instead of B because E can directly sue A, so that B's disposition of his subsisting equitable interest seems to need to satisfy s 53(1)(c)[17].

Where A has conveyed land to B for C without signing a contemporaneous declaration of trust for C, then it seems to be B as the apparent landowner who needs to produce subsequent signed writing in C's favour[18]. It seems to be assumed that A cannot supply the written evidence subsequently to the conveyance to B, but because there is a valid but unenforceable trust why cannot A later supply the written evidence to make such trust enforceable, while also allowing B as A's authorised agent (until A revokes his mandate) to supply the written evidence? After all, until such written evidence is provided B must hold on a resulting trust for A[19], who ordinarily would then need to satisfy the tougher s 53(1)(c) to dispose of his equitable interest but who, exceptionally, because of the earlier transfer of the legal title to B on an unenforceable valid oral trust for C, ought retrospectively to be able to make such trust enforceable by providing the written evidence. If A had conveyed land (or other property) to B to hold to A's order and subsequently A told B to hold on trust for C this would amount to A disposing of his subsisting equitable interest and so would need to satisfy s 53(1)(c)[20].

Where land has been conveyed by A to B on oral trusts for C or for A the interests of C or A are, in the absence of writing signed by B, fully protected against B by the maxim that Equity will not allow a statute to be used as an instrument of fraud[1]. However, in a competition between A and C the better view[2] is that C cannot prove his claim due to the absence of writing satisfying

13 For example, in correspondence *Forster v Hale* (1798) 3 Ves 696; *Childers v Childers* (1857) 1 De G & J 482, CA; in a telegram *McBlain v Cross* (1871) 25 LT 804; a recital *Re Hoyle* [1893] 1 Ch 84, CA; an affidavit *Barkworth v Young* (1856) 26 LJ Ch 153; an answer to interrogatories *Wilson v Dent* (1830) 3 Sim 385.

14 *Smith v Matthews* (1861) 3 De GF & J 139 at 151; *Morton v Tewart* (1842) Y & C Ch Cas 67 at 80.

15 *Forster v Hale* (1798) 3 Ves 696; *Oliver v Hunting* (1890) 44 Ch D 205.

16 *Tierney v Wood* (1854) 19 Beav 330; *Kronheim v Johnson* (1877) 7 Ch D 60.

17 *Grey v IRC* [1958] Ch 375 at 382; revsd [1958] Ch 690 at 715, p 238, post.

18 *Gardner v Rowe* (1828) 5 Russ 258; *Smith v Matthews* (1861) 3 De GF & J 139; *Mountain v Styak* [1922] NZLR 131; T. G. Youdan [1984] Camb LJ 306 at 316–320.

19 See p 255, post.

20 *Grey v IRC* [1960] AC 1, [1959] 3 All ER 603, HL.

1 See pp 254–257, post.

2 See p 256, post.

s 53(1)(b), so that B holds on a resulting trust for A (assuming that C has not acted to his detriment in reliance upon having the equitable interest so as to obtain an equitable proprietary interest) for, otherwise, the impact of s 53(1)(b) would be restricted to cases where the settlor declares himself trustee of his own land[3].

A declaration of trusts of property other than interests in land need satisfy no special formalities: thus unsigned writing, word of mouth or conduct will suffice[4].

Dealings with equitable interests

Dealings by a person, S, in respect of his equitable interest under a trust create problems requiring special care to be taken. It may be that S purports to declare that he himself is henceforth to hold the equitable interest on trust for a person or persons or S may direct the trustees that they are henceforth to hold the trust property not for himself but for certain other persons. It is crucial to determine whether S is declaring or creating trusts within s 53(1)(b) or whether, in reality, he is disposing of his equitable interest when s 53(1)(c) will apply, laying down that 'a disposition of an equitable interest [in realty or personalty] subsisting at the time of the disposition must be in writing signed by the person disposing of the same, or by his agent lawfully authorised in writing or by will'.

Sub-trust or assignment?

Take the situation where T holds property on trust for S, when S declares that he is henceforth holding his equitable interest on trust for B absolutely. Here, if B is of full capacity, S is a simple or bare trustee so it seems he disappears from the picture leaving T holding on trust for B[5] whereas before T held on trust for S. Thus S had divested himself of his equitable interest which he has passed to B. This means that S's declaration is treated as a disposition of his equitable interest which must actually itself be in writing or be void owing to the Law of Property Act 1925, s 53(1)(c). However, if S's declaration had left him with active duties to perform so as not be a bare simple trustee then it would be a true declaration creating a sub-trust with S as sub-trustee holding the equitable interest for his beneficiaries with their subsidiary equitable interests[6], eg if S declared himself trustee for B for life with remainder to C, or discretionary trustee of discretionary trusts for D, E and F and their wives and children. In this latter case no formalities would need to be satisfied unless S's interest was in land and even then the

---

3 *Wratten v Hunter* [1978] 2 NSWLR 367; *Morris v Whiting* (1913) 15 DLR 254.
4 *Re Vandervell's Trusts (No 2)* [1974] Ch 269, [1974] 3 All ER 205; *Paul v Constance* [1977] 1 All ER 195, [1977] 1 WLR 527; *Rowe v Prance* [2000] WTLR 249.
5 *Grey v IRC* [1958] Ch 375 at 382, per Upjohn J; revsd [1958] Ch 690 at 715 per Evershed MR, CA; *Grainge v Wilberforce* (1889) 5 TLR 436; *Re Lashmar* [1891] 1 Ch 258. Under the principle in *Saunders v Vautier* (1841) 4 Beav 115, B should be able to bring an action directly against T so as to ensure that T vests the property in B. However, where T holds on trust for S, who declares he hold his interest on trust for B, one can argue that until B directs T to hold on trust for B instead of S, S holds his old equitable chose in action against T on a true trust for B who has a new equitable close in action against S who has thereby made a part disposal for capital gains tax purposes of his old equitable interest: see B. Green (1984) 47 MLR 385 at 397–398.
6 *Onslow v Wallis* (1849) 1 Mac & G 506; *Re Lashmar* [1891] 1 Ch 258.

s 53(1)(b) formalities would only be evidential and not prerequisite to the very validity of the trusts declared by S.

Beneficiary directing T to hold for another

The other way in which S may purportedly declare trusts of his equitable interest arises where T1 and T2 are trustees of property for S and S directs them to hold the property on trust for B instead of S. The essence of this direction is that S divests himself of his equitable interest and vests it in B. Thus S's direction is treated as a disposition of his equitable interest which must actually itself be in writing or be void owing to the Law of Property Act 1925, s 53(1)(c).

The leading case is *Grey v IRC*[7] where S had already created six settlements (each with the same persons as trustees) and wished to transfer 18,000 shares to those trustees in such a way as only to pay nominal stamp duty, a tax levied on *documents* effecting transactions. Thus, on 1 February he transferred the 18,000 shares to the trustees as nominees holding the shares to his order, so that since he had not divested himself of his equitable interest the trustees held the shares on trust for him[8]. On 18 February he orally directed the trustees to divide the shares into six blocks of 3,000 each to be appropriated to each of the six pre-existing settlements. On 25 March the trustees executed documents confirming that as from 18 February they held the blocks of the shares on the trusts of the relevant settlements and S also executed these documents, though not expressed to be a party thereto.

No stamp duty was payable if the oral direction of 18 February created the trust as it would if it truly amounted to a declaration of trust of personalty. However, if the direction really amounted to an assignment or disposition of S's equitable interest then this was void until effected in writing on 25 March, in which case stamp duty would be payable on the instruments of 25 March[9].

The House of Lords unanimously held that S's oral direction was a disposition of S's equitable interest since S intended thereby to divest himself of his equitable interest and vest it in the beneficiaries under his six pre-existing settlements. As such, the oral direction was void, so that it was the documents of 25 March signed by S that validly disposed of S's equitable interest and thus ad valorem stamp duty was payable.

Exercise of T's overriding powers

By way of contrast, if property is held by trustees upon such trusts as the settlor or the trustees shall from time to time declare (such power of the trustees being valid if restricted expressly or by necessary implication to a limited class of objects or even if open to be exercised in favour of anyone in the world other than the trustees), and the *trustees* declare or appoint trusts,

---

7 *Grey v IRC* [1960] AC 1, [1959] 3 All ER 603, HL. Like so many cases on formalities the problems arose from trying to avoid ad valorem stamp duty payable on documents. Conveyances or transfers by way of gift are no longer subject to ad valorem duty: Finance Act 1985, s 82.

8 The trust was probably express, though it may have been resulting, but no court treated the matter as of any significance.

9 The 25 March documents were regarded not as ineffective subsequent written evidence but as a 'belt and braces' device capable of making a disposition as of that date insofar as necessary if the 18 February disposition were void: *Grey v IRC* [1958] Ch 690 at 706–707, CA and B Green (1984) 47 MLR 385 at 391–392.

thereby divesting the existing beneficiaries of their equitable interests and vesting equitable interests in the new beneficiaries, this is not a disposition of subsisting equitable interests within s 53(1)(c): it is the creation of new equitable interests automatically extinguishing the old equitable interests. If, however, the *settlor* declared or appointed new trusts *and he* happened to be the beneficiary under an express or resulting trust, so that he was divesting himself of his equitable interest in favour of the newly declared beneficiaries, then it seems this should be a disposition within s 53(1)(c)[10]; indeed, Viscount Simonds in *Grey v IRC*[11] stated, 'If the word disposition is given its natural meaning it cannot be denied that a direction given by [the settlor-beneficiary] whereby the beneficial interest theretofore vested in him became vested in another is a disposition.'

Re Vandervell's Trusts (No 2)[12] is the case in point, though somewhat enigmatic. V wished to endow a Chair of Pharmacology at the Royal College of Surgeons by providing it with about £150,000. To this end, in 1958 he had 100,000 'A' shares in his private company transferred to the College, so that he might declare dividends on the shares amounting to £145,000 in the next few years, and he had the College grant an option to the trustee company of V's children's settlement enabling the 100,000 shares to be acquired for £5,000. Nothing was stated as to the trusts on which the trustee company was to hold the option. Thus, the House of Lords in the earlier *Vandervell v IRC*[13] held that the option was held by the trustee company on a resulting trust for V so that V, not having divested himself absolutely of all interest in the shares, was personally liable for surtax on all the dividends paid to the College in the period from 1958 until 1961, when the option was exercised, the appropriate amount of dividends having then been paid to endow the Chair.

The trustee company used £5,000 of the children's settlement moneys to exercise the option and acquire the 100,000 shares. The trustee company and V then believed, and acted on the footing, that the shares were held on the trusts of the children's settlement (erroneously believing that the option had been so held) so that V's private company declared £770,000 dividends on the shares and the dividends were added to the funds of the children's settlement in the period 1961 onwards.

However, doubts arose as to whether or not V had effectively divested himself absolutely of all interest in the shares so the Revenue claimed that V was still personally liable for surtax on dividends paid to the children's settlement from 1961. In 1965 V made sure he had divested himself of all interest by executing a deed transferring all his interest to the trustee company on the trusts of the children's settlement.

In 1967, probably worn out by his Revenue problems, V died, leaving his personal representatives allegedly responsible for £628,000 tax due on the dividends paid to the children's settlement 1961–1965.

---

10 There are unsound dicta of Lord Denning to the contrary in *Re Vandervell's Trusts (No 2)* [1974] Ch 269, [1974] 3 All ER 205, which cannot be supported even if restricted to a resulting trust in the settlor's favour – distinguishing between a resulting and an express trust in this context appears to fly in the face of *Grey v IRC* [1960] AC 1, [1959] 3 All ER 603 and of Lord Denning in *Oughtred v IRC* [1960] AC 206 at 233, HL where he considered that dispositions of equitable interests under a constructive trust needed to satisfy s 53(1)(c).

11 [1960] AC 1 at 12.

12 [1974] Ch 269 on which see [1979] Conv 17 (G Battersby) and (1975) 38 MLR 557 (JW Harris).

13 [1967] 2 AC 291, [1967] 1 All ER 1.

The personal representatives were thus forced to claim these dividends back from the trustee company on the basis that the option, and then the shares (after the exercise of the option), were held on a resulting trust for V until V executed the 1965 deed since (1) there was insufficient evidence of any intention to have the option and then the shares held on trust for the children's settlement, or (2) even if there were sufficient evidence, V could divest himself of his equitable interest in favour of the children only by signed writing within s 53(1)(c) and no such document came into existence until 1965.

The Revenue claim against the personal representatives for the £628,000 tax was stood over pending the outcome of the personal representatives' claim against the trustee company. After all, if the personal representatives' claim against the trustee company failed this would be on the basis that V had effectively divested himself of his equitable interest in the shares in 1961 so that no tax assessment should lie against the personal representatives in respect of the dividends on the shares paid to the trustee company. However, if the Revenue felt that the personal representatives had not pressed their claim against the trustee company hard enough then the Revenue, not being a party to that action[14], would not be bound by its findings and so could still pursue its claim. As things turned out the personal representatives' claim against the trustee company succeeded before Megarry J but, on a new ground, failed according to all three judges in the Court of Appeal, and the Revenue accepted this failure, so there was no need for the personal representatives to take the case to the House of Lords to impress the Revenue with their good faith. The net result of the *Re Vandervell (No 2)* litigation was that the Revenue lost and the Vandervell family won, though the Revenue had won in respect of the 1958–61 period in *Vandervell v IRC*.

In *Re Vandervell (No 2)* the Court of Appeal held that the additional evidence available since *Vandervell v IRC* did not change the inference drawn by Lord Upjohn[15] (with whom Lord Pearce agreed) that the option and, after its exercise, the shares, were to be held by the trustee company on such trusts as V *or the trustee company* should from time to time declare. Further, there was sufficient evidence that the trustee company had declared new trusts at the time of exercising the option in October 1961 since it had paid the £5,000 from the children's settlement, its solicitors in November had written to the Revenue so informing them stating, 'Consequently such shares will henceforth be held by the company upon the trusts of the settlement', and the trustee company thenceforward paid all dividends received into the children's settlement. Of course, the company's declaration of trust (which was probably restricted by necessary implication to exercising such power only in favour of beneficiaries under trusts of which the private trust company was trustee, as believed by the directors of the trust company according to paragraph 9(3) of the facts found by the Special Commissioners), since it concerned personalty, did not need to be in any special written form but could be manifested orally or by conduct[16].

14 In *Vandervell Trustees v White* [1971] AC 912, HL, the trustee company had successfully resisted the personal representatives' claim to join the Revenue as a party so that the Revenue would be bound by the findings of the facts. The Rules of the Supreme Court were then changed to allow the Revenue to be joined in future cases if they consent.

15 [1967] 2 AC 291 at 315, 317.

16 However, there are 'difficulties in the way of a limited company declaring a trust by way of parol or conduct and without a resolution of the board of directors' per Stephenson LJ

The trustee company's declaration of valid trusts in favour of the children extinguished V's equitable interest under the resulting trust in his favour. Thus s 53(1)(c) was inapplicable since it required only that 'a disposition of an equitable interest subsisting at the time of the disposition must be in writing signed by the person disposing of the same'. After all, V did not dispose of his existing equitable interest: the trustee company did not dispose of an existing equitable interest, but created a new equitable interest thereby automatically extinguishing V's old equitable interest.

Unfortunately some of Lord Denning's remarks in the case are couched in misleading broad terms sufficient to lead the unwary to believe that s 53(1)(c) is inapplicable, and so no formalities are required, where property is held on a resulting trust for the settlor and the *settlor* terminates the resulting trust by directing the trustees to hold on new trusts for new beneficiaries. In such a case s 53(1)(c) is applicable as made plain by *Grey v IRC* where trustees held shares for the settlor and were then orally told by him to hold the shares for certain beneficiaries, and the House of Lords held that this amounted to a disposition by the settlor of the settlor's equitable interest to the new beneficiaries which was void for lack of the writing required by s 53(1)(c).

Lord Denning and Lawton LJ[17] were also quite ready to hold that V during his lifetime (so binding his personal representatives) had by his conduct estopped himself from denying the existence of his children's beneficial interest in the shares acquired upon exercise of the option. However, they made no attempt to meet the difficulties over this, as fully set out in the judgment of Megarry J. Essentially, how could V be shown to have acted unconscionably or inequitably in letting the option be exercised for the benefit of the children's settlement and letting them receive the dividends on the shares acquired by exercising the option, when at the relevant time he believed he had no right to the option or dividends entitling him to object? Since Megarry J made this point it has become established that (whilst this point may still be valid where V has merely negatively acquiesced in what has occurred) where someone like V has positively encouraged particular conduct it is not necessary for him to know that he has a legal right to prohibit such conduct[18]. However, even if V's encouragement of the trustees spending £5,000 of the moneys of the trust for V's children upon purchasing the shares is capable of founding an estoppel, one would have thought that the requi-

[1974] Ch 269 at 323. Furthermore since the trustee company thought they were already trustees of the option for the children (rather than V) and thus automatically became trustees for the children of the shares acquired upon exercising the option, it is difficult to find an intention to create a new trust in favour of the children to displace the old trust in favour of V.

17 Lawton LJ was also prepared to base his judgment on an unrealistic distinction between the option held on a resulting trust and the shares acquired upon exercising the option: after the option had been exercised it had been extinguished, so the resulting trust had been extinguished so no old equitable interest existed to be capable of assignment, so that only new equitable interests could be created. However, the option is surely not distinct from the shares but merely a limited right created out of the larger bundle of rights inherent in the ownership of the shares; for this very reason the House of Lords in *Vandervell v IRC* held that V, as beneficial owner of the *option*, had failed to divest himself absolutely of the shares which it controlled. Moreover, if the right to the shares under the option was held by the trustee company not for itself, but for V, then surely the actual shares acquired by exercising the right were held for V.

18 *Taylor Fashions Ltd v Liverpool Victoria Trustees Co Ltd* [1982] QB 133n, [1981] 1 All ER 897, approved in *Habib Bank Ltd v Habib Bank AG Zurich* [1981] 2 All ER 650 at 666; *Amalgamated Investment and Property Co v Texas Commerce International Bank Ltd* [1982] QB 84 at 104; *Lim Teng Huan v Ang Swee Chuan* [1992] 1 WLR 113 at 117.

site minimum equity to do justice to the children's settlement was to order repayment of the £5,000 with interest rather than allowing the children's settlement to retain the £770,000 still in the settlement trustee's hands[19].

Beneficiary directing T to transfer to X absolutely

Further problems concerning s 53(1)(c) arise where T holds property on trust for A absolutely and A directs T to transfer the property to X to the intent that X shall have the full legal and beneficial interest therein. Whilst there is something to be said for the view that since A formerly had a separate equitable interest, which he no longer has, he must have disposed of his equitable interest to X, *Vandervell v IRC*[20] provides clear House of Lords' authority that where the legal title to the property is transferred at the direction of the absolutely entitled beneficiary (or the beneficiaries together entitled to the entire beneficial interest) no separate assignment within s 53(1)(c) is required of the equitable interest co-extensive with the legal title.

The reasoning in the speeches of Lord Upjohn[1] and Lord Donovan[2] is based on likening A's position as absolutely entitled equitable owner to the position of an absolute *legal* beneficial owner, O, who transfers property, when there is clearly no need for O to sign a separate written assignment of the beneficial[3] interest. This accords with the object of s 53(1)(c) which 'is to prevent hidden oral transactions in equitable interests ... and making it difficult, if not impossible, for the trustee to ascertain who are in truth his beneficiaries'[4]. However, the reasoning is not very convincing because in the case of transfer by the legal beneficial owner the beneficial interest is subsumed or merged in the legal interest, whereas where T holds the legal title on trust for A the legal and equitable interests are obviously separated and the issue is whether they can be joined without a separate assignment or surrender by A, so that the legal and equitable interest may become at home in T and so be transferred by T to X. It seems that the position might be better justified on the ground that where T does transfer the legal title to X at the instigation of, or with the concurrence of, A then A's interest is overreached[5] and he cannot claim there has been a breach of trust and assert his interest against the new legal owner, X. By operation of law outside s 53(1)(c) A's equitable interest is extinguished[6] just as much as it would have been extinguished if A in signed writing had expressly surrendered his equitable interest to T, so that T might then pass the legal (and thus automatically the co-extensive equitable) interest to X[7].

On either basis it would seem to follow that it is the transfer by T to X that

---

19 B Green (1984) 47 MLR 385 at 418.
20 [1967] 2 AC 291.
 1 [1967] 2 AC 291 at 311.
 2 [1967] 2 AC 291 at 317.
 3 O is not regarded as having separate legal and equitable interests, his beneficial interest being subsumed in the legal interest: *Westdeutsche Landesbank v Islington London Borough Council* [1996] AC 669 at 706; *DKLR Holding Co v Comr for Stamp Duties* (NSW) (1982) 149 CLR 431.
 4 [1967] 2 AC 291 at 311.
 5 See R C Nolan [2002] Camb LJ 169.
 6 (1967) 31 Conv 175 (SM Spencer); [1979] Conv 17 (G Battersby). The position of X will be even stronger if he provided consideration in reliance upon acquiring title.
 7 Where T holds on trust for A it seems possible for A orally to direct T that he is to hold on trust for A until A or T declares new trusts so if it is T who declares new trusts, then T's declaration need not satisfy s 53(1)(c): conferring such a power does not confer an interest in property: see *Townshend v Harrowby* (1858) 27 LJ Ch 553; *Melville v IRC* [2002] 1 WLR 407, CA.

is crucial and not the earlier direction by A to T to make the transfer, so that A does not cease to be equitable owner upon giving his gratuitous oral direction to T. What if A dies before T carries out his direction or revokes his direction where the transaction is voluntary?[8] In the case of shares, where the legal title is transferred only upon the company registering the transferee on the register of members of the company, there must be considered the *Re Rose* principle[9] which treats gifts as complete when the donor has done all that is necessary, according to the nature of the property, that is required to be done by him. What if X has received the share certificates in question and the duly executed share transfer form but at the time of A's death or revocation of his voluntary direction X has not sent the document to the company or the company has not yet registered X as the new member? Strictly, it would seem that since T originally has the legal interest and since A originally has the equitable interest (until assigned under s 53(1)(c) or extinguished upon a transfer to a third party with A's concurrence) A has not done everything possible within his power to transfer his equitable interest for he has not taken advantage of s 53(1)(c). Thus, in the case of voluntary transactions A's death or revocation of his direction before the legal interest is effectively transferred from T to X should ensure that the equitable interest does not pass to X. However, it seems likely that a more liberal view will be taken, treating A as if he were the legal as well as the equitable owner so that X will obtain the equitable interest on *Re Rose* principles[10].

Beneficiary directing T to transfer to TT for another

Finally, there must be considered the position where T holds property on trust for A absolutely and A directs T to transfer the property to X who is to hold on trust for B[11]. Nothing was said of this position in *Vandervell v IRC*[12]. However, if, as there, the position of the absolutely entitled A is likened to the position of an absolute legal beneficial owner, O, who transfers property to X on trust for B, it is clear that O would not need to execute a separate written assignment of O's equitable interest to B: O's transfer of the legal title to X would have to satisfy the requisite formalities for the nature of the transferred property but the trusts declared by O at the time of the transfer could be oral, though if land were involved subsequent written evidence thereof would be required under s 53(1)(b). Here the analogy between A and O is obviously less convincing than in *Vandervell v IRC* especially when such an argument would undermine the decision in *Grey v IRC*[13], based on the need for trustees and their successors in title to have a paper trail where a separate equitable interest subsists, so as to know where they stand without any problems of oral evidence, so avoiding the mischief against which

---

8 See p 166, ante.

9 See p 154, ante.

10 Per Lord Wilberforce in *Vandervell v IRC* [1967] 2 AC 291 at 330; (1967) 30 MLR 461 (N Strauss) but see B Green (1984) 47 MLR 385 at 410.

11 The trust for B must commence with X's title to the property, otherwise X will hold on a resulting trust for A so that if X is subsequently to hold for B A will be making a disposition within s 53(1)(c); *Grey v IRC* [1960] AC 1, [1959] 3 All ER 603, HL.

12 [1967] 2 AC 291, [1967] 1 All ER 1, HL. The statement of Harman LJ in [1966] Ch at 296, 's 53(1)(c) in dealing with dispositions of an equitable interest only applies where the disposer is not also the controller of the legal interest' is misleadingly succinct since it contradicts *Grey v IRC* [1960] AC 1, [1959] 3 All ER 603, HL.

13 [1960] AC 1, HL.

s 53(1)(c) is directed. In *Vandervell v IRC* the effect of the disposition was that the legal and beneficial interest was at home in X, while in *Grey v IRC* and the present case, where the transferee X is to hold on trust for B, there is a clear separation of the legal interest from the equitable interest which has passed from its owner, A, to B by virtue of A's direction, thereby falling within s 53(1)(c). Indeed, in *Grey v IRC*, while the factual position was that T1 and T2 held shares on trust for A and were directed by A to hold them instead, in their existing capacities as trustees, for B, the legal position was that A directed his trustees to transfer shares to trustees of a trust for B, nowadays being a capital gains tax disposal from one set of trustees to a new set absolutely entitled against the other set, it being immaterial that the same individuals happen to comprise both sets of trustees[14].

Registers or databases of equitable interests

What is the position where there is an unincorporated society which keeps a register of members interested under a bare trust of the society's assets or where a nominee holder of securities maintains a register or database of the persons for whom it holds the securities from time to time? Does s 53(1)(c) as interpreted in *Grey v IRC* create insuperable problems? At first sight it does, but the practical inconvenience thereof (a point fundamental to *Vandervell v IRC*) indicates that the courts are likely to circumvent s 53(1)(c) on the basis that, as a matter of contract law, agreed acts of the member or beneficiary amount to authority to the society's trustees or the nominee to recognise that he no longer has any equitable interest and that some other person or persons now have enlarged equitable interests or new equitable interests, so that he is prevented from asserting any claim[15].

'Dispositions' within section 53(1)(c)

'Disposition' within s 53(1)(c) includes a conveyance which is defined[16] to include a mortgage, charge, lease, assent, vesting declaration, vesting instrument, disclaimer, release and every other assurance of property unless the context otherwise requires. However, the Court of Appeal in *Re Paradise Motor Co Ltd*[17] briefly held that s 53(1)(c) is inapplicable to a disclaimer since 'a disclaimer operates by way of avoidance and not by way of disposition'[18]. The case concerned A making a gift of shares to B, B's name being registered in the company's register of members. Within a reasonable time of learning

---

14 *Hoare Trustees v Gardner* [1978] 1 All ER 791; Taxation of Capital Gains Act 1992, s 71.

15 *Ashby v Blackwell and the Million Bank Co* (1765) Amb 503; K F Sin *The Legal Nature of the Unit Trust* (Oxford University Press, 1997); *Clarke v Dunraven* [1897] AC 59, HL; Contracts (Rights of Third Parties) Act 1999. To put matters beyond doubt, dispositions of equitable interests in shares within the CREST system and dealings in gilt-edged securities settled through the Central Gilts Office are exempted from compliance with s 53(1)(c) by the Uncertified Securities Regulations 1995, SI 1995/3272, reg 32(5) and Stock Transfer Act 1982, s 1(2). Where the declarer of a gratuitous trust for B of full capacity remains on the register or database it seems writing is required within LPA 1925, s 53(1)(c) normally (see p 238, ante) unless such disposition of the declarer's interest is exempted as under SI 1995/3272, reg 32(5).

16 Law of Property Act 1925, s 205(1)(ii).

17 [1968] 2 All ER 625, [1968] 1 WLR 1125, CA; and see *Dewar v Dewar* [1975] 1 WLR 1532; *Re Smith* [2001] 3 All ER 552; *Sembalunk v Sembalunk* (1985) 15 DLR (4th) 303 at 309–310. Note also that disclaimer of a unilateral transfer of land may be oral: *Re Birchall* (1889) 40 Ch D 436, CA.

18 [1968] 2 All ER 625 at 632, [1968] 1 WLR 1125, at 1143.

of this B orally disclaimed any interest. His subsequent claim that this disclaimer was ineffective for failure to satisfy s 53(1)(c) failed on the short ground given above by the court. No fuller explanation was given by the court.

It would seem that the court must have assumed that only the legal title to the shares had passed to B and that the equitable interest would only pass to B when, having become aware of the gift, he failed to disclaim it within a reasonable time: his disclaimer within a reasonable time prevented the equitable interest passing to him and since he avoided having the equitable interest he could not be treated as having disposed of it[19]. Thus the essence of disclaimer is that it is a refusal to accept an intended gift, not a disposal of property.

Where a release or surrender is concerned it may be argued that it takes effect by way of extinguishing the existing equitable interest and that extinction is not disposition[20] just as avoidance (in the case of disclaimer) is not disposition. Indeed, some support may be obtained from *Vandervell v IRC*[1] where T held on trust for A absolutely and A directed T to transfer the whole legal and beneficial interest to B and there was held to be no disposition within s 53(1)(c) on the part of A, though the result was that the whole interest was in B so that A's interest had somehow been released, surrendered or otherwise extinguished. However, *Vandervell v IRC* is likely to be restricted to the situation where an absolutely entitled beneficiary, A, directs a disposition of the legal estate and the beneficial interest therewith. Take the case before 1985 where O transferred property to T to hold on trust for O, so only nominal stamp duty was payable, but where O really wanted to make a gift to T escaping ad valorem duty. Could O achieve this end by then taking the step of orally releasing his equitable interest so that T became full beneficial owner? It would be extraordinary if this were the case since O was dealing just with his equitable interest[2]. Thus writing is probably required under s 53(1)(c). This is supported by the view of the House of Lords[3] that the surrender of a lease would be a disposition within s 37 of the Matrimonial Causes Act 1973.

Variations of trusts by the court under the Variation of Trusts Act 1958 do not have to satisfy s 53(1)(c)[4], nor, apparently, nominations made under a staff pension fund allowing a beneficiary to nominate a beneficiary to take on his death what would otherwise vest in his personal representatives[5]. Similarly, if a person takes out a policy on his own life where rights to a money payment only crystallise on death, there is no disposition of a subsisting equitable interest if he orally nominates X to receive the money to which he

---

19 *Re Stratton's Disclaimer* [1958] Ch 42, [1957] 2 All ER 594, CA.
20 [1960] BTR 20 (JG Monroe); *Re Tancred's Settlement* [1903] 1 Ch 715 at 725; *Re Earl Leven* [1954] 3 All ER 81, [1954] 1 WLR 1228.
1 [1967] 2 AC 291, [1967] 1 All ER 1, HL.
2 Is it not 'the disposition of an equitable interest as such' in the words of Lord Donovan in *Vandervell v IRC* [1967] 2 AC 291 at 317. Moreover, as observed by Viscount Simonds in *Grey v IRC* [1960] AC 1 at 12, 'If the word disposition is given its natural meaning it cannot be denied that a direction given by [the beneficiary] whereby the beneficial interest in the shares theretofore vested in him became vested in another is a disposition.' See also *IRC v Buchanan* [1958] Ch 289, [1957] 2 All ER 400, CA.
3 [1999] 1 AC 313, HL.
4 *Re Holt's Settlement* [1969] 1 Ch 100, [1968] 1 All ER 470.
5 *Re Danish Bacon Co Staff Pension Fund Trusts* [1971] 1 WLR 248; *Baird v Baird* [1990] 2 AC 548.

is contractually entitled and hold it on trust for B and C[6].

Where s 53(1)(c) does apply to an assignment in writing of an equitable interest and the assignee is to take as trustee the assignment is valid without the need to disclose particulars of the trust[7]. Furthermore, the requirement for signed writing can be satisfied as for ss 40 and 53(1)(b) by two or more sufficiently interconnected documents[8].

Testamentary trusts

Clearly, when a testator is intending in his will or codicil to create trusts of property to take effect on his death such trusts will only take effect if the Wills Act 1837 formalities are satisfied as respects the trust property and the intended beneficiaries by virtue of the testator's signature being attested by two witnesses present together. An apparent inter vivos trust will only be regarded as testamentary in nature if it has no immediate effect on the settlor's full beneficial ownership and purports to dispose of such equitable interest only on his death, eg a transfer to trustees of property to be held on trust in S's lifetime as to income *and capital* for S or such persons as he directs and on his death for X or such other person signified to the trustees by S in signed writing in his lifetime or by will[9]. If such trust happened to comply with testamentary formalities it would only take effect (other than as a bare trust for S) on S's death – if not revoked by some later will – when its subject matter, being whatever is left at S's death after S has done whatever he wanted with it, will be certain.

In contrast, there will be an effective inter vivos trust where S transfers property in his lifetime to trustees on trust for S for life, remainder to B or such other persons signified to the trustees by S in signed writing in his lifetime or by will, even if the trustees or S have power to revoke the trust or to appoint the property to anyone other than the trustees[10]. B has a defeasible vested interest in remainder capable of passing to his trustee in bankruptcy if he becomes bankrupt or of being disposed of by B inter vivos or by

---

6   *Gold v Hill* (1998–99) 1 ITELR 27, [1999] 1 FLR 54, while as pointed out in *Kasperbauer v Griffiths* [2000] WTLR 333 at 347, the doctrine of secret trusts has no application to nominations of beneficiaries under life policies.

7   *Re Tyler Funds Trusts* [1967] 3 All ER 389, [1967] 1 WLR 1269.

8   *Re Danish Bacon Co Staff Pension Fund* [1971] 1 All ER 486, [1971] 1 WLR 248.

9   See *Anderson v Patton* [1948] 2 DLR 202 where three judges in the Alberta Court of Appeal upheld the trial judge's construction of a trust as a gift of $5000 to a trustee upon trust for the settlor for life, then for X and Y, with a power of revocation in the settlor, so there was a valid trust, while two judges held the trust to be of capital and income for the settlor absolutely but if he did not demand the money in his lifetime then it was to pass to X and Y, so there was a void testamentary disposition. As Dixon and Evatt JJ stated in *Russell v Scott* (1936) 55 CLR 440 at 454, 'What can be accomplished only by will is the voluntary transmission on death of an interest which up to the moment of death belongs absolutely [and indefeasibly] to the deceased.' The bracketed words are correct if referring to an interest defeasible by the death of the deceased but not by some subsequent event. Also see *Governors of Foundling Hospital v Crane* [1911] 2 KB 367 at 379–380.

10   *Kauter v Hilton* (1953) 90 CLR 86 at 98–99 and 100–101; *Young v Sealey* [1949] Ch 278 at 284 and 294, Scott on *Trusts* (4th edn) para 57.1, but if the settlor retains such control that the trust is a sham in his lifetime the dispositions after his death will be testamentary: *Scott on Trusts* (4th edn) para 57.2. Where S in his lifetime sets up a joint account of cash or investments for S and B jointly then, in the absence of any resulting trust, B will become automatically entitled to the cash or investments on S's death: *Aroso v Coutts & Co* [2001] WTLR 797.

will, while S has a defeasible vested life interest entitling him to the income until exercise of the power of revocation or appointment.

Equitable proprietary estoppel

Equity is seen as its flexible best or worst in its doctrine that if a defendant encourages, or acquiesces in, the claimant acting to his detriment, in the belief that the defendant's property is the claimant's property or that the defendant has given or will give the claimant the property or an interest therein, then equity will estop the defendant (and his personal representatives) from asserting his full legal and beneficial ownership and from claiming that non-compliance with statutory formalities under the Law of Property Act 1925 or the Wills Act 1837 bars the claimant's claim. Such estoppel gives the claimant an equitable right which may be for a sum of money[11], perhaps supported by an equitable lien on the defendant's property for the claimant's expenditure[12] or the value of his improvements[13] or lost expected occupancy rights[14], or a decree perfecting the defendant's imperfect gift by ordering the defendant to convey[15] or lease[16] land to the claimant, or grant the claimant an easement[17] or a licence to use the premises as long as the claimant permanently resides there[18] or until the claimant receives compensation from the defendant[19].

The question arises whether, in the event of detrimental reliance, the court should order a remedy which fulfils the expectations of the claimant so as to perfect imperfect gifts (just like a contract is fully enforced irrespective of the consideration therefor being relatively slight) or a remedy which merely reverses the claimant's detriment. It seems that the aim is 'the minimum equity to do justice to'[20] the claimant so that the Australian courts' approach[1]

11 *Jennings v Rice* [2002] EWCA Civ 159, [2002] All ER (D) 324 (Feb).
12 *Unity Joint Stock Mutual Banking Association v King* (1858) 25 Beav 72; *Morris v Morris* [1982] 1 NSWLR 61; *Lee-Parker v Izzet (No 2)* [1972] 2 All ER 800 at 804–805; *Burrows v Sharp* (1989) 23 HLR 82; *Baker v Baker* (1993) 25 HLR 408.
13 *Raffaele v Raffaele* [1962] WAR 29; (1963) 79 LQR 228 (D E Allen).
14 *Campbell v Griffin* [2001] EWCA Civ 990, [2001] WTLR 981.
15 *Pascoe v Turner* [1979] 2 All ER 945, [1979] 1 WLR 431, CA; *Dillwyn v Llewelyn* (1862) 4 De GF & J 517; *Thomas v Thomas* [1956] NZLR 785; *Re Basham* [1987] 1 All ER 405; *Voyce v Voyce* (1991) 62 P & CR 290; *Lim Teng Huan v Ang Swee Chuan* [1992] 1 WLR 113 (where the transfer to the claimant was conditional upon payment of suitable compensation).
16 *Taylor Fashions Ltd v Liverpool Victoria Trustees Co Ltd* [1982] QB 133n, [1981] 1 All ER 897; *Siew Soon Wah v Yong Tong Hong* [1973] AC 836, [1973] 2 WLR 713, PC; *Griffiths v Williams* (1977) 248 Estates Gazette 947, CA.
17 *Ward v Kirkland* [1967] Ch 194, [1966] 1 All ER 609; *Ives Investments Ltd v High* [1967] 2 QB 379, [1967] 1 All ER 504, CA; *Crabb v Arun District Council* [1976] Ch 179, [1975] 3 All ER 865, CA.
18 *Inwards v Baker* [1965] 2 QB 29, [1965] 1 All ER 446, CA; *Greasley v Cooke* [1980] 3 All ER 710, [1980] 1 WLR 1306, CA; *Williams v Staite* [1979] Ch 291, [1978] 2 All ER 928, CA; *Maharaj v Chand* [1986] AC 898, [1986] 3 All ER 107, PC; *Matharu v Matharu* [1994] 2 FLR 597, CA. Before TLATA 1996, if the court found the plaintiff to have a life interest, as opposed to a licence then the plaintiff became a Settled Land Act tenant for life: *Ungurian v Leshoff* [1990] Ch 206.
19 *Re Sharpe (a bankrupt)* [1980] 1 All ER 198, [1980] 1 WLR 219; *Hussey v Palmer* [1972] 3 All ER 744, [1972] 1 WLR 1286, CA; *Dodsworth v Dodsworth* (1973) 228 Estates Gazette 1115; *Taylor v Taylor* [1956] NZLR 99; *Stratulatos v Stratulatos* [1988] 2 NZLR 424.
20 *Crabb v Arun District Council* [1976] Ch 179; *Pascoe v Turner* [1979] 1 WLR 431; *Baker v Baker* (1993) 25 HLR 408; *Sledmore v Dalby* (1996) 72 P & CR 196, CA; *Gillett v Holt* [2001] Ch 210.
 1 *Waltons Stores (Interstate) Ltd v Maher* (1988) 164 CLR 387; *Commonwealth of Australia v Verwayen* (1990) 170 CLR 394.

is to reverse detriment or prevent unjust enrichment, because it would normally be inequitable to assist a volunteer by providing a remedy which is disproportionate to the detriment. However there may be exceptional reasons for going further in some cases, as in *Pascoe v Turner*, where according to the Court of Appeal[2], 'The court must decide what is the minimum equity to do justice to [the claimant, Mrs Turner] having regard to the way in which she changed her position for the worse by reason of the acquiescence and encouragement of the legal owner.' This was a Mr Pascoe who had told Mrs Turner, 'The home is yours', when he left her to move in with another woman. Believing the house was now hers Mrs Turner spent £230 on improvements to it over three years, such expenditure representing a significant part of her small capital. Mr Pascoe's 'ruthless disregard of the obligations binding on his conscience' led him to try to recover the house but the court ordered him to convey the fee simple to Mrs Turner. Otherwise, she might be at risk of him selling to a bona fide purchaser of the legal estate for value without notice (when she was away, ill or on holiday) and would not have a mortgageable interest as security for loans for repairs and improvements.

From *Jennings v Rice*[3] the Court of Appeal approach now appears to be to look at the claimant's expectation as indicating the maximum extent of the equity but the court's award is a proportionate one taking account of the combination of expectations, detrimental reliance and the unconscionableness of allowing the benefactor-defendant (or the deceased benefactor's estate) to go back on his assurances. The court also takes account of any misconduct of the claimant[4], any particularly oppressive conduct of the defendant[5] and the difficulties in compelling people to live under one roof so that there may be a need for a clean break[6].

Where the assurances and the claimant's reliance have a consensual character relating to specific property the court will normally vindicate the claimant's expectations[7]. However, where the expectations are uncertain or extravagant or out of all proportion to the detriment which the claimant has suffered the court will satisfy the equity in another more limited way[8].

Development of broad approach

The starting point for proprietary estoppel claims used to be the five *probanda* of Fry J in *Willmott v Barber*[9]:

'In the first place the plaintiff must have made a mistake as to his legal rights. Secondly, the plaintiff must have expended some money or must have done some

---

2 *Pascoe v Turner* [1979] 2 All ER 945 at 950, CA, endorsing the approach of Scarman LJ in *Crabb v Arun District Council* [1976] Ch 179, [1975] 3 All ER 865, CA.
3 [2002] EWCA Civ 159, [2002] WTLR 367.
4 *J Willis & Son v Willis* [1986] 1 EGLR 62; *Williams v Staite* [1979] Ch 291, CA.
5 *Pascoe v Turner* [1979] 1 WLR 431, CA; *Crabb v Arun District Council* [1976] Ch 179, CA.
6 *Campbell v Griffin* [2001] EWCA Civ 900, [2001] WTLR 981; *Burrows v Sharp* (1991) 23 HLR 82; *Baker v Baker* [1993] 2 FLR 247, CA.
7 *Yaxley v Gotts* [2000] Ch 162 (proprietary estoppel and common intention constructive trusts often co-existing). A typical case will involve an elderly benefactor and a carer residing with him under a common understanding the latter will inherit the benefactor's house or will have a home for life: *Jennings v Rice* [2002] EWCA Civ 159, para [45].
8 *Jennings v Rice* [2002] EWCA Civ 159, para [50]; *Campbell v Griffin* [2001] EWCA Civ 900, [2001] WTLR 981; *Gillett v Holt* [2001] Ch 210, CA.
9 (1880) 15 Ch D 96 at 105–106.

act (not necessarily upon the defendant's land) on the faith of his mistaken belief. Thirdly, the defendant, the possessor of the legal right, must know of the existence of his own right which is inconsistent with the right claimed by the plaintiff. If he does not know of it he is in the same position as the plaintiff, and the doctrine of acquiescence is founded upon conduct with a knowledge of your legal rights. Fourthly, the defendant, the possessor of the legal right, must know of the plaintiff's mistaken belief of his rights. If he does not, there is nothing which calls upon him to assert his own rights. Lastly, the defendant must have encouraged the plaintiff in his expenditure of money or in the other acts which he has done, either directly or by abstaining from asserting his legal right ... Nothing short of this will do.'

The courts originally considered matters from the viewpoint of the defendant, the possessor of the legal right, so that he had to be at fault in some way before the claimant could claim an equity. Thus, if the defendant did not know the true position and so did not know of his right to object when he either acquiesced in or encouraged the claimant's belief then he was not estopped from subsequently asserting his rights against the claimant[10]. This may still be the case where he has merely acquiesced whilst his rights were being infringed at a time when he did not realise he had such rights[11].

In cases of encouragement the court now seems to regard matters from the claimant's viewpoint. It is not fault on the defendant's part that is significant: attention is directed at how unconscionable it would be if the claimant were to suffer from the defendant asserting his strict legal rights. The court adopts a broad approach[12] 'directed at ascertaining whether in particular circumstances it would be unconscionable for a party to be permitted to deny that which, knowingly or unknowingly, he has allowed or encouraged another to assume to his detriment'. The defendant's ignorance is merely one of the relevant factors in the overall inquiry.

Detrimental reliance

It is necessary to prove that the plaintiff acted to her detriment in the belief that she had or would have an interest in the defendant's property[13]. The detrimental acts do not need to be expenditure of money or be inherently referable to the property[14]. Once the claimant shows that the defendant assured the claimant she was to have an interest in the property and that the claimant suffered detriment it will be presumed that the claimant acted to

---

10   *Willmott v Barber* (1880) 15 Ch D 96; *Falcke v Scottish Imperial Insurance Co* (1886) 34 Ch D 234 at 243, 253, CA; *Re Vandervell's Trusts (No 2)* [1974] Ch 269 at 300–301.

11   *Taylor Fashions Ltd v Liverpool Victoria Trustees Co Ltd* [1982] QB 133n at 147; *Amalgamated Investment and Property Co Ltd v Texas Commerce International Bank Ltd* [1982] QB 84 at 204, CA.

12   *Taylor Fashions Ltd v Liverpool Victoria Trustees Co Ltd* [1982] QB 133n at 151, approved in *Habib Bank Ltd v Habib Bank Ag Zurich* [1981] 2 All ER 650 at 666, CA; *Appleby v Cowley* (1982) Times, 14 April; *A-G of Hong Kong v Humphreys Estate Ltd* [1987] 2 All ER 387 at 392, PC; *Lim Teng Huan v Ang Swee Chuan* [1992] 1 WLR 113 at 117, PC. Cf the broad approach to consents to breach of trust in *Re Pauling's Settlement Trusts* [1962] 1 WLR 86 at 208 endorsed by the Court of Appeal in *Re Freeston's Charity* [1979] 1 All ER 51, [1978] 1 WLR 741, CA.

13   *Greasley v Cooke* [1980] 1 WLR 1306 at 1313–1314, CA; *Watts and Ready v Storey* (1983) 134 NLJ 631, CA cited in Maudsley & Burn's *Land Law: Cases & Materials* (6th edn) p 575; *Grant v Edwards* [1986] 2 All ER 426 at 439; *Brinnand v Ewens* (1987) 19 HLR 415. *Midland Bank v Dobson* [1986] 1 FLR 171.

14   *Grant v Edwards* [1986] 2 All ER 426 at 439, CA; *Jones v Jones* [1977] 2 All ER 231; *Greasley v Cooke* [1980] 1 WLR 1306; *Re Basham* [1987] 1 All ER 405, [1986] 1 WLR 1498.

her detriment in reliance on the assurance: the onus of rebutting this pre-sumption of reliance will then be on the defendant[15].

In *Grant v Edwards*[16] Browne-Wilkinson V-C stated obiter:

'In many cases it is impossible to say whether or not the claimant would have done the act relied on as a detriment even if she thought she had no interest in the house. Setting up house together, having a baby and making payments to general housekeeping expenses (not strictly necessary to enable the mortgage to be paid) may all be referable to the mutual love and affection of the parties and not speci-fically referable to the claimant's belief that she has an interest in the house. Once it has been shown that there was a common intention that the claimant should have an interest in the house, any act done by her to her detriment relating to the joint lives of the parties is sufficient detriment to qualify. The acts do not have to be inherently referable to the house. The holding out to the claimant that she had a beneficial interest in the house is an act of such a nature as to be part of the inducement to her to do the acts relied on. Accordingly, in the absence of evidence to the contrary, the right inference is that the claimant acted in reliance on such holding out and the burden lies on the legal owner to show that she did not do so.'

Earlier, a tough approach had been taken in *Coombes v Smith*[17] where the claimant's belief, encouraged by the defendant house-owner whilst she was his mistress, that he would always provide her with a roof over her head was held to be something quite different from a belief that she had an interest in the house. Even if she had had such a belief the judge was of the view that the claimant had failed to prove that her following acts constituted detriment in the context of proprietary estoppel:

(1) leaving her husband and moving to a house owned but not occupied by the defendant[18] (who lived elsewhere with his wife and children, though indicating for ten years he would shortly be leaving them to live with the plaintiff);

(2) allowing herself to become pregnant and giving birth to their child Clare[19];

(3) looking after and redecorating the house, looking after Clare and being ready for the defendant's visits[20];

(4) taking no other steps like looking for a paid job (or, presumably, a rich husband) to provide for herself and Clare, when the defendant was happy to pay all the bills and pay an allowance to her and Clare[1].

Nowadays, a more sympathetic approach is taken to the question of det-rimental reliance. As Robert Walker LJ states in *Gillett v Holt*[2]:

'Detriment is required. But the authorities show that it is not a narrow or technical concept. The detriment need not consist of the expenditure of money or other quantifiable financial detriment, so long as it is something substantial. The requirement must be approached as part of a broad inquiry as to whether repu-diation of an assurance is or is not unconscionable in all the circumstances ...

15 *Greasley v Cooke* [1980] 1 WLR 1306, CA; *Coombes v Smith* [1986] 1 WLR 808 at 821.

16 [1986] 2 All ER 426 at 439, CA.

17 [1986] 1 WLR 808.

18 She preferred to have a relationship with, and a child by, the defendant rather than continue living with her husband.

19 She wished to bear his child.

20 She was the occupier of the house, Clare's mother and his mistress.

1 The deputy judge, Jonathan Parker QC, considered her omission to look for a job, once Clare was born, as 'more readily arguable' as beneficial then detrimental since this meant the defendant provided her with the money she needed: sed quaere [1986] Camb LJ 394 (D J Hayton).

2 [2001] Ch 210 at 232.

There must be sufficient causal link between the assurance relied on and the detriment asserted. The issue of detriment must be judged at the moment when the person who has given the assurance seeks to go back on it. Whether the detriment is sufficiently substantial is to be tested by whether it would be unjust or inequitable to allow the assurance to be disregarded - that is, again, the essential test of unconscionability. The detriment alleged must be pleaded and proved.'

Once it is proved that the assurance was made and that there has been conduct by the claimant of such a nature that inducement may be inferred, then the burden of proof switches to the defendant to establish that the claimant did not rely on the assurance[3].

In *Wayling v Jones*[4] the claimant chef was promised by his homosexual cohabitee that the latter's hotel (where the chef worked for inadequate wages) would be devised to him. It was, but a new hotel was bought without the will being altered to take account of this, so the old devise was adeemed. The new hotel was sold on the owner's death but the claimant successfully obtained the proceeds of sale to satisfy his equity, despite having answered 'Yes' in cross-examination to the question, 'If he had not made the promise to you would you have stayed.' This indicated that he stayed for low wages because he loved the hotel owner, not because he had been promised the hotel on the owner's death. However, the Court of Appeal held that since the owner had made the promise to his chef-lover who, in evidence, had said that if the owner had reneged on his promise he, the chef, would have left to find a job elsewhere, this was sufficient to prevent the owner's executors from showing that the chef had not relied upon the promise[5].

In the testamentary context where the benefactor assures the claimant that the benefactor will leave all his estate or a particular house to the claimant-carer or will see to it in his will that the claimant will be all right, the Court of Appeal[6] has rejected the view[7] that a claimant relies on testamentary promises at his own risk (because wills are always ambulatory and revocable) unless the benefactor has created or encouraged the claimant to believe he would not revoke his promise. After all, because estoppel claims concern promises unsupported by contractual consideration they must always be initially revocable: it is the claimant's detrimental reliance that thereafter makes the promises binding and irrevocable.

Thus in *Gillett v Holt*[8] the defendant landowner of substantial means had repeatedly made assurances to the claimant that he would inherit the defendant's farming business. On this basis the claimant as friend and then farm manager worked for the defendant from the age of 16 and deprived himself of the opportunity to better himself. After nearly 40 years the defendant unjustifiably sacked the claimant, made gifts to a new favourite and altered his will (under which the residuary estate went to the claimant) so as to make no provision for the claimant. The Court of Appeal awarded the claimant one of the defendant's three farms (a farmhouse and 42 hectares of land) and £100,000 to compensate him for exclusion from the rest of the defendant's farming business.

3 *Wayling v Jones* (1993) 69 P & CR 170.
4 (1993) 69 P & CR 170.
5 The court could just as easily have held that such leaving of the defendant was in reliance upon the ending of the loving relationship between the parties.
6 *Gillett v Holt* [2001] Ch 210.
7 *Taylor v Dickens* [1998] 1 FLR 806.
8 [2001] Ch 210.

Status of estoppel from purchasers' viewpoint

When the court's order creates a recognised property interest the position is clear thereafter, but beforehand there will be uncertainty over how the court will tailor the remedy to fit the circumstances under its flexible jurisdiction which, increasingly, seems concerned not simply with upholding already existing rights but with a complex exercise of discretion which may confer not a property right but a licence or just a right to compensation. If the court ultimately confers a property interest or a licence it matters not to the parties involved (as representor and representee) what the position was before the court order. Clearly, the representee had no rights before the relevant act of detrimental reliance occurred. Thereafter, can one say that the estoppel interest is too uncertain and unstable to qualify at all as a property interest[9] before the court decree, or can it rank as a mere equity, ancillary to and dependant upon an interest in land, so as to be capable of binding a purchaser of any legal or equitable interest with notice[10], or can it retrospectively be treated as having the characteristics of a full equitable interest once the court order crystallises such a property interest?[11]

So far, the courts have not had to address these issues though, inevitably, there are various obiter dicta[12] assuming that donees and purchasers with notice will be bound by inchoate estoppel interests. When the point comes to be fully argued it is possible that the court decree should only have prospective effect unless the court in its in personam jurisdiction to restrain unconscionable conduct decrees that a third party should be subject to the property interest or even licence decreed to exist between the representor and representee[13]. For the third party's conscience to be affected, so as to bring down upon him the in personam jurisdiction, it should suffice that he has actual knowledge of the estoppel claim or would have had such knowledge but for turning a Nelsonian blind eye or but for deliberately or recklessly failing to make the inquiries an honest reasonable man would have made in all the circumstances[14].

Take the sole legal beneficial owner of a house, M, who represented to F, who became his cohabitee, that she would have a half share or a life interest in the house, so leading her to act to her detriment in reliance thereon. If she is warned about M obtaining a mortgage from X having priority over her, she can have M expressly grant her a prior property interest before creating the mortgage or, if M refuses, she can issue a writ (protected as a *lis pendens*)

9 *National Provincial Bank Ltd v Ainsworth* [1965] AC 1175, D J Hayton [1990] Conv 370 at 380–384, P Ferguson (1993) 109 LQR 114; N Glover and P Todd (1996) 16 LS 325 at 342.

10 J Warburton (1991) 5 Trust Law Int 9. It is more uncertain than a mere equity to set aside a deed or rectify a deed where the ultimate court decision is predestined if the case is established.

11 G Battersby [1991] Conv 36.

12 *Lloyds Bank v Carrick* [1996] 4 All ER 630 at 642; *Voyce v Voyce* (1991) 62 P & CR 290 at 294; *Sen v Headley* [1991] Ch 425 at 440; *Re Sharpe* [1980] 1 WLR 219 at 224; *Ives Investments Ltd v High* [1967] 2 QB 379.

13 *Ashburn Anstalt v Arnold* [1989] Ch 1; *United Bank of Kuwait plc v Sahib* [1997] Ch 107 at 142. This can explain cases like *Duke of Beaufort v Patrick* (1853) 17 Beav 60 and *Ives Investments Ltd v High* (supra).

14 Cf actual 'Nelsonian' and 'naughty' knowledge sufficing for the want of probity needed to make a defendant personally liable to account for dishonestly assisting in a breach of trust or other fiduciary duty: *Nimmo v Westpac Banking* [1993] 3 NZLR 218 explaining the effect of English cases like *Agip (Africa) Ltd v Jackson* [1990] Ch 265 and *Polly Peck v Nadir (No 2)* [1992] 4 All ER 769; see Art 100, post.

claiming a proprietary estoppel interest against M and an injunction restraining him from proceeding with the mortgage. If X deliberately or recklessly failed to take the elementary conveyancing precaution of asking F as occupier whether she claimed any interest in the house and thereby divested her of the opportunity she would otherwise have had to take the only sensible precaution of taking the legal proceedings mentioned, is it not clearly unconscionable if X can then take advantage of his own wrong to have priority for his interest over whatever interest the court subsequently confers on F?

Indeed, it seems nowadays that the courts are prepared to treat proprietary estoppel interests arising between parties involved in land acquisition enterprises as if essentially the same as common intention constructive trusts[15], where it is assumed an equitable proprietary interest arises once detrimental reliance has occurred, thereby protecting F in the above example. However, if the interest is of a family overreachable type then it may be overreached by a disposition to two trustees or a trust corporation[16].

Section 116 of the Land Registration Act 2002, when in force, is intended to clarify matters in the case of registered land so that an equity by estoppel will have effect as a proprietary interest 'from the time the equity arises as an interest capable of binding successors in title (subject to the rules about the effect of dispositions on priority)', such time presumably being the time of the detrimental reliance[17]. The bracketed clause relates to the new priority rule that mere equities are to be treated like full equitable interests, with both being incapable of being defeated by a purchaser of a later equitable interest in registered land[18].

Statute may not be used as an instrument of fraud

As Lord Westbury stated in *McCormick v Grogan*[19]:

> 'the court has, from a very early period, decided that even an Act of Parliament shall not be used as an instrument of fraud; and that equity will fasten on the individual who gets a title under that Act, and impose upon him a personal obligation, because he applies the Act as an instrument for accomplishing a fraud. In this way a court of equity has dealt with the Statute of Frauds, and in this manner, also, it deals with the Statute of Wills.'

Inter vivos trusts

Where written evidence is required under Law of Property Act 1925, s 53(1)(b) of declarations of trust respecting land and A unilaterally transfers land to B to hold on trust for A, there is a perfect express trust if the trust for A is in signed writing, even if B knows nothing of the transfer, so that he can disclaim the trust if he wishes as soon as he discovers it[20].

However, if B had orally agreed to hold the land on trust for A he cannot disclaim the trust nor can he claim to be beneficial owner of the land.

---

15 *Yaxley v Gotts* [2000] Ch 162 at 176; *Banner Homes Holdings Ltd v Luff Developments Ltd* [2000] Ch 372 at 384; *Birmingham Midshires Mortgage Services v Sabherwal* (1999) 80 P & CR 256 at 263.
16 *Birmingham Midshires Mortgage Services v Sabherwal* (1999) 80 P & CR 256.
17 See Law Com no 271, *Land Registration for the 21st Century*, paras 5.30–5.31.
18 Law Com no 271, *Land Registration for the 21st Century*, para 5.36.
19 (1869) LR 4 HL 82 at 97.
20 See pp 150, 449.

According to Lindley LJ in *Rochefoucauld v Boustead*[1], the equitable principle preventing statute being used as an instrument of fraud prevents B from exploiting the statute, so that it is an express trust (within s 25(2) of the Judicature Act 1873 and so not statute-barred as a constructive trust under the Statute of Limitations) that is enforced. However, Millett LJ in *Paragon Finance plc v Thakerar & Co*[2] in a detailed historical examination of Limitation Statutes pointed out[3] that 'before 1890 constructive trusts of the first kind were treated in the same way as express trusts and were often confusingly described as such', having categorised as constructive trusts of the first kind cases where the defendant received property not in his own right but by a transaction by which both parties intended to create a trust from the outset, so that the defendant's ownership is coloured from the first by the trust and confidence by means of which he obtained it[4].

Section 53(2) of the Law of Property Act 1925 expressly exempts constructive and resulting trusts from the formalities prescribed in s 53(1), and the case where A transfers land to B on oral trusts for A can also be regarded as a resulting trust[5] in the absence of A's intent to part with the beneficial interest.

The equitable principle preventing statutes being used as instruments of fraud and leading to the imposition of a constructive trust is not confined to cases in which the conveyance was itself fraudulently obtained. 'The fraud which brings the principle into play arises as soon as the absolute character of the conveyance is set up for the purpose of defeating the beneficial interest.'[6] Thus, if A sells her two adjoining cottages to B for below market value and they agree orally that she is to be allowed to live in a particular cottage for the rest of her life B will be compelled to hold that cottage on trust for her if later he attempts to defeat her interest by relying on s 53(1)(b).

It can be argued that the equitable principle extends to the case where A's oral understanding with B is that B will hold the land on trust not for A but for C[7]. After all, if B were to append his signature to an appropriate document this would make enforceable[8] what had hitherto been an unenforceable but valid trust and B's act or omission should not determine whether B holds on trust for A or for C. Also, if A had conveyed the land to B as a beneficial gift A would have effectively divested himself of all interest and it should make no difference that the beneficial gift was to C with the interposition of B's trusteeship[9].

---

1 [1897] 1 Ch 196.
2 [1999] 1 All ER 400.
3 [1999] 1 All ER 400 at 409.
4 [1999] 1 All ER 400 at 409, where Millett LJ stated, 'Well-known examples of such a constructive trust are *McCormick v Grogan* (1869) LR 4 HL 82 (a case of a secret trust); *Rochefoucauld v Boustead* [1897] 1 Ch 196 (where the defendant agreed to buy property for the plaintiff but the trust was imperfectly recorded) and *Pallant v Morgan* [1953] Ch 43 (where the defendant sought to keep for himself property which the plaintiff trusted him to buy for both parties).'
5 *Hodgson v Marks* [1971] Ch 892, CA, subject to LPA 1925, s 60(3): p 368, post.
6 *Bannister v Bannister* [1948] 2 All ER 133 at 136.
7 *Lyus v Prowsa Developments Ltd* [1982] 2 All ER 953 at 962, though this involved not a gift but a sale of land by A to B so that A lost all his interest and it would have been fraudulent for B to claim that C's rights (subject to which A had sold the land) were unenforceable against him: see *Ashburn Anstalt v Arnold* [1989] Ch 1.
8 *Gardner v Rowe* (1828) 5 Russ 258; *Smith v Matthews* (1861) 3 De GF & J 139; *Mountain v Styak* [1922] NZLR 131.
9 T G Youdan [1984] Camb LJ 306 at 335–336.

Against this it can be argued that if A had orally declared himself a trustee of the land for C he would not have divested himself of his beneficial interest because s 53(1)(b) precludes C relying on oral evidence: it should make no difference that A transferred the land to B and declared oral trusts for C or there would hardly be any scope for the application of s 53(1)(b). Moreover, B's authority to sign the requisite writing can be revoked at will by A or by A's death[10] because A's failure to satisfy s 53(1)(b) means that his beneficial entitlement remains with him, C being incapable of proving the contrary and so not being unjustly deprived of something that he can prove is his. No constructive trust in favour of C can be imposed because it is not unconscionable for A to assert his own beneficial interest in the property.

C may invoke as analogous the case where X by will devises land to Y on the oral understanding with Y that Y will hold the land on trust for Z when X's fully secret trust in favour of Z will be enforced against Y. However, here X had died happy in the belief that he has done all he can to benefit Z while A is alive and kicking against C being benefited. The better view is thus that B holds on trust for A where s 53(1)(b) is not complied with[11], the doctrine of secret trusts not applying to inter vivos trusts, though, perhaps, such doctrine might be extended to cover the case where A died happy in the belief that he had created effective oral trusts in favour of C so as liberally to effectuate A's intentions.

The equitable principle against fraudulent use of statutes has been applied not just to the transferee-trustee but to volunteers claiming under him[12]. Indeed, it has been applied[13] to a purchaser for value without notice at the time of his purchase when subsequently he attempted to set up the absolute nature of the title of his vendor to defeat the equitable interest of the vendor's beneficiary. However, surely the equitable interest which is allowed to be proved despite s 53(1)(b) will in any case be void against a bona fide purchaser for value without notice, just as trusts satisfying s 53(1)(b) will be void against a purchaser without notice.

Where certain interests are required to be registered or protected by entry on a register such as under the Land Charges Act 1972[14] or the Land Registration Act 1925[15] or 2002 or the Companies Act 1985[16] on pain of a purchaser[17] taking free from such interests, it is not fraud for the purchaser to take advantage of his strict statutory rights by relying on the absence of the registration or protection stipulated for in the statute.

10 *Rudkin v Dolman* (1876) 35 LT 791; *Scheuerman v Scheuerman* (1916) 52 SCR 625 at 636.
11 Ford & Lee, *Principles of Law of Trusts* (2nd edn) pp 209–211, Hanbury & Martin, *Modern Equity* (16th edn) p 82, J D Feltham [1987] Conv 246. Also compare the *Strong v Bird* principle discussed p 157, ante that only operates where the deceased died happy with a continuing intention to make the gift to the person who becomes his personal representative.
12 *Re Duke of Marlborough* [1894] 2 Ch 133.
13 By Ungoed-Thomas J in *Hodgson v Marks* [1971] Ch 892 at 909, [1970] 3 All ER 513 at 522, but see inconsistency with *Dodds v Hill* (1865) 2 Hem & M 424, endorsed in *Macmillan v Bishopsgate (No 3)* [1995] 3 All ER 747 at 773; also see *Russell v Jackson* (1852) 10 Hare 204 at 212.
14 *Hollington Bros Ltd v Rhodes* [1951] 2 TLR 691; *Miles v Bull (No 2)* [1969] 3 All ER 1585; *Kitney v MEPC Ltd* [1978] 1 All ER 595, [1977] 1 WLR 981; *Midland Bank Trust Co Ltd v Green* [1981] AC 513, [1981] 1 All ER 153, HL.
15 *De Lusignan v Johnson* (1973) 230 Estates Gazette 499; *Freer v Unwins Ltd* [1976] Ch 288, [1976] 1 All ER 634; *Williams & Glyn's Bank v Boland* [1981] AC 487, [1980] 2 All ER 408, HL.
16 *Re Monolithic Building Co* [1915] 1 Ch 643, CA.
17 A genuine purchaser, not just the alter ego of a vendor, for example, trying to escape an estate contract entered into by him with X, but unprotected on the register, by selling to the vendor's controlled company; *Jones v Lipman* [1962] 1 All ER 442, [1962] 1 WLR 832.

Testamentary trusts

The equitable principle applies not just to inter vivos transactions but also to testamentary gifts. Indeed, originally the Statute of Frauds provided formalities for inter vivos and testamentary gifts though testamentary gifts are now covered by the Wills Act 1837 and inter vivos transactions by the Law of Property Act 1925.

Just as there is some old authority[18] that it is an express trust that the court enforces when it applies the equitable principle to prevent the intended inter vivos trustee setting up the Statute of Frauds or the Law of Property Act as a defence, so it so there is some old authority that it is an express trust that the court enforces when it applies the equitable principle to prevent the intended testamentary trustee setting up the Statute of Frauds or the Wills Act as a defence[19]. However the better modern approach is to treat secret trusts as based on enforcing a gratuitous promise because it would be fraudulent or unconscionable to allow the person who had agreed to carry out the obligation in another's favour to refuse to do so. After all, there is not just a fraud on the testator in betraying his confidence but there is a fraud on the secret beneficiary who would be deprived of the benefit which, but for the trustee agreeing to carry out the testator's wishes, would have been secured to him by other means[20]. Indeed, the requirement for the intended trustee's consent distinguishes secret trusts (and mutual wills) from express trusts, so the better view is that the court is imposing a constructive trust in favour of the secret beneficiaries though in some circumstances there may be an automatic resulting trust in favour of the deceased settlor's estate, eg where a devisee or legatee takes absolutely beneficially on the face of a will, though having orally agreed to hold on trusts communicated to him by the testator, and no communication of any trusts was made to him in the testator's lifetime[1].

Whilst the existence of the two approaches concerned with an express trust on the one hand and a constructive or resulting trust on the other hand is recognised by Lord Cairns, the Lord Chancellor, in *Jones v Badley*[2] in connection with testamentary trusts and by the Court of Appeal[3] in connection with inter vivos trusts the distinction between the two approaches has been lost sight of in many cases concerned with testamentary trusts. The distinction is no longer significant for limitation period purposes, while because a constructive trust is exempt from formalities by s 53(2) of the Law of Property Act 1925, judicial utilisation of it avoids the embarrassment of Equity refusing to implement a statute. Secret trusts should be categorised as constructive trusts[4] even though being treated here within the Division dealing with 'express trusts' because of the close affinity with express trusts that many secret trusts have.

---

18 *Rochefoucauld v Boustead* [1897] 1 Ch 196, explained at p 255 ante.
19 See *Jones v Badley* (1868) 3 Ch App 362 at 364; *McCormick v Grogan* (1869) LR 4 HL 82 at 88–89; *Wallgrave v Tebbs* (1855) 2 K & J 313 at 321–322; *Re Baillie* (1886) 2 TLR 660 at 661 though the express oral half-secret trust of land should have been saved under the principle that equity does not allow a statute to be used as an instrument of fraud: *Rochefoucauld v Boustead* [1897] 1 Ch 196; *Lyus v Prowsa Developments Ltd* [1982] 2 All ER 953 at 962.
20 See D R Hodge [1980] Conv 341.
1 *Re Boyes* (1884) 26 Ch D 531.
2 (1868) 3 Ch App 362 at 364.
3 *Rochefoucauld v Boustead* [1897] 1 Ch 196; *Hodgson v Marks* [1971] Ch 892, [1971] 2 All ER 684, CA.
4 *Paragon Finance plc v Thakerar & Co* [1999] 1 All ER 400 at 409 per Millett LJ; *Kasperbauer v Griffith* [2000] WTLR 333 at 343, per Peter Gibson LJ.

Distinction between fully and half-secret trusts

A testamentary trust is fully secret where a testator leaves property by will to X, who takes the property beneficially on the face of the will, or where a person dies intestate so that by operation of the intestacy rules X takes property beneficially, but where the deceased intended X to hold the property on trusts, communicated this intention in his lifetime to X, who agreed so to hold the property.

A testamentary trust is half-secret where a testator leaves property by will to X in such manner that X appears to take as trustee on the face of the will, though the terms of the trust are not apparent from the will itself or any document incorporated as part of the will under the probate doctrine of incorporation by reference. This doctrine admits to probate with the will a document referred to in the will as being already in existence if it is sufficiently described in the will to enable it to be identified from the will itself, eg 'to hold according to the directions contained in my letter to him dated 5 May 1984'[5]. Confusion of half-secret trusts with the doctrine of incorporation by reference[6] has probably led to the requirements that communication of the trust terms to the intended trustee must comply strictly with any terms regarding such communication expressed in the will and must occur prior to, or contemporaneously with, the execution of the will.

In *Re Keen's Estate*[7] £10,000 was left to the testator's executors and trustees, H and E, 'to be held upon trust and disposed of by them among such person, persons or charities as may be notified by me to them or either of them during my lifetime'. Some time before making the will the testator had given a sealed envelope to E directing that it be not opened till his death. It was then found to contain the name of a lady. However, the Court of Appeal held that the £10,000 had to be held for the residuary beneficiaries.

Lord Wright, giving the judgment of the Court of Appeal, held that communication of the trust had occurred when the sealed envelope had been delivered to E prior to execution of the will and such communication was inconsistent with the express terms of the will which contemplated future communication only, so that evidence of the earlier communicated trust was inadmissible. Even if the terms of the will could have been construed as contemplating past and future communications this would not have helped to establish a valid half-secret trust for 'the trusts referred to, but undefined in the will, must be described in the will as established prior to, or at least contemporaneously with, its execution'[8].

The objection to allowing communication to be made to the half-secret trustee after execution of the will is that this would enable the testator to 'give the go-by' to the provisions of the Wills Act by reserving to himself a power of making future testamentary dispositions orally or by unattested writing[9]. However, in the case of fully secret trusts the testator is allowed to reserve to himself such a power to 'give the go-by' to the Wills Act[10].The principle that

---

5 *Re Smart* [1902] P 238; *Re Garnett* [1894] P 90; *Re Schintz' Will Trusts* [1951] Ch 870, [1951] 1 All ER 1095.
6 For the differences see Hayton and Marshall, *Cases and Commentary on the Law of Trusts* (11th edn), paras 2–113 to 2–115.
7 [1937] Ch 236, [1937] 1 All ER 452.
8 [1937] Ch 236 at 247; *Re Bateman's Will Trusts* [1970] 3 All ER 817, [1970] 1 WLR 1463; *Johnson v Ball* (1851) 5 De G & Sm 85.
9 *Blackwell v Blackwell* [1929] AC 318 at 339; *Re Keen's Estate* [1937] Ch 236 at 246.
10 *McCormick v Grogan* (1869) LR 4 HL 82.

equity will not allow a statute to be used as an instrument of fraud is the very basis for giving the 'go-by' to statutes[11].

Furthermore, should strict compliance with the terms of the will really be necessary? If T leaves property on a half- secret trust to A, B, C and D 'to be dealt with in accordance with my wishes which I have made known to them' why should the trust for the secret beneficiaries fail[12] if it turns out that by an oversight T had only informed three of his four trustees of his wishes? Secret trusts seem to rest on the assumption that the will must first operate so as to vest the secret trust property in the fully or half-secret trustee but then the secret trusts themselves arise outside the will for equity 'makes him do what the will in itself has nothing to do with; it lets him take what the will gives him and then makes him apply it as the court of conscience directs, and it does so in order to give effect to the wishes of the testator which would not otherwise be effectual'[13]. It is thus illogical[14] for the court to concern itself so strictly with the wording of the will and also to claim, in the case of half-secret trusts, that oral evidence of communication and acceptance made after execution of the will but in the testator's lifetime should be inadmissible as allowing the Wills Act to be avoided.

Parol or extrinsic evidence may not be adduced to vary or contradict a will

The rule that is intended to prevent the 'go-by' from being given to the Wills Act is the rule that parol or extrinsic evidence may not be adduced to vary or contradict a will.

However, this rule has no application in the case of fully secret trusts where the will gives property to X apparently absolutely beneficially[15]. The standard of proof on the person seeking to establish the trust is the ordinary civil standard of proof on a balance of probabilities unless fraud is involved when a higher standard is required[16]. Where the will uses precatory words insufficient to make X a trustee of a half-secret trust the claimant will have to prove why the communication of the testator's wishes should not be treated as merely fulfilling a precatory intention rather than a trust intention[17]. If, indeed, the will leaves property to X and Y 'relying, but not by way of trust, on their applying' it as informed by the testator, it will be even harder for a claimant to prove that a fully secret trust existed outside the will but not impossible as held by the Court of Appeal in *Re Spencer's Will*[18].

11 *Re Pitt-Rivers* [1902] 1 Ch 403 at 407.

12 *Re Spence* [1949] WN 237.

13 *Blackwell v Blackwell* [1929] AC 318 at 335; *Cullen v A-G for Ireland* (1866) LR 1 HL 190 at 198. Dispositions taking effect outside the confines of the will are still testamentary: P Critchley (1999) 115 LQR 631 at 639–641.

14 (1951) 67 LQR 413 (LA Sheridan); (1937) 53 LQR 501 (Holdsworth); *Re Browne* [1944] IR 90; *Restatement of Trusts*, para 55(c)(h); *Legerwood v Perpetual Trustee Co Ltd* (1997) 41 NSWLR 532.

15 *Blackwell v Blackwell* [1929] AC 318.

16 *Re Snowden* [1979] 2 All ER 172 at 179 where Megarry V-C rejected the view of Brightman J in *Ottaway v Norman* [1972] Ch 698, [1971] 3 All ER 1325 that the standard was that required for rectification of written documents. One might have thought it logical for the standard of proof of intention to create a trust to depend always on a balance of probabilities, regardless of other circumstances: C Rickett [1979] Camb LJ 260, *Re Cleaver* [1981] 2 All ER 1018 at 1024.

17 *Hayman v Nicoll* [1944] 3 DLR 551.

18 (1887) 57 LT 519, CA. Cf *Re Falkiner* [1924] 1 Ch 88; *Re Stirling* [1954] 2 All ER 113, [1954] 1 WLR 763.

In the case of a half-secret trust where the trust property is left expressly to X on trust for purposes communicated to him, then parol evidence is inadmissible to allow the trustee to prove that he was intended to have some part of the property for himself beneficially[19]. It is said not to be in the public interest to admit an exception to the parol evidence rule so that a trustee's personal interest might conflict with his duty qua trustee[20]. However in some circumstances the court may be able to find that X was intended not to take as trustee but was intended to take a beneficial interest himself subject to satisfying some condition or equitable charge[1].

Fully secret trusts

The three necessary requirements are an *intention* on the part of the deceased to create a trust (despite the property passing apparently beneficially to the recipient under the will or the intestacy rules), *communication* thereof to the intended recipient of the property and *acceptance* thereof by the intended recipient, provided these requirements are satisfied in the deceased's life-time[2]. Acceptance by the recipient is readily inferred once communication occurs unless he protests[3].

Where intention is present but not the other requirements, as where after the testator's death an unattested set of instructions is found addressed to the person taking apparently beneficially on the face of the will, then that person does so take since no trust is established[4].

Where communication of the fact that the property is to be held upon trust is made and agreed to, but the terms of the trust are not communicated at all or are not communicated until after the deceased's death (eg when found in a letter in the deceased's bureau) then the property is held on a resulting trust for the deceased's estate, so benefiting the residuary bene-ficiaries or, if the property was itself the residuary property, the statutory next of kin[5]. If the intended trustee happens to be the residuary beneficiary or next of kin, as the case may be, there is the obvious possibility that he might be tempted to make self-serving statements, where other evidence prevents him from going so far as to claim that he was not even informed of the fact that he was intended to hold on some sort of trust. However, in the case of fully secret trusts the testator obviously runs risks with his trustee (unless having the trustee sign a witnessed document delivered into the hands of the intended beneficiaries) and his donee-volunteers claiming under him should perhaps run the same risks. It seems the court should allow all possible evidence to clarify the situation rather than impose an arbitrary salutary rule removing all temptation by prohibiting an intended fully secret trustee from

---

19 *Re Rees Will Trusts* [1950] Ch 204, [1949] 2 All ER 1003; *Re Pugh's Will Trusts* [1967] 3 All ER 337, [1967] 1 WLR 1262.

20 However, a settlor may expressly and validly create a trust under which T is a trustee and also a beneficiary. One will naturally be suspicious if a half secret trustee claims some beneficial interest but why should he not have a beneficial interest if the evidence is clear enough eg a non-testamentary document in the testator's signed handwriting or an oral statement in the presence of an independent witness? Cf *Re Tyler's Fund Trusts* [1967] 3 All ER 389, [1967] 1 WLR 1269.

1 *Irvine v Sullivan* (1869) LR 8 Eq 673; *Re Foord* [1922] 2 Ch 519.

2 *Ottaway v Norman* [1972] Ch 698, [1971] 3 All ER 1325; *Moss v Cooper* (1861) 1 John & H 352; *Re Boyes* (1884) 26 Ch D 531.

3 *Moss v Cooper* (1861) 1 John & H 352; *Tee v Ferris* (1856) 2 K & J 357.

4 *Wallgrave v Tebbs* (1855) 2 K & J 313.

5 *Re Boyes* (1884) 26 Ch D 531.

ever being able to benefit from failure of the trust qua residuary legatee or qua next of kin. If, however, the intended trustee appeared to be lying and it was otherwise impossible to ascertain the terms of the intended trust then public policy must prevent the intended trustee from obtaining any advantage from his own wrong[6].

Communication of the terms of the intended trust need not be made so that the intended trustee actually knows all the terms in the deceased's lifetime, so long as the terms are expressed in the deceased's lifetime and the intended trustee has the means of discovering them once the deceased dies, having been informed in the deceased's lifetime that he is to take as trustee. Thus, delivery to the intended trustee of a sealed envelope containing the terms of the trust will suffice if done in the deceased's lifetime though the envelope is directed not to be opened till the deceased's death[7]. The same principle will apply if a key to a locked box containing a letter with the terms of the trust is delivered by the deceased to the intended trustee[8].

Communication to the legatee/devisee must make it clear how much property is to vest in the legatee/devisee. Thus if £5,000 is bequeathed to X and Y absolutely and they agree to hold it on certain secret trusts communicated to them by the testator and, later, the testator in terms increases the legacy to £10,000, X and Y will only hold £5,000 qua secret trustees, the other £5,000 being taken by them beneficially[9]. Presumably, if the testator in terms reduces the legacy to £2,500 there will be a valid secret trust of the £2,500, the greater including the lesser figure. It would also seem that if the intended trustees agreed with the testator to hold whatever they obtain under the testator's will, then changes in the nature or value of the property resulting from codicils or fresh wills should not affect the validity of the secret trust arising on the testator's death.

Half-secret trusts

The same requirements have to be satisfied as in the case of fully secret trusts (discussed above) except there are two further requirements in that the communication must conform strictly to the language of the will and must be made prior to, or contemporaneously with, the execution of the will[10]. As already seen the justification for these two refinements is not convincing but the refinements must be taken as established law unless the House of Lords or a strong-minded Court of Appeal holds otherwise. Presumably, revocation by a testator of a half secret trust (agreed to before or at the time of the will) after making his will should be effective because it will not then be fraudulent or unconscionable for the legatee-trustee to disregard his earlier undertaking[11]. However, if it is not a simple revocation but revocation by virtue of replacing one secret beneficiary with another, it seems that effect should not be given to such revocation if conditional on the replacement trust being effective[12].

---

6 *Re Sigsworth* [1935] Ch 89.
7 *Re Keen's Estate* [1937] Ch 236; *Re Boyes* (1884) 26 Ch D 531.
8 *McDonald v Moran* (1938) 12 MPR 424 (Prince Edward Island).
9 *Re Cooper* [1939] Ch 811, [1939] 3 All ER 586.
10 *Re Keen's Estate* [1937] Ch 236, [1937] 1 All ER 452; *Re Spence* [1949] WN 237; *Re Bateman's Will Trusts* [1970] 3 All 817, [1970] 1 WLR 1463.
11 See *Guest v Webb* [1965] VR 427 at 432.
12 Cf conditional revocation of wills, eg *Re Finnemore* [1992] 1 All ER 800.

In the case of half-secret trusts ex hypothesi a trust must exist. If the specific terms of the trust are not communicated in accordance with the language used in the will[13] or are not communicated prior to or contemporaneously with the execution of the will, then the trust will be a resulting trust for the testator's estate and not an express trust for the intended beneficiaries[14]. If the half-secret trustee himself is a beneficiary under the resulting trust qua residuary legatee or next of kin there is an obvious temptation for him to allege there was either no communication to him at all or there was communication but it was after the date of the will or did not comply with the terms of the will, eg because oral and not written. Some dicta of Lord Buckmaster[15] suggest that the trustee should be excluded from benefiting under the resulting trust. However, this seems difficult to justify except where the court takes the view that there probably was a proper communication of full details of the trusts before the execution of the will despite the trustee's evidence to the contrary, in which case where the trust details cannot be ascertained public policy should prevent the trustee benefiting from his own wrongful conduct[16].

In *Re Baillie*[17] the view was taken that a half secret trust of land needs to satisfy s 53(1)(b) of the Law of Property Act, whereas it was assumed without argument in *Ottoway v Norman*[18] that a fully secret trust of land need not satisfy s 53(1)(b), presumably because fully secret trusts are clearly constructive trusts imposed to prevent the legatee-trustee taking beneficially. However, fully secret trusts, like half-secret trusts, go further in requiring the legatee-trustee not to hold on a resulting trust for the deceased's estate but to hold for the intended beneficiaries, so that both give effect to gratuitous promises that it would be fraudulent or unconscionable for the promisor to dishonour[19]. Both types of secret trust can therefore be treated as constructive trusts exempted from formal requirements by s 53(2).

Gifts to several intended trustees without communication to all

Farwell J laid down the position as follows where fully secret trusts are concerned[20]:

> 'If A induced B either to make, or leave unrevoked, a will leaving property to A and C as *tenants in common*, by expressly promising or tacitly consenting, that he and C will carry out the testator's wishes and C knows nothing of the matter until after the testator's death, A is bound but C is not bound: *Tee v Ferris*[1]; the reason stated being, that to hold otherwise would be to enable one beneficiary to deprive the rest of their benefits by setting up a secret trust. If however the gift were to A and C as *joint tenants*, the authorities have established a distinction between those cases in which the will is made on the faith of an antecedent promise by A and those in which the will is left unrevoked on the faith of a subsequent promise. In the former case the

13 *Re Spence* [1949] WN 237.
14 *Johnson v Ball* (1851) 5 De G & Sm 85; *Re Keen's Estate* [1937] Ch 236, [1937] 1 All ER 452.
15 *Blackwell v Blackwell* [1929] AC 318 at 341 respectively.
16 *Re Sigsworth* [1935] Ch 89.
17 (1886) 2 TLR 660.
18 [1972] Ch 698.
19 Fraud can be perpetuated without gain to the perpetrator: *Re Dale* [1994] Ch 31; *Twinsectra Ltd v Yardley* [2002] UKHL 12, [2002] 2 All ER 377 at paras [41] and [137].
20 *Re Stead* [1900] 1 Ch 237 at 241.
 1 (1856) 2 K & J 357.

trust binds both A and C: *Russell v Jackson*[2]; *Jones v Badley*[3], the reason stated being that no person can claim an interest under a fraud committed by another; in the latter case A and not C is bound: *Burney v Macdonald*[4] and *Moss v Cooper*[5], the reason stated being that the gift is not tainted with any fraud in procuring the execution of the will. Personally, I am unable to see any difference between a gift made on the faith of an antecedent promise and a gift left unrevoked on the faith of a subsequent promise to carry out the testator's wishes.'

However, a case can be made out that the only question to be asked is: was the gift to C induced by A's promise? If yes, C is bound, if no he is not bound. It can be said that whether A and C are tenants in common or joint tenants[6] 'C is not bound if his gift was not induced by the promise of A because to hold otherwise would be to enable A to deprive C of his benefit by setting up a secret trust; but C is bound if his gift was induced by the promise of A because he cannot profit by the fraud of another; and if the trust was communicated to A after the will was made, then C takes free if [as will almost certainly be the case] his gift was not induced by the promise of A because if there is no inducement there is no fraud affecting C.'

In the case of half-secret trusts communication must comply strictly with the terms of the will but if the will permits communication to be made to one only of several trustees a communication made to one trustee before or at the time of the execution of the will binds all of them, the trust being a joint office[7]. A subsequent communication is ineffective[8].

Secret beneficiary predeceasing testator

If D by will leaves property to T on trust expressly for B, and B predeceases D, the gift to B lapses[9]. One would expect the position to be the same if D, having obtained T's agreement to hold the property on trust for B, leaves property 'to T absolutely' or 'to T upon trusts which I have communicated to him'. However, in *Re Gardner*[10] Romer J held that B's interest did not lapse since B obtained an interest as soon as D communicated the terms of the trust to T and T accepted the trust.

D communicated the trust terms to T in 1909 and D died in 1919, B having died in the interval. It is difficult to understand Romer J's reasoning since no completely constituted trust of D's property could arise till D died without having revoked or altered the will and without having become insolvent, so that B would only have a mere spes till D died. However, if B had an absolute vested interest in a 1909 settlement and funds accruing under a will taking effect in 1919 were treated as an accretion to the 1909 settlement (rather than comprising a separate 1919 referential settlement) then if B died before

---

2 (1852) 10 Hare 204.
3 (1868) 3 Ch App 362.
4 (1845) 15 Sim 6.
5 (1861) 1 John & H 352.
6 (1972) 88 LQR 225 (B Perrins).
7 *Blackwell v Blackwell* [1929] AC 318; *Re Spence* [1949] WN 237; *Ward and Pemberton v Duncombe* [1893] AC 369.
8 *Re Keen's Estate* [1937] Ch 236.
9 However, if B is D's child and leaves issue of his own surviving D the gift takes effect in favour of B's issue: Wills Act 1837, s 33 as amended by Administration of Justice Act 1982, s 19.
10 [1923] 2 Ch 230.

1919 the funds would accrue to his estate[11]. Romer J did state[12]:

'The rights of the parties appear to me to be exactly the same as though the husband (T), after the memorandum had been communicated to him by the testatrix (D), in 1909 had executed a declaration of trust binding himself to hold any property that should come to him under his wife's (D's) partial intestacy upon trust as specified in the memorandum.'

Such a declaration, however, does not create a completely constituted trust since the subject is future property, a spes[13]. Thus, the beneficiaries could have had no rights in 1909 particularly since they were volunteers. Furthermore, even if T could be treated as declaring trusts in favour of the secret beneficiaries as soon as D died in 1919 this could not assist a predeceasing beneficiary[14] (assuming the trusts declared were not for the beneficiaries or their estates). The authority of *Re Gardner*, is thus exceptionally doubtful.

The extent to which secret trusts operate independently of settlor's will

In *Re Gardner*[15] Romer J treated the predeceasing beneficiary's interest as arising independently of the will so as not to lapse. In *Re Young*[16] Danckwerts J held that the beneficiary under a half-secret trust may take the interest intended for him even though he acted as a witness to the will so as prima facie to fall foul of Wills Act 1837, s 15, which makes void beneficial gifts to attesting witnesses of wills. He stated[17]:

'The whole theory of the formation of a secret trust is that the Wills Act has nothing to do with the matter because the forms required by the Wills Act are entirely disregarded, since the persons do not take by virtue of the gift in the will, but by virtue of the secret trusts imposed upon the beneficiary who does in fact take under the will.'

Secret trusts thus give the 'go-by' to s 15[18].

If this view is taken to its logical conclusion issue will not need to bring their secret trust beneficial interests into hotchpot under Administration of Estates Act 1925, s 49(1)(a), and the issue of a testator's child taking as secret beneficiary but who predeceases the testator leaving issue alive at the testator's death will not benefit under the exception to the doctrine of lapse in Wills Act 1837, s 33[19].

On the other hand in *Re Maddock*[20] residuary personalty was left to T absolutely but T undertook to hold a specified portion thereof for certain

---

11 *Re Playfair* [1951] Ch 4, sub nom *Re Hickman's Will Trusts, Re Playfair, Palmer v Playfair* [1950] 2 All ER 285.

12 [1923] 2 Ch 230 at 233.

13 *Re Ellenborough* [1903] 1 Ch 697; *Re Northcliffe* [1925] Ch 651; *Williams v IRC* [1965] NZLR 395; *Brennan v Morphett* (1908) 6 CLR 22. Further see p 175, ante.

14 If B is dead when an interest is purported to be created in his favour under an inter vivos disposition the interest fails: *Re Corbishley's Trusts* (1880) 14 Ch D 846; *Re Tilt* (1896) 74 LT 163.

15 [1923] 2 Ch 230.

16 [1951] Ch 344.

17 [1951] Ch 344 at 346.

18 Danckwerts J treated fully and half-secret trusts on the same footing, refusing to follow *Re Fleetwood* (1880) 15 Ch D 594 where Hall V-C held that a half-secret trust in favour of a secret beneficiary failed by reason of the beneficiary being an attesting witness.

19 Assuming *Re Gardner* [1923] 2 Ch 230 is erroneous in itself creating an equitable exception to the doctrine of lapse so that recourse to s 33 is necessary.

20 [1902] 2 Ch 220.

secret beneficiaries. In paying the testator's debts the Court of Appeal held that debts should not be paid out of the residuary personalty as a whole, but that they should be paid primarily out of that part of residuary personalty intended for T beneficially, and, if that were exhausted, then resort could be had to the secret trust portion of residue as if there had been a specific legacy of the amount of that portion set out in the will, though this should be resorted to for payment of debts before any specific legacies actually expressed in the will.

In principle, there is much to be said for the view that all secret trusts are testamentary in character[1] since they are dispositions of property (albeit operating outside the confines of the will) to take effect on death. However in Viscount Sumner's words[2], 'the doctrine must, in principle, rest on the assumption that the will has first operated according to its terms'.

Thus, secret trusts must fail if the testator revokes the relevant clause in his will or if the testator dies insolvent or the relevant property is not available due to ademption or abatement.

If a fully secret trustee dies it would seem that the secret trusts should fail[3] on the basis that the will cannot operate according to its terms whether due generally to the predecease of an apparently absolutely entitled beneficiary or to the predecease of a person whose personality was fundamental to the trusteeship. Whether secret trusts should fail if the will fails due to technicalities over the attestation procedures yet the intended trustee obtains the intended secret trust property qua statutory next of kin will depend upon whether his equitable obligations strictly relate only to what he received under the will or extend to property whether received under the will or under the intestacy rules. Presumably, if the fully secret trustee happened to attest the will the secret trust should fail since a beneficial interest is given *by the will* to the fully secret trustee though outside the will trusts are intended to operate.

In the case of half-secret trusts the death of the trustee before the will takes effect cannot affect the position (unless his personality was vital to the trusteeship or unless all knowledge of the trusts died with him) for equity will not allow a trust to fail for want of a trustee. Any attestation of the will by the half-secret trustee would fall outside Wills Act 1837, s 15. Any disclaimer by the half-secret trustee would normally be immaterial owing to Equity not allowing a trust to fail for want of a trustee.

Disclaimer by a fully secret trustee was treated by Cozens-Hardy LJ obiter[4] as causing the fully secret trusts to fail though preferable obiter dicta[5] of Lords Buckmaster and Warrington treat disclaimer as not invalidating the secret trusts which are assumed to take effect on the testator's death[6] making

---

1 P Critchley (1999) 115 LQR 631 at 639–641.
2 [1929] AC 318 at 334. Also Romer J in *Re Gardner* [1923] 2 Ch 230 at 232, 'The obligation can be enforced *if the donee becomes entitled*'. In *Re Snowden* [1979] 2 All ER 172 at 177 Megarry V-C said, 'The whole basis of secret trusts is that they operate outside the will, changing nothing that is written in it and allowing it to operate according to its tenor, but then fastening a trust on the property in the hands of the recipient.'
3 'If the legatee dies in the lifetime of the testator the persons claiming under the memorandum [ie the secret trusts] can take nothing' per Cozens-Hardy LJ in *Re Maddock* [1902] 2 Ch 220 at 231. However, the contrary was held to be the case in *Lord Inchiquin v French* (1745) 1 Cox Eq Cas 1.
4 *Re Maddock* [1902] 2 Ch 220 at 231.
5 [1929] AC 318 at 328 and 341 respectively.
6 Cf mutual wills being effective on death: *Re Dale* [1994] Ch 31.

it a fraud or breach of trust for the secret trustee to renounce the legacy. Disclaimer would, it seems, be fully effective if the testator's communication to his legatee were construed not as imposing trusts but as conferring a gift subject to a condition[7].

Revocation of his acceptance of the trust by the intended secret trustee raises further problems. If revocation occurs when the testator has plenty of time to alter his will but he fails to do so then the fully secret trustee should be allowed to take beneficially. In the case of a half-secret trustee it would seem that he should not be allowed to make the trusts fail by retracting his acceptance of the intended trusts, so that the maxim, equity will not allow a trust to fail for want of a trustee, should come into play if on the testator's death he claims to have earlier renounced his acceptance of the trust. If the testator has not reasonable time to alter his will, taking into account any physical or mental illness, then the trusts should be enforced whether fully or half-secret.

Secret 'floating' trusts

The obligation on the intended secret trustee is usually to hold specific property for a secret beneficiary absolutely, resulting normally in the trustee making an inter vivos transfer to the beneficiary. However, the obligation may be that the secret trustee is to make a will in favour of the secret beneficiary transferring to him property formerly belonging to the settlor/testator but left to the secret trustee absolutely. In *Ottaway v Norman*[8] Brightman J was prepared to assume, but without so deciding,

'that if property is given to the [trustee] on the understanding that the [trustee] will dispose by his will of such assets, if any, as he may have at his command at his death in favour of the [secret beneficiary], a valid trust is created in favour of the [secret beneficiary] which is in suspense during the lifetime of the [trustee] but attaches to the estate of the [trustee] at the moment of the latter's death.'

In such a case it would appear that the trustee takes an absolute interest in the property subject to an equitable fiduciary obligation of good faith during his lifetime neither to transfer the property nor to contract to transfer the property with destructive intent to prevent the property passing to the secret beneficiary[9], but otherwise he can resort to capital for his own purposes.

In *Healey v Brown*[10] in separate mutual wills H and W left all to the survivor of them absolutely, with a specific jointly-owned flat (or the subsequent matrimonial home) to be devised to N by the survivor. H became sole owner of the flat as surviving joint tenant but transferred it into the names of himself and his son, S, as joint tenants, so S owned the flat on his death. N claimed that S held the flat on constructive trust for her. While H had not revoked or amended his will in contravention of his agreement, the judge held that his gift of the flat was calculated to defeat the intention of the mutual contract between H and W that gave rise to a constructive trust. One would have expected that the constructive trust would affect the whole flat to prevent the fraudulent frustration of W's dying belief, encouraged by H's

---

7 See p 136, ante.

8 [1972] Ch 698 at 713.

9 Further see p 82, ante and *Birmingham v Renfrew* (1937) 57 CLR 666 at 689 approvingly cited in *Re Cleaver* [1981] 2 All ER 1018 at 1023–1024. Cf Inheritance (Provision for Family and Dependants) Act 1975, s 10. Also see *Edell v Sitzer* (2001) 4 ITELR 149 at 169–170.

10 [2002] WTLR 789.

contract with her. Oddly the judge held that the constructive trust only extended to W's half share as if there had been a secret trust accepted by H which would only cover W's property (including property of which she could easily have made herself tenant in common by severing her joint tenancy) and not property owned by H, as Morritt LJ had pointed out in *Re Goodchild*[11] where no contractual agreement not to revoke the will had been found. However, here there was such a contractual agreement that extended to H's property so the constructive trust should have extended to the whole flat. It should have been immaterial that the contract (appearing clearly from formal wills) as such was void for a technical failure to comply with the formalities for contracts relating to land, as explained at pages 429–430 below.

11 [1997] 1 WLR 1216 at 1231.

CHAPTER 3

Validity of declared trusts in relation to latent matters

Article
13 Who may be a settlor or trustee   268
14 Who may be beneficiaries   272
15 When a trust is voidable for failure of consideration or purpose or for mistake, or fraud   273
16 Effect of the bankruptcy of the settlor on the validity of a settlement   287
17 Effect of settlements intended to prejudice creditors apart from bankruptcy   291
18 When a trust designed to defeat dependants may be set aside pro tanto under a court order   295
19 Miscellaneous instances where a trust may be set aside to thwart criminals   297

ARTICLE 13

Who may be a settlor or trustee

Every person, male or female, married or unmarried, human or corporate, who has power to hold and dispose of any legal or equitable[1] estate or interest in property can create a trust in respect thereof, and can be a trustee thereof.

Minors

An infant, or minor in the modern parlance, attains full age on attaining 18 instead of 21 which was the case until 1 January 1970[2].

Since 1925 a minor cannot hold a legal estate in land and so cannot settle it[3]. Otherwise capacity to settle is treated in the same way as capacity to contract. Thus settlements that are obviously prejudicial will be wholly void[4]

---

1 *Gilbert v Overton* (1864) 2 Hem & M 110; *Kekewich v Manning* (1851) 1 De GM & G 176; *Donaldson v Donaldson* (1854) Kay 711; *Re Ralli's Will Trust* [1964] Ch 288, [1963] 3 All ER 940.
2 Family Law Reform Act 1969, ss 1, 12.
3 Law of Property Act 1925, ss 1 (6), 19. He may settle his equitable interest.
4 *IRC v Mills* [1975] AC 38, [1974] 1 All ER 722, HL; *De Francesco v Barnum* (1890) 45 Ch D 430.

whilst the minor may plead non est factum if too young to understand the nature of the arrangement he purported to make[5]. Otherwise an inter vivos settlement made by an infant which, if made by an adult, would bind the property itself, is voidable but not void; and, unless the infant repudiates it on or shortly after attaining his majority, it will be binding[6], and this is so whether the property settled is reversionary or not[7]. But where by the law of the infant's domicile or the proper law of the settlement ratification is not allowed, the settlement will not be binding, even though not expressly repudiated[8].

A minor cannot make a settlement by will unless he is a privileged testator, ie a soldier or airman in actual military service or a mariner or seaman at sea: Wills Act 1837 as amended by Wills (Soldiers and Sailors) Act 1918.

By s 20 of the Law of Property Act 1925 the appointment of an infant to be a trustee in relation to any settlement or trust is void.

Persons of unsound mind

A person of unsound mind cannot be a trustee[9], nor can he create a testamentary trust unless he possesses sufficient intelligence to recall the nature and extent of his property, and the persons who have a claim on his bounty, and a judgment sufficiently free from morbid aberration and external control to judge those claims[10]. The Court of Protection has power to make a will for a mental patient creating testamentary trusts[11].

Where a receiver has been appointed to deal with the affairs of a mental patient under the Mental Health Act 1983 it seems that any purported inter vivos settlement made by the patient will be void[12]. If a receiver has not been appointed but it is shown that the settlor is of unsound mind then again the

---

5 *IRC v Mills* [1975] AC 38, [1974] 1 All ER 722. The House of Lords unanimously reversed the view of the Court of Appeal [1973] Ch 225 at 240 and 247 that a contract or settlement was void if made by a person below the age of discretion (14 years for boys and 16 years for girls) when he is presumed by law not to have sufficient understanding to know what it involved or, at any rate, not a sufficient discretion to exercise a sound judgment on it.

6 *Duncan v Dixon* (1890) 44 Ch D 211; *Edwards v Carter* [1893] AC 360, HL; *Chaplin v Leslie Frewin (Publishers) Ltd* [1966] Ch 71 at 89 per Lord Denning MR.

7 *Carnell v Harrison* [1916] 1 Ch 328, overruling *Re Jones* [1893] 2 Ch 461; and see *Hamilton v Hamilton* [1892] 1 Ch 396. The Infants Relief Act 1874, s 2, has no application as it only prohibits action on a ratification: cf *Edwards v Carter* [1893] AC 360, HL; *Re Hodson* [1894] 2 Ch 421; and see *Harle v Jarman* [1895] 2 Ch 419 at 428.

8 *Viditz v O'Hagan* [1900] 2 Ch 87, CA.

9 *Re East* (1873) 8 Ch App 735; *Re Blake* [1887] WN 173, CA.

10 *Banks v Goodfellow* (1870) LR 5 QB 549; *Roe v Nix* [1893] P 55; *Boughton v Knight* (1873) LR 3 P & D 64. Further see Williams, Mortimer & Sunnucks, *Executors, Administrators and Probate* (17th edn), pp 158–170.

11 Mental Health Act 1983, ss 96, 97; *Re C* [1991] 3 All ER 866; *Re S* [1997] 1 FLR 96; *Re HMF* [1976] Ch 33, [1975] 2 All ER 795; *Practice Direction* [1987] 1 All ER 403. A 'patient' is a person who by reason of mental disorder is incapable of managing and administering his property and affairs: Mental Health Act 1983, s 94(2); 'mental disorder' means mental illness, arrested or incomplete development of mind, psychopathic disorder and any other disorder or disability of the mind: s 1(2) on which see the detail of *Masterman-Lister v Jewell* [2002] EWHC 417 (QB), [2002] All ER (D) 247 (Mar).

12 *Re Marshall* [1920] 1 Ch 284; *Re Walker* [1905] 1 Ch 160, CA; *Re Beaney* [1978] 2 All ER 595 at 600.

settlement will be void[13] unless the settlement was made in a lucid interval[14] when the settlor had capacity to understand the nature of the transaction.

> 'At one extreme, if the subject matter and value of a gift are trivial in relation to the donor's assets a low degree of understanding will suffice. But, at the other, if its effect is to dispose of the donor's only asset of value and thus for practical purposes to pre-empt the devolution of his estate under his will or on his intestacy, then the degree of understanding required is as high as that required for a will and the donor must understand the claims of all potential donees and the extent of the property to be disposed of.'[15]

However, where a person who is of unsound mind in fact, but is not known to be so to persons privy to valuable consideration, executes a settlement, it would seem that it would not be set aside, either at law or in equity[16]. A voidable marriage[17] entered into by a person of unsound mind is probably valuable consideration for a marriage settlement.

Foreigners

Testamentary trusts of English movables (but not English immovables) created by a testator domiciled abroad are only valid to the extent that the testator's *lex domicilii* (as his *lex successionis* according to the English forum) allows such to be disposed of free from mandatory rules protecting the interests of the testator's children or other relatives or dependants[18]. Inter vivos trusts of English movables and immovables transferred validly under the *lex situs* to trustees of an English or other trust by a settlor of foreign domicile, habitual residence or nationality are valid and unimpeachable[19] except, perhaps, to the extent that the settlor reserved a general power of appointment or revocation and his *lex successionis* at his death has mandatory rules protecting the interests after his death of his children or other relatives or dependants[20].

Corporations

A corporation is an artificial person having no capacity beyond its express objects and powers[1] set out in its memorandum of association and those implied objects and powers that are reasonably incidental to the carrying on

---

13 *Re Beaney* [1978] 2 All ER 595; *Simpson v Simpson* [1992] 1 FLR 601. Settlements for a consideration may only be voidable against a person with knowledge of the incapacity unless non est factum could have been pleaded: *Gibbons v Wright* (1954) 91 CLR 423 which was extended to gratuitous settlements in *Crago v McIntyre* [1976] 1 NSWLR 729.

14 *Elliot v Ince* (1857) 7 De GM & G 475; *Daily Telegraph Newspaper Co Ltd v McLaughlin* [1904] AC 776; but cf *Manning v Gill* (1872) LR 13 Eq 485. The Court of Protection has power to settle a patient's property under Mental Health Act 1983, s 96. An enduring power of attorney is not invalid by reason of the fact that at the time of execution of the power the donor was incapable by reason of mental disorder from managing his affairs if he understood the nature and effect of the power: *Re K* [1988] Ch 310.

15 *Re Beaney* [1978] 2 All ER 595 at 601 applied in *Re Morris* [2001] WTLR 1137.

16 *Molton v Camroux* (1848) 2 Exch 487 at 503; affd (1849) 4 Exch 17; and *Price v Berrington* (1851) 3 Mac & G 486; *Niell v Morley* (1804) 9 Ves 478. Also see *Hart v O'Connor* [1985] AC 1000, [1985] 2 All ER 880, PC.

17 Nullity of Marriage Act 1971, ss 11, 12.

18 *Re Annesley* [1926] Ch 692.

19 *Re Megret* [1901] 1 Ch 547; *Pouey v Hordern* [1900] 1 Ch 492: see pp 1047–1048, post.

20 See p 232, ante.

 1 *Bell Houses Ltd v City Wall Properties Ltd* [1966] 2 QB 656, [1966] 2 All ER 674, CA.

of the corporation's business[2]. The creation of trusts especially for the benefit of employees of the company[3] and perhaps even for endowing a professorship[4] may be intra vires the company where conducive to the continued progress of the company's business.

By s 35 of the Companies Act 1985 substituted by s 108 of the Companies Act 1989 with effect from 4 February 1991:

(1) The validity of an act done by a company shall not be called into question on the ground of lack of capacity by reason of anything in the company's memorandum.

(2) A member of a company may bring proceedings to restrain the doing of an act which but for sub-s (1) would be beyond the company's capacity; but no such proceedings shall lie in respect of an act to be done in fulfilment of a legal obligation arising from a previous act of the company.

By s 35A:

(1) In favour of a person dealing with a company in good faith, the power of the board to bind the company, or authorise others to do so, shall be deemed to be free of any limitation under the company's constitution.

(2) For this purpose
   (a) a person deals with a company if he is a party to any transaction or other act to which the company is a party;
   (b) a person shall not be regarded as acting in bad faith by reason only of knowing that an act is beyond the powers of the directors under the company's constitution; and
   (c) a person shall be presumed to have acted in good faith unless the contrary is proved.

By s 35B:

A party to a transaction is not bound to enquire as to whether it is permitted by the company's memorandum or as to any limitation on the powers of the board of directors to bind the company or authorise others to do so.

Shareholders may thus still restrain a proposed ultra vires matter and directors may still be liable for breach of duty. The section does not affect the possibility of personal liability to account as a constructive trustee if the facts otherwise give rise to such liability[5].

Regulation under Financial Services and Markets Act 2000

While trust corporations (other than those established to act only as trustee of trusts established by one family or one settlor) are required to be registered and licensed in some off-shore trust jurisdictions (eg Bermuda, Turks and Caicos Islands, Jersey, Guernsey, Isle of Man, Cayman Islands) if resident there or carrying on business there, no such requirement exists in England. However, if a trustee deals in investments or arranges deals in investments or manages investments or safeguards and administers assets belonging to

---

2 *Charterbridge Corpn v Lloyds Bank Ltd* [1970] Ch 62, [1969] 2 All ER 1185; *Re Lee Behrens & Co Ltd* [1932] 2 Ch 46; *Rolled Steel Products (Holdings) Ltd v British Steel Corpn* [1982] Ch 478, [1982] 3 All ER 1057; reversed in part on appeal [1986] Ch 246, [1985] 3 All ER 52, CA.
3 See Inheritance Tax Act 1984, ss 72, 75; Taxation of Chargeable Gains Act 1992, ss 227–231 for some tax advantages.
4 *Evans v Brunner Mond & Co* [1921] 1 Ch 359.
5 *International Sales and Agencies Ltd v Marcus* [1982] 3 All ER 551.

another[6] it will need to be authorised under the Financial Services and Markets Act 2000 and to comply with rules laid down by the Financial Services Authority.

If the trustee restricts itself to managing investments it will fall outside the 1986 Act if (a) it does not hold itself out as offering investment management services, or (b) is not remunerated for providing such services 'in addition to any remuneration' received for discharging its duties as a trustee, and for these purposes a person is not to be regarded as receiving additional remuneration merely because his remuneration is calculated by reference to time spent[7]. It might be argued that (a) seems capable of catching all trustees who hold themselves out as professional trustees (ie carrying on business as trustee) since investment management is one of the two major inherent functions of trusteeship, the other function being the trustee's distributive function which can only operate in respect of the results of the investment function. However, this would afford such little scope to the exemption that a purposive interpretation should lead the court to restrict (a) to those professional trustees who advertise their investment management expertise, though this will catch most trustees who try to attract business by marketing themselves.

For (b) to exempt a trustee, investment management services must not be remunerated in addition to remuneration for trusteeship duties. Thus, it seems that a trustee who charges not on a time basis but by way of a fixed percentage of the trust fund's value will be outside the Financial Services Act 1986.

Where a trustee is regulated under the Financial Services and Markets Act 2000 the ordinary Conduct of Business Rules will not apply to the trustee if delegating investment management to a Permitted Third Party[8].

A Permitted Third Party is an authorised or an exempt person under the 2000 Act or lawfully carrying on a regulated activity in another European Economic Area State.

ARTICLE 14

Who may be beneficiaries

Every person who would be capable of owning property if of full age and sound mind may be a beneficiary under a trust even if not of full age and sound mind.

---

6 Financial Services and Markets Act 2000, ss 19, 22 and Sch 2.
7 Financial Services and Markets Act 2000 (Regulated Activities) Order 2001, SI 2001/544, art 66.
8 Conduct of Business Rules, Chapter 11, particularly section 11.6.

Aliens

Aliens[9] have the same capacity as British subjects to hold, and therefore may be beneficiaries under trusts of, real and personal property of every kind save that they cannot be owners of British ships[10], and British ships cannot be held in trust for them, although citizens of European Union Countries have such rights under Articles 5, 6, 52 and 221 of the EU Treaty of Amsterdam[11].

Minors and persons of unsound mind

Although a minor is incapable of holding a legal estate in land[12] he can be a beneficiary under a trust of property of any kind, as can a person of unsound mind, though incapable of acting as a trustee.

Settlors and trustees

A settlor may be the beneficiary or one of the beneficiaries under the trust he creates. A trustee may also be a beneficiary, but a sole trustee cannot hold on trust for himself as sole beneficiary since it is impossible to have rights and duties at home in one person[13]. No trust can exist where the entire property, legal and equitable, is vested in one person[14]. Indeed, no separate equitable interest exists where O is absolute legal beneficial owner[15], and O does not need to comply with s 53(1)(c) of the Law of Property Act 1925 (which is concerned with a person disposing of his subsisting equitable interest) when he fully disposes of his property[16] or creates a trust of it in favour of others, thereby creating a fresh equitable obligation.

ARTICLE 15

When a trust is voidable for failure of consideration or purpose, or for mistake or fraud

(1) The court will cancel a trust at the suit of the settlor or his representatives[17], if the object for which the trust was created has failed[18];

---

9 The definition of 'alien' in the British Nationality Act 1981, s 50, is a 'person who is neither a Commonwealth citizen nor a British protected person nor a citizen of the Republic of Ireland'. By the Ireland Act 1949, s 3(1)(a)(i), the operation of the provisions of the British Nationality Act is not affected by the fact that the Republic of Ireland is not a foreign country though no part of Her Majesty's dominions.

10 Status of Aliens Act 1914, s 17 (the short title of which Act was altered by the omission of the words 'British Nationality and' by the British Nationality Act 1948, s 34, Sch 4). Trustees for aliens must also, in appropriate cases, bear in mind the provisions of the Trading with the Enemy Act 1939.

11 *R v Secretary of State for Transport, ex p Factortame Ltd* [1991] ECR I–3905.

12 See p 268, ante, where the reduction in the age of majority from 21 to 18 by the Family Law Reform Act 1969 is also noted.

13 *Rye v Rye* [1962] AC 496, [1962] 1 All ER 146, HL (B cannot grant a lease to B).

14 *Re Cook* [1948] Ch 212, [1948] 1 All ER 231; *Re Heberley* [1971] NZLR 325; *DKLR Holding Co (No 2) Pty Ltd v CSD (NSLU)* (1982) 40 ALR 1 at 26.

15 *Westdeutsche Landesbank v Islington London Borough Council* [1996] AC 669 at 706.

16 *Vandervell v IRC* [1967] 2 AC 291, [1967] 1 All ER 1, HL.

17 *Anderson v Elsworth* (1861) 3 Giff 154; *Tyars v Alsop* (1889) 37 WR 339, CA; *Morley v Loughnan* [1893] 1 Ch 736.

(2) the court will cancel or rectify (as the case may require) a settlement executed under duress or in ignorance or mistake[19], or procured by fraud, misrepresentation[20], or undue influence[1], provided that the settlor has not acquiesced in the settlement after the influence has ceased, or after he has become aware of its legal effect[2], and that the parties can be restored to their original positions[3].

PARAGRAPH 1

Total failure of consideration or purpose

In *Essery v Cowlard*[4] by a settlement in consideration of a then intended marriage, executed in 1877, it was declared that a sum of stock, which had been transferred by the intended wife to trustees, should be held by them on trusts for her benefit and that of the intended husband and the issue of the intended marriage. The marriage was not solemnised, but the parties cohabited without marriage, and three children were born. In 1883 an action was brought by the father and mother of these children against the trustees to have it set aside. It was held that, the contract to marry having been absolutely put an end to, the settlement ought to be cancelled. Similar decisions were arrived at in *Bond v Walford*[5], where an intended marriage had been simply broken off, and *Re Garnett*[6], where a decree of nullity of marriage had been made. However, a decree of nullity no longer has retrospective effect, so that such decree, like a decree of divorce, should not bring about a failure of the trust in respect of which the courts have a broad jurisdiction to make orders under the Matrimonial Causes Act 1973[7].

It seems that failure of consideration has not the same meaning as in the context of contract[8]. The above cases all concern failure of marriages but the principle seems capable of wider application as recognised by Browne LJ in *Burgess v Rawnsley* as follows[9]:

'It is clear that where a person creates a trust for a particular purpose or in con-

---

18 *Essery v Cowlard* (1884) 26 Ch D 191; *Bond v Walford* (1886) 32 Ch D 238; *Burgess v Rawnsley* [1975] Ch 429, [1975] 3 All ER 142, CA.

19 *Phillips v Mullings* (1871) 7 Ch App 244; *Forshaw v Welsby* (1860) 30 Beav 243; cf *North Ocean Shipping Co Ltd v Hyundai Construction Co Ltd, The Atlantic Baron* [1979] QB 705, [1978] 3 All ER 1170; *Re Daniel's Settlement* (1875) 1 Ch D 375; *Clark v Girdwood* (1877) 7 Ch D 9; *Re Hargreaves' Trusts* [1937] 2 All ER 545; *Lady Hood of Avolon v Mackinnon* [1909] 1 Ch 476; *Gibbon v Mitchell* [1990] 3 All ER 338.

20 *Re Glubb* [1900] 1 Ch 354.

1 *Osmond v Fitzroy* (1731) 3 P Wms 129; *Huguenin v Baseley* (1807) 14 Ves 273; *Dent v Bennett* (1839) 4 My & Cr 269; *Hoghton v Hoghton* (1852) 15 Beav 278; *Cooke v Lamotte* (1851) 15 Beav 234; *Bullock v Lloyds Bank Ltd* [1955] Ch 317, [1954] 3 All ER 726.

2 *Davies v Davies* (1869) LR 9 Eq 468, and cases cited; *Allcard v Skinner* (1887) 36 Ch D 145, CA; *Bullock v Lloyds Bank Ltd* [1955] Ch 317, [1954] 1 All ER 726.

3 *Johnston v Johnston* (1884) 52 LT 76.

4 (1884) 26 Ch D 191; and see *Chapman v Bradley* (1863) 4 De GJ & Sm 71.

5 (1886) 32 Ch D 238.

6 (1905) 93 LT 117; *Re Wombwell's Settlement* [1922] 2 Ch 298; *Re Ames' Settlement* [1946] Ch 217, [1946] 1 All ER 689.

7 Part II, as amended by the Family Law Act 1996.

8 *Burgess v Rawnsley* [1975] Ch 429 at 442.

9 *Burgess v Rawnsley* [1975] Ch 429 at 441, [1975] 3 All ER 142 at 149. Also see *Westdeutsche Landesbank Girozentrale* [1996] AC 669 at 683.

templation of a particular event and that purpose fails or that event does not happen, there is a resulting trust for the settlor. Lord Denning has already referred to Underhill on Trusts[10].

The same would also apply where two people join in creating a trust both having the same purpose or contemplating the same event. The resulting trust in such a case is for each settlor in proportion to the amount he or she put into trust.'

The case concerned H, a 63 year-old tenant of the lower flat of a house divided into two flats and his friend Mrs R, a 60-year-old widow. They purchased the house paying half each and took the conveyance jointly upon trust for sale for themselves as joint tenants. H's purpose was marriage to her though he had not mentioned this to her. In Lord Denning's opinion Mrs R's purpose was to have the upper flat to live in and H refused to let her move in when, after the purchase, she refused to marry him. If a common purpose had failed a resulting trust for each in half shares would have arisen and the fact that each had a different purpose which failed should make no difference, so that on H's death Mrs R was not entitled to the whole property.

Browne LJ and Sir John Pennycuick disagreed: a common purpose which fails must be established; or, at any rate, a failure of purpose of one settlor, not communicated to the other, cannot destroy a trust; and, in any event, Mrs R's purpose had not failed since it was not just to obtain the upper flat to live in but to take an interest in the whole house as beneficial joint tenant, as expressed in the conveyance, incidentally sharing the house in a particular manner. However, further facts showed H and Mrs R had effectively orally severed the joint tenancy.

It remains to be seen how fundamental a purpose or event must be for its failure to vitiate a trust and where the dividing line is to be drawn between a relevant purpose and an irrelevant motive[11].

Muschinski v Dodds[12] contrasts with *Burgess v Rawnsley*. An unmarried couple, who lived together, bought land on which they were to erect a house for themselves and on which stood an old cottage that they were to restore and make into an arts and craft centre. The land was conveyed to them to hold as tenants in common equally, the woman contributing $25,259 and the man $2,549 though he was expected to make a very significant contribution using his time, skill, and labour in the joint venture. The venture did not get off the ground since they split up. The Australian High Court held the parties held the property on trust to repay each other their respective financial contributions and to divide any surplus equally between them. The court applied the general principle underlying the proportionate repayment of capital contributions to a joint venture on the failure of the venture[13].

Paragraph 2

Cancellation for ignorance or mistake

Cancellation on the ground of ignorance, mistake, fraud, or undue influence

---

10 12th edn, pp 135 to 136, reproduced as Article 15(1) in the current edition.
11 As with contracts, so trusts should not be set aside because the settlor was disappointed in his motive for creating the trust or because he was mistaken on some peripheral matter.
12 (1985) 62 ALR 429.
13 *Atwood v Maude* (1868) 3 Ch App 369. For another failed venture case see *Rowan v Dann* [1991] EGCS 19 (Millett J); affd (1991) 64 P & CR 202, CA.

is more frequently sought in the case of voluntary settlements than those made for consideration. The remedy of cancellation is not, however, confined to voluntary settlements, although the court will more readily cancel a settlement for which no consideration was given than one based on value.

It is now settled that where the settlor invokes the aid of the court to set aside a voluntary settlement the *onus* of showing mistake, fraud, or undue influence is upon him[14], except:

(1) where the provisions of the settlement are so absurd and improvident as to raise a presumption that no sane person would have agreed to them knowingly[15], and

(2) where the beneficiary occupied at the date of the settlement a fiduciary position towards the settlor, in which case there is a strong prima facie presumption of undue influence[16].

The absence of a power of revocation will not operate to transfer the onus of proof from the settlor to the beneficiary[17].

On the other hand, where the beneficiaries set up the deed against the settlor the onus is on them to show that he thoroughly understood it[18].

Mistake

Although a settlor cannot obtain the setting aside or variation of a voluntary trust for the mere asking, yet some relief will be given to him where he can show that he misunderstood, or did not understand, the effect thereof. In the case of *James v Couchman*[19] it appeared that the plaintiff had, by a voluntary settlement (made with the object of protecting himself against extravagant habits), assigned property to trustees, upon trust for himself for life, remainder to his wife (if any) for life, remainder to his issue, and in default of issue to his *paternal* next of kin. North J, while refusing to set aside the settlement, thought that the ultimate limitation was unusual, and that the settlor's attention was not called to it, and that he did not understand the effect of it; and accordingly his Lordship ordered the settlement to be rectified so as to give the settlor a power of appointment in default or failure of issue. His Lordship, however, was careful to add:

---

14 *Henry v Armstrong* (1881) 18 Ch D 668.

15 *Dutton v Thompson* (1883) 23 Ch D 278. A sale at an undervalue or settlement may be set aside if of an improvident unconscionable character made by a poorly educated person acting without independent advice: *Fry v Lane* (1888) 40 Ch D 312. This principle has had a new lease of life where a wife in circumstances of emotional strain transfers her interest in the matrimonial home: *Backhouse v Backhouse* [1978] 1 All ER 1158, [1978] 1 WLR 243; *Cresswell v Potter* [1978] 1 WLR 255n; *Butlin-Sanders v Butlin* [1985] FLR 204, [1985] Fam Law 126. In *Watkin v Watson-Smith* (1986) Times, 3 July, Michael Wheeler QC as deputy judge opined that a vendor's desire for a quick sale and his old age with accompanying diminution of capacity and judgment would suffice in place of poverty and ignorance for *Fry v Lane* principles. Further see *Simpson v Simpson* [1992] 1 FLR 601; *Crédit Lyonnais v Burch* [1997] 1 All ER 144 at 151, per Nourse LJ and *Portman Building Society v Dusangh* [2001] WTLR 117, CA. The unconscionable bargains doctrine does not apply to gifts so that undue influence or mistake will need to be relied upon to upset gifts: *Langton v Langton* [1995] 2 FLR 890.

16 *Huguenin v Baseley* (1807) 14 Ves 273; *Hylton v Hylton* (1754) 2 Ves Sen 547; *Hunter v Atkins* (1834) 3 My & K 113; *Tate v Williamson* (1866) 2 Ch App 55, CA; *Allcard v Skinner* (1887) 36 Ch D 145; *Morley v Loughnan* [1893] 1 Ch 736.

17 *Hall v Hall* (1873) 8 Ch App 430, overruling *Coutts v Acworth* (1869) LR 8 Eq 558; *Wollaston v Tribe* (1869) LR 9 Eq 44; *Everitt v Everitt* (1870) LR 10 Eq 405.

18 *Phillips v Mullings* (1871) 7 Ch App 244.

19 (1885) 29 Ch D 212; and see *Cavendish v Strutt* (1903) 19 TLR 483.

'The fact that a usual power was omitted here would not weigh with me in the least if I were satisfied that the omission of such power had been brought to the attention of the settlor, as he would then have been competent to judge for himself. But it seems to me that in the present case his attention was not called to the omission'.[20]

Where a person, apparently at the point of death, executed a voluntary settlement, of which he recollected nothing, which was never read to him, and in which a power of revocation was purposely omitted by the solicitor on the ground that he knew the variable character of the settlor, and there was also evidence that the settlor thought that he was executing the settlement in place of a will, it was held that the settlement was revocable[1].

Even where there is valuable consideration given, but the settlor is infirm and ignorant, and there is reason to suppose that he did not fully understand the transaction, it will be set aside, unless it be proved that full value was given[2].

Millett J summarised the cases as showing[3] 'that, wherever there is a voluntary transaction by which one party intends to confer a bounty upon another, the deed will be set aside if the court is satisfied that the disposer did not intend the transaction to have the effect which it did. It will be set aside whether the mistake is of law or of fact, so long as the mistake is to the effect of the transaction itself and not merely as to its consequences or the advantages to be gained by entering into it.' He thus set aside a voluntary deed whereby G purported to surrender his protected life interest under a protective trust so forfeiting his interest and causing discretionary trusts to spring up, under the mistaken view that his surrender would be effective to give the remaindermen, his children, as immediate absolute entitlement.

The jurisdiction is not limited to voluntary settlements so it can extend to a pension trust, eg to set aside an employer's mistaken consent to the trustees' exercise of a power to amend the trust[4].

Rectification: unilateral transaction or bargain

If a settlement involves bargaining between the parties then rectification may be obtained where it is clearly proved by convincing evidence[5] that owing to a

20 But in *Bullock v Lloyds Bank Ltd* [1955] Ch 317, [1954] 3 All ER 726; where such a power was omitted, the settlement was set aside altogether, though undue influence was also established.

1 *Forshaw v Welsby* (1860) 30 Beav 243; *Re Flamank* (1889) 40 Ch D 461; *Re Blake* (1889) 37 WR 441. See also *Constantinidi v Ralli* [1935] Ch 427, where it was sought, without success, to compromise an action for rectification of a settlement brought upon the ground that the settlor, a foreigner, did not understand the true effect of the settlement, it being held on the evidence that she took part in the negotiations for the settlement and that it was her deed. In the same case it was held that rectification will not be made on affidavit evidence, but in s clear-cut case rectification can be ordered on affidavit evidence as in *Frey v Royal Bank of Scotland (Nassau) Ltd* (2001) 3 ITELR 775 (settlement of Marc Bolan rectified 24 years after his death to extend to illegitimate children of the rock star or his wife); *Hanley v Pearson* (1879) 13 Ch D 545.

2 *Baker v Monk* (1864) 33 Beav 419; affd (1864) 4 De GJ & Sm 388; *Clark v Malpas* (1862) 31 Beav 80; *Longmate v Ledger* (1860) 2 Giff 157; and see *O'Rorke v Bolingbroke* (1877) 2 App Cas 814, HL; and *Re Fry v Lane* (1888) 40 Ch D 312.

3 *Gibbon v Mitchell* [1990] 3 All ER 338 at 343, applied in *Dent v Dent* [1996] 1 WLR 683 and in *Anker-Petersen v Christensen* [2002] WTLR 313 (deed of assignment to trustees of Jersey discretionary trust set aside).

4 *AMP (UK) plc v Barker* [2001] WTLR 1232.

5 *AMP (UK) plc v Barker* [2001] WTLR 1232 at 1256.

mistake of the draftsman the settlement does not express the real intention of the parties: the mistake must thus be mutual[6]. Exceptionally where the bargaining parties had a common intention and it is shown (i) that the claimant erroneously believed that the instrument gave effect to that intention (ii) that the defendant knew that it did not because by reason of the claimant's mistake the instrument contained or omitted something (iii) that the defendant failed to bring the mistake to the claimant's notice, and (iv) that the mistake would benefit the defendant or, perhaps, merely be detrimental to the claimant, then rectification will be ordered to give effect to the common intention, despite the fact that the mistake was merely a unilateral mistake[7].

In the case of a unilateral transaction it is necessary only to prove that the settlement fails to express the real intention of the settlor. In *Re Butlin's Settlement Trust* Brightman J summarised the law as follows[8]:

'In the absence of an actual bargain between a settlor and trustees: (i) a settlor may seek rectification by proving that the settlement does not express his true intention, or the true intention of himself and any party with whom he has bargained, such as a spouse in the case of an antenuptial settlement; (ii) it is not essential for him to prove that the settlement fails to express the true intention of the trustees if they have not bargained; but (iii) the court may in its discretion decline to rectify a settlement against a protesting trustee who objects to rectification.'

The settlor had intended his voluntary discretionary settlement to contain a power for a majority of trustees to bind a minority in more situations than allowed for by the settlement as finally executed. Brightman J held that rectification (which has retrospective effect) was 'available not only in a case where particular words have been added, omitted or wrongly written as the result of careless copying or the like' but 'also where the words of the document were purposely used but it was mistakenly considered that they bore a different meaning from their correct meaning as a matter of construction'[9]. Applying his summary of the law (above) he ordered rectification despite the trustees' absence of intention and despite the opposition of one trustee, though not swearing any affidavit to disclose the reasons for her opposition.

Where rectification is sought which will attract tax benefits the caselaw[10]

---

6 *Re Butlin's Settlement Trusts* [1976] Ch 251, [1976] 2 All ER 483; *Joscelyne v Nissen* [1970] 2 QB 86, [1970] 1 All ER 1213.

7 *Thomas Bates & Son Ltd v Wyndham's (Lingerie) Ltd* [1981] 1 All ER 1077, [1981] 1 WLR 505, CA; *Commission for New Towns v Cooper (GB) Ltd* [1995] 2 All ER 929.

8 [1976] Ch 251 at 262, [1976] 2 All ER 483 at 489. See also *Behrers v Heilbut* (1956) 222 L Jo 290; *Re Walton's Settlement* [1922] 2 Ch 509, CA.

9 [1976] Ch 251 at 260, [1976] 2 All ER 483 at 487. Whilst a mistake as to the interpretation of words used can be rectified, so that 'children' in a Bahamian trust can be rectified to include illegitimate children (*Frey v Royal Bank of Scotland (Nassau) Ltd* (2001) 3 ITELR 775), a mistake as to material facts which led to the words used cannot be rectified: *Frederick Rose Ltd v William Pim Junior & Co Ltd* [1953] 2 QB 450, [1953] 2 All ER 739, CA ('horsebeans' used in contract under mistaken belief it meant the same as 'feveroles'). For a refusal to rectify a settlement see *Tankel v Tankel* [1999] 1 FLR 676 where appointments had been made in favour of the settlor's daughters, who were beneficiaries who had become two of the trustees in whose favour no distributions of income or capital could be made, due to a prohibitory clause of which rectification was sought so as retrospectively to validate the appointments. It is not possible to invoke the *Hastings-Bass* principle to declare the appointment of the two younger daughters as trustees to be void: see *Re Duxbury's ST* [1995] 1 WLR 425, CA.

10 *Whiteside v Whiteside* [1950] Ch 65, CA; *Re Slocock's Will Trust* [1979] 1 All ER 358; *Sherdley v Sherdley* [1986] 1 WLR 732, *Lake v Lake* [1989] STC 865.

has been summarised by Vinelott J as follows[11]: 'the court will make an order for the rectification of a document if satisfied that it does not give effect to the true agreement or arrangement between the parties, or to the true intention of a grantor or covenantor and if satisfied that there is an issue, capable of being contested, between the parties or between a covenantor or grantor and the person he intended to benefit, it being irrelevant first that rectification is sought or consented to by them all and second that rectification is desired because it has beneficial fiscal consequences. On the other hand, the court will not order rectification of a document as between the parties or as between a grantor or covenantor and an intended beneficiary, if their rights will be unaffected and if the only effect of the order will be to secure a fiscal benefit.'

Rectification is a last resort and it may be possible where words have been omitted from a deed by inadvertence so to construe a deed as to give effect to the clear intentions of the parties where it is clear what correction was required to carry out the intentions of parties[12]. Thus is *Schnieder v Mills*[13] a clause was construed with the implication therein of the words 'which has arisen prior to the date hereof' after the word 'income' so as to reflect the fact that deeds of variation of wills executed within two years of a testator's death are retrospective for the purposes of inheritance tax[14] and capital gains tax[15] but not income tax.

Rectification of marriage settlements or pension trusts

Even a marriage settlement or pension trust where valuable consideration has been provided will be rectified on clear evidence of mistake.

Thus in *Banks v Ripley*[16], Morton J ordered the rectification of a marriage settlement by the insertion of words of limitation even though the only evidence that they had been omitted by mistake was afforded by the document itself. There was also rectification of a marriage settlement in *Re Alexander's Settlement*[17] where by mistake a gift over was directed in the event of a son becoming tenant in tail male under the will of a deceased person, it appearing that under that will a son could only become tenant in tail general.

In *AMP(UK) Ltd v Barker*[18] trustees of a pension trust, with the requisite consent of the employer, exercised their power to amend the trust in terminology intended to increase benefits of members retiring early through incapacity but mistakenly extending to all early leavers. Convincing evidence of the separate intentions of the trustees and of the employer to affect only incapacity benefits justified retrospective rectification without the need to show that there was some outward expression of any agreement or accord between the trustees and the employer (although it was possible on the facts to find that 'there was in effect such an accord'[19]). Early leavers for reasons

---

11 *Racal Group Services Ltd v Ashmore* [1995] STC 1151, CA.
12 *Re Whitrick* [1957] 1 WLR 884; *Re Bacharach's Will Trust* [1959] Ch 245; *Fitzgerald v Masters* (1956) 95 CLR 420; *Wolverhampton and Dudley Breweries plc v Trusthouse Forte Catering Ltd* [1984] 2 EGLR 141.
13 [1993] STC 430.
14 Inheritance Tax Act 1984, s 142.
15 Taxation of Chargeable Gains Act 1992, s 62(6).
16 [1940] Ch 719, [1940] 3 All ER 49.
17 [1910] 2 Ch 225.
18 [2001] WTLR 1237.
19 [2001] WTLR 1237 at 1259.

unrelated to their incapacity could not resist rectification as bona fide purchasers, not having given any additional consideration for the rights mistakenly conferred on them, so that it was wholly unrealistic to treat them as purchasers of anything other than such rights as were properly granted under the pension trusts.

Rectification of wills

By s 20 of the Administration of Justice Act 1982 it is now possible for a court to rectify a will if it is satisfied that the will fails to carry out the testator's intentions in consequence of a clerical error or a failure to understand his instructions[20]. The words 'clerical error' are wide enough to include a solicitor's omission to record or include a clause from a previous will[1]. The application for rectification cannot be made, except with the court's leave, more than six months after the date on which the grant of representation to the estate was taken out. If after the six months the personal representatives distribute the estate they will not be liable for failing to take into account the possibility of the court allowing an application for rectification out of time: the estate will be recoverable from its recipients, so long as they are not bona fide purchasers[2].

Apart from this statutory power a court may rectify a will in the case of fraud[3]. It is also possible that a court as a matter of construction may be able to correct an obvious mistake or error appearing on the face of the will[4], especially now that by s 21 of the 1982 Act extrinsic evidence, including evidence of the testator's intention, may be admitted to assist in the interpretation of a will in so far as it is meaningless or the language used is ambiguous on the face of it or in so far as evidence, other than evidence of the testator's intention, shows that the language used is ambiguous in the light of the surrounding circumstances.

Potential negligence liability of legal advisers

While a solicitor may be liable for negligent breach of contract for any loss caused to the person instructing him to prepare a deed or a will, he may also be liable for the tort of negligence to third party beneficiaries suffering a loss through the solicitor's failure to achieve what he was instructed to achieve, eg negligently failing to advise a testator that a beneficiary's spouse should not attest the will[5] or negligently failing to prepare an ill elderly testator's will timeously[6] or negligently failing to use the appropriate wording or to have

---

20 If the testator has misunderstood the effect of the wording he has used then s 20 is not available so decisions like *Collins v Elstone* [1893] P 1, may still occur. If a person understood the instructions but failed to carry them out then s 20 is not available if no clerical error is involved.

1 *Wordingham v Royal Exchange Trust Co* [1992] Ch 412, [1992] 3 All ER 204; *Re Segelman* [1996] Ch 171.

2 Whether on tracing principles (Art 101, post) or under the in personam action vindicated by *Ministry of Health v Simpson* [1951] AC 251, [1950] 2 All ER 1137, HL (pp 977 and 997, post).

3 *Collins v Elstone* [1893] P 1.

4 *Re Bacharach's Will Trusts* [1959] Ch 245, [1958] 3 All ER 618; *Re Doland's Will Trust* [1970] Ch 267, [1969] 3 All ER 713; *Re Reynette-James* [1975] 3 All ER 1037, [1976] 1 WLR 161; *Re Chambers* [2001] WTLR 1375.

5 *Ross v Caunters* [1980] Ch 297.

6 *White v Jones* [1995] 2 AC 207, HL.

the will validly executed[7], or, it would seem[8], negligently failing to create an effective inter vivos trust for X after the death of the settlor, when, instead, a bare trust for the settlor containing an unattested testamentary disposition for X was actually created. While claimants have a duty to mitigate losses, there is no rule that rectification must be sought before suing the solicitor for negligence[9].

Fraud

If ignorance or mistake suffices to invalidate a settlement, a fortiori it will be cancelled where the settlor has been induced to make it by fraud; as, for instance, where a wife by falsely denying her previous adultery induces her husband to execute a deed of separation containing a stipulation not to take proceedings in respect of previous offences[10].

Undue influence

A gift or settlement may be set aside on the ground of undue influence not on the principle that it is right and expedient to save persons from the consequences of their own folly but on the principle that it is right and expedient to save them from being taken advantage of by other people[11].

As a result of the House of Lords' scrutiny[12] of two of their earlier decisions[13], one can state that there are two categories of undue influence. The first category is that of actual undue influence where the claimant proves affirmatively that the wrongdoer exerted undue influence on the claimant to have the latter enter into the particular impugned transaction; such influence may arise from conduct including duress or misrepresentations[14].

The second category arises where undue influence is presumed on a *res ipsa loquitur* basis[15] which switches the evidential burden from the claimant to the defendant, so that the defendant needs to show that actually there was no undue influence eg because of independent legal advice given to the claimant. For such switch of the evidential burden it is necessary first to show that the relationship between the parties to the transaction was (A) one where the law *de iure* presumes there to have been a relationship of trust and confidence[16] (eg always between parent and child[17], guardian and ward[18],

---

7 *Corbett v Bond Pearce* [2001] WTLR 419, CA.
8 *White v Jones* [1993] 3 All ER 481 at 492–493, *Hemmens v Wilson Browne* [1993] 4 All ER 826.
9 *Horsfall v Haywards* [1999] 1 FLR 1182, CA.
10 *Brown v Brown* (1868) LR 7 Eq 185; and see *Evans v Carrington* (1860) 2 De GF & J 481; *Evans v Edmonds* (1853) 13 CB 777; *Gordon v Gordon* (1821) 3 Swan 400. Restitutio in integrum must be possible: *Johnston v Johnston* (1884) 52 LT 76 (marriage settlement could not be set aside).
11 *Allcard v Skinner* (1887) 36 Ch D 145 at 182–183 endorsed in *National Westminster Bank plc v Morgan* [1985] AC 686 at 705, HL; *Hammond v Osbourn* [2002] WTLR 1125, CA.
12 *Royal Bank of Scotland plc v Etridge (No 2)* [2001] UKHL 44, [2001] 4 All ER 449.
13 *Barclays Bank plc v O'Brien* [1994] 1 AC 180, HL; *National Westminster Bank v Morgan* [1985] AC 686.
14 *Royal Bank of Scotland plc v Etridge (No 2)* [2001] 4 All ER 449 at para 103.
15 *Royal Bank of Scotland plc v Etridge (No 2)* [2001] 4 All ER 449 at paras 16, 107 and 161.
16 *Royal Bank of Scotland plc v Etridge (No 2)* [2001] 4 All ER 449 at paras 18, 105, 157 and 161 for Class 2A cases within the *Barclays Bank plc v O'Brien* [1994] 1 AC 180 classification.
17 *Lancashire Loans Ltd v Black* [1934] 1 KB 380; *Powell v Powell* [1900] 1 Ch 243; *Bainbrigge v Browne* (1881) 18 Ch D 188.
18 *Hatch v Hatch* (1804) 9 Ves 292.

solicitor and client[19], trustee and beneficiary[20], doctor and patient[1], spiritual mentor and disciple[2]) or (B) one where the claimant proves *de facto* there was a relationship of trust and confidence[3] (eg often between husband and wife[4] or sometimes between siblings or banker and customer[5] or employer and employee[6]). Second, to produce the equitable equivalent of the common law *res ipsa loquitur*, the impugned transaction must be shown to be so bountiful to the recipient or so detrimental to the donor as to seem explicable only on the basis that undue influence had been exercised to procure it[7].

Once the disadvantage to the settlor-donor is sufficiently grave to raise the inference that undue influence has probably been exerted the onus is thrown on the donee-beneficiary to prove affirmatively that there was no undue influence exerted. This will normally require proof that the settlor had independent advice[8] or was strongly urged to obtain such advice and that the settlement contains all usual and proper powers and provisions; and, if there are any unusual provisions, that they were brought to the notice of and understood by the settlor[9]. Exculpatory clauses benefiting the trustee should clearly be brought to the attention of the settlor, the trustee prior to creation of the trust being in a fiduciary position where there is a conflict of interest preventing him from taking advantage of his position[10].

Undue influence in relation to wills

It must be understood that the onus of proof stated above only applies in the case of settlements and gifts inter vivos. With regard to dispositions by will when once it has been proved that a will has been executed with due solemnities by a person of competent understanding, and apparently a free agent, the burden of proving that it was executed under undue influence rests on the person who so alleges[11]. Thus in *Parfitt v Lawless*[12] no presumption of undue influence arose where T left her residuary estate to a Catholic

---

19 *Wright v Carter* [1903] 1 Ch 27, CA; *Wintle v Nye* [1959] 1 WLR 284, HL.
20 *Liles v Terry* [1895] 2 QB 679 at 686; *Re Brocklehurst* [1978] 1 All ER 767 at 785.
 1 *Re CMG* [1970] Ch 574.
 2 *Allcard v Skinner* (1887) 36 Ch D 145, CA.
 3 *Royal Bank of Scotland plc v Etridge (No 2)* [2001] 4 All ER 449 at paras 14,16, 18, 106-107, 153, 156 and 161.
 4 *Barclays Bank plc v O'Brien* [1994] 1 AC 180, HL.
 5 *Lloyds Bank Ltd v Bundy* [1975] QB 326, CA.
 6 *Goldsworthy v Brickell* [1987] Ch 378; *Crédit Lyonnais Bank v Burch* [1997] 1 All ER 144; *Re Craig* [1971] Ch 95.
 7 *Royal Bank of Scotland plc v Etridge (No 2)* [2001] 4 All ER 449 at paras 24, 25, 29, 104, 106, 107 and 161; *Hammond v Osbourn* [2002] WTLR 1125, CA.
 8 Whether it will be proper to infer that such advice had an emancipating effect, so that the transaction was not brought about by the exercise of undue influence, is a question of fact to be decided having regard to all the evidence: *Royal Bank of Scotland plc v Etridge (No 2)* [2001] 4 All ER 449 at paras 20 and 153.
 9 *Everitt v Everitt* (1870) LR 10 Eq 405; *Bester v Perpetual Trustee Co Ltd* [1970] 3 NSWLR 30; *Huguenin v Baseley* (1807) 14 Ves 273; *Re Lloyds Bank Ltd* [1931] 1 Ch 289; *Bullock v Lloyds Bank Ltd* [1955] Ch 317, [1954] 3 All ER 726.
10 *Bogg v Raper* (1998) 1 ITELR 267, CA; *Scott on Trusts* (4th edn) para 222.4; also see *Baskerville v Thurgood* (1992) 100 Sask LR 214, CA where a fiduciary in breach of his obligations could not rely on an exclusion clause.
11 *Craig v Lamoureux* [1920] AC 349; (1970) 86 LQR 447.
12 (1872) LR 2 P & D 462.

priest who resided with her as her domestic chaplain and confessor. Actual coercion must be proved rather than mere persuasion[13].

Undue influence by solicitor

A gift made by a client to a solicitor, while the relation of solicitor and client exists, if of such amount as not to be a small gift but one large enough to seem explicable only on the basis of the exertion of undue influence[14] is presumed voidable. Although such gift may be ratified after the relation has ceased to exist, yet, in order to establish ratification, it must be proved to the satisfaction of the court that the donor, at the time when he was a free agent, and knew of his right to recall the gift, intentionally determined to forgo that right. In the absence of such evidence, the gift may be avoided, not only by the donor, but by his personal representatives[15]. As Cotton LJ said[16]:

> 'We must find something equivalent to a present gift when the influence arising from the existence of the relationship had ceased to exist: in the words of Turner LJ in *Wright v Vanderplank*[17], there must be "a fixed, deliberate, and unbiased determination that the transaction should not be impeached". In the case of a gift to a solicitor, the court looks most carefully to see if there has been a fixed, deliberate, and unbiased determination on the part of the donor that the transaction should not be impeached.'

Indeed, the Court of Appeal has laid it down that, in the absence of independent advice, the presumption that the settlor was unduly influenced is absolute and irrebuttable[18]; and has also extended the doctrine not only to gifts to the solicitor himself, but also to his wife[19], or his son[20]. The same principle applies to an option to purchase given by a client to his solicitor[1].

Undue parental influence

The expression 'undue influence' is not confined to cases in which the influence is exerted to secure a benefit for the person exerting it, but extends also to cases in which a person of imperfect judgment is placed, or places himself, under the direction of one possessing not only greater experience but also such force as that which is inherent in such a relationship as that between a father and his own child[2]; and the influence may be exerted not directly by the parent but through his solicitor[3]. A fortiori undue influence will be presumed where the deed confers a benefit on the parent. Thus it

---

13 *Hall v Hall* (1868) LR 1 P & D 481; *Craig v Lamoureux* [1920] AC 349; *Killick v Pountney* [2000] WTLR 41 at 66–69.
14 *Royal Bank of Scotland plc v Etridge (No 2)* [2001] 4 All ER 449 at paras 24, 92, 104 and 156.
15 *Tyars v Alsop* (1889) 37 WR 339, CA.
16 *Tyars v Alsop* (1889) 37 WR 339 at 340, CA; and see also *Nanney v Williams* (1856) 22 Beav 452; and *Wright v Carter* [1903] 1 Ch 27, CA.
17 (1856) 8 De GM & G 133; and see also *Mitchell v Homfray* (1881) 8 QBD 587, CA.
18 *Liles v Terry* [1895] 2 QB 679, CA; *Barron v Willis* [1900] 2 Ch 121, CA; *Wright v Carter* [1903] 1 Ch 27 at 57.
19 *Liles v Terry* [1895] 2 QB 679; *Wright v Carter* [1903] 1 Ch 27.
20 *Barron v Willis* [1900] 2 Ch 121; affd sub nom *Willis v Barron* [1902] AC 271; *Wright v Carter* [1903] 1 Ch 27, CA; but contra in Scotland, *Burrell v Burrell's Trustees* 1915 52 SLR 312.
1 *Demerara Bauxite Co Ltd v Hubbard* [1923] AC 673.
2 *Bullock v Lloyds Bank Ltd* [1955] Ch 317, [1954] 3 All ER 726; and see *Lancashire Loans Ltd v Black* [1934] 1 KB 380, CA.
3 *Bullock v Lloyds Bank Ltd* [1955] Ch 317, [1954] 3 All ER 726.

seems that where a deed conferring a benefit on the settlor's father is executed by a child who is not yet emancipated[4] from his father's control, and the deed is subsequently impeached by the child, the onus is on the father to prove that the gift was the result of the free exercise of independent will, and this may most readily be done by showing that the child had independent advice[5], and that he executed the deed with full knowledge of its contents, and with the full intention of giving the father the benefit conferred by it[6].

Where the settlor has been advised 'carefully, deliberately, separately and independently'[7], the fact that he has not taken the advice he has been given is not fatal to the deed.

The above rules as to rebutting the presumption of undue influence were formulated in the Privy Council case of *Inche Noriah v Shaik Allie Bin Omar*[8]. Lord Hailsham, delivering the judgment of the Board said:

> 'their Lordships are not prepared to accept the view that independent legal advice is the only way in which the presumption [of undue influence] can be rebutted; nor are they prepared to affirm that independent legal advice, when given, does not rebut the presumption, unless it be shown that the advice was taken. It is necessary for the donee to prove that the gift was the result of the free exercise of independent will. The most obvious way to prove this is by establishing that the gift was made after the nature and effect of the transaction had been fully explained to the donee by some independent qualified person so completely as to satisfy the court that the donor was acting independently of any influence from the donee and with the full appreciation of what he was doing and in cases where there are no other circumstances this may be the only means by which the donee can rebut the presumption. But ... if evidence is given of circumstances sufficient to establish this fact (ie that the gift was the result of a free exercise of the donor's will) their lordships see no reason for disregarding them merely because they do not include independent advice from a lawyer.'

Trustees need beware undue parental (or other) influence

In *Re Pauling's Settlement Trusts*[9] the Court of Appeal put forward the view (but

---

4 Marriage of a daughter even when she has gone to live with a husband is not conclusive proof of emancipation *Lancashire Loans Ltd v Black* [1934] 1 KB 380, CA. The presumption of undue influence of a parent over his child endures for a 'short time' (its precise length being in each case a question of fact) after the child has attained 21: *Re Pauling's Settlement Trusts* [1964] Ch 303, [1963] 3 All ER 1, CA, or 18 after 1969.

5 *Powell v Powell* [1900] 1 Ch 243 (approved in *Wright v Carter* [1903] 1 Ch 27, CA), independent legal advice was regarded as essential. The common law judges have been inclined to rely more on individual proof than on general presumption, and to consider the nature of the relationship and presence of independent advice as important but not essential matters to be considered on the question whether the transaction can be supported, cf *Inche Noriah v Shaik Allie Bin Omar* [1929] AC 127, PC; see *Lancashire Loans Ltd v Black* [1934] 1 KB 380 at 404, [1933] All ER Rep 201 at 208, per Scrutton LJ. It seems that there are some circumstances in which independent legal advice is essential; see *Bullock v Lloyds Bank Ltd* [1955] Ch 317, [1954] 3 All ER 726.

6 *Bainbrigge v Browne* (1881) 18 Ch D 188; and see *Tate v Williamson* (1866) 2 Ch App 55; *Kempson v Ashbee* (1874) 10 Ch App 15, and cases cited; and *Tucker v Bennett* (1887) 38 Ch D 1, CA.

7 *Bullock v Lloyds Bank Ltd* [1955] Ch 317 at 326, [1954] 3 All ER 726 at 730, per Vaisey J.

8 [1929] AC 127 at 135, approved *Lancashire Loans Ltd v Black* [1934] 1 KB 380 at 413, [1933] All ER Rep 201 at 213, CA, per Lawrence LJ. See also *Bruty v Edmundson* (1915) 85 LJ Ch 568; *Re Coomber* [1911] 1 Ch 723 and *Kali Bakhsh Singh v Ram Gopal Singh* (1913) 30 TLR 138, PC. Further see *Royal Bank of Scotland plc v Etridge (No 2)* [2001] 4 All ER 449 at paras 20 and 153 per Lords Nicholls and Scott.

9 [1964] Ch 303, [1963] 3 All ER 1, CA.

without expressing a final opinion) that a trustee who is carrying out a transaction in breach of trust will not escape liability by obtaining the consent of the beneficiary concerned if the trustee knew, or should have known, that the consent was, or might be presumed to be, induced by undue influence; but that the trustee would escape liability if it could not be shown that he knew or should have known this.

Independent advice to youthful settlors

The duty of the person tendering independent advice to a young intending settlor was laid down by Vaisey J in *Bullock v Lloyds Bank Ltd* as follows[10]:

'Such a settlement as this can, in my judgment, only be justified after prolonged consideration, being made, as it was, by a young girl only just of age, and can only stand if executed under the advice of a competent adviser capable of surveying the whole field with an absolutely independent outlook, and who explains to the intending settlor, first, that she could do exactly as she pleased, and, secondly that the scheme put before her was not one to be accepted or rejected out of hand, but to be discussed, point by point, with a full understanding of the various alternative possibilities.'

Acquiescence by settlor

The settlor will get no relief if he has knowingly acquiesced in the settlement. Thus where a father induced a young son, who was still under his roof, and subject to his influence, to make a settlement in favour of his stepbrothers and sisters, it was held that, if the son had applied promptly, the court would have set it aside. But as he had remained quiescent for some years, and had made no objection to the course which he had been persuaded to follow, he was not entitled to relief. For by so doing he had in his more mature years practically adopted and confirmed that which he had done in his early youth[11]. Nor will the court interfere where the settlor subsequently acts under the deed, or does something which shows that he recognises its validity; unless, indeed, he was ignorant of the effect of the settlement at the date of such recognition[12].

So where a lady entered a religious sisterhood, and, under circumstances which amounted to undue influence, made a voluntary settlement in its favour, but omitted, for more than six years after severing her connection with it, to seek to have the settlement set aside, it was held that her acquiescence barred her claim for relief. As Lindley LJ said[13]:

'In this particular case the plaintiff considered when she left the sisterhood what course she should take, and she determined to do nothing, but to leave matters as they were. She insisted on having back her will, but she never asked for her money

---

10 [1955] Ch 317 at 326, [1954] 3 All ER 726 at 730. See also *Re Pauling's Settlement Trusts* [1964] Ch 303, [1963] 3 All ER 1, CA; *Re Coomber* [1911] 1 Ch 723; *Bester v Perpetual Trustee Co Ltd* [1970] 3 NSWLR 30. A solicitor acting for both parties cannot give independent advice: *Powell v Powell* [1900] 1 Ch 243.

11 *Turner v Collins* (1871) 7 Ch App 329.

12 *Jarratt v Aldam* (1870) LR 9 Eq 463; *Motz v Moreau* (1860) 13 Moo PCC 376; *Davies v Davies* (1869) LR 9 Eq 468. As to ignorance, see *Lister v Hodgson* (1867) LR 4 Eq 30. Ignorance of the *right* to rescind is no bar to the defence of acquiescence: *Goldsworthy v Brickell* [1987] 1 All ER 853 at 873, CA.

13 *Allcard v Skinner* (1887) 36 Ch D 145, CA. See also *Mitchell v Homfray* (1881) 8 QBD 587, CA.

until the end of five years or so after she had left the sisterhood. In this state of things I can only come to the conclusion that she deliberately chose not to attempt to avoid her gifts but to acquiesce in them. . . . I regard this as a question of fact, and upon the evidence I can come to no other conclusion than that which I have mentioned.'

On the other hand, in *Bullock v Lloyds Bank Ltd*[14], relief was granted to a settlor who had been aware of objections to the validity of a settlement for four years before the issue of the writ, but during those four years had been endeavouring to recover her property by obtaining the trustee's consent to the exercise by her of a power of revocation which was only exercisable with the consent of the trustee. Moreover, in *Bester v Perpetual Trustee Co Ltd*[15] a woman had a settlement made 20 years earlier when she was 21 set aside, the defence of laches being rejected because no persons other than the two trustees had altered their position on the faith of the validity of the settlement.

Change of status: restitutio in integrum

Even a settlement induced by most serious misrepresentations will not be cancelled unless the parties can be replaced in their original position. In one case[16], a settlor had married a lady who represented to him that she had divorced her first husband for adultery and cruelty, whereas, in point of fact, she herself had been divorced for adultery at his suit. The settlor, on discovering this, commenced an action to have the settlement set aside. Pearson J dismissed it as being frivolous and vexatious; and the Court of Appeal confirmed his decision, on the ground that the plaintiff could not set aside the settlement and yet keep the only consideration which was given for it, namely, the marriage; one essential condition of cancellation being (as Fry LJ observed) restitutio in integrum, which was there impossible.

However, nowadays where no change of status is involved rescission will be ordered if 'the situation is such that by the exercise of its power including the power to take account of profits and to direct inquiries as to allowances for deterioration [the court] can do what is practically just between the parties and restore them substantially to the status quo.'[17] In special circumstances where rescission is impossible equitable compensation may become payable[18].

Absolute right of claimant or only on making counter-restitution?

In *TSB v Camfield*[19] the Court of Appeal has taken the strict view that if a claimant establishes a right to set aside a transaction for undue influence or misrepresentation, then it must be set aside entirely, even where she would have agreed to the mortgage on the matrimonial home for £x rather than the

---

14 [1955] Ch 317, [1954] 3 All ER 726. See also *Re Pauling's Settlement Trusts* [1964] Ch 303, [1963] 3 All ER 1, CA.
15 [1970] 3 NSWLR 30 where under her voluntary settlement she was merely a protected life tenant with no access to capital, no right of revocation being reserved.
16 *Johnston v Johnston* (1884) 52 LT 76.
17 *Alati v Kruger* (1955) 94 CLR 216 at 223–224 applied in *O'Sullivan v Management Agency and Music Ltd* [1985] QB 428, CA; *Goode and Durrant Administration v Biddulph* [1994] 2 FLR 551.
18 *Mahoney v Purnell* [1996] 3 All ER 61.
19 [1995] 1 All ER 951, CA.

actual £2x. The Australian High Court[20] has rejected this so that in such a case the mortgage for £2x would be set aside only on terms that the wife joins in a valid mortgage for £x. It seems likely that the English House of Lords will follow the view of their Australian counterparts. Indeed, Millett J (as he then was) has already indicated[1] the need for counter-restitution to the extent it is proved that the wife actually benefited from the loan that is set aside.

Third parties

On general principles of property law[2] a court will make no order that would prejudice a person who proves that he or she is a purchaser of a legal or equitable interest in the property for value without notice of the claim to avoid the trust affecting the property or a purchaser protected by statutory overreaching or registration provisions.

Where co-owners of a home charge their home to a bank as security for a loan to one co-owner or the company which he operates as a business[3], the issue arises whether or not the other co-owner is to be bound by her apparent consent to the grant of security to the bank if such consent has been vitiated by her co-owner's conduct. The House of Lords[4] has held that this is not a question of priority of competing proprietary interests but one of suretyship contracts, where the burden is on the innocent co-owner to prove that it is unconscionable for the bank-chargee to be able to enforce its charge against her because it had failed to take reasonable steps to satisfy itself that there was no vitiating factor like undue influence or misrepresentation.

ARTICLE 16

Effect of the bankruptcy of the settlor on the validity of a settlement

(1) Where
(a) an individual[5], 'the settlor', has subjected property to a trust gratuitously or in consideration of marriage or for a consideration the value of which, in money or money's worth, is significantly less than the value, in money or money's worth, of the settlor's consideration[6]; and
(b) he is adjudged bankrupt either (i) having made such disposition within the period of two years ending with the day of the pre-

---

20 *Vadasz v Pioneer Concrete SA Pty Ltd* (1995) 184 CLR 102; also see *Maguire v Makaronis* (1997) 188 CLR 449.

1 *Dunbar Bank v Nadeem* [1998] 3 All ER 876.

2 Subject to Land Registration Act 2002, s 116 which, when in force, will make earlier mere equities to set aside dispositions of registered land bind later purchasers of equitable interests: Law Com no 271, *Land Registration for the 21st Century*, paras 5.32–5.36.

3 No problem arises if the loan appears to be for the benefit of both co-owners; *CIBC Mortgages plc v Pitt* [1994] 1 AC 200, HL.

4 *Royal Bank of Scotland plc v Etridge (No 2)* [2001] 4 All ER 449 at paras 40–43, 101, 144-146. Their Lordships detailed the reasonable steps required but they fall outside the scope of a trusts book.

5 For corporate settlors see Insolvency Act 1986, ss 238 and 239.

6 Insolvency Act 1986, s 339(3).

sentation of the bankruptcy petition[7] or (ii) having made such disposition no less than two years nor more than five years from the day of the presentation of the bankruptcy petition[8] and it is shown that he was insolvent[9] at the time of the disposition or became insolvent in consequence of the disposition, such being rebuttably presumed to be the case where the disposition was in favour of his associates[10],

then, on the application of the trustee of the bankrupt's estate, the court must make such order as it thinks fit for restoring the position to what it would have been if the settlor had not made the disposition[11].

(2) Where

(a) the settlor creates a settlement which desiredly[12] has the effect of putting one of his creditors or a surety or guarantor for any of his debts or liabilities into a position which, in the event of the settlor's bankruptcy, will be better than the position he would have been in if the settlement had not been created; and[13]

(b) the settlor is adjudged bankrupt either (i) having given such preferential treatment to an associate of his within two years of the day of the presentation of the bankruptcy petition[14] or (ii) having given such preferential treatment in any other case within six months of the day of the presentation of the bankruptcy petition[15]; and

(c) the settlor at the time of the preferential treatment was insolvent or became insolvent in consequence of such preference[16], then on the application of the trustee of the bankrupt's estate the court must make such order as it thinks fit for restoring the position to what it would have been if the settlor had not given such preferential treatment[17].

(3) A court order cannot prejudice any interest in property which was acquired from a person other than the settlor and was acquired in good faith for value and without notice of the relevant circumstances, nor prejudice any interest deriving from such an interest, nor require a person who received a benefit from the disposition in good faith for value and without notice of the relevant circumstances to pay a sum to

---

7 Insolvency Act 1986, ss 339(1), 341(1)(2). Where the settlor has been made criminally bankrupt under s 264(1)(d) it is only necessary that the disposition was made on or after the date specified for the purposes of s 341(4) in the criminal bankruptcy order.

8 Insolvency Act 1986, ss 339(1), 341(1)(2).

9 Insolvency Act 1986, s 341(3).

10 Insolvency Act 1986, s 435.

11 Insolvency Act 1986, s 339(2).

12 Insolvency Act 1986, s 340(4); *Re M C Bacon Ltd* [1991] Ch 127. Preferences in favour of an associate are rebuttably presumed to be desired to improve his position. The section has extra-territorial effect as concerns persons preferred: *Re Paramount Airways Ltd* [1993] Ch 223: s 340(5).

13 Insolvency Act 1986, s 340(3).

14 Insolvency Act 1986, s 341(1)(b).

15 Insolvency Act 1986, s 341(1)(c).

16 Insolvency Act 1986, s 341(2).

17 Insolvency Act 1986, s 340(2).

the trustee of the bankrupt's estate except where he was a party to the disposition[18].

The Insolvency Act 1986

Sections 339, 341 and 342 of the Insolvency Act 1986 have replaced provisions, formerly in s 42 of the Bankruptcy Act 1914, which enabled dispositions to be set aside pro tanto where the dispositions were made within two years of the bankruptcy or after two but within ten years where the bankrupt was not solvent at the date of the disposition without the aid of the property comprised in it. The old case law on what amounts to a gratuitous disposition still remains good so that the new provisions will catch a house purchased by H in the name of W[19] or an agreement that a house purchased by H in H's name will be owned by them jointly so leading W to act to her detriment, though not having provided half the purchase moneys for the half share she is intended to have[20]. Similarly, in estimating solvency where the settlor reserves for himself a life interest out of the disposition it seems that the life interest should still be taken into account[1]. Where H lets out his farmhouse and land to W at a full market rent the court will still look to the transaction as a whole (eg the safeguarding of the family home and the farming business and the 'ransom' surrender value to permit H's mortgagee to take vacant possession and enforce the security) and so set aside the transaction[2].

The Court of Appeal decision in *Clarkson v Clarkson*[3] is illuminating on the ambit of s 339. A, B and C were directors and equal shareholders in ABC Ltd which they valued at £1.5 million. To cater for the death of any of them and provide the cash to buy out the deceased they each took out in 1989 an insurance policy for £0.5 million. C's policy was held on trust by A, B and C with power to appoint to C's spouse and issue or A and B, and in default of appointment for A and B equally. The premiums in respect of the policy that C took out were deducted from his remuneration by the company, and afterwards paid for directly by C and after his bankruptcy by his family. ABC Ltd had become insolvent in 1991 and had gone into administrative receivership. The guarantees of A, B and C for the company's indebtedness were invoked in October 1991. In November 1992 A, B and C as trustees appointed the proceeds of the policy to Mrs C. In February 1993 A, B and C were adjudicated bankrupt.

It was argued against Mrs C that she had benefited from a transaction at an undervalue within two years of the bankruptcy of A, B and C within s 339. After all, A, B and C could have appointed everything to A and B, or by refusing to co-operate in any proposed appointment by C, A and B could have engineered matters so that they took in default of appointment.

The Court of Appeal held that the creation of the trust in 1989 by C was a gift by C, and the appointment in 1992:

'was merely the exercise of a fiduciary power to select the person to whom the gift should go. It has been for centuries a principle that an appointment under a special

---

18 Insolvency Act 1986, s 342(2).
19 *Re A Debtor* [1965] 3 All ER 453, [1965] 1 WLR 1498.
20 *Re Densham (a bankrupt)* [1975] 3 All ER 726, [1975] 1 WLR 1519.
1 *Re Lowndes* (1887) 18 QBD 677.
2 *Agricultural Mortgage Corpn v Woodward* [1996] 1 FLR 226, CA.
3 (26 April 1994, unreported).

power takes effect as if it had been written into the instrument creating the power. The appointee takes the property of the settlor and not that of the donee of the power. So, if the settlement had been made less than two years before the bankruptcy petition was presented it would have been open to attack under section 339. But since it was made earlier and at a time when Mr Clarkson was solvent it cannot be set aside ... This is a very simple case. Mr Clarkson made a gift into settlement which has vested in his wife. That gift is unaffected by his subsequent bankruptcy more than two years later, and the fact that the trustees who jointly exercised the power in favour of the wife became bankrupt less than two years afterwards is irrelevant.'

The new provisions have much more flexibility than the old provisions. To restore the position the court can require any property transferred as part of the transaction to be vested in the trustee of the bankrupt's estate as well as any property representing in any person's hands the application either of the proceeds of sale of property so transferred or of money so transferred[4]. The court can also require any person to pay in respect of benefits received by him (eg as beneficiary under the settlor's settlement) such sums to the trustee of the bankrupt settlor's estate as the court may direct[5]. The court may provide for a person against whom it makes an order to be able to prove in the settlor's bankruptcy, eg for debts incurred for less than full consideration[6].

Dispositions in the two to five year period

An individual is treated as insolvent if (a) he is unable to pay his debts as they fall due or (b) the value of his assets is less than the amount of his liabilities, taking into account his contingent and prospective liabilities[7]. For the presumption of insolvency, where the transaction at an undervalue is with an associate of the settlor, there is a broad and lengthy statutory definition[8] of an associate, but a person who is an associate by reason only of being the settlor's employee is deemed not to be an associate[9]. For present purposes it suffices that an associate of the settlor includes his spouse, his relatives and their spouses, her relatives and their spouses, his partners and their spouses and relatives. A person in his capacity as trustee of a trust is an associate of X if the trust beneficiaries include, or the trust terms confer, a power that may be exercised for the benefit of X or an associate of X[10].

Unfair preferences

The principles just discussed deal with transactions at an undervalue and not with the case where full consideration has been provided. Where an individual[11] has many creditors for value it is clearly unfair for him to give preferential treatment to some creditors (eg by creating a settlement on a

4 Insolvency Act 1986, s 342(1)(a) and (b).
5 Insolvency Act 1986, s 342(1)(d).
6 Insolvency Act 1986, s 342(1)(g).
7 Insolvency Act 1986, s 341(2). Such liabilities would not seem to extend to future uncertain liabilities.
8 Insolvency Act 1986, s 435.
9 Insolvency Act 1986, s 341(2).
10 Insolvency Act 1986, s 435(5). But there is an exception where the body of trustees manages a pension trust or an employee share scheme: *Re Thirty-Eight Building Ltd* [1999] 1 BCLC 416.
11 For companies see s 239.

creditor, his spouse and issue in satisfaction of the debt) at a time when he is insolvent so that the remaining creditors will be prejudiced in the event of his bankruptcy. Thus the Insolvency Act 1986 in ss 340, 341 and 342 extends to cover unfair preferences as well as transactions at an undervalue[12]. A preference will only be unfair if there was a subjective positive desire to improve the creditor's position[13].

No prejudice to persons without notice of relevant circumstances

A problem arises from the fact that a purchaser from a donee of unregistered land will inevitably have notice of relevant circumstances so freezing the land in his hands for two or perhaps, five years. Thus the Insolvency (No 2) Act 1994 amends s 342 so that a purchaser will only be vulnerable if he was either an associate of the person initiating the undervalue transaction or preference or of the person benefiting under it, or if he can be shown to have had knowledge of the bankruptcy or pending bankruptcy.

Criminal offences

By virtue of ss 357 and 352 of the Insolvency Act 1986 a bankrupt is guilty of an offence if in the five years before his bankruptcy commenced he made or caused to be made any gift or transfer of or any charge on his property unless he proves that at the time of such conduct he had no intent to defraud or to conceal the state of his affairs. Conduct defrauding creditors covers transactions entered into for the purpose of putting assets beyond the reach of a person who is making, or may at some time make, a claim against him or of otherwise prejudicing the interests of such a person in relation to the claim which he is making or may make as appears from s 423(3) discussed below in Article 17. Assisting a person to commit such a crime will be an offence under the general aiding and abetting offence in the Accessories and Abettors Act 1861, s 8 as amended by the Criminal Law Act 1977; those involved in asset protection trusts must beware.

ARTICLE 17

Effect of settlements intended to prejudice creditors apart from bankruptcy

(1) Where
(a) a person, 'the settlor', has subjected property to a trust gratuitously or in consideration of marriage or for a consideration the value of which, in money or money's worth, is significantly less than the value, in money or money's worth, of the settlor's consideration[14], and;
(b) the court is satisfied that the settlement was entered into for the purpose[15] of putting assets beyond the reach of a person[16] who is

---

12 On 'undervalue' see *Re Kumar* [1993] 2 All ER 700.
13 *Re M C Bacon Ltd* [1991] Ch 127.
14 Insolvency Act 1986, s 423(1).
15 As to 'dominant' or 'substantial' or 'significant purpose' see *IRC v Hashmi* [2002] WTLR 19 at 28–29, reversed on other grounds: [2002] WTLR 1027, CA.

making or may at some time make a claim against the settlor, or of otherwise prejudicing the interests of such claimant or potential claimant[17], then the court may make such order as it thinks fit for restoring the position to what it would have been if the settlement had not been entered into and for protecting the interests of prejudiced persons[18].

(2) A court order cannot prejudice any interest in property which was acquired from a person other than the settlor and was acquired in good faith for value and without notice of the relevant circumstances, nor prejudice any interest deriving from such an interest, nor require a person who received a benefit from the settlement in good faith for value and without notice of the relevant circumstances to pay any sum unless he was a party to the settlement[19].

Insolvency cases

In a case where the settlor has been adjudged bankrupt or is a company which is being wound up or in relation to which an administration order is in force, the application for an order under s 423 of the Insolvency Act 1986 must be by the Official Receiver, by the trustee of the bankrupt's estate or the liquidator or administrator of the company or, with the leave of the court, by a person who is, or is capable of being, prejudiced by the settlement[20].

In a case where a person who is, or is capable of being, prejudiced by the settlement is bound by a voluntary arrangement under Pts I or VIII of the Insolvency Act 1986, the application must be by the supervisor of the voluntary arrangement or by any person who (whether or not so bound) is, or is capable of being, so prejudiced[1].

Other cases

In any other case any person who is or is capable of being prejudiced by the settlement may apply to the court, but whenever an application is made in relation to a settlement it is treated as made on behalf of every person who is, or is capable of being, prejudiced by the settlement[2]. A trustee against whom hostile litigation has been brought challenging the validity of the settlement does not have a duty to defend the trust but is obliged to remain neutral and offer to submit to the court's directions where there are rival claimants to the beneficial interest able to fight their own battles, though he will be entitled to an indemnity and a lien for his costs necessarily and properly incurred in serving a defence, agreeing to submit to the court's direction and in making discovery[3].

---

16 Any person anywhere: *Re Paramount Airways Ltd* [1993] Ch 223, CA. Leave to serve outside the jurisdiction needs to be sought, eg under CPR 6.20(10) if the claim relates to property located within the jurisdiction: *Banca Carige v Banco Nacional de Cuba* [2001] 3 All ER 923.
17 Insolvency Act 1986, s 423(3).
18 Insolvency Act 1986, s 423(2).
19 Insolvency Act 1986, s 425(2).
20 Insolvency Act 1986, s 424(1)(a).
1 Insolvency Act 1986, s 424(1)(b).
2 Insolvency Act 1986, s 424(1)(c), (2).
3 *Alsop Wilkinson v Neary* [1995] 1 All ER 431; see 842, post.

Onus of proof

The onus of proof is on the applicant[4] to show that the settlement was a transaction entered into for the purpose of putting assets beyond the reach of a person who is making or may make a claim against the settlor or of otherwise prejudicing the interests of such claimant or potential claimant. However, once the applicant has established his case[5], then it seems that a person seeking escape from having an order made against him must discharge the onus of showing that he falls within the protection afforded by s 425(2), eg proving good faith, value and lack of notice of the relevant circumstances, which will include the debtor's dominant purpose to prejudice creditors[6].

Flexible orders

Inter alia court orders may provide for any property transferred as part of the settlement to be vested in any person either absolutely or for the benefit of all the persons on whose behalf the application is treated as made[7], or for any property to be so vested if it represents in any person's hands the application either of the proceeds of sale of property so transferred or of money so transferred[8]. The order may also require any person to pay to any other person in respect of benefits received from the settlor such sums as the court may direct[9].

Impeachable settlements without limit of time

The new statutory section avoids the difficulties of interpretation that surrounded s 172 of the Law of Property Act 1925[10]. It probably encapsulates the effect of the old case law[11] so that an attempt to prejudice future creditors, even though there may be no existing creditors, will suffice to make a transaction impeachable, eg where H transfers his house to trustees on trust for his wife, remainder to his children or purchases a house in the name of his wife alone or puts his house into the joint names of himself and his wife on trust for each other equally. As Jessel MR stated[12],

> 'a man is not entitled to go into a hazardous business, and immediately before doing so, settle all his property voluntarily, the object being this: "If I succeed in business, I make a fortune for myself. If I fail, I leave my creditors unpaid. They will bear the loss." That is the very thing the Statute of Elizabeth[13] was meant to prevent.'

4   *Law Society v Southall* [2001] WTLR 719 at 729–730, per Hart J.
5   On requisite evidence see *Law Society v Southall* [2001] EWCA Civ 2001, [2002] WTLR 1151, reversing Hart J's refusal to strike out the claim.
6   *Lloyds Bank Ltd v Marcan* [1973] 3 All ER 754, [1973] 1 WLR 1387 on Law of Property Act 1925, s 172 (now repealed due to the broader effect of s 423 of the 1986 Act). Notice will include constructive notice, cf *Lloyds Bank Ltd v Marcan* [1973] 2 All ER 359 at 369 per Pennycuick V-C.
7   Insolvency Act 1986, s 425(1)(a). See *Law Society v Southall* [2001] WTLR 719 at 726–727 and *Chohan v Saggar (No 2)* [1992] BCC 750.
8   Insolvency Act 1986, s 425(1)(b).
9   Insolvency Act 1986, s 425(1)(d).
10   See 13th Edition hereof pp 211–219.
11   *Mackay v Douglas* (1872) LR 14 Eq 106; *Re Butterworth* (1882) 19 Ch D 588, CA; *Cadogan v Cadogan* [1977] 1 All ER 200, [1977] 1 WLR 1041.
12   *Re Butterworth* (1882) 19 Ch D 588 at 598; *Midland Bank v Wyatt* [1995] 1 FLR 697.
13   The predecessor of Law of Property Act 1925, s 172.

Thus, if a professional man about to become a partner is worried that the amount of professional indemnity assurance cover may prove insufficient for possible future claims so that he had better preserve his house as his major asset, and so vests it in his wife as sole absolute beneficial owner or on trust for his wife for life, remainder to their children, then it seems that the transaction will be impeachable, irrespective of any time limits[14] or of the man being adjudged bankrupt and so quite apart from investigating any possibilities under the Insolvency Act 1986 ss 339, 341 and 342. If the conscience of an existing partner is pricked by fear that certain events that have already occurred may lead to a negligence claim then the partner will clearly fall within s 423 if he then off-loads significant assets on to trustees for his family. After all, there is a clear actual fraudulent intent aimed at the particular subsequent creditor rather than a predominant anxiety that any person may somehow someday make a claim. It seems harsh that the latter suffices to make settlements impeachable indefinitely according to *Re Butterworth*. If circumstances arise to highlight such harshness, it may be that *Re Butterworth* might be able to be circumvented if the court is prepared to find that the reference in s 423(3) to purposely putting assets beyond the reach of 'a person' [not 'any person'] requires the purpose of prejudicing a particular subsequent creditor whose debt was in contemplation at the time of the prejudicial transaction[15]. This point was not argued in *Midland Bank plc v Wyatt* where s 423 was held to cover the voluntary disposition of assets to avoid future but unknown creditors and whether or not the transferor was about to enter into a hazardous business or whether his business was as sole practitioner or as partner or as participant in a limited liability company where personal guarantees are normally required.

Purpose: predominant, substantial or significant

The claimant must prove 'that the transaction was entered into for the purpose of putting assets beyond the reach of'[16] an existing or potential creditor or 'of otherwise prejudicing the interests of such a person'. Purpose seems to have the same meaning as 'object', 'end' or 'with a view to' and stops short at what was in a man's mind[17] so that it does not include the necessary effect of an act[18]. Thus, identical transactions carried out by different settlors may have different results[19]. Putting assets beyond the reach of creditors, or otherwise prejudicing them may be a necessary effect of a transaction without it being a purpose of the transaction. If the settlor had more than one purpose (eg where another purpose is to minimise liability to inheritance tax) the settlement will be impeachable if the predominant[20] or

---

14 *Law Society v Southall* [2001] EWCA Civ 2001, para 6.
15 *Law Society v Southall* [2001] WTLR 719 at 730.
16 Cf the language used by Russell LJ in *Lloyds Bank Ltd v Marcan* [1973] 3 All ER 754 at 759.
17 This is a question of fact.
18 In a tax context see *IRC v Brebner* (1966) 43 TC 705 at 713 per Lord Clyde and Lord Pearce [1967] 2 AC 18 at 27–28, HL 'that which has to be ascertained was the object (not the effect) of each interrelated transaction in its actual context', and *Mallalieu v Drummond (Inspector of Taxes)* [1983] 2 AC 861 at 870, HL 'The object of the taxpayer in making the expenditure must be distinguished from the effect of the expenditure.' Intention goes beyond purpose in including necessary effects and so is objective: *Re M C Bacon Ltd* [1991] Ch 127.
19 *Philippi v IRC* [1971] 3 All ER 61, [1971] 1 WLR 1272, CA.
20 *Chohan v Saggar* [1992] BCC 306 at 323; *Midland Bank plc v Wyatt* [1995] 1 FLR 697.

substantial[1] purpose was prejudicing creditors, substantial purpose extending to a purpose of equal power with another purpose[2], and it is possible that it would be impeachable if prejudicing creditors was a significant purpose but of less power than another purpose[3]. Some hallmarks of such purpose may include the following[4]: virtually all the settlor's assets may have been settled, the settlement may have been carried out secretly or in great haste, false statements may be found in the recitals, the settlor may continue to remain in possession of the settled property or retain some advantage under the terms of the settlement. In *Agricultural Mortgage Corpn v Woodward*[5] the Court of Appeal held that where a farmer granted a protected agricultural tenancy of his farm to his wife at full market value in order to prevent his major creditor from obtaining vacant possession of the farm with a view to enforcement of the debt, the transaction could be set aside under s 423. The wife achieved benefits greater than those conferred by the value of the consideration provided by her, namely the safeguarding of the family home, the carrying on of the family farming business and a 'ransom' surrender value against the creditor: the substantial detriment incurred by the creditor was largely matched by the substantial benefit conferred on the wife beyond the rights conferred by the tenancy agreement for which she provided full market value.

Lawyer-client privilege from disclosure of documents cannot be claimed by the client where there is a strong prima facie case that the purpose of the transaction involving the use of the solicitor was to prejudice a creditor[6].

ARTICLE 18

When a trust designed to defeat dependants may be set aside pro tanto under a court order

(1) Under the Matrimonial Causes Act 1973, s 37, a reviewable disposition of property may be set aside by the court if made with the intention of defeating a person's claim for financial relief under ss 22, 23, 24, 27, 31 (except sub-s 6) and 35 of the said Act. Any disposition of property, eg to trustees, is a reviewable disposition[7] unless made for valuable consideration (other than marriage) to a person who, at the time of the disposition, acted in relation to it in good faith and without notice of any intent to defeat a claim for financial relief;
(2) Under the Inheritance (Provision for Family and Dependants) Act 1975, s 10, a disposition of property, eg to trustees, may be set aside by the court if (i) made less than six years before his death by the

---

1 *Royscott Spa Leasing Ltd v Lovett* [1995] BCC 502, CA.
2 It would be odd if a claim failed because although the statutory purpose exists another purpose exists of equal power: *IRC v Hashmi* [2002] WTLR 19 at 29 endorsing *Pinewood Joinery v Starelm Properties Ltd* [1994] 2 BCLC 412 at 418.
3 *IRC v Hashmi* [2002] WTLR 19 at 28–29.
4 *Twyne's Case* (1602) 3 Co Rep 80b; *Re Sinclair* (1884) 26 Ch D 319, CA; *Lloyds Bank Ltd v Marcan* [1973] 3 All ER 754, [1973] 1 WLR 1387.
5 [1995] 1 BCLC 1.
6 *Barclays Bank plc v Eustice* [1995] 1 WLR 1238, CA.
7 Matrimonial Causes Act 1973, s 37(4).

deceased with the intention of defeating an application for financial provision under the said Act and (ii) if full valuable consideration[8] for the disposition was not given by the person to whom or for the benefit of whom the disposition was made ('the donee') and (iii) if the exercise of the court's power to set aside the disposition pro tanto by ordering a sum of money or other property to be provided will facilitate the making of financial provision for the applicant under the said Act. Similarly a contract to leave property by will cannot defeat an application for financial provision under the said Act unless made for full valuable consideration[9].

PARAGRAPH 1

An intent to defeat a person's claim for financial relief is an intent to prevent financial relief from being granted to that person or to that person for the benefit of a child of the family or to reduce the amount of any financial relief that might be so granted or to frustrate or impede the enforcement of any court order which might be or has been made[10].

Where the application to the court is made within three years of the disposition it is to be presumed, unless the contrary is shown[11], that the disposition was made with intent to defeat the applicant's claim for financial relief[12]. The intent does not need to be the respondent's sole intent[13]. The court may give consequential directions[14] for giving effect to its order which may cover property abroad[15] though, it seems, not the proceeds of sale of property previously disposed of by a purchaser with notice of a husband's intent to defeat his wife's claim by selling property to the purchaser[16]. For a purchaser to lack good faith requires 'something akin to fraud: at the very least it connotes a lack of honesty'[17]. Notice covers constructive notice[18] as well as actual notice.

'Disposition' does not include any provision in a will or codicil but otherwise includes any conveyance, assurance or gift of property of any description whether made by an instrument or otherwise[19].

---

8 On the meaning of this see *Re Wilkinson* [1978] Fam 22, [1978] 1 All ER 221. Marriage is not valuable consideration: s 25(1).

9 Inheritance (Provision for Family and Dependants) Act 1975, ss 11 and 12(2).

10 Matrimonial Causes Act 1973, s 37(1).

11 As in *Shipman v Shipman* [1991] 1 FLR 250.

12 Matrimonial Causes Act 1973, s 37(5); *Whittingham v Whittingham* [1979] Fam 9, [1978] 3 All ER 805.

13 *Re Kennedy* [1980] CLY 2820; *Kemmis v Kemmis* [1988] 1 WLR 1307, CA.

14 *Green v Green (Barclays Bank, Third Party)* [1981] 1 All ER 97, [1981] 1 WLR 391 holding these are incidental ancillary powers.

15 *Hamlin v Hamlin* [1986] Fam 11, [1985] 2 All ER 1037, CA.

16 *Sherry v Sherry* [1991] 1 FLR 307, CA; J Fortin [1991] Conv 370.

17 *Whittingham v Whittingham* [1979] Fam 9 at 12, [1978] 3 All ER 805 at 808.

18 *Kemmis v Kemmis* [1988] 1 WLR 1307, CA; *Sherry v Sherry* [1991] 1 FLR 307.

19 Matrimonial Causes Act 1973, s 37(6). The section does not apply to a disposition made before 1 January 1968 nor to the case where H and W are leasehold joint tenants and H serves a notice to quit on the landlord (which could be a body of trustees): *Newlon Housing Trust v Al-Sulaimen* [1999] 1 AC 313; but the court can grant an injunction to restrain serving such a notice or require an undertaking to be given to it: *Bater v Bater* [1999] 4 All ER 944.

PARAGRAPH 2

An arbitrary six year time limit applies here[20]. The requisite intent will be present if the court is of opinion that on a balance of probabilities the intention of the deceased (though not necessarily his sole intention)[1] in making the disposition or contract was to prevent an order for financial provision being made or to reduce the amount of the financial provision that might otherwise be made[2]. A disposition does not include an appointment under a special power of appointment so the appointee will be safe so long as the settlement was made more than six years before the death of the deceased settlor[3].

Where an application is made under s 10 of the 1975 Act in respect of a disposition made by the deceased to trustees or, under s 11, in respect of any payment made or property transferred, in accordance with a contract made by the deceased, to trustees then the court's powers are expressly limited[4]. The amount of money or the value of any property that the court can order to be provided *cannot*

(i)   in the case of a disposition or contract consisting of the payment of money, exceed the aggregate of so much of that money as is at the date of the court order in the hands of the trustees and the value at that date of any property which represents that money or is derived therefrom and is at that date in the hands of the trustees;

(ii) in the case of a disposition or contract consisting of the transfer of property (other than money), exceed the aggregate of the value at the date of the court order of so much of that property as is at that date in the hands of the trustee and the value at that date of any property which represents the first-mentioned property or is derived therefrom and is at that date in the hands of the trustees.

Furthermore, the trustees are not to be liable for having distributed any money or other property on the ground they ought to have taken into account the possibility that an application might be made under ss 10 or 11 of the 1975 Act[5]. Of course, beneficiaries receiving such money or other property may be subject to a court order[6].

ARTICLE 19

Miscellaneous instances where a trust may be set aside to thwart criminals

There are miscellaneous legislative instances where the court can confiscate what are, or are regarded as, the proceeds of crime in a trust fund created by a criminal.

Outside the scope of this work are wide-ranging tracing and confiscation

---

20 Inheritance (Provision for Family and Dependants) Act 1975, s 10(2)(a). Generally see [1978] Conv 13 (CH Sherrin).
1 *Re Dawkins, Dawkins v Judd* [1986] 2 FLR 360, [1986] Fam Law 295.
2 Inheritance (Provision for Family and Dependants) Act 1975, s 12(1).
3 Inheritance (Provision for Family and Dependants) Act 1975, s 10(7).
4 Inheritance (Provision for Family and Dependants) Act 1975, s 13(1).
5 Inheritance (Provision for Family and Dependants) Act 1975, s 13(2).
6 Inheritance (Provision for Family and Dependants) Act 1975, ss 10(2)(b), 11(2)(c).

provisions in statutes concerned with the proceeds of drug-trafficking, terrorism and other serious crimes, whether in the hands of the criminal or of trustees of trusts created by the criminal or of beneficiaries of such trusts[7]. Even 'clean' money can be attacked so as to deal with the criminal who lives off his 'black' criminal money, so that he can afford to put his 'white' money, earned or inherited by him, into the trust. Various assumptions against the criminal are made where he had a criminal lifestyle[8].

7 Part IV Criminal Justice Act 1988 as amended by Pt III Criminal Justice Act 1993, and Proceeds of Crime Acts 1995 and 2002; Anti-terrorism, Crime and Security Act 2001 (enabling gains of trustees to be traced and recovered rather than only the original value of the benefit received as under the CJA 1988 as amended).
8 Proceeds of Crime Act 2002, s 11.

CHAPTER 4

The interpretation of executory trusts

Article
20 Executory trusts not construed as strictly as executed trusts   299
21 Distinction between executory trusts arising under marriage articles and wills respectively   302
22 How far the wife is bound by covenants to settle property   305
23 Property which is prima facie excluded from a covenant to settle other or after-acquired property   306
24 What property is comprised in a general covenant to settle property to which the wife is presently entitled   310
25 What is comprised in a covenant to settle after-acquired property of the wife   310
26 Covenants to settle a definite interest in property   314
27 Covenants to settle property exceeding a certain value   315

ARTICLE 20

Executory trusts not construed as strictly as executed trusts

(1) In the construction of executed trusts, technical terms are construed in their legal and technical sense[1];

(2) In the construction of executory trusts (as defined in Article 6), the court is not confined to the language used. Where, therefore, such language is improper or informal[2], or would create an illegal trust[3], or one which is impossible to execute[4], or would otherwise defeat the settlor's intentions, as gathered from the motives which led to the settlement, and from its general object and purpose, or from other instruments to which it refers, or from any circumstances which may have influenced the settlor's mind[5], the court will direct a settlement to be executed in such form as will best answer the intent of the

---

1 *Wright v Pearson* (1758) 1 Eden 119; *Austen v Taylor* (1759) 1 Eden 361; *Brydges v Brydges* (1796) 3 Ves 120; *Jervoise v Duke of Northumberland* (1820) 1 Jac & W 559; and see *Re Whiston's Settlement* [1894] 1 Ch 661.
2 See *Earl Stamford v Hobart* (1710) 3 Bro Parl Cas 31.
3 *Humberston v Humberston* (1716) 1 P Wms 332.
4 *Re Shelton's Settled Estates* [1945] Ch 158, [1945] 1 All ER 283.
5 See per Lord Chelmsford in *Sackville-West v Viscount Holmesdale* (1870) LR 4 HL 543.

parties[6], unless the executory trust instrument required the consent of some third party who refused consent in circumstances where the court could not find that such refusal was in breach of a fiduciary obligation or a contractual obligation not unreasonably to withhold consent[7].

PARAGRAPH 1

The general rule with regard to executed trusts is as stated above, and the omission of apt words of limitation from equitable estates in land created by deed before 1926 was held by the Court of Appeal in *Re Bostock's Settlement*[8] to reduce the estate so given to a life estate only, even though a clear intention to pass the fee simple could be found. There appears to be an exception to this where the operative clause is not in strict conveyancing language for in *Re Arden*[9], Clauson J held that the word 'absolutely' in an appointment of land under a testamentary power was sufficient to carry the equitable fee simple to the appointees, although if that word had been omitted they could have taken life interests only. The true rule, therefore, seems to be that in the absence of words of limitation (whether technical or popular) they will not be implied merely by reason of the court being satisfied that the real intention of the appointor or grantor was to pass the fee simple; but that where he has expressed that intention in popular words (such as 'absolutely') the fact that such word would not pass a legal estate in fee simple, does not prevent it from passing the equitable fee.

The point is not now of great practical importance since the necessity for words of limitation was abolished in deeds executed after 1925 by s 60 of the Law of Property Act 1925[10] and, moreover, the court will in appropriate cases rectify a settlement by the insertion of words of limitation where it is satisfied on the evidence afforded by the document that they were omitted by mistake, and without them the document would not give effect to the intention of the parties[11].

PARAGRAPH 2

Distinction between executed and executory trusts well settled

This rule has been acted on for over 200 years, and was stated by Lord

---

6 *Earl Stamford v Hobart* (1710) 3 Bro Parl Cas 31; *Surtees v Surtees* (1871) LR 12 Eq 400; and see *Cogan v Duffield* (1876) 2 Ch D 44. As to the construction to be placed on an executory trust of heirlooms, see *Re Beresford-Hope* [1917] 1 Ch 287, where the form of settlement is indicated, and *Re Steele's Will Trusts* [1948] Ch 603, [1948] 2 All ER 193.

7 *Davis v Richards and Wallington Industries Ltd* [1991] 2 All ER 563 at 589 where a definitive pension trust deed required the consent of the trustees as fiduciaries and the consent of the employer-company's subsidiary companies not as fiduciaries but as a contractual obligation.

8 [1921] 2 Ch 469, CA, applying the principle in *Re Whiston's Settlement* [1894] 1 Ch 661, and overruling *Re Tringham's Trusts* [1904] 2 Ch 487.

9 [1935] Ch 326.

10 Also ss 130, 131. However, for entails strict language was still required for executed trusts though probably not for executory trusts as pointed out in Article 6. No new entails may be created: Trusts of Land and Appointment of Trustees Act 1996, s 2 and Sch 1, para 5.

11 *Banks v Ripley* [1940] Ch 719, [1940] 3 All ER 49.

Cowper[12] in 1710 in the following words:

> 'In matters executory, as in the case of articles or a will directing a conveyance, where the words of the articles or will are improper or informal, this court will not direct a conveyance according to such improper or informal expressions in the articles or will, but will order the conveyance or settlement to be made out in a proper and legal manner, so it may best answer the intent of the parties.'

Executed and executory trust in same instrument construed differently

The rule is strikingly exemplified by the ancient case of *Papillon v Voice*[13], where a testator had bequeathed money to trustees upon trust to purchase real estate and settle it upon A for life, with remainder to trustees to preserve contingent remainders, with remainders to the heirs of A's body, with power to jointure. He also devised his own lands to precisely similar uses. Yet it was held that, as he had manifested an intention to give A a life estate only (which the rule in *Shelley's Case* by creating an entail[14] had defeated in the case of the devised lands), the court would so model the executory trust as to carry out his intention by giving him a life estate with remainder to his first and other sons successively in tail. In fact, any indication in an executory trust that an apparent devisee in tail is only to take a life estate will be given effect to; as, for instance, a direction that he is to be unimpeachable for waste, or that he shall not have the power to bar the entail, or that if he should die without leaving issue the property should go to other persons or the like[15].

Where strict construction would make execution impossible or the trust illegal

Equity will not permit a referential trust to fail and the intentions of the settlor to be frustrated for want of the necessary ingenuity of adaptation and will direct it to be executed cy-près where execution modo et forma is impossible[16]; but this power of adaptation will not be resorted to merely to suit altered circumstances where execution of the original trusts remains possible[17].

Similarly, the words of an executory trust will be departed from where a strict construction would render the trust illegal. Thus, in an early case[18] a testator devised lands to a corporation, in trust to convey to A for life, and afterwards, upon the death of A, to his first son for life, and then to the first son of that first son for life, with remainder (in default of issue male of A) to B for life, and to his sons and their sons in like manner. That was, of course, an attempt to create a perpetuity, yet Lord Cowper held that the device ought to be complied with, so far as was consistent with the rules of law, and he

12 *Earl Stamford v Hobart* (1710) 3 Bro Parl Cas 31.
13 (1728) 2 P Wms 471; and see also *Trevor v Trevor* (1847) 1 HL Cas 239; *Parker v Bolton* (1835) 5 LJ Ch 98; and *Thompson v Fisher* (1870) LR 10 Eq 207. But cf *Re Davison's Settlement* [1913] 2 Ch 498, where it was held that the rule in *Shelley's Case* did not apply.
14 The rule in *Shelley's Case* was abolished by Law of Property Act 1925, s 131.
15 *Papillon v Voice* (1728) 2 P Wms 471; *Parker v Bolton* (1835) 5 LJ Ch 98; *Thompson v Fisher* (1870) LR 10 Eq 207; *Lord Glenorchy v Bosville* (1733) Cas temp Talb 3; 2 White & Tud LC 778.
16 *Re Shelton's Settled Estates* [1945] Ch 158, [1945] 1 All ER 283.
17 *Re Benett-Stanford Settlement Trusts* [1947] 1 All ER 888.
18 *Humberston v Humberston* (1716) 1 P Wms 332; *Williams v Teale* (1847) 6 Hare 239. See also *Re Mountgarret* [1919] 2 Ch 294. 'Wait and see' for the perpetuity period of statutory lives plus 21 years is now the case under the Perpetuities and Accumulations Act 1964 if the trust would have been void at common law, but the court will construe the executory trusts so as to oust a resulting trust on expiry of the 'wait and see' period.

directed that all the sons already born at the testator's death should take estates for life, with limitations to their unborn sons in tail. It must, however, be remembered that where the words of an instrument are plain they are construed as they stand, and without regard to the consequences of the rule against perpetuities when applied thereto. It is only where the meaning of the words used is not plain and unambiguous that the court will in construing the instrument have regard to such consequences[19].

ARTICLE 21

Distinction between executory trusts arising under marriage articles and wills respectively

(1) In the case of marriage articles there is a very strong presumption that the motive was to provide for the issue of the marriage. Consequently, provisions which, if construed literally, would defeat that object will be bent in order to give effect to the presumed intention; (2) In the case of other deeds and wills directing the creation of trusts, there is no such inherent presumption, and, consequently, some intention must either be verbally manifested, or be inferred from the object of the instrument, or from other instruments to which it refers.

PARAGRAPH 1

Distinction between executory trusts arising under marriage articles and those arising under wills

The preceding article shows the liberal interpretation which the court gives to executory trusts generally in order to comply with the inherent evidence of intention. The present article is directed to that evidence; and here there is a distinction to be observed between executory trusts contained in contracts for settlements on marriage, commonly known as marriage articles, and executory trusts directed by other instruments. This is because marriage articles by their very nature furnish more emphatically a clue to the persons intended to be provided for (namely, the spouses and issue of the marriage) than do wills or contracts for settlements on occasions other than marriage. It is, therefore, a well-settled principle that an intention to provide for issue will, in the absence of a contrary intention, be presumed in the case of executory trusts in marriage articles[20]. Such articles have, however, fallen out of use in preference for executed trusts so as to leave no room for implication.

---

19 *Re Flavel's Will Trusts* [1969] 2 All ER 232, [1969] 1 WLR 444.
20 *Jervoise v Duke of Northumberland* (1820) 1 Jac & W 559 at 574, per Lord Eldon LC; *Stonor v Curwen* (1832) 5 Sim 264; *Davies v Davies* (1841) 4 Beav 54; *Lambert v Peyton* (1860) 8 HL Cas 1; *Highway v Banner* (1785) 1 Bro CC 584; *Rossiter v Rossiter* (1863) 14 I Ch R 247.

Proper form where marriage articles provide for settlement of wife's personalty

With regard to marriage articles relating to the lady's personal property, Lord Justice Baggallay made the following remarks in *Cogan v Duffield*[1]:

> 'The mode of settling a wife's fortune which is approved by the court is to give her the first life interest for her separate use, then a life interest to the husband, then (subject to powers given to the husband and wife of appointing the fund) among the issue of the marriage, it is given equally to such of the children as being sons attain twenty-one, or being daughters attain that age or marry, or else to the children equally, with gifts over in favour of the others if any of them being sons die under twenty-one, or being daughters die under that age and unmarried; if there is no child who being a son attains twenty-one, or being a daughter attains twenty-one or marries, then if the wife survives the fund is limited to her, but if she dies in the husband's lifetime she has a general power of appointment over it, and in default of any exercise of that power it is given to her next of kin as if she had died intestate and without having married.'

It is also settled that the power of appointment among issue should be given to the spouses *and the survivor of them,* and that the settlement ought to contain the usual powers of maintenance and advancement[2]; but not an after-acquired property clause, even where the articles provide for 'such other agreements, clauses, and provisions as are usually inserted in settlements of a like nature'[3].

Paragraph 2

Executory will trusts

In a will, it is obvious that the same presumption will not arise as in the case of marriage articles. So where a testator directed that his daughters' shares should 'be settled on *themselves strictly'*, it was held that, there being no particular intention to benefit their issue, each daughter's share should be paid to her for her separate and inalienable use, and that, if she died before her husband, then her share should go as she should by will appoint, and in default of appointment to her next of kin, but if she survived her husband, then the share should belong to her absolutely[4]. This, however, was a decision upon the words of the particular will, and in other cases directions in a

---

1 The court would formerly have restrained the wife from anticipating her income; *Re Parrott* (1886) 33 Ch D 274, CA. After restraints on anticipation could no longer be imposed by reason of the Law Reform (Married Women and Tortfeasors) Act 1935 some practitioners, in settling drafts of marriage settlements, were inclined to substitute a 'protected life interest' for the lady but the tendency soon became not to impose such restrictions, at any rate where there was no reason to suppose that the wife or husband was not a responsible person. The age of majority is now eighteen and the vesting event of the prior marriage of a daughter as opposed to a son is anachronistic. Parents are, however, reluctant to let their children take absolute interests at 18 years and, for this reason, accumulation and maintenance settlements on children or grandchildren may obtain favourable inheritance tax treatment even if the contingent age is 25 years: Inheritance Tax Act 1984, s 71. Marriage articles should specify the requisite age.
2 *Re Gowan* (1880) 17 Ch D 778.
3 *Re Maddy's Estate* [1901] 2 Ch 820.
4 *Loch v Bagley* (1867) LR 4 Eq 122. Also see *Sweetapple v Bindon* (1705) 2 Vern 536; *Re Howarth* [1916] WN 50.

will for the settlement of shares of daughters have been held not to be sufficiently precise to raise an executory trust[5].

There is, however, no difference between the construction to be put on an executory trust created by marriage articles, and on an executory trust created by will, except so far as the former (by their very nature) furnish more emphatically the means of ascertaining the intention of those who created the trust. In *Sackville-West v Viscount Holmesdale*[6], Lord Chelmsford said:

'The best illustration of the object and purpose of an instrument furnishing an indication of intention in the case of executory trusts, is to be found in the instance of marriage articles, where the object of the settlement being to make a provision for the issue of the marriage, no words, however strong, which in the case of an executed trust would place the issue in the power of the father, will be allowed to prevail against the implied intention.'

So, as Sir W Grant said, in *Blackburn v Stables*[7], in the case of a will:

'if it is clearly to be ascertained from anything in the will that the testator did not mean to use the expressions, which he has employed, in their strict, proper, technical sense, the court in decreeing such settlement as he has directed will depart from his words in order to "execute his intention".'

It was, therefore, held that a direction to settle land 'in a course of entail to correspond as near as may be with the limitations' of a barony, would be properly executed, not by giving the baron an estate tail, but by giving him a life estate only, with remainders to his first and other sons successively in tail male[8].

Where the settlement subsequently executed does not exactly carry out the intentions expressed in the testator's will, the fact that the will trustees are satisfied with it will not make it a sufficient compliance with the testator's directions[9].

Direction to settle a female's legacy 'on marriage'

Where a direction in a will refers to a settlement *on marriage*, or in any other ways shows an intention to benefit the issue of the legatee, effect will be given to it. The case of *Re Spicer*[10] is a good example of this, where the will declared that no daughter of the testator should be entitled to receive her share, but only the income, with power to dispose of the principal by will if unmarried. But in the event of any daughter marrying, he empowered his trustees to see that her share was 'duly and properly settled upon her by deed so that the

---

5 *Re Bannister* (1921) 90 LJ Ch 415 (where the words were 'to be equally divided amongst and settled for their own and sole use upon' the testator's children); *Magrath v Morehead* (1871) LR 12 Eq 491.
6 (1870) LR 4 HL 543; and see also *Christie v Gosling* (1866) LR 1 HL 279. See also *Re Howarth* [1916] WN 50.
7 (1814) 2 Ves & B 367. See also *Re Beresford-Hope* [1917] 1 Ch 287 and *Bastard v Proby* (1788) 2 Cox Eq Cas 6.
8 *Sackville-West v Viscount Holmesdale* (1870) LR 4 HL 543. See also *Thompson v Fisher* (1870) LR 10 Eq 207.
9 *IRC v Raphael; IRC v Ezra* [1935] AC 96, HL; and see also *Re Potter's Will Trusts; Re Thomson's Settlement Trusts* [1944] Ch 70, [1943] 2 All ER 805, CA.
10 (1901) 84 LT 195; and see also *Re Parrott* (1886) 33 Ch D 274; and *Re Potter's Will Trusts, Re Thompson's Settlement Trusts* [1944] Ch 70, [1943] 2 All ER 805, CA, where it was held that, on the true construction of the will, the settlement ought to have made provision for the issue of subsequent marriages also.

same should be preserved for her separate use independently of her hus-band'.

In giving judgment, Buckley J pointed out that the settlement was only directed in the event of marriage, and that, therefore, the parties could not avail themselves of the doctrine in *Loch v Bagley*[11] where the words were simply 'the girls' share to be settled on themselves strictly' and there were no words relating to marriage. He therefore directed a settlement on the footing of giving the daughter a life estate for her separate and inalienable use, with no life estate to the husband, and the usual trusts in favour of issue, and in default of issue for such persons as the daughter should appoint by will, and subject thereto for the lady's next of kin, if she left a husband, or for her absolutely if she died a widow. It would seem, however, that a direction to settle on a lady 'and her children' without reference to marriage, would be construed to give a life interest to a surviving husband, and a joint power to husband and wife to appoint among issue, and a like power to the survivor, extending, in the event of the lady being the survivor, to the issue of a second marriage, with all such other powers and trusts as are set out on p 303, ante[12].

Direction to settle on marriage of man

Where a fund was bequeathed to a man until marriage, and then directed 'to be settled on his wife and children, and in default of issue to revert' to the testator's estate, the court directed that the trusts should be in favour of the man for life, with remainder to the wife for life, with remainder to the children as the husband and wife or the survivor should appoint, but if the husband should be the survivor his power was to extend to the children of a future marriage, with an ultimate trust in default of appointment for all the children *of the husband* attaining 21 or in case of daughters attaining that age or marrying, and in default of children attaining a vested interest the fund to revert to the testator's estate[13].

Nowadays there is no need to treat women differently from men: see Art 5 of the 7th Protocol to the European Convention on Human Rights.

ARTICLE 22

How far the wife is bound by covenants to settle property

(1) A wife is bound by a covenant contained in a marriage settlement, to which she is a party, to settle her other, or her after-acquired property not just where she is a covenantor but also if the words used consist of an agreement or declaration, or even a covenant by the husband alone, that the wife's property 'shall be settled' or that he, *and his wife*, or that he and all necessary parties, will settle the property;
(2) If the covenant would be binding on the wife but for her minor-ity[14], it will be voidable only and not void; and if she wishes to repudiate it, she must do so promptly;
(3) Breach of such covenants may give rise to an ordinary claim for

---

11 (1867) LR 4 Eq 122; see p 303, ante.
12 *Re Parrott* (1886) 33 Ch D 274, CA; see also *Nash v Allen* (1889) 42 Ch D 54.
13 *Re Gowan* (1880) 17 Ch D 778, where the form of order is given in full.
14 The Family Law Reform Act 1969 lowered the age of majority from 21 to 18.

damages. by those within the marriage consideration but not by or on behalf of volunteers[15].

PARAGRAPH 1

The position under the old case law was complicated by the rule that the wife's property, unless held for separate use, automatically belonged to the husband, the wife and husband being one and that one being the husband. Old principles still applicable are the principle that a declaration binds all parties to the deed[16] and that if a wife is an assenting party to a covenant she cannot afterwards obstruct its performance[17].

On the other hand, a covenant by the husband as to acts to be done by him will not bind the wife[18].

PARAGRAPH 2

Assuming that a woman, who is a minor[19], purports to covenant to settle her after-acquired property, and subsequently becomes entitled to property is she bound? The answer is yes, unless she has, after attaining her majority, and becoming aware of her right to repudiate, promptly disaffirmed her liability[20].

ARTICLE 23

Property which is prima facie excluded from a covenant to settle other or after-acquired property

Prima facie, covenants to settle other or after-acquired property (not definitely described) do not comprise:
(1) income, or (semble) capitalisations of income;
(2) immovable property which cannot by the lex situs be vested in trustees;
(3) property over which the covenantor has merely a general power of appointment, or which she has a statutory power of making her own, unless she exercises such powers in her own favour;
(4) [possibly] gifts made by her husband;
(5) [probably] property substituted for that which she possessed at the

---

15 *Re Cavendish Browne's Settlement Trusts* [1916] WN 341; and see *Cannon v Hartley* [1949] Ch 213, [1949] 1 All ER 50. See discussion pp 179–182, ante.
16 *Townshend v Harrowby* (1858) 27 LJ Ch 553.
17 *Butcher v Butcher* (1851) 14 Beav 222; *Re De Ros' Trust* (1885) 31 Ch D 81; *Re Haden* [1898] 2 Ch 220; *Lee v Lee* (1876) 4 Ch D 175.
18 *Dawes v Tredwell* (1881) 18 Ch D 354; and see *Re Smith* [1900] WN 75 (covenant by husband that he and all other necessary parties would settle; held to include only persons that the husband had a right to call on to join, and not to include the wife).
19 See note 14 (supra).
20 See *Wilder v Pigott* (1882) 22 Ch D 263; *Greenhill v North British and Mercantile Insurance Co* [1893] 3 Ch 474; and *Re Hodson* [1894] 2 Ch 421; and see Article 13, ante.

date of the marriage[1];
(6) property expressly excepted by the terms of the covenant[2];
(7) any interest of the wife in the settled property which is excluded from the settlement[3];
(8) property which is already in the settlement and on which the settlement has operated[4];
(9) property which the covenantor would forfeit if the covenant applied to it[5].

PARAGRAPH 1

Ordinary covenant binds corpus only, and not income

A settlement was made by a husband of all his personal estate to which he was then or might thereafter become entitled, in trust for himself for life with remainders over: it was held not to comprise his interest in a fund bequeathed to him for life[6].

The same principle applies to an annuity bequeathed to a wife[7]. But, of course, such limited interests may be caught by the covenant where it is plainly intended that they should be[8].

Whether covenant binds property purchased out of savings of income

Where a woman covenants to settle after-acquired property she contemplates merely the settlement of property which may come to her by gift or bequest, and not property which she may acquire out of the savings of her income, so the covenant should not extend to such savings[9]. She should not be penalised for saving her income instead of spending it as she received it.

PARAGRAPH 2

Immovable property incapable of being vested in trustees by the lex situs

In *Re Pearse's Settlement*[10] it was held that since land in Jersey could not be conveyed by a married woman to someone except for adequate pecuniary

---

1 *Re Biscoe* [1914] WN 302.
2 *Re Thorne* [1917] 1 Ch 360; *Vanneck v Benham* [1917] 1 Ch 60 (any property which the donor expresses a wish should not be brought into settlement).
3 *Re Wyatt* (1889) 60 LT 920.
4 *Re Roger's Settlement* [1951] Ch 450, [1951] 1 All ER 236.
5 *Re Smith* [1928] Ch 10.
6 *St Aubyn v Humphreys* (1856) 22 Beav 175; *Townshend v Harrowby* (1858) 27 LJ Ch 553; *Lewis v Madocks* (1810) 17 Ves 48; *Re Dowding* [1904] 1 Ch 441.
7 *Re Dowding* [1904] 1 Ch 441.
8 *Scholfield v Spooner* (1884) 26 Ch D 94, explained in *Re Dowding* [1904] 1 Ch 441; *Beatty v Vance* [1916] 1 IR 66.
9 So held in *Finlay v Darling* [1897] 1 Ch 719 and *Re Clutterbuck's Settlement* [1905] 1 Ch 200 (rejecting *Re Bendy* [1895] 1 Ch 109). Cf *Churchill v Denny* (1875) LR 20 Eq 534.
10 [1909] 1 Ch 304. Jersey law now recognises trusts of movables but not of Jersey immovables. A covenant will thus be construed as not intended to include Jersey immovables unless expressly extending to foreign immovables, in which case it may well be that the equitable in personam jurisdiction might force the covenantor to transfer the land to the trustees as apparent beneficial co-owners or to sell the land and vest the proceeds in the trustees as trustees.

compensation her after-acquired property covenant should be construed as not intended to include within its scope after-acquired Jersey land.

PARAGRAPH 3

Covenant to settle after-acquired property does not oblige donee of general power to appoint the property to herself

In *Townshend v Harrowby*[11] the wife had joined in a covenant to settle after-acquired property. She subsequently became the donee of a general power of appointment over some property; but it was held that the covenant did not apply to it so as to oblige her to exercise the power in favour of herself or the trustees of the settlement.

Kindersley V-C said:

> 'It was very important to uphold the broad distinction between property and power, and he (the Vice-Chancellor) had always endeavoured to do so. It was true that power might result in property, and the exercise of it, if general, might affect property in an indirect manner; but so long as it was unexercised it was distinct from property. In one sense it was interest in property, because if there was a power it could not be said that there was not some interest. Technically, however, in the eye of a court of law or equity, a power was not an interest, and an interest was not a power. This covenant[12] was clearly not intended to apply to a mere power.'

But where property was given for such purposes as A should appoint, and in default of appointment to her absolutely, it was held that she could not defeat a covenant in her marriage settlement to settle after-acquired property exceeding £200 by making a succession of appointments to herself of £199 each[13]. It would indeed seem that wherever there is *a gift to the lady herself in default of appointment* the fund is caught by the covenant since she has a vested interest capable of being divested only by her own act[14].

On the other hand, a wife was not bound to disentail an estate tail in order to convey the fee simple to the trustees of her settlement[15].

PARAGRAPH 4

Whether covenants to settle after-acquired property extend to gifts made by husband himself

Whether such covenants prima facie exclude gifts made by the husband to the wife is at present doubtful. In *Coles v Coles*[16], Joyce J held that such gifts

11 (1858) 27 LJ Ch 553; and see also *Ewart v Ewart* (1853) 11 Hare 276; *Bower v Smith* (1871) 19 WR 399.
12 The definition clause in a settlement could give an extended meaning to property so as to include 'rights and interests of any description' as in Inheritance Tax Act 1984, s 272 which was held to cover a general power of appointment in *Melville v IRC* [2001] EWCA Civ 1247, [2002] 1 WLR 407.
13 *Re O'Connell* [1903] 2 Ch 574; but see *Bower v Smith* (1871) 19 WR 399, explained in *Steward v Poppleton* [1877] WN 29; and *Re Lord Gerard* (1888) 58 LT 800, observed upon in *Re O'Connell*, above; and see also Article 25, post.
14 For example, *Re Brook's Settlement Trusts* [1939] Ch 993 at 996–997.
15 *Hilbers v Parkinson* (1883) 25 Ch D 200; *Re Dunsany's Settlement* [1906] 1 Ch 578.
16 [1901] 1 Ch 711, following Malins V-C in *Dickinson v Dillwyn* (1869) LR 8 Eq 546 at 551, and followed by the Irish court in *Kingan v Matier* [1905] 1 IR 272.

were excluded. On the other hand, in *Re Ellis' Settlement*[17], Swinfen Eady J held the contrary view, and said that he did not think that Joyce J meant to lay down any general rule; and in *Re Plumptre's Marriage Settlement*[18] Eve J (while admitting that it seemed somewhat anomalous), followed the view of Swinfen Eady J. Sir Arthur Underhill took the view that Joyce J did lay down a general rule of prima facie interpretation, and that he was right in that view. These covenants are (as decided by Eve J in *Re Plumptre's Marriage Settlement*) purely executory, and should therefore, like marriage articles, be construed so as to answer the presumed intentions of the parties. But if so, it is difficult to believe that any man and woman, about to marry, ever intended by such covenants to preclude the husband making a present to his wife. A covenant so construed might embrace every chattel (such as a diamond necklace, a motor car, a ring, or even a dog) which the husband might wish to give to his wife for her personal use and enjoyment, and every cheque which he might give her to take a trip on the Continent, which is, it is submitted, a reductio ad absurdum. Moreover, the original object of these covenants, as stated by James LJ in *Re Edwards*[19] was to protect the wife against the old common law doctrine which handed her chattels to her husband absolutely and her lands to him for his life. Swinfen Eady J seems to have dissented from this last view, and said that such covenants were also intended for the benefit of the issue. No doubt the issue are within the valuable consideration which supports them, for otherwise the issue could not enforce them; but the view that these covenants are intended for the benefit of the issue seems to be inconsistent with the cases in which it has been held that they apply only to property falling to the wife during the coverture although they extend to property falling to the husband jure mariti after the coverture has been determined by death or divorce (see Article 24, post), the ratio decidendi of which is that these covenants are intended for the wife's protection. However, since the wife now needs no protection, being treated as a full separate independent person, it seems the covenants are better regarded as for the benefit of the issue.

If it be argued that these covenants may exclude personal chattels, but not gifts of money or securities, it is answered that such exclusion can only be justified by implied intention and that it is a safer and more logical rule to apply the intention to all gifts made by a husband than to some only. It must also not be forgotten that, before the Married Women's Property Acts a husband was incapable of making a common law gift to his wife; so that, as a matter of law, such apparent gifts remained his property, and could not be caught by such covenants; and it would be a strange effect of the Act to bring within such covenants common law gifts which the law previously excluded from them.

The question is one which can only be settled by the Court of Appeal, but it seems unlikely to arise nowadays: all well-drafted covenants contain an exception for gifts from the husband[20].

---

17 [1909] 1 Ch 618.
18 [1910] 1 Ch 609, followed in *Leigh-White v Ruttledge* [1914] 1 IR 135.
19 (1873) 9 Ch App 97 at 100.
20 Cf 40 Encyclopaedia of Forms & Precedents (5th edn) form 13.

PARAGRAPH 8

Property already in the settlement

Where successive life interests were given to husband and wife and, in the events which happened, the reversion expectant on the death of the survivor was irrevocably appointed to the son of the marriage who died an infant, it was held that the moiety of the son's reversionary interest to which the wife became entitled on his death was not caught by her covenant to settle after-acquired property.

In that case[1] Harman J said:

> 'It would be ridiculous that property already in the settlement should come into the settlement again and go on the limitations of the settlement and so on, in an everlasting succession. I cannot think that that is what the after-acquired property clause was intended to do. Although the wife acquired this property after the date of the settlement on her son's death ... , this was the very property in which, under the settlement itself, she had a life interest already, and it is ridiculous to suppose that she would have to re-settle in order to give herself another life interest in the same property.'

ARTICLE 24

What property is comprised in a general covenant to settle property to which the wife is presently entitled

Where the covenant is to settle property to which the wife 'is now entitled', or words to that effect, all property to which she then has any title, whether it be in possession, reversion, or contingency, is bound.

In *Re Jackson's Will*[2] the covenant was, 'that if at the time of the solemnisation of the said intended marriage, the wife shall be, or if at any time thereafter, and during the joint lives of the husband and wife she or her husband in her right shall become beneficially entitled ... to any real or personal property, estate, or effects ... for any estate or interest whatsoever ... then and in every such case' it should be settled.

It was held that a reversionary interest in personalty which was vested in the wife at the date of the marriage, but was liable to be divested by the exercise of a power of appointment, was included in the covenant, although it did not fall into possession until after the husband's death[3].

ARTICLE 25

What is comprised in a covenant to settle after-acquired property of the wife

(1) A covenant to settle after-acquired property of the wife is limited, prima facie, to property acquired during the marriage;

---

1 *Re Rogers' Settlement* [1951] Ch 450 at 455, [1951] 1 All ER 236 at 238.
2 (1879) 13 Ch D 189.
3 See also *Re Mackenzie's Settlement* (1867) 2 Ch App 345; *Agar v George* (1876) 2 Ch D 706; *Cornmell v Keith* (1876) 3 Ch D 767; and *Sweetapple v Horlock* (1879) 11 Ch D 745.

(2) A covenant to settle property to which the wife *shall* become entitled is equivalent to a covenant to settle property to which she becomes entitled in possession or reversion[4], and binds:
(a) property to which she is then only contingently entitled, provided that she attains a vested interest during the period covered by the covenant; and
(b) property to which she has no title at the date of the marriage, but in which she acquires a reversionary or contingent interest during the period covered by the covenant, even although it may not fall into possession during that period.

But it does not bind property in which she has a vested (or a vested but defeasible)[5] interest in reversion at the date of the marriage.

PARAGRAPH 1

Wife's covenant limited to property acquired during marriage

In *Re Edwards*[6], James LJ said:

'The primary object of a covenant to settle the future property of a wife is to prevent its falling under the sole control of the husband, and it therefore prima facie is to be supposed not to be intended to apply to property the wife's title to which does not accrue until after the husband's death. We have consulted the Lord Chancellor [Selbourne] on the case, and he agrees with us in the opinion that, in the absence of any expression showing that a covenant of this nature was intended to have a more extended operation, it is to be construed as if the usual words, "during the said intended coverture", had been inserted.'

The rule was subsequently carried to its logical conclusion, the court holding that it applies where the coverture has been determined either by divorce or judicial separation[7].

But where the husband survives, it binds him to settle property acquired jure mariti after the wife's death

The rule, as above stated, was however, expressed somewhat too broadly by James LJ; for a general covenant by a husband and wife (or a husband alone) to settle a wife's property will not be restricted to property falling in during the coverture if the *husband* survives, though it will be so restricted when the wife survives. In *Fisher v Shirley*[8] the wife was entitled to a vested reversionary interest in personal estate, which fell into possession after her death, and was claimed by her husband jure mariti.

Stirling J, however, held that it was bound by the husband's covenant to settle the wife's after-acquired property. The learned judge, commenting upon Lord Justice James' judgment in *Re Edwards*, above, said:

---

4 *Blythe v Granville* (1842) 13 Sim 190; *Re Maltby Marriage Settlement* [1953] 2 All ER 220, [1953] 1 WLR 765. See also *Re Peel's Settlement Trusts* [1964] 3 All ER 567, [1964] 1 WLR 1232.
5 *Re Peel's Settlement Trusts* [1964] 3 All ER 567, [1964] 1 WLR 1232.
6 (1873) 9 Ch App 97 at 100.
7 *Davenport v Marshall* [1902] 1 Ch 82; *Re Simpson* [1904] 1 Ch 1. But not where there has merely been a decree nisi; *Sinclair v Fell* [1913] 1 Ch 155.
8 (1889) 43 Ch D 290.

'No doubt the concluding words of the Lord Justice in that judgment at first sight support the contention on behalf of the husband. But when the literal construction of a covenant is departed from one ought to look at the reason for so doing, and the reason assigned is that the object of the covenant is to protect the property, the subject of the covenant, from the husband's marital right, and preserve it for the benefit of the wife and children. There is no need to protect property against the husband's marital right[9] where the wife does not become entitled until after the husband's death: but there is need of such protection where the husband is the survivor, and the property falls in after the wife's death. If effect were given to the husband's claim his marital right would be enforced instead of the wife's property being protected against it, and the very object of the covenant would be defeated. The words of the covenant in the present case are quite general, and the reason assigned for limiting them does not appear to apply, and, in my opinion, they cannot in the present case be limited as suggested.'

A fresh approach?

It is clear, then, that the basis for the view that covenants of this kind operate (at least in the case of the wife) only during coverture is that their purpose is to protect the wife's property from falling into the hands of the husband. In *Re Peel's Settlement Trusts*[10], Buckley J commented:

'There is authority for the view that in the absence of an express contrary intention a covenant of this kind will operate only during coverture, although it does not say so expressly (*Re Edwards* (1873) 9 Ch App 97); but it seems to me at least arguable that the basis for this view has disappeared with the enactment of the Married Women's Property Act 1882. This point has not been fully argued before me and I do not propose to express any concluded view on it.'

Nowadays, a court may very well consider that a particular covenant in context was intended to protect the issue of the marriage and so extend beyond coverture. The draftsman should expressly specify the duration of the covenant.

PARAGRAPH 2

If the covenant only relates to future property, the question arises what future property is bound

Assuming that the covenant is restricted to *future* property of the wife, the question then arises, what constitutes *future* property. The cases are not easy to reconcile, but paragraph (2) is believed to state the modern view.

A covenant to settle future-acquired property (without more) is sufficiently wide to embrace:
(1) that which may be thereafter acquired in both title and possession; and
(2) that which may be acquired in title only, although possession may never be obtained during the coverture[11]; but it does not embrace that to which

---

9 *Re Bower Williams* [1927] 1 Ch 441, where property devolving on a husband on his wife's intestacy was held to be within the exception in s 42(1) of the Bankruptcy Act 1914 accruing to him 'in right of his wife'. Nowadays it seems only such property can accrue jure mariti though by virtue of statute.
10 [1964] 3 All ER 567, [1964] 1 WLR 1232.
11 *Hughes v Young* (1862) 32 LJ Ch 137; *Dickinson v Dillwyn* (1869) LR 8 Eq 546; *Cowper-Smith v Anstey* [1877] WN 28; *Cannon v Hartley* [1949] Ch 213, [1949] 1 All ER 50.

a *title* has already been acquired, whether or not that title is followed during the coverture by the actual right to possession.

A reversion vested at the marriage apparently not bound

The authorities are clear that where a vested reversion, to which the wife is entitled at the date of the settlement, does *not* fall in during the marriage or the life of the husband (if he be survivor), it will not be bound by the covenant to settle future-acquired property[12]. On the question whether a reversion which is vested at the date of the settlement and falls into possession during the marriage (or, where the period for which the covenant is to be operative is not named, during the life of the husband)[13] is bound, the better view appears to be that *property which was vested in interest at the date of the settlement is not caught* irrespective of the date when it falls in[14]. The same is true of property which was vested in interest, but defeasibly, at the date of the settlement[15].

Contingent interests

Where the wife has a contingent interest at the date of the marriage which both becomes vested and falls into possession during the marriage, it is bound by the covenant[16]. It seems, however, that a contingent interest which, though it becomes vested during the marriage, does not fall into possession until afterwards is not bound[17].

Transformed interests

Even if a particular interest does not (for example, because it is vested at the time when the covenant was made) fall within the ambit of a covenant to settle future property, it seems that it may do so if it is later transformed into something new. Thus in a case[18] where the trusts of a settled fund in which a wife was interested were terminated with the court's approval by family arrangements and the fund divided among the beneficiaries, Buckley J said that what the wife received under the arrangements:

' ... was not the fruition of any rights which she had under the relevant trusts, but something new, to which she became entitled for the first time under and in consequence of the arrangements, that is, after the date of her marriage. It is consequently clear, in my opinion, that what she so received was caught by the covenant ... '

---

12 See *Re Jone's Will* (1876) 2 Ch D 362; *Re Pedder's Settlement Trusts* (1870) LR 10 Eq 585; *Re Clinton's Trust* (1871) LR 13 Eq 295.
13 *Fisher v Shirley* (1889) 43 Ch D 290.
14 *Re Maltby Marriage Settlement* [1953] 2 All ER 220, [1953] 1 WLR 765; following *Re Bland's Settlement* [1905] 1 Ch 4, and not following *Re Clinton's Trust* (1871) LR 13 Eq 295; *Re Crook's Settlement* [1923] 2 Ch 339. See also *Re Williams' Settlement* [1911] 1 Ch 441, as explained in *Re Maltby Marriage Settlement*, above. *Re Maltby Marriage Settlement*, above, was followed in *Re Peel's Settlement Trusts* [1964] 3 All ER 567, [1964] 1 WLR 1232, where the covenant was not expressly limited within the period of the continuance of the marriage.
15 *Re Peel's Settlement* [1964] 3 All ER 567, [1964] 1 WLR 1232.
16 *Archer v Kelly* (1860) 1 Drew & Sm 300; *Brooks v Keith* (1861) 1 Drew & Sm 462; *Re Williams' Settlement* [1911] 1 Ch 441; and see *Re Maltby Marriage Settlement* [1953] 2 All ER 220, [1953] 1 WLR 765 and *Re Peel's Settlement Trusts* [1964] 3 All ER 567, [1964] 1 WLR 1232.
17 *Re Michell's Trusts* (1878) 9 Ch D 5, CA concerned with the clause 'come to or devolve upon the wife'. Also see *Re Peel's Settlement Trusts* [1964] 3 All ER 567 at 576.
18 *Re Peel's Settlement Trusts* [1964] 3 All ER 567 at 574.

ARTICLE 26

Covenants to settle a definite interest in property

Where the covenant is to settle a definite estate or interest in property which subsequently becomes enlarged, the covenant does not bind the enlarged interest; and, conversely, if the definite interest fails, but the covenantor acquires the property under another title, it will not be bound.

In *Sweetapple v Horlock*[19] (corrected in *Re Jackson's Will*[20]) the intended wife, being entitled to a reversionary interest under her parents' settlement, liable to be defeated by the exercise by her father of a power of appointment, covenanted to settle all property which she was '*then* seised of or interested in or entitled to'. The father subsequently exercised his power, and appointed to her exactly the same proportion of the property which she would have taken in default of appointment.

On these facts, Jessel MR held that the wife's covenant did not comprise the appointed share, although it would have done so if the share had come to her in default of appointment, saying:

'A conveyance by a person by an innocent assurance of an interest expressed as being subject to be defeated by the exercise of a power, does not convey an interest which that person might take under the power. This is not like a settlement of all property which might come to the wife in any event, but only of that which was then vested in or belonging to her.'

So, in *Smith v Osborne*[1], it was laid down that where a man, in his marriage settlement, describes himself as entitled to an expectant estate in remainder in two pieces of land, and covenants that when 'such remainder' shall become vested in possession he will convey it to the uses of his settlement, the covenant will not bind him if he becomes possessed of either of these pieces of land by a title different from that described in the covenant. As Lord Wensleydale put it, the point resolved itself into this:

'Is this a covenant to convey the townlands of Stonehouse to the trustees absolutely, whenever the covenantor was entitled to them in possession? Or is it a bargain only with respect to the contingent interest, or spes successionis, or more correctly, a bargain to convey the estates conditionally, if they should vest in possession in Mr Boyse Osborne, the covenantor, under the will of the grandfather Thomas Carr?'

His lordship then pointed out that, in the words of the covenant, it was only to take effect if the estates became vested in the covenantor under the will of his grandfather, and that, as a matter of fact, they became vested in him in defiance of that will, by gift from a tenant in tail under that will, who had disentailed. He further remarked (in reference to an argument of the trustee's counsel that there was an obvious intention to settle the estates themselves) that that was:

'to apply a wrong rule of construction. It is to interpret the covenant, not according to the meaning of the words used, but according to what the parties may be reasonably supposed (judging from the circumstances in which they were placed) to

19 (1879) 11 Ch D 745.
20 (1879) 13 Ch D 189.
1 (1857) 6 HL Cas 375.

have been likely to intend to do when they entered into the contract. ... The only safe rule of construction is to ascertain the meaning of the words used, and in this case I think it is too clear to admit of any doubt.'

ARTICLE 27

Covenants to settle property exceeding a certain value

Where the covenant is to settle property exceeding a certain value:
(1) that value is normally the actual value of the property itself after deducting estate duty or capital transfer tax or inheritance tax[2], and not the actuarial value of the covenantor's interest in it; and
(2) that value is, prima facie, construed to mean the value of funds derived from the same source: two legacies under the will of the same testator are so derived[2];
(3) where part of an estate falls under the covenant it must be valued, and where the covenant excludes specified chattels, yet they will be included if they merely form part of a residuary estate[3].

Where the covenant is to settle property which is worth more than a minimum sum, it is a matter of construction whether the property itself or the value of the covenantor's interest in it governs the question

In *Re Mackenzie's Settlement*[4] a marriage settlement contained a covenant that, if the wife then was, or should at any time during the coverture become, entitled to any real or personal estate of the value of £400, for any estate or interest, it should be settled. At the date of the settlement she was entitled (under a prior settlement) in remainder, expectant on her mother's death, to (a) a share of a sum of stock in her own right, and (b) a further share of the same stock as one of the next of kin of a deceased brother. The value of the two shares taken together was above £400, but the actuarial value of the wife's reversionary interest in them, at the date of the settlement, was considerably less than £400. It was held that both shares were included in the settlement, the true interpretation of the covenant being that it referred to the value of the property itself, and not to the value of the wife's reversionary interest in it. In giving judgment, Cairns LJ said:

'It is admitted that the share payable to her out of the fund on her mother's death would exceed £400 after all deductions, but it is said that the value of this share in the year 1861 [the date of the marriage] was under £400. The covenant, however, in my opinion, does not refer to the value of her interest in the fund, but to the value of the fund in which she has an interest; just as we should say that a man was

---

2 *Re Pares* [1901] 1 Ch 708. But cf *Re Harcourt* [1911] WN 214, where Swinfen Eady J held that an endowment policy effected by the husband in favour of the wife was not caught, because it was not worth the limit at the date when she first became entitled to the policy, and the marriage had necessarily determined when the money (beyond the limit) became payable.
3 *Vanneck v Benham* [1917] 1 Ch 60. For a case where chattels were excluded and £1,000 was bequeathed to the wife to purchase a necklace, see *Re Thorne* [1917] 1 Ch 360.
4 (1867) 2 Ch App 345.

entitled to an estate of the value of £100,000 on the death of his father, merely to describe the value of the estate, and not the interest in the estate.'

But in such a case, the value is the value when it falls into possession, so that if there is a depreciation of a reversionary interest so as to bring it below the stipulated minimum at the date when it falls into possession it will be excluded from the covenant[5].

In *Cannon v Hartley*[6], a separation deed contained a covenant to settle 'any money or property exceeding in net amount or value £1,000'. After the date of the deed the covenantor became entitled to a reversionary interest in certain property and it was conceded that both the property itself and the reversionary interest were worth more than £1,000. Romer J, however, who was careful to point out that his judgment proceeded entirely on the actual language used, appears to have assumed that the 'net amount or value' on which the liability to settle depended was the amount or value of the reversionary interest itself.

Implied term that the prescribed value refers to property derived from the same source

It will be seen that, in *Re Mackenzie's Settlement* (above), the aggregate of the two funds was held to be bound, although singly they were of insufficient amount. But although they accrued to the lady under two titles, they were derived from the same source, namely, the original settlement. Care must, however, be taken to distinguish between covenants where nothing is said upon this point, and those in which the question is distinctly dealt with. For instance, in *Re Mackenzie's Settlement* it appeared that there were two distinct funds, neither of which taken alone would have fallen under the covenant, but which, taken together, exceeded the value mentioned in the covenant, and although they came to the lady under different titles, they were held to be bound by the covenant. Nevertheless, it seems to be well settled that in such cases the fund will not be bound unless all its parts are derived from *the same source*[7]. The same source, however, does not necessarily mean under the same title. In *Re Mackenzie* both funds were derived from the same source (namely, the prior settlement) although part was derived by the lady directly and part as the next of kin of her brother. And in the same way two legacies derived from the same testator are derived from the same source[8].

Cases where the covenant limits the fund to be settled to funds acquired 'at one time'

Care must also be taken to distinguish between covenants such as those in *Re Hooper's Trusts*[9] and *Hood v Franklin*[10], where nothing is said upon the point, and those in which the fund to be settled is expressly declared to be a minimum sum derived from one and the same source and 'at one and the same time'. For instance, in *Bower v Smith*[11]:

---

5 *Re Hughes Settlement* [1924] 2 Ch 356.
6 [1949] Ch 213, [1949] 1 All ER 50.
7 *Re Hooper's Trusts* (1865) 13 WR 710; *Hood v Franklin* (1873) LR 16 Eq 496; *Re Hughes' Settlement* [1924] 2 Ch 356.
8 *Re Pares* [1901] 1 Ch 708.
9 (1865) 13 WR 710.
10 (1873) LR 16 Eq 496.
11 (1871) 19 WR 399 (the report in LR 11 Eq 279 is misleading and incorrect; see *Steward v Poppleton* [1877] WN 29).

the covenant was to settle property exceeding £500 in value which the wife should acquire 'at any one time'. She afterwards became the donee of a general power of appointment over a fund of £5,499 19s 1d. This power she exercised by eleven successive appointments in favour of herself for sums under £500 each.

On these facts it was held that the appointed funds were not bound, for although they were all derived from the same source, they were not acquired at the same time, ie at the same moment.

Sums already advanced out of the fund

Where the fund originally exceeds the minimum named in the covenant, but, by reason of advances made to the lady while it was still reversionary, the fund has been reduced below that minimum, the amount so advanced must be included for the purpose of determining whether the fund is large enough to be brought into settlement[12].

Conclusion

The whole subject of covenants to settle future property is in an unsatisfactory state, although skilled drafting can avoid the pitfalls emerging in this Chapter. In the light of the Married Women's Property Acts, and the Law Reform (Married Women and Tortfeasors) Act 1935 (which collectively have taken away the jus mariti of husbands in respect of their wives' capital except under their intestacies), such covenants ought not to be inserted in marriage settlements except after due consideration[13], taking into account the utility of preserving the family 'nest egg' for three or four generations and the ability to vary such trusts uder the Matrimonial Causes Act 1973, s 24[14].

---

12 *Hood v Franklin* (1873) LR 16 Eq 496.
13 *Re Maddy's Estate* [1901] 2 Ch 820 (such covenants not being usual covenants even in 1901).
14 *Brooks v Brooks* [1996] AC 375.

DIVISION THREE

Trusts implied by law

Chapter
5   Introduction   321
6   Resulting trusts   329
7   Constructive trusts   379

CHAPTER 5

Introduction

Analysis of trusts of property implied by law

(1) Trusts of property implied by law[1] arise where property is held by T, the person having title to the property, either:

(i) on resulting trust for B, the transferor of the property or the provider of the purchase price for the vendor to transfer title to the property, such trust arising at the time of the transfer to the transferee, T, and being founded on the automatically presumed intention of B, so as to locate the beneficial ownership of the property in B in the absence of any evidence that B intended to make a gift or a simple loan to T or to abandon all interest in the property, or

(ii) on constructive trust for X against the wishes of T, despite T in some cases having appeared to intend to be a trustee for X: such trust may often arise when T first acquires title to the property but it may arise at any time during the period of T's ownership if in accepted categories of circumstances it is considered unconscionable for T to retain the property for his own benefit to the exclusion of X.

(2) Resulting trusts of property arise in the two following cases, namely:

(a) when property is transferred to a trustee, upon trusts which do not wholly effectively dispose of the beneficial interest[2];

(b) when a purchase has been made in the name of some other person than the true purchaser[3], or personal property has been

---

1 On this classification see p 53, ante. In *Air Jamaica v Charlton* [1999] 1 WLR 1399 at 1412, Lord Mitchell stated, 'Like a constructive trust a resulting trust arises by operation of law, although unlike a constructive trust it gives effect to intention'. Such intention seems automatically to be imposed once, in the particular factual circumstances, there is an absence of actual evidence to make a gift or loan to the transferee or of actual evidence to abandon all interest in property transferred to a trustee on trusts which fail wholly or partly, see E Simpson in P Birks and F Rose, *Restitution and Equity Volume 1: Resulting Trusts and Equitable Compensation* (LLP Professional Publishing, 2000). Also see Millett LJ in (1998) 114 LQR 399 at 402, note 17.

2 Articles 29 and 30, post.

3 Article 31, post.

transferred to a stranger in blood without consideration, and there is no evidence that such persons were intended to take beneficially.

(3) Constructive trusts of property arise:

(a) when the traceable product of trust or other fiduciary property or of the breach of a fiduciary obligation not to make an unauthorised profit, particularly where there is a conflict between duty and self interest, is found in the ownership of the trustee or fiduciary[4];

(b) when trust or other fiduciary property or its traceable product has wrongfully been transferred by the fiduciary to a stranger not protected by statutory overreaching provisions or exceptions to the rule *nemo dat quod non habet* or the defence of change of position or bona fide purchaser of a legal interest for value without notice[5];

(c) when a property-owner fraudulently or unconscionably attempts to take advantage of statutory provisions or other fundamental legal principles[6] to deny the beneficial interest therein of another;

(d) when a vendor of property has entered into a specifically enforceable contract[7].

(4) This Chapter is concerned only with resulting trusts *of property* and beneficiaries' *proprietary* interests and not with the personal accountability of strangers to a trust who, in some circumstances[8] (eg if they dishonestly assist in a breach of trust), can be made *personally* liable to account as if they had been trustees, such liability being referred to traditionally as 'personal accountability as a constructive trustee' as a formula for equitable relief. Such terminology 'as a constructive trustee' should now be discarded so as to avoid confusion of personal and proprietary liability[9]. Personal accountability of strangers to a trust is covered in Article 100 below.

Resulting and constructive trusts of property

Resulting trusts only arise either in respect of express trusts of property, where there has been a failure effectively to dispose wholly of the settlor's interest or in respect of purchases or gifts of property where the apparent new owner was not intended to have the beneficial interest in the property. In both cases the beneficial interest forthwith results back to, or rather remains in, the person who provided the value transferred, whether by directly providing the property transferred or by providing the resources to enable another to vest the property in the transferee's name. Resulting trusts are a default mechanism that is part of the law of property to locate the

---

4 Article 33, post.
5 Article 34, post.
6 Article 35, post; *Paragon Finance v Thakerar* [1999] 1 All ER 400 at 409.
7 Article 36, post.
8 Article 100, post.
9 Lord Millett when Millett LJ in (1998) 114 LQR 399 at 400 and *Paragon Finance Ltd v Thakerar* [1999] 1 All ER 400 at 409 and 414; Lord Nicholls in Cornish, Nolan, O'Sullivan & Virgo (eds) *Restitution: Past, Present and Future* (Hart Publishing, 1998) pp 243–244.

beneficial ownership of property[10]. They are not based on the prevention of unjust enrichment[11], so as to create a flexible remedy where the transferor's intent to benefit the transferee was vitiated by some mistake or representation so there really was an absence of any truly based intention to benefit the transferee. If X's real or mistaken intent was for Y to treat X's assets as a freely available part of Y's general assets this is inconsistent with any proprietary trust relationship arising[12].

Constructive trusts of property originated in respect of express trusts, as a vindication of a pre-existing equitable interest, but have been extended so as to arise in respect of other fiduciary relationships concerning property and to prevent unconscionable conduct in relation thereto. They may retain or return value whether for the benefit of the person providing the value in the fiduciary property or for the benefit of persons he intended to benefit, but, unlike resulting trusts, they cannot be ousted by evidence of the real intention of the relevant party, although real intentions can be taken into account in preventing unconscionable behaviour. They may remedy unjust enrichment (so that the defendant is not enriched by the receipt of a benefit at the claimant's expense in circumstances where it would be unjust to allow the defendant to retain that benefit[13]) but they may go further and fulfil expectations or deter wrongdoing[14].

Personal accountability as express, resulting or constructive trustee of property and personal accountability of strangers to a trust

An express trustee is liable to a real and a personal action. A real action lies against him in respect of the trust property and its fruits so that he is liable to a proprietary remedy, while a personal action lies against him to account for the losses and profits arising out of his stewardship of the trust property. Once a person knows that he is an express or resulting or constructive trustee of property[15] he then becomes personally liable to account for such property but not before that, even though liable to proprietary remedies without

---

10 *Westdeutsche Landesbank v Islington London Borough Council* [1996] AC 669 at 689, 703, 709, 718, 720 and 738; WJ Swadling (1996) 16 Legal Studies 110; C F Rickett & R Grantham (2000) 116 LQR 15 at 19.

11 As favoured by P B H Birks 'Restitution and Resulting Trusts' in S Goldstein (ed) *Equity and Contemporary Legal Developments* (Hebrew Univ of Jerusalem, 1992).

12 *Westdeutsche Landesbank v Islington London Borough Council* [1996] AC 669; Lord Millett in (1998) 114 LQR 399 at 406–407 and 416.

13 On 'unjust enrichment' generally see P Birks (ed) *English Private Law* (OUP 2000), Chapter 15; P B H Birks *Introduction to the law of Restitution* (Oxford, 1985); Goff & Jones *Law of Restitution* (5th edn) pp 11 et seq; M Cope *Constructive Trusts* (Law Book Co of Australia) pp 25–26, 31–33 and the Canadian Supreme Court in cases like *Pettkus v Becker* (1980) 117 DLR (3rd) 257; *Sorochan v Sorochan* (1986) 29 DLR (4th) 1; *Peter v Beblow* (1993) 101 DLR (4th) 621 and *Korkontzilas v Saulos* (1997) 146 DLR (4th) 214, but they seem prepared erroneously to extend the concept of unjust enrichment beyond reversing detriment to fulfilling expectations.

14 See D J Hayton 'Constructive trusts: is the remedying of unjust enrichment a satisfactory approach?' in Youdan (ed) *Equity, Fiduciaries and Trusts* (1989, Carswell) pp 205–246; M Cope, *Constructive Trusts* pp 37–49. G Elias, *Explaining Constructive Trusts* (Clarendon Press, 1990) pp 1–7, 48–85 reveals that constructive trusts have different justifications, some pursuing the goal of 'perfection' to perfect a commitment that the defendant has made and should honour, others the goal of effecting reparation for loss, others the goal of restitution for unjust enrichment.

15 A settlor may transfer such property without the transferee-trustee knowing this or such property may be received without being known to be trust property.

knowing this[16]. He may disclaim the trust property if he decides not to accept the trusteeship, but if title has vested in him, then he must transfer it to the absolutely entitled beneficiary or to the trustees for the beneficiaries. Any person who receives property subject to a trust or other fiduciary relationship (without being protected, eg as a bona fide purchaser) is liable to a proprietary remedy, to the extent he has the property or its traceable product, and to a personal liability to account in Equity. Liability to account, via a surcharging, or a strict falsification, of accounts, was Equity's remedy superior to common law damages and, of course was the only personal liability where the defendant could not be sued at common law because involved with an equitable or fiduciary relationship exclusively within the province of the Courts of Equity.

Indeed, even if the defendant had not received trust or other fiduciary property but had dishonestly assisted the trustee or other fiduciary in a breach of duty, Equity, as a fictitious formula for equitable personal liability, was prepared constructively to treat him as if he had been an express trustee of the relevant property so as to make him liable 'as a constructive trustee'.

It will be seen that the plaintiff's claim to make the defendant personally liable to compensate the plaintiff need be no more than just that. It is time the courts dispensed with the confusing historical terminology of personal liability to account 'as constructive trustee'[17].

Institutional and remedial constructive trusts of property

There is much discussion[18] whether the constructive trust is a substantive institution or a remedial device without such terminology being clarified. However, where, as a formula for equitable relief, a defendant, though not a trustee, was constructively treated as if he had been a trustee, so that he could be made personally liable to account 'as a constructive trustee', this was an example of the imposition of a remedial constructive *trusteeship*. As has already been emphasised, this has nothing to do with a constructive trust *of property* and should simply be considered an instance of a personal liability to account in equity, the defendant's account of his involvement being liable to be surcharged or falsified, so as to ascertain the amount of compensation to be made to restore the value of the trust fund to its proper value.

An institutional constructive trust automatically arises in defined circumstances in accordance with settled principles of Equity, as a way of protecting or vindicating a pre-existing equitable interest in property[19], eg where

---

16 *Westdeutsche Landesbank v Islington London Borough Council* [1996] AC 669, and see p 56 ante.

17 Millett J (as he then was) and P B H Birks in McKendrick (ed) *Commercial Aspects of Trusts and Fiduciary Obligations* pp 3 and 153–155 respectively; *Paragon Finance Ltd v Thakerar* [1999] 1 All ER 400 at 409 and 414 per Millett LJ; and Lord Nicholls in Cornish, Nolan, O'Sullivan & Virgo (eds) *Restitution: Past, Present and Future* (Hart Publishing, 1998) pp 243–244.

18 See D W M Waters 'The remedial constructive trust', S Gardner 'Remedial constructive trusts: the element of discretion' and P B H Birks 'Proprietary rights as remedies' in Birks (ed) *Frontiers of liability* II (OUP, 1994); M Cope *Constructive Trusts* Chapters 1 and 2; A J Oakley *Constructive Trusts* (3rd edn) pp 19–28; *Lewin on Trusts* (17 edn) paras 7–11 to 7–23; G Elias, *Explaining Constructive Trusts* pp 156–168; D Wright *The Remedial Constructive Trust* (Butterworths Australia, 1998), as reviewed by P Birks (1999) 115 LQR 681.

19 Scott & Fratcher: *The Law of Trusts* (4th edn) Vol 5 (Boston 1989) para 462.4; *US v Fontana* 528 F Supp 137 (1981); *Rawluk v Rawluk* (1990) 65 DLR (4th) 161; *Re Sharpe* [1980] 1 All ER 198 at 203, [1980] 1 WLR 219 at 225; *Chase Manhattan Bank v Israel-British Bank (London)* [1981] Ch 105; *Re Jonton Pty Ltd* [1992] 1 Qd R 105.

property is settled on B for life remainder to C, and the trustee, T, purports to keep for himself dividends and bonus shares arising in respect of trust property or a bribe paid to him, or a company claims from a director (a fiduciary) a bribe paid to him; or X, to whom T wrongly gave trust property, purports to keep it or its product for himself; or Y, to whom S bequeathed property on Y's agreement to hold it for A for life, remainder to B absolutely, purports on S's death to keep it for himself or on resulting trust for the residuary beneficiary in S's estate; or where H and W each made wills, agreeing not to revoke them, in favour of the survivor for life, remainder to Z and then, after H's death, W revokes her will purporting to leave everything not to Z but to her new husband; or where L, as registered owner of shares in a private company having done everything he needs to do to transfer legal title to M (by handing the share certificate together with the signed transfer form) so that Equity regards the equitable title as having passed, purports as legal owner to keep the dividends for himself, having changed his mind and the company having refused (as it can) to register M as shareholder. In all these cases, inevitably, the result of the court's intervention will be the retrospective assertion or vindication of pre-existing equitable rights.

However, a 'remedial' constructive trust[20] is not automatically engendered by the facts (which in tracing claims will include the claimant's election for a constructive trust rather than an equitable lien) but is imposed by the court in its discretion against the defendant-owner of particular property, thereby conferring on the plaintiff a specific interest therein as a remedy for the defendant's breach of fiduciary obligation relating to that property. It seems that the court decree will create a new interest in property or crystallise an inchoate right in property, so supporting pre-existing rights that were not themselves enforceable equitable interests[1]: the decree may thus be prospective or retrospective against specified parties. Indeed, it seems it may even be in personam against a particular defendant's conscience while owning land, so that a defendant-purchaser may take subject to a mere contractual licence if in the circumstances it would be unconscionable for him to take free from such licence[2].

Lord Browne-Wilkinson has explained the gulf between the institutional and remedial constructive trust of property as follows[3]:

'Under an institutional constructive trust, the trust arises by operation of law as from the date of the circumstances which gave rise to it: the function of the court is merely to declare that such trust has arisen in the past. The consequences that flow from such trust having arisen (including the possibly unfair consequences to third parties who in the interim have received the trust property) are also determined by rules of law, not under a discretion. A remedial constructive trust is different. It is a judicial remedy giving rise to an enforceable equitable obligation: the extent to

---

20 As discussed but not applied in *Re Goldcorp Exchange Ltd* [1994] 2 All ER 806 at 822, PC; *Metall und Rohstoff AG v Donaldson Lufkin & Jenrette Inc* [1990] 1 QB 391 at 479 (overruled on another point by *Lonrho plc v Al Fayed* [1992] 1 AC 448); *Lonrho plc v Al Fayed (No 2)* [1992] 1 WLR 1 at 9; Millett J (as he then was) in (1991) 107 LQR 71 at 85 and [1993] Restitution LR 7 at 9.

1 See Michael Crystal QC in *Lloyds Bank plc v Rosset* [1991] 1 AC 107 at 115 but co-ownership estoppel interests are now equated with common intention constructive trusts: see p 426, post.

2 *Ashburn Anstalt v Arnold* [1989] Ch 1, CA.

3 *Westdeutsche Landesbank v Islington London Borough Council* [1996] AC 669 at 716; also *Fortex Group Ltd v Macintosh* [1998] 3 NZLR 171 at 172–173, CA. Also see Millett LJ 'Restitution and Constructive Trusts' (1998) 114 LQR 399.

which it operates retrospectively to the prejudice of third parties lies in the discretion of the court.'

A traditional doctrine which might have been considered to fall within remedial constructive trusts is that of equitable proprietary estoppel claims, leading to the discretionary award of some type of proprietary interest in land, where one could argue that the court is tailoring the remedy to fit all the circumstances right up to the date of the hearing rather than crystallising (inchoate) rights of a proprietary nature[4]. However, common intention constructive trust claims have come to be regarded as institutional trusts[5], and equitable proprietary estoppel claims to co-ownership of land have been equated[6] with such institutional trusts, while s 116 of the Land Registration Act 2002 appears designed to treat equitable proprietary estoppel interests as not arising at the date of the court order but at the date of the detriment of the claimant that enables the relevant proprietary interest to be claimed.

The remedial trust is well established in Canada[7] and in New Zealand[8] and is, perhaps, beginning to be established in Australia[9]. In England it is recognised that[10] 'Equity must retain what has been called its "inherent flexibility" and capacity to adjust to new situations by reference to the mainsprings of the equitable jurisdiction'. Equity intervenes to grant relief against fraud and unconscionable behaviour 'so when appropriate, the court will grant a proprietary remedy to restore to the plaintiff property of which he has been wrongly deprived, or to prevent the defendant from retaining a benefit which he has obtained by his own wrong ... But its intervention must be based on principle; there must be some relationship between the relief granted and the circumstances which give rise to it'.

Extra-judicially, Millett J (as he then was) has pointed out[11]:

'The question is whether proprietary remedies should be granted only in defined circumstances and then as a matter of course, so that rights of property may be fixed and ascertainable in advance; or whether they should be granted whenever the justice of the case so requires, with the result that rights of property may depend on the exercise by the court of a general discretion and cannot be known in advance. It is unlikely that the remedial constructive trust in the latter sense will gain acceptance in England. It is a counsel of despair which too readily concedes the impossibility of propounding a general rationale for the availability of a proprietary remedy. The advantage which such a remedy affords the plaintiff over the unsecured creditors of an insolvent defendant makes it imperative that the circumstances in which it will be granted should be known in advance. It is the

---

4 See *Stokes v Anderson* [1991] 1 FLR 391 at 399 per Nourse LJ; P Ferguson (1993) 109 LQR 114; D J Hayton (1993) 109 LQR 485 and Lord Browne-Wilkinson's Birmingham Univ Holdsworth Lecture 'Constructive trusts and unjust enrichment' (1996) 10 Trust LI 98.

5 Courts assume that they are recognising the claimant's already existing proprietary interest which binds a subsequent mortgagee: *Midland Bank plc v Cooke* [1995] 4 All ER 562, CA; *Lloyds Bank v Rosset* [1989] Ch 350 (but no proprietary interest on appeal).

6 *Yaxley v Gotts* [2000] Ch 162 at 176; *Banner Homes Holdings Ltd v Luff Developments Ltd* [2000] Ch 372 at 384; *Birmingham Midshires Mortgage Services v Sabherwal* (1999) 80 P & CR 256 at 263.

7 *LAC Minerals Ltd v International Corona Resources Ltd* (1989) 61 DLR (4th) 14; *Peter v Beblow* (1993) 101 DLR (4th) 621; *Korkontzilas v Saulos* (1997) 146 DLR (4th) 214.

8 *Gillies v Keogh* [1989] 2 NZLR 327; *Powell v Thompson* [1991] 1 NZLR 597; *Phillips v Phillips* [1993] 3 NZLR 159; *Commonwealth Reserves v Chodar* [2001] 2 NZLR 374.

9 *Muschinski v Dodds* (1985) 160 CLR 583; *Baumgartner v Baumgartner* (1987) 164 CLR 137; *Giumelli v Giumelli* (1999) 73 ALJR 547, (1998/99) 1 ITELR 603; Sir Anthony Mason (1994) 110 LQR 238 at 251.

10 *Lonrho plc v Fayed (No 2)* [1991] 4 All ER 961 at 969 per Millett J.

11 [1993] Restitution LR 7 at 9–10. Also see (1998) 114 LQR 399.

potential impact on creditors which makes it unacceptable that rights of property should depend upon vague and ill-defined notions of fairness.'

Accordingly, the Court of Appeal[12] has since rejected the possibility of imposing a remedial constructive trust on particular property of an insolvent defendant: it is not open to the judiciary thereby to oust the effect of the statutory insolvency priority rules. In the case of a solvent defendant it remains open to the English court[13] to impose a remedial constructive trust over specific property, but this would appear to be of little significance where the defendant is solvent and so can pay any compensation demanded.

Finally it needs to be appreciated that instead of using 'constructive trust' in an institutional sense, contrasted with an express or resulting trust, it may be used in a remedial sense contrasted with other proprietary remedies[14] such as an equitable lien or subrogation (or personal remedies like equitable liability to account[15] or equitable compensation[16]). Thus, if the claimant can show that the traceable product of his property is in the ownership of the defendant, the latter is liable to transfer it *in specie* to the claimant and so is constructive trustee thereof[17]. If the defendant had not used the claimant's money to acquire property but only to improve the defendant's property the court may impose an equitable lien over the property as security for repayment of the claimant's money. If the claimant's money had been used to discharge the defendant's mortgage over the defendant's house the court may treat the house as subject to a charge by way of subrogation in favour of the claimant as security for repayment of the claimant's money.

Purchaser's undertaking to respect a contractual licence

If P undertakes with V, a vendor of land, that P will take the property positively subject to the rights of C, a contractual licensee from V, then once P becomes registered proprietor it becomes unconscionable[18] for P to evict C on the basis C's licence is not a proprietary interest capable of binding P, but only a personal contractual interest binding V alone[19]. It is thus said that a constructive trust is imposed on P's conscience, C having an *in personam* right binding P but not a proprietary interest binding P's property: there is no constructive trust of property so as to confer a proprietary interest upon C. If, however, C had an estate contract (including an option to purchase a freehold) in circumstances where P had led C to act to his detriment in the belief such contract was valid rather than void for non-registration so that an

12 *Re Polly Peck International plc (No 2)* [1998] 3 All ER 812. See also *Commonwealth Reserves v Chodar* [2001] 2 NZLR 374 (solvency of defendant enabled imposition of remedial constructive trust over yacht and house).

13 *Westdeutsche Landesbank v Islington London Borough Council* [1996] AC 669 at 716, per Lord Browne-Wilkinson.

14 *Boscawen v Bajwa* [1995] 4 All ER 769 at 777, [1996] 1 WLR 328 at 334, CA.

15 See Art 89 post.

16 *Mahoney v Purnell* [1996] 3 All ER 61; *Swindle v Harrison* [1997] 4 All ER 705, CA.

17 *Boscawen v Bajwa* [1996] 1 WLR 328 at 334, [1995] 4 All ER 769 at 777, CA; *Giumelli v Giumelli* (1998/99) 1 ITELR 603, (1999) 61 ALR 473.

18 *Ashburn Anstalt v Arnold* [1989] Ch 1, CA. If a sale were expressed to be subject to whatever rights C might happen to have, so as defensively to protect V rather than to assist C, no constructive trusteeship would be imposed on P.

19 In some circumstances C may have a right binding P under Contracts (Rights of Third Parties) Act 1999.

equitable proprietary estoppel arose, this can lead to the imposition of a constructive trust over P's property[20].

---

20 *Yaxley v Gotts* [2000] Ch 162, CA. More commonly, P will be estopped from denying the validity of the non-registered interest, leading to P being compelled to grant the relevant interest to C or being regarded in equity as owning the land subject to C's interest: *Lyus v Prowsa Developments Ltd* [1982] 1 WLR 1044; *Crabb v Arun District Council* [1976] Ch 179, CA; *Taylor's Fashions Ltd v Liverpool Victoria Trustees Co Ltd* [1982] QB 133n.

CHAPTER 6

Resulting trusts

Article
29 Automatic resulting trusts where equitable interest not wholly disposed of, so there is some failure of the trusts   329
30 Resulting trusts arising where trusts declared illegal   343
31 Resulting trusts where purchase made in another's name or property voluntarily transferred to another   349
32 To whom property results   369

ARTICLE 29

Automatic resulting trusts where equitable interest not wholly disposed of, so there is some failure of the trusts

(1) When it appears to have been the intention of a donor that the donee should not take beneficially[1], but as trustee and there is no evidence that the donor had expressly or by necessary implication abandoned any beneficial interest in the trust property[2], there will automatically be a resulting trust in favour of the donor or his representatives where the trust declared do not exhaust the whole beneficial interest[3] as exemplified by the following cases, namely:

(a) if the donor fails to declare comprehensive trusts upon which the property is to be held; or

(b) if the donor directs that the property shall be applied for a particular purpose (as distinguished from merely being subjected to a

---

1 Lord Reid in *Vandervell v IRC* [1967] 2 AC 291 at 307 citing the 11th edition hereof; also *Hill v Bishop of London* (1738) 1 Atk 618; *Walton v Walton* (1807) 14 Ves 318; *King v Denison* (1813) 1 Ves & B 260.

2 See Lord Browne-Wilkinson in *Westdeutsche Landesbank v Islington London Borough Council* [1996] AC 669 at 708. Such rare evidence would rebut the otherwise automatic presumption that the donor must intend to retain a beneficial interest to the extent he has not effectively divested himself of the whole beneficial interest.

3 See *Westdeutsche Landesbank v Islington London Borough Council* [1996] AC 669 at 708; *Vandervell v IRC* [1967] 2 AC 291 at 313, 329.

charge for such purpose)[4] which turns out to be insufficient to exhaust the property; or

(c) if an express trust cannot wholly be carried into effect[5], though if this is because of illegality special considerations arise[6].

(d) if there is a *Quistclose*[7] trust where money is lent to a borrower for a specific purpose where the borrower is bound in equity not to use the money for any other purpose (so as not to be beneficial owner thereof), then, on the money being used for the specific purpose, the lender only has his normal remedy in debt, but otherwise the money is held on a resulting trust for the lender, the borrower having a power or duty to use it until the purpose cannot be carried out or a specified period elapses or the lender countermands the mandate, depending on the terms of their contract[8].

(2) Where the non-beneficial character of the gift appears on the face of the instrument, no evidence to the contrary is admissible[9]. But where it is merely presumed from the general scope of the instrument, parol evidence is admissible both in aid and in contradiction of the presumption[10].

(3) A resulting trust is a trust which the court can execute even though all that is required is the transfer of the property back to the settlor[11].

Paragraph 1

Broad propositions of Megarry J

The relevant points on resulting trusts were put in a series of propositions by Megarry J in *Re Vandervell's Trusts (No 2)* as follows[12]:

'(1) If a transaction fails to make any effective disposition of any interest it does nothing. This is so at law and in equity, and has nothing to do with resulting trusts.

(2) Normally the mere existence of some unexpressed intention in the breast of the owner of the property does nothing: there must at least be some expression of that intention before it can effect any result. To yearn is not to transfer.

(3) Before any doctrine of resulting trust can come into play, there must at least be some effective transaction which transfers or creates some interest in property.

---

4 *Watson v Hayes* (1839) 5 My & Cr 125; *Wood v Cox* (1837) 2 My & Cr 684; *Cunningham v Foot* (1878) 3 App Cas 974; *Re West* [1900] 1 Ch 84.
5 *Stubbs v Sargon* (1838) 3 My & Cr 507; *Ackroyd v Smithson* (1780) 1 Bro CC 503.
6 See Article 30.
7 *Barclays Bank Ltd v Quistclose Investments Ltd* [1970] AC 567, HL; see p 116 ante.
8 *Twinsectra Ltd v Yardley* [2002] UKHL 12, [2002] 2 All ER 377.
9 See *Langham v Sanford* (1811) 17 Ves 435 at 442; *Irvine v Sullivan* (1869) LR 8 Eq 673; *Re Rees' Will Trusts* [1949] Ch 541, [1949] 1 All ER 609; affd [1950] Ch 204, [1949] 2 All ER 1003; *Vandervell v IRC* [1967] 2 AC 291 at 312.
10 Statute of Frauds 1677, s 8; Law of Property Act 1925, s 53 (2); *Gascoigne v Thwing* (1685) 1 Vern 366; *Willis v Willis* (1740) 2 Atk 71; *Cook v Hutchinson* (1836) 1 Keen 42. As to parol evidence explanatory of a *testator's* intention, see *Docksey v Docksey* (1708) 2 Eq Cas Abr 506; *North v Crompton* (1671) 1 Cas in Ch 196; *Walton v Walton* (1807) 14 Ves 318; *Langham v Sanford* (1811) 17 Ves 435; *Lynn v Beaver* (1823) Turn & R 63; *Biddulph v Williams* (1875) 1 Ch D 203; *Vandervell v IRC* [1967] 2 AC 291 at 312 and Administration of Justice Act 1982, s 21.
11 *Re Sayer* [1957] Ch 423, [1956] 3 All ER 600.
12 [1974] Ch 269 at 294.

(4) Where A effectually transfers to B (or creates in his favour) any interest in any property, whether legal or equitable, a resulting trust for A may arise in two distinct classes of case. For simplicity, I shall confine my statement to cases in which the transfer or creation is made without B providing any valuable consideration, and where no presumption of advancement can arise; and I shall state the position for transfers without specific mention of the creation of new interests.

    (a)   The first class of case is where the transfer to B is not made on any trust. If, of course, it appears from the transfer that B is intended to hold on certain trusts, that will be decisive, and the case is not within this category; and similarly if it appears that B is intended to take beneficially. But in other cases there is a rebuttable presumption that B holds on a resulting trust for A. The question is not one of the automatic consequences of a dispositive failure by A, but one of presumption: the property has been carried to B, and from the absence of consideration and any presumption of advancement B is presumed not only to hold the entire interest on trust, but also to hold the beneficial interest for A absolutely. The presumption thus establishes both that B is to take on trust and also what that trust is. Such resulting trusts may be called "presumed resulting trusts".

    (b)   The second class of case is where the transfer to B is made on trusts which leave some or all of the beneficial interest undisposed of. Here B automatically holds on a resulting trust for A to the extent that the beneficial interest has not been carried to him or others. The resulting trust here does not depend on any intentions or presumptions, but is the automatic consequence of A's failure to dispose of what is vested in him. Since ex hypothesi the transfer is on trust, the resulting trust does not establish the trust but merely carries back to A the beneficial interest that has not been disposed of. Such resulting trusts may be called "automatic resulting trusts".

(5) Where trustees hold property in trust for A, and it is they who, at A's direction, make the transfer to B, similar principles apply, even though on the face of the transaction the transferor appears to be the trustees and not A. If the transfer to B is on trust, B will hold any beneficial interest that has not been effectively disposed of on an automatic resulting trust for the true transferor, A. If the transfer to B is not on trust, there will be a rebuttable presumption that B holds on a resulting trust for A.'

Significantly, there is no heading (6) where trustees hold property in trust for A, and, *without A's consent or knowledge,* transfer the property in breach of trust to B. Here, it is the trustees (and not A[13]) who are the real transferors and they intend to pass full legal beneficial ownership to B, so ousting any resulting trust[14]. However, if B is not a bona fide purchaser without notice of the trust nor protected by statutory overreaching provisions, then, because under property law rules of priorities B forthwith holds the property subject to A's continuing subsisting equitable interest, B will hold the property on a constructive trust vindicating A's equitable interest, although B will be under

---

13 Lord Upjohn in *Vandervell v IRC* [1967] 2 AC 291 at 312 restricting resulting trusts also to 'where A transfers or directs a trustee for him to transfer the legal estate to B'.
14 Although Lord Millett favoured a resulting trust here in *El Ajou v Dollar Land Holdings plc* [1993] 3 All ER 717 at 734 and in (1998) 114 LQR 399 at 401 but a constructive trust in *Boscawen v Bajwa* [1995] 4 All ER 769 at 777, while in *Twinsectra Ltd v Yardley* [2002] UKHL 12; [2002] 2 AC 164 at para 91 he accepted no resulting trust arose where property was transferred intending it to become the transferee's absolutely.

no fiduciary or equitable obligations as a trustee so long as he has no knowledge of A's interest[15].

Resulting trust 'automatic' because virtually irrebuttable

It has been pointed out by Lord Browne-Wilkinson[16] that 'automatic' resulting trusts where trusts fail are not necessarily irrebuttable because the undisposed-of beneficial interest could vest in the Crown as *bona vacantia* if the settlor had expressly or by necessary implication abandoned any beneficial interest in the trust property. This possibility seems theoretical rather than real[17], the courts being very reluctant[18] to find such an intention that provides a windfall benefit for the Crown. Moreover, it seems better to regard such rare actual evidence as ousting any question of resulting trust arising, rather than being in rebuttal of a resulting trust that has arisen.

Disposition to trustees

If property is given to trustees or left by will to trustees but no defined trusts are delimited then there is a resulting trust for the settlor or his estate, when the residuary beneficiary or the next of kin will benefit depending whether the property was the subject of a specific gift or of a residuary gift[19]. In *Vandervell v IRC*[20], a settlor transferred certain shares to an institution so that the institution would receive the dividends. By arrangement with him, the institution granted to the trustees of the settlor's family settlement an option to buy back the shares for £5,000, but the trusts on which the trustees were to hold the option were not declared. The Inland Revenue claimed that the settlor had not divested himself absolutely of all interest in the shares within s 415(1)(d) and (2) of the Income Tax Act 1952. It was held that the settlor should be treated as having settled the option on the settlement trustees and that these trustees held the option on a resulting trust for the settlor, and that he had therefore not divested himself of all interest in the shares.

Uncertainty or failure of express trust

If a declared trust is too uncertain or vague to be executed[1] or cannot be carried out by reason of lapse[2] or of complete failure of beneficiaries[3] or

---

15 No accountability arises until B's conscience is affected: *Westdeutsche Landesbank v Islington London Borough Council* [1996] AC 669 at 705–706, 707, 709 and Lord Millett in (1998) 114 LQR 399, 403–406.

16 *Westdeutsche Landesbank v Islington London Borough Council* [1996] AC 669 at 708.

17 Lord Browne-Wilkinson cited *Re West Sussex Constabulary's Benevolent Fund Trusts* [1971] Ch 1 without noting that much of it has been undermined by *Re Buckinghamshire Constabulary Fund Friendly Society (No 2)* [1979], 1 All ER 623, p 340, post.

18 For example, *Air Jamaica Ltd v Charlton* [1999] 1 WLR 1399, PC.

19 *Rudkin v Dolman* (1876) 35 LT 791; *Re Boyes* (1884) 26 Ch D 531; *Re Chapman* [1922] 1 Ch 287; *Re Pugh's Will Trusts* [1967] 3 All ER 337, [1967] 1 WLR 1262.

20 [1967] 2 AC 291, [1967] 1 All ER 1; *Re Vandervell's Trusts (No 2)* [1974] Ch 269, [1974] 3 All ER 205; and see pp 240–244, ante.

1 *Morice v Bishop of Durham* (1804) 9 Ves 399; on appeal (1805) 10 Ves 522; *Re Osmund* [1944] Ch 66, [1944] 1 All ER 12; *Re Pugh's Will Trusts* [1967] 3 All ER 337, [1967] 1 WLR 1262; *Re Atkinson's Will Trusts* [1978] 1 All ER 1275, [1978] 1 WLR 586.

2 *Ackroyd v Smithson* (1780) 1 Bro CC 503.

3 *Hedderwick's Trustees v Hedderwick's Executors* 1910 SC 333.

becomes in the event void for remoteness[4] then since it appears from the face of the instrument that the trustee was not intended to take beneficially, there will be a resulting trust. Similarly if the declared trust fails to satisfy the requisite formalities[5].

If a settlement is executed in contemplation of a marriage and the contract to marry is definitely and absolutely put an end to, so that there is a total failure of the consideration for, or purpose of, the settlement the trustees hold on a resulting trust for the settlor[6].

Failure of life interest

A resulting trust will be implied on failure of a life interest in cases where the interest in remainder does not take effect forthwith under the doctrine of acceleration. To bring this doctrine into effect there must be something equivalent to the gift of a vested remainder[7] to a person expressed to take effect on the death of the first taker[8] so that the postponement of the subsequent interest is merely in order that the life interest may be enjoyed. The principle was first established in regard to remainders in real estate[9], but has been extended to personalty and to partial as well as residuary interests[10], and it applies to settlements inter vivos as well as to wills[11]. There will, however, be no acceleration where the character of the disposition made by the settlement shows that the settlor's intention was that the person interested in remainder should take no benefit until the actual death of the person entitled to the life interest[12], or where the interests in remainder are still contingent at the determination of the life interest[13]. However, when the contingent interest becomes vested acceleration will occur[14].

In regard to instruments taking effect after 16 July 1964, it is expressly provided by s 6 of the Perpetuities and Accumulations Act 1964 that the vesting of an interest shall not be prevented from being accelerated on the

---

4 *Tregonwell v Sydenham* (1815) 3 Dow 194 at 210; *Re Drummond's Settlement* [1986] 3 All ER 45, [1986] 1 WLR 1096; *Air Jamaica Ltd v Charlton* [1999] 1 WLR 1399, PC.

5 *Hodgson v Marks* [1971] Ch 892, [1971] 2 All ER 684, CA.

6 *Essery v Cowlard* (1884) 26 Ch D 191; also see *Burgess v Rawnsley* [1975] Ch 429, [1975] 3 All ER 142, CA.

7 *Re Flower's Settlement Trusts* [1957] 1 All ER 462, CA.

8 Even though liable to be divested, see *Re Taylor* [1957] 3 All ER 56, [1957] 1 WLR 1043.

9 A distinction was made between legal remainders which could not be accelerated, see *Re Scott* [1911] 2 Ch 374, and equitable remainders which could (*Re Conyngham* [1921] 1 Ch 491) but even if this distinction was valid, as to which there is some doubt, the legislation of 1925 has swept away distinctions of this kind between legal and equitable limitations (*Re Hatfeild's Will Trusts* [1958] Ch 469, [1957] 2 All ER 261).

10 *Re Hodge* [1943] Ch 300, [1943] 2 All ER 304.

11 *Re Flower's Settlement Trusts* [1957] 1 All ER 462, [1957] 1 WLR 401, CA, but it may be more difficult to collect the intention necessary to bring the principle of acceleration into play in the case of a settlement than a will (*Re Flower's Settlement Trusts*, above). See also *Re Harker's Will Trusts* [1969] 3 All ER 1, [1969] 1 WLR 1124 showing that acceleration probably does not close class gifts despite *Re Davies* [1957] 3 All ER 52, [1957] 1 WLR 922; [1973] CLJ 246 (A M Prichard).

12 *Re Flower's Settlement Trusts* [1957] 1 All ER 462, [1957] 1 WLR 401, CA.

13 *Re Townsend's Estate* (1886) 34 Ch D 357; *Re Taylor* [1957] 3 All ER 56, [1957] 1 WLR 1043; *Re Scott* [1975] 2 All ER 1033, [1975] 1 WLR 1260.

14 *Re Townsend's Estate* (1886) 34 Ch D 357.

failure of a prior interest merely because the prior interest failed for remoteness. It is doubtful whether this provision makes any change in the law[15].

Residue after satisfaction of express trust

Where there is a devise to A upon trust to pay debts, or to answer an annuity, there is a resulting trust of what remains after payment of the debts or satisfaction of the annuity[16]. And, on similar principles where income under a settlement was payable to the wife so long as she lived with her husband and on her death, or the prior determination of the trust in her favour, to the husband during his life with a gift over on the death of the survivor, it was held that, the wife having ceased to live with the husband during the subsistence of the marriage but having survived him, there was a resulting trust of income during the rest of her life since the court could not see clearly what words ought to be written into the settlement to provide for the eventuality for which the settlement made no provision[17]. Where, however, the court can see from the document itself what words should be supplied it will fill the gap and thus prevent a resulting trust from arising[18].

Even though it may appear, at the time of execution, that a settlement effectively disposes of the whole of the settlor's interest in the property comprised in it, later events may none the less give rise to a resulting trust. This may be so if the beneficial interests fail for want of beneficiaries. Equally, it may be so if a beneficiary, though qualified to take his interest, chooses instead to surrender or release it without declaring trusts in respect of it and in such circumstances that the subsequent interests (if any) under the settlement are not accelerated. Thus in *Re Guinness's Settlement*[19], a tenant for life executed a deed which released her life interest to the settlement trustees but did not declare trusts in respect of it. Goff J held that the income must be held on a resulting trust for the settlor: it was very unlikely that the life tenant had intended this, but then ' ... it is rarely, if ever, that anyone intends to create a resulting trust'.

No resulting trust where it appears that donee was to take beneficially

On the other hand, there will be no resulting trust where an intention to exclude the settlor can be collected. Thus, where debtors assigned their property to trustees in trust to sell, and *divide the proceeds* amongst their creditors in rateable proportions according to the amounts of their respective debts, it was held by the House of Lords that there was no resulting trust

---

15 See *Re Coleman* [1936] Ch 528, [1936] 2 All ER 225; *Re Allan's Will Trusts* [1958] 1 All ER 401, [1958] 1 WLR 220; and *Re Hubbard's Will Trusts* [1963] Ch 275, [1962] 2 All ER 917.

16 *King v Denison* (1813) 1 Ves & B 260; *Watson v Hayes* (1839) 5 My & Cr 125; but see contra *Croome v Croome* (1889) 61 LT 814.

17 *Re Cochrane* [1955] Ch 309, [1955] 1 All ER 222; see also *Re Wyatt* (1889) 60 LT 920; though the assumption in that case that the gift over only took effect on death seems to have been wrong on the authorities and as a matter of interpretation, see *Upton v Brown* (1879) 12 Ch D 872; and *Underhill v Roden* (1876) 2 Ch D 494, and cases there cited; and *Re Akeroyd's Settlement* [1893] 3 Ch 363.

18 *Re Akeroyd's Settlement* [1893] 3 Ch 363; *Re Cochrane* [1955] Ch 309, [1955] 1 All ER 222; and cf *Re Cory* [1955] 2 All ER 630, [1955] 1 WLR 725; distinguished *Re Follett* [1955] 2 All ER 22, [1955] 1 WLR 429, CA.

19 [1966] 2 All ER 497, [1966] 1 WLR 1355. Also *Re Scott* [1975] 2 All ER 1033, [1975] 1 WLR 1260.

in favour of the debtors, in the event of there being more than sufficient to pay twenty shillings in the pound[20]. This decision, was, however, founded entirely on the construction of the particular deed, and turned apparently to some extent upon the fact that all the best precedents contained an *express* trust of any surplus in favour of the debtors. It must, therefore, not be rashly assumed that the same decision would be arrived at if, on the language of another creditor's deed, it should appear that the object was to *pay debts* (or a dividend on debts), and not to assign the property for better or for worse by way of accord and satisfaction. It may be observed that where, under a similar assignment to that mentioned in the last illustration, there is not enough to pay all the creditors in full, any unclaimed dividends must be applied in augmentation of the dividends of those creditors who have claimed[1].

Where there is a devise to A, *charged* with the payment of debts and legacies[2], or charged with the payment of a contingent legacy[3] which does not take effect, there will be no resulting trust; but the whole property will go to the devisee beneficially, subject only to the charge. And the same result will follow even where property is devised to A 'upon trust' to pay specific legacies, if on the whole will it appears that the testator merely meant to charge the legacies on the property[4]. In all such cases the inference is that the donee was to take everything not required to satisfy the *charge*. Thus in *Re Foord*[5] where a testator left his estate to his sister absolutely on trust to pay his widow an annuity and the estate income exceeded the annuity the sister was held beneficially entitled to the balance.

In *Re Osoba*[6] the Court of Appeal held that a testator's bequest to his widow upon trust 'for her maintenance and for the training of my daughter Abiola up to university grade and for the maintenance of my aged mother' was a trust for the three females absolutely as joint tenants. There was no resulting trust when, after the deaths of the testator's widow and mother, Abiola finished her education, so that Abiola was absolutely entitled to the property. The specified purposes were regarded merely as the testator's motives for making an absolute gift.

Where a bank made a loan of money to a local authority under a special swaps agreement, believing the authority to have power to enter into such an arrangement but it turned out to be *ultra vires* the authority, the House of Lords held[7] that no question of any resulting (or constructive) trust could arise because the lender intended the borrower to become absolute beneficial owner of the loaned money free to use it as it wished. An intention, even if based upon a mistake, of X to transfer money to Y to be freely available for

---

20 *Smith v Cooke* [1891] AC 297. It is difficult, if not impossible, to reconcile this case with *Green v Wynn* (1869) 4 Ch App 204, which does not seem to have been quoted to their lordships. Lord Halsbury spoke, in his judgment, of it being the 'ordinary and familiar method in such cases to *express a resulting* trust on the fact of the instrument'. This, at first sight, seems to be inconsistent with the idea of a resulting trust; but doubtless his lordship used the phrase 'resulting trust', not in the narrow technical sense of an implied resulting trust, but in the wider original etymological sense, of a trust (whether express or implied) springing back, or resulting, to its creator.

1 *Wild v Banning* (1866) LR 2 Eq 577.
2 *King v Denison* (1813) 1 Ves & B 260; *Wood v Cox* (1837) 2 My & Cr 684.
3 *Tregonwell v Sydenham* (1815) 3 Dow 194.
4 *Croome v Croome* (1889) 61 LT 814; *Re West* [1900] 1 Ch 84.
5 [1922] 2 Ch 519; contrast the resulting trust in *Re West* [1900] 1 Ch 84.
6 [1979] 2 All ER 393, [1979] 1 WLR 247, CA.
7 *Westdeutsche Landesbank v Islington London Borough Council* [1996] AC 669, HL.

Y's purposes as absolute beneficial owner thereof is surely inconsistent with any proprietary trust relationship and should only give rise to a personal remedy or the working out of an equitable right to rescind[8].

Resulting trusts of voluntary contributions for assisting distressed individuals

It is sometimes a question of difficulty whether the balance of a fund formed by means of voluntary contributions for the relief of particular individuals (and therefore not falling within the legal conception of a charitable trust, in which latter case the presence of general charitable intention will exclude a resulting trust)[9], results pro rata to the contributors or not. In *Re Abbott's Trust*[10]: a fund had been subscribed for the maintenance of two distressed ladies, and on the death of the survivor, Stirling J held that the balance resulted to the subscribers. On the other hand, in *Re Andrew's Trust*[11]: where a fund had been subscribed solely for the education of the children of a distressed clergyman and 'not for equal division among them', Kekewich J held that when their education was completed there was no resulting trust of the balance, and that it was divisible equally among the children, on the ground that education was merely the special purpose assigned for the gift—the motive—and that the subscribers parted with all interest in the money when they gave it. This seems to be common sense, but the distinction between the two cases is somewhat fine and seems to consist only in the fact that the first fund was subscribed for the personal support of living ladies and not for the benefit of their next of kin, whereas in the second case the money was given for the benefit of living children generally with special reference to their education.

The fact that the fund was contributed by a large number of anonymous small donors does not prevent a resulting trust from arising in their favour or entitle the Treasury Solicitor to come in and claim the balance as bona vacantia. The trustees must in such a case pay the balance into court like any other trustee who cannot find his beneficiary[12].

---

8 [1996] AC 669 at 714 per Lord Browne-Wilkinson and Millett LJ's extra-curial comments in (1998) 114 LQR 399, 406–407, 416, both being critical of *Chase Manhattan Bank v Israel-British Bank (London) Ltd* [1981] Ch 105 (where Goulding J held the payer had an equitable proprietary interest in a second payment made in ignorance of the due payment having already been made).

9 See p 341, post.

10 [1900] 2 Ch 326 and *Re Sanderson's Trust* (1857) 3 K & J 497. Also see *Re British Red Cross Balkan Fund* [1914] 2 Ch 419, where in the absence of the Attorney-General a resulting trust was erroneously admitted: *Re Welsh Hospital (Netley)* [1921] 1 Ch 655 at 622; and *Re Customs and Excise Officers' Mutual Guarantee Fund* [1917] 2 Ch 18, in both of which a resulting trust was found. Where the balance of a mutual benevolent fund is returned to the subscribers those who have received benefits out of the fund must bring them into hotchpot (*Re Hobourn Aero Components Ltd's Air Raid Distress Fund* [1946] Ch 86, [1945] 2 All ER 711; affd [1946] Ch 194, [1946] 1 All ER 501, where this point was not raised). Society rules, nowadays, often provide for equal division amongst those who are members at the date of dissolution, irrespective of benefits earlier received: *Re Sick and Funeral Society of St John's Sunday School, Golcar* [1973] Ch 51, [1972] 2 All ER 439.

11 [1905] 2 Ch 48 at 52–53 applied in *Re Osoba* [1979] 2 All ER 393, [1979] 1 WLR 247, CA.

12 *Re Gillingham Bus Disaster Fund* [1958] Ch 300, [1958] 1 All ER 37; affd [1959] Ch 62, [1958] 2 All ER 749, CA, where this point was not under consideration.

Bona vacantia

Where a donor has parted with his money out and out in pursuance of some contract this normally suffices to prevent any resulting trust arising so that the money will either be owned according to the terms of the contract (eg the constitution of a members' club) or be bona vacantia.

Thus no resulting trust will arise where the donors part absolutely with their moneys for tickets contractually entitling them to participate in raffles, sweepstakes, beetle drives, whist drives, discotheques or to watch films or live entertainment, and the purposes for which the profits from such moneys have been used fail to exhaust the profits[13].

If the contractual element is absent then it is difficult where money is raised for certain purposes to show that the donors had a general intention to part with their money absolutely beyond all recall rather than merely to part with their money sub modo to the intent that only their particular purposes should be carried into effect. However, the modern trend where street collections are concerned with thousands of anonymous small donors is for the court to be increasingly ready to find a general intention to part with money absolutely beyond all recall so as to exclude any resulting trust[14]. In such a case if the purpose does not exhaust the money then the money will pass to the Crown as bona vacantia except where the purpose was charitable, so the property is applied cy-près (see p 341, post) or the money was paid to an unincorporated association which is not moribund (see p 340, post) 'when it will pass to the members according to the association's constitution'.

In *Davis v Richards & Wallington Industries Ltd*[15] Scott J held that the contractual origin of rights under a pension trust was not necessarily conclusive against a resulting trust in favour of the providers of the trust fund. The trust deed may expressly exclude a resulting trust or such might be implied in suitable circumstances. Thus, surplus funds where the employer's obligation was to top up employee's contractually fixed contribution if the trust fund was not adequate to provide benefits in full, were held on a resulting trust for the employer to the extent they represented its contributions. However, so far as the surplus reflected employee's contributions, Scott J surprisingly found that the employees impliedly intended to exclude any resulting trust in their favour so that their share of the surplus passed as bona vacantia to the Crown or would have done, but for the learned judge's prior holding that a defective deed executed after the pension trust scheme had been terminated was effective with its power to use surplus funds to augment members' benefits.

Scott J found[16] an implied intention to exclude a resulting trust because an intent to have a resulting trust would be unworkable (the value of individual's benefits being so various and involving complex calculations) and would give

---

13 *Re West Sussex Constabulary's Widows, Children and Benevolent (1930) Fund Trusts* [1971] Ch 1, [1970] 1 All ER 544. The funds came from (1) contributions of past and present members, (2) entertainments, raffles, sweepstakes, collecting boxes, (3) outside donations and legacies and Goff J held that (1) and (2) were bona vacantia though (3) were held on resulting trusts for the donors but it appears from *Re Buckinghamshire Constabulary Widows' and Orphans' Fund Friendly Society (No 2)* [1979] 1 All ER 623, [1979] 1 WLR 936 that all three sources of funds belonged to the society and so to the members of the society equally: see p 340, post.
14 *Re West Sussex Constabulary's Widows, Children and Benevolent (1930) Fund Trusts* [1971] Ch 1, [1970] 1 All ER 544; cf *Re Gillingham Bus Disaster Fund* [1958] Ch 300, [1958] 1 All ER 37.
15 [1991] 2 All ER 563.
16 [1991] 2 All ER 563 at 595.

the employees more than the maximum intended by Parliament in the statutory requirements for benefits under exempt approved schemes. Would these thoughts have entered the employees' minds? Would not they expect to be able to have worked out for them what each was entitled to and why should Parliament's intention provide evidence of the employees' intention?

A further criticism is that he accepted *Re West Sussex Constabulary's Widows Children and Benevolent Fund Trusts*[17] as authority for surplus moneys either passing as bona vacantia or on resulting trust without considering the third alternative preferred in *Re Buckinghamshire Constabulary Widows' and Orphans Fund Friendly Society*[18], namely, that the surplus should be divided between the members of an unincorporated society or by analogy between the employee contributors.

Lord Millett in *Air Jamaica Ltd v Charlton*[19] was critical of Scott J's opinion in *Davis v Richards & Wallington Industries Ltd* because he believed tax considerations should not distort legal principle and it seemed more likely that the employees lacked intentions (rather than being capable of having rather artificial intentions being inferred), lack of intention provoking the response of a resulting trust. For tax-relief reasons the trust deed stated, 'No moneys which at any time have been contributed by the Company under the terms hereof shall in any circumstances be repayable to the Company'. Despite this, Lord Millett, giving the Privy Councils reasons, held that this clause was not intended to cover what happened outside, rather, than within, the terms of the pension scheme. The surplus moneys upon the trust being void for perpetuity were[20] 'held on resulting trust for those who provided it ... contributions were payable by the Members with matching contributions by the Company ... the surplus must be treated as provided as to one half by the Company and as to one half by the Members'.

Lord Millett rejected the Jamaica Government's claim to the Members' half share as *bona vacantia*. The Members had not received what they had contracted for when the provisions as to surplus funds on discontinuance of the pension scheme were void for perpetuity. Their 200 million dollars half share should not be *bona vacantia* but should be divided proportionately among the Members and the estates of deceased Members in proportion to the contributions made by each Member, without regard to the benefits received by each of them and irrespective of the dates on which contributions were made.

Dissolution of clubs or societies

Where a members' club (viz a club existing for the members' own personal benefit) is dissolved it is now clear that resulting trust principles are of no application.

'Membership of a club or association is primarily a matter of contract. The members make their payments and in return they become entitled to the benefits of membership in accordance with the rules. The sums they pay cease to be their individual property and so cease to be subject to any concept of resulting trust. Instead, they become the property, through the trustees of the club or association,

17 [1971] Ch 1; [1970] 1 All ER 544.
18 [1979] 1 All ER 623; [1979] 1 WLR 936.
19 [1999] 1 WLR 1399.
20 [1999] 1 WLR 1399 at 1411.

of all the members for the time being, including themselves. A member who, by death or otherwise ceases to be a member thereby ceases to be part owner of any of the club's property: those who remain continue owners. If, then, dissolution ensues there must be a division of the property of the club or association among those alone who are owners of that property to the exclusion of former members.'[1]

Division will be to existing members equally per capita or, in the case of societies with rules contemplating advantages related to contributions, rateably per contributions, assuming no society rule (contractually binding all members) provides for surplus assets on a dissolution to be distributed in some other way[2].

Where a club is formed to benefit non-members (eg widows and orphans of members) the destination of surplus assets on a dissolution or when the substratum or purpose of the club no longer subsists is very probably the same as in the case of members' clubs since gifts to clubs, unless expressly on an endowment trust for the club[3], are construed as gifts to the current members by way of accrual to the property already held on a bare administrative trust for them according to the contractually binding rules of the club[4].

One must first deal with *Cunnack v Edwards*[5] where a society, formed to provide annuities for widows of deceased members, had surplus assets after the death of the last member and the last widow, and the assets were held to pass to the Crown as bona vacantia. Lord Halsbury and A L Smith LJ held there could be no resulting trust for members' personal representatives since the members in paying their subscriptions intended to part with their moneys out-and-out subject only to their collective power (unexercised) to change the society's rules for their own benefit subject to then existing contractual rights. Rigby LJ concerned himself with the Friendly Societies Act 1829 under which the society had been registered and which in his judgment required the society's rules expressly to provide for the surplus assets to pass to members if such was to happen, so that in default thereof the surplus had to pass as bona vacantia.

In *Re West Sussex Constabulary's Widows, Children and Benevolent (1930) Fund Trusts*[6] Goff J followed *Cunnack v Edwards* in holding that surplus funds (in the form of past and present members' subscriptions and the proceeds of entertainments, sweepstakes, raffles and collecting boxes) of a police fund for their widows and orphans passed to the Crown as bona vacantia subject to any existing contractual claims on the funds. He rejected the proprietary

---

1 *Re Sick and Funeral Society of St John's Sunday School, Golcar* [1973] Ch 51 at 59–60. Cf *Re Recher's Will Trusts* [1972] Ch 526 at 538–539.
2 *Re Sick and Funeral Society of St John's Sunday School, Golcar* [1973] Ch 51, [1972] 2 All ER 439; *Re St Andrew's Allotment Association Trusts* [1969] 1 All ER 147, [1969] 1 WLR 229; *Re William Denby & Sons Ltd Sick and Benevolent Fund* [1971] 2 All ER 1196, [1971] 1 WLR 973; *Re GKN Bolts and Nuts Ltd Sports and Social Club* [1982] 2 All ER 855, [1982] 1 WLR 774.
3 An endowment trust for the benefit of club members from time to time within a specified valid perpetuity period will need to be held by club officers separate from general assets of the club.
4 See pp 123–129, ante; *Re Recher's Will Trusts* [1972] Ch 526, [1971] 3 All ER 401; *Re Lipinski's Will Trusts* [1976] Ch 235, [1977] 1 All ER 33; *Universe Tankships Inc of Monrovia v International Transport Workers Federation* [1983] 1 AC 366, [1982] 2 All ER 67, HL; *Re Buckinghamshire Constabulary Widows' and Orphans' Fund Friendly Society (No 2)* [1979] 1 All ER 623, [1979] 1 WLR 936.
5 [1896] 2 Ch 679.
6 [1971] Ch 1, [1970] 1 All ER 544.

claim to the surplus funds of the members existing at the date of dissolution since the society was not a members' club.

In *Re Buckinghamshire Constabulary Widows and Orphans' Fund Friendly Society (No 2)*[7] Walton J distinguished the *West Sussex Constabulary* case but otherwise he would have refused to follow it.

He distinguished the case on the footing that he was concerned with a friendly society registered under the Friendly Societies Act 1896. Section 49(1) in his judgment ensured that, in the absence of any provision to the contrary in the society's rules, any assets belonged to the existing members subject only to any contractual rights created against the assets or to any trusts expressly declared of the assets.

Otherwise, he considered that *Cunnack v Edwards* hinged on the Friendly Societies Act 1829 or the fact that no surviving members existed when the society became defunct, whilst the *West Sussex Constabulary* case made an invalid distinction between members' club cases and other cases. After all, all cases of persons forming societies (whether members' clubs for social or sporting purposes, or societies establishing a widows and orphans fund or formed to obtain a separate Cornish Parliament or to further the advance of alchemy) involve a contract between the members whereunder the only persons interested in the society's property are the current members to the extent that no trusts thereof are expressly declared and no contractual rights therein are given to third parties. The members, subject to any such trusts or contractual rights, are in complete control of the society's property and can alter the society's rules and appropriate the property for themselves if they see fit[8]. Thus members in existence at the date of dissolution take the society's assets to the total exclusion of any bona vacantia claim by the Crown. Only if the society has become moribund with no existing members or only one member can the Crown claim the assets. This approach of Walton J seems more consistent with principle than the approach of Goff J in the *West Sussex Constabulary* case. It has the advantage of refusing to recognise any distinction between inward-looking and outward-looking clubs and of avoiding problems of distinguishing between members' club cases and friendly society and other cases: the uncertain questions of degree involved in ascertaining when a club or society is moribund are inevitable in all club cases.

Effect of liquidation or bankruptcy of debtor after creation of a voluntary arrangement for benefit of creditors

If the voluntary arrangement of a company's or individual's assets for the benefit of creditors does provide for what is to happen on liquidation or bankruptcy then effect must be given to such provision, but otherwise, the trust will continue notwithstanding the liquidation or bankruptcy and must take effect according to its terms[9] (subject to the exercise of *Saunders v Vautier* termination rights by all the beneficiaries acting unanimously). The creditor-

---

7 [1979] 1 All ER 623, [1979] 1 WLR 936. In *Re Buckinghamshire Constabulary Widows' and Orphans' Fund Friendly Society* [1978] 2 All ER 571, [1978] 1 WLR 641, Megarry V-C had already held that Friendly Societies Act 1896, s 79 (4), conferred no power to distribute surplus assets among those not entitled under the general law.

8 See also *Re Sick and Funeral Society of St John's Sunday School, Golcar* [1973] Ch 51 at 59–60; *Re Recher's Will Trusts* [1972] Ch 526 at 538–539; *Re Grant's Will Trusts* [1979] 3 All ER 359 at 365.

9 *Shierson v Tomlinson* [2002] EWCA Civ 404; [2002] 3 All ER 474.

beneficiaries can prove in the liquidation or bankruptcy for so much of their debt as remains after payment of what is recovered under the trust.

Resulting trusts of contributions to charitable funds

Once property has been given to a charitable institution or to trustees of charitable purpose trusts which are carried into effect (as opposed to failing at the outset due to insufficiency of funds, unavailability of an appropriate site or whatever) then the property is forever dedicated to charity, so that the property will be applied cy-près if the institution is subsequently dissolved or surplus funds are available after particular purposes have been effected. As Jenkins LJ remarked[10], 'once the charity for which the fund was raised had been effectively brought into action the fund was to be regarded as permanently devoted to charity to the exclusion of any resulting trust'.

Where there is initial failure of a charitable gift there is a resulting trust of contributions to a charitable fund if no general charitable intention was present[11]. Only if the property were given with a general charitable intention will the property be applicable cy-près.

Where the source of funds for charitable trusts that have failed at the outset has been the proceeds of cash collections or the profits from some lottery, competition, entertainment, sale, or similar money-raising activity special considerations arise. It is possible to treat cash put in a collecting box as an out and out gift made with a general charitable intention[12], so that cy-près application thereof is possible, or, more likely, as an out and out gift without any general charitable intention[13], so that it becomes bona vacantia, when the Crown usually waives its rights so that the money is applied cy-près. It is very unlikely, nowadays, that the cash will be treated as given only for a specific purpose so that on failure of such purpose it will be held on resulting trust for the donor[14] (who, of course, almost invariably will be anonymous). Profits from money-raising activities cannot possibly be held on resulting trust for the subscribers who will have received their contractual consideration[15]: such profits will be bona vacantia allowed by the Crown to be applied cy-près.

Before the above principles became clear s 14 of the Charities Act 1960 (now 1993) tried to deal with the problems of cash collections and profits from money- raising activities by treating a general charitable intention as present so that the property could be applied cy-près. However, the section

---

10 *Re Ulverston and District New Hospital Building Trusts* [1956] Ch 622 at 637, CA endorsing *Re Wokingham Fire Brigade Trusts* [1951] Ch 373, [1951] 1 All ER 454; and see also *Re Cooper's Conveyance* [1956] 3 All ER 28, [1956] 1 WLR 1096. It is thus unnecessary for courts to exclude a resulting trust by finding (as they did in *Re Welsh Hospital (Netley) Fund* [1921] 1 Ch 655; *Re North Devon and West Somerset Relief Fund Trusts* [1953] 2 All ER 1032, [1953] 1 WLR 1260; *Re British School of Egyptian Archaeology* [1954] 1 All ER 887, [1954] 1 WLR 546) that the subscribers intended to give their money outright under a general charitable intention, so that the property may be applied cy-près.
11 *Re University of London Medical Sciences Institute Fund* [1909] 2 Ch 1, CA.
12 *Re Hillier* [1954] 2 All ER 59, [1954] 1 WLR 700, CA.
13 *Re Ulverston and District New Hospital Building Trusts* [1956] Ch 622, [1956] 3 All ER 164, CA.
14 *Re West Sussex Constabulary's Widows, Children and Benevolent (1930) Fund Trusts* [1971] Ch 1, [1970] 1 All ER 544.
15 *Re West Sussex Constabulary's Widows, Children and Benevolent (1930) Fund Trusts* [1971] Ch 1, [1970] 1 All ER 544.

only applies[16] 'where any difficulty in applying property to charitable purposes makes that property or the part not applicable cy-près available to be
returned to the donors', presumably by virtue of a resulting trust. There thus
seems hardly any scope for s 14 to apply, but this scarcely matters since the
cash collections or the profits from the money-raising activities will, in any
event, be applicable cy-près.

Quistclose trusts of money

Where L lends money to B (or to T on behalf of B) for a specific purpose in
sufficiently certain terms for a court to adjudge whether or not that purpose
can be, or has been, carried out and where B (or T) is bound in equity not to
treat the money as beneficially owned by B (or T) but to be kept apart to be
used only for the specific purpose[17] then, on the money being applied for
that purpose, L only has a personal remedy in debt[18]. Otherwise, the money
from the outset is held on a resulting trust for the lender. It will depend on
the terms of the contract whether B (or T) has a power or, in some circumstances, a duty to apply the money for the specific purpose and whether
the power or duty ceases when the purpose becomes incapable of achievement or when a specified period has elapsed or when L countermands his
mandate.

Evidence not admissible where donee is trustee and not a beneficiary on face of settlement

In *Re Rees' Will Trusts*[19] the testator bequeathed his residuary estate to his
'trustees absolutely, they well knowing my wishes concerning the same.'
Before signing his will the testator had orally communicated to the trustees
certain wishes which he desired them to implement, but which were not
sufficient to exhaust the residuary estate and told them that any surplus was
to be retained by them for their own benefit. It was held that the gift having
been made to the trustees the oral evidence that they were intended to take
some part beneficially must be disregarded and the surplus, after implementing the testator's other wishes, must be held on trust for the testator's
statutory next of kin.

The Court of Appeal distinguished *Irvine v Sullivan*[20]. There the testator
appointed A, B and C as trustees and gave them his property on trust for sale.
Then he gave the residue to D the lady to whom he was betrothed 'trusting
she will carry out my wishes with regard to the same with which she is fully
acquainted', and it was held that D was beneficially entitled to the surplus
remaining after satisfying the purposes communicated to her by the testator.
After all trustees, of whom D was not one, were appointed to carry out the

---

16 Section 14(5) of the 1960 Act and s 14(7) of the 1993 Act; see D Wilson [1983] Conv 40.
17 *Twinsectra Ltd v Yardley* [2002] UKHL 12, [2002] 2 All ER 377 explaining *Barclays Bank v Quistclose Investments Ltd* [1970] AC 567, HL; see pp 12 and 117, ante.
18 It would seem that the principle can extend to a gift of money to buy specific equipment so
   that once such equipment has been bought the gift is completely constituted and the money
   irrecoverable, but, until then, there is a resulting trust for the intending donor.
19 [1950] Ch 204, [1949] 2 All ER 1003; followed in *Re Pugh's Will Trusts* [1967] 3 All ER 337,
   [1967] 1 WLR 1262, distinguished in *Re Tyler's Fund Trusts* [1967] 3 All ER 389, [1967] 1 WLR
   1269. A trust deed may expressly confer beneficial interests on trustees.
20 (1869) LR 8 Eq 673.

trusts, and D who was engaged to be married to the testator was the sort of person for whom one would assume he would wish to provide so that D did not take as trustee on the face of the will.

Evidence admissible in other cases

Where a person purchased sums of stock in the names of herself and the son of her daughter-in-law, parol evidence was admitted to rebut the presumption of a resulting trust (see Article 31, post) because there was nothing to show on the face of the instrument that the son of the daughter-in-law was merely a trustee. James LJ said:

> 'Where the Court of Chancery is asked, *on an equitable assumption of presumption*, to take away from a man that which by the common law of the land he is entitled to, he surely has a right to say: "Listen to my story as to how I came to have it, and judge that story with reference to all the surrounding facts and circumstances".'[1]

So evidence is admissible to rebut the legal presumption as to part only—for instance, to prove that the donee was intended to take a *life interest*, although there is a resulting trust as to the remainder; and vice versa[2].

ARTICLE 30

Resulting trusts arising where trusts declared illegal

When a person has intentionally created an executed trust[3] for an illegal consideration or purpose which therefore fails, then a resulting trust will only be implied in favour of the settlor if:

(a) he voluntarily withdrew from the illegal purpose before it was wholly or partly carried into execution[4]; or

(b) he does not have to disclose the illegal purpose in order to rebut the presumption of advancement but can simply rely on the presumption of resulting trust arising on the transfer or purchase of property[5], it being irrelevant whether or not the illegal purpose had been wholly or partly carried into effect[6]; or

(c) the effect of allowing the trustee to retain the property might be to

---

1 *Fowkes v Pascoe* (1875) 10 Ch App 343 at 349.
2 *Lane v Dighton* (1762) Amb 409; *Rider v Kidder* (1805) 10 Ves 360; *Benbow v Townsend* (1833) 1 My & K 506; *London and County Banking Co v London and River Plate Bank* (1888) 21 QBD 535 at 542, CA; *Re Blake* (1889) 60 LT 663.
3 Where an illegal trust (or contract) is executory it simply cannot be enforced: *Tinsley v Milligan* [1994] 1 AC 340, [1993] 3 All ER 65, HL.
4 *Tribe v Tribe* [1996] Ch 107 at 135, no genuine repentance being required; *Symes v Hughes* (1870) LR 9 Eq 475; *Childers v Childers* (1857) 1 De G & J 482; *Davies v Otty (No 2)* (1865) 35 Beav 208; *Birch v Blagrave* (1755) Amb 264; *Platamone v Staple* (1815) Coop G 250.
5 *Tinsley v Milligan* [1993] [1994] 1 AC 340, 3 All ER 65, HL, applied in *Silverwood v Silverwood* (1997) 74 P & CR 453, CA; *Macdonald v Myerson* [2001] EWCA Civ 66, [2001] NPC 20; and *Lowson v Coombes* [1999] Ch 373, CA.
6 *Gorog v Kiss* (1977) 78 DLR (3d) 690 endorsed by *Tinsley v Milligan* [1994] 1 AC 340 at 376; and *Tribe v Tribe* [1996] Ch 107 at 111 per Nourse LJ.

effectuate an unlawful object, to defeat a legal prohibition, or to protect a fraud[7].

Conveyance to qualify for game licence

Thus where a father granted land to his son, in order to give him a colourable qualification to shoot game under the old game laws, and without any intention of conferring any beneficial interest upon him, the court would not enforce any resulting trust in favour of the father, for he and the son were in pari delicto, and there was no detriment to the public in allowing the son to retain the estate[8]. Of course, if there had been no illegality (if, for instance, a bare legal estate had been a sufficient qualification), there would have been a resulting trust[9].

Settlement for illegal consideration

In *Ayerst v Jenkins*[10] a widower, two days before going through the ceremony of marriage with his deceased wife's sister (which ceremony was invalid under the law then in force and was known so to be by both parties), executed a settlement reciting that he was desirous of making a provision for the lady, and had transferred certain shares into the names of trustees, upon the trusts thereinafter declared, being the separate and inalienable use of the lady during her life, and after for her death as she should by deed or will appoint. They afterwards lived together as man and wife until the widower's death. Some time afterwards, his personal representatives instituted a suit to set aside the settlement, on the ground that it was founded on an immoral consideration, being to secure her future cohabitation with him.

Lord Selborne, however, said:

'Relief is sought by the representative, not merely of a particeps criminis, but of a voluntary and sole donor, on the naked ground of the illegality of his own intention and purpose; and that, not against a bond or covenant or other obligation resting in fieri, but against a completed transfer of specific chattels, by which the legal estate in those chattels was absolutely vested in trustees ... for the sole benefit of the defendant. I know of no doctrine of public policy which requires, or authorises, a court of equity to give assistance to such a plaintiff under such circumstances. When the immediate and direct effect of an estoppel in equity against relief to a particular plaintiff might be *to effectuate an unlawful object, or to defeat a legal prohibition, or to protect a fraud*, such an estoppel may well be regarded as against public policy. But the voluntary gift of part of his own property by one particeps criminis to another, is

---

7 See per Lord Selborne in *Ayerst v Jenkins* (1873) LR 16 Eq 275 at 283; and see per Knight-Bruce LJ in *Reynell v Sprye* (1852) 1 De Gm & G 660, where he said: 'Where the parties are not *in pari delicto*, and where public policy is considered as advanced by allowing either party, or at least the more excusable of the two, to sue for relief, relief is given to him'. And see also, to same effect, *Law v Law* (1735) 3 P Wms 391, and *Lord St John v Lady St John* (1803) 11 Ves 526. Confiscation of the proceeds of crime is now a possibility under the Criminal Justice Act 1988 as amended by the Criminal Justice Act 1993, Pt III or the Proceeds of Crime Acts 1995 and 2002, or the Anti-terrorism, Crime and Security Act 2001.

8 *Brackenbury v Brackenbury* (1820) 2 Jac & W 391. See also *Chettiar v Chettiar* [1962] AC 294, [1962] 1 All ER 494, PC, where a Malayan father conveyed 40 acres of his 139 acres of rubber land to his son in order to evade certain regulations which applied to those who owned more than 100 acres. In order to rebut the presumption of advancement the father had to disclose his illegal purpose, and the court refused to declare a resulting trust.

9 *Childers v Childers* (1857) 1 De G & J 482.

10 (1873) LR 16 Eq 275.

in itself neither fraudulent nor prohibited by law; and the present is not the case of a man repenting of an immoral purpose before it is too late, and seeking to recall, while the object is yet unaccomplished[11], a gift intended as a bribe to iniquity. If public policy is opposed (as it is) to vice and immorality, it is no less true, as was said by Lord Truro in *Benyon v Nettlefold*[12], that the law, in sanctioning the defence of "*particeps criminis*", does so "on the grounds of public policy, namely, that those who violate the law must not apply to the law for protection".'

In *Phillips v Probyn*[13], North J distinguished *Ayerst v Jenkins* on the ground that in the case before him the settlement was made *in consideration* of a contemplated and then invalid *marriage* with a deceased wife's sister, and that there was a total failure of consideration. It is, however, humbly submitted that the settlement in *Ayerst v Jenkins* was also made in contemplation of, and as part of, the arrangements consequent on such a marriage, and that there is really no valid distinction between the two cases. In the very changed social and sexual climate today courts will be very averse to find a transaction tainted with illegality because in consideration of future immoral cohabitation: at the least a court is likely to find a valid consideration severable from the immoral consideration[14].

Moreover in *Tinsley v Milligan*[15] it seems that a trust set up for an illegal consideration is valid and enforceable by any beneficiary unless the beneficiary needs to lead evidence of the illegality to establish his claim. It seems he will only need to lead evidence of the declaration of trusts and of the acquisition of trust property by the trustee and so always be able to enforce the trust.

Fraudulent conveyance

But where an illegal purpose is only contemplated, there is a locus poenitentiae[16]. Thus, in *Symes v Hughes*[17] the plaintiff, being in pecuniary difficulties, assigned certain leasehold property to a trustee with a view to defeating his creditors. Two and a half years afterwards he was adjudicated bankrupt, but obtained the sanction of his creditors to an arrangement by which his estate was revested in him, he covenanting to prosecute a suit for the recovery of the assigned property, and to pay a composition to two-and-sixpence in the pound to his creditors, in case his suit should prove successful.

Lord Romilly MR in delivering judgment, said:

'Where the purpose for which the assignment was given is not carried into execution, and nothing is done under it, the mere intention to effect an illegal object when the assignment was executed does not deprive the assignor of his right to recover the property from the assignee who has given no consideration for it.'

---

11 As in *Symes v Hughes* (1870) LR 9 Eq 475.
12 (1850) 3 Mac & G 94 at 102.
13 [1899] 1 Ch 811.
14 See *Chitty on Contracts* (25th edn) para 1085 and *Tanner v Tanner* [1975] 3 All ER 776, [1975] 1 WLR 1346, CA.
15 See [1994] 1 AC 340 at 373, per Lord Browne-Wilkinson and *Ayerst v Jenkins* (1873) LR 16 Eq 275 at 283–284. Also see Law Com CP No 154 'Illegal Transactions', para 3.54.
16 *Chettiar v Chettiar* [1962] AC 294 at 302, PC; *Perpetual Executors and Trustees Association of Australia Ltd v Wright* (1917) 23 CLR 185 (Aust HC); *Martin v Martin* (1959) 110 CLR 297 (Aust HC; *Tinsley v Milligan* [1994] 1 AC 340, [1993] 3 All ER 65, HL.
17 (1870) LR 9 Eq 475. Contrast *Chettiar v Chettiar* [1962] AC 294, [1962] 1 All ER 494, PC.

So, again in *Davies v Otty*[18] the plaintiff, being apprehensive of an indictment for bigamy (conviction for which then involved forfeiture of property), conveyed his real estate to the defendant, on a parol agreement to re-transfer when the difficulty should have passed over. It subsequently transpired that the plaintiff was not liable to be indicted, and thereupon he filed a bill praying for a re-transfer of his property.

It was held, that although there was no enforceable express trust (inasmuch as there was no written proof of it), yet there was a resulting trust to which the statute did not apply; and as there was no illegality in fact, but only in intention, the court ordered the transfer prayed for.

Similarly in *Tribe v Tribe*[19] the claimant father transferred his major shareholding in a company to his son to deceive his creditors and protect his assets. In the event he did not have to carry out repairs as tenant of property used by his company and the need to deceive his creditors did not arise. He claimed to recover the shares from his son who refused to return them. The Court of Appeal held he could lead evidence of his illegal purpose to rebut the presumption of advancement. No genuine repentance was needed, it being sufficient to withdraw voluntarily from the illegal transaction when it had ceased to be needed.

Spouses' fraudulent designs

In *Gascoigne v Gascoigne*[20] a husband transferred land into his wife's name solely in order to protect the land from his existing and future creditors and tax was paid on the basis the land belonged to his wife, but it was held he could not succeed in his claim that she held the land not for herself but on trust for him. He could not be allowed to rebut the presumption that he had made an advancement or gift in his wife's favour by producing evidence of his fraudulent design even though his wife was a party to it. Similarly in *Re Emery's Investment Trust*[1] where a husband had registered some American securities in his wife's name, though it was intended that she should hold them in trust for herself and him in equal shares, evidence to this effect so as to rebut the presumption of advancement was not allowed when the rationale and effect of the transaction was to evade American withholding tax in respect of the husband's half share.

These cases were approved in *Tinker v Tinker*[2] where a husband on purchasing the matrimonial home had it conveyed into his wife's name to protect it from creditors if his new garage business failed.

'As against his wife he wants to say that it belongs to him. As against his creditors that it belongs to her. That simply will not do. The presumption is that it was

---

18 *Davies v Otty (No 2)* (1865) 35 Beav 208. See also *Sekhon v Alissa* [1989] 2 FLR 94, [1989] Fam Law 355 (where a mother recovered a share in her house conveyed into her daughter's name where her alleged purpose of capital gains tax evasion had not been carried out because the house had not been sold) and *Rowan v Dann* (1991) 64 P & CR 202, CA (where R, who had granted a lease to D with a view to a joint venture with D and to prejudicing R's creditors recovered the property by way of resulting trust when the joint venture failed to materialise and no creditors had been prejudiced).

19 [1996] Ch 107 [1995] 4 All ER 236. No recovery where purpose effectuated: *Collier v Collier* [2002] EWCA Civ 1095.

20 [1918] 1 KB 223; *Elford v Elford* (1922) 69 DLR 284.

1 [1959] Ch 410, [1959] 1 All ER 577.

2 [1970] P 136, [1970] 1 All ER 540 applied to man and mistress in *Cantor v Cox* (1975) 239 Estates Gazette 121. See also *Lowson v Lowson* [1999] Ch 373, CA.

conveyed to her for her own use, and he does not rebut the presumption by saying that he only did it to defeat his creditors.'[3]

Where property is purchased in the wife's name to avoid tax or defeat creditors the husband has to face the argument that since the design could not honestly be achieved unless the equitable beneficial ownership was conferred with the legal title on the wife the presumption is strengthened that it was so conferred.

Perhaps, mention should be made of *Heseltine v Heseltine*[4] where a husband persuaded his wealthy wife to transfer £20,000 to him in order to enable him to become a 'name' at Lloyd's and to transfer £40,000 to him to save estate duty if she predeceased him.

'The wife here has done no wrong. She only did what her husband asked her. That should not be taken against her. The court can and should impute a trust by him for her.'[5]

However, in imputing this trust the Court of Appeal seem to have been imposing a constructive trust on the ground that it would be inequitable to allow the husband to deny the wife the equitable interest in the sums. This would certainly have been the case if the husband had exercised undue influence but otherwise it is difficult to justify a constructive trust in favour of the wife so permitting her to trace the moneys and preferring her over the general creditors of the husband. A resulting trust would seem to be out of the question since the spouses knew that the husband could only become a 'name' at Lloyd's if the beneficial interest passed to him and estate duty could only be saved if the beneficial interest passed to him.

Recently in *Lowson v Coombes*[6] the claimant and his mistress together bought a house in the mistress' name to defeat claims of the claimant's wife if divorcing him, under s 37 of the Matrimonial Causes Act 1973. There was no room for any presumption of advancement as in *Tinker v Tinker*, so the claimant could rely on a resulting trust, the defendant holding the house on resulting trust for herself and the claimant in equal shares.

Crucial significance of presumption of advancement

In *Tinsley v Milligan*[7] two females, T and M, jointly purchased a house which they registered only in T's name to enable M, with the knowledge and assent of T, to make false social security benefit claims for the benefit of both of them cohabiting as lovers. On M claiming half the house, their Lordships held 3:2 in M's favour on the basis that an equitable interest under a resulting trust was presumed to arise in favour of M without the need for M to rely in any way on the underlying illegality. Lord Browne-Wilkinson for the majority emphasised, however, that if a presumption of advancement arises where A has transferred property to B (eg A being the husband or father of

---

3 *Tinker v Tinker* [1970] P 136 at 141, [1970] 1 All ER 540 at 542, per Lord Denning MR.
4 [1971] 1 All ER 952, [1971] 1 WLR 342. See (1973) Current Legal Problems 17 (A J Oakley); (1971) 115 Sol Jo 614 (S Cretney).
5 [1971] 1 All ER 952 at 955. Such broad approach has now been overridden by a stricter approach; *Grant v Edwards* [1986] Ch 638; *Lloyds Bank plc v Rosset* [1991] 1 AC 107.
6 [1999] Ch 373, CA.
7 [1994] 1 AC 340, [1993] 3 All ER 65. M had made her peace with the Department of Social Security, having told it what she had done; T had been prosecuted convicted and fined and had had to make some repayments to the Department.

B) then A will need to rebut the presumption by leading evidence of the true purpose of the transfer and if such purpose be illegal then he cannot plead it, so that the property will remain with B and A's claim will fail:

> 'A party to an illegality can recover by virtue of a legal or equitable property interest if, but only if, he can establish his title without relying on his own illegality. In cases where the presumption of advancement applies, the plaintiff is faced with the presumption of gift and therefore cannot claim under a resulting trust unless and until he has rebutted that presumption of gift: for those purposes the plaintiff does have to rely on the underlying illegality and therefore fails.'[8]

Hitherto, it had been of little relevance whether the presumption of resulting trust or the presumption of advancement applied because a consideration of all the circumstances would normally reduce the presumptions to insignificance. Thus the courts did not have to decide whether in the modern socio-economic context the presumption of advancement for transfer from husband to wife and father to child should equally apply to transfers from wife to husband and mother to child[9].

Reliance on resulting trust after carrying out illegal purpose

As Nourse LJ has pointed out[10], 'It is inherent in [*Tinsley v Milligan*] that it makes no difference whether or not the illegal purpose has been carried into effect, as it clearly had been in that case'. Thus, once the coast is clear and the transferor has defrauded his creditors etc., he can recover his property simply by relying on a resulting trust if there is no applicable presumption of advancement. Such iniquitous result led Millett LJ to suggest that if X transfers property to his nephew N to conceal it from creditors and, then, settles with his creditors on the basis he owns no interest in the property, then 'the transferor's own conduct would be inconsistent with the retention of any beneficial interest in the property', so there should be no resulting trust for him. However, this suggestion seems inconsistent with *Tinsley v Milligan* where Miss Milligan had dealt with the DHSS on the basis she had no ownership of the house owned by Miss Tinsley and where *Gorog v Kiss*[11] was endorsed.

Statutory reform seems necessary to remedy the arbitrariness and lack of any convincing rationale for the current legal position[12].

Claimants through transferor or settlor

If the transferor or settlor cannot recover then his personal representative should be in no better position[13] even though not personally in delicto. His trustee in bankruptcy should be in no better position unless public policy

---

8 [1993] 3 All ER 65 at 90 and 148; see further N Enonchong (1995) 111 LQR 135 at 148–155.
9 See p 362, post.
10 *Tribe v Tribe* [1996] Ch 107 at 111.
11 (1977) 78 DLR (3d) 690, Ontario CA.
12 See Law Com CP No 154 'Illegal Transactions: The Effect of Illegality on Contracts and Trusts' and N Enonchong, 'Illegal Transactions: The Future' [2000] RLR 82 at 99–104.
13 *Ayerst v Jenkins* (1873) LR 16 Eq 275 at 281 per Lord Selborne LC: the contrary view of Lord Eldon in *Muckleston v Brown* (1801) 6 Ves 52 at 68 seems unsound in principle.

considerations dictate otherwise[14], despite the availability of statutory provisions in the Insolvency Act 1986.

Attempt to evade rule against perpetuities or accumulations

There will also be a resulting trust where otherwise the illegal object might be attained. Thus, where a settlor attempts to settle property so as to infringe the law against perpetuities, the offending trusts will not only not be carried into effect, but the person nominated to carry them out will be held to be a mere trustee for the settlor or his representatives. This is because the attempt must have been made either through ignorance or carelessness, or else with a direct intention to contravene the law. In the former case, as there would be no delictum, the usual maxim would not apply. In the latter, equity would not allow the trustee to retain the property, and so put it in his power to carry out the illegal intention of the testator, and to defeat the policy of the law[15]. So where the settlor directs accumulations beyond the statutory period, there is a resulting trust between the end of the 21 years and the period for which the accumulations were directed[16].

ARTICLE 31

Resulting trusts where purchase made in another's name or property voluntarily transferred to another

(1) When real or personal property[17] is conveyed to a purchaser jointly with others, or to one or more persons other than the purchaser, a resulting trust will be presumed in favour of the person who is proved (by parol[18] or other evidence) to have paid the purchase-money[19] in the character of purchaser (as opposed to that of donor or lender)[20].

(2) This presumption may easily be rebutted:

(a) by parol[1] or other evidence that the purchaser intended to benefit the others; or

(b) by the fact that the person in whom the property was vested was

---

14 Cf *Trautwein v Richardson* [1946] ALR 129 at 134 per Dixon J; *Ayerst v Jenkins* (1873) LR 16 Eq 275 at 283.

15 *Carrick v Errington* (1726) 2 P Wms 361; *Tregonwell v Sydenham* (1815) 3 Dow 194; *Gibbs v Rumsey* (1813) 2 Ves & B 294.

16 *Re Travis* [1900] 2 Ch 541, CA.

17 *Dyer v Dyer* (1788) 2 Cox Eq Cas 92; *Ebrand v Dancer* (1680) 2 Cas in Ch 26; *Wheeler v Smith* (1859) 1 Giff 300.

18 *Ryall v Ryall* (1739) 1 Atk 59; *Lench v Lench* (1805) 10 Ves 511; *Rochefoucauld v Boustead* [1897] 1 Ch 196.

19 *Dyer v Dyer* (1788) 2 Cox Eq Cas 92; *Wray v Steele* (1814) 2 Ves & B 388.

20 *Rochefoucauld v Boustead* [1897] 1 Ch 196.

1 *Rider v Kidder* (1805) 10 Ves 360; *Standing v Bowring* (1885) 31 Ch D 282. The onus is on the grantee to prove the purchase-money-provider intended to be a donor if alleging this: *Seldon v Davidson* [1968] 2 All ER 755, CA.

the lawful[2] wife[3] or fiancée[4] or child of the purchaser[5] or was some person towards whom he stood in loco parentis[6], or, it seems nowadays[7], was the lawful husband or fiancée or child or some other person to whom a female purchaser stood in loco parentis, or was trustee of a settlement by which he previously settled property[8].

In any of these cases a prima facie (but rebuttable)[9] presumption will arise that the purchaser intended the ostensible grantee or grantees to take beneficially, or, in the last mentioned case, upon the trusts of the settlement in question.

(3) Similar principles apply to voluntary transfers of property except to the extent that section 60 (3) of the Law of Property Act 1925 alters the position concerning land[10].

PARAGRAPH 1

Where purchase-money contributed by two persons

Where the purchase-money is contributed, partly by the person in whose name the property is taken, and partly by another, then, if they contribute it in equal shares, they will (in the absence of evidence or circumstances showing a contrary intention[11]) take as joint tenants, because the advance being equal the interest is equal; but if in unequal shares, then a trust results to each of them of an undivided share in proportion to his advance[12] where

---

2 See *Re Scottish Equitable Life Assurance Society (Policy No 6402)* [1902] 1 Ch 282.
3 *Re Eykyn* (1877) 6 Ch D 115; *Drew v Martin* (1864) 2 Hem & M 130; *Calverley v Green* (1984) 56 ALR 483 (Aust HC); *Re Condrin* [1914] 1 IR 89.
4 *Mossop v Mossop* [1989] Fam 77, [1988] 2 All ER 202, Law Reform (Miscellaneous Provisions) Act 1970, s 2(1).
5 *Soar v Foster* (1858) 4 K & J 152; *Beckford v Beckford* (1774) Lofft 490; *Webb v Webb* [1992] 1 All ER 17 at 27.
6 *Beckford v Beckford* (1774) Lofft 490; *Current v Jago* (1844) 1 Coll 261; *Tucker v Burrow* (1865) 2 Hem & M 515; *Forrest v Forrest* (1865) 13 WR 380; *Re Paradise Motor Co Ltd* [1968] 1 WLR 1125.
7 *Brown v Brown* (1993) 31 NSWLR 582 at 591 CA (mother and child); *Nelson v Nelson* (1995) 184 CLR 538 (mother and child); *Calverley v Green* (1984) 155 CLR 242, 268–269; *Dullow v Dullow* [1985] 3 NSWLR 531 at 536 and European Convention on Human Rights Seventh Protocol, Art 5.
8 *Re Curteis* (1872) LR 14 Eq 217; *Muggeridge v Stanton* (1859) 1 De GF & J 107.
9 *Tumbridge v Care* (1871) 19 WR 1047; *Williams v Williams* (1863) 32 Beav 370; *Westdeutsche Landesbank v Islington London Borough Council* [1996] AC 669 at 708. On the other hand, if there is actual evidence of a gift, this solves the issue before any recourse needs to be made to the long-stop of a resulting trust, as emphasised by E Simpson in P Birks and F Rose *Restitution and Equity Vol 1, Resulting Trusts and Equitable Compensation* (2000) LLP, Chapter 1.
10 As to personal estate see *Vandervell v IRC* [1967] 2 AC 291, [1967] 1 All ER 1, and per Cotton LJ in *Standing v Bowring* (1885) 31 Ch D 282; and per Jessel MR in *Fowkes v Pascoe* (1875) 10 Ch App 343.
11 See *Robinson v Preston* (1858) 4 K & J 505; *Edwards v Fashion* (1712) Prec Ch 332; *Lake v Gibson* (1729) 1 Eq Cas Abr 290; *Bone v Pollard* (1857) 24 Beav 283; Megarry and Wade: *Law of Real Property* (6th edn) para 9–022; *Delehunt v Carmody* (1986) 161 CLR 464.
12 *Lake v Gibson* (1729) 1 Eq Cas Abr 290; *Rigden v Vallier* (1751) 3 Atk 731; *Crisp v Mullings* (1975) 239 Estates Gazette 119, CA; *Re Densham (a bankrupt)* [1975] 3 All ER 726, [1975] 1 WLR 1519; *Pettit v Pettit* [1970] AC 777 at 814.

this can be calculated with reasonable certainty[13]. Since undivided shares in land can now only take effect behind a trust[14] persons contributing to the purchase of land conveyed to one of them are equitable tenants in common, so that each is entitled concurrently with the other to possession of the land and use and enjoyment of it in a proper manner[15].

Payments of an income (as opposed to capital) nature for the use of property, eg rent and bills for everyday living expenses do not give the payer any interest in the property. Thus in *Savage v Dunningham*[16], where a tenancy agreement was in the name of the defendant, who had the plaintiffs living with him sharing the rent and other day-to-day expenses, it was held that no resulting trust arose in favour of the plaintiffs so as to enable them to have an interest in the freehold reversion which the defendant subsequently purchased.

Title taken in one name

At the time when property is bought[17] by A and B in the name of A the parties are presumed to intend that they are to obtain the share that they then paid for in the absence of any evidence in A's favour of gift or the application of an unrebutted presumption of advancement[18] and in the absence of an express written declaration of trust[19]. Thus, if the property cost £100,000 and A paid £60,000 and B paid £40,000 the property will be held by A on resulting trust for A and B in the proportions 3:2. The position will be the same if the property is worth £100,00 but a discount worth £60,000 is allowed to A as sitting tenant so that A only needs to pay the £40,000 provided by B[20], so long as A and B intended each to have some beneficial interest rather than A, as B's aged mother, intending to gift the benefit of her discount to B[1]. The position remains the same if A, as legal owner, mortgages the legal title in order to provide his £60,000 contribution[2]. A's and B's equitable interests under resulting trusts are fixed at the time they purchased the property by paying the purchase price. They get the shares they paid for when they

13 *Diwell v Farnes* [1959] 2 All ER 379, [1959] 1 WLR 624, CA and *Finch v Finch* (1975) 119 Sol Jo 793, CA indicating that where precise quantification is impossible it seems that the principle is that 'Equity delighteth in equality' though reliance on this should be a last resort: *Gissing v Gissing* [1971] AC 886 at 897 and 903, HL.

14 Law of Property Act 1925, s 34(1); Settled Land Act 1925, s 36(4), as amended by the Trusts of Land and Appointment of Trustees Act 1996, Schs 2 and 3.

15 *Bull v Bull* [1955] 1 QB 234, [1955] 1 All ER 253, CA; *Jones v Jones* [1977] 2 All ER 231, [1977] 1 WLR 438, CA; *Williams & Glyn's Bank v Boland* [1981] AC 487, subject to the Trusts of Land and Appointment of Trustees Act 1996, ss 12 and 13.

16 [1974] Ch 181, [1973] 3 All ER 429.

17 *The Venture* [1908] P 218 at 230; *Gissing v Gissing* [1971] AC 886 at 897, 900, 905; *Bernard v Joseph's* [1982] Ch 391 at 404; and the approach of the Court of Appeal in *Huntingford v Hobbs* [1993] 1 FLR 736, 24 HLR 65; *Springette v Defoe* (1992) 65 P & CR 1, 24 HLR 552; *Sekhon v Alissa* [1989] 2 FLR 94.

18 See pp 361–367, post.

19 *Goodman v Gallant* [1986] Fam 106, [1986] 1 All ER 311, CA; *Turton v Turton* [1988] Ch 542, [1987] 2 All ER 641, CA.

20 *Springette v Defoe* (1992) 65 P & CR 1, 24 HLR 552 CA; *Abbey National Building Society v Cann* (1989) 57 P & CR 381, CA.

1 *Ashe v Mumford* (2000) 33 HLR 756 at 769 (para 50), a declaration of trust by A of holding on trust for herself for life, remainder to B's son, C and a surrender of A's life interest being disregarded by the Court of Appeal as shams, A and C fronting B's transactions (paras 19 and 54).

2 *Huntingford v Hobbs* [1993] 1 FLR 736, 24 HLR 65, CA.

provided the purchase price[3], whether by way of their own cash (whether saved, inherited, or borrowed on mortgage) or a discount arising from their status. Exceptionally, it seems that if at the time of purchase A and B agreed that B would undertake responsibility for the mortgage payments, then A will hold on resulting trust for B as to the proportion of the price provided by the mortgage, equity regarding as done that which has to be done by B[4]. It also seems that capital acquisition costs like legal fees, survey fees and stamp duties should be treated as part of the cost of purchase as for capital gains tax[5].

If B did not contribute to the cost of purchase when the property was bought on mortgage by A, but subsequently provides £10,000 whether towards discharging A's mortgage liability for capital moneys or in paying for a capital improvement like a conservatory, this is regarded as a gift and will not confer on B a one-tenth or other proportionate share in the property[6] unless an agreement with A or a representation by A enables B to claim an equitable interest under a common intention constructive trust or proprietary estoppel principles. The position is *a fortiori* if B's £10,000 happens to represent periodic contributions to interest due under the mortgage or to premiums on the endowment policy that on maturity will ensure that the capital moneys due under the mortgage will be repaid. Lax use of language and confusion between resulting and constructive trusts has, however, led some judges to treat subsequent mortgage payments as giving rise to resulting trusts rather than constructive trusts or proprietary estoppel interests.

Where A purchases property in the name of a company or trust controlled by him the normal natural inference is that beneficial ownership was inten-

---

3 See 'Constructive trusts and unjust enrichment' (1996) 10 Trust LI 98 at 100 where Browne-Wilkinson VC stated, 'Under a resulting trust the existence of the trust is established once and for all at the date on which the property is acquired'. *Calverley v Green* (1984) 155 CLR 242; *Crisp v Mullings* (1975) 239 Estates Gazette 119, CA; *Huntingford v Hobbs* [1993] 1 FLR 736, 24 HLR 65, CA; *Harwood v Harwood* [1991] 2 FLR 274 at 292. The mortgage instalments are not part of the price already paid to the vendor but are sums paid for discharging the mortgagor's personal obligations and ultimately the incumbrance on the property: *Carlton v Goodman* [2002] EWCA Civ 545, [2002] 2 FLR 259 at para 22(vii) per Mummery LJ. For common intention constructive trusts or proprietary estoppel, payments of mortgage instalments, most of which will represent interest in the early years of the mortgage, or of interest and premiums on endowment policies to pay off the mortgage on maturity will be taken into account: *Gissing v Gissing* [1971] AC 886 at 906; *Grant v Edwards* [1986] Ch 638, CA; *Stokes v Anderson* [1991] 1 FLR 391, CA; *Lloyds Bank v Rosset* [1991] 1 AC 107.
4 *Kronheim v Johnson* (1877) 7 Ch D 60 (title in A); *Ivin v Blake* (1993) 67 P & CR 263, CA, where the resulting trust in B's favour was not ousted by a common intention trust in favour of A, the title holder; and *Huntingford v Hobbs* [1993] 1 FLR 736 and *Springette v Defoe* (1992) 65 P & CR 1 (title in A and B).
5 *Huntingford v Hobbs* [1993] 1 FLR 736; *Currie v Hamilton* [1984] 1 NSWLR 687 at 691.
6 *Winkworth v Edward Baron Developments Ltd* [1987] 1 All ER 114 at 117, [1986] 1 WLR 1512 at 1515, HL payment not referable to acquisition of house 'which had already been bought and paid for in full'; *Pettit v Pettit* [1970] AC 777 at 818; *Davis v Vale* [1971] 1 WLR 1022 at 1025; *Harwood v Harwood* [1991] 2 FLR 274 at 294; *Falcke v Scottish Imperial Insurance Co* (1886) 34 Ch D 234. However, if A and B were married or engaged to be married and contributed money or money's worth to the improvement of the property B could claim a beneficial interest under s 37 of the Matrimonial Proceedings and Property Act 1970, but this section is not available if A and B are beneficial joint tenants: *Barclays Bank Ltd v Abbas* (7 May 1985, unreported), Nicholls J. If one party pays more than his share of the mortgage payments he may recover them from the other on equitable accounting principles: see *Re Gorman* [1990] 1 All ER 717; *Currie v Homilton* [1984] 1 NSWLR 687; and p 355, post. B may by subsequently paying off A's mortgage obtain a charge by way of subrogation on the property: *Re Nicholson* [1974] 2 All ER 386 at 391.

ded to pass to the company or trustee[7], but if A transfers property from his name into that of a company or trust controlled by him, the court is ready to infer that in the circumstances the transferee was to be a nominee for A[8].

Title taken in both names

At the time when property is bought by A and B in their joint names the parties also are presumed to intend that they are to obtain the share that they *then* paid for, in the absence of an express written declaration of trust and of any evidence of gift or the application of an unrebutted presumption of advancement. Because A and B have legal title any mortgage moneys will be a joint and several liability, so giving A and B joint or equal shares in the proportion of the property purchased with the mortgage moneys unless A and B have agreed that one of them undertakes all mortgage liability or, say 75% of liability under the mortgage, when the 'undertaker' will acquire an equitable interest under a resulting trust in the proportion that the amount of his liability bears to the acquisition cost of the property[9]. If any subsequent improvements to the property paid for by one party or any subsequent payments greater than his share are alleged to give the payer a greater interest in the property, then again[10], this can only be on the basis of some agreement or representation generating a common intention constructive trust or a proprietary estoppel interest.

Where purchase money provided by one person

Of course, if A buys property in B's name A will be beneficially entitled thereto unless intending to make a gift to B. Thus, where a named couple, A and B, each subscribed for a one-fifteenth share in a National Lottery syndicate but, on separating, A continued to pay B's share as well as her own, so that B's name was ticked off the list each week, Lindsay J held[11] there to be an unrebutted presumption of resulting trust, so B's fifteenth share of the lottery winnings was held for A beneficially. There was acceptable evidence that B had rudely refused to continue paying his share and that A intended herself to benefit as to both one fifteenth shares for which she was paying.

Resulting and constructive trusts contrasted

A purchaser under a resulting trust acquires at the outset an equitable interest representing the share he or she provided for the vendor at the time the property was bought. Thus, if one party (often the woman due to the exigencies of low pay, child-bearing and child-rearing) seeks a larger share than originally paid for, especially where subsequent direct or indirect

---

7 *Nightingale Mayfair Ltd v Mehta* [2000] WTLR 901 at 925–926, per Blackburne J.
8 *United Overseas Bank Ltd v Iwuanyanwu* (20 March 2001, unreported), Robert Englehart QC.
9 *Huntingford v Hobbs* [1993] 1 FLR 736; *Springette v Defoe* (1992) 65 P & CR 1; *Carlton v Goodman* [2002] EWCA Civ 545, [2002] 2 FLR 259, where no resulting trust arose in B's favour over a house bought in the names of A and B by virtue of a joint mortgage by them, where the purchase from A's landlady was only for A's occupation where A alone could not obtain the relevant mortgage and B's function was as a facilitator, likely to 'come off' the mortgage within a year or so, and whose contribution to such arrangement was regarded as a gift and her payments of mortgage instalments after A's death payments as trustee for which she was entitled to be indemnified.
10 See note 6 above.
11 *Abrahams v Abrahams* [2000] WTLR 593.

financial contributions to mortgage payments have been made or the man has represented to the woman that she is to have a half share, and in reliance thereon, she acts significantly to her detriment, such party will have to rely on a common intention constructive trust or an equitable proprietary estoppel interest.

A person with an equitable interest under a purchase money resulting trust is fully a purchaser so as to be protected in the event of the bankruptcy of the other co-owner, while a person with an equitable interest under a constructive trust or a proprietary estoppel will be regarded as a donee or a purchaser at an undervalue[12].

The interest that the non-owning cohabitee expects to have under a constructive trust may be specified at the outset or it may be specified at a later date or it may be what will represent a fair share at the date the parties separate or the property is sold, taking account of the parties' direct and indirect financial contributions[13]. Detrimental reliance is crucial to both common intention constructive trusts and proprietary estoppel and in both instances there can be much uncertainty as to what interest arises, when it arises and how it is quantified because, essentially, the court appears to be tailoring a remedy to fit the circumstances. Both are based on conduct subsequent to the purchase so that a strong case can be made out for such being different appellations for the same doctrine[14] which could be regarded as normally having prospective remedial effects rather than as vindicating pre-existing equitable interests[15], though, so far, courts have traditionally assumed in constructive trust cases that they are somehow quantifying existing interests[16]. Indeed some judges have indicated that equitable proprietary estoppel interests should be regarded as arising at the date of detrimental reliance[17] and, for registered land, this appears to have been confirmed by the Land Registration Act 2002, s 116.

Finally, one needs to be aware that the courts often use the terminology of resulting or of constructive trusts as if the terms were interchangeable, both being concerned with common intentions[18] and both being exempt from any formalities requirements by s 53(2) of the Law of Property Act 1925 so that normally the terminology does not matter. Indeed, this has led some judges to treat subsequent payments of mortgage instalments which are potentially relevant for constructive trusts as being relevant for resulting trusts. This

---

12 *Re Densham* [1975] 3 All ER 726, [1975] 1 WLR 1519. One-ninth share under a resulting trust valid against husband's trustee in bankruptcy but the one-half share under a constructive trust was voidable as a voluntary settlement; see now Insolvency Act 1986, ss 339, 340.

13 *Austin v Keele* (1987) 61 ALJR 605, PC; *Stokes v Anderson* [1991] 1 FLR 391, CA.

14 As accepted in *Yaxley v Gotts* [2000] Ch 162 at 176, CA, endorsed by the Court of Appeal in *Banner Homes v Luff Developments Ltd* [2000] Ch 372 at 384; *Birmingham Midshires Mortgage Services v Sabherwal* (1999) 80 P & CR 256 at 263; and *Chan v Leung* [2002] EWCA Civ 1075 at para 91.

15 D J Hayton [1990] Conv 370; J Hayes (1993) So Jo 606, Lord Browne-Wilkinson Birmingham Univ Holdsworth Lecture (1996) 10 Trust L I 98 at 100; D J Hayton (1993) 109 LQR 485, see pp 425–427, post.

16 P Ferguson (1993) LQR 114; *Turton v Turton* [1988] Ch 542 at 555; *Grant v Edwards* [1986] Ch 638 at 652.

17 See p 253, ante.

18 See Lord Browne-Wilkinson in *Westdeutsche Landesbank v Islington London Borough Council* [1996] AC 669 at 708 reflecting his view in *Tinsley v Milligan* [1994] 1 AC 340. It is, however, submitted that the preferable view is that resulting trusts are an automatic response to a lack of evidence of actual intention to make a gift or a loan or to abandon any beneficial interest in the property.

ignores the essence of resulting trusts which can be summarised as the claimant having a share in the property proportionate to the share of the purchase price that she paid or undertook to pay at the time the purchase price was paid over: she gets what she then paid for or undertook to pay for. If a resulting trust claim is therefore unavailable or would result in only a small share then she can try to rely upon a common intention constructive trust[19] or an equitable estoppel claim to seek what she was led to believe she would acquire.

Express declaration of trust advisable

To avoid problems appertaining to resulting and constructive trusts and concomitant court proceedings, the Court of Appeal has emphasised many times how advisable it is for there to be an express declaration of trust setting out the equitable interests conclusively in the absence of fraud or mistake[20], although those who were not parties to the declaration of trust cannot be prejudiced by such a declaration if they have contributed to the purchase price[1].

Declarations of trust of land require to be evidenced in signed writing but where a transfer of registered land stated, 'It is hereby agreed and declared that the transferees are entitled to the land for their own benefit and that the survivor of them can give a valid receipt for capital money arising on a disposition of land' and was not signed by the transferees, it was still held to be conclusive evidence of the parties' intention to be beneficial joint tenants[2]. However, if the printed form contains the statement, 'The transferees declare that the survivor of them can/cannot give a valid receipt for capital money arising on a disposition of the land' and cannot is deleted such statement is not treated as a declaration of trust of a beneficial joint tenancy[3].

Equitable accounting

Whether the co-ownership interests arise under an express or resulting or constructive trust, equitable accounting principles will apply where the parties have split up and one has then made all the mortgage payments and spent money improving the property although enjoying rent-free occupation of the property[4]. Some cases will illustrate how these accounting principles operate: they apply to joint tenants as well as to tenants in common[5].

In *Bernard v Josephs*[6] in October 1974 an unmarried couple, M and W, bought a house in their joint names for £11,750 and took a 100% mortgage

---

19 Indeed, in *Tinsley v Milligan* [1993] 3 All ER 65 at 86 Lord Browne-Wilkinson regarded common intention constructive trusts based on financial contributions as a 'development of the old law of resulting trust'. Lord Bridge in *Lloyds Bank v Rosset* [1991] 1 AC 107 considered that 'payment of mortgage instalments will readily justify the inference necessary to the creation of a constructive trust' though, confusingly, taking the same view of initial contributions to the purchase price which, of course, give rise to a purchase money resulting trust.

20 *Goodman v Gallant* [1986] Fam 106, CA; *Turton v Turton* [1988] Ch 542, CA; *Carlton v Goodman* [2002] EWCA Civ 545, [2002] FLR 259 at para 44.

1 *City of London Building Society v Flegg* [1988] AC 54, HL.

2 *Re Gorman* [1990] 1 All ER 717, DC; *Roy v Roy* [1996] 1 FLR 541, CA.

3 *Huntingford v Hobbs* [1993] 1 FLR 736, CA; *Harwood v Harwood* [1991] 2 FLR 274.

4 For example, *Re Pavlou* [1993] 3 All ER 955; *Re Gorman* [1990] 1 All ER 717; *Bernard v Josephs* [1982] Ch 391. Further see E Cooke 'Equitable Accounting' [1995] Conv 391.

5 *Re Pavlou* [1993] 3 All ER 955.

6 [1982] Ch 391, [1982] 3 All ER 162, CA.

jointly in order to purchase the house. M contributed £650 and W £200 to the costs incidental to the conveyance, the mortgage and the moving in. Their intention was to pay the mortgage by taking in tenants, and M spent £2,000 on decorations and repairs to enable part of the house to be let. The resulting rents were used towards the mortgage payments which were made by M throughout, though they treated their resources primarily as pooled, W working all the time and using her money for joint household expenses, M for a time being unemployed. As a result of M's violence W left him in July 1976. M continued to live in the house, taking rents and paying the mortgage.

The Court of Appeal held that there was a common intention constructive trust in equal shares, M and W being regarded as having contributed to the mortgage, and thus the purchase price, in substantially equal shares, with a common intention that they should receive credits for their initial contributions and sums spent on improvements. The balance of the equity value of the house after deduction of the outstanding mortgage was about £15,000 so W was prima facie entitled to half this. However, M had to be given credit for £2,450 (being the £650 at acquisition plus £2,000 on improvements less W's £200 at acquisition). He was entitled to a further credit because, since W left, M had paid £4,743 on mortgage instalments though receiving £2,080 rent, leaving a balance of £2,663. M was credited with half this, ie £1,331.50 (in effect, paying an occupation rent for ousting his co-owner)[7]. M's total credit of £3,781.50 was rounded up to £3,800 so that deducting this from the £15,000 left £11,200, of which W's half share amounted to £5,600, which the court rounded up to £6,000 in view of the growth of property values since the proceedings began. If M did not pay W this sum within four months then the house was to be sold[8] so that W could realise her share.

Here the court did not distinguish between the capital and interest parts of the instalments of the repayment mortgage, though the usual practice as appears from *Suttill v Graham*[9] is just to set off the interest element against a notional occupational rent so that they cancel each other out and to credit the occupying payer of the mortgage with the capital element. This is a rule of convenience because much will depend upon the amount of the mortgage debt and the value of the property providing the basis for the notional occupation rent: in *Re Gorman*[10] Vinelott J was thus prepared to set off against half the notional rent half the actual mortgage instalments paid. More recently, in *Re Pavlou*[11] Millett J was prepared to order inquiries to ascertain the notional rent and then to set off against it actual mortgage payments if the trustee in bankruptcy was not agreeable to the interest element of mortgage instalments being taken to match the notional rent, or if it could not be seen in advance that the taking of the two accounts would be a waste

---

7 A co-owner if in sole occupation did not have to pay rent to the other co-owner unless he had ousted her *Dennis v McDonald* [1982] Fam 63, [1982] 1 All ER 590, CA or, perhaps, as a matter of equitable accounting until discretion was conferred on the court by Trusts of Land & Appointment of Trustees Act 1996, ss 13 and 14. In *Re Pavlou* [1993] 3 All ER 955 at 959 Millett J stated, 'A court of equity will order an inquiry and payment of an occupation rent, not only in the case where the co-owner in occupation has ousted the other, but in any other case in which it is necessary in order to do equity between the parties that an occupation rent should be paid.'

8 W had sought a declaration that she had a half share and that the house ought to be sold under Law of Property Act 1925, s 30, p 479, post.

9 [1977] 3 All ER 1117, [1977] 1 WLR 819.

10 [1990] 1 All ER 717, [1990] 1 WLR 616.

11 [1993] 3 All ER 955, [1993] 1 WLR 1046.

of time because the amounts would be likely to be so similar. He also held that the bankrupt's wife, an express joint tenant, was entitled to credit for one-half of any repairs or improvements paid for by her since her husband had left her or, if it were lesser, one-half of the increase in value of the property realised by such repairs or improvements.

Loans

Where the purchase money is provided by a third party at the request of and by way of loan to the person to whom the property is conveyed, there is no resulting trust in favour of the third party, for the lender did not advance the purchase-money as purchaser[12], but merely as lender.

In *Hussey v Palmer*[13] this last sentence was accepted as a correct statement of the law by Cairns LJ though in a dissenting judgment. The case is a very unsatisfactory one, partly due to the course events took in the county court before the registrar and then the judge. The plaintiff, the defendant's mother-in-law, having sold her condemned house, was invited by the defendant to live with the defendant and his wife. The house was rather small so an extra bedroom was built on for £607 which the plaintiff paid directly to the builder, having agreed with the defendant that this was to be treated as a loan to him.

Differences arose so the plaintiff left the house and later claimed repayment of the loan. She submitted to a non suit before the registrar when he intimated he thought she should not be claiming for money lent. A fresh plaint claimed the £607 on resulting trust principles but the judge rejected this since he found the money had been lent. Unfortunately, he rejected the plaintiff's application to amend the particulars to a claim for money lent. The plaintiff appealed against the rejection of the resulting trust and the refusal of the amendment.

Cairns LJ held[14] 'as it was a loan it is quite inconsistent with that to say that it could create a resulting trust at the same time' so that she could only claim for money lent for which amendment of her particulars should be allowed.

Surprisingly, Phillimore LJ[15] held that the loan would not be 'inconsistent with the transaction also being or involving a resulting trust' so that the plaintiff had an interest in the house proportionate to the £607 she had paid. However, a transaction of paying money over qua lender is quite different from a transaction of paying money over qua purchaser: a lender can recover just the money lent[16] whilst a purchaser acquires a proportionate interest in the property usually being an appreciating interest. The two transactions are thus mutually exclusive. This is not to say that a loan arrangement cannot commence as a primary temporary trust to carry out a purpose which, if carried out, results in a pure loan relationship excluding any trust, but which if not carried out gives rise to a secondary but final express or resulting trust: see *Barclays Bank Ltd v Quistclose Investments Ltd*[17].

---

12 *Aveling v Knipe* (1815) 19 Ves 441.
13 [1972] 3 All ER 744, [1972] 1 WLR 1286 criticised (1973) 89 LQR 2, (1973) 37 Conv 65; and see *Re Sharpe (a bankrupt)* [1980] 1 All ER 198 at 201; *Spence v Browne* [1988] Fam Law 291.
14 [1972] 3 All ER 744 at 749.
15 [1972] 3 All ER 744 at 748.
16 As emphasised by *Westdeutsche Landesbank v Islington London Borough Council* [1996] AC 669, HL.
17 [1970] AC 567, [1968] 3 All ER 651 discussed pp 12 and 116, ante.

Lord Denning in a robust judgment flying in the face of the plaintiff's evidence of a loan arrangement, held that there was no loan but that a constructive trust existed proportionate to the plaintiff's contribution because 'justice and good conscience required it'[18]. With respect, this is far too broad an approach to the use of constructive trusts and is now discredited[19]. A further justification put forward by Lord Denning was the equitable proprietary estoppel principle illustrated by cases such as *Chalmers v Pardoe*[20] and *Inwards v Baker*[1] though he overlooked the requirement that there must be words or conduct on the part of the defendant from which the plaintiff can reasonably assume that he is to have an interest proportionate to his contribution to the defendant's property. No such words or conduct were proved by the plaintiff as inducing the required expectation on her part and in the absence of such, as Lord Upjohn has said[2] 'It has been well settled that if A expends money on the property of B prima facie A has no claim on such property'. Indeed in *Davis v Vale*[3] Lord Denning himself assumed this was the law.

Risch v McFee[4], however was an exceptional case where a female not seeking repayment of her loan (and therefore making a gift) to a male house owner with whom she cohabited was found to be thereby acting to her detriment in reliance on a common intention that she should acquire a beneficial interest in the house: she thus had a pro tanto share in the house under a constructive trust.

PARAGRAPH 2

Evidence of intention to benefit

In *Standing v Bowring*[5] the plaintiff, a widow, in the year 1880 transferred £6,000 consols into the joint names of herself and her godson, the defendant. This she did *with the express intention* that the defendant, in the event of his surviving her, should have the consols, but that she herself should retain the dividends during her life. She had been previously warned that her act was irrevocable.

In delivering judgment, Cotton LJ said:

'The rule is well settled that where there is a transfer by a person into his own name jointly with that of a person who is not his child, or his adopted child, then there is prima facie a resulting trust for the transferor. But that is a presumption capable of being rebutted by showing that at the time the transferor intended a benefit to the transferee, and in the present case there is ample evidence that at the time of the transfer, and for some time previously, the plaintiff intended to confer a benefit by this transfer on her late husband's godson.'

Thus the resulting trust was rebutted for the period after the plaintiff's

---

18 [1972] 3 All ER 744 at 747.
19 See p 413, post.
20 [1963] 3 All ER 552, [1963] 1 WLR 677. On this principle see pp 248–254, ante.
1 [1965] 2 QB 29, [1965] 1 All ER 446.
2 [1970] AC 777 at 818.
3 [1971] 1 WLR 1022 at 1025.
4 (1991) 61 P & CR 42, CA.
5 (1885) 31 Ch D 282; and see also *Wheeler v Smith* (1859) 1 Giff 300; and *Fowkes v Pascoe* (1875) 10 Ch App 343.

death as was the case in *Fowkes v Pascoe*[6] where the circumstances of a wealthy widow, with plenty of consols already in her own name, putting £250 of consols into the names of herself and her lady companion and of herself and the young son of her daughter-in-law were held after her death to be explicable only on the basis of an intent to make a gift. Unfortunately, this case was not drawn to the attention of Farwell J in *Re Vinogradoff*[7] where Mrs Vinogradoff had transferred £800 of war loan stock into the joint names of herself and her four year old granddaughter but Farwell J held there was resulting trust for Mrs Vinogradoff's estate when one would have thought that the transaction could only be explicable on the basis that a gift was intended.

Banking or portfolio accounts in joint names

Where a bank balance has been transferred into joint names similar principles have been applied even though the transferor has retained dominion and control over the account during his life, so that all the donee could take by survivorship was the balance standing to the credit of the account at the donor's death[8]. The point that, where the donor retains not only the right to income but the right to use, during his life, the substance of the gift itself, the gift is of a testamentary character not made in conformity with the Wills Act 1837, does not appear to have been raised in any reported English case before *Young v Sealey*[9]. There, after reviewing certain cases in the Supreme Court of the Irish Free State[10] and the Canadian Courts[11], where it had been held that the transfer into joint names was in substance and in fact a testamentary disposition and, as such, ineffectual, Romer J said that their reasoning appealed to him. But he declined to apply such reasoning on the grounds that:

> ' ... the cases which have come before the courts of this country in which a depositor has put funds in the joint names of himself and another, intending to retain control over the funds, and to withdraw them if he thought proper, but with the further intention that the other party (if surviving) should take beneficially whatever might be left of the funds at the death of the depositor have all, so far as I am aware, resulted in the surviving beneficiary taking free from any trust, and it is impossible to say that the point was not raised in any of those cases although it is not mentioned in any report.
>
>   Further, the Appellate Division of the Supreme Court of Ontario had the point before it[12] but did not accept it.'

He went on to say that, in these circumstances, and having regard to the disturbing effect which an acceptance of the arguments might have on existing titles, any change in the current of English authority must be made,

6 (1875) 10 Ch App 343.

7 [1935] WN 68.

8 See *Marshal v Crutwell* (1875) LR 20 Eq 328 at 330, per Jessel MR; *Re Harrison* (1920) 90 LJ Ch 186. The first of these two cases was distinguished, and the second followed, in *Re Figgis* [1969] 1 Ch 123, [1968] 1 All ER 999.

9 [1949] Ch 278, [1949] 1 All ER 92. This case was considered in *Re Figgis* [1969] 1 Ch 123, [1968] 1 All ER 999.

10 *Owens v Greene* [1932] IR 225 overruled by *Lynch v Burke* [1995] 2 IR 159 so as no longer to amount to testamentary dispositions.

11 *Hill v Hill* (1904) 5 OWR 2; *Shortill v Grannen* (1920) 47 NBR 463; *McKnight v Titus* (1933) 6 MPR 282. See also *Russell v Scott* (1936) 55 CLR 440.

12 *Re Reid* (1921) 64 DLR 598.

if at all, by the Court of Appeal, and there the matter now stands. *Re Figgis*[13] has endorsed the *Young v Sealey* approach, finding that there is 'an immediate gift [at the opening of the account] of a fluctuating asset consisting of the chose in action for the time being constituting the balance in the bank account'. While this analysis is appropriate for cash deposits there are difficulties in applying it to a changing portfolio of investments but there has been held[14] to be no conceptual difficulty in a gift via a joint portfolio investment account extending to assets actually acquired by the bank and placed to the credit of the joint account-holders. In such a case the surviving donee needs to do nothing more to constitute his title and can give instructions to the bank in accordance with the mandate.

Joint banking account of husband and wife

Where husband and wife have a joint bank account, the beneficial ownership of money in it, and of assets acquired from it, will depend upon their intention. When their intention is that the account is to be a pool of their joint resources, the money in it will be treated as belonging to them jointly, and no attempt will be made to divide it between them according to their respective contributions to it. This was established by *Jones v Maynard*[15], in which Vaisey J also held that since the spouses had agreed that investments thereout were to be 'our savings' then if investments were purchased out of such an account in the name of the husband, he would hold one half of them as trustee for the wife. But he went on to suggest, obiter, that if investments were purchased in the sole name of the wife they would belong to her absolutely because the presumption of advancement would apply.

In *Re Bishop*[16], Stamp J questioned this last point and suggested that if money in an account was intended to belong to the spouses equally, and that investments purchased out of that money should also belong to them equally, it would not be possible to presume a trust of investments purchased in the husband's name for both spouses without presuming a similar trust in respect of those purchased in the name of the wife. This latter case also made it clear that in so far as the decision in *Jones v Maynard* related to investments, it was based upon its own facts particularly the common intention that investments were to be treated as 'our savings'. In general, where spouses open a joint account on terms that cheques may be drawn by either, then (unless the account is kept for some specific or limited purpose) each spouse can draw on it for his or her own benefit and any investment purchased out of the account belongs to the spouse in whose name the purchase was made. If an investment is purchased by one spouse in the joint names, there is no equity to displace the joint legal ownership and they do not hold it 'as trustees [for themselves] in equal or some other shares'[17]. On the husband's

---

13 [1969] 1 Ch 123 at 149, per Megarry LJ.
14 *Aroso v Coutts & Co* [2001] WTLR 797 (account in name of donor and his cousin's son).
15 [1951] Ch 572, [1951] 1 All ER 802 (approved in *Rimmer v Rimmer* [1953] 1 QB 63, [1952] 2 All ER 863, CA). But in *Re Cohen* [1953] Ch 88, [1953] 1 All ER 378, a cache of notes found secreted in the matrimonial home after the deaths of both spouses (who died within a few months of each other) was, in the absence of evidence of ownership, held to be the property of the wife to whom the residence belonged.
16 [1965] Ch 450, [1965] 1 All ER 249.
17 See also *Re Young* (1885) 28 Ch D 705, and *Gage v King* [1961] 1 QB 188, [1960] 3 All ER 62.

death, money standing to the credit of the account will belong to the wife[18].

When a joint account is opened by a husband in the names of his wife and himself, and the only money paid into the account is that of the husband, the question whether the presumption of advancement applies in favour of the wife may be difficult to answer. If the joint account was opened merely for convenience, the wife will not have the benefit of this presumption and will not be entitled to the money standing to the credit of the account on the husband's death[19]. But if it was opened with the intention of making provision for the wife (an intention which will be more readily inferred if the only person to operate the account was the husband), then the wife will be so entitled[20].

Presumption of advancement

The rule was stated thus by Viscount Simonds in *Shephard v Cartwright*[1]:

'The law is clear that, on the one hand, where a man purchases shares and they are registered in the name of a stranger, there is a resulting trust in favour of the purchaser; on the other hand, if they are registered in the name of a child or one to whom the purchaser then stood in loco parentis there is no such resulting trust, but a presumption of advancement. Equally it is clear that the presumption may be rebutted but should not give way to slight circumstances.'

The presumption is particularly strong for property bought in the name of a child who is a minor[2] and it seems it should make no difference whether the child is legitimate, legitimated or adopted[3].

Where the presumption has arisen and not been rebutted it will not be destroyed by anything (such as change of mind on the part of the donor) that happens subsequently.

Thus in *Crabb v Crabb*[4] a father transferred a sum of stock from his own name into the joint names of his son and of a broker, and told the latter to carry the dividends to the son's account. The father, by a codicil to his will, executed subsequently, bequeathed the stock to another; but it was held that the son took absolutely. Lord Brougham LC said:

'If the transfer is not ambiguous, but a clear and unequivocal act, as I must take it to be on the authorities, for explanation there is plainly no place. ... The transfer being held an advancement, nothing contained in the codicil, nor any other matter ex post facto, can ever be allowed to alter what has been already done.'

Similarly it has been held that even in the days when a nullity decree had

---

18 *Re Bishop* [1965] Ch 450, [1965] 1 All ER 249.
19 *Marshal v Crutwell* (1875) LR 20 Eq 328; *Thompson v Thompson* (1970) 114 Sol Jo 455, CA; *Hoddinott v Hoddinott* [1949] 2 KB 406; *Heseltine v Heseltine* [1971] 1 All ER 952, [1971] 1 WLR 342, where H purchased 4 houses in his own name, paying for them out of a joint account the money in which had been wholly provided by W, and the CA held the joint account had been opened purely for convenience and not with the intention that W should make a gift to H, so H held the houses on trust for W.
20 *Re Figgis* [1969] 1 Ch 123, [1968] 1 All ER 999. Further see (1969) 85 LQR 530 (M C Cullity).
1 [1955] AC 431 at 445, [1954] 3 All ER 649 at 652, HL; *Pettitt v Pettitt* [1970] AC 777 at 815.
2 *Shephard v Cartwright* [1955] AC 431 at 452.
3 Legitimacy Act 1976, ss 2, 8; Adoption Act 1976, s 39; *Seldon v Davidson* [1968] 2 All ER 755 at 758.
4 (1834) 1 My & K 511; and see also *Birch v Blagrave* (1755) Amb 264; and *Batstone v Salter* (1875) 10 Ch App 431, where a mother transferred stock into the joint names of herself, her daughter, and her son-in-law.

retrospective effect a subsequent decree of nullity of marriage did not destroy the presumption of advancement which existed where the husband had transferred property into the name of the wife[5].

The presumption arises where a man transfers property to his wife or his fiancée whom he subsequently marries[6], or after 1970 even if he does not[7], but not where he transfers property to his mistress or a woman with whom he cohabits as if they were man and wife[8]. It also applies where a man transfers property to his child or a person to whom he stands in loco parentis[9] or to trustees of a settlement by him on his children[10], but it must be the man's own property not just property belonging to a company controlled by the man[11].

In these days of sexual economic equality it is surely time that the presumption of advancement also operated for transfers by a wife to her husband or by a mother to her child[12].

Rebutting presumption of advancement

A declaration made by the father, *at or before* the date of the purchase, is admissible to rebut the presumption, although it might not be enforceable as a declaration of trust, on account of its not being reduced into writing in the case of land. The reason for this is that, as the trust would result to the father were it not rebutted by the relation of father and son as a circumstance of evidence, the father may counteract that circumstance of evidence by his parol declaration[13]. The transferor cannot, however, rebut the presumption of advancement by evidence showing that he intended to retain the beneficial interest in the property and made the transfer to effect a fraudulent or illegal purpose[14], unless he repented before such purpose had been partially achieved.

Surrounding circumstances

Surrounding circumstances may also tend to rebut the presumption. Thus a father, upon his son's marriage, gave him a considerable advancement, though there were several younger children who had no provision. He subsequently sold an estate, but £500 only of the purchase-money being paid, he took a security for the residue in the joint names of himself and his said son.

---

5 *Dunbar v Dunbar* [1909] 2 Ch 639.

6 *Moate v Moate* [1948] 2 All ER 486; *Ulrich v Ulrich and Felton* [1968] 1 All ER 67, [1968] 1 WLR 180. Nowadays the presumption is a very weak one as a judicial instrument of last resort if there is not even circumstantial evidence to clarify the transferor's intentions: *McGrath v Wallis* [1995] 2 FLR 114, CA.

7 Section 2 of Law Reform (Miscellaneous Provisions) Act 1970; *Mossop v Mossop* [1989] Fam 77 [1988] 2 All ER 202, CA.

8 *Rider v Kidder* (1805) 10 Ves 360; *Crisp v Mullings* (1974) 233 Estates Gazette 511; *Calverley v Green* (1984) 56 ALR 483 (Aust HC).

9 *Shephard v Cartwright* [1955] AC 431 at 445, HL. For a woman and her child see p 364, post.

10 *Re Curteis* (1872) LR 14 Eq 217.

11 *Re Vandervell's Trusts (No 2)* [1974] Ch 269 at 302–303, [1974] 1 All ER 47 at 75–76 per Megarry J.

12 See Art 5 of Seventh Protocol to European Convention on Human Rights; *Nelson v Nelson* (1995) 184 CLR 538 (presumption of advancement by mother to her child); *Brown v Brown* (1993) 31 NSWLR 582 at 591, CA; *Calverley v Green* (1984) 155 CLR 242 at 268–269.

13 *Williams v Williams* (1863) 32 Beav 370; *Warren v Gurney* [1944] 2 All ER 472, CA.

14 See p 348, ante and *Tinsley v Milligan* [1994] 1 AC 340, [1993] 3 All ER 65, HL.

He himself, however, received the interest and a great part of the principal without any opposition from the son, as did his executrix after his death, the son writing receipts for the interest.

In these circumstances it was held that the son took nothing, the Lord Chancellor (Lord Hardwicke) saying:

> 'Where a father takes an estate in the name of his son, it is to be considered as an advancement; but that is liable to be rebutted by subsequent acts. So if the estate be taken jointly, so that the son may be entitled by survivorship, that is weaker than the former case, and still depends on circumstances. The son knew here that his name was used in the mortgage, and must have known whether it was for his own interest or only as a trustee for the father; and instead of making any claim, his acts are very strong evidence of the latter; nor is there any colour why the father should make him any further advancement when he had so many children unprovided for.'[15]

The 'subsequent acts' referred to in this dictum are not subsequent acts *of the father*, which were only admissible against, and not for, him[16], but subsequent acts of the son and these are only admissible when there is nothing to show that the father did actually intend to advance the son[17]. Evidence of acts which, though not part of the same transaction, indicate a course of dealings is not admissible. In determining whether subsequent events can be regarded as forming part of the original transaction so as to be admissible evidence of intention there is no universal criterion by which a link can be established between one transaction and another. Evidence of subsequent conduct of a child amounting to an admission of his parent's original intention may be admitted in a proper case, but should be regarded jealously, and it is an indispensable condition of such conduct being admissible that it was performed with knowledge of the material facts[18].

The fact that the father had previously made provision for the son, would not of *itself* be sufficient to rebut the usual presumption, although, taken together with other circumstances, it may be a strong link in the chain[19]. Similarly, the retention by the father of the title deeds (the 'sinews of the land') of property purchased in the name of a child is not of itself conclusive to rebut the presumption of advancement but is of great significance when coupled with contemporaneous declarations by the father[20]. 'The acts and declarations of the parties before or at the time of the purchase, or so immediately after it as to constitute a part of the transaction are admissible in evidence either for or against the party who did the act or made the declaration; subsequent acts and declarations are only admissible as evidence against the party who made them and not in his favour.'[1]

The fact that a son permits his father to receive income (eg rents, dividends) from the property has been said to be insufficient to rebut the pre-

---

15 *Pole v Pole* (1748) 1 Ves Sen 76; *Stock v McAvoy* (1872) LR 15 Eq 55; *Marshal v Crutwell* (1875) LR 20 Eq 328; *McGrath v Wallis* [1995] 2 FLR 114, CA, emphasising that the presumption is a 'judicial instrument of last resort'. Further see *Damberg v Damberg* (2001) 4 ITELR 65 (NSWCA).

16 *Redington v Redington* (1794) 3 Ridg Parl Rep 106 at 177; *Shephard v Cartwright* [1955] AC 431, [1954] 3 All ER 649, HL.

17 *Sidmouth v Sidmouth* (1840) 2 Beav 447; *Hepworth v Hepworth* (1870) LR 11 Eq 10.

18 *Shephard v Cartwright* [1955] AC 431, [1954] 3 All ER 649, HL.

19 See per Lord Loughborough, *Redington v Redington* (1794) 3 Ridge Parl Rep 106 at 190; *Hepworth v Hepworth* (1870) LR 11 Eq 10.

20 *Warren v Gurney* [1944] 2 All ER 472, CA.

1 *Abrahams v Abrahams* [2000] WTLR 593 at 607.

sumption of advancement for it is an 'act of reverence and good manners'[2] though it will be most significant if the father retains the share certificates or title deeds[3] and significant if the son returns the share certificates or deed to his father[4]. In present irreverent times a court may well be prepared to treat it as significant in the father's favour if the adult son does allow his father to receive all income from the property.

The relationship of solicitor and client between the son and the parent has been considered a circumstance that will rebut the presumption of advancement[5] unless there is clear evidence of intention to make a gift.

Augmentation of settled property

In one case[6] a sum of consols was vested in the trustees of a marriage settlement upon the usual trusts. The husband directed the bankers who received the dividends (and paid them to him as tenant for life under a power of attorney from the trustees) to invest an additional sum of £2,000 consols in the names of the same trustees, so that they might receive the dividends as before. This was done, and the husband received the income of the whole during his life. No notice of the new investment was ever given to the trustees. It was held that there was no resulting trust of the £2,000 to the husband, but that it became subject to the trusts of the settlement as an augmentation of the trust fund.

Presumption of advancement: mother and child

In *Re De Visme*[7] it was laid down that, where a married woman had, out of her separate estate, made a purchase in the name of her children, no presumption of advancement arose, inasmuch as a *married* woman was under no obligation to *maintain* her children. This case was followed by Sir George Jessel MR in *Bennet v Bennet*[8], where a mother was entitled to property under the Married Women's Property Act 1870 by which married women were made as liable *as widows* for the maintenance of their children. The Master of the Rolls, however, gave it as his opinion that the presumption of intention to advance depended, not on the *liability to maintain,* but on the moral obligation on the part of a father to provide a provision or fortune for a child; and that there was no such obligation recognised on the part of a mother. If that be so, the law still remains the same, notwithstanding that the *statutory* liability for the maintenance of children has for some time been the same in the case of both spouses[9]. However, it is conceived that the point is still an open one, as Sir George Jessel's judgment is admittedly in direct conflict with that of Vice-Chancellor Stuart in *Sayre v Hughes*[10], where the presumption of

---

2 *Grey v Grey* (1677) 2 Swan 594; *Stamp Duties Comrs v Byrnes* [1911] AC 386, PC.

3 *Warren v Gurney* [1944] 2 All ER 472, CA.

4 *Re Gooch* (1890) 62 LT 384; *Stock v McAvoy* (1872) LR 15 Eq 55.

5 *Garrett v Wilkinson* (1848) 2 De G & Sm 244.

6 *Re Curteis* (1872) LR 14 Eq 217.

7 (1863) 2 De GJ & Sm 17.

8 (1879) 10 Ch D 474.

9 See Supplementary Benefits Act 1976, s 17 and Children Act 1989, s 2, each having parental responsibility for their child.

10 (1868) LR 5 Eq 376. This was the case of a *widowed* mother, but the principle appears to be the same. See also *Re Orme* (1883) 50 LT 51 and *Gore-Grimes v Grimes* [1937] IR 470.

intention to benefit was based by the Vice-Chancellor rather on motive than on duty. His lordship said:

> 'Maternal affection, *as a motive* of bounty, is, perhaps, the strongest of all, although *the duty* is not so strong as in the case of a father, inasmuch as it is the duty of a father to advance his child. That, however, is a moral obligation, and not a legal one.'

On the whole, it is with much diffidence conceived that if the authorities should ever come to be reviewed, the views of Vice-Chancellor Stuart would be found to have as much to be said in their favour as those of Sir George Jessel. Neither judge bases the presumption on legal obligation. Both admit that the presumption is found on a moral presumption of intention. But, if so, surely there is as much moral presumption of an intention by a mother to benefit her offspring as there is in the case of a father. And if neither law nor equity imposes any obligation on a father to advance his child, it is difficult to see on what principle an equity judge should invent an imperfect obligation of this kind as a foundation for a presumption of intention to benefit, while at the same time rejecting a similar moral obligation on the part of a wealthy mother. In reason and in custom there is assuredly as much obligation on the part of a mother who has the command of money to benefit her children with it as there is in the case of a father. It must in any case be borne in mind (even if the view of Jessel MR, be the correct one) that if it be proved by other evidence, as will often be the case, that the mother did in fact intend to benefit her offspring, there will be no resulting trust. Nowadays, the presumption of advancement ought to apply to the mother-child relationship whether in a stable marital relationship or in a single unmarried mother's relationship with her child where she is in loco parentis[11].

Indeed in *Gross v French*[12] the Court of Appeal held that even if the presumption of advancement operates against a mother in favour of her child there was sufficient evidence to rebut any such presumption. It will be a rare case indeed where there is no evidence available to affirm or negative any presumption, especially where the property in question is valuable.

Prima facie presumption of resulting trust in favour of a wife whose money is invested in husband's name

Although, where a man purchases property in the name of his wife or intended wife[13], there is a prima facie presumption of an intention to advance the wife[14], the converse does not hold good according to traditional case law which must be assumed to be applicable[15] until a bold court takes a sensible modern view requiring equality of treatment for spouses. Therefore, if property is purchased in the name of the husband wholly or partly out of money belonging to his wife, there is a presumption of a resulting trust in favour of the wife, which is, of course, like all other cases of resulting trust,

---

11 *Brown v Brown* (1993) 31 NSWLR 582 at 591. See also *Nelson v Nelson* (1995) 184 CLR 538 (presumption of advancement from mother to child).

12 (1975) 238 Estates Gazette 39, CA; in *Sekhon v Alissa* [1989] 2 FLR 94 there was sufficient evidence to clarify the matter between mother and daughter though a resulting trust appeared to be presumed.

13 *Moate v Moate* [1948] 2 All ER 486. For fiancées see *Mossop v Mossop* [1989] Fam 77 at 82 and Law Reform (Miscellaneous Provisions) Act 1970, s 2(1).

14 *Silver v Silver* [1958] 1 All ER 523, [1958] 1 WLR 259, CA.

15 As in *Abrahams v Abrahams* [2000] WTLR 593.

capable of being rebutted by parol or other evidence showing that it was intended to be a gift or, where the purchase-money has been contributed by the spouses, that it was intended that they should be entitled to the proceeds of sale in the proportions in which they found the purchase price[16] or, where it is not possible to quantify their interests, in equal shares[17]. It was formerly thought that the presumption of a resulting trust for the wife only applied where the property was purchased with the wife's capital, and not where it was purchased with her income. But in *Mercier v Mercier*[18], the Court of Appeal laid it down that there is no such inherent distinction between capital and income except in degree. Romer LJ said:

'No doubt in certain cases, in considering whether a gift was intended, the fact of the money having been income received by him with her consent may be material in respect of the weight of evidence; but there is no other distinction, so far as I am aware, between capital and income.'

In short, it would seem that where there is no evidence one way or the other, a resulting trust will be presumed, whether the property was paid for out of capital or income; but that where there is some evidence of intention to benefit the husband, then the fact that the payment was made out of income will, to some extent, support that evidence.

In *Pettitt v Pettitt*[19] three of the Law Lords took the view that the changing conditions of society had much diminished the usefulness of the presumptions of resulting trust and advancement at least in property disputes between husband and wife. Thus the presumptions will be applied only as a last resort and greater efforts will be made to ascertain from direct or even circumstantial evidence what the parties really intended[20]. However, the Law Lords in *Tinsley v Milligan*[1] have made the existence or not of a presumption of advancement crucial where a transferor had an illegal purpose: his claim to recover the property will fail if the application of the presumption of advancement forces him to plead his illegal purpose, while he will succeed if he can simply rely on a resulting trust.

Advancement by persons in loco parentis

The presumption of advancement in favour of persons to whom the purchaser stands in loco parentis, has been held to arise in the case of an illegitimate child[2], a grandchild *whose father was dead*[3], the nephew of a wife who had been practically adopted by the husband as his child[4], and a stepson who had not come to live with the person alleged to have been in loco

---

16 *Re Rogers' Question* [1948] 1 All ER 328, CA.
17 *Rimmer v Rimmer* [1953] 1 QB 63, [1952] 2 All ER 863, CA; *Fribance v Fribance* [1957] 1 All ER 357, [1957] 1 WLR 384, CA; *Macdonald v Macdonald* [1957] 2 All ER 690; *Finch v Finch* (1975) 119 Sol Jo 793, CA.
18 [1903] 2 Ch 98, CA.
19 [1970] AC 777 at 793, 811 and 824, but cf Lord Upjohn at 813.
20 For example *Falconer v Falconer* [1970] 3 All ER 449, [1970] 1 WLR 1333.
1 [1994] 1 AC 340, [1993] 3 All ER 65 discussed p 347, ante.
2 *Beckford v Beckford* (1774) Lofft 490; *Kilpin v Kilpin* (1834) 1 My & K 520 at 542, *sed quaere Soar v Foster* (1858) 4 K & J 152.
3 *Ebrand v Dancer* (1680) 2 Cas in Ch 26.
4 *Currant v Jago* (1844) 1 Coll 261; and see *Re Howes* (1905) 21 TLR 501, the case of a niece.

parentis until he was 16 years old[5]. But it would seem that the person alleged to have been in loco parentis must have intended to put himself in the situation of the person described as the natural father of the child with reference to those parental offices and duties which consist in *making provision for a child*. The mere fact that a grandfather took care of his daughter's illegitimate child and sent it to school, has been held to be insufficient to raise the presumption, Page-Wood V-C saying:

> 'I cannot put the doctrine so high as to hold that if a person educate a child to whom he is under no obligation either morally or legally the child is therefore to be provided for at his expense.'[6]

PARAGRAPH 3

Gifts of property

Gifts by a person in loco parentis to a child or by a man to his wife or children (and, if new case law will reflect the current sexual socio-economic equality of women, by a wife to her husband or children) are subject to the presumption of advancement and so are treated as gifts: other gifts give rise to a presumption of resulting trust except it seems where land is concerned.

In *Standing v Bowring*[7], Cotton LJ said:

> 'The rule is well settled that where there is a transfer by a person into his own name jointly with that of a person who is not his child, or his adopted child, then there is *prima facie* a resulting trust for the transferor. But that is a presumption capable of being rebutted by showing that at the time the transferor intended a benefit to the transferee.'

So in *Re Vinogradoff*[8], where a testatrix had transferred £800 War Loan into the joint names of herself and her four year old granddaughter but continued to receive the dividends until her death, Farwell J held that after the testatrix's death the granddaughter held the War Loan on a resulting trust for the testatrix's estate (although the judge did not have the benefit of having cited to him cases[9] indicating that a strong inference from the circumstance of the transferee only being a minor is that a gift was intended).

There is also a slight presumption of a resulting trust where there is a voluntary transfer of personalty into the name of another alone[10]. Much will depend on the nature of the property in question, eg personal jewellery or clothing on the one hand or property like stocks and shares where legal title

---

5 *Re Paradise Motor Co Ltd* [1968] 2 All ER 625, [1968] 1 WLR 1125, CA. In this case the Court of Appeal gave express approval to the statement of the law which is contained in this section of the text.

6 *Tucker v Burrow* (1865) 2 Hem & M 515; and see per Jessel MR in *Bennet v Bennet* (1879) 10 Ch D 474 at 477. In *Kirpalani v Hathiramani* (1992) 46 Estates & Trusts R (Ontario) it was held that a person is not in loco parentis towards another so as to displace the presumption of resulting trust unless he provides regular and systematic assistance and undertakes a moral obligation to ensure the welfare of that other.

7 (1885) 31 Ch D 282.

8 [1935] WN 68. See also *Re Howes* (1905) 21 TLR 501; *Re Muller* [1953] NZLR 879; and *Young v Sealey* [1949] Ch 278, [1949] 1 All ER 92.

9 *Fowkes v Pascoe* (1875) 10 Ch App 343; also see *Shephard v Cartwright* [1955] AC 431 at 452.

10 *Vandervell v IRC* [1967] 2 AC 291, [1967] 1 All ER 1; *Re Vandervell's Trusts (No 2)* [1974] Ch 269, [1974] 3 All ER 205, *Fowkes v Pascoe* (1875) 10 Ch App 343 at 348; *Hepworth v Hepworth* (1870) LR 11 Eq 10; *Crane v Davis* (1981) Times, 13 May.

and beneficial ownership are often divorced. If it is alleged by the recipient that moneys were provided by way of gift in respect of a house bought by the recipient and not by way of loan or purchase then the onus is on him to prove this[11]. However, in the simpler case of payment of money (by cash, cheque or bank transfer) to another this, it seems, is presumed to be to satisfy a debt or some other obligation[12].

Where land is concerned the position is somewhat controversial. Before 1925 a voluntary conveyance of freehold land 'unto the grantee and his heirs' raised a resulting use to the grantor which the Statute of Uses executed so that the legal estate forthwith reverted to the grantor. If the gift of land were 'unto and to the use of the grantee and his heirs' this prevented there being a resulting use to be executed so as to place the legal estate in the grantor and, instead, the legal estate was effectively vested in the grantee. Whether this grantee then held the legal estate on trust for himself or on resulting trust for the grantor was never decided[13].

The Law of Property Act 1925 repealed the Statute of Uses so that it is no longer necessary to transfer the fee simple 'unto and to the use of' the grantee to prevent a resulting use or trust in favour of the grantor. Then s 60(3) oracularly provides:

'In a voluntary conveyance a resulting trust for the grantor shall not be implied merely *by reason that* the property[14] is not expressed to be conveyed for the use or benefit of the grantee.'

As Russell LJ remarked in *Hodgson v Marks*[15] it is now a 'debatable question whether on a voluntary transfer of land by A to stranger B there is a presumption of resulting trust'. Is a resulting trust to be implied *by reason that* there is nothing to show that the equitable interest is to pass[16]? However, the fact that no use or trust is expressed is the reason why there is nothing to show that the equitable interest is to pass and when A is dealing with valuable land by transferring it to B, surely he would indicate it if he were retaining the beneficial interest rather than conferring it upon B. A voluntary transfer 'to B for his own benefit' clearly ousts any resulting trust, but a resulting trust is not to be implied from the absence of such words where the transfer is simply to B in fee simple. Thus the better view[17] is that no presumption of a resulting trust arises where A voluntarily conveys freehold or leasehold land to B or, probably, to A and B, though further evidence will normally be available to clarify the position as in *Hodgson v Marks*.

---

11 *Seldon v Davidson* [1968] 2 All ER 755, [1968] 1 WLR 1083, CA; *Dewar v Dewar* [1975] 2 All ER 728, [1975] 1 WLR 1532.

12 *Re Cooper* [1882] WN 96, CA.

13 Against a resulting trust are dicta in *Fowkes v Pascoe* (1875) 10 Ch App 343 at 348; *Young v Peachy* (1742) 2 Atk 254 at 257 whilst in favour are *Maitland's Equity* (2nd edn) p 77; White and Tudor, *Leading Cases in Equity* (9th edn) Vol 2, p 762 and *Neazor v Hoyle* (1962) 32 DLR (2d) 131.

14 In context this seems to mean land only. See Law of Property Act 1925, s 205(1)(ii) and (xx).

15 [1971] Ch 892 at 933. Also see *Tinsley v Milligan* [1993] 3 All ER 65 at 87 per Lord Browne-Wilkinson.

16 See 12th edn hereof, p 219.

17 As held in *Lohia v Lohia* [2001] WTLR 101 at 112, but left open on appeal [2001] EWCA Civ 1691, [2001] All ER (D) 375 (Oct), yet endorsed in *Ali v Khan* [2002] EWCA Civ 974.

ARTICLE 32

To whom property results

(1) Where a resulting trust arises under an instrument inter vivos, the beneficial interest results to the settlor himself[18]. Where the instrument is a will, the property results to the testator's estate, passing as part of his residuary estate if the failed gift was a specific or general gift or passing as undisposed of property (to his statutory next of kin under the intestacy rules) if the failed gift was of the whole or part of the residuary estate. No distinction is now made between the devolution of real estate and personal estate upon intestacy, but if the testator devised residuary real estate to R separately from his bequest of personal estate to P, then a failed gift of real estate will result to R, while a failed gift of personal estate will result to P[19], whether or not the will directed a conversion of the subject matter of the failed gift as by subjecting it to a trust for sale[20];

(2) provided that where, on the true interpretation of the instrument, property is first given to A absolutely, and then trusts are engrafted or imposed on that absolute interest which fail, the property (whether it be real[1] or personal estate) results to A absolutely to the exclusion of the donor or the persons entitled under his will or on his intestacy[2];

(3) provided also that where after waiting and seeing for the appropriate perpetuity period the event has not occurred that would make the property result to the settlor or his estate, then the interest in the property becomes absolute to the exclusion of the donor or the persons entitled to his estate under his will or intestacy[3];

(4) where a resulting trust has once arisen under an instrument which directs a conversion, and the person to whom it results dies before getting it in, then as between persons entitled to his real and personal estate it devolves (whether actually converted at the date of his death or not) as if it were actually converted, where money was directed to be laid out in the purchase of realty, unless the trust for conversion has wholly failed[4]; except that in other cases of conversion where realty is held on trust for sale or personal property is subject to a trust for sale

---

18 *Symes v Hughes* (1870) LR 9 Eq 475; *Davies v Otty (No 2)* (1865) 35 Beav 208; *Rowan v Dann* (1991) 64 P & CR 202, CA.

19 *Ackroyd v Smithson* (1780) 1 Bro CC 503; 1 Wh & Tud LC (8th edn) 394, and cases there cited.

20 *Curteis v Wormald* (1878) 10 Ch D 172; *Ackroyd v Smithson* (1780) 1 Bro CC 503.

1 *Moryoseph v Moryoseph* [1920] 2 Ch 33.

2 *Lassence v Tierney* (1849) 1 Mac & G 551; *Hancock v Watson* [1902] AC 14; *Re Cohen* [1915] WN 361; *O'Connor v Tanner* [1917] AC 25; *Re Marshall* [1928] Ch 661; *A-G v Lloyds Bank Ltd* [1935] AC 382; *Re Hatch* [1948] Ch 592, [1948] 2 All ER 288; *Watson v Holland (Inspector of Taxes)* [1985] 1 All ER 290, [1984] STC 372.

3 Perpetuities and Accumulations Act 1964, s 12 where the settlor's disposition was after 15 July 1964.

4 *Re Richerson* [1892] 1 Ch 379; *Curteis v Wormald* (1878) 10 Ch D 172; *Cogan v Stephens* (1835) 5 LJ Ch 17; *Clarke v Franklin* (1858) 4 K & J 257; *Re Lord Grimthorpe* [1908] 2 Ch 675; *Re Ffennell's Settlement* [1918] 1 Ch 91; *Re Lyne's Settlement Trusts* [1919] 1 Ch 80.

in order that the trustees may acquire realty no conversion takes place after 1996[5];

(5) where there is no other person to whom the trust property can result, it is held in trust for the Crown[6].

Historical background

Under the Administration of Estates Act 1925, both real and personal estate devolve on intestacy in the same way instead of realty passing to the heir and personalty passing to the next of kin. In the case of deaths after 1925, therefore, no questions arise as between heirs and next of kin. Nevertheless, questions may arise where a testator has devised his residuary real estate to A and his residuary personal estate to B. For this reason the old cases are retained in this edition (even where they dealt with the rival claims of heirs and next of kin) as illuminating cases where the rival claimants are devisees of real estate and legatees of personal estate.

PARAGRAPH 1

Examples

Resulting trust of surplus moneys

Where expressed trusts do not exhaust the trust property there is a resulting trust in favour of those subscribing the moneys rateably in proportion to the amounts subscribed by them. Thus in *Re British Red Cross Balkan Fund*[7] an unexpected surplus at the close of the Balkan War was held to belong to the subscribers in proportion to their subscriptions: the 'first in first out' rule in *Clayton's Case*[8] was not applied although the subscriptions had been paid at various times and the moneys had been spent while the subscriptions were coming in.

However, there can be no resulting trust where the original purpose that was carried into effect was charitable for the surplus moneys will then be applied cy-près[9].

Resulting trust under marriage settlement

By a marriage settlement, real estate of the husband, and personal estate of the wife, are vested in trustees, in trust for the husband for life, with remainder in trust for the wife for life, with remainder upon the usual trusts

---

5 Trusts of Land and Appointment of Trustees Act 1996, s 3.

6 *Re West Sussex Constabulary's Widows Children and Benevolent Fund Trusts* [1971] Ch 1; *Davies v Richards & Wallington Industries Ltd* [1990] 1 WLR 1511 overlooking the possibility of members' ownership apparent from *Re Buckinghamshire Constabulary's Widows' & Orphans' Fund Friendly Society (No 2)* [1979] 1 WLR 936 and so considering only the options of either a resulting trust or bona vacantia. See, as to both real and personal estate, Administration of Estates Act 1925 ss 45 et seq and as to estates vested in a company at the date of dissolution and not subject to any trust, see Companies Act 1985, s 654.

7 [1914] 2 Ch 419 where in the absence of the Attorney-General a resulting trust was erroneously admitted; *Re Welsh Hospital (Netley) Fund* [1921] 1 Ch 655 at 662.

8 See pp 892 and 994, post.

9 See p 341, ante.

in favour of the issue of the marriage, without any gift over in default of issue. Upon the death of the wife without issue, the real estate will result to the husband; and similarly, on the death of the husband without issue, the personal estate will result to the wife.

Resulting trust under will where no conversion directed

A testator by his will gives real and personal estate to trustees, upon trust for certain persons for life, with an ultimate remainder in trust for the testator's two nephews B and C as tenants in common in equal shares, and devises his residuary real estate to X and bequeaths his residuary personal estate to Y. B dies in the testator's lifetime. His share of the real estate results to X as residuary devisee, and his share of the personalty to Y as residuary legatee.

Resulting trust where conversion directed

The preceding examples speak for themselves, and require no comment. But the following case at first sight presents more difficulty. A testator specifically devises real estate to trustees, *upon trust to sell* and divides the proceeds between his nephews B and C. If B should die in the testator's lifetime, his share of the proceeds of the sale will lapse, and before 1926 would have resulted to the testator's heir or residuary devisee, and not to his next of kin or residuary legatees, although the trust for sale was still effective and had turned the land into pure personalty. After 1925, it will go to the residuary devisee, or, where the testator leaves no residuary devisee, to the persons entitled to any estate as to which he dies intestate.

The principle from which this proceeds (settled by the leading case of *Ackroyd v Smithson*[10]) is that conversion directed by a will is presumed to be intended only for the purposes therein expressed; and, so far as these purposes fail, equity presumed that the testator did not intend to rob his heir or residuary devisee of property which, but for those objects, would have been his, and to give such property to his next of kin or residuary legatees, whose only possible ground of claim arises from the fact that the testator's expressed intentions have been disappointed. Moreover, so far as the heir at law was concerned, this presumption was not rebutted even by a declaration that the proceeds of the sale of realty were to be personalty *for all purposes*[11], the latter words being construed as meaning all purposes *of the will.* But whether this would be so where the question in dispute is between residuary devisees and residuary legatees may be open to question.

The question was explained by Sir George Jessel MR in *Curteis v Wormald*[12]. Where personal estate had been bequeathed upon trust to purchase real estate which was to be held on trusts some of which eventually failed. It was held that land, purchased before the failure, resulted in favour of the testator's next of kin, and not his heir[13]. The Master of the Rolls, in giving judgment, after stating the facts, said:

10 (1780) 1 Bro CC 503, 1 Wh & Tud LC (8th edn) 394.
11 *Shallcross v Wright* (1850) 12 Beav 505; *Taylor v Taylor* (1853) 3 De GM & G 190; and see also *Fitch v Weber* (1848) 6 Hare 145.
12 (1878) 10 Ch D 172. As to settled land ordered to be sold by the court, see *Pole v Pole* [1924] 1 Ch 156, CA.
13 This case can, of course, never occur where the testator dies after 1925, as the same persons are now heirs and next of kin.

'The limitations took effect to a certain extent, and then, by reason of failure of issue of the tenants for life, the ultimate limitations failed, and there became a [resulting] trust for somebody. Now, for whom? According to the doctrine of the court of equity ... this kind of conversion is a conversion for the purposes of the will, and does not affect the rights of the persons who take by law *independent of the will*. If, therefore, there is a trust to sell real estate for the purposes of the will, and the trust takes effect, and there is an ultimate beneficial interest undisposed of, that undisposed-of interest goes to the heir. If, on the other hand, it is a conversion of personal estate into real estate, and there is an ultimate limitation which fails of taking effect, the interest which fails results for the benefit of the persons entitled to the personal estate, that is, the persons who take under the Statute of Distribution as next of kin[14]. Their right to the residue of the personal estate is a statutory right independent of the will.'

However, for testators who died after 1996 having in their wills created trusts to sell land or trusts to buy land, s 3(1) of the Trusts of Land and Appointment of Trustees Act 1996 states, 'where land is held by trustees subject to a trust for sale, the land is not to be regarded as personal property; and where personal property is subject to a trust for sale in order that the trustees may acquire land, the personal property is not to be regarded as land'. This section is poorly drafted[15] not being apt to cover a testamentary trust of money, say £100,000, to be laid out in the purchase of land, while there is an overlap between 'land' and 'personal property' since leaseholds fall into both categories; and it would have been better not to focus on the trustees' interest but on the beneficiary's interest, so that the interest of a beneficiary under a trust for sale of realty should have been treated for the future as an interest in realty until sale – and an interest of a beneficiary under a trust of personalty to be used for the purchase of realty should have been treated for the future as an interest in personalty until sale. However, on a purposive construction, the section should be held to abolish the doctrine of conversion[16] where freehold land (realty) is held on trust for sale or where pure personalty is held on trust to sell it to acquire freehold land (realty) but not, it seems, where money is held on trust to be laid out in the purchase of realty[17]. However, as seen in the preceding paragraph, any conversion directed by the will is ignored in any event where the will trusts fail eg for lack of a surviving beneficiary.

PARAGRAPH 2

Rule in *Lassence v Tierney*

This principle usually known as the Rule in *Lassence v Tierney*[18], but more accurately as the Rule in *Hancock v Watson*[19] is well exemplified by the latter

---

14 *Cogan v Stephens* (1835) 5 LJ Ch 17; *Bective v Hodgson* (1864) 10 HL Cas 656.
15 See P Matthews (1996/97) 5 PTPR 87 and also P H Pettit (1997) 113 LQR 207.
16 As indicated by the head-note to s 3 which has no legislative force but may be taken into account: *Stephens v Cuckfield RDC* [1960] 2 QB 373 at 383 per Upjohn LJ.
17 Query the position where T did not leave enough cash in a deposit account, so that his executor and trustee is obliged to sell personalty to provide enough cash to buy a house so there is an implied trust for sale, when it would be odd to have the original cash part dealt with differently from the part of the purchase price provided by selling personalty.
18 (1849) 1 Mac & G 551.
19 [1902] AC 14. See also *Re Bernard's Settlement* [1916] 1 Ch 552, where there was a good appointment to a daughter by will, and an attempt to settle it on her and her issue by codicil

case where a testator directed his estate to be divided into five portions and then said 'to SD I give two of such portions'. He then directed that the two portions given to SD should remain in trust for her for life, and after her decease for her children upon attaining 25 if sons, or upon attaining 21 or marrying in the case of daughters, 'but in default of any such issue' there was a gift over to the children of C. It was held that the limitation after the life estate to SD being void for remoteness, the original gift to her remained intact and passed to her representatives and did not go to the testator's next of kind under a partial intestacy. Lord Davey said:

> 'In my opinion, it is settled law that if you find an absolute gift to a legatee in the first instance, and trusts are engrafted or imposed on that absolute interest which fail, either from lapse or invalidity or any other reason, then the absolute gift takes effect so far as the trusts have failed to the exclusion of the residuary legatee or next of kin as the case may be. Of course, as Lord Cottenham has pointed out in *Lassence v Tierney*[20], if the terms of the gift are ambiguous, you may seek assistance in constructing it – in saying whether it is expressed as an absolute gift or not – from the other parts of the will, including the language of the engrafted trusts. But when the court has once determined that the first gift is in terms absolute, then if it is a share of residue (as in the present case) the next of kin are excluded in any event. In the present case I cannot feel any doubt that the original gift of two-fifths of the residuary estate to SD was in terms an absolute gift to her. ... In other words, as between herself and the estate there is a complete severance and disposition of her share so as to exclude an intestacy, though as between her and the parties taking under the engrafted trusts she takes for life only.'[1]

Subsequently, the rule was considered by the House of Lords in the Scottish case of *Fyfe v Irwin*[2]. There Lord Romer said:

> 'the court endeavours to reconcile the two inconsistent dispositions made by the trust on the one hand and the absolute gift on the other hand, and it does so by imputing to the testator the intention to modify the absolute gift only so far as is necessary to give effect to the trusts, whatever those trusts may be. ... The fact that the engrafted trusts are more than usually inconsistent with the idea that an absolute interest has been given to the legatee is not a reason for denying that such an interest has been conferred.'

So where there is a gift to A for life with remainder to his children, with a proviso that if any child dies in A's lifetime then the property shall go to the issue of that child, the original gift to a child of A remains absolute if he dies in A's lifetime *without issue*[3]. Similarly where there is a devise to A in fee simple, with an executory limitation over to B *for life* if A dies without issue, the fee simple remains in A, subject to letting in B's life estate[4].

In every case before it applies the rule the court must find something that is in form an absolute initial gift. A direction to divide a fund into parts and appropriate one of such parts to each of the beneficiaries may amount to

---

which was void for remoteness. The doctrine is equally applicable whether the fund is bequeathed to a trustee for the legatee and then settled, or it is bequeathed directly to the legatee and trusts declared of it (*Re Harrison* [1918] 2 Ch 59).

20 (1849) 1 Mac & G 551.

1 See also *Kellett v Kellett* (1868) LR 3 HL 160; *Re Marshall* [1928] Ch 661; *Re Gatti's Voluntary Settlement Trusts* [1936] 2 All ER 1489; *Re Hatch* [1948] Ch 592, [1948] 2 All ER 288. But contrast *Re Goold's Will Trusts* [1967] 3 All ER 652.

2 [1939] 2 All ER 271.

3 *Smither v Willock* (1804) 9 Ves 233; *Hodgson v Smithson* (1856) 8 De GM & G 604.

4 *Gatenby v Morgan* (1876) 1 QBD 685.

such a gift so that the rule will be applied on failure of the trusts declared of an appropriated part[5].

Peter Gibson J has summarised the guidance to be obtained from the cases as follow[6]:

'(1) in each case the court must ascertain from the language of the instrument as a whole whether there has been an initial absolute beneficial gift onto which inconsistent trusts have been engrafted[7];

(2) if the instrument discloses no separate initial gift but merely a gift coupled with a series of limitations over so as to form one system of trusts, then the rule will not apply[8];

(3) in most of the cases where the rule has been held to apply, the engrafted inconsistent trusts have been separated from the absolute gift either by being placed in a separate clause or sentence or by being introduced by words implying a contrast, such as a proviso or words such as "but so that"[9] But this is not an essential requirement, and in an appropriate context the engrafted trusts may be introduced by the word "and" or the words "and so that" ...[10];

(4) references in parts of the instrument, other than the initial gift claimed to be absolute, to the share of the donee are usually[11] treated as indicative that the share is owned by the donee ... ;[12]

(5) if a donor, by the trusts which follow the initial gift, has sought to provide for every eventuality by creating what prima facie are exhaustive trusts, it is the more difficult to construe the initial gift as an absolute gift.'[13]

Gift to a class or such of them as shall survive A goes to all if none survives A

A bequest to several, or to a class, 'or to such of them as shall be living at' the period of distribution or any other specified time, is a vested gift to all, subject to being divested for the benefit of those living at the time indicated. Consequently, if *none* survives, the original vested gift will remain intact, and all will be held to have taken as tenants in common[14]. The rule equally applies where there is an absolute gift by will which is afterwards settled by a codicil[15].

5 *Re Burton's Settlement Trusts* [1955] Ch 348, [1955] 1 All ER 433, CA; but cf *Re Payne* [1927] 2 Ch 1, where on similar words Astbury J found that there was no absolute gift and also *Re Cohen's Will Trusts* [1936] 1 All ER 103.

6 *Watson v Holland (Inspector of Taxes)* [1985] 1 All ER 290 at 300.

7 For example *Lassence v Tierney* (1849) 1 Mac & G 551 at 562; *Re Burton's Settlement Trusts* [1955] Ch 348 at 360, CA.

8 For example *Rücker v Scholefield* (1862) 1 Hem & M 36.

9 For example *Hancock v Watson* [1902] AC 14, HL; *A-G v Lloyds Bank Ltd* [1935] AC 382, HL.

10 For example *Re Johnson's Settlement Trusts* [1943] Ch 341, [1943] 2 All ER 499; *Re Norton, Wyatt v Bain* [1949] WN 23.

11 *Re Goold's Will Trusts* [1967] 3 All ER 652, Buckley J held that an express provision that the share was not to be held in trust for a beneficiary was decisive.

12 For example *A-G v Lloyds Bank Ltd* [1935] AC 382 at 345, HL; *Fyfe v Irwin* [1939] 2 All ER 271 at 282–283; *Re Burton's Settlement Trusts* [1955] Ch 348 at 356, 361, CA.

13 *Lassence v Tierney* (1849) 1 Mac & G 551 at 567; *A-G v Lloyds Bank Ltd* [1935] AC 382 at 395, HL.

14 *Browne v Lord Kenyon* (1818) 3 Madd 410; *Sturgess v Pearson* (1819) 4 Madd 411; *Belk v Slack* (1836) 1 Keen 238; *Re Sanders' Trusts* (1866) LR 1 Eq 675; *Marriott v Abell* (1869) LR 7 Eq 478; *Monck v Croker* [1900] 1 IR 56.

15 *Re Wilcock* [1898] 1 Ch 95.

Rule equally applicable to settlements inter vivos

The rule is not confined to wills[16]. Thus, where on the marriage of his daughter a father settled £800 on her and her children, it being held that on the true construction of the settlement he gave her the £800 on condition of it being settled, it followed that on her death without issue the £800 resulted to her estate and not to the father[17].

Applications of rule to accrued shares

In *Re Litt's Will Trusts*[18] it was held that the rule applied to shares passing under an accruer clause in the same way as to original shares; Lord Greene saying:

> 'I can see no logical reason whatsoever why a trust engrafted upon an absolute interest should not, among the trusts which are so engrafted, include a further absolute interest, which is in its turn subject to settlement.'

In that case the accruer clause directed that the share of a child dying without issue who attained a vested interest and any additional share or shares which might accrue or be added thereto should 'go and accrue to such of my children as shall be living at the death of such child of mine ... and so that the share which shall accrue to any child of mine ... shall be held upon the trusts' of his or her original share. But where there was no absolute gift in the accruer clause, but a mere direction that the share should accrue *to the share* of another child and be held upon the trusts of that share, and the trusts of both shares failed, Upjohn J[19] held that the accruer clause was itself part of the engrafted trusts which failed, and that the original absolute interest prevailed on the principle of *Lassence v Tierney*[20].

Initial difficulty in all cases is to determine whether the gift over is a divesting gift or a gift in remainder

In all cases, however, the initial difficulty must be borne in mind of determining whether, on the true interpretation of the instrument, there really was an absolute gift afterwards partially divested, or whether all that the beneficiary was intended to take was the restricted interest[1]. Of course, where the gift is by will, and the partial divesting is by a codicil, there is no difficulty[2], nor where, as in *Hancock v Watson*[3], there are clear words of gift and allotment. But there are numerous cases on the border line which nothing

---

16 See, for example, *Re Burton's Settlement Trusts* [1955] Ch 348, [1955] 1 All ER 433, CA.
17 *Doyle v Crean* [1905] 1 IR 252; but cf *Re Connell's Settlement* [1915] 1 Ch 867, where Sargant J held that a sum of £1,670 Consols settled by a father on his daughter's marriage resulted to him, but that a share of his residuary estate bequeathed to the trustees of that settlement resulted to her, the distinction being that there was no antecedent gift of the Consols to the daughter, but that the share of residue was referred to in the will as the daughter's share.
18 [1946] Ch 154, [1946] 1 All ER 314, CA.
19 *Re Atkinson's Will Trust* [1957] Ch 117, [1956] 3 All ER 738. In *Re Burton's Settlement Trusts* [1955] Ch 60, [1954] 3 All ER 231; reversed on appeal [1955] Ch 348, [1955] 1 All ER 433; Roxburgh J inclined to the same view of the accruer clause in the settlement before him, but the Court of Appeal did not find it necessary to decide the point.
20 (1849) 1 Mac & G 551.
1 As in *Re Goold's Will Trusts* [1967] 3 All ER 652.
2 *Norman v Kynaston* (1861) 3 De GF & J 29.
3 See p 373, ante.

but verbal criticism of the particular instrument will solve; and, as was said in *Lassence v Tierney*[4], in the case of a will containing such a disposition, the intention of the testator:

> 'is to be collected from the whole of the will, and not from there being words which, standing alone, would constitute an absolute gift.'

In doubtful cases, the subsequent disposition of the subject-matter of the gift in every possible event which can arise, forms an important consideration in putting a construction on the instrument; such a disposition being apparently inconsistent with the intention of giving an absolute interest in the first instance[5].

PARAGRAPH 3

No resulting trust where gift becomes void for remoteness

Possibilities of reverter or of resulting trust under dispositions taking effect before 16 July 1964 could validly take effect in favour of the settlor's estate after an interest terminated, even where an express gift over after that interest would be void for perpetuity[6]. For dispositions after 15 July 1964 one waits and sees[7] if the interest terminates within the statutory perpetuity period for, if it does so, then there will be a valid reverter or resulting trust in favour of the settlor or his estate[8]. If the interest does not so terminate then the interest becomes absolute to the exclusion of the settlor and his estate[9].

PARAGRAPH 4

How the person to whom converted property results holds it

Where the person, taking under a resulting trust property which is subject to conversion, dies before he has received the property, having made a will giving his real estate to A and his personal estate to B, or, as sometimes happens, having effectively disposed of his personal estate only so that there is intestacy as to his real estate, a question may still arise as to whether it results to him as realty or personalty. In *Curteis v Wormald*[10] Sir George Jessel MR said:

> 'Then the next question which arises is, how does the heir-at-law [now the residuary devisee] in the first case, or the next of kin [now the residuary legatee] in the second, take the undisposed-of interest? The answer is, *he takes it as he finds it.* If the heir-at-law becomes entitled to it in the shape of personal estate, and dies, there is

---

4 (1849) 1 Mac & G 551.
5 Examples will be found in *Rücker v Scholefield* (1862) 1 Hem & M 36; *Gompertz v Gompertz* (1846) 2 Ph 107; *Re Richards* (1883) 50 LT 22; *Waters v Waters* (1857) 26 LJ Ch 624; *Harris v Newton* (1877) 46 LJ Ch 268; *Re Payne* [1927] 2 Ch 1; and *Re Cohen's Will Trusts* [1936] 1 All ER 103; and see *Re Bickerton's Settlement* [1942] Ch 84, [1942] 1 All ER 217; where the existence of an ultimate trust for the settlor excluded the application to the rule.
6 *Re Cooper's Conveyance Trusts* [1956] 3 All ER 28, [1956] 1 WLR 1096.
7 Of course, one only needs to wait and see under the 1964 Perpetuities and Accumulations Act if the trust is not expressly restricted to a valid common law perpetuity period: see p 195, ante.
8 Perpetuities and Accumulations Act 1964, ss 3, 12.
9 Perpetuities and Accumulations Act 1964, ss 3, 12.
10 (1878) 10 Ch D 172.

no equitable reconversion as between his real and personal representatives, and consequently his executor takes it as part of his personal estate. On the other hand, if the next of kin, having become entitled to a freehold estate [under a resulting trust of converted personalty], dies, there is no equity to change the freehold estate into anything else on his death.'

The broad statement quoted above that the party to whom property results 'takes it as he finds it', is apt to mislead the unwary. It would be more accurate to say that he takes it as he *ought* to find it. That is to say, if the trust for conversion *wholly* fails, he takes it as unconverted[11], but if it only partially fails, then, as the conversion dates from the death of the testator (even though it is directed to be made at a future date)[12], he takes it as converted, and it devolves accordingly, notwithstanding that in point of fact the conversion is not, as it ought to be, carried out in accordance with the trust[13].

However the effect of s 3 of the Trusts of Land and Appointment of Trustees Act 1996 is that for testators dying after 1996 no conversion takes place for land held on trust for sale or personal property held on trust for sale in order that the trustees may acquire land, but it seems it can still take place for money directed to be used to acquire realty[14] if such trusts only fail partially.

Same rules applicable to instruments inter vivos

Precisely the same rule applies where property results on failure of trusts, whenever created by instruments inter vivos. As has been pointed out above, such property results to the settlor in the first instance; but the character in which he retains it is determined by the same principles as have been indicated in the last illustration, so that, nowadays, the settlor will take the property resulting to him in its actual state except for the case of moneys directed to be used to purchase realty where the trusts only fail partially.

PARAGRAPH 5

Rights of the Crown

By the Administration of Estates Act 1925, s 45, all existing modes, rules and canons of descent and devolution and escheat for want of heirs were abolished, and by s 46(1)(vi) of that Act, as set out in the First Schedule to the Intestates' Estates Act 1952, it is provided that in default of any person taking an absolute interest under the foregoing provisions of that section as to distribution of real and personal estate[15] on intestacy the residuary estate of an intestate shall belong to the Crown or to the Duchy of Lancaster or to the Duke of Cornwall for the time being, as the case may be, as bona vacantia and in lieu of any right to escheat.

---

11 *Re Lord Grimthorpe* [1908] 2 Ch 675; cf *Re Newbould* (1913) 110 LT 6, CA; *Re Hopkinson* [1922] 1 Ch 65.
12 *Clarke v Franklin* (1858) 4 K & J 257.
13 *Re Richerson* [1892] 1 Ch 379, and cases there cited; distinguished in *Re Hopkinson* [1922] 1 Ch 65.
14 See p 372, ante.
15 See the definition of 'the residuary estate of intestate' in Administration of Estates Act 1925, s 33(4). The persons who can take an interest are extended by the Family Law Reform Act of 1969 and of 1987 to include persons related to the intestate through illegitimacy.

It follows that if when a resulting trust arises the settlor has died intestate leaving no persons entitled to his estate under s 46(1)(i)–(v) of the Administration of Estates Act 1925, as set out in the First Schedule to the Act of 1952, the beneficial interest results to the Crown.

The Crown will also receive property as bona vacantia where a donor has parted with his money (or other property) out and out in circumstances excluding any resulting trust and where the trusts for use of the money fail in circumstances where the money does not belong to the members of an incorporated association and no general charitable intention exists to found the cy-près jurisdiction[16].

---

16 See pp 336–341, ante.

CHAPTER 7

Constructive trusts

Article
33 Constructive trusts of traceable products owned by persons in fiduciary positions   379
34 Constructive trusts of trust property or its traceable product owned by strangers to the trust   406
35 Constructive trusts of property to prevent fraudulent or unconscionable conduct   409
36 Constructive trusts imposed upon a vendor under a specifically enforceable contract   438

ARTICLE 33

Constructive trusts of traceable products held by persons in fiduciary positions

Where a person has the management of property, either as an express trustee owning the property or a trustee de son tort or partner or director or other person clothed with a disinterested fiduciary character, he is not permitted to gain any personal profit, whether from such property or from exploiting his position; and he is a constructive trustee of such profit and any traceable product thereof for the benefit of the persons equitably entitled to the property[1].

It will be a defence to prove that the profit was duly authorised or was made with the informed consent of all the beneficiaries[2].

Constructive trust and tracing

Where a trustee or other fiduciary is under a duty to keep property subject to

---

1 *Williams v Barton* [1927] 2 Ch 9 at 11; *Re Edwards* [1981] 2 All ER 941 at 950, CA; *A-G v Guardian Newspapers (No 2)* [1990] 1 AC 109, 161, 211, 262–263, 288: *A-G for Hong Kong v Reid* [1994] 1 AC 324, PC (where bribes were traced into land in New Zealand); *Don King Productions Inc v Warren* [2000] Ch 291 at 322, 341–342, CA (boxing contracts renewed after dissolution of partnership held by partner on constructive trust for partnership). For tracing see Articles 92 and 101, post.
2 See p 401, post.

fiduciary obligations separate from his own in order disinterestedly to promote the interests of his beneficiaries as opposed to his own interests, he cannot be allowed to undermine those obligations, eg by renewing a trust lease for his own benefit or by having dividends on trust shares paid into his account and then invested for himself in Whizzo Ltd shares or by taking a bribe and investing it in Fantastico Ltd shares for his own benefit. Equity has identification rules enabling beneficiaries of a fiduciary relationship to trace[3] what at the outset is fiduciary property or what ought to be fiduciary property as soon as received, because 'Equity considers as done that which ought to have been done', into the traceable product of such property. The beneficiaries will then have an equitable lien or charge over such traceable product to the extent of their claim or, if a profit has been made the traceable product will be held on constructive trust for them. Temptation is thus put beyond the reach of the fiduciary by the absolute automatic appropriation to his beneficiaries of the fruits of his breaches of duty. The constructive trust imposed with the assistance of tracing principles thus fulfils a crucial role in underpinning express and resulting trusts and similar fiduciary relationships.

Property rightfully dealt with by a trustee or other fiduciary in accordance with his duties is held for the benefit of his beneficiaries, as is property wrongfully dealt with in innocent or dishonest breach of trust or other fiduciary duty. As Lord Templeman states[4], 'Property acquired by a trustee innocently but in breach of trust and the property from time to time representing the same belong in equity to the *cestui que trust* and not to the trustee personally, whether he is solvent or insolvent. Property acquired by a trustee as a result of a criminal breach of trust and the property from time to time representing the same must also belong in equity to his *cestui que trust* and not to the trustee, whether he is solvent or insolvent'. In essence, the trust property comprises the original trust property, property subsequently added to the trust and the property from time to time representing the original or added property. This is necessarily implicit if not made explicit in the definition of the 'Trust Fund' in the trust instrument, as often is the case. As Dillon LJ states[5], 'It is a long-established principle of Equity that if a person who is a trustee receives money or property because of, or in respect of, trust property, he will hold what he receives as constructive trustee on the trusts of the original trust property'. Oliver LJ succinctly summarises the position[6], 'That which is the fruit of trust property or of the trusteeship is itself trust property', so that profits made from exploiting the trust property or the office of trustee are held on constructive trust for the beneficiaries. The trustee is not allowed to take advantage of his own wrong, so he cannot deny the beneficiaries' claim that he acted on behalf of the beneficiaries[7] (eg so that unauthorised sales and purchases are treated as if authorised overreaching dispositions).

The position can be summarised as follows[8]:

---

3 See Articles 92 and 101, post.
4 *A-G for Hong Kong v Reid* [1994] 1 AC 324 at 331.
5 *Re EVTR* [1987] BCLC 646 at 651
6 *Swain v Law Society* [1981] 3 All ER 797 at 813.
7 *A-G for Hong Kong v Reid* [1994] 1 AC 324 at 337 endorsing Sir Peter Millett, 'Bribes and Secret Commissions' [1993] Restitution LR 7 at 20.
8 By Deane J in *Chan v Zachariah* (1984) 154 CLR 178 at 198 endorsed and applied by Morritt LJ in *Don King Productions Inc v Warren* [2000] Ch 291 at 341and Neuberger J in *Gencor ACP Ltd v Dalby* [2001] WTLR 825 [2000] 2 BCLC 734.

'The principle of Equity is that a person who is under a fiduciary obligation must account to the person to whom the obligation is owed for any benefit or gain (1) which has been obtained or received in circumstances where a conflict or significant possibility of conflict existed between his fiduciary duty and his personal interest in the pursuit or possible receipt of such a benefit or gain or (2) which was obtained or received by use or by reason of his fiduciary position or of opportunity or knowledge resulting from it. Any such benefit or gain is held by the fiduciary as constructive trustee.'

Distinct proprietary and personal liability

The fiduciary is personally accountable to his beneficiaries for the profits (or losses) made by him in breach of his duties as well as having his traceable profit caught by a proprietary constructive trust. If he is sufficiently solvent then the beneficiaries will normally be happy to elect for payment to them of the appropriate amount of profit, thereby leaving the fiduciary, as purchaser, entitled to the particular assets that represent such profit. Of course, if the fiduciary be insolvent then the beneficiaries should insist on their proprietary rights under a constructive trust because their personal remedy will be worth very little.

Trustees de son tort

As A L Smith LJ stated in *Mara v Browne*[9],

'If one, not being a trustee and not having authority from a trustee, takes upon himself to intermeddle with trust matters or to do acts characteristic of the office of trustee he may thereby make himself what is called in law a trustee of his own wrong, ie a trustee de son tort, or as it is also termed, a constructive trustee.'

Distinguishing features of a trustee de son tort are that he does not claim to act in his own right but for the beneficiaries and his assumption to act as trustee is not of itself a ground of liability (save in the sense of liability to account and for any failure in the duty so assumed) so that his status as trustee precedes the occurrence which may be the subject of a claim against him[10]. It matters not that the intermeddler was honest and well intentioned, a busybody of excessive probity[11]. From the outset he will be constructive trustee of trust property received by him and thereafter he may be liable for any breach of these duties of administration. His conduct is equated to a declaration of himself as a trustee[12]. Thus in *Lyell v Kennedy*[13] it took 22 years to discover the identity of a deceased landowner's heir. In this period the defendant, who had managed the land for its owner, continued to collect the rents and place them in a separate bank account. The House of Lords held that these moneys as the product of the trust property were held on constructive trust for the heir[14].

---

9 [1896] 1 Ch 199 at 209.
10 See per Ungoed-Thomas J in *Selangor United Rubber Estates Ltd v Cradock (No 3)* [1968] 1 WLR 1555 at 1579.
11 *Lyell v Kennedy* (1889) 14 App Cas 437 at 459; *Life Association of Scotland v Siddal* (1861) 3 De GF & J 58. For a self-appointed agent, see *Montrod v Grundkotter Gmbh* [2001] EWCA Civ 1954, para 78.
12 *Life Association of Scotland v Siddal* (1861) 3 De GF & J 58 at 72 per Turner LJ.
13 (1889) 14 App Cas 437.
14 Similarly a solicitor or other agent investing trust funds while there are no trustees will be constructive trustee of the investments: *cf Blyth v Fladgate* [1891] 1 Ch 337.

One should be alert to the fact that some authors and judges have formerly used the expression 'trustee de son tort' to cover someone who has dishonestly assisted the trustees in a breach of trust and who has therefore been treated as a constructive trustee for the purpose of being made personally liable to account, though having no specific trust property of which he could be said to be constructive trustee, as discussed in Article 100, post.

Executors de son tort

An executor de son tort is a person who[15], 'to the defrauding of creditors or without full valuable consideration, obtains, receives or holds any real or personal estate of a deceased person or effects the release of any debt or liability close to the estate of the deceased'. Where he appears to be acting for the benefit of the beneficiaries then, like a trustee de son tort[16], he is regarded as a constructive trustee and cannot plead that an action against him is barred by a fixed limitation period[17]. However, if he appears to be solely acting in his own interest he may plead such a limitation period[18].

Trustee taking renewal of lease to himself

In the leading case of *Keech v Sandford*[19] a lessee of the profits of a market had devised the lease to a trustee for an infant. On the expiration of the lease, the trustee applied for a renewal; but the lessor would not renew, on the ground that the infant could not enter into the usual covenants. Upon this, the trustee took a lease to himself for his own benefit. It was, however, decreed by Lord King that he must hold it in trust for the infant; his Lordship saying:

> 'If a trustee, on the refusal to renew, might have a lease to himself, few trust estates would be renewed to cestuis que trust.'

The same principle is equally applicable to renewals by the husband or wife of a trustee[20]. It seems executors will be treated the same as trustees[1].

The same beneficial trusts as apply to the original equity of the original lease apply to the extension of that equity obtained by renewal, whether the original lease itself contains a right to call for a renewal, or the trustee obtains a renewal merely by virtue of his position as a sitting tenant[2].

Where the demised property consists of business premises the trustee will be accountable for the whole profits of the business carried on by him though the form of inquiry will vary according to the circumstances. Thus, in

---

15 Administration of Estates Act 1925, s 28.
16 *Paragon Finance Ltd v Thakerar* [1999] 1 All ER 400 at 408, CA; *Soar v Ashwell* [1893] 2 QB 390 at 396, 402 and 405.
17 *Jones v Williams* [2000] Ch 1, CA.
18 *Paragon Finance Ltd v Thakerar* [1999] 1 All ER 400 at 408, such distinction being ignored in *Jones v Williams* [2000] Ch 1, as well as *Pollard v Jackson* (1993) 67 P & CR 327: just because a person knows another person is entitled to the property does not mean he should be presumed to be acting on that person's behalf.
19 (1726) Sel Cas Ch 61; *Fitzgibbon v Scanlan* (1813) 1 Dow 261; and see *Re Morgan* (1881) 18 Ch D 93; *Re Lulham* (1885) 53 LT 9; and *Re Biss* [1903] 2 Ch 40, where the whole subject is elaborately discussed.
20 *Ex p Grace* (1799) 1 Bos & P 376; explained in *Re Biss* [1903] 2 Ch 40 at 58.
1 *Re Morgan* (1881) 18 Ch D 93; *James v Dean* (1808) 15 Ves 236.
2 *Re Knowles' Will Trusts* [1948] 1 All ER 866.

Re Jarvis[3] one executrix obtained a new lease to herself of premises, where the testator had carried on business until they suffered war damage, and resurrected the testator's business there. Upjohn J held that but for the laches, acquiescence and delay of the other beneficiary, she would have been accountable as constructive trustee of the business, subject to all just allowances for her own time, energy and skill, for certain assets which she had contributed, and for certain payments she had made to an annuitant.

Where business premises held upon trust are occupied by beneficiaries under the trust the trustees have the same right to security of tenure as if they were themselves in occupation[4]. As to their similar powers under the Leasehold Reform Act 1967, see p 457, post.

Tenant for life of leaseholds renewing to himself

A tenant for life of leaseholds (even though they be held under a mere yearly tenancy[5]), who claims under a settlement, cannot renew them for his own sole benefit. For he is not permitted to avail himself of his position, as the person in possession under the settlement, to get a more durable term, and so to defeat the probable intentions of the settlor that the lease should be renewed for the benefit of *all* persons claiming under the settlement[6].

In *Longton v Wilsby*[7], Stirling J is reported to have said that the above cases must be restricted to leases where there was a *right* of renewal either by custom or contract; but Warrington J pointed out[8] that this is an obvious mistake, and that the learned judge was only referring to the purchase of *reversions on*, and not to the *renewal* of, leases. As to the former, however, see below.

Fiduciary lessee purchasing the reversion expectant on the lease

Whether a trustee or other fiduciary person is equally precluded from purchasing for his own benefit the reversion expectant on a lease of which he is trustee, is not quite so clear. Until *Protheroe v Protheroe*[9], the authorities suggested that he was not[10], unless the lease was one which was renewable by contract or, short of that, was one in respect of which a long-standing custom of granting renewals made it possible to infer that a renewal would be highly

---

3 [1958] 2 All ER 336, [1958] 1 WLR 815.

4 Landlord and Tenant Act 1954, s 41(1). The occupation of the beneficiaries must derive its existence from the trust and not, eg from a sub-tenancy (*Frish Ltd v Barclays Bank Ltd* [1955] 2 QB 541 at 548, [1955] 3 All ER 185 at 188, CA, per Sir Raymond Evershed MR. As to the position under the Act where the landlord's interest is held on trust, see the Landlord and Tenant Act 1954, s 41(2).

5 *James v Dean* (1808) 15 Ves 236.

6 *Eyre v Dolphin* (1813) 2 Ball & B 290; *Mill v Hill* (1852) 3 HL Cas 828; *Yem v Edwards* (1857) 1 De G & J 598; *James v Dean* (1808) 15 Ves 236; *Lloyd-Jones v Clark-Lloyd* [1919] 1 Ch 424. The reader is also referred to *Re Payne's Settlement* (1886) 54 LT 840; and Article 34, post. But cf *Blake v Blake* (1786) 1 Cox Eq Cas 266.

7 (1897) 76 LT 770, strangely omitted from the authorised reports. See also *Holmes v Williams* [1895] WN 116.

8 *Bevan v Webb* [1905] 1 Ch 620. For other cases of renewals of leases by fiduciary persons, see *Smyth v Byrne* [1914] 1 IR 53; *Hahesy v Guiry* [1917] 1 IR 371; affd [1918] 1 IR 135; *Re Smith* (1918) 52 ILT 113; *Kiernan v M'Cann* [1920] 1 IR 99; and *Brady v Brady* [1920] 1 IR 170.

9 [1968] 1 All ER 1111, [1968] 1 WLR 519, CA.

10 *Randall v Russell* (1817) 3 Mer 190; *Hardman v Johnson* (1815) 3 Mer 347; *Longton v Wilsby* (1897) 76 LT 770; *Bevan v Webb* [1905] 1 Ch 620. But cf *Re Lord Ranelagh's Will* (1884) 26 Ch D 590.

probable[11]. This view of the law found support in a dictum of Wilberforce J at first instance in the case of *Phipps v Boardman*[12], when he said:

> 'By contrast with the familiar case of a renewal of the lease, typified by *Keech v Sandford*, which, if made by a person in a fiduciary position, becomes the property of the trust, the purchase of a reversion does not have this effect, unless the lease is renewable by contract or by custom … '

But in *Protheroe v Protheroe* the Court of Appeal based its decision on the view that no trustee of a lease could in any circumstances purchase the freehold for his own benefit. Lord Denning MR, who delivered the only judgment, said simply[13]:

> 'There is a long established rule of equity from *Keech v Sandford* downwards that if a trustee who owns the leasehold, gets in the freehold, that freehold belongs to the trust and he cannot take the property for himself.'

In this case, a husband and wife had purchased a leasehold house as their matrimonial home and, although the assignment was taken in the husband's name alone, it was admitted that he held on trust for himself and his wife in equal shares. The parties had separated, the wife had petitioned for divorce, and the husband had then bought the freehold reversion for a sum raised by a mortgage. It was held that, because of the Rule in *Keech v Sandford*, the wife was entitled equally with the husband to the proceeds of sale of the freehold property, but that the husband was entitled to be repaid the cost of the reversion and his expenses in acquiring it. Although this does not appear with certainty, it seems that the lease was not renewable, either by contract or by custom: certainly the court's decision did not rest on the ground that it was. No cases at all were cited in argument, and the only case mentioned in the judgment, *Keech v Sandford* itself, was of course concerned with the renewal of a lease, not with the purchase of a reversion. Moreover, the fact that *Protheroe v Protheroe* was a case concerning husband and wife may perhaps have given rise not only to the neglect, by counsel and the court, of the earlier cases (concerned, as they were, with the rights of beneficiaries and trustees who were at arm's length), but also to a desire on the part of the court to do justice as between the spouses rather than to seek and apply the principles of law which were strictly applicable as between trustee and beneficiary.

It would seem, however, that the case can be justified by the need to prevent the conflict of interest arising where otherwise the trustee would personally be the landlord of the trust tenancy and so have to deal with himself[14]. *In Thompson's Trustees in bankruptcy v Heaton*[15] Pennycuick V-C merely followed *Protheroe v Protheroe*. The Court of Appeal[16] has since applied *Thompson's Trustees* so that in *Don King Productions Inc v Warren*[17] Morritt LJ

---

11 *Phillips v Phillips* (1885) 29 Ch D 673; *Bevan v Webb* [1905] 1 Ch 620.
12 [1964] 2 All ER 187 at 201–202. In the case of a renewal the trustee is in effect buying a part of the trust property; in the case of a reversion this is not so: it is a separate item altogether.
13 [1968] 1 All ER 1111 at 1112.
14 See the concern with this in *Re Thompson's Settlement* [1986] Ch 99, [1985] 2 All ER 720.
15 [1974] 1 WLR 605.
16 *Popat v Shonchhatra* [1997] 1 WLR 1367.
17 [2000] Ch 291 at 340. In *Ward v Brunt* [2000] WTLR 731 the reversion would have been held on constructive trust by a partner but for having been acquired by her pursuant to an option under the will of the freeholder, her grandfather, rather than *qua* partner.

rejected counsel's suggestion that it was still an open question whether the rule in *Keech v Sandford* applied to the purchase of the reversion.

Renewal of leases by partial owners other than tenants for life

In the case of renewals of leases by trustees or tenants for life, the presumption against the validity of the renewal for the sole benefit of the party renewing, is absolute and irrebuttable[18]. But when we come to consider renewals by mortgagees[19] mortgagors[20], equitable co-owners not holding the legal estate as trustees or trustees for sale[1] and perhaps partners[2], the proposition requires modification. In such cases there is no irrebuttable presumption of law against the validity of the transaction, but at most a rebuttable presumption of fact that it lies on the party renewing to show that he acted bona fide, and took no undue advantage of the other parties interested[3]. If, therefore, on the evidence, the court considers that there was no bad faith and no undue advantage taken, the renewer will be allowed to retain the benefit of the renewed lease. For instance, where a lease formed part of the personal estate of an intestate, and the lessor refused to renew to the administratrix, a subsequent renewal obtained by one of the next of kin was held to be unimpeachable[4].

Tenant for life of mortgaged property purchasing interest of mortgagee

The principle precluding a tenant for life from renewing a lease for his own benefit, equally precluded a tenant for life of an equity of redemption under the old law from purchasing the fee simple from the mortgagee. It is thought that a tenant for life of mortgaged property taking an assignment of the mortgage would hold it upon the trusts of the settlement subject, of course, to a charge for what he had paid[5].

Additions to trust property

It need scarcely be said that any property acquired by trustees by reason of their legal ownership of the trust property (for instance, a Crown grant of salmon fishings opposite the trust property[6]), must be held by them as

---

18 *Re Biss* [1903] 2 Ch 40.
19 *Rushworth's Case* (1676) Freem Ch 13.
20 *Leigh v Burnett* (1885) 29 Ch D 231.
  1 *Palmer v Young* (1684) 1 Vern 276; *Holmes v Williams* [1895] WN 116; *Hunter v Allen* [1907] 1 IR 212; *Kennedy v De Trafford* [1897] AC 180; *Re Biss* [1903] 2 Ch 40; *Re Jarvis* [1958] 2 All ER 336, [1958] 1 WLR 815. The Law of Property Act 1925, ss 34–36, makes express trustees of persons taking legal title to land as co-owners.
  2 *Featherstonhaugh v Fenwick* (1810) 17 Ves 298; *Clegg v Fishwick* (1849) 1 Mac & G 294; *Re Biss* [1903] 2 Ch 40; *Clegg v Edmondson* (1857) 8 De GM & G 787 at 807; *Bell v Barnett* (1872) 21 WR 119; *Dean v MacDowell* (1878) 8 Ch D 345; *Piddocke v Burt* [1894] 1 Ch 343; *Bevan v Webb* [1905] 1 Ch 620 at 625; *Gordon v Gonda* [1955] 2 All ER 762, CA; *Thompson's Trustees in Bankruptcy v Heaton* [1974] 1 All ER 1239, [1974] 1 WLR 605.
  3 *Re Biss* [1903] 2 Ch 40.
  4 *Re Biss* [1903] 2 Ch 40.
  5 It is submitted that the principle is the same as where the tenant for life of an equity of redemption purchased the fee simple from the mortgagee as to which see *Griffith v Owen* [1907] 1 Ch 195.
  6 *Aberdeen Town Council v Aberdeen University* (1877) 2 App Cas 544.

trustees only. As Oliver LJ said in *Swain v Law Society*[7] 'that which is the fruit of trust property or of the trusteeship is itself trust property'. Similarly, where trust moneys were lent on a mortgage and the mortgagor, an eccentric, in devising properties to persons unknown to him, devised the equity of redemption to 'the mortgagee' it was held that, although the mortgagor did not know the mortgagee was a trustee, the mortgagor's intention was to increase the interest which the mortgagee already had in the property so that the equity of redemption belonged to the trust and not to the trustee beneficially[8]. If the devise had been intended personally for the trustee it seems he could have retained it beneficially since it would have come to him without his volition[9].

Tenant for life receiving money in relation to settled land

Upon similar grounds, if a tenant for life accepts money in consideration of his allowing something to be done which is prejudicial to the trust property (as, for instance, where for a consideration he refrains from opposing a private Bill prejudicial to the trust estate), he will be a trustee of such money for all the persons interested under the settlement[10], but it seems that it would be otherwise where moneys come to him without his volition[11]. Where a tenant for life has refunded to him out of capital moneys the cost of improvements effected by him, he is nevertheless entitled to retain for his own benefit reliefs or allowances for income tax purposes obtained by him in respect of such improvements, since he is entitled to the whole income of the settled property[12].

Profits made by trustee or fiduciary from property or position

As Lord Reid stated in *Brown v IRC*[13], 'If the person in a fiduciary position does gain or receive any financial benefit arising out of the use of the property of the beneficiary he cannot keep it unless he can show authority', eg by the trust deed or by contract or by the assent of all the beneficiaries. There the House of Lords held that interest earned on a solicitor's clients' moneys put in a deposit account earmarked for clients generally belonged to the clients and never belonged to the solicitor: the moneys and the interest thereon were held on an express and constructive trust respectively.

Of course, if A holds no money of B but is merely under an obligation to account to B for a certain amount of money then A can retain profits made from the use of what is his own money subject to his obligation to account for the principal sum to B and for such interest, if any, as may have been agreed with B[14]. Similarly, if A by fraudulent misrepresentations borrows £x from B secured by a mortgage over the house purchased with the £x, A cannot be

---

7   [1981] 3 All ER 797 at 813.
8   *Re Payne's Settlement* (1886) 54 LT 840; cf *Re Bagnall's Trusts* [1901] 1 IR 255.
9   *Re Northcote's Will Trusts* [1949] 1 All ER 442.
10 *Re Thorpe* [1891] 2 Ch 360; see also *Fawcett v Whitehouse* (1829) 1 Russ & M 132 and *Owen v Williams* (1733) Amb 734 where trustee benefited self instead of acting in the best interests of his beneficiaries.
11 *Re Northcote's Will Trusts* [1949] 1 All ER 442.
12 *Re Pelly* [1957] Ch 1, [1956] 2 All ER 326, CA.
13 [1965] AC 244, [1964] 3 All ER 119; see also *Reid-Newfoundland Co v Anglo-American Telegraph Co Ltd* [1912] AC 555 and *A-G v Guardian Newspapers (No 2)* [1990] 1 AC 109.
14 *Kirkham v Peel* (1881) 44 LT 195; *York and North Midland Rly Co v Hudson* (1853) 16 Beav 485.

liable to B beyond his liability to repay £x with interest even if the house has doubled in value[15].

A fiduciary[16], as part of the wider rule that a fiduciary must not place himself where his fiduciary duty and his private interest may conflict[17], is under very strict obligations or disabilities[18] that prevent him from obtaining any profit from his fiduciary relationship unless duly authorised[19]. This is to deliver him from any temptation to misuse his fiduciary position[20]. He is liable to account (so long as not holding the property subject to the relationship as debtor only) to his principal for such profit. It is immaterial that the principal could not otherwise have obtained the profit, that the fiduciary acted honestly and in his principal's best interest, that the principal benefited from the fiduciary's actions, and that the profit was obtained through use of the fiduciary's own assets and resulted from the fiduciary's personal skills[1]. Indeed, the fiduciary will be constructive trustee of the profit even if arising from misuse of his position (as opposed to the fiduciary property) as where he takes advantage of information obtained by him qua fiduciary[2] or where he takes a bribe or secret commission[3] or uses the opportunity and facilities arising by virtue of his fiduciary position to make profits for himself instead of for his principal[4]. Once the profit, in the form of specific property or cash, held on constructive trust is used to acquire property the equitable tracing process will be available, making the fiduciary hold the property on trust for the claimants. However, if the fiduciary is good for the money it will be necessary only to make him personally liable to account as was the case in *Swain v Law Society*[5], where Oliver LJ stated

> 'What one has to do is to ascertain first of all whether there was a fiduciary relationship and, if there was, from what it arose and what, if there was any, was the trust property; and then to inquire whether that of which an account is claimed either arose, directly or indirectly, from the trust property itself or was acquired not only in the course of, but by reason of, the fiduciary relationship.'

On appeal Lord Brightman (with whom the others agreed) endorsed[6] this approach but held that no fiduciary relationship existed since the Law Society was performing a public duty under s 37 of the Solicitors Act 1974 when it received large commission in respect of premiums paid by solicitors

---

15 *Halifax Building Society v Thomas* [1996] Ch 217, CA.
16 For who is a fiduciary see p 20, ante.
17 *Boardman v Phipps* [1967] 2 AC 46 at 123, per Lord Upjohn; *Re Thompson's Settlement* [1985] 2 All ER 720 at 730. If there be a conflict then he must subordinate his private interest to his fiduciary duty: *Swain v Law Society* [1981] 3 All ER 797 at 813; *Bristol & West Building Society v Mothew* [1998] Ch 1 at 19, CA.
18 *Tito v Waddell (No 2)* [1977] 3 All ER 129 at 247, per Megarry V-C.
19 See p 401, post.
20 *Swain v Law Society* [1981] 3 All ER 797 at 809.
 1 *Boardman v Phipps* [1967] 2 AC 46, [1966] 3 All ER 721, though in exceptional circumstances (as there) the fiduciary may be awarded an allowance for his expertise: see pp 657–658, post.
 2 *Boardman v Phipps* [1967] 2 AC 46, [1966] 3 All ER 721 as interpreted in *A-G for Hong Kong v Reid* [1994] 1 AC 324, PC.
 3 *A-G for Hong Kong v Reid* [1994] 1 AC 324, PC, rejecting *Lister v Stubbs* (1890) 45 Ch D 1, CA. A principal can recover the bribe from his agent whether he affirms or repudiates the contract between the agent and the briber, and is not obliged to return the bribe to the briber if he repudiates the contract: *Logicrose Ltd v Southend United Football Club Ltd* [1988] 1 WLR 1256.
 4 *A-G for Hong Kong v Reid* [1994] 1 AC 324 implicitly rejecting *A-G's Reference (No 1 of 1985)* [1986] QB 491, CA: see J C Smith (1994) 110 LQR 180.
 5 [1981] 3 All ER 797 at 813–814, [1982] 1 WLR 17 at 37.
 6 [1983] 1 AC 598 at 619, [1982] 2 All ER 827 at 838, HL.

under the Solicitors' Indemnity Assurance Scheme. In *Appleby v Cowley*[7] Megarry V-C held that the head of a barrister's set of chambers was in a fiduciary position to the members thereof, but that he did not hold the building he had purchased for chambers on constructive trust for the members since he purchased the building on his own account and not as agent or delegate of the members. The building was purchased in the course of the fiduciary relationship but not by reason of that relationship. Similarly, in *Ward v Brunt*[8] the freehold reversion to a lease to a partnership was purchased by a partner, not qua fiduciary partner, but as devisee of an option to purchase the freehold under the will of her grandfather-owner of the freehold.

Profits made by trustee's parent company

If a corporate trustee places business with its parent company, eg invests trust moneys in a fund managed for a fee by the parent company will this amount to a breach of trust making the trustee or its parent company liable? In *Jones v AMP Perpetual Trustee Co NZ Ltd*[9], where the trustee was a trustee company but not a fund manager, Thomas J held that the trustee was not liable (from which it would seem to follow that its parent could not be liable). He regarded the rule preventing a trustee from profiting as arising from the more general principle that no one who has a duty to perform shall place himself in such a position that his interest will conflict with his duty and that, if interest and duty do conflict, interest must give way. As a matter of fact and degree he held that no real sensible possibility of conflict arose which could impair the trustee's ability to serve the best interests of the beneficiaries: the parent company was a pre-eminent company with an attractive investment record, while the equivalent fee would be payable to any similar company selected to be investment manager. An alternative approach in line with *Swain v Law Society*[10] is to regard the trustee as providing its parent with the opportunity to profit in the course of its management of the trust property but not by reason of that management relationship. One needs to bear in mind the warning uttered by Lord Selborne in *Barnes v Addy*[11] that 'there is no better mode of undermining the sound doctrines of equity than to make unreasonable and inequitable applications of them'.

Trustee obtaining directorship fees by use of trust shareholding

As Cohen J said in *Re Macadam*[12]:

> 'The root of the matter really is: Did the trustee acquire the position in respect of which he drew the remuneration by virtue of his position as trustee?'

---

7 (1982) Times, 14 April. Also see *Hanson v Lorenz and Jones* [1986] NLJ Rep 1088, [1987] 1 FTLR 23, where CA held a solicitor was under no duty to account to a client for his profit from a joint venture (purchase, renovation and sale of a house through medium of companies controlled by him and by his client) in circumstances where the business or financial prudence of the deal was outside the scope of the solicitor-client relationship, and the client understood the terms of the venture agreement, which were fair in any event.
8 [2000] WTLR 731.
9 [1994] 1 NZLR 690.
10 [1981] 3 All ER 797 at 813–814 per Oliver LJ endorsed by Lord Brightman, [1983] 1 AC 598 at 619, discussed p 387, ante.
11 (1874) 9 Ch App 244 at 251.
12 [1946] Ch 73 at 82.

Harman J (as he then was) reviewed the case law thoroughly in *Re Gee*[13] concluding:

'A trustee who either uses a power vested in him as such to obtain a benefit as in *Re Macadam*[14] or who (as in *Williams v Barton's* case)[15] procures his co-trustees to give him, or those associated with him, remunerative employment must account for the benefit obtained. Further, a trustee who has the power by the use of trust votes to control his own appointment to a remunerative position and refrains from using them, with the result that he is elected to a position of profit, would also be accountable. On the other hand, it appears not to be the law that every man who becomes a trustee, holding, as such, shares in a limited company is made ipso facto accountable for remuneration received from the company independently of any use by him of the trust holding, whether by voting or refraining from so doing. For instance, A, who holds the majority of shares in a limited company becomes the trustee of the estate of B, a holder of a minority interest. This cannot, I think, disentitle A to use his own shares to procure his appointment as an officer of the company nor compel him to disgorge the remuneration he so receives, for he cannot be disentitled to the use of his own voting powers nor could the use of the trust votes in a contrary sense prevent the majority prevailing. Many other instances could be given of a similar kind. Of these *Re Dover Coalfield Extension Ltd*[16] is really one. There the trustees did not earn their fees by virtue of the trust shares[17] though, no doubt, the continued holding of those shares was a qualification necessary for the continued earning of the fees.'

Thus, a trustee will not be a constructive trustee of director's fees if using his own shares in his own favour but using the trust shares against himself he happens to be appointed to the directorship. Otherwise, he will be constructive trustee of the fees and liable to account unless, of course, authorised by the trust instrument to become director and expressly or implicitly made not liable to account for director's fees[18].

Trustee obtaining commission

As Fox LJ stated in *Swain v Law Society*[19]:

'I do not think that the fact that a trustee receives a benefit otherwise than from some direct dealing with the trust property or from the exercise of a trust power is conclusive of the question whether he has to account to the beneficiaries for the benefit he has received. If, for example, a trustee propounds a tax saving scheme to beneficiaries under which they are required to effect at their own expense policies on their own lives, I apprehend that if the trustee took commission from the insurers in respect of such policies he would be liable to account for the commission, even though he received the commission without any exercise of his powers as trustee and even though the commission did not derive from a dealing with the trust fund itself.'

Earlier[20] he had made it clear that the fact that the contract under which a fiduciary received a benefit by virtue of his trust was a contract which antedated the trust would not affect his obligation to account. If a man enters

---

13 [1948] Ch 284 at 295.
14 [1946] Ch 73, [1945] 2 All ER 664.
15 [1927] 2 Ch 9.
16 [1908] 1 Ch 65.
17 They became directors before they held any trust shares.
18 *Re Llewellin's Will Trusts* [1949] Ch 225.
19 [1981] 3 All ER 797 at 823–824.
20 [1981] 3 All ER 797 at 823.

into an agreement under which he is entitled to a commission in certain circumstances and subsequently accepts a trusteeship under which he enters into such transactions and obtains a commission he is still obliged to account to the trust.

Director obtaining profits from his directorship

Directors are subject to the strict fiduciary obligation or disability preventing them from profiting from their fiduciary relationship with their company. Thus, in *Cook v Deeks*[1], where the directors diverted to themselves contracts which they should have taken up on behalf of their company, the Privy Council held that the contracts belonged to the company in equity so that the directors held the benefit of the contracts on constructive trust for the company. The company resolution in general meeting ratifying the directors' actions and secured by the directors' majority shareholding was ineffective: the directors could not make a present to themselves of company property and defraud the minority shareholders.

In *Industrial Development Consultants v Cooley*[2] the managing director of the plaintiff company was found to be a constructive trustee of the benefit of a contract with the Eastern Gas Board and was made liable to account for the profits thereof. The Gas Board had privately told the managing director that he would not obtain a contract from them for the benefit of his company, but that he would have a good chance of privately obtaining the contract for himself if he severed his connection with the company. Pretending poor health and concealing his true reason he secured his release from employment by the company. He then obtained for himself the contract with the Gas Board that he had unsuccessfully tried to obtain for the plaintiff company. He was held liable to account for all the profit, even though the chance of his persuading the Gas Board to change their stance and contract with the plaintiff company was no greater than 10%.

Regal (Hastings) Ltd v Gulliver[3] is a particularly salutary case where the fiduciaries acted honestly in the best interests of the company, which received a totally unmerited windfall. The company formed a subsidiary company to take up leases of some cinemas. The landlord required the directors personally to guarantee the rents unless the subsidiary had a paid up capital of £5,000. The directors did not wish to give guarantees since they intended that the company and the subsidiary company should sell their properties in the near future. The company could only afford to subscribe for £2,000 paid up capital of the subsidiary. Acting honestly and in the best interests of the company, the directors ensured that the remaining £3,000 capital was subscribed for by themselves, by the chairman as nominee for someone else and by the company's solicitor. It does not seem that they considered themselves lending (or guaranteeing a loan of) the £3,000 to the company to enable it to subscribe for the shares, nor did they approach the other fifteen shareholders to let them in on the probable future profits. A

---

1 [1916] 1 AC 554.
2 [1972] 2 All ER 162, [1972] 1 WLR 443. Also see *Pre-Cam Exploration and Development Ltd v McTavish* (1966) 57 DLR (2d) 57; *Canadian Aero Service Ltd v O'Malley* (1973) 40 DLR (3d) 371 and *Abbey Glen Property Corpn v Stumborg* (1976) 65 DLR (3d) 235.
3 [1942] 1 All ER 378 later reported in [1967] 2 AC 134n.

proposed sale of the property of the company and the subsidiary company fell through, but a later sale was arranged involving the purchaser buying all the shares in the two companies and thereby obtaining the companies' property. Since the 5,000 £1 shares in the subsidiary company were sold at £3 16s 1d each, the directors, the chairman's beneficiary, and the solicitor made quite a profit on the 3,000 shares they had subscribed for at £1 each.

The purchaser, as controller of the company, had the audacity to bring an action in the company's name to make the former directors, chairman and solicitor liable to account for the profit which had been made by them taking advantage of their position: a rather sharp way of recovering part of the purchase price!

The action failed against the solicitor since he subscribed for the shares from which the profit arose not only with the knowledge and consent of the plaintiff company (as represented by its directors) but at its request. The action also failed against the chairman since, as nominee, the shares and the profits never belonged to him (and no proprietary claim via the tracing process was made against the persons for whom he was nominee[4]). However, it succeeded against the directors[5] since 'the directors, standing in a fiduciary relationship to (the plaintiff company) in regard to the exercise of their powers as directors, and having obtained these shares by reason and only by reason of the fact that they were directors and in the course of the execution of that office, are accountable for the profits which they have made out of them'.

As Lord Russell said[6]:

'The rule of equity which insists on those who by use of a fiduciary position make a profit, being liable to account for that profit in no way depends on fraud or absence of bona fides; or upon such questions or considerations as whether the profit would or should otherwise have gone to the plaintiff, or whether the profiteer was under a duty to obtain the source of the profit for the plaintiff, or whether he took a risk, or acted as he did for the benefit of the plaintiff, or whether the plaintiff has in fact been damaged or benefited by his action. The liability arises from the mere fact of a profit having in the stated circumstances been made. The profiteer, however honest and well intentioned, cannot escape the risk of being called upon to account.'

Since the claim was pleaded as a personal claim to account for moneys had and received, the defendants being good for the money, there was no need to determine whether the shares were held on constructive trust so as to lay the foundations for a tracing claim for the proceeds of sale mixed with other moneys of the defendants. However, it was assumed by Lords Russell and Wright that if the directors had held a general meeting to ratify their conduct then the defendants would have been able to retain their profits. This assumes that the shares were not held on constructive trust for the plaintiff company because, as *Cook v Deeks* makes clear, no resolution at general

---

4 As donees they could be in no better position than the chairman, if, as fiduciary, he had retained the profit for himself in breach of the fiduciary duty – cf the innocent donees in *Foskett v McKeown* [2001] 1 AC 102.

5 The chairman and the solicitor, the prime movers, thus escaped. For further details of their involvement see *Luxor (Eastbourne) Ltd v Cooper* [1941] AC 108, [1941] 1 All ER 33, HL; especially [1939] 4 All ER 411 at 416, CA.

6 [1967] 2 AC 134n at 144–145 endorsed by *Warman International v Dwyer* (1995) 69 ALJR 362.

meeting can ratify an act of expropriation of company property by the majority to the detriment of the minority[7].

If this be correct then there is only a personal liability to account where the fiduciary is a director who has taken advantage of his position (as opposed to taking advantage of property that is the subject matter of the fiduciary relationship). However, it seems anomalous and inconsistent with *A-G for Hong Kong v Reid*[8] to have such a distinction between use of position and use of property. It is thus submitted that if the issue had been raised and argued in *Regal (Hastings) Ltd v Gulliver* the directors' shares should have been held on a constructive trust.

In *Queensland Mines Ltd v Hudson*[9] the Privy Council took a liberal view in stark contrast to the strict approach of the House of Lords in earlier cases. Queensland was formed to exploit the anticipated award of mining licences. Hudson was its managing director. At the last minute Queensland's financial backing collapsed so Hudson in 1961 took the licences in his own name and resigned as managing director, though remaining a director for 10 more years. At a 1962 board meeting Hudson honestly admitted he held the licences for Queensland but candidly warned of the risks attendant upon attempting to exploit the licences. The board then resolved not to pursue the matter further, so leaving Hudson free to go it alone. It was held that Hudson was not liable for his profits in successfully exploiting the licences either because the board had given a fully informed consent or because the board had placed the licences venture outside the scope of Hudson's fiduciary relationship. However, the consent of the board members (especially if they were Hudson's cronies) is surely not enough, especially when the consent of all the directors of Regal (Hastings) Ltd was not sufficient to protect them. However, because Queensland Mines Ltd had only two (corporate) shareholders, both of whom were represented on the board of directors, and Hudson was a representative of the shareholder with a 49% holding, the board's decision may be treated as a decision of the shareholders where the majority was not controlled by the defendant[10].

As for the second reason, to allow fiduciary managers to define the scope of their own fiduciary obligations, and so immunise themselves from liability, is startling when there is obviously such a conflict of interest if the directors can acquire for themselves what they have rejected on behalf of the company, though, in exceptional circumstances, it may be that such a resolution could be passed bona fide in the interests of the company[11]. Nowadays, approval for otherwise objectionable benefits to be conferred on directors can be given by the company in general meeting under ss 320 and 322A of the Companies Act 1985.

7 *Prudential Assurance Co v Newman Industries (No 2)* [1980] 3 WLR 543 at 568 Vinelott J suggested that a ratification by a company in general meeting will only be effective if the directors in question do not control the majority of votes and it may have been that that was the position of the directors in *Regal Hastings* though the editorial note in [1942] 1 All ER 378 at 379 assumed the directors did have the majority of votes.

8 [1994] 1 AC 324.

9 (1978) 18 ALR 1, PC cogently criticised by G R Sullivan (1979) 42 MLR 711. See also *Peso-Silver Mines Ltd v Cropper* (1966) 58 DLR (2d) 1 criticised (1967) 30 MLR 450 (D Prentice), (1971) 49 Can BR 80 (S M Beck).

10 This satisfies the test suggested by Vinelott J in *Prudential Assurance Co v Newman Industries (No 2)* [1980] 3 WLR 543 at 568.

11 See *Rolled Steel (Holdings) Ltd v British Steel Corpn* [1986] Ch 246 and Gower *Principles of Modern Company Law* (5th edn) p 595.

In *Guinness plc v Saunders*[12] the House of Lords reaffirmed the impossibility of a director profiting from his fiduciary position unless duly authorised[13], so that unauthorised remuneration of £5.2 million was received by the defendant as constructive trustee thereof so that he was personally accountable therefor.

Profits made by agents

As James LJ stated in *Parker v McKenna*[14]:

> 'No agent in the course of his agency, in the matter of his agency, can be allowed to make any profit without the knowledge and consent of his principal; that rule is an inflexible rule, and must be applied inexorably by this Court which is not entitled, in my judgment, to receive evidence, or suggestion, or argument as to whether the principal did or did not suffer any injury in fact by reason of the dealing of the agent; for the safety of mankind requires that no agent shall be able to put his principal to the danger of such an inquiry as that.'

Except to the extent the agent-principal relationship is a debtor-creditor relationship the agent is a fiduciary for the purpose of imposing constructive trusteeship, liability to account and of allowing the proprietary remedies via the tracing process[15].

The leading case is *Boardman v Phipps*[16]. Assets were held upon trust to provide an annuity for the testator's widow and subject thereto for the testator's children. The trustees were an accountant, Fox, the deceased's daughter and the deceased's widow. The active trustee, Fox, was unhappy with the trust's sizeable minority shareholding in a private textile company. The solicitor to the trustees, Boardman, and a beneficiary knowledgeable in the textile business, Tom Phipps, as agents of the trust tried unsuccessfully at a general meeting to pave the ground for improvement. Boardman and Tom Phipps reckoned that a purchase of a majority holding in the company would be advisable and necessary if things were to improve, assuming a detailed investigation of the situation did not prove unsatisfactory. They so informed Fox but he made it clear that it was entirely out of the question for the trust to attempt to obtain a majority shareholding. Fox and the daughter-trustee both agreed that Boardman and Tom Phipps could go ahead and themselves personally attempt to acquire a majority shareholding. The widow-trustee was virtually senile and so was left out of the picture.

Purporting to act on behalf of the trust with its sizeable minority holding, Boardman and Tom Phipps had detailed negotiations with the company directors which provided them with information they would not otherwise have obtained. They then realised what worthwhile advantages might well flow from acquiring control of the company, reorganising its structure and realising its assets. They then put the trust beneficiaries in the picture, the

---

12 [1990] 2 AC 663.
13 Such authorisation is not precluded by Companies Act 1985, s 310: *Movitex Ltd v Bulfield* [1988] BCLC 104.
14 (1874) 10 Ch App 96 at 124–125.
15 *New Zealand Netherlands Society Oranje Inc v Kays* [1973] 2 All ER 1222, [1973] 1 WLR 1126; *Boardman v Phipps* [1967] 2 AC 46, [1966] 3 All ER 721, HL; *Re Hallett's Estate* (1880) 13 Ch D 696; *Sinclair v Brougham* [1914] AC 398 at 420; *Burdick v Garrick* (1870) 5 Ch App 233; *Metropolitan Bank v Heiron* (1880) 5 ExD 319, CA; *Lister & Co v Stubbs* (1890) 45 Ch D 1; *Makepeace v Rogers* (1865) 4 De GJ & Sm 649, CA.
16 [1967] 2 AC 46, [1966] 3 All ER 721.

widow having died so the beneficiaries were absolutely entitled under a bare trust, but not sufficiently enough for a fully informed consent to be given as the court subsequently held[17]. With much time, trouble and skill Boardman and Tom Phipps succeeded in their design so that the trust made roughly £47,000 profit from its shareholding and they made roughly £75,000 profit from their personal shareholdings.

The plaintiff beneficiary, Tom's brother John, entitled to a five-eighteenths share of the trust assets, then had the audacity to claim that Boardman and Tom Phipps held the shares, which they had acquired by virtue of exploiting an opportunity arising by virtue of their fiduciary position, as constructive trustees as to five-eighteenths of them for the plaintiff and that they were liable to account for profits made from the shares. He sought an order that the defendants should transfer to him the shares held by them as constructive trustee for him (subject to satisfying their lien for the money they had paid for the shares) or should pay him five-eighteenths of the profit found on the taking of the account.

The plaintiff succeeded in his claim but an inquiry was directed to allow the defendants on a liberal scale a sum in respect of their work and skill in obtaining the shares and making a profit therefrom.

All Law Lords agreed that Boardman was a fiduciary as solicitor to the trustees and as purporting to act as agent for the trust in the negotiations which provided the extra information for going on with the takeover. His opportunities thus arose by virtue of his fiduciary position. Tom Phipps did not seek to be treated any differently from Boardman. All agreed that the defendants would not have been able to obtain the information on which they based their successful takeover but for their ability to represent that they were acting for the trust with a sizeable minority shareholding.

Lords Hodson and Guest therefore held that the information was trust property and since the defendants had made a profit out of using this property they were clearly liable to account for the profit. Lord Cohen, however, stated[18]:

'Information is not property in the strict sense of that word and it does not necessarily follow that because an agent acquired information and opportunity while acting in a fiduciary capacity he is accountable to his principals for any profit that comes his way as the result of the use he makes of that information and opportunity. His liability to account must depend on the facts of the case. In the present case much of the information came the [defendants'] way when Mr Boardman was acting on behalf of the trustees on the instructions of Mr Fox, and the opportunity for bidding for the shares came because he purported for all purposes except for making the bid to be acting on behalf of the owners of the 8,000 shares in the company. In these circumstances the principle of *Regal (Hastings) Ltd v Gulliver* applies.'

Lords Cohen, Hodson and Guest further applied the broad principle (of which the rule that a fiduciary may not make a profit out of his trust is a part[19]) that[20] 'an agent is liable to account for profits which he makes out of the trust property if there is a possibility of conflict between his interest and his duty to his principal'. After all, the trustees might have sought Board-

17 Wilberforce J so held and no appeal from this was made.
18 [1967] 2 AC 46 at 102–103, [1966] 3 All ER 721 at 743.
19 [1967] 2 AC 46 at 123, [1966] 3 All ER 721 at 756, per Lord Upjohn.
20 [1967] 2 AC 46 at 103, [1966] 3 All ER 721 at 743, per Lord Upjohn.

man's advice on an application to the court to acquire power to purchase the outstanding shares in the company; they would need not just legal advice but practical advice as to the likelihood of the assured success of the proposed takeover and reorganisation of the company. Boardman would not have been able to give unprejudiced advice if, when his plans were well advanced ('at the third phase'), he had been consulted by the trustees as to whether they should then try to take advantage of what he had done so as to obtain profits otherwise passing to him, thereby dashing the cup of profit from his lips.

Viscount Dilhorne and Lord Upjohn dissented. They took the view that the information obtained by the defendants purporting to be agents of the trust was not trust property. Viscount Dilhorne treated information as not being trust property unless use of the information was of value to the trust and was a use in which the trust was interested: the trust had no power (except upon applying to court) to purchase further shares in the company and Fox had made it clear that the trustees did not want any involvement in purchasing shares, waging a takeover bid and reorganising the company. Lord Upjohn[1] made the good point that information 'is not property in any normal sense but equity will restrain its transmission to another if in breach of some confidential relationship' which was not the case before him.

'The real rule is that knowledge learnt by a trustee in the course of his duties as such is not in the least property of the trust and in general may be used by him for his own benefit or for the benefit of other trusts unless it is confidential information which is given to him (i) in circumstances which, regardless of his position as a trustee, would make it a breach of confidence for him to communicate to anyone, for it has been given to him expressly or impliedly as confidential; or (ii) in a fiduciary capacity and its use would place him in a position where his duty and his interest might possibly conflict.'[2]

Viscount Dilhorne and Lord Upjohn concurred also in the view that there was no conflict between the defendants' private interest and their fiduciary duty to the trust. Lord Upjohn considered that a conflict requires[3]:

'that the reasonable man looking at the relevant facts and circumstances of the particular case would think that there was a real sensible possibility of conflict not that you could imagine some situation arising which might in some conceivable possibility in events not contemplated as real sensible possibilities by any reasonable person, result in a conflict.'

At the outset, Fox had refused to consider purchasing shares to obtain a majority shareholding and the trustees had no power to purchase further shares and the whole venture would have been too speculative. At the later stage when the defendants had discovered the information that made them consider it worthwhile taking over the company and reorganising its business, though they did not approach Fox, which they ought to have done, the venture was still rather speculative, so no court would have sanctioned the trust purchasing the shares to take over the company, unless Tom Phipps was willing to enter into a contract to run the company. Fox was an experienced

1 [1967] 2 AC 46 at 128, [1966] 3 All ER 721 at 759. Further on confidential information see *De Maudsley v Palumbo* [1996] EMLR 460; *Fraser v Thames Television Ltd* [1984] QB 44, [1983] 2 All ER 101; *Faccenda Chicken Ltd v Fowler* [1987] Ch 117, [1986] 1 All ER 617. In *Satnam Investments Ltd v Dunlop Heywood Ltd* [1999] 3 All ER 652 at 669–671, CA, confidential information was regarded as property.
2 [1967] 2 AC 46 at 128–129, [1966] 3 All ER 721 at 759.
3 [1967] 2 AC 46 at 124, [1966] 3 All ER 721 at 756.

accountant with as much knowledge of the company's situation as Boardman and in evidence had stated that he would not consider the trustees buying the shares in any circumstances. There was thus no reasonable sensible possibility of conflict of interest: indeed, Fox thought it would be to the advantage of the trust if the defendants themselves purchased the shares and took over the company.

Both the majority and the minority agreed that it could not be said that all information received by a fiduciary in his fiduciary capacity was trust property so that it could never be used by the fiduciary for his own benefit—that would place a trustee of more than one trust in an impossible position. The essential difference between the majority and the minority was that the majority favoured the traditional strict deterrent approach, so that (*non-de-minimis*) possibility of a conflict between private interest and fiduciary duty arising out of use of information received in a fiduciary capacity should give rise to constructive trusteeship of the shares purchased as a result of such information, whilst the minority favoured a liberal reasonable approach[4] that only a real sensible possibility of a conflict should give rise to a constructive trusteeship of the shares and there was not such a real sensible possibility (though the majority decision can, perhaps, be justified on the basis that it was possible to take the view that there was such a real sensible possibility on the facts[5]).

It would seem that the question of possibility of conflict or not must be judged at the time when the fiduciary carried out the acts leading to the making of the profit (the third phase in *Boardman v Phipps*) so that the fiduciary can then judge whether he needs to seek the sanction of the trustees or beneficiaries or the court. As Lindley LJ said in *Re Hurst*[6], 'The conduct of trustees ought to be regarded with reference to the facts and circumstances existing at the time when they had to act and which were known or ought to have been known by them at that time.'

It is submitted the strict deterrent approach of the majority in *Boardman v Phipps* is to be supported with its clear practical advantage that should save much litigation. It protects the beneficiaries who will usually be at a substantial informational disadvantage vis-à-vis the trustees or other fiduciary who could have avoided the problem by obtaining an informed consent or court approval before commencing the activity leading to the making of the profit or otherwise by refraining from such activity and any risk of loss to the trust fund resulting therefrom.

In *A-G for Hong Kong v Reid*[7] the Privy Council endorsed *Boardman v Phipps* 'which demonstrates the strictness with which equity regards the conduct of a fiduciary and the extent to which equity is willing to impose a constructive trust on property obtained by a fiduciary by virtue of his office' before holding that 'if a fiduciary acting honestly and in good faith and making a profit which his principal could not make for himself becomes a trustee of

---

4 Favoured in *Manufacturers Trust Co v Becker* 338 US 304, 70 Sup Ct 127 (1949); *Peso-Silver Mines Ltd v Cropper* (1966) 58 DLR (2d) 1; (1967) 30 MLR 450 (D.D. Prentice) and in *Consul Development Pty Ltd v DPC Pty Ltd* (1975) 49 ALR 74. See also *Pine Pass Oil and Gas Ltd v Pac Petroleum Ltd* (1968) 70 DLR (2d) 196 and (1968) 84 LQR 472.

5 On the other hand, in the remote possibility of the trustees seeking the solicitor-defendant's advice at the time of the crucial third phase he could have openly declared his interest and declined to advise them other than to seek the advice of another solicitor.

6 (1892) 67 LT 96 at 99; also *Nestlé v National Westminster Bank plc* [1993] 1 WLR 1260, CA.

7 [1994] 1 AC 324 at 338.

that profit, then a fiduciary acting dishonestly who accepts a bribe must also be a constructive trustee [thereof].'

An agent who has been employed by his principal to purchase land cannot purchase it for himself, so if he does so he will be constructive trustee thereof for his principal[8]. Where he contracts to purchase land for himself which he should have bought for his principal and then assigns the benefit of the contract to a purchaser, then the equitable interest of the principal will have priority over the later equitable interest of the assignee-purchaser as Jessel MR held in *Cave v Mackenzie*[9].

In *English v Dedham Vale Properties Ltd*[10] self-appointed agents were held liable to account for profits. The plaintiff had sold her bungalow and four acres to the defendant for £7,750. However, seven days before contracts had been exchanged the defendant had applied for planning permission for one acre, making the application in the plaintiff's name and signed by the defendant as agent for the plaintiff. Under the Planning Acts the plaintiff did not then need to be notified of the application or informed of its outcome. Planning permission was granted after exchange of contracts but before completion. It was only after completion that the plaintiff learnt about the application. She thereupon brought an action claiming inter alia an account of profits for breach of fiduciary relationship.

Slade J held[11]:

'(1) Where, during the course of negotiations for a contract for the sale and purchase of property, the proposed purchaser in the name of and purportedly as an agent on behalf of the vendor, but without the consent or authority of the vendor, takes some action in regard to the property (whether it be the making of a planning application, a contract for the sale of the property or anything else) which, if disclosed to the vendor, might reasonably be supposed to be likely to influence him in deciding whether or not to conclude the contract, a fiduciary relationship arises between the two parties. (2) Such fiduciary relationship gives rise to the consequences that there is a duty on the proposed purchaser to disclose to the vendor before the conclusion of the contract what he has done as the vendor's purported agent, and correspondingly, in the event of non-disclosure, there is a duty on him to account to him for any profit made in the course of the purported agency, unless the vendor consents to his retaining it. In such circumstances, the person who, for his private purpose, uses the vendor's name and purports to act as his agent cannot reasonably complain if the law subjects him to the same consequences vis-à-vis his alleged principal as if he actually had the authority which he purported to have.'

Since the plaintiff's name was used in respect of the plaintiff's property, the defendant was clearly liable to account for his profit ultimately received as a result of the making of the application for planning permission. If it had been material it seems likely that the defendant could have been held to be constructive trustee of the benefit of the planning permission so that upon a sale of the acre plot with a dwelling house thereon, if the proceeds (including the profit resulting from the planning permission) had been mixed with other moneys of the defendant, an equitable tracing claim would

---

8 *Longfield Parish Council v Robson* (1913) 29 TLR 357. Similarly, if an agent is employed to find another person as purchaser of a house, but by fraudulent misrepresentations has the owner transfer the house into the name of an alias of the agent, such house will be held on constructive trust for the owner: *Collings v Lee* [2001] 2 All ER 332.
9 (1877) 46 LJ Ch 564.
10 [1978] 1 All ER 382, [1978] 1 WLR 93.
11 [1978] 1 All ER 382 at 399.

have been available if the defendant had become bankrupt, so giving the plaintiff a prior interest in the defendant's assets. Indeed, Slade J stated[12]:

> 'If the plaintiffs had learned of the application which had been made in their names and in respect of their property before contracts had been exchanged they would have been entitled to say to the defendants: "We ratify and adopt this application, which has been made in our names as our own application, and neither of you are to have anything more to do with it". Furthermore, this is, I think, effectively the course which the plaintiffs would actually have adopted unless a more favourable form of contract had been offered to them. This being so, I do not think that a court of equity should, or will, allow the defendants to be in a better position than that in which they would have found themselves if, before exchange of contracts, the defendants had told the plaintiffs of the application which had been made in their names as I think they should have told them.'

This seemingly treats the benefit of the planning application as belonging in equity to the plaintiffs[13].

Indeed, though Slade J assumed that ratification was impossible after contracts had been exchanged, there seems no reason why ratification could not have occurred. The plaintiffs were full legal and equitable owners at the time of submission of the planning application in their name, and the rule that a principal loses his right to ratify the act done on his behalf if, since the act, property rights have become vested only relates to the vesting of rights in third parties, so that the self-appointed agent cannot plead the vesting of rights in himself as a bar to ratification. Thus, on ordinary agency principles the plaintiffs should have been entitled to the benefit of the planning application and the profits flowing therefrom.

Profits by partners or prospective partners

A partner, though a fiduciary, may profit personally from information received by him qua partner so long as the use made by him of the information is outside the scope of the partnership business[14]. Where the use is for a purpose within the scope of the partnership business then the profits belong to the partnership. Profits made out of partnership property must also be held on constructive trust for the partnership[15].

A prospective partner or joint venturer who is given confidential information not to be exploited other than pursuant to the prospective partnership or joint venture will be constructive trustee of that which he obtains through using such confidential information after negotiations between the parties have failed to lead to a partnership or joint venture agreement[16].

Profits by tippees

Where information acquired by a fiduciary is confidential (so that its disclosure could be prevented by a court injunction) and is passed on to

---

12 [1978] 1 All ER 382 at 398.
13 Like the benefit of the contracts in *Cook v Deeks* [1916] 1 AC 554.
14 *Aas v Benham* [1891] 2 Ch 244 approved in *Boardman v Phipps* [1967] 2 AC 46, [1966] 3 All ER 721, HL.
15 *Don King Productions Inc v Warren* [2000] Ch 291 at 341–342, CA; *Gordon v Gonda* [1955] 2 All ER 762 at 766, where 'not' in line 33 in the clause 'would not be held' on trust for the firm seems to have been inserted by mistake in a long convoluted sentence.
16 *LAC Minerals Ltd v International Corona Resources Ltd* (1989) 61 DLR (4th) 14.

another (the 'tippee') who exploits it, then just as the profit if directly made by the fiduciary would be held on constructive trust, so should the profit made by the tippee[17]. Indeed, use by a tippee of knowledge of an opportunity of a non-confidential but special nature, like that in *Boardman v Phipps* (whose strictness has been endorsed twice by the Privy Council[18]) may well give rise to accountability and to a constructive trust[19].

Employee inventions

Under s 39 of the Patents Act 1977 an invention is taken to belong to the employer in three situations[20]. First, if it was made in the course of the normal duties of the employee or, second, outside his normal duties[1] but during the course of duties specifically assigned to him. In both cases the circumstances must be such that an invention might normally be expected to result from the carrying on of such duties[2]. Third, if the invention was made in the course of the employee's duties and, because of the nature of his duties and the particular responsibilities arising therefrom, he had a special obligation to further the interests of the employer's undertaking[3]. If the employer is unable to establish that the invention comes within one of the above three situations the invention is taken to belong to the employee. This is so even if the invention is made during the hours of, or at the place of, employment or by use of the employer's time and facilities[4].

Section 40 provides for circumstances where, notwithstanding a patent belonging to the employer, an employee may receive compensation if the patent is of outstanding benefit to the employer.

For inventions made after 1 June 1978 any term in a contract made before the invention is to be unenforceable against an employee to the extent it diminishes his rights in respect of inventions[5] but this is not to absolve the

---

17 *Nanus Asia Inc v Standard Chartered Bank* [1990] HKLR 396; *A-G v Guardian Newspapers (No 2)* [1990] 1 AC 109, 161, 211, 262–263, 278, 288. However, if the information shortly becomes readily available in the public domain so the tippee could have made the profit by relying on that, then there will be no liability: *Satnam Investments Ltd v Dunlop Heywood & Co Ltd* [1999] 3 All ER 652 at 672, CA.

18 *New Zealand Netherlands Society Oranje Inc v Kays* [1973] 1 WLR 1126; *A-G for Hong Kong v Reid* [1994] 1 AC 324.

19 An alternative explanation for *Nanus Asia* [1990] HKLR 396; but courts are reluctant to find a third party liable unless dishonest or becoming a fiduciary: *Satnam Investments Ltd v Dunlop Heywood & Co Ltd* [1999] 3 All ER 652 at 672, CA. In *Fyffes Group Ltd v Templeman* [2000] Lloyd's Rep 643 at 672 it was held that the briber of an agent may be required to account to the principal for benefits obtained from the corruption of the agent.

20 Generally see K Hodkinson (1986) 7 Company Lawyer 146.

1 This seems to mean the duties normally carried out by the employee rather than any duties contractually agreed to be carried out so that the category of specifically assigned duties outside normal duties can still be duties falling within the contract of employment.

2 *Reiss Engineering Co Ltd v Harris* [1985] IRLR 232 a middle management salesman employed to sell valves, ensure after sales service and report back problems which arose (but not to solve those problems), invented a valve which solved a specific design problem encountered by his employers. Held: the invention was not made within the course of his normal duties nor was it made in circumstances where an invention might reasonably be expected to result from carrying out his normal duties.

3 Cf *Fine Industrial Commodities Ltd v Powling* (1954) 71 RPC 253; *Cranleigh Precision Engineering Ltd v Bryant* [1964] 3 All ER 289, [1965] 1 WLR 1293.

4 *Worthington Pumping Engine Co v Moore* (1902) 20 RPC 41.

5 *Triplex Safety Glass Ltd v Scorah* [1938] Ch 211, [1937] 4 All ER 693; *Electrolux Ltd v Hudson* [1977] FSR 312.

employee from any duty of confidentiality owed to his employer. There is an exception to the prohibition against contracting out where a relevant collective agreement provides for compensation.

Commercial transactions

The courts should be very wary of extending the ambit of fiduciary obligations (with the concomitant liability to account for, and constructive trusts of, profits). Such obligations should only arise in a relationship[6] involving some inequality of footing or opportunity between the parties arising out of a particular relationship or special circumstances surrounding such relationship. If experienced businessmen with access to legal advice contract at arms' length then their relationship should not be held to be a fiduciary one, even if a continuing business relationship is contemplated and one party as a result of the business generated by the contract knows that he will receive, unknown to the other, valuable commissions and discounts from third parties[7]. The contractual position should exclusively be the position, while 'the essence of a fiduciary obligation is that it creates obligations of a different character from those deriving from the contract itself'[8]. However, property acquired in breach of confidence by a prospective partner or co-venturer will be held on constructive trust[9].

Businessmen should be regarded as voluntarily taking the risk of sharp practice of other businessmen: they are free to take extensive legal advice on their responsibilities during negotiations for contracts and can enter into a pre-contract bargaining agreement defining their duties and liabilities in respect of information acquired in the course of negotiations[10]. The courts should not allow the device of fiduciary obligations in a relationship to be extended to create a degree of uncertainty and vagueness that will jeopardise the operation of commercial transactions and inhibit the parties' ability to determine their legal relations quickly and cheaply. These practical problems are well brought out in a passage from the judgment of Robert Goff LJ (as he then was) in *Scandinavian Trading Tanker Co AB v Flota Petrolera Ecuatoriana*[11] which Lord Diplock (with whom the others concurred) cited[12] in extenso on appeal:

> 'The courts should so far as possible desist from placing obstacles in the way of either party ascertaining his legal position, if necessary with the aid of advice from a qualified lawyer, because it may be commercially desirable for action to be taken

---

6 See p 20, ante and PBH Birks 'The Content of Fiduciary Obligation' (2002) 16 Trust LI 34: a trustee's fiduciary obligation is to promote the beneficiaries' interests disinterestedly (making no unauthorised profit and avoiding conflicts of interest or preferring his beneficiaries' interests to his own) and such obligation can be imposed on others in special circumstances.

7 See eg *Jirna Ltd v Mister Donut of Canada Ltd* (1971) 22 DLR (3d) 639, (Ont CA); affd (1973) 40 DLR (3d) 303, Can SC and *Hanson v Lorenz and Jones* [1986] NLJ Rep 1088, [1987] 1 FTLR 23 where a solicitor was held by CA not to be liable to account for his profit from a joint venture (concerning purchase renovation and sale of a house) between himself and a business client where the client fully understood a fair agreement.

8 *Re Goldcorp Exchange Ltd* [1994] 2 All ER 806 at 821, PC; also *Clark Boyce v Mouat* [1993] 4 All ER 268 at 275, PC; and *Kelly v Cooper* [1993] AC 205, post p 403.

9 *LAC Minerals Ltd v International Corona Resources Ltd* (1989) 61 DLR (4th) 14.

10 *Hospital Products Ltd v United States Surgical Corpn* (1985) 55 ALR 417 (Aust HC) (liability for breach of contract, no liability to account for profits).

11 [1983] QB 529 at 540–541, [1983] 1 All ER 301 at 308–309.

12 [1983] 2 AC 694 at 713–714, [1983] 2 All ER 763 at 768–769.

without delay, action which may be irrevocable and which may have far-reaching consequences. It is for this reason that the English courts have time and again asserted the need for certainty in commercial transactions, for the simple reason that the parties are entitled to know where they stand and to act accordingly. [It is no answer that the] problem may in a particular case prove to be capable of solution by entering into a without prejudice agreement with the [other party]. This is not always possible ... Nor is it an answer that the parties can immediately apply to arbitrators or to a court for a decision. For, quite apart from the fact that some delay inherent in the legal process, if the question to be decided is whether the tribunal is to grant equitable relief, investigation of the relevant circumstances and the collection of evidence for that purpose cannot ordinarily be carried out in a very short period of time.'

Significantly in *Satnam Investments Ltd v Dunlop Heywood & Co Ltd*[13] the Court of Appeal reversed the trial judge's holding that a development company, which bought a site through taking advantage of disclosures made to it by a surveyor in breach of fiduciary duty to its principal, held the site on trust for the principal (subject to being repaid the purchase price of the site). There had been no finding that the company had come under any fiduciary obligation as a result of receiving the disclosed confidential information, nor that it had encouraged or participated in the agent's breach of duty. Thus, the Court of Appeal considered it would be contrary to commercial sense that the company should disgorge property which it had acquired merely through an opportunity provided by a breach of fiduciary duty of another in which it itself was not implicated.

Defences to constructive trust claim

Due authorisation

No constructive trusteeship of profits will arise if the conduct generating the profit is authorised by the trust instrument or by the contract of agency, or by the deed of partnership or by the original articles of a company providing the contractual basis upon which persons become members of the company[14].

A further defence is for a trustee or fiduciary to show he had the informed consent of all the beneficiaries being each of full age and capacity and between them absolutely entitled to the trust property[15] or that he had the sanction of the court[16]. The court may authorise a trustee to sell his property to the trust and retain his profit, while it may also allow a trustee remuneration for his skill and labour in making a profit for which he is accountable to the trust[17]. A partner will need the informed consent of the other partners. A director will need the informed consent of all the members of the

13 [1999] 3 All ER 652 criticised by Goff and Jones *Law of Restitution* (5th edn) Supplement to p 716.
14 *Boardman v Phipps* [1967] 2 AC 46, [1966] 3 All ER 721, HL; *Brown v IRC* [1965] AC 244, [1964] 3 All ER 119; *New Zealand Netherlands Society Oranje Inc v Kuys* [1973] 2 All ER 1222, [1973] 1 WLR 1126; *Phillips v Manufacturers Securities Ltd* (1917) 116 LT 290, CA. See also *Re Drexel Burnham Lambert* [1995] 1 WLR 32.
15 *Boardman v Phipps* [1967] 2 AC 46, [1966] 3 All ER 721; *Borland's Trustees v Steel Bros & Co Ltd* [1901] 1 Ch 279; *Boulting v Association of Cinematograph, Television and Allied Technicians* [1963] 2 QB 606 at 636.
16 *Farmer v Dean* (1863) 32 Beav 327; *Boardman v Phipps* [1967] 2 AC 46, [1966] 3 All ER 721; Trustee Act 1925, s 42.
17 *Phipps v Boardman* [1967] 2 AC 46 at 104, 112; *Guinness v Saunders* [1990] 2 AC 663 at 694, 701; *Badfinger Music v Evans* [2001] WTLR 1 at 13–17.

company[18] or of a majority acting bona fide in the interests of the company[19] except where advantage is taken of ss 320 and 322A of the Companies Act 1985[20].

It would seem that someone employed by trustees in a fiduciary position (eg a solicitor, discretionary portfolio manager, surveyor, land agent, or accountant) or a beneficiary acquiring special information whilst purportedly representing the trust so as to be treated as a fiduciary, may be able to escape liability as constructive trustee by obtaining the informed consent of independent trustees[1] as an alternative to obtaining the informed consent of all the beneficiaries. Indeed, where the business reality is such that profits could never have been earned at all as between fully independent persons except on a profit-sharing basis then a fiduciary may be allowed a share of the profits[2].

It will always be a defence to a claim by a particular plaintiff that that particular plaintiff himself gave his fully informed consent to the conduct in question of the defendant[3].

Mere use of knowledge or opportunity acquired qua fiduciary: problems of trustees of two or more trusts

There must be more than *mere* use of any knowledge or opportunity which comes to the fiduciary in the course of his fiduciary relationship[4].

Lord Upjohn in *Boardman v Phipps* stated[5]:

'There is no general rule that information learnt by a trustee during the course of his duties is property of the trust and cannot be used by him. If this was to be the rule it would put the Public Trustee and other corporate trustees out of business and make it difficult for private trustees to be trustees of more than one trust. This would be the greatest possible pity for corporate trustees and others may have much information which they may initially acquire in connection with some particular trust but, without prejudice to that trust, can make it readily available to other trusts to the great advantage of those other trusts.

The real rule is that knowledge learnt by the trustee in the course of his duties as

---

18 *Cook v Deeks* [1916] 1 AC 554; *Borland's Trustees v Steel Bros & Co Ltd* [1901] 1 Ch 279.
19 *Rolled Steel Products Ltd v British Steel Corpn* [1986] Ch 246, CA.
20 Gower, *Principles of Modern Company Law* (6th edn) p 202–206.
  1 *Regal (Hastings) Ltd v Gulliver* (1942) [1967] 2 AC 134n, [1942] 1 All ER 378, HL; *Boardman v Phipps* [1967] 2 AC 46 at 93, 117, and implicit in Lord Upjohn's speech at 130–133. See also *Anson v Potter* (1879) 13 Ch D 141. The trustees should be independent just as company directors must be if disclosure to them is to protect a promoter; *Gluckstein v Barnes* [1900] AC 240. In *Boardman v Phipps* [1967] 2 AC 46 at 104 Lord Cohen indicates that where a fund is to the fiduciaries' knowledge distributable, because the beneficiaries are each sui juris and between them absolutely entitled to call for the capital, then the informed consent of the beneficiaries is required.
  2 *O'Sullivan v Management Agency and Music Ltd* [1985] 3 All ER 351 at 373, CA; *Badfinger Music v Evans* [2001] WTLR 1; cf *Warman International Ltd v Dwyer* (1995) 128 ALR 201 at 211 and see p 658, post.
  3 See Article 97, post.
  4 *Boardman v Phipps* [1967] 2 AC 46 at 88, 89–90, 100, 102–103, 107, 126, 128–129. Directors are treated leniently so long as not acting in breach of contract or confidence: see *London and Mashonaland Exploration Co Ltd v New Mashonaland Exploration Co Ltd* [1891] WN 165; *Bell v Lever Bros Ltd* [1932] AC 161, HL; cf *Hivac Ltd v Park Royal Scientific Instruments Ltd* [1946] Ch 169, [1946] 1 All ER 350, CA; *Marshall (Thomas) Exports Ltd v Guinle* [1979] Ch 227, [1978] 3 All ER 193. As emphasised by Oliver LJ in the passage cited at p 387, ante the profits have to have been acquired not only in the course of, but *by reason of,* the fiduciary relationship.
  5 [1967] 2 AC 46 at 128–129.

such is not in the least property of the trust and in general may be used by him for his own benefit or for the benefit of other trusts unless it is confidential information which is given to him (i) in circumstances which, regardless of his position as a trustee would make it a breach of confidence for him to communicate it to anyone, for it has been given to him expressly or impliedly as confidential; or (ii) in a fiduciary capacity, and its use would place him in a position where his duty and his interest might possibly conflict. Let me give examples. A, as trustee of two settlements X and Y holding shares in the same small company, learns facts as trustee of X about the company which are encouraging. In the absence of special circumstances (such, for example, that X wants to buy more shares) I can see nothing whatever which would make it improper for him to tell his co-trustees of Y who feel inclined to sell that he has information that this would be a bad thing to do. Another example: A as trustee of X learns facts that make him and his co-trustees want to sell. Clearly he could not communicate this knowledge to his co-trustees of Y until at all events the holdings of X have been sold for there would be a plain conflict, reflected in the prices that might or might possibly be obtained.'

An equitable obligation of confidence arises from the receipt of confidential information in the knowledge that it is to be kept confidential[6]. Indeed 'if the circumstances are such that any reasonable man standing in the shoes of the recipient of the information would have realised that upon reasonable grounds the information was being given to him in confidence then this should suffice to impose upon him the equitable obligation of confidence'[7]. Thus, if a trustee of two settlements, X and Y, obtains as trustee of Y information subject to the equitable obligation of confidence then he cannot use it for the benefit of X and, it seems, even if he was trustee of X before he became trustee of Y, he cannot be sued by the X beneficiaries for breach of trust for failing to take advantage of the confidential information obtained qua trustee of Y[8]. After all, where clients of auditors consent to them acting for competing clients the auditors 'must of course keep confidential the information obtained from their respective clients'[9].

Contractual ouster of financial obligations

Kelly v Cooper[10] provides further assistance for professional trustees who act as trustee of many trusts. The case concerned an estate agent, employed to sell two adjoining properties, who, having obtained X to purchase one property, did not so inform the vendor of the other property when communicating to him X's offer of purchase, so depriving such vendor of the opportunity to obtain a higher price. The Privy Council held that there must be an implied term of the contract with the agent (known to act often for competing principals where properties are of similar description) that he is entitled to act for other principals selling competing properties and to keep confidential

---

6 *Seager v Copydex* [1967] 2 All ER 415, [1967] 1 WLR 923, CA; *De Maudsley v Palumbo* [1996] EMLR 460; *Fraser v Evans* [1969] 1 QB 349, [1969] 1 All ER 8, CA; *A-G v Jonathan Cape Ltd* [1976] QB 752, [1975] 3 All ER 484; *Dunford and Elliot Ltd v Johnson and Firth Brown Ltd* [1977] 1 Lloyd's Rep 505, CA. Generally see F Gurry, *Breach of Confidence* on this topic which falls outside the scope of this work.
7 *Coco v A N Clark (Engineers) Ltd* [1969] RPC 41 at 48, per Megarry J.
8 Cf *North and South Trust Co v Berkeley* [1971] 1 All ER 980, [1971] 1 WLR 470; [1978] Conv 114 (B Rider).
9 *Bolkiah v KPMG* [1999] 1 All ER 517 at 526–527, per Lord Millett.
10 [1993] AC 205.

the information obtained from each of his principals. Moreover[11], 'the scope of the fiduciary duties owed by the defendants to the plaintiff (and in particular the alleged duty not to put themselves in a position where their duty and their interest conflict) are to be defined by the terms of the contract of agency'. The Privy Council endorsed the following dicta of Mason J[12]:

'That contractual and fiduciary relationships may co-exist between the same parties has never been doubted. ... In these situations it is the contractual foundation which is all important because it is the contract that regulates the basic rights and liabilities of the parties. The fiduciary relationship, if it is to exist at all, must accommodate itself to the terms of the contract so that it is consistent with, and conforms to, them. The fiduciary relationship cannot be superimposed upon the contract in such a way as to alter the operation which the contract was intended to have upon its true construction.'

Thus in *Clark Boyce v Mouat*[13] the Privy Council held that a fiduciary duty cannot be prayed in aid to enlarge the scope of contractual duties so that, there being no contractual duty on the solicitor to advise the plaintiff on the wisdom of entering into the relevant transaction, the plaintiff could not claim that he nevertheless owed her a fiduciary duty to give advice.

Partners are not at such a disadvantage as many other fiduciaries (eg trustees) for a partner may make a profit from information obtained in the course of the partnership business where he does so in another firm with business outside the scope of the partnership business[14]. As Lord Hodson stated in *Boardman v Phipps*[15]:

'The case of partnership is special in the sense that a partner is the principal as well as the agent of the other partners and works in a defined area of business so that it can normally be determined whether the particular transaction is within or without the scope of the partnership. It is otherwise in the case of a general trusteeship or fiduciary position such as was occupied by Mr Boardman, the limits of which are not readily defined.'

Fiduciary cannot use the equitable principle as a shield

Upjohn LJ made it clear in *Boulting v Association of Cinematograph, Television and Allied Technicians*[16] that the principle that a trustee or other person with fiduciary duties to perform should not place himself in a position where his private interest might conflict with his fiduciary duties is a principle for the protection of the person to whom the fiduciary duties are owed, not for the benefit of the trustee or fiduciary. The person to whom the duties are owed may relax them if he sees fit but the trustee or fiduciary cannot invoke the principle for some ulterior purpose of his own.

Can strict rule be flexibly diluted?

Some flexibility is inherent in the leeway afforded to the court to find that the alleged possibility of conflict was fanciful or insignificant in all the par-

11 [1993] AC 205 at 215.
12 *Hospital Products Ltd v United States Surgical Corpn* (1984) 156 CLR 41 at 97.
13 [1993] 4 All ER 268 at 275.
14 *Aas v Benham* [1891] 2 Ch 244, CA.
15 [1967] 2 AC 46 at 108.
16 [1963] 2 QB 606 at 636–637.

ticular circumstances[17], because this will oust any liability. There is also flexibility in defining the scope of a fiduciary relationship which may make a person a fiduciary for part of his activities but not for other parts and in ascertaining whether the profit was actually acquired by reason of the fiduciary relationship[18].

There is scope to mitigate the harsh effects of the rule by making an equitable allowance in favour of the defendant constructive trustee[19]. In Canada[20], Australia[1], and New Zealand[2] there are suggestions that equity in its discretion in particular circumstances should not automatically impose a constructive trust but a lesser remedy such as a lien or a personal liability to account and, perhaps, just for a share of the profits[3]; the policy underlying liability should help determine what remedies will best further that policy and the honesty and solvency of the defendant should be important factors. No doubt, more will be heard of this in England[4] and, perhaps, flexible relief may be available under s 61 of the Trustee Act 1925. Interestingly, where it was held[5] that the briber of an agent could be required to account to the principal for benefits obtained from the corruption of the agent, the court did not make him account, because it was highly probable that the claimant-principal would have entered into the relevant contract with the briber if there had been no bribe. In so far as the contractual terms enabled the briber to make an ordinary profit it was not caused by the bribery but was profit for the provision of services for which there would have been a contract in any event. In so far as the terms were more favourable to the briber and enabled an extra profit to be made, common law damages had been ordered to be assessed.

'Chinese Walls' or information barriers

To avoid conflicts of interests and liabilities arising therefrom large companies or firms may well erect physical or geographical barriers between particular departments to try to deal with the general rule that the knowledge of a company or firm depends on the knowledge of all its employees with authority to acquire or receive such knowledge[6], but one cannot put the knowledge of one employee in one department together with the knowledge of another employee in a separate department where each acts honestly so as to conclude that the company acted dishonestly because, had the two

---

17 See *Industrial Development Consultants Ltd v Cooley* [1972] 2 All ER 162; *Jones v AMP Perpetual Trustee Co* [1994] 1 NZLR 690.
18 *Queensland Mines v Hudson* (1978) 52 ALJR 399; *New Zealand Netherlands Society Oranje Inc v Kuys* [1973] 1 WLR 1126; *Arklow Investments Ltd v Maclean* [2000] 1 WLR 594.
19 *Boardman v Phipps* [1967] 2 AC 46, HL; *O'Sullivan v Management Agency and Music Ltd* [1985] QB 428; *Badfinger Music v Evans* [2001] WTLR 1 at 13–17; see p 657, post.
20 *LAC Minerals Ltd v International Corona Resources Ltd* (1989) 61 DLR (4th) 14; *Canson Enterprises Ltd v Boughton* (1991) 85 DLR (4th) 129.
1 *Chan v Zacariah* (1984) 154 CLR 178 at 204–205.
2 *Official Assignee of Collier v Creighton* [1993] 2 NZLR 534, CA.
3 *Warman International Ltd v Dwyer* (1995) 128 ALR 201 at 211 (Australian High Court).
4 Eg *Goff & Jones, Law of Restitution* (5th edn) pp 716–718.
5 *Fyffes Group Ltd v Templeman* [2000] 2 Lloyd's Rep 643 at 652.
6 *Lloyds Bank Ltd v Savory & Co* [1933] AC 201; *Harrods Ltd v Lemon* [1931] 2 KB 157, CA; *El Ajou v Dollar Land Holdings plc* [1994] 2 All ER 685, CA.

employees pooled their information, they would have discovered an act was dishonest[7].

In the case of solicitors and of accountants providing litigation support services they owe a continuing professional duty to a former client following termination of the client relationship to preserve the confidentiality of information imparted during the relationship. Such former client can obtain an injunction preventing the professional firm from acting for someone with an adverse interest to him, assuming it is shown that the firm is in possession of confidential information, unless the firm can prove effective measures had been taken to ensure no disclosure would occur and there was no risk of the information coming into the possession of those acting for the other client. The risk must be a real one, and not merely fanciful or theoretical, but it need not be substantial. There is a presumption that unless special measures are taken information moves within a firm. The court should restrain the firm from acting for the other client unless there is clear and convincing evidence that effective measures have been taken to ensure the other client receives no confidential information[8]. An effective Chinese wall needs to be an established part of the organisational structure of the firm, not artificially created ad hoc and dependent on the acceptance of evidence sworn for the purpose by persons engaged in the relevant work[9]. However, no Chinese wall can affect the situation as between existing clients due to the inescapable conflict of interest inherent in such situation, which is also the case where a trustee will be contravening the fundamental rule against self-dealing[10] (in purchasing trust property for himself or selling his own property to the trust). If it is only the fair-dealing rule[11] that applies (as where a trustee purchases the beneficial interest of a beneficiary) then a Chinese wall can help to show that no advantage was taken of the trustee's position and the transaction was proper and reasonable.

ARTICLE 34

Constructive trusts imposed upon strangers holding trust property or its traceable product

Equity imposes a constructive trust upon trust or other property subject to a fiduciary relationship or upon its traceable product where such property has wrongfully been transferred by the fiduciary to a stranger, so long as the stranger is not protected by statutory overreaching provisions[12] or exceptions to the rule *nemo dat quod non*

---

7 *Galmerrow Securities Ltd v National Westminster Bank* [2002] WTLR 125.

8 *Bolkiah v KPMG* [1999] 2 AC 222, HL

9 *Re Firm of Solicitors* [2000] 1 Lloyd's Rep 31 (effective Chinese wall); also see *Halewood International v Addleshaw Booth* [2000] Lloyd's Rep PN 298. Further see C Hollander & S Salzedo *Conflicts of Interest and Chinese Walls* (2000, Sweet & Maxwell) and review thereof by Waller LJ in (2001) 117 LQR 335–340; *Laker Airways v FLS Aerospace Ltd* [2000] 1 WLR 113 and *Koch Shipping Inc v Richards Butler* [2002] EWCA Civ 1280.

10 See p 661 post.

11 See p 671 post.

12 Law of Property Act 1925, ss 2, 27.

habet[13] or the defence of change of position[14] or is not a bona fide purchaser of a legal interest for value without notice or a registered proprietor of land protected under the Land Registration Act 1925 or 2002[15]. However, the stranger only becomes subject to personal duties and liabilities from the time he knows of the claimant's proprietary interest or would have known but for turning a blind eye to what would otherwise be obvious or from the time when his suspicions were aroused that the transfer to him might well have been improper but he deliberately or recklessly failed to make the inquiries an honest and reasonable person would make in the circumstances[16].

The law of priorities underpinned by tracing principles

The foundation for the fundamental principle enshrined in the above Article is based on the property law rules for the priorities of competing interests supplemented by the equitable tracing rules discussed in Article 101. If T holds property on trust for A for life, remainder to B absolutely, but wrongfully makes a gift of it to G, who subsequently sells it and purchases with the proceeds a valuable painting, then the court will treat the gifted property as held on constructive trust by G from the moment of receipt[17] so that any income arising therefrom will similarly be held on constructive trust, as will the proceeds of sale and, then, the painting[18]. Thus G, when the facts are discovered, must account to A and B for everything that has happened in respect of the property since he received it, thereby assisting them in their proprietary claim via the tracing process. However, as Millett J has observed[19]:

> 'It is a mistake to suppose that in every situation in which a constructive trust arises the legal owner is necessarily subject to all the fiduciary obligations and disabilities of an express trustee.'

Lord Browne-Wilkinson has also made it clear[20] that no personal liability to account ('as a constructive trustee' in the old misleading terminology) can arise until the defendant's conscience is affected by actual 'Nelsonian' or 'naughty'[1] knowledge of the claimant's interest. Thus, so long as G remains an innocent volunteer without cognisance of the trust, he will owe no duties

---

13 Eg Factors Act 1889, Sale of Goods Act 1979, Hire Purchase Act 1964.
14 See pp 978–979, post.
15 LRA 1925, ss 5, 9, 20(1), 23(1), 59(6) or LRA 2002, ss 11, 12, 28, 29 and 30.
16 *Re Montagu's Settlement* [1987] Ch 264; *Westdeutsche Landesbank v Islington London Borough Council* [1996] AC 669 at 705–707; *Re Diplock* [1948] Ch 465 at 478, CA.
17 See *Re Sharpe* [1980] 1 All ER 198 at 203h; *A-G for Hong Kong v Reid* [1994] 1 AC 324 at 331; *Guiness v Saunders* [1990] 2 AC 663 at 696 and 701; Lord Millett in (1998) 114 LQR 399 at 402, 404–406.
18 See Article 101.
19 *Lonhro plc v Al Fayed (No 2)* [1992] 1 WLR 1 at 12. Further see his remarks in (1998) 114 LQR 399 at 404–406.
20 *Westdeutsche Landesbank v Islington London Borough Council* [1996] AC 669 at 705–707. Indeed he would prefer the recipient subject to the claimant's equitable interest from the time of receipt not to be termed a constructive trustee until the time he becomes personally liable but to be treated just like a transferee of land subject to an equitable charge or easement or restrictive covenant. However, since he is subject of equitable interests of beneficiaries under a trust it seems reasonably preferable to regard him as a constructive trustee for such beneficiaries from the outset.
1 This arises, where, despite being suspicious, the defendant deliberately or recklessly fails to make the inquiries an honest reasonable person would make: see p 974 post.

to safeguard or sensibly invest the property[2] and he will have the defence of change of position available to him[3].

If G were a purchaser and not a donee then he could take advantage of any statutory protection accorded to purchasers or the defence of bona fide purchaser of a legal interest without notice, if such defence be not ousted by statute as in the case of registered land. In the commercial context, not involving the conveyancing aspects of the purchase of land the courts are very reluctant to inhibit commercial dealings, so that a purchaser will only be treated as having constructive notice if he turned a Nelsonian blind eye to what would otherwise be obvious or if he deliberately or recklessly failed to make the inquiries that an honest, reasonable man would have made, though considering that there was something suspicious about the honesty of the circumstances but not wanting to probe matters for fear of what he might then discover[4]. In the case of the purchase of unregistered land there are well-established standard procedures that justify treating a purchaser as having constructive notice of those matters he would have discovered if he had followed such procedures rather than negligently failed to do so[5]. In the case of registered land[6] the new registered proprietor for value of the land or a charge over the land will not take subject to interests of beneficiaries unless they are protected by entry on the register or by being overriding interests or by the application of the principle that equity will not allow a statute to be used as an instrument of fraud[7].

Distinguish a resulting trust

It has been suggested[8] that a resulting trust arises in the above circumstances rather than a constructive trust because T, the trustee and transferor, has not effectively disposed of the equitable interests which must remain in the beneficiaries A and B. However, T did intend (though wrongfully) to transfer full legal and beneficial ownership to G (who could have passed such full ownership effectively to a purchaser, P, protected on property law principles, though the proceeds of sale would belong beneficially to A and B). This should therefore oust any resulting trust[9] and a constructive trust arises to vindicate the pre-existing equitable proprietary interest. As Robert Walker LJ states[10], 'where money subject to one express trust is paid improperly (and without valuable consideration) to another trust [or to X] the money or its traceable proceeds still belong in equity to the first trust and its trustees have a proprietary claim to recover them'. while Millett LJ states[11] that where such a proprietary claim succeeds, 'the court will treat the defendant as holding the property on constructive trust for the plaintiff and will order the defendant to transfer it *in specie* to the plaintiff'.

---

2 *Re Diplock* [1948] Ch 465 at 477–479; *Re Montagu's Settlement* [1987] 2 WLR 1192 at 1211.
3 See pp 978–979, post.
4 *Polly Peck International plc v Nadir (No 2)* [1992] 4 All ER 769 at 778–779.
5 Law of Property Act 1925, s 199.
6 Land Registration Act 1925, ss 5, 9, 20, 23, 70; LRA 2002, ss 11, 12, 28, 29, 30, Schs 1 and 3.
7 *Lyus v Prowsa Developments Ltd* [1982] 1 WLR 1044.
8 (1991) 107 LQR 71 at 80 and 81 per Millett J extra-judicially and also in (1998) 114 LQR 399 at 401 and *El Ajou v Dollar Land Holdings plc* [1993] 3 All ER 717 at 734.
9 See p 331 ante.
10 *Allan v Rea Bros Trustees Ltd* [2002] WTLR 625 at 641.
11 *Boscawen v Bajwa* [1995] 4 All ER 769 at 777.

ARTICLE 35

Constructive trusts arising from fraudulent or unconscionable conduct

(1) Equity imposes a constructive trust upon property which a person might attempt to obtain or retain for himself exclusively (or might prevent the equitable interest therein passing to persons for whom he had agreed to hold the property[12]) by fraudulently or unconscionably taking advantage of statutory provisions[13] or other fundamental legal principles, eg the *ius accrescendi* in a joint tenancy and the need for certainty of subject-matter of trusts. The constructive trust will be in favour of those to whose disadvantage the invocation of the provisions or principles would otherwise operate.

(2) In particular, but without prejudice to the generality of the foregoing, equity imposes a constructive trust on property:

(a) where it was the common but otherwise unenforceable intention (due to non-compliance with formalities requirements) or understanding, express or inferred (but not imputed) of the proprietor and the claimant that the claimant was to have some beneficial interest in the property and the claimant acted to his detriment in reliance thereon;

(b) where two persons, concerned with disposing of their estates on their death, enter into a contractual arrangement to subject property to a legally binding arrangement and make mutual wills pursuant to the arrangement, which is intended irrevocably to take effect on the first death, and that death occurs without the survivor having repudiated the arrangement to the deceased's knowledge (it would seem in sufficient time to enable the deceased to alter his will);

(c) where, on D's death, T becomes entitled to property, arranged by D to pass to T under D's will or intestacy, on the understanding that T is to hold on trust for a beneficiary or beneficiaries where otherwise the trust would fail for lack of compliance with formalities requirements;

(d) where a donor having legal title to property does everything he needs to do to transfer that title to a donee and that donee has not become registered with that legal title or where the donor has made an effective *donatio mortis causa* without having effectively vested legal title in the donee;

(e) where such property would otherwise belong to a person involved in an unlawful killing as a result of his crime (eg benefiting under his victim's will or intestacy or assurance policy or a joint tenancy with the victim);

(f) where a transferor's legal and beneficial title to his property has

---

12 For example, secret trusts and mutual wills.
13 For example, Wills Act 1837; Law of Property Act 1925, s 53; Administration of Estates Act 1925, s 46.

passed to the transferee according to basic principles of property law but in circumstances (eg involving fraud, misrepresentation, mistake, undue influence) where the transferor has an equitable right (ie a mere equity) to recover the property by having the transfer set aside, and the court declares that the property must be transferred *in specie* to the transferor;

(g) where money has been received by an agent and it would be unconscionable for the agent to claim beneficial title against the principal having regard to the insolvency problems of the agent when there is no express trust, or *Quistclose* purpose trust for the principal;

(h) where property not owned by the seller when he contracted to assign it to the purchaser is received by the seller, having already received the consideration from the purchaser.

Fraudulent or unconscionable abuse of statutory provisions

Where statute has prescribed formalities for wills and for dispositions of land the courts have long applied the maxim, 'Equity will not allow a statute to be used as an instrument of fraud'. Thus, as has been seen in dealing with secret trusts[14], an apparently absolutely entitled beneficiary on the face of a will can be compelled to hold his legacy on a trust communicated to him and accepted by him before the testator's death: it would be fraudulent for him to retain the property for himself. A person taking as trustee on the face of a will, disclosing no beneficiaries for whom the trustee is to hold the willed property, can be compelled to hold for beneficiaries disclosed to him outside the will before or at the time the testator made the will: as a trustee he cannot retain the property for himself, but it would be unconscionable to deny the secret beneficiaries their benefits which, but for the trustee agreeing to carry out the testator's wishes, would have been secured to them by other means. Indeed, in *Bulkley v Wilford*[15] a solicitor had his client enter into a transaction (levying a fine) that revoked the client's will but failed to advise the client to make a new will. The solicitor then happened to benefit upon the intestacy of his client. The House of Lords held it would be unconscionable if the solicitor were to do anything other than hold his interest in his client's estate for the beneficiaries under the revoked will.

In an inter vivos disposition case, *Bannister v Bannister*[16], a constructive trust was imposed by the Court of Appeal upon the defendant cottage owner to hold the cottage for the plaintiff for life: the defendant failed in his claim that the absence of a written declaration of trust enabled him to take free of the life interest he had orally agreed the plaintiff was to have when she sold him the cottage and an adjoining property at a lower price than would have otherwise been the case.

However, it appears from *Hodgson v Marks*[17] that a plaintiff can plead as

14 See p 257, ante.
15 (1834) 2 CL & Fin 102.
16 [1948] 2 All ER 133. The plaintiff was held to be a Settled Land Act tenant for life and the Court of Appeal by a majority followed this in *Binions v Evans* [1972] Ch 359, [1972] 2 All ER 70. See also *Ungurian v Lesnoff* [1990] Ch 206.
17 [1971] Ch 892, [1971] 2 All ER 684.

alternatives the application of the equitable principle that equity will not allow a statute to be used as an instrument of fraud and the imposition of a constructive trust.

Neither alternative plea will succeed where the statute (eg the Land Charges Act 1972, the Land Registration Act 1925 or 2002, the Companies Act 1985) expressly requires certain interests to be registered or protected by entry on a register upon pain of a purchaser taking property free from such interests. It is not fraudulent or unconscionable for a purchaser[18] to take advantage of his strict statutory rights by relying on the absence of the registration or protection stipulated for in the statute[19] unless he misled the plaintiff so as to make it unconscionable to allow him to insist on the position being different from what he led the plaintiff to believe[20].

Fraudulent or unconscionable use of property principles

Just as A cannot take advantage of the *ius accrescendi* of a joint tenant by killing B, where A and B hold land on trust for themselves as joint tenants, so as to claim the land exclusively for himself[1], so A cannot evict B where B merely has a contractual licence over land purchased by A from X if A had positively undertaken with X to take such land subject to B's contractual licence, thereby paying X a lower price and saving X from being sued by B for breach of contract[2]. Although, as a matter of property law, a contractual licence is not an interest in property capable of binding third parties like A, equity will regard B as having a right personally binding A's conscience so that A will be compelled to recognise B's personal rights under the contractual licence[3]. This would also seem to be the case if A's undertaking had been with B and caused B to act to his detriment[4].

However, if V sells property to P and in defensive fashion makes the sale subject to such property rights, if any, that B may happen to have, so as to satisfy V's obligations to disclose all possible incumbrances and so protect V against possible claims from P, then P is not bound by B's rights as a contractual licensee which are merely personal and not proprietary[5].

Where a defendant unconscionably tries to take advantage of uncertainty of subject matter of a trust (eg a trust of a 'fair share' of a house) the court will not allow him such advantage but find some means to prevent it (eg

---

18 There must be a genuine purchaser and not someone agreeing to take property as trustee for the unprotected person or someone who is the alter ego of the vendor endeavouring to evade the grasp of the unprotected person: *Peffer v Rigg* [1978] 3 All ER 745, [1977] 1 WLR 285 though probably erroneous on another point which cannot now stand with *Williams & Glyn's Bank Ltd v Boland* [1981] AC 487, [1980] 2 All ER 408, HL and see [1977] Camb LJ 227 and [1978] LQR 239; *Jones v Lipman* [1962] 1 All ER 442, [1962] 1 WLR 832.

19 *Hollington Bros Ltd v Rhodes* [1951] 2 TLR 691; *Miles v Bull (No 2)* [1969] 3 All ER 1585; *Kitney v MEPC Ltd* [1978] 1 All ER 595, [1977] 1 WLR 981; *De Lusignan v Johnson* (1973) 230 Estates Gazette 499; *Re Monolithic Building Co* [1915] 1 Ch 643; *Midland Bank Trust Co Ltd v Green* [1981] AC 513, [1981] 1 All ER 153, HL; *Lloyds Bank plc v Carrick* [1996] 4 All ER 630, CA.

20 *Lyus v Prowsa Developments Ltd* [1982] 1 WLR 1044; *Taylor Fashions Ltd v Liverpool Victoria Trustees Co Ltd* [1982] QB 133n.

1 *Rasmanis v Jurewitsch* [1968] 2 NSWR 166; *Re Stone* [1989] 1 Qd R 351.

2 *Ashburn Anstalt v Arnold* [1989] Ch 1, [1988] 2 All ER 147, CA. Further see Contracts (Rights of Third Parties) Act 1999.

3 *Ashburn Anstalt v Arnold* [1989] Ch 1, [1988] 2 All ER 147, CA.

4 Equitable estoppel principles come into play here: see pp 248–254, ante.

5 *Ashburn Anstalt v Arnold* [1989] Ch 1; *Bahr v Nicolay (No 2)* (1988) 62 ALJR 268.

somehow ascertain a fair share in all the circumstances[6]). Similarly, the court will intervene to prevent a defendant claiming to be absolute beneficial owner of a property acquired by him in furtherance of a pre-acquisition unenforceable[7] arrangement with the claimant for the claimant to acquire some interest in the property: the advantage to the defendant or the detriment of the claimant makes it unconscionable to allow the defendant to retain the property for himself inconsistently with the arrangement which enabled him to acquire it[8]. If the defendant cannot agree with the claimant what precise part of the property should be held on trust for the claimant or be transferred to the claimant, then the court will order a sale of the property and, usually, an equal division of the proceeds[9].

PARAGRAPH 2(A)

Common intention constructive trusts

A constructive trust may be imposed on specific property, such as a house in M's name, in order to give effect to an express or inferred common intention of M and W (whether at the time of the purchase or subsequently[10]) that W is to have a beneficial interest therein, so leading W to act to her detriment in reliance on that intention, so making it unconscionable to allow M to deny W any interest by pleading the lack of the necessary written formalities for a valid declaration of trust[11] or contract[12]. In such circumstances, the positive common intention can oust any prima facie resulting trust treating M and W as acquiring the shares they paid for at the time they completed the purchase with their saved, inherited or borrowed money, so that if M bought the house in his name with a mortgage (in his name, of course) having paid the deposit with his money, he will be sole legal beneficial owner, though if W provided the deposit and at the outset undertook with M to provide all the mortgage payment M will hold on resulting trust for her[13].

If the common intention was that W was to have a specific interest, eg a half or a quarter, or a share to be quantified on sale of the house or earlier separation of the parties as a fair share[14], taking account of W's financial contributions or their real and substantial equivalent to the acquisition of the house (without penalising her or him when prevented from making their usual contributions eg because of childbirth or illness), there will be a constructive trust of the specified share or of a fair share. Case law based on Lord Diplock's leading speech in *Gissing v Gissing* tends to stress the element of

---

6 *Passee v Passee* [1988] 1 FLR 263 at 271; *Stokes v Anderson* [1991] 1 FLR 391, CA.

7 Whether because not contractual or too uncertain.

8 *Banner Homes Group plc v Luff Developments Ltd* [2000] Ch 372, CA.

9 *Pallant v Morgan* [1953] Ch 43, [1952] 2 All ER 951; *Banner Homes Group plc v Luff Developments Ltd* [2000] Ch 372 at 388, 391, 393 and 396,CA.

10 *Austin v Keele* (1987) 61 ALJR 605, PC; *Lloyds Bank plc v Rosset* [1991] 1 AC 107 at 132.

11 *Yaxley v Gotts* [2000] Ch 162.

12 *Lloyds Bank plc v Rosset* [1991] 1 AC 107, [1990] 1 All ER 1111, HL; *Gissing v Gissing* [1971] AC 886, [1970] 2 All ER 780, HL; *Burns v Burns* [1984] Ch 317, [1984] 1 All ER 244, CA; *Grant v Edwards* [1986] Ch 638, [1986] 2 All ER 426 approved by PC in *Maharaj v Chand* [1986] 3 WLR 440 at 446, PC.

13 *Ivin v Blake* (1993) 67 P & CR 263, CA and see p 352, ante.

14 *Gissing v Gissing* [1971] AC 886 at 909, [1970] 2 All ER 780, HL; *Burns v Burns* [1984] Ch 317 at 327, [1984] 1 All ER 244 at 251, CA; *Grant v Edwards* [1986] Ch 638, [1986] 2 All ER 426, CA; *Stokes v Anderson* [1991] 1 FLR 391, CA common intention and detrimental reliance thereon so as to impose a constructive trust, rather than a resulting trust, since the flexibility of constructive trust principles affords more scope for achieving a just result.

Indeed, Lord Denning developed what he called 'a constructive trust of a new model'[15] by imposing a constructive trust 'whenever justice and good conscience required it'[16]: 'the shares may be half and half or any such other proportion as in the circumstances of the case appears to be fair and just'.[17] He was able to do this by imputing or ascribing to the parties a common intention they ought to have formed as reasonable persons if they had thought about the matter. This ignored what the House of Lords, and Lord Diplock in particular, had laid down in *Gissing v Gissing*[18]. The Court of Appeal in *Burns v Burns*[19] and *Grant v Edwards*[20] and the House of Lords in *Lloyds Bank plc v Rosset*[1] have now rejected Lord Denning's views and made it very clear that if there is no express or inferred common intention then the court cannot impute or ascribe a common intention to the parties in an attempt to produce a fair and just result. However, the principles underlying proprietary estoppel may provide some flexibility in the light of Lord Oliver's view[2] that, 'in essence, the common intention doctrine is an application of proprietary estoppel', Lord Browne-Wilkinson's preference[3] for the use of proprietary estoppel and Lord Bridge's three references[4] to 'constructive trust or proprietary estoppel', as if they both arise wherever there is a common intention followed by detrimental reliance, in his speech in *Lloyds Bank plc v Rosset* (with which the other Lords simply concurred). He there laid down[5]:

'Neither a common intention that a house is to be renovated as a joint venture nor a common intention that the house is to be shared by parents and children as the family home throws any light on their intentions with respect to the beneficial ownership of the property . . .

The first and fundamental question which must always be resolved is whether, independently of any inference to be drawn from the conduct of the parties, there has at any time prior to acquisition, or exceptionally at some later date, been any agreement, arrangement or understanding reached between them that the property is to be shared beneficially. The finding of an agreement or arrangement to share in this sense can only be based on evidence of express discussions between

---

15 *Eves v Eves* [1975] 3 All ER 768 at 771.

16 *Hussey v Palmer* [1972] 3 All ER 744 at 747, CA. Also see *Hardwick v Johnson* [1978] 2 All ER 935 at 938, CA.

17 *Bernard v Josephs* [1982] Ch 391 at 399, [1982] 3 All ER 162 at 167, CA, where he erroneously treated *Hine v Hine* [1962] 3 All ER 345, [1962] 1 WLR 1124, CA discredited by *Pettitt v Pettitt* [1970] AC 777, [1969] 2 All ER 385, HL as still being good law.

18 [1971] AC 886 at 898, 900, 904, [1970] 2 All ER 780 at 784, 786, 789.

19 [1984] Ch 317, [1984] 1 All ER 244, CA.

20 [1986] Ch 638, [1986] 2 All ER 426 accepted by PC in *Maharaj v Chand* [1986] AC 898, at 907, PC.

1 [1991] 1 AC 107, [1990] 1 All ER 1111.

2 *Austin v Keele* (1987) 61 ALJR 605 at 609, PC.

3 *Grant v Edwards* [1986] Ch 638, (1991) Birmingham University Holdsworth Lecture, 'Constructive trusts and unjust enrichment', published in (1996) 10 Trust LI 98. Also see Nicholls LJ in *Lloyds Bank v Rosset* [1989] Ch 350 at 387.

4 [1991] 1 AC 107 at 129, 132 and 133, [1990] 1 All ER 1111 at 1116 and 1119. Further on equation of constructive trusts and proprietary estoppel see *Yaxley v Gotts* [2000] Ch 162 at 176, CA and *Birmingham Midshires Mortgage Services Ltd v Sabherwal* (1999) 80 P & CR 256 at 263 and for a flexible approach to detrimental reliance see *Gillett v Holt* [2001] Ch 210, CA.

5 [1991] 1 AC 107 at 130 and 132–133. It matters not that the man does not have legal title himself but has it vested in a company he controls: *Re Schuppan* [1997] 1 BCLC 256 at 268.

the partners, however imperfectly remembered and however imprecise their terms may have been. Once a finding to this effect is made it will only be necessary for the partner asserting a claim to a beneficial interest against the partner entitled to the legal estate to show that he or she has acted to his or her detriment or significantly altered his or her position in reliance on the agreement in order to give rise to a constructive trust or proprietary estoppel.

In sharp contrast with this situation is the very different one where there is no evidence to support a finding of an agreement or arrangement to share however reasonable it might have been for the parties to reach such an agreement if they had applied their minds to the question, and where the court must rely entirely on the conduct of the parties both as the basis from which to infer a common intention to share the property beneficially and as the conduct relied on to give rise to a constructive trust. In this situation direct contributions to the purchase price by the partner who is not the legal owner, whether initially or by payment of mortgage instalments, will readily justify the inference necessary to the creation of a constructive trust. But, as I read the authorities, it is at least extremely doubtful whether anything less will do.'

Thus, he makes a crucial distinction between express and inferred common intention constructive trusts though his instance of an inferred constructive trust arising from direct contributions to the purchase price initially paid to the vendor should be classified as a presumed purchase-money resulting trust[6]: he was not a Chancery lawyer.

Express common intention

Lord Bridge placed primary emphasis on searching for express agreement arising out of express discussions, so that in *Hammond v Mitchell*[7] Waite J emphasised that as much particularity as possible of such discussion should be pleaded, although this 'means that the tenderest exchanges of courtship may assume an unforeseen significance many years later when they are brought under equity's microscope and subjected to an analysis under which many thousands of pounds of value may be liable to turn on fine questions as to whether the words were spoken in earnest or in dalliance and with or without representational effect.'

As Lord Diplock emphasised in *Gissing v Gissing*[8]:

'The relevant intention of each party is the intention which was reasonably understood by the other party to be manifested by that party's words or conduct, notwithstanding that he did not consciously formulate that intention in his own mind or even acted with some different intention which he did not communicate to the other party. On the other hand, he is not bound by any inference which the other party draws as to his intention unless that inference is one that can reasonably be drawn from his words or conduct.'

There will thus be sufficient direct evidence of an express common intention not just where the parties treated the house as 'our house' and had 'a principle of sharing everything'[9], but also where the man put up an excuse for not putting the house in joint names which he says he would otherwise

---

6 See p 351 ante.
7 [1991] 1 WLR 1127 at 1139.
8 [1971] AC 886 at 906, [1970] 2 All ER 780 at 790, HL; *Burns v Burns* [1984] Ch 317 at 336, [1984] 1 All ER 244 at 258, CA.
9 *Midland Bank plc v Dobson and Dobson* [1986] 1 FLR 171, [1986] Fam Law 55, 75, CA.

have done[10]: if there was no apparent common intention that the woman was to have a proprietary interest then the man would not have needed to put up an excuse.

However, it does not suffice that each party happened separately to form the same intention because a common intention means one that is communicated between them[11]. The court will consider the parties' common intention when the property was initially purchased but a subsequent common intention will suffice if followed by detrimental reliance[12].

Inferred common intention

In inferring a common intention from the conduct of the parties the court must look at the true state of affairs and cannot impute to the parties an intention they never actually possessed[13]. However, in the case of a couple who are married or engaged, s 37 of the Matrimonial Proceedings and Property Act 1970 is available to enable the contributor in money or money's worth to acquire a share or an enlarged share in the property, depending on the extent to which it seems just to the court, eg the share represented by the value added by the contribution[14].

Much significance has to be given to the obiter dicta of Lord Bridge (with whose speech the other Lords simply concurred) in *Lloyds Bank v Rosset*[15]. Here H and W decided to buy as their family home a derelict farmhouse for £57,000 using money provided by trustees of a family trust for H (inter alia) and who insisted that the property be bought in H's name alone. Without W's knowledge H mortgaged the property to Lloyds Bank to secure a £15,000 loan with interest. W spent some time supervising builders doing renovation work, did some preparatory cleaning work herself and some painting and decorating. It was held that there was no express common intention that W was to have an interest but even if there had been, the value of her work in relation to a farmhouse costing £72,000 was so trifling (as to be almost de minimis) that there was 'considerable doubt'[16] whether such work would amount to detrimental reliance linked to acquisition of the property so as to support a constructive trust[17]:

> 'In these circumstances [of trying to have the home ready for occupation by Christmas] it would seem the most natural thing in the world for any wife, in the absence of her husband [a courier] abroad, to spend all the time she could spare and to employ any skills she might have in doing all she could to accelerate progress

---

10 *Eves v Eves* [1975] 3 All ER 768, [1975] 1 WLR 1338, CA (alleged 20 year old girl needed to be 21 to have house in joint names); *Grant v Edwards* [1986] Ch 638, [1986] 2 All ER 426 (alleged her matrimonial proceedings be prejudiced if house put in joint names); *Hammond v Mitchell* [1991] 1 WLR 1127 (in his sole name for tax reasons, though he also said, 'Don't worry about the future because when we are married it will be half yours anyway').

11 *Springette v Defoe* (1992) 24 HLR 552, CA. Also *Mollo v Mollo* [2000] WTLR 227 at 241–242.

12 *Bernard v Josephs* [1982] Ch 391 at 404, [1982] 3 All ER 162 at 171; *Burns v Burns* [1984] Ch 317, [1984] 1 All ER 244 at 251; CA. *Austin v Keele* (1987) 61 ALJR 605, PC. The legal owner must implicitly agree that the contributor of finance is to be a purchaser and not a donor for 'It has been well settled that if A expends money on the property of B prima facie he has no claim on such property': *Pettitt v Pettitt* [1970] AC 777 at 818, HL, per Lord Diplock and *Davis v Vale* [1971] 1 WLR 1022 at 1025, CA, per Lord Denning.

13 *Grant v Edwards* [1986] 2 All ER 426; *Lloyds Bank plc v Rosset* [1991] 1 AC 107

14 See p 352, ante.

15 [1991] 1 AC 107, [1990] 1 All ER 1111.

16 [1991] 1 AC 107 at 131 and 1118.

17 [1991] 1 AC 107 at 131, [1990] 1 All ER 1111 at 1118.

of the work, quite irrespective of any expectation she might have of enjoying a beneficial interest in the property. The judge's view that some of this work was work "on which she could not reasonably have been expected to embark unless she was to have an interest in the house" seems to me quite untenable.'

Thus, there could be no inferred common intention. In the situation where the court must rely entirely on the conduct of the parties both as the basis from which to infer a common intention to share the property beneficially and as the detrimental conduct relied upon to give rise to a constructive trust[18]:

'direct contributions to the purchase price by the partner who is not the legal owner, whether initially or by payment of mortgage instalments, will readily justify the inference necessary to the creation of a constructive trust. But, as I read the authorities, it is at least extremely doubtful whether anything less will do.'

Of course, initial payments will give rise to a resulting trust anyhow[19], while some consider that subsequent mortgage payments can create or enlarge a share under a resulting trust by being regarded as deferred payment of the price (rather than repayment of the moneys paid as the purchase price to the purchaser on completion of the purchase), though the better view is that for subsequent mortgage payments to displace the resulting trust shares arising at the time of purchase there must be a common intention to such effect[20].

Lord Bridge then examined *Eves v Eves*[1] and *Grant v Edwards*[2] as 'outstanding examples'[3] where the 'indirect contributions to the acquisition or enhancement of the value of the houses made by the female partners' were 'sufficient to give rise to a constructive trust or proprietary estoppel' because of direct evidence of a common intention that the female was to have some share in the house but 'fell far short of such conduct as would by itself have supported the claim in the absence of an express representation by the male partner that she was to have an interest'.

In *Eves v Eves*[4] Stuart led Janet to believe that she was to have a fair share in the dilapidated house purchased in his name, taking account of her renovatory work. She cleaned the house and did extensive decorative work, painted the brickwork at the front of the house, wielded a 14lb sledgehammer to demolish the concrete front garden, disposed of the rubble and prepared the front garden for turfing, and helped renovate the back garden demolishing an old shed and replacing it with a new shed. The Court of Appeal held that Stuart held the house on constructive trust for himself and Janet in the proportions 3:1, the equity of redemption being worth about £10,000. Thus, in view of Lord Bridge's remarks, odd-job work even if cumulatively quite significant does not, of itself, enable any inference to be drawn of a common intention that such conduct is to be sufficient for acquiring an interest in the property: it is regarded as the 'most natural thing in the world'[5] for Janet to spend her time to have a nicer place to live in for the benefit of her relationship.

---

18 [1991] 1 AC 107 at 133 and 1119.
19 See pp 349–356, ante.
20 See pp 352–353, ante; *Bernard v Josephs* [1982] Ch 391 at 404; *Ivin v Blake* (1993) 67 P & CR 263.
 1 [1975] 3 All ER 768, [1975] 1 WLR 1338, CA.
 2 [1986] Ch 638, [1986] 2 All ER 426.
 3 [1991] 1 AC 107 at 133.
 4 [1975] 3 All ER 768.
 5 [1991] 1 AC 107 at 131 and [1990] 1 All ER 1111 at 1118.

In *Grant v Edwards*[6] the man led the woman to believe that she would have a beneficial interest in the house purchased in his name, saying it would have been taken in their joint names but for a particular excuse. For most of the time, except for three years when she had two young babies to look after, she went out to work and earned roughly the same as he did. He paid all the mortgage instalments but he would not have been able to do so and maintain the family standard of living but for her substantial contributions to household expenses, so that she could indirectly be regarded as having paid roughly half the mortgage instalments. Moreover, the £1,037 balance of a fire insurance claim paid in respect of the house was paid into a joint account. The Court of Appeal held that the man held the house on constructive trust for himself and the woman equally. Lord Bridge's remarks indicate a strong belief that the woman's conduct would not nowadays justify an inferred common intention that she was to have an interest in the house (without dealing with the contrary views of Fox LJ in *Burns v Burns*[7]) so that substantial indirect contributions to mortgage payments, via payments of household expenses freeing up the man's moneys for paying the mortgage instalments, only count where an express common intention is found that they are to be treated as contributions to the purchase price or can be inferred from a direct initial contribution to the purchase indicating a common intention that some beneficial interest is to be acquired[8].

It may well be that the leeway afforded to a judge in his fact-finding function may enable him to find just sufficient evidence of an express intention that the woman was to acquire a fair or half beneficial interest where she has made no part payment of the deposit nor directly contributed to paying off the purchase price by directly paying all or part of mortgage instalments. She will need to show more than that she has continued as before to contribute out of her earnings or private income to other household expenses, as this is consistent merely with sharing such household expenses while retaining a separate interest in capital assets acquired with their own moneys[9]. Payment of such household expenses needs to be referable to acquiring an interest in the house which can be revealed by an upwards adjustment of her contribution to such expenses in order to enable the man afford the mortgage payments[10].

In *McHardy v Warren*[11] the Court of Appeal was happy to infer that the man held on constructive trust for himself and his wife equally where the man's parents were regarded as giving him and his wife £650 in paying the £650 deposit on a house bought in the man's name when his wife was a minor. Subsequent replacement houses were bought in the man's name, but a £5,000 personal loan was made to both jointly, while the mortgage instal-

---

6 [1986] Ch 638.
7 [1984] Ch 317 at 319 (per Fox LJ). Note that at pp 344–345, May LJ restricted the taking account of indirect contributions via payment of household expenses (other than mortgage payments) to the situation where there had been a contribution to the initial deposit, revealing a common intention that she was to have some beneficial interest, as previously indicated by Lord Diplock in *Gissing v Gissing* [1971] AC 886 at 907–908.
8 *Gissing v Gissing* [1971] AC 886 at 903 and 908, [1970] 2 All ER 780 at 788 and 792; *Burns v Burns* [1984] Ch 317 at 345, [1984] 1 All ER 244 at 265.
9 *Gissing v Gissing* [1971] AC 886 at 909; *Mollo v Mollo* [2000] WTLR 227.
10 *Gissing v Gissing* [1971] AC 886 at 909; *Mollo v Mollo* [2000] WTLR 227. Cf *Le Foe v Le Foe* [2001] 2 FLR 970 in note 13 below.
11 [1994] 2 FLR 338 endorsed in *Halifax Building Society v Brown* [1996] 1 FLR 103, CA and applied in *Drake v Whipp* [1996] 1 FLR 826, CA.

ments and the £5,000 loan were always paid or repaid out of a joint account. Thus, the wife did not obtain just a proportionate 8.97% share on resulting trust principles[12].

The position was developed in *Midland Bank plc v Cooke*[13] where the husband's parents contributed £1,000 to the purchase of the house in his name where the money was again held to be a gift to husband and wife equally. This direct contribution of 6.47% under resulting trust principles was held by the Court of Appeal to indicate a common intention that the wife was to have some beneficial interest and the court was 'free to attribute to the parties an intention to share the beneficial interest in some different proportions'[14], *despite* the fact that both parties had in their evidence expressly stated on oath that they had neither made, nor intended, any agreement. Adopting a holistic approach of looking at the parties' global dealings over the span of their ownership of the property, 'one could hardly have a clearer example of a couple who had agreed to share everything equally ... the conclusion becomes inescapable that their presumed intention was to share the property in equal shares'[15].

In essence, from the springboard of a resulting trust (arising from the wife's lack of intention to make a gift of her share of the money to her husband), the Court of Appeal imposed[16] on the parties a common intention that the wife was to have some beneficial interest in the house which was to be a fair interest in all the circumstances during their ownership thereof, which amounted to a half interest held on constructive trust for her.

In the absence of a deposit or other payment to found a resulting trust and of direct payments of mortgage instalments to found an inferred common intention trust, the court will not assist a woman who acted as the man's unpaid assistant, supported him in his speculative ventures and looked after the home and their children[17] nor a daughter who worked full time in her mother's public house for pocket money only, thereby assisting her mother make profits facilitating the purchase of a house[18]. This can produce harsh results, but the Law Commission in its Discussion Paper, 'Sharing Homes', in July 2002 has not proposed any statutory reforms considering it impossible to do this satisfactorily when the range of circumstances of home-sharers (going beyond sexual cohabitees) is so extensively variable.

---

12 Contrast *Springette v Defoe* (1992) 65 P & CR 1, CA, (no more than resulting trust percentage).
13 [1995] 4 All ER 562, CA, applied in *Mollo v Mollo* [2000] WTLR 227 and *Le Foe v Le Foe* [2001] 2 FLR 970 where the deputy judge surprisingly found an inferred common intention merely from payment of household expenses, but could have relied on the wife's use of a substantial inheritance to discharge the mortgage to found such intention.
14 [1995] 4 All ER 562 at 574.
15 [1995] 4 All ER 562 at 576.
16 Despite *Gissing v Gissing* [1971] AC 886 at 898 per Lord Morris, 'The court cannot devise agreements which the parties never made. The court cannot ascribe intentions which the parties in fact never had.' Logically, there should by operation of law have been only a 6.47% share under a resulting trust, following *Springette v Defoe* (1992) 65 P & CR 1, CA, but Waite LJ was keen to formulate 'a fair presumed basis for the sharing of beneficial title': [1995] 4 All ER 562 at 575 (perhaps justifiable on flexible proprietary estoppel principles based on holding-out conduct of the husband).
17 *Hammond v Mitchell* [1992] 2 All ER 109 for Spanish house.
18 *Ivin v Blake* (1993) 67 P & CR 263 at 276, CA, endorsing *McFarlane v McFarlane* [1972] NI 59 (already endorsed by *Lloyds Bank plc v Rosset* [1991] 1 AC 107 at 133), but see deputy judge in *Haywood v Haywood*, (13 July 2000, unreported).

Detrimental reliance—express common intention

Where there has been direct evidence of an express common intention that W is to have a specific share or a fair share in return for an explicit or implicit undertaking[19] to act in a particular way, W's conduct only needs to be that undertaken. It is immaterial whether it takes the form of a contribution to the costs of acquiring the property or is of quite a different character[20]. Whatever the court decides the quid pro quo to have been, it will suffice if the claimant has furnished it[1]. Expenditure or other detrimental acts insufficiently referable to acquisition of the house and insufficient to support an inferred common intention may thus be sufficient detriment to enable a claimant to succeed upon proving an express common intention that such expenditure or other acts were to entitle her to an interest[2].

Where the express common intention was that W was to acquire over the years a fair share based on her financial contributions to the costs of acquisition or improvement of the house (without penalising her or M when prevented from making their usual contribution, eg because of childbirth or illness[3]) then W obviously needs to prove she made such contributions.

In order to show that W acted to her detriment in reliance upon the common intention there has to be some 'link' or 'referability' between the common intention and the conduct claimed to have been based upon that intention. Where W was supposed to provide a clear quid pro quo for the intended share of the house then the provision of this will suffice in itself even if, apart from the clear agreement, it would not of itself be an act inherently referable to acquisition of a house[4].

It further seems that if in the case of a quid pro quo common intention W does not provide the quid pro quo but does act to her detriment, believing she will be acquiring an interest in the home through subsequently doing what was envisaged, then the courts will be ready to grant W an interest in the home.

After all, the court will grant W an interest where there is no quid pro quo common intention (ie no bargain) but only M's unilateral declaration of intention to create a trust which is made known to W, so that M and W have an understanding or agreement that W has a share in the home[5]. As Lord Bridge stated[6]:

'Once a finding to this effect is made it will only be necessary for the partner asserting a claim to a beneficial interest to show that he or she has acted to his or her detriment or significantly altered his or her position in reliance on the agreement in order to give rise to a constructive trust or a proprietary estoppel.'

Further in *Grant v Edwards*[7], in a passage endorsed by Nicholls LJ in *Lloyds Bank plc v Rosset*[8] and by the Privy Council in *Maharaj v Chand*[9], Sir Nicholas

---

19 *Grant v Edwards* [1986] Ch 638 at 652.
20 *Grant v Edwards* [1986] 2 All ER 426 at 435–436.
1 *Grant v Edwards* [1986] 2 All ER 426 at 435–436.
2 *Grant v Edwards* [1986] 2 All ER 426 at 432, 435, 437; *Ogilvie v Ryan* [1976] 2 NSWLR 504.
3 This may help instead to establish an inferred intention for a half share: *Gissing v Gissing* [1971] AC 886 at 908–909, [1970] 2 All ER 780 at 793, HL.
4 *Grant v Edwards* [1986] 2 All ER 426.
5 *Lloyds Bank plc v Rosset* [1989] Ch 350 at 381.
6 *Lloyds Bank plc v Rosset* [1991] 1 AC 107 at 133.
7 [1986] Ch 638.
8 [1989] Ch 350 at 381 (Mustill LJ agreed at 388).
9 [1986] AC 898 at 907.

Browne-Wilkinson V-C stated[10]:

> 'Once it has been shown that there was a common intention that the claimant should have an interest in the house, any act done by her to her detriment relating to the joint lives of the parties is sufficient detriment to qualify. The acts do not have to be inherently referable to the house. The holding out to the claimant that she had a beneficial interest in the house is an act of such a nature as to be part of the inducement to her to do the acts relied on. Accordingly, in the absence of evidence to the contrary, the right inference is that the claimant acted in reliance on such holding out and the burden lies on the legal owner to show that she did not do so: *Greasley v Cooke.*'

However, subsequently in *Lloyds Bank plc v Rosset*[11] the Law Lords opined that even if Mr and Mrs Rosset had an express common intention that she was to have some interest in the house they had 'considerable doubt' whether Mrs Rosset's assistance with renovating work would amount to detriment or a significant alteration of position when 'it would seem the most natural thing in the world for any wife' to assist with such work. Their Lordships, none the less, had no doubt that the woman's conduct in *Eves v Eves*[12] and the woman's substantial contributions to household expenses in *Grant v Edwards*[13] clearly amounted to sufficient detrimental reliance to justify the imposition of a constructive trust where there was evidence of an express common intention, although in both such cases the behaviour of the woman[14] 'fell far short of such conduct as would by itself have supported the claim' by enabling an inferred common intention to be discovered.

Detrimental reliance—inferred common intention

Where the court has to rely entirely on the conduct of the parties both as the basis from which to infer a common intention to share the property beneficially and as the detrimental conduct Lord Bridge[15] has made it clear that:

> 'direct contributions to the purchase price by the partner who is not the legal owner, whether initially or by payment of mortgage instalments, will readily justify the inference necessary to the creation of a constructive trust'

though in his opinion, 'it is at least extremely doubtful whether anything less will do'.

In his review of *Grant v Edwards*[16] it is clear that he considers that indirect assistance with the payment of mortgage instalments falls far short of conduct enabling a common intention to be inferred where without the woman's substantial contribution to household expenses the man's means are insufficient to keep up the mortgage payments and keep the household going. However, if the woman initially paid part of the deposit, so as to justify the inference of a common intention, then it seems that her subsequent indirect contributions to payment of mortgage instalments will strengthen such inference while amounting to detrimental conduct that will be taken into

---

10 [1986] Ch 638 at 657.
11 [1991] 1 AC 107 at 131.
12 [1975] 3 All ER 768.
13 [1986] Ch 638.
14 [1991] 1 AC 107 at 133. Lord Bridge echoes Lord Diplock's views in *Gissing v Gissing* [1971] AC 886 at 909, [1970] 2 All ER 780 at 793.
15 [1991] 1 AC 107 at 133.
16 [1986] Ch 638.

account in ascertaining the size of her share[17].

It would seem that where the woman pays for a substantial capital improvement (eg the addition of a conservatory or a garage with a bedroom above it) then this could be regarded as conduct upon which W could not reasonably be expected to embark unless she was to have some sort of interest in the house[18], though prima facie the law regards her as making a gift to the houseowner[19]. The actual carrying out of such major works[20] by W could be regarded similarly as the 'real and substantial equivalent'[1] of paying for part of the capital acquisition and so similarly referable to acquiring some interest in the house. Indeed, where such very significant money or effort is being expended it is unlikely that there were no discussions to found some evidence of common intention.

It seems clear that conduct not specifically referable to a belief that W has or will have an interest in the home, but naturally referable to W's love for M and their children and a desire to live well in a smart, tidy and pleasant environment will not suffice to justify any inference of a common intention that she was to have some share in the home[2].

Where legal title is in both names instead of one

Where the legal title is taken in both names, but there is no express declaration of beneficial interests, the beneficial interest will prima facie be shared[3]. Where the house is bought outright without the assistance of any mortgage then the extent of the respective shares will depend on the proportion of the purchase price respectively contributed[4].

Where, as is much more usual, the house is bought with the assistance of a mortgage then the parties will have a joint and several liability for the mortgage money that became their money and was paid over as part of the purchase price due to the vendor upon completion of the purchase. Such money, together with the money paid by way of deposit and for stamp duty

---

17 *Burns v Burns* [1984] Ch 317 at 345, [1984] 1 All ER 244 at 265; *Gissing v Gissing* [1971] AC 886 at 908, [1970] 2 All ER 780 at 792; *McHardy v Warren* [1994] 2 FLR 338, CA.

18 *Burns v Burns* [1984] Ch 317 at 344–345, [1984] 1 All ER 244 at 264–265; *Bernard v Josephs* [1982] 3 All ER 162 at 171; *Stokes v Anderson* [1991] 1 FLR 391; *Passee v Passee* [1988] 1 FLR 263. Such payment could well dwarf the amount of one or two mortgage payments which would seem automatically to suffice for inferring a common intention to have some beneficial interest. If W is married or engaged to M she will obtain whatever interest the court thinks just under Matrimonial Proceedings and Property Act 1970, s 37: see p 415, ante.

19 *Winkworth v Edward Baron Developments Ltd* [1986] 1 WLR 1512 at 1515; *Pettitt v Pettitt* [1970] AC 777 at 818; *Harwood v Harwood* [1991] 2 FLR 274 at 294.

20 More significant than Janet Eves' work in *Eves v Eves* [1975] 1 WLR 1338, CA, and requiring much more commitment than paying one or two mortgage instalments.

1 *Burns v Burns* [1984] Ch 317 at 344–345, [1984] 1 All ER 244 at 264.

2 *Burns v Burns* [1984] Ch 317; *Gissing v Gissing* [1971] AC 886; *Layton v Martin* [1986] 2 FLR 227; *McFarlane v McFarlane* [1972] NI 59 endorsed in *Lloyds Bank plc v Rosset* [1991] 1 AC 107, HL and *Ivin v Blake* (1993) 67 P & CR 263, CA.

3 *Pettitt v Pettitt* [1970] AC 777 at 813–814; *Bernard v Josephs* [1982] Ch 391; *Burns v Burns* [1984] Ch 317; *Springette v Defoe* (1992) 65 P & CR 1; *Mortgage Corpn Ltd v Shaire* [2001] Ch 743 at 751 and 754, also pointing out that an express declaration of the extent of the beneficial interest is conclusive (in the absence of fraud or undue influence: *Goodman v Gallant* [1986] Fam 106). A land registry form that the survivor of the joint registered proprietors can give a valid receipt for capital moneys is not equivalent to a declaration of a beneficial joint tenancy (*Mortgage Corpn Ltd v Shaire* [2001] Ch 743): in addition, one needs a statement that the transferees are entitled 'for their own benefit' (*Re Gorman* [1990] 1 All ER 717).

4 *Burns v Burns* [1984] Ch 317 at 344–345, [1984] 1 All ER 244 at 264.

and legal costs, should be taken into account for establishing a beneficial interest under a resulting trust[5].

Exceptionally, if M and W agreed at the outset that M was to pay all or 75% of the mortgage payments then M will be treated as providing all or 75% of the borrowed money for the purposes of establishing a proportionate interest under a resulting trust[6] (or it may be possible to find a common intention that irrespective of deposit payments etc M was to be 100 or 75% equitable owner)[7]. The fact that subsequently W actually paid 30% of the mortgage payments should not alter the beneficial interests established originally[8] under the resulting (or constructive) trust, unless paid pursuant to a common intention that W was to have a beneficial interest or an increased beneficial interest, though an equitable accounting between the parties may be required in respect of the proceeds of sale when the house is sold[9].

Of course, it is also possible that M and W equally provided for the deposit and legal costs and undertook liability under the mortgage, but agreed that each was to have a fair share taking account of who directly or indirectly contributed to payments of the mortgage. Here the court has to assess each of the parties' contributions in a broad sense but 'nevertheless the court is only entitled to look at the financial contributions or their real and substantial equivalent.'[10] Payments of mortgage instalments out of pooled earnings or a joint account clearly will support a claim for a half share[11].

Size of share

It is necessary to distinguish between cases involving reliance on an express common intention and cases involving reliance on an inferred common intention[12]. In dealing with express common intention cases it further seems necessary to distinguish between cases where the claimant is relying on having performed the quid pro quo of a quid pro quo common intention and cases where the quid pro quo has not been performed or there was no quid pro quo required[13]. Finally, it is important whether the claimant, W, was led to believe she would acquire a specific (eg half or quarter) share or a vague fair share[14].

W's position will be strongest where there was an express agreement that she was to have a specific share, say a half share, if she acted in a certain way, eg gave birth to M's child (the agreement, even if a contract not being in signed writing as required by s 2 of the Law of Property (Miscellaneous Provisions) Act 1989). Here, once W has acted as promised, so that M should be holding the house on trust for them equally, but has provided no signed writing to satisfy s 53(1) (b) of the Law of Property Act 1925, it seems that

5 *Huntingford v Hobbs* [1993] 1 FLR 736, CA; *Springette v Defoe* (1992) 65 P & CR 1, CA; see p 351, ante.
6 *Huntingford v Hobbs* [1993] 1 FLR 733, CA; *Springette v Defoe* (1992) 65 P & CR 1, CA; see also *Ivin v Blake* (1993) 67 P & CR 26, CA.
7 *Bernard v Josephs* [1982] Ch 391 at 403, [1982] 3 All ER 162 at 170.
8 *Re Gorman* [1990] 1 All ER 717 at 724; *Currie v Hamilton* [1984] 1 NSWLR 687 at 691.
9 *Re Gorman* [1990] 1 All ER 717; *Currie v Hamilton* [1984] 1 NSWLR 687, and see p 355, ante.
10 *Burns v Burns* [1984] Ch 317 at 344, [1984] 1 All ER 244 at 264.
11 *Burns v Burns* [1984] Ch 317; *McHardy v Warren* [1994] 2 FLR 338.
12 *Lloyds Bank plc v Rosset* [1991] 1 AC 107.
13 *Grant v Edwards* [1986] Ch 638, CA.
14 *Gissing v Gissing* [1971] AC 886, HL; *Passee v Passee* [1988] 1 FLR 263, CA; *Stokes v Anderson* [1991] 1 FLR 391, CA.

almost as of course equity will impose a constructive trust upon M[15] so as to provide[16] 'the remedy by which [W] seeks to vindicate an express trust founded upon a common intention which [M] later repudiates.' Indeed, it would seem to be open to a court to hold that the doctrine of part performance preserved by the Law of Property Act 1925, s 55(d) enables the express trust to be enforced despite the lack of signed writing[17]. Thus W will obtain a half share.

Where there has been an express oral agreement it is open to the court to depart from the agreement only if there is a very good reason for doing so[18]. What, therefore, if W only had done one-half of what she was supposed to do, eg where she had agreed to contribute whatever she could to help with mortgage payments and household expenses (taking account of the exigencies of child-bearing and child-rearing) and she had held back for her secret nest-egg some money she had inherited so as only to have contributed half of what she could have contributed? There would seem to be flexibility to award her only a quarter share. Indeed, if, due to becoming unemployed shortly after acquisition of the home, the childless W had contributed very little and a year later ran off with X there would seem to be sufficient flexibility to award her little, if anything. When detrimental acts may be placed on a scale from 1 to 99 should a tiny scale 5 detriment really entitle W to the full half interest? Surely not.

This scale of detriment will be take into account where the parties have agreed that W is to have a fair share or some share when equity will give effect to this and not allow M to claim that W's interest is void for uncertainty, because this would be unconscionable[19]. As Lord Diplock has stated[20]:

'There is nothing inherently improbable in their acting on the understanding that the wife should be entitled to a share which was not to be quantified immediately on the acquisition of the home but should be left to be determined when the mortgage was repaid or the property disposed of, on the basis of what would be fair having regard to the total contributions, direct or indirect, which each spouse had made by that date. ... it would be for the court to give effect to the common intention of the parties by determining what in all the circumstances was a fair share.'

After citing these dicta of Lord Diplock Nourse LJ has stated[1]:

'Those observations ... support a more general proposition that all payments made and acts done by the claimant are to be treated as illuminating the common intention to the extent of the beneficial interest ... . The court must supply the

---

15 *Gissing v Gissing* [1971] AC 886 at 908.
16 *Allen v Snyder* [1977] 2 NSWLR 685 at 699.
17 W's conduct would need to be unequivocally referable to some such agreement as alleged: *Steadman v Steadman* [1976] AC 536, HL; *Wakeham v Mackenzie* [1968] 1 WLR 1175.
18 *Mortgage Corpn Ltd v Shaire* [2001] Ch 743 at 750; *Clough v Killey* (1996) 72 P & CR D 22 at 24, CA; *Grant v Edwards* [1986] Ch 638 at 657, explaining why Janet Eves received only a quarter share in *Eves v Eves* [1975] 3 All ER 768, CA, drawing an analogy with the flexible approach in proprietary estoppel cases, while common intention constructive trusts of family homes and proprietary estoppel interests in such homes are now regarded as involving interchangeable principles: *Yaxley v Gotts* [2000] Ch 162 at 176 (endorsed in *Banner Homes Holdings Ltd v Luff Developments* [2000] Ch 372 at 384; *Mollo v Mollo* [2000] WTLR 227 at 245; *Birmingham Midshires Mortgage Services Ltd v Sabherwal* (1999) 80 P & CR 256 at 263.
19 *Gissing v Gissing* [1971] AC 886 at 908; *Pallant v Morgan* [1953] Ch 43; *Chattlock v Muller* (1878) 8 Ch D 177 at 181.
20 *Gissing v Gissing* [1971] AC 886 at 908.
1 *Stokes v Anderson* [1991] 1 FLR 391 at 400.

common intention by reference to that which all the material circumstances have shown to be fair ... I think that both *Eves v Eves*[2], where no financial contribution was made by the claimant, and *Grant v Edwards*[3], where the claimant had made substantial indirect contributions to the mortgage repayments and the balance of the fire insurance moneys had been equally divided, are explicable on this basis, albeit that neither was clearly expressed to be so decided.'

Significantly, after Lord Bridge commented on these last two cases he recognised that[4] 'in no sense could these shares have been regarded as proportionate to what the judge in the instant case described as a "qualifying contribution" in terms of the indirect contributions to the acquisition or enhancement of the value of the houses made by the female partners'. In *Eves v Eves* W's odd-job work produced for her a quarter interest in an equity of redemption worth £10,000 in 1975 though she had borne two children for M, while in *Grant v Edwards* indirect contributions of less than half, due to W having M's babies in the first three years at the house, produced a half interest for W.

Thus, where the courts find that there was an express agreement or understanding they are prepared when awarding a precise share on a rough and ready broad basis[5] to take account of 'all payments made and acts done by the claimant'.[6] Strictly speaking, it seems a 'fair' share requires the taking into account only of direct and indirect financial contributions[7] or their real and substantial equivalent[8], but the court has leeway, in investigating all the circumstances where there was an express intention that W was to have some share, to find that the intention was really to have a half or quarter share[9].

Where W's claim is based on an inferred common intention in ascertaining the size of her share, one first focuses upon her direct financial contributions, whether to the initial purchase (eg deposit, stamp duty and legal costs) or to subsequent mortgage payments[10]. However, once an inferred common intention that she should have some share in the home has arisen by virtue of her contribution to the initial purchase, then subsequent indirect contributions to mortgage payments (arising from her payment of household expenses without which M could not have afforded to pay the mortgage and keep the household going) should be taken into account in ascertaining the size of her share[11].

Further, according to the Court of Appeal in *Midland Bank plc v Cooke*[12] one

---

2 [1975] 3 All ER 768, CA.

3 [1986] Ch 638.

4 *Lloyds Bank plc v Rosset* [1991] 1 AC 107 at 133.

5 'There is, of course, an air of unreality about the whole exercise': per Griffith LJ in *Bernard v Josephs* [1982] Ch 391 at 404, [1982] 3 All ER 162 at 170.

6 *Stokes v Anderson* [1991] 1 FLR 391 at 400. No distinction is made between capital and interest elements of mortgage payments: *Passee v Passee* [1988] 1 FLR 263, CA.

7 *Gissing v Gissing* [1971] AC 886 at 909; *Grant v Edwards* [1986] Ch 638 at 657, [1986] 2 All ER 426 at 439.

8 *Burns v Burns* [1984] Ch 317 at 344.

9 This seems reasonable in *Grant v Edwards* [1986] Ch 638 but artificial in *Eves v Eves* [1975] 3 All ER 768, which, perhaps, would be better justified as an intention for joint legal and equitable ownership (but not fair equitable ownership), but where equity did not perfect the imperfect gift because the minimum equity to do justice and undo the defendant's unconscionable conduct only required a quarter share.

10 *Lloyds Bank plc v Rosset* [1991] 1 AC 107.

11 *Gissing v Gissing* [1971] AC 886 at 908; *Burns v Burns* [1984] Ch 317 at 345.

12 [1995] 4 All ER 562, criticised by P O'Hagan (1997) 60 MLR 420 and M Dixon [1997] Conv 66.

can go beyond the direct or indirect financial contributions, where the parties have been honest enough to admit that they never gave ownership a thought nor reached any agreement about it, and formulate 'a fair presumed basis'[13] for the sharing of the beneficial title upon surveying the parties' whole course of dealings relating to the property, including non-financial conduct. 'That scrutiny will not confine itself to the limited range of acts of direct contribution that are needed to found a beneficial interest in the first place. It will take into consideration all conduct which throws light on the question what shares were intended. Only if that search proves inconclusive does the court fall back on the maxim "equality is equity"'[14]. The court was fortified by the flexibility in the analogous case of proprietary estoppel[15].

Date of valuation of interest

Once it has been established that W is entitled to a specific share (eg a half) it follows that the value[16] 'must be determined at the date when the property is sold, but that may have to give way to circumstances, eg one of the parties may buy out the other, in which case the value of the party's interest may have to be determined at a different date'. Valuation is not to be made as at the date when W and M separate (unless, unusually, M and W had so agreed) though separation will often bring the purpose of the trust to an end[17], but not the trust itself. Events after separation may be taken into account for the purpose of equitable accounting in respect of the proceeds of sale, eg H may be credited with mortgage instalments paid while staying in possession but debited with a notional occupation rent for using the ousted W's share of the house[18].

Constructive trusts and equitable estoppel

The above flexibility in determining the size of the interest to be awarded to W leads one to consider whether the doctrine of the common intention constructive trust should be regarded as subsumed within the broader head of equitable estoppel or proprietary estoppel[19], which is concerned with the discretionary prevention of unconscionable conduct arising out of a defen-

---

13 [1995] 4 All ER 562 at 575.

14 [1995] 4 All ER 562 at 574 and 576. Applied in *Le Foe v Le Foe* [2001] 2 FLR 970 and *Mollo v Mollo* [2000] WTLR 227.

15 [1995] 4 All ER 562 at 573–574, relying on *Grant v Edwards* [1986] Ch 638 at 657–658, Also see *Mollo v Mollo* [2000] WTLR 227 at 245.

16 *Maugh v Von Sternberg* [1986] 1 FLR 526; *Gordon v Douce* [1983] 2 All ER 228 at 230; *Turton v Turton* [1988] Ch 542, CA disapproving authority favouring date of separation.

17 Enabling a sale to be sought under Trusts of Land and Appointment of Trustees Act 1996, ss 14 and 15; see p 479 post.

18 See *Re Gorman* [1990] 1 All ER 717; *Re Pavlou* [1993] 3 All ER 955: see p 356, ante.

19 'In essence the doctrine is an application of proprietary estoppel' per Lord Oliver in *Austin v Keele* (1987) 61 ALJR 605 at 609. Further support is provided by Browne-Wilkinson V-C in *Grant v Edwards* [1986] Ch 638 and in his 1991 Holdsworth Lecture 'Constructive trusts and Unjust Enrichment', reprinted in (1996) 10 TLI 98, Nicholls LJ in *Lloyds Bank plc v Rosset* [1989] Ch 350, Nourse LJ in *Stokes v Anderson* [1991] 1 FLR 391, and in his Hong Kong *Law Lectures for Practitioners* 1991 Lecture 'Unconscionability and the Unmarried Couple' discussed by Cooke P in *Phillips v Phillips* [1993] 3 NZLR 159 at 168, while Lord Bridge in *Lloyds Bank plc v Rosset* [1991] 1 AC 107 in three places (pp 129, 132 and 133) refers to 'constructive trusts or proprietary estoppels' but avoids dealing with the reported arguments thereon of M Crystal QC.

dant, M, having induced the claimant, W, to act to her detriment in respect of specific property, eg by making an informal unenforceable gift of part of his property to W[20]. After all, in any case where the elements necessary to found a common intention constructive trust are present so are the elements necessary to found a proprietary estoppel[1], namely, that M, by virtue of his bilateral agreement with W or of his unilateral representation to W, has created an expectation or belief that W has or will have an interest in the house and on the basis of that expectation or belief W has acted to her detriment with M's encouragement or acquiescence. Thus in *Yaxley v Gotts*[2], Robert Walker LJ has stated, 'In the area of a joint enterprise for the acquisition of land the two concepts coincide'.

The estoppel approach has many advantages[3]. It avoids the search for an express or inferred common intention, which is often a difficult and somewhat artificial exercise when cohabitees often do not give detailed consideration to the matter, if, indeed, any consideration is really given. Instead, if to M's knowledge, because of M's behaviour W thinks that the house is partly hers, then good conscience requires that M should not stand by allowing W to act to her detriment or significantly alter her position on a mistaken basis or, if he does, then equity may intervene in some appropriate fashion to counteract his unconscionable behaviour. Moreover, not just financial detriment should be taken into account but any act done by her to her detriment relating to the joint life of the parties based on their home[4]. Furthermore, the flexibility of equity revealed in proprietary estoppel cases will afford the court leeway to deny a claimant the agreed interest and confer a smaller interest if award of the agreed interest would be inequitable and disproportionate in all the circumstances[5].

Just as an interest under a common intention constructive trust arises when the claimant first acts to his detriment[6], so an equitable proprietary estoppel interest will be treated as arising when the claimant first acted to his detriment[7], even though the precise size of such interest will not be ascertained until the court decides the issue. This has the advantage of protecting co-owning occupiers with only an equitable interest from subsequent mortgagees, though, in any event, even if such an occupier had no proprietary interest until the date of the court hearing, the court could have held the

---

20 See pp 248-254, ante.

 1 As recognised by Browne-Wilkinson V-C in note 19 (supra).

 2 As recognised by Browne-Wilkinson V-C in his Holdsworth Lecture (note 19 supra).

 3 [2000] Ch 162 at 176–177 (citing *Gissing v Gissing* [1971] AC 896 at 905; *Lloyds Bank v Rosset* [1991] 1 AC 107 at 132; *Grant v Edwards* [1986] Ch 638 at 656), endorsed by Chadwick LJ in *Banner Homes Group plc v Luff Developments* [2000] Ch 372 at 384. Overreaching applies to co-owned interests whether established under resulting or constructive trusts or equitable estoppel principles: *Birmingham Midshires Mortgage Services Ltd v Saberhwal* (1999) 80 P & CR 256, CA.

 4 See *Midland Bank v Cooke* [1995] 4 All ER 562, discussed at pp 418 and 424 ante.

 5 See p 248 ante.

 6 *Turton v Turton* [1988] Ch 542 at 55; *Lloyds Bank plc v Rosset* [1989] Ch 350 at 386, 393 and 402, per Nicholls , Mustill and Purchas LJJ respectively.

 7 *Voyce v Voyce* (1991) 62 P & CR 290 at 294, 296; *Lloyds Bank plc v Carrick* [1996] 4 All ER 630 at 642 (but cf *United Bank of Kuwait plc v Sahib* [1997] Ch 107 at 142). For registered land, Land Registration Act 2002, s 116 seems to make an equitable interest arise from the date of detrimental conduct of the claimant.

subsequent mortgagee's conscience to be bound by the co-owner's rights as ultimately laid down by the court[8].

Availability of Matrimonial Causes Act 1973 for spouses

The uncertainties and, at times, artificiality of applying principles of resulting trusts and constructive trusts and proprietary estoppel principles to ascertain the precise property rights of the parties should not concern spouses unless facing a claim by a creditor. This is because until the applicant remarries or the respondent dies matters should be resolved in the Family Division[9] under the jurisdiction conferred by s 24 of the Matrimonial Causes Act 1973, whereby there is a broad discretion to make orders as to property (taking into account the wife's contribution to looking after the children and the home) without the need first to ascertain precisely the beneficial shares in the property[10].

PARAGRAPH 2(B)

Mutual wills

To prevent the fraudulent or unconscionable revocation of a will in certain circumstances Equity has developed the doctrine of mutual wills which relies upon the imposition of a constructive trust upon the death of the first testator to die[11].

Where two persons (eg husband and wife or brother and sister) make a contractually binding arrangement as to the disposal of their property and make mutual wills pursuant to that arrangement, which they agree are to be unalterable, then, if one person dies but the survivor subsequently alters his testamentary dispositions in breach of the arrangement, the survivor's personal representatives will be granted probate (or letters of administration) in the ordinary way. However, they will hold the relevant part of his estate on constructive trust to give effect to the arrangement effected by the mutual wills[12]. If instead of executing separate mutual wills the parties make a joint will agreeing that the arrangement embodied therein shall be unalterable then the arrangement will also be binding on the survivor under a constructive trust[13]. It would seem that the principles underlying mutual wills should extend to cases where there are more than two parties (eg to wills of 70-year-old triplets), to where the agreement is subsequent to the making of the wills[14] (eg if it could be proved that A expressly agreed with B that he

---

8 See Hayton & Marshall *Commentary and Cases on Law of Trusts and Equitable Remedies* (11th edn, 2001), paras 6–116 to 6–117.

9 *Tee v Tee* [1999] 2 FLR 613, CA; *Williams v Williams* [1976] Ch 278, [1977] 1 All ER 28, CA; *Fielding v Fielding* [1978] 1 All ER 267, [1977] 1 WLR 1146n, CA.

10 Eg *P v P* [1978] 3 All ER 70, [1978] 1 WLR 483, CA.

11 *Dufour v Pereira* (1769) 1 Dick 419; *Birmingham v Renfrew* (1937) 57 CLR 666; *Re Cleaver* [1981] 2 All ER 1018, [1981] 1 WLR 939; *Re Dale* [1994] Ch 31.

12 *Re Oldham* [1925] Ch 75; *Gray v Perpetual Trustee Co* [1928] AC 391; *Birmingham v Renfrew* (1937) 57 CLR 666. See also (1951) 14 MLR 140 (J.D.B. Mitchell); (1970) 34 Conv 230 (R Burgess); A J Oakley *Constructive Trusts*, pp 131–140.

13 *Re Hagger* [1930] 2 Ch 190. However the practical and legal problems are such that joint wills are to be deprecated and practitioners should do their utmost to ensure that separate wills are drafted.

14 *Re Fox* [1951] 3 DLR 337, [1951] OR 378, (agreement to alter their wills).

would not revoke his will if she agreed not to revoke her will and she agreed), to where the agreement is not the same mutatis mutandis (eg I will leave my property to you for life, remainder to X if you leave your property to me for life, remainder to Z), and where there is an agreement between joint tenants of property not to sever their interest on condition the survivor disposes of the property in an agreed manner[15].

While the cases concentrate on whether or not the parties agreed not to revoke or amend their agreed wills, the crux of the obligation is not dealing with the relevant property contrary to the agreement[16], so that the survivor should still be bound by the agreement if the first to die revoked or altered the will but the relevant property continued to be dealt with in accordance with their agreement – unless the will is restrictively worded, eg 'I shall not amend nor revoke my will after the death of my spouse if the will [dated — day of —] of my spouse has not been amended nor revoked before death'. Such wording is fine where a spouse's *whole* estate is left absolutely to the surviving spouse but for the latter to bequeath or devise what remains of specific property to X, but if *part* only of the spouse's estate is to be subject to the agreed obligation then the survivor should be placed under a binding obligation in respect of that part 'if the will of my spouse has not been amended nor revoked before death so as to deal with [specified property] inconsistently with [clause 3 of her will dated — day of —]'.

Binding agreement for survivor to carry out agreed arrangement

It is vital to show on a balance of probabilities that each person agreed that if he was the survivor then he would be legally bound to carry out the agreed arrangement[17]. The agreement is a contractual one made in consideration of the mutual promises of the parties[18], though for the benefit to some extent of persons who are neither parties to the contract nor suppliers of consideration, eg where the testator's will leaves a life interest to the other mutual testator with remainders over or a limited type of 'absolute' ownership to the other with remainders over[19]. It depends on the construction of the contract whether a breach arises (i) if one party openly tells the other that he no longer is going to give effect to the arrangement for he is to change his will, or (ii) if the party's will is revoked automatically by remarriage and a new will is not made to give effect to the arrangement, or (iii) if the party revokes his will without informing the other but predeceases the other so that his secret becomes public. Usually, the contract will be presumed revocable upon notice to the other party or upon the will becoming revoked by operation of law so as not to be broken if such circumstances materialise[20]. Even where a

15 *Healey v Brown* [2002] WTLR 155; *University of Manitoba v Sanderson Estate* (1998) DLR (4th) 40.

16 *Lewis v Cotton* [2001] WTLR 1117 at 1129, NZCA.

17 *Re Cleaver* [1981] 2 All ER 1018, [1981] 1 WLR 939.

18 This is a factor which distinguishes mutual wills from secret trusts which involve voluntary undertakings. Further see *Re Goodchild* [1997] 3 All ER 63, CA and *Re Dale* [1994] Ch 31, [1993] 4 All ER 129 holding that it is not a necessary condition for the imposition of a constructive trust that the testators should confer benefits on each other.

19 See p 431, post, for such 'absolute ownership'.

20 *Dufour v Pereira* (1769) 1 Dick 419 at 420; *Stone v Hoskins* [1905] P 194 at 197; *Re Marsland* [1939] Ch 820, CA; *Birmingham v Renfrew* (1937) 57 CLR 666 at 682–683. Further see *Re Newey* [1994] 2 NZLR 590 at 593 and *Bigg v Queensland Trustees Ltd* [1990] 2 Qd R 11, critically noted by C E F Rickett (1991) 54 MLR 581, emphasising that the constructive trust remedy only breach arises during the lifetime or on the death of one party the uncertain variables make it difficult to see what the survivor's measure of damages would be[1], especially since he would then be free to rearrange his own will as he wished[2].

It is necessary to prove that the arrangement was intended to affect legal relations and was intended to bind the surviving party after the death of the other party so that the survivor could not revoke his will unless he made a new will continuing to give effect to the arrangement[3]. Thus, the arrangement must be more than an agreement to make wills in almost identical terms[4]. A recital or declaration in the wills that no alteration or revocation is to be made except by mutual consent will be sufficient[5] as will similar proof obtained outside the four corners of the will, eg in family conversations[6].

An agreement not to revoke a testamentary disposition of land is the same in effect as a promise to make such a disposition, so that it falls within the Law of Property (Miscellaneous Provisions) Act 1989, s 2(1) so that a problem arises where there is not a joint will signed by them both but separate mutual wills not containing identical terms and not signed by both parties. As a result, in *Healey v Brown*[7] the Deputy Judge held that land owned by the survivor was not subject to a valid contract, and so could not be held on any constructive trust under the mutual wills doctrine because such doctrine was founded on there being an enforceable contract. He did, however, hold that land owned by the first to die was held on constructive trust under secret trust principles which are not dependent on any contract but on a voluntary undertaking. The land in question was their matrimonial home when the first died and was a flat beneficially owned by them as joint tenants so as to pass automatically on death to the survivor.

Shortly after Mrs Brown's death Mr Brown had vested the flat in himself and his son as beneficial joint tenants so that two years later, on Mr Brown's death, his son acquired the flat as surviving joint tenant. As the judge said[8] '[This] could scarcely run more directly and fully counter to the intention of the mutual will compact that the flat should pass to his deceased wife's niece on his own death'. 'It would in my judgment be entirely inequitable now to frustrate Mrs Brown's expectation and it was unconscionable for Mr Brown to do so after her death in seeking to pass the flat to the First Defendant'[9], his son. Yet the failure to comply with the 1989 Act formalities led the judge to hold that the niece only acquired a half interest in the flat, despite the fact that Equity does not allow statutes to be used as an instrument of fraud and

becomes available after the death of the first party having performed the agreement. If such party dies failing to perform the agreement the survivor's action against the deceased's executor can only be a breach of contract action or an equitable estoppel claim if the survivor had earlier acted to his detriment in reliance on the other's promises.

1 *Lewis v Cotton* [2001] WTLR 1117 at 1129, NZCA.
2 See *Re Hobley* (1997) Times, 16 June (codicil revoking devise of property within the agreement held to leave survivor free to dispose of all property as she wished).
3 *Re Oldham* [1925] Ch 75; *Gray v Perpetual Trustee Co* [1928] AC 391 where the mere fact that husband and wife simultaneously had made wills mutatis mutandis in identical form was not of itself sufficient evidence to raise a constructive trust binding the survivor. With joint mutual wills the court is more ready to find sufficient evidence: *Re Gillespie* (1969) 3 DLR (3d) 317.
4 *Lewis v Cotton* [2001] WTLR 1117, NZCA; *Birch v Curtis* [2002] WTLR 965.
5 *Re Green* [1951] Ch 148, [1950] 2 All ER 913.
6 *Re Heys* [1914] P 192 at 194; *Re Cleaver* [1981] 1 WLR 939; *Re Newey* [1994] 2 NZLR 590.
7 [2002] WTLR 849.
8 [2002] WTLR 849 para 14.
9 [2002] WTLR 849 para 26.

will impose a constructive trust over particular property to prevent the owner retaining exclusive beneficial ownership where this would be unconscionable – and s 2(5) of the 1989 Act provides an exception for constructive trusts.

In *Dufour v Pereira*[10] Lord Camden stated the basis for imposing a constructive trust:

> 'The instrument itself is the evidence of the agreement; and he that dies first, does by his death carry the agreement on his part into execution. If the other then refuses he is guilty of a fraud, can never unbind himself, and becomes a trustee of course. For no man shall deceive another to his prejudice. By engaging to do something that is in his power, he is made a trustee for the performance, and transmits that trust to those that claim under him...there is not an instance to be found since the jurisdiction was established where one man has ever been released from his engagement after the other has performed his part' [until *Healey v Brown*].

Thus, Mr Brown and, then, his son should have been found to hold the flat on constructive trust for Mrs Brown's niece absolutely. Mrs Brown had died, reasonably believing that Mr Brown was under a legally binding agreement to give effect to what they had both believed to be a legally binding obligation. It should have been immaterial that unknown to them the agreement happened not to satisfy the formalities required by s 2(1) of the 1989 Act: its certain existence should have led to a legally binding obligation under a constructive trust.

Trust giving effect to arrangement

Assuming the terms of the mutual arrangement were not unusual in expressly providing that the survivor was only bound to give effect to the arrangement *if* he accepted property passing under the will of the deceased party, the survivor is bound as from the death of the deceased, irrespective of taking any property under the will[11]. After all, in the usual case the benefit that the ultimately surviving party contracted for was to have the ultimately predeceasing party make testamentary dispositions in the agreed form and die without altering them. Once this party dies with testamentary dispositions in the agreed form, thus having deprived himself of the chance to make alternative testamentary dispositions, then the surviving party obtains the contracted for benefit so that it would be a fraud if thereafter the survivor made testamentary dispositions inconsistent with those previously mutually agreed[12].

Thus, while Equity does not interfere with the fundamental principle that all wills are revocable till death[13] it does, if the survivor revokes his will without making a new one giving effect to the mutual arrangement, impose a constructive trust on the property subject to the arrangement that passes to the survivor's personal representatives under his new will or intestacy. The constructive trust is in favour of the mutually agreed beneficiaries. In such manner Equity is able to prevent the survivor fraudulently frustrating the arrangement with the deceased and to benefit the third party beneficiaries of

---

10 (1769) 2 Hargrave's Judicial Arguments 304 at 310.
11 Especially if disclaimer under the will enables the disclaiming party to take under the intestacy rules: cf secret trusts, pp 262 and 265, ante.
12 *Re Dale* [1994] Ch 31, [1993] 4 All ER 129.
13 *Stone v Hoskins* [1905] P 194.

the arrangement, who themselves can enforce the constructive trusts[14].

It follows that if a third party beneficiary of the mutual arrangement survives one party, but predeceases the surviving party, then the third party's interest does not lapse since it arose under the constructive trust imposed at the date of death of the first party to die. Thus in *Re Hagger*[15] H and W executed a joint mutual will leaving their moiety of their property at Wandsworth to the survivor for life, with remainder to various beneficiaries including a certain EP. It happened that W died in 1904, EP died in 1923, and H died in 1928, having made a will inconsistent with the mutually agreed arrangement. Clauson J held that EP had a vested interest in remainder in the Wandsworth property (both W's moiety passing under W's will *and H's own moiety*) as from 1904.

The property subject to the trust

In *Re Hagger* it was clear that the Wandsworth property was the subject matter of the trust and that H was, after W's death, to take a life interest in W's moiety and his own moiety. Where the mutual agreement is clear as to the property intended to be subject to the agreement and the interest to be taken therein then obviously there are no problems. The agreement may provide only for certain property of the first to die to be affected or it may also provide for the survivor's property to be affected[16].

In the former case there is no problem where a life interest is expressly conferred on the survivor. Problems, however, arise as to the scope of the survivor's obligation where an apparently 'absolute' interest in the deceased's property is conferred on the survivor who is then intended to be subject to some equitable obligation to pass the interest on to third parties after his death.

In the latter case there is no problem if the survivor takes a life interest in some part of his own property, though practical problems arise if he takes a life interest in all his property unless he has power to resort to capital and wide powers of investment. Furthermore, it must be ascertained whether all his property at the date of the deceased party's death is intended or all his property including after-acquired property. These problems become more acute where the survivor is apparently intended to retain an 'absolute' interest in his own property but subject to some equitable obligation to pass the interest on to third parties after his death.

In the case of 'absolute' interests if the courts are not to hold that a mere moral obligation exists it will be necessary for them to find an implied life interest with implied power to resort to capital and implied wide powers of investment as absolute owner or to introduce some new concept such as a floating trust as envisaged by Dixon J in *Birmingham v Renfrew*[17] in stating:

---

14 They may also have rights under the Contracts (Rights of Third Parties) Act 1999 which leave unaffected, rights under constructive trusts: see s 10 of the 1999 Act.

15 [1930] 2 Ch 190. The interest could be protected by an entry on the land register: *Fisher v Mansfield* [1997] 2 NZLR 230.

16 See *Re Green* [1951] Ch 148, [1950] 2 All ER 913; *Re Goodchild* [1997] 3 All ER 63 at 75; *Healey v Brown* [2002] WTLR 849.

17 (1937) 57 CLR 666 at 689 endorsed by Nourse J in *Re Cleaver* [1981] 2 All ER 1018, [1981] 1 WLR 939 who also pointed out, 'No objection could normally be taken to ordinary gifts of small value.' Further see endorsement and discussion in *Edell v Sitzer* (2001) 4 ITELR 149 at 169–170.

'The purpose of an arrangement for corresponding wills must often be to enable the survivor during his life to deal as absolute owner with the property passing under the will of the party first dying. That is to say the object of the transaction is to put the survivor in a position to enjoy for his own benefit the full ownership so that, for instance, he may convert it and expend the proceeds if he choose. But when he dies he is to bequeath what is left in the manner agreed upon. It is only by the special doctrines of equity that such a floating obligation, suspended, so to speak, during the lifetime of the survivor can descend upon the assets at his death and crystallize into a trust. No doubt gifts and settlements inter vivos, if calculated to defeat the intention of the compact, could not be made by the survivor and his right of disposition, inter vivos, is therefore not unqualified. But, substantially, the purpose of the arrangement will often be to allow full enjoyment for the survivor's own benefit and advantage upon condition that at his death the residue shall pass as arranged.'

Does the third party beneficiary then have a 'quasi' defeasible vested equitable interest in remainder under a quasi certain trust and, if such beneficiary having survived the 'settlor' predeceases the 'trustee', is the trustee then entitled to make larger inroads into the capital for whatever purposes he wishes, or, indeed, is the beneficiary's interest really contingent upon being alive at the survivor's death? Many matters remain to be resolved unless great care is taken in drafting mutual wills in those relatively rare circumstances where they may be justified.

In the sole English case[18] the position was clear-cut. H and W left all their property to each other absolutely, except the survivor was to leave their matrimonial home and the proceeds thereof to W's niece, N: they agreed not to amend or revoke these wills. Their home was owned as beneficial joint tenants, so on W's death H became sole beneficial owner. Shortly thereafter he transferred the home into the name of himself and his son, S, as beneficial joint tenants, so that two years later, on H's death, S became sole beneficial owner to the apparent exclusion of N. This could scarcely run more directly and fully counter to the intention of the mutual will compact so S could not rely on being beneficial sole owner as seen at p 849 ante.

Affinity with secret trusts

There is much affinity between mutual wills and secret trusts except that the arrangement giving rise to the trust is in the former case contractual[19] and in the latter case voluntary.

As Nourse J has stated[20]:

'These cases of mutual wills are only one example of a wider category of cases, for example, secret trusts, in which a court of equity will intervene to impose a constructive trust .... The principle of all these cases is that a court of equity will not permit a person to whom property is transferred by way of gift, but on the faith of an agreement or clear understanding that it is to be dealt with in a particular way for the benefit of a third person, to deal with that property inconsistently with that agreement or understanding.'

---

18 *Healey v Brown* [2002] WTLR 849.

19 Despite *Healey v Brown* [2002] WTLR 849 it ought to be immaterial that the contract turns out to be void for lack of complying with the requisite formalities under s 2(1) of the Law of Property (Miscellaneous Provisions) Act 1989: see p 430 ante and also M Cope, *Constructive Trusts* (Law Book Co, Australia 1992) Chap 12.

20 *Re Cleaver* [1981] 2 All ER 1018 at 1024.

PARAGRAPH 2(C)

Secret trusts

Secret trusts arising on a deceased's testacy or intestacy have already been fully dealt with and the fraud noted (which justifies the imposition of a constructive trust) where the deceased's wishes would be frustrated and the secret beneficiary be deprived of the benefit which, but for the trustee's agreement, would have been secured to him by the deceased by other means[1].

In the case of an inter vivos trust where A transferred land to B on the oral understanding that B is to hold it for C it seems that it should not be regarded as fraudulent for A to plead Law of Property Act 1925, s 53(1)(b) and retain his interest, not having made a perfect gift and not having died happy in the belief that he had made such a gift[2].

PARAGRAPH 2(D)

Donor doing all he is obliged to do to transfer legal title or make a donatio mortis causa

In the case of shares and registered land legal title only passes when the transferee becomes registered as shareholder or proprietor of the land, the latter being deemed to occur when all the relevant documents have been delivered to the appropriate Land Registry office, although it will occur electronically in due course. Company directors of private companies may refuse to register a transferee. The acquisition of the equitable title may be important for the three to seven year survival period required for potentially exempt transfers under inheritance tax or for the transferee to require further assistance from the transferor if the transfer form should happen to be lost or destroyed after the transferee had received it.

As already discussed a constructive trust arises as soon as the transferor has done all which it is obligatory for him to do to make the transfer effective[3], eg signed and handed over the transfer form together with the share certificate or the land certificate to the transferee or the transferee's agent, so that the transferor no longer has power to prevent delivery of the requisite documents for registration of the transferor as legal owner. Once this has happened it becomes unconscionable for the transferor to insist in being regarded as still beneficial owner so the transferee then obtains equitable title entitling him to dividends, rents and, presumably, a freshly executed transfer form if the earlier one were lost or burnt, the transferor being his nominee under *Saunders v Vautier*[4].

To make an effective donatio mortis causa there must be delivery of the subject matter of the gift or the essential indicia of title in circumstances amounting to a parting with dominion and not mere physical possession over the subject matter of the gift. Where legal title remains in the donor and passes to his personal representatives they will hold it on constructive trust

---

1 See p 257 and *Re Dale* [1994] Ch 31 at 48–49, [1993] 4 All ER 129 at 142.
2 See p 256, ante.
3 See pp 154–156.
4 (1841) 4 Beav 115.

for the donee of the effective donatio mortis causa[5]. It makes no difference that in the case of shares the company directors may refuse to register the transferee as shareholder.

No criminal may benefit from his crime

As Fry LJ stated in *Cleaver v Mutual Reserve Fund Life Association*[6]

> 'No system of jurisprudence can with reason include among the rights which it enforces rights directly resulting to the person asserting them from the crime of that person.'

Thus, when Crippen was hanged for murdering his wife it was held that the property passing on his wife's intestacy did not pass to him and through his will to his mistress, Miss Le Neve, but, instead passed to his wife's blood relatives[7]. Here, as in other English instances[8], the property was intercepted before passing to the criminal. However, it seems, as established in American and Commonwealth jurisdictions, that if the property did vest in the criminal then he would hold the property on constructive trust for those really entitled to the property[9] who would thus have priority in the event of the criminal's bankruptcy and also the right to trace the property if transferred to others. A transferee would be safe if a bona fide purchaser of the legal interest for value or protected by the change of position defence[10].

Where one joint tenant murders another it seems the criminal should hold the property as constructive trustee for himself and his victim in equal shares[11]. If the remainderman murders the life tenant it seems that the victim should be deemed to have lived as long as predicted by actuarial mortality tables (except for death-bed killings, eg 'mercy' killings) so that for this notional period the victim's interest should be held on a constructive trust for the victim's estate and, thereafter, the remaining interests should devolve normally[12].

It is not only murder that invokes the principle but also manslaughter[13]

---

5 *Sen v Headley* [1991] Ch 425 at 439–440, [1991] 2 All ER 636 at 646–647, CA.

6 [1892] 1 QB 147 at 156 but in special circumstances bigamists may have rights to ancillary statutory relief: *Rampal v Rampal (No 2)* [2001] 2 FLR 1179, CA.

7 *Re Crippen* [1911] P 108; *Re Sigsworth* [1935] Ch 89. In *Re DWS (deceased)* [2001] Ch 568 where X murdered his parents who died intestate leaving no other children, the Court of Appeal rejected the claim of X's only child, Y, under s 47 of the Administration of Estates Act 1925, refusing to treat the situation as if X had predeceased his parents: the property devolved on the class of next of kin ranking after issue of the intestate.

8 For example, *Davitt v Titcumb* [1990] Ch 110, [1989] 3 All ER 417 (proceeds of life assurance policy payable on death of murderer's co-owner).

9 *Schobelt v Barber* (1966) 60 DLR (2d) 519; *Rasmanis v Jurewitsch* [1970] 1 NSWR 650; *Re Pechar* [1969] NZLR 574.

10 *Bradley v Fox* Ill App 2d 106, 129 NE 2d 699 (1955); *Beresford v Royal Insurance Co Ltd* [1938] AC 586 at 600.

11 *Rasmanis v Jurewitsch* [1970] 1 NSWR 650; *Re K* [1985] Ch 85 (affd [1986] Ch 180 without considering this point); (1973) 89 LQR 235 (T G Youdan); (1974) 37 MLR 481 (Earnshaw and Pace); *Re Dreger* (1976) 69 DLR (3d) 47. If X, Y and Z are joint tenants and X kills Y then X should become tenant in common of one-third and Z of two-thirds. Generally see M Cope *Constructive Trusts* (Law Book Co, Australia 1992) Chap 13.

12 (1973) 89 LQR 235 at 250–251 (T G Youdan).

13 *Re Estate of Hall* [1914] P 1, CA; *Re Giles* [1972] Ch 544, [1971] 3 All ER 1141.

including manslaughter by reason of diminished responsibility[14]. However, the principle does not apply to insane killers[15].

Possible relief under Forfeiture Act 1982

Where the court is satisfied that in all the circumstances the justice of the case requires it[16], the court can modify the effect of the forfeiture rule as it applies to the 'offender' ie the unlawful killer or the person who has unlawfully aided, abetted, counselled or procured the victim's death[17], but not someone who has been convicted of murder[18]. The offender must bring proceedings within three months of conviction[19]. The Act applies to killings even before it came into operation on 13 October 1982 unless, in consequence of the forfeiture rule, the property had before then been acquired by someone else[20]. 'Acquired' denotes property which has actually been transferred to a person or to which a person has acquired an indefeasible right to have it transferred to him[1]. The Act applies to benefits under the deceased's will, nomination, intestacy, or donatio mortis causa, and to property held on trust before the death which would devolve on the offender as a result of the death[2].

PARAGRAPH 2(F)

Rescission of voidable property transfers

Where C deliberately transfers legal and beneficial ownership in particular property to D, but C's intention was vitiated by some factor such as fraud, undue influence, mistake or misrepresentation, C can elect to rescind the transfer[3]. In fixing upon the appropriate remedy the court may order D or a donee from D to transfer the property or its traceable product to C (so that D or his donee is regarded as a constructive trustee[4]) or payment of compensation may only be possible or may be more appropriate. Thus, if the vitiated transaction was a contract of loan, C cannot be placed in a better position than if the loan had been valid and so can only be a personal creditor for the amount lent[5].

However, if D's fraudulent misrepresentation or undue influence resulted

---

14 *Re Giles* [1972] Ch 544, [1971] 3 All ER 1141 and *Dunbar v Plant* [1998] Ch 412 at 436 and 437, [1997] 4 All ER 289 at 310 and 311, per Phillips LJ. See further (1973) LQR 235 at 237–248 (T G Youdan); (1974) 37 MLR 481 at 492–496 (Earnshaw and Pace).

15 *Re Houghton* [1915] 2 Ch 173; *Re Pitts* [1931] 1 Ch 546; Criminal Procedure (Insanity) Act 1964, s 1 (verdict now not guilty by reason of insanity).

16 Forfeiture Act 1982, s 2(1). See *Dunbar v Plant* [1998] Ch 412, CA. Contrast *Re H* [1990] 1 FLR 441 with *Jones v Roberts* [1995] 2 FLR 422, High Court, discussed by R A Buckley (1995) 111 LQR 196.

17 Forfeiture Act 1982, s 1(2). *Re Paterson, Petitioner* 1986 SLT 121.

18 Forfeiture Act 1982, s 5.

19 Forfeiture Act 1982, s 2(3).

20 Forfeiture Act 1982, s 2(7).

1 *Re K* [1986] Ch 180, [1985] 2 All ER 833, CA.

2 Forfeiture Act 1982, s 2(4).

3 Generally see Meagher Gummow & Lehane *Equity: Doctrines and Remedies* (3rd edn 1992) Chapter 24, Hanbury & Martin *Modern Equity* (16th edn 2001), Chapter 26.

4 See p 327 ante.

5 *Halifax Building Society v Thomas* [1996] Ch 217; *Daly v Sydney Stock Exchange* (1986) 160 CLR 371; *Westdeutsche Landesbank v Islington London Borough Council* [1996] AC 669.

in C transferring a house or a painting to D[6] then, clearly, C should be able to obtain an order for the reconveyance to C of the house or painting and such order should also be made against a donee from D. Indeed, if D had sold the house or painting and used the proceeds to buy another asset, then such traceable asset should be conveyed to C by D or by a donee thereof from D[7].

Once C's rescission has been made known to D or a donee from him, then clearly D and the donee should be regarded retrospectively from that date as constructive trustees when the court makes its order for the property to be transferred to C[8]. Indeed, because D's conscience as a fraudster or undue influencer is affected from the time he made C part with C's property, he should be constructive trustee from that time and personally accountable for any profits made out of the transferred property[9].

If D's fraudulent misrepresentations led C to believe that he had not already paid D a debt of £x, so that C paid D a further £x, which D used to purchase an asset, then C should be able to trace that £x into the asset and obtain an order for transfer of the asset to himself[10].

Controversially, in *Chase Manhattan Bank v Israel-British Bank*[11] the same was held to be the case where C's own clerical error led C mistakenly to pay D twice, Goulding J stating[12], 'A person who pays money to another under a factual mistake retains an equitable property in it and the conscience of that other is subjected to a fiduciary duty to respect his proprietary right'.

Lord Browne-Wilkinson[13] and Lord Millett[14] have rejected this on the basis that the payee became the full legal beneficial owner of the money to the exclusion of any equitable proprietary interest of the payer. The payee should only be liable to a personal common law action for money had and received, although it could also have become personally accountable in equity[15] two days after the payment when it realised there had been a double payment.

6　Where D is a fiduciary apparently authorised by C so as to fall outside the constructive trust automatically arising under Article 33 it seems he should be estopped from taking advantage of his own wrongdoing by relying on such consent, which he knew was not a true consent.

7　Where no constructive trust automatically arises against a fiduciary under the preceding footnote, it seems C only has a mere equity (*Phillips v Phillips* (1862) 4 De G F & J 208 at 218 and 222 endorsed by Lord Millett in (1998) 114 LQR 399 at 416 but see *Eyre v Burmester* (1862) 10 HL Cas 90 and *Gresley v Mousley* (1859) 4 De G & J 78 at 86) so it binds all but a bona fide purchaser of a legal or equitable interest for value without notice.

8　*El Ajou v Dollar Land Holdings plc* [1993] 3 All ER 717 at 734; *Bristol and West Building Society v Mothew* [1998] Ch 1 at 23 [1996] 4 All ER 698 at 716, CA; *O'Sullivan v Management Agency and Music Ltd* [1985] QB 428 at 457, CA; Lord Millett (1998) 114 LQR 399 at 416.

9　*Westdeutsche Landesbank v Islington LBC* [1996] AC 669 at 705–706, 707, 709.

10　*Westdeutsche Landesbank v Islington LBC* [1996] AC 669 at 716.

11　[1981] Ch 105.

12　[1981] Ch 105 at 119.

13　*Westdeutsche Landesbank v Islington LBC* [1996] AC 669 at 715.

14　(1998) 114 LQR 399 at 412-413 and Commentary thereon of A J Oakley in *Restitution, Past Present and Future* (1998), (eds Cornish, Nolan, O'Sullivan & Virgo) pp 228–230.

15　Lord Browne-Wilkinson used the traditional but misleading terminology of constructive trust in note 13 above to indicate in context that there could have been a personal liability to account as constructive trustee: see Hayton & Marshall *Commentary & Cases on Law of Trusts and Equitable Remedies* (11th edn 2001) para 6-89.

PARAGRAPH 2(G)

Unconscionable money receipts by agents with insolvency problems where principal cannot be benefited

In *Neste Oy v Lloyds Bank plc*[16] claimant ship owners made regular payments to the general bank account of PSL, their agents, to discharge present and future liabilities relating to services provided for their ships. '[The last] payment was credited to PSL at a time when Peckston Group Ltd had already resolved that it and its group companies should cease trading immediately (one of the directors supporting the resolution being a director of PSL) at a time when PSL had not paid for the services for which the funds had been remitted and at a time when, in all the circumstances, there was no chance that PSL could pay for the services'[17]. It thus appears that the directors of PSL would have been liable for wrongful trading if they had continued PSL's business. Bingham J held[18], 'Given the situation of PSL when the last payment was received, any honest and reasonable directors (or the actual directors had they known of it) would, I feel sure, have arranged for the repayment of that sum to the plaintiffs without hesitation or delay ... and, accordingly, a constructive trust is to be inferred'. Therefore, the defendant Bank could not set-off the plaintiffs' payment to PSL against money due from PSL to the Bank, which had notice of the trust.

In *Re Japan Leasing (Europe) plc*[19], a purchaser paid an instalment payment for purchase of an aeroplane to A Ltd, the head vendor, to divide the instalment between itself and three other companies, co-vendors with A Ltd. The intended beneficial payment to A Ltd discharged the purchaser of its liability to the four co-vendors under contractual arrangements which also expressly excluded any trust relationship arising between A Ltd and the other three co-vendors in respect of instalments received by A Ltd: it was only under a personal contractual obligation as agent to account to each of the three co-vendors in respect of such instalments. However, the judge held that the exclusion clause did not help A Ltd for the instalment received after its financial problems had led to it going into administration. Such clause excluded an express trust but not the constructive trust that the judge held to arise by operation of law against A because[20] 'it would be unconscionable for the Company [A Ltd], as agent, to receive money as agent knowing that it could not account for it to its principal [the other three co-vendors]'. The instalment was held on constructive trust for the four co-vendors.

PARAGRAPH 2(H)

Assignments for value of future property

As Swinfen–Eady LJ stated in *Re Lind*[1]:

---

16 [1983] 2 Lloyd's Rep 658.
17 [1983] 2 Lloyd's Rep 658 at 666.
18 [1983] 2 Lloyd's Rep 658 at 665.
19 [2000] WTLR 301.
20 [2000] WTLR 301 at 316.
 1 [1915] 2 Ch 345 at 360; also see *Re Gillott's Settlement* [1934] Ch 97 at 108–109 and *Pullan v Koe* [1913] 1 Ch 9.

'an assignment for value of future property actually binds the property itself directly it is acquired—automatically on the happening of the event, and without any further act on the part of the assigner—and does not merely rest in, and amount to, a right in contract, giving rise to an action. The assignor having the consideration, becomes in equity, on the happening of the event, trustee for the assignee of the property devolving upon or acquired by him, and which he had previously sold and been paid for.'

The constructive trust arises as a result of the maxim 'Equity regards as done that which ought to be done'[2], the assignor being bound to hold the materialised former future property on trust for the assignee by virtue of his earlier receipt of consideration from the assignee. As Dixon J stated in *Palette Shoes Pty Ltd v Krohn*[3]:

'Because value has been given on the one side, the conscience of the other party is bound when the subject matter comes into existence, that is, when, as is generally the case, the legal property vests in him. Because his conscience is bound in respect of a subject of property, equity fastens upon the property itself and makes him a trustee of the legal right or ownership for the assignee. But although the matter rests primarily in contract, the prospective right in property which the assignee obtains is a higher right than to have specific performance of a contract and it may survive the assignor's bankruptcy because it attaches without more *eo instanti* when the property arises and gives the assignee an equitable interest therein.'

ARTICLE 36

Constructive trusts imposed upon a vendor under a specifically enforceable contract

So long as the vendor enters into a specifically enforceable contract for the sale of property he becomes a constructive trustee thereof for the purchaser until the contract is completed by transfer of the property to the purchaser or to the order of the purchaser[4]. Once the purchaser has wholly fulfilled his side of the contract (eg by paying over the purchase price) but the vendor still has title to the property then the vendor holds the property on a bare trust for the absolutely entitled purchaser[5]. Until then the vendor's trusteeship is a highly self-interested modified form of trusteeship.

---

2 'The principle that is applied is not a principle depending upon the possibility of a court of equity decreeing specific performance. The relevant principle is that equity considers as done that which ought to be done': Latham CJ in *Palette Shoes Pty Ltd v Krohn* (1937) 58 CLR 1 at 16; Meagher Gummow & Lehane *Equity: Doctrines & Remedies* (3rd edn) paras 340, 654. 663.
3 (1937) 58 CLR 1 at 27. Also see *Associated Alloys Pty Ltd v ACN 001 452 106 Pty Ltd* [2001] HCA 25, (2000) 74 ALJR 862.
4 *Wall v Bright* (1820) 1 Jac & W 494 at 503; *Shaw v Foster* (1872) LR 5 HL 321; A-J Oakley *Constructive Trusts* (3rd edn) Chap 6, M Cope *Constructive Trusts* (Law Book Co of Australia, 1992) Chap 25.
5 *Shaw v Foster* (1872) LR 5 HL 321 at 349 and 356; *Bridges v Mees* [1957] Ch 475, [1957] 2 All ER 577; *Williams on Title* (4th edn) p 713.

The effect of the doctrine of conversion

Where the contract for sale is specifically enforceable the equitable doctrine of conversion looks on that as done which ought to be done. Thus equity looks on the purchaser as owner of the property the subject of the contract (eg specific real property) and the vendor as the owner of the purchase money (ie personal property)[6]. However, the vendor retains the legal title to the property (or the primary equitable title if he is selling an equitable interest) until full performance of the contract. By operation of law the vendor then holds the property on constructive trust for the purchaser[7]. Owing to absence of the necessary certainty of subject matter the purchaser does not hold the purchase money on a corresponding constructive trust for the vendor; instead, the vendor has a lien or charge on the property for the unpaid purchase money[8]. Only if the contract had been one of exchange of properties (eg if V sold Blackacre to P in exchange for P selling Whiteacre to V) would reciprocal constructive trusts have arisen.

Once the equitable doctrine of conversion has operated the vendor is subject to certain trusteelike obligations in respect of the property, whilst the purchaser becomes liable for risks inherent in the nature of ownership of the property, eg if destroyed by fire. If freehold land is the subject of the contract under the doctrine of conversion the vendor's interest is treated as one in pure personalty (the purchase proceeds) whilst the purchaser's interest is treated as one in land[9]. This can be crucial where a testator leaves his realty and personalty (or land and pure personalty) to different persons[10].

When doctrine of conversion operates

The doctrine of conversion operates from the time a contract is specifically enforceable. Few contracts for the sale of goods will be specifically enforceable since the equitable remedy of specific performance will only be granted if the breach of contract is incapable of being adequately compensated by an award of damages, eg in the case of a contract to sell a rare antique. From the moment of entering such a contract the remedy of specific performance will be available so that a constructive trust immediately arises.

---

6 For example *Re Birmingham* [1959] Ch 523, [1958] 2 All ER 397.

7 Whether the vendor's property is a legal or equitable interest: *Oughtred v IRC* [1958] Ch 383, [1958] 1 All ER 252; affd [1960] AC 206, [1959] 3 All ER 623, HL (Viscount Radcliffe and Lord Cohen); *Re Holt's Settlement* [1969] 1 Ch 100, [1968] 1 All ER 470; *DHN Food Distributors Ltd v London Borough of Tower Hamlets* [1976] 3 All ER 462, [1976] 1 WLR 852. Where there is a vendor and a purchaser and a sub-purchaser (as distinct from an assignee of the purchaser's contract) Stamp LJ has taken the view that the vendor is not a trustee for the sub-purchaser and the sub-purchaser cannot sue the vendor for specific performance. However, Goff LJ thought the sub-purchaser had acquired an equitable interest which the vendor was bound to recognise and the vendor and purchaser could not with notice of the sub-purchaser's claim agree to rescind or vary the head contract leaving the sub-purchaser with no more than a remedy against the purchaser. See *Berkley v Poulett* (1976) 242 Estates Gazette 39, CA. The absence of mutuality, because the vendor is not entitled to sue the sub-purchaser directly even if the sub-purchaser could sue such vendor, should prevent there being a specifically enforceable obligation between then so that the view of Stamp LJ seems preferable.

8 *Nives v Nives* (1880) 15 Ch D 649; *London and Cheshire Insurance Co Ltd v Laplagrene Property Co Ltd* [1971] Ch 499, [1971] 1 All ER 766.

9 *Re Birmingham* [1959] Ch 523, [1958] 2 All ER 397.

10 Before 1926 the doctrine of conversion was more crucial since on intestacy realty passed to the heir and personalty to the next of kin. Section 3 of the Trusts of Land and Appointment of Trustees Act 1996 only abolishes conversion for trusts for sale of land: see p 372 ante.

Every piece of land is regarded as unique so as to make damages inadequate as compensation for the loss of an interest in land so that specific performance is prima facie available as a remedy. However, a contract for sale of land is only enforceable if either the vendor is in a position to make title in accordance with the contract or the purchaser agrees to accept the title notwithstanding that it is not in accordance with the contract[11]. Only after the contract has been concluded does the purchaser investigate the title so that the contract will only become enforceable some period thereafter. The question arises whether conversion only occurs when the contract has become enforceable (upon the vendor being able to make title in accordance with the contract or the purchaser otherwise accepting the title the vendor has).

The authorities[12] establish that no conversion will occur if the vendor cannot make title in accordance with the contract and the purchaser does not agree to accept such other title as the vendor has. If the vendor can make title in accordance with the contract or if the purchaser otherwise accepts the title the vendor has, then conversion occurs with retrospective effect from the conclusion of the binding contract[13]. In fact, where the purchaser accepts the title the vendor has (the vendor not having been able to make title in accordance with the contract) there is no authority deciding that conversion is retrospective so that it has been suggested that conversion should only be retrospective when the vendor is able to make title in accordance with the contract and not where the purchaser agrees to accept some other title[14]. It is submitted that there should be retrospectivity in both cases. The date of concluding a binding contract (usually the date of exchange of contracts) will usually occasion no difficulty, whilst the ascertainment of the day when the purchaser agrees to accept what title the vendor has may well occasion difficulty. Moreover, if retrospectivity did not occur then the vendor would be under no trusteeship obligation in respect of the property till the purchaser accepted the vendor's actual title, so that before accepting such title, the purchaser ought to carry out a further inspection of the property to ensure that it had not deteriorated since conclusion of the contract. Since this would afford scope to the purchaser to withdraw from the contract if deterioration had occurred, the vendor de facto would need to preserve the property from deterioration, so there seems no reason why this situation shall not be regularised de jure by making the vendor under a trusteeship obligation from the date of the contract if the purchaser accepts title from the vendor otherwise than in accordance with the contract.

Conversion should thus occur from the conclusion of a binding contract of sale of land once the vendor has been able to make title in accordance with the contract or the purchaser has otherwise accepted the vendor's title. Exceptionally and anomalously, owing to *Lawes v Bennett*[15], conversion is retrospective not just to the conclusion of a binding contract but to the date of grant of an option to purchase an interest in land where such an option

---

11 *Lysaght v Edwards* (1876) 2 Ch D 499 at 506–507.
12 *Re Thomas* (1886) 34 Ch D 166; *Broome v Monck* (1805) 10 Ves 597; *Plews v Samuel* [1904] 1 Ch 464.
13 *Lysaght v Edwards* (1876) 2 Ch D 499 at 506–507, 510, 518.
14 P H Pettit (1960) 24 Conv (NS) 47, D W M Waters *The Constructive Trust*, pp 76–87.
15 (1785) 1 Cox Eq Cas 167 applied in *Townley v Bedwell* (1808) 14 Ves 591; *Weeding v Weeding* (1861) 1 John & H 424; *Re Blake* [1917] 1 Ch 18; *Re Carrington* [1932] 1 Ch 1.

has been granted and then exercised[16]. The exception has been restricted so as not to apply as between those interested in the estate of the grantee of the option[17] nor between the grantor and the grantee of the option so as to make the grantor liable as trustee between the grant and exercise of the option[18] nor where the property in question is the subject matter of a specific devise after the grant of the option so that the testator can be taken to have intended to pass to the devisee the entire interest therein, no matter what its nature[19]. Although many regard the rule in *Lawes v Bennett* as anomalous in redeeming specific devises in wills made before the grant of an option relating to the devised property Nicholls J[20] accepted it as well-established and extended it to a conditional contract entered into after the date of the testator's will where the condition was only fulfilled after the testator's death.

The nature of the vendor's trusteeship

The vendor's trusteeship is of an unusual nature. As Lord Cairns remarked in *Shaw v Foster*[1]:

> 'There cannot be the slightest doubt of the relation subsisting in the eye of a court of equity between the vendor and the purchaser. The vendor was a trustee of the property for the purchaser; the purchaser was the real beneficial owner in the eye of a court of equity of the property, subject only to this observation, that the vendor, whom I have called a trustee, was not a mere dormant trustee, he was a trustee having a personal and substantial interest in the property, a right to protect that interest, and an active right to assert that interest if anything should be done in derogation of it. The relation, therefore, of trustee and cestui que trust subsisted, but subsisted subject to the paramount right of the vendor and trustee to protect his own interest as vendor of the property.'

The vendor, unless the contract otherwise provides, has the following rights. He has a right to remain in possession of the property until completion and he has an equitable lien on the property for payment of the purchase money[2]. He has a right to rents and profits due before the contractual completion date[3], but is under a corresponding duty to discharge outgoings (eg rates) payable in respect of the property[4]. Once the vendor has received the purchase price he will become a bare trustee pending transfer of his legal title and will have to pass on all benefits to the purchaser.

The vendor is under a duty to 'use reasonable care to preserve the property in a reasonable state of preservation, and, so far as may be, as it was when the contract was made' or 'to take reasonable care that the property is not deteriorated in the interval before completion'[5]. He must keep the property in repair[6] and must not himself damage the property[7] or let others damage

---

16 Even if the purchase does not subsequently go through: *Re Blake* [1917] 1 Ch 18.
17 *Re Adams and Kensington Vestry* (1884) 27 Ch D 394.
18 *Edwards v West* (1878) 7 Ch D 858.
19 *Weeding v Weeding* (1861) 1 John & H 424; *Emuss v Smith* (1848) 2 De G & Sm 722 (codicil after option republishing the will); *Re Pyle* [1895] 1 Ch 724 (will and option grant on same day).
20 *Re Sweeting* [1988] 1 All ER 1016.
1 (1872) LR 5 HL 321 at 338.
2 *Phillips v Silvester* (1872) 8 Ch App 173; *Re Birmingham* [1959] Ch 523, [1958] 2 All ER 397.
3 *Cuddon v Tite* (1858) 1 Giff 395.
4 *Barsht v Tagg* [1900] 1 Ch 231; *Re Highett and Bird's Contract* [1902] 2 Ch 214.
5 *Clarke v Ramuz* [1891] 2 QB 456 at 460, 468.
6 *Royal Bristol Permanent Building Society v Bomash* (1887) 35 Ch D 390.
7 *Phillips v Lamdin* [1949] 2 KB 33, [1949] 1 All ER 770.

the property through lack of reasonable precautions on his part[8]. He must not withdraw any application for planning permission[9] and it seems that if the purchaser is not buying for his own occupation but for speculation, then the vendor may well be under a duty to pass on to the purchaser higher offers for the property received by the vendor[10].

Where land is sold subject to tenancies which come to an end before the contract is completed the vendor has a duty to inform the purchaser, so that a vendor who re-lets the property without informing the purchaser will be liable for any loss thereby suffered[11]. If the purchaser directs the vendor not to re-let and undertakes to compensate the vendor for any loss thereby suffered then the vendor should not re-let. If the purchaser does not respond to notification that the property (or part thereof) has fallen vacant and that the vendor is considering re-letting then the vendor should re-let[12] unless it is in his best interests to retain the property with vacant possession the better to assist a re-sale at a good price if the sale falls through. Whether the whole or only a small part of the premises falls vacant will often be crucial. If the whole becomes vacant then it will very often be in the interest of both vendor and purchaser not to re-let before completion. Where the premises comprise several lettings and have been purchased for their rental income then re-letting of the vacated part will often be best, though the purchaser may be happy to do this himself after completion, in which case he should offer to compensate the vendor for what the vendor may lose through not re-letting before completion.

The vendor's duties should be performed as much in his interest as in the purchaser's interest since the sale may fall through and, as a result, the vendor is not entitled to be reimbursed for any expenses thereby incurred[13].

The purchaser's position

Unless the purchaser has expressly waived his rights he can sue the vendor for breach of the vendor's trusteeship duties even after completion of the contract: the duties do not merge in the conveyance and completion does not amount to waiver of any breach of the vendor's trusteeship duties[14].

Since the purchaser is regarded under the doctrine of conversion as the owner of the property, the subject of the contract, he takes the benefit and burden of gains and losses of a capital nature accruing to the property itself.

Except in unforeseen extreme circumstances, a contract for the sale of land cannot be frustrated[15]. Thus (in the absence of a contrary contractual

8 *Clarke v Ramuz* [1891] 2 QB 456; *Davron Estates Ltd v Turnshire Ltd* (1982) 133 NLJ 937, CA; *Cedar Transport Group Ltd v First Wyvern Property Trustee Co Ltd* (1980) 258 Estates Gazette 1077 (damage by vandals); *Lucie-Smith v Gorman* [1981] CLY 2866 (burst pipe).
9 *Sinclair-Hill v Sothcott* (1973) 226 Estates Gazette 1399.
10 *Lake v Bayliss* [1974] 2 All ER 1114 at 1118.
11 *Earl Egmont v Smith* (1877) 6 Ch D 469.
12 *Abdulla v Shah* [1959] AC 124, [1959] 2 WLR 12, PC; (1959) 23 Conv 178 (V G Wellings).
13 *Re Watford Corpn's and Ware's Contract* [1943] Ch 82, [1943] 1 All ER 54.
14 *Clarke v Ramuz* [1891] 2 QB 456 at 561; *Cumberland Consolidated Holdings Ltd v Ireland* [1946] KB 264 at 269.
15 *Wong Lai-Ying v Chinachem Investments Co Ltd* [1978] HKLR 1, PC; *Cricklewood Property and Investment Trust Ltd v Leighton's Trust Ltd* [1945] AC 221, [1945] 1 All ER 252; *Total Oil Great Britain Ltd v Thompson Garages (Biggin Hill) Ltd* [1972] 1 QB 318, [1971] 3 All ER 1226, CA; *Hillingdon Estate Co v Stonefield Estates Ltd* [1952] Ch 627 at 631; *National Carriers Ltd v Panalpina (Northern) Ltd* [1981] AC 675, [1981] 1 All ER 161, HL; *Amalgamated Investment and Property Co v John Walker & Sons* [1977] 1 WLR 164, CA.

provision like that in Standard Conditions of Sale Condition 5.1) a purchaser bears the risk, for example, of total destruction of the buildings by fire as long as not caused by breach of the vendor's trusteeship duties[16]. If a purchaser has been foolish enough not to have insured the property he cannot, if the vendor has insured the property, recover insurance moneys from the vendor[17]. He will have to pay the purchase money to the vendor's insurance company who, having satisfied the vendor's claim, will be subrogated to the vendor's right to the purchase price[18].

Section 83 of the Fires Prevention (Metropolis) Act 1774, where buildings have been destroyed or damaged by fire, enables any person interested to require the insurance company to lay out the insurance money towards rebuilding or reinstating the building in question so long as the money has not already been paid to the assured. However it seems that this obligation only arises where the assured was under an obligation to the person interested to reinstate the premises (eg where a landlord has so covenanted with a tenant)[19]: this is unlikely as between vendor and purchaser. Section 47 of the Law of Property Act 1925 could also assist a purchaser. It enables a purchaser on or after completion to recover from the vendor any insurance money paid 'in respect of any damage to or destruction of property included in the contract' (whether caused by fire or not). However, this is subject to any contrary stipulation in the contract, any requisite consent of the insurance company, and the payment by the purchaser of the proportionate part of the premium from the date of the contract. The Law Society General Conditions of Sale and the Standard Condition of Sale exclude s 47, leaving it up to the purchaser or vendor to make appropriate insurance arrangements.

The purchaser is entitled to all gains or benefits of a capital nature *accruing to the property itself*, eg improvements financed by the vendor[20]. He is not entitled to benefits accruing to the vendor qua vendor unless expressly provided for by the contract for sale. Thus the vendor, in the absence of statutory intervention or a contrary contractual term, can retain insurance money payable to him[1]. He can retain sums due in respect of dilapidations arising between contract and conveyance payable under a lease expiring in that period[2]. In *Re Hamilton-Snowball's Conveyance*[3] H-S, occupying a requisitioned house, contracted to buy it from its owner, the conveyance to him going to have the effect of derequisitioning the house. Later the same day H-S contracted to re-sell the house to the purchaser at a much higher price, not mentioning the requisitioning since the subsequent conveyance to H-S would derequisition the house. The house was conveyed to H-S, derequisitioned, and then conveyed by H-S to the purchaser. As houseowner at the time of derequisitioning H-S received a substantial sum under the Compensation (Defence) Act 1939. The purchaser's claim that H-S held this sum as constructive trustee for the purchaser failed since the sum was not paid as

---

16 *Rayner v Preston* (1881) 18 Ch D 1, CA; *Paine v Meller* (1801) 6 Ves 349.
17 *Rayner v Preston* (1881) 18 Ch D 1, CA.
18 *Castellain v Preston* (1883) 11 QBD 380, approved by House of Lords in *Napier and Ettrick v Kershaw* [1993] AC 713.
19 *Lonsdale & Thompson Ltd v Black Arrow Group plc* [1993] Ch 361.
20 *Monro v Taylor* (1848) 8 Hare 51 at 60.
 1 *Rayner v Preston* (1881) 18 Ch D 1, CA.
 2 *Re Lyne-Stephens and Scott-Miller's Contract* [1920] 1 Ch 472. If the sale had been subject to, but with the benefit of, an existing lease the position would have differed.
 3 [1959] Ch 308, [1958] 2 All ER 319.

an accrual to the property that was the subject matter of the purchaser's contract.

Since the vendor holds the property as constructive trustee for the purchaser it follows that, if the vendor in breach of trust sells the property to a third party, the purchaser may trace the property into the proceeds of sale received by the vendor from the third party[4]. This will be useful where the purchaser has no claim against the third party for want of protecting his estate contract on the appropriate register and where the contractual claim against the vendor for damages is not worthwhile, eg because the vendor is bankrupt or because more financial benefit can be obtained from the tracing claim than from the damages claim.

4 *Lake v Bayliss* [1974] 2 All ER 1114, [1974] 1 WLR 1073.

DIVISION FOUR

The administration of a trust

Chapter
8   Disclaimer and acceptance of trusts   447
9   The estate of the trustee and its incidents   454
10 Trusts of land   463
11 The trustee's duties   484
12 The powers of the trustee   688
13 Powers of the beneficiaries   729
14 The death, retirement, or removal of trustees and the appointment of new trustees   740
15 Appointment of a judicial trustee   785
16 The Public Trustee   789
17 Administration of new trusts created under limited powers in the original settlement   803
18 The rights of the trustee   810
19 The right of trustees and beneficiaries to seek the assistance of the Public Trustee or the court in auditing or in administering the trust   831

CHAPTER 8

Disclaimer and acceptance of trusts

Article
37 The number of trustees permissible   447
38 Disclaimer of a trust   449
39 Acceptance of a trust   451

ARTICLE 37

The number of trustees permissible

As a general rule the number of trustees is unlimited by law, one being sufficient, and any greater number permissible. But there is an exception in the case of trusts of land and trustees for the purposes of the Settled Land Act, in which cases the maximum number is four and the minimum for giving a good receipt for purchase-money two, unless the sole trustee is a trust corporation.

Section 34 of the Trustee Act 1925 provides that:

(1) Where, at the commencement of this Act, there are more than four trustees of a settlement of land, or more than four trustees holding land on trust for sale, no new trustees shall (except where as a result of the appointment the number is reduced to four or less) be capable of being appointed until the number is reduced to less than four, and thereafter the number shall not be increased beyond four.

(2) In the case of settlements[1] and dispositions creating trusts[2] of land made or coming into operation after the commencement of this Act—

   (a) the number of trustees thereof shall not in any case exceed four, and where more than four persons are named as such trustees, the four first named (who are able and willing to act) shall alone be the

---

1 Under the Settled Land Act 1925: Trusts of Land and Appointment of Trustees Act 1996, s 23(1), Law of Property Act 1925, s 205(1)(xxvi), Settled Land Act 1925, s 117(1)(xxiv), Trustee Act 1925, s 68(1), (15). No new SLA settlements can be created after 1996: see s 2 of the 1996 Act.

2 See Sch 3, para 3(9) of the Trusts of Land and Appointment of Trustees Act 1996 substituting 'creating trusts of land' for 'on trust for sale of land', the former expression covering any trust of land (including trusts for sale) other than SLA settled land: s 1(1)(a) of the 1996 Act.

trustees, and the other persons named shall not be trustees unless appointed on the occurrence of a vacancy;

(b) the number of the trustees shall not be increased beyond four.

(3) This section applies to settlements and dispositions of land, and the restrictions imposed on the number of trustees do not apply—

(a) in the case of land vested in trustees for charitable, ecclesiastical, or public purposes; or

(b) where the net proceeds of the sale of the land are held for like purposes; or

(c) to the trustees of a term of years absolute limited by a settlement on trusts for raising money, or of a like term created under the statutory remedies relating to annual sums charged on land.

The minimum number of two trustees[3] (unless a trust corporation is sole trustee) to *give a good receipt for the purchase-money of English and Welsh land* is prescribed by statute whether the sale be by trustees or by a tenant for life or statutory owner selling under the powers of the Settled Land Act[4]. This is further referred to in Article 63, post.

There is no restriction on the number of tenants for life in whom settled land may be vested as joint tenants.

Where a trust initially is not a trust of land, but English and Welsh land is later acquired by the trustees, then a trust of land will arise so there is a problem if beforehand there are more than four trustees. Such land should not be vested in more than four persons as trustees, so retirement[5] of sufficient trustees to reduce their number to four should take place: otherwise, it would seem that the first four named would become trustees to the exclusion of the others[6].

When a trust of land ceases to be a trust of land because the land has been distributed to one or more beneficiaries or has been sold, so that the trustees are holding money on deposit and investments other than land, then the restriction on the number of trustees will cease[7].

---

3 This applies to Settled Land Act trustees: Settled Land Act 1925, s 18. Exceptionally, a sole personal representative acting as such may give valid receipts for capital moneys: Law of Property Act 1925, s 27(2).

4 As to trustees by s 27(2) of the Law of Property Act 1925, and as to Settled Land Act trustees by s 94 of the Settled Land Act 1925. A 'trust corporation' is defined in the statutes as 'the Public Trustee or a corporation either appointed by the Court [or the Charity Commissioners] in any particular case to be a trustee or entitled by rules made under subsection (3) of section 4 of the Public Trustee Act 1906 to act as custodian trustee' (Law of Property Act 1925, s 205(1)(xxviii); Settled Land Act 1925, s 117(1)(xxx); Trustee Act 1925, s 68(18) and by the Law of Property (Amendment) Act 1926, s 3 and Charities Act 1993, s 35, the definition was extended to include the Treasury Solicitor, the Official Solicitor, and certain other official persons and trustees of charitable, ecclesiastical and public trusts. See also the Public Trustee Rules 1912, r 30 as substituted by the Public Trustee (Custodian Trustee) Rules 1975 under SI 1975/1189 as amended by SI 1987/1891 and SI 1994/2519, which require the company to be a company constituted under the law of a European Union Member State and to have an issued share capital of £250,000 (or its foreign currency equivalent) of which not less than £100,000 (or its equivalent) paid up and to have a place of business in the UK (and, of course, be empowered under its constitution to undertake trust business): see p 797 post. It must also be authorised under the Financial Services and Markets Act 2000.

5 See Trustee Act 1925, s 39, p 746, post.

6 Trustee Act 1925, s 34(2)(a). To preserve all the trustees it would be necessary to acquire the land through a holding company owned by all the trustees.

7 See ss 17(3) and 1(1) of the 1996 Act.

ARTICLE 38

Disclaimer of a trust

No one is bound to accept the office of trustee[8]. Both the office and the estate may be disclaimed before acceptance (but not afterwards[9]) by deed or by conduct tantamount to a disclaimer[10]. The disclaimer should be made within a reasonable period, having regard to the circumstances of the particular case[11]. Part of a trust cannot be disclaimed if other parts be accepted[12]. The onus of proving disclaimer is on those who assert it[13].

Consent to undertake future trust not binding

Thus, even though a person may have agreed in the lifetime of a testator to be his executor, he is still at liberty to resile from his promise at any time before proving the will[14]. However, a person can be made a constructive or resulting trustee against his will, eg under secret trusts[15] and mutual wills[16].

Methods of disclaiming

A prudent person will, of course, always disclaim by deed[17], in order that there may be no question of the fact; but a disclaimer by counsel at the bar[18], or even by conduct inconsistent with acceptance, is sufficient[19]. In *Re Birchall*[20] the Court of Appeal held that a trustee had by conduct disclaimed the office; and that having disclaimed the office, he must of necessity have also disclaimed the estate.

Where a deed is executed with the intention that it shall operate as a disclaimer, it will have that effect, notwithstanding that the disclaiming trustee purports to convey or release his estate to the accepting trustees, an

---

 8 *Robinson v Pett* (1734) 3 P Wms 249, 2 White & Tud LC 605.
 9 *Re Lister* [1926] Ch 149; *Re Sharman's Will Trusts* [1942] Ch 311, [1942] 2 All ER 74, where this Article was cited with approval by Bennett J.
10 *Stacey v Elph* (1833) 1 My & K 195; *Townson v Tickell* (1819) 3 B & Ald 31; *Begbie v Crook* (1835) 2 Bing NC 70; *Bingham v Lord Clanmorris* (1828) 2 Mol 253; and *Re Birchall* (1889) 40 Ch D 436.
11 See *Doehd Chidgey v Harris* (1847) 16 M & W 517 at 522; *Paddon v Richardson* (1855) 7 De GM & G 563; *James v Frearson* (1842) 1 Y & C Ch Cas 370. However, it seems mere inaction over a long period may be evidence of disclaimer: *Re Clout and Frewer's Contract* [1924] 2 Ch 230.
12 *Re Lord and Fullerton's Contract* [1896] 1 Ch 228. See p 453, post. Cf *Wellesley v Withers* (1855) 4 E & B 750. If appointed trustee of two separate trusts he may accept one and reject the other unless this would be contrary to the settler's intention.
13 See *Re Arbib and Class's Contract* [1891] 1 Ch 601, CA: also p 452 post.
14 *Doyle v Blake* (1804) 2 Sch & Lef 231.
15 See p 410, ante.
16 See p 427, ante.
17 The proper mode is by deed poll (*Re Schar* [1951] Ch 280 at 284, [1950] 2 All ER 1069 at 1071). Married women are in the same position as men: Statute Law (Repeals) Act 1969, Sch, Pt III, repealing Law of Property Act 1925, ss 167–170.
18 *Norway v Norway* (1834) 2 My & K 278; *Bray v West* (1838) 9 Sim 429.
19 *Foster v Dawber* (1860) 8 WR 646; *Stacey v Elph* (1833) 1 My & K 195; *Re Gordon* (1877) 6 Ch D 531.
20 (1889) 40 Ch D 436; and see *Lancashire v Lancashire* (1848) 2 Ph 657; and *Re Clout and Frewer's Contract* [1924] 2 Ch 230.

action which logically raises the inference that he has accepted the estate[1]. However it is best to execute a deed poll expressed as a disclaimer.

Costs of disclaimer

A person nominated to be a trustee who refuses to accept the office ought not to be put to expense. He is therefore entitled, as a condition of executing a deed of disclaimer, to be paid out of the trust estate all his costs of and incident thereto, including the costs of taking counsel's opinion[2]. If (not having previously disclaimed) he is made a defendant to an action concerning the trust, he should, generally speaking, disclaim at once and offer to execute all necessary documents on his costs being paid. He will then be entitled to have the action against him dismissed, with costs, but probably only on the standard basis which has replaced party and party costs[3]. What would happen in the case of a person nominated as trustee who unreasonably refuses either to accept or disclaim seems never to have been decided in any reported case. It is apprehended, however, that he would get no costs of any proceedings rendered necessary by his ill-conditioned conduct, though it is difficult to see how he could be ordered to pay costs. Indeed, in one case (before the present wide judicial discretion as to costs) where the executrix of a deceased trustee refused to act in the trust (she could not disclaim) she was allowed her costs of a suit for the appointment of new trustees and a transfer of the trust property[4].

Effect of disclaimer

The effect of disclaimer is to avoid the devise, bequest, or grant *ab initio*, so that where there are two trustees and one disclaims, the title of the other who accepts is complete *ab initio*, and devolves on his death as such[5]. If a person appointed sole trustee disclaims (unless his personality was regarded by the settlor as critical to the running of the trust[6]), the trust does not fail: the property is held by the settlor or, if he is dead, his personal representatives upon the trusts specified in the settlement or will[7].

---

1 *Nicloson v Wordsworth* (1818) 2 Swan 365 at 370–371, 372.
2 *Re Tryon* (1844) 7 Beav 496.
3 See *Benbow v Davies* (1848) 11 Beav 369; *Norway v Norway* (1834) 2 My & K 278; *Bray v West* (1838) 9 Sim 429. As to where he is a defendant in a foreclosure action by a mortgagee of the trustee estate, see *Ford v Lord Chesterfield* (1853) 16 Beav 516.
4 *Legg v Mackrell* (1860) 2 De GF & J 551.
5 *Peppercorn v Wayman* (1852) 5 De G & Sm 230; *JW Broomhead (Vcc) Pty Ltd v JW Brownhead Pty Ltd* [1985] VR 891; *Re Paradise Motor Co Ltd* [1968] 2 All ER 625, [1968] 1 WLR 1125, CA This equally applies to powers annexed to the office: *Browell v Reed* (1842) 1 Hare 434; *Adams v Taunton* (1820) 5 Madd 435, but not to personal powers (*Wetherell v Langston* (1847) 1 Exch 634; *Crawford v Forshaw* (1890) 43 Ch D 643).
6 *Re Lysaght* [1966] Ch 191.
7 *Mallott v Wilson* [1903] 2 Ch 494, accepted by CA in *Harris v Sharp* (21 March 1989, unreported). P Matthews [1981] Conv. 141 has contended that a disclaimer of an inter vivos transfer to a sole trustee would make the transfer void and the trust fail but one may treat the transferor as a constructive trustee on *Re Rose* [1952] Ch 499, [1952] I All ER 1217, CA principles, p 154, ante or treat the vesting of the property in the trustee until he disclaims as sufficient: cf *Standing v Bowring* (1885) 31 Ch D 282 at 288. Further on the unilateral and bilateral nature of gifts see J Hill (2001) 117 LQR 127.

ARTICLE 39

Acceptance of a trust

A person may accept the office of trustee expressly, or he may do so constructively by doing such acts as are only referable to the character of trustee or executor, or he may do so by long acquiescence. In the absence of evidence to the contrary, acceptance will be presumed[8].

Express acceptance

A trustee expressly accepts the office by executing the settlement[9], or by making an express declaration of his assent[10].

Acceptance by acquiescence

Permitting an action concerning the trust property to be brought in his name[11], or otherwise allowing the trust property to be dealt with in his name[12], is such an acquiescence as will be construed to be an acceptance of the office.

Acceptance by acts of ownership

Exercising any act of ownership, such as advertising the property for sale, giving notice to the tenants to pay the rents to himself or an agent, or requesting the steward of a manor to enrol a deed in relation to the trust property, and a fortiori active interference in the affairs of the trust[13], is sufficient to constitute acceptance of a trust[14].

Acceptance by taking out probate

Where the office of executor is clothed with certain trusts, or where the executor is also nominated the trustee of real estate under a will, he is

---

8 In *Re Sharman's Will Trusts* [1942] Ch 311, [1942] 2 All ER 74, Bennett J cited this Article, for which authority is to be found in *Townson v Tickell* (1819) 3 B & Ald 31; *Re Arbib and Class's Contract* [1891] 1 Ch 601.

9 *Buckeridge v Glasse* (1841) Cr & Ph 126; *Jones v Higgins* (1866) LR 2 Eq 538.

10 *Doe d Chidgey v Harris* (1847) 16 M & W 517.

11 *Lord Montfortd v Lord Cadogan* (1810) 17 Ves 485.

12 *James v Frearson* (1842) 1 Y & C Ch Cas 370.

13 *Doyle v Blake* (1804) 2 Sch & Lef 231; *Harrison v Graham* (unreported cited in 1 P Wms (6th edn) 241n; *Urch v Walker* (1838) 3 My & Cr 702.

14 *Bence v Gilpin* (1868) LR 3 Exch 76. As to acceptance of executorship by intermeddling, and its effect on subsequent devastavit by administrator, see *Doyle v Blake* (1804) 2 Sch & Lef 231. In *Holder v Holder* [1968] Ch 353; on appeal [1968] 1 All ER 665, CA, an executor signed cheques on an account opened in the name of all three executors named in the will, and with the other executors endorsed some of the deceased's insurance policies and instructed solicitors to act for the estate. It was conceded by counsel that this was an acceptance of the executorship (eg *Cummins v Cummins* (1845) 3 Jo & Lat 64, not cited to CA) so preventing a subsequent purported renunciation of the executorship from being effective. Surprisingly, all three Lords Justices doubted the correctness of the concession.

construed to have accepted the office of trustee if he takes out probate to the will[15].

Acceptance by conduct

In *Conyngham v Conyngham*[16] one Colman was appointed trustee of a will, but he never expressly accepted the appointment. One of the trusts was in respect of the rents of a plantation then in lease to the testator's son. Coleman acted as agent of the son, who was also heir-at-law, and received the rents of the estate from him. It was held that, by so interfering with the trust property, he could not repudiate the trust and say that he merely acted as the son's agent. He received the rents; and it was incumbent on him, if he did not desire to act as trustee, to disclaim expressly, and not to leave himself at liberty to say he acted as trustee or not. It is, however, not every interference with trust property which will be construed as an acceptance of the office of trustee; for if such interference be plainly (not ambiguously) referable to some other ground, it will not operate as an acceptance[17]. It was said in an old case that merely taking charge of a trust until a new trustee can be found does not constitute, of itself, a constructive acceptance[18]. However, it is considered that this view would be rejected nowadays especially where such acts, would make even a stranger a trustee or executor de son tort (see pp 951–952, post).

In another dubious case, the joining in the legacy duty receipt for the trust fund, unaccompanied by the actual receipt of the money, was held to be of itself insufficient to fix a trustee, who desired to disclaim, with acceptance of the trusteeship, though he need not have signed if he were not a trustee[19].

Acceptance by long silence

There is a prima facie presumption of acceptance; so that where a trustee, with notice of the trust, has indulged in a passive acquiescence for some years, he will be presumed to have accepted it, in the absence of any satisfactory explanation[20]. And where a testator nominated A, who was living in Australia, to be one of his trustees if he should return to England, and some years after the testator's death he did return for a temporary visit, and there was no evidence of disclaimer, it was held that the prima facie presumption of acceptance had not been rebutted, and that a title could not be made by the other trustees[1]. There was, however, some evidence that whilst in Australia A intended to become a trustee. In *Re Clout and Frewer's Contract*[2] Lord Buckmaster, sitting in the High Court, took the view that a long period of

---

15 *Mucklow v Fuller* (1821) Jac 198; *Ward v Butler* (1824) 2 Mol 533; *Booth v Booth* (1838) 1 Beav 125; *Styles v Guy* (1849) 1 Mac & G 422; *Re Sharman's Will Trusts* [1942] Ch 311, [1942] 2 All ER 74.

16 (1750) I Ves Sen 522; and see *Re Sharman's Will Trusts* [1942] Ch 311, [1942] 2 All ER 74.

17 *Stacey v Elph* (1833) I My & K 195; *Dove v Everard* (1830) I Russ & M 231; *Lowry v Fulton* (1839) 9 Sim 104.

18 *Evans v John* (1841) 4 Beav 35.

19 *Jago v Jago* (1893) 68 LT 654.

20 *Wise v Wise* (1845) 2 Jo & Lat 403; *Re Uniacke* (1844) 1 Jo & Lat 1; *Re Needham* (1844) 1 Jo & Lat 34; *Doehd Chidgey v Harris* (1847) 16 M & W 517.

1 *Re Arbib and Class's Contract* [1891] 1 Ch 601.

2 [1924] 2 Ch 230. See also *JW Broonhead (Vic) Pty Ltd v JW Broomhead Pty Ltd* [1985] VR 891 at 931–932.

silence and inaction could rebut the presumption of acceptance, casting doubt on *Re Uniacke*[3] and *Re Needham*[4] and preferring views expressed in *Re Gordon*[5] and *Re Birchall*[6]. After all, to presume that inaction amounts to acceptance is to presume an intention to neglect a duty to act: is it not better to presume from long inaction an intention never to be under any duty?

Acceptance of part and attempted disclaimer of other part

Acceptance of part of a trust is acceptance of the whole, notwithstanding any attempted disclaimer of part. Thus, where a testator, having property here and abroad, gave the whole to trustees upon the same trusts, it was held that one of the trustees could not disclaim the English property while accepting the trusts of the foreign property. Consequently he was a necessary party to a sale of the former[7]. However it would seem that a person appointed by the same settlor to be trustee of two separate trusts could accept one and disclaim the other, unless this would be against the intention of the settlor.

Lastly, when once a trust has been effectually disclaimed, interference by the disclaiming trustee will not cancel the disclaimer or raise an inference of acceptance of the trust—as, for example, where he acts as agent for the trustees or adviser to the family[8].

The position of a trustee de son tort (ie a person not nominated as trustee who gets possession of trust property with notice of the trust) is dealt with elsewhere[9].

3 (1844) 1 Jo & Lat 1.
4 (1844) 1 Jo & Lat 34.
5 (1877) 6 Ch D 531.
6 (1889) 40 Ch D 436.
7 *Re Lord and Fullerton's Contract* [1896] 1 Ch 228; *Re Lister* [1926] Ch 149 at 166.
8 *Dove v Everard* (1830) 1 Russ & M 231; *Lowry v Fulton* (1839) 9 Sim 104; *Stacey v Elph* (1833) 1 My & K 195.
9 See pp 951–952, post.

CHAPTER 9

The estate of the trustee and its incidents

Article
40 Estate taken by the trustee   454
41 The incidents of the trustee's estate   456
42 The effect of the Limitation Act 1980 on the trustee's estate   458
43 The effect of the trustee's bankruptcy   460

ARTICLE 40

Estate taken by the trustee

The trustee takes such legal or equitable estate in the trust property as the settlor (or testator) has power to dispose of and as may be expressed to be vested in him by conveyance, assignment or other form of transfer inter vivos appropriate to property of the nature of the trust property[1], assent, vesting declaration[2], vesting order[3] or vesting deed[4] or as may be already vested in him.

Legal or equitable estate

The only estates in land capable of subsisting or of being conveyed *at law* are an estate in fee simple absolute in possession and a term of years absolute. An attempt to create any other estate in land operates only to create equitable interests[5].

Assent

A personal representative may assent to the vesting in any person who (whether by devise, bequest, devolution, appropriation or otherwise) may be entitled thereto as trustee of any estate or interest in freehold or leasehold

1 Eg the usual form of share transfer.
2 See p 776, post.
3 See p 779, post.
4 This will only be appropriate where settled land is vested in the Settled Land Act trustees as statutory owners, see Settled Land Act 1925, s 9(2).
5 Law of Property Act 1925, ss 1, 4.

property which devolved upon the personal representative[6]. In order to pass a legal estate the assent must be in writing signed by the personal representative, and name the person in whose favour it is made[7].

When land whether freehold or leasehold is given by will, or devolves on intestacy, in such a way that it is to be held upon trusts which continue after the administration of the estate has been completed and the personal representatives are also appointed (expressly or impliedly) as trustees, the question arises as to whether a written assent is necessary before the legal estate passes to them as trustees. Although it has always been considered prudent for them to mark the change in the character in which they held the property by making a written assent, the conventional view was that no assent was strictly necessary because there was in such circumstances no 'passing' of the legal estate. The principal case supporting, if not positively confirming, this view was that of *Re Cockburn*[8].

However, *Re King's Will Trusts*[9] is direct authority to the opposite effect. In that case an executor who was also trustee of a will, but who had made no written assent to himself in the latter capacity, executed a Deed of Appointment by which he appointed another person to act as trustee jointly with himself. Pennycuick J held that the executor had not acquired the legal estate in the trust property in his capacity as trustee, since he could not do this otherwise than by a written assent. Nor could the Deed of Appointment itself be construed as including an assent. Consequently the Deed of Appointment did not operate to vest the legal estate in the new trustee (or in the new trustee jointly with the executor in his capacity as trustee). Of course, the effect of this decision is not that the executor was not a trustee, but merely that he had not acquired the legal estate in that capacity; similarly, it seems that the Deed of Appointment did not fail to constitute the other person a joint trustee, but merely that it failed to vest the legal estate in him. The case of *Re Cockburn*, above, which, if not precisely in point, was clearly very relevant, does not appear to have been cited in *Re King's Will Trusts*, but the latter case, although it has aroused some criticism on this and other grounds, must for the moment be accepted as correct. It was not challenged in *Re Edwards' Will Trusts*[10] where the Court of Appeal held that the *equitable* interest in land may pass under an assent inferred from conduct where the deceased landowner's husband was both her personal representative and beneficiary and treated himself as sole beneficial owner for twenty years after her death.

Since April 1998 any disposition of unregistered land effected by an assent has triggered the requirement of compulsory registration of the land[11]. If the land was registered by the owner's death, the personal representatives should become registered themselves, whether as trustees or personal representa-

---

6 Administration of Estates Act 1925, ss 36(1), 55(1)(xix).
7 Administration of Estates Act 1925, s 36(4).
8 [1957] Ch 438, [1957] 2 All ER 522; and CVIII Law Journal 36 et seq.
9 [1964] Ch 542, [1964] 1 All ER 833. As to this case, see also pp 20, ante, 778 post, and JT Farrand 1964 Sol Jo 698 and 719; R R Walker (1964) 80 LQR 328; J F Garner (1964) 28 Conv 298; E C Ryder (1976) 29 Current Legal Problems 60 and *Williams on Title* (4th edn) pp 354–361.
10 [1982] Ch 30, [1981] 2 All ER 941, CA, discussed [1981] Conv 450 and [1982] Conv 4. *Re Kings Will Trusts* has not been followed in Ireland: *Mohan v Roche* [1991] IR 560.
11 Land Registration Act 1997, s 1; Land Registration Act 2002, s 4(1)(a).

tives, or a sole executor-beneficiary should become registered as sole proprietor[12].

ARTICLE 41

The incidents of the trustee's estate

At law the estate of the trustee is subject to the same incidents, whether privileges or burdens, as if he were also beneficial owner, except where such incidents are modified by statute.

Power to commence actions

Thus, he is the proper person to bring actions arising out of wrongs formerly cognisable by common law courts, and which necessitated the possession of the legal estate in those bringing them[13].

Trustee's right to prove in bankruptcies

Where a debtor to the trust estate becomes bankrupt, the trustee is the proper person to prove without the concurrence of the beneficiaries[14], except in the case of a simple trust. Where, however, it is probable that the debtor has paid the beneficiaries direct, it lies in the discretion of the judge to require their concurrence in the proof[15].

Trustee liable for rates and taxes

The trustee of a private trust is, as legal owner of land, liable to pay rates or council tax in respect of the trust property[16]. A trustee may also be liable in certain circumstances for income tax, capital gains tax, inheritance tax and value added tax. The law relating to a trustee's liability for such taxes is so detailed that examination of these matters should proceed from the standard works on the various taxes. A trustee must be very wary where he is trustee of a head trust and considering creating separate sub-trusts with separate non-resident trustees since he may remain liable for capital gains made by the separate trustees, the body of trustees comprising the head trustees together with the sub-trusts trustees[17]. A prospective new trustee of the head trust needs to be aware of his potential liability if capital gains are subsequently made. Care must also be taken in case the retirement or appointment of a trustee converts a non-resident trust into a resident trust[18].

---

12 Land Registration Act 1925, s 41; Land Registration Act 2002, ss 24, 27(5)(a).
13 *May v Taylor* (1843) 6 Man & G 261; *Schalit v Joseph Nadler Ltd* [1933] 2 KB 79.
14 *Ex p Green* (1832) 2 Deac & Ch 113.
15 *Ex p Dubois* (1787) 1 Cox Eq Cas 310; *Ex p Gray* (1835) 4 Deac & Ch 778.
16 *R v Sterry* (1840) 12 Ad & El 84; *R v Stapleton* (1863) 4 B & S 629.
17 *Roome v Edwards (Inspector of Taxes)* [1982] AC 279, [1981] 1 All ER 736, HL.
18 *Green v Cobham* [2000] WTLR 1101 but the judge was persuaded that the relevant appointment should be treated as void on applying the *Re Hastings-Bass* [1975] Ch 25 principle (see p 694 post).

Trustee of a business liable to creditors

If the trustee, in pursuance of the trust, carries on a business for the benefit of the beneficiaries, he will yet be personally liable to the creditors of the business[19], and may be made a bankrupt[20].

Trustee entitled to custody of deeds

A trustee in whom the legal estate is vested is entitled to the custody of the deeds[1]; but the beneficiaries are entitled, at all reasonable times, to inspect them[2].

Rights under Town and Country Planning Act 1990

Regulations provide that where the right to claim compensation under Part V of the Town and Country Planning Act 1990 (which deals with planning decisions restricting new development) becomes exercisable by reference to an interest in land which is, at the time when the right is exercisable, subject to a settlement, then (a) the right to make the claim is exercisable by the trustees; and (b) where a claim has been made by reference to such an interest as aforesaid and compensation falls to be paid, the principal amount of the compensation is payable to the trustees, and to the extent that it ought (as between the beneficiaries) to be treated as capital it is applicable as capital money under the Settled Land Act 1925, or as proceeds of sale arising under a trust of land, as the case may be[3].

Individual rights of tenants of houses to freehold or extended lease and of tenants of flats to a new 90 year lease[4]

The Leasehold Reform Act 1967, as amended by the Housing Act 1996 and the Commonhold and Leasehold Reform Act 2002 (the 'CLRA'), makes it possible for trustees of land to purchase the freehold or an extended lease if the long lease of the house has been held subject to the trust for two years. The Leasehold Reform, Housing and Urban Development Act 1992 ('the LRHUDA'), as amended by the CLRA, makes it possible for trustees holding the tenancy of a flat to purchase a new 90 year lease from the expiry date of the existing long lease if such has been held subject to the trust for two years.

Collective enfranchisement rights of tenants of flats[5]

The tenants of a block of flats have a right to have the freehold thereof acquired on their behalf by a company known as a 'RTE company' at a price determined in accordance with a statutory formula, so long as notice to the

---

19 *Farhall v Farhall* (1871) 7 Ch App 123; *Owen v Delamere* (1872) LR 15 Eq 134. But of course he has a right of indemnity, as to which see Article 83, post.

20 *Wightman v Townroe* (1813) 1 M & S 412; *Ex p Garland* (1804) 10 Ves 110; *Farhall v Farhall* (1871) 7 Ch App 123. See Article 83, post.

1 *Evans v Bicknell* (1801) 6 Ves 174.

2 *Wynne v Humberston* (1858) 27 Beav 421.

3 Town and Country Planning Act 1990, s 135.

4 See Hill & Redman's *Law of Landlord & Tenant* on the immense technical detail; and the broad powers of trustees of land in Trusts of Land and Appointment of Trustees Act 1996, s 6.

5 See footnote 4 above.

freeholder is given by the RTE company – having amongst its participating members those having tenancies of no less than half of the total number of flats in the premises. The LRHUDA[6], as amended by the CLRA, makes it possible for trustee-tenants to be involved in such purchase at the expense of the trust fund.

Right to manage block of flats[7]

The CLRA gives leaseholders under long leases of flats the right to manage their block of flats via a company known as a 'RTM company' without having to prove shortcomings on the landlord's part and without having to pay him compensation. Trustee-tenants are enabled to be involved in such enterprise[8]. The right to manage does not extend to premises which have a resident landlord and do not contain more than four flat units, the residence of a person having an interest under the trust ranking as that of the landlord where the actual landlord is a body of trustees[9].

Commonhold ownership[10]

The CLRA provides for the ownership of the freehold of interdependent properties, 'units', and the corporate ownership and management of the associated common parts by the unit owners as a commonhold association. Each unit-holder owns the freehold in his own unit, while the commonhold association owns the freehold in the common parts. A commonhold community statement governs the use and maintenance of the units and common parts. Where there are joint unit-holders, only one (nominated by one of themselves) can be registered as a member of the commonhold association, but in default, the person whose name first appears on the proprietorship register will be the registered owner[11].

ARTICLE 42

The effect of the Limitation Act 1980 on the trustee's estate

(1) A trustee of land is divested of the legal estate by the exclusive possession of a beneficiary solely and absolutely entitled to the land or the proceeds of sale thereof for the statutory period. But where land is in the possession of a beneficiary not solely and absolutely entitled to the land or the proceeds thereof, time does not run either against the trustee or against any other person having a beneficial interest in the land or the proceeds of sale thereof[12].

(2) a trustee, like a beneficial owner, may be barred by the adverse possession of a stranger; and if he be so barred, his beneficiaries will

6 Section 93A, CLRA, Sch 8, para 33.
7 See footnote 4 above.
8 CLRA, s 109.
9 CLRA, Sch 6 para 3(7).
10 On this topic see eg T Aldridge, *Commonhold* or D Clarke, *Commonhold*.
11 CLRA, Sch 3 para 8.
12 Limitation Act 1980, Sch 1, para 9.

be barred also. But the legal estate of trustees will not be extinguished until every right of action of the persons beneficially interested (who for this purpose are deemed to be entitled to the same right of action to recover the land as if their estates were legal and not equitable) is barred.

(3) An action to recover land held on trust may be brought by the trustees on behalf of any person entitled to a beneficial interest in possession in the land or proceeds of sale whose right is not barred notwithstanding that the trustees' right of action would otherwise be barred.

(4) Once sections 96 and 97 of the Land Registration Act 2002 are brought into force the registered title to land cannot be lost by adverse possession alone, while a person is not to be regarded as being in adverse possession of registered land subject to a trust unless the interest of each of the beneficiaries is an interest in possession.

PARAGRAPH 1

Exclusive possession of a beneficiary

Paragraph 9 of Sch 1 to the Limitation Act 1980 (replacing s 7(5) of the 1939 Act) expressly provides that a beneficiary[13] cannot adversely possess and so cannot acquire statutory title against his fellow beneficiaries or the trustees. However, the paragraph only applies to a trust of land (including land held on trust for sale) and to settled land, and it is apprehended that any trustee, including a constructive trustee (as, for example, a vendor under an uncompleted contract), is liable to be divested of the legal estate by possession of a person entitled in equity in exactly the same way as if the latter were a stranger[14]. But where a purchaser acknowledges that he is in possession under an uncompleted contract time will not run against the unpaid vendor since the purchaser's possession is not adverse[15].

PARAGRAPH 2

Adverse possession of a stranger

This paragraph is believed to state the effect of s 18 of the Limitation Act 1980. It had long ago been held by the courts that:

> 'the rule that the Statute of Limitations does not bar a trust estate, holds only as between cestui que trust and trustee, and between the cestuis que trust inter se, and not between cestui que trust and trustee on the one side and strangers on the other

---

13 Not being a person solely or absolutely entitled. Thus, time runs against a bare trustee, which includes a fully paid vendor still holding the legal title: *Bridges v Mees* [1957] Ch 475, [1957] 2 All ER 577.

14 This statement was expressly approved in *Bridges v Mees* [1957] Ch 475, [1957] 2 All ER 577, by Harman J, in dealing with s 7(5).

15 *Hyde v Pearce* [1982] 1 All ER 1029, [1982] 1 WLR 560, CA. It may be the purchaser is a licensee. *Bridges v Mees* (supra) was not cited.

... and therefore, where a cestui que trust and his trustee are both out of possession for the time limited, the party in possession has a good bar against them both.'[16]

The 1980 Act makes it clear that, though the trustee's right of action may be barred, his estate is not to be divested until the right of action of every beneficiary has been barred, and that even after his right of action would otherwise be barred he may sue to recover the land on behalf of a person beneficially interested in possession. Time begins to run against a beneficiary when his right of action first accrues: in the case of a future interest, the right of action first accrues when the interest falls into possession[17]. If land is held on trust for sale for A for life remainder to B, 12 years' adverse possession of the land by S will bar A's equitable interest but time will not begin to run against B until A's death. After expiry of the twelve years the trustees will hold the legal estate on trust for B as from A's death. On A's death B if of full age and sound mind or the trustees will be able to recover the land.

When ss 96 and 97 of the Land Registration Act 2002 are brought into force for registered land, there will be a new regime for the registration of an adverse possessor of an estate in land who may apply to the registrar to be registered as proprietor if he has been in adverse possession for a period of ten years ending on the date of the application[18]. The registrar will send notices of this to the registered proprietor and mortgagees; an objection from one of them will prevent registration of the adverse possessor unless this would be unconscionable (eg on proprietary estoppel principles) or he occupied the land under a reasonable mistake about the boundary or he has some other entitlement to be registered, eg as unpaid vendor or devisee under a will[19]. The registered proprietor has two years from the date of objection to take possession proceedings; otherwise the adverse possessor can apply a second time and be registered as proprietor pursuant to that application[20]. It will, however, no longer be possible for there to be any adverse possession[1] of land subject to a trust unless the interest of each of the beneficiaries is an interest in possession[2]. Thus, it becomes impossible to use adverse possession to resolve boundary disputes if the land is held in trust for successive interests.

ARTICLE 43

The effect of the trustee's bankruptcy or liquidation

(1) The property of a bankrupt divisible among his creditors does not

---

16 Per Lord Hardwicke in *Lewellin v Mackworth* (1740) 2 Eq Cas Abr 579; and to same effect per Lord Redesdale in *Hovenden v Lord Annesley* (1806) 2 Sch & Lef 607; and per Lord Manners in *Pentland v Stokes* (1812) 2 Ball & B 68 at 75. As to whether a purchaser of the equitable interest of a beneficiary gets the legal estate by 12 years' possession, see *Re Cussons Ltd* (1904) 73 LJ Ch 296, and *Bolling v Hobday* (1882) 31 WR 9.

17 Limitation Act 1980, s 15. As an alternative to the 12-year period there is a period of six years from the falling into possession of a remainderman's interest: s 15(2). On 'adverse possession' see definitive *Pye (Oxford) Ltd v Graham* [2002] UKHL 30 [2002] 3 WLR 221 on need for 'factual possession' and 'need to possess'.

18 Land Registration Act 2002, Sch 6, para 1.

19 Land Registration Act 2002, Sch 6, paras 2, 3 and 5.

20 Land Registration Act 2002, Sch 6, paras 6 and 7.

 1 Land Registration Act 2002, Sch 6, para 11.

 2 Land Registration Act 2002, Sch 6, para 12.

comprise property held by him as trustee for any other person[3], notwithstanding that it is property in his order and disposition at the commencement of the bankruptcy[4]; property held on trust by a company at the commencement of winding-up is similarly not divisible among the company's creditors[5];

(2) if the trustee has converted trust property into money or other property which would be subject to the trust in the hands of the trustee, it will remain so subject notwithstanding the trustee's bankruptcy or liquidation[6].

PARAGRAPH 1

If some person other than the trustee has a beneficial interest in property held by the trustee, the property will not vest in the trustee in bankruptcy. This was so held in relation to a solicitor's client account by Roxburgh J who said:

> 'It is to be noted that the only property which vests in the trustee [in bankruptcy] is property divisible amongst his [the bankrupt's] creditors, because section 38 [of the Bankruptcy Act 1914] points out what is meant in this Act by "the property of the bankrupt"; accordingly this client account is not vested, and will not vest, in the trustee if it is property held by the bankrupt on trust for any other person. The words "on trust for any other person," in my judgment, are of very wide import ... If it can be said of any asset that though the title is in the bankrupt, a beneficial interest therein resides in some person other than the bankrupt, even though the bankrupt himself may also have a beneficial interest therein, the asset does not vest in the trustee [in bankruptcy], though the beneficial interest, if any, which the bankrupt himself has would vest in the trustee.[7]'

In the case of a corporate trustee in liquidation the trust property does not automatically vest in the liquidator, but remains vested in the company until disposed of the course of winding-up or the company is dissolved.

An insolvent trustee, unless the trust instrument otherwise provides, remains a trustee until retirement or replacement (or dissolution if a corporation). A bankrupt trustee will often be 'unfit to act' within s 36 of the Trustee Act 1925 but this need not be the case[8]: if doubts exist and the

---

3 Insolvency Act 1986, s 283(3). If a trustee holding money in one capacity on trust for B is authorised to invest the money in a deposit account run by the trustee in another capacity then the invested money no longer represents property held on trust for B who will only be an unsecured creditor: *Space Investments Ltd v Canadian Imperial Bank Commerce Trust Co (Bahamas) Ltd* [1986] 3 All ER 75, [1986] 1 WLR 1072, PC.

4 *Re Fox, ex p Barry* (1873) LR 17 Eq 113; *Ex p Marsh* (1744) 1 Atk 158. As to constructive trustees, see *Re Boldero, ex p Pease* (1812) 19 Ves 25 at 46, and *Whitfield v Brand* (1847) 16 M & W 282.

5 For example, *Barclays Bank Ltd v Quistclose Investments Ltd* [1970] AC 567, HL; *Re Kayford Ltd* [1975] 1 WLR 279.

6 *Frith v Cartland* (1865) 2 Hem & M 417; *Re Hallett's Estate* (1880) 13 Ch D 696 at 719.

7 *Re A Solicitor* [1951] M 234, [1952] Ch 328, [1952] 1 All ER 133. Distinguish *St Thomas's Hospital (Governors) v Richardson* [1910] 1 KB 271, CA, where the legal estate in property held on an onerous lease by a husband, who had contracted to sell it to his wife for a price which she had paid, was held to have vested in the husband's trustee in bankruptcy, apparently on the ground that the husband's right of indemnity against the rent and covenants would have entitled him in the particular circumstances of that case to retain all the rents as an indemnity fund; see per Farwell LJ at 283–284.

8 For example, *Re Barker's Trusts* (1875) 1 Ch D 43; *Re Betts* (1897) 41 Sol Jo 209.

trustee is happy to retire then it is best to replace him on the grounds of retirement. A liquidator[9] of a corporate trustee in liquidation or the administrator[10] of a corporate trustee in administration has power to conduct a trusteeship vested in the company, and the power of the company to appoint new trustees is exercisable by the liquidator or administrator[11]. The costs and expenses of winding-up (including the liquidator's remuneration) are payable out of the company's own assets and not out of assets held on trust[12], though the latter assets are available for fees and expenses incurred in continuing to manage the trust as opposed to winding-up the corporate trustee. In a special case[13] where the company's liabilities have all been incurred in discharging the duties imposed by a trust then the costs of winding-up may be regarded as incurred in discharging such duties, eg if the company had been specially formed to administer a particular trust.

PARAGRAPH 2

The doctrine of tracing trust property into other property into which it has been converted is fully dealt with in Articles 92 and 101, post.

9 *Re Cyest Realty* [1977] 1 NSWLR 664; *Re Berkeley Applegate (Investment Consultants) Ltd* [1989] Ch 32; *Re William Makin & Sons Ltd* [1993] BCC 453.
10 *Polly Peck International plc v Henry* [1999] 1 BCLC 407.
11 *Denny v Yeldon* [1995] 3 All ER 624. For pension trusts there is a need for an independent trustee: Pensions Act 1995, ss 22–25.
12 *Re Berkeley Applegate (Investment Consultants) Ltd* [1989] Ch 32 at 40–41; *Re Byrne Australia Pty Ltd (No 2)* [1981] 2 NSWLR 364; *Re Matheson* (1994) 121 ALR 605 at 615.
13 See *Re Saco Gold Pty Ltd* (1983) 33 SASR 99.

CHAPTER 10

Trusts of land

Article
44 Pre-1997 'old' Settled Land Act Settlements   463
45 Post-1996 Trusts of Land   465

ARTICLE 44

Pre-1997 'old' Settled Land Act Settlements

(1) Before 1997 if a legal estate in land was not vested in trustees for sale[1] (with the proceeds of sale and the rents and profits till sale being held on trust for beneficiaries) but land was intended to be enjoyed by persons in succession or by a minor when adult or to be subject to family (as opposed to commercial) charges, then a settlement arose under the Settled Land Act 1925 ('SLA 1925')[2], the trust instrument being required to be supported by a second document, a 'vesting' deed or assent vesting the legal estate[3] in the tenant for life[4] (or, exceptionally, the statutory owner[5]), who had unfettered[6] statutory powers of disposition[7], although capital money had to be paid[8] to two Settled Land Act trustees (or a trust corporation acting as SLA trustee), but the investment or other application of the money had to be made according to the direction of the tenant for life (or statutory owner)[9].

(2)(i) After 1996, old SLA settlements continue but no new SLA settlements can be created[10], except under powers contained in an old

---

1 Settled Land Act 1925 ('SLA 1925'), s 1(7), so there were two mutually exclusive methods for settling land.
2 SLA 1925, s 1(1).
3 SLA 1925, ss 4–10.
4 SLA 1925, ss 19–21.
5 SLA 1925, ss 23, 24 and 117(1)(xxvi), as where the tenant for life was a minor.
6 SLA 1925, ss 104, 106 and 108.
7 For example, sale: SLA 1925, ss 38, 39; limited leasing powers: SLA 1925, ss 41–48.
8 SLA 1925, s 18(1)(c).
9 SLA 1925, s 75(2).
10 Trusts of Land and Appointment of Trustees Act 1996 ('TLATA 1996'), s 2(1).

SLA settlement[11] if no express election be made that the exercise of such powers is not to create a SLA settlement[12], although, in any event, no new entailed interests can be created after 1996[13]. Since 1 February 2001 section 75(2) of the Settled Land Act 1925 has been amended so that the investment or other application of capital money is to be made according to the discretion of the SLA trustees[14], and investments (but not land occupied by the tenant for life) must be in the names or under the control of the trustees[15]; however, the trustees are subject to any consent required by the settlement[16] and must, so far as practicable, consult the tenant for life and, so far as consistent with the general interest of the settlement, give effect to his wishes[17].

(ii) An old SLA settlement will cease to be such if there is a deed of discharge executed by the trustees[18] or if a conveyance or assent of the land does not state who are the SLA trustees[19] or, after 1996, if there is no relevant land or heirlooms subject to the settlement[20] (eg where the whole of the settled land and heirlooms, if any, have been sold).

(3) Charitable, ecclesiastical and public trusts of land, whether deemed before 1997 to be SLA settlements[1] or created after 1996, now rank as trusts of land[2], although exempted from some of the trusts of land regime[3] and subject to sections 37 to 39 of the Charities Act 1993.

(4) From 1 January 1997 a new 'trust of land'[4] regime has been introduced by the Trusts of Land and Appointment of Trustees Act 1996 ('TLATA 1996') whereby land is vested in trustees, whether for charitable ecclesiastical or public purposes or for a person or persons absolutely or successively, and whether under a trust for sale[5] or a complex trust or a bare trust[6] (as will be dealt with in Article 45 following this Article). This trust of land regime applies to any trust of property which consists of or includes land, whenever it was created[7], so long as it was not a pre-1997 old Settled Land Act 1925 settlement.

Old Settled Land Act 1925 settlements are of a 'special and complicated statutory character'[8] that all previous editions omitted to deal with in detail, since this real property and conveyancing topic 'would unreasonably

---

11 TLATA 1996, s 2(2).
12 TLATA 1996, s 2(3).
13 TLATA 1996, Sch 1, para 5.
14 Trustee Act 2000, Sch 1, para 10(1)(a).
15 Trustee Act 2000, Sch 1, para 10(1)(b).
16 Trustee Act 2000, Sch 1, para 10(1)(a).
17 Trustee Act 2000, Sch 1, para 10(2).
18 SLA 1925, s 17.
19 SLA 1925, s 110(5).
20 TLATA 1996, s 2(4).
 1 SLA 1925, s 29.
 2 TLATA 1996, s 2(5).
 3 For example, TLATA 1996, ss 8(3), 11 and 16(6).
 4 TLATA 1996, s 1.
 5 Land held on trust for sale is no longer personalty due to no conversion now taking place: TLATA 1996, s 3 and p 372 ante.
 6 TLATA 1996, s 1(2)(a).
 7 TLATA 1996, s 1(2)(b).
 8 See 15th edition hereof at p 451.

encumber this work if treated in any detail"[9], while there will be increasingly fewer of these relatively rare[10] settlements.

Reference should therefore be made to Megarry & Wade, *Law of Real Property* (6th edn); *Emmett on Title* (looseleaf); Ruoff & Roper, *Law and Practice of Registered Conveyancing* (looseleaf) and *Lewin on Trusts* (17th edn).

Most practitioners were happy to see the demise of the complexities of the Settled Land Act settlement where the tenant for life owned the freehold or leasehold land and was 'king of the castle'[11], though capital moneys had to be paid to the SLA trustees. Under the trusts of land regime the trustees (being two or a trust corporation) have in relation to the land all the powers of an absolute owner[12]. If, for example, a spouse on divorce obtains a life interest in the former matrimonial home and wants to have absolute control over sale and purchase of her home, then it may well be that Equity would enforce a right of direction conferred upon her against the trustees[13], just as in a trust of personalty a settlor may confer upon himself or a designated protector the right to direct the trustees in respect of certain prescribed functions of the trustees. In any event, it is absolutely clear that the spouse's consent to any disposition of the trustees can be a binding precondition[14], while the trustees can be required to consult her on exercise of their powers and the use of the capital money on a sale and to give effect to her wishes[15], especially where the terms of the trust make clear the purpose of providing accommodation for her wherever she desires in her lifetime. Indeed, in such circumstances it would seem that the trust instrument could expressly require the trustees to exercise their power to delegate by power of attorney[16] their power of sale to the spouse, though proceeds of sale would still need to be paid to the trustees[17], whose function in respect of the proceeds is not capable of delegation under TLATA 1996[18].

ARTICLE 45

Post-1996 Trusts of Land

(1) A trust of land is any trust[19] of property which consists of or includes land other than land which is land[20] to which the Universities and College Estates Act 1925 or the Settled Land Act 1925 applies as

---

9 See 15th edition hereof at p 451.

10 See *Transfer of Land: Trusts of Land* (Law Com No 181, June 1989), para 4.3 note 72 on result of consultation with practitioners.

11 See SLA 1925, ss 104, 106 and 108, while the courts were remarkably liberal in the leeway afforded to the tenant for life, despite his fiduciary position under s 107, eg *Re Thornhills Settlement* [1941] Ch 24; *England v Public Trustee* (1967) 112 Sol Jo 70; *Re Boston's Will Trusts* [1956] Ch 395 at 405.

12 TLATA 1996, s 6(1).

13 TLATA 1996, s 6(6).

14 TLATA 1996, ss 6(8), 8(2), 10(1).

15 TLATA 1996, s 11(1).

16 TLATA 1996, s 9(1).

17 TLATA 1996, s 9(7).

18 Section 9(1) only permits delegation of 'functions as trustees which relate to the land'.

19 Whether express, resulting or constructive and including a trust for sale and a bare trust: TLATA 1996, s 1(2)(a).

20 TLATA 1996, s 1(3).

explained in Article 44.

(2) Such a trust may be created in one's lifetime or by will. In the former case it is the practice, though not essential, to use two deeds, one vesting the title to the land in the trustees and the other declaring the detailed trusts, thus keeping the trusts off the title.

(3) Where a trust of land is land subject to an immediate trust for sale there is implied, despite any contrary provision, a power for the trustees to postpone sale of the land[1]; and the trustees are not liable in any way for postponing sale of the land, in the conscious exercise of their discretion, for an indefinite period[2].

(4) The doctrine of conversion no longer applies to regard land held on trust for sale as personal property and to regard as realty personal property directed to be sold in order that realty be acquired[3].

(5) Trustees of land, for the purpose of exercising their functions as trustees, have in relation to the land subject to the trust all the powers of an absolute owner[4], which need to be exercised in accordance with the duty of care under section 1 of the Trustee Act 2000[5].

(6) Trustees of land have power to acquire 'freehold or leasehold land' in the UK as an investment or for occupation by a beneficiary or for any other reason[6], as explained in Article 53(5), and subject to the duty of care in section 1 of the Trustee Act 2000.

(7) Trustees of land have power to partition land subject to the trust and provide (by way of mortgage or otherwise) for the payment of any equality money but only where beneficiaries of full age are absolutely entitled in undivided shares to the land and consent[7].

(8) Trustees of land have power compulsorily to transfer land subject to the trust to the beneficiaries interested in the land where they are each of full age and capacity and between them absolutely entitled to the land[8].

(9) The above powers of trustees of land cannot be exercised in contravention of any enactment or subordinate legislation or any rule of law or equity[9], but they can be restricted or excluded[10] or be made subject to a requirement of consent[11].

(10) Trustees of land may, by power of attorney, delegate to any beneficiary or beneficiaries of full age and beneficially entitled to an interest in possession in land subject to the trust any of their functions as trustees which relate to the land[12] (as opposed to the proceeds of

---

1 TLATA 1996, s 4(1).
2 TLATA 1996, s 4(1). This does not affect any liability incurred before 1997: s 4(3).
3 TLATA 1996, s 3.
4 TLATA 1996, s 6(1).
5 TLATA 1996, s 6(9).
6 TLATA 1996, s 6(3) as substituted by Trustee Act 2000, Sch 2, para 45(1).
7 TLATA 1996, s 7.
8 TLATA 1996, s 6(2).
9 TLATA 1996, s 6(6).
10 TLATA 1996, s 8(1), but not applicable to charitable, ecclesiastical or public trusts.
11 TLATA 1996, s 8(2).
12 TLATA 1996, s 9.

sale and receipts therefor), with the duty of care under section 1 of the Trustee Act 2000 applying to the trustees in deciding whether to delegate, in keeping the delegation under review and in intervening if need be[13], as explained in Article 55(1)(e) and (2).

(11) Where the consent of more than two persons is required under the trust to the exercise by the trustees of any function relating to the land, the consent of any two is sufficient for the protection of a purchaser[14]; and if a person whose consent is required is not of full age a purchaser can ignore the need for such consent, though the trustees should obtain the consent of a parent having parental responsibility for him or of a guardian[15].

(12) In the exercise of any function relating to land subject to the trust, the trustees of land must, so far as practicable, consult the beneficiaries of full age and beneficially entitled to an interest in possession in the land and, so far as consistent with the general interest of the trust, give effect to the wishes of those beneficiaries, or (in case of dispute) of the majority (according to the value of their combined interests)[16]. This obligation applies to all trusts of land created after 1996 except where the disposition provides to the contrary or the trust arises under a will made before 1997[17]. For trusts created before 1997 no duty to consult exists unless provision that it should is made by a deed executed by the settlor or settlors if of full capacity and alive[18].

(13) A beneficiary who is beneficially entitled to an interest in possession in land subject to a trust of land is entitled by reason of his interest to occupy the land at any time if at that time either (a) the purposes of the trust include making the land available for his occupation (or for the occupation of beneficiaries of a class of which he is a member or of beneficiaries in general) or (b) the land is held by the trustees so as to be so available[19]; but a beneficiary has no such right to occupy land if it is either unavailable or unsuitable for occupation by him[20].

(14) Where two or more beneficiaries would be entitled to occupy the land, the trustees may exclude or restrict the entitlement of any one or more (but not all) of them[1], but the trustees must act reasonably[2] and they may impose reasonable conditions[3], having taken account of the settlor's intentions, the purposes for which the land is held and the

---

13 TLATA 1996, s 9A inserted by Trustee Act 2000, Sch 2, para 47.
14 TLATA 1996, s 10(1).
15 TLATA 1996, s 10(3).
16 TLATA 1996, s 11(1).
17 TLATA 1996, s 11(2).
18 TLATA 1996, s 11(3).
19 TLATA 1996, s 12(1).
20 TLATA 1996, s 12(2).
 1 TLATA 1996, s 13(1).
 2 TLATA 1996, s 13(2).
 3 TLATA 1996, s 13(3).

circumstances and wishes of each of the beneficiaries seeking to occupy the land[4].

(15) Any person who is a trustee of land or has an interest in property subject to a trust of land may apply to the court for an order relating to the exercise by the trustees of any of their functions (including an order relieving them of any obligation to obtain the consent of, or to consult, any person concerning exercise of any of their functions) or an order declaring the nature or extent of a person's interest in the trust property[5], but this provision does not enable the court to make any order as to the appointment or removal of trustees[6]. The court must have regard to[7] (a) the intentions of the settlor, (b) the purposes for which the property subject to the trust is held, (c) the welfare of any minor who occupies, or might reasonably be expected to occupy, any trust land as his home (d) the interests of any secured creditor of the beneficiary and[8] (e) the circumstances and wishes of any beneficiaries of full age entitled to an interest in possession in trust property or (in case of dispute) of the majority according to the value of their combined interest, unless the application is made by a trustee of a bankrupt's estate. Then, the court makes such order as it thinks just and reasonable having regard to[9] (a) the interests of the bankrupt's creditors and (b) where the application relates to the home of the bankrupt or his spouse or former spouse, to (i) the conduct of the spouse or former house, so far as contributing to the bankruptcy, (ii) the needs and financial resources of the spouse or former spouse and (iii) the needs of any children, and (c) all the circumstances of the case other than the needs of the bankrupt. Where the application is made one year after the first vesting of the bankrupt's estate in a trustee, the court must assume, unless the circumstances of the case are exceptional, that the interests of the bankrupt's creditors outweigh all other considerations[10].

(16) Purchasers of land from trustees of land are not concerned to see whether or not any duty to consult beneficiaries has been complied with[11], and so long as capital monies are paid to two trustees or a trust corporation or a sole personal representative acting as such, interests under the trust of land will be overreached[12] unless, in the case of unregistered land, the purchaser or his agent had actual notice that the trustees were exceeding their powers (by ignoring any exclusion or

---

4 TLATA 1996, s 13(4).
5 TLATA 1996, s 14(1) and (2).
6 TLATA 1996, s 14(3).
7 TLATA 1996, s 15(1).
8 TLATA 1996, s 15(4).
9 TLATA 1996, s 15(4); Insolvency Act 1986, s 335A.
10 Insolvency Act 1986, s 335A(3).
11 TLATA 1996, s 16(1).
12 Law of Property Act 1925, ss 2 and 27 as amended by TLATA 1996, Sch 3, para 4.

restriction placed upon them)[13] or, in the case of registered land, there was an entry in the register limiting the trustees' powers[14].

Trusts of Land

Settled Land Act settlements created before 1997 continue, and powers exercised thereunder may create Settled Land Act settlements if no election is made that such are not to be Settled Land Act settlements. Otherwise, if land is not subject to the Universities and College Estates Act 1925 it will be a 'trust of land' covered by the Trusts of Land and Appointment of Trustees Act 1996 ('TLATA 1996'). Personal property, however, may well be within a 'trust of land', such being defined to cover 'any trust of property which consists of or includes land'[15], while the reference to 'trust' is to any description of trust (whether express, implied, resulting or constructive) including a trust for sale and a bare trust[16].

Implied trusts of land arise by virtue of statute where a person dies intestate leaving land[17] or where two or more persons are entitled to land as joint tenants or tenants in common but no express trust for them has been created[18]. Prior to 1997 all co-owned land was subject either to express or to statutorily implied trusts[19] for sale with a power to postpone sale (unless ousted expressly or by necessary implication)[20]. Thus, there was a duty to sell unless the trustees unanimously exercised their power to postpone sale so, in the absence of unanimity, the courts would enforce the letter of the trust for sale unless so to do would defeat the spirit or purpose of the trust[1].

After 1996 a settlor can still deliberately create an express trust for sale, although he can no longer oust the trustees' power to postpone sale[2].

Desirability of two deeds for lifetime trusts of land

A major object of the 1925 Property Legislation was to simplify conveyancing and facilitate sales by keeping trusts off the title or behind a curtain past which a purchaser could not peep. The Settled Land Act system required the use of two deeds, a simple one for purchasers to see who the legal title-owner was and a complex one detailing the trusts; and conveyancing practice for land held on trusts for sale made it desirable, but not compulsory, to use two deeds, only the conveyance to the trustees on unspecified trusts for sale

---

13 TLATA 1996, s 16(2) and (3).
14 Land Registration Act 2002, s 26, resolving the problem identified by Ferris & Battersby in [1998] Conv 168.
15 TLATA 1996, s 1(1)(a).
16 TLATA 1996, s 1(2)(a).
17 Administration of Estates Act 1925, s 33 as amended by TLATA 1996, Sch 2, para 5.
18 Law of Property Act 1925, ss 34 and 36 as amended by TLATA 1996, Sch 2, paras 3 and 4.
19 See Administration of Estates Act 1925, s 33 and Law of Property Act 1925, ss 34 and 36 before amendment by TLATA.
20 Law of Property Act 1925, s 25(1).
 1 *James v Challenger* [1961] 1 QB 176; *Re Buchanan-Wollaston's Conveyance* [1939] Ch 738.
 2 TLALTA 1996, s 4(1).

needing to be abstracted and produced on the sale taking place.

This desirable practice has continued and is recognised in s 35 of the Trustee Act 1925, as amended by TLATA 1996: 'Appointments of new trustees of land and of new trustees of any trust of the proceeds of sale shall, subject to any order of the court, be effected by separate instruments, but in such manner that the same persons become trustees of land and trustees of the proceeds of sale'. Thus, as also recognised in s 24 of the Law of Property Act 1925, the same persons will be appointed in one deed to be trustees of the conveyance of the legal title and in another deed to be trustees of the detailed trust of land and any proceeds thereof.

Where there is a testamentary trust so that the legal estate is vested in the personal representatives they should, on completing the administration of the estate, assent to the legal estate simply vesting in themselves as trustees[3], if the two offices are united, or in other persons as trustees, thereby keeping the testamentary trusts off the title[4].

If a purchaser or his agent sees the trust instrument and it contains exclusions or restrictions upon the trustees' powers, then a purchaser will not take a good title if he ignores those limits on the trustees' powers[5].

PARAGRAPH 3

Trusts for sale of land

Where a disposition expressly creates a trust for sale of land then, if it does not expressly create a power to postpone sale there must be implied a power for the trustees to postpone sale of the land[6] – and this implied power cannot be ousted by any provision to the contrary in the disposition, whether before or after TLATA came into force[7]. Disposition[8] should be regarded as broad enough to cover trusts for sale whether created by a transfer to trustees or by the settlor declaring himself trustee of his own designated property and whether created in writing or orally but subsequently evidenced in writing: there is no reason at all to treat any of those trusts differently from any other of them.

Trust for sale means an immediate trust for sale, whether or not exercisable at the request or with the consent of any person[9]. Until a trust for sale becomes an immediate one there is no need for any power to postpone sale, but such power will arise as soon as the trust becomes immediate eg upon the happening of some specified future event.

Curiously, the Act provides[10] that 'the trustees are not liable in any way for

---

3 *Re King's Will Trusts* [1964] Ch 542; Administration of Estates Act 1925, s 36(4).
4 The assent should be registered with the Land Registry within two months: Land Registration Act 2002, s 4 replacing Land Registration Act 1997, s 1.
5 If title is registered then a purchaser is protected if no entry of any exclusions or restrictions appears on the register: Land Registration Act 2002, s 26 resolving the difficulty identified by Ferris & Battersby in [1998] Conv 168.
6 TLATA 1996, s 4(1).
7 TLATA 1996, s 4(2) but by s 4(3) his does not affect any liability incurred by trustees before 1997.
8 TLATA 1996, s 23(2); Law of Property Act 1925, s 205(1)(ii).
9 Law of Property Act 1925, s 205(1)(xxi) as amended by TLATA 1996, Sch 4 and incorporated by TLATA 1996, s 23(2).
10 TLATA 1996, s 4(1).

postponing sale of the land, in the exercise of their discretion, for an indefinite period,' so is there an implication that they can be liable if they improperly postpone for a lengthy definite period? After all trustees are not allowed to fetter their own discretions[11] eg by deciding not to exercise their power of sale till expiry of five years, although it seems equally improper to decide not to exercise their power of sale for an indefinite period which could extend to five years if they do no return to consider the issue for five years.

On a purposive interpretation it seems the intention should be to exempt trustees from liability if, from time to time as they review matters[12], they consciously exercise their discretion to postpone sale of the land, so that sale is postponed indefinitely until the time comes when they ultimately decide to sell. 'The exercise of their discretion' clearly requires a conscious exercise thereof[13], but it cannot be implicitly restricted to 'the proper exercise of their discretion' since they could not then be liable anyhow. Perhaps one can implicitly restrict the clause to 'the bona fide exercise of their discretion' so that, for example, if within 12 months of B's death the house has not been sold by private treaty or by auction as directed by the settlor within that period, the trustees can be made liable if postponing the sale is not bona fide. In any event, if one trustee refuses to postpone, the power to postpone cannot be validly exercised since this requires unanimity, while applications can be made to the court for an order for sale under s 14, taking account of the settlor's directions.

PARAGRAPH 4

No conversion under trusts for sale of land or of personalty

Except where a trust was created by the will of a testator who died before 1997[14], a trust for sale of land does not amount under the equitable doctrine of conversion to an interest in personalty (the notional proceeds of sale), nor does a trust to sell personalty in order to acquire realty amount to an interest in realty (the notionally acquired realty)[15].

PARAGRAPHS 5, 6 AND 9

Trustees of land have all the powers of a absolute owner

For the purposes of exercising their functions as trustees, the trustees of land have in relation to the land subject to the trust all the powers of an absolute owner[16]. They also have power to acquire UK land under s 8 of the Trustee Act 2000 as an investment or for occupation by a beneficiary or for any other reason[17] and have all the powers of an absolute owner in relation to this

---

11 See p 690 post.
12 Breach of their duty to review whether to exercise their powers to sell or retain trust assets can give rise to liability
13 For example, *Rowlls v Bebb* [1900] 2 Ch 107; *Re Guinness's Settlement* [1966] 2 All ER 497.
14 TLATA 1996, s 3(2).
15 TLATA 1996, s 3(1) and (3).
16 TLATA 1996, s 6(1).
17 TLATA 1996, s 6(3) as amended by Trustee Act 2000, Sch 2, para 45(1).

land[18]. All those powers must not be exercised in contravention of any legislation or any rule of law or equity or any order of the court or of the Charity Commissioners[19]. Moreover, they can be excluded or restricted by the terms of the disposition creating the trust of land[20].

Thus, trustees cannot make gifts of trust land to persons who are not beneficiaries or objects of powers of appointment in the trust instrument, while if investing in land they must comply with the duty to take advice, taking account of the standard investment criteria[1]. In exercising any function relating to land they must consult the beneficiaries so far as practicable and give effect to their wishes so far as consistent with the general interest of the trust[2], unless the trust instrument precludes this or the trust is a pre-1997 trust[3].

The trust instrument can also exclude or restrict the trustees' powers eg by requiring consents of a specific person or persons before any particular function is exercised[4] or by requiring particular trust land to be inalienable for the duration of the trust or some lesser period or, it would seem, by stipulating that the trustees must sell the trust land or any part thereof when directed by the life tenant and not before then and must use the proceeds as directed by the life tenant in the acquisition of land or other property[5]. In an extreme situation where such exclusion or restriction was particularly disadvantageous and more prejudicial than probably contemplated by the settlor, it seems that the court could either override any restrictions[6] or confer a requisite power[7].

When exercising their powers the trustees are subject to the duty of care[8].

PARAGRAPHS 7 AND 9

Partition by trustees

Where beneficiaries of full age[9] are absolutely entitled in undivided shares to land subject to the trust, the trustees may partition the land, or any part of it, and provide for the payment of any equality money by way of mortgage or otherwise[10], but only if each of the beneficiaries consents[11]. In case of disagreements application may be made to the cout which may make such order

---

18 Trustee Act 2000, s 8 (3). Further see pp 607–609 post.

19 TLATA 1996, s 6(6).

20 TLATA 1996, s 8(1) but inapplicable to charitable, ecclesiastical or public trusts.

 1 Trustee Act 2000, ss 4 and 5.

 2 TLATA 1996, s 11(1).

 3 TLATA 1996, s 11(2). Law of Property Act 1925, s 26(3) requiring statutory trustees for sale to consult beneficiaries was repealed by TLATA.

 4 See TLATA 1996, s 10.

 5 See TLATA 1996, s 6(6) preserving rules of equity coupled with s 8(1) and the possibility of the settlor or his designated protector expressly having the right to direct the trustees in respect of particular prescribed functions.

 6 TLATA 1996, s 14(1); *Re Beale's Settlement Trusts* [1932] 2 Ch 15.

 7 Trustee Act 1925, s 57; cf *Re Cockerell's Settlement Trusts* [1956] Ch 372.

 8 TLATA 1996, s 6(9) inserted by Trustee Act 2000, Sch 2, para 45(3).

 9 If a beneficiary is a minor, however, the trustees can act on his behalf to carry out a partition as if he had been a consenting adult: TLATA 1996, s 7(5).

10 TLATA 1996, s 7(1), but an interest in part only of a commonhold unit cannot be created: Commonhold and Leasehold Reform Act 2002, Sch 5, para 8.

11 TLATA 1996, s 7(3).

as it thinks fit[12], eg an order for sale or to partition the land. On partition accounts may need to be taken as if there had been a sale eg taking account of who paid for improvements[13].

Effect is given to the partition by conveying relevant parts of the land to the person entitled thereto, whether absolutely or as a trustee[14]. Where a share is vested in a beneficiary who is a minor the trustees can act in his behalf and retain land or other property representing his share upon trust for him[15].

PARAGRAPHS 8 AND 9

Compulsory transfer to absolutely entitled beneficiaries

Without the need to consult the beneficiaries[16], let alone obtain their consent, the trustees (unless precluded by the terms of the trust instrument[17]) can off-load their trusteeship of the land (under s 6(2) of TLATA 1996) where 'each of the beneficiaries interested in the land is a person of full age and capacity who is absolutely entitled to the land'. Thus, where land is held on trust for A for life, remainder to B, C and D (whether equally or jointly), it is not until A dies that the trustees can convey the land to B, C and D on trust for themselves as joint tenants or as tenants in common in equal shares, as appropriate. The beneficiaries must do whatever is necessary to secure that the land vests in them (eg execute the conveyance, entering into covenants therein) and, if they fail to do so, the court may make an order requiring them to do so[18].

It is noteworthy, however, that under s 19 of TLATA 1996 where 'the beneficiaries under the trust are of full age and capacity and (taken together) are absolutely entitled to the property subject to the trust' they can compel the trustees to retire in favour of new trustees specified by the beneficiaries (if the power of appointing new trustees is not vested in a person, like the settlor, designated in the trust instrument). Thus, the beneficiaries can proactively intervene to prevent themselves becoming the new trustees, while once they are trustees they will normally have the statutory[19] power to appoint new trustees in their place.

It will be noted that there is a subtle difference in wording between s 19 covering beneficiaries with *Saunders v Vautier* rights to terminate a trust[20] and s 6(2) which is not intended to apply where one of the beneficiaries has a limited interest as opposed to an absolute interest, but is intended to apply where all beneficiaries are of full age and capacity and each have absolute interests in the land, and so as between themselves to be absolutely entitled to the land whether such absolute interests are beneficially owned or held on trust[1] for others. Unfortunately, s 6(2) is not drafted as unambiguously as

---

12 TLATA 1996, s 14; *Rodway v Landy* [2001] EWCA Civ 471, [2001] Ch 703, CA.
13 For example, *Re Pavlou* [1993] 3 All ER 955, [1993] 1 WLR 1046.
14 TLATA 1996, s 7(2).
15 TLATA 1996, s 7(5).
16 TLATA 1996, s 11(2)(c).
17 TLATA 1996, s 8(1).
18 TLATA 1996, s 6(2).
19 Trustee Act 1925, s 36.
20 See Article 69, post.
1 TLATA 1996, s 22(1).

ought to be the case but, looking at the parliamentary debates[2] the Lord Chancellor made it clear[3] that the section is concerned only with concurrent interests as joint tenants or tenants in common.

While the plural can include the singular under the Interpretation Act, it seems in context that the statutory power is confined to the situation where there are two or more beneficiaries under a continuing trust of land[4]. Where trustees convey to a sole beneficiary absolutely entitled to the land that trust terminates and it does not seem that any statutory authority is needed for the trustees to execute such a conveyance.

PARAGRAPH 10

Delegation to interest in possession beneficiaries

This topic is fully dealt with in Article 55 1(e) and 2, below.

PARAGRAPH 11

Requisite consents for trustees or purchasers

Trustees commit a breach of trust if the terms of the disposition creating the trust of land require the consent of a person to the exercise of a particular function relating to the land but the trustees proceed to exercise such function without such requisite consent. Because this can make it difficult to market the land s 10(1) of TLATA 1996 protects purchasers in whose favour trustees of land exercise their functions by providing that it is sufficient if the consent of any two requisite persons is obtained[5] (except in the case of charitable, ecclesiastical or public trusts[6]). Moreover, if the person whose consent is requisite is a minor, his consent is not, in favour of a purchaser, required to the exercise of the trustees' function[7]. However, the trustees will be liable for a breach of trust unless obtaining the consent of the minor's parent who has parental responsiblity for him (within the meaning of the Children Act 1989) or of a guardian of his[8].

Where the person whose consent is requisite has no power to consent due to a mental disorder then, unless the consent of two others is requisite and they give their consent, a purchaser will need to check that a receiver of the mental patient's property under s 99 of the Mental Health Act 1983 has given a duly authorised consent or that consent has been given by an attorney under an enduring power of attorney.

If problems arise over a requisite consent not being forthcoming, then application can be made to the court by a trustee of land or any person with

---

2 Under *Pepper v Hart* [1993] AC 593, HL.
3 HL Official Report (5th Series) col 957, April 22, 1996.
4 See Megarry & Wade *Law of Real Property* (6th edn) by C Harpum, (Law Commissioner responsible for TLATA) para 8-138.
5 However, it seems that a non-consenting requisite person could seek an injunction to restrain a disposition proceeding in breach of trust.
6 TLATA 1996, s 10(2): see also Sch 1 para 4.
7 TLATA 1996, s 10(3)(a). 'Purchaser' means a person who acquires an interest in, or charge on, property for money or money's worth: s 23(1).
8 TLATA 1996, s 10(3)(b). Presumably a parental consent, like that of a receiver or attorney for a mental patient, could count towards the two requisite consents under s 10(1).

an interest in property subject to a trust of land for an order relating to the exercise by the trustees of any of their functions, including an order relieving them of their obligation to obtain the consent of a particular person in connection with the exercise of any of their functions[9]. Often, however, the settlor will have intended the beneficiary (eg if a life tenant occupying the house) to be entitled to veto a sale pursuant to selfish personal interests, so that no court order will be made unless such beneficiary is unreasonably acting to the prejudice of all beneficiaries including himself and so exercising his power to withhold consent beyond the parameters contemplated by the settlor[10].

Paragraph 12

Due consultation with interest in possession beneficiaries

Except when compulsorily transferring land to the beneficiaries absolutely entitled thereto[11], trustees of land in the exercise of any function relating to the land[12] subject to the trust must, so far as is practicable, consult the beneficiaries of full age and 'beneficially entitled to an interest in possession in the land'[13] and, so far is consistent with the general interest of the trust, give effect to the wishes of those beneficiaries or of the majority according to the value of their combined interests[14]. This duty applies to all post-1996 trusts of land except those existing under a pre-1997 will, unless the terms of the disposition on trusts of land provide to the contrary, as is customary practice[15]. For pre-1997 trusts (and property added thereto) no duty to consult exists unless provision for such duty is made by a deed executed by the settlor or settlors if still alive and of full capacity[16], when such deed is irrevocable[17]. The duty is to listen to the views of those adult beneficiaries with interests in possession whom it has proved practicable to contact, but the views of the majority according to the value of their beneficial interests in possession can be rejected if the trustees consider them not to be consistent with the general interest of the trust[18], taking account of the interests of beneficiaries who are not consulted because minors or unborn or interested in remainder.

The duty only applies to the exercise of any function relating to trust land,

---

9 *Re Beale's Settlement Trusts* [1932] 2 Ch 15.
10 A fraud on the power.
11 TLATA 1996, s 11(2)(c).
12 But not any personalty comprised within the trust of land.
13 This meaning is examined in Article 55(1)(e) and does not extend to interests under discretionary trusts or the tax-favoured accumulation and maintenance settlements or under pension trusts on which see *Wrightson Ltd v Fletcher Challenge Nominees* [2001] UKPC 23 [2001] OPLR 249 at para 28.
14 TLATA 1996, s 11(1), widening provisions formerly applying to implied statutory trusts for sale by Law of Property Act 1925, s 26(3) which TLATA 1996 repealed. Query whether three equally entitled life tenants' interests should be of the same value or whether the actuarial value of younger life tenants should be taken into account.
15 TLATA 1996, s 11(2).
16 TLATA 1996, s 11(3). The real economic creator of the trust needs to execute the deed, so that if it were the trustee which declared the trust as apparent 'dummy' creator it should not be the trustee which has to execute the necessary deed.
17 TLATA 1996, s 11(4).
18 *Smith v Smith* (1975) 120 Sol Jo 100.

and the Court of Appeal[19] has held that the giving of notice by one joint tenant, A, terminating a joint periodic leasehold tenancy held by A and B on trust for A and B is not any such function: 'it is no more than the exercise by the joint tenant of his or her right to withhold his or her consent to the continuation of the tenancy into a further period'[20].

The court was influenced by the consideration that it would be artificial and pointless to require one of the two cohabitees who had broken up with the other joint tenant to consult with that opposing person, and most unlikely that Parliament would have intended the time, trouble and cost of proceedings under s 14 of TLATA 1996 to be capable of invocation[1].

It may well be that the court's decision can be justified on the basis that the duty to consult only applies to joint functions of trustees qua trustees[2] and not to the case where one of the trustees has a right to act in his or her own interest and to the prejudice of other beneficiaries[3], as is taken to be necessarily authorised by the settlor-trustee-beneficiaries when they set up the situation where they held a periodic residential tenancy on trust for themselves as cohabitees.

PARAGRAPHS 13 AND 14

Right to occupy of beneficiary with interest in possession

By s 12(1) a beneficiary who is beneficially entitled to an interest in possession in land subject to the trust is entitled by reason of his interest to occupy the land at any time if at that time (a) the purposes of the trust include making the land available for his occupation (or for the occupation of beneficiaries of a class including him or of beneficiaries in general) or (b) the land is held by trustees so as to be so available. There can be no right of occupation if the land is either unavailable or unsuitable for occupation by him[4]. The right is subject to the trustees' powers under s 13(1) to exclude or restrict the entitlement where two or more beneficiaries would qualify under s 12, and to the trustees' powers under s 13(3) to impose reasonable conditions on any beneficiary.

The meaning of 'beneficially entitled to an interest in possession in land subject to the trust' is considered in Article 55(1)(e)[5], and in the present context it is most important whether or not a beneficiary with a beneficial

---

19 *Notting Hill Housing Trust v Brackley* [2001] EWCA Civ 601, [2002] HLR 10.
20 *Notting Hill Housing Trust v Brackley* [2001] EWCA Civ 601, [2002] HLR 10 at para 23. B has a sufficient interest in the home to be protected by Article 8(1) of the Human Rights Convention (*Qazi v Harrow LBC* [2001] EWCA Civ 1634, [2002] HLR 14) but it seems interference with such will be justifiable under Art. 8(2).
1 *Notting Hill Housing Trust v Brackley* [2001] EWCA Civ 601, [2002] HLR 10 at para 26.
2 For example, *Harris v Black* (1983) 426 P & CR 366, CA, joint business tenants holding partnership assets must join in giving notices exercising statutory rights of continuation.
3 Contrast *Sykes v Land* (1984) 271 Estates Gazette 1264 at 1266 per Fox LJ, 'In general, it must be the duty of trustees to preserve trust property for the benefit of the ultimate beneficiaries and not let it be destroyed ... if Mr Sykes required Ms Land to consent to the service of a counter-notice it would be her duty to comply, and that if necessary the court in the exercise of its general jurisdiction over trustees would order her to do so.'
4 TLATA 1996, s 12(2).
5 See p 639 post.

interest in possession in an undivided share in land[6] under a sub-trust has an interest in the trust of land eg where A and B are co-owners of land with undivided equal shares and A dies leaving his share on trust for his children equally or for his son X for life remainder to Y absolutely. A purposive, rather than a narrow, interpretation would enable B not to be the only person with a right of occupation. Indeed, as pointed out in *Lewin on Trusts*[7] it would be particularly odd if A, by settling his half share on himself for life, remainder to Y, would thereby lose his former right of occupation.

The settlor's purposes within s 12(1)(a) in creating the trust are ascertained from the trust instrument itself and the circumstances in which it was made e.g. to purchase land adjoining the properties of four home-owners to preserve it as open space[8], to purchase land for the joint occupation of the male and female purchasers and, perhaps, any family they may have[9], to have the testator's bungalow sold and the proceeds divided between his five children, one of whom happens to be living with him in the bungalow[10], transferring the family home, where the testator and his wife resided and which by survivorship vested in the widow, from the widow into the names of herself and her daughter jointly, but to enable the widow to stay residing there on her own for as long as she wished[11].

If the purposes of the trust do not include making the land available for occupation of some beneficiary or beneficiaries, then, to have a right to occupy, a beneficiary with an interest in possession will need to show that the land is held by the trustees so as to be available for occupation by some beneficiary or beneficiaries[12]. It will not be so available if the trustees are marketing it for sale with vacant possession so as to have proceeds of sale to divide between the beneficiaries as directed by the testator-settlor[13]. However, if to obtain the best price the trustees or personal representatives seek in November not to market the house till May then it is available for them to permit a beneficiary to reside there, though probably on condition[14] he pays an appropriate percentage of a fair occupation rent so as not to have preferential treatment over his co-beneficiaries. Again, if leased commercial and residential premises are held on trust for a testator's widow for life but, after a few years she finds her own country house to be too large and inconvenient at a time when a nice city flat of the trustees has just become vacant, then it seems that if she sold the house the flat would be held by the trustees so as to be available for her occupation[15].

Of course, the beneficiary will have no right to occupy the land if it is unavailable (eg because leased out to a tenant) or if it is unsuitable for him[16] (eg because of personal physical disabilities or it is farmland and he has no farming experience whatever).

---

6 An undivided share in land qualifies as land, the exclusion of undivided shares from the Law of Property Act 1925 definition of land being repealed by TLATA 1996, Sch 4.
7 (17th edn), para 37-55.
8 *Re Buchanan-Wollaston's Conveyance* [1939] Ch 738.
9 *Jones v Challenger* [1961] 1 QB 176, CA; *Rawlings v Rawlings* [1964] P 398, CA.
10 *Barclay v Barclay* [1970] 2 QB 677, CA
11 *Abbey National plc v Moss* (1993) 26 HLR 249, CA.
12 TLATA 1996, s 12(1)(b). Note the present tense 'is held' as emphasised in *Rodway v Landy* [2001] Ch 703, CA.
13 Cf *Barclay v Barclay* [1970] 2 QB 677, CA.
14 TLATA 1996, s 13(3) and (6).
15 See *Lewin on Trusts* (17th edn) para 32-56.
16 TLATA 1996, s 12(2).

If only one beneficiary has the statutory right to occupy the trust land, the right cannot be excluded or restricted though reasonable conditions can be imposed. Thus, if the beneficiary had only an interest in 5% of the land[17], the rest being held on discretionary trusts or accumulation and maintenance trusts he would be treated as life tenant in 100% if allowed to occupy rent free. Under their duty to act fairly between the beneficiaries the trustees should require payment of a 95% fair occupation rent unless, for instance, such beneficiary's minor children resident with him happen to be the beneficiaries under the accumulation and maintenance trusts.

Where two or more beneficiaries qualify under s 12(1) the trustees may exclude or restrict their rights of occupation so long as this is not unreasonable and so long as the restriction is not to an unreasonable extent; and they may impose reasonable conditions on any of the beneficiaries[18]. Statute specifically refers to conditions requiring a beneficiary allowed into occupation to pay any outgoings or expenses in respect of the land or to assume any other obligations in relation to the activity which is or is proposed to be conducted there[19]. Thus, a house can be divided into two self-contained flats with the beneficiaries sharing the burden of the conversion costs and taking over payment of outgoings and expenses in relation to their particular flat[20].

Moreover, where the entitlement of any beneficiary to occupy has been excluded or restricted, then the occupying beneficiary can be required to make payments by way of compensation to the excluded or restricted beneficiary or to forgo any payment or other benefit to which he would otherwise be entitled under the trust so as to benefit that beneficiary[1].

In exercising all the above powers the trustees must have regard to the intentions of the settlor, the purposes for which the land is held, and the circumstances and wishes of each of the beneficiaries who is, or would otherwise be, entitled to occupy trust land under s 12[2]. Thus the settlor's intentions are not the decisive factor: the circumstances of a beneficiary may be more crucial as in the case of the testator's widow discussed above[3].

Finally, protection is conferred upon any beneficiary already in occupation of land and anyone occupying the land with him like a spouse or elderly parent. The trustees' powers under s 13 cannot be exercised to prevent such a person from occupying the land or result in such cesser of occupation unless the occupant consents or the court has given approval[4]. However, if the trustees' exercise of a power of appointment causes cesser of the beneficial interest entitling the occupant to occupy the land with his family members, then the land will have to be vacated, as also if the beneficiary's determinable interest in possession determines on the happening of the prescribed event.

---

17 Cf *IRC v Eversden* [2002] EWHC 1360 (Ch), [2002] STC 1109.
18 TLATA 1996, s 13(2).
19 TLATA 1996, s 13(5).
20 *Rodway v Landy* [2001] EWCA Civ 471, [2001] Ch 703.
 1 TLATA 1996, s 13(6).
 2 TLATA 1996, s 13(4).
 3 See p 477 ante.
 4 TLATA 1996, s 13(7), taking account of the settlor's intentions, the purposes for which the land is held and the circumstances of the beneficiaries qualifying within s 12(1): ss 13(8) and 15(2). See *Rodway v Landy* [2001] EWCA Civ 471, [2001] Ch 703, CA.

Paragraph 15

Court assistance for trustees and persons interested in trust property

The old law

Before TLATA 1996 land held on trust, that was not settled land within the Settled Land Act 1925 or a bare trust, was held on trust for sale with a power to postpone sale (unless ousted expressly or by necessary implication), and, of course, powers of trustees must always be exercised unanimously[5] (unless otherwise authorised by statute or by the trust instrument). Then, under s 30 of the Law of Property Act 1925, 'If the trustees for sale refuse to sell or to exercise any of the powers conferred [by ss 28 and 29], or any requisite consent cannot be obtained, any person interested may apply to the court for a vesting or other order for giving effect to the proposed transaction or for an order directing the trustees for sale to give effect thereto, and the court may make such order as it thinks fit.'

Because there was a trust or duty to sell, the court concentrated upon the need to sell the land unless this would defeat the spirit or purpose of the trust[6]; and, of course, if the trustees did not unanimously exercise the power to postpone sale, the duty to sell automatically arose, as where M and F held on trust for sale for themselves but terminated their cohabitation.

The new statutory powers

Section 14 of TLATA 1996 is much broader than the old s 30, except in only applying to trustees and not to personal representatives[7], and provides more guidance for the exercise of the court's discretion. It provides:

'(1) Any person who is a trustee of land or has an interest in property subject to a trust of land may make an application to the court for an order under this section.

(2) On an application for an order the court may make any such order–
    (a) relating to the exercise by the trustees of any of their functions (including an order relieving them of any obligation to obtain the consent of, or to consult, any person in connection with the exercise of any of their functions), or
    (b) declaring the nature or extent of a person's interest in property subject to the trust,
    as the court may think fit.

(3) The court may not under this section make any order as to the appointment or removal of trustees'.

Guidance for the court is provided in s 15–

'(1) the matters to which the court is to have regard in determining an application for an order under section 14 include–
    (a) the intentions of the person or persons (if any) who created the trust,
    (b) the purposes for which the property subject to the trust is held,
    (c) the welfare of any minor who occupies or might reasonably be expected to occupy any land subject to the trust as his home, and
    (d) the interests of any secured creditor of any beneficiary

...

---

5 *Re Mayo* [1943] Ch 302.
6 *Jones v Challenger* [1961] 1 QB 176 CA; *Re Buchanan-Wollaston's Conveyance* [1939] Ch 738.
7 TLATA 1996, s 18(1).

(3) ...the matters to which the court is to have regard also include[8] the circumstances and wishes of any beneficiaries of full age and entitled to an interest in possession in property subject to the trust or (in case of dispute) of the majority (according to the value of their combined interests).

(4) This section does not apply to an application if section 335A of the Insolvency Act 1986 applies to it.'

Under s 17(2), s 14 applies in relation to a trust of proceeds of sale of land and trustees of such a trust as in relation to a trust of land and trustees of land. A trust of proceeds of sale of land[9] is any trust of property (other than a trust of land) which consists of, or includes, any proceeds of a disposition of land held in trust (including settled land unless the proceeds remain subject to the Settled Land Act 1925) or any property representing any such proceeds.

Locus standi to apply to court

Those who are entitled to apply to the court are the trustees (but not personal representatives)[10], and any person who 'has an interest in property' (which could be personal property[11]) subject to the trust of land or of its proceeds or property representing such proceeds. Only an interest is required, not an interest in possession nor an interest as a beneficiary. Thus, applicants may be a beneficiary under a discretionary trust[12], an annuitant[13], a creditor with a charge or a charging order over a beneficiary's interest[14], a spouse with a charge under the Matrimonial Homes Act 1983, and the trustee in bankruptcy of a beneficiary[15], though probably not a receiver by way of equitable execution who was held[16] not to be a 'person interested' for the purposes of s 30 of the Law of Property Act 1925.

Determination of applications other than under Insolvency Act 1986, s 335A

Orders as the court thinks fit may be made so as to declare, but not vary[17] the nature or extent of a person's interest in trust property[18] or affect the exercise of any of the functions of the trustees, including orders relieving them of any obligation to obtain the consent of, or to consult, any person, even, as under the old s 30, where such person has expressly told the trustees not to do what they propose. It would seem that not only can the court override refusals of consents but also any exclusions by the settlor of the powers

---

8 *Mortgage Corpn v Shaire* [2001] Ch 743.

9 TLATA 1996, s 17(3) and (5).

10 TLATA 1996, s 18(1).

11 TLATA 1996, s 1(1)(a).

12 As indicated in Megarry & Wade *Law of Real Property* (6th edn) by C Harpum, the Law Commissioner responsible for TLATA 1996, para 8-142; *Gartside v IRC* [1968] AC 553, HL.

13 Like a chargee and only excluded from having an interest in possession by TLATA 1996, s 22(3).

14 *Bank of Ireland Home Mortgages Ltd v Bell* [2001] 2 FLR 809 (equitable charge) as for Law of Property Act 1925, s 30 in *Midland Bank plc v Pike* [1988] 2 All ER 434; *Lloyds Bank v Byrne* [1993] 1 FLR 369, CA; and see TLATA 1996, s 15(1)(d).

15 *Re Solomon* [1967] Ch 573; *Re Ng* [1997] BCC 507.

16 *Stevens v Hutchinson* [1953] Ch 299.

17 See Law Commission Discussion Paper 'Sharing Homes' (July 2002) para 2.26. No varying power existed under Law of Property Act 1925, s 30: *Stott v Ratcliffe* (1982) 126 Sol Jo 310; *Ahmed v Kendrick* (1987) 56 P & CR 120 at 127.

18 Proprietary estoppel principles may make a person's interest uncertain so as to need to be determined and declared.

conferred upon trustees by TLATA 1996 in a very exceptional case where such exclusions wholly undermine the trustees' fundamental functions to act in the best interests of the beneficiaries as a whole and to further the purposes of the trust, acting fairly between income and capital beneficiaries (except to the extent clearly ousted by the trust instrument)[19].It is in the sphere of co-owned land that most applications to the court are made. Case law under s 30 of the Law of Property Act 1925 established that the courts commenced with favouring enforcement of the letter of the trust for sale, once the power to postpone sale was not unanimously exercised by the cohabiting, co-owning trustees. However, the courts did look at the intentions of the settlor-trustees when becoming co-owners of the house or flat and the purposes for which they held such property, to see whether enforcing the letter of the trust for sale would defeat the purpose of the trust[20].

Many judges[1] found that the purpose was to provide a matrimonial or quasi-matrimonial home for the two settlor-trustee-beneficiaries so that the purpose did not continue once they separated, even if the home housed one parent and their children, so the welfare of the children was only an incidental factor affecting postponement of a sale only for a short period. Some judges[2], however, were prepared to find that the purpose was to provide a family home so that such purpose persisted when one parent had left the home occupied by the other parent and the children.

In any event, the voice of a secured creditor or of the trustee in bankruptcy would prevail unless the circumstances were most exceptional[3].

It has been held[4] that s 15 has changed the law giving the court greater flexibility in having always to consider whether any matters mentioned therein are present and in having greater discretion as to the weight to be given such matters in deciding what order to make, except where s 335A of the Insolvency Act 1986 applies to applications of a trustee of a bankrupt beneficiary. The authorities on s 30 have now to be treated with caution and in many cases they are unlikely to be of great assistance[5]. Certainly for trusts for sale created before 1997 as a matter of standard conveyancing practice, there should be no presumption of sale; though if an express trust for sale were deliberately imposed after 1996 this indicates the settlor's intention that there should be a sale and the purpose of the trust at the time of its creation, so there may well be a presumption in favour of sale, although the other matters mentioned in s 15 must also be considered, noting that it is the purposes for which the property *is* held at the time of the application which are relevant[6].

While the interests of secured creditors are not almost invariably conclusive as under s 30[7], a powerful consideration swaying the court is the

---

19 As indicated in Megarry & Wade *Law of Real Property* (6th edn) by C Harpum, the Law Commissioner responsible for TLATA 1996, para 8-142.
20 *Jones v Challenger* [1961] 1 QB 176, CA.
1 *Burke v Burke* [1974] 1 WLR 1063, CA; *Re Holliday* [1981] Ch 405, CA.
2 *Williams v Williams* [1976] Ch 278, CA; *Re Evers's Trust* [1980] 1 WLR 1327, CA.
3 *Re Citro* [1991] Ch 142, CA; *Lloyds Bank v Byrne* [1993] 1 FLR 369, CA.
4 *Mortgage Corpn v Shaire* [2001] Ch 743 at 757; *Bank of Ireland Home Mortgages Ltd v Bell* [2001] 2 FLR 809 at 816 per Peter Gibson LJ.
5 *Mortgage Corpn v Shaire* [2001] Ch 743 at 761.
6 *Rodway v Landy* [2001] EWCA Civ 471, [2001] Ch 703 at 711 per Peter Gibson LJ.
7 See cases cited in footnote 2 above.

unfairness of keeping such a creditor out of his money if he is not receiving proper recompense for this[8].

The welfare of any minor who occupies or might reasonably be expected to occupy land as his home is a factor always to be taken into consideration, so that there is scope to give more prominence to this than before when considering the interests of any secured creditor[9]. However, as before, where the trustees are married and there are children of a marriage matters should still be dealt with so far as possible under the flexibility of the Matrimonial Homes Act 1973[10] rather that under TLATA 1996.

Trustee in Bankruptcy's application under Insolvency Act 1986, s 335A[11]

An application by a trustee of a bankrupt's estate under s 14 has to be made to the bankruptcy court which must make such order as it thinks just and reasonable having regard to–
(a) the interests of the bankrupt's creditors;
(b) where the application concerns the home of the bankrupt or the bankrupt's spouse or former spouse–
    (i)   the conduct of the spouse or former spouse, so far as contributing to the bankruptcy;
    (ii) the needs and financial resources of the spouse or former spouse, and
    (iii) the needs of any children; and
(c) all the circumstances of the case other than the needs of the bankrupt.

Crucially, where the application is made after one year has elapsed since the bankrupt's estate first vested in a trustee, the court must assume, unless the circumstances of the case are exceptional, that the interests of the bankrupt's creditors outweigh all other considerations[12]. Exceptional circumstances, where the court may refuse a sale or postpone it temporarily, cover the serious illness of the bankrupt's spouse[13], or the case[14] where the bankrupt had petitioned for his own bankruptcy and there would be enough equity in the house to satisfy creditor's claims for capital and interest if it were sold five years after the wife and the school children had continued living there in that period. It is not exceptional that the wife and children will be displaced and unable to find a comparable home, such being the familiar melancholy consequences of debt and improvidence[15].

Equitable Accounting after sale

As already seen[16], accounts may need to be settled between co-owners after sale of their property, taking into account of any co-owner bearing a disproportionate part of the mortgage payments or being entitled to an occupation rent having been forced out of the property well before the sale or being entitled to an allowance for improvements to the property.

---

8 *Williams v Williams* [1976] Ch 278, CA.
9 *Mortgage Corpn v Shaire* [2001] Ch 743 at 760.
10 *Williams v Williams* [1976] Ch 278, CA; *Tee v Tee* [1999] 2 FLR 613, CA.
11 Inserted by TLATA 1996, Sch 3, para 23.
12 Insolvency Act 1986, s 335A(3).
13 *Judd v Brown* [1998] 2 FLR 360 (refusal); *Re Raval* [1998] 2 FLR 718 (postponement).
14 *Re Holliday* [1981] Ch 405, CA, as explained in *Re Citro* [1991] Ch 142, CA.
15 *Re Citro* [1991] Ch 142 at 157; *Re Lowrie* [1981] 3 All ER 353 at 356.
16 See pp 355–357.

Paragraph 16

Protection of Purchasers

A purchaser (meaning a person who acquires an interest in land or charge on property for money or money's worth) need not be concerned to see that the trustees have complied with their duty under s 6(5) to have regard to the rights of the benficiaries and to consult them under s 11(1) (if not ousted) nor to see that they had obtained the consent of each beneficiary to any earlier partition of the land[17].

So long as capital money is paid to two trustees or a trust corporation or a sole personal representative acting as such[18], interests under the trust of land will be overreached unless, in the case of unregistered land, the purchaser or his agent had actual notice that the trustees were exceeding their powers (by ignoring any limitations thereon in s 6(6) and (8)[19] or, in the case of registered land, there was an entry in the register limiting the trustees' powers[20].

To save the need to investigate the underlying equitable interests, where the trustees have conveyed their land to the persons believed by them to be beneficiaries of full age and capacity and have executed a deed of discharge declaring themselves discharged from the trust in relation to that land, then a purchaser is entitled to assume that the land has been free from that trust since the date of the deed of discharge[1] – unless he has actual notice that the trustees were mistaken in their belief[2].

---

17 TLATA 1996, s 16(1).
18 Law of Property Act 1925, ss 2 and 27 as amended by TLATA 1996, Sch 3, para 4.
19 TLATA 1996, s 16(2) and (3).
20 Land Registration Act 2002, s 26, resolving the problem identified by Ferris & Battersby in [1998] Conv 168.
1 Cf Settled Land Act 1925, s 17.
2 TLATA 1996, s 16(5).

CHAPTER 11

The trustee's duties

Article

46 Duty of trustee concerning acceptance of trust or additional trust property   485

47 Duty of trustee to obey the directions of the settlement unless deviation sanctioned by the court   493

48 Duty of trustee to act impartially in the sense of fairly and disinterestedly, between the beneficiaries   529

49 Duty of trustee to sell improper property   548

50 Duty of trustee, as between tenant for life and remainderman, in relation to property pending conversion   552

51 Duty of trustee in relation to the payment of outgoings out of corpus and income respectively   563

52 Duty of trustee to exercise reasonable care and skill   575

53 Powers and duties of trustee in relation to the investment of trust funds   597

54 Duty of trustee to see that he transfers trust property only to beneficiaries or to object of a power of appointment or only to persons authorised under the trust instrument or the general law to receive such property (eg as custodian or portfolio manager)   623

55 Duty of trustees not to delegate their duties or powers unless authorised   631

56 Duty of trustees to act jointly where more than one   644

57 Duty of trustee not to set up jus tertii   648

58 Duty of trustee to act gratuitously unless otherwise authorised, as is usual nowadays   651

59 Duty of trustee not to traffic with or otherwise profit by trust property nor to cause loss from a conflict between his fiduciary duty and his self-interest   659

60 Duty of trustee to be ready with his accounts   671

ARTICLE 46

Duty of trustee concerning acceptance of trust or additional trust property

(1) Before accepting a trust or additional trust property, the potential or actual trustee ought to discover:

(i) if he might be about to put himself in a position where there would be a sensible possibility of a conflict between his personal self-interest and his fiduciary duty, because in such event he should refuse the trusteeship unless such conflict is authorised by the trust instrument (or by all the beneficiaries of full age and capacity who between them are absolutely beneficially entitled to the trust property);

(ii) how onerous the task is likely to be, taking account of the value and nature of the trust property, the range of the beneficiaries and of the trustees' powers, the provisions for remuneration and for exculpation from liability, and the possibilities for dissension and animosity among beneficiaries or classes of beneficiaries;

(iii) whether there is a sensible possibility that the validity of the trust or a transfer of property to the trustees could be attacked;

(iv) whether there is a sensible possibility that he could find himself criminally liable under extensive anti-money-laundering legislation.

(2) Having accepted the trust, it is the duty of the trustee to acquaint himself, as soon as possible, with the nature and circumstances of the trust property, the terms of the trust, and the contents of the documents handed over to him relating to the trust. Where necessary, he should obtain a transfer of the trust property to himself, and (subject to the provisions of the settlement) get in debts and trust money invested on insufficient or hazardous security[1].

PARAGRAPH 1(I)

Avoidance of conflict between fiduciary duty and self-interest

If a prospective original trustee is related by blood or marriage to a beneficiary or owed a significant sum by a beneficiary[2] or may want to purchase for himself trust property at some stage (eg the large house from which he and the testator-settlor have conducted a dental or medical practice), then the trusteeship of the lifetime or testamentary trust should be refused unless the trust instrument confers express authority for such conflicts of interest or

---

1 Eg in trade: *Kirkman v Booth* (1848) 11 Beav 273; *Re Strahan* (1856) 8 De GM & G 291.
2 *Peyton v Robinson* (1823) 1 LJOS Ch 191. A bargain between a trustee and a beneficiary that payment of trust money will only be made if the trustee then receives thereout payment of his debt will be a fraud on the power of payment (so the payment will be void) unless the power expressly authorises payment on such terms, so indirectly allowing the trustee to be a beneficiary to the extent of debts due from a beneficiary to him.

self-dealing[3], eg so long as there are co-trustees who concur in the payment to a related beneficiary or the self-dealing. Where the relevant facts were known to the settlor, who still went ahead with appointing the interested person as an original trustee, the courts are easily persuaded to find a necessarily implied authority for conflicts of interest[4], except where such conflict is at its greatest in the case of self-dealing[5], but it is always better to avoid possible problems with an express authority in the trust instrument.

Where a person is asked to become new trustee of an established trust, then, unless there is some broad general authority in the trust instrument that can be relied upon, the only foolproof protection in the event of a conflict of interest is if all the beneficiaries of full age and capacity, who between them are absolutely beneficially entitled to the trust property, agree to the impeachable transaction[6]. Such a situation is, in practice, very rare because the lengthy duration of most trusts means that all the beneficiaries will not have been ascertained at the relevant time, so that a subsequently born or ascertained beneficiary may subsequently bring legal proceedings.

PARAGRAPH 1 (II)

Avoiding onerous responsibilities that are not worthwhile

As a matter of commonsense, a prospective trustee should consider the value and nature of the actual or potential trust assets and the terms of the trust instrument to ascertain how complex and difficult his task will be and how extensive his potential liability may be. Particular regard should be paid to clauses concerned with remuneration and with exculpation from liability, and he may well wish to be able to retire without the consent of his co-trustees[7], although if his co-trustees can also do this, then this is double-edged, involving a possibility of benefit or of burden. Caution is also needed if there is, or there is to be, a protector, in considering the relationship between the trustee and the protector and the impact of any powers of supervision or removal vested in the protector. Difficulties can also arise if there is only one trust for the issue of three or four marriages of the settlor or only one trust for the benefit of a settlor's family as well as for employees and ex-employees of the settlor's company and their families.

PARAGRAPH 1 (III)

Vitiated transfers to trustees or vitiated trusts

The settlor's transfer of property to trustees will be vitiated if the settlor was not the beneficial owner thereof[8] or made the transfer to prejudice his

---

3 See Art 59 post.
4 As where the settlor and spouse are trustees for their children and grandchildren or the settlor makes X and Y trustees for their children and grandchildren. For other instances see *Sargeant v National Westminster Bank* (1990) 61 P & CR 518, CA; *Edge v Pensions Ombudsman* [2000] Ch 602 at 621–622, 632–633.
5 See Art 59 post.
6 *Saunders v Vautier* (1841) 4 Beav 115, Art 69 post.
7 Trustee Act 1925 ('TA 1925'), s 39.
8 The real owner may follow or trace the property so as to recover it.

creditors[9] or under undue influence[10] or when he had no capacity[11]. Where there was a valid transfer of property to trustees the trust may be void for uncertainty[12] or administrative unworkability[13] or as a non-charitable purpose trust[14], or it may be that the trust was a sham trust for the designated beneficiaries, really being a trust of property for the settlor[15], with any dispositive provisions taking effect on the settlor's death being testamentary ones requiring compliance with the Wills Act 1837. Certain trusts subject to an exotic foreign governing law may stretch the elasticity of the trust concept beyond that permitted by English public policy or that required for the irreducible core content of a trust, so that the trust is a 'limping trust', valid under its governing law but a resulting trust of assets situated in England or other traditional trust jurisdictions[16].

If a prospective trustee believes that there is a sensible possibility that he will become involved in the time, trouble and expense of litigation, then it is only common sense to refuse the trusteeship. In addition, he could be personally liable if he had actual Nelsonian or naughty knowledge that the settlor's transfer to him was a breach of the settlor's fiduciary duty[17], while there may be problems over recourse to the trust fund for liabilities incurred in performance of the trusts or in defending the trust fund against third parties, particularly where those parties' claims succeed[18].

PARAGRAPH 1(IV)

Criminal liabilities under anti-money-laundering legislation

Money laundering[19] is an act which:
(a) constitutes an offence under ss 322, 323 or 324 of the Proceeds of Crime Act 2002;
(b) constitutes an attempt, conspiracy or incitement to commit an offence within (a);
(c) constitutes aiding, abetting, counselling or procuring the commission of an offence within (a); or
(d) would constitute an offence within (a), (b) or (c) if done in the UK.

Under s 322 a person commits an offence if he conceals, disguises, converts or transfers criminal property or removes criminal property from England and Wales or from Scotland or from Northern Ireland. 'Concealing or disguising' criminal property includes concealing or disguising its nature, source, location, disposition, movement or ownership or any rights with respect to it[20], while property is 'criminal property' if[1] (a) it constitutes any person's benefit from 'criminal conduct' or it represents such a benefit (in

---

9 See p 291 ante.
10 See pp 281–285 ante.
11 See pp 268–270 ante.
12 See Art 8(1) ante.
13 See pp 91–93 ante.
14 See pp 110–115 ante
15 See pp 59–61 ante.
16 See p 1052 post.
17 See p 974 post.
18 See p 842 and Art 83 post.
19 Proceeds of Crime Act 2002 ('PCA 2002'), s 335(11). 14 years is the maximum sentence for ss 322, 323 and 324 offences: see s 329.
20 PCA 2002, s 322(3).
 1 PCA 2002, s 335(3).

whole or part and whether directly or indirectly eg via the tracing process), and (b) the alleged offender knows or suspects that it constitutes or represents such a benefit. 'Criminal conduct' is conduct[2] which (a) constitutes an offence in any part of the UK or (b) would constitute an offence in any part of the UK if it occurred there.

Under s 323 a person commits an offence if he enters into or becomes concerned in an arrangement which he knows or suspects facilitates (by whatever means) the acquisition, retention, use or control of criminal property by or on behalf of another person. Under s 324 a person commits an offence if he acquires, uses or has possession of criminal property, unless he be a purchaser for adequate consideration[3], when the provision by a person of goods or services which he knows or suspects may help another to carry out criminal conduct is not consideration[4].

It is a defence[5] to ss 322, 323 and 324 that the alleged offender on his own initiative as soon as practicable had made an authorised disclosure under s 333 (eg to someone authorised by the National Criminal Intelligence Service or a person nominated by his employer under an established procedure) or he had intended to make such a disclosure but had a reasonable excuse for not doing so, or the act he did was done in carrying out a function he has relating to the enforcement of any provision of the 2002 Act or of any other Act relating to criminal conduct.

Where the potential defendant made the authorised disclosure before performing the act constituting an offence under ss 322, 323 or 324 and obtained an appropriate consent then no offence has been committed[6]. The appropriate consent is the consent of the officer nominated by the employer or of someone authorised by the NCIS to do a prohibited act after receiving an authorised disclosure[7]. In the case of a person authorised by the NCIS, the consent will be deemed to have been given either if notice refusing consent is not received within seven working days of disclosure to such person (starting with the first working day after disclosure) or such notice was received but thirty-one days have elapsed since receipt of such notice[8]. In the case of a nominated officer, he must not give the appropriate consent unless authorised by some person authorised by the NCIS or unless notice refusing consent is not received from such person within seven working days of disclosure to him or unless such notice of refusal was received but thirty-one days have elapsed since receipt of such notice[9].

An offence of failure to make an authorised disclosure occurs[10] if:
(i) the defendant knows[11] or suspects[12] or has *reasonable grounds for* knowing

---

2 PCA 2002, s 335(2).
3 PCA 2002, s 324(2).
4 PCA 2002, s 324(3).
5 PCA 2002, ss 322(2), 323(2), 324(2) and (3).
6 PCA 2002, ss 322(2)(a), 323(2)(a), 324(2)(a).
7 PCA 2002, s 330(1).
8 PCA 2002, s 330(2)–(6).
9 PCA 2002, s 331.
10 PCA 2002, s 325: 5 years is the maximum sentence: s 329.
11 It suffices that the defendant deliberately refrained from inquiry because he suspected the truth but did not want to have his suspicion confirmed: *Westminster City Council v Croyalgrange* [1986] 2 All ER 353 at 359, HL, per Lord Bridge.
12 Suspicion requires some foundation, as opposed to speculation, but not prima facie proof and can take account of matters that could not be put in evidence: *Hussein v Chong Fook Kam* [1970] AC 942, PC; *Welsh v Loughman* (1991) 2 VR 351.

or *suspecting* that another person is engaged in money-laundering; and
(ii) the information or other matter on which his knowledge or suspicion is
based or which gives reasonable grounds for such knowledge or suspicion came to him in the course of a business in the regulated financial
sectos[13]; and
(iii) he fails to make the authorised disclosure as soon as practicable without a
reasonable excuse.

It is a defence that the defendant was a professional legal adviser and the
information or other matter came to him in privileged circumstances (and so
was not communicated or given with the intention of furthering a criminal
purpose)[14]. In determining whether a person knows or suspects or has reasonable ground for knowing or suspecting money-laundering, the court must
consider whether the defendant had followed any relevant guidance issued
by a supervisory or other appropriate body and published in a manner in its
opinion appropriate to bring the guidance to the attention of persons likely
to be affected by it[15]. Indeed, the defendant will be safe if he does not know
or suspect another person is engaged in money-laundering if he had not
been provided by his employer with such training as is specified by the
Secretary of State for the purposes of s 325[16].

Tipping off the alleged moneylaunderer is a further offence[17] once the
defendant knows or suspects that a disclosure has been made to the relevant
person (eg to the NCIS or the person designated by the employer) unless[18]
he did not know or suspect that his tipping-off conduct was likely to be
prejudicial to investigation of the alleged money launderer or such conduct
occurred in carrying out a function relating to enforcement of the 2002 Act
or any other Act relating to criminal conduct or he was a professional legal
adviser advising the alleged criminal but not with the intention of furthering
a criminal purpose[19].

Property that is not criminal property within the Proceeds of Crime Act
2002 but which is 'terrorist property'[20], extending to property not acquired by
criminal conduct but likely to be used for the purposes of terrorism
(including any resources of a proscribed organisation), is governed by the
Terrorism Act 2000. A person commits an offence if he enters into or
becomes concerned in an arrangement which facilitates the retention or
control by or on behalf of another person of terrorist property by concealment, by removal from the jurisdiction, by transfer to nominees or in any
other way, unless he can prove he did not know and had no reasonable cause
to suspect that the arrangement related to terrorist property[1]. The Anti
terrorism, Crime and Security Act 2001 further introduced into the 2000 Act
a s 21A offence of failure to disclose that he knows or suspects or has reasonable grounds for knowing or suspecting that another person has com-

---

13 PCA 2002, Sch 6, Pt I defines the regulated sector essentially to cover persons regulated under
the Financial Services and Markets Act 2000.
14 PCA 2002, s 325(6), (10) and (11).
15 PCA 2002, s 325(8).
16 PCA 2002, s 325(7).
17 PCA 2002, s 328(1): 5 years is the maximum sentence under s 329. For resolution of practical
difficulties see *Bank of Scotland v A Ltd* [2001] 3 All ER 58, CA.
18 PCA 2002, s 328(3) and (4).
19 PCA 2002, s 328(3) and (4).
20 Terrorism Act 2000, s 14.
 1 Terrorism Act 2000, s 18.

mitted an offence under ss 15 to 18 of the 2000 Act[2]. Similar defences exist as under the Proceeds of Crime Act 2002[3].

Suspicious transaction reports: professional trustees and advisers

Professional trustees and their advisers need to be aware of the extensive width of the Proceeds of Crime Act 2002 and the Terrorism Act 2000 (as amended) so as to consider whether they need to make a suspicious trans-action report to the NCIS. After all, they need only to have reasonable grounds for suspecting[4] that a person is involved in money-laundering 'criminal property' or 'terrorist property'. Moreover, criminal property is so broadly defined[5] as to cover not just false accounting or forgery or obtaining benefits by fraud but also the benefits obtained from pure tax evasion (like non-declaration of taxable income or capital), while conduct occurring anywhere is 'criminal conduct' (potentially giving rise to 'criminal property') if it 'would constitute an offence in any part of the UK if it occurred there'. Relying on analogous extradition provisions[6], prosecution authorities are prepared to argue that the courts will transpose conduct amounting to cheating the Taxopian revenue (eg by non-disclosure), whether occurring in Taxopia or in England, into conduct amounting to cheating the national revenue, which would constitute an offence if occurring in England, but there is much to be said for respecting human rights by treating conduct cheating the Taxopian revenue as not constituting an offence in England if occurring in England or Taxopia. However, breach of another jurisdiction's exchange controls cannot amount to 'criminal conduct'.

Finally, in the regulated financial sector the due diligence requirements to help prevent money-laundering may well lead to information being available that provides reasonable grounds for money-laundering suspicions so that a suspicious transaction report should be made to the NCIS. However, finan-cial institutions can reasonably assume their clients will meet their tax liabilities unless there is some reason to suspect otherwise and are not to be bloodhounds investigating clients' affairs to ascertain whether any criminal conduct has occurred[7].

PARAGRAPH 2

Inquiries as to the property and the trusts and the trust documents

A person who undertakes to act as a trustee takes upon himself serious and onerous duties; and when, as too often happens, he adopts a 'policy of masterly inactivity', he entirely misapprehends the nature of the office to

---

2 These concern fund-raising, use and possession of property for purposes of terrorism, being concerned in arrangements to make property available to another for purposes of terrorism as well as money-laundering, so long as there is reasonable cause for suspicion.

3 Terrorism Act 2000, ss 19, 20, 21 and 21A.

4 Terrorism Act 2000, s 21A; PCA 2002, s 325(2).

5 PCA 2002, s 335.

6 *R v Chief Metropolitan Stipendiary Magistrate, ex p Secretary of State for Home Department* [1988] 1 WLR 1204.

7 UK Joint Money Laundering Steering Group's Guidance Notes for the Financial Sector, Dec 2001.

which he has been appointed. As Kekewich J said in *Hallows v Lloyd*[8]:

'What are the duties of persons becoming new trustees of a settlement? Their duties are quite onerous enough, and I am not prepared to increase them. I think that when persons are asked to become new trustees, they are bound to inquire of what the property consists that is proposed to be handed over to them, and what are the trusts. They ought also to look into the trust documents and papers to ascertain what notices appear among them of incumbrances and other matters affecting the trust.'

So that the new trustees may carry out these duties, they are entitled to require the old trustees to produce all trust documents, papers, and memoranda relating to the administration of the trust (including any letter of wishes necessary to be considered before exercising any flexible discretionary functions), and where there was previously a corporate trustee, the documents to be produced may include internal correspondence and memoranda. But what should be so produced, and whether it should be only produced or actually handed over depends upon the circumstances of each case and the nature and contents of the document[9]. Everything relating to the management and administration of the trust property should be produced, at the least, but so far as concerns documents relating to discretionary distributive functions it would seem that only those of them that should be take into account when considering fuure exercise of such functions need to be produced. It would seem that a former trustee should be obliged to supply information to the new trustee on matters not clear from the trust papers[10], just as he would be so obliged to a beneficiary of full age and capacity[11], the new trustee being no worse off than the beneficiaries to whom he owes a duty to collect in and safeguard all the property for which the former trustee should account.

If there are any doubts as to the scope of the trustees' powers, eg of investment then steps must be taken to obtain legal advice[12].

Inquiries as to acts of predecessors

New trustees should further ascertain that the trust fund is properly invested and review the trust investments[13], to see that the trust portfolio comprises not just authorised investments but is sensibly balanced as far as capital and income growth is concerned taking account of the terms, purposes and distribution requirements of the trust. They do not need to incur time, trouble and expense to hunt for breaches of trust committed by former trustees[14], since they can assume their predecessors acted properly in the absence of circumstances indicating a breach of trust or possible breach[15]. If, through not inquiring into suspicious circumstances, the trust estate should suffer, a new trustee may be liable, although he himself took no part, and

---

8 (1888) 39 Ch D 686 at 691. Precisely the same duties are binding on persons appointed as *original* trustees.
9 *Tiger v Barclays Bank Ltd* [1952] 1 All ER 85, CA. See also Article 60, post.
10 *Mond v Hyde* [1999] QB 1097 at 1104 per Bedlam J.
11 See Article 60, post.
12 *Nestlé v National Westminster Bank* [1993] 1 WLR 1260 at 1265.
13 *Nestlé v National Westminster Bank* [1993] 1 WLR 1260: there is a duty to make periodic reviews of the investments.
14 *Re Forest of Dean Coal Mining Co* (1878) 10 Ch D 450 at 453–454, per Jessel MR.
15 *Ex p Geaves* (1856) 8 De GM & G 291 at 309.

could have taken no part, in committing the original breaches of trust[16]. There is, however, no obligation upon a new trustee to make a new investigation of the title to, or value of, existing securities of a nature authorised by the trust[17].

Duty of new trustees to inquire as to losses

Where part of the trust estate has been lost, it is the duty of new trustees to inquire as to the circumstances, and as to whether there is a probability of recovering the loss or any part of it by appropriate proceedings[18]. Nor can new trustees escape this duty by purporting to be appointed trustees of what remains of the estate only[19], for the effect of doing so might be to discharge parties who were liable for breach of trust from their liability, or at least to interpose difficulties in the way of the beneficiaries recovering the loss. The proper course in such cases is to appoint the new trustees to be trustees of the whole, and for them then to take out a summons for directions as to whether any and, if so, what steps ought to be taken at the cost of the estate for the recovery of the loss[20].

Effect of not searching for notices of incumbrances

A new trustee is liable to make good moneys which he may have honestly paid to a beneficiary, if the papers relating to the trust contain a notice of an incumbrance created by that beneficiary; for if the trustee had acquainted himself, as he was bound to do, with the trust documents and papers, he would have found what was the true state of the case[1]. Where, however, no amount of search would have disclosed the notice, the trustee would, of course, not be liable, as his liability entirely depends upon his failure to perform the duty of search which the law casts upon him[2].

This is because trustees are not insurers, and their conduct ought to be judged with reference to the facts and circumstances existing at the time when they have to act, and which either are known *or ought to be known* by them at that time[3]. Moreover, a new trustee is not bound to inquire of the old trustees whether they have received notice of any incumbrances[4]. Old case law establishes that he is not even liable if he honestly, but erroneously (eg from forgetfulness), informs an intended incumbrancer that he has no knowledge of any prior incumbrancer[5].

However, under Law of Property Act 1925, s 137(3) and (8) written notices are required to be given to trustees in respect of any dealings with an equitable interest in real or personal property if it is to affect priorities of competing claims; the trustees from time to time are entitled to custody of such notices and, subject to the payment of costs, any person interested in the

---

16 *Harvey v Olliver* (1887) 57 LT 239; and see *Millar's Trustees v Polson* (1897) 34 SLR 798; *Re Strahan* (1856) 8 De GM & G 291.
17 *Rawsthorne v Rowley* [1909] 1 Ch 409n, (1907) 24 TLR 51.
18 *Bennett v Burgis* (1846) 5 Hare 295.
19 See *Bennett v Burgis* (1846) 5 Hare 295.
20 *Bennett v Burgis* (1846) 5 Hare 295. Further on *Beddoes* applications see Article 87, post.
 1 See *Hollows v Lloyd* (1888) 39 Ch D 686.
 2 *Hollows v Lloyd* (1888) 39 Ch D 686.
 3 *Re Hurst* (1892) 67 LT 96; *Youde v Cloud* (1874) LR 18 Eq 634.
 4 *Phipps v Lovegrove* (1873) LR 16 Eq 80.
 5 *Low v Bouverie* [1891] 3 Ch 82; *Porter v Moore* [1904] 2 Ch 367.

equitable interest may require production of the notice(s). An intending assignee or incumbrancer may very well be a person interested, which will certainly cover a person contractually bound to acquire the intended interest subject to there being no notices other than those of which he was aware at the date of the contract, while *Hedley Byrne v Heller*[6] has extended liability in negligence for honest mis-statements where reliance is placed on a person in a specially knowledgeable position. Thus, nowadays a trustee who honestly but negligently fails to inform an intending incumbrancer of a written notice in his custody is likely to find himself liable for loss thereby suffered.

Obtaining control of trust property and properly investing it

A trustee who leaves the trust fund in the sole name, or under the sole control, of his co-trustee will be liable if it be lost[7]. Thus trust property must be brought under the joint control of the trustees, with trust property being placed in the joint names of the trustees unless they take advantage of express or statutory powers to employ and remunerate nominees or custodians. Trustees should, of course, ensure that trust funds are properly invested in authorised investments[8].

A trustee who keeps money for an unreasonable length of time without investing it is liable if it be lost, however pure his motives may have been[9].

ARTICLE 47

Duty of trustee to obey the directions of the settlement unless deviation sanctioned by the court

(1) A trustee must obey the lawful directions of the settlement if practicable, except so far as these directions are modified by the consent of all the beneficiaries collectively (if they can all be ascertained and are of full age and capacity), or by the trustees of a pension fund for authorised purposes within section 68 of the Pensions Act 1995 if the employer consents or by the Occupational Pensions Regulatory Authority for authorised purposes within section 69 of the 1995 Act, or by the exercise of a power of amendment conferred by the trust instrument, or by the court. Consent may be given by the court on behalf of any beneficiary who is not sui juris, or potential beneficiaries who are incapable of ascertainment, or are unborn[10].

(2)

(i) Where in the management or administration of any property vested in trustees, any disposition, or any transaction, is, in the opinion of the court, expedient, but cannot be effected by reason of the absence of any power for that purpose vested in the trustees

---

6 [1964] AC 465; *Mutual Life and Citizens' Assurance Co Ltd v Evatt* [1971] AC 793; *Pirelli General Cable Works Ltd v Oscar Faber & Partners* [1983] 2 AC 1.
7 *Lewis v Nobbs* (1878) 8 Ch D 591; *Underwood v Stevens* (1816) 1 Mer 712.
8 See Article 53, post.
9 *Moyle v Moyle* (1831) 2 Russ & M 710.
10 Variation of Trusts Act 1958, s 1.

by the trust instrument, if any, or by law, the court may by order confer upon the trustees, either generally or in any particular instance, the necessary power for the purpose, on such terms, and subject to such provisions and conditions, if any, as the court may think fit and may direct in what manner any money authorised to be expended, and the costs of any transaction, are to be paid or borne as between capital and income[11];

(ii) the jurisdiction of the court to sanction the above dispositions or transactions includes power in certain circumstances to make an order authorising any expense of action taken or proposed in or for the management of land held on trust for sale to be treated as a capital outgoing, notwithstanding that in other circumstances that expense could not properly have been so treated[12];

(3) A trustee who ventures (without the sanction of the court) to deviate from the letter of his trust, does so at the peril of afterwards having to satisfy the court that the deviation was necessary and beneficial or amounted to honest conduct covered by an exemption clause in the trust instrument[13].

PARAGRAPH 1

Duty to obey directions of settlement

This is the most important of all the rules relating to the duties of trustees. Although trustees have full power as individuals or as companies to transfer their legal title to others[14], they must not act beyond the limits of the powers conferred upon them by law or the terms of the trust instrument, so that they are strictly obliged to comply with such terms, although it may be that an exemption clause in the trust instrument may excuse them from liability[15], while the court has a discretion to relieve them from liability if they acted honestly and reasonably and ought fairly to be excused for the breach and for omitting to obtain the directions of the court in the matter in question[16]. Thus, if trustees act beyond the capacity conferred upon them by law or the trust instrument and a loss be sustained then such trustees or executors 'will be liable to make it good, however unexpected the result, however little likely

---

11 The power referred to in para (2)(i), above, is conferred by the TA 1925, s 57(1), which specifically refers to 'any sale, lease, mortgage, surrender, release or other disposition, or any purchase, investment, acquisition, expenditure or other transaction'. For Settled Land Act settlements see ampler powers conferred by the Settled Land Act 1925 ('SLA 1925'), s 64.

12 Settled Land and Trustee Acts (Courts' General Powers) Act 1943, s 1, as permanently continued and amended by Emergency Laws (Miscellaneous Provisions) Act 1953, s 9.

13 *Harrison v Randall* (1851) 9 Hare 397; *Armitage v Nurse* [1998] Ch 241, CA; *Walker v Stones* [2001] QB 902. See also TA 1925, s 61.

14 *Rolled Steel Products (Holdings) Ltd v British Steel Corpn* [1986] Ch 246 at 303, per Browne-Wilkinson LJ.

15 *Armitage v Nurse* [1998] Ch 241, CA.

16 TA 1925, s 61; see Art 95 post.

to arise from the course adopted and however free such conduct may have been from any improper motive'[17].

The rule is, as we have seen[18], not binding upon a trustee where the directions of the settlement are illegal. Other exceptions necessarily arise where the directions of the settlement are impracticable (eg if it directs an immediate sale, and no purchaser can be found) or are varied or rendered impossible of fulfilment by statute[19], or are uncertain so that no valid trust is created[20].

Duty to act in accordance with actuary's advice

Where pension fund trusts provide for the trustees to act only in accordance with the advice or determination of the duly appointed actuary then they must so act. As Buckley J said in *Re George Newnes Group Pension Fund*[1], 'where a discretion of this kind is reposed in an expert, the burden rests on any party who criticises the decision of the expert to show that the expert has acted fraudulently or with some improper motive or that he has been guilty of some mistake of a substantial character or has materially misdirected himself ... The court should be very slow to criticise or seek to control the exercise of any discretion or judgment reposed in or required of an expert of this kind.' As Walton J emphasised in *Re Imperial Food Ltd's Pension Scheme*[2], 'The function of an actuary in any situation which is not governed precisely by the provisions of the trust deed is to achieve the greatest possible degree of fairness between the various persons interested under the scheme.' He then upheld an actuary's valuation of the portion of a group fund to pass to purchasers of subsidiaries in the group, where the valuation was based on the 'past service reserve method' which gave rise to a lower figure than an alternative possible valuation based on the 'share of fund method' which would have taken account of a share of the group fund's surplus over the amount required to cover actuarial liabilities. It seems that either view could be held by a competent actuary so that was the end of the case. However, he did indicate obiter that if the choice of method had been for him to make (as it was not) he had no doubt that the 'past service reserve method' was the method to adopt. It still seems[3] that it is open to a competent actuary who has read Walton J's judgment to disagree with it when reviewing all the circumstances and to make a binding valuation on the 'share of fund method'.

Where trustees are to transfer part of the trust fund as certified by the actuary into another pension scheme, but a significant delay occurs during

---

17 *Clough v Bond* (1838) 3 My & Cr 490 at 496–497; *Target Holdings Ltd v Redferns* [1996] AC 421 at 434, HL. Technically, the trustee's accounts are falsified, with new accounts being drawn up to reflect the position if the trustees had not acted beyond their powers; if they act within such powers but act negligently, then the accounts will be surcharged to reflect what would have been the position but for such negligence: see Art 89 post.

18 Articles 11 and 30, ante.

19 Eg under the National Health Service Act 1946, s 7(2); or where the trusts of premises used for the purposes of a voluntary school were modified by the Minister of Education under the powers conferred by the Education (Miscellaneous Provisions) Act 1953, s 14.

20 See Art 8(1) ante.

1 [1986] 2 All ER 802; (1969) 98 J Inst of Actuaries 251; and see *Dean v Prince* [1954] Ch 409, [1954] 1 All ER 749, CA.

2 [1986] 2 All ER 802, [1986] 1 WLR 717.

3 See on trustees' discretion *Wrightson Ltd v Fletcher Challenge Nominees Ltd* [2001] UKPC 23, [2001] OPLR 249, PC at para 29.

which there is a significant change in the value of the trust fund, with resulting implications for the alternative actuarial valuation principles, then the trustees will need to have the position reviewed by the actuary if the transferred amount is to be properly determined[4].

Failure to purchase or sell where directed to do so

If trustees are, by the settlement, directed to call in trust moneys, and to lay them out on a purchase, and they fail to do so, and the fund is lost, they are liable for the loss[5]. Similarly if a trustee for sale omits to sell property as soon as convenient and an event occurring after the convenient period causes loss, although without any default on his part, he is liable for the loss, which would not have happened had he not failed in performing the prescribed duty[6]. Again if a trustee fails to sell real property within a directed 21 year period so that it is producing mining rents for the life tenant that are higher than a reasonable percentage yield the life tenant will be entitled only to a reasonable yield from expiry of the 21-year period[7].

Payment to beneficiaries

Trustees must pay income and capital to the persons entitled without any demand[8]. If there is a permissive power to distribute income amongst a discretionary class with trusts to take effect in default of exercise of the power then failure to exercise the power within a reasonable time of receiving the income extinguishes the power in respect of such income which thereupon is held upon the default trusts[9]. Where there is a compulsory duty to distribute amongst a discretionary class the failure to execute this trust duty leaves the unfulfilled duty still in existence[10].

Direction to invest on particular securities

Where the settlement orders trust funds to be invested on particular securities, but does not clearly restrict the trustee's powers of investment *only* to such securities, the trustees are bound to invest in such securities *or* in those prescribed by statute[11].

Trustees must observe conditions imposed on their discretionary powers

Where there are any conditions attached to the exercise of any of their functions, trustees must strictly perform those conditions. For instance, where they are authorised to lend to a husband with the consent of his wife, they cannot make the advance without first obtaining the required consent,

---

4 *Stannard v Fisons Pension Trust Ltd* [1992] IRLR 27, CA.
5 *Craven v Craddock* [1868] WN 229 (actual decision reversed by CA (1869) 20 LT 638, on the interpretation of a will).
6 *Fry v Fry* (1859) 27 Beav 144.
7 *Wentworth v Wentworth* [1900] AC 163, PC.
8 *Hawksley v May* [1956] 1 QB 304, [1955] 3 All ER 353.
9 *Re Allen-Meyrick's Will Trusts* [1966] 1 All ER 740, [1966] 1 WLR 499; *Re Gulbenkian's Settlement Trusts* (No 2) [1970] Ch 408, [1969] 2 All ER 1173.
10 *Re Locker's Settlement Trusts* [1978] 1 All ER 216, [1977] 1 WLR 1323.
11 Trustee Act 2000 ('TA 2000'), ss 6(1), 7 and 9.

even though they subsequently get it[12].

In one case trustees were empowered to vary investments with the consent of the tenant for life. They sold consols, and first made an investment with such consent upon a contributory mortgage (which was not an authorised security), and subsequently called the money in, and *without* such consent reinvested it upon a mortgage which was an authorised one. It was held that, although there was no loss of capital, they were nevertheless bound to *replace the consols* which had since risen in price. For they sold the consols for the purpose of investing in an unauthorised security, which was contrary to the directions of the settlement; and then, when they realised that investment, they reinvested the proceeds without the consent of the tenant for life, which was again contrary to the directions of the settlement. In both transactions, therefore, they disobeyed the rule now under consideration, and consequently committed breaches of trust, and were bound to place the beneficiaries in the same position as they would have occupied if no such breach had been committed[13].

Trustee acting on expert's advice

If trustees are required not to act without obtaining and considering expert advice[14] (eg that of a financial intermediary authorised under the Financial Services and Markets Act 2000 before disinvesting or investing) then, of course, they must obtain and consider such advice, though they need not follow it if in their honest judgment there appear to be reasonable grounds for such. Failure to obtain such advice before selling a particular investment to purchase a new investment will not it seems make such activity unauthorised and the trustees strictly liable to replace the sold investment unless, fortuitously, the new investment is of better value[15]. If a trust deed, for example, requires pension fund trustees to act in accordance with the advice of an actuary, then the trustees and the beneficiaries are bound by such advice if the actuary's valuation (or apportionment of long term surplus between classes of beneficiaries) is based upon a method that could be used by a competent actuary and there has been no mistake or improper motive on his part[16].

Modification by beneficiaries

As will be seen in Article 69, the rule that trustees must obey the directions of the settlement is subject to modification if all parties beneficially interested

---

12 *Bateman v Davis* (1818) 3 Madd 98; but see *Stevens v Robertson* (1868) 37 LJ Ch 499, where it was held that a consent as to the mode of investing the trust fund might be given, ex post facto. It would seem that where there is a trust for sale *at such time* as A shall approve, the trustees may sell after the death of A, see *Re Powell (No 2)* (1918) 144 LT Jo 459, following *Pearce v Gardner* (1852) 10 Hare 287, 292; and also *Re Ffennell's Settlement* [1918] 1 Ch 91.

13 *Re Massingberd's Settlement* (1890) 63 LT 296; and see also *Re Bennison* (1889) 60 LT 859; and *Stokes v Prance* [1898] 1 Ch 212.

14 TA 2000, s 5.

15 See pp 604–605, post.

16 *Re Imperial Foods Ltd's Pension Scheme* [1986] 2 All ER 802, [1986] 1 WLR 717; *Re George Newnes Group Pension Fund* (1969) 98 J Inst of Actuaries 251.

are of full age and capacity[17], and concur in putting an end to or amending the trust. For the beneficiaries collectively, being the only parties beneficially interested, are entitled, at any moment, provided that they are of age and not under any disability, to depose the trustee, and distribute the trust property between themselves as they may think fit, though (except for exercising their right[18] to replace the trustees with nominated new trustees) they cannot control the exercise by the trustees of their fiduciary powers without putting an end to the trusts altogether[19]. The trustees are nevertheless entitled, if they think fit, to accept the collective directions of the beneficiaries and to act upon them without requiring the trusts to be brought to an end, and a new trust to be constituted. In the case of a modification which involves the distribution of trust property, the trustees should, for their own protection, ensure that any capital gains tax or inheritance tax payable is properly provided for.

If the trust instrument (eg a debenture trust deed or a unit trust deed) expressly provides for its terms to be varied upon a majority vote of voting beneficiaries then, of course, a variation so obtained will be effective[20].

Power of amendment in trust instrument

Powers of revocation, general powers of appointment, special powers of appointment (enabling re-settlements or only sub-settlements)[1] and powers of advancement[2] have been well-known features of trusts. In the last few decades powers of amendment have become features of many trusts, especially pension trusts (which can last indefinitely and where many significant changes can occur in the circumstances of the employer and the number of beneficiaries) and broad discretionary trusts (where circumstances can change dramatically in the course of a trust period of 80 years or more).

An occupational pension scheme will usually contain a very wide power of amendment eg 'The Trustees may at any time by deed with the consent of the Principal Company amend, extend, modify, revoke or replace all or any of the trusts powers and provisions of this Deed or of the Rules with effect from such date as is specified in that deed to the effect that any such amendment, extension, modification, revocation or replacement may be retrospective or retroactive in effect'.

A discretionary trust will often contain a power for the settlor, and the trustees after his death, to add persons to the class of persons who are beneficiaries under a discretionary trust or objects of a discretionary power of appointment as well as a power to exclude persons from such a class. The discretionary trustees will often be given power to vary or revoke any of the administrative powers and provisions of the settlement or to add any further administrative powers and provisions as the trustees may consider expedient (including provisions as to the incidence of costs and expenses between

---

17 This phrase must now be understood in the light of s 1 of the Family Law Reform Act 1969, which came into force on 1 January 1970, providing that as from that date a person attains full age (so ceasing to be an infant) on attaining the age of 18. If on that date a person had attained 18 but not 21, he attained full age on that date.
18 Trusts of Land and Appointment of Trustees Act 1996 ('TLATA 1996'), s 19.
19 *Re Brockbank* [1948] Ch 206, [1948] 1 All ER 287.
20 *Graham Australia Pty Ltd v Perpetual Trustees Ltd* [1992] PLR 193.
 1 See Art 82 post.
 2 See pp 722–724 post.

income and capital)[3].

Often there will be restrictions on the exercise of such powers to ensure that there are no adverse tax consequences for the settlor[4] or the beneficiaries[5], while such powers may well be fiduciary powers[6] preventing those powers from being exercised to benefit the exerciser (except as authorised expressly or by necessary implication) or a personal power vested in an employer subject to the obligation not to exercise it in a way that could damage the relationship of confidence between employer and employee[7]. The power may be exercisable only with the consent of X, whose power to withhold consent can be a fiduciary power or merely a personal power[8] or a personal power subject to the employer-employee relationship of confidence.

The scope of the relevant power and the obligations attaching to its exercise are a matter of construction of the wording of the clause in question in accordance with the surrounding context and in the light of admissible extrinsic evidence[9]. The matrix of facts relating to pension schemes leads to a particularly practical and purposive approach to construction.

There seems[10] a rebuttable presumption that a power of amendment cannot be used to extend its own scope or amend its own terms, particularly where there are express restrictions or limitations on the exercise of such power eg the requisite consent of a third party. On whether exercise of such a power can be retrospective the courts seem to be open-minded in construing the clause in its practical context where a likely need for retrospective amendment may well incline the court to permit this[11].

Deviation sanctioned by the court

It frequently happens that it is not possible to obtain the concurrence of all the beneficiaries, either because some of them are not of age or are otherwise under disability, or because potential beneficiaries include unascertained or unborn persons. Pressure of economic circumstances and the burden of heavy taxation, particularly since the Second World War, have, moreover,

---

3 Cf TA 1925, s 57.
4 For example, Income and Corporation Taxes Act 1988, ss 672, 675; Taxation of Chargeable Gains Act 1992, s 86.
5 Inheritance Act 1984, s 71. In the favoured accumulation and maintenance trusts it is common to provide power to vary the shares of the trust fund to which the beneficiaries will become entitled on or before attaining the age of 25 years: see J Kessler *Drafting Trusts & Will Trusts* (6th edn) paras 14-6 and 14-15 et seq.
6 See pp 29–34 ante.
7 *Imperial Group Pensions Trust Ltd v Imperial Tobacco Ltd* [1991] 1 WLR 589; *British Coal Corpn v British Coal Staff Superannuation Scheme Trustees Ltd* [1995] 1 All ER 912 (overruled in part by *National Grid Co plc v Mayes* [2001] 2 All ER 417).
8 See p 29 ante.
9 *Re Courage Group's Pension Schemes* [1987] 1 WLR 495 at 505–506; *Mettoy Pension Trustees Ltd v Evans* [1990] 1 WLR 1587; *Investors Compensation Scheme Ltd v West Bromwich Building Society* [1998] 1 All ER 98 at 114–115 per Lord Hoffmann; *Cameron v M&W Mack (ESOP) Trustee Ltd* [2002] WTLR 647 at 663–667; *National Grid Co plc v Mayes* [2001] UKHL 20, [2001] 2 All ER 417 paras 16–63 per Lord Hoffmann.
10 *Aitken v Christy Hunt plc* [1991] PLR 1; *British Coal Corpn v British Coal Staff Superannuation Scheme Trustees Ltd* [1995] 1 All ER 912. It seems a power to alter any provision or to amend any provision will permit the addition of new beneficiaries: *Kearns v Hill* (1990) 21 NSWLR 107, CA, cited with apparent approval in *Napier and Ettrick v R F Kershaw Ltd (No 2)* [1999] 1 WLR 756, HL.
11 For example, in the context of pension trusts and, now, Pensions Act 1995, s 71; also unit trusts in *Graham Australia Pty Ltd v Perpetual Trustees Ltd* [1992] PLR 193.

diminished the attractions of rigid settlements and much ingenuity has been devoted to the production of schemes by which trust funds might be divided up, or trusts rearranged, to the mutual advantage of those interested in income and capital respectively, often at the expense of the Revenue. Many such schemes were, it is believed, sanctioned by judges of the Chancery Division in chambers, and a belief that the jurisdiction to do so was unlimited was growing[12], when a sharp rebuff was administered by the House of Lords in *Chapman v Chapman*[13], affirming the decision of the Court of Appeal[14] but further narrowing the jurisdiction therein recognised.

It may now be taken to be settled that, apart from statute, the court's jurisdiction to sanction a deviation from the terms of the trust is limited to three cases which may conveniently be grouped under the following heads:

(1) cases in which the court has allowed the trustees to enter into some business transaction, or to make some investment, which was not authorised by the settlement[15];

(2) cases in which the court has allowed maintenance out of income, which the settlor or testator directed to be accumulated[16];

(3) cases in which the court has approved a compromise on behalf of minors and possible after-born beneficiaries.

The first two groups of cases are dealt with subsequently, but there remains the power of the court to sanction a compromise. It was decided by the majority of the House of Lords in *Chapman v Chapman*[17] that the court's jurisdiction in this regard is limited to cases where the beneficial interests are in dispute, and have not yet been ascertained: it is not a jurisdiction to alter ascertained interests. It was said by Lord Morton of Henryton[18] that—

'If ... there is no doubt as to the beneficial interests, the court is ... exceeding its jurisdiction if it sanctions a scheme for their alteration, whether the scheme is called a "compromise in the wider sense" or an "arrangement" or is given any other name ... I think that Farwell J ... was right when in 1901 he used the words ... "I decline to accept any suggestion that the court has an inherent jurisdiction to alter a man's will because it thinks it beneficial. It seems to me that is quite impossible"'[19].

It was accordingly held that orders sanctioning compromises in a number of cases[20] where the beneficial interests were undisputed and were ascer-

---

12 See, eg the arguments of counsel for the trustees, and the dissenting judgment of Denning LJ in *Re Chapman's Settlement Trusts* [1953] Ch 218 at 226, 227 [1953] 1 All ER 103 at 129, CA; and the argument of counsel for the appellant trustees in *Chapman v Chapman* [1954] AC 429 at 433 et seq, [1954] 1 All ER 798; *Re Duke of Leeds and the Coal Acts 1938 to 1943* [1947] Ch 525 at 557, [1947] 2 All ER 200 at 216.

13 [1954] AC 429, [1954] 1 All ER 798.

14 *Re Chapman's Settlement Trusts* [1953] Ch 218, [1953] 1 All ER 103.

15 This jurisdiction has been almost entirely superseded by the statutory jurisdiction to vary trusts under the Variation of Trusts Act 1958, below, and by that under the TA 1925, s 57, and the SLA 1925, s 64, and is further considered in the notes to paragraph (2) of this Article; p 524, post. Trustees' powers of investment have been greatly widened by the TA 2000: see Art 53, post.

16 *Re Collins* (1886) 32 Ch D 229; *Re Alford* (1886) 32 Ch D 383; see further pp 709–717 et seq, post.

17 [1954] AC 429, [1954] 1 All ER 798.

18 [1954] AC 429 at 461, [1954] 1 All ER 798 at 814.

19 *Re Walker* [1901] 1 Ch 879 at 885.

20 For example, *Re Duke of Leeds and Re the Coal Acts 1938 to 1943* [1947] Ch 525, [1947] 2 All ER 200. The decisions in *Re Downshire Settled Estates,* and *Re Blackwell's Settlement Trusts* [1953] Ch 218, [1953] 1 All ER 103 (which were heard by the Court of Appeal at the same time as *Re* tained, had been made without jurisdiction.

The inconvenience and anomalies resulting from this decision[1] led to the enactment of the Variation of Trusts Act 1958.

Variation of Trusts Act 1958

This Act (which does not extend to Scotland or Northern Ireland) applies whenever any property, real or personal, is held on trusts arising under any will, settlement or other disposition, other than trusts affecting property settled by Act of Parliament[2]. It authorises the court[3] order to approve on behalf of a person who comes within any one of four specified categories of persons any arrangement (by whomsoever it is proposed, and whether or not there is any other person beneficially interested who is capable of assenting to it) varying or revoking all or any of the trusts or enlarging the powers of the trustees of managing or administering any of the property subject to the trusts.

Persons on whose behalf approval may be given

The categories of persons are thus specified in the Act[4]:

'(1) (a)   any person having, directly or indirectly, an interest, whether vested or contingent, under the trusts who by reason of infancy or other incapacity is incapable of assenting, or

(1) (b)   any person (whether ascertained or not) who may become entitled, directly or indirectly, to an interest under the trusts as being at a future date or on the happening of a future event a person of any specified description or a member of any specified class of persons, so however that this paragraph shall not include any person who would be of that description, or a member of that class, as the case may be, if the said date had fallen or the said event had happened at the date of the application to the court, or

(1) (c)   any person unborn, or.

(1) (d)   any person in respect of any discretionary interest of his under protective trusts where the interest of the principal beneficiary has not failed or determined'[5].

Broadly the effect of the Act is to enable the court to give approval on behalf of persons who are unable to give approval for themselves (eg because

---

Chapman's Settlement Trusts), though overruled so far as they rested on the inherent jurisdiction to sanction compromises, may, perhaps, be supported as an exercise of the statutory jurisdiction to sanction a 'transaction' under s 64 of the SLA 1925; see p 527, post.

1 Cf *Re Harrison's Share under a Settlement; Re Williams' Will Trusts; Re Ropner's Settlement* [1955] Ch 260, [1954] 2 All ER 453, where Roxburgh J recalled certain orders made but not drawn up before the House of Lords decision.

2 Variation of Trusts Act 1958, s 1(1), (5).

3 See pp 520–521, post.

4 Variation of Trusts Act 1958, s 1(1).

5 'Protective trusts' means the trusts specified in s 33(1)(i) and (ii) of the TA 1925 or any like trusts, and 'the principal beneficiary' has the same meaning as in that section; 'discretionary interest' means an interest arising under s 33(1)(ii) of the TA 1925, or any like trust: Variation of Trusts Act 1958, s 1(2). As to protective trusts, see pp 210–214, ante. Of 'like trusts' Megarry J in *Re Wallace's Settlement* [1968] 1 WLR 711 at 716, said, 'The word "like" requires not identity but similarity; and similarity in substance suffices, without the need for similarity in form or detail or wording'. In *Re Bristol's Settled Estates* [1965] 1 WLR 469, where discretionary trusts were to arise for six months on the life tenant's death whether or not there had been a forfeiture, the trusts were held to be outside paragraph (d).

minors or unborn or not yet ascertained) so long as for the benefit of such persons, unless those persons are only potentially interested as beneficiaries of the discretionary trust that springs up on failure of the principal beneficiary's interest, but which has not sprung up.

As Mummery LJ states[6], 'The court is merely contributing on behalf of infants and unborn and unascertained persons the binding assents to the arrangements which they, unlike an adult beneficiary, cannot give. The 1958 Act has thus been viewed by the courts as a statutory extension of the consent principle embodied in the rule in *Saunders v Vautier*. The principle recognises the rights of beneficiaries who are *sui juris* and together absolutely entitled to the trust property, to exercise their proprietary rights to overbear and defeat the intentions of a testator or settlor'. Lord Maugham LC has also emphasised[7] that, 'The rule has no application unless all the persons who have any present or contingent interest in the property are *sui juris* and consent.' It would seem that Lord Maugham was concerned with 'vested' or contingent interests, since present interests may be vested or contingent, (as where B, aged 26 years, currently owns a vested life interest and a life interest contingent on attaining 30 years of age) but not with persons only having hopes, like objects of a power of appointment.

A distinction needs to be drawn between a contingent interest, which is property capable of being assigned or subjected to trusts, and a mere expectancy or *spes* incapable of being so assigned or subjected[8], although it can be the subject of a contract for value[9].

A trust in favour of A, if on the death of B he shall be the heir of B, (so becoming the holder of any peerage or baronetcy of B), or one of the next of kin of B or the spouse of B or a member of the Athenaeum club, confers on A a present contingent interest, which becomes vested if on B's death A has the required characteristic. In contrast, a trust in favour of whomsoever shall at the death of B be the spouse or heir of B or one of his next of kin or a member of the Athenaeum, confers no interest contingent or otherwise on anyone until the death of B, whereupon a proprietary interest is acquired by any person with the required characteristic[10]. Until then such person has no more than an expectancy or hope of qualifying as a person with the relevant characteristic, but if he does so qualify then he obtains a proprietary interest to which the trustees must give effect.

Such a presumptive person is thus not in the same position as someone who is merely an object of a power of appointment and who hopes it will be exercised in his favour some day[11]. The difference is that a person who is an object of a power is already a person of the specified description or a member of the specified class and is ready to benefit as soon as the trustees wish to exercise the power in his favour, but they are under no obligation to exercise such power. A presumptive person has to wait and see if on the specified future date or event he will become entitled to an interest under the trust as then a person of the specified description or a member of the specified class, when the trustees *must* benefit him as required under the trust. Thus, the

---

6 *Goulding v James* [1997] 2 All ER 239 at 247.

7 *Berry v Geen* [1938] AC 575 at 582. Further see Article 69 post.

8 *Re Brooks' Settlement Trusts* [1939] Ch 993; *Lovett v Lovett* [1898] 1 Ch 82.

9 *Holroyd v Marshall* (1862) 10 HL Cas 191; *Re Ellenborough* [1903] 1 Ch 697 at 200; *Williams v IRC* [1965] NZLR 395, CA.

10 *Re Earl of Midleton's Will Trusts* [1969] 1 Ch 600 at 607.

11 *Re Brooks' Settlement Trusts* [1939] Ch 993.

consent of the presumptive person is required before the trust property can be dealt with in any way prejudicial to the proprietary rights such person is bound to acquire if qualifying as a person of the specified description or class. It will be seen that paragraph (b) enables the court to consent on behalf of presumptive persons, except where persons of full age and capacity have been ascertained who would be qualifying persons if the future date or future event had occurred at the date of the application to the court, so that they can decide for themselves whether or not to consent.

Paragraph (a)

The effect of paragraph (a) is to enable the court to give approval on behalf of a minor or a mental patient[12] who has, 'directly or indirectly'[13], an interest, whether vested or contingent, under the trusts', but not on behalf of a person of full age and capacity with such 'an interest'. 'An interest' and 'a discretionary interest of his under protective trusts' are used in paragraphs (b) and (d), so that an interest should clearly cover not just vested or contingent fixed interests but also interests of a beneficiary under a discretionary trust[14], especially when a discretionary trust can be terminated if all the discretionary beneficiaries between them entitled to the equitable proprietary interest in the trust property so agree, being of full age and capacity[15].

It seems, as Warner J has pointed out[16], that 'interest' has a technical legal meaning that excludes a mere expectancy or *spes*, eg a hope of benefiting as the object of a power of appointment. This makes good sense if the consent of any objects of any power of appointment is not necessary to the termination of a trust by all the persons of full age and capacity with vested or contingent proprietary interests, including interests as beneficiaries under discretionary trusts. In *Vandervell v IRC* Lord Upjohn[17], a distinguished Chancery lawyer, remarked at the end of his speech that if a trustee held property on a trust (express or resulting) for the settlor, but with the trustee having a valid special power of appointment over the trust property, the settlor could at any time revoke that power. He could then recover absolute legal and beneficial ownership of the property from the trustee.

An explanation for the right to revoke the power could be that the settlor had not made a completed perfect gift of the whole bundle of his legal and beneficial proprietary rights in the property, but had only made it possible for someone to receive a future gift by authorising the trustee to make such a gift. This gratuitous authority could be revoked at will by the settlor: the

---

12 Under s 1(3) of the VTA 1958 the Court of Protection needs to determine the question of benefit eg *Re CL* [1969] 1 Ch 587.

13 For example, under a sub-settlement.

14 As assumed in *Re Clitheroe's Settlement Trusts* [1959] 1 WLR 1159; *Re Bristol's Settled Estates* [1965] 1 WLR 469; *Re Steed's Will Trusts* [1960] Ch 407 at 420 per Lord Evershed MR. Contrast the meaning of 'interest, whether vested or contingent' in TA 1925, s 32(1)(c): *Re Beckett's Settlement* [1940] Ch 279.

15 *Re Smith* [1928] Ch 915; *Re Beckett's Settlement* [1940] Ch 279 at 285.

16 *Knocker v Youle* [1986] 2 All ER 914 at 916–917; *Gartside v IRC* [1968] AC 553 at 606 and 617–618. Section 22 of the TLATA 1996 defines 'beneficiary' for the purpose of a *Saunders v Vautier* removal of trustees under s 19 as 'any person who under the trust has an *interest* in property subject to the trust'.

17 [1967] 2 AC 291 at 317.

conferment of a special power to make a gift is not itself a gift of any property[18].

An alternative explanation is that the rule in *Saunders v Vautier* enables the sole beneficial owner or all those persons who are of full age and capacity and between them own all the vested and contingent equitable proprietary interests in the trust property[19] to terminate the trust and divide the property between themselves as they all unanimously agree, unless those interests are defeasible by a person (whether ascertained or not) who may become entitled to a proprietary interest under the trust as being on a future date or event a person of a specified description or a member of a specified class (eg on X's death heir or spouse or next of kin of X or member of the Athenaeum): the interests of such persons are very close to contingent entitlements under contingent gifts[20], as opposed to mere hopes of persons awaiting the discretionary exercise of a power which may never be exercised in their favour, (especially if the terms of the trust instrument expressly or by necessary implication reveal that such persons are very peripheral objects of a power of appointment, not having any rights to see the trust accounts and make the trustees account for their trusteeship, such rights in the beneficiaries entitled in default of exercise of the power being sufficient on their own for the irreducible obligation to account at the core of the trust concept)[1]. However, in *Re Sharp's Settlement Trusts*[2] Pennycuick V-C (albeit in the context of 'absolutely' within s 31(2)(i)(b) of the Trustee Act 1925 and without considering the above points) held that absolutely entitled meant indefeasibly entitled free from any power of appointment which may in the future defeat such entitlement.

Only if the alternative explanation be the correct one will beneficiaries under a trust created by S be able on their own to terminate it under the *Saunders v Vautier* rule if the trustees have a fiduciary power of appointment (that they cannot validly release[3]) in favour of X (whether an adult or minor) or some person(s) satisfying a description. The hopes of X or such person(s) as objects of a power of appointment conferring authority on the trustee to make future gifts of property on S's behalf and so conferring no immediate proprietary interest, will then last only for so long as the trust endures. The trust will not terminate till all the beneficiaries, whose vested and contingent equitable proprietary interests cover the whole of the trust property, are all of full age and capacity and unanimously decide to terminate the trust, which will only be after the date of some future date or event occasioning a person

---

18 *Melville v IRC* [2001] EWCA Civ 1247, [2002] 1 WLR 407; *Re Armstrong* (1886) 17 QBD 521, CA. Where S has created a discretionary trust for the descendants of B for 80 years and, due to a calamity, such class dies out after 10 years, so there is a resulting trust for S, it seems harsh if S cannot terminate the trust and recover the trust property if he had happened to insert into the trust a power to appoint income or capital to the Red Cross. While an irrevocable trust for the descendants of B had been created, perhaps the 'vicarious' special power (*Re Wills Trust Deed* [1964] Ch 219 at 228–229) should be construed to be an irrevocable power only so long as there subsisted the trust for descendants of B. Otherwise S should appoint compliant trustees under s 19 of the TLATA 1996.

19 See cases cited in footnotes 6 and 7 above.

20 See text to footnote 10 above.

1 *Re Angora Trust, Rosewood Trust Ltd v Schmidt* [2001] WTLR 1081; and see p 673 post.

2 [1973] Ch 331.

3 Personal powers may be released to avoid problems as in *Re Christie-Miller's Settlement Trusts* [1961] 1 All ER 855n; *Re Courtauld's Settlement* [1965] 2 All ER 544n, and *Re Ball's Settlement Trusts* [1968] 2 All ER 438, but fiduciary powers cannot be released without authority in the trust instrument: *Re Wills Trust Deeds* [1964] Ch 219.

becoming entitled to an equitable proprietary interest where there is such a person who may become so entitled on some future date or event as being a person of a specified description or a member of a specified class.

If, in the light of *Re Sharp's Settlement Trusts*, the beneficiaries cannot exercise *Saunders v Vautier* rights without the consent of all the objects of any power of appointment[4], it becomes odd that it does not seem that the court can provide such consent for an infant under paragraph (a) when it can if the infant were in the stronger position of having a fixed vested or contingent interest or an interest under a discretionary trust. It also becomes odd that under paragraph (b) the court can consent on behalf of unascertained presumptive persons who may become entitled to an interest under the trust as being on a future date or event a person of any specified description or a member of a specified class but not on behalf of an unascertained object of a power of appointment, because such an object is already qualified as a person of a specified description or a member of specified class and so already entitled to benefit before any future date or event if the trustee in its discretion decides to benefit him, without being obliged in any way in that behalf. Thus, trusts can never be varied under the 1958 Act so as to affect trustees' powers to appoint to objects who are minors or unborn or otherwise unascertained (or to objects of full age and capacity who object). Even if they could, it is hard to see how deletion of the power could confer any benefit on the objects, so perhaps the 1958 Act should be amended so as then not to require any benefits as for interests under discretionary trusts within paragraph (d) that only arise on termination of a life interest under a protective trust.

Paragraph (b)

As already discussed, the effect of paragraph (b) is that the court can consent to an arrangement if for the benefit of persons who will presumptively become entitled, directly or indirectly, to an interest under a trust (but not a *spes*) as being on a future date or event a person of any specified description (eg the heir or widow of a living person) or a member of any specified class of persons (eg the next of kin of a living person or a member of the Athenaeum club). However, no consent can be given in respect of such a presumptive person if already ascertained on the basis that the future date or event had occurred at the date of the application to the court.

A case which illustrates paragraph (b) is *Re Suffert's Settlement*[5]. There a trust fund was held on protective trusts for the applicant during her life and after her death on trust for any children of hers who should attain twenty-one. If no child attained a vested interest, the applicant had a general testamentary power of appointment and, subject to that, the fund was to be held after her death on trust for her statutory next of kin. The applicant was a spinster aged 61 and sought the court's approval to an arrangement. Of the three people who would have been her statutory next of kin at the time of the case, all were

---

4 This is quite a problem if there is a power to appoint to (or add to a class of beneficiaries or objects) a large class of persons which could extend to anyone in the world except the trustees, the settlor and his spouse – unless one could construe such power, even if vested in trustees, as not a fiduciary justiciable power but an inherently releasable personal power unchallengeable in its exercise unless involving a fraud on the power: but see p 97 ante and p 734 post.

5 [1961] Ch 1, [1960] 3 All ER 561 (where it was assumed without any discussion that consent could be given on behalf of unascertained objects of power).

of full age and capacity but only one had consented. Buckley J held that he had no power to give approval on behalf of, and thus to bind, the other two people because they fell within the ambit of the concluding words of paragraph (b).

A similar case is *Re Moncrieff's Settlement Trust*[6]. There a trust fund was held on trust for the settlor for life, with remainder to such persons or purposes as the settlor should by will or codicil appoint and in default of appointment for her statutory next of kin if she had died an intestate widow. The settlor applied for an order approving apportionment of the fund between those contingently entitled and herself. She had one adopted son who would become entitled as statutory next of kin under the default clause if he survived her. Buckley J held he had no power to give approval on behalf of the adopted son since the son fell within the ambit of the concluding words of paragraph (b), but he could give approval on behalf of all other possible next of kin who could only become entitled if the adopted son predeceased the settlor since they fell outside the ambit of the concluding words of paragraph (b): the only possible next of kin on the hypothesis that the settlor had died at the date of the application was the adopted son.

These two cases were followed by Warner J in *Knocker v Youle*[7] where ultimately the issue of the settlor's four sisters were to take the trust fund in certain remote contingencies defeasible by A or B exercising a testamentary power of appointment. At the date the originating summons was issued A and B (still alive) had made wills fully exercising their powers of appointment. It was held that since such issue *now* had contingent defeasible interests they could not fall within (b) as persons 'who *may become* entitled to an interest', so (b) only covers persons who have an interest in the eyes of the law. Even if they had prima facie fallen within (b), they would have been excluded by the proviso, since there were 17 cousins who would have satisfied the class description at the date of the application to the court if all prerequisites had been satisfied at that date. It mattered not that A and B had made wills exercising their powers of appointment since the proviso was merely designed to identify the presumptive members of the class and did not advert to the question whether they would or would not have become entitled at the date of the application.

The provisions outlined above give rise to several difficulties. It has been assumed[8] that 'at the date of the application to the court' in paragraph (b) means the date on which the originating summons or, nowadays, the claim form was issued, so that the relevant parties can then be ascertained. However, take the case where there is a trust for A for life, remainder if she dies without having been made bankrupt during her lifetime to A absolutely and, subject thereto, to her statutory next of kin living at her death in equal shares, otherwise for the Red Cross absolutely. A's spouse is deceased, like her parents, and she has a daughter, D, and a 45 years old sister, S, 12 years younger than herself. Under paragraph (b) the court can approve on S's behalf but not D's behalf since D is alive at the date of the issue of the claim form. But what if D dies of a terminal disease just before the court hears the VTA application? Can the court ignore S or, upon hearing S refuses to consent, override her refusal? Under s 3(1) of the Human Rights Act 1998

6 [1962] 3 All ER 838n, [1962] 1 WLR 1344.
7 [1986] 2 All ER 914, [1986] 1 WLR 934.
8 *Re Suffert's Settlement* [1961] Ch 1 at 5; *Knocker v Youle* [1986] 1 WLR 934 at 938.

ambiguous legislation must be interpreted, so far as possible, compatibly with the Human Rights Convention (and Article 1 of the First Protocol protecting persons from being deprived of their possessions) so that the court could well construe 'at the date of application to the court' as covering the date of the court hearing.

Another difficulty lies in the relationship of paragraph (a) to paragraph (b). On the face of it, they appear to be mutually exclusive, the first applying where a person has an interest under the trusts, the second where he has no actual interest but some kind of presumptive *spes successionis*. But this leads to strange consequences. Suppose an infant with a *spes successionis* within the terms of paragraph (b) fell within the ambit of the concluding words of that paragraph, so that the court had no power under paragraph (b) to give approval on his behalf. Would the court then have power to give it under paragraph (a)? Buckley J in *Re Suffert's Settlement*[9] expressed the opinion obiter that it would: he said that the persons on whose behalf the court was precluded by the concluding words of paragraph (b) from giving approval under that paragraph did not include 'infants, because they come under a different heading in the Act'. Yet it is not clear from the wording of the Act that this is so. Counsel had argued that it was not (at the same time raising other points of difficulty) and the learned judge did not deal with his arguments. The view of Buckley J is certainly a commonsense one, since it would be extraordinary if the court could bind an infant with an actual interest but could not bind one with a mere presumptive *spes successionis*.

On the face of it, doubts might also arise as to whether the Act authorised the court to give approval to an arrangement on behalf of unascertained future spouses under paragraph (b). Any unmarried woman over sixteen years of age is a person who would be the wife of a propositus if the event of the marriage had happened at the date of the application to the court so that such a person would prima facie appear to be excluded by the closing words of paragraph (b) from the jurisdiction of the court. However, the courts have tacitly assumed they have power to approve arrangements on behalf of unascertained future spouses[10]. This can be supported by construing 'any person' as meaning 'any ascertained person' in view of the fact that 'any person' is not as in the opening words of paragraph (b) qualified by the words (whether ascertained or not).

Paragraph (c)

Consent can be given by the court in respect of any person unborn without any restrictions as to prospective interests or expectancies so the problems canvassed in relation to paragraphs (a) and (b) do not arise.

Paragraphs (a), (b) and (c) generally

Since the paragraphs (a), (b), (c) and (d) are listed in the alternative if beneficiaries fall within paragraph (d), as well as earlier paragraphs, approval may be given under paragraph (d) so as to dispense with the need to prove

---

9 [1961] Ch 1 at 5.
10 *Re Clitheroe's Settlement Trusts* [1959] 3 All ER 789, [1959] 1 WLR 1159; *Re Roberts' Settlement Trusts* (1959) Times, 8 April; *Re Steed's Will Trusts* [1960] Ch 407 at 420; *Re Lister's Will Trusts* [1962] 3 All ER 737, [1962] 1 WLR 1441. Further see JW Harris, *Variation of Trusts* (1975) pp 36–40.

benefit in respect of the beneficiaries' interests under the protective trusts[11].

The jurisdiction of the court under the Act is, it is thought, limited to authorising an arrangement which the beneficiaries themselves could have authorised if they had all been ascertained and of full age and capacity. Certainly, the court has no power to override the objections (however unreasonable), or to dispense with the consent, of persons on whose behalf the Act does not expressly authorise it to give approval, even when such persons are very numerous and difficult to ascertain[12]. If a beneficiary has disappeared in circumstances where his death is very probable but not certain it may be that a court might make more use of a Benjamin order[13], permitting a variation affecting the beneficiary's interest and so freeing the trustees from potential personal liability but preserving for the beneficiary the right to trace.

The court has power to approve an arrangement which the trustees do not consider desirable, though the views of the trustees are entitled to respect and will be considered[14]. Nor need the court be satisfied that the arrangement is for the benefit of the person who proposes it[15] or for that of other beneficiaries who are of full age and capacity and consent on their own behalf[16]. Except for applications involving protective trusts, the views of the settlor have little, if any, relevance or weight[17].

Beneficial Arrangements for which approval may be given

The power of the court is to approve 'if it thinks fit'

> 'any arrangement ... varying or revoking all or any of the trusts, or enlarging the powers of the trustees of managing or administering any of the property subject to the trusts: Provided that except by virtue of paragraph (d) ... the court shall not approve an arrangement on behalf of any person unless the carrying out thereof would be for the benefit of that person.'

'ARRANGEMENT'. First, then, what is an arrangement? Apparently the meaning of this word is not confined to an arrangement inter partes—a scheme which two or more people have worked out. Lord Evershed MR said in *Re Steed's Will Trusts*[18]:

> 'I think that the word ... is deliberately used in the widest possible sense so as to cover any proposal which any person may put forward for varying or revoking the trusts.'

(Or, presumably, for enlarging the powers of the trustees.)

'VARYING OR REVOKING'. So far as the trusts are concerned, the arrangement must be one which either varies or revokes[19] them. It seems that it cannot be one which replaces the trusts with quite different ones, because this would amount neither to a variation nor to a simple revocation. But the

11 *Re Turner's Will Trusts* [1960] Ch 122 at 127.
12 As, for instance, the class of beneficiaries in *Re Eden* [1957] 2 All ER 430, [1957] 1 WLR 788 and *Knocker v Youle* [1986] 2 All ER 914, [1986] 1 WLR 934.
13 *Re Benjamin* [1902] 1 Ch 723; *Re Green's Will Trusts* [1985] 3 All ER 455.
14 *Re Steed's Will Trusts* [1960] Ch 407, [1960] 1 All ER 487, CA.
15 *Re Steed's Will Trusts* [1960] Ch 407, [1960] 1 All ER 487, CA.
16 *Re Berry's Settlement* [1966] 3 All ER 431n, [1966] 1 WLR 1515.
17 *Goulding v James* [1997] 2 All ER 239 at 251, per Mummery LJ, but cp CPR r 64.4(2).
18 [1960] Ch 407, [1960] 1 All ER 487, CA.
19 For a case involving revocation, see *Re Seale's Marriage Settlement* [1961] Ch 574, [1961] 3 All ER 136.

line dividing variation from replacement is sometimes indistinct. Thus in one case[20], although the proposed arrangement would revoke all the prior trusts and establish new ones, it was held to amount only to a variation because the new trusts would in many respects be similar to the old. Megarry J said that

'... the old trusts may fairly be said to be varied by the arrangement whether the variation is effected directly by leaving some of the old words standing and altering others, or indirectly, by revoking all the old words and then setting up new trusts partly, though not wholly, in the likeness of the old.'

In a later case[1] the same judge went still further, saying:

'If an arrangement changes the whole substratum of a trust, then it may well be that it cannot be regarded merely as varying that trust. But if an arrangement, while leaving the substratum, effectuates the purpose of the original trust by other means, it may still be possible to regard that arrangement as merely varying the original trusts, even though the means employed are wholly different and even though the form is completely changed.'

In this latter case, Megarry J expressly distinguished the case of *Re T's Settlement Trusts*[2]. In that case Wilberforce J had declined to approve a proposed arrangement on the ground that it amounted to a completely new re-settlement, not to a variation, and that there was therefore no jurisdiction under the Act to approve it. But this was only one of the grounds on which he rested his decision, the other being that even if the court did have such jurisdiction it should none the less refuse approval in the particular circumstances of the case.

ENLARGEMENT OF POWERS. In cases in which the arrangement has proposed to enlarge the powers of the trustees, the most frequent desire appears to have been to enlarge their powers of investment[3]. However the Trustee Act 2000 now confers extensive powers of investment so the need for extra powers is very limited, eg to permit purchase of land outside the UK[4] or the acquisition of an asset that is not the 'making of an investment' but the 'application' of trust funds[5].

Cases in which the court will approve an arrangement enlarging the powers of the trustees are not, of course, confined to those involving investment. Thus in one case[6] approval was given to the retention of remuneration by director-trustees; and in another[7], involving the trusts of a will where the testator had died before 1926, approval was given to an arrangement which gave the trustees the power of advancement contained in s 32 of the Trustee Act 1925[8].

Nowadays, where no alteration of beneficial interests is sought so that it is only wider administrative powers that are sought, it is more convenient to use s 57 of the Trustee Act 1925 as emphasised in *Anker-Petersen v Anker-Petersen*[9].

20 *Re Holt's Settlement* [1969] 1 Ch 100, [1968] 1 All ER 470.
 1 *Re Ball's Settlement* [1968] 2 All ER 438, [1968] 1 WLR 899.
 2 [1964] Ch 158, sub nom *Re Towler's Settlement Trusts* [1963] 3 All ER 759.
 3 *Trustees of the British Museum v A-G* [1984] 1 WLR 418; *Steel v Wellcome Custodian Trustees* [1988] 1 WLR 167; *Anker-Petersen v Anker-Petersen* [2000] WTLR 581.
 4 TA 2000, s 8(1).
 5 TA 2000, s 3(1).
 6 *Re Cooper's Settlement* [1962] Ch 826, [1961] 3 All ER 636.
 7 *Re Lister's Will Trusts* [1962] 3 All ER 737, [1962] 1 WLR 1441.
 8 See Article 67, post.
 9 [2000] WTLR 581.

The advantages of s 57 are that the trustees are normally the applicants (unlike the position under the 1958 Act[10]), it is not essential to obtain the consent of every beneficiary of full age and capacity, the court is not required to given consent on behalf of every category of beneficiary separately but considers their interests collectively in income on the one hand and in capital on the other, so that s 57 applications are cheaper and more straight-forward, especially because they are taken in chambers while 1958 Act applications are taken in open court.

'BENEFIT': STATEMENT OF GENERAL RULE AND EXCEPTION. Having noted the extent of the court's power under the Act, it is appropriate to consider its exercise. The power is of course discretionary and the only guidance which the Act gives on its exercise is that the courts shall not approve an arrangement on behalf of any person unless the carrying out of that arrangement would be for his benefit. To this, however, there is one exception: where the arrangement is approved by virtue of paragraph (d) of s 1(1)–that is, on behalf of a person who has a discretionary interest–under protective trusts where the interest of the principal beneficiary has not failed or determined—no benefit need be shown to accrue to the person on whose behalf approval is given.

'BENEFIT': THE EXCEPTION DISCUSSED. This exception means that the provision of a 'compensation fund' for persons who fall within its terms, as was customary in some schemes presented to the court before the passing of the Act, is not an essential pre-requisite to the court's approval. But this does not imply that the interests of such persons can be ignored entirely; and the court must consider not only their interests but also the reason why they figure in the trust at all—in other words, the settlor's intention in providing the principal beneficiary with a protected rather than a full life interest[11]. The exception does not, therefore, lessen the extent of the court's discretion[12]. Thus even where, in the case of a spinster with a protected life interest, the only persons interested under the prospective discretionary trust are issue (whose advent is made very unlikely by the age of the life tenant) and a future husband (whose existence is made unlikely by the life tenant's lack of desire to marry) the court will still refuse to give approval on behalf of the 'spectral' discretionary beneficiaries to an arrangement which would frustrate the settlor's intention to protect the life tenant against her own possible improvidence[13]. And where a compensation fund *is* provided for the prospective discretionary beneficiaries, provisions affecting it must be fair: thus, the court may refuse to approve an arrangement which benefits only those beneficiaries who are already born and ignores entirely the possibility of unborn beneficiaries[14]. Where property is held on protective trusts and the protected life tenant applies to the court to vary them evidence, including evidence of the financial position of the applicant and the applicant's spouse, must be put before the court to show to what extent the protective trusts

10 *Re Druce's Settlement Trusts* [1962] 1 WLR 363.
11 *Re Steed's Will Trusts* [1960] Ch 407, [1960] 1 All ER 487, CA; *Re Burney's Settlement Trusts* [1961] 1 All ER 856, [1961] 1 WLR 545; *Gibbon v Mitchell* [1990] 3 All ER 338 at 343; *Goulding v James* [1997] 2 All ER 239, CA.
12 *Re Steed's Will Trusts* [1960] Ch 407, [1960] 1 All ER 487, CA; *Re Burney's Settlement Trusts* [1961] 1 All ER 856, [1961] 1 WLR 545; *Gibbon v Mitchell* [1990] 3 All ER 338 at 343; *Goulding v James* [1997] 2 All ER 239, CA.
13 *Re Steed's Will Trusts* [1960] Ch 407, [1960] 1 All ER 487, CA.
14 *Re Poole's Settlement's Trusts* [1959] 2 All ER 340, [1959] 1 WLR 651.

continue to serve any useful purpose[15].

It should be noted that the exception applies only to discretionary trusts which will arise on the forfeiture of a protected life interest. It does not apply to discretionary trusts which, though still future ones, are not framed to arise in this way, or are not framed to arise *only* in this way[16]. Still less does it apply to immediate discretionary trusts[17]. In cases where it does not apply, the arrangement proposed must therefore be shown to be for the benefit of the discretionary beneficiaries[18]. But where the discretionary trust does fall within the terms of paragraph (d), the court has power to approve it under that paragraph on behalf of potential beneficiaries who are unborn as well as those who are already in existence[19]. It should also be noted that the protective trusts must be either those specified in s 33(1)(i)–(ii) of the Trustee Act 1925 'or any like trusts'[20]. As to the last four words, see the discussion in *Re Wallace's Settlements*[1], where Megarry J said:

> 'The word "like" requires not identity but similarity; and similarity in substance suffices, without the need of similarity in form or detail or wording.'

'BENEFIT': THE GENERAL RULE DISCUSSED. Having considered the exception, it is necessary to return to the general rule: that the court cannot approve an arrangement on behalf of any person unless it is for his benefit.

In deciding whether a scheme is for a person's benefit the court will consider it as a whole. Typically a scheme will enhance a protected life interest into an ordinary life interest, eliminate the interests of unborn children unlikely to come into existence, insert a new perpetuity or accumulation period into the new trust arising by virtue of the 1958 Act, postpone the vesting of capital or, even income in a young person, or avoid or mitigate taxation by modifying or deleting discretionary powers or by partitioning the trust fund between income and capital beneficiaries. In the latter event the emphasis is on tax savings and not just the actuarial value of the interests of the various capital beneficiaries but also the sudden death values, the scheme being disadvantageous to them to the extent that the risk materialises of an income beneficiary failing to survive for his normal life expectancy, so that provision for any shortfall is normally required to be made via insurance or a personal covenant. However, the word 'benefit' is not to be narrowly interpreted or restricted to matters of finance. Thus:

(a) If a person derives no financial benefit from a proposed arrangement the court may still approve it on his behalf. In one case[2] a settlement provided that a beneficiary should be entitled absolutely to certain capital at the age of 21. The beneficiary had shown herself to be immature and irrespon-

---

15 *Re Baker's Settlement Trusts* [1964] 1 All ER 482n, [1964] 1 WLR 336n.
16 *Re Bristol's Settled Estates* [1964] 3 All ER 939, [1965] 1 WLR 469.
17 *Re Clitheroe's Settlement Trusts* [1959] 3 All ER 789, [1959] 1 WLR 1159.
18 *Re Bristol's Settled Estates* [1964] 3 All ER 939, [1965] 1 WLR 469.
19 *Re Turner's Will Trusts* [1968] 1 All ER 321, [1968] 1 WLR 227. Strictly, the views expressed on this point by Danckwerts J in this case were obiter, but later cases have been decided on the implicit assumption that the position is as stated in the text, and there would certainly seem to be no sensible reason why benefits should have to be proved in the case of unborn beneficiaries but not in the case of those already in existence.
20 1958 Act, s 1(2).
 1 [1968] 2 All ER 209, [1968] 1 WLR 711 and see *Thomas v IRC* [1981] STC 382 at 390.
 2 *Re T's Settlement Trusts* [1964] Ch 158, sub nom *Re Towler's Settlement Trusts* [1963] 3 All ER 759, followed in *Re Holt's Settlement* [1969] 1 Ch 100 at 121 Megarry J stating, 'The word "benefit" is plainly not confined to financial benefit but may extend to moral or social benefit'.

sible as regards money and the court was asked, just before she attained 21, to approve on her behalf an arrangement which would deprive her of her right to capital entirely and give her a mere protected life interest instead. Wilberforce J refused approval to this, but he did approve on her behalf a less drastic scheme which had the effect of postponing her right to the capital for a period and giving her a protected life interest during that period. It could no doubt be argued that, although the immediate effect of this arrangement was one of financial deprivation, it was however for the beneficiary's financial benefit in the long term and thus that the decision does not conclusively support the proposition just advanced. The point has, however, been considered in two other reported cases: *Re Tinker's Settlement*[3] and *Re C L*[4].

In the first of these a male beneficiary was to receive his share of settled capital absolutely on attaining 30. If he died under that age, his share was to accrue to his sister's share, which was settled on her for life with remainder to her children. Apparently through a drafting error, a provision that if the male beneficiary died under 30 leaving children his share should go to those children rather than accrue to the share of the sister had been omitted. The court was asked to approve, on behalf of the sister's unborn children, an arrangement whereby this provision would be inserted on the ground that, although this could not be for their financial benefit and might be to their financial detriment, it was 'reasonable and fair'. Russell J refused approval, saying that he could not bring himself to think that he would be benefiting the children if he gave away property which might accrue to them. But in *Re C L* a patient who was of advanced age and mentally ill[5] owned substantial property and had a large income. A small part of this income was derived from property in which she had a protected life interest under a settlement made by her late husband. Her adopted daughters applied to the court for approval on her behalf to an arrangement whereby she would give up her protected life interest and all other interest under the settlement in order to benefit them. Cross J gave approval, saying that although the arrangement would involve the patient in financial loss this was comparatively small and it was for her benefit to do what she herself would have done had she been of full capacity. He distinguished *Re Tinker's Settlement* above (though agreeing with it) on the basis that there one could not say that the relevant beneficiaries, if of full capacity, would in all probability have consented to the proposed variation of the settlement[6]. He added:

> 'If and so far, however, as the judge was saying that there must always be some element of financial advantage to the infant or otherwise incapable person in question before an arrangement can be said to be for his benefit, I think he went too far.'

In *Re Remnant's Settlement Trusts*[7] the children of two sisters, Dawn and Merrial, had contingent interests under a testamentary trust which contained a forfeiture provision in respect of any child who practised Roman Catholicism or was married to a Roman Catholic at the time of vesting, with an accruer provision in favour of the children of the other sister. Dawn's children were Protestant whilst Merrial's children were Catholic. In the interests

---

3 [1960] 3 All ER 85n, [1960] 1 WLR 1011.
4 [1969] 1 Ch 587, [1968] 1 All ER 1104.
5 As to the special provisions applicable to certain patients who are mentally ill, see p 521, post.
6 See also *Re Mr & Mrs N's 1989 Settlement* (1998/99) 1 ITELR 803.
7 [1970] Ch 560, [1970] 2 All ER 554. See also *Re Zekelman* (1971) 19 DLR (3d) 652.

of family harmony an application was made inter alia for deletion of the forfeiture provision.

Pennycuick J acceded to the application, though defeating the testator's clear intentions and though financially disadvantageous to Dawn's children who otherwise had a good chance of gaining under the accruer clause. Pennycuick J was much influenced by the fact that the forfeiture clause operated as a deterrent in the selection of a spouse and was the source of possible family dissension. He emphasised that 'benefit' included educational and social benefit in a broad sense:

> 'I think I am entitled to take a broad view of what is meant by "benefit", and so taking it, I think this arrangement can be fairly said to be for [the children's] benefit ... I think the court is entitled and bound to consider not merely financial benefit but benefit of any other kind'[8].

Unfortunately, *Re Tinker's Settlement*[9] was not cited to Pennycuick J and no counsel seems to have presented submissions against the proposed arrangement where the judge took on a paterfamilial role in sublimating the individual interests to broader family interests without considering, as Cross J had suggested[10], whether the Protestant children, when adult, would in all probability be happy to forgo a larger share in the trust funds resulting from their cousins' Roman Catholicism.

(b) Conversely, the mere fact that a person does derive financial benefit from a scheme does not necessarily mean that the court will sanction it on his behalf. For one thing, the financial benefit, though present, may be unfairly small, so that the scheme is not—in the wider sense—beneficial to the person concerned. Thus Ungoed-Thomas J pointed out in one case[11] that if a proposed arrangement would give infants and unborn persons an entitlement which is actuarially greater than their entitlement under the existing trusts, but which is still not as great as their bargaining strength should have enabled them to obtain, the court should not approve it. In the event, the judge did approve the arrangement in question because he held, with some hesitation, that the benefit was sufficient. It is apprehended that there may be difficulties here, unless the court can be sure that the refusal of its approval will result in the proposal being made more beneficial to the persons concerned; for otherwise the refusal may merely deprive them of the benefit, however small, which they would have obtained. For another thing, the financial benefit to a person may be outweighed by disadvantages of a different kind. Thus in *Re Weston's Settlements*[12], approval was sought on behalf of infant and unborn persons to the insertion in certain English settlements of a power for the trustees to discharge the trust property from the settlements and to subject it to the trusts of new Jersey settlements containing substantially the same beneficial trusts. The purpose behind the proposed arrangement was to establish the settlements in Jersey (where the adult beneficiaries claimed already to have taken up permanent residence and

---

8 [1970] Ch 560 at 566. *In theory* either side of the family might benefit.
9 [1960] 3 All ER 85n, [1960] 1 WLR 1011.
10 *Re CL* [1969] 1 Ch 587 at 599. One might try to reconcile *Re Remnant's Will Trusts* with *Re Tinker's Settlement* on the basis that in the former both sides of the family could benefit in theory while in the latter only one side could benefit.
11 *Re Van Gruisen's Will Trusts* [1964] 1 All ER 843n, [1964] 1 WLR 449.
12 [1969] 1 Ch 223, [1968] 3 All ER 338, CA. Further see tax avoidance discussion at pp 514–515 post

acquired a domicil) and so save capital gains tax and estate duty. Although the arrangement would thus have brought financial benefit to the persons on whose behalf its approval was sought, the court refused approval; and Lord Denning MR, with whom Danckwerts LJ agreed, based this refusal on the view that:

> '... the court should not consider merely the financial benefit to the infants or unborn children but also their educational and social benefit. There are many things in life more worth-while than money. One of these things is to be brought up in this our England, which is still "the envy of less happier lands". I do not believe it is for the benefit of children to be uprooted from England and transported to another country simply to avoid tax.'

This case also brings out the fact that the court may often be able to refuse its approval on either one of two grounds: it may either decide, as did Lord Denning here, that the arrangement is not for the benefit of the persons concerned, perhaps interpreting the word 'benefit' widely for this purpose; or it may by-pass the question of benefit, as Harman LJ seems to have done in the same case, and simply decide that (whether there is a benefit or not) the arrangement is not one which the court 'thinks fit' to approve.

The general requirement that an arrangement must be for a person's benefit if it is to be approved on his behalf by the court does not mean, of course, that all its provisions must be beneficial to him: it is enough if the provisions, taken as a whole and (if necessary) balanced one against another, are beneficial to him[13]. Benefit may sometimes be found on the principle that a bird in the hand is worth two in the bush: thus an arrangement under which a beneficiary would receive £100 a year certain instead of remaining a member of a class of discretionary beneficiaries has been held to be beneficial[14].

The court must consider individually each person on whose behalf it is asked to give approval. Thus it is not sufficient that the proposed arrangement is for the benefit of a class of persons, considered together, if some members of the class—ie those born after a certain date—would not participate in that benefit; and this is so even if the arrangement is likely to result in more persons being born in time to qualify, or in greater benefits for those who do qualify[15].

Although arrangements must generally be for the benefit of those on whose behalf the court approves them, it is not essential that this benefit should be the inevitable result of the arrangement provided that it is an overwhelmingly likely one: the court will be prepared to take, on behalf of those for whom its approval is sought, the kind of risk which an adult beneficiary of full capacity would take on his own behalf[16]. The court may take a broad, reasonable view but not a galloping, gambling view as Templeman J pointed out in *Re Robinson's Settlement Trusts*[17]. Insurance can usually take care of most risks.

TAX AVOIDANCE. It is clear that there is in principle no objection to schemes designed to avoid taxation by lawful means. In *Chapman v Chap-*

13 *Re Lister's Will Trusts* [1962] 3 All ER 737, [1962] 1 WLR 1441.
14 *Re Clitheroe's Settlement Trusts* [1959] 3 All ER 789, [1959] 1 WLR 1159.
15 *Re Cohen's Settlement Trusts* [1965] 3 All ER 139, [1965] 1 WLR 1229.
16 *Re Cohen's Will Trusts* [1959] 3 All ER 523, [1959] 1 WLR 865.
17 [1976] 3 All ER 61, [1976] 1 WLR 806.

man[18], decided before the Act of 1958, Lord Morton of Henryton deprecated the alteration by the court of settlements for the purpose of avoiding tax, saying that if the court had power to approve, and did approve, schemes for that purpose 'the way would be open for a most undignified game of chess between the Chancery Division and the legislature'. But substantially the same scheme was later approved by the court under the 1958 Act[19], and having regard to the fact that (subject to the exception already mentioned) any arrangement must be for the benefit of all the beneficiaries (either, in the case of those on whose behalf the court's approval is given, because the Act so provides or, in the case of the others, because they would not otherwise be likely to agree to it) it is perhaps inevitable that some of this benefit must often be gained at the expense of the revenue. Indeed in *Re Weston's Settlements*, Harman LJ above went so far as to say that[20]:

'... it is well known that much and perhaps the main use which has been made of the Variation of Trusts Act 1958 has been to produce schemes which will have the effect of reducing the liabilities either on capital[1] of the trusts or the income[2] of the beneficiaries.'

And when the court does approve a scheme the benefit of which depends on estate duty (or, now, inheritance tax) being avoided, it will seek to ensure that its avoidance is not jeopardised by future acts: thus in a case[3] where the incautious exercise of a power of appointment might result in a liability to estate duty which the arrangement was designed to avoid, the court required the documents to provide that the power:

'... shall not be exercisable without the consent of the trustees which consent the trustees shall not withhold if advised by counsel of not less than ten years standing [at the Bar] that any proposed appointment will not under the law in force for the time being give rise to any claim for estate duty on the reversioners' fund or any part thereof on the death of [the appointor].'

But the case of *Re Weston's Settlements*, above, indicates that a line may have to be drawn somewhere. The main facts of this case have already been mentioned. At first instance[4], Stamp J refused his approval and rested this refusal at least partly on the ground that the scheme was an artificial one designed solely to save tax, saying:

'I am not persuaded that this application represents more than a cheap exercise in tax avoidance which I ought not to sanction, as distinct from a legitimate avoidance of liability to taxation.'

With respect, however, the distinction between these two activities is difficult to define and seems to consist only in the differently coloured language in which they are described. The Court of Appeal[5] affirmed the decision at first instance, but it is not easy to decide how much weight it placed, in

18 [1954] AC 429 at 468, [1954] 1 All ER 798 at 818, HL.
19 *Re Chapman's Settlement Trusts (No 2)* [1959] 2 All ER 47n, [1959] 1 WLR 372.
20 See also the remarks of Lord Denning MR [1969] 1 Ch 223 at 245, [1968] 3 All ER 338 at 342.
 1 As in *Re Drewe's Settlement* [1966] 2 All ER 844n, [1966] 1 WLR 1518, and *Re Lloyd's Settlement* [1967] 2 All ER 314n, [1967] 2 WLR 1078.
 2 As in *Clitheroe's Settlement Trusts* [1959] 3 All ER 789, [1959] 1 WLR 1159 (income tax and surtax), and *Re Sainsbury's Settlement* [1967] 1 All ER 878, [1967] 1 WLR 476 (capital gains tax).
 3 *Re Drewe's Settlement* [1966] 2 All ER 844n, [1966] 1 WLR 1518.
 4 [1969] 1 Ch 223, [1968] 1 All ER 720.
 5 [1969] 1 Ch 223, [1968] 3 All ER 338, CA.

dismissing the appeal, upon the tax avoiding nature of the arrangement. Certainly this played a large part in the judgments of Lord Denning MR and Harman LJ with both of which Danckwerts LJ agreed, as did the fact that the beneficiaries' move to Jersey had apparently been prompted solely by the hope of obtaining the tax advantage in question. In this latter respect, the case was contrasted with that of *Re Seale's Marriage Settlement*[6] where, although the scheme sanctioned did involve the transfer of a settlement to another country and the consequent avoidance of tax, the beneficiaries had emigrated to the other country some time before and for reasons quite unconnected with the scheme. And indeed in *Re Windeatt's Will Trusts*[7], a case decided since the *Weston* case, Pennycuick J applied *Seale* and distinguished *Weston* in order to approve an arrangement which was similar to that proposed in *Weston* but which concerned beneficiaries who had already been resident in Jersey for 19 years and seemed clearly to have acquired a domicile there. Equally certainly, however, the *Weston* case does not mean that schemes which have tax avoidance as their sole purpose will no longer be approved by the courts. All that can be said, perhaps, is that the courts prefer such schemes to be presented with decorum. Where this is the only purpose of a proposed arrangement, and the arrangement itself is particularly artificial or reveals its purpose in too blatant a way, the court may be ready to refuse its approval, if not on the express ground that the scheme is simply an exercise in tax avoidance, then on the ground that it is not truly for the benefit of the beneficiaries on whose behalf approval is sought or on the ground that the court does not 'think fit' to approve it.

In *Re Chamberlain*[8] Walton J approved an arrangement transferring assets of a trust, the proper law of which was English, to trustees of a Guernsey trust where the primary beneficiaries were domiciled and resident in France and the remaindermen were domiciled and resident in Indonesia. Unlike *Re Seale's Marriage Settlement* and *Re Windeatt's Will Trusts* the beneficiaries under the settlement had no connection with the country to which the settled funds were to be exported so as to become subject to an alien proper law. The settlement had been created many years previously by an English domiciled settlor so as to remain liable to UK capital transfer tax. Foreign trustees had been appointed in place of UK trustees and the trust assets had been switched into exempt gilts so that no capital transfer tax arose on determining the settlement and once the assets had been received into the Guernsey settlement no capital transfer tax would subsequently arise: no exchange control problems arose since Guernsey is in the sterling area. Trust exporting for the purpose of avoiding tax is thus still possible despite *Re Weston* which must be restricted to its special facts.

In *Richards v Mackay*[9] Millett J contrasted cases where the court is asked to exercise an original discretion of its own (as under the 1958 Act) with those where the proposed export of a trust or other arrangement is to be carried out by the trustees in exercise of their own discretion. In the former case the

6 [1961] Ch 574, [1961] 3 All ER 136.
7 [1969] 2 All ER 324, [1969] 1 WLR 692 where Lord Denning MR stated, 'Nearly every variation that has come before the court has tax avoidance for its principal object and no-one has ever suggested that this is undesirable or contrary to public policy'.
8 (1976) 126 NLJ 104 reported in an article by JB Morcom, barrister.
9 (1990) 1 Offshore Tax Planning Review 1, (R. Bramwell QC) and (1997) 11 Trust LI 123, applied by Vinelott J in *Re Beatty's Will Trusts (No 2)* (28 February 1991, unreported, except in 11 Trust LI 77).

applicants have to make out a positive case for the exercise of a judicial discretion and 'the court is unlikely to assist them where the scheme is nothing more than a device to avoid tax and has no other advantages of any kind'. In the latter case the court only needs to be satisfied that the proposed appointment of foreign trustees or other arrangement is not so inappropriate that no reasonable trustee could entertain it. It is also significant that since *Re Weston* was decided Parliament has intervened with substantial provisions for preventing capital gains tax being avoided by means of exporting trusts[10], so that naked tax avoidance will rarely be involved where trusts are exported.

WOMEN PAST CHILDBEARING. The Act has no special effect in cases where a woman, although in theory capable of having children who would or might become beneficiaries under a trust, is thought to be, or is in fact, past the age of childbearing. Of course, the court's power to approve an arrangement on behalf of unborn persons allows it to approve an arrangement on behalf of children who may be born to a middle-aged mother just as much as those who may be born to a younger one. But when the woman concerned is clearly past the age of childbearing it is inappropriate to apply under the Act for approval on behalf of her potential children of an arrangement whereby the trust property can be dealt with on the assumption that they will not in fact be born. This was made clear by Pennycuick J in *Re Pettifor's Will Trusts*[11], where it was proposed to take out an insurance policy against the possibility of future children in such a way that the insurance money would benefit such children if they were born and thus make up their loss. He said that where the woman in question is clearly past the age of childbearing, eg 70 years old, the trustees will normally be prepared to act, without any insurance cover, on the assumption that no children will in fact be born; but if the intervention of the court is to be sought at all, an application should be made to it in its administrative jurisdiction for leave to carry out the existing trusts on the basis that no children will be born. He added that:

'... it is well established that in administration the court will allow funds to be distributed on the footing that at a certain age, normally in the late or middle fifties, a woman has become incapable of childbearing.'

A distinction must of course be drawn between cases like that described above, where the court is asked to approve on behalf of the unborn children of a woman past the age of childbearing an arrangement which allows the trustees to proceed on the assumption that they will not be born, and cases in which an arrangement has been drawn up for some larger purpose but has as one of its elements the assumption that children will not be born to a woman past the age of childbearing. In one such case[12] it was not proposed to give any benefit to such children, so that the court could not in any case approve the proposed arrangement on their behalf, but the court was asked to approve it on behalf of the other beneficiaries. The court did so, and authorised the trustees to deal with the trust fund on the basis that the woman in question was past the age of childbearing, but without extinguishing any rights that her potential children might have.

10 [1966] Ch 257, [1966] 1 All ER 913. Taxation of Chargeable Gains Act 1992, ss 80–84, 87.
11 [1966] Ch 257, [1966] 1 All ER 913; also see *Re Westminster Bank's Declaration of Trust* [1963] 1 WLR 820 (VTA order for woman aged 50).
12 *Abbott v Service* (1963) 107 Sol Jo 681.

PUBLIC POLICY. The court will not approve an arrangement which is contrary to public policy, eg which amounts to a general restraint of marriage[13].

FRAUD ON A POWER OF APPOINTMENT. Powers of appointment may be either exercised or released in order to prepare the ground for an arrangement to be submitted to the court. When the power has been released (so that the default beneficiaries take) no question of fraud on a power can, of course, arise. But when it has been exercised this question may be pertinent. If the appointment has been made in order (or partly in order) to benefit the appointor, either directly, or indirectly by creating a situation in which the court might be expected to approve an arrangement which is for his benefit and which it would not otherwise have approved, or to approve an arrangement more favourable to him than it would otherwise have approved, then the appointment will be invalid and an arrangement based upon it will not be approved[14]. But the mere fact that the appointment does benefit the appointor in any of these ways is not enough of itself to make it fraudulent, and if the court does not find, or infer, an intention to exercise it *for that purpose* the appointment will be valid and can form the basis of an arrangement which the court will approve[15].

Although it is clear that a power of appointment may be released without any question of fraudulent intention being raised, the courts have none the less been confronted in several cases under the Act with the question of how this release can be effected. If the power of appointment has not been released, expressly and by deed, before the application under the Act comes to court, but the arrangement proposed is inconsistent with the continued existence of the power, does the application itself, or the court's approval of the arrangement, amount to a release of the power? It is clear that, although an express release must be by deed[16], the donee of a power makes an effective implied release if he deals with the property in a way which is inconsistent with its exercise. It has been suggested that the donee of a power may therefore, by applying for the court's approval of an arrangement inconsistent with its continued existence, or even by merely concurring in such a scheme, release the power. In *Re Christie-Miller's Settlement Trusts*[17] Wilberforce J left this question open and accepted an oral release by the donee's counsel. In *Re Courtauld's Settlement*[18] Plowman J pointed out that an oral release of this kind could be of only evidential value and approved an arrangement on the basis that the mere fact that the donee had propounded it was enough to release the power. He said, however, that he could not decide this point in such a way as to bind persons who were not parties to the proceedings. Finally, in *Re Wallace's Settlement*[19], Megarry J was asked to approve an arrangement which revoked certain clauses in a settlement, including one conferring a power of appointment which had not been expressly released. He held that the revocation could not amount to an express release of the power. He added, referring to *Re Courtauld's Settlement*, above, that there might well be an implied release but said: 'The difficulty in such cases may

---

13 *Re Michelham's Will Trusts* [1964] Ch 550, [1963] 2 All ER 188.
14 *Re Brook's Settlement* [1968] 3 All ER 416, [1968] 1 WLR 1661.
15 *Re Robertson's Will Trusts* [1960] 3 All ER 146n, [1960] 1 WLR 1050.
16 Law of Property Act 1925 ('LPA 1925'), s 155.
17 [1961] 1 All ER 855n, [1961] 1 WLR 462.
18 [1965] 2 All ER 544n, [1965] 1 WLR 1385.
19 [1968] 2 All ER 209, [1968] 1 WLR 711.

be, however, that an implied release will not, as in *Re Courtauld's Settlement*, necessarily bind all persons'. These words may give rise to some confusion. It seems clear enough that if an implied release is in fact made it will bind all persons in just the same way as an express one would do. What Plowman J said in *Re Courtauld's Settlement* was merely that his *decision* that the implied release *was* made would not bind anyone who was not a party to the proceedings. At all events, Megarry J said that it was preferable that the power should be expressly released by deed, so that this is the proper course to take, Megarry J in *Re Ball's Settlement Trusts*[20] requiring an express release of the power.

In *IRC v Cookson*[1] Stamp LJ laid down the general law on implied release of powers as follows:

'In the absence of words which actually have that effect an instrument or the transaction which it effects will only operate to release a power if it operates in such a way that the power cannot thereafter be exercised without interfering with the operation of the earlier instrument or transaction. However probable it may be that the author of the instrument intended to destroy a power you must, in order to destroy it, find words which have that effect or something which shows by necessary implication an intention so to do.'

The effect of the court's approval

On the precise effect of the court's approval, and of the order by which this is expressed, there has been a conflict of judicial opinion. The following propositions can, it is submitted, be deduced from the cases, some more tentatively than others:

(a) whatever the precise way in which the result is achieved (and this is discussed below) the arrangement, to which those beneficiaries who act on their own behalf have assented, coupled with the order by which the court approves it on behalf of the other beneficiaries, has the immediate effect of varying or revoking the trusts (or enlarging the powers of the trustees, as the case may be). It is therefore not necessary or appropriate for the court to add to its order a direction that the arrangement shall be carried into effect, for it becomes effective automatically. The action of Vaisey J, in making such an addition to the order in the case of *Re Joseph's Will Trusts*[2] must, in the light of the cases mentioned below, be considered mistaken;

(b) but some doubt remains as to the exact way in which the variation (or revocation or enlargement) is made. In *Re Viscount Hambleden's Will Trusts*[3], Wynn-Parry J said that it was made by the court's order of approval: 'If I approve an arrangement, I vary the trusts'. But this view was rejected by Megarry J in *Re Holt's Settlement*[4] where he held (and his view is supported by dicta of the House of Lords in *IRC v Holmden*[5]) that it was the arrangement, made binding on certain beneficiaries by the court's order, which varied the trusts and not the order itself. This must therefore be considered the better view;

20 [1968] 2 All ER 438.
 1 [1977] 2 All ER 331 at 335.
 2 [1959] 3 All ER 474n, [1959] 1 WLR 1019.
 3 [1960] 1 All ER 353n, [1960] 1 WLR 82.
 4 [1969] 1 Ch 100, [1968] 1 All ER 470. See also *Spens v IRC* [1970] 1 WLR 1173 at 1183–1184.
 5 [1968] AC 685 at 701, 710–711, 713. See also *Thorn v IRC* [1976] 2 All ER 622 at 631, per Walton J.

(c) it would be wrong to conclude, however, that the sole effect of the Act is to allow the court to make good the lack of assent to an arrangement of beneficiaries who are unborn or lacking in capacity. The arrangement, after all, is not a written document signed by the beneficiaries and if the Act merely allowed the court, as it were, notionally to supply the signatures of some of the beneficiaries, it would still lack those of the others. In particular it would in many cases fail to meet the requirements of s 53(1)(c) of the Law of Property Act 1925 which provides that:

'a disposition of an equitable interest or trust subsisting at the time of the disposition, must be in writing signed by the person disposing of the same, or by his agent thereunto lawfully authorised in writing or by will.'

In *Re Holt's Settlement*, above, Megarry J acceded to the argument of counsel that by enacting the Variation of Trusts Act the legislature had provided an implied exception to these requirements where the order of the court re-worded the consent of the parties by their counsel to the arrangement. The Act contemplated that the court's order should conclude all the steps necessary to make the variation effective and 'one should construe the Act ... as authorising an order which is efficacious to achieve its avowed object'. In his judgment, Megarry J gave assent also to an alternative means of escape under s 53(2)[6] from the provisions of s 53(1)(c) of the 1925 Act, namely:

'Where ... the arrangement consists of an agreement made for valuable consideration, and that agreement is specifically enforceable, then the beneficial interests pass to the respective purchasers on the making of the agreement ... by virtue of the species of constructive trust made familiar by contracts for the sale of land, whereunder the vendor becomes a constructive trustee for the purchaser as soon as the contract is made ... '

Another point decided by Megarry J in the same case is that the arrangement coupled with the court's order constitutes an 'instrument' for the purposes of s 15(5) of the Perpetuities and Accumulations Act 1964[7], so that provisions which derive their validity from that Act may be included in the arrangement, the perpetuity and accumulation period starting afresh.

It is normally desirable that the court's order should give approval on behalf of, and thus bind all the beneficiaries who are not able to assent on their own behalf. Indeed Stamp J has doubted[8], obiter, whether it would be right to approve an arrangement which would not bind all the beneficiaries, since such approval might also fail to bind the Inland Revenue.

Jurisdiction and practice

The jurisdiction conferred by the Act is exercisable by the High Court, except

---

6 This is a little difficult to reconcile with the majority view in *Oughtred v IRC* [1960] AC 206, [1959] 3 All ER 623 (see J W Harris, *Variation of Trusts*, pp 107–109) but it has subsequent support from *DHN Food Distributors Ltd v Tower Hamlets* [1976] 1 WLR 852 and *Neville v Wilson* [1997] Ch 144, CA, though contracts for sale of interests in land are now void unless all their terms are in writing signed by both parties due to the Law of Property (Miscellaneous Provisions) Act 1989, s 2, so the remarks of Megarry J now have to be confined to personalty unless one can impose a constructive trust within s 2(5) of the 1989 Act to prevent unconscionable behaviour on proprietary estoppel grounds, as in *Yaxley v Gotts* [2000] Ch 162.

7 See also Article 11, para 1(a), ante and *Re Lansdowne's Will Trusts* [1967] Ch 603.

8 *Re Brook's Settlement* [1968] 3 All ER 416, [1968] 1 WLR 1661. But see eg *Re Clarke's Will Trusts* [1961] 3 All ER 1133, [1961] 1 WLR 1471. No doubt this may depend upon the kind of variation proposed.

that the question whether the carrying out of any arrangement would be for the benefit of a person falling within s 1(1)(a) is to be determined by order of the authority having jurisdiction under Pt VII of the Mental Health Act 1983 if that person is a patient within the meaning of that Part of that Act. But the county court has all the jurisdiction of the High Court to hear and determine proceedings under s 1 of the Variation of Trusts Act where the estate or fund subject to the trust does not exceed £30,000 in amount or value, and in these proceedings the country court judge has, in addition to any other powers and authorities which he possesses, all the powers and authorities of a judge of the Chancery Division of the High Court[9].

In regard to the exception which applies to a beneficiary who is a patient within Pt VII of the Mental Health Act 1983, it should be noted that the procedure required is for the Court of Protection to approve the arrangement on behalf of the patient as being for his benefit: it is not appropriate for the Court of Protection to direct the patient's receiver to consent to the arrangement on the patient's behalf[10]. But if the arrangement subsequently comes before the Chancery Division for approval on behalf of other beneficiaries, an order may be made that the costs in the Court of Protection shall be paid out of the trust estate[11].

The court's jurisdiction to vary trusts is not confined to those to which English law applies. Thus it extends to a Northern Ireland settlement[12], and indeed to a settlement governed by any law, though careful consideration is given to the question of whether it is proper to exercise this jurisdiction 'where there are substantial foreign elements in the case'[13], and in particular to the effectiveness of any order which the court may make[14] eg, whether the trustees and the trust property are situate in England and whether there is any possibility of 'limping' trust provisions valid under the English Act but void under some applicable law governing validity. The Recognition of Trusts Act 1987, implementing Article 8 of The Hague Convention on Trusts, allows trusts to be varied by the English court under its VTA jurisdiction but only if variation by a court is permitted to be effective by the law governing validity of the trust if alteration of beneficial interests is involved, or the law governing administration if alteration or deletion or enlargement of administrative powers is involved[15]. Obviously it will normally be best and most appropriate to vary the trust in the jurisdiction of the applicable law for validity and/or administration.

Section 1(1) of the Act gives the court power to approve any arrangement 'by whomsoever proposed'. But in applications to vary beneficial interests the beneficiaries, and not the trustees, should generally be the applicants unless the trustees are satisfied that the proposed arrangement is beneficial to the beneficiaries and that no beneficiary is willing to make the application. This was said by Russell J in *Re Druce's Settlement Trusts*[16], and he added:

'In particular it would not be right if it became the general practice for such

---

9 County Courts Act 1984, s 23. The £30,000 limit on the county court jurisdiction cannot be exceeded even if all the parties agree: County Courts Act 1984, s 24(3).
10 *Re CL* [1969] 1 Ch 587, [1968] 1 All ER 1104.
11 *Re Sanderson's Settlement Trusts* [1961] 1 All ER 25n, [1961] 1 WLR 36.
12 *Re Ker's Settlement Trusts* [1963] Ch 553, [1963] 1 All ER 801.
13 Per Cross J in *Re Paget's Settlement* [1965] 1 All ER 58, [1965] 1 WLR 1046 (New York Trust).
14 *Re Paget's Settlement* [1965] 1 All ER 58, [1965] 1 WLR 1046.
15 See p 1043 post.
16 [1962] 1 All ER 563, [1962] 1 WLR 363.

applications to be made by the trustees on the supposition that should the application fail it will be more probable ... that the costs of all parties will be directed to be paid out of the trust funds.'

It is not proposed to deal here in any more detail with matters which relate purely to practice under the Variation of Trusts Act. The relevant rules and practice directions[17] are fully summarised and discussed in the established works on practice[18].

Other powers are not limited by the Act

It is expressly provided[19] that the Act is not to limit 'the powers conferred by s 64 of the Settled Land Act 1925, s 57 of the Trustee Act 1925[20] or the powers of the authority having jurisdiction under Pt VII of the Mental Health Act 1983'[1]. Since these powers do not require unanimity on the part of all beneficiaries who are ascertainable and of full age and capacity they will doubtless still be resorted to in many cases to which they are appropriate[2]. But the jurisdiction under the Act of 1958 has the advantage that under it the powers of the trustees of management and administration may be enlarged at the same time as dealing with the alteration of beneficial interests. If no such alteration is required then it is cheaper, more convenient and more straightforward to have particular transactions or an enlargement of management and administrative powers authorised in Chambers under the Trustee Act 1925 or the Settled Land Act 1925[3].

PARAGRAPH 2

Jurisdiction before 1926

Before 1926 the power of the court to authorise trustees to carry out transactions not expressly authorised by the settlement was derived from the inherent administrative jurisdiction of the court, and until 1901 the extent of such jurisdiction was a matter of considerable doubt.

In *Re Morrison*[4] Buckley J held that he had no jurisdiction to sanction an agreement by which trustees concurred in the conversion into a limited company of a business in which the testator was a partner, on the terms of the testator's share in the business being exchanged for shares and debentures in the new company, which were not investments authorised by the will. On the other hand, in *West of England and South Wales District Bank v Murch*[5] Fry J found it possible to sanction such an agreement.

---

17 Eg Civil Procedure Rules 1998, rr 19.7, 21.2 and 21.10 and recent rr 64.2(c) and 64.4(2).

18 Atkin's *Encyclopaedia of Court Forms* Vol 41; *Chancery Practice and Procedure* (Jordans, 2001); *Lewin on Trusts* (17th edn) paras 45–79 to 45–96; E Campbell *Changing the Terms of Trusts* (Butterworths 2002), Ch 4, paras 4.94 to 4.129.

19 Section 1(6) of the 1958 Act, as amended by Mental Health Act 1959, s 149(1), Sch 7, Pt I and Mental Health Act 1983, s 148, Sch 4, para 14.

20 As to this, see also the notes to Paragraphs 2 and 3 of the present Article.

 1 Sections 95 and 96, especially s 96(3) replacing s 103(4) of the Mental Health Act 1959 on which see *Re CWHT* [1978] Ch 67, [1978] 1 All ER 210.

 2 Eg *Mason v Farbrother* [1983] 2 All ER 1078.

 3 *Anker-Petersen v Anker-Petersen* [2000] WTLR 581.

 4 [1901] 1 Ch 701; and see, to same effect, *Re Crawshay* (1888) 60 LT 357.

 5 (1883) 23 Ch D 138.

Decision of the Court of Appeal in *Re New*

In July 1901, however, the leading case of *Re New*[6] came before the Court of Appeal, which, in the exercise of its general jurisdiction, authorised the trustees of three separate trust instruments to concur in a shareholders' scheme for the reconstruction of a limited company, under which shares settled in specie were to be exchanged for shares in a new company which the trustees were not, by their settlements, authorised to hold; the court imposed on them an undertaking to apply for leave to retain the new shares and debentures if they desired to do so beyond one year.

Although the jurisdiction invoked in that case is now largely superseded by the statutory jurisdiction discussed below (and by the rather different jurisdiction under the Variation of Trusts Act 1958, discussed in the preceding pages), the inherent jurisdiction still remains, and the principles enunciated in the judgment of the court delivered by Romer LJ still command respect, and may still afford some guidance in the exercise of the statutory jurisdiction. The following passage from the judgment was cited at length and with approval by Lord Morton of Henryton in *Chapman v Chapman*:

'As a rule, the court has no jurisdiction to give, and will not give, its sanction to the performance by trustees of acts with reference to the trust estate which are not, onthe face of the instrument creating the trust, authorised by its terms ... But in themanagement of a trust estate, and especially where that estate consists of a business or shares in a mercantile company, it not infrequently happens that some peculiar state of circumstances arises for which provision is not expressly made by the trust instrument, and which renders it most desirable, and it may be even essential, for the benefit of the estate and in the interest of all the cestuis que trust, that certain acts should be done by the trustees which in ordinary circumstances they would have no power to do. In a case of this kind, *which may reasonably be supposed to be one not foreseen or anticipated by the author of the trust*, where the trustees are embarrassed by the emergency that has arisen and the duty cast upon them to do what is best for the estate, and the consent of all the beneficiaries cannot be obtained by reason of some of them not being sui juris or in existence, then it may be right for the court, *and the court in a proper case would have jurisdiction*, to sanction on behalf of all concerned such acts on behalf of the trustees as we have above referred to. By way merely of illustration, we may take the case where a testator has declared that some property of his shall be sold at a particular time after his death, and then, owing to unforeseen change of circumstances since the testator's death, when the time for sale arrives it is found that to sell at that precise time would be ruinous to the estate, and that it is necessary or right to postpone the sale for a short time in order to effect a proper sale: in such a case the court would have jurisdiction to authorise, and would authorise, the trustees to postpone the sale for a reasonable time. It is a matter of common knowledge that the jurisdiction we have been referring to, which is only part of the general administrative jurisdiction of the court, has been constantly exercised, chiefly at chambers. Of course, the jurisdiction is one to be exercised with great caution, and the court will take care not to strain its powers. It is impossible, and no attempt ought to be made, to state or define all the circumstances under which, or the extent to which, the court will exercise the jurisdiction; but it need scarcely be said that the court will not be justified in sanctioning every act desired by trustees and beneficiaries *merely because it may appear beneficial to the estate*; and certainly the court will not be disposed to sanction transactions of a speculative or risky character. But each case brought before the court must be considered and dealt with according to its special cir-

6 [1901] 2 Ch 534, approved by the House of Lords in *Chapman v Chapman* [1954] AC 429, [1954] 1 All ER 798.

cumstances. As a rule, these circumstances are better investigated and dealt with in chambers. Very often they involve matters of a delicate and private nature, the publication of which is not requisite on any good ground and might cause great injury to the trust estate.'

From this statement it clearly appears that even the limited and exceptional jurisdiction to sanction transactions in the nature of 'salvage' of the trust property must be exercised with the greatest caution, and does not extend to any alteration of the beneficial interests[7].

Applying the principle laid down in *Re New*[8], orders were made before 1926 to authorise or approve making advances out of capital for the benefit of an infant[9]; carrying on a business which was not presently saleable until it could be sold as a going concern; selling a business to a company in exchange for shares therein, and holding such shares for a limited period; holding, for a period, land which had been mortgaged to the trustees, and which mortgage they had foreclosed; the raising of money by mortgage of the trust property, where the estate would be ruined if money were not expended on it, or a settled policy would lapse if premiums were not paid[10]; a sale of a trust policy where it had become impossible to pay the premiums[11]; a compromise or scheme of family arrangement on behalf of infants interested under the trust[12] and making to an infant a larger allowance for maintenance than the settlor had named where the result would otherwise have been to injure the infant's prospects or to cause real property belonging to him to fall into ruin[13]. In the last-mentioned case the court even went to the extent of allowing subscriptions to charities, on the ground that the testator must have intended that the infant should be brought up and the property maintained in the mode usual amongst gentlemen holding the position to which he was born, so as to keep up the reputation of the family and estate which incidentally involved the payment of subscriptions to local charities[14].

Modern inherent and statutory powers to sanction deviation

The Court of Appeal[15] recently utilised the inherent salvage jurisdiction to provide the key to release of retention trust money in a building construction contract where an impasse had been reached (the unobtainability of a necessary certificate frustrating the purpose of the trust) which could not be resolved under the terms of the contract. Most of the inherent jurisdiction is now to be found in s 57 of the Trustee Act 1925, the substance of which is

---

7 Cf *Re Forster's Settlement* [1954] 3 All ER 714, [1954] 1 WLR 1450, and the majority judgment in *Re Downshire Settled Estates; Re Chapman's Settlement Trusts; Re Blackwell's Settlement Trusts* [1953] Ch 218 at 236, [1953] 1 All ER 103 at 112, CA; approved in *Chapman v Chapman* [1954] AC 429 at 465, [1954] 1 All ER 798 at 816, HL.

8 [1901] 2 Ch 534.

9 Per Kekewich J in *Re Tollemache* [1903] 1 Ch 457; affd [1903] 1 Ch 955.

10 *Neill v Neill* [1904] 1 IR 513, and *Moore v Ulster Bank* (1909) 43 ILTR 136.

11 *Hill v Trenery* (1856) 23 Beav 16; *Beresford v Beresford* (1857) 23 Beav 292; *Re Wells* [1903] 1 Ch 848.

12 *Re Wells* [1903] 1 Ch 848.

13 *Re Walker* [1901] 1 Ch 879; and see also *Griggs v Gibson* (1866) 14 WR 538; *Havelock v Havelock* (1881) 17 Ch D 807; *Re Collins* (1886) 32 Ch D 229; *Bennett v Wyndham* (1857) 23 Beav 521; *Revel v Watkinson* (1748) 1 Ves Sen 93; *Greenwell v Greenwell* (1800) 5 Ves 194; and *Barnes v Ross* [1896] AC 625.

14 See note 13, above.

15 *Rafidain Bank v Saipem* (2 March 1994, unreported), CA.

stated in paragraph (2), above, and with regard to settled land in s 64 of the Settled Land Act 1925, the substance of which is also stated in paragraph (2), above.

Jurisdiction under Trustee Act 1925, s 57

With regard to s 57 of the Trustee Act 1925, it was held by the majority of the Court of Appeal in *Re Downshire's Settled Estates, Re Chapman's Settlement Trusts* and *Re Blackwell's Settlement Trusts*[16], that it must be presumed to have been the intention of Parliament in enacting the section to confer new powers on the court rather than to codify or define existing powers, though it may well be that the jurisdiction thereunder does in some degree overlap the pre-existing inherent jurisdiction. The section envisages (1) an act unauthorised by the trust instrument, (2) to be effected by the trustees, (3) in the management or administration of the trust property, (4) which the court will empower them to perform, (5) if in its opinion the act is expedient. The key words here are 'management' and 'administration', and though it is possible that each is capable of some shade of meaning which could not properly be attributed to the other, the subject matter of both is trust property which is vested in trustees, and this cannot, by any legitimate use of language, include the equitable interests which the settlor has created in that property. The object of s 57 is to secure that trust property should be managed as advantageously as possible in the interests of the beneficiaries and, with that object in view, to authorise specific dealings or types of dealings with the property which the court might have felt itself unable to sanction under the inherent jurisdiction, either because no actual 'emergency' had arisen, or because of inability to show that the position which called for intervention was one which the creator of the trust could not reasonably have foreseen, but it was no part of the legislative aim to disturb the rule that the court will not re-write a trust or to add to such exceptions to that rule as had already found their way into the inherent jurisdiction.

The jurisdiction under s 57 co-exists side by side with that under the Variation of Trusts Act 1958[17] and, as has been seen[18], where proposals involve only the management and administration of the settled property (as opposed to the attention of beneficial interests therein) application to the court to sanction departure from the terms of a trust may be made more conveniently under s 57 than under the Act of 1958[19].

Application to the court under s 57 may be made by the trustees or a beneficiary[20] and the court may from time to time vary or rescind any order made under s 57 or may make a new or further order[1].

---

16 *Re Chapman's Settlement Trusts* [1953] Ch 218, [1953] 2 All ER 103, CA; affd sub nom *Chapman v Chapman* [1954] AC 429, [1954] 1 All ER 798, HL; counsel stated that they could not contend that s 57 of the TA 1925, had any application. None of their Lordships either affirmed or disapproved the part of the judgment of the majority of the Court of Appeal, summarised above, and, accordingly, this must be taken to be good law.

17 See pp 501 et seq, ante.

18 See p 509, ante.

19 See eg *Re Shipwrecked Fishermen and Mariners' Royal Benevolent Society Charity* [1959] Ch 220, [1958] 3 All ER 465 (extension of a charity's investment powers) applied in *Mason v Farbrother* [1983] 2 All ER 1078; and *Anker-Petersen v Anker-Petersen* [2000] WTLR 581.

20 TA 1925, s 57(3).

1 TA 1925, s 57(2).

Transactions sanctioned under Trustees Act 1925, s 57

In order that it may be sanctioned by the court under s 57 of the Trustee Act 1925, the proposed transaction must be for the benefit of the whole trust and not of one beneficiary only[2] and must not be one which could be effected without praying in aid the jurisdiction of the court under the section[3].

Apart from using its jurisdiction under the section to sanction a partition or sale to which the necessary consent could not be obtained[4] the court has made orders thereunder enabling the trustees of the wills of two testatrices, who had made identical residuary bequests for the foundation of a poor person's home, to blend the residuary estates into a single fund[5]; authorising a transaction involving the expenditure of capital in the purchase at a low price of the life tenant's interest thus making it possible to pay off certain mortgages of the reversionary interests, which had been sanctioned by the court, and a sum owing for estate duty on the death of a former life tenant and to preserve something for distribution among the reversioners[6]; authorising the sale by trustees of a reversionary interest, which they had no power under the settlement to sell until it fell into possession[7]; and conferring on the trustees power to invest in certain shares which were not included amongst the investments authorised by the settlement[8].

In considering what extended powers of investment should be conferred the court should consider the object of the trust (eg if capital appreciation were sought to enable capital purchases), the size of the trust fund (more latitude for larger funds), the width and efficacy of provisions for advice and control, while the wider the proposed powers the more should consideration be given to restricting them to a specific fraction of the fund.

In *Anker-Petersen v Anker-Petersen*[9] involving a trust fund of over £4 million the court authorised under s 57 many transactions, so enabling the trustees to take full advantage of the services of a discretionary portfolio manager authorised under the Financial Services Act 1986. First, the trustees were given power to invest in assets of any kind anywhere as if they were beneficial owners, subject to obtaining advice from an Investment Adviser, being from any person reasonably believed by the trustees to be qualified by his ability in and practical experience of financial matters to advise them on investment matters, and having regard to the need for diversification, the suitability of investments, the desirability of diminishing the risk of loss and need to strike

---

2 *Re Craven's Estate* [1937] Ch 431, [1937] 3 All ER 33.
3 *Re Basden's Settlement Trusts* [1943] 2 All ER 11; *Re Pratt's Will Trusts* [1943] Ch 326, [1943] 2 All ER 375.
4 *Re Hope's Will Trusts* [1929] 2 Ch 136; *Re Thomas* [1930] 1 Ch 194; *Re Beale's Settlement Trusts* [1932] 2 Ch 15.
5 *Re Harvey* [1941] 3 All ER 284. In each case the testatrix had directed that the home should have the same name.
6 *Re Forster's Settlement* [1954] 3 All ER 714, [1954] 1 WLR 1450.
7 *Re Cockerell's Settlement Trusts* [1956] Ch 372, [1956] 2 All ER 172, distinguishing *Re Heyworth's Contingent Reversionary Interest* [1956] Ch 364, sub nom *Re Heyworth's Settlements* [1956] 2 All ER 21; but a transaction similar to that which Upjohn J was unable to sanction in the latter case for want of jurisdiction could now be approved under the Variation of Trusts Act 1958, pp 501 et seq, ante.
8 *Re Brassey's Settlement* [1955] 1 All ER 577, [1955] 1 WLR 192. Also see *X v A* [2000] 1 All ER 490 at 495.
9 [2000] WTLR 581. It must be remembered that even if trustees have power to do something they must still exercise the appropriate degree of care in deciding whether or not to do what they have power to do.

a balance between income yield and capital appreciation. Second, the trustees were given power to hold investments in the name of nominees. Third, the trustees were given a general power to borrow money. Fourth, the trustees were empowered to employ an Investment Adviser to act as discretionary portfolio manager (thereby delegating their crucial investment role), subject to an annual review of this delegation, subject to laying down policy guidelines for the manager and using reasonable endeavours to ensure that the guidelines were observed and subject to the trustees being liable for any failure to take reasonable care in selecting a manager, fixing or enforcing the terms on which he was employed, or remedying any breaches of those terms or otherwise in supervising the manager, but not otherwise being liable for the acts or defaults of the manager. Little scope for resort to s 57 now remains after the Trustee Act 2000 conferred on trustees the powers of investment and delegation to agents, custodians or nominees.

Jurisdiction under the Settled Land Act 1925, s 64

It was held by the majority of the Court of Appeal in *Re Downshire's Settled Estates*[10] that the jurisdiction under s 64 of the Settled Land Act 1925 was ampler than that under s 57 of the Trustee Act 1925. In order that a transaction may be sanctioned under the former section, it is only necessary that it should (a) be one to be effected by the tenant for life, (b) be for the benefit of the settled land or some part thereof or of the persons interested under the settlement[11] but not necessarily of both, and (c) affect or concern the settled land or other land, in England or abroad, and whether settled or not. The last requirement could, in the view of the majority of the Court of Appeal, be satisfied by transactions only indirectly operating on the settled land providing that such operation was real and substantial by ordinary commonsense standards.

Section 64 has also been held[12] wide enough to enable trustees to transfer part of their trust property to another settlement in order to help maintain other settled property vested in the trustees, notwithstanding that such transaction might benefit some persons who were not beneficiaries under the trust. It has also been used to deal with the Duke of Marlborough's parliamentary estate at Blenheim when the Eleventh Duke and the trustees concluded that the Eleventh Duke's son as likely successor as tenant in tail would not be capable of managing the Blenheim estate. To provide for the proper future management of the estate it was held that the court could approve the Eleventh Duke conveying the estate to trustees of a new settlement on trust for sale for himself for life, then upon protective trusts for his son for life, thereafter upon the trusts of the parliamentary settlement[13].

---

10 [1953] Ch 218, [1953] 1 All ER 103, CA. There was no appeal from the Court of Appeal's decision in this case, and the SLA 1925, s 64, was not referred to by the House of Lords in *Chapman v Chapman* [1954] AC 429, [1954] 1 All ER 798, HL. 'Trusts of land' cannot benefit from s 64 although trustees for sale of land could, until the 1996 repeal of LPA 1925, s 28 which had been held to enable reliance on s 64: *Re Simmon's Trusts* [1956] Ch 125.

11 See *Re White-Popham Settled Estates* [1936] Ch 725, [1936] 2 All ER 1486, CA; *Re Earl Mount Edgcumbe* [1950] Ch 615, [1950] 2 All ER 242.

12 *Raikes v Lygon* [1988] 1 All ER 884, [1988] 1 WLR 281.

13 *Hambro v Duke of Marlborough* [1994] Ch 158, [1994] 3 All ER 332.

Extension of powers under Trustee Act 1925 and Settled Land Act 1925

The powers conferred by s 57 of the Trustee Act 1925 and s 64 of the Settled Land Act 1925 have been extended by the Settled Land and Trustee Acts (Courts' General Powers) Act 1943[14] as stated in this paragraph.

Section 1 of this Act, as subsequently amended by s 9 of the Emergency Laws (Miscellaneous Provisions) Act 1953, provides that those powers shall include power, in the circumstances specified in subs (2), to make an order authorising any expense of action taken or proposed in or for the management of settled land or of land subject to a trust of land to be treated as a capital outgoing notwithstanding that in other circumstances it could not properly have been so treated. The Act then goes on:

(2)   The said circumstances are that the court is satisfied
  (a)   that the action taken or proposed was or would be for the benefit of the persons entitled under the settlement, or under the trust of land, as the case may be, generally; and either
  (b)   that the available income from all sources of a person who, as being beneficially entitled to possession or receipt of rents and profits of the land or to reside in a house comprised therein, might otherwise have been expected to bear the expense of the action taken or proposed has been so reduced by reason of circumstances as to render him unable to bear the expense thereof, or unable to bear it without undue hardship; or
  (c)   in case in which there is no such person as aforesaid, that the income available for meeting that expense has become insufficient.
(3)   In determining whether to make such an order as aforesaid the court shall have regard to all the circumstances of the case, including the extent of the obligations, whether legally enforceable or not and whether or not relating to the land, of the person referred to in paragraph (b) of the last preceding subsection, the extent to which other persons entitled under the settlement or trust of land are likely to benefit from the action taken or proposed or from the relief which would accrue to that person from the making of the order, and the extent to which the making of the order would be likely to involve a loss to any other person so entitled without his receiving any corresponding benefit.
(4)   Such an order as aforesaid may be made notwithstanding that the action in question was taken, or the expense thereof discharged, before the passing of this Act or before the application for the order, and the court may direct such adjustments of accounts and such repayments to be made as may appear to the court to be requisite for giving full effect to the purposes of any such order.
(5)   In this section the expression 'management' includes all the acts referred to in subsection (2) of section one hundred and two of the Settled Land Act, 1925, and references in this section to expense of management include references to the expense of the employment of a solicitor, accountant, surveyor, or other person in an advisory or supervisory capacity.

The object of this extension of powers is to enable the court to authorise the use of capital for meeting expenses which would otherwise be income expenses. Since the intention is not merely to relieve the person entitled to income but to maintain the estate for the general benefit of all persons interested under the trust, the power of the court is carefully hedged about by the provisions of subsections (2) and (3).

In *Re Scarisbrick Re-settlement Estates*[15] it was argued that the effect of the section was to restrict and not to extend the powers of the court under s 64 of

---

14 Made permanent by the Emergency Laws (Miscellaneous Provisions) Act 1953, s 9 and amended by the Trusts of Land and Appointment of Trustees Act 1996, Sch 3, para 8.
15 [1944] Ch 229, [1944] 1 All ER 404.

the Settled Land Act 1925 since all that is authorised is the application of capital moneys in 'management' as defined by subsection (5), and that any other application of capital moneys which was formerly authorised by the 1925 Act must be treated as excluded by the 1943 Act. This contention was, however, rejected and the extent of the jurisdiction formerly exercised under section 64 of the Settled Land Act 1925 was confirmed.

Paragraph 3

As Sir GJ Turner stated in *Harrison v Randall*[16]:

> 'A trustee is not, in all cases, to be made liable upon the mere ground of his having deviated from the strict letter of his trust. The deviation may be necessary, or may be beneficial to the interests of the cestuis que trust, but when a trustee ventures to deviate from the letter of his trust, he does so under the obligation and at the peril of afterwards satisfying the court that the deviation was necessary or beneficial.'

It may be that the trust instrument contains a clause exempting a trustee from liability for any breach of trust unless dishonest or reckless[17]. Such a clause will protect a trustee from liability for a deliberate breach of trust honestly believed to be in the best interests of the beneficiaries unless such belief is so unreasonable that no honest reasonable person in the shoes of the particular trustee could have held such belief[18].

ARTICLE 48

Duty of trustee to act impartially in the sense of fairly and disinterestedly, between the beneficiaries

(1) A trustee must act fairly and disinterestedly in the execution of his trust, and not exercise his powers so as to confer an advantage on one beneficiary or class of beneficiary at the expense of another unless this apparent partiality results from the exercise of the power in question for the purpose for which it was given, affording proper consideration to the matters which are relevant and excluding from consideration matters which are irrelevant[19]; he must act fairly in making investment decisions which may have differing consequences for differing classes of beneficiaries[20];

(2) where the capital of the trust property is in any way augmented, the augmentation accrues for the benefit of all the beneficiaries, and

---

16 (1851) 9 Hare 397. Also see *Re New* [1901] 2 Ch 534, p 523, ante.

17 Such clauses are valid: *Armitage v Nurse* [1998] Ch 241, CA.

18 *Walker v Stones* [2001] QB 902, CA.

19 *Edge v Pensions Ombudsman* [2000] Ch 602 at 618 and 627. Also see *Lloyds Bank plc v Duker* [1987] 1 WLR 1324 where the duty of the trustee was to reject the claim of D, entitled to forty-six eightieths of the trust fund including 999 shares in a private company with share capital of 1000 shares, to have 574 of the 999 shares transferred to him, the trustees having to sell the 999 shares and then transfer forty-six eightieths of the proceeds of sale to D, so that D could not acquire a greater amount by acquiring the majority shareholding and selling it.

20 Per Hoffmann J in *Nestle v National Westminster Bank plc* [2000] WTLR 795 at 803.

is accordingly to be treated as capital and not as income[1];

(3) a trustee may pay over a share to a beneficiary to whom it is presently payable without liability for any subsequent inequality which may occur by reason of the depreciation of the investments of one share, or the appreciation of the investments of another, although in the absence of an express or statutory power of appropriation it seems a trustee should not appropriate a share of income of the trust property to beneficiaries without seeking the guidance of the court;

(4) where advances have to be brought into hotchpot, then, in the absence of a direction to the contrary, the necessary valuation must be made as at the date of actual distribution[2] and, between the date for notional distribution and the actual payment or appropriation of the property to or among the persons entitled, interest at 4% per annum must for the purposes of computation be charged against the advances and added to the income of the whole estate which is then divisible, each advanced person taking his share of the income less the 4% on his advance[3].

PARAGRAPH 1

Discretionary distributive powers

Where trustees are trustees for a class of discretionary beneficiaries with wide-ranging powers of appointment or are trustees of a pension scheme with flexible powers capable of benefiting the employer or current employees or pensioners or particular classes thereof, it is envisaged that the trustees will benefit some persons or classes of persons more than others where the trustees consider it appropriate. As Chadwick LJ has stated[4]:

> 'Properly understood, the so-called duty to act impartially is no more than the ordinary duty which the law imposes on a person who is entrusted with the exercise of a discretionary power: that he exercises the power for the purpose for which it is given, giving proper consideration to the matters which are relevant and excluding from consideration matters which are irrelevant. If trustees do that, they cannot be criticised if they reach a decision which appears to prefer the claims of one interest over others. The preference will be the result of a proper exercise of the discretionary power.'

Scott V-C has pointed out[5]:

1 *Re Barton's Trust* (1868) LR 5 Eq 238; *Bouch v Sproule* (1887) 12 App Cas 385, HL. As to apportionment of income on death of life tenant, see *Re Jowitt* [1922] 2 Ch 442. It cannot be left to trustees to resolve problems by determining whether an augmentation is to capital or to income, so ousting the jurisdiction of the court: *Re Raven* [1915] 1 Ch 673 at 677; *Re Bromson* (1958) 14 DLR (2d) 51. However, the settlor can confer power on his trustees to allocate augmentations, whether objectively capital or income augmentations, to the income or capital accounts, so leaving the trustees unhampered in their efforts to act impartially or fairly between income and capital beneficiaries.

2 *Re Hillas-Drake* [1944] Ch 235, [1944] 1 All ER 375, and *Re Slee* [1962] 1 All ER 542, [1962] 1 WLR 496, not following *Re Gunther's Will Trusts* [1939] Ch 985, [1939] 3 All ER 291; *Re Oram* [1940] Ch 1001, [1940] 4 All ER 161.

3 *Re Forster-Brown* [1914] 2 Ch 584; and *Re Cooke* [1916] 1 Ch 480, and cases there cited.

4 *Edge v Pensions Ombudsman* [2000] Ch 602 at 627.

5 [2000] Ch 602 at 618. Further see Article 61 below.

'The judge may disagree with the manner in which the trustees have exercised their discretion but, unless they can be seen to have taken into account irrelevant, improper or irrational factors, or unless their decision can be said to be one that no reasonable body of trustees properly directing themselves could have reached, the judge cannot interfere. In particular, he cannot interfere simply on the ground that the partiality showed to the preferred beneficiaries was, in his opinion, undue.'

Choice of investments

Again, where trustees have a choice of investments, they must not exercise that choice for the *sole* benefit of the tenant for life, by investing upon a highly productive but insecure property[6]. 'The obligation of a trustee is to administer the trust fund impartially or fairly, having regard to the different interests of beneficiaries'[7]. He can take into account the income needs of a life tenant and the fact that the life tenant was close to the settlor (eg his widow) and a primary object of the trust, whilst the remainderman is a remoter relative or stranger who is fairly wealthy, so as to tilt the balance in favour of the penurious life tenant even if this could lead to the real value of the capital being eroded[8].

However, if to benefit the testator's widow as life tenant of a testamentary trust, the trustees sell the main asset, a farm, and invest the proceeds solely in fixed interest securities to produce a high income, without diversifying into stocks and shares for capital growth purposes, the trustees will be liable for breach of trust[9].

A trustee can even take its own position into account where it has an equitable lien over the trust fund covering its liabilities as trustee to third parties, but it must act in a fair even-handed fashion as between the beneficiaries and itself[10].

Discretionary distribution of capital growth as if income

In trust law capital is to income as land is to the harvest therefrom and as a tree is to the fruit thereof, while economists and investors consider income to be the maximum amount a person can spend in a year and still expect to be as well off at the end of the year as at the beginning. This is the concept of

---

6 *Raby v Ridehalgh* (1855) 7 De GM & G 104; and *Stuart v Stuart* (1841) 3 Beav 430; cf *Beauclerk v Ashburnham* (1845) 8 Beav 322. The first of these cases was applied in *Re Pauling's Settlement, Younghusband v Coutts & Co (No 2)* [1963] Ch 576, [1963] 1 All ER 857. There, Wilberforce J made it clear that the trustee's duty in matters of investment to hold an equitable balance between capital and income is paramount. A trustee who has committed a breach of trust and claims that this was instigated by the life tenant and that he has therefore a right to recoup his liability out of the trust income, has no right to regulate investment policy for the purpose of ensuring that the income is substantial enough to cover this liability; still less to oppose the appointment by the court of other trustees to replace him on the ground that it would prevent him from exercising such a right. A trustee's right of recoupment does not end with his trusteeship.

7 *Nestlé v National Westminster Bank* [1994] 1 All ER 118 at 136 per Staughton LJ. This may require sale of a shareholding settled by S on his mother for life, remainder to himself where income is low though capital appreciation is high: *Re Smith* (1971) 16 DLR (3d) 130; affd (1971) 18 DLR (3d) 405.

8 *Nestlé v National Westminster Bank* [1994] 1 All ER 118 at 137 and by Hoffmann J at first instance [2000] WTLR 795 where he emphasised that the trustees must not be judged on individual investments but on the whole portfolio of investments.

9 *Re Mulligan* [1998] 1 NZLR 481.

10 *X v A* [2000] 1 All ER 490 at 495.

total return consisting of income yield plus capital growth[11]. Thus, if £1 million of trust assets appreciate to be worth £1,100,000 at the end of the year and yield income of £40,000, then the total return of £140,000 (less an amount for inflation) can be distributed as if it were income, and not just the actual £40,000 income, if the terms of the trust permit payment of capital (at least to the extent of £100,000) to income beneficiaries. While the trustee is obliged to pay out the actual £40,000 income to income beneficiaries, it has a discretion as to what extent, if any, it exercises any discretionary power to distribute capital to income beneficiaries. It must bear in mind that if, in its discretion pursuant to a power in that behalf, it distributes the whole of the total return each year, then the value of the trust fund will not grow so as to protect the capital beneficiaries from inflation.

It may be that the trustee forms an investment company to hold the portfolio of investments or that such a company with an extensive portfolio of investments is transferred to the trustee to create the trust property. If the company accounts are properly drawn up on the basis that profits and gains on investments are income of the company, this does not mean that such profits and gains are to be regarded as income of a life tenant under the trust that owns the company. However, dividends declared by such company out of the company's available income (including profits and gains) would rank as income of the trust to be distributed to the life tenant, but the trustee controlling the company under a duty as trustee to act fairly is not obliged to distribute by way of dividend all profits and gains on investments, although it should so distribute for the benefit of the life tenant the actual income yield from the investments owned by the company[12] as income to which the life tenant is entitled on trust accountancy principles.

Trustee must not exert influence against the interest of a beneficiary

On the principle enunciated in the article now under consideration, trustees must not threaten to exert their influence with third parties to the prejudice of one of their beneficiaries, in order to coerce him into consenting to a disposition of the trust property more favourable to another of the beneficiaries than would be the case if the settlement were strictly performed[13].

Annuities

On the principle that one beneficiary should not be preferred at the expense of another, where an annuity is payable out of income, the trustees will often have no power to accumulate surplus income for the purpose of better securing the annuity[14]. But the question is one of intention, and the position will usually be different if the annuity constitutes a continuing charge on

---

11 *Cowan v Scargill* [1985] Ch 270 at 287; *Anker-Petersen v Anker-Petersen* [2000] WTLR 581, Lord Nicholls in 'Trustees and their Broader Community' (1995) 9 Trust LI 71 at 75; *JW v Morgan Trust Co of the Bahamas Ltd* (2002) 4 ITELR 541.

12 *JW v Morgan Trust Co of the Bahamas Ltd* (2002) 4 ITELR 541; and *see Lloyds Bank plc v Duker* [1987] 1 WLR 1324. If there was a power in the trust instrument for the trustees not to exercise their controlling rights to ensure the company declares a dividend (often a standard power), then the trustees would not be obliged to declare a dividend of the actual income yield unless they considered this appropriate in all the circumstances.

13 *Ellis v Barker* (1871) 7 Ch App 104.

14 *Re Platt* [1916] 2 Ch 563. See also *Re Chance* [1962] Ch 593, [1962] 1 All ER 942.

income: thus Russell LJ said in *Re Berkeley*[15]:

'It is well settled that in the ordinary case where a testamentary annuity is charged on both income and capital of the estate, the annuitant is entitled to require the executors not to part with any income or capital of residue lest it should turn out later that the estate is in fact otherwise insufficient to meet the annuity: see *Re Coller's Deed Trusts*[16]. This right is not, however, absolute, and distribution is not held up where it could not prejudice the annuitant: see *Re Coller.*'

Where resort may be had to capital for the payment of an annuity if the income of a fund is insufficient to discharge it, and the trustees have had such resort, the capital beneficiaries are not entitled to be recouped from surplus income of subsequent years the amounts of capital applied in this way[17].

Where the payment of an annuity falls into arrears because there is insufficient income to pay it, and the income of the trust fund later increases, the arrears must be discharged but the annuitant cannot claim interest on them[18].

An annuitant is not entitled to require the capitalised value of his annuity to be paid to him[19]. But if T by will directs that an annuity be purchased for A for life A is entitled to take the purchase money instead of the annuity[20]. If, instead, T had conferred a power on his executors and trustee to purchase an annuity for A, the executor and trustee has power to pay the purchase money to A instead of purchasing an annuity[1].

Tax-free annuities: rule in *Re Pettit*

An annuitant under a trust is in the same position with regard to income tax as any other annuitant. The annuity is a separate source of taxable income[2] from which, whether or not it is paid out of taxed income, tax at the basic rate is deductible on payment by the trustees to the annuitant[3].

An agreement for the payment of an annuity without deduction of tax is void[4], but this rule applies only to agreements to pay in full without allowing for the deduction of tax[5], and does not apply when the true agreement is merely that the payer, and not the payee, is to bear the tax. Provisions for the payment of an annuity 'free of tax' have been construed in this way and held valid[6], and the House of Lords has confirmed this construction and indicated that it should be applied to all such provisions[7]. An annuity incorporating a provision of this kind is therefore considered as an annuity of a gross sum

---

15 [1968] Ch 744, [1968] 3 All ER 364, CA.

16 [1939] Ch 277, [1937] 3 All ER 292, CA.

17 *Re Croxon* [1915] 2 Ch 290, followed in *Re Berkeley* [1968] Ch 744, [1968] 3 All ER 364, CA.

18 *Torre v Browne* (1855) 5 HL Cas 555, followed in *Re Berkeley* [1968] Ch 744, [1968] 3 All ER 364, CA.

19 *Wright v Callender* (1852) 2 De GM & G 652. Only if those entitled to capital consented could the annuitant obtain the capitalised value of his annuity.

20 *Stokes v Cheek* (1860) 28 Beav 620; *Re Robbins* [1907] 2 Ch 8.

1 *Messeena v Carn* (1870) LR 9 Eq 260; *Re Mabbett* [1891] 1 Ch 707.

2 Schedule D, Case III (Income and Corporation Taxes Act 1988, s 18(3)).

3 Income and Corporation Taxes Act 1988, s 348.

4 Taxes Management Act 1970, s 106(2).

5 *Ferguson v IRC* [1970] AC 442, [1969] 1 All ER 1025, HL.

6 *Festing v Taylor* (1862) 3 B & S 217; *Burroughes v Abbott* [1922] 1 Ch 86; *Re Goodson's Settlement* [1943] Ch 101, [1943] 1 All ER 201.

7 *Ferguson v IRC* [1970] AC 442, [1969] 1 All ER 1025, HL.

from which tax at the basic rate has been deducted on payment[8]. The beneficiary's circumstances (with personal allowances and reliefs) may, however, be such as not to render him liable to suffer tax at the basic rate on the whole annuity, and in that event he is accountable to the trustees for so much of the repayment received as is attributable to the annuity in accordance with the rule in *Re Pettif*[9]. This rule applies only where the annuity is free of tax at the annuitant's effective rate (ie a rate dependent on the annuitant's personal circumstances); where the annuity is free of tax at the basic rate irrespective of the annuitant's personal circumstances, no refund of tax recovered falls to be made by the annuitant to the trustees[10]. This distinction must be drawn upon a proper interpretation of the wording of the will or settlement[11]. The question whether the annuity is or is not free of higher rate tax requires to be settled similarly.

Where the rule applies the annuitant is obliged[12] to claim the allowances and reliefs[13] due to him and to pay to the trustees the whole or part of any refund of tax so received, the proportion being calculated in accordance with the method laid down in *IRC v Cook*[14]. The annuitant's refund to the trustees is calculated from the value of his personal allowances and reliefs which is apportioned between the gross annuity and the annuitant's total income; the part apportioned to the annuity is refunded to the trustees. The refund so received by the trustees may be regarded as net income of the trust in the year in which it is received by the trustees. It may be distributed to beneficiaries as a net sum which has borne tax, and, in appropriate cases, will reduce any liability under s 3 of the Income and Corporation Taxes Act 1988 if the gross amount of the annuity exceeds the taxed income of the trust. If the annuitant is liable to higher rate tax (or the investment income surcharge if reintroduced) he is entitled to claim a proportion of his excess liability

8 See per Lord Sands in *Hunter's Trustees v Mitchell* 1930 SC 978, approved in *IRC v Cook* [1946] AC 1, [1945] 2 All ER 377, HL.
9 [1922] 2 Ch 765.
10 *Re Jones* [1933] Ch 842.
11 In *Re Pettit* [1922] 2 Ch 765, an annuity 'free of tax' was held to mean free of tax at the annuitant's effective rate. Decisions to the same effect were reached in *Re Maclennan* [1939] Ch 750, [1939] 3 All ER 81, CA, on the words 'clear of all deductions for income tax'; in *Re Jubb* (1941) 20 ATC 297, on the words 'free of death duties and all other taxes'; and in *Re Tatham* [1945] Ch 34, [1945] 1 All ER 29, where the annuitant was held accountable, inter alia, for postwar credits. In *Re Jones* [1933] Ch 842, the words 'such annuity as after deducting income tax at the current rate for the time being would amount to a clear yearly sum of ... ' was held to mean free of tax at the standard rate; cf *Re Eves* [1939] Ch 969, where an annuity free of income tax at the current rate for the time being deductible at source was considered to be free of tax at the annuitant's effective rate. For cases where the tax-free element was restricted to a certain rate by the instrument itself, see *Re Bates' Wills Trust* [1946] Ch 83, [1945] 2 All ER 688; *Re Arno* [1947] Ch 198, [1947] 1 All ER 64, CA.
12 *Re Kingcome* [1936] Ch 566, [1936] 1 All ER 173.
13 As to the allowances and reliefs which come within the rule, see Simon's Taxes, E 2.1123 et seq.
14 [1946] AC 1, [1945] 2 All ER 377, HL. The calculation of the refund is explained in detail in Simon's Taxes E 2.1125 et seq from which the following comment is quoted: 'It is apparent from a study of the speeches of the majority (Viscount Maugham, Lord Thankerton and Lord Porter) and of the dissenting speeches (Lord Russell of Killowen and Lord Simonds) in *IRC v Cook* [1946] AC 1, [1945] 2 All ER 377 and from the formula employed before that decision, that the whole method of calculation is fraught with difficulty. It would appear that no method suggested in argument or in speeches completely carries out the intention of the testator and is at the same time completely in accordance with the provisions of the Income Tax Acts. But the present method of calculating the gross annuity, whatever the results and complications in applying it, is in itself simple and definite.'

(that is, the liability in excess of tax at the basic rate) from the trustees, calculated in the ratio which the gross annuity bears to his total income.

Depreciation reserves

Where trustees are lawfully managing a business the trustees are justified in setting aside part of the profits for depreciation before determining net profits[15], though where trustees own a company carrying on a business it is the dividends declared in respect of shares in the company that are the income of the trust[16]. There seems scope for developing the trustees' duty of fairness or impartiality so as to justify taking a depreciation reserve where assets in the trust fund are in fact depreciating to the point where the remainderman is suffering an actual disadvantage in relation to the income beneficiary[17], particularly if the trustees have power in the trust instrument to allocate receipts or expenditure to income or capital as they deem appropriate.

PARAGRAPH 2

Augmentation of capital[18]

Where a company, out of a reserve fund, pays up unissued capital, and allots it credited as fully paid among old shareholders, any shares so allotted to trustees will be held by them as capital and as an accretion to the shares originally held by them, and will not belong to the person entitled to the trust income[19]. This is only logical when it is remembered that the true effect of the new issue is not to increase the holding because the persons to whom the new shares are issued will continue to hold the same proportion of the capital[20].

Bonuses

So where bonuses are paid *as part of capital*, they will be retained as capital by the trustee; but where bonuses are mere expressions for extra dividend income, this will not be the case. As Fry LJ said in *Re Bouch*[1] in a passage quoted with approval by Lord Herschell in giving judgment on the same case in the House of Lords (where the House of Lords rejected the Court of Appeal's inference of fact that the company intended the bonuses to be income rather than capital)[2]:

15 *Re Crabtree* [1912] WN 24, 106 LT 49, CA; *McBride v Hudson* (1962) 107 CLR 604 at 623; *Re Hunter* [1958] 77 NZLR 654 at 660; *Re Katz* (1981) 112 DLR (3d) 529.
16 *Comr of Taxes v Pratt Estate Co Ltd* [1934] NZLR 347.
17 *Re Zive* (1977) 77 DLR (3d) 669 at 680 where the trust fund consisted almost entirely of 19 investment properties leased to tenants.
18 The notes to this paragraph deal with the question of when an accretion to the trust fund is to be treated as capital, and when as income.
19 *Bouch v Sproule* (1887) 12 App Cas 385, HL; *Re Northage* (1891) 60 LJ Ch 488; *Re Joel* [1936] 2 All ER 962; *Re Wright's Settlement Trusts* [1945] Ch 211, [1945] 1 All ER 587.
20 *Re Whitfield* [1920] WN 256.
 1 (1885) 29 Ch D 635 at 653; For capital intentions see *Re Evans* [1913] 1 Ch 23; *Re Ogilvie* (1919) 35 TLR 218; *IRC v Blott* [1921] 2 AC 171, HL; *Re Taylor* [1926] Ch 923; *IRC v Wright* [1927] 1 KB 333, CA.
 2 (1887) 12 App Cas 385 at 397.

'When a testator or settlor directs or permits the subject of his disposition to remain as shares or stock in a company which has the power either of distributing its profits as dividend, or of converting them into capital, and the company validly exercises this power, such exercise of its power is binding on all persons interested under him, the testator or settlor, in the shares, and consequently what is paid by the company as dividend goes to the tenant for life, and what is paid by the company to the shareholder as capital, or appropriated as an increase of the capital stock in the concern, enures to the benefit of all who are interested in the capital'[3].

To understand problems in ascertaining, in the light of case law, what a company's intentions were, it is necessary to appreciate that by virtue of s 25 of the Companies Act 1867 the procedure adopted in *Bouch v Sproule* (and cases after the Companies Act 1900 where old habits died hard) in issuing new shares involved the company: (a) declaring a dividend and issuing a dividend warrant to its shareholders; (b) allotting the new shares to those shareholders; and (c) giving the shareholders the option either to cash the dividend warrant or have the dividend applied in paying up the allotted shares.

An illuminating explanation of *Bouch v Sproule* was given in the Privy Council case of *Hill v Permanent Trustee Co of New South Wales*[4], where Lord Russell of Killowen laid down the following principles:

'(1) A limited company when it parts with moneys available for distribution among its shareholders is not concerned with the fate of those moneys in the hands of any shareholder. The company does not know and does not care whether a shareholder is a trustee of his share or not. It is of no concern to a company which is parting with moneys to a shareholder whether that shareholder (if he be a trustee) will hold them as trustee for A absolutely or as trustee for A for life only.

(2) A limited company not in liquidation can make no payment by way of return of capital to its shareholders except in an authorised reduction of capital. Any other payment made by it by means of which it parts with moneys to its shareholders must and can only be by way of dividing profits. Whether the payment is called "dividend" or "bonus", or any other name, it must still remain a payment on division of profits.

(3) Moneys so paid to a shareholder will (if he be a trustee) prima facie belong to the person beneficially entitled to the income of the trust estate. If such moneys or any part thereof are to be treated as part of the corpus of the trust estate there must be some provision in the trust deed which brings about that result ...

3 For income intentions see *Re Northage* (1891) 60 LJ Ch 488; *Re Tindal* (1892) 9 TLR 24; *Re Malam* [1894] 3 Ch 578; *Re Despard* (1901) 17 TLR 478 and *Re Hume Nisbet's Settlement* (1911) 27 TLR 461, where Eve J admitted that but for *Re Northage* (supra) (which may, in any event, be distinguished as a more complex scheme where the option to take bonus shares was not available to all shareholders receiving the dividend) he would have had difficulty in distinguishing his case from *Bouch v Sproule* (supra) where a capital intention was found: perhaps the income cases other than *Re Northage* were wrongly decided. As to the principles on which profits ought to be ascertained by companies, see *Lubbock v British Bank of South America* [1892] 2 Ch 198; and *Re Taylor* [1926] Ch 923. In *Re Outen's Will Trusts* [1963] Ch 291, [1962] 3 All ER 478, Plowman J held, following *Bouch v Sproule*, above, that a company's decision to capitalise reserves of profits by issuing loan stock to ordinary shareholders effected a capitalisation of the profits which was binding on the shareholders so as to make the loan stock capital in the hands of trustees.

4 [1930] AC 720 at 730–732; following *Re Bates* [1928] Ch 682L. *Re Ward's Will Trusts* [1936] Ch 704, [1936] 2 All ER 773, appears not to be good law; see *Re Doughty* [1947] Ch 263, [1947] 1 All ER 207, CA; *Hill v Permanent Trustee Co of New South Wales*, above, was distinguished in *Re Outen's Will Trusts* (see note 3, above).

(4) Other considerations arise when a limited company with power to increase its capital and possessing a fund of undivided profits, so deals with it that no part leaves the possession of the company, but the whole is applied in paying up new shares which are issued and allotted proportionately to the shareholders, who would have been entitled to receive the fund had it been, in fact, divided and paid away as dividend.

(5) The result of such a dealing is obviously wholly different from the result of paying away the profits to the shareholders. In the latter case the amount of cash distributed disappears on both sides of the company's balance sheet ... the cash necessary to provide the dividend is raised and paid away, the company's assets being reduced by that amount. In the former case the assets of the company remain undiminished ... '

Moneys received by trustees on the distribution amongst shareholders of a share premium account through the medium of a reduction petition are capital assets in their hands. Section 130 of the Companies Act 1985, which requires all premiums on the issue of shares to be placed to the credit of a share premium account which can only be applied in specified ways, takes the moneys in the account out of the category of divisible profit and prevents them from being distributed by way of dividend. The only way in which they can be distributed among the shareholders is by a transaction to which the provisions relating to reduction of capital apply or in the guise of the premium payable on the redemption of redeemable preference shares. In the former case there is a reduction in the value of every share and thus a reduction of capital though not of share capital[5].

Where shares are transferred under a scheme of arrangement or debentures are issued in lieu of arrears of dividend or interest they must be treated as income even although an additional bonus of 1% is added as a solatium[6], and the same course is adopted on the distribution of a reserve fund which has never been capitalised[7]. And where, under a scheme sanctioned by the court under what is now s 425 of the Companies Act 1985, cash and debentures of another company were issued to trustees in satisfaction of amounts due to them from a company under debentures in respect of both capital and arrears of interest (and in respect of interest agreed to be paid on these arrears), it was held that a fraction of the assets thus received by the trustees should be treated as income, the fraction bearing the same proportion to the whole of the assets received as the arrears of interest (and the interest thereon) bore to the total amount of principal and arrears of interest (and interest thereon) secured by the original debentures when the scheme was approved[8].

As Lord Reid stated in *Rae v Lazard Investments Co Ltd*[9] the current position is that 'there is no doubt that every distribution of money or money's worth by an English company must be treated as income in the hands of the shareholders unless it is either a distribution in a liquidation, a repayment in respect of reduction of capital (or a payment out of a special premium account) or an issue of bonus shares (or it may be bonus debentures)'. To

5 *Re Duff's Settlement Trusts* [1951] Ch 923, [1951] 2 All ER 534, CA.
6 *Re Pennington* [1915] WN 333; *Re Sandbach* [1933] Ch 505; *Re Smith's Will Trusts* [1936] 2 All ER 1210.
7 *Re Thomas* [1916] 2 Ch 331, CA.
8 *Re Morris' Will Trusts* [1960] 3 All ER 548, [1960] 1 WLR 1210, following *Re Atkinson* [1904] 2 Ch 160, CA, and *Smith v Law Guarantee and Trust Society Ltd* [1904] 2 Ch 569, CA, and explaining and distinguishing *Re Pennington* [1914] 1 Ch 203, CA.
9 [1963] 1 WLR 555 at 565.

these exceptions must be added, by analogy with reductions of share capital, the proceeds of a purchase by a company of its own shares; also the declaration of a dividend immediately used to satisfy a contemporaneous call of unpaid share capital[10] and the type of indirect merger dealt with in *Sinclair v Lee*[11], which can be understood after considering the 'capital profits dividends' cases arising out of the nationalisation of Thomas Tilling & Co Ltd.

'Capital profits dividends'

In *Re Doughty*[12] a company had declared an 'additional dividend or distribution' out of capital profits, ie profits resulting from the realisation of capital assets, and it was held that they fell under the word 'income' in the will in question, although not subject to income tax in the hands of the recipient.

The distribution of a sum of British Transport Stock by way of 'capital profits dividend' upon the nationalisation of a part of the undertaking of Thomas Tilling & Co Ltd led to a number of applications to the court[13].

In *Re Sechiari*[14] and *Re Kleinwort's Settlements*[15], in neither of which cases any special circumstances existed, it was held that the British Transport Stock was received by trustee shareholders as income and not as capital and, accordingly, it belonged to the tenant for life, but Romer J in the one case, and Vaisey J in the other, indicated that jurisdiction to apportion existed and would be exercised in a proper case.

In *Re Rudd's Will Trusts*[16] it was held that the failure of the trustees to sell the whole or part of the Tilling Stock before it went ex-dividend and thus realise a large profit for capital was not a breach of trust such as would bring the jurisdiction to apportion into play, and that no part of the British Transport Stock ought to be apportioned to capital.

In *Re Winder's Will Trusts*[17] the application was made by trustees of the will of a testator who had died before the distribution of British Transport Stock, but after the right to it crystallised so that it formed an asset of his estate before his death. It was held by Romer J that in the circumstances the stock when received ought to be treated as capital for the purposes of the trusts of the will.

In *Re Maclaren's Settlement Trusts*[18] the tenant for life assented to the purchase as a capital investment of stock of Thomas Tilling & Co Ltd at a time when it was known that that company proposed to distribute the British Transport Stock it received amongst its stockholders. He subsequently requested the sale of both the Tilling Stock and British Transport Stock and its re-investment in the purchase of a freehold house as a residence for himself. It was held that in the circumstances the Transport Stock and the proceeds of its sale had 'assumed the guise of capital'.

10 *Re Hatton* [1917] 1 Ch 357.
11 [1993] Ch 497.
12 [1947] Ch 263, [1947] 1 All ER 207.
13 See CII Law Journal 270.
14 [1950] 1 All ER 417.
15 [1951] Ch 860, [1951] 2 All ER 328.
16 [1952] 1 All ER 254.
17 [1951] Ch 916, [1951] 2 All ER 362.
18 [1951] 2 All ER 414.

Demergers

A demerger involves a company hiving off part of its business to a new company and arranging for its shareholders to receive the shares in the new company. Thus one capital asset, the shares in the distributing company, is converted into two capital assets, the shares in the distributing company plus the shares in the new demerged company. A direct demerger involves the distributing company hiving off a part of its business to a subsidiary and then distributing shares in the subsidiary or a holding company thereof by way of an in specie dividend to its shareholders. In such a case the receipt by trustees of shares in the demerged company will continue to be an income receipt following *Re Sechiari*[19], *Re Kleinworts Settlements*[20] and *Briggs v IRC*[1] unless the House of Lords on appeal can be persuaded to take a more realistic course.

In the case of indirect demergers Nicholls V-C[2] was able to distinguish the above cases to take the realistic course of holding the shares in the new indirectly demerged company to be capital, it being crucial in such an indirect demerger that the distributing company does not own the shares in the demerged company which are transferred to its shareholders.

Enhanced scrip dividends

With conventional scrip dividends a company declares a dividend but gives each shareholder the option to take the dividend either as cash or as bonus shares. The receipt is income in nature, even if the shareholder elects to take the bonus shares because the company's intention was to pay a dividend and not to capitalise its profits: the number of bonus shares is calculated by dividing the amount of the dividend receivable by the ex-dividend market value of the shares. Enhanced scrip dividends differ because the bonus shares are issued at a price below their current market value, so that if a shareholder elects to receive shares he will get assets of greater value than the cash dividend. Indeed, the company often arranges for a third party to be ready to purchase the bonus shares at market value so that the shareholders can quickly realise the cash value of the shares. In ascertaining the company's intention as required by *Bouch v Sproule* it seems that for various reasons (like avoiding Advance Corporation Tax, before its abolition, while maintaining a regular distribution policy) the company intends shareholders to take scrip, because it is deliberately made worth much more than the cash dividend, so that the bonus shares, and the proceeds of sale thereof, are capital[3].

To obtain most for the trust the trustees should take the bonus shares but to reimburse the life tenant for lost income they could exercise, if it exists, a power to pay out of capital a sum corresponding to the amount of cash dividend. Alternatively, because the Revenue have accepted[4] that *Re Malam*[5] can be applied to capital profits, the trustees can elect to allow the life tenant a lien over the bonus shares to the amount of the cash dividend, and satisfy

19 [1950] 1 All ER 417.
20 [1951] Ch 860.
 1 (1932) 17 TC 11 and *Re Doughty* [1947] Ch 263.
 2 *Sinclair v Lee* [1993] Ch 497.
 3 *Hawkins v Hawkins* (1920) SRNSW 550.
 4 SP4/94.
 5 [1894] 3 Ch 578.

the lien out of capital cash.

It is, however, possible for trustees to take the factual view that the company with its enhanced scrip dividend policy was not, as in the *Bouch v Sproule* capitalisation cases, concerned to find a way of capitalising profits and issuing new shares, but had a policy developed from the conventional scrip dividend scheme where the intention is to pay dividend income but with the difference that the bonus shares are issued well below market value, such being part of a regular distribution policy so as not to be a 'special' or 'bonus' dividend.

The Revenue will accept the capital approach, the *Malam* approach or the income approach if supportable, as will often be the case on the particular facts involved, so that the tax consequences will much influence the approach to be adopted.

Profit on realisation of investments

It need scarcely be pointed out that where, on a change of investment, trust securities realise more than was given for them originally, the profit accrues to capital, and is not considered as income payable to the tenant for life. In the same way, where trustees of a mortgage debt foreclose, and subsequently sell the property for more than the debt and arrears of interest and costs, the balance is to be held by them as an augmentation to the capital of the trust fund. For as any diminution of the trust property would have to be borne by all the beneficiaries, and would not fall on the tenant for life only, so it is only fair that any casual augmentation should belong to all, and not merely to the life tenant.

Stocks purchased or sold by trustees 'cum dividend'

When trustees invest capital in the purchase of stocks or shares, on which, at the date of purchase, dividends have been earned and declared, but not paid, such dividends must be carried to capital and not paid as income[6]. The fairness of this is obvious. But it is also settled (with less obvious fairness) that, in the absence of special circumstances, no apportionment of income will be made where stocks are sold between two dividend days[7]. This appears to be founded merely on convenience, for Kindersley V-C in *Scholefield v Redfern*[8], while admitting that much might be said in favour of apportionment in such cases, said:

> 'When we consider a little further, it is obvious, that if the tenant for life is to have something out of the sale money, as representing income, then when the trustees invest the money, unless they invest it on the very day on which the dividend has just accrued due, the same equity ought to be administered the other way, and we ought to take from the tenant for life something of his next dividend ... and add that to the capital, in order to make things equal as between him and the remainderman. It is clear that if there is an equity one way, there is an equity the other way. It is obvious that the reason why such equity on either side has never been administered habitually by this court is, that by attempting it, a grievous burden would be

---

6 *Re Sir Robert Peel's Settled Estates* [1910] 1 Ch 389.

7 *Bulkeley v Stephens* [1896] 2 Ch 241; *Scholefield v Redfern* (1863) 2 Drew & Sm 173; *Freman v Whitbread* (1865) LR 1 Eq 266; *Re Henderson* [1940] Ch 368, [1940] 1 All ER 623.

8 (1863) 2 Drew & Sm 173 at 182.

imposed upon the estates of testators, by reason of the complex investigations which it would lead to.'

Again, in *Re Henderson*[9] Morton J pointed out the difficulty of ascertaining by what sum the purchase price was increased by reason of the fact that a dividend was accruing, and said:

'Let me assume that the dividend was paid half-yearly, that the tenant for life dies when three months of the half-year have expired, and that the investment is sold two months later. Can it ever be ascertained with accuracy what portion of the purchase-price represents five-sixths of the half-yearly dividend which is accruing?'

But the practice does not hold where the dividend is declared, but not paid at the date of the sale[10].

In *Re Winterstoke's Will Trusts*[11] Clauson J with a view to preserving the rights between tenant for life and remainderman, declared that the trustees ought to apportion the purchase price of shares in a certain way between capital and income. His decision was shortly afterwards criticised in *Re Firth*[12] by Farwell J who said that only very special circumstances would justify the process applied by Clauson J and found no such circumstances in the case before him.

These two cases were considered in *Re MacLaren's Settlement Trusts* by Harman J who said[13]:

'The court can, then, in special circumstances apportion between capital and income on sale or purchases of stock cum dividend or ex dividend, although it is not the practice to do so in the ordinary way because the various persons interested under settlements ought to take the rough with the smooth, and in order to ease the burden falling on trustees. The jurisdiction, however, exercised in special circumstances seems to be only the exercise of a right to make a more exact distinction of income from capital. As a matter of convenience, the practice is in the ordinary case that no apportionments are made, with the result that capital sometimes gets what, on a more exact scrutiny, would prove to be income or vice versa. Where this produces a glaring injustice, the court will cause a more exact calculation to be made, but it does not treat as income that which is capital, or as capital that which is income.'

In *Re Ellerman*[14] Nourse J therefore considered *Re Winterstoke's WT* to be wrong so that it ought not to be followed.

Where stocks were directed to be transferred in specie to a class on the death of a life tenant, but for convenience of division were sold and the proceeds divided, then, as his personal representatives would, under the Apportionment Act, have been entitled to an apportionment of the income up to his death if the trust had been strictly carried out, the court directed that a similar apportionment should be made in respect of the proceeds of the sale[15]. On the other hand, where there has been no dividend paid during the tenancy for life on cumulative preferred shares, it has been held that the

 9 [1940] Ch 368, [1940] 1 All ER 623.
10 *Re Sir Robert Peel's Settled Estates* [1910] 1 Ch 389.
11 [1938] Ch 158, [1937] 4 All ER 63.
12 [1938] Ch 517, [1938] 2 All ER 217; explained, *Re Henderson* [1940] Ch 368, [1940] 1 All ER 623.
13 [1951] 2 All ER 414 at 420; p 538, ante.
14 [1984] LS Gaz R 430, more fully reported sub nom *Hitch v Ruegg* [1986] TL & P 62.
15 *Bulkeley v Stephens* [1896] 2 Ch 241; *Re Muirhead* [1916] 2 Ch 181; *Re Oppenheimer* [1907] 1 Ch 399; and see *Re Henderson* [1940] Ch 368, [1940] 1 All ER 623.

life tenant's executors have no claim to any part of the dividends paid after his death[16].

Where executors sell stocks to a beneficiary pursuant to a direction in the will no question of apportionment of accruing dividends arises, for the beneficiary, like any other purchaser, 'has bought the tree, and with it the fruits that are ripening on the tree'[17].

Profit on reconstruction of company

In *Re Armitage*[18] a testator gave his estate upon the usual trusts for conversion, with power to postpone, and directed that, pending conversion, the income actually produced should be treated as income. Part of the residue consisted of shares in a company with £8 per share paid up. The company was reconstructed, and the new company paid £9 5s for each of the old shares. The £1 5s was the proceeds partly of the regular reserve fund, and partly of profits which the directors had retained to meet contingencies. It was held that the right of a tenant for life of shares is only to receive dividends and *bonuses in the shape of dividends*, and that, although £1 5s was profits, it was under the circumstances not payable as income.

Director's fee

If trustees are accountable for their fees as directors, having unauthorisedly obtained the directorships by using shares owned as trustee, then the fees are capital of the trust[19].

Unit trusts

In *Re Whitehead's Will Trusts*[20] it was held that trustees who own units in a unit trust need to inquire whether the source of any alleged capital distribution by the managers of the unit trust requires such distribution to be treated as of income or capital, just as if the trustees directly owned the shares in the portfolio of the unit trust, applying the rules earlier explained in relation to distributions by companies where the intentions of the directors of the companies need to be ascertained. This is a difficult task and one that is often overlooked.

PARAGRAPH 3

Whether trustees can safely pay the share of one beneficiary before paying the others

The question sometimes arises whether trustees can safely pay the share of one beneficiary who has attained a vested interest in possession, before paying the other beneficiaries who may not have attained a vested interest or

---

16 *Re Sale* [1913] 2 Ch 697; and *Re Grundy* (1917) 117 LT 470; following *Re Taylor's Trusts* [1905] 1 Ch 734; and distinguishing *Re Griffith* (1879) 12 Ch D 655; *Re Wakley* [1920] 2 Ch 205, CA.
17 *Re Wimbush* [1940] Ch 92, [1940] 1 All ER 229.
18 [1893] 3 Ch 337.
19 *Re Macadam* [1946] Ch 73 at 76–77.
20 [1959] Ch 579.

whose shares (by reason of incapacity or otherwise) are not presently payable[1]. If they do so, it may happen that, by reason of subsequent depreciation of securities, the balance retained by the trustee may be insufficient to pay the other beneficiaries in full, in which case the first beneficiary will have more than the others. It appears, however, to be well settled that if, when the first payment was made, the trustees have, and retain in their hands, assets which, fairly valued, are then sufficient to meet shares which are not presently payable, but have to be held in trust, they are justified in paying other shares payable pari passu but payable at once, and are not liable if the assets so retained should, in the event, prove insufficient to pay the unpaid beneficiaries in full[2]. This is because the sui juris beneficiary has a right to call for his appropriate share[3] and the conduct of trustees is regarded with reference to the facts and circumstances existing at the time when they have to act; and therefore, if they make the variation impartially at that time, they are not liable for an unforeseen loss[4]. Trustees should employ a duly qualified valuer, taking advantage of ss 11(2)(a) and 23(1) of the Trustee Act 2000 or s 22(3) of the Trustee Act 1925.

Appropriation to answer particular shares

Another question which sometimes arises is whether trustees of a settlement or will can treat their trust as several trusts, appropriating specific securities to each; or whether they must treat the trust property as one undivided fund until it becomes necessary, on the death of a life tenant, to pay and distribute his share among his children. For instance, where a settlor settles money either in a specific sum or as a share of residue upon each of his daughters for life, with remainder for her children, ought the trustees to treat the daughters' fortunes as one trust, or as several? If a severance and appropriation of securities be lawful, it may sometimes be convenient; but on the other hand the result may obviously be that (by reason of the appreciation of one appropriated set of securities, or the depreciation of another, or from both such causes) one family may get less, and the other more, than their due proportion of the entire fund. Where the trust is a trust of specific sums (eg £50,000 to be held upon trust for a settlor's daughter A for life, with remainder for her children equally, and £50,000 to be held upon a similar trust for his daughter B and her children), an appropriation is not only undoubtedly legitimate, but ought to be made[5].

---

1 Where the trustees do this and the beneficiary takes the distribution in the form of investments rather than cash the beneficiary will be treated as having received the cash value of these investments (*Re Gollins Declaration of Trust* [1969] 3 All ER 1591, [1969] 1 WLR 1858) unless the investments were specifically appropriated as having a value equivalent to a specific proportion of the whole trust fund: *Re Leigh's Settlement Trusts* [1981] CLY 2453.
2 Per Lindley LJ in *Re Hurst* (1892) 67 LT 96 at 99; *Re Swan* (1864) 2 Hem & M 34 at 37; *Re Winslow* (1890) 45 Ch D 249; *Fenwick v Clarke* (1862) 4 De GF & J 240; *Re Lepine* [1892] 1 Ch 210; and see also *Re Hall* [1903] 2 Ch 226; *Re Gardiner* [1942] NZLR 199; *Re Chirnside* [1974] VR 160.
3 See Art 69, p 729, post.
4 Cf Administration of Estates Act 1925, s 41 which authorises appropriation by personal representatives, subject to certain conditions, of part of the estate of the deceased to answer legacies, including annuities and other shares and interests in the estate: see p 545, post.
5 *Fraser v Murdoch* (1881) 6 App Cas 855; *Re Walker* (1890) 62 LT 449; and see also *Re Lepine* [1892] 1 Ch 210; *Barclay v Owen* (1889) 60 LT 220; *Re Nicholson's Will Trusts* [1936] 3 All ER 832. Unlike the position under the statutory power of appropriation conferred by the Administration of Estates Act 1925, s 41, an appropriation of securities is only valid if the

Where property is left on trust for sale or there is a trust of laand within s 1 of the Trusts of Land and Appointment of Trustees Act 1996, and there is nothing in the trust instrument indicating that no appropriation between the beneficiaries is to be made until some specified event (eg the death of a life tenant interested in one quarter of a fund) then it seems an appropriation can be made[6]. After all, the property could be sold to the beneficiary so he can have the property appropriated to him, being credited with its value at the time[7]. However, it seems that infant beneficiaries incapable of consenting to the appropriation could be bound to an appropriation in their favour if done fairly upon a proper valuation[8].

Doubts now exist in the case of income interests since it has been held that 'an interest in half the income of an undivided fund is quite different from the whole income of a divided half of that fund'[9] so that an appropriation varies the beneficial interests necessitating an application under the Variation of Trusts Act[10] if the statutory power conferred on personal representatives by s 41 of the Administration of Estates Act 1925 is not available and there is no express power of appropriation contained in the trust instrument. A properly drawn trust instrument should contain express powers of appropriation unless the settlor specifically desires no appropriation to take place until the time for distribution to absolutely entitled beneficiaries.

When the appropriation is made the beneficiary absolutely entitled can call for a transfer of the appropriated securities[11]. On similar principles it has been held that the court has jurisdiction to distribute in specie real estate directed to be sold even where there are settled shares if the trustees have power to invest in the purchase of land[12].

Appropriation at cash value or as proportion of trust fund

The general principle is that an appropriation of assets to satisfy the interest of a beneficiary is treated as payment of the cash equivalent to the beneficiary[13]. This may prove unsatisfactory and frustrate the settlor's real intentions if this cash sum is brought into account on final division of the trust

---

appropriated securities were both authorised and sufficient at the date of the appropriation; see *Re Waters* [1889] WN 39. See also *Re Forster-Brown* [1914] 2 Ch 584. It is not, however, necessary that where a trustee appropriates securities to one beneficiary he should appropriate contemporaneously to all (*Re Richardson* [1896] 1 Ch 512; *Re Nickels* [1898] 1 Ch 630) though he should consider whether equality is not best achieved by contemporaneous appropriations.

6 *Re Nickels* [1898] 1 Ch 630; *Re Brooks* (1897) 76 LT 771. Of course an appropriation must be made if directed by the trust instrument, eg *Pexton (Inspector of Taxes) v Bell* [1976] 2 All ER 914 at 949.

7 *Re Beverly* [1901] 1 Ch 681, *followed Re Craven* [1914] 1 Ch 358. Trustees of UK land have all the powers of an absolute owner in relation to the land and so have a power of partition: see TA 2000, s 8(3).

8 *Re Ruddock* (1910) 102 LT 89, CA. TA 1925, s 22(3).

9 *Re Freeston's Charity* [1978] 1 WLR 741 at 751, per Goff LJ stating the effect of *Macculloch v Anderson* [1904] AC 55.

10 See *Re Freeston's Charity* [1978] 1 WLR 741 at 752, per Goff LJ.

11 *Re Marshall* [1914] 1 Ch 192. As to stamp duty, see *Jopling v IRC* [1940] 2 KB 282, [1940] 3 All ER 279.

12 *Re Wragg* [1919] 2 Ch 58; and see also *Re Cooke's Settlement, Tarry v Cooke* [1913] 2 Ch 661. For the statutory power now to acquire land in the UK, see TA 2000, s 8.

13 *Re Gollins Declaration of Trust* [1969] 3 All ER 1591, [1969] 1 WLR 1858.

fund many years later[14]. It will often be better for the trustees to treat the appropriated assets as having a value equivalent to a specified proportion of the trust fund and to obtain the beneficiary's consent to this or the leave of the court[15]. If such consent or leave had not been obtained then on final division it may be possible with leave of the court to bring actual or notional cash sums into account at final division at their value at the time of the beneficiary's receipt multiplied by the increase in the retail price index[16].

Statutory power of appropriation

By s 41 of the Administration of Estates Act 1925 a *personal representative* (which expression does not comprise a trustee)[17] may appropriate any part of the real or personal estate of the deceased in the actual condition or state of investment thereof at the time of appropriation[18] in or towards satisfaction of any legacy bequeathed by the deceased or of any other interest or share in his property, *whether settled or not*, as to the personal representative may seem just and reasonable according to the respective rights of the persons interested in the property of the deceased, but an appropriation may not be made so as to affect prejudicially any specific devise or bequest. When an appropriation is made in respect of any settled legacy share or interest the consent must be obtained either of the trustee thereof, if any (not being also the personal representative himself), or of the person who may for the time being be entitled to the income, or, if the latter is an infant or is incapable, by reason of mental disorder within the meaning of the Mental Health Act 1983, of managing and administering his property and affairs, of his guardian or receiver (if any), or of the court. No consent (save that of that trustee, if any) is required of any person coming into existence after the appropriation, and no consent of any such guardian or receiver is required if the appropriated property is an investment authorised by law or by the trust. Any property so appropriated (though until then not an investment authorised by law or the will) is thereafter to be treated as an authorised investment and may be retained.

The personal representative may ascertain and fix the value of the respective parts of the real and personal estate and the liabilities of the deceased as he may think fit, employing a duly qualified valuer where necessary, and may make any conveyance (including an assent) which may be required for giving effect to the appropriation. The appropriation will bind all parties interested, but in making it the personal representative is to have due regard to the rights of persons who may subsequently come into existence. This statutory power of appropriation is not to prejudice any other power of appropriation conferred by law, or by the will of the deceased, and the property appropriated is to be subject to all trusts for sale and powers of

---

14 Law Reform Committee (23rd Report) Cmnd 8733, para 4.43.
15 *Re Leigh's Settlement Trusts* [1981] CLY 2453.
16 Cmnd 8733, para 4.47.
17 But an express power of appropriation is often conferred upon *trustees* of wills by reference to this section: otherwise personal representatives should consider exercising the power before fully administering the estate and becoming trustees, eg by assenting in favour of themselves as trustees.
18 The deceased's property being appropriated must be revalued at the date of appropriation: *Re Charteris* [1917] 2 Ch 379 at 386; *Re Collins* [1975] 1 WLR 309; *Re Gollins Declaration of Trust* [1969] 3 All ER 1591, [1969] 1 WLR 1858.

leasing, disposition and management in varying investments which would have been applicable if no appropriation had been made. Any appropriation *purporting to have been made under this statutory power* is, in favour of a purchaser, to be deemed to have been made in accordance with the requirements of the section. For the purposes of the section 'settled legacy, share or interest' includes any legacy share or interest to which a person is not absolutely entitled in possession at the date of the appropriation. It will be observed that the statute does not expressly authorise the trustee of the settled property to consent to the appropriation, but it is conceived that it impliedly does so and that it is left to his discretion whether he will consent or not, and that he runs no risk in giving consent so long as it is reasonable to do so.

Paragraph 4

Application of hotchpot provisions

Cases in which children have to bring sums, whether advances or loans[19], into hotchpot sometimes present great difficulty. An express hotchpot clause should be drawn up in clear terms resolving potential difficulties. Beneficiaries may also have to bring property into hotchpot as a result of the application of the equitable presumption against double portions[20], but since January 1996 spouses and issue of a person dying wholly or partly intestate no longer are subject to the hotchpot provisions in s 47(1)(iii) or s 49(1)(a) of the Administration of Estates Act 1925 which were repealed by the Law Reform (Succession) Act 1995.

The actual amount brought into hotchpot is normally the value of the portion or advancement as at the date received by the beneficiary[1].

It seems the impact of inheritance tax should be dealt with by bringing into account the net value of the benefit to the beneficiary against the net estate of the deceased where it is the deceased's estate that is distributable[2]. Where a trust fund is distributable on some event occurring (such as a life tenant's death) it seems likely that the gross amount (subject to inheritance tax) advanced to the beneficiary should be brought into account against the gross amount available on eventual distribution[3]. In a hotchpot calculation it is crucial whether the value of the distributable assets is to be reckoned as of the date of actual distribution or of the date of notional distribution. The date of notional distribution will usually be the date of a testator's death or of a life tenant's death or of a beneficiary satisfying some contingency. The date of actual distribution is the subsequent date when the distributable assets are actually distributed. In the absence of some indication in the will or trust deed that the distributable assets are to be valued at the date for notional

---

19 *Re Horn* [1946] Ch 254, [1946] 2 All ER 118, CA, affords a good example of a hotchpot clause adapted to meet the case of outstanding loans. Generally see (1961) 25 Conv 468 (JT Farrand); *Theobald on Wills* (15th edn) pp 757 et seq.

20 A legacy or share of residue is presumed adeemed if the testator made an earlier gift by way of portion when in loco parentis: generally see *Re Cameron* [1999] Ch 386 applied to a half share in realty in *Race v Race* [2002] WTLR 1193.

1 *Watson v Watson* (1864) 33 Beav 574; *Re Innes* (1908) 125 LT Jo 60; *Re Crocker* [1916] 1 Ch 25.

2 *Re Beddington* [1900] 1 Ch 771; *Re Crocker* [1916] 1 Ch 25; *Re Turner's Will Trusts* [1968] 1 All ER 321, [1968] 1 WLR 227; (1961) 25 Conv 468 at 487 (JT Farrand).

3 *Re Tollemache* [1930] WN 138; *Re Slee* [1962] 1 All ER 542, [1962] 1 WLR 496.

distribution[4] valuation is taken as of the date of actual distribution[5]. So far as hotchpot on intestacy is concerned it would seem that since the advancement is to be valued at the intestate's death this is an indication that the distributable assets are also to be valued at death[6].

So far, only the capital side of hotchpot calculations has been considered but there will be income accruing from the capital between the notional time for distribution and the actual time of distribution. The date of the valuation of the distributable capital assets controls not only the division of the capital but also the mode of controlling the intermediate income.

If the valuation of the capital is reckoned at the date of notional distribution the advancement is brought into account to reduce the gross share of capital otherwise passing to the advanced beneficiary so that, for example, as from the date of notional distribution the beneficiary is treated as entitled to a net one-third share of the capital and not a gross one-half share. He is thus entitled to one-third of the income for the period between the notional and actual distribution[7].

If valuation of the capital is not reckoned till the date of actual distribution then interest at 4% on the sums brought into hotchpot is added to the income for the period between notional and actual distribution: the total is then divided between the beneficiaries according to their gross shares of capital but the shares of the advanced beneficiaries are then debited with the 4% interest notionally payable in respect of the advanced sums[8].

The computation should be made on the basis of the gross amount of the income actually produced by the distributable capital and the gross notional 4% payable in respect of the sums brought into hotchpot as laid down in *Re Foster*[9]. However, without argument, the computation has been made on the basis of net amounts after tax[10].

Funds appointed by the deceased under a special power of appointment do not have to be brought into statutory hotchpot under s 47(1)(iii) of the Administration of Estates Act 1925[11] though they do have to be brought into equitable hotchpot arising from the application of the presumptions against double portions[12].

Whether a person brings into hotchpot benefits received by him or also benefits received by his issue depends on the wording of the hotchpot clause. If he only has to bring into hotchpot a life interest (and not a remainder passing to his issue) then the life interest will be valued on actuarial principles[13]. Under s 49(1)(a) beneficial interests acquired by issue had to be

---

4 *Re Hargreaves* (1903) 88 LT 100; *Re Mansel* [1930] 1 Ch 352; *Re Gunther's Will Trusts* [1939] Ch 985; *Re Oram* [1940] Ch 1001, [1940] 4 All ER 161.

5 *Re Poyser* [1908] 1 Ch 828; *Re Forster-Brown* [1914] 2 Ch 584; *Re Cooke* [1916] 1 Ch 480; *Re Tod* [1916] 1 Ch 567; *Re Wills* [1939] Ch 705, [1939] 2 All ER 775; *Re Hillas-Drake* [1944] Ch 235, [1944] 1 All ER 375; *Re Slee* [1962] 1 All ER 542, [1962] 1 WLR 496.

6 *Re Slee* [1962] 1 All ER 542, [1962] 1 WLR 496; (1961) 25 Conv 468 (JT Farrand).

7 See note 4, above.

8 See note 5, above.

9 [1920] 1 Ch 391.

10 *Re Wills* [1939] Ch 705, [1939] 2 All ER 775; *Re Hillas-Drake* [1944] Ch 235, [1944] 1 All ER 375.

11 *Re Reeve* [1935] Ch 110.

12 *Re Peel's Settlement* [1911] 2 Ch 165.

13 *Re Gordon* [1942] Ch 131, [1942] 1 All ER 59; *Re West* [1921] 1 Ch 533.

taken into account[14], but the equitable presumption against double portions only requires benefits received by the donee of the portion to be brought into hotchpot.

ARTICLE 49

Duty of trustee to sell improper property

Where *residuary personal estate* is settled by will for the benefit of persons in succession, all such parts of it as consist of improper securities must be converted into proper authorised securities being property of a sensible and prudent character satisfying the trustee's obligations under the Trustee Act 2000, unless the will reveals a contrary intention, eg

(a) the will contains a direction or implication that the life tenant is to enjoy the income from the property in specie; or

(b) the will confers on the trustee a discretion to postpone such conversion, not merely as an ancillary power for the more convenient realisation of the estate but as an independent power for the benefit of the life tenant, and the trustee bona fide and impartially consciously exercises the discretion.

Rule in *Howe v Lord Dartmouth*

The above rule, known as the rule in *Howe v Earl of Dartmouth*[15], is really a corollary of the principle stated in Article 48, namely, that the trustee must act impartially between the beneficiaries, for if unauthorised or improper investments[16] producing a high rate of interest but with little capital security were to be retained, the tenant for life would profit at the expense of the remaindermen, and if unauthorised or improper investments producing no income, only capital appreciation, were not converted the remaindermen would profit at the expense of the tenant for life. It must, however, be borne in mind that the rule is based upon an implied or presumed intention of the testator that the legatees shall succesively enjoy the same fund, with neither life tenant nor remainderman benefiting at the expense of the other. Courts of equity have, consequently, always declined to apply the rule in cases where the settlor has indicated an intention that the property should be enjoyed in specie, though he may not have said so in express words. The real question, therefore, in all such cases, is whether the settlor has, with sufficient distinctness, indicated his intention that the property should be enjoyed in

---

14 *Re Grover's Will Trusts* [1971] Ch 168, [1970] 1 All ER 1185; *Re Young* [1951] Ch 185, sub nom *Re Young's Will Trusts, Young v Young* [1950] 2 All ER 1040.

15 (1802) 7 Ves 137, 1 White & Tud LC 68; and see also *Hinves v Hinves* (1844) 3 Hare 609; and *Pickering v Pickering* (1839) 4 My & Cr 289.

16 The huge width of unauthorised investments (in the absence of broad express powers of investment) was reduced by the TA 1925, significantly reduced by the Trustee Investments Act 1961, and almost abolished by the TA 2000 (in the absence of express restriction in the trust instrument); however investments within the range of authorised investments will be improper ones if breaching the trustees' duties under the TA 2000 if retained or purchased by them for the trust.

specie[17], for the burden of showing this lies upon the party who desires that the rule in *Howe v Earl of Dartmouth* should not be applied[18].

The rule in *Howe v Earl of Dartmouth*, as well as requiring conversion, has certain financial apportionment consequences as between life tenant and remainderman (see Article 50, post) and reference to the rule is often made in order to allude both to the duty to convert and to these financial consequences. Understood in this sense, therefore, the rule applies to cases where the testator has expressly directed conversion (because, although there is no room for any implied duty to convert, the financial consequences of the rule still normally apply). Although the rule can be excluded by the use of appropriate words, it is not excluded merely by the addition of an express power for the trustees to postpone conversion for the more convenient realisation of the estate[19].

Impact of Trustee Act 2000 vast extension of authorised investments

Under the Trustee Act 2000[20] a trustee or personal representative is authorised to make any kind of investment that he could make if he were absolutely entitled to the assets of the trust, except that he cannot invest in land (other than in loans secured on land) except for freehold or leasehold land in the UK which, under s 8(1), can be acquired as an investment or for occupation by a beneficiary or for any other reason.

The philosophy is for trustees to have vast powers of investment, but subject to significant safeguards requiring exercise of such powers to be subject to equitable and statutory duties. Moreover, trustees, like wealthy individual investors, are entitled to be judged by the standards of modern portfolio theory which emphasises the risk level of the entire portfolio. Each particular investment is not taken in isolation but in the context of the overall portfolio[1]. Traditional warnings against the need for trustees to avoid speculative or hazardous investments are not to be read as inhibiting trustees from maintaining a portfolio which contains a sensible and prudent mixture of low risk and higher risk securities and of high-yielding investments with capital growth investments with no or little yield[2].

If it so happens that in exercising its powers within the vast range of possible investments the trustee breaks its duty of care[3] or to act fairly and disinterestedly[4], then the trustee is personally liable, whether to all the beneficiaries or just to the life tenant or just to the remainderman.

The question arises whether the rule in *Howe v Dartmouth* should not apply where the testator's will (or an intestacy) is treated as if expressly conferring the Trustee Act 2000 authority on a personal representative or trustee to invest in any kind of investment (other than in land outside the UK) on the

---

17 Per Baggallay LJ in *Macdonald v Irvine* (1878) 8 Ch D 101 at 112, CA.

18 Per James LJ in *Macdonald v Irvine* (1878) 8 Ch D 101 at 112; *Re Wareham* [1912] 2 Ch 312 at 315, CA.

19 *Re Berry* [1962] Ch 97, [1961] 1 All ER 529. In this case Pennycuick J said that in so far as *Re Fisher* [1943] Ch 377, [1943] 2 All ER 615, had decided that a mere power to postpone was enough to exclude the rule it was 'contrary to the whole current of authority'.

20 Section 3

1 *Nestle v National Westminster Bank* [2000] WTLR 795 at 802.

2 See Lord Nicholls (1995) 9 Trust LI 71 at 73, and see pp 601–602 post.

3 TA 2000, ss 1 and 2, Sch 1.

4 *Edge v Pensions Ombudsman* [2000] Ch 602, CA; *Nestle v National Westminster Bank* [2000] WTLR 795.

basis that this indicates that the testator is prepared for his executor to retain such investments of the deceased until he considers it expedient to replace them[5]. Thus, the testator should not be regarded as requiring them to be sold forthwith under an implied trust for sale only in order for the same kind of investments possibly to be purchased as authorised investments.

However, an investment within the range of statutory or, even, expressly authorised investments only becomes a proper one once the executor or trustee has obtained and considered advice[6] (unless he reasonably concludes that in all the circumstances it is unnecessary or inappropriate to do so[7]). Thus, the key issue is whether the testator can be taken to have intended the life tenant to receive all income actually produced by the residuary investments before the executors' or trustees' conscious investment decisions were duly taken. In the absence of some special wording in the testator's will which might permit the court to reach such a convenient construction, it seems that the testator's intention will be for the life tenant to receive the income from those residuary investments that the executor or trustee duly decides to retain as proper investments[8], but not the other investments that are duly sold. Therefore, it will be advisable for a testator's will to spell out an intention to permit enjoyment *in specie* of income from existing residuary investments from his death if so intending.

Small scope for implied trust for sale under *Howe v Dartmouth*

From the above it seems likely that only in respect of residuary personalty that the trustee decides not to retain or only if the testator expressly or by necessary implication restricts the range of investments otherwise permitted by the Trustee Act 2000 to a restricted class, but dies owning assets outside the restricted class, will there be room for an implied trust for sale. Even then, the old case law reveals that no such trust for sale arose if the property[9] were real property or the subject of a specific (as opposed to a residuary) bequest[10], the court in such cases presuming the testator's intention to be that the property be enjoyed *in specie*[11].

PARAGRAPH (A), (B)

Rule in *Howe v Lord Dartmouth* not applicable where contrary intention expressed

As already stated, the rule in *Howe v Earl of Dartmouth* will yield to any contrary

5 See *Brown v Gellatly* (1867) 2 Ch App 751 at 758; *Re Pitcairn* [1896] 2 Ch 199 at 209; *Re Nicholson* [1909] 2 Ch 111; J Kessler *Drafting Trusts and Will Trusts* (6th edn) para 20.32.
6 TA 2000, ss 4, 5 and 35; and see p 602 post. Until the executor or trustee does this and decides to retain an investment within the authorised range such investment is an improper one and so (in the absence of contrary intent) subject to *Howe v Dartmouth* (see *Re Rowlls* [1900] 2 Ch 107 and *Re Guinness' Settlement* [1966] 1 WLR 1355 and R Mitchell [1999] Conv 84 at 99–103).
7 TA 2000, s 5(3).
8 *Re Sheldon* (1888) 39 Ch D 50.
9 *Re Woodhouse* [1941] Ch 332.
10 *Macdonald v Irvine* (1878) 8 Ch D 101, CA; *Re Van Straubenzee* [1901] 2 Ch 779.
11 Lifetime settlements inevitably deal specifically with particular property and so an *in specie* intention is present: *Re Van Straubenzee* [1901] 2 Ch 779.

intention which may be expressed or implied in the settlement. Moreover, it is immaterial whether the contrary intention is imperatively expressed, or whether a discretion to convert or not is expressly given to the trustees; for the court will not interfere with a discretion so long as trustees exercise it in good faith[12]. Thus, in one case a testator gave his residuary estate, which included several leasehold houses (held upon short terms), to trustees, upon trust to pay the income to his wife for life, with remainder to his grand-children, and gave his trustees *power to retain any portion of his property in the same state in which it should be at his decease*, or to sell and convert the same as they should think fit. It was held that the special power to retain existing investments took the case out of the general rule as to conversion of per-ishable property, and that the trustees were at liberty to retain the short leaseholds, and any other investments held by the testator, for such period as they should think fit[13]. A similar decision was arrived at where a testator authorised his trustees to postpone the sale of his business[14].

So, again, where the testator devised wasting property to trustees, upon trust to sell 'when in their discretion they should deem it advisable', it was held that the trustees were not bound to sell until they thought fit[15].

Rule not applicable where impliedly negatived

The above cases are instances of an express intention that the trustees should have a discretion; but the same result will follow where that intention, though not expressed in so many words, can be implied. Thus, a testator, after a special bequest, gave all his residuary estate, both real and personal, to trustees, upon trust, to *sell as much and such part thereof as they might think necessary for paying all his mortgage and other debts and funeral and testamentary expenses*, and to invest the balance of the proceeds, and to stand possessed of such investments, *and all other his residuary estate*, upon trust for several per-sons successively for their respective lives, with remainders over. Part of the testator's estate consisted of leaseholds, which were retained unsold. On this state of facts it was held that, on the construction of the will, the trustees had a discretion as to what part of the testator's estate should be converted, and that the court could not interfere with the exercise of such discretion[16].

So it has been held that an express direction for sale at a particular period indicates an intention that there should be no previous sale[17] and even a *power* to sell all or any part of the estate in the absolute discretion of the trustees, has been held to negative the prima facie duty of selling wasting or reversionary property forthwith[18]. A similar view has been taken of a discre-tion to *divide* property after the death of the life tenant[19], though it has

---

12 *Gisborne v Gisborne* (1877) 2 App Cas 300; *Tabor v Brooks* (1878) 10 Ch D 273; *Re Rogers* [1915] 2 Ch 437; and *Re Slater* (1915) 113 LT 691.
13 *Gray v Siggers* (1880) 15 Ch D 74; *Re Fisher* [1943] Ch 377, [1943] 2 All ER 615.
14 *Re Crowther* [1895] 2 Ch 56; followed in *Re Elford* [1910] 1 Ch 814; but see *Re Smith* [1896] 1 Ch 171.
15 *Miller v Miller* (1872) LR 13 Eq 263; *Thursby v Thursby* (1875) LR 19 Eq 395; and see also *Re Chancellor* (1884) 26 Ch D 42; and *Re Crowther* [1895] 2 Ch 56, in both of which cases the property consisted of a business.
16 *Re Sewell's Estate* (1870) LR 11 Eq 80; and see also *Simpson v Earles* (1847) 11 Jur 921.
17 *Alcock v Sloper* (1833) 2 My & K 699; *Daniel v Warren* (1843) 2 Y & C Ch Cas 290; *Re North* [1909] 1 Ch 625.
18 *Re Pitcairn* [1896] 2 Ch 199.
19 *Collins v Collins* (1833) 2 My & K 703.

subsequently been held that a mere provision that residue is to be divided between certain persons after the life tenant's death does not exclude the rule where the division may be of the residue as converted under the rule[20]. So, in some cases, it has been decided that a trust to pay *rents* to the tenant for life, *where the testator has only leaseholds*[1], or a direction that the trustees should give a power of attorney to the life tenant to receive the income[2], is a sufficient indication of a contrary intention to take the case out of the general rule.

ARTICLE 50

Duty of trustee, as between tenant for life and remainderman, in relation to property pending conversion

(1) Where property ought to be converted, and the proceeds invested, either under an implied *Howe v Dartmouth* trust for sale or under an express trust for sale, the tenant for life is entitled, pending actual conversion, to the whole net income of income-bearing property, if a direction to that effect is expressed in or can be implied from the trust[3] or if the trust is of land[4];

(2) but in the absence of any such direction or implication, he is entitled to receive or be credited with income in accordance with the following rules, namely:

(a) where the property is personal estate (other than leaseholds), he is only entitled to a fair equivalent for the income which he would have received if the property had been sold and invested in trustee securities[5];

(b) where the property is of a reversionary nature, he is entitled, when it falls in, to a proportionate part of the capital, representing compound interest (with yearly rests[6]) on the true actuarial value of the property at the testator's death, calculated on the assumption that the actual date when the property fell into possession could have been then predicted with certainty[7];

(3) upon complete realisation of an insufficient investment, where interest is in arrears, the money realised must be divided between

20 *Re Evans' Will Trusts* [1921] 2 Ch 309.
  1 *Goodenough v Tremamondo* (1840) 2 Beav 512; *Cafe v Bent* (1845) 5 Hare 24; *Vachell v Roberts* (1863) 32 Beav 140; *Re Wareham* [1912] 2 Ch 312, CA.
  2 *Neville v Fortescue* (1848) 16 Sim 333.
  3 See *Re Sheldon* (1888) 39 Ch D 50; *Re Thomas* [1891] 3 Ch 482. Where the property is of a non-wasting nature, the court will accept very slight evidence of implied intention.
  4 *Re Oliver* [1908] 2 Ch 74; *Re Earl of Darnley* [1907] 1 Ch 159; *Re Berton* [1939] Ch 200; before LPA 1925, s 28 repealed for position to be governed by TLATA 1996, s 4 and TA 2000, s 8.
  5 *Brown v Gellatly* (1867) 2 Ch App 751; See p 557, post; *Meyer v Simonsen* (1852) 5 De G & Sm 723; *Wentworth v Wentworth* [1900] AC 163.
  6 See *Re Goodenough* [1895] 2 Ch 537; *Re Morley* [1895] 2 Ch 738; *Re Hobson* (1885) 53 LT 627; and *Re Duke of Cleveland's Estate* [1895] 2 Ch 542; *Rowlls v Bebb* [1900] 2 Ch 107, CA. As to the rate of interest, see p 589, post.
  7 *Re Earl of Chesterfield's Trusts* (1883) 24 Ch D 643; followed, with variations as to rate of interest, in *Re Goodenough* [1895] 2 Ch 537; *Re Morley* [1895] 2 Ch 738; *Re Hobson* (1885) 53 LT 627; and *Re Duke of Cleveland's Estate* [1895] 2 Ch 542.

tenant for life and remainderman in proportion to the amount due for arrears of interest and the amount of capital remaining due[8]; but this does not apply to settled shares or stock of such a nature that dividend is payable only if earned[9];

(4) this article has no application to investments made by trustees in breach of trust where no loss results; but is confined to cases where unavoidable delay takes place in converting property in due course of administration[10], and to cases where a security (whether authorised or not) has turned out to be insufficient.

Not confined to settled residue

This article is a further corollary of Article 48, and its main principle forms the second part of the rule in *Howe v Earl of Dartmouth*, namely, that, pending a conversion which ought to be made, the tenant for life is, prima facie, entitled only to the income which would have been produced by the proceeds of the conversion if it had in fact been made.

It is not (like the main rule) confined to settled residuary personal estate under a will, but is equally applicable to all settled personal property which is subject to a direction for sale exercisable forthwith. However, it does not apply where the sale is only to take place at a future date, for in that case the intention must have been that until that date arrived the tenant for life should enjoy the property in specie, though a mere power to postpone conversion, without more, is normally not enough to indicate such an intention[11].

A question of interpretation of the trust instrument

Where it is possible that the rule applies, the first question that arises is one of fact, namely, whether on the true interpretation of the trust instrument the tenant for life is either expressely or impliedly intended to take the actual income pending the sale. If that question is answered in the affirmative, cadit quaestio. But if no such intention is expressed or can reasonably be inferred, the question becomes one of law, to be answered in accordance with the rules in paragraph (2).

Paragraph 1

Rules have no application where a future sale is directed

The rules in paragraph (2) have no application where only a *future* sale is directed. In *Re North*[12] a testator, part of whose property consisted of land

---

8 *Re Atkinson* [1904] 2 Ch 160; over-ruling *Re Foster* (1890) 45 Ch D 629; and *Re Phillimore* [1903] 1 Ch 942; and see *Re Walker's Settlement Trusts* [1936] Ch 280; *Re Atkinson*, above, was applied in *Re Morris' Will Trusts* [1960] 3 All ER 548, [1960] 1 WLR 1210 (see p 537, ante).

9 See *Re Taylor's Trust* [1905] 1 Ch 734. Cf *Re Sale* [1913] 2 Ch 697; *Re Grundy* (1917) 117 LT 470; *Re Wakley* [1920] 2 Ch 205, CA; and *Re Marjoribanks* [1923] 2 Ch 307.

10 See per Byrne J in *Re Appleby* [1903] 1 Ch 565 at 566; and *Stroud v Gwyer* (1860) 28 Beav 130; but cf *Re Hill* (1881) 50 LJ Ch 551; *Slade v Chaine* [1908] 1 Ch 522; *Re Hoyles* [1912] 1 Ch 67.

11 *Re Berry* [1962] Ch 97, [1961] 1 All ER 529.

12 [1909] 1 Ch 625. For a case where a direction for a future sale was implied, see *Re Barratt* [1925] Ch 550.

with brick earth upon it which was being worked under a lease granted by him at a royalty, gave his real estate to trustees upon trust 'to pay the rents issues and profits' to certain persons for life, with remainder *after the death of the last surviving life tenant* upon trust for sale. It was held that the trustees had power, after the expiration of the lease, to let the brick earth from year to year at a royalty, and that the life tenants were entitled to the whole of such royalty. No one seems to have suggested (nor indeed could have suggested) that the rules in paragraph (2) applied, the argument being mainly directed to the power of the trustees to let the brick earth at all, and the fact that if the tenants for life had let it under the powers of the Settled Land Acts, a proportion of the royalties would have had to be carried to capital account. The judge holding, on the interpretation of the will, that the trustees had power to continue the letting of the brick earth, it followed that the tenants for life were entitled to the royalties, there being no immediate trust for conversion.

Similarly, where a testator devised and bequeathed 'a life rent in all my property' to his wife, and gave his trustees a mere power to sell and invest the proceeds, it was held that the wife was entitled to the whole of the income[13].

Exclusion of rules in the case of intestacy

By the Administration of Estates Act 1925, s 33(5), it is provided that the income of so much of the real and personal estate of the deceased as may not be disposed of by will, or may not be required for administration purposes, may, however the estate is invested, be treated and applied as income as from the death of the deceased[14].

Rules may be expressly or impliedly negatived

Even where mineral property is subject to a trust for immediate sale, yet, if the trust expressly or impliedly gives the whole of the royalties pending sale to the tenant for life, he will be entitled to them. Thus where a testator devised his brickfield to trustees upon trust to sell when in their discretion it might seem advisable, and directed that the rents and profits should until sale be *applicable and applied in the same manner as the dividends or interest to arise from the investments of the sale moneys,* it was held that the tenant for life was entitled to the whole of the royalties paid by tenants of the brickfield, although the trustees did not sell the property for ten years[15]. If, however, the italicised words had not been inserted in the will, it seems plain that the power to postpone conversion would not of itself have authorised the payment of the whole of the royalties to the tenant for life. For, in that case, the inference would have been that the power to postpone conversion was for the purpose of efficiently selling the estate, and not for the benefit of the tenant for life[16]. And the words used must be clear: thus a declaration in a will

---

13 *Re Bentham* (1906) 94 LT 307; see also *Gray v Siggers* (1880) 15 Ch D 74.
14 See and cf *Re Trollope's Will Trusts* [1927] 1 Ch 596; and *Re Sullivan* [1930] 1 Ch 84.
15 *Miller v Miller* (1872) LR 13 Eq 263; and see also *Thursby v Thursby* (1875) LR 19 Eq 395; where the whole of colliery royalties were held to be payable to the tenant for life, and *Re Crowther* [1895] 2 Ch 56.
16 *Re Woods* [1904] 2 Ch 4. See *Re Carter* (1892) 41 WR 140; *Brown v Gellatly* (1867) 2 Ch App 751; *Re Owen* [1912] 1 Ch 519; and *Re Aste* (1918) 87 LJ Ch 660. See also *Re Berry* [1962] Ch 97, [1961] 1 All ER 529.

against apportionment of 'dividends rents interests of moneys of the nature of income' has been held *not* to exclude the rule in relation to the profits of a business carried on by the testator[17].

Sale of business directed as soon as practicable

A case illustrating this part of the rule is *Re Elford*[18] where a testator directed the sale of his business as soon as practicable, but in a subsequent clause declared that pending conversion 'all the income arising from my estate' shall be applied as if it were income arising from the proceeds of the conversion. It was held, that the tenant for life was entitled to the whole of the profits of the business. It is conceived, however, that even in such a case the trustees ought to set aside a reasonable sum of profits for depreciation[19].

Purchase of land directed with all convenient speed

On the other hand, where a testator directs that a fund shall be invested in the purchase of land 'with all convenient speed', and that in the meantime the income shall be accumulated, the rule of the court is that a year is a reasonable time, and that if the purchase is not made within such year the accumulations stop, and the income is payable to the tenant for life of the land[20].

The question is really one of construction, namely, whether the testator intended that the power to postpone should be exercised for the benefit of the tenant for life, or merely for the more convenient realisation of the estate; and, if the former intention is found, no distinction is made by the court between unauthorised securities of a wasting and those of a permanent nature[1].

Settlement implying that income is to be enjoyed in specie

In one case[2] a testator empowered his trustees, at their discretion, *to continue* all or any part of his personal estate in the state of investment in or upon which the same should be at his death; or to convert it, and invest the proceeds in the names of the trustees in certain specified securities. Part of the personal estate consisted of securities not specially authorised, which were retained. It was held that the tenants for life were entitled to receive the actual income of those securities which were retained. It will be perceived that the testator authorised the *continuance* of securities and not merely the

---

17 *Re Berry* [1962] Ch 97, [1961] 1 All ER 529.
18 [1910] 1 Ch 814; following *Re Chancellor* (1884) 26 Ch D 42; and *Re Crowther* [1895] 2 Ch 56. A direction that pending sale the whole income is to be paid to a tenant for life does not negative the Apportionment Act 1870 (*Re Edwards* [1918] 1 Ch 142); *Re Elford*, above, was distinguished in *Re Berry* [1962] Ch 97, [1961] 1 All ER 529.
19 See *Re Crabtree* [1912] WN 24.
20 *Parry v Warrington* (1820) 6 Madd 155; followed by Jessel MR in *Wing v Wing* (1876) 34 LT 941; and see *Sitwell v Bernard* (1801) 6 Ves 520.
1 *Re Nicholson* [1909] 2 Ch 111. This statement of the law was approved and adopted by Neville J in *Re Inman* [1915] 1 Ch 187.
2 *Re Sheldon* (1888) 39 Ch D 50; *Gray v Siggers* (1880) 15 Ch D 74; *Re Bates* [1907] 1 Ch 22; (power 'to retain'); and *Re Wilson* [1907] 1 Ch 394; and *Re Nicholson* [1909] 2 Ch 111, to same effect. See also *Re Rogers* [1915] 2 Ch 437; *Re Slater* (1915) 113 LT 691; and *Re Fisher* [1943] Ch 377, [1943] 2 All ER 615; But cf *Re Wareham* [1912] 2 Ch 312, CA.

temporary postponement of their conversion; otherwise the decision would have been different, as was the case in *Re Chaytor*[3], where the testator only authorised the *continuance pending a favourable opportunity for selling*. The real point in such cases is whether the power to continue or retain is to be construed as a power to continue or retain permanently, or only until the trustees can sell advantageously. In the first case, the inference is that the power was for the benefit of the tenant for life; in the latter, the inference is that it was merely for the convenient administration of the estate.

Another example of an implied intention that income should be enjoyed in specie pending conversion is afforded by the case of *Re Thomas*[4]. A testator gave his residuary estate to trustees upon trust for conversion and investment of the proceeds in specified securities; with power to the trustees in their absolute discretion to retain any securities or property belonging to him at his death unconverted, for such period as they should think fit. He then declared that they should stand possessed of 'the stocks, funds, shares, and securities for the time being *constituting* or representing the residuary personal estate and effects therein before bequeathed *and of the income thereof*, upon trust to pay the income to certain persons for life with remainders over. The estate comprised certain American bonds, which were not included among the securities authorised by the will as investments, but were retained by the trustees in exercise of the discretion given to them. It was held that, on the true construction of the will, the tenants for life were entitled to the whole income of the bonds in specie. In giving judgment, Kekewich J said:

> 'I am not prepared to hold that where there is a direction for conversion of personal estate, followed by a power of retention of existing securities in the absolute discretion of the trustees, and then there are trusts for tenants for life, and afterwards for remainderman, the power of retention *necessarily* gives the tenants for life the enjoyment in specie of the securities retained by the trustees in the exercise of their discretion ... But I have no doubt that one looks out with an expectant eye for a direction to the trustees to retain securities, or any indication of the testator's intention that they shall retain indefinitely for so long as they may think fit.'

Discretionary power to retain

Even when the power to retain investments is such that it does imply the exclusion of the rule, the rule will not be excluded in fact unless and until the trustees consciously determine to exercise the power. Thus in *Re Guinness's Settlement*[5] the trustees, who had a general power to retain assets, had not exercised it in relation to one particular asset because they did not know that it applied to this asset although they had in fact retained the asset, and it was held that until they actually decided to retain the asset in exercise of their discretion, its income fell within the ambit of the rules discussed in this Article.

---

3 [1905] 1 Ch 233; and see cases under paragraph 2(b), post. Cf *Re Johnson* [1915] 1 Ch 435. But see *Re White's Settlement* [1930] 1 Ch 179.
4 [1891] 3 Ch 482; followed by Warrington J in *Re Godfree* [1914] 2 Ch 110.
5 [1966] 2 All ER 497, [1966] 1 WLR 1355.

PARAGRAPH 2(A)

Tenant for life not entitled to whole income of wasting property or unauthorised investments if settlement silent

In the leading case of *Brown v Gellatly*[6] the testator, who was a shipowner, directed his trustees to convert his personal estate into money, when and in such manner as they should see fit, and *gave them power to sail his ships until they could be disposed of satisfactorily*. The proceeds of his personal estate were then settled upon tenants for life, with remainders over. The will contained a wide power of investment in specified securities. On his death, the testator possessed: (1) numerous ships; (2) securities falling within those authorised by the will; and (3) shares and investments not so authorised. The ships could not be immediately sold, nor could the unauthorised securities. Both, pending sale, produced a high rate of income; and the question arose whether the tenants for life were entitled to the whole of that income, or only to some, and, if so, what, proportion thereof.

In giving judgment, Lord Cairns said:

'We find no indication whatever of an intention that the ships were to remain unconverted for any specific time. The testator, who had been engaged in the shipping business, knew perfectly well, and shows that he knew, that some time would necessarily be taken in converting the ships, and therefore he very wisely provided that until they were sold the executors should have power which otherwise they would not have possessed, namely, the power to sail the ships for the purpose of making profit, but in giving that power, he does not *give it as a power to be exercised for the benefit of the tenant for life as against the parties in remainder*, or for the benefit of the parties in remainder as against the interest of the tenant for life, but says that it is to be exercised for the benefit of the estate, meaning as I apprehend, for the benefit of the estate generally, without disarranging the equities between the successive takers. ... In that state of things, it seems to me that the case falls exactly within the third division pointed out by Sir James Parker in the case of *Meyer v Simonsen*[7], and that a value must be set upon the ships as at the death of the testator, and the tenant for life must have 4% on such value, and the residue of the profits must of course beinvested, and become part of the estate. Then, secondly, as to the authorisedsecurities. ... The tenant for life is, in my opinion, entitled to the specific income of the securities, just as if they had been £3 per cent consols. I understand the words of the will as amounting to the constitution by the testator of a larger class of authorised securities than this court itself would have approved of, and the court has merely to follow his directions, and treat the income accordingly, as being the income of authorised securities. Then comes the third question in the case, the securities not ranging themselves under any of those mentioned in the last clause of the will. ... As they do not come within the class of authorised securities it was the duty of the trustees to convert them at the earliest moment at which they properly could be converted. I do not mean to say that the trustees were by any means open to censure for not having converted them within the year [after testator's death], but I think that the rights of the parties must be regulated as if they had been so converted. I think the proper order to make is that which was made in *Dimes v Scott*[8], followed by Wigram V-C in the case of *Taylor v Clark*[9], namely, to treat the tenant for

---

6 (1867) 2 Ch App 751; and see also *Hume v Richardson* (1862) 4 De GF & J 29; *Re Lynch Blosse* [1899] WN 27; and *Mousley v Carr* (1841) 4 Beav 49. Followed in *Re Hazeldine* [1918] 1 Ch 433; *Re Trollope's Will Trusts* [1927] 1 Ch 596.

7 (1852) 5 De G & Sm 723.

8 (1828) 4 Russ 195.

9 (1841) 1 Hare 161.

life as entitled, during the year after the testator's death, to the dividends upon so much 3% stock as would have been produced by the conversion and investment of the property at the end of the year.'

The first branch of this decision, that relating to the ships where the trust for sale *was subject to a power to postpone sale*, was considered in *Re Parry*[10], where Romer J said:

'And, finally, not only was the order regarding the ships not inconsistent with previous authority, but it seems to me that it was plainly right. Notional conversion is very understandable when the executors are under a duty, express or implied, to sell; such a duty readily lets in the doctrine that equity regards that as done which ought to be done and the notional conversion arising from the doctrine (subject to a year's grace) acted as a convenient medium for preserving the balance between life tenant and remainderman. If no duty exists, however, the medium is not available, and another has to be found in its place. If there is no duty upon the executor to sell at once, or within a year, or at any other time, I can see no reason for assuming a notional conversion at once, or within a year, or at any other time. The essential equity, however—the balance between the successive inter-ests—remains equally compelling even where there is no immediate obligation to convert and property is retained for the benefit of the estate as a whole; it is accordingly rational, and indeed obvious, to substitute a valuation of the testator's assets in the place of a hypothetical sale, and, if so, it is difficult to think of a better date for the valuation than *the day when the testator died* and the assets passed to his executors.'

Thus, where residuary personalty is subject to a power to postpone sale, one has to wait until the residuary estate is ascertained (after collecting in all assets and paying debts, taxes and expenses) and then make a retrospective valuation at the testator's death. It might have been better to restrict *Brown v Gellatly* to a power to postpone the sale of specific assets comprised within residuary personalty and conveniently have the end of the executor's year as the date of valuation of the residuary state which should have been ascertained by them.

This is the basic rule laid down in *Re Fawcett*[11] where Farwell J laid down the following rules as to the respective rights of persons entitled to the capital and income of a residuary estate comprising unauthorised investments *where there is no express power to postpone conversion*:

(1) In the case of investments retained more than one year after the death of the testator the tenant for life is entitled to interest at 4% from the death till realisation on their value one year after the death. [As to the rate of interest see p 559, post.]
(2) In the case of investments sold within one year from the death the tenant for life is entitled to the interest on the net proceeds of sale from the date of the death till completion of the sale.
(3) The unauthorised investments for the time being unsold must be treated en bloc as one aggregate for the purpose of the rule in *Howe v Lord Dartmouth*[12].
(4) In applying that rule the Apportionment Act 1870 ought not to be applied to income accounts with reference to unauthorised investments.
(5) Any excess income from unauthorised investments over that payable to the tenant for life ought to be invested in authorised investments and the sub-sequent income thereof paid to the tenant for life.

10 [1947] Ch 23, [1946] 2 All ER 412.
11 [1940] Ch 402.
12 (1802) 7 Ves 137.

(6) If actual income from unauthorised investments is less than 4% payable to the
tenant for life then the tenant for life is entitled to have his income made up at
4% simple interest (less tax) out of excess income subsequently arising from
unauthorised investments or from the proceeds of subsequent sale of unauthorised investments. The deficit cannot be made up out of past excess income
from unauthorised investments since such excess income will have become
authorised capital.

Annuities of varying amount or uncertain duration

Where the property consists of an annuity of varying amount or uncertain
duration (so that no reasonably accurate valuation can be made) then each
instalment must be treated as a reversion falling in, as in *Re Earl of Chesterfield's
Trusts*[13] and *Re Busfield*[14].

Income derived from property of which testator was mortgagee in possession

On the same principle, where part of a testator's residuary estate consisted of
a colliery of which he was mortgagee in possession, the question arose as to
how accumulations of the income, derived from working the colliery since
the testator's death, were to be apportioned between tenant for life and
remaindermen. It was held that the proper principle was that so much as
would, if invested at the testator's death at 4% with yearly rests, have
amounted to the sum in the hands of the trustees, should be treated as
capital, and the rest as income[15].

Rate of interest allowed to tenant for life

It will be perceived that in all the above cases the rate of interest on the
capital value allowed to the life tenant was 4%. About the turn of the century,
owing to the drop in the current rate of interest, 3% was substituted for
four[16], but 4% was reverted to in 1920[17], and this was the rate allowed as late
as 1946 in relation to a death occurring in 1936[18]. But in *Wentworth v Wentworth*[19] the Privy Council stated that they did not think it expedient to hamper
the court by laying down any fixed rule as to the rate of interest to be allowed
to tenants for life on the estimated value of the capital of the property and
directed an inquiry as to what annual sum would, under all the circumstances
of the case, be fair. On the other hand, Eve J in *Re Beech*[20] pointed out that:

'a departure from a salutary rule in matters of this kind introducing as it does an
element of uncertainty in practice and administration can only be justified if the
changed conditions on which it is founded continue at least as constant as those
upon which the rule was itself framed.'

---

13 (1883) 24 Ch D 643.
14 (20 February 1919, unreported) per Sargant J; *Michael v Callil* (1945) 72 CLR 509.
15 *Re Godden* [1893] 1 Ch 292.
16 *Re Goodenough* [1895] 2 Ch 537; and *Re Duke of Cleveland's Estate* [1895] 2 Ch 542. But cf *Re
Owen* [1912] 1 Ch 519.
17 *Re Beech* [1920] 1 Ch 40; *Re Baker* [1924] 2 Ch 271.
18 *Re Parry* [1947] Ch 23 at 46, [1946] 2 All ER 412 at 423.
19 [1900] AC 163; also see *Re Lauer and Stekl* (1974) 47 DLR (3d) 286, affd sub nom *Lauer v Stekl*
(1975) 54 DLR (3d) 159n.
20 (1920) 1 Ch 40 at 44; and cf *Re Parry* [1947] Ch 23 at 47, [1946] 2 All ER 412 at 422; and *Re
Ellis* [1935] Ch 193 at p 200.

The period of low interest rates which followed the Second World War proved to lack that constancy, and no instance has been reported in which the court adopted a rate of interest lower than 4%. This time-honoured 4% rate was confirmed in 1961[1]. Since then there have been periods when 4% may have been regarded as the 'real' rate of interest when higher actual rates of interest have reflected compensation for loss of capital value due to high rates of inflation[2]: indeed, in one case[3] actual interest at the court's special account rate in respect of lost capital was divided equally between life tenant and remainderman. It is now clear that the courts are well aware of the impact of inflation and so will be much concerned with 'real' interest rates as opposed to high actual interest rates[4], though low rates are now current.

PARAGRAPH 2(B)

Tenant for life entitled to part of corpus of non-income-bearing property when realised

In the above cases the income actually received by the trustees exceeded that which they were authorised to pay to the tenant for life. But the same principle applies in favour of the tenant for life where personal[5] property is not presently saleable or realisable except at an unreasonable loss, and, pending realisation, produces no income; for instance, where part of the estate consists of a policy of assurance on another's life which does not fall in for some years after the testator's death, or a reversion in the strict sense of that word[6]. This is true even though, when the asset in question does fall in, a sum is received in respect of interest in addition to the cash or other property representing its capital value[7]. In such cases, unless the settlor contemplated that it should not be sold[8], it would be unfair to the tenant for life that he should lose intervening income. Therefore, when it does fall in, the money must be apportioned, as between capital and income, by ascertaining the sum which, put out at 4% per annum[9] on the day of the testator's death, and accumulated at compound interest with yearly rests, and deducting income tax, would, with the accumulations, have produced the amount actually received. The sum so ascertained must be treated as capital, and retained by the trustees. The residue is income, and must be paid to the tenant for life[10]. The same principle applies where a debt due to the estate is recovered by the trustees without interest[11]. It has no application to trust property consisting of an absolute interest in possession subject to a charge on income[12].

1 *Re Berry* [1962] Ch 97, [1961] 1 All ER 529.
2 *Bartlett v Barclays Bank Trust Co* [1980] Ch 515 at 547.
3 *Jaffray v Marshall* [1994] 1 All ER 143 at 154.
4 *Jaffray v Marshall* [1994] 1 All ER 143; *Wright v British Railways Board* [1983] 2 AC 773.
5 See *Re Woodhouse* [1941] Ch 332, [1941] 2 All ER 265.
6 *Re Hobson* (1885) 53 LT 627; *Rowlls v Bebb* [1900] 2 Ch 107, CA.
7 *Re Chance's Will Trusts* [1962] Ch 593, [1962] 1 All ER 942, where Wilberforce J considered this part of the text of the 11th edition of this book.
8 *Re Pitcairn* [1896] 2 Ch 199; but cf *Re Hubbuck* [1896] 1 Ch 754.
9 As to the rate of interest, see p 559, ante.
10 *Re Earl of Chesterfield's Trusts* (1883) 24 Ch D 643; and see also *Massy v Gahan* (1889) 23 LR Ir 518; *Re Morley* [1895] 2 Ch 738; and *Wilkinson v Duncan* (1857) 23 Beav 469.
11 *Re Duke of Cleveland's Estate* [1895] 2 Ch 542. It also applies to instalments of purchase-money payable over a series of years.
12 *Re Holliday* [1947] Ch 402, [1947] 1 All ER 695.

Where a testator's estate includes national savings certificates the tenant for life is not entitled to any part of the sum received on encashment which represents interest earned before the death, since there is an agreement between the purchaser of the certificates and the government that, unless they are encashed, a sum shall be added to the principal month by month with the result that at the end of each completed month the addition is capitalised[13].

Rule may be negatived expressly or by inference

This branch of the rule, like all the others, is subject to any express or implied direction to the contrary in the trust instrument; and it is now common to find in wills a clause expressly providing that, pending sale, calling in, and conversion of property, the whole of the income shall be applied as income, and on the other hand that no part of the proceeds of the sale, calling in, or conversion of reversionary property or policies of assurance shall be paid or applied as income[14]. A usual form of the clause[15] is:

> 'The income of my estate, however invested, and whether received in respect of a period wholly or only partly prior to my death but actually received after my death shall form part of and be applied as if the same were income of authorised investments thereof[16] and a reversionary or other future interest forming part of my residuary estate shall not be sold before falling into possession unless my trustees shall see special reason for such earlier sale.'

Sometimes the latter part of such a clause is so worded that:

> 'no property not actually producing income shall be treated as producing income or as entitling any tenant for life to the receipt of income.'

This form is not, however, desirable, as it may raise awkward questions as to whether it extends beyond the case of reversionary property, eg to interest in arrear or to interest which is only payable at a future date. Thus, in one case, where the testator used the above form of words, the question arose whether they applied to a mortgage made in the testator's favour, where the principal, together with simple interest, was only to be paid on the mortgagor's death. It was held that they did not, however, on the ground that such clauses only apply to property which is not *producing* income, and not to property which is *producing* income, payment of which is merely postponed[17].

In cases where the testator does not exclude the rule entirely but gives the trustees a discretionary power to retain assets which do not produce income the rule will be excluded in respect of any particular asset when, but not until, the trustees consciously determine to exercise this power of retention in respect of that asset[18].

---

13 *Re Holder* [1953] Ch 468, [1953] 2 All ER 1.
14 Cf Administration of Estates Act 1925, s 33(5), which relates to intestacy.
15 See 42 *Encyclopaedia of Forms and Precedents* (5th edn) Forms 341–343. See also Form 8 of Statutory Will Forms 1925.
16 These words will not exclude also the rule in *Allhusen v Whittell* (1867) LR 4 Eq 295; as to which see p 565, post (*Re Ullswater* [1952] Ch 105, [1951] 2 All ER 989).
17 *Re Lewis* [1907] 2 Ch 296.
18 *Re Guinness's Settlement* [1966] 2 All ER 497, [1966] 1 WLR 1355.

Paragraph 3

Proceeds of insufficient security are divided between capital and income if latter in arrear

Where a trust security turns out to be insufficient, and interest is in arrear, the sum ultimately realised by the depreciated security is divisible between capital and overdue income—even where the settlor has directed that the actual income of his estate pending conversion shall be treated as income, but that no property not actually producing income shall be treated as producing any[19]. The principles on which such division ought to be made were settled by the Court of Appeal in *Re Atkinson*[20] where it was held that the sum realised ought to be apportioned between tenant for life and remainderman in the proportion which the amount due for arrears bears to the amount due in respect of the capital debt.

Prior to realisation of insufficient security tenant for life entitled to whole of income actually received

The rule only applies where the insufficient security has been realised. Until then, the tenant for life is entitled to keep all the interest actually paid, or which is in hand ready to be paid[1]. Thus, where the trustees were mortgagees in possession of property, and interest was in arrear at their testator's death, it was held that they must first apply each instalment of rent in satisfaction of the arrears of interest due to the testator, and then distribute the balance as income up to but not exceeding the interest accrued since the testator's death on the mortgage, and apply any excess as capital[2].

The rule has no application where an investment is of such a nature (eg preference shares specifically settled) that a dividend is only payable if earned; and this is so even in the case of cumulative preference shares where the dividend which is unpaid in one year has to be made good out of the profits earned in a subsequent year. In all such cases the actual dividends declared belong to the tenant for life at the time when the dividend is declared, and the representatives of a deceased tenant for life have no claim to have arrears made good out of the dividend[3].

Paragraph 4

How far rule applies to unauthorised investments made by trustee

The rule as to the tenant for life being only entitled to 4% on investments made by the settlor which ought to be converted, does not apply to invest-

---

19 *Re Hubbuck* [1896] 1 Ch 754; and *Re Lewis* [1907] 2 Ch 296.
20 [1904] 2 Ch 160; and see *Re Walker's Settlement Trusts* [1936] Ch 280. See also *Re Morris' Will Trusts* [1960] 3 All ER 548, [1960] 1 WLR 1210.
1 *Re Broadwood's Settlement* [1908] 1 Ch 115.
2 *Re Coaks* [1911] 1 Ch 171. Ought it not to be net rental income after payment of management expenses?
3 *Re Taylor's Trusts* [1905] 1 Ch 734; *Re Sale* [1913] 2 Ch 697; *Re Wakley* [1920] 2 Ch 205, CA; *Re Marjoribanks* [1923] 2 Ch 307. For a case where under a scheme by the court ordinary shareholders had surrendered some of their shares to preference shareholders whose dividends were in arrear, see *Re MacIver's Settlement* [1936] Ch 198.

ments made by the trustee in breach of trust. In these circumstances, if no loss of capital is sustained, the remainderman is not entitled to have the capital increased by adding to it the difference between the income actually paid to the tenant for life and 4%, or such other rate as is for the time being allowed[4]; the reason being that in such cases (herein differing from speculative or wasting property settled by the settlement) the amount of the trust fund is definitely ascertained, and if it has not in fact been depreciated by the breach of trust the remainderman has no equity to have it appreciated at the expense of the life tenant. This principle holds good where no loss has been sustained, even although the tenant for life was also one of the trustees[5].

Where, however, by reason of a breach of trust, the capital has become depreciated, then when it is realised, although the tenant for life, who was no party to the breach, cannot be ordered to refund income, yet he will not get any part of the amount realised to make up arrears (if any), without bringing into hotchpot all the income he has received from the security during its entire continuance. For that is the only way of placing the beneficiaries in the approximate positions in which they would have been if no breach had been committed[6].

ARTICLE 51

Duty of trustee in relation to the payment of outgoings out of corpus and income respectively

Subject to particular statutes[7] a trustee has a general discretion to allocate outgoings out of income or capital as he sees fit but using his powers to effectuate the settlor's purposes and in accordance with his duty to keep a fair balance between the interests of income beneficiaries and capital beneficiaries and so taking account of the following traditional principles governing the incidence of outgoings after the trustees have taken advantage of their initial right to resort to capital or income as they find easiest to discharge outgoings:

(a) the corpus bears capital charges incurred for the benefit of the whole trust estate, and the income bears the interest on them[8], while if the current income is insufficient, arrears of interest on capital charges must be paid out of subsequent income[9];

(b) the income usually bears current expenses[10], including the entire

4 Per Byrne J in *Re Appleby* [1903] 1 Ch 565 at 566; *Stroud v Gwyer* (1860) 28 Beav 130; but cf *Re Hill* (1881) 50 LJ Ch 551; which was distinguished in *Slade v Chaine* [1908] 1 Ch 522.

5 *Re Hoyles* [1912] 1 Ch 67.

6 *Re Bird* [1901] 1 Ch 916; and comments thereon of Warrington KC arguendo in *Re Alston* [1901] 2 Ch 584 at 587.

7 Eg the War Damage Act 1943.

8 *Marshall v Crowther* (1874) 2 Ch D 199; *Whitbread v Smith* (1854) 3 De GM & G 727; and see and consider *Norton v Johnstone* (1885) 30 Ch D 649.

9 *Honywood v Honywood* [1902] 1 Ch 347; *Frewen v Law Life Assurance Society* [1896] 2 Ch 511.

10 *Fountaine v Pellet* (1791) 1 Ves 337 at 342 (rates and taxes); *Shore v Shore* (1859) 4 Drew 501 (receiver's commission and expenses of passing account); *Carver v Duncan (Inspector of Taxes)* [1985] AC 1082 at 1120 per Lord Templeman.

cost of keeping leaseholds in repair[11];
(c) where repairs to trust freeholds are necessary to save them from destruction[12], or fines become payable for the renewal of leases[13], or for putting in repair leasehold property which was out of repair at the date of the creation of the trust[14], the court may empower the trustees to raise the necessary amount in such a way as will be equitable between income and corpus;
(d) all costs incident to the administration and protection of the trust property, including legal proceedings, are borne by corpus[15], unless they relate exclusively to the tenant for life[16], the corpus bearing all costs, charges and expenses incurred for the benefit of the whole estate.

Section 31(1) Trustee Act 2000 general discretion

By s 31(1) 'a trustee (a) is entitled to be reimbursed from the trust funds or (b) may pay out of the trust funds expenses properly incurred by him when acting on behalf of the trust', while 'trust funds' is defined in s 39 for the purposes of the Trustee Act 2000 as 'income or capital funds of the trust'. This right of reimbursement or exoneration has always operated as a first charge on the capital and income within the trust, so that the trustees can use whatever is to hand and then make later adjustments to the accounts so as to throw the ultimate incidence of the expense on income or capital as appropriate[17] in accordance with well-established equitable principles developed on a case-by-case basis or in accordance with statute (eg the old s 19 of the Trustee Act 1925 before the new one substituted by s 34 of the Trustee Act 2000).

The old s 19 only permitted premiums to be paid out of income, but the substituted s 19(5) states that 'trust funds' means 'any income or capital funds of the trust' and the Law Commission[18] clearly intended the trustees to have a discretion as to the ultimate incidence of those premiums. The Law Commission[19] also clearly intended that the cost of employing a nominee or custodian or other agent should ultimately be allocated as the trustees decided in their discretion and believed that the s 39 definition of 'trust funds' as 'income or capital funds of the trust' achieved this.

There seems no reason to restrict the operation of 'income or capital funds of the trust' to the initial payment of outgoings so as not to cover the ultimate

---

11 See *Re Gjers* [1899] 2 Ch 54; and *Re Betty* [1899] 1 Ch 821; but cf *Re Baring* [1893] 1 Ch 61; and *Re Owen* [1912] 1 Ch 519; distinguished in *Re Shee* [1934] Ch 345.
12 *Re Courtier* (1886) 34 Ch D 136; per Cotton and Lindley LJJ in *Re Hotchkys* (1886) 32 Ch D 408.
13 *White v White* (1804) 9 Ves 554; *Nightingale v Lawson* (1785) 1 Bro CC 440.
14 *Re Copland's Settlement* [1900] 1 Ch 326.
15 *Lord Brougham v Lord Poulett* (1855) 19 Beav 119 at 135; *Sanders v Miller* (1858) 25 Beav 154; *Re Earl De La Warr's Estates* (1881) 16 Ch D 587; *Stott v Milne* (1884) 25 Ch D 710; explained in *Re Weall* (1889) 42 Ch D 674.
16 See *Re Marner's Trusts* (1866) LR 3 Eq 432; *Re Evans' Trusts* (1872) 7 Ch App 609; *Re Smith's Trusts* (1870) LR 9 Eq 374.
17 *Stott v Milne* (1884) 25 Ch D 710 at 715 per Lord Selborne LC; *Carver v Duncan* [1985] AC 1082 at 1120 per Lord Templeman. And see cases in note 7, p 573 post.
18 Law Com No 260 'Trustees' Powers and Duties' at paras 6.6, 8.39, and at p119 note on cl 34 draft Bill.
19 Law Com No 260 at paras 5.13, 8.33, and p 117 note on clauses 31 and 32 of draft Bill.

incidence of outgoings. The words should be taken at their face[20] value in accordance with the modern philosophy (eg with broad powers of investment) to confer very flexible discretionary powers on trustees but subject to the safeguards of the duties imposed on trustees when coming to exercise those powers eg the duty to act fairly between life tenant and remainderman, enabling the remainderman to challenge apportioning the cost of collecting rental income onto capital and the life tenant to challenge any attempt to apportion the cost of selling a capital asset onto income.

PARAGRAPH (A)

Charges and incumbrances

Where a capital sum is secured on property, it is payable out of corpus; but the interest on it is payable out of income[1] arising not only from the incumbered property, but from all other property subject to the same trust. If the current income is insufficient to keep down the interest, the arrears are payable out of subsequent income[2], and this is so, even where the charge in respect of which the arrears have arisen has been paid off by means of a sale of part of the property[3].

The rule as to capital charges being borne by corpus prevails even where a debt is secured by, or is payable as, an *annuity* or by instalments. In such a case the tenant for life will have to contribute an amount equal to interest on the capital value[4].

---

20 As indicated in J Kessler *Drafting Trusts and Will Trusts* (6th edn), para 20.28, although the contrary view has been taken by *Lewin on Trusts* (17th edn) para 25-26B. The power in TA 2000, s 31(1) and in TA 1925, s 19 is merely an administrative power, like that in TA 1925, s 22(4), and so will not prevent a life tenant having an interest in possession for tax purposes.

1 *Marshall v Crowther* (1874) 2 Ch D 199; *Whitbread v Smith* (1854) 3 De GM & G 727; and see *Allhusen v Whittell* (1867) LR 4 Eq 295. *Allhusen v Whittell* deals with the situation where a testator leaves his residuary estate to A for life, remainder to B absolutely and in accordance with the general law debts, expenses and legacies have to be paid out of the residue. The payments are treated as coming partly from income and partly from capital. That sum has to be ascertained which together with interest for the year succeeding death would amount to the total expended on debts, expenses and legacies: the sum so ascertained is borne by B entitled to capital and the excess of the total expenditure over the sum is borne by A entitled to income. The rate of interest to be used depends on the ratio subsisting between the actual net income after tax for the year succeeding death and the value of the residuary estate: *Re Oldham* [1927] WN 113. The calculation should be modified if payment of debts, etc is significantly before or after the end of the executor's year: rough and ready calculations will suffice: *Re Wills* [1915] 1 Ch 769. For words inappropriate to exclude the rule in *Allhusen v Whittell*, see *Re Ullswater* [1952] Ch 105, [1951] 1 All ER 989. Also see *Re Hogg* [1983] LS Gaz R 2838.

2 *Honywood v Honywood* [1902] 1 Ch 347; *Frewen v Law Life Assurance Society* [1896] 2 Ch 511; *Re Hotchkys* (1886) 32 Ch D 408.

3 *Honywood v Honywood* [1902] 1 Ch 347; *Frewen v Law Life Assurance Society* [1896] 2 Ch 511; *Re Hotchkys* (1886) 32 Ch D 408. Capital must be reimbursed if used to discharge an income expense when insufficient income was available.

4 *Bulwer v Astley* (1844) 1 Ph 422; *Playfair v Cooper* (1853) 17 Beav 187; *Ley v Ley* (1868) LR 6 Eq 174; *Re Muffett* (1888) 39 Ch D 534 (purchase-money consisting of a life annuity). But this does not apply to the case of a jointure, or other charge, where there is no covenant and therefore no debt: *Re Popham* [1914] WN 257; *Re Darby* [1939] Ch 905, [1939] 3 All ER 6.

How the respective liabilities of corpus and income are computed

There has, however, been a curious conflict of judicial authority as to how the respective contributions of capital and income ought to be computed in such cases. In *Re Bacon*[5] and *Re Henry*[6], Kekewich J laid it down that the proper way was to raise the required amount out of corpus as required, in which way the tenant for life would lose a corresponding amount of income. This view was, however, dissented from by Swinfen Eady J in *Re Dawson*[7], where his Lordship held that the successive instalments of the annuities must be borne by income and capital in proportion to the actuarial values of the life estate and reversion at the testator's death. But in the subsequent case of *Re Perkins*[8] where it was pointed out that this actuarial method would act unfairly, the same judge directed that each instalment of the annuity should be met by calculating what sum with 3% simple interest from the commencement of the life tenancy to the day of payment would have met the instalment, the sum so ascertained to come out of capital and the balance out of income. This case was subsequently followed by Joyce J in *Re Thompson*[9], by Parker J in *Re Poyser*[10] and by the Court of Appeal in *Re Berkeley*[11] and may now be taken as establishing the recognised rule[12].

Purchase of annuities

If, for example, a testator settles his residuary estate but directs that an annuity be purchased for A for life, then A is entitled to take the amount of money required to produce such annuity[13]. A has a vested legacy as from the testator's death and is entitled to interest thereon from such date[14]. In the absence of a gift over, a direction that A shall not receive the capital value of the annuity or shall not alienate the annuity is void as a naked in terrorem prohibition and probably also as repugnant to A's absolute interest in the capital value[15]. If the annuity is charged on the whole income or the whole income and corpus A is not entitled to anything except the annuity and having sufficient assets set aside to cover the annuity[16]. If there is a further provision empowering the trustees on sale of corpus to purchase annuities for annuitants and the trustees decide to exercise this power then on completion of the sale when the trustees receive the capital moneys A will have a vested right to the amount of capital required to produce the annuity[17].

Local government charges

Expenses incurred by a local authority in sewering, paving and flagging a new

 5 (1893) 62 LJ Ch 445.
 6 [1907] 1 Ch 30.
 7 [1906] 2 Ch 211.
 8 [1907] 2 Ch 596.
 9 [1908] WN 195.
10 [1910] 2 Ch 444; and *Re Craven* [1914] 1 Ch 358; and *Re Tod* [1916] 1 Ch 567.
11 [1968] 3 All ER 364.
12 But as to the rate of interest, see p 559, ante.
13 *Stokes v Cheek* (1860) 28 Beav 620.
14 *Re Robbins* [1907] 2 Ch 8, CA; *Re Brunning* [1909] 1 Ch 276.
15 *Woodmeston v Walker* (1831) 2 Russ & M 197; *Re Mabbett* [1891] 1 Ch 707.
16 *Harbin v Masterman* [1896] 1 Ch 351, CA; *Re Coller's Deed Trusts* [1939] Ch 277, CA.
17 *Re Mabbett* [1891] 1 Ch 707 (where A received nothing when dying before completion of the contract for sale).

street, and charged by statute on the adjacent land, are a charge on corpus and not income, even although they, with interest, are repayable to the local authority by instalments[18], and by s 213 of the Highways Act 1980 any person who could sell such lands under the Compulsory Purchase Act 1965 may mortgage them for raising the charge.

Arrears of interest accrued during the settlor's life

Arrears of interest on incumbrances accrued in the lifetime of the settlor before the tenant for life became such, are a charge on corpus, the tenant for life merely paying interest on them[19].

The strong inclination of the court to saddle capital charges on corpus was well exemplified by *Norton v Johnstone*[20] where a testator had directed that the income of certain estates should be accumulated until the amount of the accumulations should be sufficient to pay off existing mortgages; and that, subject thereto, the property should be held to the use of the plaintiff for life, with remainders over. Before the accumulations were sufficient to discharge the mortgages, the mortgagees sold a part of the property; and with the moneys so produced, and part of the moneys already accumulated, the mortgages were paid off. The tenant for life then claimed to be let into possession, and also to have the balance of the accumulations paid to him. On the other hand, the remainderman urged that, inasmuch as the mortgage debt had been paid off by means of a sale of the corpus (which was not what was contemplated by the testator), the accumulation of rents ought to continue, until such a sum was obtained as would be equal to the amount raised by the sale; and that the sum thus obtained ought to be employed in recouping the inheritance, the tenant for life receiving only the interest of it.

Pearson J, however, decided in favour of the tenant for life, on the ground that the mortgage debts had been paid in a way different from that which the testator intended, that he had not provided for that event, and that, consequently, the ordinary rule as to the incidence of capital charges must govern the case.

Where, however, on the expiration of a lease granted by the settlor, the tenant for life is obliged to pay compensation for improvements to the outgoing lessee *under a covenant in the lease*, he has no claim to saddle the compensation on corpus. For, as Jessel MR said,

'If he lives long enough he will let the land again and get the outlay from the incoming tenant, and so if he recovered it now ... he would be repaid it twice over'[1].

But this seems to assume that the life tenant is empowered to require (and keep for his own use) a premium from the new lease. However, this rule does not apply to compensation payable under the Agricultural Holdings Act 1986, as such compensation is expressly provided for by ss 86 and 87 of that Act. Under s 86(1) a landlord can obtain from the Minister of Agriculture an order charging the holding with repayment of compensation and the

---

18 *Re Legh's Settled Estate* [1902] 2 Ch 274; but cf Highways Act 1980, ss 212, 213.
19 *Revel v Watkinson* (1748) 1 Ves Sen 93; *Playfair v Cooper* (1853) 17 Beav 187.
20 (1885) 30 Ch D 649; and see also *Re Harrison* (1889) 43 Ch D 55; and *Re Brandon* (1932) 49 TLR 48.
1 *Mansel v Norton* (1883) 22 Ch D 769.

trustees can redeem this charge out of capital moneys pursuant to s 73(1)(ii) of the Settled Land Act 1925[2].

Calls on shares

Calls on shares which form part of a trust estate are outgoings attributable to capital and not to income, and are accordingly payable out of corpus[3].

PARAGRAPH (B)

Current annual charges

All charges of an annual character, except annual charges to secure capital sums, are payable out of income, for otherwise the corpus would inevitably decrease year by year, and would ultimately be swallowed up. As Lord Templeman said in *Carver v Duncan*[4], 'The general rule is that income must bear all ordinary outgoings of a recurrent nature, such as rates and taxes, and interest on charges and incumbrances'. It has been held that the income must bear rates and taxes[5]; the commission of house agents for obtaining tenants[6]; the rent payable for, and the expenses incident to the observance and performance of the covenants and conditions in relation to, leasehold hereditaments[7]. But a tenant for life is not liable to have his income taken for breaches of covenant not occurring in his time[8]. It would seem that even the cost of complying with a sanitary notice under the Public Health (London) Act 1936[9], or a dangerous structure notice under the London Building Act 1930, are, as a rule, payable by the tenant for life; but not, apparently, the cost of a thorough reconstruction of the sewers of a house[10], or other permanent improvements insisted on by the local authority[11]. Of course, annuities charged on income[12], the commission or poundage payable to a receiver, and the expenses incident to the preparation and passing of his accounts must be borne by income[13].

Insurance premiums

Where a life policy is maintained for the benefit of capital, the premiums are (in the absence of express direction) payable out of capital raised from time

---

2 *Re Duke of Wellington's Parliamentary Estates* [1972] Ch 374, [1971] 2 All ER 1140.

3 *Todd v Moorhouse* (1874) LR 19 Eq 69; and now TA 1925, s 11(2).

4 [1985] AC 1082 at 1120, HL.

5 *Fountaine v Pellet* (1791) 1 Ves 337, 342; including income tax even where there is a direction to pay income not exceeding £x per annum to A (*Re Cain's Settlement*) [1919] 2 Ch 364.

6 *Re Leveson-Gower's Settled Estate* [1905] 2 Ch 95. But see *Re Watson* [1928] WN 309.

7 *Re Gjers* [1899] 2 Ch 54; *Re Betty* [1899] 1 Ch 821; cf *Re Tomlinson* [1898] 1 Ch 232.

8 *Re Betty* [1899] 1 Ch 821.

9 See *Re Copland's Settlement* [1900] 1 Ch 326; and *Re Lever* [1897] 1 Ch 32. See now London Government Act 1963, s 40.

10 *Re Thomas* [1900] 1 Ch 319; and see pp 571 et seq, post; and *Re McClure's Trusts* [1906] WN 200.

11 See *Re Farnham's Trusts* [1904] 2 Ch 561. The cost of private street works is specially provided for by the Highways Act 1980, ss 212, 213.

12 *Playfair v Cooper* (1853) 17 Beav 187 at 193; *Miller v Huddlestone* (1851) 3 Mac & G 513.

13 *Shore v Shore* (1859) 4 Drew 501. Where leaseholds have to be let at a loss, the loss falls on income (*Re Owen* [1912] 1 Ch 519).

to time by a charge on the policy[14]. In practice such premiums are usually paid in the first instance out of income, and are then repayable to the tenant for life when the policy falls in with interest at 4%[15]. Of course, where a policy is specifically settled, express directions are almost invariably given for payment of the premiums; and where they are directed to be paid out of income, and for some reason the policy lapses without breach of trust, the amounts which would have been paid for keeping it up must thenceforth be paid to capital account[16].

As a result of s 34 of the Trustee Act 2000, s 19 of the Trustee Act 1925 now confers on trustees of all trusts (including bare trusts[17]) power to insure any trust property against risks of loss or damage due to any event and to pay the premiums out of the 'trust funds' defined[18] to mean 'any income or capital funds of the trust'. A trustee of land in the UK, who has all the powers of an absolute owner in relation to the land[19], will thereby incidentally have a further power to insure the land against any risks.

Trustees exercising these statutory administrative powers may initially pay premiums out of either capital or income, as is most administratively convenient, before allocating the burden of the premiums taking account of the general principle that the insurance is for the benefit of the whole estate capital and so should normally be borne by capital in the absence of express provision as to the incidence of premiums[20]. However, where there are not different beneficiaries or classes of beneficiaries interested in income and capital but, for example, co-owners of income-yielding land then premiums should be paid out of income and not out of capital necessitating sale or mortgage of the land.

When exercising a statutory or an express power to insure, the statutory duty of care applies[1] (unless excluded by the trust instrument[2]) but it does not seem that it applies to the decision whether or not to exercise the power[3].

It seems that, nowadays, a trustee, having extensive powers of insurance, is under an equitable duty to insure property to the extent that an ordinary prudent business person would have insured his or her own property in the circumstances[4], taking account of the value and liquidity of the trust capital and the cost of premiums. The trustee should be afforded reasonable leeway

---

14 *Carver v Duncan (Inspector of Taxes)* [1985] AC 1082 at 1180, HL; *Macdonald v Irvine* (1878) 8 Ch D 101, CA. Expenditure for the benefit of the whole estate is a capital expense so premiums in respect of inheritance tax protection and endowment policies are capital expenses.

15 *Re Morley* [1895] 2 Ch 738.

16 *Re Fitzgerald* (1904) 90 LT 266 at 274, CA.

17 When the *Saunders v Vautier* beneficiaries can collectively direct the trustees as to the exercise or not of the statutory power: a trustee with an equitable lien ranks as a beneficiary (see Art 83 post) so that the other beneficiaries will need his consent to their proposals.

18 TA 2000, s 19(5).

19 TA 2000, s 8(3).

20 *Re Betty* [1899] 1 Ch 821 at 829; *Re McEacharn* (1911) 103 LT 900 at 902; *Carver v Duncan* [1985] AC 1082, HL. As seen at p 564 ante, the substituted TA 1925, s 19(5) confers upon trustees much discretion on the ultimate incidence of premiums, subject to their duty to act fairly.

1 TA 2000, Sch 1, para 4.

2 TA 2000, Sch 1, para 5.

3 'Trustees' Powers and Duties' Law Com No 260 (1999) para 6.9 and see terminology 'in deciding' in TLATA 1996, s 9A inserted by TA 2000, Sch 2, para 47.

4 *Re Betty* [1899] 1 Ch 821 at 829; *Kingham v Kingham* [1897] 1 IR 170 at 174; 'Trustees' Powers and Duties' Law Com No 260 (1999) p 163; *Lewin on Trusts* (17th edn) para 34-37; P Reed & R Wilson *The Trustee Act 2000: A Practical Guide* (Jordans 2001) paras 7.11–7.14.

in balancing the risk of substantial loss against the burden of very expensive insurance, so that it may be proper to take out an insurance policy with a high excess to be borne first by the trust and only to cover some basic risks rather than all risks or even not to insure, although it would then be wise to obtain the written consents thereto of existing beneficiaries of full age and capacity[5].

Trustees have to exercise their powers unanimously (unless otherwise authorised by the trust instrument or by statute) so that one trustee can prevent his co-trustees from exercising the power of insurance to any greater extent than he wishes. His co-trustees cannot then be liable for any breach of trust unless his view was outside the reasonable limits for the exercise of the trustees' discretion such that they should have applied to the court for directions pursuant to their paramount duty to act in the best interests of present and future beneficiaries[6].

Money paid for redemption of rentcharge

Where a rentcharge is redeemed by the tenant for life, he is only entitled to be recouped, out of corpus, the amount paid, less the value of the redemption of his life estate[7].

Losses on trust business

Where a business is vested in trustees in trust for successive tenants for life and a remainderman, the net losses on one year's trading must generally be made good out of the profits of subsequent years, and not out of capital[8]. This is because the outgoings of a business are part of the regular current expenses, and there can be no profits until all losses are paid, whether such losses are incurred in a year in which gross profits exceed the losses, or were incurred in prior years. This rule, however, will not apply where a business is not carried on under a direction in the settlement, but all interested parties do not want a sale at a loss to occur so that the business is merely carried on temporarily until it can be sold profitably and the remaindermen concede that a *Re Earl of Chesterfield* appointment[9] is appropriate. In such cases the annual loss or profit (if any) ought to be apportioned between capital and income as follows. Calculate the sum which, put out at interest at 4% per annum on the day when the business ought to have been sold (if it could have been) and accumulated at compound interest at the like rate, with yearly rests, would, together with such interest and accumulations, after deducting income tax, be equivalent at the end of each year to the amount of the loss or profit sustained or made during that year. The sum so ascertained will be charged against, or credited to, capital, and the rest of the loss will be charged against, or the rest of the profit will be credited to, income[10].

---

5 Then they cannot sue for the breach of the trust and they are liable to indemnify the trustee.
6 *Cowan v Scargill* [1985] Ch 270 at 286–287.
7 *Re Duke of Leinster* (1889) 23 LR Ir 152.
8 *Upton v Brown* (1884) 26 Ch D 588.
9 See p 560, ante.
10 *Re Hengler* [1893] 1 Ch 586. Cf *Re Owen* [1912] 1 Ch 519.

Where intention can be implied that losses shall be borne by capital

However, where, on the facts, it appears to have been the settlor's intention that losses in a trust business should be borne by capital, effect will be given to that intention. For instance, where *it has been the custom of a partnership* to write off the losses of unprosperous years from each partner's share of capital, that custom will be continued, even as between a tenant for life and remainderman after the death of a partner who has bequeathed his share to persons in succession[11].

So, where the settlement empowers trustees to make improvements out of capital or income, they must exercise a fair discretion, and not throw the cost wholly on income[12].

PARAGRAPH (C)

Repairs

Well-drawn settlements of house property on trust usually provide that the trustees shall keep it in repair, and insured against loss or damage by fire, out of the rents and profits.

Before 1997, s 28(2) of the Law of Property Act 1925 otherwise provided that:

> (2) Subject to any direction to the contrary in the disposition on trust for sale or in the settlement of the proceeds of sale, the net rents and profits of the land until sale, after keeping down costs of repairs and insurance and other out-goings shall be paid or applied, except so far as any part thereof may be liable to be set aside as capital money under the Settled Land Act 1925 in like manner as the income of investments representing the purchase-money would be payable or applicable if a sale had been made and the proceeds had been duly invested[13].

Maugham J in *Re Smith*[14] held that the subsection did not take away the discretion of the court to decide in a proper case[15] that the cost of certain repairs ought to be borne by capital. Section 1 of the Settled Land and Trustee Acts (Courts' General Powers) Act 1943[16] then extended the courts' jurisdiction under s 57 of the Trustee Act 1925 and s 64 of the Settled Land Act 1925 (which applied to land held on trust for sale as a result of s 28(1) of the Law of Property Act 1925[17]) so as to enable it to order that the cost of any repairs shall be treated as a capital outgoing when they are for the benefit of all persons beneficially interested and the income out of which their cost would ordinarily have been payable has become inadequate for the purpose.

After 1996 and, now as a result of s 8(3) of the Trustee Act 2000[18], trustees

---

11 *Gow v Foster* (1884) 26 Ch D 672.
12 *Re Earl of Stamford and Warrington* [1916] 1 Ch 404.
13 See also the SLA 1925, s 102, applicable to the trusts for sale by LPA 1925, s 28(1) until 1997.
14 [1930] 1 Ch 88.
15 See *Re Hotchkys* (1886) 32 Ch D 408; *Re Farnham's Trusts* [1904] 2 Ch 561.
16 Set out on p 528, ante, as amended and made permanent by the Emergency Laws (Miscellaneous Provisions) Act 1953.
17 *Re Simmons* [1956] Ch 125.
18 Replacing s 6(1) of the TLATA 1996.

of land[19] have all the powers of an absolute owner in relation to the land and so can carry out repairs and improvements. Whether such expenditure should be borne by capital or income now depends on equitable principles.

It has been held that trustees may, without any order, do such repairs to leasehold property as are necessary to prevent a forfeiture of the lease, and repay themselves out of the income[20], but without prejudice to the rights of tenant for life and remainderman inter se[1], on the ground that trustees may expend money by way of salvage, and have a lien both on income and corpus for expenses properly incurred by them, as will be seen later on[2].

The following propositions founded on the practice prior to 1926 are submitted as offering some guidance as to the principles on which the court might be expected to act in the exercise of its jurisdiction to throw the cost of repairs on to capital and upon which the trustees should base the proper exercise of their discretion[3]:

(1) where the property was in disrepair when the tenant for life came into possession, then, whatever its tenure may be, the court would probably not throw the cost exclusively on him, but would sanction a mortgage, equitably apportioning the ultimate cost between corpus and income[4]. There is, however, no reported case showing how this equitable apportionment will be carried out; but in one case in which Sir Arthur Underhill appeared before Romer J in chambers, that learned judge approved a scheme under which the trustees were to pay for a new roof in a tropical climate (which was estimated to last for twenty years only) by a sinking fund extending over that period. And where trustees, under a power, invested money in the purchase of real estate out of repair, the cost of putting it in repair was thrown exclusively on capital[5]. On the other hand, cases have been known where the judge made a rough and ready apportionment, such as an arbitrator might make. There is in fact no technical rule—the judge directs what he considers to be fair and reasonable;

(2) where the property was not in disrepair when the tenant for life came into possession, the question is governed by the maxim he who takes the benefit ought also to bear the burden, unless it becomes a clear case of salvage; and as regards leaseholds the person entitled to enjoy the income of the property must perform the conditions of the lease as to repairs[6];

---

19 The SLA 1925 as amended by the TA 2000, Sch 2, paras 7–17 governs the position of tenant for life and the SLA trustees. Many repairs to freehold land amount to improvements which can be thrown onto capital under SLA 1925 as amended by the Agricultural Holdings Act 1986: see p 573 post.

20 *Re Fowler* (1881) 16 Ch D 723.

1 *Re Hotchkys* (1886) 32 Ch D 408.

2 Article 83, post.

3 For further examples see *Re Jackson* (1882) 21 Ch D 786; *Re Hawker's Settled Estates* (1897) 66 LJ Ch 341; *Re Lord Sherborne's Settled Estate* [1929] 1 Ch 345; *Re Smith* [1930] 1 Ch 88; *Re Whitaker* [1929] 1 Ch 662; *Re Conquest* [1929] 2 Ch 353; *Re Jacques Settled Estates* [1930] 2 Ch 418; and *Re Borough Court Estate* [1932] 2 Ch 39. For a case involving special circumstances, see *Re Earl Berkeley* [1968] Ch 744, [1968] 3 All ER 364, CA.

4 *Re Courtier* (1886) 34 Ch D 136; as explained in *Re Redding* [1897] 1 Ch 876; *Re Betty* [1899] 1 Ch 821; and *Re Kingham* [1897] 1 IR 170; acquiesced in by Kekewich J in *Re Gjers* [1899] 2 Ch 54; contrary to his previous decision in *Re Tomlinson* [1898] 1 Ch 232.

5 *Re Freman* [1898] 1 Ch 28; but cf *Re Lord De Tabley* (1896) 75 LT 328; *Re Freman*, above, was distinguished by Eve J in *Re Jervis* (1919) 146 LT Jo 215.

6 *Re Kingham* [1897] 1 IR 170; *Re Redding* [1897] 1 Ch 876; *Re Betty* [1899] 1 Ch 821; *Re Gjers* [1899] 2 Ch 54; and see *Re Partington* [1902] 1 Ch 711, as to re-drainage of a leasehold house being borne by income.

(3) the fact that the trustees are expressly authorised to pay for repairs out of income or capital will not justify them in throwing on to capital the cost of repairs which ought to be borne by income for the purpose of relieving the person entitled to that income, such powers being prima facie intended for the benefit of the estate and to be used so as to adjust the burden equitably[7].

Alterations in the nature of repairs under the Settled Land Act

By the Third Schedule to the Settled Land Act 1925 improvements on which capital moneys are authorised by that Act to be expended[8] are to include structural or other[9] *additions to* or *alterations in* buildings reasonably necessary or proper to enable the same to be let, and also the rebuilding of the principal mansion house. But, in the latter case, the sum to be applied out of capital money is not to exceed one-half of the annual rent of the settled land. Under a similar provision in the Settled Land Act 1890 it was held, that although mere repairs and improvements will not amount to a 'rebuilding' of the principal mansion house[10]; yet reconstruction, alteration, and enlargement of a considerable part of the house may[11]. For instance, the Act was held to apply where the house had become infested with dry rot, and portions had to be rebuilt in order to save the whole[12]. It has likewise been held that the substitution of a block floor over concrete for ordinary floor boards in order to keep dry rot out of the basement of a large house let in separate offices was an alteration reasonably necessary or proper to enable the same to be let[13]. By virtue of the Agricultural Holdings Act 1986, s 89(1), and Seventh Schedule, the improvements authorised by the Settled Land Act 1925, s 83 and Third Schedule[14], include repairs to fixed equipment reasonably necessary for the proper farming of agricultural land.

Fencing of unfenced land

Where the question arises as to the incidence of the cost, not of mere repairs, but of putting property into a better condition than it was in originally, it would seem that no part of the cost falls on income. Thus, the expense of

---

7 *Re Lord De Tabley* (1896) 75 LT 328; *Re Earl of Stamford and Warrington* [1916] 1 Ch 404; *Re Lord Boston's Will Trusts* [1956] Ch 395.
8 SLA 1925, ss 73(1)(iii), 83 and Sch 3. See also *Re Duke of Wellington's Parliamentary Estates* [1972] Ch 374, [1971] 2 All ER 1140.
9 *Re Lindsay's Settlement (No 2)* [1941] Ch 119, [1941] 1 All ER 143.
10 *Re De Teissier's Settled Estates* [1893] 1 Ch 153; *Re Lord De Tabley* (1896) 75 LT 328; *Re Wright's Settled Estates* (1900) 83 LT 159.
11 *Re Walker's Settled Estate* [1894] 1 Ch 189; and see *Re Leveson-Gower's Settled Estate* [1905] 2 Ch 95.
12 *Re Legh's Settled Estate* [1902] 2 Ch 274.
13 *Stanford v Roberts* [1901] 1 Ch 440; and see also *Re Clarke's Settlement* [1902] 2 Ch 327; *Re Gaskell's Settled Estates* [1894] 1 Ch 485; both approved by Court of Appeal in *Re Blagrave's Settled Estates* [1903] 1 Ch 560; *Standing v Gray* [1903] 1 IR 49; *Re Battle Abbey Settled Estate* [1933] WN 215; and *Re Swanwick House, Prestbury* [1939] 3 All ER 531; where the cost of conversion into flats was held to be proper expenditure to enable the property to be let to the greatest advantage.
14 See *Re Duke of Northumberland* [1951] Ch 202, [1950] 2 All ER 1181; *Re Sutherland Settlement Trusts* [1953] Ch 792, [1953] 2 All ER 27; *Re Lord Brougham and Vaux's Settled Estates* [1954] Ch 24, [1953] 2 All ER 655.

fencing waste lands granted to a trustee for the benefit of the estate must be paid out of corpus exclusively[15].

Paragraph (d)

General costs incident to administration

Legal expenses or investment advice incident to the administration of a trust almost exclusively fall on capital, unless the settlor has expressly provided for them, for they are for the benefit of all persons interested. Thus:

the costs of the appointment of new trustees[16],
the costs incident to the investment or change of investment of trust funds[17],
the costs of obtaining investment advice, since such affects the future value of corpus and the future level of income[18],
the costs of obtaining legal advice[19], and of taking the direction of the court[20],
the costs of an administration action[1],
the costs of paying money into court under the Trustee Act[2],
the costs of bringing or defending actions against third parties for the protection of the estate[3] (eg lessees for breach of their covenants to repair[4]), and the like,

have all been held to be payable out of corpus. Even where the costs of management are directed by the settlement to be paid out of income, the court may, in exceptional cases, order them to be paid out of corpus[5]. On the other hand, where money is paid into court under the Trustee Act, the costs of all necessary parties to a petition for obtaining an order for the payment of the *income* to the tenant for life have been held to be payable out of income[6].

Trust accounts and audit

If trust accounts are audited no more than once in every three years, the trustees have a discretion under s 22(4) of the Trustee Act 1925 as to the

---

15 *Earl of Cowley v Wellesley* (1866) LR 1 Eq 656; and see SLA 1925, s 83, and judgment of Kekewich J in *Re Verney's Settled Estates* [1898] 1 Ch 508.
16 *Re Fellows' Settlement* (1856) 2 Jur NS 62; *Re Fulham* (1850) 15 Jur 69; *Ex p Davies* (1852) 16 Jur 882.
17 But not of petition to vary investment of funds in court, see *Equitable Reversionary Interest Society v Fuller* (1861) 1 John & H 379.
18 *Carver v Duncan* [1985] 2 All ER 645 at 653, HL.
19 *Poole v Pass* (1839) 1 Beav 600.
20 *Re Elmore's Will Trusts* (1860) 9 WR 66; *Re Leslie's Settlement Trusts* (1876) 2 Ch D 185.
 1 *Re Turnley* (1866) 1 Ch App 152.
 2 *Re Whitton's Trusts* (1869) LR 8 Eq 352.
 3 *Stott v Milne* (1884) 25 Ch D 710; *Hamilton v Tighe* [1898] 1 IR 123; and see also *Re Earl De La Warr's Estates* (1881) 16 Ch D 587, and *Re Earl of Berkeley's Will* (1874) 10 Ch App 56. And as to defending foreclosure actions and obtaining transfers of the mortgage, see *More v More* (1889) 37 WR 414.
 4 *Re McClure's Trusts* (1906) 76 LJ Ch 52. Here corpus did not exclusively bear the burden of £200 incurred in survey fees and legal fees for serving notices of disrepair: Kekewich J said, 'The burden is to be cast not wholly upon the tenant for life nor upon the remainderman but is to be borne by each in fair proportion. That can be done by raising the amount required by mortgage of the property, the tenant for life bearing the burden of the interest payments.'
 5 See *Re Tubbs* [1915] 2 Ch 137, CA; and *Re Hicklin* [1917] 2 Ch 278.
 6 *Re Marner's Trusts* (1866) LR 3 Eq 432; *Re Evans' Trusts* (1872) 7 Ch App 609; *Re Whitton's Trusts* (1869) LR 8 Eq 352; *Re Smith's Trusts* (1870) LR 9 Eq 374; *Scrivener v Smith* (1869) LR 8 Eq 310; *Longuet v Hockley* (1870) 22 LT 198; but see *Eady v Watson* (1864) 12 WR 682.

incidence of the cost between capital and income, but in default of exercise of such discretion costs attributable to capital shall be borne by capital and those attributable to income by income, so that the auditor should be asked to advise on such attribution. If accounts are audited more than once in every three years because the nature of the trust or any special dealings with the trust property make a more frequent exercise of the right reasonable, s 22(4) continues to apply. On principle, the cost should fall on capital because the audit is for the benefit of the estate as a whole to ensure that after falsification and surcharge of the accounts, if necessary, the due amount of capital is present, but this provides the basis for checking that the due amount of income was, and should be, provided, so that it would be difficult for an income beneficiary to complain if there was an apportionment according to the default provision in s 22(4).

With professionally prepared annual trust accounts, it is common to pay for them out of the income available for the income beneficiaries (especially if there are liquidity problems with capital assets) without complaint from such beneficiaries. However, where, as should be the case, the accounts include balance sheets and capital accounts for the benefit of the estate as a whole and the capital beneficiaries in particular, it is wholly justifiable[7] to charge the costs thereof to the capital beneficiaries and the costs of the income accounts to the income beneficiaries in accordance with the default provision in s 22(4) for the analogous costs of independent audits.

ARTICLE 52

Duty of trustee to exercise reasonable care and skill

(1) Trustees are not insurers[8], and, except where courts of equity have imposed distinct and stringent duties upon them (which duties are mentioned in the succeeding Articles of this Chapter) not to breach their obligation of undivided disinterested loyalty nor to act beyond the powers conferred upon them by the trust instrument or by law[9], a trustee must exercise such care and skill as is reasonable in the circumstances, having regard in particular (a) to any special knowledge or experience that he has or holds himself out as having and (b), if he acts as trustee in the course of a business or profession, to any special knowledge or experience that it is reasonable to expect of a person acting in the course of that kind of business or profession[10].

(2) the conduct of trustees is to be judged with reference to the facts and circumstances existing at the time when they had to act and which

---

7 *Shore v Shore* (1859) 4 Drew 501 and *Earl of Cowley v Wellesley* (1866) LR 1 Eq 656 are not authority to the contrary because the costs there related respectively to the costs of a receiver of rents to which the income beneficiary was entitled and to the costs of accounts for succession duty payable by the life tenant.
8 *Re Hurst* (1892) 67 LT 96; *Re Chapman* [1896] 2 Ch 763 at 775, per Lindley LJ; *Bartlett v Barclays Bank Trust Co Ltd* [1980] Ch 515, [1980] 1 All ER 139.
9 For strict liability on falsification of account for acting ultra vires see Art 89 post.
10 TA 2000, ss 1, 2, Sch 1.

were known or ought to have been known to them at the time[11]; (3) though it cannot oust the jurisdiction of the court to determine matters of law, the trust instrument may to a greater or lesser extent qualify or exclude the duties otherwise imposed by equity upon the trustees, so long as there remains a sufficient inner core of duties owed to the beneficiaries to enable a trust to subsist (as opposed to an agency or nomineeship arrangement on behalf of the settlor), while exemption may expressly be granted to trustees against liability for a breach of duty which is not dishonest, unless the trustee's belief is so unreasonable that no honest reasonable person with the objective attributes of the trustee in question (eg a solicitor paid to act as trustee) could have held such belief.

PARAGRAPH 1

The duty of care under Trustee Act 2000

The Trustee Act 2000 in enacting[12]'the duty of care', which applies[13] to the extensive range of powers derived from the 2000 Act and ss 15, 19 and 22 of the Trustee Act 1925 as well as to equivalent types of powers derived from the trust instrument and to the investment and reviewing duties imposed by ss 4, 5 and 22 of the 2000 Act, seems to codify the general equitable duty of care[14], breach of which enables the trust accounts to be surcharged[15] with the amount of income or capital that would have been trust income or capital but for the trustee's breach of the equitable duty of care in acting within the powers conferred by law or the trust instrument. It applies to trusts in existence when it came into force on 1 February 2001 but *ex abundante cautela* does not apply to acts or omissions before then.

The general equitable duty of care was a developing one which had not been laid down with precision. The general duty was to take the care of an ordinary prudent businessman in managing his own affairs[16], except that in selecting investments he had to consider that he was making an investment for the benefit of other people for whom he felt morally obliged to provide[17], so that there could be no question of making a speculative investment that an ordinary prudent businessman might occasionally make for himself: 'safety first' was the cardinal principle[18]. A paid trustee was expected to exercise a

---

11 *Re Hurst* (1892) 67 LT 96 at 99 per Lindley LJ, CA; *Nestlé v National Westminster Bank* [1994] 1 All ER 118 at 134 per Staughton LJ: 'the trustees performance must not be judged with hindsight'.

12 TA 2000, s 1.

13 TA 2000, Sch 1, extending to powers of investment, acquisition of land, appointment of agents, nominees and custodians, compounding liabilities, insurance, and valuing interests.

14 As intended by Law Com Report No 260 (1999) 'Trustees' Powers and Duties', para 2.35.

15 See Art 89 post.

16 *Brice v Stokes* (1805) 11 Ves 319; *Massey v Banner* (1820) 1 Jac & W 241; *Bullock v Bullock* (1886) 56 LJ Ch 221; *Speight v Gaunt* (1883) 22 Ch D 727 at 736 and 754; affd sub nom *Speight v Gaunt* (1883) 9 App Cas 1, at 19 per Lord Blackburn.

17 *Re Whiteley* (1886) 33 Ch D 347 at 355 and 358; *Cowan v Scargill* [1985] Ch 270 at 288; *Nestlé v National Westminster Bank* [1994] 1 All ER 118 at 126 and 140, CA; Lord Nicholls in (1995) 9 Trust LI 71 at 73.

18 See *Nestle v National Westminster Bank* [1994] 1 All ER 118 at 142 per Leggatt LJ.

higher standard of diligence and knowledge than an unpaid trustee[19], while a professional corporate trustee was expected to use the special care and skill which it professed itself to have in its advertising literature and its dealings with the settlor[20].

The statutory duty of care is to 'exercise such care and skill as is reasonable in the circumstances', which will include the fact that in his investment function a trustee is investing not for his own benefit but for the benefit of others and also the fact that he is acting gratuitously or being paid for his services. In particular, regard must be had under s 1(1)(a) to any special knowledge or experience that the trustee subjectively has or holds himself out as having and under s 1(1)(b), if he 'acts as a trustee in the course of a business or profession' (and so is a paid trustee), to any special knowledge or experience that it is objectively reasonable to expect of a person acting in the course of that kind of business or profession.

Section 1(1)(b) of the 2000 Act imposes an objective minimum standard on a solicitor or accountant or fund-manager acting as a paid trustee, but s 1(1)(a) raises that standard if such trustee has or holds himself out as having special knowledge or experience.

Trustees of pension schemes, common investment schemes for charities and authorised unit trusts; bare trustees and constructive trustees.

The statutory duty of care does not apply to many functions of pension scheme trustees already covered by the Pensions Act 1995[1], while many of the powers conferred by the 2000 Act or their corresponding express powers are inappropriate for trustees of authorised unit trusts[2] or of common investment schemes for charities[3] or are regulated by other laws.

Otherwise, any trustee having statutory or express powers of investment or of acquisition of land or of appointing agents, nominees and custodians or of compounding liabilities or of insuring or of valuing assets, is subject to the statutory duty of care[4] (except to the extent excluded by the trust instrument[5]) when exercising any of those powers. 'Trustee' is not defined anywhere in the 2000 Act, although its substitution of a new s 19 power to insure into the 1925 Act is in terminology apt to cover a bare trustee in that context because the substituted s 19(2) creates a special exception from s 19(1) for property held on a bare trust. On the other hand, s 16 of the 2000 Act, in permitting trustees to appoint a nominee unless there is already a custodian trustee, indicates that a nominee is not to be regarded as being a trustee with the powers of a trustee under the 2000 Act subject to the duty of care in their exercise. Where T has agreed to be nominee or bare trustee for B, T should have no power to do anything other than as directed by B[6], but if B, subject to revocation by B, confers powers on T then T becomes subject to the statutory duty of care[7]. It should be noted that if T has a prior beneficial lien to cover

19 *Re Waterman's Will Trusts* [1952] 2 All ER 1054 at 1055; *National Trustees Co of Australia v General Finance Co* [1905] AC 373 at 381.
20 *Bartlett v Barclays Bank Trust Co Ltd* [1980] Ch 515 at 534.
1 TA 2000, s 36.
2 TA 2000, s 37.
3 TA 2000, s 38.
4 TA 2000, Sch 1, paras 1–6.
5 TA 2000, Sch 1, para 7.
6 See p 58 ante.
7 TA 2000, Sch 1.

T's liabilities, then the other beneficiaries cannot terminate the trust: T is entitled to continue managing so much of the trust property as he retains with the same powers as were conferred in the trust instrument[8].

Where a person is a constructive trustee of property as trustee *de son tort*, having undertaken to act as if trustee though not validly appointed as such, then the statutory duty of care will apply. Otherwise, it is only from the time that the conscience of the constructive trustee of property was affected (viz such person had actual, Nelsonian or 'naughty' knowledge of the trust) that there can be personal liability for breach of any duty of care[9]. If express trustees are extant or all the beneficiaries collectively entitled are present and demanding the property, then the constructive trustee's duty is to transfer the property as soon as practicable to the trustees or the beneficiaries as the case may be, the trustee merely being a nominee. If there are no trustees and the beneficiaries include minor or unborn persons, then it seems the constructive trustee will have to fulfil the role of a trustee until the property can be vested in new trustees, and the duty of care will apply.

Realisation of debts

It is the duty of a trustee to realise debts owing to the trust estate with all convenient speed[10]. He should not only press for payment, but, if they are not paid within a reasonable time, should enforce payment by means of legal proceedings[11]. However, one trustee ought not to commence proceedings without consulting his co-trustees; and if he does so and is condemned in costs to a third party he will have to bear them himself[12]. Under the Trustee Act 1925, s 15 until 1 February 2001, trustees who had failed to take proceedings to get in a debt were not liable for failure so to do where they had acted in good faith. 'Good faith,' however, involves the exercise of 'active discretion' on the part of the trustees, so they would be liable for loss arising from supineness or carelessness[13]. Since 1 February 2001[14] trustees in compounding, compromising or abandoning claims under the Trustee Act 1925, s 15 are not to be liable for any loss thereby occasioned if they had discharged their statutory duty of care.

In one very old case where a beneficiary would have been ruined by the immediate realisation of a debt due from him to the trust estate, and other beneficiaries (his children) would have been seriously prejudiced, the House of Lords held that the trustee exercised a reasonable discretion in refraining from suing the debtor and in allowing him time, and that the trustee was

---

8 *X v A* [2000] 1 All ER 490.

9 *Westdeutsche Landesbank v Islington London Borough Council* [1996] AC 669 at 705 and 707.

10 *Buxton v Buxton* (1835) 1 My & Cr 80.

11 *Re Brogden* (1888) 38 Ch D 546; and *Millar's Trustees v Polson* (1897) 34 SLR 798; *Fenwick v Greenwell* (1847) 10 Beav 412; *Grove v Price* (1858) 26 Beav 103.

12 *Re England's Settlement Trusts* [1918] 1 Ch 24.

13 *Re Greenwood* (1911) 105 LT 509 (where a debt was uncollected and no action brought for seven years although the debtor was possessed of considerable means). Overdue payments under a covenant are income of the trust for the year in which the payments were due, so a claim for repayment of tax made later than 6 years after a covenanted payment fell due will be out of time. Trustees must bear in mind that delay in enforcing a covenant may result in loss of a claim for repayment of tax: *IRC v Crawley* [1987] STC 147.

14 TA 2000, Sch 2, para 20.

consequently discharged from liability for any consequent losses[15]. Where a trustee needs reassurance that it will be a proper unimpeachable exercise of its s 15 powers to compromise a debt, it should obtain the directions of the court that this will be the case. This will require the court to be satisfied[16] that the trustee has in fact formed the opinion in good faith, that the special circumstances render it desirable and proper to take the particular course of action, the opinion is one at which a reasonable trustee, properly instructed, could have arrived and the opinion is not vitiated by any actual or potential conflict of interest. This would be appropriate where the debt was owed to trustees by the deceased settlor's family company in which the trustees held a significant shareholding upon trust for the settlor's issue, some of whom were in the employ of the company, and where postponement of calling in the debt might either see the company through a difficult situation or lose the debt upon the company's subsequent liquidation, though suing for the debt, whilst occasioning a short-term benefit, might precipitate events leading to liquidation of the company. Indeed such steps were recently taken[17] where trustees of a pension scheme sought to use s 15 to compromise a claim against the employer to fund the scheme up to the statutory minimum funding requirements.

Trustees bound to realise an investment which has ceased to be authorised

Section 4 of the Trustee Act 1925 provided that:

> 'A trustee shall not be liable for breach of trust by reason *only* of his continuing to hold an investment which has ceased to be an investment authorised by the trust instrument or by the general law.'

However there was a duty to conduct regular reviews of investments[18], so that once such review indicated an investment had become unauthorised, then it needed to be sold as soon as reasonable practicable, not necessarily immediately[19]. The Trustee Act 2000 repealed s 4 as from 1 February 2001, taking account of the immensely wide powers of investment generally and of acquisition of land in particular, so that (unless restricted by the trust instrument) investments in any assets other than non-UK land, will be authorised if the trustees obtain and consider proper advice having regard to the standard investment criteria of s 4 of the Trustee Act 2000 and the need to review investments regularly under s 4(2).

Allowing rents to fall in arrears

Where trustees allowed rents to get in arrears, it was held that they were liable to make good the arrears, though without interest[20].

---

15 *Ward v Ward* (1843) 2 HL Cas 777n at 784; *Clack v Holland* (1854) 19 Beav 262; and see *Re Hurst* (1892) 67 LT 96.

16 See *Public Trustee v Cooper* [2001] WTLR 901 at 925 applied in *Representation of I* (2001) 4 ITELR 446.

17 *Bradstock Group Pension Scheme Trustees Ltd v Bradstock Group plc* [2002] EWHC 1461 (Ch), [2002] PLR 327. The beneficiaries need to be informed of the Part 8 application and the proposed compromise: *Re Owens Corning Fiberglass (UK) Pension Plan Ltd* (2002) Times, 8 July [2002] PLR 323.

18 *Nestlé v National Westminster Bank plc* [1994] 1 All ER 118, CA.

19 See *Wright v Ginn* [1994] OPLR 83; *Re Medland* (1889) 41 Ch D 476.

20 *Tebbs v Carpenter* (1816) 1 Madd 290; and see as to interest, *Lowson v Copeland* (1787) 2 Bro CC 156; *Wiles v Gresham* (1854) 2 Drew 258; *Rowley v Adams* (1849) 2 HL Cas 725.

Bankrupt trustee indebted to trust

Where a trustee, indebted to the trust, becomes bankrupt, it is his duty to prove the debt; and if he neglects to do so he will be liable for the loss[1]. If he absconds, the beneficiaries may prove[2]; and if a co-trustee has paid part, the beneficiaries may nevertheless prove for the whole[3].

Life policies

Where part of the trust property was a life policy, and default was made in payment of the premium for keeping it alive, the trustees were held liable for not surrendering the policy and obtaining the surrender value[4].

Neglect to register when necessary

Again, it has been held that a trustee will be liable if he fails to register the trust instrument (where it requires to be registered), and the settlor is thereby enabled to effect a mortgage on the property[5].

Joining in sale of contiguous properties

Trustees must use their best endeavours to sell to the best advantage[6]. They should, therefore (in general), abstain from joining with the owners of contiguous property in a sale of the whole together, unless such a course would be clearly beneficial to their beneficiaries. For, by doing so, they expose the trust property to deterioration on account of the flaws, or possible flaws, in the title to the other property. But:

> 'suppose there were a house belonging to trustees, and a garden and forecourt belonging to somebody else; it must be obvious that those two properties would fetch more if sold together than if sold separately. You might have a divided portion of a house belonging to trustees and another divided portion belonging to somebody else. It would be equally obvious, if these two portions were sold together, that a more beneficial result would thereby take place. ... But in those cases where it is not *manifest on a mere inspection* of the properties that it is more beneficial to sell them together, then you ought to have reasonable evidence ... that is is a prudent and right thing to do, and that evidence, as we know by experience, is obtained from surveyors and other persons who are competent judges'[7].

The trustees must, of course, ensure that their apportioned part of the purchase price is duly paid to them alone.

Where trustees are reversioners, it is obvious that they may in general join in a sale; for everybody knows that as a general rule (of course there are

1 *Orrett v Corser* (1855) 21 Beav 52.
2 *Re Bradley* (1910) 54 Sol Jo 377.
3 *Edwards v Hood-Barrs* [1905] 1 Ch 20.
4 *Re Godwin's Settlement* (1918) 87 LJ Ch 645.
5 *Macnamara v Carey* (1867) IR 1 Eq 9; and as to neglect to give notice to an assurance company of an assignment to the trustees of a policy, see *Kingdon v Castleman* (1877) 25 WR 345. But *query* whether these neglects of a skilled agent would now be held to fall on the trustee. Further see TA 1925, s 61, Art 95, post.
6 See *Buttle v Saunders* [1950] 2 All ER 193, (1950) 14 Conv (NS) 228 (EH Bodkin); (1975) 39 Conv (NS) 177 (A Samuels).
7 Per Jessel MR in *Re Cooper and Allen's Contract for Sale to Harlech* (1876) 4 Ch D 802 at 816, 817. See also *Rede v Oakes* (1864) 4 De GJ & Sm 505; *Re Parker and Beech's Contract* [1887] WN 27.

exceptions to every rule) the entirety of freehold estate fetches more than the sum total of the separate value of the particular estate and reversion[8]. This view has since received the express sanction of the legislature[9]. Likewise, trustees of an undivided share in the proceeds of land directed to be sold, or in any other property are empowered by statute to concur in a sale jointly with the persons entitled to or having power in that behalf over the other share or shares[10].

Depreciatory conditions of sale

Trustees ought not to do any act which will depreciate the property. No sale made by a trustee can be impeached on the ground that any of the conditions was unnecessarily depreciatory unless the beneficiaries prove that the consideration was thereby rendered inadequate; and, after the execution of the conveyance, no such sale can be impeached at all as against the purchaser, unless the beneficiaries also prove that such purchaser was acting in collusion with the trustee at the time when the contract for sale was made[11].

Improvident sale

If trustees for sale fail in reasonable diligence in inviting competition, or if they contract to sell under circumstances of great improvidence or waste, they will be personally responsible[12], and the onus of proving that they acted reasonably is upon them[13]. It is, therefore, the duty of trustees for sale to inform themselves of the real value of the property and to fix a reserve price, and for that purpose to employ, if necessary, some independent experienced person to value it[14]. Planning permission or planning potential should be emphasised in the sale particulars[15]. But if they perform this duty, they will not be responsible if the beneficiaries seek to impeach the sale as improvident[16].

Non-renewal of fixed or periodic tenancies

While it is the duty of trustees to preserve the trust assets, they need not necessarily renew a fixed term business tenancy or allow a periodic tenancy to continue. Thus, if A and B Ltd hold a tenancy on trust for themselves, but they are partners in a firm which they have dissolved and are at loggerheads with each other, one cannot obtain an interlocutory order to force the other to join in serving a counter-notice under the Landlord and Tenant Act 1954

---

8 Per Jessel MR in *Re Cooper and Allen's Contract for Sale to Harlech* (1876) 4 Ch D 802 at 816, 817. See also *Rede v Oakes* (1864) 4 De GJ & Sm 505; *Re Parker and Beech's Contract* [1887] WN 27.
9 TA 1925, s 12. Also see TA 2000, s 8(3).
10 TA 1925, s 24. Also see TA 2000, s 8(3).
11 TA 1925, s 13.
12 *Ord v Noel* (1820) 5 Madd 438; and *Anon* (1821) 6 Madd 10; *Pechel v Fowler* (1795) 2 Anst 549; cf *Cuckmere Brick Co Ltd v Mutual Finance Ltd* [1971] Ch 949, [1971] 2 All ER 633; *Downsview Nominees v First City Corpn* [1993] AC 295, [1993] 3 All ER 626, PC.
13 *Norris v Wright* (1851) 14 Beav 291.
14 *Oliver v Court* (1820) 8 Price 127; *Campbell v Walker* (1800) 5 Ves 678; and see per Jessel MR in *Re Cooper and Allen's Contract for Sale to Harlech* (1876) 4 Ch D 802 at 816.
15 *Cuckmere Brick Co Ltd v Mutual Finance Ltd* [1971] Ch 949, [1971] 2 All ER 633.
16 *Grove v Search* (1906) 22 TLR 290; and cf *Reliance Permanent Building Society v Harwood-Stamper* [1944] Ch 362 at 369 et seq, [1944] 2 All ER 75 at 79, per Vaisey J.

to enable the business tenancy to be renewed: the court considered it unlikely that at the trial of the action it would be held to be a breach of trust to fail to join in the application for a new tenancy[17].

Indeed, where A and B were cohabitees and their relationship had broken down, the Court of Appeal[18] has held it not to be a breach of trust for A[19] (who has no need to consult B[20] under s 11 of the Trusts of Land and Appointment of Trustees Act 1996) to serve a notice to quit in respect of their joint periodic tenancy (held on a statutory trust) so as to bring the tenancy to an end for both of them. Thus, the landlord local authority could evict B, such conduct not amounting to dishonest assistance in a breach of trust or knowing inconsistent dealing with trust property[1].

The landlord's position is not affected if B had obtained against A a standard non-molestation and non-exclusion court order prohibiting A from molesting B or excluding B from the premises, the court order applying only so long as A has a proprietary interest in the premises entitling A to take action to exclude B, as the House of Lords held in *Harrow LBC v Johnstone*[2]. Since the non-exclusion order had there been made in divorce proceedings between A and B it is submitted that to prevent the landlord being able to evict B, B should have claimed a transfer of the tenancy to B alone and until such claim was resolved A should have been restrained from serving a notice to quit on the landlord. Once notice to quit has been served, A has no property of which to dispose so that it cannot amount to a reviewable disposition of property that B can attack under s 37 of the Matrimonial Causes Act 1973[3].

Dishonourable duty to 'gazump'

Where trustees who have entered into negotiations for the sale of the trust property receive a subsequent higher offer from another party, they should at least probe the subsequent offer irrespective of any questions of commercial morality which might have led a vendor who was not a trustee to close the deal with the original purchaser. Nevertheless the trustees retain such a discretion as will allow them to act with proper prudence, and may pray in aid the commonsense rule underlying the old proverb 'A bird in the hand is worth two in the bush'; so that there may be cases in which they could properly refuse a higher offer and proceed with a lower one[4].

---

17 *Harris v Black* (1983) 46 P & CR 366, CA.
18 *Crawley Borough Council v Ure* [1995] 1 FLR 806, [1996] QB 13.
19 *Hammersmith & Fulham London Borough Council v Monk* [1992] 1 AC 478, [1992] 1 All ER 1, HL (notice by one joint tenant suffices to terminate for all).
20 *Notting Hill Housing Trust v Brackley* [2001] EWCA Civ 601, [2002] HLR 10, CA. In *Quazi v Harrow London Borough Council* [2001] EWCA Civ 1834, [2002] HLR 14, the Court of Appeal held that B has sufficient interest in the family home where he lives to fall within the Human Rights Act 1998, Sch 1, Pt I, art 8(1), though interference with such right is likely to be justified under Article 8(2).
1 See Art 100 post.
2 [1997] 1 All ER 929, HL.
3 *Newlon Housing Trust v Alsulaimen* [1999] 1 AC 313, HL.
4 *Buttle v Saunders* [1950] 2 All ER 193; *Cowan v Scargill* [1984] 2 All ER 750 at 761, 193; *Selby v Bowie* (1863) 8 LT 372; *R v Commission for New Towns, ex p Tomkins* [1988] RVR 106; affd (1989) 58 P & CR 57.

Improvident leasing or letting

Precisely the same principles apply to the leasing or letting of trust property; and if the trustees do not take proper steps, by consulting a practical valuer, to ascertain the proper rent, or, a fortiori, knowing the proper rent accept a lower rent, they will be liable to make good the difference[5]. Nowadays, indeed, trustees should seriously consider whether it is in the best interests of a trust to let or re-let property (rather than sell with vacant possession) balancing the capital growth potential and the actual realisable income, taking into account repairing obligations and the statutory protection as to tenure of, and rents payable by, tenants.

Grant of leases and options as if absolute owner

Having, for the purpose of exercising his functions as a trustee, all the powers of an absolute owner in relation to trust land, a trustee of land can grant leases or options on such terms (eg rent review clauses, break clauses, option to purchase at market value as ascertained by a properly qualified third party, a price other than money) as satisfy the statutory duty of care, without being restricted by the wording of sections of earlier statutes. Proper advice, however, must be taken and considered.

Improvident purchase

The same principles hold good in the case of trustees of a trust for the purchase of land or of trustees exercising their statutory or other powers to acquire land, who ought clearly to satisfy themselves of the value of the property, and for that purpose to employ a valuer of their own, and not trust to the valuer of the vendor. For a man may bona fide form his opinion, but he looks at the case in a totally different way when he knows on whose behalf he is acting; and if the trustees rely upon the vendor's valuer, and he, however bona fide, values the property at more than its true value, they will be liable[6].

Trustees for purchase should also take reasonable care that they get a good marketable title, and that they do not, by conditions of sale, bind themselves not to require one[7]; and they should never purchase without getting the legal estate unless they are expressly authorised[8] to acquire an equitable interest, when all precautions should be taken to protect the vulnerability of such interest if the land be sold to a bona fide purchaser or to a new registered proprietor.

Purchasing with the assistance of a mortgage

It seems that when trustees are acquiring land under s 8(1) of the Trustee Act 2000 they have power to purchase it with the assistance of a mortgage over it[9],

---

5 *Ferraby v Hobson* (1847) 2 Ph 255.
6 *Ingle v Partridge* (1865) 34 Beav 411; and see also *Fry v Tapson* (1884) 28 Ch D 268; *Waring v Waring* (1852) 3 I Ch R 331.
7 *Eastern Counties Rly Co v Hawkes* (1855) 5 HL Cas 331.
8 The TA 2000 extends to acquisition of legal estates (s 8(2) thereof) which probably covers legal interests like legal rentcharges: see pp 607–608.
9 See Law Com Report No 260, 'Trustees' Powers and Duties' para 2.44; *Lewin on Trusts* (17th edn) para 35-194L.

the acquisition of the legal estate and the legal charge thereon being one indivisible transaction[10] by the trustees with all the powers of an absolute owner in relation to the land they are acquiring.

Indeed, for the purpose of exercising their functions as trustees they have all the powers of an absolute owner in relation to the land that they acquire. Because an absolute owner can mortgage his subsisting legal estates in land in order to help purchase new investments, can trustees mortgage trust land in order to help purchase new investments in exercising their investment functions? This creation of a new liability imposed on subsisting trust land to create a new fund of money to be invested in the purchase of new investments seems one step removed from a power to invest as if an absolute owner, which seems implicitly restricted to making investments out of subsisting cash or investments currently available for the purchase or exchange of investments[11]. Thus, it would seem that 'gearing up' is not possible under the 2000 Act unless there is an express power in that behalf.

Error of judgment

Even apart from s 61 of the Trustee Act 1925 which gives the court power to excuse a trustee who has acted reasonably and honestly and ought fairly to be excused for the breach and for omitting to obtain the directions of the court in the matter, a trustee is not responsible for a mere error of judgment, if he has exercised a reasonable discretion and acted with diligence and good faith. Thus, where an executor omitted to sell some foreign bonds for a year after the testator's death, although there was a direction in the will to convert with all reasonable speed, he was held not to be responsible for a loss caused by the bonds falling in price, for although the conclusion he came to was unfortunate, yet having exercised a bona fide discretion, the mere fact of the loss was not sufficient to charge him[12]. A fortiori will this be so where there is power to postpone a sale[13]. As to what constitutes a reasonable delay, this depends on the particular circumstances affecting each case. Prima facie, a trustee ought not to delay realisation beyond a year, even where he has apparently unlimited discretion[14]; and, if he procrastinates beyond that period, the onus will be cast upon him of proving that the delay was reasonable and proper[15]. If he considers further delay very desirable he should apply to the court[16].

In *Re Chapman*[17] Lopes LJ said:

> 'A trustee who is honest and reasonably competent is not to be held responsible for a mere error in judgment when the question which he has to consider is whether a security for a class authorised, but depreciated in value, should be retained or realised, provided he acts with reasonable care, prudence and circumspection.'

---

10 *Abbey National Building Society v Cann* [1991] 1 AC 56, HL.
11 *Re Suenson-Taylor's Settlement* [1974] 3 All ER 397.
12 *Buxton v Buxton* (1835) 1 My & Cr 80; and see *Paddon v Richardson* (1855) 7 De GM & G 563.
13 *Re Schneider* (1906) 22 TLR 223.
14 *Sculthorpe v Tipper* (1871) LR 13 Eq 232; and as to the propriety of an executor allowing the testator's money invested on mortgage to remain so until wanted, see *Orr v Newton* (1791) 2 Cox Eq Cas 274, PC; *Robinson v Robinson* (1851) 1 De GM & G 247.
15 See per Wood LJ in *Grayburn v Clarkson* (1868) 3 Ch App 605 at 606; and *Hughes v Empson* (1856) 22 Beav 181.
16 See *Morris v Morris* (1858) 4 Jur NS 802.
17 [1896] 2 Ch 763 at 778.

Brightman J in *Bartlett v Barclays Bank Trust Co Ltd*[18] endorsed this, saying, 'Nor must the court be astute to fix liability on a trustee who has committed no more than an error of judgment, from which no business man, however prudent, can expect to be immune'.

In *Re Lucking's Will Trusts*[19] Mr Lucking as active trustee and main beneficiary under a trust which had a controlling shareholding in the Lucking family company and as director of that company brought in D to manage the business. From D's appointment in 1954 to his dismissal in 1961 he was allowed to remain living in Stirling in Scotland though the company business was in Chester: he was thus allowed hotel expenses in Chester and travelling expenses to and from Chester in addition to his salary. Of this Cross J said, 'It may very well have been an unnecessary concession and an error of judgment, but not, in my judgment, a breach of trust'. The learned judge went on to hold that signing blank cheques on the No 2 account was also not a breach of trust so long as Mr Lucking had no reason to think that D was abusing the confidence reposed in him, ie until the summer of 1957 when Mr Lucking realised that D was overdrawing at a rate of £1,400 p a on top of his salary and his expenses and his travel allowance.

Theft of trust property

A trustee will not be liable if the trust property be stolen, provided he has taken reasonable care of it[20], even although the thief be his own servant, if, on the facts proved, it appears that the trustee was justified in entrusting the custody of the property to such servant as for example in the managing of a trust business[1]. On the other hand, it has been held that a trustee is liable if he is induced by fraud or forgery to hand it over to the wrong person[2] because he is then acting beyond his powers as as to be strictly liable upon falsification of the accounts unless protected by an exemption clause in the trust instrument or afforded relief by the court under s 61 of the Trustee Act 1925[3]. As has been shown in this article, a trustee is in the position of a bailee; he must take reasonable care of the trust property, and if it is lost or stolen he is discharged from responsibility provided that he was not guilty of negligence, which would lead to surcharging of the accounts.

Neglect in keeping trust securities

Where a trustee of a policy of insurance neglected to indorse on it a memorandum of the trust, or to give notice to the office, and by his subsequent carelessness allowed it to get into the hands of the settlor, who mortgaged it to a third party, the trustee was held liable[4]. Again, where part of the trust property was a policy of assurance on the settlor's life which he failed to keep on foot, and the trustees neglected to get the surrender value, they were held

---

18 [1980] 1 All ER 139 at 150.
19 [1967] 3 All ER 726, [1968] 1 WLR 866.
20 *Jones v Lewis* (1751) 2 Ves Sen 240; *Job v Job* (1877) 6 Ch D 562.
 1 *Jobson v Palmer* [1893] 1 Ch 71; and see also *Weir v Bell* (1878) 3 Ex D 238, CA. Compare *Re Lucking's Will Trusts* [1967] 3 All ER 726.
 2 See Art 54 and Illustrations thereto, pp 624–625 post.
 3 See Art 95, post; *Re Smith* (1902) 71 LJ Ch 411.
 4 *Kingdon v Castleman* (1877) 25 WR 345; and see *Barnes v Addy* (1874) 9 Ch App 244; and *Hobday v Peters (No 3)* (1860) 28 Beav 603.

liable[5], but a trustee was held not to be liable where he kept up the policy, but forgot the receipt, and the company wrongly refused to pay in consequence[6].

Where trustees hold securities payable to bearer, they must appoint a person to act as custodian of the securities unless otherwise authorised in the trust instrument[7].

Inventory of chattels

A trustee of chattels should make and keep an inventory of them, so that, if lost by the neglect or fraud of others, proper evidence of the nature and value of the chattels may be preserved[8].

Neglect to invest trust fund

A trustee ought to invest moneys in his hands subject to the trust within a reasonable time; and if he omits to do so, he will be charged interest[9]; and if the fund be lost, he will be liable to make it good[10]. A fortiori will he be liable where he has left the trust fund in the sole custody of his co-trustee[11]. And, on similar grounds, trustees ought to accumulate the income of infants' property (in so far as it is not applied for maintenance, etc) by way of compound interest[12].

Controlling interest in private company

The duties of trustees whose investment holdings give them a controlling interest in a private company were considered in *Re Lucking's Will Trusts*[13]. In that case a sole trustee had, by virtue of such an interest, appointed a manager of the company business who also became a director. Losses occurred through the misconduct of the manager and the trustee was held liable because he had failed adequately to supervise the manager's drawings from the company after the summer of 1957 when it had become apparent that some check ought to be imposed on such drawings. But a second trustee, who had been appointed in the meantime and had relied on what the first trustee told him, was held in the circumstances not to have failed to exercise ordinary prudence. Cross J stated:

5 *Re Godwin's Settlement* (1918) 87 LJ Ch 645.
6 *Re McGaw* [1919] WN 288.
7 TA 2000, s 18 but this does not apply if the trust has a custodian trustee or securities are vested in the official custodian for charities.
8 *Temple v Thring* (1887) 56 LJ Ch 767.
9 See *Gilroy v Stephens* (1882) 30 WR 745; *Stafford v Fiddon* (1857) 23 Beav 386; and *Re Jones* (1883) 49 LT 91. In *Cann v Cann* (1884) 51 LT 770, Kay J considered that six months was the maximum period. Cf also *Midland Bank Trustee (Jersey) Ltd v Federated Pension Services* [1996] PLR 179 and *Re Waterman's Will Trusts* [1952] 2 All ER 1054; where, however, no beneficiary desired to attack the trustee on the basis of breach of trust in failing to invest. Nowadays, there seems little excuse for not investing money forthwith in a deposit account unless a particular investment is to be made within days, requiring money to be available in a current account.
10 *Moyle v Moyle* (1831) 2 Russ & M 710; *Cann v Cann* (1884) 33 WR 40; *Astbury v Beasley* (1868) 17 WR 638.
11 *Lewis v Nobbs* (1878) 8 Ch D 591; or left it with his law agent for five months: *Wyman v Paterson* [1900] AC 271.
12 TA 1925, s 31(2); and see Article 66 where the provision itself is more fully discussed.
13 [1967] 3 All ER 726, [1968] 1 WLR 866.

'I do not look on him as a passive trustee who has allowed his co-trustee to decide for him matters on which they ought to have exercised a joint discretion. He was entitled to rely on what Mr Lucking told him about the company's affairs as being accurate and adequate unless he had some positive reason to think the contrary which he had not.'

Earlier Cross J had considered the general position:

'What steps, if any, does a reasonably prudent man who finds himself a majority shareholder in a private company take with regard to the management of the company's affairs? He does not content himself with such information as to the management of the company's affairs as he is entitled to as shareholder, but ensures that he is represented on the board. He may be prepared to run the business himself as managing director or, at least, to become a non-executive director while having the business managed by someone else. Alternatively, he may find someone who will act as his nominee on the board and report to him from time to time as to the company's affairs. In the same way trustees holding a controlling interest ought to ensure so far as they can that they have such information as to the progress of the company's affairs as directors would have. If they sit back and allow the company to be run by the minority shareholder and receive no more information than shareholders are entitled to, they do so at their risk if things go wrong.

In this case the trust was represented on the board by Mr Lucking. One ought not to regard him as performing a duty to the trust which it was incumbent on the trustees to perform personally, so that [the second trustee] became automatically responsible for any deficiences of Mr Lucking as does a passive trustee who allows his co-trustee to exercise alone discretions which it is their duty to exercise jointly. If these trustees had decided, as they might have done, to be represented on the board by a nominee they would have been entitled to rely on the information given them by the nominee even though such information was inaccurate or inadequate, unless they had reason to suspect that it was inaccurate or inadequate. [The second trustee] cannot have been in a worse position because his co-trustee was the trust's representative on the board than he would have been if the trust's representative had not been a trustee at all.'

In *Re Miller's Deed Trusts*[14] Oliver J did not read Cross J's judgment as imposing on trustees having a controlling interest in a private company a necessary requirement that one of them or a nominee must be on the board of directors where one trustee was an accountant whose firm acted as auditors to the company and who, or a member of his staff, was normally in regular monthly attendance at the company's premises dealing with accounts.

In *Bartlett v Barclays Bank Trust Co Ltd*[15] Brightman J endorsed this saying:

'[Cross J] was merely outlining convenient methods by which a prudent man of business (as also a trustee) with a controlling interest in a private company can place himself in a position to make an informed decision whether any action is appropriate to be taken for the protection of his asset. ... Alternatives which spring to mind are the receipt of copies of the agenda and minutes of board meetings, the receipt of monthly management accounts in the case of a trading concern or quarterly reports. Every case will depend on its own facts. ... *The purpose to be achieved* is not that of monitoring every move of the directors, but of *making it reasonably probable ... that the trustees or one of them will receive an adequate flow of information in time to enable the trustees to make use of their controlling shareholding should this be necessary*

---

14 [1978] LS Gaz R 454.
15 [1980] Ch 515 at 533–534.

for the protection of their trust asset, namely the shareholding[16]. . . . It was not proper for the bank to confine itself to the receipt of the annual balance sheet and profit and loss account, detailed annual financial statements and the chairman's report and statement, and to attendance at the annual general meetings and the luncheons that followed, which were the limits of the bank's regular sources of information. Had the bank been in receipt of more frequent information it would have been able to step in and stop, and ought to have stopped the board embarking on the Old Bailey project.'

Bound to insure against risks in many circumstances

As already discussed[17], nowadays trustees should exercise their powers (as absolute owner of land under s 8(3) of the Trustee Act 2000 or their sub-stituted[18], s 19 of the Trustee Act 1925 powers) to insure any trust property against risks of loss or damage due to any event, when exercising the care and skill of an ordinary prudent businessman in furthering the financial interests of present and future beneficiaries. The extent of such cover will take account of the value and liquidity of the trust capital and the cost of premiums in balancing the risk of substantial loss against the expense of the premiums.

Application of insurance money where policy kept up under any trust, power or obligation

And by s 20 it is provided that:

(1) Money receivable by trustees or any beneficiary under a policy of insurance against the loss or damage of any property subject to a trust or to a settlement within the meaning of the Settled Land Act, 1925, shall, where the policy has been kept up under any trust in that behalf or under any power statutory or otherwise, or in performance of any covenant or of any obligation statutory or otherwise, or by a tenant for life impeachable for waste, be capital money for the purposes of the trust or settlement, as the case may be.

(2) If any such money is receivable by any person, other than the trustees of the trust or settlement, that person shall use his best endeavours to recover and receive the money, and shall pay the net residue thereof, after discharging any costs of recovering and receiving it, to the trustees of the trust or settlement, or, if there are no trustees capable of giving a discharge therefore, into court.

(3) Any such money—

    (a) if it was receivable in respect of settled land within the meaning of the Settled Land Act 1925 or any building or works thereon, shall be deemed to be capital money arising under that Act, from the settled land, and shall be invested or applied by the trustees, or, if in court, under the direction of the court, accordingly;

    (b) if it was receivable in respect of personal chattels settled as heirlooms within the meaning of the Settled Land Act 1925 shall be deemed to be capital money arising under that Act, and shall be applicable by the trustees, or, if in court, under the direction of the court, in like manner as provided by that Act with respect to money arising by a sale of chattels settled as heirlooms as aforesaid;

    (c) if it was receivable in respect of property held upon trust for sale, shall be held upon the trusts and subject to the powers and provisions applicable

---

16 Editor's italics.
17 At p 569 ante.
18 See TA 2000, s 34.

to money arising by a sale under such trust;
(d)   in any other case, shall be held upon trusts corresponding as nearly as may be with the trusts affecting the property in respect of which it was payable.
(4)   Such money, or any part thereof, may also be applied by the trustees, or, if in court, under the direction of the court, in rebuilding, reinstating, replacing, or repairing the property lost or damaged, but any such application by the trustees shall be subject to the consent of any person whose consent is required by the instrument, if any, creating the trust to the investment of money subject to the trust, and, in the case of money which is deemed to be capital money arising under the Settled Land Act, 1925, be subject to the provisions of that Act with respect to the application of capital money by the trustees of the settlement.
(5)   Nothing contained in this section prejudices or affects the right of any person to require any such money or any part thereof to be applied in rebuilding, reinstating, or repairing the property lost or damaged, or the rights of any mortgagee, lessor, or lessee, whether under any statute or otherwise.
(6)   This section applies to policies effected either before or after the commencement of this Act, but only to money received after such commencement.

These sections do not, however, apply to property held by bare trustees on trust for beneficiaries absolutely entitled.

If trustees do not insure, and a beneficiary does so out of his own moneys, he may keep whatever is paid under the policy for himself[19]; but not where the premiums are paid out of the trust income[20].

Liability for repairs

Trustees are generally bound to see that trust premises do not fall into decay[1]. But, as we have seen, the cost of repairs is not necessarily thrown exclusively on income[2], and trustees should apply to the court for directions as to raising the necessary money[3]. It has, however, been decided that when *leasehold* houses are held in trust to receive the rents and pay them to A for life, and after his death in trust for B, the trustees, in order to avoid forfeiture, are entitled to apply the rents in keeping the houses in a proper state[4]. But this is without prejudice to the ultimate incidence of the cost[5].

Liability of retired trustee

A retired trustee, while remaining liable for breaches of trust committed during his trusteeship, will not be liable for breaches of trust after his retirement except that where a trustee retires from the trust in order, as he thinks, to relieve himself from the responsibility of a wrongful act which his co-trustee has in mind, he will be held as fully responsible as if he had been particeps criminis[6]. To make him responsible however it must be proved that

---

19 *Gaussen v Whatman* (1905) 93 LT 101.
20 Section 20(1); *Re Quicke's Trusts* [1908] 1 Ch 887.
 1 Per Cotton LJ in *Re Hotchkys* (1886) 32 Ch D 408.
 2 Art 51, ante.
 3 *Re Fowler* (1881) 16 Ch D 723. But see *Re Courtier* (1886) 34 Ch D 136; and also Art 51, ante.
 4 *Re Fowler* (1881) 16 Ch D 723. But see *Re Courtier* (1886) 34 Ch D 136; and also Art 51, ante.
 5 *Re Courtier* (1886) 34 Ch D 136 and *Re Hotchkys* (1886) 32 Ch D 408; and see pp 571 et seq, ante.
 6 *Norton v Pritchard* (1845) 5 LTOS 2; *Webster v Le Hunt* (1861) 9 WR 918; *Palairet v Carew* 32 Beav 564; *Clark v Hoskins* (1868) 37 LJ Ch 561.

the very breach of trust which was in fact committed was not merely the outcome of, or rendered easy by, the retirement, but was contemplated by the trustee who retired[7].

Liability of trustee where loss results from act or default of agents nominees or custodians

Trustees will often employ agents nominees or custodians under the Trustee Act 2000[8] or express powers in the trust instrument. When trustees act within such powers they are not automatically responsible for any act or default of such persons: they are only liable for any personal failure to comply with their duty of care when entering into the arrangements under which another person acts as agent, nominee or custodian and when keeping those arrangements under review[9] (needing to consider if they need to intervene by giving directions to or dismissing such a person and so acting if there is such a need[10]). Any right of action against the agent, nominee or custodian will be an asset of the trust which the trustees should seek to realise, if appropriate[11], on pain of personal liability if not complying with their own duty of care and skill.

PARAGRAPH 2

Relevant time for judging trustees' conduct

As Lindley LJ stated in *Re Hurst*[12]:

'The conduct of trustees ought to be regarded with reference to the facts and circumstances existing at the time when they had to act and which were known or ought to have been known by them at the time.'

In *Nestlé v National Westminster Bank* Hoffmann J emphasised[13] that, 'in reviewing the conduct of trustees over a period of more than 60 years one must be careful not to endow the prudent trustee with prophetic vision or expect him to have ignored the received wisdom of his time'.

PARAGRAPH 3

No ousting the jurisdiction of the court

On matters of law, the jurisdiction of the court cannot be ousted by provisions in the trust instrument[14] eg a specific power to decide whether a receipt

---

7 *Head v Gould* [1898] 2 Ch 250.
8 See Art 55 post.
9 TA 2000, s 23(1).
10 TA 2000, s 22.
11 Taking account of the wealth of the defendant and the strength of the trustee's claim and the possibility of compromising the matter under s 15 of the TA 1925: a *Beddoe* application will usually be appropriate (see p 845 post).
12 (1892) 67 LT 96 at 99, CA; *Re Chapman* [1896] 2 Ch 763 at 777–778, CA; *Nestlé v National Westminster Bank (No 2)* [1993] 1 WLR 1260, [1994] 1 All ER 118, CA.
13 [2000] WTLR 795 at 802.
14 *Re Wynn* [1952] Ch 271; *Re Raven* [1915] 1 Ch 673; *Re Bronson* (1958) 14 DLR (2nd) 51; *Boe v Alexander* (1988) 41 DLR (4th) 520.

is an income or capital receipt or a general power to determine all questions arising in the execution of the trust provisions. However, trustees may be authorised to distribute receipts whether of a capital or income nature as they see fit in their discretion, irrespective of whether the recipient is otherwise only interested in capital or only in income.

Excluding duties in respect of particular property

If a very wealthy testator wants to be kind to his brother and sister living in one of his houses and wants to avoid any death duties payable on their deaths he may provide in his will trust, 'My trustees shall have no responsibility or duty with respect to such house' until both are dead, though subject thereto the testator's estate is left on trust for sale (with power to postpone sale) for the testator's children with remainders over. At the testator's death his brother and sister were 92 and 87 and the property market was falling. The Privy Council in *Hayim v Citibank*[15] upheld the testator's clause, so rejecting the children's claim for breach of trust when the house was sold after the death of the last surviving sibling for much less than would have been obtained if a speedy sale had occurred. The provision was:

> 'in the circumstances designed to enable Albert and Marie to remain in the house so long as [the trustee] saw fit. ... If clause 10 were exploited for any other purpose the beneficiaries could complain and the court could find that [the trustee] had not properly exercised the discretion conferred on it to postpone sale either in the interests of the beneficiaries or of Albert and Marie.'

Here the house was only a small part of the testator's estate and some residual duties (eg not to use the house for the trustee's own purposes) remained even in respect of the house.

However, there are implications for the case where the trust property consists almost wholly of a company transferred by the settlor to the trustees, whether the settlor's trading company or investment company, where the settlor or the settlor's nominee is intended to continue running the company. Most of the trustees' duties, under *Bartlett v Barclays Bank Trust Co*[16], *Cowan v Scargill*[17] and the Trustee Act 2000[18] will be capable of exclusion.

The settlor's trust instrument can provide, for example, that the controlling shareholding in the settlor's company that is to be the trust's only significant asset is to be retained and not sold until its value falls a specified percentage below its value when transferred to the trustee or until a specified person consents, but whose power to withhold consent is not to be a fiduciary power, only a personal one incapable of challenge unless amounting to a fraud on the power. Thus, the duty to consider diversification is negated.

The settlor could also exclude the trustee's duty to take such steps as make it reasonably probable that the trustee will receive an adequate flow of information in time to enable it to use its controlling interest to protect the beneficiaries' interests if necessary. Indeed, he could go on to exclude the trustee's duty to interfere in the affairs of the company in any way whatsoever unless it has actual knowledge that one or more of the directors is acting dishonestly in the running of the company.

---

15 [1987] AC 730.
16 [1980] Ch 515.
17 [1985] Ch 270.
18 Sections 6(1), 21(3), 26 and Sch 1, para 7.

However, the trustee does have *power* to obtain information and interfere (by virtue of its controlling shareholding) so far as necessary to protect beneficiaries' interests, while it seems that the trustee has an overriding duty to exercise its powers so as to safeguard and further the beneficiaries' interests as a whole[19] and that this duty at the core of the trust cannot be ousted[20]. Thus, the trustee would need to exercise its power to obtain information, so as to be able to interfere before obtaining actual knowledge of dishonesty on the part of directors, because by that time it will almost always be too late to protect the beneficiaries' interests, dishonest persons often dissipating their assets so as to have nothing left to satisfy creditors.

To exclude the trustee's power to intervene and replace the directors of the company, the settlor would need to arrange for the company to be created under a foreign law[1] under which the managing director (being the settlor's nominee or the settlor himself) cannot be removed until certified mentally incompetent by two qualified medical practitioners in the foreign jurisdiction, so staying on until resigning or dying, with directors being removable only by the managing director. This will mean that the settlor has transferred a flawed asset (a pig in a poke) to the trustee for the beneficiaries, who will not be able to complain that all they have is a flawed asset as intended by the settlor, the trustees having run the trust to the extent income materialised from company dividends but the settlor or his nominee having run the company owned by the trustee. However, if significant income has not been made available to give the trustee something to do, the company having power to make gifts or loans to the settlor's family, relatives and friends, then the trust should normally be regarded as a sham.

Where the settlor wants himself or his nominee to perform the role of discretionary portfolio manager he may (like a billionaire who has just won £5 million lottery money) provide, 'The Trustee shall speculate with the Trust Fund (but have power to invest[2] it while awaiting speculative opportunities) as if he were an absolutely entitled beneficial owner speculating on his own behalf in circumstances where he could afford to lose the whole Fund in acquiring any assets of whatsoever nature anywhere without it affecting his standard of living one iota; and the Trustee shall be under no duty to exercise care and skill mindful that he is acting for the benefit of others but shall only be liable for losses caused by his own dishonesty'[3]. To protect the Trustee and to further the settlor's interests, the trust instrument may also provide, 'The Trustee must employ the settlor as discretionary manager of the Fund (without payment of any fee and without authority to

19 *Cowan v Scargill* [1985] Ch 270; *Beauclerk v Ashburnham* (1845) 8 Beav 322.

20 This is surely part of 'the duty of the trustees to perform the trusts honestly and in good faith for the benefit of the beneficiaries' (*Armitage v Nurse* [1998] Ch 241 at 253) so they should not ignore a significant drop in profits from a preceding year. If they then relied on the presence of an exemption clause exempting them from liability for a breach of trust unless dishonest to justify refusing to inquire about such a fall crying out for an explanation, they should lose its protection because in so refusing they acted recklessly which equates to dishonesty: *Armitage v Nurse* [1998] Ch 241 at 254.

1 For example, British Virgin Islands.

2 This would be a power of investment within TA 2000, s 4(1) but it is very doubtful whether the duty to speculate could be so regarded, although, in any event, the power to make an authorised investment after proper advice having regard to the standard investment criteria can be subject to any restriction or exclusion imposed by the trust instrument: TA 2000, s 6(1)(b).

3 *Armitage v Nurse* [1998] Ch 241; TA 2000, Sch 1, para 7.

self-deal directly or indirectly so as to benefit himself or his spouse in any way) until the settlor resigns such post or dies or is certified as a mental patient, so that in all the circumstances it is unnecessary and inappropriate for the Trustee to review the investments and other assets comprising the fund'[4].

Non-excludable duties: irreducible core content of a trust

As Millett LJ has stated[5], 'There is an irreducible core of obligations owed by the trustees to the beneficiaries and enforceable by them which is funda-mental to the concept of a trust. If the beneficiaries have no rights enforceable against the trustees there are no trusts'. The Court of Appeal[6] has held that these core obligations do not include the duties of care and skill, prudence and diligence, and so has upheld a clause exempting a trustee from liability for loss or damage unless caused by the trustee's own actual fraud, but they do include the duty to perform the trusts honestly and in good faith for the benefit of the beneficiaries[7]. To enforce this duty the beneficiaries have a right to see the trust accounts[8] so that they are then able to falsify or surcharge those accounts.

Thus, if a clause stated that the trustees are not to account to the bene-ficiaries[9] for anything happening in the lifetime of the settlor or that the beneficiaries are to have no right to sue the trustees for any alleged breach of trust occurring in the settlor's lifetime, there is no trust for the beneficiaries while the settlor is alive, the substance of the matter simply being that the trust fund is held to his order[10]; on his death a trust of whatever remains may be intended to arise, but this will be a testamentary trust that will be void if not complying with the formalities required for a valid will[11].

Exemption from liability for breach of duty unless dishonest

The benefit of an exemption clause conferred by the settlor on the trustee is construed so as to cover no more than its wording is apt to cover[12] but not so as restrictively to cover less than would appear on a fair reading of the

---

4 Because employment is required by the trust instrument, delegation is not under TA 2000, Pt IV but even if it were the duty to review can be ousted: TA 2000, s 21(3).
5 *Armitage v Nurse* [1998] Ch 241; also D J Hayton 'The Irreducible Core Content of Trustee-ship', Chapter 3 in A J Oakley (ed) *Trends in Contemporary Trust Law* (Oxford, 1996).
6 *Armitage v Nurse* [1998] Ch 241.
7 *Armitage v Nurse* [1998] Ch 241 at 253.
8 See Article 60. Objects of a power of appointment, however, may be excluded expressly or by necessary implication from having any right to see the trust accounts and to make the trustees account for their trusteeship: *Re Angora Trust* [2001] WTLR 1081.
9 A clause intended to prevent any meaningful right to account from arising (eg 'The Trustee shall keep this Trust Deed secret and confidential to itself alone and shall not inform any beneficiary that he or she be a beneficiary and shall always ensure that benefits provided to any beneficiary are provided in untraceable fashion so far as possible') would also be repugnant to the trust concept: *Cf Scally v Southern Health and Social Services Board* [1992] 1 AC 294 at 306–307 and *Re Murphy's Settlement* [1998] 3 All ER 1
10 Since the settlor did not intend the beneficiaries to have any rights in his lifetime nor did he intend the trustees to be beneficial owners, there is a resulting trust in his favour with a power, which he can revoke (*Vandervell v IRC* [1967] 2 AC 291 at 317) to benefit the so-called beneficiaries.
11 *Re Pfrimmer Estate* [1936] 2 DLR 123; *Baird v Baird* [1990] 2 AC 548, PC.
12 For example, *Wight v Olswang (No 1)* (1999) 1 ITELR 783; *Bogg v Raper* (1998) 1 ITELR 267; *Walker v Stones* [2001] QB 902 at 935.

wording. Thus, a clause exempting from loss or damage not caused by the trustee's own fraud will not extend to a beneficiary claiming to recover trust property purchased by the trustee in breach of the 'no self-dealing' rule[13]. However, a clause exempting trustees for liability for 'omissions made in good faith' is taken at its face value to cover both non-negligent and negligent omissions[14], rather than restricted under a *contra proferentem* construction to cover non-negligent omissions only where strict liability arises on falsification of the accounts[15].

The Court of Appeal[16] has accepted that an aptly worded exemption clause can protect a trustee from liability for any breach of trust other than a dishonest (including reckless[17]) breach of trust, it not being repugnant to the core concept of a trust nor contrary to public policy to exempt a trustee from liability for negligence extending to gross negligence. Such view may still be challenged[18] because the court did not have cited to it English cases[19] that distinguish gross negligence from ordinary negligence, so the court, believing that 'English lawyers have always had a healthy disrespect for the distinction'[20], regarding gross negligence as 'ordinary negligence with a vituperative epithet'[1], assumed that such distinction could not be made. Exemption from negligence of all degrees therefore had to be accepted or rejected, and, in modern times, when exemption from negligence is commonplace in the contractual context and the trust context, one could hardly justify outlawing exempting liability for negligence[2]. The Law Commission has recently issued a Consultation Paper to see whether the liability of paid professional trustees for negligence should be outlawed, the Trustee Act 2000[3] having deliberately permitted ouster of its duty of care until the Law Commission investigated the matter further.

Exemption from liability for deliberate breaches

Lord Nicholls[4] considered that it was dishonest for a trustee to act beyond his

---

13 *Armitage v Nurse* [1998] Ch 241 at 253.
14 *Bogg v Raper* (1998) 1 ITELR 267, CA, and *Walker v Stones* [2001] QB 902 at 941, CA. It should follow that a clause exempting a trustee from liability 'for any negligent breach of trust' should cover gross and ordinary negligence.
15 As held under a restrictive approach by the Minnesota CA in *Re Williams Trust* (2000) 2 ITELR 313.
16 *Armitage v Nurse* [1998] Ch 241 at 253.
17 *Armitage v Nurse* [1998] Ch 241 at 251, 'dishonesty' covering a trustee pursuing a course of action recklessly indifferent whether or not it is contrary to the beneficiaries' interests. A trustee relying on a clause exempting him from liability for breach to justify what he is about to do is acting recklessly ie dishonestly: *Armitage v Nurse* [1998] Ch 241 at 254.
18 As in the appeal to the Privy Council from the Jersey CA in *Midland Bank Trustee (Jersey) Ltd v Federated Pension Services* [1996] PLR 179 which settled on the morning it was to be opened in the PC.
19 Bailment cases where gratuitous bailees can only be liable if guilty of gross negligence (*Giblin v McMullen* (1868) LR 2 PC 317; *Beal v South Devon Rly Co* (1864) 3 H & C 337) and mortgage cases postponing a legal mortgagee's priority if guilty of gross negligence (eg *Colyer v Finch* (1856) 5 HL Cas 905, 928-929). The court also believed Scots law permitted exemption from liability for gross negligence but it does not: *Lutea Trustees Ltd v Orbis Trustees Guernsey Ltd* SCLR 735, 1998 SLT 471.
20 *Armitage v Nurse* [1998] Ch 241 at 254.
1 *Armitage v Nurse* [1998] Ch 241.
2 *Armitage v Nurse* [1998] Ch 241.
3 TA 2000, Sch 1, para 7.
4 *Royal Brunei Airlines v Tan* [1995] 2 AC 378 at 390, PC.

powers and so take a risk to the prejudice of another's rights, which risk is known to be one which there is no right to take. If the risk materialises and causes loss then the trustee who knowingly took the risk will be accountable accordingly. However, Millett LJ[5] considered that if trustees deliberately commit a breach of trust but in good faith in the honest belief that they are acting in the best interests of the beneficiaries their conduct is not dishonest.

In *Walker v Stones*[6] Rattee J followed the view of Millett LJ so as to allow a trustee to rely on an exemption clause exempting him from liability unless dishonest. On appeal[7], the Court of Appeal considered 'it most unlikely that [Millett LJ] would have intended his dicta to apply to a case where [as here] a solicitor-trustee's perception of the interests of the beneficiaries was so unreasonable that no reasonable solicitor-trustee could have held such belief. Indeed, in my opinion, such a construction of the clause could well render it inconsistent with the very existence of an effective trust'. After all, a settlor intends the trustee only to have the powers conferred by law and the settlor upon the trustee, and not also to have power to do anything else that the trustee subjectively honestly believes to be in the interests of the beneficiaries even if no reasonable trustee could possibly have held such belief.

Thus, a clause exempting a trustee from liability for breaches of trust, other than dishonest breaches, does not extend to a deliberate breach committed in the genuine belief that the course taken was in the interests of the beneficiaries if such belief was so unreasonable that no reasonable trustee of the actual trustee's type could have held that belief.

Ouster of duty better for trustees than exemption from liability for breach of duty

Ouster of a duty is preferable for a trustee than exemption from liability for a breach of trust. A trustee can be removed for a breach of trust even if exempted from liability therefor. More importantly, a trustee who deliberately relies on an exemption clause so as to proceed to commit a breach of trust is acting recklessly which amounts to acting dishonestly, against which no exemption clause can be effective. However, if a provision expressly provides that the trustee is not placed under a duty otherwise applicable under trust law, then a trustee relying on the absence of such a duty cannot be made liable for such conduct.

Statutory prohibitions on exemption clauses in trust instruments

Where there is a trust deed for securing an issue of debentures any provision therein is void[8], 'in so far as it would have the effect of exempting a trustee from, or indemnifying him against, liability for breach of trust where he fails to show the degree of care and diligence required of him as trustee, having regard to the provisions of the trust deed conferring any powers, authorities or discretions'; but a three-quarters majority of debenture holders may release him from liability[9].

---

5 *Armitage v Nurse* [1998] Ch 241 at 252, and subsequently as Lord Millett in *Three Rivers District Council v Governor of Bank of England (No 3)* [2000] 2 WLR 1220 at 1274.
6 [2000] WTLR 795 striking out the beneficiaries' claim.
7 [2001] QB 902 at 941; leave to appeal given by HL.
8 Companies Act 1985, s 192(1).
9 Companies Act 1985, s 192(2).

For authorised unit trusts any provision is void[10] so far as it would have the effect of exempting the trustee or the manager from liability for any failure to exercise due care and diligence in discharge of his functions.

In the case of pension trust schemes liability for breach of any obligation to take care or exercise skills in the performance of any investment functions cannot be excluded or restricted by an instrument or agreement[11] where the function is exercisable by a trustee or by a person to whom any investment function has been delegated under s 34 of the Pensions Act 1995 (permitting discretionary investment functions to be delegated eg to a portfolio fund manager).

Trusts are not contracts, trustees as an incident of their office being entitled to charge remuneration provided for in the trust instrument or by law; so trusts are unaffected by the Unfair Contracts Terms Act 1977[12] and so far, have not been affected by regulations made under the European Directive[13].

The effect of undue influence or breach of fiduciary duty

Fiduciary duties can exist before formal creation of the trust relationship[14] and it will be wise to minimise the chances of the settlor or a beneficiary alleging that an exemption clause had been included in the trust instrument as a result of a breach of fiduciary duty or by means of undue influence such that the trustee cannot be allowed to rely on the terms of such clause[15]. The settlor's attention must be drawn to the clause and the effect of the clause and until *Bogg v Raper*[16] it would have been thought wise to take the precaution of advising the settlor to consult an independent lawyer[17]: a document signed by the settlor acknowledging such matters would provide helpful evidence. In the light of *Bogg v Raper* it is only necessary to show that the settlor-testator knew and approved the clause, the Court of Appeal considering[18] that an exemption clause, unlike a remuneration clause, did not confer a benefit on the solicitor preparing his client's will trust of which the solicitor was to be an executor and trustee, However, there is much to be said for the view that the solicitor was unjustly enriched at the expense of the beneficiaries in saving himself from paying the requisite insurance premiums

---

10 Financial Services and Markets Act 2000, s 253 re-enacting Financial Services Act 1986.
11 Pensions Act 1995, s 33.
12 Sir William Goodhart 'Trust Law for the 21st Century' in AJ Oakley (ed) *Trends in Contemporary Trust Law* (Oxford 1996) p 270. A *contra proferentem* approach applies to exemption clauses in contracts but not in trusts: see p 594 ante.
13 Council Directive 93/13 EEC; Law Commission Consultation Paper, 'Trustee Exemption Clauses', Nov 2002.
14 *Swain v Law Society* [1982] 1 WLR 17 at 26, [1981] 3 All ER 797 at 805–806 per Stephenson LJ; *Galmerrow Securities Ltd v National Westminster Bank* [2002] WTLR 125 at 148; *Bogg v Raper* (1998) 1 ITELR 267, CA.
15 To this effect see *Rutanen v Ballard* 424 Mass 723 at 733 (1997); *Baskerville v Thurgood* (1992) 100 Sask LR 214, CA; *Jothann v Irving Trust Co* 270 NYS 721, 277 NYS 955 (1934) and *Scott on Trusts* Vol III para 222.4.
16 (1998) 1 ITELR 267.
17 Eg precautions suggested by *Barclays Bank v O'Brien* [1994] 1 AC 180 and *Royal Bank of Scotland v Etridge (No 2)* [2001] UKHL 44, [2001] 3 WLR 1021, HL.
18 (1998) 1 ITELR 267 at 285.

to cover possible liability and saving himself from the claimant's claim for £8 million[19].

It would seem that successor trustees as donees of the legal title with an equitable interest under exemption and remuneration clauses will only require the benefit of such clauses as already vitiated by the circumstances surrounding their creation[20].

ARTICLE 53

Powers and duties of trustee in relation to the investment of trust funds

(1) Trustees cannot lawfully invest trust funds upon any securities other than those authorised by the settlement or by statute (or, in rarer cases, by the court).

(2) Statutory powers of investment are now contained almost entirely in the Trustee Act 2000 except[1] for trustees of occupational pension schemes[2], authorised unit trusts and charitable common investment schemes. Whether any provision relating to the powers of trustees which is contained in the settlement or other relevant instrument can limit the powers of investment conferred by the Act will depend upon the date and nature of the instrument. Unless the instrument is an enactment or instrument made under an enactment, in which case it may limit those powers whatever its date, it can limit them only if it is made after the passing of the Trustee Investments Act on 3 August 1961[3].

(3) Under section 3 of the Trustee Act 2000 a 'general power of investment' is conferred upon a trustee so that he 'may make any kind of investment that he could make if he were absolutely entitled to the assets of the trust', but[4] this power does not permit him to make investments in land, other than in loans secured on land, because powers to acquire legal estates in land in the UK are conferred by section 8.

---

19 The saving of expense is a benefit or enrichment: *Peel v Canada* (1993) 98 DLR (4th) 140; *Peter v Beblow* (1993) 101 DLR 621 at 645; A Burrows *Law of Restitution* (3rd edn) p 8; Goff & Jones *Law of Restitution* (5th edn) pp 16, 27.

20 Successor trustees should not be regarded as purchasers: remuneration clauses are regarded as gifts subject to a condition (*Re Pooley* (1880) 40 Ch D 1; *Re White* [1898] 2 Ch 217; *Re Brown* [1918] WN 118; *Re Duke of Norfolk's Settlement Trusts* [1982] Ch 61) while exemption clauses may be regarded as conferring a bounty upon the trustees at least to the cost of insuring against the liabilities relieved. The first equity prevails against the later equity: *Cave v Cave* (1880) 15 Ch D 639.

1 TA 2000, ss 36, 37 and 38.

2 Pensions Act 1995, ss 34 and 35.

3 TA 2000, ss 6(2) and 7. See also p 599, post. In the case of a will, the date on which it is made will be the date of its execution, not that of the testator's death; but it seems that a will confirmed by a codicil is for this purpose 'made' at the date of execution of the codicil (see the Wills Act 1837, s 34 though this section applies only 'for the purposes of the Act'; and see *Berkeley v Berkeley* [1946] AC 555, [1946] 2 All ER 154, HL). Support is lent to this view by the fact that the draftsman of the Family Law Reform Act 1969 felt it necessary expressly to negative this construction: see s 1(7) of the Act.

4 TA 2000, s 3(3).

(4) Before exercising any power of investment, whether the general power of investment or an express power of investment, a trustee must obtain and consider 'proper advice' about the way in which, having regard to the 'standard investment criteria', the power should be exercised[5] unless he reasonably concludes that, in all the circumstances, it is unnecessary or inappropriate to do so[6]; this is also the case[7] when a trustee is performing his duty[8] from time to time to review the investments of the trust.

(a) 'Proper advice' is the advice of a person who is reasonably believed by the trustee to be qualified to give it by his ability in and practical experience of financial and other matters relating to the proposed investment[9].

(b) The 'standard investment criteria' are[10]:

   (i)   the suitability to the trust of investments of the same kind as any particular investment proposed to be made or retained and of that particular investment as an investment of that kind, and

   (ii) the need for diversification of investments of the trust, in so far as is appropriate to the circumstances of the trust.

(5) Under section 8(1) of the Trustee Act 2000, except for trusts governed by the Settled Land Act 1925 or the Universities and College Estates Act 1925, a trustee may acquire 'freehold or leasehold land' in the UK whether as an investment or for occupation by a beneficiary or for any other reason; 'freehold or leasehold land' covers a legal estate or interest in English or Welsh land[11], and, in relation to Scotland, (i) the estate or interest of the proprietor of the *dominium utile* or, in the case of land not held on feudal tenure, the estate or interest of the owner or (ii) a tenancy, and, in relation to Northern Ireland, a legal estate in land, including land held under a fee farm grant.

(6) A trustee of land initially settled upon him or a trustee of land or of pure personalty acquiring land under section 8(1) has, for the purpose of exercising his functions as a trustee, all the powers of an absolute owner in relation to the land[12]; but in the case of pre 1997 Settled Land Act settlements[13] the inter-related position of the tenant for life and the Settled Land Act trustees is governed by the Settled Land Act 1925 as amended by the Trustee Act 2000 Schedule 2 paras 7–17.

(7) Wide express powers of investment are very common so as to confer wider powers than those conferred by the Trustee Act 2000,

---

5 TA 2000, s 5(1).
6 TA 2000, s 5(3).
7 TA 2000, s 5(2).
8 TA 2000, s 4(2).
9 TA 2000, s 5(4).
10 TA 2000, s 4(3).
11 TA 2000, s 8(2)(a) and presumably LPA 1925, s 1(4) as for TLATA 1996, s 6(3) by s 23(2) thereof: see p 608 post.
12 TA 2000, s 8(3).
13 See Article 44 ante.

and the courts[14] are not astute to limit the scope of these express powers if the natural and proper meaning of the words used allows for wide powers of investment or other application of trust property by trustees in the exercise of their managerial and administrative functions.

(8) Trustees act beyond their powers if investing in unauthorised investments so that their accounts can be strictly falsified[15], but even if they invest in authorised investments their accounts can be surcharged[16] if the value of the trust fund would have been higher but for their breach of any equitable or statutory duty in exercising their powers of investment[17].

(9) Trustees will often transfer trust investments[18] to a nominee[19] or a custodian[20] or purchase investments in the name of a nominee or custodian, either under express powers in that behalf or under powers in the Trustee Act 2000[1], while bearer securities must be deposited with a qualifying custodian[2] unless there is a sole trustee which is a trust corporation[3] or the trust instrument otherwise provides[4].

(10) Trustees will often delegate their asset management functions to a discretionary portfolio manager or a land manager, either under express powers in that behalf or under the powers contained in the Trustee Act 2000[5].

PARAGRAPHS 2, 3 AND 4

Availability of the general power of investment

The general power of investment is conferred on trustees (except for trustees of pension schemes, authorised unit trusts and charitable common investment schemes[6] and, probably, bare trustees[7]) in addition to powers conferred on trustees otherwise than by the Trustees Act 2000, but subject to any restriction or exclusion imposed by the trust instrument[8] if made after 2 August 1961 or by any enactment or subordinate legislation[9]. However, a

---

14 For example, *Re Harari's Settlement Trusts* [1949] 1 All ER 430; *Re Peczenik's Settlement* [1964] 2 All ER 339; *R v Barlow Clowes (No 2)* [1994] 2 All ER 316, CA.
15 See Art 89(1) post.
16 See Art 89(2) post.
17 *Nestlé v National Westminster Bank* [1994] 1 All ER 118, CA; *Re Mulligan* [1998] 1 NZLR 481.
18 A transferee may have custody of tangibles but title to intangibles must be transferred, title and custody being inseparable for intangibles ie choses in action.
19 TA 2000, s 16.
20 TA 2000, s 17.
 1 TA 2000, ss 16–23.
 2 TA 2000, ss 18 and 19.
 3 TA 2000, s 25(2).
 4 TA 2000, s 18(2).
 5 TA 2000, ss 11–15.
 6 TA 2000, ss 36, 37 and 38.
 7 See p 577 ante.
 8 TA 2000, s 6(1). In the absence of a definition of 'trust instrument' such instrument is capable of extending to an instrument exercising a special power of appointment in the original trust deed: *Lewin on Trusts* (17th edn) para 35-01D.
 9 TA 2000, s 7(2).

power to invest only in authorised investments or in investments authorised under the Trustee Investments Act 1961 is treated as conferring the general power of investment on the trustee[10]. A post-1961 power to invest in any UK securities will not work as a restriction or exclusion imposed by the trust instrument despite the necessary implication that it is forbidden to invest in non-UK securities[11]. However, the express addition of the words 'but not in any non-UK securities' would appear to amount to an exclusion or restriction of the general power[12]. It is then most likely that an application to the court under s 57 could successfully be made for conferment of the general power, a settlor conferring the power in 1962 in substance conferring as an addition to power to invest in investments authorised under the 1961 Act the power to invest in any UK securities not so authorised – so not having any excluding or restrictive intent in respect of investments then ranking as authorised investments.

Trustees of occupational pension schemes

Section 34(1) of the Pensions Act 1995 ensures that trustees of a pension trust scheme[13]'have, subject to any restrictions imposed by the scheme, the same power to make an investment of any kind as if they were absolutely entitled to the assets of the scheme'. The Trustee Act 2000[14] followed this model in conferring on a trustee power to 'make any kind of investment that he could make if he were absolutely entitled to the assets of the trust'.

It is noteworthy that subjective, and not objective, powers of an absolute beneficial owner are conferred, so that the statutory powers of a corporate trustee may be limited if it is limited in what it can do with its own beneficially owned assets. Furthermore, no clarification of the meaning of investment[15] is given so as to make clear that non-income-yielding assets may be purchased in accordance with modern portfolio theory.

Trustees of a pensions trust scheme can delegate discretionary portfolio management to a fund manager[16] authorised under s 192(1)(a)–(c) of the Financial Services Act 1986 or, now, art 4 of the Financial Services and Markets Act 2000 (Carrying on of Regulated Activities by Way of Business) Order 2001 and, subject to taking certain limited precautions in the appointment and supervision of such manager, are protected from liability for the manager's acts or defaults[17]. They can also delegate to a manager not so authorised or to two of themselves the exercise of investment discretions but they then remain liable for the acts or defaults of such persons as if their own[18].

Unless exempted[19], the trustees must ensure that there is prepared, maintained and from time to time revised a written statement of the prin-

---

10 TA 2000, s 7(3).
11 Cf *Re Burke* [1908] 2 Ch 248.
12 Cf *Ovey v Ovey* [1900] 2 Ch 524.
13 Defined in Pensions Act 1995, s 124(1).
14 TA 2000, s 3(1).
15 See p 601 post.
16 Pensions Act 1995, s 34(2).
17 Pensions Act 1995, s 34(3).
18 Pensions Act 1995, s 34(5).
19 Pensions Act 1995, s 35(7).

ciples governing investment decisions[20] setting out the kinds of investments
to be held, the balance between different kinds of risk, expected return,
realisation of investments and such other matters as may be prescribed[1]. Such
statement must also cover the trustees' policy for securing compliance with s
36 and the minimum funding requirements of s 56[2].

Section 36 is concerned to ensure the trustees or fund manager consider
the need for diversification and the suitability of the kind of investment
proposed and the particular one of that kind[3]. The trustees, before investing
in any manner, must obtain and consider proper advice taking account of the
above criteria and the above written statement[4], while in retaining investments they must determine at what intervals to obtain proper advice and
then obtain and consider it accordingly[5].

The trustees' power of investment cannot be restricted by reference to the
consent of the employer[6], and tight restrictions are imposed[7] on the proportion of the trust fund that may be invested in 'employer-related investments'.

Ambit of the general power of investment

Section 3 empowers a trustee (subject to ss 4, 5, 6 and 7) to 'make any kind of
investment that he could make it he were absolutely entitled to the assets of
the trust', except for 'investments in land [dealt with in s 8] other than in
loans secured on land'. Many years ago an investment was considered to be
an asset acquired for the sake of the income it would yield[8], but nowadays
with the emphasis placed on 'total return', taking account of income yield
and capital appreciation[9] in accordance with modern portfolio theory[10], an
investment is considered to cover any asset acquired for a portfolio for the
sake of its income yield or anticipated capital profit or both. Thus, the
purchase by trustees of depreciating chattels for a villa that is trust property
or the purchase of a depreciating car for use by a beneficiary would not
amount to an investment.

However, because investing in investments covers the 'laying out of money
in anticipation of a profitable capital or income return'[11] the purchase of a
valuable painting or a rare stamp or antique desk that the trustees believe to

---

20 Pensions Act 1995, s 35(1). Proper advice needs to be obtained and the employer must be
consulted: s 35(5).

1 Pensions Act 1995, s 35(3). For example, the extent to which social environmental or ethical
considerations are taken into account and the trustees' policy as to the exercise of voting
rights attached to investments: SI 1999/1849.

2 Pensions Act 1995, s 35(2).

3 Pensions Act 1995, s 36(1).

4 Pensions Act 1995, s 36(3).

5 Pensions Act 1995, s 36(4).

6 Pensions Act 1995, s 35(4).

7 Pensions Act 1995, s 40; SI 1996/3127.

8 *Re Somerset* [1894] 1 Ch 231 at 247; *Re Wragg* [1919] 2 Ch 58 at 65.

9 *Harries v Church Comrs* [1992] 1 WLR 1241 at 1246, 'the purposes of the trust will be best
served by the trustees seeking the maximum return, whether by way of income or capital
growth, which is consistent with commercial prudence'; Lord Nicholls (1995) 9 Trust LI 71 at
73; *Cowan v Scargill* [1985] Ch 270 at 287.

10 See J Langbein (1996) 81 Iowa LR 641; I N Legair (2000) 14 Trust LI 75.

11 *Cook v Medway Housing Society* [1997] STC 90 at 98 per Lightman J.

have a good chance of capital appreciation will be an investment[12].

It may be argued that if a trustee can 'make any kind of investment that he could make if he were absolutely entitled to the assets of the trust', then he can not only use money donated by the settlor and the proceeds of the sale of investments to purchase new investments, but he can exchange an old investment to substitute a new investment therefor, and even mortgage an old investment so as to raise new money to make a new investment. After all, an absolute owner of assets can sell those assets or exchange those assets or mortage those assets in order to make a new investment.

On the other hand, it can be argued that the making of any kind of investment implicitly needs to be made out of subsisting cash or investments that currently are trust assets available for the purchase or exchange of investments, so that the creation of a mortgage liability imposed on old trust assets to create a new fund of money to be used in the purchase of a new investment is one step removed from the power conferred by s 3 of the Trustee Act 2000. This argument seems the better one in the light of *Re Suenson-Taylor's Settlement*[13] although, in any event, such gearing-up would not be authorised unless proper advice had been obtained and considered[14] in the light of the statutory duty of care[15], to the extent not excluded in the trust instrument[16]. In many circumstances it would be unlikely that gearing-up would be advised in the light of the duty of care.

Condition precedent to exercise of the general power of investment or of express powers

By s 5(1) of the Trustee Act 2000 'before exercising any power of investment, whether arising under this Part or otherwise, a trustee must (unless the exception applies) obtain and consider proper advice about the way in which, having regard to the standard investment criteria, the power should be exercised'. The exception[17] is that 'a trustee need not obtain such advice if he reasonably concludes that in all the circumstances it is unnecessary or inappropriate to do so'. The trustee's conclusion needs to be objectively reasonable[18], taking account of all the circumstances eg the financial experience of the trustee, the amount of cash or the value of investments involved, the nature of the investment being considered. The trustee, to protect himself, should provide contemporaneous written evidence of the reason(s) for considering the exception applied.

Obtaining and considering proper advice is needed if there are doubts over the applicability of the exception. 'Proper advice'[19] is 'the advice of a person who is reasonably believed by the trustee to be qualified to give it by his ability in, and practical experience of, financial and other matters relating to the proposed investment'. The advisor must be subjectively believed by the trustee to be qualified on objective reasonable grounds so that the choice of

---

12 Law Com No 260 'Trustees' Powers and Duties' page 22 note 56 and Explanatory Notes to TA 2000, paras 22 and 23.
13 [1974] 3 All ER 397, [1974] 1 WLR 1280.
14 TA 2000, ss 4 and 5.
15 TA 2000, ss 1 and 2.
16 TA 2000, Sch 1, para 7.
17 TA 2000, s 5(3).
18 See next but one footnote.
19 TA 2000, s 5(4).

adviser was one which a reasonable trustee could have made in all the circumstances even if the court might have taken a different view[20]. The advice need not be given or confirmed in writing but it will be wise for the trustees to require such in case problems arise later. There are no provisions similar to those in s 4(4) and (6) of the Trustee Investments Act 1961 concerning a trustee being advised by a co-trustee or an officer or servant of a corporate trustee, but it would seem that the advice of a co-trustee reasonably believed to be duly qualified could be 'proper advice'. It is less clear whether the advice of a senior employee of a corporate sole or co-trustee is capable of being proper advice. It should probably suffice when an individual sole trustee who is duly qualified can act without[1] taking proper advice. The advice obtained has to be considered, not followed, so it need not be followed, but it is wise to provide contemporaneous written evidence as to why the advice was not followed in case of subsequent complaints from beneficiaries.

A trustee must from time to time review the investments of the trust[2] and then (unless the s 5(3) exception applies) obtain and consider proper advice about whether, having regard to the standard investment criteria, the investments should be varied[3].

The standard investment criteria to which a trustee must have regard are[4]:

'(a) the suitability to the trust of investments of the same kind as any particular investment proposed to be made or retained and of that particular investment as an investment of that kind, and

(b) the need for diversification of investments of the trust, in so far as is appropriate to the circumstances of the trust'.

Thus, trustees need to consider the different types of investment open to them (eg land, quoted stocks and shares, unit trusts, investment trusts, mortgages, bonds, building society deposits, tax reserve certificates) and to consider that the more diversified the portfolio of investments the lower the overall level of risk for the portfolio, the trustees being entitled to be judged according to modern portfolio theory[5]. However, the circumstances of the case must be taken into account eg restrictions on sale (whether by articles of a private company or by a consent required in the trust instrument), the settlor's purposes as, for example, indicated in his letter of wishes, especially where beneficiaries may have interests as employees in the family company controlled by the trustees[6].

The statutory duty of care applies to a trustee[7] 'when exercising the general power of investment or any other power of investment, however conferred' and 'when carrying out a duty to which he is subject under ss 4 or 5 (Duties relating to the exercise of a power of investment or to the review of investments'.

---

20 *Edge v Pensions Ombudsman* [2000] Ch 602 at 618–619, 627 and 630.
1 TA 2000, s 5(3).
2 TA 2000, s 4(2).
3 TA 2000, s 5(2).
4 TA 2000, s 4(3).
5 *Nestlé v National Westminster Bank* [2000] WTLR 795 at 802; *JW v Morgan Trust Co of the Bahamas Ltd* (2002) 4 ITELR 541, Lord Nicholls, 'Trustees and their Broader Community' (1995) 9 Trust LI 71 at 75.
6 For example, *Public Trustee v Cooper* [2001] WTLR 901.
7 TA 2000, Sch 1, para 1.

Exclusions or restrictions relating to investment powers

The 'general power of investment' is in addition to powers conferred on trustees otherwise than by the Trustee Act 2000 but is subject[8] to any restriction or exclusion imposed by the trust instrument after 2 August 1961[9] or by any enactment or subordinate legislation, while the statutory duty of care does not apply in so far as it appears from the trust instrument that the duty is not meant to apply[10].

The 'general power of investment' is[11] the power of a trustee to make any kind of investment that he could make if he were absolutely entitled to the assets of the trust 'subject to the provisions of this Part' viz ss 4, 5, 6 and 7. Thus, the general power of investment is the power so to invest only if the trustee has obtained and considered proper advice, having regard to the standard investment criteria, and it is this that is subject to exclusion or restriction expressly or by necessary implication, as where an express power of investment in a wider range of assets than those permitted by the general power of investment is subject to an exclusion or restriction which should apply *a fortiori* to the narrower general power of investment.

It follows that a settlor can exclude any duty to consider the need for diversification eg for so long as the trustees retain the controlling share-holding in a particular company, or can exclude any duty to take proper advice, eg for so long as the trustees consult the settlor before making any investment decision.

Status of investments purchased without requisite proper advice

The key issue is whether investments within the range permitted by the general power of investment or an express power of investment, but which are purchased without the requisite 'proper advice', amount to unauthorised investments, the trustees having acted beyond their powers, or amount to merely improper investments, the trustees having acted improperly in breach of trust but within their powers. In the case of unauthorised investments the trustees are strictly liable upon a falsification of the trust accounts[12], while in the case of improper investments the accounts will be surcharged in the amount of any loss which would not have been incurred but for the improper conduct of the trustees[13].

It seems that a general power of investment or an express power of investment can be likened to a mortgagee's statutory power of sale[14]. The power of investment arises under s 3 of the Trustee Act 2000 or the trust instrument but does not become exercisable until the requisite proper advice has been obtained and considered under ss 4 and 5 of the 2000 Act. It is significant that ss 4(1) and 5(1) use the terminology of '*exercising* any power

---

8 TA 2000, s 6(1).
9 TA 2000, s 7(2).
10 TA 2000, Sch 1, para 7.
11 TA 2000, s 3(1) and (2).
12 See Art 89(1) post. Good title will pass to a purchaser because the individual trustees (or a corporation with a broad objects clause) have power or capacity as such to transfer title: *De Vigier v IRC* [1964] 2 All ER 907 at 914, HL; *Hammersmith & Fulham London Borough Council v Monk* [1992] 1 AC 478 at 493; *Rolled Steel Products (Holdings) Ltd v British Steel Corpn* [1985] 3 All ER 52 at 91 [1986] Ch 246 at 303, CA.
13 See Art 89(2) post.
14 LPA 1925, ss 101 at 103.

of investment, whether *arising* under this Part of otherwise'. It also makes sense that strict liability by way of falsification of accounts should only be imposed in clearly defined, easily ascertainable circumstances and not in circumstances, like those involved in ss 4 and 5, where the opposite may well be the case.

Investment in loans secured on land

Trustees can invest in a loan secured on land if they have rights under any contract under which they provide another with credit and the obligation of the borrower to repay is secured on land[15]. Such an investment falls within the trustee's power[16] to 'make any kind of investment that he could make if he were absolutely entitled to the assets of the trust'.

Such powers to invest in a loan secured on land are broad enough to enable trustees to be sole or co-lenders and sole or co-mortgagees or co-chargees[17] and to invest not just in legal mortgages or charges over freehold or leasehold land or in legal sub-mortgages, but also equitable mortgages or charges or sub-mortgages and, even, in second or subsequent mortgages or charges or sub-mortgages as opposed to first mortgages or charges or sub-mortgages.

Traditionally[18], trustees could not invest in contributory mortgages, second mortgages or equitable charges of freeholds or leaseholds nor on first legal mortgages of leaseholds with fewer than 60 years to run. The potential inadequacy or vulnerability of such types of mortgage meant they had to be avoided at all costs. Nowadays, there may well be circumstances where some such types of mortgage can be invested in in accordance with the duties imposed on trustees to safeguard their beneficiaries' interests.

Sections 8, 9 and 10 of the Trustee Act 1925, until repealed by the Trustee Act 2000, provided assistance for trustees lending on mortgage by permitting dispensing with production of the lessor's title where the lessee was mortgaging the leasehold interest to the trustees[19], permitting loaned money not to be called in for a period not exceeding seven years[20], permitting up to two thirds of the sale price of trust land to be secured by a legal mortgage[1], and protecting trustees from liability for loss arising by reason only of the loan exceeding two thirds of the value of the property if certain precautions had been taken[2] or making trustees only liable to the extent the amount advanced was larger than the proper amount that should have been lent on mortgage[3]. The repeal of ss 8 and 9 does not affect their operation[4] in relation to loans made before 1 February 2001[5].

---

15 TA 2000, s 3(3) and (4). For 'land' see under paras (5) and (6) post.

16 TA 2000, s 3(1).

17 See Law Com Report No 260 'Trustees' Powers and Duties' para 2.28.

18 See 15th edn hereof pp 603–605.

19 TA 1925, s 8(2) in light of LPA 1925, s 44(2), but registration of the superior title under the Land Registration Acts 1925 and 2002 increasingly simplifies matters by enabling the inferior title to be title absolute, not just good leasehold title.

20 TA 1925, s 10(1).

1 TA 1925, s 10(2).

2 TA 1925, s 8(1).

3 TA 1925, s 9.

4 On these sections see 15th edn hereof pp 587–589 and 605–608.

5 TA 2000, s 40(2), Sch 3, paras 2 and 3.

Particular duties when investing in mortgages or charges

Trustees need to focus upon the title of the borrower (so that it is readily saleable if need be) and upon the value of the property and its sufficiency for the amount of the loan once they have made the preliminary decision that an investment by way of mortgage, as opposed to any other kind of investment, is appropriate for the portfolio of trust assets. Thus, unless themselves having particular expertise, they will need to take the advice of a financial consultant on the balance of the portfolio and, then, of a surveyor-valuer and a solicitor.

Case law and s 8 of the Trustee Act 1925 indicate that compliance with the duty of care will require the trustees to give written instructions to the valuer (preferably a local one or, otherwise, with the assistance of the trustees he will need to take extra time to familiarise himself with all material circumstances affecting the locality[6]). They should select as valuer someone they adjudge on reasonable grounds to be an able practical valuer and who is independent of the mortgagor and whose fee is not dependent on the mortgage transaction being completed[7]. The valuer should be instructed that his valuation is for the trustees for the purpose of considering the advisability of investing trust funds on the security of the property (so any matters tending to decrease the present or future value of the property should be stated) and that he must advise the trustees in the light of his valuation as to what amount could safely be lent upon the security of the property[8]. Section 8 used to provide protection for advances up to two thirds of the value of the property if so advised, but there is now no hard and fast rule. Thus trustees, therefore, ought to be regarded as complying with their duty of care if their valuer recommends that an amount of three quarters of his valuation can safely be advanced on the security of the well-located residential property which he has conservatively valued.

Possible problems in replacing Trustee Act 1925, Pt I with general power of investment

As just seen s 10 of the Trustee Act 1925 has been repealed. Under s 10(3) trustees holding securities in a company had power to 'concur in any scheme or arrangement.

(a) for the reconstruction of the company;
(b) for the sale of all or any part of the property and undertaking of the company to another company;
(bb) for the acquisition of the securities of the company, or of control thereof, by another company;
(c) for the amalgamation of the company with another company;
(d) for the release, modification or variation of any rights, privileges or liabilities attached to the securities or any of them

in like manner as if they were entitled to such securities beneficially[9], with power to accept any securities of any denomination or description of the reconstructed or purchasing or new company in lieu of or in exchange for all or any of the first mentioned securities'.

---

6 *Fry v Tapson* (1884) 28 Ch D 268.
7 *Re Walker* (1890) 59 LJ Ch 386; *Re Somerset* [1894] 1 Ch 231; *Re Dive* [1909] 1 Ch 328.
8 *Re Solomon* [1912] 1 Ch 261 compromised [1913] 1 Ch 200, CA; *Shaw v Cates* [1909] 1 Ch 389.
9 But consent was required of anyone whose consent would be required to a change of investments: TA 1925, s 10(5).

The general power of a trustee to 'make any kind of investment that he could make if he were absolutely entitled to the assets of the trust' appears to cover (a), (bb) and (c), but not (b) and (d). In (b) where it is the company selling its assets or undertaking and it cannot do this without the concurrence of its shareholders (as in the case of a reconstruction under s 110 of the Insolvency Act 1986) it seems the trustees will not by their concurrence be making an investment. However, in dissenting from the reconstruction they can require their shares to be purchased, having of course power to sell those investments in order to make a new investment. In (d) it does not seem that releasing modifying or varying rights for no consideration can amount to the making of an investment.

Thus trust deeds should expressly confer on trustees the powers of an absolute beneficial owner to exercise any rights attached to trust investments or expressly confer powers in the terms of s 10(3).

Section 11 has also been repealed. Subsection (1) conferred power pending the making of an investment to pay any trust money into a bank to a deposit or other account (with the interest thereon being applied as income) separate from the trustee's personal account, of course. This seems to have been declaratory of the general law[10] and such temporary income-yielding investment before making a longer term investment would seem, in any event, to fall within the ambit of the general power of investment.

Section 11(2) permitted trustees to 'apply capital money subject to a trust in payment of the calls on any shares subject to the same trust'. The general power to make any kind of investment a trustee could make if he were absolutely entitled to the assets of the trust clearly extends to him purchasing shares issued partly paid, but subject to the obligation to pay the amount unpaid when called upon, where the trustees were the original subscribers to whom the shares were first issued, and there seems no reason why it should make any difference that the trustees purchased the partly-paid shares from the original subscriber or a successor in title thereto: in each case the purchase is in exchange for some money to be paid forthwith and for incurring the obligation to pay the remainder when duly called for.

PARAGRAPHS 5 AND 6

Specific power of trustees to acquire 'freehold or leasehold land' in UK in respect of which the trustees have all the powers of an absolute owner

Trustees may, under s 8(1) of the Trustee Act 2000, 'acquire freehold or leasehold land in the UK (a) as an investment (b) for occupation by a beneficiary or (c) for any other reason'. Such English or Welsh land must be a legal estate, as for Northern Irish land but this includes land held under a fee farm grant. Such Scots land must be the estate or interest of the proprietor of the *dominium utile* or of the owner of land not held on feudal tenure or must be a tenancy. For trustees who acquire land other than under s 8(1), eg because they already have land settled on them initially by the settlor[11], the amended s 6(3) of the Trustees of Land and Appointment of Trustees Act 1996 provides, 'The trustees of land have power to acquire land

---

10 *Ex p Belchier* (1754) Amb 218; *Massey v Banner* (1820) 1 Jac & W 241 at 248; *Ex p Kingston* (1871) 6 Ch App 632.
11 Not being settled land under the SLA 1925; see Article 44 ante.

under the power conferred by section 8 of the Trustee Act 2000'. Under
s 8(3), 'For the purpose of exercising his functions as a trustee, a trustee who
acquires land under this section has all the powers of an absolute owner in
relation to the land'. To cover land initially settled on the trustees and not
subsequently acquired by them, s 6(1) of the 1996 Act provides, 'For the
purpose of exercising their functions as trustees, the trustees of land have in
relation to the land subject to the trust all the powers of an absolute owner.'
Such powers necessarily enable trustees to be co-purchasers if otherwise
complying with their duties of care.

In exercising their powers as an absolute owner the trustees of land or just
of movables can purchase land (together with appurtement easements
profits and restrictive covenants) by way of mortgage *over that land,* acquiring
the benefit of the legal estate in land at the same time as incurring the
burden of the mortgage without which the legal estate could not have been
acquired[12], but they cannot create a liability by mortgaging *other trust property*
in order to generate money to be used in the acquisition of further investments, whether purchased outright or with the assistance of a mortgage over
them[13].

'Land' is not defined in the Trustee Act 2000[14], but by the Interpretation
Act 1978[15], unless the contrary intention appears, ' "land" includes buildings
and other structures, land covered with water, and any estate, *interest, easement, servitude* or right in or over land'. 'Legal estate' is not defined in the
2000 (or the 1978) Act but, presumably, should have the meaning set out in s
1(4) of the Law of Property Act 1925[16] so as to include not just legal estates
but also interests and charges like legal profits relating to game-shooting or
legal rentcharges, as was the case for trustees of land under s 6(3) of the
Trust of Land and Appointment of Trustees Act 1996 having powers to
purchase a 'legal estate in any land', with the LPA 1925 definitions applying
to such terminology, until such powers were replaced by the powers in s 8 of
the 2000 Act. It would, indeed, be most strange if trustees investing under the
1996 Act in perpetual rentcharges[17] or in shooting rights over estates in the
nature of a legal profit or in acquiring a useful legal easement from the new
owner of neighbouring land could no longer do so after January 2001 and
would need to sell such existing assets[18].

'Freehold or leasehold land' means 'a legal estate in land', but, in the light
of the above, this should extend beyond a freehold or leasehold estate to a
legal rentcharge or a legal easement or profit, because it seems likely that
legal estate does not have the narrow meaning in s 1(1) of the Law of

---

12 *Abbey National Building Society v Cann* [1991] 1 AC 56, HL.
13 See p 602 ante.
14 Which refers to Scots and Northern Ireland land as well as English and Welsh land.
15 Sch 1.
16 s 205(1)(x).
17 Perpetual rentcharges were even authorised under Trustee Investments Act 1961, Sch 1, Pt II,
   para 14 as well as s 6(3) of the TLATA 1996.
18 Section 8 of the TA 2000 was intended in similar terms to replace s 6(3) of the 1996 Act
   without changing matters: Law Com Report No 260 'Trustees' Powers and Duties' page 101
   Explanatory Note. It would seem that the draftsperson of Sch 3, para 7(1) of the 2000 Act,
   worried about the repeal of the Trustee Investments Act 1961, put in a provision for continuing to hold rentcharges without appreciating that this was unnecessary because, as legal
   interests, they fell within the definition of legal estates: if it had been necessary, then all other
   legal interests should have been similarly protected.

Property Act 1925 restricting legal estate to freeholds and leaseholds[19] but the broad meaning in s 1(4) thereof.

Acquisition as investment or for occupation or other reasons

When land is acquired by way of 'investment' then as earlier discussed[20], the duties to take advice, having regard to the standard investment criteria, and the equitable duty to act fairly between the beneficiaries will need to be complied with. While leaseholds of any duration may be acquired, the acquisition of leaseholds of short duration that are wasting assets will normally be out of the question having regard to such duties.

Originally, land purchased for occupation by a beneficiary was not regarded as an investment because it was not intended to produce income[1], although if purchased also with a view to capital growth as part of a balanced portfolio in accord with modern portfolio theory it might nowadays be regarded as an investment. Acquisition 'for occupation by a beneficiary' is now expressly permitted, but since it may well be regarded as also an investment the trustees should take advice as with any other investment and fairly consider the potential impact on all beneficiaries.

Clearly, occupation by a beneficiary cannot extend to a beneficiary with an interest in remainder after an interest in possession. Only the beneficiary with an interest in possession could occupy the land because to oust his interest in favour of the interest of the remainderman would be for the trustees to alter the beneficial interests laid down by the settlor. Purchasing for occupation by a beneficiary is merely an administrative power, not a distributive one permitting the trustees to distribute to the remainderman a benefit intended only for the life tenant. However, trustees should be able to purchase land for occupation by beneficiaries interested in income under a discretionary trust[2]. Thus, trustees could purchase a house for occupation of a discretionary income beneficiary and his family and permit him a licence to live there which is revocable at the whim of the trustees, although if there is a power to appoint income in a sufficient amount of capital to such a beneficiary so as to confer upon him an interest in possession therein, then he may have an interest in possession in the house[3]. Indeed, the trustees may acquire a house in the Lake District or Cornwall to be used as a holiday home from time to time by discretionary beneficiaries and their families.

In the case of mere object of a power of appointment it would seem that a house cannot be acquired for occupation for such a person until, pursuant to the power, an income interest is appointed in the capital used to acquire the house for the benefit of such person or until the power has been exercised (if

---

19 Although *Lewin on Trusts* (17th edn) para 35-194F takes this narrow view, but cf para 35-194 M on acquiring a profit.
20 See p 602 ante.
1 *Re Power's Will Trusts* [1947] Ch 572.
2 By TA 2000, s 35(2)(c) the reference to a beneficiary in s 8(1)(b) is to be read as referring to a person who, under the will of the deceased or under the law of intestacy, is beneficially interested in the estate, not merely interested in the due administration of the estate. Thus, one waits till the executors have completed their administration and themselves become trustees or transfer property to trustees whether on fixed or discretionary trusts.
3 For inheritance tax danger if an interest in possession is created see Inheritance Tax Act 1975, s 65.

it can be) to make him a discretionary beneficiary in trust income[4].

In the case of the favoured accumulation and maintenance trusts[5], where income is to be accumulated to the extent not used for maintenance of a beneficiary who is to take a beneficial interest in possession or absolute interest on or before attaining 25 years of age, it should also be permissible for trustees to buy land for occupation by such beneficiary eg buying a flat for the beneficiary-student to occupy while studying for a degree in that locality.

With the powers of an absolute owner, the trustees can impose reasonable conditions related to the occupation of the trust land. One naturally assumes that purchase 'for occupation by a beneficiary' relates to physical residence by that beneficiary and, if appropriate, his family, but it could extend to occupation for a business purpose of the beneficiary, though the trustees would need to ensure they act fairly between income and capital beneficiaries[6] in going ahead with such a proposed purchase.

In any event such a purchase for occupation for a business purpose of a beneficiary comes with s 8(1)(c) as an acquisition 'for any other reason'. This is primarily concerned with the functional purposes of charitable trusts but can otherwise authorise the trustees to acquire land not as an investment and not for residential occupation by a beneficiary currently interested in income of the trust, but for some other reason connected with furthering the interests of the beneficiaries as a whole and not the furthering of the trustees' interests at all (except to the extent otherwise authorised expressly or by necessary implication in the trust instrument). Thus, if the trustees have power under the trust instrument to carry on a business for the benefit of the beneficiaries then the trustees may acquire land for the purpose of carrying on and developing that business. In the absence of such a power, however, they cannot go off on frolic of the own so as to acquire land to commence a business role as trustee in addition to their fundamental investment role.

Settled Land Act 1925 trustees and tenant for life

Pre-1997 settlements under the Settled Land Act 1925 and new settlements made by virtue of powers thereunder unless designated not to be SLA settlements[7] are subject to the Settled Land Act 1925 regime as amended by the Trustee Act 2000[8]. While the tenant for life (or the statutory owner eg if there be no tenant for life of full age and capacity) decides whether to sell, lease, or otherwise dispose of the settled land, any capital money arising thereby which needs to be invested is invested in investments within s 73 of the Settled Land Act 1925[9] by the trustees (who must be paid the capital money), although they must so far as practicable consult the tenant for life and give effect to his wishes so far as is consistent with the general interest of the settlement[10].

---

4 Objects only have a spes or hope or expectancy and have no interest in the trust property (*Re Brooks' Settlement Trusts* [1939] Ch 993), but a beneficiary under a discretionary trust does have a proprietary interest of sorts: *Knocker v Youle* [1986] 2 All ER 914; *Re Smith* [1928] Ch 915.

5 Inheritance Tax Act 1984, s 71.

6 *Nestlé v National Westminster Bank* [1994] 1 All ER 118, CA; *Edge v Pensions Ombudsman* [2000] Ch 602; *Beauclerk v Ashburnham* (1845) 8 Beav 322.

7 TLATA 1996, s 2(3).

8 TA 2000, Sch 2, paras 7–17.

9 These extend to investments authorised under the general power of investment within s 3 of TA 2000 as well as expressly authorised investments.

10 SLA 1925, s 75(2) and (4) as substituted by TA 2000, Sch 2, para 10(1) and (2).

Such investments are held in the names of or under the control of the SLA trustees[11]. However, freehold or leasehold land with at least 60 years unexpired acquired at the request of the tenant for life for occupation by the tenant for life is vested in the tenant for life[12].

PARAGRAPH 7

Expressly and necessarily impliedly authorised investments

It is well-established that wills impliedly authorise the retention of investments that are specifically referred to in a specific bequest[13] or are intended to be capable of being retained for the benefit of the income beneficiary even if the subject of a residuary bequest[14]. However, where there is a power to retain specific shares this does not authorise the purchase of more of the same shares[15].

Where, under s 41 of the Administration of Estates Act 1925, there is an appropriation by personal representatives of a deceased's property towards satisfying a settled legacy, with the consent of the trustee or the income beneficiary, such appropriated property becomes an authorised investment so far as concerns its retention[16].

Investment clauses are now construed fairly and straightforwardly rather than in a restrictive fashion, but the court must first consider whether the relevant clause is truly an investment clause or not. Thus, in *Re Barlow Clowes (No 2)*[17] the Court of Appeal construed a clause which authorised the trustee to buy and sell British Government stock 'and to place any uninvested funds with any bank, local authority or other body on such terms and conditions as you see fit whether bearing interest or not' as authorising him to *invest* in British Government stock and merely *place* uninvested moneys temporarily pending investment in British Government stock. The words used were not intended to enable the trustee to invest in any corporate or other body he saw fit apart from investing in British Government stock.

However in *Nestlé v National Westminster Bank*[18] a lengthy clause 13 declaring 'all moneys liable to be invested may be invested upon any stocks or securities of or guaranteed by the UK Government or any British Colony or Dependency or any Foreign State or the stocks, shares, bonds, debentures or securities of any Railway or other Company established in the UK' was held to extend to investment in the purchase of ordinary shares in companies incorporated in the UK.

If the trustee be given power to invest in such securities as he sees fit, it will be construed as power to invest in such investments as he sees fit (whether or not authorised by the general law), so that any investment honestly thought

---

11 SLA 1925, s 75(2) as substituted above.
12 SLA 1925, ss 10, 73(1)(xi) for moneys to be invested 'or otherwise applied' eg for occupation; substituted s 73(2).
13 *Re Pugh* [1887] WN 143; *Re Whitfield* [1920] 125 LT 61.
14 *Re Pitcairn* [1896] 2 Ch 199; *Brown v Gellatley* (1867) 2 Ch App 751.
15 Hence the need in *Boardman v Phipps* [1967] 2 AC 46 for the trustees to obtain court permission under TA 1925, s 57 if they were to purchase more shares in Lester & Harris Ltd.
16 Administration of Estates Act 1925, s 41(2).
17 [1994] 2 All ER 316 at 327–330, CA.
18 [1994] 1 All ER 118, CA.

to be in the interests of the beneficiaries will be authorised[19], except, according to an old case of doubtful authority nowadays[20] a loan of money at interest on a mere personal contract to repay it with interest. If the power is to invest in investments in his absolute discretion in all respects as if he were the absolute beneficial owner of the Trust Fund this does not exempt him from the need to satisfy the duty of care[1].

If, to avoid doubt, express power to lend money at interest is to be conferred on trustees its terms should make clear whether a bond or promissory note from the borrower will suffice or whether the loan should only be made on the security of real or personal property[2]. Where there is an express power to lend, with or without security for such loan, the trustee must not make it merely to accommodate the borrower but must consider whether such loan is in the best financial interests of the beneficiaries as a whole, especially if the borrower is a beneficiary[3]. If the loan can only be made to a specified partnership then upon a change in the membership of the partnership the loan becomes unauthorised unless the terminology of the power can be construed as permitting the loan to be made to the firm known as 'X and partners' irrespective of who are the partners from time to time[4].

For over thirty years it has been common to use very wide express investment powers and such continue to be used due to the limits of the statutory default powers in the Trustee Act 2000. Thus, to avoid uncertainties in construing the 2000 Act and to extend the powers upon trustees for the next eighty or more years and relying on the safeguards provided by the trustees' equitable and statutory duties[5], many trust instruments contain a broad power along the following lines: 'In performing their managerial or administrative functions the Trustees may apply or invest the Trust Fund as if they were the absolute beneficial owners thereof in the purchase or acquisition or protection of assets or investments of whatsoever nature and wherever situated, and whether or not yielding income, [or of a speculative or hazardous nature] [and including the acquisition of derivatives but only for the purpose of limiting risks and not for the purpose of speculation]'.

Without the optional clauses in brackets such express power solves any problems caused by the repeal of s 10(3) of the Trustee Act 1925 and the ambit of the restrictions concerning acquisition of interests in land in s 8 of the Trustee Act 2000, and should extend to permitting unsecured loans and to mortgaging some of the trust property in order to acquire money to enable further trust property to be purchased. However, many draftspersons play safe by expressly including specific powers for the avoidance of any doubt.

19 *Re Douglas' Will Trusts* [1959] 2 All ER 620; *Re Harari's Settlement Trusts* [1949] 1 All ER 430; *Re McEachern's Settlement Trusts* [1939] Ch 858; *Re Peczenik's Settlement Trusts* [1964] 2 All ER 339.

20 *Khoo Tek Keong v Ch'ng Joo Tuan Neoh* [1934] AC 529, PC. If a secured loan is an investment it is difficult to see why an unsecured loan is not also an investment that could form part of a well-balanced portfolio if balanced by little or no risk investments; especially where the loan was an urgent one made in the subsequently unfulfilled expectation that security would be provided.

1 *Bartlett v Barclays Bank Trust Co Ltd* [1980] Ch 515 at 536.

2 *Re Laing's Settlement* [1899] 1 Ch 593.

3 *Re Laing's Settlement* [1899] 1 Ch 593. Joint trustees cannot lend to one of themselves in breach of their undivided duty of loyalty unless authorised by the trust deed.

4 *Re Tucker* [1894] 1 Ch 724; affd [1874] 3 Ch 429; *Smith v Patrick* [1901] AC 282, HL.

5 Many of these duties, however, may be expressly ousted: see p 591 ante.

PARAGRAPH 8

Trustees not necessarily protected by investing in authorised securities

A trustee is not necessarily safeguarded merely because the investments he makes are authorised by the settlement or by statute. To invest in any other way would, of itself, be a breach of trust leading to a strict falsification of the trust accounts. However, a breach of trust will arise if he fails to obtain and consider proper advice, having regard to the standard investment criteria, or fails from time to time to review the investments with a view to vary them[6] or fails to exercise the duties of care[7] and fairness[8] when exercising his powers of investment or carrying out his duties to obtain and consider proper advice and to review the trust investments from time to time. If such a breach causes a loss (including a loss of profit), then the trusteeship accounts will be surcharged with the amount of the loss[9].

Where, however, the trustees are required by the settlement to comply with the directions as to investment of one of the beneficiaries, then if this power of direction be a personal power as opposed to a fiduciary power[10], and the beneficiary is not acting in wholly unreasonable fashion[11] beyond that contemplated by the settlor, their only responsibility is to see that they are not paying a higher price than is reasonable and proper[12]. Nevertheless, if the trust is a trust of land, then if the trustees believe the direction to be one that no reasonable beneficiary should give or if his consent to their action is requisite and no reasonable beneficiary should withhold his consent, the trustees may apply to the court for such order as the court thinks fit under ss 14 and 15 of the Trusts of Land and Appointment of Trustees Act 1996[13]. If the trustees believe a fiduciary power is being exercised in breach of fiduciary duty and fear liability as accessory to such breach, they can obtain directions from the court[14].

Trustees' duties and standard of care

In *Cowan v Scargill*[15], where trustees had very wide powers of investment, Megarry V-C made the following points.

---

6 TA 2000, ss 4 and 5.
7 TA 2000, ss 1, 2, Sch 1, paras 1 and 2.
8 *Nestlé v National Westminster Bank* [1994] 1 All ER 118, CA.
9 Loss can cover loss of profit if proved: *Nestlé v National Westminster Bank* [1994] 1 All ER 118, CA, applied in *Re Mulligan* [1998] 1 NZLR 481.
10 Nowadays, it seems clear wording would be needed to justify a power of a beneficiary or a third party to be merely a personal power when concerned with investment of the trust property at the heart of the trust: *Vestey's Executors v IRC* [1949] 1 All ER 1108 at 1115, HL; *Comr of Stamp Duties v Way* [1942] 1 All ER 191, PC.
11 A fraud on the power. Indeed, *Beauclerk v Ashburnham* (1845) 8 Beav 322 at 328 indicates that the trustees should seek directions from the court if directed to lay out the trust moneys in a low, bad and deteriorating situation, eg purchasing land in Ireland in 1886 as required by the trust instrument but excused by the court in *Re Maberly* (1886) 33 Ch D 455.
12 *Re Hart's Will Trust* [1943] 2 All ER 557.
13 *Re Beale's Settlement Trust* [1932] 2 Ch 15.
14 *Finers v Miro* [1991] 1 All ER 182; *Re Arnott* [1899] IR 201; the complaining power exerciser can also issue a claim seeking directions: *Re Sutherland's Settlement Trust* [1953] Ch 792.
15 [1985] Ch 270, [1984] 2 All ER 750. This has been applied in *Martin v City of Edinburgh District Council* [1988] SLT 329, (1989) 1 Pensions LR 9; *Harries v Church Comrs* [1992] 1 WLR 1241 (though accepting that in charitable trusts there is more scope for taking account of ethical considerations) and *Jones v AMP Perpetual Trust to NZ Ltd* [1994] 1 NZLR 690.

1. 'It is the duty of trustees to exercise their powers in the best interest of the present and future beneficiaries of the trust, holding the scales impartially between the different classes of beneficiaries ... When the purpose of the trust is to provide financial benefits for the beneficiaries, as is usually the case, the best interests of the beneficiaries are normally their best financial interests. The power must be exercised so as to yield the best return for the beneficiaries, judged in relation to the risks of the investments in question; and the prospects for the yield of income and capital appreciation both have to be considered in judging the return from the investment'[16]. Only if investments are of equal financial merits can moral considerations influence the choice of investment. Otherwise, trustees must put on one side their own social or political views. Where trusts are set up to provide financial benefits then financial considerations are paramount except for the very rare case eg where all the beneficiaries are adult, teetotal, non-smoking, peace campaigners with the same moral attitude to investment in alcohol, tobacco or armaments.

2. The trustees must 'take such care as an ordinary prudent man would take if he were minded to make an investment for the benefit of other people for whom he felt morally bound to provide. This duty includes the duty to seek advice on matters which the trustee does not understand, such as the making of investments, and, on receiving that advice, to act with the same degree of prudence. Although a trustee who takes advice on investments is not bound to accept and act on that advice, he is not entitled to reject it merely because he sincerely disagrees with it, unless in addition he is acting as an ordinary prudent man would act'[17].

3. The trustees must consider the need for diversification of investments and the suitability of the investments proposed as laid down by s 6 of the Trustee Investments Act 1961, now s 4 of the Trustee Act 2000.

4. If trustees are deadlocked on investment policy because five favour one policy and five another and no casting vote is available, then the court has jurisdiction to intervene and determine which policy is appropriate.

On the facts Megarry V-C held the five defendant trustees to be in breach of their fiduciary duties in their attempt to restrict the investment policy of the trustees of the mineworkers' pension fund in such fashion as to ensure the general prosperity of the coal industry eg prohibiting investment in competing industries and reducing overseas investment. If such restrictions are desired then they should be inserted in the original trust deed.

It is not considered that the Trustee Act 2000 has changed the position as set forth by Megarry V-C. It leaves unaffected the duty to maximise financial returns holding the scales fairly[18] or impartially between different classes of beneficiaries. It spells out[19] the duty[20] from time to time to review the investment portfolio with a view to varying it and the duty to obtain and

---

16 [1985] Ch 270 at 286–287. In selling land where no written contract yet subsists trustees must negotiate with a serious bidder making a higher offer, even if as honourable men they would prefer to stick with their original bargain: *Buttle v Saunders* [1950] 2 All ER 193.

17 [1985] Ch 270 at 289, also saying 'Honesty and sincerity are not the same as prudence and reasonableness'.

18 As emphasised by the Court of Appeal in *Nestlé v National Westminster Bank* [1994] 1 All ER 118 and *Edge v Pensions Ombudsman* [2000] Ch 602.

19 TA 2000, s 4(2).

20 *Nestlé v National Westminster Bank* [1994] 1 All ER 118, CA, where there was a blatant breach of this duty.

consider proper advice[1] having regard to the standard investment criteria[2] (diversification of investments and suitability to trust of proposed investments).

The Trustee Act 2000[3] does lay down the duty of care of trustees, so far as not excluded by the trust instrument, so that a trustee 'must exercise such care and skill as is reasonable in the circumstances, having regard in particular (a) to any special knowledge or experience that he has or holds himself out as having, and (b) if he acts as trustee in the course of a business or profession, to any special knowledge or experience that it is reasonable to expect of a person acting in the course of that kind of business or profession'.

Because this statutory duty of care is deliberately worded flexibly in imposing a duty to 'exercise such care and skill as is reasonable in all the circumstances' it permits taking account of whether or not the trustee is a paid professional, whether or not he has held himself out as having higher abilities than other trustees, and the circumstance that he is selecting investments for sale or purchase not for himself but for other persons, who may be much worse off than himself and very dependent on the trust for their support. Thus, it is not considered that a trustee's duty of care in selecting appropriate investments has been reduced by the Trustee Act 2000 to a duty only to take as much care as if he were investing on his own behalf. It remains at the level indicated by Megarry V-C[4].

Exercising such care and skill as is reasonable in all the circumstances should involve the trustees taking account of considerations like the following spelled out in the American Uniform Prudent Investor Act:
(1) general economic conditions;
(2) the possible impact of inflation or deflation;
(3) the expected tax consequences of investment decisions or strategies;
(4) the role that each investment or course of action plays within the overall portfolio;
(5) the expected total return from income and the appreciation of capital;
(6) other resources of the beneficiaries;
(7) needs for liquidity, regularity of income, and preservation or appreciation of capital; and
(8) an asset's special relationship or special value, if any, to the purposes of the trust or to one or more of the beneficiaries.

Of course, the trustees should make reasonable efforts to verify facts relevant to the investment and management of the trust assets[5] eg wealth of beneficiaries, domicile if relevant to tax treatment of assets on beneficiary's death, residence if cared for in residential accommodation (especially if the trust income would all be used to defray expenses under the National Assistance (Assessment of Resources) Regulations, so it would be better to invest only for capital appreciation).

Where confrontation is not sought between the trustees and the beneficiaries (unlike the *Cowan v Scargill* situation) there is still much scope for trustees quietly to take into account the moral, social and political views of

1 TA 2000, s 5.
2 TA 2000, s 4(3).
3 TA 2000, s 1 and Sch 1.
4 *Cowan v Scargill* [1985] Ch 270 at 289, endorsed by Lord Nicholls in 'Trustees and their Broader Community', (1995) 9 Trust LI 71 at 73.
5 *Nestlé v National Westminster Bank* [1994] 1 All ER 118, CA.

beneficiaries and of themselves[6], since it will in practice be difficult to prove that at the time a particular investment was made it was not as equally financially meritorious as certain other possible investments. The inevitable uncertainty in the stock market makes it difficult to assess which particular investment or type of investment would be the best in terms of capital growth, income and risk: a reasonable amount of leeway must be afforded to trustees.

Indeed the difficulty that faces a beneficiary who wishes to complain that the selection of a particular type of investment was, in terms of capital growth, infelicitous was illustrated in *Nestlé v National Westminster Bank plc*[7] where the trustee, having wider powers of investment than it had appreciated, failed to seek advice on the true extent of its powers under the trust instrument and accordingly restricted its actual investments to those of a type which, in the event, resulted not merely in a failure to achieve the kind of capital growth that more adventurous investment in equities rather than gilts would have achieved but also a depreciation in real terms of the capital value of the fund. It also failed to conduct regular reviews of the investment portfolio between 1922 and 1959. Whilst finding that the bank had acted in breach of trust the Court of Appeal held that it could not fix the trustee with liability for default. Staughton LJ held that failure to to diversify up to 1960 was not a breach of trust because he could not accept that at that time failure to diversify 'was a course which no prudent trustee would have followed'[8]. Leggatt LJ stated:

> 'The appellant ... had to prove that a prudent trustee, knowing of the scope of the bank's investment powers and conducting regular reviews, would so have invested the trust funds as to make it worth more than it was worth when the plaintiff inherited it.'[9]

She failed to produce enough evidence to prove any 'loss' incurred by making a gain less than would have been made by trustees acting as prudent businessmen investing for persons for whom they felt morally obliged to provide. Because there was no loss there was no cause of action.

At first instance, Hoffmann J had taken the opportunity to restate what he took to be the duty of a trustee in balancing the interests of life tenant and remainderman as regards selection of the type of investment. He had said:

> 'Modern trustees acting within their investment powers are entitled to be judged by the standards of current portfolio theory, which emphasises the risk level of the entire portfolio rather than the risk attaching to each investment taken in isolation ... A trustee must act fairly in making investment decisions which may have dif-

---

6 Indeed, pension trustees need have regard to their beneficiaries on the extent to which they have taken account of ethical and environmental considerations. Charitable trustees should not invest in companies whose products (eg armaments or alcohol) are incompatible with the purposes of the charity (eg Society of Friends, Alcoholics Anonymous) or where shareholdings in particular companies might well hamper a charity's work by making potential recipients of aid unwilling to be helped, or by alienating those who support the charity financially or by voluntary work: *Harries v Church Comrs* [1993] 2 All ER 300.

7 [1994] 1 All ER 118, CA.

8 [1994] 1 All ER 118 at 138. Nowadays, it would appear to be reckless if a trustee failed to consider diversification for a decade and it ought to be the case that such recklessness, a type of dishonesty (according to *Armitage v Nurse* [1998] Ch 241, CA) should lead to a presumption that loss flowed from such recklessness unless disproved by the trustee, everything being presumed against a dishonest trustee (see pp 885–887 post).

9 [1994] 1 All ER 118 at 141.

ferent consequences for differing classes of beneficiaries ... The trustees have a wide discretion. They are, for example, entitled to take into account the income needs of the tenant for life or the fact that the tenant for life was a person known to the settlor and a primary object of the trust whereas the remainderman is a remoter relative or a stranger. Of course, these cannot be allowed to become the overriding considerations but the concept of fairness between classes of beneficiaries does not require them to be excluded. It would be an inhuman rule which required trustees to adhere to some mechanical rule for preserving the real value of capital when the tenant for life was the testator's widow who had fallen upon hard times and the remainderman was young and well off'[10].

The Court of Appeal, not finding it necessary to comment on his reformulation of the test laid down by Megarry V-C (in terms of 'holding the scales impartially')[11] to permit the trustee to aim at 'fairness' between the classes of beneficiaries, none the less agreed in substance that the personal circumstances of the life tenant might be taken into account in, for example, deciding to choose a high-income yield investment, inevitably at the expense of the remainderman to the extent that a high growth investment might, instead, have been chosen[12].

In dealing with the investment of proceeds of sale of the family home the Court of Appeal rejected the appellant's prima facie strong claim by applying the view of Megarry V-C[13]:

'If trustees make a decision on wholly wrong grounds, and yet it subsequently appears, from matters which they did not express or refer to, that there are in fact good and sufficient reasons for supporting their decisions, then I do not think that they would incur any liability for having decided the matter on erroneous grounds, for the decision itself was right.'

The appellant, having a difficult and costly onus of proof to discharge in *Nestle v National Westminster Bank* despite having the advantage of deficient behaviour by the trustee, may have been entitled to feel aggrieved, but not the claimants in *Galmerrow Securities Ltd v National Westminster Bank*[14] where in the context of a clause absolving the trustee of a unit trust for liability for loss that might arise from 'the exercise or non-exercise' of its powers, except in the cases of fraud or negligence, the question arose whether it was negligent not to have removed the property fund manager, whose investment strategy had, because of the London property market crash of 1974, been unsuccessful. As, on the facts, the unit holders needed to vary the trust deed to provide better remuneration terms, the trustee would have been unable to replace the manager sufficiently quickly, so it had not been negligent:

'The venture was a speculation and like all speculations carried with it the risk of failure. It would not be right to visit the consequences of that misjudgment of the market upon NatWest which is not shown to have had any power open to it which would remedy or mitigate the consequence ... it is not negligent to fail to act where no alternative course of conduct to the continuance of the present arrangement is proved to have been available to the person who has a power to act.'[15]

10 [2000] WTLR 795 at 802–803.
11 *Cowan v Scargill* [1985] Ch 270 at 286.
12 *Nestle v National Westminster Bank plc* [1993] 1 WLR 1260 at 1270–1272, 1279. See also *Karger v Paul* [1984] VR 161 and *Re Saunders and Halom* (1986) 32 DLR (4th) 503.
13 [1985] Ch 270 at 294.
14 [2002] WTLR 125.
15 [2002] WTLR 125 at 155.

Essentially[16], to succeed in a claim that negligent or unfair investment of the trustees caused loss, a claimant beneficiary has to prove that no trustee, acting with the requisite minimum care and skill and suffering from the bad luck[17] that can affect investors, could possibly have ended up with a trust fund of the complained-of value. Thus in *Re Mulligan*[18], to favour the life tenant-widow of the testator-settlor, the trustees did not diversify at all by investing in equities, but invested the proceeds of the testator's farm in high-yielding investments allowing depreciation of the value of capital. The New Zealand High Court held that the trustees should in 1972 have diversified to the extent of investing 40% of the capital in equities which would have appreciated not at 100% of an appropriate index of equities but only at 75% thereof, taking account of dealing costs and the fact that the fund was not large enough for the trustees to be able to rival the index.

In *Re Smith*[19] only Imperial Oil Company Stock was held on trust for S's mother for life, remainder to S. From the outset there was only an average dividend of two and a half per cent for the mother, when returns of up to 8 to 10 per cent were available in respect of good quality bonds and mortgages. The trustee ignored the mother's requests for diversification and a better income when S preferred retention of the stock. The Ontario Court of Appeal held there had been a breach of trust and replaced the trustee.

In *Bartlett v Barclays Bank Trust Co Ltd*[20] trustees with power to invest in investments that an absolute beneficial owner might invest in were held liable for hazarding money in a development project concerning a site near the Old Bailey. This project 'was a gamble because it involved buying into the site at prices in excess of the investment values of the properties, with no certainty or probability, with no more than a chance, that planning permission might be obtained for a financially viable redevelopment, that the numerous proprietors would agree to sell out or join in the scheme, that finance would be available on acceptable terms, and that the development would be completed, or at least become a marketable asset, before the time came to start winding up the trust'. In fact it was a company which was controlled by the trustees with a 99.8% shareholding that actually carried out the hazardous speculation leading the company to lose over half a million pounds but this did not alter the liability of the trustees. The trustees had failed to use their controlling shareholding to ensure that they received an adequate flow of information concerning the intentions and activities of the company, and, if they had received such information, they would have been under a duty to use their controlling shareholding to stop the speculative project. No prudent businessman, mindful he was trustee for the benefit of others, would have failed to stop the speculative project[1].

16 *Wight v Olswang (No 2)* [2001] WTLR 291 CA, following the lead in the court below [2000] WTLR 783, taking account of *Bristol & West Building Society v Mothew* [1998] Ch 1.

17 See Staughton LJ in *Nestlé v National Westminster Bank* [1994] 1 All ER 118 at 133.

18 [1998] 1 NZLR 481.

19 (1971) 16 DLR (3d) 130; affd (1971) 18 DLR (3d) 405.

20 [1980] Ch 515, [1980] 1 All ER 139. For a further case of hazardous investment via a controlled company so as to cause loss to the beneficiaries under the trust, see *Walker v Stones* [2001] QB 902, CA.

1 For clauses to protect trustees in such a situation see p 591 ante.

PARAGRAPH 9

Holding investments in name of nominee or custodian

Originally, when investment was relatively simple and leisurely, all investments had to be held in the names of all the trustees[2], unless otherwise expressly authorised in the trust instrument. However, changes in trust law had to follow upon changing investment practices. Speed in making and acting upon investment decisions became crucial, while the time for settlement of transactions on the London Stock Exchange has gradually been reduced to three working days. Indeed, to cut costs and speed up transactions, the holding of many securities has been dematerialised via an electronic database, so that securities are held in uncertificated form and settlement of dealings takes place electronically[3]. This is a system called CREST governing dealings in most public companies' shares.

Trustees may become system-members of CREST having direct access to the system or sponsored members, who act by instructing system-members to act as their agent in implementing their instructions and debiting their bank account. The dematerialised securities will be held in the name of the trustees[4]. However, if the trustees act via a sponsored member they may require their shares to be certificated[5], although extra cost and time will be taken up for subsequent sales of the shares needing to be in dematerialised form.

Often it is easier for trustees to hold interests in securities via a nominee or custodian which is a member of CREST or to hire a discretionary portfolio manager[6] which holds all its interests in securities via such a nominee or custodian. It would appear that authorisation of the trustees to invest in foreign securities will necessarily authorise the acquisition of dematerialised securities in the names of the trustees where a dematerialised system is in operation or in the name of a nominee if so required by the foreign system. However, use of a nominee or custodian under ss 16 to 20 of the Trustee Act 2000 will normally be desirable in any event.

Statutory powers to appoint nominees and custodians

By s 16 trustees (other than of pension schemes, authorised unit trusts or charitable common investment schemes[7]) may appoint a person to act as their nominee in relation to such of the trust assets as they determine (other than settled land within the Settled Land Act 1925) and then take such steps as are necessary to secure that those assets are vested in the nominee. The appointment must be in or evidenced in writing but cannot be made if the trust has a custodian *trustee*[8] or the assets are vested in the official custodian for charities.

Custodians undertake the safe custody of assets or of any documents or

---

2 *Lewis v Nobbs* (1878) 8 Ch D 591; *Re Flower and Metropolitan Board of Works* (1884) 27 Ch D 592.
3 Companies Act 1989, s 207; Uncertificated Securities Regulations 1995, SI 1995/3272. Dispositions of equitable interests in such securities are exempted by reg 32(5) thereof from the need for signed writing within LPA 1925, s 53(1)(c) but overreaching authorised sales or gifts by trustees take effect without such need, anyhow: R C Nolan [2002] Camb LJ 169.
4 Authorised directly and indirectly by reg 33(1)(c).
5 Uncertificated Securities Regulations 1995, Sch 1, para 13.
6 See pp 621 and 638 post.
7 See TA 2000, ss 36, 37, 38.
8 See p 796 post.

records concerning the assets and normally fulfil many administrative tasks e.g. keeping track of dividend payments, bonus issues, and of any tax repayment claims. Trustees[9] (other than of pension schemes, authorised unit trusts or charitable common investment schemes) may appoint a person to act as custodian in relation to such of the trust assets as they determine[10] and, unless otherwise authorised, must appoint a custodian of any bearer securities of the trust[11]. The appointment must be in or evidenced in writing but cannot be made if the trust has a custodian trustee or the assets are vested in the official custodian for charities.

To be eligible for appointment as a nominee or custodian[12] or as nominee and custodian and agent[13] if so desired, a person must either (a) carry on a business which consists of or includes acting as a nominee or custodian, or (b) be a body corporate controlled by the trustees, or (c) a body corporate recognised under s 9 of the Adminstration of Justice Act 1985 (by the Council of the Law Society for the provision of such professional services), although trustees of a charity (other than an exempt charity) must act in accordance with any guidance given by the Charity Commissioners[14]. Trustees may appoint one of themselves if a trust corporation, or two or more of themselves acting jointly[15].

The terms of appointment are such terms as to remuneration and other matters as the trustees may determine[16]. However, unless it is objectively reasonably necessary for them to do so, they must not include terms permitting the nominee or custodian to appoint a substitute, or restricting the liability of the nominee or custodian or his substitute to the trustees or to any beneficiary, or permitting the nominee or custodian to act in circumstances capable of giving rise to a conflict of interest[17].

It will be wise to have written evidence recording why the trustees considered it reasonably necessary to include any of the proscribed terms in case there arises the question of fact as to whether or not such terms were at that time reasonably necessary. The trustees are only allowed to remunerate the nominee or custodian out of trust funds if there is a term for payment of remuneration and the amount does not exceed such remuneration as is objectively reasonable in the circumstances for the provision of the relevant services[18]. The trustees may reimburse the nominee or custodian out of trust funds for any expenses properly incurred by him acting as such[19].

If the trustees fail to act within the limits of the above statutory powers in appointing a nominee or custodian this does not invalidate the appoint-

---

9 TA 2000, s 17. The powers in ss 16 and 17 are additional to any express powers: s 26(a).

10 Settled Land Act trustees' investments (other than land vested in the tenant for life) can thus be vested in a custodian.

11 TA 2000, s 18. Under s 25 (2) there is no such duty on a sole trustee if it be a trust corporation. Where there are two trustees, one of which is a trust corporation, they can appoint the trust corporation to be custodian of bearer securities: s 19(5).

12 TA 2000, s 19(1) and (2).

13 TA 2000, s 19(6) and (7).

14 TA 2000, s 19(4).

15 TA 2000, s 19(5).

16 TA 2000, s 20(1).

17 TA 2000, s 20(2).

18 TA 2000, s 32(2). The excess amount will have to be paid by the trustees out of their own pockets.

19 TA 2000, s 32(3).

ment[20], so protecting persons dealing with the appointee, but the trustees remain liable to the beneficiaries for acting beyond their powers.

Duty of care

The statutory duty of care applies[1] (subject to contrary intention in the trust instrument[2]) to a trustee when 'entering into arrangements' under which a person is appointed as agent, nominee or custodian under the Trustee Act 2000 powers or any other powers (eg in the trust instrument) and when carrying out the duty to review the arrangements and how they are being put into effect. 'Entering into arrangements' includes selecting the person who is to act and determining the terms on which he is to act[3].

In reviewing matters, if circumstances make it appropriate to do so, the trustees must consider whether there is a need to intervene by giving directions or even by revoking the arrangements and, if there is such a need, they must so intervene[4].

A trustee is not liable for any act or default of the agent nominee or custodian unless he personally failed to comply with the above duty of care[5].

Restriction or exclusion of statutory provisions

Not only the statutory duty of care can be ousted[6] (up to the point of excluding liability for all breaches of trust except dishonest or reckless breaches[7]) but the power-conferring provisions concerning nominees, custodians and agents are subject to any restriction or exclusion imposed by the trust instrument[8], while the reviewing duties and liabilities in ss 22 and 23 are capable of being ousted by inconsistent terms in the trust instrument or subordinate legislation[9].

PARAGRAPH 10

Delegation of asset management functions

Where trustees are not themselves skilled portfolio managers they may very well prefer to delegate discretionary portfolio management, rather than making their own discretionary decisions after having obtained and considered proper advice[10], leaving them leeway necessitating the exercise of

---

20 TA 2000, s 24.
 1 TA 2000, Sch 1, para 3(1).
 2 TA 2000, Sch 1, para 7.
 3 TA 2000, Sch 1, para 3(2).
 4 TA 2000, s 22(1), (4), unless ousted by inconsistent terms in the trust instrument: s 21(3).
 5 TA 2000, s 23, unless ousted as above.
 6 TA 2000, Sch 1, para 7.
 7 *Armitage v Nurse* [1998] Ch 241.
 8 TA 2000, s 26(b). Also by s 26(a) the statutory powers only need be relied upon if no express power is available eg to employ nominees, custodians and agents on whatever terms the trustees honestly believe to be appropriate to help them fulfil their investment functions.
 9 TA 2000, s 21(3).
10 TA 2000, s 5.

some discretion[11]. A discretionary portfolio manager can then make and implement decisions instantaneously at a particular market price, without needing to consult the trustees, by which time the market could well have moved against them.

Before the Trustee Act 2000 came into force on 1 February 2001 there was no power to employ a discretionary portfolio manager unless there was an express power in the trust instrument[12] or unless s 25 of the Trustee Act 1925[13] was exploited to permit delegation of discretions by power of attorney for up to twelve months at a time (though there was then automatic liability for the acts or defaults of the delegate)[14].

The Trustee Act 2000, taking inspiration from the Pensions Act 1995[15], now authorises delegation of the 'asset management functions' of trustees[16] consisting of 'the investment of assets subject to the trust, the acquisition of property which is to be subject to the trust, and managing property which is subject to the trust and disposing of, or creating or disposing of an interest in, such property'. However, before authorising a delegate to exercise any such functions, they must have prepared a 'policy statement' and the agreement in, or evidenced in, writing must include a term requiring compliance with such statement or any revised statement after a regular review.

This power, therefore, does not arise unless and until the policy statement has been prepared and there is some writing containing a term for securing compliance with such statement. However, a failure by the trustees to act within the limits of the powers capable of being conferred[17] by the Trustee Act 2000 in authorising a person to exercise any function of theirs as an agent does not invalidate the authorisation[18].

An express power to delegate asset management functions that is broader than the statutory power, not containing the restrictions attached to the statutory power, may be relied upon by the trustees, the statutory power being in addition to express powers[19]. Alternatively, it seems that the trust instrument may impose a restriction or exclusion on the statutory power to delegate[20].

In deciding whether or not to exercise their powers of delegation the trustees can suit themselves and do not need to prove it was reasonably necessary or in the best interests of the beneficiaries. However, once they have decided to delegate they come under extensive duties of care in selecting and supervising such delegates as dealt with below in Article 55.

---

11 If the adviser came up with 'take it or leave it' advice which the trustees always took, they would be very vulnerable to the allegation that they had wrongfully delegated investment management to the adviser and had not consciously exercised their own discretion.
12 Hence the need for applications to the court under TA 1925, s 57 to obtain the requisite powers eg *Anker-Petersen v Anker-Petersen* [2000] WTLR 581.
13 As substituted by Powers of Attorney Act 1971, s 9(2).
14 TA 2000, s 25(5).
15 Pensions Act 1995, ss 34–36.
16 TA 2000, ss 11 and 15.
17 If they were actually conferred there would be no *ultra vires* problem.
18 TA 2000, s 24. The delegate may however be liable for dishonestly assisting in a breach of trust if having actual, Nelsonian or naughty knowledge (see p 974 post) of failure to comply with the statutory requirements.
19 TA 2000, s 26(a).
20 TA 2000, s 26(b).

ARTICLE 54

Duty of trustee to see that he transfers trust property only to beneficiaries or to objects of a power of appointment or only to persons authorised under the trust instrument or the general law to receive such property (eg as custodian or portfolio manager)

(1) The responsibility of handing the trust property to the persons entitled lies upon the trustee, so that if he acts beyond his powers his accounts are falsified. However, if he acts within his powers (eg in transferring trust property to a nominee, custodian or discretionary portfolio manager) his accounts can only be surcharged to the extent that but for his failure to observe some equitable or statutory duty the trust fund would not have suffered the particular loss in question. Formerly neither mistake[1] nor fraud[2] afforded any excuse against the strict liability arising upon falsification of conduct that was beyond the trustee's powers, but now the court has power to excuse such a mistake made honestly and reasonably[3], and by section 27 of the Trustee Act 1925 a trustee is granted further protection by giving notice by advertisement. Nevertheless, in cases of doubt the trustee should apply to the court for its direction[4]. To deal with problems otherwise arising in the case of legitimated or adopted persons some statutory protection is granted to trustees and personal representatives[5];

(2) if, however, the person who is really entitled to trust property is not the beneficiary who appears on the face of the settlement (but someone who claims through him), and the trustees have neither express nor constructive notice of such derivative title, they cannot be made to pay over again[6];

(3) on the other hand, if they have notice of the derivative title, they cannot refuse to pay to the person entitled under it on the ground that such title has been improperly obtained and is liable to be set aside[7], unless it is on the face of it prima facie voidable, or is the result of an appointment under a power in the trust instrument which they suspect is a fraud on the power.

---

1 *Re Hulkes* (1886) 33 Ch D 552. As to fraud, see *Re Bennison* (1889) 60 LT 859. See comments, p 585, ante.

2 *Eaves v Hickson* (1861) 30 Beav 136.

3 If the court also feels he ought fairly to be excused for omitting to obtain the directions of the court. TA 1925, s 61; as to which see Article 95, post.

4 *Talbot v Earl of Radnor* (1834) 3 My & K 252; *Merlin v Blagrave* (1858) 25 Beav 125; *Ashby v Blackwell* (1765) 2 Eden 299; *Eaves v Hickson* (1861) 30 Beav 136; *Sporle v Barnaby* (1864) 10 Jur NS 1142.

5 Adoption Act 1976, s 45; Legitimacy Act 1976, s 7.

6 *Cothay v Sydenham* (1788) 2 Bro CC 391; *Leslie v Baillie* (1843) 2 Y & C Ch Cas 91; *Re Lord Southampton's Estate* (1880) 16 Ch D 178.

7 *Devey v Thornton* (1851) 9 Hare 222 at 231.

Paragraph 1

Duty to inform beneficiaries of their interests

Trustees are under a fundamental primary duty to distribute the trust property only to a beneficiary or object of a power of appointment, and to the right beneficiary or object and only to transfer trust property to another person if they have power under the trust instrument or the general law to do so (eg so as to avail themselves of the services of a discretionary portfolio manager or a custodian). For such duty to be an enforceable meaningful obligation[8], a beneficiary of full age and capacity has a right to be told by the trustees that he is a beneficiary[9] and, indeed, a right to be told by the settlor the name and address of the trustees to whom demands for accounts and requests for discretionary distributions can be sent[10]. Every beneficiary is entitled to see the trust accounts, with a view to falsification of such accounts if trust property has been transferred to a person who is not a beneficiary or an object of a power of appointment or who is not an authorised managerial or administrative recipient, such as a portfolio manager or a custodian. It matters not that the beneficiary's interest is vested or contingent, or in possession or not, or that of a beneficiary under a discretionary trust[11]. However, whether or not a mere object of a power of appointment has a right to see the accounts and to bring an action of account depends upon the settlor's intention, so such right may be excluded expressly or by necessary implication[12].

Trustees are not, however, required to give the beneficiaries legal advice or to inform them of rights such as a right to sever a joint tenancy[13]. Executors have been held to be under no duty to inform will beneficiaries of their interests since wills are open to public inspection[14] but there is much to be said for the view that once the executors completed their administration so as to become trustees[15], and certainly once they have assented to property vesting in themselves or others as trustees, then the trustees should be in the same position as trustees of inter vivos trusts.

Payment under a forged document

Where a trustee made a payment to one who produced a forged authority from the beneficiary, it was held that the trustee and not the beneficiary had to bear the loss, for, as was said by Lord Northington[16]:

---

8 Cf *Scally v Southern Health & Social Services Board* [1992] 1 AC 294, 304–306.
9 *Hawkesley v May* [1956] 1 QB 304, 332. Further see Article 60, post.
10 *Re Murphy's Settlement* [1998] 3 All ER 1.
11 *Armitage v Nurse* [1998] Ch 241 at 253 and 261; *Re Tillott* [1892] 1 Ch 86; *A-G of Ontario v Stavro* (1994) 119 DLR (4th) 750; *Re Murphy's Settlement* [1998] 3 All ER 1.
12 *Re Angora Trust* [2001] WTLR 1081. In ordinary family discretionary trusts where objects of the power of appointment are family members the settlor will be presumed to intend them to have accounting rights although they may also have such rights as contingent discretionary beneficiaries: *Spellson v George* (1987) 11 NSWLR 300 at 315–316; *Re Murphy's Settlement* [1998] 3 All ER 1 at 3 and 9.
13 *Hawksley v May* [1956] 1 QB 304, [1955] 3 All ER 353 on which see (1970) 34 Conv 29 (A Samuels).
14 *Re Mackay* [1906] 1 Ch 25.
15 *Re Cockburn* [1957] Ch 438.
16 *Ashby v Blackwell* (1765) 2 Eden 299; but see *Re Smith* (1902) 71 LJ Ch 411.

'A trustee, whether he be a private person or a body corporate, must see to the reality of the authority empowering him to dispose of the trust money; for if the transfer is made without the authority of the owner, the act is a nullity.'

So, again, trustees who paid over the trust fund to wrong persons, upon the faith of a forged marriage certificate, were made responsible for so much of the trust fund as could not be recovered from those who had wrongfully received it[17], or from the father responsible for altering the marriage certificate so as to make his children appear to be legitimate and thus be beneficiaries.

The question whether an honest and reasonable mistake as to the nature of a forged document, or as to the construction of an obscure one, would now be excused under s 61 of the Trustee Act 1925, is discussed in Article 95, post.

Non-delegable nature of distributive functions of trustees

Section 11(2)(a) of the Trustee Act 2000 does not authorise trustees to delegate any functions relating to whether, or in what way, any assets of the trust should be distributed to beneficiaries or to objects of powers of appointment. Thus it is solely the responsibility of the trustees to distribute trust assets correctly subject to any protection from an exemption clause or relief from the court under the Trustee Act 1925, s 61.

Transfer to unauthorised person

If trustees or executors with no authority to entrust trust funds to the management of a third party do so entrust the funds and a loss is sustained, then such trustees or executors 'will be forced to make it good, however unexpected the result, however little likely to arise from the course adopted and however free such conduct may have been from any improper motive'[18]. Mitigation of such strict liability may be possible under s 61 of the Trustee Act 1925 or by a clause in the trust instrument exempting trustees from liability for negligence if the conduct be negligent rather than reckless or deliberate.

Duty to pay at right time on satisfaction of a condition

Where a solicitor holding a lender's money on trust to pay it over on the completion of a purchase by the borrower and in return for receiving documentary security, deliberately in breach of trust paid the money over to the borrower ten days early, he became strictly liable to replace such money. However, falsification of accounts ceased to be available when three weeks later completion of the purchase took place and the solicitor obtained the required documentary security for the lender. To surcharge the accounts it was necessary to show that but for the early payment the alleged loss would not have occurred: a trial would be necessary to establish this so the application for summary judgment was rejected by the House of Lords[19].

---

17 *Eaves v Hickson* (1861) 30 Beav 136; and see also *Bostock v Floyer* (1865) LR 1 Eq 26; and *Sutton v Wilders* (1871) LR 12 Eq 373.
18 *Clough v Bond* (1838) 3 My & Cr 490 at 496–497.
19 *Target Holdings Ltd v Redferns* [1996] AC 421 as explained by Lord Millett in (1998) 114 LQR 214 at 225–227. The plaintiff simply had claimed the £1,500,000 loan less the £500,000 received on selling the property which had been fraudulently valued at £2 million.

Statutory protection for illegitimate, legitimated and adopted persons

Where illegitimate persons or their relatives are entitled to property by reason of ss 14 to 16 of the Family Law Reform Act 1969 protection was afforded under s 17 thereof to trustees and personal representatives who, without notice of a claim, distributed the property without having ascertained that no person was entitled under ss 14 to 16. However, s 17 has been repealed in the belief that protection by advertisement under s 27 of the Trustee Act 1925 should be sufficient[20].

However, a trustee or personal representative is not under a duty to inquire before distributing any property whether any adoption had been effected or revoked or whether any person is illegitimate or has been adopted by one of his natural parents or could be legitimated (or, if deceased, treated as legitimated) if that fact could affect entitlement to the property[1]. The fiduciary is not to be liable for any distribution of property made without regard to any such fact if he has not received notice thereof before such distribution[2].

None of the above statutory protection afforded to trustees and personal representatives is to prejudice the right of any person to follow the property, or any property representing it, into the hands of another person, other than a purchaser, who has received it[3].

Mistake as to construction of settlement

A trustee who, by mistake, pays the capital to the tenant for life, instead of investing it and paying him the income only, will in general have to make good the loss to the estate, although he will, as will be seen hereafter, be entitled to be recouped out of the life estate[4]. Similarly, trustees who had distributed a trust fund upon what turned out to be an erroneous, although bona fide, construction of the trust instrument were formerly always held liable to refund the property distributed, together with interest thereon at 4%[5], and this notwithstanding that they have acted under the advice of counsel[6]. But now the court has power[7], which it will exercise in a proper case, of excusing a trustee who has acted on legal advice in such a case[8].

Reliance on counsel's opinion and court authorisation

Where a question of construction has arisen out of the terms of a will or a trust and an opinion in writing of a barrister of at least ten years' standing has been obtained thereon by the personal representatives or trustees, then such persons can safely proceed to take such steps in reliance on the opinion as

---

20 Family Law Reform Act 1987, s 20 commented upon by G. Miller [1988] Conv 410 at 417–419.
1 Adoption Act 1976, s 45; Legitimacy Act 1976, s 7.
2 Adoption Act 1976, s 45; Legitimacy Act 1976, s 7.
3 Adoption Act 1976, s 45(3); Legitimacy Act 1976, s 7(3).
4 *Barratt v Wyatt* (1862) 30 Beav 442; *Davies v Hodgson* (1858) 25 Beav 177; *Griffiths v Porter* (1858) 25 Beav 236.
5 *Hilliard v Fulford* (1876) 4 Ch D 389; and see also *Re Ward* (1878) 47 LJ Ch 781; and *Re Hulkes* (1886) 33 Ch D 552.
6 See *National Trustees Co of Australasia v General Finance Co of Australasia* [1905] AC 373.
7 Under s 61 of the TA 1925. See Article 95, post.
8 *Re Allsop* [1914] 1 Ch 1, CA.

the High Court specifies without hearing argument[9]. The High Court will not make an order under this summary procedure if it appears that a dispute exists which would make it inappropriate for the court to make the order without hearing argument[10].

Protection by means of advertisements

Trustees and personal representatives may protect themselves against their strict liability by advertising for 'interested' persons (viz beneficiaries[11] and creditors of the estate) whose claims they are not aware of, although, oddly, the statutory protection does not extend to trusts of property not comprising any land[12] and not subject to a trust for sale. By s 27 of the Trustee Act 1925, as amended by the substitution of the words between square brackets in sub-s (1), by the Law of Property (Amendment) Act 1926, s 7 and Schedule, it is enacted as follows:

(1) With a view to the conveyance to or distribution among the persons entitled to any real or personal property, the trustees of a settlement, trustees of land, trustees for sale of personal property or personal representatives, may give notice by advertisement[13] in the Gazette, and [in a newspaper circulating in the district in which the land is situated], and such other like notices, including notices elsewhere than in England and Wales, as would, in any special case, have been directed by a court of competent jurisdiction in an action for administration, of their intention to make such conveyance or distribution as aforesaid, and requiring any person interested to send to the trustees or personal representatives within the time, not being less than two months, fixed in the notice or, where more than one notice is given, in the last of the notices, particulars of his claim in respect of the property or any part thereof to which the notice relates.

(2) At the expiration of the time fixed by the notice the trustees or personal representatives may convey or distribute the property or any part thereof to which the notice relates, to or among the persons entitled thereto, having regard only to the claims, whether formal or not, of which the trustees and personal representatives then had notice and shall not, as respects the property so conveyed or distributed, be liable to any person of whose claim the trustees or personal representatives have not had notice at the time of conveyance or distribution; but nothing in this section—

    (a) prejudices the right of any person to follow the property, or any property representing the same, into the hands of any person, other than a purchaser, who may have received it; or

    (b) frees the trustees or personal representatives from any obligation to make searches or obtain official certificates of search similar to those which an intending purchaser would be advised to make or obtain.

(3) This section applies notwithstanding anything to the contrary in the will or other instrument, if any, creating the trust.

Application may be made to the court in the administration of the estate of a deceased person for an inquiry what notices or advertisements should be

---

9 Administration of Justice Act 1985, s 48(1). See Practice Direction – Pt 8, section A, paras A.1(1) and A.2(1) and CDPD 12, section A.

10 Administration of Justice Act 1985, s 48(2).

11 *Re Aldhous* [1955] 2 All ER 80, [1955] 1 WLR 459.

12 Trustees are 'trustees of land' if any part of the trust property is land: TLATA 1996, s 1(1)(b).

13 The advertisement should follow accurately the wording of the statute and should indicate that it is not only the claims of creditors but also those of beneficiaries which are required to be sent in (*Re Aldhous* [1955] 2 All ER 80, [1955] 1 WLR 459). For a form to use, see *Law Society's Gazette*, for July 1955, p 307; 42 *Encycl Forms & Precedents* (5th edn) Form 537.

issued in a special case[14]; a like application may, it is thought, properly be made by trustees seeking to avail themselves of the protection of s 27, above, in a case where the circumstances are special.

Payment under a power of attorney

Section 29 of the Trustee Act 1925 used specifically to provide protection for trustees making a distribution to an agent of a beneficiary. Now the section has been repealed and the position is governed generally by s 5 of the Powers of Attorney Act 1971 which is as follows:

> 5(1) A donee of a power of attorney who acts in pursuance of the power at a time when it has been revoked shall not, by reason of the revocation, incur any liability (either to the donor or to any other person) if at that time he did not know that the power had been revoked.
>
> (2) Where a power of attorney has been revoked and a person [eg a trustee or executor], without knowledge of the revocation, deals with the donee of the power, the transaction between them shall, in favour of that person, be as valid as if the power had then been in existence.
>
> (3) Where the power is expressed in the instrument creating it to be irrevocable and to be given by way of security then, unless the person dealing with the donee knows that it was not in fact given by way of security, he shall be entitled to assume that the power is incapable of revocation except by the donor acting with the consent of the donee and shall accordingly be treated for the purposes of subsection (2) of this section as having knowledge of the recovation only if he knows that it has been revoked in that manner.
>
> (4) Where the interest of a purchaser depends on whether a transaction between the donee of a power of attorney and another person was valid by virtue of subsection (2) of this section, it shall be conclusively presumed in favour of the purchaser that that person did not at the material time know of the revocation of the power if—
>
>   (a) the transaction between that person and the donee was completed within twelve months of the date on which the power came into operation; or
>
>   (b) that person makes a statutory declaration, before or within three months after the completion of the purchase, that he did not at the material time know of the revocation of the power.
>
> (5) Without prejudice to subsection (3) of this section, for the purposes of this section knowledge of the revocation of a power of attorney includes knowledge of the occurrence of any event (such as the death of the donor) which has the effect of revoking the power.

PARAGRAPH 2

Trustees not bound to know of derivative title

In *Leslie v Baillie*[15] a testator who died, and whose will was proved in England, bequeathed a legacy to a married woman whose domicile, as well as that of her husband, was in Scotland. The husband died a few months after the testator. After his decease, the executors of the testator paid the legacy to the widow. It was proved that, according to Scots law, the payment should have

---

14 *Re Letherbrow* [1935] WN 34; *Re Holden* [1935] WN 52. Where it is impracticable to advertise in a foreign country where the deceased resided the court may authorise distribution without advertisements there: *Re Gess* [1942] Ch 37.

15 (1843) 2 Y & C Ch Cas 91; and see also *Re Cull's Trusts* (1875) LR 20 Eq 561.

been made to the husband's personal representatives. It was, however, held that, in the absence of proof that the executors of the settlor knew the Scots law on the subject, the payment to the widow was a good payment.

Where B is a person entitled in default of an appointment by the life tenant who has died, then the trustees can safely pay the trust fund to B if the life tenant's solicitor swears that to his knowledge no appointment was ever made[16]. If a power of appointment has been exercised, apparently properly, in favour of Y so that the trustees, having made reasonable inquiries, pay the trust funds to Y, then the trustees will not be liable to pay the money again to Z if it turns out there was a prior appointment in Z's favour[17].

Disputes between beneficial claimants

Trustees are not bound to hand over the trust fund to the mortgagee of their beneficiary, where accounts are pending between the mortgagee and mortgagor[18].

Effect of not searching for notices of incumbrances

On the other hand, a new trustee is liable to make good moneys paid by him bona fide to a beneficiary, if the papers relating to the trust include a notice of an incumbrance created by that beneficiary depriving him of the right to receive the money[19], and so is a trustee who dispenses with an investigation of the title of an alleged assign whose title is in fact bad[20]. Kekewich J held that this is none the less so if the alleged assign is the trustee's own solicitor[1], on the ground that if the trustee had acquainted himself, as he was bound to do with the trust documents and papers, he would have found what the true state of the case was. But the Court of Appeal has since held[2] that at all events it would be good ground for excusing the trustee from the consequences of such a technical breach under section 61 of the Trustee Act 1925, as to which see Article 95, post. Where no amount of search would have disclosed the notice, the trustee would, of course, not be liable.

Trustee not entitled to the deed of assignment

Where a person claims as the assign of a beneficiary, it might be thought that the trustee would, on payment, be entitled to the custody of the deed of assignment as evidence of authority for paying the assign. But this is not so[3],

---

16 *Re Cull's Trusts* (1875) LR 20 Eq 561.

17 *Cothay v Sydenham* (1788) 2 Bro CC 391: cf *Re Lord Southampton's Estate* (1880) 16 Ch D 178. It could be submitted that this situation falls within Art 54 para 1 for it is difficult to distinguish between a payment made on the faith of a void forged marriage certificate and a payment made on the faith of a void appointment in favour of Y. In any event a trustee in such a case should have the protection of TA 1925, s 61 if not protected by an exemption clause.

18 *Hockey v Western* [1898] 1 Ch 350.

19 *Hallows v Lloyd* (1888) 39 Ch D 686. This is so even where the trustees have a discretion to pay the income to or for the benefit of the assignor, 'his wife or children', if they do in fact pay it to the assignor: *Re Neil* (1890) 62 LT 649; *Lord v Bunn* (1843) 2 Y & C Ch Cas 98. See also *Burrowes v Lock* (1805) 10 Ves 470; and *Re Coleman* (1888) 39 Ch D 443.

20 *Davis v Hutchings* [1907] 1 Ch 356.

1 *Davis v Hutchings* [1907] 1 Ch 356.

2 *Re Allsop* [1914] 1 Ch 1.

3 *Re Palmer* [1907] 1 Ch 486.

although it would seem that he is entitled to the statutory acknowledgment for production and undertaking for safe custody, and he would be wise also to take an attested copy. As Swinfen Eady J said in *Re Palmer*[4]:

'Where money is paid by a trustee to a person who receives it under a power of attorney, the trustee cannot claim that the power of attorney should be given up to him. It was said that the trustee would be in a very unfortunate position if an action were brought against him for the fund and he had not the deeds; but it might equally be said that the company [the assigns] would be in a very unfortunate position if they handed over the deeds and the assignor disputed the assignment and brought an action against the company to set it aside.'

PARAGRAPH 3

Whether a trustee is to investigate where he merely suspects mala fides by assignee of beneficiary

The question of how far a trustee can refuse to pay an assign where he suspects unfair dealing, is by no means easy.

It appears to be well settled, that, where his beneficiary is dead, he cannot refuse to pay his personal representative on the ground that he obtained probate or administration unfairly[5]. It is for other persons interested to take action in such a case, and not the trustee.

The same principle also seems to apply to an assignment inter vivos. It is not for the trustee to question its validity if the assignor does not do so. If the deed is not a forgery it stands good until it is cancelled by the court, and it cannot be cancelled by the court at the instance of the trustee[6]. This class of cases would, it seems, cover assignments and mortgages by reversioners where the trustees may suspect unfair dealing or undue influence.

But the problem becomes much more difficult when we approach transactions which are either:

(1) prima facie invalid, or
(2) appointments in the exercise of powers contained in the trust instrument.

Generally where a reasonable doubt arises as to the claimant's title the prudent course is to apply to the court for directions. If the trustee is forced to defend a claim he could well be at risk of being ordered personally to pay the costs of both sides[7] or of being deprived of a right to reimburse his own costs from the trust fund[8].

Trustee bound to investigate where instrument is prima facie invalid

(1) With regard to instruments prima facie invalid, one may take, as typical, an assignment, whether voluntary or for value, by a beneficiary to one of the trustees. It is apprehended that in such a case the other trustees would not only be justified, but bound, to refuse payment to their co-trustee without an order of the court; for res ipsa loquitur and the deed, on the face of it,

4 [1907] 1 Ch 486 at 488.
5 *Devey v Thornton* (1851) 9 Hare 222 at 226.
6 *Devey v Thornton* (1851) 9 Hare 222 at 226.
7 *Re Knox's Trusts* [1895] 2 Ch 483; *Moss v Integro Trust (BVI) Ltd* (1998) 1 OFLR 427.
8 *Griffin v Brady* (1869) 39 LJ Ch 136.

cannot be supported without some outside evidence that the parties were at arms' length, and that no unfair advantage was taken by the assign. Anyhow, it is scarcely open to doubt that, in such a case, the co-trustee would be justified in seeking the direction of the court.

Trustee suspecting a fraud on a power

(2) Where the trustee has reasonable ground for suspicion that an appointment made by a predecessor or a third party is a fraud on a power[9] in the trust instrument, he certainly ought not to pay without the direction of the court. For, as pointed out by Farwell LJ in *Cloutte v Storey*[10], an appointee can only claim an equitable right if the appointment is valid. If it is not valid it passes nothing, and the property remains the property of the person who takes in default of appointment. It is, therefore, the duty of a trustee to satisfy himself that an alleged appointment is valid before acting on it; and if he has reasonable doubts, he is not only justified in acting but bound to act under the direction of the court[11].

One may perhaps ask: if a fraudulent appointment is futile and void ab initio, is not a trustee who acts upon it, although without knowledge of the fraud, paying to the wrong beneficiary, and if so, are his accounts not falsified so that he is stricly liable? It is apprehended that this would be so but for the possibility of relief under s 61 of the Trustee Act 1925, as it is difficult to distinguish between a payment made on the faith of a fraudulent certificate of marriage, and one made on the faith of an appointment which turns out to be fraudulent. There can, however, be no reasonable doubt that under s 61, a trustee who innocently, and reasonably, assumed the bona fides of an appointment would be excused[12] if not already protected by a broad exemption clause.

ARTICLE 55

Duty of trustees not to delegate their duties or powers unless authorised

1 Trustees must not collectively delegate their duties or powers either to a stranger or to a beneficiary or to a co-trustee[13], unless authorised

---

9 Essentially an appointment is a fraud on a power if made for a corrupt or foreign purpose outside the intended scope of the power: further see *Lawrie v Bankes* (1858) 4 K & J 142; *Vatcher v Paull* [1915] AC 372, HL; *Re Crawshay* [1948] Ch 123 at 133 et seq, CA; *Re Simpson* [1952] Ch 412; but see *Re Burton's Settlement* [1955] Ch 82, [1954] 3 All ER 193. The doctrine of frauds on powers does not apply to an exercise of a power of revocation contained in a revocable appointment: *Re Greaves' Will Trusts* [1954] Ch 434. As to frauds on a power in relation to the Variation of Trusts Act 1958, see p 518, ante.

10 [1911] 1 Ch 18 at 32 and 33; and see *Duke of Portland v Topham* (1864) 11 HL Cas 32; and see order thereon, Seton on Judgments (7th edn) p 1672; and see also *Hopkins v Myall* (1830) 2 Russ & M 86; *Cocker v Quayle* (1830) 1 Russ & M 535; *Reid v Thompson and M'Namara* (1851) 2 1 Ch R 26; *Cochrane v Cochrane* [1922] 2 Ch 230.

11 See *Hannah v Hodgson* (1861) 30 Beav 19; *King v King* (1857) 1 De G & J 663.

12 See *Re Smith* (1902) 71 LJ Ch 411; *Re Allsop* [1914] 1 Ch 1; and Art 95, post.

13 *Adams v Clifton* (1826) 1 Russ 297; *Chambers v Minchin* (1802) 7 Ves 186; *Wood v Weightman* (1872) LR 13 Eq 434; *Re Bellamy and Metropolitan Board of Works* (1883) 24 Ch D 387; *Langford v Gascoyne* (1805) 11 Ves 333; *Clough v Bond* (1838) 3 My & Cr 490; *Cowell v Gatcombe* (1859) 27 Beav 568; *Eaves v Hickson* (1861) 30 Beav 136; *Re Flower and Metropolitan Board of Works* (1884) 27 Ch D 592.

by the settlement[14], except in the following cases, namely:
(a) they may engage and pay reasonable remuneration[15] to a person to act as nominee or custodian under sections 16 to 20 of the Trustee Act 2000, as already discussed within Article 53;
(b) subject to (c), (d) and (e), they may engage and pay reasonable remuneration to any person (including a co-trustee[16] but not a beneficiary[17]) as agent to exercise any or all of their 'delegable functions' which in the case of a trust other than a charitable trust, consist of any function other than[18]
    (i)   any functions relating to whether or in what way any assets of the trust should be distributed,
    (ii) any power to decide whether any fees or other payment due to be made out of the trust funds should be made out of income or capital,
    (iii) any power to appoint a person to be a trustee of the trust, or
    (iv) any power conferred by any other enactment or the trust instrument which permits the trustee to delegate any of their functions or to appoint a person to act as a nominee or custodian,
   but in the case of a charitable trust consist of[19]
    (i)   any function consisting of carrying out a decision the trustees have taken,
    (ii) any function relating to the investment of assets subject to the trust,
    (iii) any function relating to the raising of funds for the trust otherwise than by means of profits of a trade which is an integral part of carrying out the trusts charitable purposes, and
    (iv) any other function prescribed by an order made by the Secretary of State;
(c) they may not authorise a person to act as agent on terms permitting the agent to appoint a substitute or to act in circumstances capable of giving rise to a conflict of interest or restricting the liability of the agent or his substitute to the trustees or any beneficiary, unless it is reasonably necessary for them to do so[20];
(d) in the case of asset management functions, they may not delegate except by an agreement which is in, or evidenced in, writing[1] and unless[2]
    (i)   they have prepared a policy statement, in, or evidenced in

---

14 *Kilbee v Sneyd* (1828) 2 Moll 186; *Doyle v Blake* (1804) 2 Sch & Lef 231; *Re Airey* [1897] 1 Ch 164 at 170. For delegation via the exercise of a special power of appointment see Article 82 below.
15 TA 2000, s 32.
16 TA 2000, s 12(1).
17 TA 2000, s 12(3).
18 TA 2000, s 11(2).
19 TA 2000, s 11(3).
20 TA 2000, s 14(2).
 1 TA 2000, s 15(1).
 2 TA 2000, s 15(2).

writing, giving guidance as to how the functions should be exercised, and

(ii) there is a term in the agreement that the agent will secure compliance with the policy statement and any revised or replacement policy statement;

(e) in the case of trusts of land, they may, by power of attorney, delegate to any beneficiary or beneficiaries of full age and beneficially entitled to an interest in possession in land subject to the trust, any of their functions as trustees which relate to the land, the beneficiary or beneficiaries then being in the same position as the trustees as to duties and liabilities except for the purpose of any enactment permitting the delegation of functions by trustees or imposing requirements relating to receipts for capital money[3].

2 (a) Except in respect of delegation under (e) above, trustees owe no duty of care in deciding whether or not to exercise their statutory or express powers of delegation, but they do owe a duty of care (unless ousted in the trust instrument[4]) when entering into arrangements[5] for delegating to agents, nominees or custodians under statutory or express powers and when carrying out[6] their duty[7] to review the arrangements under which such delegates act (including the policy statement for asset management) with a view to intervening if need be; they will not be personally liable for any act or default of the agent, nominee or custodian unless they failed to comply with their duty of care[8].

(b) In respect of trustees of land delegating by power of attorney to currently entitled beneficiaries, the trustees are under a duty of care in deciding whether to delegate any of their functions on particular terms[9] and, if they delegate, they are under a duty to keep the delegation under review[10] with a view to intervening if need be, a duty of care applying[11] to such reviewing duty; they will not be personally liable for any act or default of the beneficiary unless they failed to comply with their duty of care[12].

3 Each trustee individually may by power of attorney[13] delegate for a period not exceeding twelve months the execution or exercise of all or any of the trusts, powers and discretions vested in him as trustee[14]: he

---

3 TLATA 1996, s 9.
4 TA 2000, Sch 1, para 7.
5 TA 2000, Sch 1, para 3(1)(a)–(d).
6 TA 2000, Sch 1, para 3(1)(e).
7 TA 2000, s 22, unless ousted by trust instrument: TA 2000, s 21(3).
8 TA 2000, s 23(1).
9 TA 2000, Sch 2, para 47 inserting s 9A into the TLATA 1996.
10 TLATA 1996, s 9A(3).
11 TLATA 1996, s 9A(5).
12 TLATA 1996, s 9A(6).
13 The Trustee Delegation Act 1999, ss 1, 2 and 3 makes special provision for co-owners of land so that a trustee with a beneficial co-ownership interest in trust land can simply grant a power of attorney under the Powers of Attorney Act 1971 or an enduring power to his co-owner, but s 7 requires compliance with the Law of Property Act 1925, ss 2 and 27.
14 TA 1925, s 25 as substituted by the Trustee Delegation Act 1999, s 5.

is, however, liable for the acts or defaults of the donee of the power of attorney as if they were his own acts or defaults[15].

The original position

Originally the rule was strictly observed that an agent could only be properly employed where such employment was expressly authorised by the settlement, or where ex necessitate rei it was impossible for the trustee satisfactorily to do the act himself[16], or where the act was merely ministerial and employment of an agent was not the delegation of a function but the performance of a function though an agent, normally necessary or in the ordinary course of affairs from the point of view of a prudent man of business[17]. The care of a prudent businessman had to be exercised in the choice of agent (who had to be employed within the scope of his expertise[18]) and in the supervision of the agent[19]. An express or statutory provision authorising wider use of agents and exempting a trustee from liability for loss caused by the acts or defaults of an agent unless the loss occurred by reason of the trustee's 'wilful default' did not relieve the trustee of his duty to exercise the care of the prudent man of business in the appointment and in the supervision of agents: a beneficiary's action would still succeed if he could prove 'wilful default which includes want of ordinary prudence on the part of the trustees' as where trustees negligently appointed an unsuitable agent or negligently supervised an agent[20].

The effect of the Trustee Act 1925

The Trustee Act 1925 radically enlarged trustees' collective powers to delegate implementation of their decisions[1], but not their own discretionary decision-making powers to agents. Section 23 enabled them to delegate, whether or not there was any reasonable need for this, so lazy trustees could even delegate matters they could have seen to personally. It was clear that, as before, trustees who in good faith employed an agent whom they had power to employ under the general law or s 23, would not be automatically liable for the acts or defaults of such agent. It was, however, uncertain whether trustees still owed a duty to select and supervise such agents with the care of a prudent businessman[2].

Traditionalists considered such duty continued after 1925 so that trustees would still be personally liable if themselves personally guilty of wilful default in the traditional equitable sense which covered deliberate, reckless and negligent conduct.

Modernists, believing in a literal, rather than an historical interpretation of

---

15 TA 1925, s 25(7).

16 For example, trusts of property in the far-flung British Empire where a local manager could run huge plantations and make maintenance payments for beneficiaries out there who were children: recognised in TA 1925, s 23(2).

17 *Speight v Gaunt* (1883) 9 App Cas 1; *Re Parsons, ex p Belchier* (1754) Amb 218.

18 *Fry v Tapson* (1884) 28 Ch D 268.

19 *Re Weall* (1889) 42 Ch D 674; *Mathew v Brise* (1845) 15 LJ Ch 39.

20 *Underwood v Stevens* (1816) 1 Mer 712; *Rehden v Wesley* (1861) 29 Beav 213; Law of Property (Amendment) Act 1859, s 31; Trustee Act 1893, s 24; *Re Chapman* [1896] 2 Ch 763 at 776; *Re Brier* (1884) 26 Ch D 238 at 243; *Speight v Gaunt* (1883) 9 App Cas 1 at 13–15 and 22–23.

1 See 15th edn hereof, pp 620–624 on TA 1925, ss 23 and 30.

2 See 15th edn hereof, pp 620–624 on TA 1925, ss 23 and 30.

ss 23(1) and 30(1) of the Trustee Act 1925, considered trustees would only be personally liable in respect of acts or defaults of agents if themselves guilty of wilful default in the common law sense of deliberate or reckless, but not negligent conduct. In *Armitage v Nurse*[3] the Court of Appeal, in *obiter dicta* without full argument, accepted the modernist interpretation that permits trustees to get away with negligent conduct in the selection and supervision of agents. This helped to provide momentum for the Trustee Act 2000 which imposes a duty of care on the trustees in the arrangements for employing and supervising agents, whether employed under statutory or express powers[4].

The Trustee Act 2000 has repealed ss 23 and 30 of the Trustee Act 1925. Section 23(2) automatically permitted discretions to be exercised by delegates authorised by the trustees in respect of non-UK trust property. whether or not it was otherwise impossible for the trustees satisfactorily to run the trust or reasonably necessary for the operation of the trust. In the light of the repeal of s 23(2) and the modern ease of communication by e-mail, phone and fax there now seems no scope for this exceptional position provided for under the general law when communications took many months[5].

PARAGRAPH 1(B)

Delegable functions of trustees

The power to employ agents under s 11 of the Trustee Act 2000 is not available to trustees of authorised unit trusts[6] or of charitable common investment schemes[7], while trustees of pension schemes[8] cannot use it in relation to any investment functions nor to authorise a person to act as their agent if being the employer in relation to the scheme or if connected with, or an associate of, such employer.

Otherwise, trustees of a non-charitable trust[9] whenever they wish can delegate functions:

'other than
(a) any function relating to whether or in what way any assets of the trust should be distributed,
(b) any power to decide whether any fees or other payment due to be made out of the trust funds should be made out of income or capital,
(c) any power to appoint a person to be trustee of the trust, or
(d) any power conferred by any other enactment or the trust instrument which permits the trustees to delegate any of their functions or to appoint a person to act as nominee or custodian.'

The clear intention behind (a) is to ensure that distributive discretions[10] concerning payment of capital to beneficiaries or to objects of powers of payment or accumulation of income are not to be delegated: only adminis-

---

3 [1998] Ch 241 at 252.
4 TA 2000, Sch 1, para 3.
5 *Stuart v Norton* (1860) 14 Moo PCC 17. Now also consider TA 2000, s 11(2)(a); and Law Com Report No 260, 'Trustees Powers and Duties', para 4.13.
6 TA 2000, s 37.
7 TA 2000, s 38.
8 TA 2000, s 37(4).
9 TA 2000, s 11(2).
10 These should extend to the exercise of powers of appropriation to individual beneficiaries or to trust funds for beneficiaries as steps on the way to a distribution.

trative or managerial functions concerning the trustees' running of the trust in the best interests of the beneficiaries are to be delegable. For the same reason, if trustees have a discretion as to paying outgoings of an income nature out of capital and vice versa, so as to have adverse distributive effect on an income or capital beneficiary, they must exercise it themselves.

As for (d) the reference to any power conferred by any *other* enactment indicates that a power conferred by the Trustee Act 2000 itself to appoint an agent[11] enables the trustees to appoint an agent whose function can include the appointment of another agent[12].

In the case of charitable trusts, delegable functions are[13]:

(a) any function consisting of carrying out trustees' decisions,
(b) any function relating to investment of trust assets (including managing any trust land and creating or disposing of an interest in such land),
(c) any fund-raising function otherwise than by trading which is an integral part[14] of carrying out the trust's charitable purposes, and
(d) any function prescribed by an order[15] made by the Secretary of State.

Eligibility as a delegate

Trustees can appoint anyone under s 11 including one of themselves[16] to exercise any of their delegable functions, but they can never under s 11 so authorise any beneficiary (even if also a co-trustee)[17]. The appointee may also act as the trustees' nominee or custodian if qualifying under statutory or other powers[18]. If trustees appoint two or more persons to exercise the same function they can only do this on the basis that such persons are to exercise the function jointly[19].

Burdens attached to trustees' specific functions attach to the delegate

A delegate exercising any particular function delegated to him by the trustees under s 11 is, of course, subject to any specific duties or restrictions attached to that function[20]. Thus, a discretionary portfolio manager must have regard to the standard investment criteria, although he will not be subject to the requirement to obtain advice as he should be the kind of person from whom it would have been proper for the trustees to obtain advice[1]. However, it is not considered that such portfolio manager is subject to the general duty to

---

11 Note that terms permitting an agent to appoint a *substitute* and restricting the liability of such substitute are not authorised unless reasonably necessary: TA 2000, s 14(2) and (3).
12 A discretionary portfolio manager may well be given power to appoint a nominee or custodian.
13 TA 2000, s 11(3).
14 A trade is an integral part of carrying out a trust's charitable purpose if, whether carried on in the UK or elsewhere, the profits are applied solely for trust purposes and either the trade is exercised in the course of the actual carrying out of a primary purpose of the trust or the work in connection with the trade is mainly carried out by beneficiaries of the trust: TA 2000, s 11(4).
15 Exercisable by a statutory instrument subject to annulment by resolution of either House of Parliament: TA 2000, s 11(5).
16 TA 2000, s 12(1).
17 TA 2000, s 12(3).
18 TA 2000, s 12(4).
19 TA 2000, s 12(2).
20 TA 2000, s 13(1).
 1 TA 2000, s 13(2).

act fairly imposed upon trustees as such and who should comply with this duty in preparing their policy statement[2] for the manager to comply with and in monitoring such statement and the conduct of the manager[3].

Where trustees of land are subject under s 11(1) of the Trusts of Land and Appointment of Trustees Act 1996 to the duty to consult with the beneficiaries it is they who must perform this duty: they cannot delegate it, and, indeed, any delegate cannot be subjected to s 11 of the 1996 Act[4]. The position is similar[5] where Settled Land Act trustees own investments and must so far as practicable consult the tenant for life and give effect to his wishes so far as consistent with the general interest of the settlement. If a discretionary portfolio manager is to operate speedily and effectively the tenant for life's consent to the policy statement guidelines, after consultation, should suffice to oust the need for consultation by the trustees before every sale or purchase by the manager.

PARAGRAPH 1(c)

Terms of delegation

Subject to complying with the duty of care[6], trustees have a very broad discretion as to the terms upon which they engage a delegate under s 11[7], so long as remuneration does not exceed such amount as is objectively reasonable in all the circumstances for the provision of the relevant services[8]. However, unless it is objectively reasonably necessary[9], the contractual terms must not include terms permitting the agent to appoint a substitute or to act in circumstances capable of giving rise to a conflict of interest or 'restricting the liability of' the agent or his substitute to the trustees or any beneficiary[10]. It would accord with the philosophy of such proscription if terms 'restricting' the liability of an agent or his substitute extended to terms 'ousting' liability by ousting duties[11] (so there can be no breach thereof to give rise to any liability) but, in any event, compliance with the duty of care could well prevent agreeing to any terms ousting liability altogether in particular circumstances.

To avoid any future problems, trustees will be wise to preserve contemporaneous written evidence of the factors that led them to think it was objectively reasonably necessary in the best interests of the beneficiaries as a whole to agree to the proscribed terms. Usually, there will be presentations by, say, three prospective discretionary portfolio managers, so that the trustees should probe the need for such terms if they are to obtain the services of

---

2 TA 2000, s 15(2), (3).
3 TA 2000, s 22.
4 TA 2000, s 13(4) and (5).
5 TA 2000, Sch 2, para 10 inserting into SLA 1925, s 75(4), (4B) and (4C).
6 TA 2000, Sch 1, para 3.
7 TA 2000, s 14(1).
8 TA 2000, s 32(2). These restrictions are inapplicable if an express power in the trust instrument is being used (TA 2000, s 26(a)) or if the trust instrument expressly restricts or excludes s 14(2) and (3) (TA 2000, s 26(b)).
9 TA 2000, s 14(2).
10 TA 2000, s 14(3).
11 If Parliament intended to proscribe terms 'restricting' liability then, *a fortiori*, terms going beyond that by 'ousting' liability should be proscribed.

the manager likely to perform best for the trust and, perhaps, attach some conditions, eg as to notification to them by the agent when it has acted in circumstances capable of giving rise to a conflict of interest.

PARAGRAPH 1(D)

Asset management delegation

Special restrictions apply if trustees exercise their s 11 power[12] to delegate any of their asset management functions defined[13] as functions relating to:

'(a) the investment of assets subject to the trust,
(b) the acquisition of property which is to be subject to the trust, and
(c) managing property which is subject to the trust and disposing of, or creating or disposing of an interest in, such property.'

One naturally thinks of a discretionary portfolio manager dealing with stocks and shares and bonds and gilts or of a land agent dealing with rented-out residential and commercial property, but the definition is broad enough to cover an estate agent or an auctioneer selling a trust house or painting for the best price reasonably obtainable.

No authority is conferred on an agent to exercise any asset management function until the trustees have (1) prepared a policy statement giving guidance as to how the function should be exercised[14] and being in writing or evidenced in writing[15] and (2) entered into an agreement, which is in writing or evidenced in writing[16], containing a term[17] that the agent will secure compliance with the policy statement, except that failure to comply with these conditions does not invalidate the authorisation of the agent[18], thereby protecting third parties and the agent. As to be expected, the guidance given in the policy statement has to be formulated with a view to ensuring that the asset management functions will be exercised in the best interest of the trust beneficiaries[19].

The above statutory power is in addition to any express power conferred by the trust instrument[20], so trustees may prefer to act pursuant to the express power rather than be subject to the statutory restrictions, although, to achieve the same end as a self-sufficient express power, it is possible[1] for the trust instrument to restrict or exclude the conditions attached to the statutory power.

---

12 The s 11 power to employ an agent for asset management only if certain conditions are satisfied is in addition to powers expressly conferred by the trust instrument (per s 26(a)) and is also subject to any restriction or exclusion in the trust instrument (per s 26(b)).
13 TA 2000, s 15(5).
14 TA 2000, s 15(2)(a).
15 TA 2000, s 15(4).
16 TA 2000, s 15(1).
17 TA 2000, s 15(2)(b).
18 TA 2000, s 24.
19 TA 2000, s 15(3).
20 TA 2000, s 26(a).
 1 TA 2000, s 26(b).

PARAGRAPH 1(E)

Delegation by trustees of land to a beneficiary

'Trustees of land may, by power of attorney, delegate to any beneficiary or beneficiaries of full age and beneficially entitled to an interest in possession in land subject to the trust any of their functions as trustees which relate to the land.'[2] It seems implicit that these functions are only administrative or managerial functions and not distributive functions involving the exercise of powers of appointment or discretionary trusts so as to favour certain persons over others. Moreover, it is only functions relating to the land that can be delegated, not functions relating to the proceeds of sale of land or investments thereof or of originally settled assets that are not land. There seems no reason why delegation may not relate to separate parts of the land so that one beneficiary then manages one part and another beneficiary another part.

Delegation may only occur where there is some beneficiary[3] entitled to an interest in possession in the relevant land. Beneficial entitlement is required so that entitlement as personal representative or as trustee, eg of a sub-trust, is not sufficient[4].

A beneficiary has an interest in possession if entitled to occupy the land or to receive the rents and profits[5] therefrom, having an immediate right to present enjoyment of the land or the rents and profits. Where a beneficiary currently has a life interest but it is subject to a power of accumulation of income vested in the trustees, the beneficiary does not have an immediate right of present enjoyment for inheritance tax purposes[6], although his interest is not in remainder or in reversion and so can be regarded as in possession. The onus will be on those alleging that interest in possession has the simple latter meaning to prove that this was intended[7] rather than the stricter inheritance tax meaning. Because the position is ambiguous there should be an express power permitting delegation to a beneficiary currently interested in income but subject to a power of accumulation if the settlor desires such flexibility.

It does seem clear that a beneficiary under an accumulation and maintenance trust, who will become entitled to income or capital upon some future event (eg on attaining 25 years of age) but, until then, the trustees are under a duty to accumulate income, so far as not applied for the maintenance of the beneficiary, does not have an interest in possession. Moreover, any beneficiary interested under a discretionary trust of income does not seem someone entitled to an interest in possession for the purposes of the

---

2 TLATA 1996, s 9(1). This cannot be an enduring power within Enduring Powers of Attorney Act 1985: see s 9(6)

3 TLATA 1996, s 22(1) for definition of a beneficiary as a person who has an interest in property subject to the trust.

4 TLATA 1996, s 22(2). Annuitants are not beneficiaries interested in possession: s 22(3).

5 TLATA 1996, s 23(2) incorporating LPA 1925, s 205(1)(xx).

6 *Pearson v IRC* [1981] AC 753, HL where, by a majority, the House of Lords notoriously held that a life tenant subject to a power of accumulation did not have an interest in possession for the purposes of capital transfer tax, now inheritance tax, though all four Chancery judges involved in stages of the appeal considered there was an interest in possession because it was not in remainder or in reversion.

7 See SLA 1925, s 20(1) and *Pearson v IRC* [1980] Ch 1 at 9 but cf *Re Earl of Stamford and Warrington* [1925] Ch 162 at 171, not challenged on appeal [1925] Ch 589 at 591.

1996 Act[8] unless and until the trustees exercise any discretionary power that they may have to appoint an interest in possession to such person.

Finally, delegation can only be to someone beneficially entitled to an interest in possession in *land,* while a trust of an undivided share in land is itself a trust of land[9] so the trustee thereof can delegate to a beneficiary with an interest in possession under the sub-trust. More significant is whether the head trustees can delegate to such a beneficiary under the sub-trust. It seems clear that they can if the sub-trust was created by the settlor of the head trust as a subsidiary part thereof or if they themselves, pursuant to powers in this behalf, created the sub-trusts within the umbrella of the head trust. However, where the beneficial co-owner of the undivided share under S's settlement created an independent settlement of his undivided share, eg on B for life, delegation to B by the trustees of S's settlement will only be permissible if a broad non-technical construction is taken of s 9, which would seem to be in keeping with the purpose of the section.

Duration of delegation

The power of attorney may be for a defined period or it may be indefinite[10], but it must be given by all the trustees jointly and then be revocable by any one or more of them (unless expressed to be irrevocable and to be given by way of security). The power is automatically revoked by the appointment of a new trustee, but not by a current trustee dying or otherwise ceasing to be a trustee[11].

When the attorney ceases to be a person beneficially entitled to an interest in possession in land the power is automatically revoked if given to him alone[12]. If given to him and two or more other beneficiaries to be exercised jointly (not separately) the power is revoked if each of the other beneficiaries ceases to be so entitled, but otherwise it remains in force for the remaining beneficiaries. If the power were given to beneficiaries to be exercised by them separately, or either separately or jointly, the power is revoked only as concerns the beneficiary ceasing to be a person beneficially entitled to an interest in possession[13].

Delegates as trustees of their functions relating to land

Beneficiaries to whom functions have been delegated by power of attorney under s 9 of the 1996 Act are, in relation to the exercise of their functions, in the same position as trustees with the same duties and liabilities, but are not regarded as trustees for any other purposes, particularly the purposes of any enactment permitting the delegation of functions by trustees or imposing requirements relating to the payment of capital money[14]. Thus, a beneficiary-attorney cannot sub-delegate the functions delegated to him by the trustees.

---

8 In context see 'entitled' in s 12 of the 1996 Act and consider the unascertainable value of a discretionary interest for purposes of s 11(1)(b).
9 TLATA 1996, s 23(2) incorporating LPA 1925, s 205(1)(ix) as amended by the 1996 Act s 25 (2) and Sch 4.
10 TLATA 1996, s 9(5).
11 TLATA 1996, s 9(3).
12 TLATA 1996, s 9(4).
13 TLATA 1996, s 9(4).
14 TLATA 1996, s.9(7).

It also seems clear that a sole life tenant or joint life tenants cannot give a valid receipt for capital money arising from the exercise of a delegated function, eg a power to sell the land or grant an easement over it. The delegated functions must relate to the land, while giving a valid overreaching receipt relates to the proceeds of sale of land. Thus, the trustees themselves must provide the receipt to satisfy s 27 of the Law of Property Act 1925 or exercise their power under s 11 of the Trustee Act 2000 to appoint an agent, eg a solicitor, to provide a receipt on their behalf.

PARAGRAPH 2

Duties of care where trustees of land delegate to a beneficiary

Trustees of land in deciding whether to delegate any of their functions relating to land to a currently entitled beneficiary under s 9 of the Trusts of Land and Appointment of Trustees Act 1996 must comply with the statutory duty of care[15] except to the extent ousted by the trust instrument[16]. Once they have decided to make and have made a delegation on particular terms that is not an irrevocable one by way of security, they must keep the delegation under review with a view to intervening and if they consider they should intervene (eg by revoking the delegation or giving directions to the delegate) they must do so[17]. The duty of care (unless ousted by the trust instrument) applies to 'trustees in carrying out any duty under sub-s (3)' to keep the delegation under review and to intervene if appropriate[18].

'Unless the trustee fails to comply with the duty of care in deciding to delegate any of the trustee's functions under section 9 or in carrying out any duty under subsection (3)' he is not liable for any act or default of the delegate[19]. It seems clear that 'in deciding to delegate' must cover the terms of delegation as an integral part of the decision to delegate, which must depend on the terms of the delegation and the attributes of the delegate-beneficiary. It also seems that 'in carrying out any duty' under subs (3) to review and, then, to intervene, if appropriate, should cover the whole nil to one hundred per cent band of the duty, thereby preventing the trustee from arguing unmeritoriously that his total failure to review the conduct of the delegate means that he cannot be liable for any act or default of the delegate. Alternatively, such argument could be trumped by holding that breach of his duty to review and then intervene, if appropriate, is a personal default of the trustee for which he is personally liable.

Duties of care where trustees delegate under s 11 of the Trustee Act 2000

The same arguments as those canvassed in the preceding paragraph arise where s 23(1) of the Trustee Act 2000 provides 'unless he has failed to comply with the duty of care applicable to him under paragraph 3 of Schedule 1 ... when carrying out his duties under section 22' to keep under review the arrangements under which an agent, nominee or custodian con-

---

15 TLATA 1996, s 9A inserted by TA 2000, Sch 2, para 47.
16 TA 2000, Sch 1, para 7.
17 TLATA 1996, s 9A(3).
18 TLATA 1996, s 9A(5).
19 TLATA 1996, s 9A(6).

tinues to act for the trustees, 'a trustee is not liable for any act or default of the agent, nominee or custodian'. To prevent the trustee from escaping all liability when he totally failed to keep the agency arrangements under review, 'carrying out his duties' must extend to the whole nil to one hundred per cent band of the duties or, otherwise, such a total breach of his duties is a personal default for which he is personally liable, unaffected by s 23(1).

Unless inconsistent with the trust instrument[20], once trustees, pursuant to their powers under the Trustee Act 2000, have entered into arrangements for someone to act as agent (or nominee or custodian) they must keep the arrangements under review, checking how those arrangements are being implemented, considering whether they need to exercise their powers to intervene (by giving directions or revoking the arrangements) and they must exercise them if there be a need[1]. In the case of an agent exercising asset management functions, the reviewing duty extends to considering whether there is any need for a revised or replacement policy statement and, if there is such a need, then to producing such a revised or replacement policy, and to assessing whether the current policy statement is being complied with[2]. The duty of care applies to these reviewing and intervention duties[3] except to the extent ousted by the trust instrument[4].

The duty of care (except to the extent ousted by the trust instrument) also applies to a trustee when 'entering into arrangements' for the appointment of an agent (nominee or custodian) under the Trustee Act 2000 or under express powers in the trust instrument[5]. 'Entering into arrangements' covers selecting the person who is to act, determining any terms on which he is to act, and, if the person is being authorised to exercise asset management functions, the preparation of a policy statement[6].

PARAGRAPH 3

Temporary delegation by a trustee of all or any of his discretions

Totally distinct from the collective power of the body of the trustees to delegate pursuant to the Trustee Act 2000 or express powers in the trust instrument is the power (under the substituted[7] s 25 of the Trustee Act 1925) of each trustee personally, by power of attorney, to 'delegate the execution or exercise of all or any of the trusts, powers and discretions vested in him as trustee either alone or jointly with any other person or persons'. This extends beyond administrative or managerial functions to every function including distributive functions. The delegate becomes the *alter ego* of the trustee in respect of the delegated functions, so the delegating trustee is automatically liable for the acts or defaults of the delegate as if they were the acts or defaults of the delegating trustee[8].

Because a trustee can delegate every function so that the delegate can

---

20 TA 2000, s 21(3).
 1 TA 2000, s 22(1).
 2 TA 2000, s 22(2).
 3 TA 2000, Sch 1, para 3(1)(e).
 4 TA 2000, Sch 1, para 7.
 5 TA 2000, Sch 1, para 3(1).
 6 TA 2000, Sch 1, para 3(2).
 7 By Trustee Delegation Act 1999, s 5.
 8 TA 1925, s 25(7).

essentially become a substitute trustee, the delegation can continue only for a period of 12 months or any shorter period stipulated in the power of attorney, the period commencing with the date of execution of the power of attorney by the trustee or as expressly provided in such power of attorney[9]. Furthermore, to give those with the power to appoint a replacement trustee the opportunity to exercise such power, the delegating trustee, before or within seven days after giving the power of attorney, must give written notice of it to each person (other than himself), if any, who has express power under the trust instrument to appoint a new trustee, and to each of the other trustees (who have statutory default powers[10] to appoint a replacement trustee)[11]. The written notice must specify the date on which the power comes into operation and its duration, the donee of the power, the reason why the power is given, and, where some only are delegated, the particular trusts, powers and discretions delegated[12]. Failure to comply with this notice requirement, however, does not, in favour of a person dealing with the donee of the power, invalidate any act done or instrument executed by the donee[13].

For the purpose of performing the delegated functions the donee may exercise any of the powers conferred on the trustee-donor by statute (eg in s 11 of the Trustee Act 2000) or the trust instrument, including power, for the purpose of transferring any inscribed stock, himself to delegate to an attorney power to transfer, but not including the power of delegation under the substituted s 25 of the Trustee Act 1925[14].

A statutory 'General Trustee Power of Attorney' is provided by s 25(6): a separate power of attorney is required for each trust to which the delegation is to apply. Otherwise, a power in a form to like effect but expressed to be made under s 25(5) can be used: it would then seem that a trustee of say, five trusts, could use that power of attorney to delegate his trusteeship functions in relation to the five singly specified trusts to a colleague of his while on a six month sabbatical from work, but it will be safer to use a separate power of attorney for each separate trust.

The persons who may be donees of the power of attorney include a trust corporation[15] or a co-trustee, but the requirement for capital money to be paid to a trust corporation or two persons continues to apply[16], eg if one of two trustees, A, delegated his functions to his co-trustee, B, who is not a trust corporation, then B cannot give a valid receipt for capital money on sale of property nor execute an overreaching deed.

The donee may recover expenses incurred in performing his duties just as his donor could have recovered such expenses if incurring them[17]. Section 25 does not make any reference to payment of reasonable remuneration to the donee, but it would be strange if the remuneration to which the donor was entitled as trustee could not be diverted to the donee performing the functions that the donor would otherwise have to perform. Indeed, if the

---

9 TA 1925, s 25(2).
10 TA 1925, s 36(1).
11 TA 1925, s 25(4). In the case of delegation by a personal representative notice must be given to each of the other personal representatives, if any, except an executor who has renounced probate.
12 TA 1925, s 25(4).
13 TA 1925, s 25(4).
14 TA 1925, s 25(8)
15 TA 1925, s 25(3)
16 Trustee Delegation Act 1999, s 7.
17 TA 1925, s 25(8).

donor-trustee is entitled to be indemnified out of trust funds for the costs of the power of attorney as properly incurred by him acting as trustee on behalf of the trust[18], should he not also be entitled to the costs of employing the donee-attorney?

Enduring Powers of Attorney and Co-owners of Land

It is possible[19] for the temporary delegation of trusteeship functions under the substituted s 25 of the Trustee Act 1925 to be by way of an enduring power of attorney under the Enduring Powers of Attorney Act 1985 so as to survive the loss of mental capacity of the donor. However, with a maximum twelve months duration, this is not very significant.

Much more significant is that where M and W hold land on trust for M and W each can confer a power of attorney on the other under s 1 of the Trustee Delegation Act 1999[20] which can be by way of an enduring power of attorney, enabling the other to exercise any trustee function of the donor, eg to sell the land. The key feature is that the donor-trustee had a beneficial interest in the land, its proceeds or income at the time of the donee's act[1]. In favour of a purchaser an 'appropriate statement' is conclusive evidence, being a signed statement of the donee when doing the act in question or within three months thereof that the donor has or had a beneficial interest in the property at the time of the donee doing the act[2].

A sole individual donee cannot give a valid receipt for capital money or execute an overreaching deed[3], but if the enduring power of attorney is registered such sole donee can appoint an additional trustee[4].

ARTICLE 56

Duty of trustees to act jointly where more than one

In the case of a non-charitable[5] trust which is not a pension trust scheme[6] where there are more trustees than one, all must join in the execution of the trust[7], save only:
(a) where the settlement[8] or a competent court otherwise directs;

---

18 TA 2000, s 31.
19 Trustee Delegation Act 1999, s 6.
20 Not under TA 1925 or an express power in the trust instrument: Trustee Delegation Act 1999, s 1(8).
1 Trustee Delegation Act 1999, s 1(1).
2 Trustee Delegation Act 1999, s 2(2), (3).
3 Trustee Delegation Act 1999, s 7.
4 Trustee Delegation Act 1999, s 8.
5 *Re Whiteley* [1910] 1 Ch 600 (majority decisions are not valid). If decision by a majority is expressly allowed it is not enough that a majority sign a paper recording the decision (unless this be authorised by the trust instrument); the trustees must meet so the matter can be considered by them: *A-G v Scott* (1750) 1 Vs Sen 413.
6 Pensions Act 1995, s 32 (majority decisions are valid unless unanimity expressly required).
7 *Luke v South Kensington Hotel Co* (1879) 11 Ch D 121; *Re Dixon* (1826) 2 GL & J 114; *Re Flower and Metropolitan Board of Works* (1884) 27 Ch D 592; but retrospective assent to the decision of the other trustees by a non-consulted trustee will validate such decision: *Messeena v Carr* (1870) LR 9 Eq 260; *Libby v Kennedy* (1998) OPLR 213.
8 *Re Butlin's Settlement Trust* [1976] Ch 251.

(b) as to the receipt of income[9];
(c) as to such matters as can be lawfully delegated under Article 55.

This article is a corollary of Article 55 for, if trustees cannot delegate their duties, it follows that they must all personally perform those duties, and not appoint one of themselves to manage the business of the trust. It is not unusual to find one of several trustees spoken of as the 'acting trustee', meaning the trustee who actively interests himself in the trust affairs, and whose decisions are merely indorsed by his co-trustees. The court, however, does not recognise any such distinction; for the settlor has trusted *all* his trustees, and it behoves each and every one of them to exercise his individual judgment and discretion on every matter, and not blindly to leave any questions to his co-trustees or co-trustee[10].

Exceptionally, as where the settlor would prefer to have X alone as trustee managing the affairs of the trust, but a second trustee, Y, is needed (because the trust assets include land, so two trustees are needed to give a good receipt and overreach the beneficiaries' interests) the trust instrument may expressly stipulate that Y, or any successor trustee, while X is a trustee, must always act as directed by X unless aware that X is thereby committing a breach of trust[11]. Similarly, there is no reason why a trust instrument should not effectively provide for X to have a casting vote if X and Y (or Y's successor) cannot agree on a matter concerning the trust[12], although if aware that X is seeking to commit a breach of trust, Y must not join X in carrying out such breach, and indeed, should seek an injunction to restrain X if X is in a position on his own, without Y's assistance, to commit a breach of trust[13].

Majority of trustees cannot bind the rest

Thus, the act of a majority of private (as opposed to charitable or pension scheme) trustees cannot bind either a dissenting minority, or the trust estate. In order to bind the trust estate the act must be the act of all unless the trust instrument expressly authorises the trustees to act according to the majority view where they are not unanimous[14]. Where there is a trust for sale of real estate with a discretionary power to postpone the sale, the property must be sold within a reasonable time, unless the trustees are unanimously in favour of a postponement[15], and the same rule applies to a trust for sale with power to retain existing investments[16]. At the same time, in such cases a trustee, if acting bona fide, may defer to what he considers to be the better judgment of his co-trustee, although he does so with reluctance[17]. On the same ground, if

9 As to shares and stocks, see Companies Act 1985, s 360; but consider *Binney v Ince Hall Coal and Cannel Co* (1866) 35 LJ Ch 363. As to rents, see *Townley v Sherborne* (1634) J Bridg 35, 2 Wh & Tu Lead Cas (8th edn) 627; *Gouldsworth v Knights* (1843) 11 M & W 337; and *Gough v Smith* [1872] WN 18.
10 *Munch v Cockerell* (1840) 5 My & Cr 178; *Re Lucking's Will Trusts* [1967] 3 All ER 726.
11 *Re Arnott* [1899] 1 IR 201. Y will be personally liable if dishonestly facilitating a breach of trust.
12 After all, the settlor can provide for majority decisions and for the chairman of the trustees to have a casting vote where the trustees are evenly divided.
13 *Booth v Booth* (1838) 1 Beav 125; *Gough v Smith* [1872] WN 18.
14 *Luke v South Kensington Hotel Co* (1879) 11 Ch D 121; *Swale v Swale* (1856) 22 Beav 584; *Re Butlins Settlement Trust* [1976] Ch 251, [1976] 2 All ER 483. It may be otherwise, however, with regard to charitable trustees; (see Charities Act 1960, ss 28 and 34) and pension trustees (Pensions Act 1995, s 32).
15 *Re Roth* (1896) 74 LT 50; *Jones v Challenger* [1961] 1 QB 176, CA.
16 *Re Hilton* [1909] 2 Ch 548.
17 *Re Schneider* (1906) 22 TLR 223.

one of several trustees incurs costs without consultation with his co-trustees, he cannot recover them from the estate where his efforts have resulted in loss[18].

Revocable or periodic obligations terminable by notice

Exceptionally, if T1 and T2 contract with C on terms which are revocable or are to continue in operation for one year in the first place and thereafter from year to year unless determined by notice at the end of the first or any subsequent year, the contract will only continue or only persist beyond the initial period so long as both T1 and T2 are willing that it should do so[19]. Thus, either T1 or T2 can alone give notice unless restrained by an injunction, as where the giving of such a notice would in the circumstances amount to a breach of trust, eg the loss of a valuable leasehold (as opposed to an unsatisfactory contract with a discretionary portfolio manager who is a friend of T2).

All trustees must join in receipt

Likewise, all the trustees must join in the receipt of money, unless, of course, the settlement authorises one of them to give good receipts and discharges, assuming capital moneys on the sale of land in England and Wales are not involved when receipt must be by two trustees or a trust corporation[20]. As Kay J said in *Re Flower and Metropolitan Board of Works*[1]:

'The theory of every trust is that the trustees shall not allow the trust moneys to get into the hands of any one of them, but that all shall exercise control over them. They must take care that they are in the hands of all, or invested in their names, or placed in a proper bank in their joint names. ... The reason why more than one trustee is appointed, is that they shall take care that the moneys shall not get into the hands of one of them alone. ... and they have no right, as between themselves and the cestuis que trust, unless the circumstances are such as to make it imperatively necessary to do so, to authorise one of themselves to receive the moneys.'[2]

In practice, trustees receiving capital money on sale of land will, under s 11 of the Trustee Act 2000[3], authorise their solicitor to receive such money on their behalf.

Investments should be in joint names

Unless advantage is taken of the Trustee Act 2000 to appoint nominees or custodians, all investments of trust moneys should be made in the joint names of the trustees, for otherwise one trustee would be able to realise and

---

18 *Re England's Settlement Trusts* [1918] 1 Ch 24.
19 *Hammersmith and Fulham London Borough Council v Monk* [1992] 1 AC 478, [1992] 1 All ER, HL, also indicating that all trustees must join in the operation of a break clause in a lease, a surrender of the lease, an application for relief against forfeiture and the exercise of an option to renew the lease.
20 LPA 1925, s 27.
1 (1884) 27 Ch D 592.
2 *See also Lee v Sankey* (1872) LR 15 Eq 204; *Clough v Bond* (1838) 3 My & Cr 490; and *Walker v Symonds* (1818) 3 Swan 1 at 61.
3 Replacing TA 1925, s 23(1) and (3).

appropriate the money[4]. But this must of course yield to necessity; as, for instance, where shares are specifically bequeathed to trustees upon certain trusts (so that retention of such shares is authorised), and it is found that by the regulations of the company the shares can only be registered in the name of one person[5]; or where investments that the trustees are authorised to purchase can only be held in the name of a nominee for the purchasers.

Income

As a general rule, however, although trustees must join in the receipt of capital, it is permissible for them to allow one of their number to receive the income. Thus, in the case of rents, the trustees may delegate the collection to one of their number or to a rent collector, for it would be impossible for them all to collect the rents[6]. If, however, there is any fear of misappropriation by the collecting trustee, the others should notify the tenants not to pay him again[7]. A similar rule applies to the receipt of dividends on stocks or shares, from the necessity of the case, where the Articles of Association of limited companies provide that trusts shall not be recognised and that payment shall be made to the first of several joint holders[8].

Trustee joining in receipt for conformity

In cases where a trustee permits his co-trustee to receive moneys owing to the estate (eg where he permits him to collect rents), then, even though he join in the receipt for such moneys, and thereby acknowledge that he has received them, he will not be liable *if he can prove*[9] that he did not in fact receive them, and that he only joined in the receipt for the sake of conformity[10].

Trustee must not permit co-trustee to retain money

Even where a trustee may safely permit his co-trustee to receive trust moneys, he will, nevertheless, be liable for breaching his duty of care if he permits him to retain them for a longer period than the circumstances of the case require[11].

---

4 *Lewis v Nobbs* (1878) 8 Ch D 591; *Swale v Swale* (1856) 22 Beav 584.
5 *Consterdine v Consterdine* (1862) 31 Beav 330.
6 *Townley v Sherborn* (1634) J Bridg 35, 2 White & Tud LC 627.
7 *Gough v Smith* [1872] WN 18.
8 Companies Act 1985, s 360; Companies (Tables A to F) Regulations 1985, SI 1985/805, Table A, arts 5 and 106.
9 *Brice v Stokes* (1805) 11 Ves 319, 2 White & Tud LC 631; *Townley v Sherborn* (1634) J Bridg 35, 2 White & Tud LC 627; *Re Fryer* (1857) 3 K & J 317.
10 *Fellows v Mitchell* (1705) 1 P Wms 81; *Re Fryer* (1857) 3 K & J 317. There is less need for this nowadays in the light of TA 2000, ss 11 and 12(1).
11 *Brice v Stokes* (1805) 11 Ves 319, 2 White & Tud LC 631. *Thompson v Finch* (1856) 8 De GM & G 560; *Walker v Symonds* (1818) 3 Swan 1; *Hanbury v Kirkland* (1829) 3 Sim 265; distinguished in *Re Munton* [1927] 1 Ch 262; *Styles v Guy* (1849) 1 Mac & G 422; *Wiglesworth v Wiglesworth* (1852) 16 Beav 269; *Egbert v Butter* (1856) 21 Beav 560; *Rodbard v Cooke* (1877) 25 WR 555; *Lewis v Nobbs* (1878) 8 Ch D 591; *Consterdine v Consterdine* (1862) 31 Beav 330; and *Carruthers v Carruthers* [1896] AC 659.

Trustee must not permit co-trustee alone to sign cheques

For like reasons, trustees in whose names trust moneys are banked should not authorise the bankers to pay cheques signed by one only of their number, for that would be equivalent to giving the sole control of the trust funds to one trustee; whereas the beneficiaries are entitled to the safeguard of the control of all[12]. A trustee may, however, entrust his co-trustee with a crossed cheque, signed by both of them, for delivery to the beneficiary[13]. He may well be at risk if he entrusts his co-trustee with a blank cheque signed by him and the co-trustee takes advantage of this for his own purposes: there will certainly be liability if he knew or ought to have known that his co-trustee had earlier obtained a similar advantage[14].

If one trustee forges the signature of the other to a cheque, and obtains payment from the bank to which the trustees had given a mandate to honour drawings signed by them both, the bank does not obtain a good discharge; but it was surprisingly held by McNair J in *Brewer v Westminster Bank Ltd*[15], that the innocent trustee cannot obtain a declaration of the bank's liability since the obligation of the bank is owed to both trustees jointly, and the delinquent trustee must be a party to the action and the forgery by him is an essential link in the claim.

Justifiably that case was not followed in *Welch v Bank of England*, by Harman J who said:

'I confess that I do not follow that decision. None of the cases in equity were cited to the judge. It may be however that this would be a good defence at law. It is certainly, I think, no defence in equity.'[16]

ARTICLE 57

Duty of trustee not to set up jus tertii

A trustee, who has acknowledged himself as such, must not set up, or aid, the adverse title of a third party against his beneficiary[17]. But he has a right to have the direction of the court as to whether he should resist an adverse claim which has been made[18] or as to what he should do in respect of an adverse potential claim which he has reasonable grounds to believe could make him personally liable to the claimant if the claimant knew what he was doing[19]; if, with notice of the adverse

12 *Clough v Bond* (1838) 3 My & Cr 490; *Trutch v Lamprell* (1855) 20 Beav 116. Note that delegable functions under TA 2000, s 11 do not extend to distribution of assets.
13 *Lake Bathurst Australasian Gold Mining Co, Re Barnard v Bagshaw* (1862) 3 De GJ & Sm 355.
14 Cf *Re Lucking's Will Trusts* [1967] 3 All ER 726, [1968] 1 WLR 866.
15 [1952] 2 All ER 650 (a case as to executors' joint banking account). It is understood that an appeal in this case was compromised.
16 [1955] Ch 508 at 532, [1955] 1 All ER 811 at 821 (a case as to forged transfers of stocks).
17 *Newsome v Flowers* (1861) 30 Beav 461; *Devey v Thornton* (1851) 9 Hare 222. Exceptionally, a trustee will be allowed to substantiate a claim that property allegedly devolving upon testamentary trusts is really his property: *Re Tucker* [1918] VLR 460; *Allen v Roughly* (1955) 94 CLR 98.
18 *Neale v Davies* (1854) 5 De GM & G 258, per Wood V-C and Turner LJ (Knight-Bruce LJ dissenting surprisingly). See also *Alsop Wilkinson v Neary* [1995] 1 All ER 431, p 842, post.
19 *Finers v Miro* [1991] 1 All ER 182 [1991] 1 WLR 35, CA.

claim, he continues to pay his beneficiaries and himself he will do so at his own peril[20].

Trustees must not contest the title of their beneficiaries

In *Newsome v Flowers*[1] a chapel was vested in trustees, in trust for Particular Baptists. Subsequently part of the congregation seceded, and went to another chapel. Still later, the surviving trustees were induced (not knowing the real object) to appoint new trustees, and vest the property in them. Immediately afterwards the new trustees—who were in fact attached to the seceding congregation—brought an action to obtain possession of the chapel. Their appointment was, however, set aside, and it was held that they could not plead the adverse claims of the seceders as a defence against the congregation of the chapel, who were their beneficiaries.

Nor, however honestly trustees may believe that the trust property belongs of right to a third party, are they justified in refusing to perform the trust they have once undertaken, or in communicating with such other person on the subject; but they must assume the validity of the title of their beneficiaries until it be negatived[2].

Obtaining the directions of the court

The above cases show that trustees are not justified in taking an actively hostile attitude towards the validity of their trust. Where they have received notice of a paramount claim, and of the intention of the claimant to hold them responsible if they deal with the fund in a manner contrary to such claim, the trustees can hardly be expected at their own personal risk to go on steadily executing the trust which they have undertaken, but must be able to apply to the court for directions and relief. Thus in *Neale v Davies*[3], Vice-Chancellor Wood and in the Court of Appeal Lord Justice Turner held that the trustees were entitled to refuse to execute the trust under such circumstances, and had a right to come to the court for its direction. Surprisingly, Knight-Bruce LJ, however, dissented.

Nowadays, it is clear that a trustee is always entitled to act under the direction of the court when he is placed in a position of difficulty or danger whether under the inherent jurisdiction or Order 85, rule 2, RSC now Part 64.2 CPR[4]. Thus, in *Finers v Miro*[5] there were reasonable grounds for believing that the defendant had defrauded X Ltd of millions of dollars indirectly held by the plaintiff solicitor through an intricate network of overseas companies, trusts and foundations held by the plaintiff on trust for the defendant absolutely. Because the plaintiff was potentially personally liable to account to X Ltd for knowing assistance in a dishonest breach of fiduciary duty, the Court of Appeal held, despite the solicitor-client relationship between plaintiff and defendant, the plaintiff was entitled to obtain the court's directions. The plaintiff was authorised to inform X Ltd sufficiently to enable

---

20 *Wright v Chard* (1859) 4 Drew 673; affd (1860) 29 LJCh 415.
 1 (1861) 30 Beav 461.
 2 *Beddoes v Pugh* (1859) 26 Beav 407.
 3 (1854) 5 De GM & G 258.
 4 See Art 87, post.
 5 [1991] 1 All ER 182, [1991] 1 WLR 35, CA.

it to decide whether or not to make a claim against the defendant's assets held by the plaintiff and frozen except for releasing 100,000 dollars to the defendant for his legal expenses.

However, in *United Mizrahi Bank v Doherty*[6] the court was not prepared to assist a firm of solicitors seeking a direction that they would have an unimpeachable title to moneys paid to them out of their client's bank account which was frozen except for payment thereout of legal expenses, the claimant alleging that the account contained money belonging to the claimant having been misappropriated from it by the defendant. The court was not prepared to close off the possibility that knowledge of someone in the firm might mean that the firm could not qualify as a bona fide purchaser without notice once all the facts emerged after the defendant's trial[7], so that the claimant might be abe to recover the payments made for legal expenses.

Notice of adverse claim

In *Carl-Zeiss-Stiftung v Herbert Smith & Co (a firm) (No 2)*[8] the Court of Appeal held that knowledge of a claim being made against a solicitor's client by the other party to the action (in which the solicitor represented the client) was not sufficient to amount to notice of a trust (the East German plaintiff company claiming that the assets of the West German defendant company were held on trust for it) and of misapplication of trust moneys by the client so as to make the solicitor constructive trustee of the moneys for the other party. The solicitor was a bona fide purchaser without notice. Significantly, the claim was a strongly disputed one involving unsolved questions of fact and difficult questions of German and of English law so that it was impossible for the solicitor to know whether or not the claim was well-founded.

In the commercial context (other than the purchase of land) it seems[9] that a purchaser of property will not have notice that it is trust property unless he has actual knowledge or deliberately turned a blind eye so as to avoid actual knowledge or deliberately or recklessly failed to make the inquiries an honest reasonable man would have made due to the circumstances appearing suspicious to him, such latter types of knowledge being regarded in shorthand as 'Nelsonian' and 'naughty' knowledge respectively. A person who dishonestly assists in a breach of fiduciary duty is personally liable to account to those suffering loss thereby[10].

---

6 [1998] 2 All ER 230, [1998] 1 WLR 435.

7 Doherty, the Bank's Chief Lending Officer, subsequently pleaded guilty and was jailed for five years: the court's ruling meant that solicitors feared the risk of having to repay fees received out of the defendant's account, so facing working for nothing.

8 [1969] 2 Ch 276, [1969] 2 All ER 367, CA but cf *Guardian Trust and Executors Co of New Zealand Ltd v Public Trustee of New Zealand* [1942] AC 115 at 125, per Lord Romer (executor with notice from next-of-kin that they intended to challenge the will was held personally liable for the amount of legacies paid thereafter when the challenge succeeded).

9 *Polly Peck International plc v Nadir (No 2)* [1992] 4 All ER 769.

10 See Art 100(2) and (3) post.

ARTICLE 58

Duty of trustee to act gratuitously unless otherwise authorised, as is usual nowadays

A trustee, other than the Public Trustee[11] or a custodian trustee[12], or an independent trustee of a pension scheme[13] or a trust corporation[14], has no right to charge for his time and trouble[15] except:
(a) where the settlement so provides[16];
(b) where he acts in a professional capacity and each other trustee has agreed in writing that he may be remunerated[17];
(c) where he has entered into a legally binding agreement with the beneficiaries being of full age and capacity who have freely and without unfair pressure entered into the agreement[18];
(d) where the trustee is a solicitor authorised under the exceptional rule in *Cradock v Piper*[19];
(e) where the court has authorised payment of remuneration under its inherent jurisdiction;
(f) where the trust property is abroad, and it is the custom of the local courts to allow remuneration[20].

Basis of the rule

While a trustee has always been entitled to be indemnified against costs and expenses properly incurred by him as trustee, he has had to perform his office gratuitously for, otherwise 'the trust estate might be loaded and made of little value'[1], his self interest in doing as much remunerated work as possible prevailing over his fiduciary duty with undivided loyalty to further the interests of the beneficiaries, unless the trust instrument authorised such conflict and provided openly for payment of remuneration as an incident[2] of the office.

---

11 By s 7 of the Public Trustee Act 1906, the Public Trustee is authorised to charge fees to be fixed by the Treasury with the sanction of the Lord Chancellor.
12 A body appointed to be a custodian trustee may charge fees not exceeding those charged by the Public Trustee; see pp 658, 792, 797, post.
13 On insolvency of the employer company, an independent trustee of the pension scheme has to be appointed: he is entitled to payment out of the Scheme's resources for his reasonable fees and expenses in priority to all other claimants: Pensions Act 1995, s 20.
14 TA 2000, s 29(1) where no express provision in the trust instrument.
15 *Robinson v Pett* (1734) 3 P Wms 249, 2 White & Tud LC 605; *Barrett v Hartley* (1866) LR 2 Eq 789.
16 *Robinson v Pett* (1734) 3 P Wms 249; *Webb v Earl of Shaftesbury* (1802) 7 Ves 480; *Willis v Kibble* (1839) 1 Beav 559. The TA 1925 although allowing trustees to employ and pay agents (s 23, p 634, ante) probably did not authorise the employment and payment of one of themselves.
17 TA 2000, s 29(2).
18 TA 2000, s 29(2).
19 *Re Sherwood* (1840) 3 Beav 338: only those beneficiaries who are party to the contract have to provide the remuneration.
20 *Chambers v Goldwin* (1804) 9 Ves 254; cf *Re Northcote's Will Trusts* [1949] 1 All ER 442.
1 *Robinson v Pett* (1734) 3 P Wms 249 at 251.
2 *Galmerrow Securities Ltd v National Westminster Bank plc* [2002] WTLR 125 at 156.

Charging may be authorised by the settlement

If, however, the settlement provides that the trustee *may* charge, he will be allowed to do so; but charging clauses were strictly construed[3] before the Trustee Act 2000. Thus, if a solicitor-trustee was authorised to make 'professional charges'[4] (even where the words 'for his time and trouble' are added[5]), he was not allowed to charge for time and trouble expended otherwise than in his position as solicitor. On the other hand, where a will authorised any trustee thereof who may be a solicitor to make:

'the usual professional, *or other proper and reasonable charges,* for all business done and time expended in relation to the trusts of the will, *whether such business is usually within the business of a solicitor or not'*,

the taxing master had power to allow to a solicitor-trustee the proper charges for business not strictly of a professional nature transacted by him in relation to the trust estate[6], although not for work altogether outside his professional vocations[7]. Thus, a well-drafted clause needed to authorise a professional trustee to charge for services which a layman could do personally.

Now, by s 28 of the Trustee Act 2000, if there is a provision in the trust instrument entitling a trustee who is 'acting in a professional capacity' or is a trust corporation to receive payment out of trust funds in respect of services provided to, or on behalf of, the trust, such provision extends to services even if they are services capable of being provided by a 'lay trustee'[8]. However, this only applies to a trustee of a charitable trust[9], if a trust corporation or an individual trustee who is not a sole trustee and who has the agreement of a majority of the other trustees. Significantly, payment for such trustee services is now not regarded as a gift[10] but as remuneration for the purposes of the Wills Act 1837 and the Administration of Estates Act 1925[11].

A 'lay trustee' is someone who is neither a trust corporation nor a person acting in a professional capacity[12]. A trustee 'acts in a professional capacity' if he acts in the course of a profession or business which consists of, or includes, the provision of services in connection with (a) the management or administration of trusts generally or a particular kind of trust or (b) any

---

3 *Re Gee* [1948] Ch 284, [1948] 1 All ER 498.
4 *Harbin v Darby* (1860) 28 Beav 325; *Re Chapple* (1884) 27 Ch D 584.
5 *Re Chalinder and Herington* [1907] 1 Ch 58.
6 *Re Ames* (1883) 25 Ch D 72. Where the trust was created by will, the solicitor's charges in such cases were considered to be general legacies for purposes of legacy duty (*Re Thorley* [1891] 2 Ch 613), and for purposes of abatement (*Re Brown* [1918] WN 118), and for him losing the legacy if he or his spouse attested the will (*Re Pooley* (1888) 40 Ch D 1) (though a solicitor who attested the will might take advantage of a charging clause if he was not appointed a trustee until after the testator's death: *Re Royce's Will Trusts* [1959] Ch 626, [1959] 3 All ER 278, CA). He could not charge at all if the estate was insolvent (*Re White* [1898] 2 Ch 217, CA) or if the estate had been exhausted by specific legacy. However, the charges were taxable as income: *Dale v IRC* [1954] AC 11, HL.
7 *Clarkson v Robinson* [1900] 2 Ch 722. If a clause were to allow a trustee to charge for services which a layman can do personally then this had to be explained to the settlor or testator: *Re Orwell's Will Trusts* [1982] 3 All ER 177 at 179.
8 Unless the trust instrument makes inconsistent provision, eg my trustees shall only charge for professional services that a layman could not provide: TA 2000, s 28(1).
9 TA 2000, s 28(3).
10 See note 6 above.
11 TA 2000, s 28(4).
12 TA 2000, s 28(6).

particular aspect of the management or administration of trusts generally or a particular kind of trust and if the services he provides fall within that description[13]. It seems that a Schedule D Case I or II taxable trade or profession is required but that a corporation, which is not a trust corporation, could qualify as a professional trust services provider[14], though it is likely that an express clause entitling any corporation to charge its scale fees from time to time[15] will be regarded as inconsistent with s 28 if in some special circumstance it sought to charge additional fees under s 28.

Cradock v Piper exception where solicitor acts for himself and another

There is a curious exception to the old rule that a solicitor-trustee cannot, in the absence of an enabling clause, charge profit costs. This exception (known as the rule in *Cradock v Piper*[16]) has been enunciated in the following terms:

> 'Where there is work done *in a suit*, not on behalf of the trustee, who is a solicitor alone, but on behalf of himself and a co-trustee, the rule will not prevent the solicitor or his firm from receiving the usual costs, if the costs of appearing for and acting for the two have not increased the expense; that is to say, if the trustee himself has not added to the expense which would have been incurred if he or his firm had appeared only for his co-trustee.'[17]

This exception is, however, limited to the costs incurred in respect of business done in an *action or matter*, and does not apply to business done out of court[18].

Trustee Act 2000, s 29 authorisation

In the absence of any provision about remuneration in legislation or in the trust instrument (which should cover a charging clause for persons other than the settlor or his spouse), not only is a trust corporation (not being trustee of a charitable trust) entitled to receive remuneration out of trust funds for trust services[19], but also any trustee who acts in a professional capacity, but is not a trust corporation, a trustee of a charitable trust or a sole trustee, if each other trustee has agreed in writing to his being remunerated for his trust services[20]. It matters not that the trust services are capable of being provided by a lay trustee[1].

Reasonable remuneration[2] is such remuneration as is reasonable in the circumstances for provision of the trust services, and in relation to the services of a trust corporation that is an authorised institution under the

13 TA 2000, s 28(5).
14 TA 2000, s 29(2) and 'person' in Interpretation Act 1978, Sch 1.
15 Express provision had to be made for standard scale fees as opposed to fees from time to time relating to specific services: *Re Cooper* [1939] 160 LT 453.
16 (1850) 1 Mac & G 664.
17 Per Cotton LJ in *Re Corsellis* (1887) 34 Ch D 675; and see to same effect *Re Barber* (1886) 34 Ch D 77.
18 *Stocken v Dawson* (1843) 6 Beav 371; *Burden v Burden* (1813) 1 Ves & B 170.
19 TA 2000, s 29(1).
20 TA 2000, s 29(2). For 'in a professional capacity' see s 28(5) discussed in the preceding paragraph.
1 TA 2000, s 29(4).
2 TA 2000, s 29(3).

Banking Act 1987 providing trust services in that capacity, the instiution's resonable charges for such services.

Those in the invidious position of having to agree to their co-trustee being remunerated and then hoping such co-trustee will agree to themselves being remunerated have been placed in that position by the Trustee Act, so that merely entering into the agreement is not in itself impeachable at one extreme[3] while at the other extreme, the agreements would be impeachable if entered into under a reciprocal arrangement whereby each agrees to the other's remuneration only on the basis that they will agree to his remuneration[4]. However, if they consider what is in the best interests of the beneficiaries, taking account of the cost of employing delegates to act on behalf of the trustees if they are unpaid and so desire to minimise their own involvement, and the possibility of the trustees resigning and replacing themselves with a trust corporation with its scale fees and difficulties in establishing close ties with the beneficiaries for some time, then there should be no problems even if there are only two trustees who are partners in the same firm of solicitors where there is a home made will trust appointing them trustees or appointing lay trustees who have appointed the two partners as trustees to replace themselves. Indeed, in the latter case it seems acceptable for the professional trustees to make it plain that they will not accept appointment unless remuneration is agreed at the time of appointment, so they know where they stand, so that the appointing lay trustees continue as trustees to appoint one professional trustee agreeing in the deed of appointment to remuneration, and, then, the three trustees appoint the other professional trustee as an additional trustee agreeing in the deed of appointment to remuneration before the two lay trustees retire.

Once remuneration has been authorised under s 29(2) due to each of the other trustees having agreed in writing to a trustee, T, being remunerated for his services, that should be where T stands for the duration of his trusteeship, irrespective of one or more of the trustees being replaced by other persons as trustees. On this basis T, having once been duly authorised to receive remuneration, one might think he should continue to be so authorised even if subsequently becoming a sole trustee. However, it may be[5] that it is only so long as T is not a sole trustee that T can continue to charge remuneration; in which case T will need to execute a deed of appointment appointing X to act in a professional capacity and to be remunerated therefor. No doubt, taking account of the trust's history, X will shortly agree in writing that T may be remunerated for trust services[6]. If the latter strict construction be correct, then statute has placed T in an invidious position having taken office believing thereafter he would be entitled to remuneration, so as probably implicitly authorising him to take account of his self-interest when looking to appoint a new trustee. To avoid such problems T should ensure that once the number of trustees falls to two then a third trustee is appointed, although the downside will be the extra costs remunerating three trustees and obtaining unanimity for decisions. Taking account of these considerations, it is hoped the courts will construe s 29(2) so that 'once duly authorised thereafter duly

---

3 *Edge v Pensions Ombudsman* [2000] Ch 602, CA.

4 A fraud on the power.

5 TA 2000, s 29(2)(b) applying throughout, not just at the time of the remuneration agreement.

6 This should be capable of authorising remuneration retrospectively for the period when T was sole trustee: *Messeena v Carr* (1870) LR 9 Eq 260; *Libby v Kennedy* (1998) OPLR 213.

authorised'. After all, a beneficiary is entitled to challenge the charges made by a professional trustee[7].

The court's inherent jurisdiction

Although much less likely to be needed after the Trustee Act 2000, the court has inherent jurisdiction to authorise prospectively or retrospectively remuneration or extra remuneration for an express resulting or constructive trustee but the jurisdiction 'should be exercised only sparingly and in exceptional cases'[8], eg where the execution of the trust is more than ordinarily burdensome and especially beneficial for the trust beneficiaries[9] or where inflation has had disastrous consequences on fixed remuneration[10].

Where the jurisdiction is invoked it should be plainly sought by direct application: there should certainly not be inserted in the terms of a compromise a remuneration provision which has nothing to do with the matter in dispute and which is directly for the trustee's benefit[11].

In *Re Duke of Norfolk's Settlement Trusts*[12] the Court of Appeal in reserved judgments reversed Walton J[13] in part and clarified the law. There was no appeal against the extra remuneration which Walton J had authorised for exceptionally burdensome work in connection with the development of Arundel Court in The Strand and which was entirely outside anything which could reasonably have been foreseen when the trustees accepted office.

Walton J had held that the court had no general inherent jurisdiction to authorise for the future any general increase in the trustee company's remuneration, eg to increase the management fee to 40p from 10p per £100 on the aggregate amount of the market values of the trust property. The Court of Appeal[14] held that:

> 'the court has an inherent jurisdiction to authorise the payment of trustees and that jurisdiction extends to increasing the remuneration authorised by the trust instrument. In exercising that jurisdiction the court has to balance two influences which are to some extent in conflict. The first is that the office of trustee is, as such, gratuitious; the court will accordingly be careful to protect the interests of the beneficiaries against claims by the trustees. The second is that it is of great importance to the beneficiaries that the trust should be well administered. If, therefore, the court concludes, having regard to the nature of the trust, to the experience and skill of a trustee and to the amounts which he seeks to charge when compared with what other trustees might require to be paid for their services and to

---

7 *Re Fish* [1893] 2 Ch 413, CA; *Re Wells* [1962] 1 WLR 397; affd [1962] 2 All ER 826; the trustee must account for the amount overcharged.
8 Per Upjohn J in *Re Worthington* [1954] 1 All ER 677, [1954] 1 WLR 526. Further, see *Re Duke of Norfolk's Settlement Trusts* [1982] Ch 61, [1981] 3 All ER 220, CA; *Marshall v Holloway* (1820) 2 Swan 432; *Re Freeman* (1887) 37 Ch D 148; *Re Masters* [1953] 1 All ER 19, [1953] 1 WLR 81.
9 *Boardman v Phipps* [1967] 2 AC 46, [1966] 3 All ER 721; *Re Duke of Norfolk's Settlement Trusts* [1982] Ch 61, [1981] 3 All ER 220, CA; *John v James* [1986] STC 352 at 358.
10 *Re Barbour's Settlement* [1974] 1 All ER 1188 at 1192.
11 *Re Barbour's Settlement* [1974] 1 All ER 1188; *Re Codd* [1975] 2 All ER 1051n, [1975] 1 WLR 1139.
12 [1982] Ch 61, [1981] 3 All ER 220, CA. Applied in *Re Drexel Burnham Lambert's Pension Plan* [1995] 1 WLR 32.
13 [1979] Ch 37, [1978] 3 All ER 907.
14 [1982] Ch 61 at 79, [1981] 3 All ER 220 at 230, CA. The consent of beneficiaries is not required as under the Variation of Trusts Act 1958, but their objections will be considered, eg *Polly Peck International plc v Henry* [1999] 1 BCLC 407.

all the other circumstances of the case, that it would be in the best interests of the beneficiaries to increase the remuneration, then the court may properly do so.'

The case was then remitted to the Chancery Division for consideration to be given to the exercise of the jurisdiction.

Unfortunately, the Court of Appeal did not mention *Re Keeler's Settlement Trusts*[15], where Goulding J had followed Walton J in *Re Duke of Norfolk's Settlement Trusts* but *Re Keeler's Settlement Trusts* can no longer be authoritative so far as regards future remuneration of trustees.

Goulding J was also asked to allow the trustees to retain past remuneration earned in directorships to which they had been elected by virtue of trust shareholdings. He held that they could only retain the fees if 'it is plainly expedient in the interests of the trust for the directorship in question to be held by a trustee' as was the case, but that a director-trustee can only 'be allowed to retain reasonable remuneration for effort and skill applied by him in performing the duties of the directorship *over and above* the effort and skill ordinarily required for a director appointed to represent the interests of a substantial shareholder. The latter is something that a prudent man of business would in general undertake in the management of his own investments, and so is in general an exertion reasonably expected of a trustee'[16]. Since there was no evidence of the scale or intensity of the director-trustees' activities their claim was rejected, but an inquiry was directed to ascertain what effort and skill had been applied over and above the effort and skill ordinarily required.

The companies were the settlor's family companies and, as he swore in an affidavit, he had envisaged that his two sons would become trustees and directors after acquiring the necessary experience in the family business. Clause 4 of the Settlement, indeed, authorised the transfer of shares into the name of a trustee to enable him to have sufficient qualifying shares to be eligible for a directorship 'if at the request of the Trustees appointed or to be appointed as director of any Company in which the Trustees have an interest'.

On the authority of *Re Llewellin's Will Trust*[17] (not cited in *Re Keeler's Settlement Trusts*) it is unfortunate that the above clause was not treated as authorising the appointment of a trustee to a remunerated office and thus retention of such remuneration. In *Re Llewellin's Will Trusts* a will authorised the trustees 'to make arrangements with the ... company ... for the appointment of my said trustees or either of them or any other person as director or managing director of the said company'. Jenkins J, observing that the company articles provided for remunerating directors, remarked that 'the testator has expressly empowered his trustees to make arrangements for the appointment of themselves to offices which can fairly be described as remunerated' and so held that the trustees could retain their directors' fees even though 'the trustees are in the invidious position of fixing their own remuneration, being completely in control of the company ... but that is the result which must inevitably ensue'[18].

15 [1981] Ch 156, [1981] 1 All ER 888.
16 [1981] Ch 156 at 162, [1981] 1 All ER 888 at 893.
17 [1949] Ch 225, [1949] 1 All ER 487.
18 [1949] Ch 225 at 229, [1949] 1 All ER 487 at 489. Further see liberal tendencies in *Sargeant v National Westminster Bank* (1990) 61 P & CR 518 at 523 and *Re Drexel Burnham Lambert's Pension Plan* [1995] 1 WLR 32.

In *Foster v Spencer*[19] the judge awarded remuneration for past services to trustees of a decaying cricket ground ultimately sold by them with planning permission for over £900,000. The services they rendered were wholly outside their contemplation when appointed as unpaid trustees and refusal of remuneration would lead to unjust enrichment of the beneficiaries at their expense. The court was happy with the retrospective application because the true extent of the trustees' tasks and services could not be known until it was possible to market and sell the land well, while no money was available for paying remuneration for a long time. Indeed, interest was awarded at 8% from the time that funds were available to pay remuneration[20].

Remuneration where breach of fiduciary duty

In *Boardman v Phipps*[1] the House of Lords upheld the trial judge's allowance of generous remuneration to the solicitor to the trustees who had been guilty of an innocent breach of trust and whose exceptional abilities had proved to be of exceptional benefit to the trust for whom the solicitor held his profits on constructive trust. In *O'Sullivan v Management Agency and Music Ltd*[2] Fox LJ stated:

> 'A hard and fast rule that the beneficiary can demand the whole profit without an allowance for the work without which it could not have been created is unduly severe. Nor do I think that the principle is only applicable in cases where the personal conduct of the fiduciary cannot be criticised. The justice of the individual case must be considered on the facts of that case. Accordingly, where there has been dishonesty or surreptitious dealing or other improper conduct then it might be appropriate to refuse relief; but that will depend on the circumstances.'

Thus, the Court of Appeal held that a fiduciary agent whose contract with his performer was set aside for undue influence was entitled to remuneration and a reasonable sum by way of profit because of a significant contribution to the performer's success[3]. In *Re Berkeley Applegate Ltd*[4] it was stated:

> 'The authorities establish a general principle that where a person seeks to enforce a claim to an equitable interest in property, the court has a discretion to require as a condition of giving effect to that equitable interest that an allowance be made for costs incurred and for skill and labour expended in connection with the adminis-tration of the property. It is a discretion which will be sparingly exercised; but factors which will operate in favour ... include the fact that if the work had not been done ... it would have had to be done either by the person entitled to the equitable interest or by a receiver appointed by the court whose fees would have been borne by the trust property, and the fact that the work has been of substantial benefit to the trust property ... '

Thus, where a company went into liquidation and held mortgage loans and funds on trust for investors (who had advanced funds to be invested in mortgages) and it was likely that the costs incurred and skill and labour expended by the liquidator in administering the trust property would greatly

---

19 [1996] 2 All ER 672.
20 No interest, however, was allowed in respect of expenses properly incurred by the trustees.
 1 [1967] 2 AC 46.
 2 [1985] QB 428 at 468 endorsed in *Cheese v Thomas* [1994] 1 All ER 35 at 43, CA; see also *Warman International Ltd v Dwyer* (1995) 69 ALJR 362.
 3 See also *John v James* [1986] STC 352 at 358.
 4 [1988] 3 All ER 71 at 83.

exceed the company's free assets, the court declared that the liquidator would be entitled to be paid his costs and remuneration out of the trust property to the extent that the company's free assets, were insufficient.

In *Guinness plc v Saunders*[5] Lord Goff made the general point that the exercise of the jurisdiction should be 'restricted to those cases where it cannot have the effect of encouraging trustees in any way to put themselves in a position where their interests conflict with their duties as trustees'. However, these dicta seem too sweeping in the light of the authorities. In *Guinness* a director's claim to reasonable equitable remuneration for work done without an intra vires authorisation from the committee of directors failed, the court not being entitled to usurp the functions conferred on the directors by the company's articles, especially when it still remained open to the company to award the director appropriate remuneration.

In *Badfinger Music v Evans*[6] the court considered that Lord Goff's dicta were too strict, the existence or absence of a conflict of interest being an important consideration but not the only factor to be taken into account. Indeed, reasonable remuneration could be calculated by reference to a percentage of profits in a case where a flat fee of similar amount (or even larger amount) could have been recoverable.

The court's statutory jurisdiction

Where the court appoints a corporation, other than the Public Trustee, to be a trustee it is empowered by s 42 of the Trustee Act, 1925, to authorise such remuneration for its services as the court thinks fit[7]. The court may also authorise remuneration for a person whom it appoints as a judicial trustee under the Judicial Trustees Act 1896, s 1(5).

The Public Trustee and custodian trustees

The Public Trustee is allowed to charge such fees as may be fixed by the Treasury[8]. A custodian trustee is allowed to charge such fees as the Public Trustee could charge for acting as custodian trustee[9]. A trust corporation could not be appointed custodian trustee and managing trustee so as to enable it to charge fees[10], but it can now charge under s 29(1) of the Trustee Act 2000 if not trustee of a charitable trust and there is no charging clause in the trust instrument.

Agreement with beneficiaries

A trustee is entitled to remuneration if the beneficiaries are all of full age and

---

5 [1990] 2 AC 663 at 701, [1990] 1 All ER 652 at 667, HL.
6 [2001] 1 WLTR 1: where the claimant's conduct was open to serious criticism though not dishonest, he was entitled to a flat fee, though a fiduciary and his sound-engineer was entitled to a percentage of the profits. Also *University of Nottingham v Fisher* [2000] ICR 1462.
7 *Re Young* (1934) 103 LJP 75; *Re Masters* [1953] 1 All ER 19, [1953] 1 WLR 81 (both cases where remuneration of an administrator was authorised); and see *Hearn v Morgan* [1945] 2 All ER 480 at 481, where the relevant terms of the orders of the court are set out in the case stated; the decision is reported on a question of liability to income tax.
8 Public Trustee Act 1906, s 9, as amended by the Administration of Justice Act 1965, s 2; Public Trustee (Fees) Act 1957 and orders made thereunder.
9 Public Trustee Act 1906, s 4.
10 *Arning v James* [1936] Ch 158; *Forster v Williams Deacon's Bank Ltd* [1935] Ch 359.

capacity and between them absolutely entitled to the settled property and so agree[11], so long as undue influence was not exercised by him[12]. If one beneficiary (eg the life tenant) agrees that the trustee may be paid out of his interest then that beneficiary will be bound and will not be able to sue for breach of trust for past payments and, if contractually bound, will be unable to revoke his agreement.

Challenging trustee's fees

Remuneration chargeable under s 29 of the Trustee Act 2000 is such remuneration as is reasonable in the circumstances[13], so that the beneficiaries may make the trustee account for the amount by which his remuneration exceeds that which is reasonable in all the circumstances. Where there is an express clause in the trust instrument authorising the trustee to charge for his services as trustee, the beneficiaries can also seek to make the trustee account for the amount by which his remuneration exceeds what is reasonable for him to charge in all the circumstances[14].

ARTICLE 59

Duty of trustee not to traffic with or otherwise profit by trust property nor to cause loss from a conflict between his fiduciary duty and his self-interest

(1) A trustee must not use or deal with trust property or exploit his position for his own private advantage for he will be strictly liable to account for his profits of which he will be constructive trustee[15] and he will similarly be personally accountable for losses arising where there is a real sensible possibility of a conflict between his fiduciary duty and his self-interest[16].

(2) A disposition of trust property to a trustee is automatically voidable by a beneficiary ex debito justitiae, however fair the transaction may be (the 'self-dealing' rule) unless:

---

11 It seems that the agreement (unless in a deed) needs to be concluded before the trustee accepts office (as indicated by *Re Sherwood* (1840) 3 Beav 338 and *Douglas v Archbutt* (1858) 2 De G & J 148) since once the trustee has accepted office he is already under a duty to the beneficiaries to act gratuitously so that no consideration exists for a contractually binding agreement. However, the acquiescence of a beneficiary prevents a beneficiary from suing for breach of trust for past payments of remuneration.

12 *Ayliffe v Murray* (1740) 2 Atk 58.

13 TA 2000, s 29(2).

14 *Re Fish* [1893] 2 Ch 413, although Lindley LJ surprisingly contemplated that the beneficiaries' accounting rights could be ousted by a provision in the trust instrument authorising a co-trustee's bona fide approval of his co-trustee's account to bind the beneficiaries: *Re Wells* [1962] 2 All ER 826, [1962] 1 WLR 874.

15 *A-G for Hong Kong v Reid* [1994] 1 AC 324, PC; *Webb v Earl of Shaftesbury* (1802) 7 Ves 480; *Ex p Lacey* (1802) 6 Ves 625; and see *Re Imperial Land Co of Marseilles* (1877) 4 Ch D 566; *Aberdeen Town Council v Aberdeen University* (1877) 2 App Cas 544; and *Rochefoucauld v Boustead* [1898] 1 Ch 550. Cf also *Brown v IRC* [1965] AC 244, [1964] 3 All ER 119, HL (but see, now, Solicitors' Accounts Rules 1991). This has been dealt with in Art 33, ante.

16 *Clark Boyce v Mouat* [1994] 1 AC 428; *Nocton v Lord Ashburton* [1914] AC 932; *Canson Enterprises Ltd v Boughton & Co* (1991) 85 DLR (4th) 129; *Glennie v McDougall & Cowans Holdings Ltd* [1935] 2 DLR 561 at 579; *Swindle v Harrison* [1997] 4 All ER 705, CA; *Bristol and West Building Society v Mothew* [1998] Ch 1.

(a) under an express or necessarily implied[17] power in the settlement; or
(b) by leave of a competent court; or
(c) under a contract or option made before the fiduciary relationship arose[18]; or
(d) carried out under section 68 of the Settled Land Act 1925 or section 39 of the Pensions Act 1995; or
(e) the beneficiary acquiesced in the transaction[19]; or
(f) exceptional circumstances exist and it is proved by the party seeking to uphold the transaction that it was a fair and reasonable one not vitiated by any conflicting interest or duty.

(3) A trustee may purchase or accept a mortgage of the equitable interest of a beneficiary in the trust property[20], but, if the transaction be impeached, it is incumbent on the trustee to prove[1] affirmatively and clearly (the 'fair-dealing' rule):

(a) that he and the beneficiary were at arm's length and that no confidence was reposed in him;
(b) that the transaction was for the advantage of the beneficiary; and
(c) that full information was given to the beneficiary of the value of the property, of the nature of his interest therein and of the circumstances of the transaction[2].

(4) A trustee cannot qualify himself to become a purchaser by retiring from the trusteeship with that view[3].

Paragraph 1

These matters have already been fully dealt with in Article 33 (concerned with constructive trusts of profits) to which reference should be made. If losses arise instead of profits then, assuming that no defence is available that would have been available if a profit had been made, the trustee or fiduciary is personally accountable for such loss. It has been said that if non-disclosure of material facts is at the heart of the breach of fiduciary duty the defendant 'cannot be heard to maintain that disclosure would not have altered the decision to proceed with the transaction, because the [claimant's] action would be surely determined by some other factor ... Once the court has determined that the non-disclosed facts were material, speculation as to what course the [claimant], on disclosure, would have taken is not relevant'[4].

---

17 *Sargeant v National Westminister Bank plc* (1990) 61 P & CR 518, CA; *Edge v Pensions Ombudsman* [2000] Ch 602, CA.
18 *Re Mulholland's Will Trust* [1949] 1 All ER 460.
19 *Holder v Holder* [1968] Ch 353, CA.
20 *Gibson v Jeyes* (1801) 6 Ves 266; *Phipps v Lovegrove* (1873) LR 16 Eq 80; *Newman v Newman* (1885) 28 Ch D 674.
1 Cases in note 15, above; and also *Randall v Errington* (1805) 10 Ves 423; *Coles v Trecothick* (1804) 9 Ves 234.
2 See *Chillingworth v Chambers* [1896] 1 Ch 685.
3 *Ex p James* (1803) 8 Ves 337; *Spring v Pride* (1864) 4 De GJ & Sm 395. But cf *Re Boles and British Land Co's Contract* [1902] 1 Ch 244.
4 *Brickenden v London Loan & Savings Co* [1934] 3 DLR 465 at 469, PC; *Farrington v Rowe McBride & Partners* [1985] 1 NZLR 83 at 99. Misrepresentations are *a fortiori* non-disclosures.

However, these remarks have been restricted[5] to a claim to rescind the transaction, although it may well be that if the defendant is being sued for an account or equitable compensation, then misrepresentation or non-disclosure by him in breach of his duty of undivided loyalty should place the onus of proof upon him to prove that the losses would have occurred even if there had been no such breach[6], particularly if his breach was fraudulent[7]. Where the trustee's conduct amounts to a failure to do what he should have done and is a breach of his undivided duty of loyalty, he will be liable (via surcharging his accounts) for losses that would not have occurred but for his breach of duty. Other fiduciaries will also be liable for such losses, but there may be more possibility to restrict the scope thereof[8].

PARAGRAPH 2

The self-dealing rule

As Megarry V-C said in a reserved judgment in *Tito v Waddell (No 2)*[9]:

'The self-dealing rule is (to put it very shortly) that if a trustee sells the trust property to himself the sale is voidable by any beneficiary ex debito justitiae, however fair the transaction.'

Vinelott J has stated[10]:

'It is clear that the self-dealing rule is an application of the wider principle that a man must not put himself in a position where duty and interest conflict or where his duty to one conflicts with his duty to another.'

Until *Holder v Holder*[11] the rule was considered to stand much more upon general principle than upon the circumstances of any individual case. It rested upon this: that 'the purchase is not permitted in any case, however honest the circumstances, the general interest of justice requiring it to be destroyed in every instance; because no court is equal to the examination and ascertainment of the truth'[12]. Consequently, under no circumstances could an active trustee, nor, indeed, a passive trustee *who had been* (at all events within a recent period) *an active one*, nor even a person who had been

---

5 *Swindle v Harrison* [1997] 4 All ER 705 at 726, per Hobhouse LJ.

6 *Bank of New Zealand v New Zealand Guardian Trust Co* [1999] 1 NZLR 664 at 687, CA.

7 *Swindle v Harrison* [1997] 4 All ER 705 at 716–717, per Evans LJ, but rejected by Tuckey LJ in *Collins v Brebner* [2000] Lloyd's Rep PN 587, CA where the defendant's ultimate obtaining of a 50% shareholding in the specified company with the claimant's £524,000 held on trust for the claimant was held to prevent the defrauded claimant from recovering for further losses unless proved to result from the defendant's fraud, following *Target Holdings v Redferns* [1996] AC 421. And see *County NatWest Ltd v Barton* [2002] 4 All ER 494, CA. It may be that where a commercial bare trust arises incidentally in the course of a contractual relationship with a fiduciary element as in the solicitor-client relationship, contractual principles should prevail (implicitly ousting equitable principles), so that a rebuttable presumption only arises against a trustee of a continuing trust and not a 'one-off' trust incidental to a contract.

8 *Swindle v Harrison* [1997] 4 All ER 705, CA; *Collins v Brebner* [2000] Lloyd's Rep PN 587, CA.

9 *Tito v Waddell (No 2)* [1977] 3 All ER 129 at 241, per Megarry V-C.

10 *Re Thompson's Settlement* [1985] 2 All ER 720 at 730 and *Movitex Ltd v Bulfield* [1988] BCLC 104 at 117.

11 [1968] Ch 353, [1968] 1 All ER 665.

12 Per Lord Eldon in *Ex p James* (1803) 8 Ves 337 at 345; and see *Beningfield v Baxter* (1886) 12 App Cas 167.

erroneously treated by all parties as a trustee[13] (ie a trustee de son tort), purchase trust property from himself or his colleagues, either directly, or through the intervention of a third party[14]. It mattered not that an independent third party fixed the purchase price. Thus in *Wright v Morgan*[15] a testator left land on trust for sale with power to postpone sale for seven years and provided that it should be offered at a price to be fixed by valuers to one of his sons, A, who was one of the trustees. A assigned his right (which was treated as an option and not a right of pre-emption) to his brother, B, who was also one of the trustees but who, unlike A, was not authorised to purchase by the terms of the will. B arranged for the sale to himself, retired from the trusteeship and purchased at a price fixed by the valuers. The Privy Council set the purchase aside: after all, B was one of those responsible for determining when the land was to be sold and prices could fluctuate over the years.

Exceptional circumstances

In *Holder v Holder*[16] the Court of Appeal refused to treat the rule as inflexible, not being impressed by Lord Eldon's view that no court is equal to the examination and ascertainment of the knowledge and intention of a trustee, since the Court of Appeal considered that courts were daily engaged in ascertaining parties' knowledge and intentions. In the case a testator had appointed his widow, daughter and son to be his executors and trustees. The son took a very few minor incidental steps at the outset in connection with the administration of the estate but then took no further part. He executed a deed of renunciation of the executorship so only the widow and the daughter took out probate. The deed was ineffective owing to his technical intermeddling with the estate. The son had a tenancy of a farm comprised in his father's estate. The farm was offered for sale at auction subject to the son's tenancy and the son purchased the freehold reversion in the farm at well above the reserve price. The Court of Appeal refused to set aside the purchase on the application of a beneficiary under the will.

The purchase was not voidable due to the following special circumstances: the son had played no real part in the administration of the estate; there was, in fact, no conflict of duty and self-interest for the beneficiaries knew the son was a prospective purchaser and did not look to him to protect their interests; the son had taken no part in instructing the valuers or in the preparations for the auction sale and was not in the position of being both vendor and purchaser; any special knowledge which the son had was acquired by him as tenant of the farm and not as executor.

Subsequently, in *Hillsdown plc v Pensions Ombudsman*[17] Knox J refused to treat the self-dealing rule as inflexible where directors of limited companies

---

13 *Plowright v Lambert* (1885) 52 LT 646. As to executor, see *Hall v Hallett* (1784) 1 Cox Eq Cas 134.
14 *Campbell v Walker* (1800) 5 Ves 678; *Knight v Marjoribanks* (1849) 2 Mac & G 10; and see *Re Walters* [1954] Ch 653, sub nom *Re Sharman, Trevenen v Pearce* [1954] 1 All ER 893. But in one case it was held that a trustee who had retired for upwards of 12 years was not precluded from purchasing part of the trust property (*Re Boles and British Land Co's Contract* [1902] 1 Ch 244).
15 [1926] AC 788.
16 [1968] Ch 353.
17 [1997] 1 All ER 862 at 895–896 two persons were directors of the relevant three companies, being the trustee of pension scheme A, the trustee of pension scheme B (to whom the pension funds of A were being transferred) and the employer.

dealing with each other are concerned, but held that the fact that negotiations have been conducted by persons one or more of whom had a conflict of duties places upon those seeking to uphold the transaction the onus of proving that it was, indeed, reasonable and proper on a full investigation of the facts.

A flexible approach was also taken in *Public Trustee v Cooper*[18] where an unconnected outsider had made a take-over offer for shares in a private company where a key shareholding was held on trust for company employees (largely opposed to the take-over) and one trustee had a substantial minority shareholding that he himself owned beneficially, while also being a trustee of a charitable trust with a minority shareholding (the charity being keen to accept the offer). Hart J held the self-dealing rule did not apply in respect of the trust for employees but the trustees thereof, if they wanted to be able to exercise their discretion without surrendering it to the court, had to discharge the onus of proving that the conflicting interest or duty had not operated in a vitiating way: the onus had been discharged.

He stated[19]:

'The beneficiary is entitled to the decision of all his trustees, but, at the same time, he is entitled to require that the decision is made independently of any private interest or competing duty of any of the trustees. Where a trustee has such a private interest or competing duty there are three possible ways in which the conflict can successfully be managed. One is for the trustee concerned to resign. This will not always provide a practical or sensible solution. The trustee concerned may represent an important source of information or advice to his co-trustees or have a significant relationship to some or all of the beneficiaries such that his departure as a trustee will be potentially harmful to the interests of the trust estate or its beneficiaries.

Secondly, the nature of the conflict may be so pervasive throughout the trustee body, that they, as a body, have no alternative but to surrender their discretion to the court.

Thirdly, the trustees may honestly and reasonably believe that, notwithstanding a conflict affecting one or more of their number, they are nevertheless able fairly and reasonably to take the decision. In this third case, it will usually be prudent, if time allows, for the trustees to allow their proposed exercise of discretion to be scrutinised in advance by the court in proceedings in which any opposing beneficial interests are properly represented, and for them not to proceed unless and until the court has authorised them to do so. If they do not do so, they run the risk of having to justify the exercise of their discretion in subsequent hostile litigation and then satisfy the court that their decision was not only one which any reasonable body of trustees might have taken but was also one that had not in fact been influenced by the conflict.'

No need for self-dealing rule if only one party or transaction not genuine

T cannot contract with himself and so cannot purchase from himself[20], nor can he make a gift of a chattel to himself or grant a lease to himself[1], nor could he convey land to himself until statute permitted this[2] (eg for an

---

18 [2001] WTLR 901, especially at 933.
19 [2001] WTLR 901 at 933–934.
20 *Williams v Scott* [1900] AC 499; *Ellis v Kerr* [1910] 1 Ch 529; LPA 1925, s 82.
 1 *Rye v Rye* [1962] AC 496.
 2 LPA 1925, s 72(4).

executor[3] to transfer land to himself beneficially or as trustee). Thus, the purported transaction is of no effect[4] except for a conveyance of land where the legal title, but not the equitable title, will pass, no overreaching of the equitable title occurring. However, a trust instrument may authorise a bank trustee to deposit money with itself by way of unsecured loan, so that the beneficiaries' equitable proprietary interest disappears to the extent of such deposit[5].

A sale or lease to a nominee does not breach the requirement for two parties to a transaction capable of overreaching the beneficiaries' interests[6].

Sale to the wife of trustee

A sale to a trustee's wife is not automatically voidable but the circumstances will be closely examined[7]. After all,

> 'there are wives and wives. In one case the trustee may have sold privately to his wife with whom he was living in perfect amity; in another the property may have been knocked down at auction to the trustee's wife from whom he has been living separate and in enmity for a dozen years.'[8]

One must look at realities to see if she should be treated as the trustee's alter ego.

Sale to company in which trustee holds shares

The rule vitiating purchases by trustees does not prevent a trustee from selling to a limited company (other than a 'one man company'[9]) in which he is a mere shareholder; for a sale by a person to a corporation of whom he is a member is not, either in form or in substance, a sale by him to himself and others. Nevertheless, in such a case, there is such a conflict of interest and duty that, if the sale be impeached by the beneficiaries, the onus will lie on the company to show affirmatively that the trustee had taken all reasonable pains to secure a purchaser at the best price, and that the price given by the company was not inadequate at the time, although a better price might have been obtained by waiting[10].

---

3 Administration of Estates Act 1925, s 36(4).

4 However, if the value of the property were less than the purchase price added to the trust fund, it seems the beneficiaries could retain the price as part of their fund if the trustee tried to recover it: it is the victim not the wrongdoer who has the remedies and the trustee should not be better off if the transaction were void rather than voidable.

5 *Space Investments Ltd v Canadian Imperial Bank of Commerce Trust Co (Bahamas) Ltd* [1986] 3 All ER 75, PC.

6 It is an unauthorised transaction, unless in a special case authorised, eg where T holds land for A absolutely and is authorised to grant a lease to A: *Ingram v IRC* [2000] 1 AC 293 at 305 and 310, HL, approving Millett LJ, below in the Court of Appeal, [1997] 4 All ER 395 at 426–427.

7 *Burrell v Burrell's Trustees* 1915 SC 333; *Re King's Will Trust* (1959) 173 Estates Gazette 627. Cf *Re McNally* [1967] NZLR 521.

8 *Tito v Waddell (No 2)* [1977] 3 All ER 129 at 241.

9 *Silkstone and Haigh Moor Coal Co v Edey* [1900] 1 Ch 167 or presumably a company of which he is managing director and (with his and his wife's shares) majority shareholder: *Re Thompson's Settlement* [1985] 2 All ER 720 at 729 where Vinelott J at pp 730–731 also indicated that sale by a trustee to a partnership of which he was a member would be automatically voidable.

10 *Farrar v Farrars Ltd* (1888) 40 Ch D 395; *Tse Kwong Lam v Wong Chit Sen* [1983] 3 All ER 54, [1983] 1 WLR 1349, PC.

Employment of parent company by subsidiary company

What happens if a company-trustee places business with its holding company, eg invests trust moneys in a fund managed by its holding company for a fee? It seems that the onus will lie on the trustee to show that the placement of its business with its holding company did not create a real sensible possibility of conflict which could impair the trustee's ability to serve the best interests of the beneficiaries, as where the holding company is a pre-eminent company with an attractive investment record and where the equivalent fee would be payable to any similar company selected to be investment manager[11].

Subsequent repurchase by trustee without collusion

The fact that a trustee has sold trust property in the hope, subsequently realised, of being able to repurchase it for himself at a future time, is not of itself a sufficient ground for setting aside the sale, where the price was not inadequate at the time, and there was no agreement or understanding existing at the time of the first sale that the purchaser should sell or reconvey the property to the trustee. The fact that the trustee many years afterwards made a handsome profit by repurchasing and selling the property makes no difference[12]. However, in the case just cited, more than twenty years had elapsed without the sale being impeached, and many of the parties were dead; and, as the court said, the presumption of law that a transaction was legal and honest is a presumption that is strengthened by lapse of time. It is, however, clear that where trustees have rightly sold to A, so long as that sale is not completed and remains executory, one of the vendor trustees cannot repurchase the property from A for himself[13].

Application of the rule to other fiduciary persons

The general self-dealing rule that a purchase by a trustee can be set aside applies to all persons in a fiduciary position, who are involved in disposing of fiduciary property to themselves or their nominee. Thus it has been held that an agent employed for the sale of an estate cannot purchase it for himself or another[14].

On the other hand where there are genuinely two parties to the transaction as where a client was very desirous of selling property, and, after vainly endeavouring to do so, finally sold it to his solicitor (who was, of course, a fiduciary) and it was proved that the transaction was fair and the price adequate, and indeed more than could have been obtained elsewhere at the time, and that the client quite understood his position, it was held that such a sale was good and binding, although it lay upon the solicitor to prove that it

---

11 *Jones v AMP Perpetual Trustee Company NZ Ltd* [1994] 1 NZLR 690 at 710–711 where Thomas J would also have excused the trustee, if necessary, from liability under the New Zealand equivalent of TA 1925, s 61, the loss of value of the investments being caused by the October 1987 stockmarket crash. Cp harsh *Re Brooke Bond & Co Ltd's Trust Deed* [1963] Ch 357.

12 *Re Postlethwaite* (1888) 37 WR 200, CA; and see also *Dover v Buck* (1865) 5 Giff 57; and *Baker v Peck* (1861) 9 WR 472; but cf *A-G v Lord Dudley* (1815) Coop G 146.

13 *Williams v Scott* [1900] AC 499; *Delves v Gray* [1902] 2 Ch 606; *Parker v McKenna* (1874) 10 Ch App 96 at 125.

14 *Ex p Bennett* (1805) 10 Ves 381; *Re Bloye's Trust* (1849) 1 Mac & G 488; affd sub nom *Lewis v Hillman* (1852) 3 HL Cas 607; *De Bussche v Alt* (1878) 8 Ch D 286.

was unimpeachable[15]. A solicitor purchasing from his client should, however, to avoid allegations of undue influence always make him employ a separate solicitor[16]; and this is so even where the solicitor purchases, not directly from the client, but from the latter's trustee in bankruptcy[17].

The rule applies even where the party from whom advice is sought is not a professional adviser; for the fact that he accepts the position of adviser places him under a fiduciary obligation towards the party seeking advice[18].

Trustee cannot lease to himself or sell or lease own property to trust

Trustees cannot lease the trust estate to one of themselves, and if they do so the lessee will have to account for the profits[19]. Just as agents cannot sell or lease their own property to their principal except with his knowledge and approval[20], so a trustee cannot sell or lease his own property to himself and his co-trustees, although there is no English case directly in point[1].

Sine qua non concurrence of trustee

In *Re Thompsons' Settlement*[2] it was held that the self-dealing rule extends to cases where a trustee concurs in a transaction (eg the grant or assignment of a lease) which cannot be effected without his concurrence and where he also has an interest in, or holds a fiduciary duty to another in relation to, the same transaction.

Mortgages

In one case concerning the property of a charity, the trustees of which could act by a majority, it was held that one of several trustees might himself become a mortgagee of the trust property and exercise over it all the rights of a mortgagee[3]. It does not appear whether the mortgagee-trustee concurred with his co-trustees in exercising their discretion.

Where trustees must act unanimously, as in the case of private trusts unless the trust instrument otherwise provides, it is clear that a conflict of duty and self-interest may arise in the case of a mortgagee-trustee so that prima facie the mortgage will be voidable in the absence of special circumstances entirely satisfying the court as to the complete propriety of the mortgage.

---

15 *Spencer v Topham* (1856) 22 Beav 573, 2 Jur NS 865; *Gibson v Jeyes* (1801) 6 Ves 266; *Johnson v Fesemeyer* (1858) 3 De G & J 13; *Edwards v Meyrick* (1842) 2 Hare 60.

16 *Cockburn v Edwards* (1881) 18 Ch D 449.

17 *Luddy's Trustee v Peard* (1886) 33 Ch D 500; and see also *Barron v Willis* [1900] 2 Ch 121; affd sub nom *Willis v Barron* [1902] AC 271.

18 *Tate v Williamson* (1866) 2 Ch App 55.

19 *Re Dumbell, ex p Hughes* (1802) 6 Ves 617; *Re John's Assignment Trusts* [1970] 1 WLR 955 at 960.

20 *Bentley v Craven* (1853) 18 Beav 75; *Re Cape Breton Co* (1885) 29 Ch D 795, CA; Goff & Jones *Law of Restitution* (5th edn) Ch 33(B) 3.

1 *Bentley v Craven* (1853) 18 Beav 75 at 76; *Re Cape Breton Co* (1885) 29 Ch D 795 at 803, CA; *Scott on Trusts* (4th edn) Vol IIA para 170.12 to 170.13; *National Trust Co Ltd v Osadchuk* [1943] SCR 89.

2 [1986] Ch 99, [1985] 2 All ER 720.

3 *A-G v Hardy* (1851) 1 Sim NS 338 accepted by Stirling J in *Re Mason's Orphanage* [1896] 1 Ch 54 at 59.

Personal representative's appropriation of deceased's assets for himself

In satisfaction of a pecuniary legacy or the statutory pecuniary legacy on intestacy or a debt due to him, the personal representative can appropriate[4] to himself, cash or the equivalent of cash (like quoted government securities and quoted shares with a clear market value) but not shares in an unquoted company[5]. The rationale is that the open market value of securities equivalent to cash could have been obtained by a sale and the proceeds then remitted to the personal representative as his own property[6]. Thus, a trustee should also be able similarly to appropriate to himself to satisfy a fixed sum due to him as beneficiary or by way of indemnity.

In satisfaction of a share in the deceased's residuary estate the cases seem to establish that an appropriation of assets can be made by the personal representative to himself if it is fairly made without an eye to obtaining for himself those assets that are more likely to appreciate than others[7].

Express or necessarily implied authorisation

A trust instrument may expressly authorise trustees to act in ways benefiting themselves where they are also beneficiaries under the trust or objects of powers therein, eg a clause entitling a trustee to act and exercise discretionary powers notwithstanding any direct personal interest therein[8]. The onus is then on those attacking the exercise of the function by the trustees, to impeach it (eg as ignoring a relevant factor or taking account of an irrelevant factor or perverse to any sensible expectation of the settlor)[9] whether the authorisation is express or necessarily implied from the circumstances[10] (eg the settlor appointed A and B to be trustees but also beneficiaries under his discretionary trust)[11].

Purchase by trustee by leave of the court

Where there are infant beneficiaries or unborn beneficiaries the court will, on the application of the trustee, allow him to purchase, if it can see that, in the circumstances, it is clearly for the benefit of the beneficiaries, but not otherwise[12]. The best course of procedure in such an application is to issue a Part 8 claim form invoking Order 85, rule 2(3)(d). The master will make an order approving the sale in clear cases and in cases of greater difficulty the summons will be adjourned to the judge (usually as a Monday morning chambers summons). The usual practice is for costs to be paid by the purchasing trustee. An alternative method would be an application under s 57 of

---

4 Administration of Estates Act 1925, s 41.
5 *Kane v Radley-Kane* [1999] Ch 274.
6 *Kane v Radley-Kane* [1999] Ch 274.
7 *Barclay v Owen* (1889) 60 LT 220; *Re Richardson* [1896] 1 Ch 512; *Kane v Radley-Kane* [1999] Ch 274. For the need to act fairly see *Lloyds Bank v Duker* [1987] 3 All ER 193 and *Edge v Pensions Ombudsman* [2000] Ch 602.
8 *Re Beatty's Will Trust* [1990] 3 All ER 844 at 846, sub nom *Re Beatty Hinves v Brooke* [1990] 1 WLR 1503 at 1506; *Blair v Vallely & Blair* [2000] WTLR 615 at 639.
9 See Article 61 below.
10 *Edge v Pensions Ombudsman* [2000] Ch 602 at 622 and 631–633, CA.
11 *Edge v Pensions Ombudsman* [2000] Ch 602 at 622 and 631–633, CA; *Re Drexel Burnham Lambert UK Pension Plan* [1995] 1 WLR 32; *Sargeant v National Westminster Bank* (1990) 61 P & CR 518, CA.
12 *Farmer v Dean* (1863) 32 Beav 327; *Campbell v Walker* (1800) 5 Ves 678.

the Trustee Act 1925[13]. It is apprehended that no such application could succeed in the face of opposition by any beneficiary, unless the court considered such opposition to be merely capricious and unreasonable.

Pensions Act 1995, s 39

Doubts subsequently assuaged by the courts[14], as to the extent members of pension trust schemes who were also trustees could exercise discretions so as to benefit themselves led to s 39 of the Pensions Act 1995, stating:

> 'No rule of law that a trustee may not exercise the powers vested in him so as to give rise to a conflict between his personal interest and his duties to the beneficiaries shall apply to a trustee of a trust scheme, who is also a member of the scheme, exercising the powers vested in him in any manner, merely because their exercise in that manner benefits, or may benefit, him as a member of the scheme.'

The trustee-member problem ceased to be one so far as concerns pension schemes of insolvent employees because the Pension Schemes Act 1993, ss 119 and 121 require independent trustees to be appointed for the exercise of discretions.

Purchase under contract made before the fiduciary relationship arose

Where the contract for purchase was made before the fiduciary relationship came into existence the creation of that relationship will not prevent the trustee from asserting his rights under the contract[15]. Thus, where a lessor had granted an option to purchase the demised premises at a fixed price it was held that the lessee was not prevented from exercising the option after the lessor's death by having become his executor[16].

Purchase by bare trustees

The rule as to selling to himself only applies where the express or constructive trustee is substantially an active trustee having the opportunity of thereby acquiring information concerning the trust property. He may purchase where he is the mere depositary of the legal estate without any duties, and without ever having had any[17], or is a person nominated trustee who has disclaimed[18]. However, a trustee who was originally an executive trustee, and has become a mere bare trustee by performance of the trusts, would, it is apprehended, be disqualified; for he would have had an opportunity of becoming acquainted with the property and its value[19].

Purchase from person to whom trustee's functions delegated

Where a collective delegation has been made to a person or persons bene-

---

13 See pp 525, et seq, ante.

14 *Edge v Pensions Ombudsman* [2000] Ch 602, CA; *Re Drexel Burnham Lambert UK Pension Plan* [1995] 1 WLR 32.

15 *Vyse v Foster* (1874) LR 7 HL 318.

16 *Re Mulholland's Will Trusts* [1949] 1 All ER 460.

17 *Sutton v Jones* (1809) 15 Ves 584. Also see *Pooley v Quilter* (1858) 4 Drew 184; *Denton v Donner* (1856) 23 Beav 295; cp *Re Brooke Bond Ltd's Trust Deed* [1963] Ch 357.

18 *Stacey v Elph* (1833) 1 My & K 195.

19 *Ex p Bennett* (1805) 10 Ves 381. But cf *Re Boles and British Land Co's Contract* [1902] 1 Ch 244.

ficially interested in possession under a trust of land[20] and a trustee seeks to purchase the land, he faces the difficulties that he may well have acquired useful information about the land while trustee and that his interest in purchasing conflicts with his duty to consider revoking the delegation which would interfere with his purchase. Thus, it is likely that his purchase will be impeachable unless with the consent of the court or of all the beneficiaries if ascertained and of full age and capacity[1].

In the case of an individual delegation by a trustee by a power of attorney it seems that the acts of the delegate are treated as acts of the trustee[2], so that any purchase by the latter will be impeachable.

Purchase by trustees of subsidiary settlement

A question sometimes arises in practice whether, on a sale by trustees, the property can be purchased beneficially by a person who is a trustee of a subsidiary settlement by which a share in the proceeds of the sale is settled. Curiously enough, this point seems never to have been decided; but it is submitted that such a purchase might be impeached, for it is the duty of the trustee of the subsidiary settlement to watch over the interests of *his* beneficiaries. It is obviously to their interest that the sale shall realise a high price, whereas it is to the interest of a purchaser that it shall be sold cheaply. By himself becoming a purchaser, therefore, the subsidiary trustee is acting in a character wholly inconsistent with his fiduciary duty; and little doubt is entertained that, if the sale were impeached by his beneficiaries, the onus would be on him under the fair-dealing rule of proving that he acted bona fide and gave an adequate price.

Acquiescence or concurrence by knowledgeable beneficiaries of full age and capacity

In *Holder v Holder*[3] an additional ground upon which a beneficiary failed to have a purchase set aside was that he had acquiesced in the purchase. It would be inequitable to allow him to assert any equity to set the auction sale aside (if he had such equity) because he had full knowledge of the sale and stood by making no attempt to stop completion, and restitutio in integrum was impossible.

In principle, a trustee should be able to purchase trust property if this is agreed by all the beneficiaries, being of full age and capacity and between them absolutely entitled to the settled property, and so long as the beneficiaries were given full information and freely gave their agreement. The onus is on the trustee to prove this and in the case of land he will normally find the property unmarketable, purchasers with constructive notice of the equity to set aside being bound by the equity[4] and not being able to be sure that fully informed free consent was given by the beneficiaries.

---

20 TLATA 1996, s 9.
1 If the delegation were made with a view to facilitating the purchase, such would be clearly impeachable.
2 TA 1925, s 25(5) as substituted by the Trustee Delegation Act 1999, s 5.
3 [1968] Ch 353, [1968] 1 All ER 655.
4 *Cookson v Lee* (1853) 23 LJ Ch 473; *Aberdeen Town Council v Aberdeen University* (1877) 2 App Cas 544.

The beneficiaries' remedies

If the trustee has resold the property at a profit the beneficiaries can adopt the sale and recover the profit[5].

If the trustee has not re-sold the beneficiaries may, if they all agree, insist that the property be reconveyed by the purchasing trustee to the vendor trustees; otherwise the property will be re-sold under the direction of the court on the footing that if it realises more than the reserve price fixed by the court the surplus belongs to the trust whereas if it realises less, then the purchasing trustee is held to his bargain[6]. All beneficiaries should be notified of the course proposed by the court on the application of a particular beneficiary so that all may have the opportunity of being heard and all will be bound. The reserve price must be calculated as the sum of the price paid by the purchasing trustee and, at least where he acted in good faith, a figure appropriate for any improvements made to the property which, it seems, should be based on the difference between the improved and the unimproved value of the property[7]. Any balance on income account should, as the case may be, be added to or deducted from the reserve. The purchasing trustee will be credited with interest at 5%[8] on the purchase price and the improvements figure and debited with a proper rent. Any excess of interest over rent will be added to the reserve whilst any deficiency will be subtracted from the reserve. If the property fetches more than the reserve and the costs of re-sale then it seems the costs are borne by the trust. If the reserve is not reached or only exceeded by an amount not covering the costs of re-sale then there is something to be said for the claimant beneficiary seeking re-sale to pay the costs in some circumstances.

Upon ordering re-sale the court has discretion to allow the purchasing trustee to bid at the auction but it will not normally exercise this discretion if any adult beneficiary objects though, in principle, there is much to be said, if the beneficiaries disagree as to this, for the view that the matter ought to be decided by the court in the interests of the trust as a whole[9].

PARAGRAPH 3

Purchase by trustee of beneficiary's equitable interest

But although a trustee is incapable of purchasing from himself or his colleagues, there is no fixed and arbitrary rule that he cannot, in any circumstances, purchase the interests of his beneficiaries from the beneficiaries

---

5 *Baker v Carter* (1835) 1 Y & C Ex 250. If the purchaser had notice of the beneficiary's equity the beneficiary may recover the property from the purchaser. If sale were to a purchaser without notice for less than the true value the beneficiaries can claim from the trustee the difference between the price paid and the true value with interest at 4%; *Lord Hardwicke v Vernon* (1799) 4 Ves 411.

6 *Holder v Holder* [1966] 2 All ER 116 at 128–131, Harman LJ in [1968] 1 All ER 665 at 669 approving the form of order obiter whilst allowing the appeal. See also *Price Waterhouse v MacCulloch* (1986) 25 DLR (4th) 126 where an executor was liable.

7 *Holder v Holder* [1966] 2 All ER 116 at 169. In principle, to prevent the trustee profiting he should only recover for improvements the lesser of (a) the actual cost of improvements or (b) the difference between the improved and unimproved value of the property.

8 *Holder v Holder* [1966] 2 All ER 116 at 130, Cross J considering that the traditional 4% would be 'unfair in present day conditions'.

9 *Tennant v Trenchard* (1869) 4 Ch App 537; *Holder v Holder* [1966] 2 All ER 116 at 130.

themselves. Thus a purchase by a trustee for sale of the interest of a beneficiary in the proceeds of sale is unobjectionable[10]. Yet the court regards such transactions with great jealousy; and, if impeached, they cannot stand unless the trustee can affirmatively and clearly show that the parties were completely at arm's length in making the bargain, that the bargain was a beneficial one to the beneficiaries, and that the trustee candidly disclosed all facts known to him which could in any way influence the vendors[11].

In *Tito v Waddell (No 2)*[12] Megarry V-C called the rule the 'fair-dealing' rule summarising it as:

> 'that if a trustee purchases the beneficial interest of any of his beneficiaries, the transaction is not voidable ex debito justitiae, but can be set aside unless the trustee can show that he has taken no advantage of his position and has made full disclosure to the beneficiary, and that the transaction is fair and honest.'

Thus, in *Hill v Langley*[13] where an executor and trustee had taken an assignment of his sister's half interest in their father's residuary estate without disclosing information relevant to the value of that interest, the assignment was set aside so that the traceable assets within the half interest could be recovered.

The rule can apply where the transaction with the beneficiary is effected not by the trustee but by some person or body which is merely the trustee's alter ego. Short of the alter ego case where they must disclose the true position, trustees are not under any duty to proffer information to their beneficiary, or to see that he has proper advice merely because they are trustees for him and know that he is entering into a transaction with his beneficial interest with some person or body connected in some way with, but independent of, the trustees such as a company in which the trustees own some shares beneficially[14].

Mortgage of equitable interest of trustee

A trustee may take a fair mortgage from his beneficiary; and, in an appropriate case, may obtain priority over prior equitable mortgagees of whose claims he had no notice when he made the advance[15].

ARTICLE 60

Duty of trustee to be ready with his accounts

(1) A trustee must:
(a) keep clear and accurate accounts of the trust property[16]; and

---

10 *Coles v Trecothick* (1804) 9 Ves 234; and *Clarke v Swaile* (1762) 2 Eden 134.
11 See per Lord Cairns in *Thomson v Eastwood* (1877) 2 App Cas 215 at 236, HL; *Williams v Scott* [1900] AC 499; *Dougan v Macpherson* [1902] AC 197, where the trustee had had a valuation made for himself which he did not communicate to the beneficiary.
12 [1977] 3 All ER 129 at 241.
13 (1988) Times, 28 January.
14 *Tito v Waddell (No 2)* [1977] 3 All ER 129 at 242–243.
15 *Newman v Newman* (1885) 28 Ch D 674.
16 *Springett v Dashwood* (1860) 2 Giff 521; *Burrows v Walls* (1855) 5 De GM & G 233; *Newton v Askew* (1848) 11 Beav 145 at 152; *Pearse v Green* (1819) 1 Jac & W 135.

(b) at all reasonable times, at the request of a beneficiary, give him full and accurate information as to the amount and state of the trust property[17], and permit him or his solicitor[18] or accountant to inspect the accounts and vouchers, and other documents (including legal advice[19]) relating to the trust[20], so long as such documents do not reveal the reasons or the reasoning process for the exercise of the trustees discretions[1] and so long as supplying the documents in an exceptional case would not prejudice the interests of the beneficiaries as a whole and the ability of the trustee to discharge its obligations under the trust, particularly management of a business[2]. Where a notice in writing of a dealing with an equitable interest in real or personal property has been served on a trustee under section 137 of the Law of Property Act 1925 any person interested in the equitable interest may require production of the notice subject to paying any costs, otherwise a trustee is under no duty to volunteer such information[3].

(2) A trustee is, nevertheless, not bound to supply copies of accounts or trust documents[4], or to supply information which necessitates expenditure[5], except at the cost of the beneficiary requiring the same.

Paragraph 1

Irreducible core of accountability to beneficiaries

As Millett LJ (as he then was) stated in *Armitage v Nurse*[6], when dealing with a private trust as opposed to a charitable trust, 'there is an irreducible core of obligations owed by the trustees to the beneficiaries and enforceable by them which is fundamental to the concept of a trust. If the beneficiaries have no rights enforceable against the trustees there are no trusts'[7]. The rights of a beneficiary to monitor and protect his proprietary interest by obtaining accounts from the trustee so that they can then be falsified or surcharged is at the very core of the trust concept.

As Millett LJ also stated[8], 'Every beneficiary is entitled to see the trust

---

17 *Re Tillott* [1892] 1 Ch 86; *Re Page* [1893] 1 Ch 304 at 309; *Talbot v Marshfield* (1868) 3 Ch App 622 (explained and distinguished in *Re Londonderry's Settlement* [1965] Ch 918, [1964] 3 All ER 855, CA); *Ryder v Bickerton* (1743) 3 Swan 80n. Particularly detailed disclosure of information is required for beneficiaries under occupational pension schemes by virtue of subordinate legislation. See also *Wilson v Law Debenture Trust Corpn* [1995] 2 All ER 337.
18 *Kemp v Burn* (1863) 4 Giff 348.
19 *Hawkesley v May* [1956] 1 QB 304, [1955] 3 All ER 353.
20 *Re Cowin* (1886) 33 Ch D 179; *Ottley v Gilby* (1845) 8 Beav 602; see also *Re Londonderry's Settlement* [1965] Ch 918, [1964] 3 All ER 855, CA: p 678, post.
 1 *Re Londonderry's Settlement* [1965] Ch 918, CA.
 2 *Re Rabbaiotti's Settlement* [2000] WTLR 953; *Rouse v 100F Australian Trustees Ltd* [2000] WTLR 111.
 3 *Low v Bouverie* [1891] 3 Ch 82 at 99.
 4 *Ottley v Gilby* (1845) 8 Beav 602.
 5 *Re Bosworth* (1889) 58 LJ Ch 432.
 6 [1998] Ch 241 at 253 and see DJ Hayton 'The Irreducible Core Content of Trusteeship', Ch 3 in A J Oakley (ed) *Trends in Contemporary Trust Law* (Oxford 1996).
 7 While there will be no trusts for beneficiaries , there will be a resulting trust for the settlor.
 8 *Armitage v Nurse* [1998] Ch 241 at 261.

accounts, whether his interest is in possession or not', so that he has the means to discover whether there has been a breach of trust which can be remedied. Thus, beneficiaries with a life interest or an interest in remainder, whether in income or in capital[9] and whether vested or contingent[10], have accounting rights, as do beneficiaries under discretionary trusts[11] and also objects of a power of appointment if so intended by the settlor[12].

Just as trusts are perfectly valid where no powers of appointment are contained therein, so trusts can be perfectly valid when containing powers of appointment where the settlor expressly or by necessary implication has excluded the objects thereof from having any accounting or enforcement rights, only conferring upon them the right to retain whatever might happen to be appointed to them[13]. The trustee-beneficiary obligation alone suffices for a valid trust fund without the need for any trustee-object obligation if the settlor does not intend to create the latter obligation. It is only vital to the trust concept that the beneficiaries as beneficial owners of the trust property, except to the extent that any appointments are made in favour of objects of a power of appointment in the trust instrument, have accounting and enforcement rights.

Often a settlor will intend objects of a power of appointment to have accounting and enforcement rights, as where for a considerable period all that can happen is for there to be appointments made to such objects, no trust arising until the end of such period, so that it is natural meanwhile for the settlor to intend the objects to have enforcement rights[14]. Indeed, if the beneficiaries entitled in default of exercise of the powers are not going to be ascertained until the end or near the end of a lengthy trust period, when their accounting and enforcement rights will enable them retrospectively to bring the trustees to account, it may well be natural for the settlor to intend objects of powers in the intervening period to have accounting and enforcement rights. However, if the settlor wishes exclusively to rely on the retrospective accounting rights of the beneficiaries when ultimately ascertained to anchor the obligations binding the trustees, he can expressly exclude the accounting rights of objects eg if he believes it to be in their best interests to be kept in the dark as to the possible extent of their good fortune.

Concomitant duty to notify beneficiaries

To give meaningful substance[15] to the duty of trustees to account to their

9 Income distribution details should not concern capital beneficiaries as they have no interest therein, but they are very interested in how the capital is invested. Capital distributions, however, do concern income beneficiaries as reducing the fund producing their income and so reducing their income.

10 *Re Tillott* [1892] 1 Ch 86; *A-G of Ontario v Stavro* (1995) 119 DLR (4th) 750.

11 *Chaine Nickson v Bank of Ireland* [1976] IR 393; *Spellson v George* (1987) 11 NSWLR 300; *Re Murphy's Settlement* [1998] 3 All ER 1.

12 *Re Murphy's Settlement* [1998] 3 All ER 1 at 9 treating the claimant like an object of a power of appointment as in *Re Manisty's Settlemement* [1974] Ch 17. Note that if the settlor's descendants are both objects of a power of appointment and contingent beneficiaries under the ultimate discretionary trust if alive at the expiry of the trust period, they will have rights to accounts qua contingent beneficiary, it being possible (as under possibilities permitted by equity under the old rule against remoteness of vesting) they could still be alive (even aged 150 years) at the expiry of the trust period.

13 *Re Angora Trust* [2001] WTLR 1081, Manx CA; *Re Manisty's Settlement* [1974] Ch 17 at 25.

14 *Spellson v George* (1987) 11 NSWLR 300.

15 See *Scally v Southern Health and Social Services Board* [1992] 1 AC 294 at 306–307, HL.

beneficiaries, the trustees are under a duty to take reasonable practicable steps to inform their beneficiaries of the trusts favouring the beneficiaries, although problems over sanctions undermine this duty of notification[16]. If a beneficiary does not know he is a beneficiary how can he enforce the trustees' duty to account? Indeed, if he does not know who are the trustees how can he exercise his rights against them? Thus, in *Re Murphy's Settlement*[17] the settlor's son, as beneficiary under a discretionary trust, obtained a court order for the settlor to give him the names and addresses of the trustees of a foreign trust (that the settlor admittedly knew) so that he could apply to them for a discretionary distribution, having fallen out with his father and being poor enough to be in receipt of legal aid for his application to the court.

Whether beneficiaries' interests are under fixed[18] or discretionary trusts[19], whether in income or capital, and whether vested or contingent, trustees are necessarily under a duty to take reasonable practicable steps to inform beneficiaries of full age and capacity of their beneficial interests. Those currently interested in income cannot be expected to look after the capital beneficiaries' interested in capital growth and, due to their personal wealth or their relationships with a trustee, might not bother monitoring what is happening to the trust fund. The sooner a capital beneficiary has any lost capital restored to the trust fund the better, the trustee's ability to restore it usually diminishing as time goes by. Moreover, a capital beneficiary may need to make out the case for a power of advancement or appointment to be exercised in his favour. Beneficiaries under discretionary trusts of income or capital also need to be able to make out a case for discretions to be exercised in their favour.

What then of the position of persons who only are objects of a power of appointment vested in the trustees and hope discretions will be exercised in their favour? If the settlor intends them to have the right to make the trustees account, with the trustees being under a duty to consider cases made to them by objects for the power of appointment to be exercised, then the trustees must take all practicable reasonable steps to notify objects they are objects. However, where the class of objects of a power comprises two sub-classes, like the settlor's descendants and employees and ex-employees of the settlor's company, then, while there will ordinarily be a duty to notify descendants within the primary class, there will not normally be a duty to notify the more remote class[20]. Where there is one huge class then one may expect there to be no duty of notification[1], but the settlor should spell out the position in the trust instrument to put matters beyond doubt.

---

16 Removal of the trustee could be sought; otherwise, since there would normally be no loss to the trust fund to account for, the claimant beneficiary would need to seek equitable compensation eg for personal loss incurred a month before the trustees paid him £1 million on a contingency being satisfied (eg attaining 30 years of age) of which he knew nothing until the payment arrived and the loss would have been avoided if he had known.
17 [1998] 3 All ER 1.
18 *Hawkesley v May* [1956] 1 QB 304; *Brittlebank v Goodwin* (1868) LR 5 Eq 545. Trustees must do everything possible to ascertain a life tenant to whom to pay income. In the case of discretionary trusts and powers they need only take reasonable practicable steps, enabling them to size up their task and invoke and deal with any applications to them: *Re Hay's Settlement Trust* [1981] 3 All ER 786.
19 *Re Murphy's Settlement* [1998] 3 All ER 1; *Stuart-Hutcheson v Spread Trustee Co Ltd* [2002] WTLR 1213.
20 *Re Manisty's Settlemement* [1974] Ch 17 at 25.
 1 *Re Angora Trust* [2001] WTLR 1081, Manx CA.

Modification of trustees' duties and beneficiaries' correlative rights

There cannot be any obligation, hence there cannot be any trust, if the trustee does not owe a duty to account to any beneficiary[2]; but, once there is such a duty, then if the trust also creates objects of a power of appointment there is no need for any duty to account to be owed to any object[3]. It matters not that there is currently no ascertained beneficiary to enforce the trustee's duty to account[4], so long as there is such a beneficiary ascertained by the end of the trust period who will retrospectively have the right to make the trustee account for the operation of the trust throughout the trust period. Thus, a settlor can create a 'blackhole trust' for objects of a power with no accounting rights and not retrospectively enforceable by a beneficiary till near the end of a lengthy trust period or, primarily for himself, he can create a 'blind trust' under which he prevents himself from having any rights as a beneficiary to see the accounts (with supporting information) for a pre-scribed period eg while he is Prime Minister or Chancellor of the Exchequer or Head of the Serious Fraud Office. If a trust instrument did not directly oust the duty of the trustees to account, but stipulated that the trust instrument was not to be disclosed to any beneficiary and any distributions to beneficiaries were to be achieved so far as practicable in untraceable fashion, (to ensure that no beneficiary could discover the existence of the trust and the whereabouts of the trustees), then this indirect ouster of the duty to account would negate the existence of any trust for the 'beneficiaries'. There would be a resulting trust for the settlor with a power to benefit the 'beneficiaries' re-characterised as objects of a power of appointment with no right to make the trustees account.

What if a settlor created a discretionary trust for his four children, his grandchildren and great-grandchildren, with the trustees having a power of appointment in favour of persons being spouses or co-habitees of beneficiaries, but there is a provision that no person capable of benefiting under the trust is to be informed of the trust except for the four children and the persons who after their death become the eldest of the next generation in each of the four branches of the family, such four children and the eldest member of each successor generation in each family branch alone to have the right to see trust accounts and bring the trustees to account for any breaches of trust? If child B dies, survived by three children, X, Y and Z, born in that order, can Y and Z, having fortuitously learned of the trust, succeed in a claim to see the trust accounts so that they can then sue in respect of any breaches of trust that may then be discovered?

Their claims should fail because there is no reason why the settlor's intentions should not be implemented. This could either be because:

(i) X alone of X, Y and Z ranks as a beneficiary with the inherent rights necessary for the status of beneficiary, so that Y and Z without such rights have to be re-characterised as merely objects of a power of appointment,

---

2 *Armitage v Nurse* [1998] Ch 241 at 253.

3 *Re Angora Trust* [2001] WTLR 1081, Manx CA.

4 For example, there may be a duty to accumulate income (with powers of appointment over income and capital) for a prescribed period, at the end of which the beneficiaries can be ascertained but not till then. In September 2002 the Lord Chancellor's Department issued a Consultation Paper 'The Rule against Excessive Accumulations' for abolishing the rule against accumulations (as recommended by the Law Commission) by means of a Regulatory Reform Order under the Regulatory Reform Act 2001. Further on 'blackhole trusts' see D J Hayton, *Modern International Developments in Trust Law* (Kluwer, 2000) Chapter 15.

or

(ii) Y and Z are 'lesser' beneficiaries, while X is a 'full' beneficiary.

The first basis seems to be in line with the views of Millett LJ in *Armitage v Nurse*.

It is true that objects of a power of appointment can have greater or lesser rights, so that objects consisting only of the settlor's grandchildren can be given full rights to see trust accounts and sue the trustees while objects consisting of a huge class need have no such rights. However, the status of beneficiaries under English trust law needs to be linked with having an equitable proprietary interest in trust property that can be protected or vindicated by the beneficiary's rights to make the trustee account for trusteeship of the trust property and to trace the traceable product of trust property so as to recover it if need be. A person without such personal and proprietary rights should not rank as a beneficiary despite the settlor labelling him a beneficiary.

The key point for a settlor who wishes persons only to benefit if a discretion is exercised by his trustees in their favour and who does not want those persons to have rights to see the trust accounts (with supporting information) and bring the trustees to account, is that he can achieve these wishes by making such persons only objects of a power of appointment and expressly stipulating that such objects have no such rights. Indeed, there seems no reason why he cannot go further and stipulate that his trustees are not to inform such objects that they are such[5] objects, and, if they decide to benefit any such object, they must, so far as practicable, transmit such benefit in untraceable fashion.

A settlor needs to be aware that if he is creating a trust for beneficiaries (as opposed to objects of powers of appointment) then those beneficiaries must have full rights to see the trust accounts and bring the trustees to account. If the settlor stipulated 'The Protector alone shall have rights to see trust accounts and documents and bring an action against the trustees' the court, rather than hold that this meant the property was held on resulting trust for the settlor with power to benefit beneficiaries as if objects of a power, would likely hold that the Protector held these rights as a fiduciary for the benefit of the beneficiaries[6] as part of the Protector's irreducible core function[7], but that these rights of the Protector were in addition to the beneficiaries' rights[8] and so exercisable by the Protector while the beneficiaries are unborn or unascertained or not of full capacity. The position would be the same if the 'Protector' were, instead, named the 'Enforcer' though if a Cayman (Special Trusts Alternative Regime) Law trust for beneficiaries were involved, where none of the beneficiaries had been appointed an enforcer, because the

---

5 *Re Manisty's Settlement* [1974] Ch 17 at 25.

6 The beneficiaries will then be entitled to see the accounts and obtain the information acquired by the Protector, will have a right to ensure he acquires such material for their benefit and that he sues the trustees if necessary: if he did not, then they themselves could sue the trustee joining the Protector as co-defendant: cf *Parker-Tweedale v Dunbar Bank plc* [1990] 2 All ER 577 at 582-583 and 587.

7 A fiduciary is bound to account to those for whom he is a fiduciary: *A-G v Cocke* [1988] 2 All ER 391 at 395. It would seem to be repugnant to, or inconsistent with, the core content of protectorship not to hold as a fiduciary the core right to make the trustee account.

8 Beneficiaries' fundamental proprietary *Saunders v Vautier* rights to terminate a trust and claim property from the trustee cannot be affected by any rights of a protector (or enforcer) where there is a valid trust governed by English law. Under a foreign law beneficiaries may have no *Saunders v Vautier* rights as in virtually all States in USA.

Cayman Statute surprisingly prescribes such beneficiaries have no interest whatsoever in the trust property and have no right to sue the trustee or the enforcer in any way whatsoever, then the English court should hold there to be a resulting trust for the settlor with power to benefit the beneficiaries re-characterised as objects of a power of appointment.

Accounting duties of trustees

Trustees must keep clear and distinct accounts of property administered as trustee[9] with supporting vouchers and other documentation[10]. They must always be ready to give full information as to the investment of trust funds, producing mortgage deeds or other appropriate documentation to support their claims[11].

Nature of beneficiaries' rights to inspect trust documents

In less complex times where trusts conferred fixed interests eg on A for life remainder to B, it was easy to consider that the right of A and B to inspect the trust documents was based on A and B having equitable proprietary rights in all trust assets which extended to trust documents[12]. Nowadays, where beneficiaries interested under complex discretionary trusts (and, if desired, objects of a power of appointment) have rights to inspect trust documents, such rights can be seen to be based not on equitable proprietary rights in such documents but on the core right to make trustees account for their trusteeship of the trust property[13].

It follows that, instead, of concentrating upon whether particular documents should be appropriately termed 'trust documents' the real question should be whether or not particular documents need to be capable of being inspected by a beneficiary if he is to be able properly to bring the trustees to account eg if stealing trust assets or for not exercising their functions for the purposes for which those functions were conferred upon them by the settlor but acting irrationally or negligently or for reasons perverse to any sensible expectation of the settlor.

Costs on failure to keep accounts

Failure by trustees to keep accounts and vouchers may lead to them having to bear their own costs even where an administration action is dismissed[14]. If, however, the action succeeds the trustee will normally[15] have to pay the claimant's costs as well[16] up to the hearing[17]. But, as the reason of this is that

  9 *Pearse v Green* (1819) 1 Jac & W 135.
  10 *Clarke v Earl of Ormonde* (1821) Jac 108 at 120.
  11 *Re Tillott* [1892] 1 Ch 86 at 88.
  12 *O'Rourke v Darbishire* [1920] AC 581 followed in *Re Londonderry's Settlement* [1965] Ch 918.
  13 *Re Rabbaiotti's Settlement Trust* [2000] WTLR 953 at 963–964; *Hartigan Nominees Pty Ltd v Rydge* (1992) 29 NSWLR 405; *Stuart-Hutcheson v Spread Trustee Co Ltd* [2002] WTLR 1213.
  14 *Payne v Evens* (1874) LR 18 Eq 356; and see to same effect, *Re Page* [1893] 1 Ch 304.
  15 If the claimant has been over hasty in seeking the assistance of the court he, or even his solicitor, may be ordered to pay the costs: *Re Dartnall* [1895] 1 Ch 474.
  16 *Eglin v Sanderson* (1862) 3 Giff 434; *Newton v Askew* (1848) 11 Beav 145.
  17 *Springett v Dashwood* (1860) 2 Giff 521; *Re Linsley* [1904] 2 Ch 785. Trustees who deliberately try to keep the beneficiaries in the dark will be liable to have costs awarded against them on the indemnity basis: *Re Den Haag Trust* (1998) 1 OFLR 495.

such costs are caused by the trustee's neglect to keep and furnish accounts, the claimant will not in general be entitled to costs against the trustee beyond the time when the account is actually rendered, or ordered by the court to be rendered. From this time, if the accounts are substantially accurate, the trustee will be entitled to his costs out of the estate[18], or, if the claimant sues alone, out of his share in the estate[19]. In one case, however, it was held that where a trustee by his gross and indefensible neglect to furnish accounts renders an originating summons necessary, he may be ordered to pay all the costs, including the costs of taking and vouching the account[20]. It is no defence that the trustees are illiterate and incapable of keeping accounts; for in that case they would be justified in employing, and be bound in point of law to employ, a competent agent to keep the accounts for them[1].

Inaccurate accounts

The importance of keeping accounts is shown by the fact that, although the court will generally saddle with costs a trustee whose only fault is that he has failed to do so, yet where a trustee has kept and furnished accounts, which, by an honest mistake, turn out to be inaccurate, he will be allowed his costs[2].

Information as to investment of trust funds

'A trustee is bound to give his cestui que trust proper information as to the investment of the trust estate, and where the trust estate is invested on mortgage, it is not sufficient for the trustee merely to say, "I have invested the trust money on a mortgage", but he must produce the mortgage deeds, so that the cestui que trust may thereby ascertain that the trustee's statement is correct, and that the trust estate is so invested. . . . Where a portion of the trust estate is invested in consols, it is not sufficient for the trustee merely to say that it is so invested, but his cestui que trust is entitled to an authority from the trustee to enable him to make proper application to the bank, . . . in order that he may verify the trustee's own statement; there may be stock standing in the name of a person who admits he is a trustee of it, which at the same time is incumbered, some other person having a paramount title may have obtained a charging order on the stock or placed a distringas upon it.'[3]

Other documents relating to the trust: Re Londonderry's Settlement

The extent of the trustee's duty to disclose other documents relating to the trust was considered by the Court of Appeal in *Re Londonderry's Settlement*[4] where a beneficiary under a discretionary trust of income, but also the object of a power of appointment over capital, disgruntled by the amount of capital proposed to be distributed to her, sought to obtain information to enable her to launch an attack on the trustees' allocation of trust capital. The right of beneficiaries to inspect Counsel's Opinions taken by the trustees at the

---

18 *Ottley v Gilby* (1845) 8 Beav 602.
19 *Thompson v Clive* (1848) 11 Beav 475.
20 *Re Skinner* [1904] 1 Ch 289; explained in *Re Holton's Settlement Trusts* [1918] WN 78.
1 *Wroe v Seed* (1863) 4 Giff 425 at 429. Any trustee may employ an agent to keep their accounts: TA 2000, s 11.
2 *Smith v Cremer* (1875) 24 WR 51.
3 Per Chitty J in *Re Tillott* [1892] 1 Ch 86 at 88.
4 [1965] Ch 918, [1964] 3 All ER 855, CA; see also *Lemos v Coutts & Co* [1992–93] CILR 460 (CA Cayman).

expense of the trust fund to guide them on their obligations as trustees was confirmed. Apart from that, the court laid down certain general propositions, making it clear, however, that they were not intended to be all-embracing and that they might not be applied inflexibly and in all circumstances. These propositions are:

(a) the principle that where the trustees have, in good faith, reached certain decisions as to the exercise of their discretionary powers over trust property they are under no duty to disclose their reasons holds good even when those reasons have been committed to paper. So they are not bound to disclose to a beneficiary the agenda of their meetings, nor any documents (including minutes of meetings) relating to the deliberations in which they engaged before taking their decisions, or disclosing their reasons for taking them or the material on which those reasons were or might have been based. The court considered that such documents were not, in fact, trust documents, adding that, even if they were, it was in the interests of all concerned that they should be confidential and the court would not order their disclosure;

(b) where trustees have power, subject to the consent of certain appointors, to appoint shares of capital to beneficiaries, no beneficiary has the right to inspect communications between individual trustees and appointors, or between any of the trustees or appointors and an individual beneficiary because, it seems, they are not trust documents;

(c) but if a solicitor advising the trustees commits to paper an aide-memoire summarising the state of the fund, or of the family concerned, and reminding the trustees of past distributions and future possibilities, it seems that this is a document which beneficiaries have a right to inspect.

Right to disclosure under Civil Procedure Rules

It should be noted that the court order was made 'without prejudice to any right of the defendant to discovery in separate proceedings against the plaintiffs'. Thus if a beneficiary bona fide instituted hostile litigation against trustees alleging improper exercise of their discretions then he could obtain discovery of documents relevant to exercise of these discretions[5] for an applicant was entitled to discovery of any document 'which may fairly lead him to a train of inquiry' that may 'either directly or indirectly enable the party either to advance his own case or to damage the case of his adversary'[6].

'Discovery' has been replaced by 'disclosure' under the Civil Procedure Rules[7]. If a claimant can make out a properly particularised claim (so that it cannot be struck out as a mere 'fishing expedition' to see if material can be discovered to support the claim) this triggers standard disclosure of documents that can advance or hinder either party's case[8]; subsequent applications can then be made in relation to specific disclosure of documents not disclosed pursuant to standard disclosure.

---

5 Eg *Talbot v Marshfield* (1865) 2 Drew & Sm 549.
6 *Compagnie Financiere du Pacifique v Peruvian Guano Co* (1882) 11 QBD 55 at 63. See (1965) 81 LQR 196 (R E Megarry).
7 CPR Pt 31 and Practice Direction thereof.
8 Under CPR, r 31.16 pre-action disclosure of documents subject to standard disclosure if the action had been commenced can be ordered by the court if desirable to assist fair expedient resolution of the dispute: *Bermuda International Securities Ltd v KPMG* [2001] EWCA Civ 269, [2001] 3 CPLR 252, CA.

Confidentiality of trustees' deliberations

It is well established[9] that trustees are not obliged to give reasons for their exercise of distributive discretions so that they are not obliged to disclose their reasons or their reasoning processes but are entitled to keep them confidential: otherwise embitterment and embarrassment could well arise and persons could well be deterred from acting as trustees. This applies not just to private family trusts but to pension trusts where the members of the pension scheme have purchased their interests under the trusts[10]. If reasons are not given then the trustees have plenty of leeway because their exercise of a discretion can only be challenged[11] if (which is often difficult) prima facie evidence can be found by a claimant to justify alleging the discretion was exercised mala fide, capriciously, spitefully, perversely to any sensible expectation of the settlor, or without any real and genuine consideration, or the trustees would not have done what was done if irrelevant considerations had not been taken into account or if relevant considerations, which were not taken into account, had been taken into account. Disclosure of documents in such litigation can then lead to the trustees' reasons becoming apparent.

Whether the trustees volunteered reasons at the outset or only later at the stage of disclosure or of cross-examination[12], the exercise of their distributive discretion should stand unless the claimant makes out any of the above allegations, in which event the trustees or new trustees, replacing the old trustees, should be free to exercise their discretion afresh but on a proper basis.

Letters of Wishes

Separate from a trust instrument, there is increasingly found in the case of very flexible discretionary trusts a letter of wishes signed by the settlor or a memorandum of wishes drawn up by the trustee to indicate the settlor's wishes. The settlor is normally not very interested in the technical trust instrument that confers immense discretions but he does spend much time and thought as to what should guide the trustees in the exercise of those discretions and he puts these thoughts into his letter of wishes (used hereafter to include a memorandum of wishes which serves the same purpose and is of the same significance). It is the letter of wishes that necessarily fleshes out the skeletal trust provisions.

Legally binding letters

In an exceptional case, the letter of wishes may be intended by the settlor and accepted by the trustees as a *legally binding* document, overriding the terms of

---

9 *Re Londonderry's Settlement* [1965] Ch 918, CA.

10 *Wilson v Law Debenture Trust Corpn plc* [1995] 2 All ER 337.

11 *Gisborne v Gisborne* (1877) 2 App Cas 300; *Re Hay's Settlement Trust* [1982] 1 WLR 202; *Turner v Turner* [1984] Ch 100; *Mettoy Pension Trustees Ltd v Evans* [1990] 1 WLR 1587; *Edge v Pensions Ombudsman* [2000] Ch 602, CA.

12 As Robert Walker LJ pointed out in *Scott v National Trust* [1998] 2 All ER 705 at 719, 'If a decision taken by trustees is directly attacked in legal proceedings, the trustees may be compelled either legally (through discovery or subpoena) or practically (in order to avoid adverse inferences being drawn) to disclose the substance of the reasons for their decision'. However, before then, if the trustees themselves are not prepared to give up the confidentiality of their reasons and reasoning processes then nothing can be done.

the trust instrument to the extent inconsistent therewith. Just as the beneficiaries have a right to see the formal trust instrument, so they have a right to see the informal letter of wishes where the legally binding terms of the trust are found by incorporating both documents[13]. Moreover, any term that the trust instrument or the legally binding letter of wishes is not to be disclosed to any beneficiary but to be kept secret and confidential would, of course, be rejected as repugnant to, or inconsistent with, the trust concept, such obligation requiring beneficiaries to have a meaningful right to make the trustees account for their trusteeship[14].

Legally significant letters

Normally, the key letter of wishes is intended to have legal significance only eg 'This letter is not intended to be legally binding upon the trustees in any way. It is intended only to provide some guidance for the trustees in exercising their functions, but, having considered whatever guidance may appear to be provided herein, they are, of course, free to exercise their independent judgment in ever-changing circumstances'.

This *legally significant* letter has to be considered by the trustees and passed on to replacement trustees, because it normally is the key document to guide the trustees in exercising very broad flexible discretions in a fairly standard-form trust deed. It will make clear to the trustees what are the purposes and expectations of the settlor in conferring such immense discretions upon the trustees.

Such crucial document would thus appear to be a 'trust document' if a court, as in *Re Londonderry's Settlement*[15], bases beneficiaries' rights to inspection of documents on such documents being 'trust documents' in which beneficiaries have some equitable proprietary rights. Alternatively, if the better view is that inspection is based on the core accountability of trustees to beneficiaries, the letter is a key document that needs to be available for inspection by beneficiaries if they are going to be in a position where it becomes possible for them to bring the trustees properly to account. If the beneficiaries cannot ascertain the purposes and expectations of the settlor how can they possibly allege that the trustees did not responsibly exercise their discretion for furthering the purposes and expectations of the settlor, but exercised their discretion arbitrarily or contrary to the settlor's purposes and expectations or irrationally, failing to take account of relevant factors or taking account of irrelevant factors? For the beneficiaries to have a meaningful right to make the trustees account for the exercise of their discretions, surely they must have a right to see the key letter of wishes as well as the trust instrument (though subject to deletion from the letter of any embarrassing personal information regarded as confidential to the settlor, his trustees and the person named in the letter)?

---

13 *Chase Manhattan Equities Ltd v Goodman* [1991] BCLC 897 at 923, the trust instrument being a sham or pretence in those parts overridden by the legally binding letter. It is thus advantageous to allege this in bringing legal proceedings.
14 *Armitage v Nurse* [1998] Ch 241 at 253; voidness of clause 15 purporting to oust accountability to beneficiaries in *Re Levy* [1960] Ch 346 at 366; *Scally v Southern Health & Social Services Board* [1992] 1 AC 294 at 306-307; and pp 673 and 677 ante.
15 [1965] Ch 918, CA, but see p 679 ante.

Express confidentiality of legally significant letters

The question then arises whether the settlor can expressly provide that the legally significant letter of wishes is not to be disclosed to any beneficiary but to be kept secret and confidential if, indeed, the inherent nature of a letter of wishes independent of the trust instrument does not make it inherently confidential and unavailable to the beneficiaries if requesting to inspect it. Opinions of foreign judges are divided on this issue[16].

In principle, it is submitted that the key letter of wishes separate from a broad, bland but skeletal trust instrument is normally intended by the settlor to be for the benefit of the settlor (dispensing vicarious benevolence via the trustees), and the beneficiaries and the trustees, so they all know the sort of music that the trustees are supposed to be playing with their immense orchestra of powers and discretions. There is thus no implied necessity to make the key letter of wishes confidential and not available to beneficiaries to inspect[17].

However, if the settlor chooses expressly to stipulate that his legally significant letter of wishes is not to be made available to beneficiaries but to be kept secret and confidential, will the law accept this? After all, it will not accept a similar stipulation in respect of the trust instrument because such stipulation preventing any obligation of accountability to beneficiaries arising is repugnant to, or inconsistent with, the concept of the trust. Does not the confidentiality of a legally significant letter of wishes, that is crucial to the operation of a bland, flexible discretionary trust, also prevent key accountability arising when, without sight of the letter of wishes making clear the purposes and expectations of the settlor as to the parameters within which he expects his trustees to exercise their immense discretions, a beneficiary cannot raise a particularised claim that the trustees exercised their discretions contrary to the purposes for which the settlor conferred the discretions and took account of irrelevant factors or ignored relevant factors? Thus, prima facie, the legally significant letter of wishes should be made available to a beneficiary upon request (though subject to deletion of any information given by a person in confidence to the settlor to be shared only with the trustees).

On the other hand, some accountability remains in respect of trustees' distributive functions if a particularised claim that the trustees had not acted in good faith can be made out, so that disclosure of the letter of wishes then occurs under the Civil Procedure Rules, while in respect of trustees' investment and managerial functions a particularised claim involving breach of statutory and equitable duties will be available if appropriate after inspecting trust accounts and supporting documents (other than any letter of wishes). There is thus substance in accountability for the investment and managerial side of trustees' functions even if, on the distributive side, accountability is nearly *de minimis* when one considers how difficult indeed it is to make out a particularised claim of lack of good faith unless one has a very extreme case

---

16 *Hartigan Nominees Pty Ltd v Rydge* (1992) 29 NSWLR 405; *Re Rabaiotti's Settlement* [2000] WTLR 953.

17 The fact that the letter, like the trust instrument, is given to the trustees and not to the beneficiaries should be a neutral indicator, though not so considered in *Re Rabbaiotti's Settlement* [2000] WTLR 953. It may be that, in some circumstances, beneficiaries have a right of access to letters of wishes affecting them under the Data Protection Act 1998: see M Shillingford 'The Data Protection Act 1998' in the TACT Review, Issue No 11, April 2000, pp 3–8.

where the facts cry out for an explanation by the trustees eg only male beneficiaries benefit or only those of a particular religion or an appointee of £250,000 capital slept with one or both trustees just before the appointment.

However, such minimal accountability is consistent with the trust concept because an exemption clause can oust liability of trustees for everything except dishonest conduct so that as Millett LJ has stated[18], 'The duty of the trustees to perform the trusts honestly and in good faith for the benefit of the beneficiaries is the minimum necessary to give substance to the trusts'. The effect of an expressly confidential letter of wishes that is not to be disclosed to the beneficiaries (except pursuant to disclosure under Civil Procedure Rules if litigation can be instituted without being struck down as a 'fishing expedition') is thus no worse than the broadest permitted exemption clause. Therefore, the better view, upon reflection, is that beneficiaries do not have a right to inspect such a confidential letter of wishes.

Morally binding letters

However, to put the position beyond doubt a settlor could make his letter of wishes merely morally binding and of no legal signficance, so that, perhaps, no disclosure even needs to be made of it if by some chance legal proceedings are duly instituted against the trustees. He could state, 'This letter is not to be regarded as a legally significant letter indicating the purposes for which the discretions in my trust deed have been conferred on my trustees because I do not want my trustees to have legal obligations placed upon them by this letter so as to be forced to go out of their way to justify the exercise of their discretions. I believe the imposition of any legal obligations by this letter would cause more difficulties than benefits to accrue, creating greater cost burdens and proving likely to upset relationships between my beneficiaries. Thus, my trustees are only under a moral obligation to take account of the following wishes of mine and shall not be accountable before the courts in relation to taking into account or failing to take into account such wishes. It is on this basis only that they have been prepared to take on the invidious task of exercising discretions under my Trust Deed.'

Protecting the confidentiality of trustees' reasoning and letters of wishes

Indeed, before leaving the topic, one needs to consider whether there should be a prohibition on making a legally significant letter of wishes available to beneficiaries in order to protect the confidentiality of the trustees' reasons and reasoning processes. Clearly, if the trust instrument itself contained 'material upon which the trustees reasons were or might have been based'[19] this would not prevent the beneficiaries from inspecting the trust instrument, although the Court of Appeal in *Re Londonderry's Settlement* considered that other documents containing such material should not be available for inspection, though such documents were prepared, not by the settlor, but by the trustees or their advisers to help the trustees in their deliberations.

It is submitted that once one appreciates that a settlor's legally significant letter of wishes is a key document produced by the settlor to flesh out his intentions, purposes and expectations not otherwise apparent from his inextricably linked trust instrument, that provides only the skeletal structure

---

18 *Armitage v Nurse* [1998] Ch 241 at 253–254.
19 [1965] Ch 918 at 940.

for the exercise of immense discretions, then it should be available to beneficiaries and trustees alike to check that the trustees are conducting their orchestra of discretions to play the sort of tunes intended by the settlor[20]. This is based on the assumption that a settlor who produces a trust instrument and a letter of wishes so as to benefit his beneficiaries will intend them not to be dependent upon the whims of the trustees but to be able to check that the trustees are acting within the parameters intended by the settlor, unless he goes out of his way to make his letter either expressly confidential and not to be disclosed to any beneficiaries or expressly morally binding only.

One also needs not to read too much into the general guidelines provided by the Court of Appeal in *Re Londonderry's Settlement*[1] when it was not faced with any letter of wishes produced by the settlor, but only documents produced by the trustees and their advisors at the time their discretions were under consideration so that, at one extreme, the court was prepared to order that there should be no disclosure of documents containing 'material upon which the trustees' reasons were or might have been based'. The whole point of a legally significant letter of wishes is to provide guidance as to the *settlor's* reasons for creating such a flexible settlement and to indicate matters that the trustees might or might not need to take into account in exercising a variety of discretions. It is not a document emanating from the trustees or their advisers at the time their discretions are under consideration to provide insight into their discretionary reasons or their discretionary reasoning process. Thus, such a document should not be kept from the beneficiaries.

Finally, even where a settlor has stipulated that his letter of wishes is confidential and is not to be disclosed to the beneficiaries by the trustees, it is likely that the courts will imply a proviso along the lines 'unless the trustees consider disclosure to a particular beneficiary or beneficiaries either to be in the interests of the particular beneficiary or beneficiaries in question and to be compatible with the proper operation of the trust as intended by the settlor or to be necessary to protect the trustees from liability to the beneficiaries;[2]' but these implications could be expressly ousted by a provision that in the settlor's lifetime the letter of wishes is not to be disclosed without the consent of the settlor, the settlor providing a separate indemnity to the trustee against any liability of the trustee thereby arising to beneficiaries. The veto of the settlor would then be conclusive unless the court considered that the letter of wishes was a legally binding one, so that the trust instrument, which the beneficiaries had a right to inspect, comprised the letter of wishes together with the trust deed to the extent the deed's provisions were compatible with those in the letter of wishes.

Trustees' discretion in exceptional case to withhold documents in interests of beneficiaries as a whole

Even where a beneficiary has a right to see trust documents, in an exceptional case the trustees may decline to provide documents and other information to a particular beneficiary if they have reasonable grounds for

---

20 See Kirby P and Sheller J A in *Hartigan Nominees Pty Ltd v Rydge* (1992) 29 NSWLR 405 but contrast Mahoney J A therein and Jersey Royal Court in *Re Rabbaiotti's Settlement* [2000] WTLR 953.

1 [1965] Ch 918 at 940.

2 For example, to help rebut inferences from facts crying out for an explanation eg retention of a significant shareholding for too long before its price collapsed.

considering that providing the relevant documents and information to that beneficiary will not be in the best interests of the beneficiaries as a whole but will be prejudicial to the ability of the trustees to discharge their obligations under the trust[3] eg a trust involving the conduct of a business where that beneficiary runs a competing business and seeks the information to provide him with a competitive advantage, or is an employee of a competing business seeking to advance his interests with his employer by providing his employer with the information in return for promotion and a pay-rise.

If a beneficiary be dissatisfied with the trustees' refusal to make documents and information available he can seek the directions of the court, so that the court can decide whether the strong presumption in favour of disclosure should be overridden in the best interests of the beneficiaries as a whole.

While an assignee of a beneficiary's interest and the personal representative of a deceased beneficiary will have the same rights as the beneficiary[4], it may be that, while the beneficiary would have had the usual full rights to trust documents and supporting documentation, the assignee or personal representative will not be allowed such full rights because endeavouring to use them for their personal ends which conflict with the interests of the beneficiaries as a whole[5].

Use of privilege against self-incrimination

One might have thought that the privilege against self-incrimination could not extend to a trustee or other fiduciary sued for breach of his duty so as to protect a criminally fraududent trustee (but not a negligent trustee). However, the Court of Appeal[6] has held that it does so extend unless, it seems, the trustee or other fiduciary expressly covenanted or contracted to waive any claim he might have to the privilege in respect of matters arising from his trusteeship or fiduciary relationship[7].

Trustee bound upon demand to give information as to notices of incumbrances

Subject to payment of any costs, any person interested in the equitable interest is entitled to see any notices of dealings with the equitable interest[8]. An intending assignee is probably a person interested in the equitable interest[9]. A trustee should take care in answering enquiries for he may be liable for honest but negligent misrepresentation[10].

---

3 *Rouse v 100F Australian Trustees Ltd* (1999) 2 ITELR 289, [2000] WTLR 111 at 128–129; *Re Rabbaiotti's Settlement* [2000] WTLR 953 at 962; *Re Lemos Trust* [1992] CILR 26.

4 For example, to ensure a life tenant received the income he should have received when alive.

5 Cf *Global Custodians Ltd v Mesh* (2000) 2 ITELR 327.

6 *Bishopsgate Investment Management Ltd v Maxwell* [1993] Ch 1, [1992] 2 All ER 856.

7 [1992] 2 All ER 856 at 881 and 991; *East India Co v Atkyns* (1720) 1 Com 346, assuming that the settlor's fair insistence upon this to protect the vulnerable beneficiaries from exploitation of the trustee's office does not amount to an Article 17 abuse of the trustee's Article 6 right to a fair trial under the Convention on Human Rights as incorporated by the Human Rights Act 1998.

8 LPA 1925, s 137(8).

9 See Wolstenholme and Cherry, *Conveyancing Statutes* (13th edn) vol 1, discussion of s 137(8), but cf (1935) 20 Conv 137 (Gower). A person would certainly be interested if contractually bound to acquire the interest subject to being relieved of his obligation if any notices materialised other than those of which he was aware at the time of the contract.

10 Misrepresentation Act 1967, s 2(1); *Hedley Byrne & Co Ltd v Heller* [1964] AC 465, [1963] 2 All ER 575, HL.

Information as to private company where substantially all shares held by trustees

In *Butt v Kelson*[11] where substantially all the shares of a private company were held upon trust and the trustees were directors of the company, it was held that the beneficiaries were subject to the restrictions imposed by the Articles which provided that no member, not being a director, should have any right to inspect any account, book or document of the company except as conferred by statute or authorised by the directors or by the company in general meeting, but Romer LJ delivering the leading judgment in the Court of Appeal, went on to say that if a beneficiary:

> 'firstly, specifies the documents of the company that he wants to see, secondly, makes out a proper case for seeing them, and, thirdly, is not met by any valid objection by the other beneficiaries or by the directors from the point of view of the company, then the directors should give inspection, not because they, as directors, can be compelled to do so, but as a short-circuit, if one may so describe it, to an order compelling them to use their voting powers so as to bring about what the plaintiff desires to achieve.'

However, it is difficult to reconcile this with the principle that, whilst all beneficiaries being of full age and capacity and between them absolutely entitled to the settled property can terminate the trust, they cannot whilst the trust continues control the trustees in the exercise of their powers and discretions under the trust[12].

It seems likely that if a beneficiary went so far as to specify documents relating to the day-to-day running of underlying companies then he would not be allowed to see them without making out a special case: the balance sheet and profit and loss accounts should normally suffice[13]; and where trustees are allowed to retain fees as directors beneficiaries must be allowed to check documents indicating the actual amount of the fees to see if such fees are reasonable and proper.

Information where trustee a partner

In *Morris v Morris*[14] a distinction was drawn from *Butt v Kelson*, namely a distinction between the information and obligations of a trustee acting as a partner with other partners, in making day-by-day discretionary decisions in relation to the running of the business, and the obligations of a trustee to the beneficiaries of the trust to provide them with information. The beneficiaries should not be able to interfere with the workings of the partnership business: thus, they were not entitled to see the books of account of the partnership business and documents relating to such business other than the balance sheets and profit and loss accounts.

---

11 [1952] Ch 197, sub nom *Butt, Re, Butt v Kelson* [1952] 1 All ER 167, CA.
12 See *Re Whichelow* [1953] 2 All ER 1558, [1954] 1 WLR 5, and *Re Brockbank* [1948] Ch 206, [1948] 1 All ER 287. This aspect is considered p 736, post.
13 *Re Ojjeh Trust* (1992–93) CILR 348.
14 (1993) 9 WAR 150.

PARAGRAPH 2

Expensive information

As above stated, a beneficiary is entitled, either personally or by his solicitor or accountant, to *inspect* the trust accounts and documents. If, however, he requires a copy of an account or document, he must either take copies himself at the trustee's office using his own portable copier or, for a reasonable fee, using an office copier, or pay the necessary expense himself; for it is not fair that it should be saddled on the trust estate, nor, of course, can the trustee be expected to incur the expense personally[15]. On the same ground, where a beneficiary demands information as to his rights under the settlement which cannot be furnished by the trustee without the assistance of a solicitor, the trustee is not bound to incur that expense (or if he be himself a solicitor, with power to charge, he is not bound to incur the loss of time), unless the beneficiary is willing to pay the reasonable costs of complying with his requisition[16].

---

15 *Ottley v Gilby* (1845) 8 Beav 602; *Kemp v Burn* (1863) 4 Giff 348; *Re Watson* (1904) 49 Sol Jo 54.
16 *Re Bosworth* (1889) 58 LJ Ch 432.

CHAPTER 12

The powers of the trustee[1]

Article
61 General principles applicable to powers of trustees   688
62 Managerial powers of trustees with particular reference to sales   703
63 Power of trustees to give receipts   705
64 Powers with regard to reversionary interests   706
65 General administrative powers of trustees   707
66 Power to allow maintenance to infants   709
67 Power of advancement   717
68 Suspension of the trustee's powers by administration action   726

ARTICLE 61

General principles applicable to powers of trustees

(1) Unless and until his powers are suspended by an administration action[2], a trustee
(a) must consider from time to time the exercise of his distributive and managerial discretions;
(b) must not fetter the future exercise of his discretions;
(c) must consciously exercise his own discretion in good faith and not passively fall in with suggestions of the settlor or his co-trustees;
(d) must exercise his discretions only within the scope of the terms of the relevant power and, then, only for the purposes for which the discretions were conferred on him by the settlor and not perverse to any sensible expectation of the settlor, thereby keeping an even hand among all the beneficiaries except in so far as he may fairly discriminate between them[3];

1 The powers of managing infants' estates or settled property conferred by the Settled Land Act 1925 on trustees for purposes of that Act, are outside the scope of this work.
2 See Article 68, post. Also, no discretionary powers can be exercised in the very rare case where the trustees have paid the trust fund into court: *Re Murphy's Trusts* [1900] 1 IR 145; *Re Nettlefold's Trusts* (1888) 59 LT 315.
3 As where the settlor intends discretionary trusts and powers to benefit some more than others and some not at all, or intends his life-tenant-widow to be the main object of his bounty and not a remote wealthy remainderman.

(e) must exercise his distributive discretions responsibly in properly informed fashion, taking account of relevant matters and ignoring irrelevant matters;

(f) must exercise his managerial discretions in accordance with the duty of care, so far as not ousted in the trust instrument;

(g) must not exercise any discretions directly or indirectly for his own benefit unless authorised by the trust instrument or by statute.

(2) If he complies with the above duties the exercise of his discretions will be unchallengeable even if the court itself would consider it reasonable and better to have exercised the discretion in different fashion.

PARAGRAPH 1(A)

Duty to keep discretions under review

In the case of a discretionary trust, the income or capital subject thereto must be distributed, but the trustees have a discretion as to which of the beneficiaries will take what amount and they must exercise this discretion within a reasonable time of the income or capital becoming distributable[4]. In the case of a discretionary power of appointment the trustees are not bound to exercise it but they must consider from time to time whether or not to exercise it, taking account of the range of objects of the power and then considering the appropriateness of individual appointments[5].

Where the trustees have managerial discretions, particularly in investing the trust fund, then they must keep the position under review, taking advice and taking account of the standard investment criteria where investments are concerned[6]. If losses to the trust fund would not have occurred but for breach of the duty to review managerial discretions or breach of specific duties in the investment function, then the trustees will have to account for such loss. Failure to carry out discretionary *trusts* of income or capital within a reasonable time leaves such still available for distribution amongst those who were possible recipient beneficiaries within such period[7]. Innocent trustees (eg awaiting resolution by the courts of the validity of the trusts) may subsequently exercise their discretions[8]. Wrongdoing trustees may be replaced by new trustees to exercise the discretions or, where distribution of funds is required, the court may direct preparation of a scheme by representative members of the beneficial class or in a simple case fix the basis of distribution itself[9].

Failure to exercise a discretionary *power* of appointment over income or capital within a reasonable time or any stipulated time leaves the income or

---

4 *Re Locker's Settlement Trust* [1978] 1 All ER 216.
5 *Re Hay's Settlement Trust* [1981] 3 All ER 786.
6 *Nestlé v National Westminster Bank* [1994] 1 All ER 118, CA; Trustee Act 2000 ('TA 2000'), ss 3, 4 and 5.
7 *Re Locker's Settlement Trust* [1978] 1 All ER 216.
8 *Re Locker's Settlement Trust* [1978] 1 All ER 216.
9 *McPhail v Doulton* [1971] AC 424 at 457.

capital belonging to the default beneficiaries[10]. Nothing can then be done by a disgruntled object except, it seems, that equitable compensation in the appointed amount will be available where the trustees actually prepared the deed of appointment but negligently executed it a day too late[11]. The court cannot intervene except to remove a trustee (as where the trustee told the object he hated him and would never make an appointment in his favour) where the power of appointment was not exercised in favour of a complaining object of such power, because the court does not positively exercise such power: it only intervenes negatively to restrain the improper exercise of such a power[12].

Exceptionally, if the object of some power like a power of advancement or a power to augment benefits under a pension scheme is also a beneficiary, then the court will intervene to direct exercise of the power in a special case eg where a trustee refused to consider exercising her discretion to advance capital to a beneficiary, her daughter, who had married against her wishes, though her co-trustee, the Public Trustee considered it to be a plain case for the advancement to be made[13] or where the employer-trustee of its pension trust for employees was in liquidation and the liquidator was in the impossible position of looking after creditors interested in the non-exercise of a power to benefit scheme members and looking after scheme-members interested in that power being exercised in their favour[14].

PARAGRAPH 1(B)

Duty not to fetter exercise of discretions

Just as powers vested in trustees ex officio cannot be released by the trustees (unless expressly authorised)[15] it is trite law that trustees cannot fetter the future exercise of powers vested in trustees ex officio[16], (although, in theory, the settlor could expressly authorise this). Any fetter is of no effect. Trustees need to be properly informed of all relevant matters at the time they come to exercise a relevant power. However, the current exercise of a particular power that has irrevocable impact on part of the trust fund is unimpeachable eg if money is invested in a bond that cannot be redeemed for five years or part of the settled property is settled revocably or irrevocably on B contingent

---

10 *Re Allen-Meyrick's Will Trust* [1966] 1 All ER 740; *Re Gulbenkian's Settlement Trust* [1970] Ch 408; or capital if the power relating thereto must be exercised before a particular date: *Breadner v Granville-Grossman* [2001] Ch 523.

11 *Breadner v Granville-Grossman* [2001] Ch 523 implications discussed by D J Hayton in PBH Birks & A Pretto *Breach of Trust* (Hart Publishing, 2002), Chapter 13 'Overview' p 388.

12 *Re Manisty's Settlement* [1974] Ch 17 at 25–26 and 27–28; *Re Hay's Settlement Trusts* [1981] 3 All ER 786 at 792; *Whishaw v Stephens* [1970] AC 508 at 525 per Lord Upjohn.

13 *Klug v Klug* [1918] 2 Ch 67; also see *White v Gane* (1854) 18 Beav 571 and *Re Lofthouse* (1885) 29 Ch D 921.

14 *Mettoy Pension Trustees Ltd v Evans* [1991] 2 All ER 513 where the remarks of Warner J at p 549 on the extensive powers of the court to carry out discretionary trusts (in ways indicated in *McPhail v Doulton* [1971] AC 424 at 457) need to be restricted to the context of powers to increase the benefits of beneficiaries who also had earned their expectations as deferred pay; and *Thrells v Lomas* [1993] 2 All ER 546.

15 *Re Wills' Trust Deeds* [1964] Ch 219.

16 *Swales v IRC* [1984] 3 All ER 16 at 24; *Re Gibson's Settlement Trust* [1981] Ch 179 at 182–183.

upon attaining 25 years, thereby providing intermediate income for the education of B, or an option is granted over part of the property[17].

PARAGRAPH 1(C)

Duty consciously to act in good faith

A discretion is not regarded as exercised by a trustee unless he consciously directs his mind to the fact that he does not have to exercise his discretion unless he considers this appropriate in all the circumstances. Thus, if a trustee automatically signs a deed of appointment placed before him by the settlor the deed will be void[18], while if trustees automatically pay all the income of the trust fund to the infant beneficiary's father without appreciating they have a discretion to pay only the amount needed for the infant's maintenance, the infant's father will have to repay all the money[19].

Any decision actuated by caprice[20] or spite[1] or a bribe[2] will be a nullity.

PARAGRAPH 1(D)

Duty to exercise discretions only for purposes intended by settlor so as fairly to benefit the beneficiaries

First, trustees must not exercise any discretionary power *ultra vires* its terms, so they must keep within the specified class of beneficiaries or objects[3] and otherwise act in accordance with the terminology of the trust instrument[4] or of statutory default powers.

Second, trustees must not exercise their powers other than for the purposes for which the settlor conferred those powers so that the trustees fulfil

---

17 Trustees now have much wider powers than previously when grants of options were impermissible as fettering trustees' functions: *Oceanic Steam Navigation Co v Sutherberry* (1880) 16 Ch D 236, CA.

18 *Turner v Turner* [1984] Ch 100, like an equitable *non est factum*.

19 *Wilson v Turner* (1883) 22 Ch D 521, CA. Similarly, a power to retain assets and not sell them had to be consciously exercised to oust a *Howe v Dartmouth* apportionment between life tenant and remainderman: *Re Guinness' Settlement* [1966] 2 All ER 497.

20 *Re Manisty's Settlement* [1973] 2 All ER 1203 at 121; *Re Pauling's Settlement Trust* [1964] Ch 303 at 333.

1 *Klug v Klug* [1918] 2 Ch 67.

2 This will also fall foul of the principle that a fiduciary power cannot be exercised in the power-holder's own favour unless authorised: *Re Skeats Settlement* (1889) 42 Ch D 522 at 526.

3 *Whishaw v Stephens* [1970] AC 508 at 518.

4 *Harris v Lord Shuttleworth* [1994] ICR 991 at 999, [1995] OPLR 79 at 86–87 per Glidewell LJ; *Wrightson Ltd v Fletcher Challenge Nominees Ltd* [2001] UKPC 23, [2001] OPLR 249 at para 11. Any requisite consents to the exercise of powers must be obtained (eg the consent of the life tenant to a power of advancement: *Re Forster's Settlement* [1942] Ch 199) unless the court can dispense with them in the case of land held on trust (Trusts of Land and Appointment of Trustees Act 1996 ('TLATA 1996'), s 14) or circumvent the matter by granting managerial powers under Trustee Act 1925 ('TA 1925'), s 57 or by the replacement of a person, such as a protector, refusing consent in breach of his fiduciary obligation (there being such inherent power if there is inherent power to appoint a protector as established in *Steele v Paz Ltd* [1993–95] Manx LR 102, and on appeal at 426).

the settlor's expectations[5]. This is of particular significance where the settlor has provided his trustees with exceptionally broad flexible powers, though expecting them to be used for relatively narrow purposes: it may be said that he provides the trustee as conductor with a large orchestra of powers in the trust instrument but he expects the trustee to play only music of the type indicated by him eg in a letter of wishes or in oral discussions with the trustees.

Where a range of beneficiaries is intended to be benefited throughout the duration of the trust, the settlor expects the trustees to act fairly in exercising their powers by holding an even hand between all the beneficiaries except where he intends different discriminatory treatment to be accorded to the beneficiaries[6]. Examples of this are where he has created extensive discretionary trusts or powers of appointment in a family trust or where trustees of a pension trust have extensive discretionary powers capable of discriminating between different classes of beneficiaries[7] or where he intends his life-tenant-widow to be well looked-after as the main object of his bounty rather than a remote wealthy remainderman, like a charity or a cousin who is next of kin[8].

It is perverse to any sensible expectation of the settlor for trustees to exercise their powers for purposes they know were not intended by the settlor so that they commit a fraud on the power[9]. However, in the area of pension trusts where beneficiaries have earned their rights and so have higher expectations than beneficiaries under family trusts, there has developed the notion enunciated by Glidewell LJ in *Harris v Lord Shuttleworth*[10] that trustees 'must not arrive at a perverse decision ie a decision to which no reasonable body of trustees could arrive'.

This is the public law, judicial review *Wednesbury* principle, named after *Associated Provincial Picture Houses Ltd v Wednesbury Corpn*[11] where it was held that the decision of a local authority or some domestic tribunal will be void if it is so unreasonable that no reasonable body could have arrived at it. Where the decision of a body of pension trustees relates to whether someone should receive a pension early, on grounds like incapacity or disablement that is likely to be irremediable, or should receive a lump sum as the deceased's cohabitee, the body is acting like a domestic tribunal[12], so it was natural in

---

5 *McPhail v Doulton* [1971] AC 424 at 449, HL; *Re Hay's Settlement Trust* [1981] 3 All ER 786 at 792; *Hayim v Citibank* [1987] AC 730 at 746, PC; *Re Beatty's Will Trust* [1990] 3 All ER 844 at 846; *Edge v Pensions Ombudsman* [1998] Ch 512 at 535 per Scott V-C and on appeal [2000] Ch 602 at 627 per Chadwick LJ.

6 Or in favour of persons who technically are not beneficiaries like the two elderly occupants of the Hong Kong house as to which the trustee-executors had no duties (other than not to benefit themselves) in *Hayim v Citibank* [1987] AC 730, PC.

7 *Edge v Pensions Ombudsman* [2000] Ch 602.

8 *Nestle v National Westminster Bank* [1994] 1 All ER 118, CA affirming Hoffmann J, reported [2000] WTLR 795. Breach only gives rise to personal accountability here (eg *Re Mulligan* [1998] 1 NZLR 481) while exercise of distributive (as opposed to investment) functions are void in equity as frauds on a power: *Cloutte v Storey* [1911] 1 Ch 18, CA.

9 For example, adding their children or friends to a class of beneficiaries where there is a broad power to add persons, transferring the trust property to a new trust under a power in that behalf where they are the new trustees with better exemption and remuneration clauses, appointing money to a beneficiary so that he can give them half or repay a debt to them.

10 [1994] ICR 991 at 999, [1995] OPLR 79 at 86–87, CA.

11 [1948] 1 KB 223, CA.

12 And see Pensions Act 1995, s 50 on procedural arrangements needing to be in place for resolution of disputes. Voidness also avoids problems with s 67 of that Act.

Harris v Lord Shuttleworth[13] expressly to adopt judicial review principles laid down in *Lee v Showmen's Guild of Great Britain*[14].

In *Edge v Pensions Ombudsman*[15] where a pension scheme's rules were amended by the trustees to take account of an actuarial surplus, but did not benefit one class of beneficiaries, Scott V-C accepted this judicial review approach stating[16]:

> 'The judge may disagree with the manner in which the trustees have exercised their discretion, but, unless they can be seen to have taken into account irrelevant, improper or irrational factors, or unless their decision can be said to be one that no reasonable body of trustees properly directing themselves would have reached, the judge cannot interfere.'

On appeal, the Court of Appeal[17] thought it 'no coincidence that courts considering the exercise of discretionary powers by those to whom such powers have been entrusted (albeit in different contexts), should reach similar and consistent conclusions and should express these conclusions in the same language'. However, it considered[18] it 'unnecessary to consider, in the present case, how far an analogy between the principles applicable in public law cases can or should be pressed in the different context of a private pension scheme'.

It is submitted that in the context of pension scheme trusts, where an employee enters into a contract of employment and as a condition thereof pays his first contribution to the trustees, thereupon making him a settlor-beneficiary[19], it is proper to regard him as having a reasonable legitimate expectation[20] that the trustees will not be permitted to make a decision adversely affecting his interests that is a decision that no reasonable body of trustees could have made: such a decision is void.

However, in the context of a private family trust where the beneficiaries are neither settlors nor parties to the transaction, it is submitted that there should be no invocation of *Wednesbury* public law principles, the beneficiaries having well-established private law fraud on a power rights that are focused upon the purposes and expectations of the settlor. Once one public law principle applies there is a danger that judges not steeped in trust law will begin to apply other public law principles, for example, concerned with natural justice and due process, as to the way in which decisions are arrived at. As has been stated[1], 'The difference between the public law and the trust approach is that the former focuses on the individual's opportunity to be heard before a decision, whereas the trust concept focuses on the information available to the person making the decision' as will now be examined.

---

13 [1994] ICR 991 at 999, [1995] OPLR 79 at 86–87, CA. Also *Wild v Pensions Ombudsman* [1996] 2 FLR 680 at 688 and 691.
14 [1952] 2 QB 329, CA.
15 [1998] Ch 512.
16 [1998] Ch 512 at 534.
17 [2000] Ch 602 at 628.
18 [2000] Ch 602 at 630.
19 *Air Jamaica Ltd v Charlton* [1999] 1 WLR 1399, PC.
20 Cf implied terms giving effect to the reasonable expectations of the mortgagor and mortgagee in *Paragon Finance plc v Staunton* [2001] EWCA Civ 1466, [2002] 2 All ER 248 at paras 36–42: mortgagee not to exercise interest-rate-changing discretion dishonestly, for an improper purpose, capriciously or arbitrarily nor in a way that no reasonable mortgagee would do.
1 *R v Charity Comrs, ex p Baldwin* [2001] WTLR 137 at 148–149

PARAGRAPH 1(E)

Duty in exercising distributive discretions to make a properly informed decision

For trustees to act responsibly they must inform themselves, before making a decision, of matters which are relevant to the decision[2]. Their decision must then take account of such relevant matters and ignore irrelevant matters[3]. However, the rules of natural justice do not apply to the exercise of a discretion by trustees (unless expressly imported by the terms of a trust), so that trustees, minded to benefit X, do not have to inform Y (for whom less will be available) so as to afford Y the opportunity to make representations against such course of action[4].

Examination is thus focused upon the matters known to, and considered by, the trustees in their decision-making process[5]. The principle *in Hastings-Bass* has developed from the decision in *Re Hastings-Bass*[6] of the Court of Appeal which stated:

> 'Where a trustee is given a discretion as to some matter under which he acts in good faith, the court should not interfere with his action, notwithstanding that it does not have the full effect which he intended unless
> (1) what he has achieved is unauthorised by the power conferred on him, or
> (2) it is clear that he would not have acted as he did (a) had he not taken into account considerations which he should not have taken into account or (b) had he not failed to take into account considerations which he ought to have taken into account.'

Over the years this statement has been taken out of context and treated as if part of a statute, so leading to some odd consequences which become worse when some courts have slipped into treating 'would' as if it only meant 'might', so making trustees' decisions more vulnerable.

Re Hastings-Bass and *Re Abrahams' Will Trust*[7], which was the basis of the judgment in *Re Hastings-Bass*, might well be explicable on the basis that the trustees' exercise of their powers of advancement 'for the benefit of' beneficiary B, appeared clearly authorised by the terms of the powers, but in *Re Abrahams' Will Trust* the exercise of the power actually was *ultra vires*, because not for the benefit of B in all the circumstances after crucial benefiting provisions turned out to be void for perpetuity, while in *Re Hastings-Bass* the exercise of the power was actually *intra vires* because sufficiently for the benefit of B, though some provisions were void for perpetuity. Thus, the exercise of the power was valid in *Re Hastings-Bass* but void in *Re Abrahams' Will Trust*.

---

2 *Stannard v Fisons Pension Trust* [1992] IRLR 27, CA; *Scott v National Trust* [1998] 2 All ER 705 at 717; *R v Charity Comrs, ex p Baldwin* [2001] WTLR 137 at 148.
3 *Re Hastings-Bass* [1975] Ch 25 at 4.
4 *Karger v Paul* [1984] VR 161 at 166 endorsed in *R v Charity Comrs, ex p Baldwin* [2001] WTLR 137 at 148; *Scott v National Trust* [1998] 2 All ER 705 at 717; *Re B* [1987] 2 All ER 475 at 478.
5 See *Stannard v IRC* [1991] PLR 225 at para 65 per Staughton LJ, applied in *Hearn v Younger* [2002] EWHC 963 Ch at para 91, [2002] WTLR 1317. However, until Civil Procedure Rules on disclosure can be invoked, it is difficult to obtain sufficient evidence as to the reasoning of the trustees to enable litigation to be instituted: see p 683 ante.
6 [1975] Ch 25 at 41.
7 [1969] 1 Ch 463.

In *Mettoy Pension Trustees Ltd v Evans*[8] Warner J took matters further. Believing that the reason for the application of the *Hastings-Bass* principle was the failure by the trustees to take into account considerations that they ought to have taken into account, he held[9] that it did not matter whether that failure was due to the overlooking of some relevant rule of law or limit on their discretion, or was due to some other cause. This seems justifiable because an apparent advancement on various trusts for B and several others might actually not be of benefit to B where the trustees were ignorant of key financial or personal circumstances of B[10].

Warner J assumed that application of the principle would result in conduct of the trustees being void, but he was prepared for the court only to declare a particular provision in a deed to be void if it was satisfied that the trustees *would* have acted in the same way if they had a proper understanding of the effect of their act but with the omission of such provision[11].

He emphasised[12], 'It is not enough for the principle to apply that it should be shown that the trustees did not have a proper understanding of the effect of their act. It must also be clear that, had they had a proper understanding of it, they would not have acted as they did'. Because it was not possible to say what the outcome would have been if the trustees had properly understood the position the deed in question remained valid.

However, in *Stannard v Fisons Pensions Trust Ltd*[13] the Court of Appeal held that trustees had to re-calculate the amount of the new pension trust fund to be set up by a distribution from the old pension fund to cover the pensions of employees transferring to the employment of another company. This was because an out-of-date valuation had led them to believe the pension fund was in deficit, when it actually was in surplus at the time of setting up the new trust fund. It so happened that Dillon LJ referred to an earlier 1986 decision, *Kerr v British Leyland (Staff) Trustees Ltd*[14], where *Re Hastings-Bass* had not been cited, involving a claim by a beneficiary under a pension trust to retire early due to a disability. The trustee's agent wrongly summarised the effect of a second medical expert's evidence and the trustees rejected the claim. Fox LJ held that no properly informed decision had been made so the trustees were ordered to reconsider the claim: if the trustees had appreciated the true position, 'I think that it might materially have affected their decision and that they might well have concluded that the proper course was to defer a decision until more was known about the effect the remedial steps were having upon Mr Kerr'[15].

Although Dillon LJ had been referred to *Re Hastings Bass* it was easy for him to say that it *might* materially have affected the trustees' decision if they had been properly informed as to the then current value of the fund and the implications of its value (for choosing a past service reserve method or total service reserve method for calculation purposes).

---

8 [1991] 2 All ER 513.
9 [1991] 2 All ER 513 at 555.
10 For example, B being much poorer than they thought and not childless as they thought, but having two non-marital children.
11 [1991] 2 All ER 513 at 555.
12 [1991] 2 All ER 513 at 555.
13 [1992] IRLR 27, CA.
14 [2001] WTLR 1071, [1989] IRLR 522, CA.
15 [2001] WTLR 1071 at 1079.

Since then, there have been two pension trust cases in which Lawrence Collins J[16] and Etherton J[17] have indicated that first instance judges should follow the later decision of the Court of Appeal in *Stannard* rather than that in *Re Hastings-Bass* itself, though in both cases the 'would' test was passed as well as the 'might' test.

Where beneficiaries are challenging a decision made by pension trustees to reject their claim, it seems proper that they can compel trustees to reconsider a decision made on incomplete evidence (so that relevant facts are missing) if the decision might be different once the evidence is complete. Beneficiaries may be regarded as having earned a legitimate reasonable expectation of this[18] in the light of becoming settlor-beneficiaries by virtue of entering into a contract of employment with a company. However, once the fully informed reconsideration has occurred, if the trustees do not change their minds, then that is an end of the matter, assuming they acted in good faith and not out of spite or malice or corruptly.

However, in the private family trust context it is submitted that, to strike the balance between the pursuit of perfectly informed decision-making and the need for practical certainty, a beneficiary's claim should only succeed if he proves that if the trustees had taken into account all the relevant considerations they *would* not have acted as they did in the exercise of their distributive functions. Even then, it is unsatisfactory that the concept of 'relevant consideration' is so open-textured: when do considerations start to become judgment-influencing considerations of some significance?

One thinks of the *Hastings-Bass* principle as one that beneficiaries invoke against the trustees, but it has been successfully invoked in two cases by the trustees so as to protect themselves from claims against them by beneficiaries and so as to undo the disastrous tax consequences of their own deliberate actions.

In *Green v Cobham*[19] the trustees made an appointment on sub-trusts in 1990 in order to benefit a particular beneficiary and to save tax. They overlooked the aggregation of head trustees and sub-trustees to determine residence based on the majority's residence in the UK or abroad[20] and took no account of one English-resident professional trustee telling them he intended shortly thereafter to retire from professional practice as a solicitor. On such retirement his *de iure*[1] non-residence would cease and his *de facto* residence in England would count in determining the residence of the head trust and associated sub-trusts.

In 1999 the trustees woke up to the disastrous tax consequences of their actions and invoked *Re Hastings-Bass* to undo their actions: obviously, if they had appreciated the effect of their deliberate appointment they would not have made it. The court accepted this, declared the 1990 appointment an invalid exercise of the trustees' power of appointment and so void in its entirety.

In *Abacus Trust Co (Isle of Man) Ltd v NSPCC*[2] leading tax counsel advised on

---

16 *AMP (UK) Ltd v Baker* [2001] WTLR 1265 (2001) 3 ITELR 414.
17 *Hearn v Younger* [2002] EWHC 963 (Ch), [2002] WTLR 1317.
18 Note also Pensions Act 1995, s 50 requiring arrangements in place for resolution of disputes.
19 [2000] WTLR 1101. The Revenue were not informed of the trustees' proceedings.
20 *Roome v Edwards* [1982] AC 279.
 1 Now Taxation of Chargeable Gains Act 1992, s 69(2), formerly Capital Gains Taxes Act 1979, s 52(2).
 2 [2001] WTLR 953. The Revenue were informed but refused to be joined as a party.

a 'flip flop' capital gains tax avoidance scheme, which required a proposed appointment in favour of the NSPCC not to be made until the start of the next tax year. Overlooking this, the trustees made the appointment just *before* expiry of the current tax year with disastrous tax consequences. Upon realising this, the trustees invoked *Re Hastings-Bass* and *Green v Cobham* to undo their actions. Patten J followed those cases to declare the appointment invalid and of no effect.

As a result Etherton J has summarised the *Hastings-Bass* principle as follows[3] 'A decision of trustees to exercise a discretion will be void if (a) the trustees have failed to take into account a material consideration, and (b) that consideration might materially have affected their decision.'

Limits upon Hastings-Bass principle

If this be the case, it is very odd that the remedies of rectification of a deed of appointment and of setting such a deed aside for mistake are not available where there was no mistake as to the appointment and the effect of it as an appointment, only a mistake as to its consequences and advantages[4], while it seems the *Hastings-Bass* principle can be exploited to declare an appointment void where there was no mistake as to the appointment and the effect of it as an appointment, only a mistake as to its consequences and advantages.

If one refers back to *Re Hastings-Bass* the formula used by the Court of Appeal was as follows[5], 'Where a trustee is given a discretion as to some matter under which he acts in good faith the court should not interfere with his action, *notwithstanding that it does not have the full effect intended* unless . . . he *would* not have acted as he did had he not failed to take into account considerations which he ought to have taken into account'. The implication is that where the action by way of exercise of a power of appointment does have the full effect intended, so there is no mistake as to the effect of the appointment as an appointment, then the court will not interfere, mistakes as to the consequences and advantages of an appointment not being of concern to the courts as supported by the law on rectification and on setting aside for mistake.

In *Re Hastings-Bass* the exercise of the power of advancement by way of a trust for the beneficiary, W, for life, with remainders over, did not have the full effect intended because the remainders were void for perpetuity (W not ranking as a life in being of this trust created out of an old trust and so having the perpetuity period appropriate to the old trust) but it was still of great benefit to W by saving much estate duty, even if the trust of capital was valid only to the extent of her life interest, so the power to make an advancement 'for the benefit of' W had been properly exercised.

It is thus submitted that the time has come to place some limits on the *Hastings-Bass* principle so that it is inapplicable where the mistake of trustees is not as to the effect of their actions as such (eg in making an appointment which as an appointment achieves what they deliberately meant to achieve) but as to the consequences and advantages thereof (eg in exacerbating tax

---

3 *Hearn v Younger* [2002] EWHC 963 (Ch) [2002] WTLR 1317 at para 86.
4 *Gibbon v Mitchell* [1990] 3 All ER 338; *AMP (UK) plc v Barker* [2001] WTLR 1237 at 1260; *Anker-Petersen v Christensen* [2002] WTLR 313 at 330-331. If the document represents the parties' true intention rectification is not possible: *Re Butlin's Settlement* [1976] Ch 251.
5 [1975] Ch 25 at 41.

liabilities rather than avoiding or mitigating them). As Park J states[6], 'It cannot be right that whenever trustees do something which they later regret and think that they ought not to have done, they can say they never did it in the first place.'

He went on to hold[7] that, while the *Hastings-Bass* principle operates to invalidate a purported exercise of a power by trustees, it does not apply with reverse effect so as to treat as valid what the trustees would have done if they had been fully informed instead of acting under a misapprehension. Thus, a power of appointment executed by them one day later than the last day for its exercise could not be treated as having been made one day earlier, as it would have been if they had appreciated the true position.

In *Re Duxbury's Settlement Trust*[8] it had already been held that a failure to take into account a material consideration when exercising a power of appointment of new trustees did not invalidate the appointment, such falling outside the *Hastings-Bass* principle. The three trustees, who retired on replacing themselves with a sole trust corporation, and that trust corporation, on retiring itself by replacing itself with the Public Trustee, had overlooked the prohibition in the trust deed upon any discretionary powers (other than the appointment of new trustees) being exercised unless there were at least two trustees. It seems the *Hastings-Bass* principle should be confined to distributive discretions involving trust capital or income being distributed to beneficiaries or to trustees for beneficiaries. Where managerial, administrative discretions are concerned, third parties dealing with trustees need to be able safely to deal with them and so be unaffected by hidden material considerations which would (and *a fortiori* which might) have influenced particular decisions.

Decisions that are not properly informed: void or voidable?

Clearly, if trustees are not informed at all but automatically sign an appointment put before them by the settlor, that appointment is void[9], as also is the case for distributions by way of appointment or otherwise that are not authorised by the terms of the trust or power[10] or that amount to a fraud on the power by going beyond the purpose of the power[11]. If a deed of appointment is rectified to give effect to what was truly intended to be present in the deed, then rectification is retrospective[12], the rectified deleted parts of the deed thus being regarded as void.

However, where the court is asked to set aside a deed of appointment or advancement for mistake the deed is voidable in equity[13], so why should a mistakenly informed decision of trustees be void rather than voidable, assuming that the decision is within the trustees' powers? In *Re Abrahams Will*

---

6 *Breadner v Granville-Grossman* [2001] Ch 523 at 543.
7 *Breadner v Granville-Grossman* [2001] Ch 523 at 543.
8 [1995] 3 All ER 145, CA.
9 *Turner v Turner* [1984] Ch 100.
10 For example, *Re Diplock* [1948] Ch 465.
11 *Cloutte v Storey* [1911] 1 Ch 18.
12 *Re Butlin's Settlement* [1976] Ch 251; *Malmesbury v Malmesbury* (1862) 31 Beav 407.
13 The court in deciding whether to rescind or set aside the deed for mistake will take account of the usual discretionary bars thereon if applicable.

Trust[14] and *Re Hastings-Bass*[15] part of the exercise of the relevant power was void under the rule against perpetuity, and in the former, but not the latter, the court went on to hold that such partial voidness of the actual advancement purportedly made for the benefit of C wholly altered the character of the advancement and meant that it was not actually for the benefit of C. The trustees could only validly exercise the power if it was actually for the benefit of C, so[16], 'In my judgment the result of that must be that there never was a valid exercise of the power of advancement.' It therefore appears, as counsel for the Revenue there argued[17], that the exercise of the power was void as being beyond the powers of the trustees.

On this basis, there was no justification in those cases[18] where the trustees acted well within their powers for the courts holding that their misinformed decisions were automatically void. They should just have been liable to be set aside in equity, subject to the usual equitable discretions where third party rights have intervened or there has been delay or acquiescence[19].

No analogies should be drawn with public law judicial review principles: trust law is an autonomous private law. Judicial review must be brought within three months of the disputed decision and decisions of bodies made on wrong grounds are regarded as made without jurisdiction so as always to be void[20]. Trust law is not so crude, having been developed over the centuries by judges steeped in equity so as to allow more leeway, both to trustees and to beneficiaries, over a graduated range of conduct from non-feasance through to increasing degrees of misfeasance.

PARAGRAPH 1(F)

Duty to exercise managerial discretions with due care

In exercising distributive discretions (involving distribution of income or capital to or for the benefit of beneficiaries under discretionary trusts or objects of powers of appointment or to or for the benefit of beneficiaries via exercise of powers of maintenance and advancement or powers of accumulation) trustees are exercising only internal functions relating to the trustee-beneficiary or trustee-object relationship. The recipients of the settlor's vicarious bounty are volunteers and so can have no protection as bona fide purchasers for value without notice although they may be protected if they

---

14 [1969] 1 Ch 463.
15 [1975] Ch 25, CA.
16 [1969] 1 Ch 463 at 485.
17 [1969] 1 Ch 463 at 483. The fact that the effect of the rule against perpetuity according to Cross J (at p 85) 'wholly altered the character of' the advancement brings the advancement document within the dictum of Lord Wilberforce in *Saunders (Executrix of Will of Gallie) v Anglia Building Society* [1971] AC 1004 at 1026, 'a document should be held to be void (as opposed to voidable) only when the transaction which the document purports to effect is essentially different in substance or kind from the transaction intended'.
18 *Green v Cobham* [2000] WTLR 1101 and *Abacus Trust Co (Isle of Man) Ltd v NSPCC* [2001] WTLR 953
19 As suggested by Robert Walker LJ (as he then was) in 'The Limits of the Rule in Re Hastings-Bass' in [2002] PCB 226, (2002) 13 KCLJ 173.
20 See R Davern in D J Hayton (ed) *Extending the Boundaries of Trusts and Similar Ring-Fenced Funds* (Kluwer, 2000) at p 439, citing *Anismic Ltd v Foreign Compensation Commission* [1969] 2 AC 147, *Secretary of State for Education v Tameside Metropolitan Borough Council* [1977] AC 1014 at 1027 and *R v Criminal Injuries Compensation Board, ex p A* [1999] 2 AC 330 at 345.

change their position as a result of such bounty. They are also 'insiders' with rights to see the trust instrument and trust accounts, so that they are in a position when receiving benefits to know whether or not the trustees are acting within the limits of the powers conferred on them by the settlor or by law and not for purposes perverse to any sensible expectation of the settlor, and they are in a position to make the trustees fully informed of their circumstances which may justify an exercise of a distributive discretion in their favour. By contrast, in exercising managerial or administrative discretions, the trustees will be dealing with third parties, who are not 'insiders' but who may well be bona fide purchasers for value without notice or be protected by statutory overreaching provisions (as where the proceeds of sale of land are paid to two trustees or to a trust corporation) or by equitable overreaching under authorisations in the trust instrument (as where jewels or shares in X Co Ltd are authorised to be sold and the proceeds are used to buy Y Co Ltd shares).

One also has to remember that the individuals who are trustees or the corporation that is trustee will have full legal ownership of the trust assets and will not be acting beyond their own powers and capacity when transferring legal title to a third party, so that legal title will validly pass[1]. If the trustees are acting beyond the limits imposed upon them by the trust instrument or the general law of trusts, then they will be acting in breach of trust, but the third party now owning the legal title will often be a bona fide purchaser thereof for value without notice of any trusts or be protected by statutory or equitable overreaching provisions despite any notice of the trusts.

Because the beneficiaries then have no remedy against the third party, the focus turns upon the internal obligations owed by the trustees to their beneficiaries. The trustees may be liable for breach of specific duties eg not having taken proper advice when making investments[2], not having taken account of the statutory standard investment criteria[3], not having provided a proper-policy statement for their asset manager[4], not having made regular reviews of investments or of delegations to others[5]. More often, the trustees will be liable for failure to observe the statutory duty of care[6] (if not ousted in the terms of the trust instrument[7]) eg in selecting investments or in selecting and supervising any delegates they employ to carry out or help carry out their managerial functions.

Breaches of specific duties and breaches of the duty of care will lead to the trustees' accounts being surcharged with an amount to make up the extra value the trust fund would have had but for their breaches of duty.

---

1 *Rolled Steel Products (Holdings) Ltd v British Steel Corpn* [1986] Ch 246 at 303 per Browne-Wilkinson LJ, *De Vigier v IRC* [1964] 2 All ER 907 at 914 per Lord Upjohn.
2 TA 2000, s 5.
3 TA 2000, s 4(3).
4 TA 2000, s 15.
5 TA 2000, ss 4(2) and 22.
6 TA 2000, s 1 and Sch 1.
7 As seen in Article 52, trustees may be exempted from liability for negligence, whether gross or ordinary, (*Armitage v Nurse* [1998] Ch 241, CA), while clauses exempting a trustee from liability unless fraudulent also protect him from deliberately committing a breach of trust if he honestly believes it to be in the best interests of his beneficiaries unless he is a lawyer (or a professional trustee) paid to act as trustee and no reasonable lawyer (or professional trustee) could have held such belief, for otherwise, a wholly unreasonable trustee could undermine the core effectiveness of the settlor's trust (*Walker v Stones* [2001] QB 902 at 941, CA).

PARAGRAPH 1(G)

Duty not to break the duty of undivided loyalty

More fundamental than not breaking prescriptive duties laid down by equity and statute is not breaking the proscriptive fiduciary obligation of undivided loyalty owed to the beneficiaries[8]. This fiduciary obligation is the obligation to put the interests of the particular beneficiaries above all other interests (unless otherwise authorised) so that no profit can be made from the trust property or the office of trustee (unless authorised) and (unless authorised) the trustee must not place himself in a position where his own interest conflicts with the interests of his beneficiaries or his duty in one capacity conflicts with his duty in another capacity or in a position where there is a sensible possibility of such conflict arising; but if there is a conflict or possibility thereof the trustee must prefer his duty to his interest save as permitted by the trust instrument to consider his interest.

Breach of fiduciary obligation connotes disloyalty or infidelity: mere incompetence is not enough[9]. To uphold the fundamental fiduciary obligation owed to vulnerable beneficiaries the trustee is strictly liable for profits[10] made in breach of the obligation and, indeed, a constructive trust is automatically imposed on the profits and the traceable product thereof[11]. There seems a reluctance to apply the logic of strict personal liability for losses, but at least the onus of proof lies on the trustees to show that the losses were not caused by the trustee's breach because they would have occurred even if there had been no such breach[12].

PARAGRAPH 2

Much discretionary leeway afforded to trustees

As the Court of Appeal pointed out in *Edge v Pensions Ombudsman*[13], if trustees exercise their discretionary power for the purpose for which it is given, giving proper consideration to the matters which are relevant and excluding from consideration matters which are irrelevant, they cannot be criticised if they reach a decision which appears to prefer the claims of one interest over others: the preference will be the result of a proper exercise of the discretionary power.

The Court of Appeal endorsed the approach of Scott V-C[14] who had emphasised that it was not for a judge to exercise the discretion of trustees unless they had surrendered it to the court in a particular situation[15]. The

---

8 See Articles 33, 58 and 59, ante.
9 *Bristol & West Building Society v Mothew* [1998] Ch 1 at 18, CA.
10 See Article 59, ante.
11 See Article 33, ante.
12 *Bank of New Zealand v New Zealand Guardian Trust Co* [199] 1 NZLR 664 at 687, CA; *Swindle v Harrison* [1997] 4 All ER 705 at 716–717 but lesser fiduciaries than trustees may justifiably be under lesser obligations.
13 [2000] Ch 602 at 627.
14 [2000] Ch 602 at 618 and 630.
15 Where trustees have decided what they want to do, but fear their exercise of their discretion in the way they have decided might be open to challenge, they can apply to the court for a declaration that their proposed discretionary decision is within the leeway afforded to them and so would be a proper exercise of their discretion: *Public Trustee v Cooper* [2001] WTLR 901 at 923; *Representation of I* (2002) 4 ITELR 446 (momentous foreign tax payment).

judge may disagree with the trustees' exercise of their discretion because he would have exercised it differently if in their shoes, but, nevertheless, he cannot interfere where the trustees had complied with the applicable duties in coming to their decision.

It is thus a 'well-established rule that where a discretion is entrusted to a trustee, the trustee is not required to give reasons for the exercise of that discretion and that, in the absence of evidence that the trustee has acted improperly, whether from an improper motive or by taking account of factors which the trustee should not have taken into account or not taking into account factors which the trustee should have taken into account, the court will not interfere with the exercise of the trustee's discretion'[16]. However, 'If a decision taken by trustees is directly attacked in legal proceedings, the trustees may be compelled either legally (through discovery or subpoena) or practically (in order to avoid adverse inferences being drawn) to disclose the substance of the reasons for their decision'[17]. Normally, if the exercise of distributive discretions is in issue it is difficult to have initial evidence to support a claim and prevent it from being struck out as a mere 'fishing expedition'.

Often trustees are given a power to distribute income or capital between members of a class as they see fit in their absolute discretion or to invest the trust fund as they see fit in their absolute discretion, but this is subject to the implicit restriction that their discretion should be exercised properly within the limits of the general law[18]. It makes no difference if 'in their uncontrollable discretion' is used[19]: such cannot be taken at its face value for that would prevent the beneficiaries having any enforceable rights so there would be no trust[20]. In carrying out their fundamental investment role and their fundamental distributive role in favour of beneficiaries, trustees must exercise their discretions within the limits of the general law.

However, without prejudice to such irreducible core content of the trust, a settlor may expressly or by necessarily implication prevent objects of a power of appointment from having the rights of beneficiaries as to accountability of the trustees[1]: and there is no reason why *powers* conferred on trustees in respect of objects of powers of appointment and of adding persons to classes of beneficiaries or of objects or deleting persons from such classes, should not be excluded from being subject to any fiduciary obligations by expressly being made personal powers, expressed to be unchallengeable in the courts unless their exercise amounts to a fraud on the power that dishonestly benefits the trustees. Indeed, it would seem that the power of trustees to add anyone in the world (except the trustees, the settlor and the settlor's spouse) to the class of beneficiaries or of objects of a power of appointment, or to appoint income or capital directly to anyone in the world, but members of such excepted class, cannot be capable of being 'policed' so as to be a

16 *Wilson v Law Debenture Trust Corpn plc* [1995] 2 All ER 337 at 343 per Rattee J based on *Re Beloved Wilkes Charity* (1851) 3 Mac & G 440 and *Re Londonderry's Settlement* [1965] Ch 918, CA.
17 *Scott v National Trust* [1998] 2 All ER 705 at 719, per Robert Walker J.
18 *Gisborne v Gisborne* (1877) 2 App Cas 300, HL; *Whishaw v Stephens* [1970] AC 508 at 518, HL; *Tempest v Lord Camoys* (1882) 21 Ch D 571, CA; *Bishop v Bonham* [1988] 1 WLR 742 at 751–752, CA.
19 *Gisborne v Gisborne* (1877) 2 App Cas 300, HL; *Whishaw v Stephens* [1970] AC 508 at 518.
20 *Armitage v Nurse* [1998] Ch 241 at 253, CA; D J Hayton, 'The Irreducible Core Content of Trusteeship', Chap 3 in A J Oakley (ed) *Trends in Contemporary Trust Law* (Oxford, 1996).
 1 *Re Angora Trust* [2001] WTLR 1081, Manx CA.

fiduciary power and so, by necessary implication, is merely a personal power unchallengeable in its exercise unless that amounts to a dishonest fraud on the power[2].

ARTICLE 62

Managerial powers of trustees with particular reference to sales

Subject to restriction or extension in the trust instrument or ad hoc legislation,
(1) trustees of land have power to manage their land as if absolute owners[3] and to employ agents in this behalf[4], while they may delegate their functions relating to the land to a beneficiary or beneficiaries of full age beneficially entitled to an interest in possession[5];
(2) trustees of property other than land have power to sell it to make any kind of investment they could make if absolutely entitled to it, but they cannot invest in land, except for loans secured on land[6], unless it is 'freehold or leasehold land' in the UK, although they can acquire freehold or leasehold land in the UK for occupation by a beneficiary or for any other reason[7]: they may employ agents[8].

PARAGRAPHS 1 AND 2

Very extensive general powers of trustees

In simpler static times, the rule had been that trustees were supposed to preserve the settled property in specie for the beneficiaries therein[9] and could not dispose of it unless directed or empowered by the trust instrument or by the court or by some statutory authority[10]. Moreover, the settlor was relying on the trustees personally to do this, so that they could not employ agents, even for the implementation of their decisions, unless this was reasonably necessary or in the ordinary course of affairs[11].

Nowadays, in view of the protective panoply of equitable and statutory duties imposed upon trustees in the exercise of their powers[12], trust instru-

---

2 See p 97 ante. However, it is probably not a fully personal power that is inherently capable of being released, while a fiduciary duty to consider exercising it will subsist.
3 TLATA 1996, s 6 and Article 45 ante.
4 TA 2000, ss 11–24, and Article 55 ante.
5 TLATA 1996, s 9 and Article 55(1)(e) ante.
6 TA 2000, s 3.
7 TA 2000, s 8.
8 TA 2000, ss 11–24.
9 Nowadays the emphasis is on preserving the capital value of the trust property, taking account of inflation, unless the settlor clearly intended the life tenant (eg his widow) to be the primary object of his bounty rather than the remainderman (eg a cousin as next of kin or some charity): *Nestlé v National Westminster Bank* [1994] 1 All ER 118 at 133, 137 and 140, CA; *Karger v Paul* [1984] VR 161; *Re Saunders and Halom* (1986) 32 DLR (4th) 503.
10 See 15th edn hereof, Article 64.
11 See Article 55 ante.
12 See Articles 48, 52, 53 and 55 ante.

ments and the Trusts of Land and Appointment of Trustees Act 1996 and the Trustee Act 2000 (in default of express powers in the relevant trust instrument) confer very extensive powers to manage the trust property[13] and purchase or acquire new trust property[14] using the services of nominees and custodians and agents[15], who may have discretionary, and not merely ministerial, functions delegated to them eg discretionary portfolio management[16]. These matters have all been considered in earlier Articles (as footnoted) dealing with the duties of trustees.

Power to raise capital money

Trustees (other than trustees of charities or Settled Land Act trustees who are not also statutory owners) who are authorised under the trust instrument or by law (eg s 32 of the Trustee Act 1925) to pay or apply capital money subject to the trust for any purpose or in any manner have power to raise the money required by sale, conversion, calling in, or mortgage of all or any part of the trust property for the time being in possession[17]. This statutory power cannot be ousted by the trust instrument[18], and a similar power will be available, anyhow, where the property is land where such power is within the general powers of trustees of land as if absolute owners thereof.

It has been held that this statutory power does not authorise trustees to raise money to purchase further investments by mortgaging existing investments[19] and, as already seen[20], the new general absolute powers do not appear apt to empower such 'gearing up' the value of the trust fund.

Conduct of sales

Where a trustee has a duty or power to sell real or personal property then, unless there is a contrary intention expressed in the trust instrument[1], he may sell or concur with any person in selling all or any part of the property, either subject to prior charges or not, and either together or in lots, by public auction or by private contract, subject to any such conditions respecting title or evidence of title or other matter as the trustee thinks fit, with power to vary any contract for sale, and to buy in at any auction, or to rescind any contract for sale and to re-sell, without being answerable for any loss[2].

Specific statutory power[3] is also conferred on trustees of land to dispose of surface and mines and minerals separately, though now covered by absolute owner powers in the Trusts of Land and Appointment of Trustees Act 1996, s 6 which also empower trustees of leases to sell via underleases at apportioned rents[4] and a sale for a price other than money.

Purchase money must be apportioned before completion where trustees

---

13 See Article 45 ante.
14 See Article 53 ante.
15 See Article 55 ante
16 See Article 55 ante, TA 2000, s 15.
17 TA 1925, s 16(1).
18 TA 1925, s 16(2).
19 *Re Suenson-Taylor's Settlement* [1974] 3 All ER 397.
20 See p 602 ante.
 1 TA 1925, s 69(2).
 2 TA 1925, s 12(1).
 3 TA 1925, s 12(2).
 4 Also see *Re Judd and Poland's Contract* [1906] 1 Ch 684, CA.

make a sale jointly with another and the purchaser must pay the apportioned trust money only to the trustees[5].

Where trustees hold an undivided share in property on trust they can execute any trust or power vested in them in relation to such share in conjunction with persons owning the other share or shares, and notwithstanding that one or more of the trustees may be entitled to an undivided share in his own right or as trustee for others[6]. The last proviso goes beyond the absolute owner powers in Trusts of Land and Appointment of Trustees Act 1996.

Specific performance will not be granted of a contract made by the trustees in breach of trust[7], while it is possible that some of the conditions of a contract of sale of land may be depreciatory conditions that may or may not amount to a breach of trust. Accordingly, s 13 of the Trustee Act 1925 provides that no sale shall be impeached by a beneficiary (or objected to by the purchaser) on the basis that any condition thereof was unnecessarily depreciatory unless thereby making the sale price inadequate, while, after conveyance, no sale can be impeached as against the purchaser on the ground that any condition was unnecessarily depreciatory unless the purchaser was acting in collusion with the trustees when the contract was made.

ARTICLE 63

Power of trustees to give receipts

(1) The receipt in writing of a trustee for any money, securities, investments or other personal property or effects payable, transferable, or deliverable to him under any trust or power is a sufficient discharge to the person paying, transferring, or delivering the same and effectually exonerates him from seeing to the application or being answerable for any loss or misapplication thereof[8].

(2) Except where the trustee is a trust corporation constituted under the law of a Member State of the European Union[9], a sole trustee cannot give a valid receipt for the proceeds of sale or other capital money arising under a trust of land[10] or for capital money arising under the Settled Land Act 1925.

(3) Paragraphs 1 and 2 of this Article apply notwithstanding anything to the contrary in the instrument, if any, creating the trust[11].

The above Article states the effect of s 14 of the Trustee Act 1925, as amended. Sub-section (2) is complementary to s 27(2) of the Law of Property Act 1925, which provides that notwithstanding anything to the contrary in the instrument (if any) creating a trust of land or affecting the net proceeds of sale of the land if it is sold, the proceeds of sale are not to be paid to or applied by the direction of fewer than two trustees except where the trustee is

---

5 *Re Cooper and Allen's Contract* (1876) 4 Ch D 802.
6 TA 1925, s 24.
7 *Dunn v Flood* (1885) 28 Ch D 586, CA.
8 TA 1925, s 14(1), as amended by TA 2000, Sch 2, para 19.
9 See the Law of Property Act 1925, s 205(1)(xxviii); see note 4, p 448, ante and p 797, post.
10 TA 1925, s 14(2), as amended by TLATA 1996, Sch 3, para 3(3).
11 TA 1925, s 14(3).

a trust corporation. However, a bona fide purchaser of a legal estate in unregistered land for value without notice of an equitable interest may obtain a good title from a sole legal owner[12]. In the case of registered land a purchaser from a sole registered proprietor will obtain a good title free from any equitable interest not ranking as an overriding interest and not protected by entry on the register[13] so long as the purchaser is not using the Land Registration Act provision as an instrument of fraud[14].

Until 1997, while the proceeds of sale of land in England and Wales can be properly paid to two persons (whether individuals or companies or one individual and one company) s 37(1)(c) of the Trustee Act 1925 prevented a trustee from being validly discharged from his trust unless there would be either a trust corporation constituted in a State within the European Union or at least two *individuals* to perform the trust (though this latter requirement could be ousted by the terms of the trust instrument)[15]. The Trusts of Land and Appointment of Trustees Act 1996, Sch 3, para 4(8)(b) then changed 'individuals' into 'persons', so closing the trap by mirroring the position under the Law of Property Act 1925, s 27(2).

ARTICLE 64

Powers with regard to reversionary interests

(1) Where trust property includes any share or interest in property not vested in the trustees, or the proceeds of the sale of any such property, or any other thing in action, the trustees on the same falling into possession, or becoming payable or transferable may:
(a) agree or ascertain the amount or value thereof[16] or any part thereof in such manner as they may think fit;
(b) accept in or towards satisfaction thereof, at the market or current value, or upon any valuation or estimate of value which they may think fit, any authorised investments;
(c) allow any deductions for duties, costs, charges and expenses which they may think proper or reasonable;
(d) execute any release in respect of the premises so as effectually to discharge all accountable parties from all liability in respect of any matters coming within the scope of such release;
without being responsible in any such case for any loss occasioned by any act or thing so done by them if they have discharged the duty of care set out in section 1 of the Trustee Act 2000.
(2) The trustees are not under any obligation and are not chargeable with any breach of trust by reason of any omission:

---

12 *Kingsnorth Trust Ltd v Tizard* [1986] 2 All ER 54; *Williams and Glyn's Bank v Boland* [1979] Ch 312 at 330, 341, [1979] 2 All ER 697 at 704, 713, CA.
13 Land Registration Act 1925, ss 20, 23; Land Registration Act 2002, ss 26, 29 and 30.
14 *Jones v Lipman* [1962] 1 All ER 442, [1962] 1 WLR 832; see also *Lyus v Prowsa Developments Ltd* [1982] 2 All ER 953.
15 *London Regional Transport Pension Fund Trust Co Ltd v Hatt* [1993] PLR 227 at 260–262.
16 See also TA 1925, s 22(3), as to valuations.

(a) to place any distringas notice[17] or apply for any stop or other like order upon any securities or other property out of or on which such share or interest or other thing in action as aforesaid is derived, payable or charged; or,

(b) to take any proceedings on account of any act, default, or neglect on the part of the persons in whom such securities or other property or any of them or any part thereof are for the time being, or had at any time been, vested; unless and until required in writing so to do by some person, or the guardian of some person, beneficially interested under the trust, and unless also due provision is made to their satisfaction for payment of the costs of any proceedings required to be taken.

(3) Nevertheless nothing in paragraphs (1) and (2) of this article relieves the trustees of the obligation to get in and obtain payment or transfer of such share or interest or other thing in action on the same falling into possession.

The above Article reproduces s 22(1) and (2) of the Trustee Act 1925 as amended by the Trustee Act 2000, Sch 2, para 22(a), substituting for 'good faith' the need to comply with the statutory duty of care. It will be noticed that it is restricted to interests in property not vested in the trustees and to choses in action.

ARTICLE 65

General administrative powers of trustees

(1) A personal representative, or two or more trustees acting together, or, subject to the restrictions imposed in regard to receipts by a sole trustee not being a trust corporation, constituted under the law of a State within the European Union[18], a sole acting trustee where by the instrument, if any, creating the trust, or by statute, a sole trustee is authorised to execute the trusts and powers reposed in him, may, if and as he or they think fit:

(a) accept any property, real or personal, before the time at which it is made transferable or payable; or

(b) sever and apportion any blended trust funds or property; or

(c) pay or allow any debt or claim on any evidence that he or they may think sufficient; or

(d) accept any composition or any security, real or personal, for any debt or for any property, real or personal, claimed; or

(e) allow any time of payment of any debt; or

(f) compromise, compound, abandon, submit to arbitration, or otherwise settle any debt, account, claim, or thing whatever relating to the testator's or intestate's estate or to the trust;

---

17 Now a stop notice: RSC Ord 50, rr 11–14.
18 See pp 448, ante, 797, post.

and for any of those purposes may enter into, give, execute, and do such agreements, instruments of composition or arrangement, releases, and other things as to him or them seem expedient, without being responsible for any loss occasioned by any act or thing so done by him or them if he has or they have discharged the duty of care set out in section 1 of the Trustee Act 2000.

This Article reproduces s 15 of the Trustee Act 1925, as amended by the Trustee Act 2000[19] so as to require not merely good faith but compliance with the statutory duty of care in exercising the extensive powers conferred by s 15.

In *Re Ezekiel's Settlement Trusts*[20] where the trustees had surrendered to the court their discretion as to whether they should accept a compromise that had been offered, the Court of Appeal directed the trustees to proceed with a compromise for £7,750 of a claim for £15,000, and Lord Greene MR pointed out that 'the court, just the same as any trustee, has to act on the balance of possibilities and the balance of apparent advantages'.

In order to justify a payment by way of compromise there must have been a claim, but it is not necessary to establish that the claim would have succeeded, for the effect of that would be to reduce the power to compromise to a nullity[1]. It seems the section only applies where the trustee has actively exercised some discretion so that loss has not arisen from passive inactivity[2].

Whilst the nature of executorship enables an executor in a proper case to compromise a claim by his co-executor against the estate[3] it seems that trustees should not compromise a claim by one of themselves against the trust property unless there is a special authority for a majority to bind the minority[4] or the court sanctions such compromise.

The power to compromise is very broad indeed. Any disparity between the beneficiaries arising upon exercise of the power is to be judged by ascertaining whether the compromise is desirable and fair as regards all the beneficiaries. Thus, where the consideration for the compromise of a claim against a party extraneous to the trust, who owned a beneficial interest in the trust, included the surrender of that interest and the consequential alteration of the beneficial interests the compromise lay within the power to compromise[5], although the power does not enable trustees to effect a variation of the trusts.

The need not to act just in good faith, but to comply with the duty of care in the Trustee Act 2000, means that trustees will often be advised to apply to the court to confirm that they will be acting properly if they decide to compromise a valuable or difficult claim as proposed to the court, and the costs of such application should be ordered to be paid out of the trust fund[6].

19 TA 2000, Sch 2, para 20.
20 [1942] Ch 230, [1942] 2 All ER 224, CA.
 1 *Re Ridsdel* [1947] Ch 597, [1947] 2 All ER 312. See also *Re Shenton* [1935] Ch 651.
 2 *Re Greenwood* (1911) 105 LT 509; *Partridge v Equity Trustees Executors and Agency Co Ltd* (1947) 75 CLR 149, Aus HC.
 3 *Re Houghton* [1904] 1 Ch 622. Administration of Estates Act 1971, s 10(2), provides some additional protection for a personal representative who pays a debt to a creditor.
 4 *Luke v South Kensington Hotel Co* (1879) 11 Ch D 121.
 5 *Re Earl of Strafford* [1978] 3 All ER 18, [1978] 3 WLR 233; affd [1980] Ch 28, [1979] 1 All ER 513, CA.
 6 *Re Owens Corning Fiberglas (UK) Pension Plan Ltd* [2002] PLR 323, (2002) Times, 8 July; *Bradstock Pension Scheme Trustees Ltd v Bradstock Group plc* [2002] PLR 327, (2002) Times, 10 July.

ARTICLE 66

Power to allow maintenance to infants

(1) Where any property is held by trustees in trust for any person for any interest whatsoever, whether vested or contingent, then, subject to any prior interests[7] or charges affecting that property, the trustees *may*, during the period when that beneficiary is under the age of 18, if his interest so long continues, make an allowance of the whole or part of the income of that property for or towards his maintenance, education, or benefit[8].

(2) This power is discretionary, but is exercisable notwithstanding that there is another fund applicable to the same purpose, or some person bound by law to provide for such maintenance or education[9].

(3) In deciding whether the whole or any part of the income of the property is, during the period when a beneficiary is under 18, to be paid or applied for the purposes aforesaid, the trustees must have regard to his age and his requirements and generally to the circumstances of the case[10], and in particular to what other income, if any, is applicable for the same purposes. Where trustees have notice that the income of more than one fund is applicable for those purposes, then, as far as practicable, unless the entire income of the funds is paid or applied as aforesaid or the court otherwise directs, a proportionate part only of the income of each fund ought to be so paid or applied[11].

(4) The trustees may pay the allowance to the parent or guardian of the beneficiary under 18, instead of expending it directly themselves[12].

(5) The balance of the income not applied for the maintenance, education, or benefit of the beneficiary under 18 *must* during the period when he remains under 18 (if his interest so long continues) be accumulated at compound interest, but the trustees may, at any time during the period when he is under 18 (if his interest so long continues) apply the accumulations or any part thereof as if they were income of the current year[13].

---

7 The question has been raised as to whether, and in what circumstances, the mere fact that remaindermen will or may become entitled to the capital of the trust fund, and thus to any accumulations of income which may augment it (so that they have an interest in ensuring that income is accumulated rather than spent), gives them a 'prior interest' within the meaning of this provision (TA 1925, s 31(1)). The point was deliberately left undecided by Clauson J in *Re Spencer* [1935] Ch 533, and by the Court of Appeal in *Re Turner's Will Trusts* [1937] Ch 15, [1936] 2 All ER 1435, CA. See also *IRC v Bernstein*, where the point was considered in relation to the power of advancement (TA 1925, s 32) at first instance [1960] Ch 444, [1960] 1 All ER 697; and on appeal [1961] Ch 399, [1961] 1 All ER 320, CA; see p 718, post.

8 In *Re Heyworth's Contingent Reversionary Interest* [1956] Ch 364 at 370, [1956] 2 All ER 21 at 23, Upjohn J said that these were words of the widest import. Also see *Allen v Coster* (1839) Beav 202.

9 Section 31(1)(i).

10 Section 31(1). As to the former law see *Wilson v Turner* (1883) 22 Ch D 521, CA.

11 See, as to the former law, *Smith v Cock* [1911] AC 317. Paragraph 3 here sets out the proviso to s 31(1) which trust instruments often exclude.

12 In pre-1970 trusts where 21 years is the norm the trustees *may* pay the beneficiary at 18.

13 Section 31(2).

(6) Even if the beneficiary on attaining the age of 18 years has not a vested interest in the income, the trustees must thenceforth pay the *income* of the property and of any accumulations thereto, made under paragraph 5 of this Article, to the beneficiary until he either attains a vested interest or dies, or until failure of his interest[14].

(7) (i) If the beneficiary:

(a) attains the age of 18 years, or marries under that age and his interest in such income while he is under 18 or until his marriage is a vested interest; or

(b) on attaining the age of 18 years or on marriage under that age becomes entitled to the property from which such income arose in fee simple, absolute or determinable, or absolutely, or for an entailed interest;

the trustees must hold the accumulations in trust for such person absolutely[15], and the receipt of such person after marriage, and though still under 18, is a good discharge[16]. This provision operates without prejudice to any provision with respect to such accumulations contained in any settlement by him made under any statutory powers during his infancy.

(ii) In any other case the trustees must, notwithstanding that such person had a vested interest in such income[17], hold the accumulations as an accretion to the capital of the property from which they arose[18]. If such property is settled land within the Settled Land Act 1925, the accumulations should be treated as if they were capital moneys.

(8) The above provisions apply to a contingent interest only if the limitation or trust carries the intermediate income of the property[19], but they apply to a future or contingent legacy by the parent of, or a person standing in loco parentis to, the legatee, if and for such period as, under the general law, the legacy carries interest for the maintenance of the legatee[20].

(9) These provisions apply to a vested annuity in like manner as if the annuity were the income of property held by trustees in trust to pay the income thereof to the annuitant for the same period for which the annuity is payable, save that in any case accumulations made whilst the

---

14 Section 31(1)(ii). The beneficiary's entitlement to income confers an interest in possession upon him so as to attract inheritance tax if he dies or assigns the interest: Capital Transfer Tax Act 1984 (alternatively named Inheritance Tax Act by Finance Act 1986, s 100) ss 51, 52; *Swales v IRC* [1984] 3 All ER 16 at 24; *Re Jones' Will Trusts* [1947] Ch 48, [1946] 2 All ER 281.

15 *Re Fulford* [1930] 1 Ch 71.

16 Section 31(2)(i).

17 The words 'notwithstanding that such person had a vested interest in such income' refer to the nature of the interest conferred by the settlement on the infant and are not an affirmation that the infant's interest in the surplus income remains a vested interest despite the alteration of his rights into a contingent interest by the subsection: *Stanley v IRC* [1944] KB 255 at 261.

18 Section 31(2)(ii).

19 Section 31(3).

20 In any such case the rate of interest (if the income available is sufficient, and *subject to any rules of court to the contrary*) is to be five pounds per cent per annum. However, it may be that RSCO 44, r 10, applicable under CPR, Pt 50, r 50.1 now makes 6% the rate payable when accounting for legacies if the income available is sufficient.

annuitant is under 18 must be held in trust for the annuitant or his personal representatives absolutely[1].

(10) These provisions do not apply where the instrument, if any, under which the interest arises came into operation before 1 January 1926, thereafter, they do apply, but with 21 years replacing 18 years where the instrument under which the interest arises came into operation before 1 January 1970, when the age of majority became 18 under the Family Law Reform Act 1969; and they may be negatived or modified by the instrument creating the trust[2], but any period of accumulation must be one permitted by statute.

Application of Trustee Act 1925, s 31

The section can only apply if the trust limitations in favour of the beneficiary in question carry the intermediate income and if no express or implied contrary intention appears in the trust instrument.

Where the section does apply the trustees must apply their discretion rather than merely pay the income automatically to the beneficiary's parent[3]. The circumstances of the beneficiary and his parents should be reviewed regularly. A special point should be made to review the position a month or so before the beneficiary attains 18 since the statutory power to apply income and accumulations thereof expires on his 18th birthday and, before then, such could be allocated to him absolutely or contingent upon attaining his majority, such being applications of money for his benefit[4].

It is apprehended that, in spite of the wide words of the section, trustees should ask the parent or guardian for some reasonable explanation as to how he intends to apply the sum allowed by them, although they are not bound to see to its application. It does not matter that parents of the infant being maintained are incidentally benefited though, of course, a trustee should not maintain an infant with the purpose of benefiting the parents[5].

The power being discretionary, the court will not interfere with the trustees' discretion so long as they exercise it bona fide and rationally[6].

Sums paid by trustees in the exercise of their discretion form part of the total income of the infant for tax purposes as soon as the trustees exercise their discretion[7].

---

1 Section 31(4).
2 Sections 31(5), 69(2); *Re Turner's Will Trusts* [1937] Ch 15, [1936] 2 All ER 1435; where a power of appointment is exercised 'the document' exercising the power is the instrument under which the appointed interest arises: *Re Dickinson's Settlement* [1939] Ch 27; *Begg-McBrearty v Stilwell* [1996] 4 All ER 205. The age of 21 years is relevant for testamentary trusts of a testator who died after 1969 but made his will before 1970: Family Law Reform Act 1969, s 1(7).
3 *Wilson v Turner* (1883) 22 Ch D 521.
4 *Re Vestey's Settlement* [1951] Ch 209, CA; *Pilkington v IRC* [1964] AC 612, HL on benefit via settlements.
5 *Re Lofthouse* (1885) 29 Ch D 921.
6 *Re Bryant* [1894] 1 Ch 324; *Re Senior* [1936] 3 All ER 196.
7 *Drummond v Collins* [1915] AC 1011, HL. Income applied for an infant unmarried child of the settlor is treated as the settlor's income. Any sum paid out of trust funds to the settlor's child is treated as income to the extent that accumulated income is available. See the Income and Corporation Taxes Act 1988, s 660B as substituted by Finance Act 1995, s, 68, Sch 17.

Statutory power not always applicable

Except for the case of a future or contingent legacy by the parent of, or of a person in loco parentis to, the legatee where under the general law[8] the legacy carries interest for the maintenance of the legatee, s 31 of the Trustee Act 1925 applies only *where the gift carries the intermediate income,* so that if, on the true construction of the settlement, that income is payable to someone else during the infancy or if there is an express direction to the trustees to accumulate the income during the minority of the contingent life tenant and to add that income to the corpus[9], the infant will not (with the exception hereinafter referred to in the case of portions charged on land) be entitled to be maintained. Consequently, the first question which the practitioner has to solve in all cases of maintenance (except as aforesaid), is whether or not the income of the fund will go along with the capital if and when the latter vests. If it will, then unless there is an express direction to accumulate all the income until the corpus vests, maintenance may be safely allowed. If it will not, then maintenance must be refused as it also must be where there is an express direction for accumulation.

Where trustees hold property on discretionary trusts before holding it for persons with vested or contingent interests and, pursuant to their discretions, the trustees allocate income absolutely to a discretionary beneficiary such income does not fall within s 31 though income arising from such income will do[10]. An infant discretionary beneficiary is thus absolutely entitled to the allocated income and does not have his interest converted into a contingent interest by the application of s 31[11].

What gifts carry actual intermediate income

An inter vivos settlement will need to be of specific property and even if a beneficiary's interest is contingent will carry the intermediate income (unless a contrary intent is present as where the income is disposed of in favour of someone else or directed to be accumulated to the capital). A testamentary contingent bequest of residuary personalty will carry intermediate income[12] unless a contrary intent is present eg where it is expressly deferred to some future date[13].

With regard to specific devises and bequests and residuary devises contained in wills coming into operation after 1925, s 175 of the Law of Property Act 1925 provides as follows:
(1) A contingent or future specific devise[14] or bequest of property, whether

8 See p 713, post.
9 *Re Stapleton* [1946] 1 All ER 323.
10 *Re Vestey's Settlement* [1951] Ch 209, [1950] 2 All ER 891.
11 For such conversion, see p 715, post.
12 *Re Adams* [1893] 1 Ch 329 at 334. The intermediate income is carried for as long as the law allows it thereby to be accumulated for the beneficiary: *Re McGeorge* [1963] Ch 544, [1963] 1 All ER 519.
13 *Re Oliver* [1947] 2 All ER 162 at 166; *Re Gillett's Will Trusts* [1950] Ch 102, [1949] 2 All ER 893; *Re Geering* [1964] Ch 136, [1962] 3 All ER 1043: such express deferral may even prevent a vested residuary bequest from carrying intermediate income.
14 In *Re McGeorge* [1963] Ch 544, [1963] 1 All ER 519, the testator had devised land to his daughter and declared that 'the ... devise ... shall not take effect until after the death of my ... wife should she survive me', going on to make substitutionary provision for the land if his daughter should die before the survivor of the testator and his wife. Cross J held that the land was the subject of a 'future specific devise' within s 175 and therefore carried the income but

real or personal, and a contingent residuary devise of freehold land, and a specific or residuary devise of freehold land to trustees upon trust for persons whose interests are contingent or executory shall, subject to the statutory provisions relating to accumulations, carry the intermediate income of that property from the death of the testator, except so far as such income, or any part thereof, may be otherwise expressly disposed of.

(2) This section applies only to wills coming into operation after the commencement of this Act.

In considering s 175 a distinction has to be drawn between gifts which are merely contingent (or vested subject to defeasance) and those which are expressly deferred to a future date. Prima facie, a gift of residue which is deferred to a future date does not carry the intermediate income whether it is vested, or vested subject to defeasance, or contingent, unless the will contains words indicating an intention that the income is to go with the capital[15].

General or pecuniary legacies that merely carry interest

It will be perceived that s 175 does not refer to contingent or future general legacies (eg 'I bequeath 1,000 ordinary shares in ICI Ltd') or pecuniary legacies (eg 'I bequeath £5,000'). The basic principle is that a general or pecuniary legacy carries interest (at 5% if the income available is sufficient[16] and there is no rule of court to the contrary[17]) from the time at which it is payable[18]. Such time if not specified by the testator will, in the case of an immediate legacy, be one year after the testator's death[19] (ie at the end of the executor's year) and in the case of a contingent or deferred legacy will be the time the contingency is satisfied or the deferred event occurs[20].

Exceptionally, interest runs from the testator's death in four instances. First, if a vested legacy is given in satisfaction of a debt[1] and, second, if a vested legacy is charged on realty alone[2]. Third, if a testator gives a legacy to a minor and in his will shows an intention to provide for the minor's maintenance or education[3] even if the legacy is contingent upon an event having no reference to the legatee's minority, eg the attainment of twenty-five years of age[4]. Fourth, if a testator gives a legacy to his minor child or to a minor to

that, since it was liable to defeasance during the lifetime of the testator's widow, the income should be accumulated and the daughter could not claim that it be paid to her under s 31(1)(ii) because (a) her interest was vested and not contingent and (b) since the gift was a future gift, the will showed a contrary intention within s 69(2).

15 *Re Geering* [1964] Ch 136, [1962] 3 All ER 1043. In this case, Cross J held that this prima facie rule was in fact rebutted by the wording of the will. But in *Re Nash* [1965] 1 All ER 51, [1965] 1 WLR 221, Ungoed-Thomas J held that no such rebuttal was to be found in the will and that the normal rule should be applied: the intermediate income was therefore ordered to be accumulated for 21 years or until the ultimate gift vested in possession (whichever period was the shorter), and if the gift failed to vest within 21 years the intermediate income which accrued after the end of that period would pass on intestacy.

16 TA 1925, s 31(3).

17 SI 1983/1181, RSCO 44, r 10, may perhaps rank as such a rule: see note 20, p 710.

18 *Re Hall* [1951] 1 All ER 1073; *Re Raine* [1929] 1 Ch 716.

19 *Re Hall* [1951] 1 All ER 1073.

20 *Re Raine* [1929] 1 Ch 716.

1 *Re Rattenberry* [1906] 1 Ch 667.

2 *Shirt v Westby* (1808) 16 Ves 393.

3 *Re Churchill* [1909] 2 Ch 431; *Re Selby-Walker* [1949] 2 All ER 178; *Re Stokes* [1928] Ch 716; *Re West* [1913] 2 Ch 345.

4 *Re Jones* [1932] 1 Ch 642 (the headnote is wrong).

whom he stands in loco parentis[5], so long as the testator makes no other provision for maintenance of the minor[6], so long as the legacy is given directly to the minor and not to trustees for the minor[7] and so long as any specified contingency has some reference to the child's minority (eg attaining an age no greater than 18 years)[8].

There is one special case where a contingent general or pecuniary legacy carries actual intermediate income: where a legacy is directed to be set apart from the rest of the testator's estate for the purpose of benefiting the minor legatee (and not merely for convenience of administration) this will carry the actual intermediate income produced by such separate fund as from the end of the executor's year[9] (or from such earlier date as the separate fund is established if such is the testator's intention[10]). If, in the third or fourth exceptional instance mentioned in the preceding paragraph, a fund to provide the legacy is set aside for the sake of convenience, then any excess of income over the applicable interest rate will fall to be distributed as part of the residuary bequest. By oversight it seems that s 31(3) only applies to the fourth exceptional instance and not to the third exceptional instance so that in the latter instance the contingent legatee will not be affected by s 31.

Portions charged on land

There is, however, an exception to the general rule with regard to contingent portions charged on land. Although such gifts do not vest until they are wanted, namely, in case of sons at full age, or in case of daughters at full age or marriage, and do not carry intermediate income, yet an infant contingent portioner is entitled to such a rate of interest or allowance in respect of his or her portion as the court may deem necessary for maintenance[11].

Residuary gift to infant

A gift of residue to an infant *makes the executor a trustee*, and enables him to allow maintenance under this Article[12].

Personal representatives have power under s 42 of the Administration of Estates Act 1925, to appoint new trustees of an infant's absolute[13] share of residue, and thereby to obtain a discharge themselves. This power may be exercised even where the personal representatives are attorneys, and trustees appointed by such attorneys have the powers of trustees constituted by English law and so may allow maintenance under the Trustee Act 1925, s 31[14].

---

5 *Re Bowlby* [1904] 2 Ch 685.
6 *Re George* (1877) 5 Ch D 837.
7 *Re Pollock* [1943] Ch 338.
8 *Re Abrahams* [1911] 1 Ch 108.
9 *Re Medlock* (1886) 55 LJ Ch 738; *Re Woodin* [1895] 2 Ch 309, CA; *Re Couturier* [1907] 1 Ch 470.
10 Until establishment of the separate fund the applicable interest rate thereon may be payable from the date of the testator's death if the exceptional circumstances referred to in the preceding paragraph are present.
11 Per Farwell J *Re Greaves' Settled Estates* [1900] 2 Ch 683.
12 *Re Smith* (1889) 42 Ch D 302. The same rule applies to an administration, see *Re Adams* (1906) 51 Sol Jo 113.
13 Upon an English intestacy the statutory trusts will involve the beneficiary if a minor in having only a contingent interest unless married.
14 *Re Kehr* [1952] Ch 26, [1951] 2 All ER 812.

Contrary intention

After some conflict of judicial opinion, it has been decided by the Court of Appeal that all the provisions of s 31 of the Trustee Act 1925, whether expressed as permissive or as imperative, are 'powers conferred by this Act' within the meaning of s 69(2) of that Act, and therefore apply if and so far only as a contrary intention is not expressed in the instrument creating the trust, and have effect subject to the terms of that instrument[15]. An express direction (as opposed to a power) to accumulate income during infancy will almost invariably, amount to a contrary intention sufficient to negative the statutory power[16], though, in any event, it may cause the gift not to carry the intermediate income, as has been seen above[17]. The statutory duty under s 31(1)(ii) to pay income to adult contingent beneficiaries has been held to be negatived by an express power for the trustees to make payments to certain of the persons who claimed its benefit 'on account of their respective expectant shares of the trust fund and the income thereof', this express power being held inconsistent with the existence of the statutory duty[18], and by a provision expressly deferring the enjoyment of a gift[19].

Where an express direction to accumulate does amount to an expression of contrary intention the fact that it is partially invalidated by s 164 of the Law of Property Act 1925 does not render s 31 applicable as from the date of the express direction becoming invalid: the income will be treated as undisposed of[20] unless carried to beneficiaries with vested interests by Law of Property Act 1925, s 164[1].

Section 31 will be excluded if its application would be inconsistent with the purport of the instrument in question. Thus the statutory duty in s 31(2)(ii) to hold accumulations as an accretion to capital will be excluded where an appointment of income to six minors 'in equal shares *absolutely*' reveals in context an intention that each is to take an indefeasible share even if dying before attaining 18 years of age[2].

Vested interests converted into contingent interests

Section 31(2)(ii) has a significant effect since accumulations of income will not pass to a beneficiary with a vested interest in income under the terms of a settlement unless he satisfies a contingency set forth in s 31(2)(i) or unless he is also entitled to the capital to which the accumulations automatically accrue. This has important tax consequences since if a beneficiary (or his personal representative if he died immediately after the income arose) is not

---

15 *Re Turner's Will Trusts* [1937] Ch 15, [1936] 2 All ER 1435, CA (overruling *Re Spencer* [1935] Ch 533, and *Re Ricarde-Seaver's Will Trusts* [1936] 1 All ER 580). And see also *Re Watt's Will Trusts* [1936] 2 All ER 1555; *Re Rees* [1954] Ch 202, [1954] 1 All ER 7.

16 *Re Turner's Will Trusts* [1937] Ch 15, [1936] 2 All ER 1435; *IRC v Bernstein* [1961] Ch 399, [1961] 1 All ER 320; *Re Erskine's Settlement Trusts* [1971] 1 All ER 572, [1971] 1 WLR 162; cf *Re Thatcher's Trusts* (1884) 26 Ch D 426; *Re Cooper* [1913] 1 Ch 350.

17 See p 712, ante.

18 *Re Geering* [1964] Ch 136, [1962] 3 All ER 1043.

19 *Re McGeorge* [1963] Ch 544, [1963] 1 All ER 519: see note 14 on p 712, ante.

20 *Re Ransome* [1957] Ch 348, [1957] 1 All ER 690; *Re Erskine's Settlement Trusts* [1971] 1 All ER 572, [1971] 1 WLR 162. In *Brotherton v IRC* [1978] 2 All ER 267 at 272 Stamp LJ giving the judgment of the Court of Appeal spoke of *Re Ransome* as follows, 'I would not wish to throw any doubt on that decision but it is right to say that it has not been considered'.

1 *Brotherton v IRC* [1978] 2 All ER 267, [1978] 1 WLR 610.

2 *Re Delamere's Settlement Trusts* [1984] 1 All ER 584, [1984] 1 WLR 813, CA.

entitled to the income then the disadvantageous income tax treatment accorded to accumulation and discretionary trusts under the Income and Corporation Taxes Act 1988, ss 686–687, applies, while absence of an interest in possession is most significant for inheritance tax purposes.

A beneficiary becomes entitled to accumulations only if (a) he attains 18 or marries thereunder and his interest beforehand was vested under the terms of the settlement, eg to B for life or (b) on attaining 18 or marrying thereunder he becomes entitled to the capital from which the income arose in fee simple absolute or determinable[3] in relation to realty, or absolutely and indefeasibly[4] in relation to personalty, or for an entailed interest in relation to realty and personalty.

In other cases the accumulations pass with the capital to the persons interested in capital so that the beneficiary (or his personal representative) only obtains the accumulations if he is entitled to the capital.

It follows that where B is an unmarried minor he only has a contingent interest in income as it arises under a 1996 settlement conferring an interest on B for life or for B in tail[5]. If personalty is settled on B absolutely then B's entitlement to capital ensures that he receives all accumulations of income not otherwise applied for his maintenance etc. However, if freehold land was settled on B absolutely then the effect of the Administration of Estates Act 1925, s 51(3), is to make B's interest contingent for if he dies unmarried before attaining majority the land and the accumulations pass as if B had merely had an entail. For inheritance tax purposes a settlement will be taxed as one where no interest in possession subsists where B is a minor and is not entitled to capital (so that he is not entitled to accumulations of income not applied for his maintenance etc)[6]. Exceptionally, B as a minor will have an interest in possession where he has a vested annuity since the Trustee Act 1925, s 31(4), entitles B or his personal representatives to accumulations.

Class gifts

The Apportionment Act 1870 requiring apportionment of income on trust assets on a day-to-day basis applies to trusts within s 31 of the Trustee Act[7]. It will apply when a beneficiary attains 18, though producing an anomalous result where income is received after such date. To the extent income is apportioned in respect of the period before such date such income 'cannot be applied for maintenance etc. because the trustees cannot exercise their discretion in advance so as to affect the income when it is received, and they cannot apply it in arrears because the infancy will have ceased'[8]. It also applies when a class member dies or is born.

Take a 1985 settlement on X's grandchildren, now alive or born within 21

---

3 It seems this means a determinable fee in the strict sense distinct from a fee simple on condition: *Re Sharp's Settlement Trusts* [1973] Ch 331, [1972] 3 All ER 151, but cf the Settled Land Act 1925, s 117(1)(iv), treating 'determinable fee' as meaning a fee determinable whether by limitation or condition.

4 The interest will not be absolute if defeasible by an overriding power or upon the fulfilment of a condition: *Re Sharp's Settlement Trusts* [1973] Ch 331, [1972] 3 All ER 151.

5 *Stanley v IRC* [1944] KB 255, [1944] 1 All ER 230; *Re Delamere's Settlement Trusts* [1984] 1 All ER 584, [1984] 1 WLR 813, CA. Entailed interests cannot be created after 1996: TLATA 1996, s 2(6).

6 See B McCutcheon, *Inheritance Tax* (3rd ed) para 17–05 paras 16–72 to 16–80.

7 *Re Joel's Will Trust* [1967] Ch 14, [1966] 2 All ER 482.

8 *Re Joel's Will Trust* [1967] Ch 14 at 29.

years if they attain twenty-six where five grandchildren now exist aged twenty-five, nineteen, twelve, seven and two. A fifth share of income must be paid to the two eldest and a fifth share of income may be used for the maintenance etc of each of the others and to the extent not so used must be accumulated. The allocations to the three minor beneficiaries must each be kept separate[9]. If a sixth grandchild is born then sixth shares are allocable. If a grandchild then dies before attaining twenty-six the relevant shares of income will be fifths once more. Income provisionally accumulated and allocated to such deceased grandchildren is treated as an accretion to the capital of the whole fund, divisible amongst all beneficiaries ultimately becoming entitled to the capital even if not alive during the period when such accumulated income arose[10]. Otherwise a beneficiary can only be maintained etc out of income attributable to the period when he was alive and allocated to him as his proportionate share of income.

ARTICLE 67

Power of advancement

(1) Trustees may at any time or times pay or apply any capital money subject to a trust, for the advancement or benefit, in such manner as they may, in their absolute discretion, think fit, of any person entitled to the capital of the trust property or of any share thereof, whether absolutely or contingently on his attaining any specified age or on the occurrence of any other event, or subject to a gift over on his death under any specified age or on the occurrence of any other event[11], and whether in possession or in remainder or reversion, and such payment or application may be made notwithstanding that the interest of such person is liable to be defeated by the exercise of a power of appointment or revocation, or to be diminished by the increase of the class to which he belongs[12].

(2) The money so paid or applied for the advancement or benefit of any person must not exceed altogether in amount one-half of the presumptive or vested share or interest of that person in the trust property. It seems that the power ceases to be exercisable in respect of a particular beneficiary once it has been exercised in respect of such beneficiary's presumptive half share, so that a subsequent appreciation of the assets remaining in the settlement will not enable any

---

9 *Re Joel's Will Trust* [1967] Ch 14, [1966] 2 All ER 482; *Re Sharp's Settlement Trusts* [1973] Ch 331, [1972] 3 All ER 151. Allocated accumulations will pass to the beneficiaries when they obtain vested interests.

10 *Re Joel's Will Trust* [1967] Ch 14, [1966] 2 All ER 482. The Law Reform Committee 23rd Report 1982 (Cmnd 8733) para 3.41 recommends abrogation of the *Re Joel's Will Trust* time apportionment: the income from the trust should be apportioned between the class of beneficiaries as constituted on the day the income is received by the trustees. A draftsman may expressly provide for this in the settlement.

11 See *Re Garrett, Croft v Ruck* [1934] Ch 477.

12 The power of revocation in Mental Health Act 1983, s 96(3) does not prevent an advancement of capital: *Re CWHT* [1978] Ch 67, [1978] 1 All ER 210 on the corresponding s 103(4) of the 1959 Act.

further advancement to be made to such beneficiary.

(3) If that person is or becomes absolutely and indefeasibly entitled to a share in the trust property the money so paid or applied must be brought into account as part of such share.

(4) No such payment or application may be made so as to prejudice any person entitled to any prior life or other interest, whether vested or contingent, in the money paid or applied unless such person is in existence and of full age and consents in writing to such payment or application.

(5) This power does not apply to money applicable as capital money for the purposes of the Settled Land Act 1925.

(6) This power does not apply to trusts constituted or created before 1 January, 1926 and may be negatived or modified by the instrument creating the trust, eg so that if the power is extended to the whole of a prospective share the consent of the life tenant remains requisite[13].

Application of statutory power

The above statutory power of advancement conferred by s 32 of the Trustee Act 1925 is to the same effect as the usual advancement clause formerly contained in most well-drafted wills and settlements[14]. Its operation may be excluded by the expression of a contrary intention in the will or settlement[15] and it only relates to trusts constituted or created after 1925.

For this purpose a trust in a will is not 'constituted or created' until the death of the testator[16]. Trusts created by a deed of appointment executed pursuant to a special power of appointment conferred by will are constituted by the will, that is, from the death of the testator since an appointment under a special power must be read into the instrument creating it[17]. It is otherwise in the case of trusts created by a deed exercising a general power of appointment given by will which derive their force from and originate in the appointment only. The result is that s 32 applies to the trusts arising on the exercise after 1925 of a general power whenever created[18].

---

13 TA 1925, s 69(2); *Henley v Wardell* (1988) Times, 29 January.

14 *Re Stimpson's Trusts* [1931] 2 Ch 77. The express power is still required in Settled Land Act settlements created under powers in pre-1997 settlements (TA 1925, s 32(2), the effect whereof is stated in para 5 of this Article).

15 TA 1925, s 69(2). See *IRC v Bernstein* [1961] Ch 399, [1961] 1 All ER 320, CA, where the statutory power of advancement was held to be impliedly excluded by the manifest intention of the settlor that there should be no distribution during his lifetime (compare *Re Henderson's Trusts* [1969] 3 All ER 769, [1969] 1 WLR 651). See also *Re Evans' Settlement* [1967] 3 All ER 343, [1967] 1 WLR 1294 where Stamp J held that although an express power of advancement did not necessarily exclude the statutory power, the express power in this case, being limited to a stated sum, did do so. For a case in which the statutory power was restricted, but not in such a way as to affect its operation in the circumstances which had arisen, see *Re Collard's Will Trusts* [1961] Ch 293, [1961] 1 All ER 821 (a provision that the power should not be exercised 'for any purposes connected with business' did not prevent its exercise for the purpose of saving estate duty).

16 *Re Darby* (1943) 59 TLR 418.

17 *Re Batty* [1952] Ch 280, [1952] 1 All ER 425; as explained in *Re Bransbury's Will Trusts* [1954] 1 All ER 605, [1954] 1 WLR 496.

18 *Re Bransbury's Will Trusts* [1954] 1 All ER 605, [1954] 1 WLR 496.

Cash or property may be advanced subject to being brought into account

The power of advancement is primarily a power to make payments of cash and can be exercised informally, though the trustees should record what they have done. The court will not insist on circuity of action: thus, instead of advancing cash to a beneficiary to enable him to purchase land forming part of the trust property, the trustees may simply transfer the land in question to him[19]. Money paid or applied by way of advancement must, of course, be brought into account when the beneficiary's share of capital becomes distributable to him, as should the money-equivalent of any assets directly advanced to the beneficiary irrespective of any depreciation or appreciation of such assets or the traceable product thereof[20].

Exhausting the exercise of the power

In *Re Marquess of Abergavenny's Estate Act Trusts*[1] the trustees had express power from time to time to advance to the life tenant any part or parts not exceeding in all one half in value of the settled fund. Goulding J held that an advance of half the value of the fund exhausted the exercise of the power, so that it ceased to be exercisable in the life tenant's favour, even though the retained settled assets had subsequently much increased in value. It is difficult to distinguish the statutory power from such express power, so that to retain flexibility the trustees should, therefore, never quite exercise the statutory power of advancement to the full value of half the settled assets at the date of exercise of the power. If a settlor would wish half of any subsequent increase in value of the settled assets retained by the trustees to be available for further advancement then the statutory power should be expressly varied by the trust instrument[2].

Purpose of the advance

The word 'benefit' is the widest possible word which could be employed and includes a payment direct to the beneficiary. That, however, does not absolve the trustees from making up their minds whether the payment in the particular manner which they contemplate is for the benefit of the beneficiary[3]. Clearly a payment direct to the beneficiary which will effect a substantial saving of tax on the death of the tenant for life will be for the benefit of the

---

19 *Re Collard's Will Trusts* [1961] Ch 293, [1961] 1 All ER 821, where Buckley J also said: 'There is no doubt that the statutory power of advancement is constantly exercised by trustees transferring to beneficiaries Stock Exchange investments by way of advancement'. See also *Pilkington v IRC* [1964] AC 612, [1962] 3 All ER 622, HL.

20 Money or assets advanced are from the date of such advancement no longer part of the trust property: *Re Fox* [1904] 1 Ch 480; *Re Pilkington's Will Trusts* [1959] Ch 699 at 705. Their value at that date is thus the relevant value: see *Re Gollin's Declaration of Trust* [1969] 3 All ER 1591 and contrast advancements caught by Administration of Estates Act 1925, s 47(1)(iii) where it is the date of the intestate's death that is the valuation date.

1 [1981] 2 All ER 643, [1981] 1 WLR 843.

2 Consideration might also be given to how advanced or appropriated property should be brought into account on final distribution: see pp 544–545, ante.

3 *Re Moxon's Will Trusts* [1958] 1 All ER 386, [1958] 1 WLR 165; *Re Pauling's Settlement Trust* [1964] Ch 303, [1963] 3 All ER 1, CA.

beneficiary[4], as may be a payment to enable him to discharge his debts[5]. Payment of capital under a scheme to provide for prospective public school fees will also be for the benefit of an infant beneficiary.

Where the statutory power did not apply, an express clause authorising the application of moneys for the 'advancement' of the beneficiary but *not* containing the wider word 'benefit'[6] has been held to authorise payments for

purchasing a commission in the army[7];

putting out as an apprentice[8];

emigrating[9];

purchasing an outfit[10];

furnishing a house[11];

payment of legacy duty[12];

establishing in business[13] (but not making a deposit with the Trustees of Lloyd's for the purpose of becoming an underwriter[14]) or even establishing a husband in business[15];

and a power to raise money for starting the testator's son in business has been held to authorise the trustees to apply money towards the purchase of a house, with or without a surgery, for him to live in while practising medicine[16].

It is plain, therefore, that if the power of advancement is exercised for the benefit of the beneficiary, its exercise will not be made improper by the fact that other people benefit incidentally as a result[17]. It has indeed been held[18] that trustees may exercise a power of advancement in the normal form to pay a sum to a charity at the request of a wealthy beneficiary: the discharge of the beneficiary's moral obligation to make charitable donations was held to be for his benefit but, said Pennycuick J it is essential:

'that the beneficiary himself should recognise the moral obligation. It is not open to trustees to pay away the beneficiary's prospective capital over his head or against his will in discharge of what they consider to be his moral obligation.'

In line with this, under an express power to apply capital for the benefit of a beneficiary it has been held proper to re-settle it on the beneficiary's

---

4 *Re Moxon's Will Trusts* [1958] 1 All ER 386, [1958] 1 WLR 165. See also *Pilkington v IRC* [1964] AC 612, [1962] 3 All ER 622, HL, per Viscount Radcliffe.

5 Cf *Lowther v Bentinck* (1874) LR 19 Eq 166.

6 A discussion of these two words is to be found in *Pilkington v IRC* [1964] AC 612, [1962] 3 All ER 622, HL.

7 *Lawrie v Bankes* (1857) 4 K & J 142.

8 *Swinnock v Crisp* (1681) Freem Ch 78; *Simpson v Brown* (1864) 13 WR 312.

9 *Re England* (1830) 1 Russ & M 488; *Re Salters Trusts* (1866) 17 I Ch R 176.

10 *Re Welch* (1854) 23 LJ Ch 344.

11 *Perry v Perry* (1870) 18 WR 482.

12 *Klug v Klug* [1918] 2 Ch 67.

13 *Re Mead* (1918) 88 LJ Ch 86, CA; also see *Hardy v Shaw* [1975] 2 All ER 1052.

14 *Re Craven's Estate* [1937] Ch 431, [1937] 3 All ER 33.

15 *Re Kershaw's Trusts* (1868) LR 6 Eq 322.

16 *Re Williams' Will Trusts* [1953] Ch 138, [1953] 1 All ER 536.

17 This was confirmed by the House of Lords in *Pilkington v IRC* [1964] AC 612, [1962] 3 All ER 622, HL. Also see *Re Hampden Settlement Trusts* [1977] TR 177 and [2001] WTLR 195 (where in the case of a wealthy beneficiary with plenty to support himself it was held for his benefit to appoint trust property on trust for his family though they were not beneficiaries) and *Re Lesser* [1947] VLR 366 (purchase of house for infant beneficiaries to live in with their parents).

18 *Re Clore's Settlement Trusts* [1966] 2 All ER 272, [1966] 1 WLR 955.

children, with a view to avoiding tax, in a case where the beneficiary was already well provided for[19].

The word 'advancement' does not imply that the interest of the beneficiary need be in any sense accelerated: thus the power of advancement may be properly exercised by the trustees settling the property advanced upon trusts which in fact defer the beneficiary's physical possession of the property longer than the original settlement would have done[20]. (As to the propriety of the trustees making an advancement by way of settlement, see below.)

In no case, however, must a power of advancement be exercised so as to procure a benefit to the trustees[1].

Although the trustees must decide, before exercising the power that there is some good reason for doing so and must, in the words of Willmer LJ[2], 'weigh on the one side the benefit to the proposed advancee, and on the other hand the rights of those who are or may ... become interested under the trusts', there is no need for the advance to be 'personal' to the beneficiary in the way suggested by the Court of Appeal in *Re Pilkington's Will Trusts*[3]. In that case, Lord Evershed MR said that the statutory power of advancement could not be exercised unless the benefit to be conferred was 'personal to the person concerned in the sense of being related to his or her own real or personal needs' and the exercise was 'an exercise done to meet the circumstances as they present themselves in regard to a person within the scope of the section whose circumstances call for that to be done which the trustees think fit to be done'. But the House of Lords in reversing (sub nom *Pilkington v IRC*[4]) the decision of the Court of Appeal, found it impossible to import a restriction of this kind into the statutory power, Lord Radcliffe saying that it seemed to him 'uncontrollably vague as a guide to a general administration'.

Ensuring purpose effected

If trustees do make an advance for a particular purpose, which they state, the question arises as to whether and how far they must ensure that it is used for that purpose. In *Re Pauling's Settlement*[5] the Court of Appeal held that in such a case the trustees can properly pay the advance to the person for whose benefit it is made if they reasonably believe that he can be trusted to carry out the purpose prescribed; but if the person concerned had, to the trustees' knowledge, applied any previous advance in some way other than the one prescribed, the trustees would not be justified in paying another advance to him for a specific purpose and should themselves apply it for the purpose for which they wished it to be used. Alternatively, the person to whom an advance is made for a stated purpose can expressly be placed under a *Quistclose* trust obligation (explained at p 116 ante) to carry out that purpose, and the trustees should not relieve him of that obligation or pay the advance to him in such a way as to leave him free to carry it out or to disregard it

19 *Re Earl of Buckinghamshire's Settlement Trusts* (1977) Times, 29 March.
20 *Pilkington v IRC* [1964] AC 612, [1962] 3 All ER 622, HL.
 1 *Molyneux v Fletcher* [1898] 1 QB 648 (advance to daughter to enable her to pay father's debt to one of the trustees).
 2 In *Re Pauling's Settlement Trust* [1964] Ch 303, [1963] 3 All ER 1, CA.
 3 [1961] Ch 466, [1961] 2 All ER 330, CA.
 4 [1964] AC 612, [1962] 3 All ER 622, HL.
 5 See note 2, above.

without any responsibility on their part to enquire as to its application.

Re Pauling's Settlement further indicates that requests from and consents of young adult beneficiaries in respect of advancements must be carefully considered since until such beneficiaries are 'emancipated' from their parents questions of undue influence arise, making it most unsafe to rely on beneficiaries' consents to a breach of trust if the advance turns out to be a breach of trust as for the benefit of a beneficiary's parent and not for the benefit of the beneficiary.

Advancement by way of settlement

Trustees exercising a power of advancement may make settlements on objects of the power if the particular circumstances of the case warrant that course as being for the benefit of the object of the power[6]. This has been confirmed by the House of Lords in *Pilkington v IRC*[7] on appeal from the contrary decision of the Court of Appeal[8], though their Lordships pointed out that the trustees should be cautious about re-settling the property so as to postpone the beneficiary's entitlement (though there may be justifiable capital gains tax or special personal reasons). The view taken by the House of Lords is indeed consonant with a long line of authority. Thus, in *Re Halsted's Will Trusts*[9] Sir Christopher Farwell J decided that under an express power of advancement in a will for the 'benefit of advancement in life' of a beneficiary trustees might settle a sum on him in order to provide for his wife and children, but on terms that the settlement was limited to benefit him, his wife and children with an ultimate trust for residue of the testator's estate.

Again, in *Re Ropner's Settlement Trusts*[10], Harman J held that it was properly conceded by counsel that under a power to apply one-quarter of trust funds 'for the advancement, preferment or benefit' of beneficiaries, trustees might properly transfer part of the trust funds to the trustees of settlements on objects of the power, the main reason being to avoid heavy death duties on the death of a man aged fifty-eight.

In at least one case[11] the court has even refused to sanction an advancement unless the beneficiary settled the sum advanced.

The provisions that may be included in a settlement were considered by Upjohn J in *Re Wills' Trusts*[12], where he opined:

'What the authorities typified by *Re May's Settlement*[13] and *Re Mewburn's Settlement*[14] establish to my mind is that any settlement made by way of advancement on an object of the power by trustees must not conflict with the principle delegatus non potest delegare. Thus, unless upon its proper construction the power of advance-

---

6 *Re Wills' Will Trusts* [1959] Ch 1, [1958] 2 All ER 472. To strengthen 'benefit' for the beneficiary for whose benefit there is to be a re-settlement it will help in the resettlement to confer powers of appointment on such beneficiary. The consent of the beneficiary to the re-settlement is not needed: *Re Cameron* [1999] 2 All ER 924 at 948–949.
7 See note 4, above.
8 See note 3, above.
9 [1937] 2 All ER 570.
10 [1956] 3 All ER 332n, [1956] 1 WLR 902. See also *Re Meux* [1958] Ch 154, [1957] 2 All ER 630; *Re Wills' Will Trusts* [1959] Ch 1, [1958] 2 All ER 472.
11 *Roper-Curzon v Roper-Curzon* (1871) LR 11 Eq 452, where the beneficiary who was already married was studying for the law.
12 [1959] Ch 1, [1958] 2 All ER 472 but the re-settlement did not contain discretionary powers.
13 [1926] Ch 136.
14 [1934] Ch 112.

ment permits delegation of powers and discretions, a settlement created in exercise of the power of advancement cannot in general delegate any powers or discretions, at any rate in relation to beneficial interests, to any trustees or other persons, and in so far as the settlement purports to do so it is pro tanto invalid. I say that without prejudice to the propriety of including ordinary powers of advancement in such settlement; see *Re Morris' Settlement Trusts.*'[15]

In *Pilkington v IRC*, however, the House of Lords held that trustees could properly exercise their statutory power of advancement by adding the property advanced to another settlement, which was already in existence and of which they themselves happened to be the trustees. Viscount Radcliffe dealt with several arguments which had been raised by the Revenue against the propriety of such an exercise, including one based on the maxim dele- gatus non potest delegare, mentioned above. In this connection he said[16]:

'I am unconvinced by the argument that the trustees would be improperly dele- gating their trust by allowing the money raised to pass over to new trustees under a settlement conferring new powers on the latter. In fact I think the whole issue of delegation is here beside the mark. The law is not that trustees cannot delegate: it is that trustees cannot delegate unless they have authority to do so. If the power of advancement which they possess is so read as to allow them to raise money for the purpose of having it settled [and the House of Lords considered that the statutory power was to be read in this way] then they do have the necessary authority to let the money pass out of the old settlement into the new trusts. No question of delegation of their powers or trusts arises. If, on the other hand, their power of advancement is read so as to exclude settled advances, cadit quaestio.'

The House of Lords considered that the statutory power of advancement in substance gave the trustees power to free money from the trust and subject it to another, whether indirectly by advancing it to the beneficiary for the binding purpose of being settled by the beneficiary on new trusts or directly by transferring it themselves new trustees of new trusts; the new trustees then are to exercise original discretions of their own, there being no question of them exercising delegated functions of the old trustees. However, rather than rely upon the latter necessary implication when there were the above cited dicta of Upjohn J and some cases[17] narrowly construing the cope of special powers of appointment so as not to authorise the creation of inde- pendent new trusts conferring extensive new discretions upon the new trustees, the conservative practice arose of expressly extending the statutory power of advancement to permit advancements to trustees of new trusts upon discretionary trusts or upon protective trusts, which may result in discre- tionary trusts arising upon forfeiture of the protected life interest, and, whether or not containing flexible powers of appointment. There is no harm in continuing such practice but there is no need for it[18].

The statutory power of advancement does not contain any express refer- ence to 'raising' money or part of the trust funds for the purpose of an advancement, although s 16 of the Trustee Act 1925 seems available for this purpose. Where such words do occur in an express power, the requirement is

15 [1951] 2 All ER 528, CA.
16 [1964] AC 612 at 639.
17 *Re Morris' Settlement Trusts* [1951] 2 All ER 528, CA; *Re Hunter's Will Trusts* [1963] Ch 372, [1962] 3 All ER 1050; *Re Hay's Settlement Trusts* [1981] 3 All ER 786, [1982] 1 WLR 202.
18 See *Lewin on Trusts* (17th edn), para 32-18; J Kessler *Drafting Trusts and Will Trusts* (6th edn), paras 10.5 and 10.11; A J Oakley (ed) Parker & Mellows *The Modern Law of Trusts* (7th edn), pp 626–627.

sufficiently met by taking specified investments out of the general trust fund and holding them upon new trusts for the benefit of the beneficiary advanced[19]. The power to 'pay or apply' is sufficiently exercised by a resolution of the trustees allocating money (or property) to a beneficiary[20] or by the trustees appropriating it to the trusts of another settlement of which they are themselves the trustees[1].

The rule against perpetuities

For the purpose of the rule against perpetuities, there is an effective analogy between powers of advancement and special powers of appointment, so that if the trustees exercise their power of advancement by imposing new trusts upon the property advanced, the validity of those new trusts from the point of view of perpetuity is to be judged in the same way as the trusts declared by the exercise of a special power of appointment (see pp 198–200, ante) because 'the new settlement is only effected by the operation of a fiduciary power which itself "belongs" to the old settlement'[2]. The Perpetuities and Accumulations Act 1964 will not apply to the advancement unless the original settlement was created after 15 July 1964 owing to s 15(5) of the 1964 Act applying by analogy.

If part of the exercise of a power of advancement is void for perpetuity and this alters the resultant effect of the advancement so drastically that it cannot reasonably be regarded as beneficial to the beneficiary intended to be advanced or that the trustees cannot reasonably be supposed to have addressed their minds to the questions relevant to the true effect of the advancement then the whole advancement is void[3]. Otherwise the part of the advancement not void for perpetuity (eg a life interest in B's favour) stands even if no effective trusts of the capital interest have been created: the fact that trustees now hold the capital for B for life is an application of capital within s 32[4].

Consent of persons having prior interests

If a person having a 'protected life interest' gives his or her consent to an advance under the above power, he or she will not forfeit his or her beneficial interest in the trust fund whether the advancement is made under an express advancement clause[5] or under the statutory power[6] except where the statutory power applies in the case of a will made before, but coming into operation after 1925[7].

19 *Re Wills' Will Trusts* [1959] Ch 1, [1958] 2 All ER 472.
20 *Re Baron Vestey's Settlement* [1951] Ch 209, [1950] 2 All ER 891, CA.
1 *Pilkington v IRC* [1964] AC 612, [1962] 3 All ER 622, HL.
2 *Pilkington v IRC* [1964] AC 612, [1962] 3 All ER 622, HL.
3 *Re Hastings-Bass* [1975] Ch 25, [1974] 2 All ER 193 (restrictively interpreting *Re Abraham's Will Trusts* [1969] 1 Ch 463, [1967] 2 All ER 1175) discussed and clarified in *Mettoy Pension Trustees Ltd v Evans* [1991] 2 All ER 513 at 552–555: see p 694, ante. For adverse tax consequences that may flow from a void advancement see *Spens v IRC* [1970] 3 All ER 295, [1970] 1 WLR 1173.
4 *Re Hastings-Bass* [1975] Ch 25, [1974] 2 All ER 193.
5 *Re Shaw's Settlement* [1951] Ch 833, [1951] 1 All ER 656; following *Re Hodgson* [1913] 1 Ch 34, and distinguishing *Re Stimpson's Trusts* [1931] 2 Ch 77.
6 *Re Rees* [1954] Ch 202, [1954] 1 All ER 7.
7 *Re Stimpson's Trust* [1931] 2 Ch 77, as explained in *Re Rees' Will Trusts* [1954] Ch 202, [1954] 1 All ER 7.

The beneficiaries under a discretionary trust are not persons 'entitled to any prior life or other interest etc', and therefore their consent to the exercise of the power is unnecessary[8]. Likewise the consent of persons who would be interested should the discretionary trusts arise out of statutory protective trusts need not be obtained[9] though the principal beneficiary with the protected life interest must give his consent.

In *IRC v Bernstein*[10] clause 2 of the settlement directed that the income of the trust fund should be accumulated during the settlor's lifetime 'in augmentation of the capital of the trust fund and for the benefit of the person or persons who shall eventually become entitled thereto'. Subsequent clauses provided that on the settlor's death the relevant portion of the fund (in fact two-thirds) should be held on trust for his wife absolutely or, if she were then dead, for the children of the marriage then living, with a further gift over. At the date of the case, no children had been born.

The main point of the case was whether the statutory power of advancement was in fact applicable to the settlement at all, and it was held at first instance and on appeal that it was not. While a duty to accumulate is necessarily inconsistent with the statutory power of maintenance, it is not necessarily inconsistent with the power of advancement, though in context it was, since the main object of the trust was to build up an intact capital fund. The question was also raised as to whether, if the power had applied, the unborn children would have had a 'prior ... interest' necessitating their consent to its exercise in the wife's favour. The argument that they did have a prior interest seems to have been based on the contention that clause 2 made a separate disposition of the accumulations of income which went to augment the capital (as distinct from the original capital itself) and that this disposition gave the wife and children an interest, in ensuring that all income was applied in augmentation of capital, which was prior to the remaining dispositions. At first instance, Danckwerts J held that they did not have prior interests, saying simply that 'the first interest seems to me to be that of the wife' and that he therefore could not see how 'the interest of possible children ... can be regarded as a prior interest at all', adding that they had 'only a contingent interest which is subject to her first interest ... '

The approach of the Court of Appeal was less robust in two respects: first, because the Court did not consider it necessary to decide this point and deliberately refrained from doing so; and secondly, because it gave more recognition to the subtlety of the argument. Thus since the 'prior interest' was alleged to exist in the accumulations of income rather than in the original capital, the Court of Appeal treated the point involved as being the same as that which was raised, but not decided, in connection with s 31 of the Act in *Re Spencer, Lloyds Bank Ltd v Spencer*[11] and *Re Turner's Will Trusts*[12]. Evershed MR, like the judges involved in those two cases, shrank from finding that the children had prior interests when they had no present right to call for income, though Harman LJ had a slight preference for the Special Commissioners' view that the children did have prior interests.

The court has no power to dispense with any consent to the exercise of an

---

8 *Re Beckett's Settlement, Re Beckett* [1940] Ch 279.
9 *Re Harris' Settlement* (1940) 162 LT 358.
10 At first instance [1960] Ch 444, [1960] 1 All ER 697; and on appeal [1961] Ch 399, [1961] 1 All ER 320, CA.
11 [1935] Ch 533.
12 [1937] Ch 15, [1936] 2 All ER 1435, CA. See p 715, ante.

express power of advancement required by the settlement[13] and, presumably, it has no power to dispense with any requisite consent to the exercise of the statutory power.

Capital Gains Tax considerations

A line can be drawn between 'resettlement' cases where an advancement is made so that new trusts, powers and provisions supersede the original trusts, powers and provisions (even if the same persons happen to be trustees of the new trusts and the original trusts) and 'sub-settlement' cases where an advancement by way of allocation of part of the capital otherwise leaves the trusts, powers and provisions of the original settlement applicable thereto[14]. In the former situation a capital gains tax charge will arise since the trustees of the separate new trust become absolutely entitled against the trustees of the original trusts within Taxation of Chargeable Gains Act 1992, s 71.

ARTICLE 68

Suspension of the trustee's powers by administration action

(1) Where a judgment has been given for the execution of the trust by the court, or (before judgment) an injunction has been granted, or a receiver appointed, the trustee can only exercise his powers with the sanction of the court[15].
(2) But, although its sanction must be obtained, the court will not interfere with a discretion reposed in a trustee and expressed to be absolute and uncontrollable, so long as it is exercised in good faith[16].
(3) A decree for administration does not absolve a trustee or personal representative from the performance of his duties[17], but he should obtain the sanction of the court to each transaction or type of transaction[18].

After judgment

Thus, a trustee or personal representative cannot, after an order for execution of the trust or for general administration (even though only one account

13 *Re Forster's Settlement* [1942] Ch 199, [1942] 1 All ER 180. Presumably, in a case appropriate for the application of equitable proprietary estoppel principles a person with a prior interest who had orally consented would not be permitted to prevent the advancement.
14 *Hoare Trustees v Gardner* [1979] Ch 10, [1978] 1 All ER 791; *Roome v Edwards (Inspector of Taxes)* [1982] AC 279, [1981] 1 All ER 736, HL; *Bond v Pickford* [1983] STC 517, CA; *Swires v Renton* [1991] STC 490. See pp 806–808, post.
15 *Mitchelson v Piper* (1836) 8 Sim 64; *Shewen v Vanderhorst* (1830) 2 Russ & M 75; *Minors v Battison* (1876) 1 App Cas 428; *Re Gadd* (1883) 23 Ch D 134. The mere issue of a claim for administration does not affect the trustee's powers (*Berry v Gibbons* (1873) 8 Ch App 747), nor does the issue of a claim under RSC Ord 85, r 3 now CPR, Pt 64, except so far as interference with or control of any power or discretion is necessarily involved in the particular relief sought.
16 *Gisborne v Gisborne* (1877) 2 App Cas 300; *Tempest v Lord Camoys* (1882) 21 Ch D 571; and see Article 65, ante.
17 *Garner v Moore* (1855) 3 Drew 277, and *Bernhardt v Galsworthy* [1929] 1 Ch 549.
18 *Re Viscount Furness* [1943] Ch 415, [1944] 1 All ER 66.

is to be proceeded with forthwith[19]) prosecute or defend legal proceedings[20], or execute a power of sale[1], or appoint trustees[2] or do repairs[3], or invest[4], or exercise any other power, or deal in any way with the assets, even in due course of administration[5], without applying to the court to sanction his doing so. It remains his duty to bring before the court questions upon which the direction of the court is required, and if he acts, or omits to act, without the direction of the court he does so at his peril[6]. However it seems a good title can be conferred on innocent purchasers[7].

It has been suggested[8] that the restrictions imposed by an administration order apply only to powers of management (eg the appointment of trustees, the transposing of investments, the sale of assets) and not to the exercise of an absolute discretionary power over beneficial distribution of the trust funds. To be on the safe side[9] it will be advisable to seek the court's confirmation of this or the court's leave, if the court should take the view that leave is necessary.

Before judgment

But where an executor or administrator, after the commencement of a creditor's administration action, and before judgment, has voluntarily paid any creditor in full, he will be held to have made a good payment, and will be allowed it in passing his accounts, even though he may have had notice of the action before payment; and, it is apprehended, the same principle would be equally applicable to trustees. To prevent such payments being made in any such case, the claimant should, immediately upon issuing his writ, apply for and obtain a receiver[10].

In *Cafe v Bent*[11] Wigram V-C stated:

'There is no reason why the mere institution of a suit which may never be prosecuted should have the effect of preventing trustees from exercising their discretion ... the mere filing of a bill cannot have the effect of preventing trustees from doing acts which are necessary to the due execution of the trust which is imposed upon them.'

Powers of appointment[12] and powers of advancement[13] survive as well as powers of management.

---

19 *Re Viscount Furness* [1943] Ch 415, [1944] 1 All ER 66.
20 *Jones v Powell* (1841) 4 Beav 96.
 1 *Walker v Smalwood* (1768) Amb 676. But the trustee can give a good title to a specific chattel to a purchaser who has no notice of the order (*Berry v Gibbons* (1873) 8 Ch App 747, as explained in *Re Viscount Furness* [1943] Ch 415, [1944] 1 All ER 66).
 2 *Webb v Earl of Shaftesbury* (1802) 7 Ves 480.
 3 *Mitchelson v Piper* (1836) 8 Sim 64.
 4 *Bethell v Abraham* (1873) LR 17 Eq 24.
 5 *Re Viscount Furness* [1943] Ch 415, [1944] 1 All ER 66.
 6 *Garner v Moore* (1855) 3 Drew 277.
 7 *Berry v Gibbons* (1873) 8 Ch App 747.
 8 AJ Hawkins (1968) 84 LQR 64 at 68–73; *Bethell v Abraham* (1873) LR 17 Eq 24 at 26 per Jessel MR.
 9 In view of obiter dicta of Morton J in *Re Viscount Furness* [1943] Ch 415, [1944] 1 All ER 66, envisaging the court's sanction as requisite to any distribution of assets.
10 *Re Radcliffe* (1878) 7 Ch D 733, and see also *Re Barrett* (1889) 43 Ch D 70.
11 (1843) 3 Hare 245.
12 *A-G v Clack* (1839) 1 Beav 467; *Thomas v Williams* (1883) 24 Ch D 558.
13 *Sillibourne v Newport* (1855) 1 K & J 602; *Talbot v Marshfield* (1867) LR 4 Eq 661; *Brophy v Bellamy* (1873) 8 Ch App 798.

Loss of powers by trustees who have paid money into court

It may be conveniently mentioned here that, where trustees have paid the trust fund into court under s 63 of the Trustee Act 1925, they can no longer exercise any of their powers, discretionary or otherwise. This is because the payment into court is, in effect, a retirement by the trustees from their office, and a relinquishment of the judgment and discretion confided to them by the settlor[14]. New trustees may be appointed or in a special case the court may even exercise discretions or powers[15].

14 *Re Nettlefold's Trusts* (1888) 59 LT 315.
15 *Re Ashburnham's Trust* (1885) 54 LT 84; *Klug v Klug* [1918] 2 Ch 67; *McPhail v Doulton* [1971] AC 424, [1970] 2 All ER 228; *Mettoy Pension Trustees Ltd v Evans* [1991] 2 All ER 513; see p 97, ante.

CHAPTER 13

Powers of the beneficiaries

Article
69 Power of a sole beneficiary or of the beneficiaries collectively to extinguish the trust   729
70 Power of one of several beneficiaries partially interested in a special trust   737

ARTICLE 69

Power of a sole beneficiary or of the beneficiaries collectively to extinguish the trust

If there is only one beneficiary, or if there are several (whether entitled concurrently or successively) and they are all of one mind, not one being under any disability[1], the specific performance of the trust may be arrested, and the trust extinguished by that beneficiary or the body of beneficiaries collectively without reference to the wishes of the settlor or the trustees. The equitable proprietors of the trust property are entitled to claim it for themselves even if the settlor wants the trustees to manage it for them for particular purposes of his own. They cannot, however, compel the trustees to continue to run the trust in a form modified by themselves, but their authority to the trustees so to run the trust, if the trustees wish, will provide the trustees with a defence to any claim that the trustees thereby committed a breach of trust. Exceptionally, section 19 of the Trusts of Land and Appointment of Trustees Act 1996 permits the beneficiaries under the trust of full age and capacity and, taken together, absolutely entitled to the trust property, to rid themselves of unwanted trustees without the need to terminate the trust, because they can compel those trustees to retire and appoint as new trustees the persons specified by all those

---

1 Ie minors and persons of unsound mind. As to the power of the court under the Variation of Trusts Act 1958 to give consent on behalf of beneficiaries under disability or not ascertainable, see pp 501 et seq, ante.

beneficiaries collectively, so long as the power of appointing new trustees is not reserved to others under the trust instrument.

Illustration in case of a simple trust

Thus, if property is devised to the trustees in fee simple, upon trust for sale and to invest the proceeds of sale and to pay the income thereof to the testator's widow for life, and after her death to hold such investments upon trust for B absolutely, B, on the death of the widow, is entitled to call upon the trustees to vest the property if still unsold in him absolutely, or may by writing declare new trusts thereof[2], for in equity B is the sole and absolute owner, and the court will not permit a person solely and absolutely entitled, to be subjected to the tutelage or interference of a trustee. The court, in fact, regards a trustee as a kind of intermediary or stakeholder, whose office is to hold the scales evenly, and to see that the rights of several persons are mutually respected. Where there is only one person interested, however, and that person is of full age and capacity, the trustee's raison d'être ceases to exist; and consequently he himself becomes merely a person in the legal possession of another person's estate[3], and if the beneficiary refuses to accept a transfer of trust funds the trustee can pay them into court just as the beneficiary can insist on a transfer to himself against the trustee's wishes[4].

Illustration in case of a special trust where parties interested elect to stop it

The above is a case of a simple trust where, even under the terms of the trust, the trustees no longer have any active duties to perform, but the same result follows even where the settlor has contemplated and intended that the trustee shall have the control of the property, if the sole party beneficially interested is of full age and capacity and in favour of 'breaking the trust', or if the parties collectively beneficially interested (if there are several of them) are all of full age and capacity and are unanimously in favour of doing so. For a trust is the equitable equivalent of a common law gift, and, when once declared, the settlor, like the donor of a gift, has no further rights over the property unless he be also one of the beneficiaries or has reserved to himself a power of revocation or appointment[5].

Thus, in one case[6] a testator gave his residuary personal estate to an infant, and directed his executors to place it out at interest to accumulate, and to pay the principal and accumulations to the infant on his attaining twenty-four, and in the meantime to allow £60 a year for his maintenance. In the event of the infant's dying under 21 the testator gave the estate to third

---

2 *Grey v IRC* [1960] AC 1, [1959] 3 All ER 603, HL.

3 *Smith v Wheeler* (1669) 1 Mod Rep 16; *Brown v How* (1740) Barn Ch 354; *A-G v Gore* (1740) Barn Ch 145; *Kaye v Powel* (1791) 1 Ves 408; and per Fry J *Re Cotton's Trustees and London School Board* (1882) 19 Ch D 624 at 627.

4 *IRC v Hamilton-Russell Executors* [1943] 1 All ER 474, CA.

5 *Re Bowden* [1936] Ch 71.

6 *Josselyn v Josselyn* (1837) 9 Sim 63; *Saunders v Vautier* (1841) Cr & Ph 240; *Wharton v Masterman* [1895] AC 186; *Re Johnston* [1894] 3 Ch 204; *Re Smith* [1928] Ch 915; *Re Nelson* [1928] Ch 920n; *Thorn v IRC* [1976] 2 All ER 622 at 631; and distinguish *Re Lord Nunburnholme* [1911] 2 Ch 510; reversed on appeal [1912] 1 Ch 489, CA, on the construction of the will; *Re Travis* [1900] 2 Ch 541, CA; *Berry v Geen* [1938] AC 575, [1938] 2 All ER 362; and *IRC v Hamilton-Russell Executors* [1943] 1 All ER 474, CA. *Talbot v Jevers* (1875) LR 20 Eq 255, appears to be inconsistent with the other cases.

persons. The court held that, on the true construction of the will, the infant took an absolute vested and transmissible interest on attaining 21; and that, consequently, being the only person beneficially interested, he could put an end to the trust, and was entitled to have the residue and accumulations at once transferred to him. For, as Page Wood V-C said, in the case of *Gosling v Gosling* (when 21 years represented the age of majority)[7]:

> 'The principle of this court has always been to recognise the right of all persons who attain the age of 21 to enter upon the absolute use and enjoyment of the property given to them by will, notwithstanding any directions by the testator to the effect that they are not to enjoy it until a later age—unless, during the interval, the property is given for the benefit of another. If the property is once theirs, it is useless for the testator to attempt to impose any fetter upon their enjoyment of it in full so soon as they attain 21.'

Section 14 of the Perpetuities and Accumulations Act 1964 applies s 2 of the Act as to presumptions of future parenthood in determining whether all beneficiaries are ascertained so as to have a right to stop accumulations.

However, the *Saunders v Vautier* principle has developed well beyond utilisation for stopping accumulations. Now, 'the principle recognises the rights of beneficiaries who are *sui juris* and together absolutely entitled to the trust property to exercise their proprietary rights to overbear and defeat the intentions of a testator or settlor'[8].

Absolute gift with superadded direction

Where a testator directed his property to be divided into nine shares and gave one and half shares each to each of his two daughters, 'to be settled on themselves at their marriage', it was held by Sir James Bacon V-C that, on the true construction of the will (inasmuch as there was no reference to grandchildren, or any intimation of the testator's desire to restrict the gift to a life interest), the daughters took absolutely; and, if so, then, under the above rule, they were entitled to have their shares paid over to them on attaining 21, free from all liability to have the same settled[9]. Whether the learned judge's construction of the will was correct may, perhaps, be respectfully doubted[10]. Anyhow, one must carefully distinguish the above case from those in which there is a direction to settle on a daughter *and her issue*[11], where, of course, she would not be the only person beneficially interested and, consequently, would not be entitled to demand the capital.

A clearer case is *Re Bowes*[12] where, in effect, a testator bequeathed money on trust to spend it upon planting trees for shelter on Blackacre held on trust for A for life, remainder to B, and North J held A and B could claim the

---

7 (1859) John 265 endorsed by Lord Herschell *in Wharton v Masterman* [1895] AC 186 at 192.
8 *Goulding v James* [1997] 2 All ER 239 at 247, per Mummery LJ, and to override the rights of any enforcer if English law (in the light of recognition of foreign trusts with enforcers with rights) developed to permit such rights to exist, eg, if for a lengthy period there are no ascertained beneficiaries of full age and capacity with rights to make the trustees account as will be possible if the rule against accumulations is abolished as recommended by a deregulatory order, in the Lord Chancellor's Department's Consultation Document of September 2002.
9 *Magrath v Morehead* (1871) LR 12 Eq 491; *Re Jordan's Trusts* [1903] 1 IR 119.
10 See *Loch v Bagley* (1867) LR 4 Eq 122.
11 See, for example, *Wise v Piper* (1880) 13 Ch D 848.
12 [1896] 1 Ch 507. Also see *Re Lipinski's Will Trust* [1976] Ch 235.

money for themselves. Similarly, if T, the founder of a family company now run by his son, A, who has a 25% shareholding in the company, leaves his 51% shareholding to A to hold on trust for A's siblings, B, C and D equally, so that A may control the 76% shareholding and keep the family business going for the benefit of A, B, C and D, then B, C and D can demand the 51% shareholding so that they can sell the company to an outsider and wholly frustrate T's intentions. To prevent this T should have granted only contingent interests to B, C and D or have made them beneficiaries under discretionary trusts for them and their unascertained unborn issue or have chosen as the applicable law that of one of many American states that prevents termination of a trust where this would be contrary to the purpose of the settlor.

Legacies to purchase annuities

Where a legacy is bequeathed to purchase an annuity the intended annuitant or his personal representative if he is dead but survived the testator, may claim the legacy be paid directly to him[13].

Need for indefeasible absolute beneficial entitlement

If property is settled on B contingent upon attaining 30 years of age B cannot claim entitlement to the property till attaining 30[14]. However, if property were settled upon B for life if attaining 30 and subject thereto for C absolutely, then B and C between them as the only persons beneficially interested in the property could compel the trustees to divide it between themselves as they directed[15].

If property were settled on discretionary trusts for D, E, F and G such that income and capital had to be distributed between them before the death of the last survivor, then D, E, F and G could terminate the trust and acquire the property in such shares as they agreed[16]. However if there is a fluctuating class, like D, E, F and G and their spouses and issue for 80 years or members of a club for 80 years so there is a fluctuating class of trust beneficiaries, then all the beneficiaries between them absolutely entitled to the property cannot be ascertained, so that the trust cannot be terminated before expiry of the 80 years[17].

In the case of a unit trust, this operates on a cash fund basis where the unit holders have a contractual right to money payments secured upon the assets[18] held by the custodian trustees, so that the unit holders cannot terminate the trust prior to its termination date[19].

Where property is settled on B for life, remainder to B's widower or to his

---

13 *Re Browne's Will* (1859) 27 Beav 324; *Stokes v Cheek* (1860) 28 Beav 620; *Re Mabbett* [1893] 1 Ch 707.
14 *Re Lord Nunburnholme* [1912] 1 Ch 489.
15 *Berry v Geen* [1938] AC 575 at 582 per Lord Maugham.
16 *Re Smith* [1928] Ch 915.
17 *Re Jefferies* [1936] 2 All ER 626; *Re Levy* [1960] Ch 346 at 363; *Re Westphal* [1972] NZLR 792 at 794–795.
18 Cf *Air Jamaica Ltd v Charlton* [1999] 1 WLR 1399, PC and *Wrightson Ltd v Fletcher Challenge Nominees Ltd* [2001] UKPC 23, [2001] All ER (D) 89 (May) at para 28 on members of pension trust schemes having no beneficial proprietary interests in the trust fund which is merely security for payment of benefits to them.
19 See K F Sin, *The Legal Nature of the Unit Trust*, (Oxford, 1997) pp 114–120 explaining the weakness of contrary dicta in *Re AEG Unit Trust (Managers) Ltd's Deed* [1957] Ch 415 at 422.

statutory next of kin, then no termination can be achieved while B is still alive, because until his death one cannot be sure who will be his widow or his next of kin[20]. His current presumptive widow or next of kin could die, so that his actual widow or next of kin turn out to be different persons.

It is clear that the *Saunders v Vautier* principle 'recognises the rights of beneficiaries who are *sui juris* and together absolutely entitled to the trust property to exercise their proprietary rights to overbear and defeat the intentions of a testator or settlor'[1] by terminating the trust and dividing the property up as they unanimously agree, so that the principle cannot apply in favour of such beneficiaries if their rights are defeasible by the rights of others that are current (eg any right of revocation reserved by the settlor) or can arise upon the happening of a future event (eg satisfaction of a condition).

What then is the position where the collective proprietary right of the beneficiaries is defeasible because the trust contains a power of appointment in favour of a class of objects which might from time to time be exercised in favour of one or more of the objects? An object has no proprietary interest until an appointment is made in his favour: before then he only has a hope that he might acquire a proprietary interest. The settlor has made a completed gift of an equitable proprietary interest to the beneficiaries collectively entitled in default of any exercise of the power but has merely provided a gratuitous mandate[2] to the trustees so as to enable them, if they wish, to confer a proprietary interest on one or more objects at some future time[3].

It is noteworthy that under s 19 of the Trusts of Land and Appointment of Trustees Act 1996 the persons who can force the trustees to retire by replacing themselves as directed are 'the beneficiaries under the trust of full age and capacity and (taken together) absolutely entitled to the property subject to the trust' where 'beneficiary' means[4] 'any person who under the trust has an interest in property subject to the trust'. It thus seems that persons who have vested or contingent interests or interests as discretionary beneficiaries are covered[5], but not persons who do not yet have proprietary interests but merely the hope that they may later obtain proprietary interests[6].

However, in *Re Sharp's Settlement Trust*[7] Pennycuick V-C held that beneficiaries had not become 'absolutely' entitled to trust property when the property remained subject to a special power of appointment vested in trustees because the beneficiaries' interests were defeasible, although the issue was not raised whether there should be a distinction between defeasi-

---

20 *Re Earl of Midleton's Will Trust* [1969] 1 Ch 600 at 607 discussed p 502 ante.

1 *Goulding v James* [1997] 2 All ER 239 at 247 per Mummery LJ. Note that while a trust may be declared of a non-assignable contract, the beneficiaries cannot call for assignment of the contract: *Don King Productions Inc v Warren* [2000] Ch 291 at 321, CA.

2 This could justify the remarks of Lord Upjohn in *Vandervell v IRC* [1967] 2 AC 291 at 317 that if trustees held property on trust for the settlor but with the trustees having a power of appointment the settlor could at any time revoke that power.

3 Conferment of a power is not a gift of property: *Re Armstrong* (1886) 17 QBD 521; *Melville v IRC* [2001] EWCA Civ 1247, [2002] 1 WLR 407, CA.

4 Trusts of Land and Appointment of Trustees Act 1996 ('TLATA 1996'), s 22(1).

5 See *Knocker v Youle* [1986] 2 All ER 914 at 916–917 albeit in context of Variation of Trusts Act 1958, s 1; and see p 503 post.

6 In *Re Gartside v IRC* [1968] AC 553 an interest under a discretionary trust was capable of being an interest in property in some circumstances, but not the estate duty context in question, but it was accepted (at p 607) that an object of a power of maintenance (where there was a trust to accumulate under Trustee Act 1925, s 31) could not be regarded as having an interest.

7 [1973] Ch 331 at 338 in particular.

bility by the rights of others and defeasibility by the hopes of others.

If there be no such distinction this raises problems that have already been discussed[8] in the context of the significance of the *Saunders v Vautier* principle for variations under the Variation of Trusts Act 1958, where powers of appointment subsist that are subject to fiduciary obligations and so cannot be released as personal powers can[9].

Position summarised in *Stephenson v Barclays Bank Trust Co Ltd*

Walton J stated as elementary principles[10]:

'(1) In a case where the persons who between them hold the entirety of the beneficial interests in any particular trust fund are all sui juris and acting together ("the beneficial interest holders"), they are entitled to direct the trustees how the trust fund may be dealt with. (2) This does not mean, however, that they can at one and the same time override the pre-existing trusts and keep them in existence. Thus, in *Re Brockbank*[11] itself the beneficial interest holders were entitled to override the pre-existing trusts by, for example, directing the trustees to transfer the trust fund to X and Y, whether X and Y were the trustees of some other trust or not, but they were not entitled to direct the existing trustees to appoint their own nominee as a new trustee of the existing trust. By so doing they would be pursuing inconsistent rights. (3) Nor, I think, are the beneficial interest holders entitled to direct the trustees as to the particular investment they should make of the trust fund. I think this follows for the same reasons as the above. Moreover, it appears to me that once the beneficial interest holders have determined to end the trust they are not entitled, unless by agreement, to the further services of the trustees. Those trustees can of course be compelled to hand over the entire trust assets to any person or persons selected by the beneficiaries against a proper discharge, but they cannot be compelled, unless they are in fact willing to comply with the directions, to do anything else with the trust fund which they are not in fact willing to do. (4) Of course, the rights of the beneficial interest holders are always subject to the right of the trustee to be fully protected against such matters as duty, taxes, costs or other outgoings; for example, the rent under a lease which the trustees have properly accepted as part of the trust property.

So much for the rights of the beneficial interest holders collectively. When the situation is that a single person who is sui juris has an absolutely vested beneficial interest in a share of the trust fund, his rights are not, I think, quite as extensive as those of the beneficial interest holders as a body. In general, he is entitled to have transferred to him (subject, of course, always to the same rights of the trustees as I have already mentioned above) an aliquot share of each and every asset of the trust fund which presents no difficulty so far as division is concerned. This will apply to

---

8 See pp 502–505 ante. Also the problem that unauthorised acquisitions by trustees cannot be adopted so as to become authorised unless all objects of powers as well as beneficiaries are ascertained and of full age and capacity and agree.

9 For example, where the settlor has expressly excluded accountability of trustees to objects of powers, the accountability to the default beneficiaries sufficing for a valid trust (*Re Angora Trust* [2001] WTLR 1081) or the power is vested not in trustees but in a widow for example. Where trustees have a power of such extensive ambit that there is a lack of justiciability eg to add any one in the world (but four excepted persons) to a class of beneficiaries or objects of powers or to appoint to any one in the world (but four persons), this should raise the necessary implication that the power is not subject to any obligations other than those covered by the fraud on a power doctrine, the duty periodically to consider exercising the power and the duty not to release powers vested in the office of trustee without express authority.

10 [1975] 1 All ER 625 at 637. See also *Booth v Ellard* [1978] 1 WLR 1443, CA applied in *Jenkins v Brown* [1989] STC 577 (no capital gains tax charge if 6 people vest their farms in a trust for themselves and one later obtains back what he put into the trust or its equivalent value).

11 [1948] Ch 206, [1948] 1 All ER 287.

such items as cash, money at the bank or an unsecured loan, stock exchange securities and the like. However, as regards land, certainly, in all cases[12], as regards shares in a private company in very special circumstances (see *Re Weiner's Will Trusts*[13]) and possibly (although the logic of the addition in fact escapes me[14]) mortgage debts (see *Re Marshall*[15] per Cozens-Hardy MR) the situation is not so simple, and even a person with a vested interest in possession in an aliquot share of the trust fund may have to wait until the land is sold, and so forth, before being able to call on the trustees as of right to account to him for his share of the proceeds.'

Possible future beneficiaries

Where it is not absolutely certain that no more beneficiaries can come into existence so as to enable the existing beneficiaries to take advantage of the *Saunders v Vautier* principle, the court may give leave to the trustees to distribute the trust property according to the directions of the existing beneficiaries (so long as the contingent rights of living persons are not prejudiced without their consent)[16]. The classic case is where the ultimate beneficiaries are the children of a living person when adopted children and children born as a result of medical advances may possibly feature. If appropriate evidence is obtained, eg as to the physical impossibility of a parent creating future children[17] and the strong possibility that there will be no adoption[18] nor exploitation of medical advances, then the court may authorise distribution in the exercise of its administrative jurisdiction[19], without prejudice to the rights of any child subsequently coming into existence. Alternatively, application can be made under the Variation of Trusts Act 1958 to approve an arrangement eliminating the interests of unborn persons, but some provision against the eventuality of birth or adoption of such persons will need to be made, eg via insurance.

Modification of trusts so as to control trustees

Although the beneficiaries acting collectively can require the trustees to transfer the trust property to themselves absolutely or to other persons upon trusts identical with, or corresponding to, or even completely different from the trusts of the settlement, it is conceived that they cannot force upon the trustees against their will modifications of the trusts which would impose

---

12 *Re Horsnaill* [1909] 1 Ch 631; *Re Kipping* [1914] 1 Ch 62.
13 [1956] 2 All ER 482, [1956] 1 WLR 579.
14 In *Crowe v Appleby* [1975] 3 All ER 529 at 537, Goff J endorsed the views of Walton J and pointed out 'the logic of the addition of mortgages is that they include not only the debt but the estate and powers of the mortgagee'.
15 [1914] 1 Ch 192 at 199.
16 *Re White* [1901] 1 Ch 570; *Davidson v Kimpton* (1881) 18 Ch D 213; *Re Widdow's Trust* (1871) LR 11 Eq 408; *Re Millner's Estate* (1872) LR 14 Eq 245; *Re Jordan's Trust* [1903] 1 IR 119; *Re Cazenove* (1919) 122 LT 181; *Re Smith* [1928] Ch 915; *Re Whichelow* [1954] 1 WLR 5 at 8; but cf *Croxton v May* (1878) 9 Ch D 388.
17 *Bullas v Public Trustee* [1981] 1 NSWLR 641 (hysterectomy); *Re Pettifor's Will Trust* [1966] Ch 257 (women over 70 years).
18 It is presumed a woman over 54 years will not adopt a child: Adoption Act 1976, s 42(5). In Australian context see *Re Cassidy* [1979] VR 369 at 372; *National Trustees Executors & Agency Co v Tuck* [1967] VR 847; *Bullas v Public Trustee* [1981] NSWLR 641.
19 In *Figg v Clarke* [1997] 1 WLR 603 the court held that children did not become absolutely entitled to trust property for capital gains tax purposes the moment their father had an accident making him incapable of having further children but only on his death. If leave to distribute had been sought after the accident it seems likely it would have been granted.

upon the trustees new duties involving an exercise of discretion nor can they, without the consent of the trustees, abrogate discretions or powers conferred upon the trustees by the instrument creating the trust, or seek to control the exercise of such discretions or powers. Thus, it has been held[20] that the beneficiaries cannot compel the retirement of a trustee or control the exercise of the statutory power of appointing new trustees conferred on a continuing trustee, although they now can under s 19 of the Trusts of Land and Appointment of Trustees Act 1996 if the powers of appointing new trustees is not conferred on someone else by the trust instrument. However, they can collectively consent or acquiesce in the trustees doing something beyond their powers whereupon they will not be able to sue for any breach of trust.

Where the trust estate included shares in a limited company of which the trustees were directors it was held by the Court of Appeal in *Butt v Kelson*[1] that the beneficiaries were not entitled to call on these directors to use their powers as directors as if they held those powers on trust for them, but that they could compel them to use their votes as shareholders as the beneficiaries should think proper, even to the extent of altering the articles of association if the trust shares carried sufficient votes. As Upjohn J (as he then was) pointed out in *Re Whichelow*[2], this decision is very difficult to reconcile with the line of cases (not cited to the Court of Appeal) establishing the principle that beneficiaries cannot compel the trustees to do as the beneficiaries wish (and so control the trustees' discretions) except so as to transfer the trust assets to persons nominated by the beneficiaries of full age and capacity and between them absolutely entitled to the entire beneficial interest. Perhaps *Butt v Kelson* might be justified on the basis that, to prevent any possibility of the trustees as directors being liable to the company for breach of duty, it was necessary for the court not merely to point out that the trustees qua shareholders could exercise their votes as they saw fit (so long as not perpetrating a fraud on minority shareholders) and so against what the directors might consider in the best interests of the company, but to direct the trustees qua shareholders to vote as desired by the beneficiaries as in their best interests since the trustees, being directors, were not in a position to exercise their discretion impartially and properly. *Butt v Kelson* should thus be restricted to trustee shareholders who are also directors. Alternatively, it has been suggested[3] that the circumstances could have been regarded as exceptional, so that the trustees had come under a duty to exercise their discretionary power as indicated so that a duty was being enforced.

20 *Re Brockbank* [1948] Ch 206, [1948] 1 All ER 287 endorsed in *Stephenson v Barclays Bank Trust Co* [1975] 1 All ER 625 at 637, p 734, ante and in *Holding & Management Ltd v Property Holding plc* [1990] 1 All ER 938 at 948 CA. Also see *Napier v Light* (1974) 236 Estates Gazette 273, CA, where the two absolutely entitled sui juris beneficiaries of a trust for sale of land could not commit their trustees to tenancies purportedly created by the beneficiaries to whom no power had been delegated by the trustees under Law of Property Act 1925, s 29.
1 [1952] Ch 197, [1952] 1 All ER 167.
2 [1953] 2 All ER 1558, [1954] 1 WLR 5, citing *Re Brockbank* [1948] Ch 206, [1948] 1 All ER 287; *Re Higginbottom* [1892] 3 Ch 132; and *Tempest v Lord Camoys* (1882) 21 Ch D 571.
3 *Lewin on Trusts* (17th edn) paras 23-09 and 24-08.

ARTICLE 70

Power of one of several beneficiaries partially interested in a special trust

(1) The authority of one of several beneficiaries interested in a special trust in general depends upon the terms of the trust as construed by the court, coupled with the powers conferred on persons entitled to equitable interests by the Settled Land Act 1925 and the Trusts of Land and Appointment of Trustees Act 1996; but a beneficiary, who is of full age and capacity, cannot be prohibited from assigning his or her interest, while such a beneficiary with an absolutely vested beneficial interest in a share of a trust fund will be entitled to an aliquot share of each and every asset of the trust fund which presents no difficulty so far as division is concerned, there being difficulties with land, mortgage debts and, in very special circumstances, shares in a private company[4].

(2) (a) In the case of a trust of land, a sole beneficiary beneficially entitled to an interest in possession in the land is entitled by reason of his interest to occupy the land at any time if then the purposes of the trust include making the land available for his occupation or the land is held by the trustees so as to be so available, unless it is unsuitable for occupation by him[5], though the trustees may impose reasonable conditions upon him[6]; where there is more than one such beneficiary they are in a weaker position[7] because the trustees may exclude or restrict the entitlement of any one or more (but not all) of them[8] so long as this is not unreasonable[9].

(b) In this behalf, trustees of land have a power revocably to delegate any of their functions as trustees which relate to the land (but not to proceeds of sale thereof)[10]; the beneficiaries can apply to the court for an order relating to the exercise by the trustees of any of their functions[11].

(c) A tenant for life under the Settled Land Act 1925 has the legal estate in the settled land vested in him[12] and so is thereby entitled to possession.

---

4 *Stephenson (Inspector of Taxes) v Barclays Bank Trust Co Ltd* [1975] 1 All ER 625 at 637, cited, p 734, ante.
5 TLATA 1996, s 12(1) and (2).
6 TLATA 1996, s 13(3).
7 Also a weaker position than before the Act: *IRC v Eversden* [2002] EWHC 1360 (Ch), [2002] STC 1109 at paras 21 and 24; *Bull v Bull* [1955] 1 QB 234; *City of London Building Society v Flegg* [1988] AC 54 at 78 and 79.
8 TLATA 1996, s 13(1).
9 TLATA 1996, s 13(2).
10 TLATA 1996, s 9.
11 TLATA 1996, s 13(7), 14(1).
12 Settled Land Act 1925, ss 4 and 6.

PARAGRAPH 1

Equitable interest of beneficiary cannot generally be made inalienable

The interest of a beneficiary cannot be made inalienable[13]. Thus a trust to apply income for another's maintenance entitles him to have the income paid to him or to his alienee, even although he be restrained from alienation; for no one in remainder is injured by it and he alone was absolutely entitled to the income being applied for his benefit as he saw it[14]. If an absolute interest in capital or income is given to a person, then it is repugnant to, or inconsistent with, the nature of that absolute interest to prevent it being dealt with as an absolute interest and so passing to the owner's trustee in bankruptcy if he becomes bankrupt[15].

Protective trusts

Where, however, there is a trust to pay income to A *until* he shall alienate it or become bankrupt etc; and, upon the happening of any of those events, a further trust to pay to him, or apply for his benefit during the remainder of his life, the whole *or so much only* of such income as the trustees may in their discretion think fit, and, subject thereto, the residue of such income (if any) is to be *paid to other persons*; then, as the trustees have an absolute discretion as to what part of the income they will apply for the benefit of the tenant for life, his alienees or creditors cannot force the trustees to pay them any part of the income[16].

Partial restraint on alienation

A provision that a beneficiary may only alienate his interest in favour of one of a small class of named persons which inevitably diminish in course of time is tantamount to a general restraint on alienation and, therefore, void[17]. Where, however, the class of permitted alienees is a large and indeterminate one (such as the beneficiary's 'family') which may increase as time goes on, a restriction against alienating outside that class may be good[18].

Right to aliquot share

A beneficiary of full age and capacity with an absolute vested beneficial interest in a share of a trust fund will be entitled to an aliquot share of each and every asset of the fund which presents no difficulty so far as division is

---

13 *Snowdon v Dales* (1834) 6 Sim 524; *Green v Spicer* (1830) 1 Russ & M 395; *Brandon v Robinson* (1811) 18 Ves 429; *Hood v Oglander* (1865) 34 Beav 513. Inalienable interests under trusts governed by a foreign law will be recognised: *Re Fitzgerald* [1904] 1 Ch 573.
14 *Younghusband v Gisborne* (1844) 1 Coll 400; affd 15 LJ Ch 355; *Snowdon v Dales* (1834) 6 Sim 524.
15 *Re Machu* (1882) 21 Ch D 838.
16 *Re Bullock* (1891) 64 LT 736; *Train v Clapperton* [1908] AC 342; and cf *Lord v Bunn* (1843) 2 Y & C Ch Cas 98; which seems contra at first sight, but really turned on a question of construction; see also *Re Laye* [1913] 1 Ch 298; and *Re Hamilton* (1921) 124 LT 737; and as to such trusts generally, see p 210, ante.
17 *Attwater v Attwater* (1853) 18 Beav 330; *Re Brown* [1954] Ch 39, [1953] 2 All ER 1342.
18 *Re Macleay* (1875) LR 20 Eq 186; (criticised by Pearson J in *Re Rosher* (1884) 26 Ch D 801).

concerned[19] eg cash, bank deposits, shares in quoted companies. He is not entitled to an aliquot share if it is in land[20] or mortgage debts[1] or in very special circumstances, in shares in a private company[2]. Thus, in *Lloyds Bank plc v Duker*[3], due to the trustees' overriding duty to act fairly and impartially, the court rejected the claim of a beneficiary to have 574 of 999 shares in a private company (representing his forty-six eightieths of a trust fund including such shares) where such majority shareholding would be worth much more than forty-six eightieths of the proceeds of sale of the 999 shares. Sale of the shares was ordered so that the proceeds could then be distributed to the relevant beneficiaries in the relevant fractions.

PARAGRAPH 2

How far beneficiary with interest in possession may claim actual possession of land

The position of a beneficiary currently entitled to an interest in possession of land is summarised in paragraph 2 itself and discussed in detail in Article 45 above.

---

19 *Stephenson v Barclays Bank Trust Co Ltd* [1975] 1 All ER 625 at 637–638, cited p 734, ante.
20 *Re Kipping* [1914] 1 Ch 62; *Crowe v Appleby* [1975] 3 All ER 529.
 1 *Re Marshall* [1914] 1 Ch 192 at 199; *Crowe v Appleby* [1975] 3 All ER 529 at 537.
 2 *Re Weiner's Will Trusts* [1956] 2 All ER 482.
 3 [1987] 3 All ER 193, [1987] 1 WLR 1324.

CHAPTER 14

The death, retirement, or removal of trustees and the appointment of new trustees

Article

71 Devolution of the office and estate on death of trustees   740
72 Retirement or removal of a trustee   743
73 Appointment of new trustees   751
74 Appointment of trustees for sale of land   775
75 Vesting of trust property in new trustees   776

ARTICLE 71

Devolution of the office and estate on death of trustees

(1) Upon the death of one of two or more trustees the office, as well as the estate, survives to the surviving trustees or trustee[1], who can carry out the trust and exercise all such powers as were given to the original trustees as such[2].

(2) Upon the death of a sole or last surviving trustee, the trust property devolves on his legal personal representative[3].

(3) Until the appointment of new trustees, the personal representatives or representative for the time being of a sole trustee, or, where there were two or more trustees, of the last surviving or continuing trustee, can exercise or perform any power or trust which was given to, or capable of being exercised by, the sole or last surviving or continuing trustee, or other the trustees or trustee for the time being of the trust[4].

(4) This article must be read subject to the restrictions imposed in

---

1 *Warburton v Sandys* (1845) 14 Sim 622; *Eyre v Countess of Shaftesbury* (1725) 2 P Wms 103; and now Trustee Act 1925 ('TA 1925'), s 18(1); *Re Harding* [1923] 1 Ch 182.
2 TA 1925, s 18(1), re-enacting 1893 Act, s 22; and *Lane v Debenham* (1853) 11 Hare 188; *Re Cookes' Contract* (1877) 4 Ch D 454; and *Re Harding* [1923] 1 Ch 182. As to whether the court will pay out trust money in court to a sole surviving trustee, see *Leigh v Pantin* [1914] 2 Ch 701.
3 See Administration of Estates Act 1925, ss 1, 3.
4 TA 1925, s 18(2).

regard to receipts by a sole trustee, not being a trust corporation[5].

(5) The person upon whom the estate devolves cannot be compelled to act in the trusts[6]; nor, on the other hand, can he insist upon doing so against the wishes of a donee of a power of appointing new trustees in substitution for deceased ones[7].

(6) In this article 'personal representative' does not include an executor who has renounced probate or has not proved[8].

PARAGRAPH 1

Death of co-trustee

The law as to survival stated in this paragraph has always applied with regard to trusts as distinguished from bare powers[9], and since 1881 has been statute law. The law as to powers incident to the office of trustee is now set forth in s 18(1) of the Trustee Act 1925[10] in the following words:

> Where a power or trust is given to or imposed on two or more trustees jointly, the same may be exercised or performed by the survivors or survivor of them for the time being.

It would seem however, that the statute applies only to powers which are fiduciary, ie incident to the office of trustee; and that it is in all cases a question of interpretation whether a discretionary power was intended to be incident to the office, or was a mere naked personal power given to the individuals who were also nominated as trustees[11]. However,

> 'every power given to trustees which enables them to deal with or affect the trust property is prima facie given them ex officio as an incident of their office, and passes with the office to the holders or holder thereof for the time being.'[12]

The mere fact that the power is one requiring the exercise of a very wide personal discretion is not enough to exclude this prime facie presumption, and little regard is now paid to such minute differences as those between such expressions as 'my trustees', 'my trustees, A & B', and 'A & B, my trustees'. In short, the testator's reliance on the individuals to the exclusion

---

5 These restrictions are in TA 1925, ss 14 and 18; Law of Property Act 1925 ('LPA 1925'), s 27; and Settled Land Act 1925, s 94.
6 *Re Benett* [1906] 1 Ch 216 at 225; *Re Ridley* [1904] 2 Ch 774; and cases there cited.
7 *Re Routledge* [1909] 1 Ch 280.
8 TA 1925, s 18(4).
9 *Warburton v Sandys* (1845) 14 Sim 622; *Eyre v Countess of Shaftesbury* (1725) 2 P Wms 103; *Lane v Debenham* (1853) 11 Hare 188. *Re Cookes' Contract* (1877) 4 Ch D 454; *Doe d Read v Godwin* (1822) 1 Dow & Ry KB 259; *Re Bacon* [1907] 1 Ch 475.
10 Re-enacting s 22 of the Trustee Act 1893, which in turn re-enacted s 38 of the Conveyancing Act 1881. The words 'unless the contrary is expressed in the instrument, if any, creating the trust' which were present in the former enactments are omitted in reliance on s 69(2) of the 1925 Act.
11 *Crawford v Forshaw* [1891] 2 Ch 261, CA; and see also *Re Perrott and King's Contract* (1904) 90 LT 156. See *Re Eades* [1920] 2 Ch 353; and *Re Willis* [1920] 2 Ch 358 per Astbury J but reversed by CA [1921] 1 Ch 44. See pp 29–34 ante.
12 Per Farwell J in *Re Smith* [1904] 1 Ch 139 at 144; cf *Re De Sommery* [1912] 2 Ch 622; and see *Re Symm's Will Trusts* [1936] 3 All ER 236 and *Re Will's Trust Deeds* [1964] Ch 219.

of the holders of the office for the time being must be expressed in clear and apt language[13].

Paragraph 2

Devolution on death of sole or last surviving trustee

Since 1925 all trust estates devolve on the general personal representatives of the sole or last surviving trustee, in whom the estate was vested, and it is conceived that a sole or last surviving trustee cannot appoint 'special executors' for the purpose of executing the trust[14]. This view receives some support from the case of *Re Cohen's Executors and LCC*[15], where the general executors were held to be alone the personal representatives within the meaning of the Land Transfer Act 1897.

Where powers and trusts have devolved upon a personal representative of a trustee the question arises whether upon the death of such personal representative (having failed to appoint further trustees) the powers and trusts can devolve further upon his own personal representative or whether such powers and trusts revert to the trustee's estate so as to be exercisable by an administrator de bonis non administratis. If the executor of the deceased personal representative is executor by representation of the trustee then he has the capacity to perform powers and trusts under the Trustee Act 1925, s 18(2)[16]. It would also seem that if the deceased personal representative had accepted the trust then he should be treated as a trustee within s 18(2) for his powers to devolve thereunder to his own personal representative[17] though the position is not free from doubt[18].

Paragraph 3

Execution of trusts by personal representatives of sole or last surviving trustee

This paragraph reproduces s 18(2) of the Trustee Act 1925 which re-enacts s 8 of the Conveyancing Act 1911 with the difference that it is not restricted to trusts which have come into operation since 1881[19]. Where a deceased trustee's powers have devolved upon his personal representative, who then dies before having appointed new trustees but having accepted the role of trustee, it seems[20] that he should be treated as trustee for his powers to devolve under s 18(2) to his own personal representative. If he was executor

---

13 Per Farwell J in *Re Smith* [1904] 1 Ch 139 at 144; cf *Re De Sommery* [1912] 2 Ch 622; and see *Re Symm's Will Trusts* [1936] 3 All ER 236 and *Re Will's Trust Deeds* [1964] Ch 219.
14 See *Re Parker's Trusts* [1894] 1 Ch 707; *Rose v Bartlett* (1633) Cro Car 292; *Clough v Dixon* (1841) 10 Sim 5 64. The devolution of settled land under the Settled Land Act 1925 is outside the scope of this work: see Megarry and Wade, *Real Property* (6th edn) paras 8-031 et seq.
15 [1902] 1 Ch 187.
16 Administration of Estates Act 1925, s 7; TA 1925, s 68(9).
17 *Williams on Title* (4th edn) p 490, Pettit *Equity and the Law of Trusts* (7th edn) p 341; (1977) 41 Conv 423 (P W Smith); *Re Timmis* [1902] 1 Ch 176.
18 Wolstenholme and Cherry, *Conveyancing Statutes* (13th edn) p 21.
19 The application of s 18(2) of the TA 1925 to trusts whenever created depends on s 69(1) of that Act.
20 See P W Smith (1977) 41 Conv 423, *Williams on Title* (4th edn) p 490.

of the deceased trustee and himself appointed an executor, who obtained probate, then his executor would be executor by representation[1] of the trustee and so have the s 18(2) powers in any event.

ARTICLE 72

Retirement or removal of a trustee

(1) A trustee can only retire:
(a) under an express or a necessarily implied[2] power;
(b) under the statutory power conferred by the Trustee Act 1925, either on the appointment of a new trustee in his place, or without such appointment if at least two trustees will continue in office or if the continuing trustee is a trust corporation;
(c) by the consent of *all* the beneficiaries, which can only be obtained where all are of full age and capacity[3]; or
(d) by order of the court[4].
(2) A trustee may be removed from his office:
(a) under an express power;
(b) by the direction of all the beneficiaries who, take together, are absolutely entitled to the trust property and all of full age and capacity if the trust instrument has not conferred power to appoint new trustees on someone else or otherwise ousted the right of the beneficiaries[5];
(c) under the statutory power of appointing new trustees contained in sections 36 and 37 of the Trustee Act 1925 in cases where he remains out of the kingdom for more than twelve months consecutively[6], refuses or is unfit to act, or is incapable of acting; or
(d) by the court[7] appointing a new trustee in his place (or, exceptionally, under its inherent jurisdiction[8] by simply removing the trustee without replacing him if sufficient trustees remain), at the instance of any trustee or beneficiary, where he has behaved improperly[9], or is incapable of acting properly[10], or from faults of

1 Administration of Estates Act 1925, s 7.
2 *Davis v Richards and Wallington Industries Ltd* [1991] 2 All ER 563 at 581.
3 *Wilkinson v Parry* (1828) 4 Russ 272; and see Art 69, ante.
4 *Re Gregson's Trusts* (1886) 34 Ch D 209; *Re Chetwynd's Settlement* [1902] 1 Ch 692.
5 Trusts of Land and Appointment of Trustees Act 1996 ('TLATA 1996'), ss 19 and 21.
6 See p 759, post.
7 Under s 41 of the TA 1925 or under its inherent jurisdiction. Procedure under the Act is by originating summons (now a Part 8 claim form) even where the trustee resists (*Re Danson* (1899) 48 WR 73) if there is no dispute of fact. Where there is a dispute of fact, the court may decline to exercise the jurisdiction under s 41 and leave the parties to invoke the inherent jurisdiction of the court over trustees in an action. See per Bennett J in *Re Henderson* [1940] Ch 764 at 767, [1940] 3 All ER 295 at 298.
8 *Re Harrison's Settlement Trusts* [1965] 3 All ER 795 at 799; *Clarke v Heathfield (No 2)* [1985] ICR 606; *Re Chetwynd's Settlement* [1902] 1 Ch 692.
9 *Millard v Eyre* (1793) 2 Ves 94; *Palairet v Carew* (1863) 32 Beav 564.
10 *Buchanan v Hamilton* (1801) 5 Ves 722; and *Re Lemann's Trusts* (1883) 22 Ch D 633; and *Re Phelp's Settlement Trusts* (1885) 31 Ch D 351, where trustees were incapable from old age and infirmity.

temper or want of tact is in a permanent condition of hostility with his co-trustees and beneficiaries[11], or has been convicted of an offence involving dishonesty or is a recent bankrupt[12], or is residing permanently, or for a long or indefinite period, abroad[13], or cannot be heard of[14], or where any other good reason exists[15];

(e) if he is a trustee of a pension trust scheme by the Occupational Pensions Regulatory Authority if it is satisfied that he is in serious or persistent breach of any of his duties under the Pensions Act 1995 or the Pension Schemes Act 1993, sections 6, 113, 175, Chapter IV of Part IV and may be suspended for a period not exceeding twelve months pending consideration being given to his removal[16], while he will cease to be a trustee[17] if he becomes disqualified under section 29 of the Pensions Act 1995.

PARAGRAPH 1

Retirement under powers of appointing new trustees

The most usual way in which a trustee retires is under a power enabling some person or persons to appoint a new trustee in his place in the event (inter alia) of his desiring to retire. This mode of retiring necessitates the appointment of a new trustee in the place of the one retiring[18]. No question, however, can ever arise as to the costs of such an appointment, inasmuch as ex hypothesi the power provides for the retirement of the trustee *if he so desires*. The costs, therefore, in such cases always fall on the estate and not on the retiring trustee. Such a power may be expressly given by the settlement, but, unless a contrary intention is expressed in the settlement, will also be implied therein by statute irrespective of the date at which the settlement came into operation. This statutory power will be discussed in the next article.

Danger of trustees not being discharged

It must be noted that by s 37(1)(c) of the Trustee Act 1925 (as amended by the Trusts of Land and Appointment of Trustees Act 1996[19] substituting 'persons' for 'individuals') even though a new trustee is appointed in place of the old trustee such old trustee will not be discharged from his trust unless there will then be either a trust corporation (incorporated only in a state of the European Union) or at least two persons to act as trustees (except where

11 *Letterstedt v Broers* (1884) 9 App Cas 371 at 386; see *Earl of Portsmouth v Fellows* (1820) 5 Madd 450.
12 *Re Adams' Trust* (1879) 12 Ch D 634; *Re Barker's Trusts* (1875) 1 Ch D 43.
13 *Buchanan v Hamilton* (1801) 5 Ves 722; *Re Bignold's Settlement Trusts* (1872) 7 Ch App 223; and *Re Moravian Society* (1858) 26 Beav 101.
14 *Re Harrison's Trusts* (1852) 22 LJ Ch 69.
15 See *Assets Realisation Co v Trustees etc Corpn* (1895) 65 LJ Ch 74; *Re Henderson* [1940] Ch 764, [1940] 3 All ER 295.
16 Pensions Act 1995, ss 3 and 4.
17 Pensions Act 1995, s 30.
18 *Adam and Co International Trustees Ltd v Theodore Goddard* [2000] WTLR 349 at 355.
19 TLATA 1996, Sch 3, para 3(12).

only one trustee was originally appointed and a sole trustee is able to give valid receipts for capital money)[20].

The question arises whether s 37(1)(c) is an inflexible mandatory rule or can be ousted by a contrary provision in the trust instrument[1]. Originally, under s 10(2)(c) of the Trustee Act 1893 trustees were not discharged unless there were 'at least two trustees to perform the trust', though by s 10(5) 'This section applies only if and so far as a contrary intention is not expressed in the instrument, if any, creating the trust and shall have effect subject to the terms of that instrument'. The Law of Property Act 1922, s 110(9) substituted for the quoted words in s 10(2)(c) 'either a trust corporation or at least two individuals to perform the trust' but, of course, contrary scope remained under s 10(5).

The Law of Property (Amendment) Act 1924 left the position as it was above, except for adding in Pt II, Sch 5, para 5(4), 'Nothing in the Trustee Acts shall authorise the appointment of a sole trustee not being a trust corporation where the trustee when appointed will not be able to give valid receipts for all capital money arising under the trust'. This was introduced to reflect the fact that the new legislation contains the inflexible mandatory rule that a sole trustee, not being a trust corporation, cannot give a valid receipt for capital money arising in respect of English or Welsh land held on trust for sale or subject to a Settled Land Act settlement.

Thus, the position then was that, if no English or Welsh land be comprised in the trust, a trust instrument could expressly provide for trustees to be validly discharged when the settlor or trustees, as the case may be, appointed as new sole trustee an individual or a body corporate.

The Trustee Act 1925 was expressly stated to be 'An Act consolidating certain enactments relating to trustees in England and Wales' (eg Trustee Act 1893, Law of Property Act 1922, Law of Property (Amendment) Act 1924) so that Parliament could enact it on the nod without discussion. Thus one expects the position under the Trustee Act 1925 to be as stated in the preceding paragraph because Parliament's intention was not to change the law.

The draftsman in his consolidation exercise boldly inserted a general contrary intention provision at the end of the 1925 Act in s 69(2):

'The powers conferred by this Act on trustees are in addition to the powers conferred by the instrument, if any, creating the trust, but those powers, unless otherwise stated, apply if and so far only as a contrary intention is not expressed in the instrument, if any, creating the trust, and have effect subject to the terms of that instrument ... '

With s 36 being headed 'Powers of appointing new or additional trustees' and s 37 headed 'Supplemental provisions as to appointment of trustees', it follows that trustees should be able validly to retire from the trust, unless the trust includes any land in England or Wales[2], when they exercise their s 36 power to appoint as successor a sole trustee if so authorised by the terms of

---

20 Ie the trust is of pure personalty and not of English or Welsh land: LPA 1925, s 27(2); TA 1925, s 14(2).

1 *Mettoy Pension Fund Trustees Ltd v Evans* [1991] 2 All ER 513 at 534.

2 Section 37(2) is mandatory: 'Nothing in this Act shall authorise the appointment of a sole trustee not being a "trust corporation" where the trustees when appointed would not be able to give valid receipts for all capital money arising under the trust' but only in relation to the statutory power of appointment in the Act and not to an express power, which can thus be used to circumvent it' as pointed out in *London Regional Transport Pension Fund Trust Co Ltd v Hatt* [1993] PLR 227 at 261.

the trust instrument. If it is the settlor who appoints a sole trustee in place of the existing trustees it should make no difference, just as it was before 1926, the 1925 Act not dealing with such powers conferred on the settlor.

The position should be the same mutatis mutandis for s 39 of the Trustee Act 1925, the Law of Property Act 1922, s 110(10) substituting corresponding words in s 11(1) of the Trustee Act 1893, leaving scope for contrary intention under s 11(3).

Helpfully, Knox J in *London Regional Transport Pension Fund Trust Co Ltd v Hatt*[3] has now held that s 37(1)(c) is subject to a contrary intention expressed in the trust instrument and this should also follow for s 39.

Retirement under statutory power without appointment of successor

Section 39 of the Trustee Act 1925 provides that:

(1) Where a trustee is desirous of being discharged from the trust, and after his discharge there will be either a trust corporation[4] or at least two persons[5] to act as trustees to perform the trust, then, if such trustee as aforesaid by deed declares that he is desirous of being discharged from the trust, and if his co-trustees and such other person, if any, as is empowered to appoint trustees, by deed consent to the discharge of the trustee, and to the vesting in the co-trustees alone of the trust property, the trustee desirous of being discharged shall be deemed to have retired from the trust, and shall, by the deed, be discharged therefrom under this Act, without any new trustee being appointed in his place.

(2) Any assurance or thing requisite for vesting the trust property in the continuing trustees alone shall be executed or done.

It would seem that the power to obtain his discharge without appointment of a successor is one of the powers conferred on trustees which under s 69(2) thereof[6] yield to the express terms of the settlement, as should the need for there to be a trust corporation incorporated in a state within the European Union or at least two individuals. A deed is required if advantage is to be taken of s 40(2) of the Trustee Act to vest relevant property in the continuing trustees alone[7].

Retirement by consent of all the beneficiaries

The method of retirement by consent of all the beneficiaries is merely a corollary of Article 69. The beneficiaries collectively being the sole owners of the property, and able to put an end to the trust, can a fortiori permit the trustee to retire, even though the result may be to leave a single individual to act as trustee. It may be doubted, however, whether the beneficiaries can permit a trustee to retire without the consent of his co-trustee or co-trustees[8].

---

3 [1993] PLR 227 at 260–262, discussed by D. Way [1993] 2 J Int P 100 and accepted in *Adam and Co International Trustees Ltd v Theodore Goddard* [2000] WTLR 349.

4 See note 4, p 448, ante. Companies incorporated outside the European Union cannot be 'trust corporations' however well capitalised. Also see p 797, post.

5 See TLATA 1996, Sch 3, para 3(13).

6 See *Re Warren* [1939] Ch 684, [1939] 2 All ER 599 and *Adam and Co International Trustees Ltd v Theodore Goddard* [2000] WTLR 349 at 355. When English or Welsh land comes to be sold, however, no valid capital receipt can be given to protect a purchaser unless there are two trustees or a trust corporation: LPA 1925, s 27(2).

7 See p 776, post.

8 Cf *Re Brockbank* [1948] Ch 206, [1948] 1 All ER 287; cited p 736, ante.

In any event, in the case of trusts of land all such beneficiaries may be able, instead, to rely on s 19 of the Trusts of Land and Appointment of Trustees Act 1996 discussed below.

Retirement by order of the court

Retirement by order of the court is now a comparatively rare method of retirement from a trust. It might arise where the trustee wishes to retire and either cannot procure a person to take his place, or, being himself the appointing party, has a dispute with his beneficiaries in relation to the person to be appointed, or where the persons to appoint are out of the country, or cannot be found[9]. In such cases he would be justified in issuing a Part 8 claim under CPR Part 54, for the appointment of a new trustee in his place and it is conceived that ordinarily he would not only be exempt from bearing the costs of the application, but would also be entitled to his own costs[10].

The court also has jurisdiction in an administration action or on a claim inter partes asking for administration or execution of the trusts (but not on a claim under the Trustee Act 1925[11]) to discharge one of two or more trustees without appointing another person to succeed him[12]. It will not do so unless there remain at least two trustees or a trust corporation to perform the trust.

Retiring trustees not released from liability

Where a trustee hands over to another trustee he is not entitled to a formal release from the trusteeship, since the only persons who can give, or are called on to give, a formal release to trustees are the beneficiaries when the trust is wound up[13].

PARAGRAPH 2(A)

Illustration of express power to remove a trustee

An instance of a trustee being removable under an express power is afforded by the form of bankers' mortgage, namely, containing a declaration by a mortgagor who has deposited his title deeds that he will hold the legal estate in trust for the mortgagees, with power for the mortgagees, during the continuance of the security, to remove him or any other trustee from the trusteeship, and to appoint themselves or any other person in his place. In such cases the mortgagees can, by a deed removing the trustee and appointing another person, without even the necessity for an express vesting declaration[14], take the legal estate out of the mortgagor, or even of an assign

9 See *Re Humphry's Estate* (1855) 1 Jur NS 921; and *Re Somerset* [1887] WN 122.

10 See *Re Chetwynd's Settlement* [1902] 1 Ch 692.

11 *Re Chetwynd's Settlement* [1902] 1 Ch 692. The device of re-appointing the continuing trustees in place of themselves and the retiring trustee (as in *Re Stokes' Trusts* (1872) LR 13 Eq 333; and *Re Harford's Trusts* (1879) 13 Ch D 135) was disapproved in *Re Aston* (1883) 23 Ch D 217; following a decision of Cotton LJ in *Re Colyer* (1880) 50 LJ Ch 79, and is not now followed.

12 See *Re Chetwynd's Settlement* [1902] 1 Ch 692, and *Re Stretton* [1942] WN 95.

13 *Tiger v Barclays Bank Ltd* [1951] 2 KB 556, [1951] 2 All ER 262; affd [1952] 1 All ER 85, CA, where this point was not in issue.

14 See p 776, post.

to whom he has conveyed it with notice[15]. Sometimes, the settlor will reserve to himself or confer on a protector the right to remove a trustee at any time and replace him with a new trustee, although this will be presumed to be a fiduciary power to be exercised in the best interests of the beneficiaries as discussed under Article 73(1)(a) below.

Problem where remove without replacing

If A, B and C are trustees and C is removed pursuant to an express power of removal that permits removal other than by replacement, legal title remains in A, B and C because s 39 does not apply to vest title in A and B alone (C not having executed a deed retiring from the trusteeship). It will thus be necessary to appoint a replacement trustee, D, who can then execute a deed of retirement benefiting from ss 39 and 40(2) of the Trustee Act so as to vest legal title in A and B alone.

PARAGRAPH 2(B)

Qualifying Requirements

Where there is at the time in question[16] no person nominated for the purpose of appointing new trustees by the trust instrument and the beneficiaries under the trust are all of full age and capacity and between them are collectively entitled to the trust property[17], then they may collectively give a written direction requiring the trustee(s) to retire and if they wish, also requiring the retiring trustee(s) to appoint the person(s) specified in the direction[18]. This right can be excluded by a provision in a post-1996 trust[19], while in the case of pre-1997 trusts it can be excluded by a provision in a post-1996 deed only if such a deed is executed by the settlor(s)[20].

The purpose of the provision is to save those beneficiaries who have collective *Saunders v Vautier* rights from having to terminate the trust (with disadvantageous tax consequences) and create a new trust on the same terms where they simply want to replace the trustees. Thus, beneficiaries under a discretionary trust with collective *Saunders v Vautier* rights should be able to force the trustees to retire in favour of new trustees nominated by the beneficiaries when 'beneficiary' is defined[1] as 'any person who under the trust has an interest in property subject to the trust (including a person who has such an interest as trustee or as a trustee or a personal representative)'.

---

15 *London and County Banking Co v Goddard* [1897] 1 Ch 642.
16 For example, if by then the person nominated in the trust instrument has died.
17 TLATA 1996, s 19(1).
18 TLATA 1996, s 19(2). The beneficiaries' collective right is personal to them so they can appoint one or more of themselves to be new trustees if they wish, and the retiring trustees should do as they are told unless aware of facts indicating that the participation of one beneficiary thereby placed in a vulnerable position has been obtained by fraud or undue influence.
19 TLATA 1996, s 21(5).
20 TLATA 1996, s 21(6). The deed is irrevocable by s 21(7).
 1 TLATA 1996, s 22(1): it includes an annuitant (whose interest in the trust property is only excluded from being an interest in possession by s 22(3)).

However, it does not seem[2] that there need be any involvement of an object of a power of appointment who only has a hope of obtaining 'an interest in property subject to the trust' if the trustees happen to exercise their discretion in his favour, the trustees not being obliged to exercise their discretion at all.

Where the interest of a beneficiary has passed by operation of law to his personal representative or to his trustee in bankruptcy or has been assigned to B beneficially or to T on various trusts, then it will be the personal representative or trustee in bankruptcy or B or T who will need to join with the other beneficiaries to force the trustees to retire.

Beneficiaries' Directions

The beneficiaries' directions may require the retirement of a trustee or trustees without any new trustee being appointed (provided there will be either a trust corporation or at least two trustees left to perform the trust) or require both the retirement of a trustee or trustees and the appointment of a new trustee or trustees (provided as above) or require the appointment of an additional trustee or trustees (subject to the usual restrictions on the number of trustees)[3]. A single direction may be given by all the beneficiaries jointly or by each of them (whether solely or jointly with one or more of the others) specifying the same person or persons for retirement and appointment[4]. A written withdrawal by any one beneficiary before compliance with the direction(s) makes the direction(s) ineffective[5]. Retirement directions need to be served on the retiring trustee(s), while appointment directions must be served on all the trustees.

Implementation of Directions

A trustee shall make a deed declaring his retirement and be deemed to have retired and be discharged from his trust where (a) he has been given a direction, (b) 'reasonable arrangements have been made for the protection of any rights of his in connection with the trust', (c) there will be a trust corporation or at least two trustees after he has retired and (d) either another person is to be appointed to be a new trustee on his retirement or the continuing trustees by deed consent to his retirement[6]. Where a trustee retires, he and the continuing trustees (together with any new trustee) must (subject to any arrangements for the protection of his rights)[7] do anything necessary to vest the trust property in the continuing trustees (or the continuing and new trustees). It thus seems that, as in the case of voluntary retirements, it is envisaged that, rather than force the retired trustee to rely solely on his equitable non-possessory lien, he and the other trustees will

---

2 In *Gartside v IRC* [1968] AC 553 in the estate duty context 'interest' did not extend to an interest as beneficiary under a discretionary trust and *a fortiori* (at 607) not to the hope of an object of a power of appointment, but 'interest' in context can extend to discretionary trust beneficiaries: *Knocker v Youle* [1986] 2 All ER 914 at 916–917.
3 TLATA 1996, s 19(2) and (3)(c). A direction may be given to the personal representative of the last trustee.
4 TLATA 1996, s 21(1).
5 TLATA 1996, s 21(1).
6 TLATA 1996, s 19(3).
7 TLATA 1996, s 19(4).

come to reasonable arrangements, eg including an indemnity given by them to him against contingent and future liabilities.

If the trustee fails to execute the requisite deed eg because not satisfied with the arrangements for his protection, then the beneficiaries may seek a mandatory order from the court, with the trustee being at risk as to the costs if he loses the case, and the court ultimately having power to nominate a person to execute the deed on his behalf[8].

A retirement without the appointment of any new trustee operates under s 40(2) of the Trustee Act 1925 to vest the trust property in the new trustees (other than property excepted by s 40(3)). While an appointment of new trustees must, at the least, be in writing[9], it will be better for it to be by deed so as to obtain the benefit of s 40 for much trust property, although specific steps will be necessary for other trust property (eg stocks and shares) to be vested in the new trustees together with any continuing trustees.

Where trustee is mentally disordered

If a trustee is incapable by reason of mental disorder of exercising his functions as trustee and there is no person entitled to appoint a replacement trustee under s 36(1) of the Trustee Act 1925, then the collectively absolutely entitled beneficiaries of full age and capacity can arrange for a replacement trustee[10]. They need to give a written direction to a receiver of the trustee or an attorney acting for him under a registered enduring power of attorney or a person authorised for the purpose by the authority (the Court of Protection) having jurisdiction under the Mental Health Act 1983, Pt VII, requiring the recipient to appoint by writing the person or persons specified in the direction to be a trustee or trustees in place of the incapable trustee[11].

PARAGRAPH 2(c) AND (D)

The removal of a trustee under the statutory power of appointing new trustees, or by the court, is so mixed up with the appointment of new trustees, that reference should be made to the next Article for further information on the subject[12].

---

8 Supreme Court Act 1981, s 39.
9 TLATA 1996, s 19(2)(b).
10 TLATA 1996, s 20(1) subject to s 21 in the same way as s 19.
11 TLATA 1996, s 20(2). If there is another trustee who is of sound mind he will normally exercise his powers under s 36(1) of the TA 1925 (but see s 36(9), so that s 20 will normally be used to appoint two or more trustees, implicitly subject to the maximum of four for land.
12 An executor who is incapable of performing his duties can, in effect, be removed by revocation of the grant of probate. See *Re Galbraith* [1951] P 422, [1951] 2 All ER 470n; but see *Re Cope's Estate* [1954] 1 All ER 698, [1954] 1 WLR 608. But the Family Division has no jurisdiction to order the removal of a trustee: *Compton (Marquess of Northampton) v Compton (Marchioness of Northampton) and Hussey* [1960] P 201, [1960] 2 All ER 70. The High Court now has jurisdiction to remove a personal representative: Administration of Justice Act 1985, s 50.

ARTICLE 73

Appointment of new trustees[13]

(1) New trustees of a settlement may be appointed:
(a) under an express or a necessarily implied[14] power;
(b) under the statutory power conferred by section 36 of the Trustee Act 1925;
(c) by the High Court (or where the trust fund does not exceed £30,000 in value, the county court[15]) on the application of any trustee or beneficiary[16], whenever it is expedient to appoint a new trustee or new trustees, and it is found inexpedient, difficult or impracticable to do so without the court's assistance; and particularly where it is desirable to appoint a new trustee in substitution for a trustee who is incapable, by reason of mental disorder within the meaning of the Mental Health Act 1983[17], of exercising his functions as trustee, or is a bankrupt, or is a corporation which is in liquidation or has been dissolved[18]. Where, however, there is a donee of a power of appointing new trustees able and willing to exercise it, the court has no power to appoint new trustees contrary to his wishes[19]; or
(d) by the authority having jurisdiction under Part VII of the Mental Health Act 1983, in cases where such authority has concurrent jurisdiction with the High Court by virtue of section 54 of the Trustee Act 1925, as amended by the Mental Health Act 1983, section 148(1) and Schedule 4[20];
(e) if a trustee of a pension trust scheme has been removed by the Occupational Pensions Regulatory Authority or has ceased to be a trustee by reason of his disqualification the Authority may appoint another trustee in his place[1].
(2) In the case of pension trust schemes an independent trustee must be appointed, where the employer is insolvent, by the insolvency practitioner in relation to such employer or the official receiver if satisfied that there is no independent trustee[2].

---

13 The appointment of a judicial trustee is treated separately in Article 76 post.
14 *Davis v Richards & Wallington Industries Ltd* [1991] 2 All ER 563 at 581.
15 County Courts Act 1959, s 52, as amended.
16 TA 1925, s 58. The court can charge the costs of such appointment, and of vesting orders, on the trust estate (TA 1925, s 60).
17 See s 1(2) of the 1983 Act.
18 TA 1925, s 41, as amended by Mental Health Act 1983, s 148(1) and Sch 4, and by Criminal Law Act 1967, s 10(2) and Sch 3, Pt III.
19 *Re Higginbottom* [1892] 3 Ch 132. But this does not relate to applications for this appointment of a judicial trustee under the Judicial Trustees Act 1896, as to which see Article 76, post, and *Douglas v Bolam* [1900] 2 Ch 749; nor, it is apprehended, to cases in which a judgment for general administration has been given, as to which see pp 726 et seq, ante.
20 For the relevant powers under the 1983 Act, see s 96 thereof. See also pp 766, 783, post.
1 Pensions Act 1995, s 7.
2 Pensions Act 1995, s 23.

(3) Every new trustee, both before and after the trust property is vested in him, has the same powers, authorities, and discretions (incident to the office of trustee)[3], and may in all respects act as if he had been an original trustee, while the newly appointed independent trustee of a pension trust scheme will have all the trustees' discretionary powers vested in him alone[4].

(4) Any person, including a corporation[5], who can hold property, is capable of being appointed to be a trustee except, in the case of pension trust schemes, a person disqualified by reason of dishonesty insolvency and other prejudicial matters within section 29 of the Pensions Act 1995; but an infant cannot be appointed, and serious consideration should be given before appointing a person who resides out of the jurisdiction of the court, or one who is a beneficiary, or husband of a beneficiary.

(5) Where there are more than four trustees of a trust of land no new trustee can be appointed (except where on the appointment the number is reduced to four or less) until the number is reduced to less than four, and thereafter the number cannot be increased beyond four[6].

(6) Where an attempted appointment is invalid the old trustee remains liable, and the invalidly appointed new trustee also becomes liable as a trustee de son tort if he intermeddles with the trust property[7].

PARAGRAPH 1(A)

Appointment of new trustees under express power

Express powers to appoint new trustees are construed somewhat strictly. Thus, where an express power to appoint new trustees is vested in:

> 'the surviving or continuing trustees or trustee, or executors or administrators of the last surviving and continuing trustee,'

and all the trustees are desirous of retiring, they cannot do so by appointing new trustees in their place by a single deed; but a new trustee must be appointed in the place of the first retiring trustee by one deed, and then the new trustee must join in a second deed appointing another new trustee in

---

3 As to the difference between powers incident to the office and powers confided to persons who are also trustees, see per Farwell J in *Re Smith* [1904] 1 Ch 139 at 144; and Art 74, ante.
4 Pensions Act 1995, s 25.
5 *Re Thompson's Settlement Trusts* [1905] 1 Ch 229.
6 TA 1925, s 34 as amended by the TLATA 1996, Sch 3, para 3(9). The restrictions do not apply in the case of land for charitable, ecclesiastical or public trusts, or to the trustees of portions terms etc. See TA 1925, s 34(3).
7 *Pearce v Pearce* (1856) 22 Beav 248; *Adam & Co International Trustees Ltd v Theodore Goddard* [2000] WTLR 349.

the place of the second retiring trustee, and so on[8].

This singular instance of verbal subtlety all turns upon the idea that trustees who are *about to retire cannot be said to be continuing*[9], but that if one retired first, the other would be a continuing trustee, although he might intend to retire the next day. If, in addition to the words 'surviving and continuing', the words 'or other trustee or trustees' had been added, the retiring trustees might have appointed new ones by the same deed[10].

So, again, the words 'unfit and incapable' are very strictly construed. Thus, where a new trustee was to be appointed if a trustee became 'incapable of acting', it was held that the bankruptcy of one of the trustees did not fulfil the condition, as it only rendered him *unfit* but not *incapable*[11]. Similarly, where the words were 'unable to act', it was held that absence in China or Australia did not *disable*[12], although it clearly unfitted[13], a trustee for the office. But where the power was to arise in case a trustee should 'be abroad', the fact of his having taken a five years' lease of a residence in Normandy was held to be sufficient to enable the donee of the power to displace him[14]. It has been held that unsoundness of mind *disables* a trustee so as to bring a power into operation[15].

With regard to a trustee becoming *unfit* to act, bankruptcy (at all events where the trust property consists of money or other property capable of being misappropriated, and where the beneficiaries desire his removal[16]) and liquidation or composition[17], or conviction of a dishonesty crime[18], are grounds for his removal *by the court*, under s 41 of the Trustee Act 1925[19]. It thus seems likely that they would enable a donee of a power of appointing new trustees to displace him in hostile proceedings on the ground of *unfitness*. Under the old law it was held that infancy was not *unfitness*, although an

---

8 *Lord Camoys v Best* (1854) 19 Beav 414; *Re Coates to Parsons* (1886) 34 Ch D 370; *Re Norris* (1884) 27 Ch D 333. This notion was strongly disapproved by Bacon V-C in *Re Glenny and Hartley* (1884) 25 Ch D 611; but the Vice-Chancellor's dicta were equally strongly disapproved by Pearson J in *Re Norris*, above, and by North J in *Re Coates to Parsons*, above.

9 With regard to appointments made under the statutory power this is not so, as the statute enacts that a continuing trustee shall include a refusing or retiring trustee, *if willing to act*, as donee of the power (TA 1925, s 36(8); but he is not a necessary party if unwilling to act (see *Re Norris* (1884) 27 Ch D 333).

10 With regard to appointments made under the statutory power this is not so, as the statute enacts that a continuing trustee shall include a refusing or retiring trustee, *if willing to act*, as donee of the power (TA 1925, s 36(8); but he is not a necessary party if unwilling to act (see *Re Norris* (1884) 27 Ch D 333).

11 *Turner v Maule* (1850) 15 Jur 761; see *Re Watts' Settlement* (1851) 9 Hare 106.

12 *Withington v Withington* (1848) 16 Sim 104; *Re Harrison's Trusts* (1852) 22 LJ Ch 69; *Re May's Will Trusts* [1941] Ch 109 (trustee resident in enemy-occupied territory not incapable of acting); but see *Re Bignold's Settlement Trusts* (1872) 7 Ch App 223.

13 *Mennard v Welford* (1853) 1 SM & G 426; and *Re Harrison's Trusts* (1852) 22 LJ Ch 69. A mere temporary absence abroad would not unfit a trustee for the office (*Re Moravian Society* (1858) 26 Beav 101).

14 *Re Earl of Stamford* [1896] 1 Ch 288.

15 *Re East* (1873) 8 Ch App 735.

16 See *Re Barker's Trusts* (1875) 1 Ch D 43; *Re Adams' Trust* (1879) 12 Ch D 634.

17 See *Re Barker's Trusts* (1875) 1 Ch D 43; *Re Adams' Trust* (1879) 12 Ch D 634.

18 *Turner v Maule* (1850) 15 Jur 761.

19 Replacing s 25 of the Trustee Act 1893. The Criminal Law Act 1967, s 1, has abolished the distinction between felonies and misdemeanours and s 10 and Sch 3, P III, therefore repeal the words in s 41 of the TA 1925 which refer specifically to a trustee being convicted of felony. It is clear none the less that the trustee's conviction for a serious crime would make it expedient to replace him.

infant would be removed by the court[20]; but by s 20 of the Law of Property Act 1925 it is provided that 'the appointment of an infant to be a trustee in relation to any settlement or trust shall be void, but without prejudice to the power to appoint a new trustee to fill the vacancy'[1]. Lastly, with regard to *incapacity*, the word is strictly limited to incapacity of the trustee arising from some personal defect[2], as illness, physical or mental[3], or infancy.

Power personal and not incident to donee's interest

Where the power is vested in a beneficiary he may exercise it even after alienating his interest by way of a mortgage assignment[4]. On the other hand, where a decree for administration by the court has been made, the donee of a power (whether express or statutory) can only appoint a new trustee under the supervision of the court, which will, however, accept his nominee, unless there be strong grounds for rejecting him[5].

Power normally fiduciary

Where a power to remove trustees by replacing them with new trustees is vested in a beneficiary who is the primary object of the settlor's bounty, especially if his power is not restricted to a few specified eventualities, the obvious inference is that the power has been conferred on the beneficiary to look after his own personal interests and not those of the beneficiaries as a whole. However, if it is someone who is not a beneficiary, but the settlor or, a *fortiori*, a designated protector, who has such power, there is a strong presumption that such power is a fiduciary one[6] to be exercised only in the best interests of the beneficiaries as a whole, because the subject-matter of the power is the office of the trustee at the very core of the trust, obliged to act in the best interests of the beneficiaries as a whole, while the function of a protector is naturally presumed to be to protect the interests of the beneficiaries as a whole. Nevertheless. the initial protector may be a beneficiary with a significant interest to protect[7] (eg the settlor's widow life-tenant or a son being managing director of the company which is a major trust asset) or the settlor's foreign lawyer, whom the settlor expects to protect a significant interest of the settlor not as beneficiary under the trust but as managing director (at a good salary with good perquisites) of a company controlled by the trustees or in which the trustees have a significant shareholding[8].

To avoid the operational problems that will arise if the purportedly replaced trustees argue that their replacement was in breach of the equitable

---

20 *Re Tallatire* [1885] WN 191. Minors, as infants are now known, attain majority at the age of 18 years under the Family Law Reform Act 1969.

1 See *Re Vinogradoff* [1935] WN 68.

2 See *Re Watts' Settlement* (1851) 9 Hare 106; *Turner v Maule* (1850) 15 Jur 761; *Re Bignold's Settlement Trusts* (1872) 7 Ch App 223.

3 *Re East* (1873) 8 Ch App 735; *Re Blake* [1887] WN 173.

4 *Hardaker v Moorhouse* (1884) 26 Ch D 417.

5 *Re Gadd* (1883) 23 Ch D 134; *Re Hall* (1885) 33 WR 508; *Re Sales* [1911] WN 194, followed, *Re Cotter* [1915] 1 Ch 307.

6 *Steele v Paz* [1993–95] Manx LR 426, CA; *IRC v Schroder* [1983] STC 480; *Re Osiris Trustees* (2000) 2 ITELR 404. See pp 29–34 ante.

7 *Rawson Trust v Perlman* Butts OCM, Vol 11, pp 35–54 (Bahamas Sup Ct); and see *Re Z Trust* [1997] Cayman ILR 248.

8 See *Von Knierem v Bermuda Trust Co* Butts OCM, Vol 1, p 116.

and fiduciary duties placed upon the donee of the power of appointment so that they remain the trustees, it will help if the trust instrument spells out the limited nature of donee's duties rather than having to fall back upon necessary implications. It also helps if the trust assets are held by a custodian trustee so the replaced old trustees need not be told who are the new trustees to whom (no trust assets needing to be transferred) and so that the trust continues to operate smoothly with the custodian trustee taking its instructions from the new trustees. This custodian trusteeship structure is also essential to the effectiveness of automatic 'flee' (or should it be 'flea') clauses where, in certain specified events, T Co Ltd in Suntopia is to cease to be a trustee and E Trust Co Ltd in Erewhon is to become trustee, for otherwise Suntopian assets can be frozen and the Suntopian trustees enjoined from any activities.

Exercise of express power by a minor

It would seem that a minor can validly exercise an express power of appointment, but a minor is not bound by an act which is either imprudent or prejudicial to his interests or which, where he is executing an authority with which he is entrusted, touches his interest. Where therefore a minor, having an express power to appoint new trustees and being himself beneficially entitled to the property on attaining twenty-five, appointed his mother, to whom the income was payable for his benefit until he attained twenty-five, as sole trustee, the court held the appointment to be invalid[9].

Exercise of express power on behalf of person who is mentally ill

Where a power of appointment is vested in a person who is incapable, by reason of mental disorder, of managing and administering his property and affairs[10], the judge[11] may exercise the power[12] and may also make consequential vesting orders[13].

PARAGRAPH 1(B)

Appointment of new trustees under the statutory power

If there be no express power, or even if there is one but the statutory power is not expressly negatived or modified[14], and the express power is for some reason inapplicable to the state of circumstances that has arisen, new trustees

---

9 *Re Parsons* [1940] Ch 973, [1940] 4 All ER 65.
10 See the Mental Health Act 1983, s 94.
11 'The judge' in this context is defined in s 94 of the 1983 Act.
12 Mental Health Act 1983, s 96(1). See also, as cases decided under ss 128, 129 of the Lunacy Act 1890 (which was replaced by the 1959 Act); *Re Shortridge* [1895] 1 Ch 278; *Re Fuller* [1900] 2 Ch 551; *Re Blake* [1887] WN 173, CA. These provisions apply whether or not the patient is a trustee. It seems that if the patient's receiver is unwilling to exercise the power (needing the authority of the judge), the surviving or continuing trustees may appoint new trustees under TA 1925, s 36.
13 Mental Health Act 1983, s 96(2). See also the preceding footnote.
14 *Cecil v Langdon* (1884) 28 Ch D 1; and *Re Wheeler and de Rochow* [1896] 1 Ch 315, followed in *Re Sichel* [1916] 1 Ch 358. If the events contemplated by a limited express power of appointment have not occurred then the statutory power applies.

may be appointed under the provisions of s 36 of the Trustee Act 1925. That section and ss 37 and 38 of the Act are in the following words:

36.—(1)
> Where a trustee, either original or substituted, and whether appointed by a court or otherwise, is dead, or remains out of the United Kingdom for more than twelve months, or desires to be discharged from all or any of the trusts or powers reposed in or conferred on him, or refuses or is unfit to act therein, or is incapable of acting therein, or is an infant, then, subject to the restrictions imposed by this Act on the number of trustees—
>
> (a) the person or persons nominated for the purpose of appointing new trustees by the instrument, if any, creating the trust[15]; or
> (b) if there is no such person, or no such person able and willing to act, then the surviving or continuing trustees or trustee for the time being, or the personal representatives of the last surviving or continuing trustee[16]:
>
> may, by writing[17], appoint one or more other persons (whether or not being the persons exercising the power) to be a trustee or trustees in the place of the trustee so deceased remaining out of the United Kingdom, desiring to be discharged, refusing, or being unfit or being incapable, or being an infant, as aforesaid.
>
> (2) Where a trustee has been removed under a power contained in the instrument creating the trust, a new trustee or new trustees may be appointed in the place of the trustee who is removed, as if he were dead, or, in the case of a corporation, as if the corporation desired to be discharged from the trust, and the provisions of this section shall apply accordingly, but subject to the restrictions imposed by this Act on the number of trustees.
>
> (3) Where a corporation being a trustee is or has been dissolved, either before or after the commencement of this Act, then, for the purposes of this section and of any enactment replaced thereby, the corporation shall be deemed to be and to have been from the date of the dissolution incapable of acting in the trusts or powers reposed in or conferred on the corporation.
>
> (4) The power of appointment given by subsection (1) of this section or any similar previous enactment to the personal representatives of a last surviving or continuing trustee shall be and shall be deemed always to have been exercisable by the executors for the time being (whether original or by representation) of such surviving or continuing trustee who have proved the will of their testator or by the administrators for the time being of such trustee without the concurrence of any executor who has renounced or has not proved.
>
> (5) But a sole or last surviving executor intending to renounce, or all the executors where they all intend to renounce, shall have and shall be deemed always to

---

15 In *Re Wheeler and de Rochow* [1896] 1 Ch 315, Kekewich J held that if there is a limited express power of appointment in certain events and no such event occurs so that reliance is placed on the statutory power, then the nominee with the limited power is not the 'person nominated for the purpose of appointing new trustees' within s 36(1)(a) so that the proper nominating person is to be found in s 36(1)(b). Neville J reluctantly followed this in *Re Sichel* [1916] 1 Ch 358. Section 36 in substance merely re-enacts Trustee Act 1893, s 10(1), so the position seems the same.

16 See *Re Shafto's Trusts* (1885) 29 Ch D 247; *Nicholson v Field* [1893] 2 Ch 511; *Re Coates to Parsons* (1886) 34 Ch D 370.

   Query whether those who have actually proved can exercise the power without the joinder of those who have not renounced; cf *Re Boucherett* [1908] 1 Ch 180. An executor who has not proved his trustee-testator's will can exercise this power, but the trustee appointed in such circumstances can only prove his title by reference to a proper grant of representation establishing that the appointor was executor under the testator's last will, so that a grant of probate or of letters of administration with the will annexed is vital in practice: *Re Crowhurst Park* [1974] 1 All ER 991, [1974] 1 WLR 583.

17 Nevertheless the power cannot be exercised by will; see *Re Parker's Trusts* [1894] 1 Ch 707. A deed will attract the benefit of s 40 of the TA 1925.

have had power, at any time before renouncing probate, to exercise the power of appointment given by this section, or by any similar previous enactment, if willing to act for that purpose and without thereby accepting the office of executor.

(6) Where in the case of any trust, there are not more than three trustees[18] –

    (a) the person or persons nominated for the purpose of appointing new trustees by the instrument, if any, creating the trust; or

    (b) if there is no such person, or no such person able and willing to act, then the trustee or trustees for the time being;

may, by writing, appoint another person or other persons[19] to be an additional trustee or additional trustees, but it shall not be obligatory to appoint any additional trustee, unless the instrument, if any, creating the trust, or any statutory enactment provides to the contrary, nor shall the number of trustees be increased beyond four by virtue of any such appointment.

(6A) A person who is either—

    (a) both a trustee and attorney for the other trustee (if one other), or for both of the other trustees (if two others), under a registered power; or

    (b) attorney under a registered power for the trustee (if one) or for both or each of the trustees (if two or three),

may, if subsection (6B) of this section is satisfied in relation to him, make an appointment under subsection (6)(b) of this section on behalf of the trustee or trustees[20].

(6B) This subsection is satisfied in relation to an attorney under a registered power for one or more trustees if (as attorney under the power)—

    (a) he intends to exercise any function of the trustee or trustees by virtue of section 1(1) of the Trustee Delegation Act 1999; or

    (b) he intends to exercise any function of the trustee or trustees in relation to any land, capital proceeds of a conveyance of land or income from land by virtue of its delegation to him under section 25 of this Act or the instrument (if any) creating the trust.

(6C) In subsections (6A) and (6B) of this section "registered power" means a power of attorney created by an instrument which is for the time being registered under section 6 of the Enduring Powers of Attorney Act 1985.

(6D) Subsection (6A) of this section—

    (a) applies only if and so far as a contrary intention is not expressed in the instrument creating the power of attorney (or, where more than one, any of them) or the instrument (if any) creating the trust; and

    (b) has effect subject to the terms of those instruments.

(7) Every new trustee appointed under this section as well before as after all the trust property becomes by law, or by assurance, or otherwise, vested in him, shall have the same powers, authorities, and discretions, and may in all respects act as if he had been originally appointed a trustee by the instrument, if any, creating the trust.

(8) The provisions of this section relating to a trustee who is dead include the case of a person nominated trustee in a will but dying before the testator, and those

---

18 As amended by TLATA 1996, Sch 3, para 3(11).

19 The appointor cannot appoint himself to be an additional trustee, though he could under sub-s (1) appoint himself to fill a vacancy (*Re Power's Settlement Trusts* [1951] Ch 1074, [1951] 2 All ER 513, CA; and see *Re Sampson* [1906] 1 Ch 435).

20 This has effect only where the power, or (where more than one) each of them, was created after commencement of the Trustee Delegation Act 1999 (on 1 March 2000) which by s 8 inserted subs (6A)–(6D). The purpose is to deal with the situation where one co-owner of land has, before losing capacity, delegated his trustee functions to the other co-owner by enduring power of attorney, and two trustees are needed to give a good receipt for the proceeds of sale of the land.

relative to a continuing trustee include a refusing or retiring trustee[1] if willing to act in the execution of the provisions of this section.

(9) Where a trustee is incapable, by reason of mental disorder within the meaning of the Mental Health Act 1983, of exercising his functions as trustee and is also entitled in possession to some beneficial interest in the trust property, no appointment of a new trustee in his place shall be made by virtue of paragraph (b) of subsection (1) of this section unless leave to make the appointment has been given by the authority having jurisdiction under Part VI of the Mental Health Act 1983.

37.—(1)

On the appointment of a trustee for the whole or any part of trust property–

(a) the number of trustees may, subject to the restrictions imposed by this Act on the number of trustees, be increased; and

(b) a separate set of trustees, not exceeding four, may be appointed for any part of the trust property held on trusts distinct from those relating to any other part or parts of the trust property, notwithstanding that no new trustees or trustee are or is to be appointed for other parts of the trust property, and any existing trustee may be appointed or remain one of such separate set of trustees, or, if only one trustee was originally appointed, then, save as hereinafter provided, one separate trustee may be so appointed; and

(c) it shall not be obligatory, save as hereinafter provided, to appoint more than one new trustee where only one trustee was originally appointed[2], or to fill up the original number of trustees where more than two trustees were originally appointed, but, except where only one trustee was originally appointed, and a sole trustee when appointed will be able to give receipts for all capital money, *a trustee shall not be discharged from his trust unless there will be either a trust corporation or at least two persons[3] to act as trustees to perform the trust*; and

(d) any assurance or thing requisite for vesting the trust property, or any part thereof, in a sole trustee, or jointly in the persons who are the trustees, shall be executed or done.

(2) Nothing in this Act shall authorise the appointment of a sole trustee, not being a trust corporation, where the trustee, when appointed, would not be able to give valid receipts for all capital money arising under the trust.

38.—(1)

A statement, contained in any instrument coming into operation after the commencement of this Act by which a new trustee is appointed for any purpose connected with land, to the effect that a trustee has remained out of the United Kingdom for more than twelve months or refuses or is unfit to act, or is incapable of acting, or that he is not entitled to a beneficial interest in the trust property in possession, shall, in favour of a purchaser of a legal estate, be conclusive evidence of the matter stated.

(2) In favour of such purchaser any appointment of a new trustee depending on the statement, and any vesting declaration, express or implied, consequent on the appointment, shall be valid.

---

1 A trustee who is compulsorily removed (eg on account of absence abroad) is not a 'refusing or retiring trustee' within this provision (*Re Stoneham's Settlement Trusts* [1953] Ch 59, [1952] 2 All ER 694).

2 Mere disclaimer by one of two trustees does not enable the other to retire and appoint one only in his place: *Earl of Lonsdale v Beckett* (1850) 4 De G & Sm 73; and see *Re Birchall* (1889) 40 Ch D 436.

3 'Persons' substituted for 'individuals' by TLATA 1996, Sch 3, para 3(12).

Inviolability of the statutory power

The court itself regards the statutory power as deserving of the greatest respect and as one with which it will not interfere, as is shown by *Re Gadd*[4]. It would not aid the beneficiaries, even when all concurred, to control the exercise of the power[5] but now the beneficiaries collectively absolutely beneficially entitled and of full age and capacity can retire and replace the trustees under s 19 of the Trusts of Land and Appointment of Trustees Act 1996[6].

When the statutory power is exercisable

It will be observed that the statutory power is exercisable in seven cases, namely:
(1) where a trustee is dead;
(2) where he remains out of the United Kingdom for more than twelve months;
(3) where he desired to be discharged;
(4) where he refuses to act;
(5) where he is unfit to act;
(6) where he is incapable of acting; and
(7) where he is an infant[7].

Deceased trustee

This head includes the case of a person nominated trustee in a will but dying before the testator. However, it should be noted that if a will creates trusts but all the intended trustees predecease the testator, so that no one has ever been a trustee, then no trustee can be appointed under this head[8] because there can then be no surviving or continuing trustees. In such a case the personal representative of the testator has title to the property[9] until the court appoints trustees[10], equity not allowing a trust to fail for want of a trustee.

Trustee residing abroad

The second ground enables a new trustee to be appointed in the place of a trustee who has been resident abroad for 12 months even against his will[11], '12 months' for this purpose meaning residence for an unbroken period of 12 months[12]. To facilitate matters whilst abroad a trustee may by power of attorney[13] delegate his duties and discretions for a period not exceeding 12 months.

4 (1883) 23 Ch D 134; and see *Re Higginbottom* [1892] 3 Ch 132.
5 *Re Brockbank* [1948] Ch 206, [1948] 1 All ER 287.
6 See pp 733 and 748 ante.
7 Reversing the decision in *Re Tallatire* [1885] WN 191. Infancy was up to the age of 21 years till 1970 when it became up to the age of 18 years.
8 *Nicholson v Field* [1893] 2 Ch 511.
9 Administration of Estates Act 1925, ss 1, 2.
10 *Re Williams* (1887) 36 Ch D 231.
11 *Re Stoneham's Settlement Trusts* [1953] Ch 59, [1952] 2 All ER 694.
12 *Re Walker* [1901] 1 Ch 259.
13 TA 1925, s 25, p 642, ante.

Trustee desiring to be discharged

The third ground is clearly applicable to the case of an executor who, having paid debts, and funeral and testamentary expenses, has assented to a settled legacy where the testator has not appointed trustees to administer it. In such cases, where the executor has assented to the legacy, he becomes functus officio qua executor, and thenceforth holds the legacy as trustee[14], and can, like any other trustee, retire, and appoint a new one in his place under the section now under consideration[15]. Further, it is now clear that the section is equally applicable where the legacy is not settled (eg a legacy to an infant for which the executor cannot get a receipt), or where an administrator holds a share of residue. This appears from the judgment of Danckwerts J in *Re Cockburn's Will Trusts*[16], where he said:

'Whether persons are executors or administrators, once they have completed the administration in due course, they become trustees holding for the beneficiaries, either on an intestacy or under the terms of the will, and are bound to carry out the duties of the trustees, though in the case of personal representatives, they cannot be compelled to go on indefinitely acting as trustees and are entitled to appoint new trustees in their place and thus clear themselves from duties which were not expressly conferred on them under the terms of the testator's will and which, for that purpose, they are not bound to accept. It seems to me that if they do not appoint new trustees to proceed to execute the trusts of the will they will become trustees in the full sense. Further, it seems to me that they have the power, under the trusts (*sic*) conferred by section 36 of the Trustee Act 1925 to appoint new trustees of the will to act in their place.'

His Lordship went on to say that it had been recognised for a great number of years, and he felt no doubt that a personal representative who had 'completed his duties in a proper manner' can appoint new trustees[17].

Filling up place of trustee who has already retired

Where one of three or more trustees has retired under s 39 of the Act of 1925[18], without a new trustee having been appointed in his place, his place can be subsequently filled up before another vacancy occurs, by virtue of s 36(6)[19], which gives power to appoint additional trustees even where there

14 See *Re Smith* (1889) 42 Ch D 302; *Re Earl of Stamford* [1896] 1 Ch 288; *Re Willey* [1890] WN 1; *Re Timmis* [1902] 1 Ch 176; and *Re De Sommery* [1912] 2 Ch 622.
15 *Re Smith* (1889) 42 Ch D 302; *Re Earl of Stamford* [1896] 1 Ch 288; *Re Willey* [1890] WN 1; *Re Timmis* [1902] 1 Ch 176; and *Re De Sommery* [1912] 2 Ch 622 and *Re Pitt* (1928) 44 TLR 371; *Re Yerburgh* [1928] WN 208; and see also *Re Moore* (1882) 21 Ch D 778; and comments thereon of Kekewich J in *Eaton v Daines* [1894] WN 32; Administration of Estates Act 1925, s 42 may be available to enable a personal representative to obtain a discharge: see p 714, ante.
16 [1957] Ch 438, [1957] 2 All ER 522. See also *Re Ponder* [1921] 2 Ch 59; *Re Pitt* (1928) 44 TLR 371. So far as the observations of the CA in *Harvell v Foster* [1954] 2 QB 367, [1954] 2 All ER 736, CA, cast any doubt on these cases they were obiter and in the view of Danckwerts J in *Re Cockburn's Will Trusts*, above, were probably unjustified.
17 In the case of land, personal representatives should execute a written assent in their own favour as trustees before they appoint new trustees; since, although the new trustees are no doubt validly appointed as such even if there has been no assent, the legal estate in the land will not vest in them under s 40 of the TA 1925 (p 776, post) unless it was vested in the appointors as trustees and this will not be so if the appointors have not made a written assent: *Re King's Will Trusts* [1964] Ch 542, [1964] 1 All ER 833. See also p 455, ante, and pp 778–779, post.
18 See p 746, ante.
19 See p 757, ante.

is no vacancy, where there are not more than three trustees and that the result of the appointment will not be to make the trustees more than four in number.

Refusal to act as trustee

It is apprehended that the fourth case, namely, refusal to act, clearly extends to the case of a disclaimer—ie to a case where the person nominated as trustee has never accepted the office[20].

Unfitness or incapacity

With regard to a trustee becoming unfit to act (eg by virtue of his bankruptcy) or incapable of acting (eg by virtue of mental disorder), see p 753, ante.

Where a trustee who is incapable through mental disorder is also entitled in possession to some beneficial interest, no appointment of a new trustee in his place under s 36(1)(b) may be made without leave of the authority having jurisdiction under Part VII of the Mental Health Act 1983[1]. Thus a co-trustee cannot replace him but the person (if any) having express power in the trust instrument may replace him under s 36(1)(a), while, if his co-owner of land is his attorney under a registered enduring power of attorney, that co-owner[2] may appoint an additional trustee under s 36(6)(b), so that there are two trustees to give a valid capital receipt for the proceeds of sale of the land under an overreaching sale.

The appointor(s)

In the above statutory cases, the appointment of new trustees must be made in writing (normally a deed to take advantage of the vesting provisions in s 40 of the Trustee Act 1925[3]) by the person(s) nominated for the purpose of appointing new trustees by the trust instrument or if there be no such person (or no such person able and willing to act) then by the surviving or continuing trustee(s) or the personal representatives of the last surviving or continuing trustee. A 'continuing' trustee includes a refusing or a retiring trustee if willing to act in making the new appointment[4]: the practice is for them to participate in the appointment if possible. A sole surviving trustee cannot appoint new trustees by his will[5] so that in such eventuality it will fall to his personal representatives to appoint new trustees.

Increase or reduction in number of trustees

By s 37 of the Trustee Act 1925[6], on an appointment under the statutory power, the number of the trustees may be increased (but not to more than

---

20 See *Re Hadley* (1851) 5 De G & Sm 67; *Re Birchall* (1889) 40 Ch D 436.
 1 Section 36(9) of the TA 1925, as amended by the Mental Health Act 1983; see p 758, ante.
 2 Section 36(6A) of the TA 1925 as amended by the Trustee Delegation Act 1999, s 8: see p 757 ante.
 3 See p 776, post.
 4 TA 1925, s 36(8).
 5 *Re Parker's Trusts* [1894] 1 Ch 707.
 6 See p 758, ante.

four in the case of trusts of land) or diminished so long as there will then be either a trust corporation (incorporated in a European Union State) or at least two persons to perform the trust[7], unless only one trustee was originally appointed and a sole trustee will be able to give valid receipts for all capital money. Thus a sole surviving trustee will not be discharged by the appointment of one only in his place unless the new trustee is a trust corporation. The question whether the number could be increased or diminished under a special power, depended on the interpretation of the power itself[8], but, as the statutory power is exercisable by the same persons as would exercise the express power, the point appears to be merely academic. The court is generally indisposed to reduce the number unless an administration action is pending, or the fund is about to be paid into court or is immediately divisible[9]. By s 36(6) of the Act of 1925[10] the number of trustees can be increased by the appointment of an additional trustee when no vacancy exists if there are not more than three trustees (none of them being a trust corporation).

Severance of trusts

The provision in s 37(1)(b) of the Trustee Act 1925[11], authorising the severance of trusts by donees of the power of appointing new trustees applies notwithstanding that the trusts, although separate for a time when there are two life tenants, may ultimately again unite in favour of one individual[12].

It is conceived that four existing trustees of a will could not split themselves into two sets, two of the trustees taking over fund A and the other two trustees taking over fund B, for there would be no appointment of a *new* trustee for the whole *or any part* of the trust property. Whether, after a total extinguishment of all the trustees, new trustees can be appointed of part of the trust property, leaving the residue in the hands of the executors of the last surviving trustee, seems doubtful, and has been answered in the negative by the Irish Courts[13].

Where donees of express power differ, or one incapable, the statutory power is available

Where there are joint donees of a power of appointment named in the settlement, and they differ as to the person to be appointed, they will be deemed to be 'unable or unwilling', to appoint, so as to vest the statutory

---

7 Unless the trust instrument authorises trustees to replace themselves and be discharged even if they appoint a trust corporation not incorporated in a European Union State, so long as no land in England and Wales is part of the trust property, when the appointment of a new sole trustee will only be valid if it is a European Union trust corporation capable of giving a valid receipt for capital moneys: see p 448, ante and p 797, post.
8 *Meinertzhagen v Davis* (1844) 1 Coll 335 at 341; *Miller v Priddon* (1852) 1 De GM & G 335; *Re Bathurst's Estate* (1854) 2 Sm & G 169; See *Earl of Lonsdale v Beckett* (1850) 4 De G & Sm 73; but cf *Re Cunningham and Bradley to Wilson* [1877] WN 258; and *West of England etc Bank v Murch* (1883) 23 Ch D 138.
9 *Re Skeats' Settlement* (1889) 42 Ch D 522; *Re Newen* [1894] 2 Ch 297; *Re Gardiner's Trusts* (1886) 33 Ch D 590.
10 See p 757, ante.
11 See p 758, ante.
12 *Re Hetherington's Trusts* (1886) 34 Ch D 211; *Re Moss's Trusts* (1888) 37 Ch D 513.
13 *Re Nesbitt* (1887) 19 LR Ir 509.

power in the surviving or continuing trustees[14]. It may be observed that the statutory power is not imperative, and imposes no obligation on the donee of the power to appoint new trustees[15]; and that it is exercisable by an express donee notwithstanding that the personal representatives of the last surviving trustee have acted as trustees[16].

PARAGRAPH 1(C)

Appointment of new trustees by the court

The court has an inherent jurisdiction to appoint trustees in proceedings where an order has been made for administration or execution of the trusts. But the jurisdiction of the court to appoint new trustees most frequently exercised is that conferred and governed by the following section of the Trustee Act 1925:

41.—(1) The court[17] may, whenever it is expedient to appoint a new trustee or new trustees, and it is found inexpedient difficult or impracticable so to do without the assistance of the court, make an order appointing a new trustee or new trustees, either in substitution for or in addition to any existing trustee or trustees, or although there is no existing trustee.

In particular and without prejudice to the generality of the foregoing provision, the court may make an order appointing a new trustee in substitution for a trustee who is incapable by reason of mental disorder within the meaning of the Mental Health Act 1983 of exercising his functions as trustee, or is a bankrupt, or is a corporation which is in liquidation or has been dissolved[18].

(2) The power conferred by this section may, in the case of a deed of arrangement within the meaning of the Deeds of Arrangement Act 1914, be exercised either by the High Court or by the court having jurisdiction in bankruptcy in the district in which the debtor resided or carried on business at the date of the execution of the deed.

(3) An order under this section, and any consequential vesting order or conveyance, shall not operate further or otherwise as a discharge to any former or continuing trustee than an appointment of new trustees under any power for that purpose contained in any instrument would have operated.

(4) Nothing in this section gives power to appoint an executor or administrator.

42.—Where the court appoints a corporation, other than the Public Trustee, to be a trustee either solely or jointly with another person, the court may authorise the corporation to charge such remuneration for its services as trustee as the court may think fit.

43.—Every trustee appointed by a court of competent jurisdiction shall, as well before as after the trust property becomes by law, or by assurance, or otherwise, vested in him, have the same powers, authorities, and discretions, and may in all respects act as if he had been originally appointed a trustee by the instrument, if any, creating the trust.

It should be noted that a corporation appointed by the court in any par-

---

14 *Re Sheppard's Settlement Trusts* [1888] WN 234.
15 *Peacock v Colling* (1885) 33 WR 528; *Re Knight's Will* (1884) 26 Ch D 82.
16 *Re Routledge* [1909] 1 Ch 280.
17 Ie the High Court, or where the trust state does not exceed £30,000 in value, the county court. See County Courts Act 1984, s 23.
18 This provision has been amended by the Mental Health Act 1983 and by the Criminal Law Act 1967.

ticular case to be a trustee ranks as a trust corporation[19] and so is able on its own to give a valid receipt for capital moneys derived from land.

Examples of cases in which application to court is proper

Application should only be made to the court to appoint new trustees in cases where, for some reason or other, it is difficult, inexpedient, or impracticable to appoint them otherwise. Thus, where the donee of a power was anxious to exercise it corruptly, the court could not *under the statutory power* appoint over his head; although, of course, in an *action* to restrain him and to administer the trust it would have been a different matter[20].

No donee of the power, or none capable of acting

However, situations still arise in which it is inexpedient or impracticable to appoint new trustees out of court. Thus, if a last surviving or a sole trustee died intestate, and left no estate, so that no one will take out letters of administration to him, and no one is named in the settlement to appoint new trustees, it may be necessary to apply to the court.

Under similar powers conferred by earlier Acts the court has replaced a trustee who has become, through old age and infirmity, incapable of acting in the trust[1].

Appointment by court where no original trustees

Where, by inadvertence, or by reason of disclaimer, death, or otherwise, there never were any original trustees of the settlement, and no express power of appointing any, the court will appoint some[2].

Appointment by court where a minor is trustee or donee of an express power

Where a person appointed to be a trustee is a minor, and the statutory power is not available[3], the court will appoint another in his place, for the appointment of a minor to be a trustee in relation to any settlement or trust is void[4]. Where the donee of an express power of appointing new trustees is an infant it will almost always be desirable to seek the aid of the court. Though it appears that a minor can exercise such a power after he has reached years of some discretion, yet an appointment he may make will be liable to be set aside, and cannot therefore safely be acted upon[5].

---

19 TA 1925, s 68(18).
20 See *Re Hodson's Settlement* (1851) 9 Hare 118. And cf *Middleton v Reay* (1849) 7 Hare 106. But sometimes where the donee neglects to appoint (*Finlay v Howard* (1842) 2 Dr & War 490).
1 *Re Lemann's Trusts* (1883) 22 Ch D 633; *Re Phelps' Settlement Trusts* (1885) 31 Ch D 351.
2 *Dodkin v Brunt* (1868) LR 6 Eq 580; *Viscountess D'Adhermar v Bertrand* (1865) 35 Beav 19; *Re Smirthwaite's Trusts* (1871) LR 11 Eq 251; *Re Davis' Trusts* (1871) LR 12 Eq 214; *Re Moore* (1882) 21 Ch D 778; *Re Williams' Trusts* (1887) 36 Ch D 231.
3 Infancy of a trustee is one of the events in which the statutory power is exercisable; see TA 1925, s 36(1), p 756, ante.
4 LPA 1925, s 20.
5 *Re Parsons* [1940] Ch 973, [1940] 4 All ER 65.

Appointment by court in cases of doubt

If there be a doubt whether the statutory (or an express) power applies, the court will solve it by appointing new trustees itself[6].

Where there are not more than three trustees, the current trustees in the absence of someone with an express power of appointing new trustees can appoint an additional trustee without waiting for a vacancy so long as the total number is not increased beyond four[7]. If there is disagreement between co-trustees then the court may appoint an additional trustee but it will not normally appoint an additional trustee against the wishes of a sole trustee appointed by the settlor, in the absence of allegations against his honesty, even at the unanimous request of the existing beneficiaries[8], except where there is a trust of land, when, unless the sole trustee is a trust corporation, a valid receipt cannot be given by less than two trustees[9]. However, in an exceptional case it could appoint an additional trustee to ensure that repeated deficiencies in the administration of the trust ceased[10].

Appointment by court where the donees of power cannot agree

It has been held that where the power of appointing new trustees was given to a husband and wife jointly, and they were judicially separated, the husband being resident in Australia, it was inexpedient or difficult to appoint new trustees without the assistance of the court which, therefore, made the appointment on the petition of the wife and her children who were the sole beneficiaries[11]. The position is the same where the donees of the power cannot agree upon the choice of the new trustees: see as to this, p 762, ante.

Appointment by the court in cases of friction

The court will not in exercise of its statutory jurisdiction remove a trustee against his will and appoint another in his place where there is a dispute as to fact; but where there is no such dispute the court may resolve friction between trustees by making an order for the substitution of a new trustee for one of the existing trustees[12]. Where there is a dispute as to any relevant fact, the proper course is to invoke the inherent jurisdiction of the court over trustees in a Part 7 claim for administration or execution of the trusts.

It is not necessary that the trustee to be removed should have been guilty of any dishonesty or other misconduct if his continuance as trustee would impede the effectual execution of the trusts. Indeed, the court will remove a trustee and appoint a new one in his stead where the only complaint against him is that, from faults of temper, it has become impossible to transact the trust business with him. This sometimes appears to be a slur upon a perfectly honest but impracticable trustee; but, as Lord Blackburn said in *Letterstedt v Broers*[13]:

---

6 *Re Woodgate's Settlement* (1856) 5 WR 448.
7 TA 1925, s 36(6); p 757, ante.
8 *Re Badger* [1915] WN 166; see *Re Rendell's Trusts* (1915) 139 LT Jo 249.
9 LPA 1925, s 27(2); and see Article 74, post.
10 See *Titterton v Oates* [2001] WTLR 319.
11 *Re Somerset* [1887] WN 122.
12 *Re Henderson* [1940] Ch 764, [1940] 3 All ER 295.
13 (1884) 9 App Cas 371 at 386, 387; and see *Earl of Portsmouth v Fellows* (1820) 5 Madd 450.

'In exercising so delicate a jurisdiction as that of removing trustees, their lordships do not venture to lay down any general rule beyond the very broad principle ... that their main guide must be the welfare of the beneficiaries. Probably it is not possible to lay down any more definite rule in a matter so essentially dependent on details often of great nicety. ... It is quite true that friction or hostility between trustees and the immediate possessor of the trust estate, is not of itself a reason for the removal of trustees. But where the hostility is grounded on the mode in which the trust has been administered, ... it is certainly not to be disregarded. ... If it appears clear that the continuance of the trustee would be detrimental to the execution of the trusts, even if for no other reason than that human infirmity would prevent those beneficially interested, or those who act for them, from working in harmony with the trustee, and if there is no reason to the contrary from the intentions of the framer of the trust to give this trustee a benefit or otherwise, the trustee is always advised by his own counsel to resign, and does so. If, without any reasonable ground he refuses to do so, it seems to their lordships that the court might think it proper to remove him.'

Appointment by court where trustee is a criminal, bankrupt or incapable

Where a trustee has been convicted of a serious crime[14] or is a bankrupt[15], and refuses to join in the appointment of a new trustee in his place, the court can and will remove him, and appoint another person if the beneficiaries desire it[16], so also where a trustee has become incapable, by reason of mental disorder within the meaning of the Mental Health Act 1983, of exercising his functions as trustee[17], or has gone to reside permanently abroad[18], or has absconded.

Removal and appointment where breach of trust

It does not necessarily follow that new trustees will be appointed to replace trustees who have been guilty of a breach of trust, even if such trustees have defended their conduct till judgment has been given against them. It is still necessary to find 'something which induces the court to think either that the trust property will not be safe, or that the trust will not properly be executed in the interests of the beneficiaries'[19]. Thus, no order removing trustees held liable for a breach of trust and appointing new trustees was made where the trust fund had become distributable between beneficiaries of full age and capacity, some of whom did not want the trustees removed, taking into account the extra costs thereby involved which it seemed unnecessary to incur[20].

---

14 See note 19 on p 753, ante.
15 As to the procedure for appointing new trustees of a bankrupt solicitor's client account, see *Re A Solicitor* [1952] Ch 328, [1951] 1 All ER 133.
16 TA 1925, s 41, as amended: see pp 763–764, ante. And see *Coombes v Brookes* (1871) LR 12 Eq 61; *Re Adams' Trust* (1879) 12 Ch D 634; *Re Foster's Trusts* (1886) 55 LT 479; *Re Danson* (1899) 48 WR 73; *Re Henderson* [1940] Ch 764, [1940] 3 All ER 295.
17 TA 1925, s 41, as amended: see p 763, ante.
18 *Re Bignold's Settlement Trusts* (1872) 7 Ch App 223. As to the length of absence abroad, see *Hutchinson v Stephens* (1834) 5 Sim 498. For a case in which the court held it proper to displace a trustee resident in enemy-occupied territory in time of war, see *Re May's Will Trusts* [1941] Ch 109.
19 *Re Wrightson* [1908] 1 Ch 789 at 803. See also *Nissen v Grunden* (1912) 14 CLR 297; *Princess Ann of Hesse v Field* [1963] NSWR 998.
20 *Re Wrightson* [1908] 1 Ch 789 at 803. See also *Nissen v Grunden* (1912) 14 CLR 297; *Princess Ann of Hesse v Field* [1963] NSWR 998.

The general rule for removal of a trustee is that his 'acts or omissions must be such as to endanger the trust property or to show a want of honesty or a want of proper capacity to execute the duties or a want of reasonable fidelity'[1]. As Dixon CJ said in *Miller v Cameron*[2]:

'The jurisdiction to remove a trustee is exercised with a view to the interest of the beneficiaries, to the security of the trust property and to an efficient and satisfactory execution of the trusts and a faithful and sound exercise of the powers conferred upon the trustee.'

If hostility between the trustees prevents them from acting unanimously (as they must unless otherwise authorised) then one or all should be removed and replaced[3].

Section 41 does not confer the power simply to remove a trustee without appointing a new trustee in his place but the court has inherent power to do so if sufficient trustees remain or a receiver is appointed to safeguard the assets[4]. Indeed, in an emergency trustees may be removed on an interim application without notifying the defendants and a receiver appointed of the trust assets until appointment of new trustees after hearing the defendants[5].

Appointment defeating trustee's rights

In *Re Pauling's Settlement Trusts*[6] the plaintiff had previously brought a successful action against the defendant bank as trustee for breach of trust, and it had been ordered that two or more persons should be appointed new trustees of the settlement under s 41. On the reference pursuant to that order, the trustee bank objected to the appointment of new trustees at a time when an appeal and a cross-appeal were pending in the main action. One objection was that such an appointment would defeat the bank's right to impound the interest of the life tenant (who was said to have instigated the breaches of trust); but Wilberforce J held that a trustee's equitable right to impound is not defeated by the appointment of new trustees because it does not depend upon the trustee being in actual possession of the trust fund, and that the right of indemnity by way of impounding under s 62 of the Trustee Act 1925 (see Article 99, post) extends in favour of a former trustee. But he held that the order for appointment of new trustees should not be implemented for the time being because (inter alia) it would deprive the bank of its security for costs and also of the funds from which to pay the estate duty for which it might (depending on the result of the appeal) be liable and remain liable even if replaced by new trustees.

Trustee charged with breach of trust appointing a new trustee against plaintiff's wishes

Where a trustee, charged with breach of trust, appointed a new trustee

1 *Letterstedt v Broers* (1884) 9 App Cas 371 at 386.
2 (1936) 54 CLR 572 at 580 followed in *Re Roberts* (1983) 70 FLR 158; *Titterton v Oates* [2001] WTLR 319 and *Monty Financial Services Ltd v Delmo* [1996] 1 VR 65.
3 *Re Consiglio's Trusts* (1973) 36 DLR (3d) 658.
4 *Re Harrison's Settlement Trusts* [1965] 3 All ER 795 at 799; *Re Chetwynd's Settlement* [1902] 1 Ch 692, *Re Henderson* [1940] Ch 764; *Clarke v Heathfield (No 2)* [1985] ICR 606.
5 *Clarke v Heathfield* [1985] ICR 203.
6 [1963] Ch 576, [1963] 1 All ER 857.

against the claimant's wishes, both were removed[7]; and a similar course was followed where the donee of a power appointed a new trustee because the old one would not commit a breach of trust[8].

Summary procedure only applicable where trust is clear

The regular procedure for the appointment of new trustees by the court under the statutory jurisdiction is by claim form under Pt 8 of the Civil Procedure Rules[9]; but it would seem that where the trust is not clear on the face of written documents (eg where a conveyance is taken in the name of some other person than the real purchaser[10]), the court first requires the trust to be established to its satisfaction by a claim under Pt 7 of the Rules so as to resolve a substantial dispute of fact, as where the inherent jurisdiction to remove a trustee is invoked.

Appointing person to perform the duties incident to office of executor

Although s 41(4) of the Trustee Act 1925[11] expressly prohibits the court from appointing an executor or administrator, yet where a testator has not appointed a trustee of trust legacies (and, consequently, the trusteeship is incident to the office of executor), the court has jurisdiction when the estate has been cleared to appoint some one to perform those fiduciary duties in his place[12].

Section 50 of the Administration of Justice Act 1985 now confers power on the High Court to appoint a substitute for, or to remove, a personal representative where application in this behalf is made by a beneficiary interested in the deceased's estate or by a personal representative.

Practice on applications to the court

With regard to the practice on applications for the appointment of new trustees, ss 58, 59, and 60 of the Trustee Act 1925 are in the following words:

Persons entitled to apply for orders

58.—(1) An order under this Act for the appointment of a new trustee or concerning any interest in land, stock, or thing in action subject to a trust, may be made on the application of any person beneficially interested[13] in the land, stock or thing in action, whether under disability or not, or on the application of any person duly appointed trustee thereof.

(2) An order under this Act concerning any interest in land, stock, or thing in

---

7 *Peatfield v Benn* (1853) 17 Beav 522.

8 *Pepper v Tuckey* (1844) 2 Jo & Lat 95.

9 Even where the trustee whom it is desired to displace opposes (*Re Danson* (1899) 48 WR 73).

10 *Re Martin's Trusts Lands etc Improvement Co v Martin* (1887) 34 Ch D 618; and see also *Re Carpenter* (1854) Kay 418; and *Re Weeding's Estate* (1858) 4 Jur NS 707.

11 See p 763, ante.

12 *Re Moore* (1882) 21 Ch D 778; *Eaton v Daines* [1894] WN 32; and *Re Willey* [1890] WN 1; *Re Earl of Stamford* [1896] 1 Ch 288; and see TA 1925, s 68(17); (interpretation of 'trust' and 'trustee'); and see also *Re Ponder* [1921] 2 Ch 59; *Re Cockburn's Will Trusts* [1957] Ch 438, [1957] 2 All ER 522.

13 Held to include a contingent beneficiary (*Re Sheppard's Trusts* (1862) 4 De G F & J 423) and a purchaser of trust property (*Ayles v Cox* (1853) 17 Beav 584).

action subject to a mortgage may be made on the application of any person beneficially interested in the equity of redemption, whether under disability or not, or of any person interested in the money secured by the mortgage[14].

Power to give judgment in absence of a trustee

59.—Where in any action the court is satisfied that diligent search has been made for any person who, in the character of trustee, is made a defendant in any action, to serve him with a process of the court, and that he cannot be found, the court may hear and determine the action and give judgment therein against that person in his character of a trustee as if he had been duly served, or had entered an appearance in the action, and had also appeared by his counsel and solicitor at the hearing, but without prejudice to any interest he may have in the matters in question in the action in any other character.

Power to charge costs on trust estate

60.—The court may order the costs and expenses of and incident to any application for an order appointing a new trustee, or for a vesting order, or of and incident to any such order or any conveyance or transfer in pursuance thereof, to be raised and paid out of the property in respect whereof the same is made, or out of the income thereof, or to be borne and paid in such manner and by such persons as to the court may seem just.

PARAGRAPH 1(D)

Concurrent mental health jurisdiction

Section 54 of the Trustee Act 1925, as amended by the Mental Health Act 1983[15], provides for the concurrent jurisdiction of the High Court and of the judge or the authority having jurisdiction under Pt VII of the 1983 Act[16] in the four cases therein mentioned, namely in relation to (a) mortgaged property of which the patient has become a trustee merely because the mortgage has been paid off, (b) matters consequent on the making of provision by such authority for the exercise of a power of appointing trustees or retiring from a trust, (c) matters consequent on the making of provision by such authority for the carrying out of any contract entered into by the patient, and (d) property to some interest in which the patient is beneficially entitled but which, or some interest in which, is held by the patient under an express, implied or constructive trust.

In these cases application may still be made to the Court of Protection and this procedure will often be advantageous upon the score of convenience and economy as compared with an application in the Chancery Division. But if there is any substantial part of the trust property in which the patient has no beneficial interest, the application should be made to the Chancery Division[17].

14 See *Re Peacock* (1880) 14 Ch D 212.
15 See p 783, post.
16 The office is known as the Court of Protection: see s 93 of the 1983 Act.
17 *Jackson v Nerman* (1933) unreported. For the practice on applications see Heywood & Massey *Court of Protection Practice* (12th edn), Ch 15.

Paragraph 2

Only such powers pass to new trustees as are incident to the office

As above stated, every new trustee has the same powers, authorities, and discretions as if he had been an original trustee. This, however, only applies to powers, authorities, and discretions which, on the true construction of the trust instrument, are incident to the office, and not to mere naked powers given to the original trustees personally. The same principles are applicable to this as those already discussed under Article 71, ante, in relation to the survivorship of powers on the death of one of several trustees. Prima facie such powers are so incident[18].

Paragraph 3

Persons proper to be appointed new trustees

In selecting persons to be new trustees, the court acts upon the following principles, and it is apprehended that donees of powers *ought* to be guided by the same considerations. However, trustee have plenty of leeway in the exercise of their discretion. So long as their exercise of their power of appointment does not amount to a fraud on the power which in the eyes of equity[19] would make the exercise void, they only commit a breach of trust if the appointment is one that no properly informed trustee could make[20].

First, regard will be paid to the wishes of the settlor as expressed in, or plainly deduced from, the settlement.

Secondly, a person will not be appointed with a view to promoting the interest of some of the beneficiaries in opposition to the interest of others. It is said to be not proper to appoint new trustees without communicating with the beneficiaries and hearing their objections; at all events where it is likely that they would object[1]. The reason for this is that the attitude of the beneficiaries towards the new trustee could create bad relationships and impair the efficiency with which fiduciary duties are performed.

Thirdly, regard will be had to the question whether the appointment will promote or impede the execution of the trust; but the mere fact of a continuing trustee refusing to act with the proposed new trustee will not be sufficient to induce the court to refrain from appointing him[2] because that would give the continuing trustee a power of veto, but it may well be necessary to remove the continuing trustee if the trust is to be operated smoothly and efficiently.

Fourthly, a person will not normally be appointed if to do so would place him in a position in which his interest and his duty would be apt to conflict

---

18 *Re de Sommery* [1912] 2 Ch 622; and see *Innes (Inspector of Taxes) v Harrison* [1954] 1 All ER 884, [1954] 1 WLR 668. Also, see pp 29–34, ante.

19 *Cloutte v Storey* [1911] 1 Ch 18 at 31, so at common law a purchaser could acquire a legal title and be protected as a purchaser thereof without notice.

20 *Richard v Mackay* (1987) 11 Tru LI 23, Millett J (as he then was) pointing out that proposed appointment would be unchallengeable if 'not so inappropriate that no reasonable trustee could entertain it'. If it were so inappropriate then it would be liable to be set aside at the instance of a beneficiary who had not consented to it: *Re Whitehead's Will Trusts* [1971] 1 WLR 833 at 837.

1 *Marshall v Sladden* (1849) 7 Hare 428, and *O'Reilly v Alderson* (1849) 8 Hare 101.

2 *Re Tempest* (1866) 1 Ch App 485.

unless the settlement contemplates the possibility of such conflict, eg where the trustee of a pension fund may well also be a beneficiary[3].

Appointment by the donee of the power of himself

It was not settled before the Trustee Act 1925 to what extent the donee of a power of appointing new trustees could appoint himself[4]. However, the point is now settled by s 36(1) of the Trustee Act 1925[5] which expressly authorises the appointment of:

'one or more other persons (*whether or not being the persons exercising the power*)',

but this does not enable donees to appoint themselves to be additional trustees where no vacancy exists[6].

Appointment of person entitled to life interest

A person entitled for life has been held to be not improperly appointed[7], but such an appointment is certainly not advisable, for one of the main objects of a trustee is to protect the reversioner against the person entitled to income.

Appointment of remainderman

It has been held[8] that a reversioner is not a person whom *the court* will appoint, at all events where there is an infant entitled for life. For the interest of a person entitled in remainder is somewhat opposed to that of a tenant for life; and it would be for his advantage to lay out trust income in making improvements on the property, instead of making accumulations for the benefit of the tenant for life. Of course, however, such an objection would be inapplicable where a tenant for life is of full age and capacity and consents to the appointment, and in special circumstances the court will appoint a beneficiary[9].

Appointment of solicitor to the trust

The solicitor to the trust is normally not a proper person to be appointed a new trustee. Such an appointment would not, however, be bad, so as to invalidate the acts of the trustee so appointed; but the court will seldom make, or sanction, such an appointment unless a very special case is made out[10]. When such an appointment is made the appointee is generally

---

3 *Re Parsons* [1940] Ch 973; *Re Drexel Burnham Lambert UK Pension Plan* [1995] 1 WLR 32.
4 See *Re Sampson* [1906] 1 Ch 435; *Montefiore v Guedalla* [1903] 2 Ch 723; *Tempest v Lord Camoys* (1888) 58 LT 221; *Re Skeats' Settlement* (1889) 42 Ch D 522; and *Re Newen* [1894] 2 Ch 297; *Re Shortridge* [1895] 1 Ch 278.
5 See p 756, ante.
6 *Re Power's Settlement Trusts* [1951] Ch 1074, [1951] 2 All ER 513, CA.
7 *Forster v Abraham* (1874) LR 17 Eq 351; and see *Briggs v Parsloe* [1937] 3 All ER 831.
8 *Re Paine's Trusts* (1885) 28 Ch D 725.
9 *Ex p Conybeare's Settlement* (1853) 1 WR 458.
10 *Re Norris* (1884) 27 Ch D 333; and *Re Earl of Stamford* [1896] 1 Ch 288. The same rule is equally applicable to appointments of trustees for purposes of the Settled Land Act: *Re Kemp's Settled Estates* (1883) 24 Ch D 485; *Re Spencer's Settled Estates* [1903] 1 Ch 75. For acceptance of the appointor's own solicitor see *Re Cotter* [1915] 1 Ch 307.

required to undertake, should he become sole trustee, forthwith to appoint another to act with him.

Appointment of beneficiaries' bankers

In *Re Northcliffe's Settlements*[11] it was held by the Court of Appeal that there is no principle which would prevent a bank being appointed trustee merely because the beneficiaries are customers of the bank and, in fact, have overdrawn accounts.

Near relations

It used to be said that the court would never appoint a near relation of a beneficiary, except in case of necessity[12]. But this seems to be a counsel of perfection, and is not now followed in practice.

Persons out of jurisdiction appointed trustee

The provision in s 36(1) of the Trustee Act 1925 which enables a trustee who remains out of the UK for more than twelve months to be replaced does not make persons resident abroad ineligible to be appointed trustees. In *Re Whitehead's Will Trusts* Pennycuick V-C in 1971 summarised the traditional position as follows[13]:

> 'The law has been quite well established for upwards of a century that there is no absolute bar to the appointment of persons resident abroad as trustees of an English trust. I say "no absolute bar" in the sense that such an appointment would be prohibited by law and would consequently be invalid. On the other hand, apart from exceptional circumstances, it is not proper to make such an appointment, that is to say, the court would not, apart from exceptional circumstances, make such an appointment; nor would it be right for the donees of such a power to make an appointment out of court. If they did, presumably the court would be likely to interfere at the instance of the beneficiaries. There do, however, exist exceptional circumstances in which such an appointment can properly be made. The most obvious are those in which the beneficiaries have settled permanently in some country outside the UK and what is proposed to be done is to appoint new trustees in that country.'

Clearly, it will be proper to appoint as new trustees persons resident in another jurisdiction if the beneficiaries are resident in that jurisdiction, the trust assets are in, or will be transferred to, that jurisdiction, and the jurisdiction has its own trust law[14] or recognises and gives effect to foreign trusts[15]. In these circumstances the English court itself will be prepared to

11 [1937] 3 All ER 804, CA.
12 *Wilding v Bolder* (1855) 21 Beav 222.
13 [1971] 1 WLR 833 at 837. See also *Re Windeatt's Will Trusts* [1969] 1 WLR 692.
14 *Re Freeman's Settlement Trusts* (1887) 37 Ch D 148; *Re Liddiard* (1880) 14 Ch D 310; *Re Cunard's Trusts* (1878) 27 WR 52; *Re Austen's Settlement* (1878) 38 LT 601; *Re Hill's Trusts* [1874] WN 228; *Re Seale's Marriage Settlement* [1961] Ch 574, [1961] 3 All ER 136; *Meinertzhagen v Davis* (1844) 1 Coll 335.
15 *Re Windeatt's Will Trusts* [1969] 2 All ER 324, [1969] 1 WLR 692; *Re Whitehead's Will Trusts* [1971] 2 All ER 1334, [1971] 1 WLR 833. In *Re Weston's Settlements* [1969] 1 Ch 223, [1968] 3 All ER 338, CA, p 513, ante, an arrangement to export to Jersey was held not for the benefit of beneficiaries who had just settled in Jersey (perhaps temporarily). Jersey now has a trust law of its own: Trusts (Jersey) Law 1983. Implementation of The Hague 1984 Convention on The Law Applicable to Trusts and on their Recognition will assist: see Article 105, post.

appoint non-resident trustees or approve an arrangement under the Variation of Trusts Act 1958 by which non-resident trustees are appointed and the trust fund is exported. Indeed, in *Re Chamberlain*[16] an arrangement was approved for the export of a trust to Guernsey with Guernsey trustees where the primary beneficiaries were domiciled in France and the remaindermen were domiciled in Indonesia.

Nowadays, when it is the trustees who are proposing to exercise their discretion so as to appoint foreign trustees and who are considering seeking the declaratory authorisation of the court that this is within the leeway afforded to them, it seems that so long as there are some grounds for the trustees to believe that the proposed appointment is for the benefit of the beneficiaries there is no need to seek the protection of the court. As Millett J stated back in 1987[17]:

'The appropriateness is for the trustees to decide, and different minds may have different views on what is appropriate in particular circumstances. Certainly, in the conditions of today when one can have an international family with international interests and where they are as likely to make their home in one country as in another and as likely to choose one jurisdiction as another for the investment of their capital, I doubt that the language of Sir John Pennycuick is really in tune with the times. In my judgment, where the trustees retain their discretion, as they do in the present case, the court should need to be satisfied only that the proposed transaction is not so inappropriate that no reasonable trustee could entertain it.'

Thus, he held that the trustees could properly transfer part of the trust fund to the trustees of an ad hoc trust to be established in Bermuda with Bermudan resident trustees even though the beneficiaries had no connection with Bermuda. Although this did not involve the appointment of new trustees of an existing trust nothing turns on this distinction as recognised in *Re Whitehead's Will Trusts*[18]. However, Millett J did contrast cases where the court is asked to exercise a discretion of its own (eg under the Variation of Trusts Act 1958 or s 41 of the Trustee Act 1925) because in these cases the applicants have to make out a positive case for the court to exercise its discretion 'and the court is unlikely to assist them where the scheme is nothing more than a device to avoid tax and has no other advantages of any kind'.

It is crucial to ensure that the English trustees are duly discharged under s 37(1)(c) of the Trustee Act 1925[19], noting that there a trust corporation only covers European Union companies carrying on trust business.

Settlements subject to a foreign trust law

Even in the case of a foreign settlement the court has inherent jurisdiction to make *in personam* orders removing and replacing foreign trustees so long as the trustees are subject to the jurisdiction of the English court[20].

In drafting a settlement, if the possibility of appointing foreign trustees is considered, a clause should expressly authorise the appointment of foreign

---

16 Discussed in (1976) 126 NLJ 1034.
17 *Richard v Mackay* (1987) 11 Tru LI 23 reporting 4 March 1987 judgment followed by Vinelott J in *Re Beatty's Will Trusts (No 2)* (28 February 1991, reported in (1991) 11 Tru LI 77.
18 [1971] 1 WLR 833 at 838.
19 See p 758 ante.
20 *Chellaram v Chellaram* [1985] Ch 409.

trustees wherever resident and exempt the appointors from any liability so long only as they act in good faith. Indeed, express power might well be conferred on the trustees (perhaps with the consent of a 'protector') to replace the law governing validity of the trust, as well as the law governing matters of administration, by another law.

Appointment of an alien

The court usually refuses to appoint an alien as trustee unless he be permanently resident in England or special circumstances are present justifying appointment of a non-resident trustee.

Appointment of a trust company

Subject to the fact that a corporation could not hold real property in trust which it could not hold for its own benefit without licence in mortmain[1] an incorporated company could always be appointed an original sole trustee; but owing to the impossibility of making it a joint tenant with a natural person, it was impracticable to appoint such a company to be one of two or more trustees. This difficulty was, however, obviated by the Bodies Corporate (Joint Tenancy) Act 1899 by which a body corporate is rendered capable of being a joint tenant. In *Re Thompson's Settlement Trusts*[2] Swinfen-Eady J held that a company could be appointed one of several trustees under a power the words of which authorised the appointment 'of a new trustee or new trustees'. It is apparent that the statutory power contained in s 36 of the Trustee Act 1925[3] equally authorises the appointment of a company, for although that section empowers the appointment of 'another person or other persons', yet by the Interpretation Act 1978 the word 'person' in an Act of Parliament includes a corporation. It seems the same result should follow under a special power in similar terms since a company is a legal person, so that one would expect the word 'individual' to be used if human persons alone are to be trustees.

Corporation sole

A corporation sole may be a trustee: there is no principle that a conveyance to a corporation sole cannot take effect when a trust is imposed[4].

---

1 *Sonley v Clock-makers' Co* (1780) 1 Bro CC 81. The Mortmain Acts are now repealed: Charities Act 1960, ss 38 and 48, and Sch 7, Pt II.
2 [1905] 1 Ch 229. As to the effect on the legal estate of a corporation trustee being wound up see *Hastings Corpn v Letton* [1908] 1 KB 378; *Re No 9 Bomore Road* [1906] 1 Ch 359; and *Re Nos 56 and 58 Albert Road, Norwood* [1916] 1 Ch 289. But distinguish *Re Queenstown Dry Docks Shipbuilding and Engineering Co* [1918] 1 IR 356; after 1925 the court has express statutory jurisdiction to create a corresponding estate and vest it in the person entitled (LPA 1925, s 181).
3 See pp 756–757, ante.
4 *Bankes v Salisbury Diocesan Council of Education Inc* [1960] Ch 631, [1960] 2 All ER 372.

PARAGRAPH 5

Effect of invalid appointment of new trustee

An illustration of this paragraph of the present article is afforded by the case of *Pearce v Pearce*[5]. There A and B were trustees when a deed was prepared appointing C a new trustee in place of B. This was executed by C but by inadvertence it was not executed by the donees of the power to appoint trustees. It was therefore invalid. The trust fund was nevertheless transferred from the names of A and B into those of A and C. Afterwards A and C authorised the husband of the life tenant to receive the fund, and it was lost.

It was held that both B and C were liable—B because he had never ceased to be a trustee, and had yet denuded himself of the trust property, and C because she had intermeddled with trust property, and therefore became a constructive trustee. Whether B would now get full or partial relief under such circumstances under s 61 of the Trustee Act 1925[6] is, of course, another matter, depending on his honesty and the reasonableness of his conduct and on whether it appears to the court that he 'ought fairly to be excused'.

ARTICLE 74

Appointment of trustees for sale of land

(1) Appointments of new trustees of land and of new trustees of any trust of the proceeds of sale of the land shall, subject to any order of the court be effected by separate instruments, but in such manner as to secure that the same persons become the trustees of land and trustees of the trust.
(2) Where new trustees of land are appointed, a memorandum of the persons who are for the time being the trustees of the land shall be endorsed on or annexed to the conveyance by which the land was vested in trustees of land; and that conveyance shall be produced to the persons who are for the time being the trustees of the land by the person in possession of it in order for that to be done when the trustees require its production.

This article states the effect of s 35(1), (3), (4), of the Trustee Act 1925 as amended by the Trusts of Land and Appointment of Trustees Act 1996, Sch 3, para 3(10).

In view of the fact that unless a trust corporation[7] is a sole trustee there must be at least two trustees to give a receipt for proceeds of sale arising on the exercise of a trust for sale of English or Welsh land[8], it should be seen that appointment of individuals as new trustees of trusts of land always result in there being at least two trustees.

---

5 (1856) 22 Beav 248. Also *Adam & Co International Trustees Ltd v Theodore Goddard* [2000] WTLR 349.
6 See Art 95, post.
7 See 448, 797, ante.
8 See Article 63, ante.

ARTICLE 75

Vesting of trust property in new trustees

(1) On a change in the trusteeship out of court, the trust property should be vested jointly in the persons who as a result of such change become the trustees[9]. This may be done:
(a) by the ordinary modes of transferring property;
(b) except for the classes of property set out in section 40(4) of the Trustee Act 1925[10], by a vesting declaration, express or implied by statute, contained in a deed of appointment of a new trustee or in a deed of discharge of a retiring trustee;
(c) where neither of the foregoing means is available, by a vesting order made by a competent court[11].
(2) On the appointment of a new trustee by the court, a vesting order will be made vesting the trust property in the new trustee or trustees, either alone, or jointly with the continuing trustee or trustees, as the case may require.

PARAGRAPH 1(B)

Vesting declarations on appointments out of court

An implied vesting declaration is imported, subject to any express provision in the deed to the contrary, into any deed of appointment or discharge of new trustees by s 40 of the Trustee Act 1925[12], which is in the following terms:

(1)   Where by a deed a new trustee is appointed to perform any trust, then—
   (a)   if the deed contains a declaration by the appointor to the effect that any estate or interest in any land subject to the trust, or in any chattel so subject, or the right to recover or receive any debt or other thing in action so subject, shall vest in the persons who by virtue of the deed become or are the trustees for performing the trust, the deed shall operate, without any conveyance or assignment, to vest in those persons as joint tenants and for the purposes of the trust the estate interest or right to which the declaration relates[13], and
   (b)   if the deed is made after the commencement of this Act and does not contain such a declaration, the deed shall, subject to any express provision to the contrary therein contained, operate as if it had contained such a declaration by the appointor extending to all the estates interests and rights with respect to which a declaration could have been made.
(2)   Where by a deed a retiring trustee is discharged under section 39 of this Act or

---

9 TA 1925, s 37(1)(d).
10 See p 777, post.
11 Normally the application will be to the Chancery Division of the High Court, but in certain cases of small trust estates the county court has jurisdiction; TA 1925, s 63A inserted by County Courts Act 1984, Sch 2, para 1.
12 Re-enacting the Trustee Act 1893, s 12, which in its turn re-enacted the Conveyancing Act 1881, s 34.
13 See also, as to legal estates, s 9(1) of the LPA 1925 so that the estate if not vested is the appointor may vest in the appointees but not so as to obviate the difficulties apparent in *Re King's Will Trusts* [1964] Ch 542 discussed, p 778, post.

section 19 of the Trusts of Land and Appointment of Trustees Act 1996[14] without a new trustee being appointed, then—

(a) if the deed contains such a declaration as aforesaid by the retiring and continuing trustees, and by the other person, if any, empowered to appoint trustees, the deed shall, without any conveyance or assignment, operate to vest in the continuing trustees alone, as joint tenants, and for the purposes the trust, the estate, interest or right to which the declaration relates; and

(b) if the deed is made after the commencement of this Act and does not contain such a declaration, the deed shall, subject to any express provision to the contrary therein contained, operate as if it had contained such a declaration by such persons as aforesaid extending to all the estates, interests and rights with respect to which a declaration could have been made.

(3) An express vesting declaration, whether made before or after the commencement of this Act, shall, notwithstanding that the estate, interest, or right to be vested is not expressly referred to, and provided that the other statutory requirements were or are complied with, operate and be deemed always to have operated (but without prejudice to any express provision to the contrary contained in the deed of appointment or discharge) to vest in the persons respectively referred to in subsections (1) and (2) of this section, as the case may require, such estates, interests and rights as are capable of being and ought to be vested in those persons.

(4) This section does not extend—

(a) to land conveyed by way of mortgage for securing money subject to the trust, except land conveyed on trust for securing debentures or debenture stock;

(b) to land held under a lease which contains any covenant, condition or agreement against assignment or disposing of the land without licence or consent, unless, prior to the execution of the deed containing expressly or impliedly the vesting declaration, the requisite licence or consent has been obtained, or unless, by virtue of any statute or rule of law, the vesting declaration, express or implied, would not operate as a breach of covenant or give rise to a forfeiture;

(c) to any share, stock, annuity or property which is only transferable in books kept by a company or other body, or in manner directed by or under an Act of Parliament.

In this subsection 'lease' includes an underlease and an agreement for a lease or underlease.

(5) For purposes of registration of the deed in any registry, the person or persons making the declaration expressly or impliedly, shall be deemed the conveying party or parties, and the conveyance shall be deemed to be made by him or them under a power conferred by this Act.

(6) This section applies to deeds of appointment or discharge executed on or after the first day of January, 18 hundred and eighty-two.

With regard to the property which does not pass by a vesting declaration, mortgages are invariably transferred without disclosing the trust, so as to keep it off the face of the mortgagor's title. Stocks, shares, etc, are transferred via the CREST system or by transfer form, duly registered with the bank or company. It may be that equitable interests requiring to be transferred by signed writing (by s 53(1)(c) of the Law of Property Act 1925) do not pass by a vesting declaration, such declaration just extending to debts or other

---

14 Inserted by the TLATA 1996, Sch 3, para 3(14). Note that s 40(1) is unrestricted, so applying to appointments by deed under express powers, while s 40(2) does not cover retirements under express powers or the removal of a trustee under an express power.

choses in action which in context may be restricted to legal (and not equitable) choses in action since a debt is a legal chose in action. On the other hand, if the section is intended to extend to legal choses in action it should *a fortiori* extend to lesser interests like equitable choses in action, which is the preferable view. Where nominees hold assets on trust for the trustees, as often is the case, it makes sense for the new and continuing trustees to ensure that the nominees' register or electronic records duly acknowledge their entitlement. If no transfer by the retiring trustee is possible then an application to the court under s 44 of the Trustee Act is necessary.

In the case of registered land the Registrar is required by Land Registration Act 1925, s 47, to give effect on the register to any vesting order or vesting declaration made on the appointment or discharge of a trustee: the provisions of the Trustee Act 1925 relating to the appointment and discharge of trustees and the vesting of trust property apply to registered land *subject to the proper entry being made on the register*. To obviate the need for the Land Registry to check on the validity of the deed of appointment and then alter the register it is more convenient for the retiring current registered proprietors to execute a transfer to the new trustees as new proprietors[15].

Declaration operative only on property vested in trustees as trustees

In *Re King's Will Trusts*[16] Pennycuick J considered, inter alia, several points turning on the interpretation of s 40. In that case a will which imposed certain trusts upon freehold land was proved by two of the persons named as executors and trustees. Later, when the administration was complete and one of the proving executors had died, the surviving executor appointed another person to act jointly with him as trustee of the will. No assent had been executed in respect of the land. The question arose as to whether, by virtue of s 40, the legal estate was currently vested in these two persons as *trustees* of the will. Since the Deed of Appointment contained no express declaration vesting the land in them, their ownership of the legal estate depended upon the operation of the vesting declaration implied by s 40(1)(b).

Two main arguments were put forward to show that the legal estate was vested in the two persons concerned. First, it was said that no written assent was necessary to transfer a legal estate in land from a person in his capacity as executor to the same person in his capacity as trustee; that since administration of the estate had been completed the surviving executor therefore held the legal estate as trustee when he made the Deed of Appointment; and that s 40 therefore operated in the usual, straightforward way.

Of this argument, which has been considered more fully at p 455, ante, it suffices to say that it was rejected, the learned judge holding that s 36 of the Administration of Estates Act 1925 makes a written assent necessary to transfer the legal estate from an executor to a trustee, even when the executor and the trustee are one and the same person. Since no written assent had been made, the legal estate was therefore vested in the appointor as *executor* when he made the appointment.

Even so it was argued, secondly, that the Deed of Appointment was, under s 40(1)(b), deemed to include a declaration by the appointor which operated

15 See Land Registration Act 2002, s 27.
16 [1964] Ch 542, [1964] 1 All ER 833. See also pp 20 and 455, ante. It has not been followed in Ireland: *Mohan v Roche* [1991] 1 IR 560.

to vest in himself and the new trustee 'any estate or interest in any land subject to the trust'; and that since the appointor was in this case also the executor the implied declaration must extend to land which he held in his capacity as executor, so that the Deed of Appointment amounted also to an assent or conveyance by which the surviving executor vested the land in himself and the new trustee as trustees of the will.

This argument was supported by a reference to s 9(1) of the Law of Property Act 1925 which, so far as material, provides that:

> '... every vesting declaration (express or implied) under any statutory power ... which is made for the purpose of vesting, conveying, or creating a legal estate, shall operate to convey or create the legal estate disposed of in like manner as if the same had been a conveyance executed by the estate owner of the legal estate ...'.

and this was said to make it clear that the Deed of Appointment must be read as containing a conveyance by the surviving executor in that capacity (he being 'the estate owner') to the two persons who were to become the trustees. But this argument was also rejected. The implied vesting declaration operates only upon 'land subject to the trust', and the learned judge held that this meant land which was already trust property and could not include land which was still vested in the executor as such.

PARAGRAPHS 1(C) AND 2

Vesting orders made by the Chancery Division

The jurisdiction of the Chancery Division to make orders vesting trust property in any part of Her Majesty's dominions except Scotland[17] in the trustees for the time being of a settlement is codified in ss 44, 45, 49, 50–56 and 58 of the Trustee Act 1925, which are set out below. For the sake of convenience comments thereon are relegated to the footnotes.

Vesting orders of land

44.—In any of the following cases, namely—
(i) Where the court appoints or has appointed a trustee or where a trustee has been appointed out of court under any statutory or express power;
(ii) Where a trustee entitled to or possessed of any land[18] or interest therein, whether by way of mortgage or otherwise, or entitled to a contingent right therein, either solely or jointly with any other person—
   (a) is under disability[19], or
   (b) is out of the jurisdiction of the High Court[20]; or
   (c) cannot be found, or, being a corporation, has been dissolved[1];

---

17 TA 1925, s 56. The width of this jurisdiction (see on 'HM's Dominions' Halsbury's Laws of England (4th edn) Vol 6, para 803) is unlikely to be invoked nowadays when the relevant overseas jurisdiction where the land or the valuable assets are situate would seem more appropriate.
18 This includes leaseholds; see definition of 'land', TA 1925, s 68.
19 This includes mental illness: see s 54, p 783, post. See also note 9, on p 782, post.
20 A mere temporary absence (eg that a sailor) is not sufficient: *Hutchinson v Stephens* (1834) 5 Sim 498.
1 This is intended to put an end to such question as arose in *Re Nos 56 and 58 Albert Road, Norwood* [1916] 1 Ch 289; and *Re Queenstown Dry Docks Shipbuilding and Engineering Co* [1918] 1 IR 356.

(iii) Where it is uncertain who was the survivor of two or more trustees jointly entitled to or possessed of any interest in land[2];

(iv) Where it is uncertain whether the last trustee known to have been entitled to or possessed of any interest in land is living or dead[3];

(v) Where there is no personal representative of a deceased trustee who was entitled to or possessed of any interest in land, or where it is uncertain who is the personal representative of a deceased trustee who was entitled to or possessed of any interest in land[4];

(vi) Where a trustee jointly or solely entitled to or possessed of any interest in land, or entitled to a contingent right therein, has been required, by or on behalf of a person entitled to require a conveyance of the land or interest or a release of the right, to convey the land or interest or to release the right, and has wilfully refused or neglected to convey[5] the land or interest or release the right for twenty-eight days after the date of the requirement;

(vii) Where land or any interest therein is vested in a trustee whether by way of mortgage or otherwise, and it appears to the court to be expedient;

the court may make an order (in this Act called a vesting order) vesting the land or interest therein in any such person in any such manner and for any such estate or interest as the court may direct, or releasing or disposing of the contingent right to such person as the court may direct:

Provided that—

(a) Where the order is consequential on the appointment of a trustee the land or interest therein shall be vested for such estate as the court may direct in the persons who on the appointment are trustees; and

(b) Where the order relates to a trustee entitled or formerly entitled jointly with another person, and such trustee is under disability or out of the jurisdiction of the High Court or cannot be found, or being a corporation has been dissolved, the land interest or right shall be vested in such other person who remains entitled, either alone or with any other person the court may appoint.

Orders as to contingent rights of unborn persons

45.—Where any interest in land is subject to a contingent right in an unborn person or class of unborn persons who, on coming into existence would, in respect thereof, become entitled to or possessed of that interest on any trust, the court may make an order releasing the land or interest therein from the contingent right, or may make an order vesting in any person the estate or interest to or of which the unborn person or class of unborn persons would, on coming into existence, be entitled or possessed in the land.

---

2 Cf s 55, p 784, post.

3 Cf s 55, p 784, post.

4 Cf s 55, p 784, post; and see *Re William's Trusts* (1887) 36 Ch D 231; *Re Rackstraw's Trusts* (1885) 52 LT 612; and *Re Pilling's Trusts* (1884) 26 Ch D 432.

5 A trustee's conduct in not conveying cannot be considered wilful, if the title of the applicant to call for a conveyance is subject to a dispute which leads the trustee to entertain a bona fide doubt as to his title (*Re Mills' Trusts* (1888) 40 Ch D 14). But if he has acted unreasonably he may have to pay the costs (*Re Knox's Trust* [1895] 1 Ch 538; affd [1895] 2 Ch 483, CA). The claim must not even be issued until the twenty-eight days have elapsed (*Re Knox's Trust*, ante). The Law Reform Committee 23rd Report (Cmnd 8733) para 5.8 recommends removal of 'wilfully' from s 44(vi) in line with s 51(1)(ii). Where one or more beneficiaries are absolutely beneficially entitled to the land so as having rights to replace the trustees under s 19 of the TLATA 1996 it seems the court will vest the land directly in such person or persons preferring the approach in *Re Godfrey's Trusts* (1883) 23 Ch D 205 to that in *Re Holland* (1881) 16 Ch D 672 and *Re Currie* (1878) 10 Ch D 93. Saving expense and circuity of action fits in with the philosophy reflected in the Civil Procedure Rules.

Effect of vesting order

49.—A vesting order under any of the foregoing provisions shall in the case of a vesting order consequential on the appointment of a trustee, have the same effect

(a) as if the persons who before the appointment were the trustees, if any, had duly executed all proper conveyances of the land for such estate or interest as the court directs; or

(b) if there is no such person, or no such person of full capacity, as if such person had existed and been of full capacity and had duly executed all proper conveyances of the land for such estate or interest as the court directs;

and shall in every other case have the same effect as if the trustee or other person or description or class of persons to whose rights or supposed rights the said provisions respectively relate had been an ascertained and existing person of full capacity, and had executed a conveyance or release to the effect intended by the order.

Power to appoint person to convey

50.—In all cases where a vesting order can be made under any of the foregoing provisions, the court may, if it is more convenient, appoint a person to convey the land or any interest therein or release the contingent right, and a conveyance or release by that person in conformity with the order shall have the same effect as an order under the appropriate provision.

Vesting orders as to stock and things in action

51.—(1) In any of the following cases, namely:—

    (i)   Where the court appoints or has appointed a trustee, or where a trustee has been appointed out of court under any statutory or express power,

    (ii)   Where a trustee entitled, whether by way of mortgage or otherwise, alone or jointly with another person to stock[6] or to a thing in action—

        (a) is under disability, or

        (b) is out of the jurisdiction of the High Court; or

        (c) cannot be found, or, being a corporation, has been dissolved; or

        (d) neglects or refuses to transfer stock or receive the dividends or income thereof, or to sue for or recover a thing in action, according to the direction of the person absolutely entitled thereto for twenty-eight days next after a request in writing has been made to him by the person so entitled; or

        (e) neglects or refuses to transfer stock or receive the dividends or income thereof, or to sue for or recover a thing in action for twenty-eight days next after an order of the court for that purpose has been served on him;

    (iii) Where it is uncertain whether a trustee entitled alone or jointly with another person to stock or to a thing in action is alive or dead;

    (iv) Where stock is standing in the name of a deceased person whose personal representative is under disability;

    (v) Where stock or a thing in action is vested in a trustee[7] whether by way of mortgage or otherwise and it appears to the court to be expedient;

the court may make an order vesting the right to transfer or call for a transfer of stock, or to receive the dividends or income thereof, or to sue for or recover

---

6 As to meaning of stock, see s 68(14).

7 Where stock is vested in the Public Trustee by virtue of the Administration of Estates Act 1925, s 9 as amended by Law of Property (Miscellaneous Provisions) Act 1994, s 14 he seems not a trustee within the meaning of this para because such vesting 'does not impose on him any duty, obligation or liability in respect of the property' so that a grant of representation will need to be taken out: *Re Deans* [1954] 1 All ER 496.

the thing in action, in any such person[8] as the court may appoint[9]:
Provided that—

(a)   Where the order is consequential on the appointment of a trustee, the right shall be vested in the persons who, on the appointment, are the trustees; and

(b)   Where the person whose right is dealt with by the order was entitled jointly with another person, the right shall be vested in the last-mentioned person either alone or jointly with any other person whom the court may appoint.

(2)   In all cases where a vesting order can be made under this section, the court may, if it is more convenient, appoint some proper person to make or join in making the transfer:

Provided that the person appointed to make or join in making a transfer of stock shall be some proper officer of the bank, or the company or society whose stock is to be transferred.

(3)   The person in whom the right to transfer or call for the transfer of any stock is vested by an order of the court under this Act, may transfer the stock to himself or any other person, according to the order, and the Bank of England and all other companies shall obey every order under this section according to its tenor.

(4)   After notice in writing of an order under this section it shall not be lawful for the Bank of England or any other company to transfer any stock to which the order relates or to pay any dividends thereon except in accordance with the order.

(5)   The court may make declarations and give directions concerning the manner in which the right to transfer any stock or thing in action vested under the provisions of this Act is to be exercised.

(6)   The provisions of this Act as to vesting orders shall apply to shares in ships registered under the Acts relating to merchant shipping as if they were stock.

Vesting orders of charity property

52.—The powers conferred by this Act as to vesting orders may be exercised for vesting any interest in land, stock, or thing in action in any trustee of a charity or society over which the court would have jurisdiction upon action duly instituted, whether the appointment of the trustee was made by instrument under a power or by the court under its general or statutory jurisdiction.

---

8 Nowadays to save expense and circuity of action, if there is a beneficiary who is absolutely entitled, it is believed that the court will normally vest the property directly in such beneficiary rather than in trustees for him as was the old practice (*Re Holland* (1881) 16 Ch D 672, CA): and see *Orwin v A-G* [1998] 2 BCLC 693, CA.

9 In *Re Harrison's Settlement Trusts* [1965] 3 All ER 795, [1965] 1 WLR 1492, Cross J considered the situation where one of the trustees has become disabled through mental illness and the court is asked to vest the trust property in the other trustees alone (under ss 44 and 51 of the TA 1925, above), without removing the disabled trustee from the trusteeship. He said that the court would very seldom take this course if the trust was a continuing one, because it was preferable to replace the disabled trustee entirely. Accordingly, following *Re Nash* (1881) 16 Ch D 503, he refused to accede to the application in the present case, which did involve a continuing trust. He referred to the cases of *Re Watson* (1881) 19 Ch D 384, and *Re Martyn* (1884) 26 Ch D 745, in which the court had acceded to such an application, but pointed out that in these cases the trusts were not continuing, the trust property being in fact due for distribution, so that the situation was different and the decisions in those cases were justified for that reason. He considered that the two reported cases in which the court had acceded to such an application in the case of a continuing trust, *Re Leon* [1892] 1 Ch 348, and *Re Lees' Settlement Trusts* [1896] 2 Ch 508, must be treated as exceptional and pointed out that the applications in those cases were unopposed.

Vesting orders in relation to infant's beneficial interests

53.—Where an infant is beneficially entitled to any property the court may, with a view to the application of the capital or income thereof for the maintenance, education, or benefit[10] of the infant, make an order—

(a) appointing a person to convey such property[11]; or

(b) in the case of stock, or a thing in action, vesting in any person the right to transfer or call for a transfer of such stock or to receive the dividends or income thereof, or to sue for and recover such thing in action, upon such terms as the court may think fit.

Jurisdiction of the High Court in regard to mental patients

54.—(1) Subject to the provisions of this section, the authority having jurisdiction under Part VII of the Mental Health Act 1983 shall not have power to make any order, or give any direction or authority, in relation to a patient who is a trustee if the High Court has power under this Act to make an order to the like effect.

(2) Where a patient is a trustee and a receiver appointed by the said authority is acting for him or an application for the appointment of a receiver has been made but not determined, then, except as respects a trust which is subject to an order for administration made by the High Court, the said authority shall have concurrent jurisdiction with the High Court in relation to—

(a) mortgaged property of which the patient has become a trustee merely by reason of the mortgage having been paid off;

(b) matters consequent on the making of provision by the said authority for the exercise of a power of appointing trustees or retiring from a trust;

(c) matters consequent on the making of a provision by the said authority for the carrying out of any contract entered into by the patient;

(d) property to some interest in which the patient is beneficially entitled but which, or some interest in which, is held by the patient under an express, implied or constructive trust.

---

10 These words are of the widest import (*Re Heyworth's Contingent Reversionary Interest* [1956] Ch 364, [1956] 2 All ER 21). They cover not merely expenditure but capital investment such as the purchase of a house to live in or a share in a partnership or even, in some cases, placing of money on deposit for an infant (*Re Baron Vestey's Settlement* [1951] Ch 209, [1950] 2 All ER 891, CA). However, to bring the jurisdiction into play there must be 'a view to the application' of the capital or income for the maintenance, education or benefit of the infant. In *Re Heyworth's Contingent Reversionary Interest*, above, what was proposed was the sale of an infant's contingent reversionary interest to the life tenant for cash, thus putting an end to the settlement. There was no suggestion that the transaction was necessary to enable the infant to be maintained till attaining full age and Upjohn J held that he had no jurisdiction under the section to sanction it. This case was distinguished in *Re Meux* ([1958] Ch 154, [1957] 2 All ER 630), where it was proposed to convey the entailed interest of an infant tenant in tail to his father the tenant for life and protector of the settlement for a proper price to be paid to trustees and settle it on virtually the same trusts as those under which the entailed interest arose except that the father would have no beneficial interest and the infant would have a contingent, as opposed to a vested interest. It was held that the settlement of the proceeds of sale, which on the authority of *Re Ropner's Settlement Trusts* [1956] 3 All ER 332n, [1956] 1 WLR 902, was an 'application', was an absolutely essential part of the transaction looked at as a whole, for no court would consider it fair merely to bar the entail and sell the property without making provision for interests subsequent to that of the infant. That led Wynn Parry J to the conclusion that he was dealing with one single transaction which was overwhelmingly in favour of the infant and that he had jurisdiction to approve it. For further cases in which the court appointed a person under s 53 to execute a disentailing deed, see *Re Bristol's Settled Estates* [1964] 3 All ER 939, [1965] 1 WLR 569, and *Re Lansdowne's Will Trusts* [1967] Ch 603, [1967] 1 All ER 888 (in which *Re Meux*, above, was applied).

11 See *Re Gower's Settlement* [1934] Ch 365, where the court authorised a mortgage of an infant's estate tail in remainder.

The Lord Chancellor may make rules[12] with respect to the exercise of the jurisdiction referred to in this subsection.

(3) In this section 'patient' means a patient as defined by section one hundred and one of the Mental Health Act 1959, or a person as to whom powers are exercisable and have been exercised under section one hundred and four of that Act.

Orders made upon certain allegations to be conclusive evidence

55.—Where a vesting order is made as to any land under this Act or under Part VII of the Mental Health Act 1983, as amended by any subsequent enactment, or under any act relating to lunacy in Northern Ireland, founded on an allegation of any of the following matters namely—

(a) the personal incapacity of a trustee or mortgagee; or

(b) that a trustee or mortgagee or the personal representative of or other person deriving title under a trustee or mortgagee is out of the jurisdiction of the High Court or cannot be found, or being a corporation has been dissolved; or

(c) that it is uncertain which of two or more trustees, or which of two or more persons interested in a mortgage, was the survivor; or

(d) that it is uncertain whether the last trustee or the personal representative of or other person deriving title under a trustee or mortgagee, or the last surviving person interested in a mortgage is living or dead; or

(e) that any trustee or mortgagee has died intestate without leaving a person beneficially interested under the intestacy or has died and it is not known who is his personal representative or the person interested;

the fact that the order has been so made shall be conclusive evidence of the matter so alleged in any court upon any question as to the validity of the order; but this section does not prevent the court from directing a reconveyance or surrender or the payment of costs occassioned by any such order if improperly obtained.

Application of vesting order to property out of England

56.—The powers of the court to make vesting orders under this Act shall extend to all property in any part of His Majesty's dominions except Scotland[13].

Persons entitled to apply for orders

58.—(1) An order under this Act for the appointment of a new trustee or concerning any interest in land, stock, or thing in action subject to a trust, may be made on the application of any person beneficially interested[14] in the land, stock, or thing in action, whether under disability or not, or on the application of any person duly appointed trustee thereof.

(2) An order under this Act concerning any interest in land, stock or thing in action subject to a mortgage may be made on the application of any person beneficially interested in the equity of redemption, whether under disability or not, or of any person interested in the money secured by the mortgage[15].

---

12 Further see Heywood & Massey *Court of Protection Practice* (12th edn).

13 Where there are investments or property situate in Scotland the court will give leave to the trustees to make application to the appropriate court in Scotland for a vesting order: See *Practice Direction* [1945] WN 80 and [1985] 1 All ER 884.

14 This includes a person contingently interested (*Re Sheppard's Trusts* (1862) 4 De GF & J 423).

15 Where the trust funds are invested in unauthorised stocks, the order will give the new trustees, *or purchasers from them*, the right to call for a transfer etc (*Re Peacock* (1880) 14 Ch D 212).

CHAPTER 15

Appointment of a judicial trustee

ARTICLE 76

Statutory power of the court to appoint a judicial trustee

(1) Where application is made to the court[1] by or on behalf of the person creating or intending to create a trust[2], or by or on behalf of a trustee or beneficiary, the court may in its discretion appoint a person (called a judicial trustee) to be a trustee for that trust, either jointly with any other person, or as sole trustee, and, if sufficient cause is shown, in place of all or any existing trustees[3]. An injunction may be granted to preserve the position until the hearing of the summons for the appointment of a judicial trustee. Where the application relates to the estate of a deceased person the court may if it thinks fit proceed as if the application were, or included, an application under section 50 of the Administration of Justice Act 1985 conferring power to appoint a substitute for, or to remove, a personal representative.

(2) Any fit and proper person nominated in the application may be appointed, including, a beneficiary, or the husband, wife, or relation of a beneficiary, or a solicitor to any of such parties or to the trust[4], or

---

1 The High Court or any county court judge to whom jurisdiction may be assigned under the Act by rules made thereunder (Judicial Trustees Act 1896, s 2). The appointment may be made by a Master of the Chancery Division.

2 The administration of the estate of a deceased testator or intestate is a trust, and his personal representative a trustee for the purposes of the Act (Judicial Trustees Act 1896, s 1(2)). The Act, however, contains no complete definition of the word 'trust', which must therefore be given its ordinary meaning, with the result that Settled Land Act trustees are trustees of a trust for the purposes of the Act. See *Re Marshall's Will Trusts* [1945] Ch 217, [1945] 1 All ER 550.

3 Judicial Trustees Act 1896, s 1(1); Judicial Trustee Rules 1983, r 3. For an instance of appointment of two banks, each as sole judicial trustee of part of the trust estate, see *Re Cohen* [1918] WN 252. But this case related to trusteeship and was distinguished in *Re Wells* [1967] 3 All ER 908, [1968] 1 WLR 44, which was concerned with executorship: it was held that the court had no power to appoint a judicial trustee to deal with part only of an estate since the executorship was indivisible and the administration of this part of the estate was not a separate trust; and in the circumstances it would not be right to appoint a judicial trustee of the whole estate.

4 Recognised originally by Judicial Trustee Rules 1897, r 5(1) which Rules were revoked and replaced by Judicial Trustee Rules (SI 1972/1096) which were revoked and replaced by Judicial Trustee Rules 1983 (SI 1983/370).

a person who is already a trustee[5]. In the absence of such nomination, or if the court disapproves it[6], the official solicitor of the court, or some other person approved by the judge, may be appointed[7]. An unofficial judicial trustee must give security by way of guarantee unless the court otherwise directs[8].

(3) Remuneration may be assigned by the court to the judicial trustee[9].

(4) The evidence in support of an application must include an affidavit containing the following particulars so far as obtainable:

(a) a short description of the trust instrument;

(b) short particulars of the trust property with an approximate estimate of its income, and capital value;

(c) short particulars of any incumbrances affecting the property;

(d) particulars as to persons possessing trust documents;

(e) names and addresses of beneficiaries and short particulars of their interests;

(f) name, address and description of the proposed judicial trustee together with remuneration proposals[10].

(5) Once in every year the accounts of a judicial trustee have to be audited by an officer of the court, or a professional accountant appointed by the court or, in the case of a corporate judicial trustee, submitted to such persons as the court may direct, whereupon only if such person or a beneficiary objects will accounts have to be lodged with the court for examination by or on behalf of the court[11].

(6) The accounts, with a note of any corrections made on the audit, must be filed as the court directs, and the judicial trustee must send a copy of the accounts, or if the court thinks fit, a summary of the accounts to such beneficiaries or other persons as the court thinks proper[12].

(7) Where a judicial trustee has failed to comply with the 1896 Act or the 1983 Rules or any direction of the court or has otherwise misconducted himself in relation to the trust the court may subsequently disallow any remuneration; if he failed to pay any sum into the trust account within a reasonable period of time the court may charge him with interest currently payable in respect of judgment debts[13].

(8) The court may direct an inquiry into the administration of the

---

5 Recognised originally by Judicial Trustee Rules 1897, r 5(1) which Rules were revoked and replaced by Judicial Trustee Rules (SI 1972/1096) which were revoked and replaced by Judicial Trustee Rules 1983 (SI 1983/370).

6 Judicial Trustees Act 1896, s 1(3).

7 *Douglas v Bolam* [1900] 2 Ch 749.

8 Judicial Trustees Act 1896, s 4(1), and Judicial Trustee Rules 1983, r 6.

9 Judicial Trustees Act 1896, s 1(5).

10 Judicial Trustee Rules, r 3.

11 Judicial Trustees Act 1896, s 1(6), and Judicial Trustee Rules, rr 9, 12, 13.

12 Judicial Trustee Rules, rr 12, 13. The beneficiaries should be sent copies of any corrections or comments made on the audit in order that they may be in a position to take such proceedings as they may be advised in respect of any matters which are open to question. See *Re Ridsdel* [1947] Ch 597, [1947] 2 All ER 312.

13 Judicial Trustee Rules, r 14.

trust by the judicial trustee[14], and may, either with or without any request, give any special or general directions in regard to the trust or its administration[15].

(9) In all cases a judicial trustee is to be subject to the control and supervision of the court as an officer thereof[16], and may at any time request the court to give him directions[17].

(10) Where a judicial trustee fails to submit his account or do any other thing which he is required to do he may be required to attend in chambers to show cause for the failure and the court may give such directions as it thinks proper including directions for the discharge of the trustee and the appointment of another and the payment of costs[18].

(11) The appointment of an official of the court as a judicial trustee is an ex officio appointment so that no further order or appointment is necessary by reason only of the person appointed dying or ceasing to hold office: any property vested in such person on his dying or ceasing to hold office vests in the person appointed to succeed him without any conveyance assignment or transfer[19].

(12) An official of the court cannot be appointed as judicial trustee;

(a) for any persons in their capacity as members or debenture holders of, or being in any other relation to, any corporation or unincorporated body; or

(b) of a trust which involves the carrying on of any trade or business unless the court, with or without special conditions, specifically directs[20].

Purpose of the Act

The object of the Judicial Trustees Act 1896 was to provide a middle course in cases where the administration of the estate by the ordinary trustees had broken down and it was not desired to put the estate to the expense of a full administration. A high degree of protection for the property is secured—

(1) by the appointment of an official, or

(2) in the alternative, of a person who gives security for his honesty, and

(3) by having his accounts audited once a year, and

(4) generally requiring him to act in concert with the court and under conditions which enable the court to supervise his transactions.

Having regard to the fact that judicial trustees are almost always appointed in chambers, it is difficult to judge as to the extent to which this Act has been utilised, but it is believed not to have found great favour. There have, how-

---

14 Judicial Trustees Act 1896, s 1(6).
15 Judicial Trustees Act 1896, s 1(4).
16 Judicial Trustees Act 1896, s 1(3).
17 Judicial Trustee Rules, r 8. This may be done quite informally by a simple letter addressed to the officer of the court. This right to apply for directions does not exclude the ordinary power of a trustee to compromise claims under the Trustee Act 1925, s 15(f). See *Re Ridsdel* [1947] Ch 597, [1947] 2 All ER 312.
18 Judicial Trustee Rules, r 14.
19 Judicial Trustee Rules, r 16.
20 Judicial Trustee Rules, r 15.

ever, been cases where the appointment of a judicial trustee has been of the greatest benefit to the beneficiaries; in one unreported case, which came to the knowledge of the late Sir Arthur Underhill, such an appointment was the means of extricating a fund and its beneficiaries from a morass of cost and complexity such that, but for the appointment of a judicial trustee, the parties would have felt constrained, having regard to their limited means, to abandon their attempt to secure the fund. For similar reasons it may be helpful and cost-efficient for members of a pension scheme trust to have a judicial trustee appointed to help unscramble the muddled affairs of the trust[1]. Again, in the well-known and complicated *Diplock* litigation[2] the appointment of a judicial trustee was clearly an advantage as was recognised by the fact that he was allowed a separate set of costs in the actions by the next of kin to recover moneys paid away by the executors under an invalid residuary bequest.

When there was no machinery for the retirement of a personal representative the machinery for the appointment of a judicial trustee in his place could be invoked, but a replacement can now more conveniently be achieved by appointment of a replacement under s 50 of the Administration of Justice Act 1985. In an application under the Judicial Trustees Act 1896 the court may now proceed as if the application were under the 1985 Act and vice versa[3].

Discretion of the court

The power of the court to appoint a judicial trustee is purely discretionary, and will not be exercised where no charge of improper conduct is made against an existing trustee who opposes the application, even where he or she is a sole trustee[4]; nor where the donee of the power of appointing trustees has appointed persons able and willing to act[5]; nor will the court as a rule appoint a judicial trustee to act with a private one[6].

Rules

In compliance with s 4 of the Act, a code of thirty-five rules was made in 1897, but the position is now governed by the Judicial Trustee Rules 1983. Remuneration has to be authorised by the court which will normally direct it to be fixed by reference to such scales or rates of professional charges as it thinks fit: see rule 11.

---

1 *McDonald v Horn judgment of Vinelott J* (1993) Times, 12 October. On appeal see [1995] 1 All ER 961, CA.
2 *Chichester Diocesan Fund and Board of Finance Inc v Simpson* [1944] AC 341, [1944] 2 All ER 60, HL; *Re Diplock* [1948] Ch 465, [1948] 2 All ER 318, CA; affd sub nom *Ministry of Health v Simpson* [1951] AC 251, [1950] 2 All ER 1137, HL. Also see *Bowen-Jones v Bowen-Jones* [1986] 3 All ER 163 where both sides agreed to the court appointing a chartered accountant to be judicial trustee to resolve the accounts and distribute property between the absolutely entitled beneficiaries.
3 Administration of Justice Act 1985, s 50(4), Judicial Trustees Act 1896, s 1(7) added by the 1985 Act.
4 *Re Ratcliff* [1898] 2 Ch 352 (an ordinary trustee was appointed instead, nominated by the sole executrix).
5 *Re Chisholm* (1898) 43 Sol Jo 43.
6 See also *Re Martin* [1900] WN 129.

CHAPTER 16

The Public Trustee

Article
77 The nature and functions of the Public Trustee, and the guarantee of the State to be answerable for his breaches of trust   789
78 The appointment of the Public Trustee as an ordinary trustee   794
79 The appointment and removal of the Public Trustee or certain corporate bodies as mere 'custodian trustee'   796
80 The respective duties, rights, and liabilities of the custodian trustee and managing trustees   799
81 Special rules relating to the Public Trustee   801

ARTICLE 77

The nature and functions of the Public Trustee, and the guarantee of the State to be answerable for his breaches of trust

(1) The Public Trustee is a corporation sole established by statute[1]. He is a salaried official, prohibited from acting for personal reward[2] and empowered to act where appointed[3]:

(a) as an ordinary trustee either alone or jointly with others[4];

(b) as a mere 'custodian trustee', or treasurer, the administration being confided to ordinary trustees called 'managing trustees';

(c) as a judicial trustee[5]; and

(d) in certain other capacities not falling within the law of private trusts[6].

(2) The Public Trustee is, on the other hand, forbidden to accept:

---

1 Public Trustee Act 1906. The statute only applies to English trusts, and the Public Trustee has no power to accept the trusts of a foreign instrument, eg a Scottish trust disposition and settlement (*Re Hewitt's Settlement* [1915] 1 Ch 228; but cf *Re Ardagh's Estate* [1914] 1 IR 5). One appointee is both Public Trustee and Official Solicitor to the Supreme Court.
2 Public Trustee Act 1906, s 11(1).
3 Public Trustee Act 1906, s 2(1).
4 Public Trustee Act 1906, s 5(1).
5 As to judicial trustees, see Article 76, ante.
6 Such as the office of executor or administrator, the administration of small estates under £1,000 (which means estates of deceased persons not trust estates) (*Re Devereux* [1911] 2 Ch 545).

(a) any trust exclusively for religious or charitable purposes[7];

(b) any trust made solely by way of security for money[8];

(c) any trust for the benefit of creditors[9];

(d) any trust involving the management or carrying on of a business[10];
save only—

   (i) where he is merely custodian trustee without power of management, and either holds no property which exposes him to risk, or the circumstances are exceptional, and he is fully indemnified; or

   (ii) where, being an ordinary trustee, the circumstances are exceptional, and he either obtains the consent of the Treasury, or accepts the trusteeship for a time not exceeding 18 months with a view only to winding up the business, and is satisfied that it can be carried on without risk or loss.

(3) The Public Trustee is only offered by the State as an alternative to ordinary private persons, and therefore can only act where appointed as mentioned in Article 78, post. Moreover, he may decline to act, or may prescribe conditions on which alone he will accept the appointment; save only that he is forbidden to decline merely on the ground that the estate is of small value[11].

(4) The Public Trustee has the same powers, duties, and liabilities, and is entitled to the same rights and immunities and is subject to the same control and jurisdiction of the court, as a private person acting in the same capacity[12], though the State guarantees the beneficiaries against his breaches of trust, including the acts and defaults of his officers[13].

(5) For the services of the Public Trustee and the State guarantee, the State charges an acceptance fee, an administration fee and a withdrawal fee in respect of all trusts together with additional fees for special services[14].

(6) Where a person dies intestate his estate vest in the Public Trustee until the grant of administration to such estate, as also is the position where a testator dies and at the time of his death there is no executor with power to obtain probate of the will or at any time before probate of the will is granted there ceases to be any executor with power to obtain probate: the vesting of the estate in the Public Trustee does not

---

7 Public Trustee Act 1906, s 2(5). This includes trusts under which the trustee has to select charitable objects (*Re Hampton* (1918) 88 LJ Ch 103).

8 Public Trustee Rules 1912, r 6.

9 Public Trustee Act 1906, s 2(4).

10 Public Trustee Act 1906, s 2(4).

11 Public Trustee Act 1906, s 2(3).

12 Public Trustee Act 1906, s 2(2).

13 Public Trustee Act 1906, s 7(1).

14 Public Trustee Act 1906, s 9; Public Trustee (Fees) Act 1957; and Public Trustee (Fees) Order 1999, SI 1999/855.

confer on him any beneficial interest in, or impose on him any duty, obligation or liability in respect of, the property[15].

Paragraph 1

Establishment of a Public Trustee

The Public Trustee Act 1906 was passed not only with the object of meeting the increasing difficulty of finding suitable persons to act as trustees, but also to safeguard beneficiaries against those fraudulent misappropriations by trustees which had previously been unpleasantly frequent. The Act also contains provisions for the appointment of what are in the Act called custodian trustees (as distinguished from those trustees who actively manage the trust), and for the auditing of trust accounts. The Act further provides for the administration of small estates not exceeding £1,000 in value by the Public Trustee in place of the court, and enables the Public Trustee to accept the offices of executor or administrator. As, however, those are matters outside the law of trusts, it is proposed in this work to confine the consideration of the Act to matters affecting the appointment of the Public Trustee (and certain corporate bodies) to trusteeships, custodian and ordinary. The provisions relating to the auditing of ordinary trust accounts by the Public Trustee will be considered later on in Article 86, post.

Paragraph 2

Trusts the Public Trustee may not accept

It is considered that the exception of trusts *exclusively* for religious or charitable purposes does not include the trusts of a will some of which are private and others charitable; eg where residue is given to the testator's widow for life, and after her death to divers charities[16].

The exception of trusts by way of security for money rules out trust deeds for securing debentures or debenture stock, and those rare mortgages which are drafted in the form of trusts. Deeds of arrangement for the benefit of creditors do not, it is conceived, include those trust deeds which are made for the convenience of the debtor rather than for the benefit of the creditors, which have been discussed at pp 140 et seq, ante.

The exception of trusts which involve the management of a business was obviously necessary, as no public official could be expected to carry on commercial undertakings.

---

15 Administration of Estate Act 1925, s 9 as substituted by Law of Property (Miscellaneous Provisions) Act 1994, s 14.
16 The Public Trustee accepted the trusts of the will of George Bernard Shaw containing gifts in aid of the reform of the alphabet, which were, however, held by Harman J not to be charitable; *Re Shaw* [1957] 1 All ER 745, [1957] 1 WLR 729; compromised on appeal [1958] 1 All ER 245n.

PARAGRAPH 3

Not compulsory

The Public Trustee is merely offered as a convenience and safeguard to those who care to avail themselves of his services, and not to all of those, as he is given a discretion as to whether or not he will accept a trust, the only restriction being that he must not refuse solely on the ground that the property is small. No appointment of the Public Trustee as a trustee should be made without his formal consent to act[17], which is usually incorporated in the deed of appointment. A testamentary appointment will only become effective if and when the formal consent is given[18].

PARAGRAPH 4

State guarantee

The Public Trustee is in exactly the same position as a private trustee with regard to the beneficiaries, with the addition that the State guarantees that it will make good *any losses which an ordinary trustee would be liable to make good*, taking into account the terms of the trust instrument as in the case of a private trustee. At one time there seems to have been an impression among the general public that the State not only gives this guarantee, but goes further, and guarantees the beneficiaries against all loss, whether arising from breach of trust or depreciation of securities. Needless to say that was a popular error. Still a guarantee which covers fraud and negligence is not to be treated lightly, particularly when it is united with that official cautious coldheartedness which precludes all chance of those frequent breaches of trust which result from tender-heartedness.

PARAGRAPH 5

Fees payable to the Public Trustee

The Public Trustee (Fees) Act 1957 provides that the power to fix fees chargeable in respect of the duties of the Public Trustee shall be exercised by orders made by statutory instrument, which must prescribe whether each fee is to be paid out of capital or income, and power is conferred on the Public Trustee, where a fee is payable out of capital, to direct, with the consent of the beneficiary entitled to the income, if he is of full age, that it shall be paid out of income[19].

The Public Trustee (Fees) Order 1999[20] contains the current fees payable. Since these fees are likely to change quite often there is little point in noting them but the fees are an acceptance fee, an administration fee and a withdrawal fee whilst additional fees are prescribed for certain particular services.

All these fees are to be paid out of capital, except the following which are

---

17 Public Trustee Rules 1912, r 8, though a subsequent formal consent will be effective if given: *Re Shaw* [1914] WN 141.
18 Public Trustee Rules 1912, r 8.
19 Public Trustees (Fees) Act 1957, s 1.
20 SI 1999/855.

to be paid out of income[1]:
(a) Fees which under s 1(3) of the Act of 1957 the Public Trustee directs to be paid out of income.
(b) The administration fee payable in respect of annuities and similar terminable payments.
(c) The insurance fee.
(d) The income-collection fee.
(e) The management fees where the Public Trustee acts as a trustee of a superannuation scheme or on behalf of the trustees of a friendly society or runs a common investment scheme.
(f) VAT where the fee in respect of which VAT is payable is itself payable out of income.

Fees to the Public Trustee which are payable out of income have to be borne rateably by the several persons entitled to the trust income[2], and not exclusively by persons entitled to the income of residue. In one case it was held that annuitants must bear their share of an income fee payable under an earlier fee order[3]. But in *Re Riddell*[4], Farwell J dissented from this (and, it is respectfully submitted, rightly) on the ground that the provision of these payments is a part of the expenses of administration and must be paid out of the estate but not out of the portions thereof given before the residue is disposed of. So where the direction was to set aside such a fund as would provide an annuity of a stated amount, the income fee was held to be payable out of the income of the fund; but the fund set aside had to be sufficient to discharge by the income thereof both the stated annuity in full and the income fee[5]. Where the Public Trustee was appointed a trustee after the appropriation of annuity funds but there was power to resort to capital if the income of any fund should be insufficient to answer the annuity, Vaisey J directed that out of the income of each fund the annuity and the Public Trustee's income fee should be paid and that in case of a deficiency of income to meet these two payments recourse should be had to the capital of the particular fund[6]. Questions as to the incidence of fees as between capital and income do not, however, arise where the Public Trustee (Fees) Order 1999 applies as that order makes express provision[7] as to such incidence. The fact that the duties are light in proportion to the fees chargeable has been held not to be a good ground for refusing to allow retiring trustees to appoint the Public Trustee[8].

---

1 Section 1(2) of the Public Trustee (Fees) Act 1957 provides that 'Every fees order made after the passing of this Act shall indicate, with respect to every fee fixed by the order, whether it is to be paid out of capital or out of income'. See also Public Trustee Act 1906, s 9(5).
2 *Re Roberts' Will Trusts* [1937] Ch 274, [1937] 1 All ER 518.
3 *Re Bentley* [1914] 2 Ch 456.
4 [1936] Ch 747, [1936] 2 All ER 1600. Cf *Re Hulton* [1936] Ch 536, [1936] 2 All ER 207, and *Re Godwin* [1938] Ch 341, [1938] 1 All ER 287.
5 *Re Godwin* [1938] Ch 341, [1938] 1 All ER 287.
6 *Re Evans' Will Trusts* [1948] Ch 185, [1948] 1 All ER 381.
7 See p 792, ante.
8 *Re Drake's Settlement* [1926] WN 132.

ARTICLE 78

The appointment of the Public Trustee as an ordinary trustee

(1) The Public Trustee may be appointed an ordinary trustee of any trust (other than those which he is forbidden to accept[9]), whether the trust was created before or since the Act, unless the instrument creating the trust contains a direction to the contrary; and even then he may be appointed if the court so orders[10].

(2) The appointment must be made either[11]:

(a) by the creator of the trust;

(b) by the person having power to appoint new trustees; or

(c) by the court.

(3) Unless appointed by the will of a settlor the consent of the Public Trustee under his official seal must be obtained before he is appointed. Where appointed by such a will the appointment does not take effect until he so consents[12].

(4) Where he is appointed to be a new trustee he may (unlike an ordinary individual) be appointed sole trustee (even where the trust instrument or a statute forbids the appointment of a sole trustee)[13], and correspondingly all his co-trustees may retire under section 39 of the Trustee Act 1925 leaving him sole trustee, and without any of the consents required by that section[14].

(5) Where, however, it is proposed to appoint the Public Trustee to be a new trustee or additional trustee, notice of the proposed appointment must, where practicable, be given to all the beneficiaries in the United Kingdom whose addresses are known or to the guardians of such of them as are infants, and any person to whom such notice has been given may within 21 days apply to the court to prohibit the appointment, which the court may do if it considers it expedient. Nevertheless, failure to give the notice does not invalidate the appointment[15].

PARAGRAPHS 1, 2, AND 3

How the Public Trustee is appointed

The Public Trustee can be appointed by will or codicil without any previous communication to him, but he does not become a trustee until he has accepted the appointment[16]. In the case of trusts created inter vivos he

---

9 Article 77(2) ante; and Public Trustee Act 1906, s 2(4), and Public Trustee Rules 1912, r 6.

10 Public Trustee Act 1906, s 5(1) and (3).

11 Public Trustee Act 1906, s 5(1).

12 Public Trustee Rules 1912, r 8(2); and see *Re Shaw* [1914] WN 141; and Public Trustee Rules 1916, r 3.

13 *Re Leslie's Hassop Estates* [1911] 1 Ch 611.

14 Public Trustees Act 1906, s 5(1) and (2).

15 Public Trustee Act 1906, s 5(4). See *Re Drake's Settlement* [1926] WN 132.

16 Public Trustee Rules 1912, r 8(2).

cannot be appointed without his previous consent given under his corporate seal, which is usually given by his execution of the instrument appointing him[17], the effect of which would seem to be to make such appointments mere offers, although when he dòes subsequently consent the appointment becomes ipso facto effective[18].

Where a person is appointed by a testator to act jointly with the Public Trustee and does not disclaim, it is his duty to communicate the Public Trustee's appointment to him as soon as practicable[19].

Appointment by the court

The tendency of the court is not to appoint the Public Trustee against the wishes of a continuing trustee, where nothing is alleged against him[20], unless for some special reason it is 'expedient'[1], or against the wishes of any considerable proportion of the beneficiaries[2].

Where it is proposed to appoint the Public Trustee in place of a retiring judicial trustee, the court ought to make an order that there shall cease to be a judicial trustee[3].

PARAGRAPH 4

Appointment as sole trustee

The Act provides that the Public Trustee may be appointed a sole trustee in cases where no other sole trustee could be appointed without breach of trust[4]. It has been held that this not only applies to cases where the appointment of a sole trustee is forbidden by law but also to cases where it is expressly directed by the settlement that the trustees shall be kept up to a prescribed number[5] or that discretions and powers cannot be exercised if there are fewer than two trustees, so that despite such directions the Public Trustee can effectively act on his own[6].

Since the Public Trustee is a trust corporation[7], he can, even though sole trustee, give a good receipt for proceeds of sale arising under a trust for sale of land[8].

17 Public Trustee Rules 1912, r 8 and Public Trustee Rules 1916, r 3.
18 *Re Shaw* [1914] WN 141.
19 Public Trustee Rules 1912, r 8(3).
20 See per Neville J *Re Kensit* [1908] WN 235.
 1 *Re Henderson* [1940] Ch 764, [1940] 3 All ER 295.
 2 *Re Drake's Settlement* [1926] WN 132.
 3 *Re Johnston* [1911] WN 234.
 4 Public Trustee Act 1906, ss 2(2), 5.
 5 *Re Leslie's Hassop Estates* [1911] 1 Ch 611; *Re Moxon* [1916] 2 Ch 595.
 6 *Re Duxbury's Settlement Trusts* [1995] 1 WLR 425, CA.
 7 Trustee Act 1925, s 68(18); Law of Property Act 1925, s 205(1)(xxviii). As to trust corporations, see p 448, ante and p 797, post.
 8 Trustee Act 1925, s 14(2); Law of Property Act 1925, s 27(2).

PARAGRAPH 5

Effect of not giving beneficiaries notice of intention to appoint Public Trustee as a new trustee

It seems that the proviso at the end of s 5(4) of the Public Trustee Act 1906 that 'failure to give the notice is not to invalidate the appointment', makes the sole effect of failure to give such notice a ground on which any beneficiary may *at any time* (and not merely within 21 days) apply to the court to remove the Public Trustee. It should be noticed that this provision as to notice is confined to cases where the Public Trustee is appointed an ordinary trustee, and has no application in the case of his appointment as a custodian trustee.

ARTICLE 79

The appointment and removal of the Public Trustee or certain corporate bodies as mere 'custodian trustee'

(1) The Public Trustee (with regard to trusts which he is not forbidden to accept[9]), if he consents to act as such, and also any banking or insurance company, or other body corporate entitled by rules under the Public Trustee Act 1906 to act as such, may be appointed custodian trustee of any trust[10].

(2) The appointment may be made[11]:

(a) by the creator of the trust;

(b) by the court on the application of anyone who could apply for the appointment of a new trustee;

(c) by the person having power to appoint new trustees, even (semble) where the trust instrument forbids it[12].

(3) The court may terminate the custodian trusteeship on the application of the custodian trustee or the managing trustee or of any beneficiary, if:

(a) it is the general wish of the beneficiaries; or

(b) it is expedient on any other grounds[13], and thereupon the court may give general directions and make the requisite vesting orders[14].

---

9 See Article 77(2), ante; and Public Trustee Act, 1906, s 2(4) and Public Trustee Rules 1912, r 7.

10 Public Trustee Act 1906, s 4(1) and (3), and Public Trustee Rules 1912, r 6(d); and with regard to other corporate trustees, r 30, as amended by the Public Trustee (Custodian Trustee) Rules 1975, SI 1975/1189 (amended by SI 1976/836; SI 1981/318; SI 1984/109; SI 1985/132; SI 1987/1891).

11 Public Trustee Act 1906, s 4(1).

12 *Re Cherry's Trusts* [1914] 1 Ch 83.

13 Eg if it is desired to appoint the custodian trustee to be managing trustee, in which case the custodian trustee must first be terminated (*Re Squire's Settlement* (1946) 115 LJ Ch 90).

14 Public Trustee Act 1906, s 4(2)(i).

Advantages of custodian trusteeship

The appointment of a custodian trustee has practical advantages, for
(1) it safeguards the capital against loss from obvious breaches of trust, whether fraudulent or not, and
(2) it saves the periodic expense caused by the necessity of transferring the trust property on every appointment of new trustees, and
(3) it makes it more likely that the trust will continue to be run effectively if the managing trustee is removed and replaced by another of whose identity it is ignorant, yet is aggrieved by its removal.

On the other hand, it leaves the management in the hands of ordinary active trustees. Custodian trusteeship has not however greatly commended itself to the public, despite the fact that it has become common to appoint either the Public Trustee or one of the great banks or insurance societies to be a corporate trustee in the full sense of a managing trustee.

Certain corporate bodies may be appointed custodian trustees

The Public Trustee Act 1906 authorises the appointment as custodian trustee not only of the Public Trustee but also of any banking or insurance company or other body corporate which is entitled by rules made under the Act to act as custodian trustee; and any such body so appointed may charge fees not exceeding those charged by the Public Trustee[15].

By virtue of the Public Trustee (Custodian Trustee) Rules 1975, SI 1975/ 1189, which substitutes a new rule for rule 30 of the Public Trustees Rules 1912.

'The following corporations shall be entitled to act as custodian trustees:
(a) the Treasury Solicitor;
(b) any corporation which:
  (i) is constituted under the law of the United Kingdom or of any part thereof, or under the law of any other Member State of the European Union or of any part thereof;
  (ii) is empowered by its constitution to undertake trust business (which for the purpose of this rule means the business of acting as trustee under wills and settlements and as executor and administrator) in England and Wales[16]:
  (iii) has one or more places of business in the United Kingdom; and
  (iv) is
       a company incorporated by special Act of Parliament or Royal Charter, or a company registered (with or without limited liability) in the United Kingdom under the Companies Act 1948 or 1985 or under the Companies Act (Northern Ireland) 1960 or in another Member State of the European Union and having a capital (in stock or shares) for the time being issued of not less than £250,000 (or its equivalent in the currency of the State where the company is registered), of which not less than £100,000 (or its equivalent) has been paid up in cash, or a company which is registered without limited liability in the United

---

15 But see *Forster v Williams Deacon's Bank Ltd* [1935] Ch 359, CA; where it was held that a bank which has been appointed to be (a) managing trustee, and (b) custodian trustee, was not entitled to charge fees under the Public Trustee Act 1906, s 4(3). Followed in *Arning v James* [1936] Ch 158.
16 See *Re Bigger* [1977] 2 All ER 644 (Bank of Ireland effectively empowered by its constitution, because Ireland had joined the European Economic Community, to undertake trust business in England and Wales).

Kingdom under the Companies Act 1948 [or 1985] or the Companies Act (Northern Ireland) 1960 or in another Member State of the European Union and of which one of the members is a company within any of the classes defined in this sub-paragraph;

(c) any corporation which is incorporated by the special Act or Royal Charter or under the Charitable Trustees Incorporation Act 1872[17] which is empowered by its constitution to act as a trustee for any charitable purposes, but only in relation to trusts in which its constitution empowers it to act;

(d) any corporation which is constituted under the law of the United Kingdom or of any part thereof and having its place of business there, and which is either:

    (i) established for the purpose of undertaking trust business for the benefit of Her Majesty's Navy, Army, Air Force or Civil Service or of any unit, department, member or association of members thereof, and having among its directors or members any persons appointed or nominated by the Defence Council or any Department of State or any one or more of those Departments, or

    (ii) authorised by the Lord Chancellor to act in relation to any charitable, ecclesiastical or public trusts as a trust corporation, but only in connection with any such trust as is so authorised;

(e) any Regional Health Authority, District Health Authority or special health authority, but only in relation to any trust which the authority is authorised to accept or hold by virtue of section 90 of the National Health Service Act 1977;

(f) the British Gas Corporation[18], or any subsidiary of the British Gas Corporation but only in relation to a pension scheme or pension fund established or maintained by the Corporation by virtue of section 36 of the Gas Act 1972;

(g) the London Transport Executive[19], but only in relation to a pension scheme or pension fund—

    (i) which is established or administered by the Executive by virtue of section 6 of the Transport (London) Act 1969, or

    (ii) in relation to which rights, liabilities and functions have been transferred to the Executive by an order under section 74 of the Transport Act 1962 as applied by section 18 of the Transport (London) Act 1969;

(h) any of the following, namely:—

    (i) the Greater London Council[20],

    (ii) the corporation of any London borough (acting by the council),

    (iii) a county council, district council, parish council or community council,

    (iv) the Council of the Isles of Scilly,

    (v) the Common Council of the City of London,

but only in relation to charitable or public trusts (and not trusts for an ecclesiastical charity or for a charity for the relief of poverty) for the benefit of the inhabitants of the area of the local authority concerned and its neighbourhood, or any part of that area.

(i) any of the following, namely:—

    (i) a metropolitan district council[1] or a non-metropolitan county council,

    (ii) the corporation of any London borough (acting by the council),

    (iii) the Common Council of the City of London,

    (iv) the Council of the Isles of Scilly,

but only in relation to any trust under which property devolves for the sole

---

17 Repealed by Charities Act 1993: see Pt VII of that Act.

18 Dissolved by British Gas Corporation Dissolution Order 1990 SI 1990/147 under Gas Act 1986: for property vesting in British Gas plc see 1986 Gas Act, Pt II, 1986 SI 1986/1317.

19 Under London Regional Transport Act 1984 London Regional Transport takes over London transport functions.

20 Abolished along with metropolitan councils by Local Government Act 1985. As to the transfer of functions, see Pt II of that Act.

1 Abolished along with metropolitan councils by Local Government Act 1985. As to the transfer of functions, see Pt II of that Act.

benefit of a person who occupies residential accommodation provided under section 21(1)(a) of the National Assistance Act 1948 by the local authority concerned or is in the care of that authority; and a corporation acting as a custodian trustee by virtue of this paragraph in relation to any trust shall be entitled to continue so to act in relation to that trust until a new custodian trustee is appointed, notwithstanding that the person concerned ceases to occupy such accommodation or to be in the care of that authority, as the case may be.

(j) the National Coal Board[2] or any subsidiary of the National Coal Board, but only in relation to a scheme or arrangements established under regulations made under section 37 of the Coal Industry Nationalisation Act 1946.'

To this list has been added any corporation in relation to it, acting as trustee of a pension scheme established or maintained by the British Broadcasting Corporation[3].

Custodian trustee making profit from trust

The rule that a trustee must not profit from his trust applies to custodian trustees although almost bare trustees, and a corporate custodian trustee has been held to be unable (without the authority of the court) lawfully to contract for its own benefit with the managing trustee[4].

ARTICLE 80

The respective duties, rights and liabilities of the custodian trustee and managing trustees

The respective functions and rights of a custodian trustee and the managing trustees are as follows[5]:

(a) the trust property must be transferred to the custodian trustee as if he were sole trustee, and for that purpose vesting orders may, where necessary, be made under the Trustee Act 1925[6]. And, subject and without prejudice to the rights of any other persons, the custodian trustee is to have the custody of all securities and documents of title relating to the trust property; but the managing trustees are to have free access thereto, and to be entitled to take copies thereof or extracts therefrom[7];

(b) the management of the trust property, and the exercise of any power or discretion exercisable by the trustees under the trust, remain vested in the managing trustee[8];

(c) the custodian trustee must concur in and perform all acts neces-

---

2 The British Coal Corporation has replaced the National Coal Board. The 1946 Act has been repealed but regulations under Coal Industry Act 1994, Sch 5, para 2, continue such pension schemes so that they remain trust corporations: Public Trustee (Custodian Trustee) Rules 1994, SI 1994/2519.
3 SI 1987/1891.
4 *Re Brooke Bond & Co Ltd's Trust Deed* [1963] Ch 357, but see pp 665 and 668.
5 Public Trustee Act 1906, s 4(2).
6 Public Trustee Act 1906, s 4(2)(a). As to such vesting orders, see pp 779 et seq, ante.
7 Public Trustee Act 1906, s 4(2)(c).
8 Public Trustee Act 1906, s 4(2)(b).

sary to enable the managing trustees to exercise their powers of management, or any other power or discretion vested in them (including the power to pay money or securities into court), unless the matter in which he is requested to concur is a breach of trust, or involves a personal liability upon him in respect of calls or otherwise. But, unless he so concurs, the custodian trustee is not liable for any act or default on the part of the managing trustees or any of them[9];

(d) all sums payable to, or out of, the income or capital of the trust property, must be paid to or by the custodian trustee: provided that the custodian trustee may allow the dividends and other income derived from the trust property to be paid to the managing trustees, or to such person as they direct, or into such bank to the credit of such person as they may direct, and in such case is exonerated from seeing to the application thereof, and is not answerable for any loss or misapplication thereof[10];

(e) the custodian trustee, if he acts in good faith, is not liable for accepting as correct, and acting upon the faith of, any written statement by the managing trustees as to any birth, death, marriage, or other matter of pedigree or relationship, or other matter of fact, upon which the title to the trust property or any part thereof may depend, nor for acting upon any legal advice obtained by the managing trustees independently of the custodian trustee[11];

(f) the power of appointing new trustees, when exercisable by the trustees, is to be exercised by the managing trustees alone, and in determining the number of trustees the custodian trustee is not to be counted, but the custodian trustee has the same right of applying to the court to appoint a new trustee as any other trustee has[12].

Management of the trust where custodian trustee appointed

The distinction between a custodian trustee and a bare trustee is a fine one, but it is a real one. A bare trustee has to do what he is told. A custodian trustee, while generally having to do or he is told, does not have to do what he is told and must not do it if it would involve him knowingly participating in a breach of trust[13]. He will so participate not only where he has actual knowledge but also, it seems, where he turns a Nelsonian blind-eye to what would otherwise appear a breach of trust or where he deliberately or recklessly fails to make the inquiries an honest and reasonable man would make despite having his suspicions aroused over the propriety of his instructions: his want of probity will justify the imposition of personal liability[14].

9 Public Trustee Act 1906, s 4(2)(d).
10 Public Trustee Act 1906, s 4(2)(e).
11 Public Trustee Act 1906, s 4(2)(h).
12 Public Trustee Act 1906, s 4(2)(f) and (g).
13 See *IRC v Silverts Ltd* [1951] Ch 521, [1951] 1 All ER 703, CA.
14 See Art 100, post; *Royal Brunei Airlines v Tan* [1995] 2 AC 378, [1995] 3 All ER 97.

ARTICLE 81

Special rules relating to the Public Trustee

(1) Any person aggrieved by any act or omission or decision of the Public Trustee in relation to the trust may apply to the court, which may make such order as it thinks fit[15]. The application is made to a judge of the Chancery Division in Chambers[16].

(2) The Public Trustee may employ, for the purposes of the trust, such solicitors, bankers, accountants, and brokers, or other persons as he may deem necessary, having regard to the interests of the trust; and in doing so must, where practicable, take into consideration the wishes of:

(a) the creator of the trust;

(b) the other trustees (if any); and

(c) the beneficiaries;

either expressed or implied from the previous practice of the creator or trustees[17]. He may also take and use professional advice and assistance in regard to legal and other matters, and act on credible information (though less than legal evidence) of facts[18].

(3) The Public trustee may make advances out of public money for the purposes of any trust estate of which he is trustee[19].

(4) The entry of the name of the Public Trustee in the books of a company does not constitute notice of the trust, nor is any one affected with notice of a trust by the mere fact of dealing with the Public Trustee[20].

(5) The Public Trustee is bound to keep a register setting out the date of acceptance, particulars of the trust property, particulars of the person entitled to the income, particulars of any notices received as to dealings with any beneficial interest or of any exercise or release of any power, and entries of any decision or opinion of the court in respect of the trust estate and of decisions of his own relating thereto of every trust of which he is trustee[1].

---

15 Public Trustee Act 1906, s 10. In *Re Wilson* [1964] 1 All ER 196, [1964] 1 WLR 214, a beneficiary had disappeared and the Public Trustee refused under the Public Trustee Rules 1912, r 27 (which enables him to refuse payment until evidence is produced that the beneficiary is alive) to make the income payments otherwise due to him. The beneficiary's wife, who had obtained a sequestration order, applied to the court under s 10, above. Ungoed-Thomas J held that the Public Trustee had a discretion under r 27 to refuse payment and since the wife (on whom the onus lay) had not produced the necessary evidence the court would not interfere with the exercise of that discretion; nor would the court interfere with the Public Trustee's decision not to apply under r 28 for the court's directions.

16 RSC Ord 93, r 2.

17 Public Trustee Act 1906, s 11(2).

18 Public Trustee Rules 1912, r 26.

19 Public Trustee Act 1906, r 25.

20 Public Trustee Act 1906, s 11(5).

1 Public Trustee Rules 1912, r 16.

Procedure by way of appeal from decisions of Public Trustee

The procedure for appealing from a decision of the Public Trustee to a judge is by Part 8 claim in the chambers of a judge of the Chancery Division, the being entitled in the matter of the will, settlement, or other trust, and in the matter of the Public Trustee Act 1906 and s 10 of that Act being specified in the body of the claim as the section under which relief is sought. If the parties desire to be heard the Public Trustee ought to hear them, before deciding a point judicially against them[2]. The section applies to all decisions of the Public Trustee in discharge of his judicial functions under the Act[3]. The practitioner is warned that the simple and inexpensive procedure for taking the opinion of the court on any question arising in the course of *any administration* without judicial proceedings under s 3(4) of the Act, has no application to cases where the Public Trustee is *acting as trustee*, but is confined to 'the administration of small estates'[4] ie of deceased persons[5]. All applications in relation to trusts must either be by beneficiaries in the nature of appeals from the Public Trustee under s 10 of the Public Trustee Act 1906 or by the Public Trustee or a beneficiary under the general law of trusts as made applicable to the Public Trustee by s 2(2).

---

2 Per Parker J *Re Oddy* [1911] 1 Ch 532.
3 *Re Oddy* [1911] 1 Ch 532 approved in *Re Utley* [1912] WN 147.
4 *Re Oddy* [1911] 1 Ch 532.
5 *Re Oddy* [1911] 1 Ch 532, and *Re Oddy* (1910) 104 LT 338.

CHAPTER 17

Administration of new trusts created under limited powers in the original settlement

ARTICLE 82

By whom new trusts created under powers of appointment are to be carried out

(1) Where the donee of a general power creates new trusts:
(a) if the appointment is made by an instrument inter vivos he can nominate new trustees for carrying them out, to whom the old trustees must transfer the property;
(b) if the appointment is made by a testamentary instrument the old trustees must transfer the property to the personal representatives of the appointor to be dealt with by them as part of his assets in due course of administration[1].

(2) Where the donee of a special power creates new trusts, it seems that he cannot create separate trusts under the administration of new trustees unless the power is in a wide form which either expressly or impliedly authorises him to do so[2]. In contrast the usual form of a power of advancement is of such width that it can, but need not necessarily, be exercised so as to create separate trusts under the administration of new trustees[3].

(3) A resettlement on separate trusts pursuant to a special power will incorporate the statutory power of advancement[4], but will not be able to contain discretionary or protective trusts or powers of appointment[5] unless the special power for the benefit of objects thereof is construed as wide enough to permit delegation of such discretions to the trustees of the settlement.

1 *Re Hoskin's Trusts* (1877) 5 Ch D 229; on appeal (1877) 6 Ch D 281; *Hayes v Oatley* (1872) LR 14 Eq 1; *Re Philbrick* (1865) 13 WR 570; *Re Peacock's Settlement* [1902] 1 Ch 552 (administration with will annexed).
2 *Bond (Inspector of Taxes) v Pickford* [1983] STC 517, CA; *Roome v Edwards (Inspector of Taxes)* [1982] AC 279, [1981] 1 All ER 736, HL; *Busk v Aldam* (1874) LR 19 Eq 16; *Von Brockdorff v Malcolm* (1885) 30 Ch D 172; *Re Tyssen* [1894] 1 Ch 56; and per Cotton LJ in *Scotney v Lomer* (1886) 31 Ch D 380.
3 *Pilkington v IRC* [1964] AC 612, [1962] 3 All ER 622, HL; *Bond v Pickford*, supra; *Roome v Edwards*, supra. See pp 722–723, ante.
4 *Re Mewburn* [1934] Ch 112; *Re Morris* [1951] 2 All ER 528 at 533, CA.
5 *Re Morris* [1951] 2 All ER 528, CA; *Re Hunter's Will Trusts* [1963] Ch 372; *Re Hay's Settlement Trusts* [1981] 3 All ER 786.

PARAGRAPH 1(A)

Donee of general power may appoint by deed to new trustees

A general power, being a power to appoint to anyone in the world, is tantamount to ownership and the donee can exercise it in whatever way he pleases[6]. It follows that the donee may, by instrument inter vivos, appoint not merely in favour of persons to take beneficially, but in favour of persons who are to hold upon new special trusts. In either case the trusts of the old settlement are spent, and the trustees functi officio, and their sole remaining duty is to transfer the property to the appointees, whether they be beneficial or fiduciary.

Exceptionally, if the general power is vested in trustees ex officio so that the power is fiduciary and not a personal beneficial power then the trustees can only exercise the power in ways contemplated by the settlor[7].

PARAGRAPH 1(B)

Where general power exercised by will, property must in first instance be transferred to personal representative

Where the appointment is made by a testamentary instrument the matter is somewhat different. In that case the appointor, by exercising the power, makes the property assets for the payment of his debts in due order of administration[8]. By the mere fact of the appointment, therefore, he gives an interest to his personal representative, who may require the fund for debts or death duties. Consequently, the trustees of the settlement must transfer the fund to the personal representative or according to his direction[9]. If the appointor has declared new trusts, and appointed new trustees for carrying them out, then, of course, it will be the duty of the personal representative to transfer or direct the transfer to such new trustees of so much as he may not require for debts or duties. In either case, however, the functions of the old trustees cease on the death of the appointor.

PARAGRAPH 2

Whether donee of special power can appoint to new trustees is a question of construction

Appointments creating new trusts under special or limited powers give rise to more difficulty. As is stated in *Farwell on Powers*[10]:

'If other indications of intention be lacking, at all events in the case of personalty, a settlor or testator who vests funds in trustees, and provides machinery for filling up vacancies in their number, may well be taken to have intended that the fund shall

6 *Re Triffitt's Settlement* [1958] Ch 852, [1958] 2 All ER 299.
7 *Re Beatty's Will Trusts* [1990] 3 All ER 844 at 846–847.
8 *Lassells v Cornwallis* (1704) 2 Vern 465; *Holmes v Coghill* (1802) 7 Ves 499; affd (1806) 12 Ves 206; *Pardo v Bingham* (1868) LR 6 Eq 485. This is the case even where the consent of the trustees is necessary to the exercise of the power: *Re Phillips* [1931] 1 Ch 347.
9 See cases cited, note 1, p 803, ante.
10 *Farwell on Powers* (3rd edn) p 374.

remain in the custody of the persons to whom he has entrusted it, until some beneficiary absolutely entitled is ready to receive it; although he has given power to another to say who the beneficiary shall be. He may well trust (say) his daughter, to select which of her children shall take the fund, and yet not desire her to nominate the trustees who are to hold it.'

Mere power of selection

Thus, in *Re Tyssen*[11]:

'under a special power in favour of children, the donees appointed in favour of one daughter upon certain trusts in favour of another daughter;'

but it was held that the fund ought not to be transferred to the first daughter as trustee under the appointment, but ought to be retained by the trustees of the settlement. The same view had been previously taken in *Busk v Aldam*[12].

Power to appoint in such manner and form as donee may think fit

On the other hand, in the subsequent case of *Re Redgate*[13] Buckley J held that, under a power to appoint to children 'for such estate or estates manner and form' as the donee of the power should direct, the power was well exercised by an appointment to new trustees upon trust for sale and distribution of the proceeds among the children. His Lordship seems to have based his judgment on the analogy of powers operating to transfer the legal estate under Statute of Uses, with regard to which it was held, in several cases[14], that such powers authorised an appointment to trustees upon trust for sale. To this it may be countered that, where a settlor has confided the property to trustees upon such trusts as another shall appoint, he has himself chosen the hands to administer the trust; whereas in the case of powers operating under the Statute of Uses he had not done so. His Lordship, however, seems impliedly to admit in his judgment that he was bound to find something in the language of the settlement justifying the appointment to new trustees; and, accordingly, fixed on the words 'manner and form', which, by contrast with the words 'estate or estates', seemed to him to imply a power to do something else than to give an estate to children: in other words to imply a power to 'give a child in some manner and form an interest in the property which shall not be an estate in the property itself'. This ingenious distinction, however, may be regarded as somewhat over subtle.

However, in a later case of *Re Adams' Trustees and Frost's Contract*[15], Warrington J came to the same conclusion, where the words 'manner and form' were absent and the settlement merely directed the trustees to transfer 'or

11 [1894] 1 Ch 56.
12 (1874) LR 19 Eq 16; and see per Cotton LJ in *Scotney v Lomer* (1886) 31 Ch D 380.
13 [1903] 1 Ch 356; distinguished by Astbury J in *Re Mackenzie* [1916] 1 Ch 125.
14 *Kenworthy v Bate* (1802) 6 Ves 793; *Cowx v Foster* (1860) 1 John & H 30; *Fowler v Cohn* (1856) 21 Beav 360; *Webb v Sadler* (1873) 8 Ch App 419; *Re Paget; Re Mellor* [1898] 1 Ch 290; *Re Ainsworth, Re Yates* [1921] 2 Ch 179, where Eve J held that such a power also authorised an appointment to trustees for sale, with power to postpone and manage and lease in the meanwhile.
15 [1907] 1 Ch 695; and see *Re Falconer's Trusts* [1908] 1 Ch 410, as to the power of a donee of a special power of appointment to enlarge the range of investments; and see also *Re Taylor*, not reported, but decided on 28 February 1912, where Parker J went a step further, and held that a donee of a power to appoint the proceeds of sale of real and *personal estate, directed to be sold* can stop the direction for sale and appoint a house to A (an object of the power) so long as she remains a spinster and inhabits it.

pay'. From these words, the learned judge inferred a power in the donee to direct a sale, and then took one step further and inferred that he might appoint his own trustees to carry out the sale notwithstanding that under the settlement the trustees thereof had an express power of sale.

In *Re Rank's Settlement Trusts*[16] Slade J held that a special power of appointment on trusts 'with such provisions for maintenance education and advancement and otherwise *at the discretion of* any person and with such gifts over and *generally in such manner* for the benefit of' certain issue conferred upon the donee of the power the authority to give new trustees all such administrative powers as were reasonably ancillary to the appointed beneficial interests, including wider powers of investment than were contained in the trust instrument conferring the power of appointment.

Special powers in the wider form

In *Bond v Pickford*[17] Slade LJ characterised as powers in the wider form 'powers to alter the presently operative trusts of a settlement which expressly or by necessary implication authorise the trustees to remove assets altogether from the original settlement (without rendering any person absolutely beneficially entitled to them)'. Powers of this nature which do not confer on the trustees such authority are regarded as 'powers in the narrower form'.

This distinction is of great importance for capital gains tax purposes. It has developed as a more precise and workable distinction than that between special powers of appointment and powers of advancement[18], especially when the latter distinction was often indistinct in the case of certain wide express powers, eg of appropriation or allocation of trust assets.

If there is a separate settlement created under a power in the wider form there will be a deemed disposal for capital gains tax purposes, the trustees of the separate settlement having become absolutely entitled to the subject matter thereof as against the trustees of the original settlement[19]. If there is no separate settlement, then the trustees of the sub-settlement and the trustees of the head settlement will be treated as a single and continuing body of trustees[20]. This means there will be no deemed disposal, but if there are two UK head trustees and the two non-resident sub-trustees realise their gains on their sub-trust assets abroad the UK trustees will be liable for CGT thereon[1].

A power in the narrower form is ex hypothesi incapable of being exercised so as to create a separate settlement. An appointment under a special power to appoint to beneficiaries in the classical form (which is frequently found as the primary provision of a discretionary settlement—the discretionary trusts being expressed to apply only until and in default of appointment) cannot create a separate settlement in the absence of further terms in the trust instrument expressly or by necessary implication authorising such creation[2].

---

16 [1979] 1 WLR 1242.
17 [1983] STC 517 at 523, CA.
18 'Advancement' has the connotation of receiving part of the capital earlier than one would expect, taking into account one's vested or contingent interest in capital.
19 Taxation of Chargeable Gains Act 1992, s 71. Further see Whiteman, *Capital Gains Tax* (4th edn) paras 26–29 to 26–41.
20 Taxation of Chargeable Gains Act 1992, s 69.
 1 *Roome v Edwards* [1982] AC 279, [1981] 1 All ER 736, HL.
 2 *Bond v Pickford* [1983] STC 517 at 522–533, 529, CA.

This reflects two basic principles of English trust law. The office of a trustee being one of personal confidence, it is well settled that a trustee may not delegate the exercise of his trusts, powers and discretions to other persons except where authorised by the trust instrument or by statute. Secondly, when a special power of appointment is exercised the limitations created under it are treated as written into the original instrument which created the power[3].

A power in the wider form is ex hypothesi capable of being exercised so as to create a separate settlement but it is also capable of being exercised in narrow fashion so as not to create a separate settlement. Such a power will include a power to appoint to anyone except certain named persons[4] or to appoint to anyone living at a specified date[5], whether or not such power is vested in joint appointors[6] or is subject to the consent of some named person[7]. Such a power includes a power to 'pay or apply the whole or any part or parts of the Capital to or for the benefit of all or any one or more of the specified class [freed and released from the trusts concerning the same][8] or [in such manner as the Trustees shall in their absolute discretion think fit]'[9]. However, a power in the narrower form was held to exist where it was a power to 'apply capital for the benefit of any one or more of the Beneficiaries by allocating or appropriating to such Beneficiary such sum out of or investments forming part of the Capital as the Trustees think fit either absolutely or contingently upon the attainment by him or her of a specified age and so that the provisions of s 31 of the Trustee Act 1925 and the powers of the Trustees to invest and vary investments shall apply to any moneys or investments so allocated or appropriated'[10].

Whether separate settlement created under wider form of power

In *Roome v Edwards*[11] Lord Wilberforce provided the following guidelines as to whether a power had been exercised so as to create a separate settlement.

'I think that the question whether a particular set of facts amounts to a settlement should be approached by asking what a person, with knowledge of the legal context of the word under established doctrine and applying this knowledge in a practical and commonsense manner to the facts under examination, would conclude. To take two fairly typical cases. Many settlements contain powers to appoint a part or a proportion of the trust property to beneficiaries; some may also confer power to appoint separate trustees of the property so appointed or such power may be conferred by the Trustee Act 1925, s 37. It is established doctrine that the trusts declared by a document exercising a special power of appointment are to be read into the original settlement. If such a power is exercised, whether or not separate

---

3 *Muir (or Williams) v Muir* [1943] AC 468, HL; *Roome v Edwards* [1982] AC 279, [1981] 1 All ER 736, HL.
4 *Re Triffitt's Settlement* [1958] Ch 852, [1958] 2 All ER 299.
5 *Re Jones* [1945] Ch 105.
6 *Re Earl of Coventry's Indentures* [1974] Ch 77, [1973] 3 All ER 1.
7 *Re Triffitt's Settlement* [1958] Ch 852, [1958] 2 All ER 299.
8 *Hart (Inspector of Taxes) v Briscoe* [1979] Ch 1, [1978] 1 All ER 791; *Swires v Renton* [1991] STC 490 (wide power exercised not so as to re-settle on separate trusts but to sub-settle by grafting new trusts on to old trusts).
9 *Bond v Pickford* [1983] STC 517, CA. This is similar to the power of advancement in Trustee Act 1925, s 32. Also see *Ewart v Taylor (Inspector of Taxes)* [1983] STC 721.
10 *Bond v Pickford* [1983] STC 517, CA.
11 [1982] AC 279, [1981] 1 All ER 736, HL.

trustees are appointed, I do not think that it would be natural for such a person as I have presupposed to say that a separate settlement had been created; still less so if it were found that provisions of the original settlement continued to apply to the appointed fund, or that the appointed fund were liable, in certain events, to fall back into the rest of the settled property. On the other hand, there may be a power to appoint and appropriate a part of the trust property to beneficiaries and to settle it for their benefit. If such a power is exercised, the natural conclusion might be that a separate settlement was created, all the more so if a complete new set of trusts were declared as to the appropriated property, and if it could be said that the trusts of the original settlement ceased to apply to it. There can be many variations on these cases each of which will have to be judged on its facts.'

The Board of Inland Revenue in a Statement of Practice has stated[12]:

'It is now clear that a deemed disposal under Capital Gains Tax Act 1979, section 54 [now TCGA 1992, s 71] cannot arise unless the power exercised by the trustees, or the instrument conferring the power, expressly or by necessary implication, confers on the trustees authority to remove assets from the original settlement by subjecting them to the trusts of a different settlement. Such powers (which may be powers of advancement or appointment) are referred to by the Court of Appeal in *Bond v Pickford* as "powers in the wider form." However, the board considers that a deemed disposal will not arise when such a power is exercised and trusts are declared in circumstances such that—

(a) the appointment is revocable
(b) the trusts declared of the advanced or appointed funds are not exhaustive so that there exists a possibility at the time when the advancement or appointment is made that the funds covered by it will on the occasion of some event cease to be held upon such trusts and once again come to be held upon the original trusts of the settlement.

Further, when such a power is exercised the Board considers it unlikely that a deemed disposal will arise when trusts are declared if duties in regard to the appointed assets still fall to the trustees of the original settlement in their capacity as trustees of that settlement, bearing in mind the provision in Capital Gains Tax Act 1979, section 52 (1) [now TCGA 1992, s 69] that the trustees of a settlement form a single and continuing body (distinct from the persons who may from time to time be the trustees).

Finally, the Board accept that a power of appointment or advancement can be exercised over only part of the settled property and that the above consequences would apply to that part.'

PARAGRAPH 3

Delegation of discretions to new trustees

Since *Pilkington v IRC*[13] the statutory power of advancement 'for the benefit of' a beneficiary, B, has been construed broadly so as to enable advancements to be made by way of resettlement on separate new trusts, freed and discharged from the old trusts, and which may confer discretions on the new trustees if this is 'for the benefit of' B, such delegation by the old trustees to the new trustees being an authorised one. If a special power of appointment is in the 'wider' form already discussed, then it may be exercised to resettle all or part of the trust property on new separate trusts which will automatically incorporate the statutory power of advancement in favour of beneficiaries

12 SP 7/84, [1983] STC 517 at 699.
13 [1964] AC 612; see p 722 ante.

interested in capital[14]. It is then a question of construing the terms of the special power to see if they are broad enough to enable the resettlement to confer discretions on the new trustees by way of creating a protective trust (which may become a discretionary trust on bankruptcy of the life tenant) or an immediate discretionary trust and whether or not containing discretionary powers of appointment. Case law reveals an out-dated restrictive Victorian approach to construction of special powers[15], whereas the modern trend is to give words like 'for the benefit of' a wide unrestricted meaning[16], although modern draftspersons have the practice of drafting special powers of appointment in the wider form which do expressly confer the widest possible power to confer discretions on the new trustees of the resettled trust property, thereby avoiding problems.

---

14 *Re Mewburn* [1934] Ch 112; *Re Morris* [1951] 2 All ER 528 at 533. Logically this would also be the case if the statutory power were extended to cover not just half, but all the capital, as pointed out in J Kessler *Drafting Trusts and Will Trusts* (6th edn) para 10-5, footnote 22 and *Lewin on Trusts* (17th edn) para 29-46 footnote 27.
15 *Re Morris* [1951] 2 All ER 528, CA; *Re Hunter's Will Trust* [1963] Ch 372; *Re Hay's Settlement Trust* [1981] 3 All ER 786.
16 *Pilkington v IRC* [1964] AC 612, HL; *Re Hampden's Settlement Trusts* [1977] TR 177, [2001] WTLR 195 (a special power); plus *Re Pocock's Policy* (1871) 6 Ch App 445. Further see G Thomas *Powers* (Sweet & Maxwell 1998), paras 7-58 to 7-83.

CHAPTER 18

The rights of the trustee

Article
83 Right to reimbursement and indemnity   810
84 Right to discharge on completion of trusteeship   827
85 Right to pay trust funds into court in certain circumstances   829

ARTICLE 83

Right to reimbursement and indemnity

(1) A trustee is entitled to be reimbursed out of the trust funds or may pay out of the trust funds[1] all expenses which he has properly incurred when acting on behalf of the trust[2], having regard to the circumstances of each particular case[3], but without interest[4], unless he has paid an interest-bearing claim, in which case he stands in the shoes of the creditor by subrogation[5]. Exceptionally, where expenses were incurred without authorisation but the trustee in good faith conferred a benefit on the trust property he will have a right of indemnity to the value of the benefit conferred[6].

(2) The trustee's lien covers present and future liabilities[7] and extends over both capital and income[8] so as to confer upon him a beneficial interest in the nature of a non-possessory equitable lien with priority

---

1 *Re Earl of Winchilsea's Policy Trusts* (1888) 39 Ch D 168.
2 Trustee Act 2000, s 31(1); *Worrall v Harford* (1802) 8 Ves 4; *Re German Mining Co* (1854) 4 De GM & G 19; *Re Grimthorpe* [1958] Ch 615, [1958] 1 All ER 765; *Holding and Management Ltd v Property Holding and Investment Trust plc* [1990] 1 All ER 938, [1989] 1 WLR 1313, CA.
3 *Leedham v Chawner* (1858) 4 K & J 458.
4 *Gordon v Trail* (1820) 8 Price 416; *Foster v Spencer* [1996] 2 All ER 672 at 678.
5 *Re Beulah Park Estate* (1872) LR 15 Eq 43; *Finch v Pescott* (1874) LR 17 Eq 554.
6 *Vyse v Foster* (1872) 8 Ch App 309 at 336–337; *Re Smith's Estate* [1937] Ch 636, [1937] 3 All ER 472; *Conway v Fenton* (1888) 40 Ch D 512 at 518: an independent restitutionary right to prevent unjust enrichment.
7 *X v A* [2000] 1 All ER 490.
8 *Stott v Milne* (1884) 25 Ch D 710; *Re Davis* (1832) 1 Deac & Ch 272; *Re German Mining Co* (1854) 4 De GM & G 19; and see *Walters v Woodbridge* (1878) 7 Ch D 504, CA (considered and explained in *Re Spurling's Will Trusts* [1966] 1 All ER 745, [1966] 1 WLR 920).

over the claims of the beneficiaries[9]. After retirement or removal of a trustee his lien automatically binds the trust fund in the hands of the successor trustees[10]. When trustees exercise discretionary powers to distribute trust funds to a beneficiary they will be regarded as over-reaching any equitable lien of themselves or any predecessors unless such lien is expressly preserved[11]. When trustees are obliged to distribute trust funds to persons absolutely entitled under the terms of the trust they have a right to retain assets to cover future liabilities[12] and a right to preserve their lien (though they may rely on personal covenants of indemnity): if they do not expressly exercise such rights, it seems they will lose them[13].

(3) Where the only beneficiary is a person of full age and capacity, who himself created the trust or accepted the beneficial ownership with knowledge that the legal ownership of the trust property was vested in the trustee, the right of the trustee to indemnity against liabilities incident to the legal ownership is not limited to the trust property, but is enforceable in equity against the beneficiary personally, unless he is in a position to disclaim the property[14]. The principle is equally applicable where all the beneficiaries between them absolutely entitled are each of full age and capacity[15].

(4) Where a trustee has committed a breach of trust, his right of indemnity is limited to the extent to which the liabilities properly incurred exceed the compensation due from him to the trust estate[16].

(5) A person against whose claims the trustee is, by the settlement, entitled to be indemnified, is allowed to stand in the trustee's place, by way of subrogation, against the fund which the settlor has authorised the trustee to use in the enterprise in question[17]. Such person will therefore need to show that the debt was properly incurred and that the state of accounts between the trustee and the beneficiaries (taking into account any losses flowing from any breach of trust) is such that there is some balance in the trustee's favour to which the right of indemnity may attach[18].

9 *Dodds v Tuke* (1884) 25 Ch D 617; *Mathias v Mathias* (1858) 3 Sm & G 552; *Re Griffith* [1904] 1 Ch 807; *Octans Investments Pty Ltd v Knight* (1979) 144 CLR 360.

10 *Dimos v Dikeakos Nominees Ltd* (1996) 68 FCR 39, (1997) 149 ALR 113; *Rothmore Farms Pty Ltd v Belgravia Pty Ltd* [1999] FCA 745, (1999) 2 ITELR 159.

11 See p 820 post.

12 *X v A* [2000] 1 All ER 490.

13 See p 820 post.

14 *Hardoon v Belilios* [1901] AC 118; *J W Broomhead (Vic) Pty Ltd (in liquidation) v J W Broomhead Pty Ltd* [1985] VR 891. The previous cases at law, such as *Hosegood v Pedler* (1896) 66 LJQB 18, are inapplicable, the right being peculiarly an equitable one; cf *Jervis v Wolferstan* (1874) LR 18 Eq 18 at 24; *Fraser v Murdoch* (1881) 6 App Cas 855 at 872; *Re German Mining Co* (1854) 4 De GM & G 19 at 54; *Hobbs v Wayet* (1887) 36 Ch D 256.

15 *Balkin v Peck* (1997) 43 NSWLR 766.

16 *Re Knott* (1887) 56 LJ Ch 318; *Re Kidd* (1894) 70 LT 648 at 649. *Re Evans* (1887) 34 Ch D 597 at 601, CA; *RWG Management Ltd v Corporate Affairs Comr* [1985] VR 385.

17 *Ex p, Garland* (1804) 10 Ves 110; *Fraser v Murdoch* (1881) 6 App Cas 855, HL.

18 See cases cited in notes 2 and 3, p 824, post.

PARAGRAPH 1

Right to indemnity

As was said by Danckwerts J in *Re Grimthorpe*[19]:

> 'It is a commonplace that persons who take the onerous and sometimes dangerous duty of being trustees are not expected to do any of the work on their own expense; they are entitled to be indemnified against the costs and expenses which they incur in the course of their office; of course, that necessarily means that such costs and expenses are properly incurred and not improperly incurred. The general rule is quite plain; they are entitled to be paid back all that they have had to pay out.'

This rule, however, applies only to costs incurred for the purpose of benefiting the trust estate. Obviously trustees are not entitled to recoup their costs on an indemnity basis in respect of hostile litigation with the beneficiaries designed to define and secure their personal rights as individuals[20]. Section 31(1) of the Trustee Act 2000[1], reflecting the position in equity given statutory force since 1859, provides 'A trustee (a) is entitled to be reimbursed from the trust funds[2] or (b) may pay out of the trust funds, expenses properly incurred by him when acting on behalf of the trust'. One tends to think of the right of indemnity as inseparable from the office of the trustee[3], and it is after the Trustee Act 2000, because s 31(1) cannot be ousted by a contrary intent as was possible under the Trustee Act 1925, s 69(2) and its predecessors, when it was thought that if the trustee were willing to accept office where the trust instrument ousted his indemnity right then there was no reason why he should not be free to do so[4]. However, where exclusion of the statutory right to claim an indemnity would frustrate a subrogation claim it was possible that equity could intervene where a fraud would otherwise be perpetrated by a settlor-beneficiary or sui-juris volunteer beneficiaries claiming to take benefits without any burdens[5].

The right to an indemnity is normally crucially important for a trustee, unless he has a very liberal right to remuneration under a charging clause. Since a trust is not a legal entity that can enter into contracts, sue or be sued, it is the trustees who are personally liable unless as a matter of contract law[6] the trustees can persuade a third party to agree that the trustees' liability should be limited or excluded and that the trustees should only pay the debt out of the trust property under the statutory right to indemnity in s 31(1) of

---

19 [1958] Ch 615 at 623, [1958] 1 All ER 765 at 769.

20 *Re Dargie* [1954] Ch 16, [1953] 2 All ER 577. They are so entitled where they successfully defend themselves against an action for breach of trust, and may even recoup that part of the costs of which they were deprived for putting forward unsuccessful arguments that prolonged the case: *Armitage v Nurse* [1998] Ch 241 at 262–263. See p 818 post.

1 Section 31(2) extends s 31(1) to a trustee exercising functions as agent, nominee or custodian.

2 Defined in s 39 to mean 'income and capital funds of the trust' thereby affording greater discretion as to the ultimate incidence of expenses than before: see p 564 ante.

3 *Worrall v Harford* (1802) 8 Ves 4 at 8; *Re Exhall Coal Co Ltd* (1866) 35 Beav 449 at 453.

4 *Re German Mining Co* (1854) 4 De GM & G 19 at 52; *RWG Management Ltd v Corporate Affairs Comr* [1985] VR 385 at 395. There may be a liberal charging clause.

5 *Re Johnson* (1880) 15 Ch D 548 at 550.

6 *Muir v City of Glasgow Bank* (1879) 4 App Cas 337 at 355, 362, HL; *Perring v Draper* [1997] EGCS 109; *Marston Thompson & Evershed plc v Benn* [1998] CL 613; *Watling v Lewis* [1911] 1 Ch 414 at 424; *Re Robinson's Settlement* [1912] 1 Ch 717 at 729. Further see Trust Law Committee Consultation Paper and the Report on 'Rights of Creditors against Trustees and Trust Funds'.

the Trustee Act 2000. Trustees can never plead their contract was ultra vires and void (as companies could plead at common law) because the trustees contract as individuals who have no restriction on their capacity as individuals[7].

Damages recovered by third parties

In *Benett v Wyndham*[8] a trustee, in the due execution of his trust, directed a bailiff, employed on the trust property, to have certain trees felled. The bailiff ordered the wood-cutters usually employed on the property to fell the trees. In doing so they negligently allowed a bough to fall on to a passer-by, who, being injured, recovered heavy damages from the trustee in a court of law. These damages were, however, allowed to the trustee out of the trust property.

Calls on shares

Where a trustee of shares has been obliged to pay calls upon them, he is entitled to be reimbursed[9]; and the right to be indemnified accrues directly the liability is proved to exist[10]. However, there must be some proof that the liability is not merely hypothetical, for a person entitled to be indemnified cannot claim a declaration of his right to indemnity before the contingency which creates the damage has arisen[11]. Therefore, although a trustee may, as such, be a member of a company which is being wound up, he cannot bring an action to establish his right to an indemnity, unless he can establish the fact that calls *must* be made[12]. And where the court makes an order for the distribution of a trust fund it will not set aside any part of the fund to indemnify the testator's executors against possible liabilities which may arise in respect of leases formerly held by him, unless there is privity of estate between the executors and the lessors[13] and no assent has been executed[14].

Liability from holding title to trust property

Unless protected by statute (as in the case of inheritance tax[15]) a trustee is personally liable to the extent of his own wealth for liabilities imposed upon

7 See Lord Upjohn in *De Vigier v IRC* [1964] 2 All ER 907 at 914, HL; *Hammersmith and Fulham LBC v Monk* [1992] 1 AC 478 at 493, per Lord Browne Wilkinson; *Rolled Steel Products (Holdings) Ltd v British Steel Corpn* [1986] Ch 246 at 303, per Browne-Wilkinson LJ.
8 (1862) 4 De GF & J 259; and see *Re Raybould* [1900] 1 Ch 199.
9 *James v May* (1873) LR 6 HL 328; *Re National Financial Co* (1868) 3 Ch App 791; *Fraser v Murdoch* (1881) 6 App Cas 855. See also, as to right of executor to recover calls from a residuary legatee, *Whittaker v Kershaw* (1890) 45 Ch D 320.
10 *Hobbs v Wayet* (1887) 36 Ch D 256.
11 *Hughes-Hallett v Indian Mammoth Gold Mines Co* (1882) 22 Ch D 561.
12 However, contrast *X v A* [2000] 1 All ER 490 where the court upheld a lien in respect of potential future liability under an Act not in force and Mason P in *Commissioner of Stamp Duties v ISPT* (1999) 2 ITELR 1 at 18, 'A trustee's right of indemnity arises at the time when a liability is incurred, and, it is at this stage that the lien over trust assets arises: *Custom Credit Corpn Ltd v Ravi Nominees Pty Ltd* (1982) 8 WAR 42 at 53–53'.
13 *Re Nixon* [1904] 1 Ch 638; *Re Owers* [1941] Ch 389, [1941] 2 All ER 589. A sum paid into court as a protection to executors will be paid out when all claims against them are barred by lapse of time (*Re Lewis* [1939] Ch 232, [1939] 3 All ER 269).
14 *Re Bennett* [1943] 1 All ER 467.
15 Inheritance Tax Act 1984, s 204(2).

him as owner of trust property, but he has a right of indemnity out of the trust property where the property was properly acquired. Liability under Pt IIA of the Environmental Protection Act 1990 for the costs of cleaning up contaminated land is of particular concern to trustees and, to this end, they may retain and manage trust assets even after beneficiaries have become absolutely entitled to the trust property[16]. Perhaps the courts may develop a principle as in the USA that the trustee's liability should be limited to the extent to which the trust fund is sufficient to indemnify him where he is without fault for the liability and for the insufficiency of the fund to be able to satisfy the liability[17].

Indemnity for liabilities incurred in carrying on trust business

So where trustees or executors have *rightly* carried on a business in accordance with the provisions of a will or settlement, they are entitled to be indemnified out of the trust estate against any liabilities which they have properly incurred[18]. This right will not, however prevail against creditors *of the testator* himself unless they have assented to the business being carried on in the interest as well of themselves as of the beneficiaries under the will, and their assent will not be assumed because they have not actively interfered with the continuance of the business[19]. But where the settlement has directed a trustee to employ a specific portion only of the estate for the purpose of carrying on the business, the rule is that, although the trustee is personally liable to creditors for debts incurred by him in carrying on the trade pursuant to the settlement, his right to indemnity is limited to the specific assets so directed to be employed[20].

Solicitor's costs

A trustee or executor will be allowed the amount of a solicitor's bill of costs which he has paid for services rendered in the matter of the trust[1], even, it would seem, where the necessity for the services arose through want of caution on the part of the trustee, eg where proceedings had to be taken by an administrator against an agent to whom he had entrusted money to make payments[2]. However, under the Solicitors Act 1974, s 71(3), beneficiaries may, at the discretion of the court, obtain an order to tax the costs of the trustee's solicitor[3].

16 *X v A* [2000] 1 All ER 490.

17 *Scott on Trusts* (4th edn), para 265.4; Restatement (Second) of Trusts, para 265; section 1010(b) Uniform Trust Code.

18 *Re Oxley* [1914] 1 Ch 604, explaining *Dowse v Gorton* [1891] AC 190; *Re Evans* (1887) 34 Ch D 597, dissenting from *Re Brooke* [1894] 2 Ch 600, and *Re Hodges* [1899] 1 IR 480. For the clearest exposition of the law see *Vacuum Oil Co Pty Ltd v Wiltshire* (1945) 72 CLR 319.

19 *Re Oxley* [1914] 1 Ch 604, explaining *Dowse v Gorton* [1891] AC 190; *Re Evans* (1887) 34 Ch D 597, dissenting from *Re Brooke* [1894] 2 Ch 600, and *Re Hodges* [1899] 1 IR 480. For the clearest exposition of the law see *Vacuum Oil Co Pty Ltd v Wiltshire* (1945) 72 CLR 319.

20 *Re Johnson* (1880) 15 Ch D 548; *Re Webb* (1890) 63 LT 545. As to the right of creditors of the business to be placed in the shoes of the trustee by way of subrogation, see p 824, post.

1 *Macnamara v Jones* (1784) 2 Dick 587.

2 *Re Davis* [1887] WN 186.

3 See *Re Miles* [1903] 2 Ch 518, *McIlwraith v McIlwraith* 24 July 2002, (2002) 152 NLJ 1414.

Basis on which costs of litigation are taxed

In cases to which trustees are parties in their capacity as such, and in which it is appropriate that they should be indemnified as to their proper costs and expenses of the proceedings, the order as to the costs of the trustees should direct taxation on the indemnity basis out of the trust fund[4].

On a taxation on the indemnity basis all costs shall be allowed except insofar as they are of an unreasonable amount or have been unreasonably incurred and any doubts as to whether the costs were reasonably incurred or were reasonable in amount should be resolved in favour of the reviewing party[5].

Other instances of costs, charges, and expenses allowed trustees

It has been held that a trustee is entitled to be reimbursed costs of former trustees, paid by him to their personal representatives before the latter transfer the trust estate[6]. He is also entitled to be reimbursed costs incurred by him prior to his appointment in obtaining a statement of the trust property and ascertaining that the power of appointing new trustees is being properly exercised[7]; and also costs incurred by the donee of the power of appointment in relation to the trustee's appointment[8].

Expenses incurred in litigation with third parties

Where a trustee takes upon himself the responsibility of defending an action in relation to the trust estate without procuring the sanction of the court, then if the action succeeds the onus lies upon him of proving that he had reasonable grounds for defending it. If he cannot prove such grounds, he is not entitled to retain out of the trust property the costs of the action beyond the amount which he would have incurred if he had applied for leave to defend[9]. The position is similar where the trustee commences an action on behalf of the trust if such action fails. In attempting to ascertain whether the costs were properly incurred the court puts itself 'in the position in which the court would have been had an application been made to the court, as it ought to have been made if it was intended to throw the costs of the proceedings on the estate before commencing the action which has been brought and tried'[10].

---

4 *McDonald v Horn* [1995] 1 All ER 961, CA.
5 See *Bowen-Jones v Bowen-Jones* [1986] 3 All ER 163 at 164 where it is pointed out that the previous five main bases of taxation set out in *EMI Records Ltd v Ian Cameron Wallace Ltd* [1983] Ch 59, [1982] 2 All ER 980 now appear to have been reduced to two. See also *Re Basham* [1986] 1 WLR 1498 at 1511. See now Civil Procedure Rules, r 44.4(2) and (3), r 48.4; and p 840 post.
6 *Harvey v Olliver* [1887] WN 149.
7 *Re Pumfrey* (1882) 22 Ch D 255. This case was considered in *De Vigier v IRC* [1964] 2 All ER 907, HL, where it was considered relevant as showing that a trustee who had made payments for trust purposes was entitled in equity to a charge on the trust property and his bank was subrogated to his rights having provided the relevant money by way of loan.
8 See penultimate note.
9 *Leedham v Chawner* (1858) 4 K & J 458; *Re Beddoe* [1893] 1 Ch 547; followed, *Re England's Settlement Trusts* [1918] 1 Ch 24.
10 *Re Yorke* [1911] 1 Ch 370; *Singh v Bhasin* [2000] WTLR 275.

A protective Beddoe application

The moral is always to apply to the court for its sanction. In *Smith v Croft*[11] Walton J pointed out:

> 'In a *Beddoe* application the trustee, who is typically a wholly independent person with no axe to grind, who has, or thinks he has, a cause of action obtains leave from the court to bring the action at the expense of the trust estate. The beneficiaries concerned are joined and basically whether or not the action proceeds is determined by a majority vote of the beneficiaries, by which the minority are bound. Even when the proposed defendant is himself a beneficiary, so that his voice is not to be counted, he is always made a party, allowed to be present and to address any arguments he may wish to the court: see *Re Moritz.*'[12]

As Lightman J pointed out in *Alsop Wilkinson v Neary*[13]:

> 'Trustees have a duty to protect and preserve the trust estate for the benefit of the beneficiaries and accordingly to represent the trust in a third party dispute ... trustees are well advised to seek court authorisation before they sue or defend. The right to an indemnity and a lien will ordinarily extend to the costs of such an application. The form of application is a separate action to which all the beneficiaries are parties (either in person or by a representative defendant). With the benefit of their views the judge thereupon exercising his discretion determines what course the interests of justice require to be taken in the proceedings (see *Evans v Evans*[14] considered in *McDonald v Horn*)[15]. So long as the trustees make full disclosure of the strength, and weaknesses of their case, if the trustees act as authorised by the court their entitlement to an indemnity and lien is secure.'

A protective clause for relying on counsel's advice

The costs and delay occasioned by a need for a *Beddoe* application make it desirable to insert a clause in the original trust instrument permitting trustees to recover their expenses out of the trust fund on an indemnity basis if they act on the advice of experienced counsel (as the judge on a *Beddoe* application does to a great extent). To this end the following clause has been suggested[16], 'A Trustee shall not be liable for acting in accordance with the advice of Counsel, of at least ten years standing, with respect to the settlement. The Trustees may in particular conduct legal proceedings in accordance with such advice without obtaining a Court Order. A Trustee may recover from the Trust Fund any expenses where he has acted in accordance with such advice'. Such 'does not apply if the trustee knows or has reasonable cause to suspect that the advice was given in ignorance of material facts; if proceedings were pending to obtain the decision of the court in the matter; in relation to a Trustee who has a personal interest in the subject matter of

11 [1986] 2 All ER 551 at 558.
12 [1960] Ch 251, [1959] 3 All ER 767. Walton J should have added *Re Eaton* [1964] 3 All ER 229n, [1964] 1 WLR 1269 since *Re Moritz* indicated the defendant should not normally be present or be furnished with the plaintiff's evidence but *Re Eaton* allowed practice to be adjusted to enable a defendant to see some of the evidence and to make representations.
13 [1995] 1 All ER 431 The *Beddoe* application failed because the application was not made in separate proceedings from the main action and the necessary parties were not before the court, but Lightman J indicated an application to defend would probably fail because no funds were available to the trustees and any defence was, at its highest, speculative. Further see p 845 post.
14 [1985] 3 All ER 289 [1986] 1 WLR 101, CA.
15 [1995] 1 All ER 961.
16 J Kessler *Drafting Trusts and Will Trusts* (6th edn), para 5.28.

the advice; or in relation to a Trustee who has committed a breach of trust relating to the subject matter of the advice'.

Unreasonable expenses disallowed

Trustees will not be allowed to reimburse themselves *every* out-of-pocket expense, but only such as are reasonable and proper under the circumstances. Thus the expenses of a trustee's journey to Paris, in order that he might be present at the hearing of a suit brought in the French courts (the sole question being one of French law, and not of fact), were disallowed[17].

Voluntary subscriptions

As a general rule, the payment, by trustees, of voluntary subscriptions for public or charitable objects is not allowed. But nevertheless they may be in exceptional cases—for instance, where the subscriptions are reasonable in amount and made in the honest belief that the payment will benefit the estate[18]. As to charitable subscriptions made under the power of advancement, see p 720, ante.

Unnecessary law costs

A trustee, although entitled to obtain legal advice in relation to the execution of the trust, is not entitled, out of an excess of caution, to charge the estate with unnecessary legal costs. For instance, on retirement he is not entitled to have an attested copy of the settlement, or of the appointment of new trustees, made at the expense of the estate[19]. And on an appeal between beneficiaries it has been said that trustees ought not, as a rule, to brief counsel[20]. However, the practice is that trustees served with notice of appeal upon the construction of a will should have their costs of appearing by counsel[1]. If trustees appeal from an order of the court they will have to pay the costs if they are unsuccessful[2]. Indeed, where trustees have sought guidance from the court so as to be protected by the court's order then it is not for them to appeal: that should be done by a beneficiary[3].

Where the dispute is essentially between claimants of the trust property on the one hand and the beneficiaries under the trust on the other hand, the trustees will obtain their costs of adopting a neutral stance and making dis-

---

17 *Malcolm v O'Callaghan* (1837) 3 May & Cr 52.
18 *How v Earl of Winterton* (1902) 51 WR 262 (subscriptions to a church school allowed, as otherwise a school board would have been necessary and the estate would have been liable for an increase in rates exceeding the amount of the subscriptions). See also *Re Walker* [1901] 1 Ch 879, where the court sanctioned the payment of charitable subscriptions.
19 *Warter v Anderson* (1853) 11 Hare 301; and see Article 84 post.
20 *Carroll v Graham* [1905] 1 Ch 478; see per contra *Catterson v Clark* (1906) 95 LT 42; and cf *Re Barry's Trusts* [1906] 2 Ch 358.
 1 See old RSC Ord 59 r 10.
 2 *Re Earl of Radnor's Will Trusts* (1890) 45 Ch D 402.
 3 *Re Londonderry's Settlement* [1965] Ch 918 at 930, [1964] 3 All ER 855 at 858 per Harman LJ (with whom, it seems, Danckwerts LJ agreed) though the non-Chancery lawyer Salmon LJ disagreed at 936 and 862 because the trustees believed an appeal was essential for the protection of the general body of the beneficiaries; the trustee's appeal was successful so they were allowed their costs out of the trust fund.

closure but will not recover their costs to the extent that they side with the losing party[4].

Interest

Although a trustee is entitled to be reimbursed his out-of-pocket costs and expenses, he is not, as a rule, entitled to interest on them—a rule not altogether in accordance with justice[5]. And although by s 66(a) of the Solicitors Act 1974, a solicitor may be allowed on taxation with respect to contentious business, interest on disbursements made for his client, this does not seem to apply to disbursements made by a solicitor trustee. There is, however, an exception to the rule, namely, that where a trustee has paid out of his own moneys an interest-bearing claim against the estate, he stands by way of subrogation in the shoes of the creditor, and is entitled to interest[6].

Expenses paid out of taxed income

The expenses of the trustees are borne out of the net income of the trust after payment of income tax[7].

PARAGRAPH 2

Trustees' paramount lien on trust property for expenses

If, in an administration action, it appears probable that the trust fund will be insufficient for the payment of the whole of the costs in full, the trustees are entitled to have inserted in the order a direction that their costs, charges, and expenses shall be paid in priority to those of the beneficiaries[8]. In short, the trustees' lien takes precedence over all beneficial interests, and this not only as against original beneficiaries but also against all purchasers or mortgagees claiming through or under them[9].

A trustee who successfully defends proceedings brought against him as trustee by a beneficiary and arising out of the execution of the trust is entitled to his costs out of the trust fund and to a lien for their payment[10].

Trustees' lien for legal costs where settlement void or avoided

In *Re Holden*[11] Holden executed a post-nuptial voluntary settlement. He

4 *Alsop Wilkinson v Neary* [1995] 1 All ER 431, p 841 post.
5 *Gordon v Trail* (1820) 8 Price 416.
6 *Re Beulah Park Estate, Sargood's Claim* (1872) LR 15 Eq 43; *Finch v Pescott* (1874) LR 17 Eq 554.
7 *Aiken v Macdonald's Trustees* (1894) 3 TC 306; *Murray v IRC* 1926 SLT 714; *Macfarlane v IRC* 1929 SC 453. Income & Corporation Taxes Act 1988, s 686; J Tiley *Revenue Law* (4th edn) pp 559 and 563.
8 *Dodds v Tuke* (1884) 25 Ch D 617. But even without this direction the trustees would be entitled to be paid in priority to the other parties (*Re Griffith* [1904] 1 Ch 807; *Re Turner* [1907] 2 Ch 126).
9 *Re Knapman* (1881) 18 Ch D 300, CA; cf *Re Andrews* (1885) 30 Ch D 159.
10 *Re Spurling's Will Trusts* [1966] 1 All ER 745, [1966] 1 WLR 920, in which *Turner v Hancock* (1882) 20 Ch D 303, and *Re Grimthorpe's* [1958] Ch 615, [1958] 1 All ER 765, were applied, *Re Dunn* [1904] 1 Ch 648, was distinguished, and *Walters v Woodbridge* (1878) 7 Ch D 504, CA, was considered and explained.
11 (1887) 20 QBD 43.

subsequently commenced an action to set it aside for undue influence, but failed in his contention, the action being dismissed with costs against him, which he did not pay. He then became bankrupt within two years of the date of the settlement, which accordingly became void under the Bankruptcy Act then in force. It was held that, although the settlement was void, yet, as it had originally been valid, but voidable, and as the trustees had incurred costs in the execution of their duty which they could not recover from the bankrupt, they were entitled to be fully indemnified out of the trust funds.

In *Alsop Wilkinson v Neary*[12] Lightman J has made it clear that where there is a dispute between rival claimants to the beneficial interest in the trust property the trustee's normal duty as 'pig in the middle' is to remain neutral and offer to submit to the court's directions, leaving it to the rivals to fight their battles. If this stance be adopted the trustee will be entitled to an indemnity and lien in respect of costs necessarily and properly incurred, eg in serving a defence agreeing to submit to the court's directions and in making discovery. If the rival claimant's cannot agree how the trust fund should be invested and managed until the claims are resolved, appropriate directions can be obtained from the court under CPR Rule 64. If the trustee actively defends the trust but fails then, unless the circumstances are exceptional[13], he will not be entitled to his costs out of the trust fund, although he will be if he succeeds in his defence.

No paramount lien where trustee has mixed his money with trust fund

Where a trustee for purchase advanced money of his own to enable a particular property to be purchased and the price of the property exceeded the whole trust fund, it was held that he had not a *first* charge on the property for reimbursing himself his advance, but that the beneficiaries had a first charge on the estate for the amount of the trust fund, and that he only had a second charge for the amount of his advance[14]. The ratio decidendi in this case would seem to have been that it was not so much a question of indemnity for *costs and expenses incurred in the performance of his duty* as of a gratuitous mixing of his own moneys with the trust moneys; and that this (as will be seen later on)[15] gave the trust estate a first and paramount charge. So where a trustee paid premiums on a settled policy out of his own pocket, instead of applying a fund provided for that purpose by the settlement, he was disallowed the payments[16].

Trustee can refuse to transfer property to new trustees or absolutely entitled beneficiaries until his lien is satisfied

By virtue of his lien a trustee has the right to retain sufficient trust assets to cover actual and contingent liabilities and also possible potential liabilities that can be identified[17]. This can lead to the trustee continuing to manage the trust property after all the beneficiaries have become entitled to it,

---

12 [1995] 1 All ER 431 at 435; see pp 841–842, post.
13 *Bullock v Lloyds Bank Ltd* [1955] Ch 317, [1954] 3 All ER 726 as explained in *Alsop Wilkinson v Neary* [1995] 1 All ER 431 at 436.
14 *Re Pumfrey* (1882) 22 Ch D 255, approved in *De Vigier v IRC* [1964] 2 All ER 907, HL.
15 Article 92, post.
16 *Clark v Holland* (1854) 19 Beav 262.
17 *X v A* [2000] 1 All ER 490; Trusts of Land and Appointment of Trustees Act 1996, s 19(3)(b).

exercising its powers under the trust instrument for the benefit of itself and those beneficiaries, fairly considering the interests of itself and of them[18].

Trustee's lien continues to bind trust property in hands of successor trustees

A trustee may choose not to exercise his right of retention if satisfied that his interests are adequately protected or may overlook some possible liability, falsely assuming that liabilities of trustees attach to the holders of the office from time to time. Where he is replaced by new trustees his beneficial interest in the nature of a non-possessory lien[19] continues to bind the trust assets just like the interests of the beneficiaries[20], and affords him an independent right of recourse to the trust assets that is not dependent in any way upon the successor trustees' right of indemnity against the trust assets.

Assets distributed to beneficiaries no longer subject to lien unless it is expressly preserved

Where a trustee exercises discretionary powers of appointment or discretionary trusts in favour of X it seems that this will overreach not just the equitable interests of beneficiaries designated in the trust instrument but also the equitable interest commensurate with any right of indemnity of a trustee[1], it being implicit – if not made explicit – that the distribution is of assets freed and discharged from the trusts affecting them[2], unless otherwise stipulated. When the trust terminates so that whatever trust assets remain must be transferred to the beneficiaries absolutely entitled to them, the trustee is a superior beneficiary who will be releasing or giving away his beneficial interest in assets he transfers to the beneficiaries freed and discharged from the trusts affecting them.

Transfer subject to indemnity from new trustees

Often, to guard against known or potential liabilities, trustees will refuse to transfer trust property to new trustees until the new trustees provide an indemnity for the old trustees by virtue of the powers conferred by s 15 of the Trustee Act 1925 or by the trust instrument. To protect themselves, the new trustees will want their liability under the indemnity to be restricted to the

---

18 *X v A* [2000] 1 All ER 490 at 494–495.

19 *Dimos v Dikeakos Nominees Ltd* (1996) 68 FCR 39 (19970 149 ALR 113; *Rothmore Farms Pty Ltd v Belgravia Pty Ltd* (1999) 2 ITELR 159.

20 There are two classes of beneficiaries: (1) the trustee with a beneficial interest commensurate with his right of indemnity, (2) the persons designated as beneficiaries in the trust instrument: see *Octans Investments Pty Ltd v Knight* (1979) 144 CLR 360; *Kemtron Industries Pty Ltd v Commissioner of Stamp Duties* [1984] 1 Qd R 576 at 590.

1 *Octans Investments Pty Ltd v Knight* (1979) 144 CLR 360; *Kemtron Industries Pty Ltd v Commissioner of Stamp Duties* [1984] 1 Qd R 576; and on authorised overreaching (explaining *Vandervell v IRC* [1967] 2 AC 291) see R C Nolan [2002] Camb LJ 169 and C Harpum [1990] Camb LJ 277.

2 In *Rothmore Farms Pty Ltd v Belgravia Pty Ltd* [1999] FCA 745 (1999) 2 ITELR 159 at para 116 counsel for the sole distributee, who was party to a scheme to evade a right of indemnity and defraud creditors, did not seek to argue that the distributee took free from an original trustee's right of indemnity that survived the appointment of the distributor as new trustee. If the trustee-distributor is guilty of a fraud on a power in exercising his discretion so as to defraud an earlier trustee the exercise of the power will be void: *Cloutte v Storey* [1911] 1 Ch 18, CA.

value of the trust fund in their hands, but to protect the old trustees, it is common to provide that in calculating that value distributions of assets out of the trust fund are only to be excluded from calculation of that value if and to the extent that the beneficiaries receiving such distributions enter into direct covenants with the old trustees to indemnify them. Because procuring such covenants is necessary for the new trustees to protect themselves they can be relied upon to do so[3].

PARAGRAPH 3

Personal indemnity by beneficiary under a simple trust

In one case[4] fifty shares in a company were placed in the plaintiff's name by his employers, who were brokers. He had no beneficial interest in them, and was merely a bare trustee for the employers. Ultimately the defendant, as successor in title of the employers, became beneficially entitled to the shares, and received the dividends. Subsequently a call was made which the plaintiff was obliged to pay and thereupon he sued the defendant, who refused to indemnify him. On these facts it was held that the plaintiff was entitled to be indemnified by the defendant personally. Lord Lindley said:

'The plainest principles of justice require that the cestui que trust who gets all the benefit of the property should bear its burdens unless he can show some good reason why his trustee should bear them himself. The obligation is equitable and not legal, and the legal decisions negativing it unless there is some contract or custom imposing the obligation, are wholly irrelevant and beside the mark. Even where trust property is settled on tenants for life and children, the right of the trustee to be indemnified *out of the whole trust estate* against any liabilities arising out of any part of it is clear and indisputable; although, if that which was once one large trust estate has been converted by the trustees into several smaller distinct trust estates, the liabilities incidental to one of them cannot be thrown on the beneficial owners of the others. ... But where the only cestui que trust is a person sui juris, the right of the trustee to indemnity by him against liabilities incurred by the trustee by his retention of the trust property has never been limited to the trust property; it extends further, and imposes upon the cestui que trust a personal obligation enforceable in equity to indemnify his trustee. This is no new principle, but as old as trusts themselves. ... Although the defendant did not create the trust, he accepted a transfer of the beneficial ownership in the shares ... with full knowledge of the fact that they were registered in the plaintiff's name as trustee for their original purchasers and their assigns, whoever they might be.'

A case of this kind arose where two partners had taken a lease, as trustees, for the firm, and ultimately the executors of one of the trustees were compelled to pay large arrears of rent. It was held that they could insist upon contribution from all the co-partners, and that the fact of the lease having been assigned to a limited company which made default in paying the rent, did not free the co-partners from the trustees' right to contribution[5].

In *J W Broomhead (Vic) Pty Ltd (in liquidation) v J W Broomhead Pty Ltd*[6] the

---

3 Further see Trust Law Committee Consultation Paper, 'The Proper Protection by Liens, Indemnities or Otherwise of those who cease to be Trustees': www.kcl.ac.uk/depsta/law/tlc
4 *Hardoon v Belilios* [1901] AC 118; and see also *Jervis v Wolferstan* (1874) LR 18 Eq 18 at 24; *Fraser v Murdoch* (1881) 6 App Cas 855; *Independent Trustee Services Ltd v Rowe* [1998] OPLR 77.
5 *Matthews v Ruggles-Brise* [1911] 1 Ch 194.
6 [1985] VR 891.

defendants formed a company to carry on a trade as trustee and to pay or apply the net income to the defendants in accordance with the number of units they had under the trust (100 units had been divided into 42, 10, 24 and 24). It was held that the defendants had personally to indemnify the company trustee, though each defendant's share of the liability was not to exceed his proportion of the beneficial interest. It mattered not that some of the beneficiaries had declared sub-trusts of their units for infant children. In principle, it would seem that persons who purchase units of a unit trust can thus be called on to indemnify the trustee unless the trust instrument excludes[7] the trustee's right to be indemnified personally by the beneficiaries.

It may be that just as a right of subrogation may subsist in respect of the right of indemnity out of the trust property so it may subsist in respect of the right of indemnity against the beneficiaries personally[8]. In principle there should be no distinction between the two rights of indemnity[9].

Limits upon right to personal indemnity

The above decisions, however, only relate to the case of simple trusts in favour of a person or persons absolutely entitled who created the trust themselves or who accepted a transfer of the beneficial ownership in the trust property with full knowledge of the facts. As Lord Lindley observed[10]:

> 'it is quite unnecessary to consider in this case the difficulties which would arise if these shares were held by the plaintiff on trust for tenants for life, or for infants, or upon special trusts limiting the right to indemnity. In those cases there is no beneficiary who can be justly expected or required personally to indemnify the trustee against the ... burdens incident to his legal ownership; and the trustee accepts the trust *knowing that under such circumstances and in the absence of special contract his right to indemnity cannot extend beyond the trust estate* ie beyond the respective interests of his cestuis que trust. In this case their lordships have only to deal with a person sui juris beneficially entitled to shares which he cannot disclaim.'

The justification for making A, B, C, and D personally liable to indemnify the trustees (and creditors subrogated to the trustees) where the property is held in trust for A, B, C and D absolutely seems to rest on the principle that A, B, C and D can terminate the trust at any time as the beneficiaries of full age and capacity between them absolutely entitled to the trust property[11]. One can thus infer a continuing request by them to the trustees to incur liabilities in duly administering the trust property. Thus A, B, C and D should also be personally liable to indemnify the trustees if of full age and capacity and between them entitled to the trust property by virtue of successive rather than concurrent interests. In *Balkin v Peck*[12] the New South Wales Court of Appeal held that where property is held on trust for A for life, remainder to B, C and D equally and English trustees had to pay overlooked inheritance

---

7 The right can be excluded: *Gillan v Morrison* (1847) 1 De G & Sm 421; *Hardoon v Belilios* [1901] AC 118, PC; *RWG Management Ltd v Corporate Affairs Comr* [1985] VR 385.

8 Unless personal liability has been excluded by the trust instrument: *McLean v Burns Philip Trustee Co Pty Ltd* (1985) 2 NSWLR 623 at 641.

9 See *Scott on Trusts* (4th edn), para 478; *Belar Pty Ltd v Mahaffey* [2000] 1 Qd R 477; *Countryside (No 3) Pty Ltd v Bayside Brunswick Pty Ltd* (20 April 1994, unreported) NSW Sup Ct, Brownie J.

10 *Hardoon v Belilios* [1901] AC 118.

11 *Saunders v Vautier* (1841) 4 Beav 115 principle discussed in Article 69, ante.

12 (1997) 43 NSWLR 706, (1998) 1 ITELR 717.

tax on the death of A, (resident in England) then the trustees had a personal right of indemnity against B, C and D in Australia to whom the trustees had transferred the trust assets.

In any event if any beneficiary of full age and capacity, whether with a life interest or only interested under a discretionary trust, requests the trustee to incur a liability the beneficiary becomes personally liable to indemnify the trustee[13]. The settlor who requests the trustee to assume the office of a trustee (from which liabilities will inevitably flow) does not thereby make himself personally liable to indemnify the trustee unless he retain such wide powers to direct the trustee that the relationship of principal and agent is established between them[14].

Trustees of clubs have no right to personal indemnity

As an illustration of the remarks in the last paragraph the case of trustees of a members' club may be cited. It is a fundamental condition of clubs that members are not legally liable to any one beyond the amount of their subscriptions. There is, therefore, in the nature of the transaction an implied bargain, unless the rules of the club provide to the contrary (as they certainly ought to do), that the members shall not as beneficiaries be liable to indemnify the trustees[15], and the trustees are taken to accept the office with knowledge of this condition.

PARAGRAPH 4

Trustee can only receive costs where he has discharged his own indebtedness to the estate

If the state of accounts between the trustee and the beneficiaries, taking account of any losses caused by any breach of trust by the trustee, is such that the trustee is in deficit then he has no right to any indemnity till that deficit has been made good[16]. This will prejudice the derivative right of any creditor seeking to be subrogated to the trustee's right of indemnity[17]. However, where there are two trustees and one is indebted to the trust but the other is not, the creditors can take advantage of the latter's right to an indemnity[18]. It sometimes happens that, in the course of an administration action or summons, a trustee is ordered to refund to the estate moneys lost by reason of some breach of trust for which he is responsible, but that he is nevertheless allowed his costs of the litigation, either in the whole, or limited to costs incurred after the judgment[19]. In all such cases, however, he will not be permitted to receive the costs in fact allowed to him (or his costs, charges, and expenses properly incurred outside the litigation) until he has made

---

13 *Balsh v Hyham* (1728) 2 P Wms 453; *Hobbs v Wayet* (1887) 36 Ch D 256; *J W Broomhead (Vic) Pty Ltd v JW Broomhead Pty Ltd* [1985] VR 891.

14 *Fraser v Murdoch* (1881) 6 App Cas 855; *Trident Holdings Ltd v Danand Investments Ltd* (1988) 49 DLR (4th) 1.

15 *Wise v Perpetual Trustee Co Ltd* [1903] AC 139.

16 *Re Johnson* (1880) 15 Ch D 548 at 552; *Re Frith* [1902] 1 Ch 342 at 345; *Re Evans* (1887) 34 Ch D 597 at 601.

17 *Ex p Edmonds* (1862) 4 De G F & J 488 at 498.

18 *Re Frith* [1902] 1 Ch 342 at 346.

19 On costs see pp 840–842, post.

good the loss to the estate caused by his breach[20]. In practice the costs are set off against the liability, the trustee either receiving or paying the balance only. The principle sometimes causes hardship to the solicitor of an insolvent trustee, as he loses the security of the estate for the costs of what may have been a costly litigation, and cannot recover them from his own insolvent client[1].

PARAGRAPH 5

Persons employed by, or who supply goods to, the trustee have no direct claim on estate but may have a subrogation claim

Persons to whom a trustee has incurred liability have no original or direct right to claim payment out of the trust estate. This question usually arises in relation to the business of a testator carried on, rightly or wrongly, by his trustees. If a testator's will is silent on the question, his business ought to be sold as a going concern, or wound up with reasonable despatch. If (as sometimes happens) trustees carry it on for the benefit of the family, they do so at their own risk; and, if losses ensue, have no right to reimbursement out of the trust property, though they may have personal claims against members of the family of full age and capacity. On the other hand, a testator not infrequently directs his business to be carried on, and authorises the employment in it of all, or a specific portion, of his assets; and in that case, of course, the trustees are entitled to reimbursement of losses out of the assets so appropriated. Now in such cases the creditors of the business have no original right to claim payment of their debts out of the *trust estate*[2], their remedy being against the trustee whom they trusted; but nevertheless, they have also a right to be *put in his place* against the trust estate by subrogation. The right, however, is strictly limited to the right of the trustee himself. Therefore, if he is (by reason of breach of trust or otherwise) himself indebted to the trust estate to an extent exceeding his claim to indemnity, then, inasmuch as he cannot be entitled to an indemnity except upon the terms of making good his own indebtedness to the trust, the creditors are in no better position, and can have no claim against the estate[3].

It seems a creditor has four hurdles to surmount, needing to show that the contractual liability incurred by the trustee was not improperly incurred (1) by lack of capacity due to limits imposed by the trust instrument; (2) by lack of due authorisation where there is power to enter into the transaction but only in accordance with some requisite internal procedure which was not observed, eg the holding of a meeting before taking the decision or a

---

20 *Re Knott* (1887) 56 LJ Ch 318.
1 *Lewis v Trask* (1882) 21 Ch D 862; *Re Basham* (1883) 23 Ch D 195; *McEwan v Crombie* (1883) 25 Ch D 175. But cf *Clare v Clare* (1882) 21 Ch D 865.
2 *Re Johnson* (1880) 15 Ch D 548; *Re Webb* (1890) 63 LT 545; *Strickland v Symons* (1884) 26 Ch D 245; and see also *Redman v Rymer* (1889) 60 LT 385; *Baroness Wenlock v River Dee Co* (1887) 19 QBD 155; *Moore v M'Glynn* [1904] 1 IR 334; and as to torts, *Re Raybould* [1900] 1 Ch 199.
3 *Re Johnson* (1880) 15 Ch D 548; *Ex p Garland* (1804) 10 Ves 110; recognised in *Re Blundell* (1890) 44 Ch D 1 at 11; *Re Frith* [1902] 1 Ch 342; *Re British Power Traction and Lighting Co* [1910] 2 Ch 470. A defaulting trustee cannot claim any beneficial interest before making good his default (*Doering v Doering* (1889) 42 Ch D 203; *Re Dacre* [1916] 1 Ch 344 at 347) is the underlying principle. Further see Trust Law Committee Consultation Paper and their Report on 'Rights of Creditors against Trustees and Trust Funds'.

unanimous (not a majority) decision, or the consent of X to a decision; (3) by breach of some equitable duty, eg to diversify investments, to exercise the duty of care in appointing and supervising agents and in making investment or managerial decisions; and that the trustee (4) is not indebted to the trust by reason of conduct totally unconnected with the creditor's transaction but by virtue of some unrelated breach of trust occurring before or after such transaction.

There is nothing a potential creditor can do about the fourth hurdle unless the trustee's power to enter into the transaction with the creditor is regarded as authorising a term in the contract which confers on the creditor a direct unsecured right of recourse to the trust fund irrespective of any indebtedness of the trustee to the trust which is unrelated to the transaction and such a term is inserted in the contract[4]. Clearly, no term in the contract can protect the creditor where the liability incurred by the trustee was improperly incurred because this would enable the trustee to commit breaches of trust wholly undermining the effectiveness of the settlor's trust. The problem for a creditor in negotiating a deal with the trustees is that the better the deal is for the creditor, the more likely the deal is in breach of the trustee's duty of care, so ousting any subrogation rights of the creditor if the trustees do not discharge their liability to the creditor.

Recourse can only be made to the right of subrogation where the personally liable trustee is insolvent or the circumstances are such as to lead to the reasonable conclusion that a judgment against the trustee would be pointless[5].

Where a testator authorises trustees to carry on a business but directs that a limited part of his estate is to be used for that purpose, then the trustees' right of indemnity and, thus, the claims of creditors subsequent to the testator's death are limited to that part[6]. Similarly, if executors exercise a power of appropriation to sever the estate so that they hold half including a business for X and her family and the other half for Y and her family there is no right of recourse against Y's half for business debts arising after the severance[7]. Old case law[8] (which may require reconsideration in modern conditions) indicates that for the right of subrogation to subsist there must have been a positive express dedication or appropriation of the property to be used for the purposes of trade. This view may be confined to cases where the trustees have not been expressly authorised to carry on the business but have had to carry it on for a period by way of salvage to enable it to be sold for a reasonable price. Even here though, the court will as between the trustees and the beneficiaries allow the trustees an indemnity out of the estate so it is difficult to see why a right of subrogation should not subsist to that extent.

Protection of third parties via direct claims on estate

Trustees may have power to create a fixed charge over specific assets com-

---

4 See J G Merralls QC (1993) Australian Bar Review 248; *Scott on Trusts* (4th edn) Vol IIIA, pp 499–500.
5 *Owen v Delamere* (1872) LR 15 Eq 134; *Re Morris* (1889) 23 LR Ir 333; *Fairland v Percy* [1875] LR 3 P & D 217.
6 *Ex p Garland* (1804) 10 Ves 110.
7 *Frazer v Murdoch* (1881) 6 App Cas 855, HL.
8 *Strickland v Symons* (1884) 26 Ch D 245; and see *Re German Mining Co* (1854) 4 De GM & G 19; and *Labouchere v Tupper* (1857) 11 Moo PCC 198. But contrast *Re Raybould* [1900] 1 Ch 199.

prised in the trust estate but may they be given express power to create a floating charge over the trust estate generally, in the sense of the assets from time to time comprised within such estate? The Law Reform Committee's Twenty-Third Report (1982)[9] saw 'no reason to doubt that a trust instrument could be so worded' to confer just that sort of power[10]. The instrument should spell out the events in which such charge will crystallise. The traditional view was that because the basis of a floating charge is contract law[11] and the burden of a contract with T1 cannot without a novation be imposed on T2, a charge of future property created by T1 will not operate upon property acquired after the appointment of T2. The deed creating the floating charge should therefore ensure that there will be no change of trustee without the chargee's consent, so as to enable a new arrangement to be entered into with the new trustee, and that the charge will automatically crystallise if a change of trustees does occur without consent. The deed should also restrict the trustee's exercise of powers that could detrimentally affect the chargee (eg distributive powers over capital); it could indeed provide for the trustee's personal liability to extend to the value of assets distributed to the beneficiaries except to the extent that such beneficiaries entered into direct covenants to indemnify the chargee.

An alternative approach, taking account of an analogy with the trustee's lien conferring upon him a beneficial interest in the trust *fund*[12] (although superior to the beneficial interests of the designated beneficiaries) is that a power to create a floating charge over the assets from time to time comprised in the trust fund, when exercised, creates an equitable interest binding the trust fund, not just in the hands of the trustee-chargors but also their successors as trustees, though the latter cannot be personally liable unless there is a novation of the contract entered into by the trustee-chargors.

Where trustee is insolvent

On insolvency the right of indemnity vests in the trustee in bankruptcy or remains with the insolvent trustee[13]. The benefit of the right of indemnity out of the trust fund is available only for payment of creditors of the trust and not the general creditors of the insolvent trustee[14].

---

9 Para 2.21.

10 It seems that a power for value to make a creditor an equitable beneficiary in the trust fund in its state from time to time until payment of the debt would in substance be held to be a security interest by way of floating charge: see p 15, ante.

11 *Holroyd v Marshall* (1862) 10 HL Cas 191; *Tailby v Official Receiver* (1888) 13 App Cas 523; *Akron Tyre Co Pty Ltd v Kittson* (1951) 82 CLR 477.

12 *Kemtron Industries Pty Ltd v Comr of Stamp Duties* [1984] 1 QdR 576 at 590; *Octavo Investments Pty Ltd v Knight* (1979) 144 CLR 360; *Dimos v Dikeakos Nominees Ltd* (1996) 68 FCR 39, (1997) 149 ALR 113.

13 *St Thomas' Hospital Governors v Richardson* [1910] 1 KB 271, CA; *Re Richardson* [1911] 2 KB 705 at 717, CA.

14 *Re Richardson* [1911] 2 KB 705; *Re Byrne Australia Pty Ltd* [1981] 1 NSWLR 394; *Re Byrne Australia Pty Ltd (No 2)* [1981] 2 NSWLR 364; *Collie v Merlaw Nominees Pty Ltd* [2001] Victoria SC 39. Also see *Rye v Ashfield Nominees Ltd* New Law Digest, 2 August 2001.

ARTICLE 84

Right to discharge on completion of trusteeship

Upon the completion of his trusteeship, a trustee is entitled to have his accounts examined and settled by the beneficiaries; and either to have a formal discharge given to him or to have the accounts taken in court. He cannot, however, as a rule, demand a release by deed[15], nor to have deeds relating to the trust, or to the title of an assign of one of the original beneficiaries, handed over to him; but it seems that he is entitled to an examined copy and to an acknowledgment for production and an undertaking for safe custody.

Release by deed cannot usually be required

A trustee, on finally transferring stock to a beneficiary, demanded from the latter a deed of release. The beneficiary, however, refused to give him anything except a simple receipt for the amount of stock actually transferred which, of course, left it open to him to say that that amount was not the amount to which he was entitled. The court held that no *deed* was demandable, but in *Chadwick v Heatley*[16], the judge said:

'Though it may not have been the right ... of the trustee to require a deed, I think that it was his right to require that his account should be settled—that is to say, that he and his family should be delivered from the anxiety and misery attending unsettled accounts.'

And *Kindersley V-C in King v Mullins*[17] said:

'In the case of a declared trust, where the trust is apparent on the face of a deed, the fund clear, the trust clearly defined, and the trustee is paying either the income or the capital of the fund, if he is paying it in strict accordance with the trusts, he has no right to require a release under seal. It is true that in the common case of *executors*, when the executorship is being wound up, it is the practice to give executors a release. An executor has a right to be clearly discharged, and not to be left in a position in which he may be exposed to further litigation; therefore he fairly says, unless you give me a discharge on the face of it protecting me, I cannot safely hand over the fund; and therefore it is usual to give a release; but such a claim on the part of a *trustee* would in strictness be improper, if he is paying in accordance with the letter of the trust. In such a case he would have no right to a release.'

Right to settlement of account restricted to the actual trust fund

Although a trustee is entitled to have his accounts settled before handing over the trust fund, this right is confined to the accounts of that particular trust. Where, therefore, a person is trustee of two distinct trusts for the same

---

15 *Chadwick v Heatley* (1845) 2 Coll 137; *Re Wright's Trusts* (1857) 3 K & J 419; *King v Mullins* (1852) 1 Drew 308; *Tiger v Barclay's Bank Ltd* [1951] 2 KB 556, [1951] 2 All ER 262; affd [1952] 1 All ER 85, CA, where this point was not in issue; and see *Re Earl of Stamford* [1896] 1 Ch 288 at 301; Law of Property (Miscellaneous Provisions) Act 1989, s 1 (now contains the formalities requirements for a deed).
16 (1845) 2 Coll 137.
17 (1852) 1 Drew 308 at 311.

beneficiaries, he cannot mix up the two, and refuse to pay over the first fund until all questions as to the second have been settled[18].

Release may be required in exceptional cases

Where trust moneys have been resettled, the trustees or executors of the original settlement or will are, it has been said, entitled to a release by deed from their beneficiaries, though they are entitled only to a mere receipt from the trustees to whom they pay the moneys[19]. On the other hand, where a person having a *general* power of appointment by will, appoints the fund in pursuance of the power and appoints executors, the trustees of the fund can safely hand it over to the executors on their receipt, and cannot demand a release by deed from the beneficiaries[20]; for, by appointing, the donee of the power makes the property assets of his own[1].

Trustee cannot demand custody of assignments of shares of the original beneficiaries

It is well settled that, on the distribution of a trust fund, a share in which has been previously assigned, the trustee has no right to require the delivery to him of the assignment and other documents of title before payment of his share to the assignee[2]; and of course it follows that a trustee cannot require a power of attorney to be handed to him[3]. However, he is entitled to retain custody of the trust instrument and of appointments of new trustees.

How far a trustee is entitled to copies of deeds, etc

This, however, does not dispose of the question whether a trustee can demand *copies* of those documents which justify him in doing what he has in fact done. This certainly does not seem unreasonable in principle, especially where he is paying money to a person who claims as attorney or assignee of one of the original beneficiaries. The authorities seem to show that he can demand plain examined copies, but not attested copies or, a fortiori, duplicates, except perhaps at his own expense. Thus in *Warter v Anderson*[4] the representative of a deceased trustee was held not to be entitled, upon transferring the property to new trustees, to be furnished at the expense of the trust with a duplicate of the appointment of the new trustees, nor even to an attested copy thereof, although the Vice-Chancellor intimated that he had a right to have an examined copy and possibly at his own expense an attested copy or even a duplicate.

Further, it would seem from the judgment of Swinfen Eady J in a subsequent case that possibly a trustee may be entitled to insist upon an acknowledgment for production and an undertaking for safe custody as well as to a copy[5].

---

18 *Price v Loaden* (1856) 21 Beav 508.
19 *Re Cater's Trusts (No 2)* (1858) 25 Beav 366.
20 *Re Hoskin's Trusts* (1877) 5 Ch D 229; on appeal 6 Ch D 281.
  1 See p 803, ante.
  2 *Re Palmer* [1907] 1 Ch 486.
  3 *Re Palmer* [1907] 1 Ch 486.
  4 (1853) 11 Hare 301; and see *Clayton v Clayton* [1930] 2 Ch 12.
  5 *Re Palmer* [1907] 1 Ch 486.

ARTICLE 85

Right to pay trust funds into court in certain circumstances

(1) Trustees, or the majority of trustees, having in their hands or under their control money or securities belonging to a trust, may pay the same into court[6].

(2) Payment into court is not, however, justifiable merely in order to raise some question which can be determined more cheaply by means of a Part 8 claim form (replacing an originating summons)[7]; nor where the equities are perfectly clear[8], and, if trustees pay into court in such circumstances, they may have to pay the costs of obtaining payment out[9].

Payment into court where beneficiaries are under disability

A trustee is justified in paying money into court where he cannot get a valid discharge; as, for instance, where beneficiaries who are absolutely entitled are infants[10] or of unsound mind[11].

Where money claimed by a representative

It has been said that a trustee may properly pay money into court where it is claimed by the representative of a beneficiary because the beneficiary may have disposed of it[12], but a Part 8 claim would seem to be the more appropriate course.

Payment to one who claims in default of appointment

A trustee ought not to hesitate to pay the money to a beneficiary who claims in default of appointment, if he has no notice of any appointment by the donee of the power, and no ground for believing that any appointment has been made. For in that case he could not be made liable if he paid over the fund, even if an appointment were subsequently discovered[13]. Anyhow, now, a trustee in such a case would only be allowed the costs of a claim.

---

6 Ie the High Court, or where the funds paid in are of less than £30,000 in value the county court; see the Trustee Act 1925, s 63, and the County Courts Act, 1984, s 23.
7 *Re Giles* (1886) 34 WR 712.
8 *Re Cull's Trusts* (1875) LR 20 Eq 561; *Re Elliot's Trusts* (1873) LR 15 Eq 194.
9 *Re Cull's Trusts* (1875) LR 20 Eq 561; *Re Elliot's Trusts* (1873) LR 15 Eq 194; *Re Leake's Trusts* (1863) 32 Beav 135; *Re Heming's Trust* (1856) 3 K & J 40.
10 *Re Cawthorne* (1848) 12 Beav 56; *Re Beauclerk* (1862) 11 WR 203; *Re Coulson's Trust* (1857) 4 Jur NS 6. It was unsafe to keep and invest an infant's legacy as if the investment depreciated the executor was liable (*Re Salomons* [1920] 1 Ch 290). After 1925 instead of paying it into court the better course is for the personal representatives to appoint trustees of the legacy under the power given by the Administration of Estates Act 1925, s 42; or to make an appropriation under s 41 thereof.
11 *Re Upfull's Trust* (1851) 3 Mac & G 281; *Re Irby* (1853) 17 Beav 334; and see *Re Carr's Trusts* [1904] 1 Ch 792.
12 *Re Lane's Trust* (1854) 24 LTOS 181; *King v King* (1857) 1 De G & J 663.
13 Per Jessel MR in *Re Cull's Trusts* (1875) LR 20 Eq 561, distinguishing *Re Wylly's Trusts* (1860) 28 Beav 458; but see also *Re Swan* (1864) 2 Hem & M 34; *Re Roberts' Trust* (1869) 17 WR 639; *Re Bendyshe* (1857) 5 WR 816; *Re Williams' Settlement* (1858) 4 K & J 87.

Reasonable doubt or claim

Again, where the trustee is uncertain as to the persons entitled[14] as when he has a bona fide doubt as to the law[15], or has received a bona fide claim sanctioned by respectable solicitors[16], he may properly pay the fund into court, unless the question can be settled by a Part 8 claim or the trustee will be protected by taking advantage of s 27 of the Trustee Act 1925 or s 48 of the Administration of Justice Act 1985. For instance, where a necessary party to a claim is out of the jurisdiction, so that the proceedings could not be served, payment into court would be justifiable.

Undue caution

Where, however, a beneficiary in reversion who had gone to Australia, and had not been heard of for some years, suddenly reappeared, and there was no reasonable doubt as to his identity, it was held that the trustee was not entitled to pay the trust fund into court, and he was ordered to *pay* the costs of all parties[17].

General warning

Lastly, warning must be given that, now that most questions of doubt or difficulty can be decided on a Part 8 claim, the right of paying money into court can only be used with safety in somewhat rare cases as a last resort and that the apparently unconditional invitation extended to trustees by the words of s 63(1) of the Trustee Act 1925 is an invitation which can only be accepted at the risk of having to pay costs.

---

14 *Re Headington Trust* (1857) 6 WR 7.
15 *King v King* (1857) 1 De G & J 663; *Re Metcalfe* (1864) 2 De GJ & Sm 122; *Gunnell v Whitear* (1870) LR 10 Eq 664.
16 *Re Maclean's Trusts* (1874) LR 19 Eq 274.
17 *Re Elliot's Trusts* (1873) LR 15 Eq 194; *Re Foligno's Mortgage* (1863) 32 Beav 131; *Re Knight's Trusts* (1859) 27 Beav 45; *Re Woodburn's Will* (1857) 1 De G & J 333; *Re Cull's Trusts* (1875) LR 20 Eq 561 and see A J Hawkins (1968) 84 LQR 64 at 65–67. As to when payment into court is justifiable, see *Re Davies' Trusts* (1914) 59 Sol Jo 234.

CHAPTER 19

The right of trustees and beneficiaries to seek the assistance of the Public Trustee or the court in auditing or in administering the trust

Article
86 Right of trustee or beneficiary to official audit of the trust through the Public Trustee   831
87 Right of trustee or beneficiary to take the direction of the court in relation to specific questions   832
88 Right under certain circumstances to have the trust administered under the direction of the court   845

ARTICLE 86

Right of trustee or beneficiary to official audit of the trust through the Public Trustee

On an application being made to the Public Trustee[1] and notice thereof given by any trustee or beneficiary[2], the condition and accounts of any trust must, unless the court orders otherwise, be investigated and audited by such solicitor or public accountant as may be agreed on by the applicant and the trustees or, in default of agreement[3], by the Public Trustee or some person appointed by him[4]. A trustee or beneficiary cannot be appointed to make the investigation or audit[5]. The Public Trustee may require a deposit from the applicant for payment of any expenses of the investigation or audit ordered by the Public Trustee to be paid by the applicant personally[6].

Except with the permission of the court, the investigation and audit must not be required within twelve months of any previous investigation and audit[7].

1 Public Trustee Rules 1912, r 31.
2 The notice must, unless the Public Trustee directs otherwise, be given to every other trustee or beneficiary (Public Trustee Rules 1912, r 12).
3 If no solicitor or public accountant has been appointed within one month from the date of the application, there is deemed to be a default of agreement and the applicant may apply to the Public Trustee accordingly (Public Trustee Rules 1912, r 34).
4 Public Trustee Act 1906, s 13(1).
5 See Public Trustee Act 1906, s 13(1).
6 Public Trustee Rules 1912, r 32.
7 See the proviso to Public Trustee Act 1906, s 13(1).

On the other hand, s 22(4) of the Trustee Act, which gives the right of having an audit to the trustees, provides that, except in special circumstances, an audit shall not be made more than once in every three years[8]. These enactments seem to be somewhat conflicting but when trustees require a more frequent audit than a triennial one it will, in practice, usually be because there are 'special circumstances' such as are contemplated by s 22(4) of the 1925 Act. The Public Trustee may restrict the investigation and audit, eg to a specified time or trust property[9].

The costs of the investigation and audit, including the auditor's remuneration[10] will normally be paid out of the trust fund, but the Public Trustee may order the applicant or trustee to pay such costs personally or partly by one and partly by the other[11]. Before making any such order, the Public Trustee should hear the parties[12]. Where an application is unreasonable and vexatious the Public Trustee would be right to make the applicant pay the costs[13]. A person aggrieved by any act or omission or decision of the Public Trustee may apply to the court. The application should be made to a judge of the Chancery Division of the High Court sitting in private[14]. It should be made by CPR Part 8 claim form.

The Law Reform Committee has recommended the repeal of s 13: it has been invoked only occasionally and its operation has not been found to be particularly effective since there are no powers to enforce the Public Trustee's findings[15].

ARTICLE 87

Right of trustee or beneficiary to take the directions of the court in relation to specific questions

(1) A claim may be brought[16] for the determination of any question arising in the execution of a trust. The following are examples of the types of claims which may be brought[17]:

---

8 Accounts may be kept by an accountant under Trustee Act 2000 s 11.
9 Public Trustee Rules 1912, r 33.
10 For fees see Public Trustees (Fees) Order 1999, SI 1999/855.
11 Public Trustee Act 1906, s 13(5).
12 *Re Oddy* [1911] 1 Ch 532.
13 *Re Oddy* [1911] 1 Ch 532; *Utley* [1912] WN 147.
14 Public Trustee Act 1906, s 10; see CPR Sch 1 RSC Ord 93 r 2.
15 Cmnd 8733 para 4.48
16 This paragraph sets out the effect of CPR Pt 64 r 64.2(1) and Practice Direction to CPR Pt 64 para 1. The old RSC Ord 85 was preserved with amendments by the new rules (CPR, r 50.1 and Sch 1). The scheduled rules were revoked by CPR Pt 64 which came into force on 2 December 2002. Any attempt to exclude this right to apply to the court (eg by a provision in a will that the determination by the trustees of any questions and matters arising in the execution of the trusts shall be conclusive and binding on all parties) is void (*Re Wynn* [1952] Ch 271, [1952] 1 All ER 341, and see *Bury v Phillips* (1696) Skin 477; *Re Raven* [1915] 1 Ch 673). Questions of fact may be left to be determined by trustees: *Re Coxen* [1948] Ch 747, [1948] 2 All ER 492; *Re Tuck's Settlement* [1978] Ch 49, [1978] 1 All ER 1047, CA. See p 89 ante.
17 Practice Direction to CPR Pt 64 para 1. It is also common practice to add a claim for the execution of the trusts under the court's direction 'if and so far as may be necessary'. This may not be wanted but to do so avoids a multitude of objections if that proves necessary (see *Re Berens* [1888] WN 95: and see also *Re Freme's Contract* [1895] 2 Ch 256; affd [1895] 2 Ch

(a) A claim for the determination of any of the following questions[18]:
  (i) any question as to the composition of any class of persons having a beneficial interest in any property subject to a trust[19];
  (ii) any question as to the rights or interests of a person claiming to be beneficially entitled under a trust.
(b) A claim for any of the following remedies[20]:
  (i)   an order requiring a trustee to provide and, if necessary, verify accounts[1];
  (ii) an order requiring a trustee to pay into court money which he holds in that capacity[2];
  (iii) an order directing a trustee to do or not to do a particular act[3];
  (iv) an order approving any sale, purchase, compromise or other transaction by a trustee[4];
  (v)   an order directing any act to be done in the execution of a trust which the court could order to be done if the trust were being executed under the direction of the court[5].
Third party disputes[6] should not be decided in this way[7]. Contingent or future questions cannot normally be decided[8]. A claim brought to determine questions arising in the execution of a trust must be made by Part 8 claim form[9].
(2) If a question of construction of a will or a trust has arisen and the opinion in writing of a person with a ten year High Court qualification[10] has been obtained, then the court on the application of the personal representatives or trustees without hearing any argument,

---

778). The court will only make an administration order if it considers that the issues between the parties cannot properly be resolved in any other way (see Practice Direction to CPR Pt 64 para 3.1).

18 Practice Direction to CPR Pt 64 para 1(1). For precedents, see 41 Atkin's Court Forms (2000 issue), forms 127–129.

19 For precedents, see 41 Atkin's Court Forms (2000 issue), Forms 130–132.

20 Practice Direction to CPR Pt 64, para 1(2).

 1 For precedents, see 41 Atkin's Court Forms (2000 issue), Forms 209, 210.

 2 *Nutter v Holland* [1894] 3 Ch 408. For precedents, see 41 Atkin's Court Forms (2000 issue), Form 141.

 3 For precedents, see 41 Atkin's Court Forms (2000 issue), Forms 137–143. This procedure is not appropriate to compel trustees to concur in a sale of property in a partition action (*Suffolk v Lawrence* [1889] 32 WR 899. See also *Re Leask* [1891] 65 LT 199. The court does not generally interfere with the exercise of trustees' powers, see Art 61 ante.

 4 For precedents, see 41 Atkin's Court Forms (2000 issue), Forms 148–153; see *Re Robinson* (1885) 31 Ch D 247.

 5 For precedents, see 41 Atkin's Court Forms (2000 issue), Forms 154–156

 6 Ie disputes with persons, otherwise than in the capacity of beneficiaries, in respect of rights and liabilities assumed by the trustees as such in the administration of the trust (see *Alsop Wilkinson v Neary* [1995] 1 All ER 431 at 434).

 7 See *Marley v Mutual Security Merchant Bank* [1991] 3 All ER 198 at 201.

 8 *Re Berens* [1888] WN 95; see p 838 post. The court will also not accept a general surrender of a discretion which is exercisable from time to time in changing circumstances (*Re Allen-Meyrick's Will Trusts* [1966] 1 WLR 499).

 9 CPR Pt 64, r 64.3. For the necessary contents of a Part 8 claim form see CPR Pt 8, r 8.2. In particular, the claim form must contain a statement showing the representative role of the trustee in the proceedings (CPR, r 8.2(d) and (e)).

10 As to which see Courts and Legal Services Act 1990, s 71(2), Sch 10 para 63.

may make an order authorising them to take such steps in reliance on the opinion as are specified in the order[11]. The court will not make such an order if it appears that a dispute exists which makes it inappropriate to make the order without hearing argument[12].

(3) Where the trustees or by analogy other parties bring a claim to have the trust instrument construed for their guidance or to have determined some question arising in the administration, the costs of all parties will normally be ordered to be paid out of the trust fund, and generally those costs will be ordered to be assessed on the indemnity basis[13]. Where the claim concerns rival claims to the trust fund or it is, in substance, hostile litigation, the court will normally order the unsuccessful party to pay the costs of the successful party[14]. A trustee, beneficiary or other person concerned in relation to the administration of a trust may apply to the court at any stage of proceedings for an order that his costs be paid out of the trust fund[15]. An application can be made to the court (a *Beddoe* application) for directions whether or not the trustee should bring or defend proceedings in his capacity as trustee[16].

(4) No claim for the determination of questions arising in the execution of a trust can be brought after the trust has been completely administered and the property handed over by the trustees; any relief claimed by beneficiaries after that must be the subject of a claim brought by standard claim form under Part 7 of CPR[17].

PARAGRAPH 1

JURISDICTION

Trustees are entitled to seek the assistance of the court in determining how the trust instrument should be construed or as to the proper administration of the trust so as to enable them to execute their duties properly. They can then act in accordance with that guidance without fear that they are in breach of trust. It is clear that a beneficiary is also entitled to seek the court's guidance[18].

11 Under Administration of Justice Act 1985, s 48(1). The claim is brought by Part 8 procedure (CPR Pt 64, r 64.3). No defendant should be named under CPR Pt 8, r 8.2A. No separate application for permission under r 8.2A need be made. For the procedure generally see Practice Direction to CPR Pt 64 para 5 and para 26.36 of the Chancery Guide.
12 Administration of Justice Act 1985, s 48(2). This procedure will not be inappropriate where the dispute is between two rival constructions of which one is obviously wrong.
13 *Re Buckton* [1907] 2 Ch 406; see CPR Pt 48, r 48.4(2). The general principles set out in *Re Buckton* have not been superseded by CPR (*see D'Arbo v Page (No 2)* (2000) Times, 10 August).
14 *Re Buckton* [1907] 2 Ch 406.
15 Practice Direction to CPR Pt 64 para 6.3. Where trustees have power to agree to pay the costs of a party, and exercise properly such a power, CPR, r 48.3 applies. In such a case, an order is not required and the trustees are entitled to recover out of the trust fund any costs which they pay pursuant to the agreement made in exercise of the power (Practice Direction at para 6.2).
16 *Re Beddoe* [1893] 1 Ch 547.
17 *Wightman v Cousins* [1932] NI 61, CA.
18 See, eg, the nature of the remedies set out in Practice Direction to CPR Pt 64 para 1(2). Protectors may also raise a claim (see *von Knierem v Bermuda Trust Co Ltd* Butts OCM Vol 1,

Where the court is asked to make a decision on a course of action proposed or actually taken by trustees, the court may be exercising its own discretion or simply protecting the trustees in an exercise of their own. The act of seeking the court's guidance does not however necessarily involve the trustees in a surrender of discretion[19]. The analysis of Robert Walker J in an unreported decision, referred to in *Public Trustee v Cooper*[20], provides guidance.

First, there are proceedings for guidance as to whether some proposed action is within the trustees' powers. That is ultimately a question of construction of the trust instrument or statute or both.

Second, there are cases in which the question is whether the proposed course of action is a proper exercise of the trustees' power but no real doubt exists as to the nature and extent of the power and the trustees have decided how they want to exercise it. The trustees wish to obtain the blessing of the court because the decision is particularly momentous. In such cases, there is no question of surrender of discretion. Indeed it is most unlikely that the court will be persuaded in the absence of special circumstances to accept a surrender of discretion on questions of that sort since the trustees are prima facie in a much better position than the court to know what is in the best interests of the beneficiaries.

Third, there are cases of surrender of discretion properly so called. There the court will only accept a surrender of discretion for a good reason, the most obvious being either that the trustees are deadlocked (but honestly deadlocked, so that the question cannot be resolved by removing one trustee rather than another) or because the trustees are disabled as a result of a conflict of interest. The difference between category (2) and category (3) is under the former the court is approving the exercise of discretion by trustees and under the latter it is exercising its own discretion.

Fourth, there are cases where trustees have actually taken action, and that action is attacked as being either outside their powers or an improper exercise of their powers.

PROCEDURE

Claim Form and Parties

A claim for the court to determine any question arising in the execution of a trust must be made by issuing a Part 8 claim form[1]. All the trustees must be

---

116; *Re Omar Family Trust* [2000] WTLR 713 at 714; *Re Hare Trust* (2001) 4 ITELR 288), presumably because a question arises or a remedy is sought like one in Article 88(1)(b)(iii) or (v) which could be determined or granted in a claim for execution of the trust under the direction of the court, and a protectorship can be an office under the trust like a trusteeship, so the court has inherent power to appoint a protector where otherwise the office would not be filled and, presumably, to replace a wrongdoing protector: *Steele v Paz Ltd* [1993-95] Manx LR 102 and, on appeal, 426.

19 *Public Trustee v Cooper* [2001] WTLR 901. Hart J followed and quoted from an unreported decision, given in private, of Robert Walker J which explained that the case of *Marley v Mutual Security Merchant Bank and Trust Co Ltd* [1991] 3 All ER 198 was not authority for the proposition that the act of seeking directions necessarily involved a trustee in a surrender of discretion.

20 *Public Trustee v Cooper* [2001] WTLR 901 at 922–924.

1 CPR Pt 64 r 64(3). If the claim involves an allegation of fraud or wilful default or other breach of trust against the trustees and there is likely to be a substantial dispute of fact, the Part 8 procedure will usually be unsuitable. The court may order at any stage the claim to continue as if begun by standard claim for under CPR Pt 7 (CPR Pt 8 r 8.13). It will then allocate to a track and give directions.

parties[2]. If the claim is brought by some of the trustees, any other trustee who does not consent to being joined as a claimant must be made a defendant[3]. A claim may be brought by or against trustees without adding as parties any beneficiaries[4]. Any judgment or order given or made in the claim will be binding on the beneficiaries unless the court orders otherwise[5]. The claimant may make parties to the claim any beneficiaries who it is appropriate to make parties having regard to the nature of the order sought[6]. If there are only two views as to the appropriate course, and one is advocated by one beneficiary who will be joined, it may not be necessary for other beneficiaries to be joined since the trustees may be able to present the other argument[7]. If the trustees are unsure as to which beneficiaries need to be joined, they may issue the claim form without naming any defendants[8] and apply for directions as to which ones should be joined in or notified of the proceedings[9].

Evidence

The trustees' evidence should be given by witness statement. In order to ensure that, if directions are given, the trustees are properly protected by the order, they must ensure full disclosure of relevant matters, even if the case is to proceed with the participation of beneficiaries as defendants[10]. One type of application which is of considerable importance in practice is for the court's guidance as to whether the trustees should or should not bring or defend litigation (a *Beddoe* application)[11]. Such applications should be supported by evidence including the advice of an appropriately qualified lawyer[12] as to the prospects of success and other matters relevant to be taken into account, including a cost estimate for the proceedings and any known facts concerning the means of the opposite party to the proceedings and a draft of any proposed statement of case[13].

The evidence should also state whether any relevant pre-action protocol has been followed and the trustees have proposed or undertaken (or intend to propose) mediation by ADR and, if not, why not[14].

All applications for directions should be supported by evidence showing the value of the trust assets, the significance of the proposed litigation or other courses of action for the trust and why directions are needed[15]. In the case of a pension trust the evidence should include the latest actuarial valuation and describe the membership profile and, if a deficit on winding

---

2 CPR r 64.4(1)(a).
3 CPR r 64.4(1)(b).
4 CPR r 19.7A(1).
5 CPR r 19.7A(2). It is not normal practice to make representation orders (under CPR r 19.7) on an application for directions. The trustees will have all the authority they need without having to join every beneficiary.
6 CPR r 64.4(1)(c).
7 Practice Direction B to CPR Pt 64, para 4.1.
8 Under CPR Part 8 r 8.2A.
9 Practice Direction B to CPR Pt 64 para 4.3.
10 *Marley v Mutual Security Merchant Bank* [1991] 3 All ER 198 at 201; see also Practice Direction B to CPR Pt 64 para 7.1 and Practice Direction to CPR Pt 64 para 6.7 (in relation to prospective costs orders).
11 [1893] 1 Ch 547.
12 As to which see Practice Direction B to CPR Pt 64 para 7.3.
13 Practice Direction B to CPR Pt 64 para 7.2.
14 Practice Direction B to CPR Pt 64 para 7.5.
15 Practice Direction B to CPR Pt 64 para 7.4.

up is likely, the priority provisions and their likely effect[16].

If a beneficiary is party to the proposed litigation, he should be a party to the claim for directions but any material which would be privileged as regards that beneficiary should be put in evidence as exhibits to the trustees' witness statement and should not be served on the beneficiary[17]. The beneficiary defendant may be excluded from part of the hearing, including that which relates to the material withheld[18]. The evidence should also explain what consultation, if any, there has been with beneficiaries[19]. The trustees will be expected to have canvassed the proposed course of action with all the adult beneficiaries of a private trust or, if there are numerous beneficiaries, with the principal adult beneficiaries.

If a child beneficiary is a defendant, the court will expect to have put before it the instructions to and advice of an appropriately qualified lawyer as to the benefits and disadvantages of the proposed, and any other relevant, course of action from the point of view of the child[20].

Case management, hearings and level of judge

The claim will be referred to the Master to consider directions for the management of the case[1]. This will happen when either a defendant has acknowledged service or the period for doing so has expired or, if no defendant is named, as soon as the claimants' evidence has been filed[2]. Such directions may be given without a hearing in some cases including directions as to parties or as to notice of proceedings.

The court will always consider whether it is possible to deal with the application on paper without a hearing[3]. The trustees must always consider whether a hearing is needed for any reason[4]. If a party considers that a hearing is needed, this should be stated and the reasons explained in his evidence or otherwise in a letter to the court[5]. If the court is minded to refuse to give directions asked for on a consideration of the papers alone, the

---

16 Practice Direction B to CPR Pt 64 para 7.4.

17 Practice Direction B to CPR Pt 64 para 7.6. See also *Re Moritz decd* [1960] Ch 251, [1959] 3 All ER 767; *Re Eaton* [1964] 1 WLR 1269, [1964] 3 All ER 299. Where, of necessity, separate from particular litigation the trustees make a *Beddoe* application in relation to recovery of the costs thereof out of the trust fund the beneficiaries must be parties even though not parties to the litigation against the trustee: *Alsop Wilkinson v Neary* [1996] 1 WLR 1220 [1995] 1 All ER 431; *STG Valmet Trustees Ltd v Brennan* [2002] WTLR 273 (CA Gibraltar comprising three retired English L.JJ.). Further see *Breadner v Granville Grossman* [2001] WTLR 377 at 390.

18 Practice Direction B to CPR Pt 64 para 7.6. See also *Re Moritz decd* [1960] Ch 251, [1959] 3 All ER 767; *Re Eaton* [1964] 1 WLR 1269, [1964] 3 All ER 299. Where, of necessity, separate from particular litigation the trustees make a *Beddoe* application in relation to recovery of the costs thereof out of the trust fund the beneficiaries must be parties even though not parties to the litigation against the trustee: *Alsop Wilkinson v Neary* [1996] 1 WLR 1220 [1995] 1 All ER 431; *STG Valmet Trustees Ltd v Brennan* [2002] WTLR 273 (CA Gibraltar comprising three retired English L.JJ.). Further see *Breadner v Granville Grossman* [2001] WTLR 377 at 390.

19 Practice Direction B to CPR Pt 64 para 7.7.

20 Practice Direction B to CPR Pt 64 para 7.10.

1 Practice Direction B to CPR Pt 64 para 5.1.

2 Practice Direction B to CPR Pt 64 para 5.1.

3 Practice Direction B to CPR Pt 64 para 6.1; see also Practice Direction to CPR Pt 64 para 6.5 (in relation to prospective costs orders).

4 Practice Direction B to CPR Pt 64 para 6.1; see also Practice Direction to CPR Pt 64 para 6.5 (in relation to prospective costs orders).

5 Practice Direction B to CPR Pt 64 para 6.1; see also Practice Direction to CPR Pt 64 para 6.5 (in relation to prospective costs orders).

parties will be notified and given the opportunity to ask for a hearing[6].

The claim will usually be listed and heard in private[7]. If confidentiality of the directions sought is important (eg directions relating to actual or proposed litigation with a third party who could find out what directions the claimants are seeking through access to the claim form[8]) the statement of the remedy[9] may be expressed in general terms[10]. The trustees must, in that case, state specifically in the evidence what directions they seek.

A master or district judge may give the directions sought though, if the directions relate to actual or proposed litigation, only if it is a plain case, and therefore usually without a hearing[11]. A master or district judge may not deal with questions of law or the construction of a document[12].

Contingent or future questions not usually decided

The court is very reluctant to decide question which have not yet arisen or may never arise, particularly where the decision affects the rights, or possible rights, of unborn persons. But exceptions are made where a beneficiary's rights under the trust depend on an event which is presently contemplated, so that until the question is decided he is practically unable to shape his conduct. Thus a daughter could raise a claim as to the validity of the trusts of her father's will forbidding marriage with a person of different faith[13]. On the other hand, in a case where Sir Arthur Underhill appeared for the trustees, the court refused to consider the question whether a tenant for life (who had been married some years and had no issue) would, if he died without issue, be absolutely entitled to the trust fund, or whether there would be a gift over to his brother's issue. His evidence was that if it was decided that he would be absolutely entitled he need not save so much of his income as would otherwise be necessary, but this was held to be insufficient. The moral seems to be that contingent questions will not be decided unless the contingent event depends on the applicant's volition, and he convinces the court that he intends to exercise that volition forthwith if the result of doing so would not deprive him of his rights under the trust. For example, if a will gave income of a trust fund to a testator's son until he quits the kingdom and then over to another, it is probable that if the son contemplated accepting an official appointment abroad the court would say whether the effect of doing so would cause a forfeiture, but it would probably not decide the question if the son had no present intention of quitting the kingdom unless the son was arguing that the contingent event was void for uncertainty[14].

---

6 Practice Direction B to CPR Pt 64 para 6.2; see also Practice Direction to CPR Pt 64 para 6.5 (in relation to prospective costs orders).

7 See CPR Pt 39, r 39.2(3)(f); see also Practice Direction to CPR Part 39 para. 1.5 (in relation to *Beddoe's* applications). Accordingly, the order made and the other documents among the court records (apart from the claim form which has been served) will not be open to inspection by third parties without the court's permission (r5.4(2)). If the matter is disposed of without a hearing, the order made will be expressed to have been made in private.

8 Under CPR Pt 5, r 5.4.

9 For the purposes of CPR, r 8.2(b).

10 Practice Direction B to CPR pt 64 para 2.

11 Practice Direction to CPR Pt 2 para 5.1(e); see also Practice Direction B to CPR 64 para 7.11.

12 Practice Direction to Pt 2 para 5.1(d).

13 See *Re Berens* [1888] WN 95; and see also *Curtis v Sheffield* (1882) 21 Ch D 1; *Re Staples* [1916] 1 Ch 322; *Re Freme's Contract* [1895] 2 Ch 256; affd [1895] 2 Ch 778.

14 Cf *Sifton v Sifton* [1938] AC 656, [1938] 3 All ER 435. But in this case, and in such English cases as *Re Gape* [1952] Ch 418, [1952] 1 All ER 827; affd [1952] Ch 743, [1952] 2 All ER 579;

PARAGRAPH 3

COSTS

Court's jurisdiction

The court's jurisdiction to deal with litigation[15] costs is based upon s 51 of the Supreme Court Act 1981. The court has a wide discretion to determine by whom and to what extent the costs are to be paid[16]. This discretion is however by no means untrammelled and must be exercised in accordance with the rules of the court and established principles[17].

Rules of the court

The CPR only provides for the assessment of costs. It does not deal with entitlement to costs out of the trust fund. If however the trustees are entitled to costs out of the trust fund, CPR, r 48.4 provides that such costs will normally be assessed on the indemnity basis[18]. The court may order otherwise if the trustee acts for his own benefit or prefers some beneficiaries to others[19]. The court will not allow costs which have been unreasonably incurred[20] or are unreasonable in amount[1]. In assessing costs on the indemnity basis, the court must have regard to all the circumstances of the case in deciding whether costs were unreasonably incurred or unreasonable in amount[2]. The court will however resolve any doubt in favour of the receiving party[3].

Established principles

The principles underlying the trustees' entitlement to costs out of the trust fund and the extension of these principles to other parties are set out in the case of *Re Buckton*[4] (summarised by Hoffman LJ in *McDonald v Horn*[5]). A

the question decided was whether the gift over was void for uncertainty or not. On academic issues see *Ainsbury v Millington* [1987] 1 All ER 929, and on the need for a current dispute rather than a hypothetical or future question see *Mercury Communications Ltd v Director General of Telecommunications* [1994] 36 LS Gaz R 36, CA.

15 Including administration of trusts (see Supreme Court Act 1981, s 51(4)).

16 Supreme Court Act 1981, s 51(3).

17 *McDonald v Horn* [1995] 1 All ER 961 at 969.

18 The costs of a claim properly brought or defended by a beneficiary will also usually be assessed on the indemnity basis (*Re Buckton* [1907] 2 Ch 406 at 414 et seq). The old Practice Direction to CPR Sch 1 Ord 85 para 9 stated that the costs of defendant beneficiaries would normally be assessed on this basis subject to their conduct in the proceedings having been proper and reasonable. This provision has been revoked without similar provisions being made in CPR Pt 64. The general principles set out in *Re Buckton* have not, however, been superseded by CPR (see *D'Arbo v Paget (No 2)* (2000) Times, 10 August 2001).

19 CPR Pt 48, r 48.4(3). See *Holding and Management Ltd v Property Holding and Investment Trust plc* [1988] 2 All ER 702, [1988] 1 WLR 644; affd [1990] 1 All ER 938, [1989] 1 WLR 1313, CA. It is however in such circumstances that the trustee would not be entitled to cost out of the trust fund in the first place.

20 On acting unreasonably see *Re Spurling's Will Trusts* [1966] 1 All ER 745, [1966] 1 WLR 920. See also *Re Knox's Trust* [1895] 2 Ch 483 and *Re Ruddock* (1910) 102 LT 89.

1 See CPR Pt 44, r 44.4(1).

2 CPR Pt 44, r 44.5(1)(b).

3 CPR Pt 44, r 44.4(3).

4 *Re Buckton* [1907] 2 Ch 406.

5 *McDonald v Horn* [1995] 1 All ER 961 at 970. For recent discussion, see *Machin v National Power plc* [1998] Pen LR 295, [2001] WTLR 741 and *Chessels v British Telecommunications plc* [2002] WTLR 719.

three-fold classification was adopted by Kekewich J in *Re Buckton*[6]. The first category was proceedings brought by trustees to have the guidance of the court as to the construction of the trust instrument or some other question arising in the course of administration. In such cases, the costs of all parties were normally treated as incurred for the benefit of the trust and ordered to be paid out of the trust fund. Second, there were cases in which the application was made by someone other than the trustees, but raising the same kind of point as in category (1) and would have justified a claim being brought by the trustees. That is treated in the same way as category (1). Third, there are cases in which a beneficiary is making a hostile claim against the trustees or another beneficiary. In such cases the unsuccessful party will usually be ordered to pay the costs of the successful party, as in ordinary litigation[7]. Categories (1) and (2) are usually concerned with friendly litigation, seeking the necessary guidance of the court on issues of difficulty in relation to the construction or management of a trust. Exceptionally such cases may, in substance, be hostile litigation in which costs should follow the event[8].

Hoffmann LJ in *McDonald v Horn* also referred[9] to *Beddoe's* applications, following the case of that name[10], in which the trustees can seek advance approval from the court for incurring litigation costs on behalf of the trust[11].

Hostile litigation

In a case where the dispute is, in substance, between rival claimants to the trust fund (category (3) in *Re Buckton*), the trustees must normally take a passive role – filing a defence that the trustees submit to the court's directions and disclosing relevant documents, in which event they will be entitled to an indemnity for their costs out of the trust fund[12]. If they adopt a partisan role arguing positively for a specific outcome in the interests of one class of beneficiary against the interests of a claimant beneficiary or class of beneficiary, the trustees if they fail are likely to be deprived of their costs and ordered to pay the costs of the successful party[13].

Trust disputes, beneficiaries' disputes and third party disputes

A different classification was adopted by Lightman J in *Alsop Wilkinson v Neary*[14]. Trustees may be involved in three types of cases[15]. The first are disputes ('trust disputes') as to the trusts on which trustees hold the subject

---

6 *Re Buckton* [1907] 2 Ch 406 at 413 et seq. Applied in *D'Abo v Carleton Paget* [2000] WTLR 863 where a beneficiary raised a point against another beneficiary that would have justified a construction claim brought by the trustees.

7 CPR Pt 44, r 44.3(2). See also *Alsop Wilkinson v Neary* [1996] 1 WLR 1220 at 1225. For a recent decision see *Breadner v Granville-Grossman* [2001] WTLR 377.

8 *See Breadner v Granville-Grossman* [2001] WTLR 377 at 389.

9 At p 970.

10 [1893] 1 Ch 547.

11 See p 844 ante.

12 *Alsop Wilkinson v Neary* [1996] 1 WLR 1220 at 1225. Exceptionally, it may be that the trustee can perform an active role eg if the claim only relates to part of the fund, the beneficiaries are unborn, unascertained or minors or cannot obtain legal aid, or the claim may be a 'try-on' susceptible to a strike out application: see *STG Valmet Trustees Ltd v Brennan* [2002] WTLR 273; *Re Hall* [1994-95] Cayman ILR 456.

13 *Breadner v Granville Grossman* [2001] WTLR 377 at 388.

14 [1996] 1 WLR 1220.

15 *Alsop Wilkinson v Neary* [1996] 1 WLR 1220 at 1223–1224.

matter of the trusts. It may be friendly litigation[16], involving the true construction of the trust instrument or some other question arising in the course of administration of the trust. It may be hostile, involving a challenge in whole or in part to the validity of the settlement by the settlor on grounds of undue influence or by a trustee in bankruptcy or a defrauded victim or creditor of the settlor so that the trustees hold as trustees for the settlor, the trustee in bankruptcy, the victim or creditor in place of or in addition to the beneficiaries.

In hostile litigation the trustees should normally remain neutral, leaving it to the rival claimants to fight their own battles and offering to submit to the court's directions. If they adopt this stance, they will be entitled to be reimbursed their costs out of the trust fund[17]. If they choose actively to defend the trust and succeed (eg in rejecting the settlor's claim to set aside for undue influence) they should be entitled to their costs out of the trust fund for preserving the interests of the beneficiaries under the trust[18]. However, if they fail they will normally not be entitled to any indemnity because they will have incurred costs in an unsuccessful attempt to prefer one class of beneficiaries (eg the specified beneficiaries) over another (eg the trustee in bankruptcy or the creditors) and so have acted unreasonably and otherwise than for the benefit of the trust estate[19].

Second, there are disputes ('beneficiaries' disputes') with one or more of the beneficiaries as to the propriety of any action which the trustees have taken or omitted to take or may or may not take in the future[20], eg an action for breach of trust and removal of trustees. Such a dispute is regarded as ordinary hostile litigation in which costs follow the event and do not come out of the trust estate[1].

Third, there are disputes ('third party disputes') with third parties, otherwise than in the capacity of beneficiary, in respect of rights and liabilities assumed by the trustees as such in the administration of the trust. The trustees have a duty to protect and preserve the trust estate and accordingly represent the trust in third party disputes. Before doing so however, they are well advised to make an application (a *Beddoe* application) to the court for permission to bring or defend proceedings at the expense of the trust fund[2].

Costs on appeal

Trustees and beneficiaries may be able to seek authoritative guidance of the High Court at the expense of the trust fund but once such guidance has been obtained, then in the absence of some special circumstances (eg difficulties arising from that decision itself) the parties have the authoritative guidance they need[3]. The fact that they do not like it will not justify the costs of appeal.

---

16 The line between friendly and hostile litigation which is relevant to costs is not always easy to draw (see *Re Buckton* [1907] 2 Ch 406 at 415; *D'Abo v Carleton Paget* [2000] WTLR 863 at 868–869 and *Alsop Wilkinson v Neary* [1996] 1 WLR 1220 at 1224).
17 *Alsop Wilkinson v Neary* [1996] 1 WLR 1220 at 1225.
18 See *Re Holden* (1887) 20 QBD 43.
19 *Alsop Wilkinson v Neary* [1995] 1 All ER 431 at 436
20 *Alsop Wilkinson v Neary* [1995] 1 All ER 431 at 434
1 *McDonald v Horn* [1995] 1 All ER 961; *Holding and Management Ltd v Property Holding & Investment Trust plc* [1990] 1 All ER 938, [1989] 1 WLR 1313 (trustee of maintenance fund for block of flats not entitled to costs out of fund where tenant-beneficiaries successfully claimed proposed works were not repairs but improvements).
2 See p 844 post.

If the trustees appeal, they do so at their own risk as to costs and will usually be ordered to pay costs if the appeal is unsuccessful. If the beneficiary appeals unsuccessfully, he will usually be ordered to pay the respondent's costs on the standard basis. The respondent trustees will usually be entitled to the difference between their costs on the standard and indemnity basis out of the trust fund[4]. The court will only order payment of the costs of an unsuccessful appeal out of the trust fund in exceptional circumstances, as where large interests, and particularly those of unborn persons, are at stake[5].

Prospective costs orders

A trustee, beneficiary, or other persons concerned, in relation to the execution of a trust, including questions of construction, questions relating to the exercise of powers conferred by the trust, or questions as to the validity of the trust, may apply to the court at any stage of proceedings for an order (a 'prospective costs order') that his costs be paid out of the trust fund[6]. In the case of the trustees' costs, the court may authorise the trustees to raise and meet such costs out of the trust fund[7]. In the case of the costs of any other party, the court may authorise or direct the trustees to pay such costs (or any part of them, or the costs incurred up to a particular time) out of the trust fund to be assessed, if not agreed by the trustees, on the indemnity basis or, if the court directs, on the standard basis, and to make payments from time to time on account of such costs[8].

In deciding whether to make a prospective costs order, the court will have regard to (1) the applicant's prospects of success of the claim or defence sought to be made or resisted, (2) the general reluctance of the court to deal with costs before, rather than after, trial unless satisfied that it is clear that the judge at trial would be bound to make an order in favour of the applicant[9], (3) the degree of risk that such an order might work injustice, and (4) the existence of any special circumstances[10].

3   *Re Earl of Radnor's Will Trusts* (1890) 45 Ch D 402 and *Re Londonderry's Settlement* [1965] Ch 918 at 930–931 per Harman LJ, at 936 per Salmon LJ and costs out of trust fund at 940, the appeal being successful. For recent decisions see *Machin v National Power plc* [2001 WTLR 746 and *Chessels v British Telecommunications plc* [2002] WTLR 735.
4   *Re Stuart* [1940] 4 All ER 80, also indicating that the appellant beneficiary should give notice to the respondents that he will ask the court to make only one order for costs against him on the basis there only needs be one ad idem representation against him. In the House of Lords trustees passively interested are not required to lodge a separate case but should ensure their position is explained in one of the cases lodged: *HL Practice and Standing Orders*, 16.11.
5   *Re Stuart* [1940] 4 All ER 80, also indicating that the appellant beneficiary should give notice to the respondents that he will ask the court to make only one order for costs against him on the basis there only needs be one ad idem representation against him. In the House of Lords trustees passively interested are not required to lodge a separate case but should ensure their position is explained in one of the cases lodged: *HL Practice and Standing Orders*, 16.11.
6   Practice Direction to CPR Pt 64 para 6.3. Where trustees have power to agree to pay the costs of a party, and exercise properly such a power, CPR, r 48.3 applies. In such a case, an order is not required and the trustees are entitled to recover out of the trust fund any costs which they pay pursuant to the agreement made in exercise of the power (Practice Direction to CPR Pt 64 para 6.2).
7   Practice Direction to CPR Pt 64 para 6.4(a).
8   Practice Direction to CPR Pt 64 para 6.4(b).
9   It is not necessary however for the applicant to show that no reasonable trial judge would have ordered otherwise (*Re British Airways Pension Schemes* [2000] Pen LR 311, 315).
10 See *National Anti-vivisection Society v Duddington* (1989) Times, 23 November; *Re Westdock Realisations Ltd* [1988] BCLC 354; see also *Re Evans* [1985] 3 All ER 289, [1986] 1 WLR 580; *Re Biddencare Ltd* [1994] 2 BCLC 160; *McDonald v Horn* [1995] 1 All ER 961; *Re British Airways*

It will often be unjust for the successful claimant to property in dispute being placed in a position where, even if he wins, property held to be his is burdened with payment of the unsuccessful parties' costs. That is a powerful consideration where the persons who would benefit from the prospective costs order are all adult and of full age and capacity[11]. In a case which depends on the determination of the question whether property is held in trust by the defendants for the claimant, the very existence of the trustee/beneficiary relationship is in issue. Since that involves hostile litigation between two rival claimants it is normally wrong for the court to fetter the discretion of the trial judge by making a prospective costs order in favour of the defendants to be paid out of the property in dispute which might operate unjustly against the claimant[12].

In one case[13], the representative members of a pension scheme obtained a prospective costs order in an action against their employers and the trustees. The representative employees did not have the resources to pursue major litigation but their claims were so strong that it was inconceivable that an independent trustee, if appointed, would not have applied for and obtained such an order. In another case[14], the court decided that it was reasonable to make a prospective costs order in favour of a representative beneficiary joined as a defendant, where he represented a significant class of members in respect of a pension scheme. There were two classes of beneficiary and, although there was no obvious conflict between them, separate legal representation was requested. The court was entitled to take into account the suspicions which existed between the two classes and the desirability of having the ultimate decision (as to whether to merge two pension schemes) accepted with good grace.

One set of costs only allowed unless severance necessary

Except under special circumstances[15], trustees should bring and defend claims jointly. They will only be allowed one set of costs between them[16], to be apportioned by the costs judge[17]. If a trustee improperly refuses to join with his co-trustee as claimant, and consequently has to be made a defendant, he

---

Pension Schemes [2000] Pen LR 311; *Weth v A-G* [2001] WTLR 155; *Machin v National Power plc* [2001] WTLR 741; *STG Valmet Trustees Ltd v Brennan* [2002] WTLR 280; and *Chessels v British Telecommunications plc* [2002] WTLR 719.

11 *Re Evans* [1986] 1 WLR 101; [1985] 3 All ER 289, CA.

12 *National Anti-vivisection Society Ltd v Duddington* (1989) Times, 23 November, Mummery J; *STG Valmet Trustees Ltd v Brennan* [2002] WTLR 273 (Gibraltar CA). In *Re Omar Family Trust* [2000] WTLR 713 the trustee obtained a prospective order for its costs to be paid out of the trust fund where the protector had brought an action to replace the trustee which was opposed by the principal beneficiary but not the trustee, since no impropriety was alleged against it, although it intended to present its concerns about the purported exercise of removal without compromising its neutrality.

13 *McDonald v Horn* [1995] 1 All ER 961.

14 *Re British Airways Pensions Schemes* [2000] Pens LR 311.

15 Trustees may properly sever their statements of case and if successful recover separate sets of costs where there are reasonable grounds for doing so. This conclusion was reached by Ungoed-Thomas J in *Re Spurling's Will Trusts* [1966] 1 All ER 745, [1966] 1 WLR 920, where, after a survey of the authorities, he gave three examples of such grounds: that one trustee has a personal interest which conflicts with his duty as a trustee; that one trustee is able to admit facts which the others do not believe to be true; and that allegations of fraud or improper conduct are made against one trustee.

16 *Hughes v Key* (1885) 20 Beav 395; *Gompertz v Kensit* (1872) LR 13 Eq 369.

17 *Re Isaac* [1897] 1 Ch 251.

may be deprived of costs altogether. But, on the other hand, where, owing to one trustee being also a beneficiary, it is necessary that one should be claimant, and the other defendant, they will each be allowed separate sets of costs on an indemnity basis[18] and the same rule prevails where hostile litigation is brought against one of the trustees, in which case he may employ two counsel[19].

Beddoe applications

Trustees may need to bring claims against, or defend claims brought by, third parties which could affect the trust estate. They have a duty to protect and preserve the trust estate and accordingly represent the trust in third party disputes[20]. If the trustees bring or defend the claim properly for the benefit of the trust, they will be entitled to be reimbursed for their costs from the trust fund, even if they lose the litigation. However, it is open to them, and prudent, to make an application (a *Beddoe* application) to the court for permission to bring or defend proceedings at the expense of the trust fund[1]. If they are given permission, they will be entitled to their costs out of the trust fund win or lose, together with any costs which they may be ordered to pay to the third party. If however they fail to obtain permission, they do so at their own risk as to costs. If they lose the litigation, they will not receive their costs unless they establish that the costs were properly incurred. Even if they have been advised by counsel, they will not receive their costs unless the court is satisfied that it would have authorised the claim or defence had an application been made[2].

In a case where the dispute is in substance between rival claimants to the entire fund the court will normally direct the trustees to take a passive role. The beneficiaries will be ordered to be joined as defendants and left to fight the claim, if they so wish, at their own expense rather than at the expense of the trust fund[3]. In the case of a trustee who is defending personal charges of misconduct or maladministration the trustee will almost always have to defend the claim, which is a personal one, at his own risk as to costs[4].

---

18 *Re Love* (1885) 29 Ch D 348; *Re Morgan* [1927] WN 180.

19 *Re Maddock* [1899] 2 Ch 588.

20 See *Alsop Wilkinson v Neary* [1996] 1 WLR 1220 at 1224, [1995] 1 All ER 431 at 434.

1 Practice Direction to CPR Pt 64 para 1(2)(b). For the procedure see p 835 ante. In a case of urgency, such as where a limitation period or period for service of proceedings is about to expire, the court may be able to give directions on a summary consideration of the evidence to cover the steps which need to be taken urgently, but limiting those directions so that the application needs to be renewed on fuller consideration at an early stage (Practice Direction B to CPR Pt 64 para 7.9).

2 *Singh v Bhasin* [2000] WTLR 275.

3 *Re Evans deceased* [1986] 1 WLR 101; *Breadner v Granville-Grossman* [2001] WTLR 377. Where there are reasonable doubts as to whether the case is an exceptional one for the trustee to take active defensive steps against a rival claimant to all or part of the trust fund as where, otherwise, there is no viable defendant, a *Beddoe* application should be made, though such application is quite different from the ordinary *Beddoe* application, having a close affinity to a prospective costs order.

4 The ordinary rules as to costs of hostile litigation apply to breach of trust claims (*McDonald v Horn* [1995] 1 All ER 961 at 972; *Alsop Wilkinson v Neary* [1996] 1 WLR 1220 at 1224).

ARTICLE 88

Right under certain circumstances to have the trust administered under the direction of the court

(1) Where the trustee reasonably wishes to be discharged from the *office of trustee*, or where difficulties arise which cannot be determined summarily under CPR Part 64, rule 2(1), or where it is dangerous to administer the trust except under the direction of the court, any trustee or any beneficiary may bring a claim for the administration of the trust under the court's direction[5]. This must now be made by a claim form under CPR Part 8[6]. The court will only make an administration order if it considers that the issues between the parties cannot properly be resolved in any other way[7].

(2) Where the equities are perfectly clear and unambiguous[8]; or a trustee-claimant merely craves to be released from caprice or laziness, or there is no real difficulty in administering the trust, and no reasonable allegation of dishonesty or incompetence against the trustees[9], the claimant will have to pay all the costs. Even where he acts bona fide but without any real cause, he will not be allowed his own costs[10]; and where he brings an action when the same object might have been obtained by payment into court or by a claim made under CPR Part 64, rule 2(1)[11], he will not be allowed the extra costs[12] occasioned thereby. He will always appeal from an order of the court at his own risk[13].

When general administration will be ordered

Claims for the actual administration of a trust by the court are now very rare, although it is quite common to add a claim for general administration, if and so far as may be necessary, to a claim under CPR Part 64, rule 2(1), so as to give the court jurisdiction to go further than that order would otherwise authorise. In such cases, although an order pro forma is made, all further proceedings are stayed. Practice Direction to CPR Part 64 paragraph 3.1 provides, however, that the court will only make an administration order if it considers that the issues between the parties cannot properly be resolved in

---

5 *Talbot v Earl of Radnor* (1834) 3 My & K 252; *Goodson v Ellisson* (1827) 3 Russ 583; and for precedents, see 41 Atkin's Court Forms, Forms (2000 issue) forms 17, 201 et seq.
6 CPR Pt 64, r 64.3.
7 Practice Direction to CPR Pt 64 para 3.1; see also *Re Blake* (1885) 29 Ch D 913; *Re De Quetteville* (1903) 19 TLR 383.
8 *Re Knight's Trusts* (1859) 27 Beav 45; *Lowson v Copeland* (1787) 2 Bro CC 156; *Re Elliot's Trusts* (1873) LR 15 Eq 194; *Re Foligno's Mortgage* (1863) 32 Beav 131; *Re Woodburn's Will* (1857) 1 De G & J 333; *Beaty v Curson* (1868) LR 7 Eq 194; *Re Hoskin's Trusts* (1877) 5 Ch D 229.
9 *Forshaw v Higginson* (1855) 20 Beav 485; *Re Stokes' Trusts* (1872) LR 13 Eq 333; *Re Cabburn* (1882) 46 LT 848.
10 *Re Leake's Trusts* (1863) 32 Beav 135; *Re Heming's Trust* (1856) 3 K & J 40; *Re Hodgkinson* [1895] 2 Ch 190; and see CPR, Pt 44, r 44.4(1).
11 *Re Giles* (1886) 34 WR 712.
12 *Wells v Malbon* (1862) 31 Beav 48; but see *Smallwood v Rutter* (1851) 9 Hare 24.
13 *Rowland v Morgan* (1848) 13 Jur 23; *Tucker v Hernaman* (1853) 4 De GM & G 395; *Re Earl of Radnor's Will Trusts* (1890) 45 Ch D 402 at 423.

any other, as mentioned in Article 87. The principles on which the court will, under Practice Direction to CPR Part 64 paragraph 3 grant or refuse general administration, have been discussed, in relation to the corresponding provision (Order 55, rule 10) of the earlier Rules, in two cases; one before Pearson J[14] and the other before the Court of Appeal[15], in which the learned Lords Justices were more inclined to restrict the right to a decree than was Pearson J. Cotton LJ in the latter case said:

> 'Where there are questions which cannot properly be determined without some accounts and inquiries or directions which would form part of an ordinary administration decree, then the right of the party to have the decree or order is not taken away[16], but the court may restrict the order simply to those points which will enable the question which requires to be adjudicated upon to be settled. That is the result of Order, 55, rule 10 [now Practice Direction to CPR Pt 64 para 3]. Then we have Order 65, rule 1 [now revoked but see Supreme Court Act 1981 s 51 and CPR, Part 44], which says: "Subject to the provisons of the Acts and these Rules, the costs of and incident to all proceedings in the Supreme Court, including the administration of estate and trusts, shall be in the discretion of the court of judge". These two rules must be read together, and we then find this: that if a party comes and insists that there is a question to be determined, and, for the purposes of determining that question, asks for an administration judgment, the court cannot refuse the judgment, unless it sees that there is no question which requires its decision; but rule 1 of Order 65 puts the party who applies for the judgment and insists upon it in this position—that if it turns out that what has been represented as the substantial question requiring adjudication is one which was not a substantial question, or that the applicant was entirely wrong in his contention as to that particular question, the court can, and, in my opinion, ought ordinarily to make the person who gets the judgment pay the costs of all the proceedings consequent upon his unnecessary or possibly vexatious application to the court.'[17]

Deduction from Lord Justice Cotton's judgment

It will be seen from the above judgment that, since almost all isolated questions of construction or administrative difficulty can be dealt with singly, cases necessitating general administration can seldom arise; except:

(1) where the trustees cannot pull together, or
(2) the circumstances of the estate give rise to ever-recurring difficulties requiring the frequent direction of the court, or
(3) where a prima facie doubt is thrown on the bona fides or the discretion of one or more of the trustees.

Possibly, also, a trustee would be held entitled to a judgment for general administration to relieve him of trouble and annoyance. where there were divers disputes as to the proper beneficiaries, out of which disputes several actions had sprung, to all of which the trustee was a necessary defendant[18]. For if he brings the money into court under the Act, he still remains a trustee; and though he would be under no liability in respect of the fund brought in, he would not be discharged from liability in respect of the past income. Moreover, he must be served with notice of all proceedings in

---

14 *Re Wilson* (1885) 28 Ch D 457.
15 *Re Blake* (1885) 29 Ch D 913; and see also *Re Gyhon* (1885) 29 Ch D 834.
16 Before the making of RSC Ord 55, r 10 (now Practice Direction to CPR Pt 64, para 3), a decree for general administration was granted to a trustee or beneficiary as of course.
17 A trustee may first seek protection under *Re Beddoe* [1893] 1 Ch 547; see p 844, ante.
18 *Barker v Peile* (1865) 2 Drew & Sm 340.

relation to the fund, and this of necessity would compel him to incur some expense in employing a solicitor.

It has also been held that the court will not necessarily order general administration because a testator has directed his trustees to commence an action for it[19]; for the court is for the benefit of the living and not the dead.

In *McLean v Burns Philp Trustee Co Pty Ltd*[20] Young J, in a thorough judgment, accepted that a general administration order would be made only in the three summarised cases deduced from Cotton LJ's judgment, but pointed out that in the second and third categories the court takes a relatively benign view and might act on relatively weak evidence because if the claimant puts forward a case which seems to require the court's investigation, and it turns out not to be a proper case, the court will visit on the plaintiff the costs of the proceedings. This heavy potential burden of costs seems to have been a prime weapon for keeping administration actions within proper bounds[1]. He emphasised that the court does not make an administrative decree if the only possible result would be that the whole trust fund would be spent in costs or where there would not be likely to be any benefit to the beneficiaries[2]. Secondly, where the trustee has been given a discretion by the trust instrument, the court does not enforce the exercise of the power against the wish of the trustees, but it does prevent them exercising it improperly[3].

19 *Wells v Malbon* (1862) 31 Beav 48.
20 [1985] 2 NSWLR 623.
  1 *Fane v Fane* (1879) 13 Ch D 228.
  2 *Re Customs and Excise Officers' Mutual Guarantee Fund* [1917] 2 Ch 18 at 26–27.
  3 *Tempest v Lord Camoys* (1882) 21 Ch D 571 at 578, CA; but see *Mettoy Pension Trustees Ltd v Evans* [1991] 2 All ER 513 and p 94 and Art 61 ante.

DIVISION FIVE

The consequences of a breach of trust

Chapter
20 The liability of the trustees   851
21 Protection accorded to trustees in case of breach of trust   913
22 Liability of third parties and beneficiaries   950

CHAPTER 20

The liability of the trustees

Article
89 The measure of the trustee's liability for breach of trust   851
90 Joint and several liability of trustees   877
91 Set-off of gain on one breach against loss on another not allowed   878
92 Property acquired by trustee or fiduciary can be traced and claimed by the beneficiaries or principal   880
93 Application by interim claim to safeguard the trust property if endangered   903
94 Dishonest breach of trust may be a crime   907

ARTICLE 89

The measure of the trustee's liability for breach of trust

(1) Where a trustee's conduct is not authorised by the terms of the trust or by law, so that he breaks his duty of fidelity to the terms of the trust or his duty of undivided loyalty to serving the best interests of the beneficiaries and not of himself or of others, he is personally liable for any loss that would not have occurred but for him so acting beyond his powers. His trust accounts are falsified and he is not allowed by way of defence to raise issues concerning remoteness of damage, *novus actus interveniens*, lack of foreseeability of damage, contributory negligence and lack of mitigation of loss[1]. Equity regards a trustee as inducing the settlor to transfer ownership of the trust property to the trustee upon the trustee's undertakings of fidelity to the trust's terms and of undivided loyalty to the beneficiaries. Thus, the trustee is not allowed to deny that he observed those core undertakings by subsequently asserting that he actually did something which he knew he was not allowed to do: he cannot take advantage of his own wrongdoing. Therefore, his accounts are falsified to restore the position to what it was before he broke his core duties, unless the

---

1 *Target Holdings Ltd v Redferns* [1996] AC 421, HL; *Re Duckwari plc* [1999] Ch 253 at 262–267, CA.

trust instrument exempts him from liability for any breach of trust, other than a dishonest breach, and he deliberately did something he was not authorised to do but honestly believed this to be in the best interests of the beneficiaries, except where no reasonable trustee in his shoes could have held such belief[2].

(2) Where a trustee's conduct is authorised but he fails to comply with the duties imposed upon him or the standard of care required of him, then the trust accounts are surcharged with the extra amount the trust fund would have had but for his improper or negligent conduct unless he is protected by a clause exempting him from liability for such a breach of trust[3]. There appears to be the same stringent 'but for' causation test[4] that applies where the trustee's accounts are falsified because he has done what he is not entitled to do. However, when he has been doing what he is entitled to do but doing it in an improper or negligent way, it seems very likely that the courts will hold that the accounts should be surcharged on the same causation basis as utilised for assessing common law damages for negligence, but taking account of loss to the trust fund and not of an individual claimant. Such common law causation basis is used for assessing the liability of persons like solicitors, partners and company directors who have acted in breach of prescriptive equitable duties of care, although such persons are liable on the stringent 'but for' causation test if in breach of their proscriptive duty of fidelity and undivided loyalty, which may give rise to a right of rescission or a right to receive a transfer of title of property (ascertained with the assistance of tracing principles) from the wrongdoing fiduciary who acquired such property in breach of such duty, or a right to equitable compensation[5].

(3) Where property has been acquired for himself by a trustee in breach of his obligation of undivided loyalty, title to such property or its traceable product must be transferred as an accretion to the trust fund (subject to the trustees' lien for reimbursing his acquisition expenses) unless the beneficiaries are content for the trustee to account to the trust fund for the trustee's profit[6]. However, where the value of such property or its traceable produce has depreciated, the beneficiaries, instead of adopting the acquisition thereof may falsify the accounts so that the trustee becomes personally liable and then exploit their lien over the property to have title to such property transferred as an accretion to the trust fund in part satisfaction of the trustee's personal liability to account[7].

(4) Where a trustee's failure properly to perform his functions causes a beneficiary to suffer an individual loss over and above any loss

---

2 *Walker v Stones* [2001] QB 902, CA; see p 595 ante.
3 On exemption clauses see pp 576 and 591–596 ante.
4 *Target Holdings Ltd v Redferns* [1996] AC 421, HL.
5 See *Bristol and West Building Society v Mothew* [1998] Ch1, CA. Also see *Swindle v Harrison* [1997] 4 All ER 705, CA and *Re Duckwari plc* [1999] Ch 253, CA.
6 *Phipps v Boardman* [1967] 2 AC 46, HL.
7 *Re Lake* [1903] 1 KB 439.

remediable through falsifying or surcharging the trust accounts and such special loss would not have occurred but for such failure, then equitable compensation in the amount of that loss will be payable by the trustee to that beneficiary.

(5) Apart from the above personal or proprietary liability of a trustee who has committed a breach of trust, such trustee may be liable to a direction[8] or declaration[9] of the court or may be injuncted by the court from particular conduct[10] or removed or replaced by another trustee[11].

PARAGRAPHS (1) AND (2)

Personal liability via the taking of accounts

At the core of the trust is the duty of trustees to produce accounts that are available for the beneficiaries to examine and, if appropriate, to seek to falsify or surcharge them. The beneficiaries are entitled to accounts and supporting documents and information without any court order[12], but they can, of course, obtain a court order for an account so as to enforce the trustees' primary duty to the beneficiaries.

There are two forms of account, with an order to pay any sum found to be due to the trust estate when the accounting process is complete: the common account and the account on the footing of wilful default. Where it transpires that the trustees have acted beyond their powers by doing something they are not authorised to do (eg distributing trust money by way of gift to themselves or to someone else who is not a beneficiary or purchasing an unauthorised asset) the accounts will be falsified, deleting unauthorised entries of disbursements or transfers or acquisitions of assets, so that the appropriate sums or assets remain in the trust fund and the trustees must reconstitute the trust fund as it would have been but for the breach of trust, it being 'well recognised that the basis on which a trustee is liable to make good a misapplication of trust moneys is strict and harsh, especially where there has been a huge depreciation in the value of the asset acquired', as where there is a dramatic fall in the property market or the stock market[13]. Where the trustees have not exceeded their powers, but have failed to act as they should have acted to comply with their equitable or statutory duties, their accounts will be

---

8 For example, Trustee Act 1925, s 61, CPR Rule 64 and Practice Directions thereon.
9 *Cowan v Scargill* [1985] Ch 270 at 286, 296, 299 per Megarry VC; *Public Trustee v Cooper* [2001] WTLR 901.
10 For example, Article 93 post.
11 *Letterstedt v Broers* (1884) 9 App Cas 371, HL.
12 See Article 59 ante.
13 *Re Duckwari plc* [1999] Ch 253 at 265 per Nourse LJ; *Pit v Cholmondeley* (1754) 2 Ves Sen 565, 28 ER 360; *Knott v Cottee* (1852) 16 Beav 77 at 79. Where unauthorised investments have been made 'the case must either be treated as if these investments had not been made, or had been made for his own benefit out of his own moneys and that he had at the same time retained moneys of the [trust] in his hands'; *Wallersteiner v Moir (No 2)* [1975] QB 373 at 397 per Buckley LJ; Lord Millett in (1998) 114 LQR 214 at 226–227.

surcharged to add the value that the trust fund would have had but for such failure[14].

While the taking of such accounts will reveal instances where a trustee acted beyond his powers by diverting to himself proceeds of sale of trust assets or dividends on trust shares, it may be that a trustee profited from his trust in a less direct manner from personal activities that conflicted with his obligation of undivided loyalty. Here the beneficiaries need to obtain an order for an account of profits springing from a particular breach[15]: this provides a remedy for specific wrongdoing and nothing more[16].

The order for an account of administration in common form is available without any allegation of wrongdoing and requires the defendant to account only for what has actually been received, what has been disbursed in management expenses and what has been distributed[17]. It is then open to the beneficiaries to falsify or surcharge items in those accounts, amending (or commencing) proceedings to seek the remedy of an account on the footing of wilful default as a response to at least one particularised breach of trust[18]. The court is ready to assume that if one breach has occurred there are likely to be others, so the defendant is generally required to account not only for what was actually received or what extra value the trust fund might have had but for the wilful default of the defendant[19], which extends to deliberate, reckless and negligent breaches of trust[20]. This affords plenty of leeway for a roaming inquiry by the Master taking the account, and casts a much more substantial burden of proof on the defendant than applies in the case of common accounts[1].

The accounts are taken to the date on which they are rendered so as then to establish the extent of the trustee's duty to restore the trust fund either *in specie* or by value[2]. This restorative obligation is often referred to as 'restitutionary', but the latter expression should be restricted to requiring defendants to give up gains not to replace losses, the measure of restitution being the defendant's gain[3].

---

14 *Re Tebbs* [1976] 2 All ER 858; *Bartlett v Barclays Bank Trust Co Ltd (No 2)* [1980] Ch 515 at 543; *Glazier v Australian Men's Health (No 2)* [2001] NSWSC 6; Lord Millett in (1998) 1145 LQR 214 at 225–226; R Chambers in Birks & Pretto (eds) *Breach of Trust* (Hart Publishing, 2002), Chapter 1 'Liability' at pp 16–20.

15 For example, *Phipps v Boardman* [1967] 2 AC 46.

16 *Glazier v Australian Men's Health (No 2)* [2001] NSWSC 6. Where an asset is received by way of a bribe or in breach of the fiduciary duty of undivided loyalty the fiduciary will be personally liable for the highest value of the asset while he owns it: *Nant-y-glo and Blaina Ironworks Co v Grave* (1878) 12 Ch D 738 accepted in *Target Holdings Ltd v Redferns* [1996] AC 421 at 440, HL.

17 *Glazier v Australian Men's Health (No 2)* [2001] NSWSC 6.

18 *Glazier v Australian Men's Health (No 2)* [2001] NSWSC 6; *Gordon v Gonda* [1955] 2 All ER 762 at 768, CA; *Coulthard v Disco Mix Club Ltd* [1999] 2 All ER 457 at 481.

19 *Glazier v Australian Men's Health (No 2)* [2001] NSWSC 6; *Re Tebbs* [1976] 2 All ER 858 (where in the circumstances the order was limited to an account only of part of the administration).

20 *Glazier v Australian Men's Health (No 2)* [2001] NSWSC 6; *Bartlett v Barclays Bank Trust Co (No 2)* [1980] Ch 515.

1 *Glazier v Australian Men's Health (No 2)* [2001] NSWSC 6.

2 *Bartlett v Barclays Bank Trust Co (No 2)* [1980] Ch 515; *Target Holdings Ltd v Redferns* [1996] AC 421, HL; Lord Millett in (1998) 114 LQR 214 at 225.

3 See Birks & Pretto (eds) *Breach of Trust* (Hart Publishing, 2002) at p xi of their Preface, and pp 13–15 (R Chambers); and C Mitchell in Birks & Rose (eds) *Restitution and Equity Vol 1* (Mansfield Press, 2000) at pp 212–213.

Restorative liability to account on a strict 'but for' causation test

The nature of a trustee's liability to account for losses is well brought out in the judgment of Street J (as he then was) in *Re Dawson*[4] in the following passage, although, now that 'restitution' and 'restitutionary' have developed as quasi-terms of art for remedies for surrendering a gain one should use 'restoration' and 'restorative' in respect of remedies compensating for loss.

'The obligation of a defaulting trustee is essentially one of effecting a restitution to the estate. The obligation is of a personal character and its extent is not to be limited by common law principles governing remoteness of damages. In *Caffrey v Darby*[5], trustees were charged with neglect in failing to recover possession of part of the trust assets. The assets were lost and it was argued by the trustees that the loss was not attributable to their neglect. The Master of the Rolls, in stating his reasons, asked "will they be relieved from that by the circumstance that the loss has ultimately happened by something that is not a direct and immediate consequence of their negligence?" His answer to this question was that, even supposing that "they could not look to the possibility" of the actual event which occasioned the loss, "yet, if they have already been guilty of negligence they must be responsible for any loss in any way to that property; for whatever may be the immediate cause the property would not have been in a situation to sustain that loss if it had not been for their negligence. If they had taken possession of the property it would not have been in his possession. If the loss had happened by fire, lightning, or any other accident, that would not be an excuse for them, if guilty of previous negligence. That was their fault." *Caffrey v Darby* is consistent with the proposition that if a breach has been committed then the trustee is liable to place the trust estate in the same position as it would have been in if no breach had been committed. Considerations of causation, foreseeability and remoteness do not readily enter into the matter. To the same effect is the case of *Clough v Bond*[6]. It was argued before Lord Cottenham LC that "the principle of the court is to charge persons in the situation of trustees as parties to a breach of trust, wherever they have acted irregularly, and the irregularity, however well intended, has in the result enabled their co-trustees to commit a breach of trust, or has been, however remotely, the origin of the loss." ... The principles embodied in this approach do not appear to involve any inquiry as to whether the loss was caused by or flowed from the breach. Rather the inquiry in each instance would appear to be whether the loss would have happened if there had been no breach ... The cases to which I have referred demonstrate that the obligation to make restitution, which courts of equity have from very early times imposed on defaulting trustees and other fiduciaries, is of a more absolute nature than the common-law obligation to pay damages for tort or breach of contract. Moreover the distinction between common law damages and relief against a defaulting trustee is strikingly demonstrated by reference to the actual form of relief granted in equity in respect of breaches of trust. The form of relief is couched in terms appropriate to require the defaulting trustee to restore to the estate the assets of which he deprived it. Increases in market values between the date of breach and the date of recoupment are for the trustee's account: the effect of such increases would, at common law, be excluded from the computation of damages but in equity a defaulting trustee must make good the loss by restoring to the estate the assets of which he deprived it notwithstanding that market values may have increased in the meantime. The obligation to restore to the estate the assets of which he deprived it necessarily connotes that, where a monetary compensation is

---

4 [1966] 2 NSWR 211. This passage has been endorsed by Brightman LJ in *Bartlett v Barclays Bank Trust Co Ltd* [1980] Ch 515 and by Lord Browne-Wilkinson in *Target Holdings Ltd v Redferns* [1996] AC 421, HL.
5 (1801) 6 Ves 488.
6 (1838) 3 My & Cr 490.

to be paid in lieu of restoring assets, that compensation is to be assessed by reference to the value of the assets at the date of restoration and not at the date of deprivation. In this sense the obligation is a continuing one and ordinarily, if the assets are for some reason not restored in specie, it will fall for quantification at the date when recoupment is to be effected, and not before.'

Lord Browne-Wilkinson has thus summarised the position as follows[7]:

'The basic rule is that a trustee in breach of trust must restore or pay to the trust estate either the assets which have been lost to the estate by reason of the breach or compensation for such loss. Courts of Equity did not award damages but, acting in personam, ordered the defaulting trustee to restore the trust estate ... If specific restitution of the trust property is not possible, then the liability of the trustee is to pay sufficient compensation to the trust estate to put it back to what it would have been had the breach not been committed (see *Caffrey v Darby*[8] and *Clough v Bond*[9]). Even if the immediate cause of the loss is the dishonesty or failure of a third party, the trustee is liable to make good that loss to the trust estate if, but for the breach, such loss would not have occurred (see Underhill & Hayton *Law of Trusts and Trustees* (14th edn) pp 734–736, *Re Dawson*[10], and *Bartlett v Barclays Bank Trust Co Ltd (No 2)*.[11] Thus the common law rules of remoteness of damage and causation do not apply. However, there does have to be some causal connection between the breach of trust and the loss to the trust estate for which compensation is recoverable viz the fact that the loss would not have occurred but for the breach.'

He went on to endorse[12] the approach of McLachlin J (as she then was) in *Canson Enterprises Ltd v Boughton & Co*[13] that 'foreseeability of loss does not enter into the calculation' and to conclude[14] that 'equitable compensation for breach of trust is designed ....to make good a loss in fact suffered by the beneficiaries and which, using hindsight and common sense, can be seen to have been caused by the breach'. As McLachlin J stated[15], 'The plaintiff will not be required to mitigate...but losses resulting from clearly unreasonable behaviour on the part of the plaintiff will be adjudged to flow from that behaviour, and not from the breach'.

In *Target Holdings Ltd v Redferns*[16] the House of Lords laid down stringent accountability rules for trustees but allowed an appeal against summary judgment given against the defendant solicitor based on falsification of the trust account because, by the time the account was taken, the defendant had done what he was authorised to do, so a trial was needed to ascertain whether the loss would not have occurred but for the defendant improperly carrying out his authorised task. The defendant solicitor was supposed to use the

---

7 [1996] AC 421 at 434. Also see *Maguire v Makaronis* (1997) 188 CLR 449 at 470.
8 (1801) 6 Ves 488.
9 (1838) 3 My & Cr 490.
10 [1966] 2 NSWR 211.
11 [1980] Ch 515.
12 [1996] AC 421 at 438.
13 (1991) 85 DLR (4th) 129 at 160.
14 [1996] AC 421 at 439.
15 (1991) 85 DLR (4th) 129 at 163. Also see *Lipkin Gorman v Karpnale plc* [1992] 4 All ER 331 at 361; *Nationwide Building Society v Balmer Radmore* [1999] PNLR 606.
16 [1996] AC 421, applied in *Collins v Brebner* [2000] Lloyd's Rep PN 587, CA. The stringent causation test, rendering a defendant liable for losses resulting from a sudden market depreciation wholly unconnected with the breach and applicable to trustees or to directors who misapply trust or company property, was applied by the Court of Appeal in *Re Duckwari plc* [1999] Ch 253 at 262 and 265.

claimant's £1,500,000 to help a client purchase freehold land with the claimant's loan secured by a mortgage thereon. The defendant paid the money over before completion and so without obtaining the requisite mortgage. Thus, the disbursement was falsified and the defendant treated as if he still had the £1,500,000 available to be paid out in return for the mortgage, which was treated as occurring when he obtained the mortgage on completion of the purchase a couple of weeks later. He could only be surcharged for improperly carrying out his authorised task with the amount of any loss that would not have been incurred but for his improper conduct[17], and this required investigation of the facts of a mortgage fraud (the land realised only £500,000) to see whether it would not have happened but for the premature payment of the £1,500,000 without security.

While *Target Holdings* is clear House of Lords authority for the stringent causation test applying to both falsification and surcharge of accounts, pressure is growing for there to be relaxation of this tough test in the case of surcharging of accounts for the negligent conduct of the trustee[18].

To underpin the trust concept and protect vulnerable beneficiaries, one can understand that Equity will not permit a trustee to take any advantage from doing what he knows he is not entitled to do and, of course, will not permit him to say that he did not know what he was entitled to do and what he was not entitled to do. Equity looks on him as having done only what he was entitled to do. If he acts beyond his powers, eg in selling an authorised asset to buy an unauthorised asset with the proceeds of sale or permitting a trust painting to be taken outside the UK, then he cannot object if the beneficiaries treat him as if he had not acted beyond his powers and still had the authorised asset or its proceeds of sale or the painting or its value[19]. Events occurring after the ultra vires act are irrelevant, except in so far as they influence the beneficiaries' election (eg to have the authorised investment restored *in specie* or to have its proceeds of sale restored to the trust fund) or in so far as the ignoring of an unauthorised act, like lending money without security, leaves the money notionally still in the account to be lent on obtaining the requisite security as an authorised transaction, leaving the account liable only to be surcharged for improperly or negligently granting a mortgage[20].

Falsification of accounts leads to the same measure of liability as for deceit at common law because Equity regards a trustee as being guilty of equitable fraud, if doing what he undertook not to do by accepting the trusteeship and

---

17 See Lord Millett in (1998) 114 LQR 214 at 227.

18 See Lord Millett in (1998) 114 LQR 214 at 226 invoking *Henderson v Merrett Syndicates Ltd* [1995] 2 AC 145 at 205 and *Bristol and West Building Society v Mothew* [1998] Ch 1 at 16–18 in the context of a solicitor-fiduciary, CA; also *Bank of New Zealand v New Zealand Guardian Trust Co Ltd* [1999] 1 NZLR 664 at 681–682 (Gault J) at 687 (Tipping J); P Birks and A Pretto (eds) *Breach of Trust* (Hart Publishing, 2002) p ix.

19 *Knott v Cottee* (1852) 16 Beav 77; *Wallersteiner v Moir (No 2)* [1975] QB 373 at 397. Section 61 of the Trustee Act 1925, replacing the Judicial Trustees Act 1896, is available to mitigate such strict liability eg if an exceptional forgery leads to money being distributed to a non-beneficiary. Directors of companies are also strictly liable if making the company act ultra vires eg by paying out ultra vires dividends, though capable of being relieved under s 727 of the Companies Act 1985: *Bairstow v Queen's Moat Houses plc* [2001] EWCA Civ 712, [2001] 2 BCLC 531, CA.

20 As in *Target Holdings Ltd v Redferns* [1996] AC 421 as explained by Lord Millett in (1998) 114 LQR 214 at 227.

inducing the settlor to transfer ownership of the trust property to him. As Viscount Haldane LC states in *Nocton v Lord Ashburton*[1]:

> 'When fraud is used in Chancery in describing cases which were within its exclusive jurisdiction, it is a mistake to suppose that an actual intention to cheat must always be proved. A man may misconceive the extent of the obligation which a Court of Equity imposes on him. His fault is that he has violated however innocently because of his ignorance, an obligation which he must be taken by the Court to have known, and his conduct has in that sense always been called fraudulent... What it really means is not moral fraud in the ordinary sense, but breach of the sort of obligation which is reinforced by a Court that from the beginning regards itself as a Court of conscience.'

Centuries ago, as appears from the influential case, *Coggs v Barnard*[2], dealing in intellectual detail with bailment cases, neglect was regarded as tantamount to decit where a bailee's agreement to take care of the bailor's property entrusted to his custody induced the bailment. That approach has been outmoded at common law for over a century and is today regarded as outmoded[3] where a person, like a solicitor, who is not in breach of his proscriptive fiduciary obligation of fidelity and undivided loyalty to his principal but is in breach of an equitable duty of care is assessed on the same basis as breach of common law duties of care where a fiduciary's principal is suing the fiduciary for loss caused by the fiduciary's negligent conduct[4].

There seems no reason to treat negligent trustees any differently from negligent fiduciaries[5], except for the fact that the trustees have to add the appropriate amount of the surcharge to the trust fund, taking account of the loss to it rather than the loss to the individual claimant like the fiduciary's principal. This has implications for paying the due amount into the trust fund without regard to any alleged contributory negligence of a current beneficiary or to beneficiaries' tax liabilities, beneficiaries' liabilities to tax arising when property is distributed out of the trust estate and not at the point of restoration of value to the trust fund[6].

However, care must be taken to keep common law negligence out of trusts where liability is exclusively equitable. Take *Froese v Montreal Trust Co*[7] decided (2:1) by the Ontario Court of Appeal. It held beneficiaries of a pension trust to be entitled to common law damages for negligence against the defendant custodian trustee. It had not chased up contributions that should have been paid to it by the employer under the pension trust set up by the employer with itself as trustee and which had gone into liquidation owing millions of dollars of unpaid contributions on behalf of itself and its employees. As provided by the terms of the trust deed, the employer as managing trustee exercised its power to appoint the custodian trustee to be custodian of money

---

1 [1914] AC 932 at 954. Earlier at 953 he stated 'In Chancery the term "fraud" thus came to be used to describe what fell short of deceit, but imported breach of duty to which equity had attached its sanction. What was laid down by Lord Eldon in *Bulkley v Wilford* (1834) 2 Cl & Fin 102 at 177 explains the nature of this duty'.

2 (1703) 2 Ld Raym 909 at 918–919, 92 ER 107 at 113.

3 *Bristol and West Building Society v Mothew* [1998] Ch 1 at 16–18; *Bank of New Zealand v New Zealand Guardian Trust Co* [1999] 1 NZLR 664, CA; *Stratford v Shayle-George* [2001] NZCA 299.

4 *Bristol and West Building Society v Mothew* [1998] Ch 1 at 16–18; *Bank of New Zealand v New Zealand Guardian Trust Co* [1999] 1 NZLR 664, CA; *Stratford v Shayle-George* [2001] NZCA 299.

5 Lord Millett in (1998) 114 LQR 214 at 226; *Bank of New Zealand v New Zealand Guardian Trust Co* [1999] 1 NZLR 664, CA; Birks & Pretto (eds), *Breach of Trust* (Hart Publishing, 2002) p ix.

6 *Bartlett v Barclays Bank Trust Co (No 2)* [1980] Ch 515.

7 (1996) 137 DLR (4th) 725.

paid to it and of investments purchased by it as directed by the managing trustee (or an investment manager appointed by it); however, the custodian trustee under the terms of its appointment was under no duty to chase up contributions due from the employer. Thus, the beneficiaries took their interests subject to the burden of the employer as managing trustee exercising its powers in such fashion, and so should not have been able to make the custodian trustee account for any loss resulting from the employer's non-payment of contributions. There was no duty to account for such contributions, and thus no order for an account of administration on the basis of wilful default could have been made, while the absence of any equitable duty owed to the beneficiaries by the custodian trustee would, anyhow, have ousted any possible common law duty, but, the trust relationship being exclusively equitable, there was no scope for any intervention at common law.

Replacement without regard to fiscal liabilities

In *Re Bell's Indenture*[8] Vinelott J held that no distinction could be drawn between the liability of an express trustee who misappropriated trust money (whether for his own or for others' benefit) and the liability for misappropriation of a person liable as constructive trustee, the liability in both cases being to replace the money without any regard to any fiscal liabilities that might have fallen on the trust fund had it not been misappropriated. Thus, estate duty that would have been payable if the trust fund had remained intact was not deductible by the defendant. The Estate Duty Office accepted that the misapplied property could not be reconstituted or recovered by tracing, so that duty would not be exacted on any money that was replaced.

In *Bartlett v Barclays Bank Trust Co Ltd (No 2)*[9] Brightman LJ rejected the Bank's contention that if the money to be accounted for to the plaintiffs were to escape taxation, which otherwise would have been payable had the breach of trust never been committed, the Bank should not have to pay over more than the requisite net sum:

> 'My reasoning is this: the obligation of a trustee who is held liable for breach of trust is fundamentally different from the obligation of a contractual or tortious wrong-doer. The trustee's obligation is to restore to the trust estate the assets of which he has deprived it. The tax liability of individual beneficiaries, who have claims qua beneficiaries to the capital and income of the trust estate, do not enter into the picture because they arise not at the point of restitution to the trust estate but at the point of distribution of capital or income out of the trust estate. These are different stages despite the fact they coalesce in the draft minutes.'

Unfortunately, the above cases were not cited in *O'Sullivan v Management Agency and Music Ltd*[10]. The plaintiff sought an account of profits flowing from the defendant's breach of fiduciary duty and procurement of a contract by undue influence. The Court of Appeal held that no deductions should be made in respect of the six most recent years when the defendant had paid tax on the improperly obtained profits since the defendant would be able to re-open the tax assessments to exclude such improper profits. However, irre-

---

8 [1980] 3 All ER 425, [1980] 1 WLR 1217.
9 [1980] Ch 515 at 543, [1980] 2 All ER 92 at 96.
10 [1985] QB 428, [1985] 3 All ER 351, CA. The defendant was not allowed to deduct tax in *Guardian Ocean Cargoes v Banco da Brasil* [1992] 2 Lloyd's Rep 193.

coverable tax paid by the defendant on improperly obtained profits in earlier years was deductible. *O'Sullivan* was thus concerned not with the plaintiff's position but with calculating compensation so as to put the defendant in the same net of tax position he would have achieved but for breach of his fiduciary duty. This is the obverse of the common law damages (*Gourley*[11]) rule requiring such damages be calculated so as to put the plaintiff in the same net of tax position.

In *John v James*[12] a similar problem arose where the defendants had retained excessive fees in breach of a fiduciary duty owed to the plaintiff. The defendants first sought to reduce the profit for which they had to account by tax that they had paid on those profits in the past. Nicholls LJ said this would mean that 'the plaintiffs would be penalised because of the defendants' breach of fiduciary duty. In principle that cannot be right'. Moreover, *Gourley* applies if non-taxable damages compensate for taxable losses, so that a mirror-image *Gourley* for defendants would seem to arise only if the profits are taxable in the defendant's hands but compensation payable by him is not deductible for tax purposes, and Nicholls LJ strongly suspected that the defendants' payments would be treated as allowable deductions. This issue was not dealt with in *O'Sullivan*.

The defendants further sought to reduce the amount of their liability by a standard *Gourley* deduction to take account of the plaintiff's exemption from tax on moneys payable in respect of loss of income that would have been taxable in his hands had it been paid at the proper time. It seemed likely that the moneys recoverable by the plaintiff and his associates should be treated as recovery of an old debt referable to a period behind the relevant six year period and so exempt from tax. Nicholls LJ did not rule on this but rejected the defendants' submission on the grounds of the complexity of the outcome and 'the impracticality of the course involved' since it would be necessary to investigate the tax position of several persons in several countries over many years. Is it really a justifiable outcome that plaintiffs suffer the *Gourley* deductions if their tax affairs are straightforward but not if they are 'impracticably complicated'?

Nicholls LJ further rejected the defendants' claim that compound interest (at the agreed rate of 1% above minimum lending rate or its equivalent) should be paid less the tax which would have been paid by the defendants (following the approach taken in *O'Sullivan*[13]) since this exercise 'also would be an impracticably complicated one'. He further stated[14], 'unlike the position where the court orders an account to be taken of the defendant's profits, a compound interest calculation is not intended or expected to correspond precisely with the amount of a defendant's profits. It is a convenient yardstick'.

To cover himself, Nicholls LJ made it clear that his case was a special one decided on its own particular facts. He refused to say whether the *O'Sullivan* decision was reached per incuriam. He distinguished it, since there the court was fixing the terms on which agreements were to be set aside in equity and thought it just that the defendant's liability should be limited to accounting for their actual profit which did not include tax paid and irrecoverable: since

---

11 *British Transport Commission v Gourley* [1956] AC 185, [1955] 3 All ER 796, HL.
12 [1986] STC 352.
13 [1985] QB 428 at 460, [1985] 3 All ER 351 at 368, CA.
14 [1986] STC 352 at 363–364.

the court's purpose was to remove from the defendants the profits to which they were not entitled, it was necessary in calculating compound interest to deduct the tax which would have been paid by the defendants thereon. It seems *O'Sullivan* was a decision turning on its own particular facts.

It is submitted that the proper approach will normally be that appearing from *Re Bell's Indenture* and *Bartlett* except where there are very special particular facts to justify equity not looking after its own as scrupulously as possible and deterring wrongdoers as much as possible.

Examples of measure of responsibility for loss

To keep persons in a fiduciary capacity up to their duty many old cases establish that equity treats a defaulting trustee or other fiduciary severely. Thus, it is not open to the trustee, where he has committed a positive breach of his proscriptive obligation of fidelity to the trust, and loss has followed, either to tender evidence that if he had strictly followed the directions of the trust an equal or greater loss would have taken place[15], or to claim that the tenant for life shall bring into hotchpot against future income all excess of past income over that which would have been received if the fund had been properly invested[16]. Moreover, where trustees are empowered to lend the trust fund to a husband with the written consent of his wife and they dispense with that consent they will be liable, and cannot tender evidence to show that if the wife had been applied to for her consent she would certainly have given it[17].

Knott v Cottee[18] laid down that unless a trustee invests in authorised securities the case is either treated:

'as if the investments had not been made, or had been made for his own benefit out of his own moneys, and that he had at the same time retained moneys of the testator in his hands. ... I cannot concur in the argument that the court must charge him as if the money had been invested in consols. If that were so, the court must charge him the other way where the funds have fallen, which it never does. ... The persons interested were entitled to earmark them [the unauthorised investments], as being bought with the testator's assets, in the same manner as if the executor had bought a house with the trust funds; and, though they do not recognise the investment, they had a right to make it available for what was due.'

Thus, where the unauthorised investments were ordered into court and sold at a loss the trustees were liable for such loss even though at the date of the subsequent court decree there would have been no loss if these investments had been retained[19]. The trustee is therefore strictly liable to restore

---

15 *Shepherd v Mouls* (1845) 4 Hare 500 at 504; *Watts v Girdlestone* (1843) 6 Beav 188; *Byrchall v Bradford* (1822) 6 Madd 235; and see also *Re Massingberd's Settlement* (1890) 63 LT 296 and *Target Holdings Ltd v Redfern* [1994] 2 All ER 337, CA.

16 See *Re Whiteley* (1886) 33 Ch D 347 at 354; affd sub nom *Learoyd v Whiteley* (1887) 12 App Cas 727; dissenting from *Fry v Tapson* (1884) 28 Ch D 268; and see also *Slade v Chaine* [1908] 1 Ch 522, where it was held that such excess could be kept by the tenant for life and was not capital.

17 *Bateman v Davis* (1818) 3 Madd 98 cf *Regal (Hastings) Ltd v Gulliver* [1942] 1 All ER 378, HL.

18 (1852) 16 Beav 77; and see *Re Whiteley* (1886) 33 Ch D 347 at 354.

19 Where trustees still have unauthorised investments that have proved profitable such investment may be adopted (and retained or be sold) on behalf of the trust so that the trust profits. If they proved unprofitable the beneficiaries can reprobate the transaction and claim compensation and take over the investment in part satisfaction of such claim; but they should make it clear that they are not approbating the transaction and are not taking over the investments as approbated authorised investments, for then the loss claim would itself be lost: cf *Thornton v Stokill* (1855) 1 Jur NS 751; *Re Lake* [1903] 1 KB 439.

the amount he positively misapplied. As Buckley LJ stated[20]:

> 'This is on the notional ground that the money so applied was in fact the trustee's own money and that he has retained the misapplied trust money in his own hands and used it for his own purposes.'

It can be said that equity thus presumes the trustee to have acted honestly and not in breach of his duty, not letting him take advantage of his own wrong. Thus if £10,000 is spent on an unauthorised asset which falls to a value below £10,000 the trustee must replace the £10,000 with interest. If an authorised investment was sold for £10,000 in order to enable purchase of an unauthorised investment the trustee must replace the authorised investment if the unauthorised investment is worth less than it, though if the authorised investment and the unauthorised investment are both worth less than £10,000, then the trustee must replace £10,000 with interest. The fact that in the intervening period (between the breach and remedying the breach) the unauthorised investment soared in value, say doubling its value, before falling below £10,000, does not enable the measure of liability to be calculated by reference to the highest value of that asset in that period[1].

As already seen in discussing *Target Holdings Ltd v Redferns*[2] endorsement was there given to Lord Cottenham's views in *Clough v Bond*[3] that if a trustee or personal representative invests funds in unauthorised securities or puts them within the control of persons who are not authorised to be entrusted with them and a loss be sustained such trustee or personal representative will be liable to make it good, however unexpected the result, however little likely to arise from the course adopted and however free such conduct may have been from any improper motive. All such loss is recoverable even though it would not have been on the application of principles derived from the law of tort relating to causation, foreseeability and remoteness[4]. On this basis if trustees delegated management of their investment portfolio to a discretionary manager where not authorised to do so, then the trustees would be automatically liable even if the loss in value of the portfolio was caused by an unforeseeable market crash. However, in cases where it is alleged that the trustee omitted to exercise the requisite degree of care it seems likely that compensation for breach of equitable duties of care will be assessed on the same basis as common law damages for negligence[5]. It is clear that there is no principle that once a failure amounting to a breach of trust is proved then the burden falls on the defaulting trustee to show that loss did not result from the breach[6].

Thus, in *Nestlé v National Westminster Bank*[7] the plaintiff proved that the

---

20 *Wallersteiner v Moir (No 2)* [1975] QB 373 at 397, [1975] 1 All ER 849 at 863.
1 See the overruling of *Jaffray v Marshall* [1994] 1 All ER 143 in *Target Holdings Ltd v Redferns* [1996] AC 421. Such calculation is possible, however, for an asset received as a secret commission or bribe: *Nant-y-glo and Blaina Ironworks v Grave* (1878) 12 Ch D 738.
2 [1996] AC 421, HL.
3 (1838) 3 My & Cr 490 at 496–497.
4 See p 856 ante, but, nowadays, it is much less likely that a trustee's conduct will be unauthorised because, in default of express authority in the trust instrument, the Trustee Act 2000 confers very wide powers of investment and of employing agents, nominees and custodians.
5 See p 855 ante.
6 *Nestlé v National Westminster Bank* [1994] 1 All ER 118; *Re Miller's Deed Trusts* [1978] LS Gaz R 454 (endorsed in *Target Holdings Ltd v Redferns* [1994] 2 All ER 337 at 352 and [1996] AC 421 at 434) where the company would, anyhow, have gone into liquidation.
7 [1994] 1 All ER 118.

Bank was in breach of trust in failing to obtain legal advice as to the scope of the investment clause, in failing to understand its broad investment powers, and in failing to conduct regular periodic reviews of the portfolio. However, she had to go on to prove that a prudent trustee knowing of the broad scope of the investment clause and conducting regular reviews would so have invested the trust funds as to make it worth more than it was worth when she became entitled to it. Until she proved any loss there was no cause of action and no recourse could be had to any presumptions against a wrongdoing trustee[8] where the trustee was merely doing badly what it was authorised to do[9].

As Dillon LJ stated[10]:

'The onus is on her to prove that she has suffered loss because from 1922 to 1960 the equities in the fund were not diversified. In some cases it is sufficient to prove loss of a chance because in such cases the outcome, if the plaintiff had not lost the chance, can never be proved. But in the present case, if the annuity fund had been invested wholly in fixed interest securities, it would have been relatively easy to prove, even though the event never happened, that the fund would have been worth much more if a substantial part had been invested in equities. Consequently, fair compensation could have been assessed. Equally, it would have been possible, if it be the fact, that the equities in the fund would have performed even better if diversified than they did as concentrated in bank and insurance shares. But Miss Nestlé has not provided any such proof. She has not even provided any material which would enable the court to assess the strength of, or value, the chance which she claims she has lost. Therefore her claim must fail.'

Dillon and Staughton LJJ directly and Leggatt LJ indirectly indicated that nineteenth-century authority to the effect that compensation should be limited to the difference between the actual performance of the fund and the very least that a trustee acting properly might have achieved was flawed.

Hence compensation must be fair, eg related to the average performance of ordinary shares in the relevant period.

As Dillon LJ emphasised[11], investment conditions were very different 50 years ago, let alone 150 years ago, so that too much weight should not be accorded to the actual decisions of the courts in those days. It seems that credence should no longer be given to decisions[12] indicating that where trustees have a choice of investments (eg real securities or Government securities) but invest in unauthorised securities the beneficiaries can only claim to have the trust fund made good with interest. It seems clear that the beneficiaries cannot choose a particular authorised security which has appreciated dramatically to claim that the trustees should have invested in that particular security[13]. Instead, they can claim 'fair compensation' based, it

---

8 [1994] 1 All ER 118 at 141.
9 If the trustee acted recklessly, so as not to be acting in good faith then it seems it would be a wrongdoer so the onus would lie on the trustee to prove the loss did not flow from his breach: see Millett LJ on recklessness and lack of good faith in *Armitage v Nurse* [1998] Ch 241, CA and *Bristol and West Building Society v Mothew* [1998] Ch 1, CA.
10 [1994] 1 All ER 118 at 127.
11 [1994] 1 All ER 118 at 126.
12 *Robinson v Robinson* (1851) 1 De GM & G 247; *Shepherd v Mouls* (1845) 4 Hare 500.
13 *Robinson v Robinson* (1851) 1 De GM & G 247; *Shepherd v Mouls* (1845) 4 Hare 500, but if the investment to be made is directed by the trust instrument and not left to the discretion of the trustees then so much of the investment as would have been obtained by a purchase at the proper time can be obtained less any outgoings (ie calls on shares) which would necessarily have been payable if the investment had been made: *Byrchall v Bradford* (1822) 6 Madd 235;

seems, on the average performance of investments within the authorised class of investments[14].

Indeed this was the approach in *Re Mulligan*[15] where the trustees favoured the life tenant by not investing in equities so as to provide capital growth and protection against inflation. The New Zealand High Court held the trustees should have diversified in 1972 to the extent of investing 40% of the capital in equities which should then be treated as appreciating at 75% of an appropriate index of equities. The 25% discount took account of dealing costs that would need to have been incurred and the fact that the fund was not large enough to be expected to rival a broad-based index. Nowadays, however, one needs to bear in mind the possibility of investing small funds in 'tracker funds' which track and reflect the index, so obviating the need for a discount based on the size of the fund in question.

Similarly if trustees do invest in authorised fashion but do not diversify sufficiently though having a broad spread of equities as well as gilts then again fair compensation should be payable, eg if trustees left five million pounds on deposit for nine months in a year like 1986 when one would have expected a 20% gain in the average price of ordinary shares in such period[16].

No problems arise over beneficiaries suing for diminution in the value of a trust shareholding caused by the trustees' failure to keep themselves fully informed of the activities of a company controlled by them or in which they have a substantial shareholding where the shares have been sold. Where the shares remain part of the trust property there is the *Prudential Assurance*[17] principle to consider, that a shareholder cannot sue for damages in respect of the diminution in value of his shares caused by a wrong to the company where the company itself has a cause of action entitling it to recover for the wrong to it. However, the Court of Appeal[18] has held that this principle does not operate where a beneficiary is suing a trustee where the breach of trust has caused loss to the trust fund or the beneficiary that is separate from any loss that may have been occasioned to the company in which the beneficiary is financially interested: the mere fact that the defendant's conduct may also have given rise to a cause of action at the suit of the company in which the beneficiary is interested will not deprive the claimant beneficiary of his right of action.

The House of Lords[19] in dealing with a breach of trust case endorsed the minority opinion of three Supreme Court of Canada Justices in *Canson Enterprises Ltd v Boughton*[20] involving not a trustee but a solicitor in breach of hi fiduciary duty of undivided loyalty. However, it seems clear that the position should be the same for a trustee who breaks such duty if independent unrelated losses flow from the breach. In *Canson Enterprises Ltd v Boughton* a solicitor's breach of his fiduciary duty, by not disclosing a secret intermediate profit, while acting for the plaintiff in the purchase and redevelopment of

---

Pride v Fooks (1840) 2 Beav 430; *Briggs v Massey* (1882) 30 WR 325 (and see also *Re Hulkes* (1886) 33 Ch D 552 and *Elder's Trustee & Executor Co Ltd v Higgins* (1965) 113 CLR 426).

14 *Nestlé v National Westminster Bank* [1994] 1 All ER 118, CA.

15 [1998] 1 NZLR 481.

16 See *Midland Bank Trustee (Jersey) Ltd v Federated Pension Services Ltd* [1995] Jer LR 352, CA, [1996] Pens LR 179.

17 *Prudential Assurance Co Ltd v Newman Industries Ltd (No 2)* [1982] Ch 204, CA.

18 *Walker v Stones* [2001] QB 902, CA; cp *Shaker v Al Bedrawi* [2002] EWCA Civ 1452 (profits claim).

19 *Target Holdings Ltd v Redferns* [1996] AC 421.

20 (1991) 85 DLR (4th) 129.

land, meant that the plaintiff purchased land which it would not otherwise have purchased. Its claim for compensation in equity for losses occasioned by the collapse of a building erected on the land was dismissed as having been caused by the intervention of engineers and pile drivers chosen by the plaintiff and who were negligent in carrying out the building operations. The plaintiff had simply lost the opportunity to acquire the property at a lower price than it paid, so it was only entitled to the difference between the lower price and the price it paid. The other losses were independent unrelated losses that were too remote to be attributed to the solicitor's breach of duty.

This result is obviously sensible but it took the Supreme Court of Canada over a year to deliver reasons. The majority opinion distinguished the solicitor's fiduciary relationship from a trust relationship and held that equity could borrow principles from the common law of tort damages to find the damage too remote. The minority opinion (favoured by the House of Lords) developed equitable principles to hold that loss is limited to that which flows from the breach via direct links so as not to be too remote, McLachlin J (with whom Lamer CJ and L'Heureux-Dube J agreed) stating[1]:

> 'Foreseeability is not a concern in assessing compensation, but it is essential that the losses made good are only those which, on a common sense view of causation, were caused by the breach. The plaintiff will not be required to mitigate, as the term is used in law, but losses arising from clearly unreasonable behaviour on the part of the plaintiff will be adjudged to flow from that behaviour and not from the breach. When the trustee's breach permits the wrongful or negligent acts of third parties, thus establishing a direct link, the resulting loss will be recoverable. Where there is no such link the loss must be recovered from third parties.'

It would thus appear if the trustees acted ultra vires by purchasing foreign land which they were not authorised to acquire and engaged contractors to erect a building on the land which then collapsed or was blown up by terrorists, the trustees would be liable for the whole loss flowing from their mortal sin unlike the vencial sin in *Canson* where the scope and purpose of the fiduciary obligation justified the limit placed on the extent of liability for losses[2].

Contributory negligence

As Handley JA has stated extra-judicially[3]:

> 'Contributory negligence has never been a defence to an action for legal or equitable fraud. A plaintiff is entitled to relief if the fraud was "a cause" of the loss even if there were more weighty causes for in this field the court does not allow an examination into the relative importance of contributory causes. The same principles must apply to that species of equitable fraud which comprises breaches of fiduciary duty.'

1 (1991) 85 DLR (4th) 129 at 146.
2 Cf approach of Mummery LJ in *Swindle v Harrison* [1997] 4 All ER 705, CA (where a loss arose that was not related to the breach of fiduciary obligation); limits on a trustee's liability may arise under an exercise of the court's discretion under s 61 of the Trustee Act 1925. Indeed, it may be that the courts will ultimately treat failure to disclose an interest as a separate category requiring less strict liability than more fundamental breaches of fiduciary obligations: *Bairstow v Queen's Moat Houses plc* [2001] EWCA Civ 712, [2001] 2 BCLC 531 at para 53.
3 PD Finn (ed) *Essays on Damages* (1992) pp 126–127, also Gummow J in TG Youdan (ed) *Equity, Fiduciaries and Trusts* (1989 Carswell, Canada) pp 82–87: C Rickett and J Gezler in Birks and Rose (eds) *Restitution and Equity Vol 1 Resulting Trusts and Equitable Compensation* (Mansfield Press, 2000), pp 179–189 and 240–245 respectively.

A claimant beneficiary is entitled to trust in his trustee and a person is entitled to trust the person owing him a fiduciary obligation of fidelity and undivided loyalty in circumstances exposing his vulnerability: neither is under a duty to check up on the person he is entitled to expect to be acting loyally in his own best interests.

However, once the claimant becomes aware that the defendant is not to be trusted or is probably not to be trusted then losses which the plaintiff could subsequently have prevented by appropriate action will not be recoverable as a matter of causation. Thus in *Lipkin Gorman v Karpnale*[4] the plaintiff's claim for losses was restricted to the period before it became aware of its partner's dishonest activities and had only itself to blame for not withdrawing his mandate to sign on its behalf. It would be inequitable to allow the claimant to claim for a loss to which it materially contributed when it could reasonably be expected to have done something to prevent it.

Where a person takes it upon himself to become a trustee he thereby undertakes to abide strictly by the terms of the trust (so as never to act ultra vires) and loyally to serve the best interests of the beneficiaries and not of himself or others (so as not to further the interests of himself or others). If he steps out of line, doing (defiantly or otherwise) what he undertook never to do, then this is his fault and no-one else's. Equity regards this as fraudulent deceitful behaviour whether or not the relevant behaviour was dishonest[5]. However, in the context of a one-to-one fiduciary obligation, where the fiduciary can prove that the claimant would have anyhow done what he did regardless of the fiduciary's breach of fiduciary duty, then the fiduciary will escape liability[6] but the fiduciary is disabled from asserting that the claimant contributed by his own want of care to the loss[7].

When one moves from breach of proscriptive fiduciary obligation to the breach of equitable duties of care in the one-to-one context then there is scope for the fiduciary to take advantage of contributory negligence of the claimant in appropriate circumstances[8]. However, in the case of a trust fund for present and future beneficiaries there can be no question of reducing the amount to be restored to the trust fund because one or two of the bene-

---

4 [1992] 4 All ER 331 at 361; and *Corporacion Nacional del Cobre v Sogemin Metals Ltd* [1997] 2 All ER 917 at 925.

5 *Nocton v Lord Ashburton* [1914] AC 932 at 953–954; *Bank of New Zealand v New Zealand Guardian Trust Co Ltd* [1999] 1 NZLR 664 at 687, CA, the trustee's conscience being sufficiently affected to incur liability under a strict 'but for' causation test whether his stepping totally out of line was dishonest or not. Evans LJ in *Swindle v Harrison* [1997] 4 All ER 705 at 717 is with respect out of line in trying to draw a difficult distinction between dishonest and honest breaches of the fiduciary obligation of fidelity and undivided loyalty. Restriction of the extent of liability of a fiduciary can best be achieved by identifying the scope of the duty and the purpose of the rule imposing a duty as pointed out by Mummery LJ at p 734. However, the approach of Evans LJ was adopted in *Nationwide Building Society v Various Solicitors (No 3)* [1999] PNLR 606.

6 *Nocton v Lord Ashburton* [1914] AC 932 at 953–954; *Bank of New Zealand v New Zealand Guardian Trust Co Ltd* [1999] 1 NZLR 664 at 687, CA, the trustee's conscience being sufficiently affected to incur liability under a strict 'but for' causation test whether his stepping totally out of line was dishonest or not. Evans LJ in *Swindle v Harrison* [1997] 4 All ER 705 at 717 is with respect out of line in trying to draw a difficult distinction between dishonest and honest breaches of the fiduciary obligation of fidelity and undivided loyalty. Restriction of the extent of liability of a fiduciary can best be achieved by identifying the scope of the duty and the purpose of the rule imposing a duty as pointed out by Mummery LJ at p 734. However, the approach of Evans LJ was adopted in *Nationwide Building Society v Various Solicitors (No 3)* [1999] PNLR 606.

7 *Nationwide Building Society v Various Solicitors (No 3)* [1999] PNLR 606.

8 *Bank of New Zealand v New Zealand Guardian Trust Co Ltd* [1999] 1 NZLR 664, CA; *Bristol and West Building Society v Mothew* [1998] Ch 1, CA.

ficiaries of full age and capacity were involved in the trustee's conduct so as to be regarded as contributorily negligent[9]: only any particular share to which such a beneficiary is entitled can be affected, and then such consenting or instigating beneficiary's interest is liable to be impounded by the trustee[10].

Compensation award compensatory not punitive

While equitable principles may make it easier for a claimant to establish a large measure of loss they are not designed to make a defendant liable for more than such loss by way of penalty. This appears clearly from cases concerned with awards of interest against defaulting trustees. Compound interest at the higher mercantile rate is awarded not as a punishment but only as fairly representing what the defendant can be presumed to have received in the circumstances[11]. At common law the opportunities for exemplary or aggravated damages are very limited while it goes against the grain for courts of equity to act in punitive fashion going beyond the claimant-friendly strict liability it imposes to uphold standards so that confidence may be maintained in the trust concept or in other fiduciary relationships. However, because compensation for nervous distress and anxiety can be available for certain sorts of contract designed to provide peace of mind and freedom from distress the question arises whether Equity should exclude the availability of such compensation for cases where to free persons from stress and anxiety can be considered a factor in making them beneficiaries under a trust. It is submitted that such argument overlooks the essential representative restorative proprietary nature of an action for breach of trust: whether such action itself be personal or proprietary its function is simply to restore to the trust estate property or the value of such property. The Jersey Royal Court[12] has refused to award exemplary damages or compensation for distress while the English court[13] is averse to the award of compensation for distress or inconvenience unless expressly or implicitly authorised by statute.

Loss of interest

A trustee who is guilty of unreasonable delay in investing trust funds will certainly be answerable to the beneficiaries for simple interest during the continuance of such delay[14]; for if he had done his duty, interest would in fact have been received. On the same ground, where an executrix allowed trust money to remain uninvested in her solicitor's hands for nine years during the

---

9 Similarly, in a pension trust there can be no question of the trusts being altered by an estoppel by convention against the trustees, no estoppel being capable of binding future beneficiary-members of the pension scheme: *Redrow v Pedley* [2002] Pens LR 339.

10 See pp 947–948 post.

11 *Guardian Ocean Cargoes v Banco de Brasil* [1992] 2 Lloyd's Rep 193; *Vyse v Foster* (1872) 8 Ch App 309 at 333; *A-G v Alford* (1855) 4 De GM & G 843 at 851.

12 *West v Lazard Bros and Co Jersey Ltd* [1993] JLR 165.

13 *Miller v Stapleton* [1996] 2 All ER 449; *Westminster City Council v Heywood* [1998] Ch 377 at 396, 410–411, CA; permitted for Pensions Ombudsman to award compensation for distress and inconvenience under Pension Schemes Act 1993, s 151(2).

14 *Stafford v Fiddon* (1857) 23 Beav 386; *Jones v Foxall* (1852) 15 Beav 388 at 392. In the light of *Nestlé v National Westminster Bank* [1994] 1 All ER 118, CA and *Midland Bank Trustee (Jersey) Ltd v Federated Pension Services Ltd* [1995] Jersey LR 352, [1996] Pens LR 179, CA, there may be an alternative claim for loss of the profit that would have been made if the trustee had exercised his power to invest in a broad range of shares.

infancy of the beneficiary, she was charged with compound interest, with half-yearly rests, as it was her duty to have accumulated the income, by investing it from time to time in consols[15]. A fortiori is this the case where there is an express trust for accumulation[16].

Rate of interest in ordinary circumstances

Where income has been lost due to the trustees' default in respect of the capital Brightman LJ has stated (at a time when inflation had led to high interest rates)[17]:

> 'In former days a trustee was as a rule charged only with interest at 4% unless there were special circumstances ... In these days I think it would be unrealistic for a court of equity to abide by the modest rate of interest which was current in the stable times of our forefathers.
>
> In my judgment a proper rate of interest to be awarded, in the absence of special circumstances, to compensate beneficiaries and trusts for non-receipt from a trustee of money that ought to have been received is that allowed from time to time on the courts' short-term investment account, established under section 6(1) of the Administration of Justice Act 1965. To some extent the high interest rates payable reflect and compensate for the continued erosion in the value of money by reason of galloping inflation. It seems to me arguable, therefore, that if a high rate of interest is payable in such circumstances, a proportion of that interest should be added to capital in order to help maintain the value of the corpus of the trust estate. It may be, therefore, that there will have to be some adjustment as between life tenant and remainderman.'

This approach was adopted in *Jaffray v Marshall*[18] where the interest was apportioned equally between income and capital.

The rate on the short-term investment account, now the special investment account under the Court Fund Rules 1987, is generally in line with that offered by National Savings. Changes are made in the rate much less frequently than those made to the clearing banks' base rate.

Higher rate in special circumstances

Bartlett and *Jaffray* both concerned money lost by the neglect of the trustees rather than by the positive misapplication of trust funds. As Buckley LJ has pointed out[19], in the latter event liability to replace the lost capital with interest arises 'on the notional ground that the money so applied was in fact the trustee's own money and that he has retained the misapplied trust moneys in his own hands and used it for his own purposes' so that the appropriate rate is the commercial rate of 1% above the London and Scottish clearing banks' base lending rates, and interest will be compounded with yearly units where such represents what the trust can be presumed to have lost or what the trustee can be presumed to have obtained[20].

Nevertheless the court has a discretion which it may exercise so as to favour

15 *Gilroy v Stephens* (1882) 30 WR 745 (Fry J); and see also *Re Emmet's Estate* (1881) 17 Ch D 142.
16 *Re Barclay* [1899] 1 Ch 674; *Raphael v Boehm* (1805) 11 Ves 92.
17 *Bartlett v Barclays Bank Trust Ltd (No 2)* [1980] Ch 515 at 547, [1980] 2 All ER 92 at 97–99.
18 [1994] 1 All ER 143, but note that the decision on liability for lost capital was overruled by *Target Holdings Ltd v Redferns* [1996] AC 421, HL.
19 *Wallersteiner v Moir (No 2)* [1975] QB 373 at 397.
20 See pp 870–871, post.

the defendant in special circumstances. Thus, in *Re Evans*[1] the defendant administrator of her intestate father's estate believed her brother was dead, not having heard from him for over 30 years. Acting on legal advice she purchased a missing beneficiary policy to cover half the estate (as better than incurring the expense of a *Benjamin*[2] order). Four years later the claimant brother appeared, claiming interest, the policy not extending to interest. The judge rejected the claim to interest at 1% above base lending rate from time to time and the defendant's claim that 6% was appropriate as the rate payable on unpaid legacies. The rate payable on the special investment court account had fluctuated between 8 and 14.5%. The judge awarded 8% interest throughout the period, taking account of the fact the defendant was a lay person and not a professional administrator.

However, a trustee who, without proper authority, calls in trust property properly invested at a higher rate than the ordinarily appropriate current rate of interest will be liable for that higher rate of interest; for although he may not actually have received that rate, he would have done so[3] but for his unauthorised act. Similarly, where the trustee actually received a higher rate he will be accountable therefore[4].

Where a trustee makes unauthorised use of trust money for his own purposes and the profits made are unascertainable or less than the amount produced by applying a commercial rate of interest of 1% above the London clearing banks' base rate then such commercial rate will be payable, perhaps at compound interest with yearly rests[5].

Mixing trust funds with trustee's own moneys

Liability for interest relating to innocent breaches of trust is supposed to be based on the actual amount of loss, but if a trustee keeps the money in his hands, meaning to appropriate it, or even to use it temporarily only (and indeed even where he does so in order that the beneficiaries may have a larger income[6]), the actual loss ceases to be the measure of his responsibility. As Lord Cranworth said in the leading case of *A-G v Alford*[7] (when 4% was the norm):

'in such a case I think the court would be justified in dealing in point of interest very hardly with an executor, *because it might fairly infer that he used the money in speculation, by which he either did make 5%, or ought to be estopped from saying that he did not:* the court would not there inquire what had been the actual proceeds, but in application of the principle, in odium spoliatoris omnia praesumuntur, would assume that he did make the higher rate, *that is, if that were a reasonable conclusion.*'

---

1 [1999] 2 All ER 777 at 788.
2 [1902] 1 Ch 723.
3 See judgment in *Jones v Foxall* (1852) 15 Beav 388; and see principles stated in *Re Massingberd's Settlement* (1890) 63 LT 296; and *Mosley v Ward* (1805) 11 Ves 581.
4 *Re Emmet's Estate* (1881) 17 Ch D 142. This should include the case where the trustee has used the trust money to reduce his overdraft and so save paying an actual interest rate: *Farnell v Cox* (1898) 19 LR NSW Eq 142.
5 *O'Sullivan v Management Agency and Music Ltd* [1985] QB 428, [1985] 3 All ER 351, CA, p 871, post.
6 *Re Davis* [1902] 2 Ch 314.
7 (1855) 4 De GM & G 843 at 852; *Stafford v Fiddon* (1857) 23 Beav 386; *Jones v Foxall* (1852) 15 Beav 388; *Re Jones* (1883) 49 LT 91; *Re Emmet's Estate* (1881) 17 Ch D 142; and *Re Davis* [1902] 2 Ch 314.

Solicitor-trustee using trust funds in his business[8]

In *Burdick v Garrick*[9] a solicitor, as the agent of the plaintiff, held a power of attorney from him, under the authority of which he received divers sums of money, and paid them into the bank to the credit of his (the solicitor's) firm. On a bill being filed by the client for an account, the Vice-Chancellor made a decree for payment of the principal with *compound interest.*

The Court of Appeal, however, reversed this decision, Lord Hatherley saying:

> 'The Vice-Chancellor has directed interest to be charged at the rate of 5%, which appears to me to be perfectly right, and for this reason that the money was retained in the defendants' own hands, and was made use of by them[10]. That being so, the court presumes the rate of interest made upon the money to be 5%. I cannot, however, think the decree correct in directing half-yearly rests, because the principle laid down in the case of *A-G v Alford* appears to be the sound principle, namely, that the court does not proceed against an accounting party by way of punishing him for making use of the plaintiff's money by directing rests, or payment of compound interest, but proceeds upon this principle, either that he has made, or has put himself into such a position as that he is to be presumed to have made, 5%, or compound interest, as the case may be.'

His Lordship then pointed out that no doubt where a trustee employs money in ordinary trade he may be made liable for compound interest, where trade capital is presumed to yield it; but that that reason had no application to capital employed in a solicitor's business, upon which a solicitor is frequently receiving no interest at all.

Trustee allowing trust fund to remain in his business

In order to charge a trustee with compound interest, or with actual profits for employing the trust funds in trade, there must be an active calling in of the trust moneys for the purpose of embarking them in the trade or speculation; a mere neglect to withdraw funds *already embarked by the settlor in the trustee's trade* is not sufficient[11].

Rate of interest to be charged against trustee using money

It will be perceived that in the old cases the rate was 5% interest[12].

However, in *Wallersteiner v Moir (No 2)*[13] the Court of Appeal, applying

---

8 The Solicitors' Account Rules are designed to prevent trust moneys from being so used. As to the enforcement of such rules, see the Solicitors Act 1974 s 32.

9 (1870) 5 Ch App 233. See also *Hale v Sheldrake* (1889) 60 LT 292; where a husband of the tenant for life was ordered to replace a trust fund, but without interest, as the wife had allowed him to receive the income.

10 See to same effect *Bate v Scales* (1806) 12 Ves 402; *Re Pilling, ex p Ogle* (1873) 8 Ch App 711; *Jones v Foxall* (1852) 15 Beav 388; *Heathcote v Hulme* (1819) 1 Jac & W 122; *Docker v Somes* (1834) 2 My & K 655; *Berwick-upon-Tweed Corpn v Murray* (1857) 7 De GM & G 497; and *Gordon v Gonda* [1955] 2 All ER 762, [1955] 1 WLR 885, CA.

11 *Vyse v Foster* (1872) 8 Ch App 309; affd (1874) LR 7 HL 318; *Smith v Nelson* (1905) 92 LT 313; *Brown v Sansome* (1825) M'Cle & Yo 427; but cf *Townend v Townend* (1859) 1 Giff 201.

12 See also *Bate v Scales* (1806) 12 Ves 402; *Re Davis* [1902] 2 Ch 314 and *Gordon v Gonda* [1955] 2 All ER 762, [1955] 1 WLR 885, CA.

13 [1975] QB 373, [1975] 1 All ER 849, CA. See further *Westdeutsche Londesbank Girozentrale v Islington Borough Council* [1994] 4 All ER 890, CA; revsd [1996] AC 669, HL and *Mather v TM Sutton Ltd* [1994] 4 All ER 793 (fiduciary relationship between pawnbroker and pawnor liable

principles applicable to trustees to a director of a company who is in a fiduciary position similar to a trustee, held that where a fiduciary used his beneficiaries' money in his own commercial transactions he should be debited with compound interest at the commercial rate of 1% above minimum lending rate (or official bank rate) with yearly rests. This commercial rate is now 1% above the London and Scottish clearing banks' base rate[14] as held by the Court of Appeal in *O'Sullivan v Management Agency and Music Ltd*[15], though awarding simple interest only since the money was used in a joint venture benefiting the plaintiff as well as the defendant. In *John v James*[16] compound interest was awarded to ensure that the defendant did not retain profits for which he ought to account. Compound interest is awarded not as a punishment but as fairly representing what the defendant is presumed to have received in the commercial context[17], though the presumption is often more readily made where stress has been laid on fraud or gross misconduct on the defendant's part[18].

The cost and difficulty of ascertaining actual profits, and thus whether or not they represent a return exceeding the commercial rate, is such that it is often best to elect for charging interest at the presumed commercial rate, with compound interest at yearly rates where the money was used by the defendant in his own business. An election must be made since the plaintiff cannot both approbate and reprobate: of course, it would also be inequitable to allow the plaintiff to claim actual profits for profitable periods and a commercial rate of interest for unprofitable periods[19].

Liability of constructive trustee

In *El Ajou v Dollar Land Holdings plc (No 2)*[20] where a third party was held personally liable to account as a constructive trustee of the plaintiff's traced money, having failed in its defence of bona fide purchaser without notice, Walker J held 'the rate of interest should mirror so far as possible the income which the plaintiff might have earned had the principal sum been paid to him in March 1988'. He ordered that the rate should be the base rate from time to time of the London clearing banks without the addition of any percentage but compounded with yearly rests.

to pay interest in equity on surplus proceeds of sale: interest rate to be fixed after inquiry as to actual high interest-bearing use of money in trade).

14 *Buckingham v Francis* [1986] 2 All ER 738 at 743–744; *Shearson Lehman Hutton Inc v Maclaine Watson & Co Ltd (No 2)* [1990] 3 All ER 723 at 732–733, though a party may prove special circumstances justifying instead LIBOR (London Inter-Bank Offer Rate) plus one-eighth, or 1% above New York prime rate: *Guardian Ocean Cargoes Ltd v Banco da Brasil (No 3)* [1992] 2 Lloyd's Rep 193.

15 [1985] QB 428, [1985] 3 All ER 351, CA.

16 [1986] STC 352.

17 *Wallersteiner v Moir (No 2)* [1975] QB 373, [1975] 1 All ER 849, CA; *Guardian Ocean Cargoes Ltd v Banco da Brasil (No 2)* [1992] 2 Lloyd's Rep 193.

18 *Jones v Foxall* (1852) 15 Beav 388; *Gordon v Gonda* [1955] 2 All ER 762, CA.

19 *Heathcote v Hulme* (1819) 1 Jac & W 122; *Vyse v Foster* (1872) 8 Ch App 309 at 334; *Tang Man Sit v Capacious Investments Ltd* [1996] 1 All ER 193, PC.

20 [1995] 2 All ER 213.

Retention of unauthorised investment or improper retention of authorised investment

A trustee who retains an unauthorised investment is liable for the difference between the price obtainable by sale at the proper time and the actual proceeds of sale. Thus in *Fry v Fry*[1] trustees were liable for the difference between the price offered for an inn in 1837 and the price to be received on sale in 1859, which would be very low due to the diversion of road traffic by the opening of a railway in 1843.

Where the trustees have a duty to sell but a power to postpone sale and in breach of trust they postpone sale for too long difficulties arise where during the period over which the trustees should have sold the asset its value has fluctuated considerably. In *Fales v Canada Permanent Trust Co*[2] the Supreme Court of Canada held the proper measure of compensation was the average of the highest and lowest prices of the asset in the period from when it could first have been sold to advantage till the date by which it should reasonably have been sold. No authority was cited for this, though it is supported by American cases[3] and is consistent with *Re Bell's Indenture*[4]. However, *Michael v Hart & Co*[5] and *Jaffray v Marshall*[6] are English authority for the defaulting trustee under a continuous obligation to restore property or its value having to pay compensation on the footing of the highest price obtainable during the relevant period, everything being presumed against the wrongdoer which seems appropriate where he profits from a breach of his prospective obligation of fidelity to the terms of his trust and of undivided loyalty to the beneficiaries[7] but not where he is only negligently doing what he is authorised to do. Lord Browne-Wilkinson[8] therefore overruled *Jaffrey v Marshall* where it seems the trustees' negligent performance of what the beneficiaries in remainder had authorised them to do to benefit their mother, the life tenant, had caused the loss.

Improper sale of authorised investment

It is a breach of trust if trustees sell an authorised investment for the purpose of investing in an unauthorised investment or of paying the proceeds to the life tenant in breach of trust[9]. The trustees are liable to replace the authorised investment or the proceeds of sale thereof, whichever is the greater burden[10]. Replacement of the authorised investment will be at its value at the date it is actually replaced, so remedying the breach, or at the subsequent

---

1 (1859) 27 Beav 144. Now no liability for conscious postponement: TLATA s 4(1).
2 (1976) 70 DLR (3d) 257.
3 See *Scott on Trusts* (4th edn) para 209.
4 [1980] 3 All ER 425 (property sold in breach of trust in 1947 resold in 1949, and the 1949 sale price was accepted as the measure of the trustee's liability when 1949 was a time at which the trustees could properly have sold).
5 [1901] 2 KB 867 at 869–870 and on appeal the observation of Collins MR at [1902] 1 KB 482 at 488.
6 [1994] 1 All ER 143 at 153, but rejected in *Target Holdings Ltd v Redferns* [1996] AC 421.
7 See *Nant-y-glo and Blaina Ironworks Co v Grave* (1878) 12 Ch D 738 (in an account of profits, fiduciary-director liable for highest value of shares given to him as a secret commission between date of receipt and the trial).
8 *Target Holdings Ltd v Redferns* [1996] AC 421 at 440.
9 *Re Bell's Indenture* [1980] 3 All ER 425, [1980] 1 WLR 1217.
10 *Shepherd v Mouls* (1845) 4 Hare 500 at 504.

date of the court judgment[11]. Exceptionally, where the authorised investment would in any event have been sold, the date when such sale should have occurred will be the relevant date for valuing the loss[12].

A strict deterrent policy underlies the decisions. Thus, where an authorised investment is sold but with a view to investing in an unauthorised investment the liability is to replace the authorised investment and not merely to make good the proceeds misapplied[13], though some argue that the latter measure of liability should suffice: although the *motive* for the sale of the authorised investment was to reinvest in an unauthorised security, the sale itself was authorised, so that liability should extend no further than making up the proceeds of such sale if the unauthorised investment has depreciated in value.

Liability of executors of deceased trustee who was party to a breach for loss incurred after his death

In *Lander v Weston*[14] two trustees, in breach of trust, sold consols and advanced the proceeds to the husband of the life tenant. He subsequently repaid the advance to the surviving trustee, who reinvested it in unauthorised stock for a few days, and then sold such stock and again lent the proceeds to the husband, with the result that the fund was lost.

It was held that not only was the surviving trustee liable for the loss (which was obvious), but so also were the executors of the deceased trustee; because but for the original sale of the stock to make the advance to the husband, that stock would have remained intact. The mere repayment by the husband to the surviving trustee and the investment in unauthorised stock did not set matters right and so condone the original breach because the original consols were not replaced, quite apart from the fact that the repayment for a few days was a sham. Consequently the executors of the deceased trustee were liable for all loss which happened (even after his death) before the fund was ultimately replaced.

PARAGRAPH 3

Accounting for profits

The substantive rule that a trustee may not profit from his trust has already been considered in Article 33. A profit can arise from a breach of trust where a trustee purchases an unauthorised investment which rises in value, or

---

11 *Re Bell's Indenture* [1980] 3 All ER 425, where it was pointed out that in *Re Massingberd's Settlement* (1890) 63 LT 296 the reference to the date of the writ rather than the date of judgment was per incuriam.
12 *Re Bell's Indenture* [1980] 3 All ER 425, [1980] 1 WLR 1217 followed by Megarry V-C in *Re Montagu's Settlements* [1987] Ch 264.
13 *Re Massingberd's Settlement* (1890) 63 LT 296; and see also *Re Bennison* (1889) 60 LT 859; and *Stokes v Prance* [1898] 1 Ch 212. In *Re Bell's Indenture* (supra) it was pointed out that the date of the judgment should replace date of the writ in *Re Massingberd's Settlement*; counsel expressly reserved the right to challenge the correctness of *Massingberd* in a higher court.
14 *Lander v Weston* (1855) 3 Drew 389; and see also *Bacon v Clark* (1836) 3 My & Cr 294; and *Clough v Bond* (1838) 3 My & Cr 490.

retains an unauthorised investment which rise in value, or receives a bribe[15] to influence his behaviour as a trustee, or diverts to himself a business opportunity offered to the trust, or uses trust funds for his own business or professional purposes. In such cases the trustee is personally accountable in respect of the trust property and profits made therefrom, and there may also be a possible proprietary remedy if the property or its traceable equivalent still subsists in the trustee's hands[16].

In the case where the trustee uses trust funds for his own business or professional purposes, instead of seeking an account of profits, the beneficiaries may seek compensation with interest at the mercantile rate already discussed at p 870, ante, eg if there are difficulties assessing how much profit was made or if it seems that not much profit was made. As already seen, an election must be made between these two inconsistent remedies[17].

Election between accounting for profits or compensation for loss

In respect of a particular breach of trust or of the self-dealing or fair-dealing rules[18], it is not possible to approbate and to reprobate, to adopt and to disavow, to blow hot and to blow cold. Suing for profits adopts the trustee's conduct whilst claiming compensation rejects such conduct. Thus, if T holds 16 houses on trust to transfer them to C, but without C's knowledge, leases them, C must elect[19] whether to sue for the actual profit made by T from renting out the houses or for the loss caused to C in not being able to rent out the houses.

An account of profits requires the trustee to give up his improper gains, whilst compensation requires the trustee to indemnify the trust against loss. In the former case it is immaterial whether or not the trust suffered any loss: in the latter it is immaterial whether or not the trustee made any gain. A trustee's gain is not to be measured by the trust's loss nor the trust's loss by the trustee's gain[20].

If a trustee breaks the self-dealing rule the beneficiary has to elect between (1) claiming the purchased property or its traceable equivalent (with whatever income it produced or should have produced) or its value before it was dissipated or given away (with interest thereafter) or (2) claiming compensation equal to the difference between actual market value at the date of the trustee's purchase and the lower price paid by the trustee, with interest on such lost capital since such date[1].

If trustees sell £10,000 of authorised shares to purchase £10,000 of unauthorised shares then which election should be made depends on the current values of these shares. If the unauthorised shares are valued at more than the authorised shares and more than £10,000, then the trustees' actions should

---

15 The trustee or other fiduciary who receives shares as a bribe or a secret commission is liable for their highest value since the date of their receipt: *Nant-y-glo and Blaina Ironworks v Grave* (1878) 12 Ch D 738.

16 See Art 104. See further *Warman International Ltd v Dwyer* (1995) 69 ALJR 362.

17 *Heathcote v Hulme* (1819) 1 Jac & W 122, p 871, ante.

18 Regarded by Megarry V-C in *Tito v Waddell (No 2)* [1977] Ch 106, [1977] 3 All ER 129 as disabilities rather than a breach of trust for Limitation Act purposes.

19 *Tang Man Sit v Capacious Investments Ltd* [1996] AC 514, PC.

20 In the context of account for profits and damages see *Warman International Ltd v Dwyer* (1995) 69 ALJR 362; *Colbeam Palmer Ltd v Stock Affiliates Pty Ltd* (1968) 122 CLR 25 at 34; and *Ansell Rubber Co Pty Ltd v Allied Rubber Industries Pty Ltd* [1972] RPC 811 at 828.

1 Cf *McKenzie v McDonald* [1927] VLR 134.

be adopted and the shares taken over as proper trust shares, making the trustees personally liable to account for these profitable shares (and the dividends thereon)[2]. If the unauthorised shares are worth less than the authorised shares which are worth more than £10,000, then the trustees' actions should be disavowed and the trustees made to replace the authorised shares that they improperly sold or pay compensation of a sum equal to such replacement cost[3]. It will be possible, if acceptable to the beneficiaries, to take over the unauthorised shares in part satisfaction of the trustees' personal liability to compensate the trust[4].

If both the authorised and unauthorised shares are worth less than £10,000, then the trustees must compensate the trust by repaying the £10,000 with interest thereon from the date of the improper sale of the authorised securities[5].

If the beneficiaries lack capacity to elect which remedy to pursue it seems that the court should enforce the most advantageous remedy available to the beneficiaries in the circumstances[6]. After all, if the unborn or minor beneficiaries were relegated to their compensation remedy, because they could not positively adopt the transaction and claim the profits, the trustees would be allowed to profit from their trust in breach of their fundamental duty[7]. However, where the profitable investment is an unauthorised investment, then it will need to be sold[8] and converted into an authorised investment, unless all the beneficiaries between them absolutely entitled to the trust property and of full age and capacity elect to adopt the investment as authorised, despite the trust restrictions on a limited class of authorised investments[9].

PARAGRAPH 4

A trustee may negligently perform his functions so as to cause no loss to the trust fund but to cause loss to a particular beneficiary. Take the case of T who, in accordance with the purposes of the settlor in creating an accumulation and maintenance trust with flexible powers, decides to make an appointment of half the trust capital to O before he attains 25 years of age on 2 August when the power of appointment will cease to be exercisable. The deed of appointment is duly prepared but is not executed by T *before* 2 August but *on* 2 August, so the deed is ineffective[10] and the beneficiaries entitled in

---

2 Cf *Boardman v Phipps* [1967] 2 AC 46, [1966] 3 All ER 721, HL; *Docker v Somes* (1834) 2 My & K 655; *Scott v Scott* (1963) 109 CLR 649.

3 *Re Bell's Indenture* [1980] 3 All ER 425, [1980] 1 WLR 1217. Interest will be payable thereon: *Re Dawson* [1966] 2 NSWLR 211 (semble on the original £4,700 rather than the replacement cost of £5,829).

4 It should be made clear that this is what is being done as opposed to adopting or ratifying the investment as if it had originally been authorised: see *Thornton v Stockill* (1855) 1 Jur NS 751 and *Re Lake* [1903] 1 KB 439.

5 *Shepherd v Mouls* (1845) 4 Hare 500 at 504.

6 *Scott on Trusts* (4th edn) para 208.5.

7 See Article 59.

8 This sale, pursuant to the trustees' duty to sell unauthorised investments will overreach the beneficiaries interests: *Re Jenkins and HE Randall & Co's Contract* [1903] 2 Ch 362.

9 *Wright v Morgan* [1926] AC 788, PC; *Re Patten and Edmonton Union* (1883) 52 LJ Ch 787; *Re Jenkins and H E Randall & Co's Contract* [1903] 2 Ch 362.

10 See the facts in *Breadner v Granville-Grossman* [2001] Ch 523, [2000] 4 All ER 705.

default of any appointment are entitled to all and not just half of the trust capital – and T must duly account to them for the whole capital. O will surely be entitled to equitable compensation in the amount of half the capital. This could be on the basis that T had negligently broken his equitable duty of care to O. Alternatively, while T actually has to account to the default beneficiaries for the whole capital, T is estopped from denying that he is personally liable to render an account to O for half the capital (and income subsequently arising therefrom) that T put himself under a duty to transfer to O, Equity looking on as done (as between T and O) that which ought to have been done before T's neglectful mistake put it out of his power to do what he ought to have done.

Another scenario is where B tells T that she is £100,000 in debt at a crippling 18% interest, so that she is desperately looking forward to receiving from T £100,000 to which she becomes entitled under the trust in two months time on attaining 35 years of age. Despite this, T does not get round to paying her the £100,000 till three months after her birthday because he and his wife were taking a four month round-the-world trip of a lifetime. While T must account for three months interest on the £100,000 at the mercantile higher than ordinary rate as if he had used the money for his own purposes, it seems clear that he will be forced by way of equitable compensation to make up the difference between that rate and the 18% paid by B.

In *Bank of New Zealand v New Zealand Guardian Trust Co Ltd*[11] a beneficiary claimed for an individual loss extraneous to the trust estate. The Bank claimed that the trustee of a secured debenture trust had failed in its duty to monitor the conduct of the company which had borrowed money from the Bank and other lenders and which had itself made unsecured advances to its subsidiaries in breach of its obligations under the debenture deed. The Bank claimed that because it was not notified of the breach it had lost the opportunity to withdraw from the loan facility at a time when it would have recovered the full amount due.

The New Zealand Court of Appeal held that the strict 'but for' test of causation did not apply because there had been no breach of the duty of fidelity and loyalty, only a breach of the duty to exercise reasonable care. There was no reason to approach the trustee's breach of its duty to act diligently in any different manner as regards causation and remoteness than would be the case if the cause of action were in contract or tort rather than in equity. On this basis the scope of the trustee's duty was to maintain (and not permit diminution of) the value of the secured debenture by monitoring the company's compliance and, if necessary, threatening to enforce or enforcing the charge over the company's property. The Bank's loss flowed not from any diminution in the value of the trust property but from the loss of opportunity to exit the loan syndicate. The scope and purpose of the trustee's duty[12] did not extend to protecting the Bank from the loss it suffered from the company's insolvency through causes unconnected with the unsecured advances to its subsidiaries which the trustee failed to detect and report. Thus, the Bank's claim failed.

Equitable compensation in the above cases payable to individual beneficiaries must be distinguished from the equitable compensation paid directly to an absolutely entitled beneficiary when the trusts relating to his share of

---

11 [1999] 1 NZLR 664, CA.
12 Also see the approach of Mummery LJ in *Swindle v Harrison* [1997] 4 All ER 705 at 733–735.

the trust fund have come to an end. The measure of the latter compensation is the same as if the trustees were liable to restore to the trust fund the relevant amount ascertained on falsification and surcharge of the accounts, but it is not necessary to increase the trust fund by the relevant amount and then to transfer to the beneficiary his entitlement therein: the amount can be ordered to be paid directly to the absolutely entitled beneficiary[13].

ARTICLE 90

Joint and several liability of trustees

(1) Each trustee is, in general, liable for the whole loss when caused by the joint[14] default of all the trustees, even although all may not have been equally blameworthy[15]; and a decree against all may be enforced against one or more only[16].

(2) But although the liability is several as well as joint, all the actual trustees or the personal representatives of the last surviving trustee are necessary parties to the action[17].

All parties to a breach are equally liable

All parties to a breach of trust are equally liable, and there is between them no primary liability[18]; and the liability for breach of trust is not confined to express trustees, but extends to all who are actually privy to the breach. Thus, where trustees delegated their trusteeship to their solicitors, who received the moneys, and did not invest them but made use of them in their business, it was held that both the trustees and the solicitors were equally liable and that judgment might be executed by the beneficiaries against the solicitors only[19]. This principle does not, however, apply to professional payments made by trustees to a solicitor or other agent who knows that the money is trust money, unless facts are brought home to him which show that, to his knowledge, the money was being applied in a manner inconsistent with the trust, or, in other words, that the solicitor or other agent was party either to a fraud, or to a breach of trust on the part of the trustees. To make an agent liable to return costs:

> 'he must be fixed with notice that, at the time when he accepted payment, the trustee had been guilty of a breach of trust such as would preclude him altogether from resorting to the trust estate for payment of costs; so that in fact the application of the trust estate in payment of costs would be a breach of trust'.[20]

13 *Target Holdings Ltd v Redferns* [1996] AC 421 at 434–435.
14 See Article 98 as to when a trustee is not answerable for the default of a co-trustee.
15 *Wilson v Moore* (1833) 1 My & K 126; *Lyse v Kingdon* (1844) 1 Coll 184; *Re Biddulph* (1869) 4 Ch App 280. This applies not only to express trustees, but to all persons who meddle with the trust property with notice of the trust. See *Cowper v Stoneham* (1893) 68 LT 18.
16 *A-G v Wilson* (1840) Cr & Ph 1 at 28; *Fletcher v Green* (1864) 33 Beav 426.
17 *Re Jordan* [1904] 1 Ch 260.
18 Per Leach MR in *Wilson v Moore* (1833) 1 My & K 126.
19 *Cowper v Stoneham* (1893) 68 LT 18; and see also *Blyth v Fladgate* [1891] 1 Ch 337, and Art 100, post, where the liability of third parties is more fully discussed.
20 Per Stirling J in *Re Blundell* (1888) 40 Ch D 370; and *Re Munton* [1927] 1 Ch 262. See *Carl-Zeiss-Stiftung v Herbert Smith & Co (a firm) (No 2)* [1969] 2 Ch 276, [1969] 2 All ER 367, p 954, post.

Beneficiaries may claim the whole from any one of the trustees

It follows from the nature of the liability being several as well as joint, that until the plaintiffs have received one hundred pence in the pound they are entitled to claim the whole debt from any one trustee in respect of his several liability, notwithstanding that they have accepted a sum from another trustee in satisfaction of *his* liability. If, therefore, the former becomes bankrupt, the plaintiffs can prove for the full amount against his estate, without first deducting the sum received from the other trustee[1]. Nevertheless a release of one trustee *may* incidentally operate as a release of the others if the beneficiary elects to accept an investment the making of which was the breach of trust complained of[2].

Contribution between trustees

A trustee who is obliged to pay out to an absolutely entitled beneficiary who has suffered loss or is obliged to restore the trust fund to the value it would have had but for a breach of the trust will normally have a right of contribution from the other trustees as discussed below in Article 99.

ARTICLE 91

Set-off of gain on one breach against loss on another not allowed

A trustee is liable only for the actual loss in each distinct and complete transaction which amounts to a breach of trust, and not for the loss in each particular item thereof[3]. A loss in one transaction or fund is not, however, compensated by a gain in another and distinct one[4].

Where breach of trust causes benefit to the estate, trustee not liable for outlay

In *Vyse v Foster*[5] a testator devised his real and personal estates upon common trusts for sale, making them a mixed fund. His trustees were advised that a few acres of freehold land which belonged to him might be advantageously sold in lots for building purposes, and that, to develop their value, it was desirable to build a villa upon part of them. They accordingly built one at a cost of £1,600 out of the testator's personal estate. The evidence showed that the outlay had benefited the estate, but Vice-Chancellor Bacon disallowed the £1,600 to the trustees in passing their accounts.

The Court of Appeal (and subsequently the House of Lords), however, reversed this, James LJ saying:

'As the real and personal estate constituted one fund, we think it neither reasonable nor just to fix the trustees with a sum, part of the estate, bona fide laid out on other part of the estate in the exercise of their judgment as the best means of increasing the value of the whole.'

1 *Edwards v Hood-Barrs* [1905] 1 Ch 20.
2 See *Blackwood v Borrowes* (1843) 4 Dr & War 441.
3 *Vyse v Foster* (1872) 8 Ch App 309; affd (1874) LR 7 HL 318.
4 *Wiles v Gresham* (1854) 2 Drew 258; affd (1854) 5 De GM & G 770; *Dimes v Scott* (1828) 4 Russ 195; *Re Leonard, ex p Lewis* (1819) 1 Gl & J 69.
5 (1872) 8 Ch App 309.

Loss on one transaction cannot be set off against gain on another

In *Wiles v Gresham*[6] on the other hand by the negligence of the trustees of a marriage settlement, a bond debt for £2,000 due from the husband was not got in, and was totally lost. Certain other of the trust funds were without proper authority invested in the purchase of land upon the trusts of the settlement. The husband, out of his own money, greatly added to the value of this land, and upon a claim being made against the trustees for the £2,000 they endeavoured to set off against that loss the gain which had accrued to the trust by the increased value of the land, but their contention was disallowed, the two transactions being separate and distinct.

Again, in *Dimes v Scott*[7] trustees had kept invested on unauthorised security at 10% a sum of money which they ought to have invested in consols, at a far lower rate of interest. The whole interest was wrongfully paid to the life tenant instead of just 3% then applicable under the rule in *Howe v Dartmouth*. Later the money was invested in consols when they were at a low price so that more consols were purchased than would have been the case if they had earlier been purchased at the proper time. The trustees claimed to set off the gain against the loss, but were not allowed to do so, because 'at whatever period the unauthorised security was realised, the estate was entitled to the whole of the consols that were then bought, and if it was sold at a later period than it ought to have been the executor was not entitled to any accidental advantage thence accruing'.

This case is at first sight difficult to distinguish from *Vyse v Foster*, but it will be perceived that the loss and gain resulted from two distinct transactions. The loss resulted from a breach of trust in not realising the securities; the gain arose from a particular kind of stock being at a lower market value than usual at the date at which the trustees bought it.

There can be difficulty in determining whether two distinct transactions occurred or only a single transaction. Thus where trustees committed a breach of trust in lending trust moneys on mortgage, and upon a suit by them the mortgaged property was sold, and the money paid into court, and invested in consols pending the suit, and the consols rose in value, the trustees were allowed to set off the gain in the value of the consols against the loss under the mortgage, for the gain and loss arose out of one transaction[8]. It is very difficult to reconcile this case with the last one, but it seems to be reasonable and in accordance with common sense and justice.

In *Bartlett v Barclays Bank Trust Co Ltd (No 2)*[9] Brightman J stated:

'The general rule is that where a trustee is liable in respect of distinct breaches of trust, one of which resulted in a loss and the other in a gain, he is not entitled to set off the gain against the loss, unless they arise in the same transaction. The relevant cases are, however, not altogether easy to reconcile. All are centenarians and none is quite like the present. The Guildford development stemmed from exactly the same policy and exemplified the same folly as the Old Bailey project. Part of the profit was used to finance the Old Bailey disaster. By sheer luck the gamble paid off handsomely on capital account. I think it would be unjust to deprive the bank of this element of salvage. My order will therefore reflect the bank's right to an appropriate set-off.'

---

6 (1854) 2 Drew 258; *Re Barker* (1898) 77 LT 712.
7 (1828) 4 Russ 195. For investment portfolio theory see p 601, ante.
8 *Fletcher v Green* (1864) 33 Beav 426.
9 [1980] Ch 515 at 538.

ARTICLE 92

Property acquired by trustee or fiduciary can be traced and claimed by the beneficiaries or principal

(1) If a trustee or other fiduciary has, in breach of trust or other fiduciary obligation, converted trust or fiduciary property into some other form, the property into which it has been so converted becomes subject to the trust or other fiduciary obligation. If *all* the beneficiaries are of full age and capacity, they can collectively elect to adopt the breach, and take the property as it then stands; but failing such election, the property must be reconverted if it is not an authorised investment. In that case any gain accrues for the benefit of the beneficiaries and any loss falls on the trustee or other fiduciary[10]. Where a trustee or other fiduciary has made an unauthorised use of the trust or fiduciary property or has otherwise exploited his position in breach of his duty[11] so as purportedly to obtain a personal profit for himself, then such profit into whatever form it may be converted is also trust property and must be invested in authorised investments and held for the trust beneficiaries unless they are all of full age and capacity and elect to take the property as it then stands.

(2) If a trustee has mixed trust moneys with his own, or has, partly with his own and partly with trust moneys, purchased other property, then the beneficiaries cannot elect to take the whole of the mixed fund or the entire property so purchased. However, the beneficiaries can trace into the mixed fund or property so purchased and either assert a proprietary claim to a proportionate share, or alternatively take a first charge on the traced assets to secure restoration of the trust fund[12]. Moreover, if there is an increase in the value of the property paid for partly with trust money, in substance, the trustee and the beneficiaries are treated as co-owners of the appreciated property in proportions corresponding to their respective contributions to the purchase price[13].

(3) Where assets of two trusts have been mixed (other than in a current banking account) any losses or gains in the value of the mixed fund are shared rateably according to the values of the mixed assets of

10 See per Pearson J in *Re Patten and Edmonton Union* (1883) 52 LJ Ch 787; *Re Hallett's Estate* (1880) 13 Ch D 696; *Taylor v Plumer* (1815) 3 M & S 562; *Frith v Cartland* (1865) 2 Hem & M 417; *Hopper v Conyers* (1866) LR 2 Eq 549; *Lane v Dighton* (1762) Amb 409; *Scales v Baker* (1859) 28 Beav 91; *Cook v Addison* (1869) LR 7 Eq 466; *Ernest v Croysdill* (1860) 2 De GF & J 175; *Re Anslow* (1880) 28 WR 522; *Wright v Morgan* [1926] AC 788.

11 *A-G for Hong Kong v Reid* [1994] 1 AC 324, [1994] 1 All ER 1, PC.

12 *Foskett v McKeown* [2001] 1 AC 102 at 131, per Lord Millett. See too *Re Hallett's Estate* (1880) 13 Ch D 696; *Re Oatway* [1903] 2 Ch 356; *Lupton v White* (1808) 15 Ves 432; *Pennell v Deffell* (1853) 4 De GM & G 372; and *Re Diplock* [1948] Ch 465, [1948] 2 All ER 318, CA; affd sub nom *Ministry of Health v Simpson* [1951] AC 251, [1950] 2 All ER 1137, HL; *El Ajou v Dollar Land Holdings plc* [1993] 3 All ER 717 at 735–736; revsd [1994] 2 All ER 685 at 701.

13 See *Re Tilley's Will Trusts* [1967] Ch 1179, [1967] 2 All ER 303; *Scott v Scott* (1963) 109 CLR 649; *Paul A Davies (Australia) Pty Ltd (in liquidation) v Davies* [1983] 1 NSWLR 440.

each trust[14]. Where mixing occurs in a current banking account the rule in *Clayton's Case* has traditionally been applied to attribute the first drawings out to the first payments in[15] unless this produces an inequitable result[16]. However there are strong reasons for thinking that this situation should not be resolved by application of the rule in *Clayton's Case*, and should instead be resolved by adopting the *Re Diplock* rateable proportion rule.

(4) Traditionally, by virtue of authority rather than principle, the equitable right to trace and to assert proprietary claims required a continuing right of property recognised in equity or its concomitant, a fiduciary or quasi-fiduciary relationship. The right to trace thus extended well beyond the pure trustee-beneficiary relationship since the concept of fiduciary or quasi-fiduciary relationship was stretched to the limit in the interests of protecting quasi-beneficiaries and it was even suggested that a thief becomes a constructive trustee of what he steals[17], so that equity in its auxiliary jurisdiction might assist a plaintiff who was sole legal beneficial owner of a stolen asset where legal remedies were inadequate in the circumstances. The tracing cases to this effect have now been superseded by the House of Lords' judgment in *Foskett v McKeown*[18] where Lord Steyn and Lord Millett both stated that there is no need to show a trust or fiduciary relationship in order to bring the 'equitable' tracing rules into play, because there is only one set of tracing rules which can be invoked by common law and equitable claimants alike.

(5) The right to trace is lost when no traceable product of trust or other fiduciary property can be identified or the traceable product is found (as Article 101 reveals) in the hands of a third party who is a bona fide purchaser of a legal interest for value without notice or who makes out the defence of change of position.

PARAGRAPH 1

Introduction

In *Foskett v McKeown*[19], Lord Millett distinguished 'tracing', 'following', and 'claiming' in these terms:

---

14 *Sinclair v Brougham* [1914] AC 398 at 442; *Re Diplock* [1948] Ch 465 at 533, 534, 539; *Foskett v McKeown* [2001] 1 AC 102 at 132, per Lord Millett.

15 *Re Hallett's Estate* (1879) 13 Ch D 696 (Fry J); *Hancock v Smith* (1889) 41 Ch D 456 at 461; *Re Stenning* [1895] 2 Ch 433; *Re Diplock* [1948] Ch 465 at 553–554.

16 *Barlow Clowes International Ltd v Vaughan* [1992] 4 All ER 22 at 39 and 44; *Re Ontario Securities Commission* (1986) 30 DLR (4th) 1; *Re Registered Securities* [1991] 1 NZLR 545.

17 *Bishopsgate Investment Management Ltd v Maxwell* [1993] Ch 1 at 70, [1992] 2 All ER 856 at 909 per Mann LJ; *Lipkin Gorman v Karpnale Ltd* [1991] 2 AC 548 at 565–566, [1992] 4 All ER 512 at 522 per Lord Templeman; *Westdeutsche Landesbank Girozentrale v Islington London Borough Council* [1996] AC 669 at 716, per Lord Browne-Wilkinson.

18 [2001] 1 AC 102 at 113 and 128.

19 [2001] 1 AC 102 at 129–130, adopting the terminology suggested in L D Smith *The Law of Tracing* (1997). See too *Boscawen v Bajwa* [1996] 1 WLR 328 at 334, CA.

'[Tracing and following] are both exercises in locating assets which are or may be taken to represent an asset belonging to the plaintiffs and to which they assert ownership. The processes of following and tracing are, however, distinct. Following is the process of following the same asset as it moves from hand to hand. Tracing is the process of identifying a new asset as the substitute for the old. Where one asset is exchanged for another, a claimant can elect whether to follow the original asset into the hands of the new owner or to trace its value into the new asset in the hands of the same owner. ... Tracing is also distinct from claiming. It identifies the traceable proceeds of the claimant's property. It enables the claimant to substitute the traceable proceeds for the original asset as the subject matter of his claim. But it does not affect or establish his claim. That will depend on a number of factors including the nature of his interest in the original asset. He will normally be able to maintain the same claim to the substituted asset as he could have maintained to the original asset. ... But his claim may also be exposed to potential defences as a result of intervening transactions.'

In Lord Millett's view, therefore, 'the rules of following and tracing ... are essentially evidential in nature', and they are essentially distinct from 'rules which determine substantive rights': the former are concerned with identifying property in other hands or in another form; the latter with the rights that a claimant can assert against the property in its present form'[20].

Where trust property has been wrongfully converted into a different form by the trustee, either by exchanging the trust property for another asset, or by mixing the trust property with other property, or by a combination of the two, and the substitute asset or mixture remains in the trustee's hands, there is no need for the beneficiaries to 'follow' their property or its traceable product into the hands of a third party, before they can assert a proprietary claim to the new asset or mixture[1]. However, it will be necessary for the beneficiaries to 'trace' the value inherent in the trust property through the trustee's substitutions or mixtures into the value inherent in the substitute asset or mixture, as they can only asset a proprietary claim to the new asset or mixture once they have established that this is the traceable product of trust property.

Stock bought with trust or fiduciary money

Where money is handed to a broker for the purpose of purchasing stock, and he invests it in unauthorised stock, and absconds, the stock which he has purchased will belong to the principal, and not to the broker's trustee in bankruptcy, for a broker is a fiduciary or constructive trustee for his principal; and, as was said by Lord Ellenborough[2]:

'the property of a principal entrusted by him to his factor for any special purpose belongs to the principal, notwithstanding any change which that property may have undergone in point of form, so long as such property is capable of being identified, and distinguished from all other property.'

Nor does a personal judgment against the trustee to make good the loss release the lien of the beneficiaries on an unauthorised investment[3].

---

20 *Glencore International AG v Metro Trading International Ltd* [2001] 1 Lloyd's Rep 284 at 329.
1 The process of following trust property or its traceable proceeds into the hands of third parties is discussed in Article 101, post.
2 *Taylor v Plumer* (1815) 3 M & S 562 clarified by L Smith (1995) LMCLQ 240 and Millett LJ in *Trustee of Property of FC Jones & Sons v Jones* [1997] Ch 159 at 169; see also *Re Strachan* (1876) 4 Ch D 123 at 128, CA; *Re Hallett's Estate* (1880) 13 Ch D 696 at 717.
3 *Francis v Francis* (1854) 5 De GM & G 108.

If a trustee makes a profit by selling shares belonging to the trust when the share price is high and buying the same shares back when the price is low and pretending that the trust has had the same shares throughout then, again, the profit should belong to the trust as trust property and be traceable.

Money produced by trust or fiduciary chattels

If goods consigned to a factor be sold by him and reduced into money, yet if the money can be traced – as, for instance, where it has been kept separate and apart from the factor's own moneys, or kept in bags, or the like[4], or has been changed into bills or notes[5], or into any other form[6], or has been paid into the factor's account at the bank[7] – the employer, and not the creditors of the factor, will, upon his bankruptcy, be entitled to the property into which it has been converted. For the creditors of a defaulting trustee can have no better right to the trust property than the trustee himself[8]. However, where a person whose business it is to act as an agent in turning to account the property of his principal, ceases to carry on this business actively, there is no general rule that he cannot keep the proceeds of the principal's property for himself, and even if the agency relationship comes to an end because the agent is forced into administrative receivership, this cannot alter the agent's right to seek outstanding sums from customers, nor can it alter the right of the agent's bank to enforce a charge against these book debts, unless this would be wholly unconscionable[9].

Money produced by misuse of fiduciary position

If in breach of fiduciary duty a fiduciary receives a bribe which he then invests in property, such bribe and then such property is held on a constructive trust for the person injured, Equity considering as done that which ought to be done[10].

Wrongful sale by vendor

A vendor who, after entering into a contract for sale of land[11], sells it to another person will hold the proceeds of sale (and anything purchased therewith) on constructive trust for the original contracting purchaser subject to that purchaser paying over the agreed purchase price[12].

Sale by trustees of property wrongfully acquired out of trust moneys

Where the trustees of a will invested trust moneys in an unauthorised purchase of land, and afterwards contracted to sell it for a largely increased

---

4 *Tooke v Hollingworth* (1793) 5 Term Rep 215.
5 *Re Jullian, ex p Dumas* (1754) 2 Ves Sen 582; *Scott v Surman* (1742) Willes 400.
6 *Frith v Cartland* (1865) 2 Hem & M 417; *Birt v Burt* (1877) 11 Ch D 773n.
7 *Re Hallett's Estate* (1880) 13 Ch D 696.
8 *Taylor v Plumer* (1815) 3 M & S 562.
9 [2000] 1 BCLC 761.
10 *A-G for Hong Kong v Reid* [1994] 1 AC 324, [1994] 1 All ER 1, PC.
11 See Art 36, ante.
12 *Lake v Bayliss* [1974] 2 All ER 1114, [1974] 1 WLR 1073.

price, it was held that they were acting properly in so doing, and that the concurrence of one beneficiary was sufficient to make a good overreaching title[13]. For, as Pearson J put it:

'I see no reason why the trustees should not now do what it was all along their duty to do, and what the court would have ordered them to do. At the same time, I agree that it would be proper to take the concurrence of one of the cestuis que trust; because, if all of them elected to take their shares of the land after it had been purchased, they would have been entitled to do so.'

The report states that the learned judge said that a good title could be made on the purchasers seeing that the purchase-money was invested in the names of the trustees as trustees; but no such requirement has been suggested in subsequent cases and it seems to be quite inconsistent with s 14 of the Trustee Act 1925, s 27 of the Law of Property Act 1925 and the language of Cozens-Hardy J in *Power v Banks*[14] where he said:

'by means of the sales ... the purchase-money got into ... the proper hands, and I cannot see what harm was done by this. To affect the purchasers ... with the consequences of any subsequent misappropriation ... would be unjust unless the sale itself was a wrongful act.'

On the same principle, where the beneficiaries or any of them are infants, the trustees can sell the wrongfully acquired unauthorised investment without anyone's consent; because in that case the beneficiaries collectively are not in a position to adopt the breach[15].

PARAGRAPH 2

Trust or fiduciary property mixed with other property so as to lose its discrete identity

The case is comparatively simple where (as in the foregoing illustrations) the trustee has spent or converted the trust property, and nothing but the trust property. It becomes more difficult when the trustee has mixed the trust moneys with his own so that uncertainty of subject-matter of the trust arises, and either kept the mixed fund or spent it in the purchase of other property. The case then turns entirely upon the question whether the mixed fund, so formed, can still be identified; or, if it has been spent, whether it can be traced into the property which has been purchased with it. As Lord Greene[16] has stated:

'The equitable remedies pre-suppose the continued existence of the money either as a separate fund or as part of a mixed fund or as latent in property acquired by means of such a fund.'

---

13 *Re Patten and Edmonton Union* (1883) 52 LJ Ch 787. See Birks and Prett (ed) *Breach of Trust* (Hart Publishing, 2002) Chapter 4 'Overreaching' by D Fox.
14 *Re Jenkins and H E Randall & Co's Contract* [1903] 2 Ch 362; and see *Power v Banks* [1901] 2 Ch 487 at 496. A purchaser would only have problems if not acting in good faith by purchasing knowingly at an undervalue: *Cowan de Groot Properties v Eagle Trust plc* [1992] 4 All ER 700.
15 *Re Jenkins and H E Randall & Co's Contract* [1903] 2 Ch 362.
16 In *Re Diplock* [1948] Ch 465 at 521, [1948] 2 All ER 318 at 347, CA; affd sub nom *Ministry of Health v Simpson* [1951] AC 251, [1950] 2 All ER 1137, HL.

However, as Lord Millett brings out[17]:

'In principle it should not matter . . . whether the trustee mixes the trust money with his own and buys the new asset with the mixed fund or makes separate payments of the purchase price (whether simultaneously or sequentially) out of the different funds. In every case the value formerly inherent in the trust property has become located within the value inherent in the new asset.'

If the trust property has ceased to have any continued existence, because it has been dissipated[18], then, as the actual property is gone, and nothing can be identified as standing in its place, the beneficiary can only proceed against the trustee personally for the breach of trust, or, if the latter be bankrupt, can prove only as a creditor[19]. For the right of the beneficiary is only to have the actual trust property or that which stands in its place, or to have a charge on it[20].

It has been suggested[1] that, even though a claimant's £x has been dissipated, the claimant should have an equitable lien or charge for £x over all the defendant fiduciary's remaining unencumbered assets which had earlier been swollen by the plaintiff's £x. This suggestion has been rejected by the Court of Appeal in *Re Hallett & Co*[2] and *Bishopsgate Investment Management Ltd v Homan*[3]: it would so dramatically affect the rights of the unsecured creditors of the defendant on his insolvency that only legislation should alter the position if a full consideration of the problems justifies such legislation or some limited legislation covering special types of defendants in specified circumstances.

Trust property mixed with trustee's property

If a trustee mixes assets with his own the onus of proof is on the trustee to distinguish the separate assets and, to the extent that he fails to do so, they belong to the trust[4]. Moreover as Staughton J stated[5], 'If the wrongdoer has destroyed or impaired the evidence by which the innocent party could show how much he has lost the wrongdoer must suffer from the resulting uncertainty.' The tracing rules which apply in this situation thus dovetail with the more general rule of evidence that where evidential uncertainty is created by wrongdoing, evidential presumptions will be made against the wrongdoer[6].

The starting point is that the beneficiaries will have a first charge for their

---

17 *Foskett v McKeown* [2001] 1 AC 102 at 130.
18 Although the payment of a debt was traditionally regarded as a dissipation, in this context (*Re Diplock* [1948] Ch 465 at 549), it now seems that the beneficiaries may 'backwards trace' through such payments into an asset, or trace into an extinguished charge which they may then acquire, by a legal fiction via subrogation. See p 902 post.
19 *Re Jullian, ex p Dumas* (1754) 2 Ves Sen 582; *Scott v Surman* (1742) Willes 400; *Re Hallett & Co* [1894] 2 QB 237; *Foskett v McKeown* [2001] 1 AC 102 at 130.
20 See *Re Diplock* [1948] Ch 465, [1948] 2 All ER 318, CA; affd sub nom *Ministry of Health v Simpson* [1951] AC 251, [1950] 2 All ER 1137, HL.
1 *Space Investments Ltd v Canadian Imperial Bank of Commerce Trust Co (Bahamas) Ltd* [1986] 3 All ER 75 at 77, [1986] 1 WLR 1072 at 1074; Goff & Jones, *Law of Restitution* (4th edn) pp 99, 132.
2 [1894] 2 QB 237 at 245.
3 [1995] Ch 211, [1995] 1 All ER 347.
4 *Lupton v White* (1808) 15 Ves 432; *Westdeutsche Landesbank Girozentrale v Islington Borough Council* [1996] AC 669.
5 *Indian Oil Corpn Ltd v Greenstone Shipping SA* [1987] 3 All ER 893 at 906.
6 *Armory v Delamirie* (1721) 1 Stra 505; *Infabrics Ltd v Jaytex Ltd* [1985] FSR 75.

money on the mixed fund and any property purchased thereout[7]. In Lord Millett's words[8], 'As against the wrongdoer and his successors, the beneficiary is entitled to locate his contribution in any part of the mixture and to subordinate their claims to share in the mixture until his own contribution has been satisfied'. Thus, if trust money is mixed with the trustee's own money in account No. 1 and the trustee then transfers money therefrom into account No 2 and account No 3 (thereby acquiring choses in action) and purchases with money in account No 1 a painting and a flat the plaintiff beneficiaries will have an equitable charge for their moneys over whatever money remains in the No 1, No 2 and No 3 accounts and over the painting and the flat. Equity imposes such charges over the new assets because they are derived from a fund which is treated as if subject to a charge in favour of the claimant beneficiaries[9]. If the defendant does not personally satisfy the claimants' claim they can assert their charge over any of the traced assets to satisfy their claim. Only if they seek more than a charge by seeking a proportionate share of an appreciated asset will they need to consider relying upon artificial presumptions against a wrongdoer, whether the presumption[10] that he acted honestly in first using his own money or the presumption[11] that he used trust money because he cannot allege he used his own money until he reinstated the trust money in a trust account.

Where mixing takes place in a current account of a bank the trustee is presumed to draw out his own moneys[12] first and not to draw on the trust moneys until his own moneys have been exhausted[13]. However, once trust moneys have been drawn upon a beneficiary cannot claim that subsequent payments in to the trustee's own account are meant to be trust moneys unless such payments represent the proceeds of sale of traceable trust property[14]. Thus a beneficiary can normally claim only against the lowest credit balance in the mixed current account[15] though he may be lucky enough to be able to trace withdrawn moneys into a valuable appreciating investment.

Where moneys are withdrawn to purchase what turns out to be a profitable investment the beneficiaries can claim such investment even if at the time of the purchase the trustee's own moneys (mixed with the trust moneys) could

---

7 *Re Hallett's Estate* (1880) 13 Ch D 696; *Re Oatway* [1903] 2 Ch 356; *Re Diplock* [1948] Ch 465 at 539, CA; *El Ajou v Dollar Land Holdings plc* [1993] 3 All ER 717 at 735; revsd [1994] 2 All ER 685 at 699, 701.

8 *Foskett v McKeown* [2001] 1 AC 102 at 132.

9 *El Ajou v Dollar Land Holdings plc* [1993] 3 All ER 717 at 736.

10 *Re Hallett's Estate* (1880) 13 Ch D 696 at 727–728.

11 *Re Oatway* [1903] 2 Ch 356.

12 *Re Tilley's Will Trusts* [1967] Ch 1179, [1967] 2 All ER 303; *Scott v Scott* (1963) 109 CLR 649; *Paul A Davies (Australia) Pty Ltd (in liquidation) v Davies* [1983] 1 NSWLR 440.

13 *Re Hallett's Estate* (1880) 13 Ch D 696 followed in *Grabowski v Grangemore Investments* [2002] EWHC 851 (Ch).

14 *James Roscoe (Bolton) Ltd v Winder* [1915] 1 Ch 62.

15 *James Roscoe (Bolton) Ltd v Winder* [1915] 1 Ch 62; *Bishopsgate Investment Management Ltd v Homan* [1995] 1 All ER 347, CA. For cases where money replaced in a trust account was the traceable proceeds of trust money previously withdrawn from the account, see L D Smith *The Law of Tracing* (1997) at 202, n 154, and also *Westdeutsche Landesbank Girozentrale v Islington LBC* [1994] 4 All ER 890 at 939. The 'lowest intermediate balance' role was unfortunately abrogated by the Ontario Court of Appeal without appreciating that the role does not resolve evidential uncertainties, but rather, helps to identify what is evidentially certain about the trustees' actions, in *Law Society of Upper Canada v Toronto Dominion Bank* (1998) 169 DLR (4th) 353, noted LD Smith (2000) 33 Cam Bus LJ 75.

have sufficed to effect the purchase[16]. The presumption that the trustee is presumed to draw out his own moneys first and the 'first in first out' principle enshrined in *Clayton's Case* cannot be invoked by the wrongdoing trustee to his own advantage to control the book-keeping and allocate profitable investments to himself. His conduct prevented proper accounts from being kept so it is up to the beneficiaries to resolve the book-keeping as they wish, and it is the trustee's own fault that his mixing of moneys prevents him from disputing such book-keeping. The beneficiaries can choose to treat withdrawals that are dissipated as representing the trustee's money and profitable withdrawals as representing the trust moneys. The trustee cannot take advantage of his own wrongdoing to put himself in the position of 'Heads I win, tails you lose'; he cannot complain that his wrongdoing enables the beneficiaries to be in that position: 'everything is presumed against him'[17].

Where a trustee mixes, say, £10,000 of trust money with £10,000 of his own, so as to purchase Whizzo Ltd shares for £20,000, then the trust beneficiaries can choose either to take a 50% ownership interest in the shares, or to take a charge over the shares to the value of £10,000, depending on which of these is most advantageous to them[18]. Exceptionally, if the trustee would not have been able to purchase the shares but for being the trustee, as where the offer was made to him qua trustee, the shares should belong exclusively to the trust, subject to him being reimbursed his own expenditure[19]. Similarly, if investments had, for example, to be in minimum £100,000 blocks which the trust, but not the trustee personally, could provide, the trustee only having £10,000 spare which he invested with £90,000 of trust moneys, then it seems that the investment should belong to the trust beneficiaries, subject to reimbursement of the £10,000 with interest. A trustee must not profit from his trust (unless authorised by the trust instrument): Equity should regard him as having done what he was duty-bound to do, namely to acquire the investments for the benefit of the trust beneficiaries and not himself.

A trustee of course may reinstate the trust fund and so right the wrong[20] and thereafter, having distinguished his own private property from the trust property, he may invest his private property profitably or unprofitably. Until he has done that he cannot prove that it was not trust moneys that were used to purchase the profitable investment[1].

---

16 *Re Oatway* [1903] 2 Ch 356. There seems no justification for restricting this claim to the situation where insufficient moneys are left in the account to cover the trust moneys, though such restriction may (accidentally?) be implicit in the final sentence of the penultimate paragraph of the judgment of Ungoed-Thomas J in *Re Tilley's Will Trusts* [1967] Ch 1179, [1967] 2 All ER 303. A subsequent fortuitous dissipation or not of the balance in the account by the trustee should be immaterial.

17 *Gray v Haig* (1855) 20 Beav 219 at 226 per *Romilly MR Jaffray v Marshall* [1994] 1 All ER 143 at 151.

18 *Foskett v McKeown* [2001] 1 AC 102; *Mitchell v O'Brien* [2002] All ER(D) 125 (Feb). See too *Re Tilley's Will Trusts* [1967] Ch 1179; *Wedderburn v Wedderburn* (1838) 4 My & Cr 41.

19 Eg *Keech v Sandford* (1726) 2 Eq Cas Abr 741.

20 [1903] 2 Ch 356 at 361. If T mixed £10,000 of trust money with his own £5,000 to purchase shares worth £15,000, which he later sells for £30,000, he can only reinstate the trust fund by paying £20,000 and not £10,000 into a designated trust account.

1 Thus if T mixes £20,000 trust money with £10,000 of his own money and spends £18,000 on a profitable investment which doubles in value the trust beneficiaries should be able to claim a £2,000 charge on the moneys remaining in the mixed account as well as the £36,000 investment representing the £18,000 balance of the £20,000 trust money. The wrongdoing trustee can hardly be heard to claim that it would be fairer to allow him to make a profit either by claiming 10 eighteenths of the investment for himself or 10 thirtieths thereof.

Causation problems and the alternative remedies

Equity's minimum remedy is the imposition of a lien or charge over the identifiable product of the plaintiff's property to satisfy the plaintiff's claim in respect of such property. However, in some circumstances Equity will impose a constructive trust over such identifiable product to the extent of such share therein as reflects the value of the plaintiff's traceable interest, thereby enabling the plaintiff to recover more than would be achieved by the imposition of a lien.

To achieve this favourable result it is submitted that a plaintiff needs to prove not just the transactional proprietary links. It is fundamental that he should also establish as a matter of causation that the defendant was unjustly enriched at the plaintiff's expense because, but for the value input from the plaintiff's property, the defendant probably would not have acquired the asset in which the plaintiff claims a whole or partial share. This is the crucial justification for the imposition of the constructive trust which captures the profit for the plaintiff and makes it unavailable to the defendant and his creditors on his insolvency.

A helpful and illuminating case is *Re Tilley's Will Trusts*[2] where Ungoed-Thomas J was prepared to find that there were transactional proprietary links to justify the imposition of a lien but held that no constructive trust of a profitable proportionate share would be imposed. The plaintiff argued that £179 of trust money had been used by the trustee in purchasing a £1,000 house and £83 in purchasing a £2,050 house because the trust moneys had been paid into the trustee's bank account whence the purchase moneys had been paid, leaving her account overdrawn, so that logically there were clear transactional links. She was a woman of substantial wealth having (in 1939) overdraft facilities of £22,000. In the 1950s her account was substantially in credit when she paid in three trust sums totalling £1,975 and later purchased houses in her name when her account contained more than enough, without regard to the trust moneys, to pay for such purchases.

Ungoed-Thomas J took the view[3] that if the trustee had been dishonest, deliberately using trust money in the purchases, then the beneficiaries would be entitled to proportionate shares in the property purchased. One can see that here there would be clear transactional and causative links because she would not be in a position (due to her intentions, quite apart from her mixing of the funds) to prove the moneys invested in the houses were not trust moneys. However, he held that the trustee, an elderly widow who was also life tenant under her spouse's will, had innocently but misguidedly intermingled trust money with her own. He then held that her wealthy financial circumstances meant that she would have bought the properties anyhow, so that the beneficiaries were not entitled to proportionate shares in the properties.

> 'The trustee's breach halted at the mixing of funds in her bank account. Although properties bought out of those funds would, like the bank account itself, ... be charged with repayment of the trust moneys ... yet the trust moneys were not invested in properties at all but merely went in reduction of the trustee's overdraft which was in reality the source of the purchase moneys.'

One can thus see that it was not a case where the defendant would not have

2 [1967] Ch 1179.
3 [1967] Ch 1179 at 1193.

bought the houses but for the trust money. Therefore she had not obtained the houses and thereby enriched herself at the expense of the trust beneficiaries, though she had obtained a benefit of £2,237 (£179 + £83 + £1,975), making her personally liable to account for the £2,237 but without interest since she was the life tenant.

Because the £2,237 was readily available out of the deceased trustee's estate the question of any lien to secure payment did not arise. However, the judge indicated[4] that he would have been prepared to impose a lien 'on the properties purchased by the widow out of the bank account as security for repayment of the £2,237 trust moneys paid into her bank account in accordance with the principle in *Re Oatway*'[5] if 'the moneys in the bank account were inadequate' to satisfy a lien on such account.

The defendant was fortunate in having as the judge Ungoed-Thomas J, renowned for his close concern for honesty and dishonesty and for his concentration upon the merits of individuals rather than upon lofty legal principles. The deterrent philosophy underpinning the integrity of trusteeship as reflected in *Boardman v Phipps*[6]; *A-G for Hong Kong v Reid*[7] and *Foskett v McKeown*[8] indicates that, as a trustee wrongfully mixing trust funds with her own, she should not have been allowed to argue that the profitable investments belonged to her and not to the trust beneficiaries and that she had done for herself what she could have done for the beneficiaries. After all, throughout her trusteeship she had acted recklessly, cavalierly and in clear breach of trust by not taking easy elementary steps to keep the trust money separate from her own, so that she could not prove that trust money had not actually been used towards the purchase of houses: she could not really disprove the causative link with the houses, as recognised by the preparedness of Ungoed-Thomas to impose a lien on the houses if her estate had not easily been able to pay the £2,237.

It is submitted that an express trustee who wrongly mixes trust money with her or his own, so that it cannot be established whose money was used to purchase particular assets, cannot be allowed to escape liability by arguing that he would have bought the assets anyway, having more than enough capacity to buy them without the assistance of the trust money, so that he is entitled to these profitable assets. Moreover, there ought not to be different approaches for lay trustees as opposed to professional trustees, or, within the category of lay trustees, for elderly housewives as opposed to entrepreneurial businessmen. Moreover, volunteers who take from wrongdoing trustees cannot be placed in a better position than the trustees themselves, as the majority of the House of Lords recently made clear in *Foskett v McKeown*[9].

However, if the defendant does not know that he is a trustee but is a constructive trustee, like the defendants in *Boardman v Phipps*[10], then he should be able to argue that he would have bought the relevant assets anyway so that he has not been unjustly enriched at the expense of the trust and no constructive trust should therefore attach to those assets. Thus, if the millionaire, Tom Boardman, had sold the shares subject to the constructive trust

---

4 [1967] Ch 1179 at 1193.
5 [1903] 2 Ch 356.
6 [1967] 2 AC 46.
7 [1994] 1 AC 324, PC.
8 [2001] 1 AC 102 at 134, HL.
9 [2001] 1 AC 102 at 127 and 131, per Lord Millett.
10 [1967] 2 AC 46.

for £50,000 and, believing the proceeds to be his, had then used them with another £50,000 of his to purchase Great Co shares which doubled in value, he should not hold half such shares on a constructive trust. Instead, he should simply hold the shares subject to a lien for £50,000 and interest.

A fortiori this should be the position for an innocent donee, D, having no actual, Nelsonian or naughty knowledge[11] that he had received trust property.

Tracing trust funds into property insurance proceeds

Problems arise over the proceeds of insurance in respect of property that is the traceable product of property of a claimant, P, where the premiums were paid by a defendant, D, out of his own money. Robert Goff J[12] considered that the 'insurance money is the product, not of the property involved, but of the premiums'. However, but for D acquiring the property he would not have had an insurable interest entitling him to pay the premiums and receive the proceeds of the policy in the event of the loss or destruction of the property. Thus, D should be personally liable for the insurance proceeds subject to a credit for the premiums paid by him. It would further seem that D should be liable to the proprietary remedy if he be an errant fiduciary under an express or implied duty[13] to insure the trust property (or even with a power to insure trust property) so that equity will look on as done that which ought to be done[14] (or estop D from denying the presumption[15] that he used his fiduciary insurance power): the insurance policy and its proceeds will then be held upon the same trusts as the insured property, subject to D having a lien for the cost of the premiums he paid himself. However, if D were an innocent donee he would be under no duty to insure the property and have no fiduciary powers that he could be presumed to have used, so that P should have no proprietary right to insurance proceeds, capable of prejudicing D's unsecured creditors upon the insolvency of D.

---

11 'Nelsonian' and 'naughty' knowledge represent the knowledge that D is deemed to have from wilfully shutting his eyes to the obvious, or from wilfully or recklessly failing to make the enquiries an honest and reasonable man would make in the suspicious circumstances, ie categories (ii) and (iii) in *Baden Delvaux v Société Generale* [1992] 4 All ER 161 at 235. See p 974 post. Strictly, an innocent volunteer means one without actual constructive or imputed notice (as assumed in *Re Diplock* [1948] Ch 465) but in line with the liberal approaches in *Re Tilley's Will Trusts* [1967] Ch 1179 and *Re Montagu's Settlements* [1987] Ch 264 it is submitted that there should be scope for D not to be in as strict a position as an express trustee, so that he can be allowed to prove that he has not actually enriched himself at the expense of beneficiaries because he would have bought the relevant asset anyway: see p 995, post.
12 *Ellerman Lines Ltd v Lancaster Maritime Co Ltd* [1980] 2 Lloyd's Rep 497 at 502 applying *Rayner v Preston* (1881) 18 Ch D 1. The House of Lords showed no inclination to reach a similar conclusion by way of analogy in the recent life insurance proceeds case of *Foskett v McKeown* [2001] 1 AC 102.
13 Nowadays, standards of care should require a trustee to insure trust property where a reasonable businessman would do so and probably to the full value rather than the three-quarters covered by the Trustee Act 1925, s 19.
14 Eg *A-G for Hong Kong v Reid* [1994] 1 All ER 1.
15 *Omnia praesumuntur rite esse acta* and 'every presumption must be made against him as a wrongdoer' as appears from *Foskett v McKeown* [2001] 1 AC 102 at 132, HL.

Purchase of property with mortgage loan

Paul A Davies Pty (Australia) Ltd (in liquidation) v Davies[16] illustrates tracing possibilities arising from loans. Take two brothers who innocently but erroneously believe they can borrow £20,000 from their private company to use as a deposit on a private venture involving purchase of a restaurant for £200,000. They go into occupation for a monthly fee and defer completion for three years on a further payment of £20,000, similarly borrowed from the company, and on agreeing to raise the purchase price from £200,000 to £250,000. After two years they complete the purchase early, taking out a mortgage on the restaurant to secure the necessary £210,000 bank loan and personally covenanting to repay the loan. A year later they sell out to a purchaser for £320,000, paying off the £210,000 loan out of the proceeds. The company is not just entitled to four twenty-fifths of the profits. After all, the company's £40,000 gave it an equitable interest in the restaurant, which the brothers then used as security for the £210,000 loan, which was repaid out of the proceeds of sale and not out of the brothers' money. Thus the company is entitled to all the profit.

PARAGRAPH 3

Trust assets mixed with assets of another trust

If the assets of Trust 'A' and the assets of Trust 'B' are mixed (other than in a current bank account) then any loss is borne rateably according to the values of the mixed assets of the two trusts, eg if £4,000 from Trust 'A' and £2,000 from Trust 'B' were used to purchase a £6,000 car now depreciated to £3,000 in value then the car would be subject to a charge in favour of 'A' and 'B' in the proportions 2 to 1[17]. Any gains should similarly be rateably shared[18].

Where mixing occurs in a current banking account prima facie, to apportion losses, the traditional view is that the rule in *Clayton's* case[19] applies whereby the first drawings out are attributed to the first payments in[20]. However, the rule will not apply if a specific withdrawal is unmixed and earmarked as particular trust money[1]. The following account will consider the present state of the authorities and then discuss the future development of the law in this area.

As matters currently stand, there is Court of Appeal authority of recent

---

16 [1983] 1 NSWLR 440; *Re Marriage of Wagstaff* (1990) 14 Fam LR 78, 99 FLR 390; *Australian Postal Corpn v Lutak* (1991) 21 NSWLR 584. In the last case the plaintiff's $20,000 had been used with an equitable mortgagee's $70,000 to buy a $90,000 house sold for $110,000 when $103,000 capital and interest were due to the mortgagee. Bryson J held the plaintiffs were entitled to $40,000, representing their $20,000 charge and the $20,000 profit, so the equitable mortgagee received only $70,000. Because the house could not have been purchased but for the mortgage it is difficult to see why the mortgagee did not have priority over the plaintiff for the $103,000: cf *Abbey National Building Society v Cann* [1991] 1 AC 56; *Equity and Law Home Loans Ltd v Prestidge* [1992] 1 WLR 137.

17 *Sinclair v Brougham* [1914] AC 398; *Re Diplock* [1948] Ch 465 at 533, 534, 539, CA.

18 *Lord Provost of Edinburgh v Lord Advocate* (1879) 4 App Cas 823.

19 (1816) 1 Mer 572.

20 *Re Hallett's Estate* (1880) 13 Ch D 696 (Fry J); *Hancock v Smith* (1889) 41 Ch D 456 at 461; *Re Stenning* [1895] 2 Ch 433.

1 *Re Diplock* [1948] Ch 465 at 551–552, CA (rescinded at 559 on the facts but not affected on the principles); *Russell-Cooke Trust Co v Prentis* [2002] EWHC 2227 (Ch) paras 39, 44.

vintage for the proposition that the rule in *Clayton's* case remains Equity's default rule for the resolution of evidential uncertainty where a trustee has wrongly mixed the assets of two trusts in a bank account[2]. However, the application of *Clayton's* case can easily lead to arbitrary unfair results. Take the following payments into T's empty bank account: (1) £2,000 from Trust X (ii) £4,000 from Trust Y (iii) £6,000 from Trust Z. Then T withdraws £4,000 which he dissipates on holiday; then T purchases shares for £8,000 which are now worth £12,000. By *Clayton's* case the withdrawn £4,000 exhausts the funds of Trust X and reduces Trust Y's funds to £2,000. Thus the £8,000 invested in shares represents £2,000 of Trust Y's funds and £6,000 of Trust Z's funds. Therefore, one quarter of the shares belongs to Trust Y and three quarters to Trust Z, whilst there is nothing for Trust X[3]. Surely, the more equitable course would be to divide the shares between Trusts X, Y and Z in the proportions 1:2:3 so that each trust would recover its original funds of £2,000, £4,000 and £6,000 respectively.

In considering the application of *Clayton's* case where there is a deficiency one must also consider the *Roscoe v Winder*[4] lowest intermediate balance rule which in its repeated application, will soon make matters complex and difficult in respect of early deposited funds, whose beneficiaries will need to try to prove that subsequent payments in, represent the traceable proceeds of sale of investments earlier purchased with early deposited funds. It is obvious that early payers suffer under *Clayton's* case but a late payer will regard this as justified. If X Trust, Y Trust and Z Trust funds are withdrawn and dissipated so as only to leave £1,200 in the account why should a subsequent payment of £12,000 from the O Trust enure for the benefit of the other three trusts.

As a result the Canadian and USA courts[5] have developed the 'rolling charge' solution to produce a manifestly fairer solution. In the words of Woolf LJ[6]:

> 'This solution involves treating credits to a bank account made at different dates and from different sources as a blend or cocktail with the result that when a withdrawal is made from the account it is treated as a withdrawal in the same proportions as the different interests in the account bear to each other at the moment before the withdrawal is made.'

To illustrate this, take £2,000, £4,000 and £6,000 paid on successive days from the X Trust, Y Trust and Z Trust into a trustee's account with a nil balance, £10,800 then being withdrawn and dissipated. The O Trust's £12,000 is then paid in (so that there is a £13,200 credit) but £6,600 is later spent on shares subsequently sold for £9,900 which is paid into the account (making a credit of £16,500). Later £16,500 is paid in from the P Trust, before £26,400 is spent (leaving a credit of £6,600) upon an asset later sold for £9,900 which is paid into the account (making a credit of £16,500) whereupon £11,220 is dissipated leaving £5,280 in the account.

Here the £10,800 debit is debited pro rata to X, Y, Z Trusts leaving them

---

2 *Barlow Clowes International Ltd v Vaughan* [1992] 4 All ER 22, CA. See too *Sheppard v Thompson* [2001] All ER (D) 07 (Dec).
3 If subsequently T sold a quarter of the shares this would not be treated as a sale of Trust Y's shares but as a sale of a shareholding made up as to one-quarter with Trust Y's shares and three-quarters with Trust Z's shares: *Re Diplock* [1948] Ch 465 at 554–555, CA.
4 [1915] 1 Ch 62.
5 Eg *Re Ontario Securities Commission* (1986) 30 DLR (4th) 1; *Gibbs v Gerberich* 1 Ohio App 2d 93 (1964).
6 [1992] 4 All ER 22 at 35.

with £200, £400 and £600 respectively. The £6,600 debit is debited pro rata to X Y Z and O Trusts in the proportion 2:4:6:120 while the £9,900 credit will be credited in the same proportions. After the addition of the P Trust's £16,500 the £33,000 will be treated as owned in the proportions 2:4:6:120:132 and the subsequent £26,400 debit, the £9,900 credit and £11,220 debit will be similarly treated, so leaving the £5,280 balance to be owned in the proportions 2:4:6:120:132, so that the X, Y, Z, O and P Trusts will respectively receive £40, £80, £120, £2,400 and £2,640.

This achieves a fairer result than that achieved by applying *Clayton's* case which would leave the P Trust with £5,280 or by the rateable approach dividing the balance in the original rateable proportions of trust moneys, namely 2,000:4,000:6,000:12,000:16,500 so that the X Y Z O and P Trusts respectively receive £261, £522, £783, £1,564 and £2,150. However, it will be appreciated it is a more complex approach and it will often be impracticable and expensive to implement it, even with the benefit of modern computer technology, as was the case in *Barlow Clowes International Ltd v Vaughan*[7].

Woolf LJ there held[8] that, while *Clayton's* case *can* be applied when trust moneys have been mixed in a bank account with other trust moneys or with the money of an innocent volunteer, it 'need only be applied when it is convenient to do so and when its application can be said to do broad justice having regard to the nature of the competing claims'. Along with Woolf LJ, both Dillon and Leggatt LJJ agreed that because the claimants expected their money to be pooled in, effectively, a collective investment scheme they should share rateably what was left in the pool. While Dillon LJ[9] was happy to follow *Re Diplock*[10] with a general rule of practice that *Clayton's* case is to be applied, Leggatt LJ stated[11]:

'As between beneficiaries to whom money in an account belongs, they should share loss in proportion to their interest in the account immediately before each withdrawal. The fairness of that course is obvious. But, if, as here, the calculation is too difficult or expensive, the beneficiaries should share rateably. It seems to me[12] that the rule in *Clayton's* case has nothing to do with tracing and therefore provides no help in the present action.'

He had to admit, however, that *Clayton's* case had been upheld by the Court of Appeal in *Re Diplock* so that it was possible if convenient to apply it.

It is submitted that the time has come for the English courts to develop the law in this area in a more positive manner. At the very least, they should take a wide view of the circumstances in which it is 'convenient and just' for them to use the rolling charge solution in preference to the rule in *Clayton's* case.

7 [1992] 4 All ER 22.
8 [1992] 4 All ER 22 at 39. He would even have excluded *Clayton's* case where BCI, in fact, created a pool, though being under an obligation to keep funds separate, because he considered one could then presume the intention of investors would be to have a pro rata distribution: see p 41. Perhaps he is attributing over-much altruism to investors disadvantaged by such presumption: does not such attribution wholly undermine *Clayton's* case so that an open rejection of it would be best, eg *Re Registered Securities* [1991] 1 NZLR 545.
9 [1992] 4 All ER 22 at 33.
10 [1948] Ch 465.
11 [1992] 4 All ER 22 at 44.
12 See [1992] 4 All ER 22 at 43 where he pointed out that *Re Diplock* 'equated the presumed intention of a person in relation to his banker with a beneficiary's intention in relation to a trustee even though they have nothing to do with each other. The relationship of a banker and customer is that of debtor and creditor. The beneficiary has no relationship with the banker who maintains the account in which the beneficiary's money has been placed.'

But they could usefully take the still more radical step of holding that the rule in *Clayton's* case simply does not apply where a trustee has wrongfully mixed the assets of two trust funds in a current bank account, and that this situation should instead be resolved by using the rateable approach, unless the timings of deposits and withdrawals from the account are so complicated that the rolling charge solution must be used. In principle, the rule in *Clayton's* case is undesirable because the results which it produces can be arbitrary and unjust. For this reason it has been rejected by the courts of many other jurisdictions[13]. The English courts should follow suit, not only on the grounds of principle, but also as a matter of authority, first because *Clayton's* case itself was not concerned with the situation under discussion, but was concerned only with a dispute centring on the appropriation of payments as between a bank and its customer[14]; and secondly because the rule in *Clayton's* case is predicated on an understanding of the nature of a bank account – that it consists of stacked units of value – that has now been superseded by Lord Millett's understanding of the nature of a bank account – that it consists of a uniform mixture of value – in *Foskett v McKeown*[15]. In Lord Millett's view[16]:

> 'We speak of money at the bank, and of money passing into and out of a bank account. But of course the account holder has no money at the bank. Money paid into a bank account belongs legally and beneficially to the bank and not to the account holder. The bank gives value for it, and it is accordingly not usually possible to make the money itself the subject of an adverse claim. Instead a claimant normally sues the account holder rather than the bank and lays claim to the proceeds of the money in his hands. These consist of the debt or part of the debt due to him from the bank. We speak of tracing money into and out of the account, but there is no money in the account. There is merely a single debt of an amount equal to the final balance standing to the credit of the account holder.'

Trust assets mixed with trustee's assets and assets of another trust

If the mixed fund contains not just the moneys of trust funds but also the trustee's own money, one must first apply the principles applicable to a trustee's own money mixed with trust money of an amount corresponding to the aggregate value of all the mixed trust funds. Once the total entitlement of those mixed funds has been determined then one applies the principles above discussed in apportioning such mixed funds between different trusts.

Paragraph 4

The need for a fiduciary relationship concerning property

As Lord Millett clearly stated in *Foskett v McKeown*[17], tracing the value inherent in property into a new asset is a separate process from asserting a proprietary claim to an asset in a defendant's hands which the claimant has identified as

---

13 *Re Ontario Securities Commission* (1986) 30 DLR (4th) 1, Ontario CA; *Re Registered Securities* [1991] 1 NZLR 545, NZCA; *Keefe v Law Society of New South Wales* (1998) 44 NSWLR 451, NSWCA; *Re Esteem Settlement* [2002] Jersey LR 53: so in *Russell-Cooke Trust Co v Prentis* [2002] EWHC 2227 (Ch) para 55 it was treated as an exception to a rateable rule.
14 For discussion, see L D Smith *The Law of Tracing* (1997), pp 183–194.
15 [2001] 1 AC 102.
16 [2001] 1 AC 102 at 127–128.
17 [2001] 1 AC 102 at 129–130.

representing the traceable proceeds of his misappropriated property. The following discussion will therefore consider two separate questions in turn: first, whether a claimant must show that property was held for him on trust, or was subject to some other fiduciary relationship, before he can invoke equitable tracing rules with a view to identifying assets as the traceable proceeds of his property; secondly, whether a claimant must show that he was the equitable owner of property before he can make an equitable proprietary claim to the traceable proceeds of this property.

Tracing

The traditional view for many years has been that there are different tracing rules in equity and at common law, and that the equitable tracing rules are more favourable to claimants than the common law tracing rules, most noticeably because it is impossible to trace through mixtures of money in bank accounts at common law, something which the equitable tracing rules allow[18]. It has also been said by the courts for many years that claimants must show that their property was held on trust or that it was subject to some other fiduciary relationship before they can take advantage of the equitable tracing rules with a view to tracing through mixtures in bank accounts[19].

As Professor Smith has lucidly explained[20], these findings were always suspect as a matter of authority. They were inconsistent with a long line of cases in which the courts did not require claimants to establish a fiduciary relationship before invoking the equitable tracing rules with a view to showing that their money had been used to pay off securities to which they sought to be subrogated[1]. They were also inconsistent with *Marsh v Keating*[2], in which the House of Lords advised by 12 common law judges was willing to accept that the common law could trace through a mixed bank account. Finally, Viscount Haldane LC's finding in *Sinclair v Brougham*[3] that there can be no tracing at common law where money has been lent and placed in a bank account was founded on a misunderstanding of Thesiger LJ's previous, undoubtedly correct statement in *Re Hallett's Estate*[4] that a claimant who makes an unsecured loan to a defendant cannot as a general rule make a proprietary claim to the defendant's assets to secure repayment of the loan.

These objections to the traditional view are now of subsidiary importance, however, following the House of Lords' landmark speeches in *Foskett v*

---

18 *Sinclair v Brougham* [1914] AC 398 at 419–420 per Viscount Haldane LC; *Banque Belge pour l'Étranger v Hambrouck* [1921] 1 KB 321 at 328 per Bankes LJ and at 330 per Scrutton LJ; *Re Diplock* [1948] Ch 465 at 518 per curiam; *Agip (Africa) Ltd v Jackson* [1991] Ch 547 at 566 per Fox LJ. See too *Taylor v Plumer* (1815) 3 M & S 562 at 575 per Lord Ellenborough, which has often been said to stand for the proposition that tracing through mixtures in bank accounts is not possible at common law, but which in fact lays down a rule about claiming – moreover, the case was ultimately decided on equitable principles, as confirmed in *Trustee of FC Jones & Son (a firm) v Jones* [1997] Ch 159 at 169 per Millett LJ.
19 *Sinclair v Brougham* [1914] AC 398 at 421 per Viscount Haldane LC; *Re Diplock* [1948] Ch 465 at 536–537 per curiam; *Agip (Africa) Ltd v Jackson* [1991] Ch 547 at 566 per Fox LJ; *Boscawen v Bajwa* [1995] 4 All ER 769 at 777 per Millett LJ.
20 L D Smith *The Law of Tracing* (1997) at pp 123–130 and 168–174.
1 For example, *Marlow v Pitfeild* (1719) 1 P Wms 558; *Baroness Wenlock v River Dee Co* (1887) 19 QBD 155; *Orakpo v Manson Investments Ltd* [1978] AC 95.
2 (1834) 2 Cl & Fin 250.
3 [1914] AC 398 at 419–421.
4 (1880) 13 Ch D 696 at 723–724. Also *Halifax Building Society v Thomas* [1995] 4 All ER 673, CA (secured loan)

McKeown[5]. Lord Steyn and Lord Millett both stated that there is now only one set of tracing rules in English law, applicable to common law and equitable claimants alike, and although their observations on this point were obiter, it seems most unlikely that they will not be followed in future cases. Hence, it is now clear that English law does not distinguish between two sets of tracing rules, and does not restrict the availability of a more claimant-friendly set of 'equitable' rules to claimants who can show that their property was held subject to a fiduciary relationship.

In the relevant part of Lord Steyn's speech, he observed that[6]:

'counsel for the purchasers from time to time invoked "the rules of tracing". By that expression he was placing reliance on a corpus of supposed rules of law, divided into common law and equitable rules. In truth tracing is a process of identifying assets: it belongs to the realm of evidence. It tells us nothing about legal or equitable rights to the assets traced. In a crystalline analysis Professor Birks ("The Necessity of a Unitary Law of Tracing", essay in *Making Commercial Law, Essays in Honour of Roy Goode* (1997), pp 239–258) explained, at p 257, that there is a unified regime for tracing and that "it allows tracing to be cleanly separated from the business of asserting rights in or in relation to assets successfully traced". Applying this reasoning Professor Birks concludes, at p 258:

"that the modern law is equipped with various means of coping with the evidential difficulties which a tracing exercise is bound to encounter. The process of identification thus ceases to be either legal or equitable and becomes, as is fitting, genuinely neutral as to the rights exigible in respect of the assets into which the value in question is traced. The tracing exercise once successfully completed, it can then be asked what rights, if any, the plaintiff can, on his particular facts, assert. It is at that point that it becomes relevant to recall that on some facts those rights will be personal, on others proprietary, on some legal, and on others equitable."

I regard this explanation as correct. It is consistent with orthodox principle. It clarifies the correct approach to so-called tracing claims. It explains what tracing is about without providing answers to controversies about legal or equitable rights to assets so traced.'

Lord Millett agreed[7]:

'Given its nature, there is nothing inherently legal or equitable about the tracing exercise. There is thus no sense in maintaining different rules for tracing at law and in equity. One set of tracing rules is enough. The existence of two has never formed part of the law in the United States: see *Scott on Trusts*, 4th ed (1989), section 515, at pp 605–609. There is certainly no logical justification for allowing any distinction between them to produce capricious results in cases of mixed substitutions by insisting on the existence of a fiduciary relationship as a precondition for applying equity's tracing rules. The existence of such a relationship may be relevant to the nature of the claim which the plaintiff can maintain, whether personal or proprietary, but that is a different matter. I agree with the passages which my noble and learned friend, Lord Steyn, has cited from Professor Birks's essay "The Necessity of a Unitary Law of Tracing", and with Dr Lionel Smith's exposition in his comprehensive monograph *The Law of Tracing* (1997): see particularly pp 120–130, 277–279 and 342–347.'

In the past, the courts have been tempted to discover fiduciary relationships between the parties to litigation not because the parties' relationship has been of the sort that would normally attract the imposition of fiduciary

---

5 [2001] 1 AC 102.
6 [2001] 1 AC 102 at 113.
7 [2001] 1 AC 102 at 129–130.

duties, but because the courts have wished to enable the claimant to take advantage of the equitable tracing rules. So, for example, it has been held that a thief owes a fiduciary duty to his victim, with the result that the victim can invoke the equitable tracing rules in order to trace through the thief's sale of the stolen property and mixing of the proceeds in a bank account, so as to make a proprietary claim to the traceable proceeds of the victim's property[8]. Findings of this sort debase the currency of the fiduciary concept, and run counter to Sopinka J's warning in the Supreme Court of Canada, in *Norberg v Weinrib*[9], that 'equitable doctrines cannot be imported simply in order to improve the nature and extent of the remedy'. One effect of the findings in *Foskett* will be to relieve the courts from the need to do this in order to give claimants access to the equitable tracing rules.

Claiming

The question as to when a claimant can make a proprietary claim to assets in a defendant's hands is a difficult and controversial subject. Two aspects of this question will be touched on here.

First, it is beyond question that trust beneficiaries are entitled to assert a proprietary claim to assets that are the traceable proceeds of misapplied trust property, but the source of this entitlement is a matter of controversy. One view is that the beneficiaries' entitlement derives from the law of unjust enrichment where the trustee has enriched himself by using their property to acquire a new asset for himself without their consent[10]. In *Foskett v McKeown*[11], however, their Lordships held that the beneficiaries' right to claim new assets which are the traceable proceeds of trust property is a right which does not lie in the law of unjust enrichment, but is rather a right to 'vindicate' their continuing proprietary entitlement to the trust property and its traceable proceeds. With respect, their Lordships' assertions to this effect presume what they seek to prove, namely that the equitable owner of an asset always has an equitable proprietary interest in a substitute asset acquired with the original asset. In their Lordships' view, it lies in the nature of equitable property rights that the owner's interest in the original asset always detaches itself from the original asset and reattaches itself to the new asset whenever the assets are exchanged – but their Lordships do not explain why the owner's interest should behave in this way. In the case of property held on an express trust, 'the trust fund' is normally defined in terms such as 'property transferred to the trustees to hold on the terms of this settlement and all the property from time to time representing the same', although the latter clause can simply be regarded as spelling out what is inevitably involved in the settlor creating a trust. When the trustees replace trust assets with other assets

---

8 *Black v Freedman* (1910) 12 CLR 105 at 110, endorsed by Lord Templeman in *Lipkin Gorman v Karpnale Ltd* [1991] 2 AC 548 at 565-6; *Bishopsgate Investment Management Ltd v Maxwell* [1993] Ch 1 at 70; *Westdeutsche Landesbank Girozentrale v Islington London Borough Council* [1996] AC 669 at 716, distinguished in *Box v Barclays Bank plc* [1998] 18 LS Gaz R 33, on the basis that the rule does not extend to fraudulently induced transfers.

9 (1992) 92 DLR (4th) 449 at 481.

10 P Birks 'Property, Unjust Enrichment, and Tracing' (2001) 54 CLP 231.

11 [2001] 1 AC 102 esp at 108 per Lord Browne-Wilkinson and at 127 per Lord Millett. Cf *Eagle Star Insurance Co Ltd v Karasiewicz* [2002] EWCA Civ 940 at para 19 per Arden LJ, considering that extinguished security rights can be acquired, by a legal fiction, via subrogation, 'by way of satisfaction of a pre-existing equitable proprietary right which is vindicated by the order for subrogation'.

in an authorised fashion, overreaching occurs, with the result that the beneficiaries' proprietary interests switch from the old assets to the new assets[12].
Where the trustees acted in an unauthorised fashion they cannot deny that
they acted in an authorised fashion if the beneficiaries seek entitlement to
the new assets, and so the position is as if the trustees had intentionally
acquired the new assets on trust for the beneficiaries. A donee of such a new
asset from the trustee can be in no better position than the trustee, taking a
derivatively defective title.

However, if the donee then sells the assets to buy, say, a painting, it can be
argued that once the beneficiaries discover what happened and claim the
painting, the donee cannot deny their claim that she should be retrospectively treated as if she had bought the painting on their behalf as
nominee for them, so that she must deliver the painting to them or to the
trustees for them. Here, however, there is a strong argument that unjust
enrichment is the reason for the beneficiaries' right to claim an equitable
interest in the painting, the donee having enriched herself at the beneficiaries' expense by using their assets to obtain the painting for herself
without their consent.

Secondly, it has been held in various cases that in some situations where
the absolutely entitled legal owner of property transfers it to a recipient in
circumstances where title to the property passes but where the recipient's
enrichment at the transferor's expense is unjust (for example, because the
transfer was due to fraud, undue influence, or a mistake), the transferor is
not merely entitled to bring a personal restitutionary claim in unjust
enrichment to recover the value of the property, but is also entitled to bring a
proprietary restitutionary claim to the extent that the property traceably
survives in the recipient's hands. Distinguishing the circumstances in which a
restitutionary claimant can have a proprietary remedy from those in which he
is confined to a personal remedy is a task that lies beyond the scope of the
present discussion[13]. However, it is proposed to comment here on Lord
Browne-Wilkinson's treatment of this question in *Westdeutsche Landesbank
Girozentrale v Islington London Borough Council*[14].

In the *Westdeutsche* case, Lord Browne-Wilkinson reviewed *Chase Manhattan
Bank v Israel-British Bank (London) Ltd*[15] where Goulding J had held that a
claimant who mistakenly pays the same sum twice to a defendant 'retains an
equitable property in [the second payment] and the conscience of [the
defendant] is subjected to a fiduciary duty to respect [the claimant's] proprietary right.' Lord Browne-Wilkinson stated[16]:

> 'I cannot agree with this reasoning. First, it is based on a concept of retaining an
> equitable property in money where, prior to the payment to the recipient bank,
> there was no existing equitable interest. Further, I cannot understand how the

---

12 further C Harpum 'Overreaching, Trustees' Powers and the Reform of the 1925 Property
   Legislation' [1990] CLJ 277, endorsed in *State Bank of India v Sood* [1997] Ch 276, CA; D Fox
   'Overreaching' in P Birks and A Pretto (eds) *Breach of Trust* (2002) p 95.
13 A wide range of views on this subject can be found in the academic literature: see eg L D
   Smith *The Law of Tracing* (1997) at pp 283–369; F D Rose (ed) *Restitution and Insolvency*
   (2000), passim; P Birks and C Mitchell 'Unjust Enrichment' in P Birks (ed) *English Private Law*
   (2000) at pp 593–603; A Burrows 'Proprietary Restitution: Unmasking Unjust Enrichment'
   (2001) 117 LQR 412; C Rotherham *Proprietary Remedies in Context* (2002).
14 [1996] AC 669.
15 [1981] Ch 105 at 119.
16 [1996] AC 669 at 714 and 715.

recipient's "conscience" can be affected at a time when he is not aware of any mistake. . . . However, although I do not accept the reasoning of Goulding J, *Chase Manhattan* may well have been rightly decided. The defendant bank knew of the mistake made by the paying bank within two days of the receipt of the moneys . . . . The judge treated this fact as irrelevant . . . but in my judgment it may well provide a proper foundation for the decision. Although the mere receipt of the moneys, in ignorance of the mistake, gives rise to no trust, the retention of the moneys after the recipient bank learned of the mistake may well have given rise to a constructive trust: see *Snell's Equity*, p 193; Pettit, *Equity and the Law of Trusts*, 7th ed (1993) p 168; *Metall und Rohstoff AG v Donaldson Lufkin & Jenrette Inc* [1990] 1 QB 391, 473–474.'

These three references indicate that his Lordship was referring to the *personal* liability of a defendant 'as a constructive trustee' where he has innocently received trust property, but has later become cognisant of the trust and has nonetheless wrongfully dealt with the property in a manner inconsistent with the trust. However, in *Chase Manhattan*, Goulding J held that the money which had been mistakenly paid to the defendant was subject to the claimant's *proprietary* entitlement, the defendant being insolvent, while in *Metall und Rohstoff* the court emphasised that personal accountability as a constructive trustee arises only in respect of property already subject to a trust, yet Lord Browne-Wilkinson considered that there was no existing equitable interest under a trust in *Chase Manhattan*, when the defendant bank received the mistaken payment.

Despite this confusion of thought with regard to personal and proprietary liability, however, it is clear that his Lordship did not intend to elevate personal claims in unjust enrichment to proprietary claims whenever the defendant becomes aware of the claimant's entitlement and the benefit he has received at the claimant's expense traceably survives in his hands. That would amount to (1) the imposition of a proprietary remedial constructive trust which in his speech he held was not part of English law[17]; (2) the recognition that *Sinclair v Brougham*[18] was rightly decided despite his rejection of it[19]; and (3) the generation of 'off-balance sheet liabilities' creating new unmanageable risks for commercial actors, something which he decried in his speech[20]. Perhaps the way ahead where dispositions are voidable for fraud, mistake, or undue influence is to focus on the equitable remedy of rescission subject to the usual equitable bars as suggested extra-judicially by Lord Millett[1].

PARAGRAPH 5

Need for identified traced product of trust or fiduciary property

The equitable remedies of an equitable charge or of a constructive trust of a proportionate share can only be imposed in respect of an identified traced product of property subject to a trust or other fiduciary relationship[2]. The plaintiff has to identify his original proprietary right in respect of a particular

---

17 [1996] AC 669 at 714–715 and 716.
18 [1914] AC 398, HL.
19 [1996] AC 669 at 713.
20 [1996] AC 669 at 705.
 1 (1998) 114 LQR 399 at 416–417.
 2 *Napier and Ettrick v Kershaw* [1993] AC 713, [1993] 1 All ER 385, HL; *Bishopsgate Investment Management Ltd v Homan* [1995] Ch 211, [1995] 1 All ER 347, CA and p 885, ante.

asset and then show that there are transactional links between such original asset and a new asset in the defendant's hands so that the value of the original asset is represented in the new asset.

A wrongdoing trustee who, deliberately or fortuitously, has transactional links occurring in foreign jurisdictions having no concept of equitable proprietary ownership cannot thereby thwart the tracing process of the English forum to determine the amount for which he is personally liable[3] nor should he thereby thwart a proprietary claim to the traced assets that establish the amount of that personal liability. Factually, nothing will be traceable if the original asset is sold and the proceeds spent on a holiday or on a horse which dies or on a painting which is destroyed in circumstances where no insurance compensation[4] is available. As a matter of law if the claimant authorises his proprietary interest to be displaced by a transaction creating only a debtor-creditor relationship he will only have a personal claim against that debtor, ie if the trustee or fiduciary is authorised to lend the claimant's money to himself[5] or to mix the claimant's resin with his own materials so as to produce chipboard[6] (there being no agreement as to the claimant then becoming a proportionate owner of the chipboard[7]).

Money and bank accounts

Once a wrongdoing fiduciary has mixed trust funds with his own in a bank account an equitable lien or charge will automatically attach to that account and therefore to moneys paid out of that account, whether into other accounts (so purchasing a chose in action) or to purchase a painting or Whizzo shares, until the fiduciary discharges the burden of showing that he has reinstated the trust fund and remedied the breach of trust[8]. Once it has been established with the help, if need be, of any presumptions against wrongdoers that a bank account or some shares or some land be subject to an equitable charge then such charge will automatically bind a transferee of such property other than a bona fide purchaser of a legal interest without notice[9].

Money passing through a clearing system raises difficulties because of the netting off that occurs between banks that are members of such systems. The

---

3 *El Ajou v Dollar Land Holdings Ltd plc* [1993] 3 All ER 717 at 736–737; revsd [1994] 2 All ER 685. The case involved personal liability, but the principle is broad enough to compel a defendant in the jurisdiction to treat assets within the jurisdiction as trust assets, if having regard to their history and his state of knowledge, it would be unconscionable for him to treat them as his own: see Millet LJ at 737h. The defendant could be compelled by an *in personam* order to bring foreign assets within the jurisdiction or transfer title to foreign immovables: cf *Webb v Webb* [1992] 1 All ER 17 [1994] QB 696; *Cook Industries v Galliher* [1979] Ch 439; *Derby v Weldon (No 6)* [1990] 1 WLR 1139. However if the defendant is an innocent donee who acquired a good clean title in a foreign *lex situs* the English court should recognise the effect of the *lex situs*.

4 See p 890, ante.

5 *Space Investments Ltd v Canadian Imperial Bank of Commerce Trust Co* [1986] 3 All ER 75, [1986] 1 WLR 1072, HL; *Re Goldcorp Exchange Ltd* [1994] 2 All ER 806; *Customs and Excise Comrs v Richmond Theatre Management Ltd* [1995] STC 257.

6 *Borden UK Ltd v Scottish Timber Products* [1981] Ch 25.

7 *Coleman v Harvey* [1989] 1 NZLR 723.

8 *El Ajou v Dollar Land Holdings plc* [1993] 3 All ER 717 at 735–736; *Foskett v McKeown* [2001] 1 AC 102 at 130.

9 *El Ajou v Dollar Land Holdings plc* [1993] 3 All ER 717 at 735–736; revsd [1994] 2 All ER 685 at 701 per Hoffmann LJ.

courts look at 'the substance of the matter'[10] to see if there is a sufficient nexus between the debit to X's account and the credit to Y's account to enable the latter to be treated as representing the former. In *Agip (Africa) Ltd v Jackson*[11] it was accepted that equity can trace money through a clearing system and even identify a credit with a debit where the credit entry was the first in time while in *El Ajou v Dollar Land Holdings plc*[12] money was traced through back to back credit facilities.

The tracing process is used to identify what is trust property[13] so that one can then tell whether or not a breach of trust has occurred in respect of that property. In clearing systems, through which pass the proceeds of sale of trust property or dividends on trust shares, it seems that there will be an equitable charge over a very valuable chose in action.

Take the C Bank with a £100 million credit with the Bank of England operating the clearing system and the D Bank with a £90 million credit with the Bank of England. During the day transactions occur such that C Bank owes D Bank £15 million while D Bank owes C Bank £20 million necessitating C Bank being credited with £5 million so that its credit stands at £105 million while D Bank's credit stands at £85 million. If a purchaser of trust property paid the £50,000 price out of his account with C Bank in favour of the trust account with D Bank, the £50,000 will be regarded as within the £15 million treated as passing[14] (despite the 'netting off') to the D Bank, so that there will be an equitable charge for £50,000 arising by operation of law over the £85 million credit balance with the Bank of England. The chose in action with the Bank of England charged with payment of the trust's £50,000 will cease to be so upon D Bank crediting the trust account with the £50,000 under an authorisation to deposit the money with itself by way of loan (enabling money to be loaned to the Bank of England). The trust will then own a chose in action against the D Bank[15] so that if the trustee then uses it by withdrawing £50,000 to buy a painting the beneficiaries will be able to trace and claim the painting.

Payment of debts with trust money

In *Re Diplock*[16], the Court of Appeal considered that a tracing process would come to an end, and that a claimant would be left with nothing into which he might trace the value inherent in his property, where the property or its traceable proceeds are used to pay off a debt. The better view, however, is that where a trustee misappropriates trust money and uses it to pay off a debt which he owes to a creditor, there are two ways in which the beneficiaries might trace into an asset to which they can then assert a proprietary claim.

10 *Agip (Africa) Ltd v Jackson* [1991] Ch 547 at 561, [1992] 4 All ER 451 at 462.
11 [1990] Ch 265; affd [1991] Ch 547, the plaintiff's banker buying on credit from Lloyds Bank a payment to Baker Oil and then debiting the plaintiff's account with the payment.
12 [1993] 3 All ER 717; revsd [1994] 2 All ER 685.
13 In *Re Hallett's Estate* (1889) 13 Ch D 696 at 708–709 Jessel MR emphasised 'there is no distinction between what is a rightful and wrongful disposition of the property so far as regards the right of the beneficial owner to follow the proceeds'.
14 *Re Harmony and Montague Tin Mining Co Ltd (Spargo's Case)* (1873) 8 Ch App 407.
15 *Space Investments Ltd v Canadian Imperial Bank of Commerce Trust Co* [1986] 3 All ER 75; *Customs and Excise Comrs v Richmond Theatre Management Ltd* [1995] STC 257. For further discussions of the issues explored here, see L D Smith 'Tracing and Electronic Funds Transfers' in F D Rose (ed) *Restitution and Banking Law* (Mansfield Press 1998) p 120.
16 [1948] Ch 465 at 549; followed in *Euroactividade AG v Mason Investments Ltd* [1994] NPC 55.

First, if the trustee's debt to the creditor was secured by a charge over the trustee's property, the beneficiaries can ask the court to treat them, by a legal fiction, as though the creditor's charge had not been extinguished after all, but had instead been assigned by the creditor to the beneficiaries, in order that the beneficiaries might enforce the charge against the trustee's property to secure restoration of the trust fund[17]. This remedy is known as subrogation. In *Boscawen v Bajwa*[18], Millett LJ (as he then was) observed that, contrary to the Court of Appeal's finding in *Re Diplock*, 'the discharge of the creditor's security is certainly not a bar to subrogation in equity; it is rather a precondition'. In *Banque Financière de la Cité v Parc (Battersea) Ltd*[19], Lord Hoffmann stressed the fictional nature of the subrogation remedy, and held that it lies in the court's discretion to tailor the remedy to fit the circumstances of a case, by varying the extent to which a claimant is entitled to be treated as though he has acquired the creditor's rights, to ensure that his fictional acquisition of these rights does not unfairly prejudice the position of third parties[20].

Secondly, if the trustee borrows £10,000 from a creditor, and uses this money towards purchasing an asset, and then uses money which he has misappropriated from the trust to pay off his debt, then the beneficiaries should be able to 'trace backwards' through the payment of the debt into the asset which was purchased with the borrowed money, and identify the value inherent in the asset as the traceable proceeds of the value inherent in the trust property. In other words, the wrongdoing trustee should not be able to deny the beneficiaries' claims to be treated as if they had been original co-purchasers. This analysis, suggested by Professor Smith[1], has support in England at Court of Appeal level[2]: from Dillon LJ *in Bishopsgate Investment Management v Homan*[3] (although in the same case it was disapproved by Leggatt LJ[4]), and from Scott V-C in *Foskett v McKeown*[5]. However, in the latter case, Scott V-C considered that it should only be possible to 'trace backwards' through a wrongdoing trustee's payment of a debt into the asset purchased with the borrowed money if it can be shown that it was the trustee's intention at the time of borrowing the money that he would later wrongfully use the trust money to repay his creditor. With respect, however, this proposed

---

17 *M'Mahon v Fetherstonhaugh* [1895] 1 IR 182; *McCullough v Marsden* (1919) 45 DLR 645. Cf *Foskett v McKeown* [1998] Ch 265 at 277, CA; revsd [2001] 1 AC 102 at 118, not because the beneficiaries were not entitled to subrogation as a matter of principle, but because there was no right to which they could be subrogated on the facts; *Eagle Star Insurance Co Ltd v Karasiewicz* [2002] EWCA Civ 940 at para 19 where Arden LJ held that as a general rule discharged security rights can be acquired via subrogation 'by way of satisfaction of a pre-existing equitable proprietary right which is vindicated by the order for subrogation'.

18 [1996] 1 WLR 328 at 340.

19 [1999] 1 AC 221 at 236.

20 For further judicial consideration of this point, see *Halifax Mortgage Services Ltd v Muirhead* (1997) 76 P & CR 418, CA, noted C Mitchell (1998) 12 Tru LI 175; *Halifax plc v Omar* [2002] EWCA Civ 121, [2002] 2 P & CR 377; *Eagle Star Insurance Co Ltd v Karasiewicz* [2002] EWCA Civ 940, [2002] All ER (D) 240 (Apr).

1 L D Smith 'Tracing into the Payment of a Debt' [1995] CLJ 290, esp pp 292–295, expanded in L D Smith *The Law of Tracing* (1997), pp 146–152.

2 Cf *Re Agricultural Credit Corpn of Saskatchewan v Pettyjohn* [1991] 3 WWR 689 (Sask CA).

3 [1995] Ch 211 at 216–217.

4 [1995] Ch 211 at 221–212. One could argue that if the trustee's personal creditworthiness enables him to become legal beneficial owner of an asset, then his full ownership should not be affected by subsequent events (other than the owner's voluntary disposition of all or part of his title).

5 [1998] Ch 265 at 283–284, not considered on appeal to HL: [2001] 1 AC 102.

restriction, in favouring the trustee, seems likely to cause evidential difficulties in practice, and, in principle, there is no compelling reason why the beneficiaries' right to 'backwards tracing' should be made contingent on the trustee's state of mind at the time of the original loan transaction.

ARTICLE 93

Application for interim remedy to safeguard the trust property if endangered

(1) Where the court is satisfied that trust property[6] is in danger:

(a) by reason of the active[7] or passive[8] misconduct of the trustees; or

(b) by reason of the trustees residing out of the jurisdiction of the court[9];

an injunction will be granted on an application[10] at the instance of any person with a right to make the trustees account[11] for the trust property (including a co-trustee[12], even if himself breached his trust[13]) either compelling the trustees to do their duty[14], or restraining them from interfering with the trust property[15], as the case may require; and, if expedient, a receiver will be appointed[16].

(2) Where a trustee has admitted that he has trust moneys in his hands, and the court considers the trust property is endangered, an interim order may be made for payment of the amount into court; but there must be an admission direct or implied, written or verbal, and no dispute as to the defendant's liability, as the court cannot try the question on an interim application[17].

---

6 As to what amounts to trust property, see *A-G for Hong Kong v Reid* [1994] 1 AC 324, [1994] 1 All ER 1, PC, discussed p 396, ante; *Eldan Services Ltd v Chandag Motors Ltd* [1990] 3 All ER 459; *A v C* [1981] QB 956n.

7 *Earl Talbot v Hope-Scott* (1858) 4 K & J 139; *Middleton v Dodswell* (1806) 13 Ves 266; *Dance v Goldingham* (1873) 8 Ch App 902.

8 *Foley v Burnell* (1783) 1 Bro CC 274; *Fletcher v Fletcher* (1844) 4 Hare 67.

9 *Noad v Backhouse* (1843) 2 Y & C Ch Cas 529; *Dickins v Harris* (1866) 14 LT 98.

10 See CPR Pt 25, r 25 for an order for the detention, custody or preservation of trust property by way of interim remedy.

11 See Article 60. In Australia an injunction was granted to preserve the interest of a child *en vetre sa mere* at the instance of the child's father who was appointed by the court to represent the child: *Yunghams v Candoora No 19 Pty Ltd* (1999) 2 ITELR 589; CPR Pt 19, r 19.7 for English representation orders.

12 *Young v Murphy* [1996] 1 VR 279 (a thorough survey); *Re Forest of Dean Coal Mining Co* (1878) 10 Ch D 450; *Space Investments Ltd v Canadian Imperial Bank of Commerce Trust Co (Bahamas) Ltd* [1986] 1 WLR 1072 at 1074, PC.

13 *Baynard v Woolley* (1855) 20 Beav 583.

14 See note 8 above.

15 See note 7, above.

16 See cases in note 8, above, and *Bennett v Colley* (1832) 5 Sim 182; Supreme Court Act 1981, s 37.

17 *London Syndicate v Lord* (1878) 8 Ch D 84 at 90; *Freeman v Cox* (1878) 8 Ch D 148; *Hampden v Wallis* (1884) 27 Ch D 251; *Dunn v Campbell* (1879) 27 Ch D 254n; *Porrett v White* (1885) 31 Ch D 52, CA; *Wanklyn v Wilson* (1887) 35 Ch D 180; *Re Beeny* [1894] 1 Ch 499; *Neville v Matthewman* [1894] 3 Ch 345, CA; *Re Benson* [1899] 1 Ch 39.

PARAGRAPH 1

Interim injunction principles

The approach prescribed by *American Cynamid Co v Ethicon Ltd*[18] needs to be followed. First, the plaintiff must show an arguable case. If an arguable case is shown then the balance of convenience should be applied. If the scale appears very evenly balanced it is then legitimate to take into account the strength or weakness of the plaintiff's case. However, even if the plaintiff's case is weak the court may grant him protection falling short of a full pre-servation order. Thus in one case[19] the Court of Appeal ordered the defendant, Central Bank of Cyprus, to earmark the £8 million, representing the plaintiff's claimed traceable money, in a separate account and to refrain from dealing with it otherwise than in the normal course of its banking business and only to the extent that no other funds were available in England for that purpose. The Bank was also required to inform the plaintiff's solicitors in advance of any proposed use to be made of the £8 million and, at the same time, to give details of all foreign currency reserves for the time being held in England. It may be that such flexibility might enable a court to preserve a proportion of the disputed assets relative to the strength of the plaintiff's case.

Loss of a portion of the trust property

The loss of a portion of the trust property affords prima facie ground for appointing a receiver on an interim application[20]; and so does reasonable anticipation of a loss.

Trust property in danger

In support of an interim injunction where the trust property is in danger, there may be claimed an interim order directing information to be provided about the location of trust property or property claimed to be trust property or the traceable product of trust property[1]. Such order can be made in respect of foreign proceedings where no claim is made over which the English court has jurisdiction[2].

If trust property is in a jurisdiction that neither recognises trusts nor would recognise an order of the English court, the court may order the property to be brought within the jurisdiction[3].

The court will appoint a receiver and grant an injunction where, from the character or condition of the trustee, he is not a fit person to have the control of the trust property; as, for instance, where he is insolvent[4], or about to

---

18 [1975] AC 396 [1975] 1 All ER 504, HL.

19 *Polly Peck International plc v Nadir (No 2)* [1992] 4 All ER 769 at 784 and 787, CA.

20 *Evans v Coventry* (1854) 5 De GM & G 911.

1 CPR Pt 25, r 25.1(1*); Norwich Pharmacal Co v Customs and Excise Comrs* [1974] AC 133, HL. Equity does not want to act in vain and wants its orders to be effective: *Banker's Trust Co v Shapira* [1980] 1 WLR 1274 at 1280, CA.

2 CPR Pt 25, r 25.4.

3 *Derby & Co Ltd v Weldon (No 6)* [1990] 1 WLR 1139, CA.

4 *Mansfield v Shaw* (1818) 3 Madd 100; *Gladdon v Stoneman* (1808) 1 Madd 143n, followed in *Bowen v Phillips* [1897] 1 Ch 174.

become bankrupt[5], or is a person of dissolute habits, or dishonest[6] or in contempt of court orders[7].

So where, there being some disagreement between three trustees, the majority acted alone and took securities in their own names, omitting the name of the dissentient trustee, it was held that the plaintiff (a beneficiary) was entitled to a receiver[8].

Now that trustees can be removed and replaced on a wide variety of grounds it will rarely be necessary to appoint a receiver except as an interim measure where the affairs of the trust are in special disorder requiring a troubleshooter to resolve matters that most trustees could not reasonably be expected to do. One such special case involved the National Union of Mineworkers during the lengthy miners' strike where the union trustees were salting money away in devious ways in various countries and were in contempt of court orders: the Court of Appeal[9] even upheld an ex parte (without notice) order for the removal of the trustees and the appointment of a receiver.

The appointment of a receiver does not necessarily involve removing the trustees since it may be a temporary expedient in the interests of continuing the management of the trust where it is needed pending resolution of a problem. As Megarry V-C said in *A-G v Schonfield*[10], 'The remedy is one to be moulded to the needs of the situation: within proper limits a receiver may be given such powers as the court considers to be appropriate to the particular case.' Thus, a receiver may even be appointed of assets worldwide[11].

Where same persons trustees under conflicting settlements

In *Earl Talbot v Hope-Scott*[12] lands were vested in trustees, by Act of Parliament, upon trust for sale, and, subject thereto, upon trusts inalienably annexing the rents to the earldom of Shrewsbury. The Earl of Shrewsbury attempted to disentail (which of course he could not do effectually), and demised the lands to the same trustees, upon trust for a particular claimant of the title. The trustees accepted this trust, and claimed to receive the rents in that character, pending proceedings by the plaintiff to establish his claim to the earldom. A receiver of the rents was, however, appointed on his application, upon the ground that the trusts of the will were in conflict with the prior trusts upon which the trustees held the estate.

Injunction granted to restrain improper sale

Again, the court will grant an injunction to restrain a sale by trustees at an undervalue[13] or a sale of land held on trust for sale without appointing a second trustee and without consulting the beneficiaries[14].

5 *Re H's Estate* (1875) 1 Ch D 276.
6 See *Everett v Prythergch* (1841) 12 Sim 363.
7 *Clarke v Heathfield* [1985] ICR 203, CA.
8 *Swale v Swale* (1856) 22 Beav 584.
9 *Clarke v Heathfield* [1985] ICR 203, CA.
10 [1980] 1 WLR 1182 at 1187.
11 *Derby & Co Ltd v Weldon (Nos 3 and 4)* [1990] Ch 65, CA.
12 (1858) 4 K & J 139; and see to same effect *Price v Loaden* (1856) 21 Beav 508.
13 *Anon* (1821) 6 Madd 10; and see *Webb v Earl of Shaftesbury* (1802) 7 Ves 480; *Milligan v Mitchell* (1833) 1 My & K 446; *Dance v Goldingham* (1873) 8 Ch App 902; *Wheelwright v Walker* (1883) 31 WR 912; *Buttle v Saunders* [1950] 2 All ER 193.

Where new trustees or co-trustees sue for redress of breach of trust

When new trustees or continuing co-trustees sue for restoration of lost assets or value to the trust fund they need not make the beneficiaries parties, because they sufficiently represent the beneficiaries interests[15] unless it seems[16], all the beneficiaries are ascertained and of full age and capacity and might wish an unauthorised investment to be retained and not sold.

PARAGRAPH 2

Payment into court ordered on application

It is obviously a severe measure to order a trustee to pay money into court pending the trial of an action. It will, therefore, only be done where the trustee has admitted that he has the money *in his hands*, or possibly where he has admitted that he has had it and has either misappropriated it or not accounted for it[17], or not invested it[18], or has invested or paid it away improperly[19], and it is clear that he has no real defence.

Practice no longer favoured

The court does not, however, favour these interim applications as readily as it once did; and the Court of Appeal laid it down in *Neville v Matthewman*[20] that:

> 'unless care is taken in making such orders a very dangerous precedent may be established. Such orders may easily become very oppressive. Under the old practice of the Court of Chancery such an order could only have been made upon an admission contained in the defendant's answer. We all know with what care answers were framed; and if by his answer the defendant admitted that he had in his hands money belonging to the plaintiff, there could be no danger in ordering him to pay it into court.'

Lord Justice Davey added that an extension of the doctrine was made by Jessel MR in *Freeman v Cox*[1], and that he (the Lord Justice) was not disposed to carry the practice any further. In his opinion such orders ought to be made only when it is made out to the satisfaction of the court that the defendant has the sum claimed *in his hands and that he has no real defence*. In *Re Benson*[2], however, North J ordered payment into court, although the trustee deposed that he had spent it.

---

14 *Waller v Waller* [1967] 1 All ER 305, [1967] 1 WLR 451.
15 CPR 64 and Practice Directions thereon; see *Re Cross* (1882) 20 Ch D 109; *Williams v Barton* [1927] 2 Ch 9; *Young v Murphy* [1996] 1 VR 279.
16 *Butler v Butler* (1877) 7 Ch D 116 at 120, CA.
17 *Freeman v Cox* (1878) 8 Ch D 148.
18 *Wiglesworth v Wiglesworth* (1852) 16 Beav 269.
19 *Bourne v Mole* (1845) 8 Beav 177; *Re Whiteley* (1886) 33 Ch D 347; affd sub nom *Learoyd v Whiteley* (1887) 12 App Cas 727; *Scott v Becher* (1817) 4 PR 346; *Meyer v Montriou* (1841) 4 Beav 343; but cf *Crompton and Evans' Union Bank v Burton* [1895] 2 Ch 711.
20 *Neville v Matthewman* [1894] 3 Ch 345 at 353, CA, per Lindley LJ. The subsequent case of *Nutter v Holland* [1894] 3 Ch 408, was an application by originating summons, now a Part 8 claim. See also *Crompton and Evans' Union Bank v Burton* [1895] 2 Ch 711.
1 (1878) 8 Ch D 148.
2 [1899] 1 Ch 39 but cf *Re Clinton's Will* (1910) 10 SRNSW 465.

ARTICLE 94

Dishonest breach of trust may be a crime[3]

(1) A trustee will be guilty of theft under the Theft Act 1968[4] if he dishonestly appropriates property belonging to another with the intention of permanently depriving the other of it[5].
(2) A trustee convicted of a criminal offence may be ordered to pay compensation for any loss or damage resulting from his offence[6].

PARAGRAPH 1

The elements of mens rea and actus reus comprising theft are amplified in ss 2 to 6 of the Act. Each of these elements must be proved before the offence can be established.

Actus reus

'Appropriates'

Any assumption of the rights of an owner amounts to an appropriation, including, after acquisition without stealing, a later assumption of a right to it by keeping or dealing with it as owner[7]. A disposal for his own purposes of goods held in trust by a trustee will constitute theft[8].

'Property'

Property includes money and all other property, real or personal, including things in action and other intangible property[9]. A trustee, unlike other persons, may steal land or anything forming part of the land where he deals with it in breach of the confidence[10] reposed in him[11].

'Belonging to another'

Property is regarded as belonging to any person having possession or control of it, or having in it any proprietary right or interest (not being an equitable interest arising solely from an agreement to grant or transfer an interest)[12]. Where property is subject to a trust, the persons to whom it belongs include

---

3 Generally, see (1975) 39 Conv NS 29 (R Brazier). As to trustees and insider trading taking advantage of price-sensitive information, see Criminal Justice Act 1993, Pt V and Financial Services and Markets Act 2000, Pt VIII.
4 11(1) Halsbury's Law (4th edn Reissue) paras. 541–550. For general commentary, see Smith, *The Law of Theft* (8th edn (1997)); Griew, *The Theft Acts* (7th edn (1995)).
5 Theft Act 1968, s 1.
6 Powers of Criminal Courts Act 1973, s 35(1).
7 Theft Act 1968, s 3(1). A transferee for value acting in good faith is protected by s 3(2) from the consequences that might otherwise arise from a defect in the transferor's title.
8 *International Factors Ltd v Rodriguez* [1979] QB 351 at 358, [1979] 1 All ER 17 at 21, CA.
9 Theft Act 1968, s 4(1).
10 'Confidence' was intended as a word of general meaning, replacing 'trust' in the Criminal Law Revision Committee's draft Bill; see 291 HL Official Report (6th series) col 22.
11 Theft Act 1968, s 4(2)(a).
12 Theft Act 1968, s 5(1).

any person having a right to enforce the trust[13]. Where a person receives property from or on account of another, and is under an obligation to the other to retain and deal with that property or its proceeds in a particular way, the property or proceeds are regarded (as against him) as belonging to the other[14].

In *R v Mainwaring*[15] in a passage endorsed by *R v Dubar*[16] Lawton LJ stated:

> 'Whether or not an obligation arises is a matter of law, because an obligation must be a legal obligation. But a legal obligation arises only in certain circumstances, and in many cases the circumstances cannot be known until the facts have been established. It is for the jury, not the judge, to establish the facts if they are in dispute. What, in our judgment, a judge ought to do is this: if the facts relied upon by the prosecution are in dispute he should direct the jury to make their findings on the facts and then say to them: if you find the facts to be such and such then I direct you as a matter of law that a legal obligation arose to which section 5(3) applies.'

Constructive trusts

As ever, one must clearly distinguish the constructive trust of specific property from the constructive trustee*ship* imposed upon a defendant so that he may be made personally liable to account as if he had been an express trustee[17]. In the case of personal liability as a constructive trustee where there is simply a debtor—creditor relationship, there being no specific trust property or its traceable equivalent, there can be no question of theft of property belonging to another[18].

Section 5(2) treats property 'as belonging to any person having in it any proprietary right or interest not being an equitable interest arising only' from a specifically enforceable contract. This must surely cover equitable interests under trusts—whether express, resulting or constructive[19]. Thus if an express trustee uses trust property to make a profit for himself and spends the profit on a holiday for his wife and himself the actus reus of theft should be satisfied. The position should be similar if a trustee privately in his own name renewed the trust lease or purchased the freehold reversion to the trust lease[20], then sold his interest at a profit and dissipated the profit in paying off his debts.

The legal position has been obscured somewhat by the Court of Appeal in

---

13 Theft Act 1968, s 5(2). In the case of charitable trusts, such person is the Attorney General: see *National Anti-Vivisection Society v IRC* [1948] AC 31 at 62, HL, per Lord Simonds. In the case of a non-charitable purpose trust recognised as valid under the Recognition of Trusts Act 1987 it will be the person nominated as enforcer under the trust instrument.

14 Theft Act 1968, s 5(3). See *R v Wills* (1990) 92 Cr App Rep 297; *R v Wain* [1995] 2 Cr App Rep 660. This should cover *Quistclose* loan purpose trusts as explained by Lord Millett in *Twinsectra v Yardley* [2002] UKHL 12, [2002] 2 All ER 377. Further see *R v Klineberg* [1999] 1 Cr App 427, CA, discussed in [1999] Crim Law Review 417–419 and (1999) 91 Crim Law 1–3 and *R v Governor of Brixton Prison* [1996] 4 All ER 350 at 364, per Beldam J.

15 (1981) 74 Cr App Rep 99 at 107.

16 [1995] 1 All ER 781 at 787 and 789.

17 See Article 100 post.

18 *A-G's Reference (No 1 of 1985)* [1986] QB 491, [1986] 2 All ER 219, CA, though see p 909, post.

19 Williams *Textbook of the Criminal Law* (3rd edn) p 753ff; JC Smith *Law of Theft* (8th edn) p 50; now see *R v Clowes (No 2)* [1994] 2 All ER 316 at 335–336 where the Court of Appeal held that even equitable interests in bank accounts, to which trust moneys can be traced and over which an equitable charge is imposed, suffice. Also see *R v Shadrokh-Cigari* [1988] Crim LR 465.

20 See Article 33, ante.

A-G's Reference (No 1 of 1985)[1] where a public house manager, with his bar-man's assistance, bought beer from a wholesaler intending to make a secret profit from the unauthorised sale of the beer to customers in the pub. They were charged with going equipped for theft when found secretly bringing their own beer into the pub, and they were acquitted.

The referred questions were 'On a charge of theft, where an employee has used his employer's premises and facilities to make a secret profit, will that secret profit be subject to a constructive trust in favour of the employer? And, if so, does that constructive trust give the employer a proprietary right or interest in the secret profit within section 5(1) of the Theft Act?' The two answers were 'If, which we do not believe, it is properly described as a trust, it is not such a trust as falls within the ambit of section 5(1)' and 'No'.

Unfortunately, the court did not appreciate that property derived from use of property entrusted to a fiduciary should be regarded as held on a pro-prietary constructive trust or did not appreciate that the manager's use of his employer's beer pumps, beer glasses, cellars, bar, heating and lighting invoked the application of proprietary constructive trust principles. The court thus overlooked *Reid-Newfoundland Co v Anglo-American Telegraph Co Ltd*[2] where the appellants were entitled to use a special telegraphic wire but not to transmit any commercial messages except for the benefit of the respondents. The appellants made a profit from using the wire for their own business purposes. The Privy Council held[3] 'an obligation in the nature of a trust arose on their part to keep an account of the profits accruing from such use of the wire and to set their profits aside as money belonging to the respondents'. As Page-Wood V-C has stated[4], 'where a chattel is entrusted to an agent to be used for the owner's benefit, all the profits which the agent may make by using that chattel belong to the owner'.

On inadequate consideration of the position the court concluded that no constructive trust of the secret profit existed, basing itself on *Lister v Stubbs*[5] which held that where a fiduciary does not use trust property but only uses his fiduciary position (eg to take a bribe) then he is only personally liable to account for the money obtained by use of such position. Since then, a strong Privy Council in *A-G for Hong Kong v Reid*[6] has rejected the difficult distinc-tion between use of fiduciary property and use of fiduciary position, has pointed out case law overlooked in *Lister v Stubbs*, and has refused to apply *Lister v Stubbs*, which can therefore now be regarded as wholly discredited[7]. Moneys like bribes and secret profits, obtained by virtue of a fiduciary posi-tion are now held on constructive trust, equity regarding as done that which ought to be done.

Surprisingly, the court then stated[8]:

'assuming that, contrary to our views, s 5(1) does import the constructive trust into the 1968 Act, on the facts of the case the employers still obtain no proprietary interest. A trustee is not permitted to make a profit from his trust. Therefore, if he

1 [1986] QB 491, [1986] 2 All ER 219, CA.
2 [1912] AC 555, PC.
3 [1912] AC 555 at 559.
4 *Shallcross v Oldhan* (1862) 2 John & H 609 at 616.
5 (1890) 45 Ch D 1, CA.
6 [1994] 1 AC 324, [1994] 1 All ER 1, discussed p 396, ante.
7 The Court of Appeal is free to follow the Privy Council decision: *Worcester Works Finance Ltd v Cooden Engineering Ltd* [1972] 1 QB 210.
8 [1986] 2 All ER 219 at 225, CA.

uses trust property to make a profit from the trust he is accountable for that profit. If and when such property is identified as a separate piece of property, he may be a constructive trustee of it. However, until the profit is identifiable as a separate piece of property it is not trust property and his obligation is to account only.'

With the greatest of respect, these dicta are wholly misconceived since they were uttered without any consideration of the equitable tracing rules which give the claimant an equitable proprietary interest in the traceable product or profit of trust property, even though such may not be a separate piece of property but part of a mixed fund or a property amalgam. The claimant will either have a charge on such fund or amalgam or, if more beneficial, he will be a co-owner thereof according to the proportion of traceable trust property therein[9]. Appreciating this, the Court of Appeal[10] has since held that beneficiaries' equitable interests in bank accounts and withdrawals from them arising from the application of equity's tracing rules are proprietary rights or interests within s 5(1) of the Theft Act 1968.

Where two or more persons are involved in fraudulent schemes to sell their own beer or sandwiches and not their employer's on his premises it is now safe[11] to charge them with common law conspiracy to defraud in addition to a statutory conspiracy involving the commission of a specific offence if appropriate. If a defendant is charged under s 25 of the 1968 Act there are problems since it may well be that passengers or customers would not have refused to purchase refreshments from the defendant if they had known he was operating a fraud on his employer so the defendant cannot be said to have been going equipped to cheat the passengers or customers[12]. If charged under s 17 there is the difficulty that since the defendant will not have used his employer's supplies but private supplies, which will not show up in the employer's accounts, there will be no false accounting[13].

Mens rea

'Dishonesty'

The issue of dishonesty is a question of fact for the jury[14]. Dishonesty does not necessarily depend upon a correct understanding by an accused of all the legal implications of his conduct: The test is that laid down in *R v Ghosh*[15], namely, whether the accused was acting dishonestly by the standards of ordinary and decent people and, if so, whether he himself must have realised that what he was doing was, by those standards, dishonest[16].

A person's appropriation of property belonging to another is not dishonest if he appropriates it believing (1) he has in law the right to deprive the other of it, (2) he would have the other's consent if the other knew of the circumstances, (3) (except where the property came to him as trustee or personal representative) that the person to whom the property belongs

9 See Article 92, ante.
10 *R v Clowes (No 2)* [1994] 2 All ER 316 at 335–336.
11 *R v Cooke* [1986] AC 909, [1986] 2 All ER 985, HL.
12 *R v Cooke* [1986] AC 909, [1986] 2 All ER 985, HL.
13 *R v Cooke* [1986] AC 909, [1986] 2 All ER 985, HL.
14 *R v Feely* [1973] QB 530, [1973] 1 All ER 341, CA.
15 [1982] QB 1053.
16 *R v Clowes (No 2)* [1994] 2 All ER 316 at 330–331, CA.

cannot be discovered by taking reasonable steps[17]. Before the Theft Act 1968 a fiduciary who abstracted money from a fund intending to repay shortly without causing any loss was guilty of larceny[18]. Now it is up to the jury to decide whether the fiduciary was acting dishonestly[19]. It has been suggested[20] that the Act might usefully be amended so that 'A person is not guilty of theft by reason only of the fact that, being in lawful control of money or a monetary fund, he appropriates the whole or part of it, intending to repay promptly, in the sure belief that he has resources presently available for virtually immediate repayment, and being certain that he will be able to repay it so as to cause no loss or inconvenience to the owner' since in such circumstances it is hardly likely that a jury would find such person was acting dishonestly.

'Intention of permanently depriving'[1]

Where the property is subject to a trust, an intention to defeat the trust is regarded as an intention to deprive of the property any person having the right to enforce the trust[2]. Borrowings do not involve permanent deprivation unless moneys or fungible goods (like bottles of claret) are involved, when the very same notes or bottles are not returned.

Other offences

There are five further offences under the Theft Act 1968[3] which may be committed by a dishonest[4] trustee[5]. These are:
(1) Obtaining property by deception[6].
(2) Obtaining a pecuniary advantage by deception[7].
(3) False accounting[8].
(4) Publication of false, deceptive or misleading statements by officers of a body corporate or unincorporated association[9].
(5) Suppression of documents[10].
  Where two or more co-trustees agree to do an unlawful act, or to do a lawful act by unlawful means, they will be guilty of conspiracy[11].

---

17 Theft Act 1968, s 2(1). The trustee cannot assert that his inability to discover the beneficiary leads to his own absolute entitlement.
18 *R v Williams* [1953] 1 QB 660.
19 *R v Feely* [1973] QB 530.
20 G Williams (1985) 5 Legal Studies 183 at 189.
1 Theft Act 1968, s 6.
2 Theft Act 1968, s 5(2); and see note 13, p 908 above.
3 See note 4, p 907, ante.
4 See note 15, above.
5 Generally, see (1975) 39 Conv NS 29 at 42–44 (Brazier).
6 Theft Act 1968, s 15.
7 Theft Act 1968, s 16.
8 Theft Act 1968, s 17.
9 Theft Act 1968, s 19.
10 Theft Act 1968, s 20.
11 See 11(1) Halsbury's Laws (4th edn) paras 59–66. The Criminal Law Act 1977, ss 1–5, abolishes the common law offence of conspiracy and creates a statutory offence. The 1977 Act does not apply to conspiracy to defraud, on which, see *Scott v Metropolitan Police Comr* [1975] AC 819, [1974] 3 All ER 1032, HL. For the relationship between common law conspiracy to defraud and statutory conspiracy under Criminal Law Act 1977, s 1 see *R v Cooke* [1986] AC 909, [1986] 2 All ER 985, HL. Now see Criminal Justice Act 1987, s 12, intended to allow common law conspiracy to defraud to have the same meaning and width as it had before the 1977 Act.

Paragraph 2

The procedure under the Powers of Criminal Courts Act 1973[12] is intended for clear and simple cases[13]. Damages awarded in subsequent civil proceedings in respect of the same loss or damage are assessed without regard to any order[14], but in determination of the award, the amount so assessed must be reduced by any amount paid under the order[15]. Where any difficult questions of title or the appropriate measure of compensation arise, it is submitted that the victim should be left to his remedy in the civil courts[16].

---

12 Powers of Criminal Courts Act 1973, ss 35–38.
13 *R v Kneeshaw* [1975] QB 57, [1974] 1 All ER 896, CA.
14 Powers of Criminal Courts Act 1973, s 38(1), (2).
15 Powers of Criminal Courts Act 1973, s 38(2).
16 See *R v Daly* [1974] 1 All ER 290, [1974] 1 WLR 133, CA; *R v Inwood* (1974) 60 Cr App Rep 70 at 73, CA; *R v Kneeshaw* [1975] QB 57, [1974] 1 All ER 896, CA.

CHAPTER 21

Protection accorded to trustees in case of breach of trust

Article
95 General protection of trustees who have acted reasonably and
    honestly   913
96 Limitation of actions by beneficiaries against trustees   920
97 Concurrence of or waiver or release by the beneficiaries   931
98 Protection against the acts of co-trustee   938
99 Trustees generally entitled to contribution inter se, but may be entitled
    to be indemnified by co-trustee or beneficiary who instigated breach
    940

ARTICLE 95

General protection of trustees who have acted reasonably and honestly

If it appears to the court that a trustee (or personal representative) is
or may be personally liable for any breach of trust, but that he:
(a) has acted honestly;
(b) has acted reasonably; and
(c) ought fairly to be excused for the breach *and* for omitting to
    obtain the directions of the court in the matter in which he
    committed such breach,
then the court may relieve him, either wholly or partly, from personal
liability for breach[1]. The onus of proving honesty and reasonableness
and that he ought fairly to be excused is cast upon the trustee[2], and
whether a trustee acted reasonably and honestly is a question of fact
depending on the circumstances of each case, no general principle or
rule being possible[3].

1 Trustee Act 1925, s 61; and see *National Trustees Co of Australasia v General Finance Co of
Australasia* [1905] AC 373. The relief could be given without the Act being pleaded: *Singlehurst v Tapscott Steamship Co Ltd* [1899] WN 133; *Re Pawson's Settlement* [1917] 1 Ch 541; but, in
view of CPR Pt 16, r 16.5(2)(a), a trustee or personal representative whose defence did not
raise the issue of s 61 and the requisite financial basis could have problems.
2 *Re Stuart* [1897] 2 Ch 583; *Marsden v Regan* [1954] 1 WLR 423.
3 *Re Turner* [1897] 1 Ch 536; *Re Barker* (1898) 77 LT 712; *Re Stuart* [1897] 2 Ch 583; and see *Re
Windsor Steam Coal Co* (1901) Ltd [1929] 1 Ch 151.

Reasonableness required as well as honesty

This statutory rule, now contained in s 61 of the Trustee Act 1925[4] was designed to protect honest trustees, and ought not to be construed in a narrow sense[5], but it will be perceived that all three circumstances must co-exist to entitle a trustee to the benefit of the section, namely,

(1) he must have acted honestly, and

(2) he must also have acted reasonably (honest folly is not excused[6]), and

(3) he ought fairly (that is to say in fairness to himself and other persons who may be detrimentally affected[7]) to be excused not just for the breach but also for omitting to obtain the directions of the court in the matter in which he committed the breach[8].

The section in its concern for the case where a trustee 'is or *may* be personally liable' extends to actual or possible past liability but not so as to authorise future liability. A trustee can thus invoke the section where he 'may' be liable for breach of trust so as to make it unnecessary to prove that there actually has been a breach of trust.

In *Re Rosenthal*[9] the defendants, who had been acting in the administration of a deceased's estate, transferred a house to the specific devisee without making any provision for payment of the estate duty which should have been borne by the house. The devisee sold the house and the proceeds were remitted to her in Israel where she lived. The defendant paid £270 of the estate duty on the house out of the residuary estate, leaving about £1,500 of estate duty still to be found. The residuary legatee obtained a declaration that the defendants were not entitled to pay the £1,500 out of the residuary estate. Plowman J held that no breach of trust had yet occurred in respect of the outstanding £1,500 to enable the defendants to invoke s 61. The £270 had been paid out of the residuary estate in breach of trust but the defendants were professional trustees and although they had acted honestly they had neither acted reasonably nor ought they fairly to be excused for such breach of trust.

The section is broad enough to enable the court to excuse not just surchargeable breaches of trust in the management of trust property[10] but also falsifiable payments to the wrong persons[11] or acquisitions or dispositions that are unauthorised[12].

---

4 The rule was originally introduced by s 3 of the Judicial Trustees Act 1896. For a useful survey of the position see (1955) 19 Conv 420 (LA Sheridan) and Birks & Pretto *Breach of Trust* (Hart Publishing, 2002) Chapter 9 'Excuses' by J Lowry and R Edmunds. For similar protection for company directors see Companies Act 1985, s 727.

5 *Re Allsop* [1914] 1 Ch 1 at 11 per Cozens-Hardy MR and *Re Grindey* [1898] 2 Ch 593 at 601 per Chitty LJ, CA. A person whose want of probity causes him to be liable as a constructive trustee (see Article 100, post) will not be able to invoke the section, but an innocent recipient of trust property who cannot take advantage of the defence of change of position in respect of his conduct or who unjustly enriched himself by unknowingly using money subject to a trust to discharge earlier incurred debts will fall outside the merits of s 61 if technically falling within it as a constructive trustee.

6 *Re Turner* [1897] 1 Ch 536; *Re Barker* (1898) 77 LT 712; *Re Stuart* [1897] 2 Ch 583.

7 *Marsden v Regan* [1954] 1 All ER 475, [1954] 1 WLR 423, CA.

8 *National Trustees Co of Australasia v General Finance Co of Australasia* [1905] AC 373.

9 [1972] 3 All ER 552, [1972] 1 WLR 1273.

10 *Re Smith* (1902) 86 LT 401.

11 *Re Allsop* [1914] 1 Ch 1. Where a trustee or personal representative pays the wrong persons because he does not have notice of illegitimate or legitimated or adopted persons he may have protection under Trustee Act 1925, s 27 (where advertisements placed), Legitimacy Act 1976, s 7 and Adoption Act 1976, s 45.

12 *Perrins v Bellamy* [1898] 2 Ch 521; affd [1899] 1 Ch 797, CA.

What conduct is reasonable

The requirement of honesty, that is, that the trustee should have acted in good faith for the welfare of the trust, needs no elaboration. As to reasonableness each case must depend upon its own facts. In another connexion it was said by Lord Normand in a Scottish appeal in the House of Lords[13]:

'Error, either of fact or law, is no more than evidence of unreasonableness or of bad faith. . . . We are concerned only with unreasonableness, but there is other evidence in the case that the trustees addressed themselves to their duty carefully, seriously and impartially, and with a real desire to perform their duty to the best of their ability. One most important fact is that they took the advice of counsel and were guided by it and acted upon it. That is powerful evidence against unreasonableness. I am not prepared to accept the view that the supposed unreasonableness of their decision or of the ground on which they reached it must outweigh more direct and satisfying evidence that they behaved as reasonable men would.'

A trustee cannot be considered to have acted reasonably, if he has neglected to obtain skilled advice. Regard must be had to the estate of which he is a trustee. In a large estate it may be only reasonable that he should consult counsel of the first rank or apply for the directions of the court, whereas it would not be reasonable to insist upon all this where the estate is small[14]. In such a case it may be reasonable to act upon the advice of a solicitor[15], without going to counsel, but merely taking advice, without more, is not necessarily a passport to relief[16]. Counsel must be adequately instructed and allowed sufficient time to give properly considered advice[17].

It appears that high standards are expected of trustees. In *Roome v Edwards*[18] a UK set of trustees was charged to capital gains tax in respect of the transactions of a Cayman Islands set of trustees appointed by the UK trustees but over which they had no control, since both sets of trustees were regarded as a single and continuing body of trustees[19] of the settlement comprising the UK and the foreign assets. Lord Roskill stated[20]:

'Your Lordships were strongly pressed with the submission that this conclusion would or might jeopardise trustees such as the taxpayers who have no legal control over the assets which were the subject of the deemed disposal. Your Lordships were assured that in the present case the taxpayers were properly and adequately protected by the beneficiaries in relation to any liability which might fall on them. My Lords, the short answer to this powerfully urged plea is surely this. Persons, whether professional men or not, who accept appointment as trustees of settlements such as these are clearly at risk under [what is now the Taxation of Chargeable Gains Act 1992] and have only themselves to blame if they accept the obligations of trustees in these circumstances without ensuring that they are sufficiently and effectively protected whether by their beneficiaries or otherwise for fiscal or other liabilities

13 *Dundee General Hospitals Board of Management v Walker* [1952] 1 All ER 896, HL.
14 *Re Allsop* [1914] 1 Ch 1 at 13. Where a barrister of at least ten years' standing has given a written opinion on a question of construction the High Court, without hearing argument, can authorise trustees or personal representatives safely to take steps in reliance on the opinion: Administration of Justice Act 1985, s 48.
15 *Re Evans* [1999] 2 All ER 777.
16 *Marsden v Regan* [1954] 1 All ER 475 at 482 per Evershed MR; and see *National Trustees Co of Australasia v General Finance Co of Australasia* [1905] AC 373, PC.
17 *Baden v Societé Generale* [1992] 4 All ER 161 at 272.
18 [1982] AC 279, [1981] 1 All ER 736, HL.
19 Taxation of Chargeable Gains Act 1992, s 69(3).
20 [1982] AC 279 at 299, [1981] 1 All ER 736 at 744.

which may fall on them personally or as a result of the obligations which they had felt able to assume.'

Of course, it was not necessary to consider the application of s 61 of the Trustee Act as it would have been if the UK trustees had created a sub-trust with Cayman Islands trustees, whose activities led to a tax charge, in respect of the Cayman property, which the UK trustees had had to pay out of the UK property to the prejudice of UK beneficiaries. The strong implication is that in such circumstances the court would be most reluctant to relieve the UK trustees under s 61 of the Trustee Act.

While this may be justifiable in the case of professional trustees there may well be a case for excusing a non-professional co-trustee like Mrs Wohlleben (a married woman with four children) in *Wohlleben v Canada Permanent Trust Co*[1] where Dickson CJ stated:

'She tried to the best of her ability to keep herself informed but Canada Permanent failed to make known to her the contents of papers which were essential to informed opinion. She made all decisions which she had to make within the limits of her experience and knowledge, and I cannot find that she failed to listen to reason or that she responded irrationally or obdurately ... this is the very sort of case for which the section was intended. Mrs Wohlleben ought fairly to be excused from her breach of trust.'

This had the effect of throwing all the liability on the professional trustee, so having the same effect as the indemnity given to a lay trustee against a co-trustee who is a solicitor, whose advice and control caused the lay trustee's participation in the breach of trust[2].

In *Re Evans*[3] the defendant administrator of her intestate father's estate wound up his estate and distributed the property to herself, assuming that her brother was dead, not having heard from him for over 30 years. On her solicitor's advice, she took out a missing beneficiary policy to cover half the estate as less expensive and more effective than procuring a *Benjamin* order[4]. Four years later her brother turned up, took the proceeds of the policy covering his capital entitlement but sued for interest. She was held liable to account for interest but was granted partial relief under s 61 being relieved to the extent that the interest claim could not be satisfied out of the proceeds of sale of a property derived from the deceased's estate which was still at the defendant's disposal. The judge took account of the relatively small size of the estate, the unwarranted expense of applying to the court, and the defendant being a lay person unaccustomed to problems of this nature who was at all times willing to abide by the advice of solicitors.

In *Segbedzi v Segbedzi*[5] the defendant army officer was one of four administrators of a Ghanaian who died intestate in Ghana, leaving Ghanaian and English estate. Because he took up a new job in Swaziland he decided to resign as administrator and this was accepted at a family meeting by the head of the family who received his letter of resignation and then wrote to him telling him that 'the Solicitor for the Estate [of the deceased] has been informed and you will be instructed as to what legal procedures to follow'.

1　(1976) 70 DLR (3d) 257 at 275 (Can SC); contrast *Re Mulligan* [1998] 1 NZLR 481.
2　*Re Partington* (1887) 57 LT 654 and pp 945–946, post.
3　[1999] 2 All ER 777, but cf P Kenny in [1999] Conv 375 at 376.
4　[1902] 1 Ch 723; p 508 ante.
5　[2002] WTLR 83. The guarantors had not been notified of the defendant's intention to resign and not act further.

Nothing further happened, but the defendant (in breach of duty) left it to the other three administrators to deal with the estate. This led to substantial losses occurring. The judge however, granted relief under s 61 to the defendant in respect of claims by those beneficially interested in the estate despite the defendant's knowledge that further formalities were required to effect his removal. As a condition of resealing the Ghanaian letters of administration, the English court had required a guarantee against losses up to £104,000 from two guarantors, who provided this at the request of the administrators, and so had an implied contractual right of indemnity from them jointly and severally. Relief under s 61 from the beneficiaries' claims could have no effect on the guarantors' right to recover their £104,000 from the defendant alone, who would then need to seek contribution from the other three administrators. The defendant's appeal was dismissed.

Clearly, a person found liable for a breach of trust which involves lack of reasonable care can satisfy a court that he acted reasonably[6].

Examples of unreasonable conduct

Where the breach of trust consisted in investing the trust funds upon insufficient mortgage security, prima facie the statutory requirements in the now repealed s 8 of the Trustee Act 1925 as to the employment of an independent surveyor constitute a standard by which reasonableness of conduct should be judged; although non-compliance with those requirements was not necessarily a fatal obstacle to an application for relief. It was also a matter of consideration whether the trustee would have acted in the same way if he had been a prudent person lending money of his own[7]. Where, therefore, the trustee acted on the valuation of a valuer employed by the solicitor *who acted for the mortgagors also*, and the valuation in one case merely stated the amount for which the property was a good security, without stating the value of the property itself, and in another, although the value was stated, the sum advanced exceeded two-thirds of that value, it was held that no relief could be given to the trustee[8].

So, again, where the trustee invested the trust fund on the security of a second mortgage in Ireland he was not excused where he took no advice on the matter, employing the mortgagor's solicitor and not really considering the risks[9].

So, also, it has been held that a trustee does not act reasonably (however honest he may have been) in allowing his co-trustee to receive trust money without inquiry as to its application[10], or in allowing his co-trustee to act without check or inquiry[11], even where he is a solicitor who transacts the trust

---

6 Cf *Re D'Jan of London Ltd* [1994] 1 BCLC 561 at 564 per Hoffmann LJ in the director's context of the Companies Act 1985, s 727.
7 *Re Turner* [1897] 1 Ch 536 at 542; *Re Lord de Clifford's Estate* [1900] 2 Ch 707 at 716.
8 *Re Stuart* [1897] 2 Ch 583; and see *Khoo Tek Keong v Ch'ng Joo Tuan Neoh* [1934] AC 529, PC where, although the power of investment was extremely wide, it was held that it was unreasonable to lend trust money merely on a personal promise to repay it with interest, although the testator had been accustomed to make such loans during his lifetime.
9 *Chapman v Browne* [1902] 1 Ch 785.
10 *Wynne v Tempest* (1897) 13 TLR 360.
11 *Re Second East Dulwich 745th Starr-Bowkett Building Society* (1899) 68 LJ Ch 196. See note 17, below.

business[12]. The section is not meant to be used as a sort of general indemnity clause for honest men who neglect their own duties as trustee[13]. Thus, a bank trustee that acted honestly obtained no relief when it acted unreasonably in failing to keep in touch with the activities of a company in which it had a 99.8% shareholding so that a large loss flowed from the company's disastrous property speculation[14]. However, the above cases, and those which follow, must only be taken as examples of the general trend of judicial opinion; for, in the words of Byrne J, it is 'impossible to lay down any general rules or principles to be acted on in carrying out the provisions of the section, and each case must depend upon its own circumstances'[15].

Examples of reasonable conduct

Trustees who acted throughout bona fide and in accordance with what was the generally held view of the law, supported by judicial authority until that authority was overruled by the House of Lords, were held to have acted honestly and reasonably and to be fairly entitled to be excused[16]. But no relief was given in a case in which a solicitor-trustee had formed a wrong view of the effect of a statute by failing to notice one of its provisions: 'A prudent man whose affairs were affected by a statute would either satisfy himself that he fully understood its effect or would seek legal advice. A solicitor-trustee could not be heard to say that it was reasonable to apply a lower standard to him'[17].

The sale of leaseholds under a mistake of law, where there was no power of sale, has been held to be reasonable and excusable[18], and so has the payment by executors to their solicitor of money for the specific purpose of paying debts and administration expenses, which the solicitor misappropriated[19]. Wilful default in not suing a debtor to the estate has been excused, where the trustee had reasonable grounds for believing the proceedings would have been ineffectual[20]; and also where the debt was small, and he reasonably believed that the debtor was a man of good credit, and that, having regard to the testator's will, he was not bound to take proceedings[1].

So where a testator left an estate of £22,000, and it appeared that his debts only amounted to £100 or so, it was held that the executor acted reasonably in paying the widow an immediate legacy of £300, and in permitting her (under the trusts of the will) to receive so much of the income of the estate as was necessary for the maintenance of herself and family, before advertising for claims, although it subsequently turned out that there was a large claim

---

12 *Re Turner* [1897] 1 Ch 536; *Williams v Byron* (1901) 18 TLR 172. If the solicitor is a co-trustee then he may be obliged to indemnify the lay trustee against loss suffered by the lay trustee liable for breach of trust: *Re Partington* (1887) 57 LT 654; *Head v Gould* [1898] 2 Ch 250, p 945, post.

13 *Williams v Byron* (1901) 18 TLR 172 at 176.

14 *Bartlett v Barclays Bank Trust Co Ltd* [1980] Ch 515, [1980] 1 All ER 139.

15 Per Byrne J in *Re Turner* [1897] 1 Ch 536, and per Romer J in *Re Kay* [1897] 2 Ch 518 at 524.

16 *Re Wightwick's Will Trusts* [1950] Ch 260, [1950] 1 All ER 689.

17 *Ward-Smith v Jebb* (1964) 108 Sol Jo 919. The co-trustee was not a lawyer but, in the absence of evidence that he was given specific advice on the point in question by the solicitor-trustee or some other legal adviser, he was not granted relief. He might have had a right of indemnity against the solicitor-trustee, but that matter was not before the court.

18 *Perrins v Bellamy* [1898] 2 Ch 521; affd [1899] 1 Ch 797, and so also has a mistaken interpretation of the trust instrument (*Re Allsop* [1914] 1 Ch 1, CA).

19 *Re Lord De Clifford's Estate* [1900] 2 Ch 707.

20 *Re Roberts* (1897) 76 LT 479; and see Art 68.

1 *Re Grindey* [1898] 2 Ch 593.

for fraudulent misappropriation of rents received and not accounted for by the testator, which caused his estate to be insolvent[2]. But the executor was not excused for allowing the widow to take the income after the claimant had issued his writ; and, apparently, Romer J felt considerable doubts as to whether he ought to have excused payment of income after the executor had notice of the claim.

Again where a testator authorised his trustees to employ agents to act for them under his will and declared that they should be indemnified for the acts and omissions of such agents, it was held that, even if such words did not authorise them to pay money to their solicitor for the discharge of death duties (which was doubtful), yet their conduct was honest and reasonable, and that they ought to be excused[3].

Honesty and reasonableness do not always suffice if court thinks the trustees nevertheless ought not to be excused

It must not be assumed, however, that where a trustee has acted both honestly and reasonably he ought to be excused as a matter of course; for relief is always within the discretion of the court and an appellate court will be reluctant to interfere with the exercise of its discretion by a lower court[4]. Unless honesty and reasonableness are proved:

'the court cannot help the trustees; but if both are made out, there is then a case *for the court to consider* whether the trustee ought fairly to be excused for the breach, looking at all the circumstances'[5].

It seems that the court will be more loath to excuse a paid professional trustee who is now[6] expected to exhibit such care and skill as is reasonable having regard to any knowledge or experience that it is objectively reasonable to expect of a professional trustee as well as to any special knowledge or experience that he subjectively has or holds himself out as having, previously having been expected to exercise a higher standard of diligence and knowledge than a gratuitous trustee[7]. Thus in *Re Windsor Steam Coal Co (1901) Ltd*[8] PO Lawrence LJ speaking of the claim of a liquidator of a company, who had neglected to apply to the court for directions before making a large payment from the company's fund, said:

'Even if the appellant had himself taken the best possible advice and had made the payment acting on such advice, I am of opinion that that would not be sufficient to excuse him having regard to the fact that he was a paid trustee, and paid for his skill and services in performing his duties.'

And in *Re Pauling's Settlement Trusts*[9], where a bank had not only accepted the office of professional trustee but had done so under a settlement created

---

2 *Re Kay* [1897] 2 Ch 518. Also see *Guardian Trust Co of New Zealand v Public Trustee of New Zealand* [1942] AC 115, [1942] 1 All ER 598, PC.
3 *Re Mackay* [1911] 1 Ch 300.
4 *Marsden v Regan* [1954] 1 All ER 475, [1954] 1 WLR 423, CA.
5 *National Trustees Co of Australasia v General Finance Co of Australasia* [1905] AC 373, PC.
6 Trustee Act 2000, s 1; p 577 ante.
7 *Re Waterman's Will Trusts* [1952] 2 All ER 1054; *Bartlett v Barclays Bank Trust Co Ltd* [1980] Ch 515, [1980] 1 All ER 139; see pp 577 and 587, ante. Further see *Re Cooper (No 2)* (1978) 90 DLR (3d) 715.
8 [1929] 1 Ch 151.
9 [1964] Ch 303, [1963] 3 All ER 1, CA. See especially pp 339 and 11 (letter F), respectively.

by one of its customers, the Court of Appeal said that since it had thus deliberately placed itself in a position where its duty as trustee conflicted with its interest as banker, the court should be very slow to relieve it under the provisions of s 61.

Where a non-professional trustee has honestly and reasonably acted on the ill-advice obtained on behalf of the trust from a solicitor, the court will not excuse him if he abstains from recovering the loss from the solicitor where the latter is responsible for negligence for such abstention will not be reasonable[10].

Breaches of trust creating profit for trustees

All the above cases concerned trustees or personal representatives seeking relief from personal liability for losses arising from a breach of trust. In theory it could extend to relief from personal liability for profits, but this would be of little assistance if proprietary liability still remained in respect of the property (and its traceable product) acquired by the trustee. Thus, in practice, relief is accorded to honest hard-working trustees by awarding them an allowance for their endeavours[11].

ARTICLE 96

Limitation of actions by beneficiaries against trustees

(1) No statutory period of limitation applies to an action by a beneficiary under a trust[12], being an action:
(a) in respect of any fraud or fraudulent breach of trust to which the trustee was party or privy; or
(b) to recover from the trustee trust property or the proceeds thereof in the trustee's possession, or previously received by him and converted to his use[13].
(2) Where a trustee who is also a beneficiary under the trust receives or retains trust property or its proceeds as his share on a distribution of trust property made honestly and reasonably, his liability under (b) above is limited to the excess over his proper share, if an action is brought to recover the trust property more than six years after the distribution[14].
(3) Subject as aforesaid, an action by a beneficiary to recover trust property or in respect of any breach of trust, not being an action for which a period of limitation is prescribed by some specific provision of

---

10 *National Trustees Co of Australasia v General Finance Co of Australasia* [1905] AC 373, PC.
11 See pp 657–658 ante.
12 This includes constructive and resulting trusts, as well as express trusts. See the Limitation Act 1980, s 38, which gives to the terms 'trust' and 'trustee' the same meaning as is given to them by s 68 of the Trustee Act 1925. However, in historical context, only one category of true constructive trust is covered: *Paragon Finance plc v DB Thakerar & Co* [1999] 1 All ER 400, CA; see p 923 post. Actions by the Attorney General to enforce charitable trusts are not 'actions by a beneficiary under a trust': *A-G v Cocke* [1988] Ch 414, [1988] 2 All ER 391.
13 Limitation Act 1980, s 21(1); *Miller v Bain* [2002] BCLC 266.
14 Limitation Act 1980, s 21(2).

the Limitation Act 1980, will be barred if brought after the expiration of six years from the date on which the right of action accrued; but a right of action is not deemed to have accrued to any beneficiary entitled to a future interest in the trust property, until the interest falls into possession[15], and a person currently interested as beneficiary under a discretionary trust or as object of a power of appointment does not have an interest in possession until the trustees in exercise of their discretion confer an interest in the trust property upon him[16].

(4) No beneficiary as against whom there would be a good defence under the Limitation Act 1980, can derive any greater or other benefit from a judgment or order obtained by any other beneficiary than he could have obtained if he had brought the action and the Act had been pleaded in defence[17].

(5) Subject to the provisions of paragraphs 1 and 2, above, no action in respect of any claim to the personal estate of a deceased person or to any share or interest therein, whether under a will or on intestacy, can be brought after the expiration of twelve years from the date when the right to receive such share or interest accrued[18] nor can any action to recover arrears of interest in respect of any legacy, or damages in respect of such arrears, be brought after the expiration of six years from the date on which the interest became due[19].

(6) An action for an account cannot be brought after the expiration of any time limit under the Act which is applicable to the claim which is the basis of the duty to account[20].

(7) All statutory limitation periods are extended where any necessary party to the action is or has been an enemy or prisoner of war, so as not to expire before the end of twelve months from his ceasing to be an enemy or to be detained as a prisoner[1].

(8) Where periods of limitation are expressly provided by statute, the doctrine of laches (as distinct from acquiescence: see p 933, post) has no application[2] but if no statutory period of limitation is laid down then laches may bar a claim.

(9) The general provisions in the Limitation Act 1980, sections 28 and

---

15 Limitation Act 1980, s 21(3). As to when the statute begins to run in cases where the plaintiff has always been in possession, but acquires a new title, see *Mara v Browne* [1895] 2 Ch 69 (reversed on another point) where a person with an interest in possession and a reversionary interest was not barred as to the latter though barred as to the former. If trustees make a valid advance to a remainderman with a future interest, it seems that his interest falls (pro tanto) into possession; but this is not so if the advance is invalid: *Re Pauling's Settlement Trusts* [1964] Ch 303, [1963] 3 All ER 1, CA, in which the Court of Appeal confirmed on this point the judgment of Wilberforce J at first instance ([1961] 3 All ER 713 at 735).
16 *Armitage v Nurse* [1998] Ch 241, CA.
17 Limitation Act 1980, s 21(4).
18 Limitation Act 1980, s 22(a).
19 Limitation Act 1980, s 22(b).
20 Limitation Act 1980, s 23.
1 Limitation (Enemies and War Prisoners) Act 1945.
2 *Re Pauling's Settlement Trusts* [1962] 1 WLR 86 at 115, per Wilberforce J; [1964] Ch 303 at 353, per Willmer LJ.

32, which extend limitation periods in cases of disability, fraud, deliberate concealment or mistake apply to actions against trustees.

The Limitation Act 1980

These paragraphs state the effect of ss 21, 22 and 23 of the Limitation Act 1980 which to a large extent restate ss 19 and 20 of the Limitation Act 1939. Express, resulting and constructive trustees of property are dealt with on the same footing[3]. There is a major distinction between (i) trustees who have been guilty of fraud or who have retained trust property (or its product) or converted it to their use and (ii) trustees who have committed an 'innocent' or 'negligent' breach of trust. In the former case no limitation period applies[4] though the trustees may plead laches or acquiescence. In the latter case a six year limitation period is prescribed as for proprietary claims against innocent strangers[5], unless it seems, such innocent strangers' title is derived from a fraudulent breach of trust[6].

Exceptionally, a 12-year period is prescribed for 'any claim to the personal estate of a deceased person' so that an underpaid or unpaid creditor, legatee or next of kin has 12 years in which to sue the personal representatives (even if they hold such estate as trustees upon completing their administration) or other persons who received such estate[7].

Oddly, ss 21(1) and (3) only apply at face value to actions by a beneficiary under a trust, so that an action by a trustee on behalf of his beneficiaries (who may be unborn or unascertained) against a co-trustee or former trustees or a third party (owning trust property or its traceable product or personally liable in respect of dishonest assistance in breach of trust or dishonest dealings with the trust property) is neither helped nor hindered, so the result of an action against such a defendant depends on whether it be brought by a beneficiary or a trustee. This cannot be justified: the courts will surely apply the six year period by analogy with the statutory period for actions by beneficiaries so that the position is as it was under the Trustee Act 1888[8]. However, it has been held that an action by the Attorney-General to enforce a charitable trust is subject to no statutory time bars[9].

---

3 Limitation Act 1980, s 38(1) referring to Trustee Act 1925, s 68(17). The pre-1939 Limitation Act distinction between express and one category of constructive trustees expounded in *Taylor v Davies* [1920] AC 636, however continues to subsist: *Paragon Finance plc v DB Thakerar & Co* [1999] 1 All ER 400, CA; p 923 post.
4 Limitation Act 1980, s 21(1).
5 Limitation Act 1980, s 21(3).
6 Limitation Act 1980, s 21(1)(a); *GL Baker Ltd v Medway Building and Supplies Ltd* [1958] 1 WLR 1216 at 1221–1222; Law Com CP No 151 Limitation of Actions, 1998, para 4.16.
7 Limitation Act 1980, s 22(a) replacing Limitation Act 1939, s 20: *Re Diplock* [1948] Ch 465 at 511–513 approved seemingly on appeal in *Ministry of Health v Simpson* [1951] AC 251 at 276, HL, Protection against such claims may be available under Trustee Act 1925, s 27, p 627, ante.
8 *Re Bowden* (1890) 45 Ch D 444. On applying the six-year period by analogy see *Companhia de Seguros Imperio v Heath (REBX) Ltd* [2001] 1 WLR 112, CA.
9 *A-G v Cocke* [1988] Ch 414.

Paragraph 1

Perpetual liability (subject to laches)

No period of limitation applies for actions in respect of any fraud or fraudulent breach of trust to which the trustee was a party or privy nor to recover from the trustee trust property or the proceeds thereof in the possession of the trustee or previously received by the trustee and converted to his use[10] eg to pay off his private debts.

The trustee needs to be a party or privy to actual dishonesty[11] viz pursuit of a course of action knowing it to be contrary to the beneficiaries' interests or being recklessly indifferent whether it is so contrary[12]. An innocent trustee is not liable for the fraud of his co-trustee[13] or of his solicitor or other agent[14].

Because s 21(1) is not restricted on its face to actions against the trustee it seems that an action against an innocent donee from the trustee may be regarded[15] as one 'in respect of any fraud or fraudulent breach of trust to which the trustee was a party or privy'. The fact that the innocent donee takes title forthwith subject to the beneficiaries' interests of which he may be ignorant for many years till being informed of their claims, does not require him to be treated as a trustee for the purposes of s 21[16]. Since there is no justification for treating an *innocent* recipient differently depending upon whether the trustee was or was not acting dishonestly when transferring title to him, it may be that the courts might restrict s 21(1) to actions against *trustees*, leaving s 21(3) for actions against third parties.

Two classes of constructive trustee

It then becomes crucial that the Court of Appeal has restricted perpetual liability (subject only to laches) to only one category of constructive trustee. The Court of Appeal[17] distinguished two classes of constructive trustee: (1) where the defendant acquired the property or control over the property as a trustee or other fiduciary in an unimpeached arrangement before the conduct complained of when he abused the trust and confidence reposed in him; (2) where the wrongful conduct of the defendant in asserting his selfish interests leads to an equitable obligation being placed upon him. Before the Trustee Act 1888 intervened, Courts of Equity treated the former category as being express trustees against which time did not run, while, when the 1888 Act expressly made clear that the express trustee position covered con-

---

10 Limitation Act 1980, s 21(1). W J Swadling in Chapter 11 'Limitation' in Birks & Pretto *Breach of Trust* (Hart Publishing, 2002) reveals there should be a different starting point for resolving the current messy situation if one examines the historical context, but the modern starting point has to be *Paragon Finance plc v DB Thakerar & Co* [1999] 1 All ER 400, CA.

11 *Armitage v Nurse* [1998] Ch 241 at 260 (though not supported by the reference to *Beaman v ARTS Ltd* [1949] 1 KB 550 at 558 which did not concern the predecessor to s 21 which was Limitation Act 1939 s 19, but concerned s 26 of the latter Act which was the predecessor to s 32 of the 1980 Act); *Thorne v Heard* [1895] AC 495, HL.

12 *Armitage v Nurse* [1998] Ch 241 at 251 and 260.

13 *Re Tufnell* (1902) 18 TLR 705.

14 *Re Fountaine* [1909] 2 Ch 382, CA; *Thorne v Heard* [1895] AC 495 (but no longer authoritative on the effect of fraud or concealment of a trustee's agent in view of Limitation Act 1980, s 32(1)(a)and (b)).

15 *GL Baker Ltd v Medway Building Supplies Ltd* [1958] 1 WLR 1216 at 1221–1222.

16 *Paragon Finance plc v DB Thakerar & Co* [1999] 1 All ER 400, CA.

17 *Paragon Finance plc v DB Thakerar & Co* [1999] 1 All ER 400 at 408–414, CA.

structive trustees, it was held that the second category of constructive trustees could still plead limitation as a defence[18]. The Court of Appeal has held this distinction was preserved in the 1939 and 1980 Limitation Acts, so constructive trustees within the second category can raise a limitation defence even in cases of fraud and retention or conversion of trust property, as for equivalent situations at common law (subject to limitation periods not running till the fraud was discovered or could with reasonable diligence have been discovered).

Persons within the first category of constructive trustee include trustees de son tort[19], an executor de son tort[20] voluntarily undertaking executorship functions, company directors[1], a controller of a company's bank account[2], secret trustees[3] and an agent like a solicitor receiving trust property agreeing to treat it as such but subsequently dealing with it inconsistently with the trusts affecting it[4]. Within the second category able to plead the Limitation Act are included persons who knowingly receive trust property in breach of trust[5], or who innocently receive trust property for their own benefit but who then insist on retaining it or dealing with it as if it were their own property after becoming aware that it was trust property that they had received, and persons who dishonestly assist in a breach of trust or other fiduciary duty[6].

Unless the courts are prepared to restrict s 21(1) to actions against trustees (including the first but not the second category of constructive trustees)[7], one reaches the unsatisfactory result that a defendant within the second category of constructive trustee who can plead a six-year limitation period under s 21(3) 'subject to the preceding provisions of this section' will not be able to take advantage of s 21(3) if the trustee's conduct involving him was dishonest but will be able to if that conduct was not dishonest.

Where an action is brought under s 21(1)(b) a trustee who remains in actual physical occupation of trust property for his own purposes cannot be heard to say that he has not received any rents or profits in respect of the

---

18 *Taylor v Davies* [1920] AC 636, PC; *Clarkson v Davies* [1923] AC 100 at 110–111, PC.
19 *Paragon Finance plc v DB Thakerar & Co* [1999] 1 All ER 400 at 408.
20 *James v Williams* [2000] Ch 1 CA in ignorance of *Paragon Finance* held no limitation period applied to an executor de son tort due to Limitation Act 1980, s 21(1)(b) but it would seem that the executor de son tort intermeddled on purely selfish (not altruistic) grounds so that he should have fallen outside s 21(1) and within s 21(3).
1 See penultimate footnote and *JJ Harrison (Properties) Ltd v Harrison* [2001] EWCA Civ 1467, [2001] WTLR 1327 at 1342.
2 *Bank of Credit & Commerce International v Jan* (17 November 1999, unreported), Jonathan Parker J.
3 *Paragon Finance plc v DB Thakerar & Co* [1999] 1 All ER 400 at 409 where Millett LJ also instanced *Rochefoucauld v Banstead* [1897] 1 Ch 196 (where the defendant agreed to buy property for the plaintiff but the trust was imperfectly recorded) and *Pallant v Morgan* [1952] 2 All ER 951 (where the defendant sought to keep for himself property which the plaintiff had trusted him to buy for both parties).
4 *Lee v Sankey* (1873) LR 15 Eq 204; *Soar v Ashwell* [1893] 2 QB 390.
5 *Taylor v Davies* [1920] AC 636, PC.
6 See Birks & Pretto *Breach of Trust* (Hart Publishing, 2002), Chapter 6 'Assistance' by C Mitchell pp 209–211.
7 In *DEG-Deutsche v Koshy* [2002] 1 BCLC 478 at para 287 Rimer J happened to state, 's 21 is concerned only with claims against express trustees or persons in a like position (true constructive trustees), being persons who were trustees (or in the position of trustees) of the relevant property before the occurrence of the transaction sought to be impugned by the claim. But it does not apply to cases in which the defendant's trust obligation only arises as a direct consequence of the unlawful transaction which is impeached by the claimant'.

property. He will be charged a notional occupation rent, and, unless he can discharge himself by showing that he has paid moneys away:

> 'he must be considered as still having it in his pocket at the material date, and, therefore, cannot escape under the provisions of the Limitation Act.'[8]

PARAGRAPH 2

Overpayment to trustees as beneficiaries

Where trustees paid themselves as beneficiaries annuities without deducting tax it was held they could not plead any limitation period in respect of these overpayments to themselves but that they could in respect of over-payments to other beneficiaries.

Under a novel provision in Limitation Act 1980, s 21(2) if a trustee, who is also a beneficiary, receives or retains trust property or its proceeds as his beneficial share on a distribution of the trust property made by him honestly and reasonably, then his liability will be limited to the excess over his proper share, if an action is brought to recover the trust property more than six years after the distribution. Thus, if T distributed one-third of the trust property to himself, honestly and reasonably believing that only three beneficiaries exist, he will be liable to a fourth beneficiary after six years not for a quarter share but only for the one-twelfth difference between the one-third share he took and the one-quarter share which was truly his.

PARAGRAPHS 3 AND 4

Six Years Period

Under s 21(3), subject to no limitation period applying because of s 21(1), an action by a beneficiary to recover trust property or in respect of any breach of trust cannot be brought after six years from the date on which the right of action accrued (unless the action is to recover land[9] or the twelve-year period in s 22 applies in the case of personal representatives who have become trustees upon completing administration of the estate[10]). Because recovering trust property from the trustee (including the first but not the second category of constructive trustee) falls within s 21(1), only recovering trust property (including its traceable product) from a third party falls within s 21(3). An innocent third party receiving title to property for his own benefit from a trustee thus appears to be safe six years after receipt of such property: he is not regarded as a trustee within s 21(1), because being within the second category of constructive trustee. However his trustee-donor falls within s 21(1)(a) so as to make him as donee liable, irrespective of time, if the transfer of title was dishonest[11], unless the court can restrict s 21(1) to actions

---

8 *Re Howlett* [1949] Ch 767 at 778, [1949] 2 All ER 490 at 495, per Danckwerts J.
9 Twelve years is normally available to recover unregistered land (Limitation Act 1980, s 15) while Land Registration Act 2002, Sch 6 contains special rules enabling an adverse possessor to apply to become registered proprietor after ten years but the current registered proprietor who must be notified can prevent this except in very limited circumstances.
10 *Re Diplock* [1948] Ch 465 at 511–513; *Ministry of Health v Simpson* [1951] AC 251 at 276–277.
11 *GL Baker Ltd v Medway Building and Supplies Ltd* [1958] 1 WLR 1216 at 1221–1222.

against trustees and not against third parties[12].

Personal actions against trustees not perpetually vulnerable under s 21(1) and personal actions against third parties involved in a breach of trust are barred six years after the right of action accrued, not from the date on which loss was first suffered eg six years from the date an unauthorised or improper investment was made[13]. The payment of the full amount of income due to the life tenant is not an acknowledgment that capital is intact so as to prevent time running against the beneficiary[14].

Although a life tenant may be barred at the expiration of six years from the date of a breach of trust (eg the date of an improper mortgage) the remainderman will not be barred until six years after his interest falls into possession. If he compels the trustees to replace the loss during the life tenancy after the life tenant has become barred, the trustees are entitled to receive for themselves the income of the sum replaced by them, but until they have replaced the whole loss the income must be accumulated towards such replacement[15].

A beneficiary who has both an interest in possession and a future interest may sue in reliance on his future interest after his interest in possession claim has become barred[16] (but not so as to receive any income which the trustees may retain for themselves) except in the case of land, where s 15(5) applies to bar the future interest once the interest in possession has been barred.

Problems for discretionary trustees

Where a beneficiary is merely interested under a discretionary trust until obtaining a life interest upon attaining 25 years the Court of Appeal[17] has held that time does not run until the beneficiary obtains an interest in possession on his 25th birthday. It matters not that at 18 a beneficiary, whether or not having an interest in possession, is entitled to see the trust accounts with supporting information so as to be able to discover whether there has been a breach of trust.

Millett LJ has stated[18] that the rationale for time not running till an interest in possession has been acquired 'is not that a beneficiary with a future interest has not the means of discovery [because he has], but that the beneficiary should not be compelled to litigate (at considerable personal expense) in respect of an injury to an interest which he may never live to enjoy. Similar reasoning would apply to exclude a person who is merely the object of a discretionary trust or power which may never be exercised in his favour'.

This means that the liability of trustees of a discretionary trust is open-ended because towards the end of the trust period there will almost always be some beneficiary under a discretionary trust or some object of a power of appointment who will not have received any trust income or capital and who will therefore be able to claim that losses from breaches of trust over the last 70 or 80 years should be restored to the trust fund (or it may be that the

12 See note 7 above.
13 *Re Somerset* [1894] 1 Ch 231, CA.
14 *Re Fountaine* [1909] 2 Ch 382, CA. On acknowledgments see Limitation Act 1980, ss 29, 30, 31.
15 *Re Somerset* [1894] 1 Ch 231, CA.
16 *Mara v Browne* [1895] 2 Ch 69 at 96–97 (reversed on another point [1896] 1 Ch 199, CA).
17 *Armitage v Nurse* [1998] Ch 241.
18 *Armitage v Nurse* [1998] Ch 241 at 261.

person ultimately absolutely receiving what remains of the trust property could sue on his own behalf alleging there would have been much more passing to him but for breaches of trust in the preceding 70 or 80 years). It thus makes sense to exclude objects of powers from having a right to make the trustees account and to appoint a small amount to each beneficiary on attaining 18 years of age but this still leaves trustees exposed, although if they arrange for an independent annual audit this will make it most unlikely that actions will be brought years later, especially if a clause in the trust instrument provides that accounts approved by independent auditors shall be regarded as conclusively correct unless any trustee, knowing there had been a breach of trust, deliberately concealed it from the auditors.

The mandatory statutory limitation rules cannot be directly ousted because this would be contrary to public policy. However, just as determinable interests enduring only until bankruptcy are valid, perhaps one could validly provide that the interests of anyone interested under the settlement in whatever should be restored to the trust fund as a result of any breaches of duty by the trustees shall endure only until six years have elapsed since the relevant breach of trust or, in the case where the trustee, knowing he had committed a breach, deliberately concealed it, until six years have elapsed since discovery of such concealed breach or the time when such concealment could with reasonable diligence have been discovered.

Alternatively, a clause in the trust instrument could provide that if anyone interested under the trust brings an action in respect of a breach of trust that occurred more than six years previously or, in the case where the trustee knowing he had committed a breach deliberately concealed it, more than six years after discovery of it or the time when it could with reasonable diligence have been discovered, then anything recovered in such action shall be held on trust for the trustee held liable for the breach. To prevent the circuity of a beneficiary exercising his right of action against the trustee, who would then be entitled to the fruits of the action, the trustee is entitled to prevent the beneficiary's action being pursued[19].

Breach of self-dealing and fair-dealing rules

In *Tito v Waddell (No 2)*[20] Megarry V-C held that the self-dealing rule (enabling beneficiaries as of right to set aside purchases of trust property) and the fair-dealing rule (enabling a beneficiary to have the purchase of his equitable interest set aside unless the trustee shows the purchase was scrupulously fair) amount to disabilities of the trustee so that infractions of such rules are not breaches of trust and so that s 21(3) of the Limitation Act 1980 is inapplicable, leaving laches as the only time-based defence. All fiduciaries are subject to these rules, not just trustees, and Megarry V-C considered that breach of trust within s 21 concerns only breaches by trustees of duties confined to trustees as such. He was also influenced[1] by the fact that he was concerned with a breach of the fair-dealing rule where the beneficiary seeks to recover his beneficial interest, while s 21(3) concerns recovery of 'trust property'.

Because the duty of undivided loyalty is so fundamental to the trust there is much to be said for breach of it to be regarded as a breach of trust. However,

19 *Ingram v IRC* [1997] 4 All ER 395 at 424 per Millett LJ.
20 [1977] Ch 106.
 1 [1977] Ch 106 at 247.

breach of the self-dealing and fair-dealing rules will often fall within s 21(1) so as to oust s 21(3), while a breach of the self-dealing rule (if not within s 21(1)) will, it seems, lead to a beneficiary seeking 'to recover trust property' within the first part of s 21(3)[2].

PARAGRAPH 5

Legacies

By s 22 of the Limitation Act 1980 it is provided that the period of limitation for all actions in respect of any claim to the personal estate of a deceased person shall be 12 years.

The wording of the section, which refers to 'actions in respect of' personal estate and not to 'actions to recover' personal estate, is important, since it has been held by the Court of Appeal[3] to be wide enough to apply not only to an action by an unpaid beneficiary against a personal representative but also to an action by an unpaid beneficiary directly against one overpaid or wrongly paid. After expressing his complete agreement with the reasoning and conclusion of the Court of Appeal in this case, when appealed to the House of Lords, Lord Simonds (with whom their other Lordships concurred) said:

> 'there is nothing in the ancestry of this section which justifies, much less requires, a narrower meaning being given to its words than they ordinarily bear.'[4]

PARAGRAPH 6

Action for account

An action for an account must not be brought after the expiration of any time limit under the Limitation Act 1980 which is applicable to the claim which is the basis of the account. It would seem[5] that this provision in s 23 of the 1980 Act should, in historical context, be restricted to claims within Equity's concurrent or auxiliary jurisdiction and not claims like those of beneficiaries under trusts within Equity's exclusive jurisdiction so their claims to accounts should fall outside s 23, as held in *A-G v Cocke*[6], though for other reasons. However, merely because a beneficiary seeks an account *simpliciter*[7] a trustee cannot be deprived of a limitation defence otherwise available to him so he can restrict the period for which he has to account if he makes out such a defence[8].

---

2 *JJ Harrison (Properties) Ltd v Harrison* [2001] WTLR 1327 at 1344 per Chadwick LJ.
3 *Re Diplock* [1948] Ch 465, [1948] 2 All ER 318, CA; affd sub nom *Ministry of Health v Simpson* [1951] AC 251, [1950] 2 All ER 1137, HL; *Re Oliver* [1927] 2 Ch 323.
4 *Ministry of Health v Simpson* [1951] AC 251 at 276–277, HL.
5 See Birks & Pretto *Breach of Trust* (Hart Publishing, 2002), Chapter 11 'Limitation' by W J Swadling, pp 336–337.
6 [1988] Ch 414, where no limitation period applied to the A-G's action.
7 See *Gwembe Valley Development Co Ltd v Koshy* [1998] 2 BCLC 613 at 621–623; *Nelson v Rye* [1996] 1 WLR 1378 at 1390 but note criticism in *Paragon Finance plc v DB Thakerar & Co* [1999] 1 All ER 400 at 415–416, CA.
8 *DEG-Deutsche Investitions Und Entwicklungsesellschaft MBH v Koshy* [2002] 1 BCLC 478, paras 279 et seq but Rimer J held no limitation period applied to the claim for profits.

PARAGRAPH 7

War-time extensions

The limitation periods prescribed by ss 21 and 22 of the Limitation Act 1980 are extended in cases where any necessary party to the action is or has been an enemy or a prisoner of war by s 1 of the Limitation (Enemies and War Prisoners) Act 1945 which, though passed to meet conditions arising in the last war, is permanent legislation, and is in the following terms:

(1) If at any time before the expiration of the period prescribed by any statute of limitation for the bringing of any action any person who would have been a necessary party to that action if it had then been brought was an enemy or was detained in enemy territory, the said period shall be deemed not to have run while the said person was an enemy or was so detained, and shall in no case expire before the end of twelve months from the date when he ceased to be an enemy or to be so detained, or from the date of the passing of this Act, whichever is the later:

Provided that, where any person was only an enemy as respects a business carried on in enemy territory, this section shall only apply, so far as that person is concerned, to actions arising in the course of that business.

(2) If it is proved that any person was resident or carried on business or was detained in enemy territory at any time, he shall for the purposes of this Act be presumed to have continued to be resident or to carry on business or to be detained, as the case may be, in that territory until it is proved that he ceased to be resident or to carry on business or to be detained in that territory at an earlier date.

(3) If two or more periods have occurred in which any person who would have been such a necessary party as aforesaid was an enemy or was detained in enemy territory, those periods shall be treated for the purposes of this Act as one continuous such period beginning with the beginning of the first period and ending with the end of the last period.

By s 2(1), 'enemy' is defined as meaning any person who is or is deemed to be an enemy for any purposes of the Trading with the Enemy Act 1939 and may therefore include British subjects resident in enemy territory; 'enemy territory' is given a very wide meaning and includes territory under the sovereignty of or occupied by an enemy Power or which the Department of Trade and Industry has directed to be treated as enemy territory, and in respect whereof no cessation order has been made; and 'statute of limitation' includes the Limitation Act 1939 and 1980.

References to the period during which any person was detained in enemy territory are by s 2(3) to be construed as including references to any immediately succeeding period during which that person remained in enemy territory.

PARAGRAPH 8

Whether doctrine of laches available

It is clear that if statute specifically provides for an express period of limitation then there is no room for the equitable doctrine of laches though there may still be scope for a defence of acquiescence to arise[9]. Equally clearly if statute altogether omits mention of any limitation period for certain circumstances then the doctrine of laches must apply, eg to claims to set aside for breach of the self-dealing or fair-dealing rules or for equitable compensation in lieu thereof[10]. Where statute specifically states as in s 21(1) of the 1980 Act, 'No period of limitation prescribed by this Act shall apply to ... ' it is considered that this is insufficient to oust the doctrine of laches especially since s 36(2) of the 1980 Act states that 'nothing in the Act shall affect any equitable jurisdiction to refuse relief on the grounds of acquiescence or otherwise'. Thus the defence of laches succeeded in *Nelson v Rye*[11].

Laches consists of a substantial lapse of time coupled with circumstances 'where it would be practically unjust to give a remedy either because the party has by his conduct done that which might fairly be regarded as equivalent to a waiver of it, or where by his conduct and neglect he has, though perhaps not waiving that remedy, yet put the other party in a situation in which it would not be reasonable to place him if the remedy were afterwards asserted'[12]. A bare trustee cannot plead laches against his beneficiary with an undisputed equitable title[13] nor can express trustees of a charitable trust for the public make out a case of laches against the public[14].

PARAGRAPH 9

Extension of limitation period

Where in the case of an action for which a limitation period is prescribed by the 1980 Act (a) an action is based upon the fraud of the defendant[15] or his agent or of any person through whom he claims[16] or his agent or (b) any fact relevant to the plaintiff's right of action has been deliberately concealed from him by any such person aforesaid or (c) the action is for relief from the consequences of a mistake[17], then the limitation period does not begin to run until the plaintiff has discovered the fraud, concealment or mistake or could with reasonable diligence have discovered it[18]. Section 32(3) and (4) provide

---

9 *Re Pauling's Settlement Trusts* [1962] 1 WLR 86 at 115; on appeal [1964] Ch 303 at 353, [1962] 1 WLR 86 at 115.

10 *Tito v Waddell (No 2)* [1977] 3 All ER 129 at 248.

11 [1996] 2 All ER 186 at 200–206, though disapproved on other points in *Paragon Finance plc v DB Thakerar & Co* [1999] 1 All ER 400 at 415–416.

12 *Lindsay Petroleum Co v Hurd* (1874) LR 5 PC 221 at 239–240, per Lord Selborne LC. Also see *Fysh v Page* (1956) 96 CLR 233 (Aust HC) (12-year delay barred claim to set aside purchase by fiduciary). Further, see Birks & Pretto (eds) *Breach of Trust* (Hart Publishing, 2002), Chapter 12 'Laches, Estoppel and Election' by G Watt.

13 *Joyce v Joyce* [1978] 1 WLR 1170; *Frawley v Neill* (1999) Times, 5 April; *Mills v Drewitt* (1855) Beav 632 at 638, 52 ER 748 at 750. Laches can bar a personal as opposed to a proprietary claim: *Bright v Legerton* (1861) 2 De GF & J 606.

14 *Brisbane City Council v A-G* [1979] AC 411, PC.

15 This requires fraud to be an ingredient essential to the cause of action: *Beaman v ARTS Ltd* [1949] 1 KB 550 at 558, CA. It seems that fraud will be regarded as unambiguously referring to dishonesty: *Armitage v Nurse* [1998] Ch 241 at 260. Historically, such extension was not needed for claims within Equity's exclusive jurisdiction: Birks & Pretto (eds) *Breach of Trust* (Hart Publishing, 2002), Chapter 11 'Limitation' by W Swindling, pp 325, 330 and 334.

16 See *Eddis v Chichester Constable* [1969] 2 Ch 345, [1969] 2 All ER 912.

17 See *Phillips-Higgins v Harper* [1954] 1 QB 411.

18 Limitation Act 1980, s 32. On reasonable diligence see *Peco Arts Inc v Hazlitt Gallery Ltd* [1983] 3 All ER 193, [1983] 1 WLR 1315. What must be discovered or known are all the facts which together constitute the cause of action: *Official Assignee of Collier v Creighton* [1993] 2 NZLR 534 at 538–540.

protection for purchasers for value without notice of the fraud, concealment or mistake.

No limitation period is prescribed for any fraud or fraudulent breach of trust involving the trustee, but facts concerning an innocent or negligent breach of trust could be deliberately concealed by acts or omissions of the trustee once he became aware that he had committed such breach[19].

Section 32(1)(b) operates to postpone the running of time wherever there is a deliberate concealment, whether such concealment was contemporaneous with or subsequent to the accrual of the cause of action[20].

ARTICLE 97

Concurrence of or waiver or release by the beneficiaries

(1) A beneficiary who has assented to, or concurred in, a breach of trust[1], or who has subsequently released or confirmed it[2], or even acquiesced in it[3], cannot afterwards charge the trustees with it. Provided:

(a) that the beneficiary was of full age and capacity at the date of such assent or release[4];

(b) that he had full knowledge of the facts, and knew what he was doing[5] and the legal effect thereof[6], though, if in all the circumstances it is not fair and equitable that, having given his concurrence or acquiescence, he should subsequently turn round and sue the trustees, it is not necessary that he should know that what he is concurring or acquiescing in is a breach of trust (provided he fully understands what he is concurring or acquiescing in) and it is

---

19 Limitation Act 1980, s 32(2) as interpreted in *Cave v Robinson Jarvis and Rolf* [2002] UKHL 18, [2002] 2 All ER 641.

20 *Sheldon v R H Outhwaite (Underwriting Agencies) Ltd* [1996] AC 102, [1995] 2 All ER 558, HL. If a life tenant wrongfully sells an heirloom and says nothing about this, this amounts to deliberate concealment: *Eddis v Chichester Constable* [1969] 2 Ch 345 at 356, CA.

1 *Brice v Stokes* (1805) 11 Ves 319; 2 White & Tud LC 631; *Wilkinson v Parry* (1828) 4 Russ 272; *Nail v Punter* (1832) 5 Sim 555; *Life Association of Scotland v Siddal* (1861) 3 De GF & J 58; *Walker v Symonds* (1818) 3 Swan 1; *Evans v Benyon* (1887) 37 Ch D 329; *Re Pauling's Settlement Trusts* [1964] Ch 303, [1963] 3 All ER 1, CA).

2 *French v Hobson* (1803) 9 Ves 103; *Wilkinson v Parry* (1828) 4 Russ 272; *Cresswell v Dewell* (1863) 4 Giff 460.

3 See *Broadhurst v Balguy* (1841) 1 Y & C Ch Cas 16; *Brewer v Swirles* (1854) 2 Sm & G 219; *Stafford v Stafford* (1857) 1 De G & J 193; *Re Jarvis* [1958] 2 All ER 336, [1958] 1 WLR 815; *Re Pauling's Settlement Trusts* [1964] Ch 303, [1963] 3 All ER 1, CA.

4 *Lord Montford v Lord Cadogan* (1816) 19 Ves 635; *Overton v Bannister* (1844) 3 Hare 503 at 506.

5 *Re Garnett* (1885) 31 Ch D 1; *Buckeridge v Glasse* (1841) Cr & Ph 126; *Hughes v Wells* (1852) 9 Hare 749; *Cockerell v Cholmeley* (1830) 1 Russ & M 418; *Strange v Fooks* (1863) 4 Giff 408; *March v Russell* (1837) 3 My & Cr 31; *Aveline v Melhuish* (1864) 2 De GJ & Sm 288; *Walker v Symonds* (1818) 3 Swan 1. Paragraph 1 of this Article, as it stood in the 1960 edition was referred to by Wilberforce J in *Re Pauling's Settlement Trusts* [1961] 3 All ER 713, [1962] 1 WLR 86; (on appeal [1964] Ch 303, [1963] 3 All ER 1, CA).

6 *Re Garnett* (1885) 31 Ch D 1; *Cockerell v Cholmeley* (1830) 1 Russ & M 418; *Marker v Marker* (1851) 9 Hare 1; *Burrows v Walls* (1855) 5 De GM & G 233; *Stafford v Stafford* (1857) 1 De G & J 193; *Strange v Fooks* (1863) 4 Giff 408; *Re Howlett* [1949] Ch 767 at 775, [1949] 2 All ER 490 at 492.

not necessary (though it is significant[7]) that he should himself have directly benefited by the breach of trust[8];

(c) that no undue influence was brought to bear upon him to extort the assent or release[9].

(2) Where a beneficiary has obtained judgment in an action for breach of trust, or merely for general administration, it is not competent for him afterwards in that action to charge the trustees with breaches of trust committed before action and not alleged in the pleadings and proved at the trial, or even to ask for their removal on that ground[10]; nor, it seems, can a fresh action be brought for that purpose without the leave of the court[11].

PARAGRAPH 1

Distinction between right to plead concurrence and the right to indemnity

One must carefully distinguish between the rules stated in the present article and those stated in Article 99, post. The present article is concerned only with the circumstances in which a trustee may plead concurrence or assent by way of defence to an action by the concurring or assenting beneficiary. Article 99, on the other hand, deals with the question as to the circumstances in which a trustee, who may possibly have no defence to an action for breach of trust, may yet call upon his co-trustee, or a concurring or assenting beneficiary, to indemnify him against the consequences of the breach.

Claimant party to breach of trust

The principle that a party concurring in a breach of trust cannot afterwards complain of it is well illustrated in an old case where stock was settled on a married woman for her separate use for life, with a power of appointment by will. The trustees, at the instance of the husband, sold out the stock, and paid the proceeds to him. The wife filed a bill to compel the trustees to replace the stock, and obtained a decree, under which the trustees transferred part of the stock into court, and were allowed time to re-transfer the remainder. The wife then died, having by her will appointed the stock to the husband. He then filed a bill against the trustees, claiming the stock under the appointment, and praying for the same relief as his wife might have had. It is needless to say that his claim was promptly rejected[12].

---

7 *Stafford v Stafford* (1857) 1 De G & J 193 (benefits from breach of trust accepted for 15 years).

8 *Holder v Holder* [1968] Ch 353 at 369, 394, 399 (CA) approving *Re Pauling's Settlement Trusts* [1962] 1 WLR 86 at 108. Also *Re Freeston's Charity* [1979] 1 All ER 51 at 62, CA.

9 *Bowles v Stewart* (1803) 1 Sch & Lef 209; *Earl Chesterfield v Janssen* (1751) 2 Ves Sen 125; *Stevens v Robertson* (1868) 18 LT 427; White & Tud LC 630. In *Re Pauling's Settlement Trusts* [1964] Ch 303, [1963] 3 All ER 1, CA, the Court of Appeal expressed the view that a trustee who carried out a transaction with the beneficiary's apparent consent might still be liable if the trustee knew or ought to have known that the beneficiary was acting under the undue influence of another, or might be presumed to have so acted, but that the trustee would not be liable if it could not be established that he knew or ought to have known. The Court added that the trustee's liability might still exist even if he had received no benefit from the breach of trust.

10 *Re Wrightson* [1908] 1 Ch 789.

11 *Re Wrightson* [1908] 1 Ch 789 at 800.

12 *Nail v Punter* (1832) 5 Sim 555.

Release need not be under seal

A formal release in a deed, or an express confirmation, will, of course, estop a beneficiary from instituting subsequent proceedings[13] except that a release which relates to a transaction that is void in equity, being beyond the trustees' power like a fraud on the power, is not binding on the beneficiary executing it[14]. It would seem that any positive act or expression indicative of a clear intention to waive a breach of trust will, if supported by valuable consideration (however slight), be equivalent to a release[15]. Thus, in *Ghost v Waller*[16] a marriage being in contemplation, the lady executed a settlement of real estate under which, in default of issue and in the event of her surviving the husband, she became once more absolutely entitled to the settled property. Between the date of the settlement and the marriage a breach of trust took place through the fraud of the trustees' agent; but in consideration of the trustees undertaking to assist in getting back part of the loss from the agent's estate she through her solicitor agreed (merely by letter) 'to give up all claims if she has any against her trustees for negligence'. Years afterwards, after the death of the husband without issue, she sought to sue the trustees, but it was held that she had effectually released them.

Section 10 of the Unfair Contract Terms Act 1977 does not affect releases or compromises relating to events that had already occurred so as to make such not binding because unreasonable: the Act is concerned only with prospective liabilities[17].

Release may be inferred from conduct

A release may be inferred from conduct. Thus, where a mother bequeathed property to her son and 'prohibited him from setting up any claim on account of any error, irregularity, or impropriety in the execution of the trusts' of her father's will, it was held that having accepted the bequest the son could not sue the executor of his grandfather's will for employing part of the estate in his own business[18].

Acquiescence

Even before the limitation periods now contained in s 21 of the Limitation Act 1980[19] were introduced[20], a beneficiary under a declared trust would disentitle himself to relief by acquiescence over a period. Thus, where a trustee with the knowledge, but without the consent, of the beneficiary, accepted a reduced rent from a lessee of the trust property, and the beneficiary complained of the abatement, but took no steps to put an end to it for some years, it was held that, after the expiration of the lease, the trustee could not be called upon to make up the deficiency[1]. Generally speaking, the

---

13 See *Re Montagu's Settlements* [1987] 2 WLR 1192 at 1212.
14 *Thomson v Eastwood* (1877) 2 App Cas 215 at 234 and 247, HL.
15 See *Stackhouse v Barnston* (1805) 10 Ves 453, per Sir W Grant, and *Farrant v Blanchford* (1863) 1 De GJ & Sm 107 at 119–120 per Lord Westbury LC.
16 (1846) 9 Beav 497.
17 *Tudor Grange Holdings Ltd v Citibank NA* [1992] Ch 53, [1991] 4 All ER 1.
18 *Egg v Devey* (1847) 10 Beav 444.
19 See Art 96, ante.
20 By the Trustee Act 1888.
1 *McDonnel v White* (1865) 11 HL Cas 570; and see to same effect *Fletcher v Collis* [1905] 2 Ch 24.

same result follows where, with full knowledge of a breach of trust, the beneficiaries take no steps for many years[2], but where the delay can be reasonably explained, and the trustees have not been damnified by it, it is otherwise[3].

Acquiescence by reversioner

It must not, however, be assumed that where a person entitled in reversion knows of a breach of trust, and protests, but takes no steps until he becomes entitled in possession, he thereby loses his remedy. In such cases it is apprehended that much must depend on the surrounding circumstances. For instance, where the reversioner was a young lady living with her mother, and the breach consisted in a loan by the trustees at the mother's request to her son (which the daughter objected to), it was held that seven years' delay was no evidence of acquiescence, having regard to her relationship to the mother and brother and the difficulty of taking proceedings without a family quarrel[4]. But where there were no similar circumstances a reversioner was held to be barred after fourteen years' acquiescence[5].

Acquiescence in a past breach does not constitute a licence for the trustee to commit future breaches[6].

When acquiescence is a bar

Although long acquiescence is a bar to relief, the reason for so holding is that the fact of lying by for a considerable period is evidence of an intention or election on the part of the beneficiary not to exercise his strict rights. Consequently, where the circumstances are such as to afford no ground for any such presumption, acquiescence, however long, will be no bar to relief:
(1) unless the Limitation Act 1980 is applicable[7], or
(2) unless in the circumstances it appears to be for the general convenience that a suit in respect of a long dormant grievance should be disallowed.

In the latter case the court will refuse relief on the ground that 'expedit reipublicae ut sit finis litium'. For instance, where a claimant seeks to set aside a purchase obtained from him by his solicitor, a delay of less than twenty years *may* bar the right to relief, if it would be inconvenient to grant it[8].

---

2 *Sleeman v Wilson* (1871) LR 13 Eq 36; and see also *Life Association of Scotland v Siddal* (1861) 3 De GF & J 58 at 72, 74 per Turner LJ; *Jones v Higgins* (1866) LR 2 Eq 538; *Broadhurst v Balguy* (1841) 1 Y & C Ch Cas 16; *Newham v Newham* (1822) 1 LJOS 23; *Griffiths v Porter* (1858) 25 Beav 236; *Davies v Hodgson* (1858) 25 Beav 177; *Hourigan v Trustees Executors and Agency Co Ltd* (1934) 51 CLR 619. See also *Nocton v Lord Ashburton* [1914] AC 932 at 944 and 958 in respect of the claim relating to a 1904 mortgage being barred by acquiescence.
3 See *Story v Gape* (1856) 2 Jur NS 706. See also *Re Pauling's Settlement Trusts* [1964] Ch 303, [1963] 3 All ER 1, CA, where the Court of Appeal held that a delay of four years was explicable on the ground that the case was a complicated one demanding exploration before proceedings could be instituted; *Reader v Fried* [2001] Victoria SC 495 and *Orr v Ford* (1989) 167 CLR 316.
4 *Phillipson v Gatty* (1848) 7 Hare 516. See also *Life Association of Scotland v Siddal* (1861) 3 De GF & J 58.
5 *Farrar v Barraclough* (1854) 2 Sm & G 231; and see also *Bate v Hooper* (1855) 5 De GM & G 338; *Browne v Cross* (1851) 14 Beav 105; *Farrant v Blanchford* (1863) 1 De GJ & Sm 107.
6 *Swain v Law Society* [1982] 1 WLR 17; revsd [1983] 1 AC 598, HL.
7 Consider *Re Cross* (1882) 20 Ch D 109.
8 *Gresley v Mousley* (1859) 4 De G & J 78; *Gregory v Gregory* (1815) Coop G 201. See also *Official Assignee of Collier v Creighton* [1993] 2 NZLR 534.

So where, in an action for an account, the plaintiff, by lying by, has rendered it impossible or very inconvenient for the defendant to render the account, he will get no relief[9].

Where the claim is against a constructive trustee on account of the profits of a business the remedy must in all cases be sought with reasonable celerity. As Knight Bruce LJ said in *Clegg v Edmondson*[10]:

> 'In such cases a man having an adverse claim in equity on the ground of constructive trust should pursue it promptly, and not by empty words only. He should show himself in good time willing to participate in possible loss as well as profit, not play a game in which he alone risks nothing.'

PARAGRAPH 1(A)

Minors incapable of release or acquiescence

A minor cannot lose his right to relief, either by concurrence or release, for the law presumes that he has not the requisite discretion to judge. Nor would this be in any way affected (at least it is so submitted) by the fact that he falsely represented himself to be of age, unless he thereby fraudulently caused the breach of trust of which he complains[11].

PARAGRAPH 1(B)

Full knowledge of beneficiary essential

Even a release in a deed (and a fortiori mere concurrence or subsequent acquiescence) will not avail the trustee unless the beneficiary had full knowledge. Thus a release to a trustee has been set aside after the lapse of more than twenty years, after the death of the trustee, on evidence of the claimant (corroborated by the tenor of the release) that it was executed in error, although no fraud was imputed[12].

So where, on the footing of a supposed illegitimacy, the title of a beneficiary to a trust legacy was disputed and denied by the trustee, and the former was thereby induced to accept from the trustee a smaller sum than that to which he was entitled under the will, and, by deed, to release the trustee from the payment of the legacy, the court would not permit the release to stand even after the lapse of more than 25 years[13].

Although there was some authority[14] for the view that a man is not bound by his concurrence or acquiescence unless and until he knows his legal rights

---

9 See per *Lord Alvanley in Pickering v Earl Stamford* (1793) 2 Ves 272; and see also *Tatam v Williams* (1844) 3 Hare 347 and *Nelson v Rye* [1996] 2 All ER 186.
10 (1857) 8 De GM & G 787. See *Re Jarvis* [1958] 2 All ER 336, [1958] 1 WLR 815.
11 See *Cory v Gertcken* (1816) 2 Madd 40; *Overton v Banister* (1844) 3 Hare 503; *Wright v Snowe* (1848) 2 De G & Sm 321.
12 *Re Garnett* (1885) 31 Ch D 1; and see also *Sawyer v Sawyer* (1885) 28 Ch D 595; and *Burrows v Walls* (1855) 5 De GM & G 233.
13 *Thomson v Eastwood* (1877) 2 App Cas 215, HL; and see *McDonnel v White* (1865) 11 HL Cas 570; *Dougan v Macpherson* [1902] AC 197, HL; and *National Trustees Co of Australasia v General Finance Co of Australasia* [1905] AC 373.
14 *Cockerell v Cholmeley* (1830) 1 Russ & M 418 at 425; *Willmott v Barber* (1880) 15 Ch D 96 at 105; *Farrant v Blanchford* (1863) 1 De GJ & Sm 107 at 119–120.

this is not a hard and fast rule. In *Re Pauling's Settlement Trusts*[15] Wilberforce J after considering older cases[16], said:

'The result of these authorities appears to me to be that the court has to consider all the circumstances in which the concurrence of the cestui que trust was given with a view to seeing whether it is fair and equitable that, having given his concurrence, he should afterwards turn round and sue the trustees: that, subject to this, it is not necessary that he should know that what he is concurring in is a breach of trust, provided that he fully understands what he is concurring in, and that it is not necessary that he should himself have directly benefited by the breach of trust.'

In the later case of *Holder v Holder*[17], these dicta were followed by Cross J at first instance, and expressly approved and applied by the Court of Appeal, Harman LJ stating[18]:

'There is, therefore, no hard and fast rule that ignorance of a legal right is a bar [to the trustee's defence] but the whole circumstances must be looked at to see whether it is just that the complaining beneficiary should succeed against the trustee.'

The dicta of Cross J and Harman LJ's statement were endorsed by the Court of Appeal in *Re Freeston's Charity*[19]. Another approach that the Court of Appeal[20] has adopted is that a claimant's right will be lost if 'it would be dishonest or unconscionable for the claimant to seek to enforce it'.

Where trustees wish to obtain the consent of beneficiaries of full age and capacity to activities that will profit the trustees particular care must be taken to ensure that the fully informed consent of the beneficiaries is obtained[1]. Where the trustees know that a breach of trust is involved they must so inform the beneficiaries.

Necessity of reciting actual breaches of trust in a deed of release

For these reasons a release, where intended to cover known breaches of trust, must contain recitals showing fully and precisely the circumstances under which the breach took place, including the amount of the loss (if any) and that such circumstances did in fact amount to a breach of trust. If this be not done, the general words will be controlled and restricted in their operation by the recitals to the matters actually stated[2]. Indeed, it is the duty of the trustees to see that the beneficiary, who is about to execute a release, is

15 [1962] 1 WLR 86 at 108.
16 *Walker v Symonds* (1818) 3 Swan 1; *Evans v Benyon* (1887) 37 Ch D 329; *Re Garnett* (1884) 50 LT 172; on appeal (1885) 31 Ch D 1, CA; *Re Somerset* [1894] 1 Ch 231; *Chillingworth v Chambers* [1896] 1 Ch 685, CA.
17 [1966] 2 All ER 116, [1966] 3 WLR 229; on appeal [1968] Ch 353, [1968]1 All ER 665, CA.
18 [1968] Ch 353 at 394, CA. Also *Goldsworthy v Brickell* [1987] 1 All ER 853 at 873, CA
19 [1979] 1 All ER 51 at 62, [1978] 1 WLR 741 at 754–755, CA.
20 *Shaw v Applegate* [1978] 1 All ER 123 at 131, [1977] 1 WLR 970 at 978, CA; *Swain v Law Society* [1981] 3 All ER 797 at 810, CA (where the defence of acquiescence succeeded for the solicitors' indemnity insurance commission paid to the Law Society prior to 1979 but not thereafter, but in the Lords [1983] 1 AC 598, [1982] 2 All ER 827, p 387 ante, the point did not arise). Further see *Knight v Frost* [1999] 1 BCLC 364 where acquiescence in a breach of fiduciary duty by a director was not established in respect of a £300,000 loan but was established in respect of a subsequent £75,000 loan though disputed by J Payne in Chapter 10 'Consent' in Birks & Pretto *Breach of Trust* (Hart Publishing, 2002).
1 *Phipps v Boardman* [1964] 2 All ER 187 at 204–205, 207. The point was not pressed in the appeals.
2 *Lindo v Lindo* (1839) 8 LJ Ch 284; *Ramsden v Hylton* (1751) 2 Ves Sen 304; *Pritt v Clay* (1843) 6 Beav 503.

properly advised as to his rights[3]. Where the trustees rely on the beneficiary having been separately advised, so as to oust a finding of undue influence, they must *prove* that he did in point of fact employ a separate solicitor, and not merely someone nominated by the trustees or their solicitor[4].

Ignorance of beneficiary where he has had the advantage of the breach

It seems that where a beneficiary has, for valuable consideration (eg marriage), had the advantage of a breach of trust, but without any knowledge of the breach, he can sue the trustee without replacing the amount which he himself has received by reason of the breach. Thus, where part of the proceeds of trust funds misappropriated by a father were made subject to the marriage settlement of his son (a beneficiary in remainder who was ignorant of the source whence the property proceeded, and thought it was a gift from his father), it was held that the son's representatives were entitled to have his share of the trust funds replaced without deducting the value of the proceeds settled[5].

PARAGRAPH 1(c)

A release made by a beneficiary who has just attained his majority will be subject to considerable scrutiny in case it was obtained by undue influence. Thus in *Wade v Cox*[6] a release executed by a twenty-three year old man in favour of his trustee was set aside eighteen years afterwards.

Similarly where beneficiaries aged between twenty-one and twenty-seven years consented to breaches of trust for the benefit of their parents the Court of Appeal held that 'a trustee carrying out a transaction in breach of trust may be liable if he knew, or ought to have known, that the beneficiary was acting under the undue influence of another, or may be presumed to have done so, but will not be liable if it cannot be established that he knew or ought to have known'[7]. When a young adult may be presumed to be fully emancipated from parental influence is a question of fact in all the circumstances of a particular case[8].

---

3 This point, and the extent of the solicitor's duty to advise, were considered in *Re Pauling's Settlement Trusts* [1964] Ch 303, [1963] 3 All ER 1, CA.
4 *Lloyd v Attwood* (1859) 3 De G & J 614.
5 *Crichton v Crichton* [1896] 1 Ch 870, reversing decision of North J [1895] 2 Ch 853; *Re Pauling's Settlement Trusts* [1964] Ch 303 at 354, 357–358 (Anthony, an innocent volunteer, did not have to account for benefits indirectly received through his mother, but Ann conceded that £300 spent directly for her benefit on furniture had to be brought into account).
6 (1835) 4 LJ Ch 105. However, times have changed so that 18 years is now the age of majority and persons normally become independent minded by the time they reach 23 years.
7 *Re Pauling's Settlement Trusts* [1964] Ch 303 at 338.
8 See *Bullock v Lloyds Bank Ltd* [1955] Ch 317 where a settlement created one month after attaining majority was set aside for undue influence, despite some lengthy but explicable delay.

ARTICLE 98

Protection against the acts of co-trustee

(1) A trustee is not vicariously answerable for the receipts, acts, or defaults of his co-trustee[9], but only for his *own* acts or defaults such as:
(a) where he *hands* the trust property to his co-trustee without seeing to its proper application[10];
(b) where he allows his co-trustee to *receive* the trust property without making due inquiry as to his dealing with it[11];
(c) where he becomes aware of a breach of trust, either committed or meditated, and abstains from taking the needful steps to obtain restitution and redress, or to prevent the meditated wrong[12].
(2) Even in the above three cases the trustee may be relieved from responsibility by express declaration in the trust deed.

Position apart from statute

In the leading case of *Wilkins v Hogg*[13] a testatrix, after appointing three trustees, declared that each of them should be answerable only for losses arising from his own default, and not for involuntary acts or for the acts or defaults of his co-trustees; and, particularly, that any trustee who should pay over to his co-trustees, or should do or concur in any act enabling his co-trustees to receive any moneys for the general purposes of her will, should not be obliged to see to the due application thereof, nor should such trustee be subsequently rendered liable by any express notice or intimation of the actual misapplication of the same moneys. The three trustees joined in signing and giving receipts to insurance companies for sums of money paid by them, but two of the trustees permitted their co-trustee to obtain the money without ascertaining whether he had invested it. This trustee having misapplied it, it was sought to make his co-trustees responsible, but Lord Westbury held that they were not, saying:

'There are three modes in which a trustee would become liable *according to the ordinary rules of law*—first, where, being the recipient, he hands over the money without securing its due application; secondly, where he allows a co-trustee to receive money without making due inquiry as to his dealing with it; and thirdly, where he becomes aware of a breach of trust, either committed or meditated, and abstains from taking the needful steps to obtain restitution or redress. The framer of the clause under examination knew these three rules, and used words sufficient to meet all these cases. There remained, therefore, only personal misconduct, in respect of which a trustee acting under this will would be responsible. He would still be answerable for collusion if he handed over trust money to his co-trustee with

---

9 Trustee Act 1925, s 30 before its repeal by the Trustee Act 2000; *Dawson v Clarke* (1811) 18 Ves 247; and see *Welch v Bank of England* [1955] Ch 508, [1955] 1 All ER 811.
10 *Walker v Symonds* (1818) 3 Swan 1; and *Bone v Cooke* (1824) 13 Price 332. The case of *Re Fryer* (1857) 3 K & J 317, merely turned upon a question of procedure, wilful default not having been pleaded.
11 See *Wynne v Tempest* (1897) 13 TLR 360; *Bradwell v Catchpole* (1700) 3 Swan 78n; *Marriott v Kinnersley* (1830) Taml 470.
12 *Millar's Trustees v Polson* (1897) 34 SLR 798.
13 (1861) 31 LJ Ch 41; and see *Pass v Dundas* (1880) 43 LT 665; *Dix v Burford* (1854) 19 Beav 409; *Mucklow v Fuller* (1821) Jac 198; *Brumridge v Brumridge* (1858) 27 Beav 5.

reasonable ground for believing or suspecting that that trustee would commit a breach of trust; but no such case as this was made by the bill.'

However, an exculpatory clause cannot protect a trustee who commits a breach of trust dishonestly (which includes reckless indifference to the beneficiaries' interests) or honestly if no reasonable trustee in his shoes could have honestly done what he did[14].

Commonly, a trustee is liable for the acts of a co-trustee where he is a passive trustee who allows his co-trustee to exercise alone discretions which it is their duty to exercise jointly so that he himself is at fault. However, where trustees who are majority shareholders in a company have one trustee representing them on the board of the company then:

'one ought not to regard him as performing a duty to the trust which it was incumbent on the trustees to perform personally so that [the trustees] become automatically responsible for any deficiencies in [him], as does a passive trustee who allows his co-trustee to exercise alone discretions which it is their duty to exercise jointly. If these trustees had decided as they might have done, to be represented on the board by a nominee they would have been entitled to rely upon the information given to them by that nominee as to the way in which the company's affairs were being managed even though such information was inaccurate or inadequate, *unless they* had some reason to suspect that it was inaccurate or inadequate.'[15]

Statutory indemnity 1859 to 2000

By s 30(1) of the Trustee Act 1925[16] it was provided as follows:

A trustee shall be chargeable only for moneys and securities actually received by him notwithstanding his signing any receipt for the sake of conformity, and shall be answerable and accountable only for his own acts, receipts, neglects, or defaults, and not for those of any other trustee, nor for any banker, broker, or other person with whom any trust money or securities may be deposited, nor for the insufficiency or deficiency of any securities, nor for any other loss[17], unless the same happens through his own wilful default.

This section replaced s 24(1) of the Trustee Act 1893 which replaced s 31 of the Law of Property (Amendment) Act 1859 which 'incorporated, into instruments creating trusts the common indemnity clause which was usually inserted in such instruments. It does not substantially alter the law as it was administered by courts of equity'[18] which construed such express indemnity clauses very strictly against trustees attempting to rely upon them. Thus 'wilful default' was construed as including 'want of ordinary prudence'[19] though in *Re Vickery*[20] Maugham J, somewhat surprisingly relying on company law cases, treated 'wilful default' as meaning only a consciousness of committing a breach of duty or a recklessness as to whether or not a breach was being committed.

---

14 *Armitage v Nurse* [1998] Ch 241, CA; *Walker v Stones* [2001] QB 902, CA.
15 *Re Lucking's Will Trusts* [1967] 3 All ER 726 at 733.
16 See *Re Munton* [1927] 1 Ch 262, CA, and *Re Windsor Steam Coal Co* (1901) Ltd [1929] 1 Ch 151; per Maugham J in *Re Vickery* [1931] 1 Ch 572 at 580.
17 Of a similar sort: *Re Vickery* [1931] 1 Ch 572 at 582.
18 *Re Brier* (1884) 26 Ch D 238 at 243, per Lord Selborne.
19 *Re Chapman* [1896] 2 Ch 763 at 776, per Lindley LJ; *Underwood v Stevens* (1816) 1 Mer 712.
20 [1931] 1 Ch 572.

Then, in *Armitage v Nurse*[1] the Court of Appeal endorsed this, before the Trustee Act 2000 repealed s 30, having made express provision concerning trustee's liabilities for agents, nominees or custodians that they employ, but leaving the question of the liability for the conduct of a co-trustee to the general law treating trusteeship as a joint office[2] and the provisions of particular trust instruments.

Post Trustee Act 2000

Repeal of the earlier statutory provision has two significant consequences. In cases formerly within s 30 a trustee is no longer protected unless guilty of 'wilful default', so that the presence or absence of an exemption clause in the trust instrument becomes crucial, while he also loses the protection of the onus of proof falling upon the beneficiary-claimants[3].

The burden of proving that he acted properly in fulfilling the functions of his joint office falls back upon him[4]. Otherwise, it is not believed that the repeal will make much difference, the earlier statutory provisions having been declaratory of the position in equity. Joining in receipts for the sake of conformity and permitting a co-trustee to receive money in the first instance will be safe behaviour, but money must not be allowed to be retained by the co-trustee for longer than reasonably necessary[5], while if the co-trustee says that the money has been duly invested this needs to be checked[6]. The safest course is for money to be paid into a joint bank account of the trustees.

ARTICLE 99

Trustees generally entitled to contribution inter se, but may be entitled to be indemnified by co-trustee or beneficiary who instigated breach

(1) As a general rule, where several trustees have been held jointly and severally liable for a breach of trust not amounting to actual dishonesty[7], those who are obliged to pay will be entitled to exact contribution from the others[8], notwithstanding that the former may be more blameworthy, or that the loss caused by the breach only occurred after the death or retirement of the trustee from whom contribution is sought[9]. This is subject to provisos that an indemnity

1 [1998] Ch 241, CA, but no detailed consideration was given to substantial criticisms of *Re Vickery's* interpretation of 'wilful default' eg by G H Jones (1959) 22 MLR 381; J E Stannard [1979] Conv 345 and 15th edn hereof pp 623–624.
2 See Article 56 ante.
3 *Re Brier* (1884) 26 Ch D 238, CA.
4 *Brice v Stokes* (1805) 11 Ves 319.
5 *Brice v Stokes* (1805) 11 Ves 319; *Lewis v Nobbs* (1878) 8 Ch D 591; *Wynne v Tempest* (1897) 13 TLR 360.
6 *Mendes v Guedalla* (1862) 2 John & H 259; *Thompson v Finch* (1856) 22 Beav 316.
7 *A-G v Wilson* (1840) Cr & Ph 1 at 28; see *Lingard v Bromley* (1812) 1 Ves & B 114; *Tarleton v Hornby* (1835) 1 Y & C Ex 333. It seems very likely that the Law Reform (Married Women and Tortfeasors) Act 1935 did not alter the position: (1948) 64 LQR 46 at 47 (P H Winfield).
8 *Lingard v Bromley* (1812) 1 Ves & B 114; *Birks v Micklethwaite* (1864) 33 Beav 409; *A-G v Daugars* (1864) 33 Beav 621. This claim to contribution is a specialty debt: Mercantile Law Amendment Act 1856, s 5.
9 *Jackson v Dickinson* [1903] 1 Ch 947; *Canada Safeway Ltd v Thompson* [1952] 2 DLR 591.

against loss may be available in the following circumstances:

(a) where one of the trustees who was guilty of the breach is, or subsequently becomes[10], a beneficiary, he will in general be unable to claim contribution from his co-trustees until he has made good to the trust estate any loss sustained up to the extent of his own beneficial interest[11]; and

(b) where one of several trustees has been guilty of dishonesty, or has been a professional person on whom his co-trustees reasonably relied, he may have to indemnify them and to bear the *whole loss* himself[12];

(c) if one of two trustees is, exceptionally, relieved from liability under section 61 of the Trustee Act then the other trustee will have to bear the whole loss himself[13].

(2) The above rule gives no right of contribution to a trustee who alone committed a breach of trust, against a new trustee (even a beneficiary) subsequently appointed, notwithstanding that if the latter had insisted upon the matter being put right on his appointment, no loss would have occurred.

(3) Where a trustee commits a breach of trust at the instigation or request[14], or with the consent in writing, of a beneficiary, the court may make such order as it deems just, for impounding all or any part of the beneficiary's interest in the trust property by way of indemnity to the trustee or persons claiming through him[15].

(4) Such contribution or indemnity may be ordered in the action in which the liability for breach of trust is established without any counter-claim[16].

PARAGRAPH 1

Contribution between trustees

In one case A, one of the trustees of a settlement, allowed his co-trustee B to have the trust fund to invest. B handed it to an 'outside broker', who misappropriated parts of it. It was held that both trustees were in pari delicto (equally blameworthy), and that B was, therefore, entitled to contribution from A, although he had taken a more active part in the transaction which led to the loss; and that, for the purpose of barring an action between the trustees, the limitation period did not begin to run until the judgment

---

10 *Evans v Benyon* (1887) 37 Ch D 329.

11 *Chillingworth v Chambers* [1896] 1 Ch 685.

12 *Bahin v Hughes* (1886) 31 Ch D 390; *Blyth v Fladgate* [1891] 1 Ch 337 at 365; *Fetherstone v West* (1871) IR 6 Eq 86; *Lockhart v Reilly* (1856) 25 LJ Ch 697; *Thompson v Finch* (1856) 22 Beav 316; and see *Butler v Butler* (1877) 7 Ch D 116; *Wynne v Tempest* [1897] 1 Ch 110.

13 *Wohlleben v Canada Permanent Trust Co* (1977) 70 DLR (3d) 257.

14 The request need not be in writing, although a mere consent must be: per Kekewich J in *Griffith v Hughes* [1892] 3 Ch 105 at 109; and per Lindley LJ in *Re Somerset* [1894] 1 Ch 231 at 266.

15 Trustee Act 1925, s 62. In *Re Pauling's Settlement Trusts (No 2)* [1963] Ch 576, [1963] 1 All ER 857, Wilberforce J said that a trustee's rights to impound, under s62 and in equity, did not depend upon his being still a trustee at the date of the impounding order.

16 *Priestman v Tindall* (1857) 24 Beav 244; *Re Holt* [1897] 2 Ch 525.

declaring them liable for breach of trust[17].

So where a large balance was found to be due jointly from a trustee and the representatives of a deceased co-trustee[18], but costs were given to both out of the trust estate, it was held (the estate of the deceased co-trustee being insolvent, and therefore unable to contribute) that the surviving trustee, upon paying the whole of the loss, was entitled to a lien for half of it on the costs awarded to the representatives of his deceased co-trustee[19].

Civil Liability (Contribution) Act 1978

This Act came into force on 1 January 1979[20]. It repeals s 6 of the Law Reform (Married Women and Tortfeasors) Act 1935 and provides for a general right of contribution. This right supersedes any other right of contribution[1] (not being an express contractual right) but nothing in the 1978 Act affects any right to an indemnity[2]. The Act does not apply where the damage in question occurred before 1979[3] and a person is not to be entitled to recover contribution or be liable to make contribution 'by reference to any liability based on breach of any obligation assumed by him' before 1979[4]. These words are entirely apt to describe the consensual acceptance of obligations under a contract or of obligations as trustee[5]. Thus persons appointed trustees before 1979 should not be affected so far as concerns breaches of trust claims by beneficiaries.

By s 1(1) any person liable in respect of any damage suffered by another person may recover contribution from any other person liable *in respect of the same damage* even if that other person has reached a bona fide settlement with the plaintiff[6].

Under s 6(1) a person is liable in respect of any damage if the person who suffered it is entitled to recover compensation from him in respect of that damage (whatever the legal basis of his liability, whether tort, breach of contract, breach of trust or otherwise). Damage means harm or loss, and not damages[7]. One must ask[8] (1) What damage has A suffered? (2) Is B liable to A in respect of that damage? (3) Is C also liable to A in respect of that damage

---

17 *Robinson v Harkin* [1896] 2 Ch 415; Limitation Act 1980, s 10.

18 It need scarcely be pointed out that the representatives of a deceased trustee are not liable for a breach of trust committed after his death, where he has left the trust fund in a proper state of investment (*Re Palk* (1892) 41 WR 28). Of course they may be liable where he has not so left it (*Gibbins v Taylor* (1856) 22 Beav 344).

19 *Fletcher v Green* (1864) 33 Beav 426; and see also *Collings v Wade* [1903] 1 IR 89, where the insolvent trustee subsequently died a rich man.

20 Section 10(2). Once B and C are each persons against whom liability had been, or could be, established in an action brought against them by A in an English court (applying the appropriate law in accordance with English private international law rules) then the Act confers on B a right of contribution against C: *Arab Monetary Fund v Hashim (No 9)* (1994) Times, 11 October; *Lister & Co v E G Thomson Ltd* [1987] 3 All ER 1032 at 1038. Also see *Petroleo Brasiliero SA v Mellitus Shipping Inc* [2001] 2 Lloyd's Rep 203.

1 Section 7(3).

2 Section 7(3).

3 Section 7(1).

4 Section 7(2).

5 *Lampitt v Poole Borough Council* [1990] 2 All ER 887 at 892, CA.

6 *Logan v Uttlesford District Council and Hammond* [1986] NLJ Rep 541.

7 *Birse Construction Ltd v Haistie Ltd* [1996] 2 All ER 1 at 8 per Rock LJ endorsed in *Royal Brompton Hospital NHS Trust v Hammond* [2002] UKHL 14, [2002] 2 All ER 801, at paras 6 and 27.

8 *Royal Brompton Hospital NHS Trust v Hammond* [2002] UKHL 14, [2002] 2 All ER 801 at para 6.

or some of it? One loss thus needs to be apportioned between those liable eg the trustees and a person dishonestly assisting the trustees in their breach of trust[9] and a recipient of trusts assets, it would seem[10], if trustees wrongly transfer money or other assets to an innocent recipient who uses the money or the proceeds of sale of the assets to discharge an earlier debt so as to enrich himself at the beneficiaries' expense and become liable to repay the money.

In any proceedings for contribution made under s 1 the amount of the contribution recoverable from any person is to be 'such as may be found by the court to be just and equitable having regard to the extent of that person's responsibility for the damage in question'[11]. However, the court has power in any such proceedings to exempt any person from liability to make contribution or to direct that the contribution to be recovered from any person is to amount to a complete indemnity[12].

How the courts will operate the Act in respect of trustees remains to be seen. Certainly, the courts can be more flexible in their treatment of trustees who have varying degrees of responsibility for a breach of trust. It is submitted, however, that it should be a very exceptional case where unequal treatment is accorded to trustees (except in indemnity cases, eg where a vulnerable passive lay trustee may be protected) since the sanction of equal liability serves a useful salutary function for breach of what is a joint obligation par excellence[13]. Moreover, trustees undertake an active joint obligation: this should not be undermined by encouraging hopes that passivity might help a trustee reduce the extent of his liability. By sitting back and leaving everything to a co-trustee, a trustee fundamentally breaks his duty of fidelity and loyalty and cannot be heard to deny that the breach would not have occurred but for him doing the opposite of what he had positively undertaken to do. This strict prophylactic approach of Equity should not be lost sight of when applying a statute passed primarily to deal with contractual and tortious claims, but which introduces useful flexibility in breach of trust cases where dishonest accessories are involved, so that a dishonest trustee or fiduciary who orchestrates a scheme using dishonest accessories can be made to bear say 87.5% of the burden and the dishonest accessory 12.5%[14].

No action to recover contribution under the 1978 Act can be brought after the expiration of two years from the date of judgment or award of damages against the person seeking contribution or, otherwise, the date such person agreed to make a payment in satisfaction of his liability[15].

---

9 *Dubai Aluminium Co Ltd v Salaam* [1999] 1 Lloyd's Rep 415; *Arab Monetary Fund v Hashim (No 9)* (1994) Times, 11 October.

10 *Friends' Provident Life Office v Hillier Parker May & Rowden* [1997] QB 85, CA, accepted by HL in *Royal Brompton Hospital NHS Trust v Hammond* [2002] UKHL 14, [2002] 2 All ER 801, though certain dicta disapproved.

11 Civil Liability (Contribution) Act 1978, s 2(1).

12 Civil Liability (Contribution) Act 1978, s 2(2).

13 See *Bahin v Hughes* (1886) 31 Ch D 390, CA for emphasis on culpability of inactive trustee. Where the trustees are authorised to act by a majority then the dissenting minority if not protected, as usual, by a clause in the trust instrument, will need to seek the directions of the court (at the expense of the trust fund) if they believe the majority may be committing a breach of trust.

14 *Arab Monetary Fund v Hashim (No 9)* (1994) Times, 11 October; also see *Dubai Aluminium Co Ltd v Salaam* [1999] 1 Lloyd's Rep 415 discussed by C. Mitchell in Birks & Rose *Restitution and Equity Vol 1 Resulting Trusts and Equitable Compensation* (Mansfield Press, 2000), Chapter 12 'Apportioning Liability for Trust Losses'.

15 Limitation Act 1980, s 10.

PARAGRAPH 1(A)

Trustee-beneficiary generally bound to indemnify co-trustee to extent of his beneficial interest

This sub-paragraph is well illustrated by the case of *Chillingworth v Chambers*[16], where the whole of the authorities were elaborately discussed by the Court of Appeal. The plaintiff and defendant, the trustees of a will, had committed breaches of trust by investing on insufficient securities, bearing a high rate of interest, and were declared to be jointly and severally liable to make good the loss to the trust estate. The plaintiff trustee, after some and before others of the investments in question had been made, became also beneficially entitled to a share in the trust estate, as the successor in title of his deceased wife. He claimed to be entitled to contribution from the defendant trustee on the ground that they were both in pari delicto.

The court, however, rejected this claim, on the ground that the rule as to the right of a trustee to contribution from his co-trustee for loss occasioned to the estate by a breach of trust for which both are equally to blame, does not apply where one of them is also a beneficiary, until he has made good any loss sustained to the extent of his own beneficial share in the property. In that case, the rule to be applied is that under which the *share or interest* of a trustee-beneficiary who has assented to a breach of trust has to bear the whole loss; and the trustee who is a beneficiary must therefore indemnify his co-trustee to the extent of his share or interest in the trust estate, and not merely to the extent of the benefit he has received. Lindley MR, in giving judgment, made the following important observations:

> 'The plaintiff and the defendant being in pari delicto, the plaintiff's right as trustee to contribution from the defendant as co-trustee to the extent of one-half the loss is established by a long series of authorities, of which it is only necessary to mention *Lingard v Bromley*[17] and *Bahin v Hughes*[18]. On the other hand, the right of the defendant as trustee to be indemnified out of the share of the plaintiff as cestui que trust against the consequences of a breach of trust committed at his request and for his benefit is equally indisputable. It was treated by Lord Eldon as clear law in his day that a cestui que trust who concurs in a breach of trust is not entitled to relief against his co-trustees in respect of it: see *Walker v Symonds*[19]. ... Lord Eldon's statement of the law was distinctly approved and followed in *Farrant v Blanchford*[20]. Moreover ... it was decided, in *Evans v Benyon*[1], that this doctrine applies to a person who becomes a cestui que trust after his concurrence. Further, in *Butler v Carter*[2], Lord Romilly stated distinctly that where one of two trustees was himself a cestui que trust he could not call upon his co-trustee to replace stock which they had both permitted to be misapplied. These cases are all based on obvious good sense; for if I request a person to deal with my property in a particular way, and loss ensues, I cannot justly throw that loss on him. Whatever our liabilities may be to other people, still, as between him and me, the loss clearly ought to fall on me. Whether I am solely entitled to the property, or have only a share or a limited

---

16 [1896] 1 Ch 685. See also *Moxham v Grant* [1900] 1 QB 88 (where directors of a company were held entitled to indemnity from shareholders who had been paid capital ultra vires) and *MacDonald v Hauer* (1976) 72 DLR (3d) 110.
17 (1812) 1 Ves & B 114.
18 (1886) 31 Ch D 390.
19 (1818) 3 Swan 1 at 64.
20 (1863) 1 De GJ & Sm 107.
 1 (1887) 37 Ch D 329.
 2 (1868) LR 5 Eq 276 at 281.

interest, still the loss which I sustain in respect of my share or interest must clearly be borne by me, not by him. . . . The plaintiff contended, on the authority of *Raby v Ridehalgh*[3], that the plaintiff's liability as cestui que trust to indemnify the defendant, and the extent of the plaintiff's inability to obtain relief against the defendant, was limited, not by the amount of the plaintiff's share in the trust estate, *but by the benefit derived by the plaintiff from the breach of trust.*'

His Lordship then showed that that case was no authority for such a proposition, and continued:

'Suppose a cestui que trust in remainder to induce his trustees to commit a breach of trust for the benefit of the tenant for life—perhaps his own father or mother—can such a remainderman compel the trustees to make good the loss or resist their claim to have it made good out of his interest when it falls in, if some other cestui que trust compels them to make the loss good? *I apprehend not; and yet, in the case supposed, the cestui que trust in remainder might not himself have derived any benefit at all from the breach.*'

Kay LJ in the same case does not seem to have been willing to commit himself to the extent of the words above italicised[4]; but decided that, as in that case, the plaintiff *had* received some benefit from the breach, he was primarily liable not merely to the extent of that benefit, but to the extent of his whole share.

PARAGRAPH 1(B)

Cases in which one trustee is bound to indemnify his less guilty co-trustees

In *Bahin v Hughes*[5], Cotton LJ said:

'On going into the authorities, there are very few cases in which one trustee, who has been guilty with a co-trustee of breach of trust and held answerable, has successfully sought indemnity as against his co-trustee. *Lockhart v Reilly*[6] and *Thompson v Finch*[7] are the only cases which appear to be reported. Now in *Lockhart v Reilly* it appears from the report of the case in the Law Journal that the trustee by whom the loss was sustained had been not only trustee, but had been and was a solicitor, and acting as solicitor for himself and his co-trustee, and it was on his advice that Lockhart had relied in making the investment which gave rise to the action of the cestui que trust[8]. . . . Of course where one trustee has got the money into his own hands, and made use of it, he will be liable to his co-trustee to give him an indemnity[9]. Now I think it wrong to lay down any limitation of the circumstances under which one trustee would be held liable to the other for indemnity, both having been held liable to the cestui que trust; but so far as cases have gone at present, relief has only been granted against a trustee *who has himself got the benefit of the breach of trust, or between whom and his co-trustees there has existed a relation, which will justify the court in treating him as solely liable for the breach of trust.*'

These italicised dicta may be invoked not just against a trustee who is a

---

3 (1855) 7 De GM & G 104.
4 *Chillingworth v Chambers* [1896] 1 Ch 685 at 707.
5 (1886) 31 Ch D 390 at 394; and see also *Robinson v Harkin* [1896] 2 Ch 415.
6 (1856) 25 LJ Ch 697.
7 (1856) 22 Beav 316; but see also *Warwick v Richardson* (1842) 10 M & W 284.
8 See also to same effect *Re Turner* [1897] 1 Ch 536; and *Re Linsley* [1904] 2 Ch 785, where Warrington J made a solicitor-trustee indemnify his co-trustee against costs, merely because he was negligent in furnishing accounts to the beneficiaries.
9 See *Fetherstone v West* (1871) IR 6 Eq 86.

solicitor but also against a trustee who is a Chancery barrister or a bank manager or a professional trustee. An 'innocent' non-professional trustee misled by the advice of such a co-trustee might alternatively be able to claim relief under s 61 of the Trustee Act 1925.

Solicitor-trustee not necessarily liable to indemnify co-trustee

It must not, however, be assumed from the above citation that a solicitor-trustee who advises the commission of a breach of trust is necessarily bound to indemnify his co-trustees; for where the co-trustee has himself been an active participator in the breach of trust, and has not participated in it merely in consequence of the advice and control of the solicitor, he will have no right to be indemnified. Thus, where a lady trustee joined in the importunities of her brother, and thus induced her co-trustee (a solicitor) to commit a breach of trust for the brother's benefit, it was held that she was not entitled to call upon the solicitor-trustee for an indemnity[10].

Professional trustee and lay trustee

In *Re Mulligan*[11] the lay trustee who was life tenant, and the trust corporation co-trustee were held jointly and severally liable to beneficiaries on the death of the life tenant, who suffered losses from the trust money on sale of a farm being invested solely in fixed interest securities for many years. The life tenant's personal representatives claimed an indemnity from the trust corporation, which itself claimed an indemnity from them on the basis the life tenant had alone benefited from the breach of trust designed to favour her over the remainderman interested in capital growth investments protecting against inflation. Surprisingly the judge found that her subjective intent to benefit herself at the expense of the remainderman was not of itself sufficient when it so happened that, objectively, her strategy had been mistaken, because a mix of fixed-interest and share investments would have enabled her to enjoy a higher income than the one actually received. On the other hand, despite her vociferousness the trust corporation as such should not have meekly acquiesced in her selfish policy[12], so one can appreciate a reluctance to permit it to be indemnified out of her estate. Her estate's claim to be indemnified by the trust corporation was rejected because she herself was a person of some business acumen whose overriding of the advice of her co-trustee was not the product of her ignorance or vulnerability. A draw was thus a fair result.

Trustee benefiting incidentally by breach not always liable to indemnify co-trustee

Although, as stated by Cotton LJ in *Bahin v Hughes*[13], a trustee who has got the trust money into his own hands and made use of it, will in general be liable to

---

10 *Head v Gould* [1898] 2 Ch 250. See also *Ward-Smith v Jebb* (1964) 108 Sol Jo 919; p 918, ante, where the question of indemnity by a solicitor-trustee who had wrongly interpreted a statute was raised but not decided.
11 [1998] 1 NZLR 481 (at 511 in particular).
12 It should have applied to the court for directions which the life tenant-trustee would have to comply with or be replaced as trustee.
13 (1886) 31 Ch D 390.

indemnify his co-trustee, yet he will not have to do so where his breach of trust is only remotely connected with the loss; unless, of course, he was guilty of actual fraud. Thus the fact of a borrower of trust funds on insufficient security repaying out of the money so borrowed a debt due from him to one of the trustees is not, of itself, sufficient to render the trustee accepting repayment liable, since the borrower is under no restriction as to its application[14].

Paragraph 2

Liability of trustee-beneficiary confined to breaches of trust to which he was privy

The primary liability of a trustee-beneficiary for a breach of trust is confined to breaches committed with his privity, and does not extend to the case where his only breach consists in failing to take steps to put the original breach right when he subsequently becomes a trustee, even although, if he had done so, it is probable that no loss would have been suffered. In such a case the trustee who committed the original breach and the beneficiary subsequently appointed to be a trustee who merely failed in his duty of not insisting on the breach being set right are not in pari delicto. Both may be liable to the other beneficiaries, but the original breach is the fons et origo mali, and the original trustee who alone committed it is primarily responsible as between himself and the trustee subsequently appointed. This was decided by Warrington J in *Re Fountaine*[15] (in which the late Sir Arthur Underhill was counsel), but the case is reported only on other points which were appealed.

It would seem that the Civil Liability (Contribution) Act 1978 would not apply as between the original trustee and the new trustee, on the basis that the damage or harm first caused by the original trustee is different from the damage or harm caused by the new trustee[16].

Paragraph 3

Breaches of trust committed at the instigation, or request, or with consent of beneficiaries

Paragraph 3 of the present Article is based on s 62 of the Trustee Act 1925[17]. As Wilberforce J (as he then was) said in *Re Pauling's Settlement Trusts (No 2)*[18] 'the statutory right is extending the equitable right and not limiting it'. To invoke the equitable jurisdiction to impound it had previously been necessary in the cases of instigation or request to prove a motive of personal

---

14 *Chillingworth v Chambers* [1896] 1 Ch 685; *Butler v Butler* (1877) 7 Ch D 116; and see also *Whitney v Smith* (1869) 4 Ch App 513.
15 [1909] 2 Ch 382.
16 *Royal Brompton Hospital NHS Trust v Hammond* [2002] UKHL 14, [2002] 2 All ER 801.
17 It replaces the Trustee Act 1893, s 45, which replaced Trustee Act 1888, s 6. With regard to the procedure where the plaintiff is an innocent beneficiary and the trustee desires to claim indemnity against another beneficiary, see *Re Holt* [1897] 2 Ch 525; *Molyneux v Fletcher* [1898] 1 QB 648 at 656.
18 [1963] Ch 576 at 584.

benefit on the part of the beneficiary[19] and in the case of consent or concurrence to prove personal benefit actually obtained by the beneficiary[20]. This is no longer the case, though the factors of motive and benefit will no doubt influence the court in exercising its discretion. Both under s 62 and in equity a trustee's right to impound does not depend upon him still being a trustee at the date of the impounding order[1].

To render beneficiary liable to indemnify trustee, he must have known all the facts amounting to a breach of trust

To make a beneficiary liable under s 62 of the Act of 1925, he or she must not only have instigated or requested or consented in writing to the breach, but must also have known all the facts which would render what was done a breach of trust, without necessarily appreciating that these facts amounted in law to a breach of trust. Thus, where a tenant for life undeniably requested trustees to invest the trust fund on a certain security, but it did not appear that he intended to be a party to a breach of trust, and in effect he left it to the trustees to determine whether the security was a proper one for the sum to be advanced, it was held that the trustees could not impound his life interest to make good the breach[2] but if the tenant for life had been proved to have *knowingly requested a breach of trust*, the decision would have been otherwise[3]. Subsequently, it has been held that, quite apart from the statute, a tenant for life who consents to the trustee handing over the capital to his (the life tenant's) wife, cannot, and neither can his trustee in bankruptcy, deny the right of the trustee who has had to replace the capital, to impound the income by way of indemnity during the life of the life tenant; and this notwithstanding that the consent was not in writing[4]. The justification for this is that the life tenant is debarred from suing for breach of trust since he consented to it[5].

No right to impound in order to make good the trustee's beneficial interest

The right of a trustee to impound the interest of beneficiaries who have instigated a breach is, however, only applicable for the purpose of indemnifying him against the claims of other beneficiaries. It does not enable him to obtain an indemnity against other losses. Thus, where a trustee subsequently became entitled to share in the trust fund as one of the next of kin of

19 *Raby v Ridehalgh* (1855) 7 De GM & G 104; *Hanchett v Briscoe* (1856) 22 Beav 496.
20 *Cocker v Quayle* (1830) 1 Russ & M 535 at 538; *Booth v Booth* (1838) 1 Beav 125; *Williams v Allen (No 2)* (1863) 32 Beav 650; *Blyth v Fladgate* [1891] 1 Ch 337 at 363.
1 *Re Pauling's Settlement Trusts (No 2)* [1963] Ch 576.
2 *Re Somerset* [1894] 1 Ch 231; *Mara v Browne* [1895] 2 Ch 69. Also see impounding of life tenant's interest in *Jaffrey v Marshall* [1994] 1 All ER 143 at 154 (though the decision was overruled on liability by *Target Holdings Ltd v Redferns* [1996] AC 421, HL).
3 *Raby v Ridehalgh* (1855) 7 De GM & G 104; *Bolton v Curre* [1895] 1 Ch 544.
4 *Fletcher v Collis* [1905] 2 Ch 24; and see for other instances of income being impounded to make good mistakes, *Re Ainsworth* [1915] 2 Ch 96; *Re Robinson* [1911] 1 Ch 502; *Re Reading* [1916] WN 262 (in which the judgment of Warrington J in *Re Horne* [1905] 1 Ch 76, was said not to be of general application); *Re Musgrave* [1916] 2 Ch 417 (income-tax, omitted to be deducted under testamentary trust to pay annuity 'without deduction', where such words do not cover income tax, recoverable out of future annuity payments, and *Re Horne* (supra) restrictively interpreted) and see *Re Gordon's Settlement* [1924] 1 Ch 146.
5 See Article 97, ante.

a beneficiary, it was held that he could not call on a beneficiary at whose instigation the breach was committed to indemnify him against loss as such next of kin, even although the beneficiary had given him an express covenant of indemnity[6]. It is submitted that the same principle would apply a fortiori to the statutory right, which is not so strong in favour of the trustee as an express covenant.

Where trustees have wrongfully parted with trust fund to trustees of subsidiary settlement

Where trustees, at the request of a beneficiary, advance the trust fund to her, with notice that she has settled it by another settlement, they cannot impound her income under such other settlement, because that income is not the interest of a beneficiary in the trust estate *of which they are the trustees*[7].

---

6 *Evans v Benyon* (1887) 37 Ch D 329; cf *Orrett v Corser* (1855) 21 Beav 52.
7 *Ricketts v Ricketts* (1891) 64 LT 263.

CHAPTER 22

Liability of third parties and beneficiaries

Article
100 Personal liability of third parties or beneficiaries who are involved in a breach of trust   950
101 Tracing and following trust property and its proceeds into the hands of third parties, and claiming assets in their hands   983

ARTICLE 100

Personal liability of third parties or beneficiaries who are involved in a breach of trust

(1) A person who is neither a trustee, nor authorised by the trustees, but who takes it on himself to intermeddle with trust matters or do acts characteristic of the office of trustee makes himself a trustee de son tort, becoming personally liable to account to the beneficiaries, in addition to holding the trust property or its traceable product as constructive trustee for the beneficiaries[1];

(2) a person who is not a trustee, but who lawfully receives trust property from the trustees in his capacity as the trustees' agent, and who subsequently deals with the property in a way that he knows to be inconsistent with the trust, will be personally liable to compensate the beneficiaries for the loss which they sustain as a result of his dishonest dealing with the trust property, or to disgorge the profits of his wrongdoing to them[2];

(3) a person who dishonestly assists in a breach of trust or other fiduciary duty will be personally liable to compensate the beneficiaries for their loss, or to disgorge the profits of his wrongdoing to them[3];

(4) a person who dishonestly receives property for his own benefit with knowledge of the fact that it is misapplied trust property, or who receives such property innocently but subsequently acquires knowl-

---

1 *Mara v Browne* [1896] 1 Ch 199; *Lyell v Kennedy* (1889) 14 App Cas 437.
2 *Lee v Sankey* (1873) LR 15 Eq 204; *Soar v Ashwell* [1893] 2 QB 390.
3 *Royal Brunei Airline Sdn Bhd v Tan* [1995] 2 AC 378; *Twinsectra Ltd v Yardley* [2002] 2 AC 164.

edge of its improper provenance and then dishonestly deals with the property for his own benefit in a way that he knows to be inconsistent with the trust, will be personally liable to compensate the beneficiaries for their loss or to disgorge the profits of his wrongdoing to them[4]; moreover, it seems likely that even if he does not know of the property's improper provenance at the time of receipt, and does not subsequently acquire such knowledge by the time when he innocently deals with it for his own benefit, he will still be personally liable to make restitution of the value of the property to the beneficiaries on the ground that he has been unjustly enriched at their expense, subject to his ability to establish a change of position defence to their claim[5];

(5) where a person is indebted to the trust estate[6] (whether by reason of his involvement in a breach of trust or in respect of a simple contract debt), and he has an equitable interest in the trust property (whether original or derivative[7]), his interest may be impounded to make good his liability, and this remedy will not only affect him personally[8], but will also affect all persons claiming under him, including purchasers for value without notice.

PARAGRAPH 1

Trustees de son tort – strangers purporting to act as trustees

As A L Smith LJ stated in *Mara v Browne*[9]:

'If one, not being a trustee and not having authority from a trustee, takes upon himself to intermeddle with trust matters or to do acts characteristic of the office of trustee he may thereby make himself what is called in law a trustee of his own wrong, ie a trustee de son tort, or as it is also termed, a constructive trustee.'

Distinguishing features of a trustee de son tort are that he does not claim to act in his own right, but for the beneficiaries, and his assumption to act as trustee is not of itself a ground of liability, save in the sense that the courts will treat him constructively as having assumed a duty to account for his management of the trust property, a breach of which duty will render him personally liable to compensate the beneficiaries for their loss[10]. Hence his status as trustee precedes the occurrence which may be the subject of a claim

4 *Belmont Finance Corpn v Williams Furniture Ltd (No 2)* [1980] 1 All ER 393; *Re Montagu's Settlement Trusts* [1987] Ch 264; *BCCI v Akindele* [2001] Ch 437.
5 *Grupo Torras SA v Al-Sabah (No 5)* [2001] Lloyd's Rep Bank 36 at 62; *Twinsectra Ltd v Yardley* [2002] 2 AC 164 at 194. See too Lord Nicholls, 'Knowing Receipt: The Need for a New Landmark', in W R Cornish et al (eds) *Restitution: Past, Present and Future* (1998) 231.
6 *Re Taylor* [1894] 1 Ch 671.
7 *Jacubs v Rylance* (1874) LR 17 Eq 341; *Doering v Doering* (1889) 42 Ch D 203; *Chillingworth v Chambers* [1896] 1 Ch 685.
8 *Woodyatt v Gresley* (1836) 8 Sim 180; *Fuller v Knight* (1843) 6 Beav 205; *M'Gachen v Dew* (1851) 15 Beav 84; *Vaughan v Noble* (1861) 30 Beav 34; *Jacubs v Rylance* (1874) LR 17 Eq 341; *Re Taylor* [1894] 1 Ch 671; *Re Weston* [1900] 2 Ch 164.
9 [1896] 1 Ch 199 at 209. Also per Danckwerts LJ in *Carl Zeiss Stiftung v Herbert Smith & Co (No 2)* [1969] 2 Ch 276 at 289.
10 *Montreal Trust Co of Canada v Hickman* [2001] NFCA 42 at para 44.

against him[11]. His conduct is equated to a declaration of himself as a trustee[12], and like an express trustee he must familiarise himself with the extent of his powers and duties on taking office, and thereafter he may be liable for a breach of these duties[13]. The liability of a trustee de son tort is not a secondary liability, in the way that the liability of those who dishonestly assist in a breach of trust is a secondary liability because it is predicated on the commission of a primary breach of trust by the trustees[14]. It is rather a primary liability which is incurred when the trustee de son tort himself breaches the trust duties which he previously constructively assumed when he intermeddled with the trust property. Thus in *Blyth v Fladgate*[15] where a sole trustee had solicitors invest trust funds in Exchequer Bills and, after his death and before appointment of any new trustees, the bills were sold by the solicitors and the proceeds invested in a loan on mortgage, the solicitors were personally accountable for the loss arising when the security proved insufficient.

There is no need to show that an intermeddler has acted dishonestly in order to fix him with liability as a trustee de son tort – he may have been honest and well intentioned, a busybody of excessive probity[16]. To show that a defendant has relevantly 'intermeddled' with the trust affairs, it is not enough to show that he has attended meetings of the trustees without participating in the trustees' decision making - he must take it on himself to assume a more active role in the management of the trust affairs than this[17].

One should be alert to the fact that some authors and judges have formerly used the expression 'trustee de son tort' to cover not the primary liability described here, but the secondary or accessory liability that is incurred by a person who dishonestly assists in a breach of trust.

PARAGRAPH 2

Elements of liability for dishonest dealing by trustees' lawful agents

To make the lawful agent of trustees personally liable for dishonest dealing it is necessary to establish:

(1) a trust or other fiduciary relationship;
(2) a lawful receipt of trust property or other fiduciary property by the agent of the trustees or fiduciary, in his ministerial capacity;

---

11 *Selangor United Rubber Estates Ltd v Cradock (No 3)* [1968] 1 WLR 1555 at 1579; *Paragon Finance plc v D B Thackerar & Co (a firm)* [1999] 1 All ER 400 at 408–409. In contrast, executors de son tort are not generally constructive trustees of the estate which they take it upon themselves to administer, but cf *James v Williams* [2000] Ch 1 (decided in ignorance of Millett LJ's twofold classification of constructive trusteeship in *Paragon Finance plc v D B Thackerar & Co (a firm)* [1999] 1 All ER 400 at 408–409), where an executor de son tort knew that he was not solely entitled to inherited property but regarded himself as such, and so was surprisingly held by the Court of Appeal to hold a proportionate share of the property on constructive trust for the others entitled to share in the estate.

12 *Life Association of Scotland v Siddal* (1861) 3 De GF & J 58 at 72.

13 *Pearce v Pearce* (1856) 22 Beav 248 at 252.

14 See p 956, post.

15 [1891] 1 Ch 337. See too *Goddard v DFC New Zealand Ltd* [1991] 3 NZLR 580.

16 *Lyell v Kennedy* (1889) 14 App Cas 437 at 459; *Mara v Browne* [1896] 1 Ch 199 at 209; *Life Association of Scotland v Siddal* (1861) 3 De GF & J 58; *Baden, Delvaux v Société Générale pour Favoriser le Développement du Commerce et de l'Industrie en France SA* [1993] 1 WLR 509n at 577.

17 *Clay v Clay* [1999] WASCA 8 at para 16.

(3) a subsequent dealing with the property by the agent that is inconsistent with the rights of the beneficiaries or the principal;
(4) a dishonest state of mind on the part of the agent at the time of this dealing.

If an agent lawfully receives trust property, but then dishonestly takes it on himself to treat the property as his own, and misapplies it for his own benefit, then he will be liable for dishonest dealing in line with Article 100(4), but it should be noted that agents can also incur liability for dishonest dealing where they have misapplied trust property while purporting to act in their agency role, and without benefiting themselves. If a defendant does not purport to act as an agent, but instead takes it on himself to do acts characteristic of the office of trustee, then there is no need to prove dishonesty against him with a view to fixing him with liability as a dishonest dealer, as he will be liable as a trustee de son tort[18]. If a defendant receives misapplied trust property from the trustees in his capacity as the trustees' agent, and then applies it in accordance with their instructions, knowing that the trustees are acting in breach of trust, then he will not incur the primary liability of a dishonest dealer, but he will incur the secondary, accessory liability of a dishonest assistant in a breach of trust[19].

Agents who lawfully receive trust property

In relation to the liability of agents who cause a loss to the beneficiaries by dealing with trust property that they have lawfully received from the trustees one must bear in mind Lord Selborne LC's warning in *Barnes v Addy* against extending the scope of their liability too far[20]:

'Those who create a trust clothe the trustee with a legal power and control over the trust property, imposing on him a corresponding responsibility. That responsibility may no doubt be extended in equity to others who are not properly trustees if they are found either making themselves trustees de son tort or actually participating in any fraudulent conduct of the trustee to the injury of the cestui que trust. But on the other hand strangers are not to be made constructive trustees merely because they act as the agents of trustees in transactions within their legal powers, transactions, perhaps, of which a Court of Equity may disapprove, unless those agents receive and become chargeable with some part of the trust property, or unless they assist with knowledge in a dishonest and fraudulent design on the part of the trustees[1]. .... If those principles were disregarded I know not how anyone could in transactions admitting of doubt as to the view which a Court of Equity might take of them, safely discharge the office of solicitor, of banker or of agent of any sort to the trustees. But, on the other hand, if persons dealing honestly as agents are at liberty to rely on the legal power of the trustees, are not to have the character of trustees constructively thrust upon them, then the transactions of mankind can safely be carried through; and I apprehend those who create trusts do expressly intend, in the absence of fraud and dishonesty, to exonerate such agents of all classes from the

18 *Blyth v Fladgate* [1891] 1 Ch 337; *Williams-Ashman v Price and Williams* [1942] Ch 219 at 228. See p 951, ante.
19 See p 956, post.
20 (1874) 9 Ch App 244 at 251–252. See too *Williams v Williams* (1881) 17 Ch D 437 at 442; *Carl Zeiss Stiftung v Herbert Smith & Co (a firm)* [1969] 2 Ch 276 at 299 and 304; *Competitive Insurance Co v Davies Investments Ltd* [1975] 3 All ER 254 at 264.
 1 NB the rule that liability for dishonest assistance can be incurred only by those who assist in a dishonest breach of trust has now been abrogated by *Royal Brunei Airlines Sdn Bhd v Tan* [1995] 2 AC 378, approved in *Twinsectra Ltd v Yardley* [2002] UKHL 12, [2002] 2 AC 164.

responsibilities which are expressly incumbent by reason of the fiduciary relation upon the trustees.'

Dishonest dealing by agents

In line with Lord Selborne LC's observations, and in line with the Privy Council's decision in *Royal Brunei Airlines Sdn Bhd v Tan*[2], with regard to the state of mind which must be established against defendants to fix them with (secondary) liability for dishonestly assisting in a breach of trust, a defendant must have acted dishonestly before he can be fixed with (primary) liability for the equitable wrong of dealing with trust property that he has lawfully received in his capacity as the trustees' agent, in a manner that is inconsistent with the terms of the trust[3]. Support for this view may be derived from various sources. In *Williams-Ashman v Price and Williams*, Bennett J considered that[4]:

'An agent in possession of money which he knows to be trust money, *so long as he acts honestly*, is not accountable to the beneficiaries interested in the trust money unless he intermeddles in the trust by doing acts characteristic of a trustee and outside the duties of an agent.'

In *Carl Zeiss Stiftung v Herbert Smith & Co (a firm)*, Sachs LJ stated that[5]:

'professional men and agents who have received moneys as such and acted bona fide are accountable only to their principals unless dishonesty as well as cognisance of trusts is established against them.'

Finally, in *Cukurooa Celik Enduustrisi AS v Hill Taylor Dickinson (a firm)*[6], Morison J followed Sachs LJ's dictum in the *Carl Zeiss* case, and held that solicitors who had lawfully received money from a client that was allegedly subject to a trust in the claimant's favour, and had placed the money it in their client account, owed duties to the client 'to pay the monies out in accordance with their instructions and to give proper advice to their clients', but could not be liable to the alleged beneficiary for dealing with the property in a manner inconsistent with the alleged trust 'unless something akin to impropriety or dishonesty is alleged'.

In *Williams-Ashman*, solicitors who followed the instructions of the sole trustee in making an unauthorised loan to the trustee's son and in making other unauthorised investments were held not to be liable to compensate the beneficiaries even though they could have checked the terms of the trust instrument, which they had drawn up themselves, placed in their safe, and forgotten. They had not acted dishonestly, and had followed the trustee's instructions in good faith. Likewise, in *Williams v Williams*[7] a settlor suppressed the existence of a settlement on his wife and children and the defendant solicitor carried out the sale of various lands which were in fact

2 [1995] 2 AC 378.
3 In Canada, the cases on this subject are grouped under the heading 'knowing dealing': *Citadel General Assurance Co v Lloyds Bank Canada* [1997] 3 SCR 805 at 821.
4 [1942] Ch 219 at 228. Emphasis added.
5 [1969] 2 Ch 276 at 299, approving the statement which appeared in the 11th edn of *Underhill* at p 599: 'Where the agent of the trustees acts honestly and confines himself to the duties of an agent then, though he will not be accountable to the beneficiaries, they will have their remedy against the persons who are the real trustees.'
6 (1 June 1996, unreported), QBD (Comm Ct).
7 (1881) 17 Ch D 437, treated in this category by Brightman J in *Karak Rubber Co Ltd v Burden (No 2)* [1972] 1 All ER 1210 at 1242.

subject to the settlement and disposed of the proceeds in accordance with the instructions of the settlor's widow and executrix. The solicitor honestly believed that there was no settlement, and although the circumstances were such that it was negligent of the solicitor to hold this belief, Kay J considered that he was not liable to compensate the beneficiaries. In *Lee v Sankey*[8], on the other hand, solicitors were found liable where they were employed by two trustees to receive the proceeds of sold trust properties, and with knowledge of the terms of the trust paid the proceeds over to only one of the trustees, who dissipated the money and died insolvent. These cases are all consistent with the view that the type of dishonesty which must be proven against a defendant is the 'conscious dishonesty' recently identified by the House of Lords in *Twinsectra Ltd v Yardley*[9] as the requisite state of mind for liability as a dishonest assistant in a breach of trust[10].

Pleading dishonesty

The courts have issued various guidelines with regard to the pleading of claims in which dishonesty is alleged against a defendant. These guidelines should be followed whether the claim is for dishonest dealing with trust property, dishonest assistance in a breach of trust, or dishonest receipt and dealing with trust property for one's own benefit.

Defendants are entitled to have their conduct judged against distinct allegations of dishonesty as pleaded[11], and 'in order to allege fraud it is not sufficient to sprinkle a pleading with words like "wilfully" or "recklessly" (but not "fraudulently" or "dishonestly") ... [as this] may still leave it in doubt whether the words are being used in a technical sense or merely to give colour by way or pejorative emphasis to the complaint'[12]. 'Where fraud has not been sufficiently pleaded, it is ... no answer to say that if it had been sufficiently pleaded no further evidence would be called for the defence', for 'the presence or absence of a charge of fraud may ... affect the whole manner in which a defence is conducted'[13]. Hence, it is 'generally no answer to a demand for particulars ... that the defendant already knows the information ... [as] the defendant is entitled to pin the [claimant] down by his or her pleading so that the case to be met will be known'[14].

'It is not necessary to use the word "fraud" or "dishonesty" [in the pleadings] if the facts which make the conduct complained of fraudulent are pleaded, but if the facts pleaded are consistent with innocence, then it is not

---

8 (1873) LR 15 Eq 204.
9 [2002] UKHL 12, [2002] 2 AC 164.
10 See p 959, post.
11 *Armitage v Nurse* [1998] Ch 241 at 251, following *Davy v Garrett* (1878) 7 Ch D 473 at 489. See too *Practice Direction*, Part 16, rule 16.2(5). Under the Bar Code of Conduct, para 606(c), counsel must have reasonably credible material to enable fraud properly to be pleaded, but the Code does not require full disclosure of this material to the defendant: *Rigby v Den Decorating Systems Ltd* (15 March 1999, unreported), CA. In the event that a defendant defeats allegations of dishonesty, claimant's counsel will not be liable to a wasted costs order, provided that a reasonable lawyer might have decided to plead dishonesty on the available material: *Brown v Bennett* [2002] 1 WLR 713.
12 *Armitage v Nurse* [1998] Ch 241 at 257.
13 *Belmont Finance Corpn Ltd v Williams Furniture Ltd* [1979] Ch 250 at 270.
14 *Montreal Trust Co v Hickman* [2001] NFCA 42 at para 60.

open to the court to find fraud'[15]. Nor is it necessary to provide particulars of knowledge in a fraud claim, provided that actual knowledge is pleaded, but it is open to the defendant to seek further particulars of such a pleading of actual knowledge, and 'if there is a pleading that a person "knew or ought to have known" particular matters, then that rolled-up plea should be particularised'[16]. It is usually harder to prove an allegation of dishonesty than an allegation of negligence, as 'the more serious the allegation the less likely it is that the event occurred and, hence, the stronger should be the evidence before the court concludes that the allegation is established on the balance of probability'[17]. Before a court is likely to reach such a conclusion in an application for summary judgment, the pleaded facts must therefore be particularly clear[18].

Paragraph 3

Elements of liability as a dishonest assistant

To make a defendant personally liable for dishonest assistance in a breach of trust or other fiduciary duty it is necessary to establish[19]:

(1) a trust or other fiduciary relationship;
(2) a breach of trust or other fiduciary duty on the part of the trustee or other fiduciary;
(3) a causal link between the breach and a loss to the beneficiaries, or between the breach and a gain to the defendant, depending on the remedy which is sought;
(4) assistance by the defendant in the breach; and
(5) a dishonest state of mind on the part of the assistant.

Each of these requirements will be discussed in turn. It should also be noted that liability for dishonest assistance in a breach of trust or other fiduciary duty 'is not dependent upon receipt of trust property' and 'arises even though no trust property has reached the hands of the accessory'[20]. Where a defendant has in fact received trust property, however, there is nothing to stop the beneficiaries from suing him for dishonest assistance if they wish to do so[1]. In practice, they will generally prefer to make a proprietary claim, or alternatively to make a claim in knowing receipt, for which the mental element is easier to prove, but they may be unable to pursue the first option if the property has been dissipated, and the second if the defendant has received the property ministerially and not beneficially[2].

---

15 *Armitage v Nurse* [1998] Ch 241 at 251, following *Belmont Finance Corpn Ltd v Williams Furniture Ltd* [1979] Ch 250 at 268.
16 *Rigby v Decorating Den Systems Ltd* (15 March 1999, unreported), CA.
17 *Re H* [1996] AC 563 at 586 per Lord Nicholls, followed in *Grupo Torras v Al-Sabah (No 5)* [2001] Lloyd's Bank Rep 36 at 45, CA.
18 *Houghton v Fayers* [2000] Lloyd's Rep Bank 145 at 149; *Gencor ACP Ltd v Dalby* [2000] 2 BCLC 734 at 758.
19 *Royal Brunei Airline Sdn Bhd v Tan* [1995] 2 AC 378; *Twinsectra Ltd v Yardley* [2002] UKHL 12, [2002] 2 AC 164.
20 *Royal Brunei Airline Sdn Bhd v Tan* [1995] 2 AC 378 at 382; *Houghton v Fayers* [2000] Lloyd's Rep Bank 145 at 149.
 1 *Baden, Delvaux v Société Générale pour Favoriser le Développement du Commerce et de l'Industrie en France SA* [1993] 1 WLR 509n at 572–573; *Equiticorp Industries Group Ltd (in stat man) v R (No 47)* [1998] 2 NZLR 481 at 539.
 2 *Twinsectra Ltd v Yardley* [2002] UKHL 12, [2002] 2 AC 164 at 194. See p 970, post.

Existence of trust or other fiduciary relationship

Claims for dishonest assistance are not limited to the situation where an express trustee has misappropriated trust property. They can also lie against defendants who have assisted in the misappropriation of property by other fiduciaries who have voluntarily assumed responsibility for managing the property to their principals – for example, company directors[3], partners[4], and other agents and/or employees[5]. Claims can also clearly lie where a defendant has helped a constructive or resulting trustee to misapply the trust property[6]. However, it is currently unclear on the authorities whether liability as a dishonest assistant can be incurred by a defendant who has assisted in a breach of trust or other fiduciary duty that does not entail the misapplication of property[7]. Authorities regarding it as an open question, whether liability can be incurred where a defendant has assisted in some other kind of breach, are: *Brown v Bennett* [1999] 1 BCLC 649 at 657–659; *Fyffes Group Ltd v Templeman* [2000] 2 Lloyd's Rep 643; *Goose v Wilson Sandford & Co (No 2)* [2000] EWCA Civ 73 at para 88; *Gencor ACP Ltd v Dalby* [2000] 2 BCLC 734 at 757. It is submitted that in principle a claim should lie in such a case, consistently with the courts' general desire to preserve the integrity of fiduciary relations.

Breach of trust or fiduciary duty

There was originally no requirement that the breach of trust in which a defendant has assisted should itself have been a dishonest breach[8], but then, in an unreserved judgment not discussing the earlier cases, Lord Selborne LC held that assistants in a breach of trust could not be liable unless (inter alia)[9]:

> 'they assist with knowledge in a dishonest and fraudulent design on the part of the trustees.'

The requirement that a defendant must have assisted in a dishonest breach of trust was confirmed by the Court of Appeal in *Belmont Finance Corpn Ltd v Williams*[10], but subsequently, in his speech for the Privy Council in *Royal Brunei Airlines Sdn Bhd v Tan*[11], Lord Nicholls refused to follow the Court of Appeal's decision on this point, holding that there is no need to show that the breach of trust assisted by a defendant was itself a dishonest breach. His

---

3 *Selangor United Rubber Estates Ltd v Cradock (No 3)* [1968] 1 WLR 1555; *Belmont Finance Corpn Ltd v Williams Furniture Ltd (No 2)* [1980] 1 All ER 393; *Heinl v Jyske Bank (Gibraltar) Ltd* [1999] Lloyd's Rep Bank 511.

4 *Alers-Hankey v Teixeira* (9 April 2002, unreported), British Columbia CA.

5 *Norwich Union Fire Insurance Society Ltd v Central Auto Salvage (London) Ltd* (30 July 1993, unreported), CA; *Brinks Ltd v Abu-Saleh (No 3)* [1996] CLC 133; *Comax Secure Business Services Ltd v Wilson* (21 June 2001, unreported), QBD.

6 *Bank Tejerat v Hong King and Shanghai Banking Corpn (CI) Ltd* [1995] 1 Lloyd's Rep 239; *Bankgesellschaft Berlin AG v Makris* (22 January 1999, unreported), QBD (Comm Ct); *Heinl v Jyske Bank (Gibraltar) Ltd* [1999] Lloyd's Rep Bank 511.

7 Authorities favouring the narrow view, that assistance liability can be incurred only where the breach of trust or fiduciary duty has entailed a misapplication of funds are: *Cowan de Groot Properties Ltd v Eagle Trust plc* [1991] BCLC 1045 at 1103; *Bankgesellschaft Berlin AG v Makris* (22 January 1999, unreported), QBD (Comm Ct); *Satnam Investments Ltd v Dunlop Heywood & Co Ltd* [1999] 1 BCLC 385 at 404; *Petrotrade Inc v Smith* [2000] 1 Lloyd's Rep 486 at 491–492.

8 *Fyler v Fyler* (1841) 3 Beav 550; *A-G v Corpn of Leicester* (1844) 7 Beav 176.

9 (1874) 9 Ch App 244 at 252.

10 [1979] Ch 250 at 257.

11 [1995] 2 AC 378.

finding in this regard has now been approved by the House of Lords, in *Twinsectra Ltd v Yardley*[12].

Causal link between the breach of trust and loss to the beneficiaries or gain to the defendant

In practice, claimants most often seek compensatory awards against dishonest assistants[13], but it is also open to them in appropriate circumstances to ask for an award which is measured not by reference to the claimants' loss, but by reference to the defendants' gain[14]. Depending on the remedy he seeks, a claimant must show not only that a breach of trust or fiduciary duty has been committed, but also that this breach has caused him a loss, or else that the dishonest assistant has been enriched as a consequence of the breach. Authority for the first of these propositions is *Brown v Bennett (No 2)*[15], in which Neuberger J struck out a claim in dishonest assistance on the ground (inter alia) that even if the claimants had made out a prima facie case that the defendants had assisted in various breaches of fiduciary duty by some company directors, they had failed to establish a causal link between these breaches and the loss in respect of which they sought to be compensated, which would have happened anyway. Authority for the second proposition is *Fyffes Group Ltd v Templeman*[16], in which Toulson J held that in principle a claimant can have an account of profits against a dishonest assistant who has enriched himself by his equitable wrongdoing, regardless of whether the breach has caused the claimant a loss, provided that there is a causal link between the breach and the defendant's gain.

Assistance

For a defendant to have assisted in a breach of trust or other fiduciary duty in a relevant way, his actions or omissions must have helped the trustee or fiduciary: a defendant cannot relevantly have assisted in a breach if his actions or omissions have either hampered the trustee or fiduciary or have been of 'minimal importance' to him[17]. There is no need for the claimant to show that the dishonest assistant's action 'inevitably [had] the consequence that a loss [was suffered]'[18], nor is it an answer to a claim that a dishonest

---

12 [2002] UKHL 12, [2002] 2 AC 164 at 171 and 195.
13 For the principles governing the assessment of quantum in the case of compensatory awards, see *Control Centre Pty Ltd v Ty* (24 July 1995, unreported), NSW Sup Ct (Eq Div) at paras 64–71; *Equiticorp Industries Group Ltd (in stat man) v R (No 47)* [1998] 2 NZLR 481, at 644–646 and 658; *News International plc v Clinger* (17 November 1998, unreported), Ch D at para 388; *Northland Bank v Willson* (1999) 249 AR 201 at 238; *Fyffes Group Ltd v Templeman* [2000] 2 Lloyd's Rep 643 at 660–668; *Alers-Hankey v Teixeira* (9 April 2002, unreported), British Columbia CA.
14 For the principles governing the assessment of quantum in the case of gain-based awards, see *Timber Engineering Co Pty Ltd v Anderson* [1980] 2 NSWLR 488 at 495; *Warman International Ltd v Dwyer* (1995) 182 CLR 544 at 562ff; *Control Centre Pty Ltd v Ty* (24 July 1995, unreported), NSW Sup Ct (Eq Div) at paras 72–76; *Fyffes Group Ltd v Templeman* [2000] 2 Lloyd's Rep 643 at 668–672.
15 (18 October 2000, unreported), Ch D.
16 [2000] 2 Lloyd's Rep 643, at 660-668. On the facts of this case, the claimant's loss and the defendant's gain were the same.
17 *Baden, Delvaux v Société Générale pour Favoriser le Développement du Commerce et de l'Industrie en France SA* [1993] 1 WLR 509n at 574.
18 *Baden, Delvaux v Société Générale pour Favoriser le Développement du Commerce et de l'Industrie en France SA* [1993] 1 WLR 509n at 575.

assistant 'only participated in a part of a chain of events all of which led to [the breach], or to assert that the [breach] would probably have occurred without his assistance'[19]. But although it is 'inappropriate' for the court 'to become involved in attempts to assess the precise causative significance of the dishonest assistance in respect of ... the breach of trust or fiduciary duty', a claimant must show that the defendant's actions or omissions have had *some* causative significance, for 'if there is no causative effect and therefore no assistance given by the [defendant] ... the requirements of conscience [do not] require any remedy at all'[20].

Hence, although a defendant might incur liability for actions or omissions which precede the commission of the breach[1], he cannot be liable if his actions or omissions only occurred after the breach was fully implemented[2]. However, where the breach has entailed the misapplication of funds, the courts are likely to hold that the breach was not fully implemented until the funds were hidden away where the beneficiaries could not find them, with the consequence that those who assist in money-laundering activities after trust funds have been removed from a trust account can be fixed with liability for dishonest assistance[3]. If a trustee or other fiduciary has committed a series of breaches, a defendant can only be liable for dishonest assistance in respect of those breaches to the commission of which his own actions or omissions have made a difference[4].

Dishonest state of mind

Until recently, the leading English case on the mental state required for liability as a dishonest assistant was *Royal Brunei Airlines Sdn Bhd v Tan*[5], a decision of the Privy Council which was not technically binding on the English courts, but which was said nonetheless by the Court of Appeal in *Bank of Scotland v A Ltd*[6], to contain the 'clearest guidance' out of 'all the authorities' on the 'test of guilty knowledge' for such liability. Lord Nicholls' discussion of this subject in *Royal Brunei* has now been glossed by the House of Lords in *Twinsectra Ltd v Yardley*[7].

Prior to *Royal Brunei*, in *Baden, Delvaux v Société Générale pour Favoriser le Développement du Commerce et de l'Industrie en France SA*[8], Peter Gibson J held that a defendant might be liable for assisting in a breach of trust even if his

---

19 *Balfron Trustees Ltd v Peterson* [2001] IRLR 758 at 761.
20 *Grupo Torras SA v Al-Sabah (No 5)* (24 June 1999, unreported), QBD (Comm Ct), affirmed on appeal [2001] Lloyd's Rep Bank 36 at 61, and again in *Casio Computer Co Ltd v Sayo* [2001] EWCA Civ 661, [2001] IL Pr 694 at paras 15 and 52.
1 R P Austin, 'Constructive Trusts' in P D Finn (ed), *Essays in Equity* (1985) 196, 236-7, discussing *Adams v Bank of New South Wales* [1984] 1 NSWLR 285. See too *Aequitas Ltd v Sparad No 100 Ltd* [2001] NSWSC 14.
2 *Brown v Bennett* [1998] 2 BCLC 97 at 105.
3 *Heinl v Jyske Bank (Gibraltar) Ltd* [1999] Lloyd's Rep Bank 511 at 523, approving *Agip (Africa) Ltd v Jackson* [1990] Ch 265 at 293. See too *Casio Computer Co Ltd v Sayo* [2001] EWCA Civ 661, [2001] IL Pr 694 at para 22.
4 *Grupo Torras SA v Al-Sabah (No 5)* (24 June 1999, unreported), QBD (Comm Ct).
5 [1995] 2 AC 378.
6 [2001] EWCA Civ 52, [2001] 1 WLR 751 at 761. See too *Three Rivers District Council v Bank of England (No 3)* [2000] 2 WLR 15 at 62.
7 [2002] UKHL 12, [2002] 2 AC 164.
8 [1993] 1 WLR 509n. Although the case was finally decided in 1983, it was not reported for another ten years.

behaviour fell short of dishonesty[9], and he accepted that any of five types of knowledge would serve to render a defendant liable as an assistant in a breach of trust: (i) actual knowledge; (ii) wilfully shutting one's eyes to the obvious; (iii) wilfully and recklessly failing to make such inquiries as an honest and reasonable man would make; (iv) knowledge of circumstances which would indicate the facts to an honest and reasonable man; (v) knowledge of circumstances which would put an honest and reasonable man on inquiry[10]. He also held that types (ii)–(v) could all be distinguished from type (i), as constituting various types of 'imputed' or 'constructive knowledge'[11]. The *Baden, Delvaux* classification of knowledge subsequently formed the starting point for discussion in a series of English cases on liability for assisting in a breach of trust. The points were made in these cases, that categories (ii) and (iii) should more properly be understood as types of actual, rather than constructive knowledge[12]; that constructive knowledge is not the same thing as constructive notice[13]; that in commercial transactions, men of business do not normally make inquiries unless the facts are such as to raise suspicion, suggesting that constructive notice, as that term is generally understood in relation to dealings with land, has only a limited role to play in the context of commercial transactions[14]; that categories (i), (ii), and (iii) certainly suffice for liability as an assistant[15]; and that categories (iv) and (v) are phrased in a way that might take in dishonest as well as negligent states of mind[16]. A consensus also emerged that, contrary to Peter Gibson J's finding on the point in *Baden, Delvaux*, a defendant must have been dishonest to incur liability[17].

The view that dishonesty is a pre-requisite for liability was not beyond doubt, however, as a line of cases pre-dating *Baden, Delvaux* and holding that a defendant can be liable if he has honestly but negligently failed to investigate the circumstances of an impugned transaction, was never overruled[18]. The body of law founded on the *Baden, Delvaux* classification also suffered from the more general problem that it was over-theorised: as Lord Nicholls subsequently put it in *Royal Brunei*, the courts had been led into 'tortuous convolutions' in their efforts to investigate the 'sort' of knowledge possessed by defendants, 'when the truth is that "knowingly" is inapt as a criterion

---

9 [1993] 1 WLR 509n at 577.

10 [1993] 1 WLR 509n at 575–587.

11 [1993] 1 WLR 509n at 576.

12 *Agip (Africa) Ltd v Jackson* [1990] Ch 265 at 293; *Cowan de Groot Properties Ltd v Eagle Trust plc* [1991] BCLC 1045 at 1103.

13 *Re Montagu's Settlement Trusts* [1987] Ch 264 at 277–299.

14 *Cowan de Groot Properties Ltd v Eagle Trust plc* [1991] BCLC 1045 at 1112; *Eagle Trust plc v SBC Securities Ltd* [1993] 1 WLR 484 at 492–493; *El Ajou v Dollar Land Holdings plc* [1993] BCLC 735 at 758.

15 *Re Montagu's Settlement Trusts* [1987] Ch 264 at 272; *Lipkin Gorman v Karpnale Ltd* [1987] 1 WLR 987 at 1005–1006, affirmed [1989] 1 WLR 1340 at 1355, not considered on appeal to HL [1991] 2 AC 548.

16 *Agip (Africa) Ltd v Jackson* [1990] Ch 265 at 293; *Cowan de Groot Properties Ltd v Eagle Trust plc* [1991] BCLC 1045 at 1112.

17 *Re Montagu's Settlement Trusts* [1987] Ch 264 at 285; *Agip (Africa) Ltd v Jackson* [1990] 1 Ch 265 at 292–293, on appeal: [1991] Ch 547 at 569; *Eagle Trust plc v SBC Securities Ltd* [1993] 1 WLR 484 at 495; *Lipkin Gorman v Karpnale Ltd* [1989] 1 WLR 1340 at 1354–1355, not considered on appeal to HL; *Cowan de Groot Properties Ltd v Eagle Trust plc* [1991] BCLC 1045 at 1101; *Polly Peck International v Nadir (No2)* [1993] BCLC 187 at 203–204; *Bank Tejerat v Hong Kong and Shanghai Banking Corp (CI) Ltd* [1995] 1 Lloyd's Rep 239 at 248.

18 *Selangor United Rubber Estates Ltd v Cradock (No 3)* [1968] 1 WLR 1555; *Karak Rubber Co Ltd v Burden (No2)* [1972] 1 WLR 602; *Rowlandson v National Westminster Bank Ltd* [1978] 1 WLR 798.

when applied to the gradually darkening spectrum where the differences are of degree and not kind.'[19]

In *Royal Brunei*, Lord Nicholls was therefore determined to start afresh. He held that knowledge is best avoided as a defining ingredient of liability, and that the *Baden, Delvaux* scale is best forgotten in this context[20]. He rejected the idea that unconscionability should be the touchstone for liability, unless it is made clear 'what, *in this context*, unconscionable *means*'[1], and he held instead that to fix a defendant with liability, it must be shown that he has acted dishonestly. In line with this decision, the English courts, along with the courts of most other Commonwealth jurisdictions other than Canada[2], no longer refer to this head of liability as liability for 'knowing assistance', and have come instead to refer to it as liability for 'dishonest assistance'[3].

In the *Royal Brunei* case, Lord Nicholls made it clear that the test for dishonesty in this context is not purely subjective, in the sense that individuals are not 'free to set their own standards of honesty in particular circumstances'[4], and must instead be judged by reference to the objective standards of right-thinking members of society. So, as the courts have put it in subsequent cases, there is no 'Robin Hood' defence to an action for dishonest assistance[5]. Lord Nicholls also clearly stated that[6]:

> 'honesty ... does have a strong subjective element in that it is a description of a type of conduct assessed in the light of what a person actually knew at the time, as distinct from what a reasonable person would have known or appreciated.'

Arguably less clear, however, is whether Lord Nicholls meant to lay down a test for dishonesty which incorporated any further subjective element than this, and more specifically, whether he meant to lay down a test which requires it to be shown not merely that a defendant's behaviour has been dishonest by the standards of right-thinking people, but also that the defendant was conscious of this fact at the time when he acted. In the language of criminal lawyers, the question therefore arises whether Lord Nicholls meant to lay down a test for dishonesty that was analogous to the test

---

19 [1995] 2 AC 378 at 391.

20 [1995] 2 AC 378 at 392.

1 [1995] 2 AC 378 at 392 (his emphasis).

2 The leading Canadian case remains *Air Canada v M & L Travel Ltd* [1993] 3 SCR 787, in which Iacobucci J held at 811 that 'the knowledge requirement for this type of liability is actual knowledge ... recklessness or wilful blindness', and at 826 that 'it is unnecessary ... to find that the [assistant] himself acted in bad faith or dishonestly'. In line with this decision, the Canadian courts have persisted with the language of 'knowing assistance': *Gold v Rosenberg* [1997] 3 SCR 767 at 780; *Citadel General Assurance Co v Lloyd's Bank Canada* [1997] 3 SCR 805 at 819; *Glenko Enterprises Ltd v Keller* [2001] 1 WWR 229 at 248.

3 England: *Gencor ACP Ltd v Dalby* [2000] 2 BCLC 734 at 756; *Walker v Stones* [2001] 2 WLR 623 at 665; *Twinsectra Ltd v Yardley* [2002] UKHL 12, [2002] 2 AC 164 at 168 and 171. Australia: *Burger King Corpn v Hungry Jack's Pty Ltd* (21 June 2001, unreported), NSWCA; *Pilmer v Duke Group Ltd (in liquidation)* [2001] HCA 31 at para 3. Hong Kong: *Bardissy v D'Souza* [1999] HKCFI 85. Malaysia: *Industrial Concrete Products Bhd v Concrete Engineering Products Ltd* [2001] 2 MLJ 332 at 363. New Zealand: *Equiticorp Industries Group Ltd (in stat man) v R (No 47)* [1998] 2 NZLR 481 at 540. Singapore: *Banque Nationale de Paris v Hew* [2001] 1 SLR 300.

4 [1995] 2 AC 378 at 389.

5 *Grupo Torras SA v Al-Sabah (No 5)* [2001] Lloyd's Rep Bank 36 at 60; *Walker v Stones* [2001] QB 902 at 939; *Twinsectra Ltd v Yardley* [2002] UKHL 12, [2002] 2 AC 164 at172. Cf *Consul Developments Pty Ltd v DPC Estates Pty Ltd* (1975) 132 CLR 373 at 398.

6 [1995] 2 AC 378 at 389.

for dishonesty laid down in the context of criminal proceedings by Lord Lane CJ in *R v Ghosh*[7] ?

There are powerful reasons for thinking that this was not Lord Nicholls' intention. One is the fact that Lord Nicholls found the defendant liable for dishonest assistance on the facts of the *Royal Brunei* case, even though the claimant never argued, and Lord Nicholls did not hold, that the defendant knew that right-thinking people would have thought his behaviour dishonest. Another is the fact that Lord Nicholls expressly stated that[8]:

> 'Whatever may be the position in some criminal or other contexts (see, for instance, *R v Ghosh* [1982] QB 1053), in the context of the accessory liability principle acting dishonestly, or with a lack of probity, which is synonymous, means simply not acting as an honest person would in the circumstances. This is an objective standard.'

It is true that Lord Nicholls also held that 'for the most part dishonesty is to be equated with conscious impropriety'[9], but the formulation 'for the most part' allows for the possibility that a defendant can also act dishonestly even though he does not appreciate that right-thinking people would consider his behaviour to be dishonest[10]. In *Grupo Torras SA v Al-Sabah (No 5)*[11], Mance J (as he then was) did not understand Lord Nicholls to have laid down a test for dishonesty which was analogous to the test in the *Ghosh* case; nor did Hart J consider him to have done so in *Criterion Properties plc v Stratford UK Properties LLC*[12]; nor was his speech interpreted in this way by many legal practitioners[13].

Notwithstanding all this, however, and notwithstanding the fact that in his dissenting speech in the House of Lords in *Twinsectra Ltd v Yardley*[14], Lord Millett was led by the foregoing reasons to conclude that Lord Nicholls did not mean to introduce a test of conscious dishonesty[15], the majority of their Lordships held in the *Twinsectra* case that in fact this was Lord Nicholls' intention. Lord Hutton[16], who gave the leading speech, interpreted Lord Nicholls' statements that dishonesty should be judged by reference to an objective standard to mean that defendants should not be permitted to rely on a 'Robin Hood' defence. He also interpreted Lord Nicholls' statements that dishonesty has a subjective element because it must be judged by reference to the defendant's personal knowledge of the circumstances to mean that the defendant must have known that his actions were dishonest.

---

7 [1982] QB 1053.

8 [1995] 2 AC 378 at 389.

9 [1995] 2 AC 378 at 389.

10 For this reason, and notwithstanding Lord Hutton's subsequent approval of her comments in *Twinsectra Ltd v Yardley* [2002] UKHL 12, [2002] 2 AC 164 at 175, it is hard to agree with Steel J's statement in *Abbey National plc v Solicitors Indemnity Fund Ltd* [1997] PNLR 306 at 310, that Lord Nicholls meant to introduce the *Ghosh* test because he 'particularly refers to a conscious impropriety' in his speech.

11 (24 June 1999, unreported), QBD (Comm Ct); affirmed on a different point [2001] Lloyd's Rep Bank 36.

12 [2002] EWHC 496 (Ch), [2002] 2 BCLC 151 at 171.

13 For example, W Blair QC, 'Secondary Liability of Financial Institutions for the Fraud of Third Parties', (2000) 30 HKLJ 74 at 83; J S K Chan, 'Dishonesty and Knowledge', (2001) 31 HKLJ 283 at 301; A Stafford QC, 'Solicitors' Liability for Knowing Receipt and Dishonest Assistance in a Breach of Trust', (2001) 17 PN 3 at 14.

14 [2002] UKHL 12, [2002] 2 AC 164.

15 [2002] UKHL 12, [2002] 2 AC 164 at 194–202.

16 [2002] UKHL 12, [2002] 2 AC 164 at 171–180. Lord Slynn and Lord Steyn agreed with him at 167; Lord Hoffmann agreed with him at 170.

With respect to Lord Hutton, this was a strained reading of Lord Nicholls' words, and considered purely as a matter of textual interpretation, Lord Millett's analysis is to be preferred. Considered as a matter of authority, however, it was obviously open to their Lordships to adopt the *Ghosh* test in this context if they wished to do so, since they were not bound by the decision in the *Royal Brunei* case, and Lord Hutton did offer one policy justification for his conclusion, namely that[17]:

> 'A finding by a judge that a defendant has been dishonest is a grave finding, and it is particularly grave against a professional man, such as a solicitor. Notwithstanding that the issue arises in equity law and not in a criminal context, I think that it would be less than just for the law to permit a finding that a defendant had been "dishonest" in assisting a breach of trust where he knew of the facts which created the trust and its breach but had not been aware that what he was doing would be regarded by honest men as being dishonest.'

Certainly, the effect of the House of Lords' decision is to make it more difficult for claimants to make out a case of dishonest assistance, and it seems likely that they will now find it particularly difficult to do this against corporate defendants, unless they are able to identify a particular individual within a defendant company who has acted with knowledge of the relevant facts and with conscious dishonesty, and whose mind should be identified with the company's 'mind' in all the circumstances of the case, pursuant to the principles governing the corporate identification doctrine which were laid down by Lord Hoffmann in his speech for the Privy Council in *Meridian Global Funds Management Asia Ltd v Securities Commission*[18]. It is true that in some Australian and New Zealand cases, the courts have been willing to aggregate the knowledge of several corporate employees, with a view to fixing the company with knowledge of particular facts[19]. However, this process has not recommended itself to the English courts when it has been urged upon them in criminal cases, and they are particularly unhappy with the notion that a consciously dishonest corporate 'mind' can be conjured up by aggregating the knowledge of several employees, none of whom, individually, is consciously dishonest[20]. Representative of this attitude is Harman J's statement in *Galmerrow Securities Ltd v National Westminster Bank plc* that[1]:

> 'knowledge held by a corporation depends on the knowledge of all its employees ... [but] one cannot put the knowledge of one employee, who acts honestly in the course of his duties, together with the knowledge of another employee in a separate department, who acts honestly in the course of his duties, and conclude that the corporation has acted dishonestly because had the two employees pooled their information it would have become apparent that an act was dishonest.'

A final issue remains to be considered here, namely whether the test for

---

17 [2002] 2 AC 164 at 174.
18 [1995] 2 AC 500 at 507. See too *London Underground Ltd v NURMTW* [2001] ICR 647 at 662, where Robert Walker LJ considered the 'essential point' of *Meridian* to be that: 'in determining the mental state of an artificial person (when some ... rule requires that rather fictional exercise to be carried out) it may be necessary to look, not only at the body's formal constitution, but also at the way it actually organises its activities, and at the scope and purpose of the ... rule'.
19 *Macquarie Bank Ltd v Sixty-Fourth Throne Pty Ltd* [1998] 3 VR 133 at 161; *Equiticorp Industries Group Ltd (in stat man) v R (No 47)* [1998] 2 NZLR 481 at 627–629.
20 *R v HM Coroner for East Kent, ex p Spooner* (1987) 88 Cr App Rep 10 at 15-17; *A-G's Ref (No 2 of 1999)* [2000] 3 WLR 195 at 211–212.
1 [2002] WTLR 125 at 151–152.

dishonesty laid down in *Royal Brunei* and *Twinsectra* requires it to be shown that the defendant knew that his actions or omissions would enable a wrong to be committed against the claimant, or whether it is sufficient that he knew his actions or omissions would enable a wrong to be committed against some person or persons unknown, or even that he thought (incorrectly) that they would enable a wrong to be committed against some particular person other than the claimant. In *Agip (Africa) Ltd v Jackson*[2], Millett J (as he then was) held that it would suffice for a finding of dishonesty that the defendants had known that they were participating in a fraud, and that it made no difference whether they knew the identity of their victim. In his view[3]:

> 'It is no defence for a man charged with having knowingly assisted in a fraudulent and dishonest scheme to say that he thought it was "only" a breach of exchange control or "only" a case of tax evasion. It is not necessary that he should have been aware of the precise nature of the fraud or even of the identity of its victim. A man who consciously assists others by making arrangements which he knows are calculated to conceal what is happening from a third party, takes the risk that they are part of a fraud practised on that party.'

Likewise, when the *Agip* case went to the Court of Appeal, Fox LJ did not think that[4]:

> 'persons who needed to demonstrate that they had acted honestly could shelter behind transactions or objects which were themselves disreputable.'

These statements marked a departure from Sachs LJ's previous finding in *Carl Zeiss Stiftung v Herbert Smith & Co (No 2)*[5], that a defendant must have had 'both actual knowledge of the trust's existence and actual knowledge that what is being done is improperly in breach of that trust'. But in *Brinks Ltd v Abu-Saleh (No 3)*[6], Rimer J stated that the defendant (who had not in any case relevantly assisted the breach of fiduciary duty in issue) could not be said to have possessed the requisite state of mind for liability because she had mistakenly believed herself to be participating in a fraudulent scheme to evade tax.

The inconsistency between *Agip* and *Brinks* was subsequently discussed by Mance J (as he then was), and again by the Court of Appeal, in *Grupo Torras SA v Al-Sabah (No 5)*[7]. In Mance J's view, Millett J's comments were deprived of general authority by the fact that in *Agip* the defendants had had ample reason to suspect a fraud on the claimant, and he preferred Rimer J's approach, stating that:

> 'The problem with which Rimer J was concerned was the not uncommon problem that, if she had assisted at all, the defendant [in *Brinks*] would plainly have been dishonest in a general sense, since it was clear that the whole purpose of the trips was dishonest tax evasion. But the answer to this problem seems to lie in recognising that, for dishonest assistance, the defendant's dishonesty must have been towards the plaintiff in relation to property held or potentially held on trust or constructive trust, rather than in the introduction of a separate criterion of knowledge of any such trust.'

2 [1990] Ch 265.
3 [1990] Ch 265 at 295, followed in *Barret v McCormack* (1999) 4 ITELR 1 at 26, and also in *Banque Nationale de Paris v Hew* [2001] 1 SLR 300 at 333–334.
4 [1991] Ch 547 at 569.
5 [1969] 2 All ER 367 at 379.
6 [1996] CLC 133.
7 (24 June 1999, unreported), QBD (Comm Ct); on appeal: [2001] Lloyd's Rep Bank 36.

On appeal, the Court of Appeal did not find it necessary to express a final view on this point, as on the facts of the *Grupo Torras* case, the appellant for whom it might have made a difference had known that the funds with which he had been concerned had belonged to, or emanated from, the claimants. Nonetheless, their Lordships stated that they were 'disposed to agree with Rimer J's observations'[8].

With respect, it is hard to agree that a defendant who knows or has good grounds for suspecting that he has assisted in fraudulent behaviour of some kind should be absolved from liability towards the claimant he has actually helped to defraud, because he did not know who his victim was, or because he thought that he was helping to defraud someone else. To allow a defendant to rely on this argument is effectively to absolve him from liability on the ground that he assumed the risk that someone other than the actual victim of his wrongdoing might pursue him through the civil – or criminal – justice system, but that he did not assume the risk that the actual victim of his wrongdoing should do so. It is hard to see why someone who has acted with conscious dishonesty should be permitted to rely on this disreputable argument. Moreover, the practical effect of the *Grupo Torras* dicta is to make it easier for defendants to escape liability for dishonest assistance by fabricating explanations of their behaviour, as an untruthful story of dishonest conspiracy is often likelier to correspond with the facts of a dishonest assistance case than an untruthful story of blameless conduct.

Vicarious liability of a defendant's partners

The question has arisen in a number of cases where a partner has dishonestly assisted in a breach of trust or fiduciary duty, whether his fellow partners might be vicariously liable for his equitable wrongdoing. In *Re Bell's Indenture*[9], Vinelott J held not, following the Court of Appeal's decision in *Mara v Browne*[10] that it is no part of the implied actual authority of a partner to make his fellow partners personally liable to account for his wrongdoing, and these cases were both followed by Tipping J, in a New Zealand case, *Estate Realties Ltd v Wignall*[11]. However, they were not cited in *Agip (Africa) Ltd v Jackson*[12], where Millett J (as he then was) held that the partner of a money-laundering accountant should be vicariously liable for his dishonest assistance in a breach of trust, and Millett J's decision on this point was upheld by the Court of Appeal[13]. This left the law in rather an uncertain state, but recently the point was considered again, in *Dubai Aluminium Co Ltd v Salaam*[14], where the Court of Appeal concluded that on the right set of facts a partner can indeed be fixed with vicarious liability for a fellow partner's dishonest assistance, under the Partnership Act 1890, s 10. However, a dishonest assistant's partners will only be caught by this section if they have actually or apparently authorised his activities; his activities will not be actually authorised if they are

---

8 (24 June 1999, unreported), QBD (Comm Ct); on appeal: [2001] Lloyd's Rep Bank 36 at 59.
9 [1980] 1 WLR 1217.
10 [1896] 1 Ch 199.
11 [1992] 2 NZLR 615 at 634–635.
12 [1990] Ch 265.
13 [1991] Ch 547.
14 [2001] QB 113. Leave to appeal granted: [2001] 1 WLR 884. Commonwealth decisions to like effect are: *Young v Murphy* [1996] 1 VR 279 at 315; *McDonic v Heatherington* (1997) 142 DLR (4th) 648. For liability for employees see *Balfron Trustees Ltd v Petersen* [2002] WTLR 157.

undertaken for a dishonest purpose, even if he could have engaged in such activities in a legitimate way; and his activities will only be apparently authorised if the partners have represented to the beneficiaries or principal that the dishonest assistant has the partners' authority to engage in these activities, and they have relied on this representation to their detriment. This situation seems most likely to arise in practice where a trustee or other fiduciary has committed an innocent breach of trust, with the dishonest assistance of a defendant whose firm has been employed by the trustee or principal[15].

Protection for suspicious agents or advisers

Banks, building societies, and other financial institutions, as well as lawyers and accountants, are now required to take many more precautions than hitherto against the possibility that their clients are engaged in laundering the proceeds of criminal activity or terrorism. Several statutes now make it a criminal offence to assist in money laundering, to fail to report information relating to the activities of money launderers, and to tip off money launderers that they are under criminal investigation. The mens rea requirements for these offences range from actual knowledge or suspicion of relevant facts, as in the Criminal Justice Act 1988, s 93A, and the Drug Trafficking Act 1994, s 50, for example, to the more draconian requirements of the Criminal Justice Act 1988, s 39C(2), of the Terrorism Act 2000, s 21A, and of the Proceeds of Crime Act 2002, s 330, which also catch defendants who have had 'reasonable grounds for knowing or suspecting' the relevant facts[16]. Even standing alone, these provisions would obviously give financial and other professional intermediaries a considerable incentive to create internal checking and monitoring procedures, with a view to protecting themselves against liability. But these institutions must additionally take due heed of the Money Laundering Regulations 1993, the Money Laundering Guidance Notes issued by the Joint Money Laundering Steering Group, and the Money Laundering Rules issued by the Financial Services Authority under powers conferred by the Financial Services and Markets Act 2000. These variously require financial institutions to establish internal procedures, eg to check the identity of customers, keep records, appoint compliance officers, train staff, or describe how to achieve best practice in these areas. Taken collectively, they represent an extensive and detailed description of how professional intermediaries ought to behave, and failure to live up to the standards which they demand seems certain to be construed by the English courts as a relevant matter when considering the honesty of an intermediary's conduct in the context of civil proceedings for dishonest assistance.

The question arises as to how agents and advisers might protect themselves in the event that they receive money from a client and become suspicious about its provenance, given that they owe contractual and fiduciary duties to their clients, and might face civil suits by their clients for breach of these

---

15 [2001] QB 113 at 133 per Evans LJ, distinguishing the facts of the *Dubai Aluminium* case on this basis from the facts of *Hamlyn v John Houston & Co* [1903] 1 KB 81 and *Lloyd v Grace, Smith & Co* [1912] AC 716.

16 Section 21A(6) of the Terrorism Act 2000, and s 330(8) of the Proceeds of Crime Act 2002, both also provide that in deciding whether a person has committed an offence under the section, 'the court must consider whether he followed any relevant guidance' approved by the Treasury or other supervisory body.

duties in the event that they fail to follow their client's instructions, but given too that they may incur criminal sanctions or civil liability for dishonest assistance in the event that they comply with them[17]. Depending on the circumstances, intermediaries in this position are advised to apply to the Serious Fraud Office for directions, as recommended by the Court of Appeal in *Bank of Scotland v A Ltd*[18], or alternatively to the court, as in *Finers v Miro*[19].

PARAGRAPH 4

Elements of liability where misapplied trust property has been received and dealt with by a defendant for his own benefit

To make a defendant personally liable where he has received misapplied trust property and dealt with the property for his own benefit it is currently necessary to establish:

(1) property held on trust or subject to some other fiduciary duty;
(2) misapplication of the property by the trustees or fiduciary in breach of trust or fiduciary duty;
(3) receipt of the property or its traceable proceeds by the defendant;
(4) causal link between the defendant's receipt and the breach of trust or fiduciary duty;
(5) dealing with the property by the defendant for his own benefit, and not in his character as agent for another party.
(6) knowledge by the defendant that the property has been transferred in breach of trust or breach of fiduciary duty, either at the time of receipt or at any other time prior to his dealing with the property for his own benefit.

Although the courts have discussed this final requirement in many cases, it still cannot be said that it has been definitively settled what states of mind will suffice to incur liability. However, some recent judicial observations on the nature of liability under this head suggest that the time is now ripe for the courts to take a more radical approach to this question[20], by recognising not only that it is a fault-based equitable wrong to receive and deal with misapplied trust property for one's own benefit with a dishonest state of mind, but also that a strict liability claim in unjust enrichment will alternatively lie against the recipients of misapplied trust property, subject to the recipients' ability to raise the defence of change of position. In the following account, each of the current requirements for liability will be considered, and the future direction of the law will then be discussed.

---

17 For cases exploring the tensions created for financial institutions wishing to avoid civil liability from these two possible directions, see *TTS International v Cantrade Private Bank* (Royal Court of Jersey, 1995), noted D Banks (1995) 4 JITCP 60; *Wavefront Trading Ltd v Po Sang Bank Ltd* [1999] HKFCI 5; *US International Marketing Ltd v National Bank of New Zealand Ltd* (20 June 2002, unreported), NZ High Ct.
18 [2001] EWCA Civ 52, [2001] 1 WLR 751.
19 [1991] 1 WLR 35. See too *C v S* [1999] 1 WLR 1551.
20 Of particular importance are Lord Nicholls' extra-judicial observations in his article 'Knowing Receipt: The Need for a New Landmark' in W R Cornish et al (eds) *Restitution: Past, Present and Future* (1998) 231. See too *Grupo Torras SA v Al-Sabah (No 5)* [2001] Lloyd's Rep Bank 36 at 62, CA; *Bank of Credit and Commerce International (Overseas) Ltd v Akindele* [2001] Ch 437 at 456, CA; *Twinsectra Ltd v Yardley* [2002] UKHL 12, [2002] 2 AC 164 at 194.

Property held on trust or subject to fiduciary duty

Liability is not confined to cases where the misapplied property has been held on trust, but may also be incurred where a defendant has received property that has been controlled by a person, such as a company director or employee, who owed fiduciary duties to a principal in respect of his handling of the property[1]. In the absence of a trust or fiduciary duty, however, liability will not arise[2].

Misapplication of property in breach of trust or fiduciary duty

It must be shown that the trustee or fiduciary who controlled the property misapplied it in breach of trust or breach of fiduciary duty, but there is no need to show that he committed this breach with a dishonest state of mind[3].

Receipt of the property or its traceable proceeds by the defendant

The defendant's receipt of the property or its traceable proceeds must not be protected by the overreaching provisions of the 1925 property legislation, nor by the exceptions to the *nemo dat quod non habet* principle such as those embodied in the Factors Act 1889, the Sale of Goods Act 1979, and the Consumer Credit Act 1974. Nor must the defendant be in a position to raise the defence of bona fide purchase for value of the legal estate without notice of the beneficiaries' interest[4].

In the absence of fraud, a company's receipt of property will not be treated as receipt by its shareholders for the purposes of fixing the shareholders with liability, even if the company is wholly owned[5]. In the case of fraud, however, 'the court is entitled to "pierce the corporate veil" and recognise the receipt of the company as that of the individual(s) in control of it if the company was used as a device or facade to conceal the true facts thereby avoiding or concealing any liability of those individual(s)'[6].

Receipt of trust property by a defendant clearly includes receipt of the traceable proceeds of the trust property, as identified in accordance with the relevant tracing rules. Thus, in *El Ajou v Dollar Land Holdings plc*, Hoffmann LJ considered that a claimant must show[7]:

---

1 *Competitive Insurance Co v Davies Investments Ltd* [1975] 3 All ER 254; *Belmont Finance Corpn Ltd v Williams Furniture Ltd (No 2)* [1980] 1 All ER 393; *Baden, Delvaux v Société Générale pour Favoriser le Développement du Commerce et de l'Industrie en France SA* [1993] 1 WLR 509n; *Rolled Steel Products (Holdings) Ltd v British Steel Corpn* [1986] Ch 246; *Precision Dippings Ltd v Precision Dippings Marketing Ltd* [1986] Ch 447; *Agip (Africa) Ltd v Jackson* [1991] Ch 547; *Heinl v Jyske Bank (Gibraltar) Ltd* [1999] Lloyd's Rep Bank 511; *CMS Dolphin Ltd v Simonet* [2001] 2 BCLC 704.

2 *Walker v Standard Chartered Bank* (27 February 1998, unreported), Ch D; *Box v Barclays Bank plc* [1998] 18 L S Gaz R 33.

3 *Polly Peck International plc v Nadir (No 2)* [1992] 4 All ER 769 at 777; *El Ajou v Dollar Land Holdings plc* [1994] 2 All ER 685 at 700; *Brown v Bennett* [1999] 1 BCLC 649.

4 *Re Diplock* [1948] Ch 465 at 535 and 544, CA; *Carl Zeiss Stiftung v Herbert Smith & Co (a firm) (No 2)* [1969] 2 Ch 276 at 289 per Danckwerts LJ; *Cowan de Groot Properties Ltd v Eagle Trust plc* [1992] 4 All ER 700 at 767.

5 *Trustor AB v Smallbone (No 2)* [2001] 3 All ER 987 at 994, per Morritt V-C following *Cowan de Groot Properties Ltd v Eagle Trust plc* [1992] 4 All ER 700 at 762, and *El Ajou v Dollar Land Holdings plc* [1993] 3 All ER 717 at 738.

6 *Trustor AB v Smallbone (No 2)* [2001] 3 All ER 987 at 995.

7 [1994] 2 All ER 685 at 700. See too *Agip (Africa) Ltd v Jackson* [1990] Ch 265 at 289–292; *Boscawen v Bajwa* [1996] 1 WLR 328 at 334; *Foskett v McKeown* [2001] 1 AC 102 at 128; *Trustor AB v Smallbone (No 2)* [2001] 3 All ER 987 at 994.

'first, a disposal of his assets in breach of fiduciary duty; secondly, the beneficial receipt by the defendant of assets which are traceable as representing the assets of the [claimant]; and thirdly, knowledge on the part of the defendant that the assets he received are traceable to a breach of fiduciary duty.'

The question arises whether the courts are tied to a strict transactional approach to identifying the traceable proceeds of trust property, or whether they might instead use a causative ('but for') approach to determining whether a defendant has received the traceable proceeds of trust property. Take the case where a trustee wrongfully gives a cheque for £10,000 drawn on a trust account to D1, and D1 pays the cheque into his own current account. The following day D1 receives a cheque from X for £10,000 for work done which he endorses in favour of his son, D2, believing that he can afford to make such a gift to D2 in the circumstances, although he would not otherwise have made such a gift. The beneficiaries have no proprietary remedy against D2 because they cannot trace *their* £10,000 into D2's hands. However, the substance of the matter is that D2 would not have received D1's endorsed cheque but for D1 having previously received the trustee's payment, and in these circumstances it is submitted that D2 should be liable to a personal claim by the beneficiaries, assuming that the knowledge requirement is satisfied[8]. This result could have been reached if D1 had paid X's cheque into his current account, and had then paid D2 out of this account, and to deny the beneficiaries a claim for knowing receipt in the situation described, on the ground that they cannot prove transactional proprietary links between the money withdrawn from the trust account and the money received by D2, is surely 'to adopt an unnecessary "proprietary analysis" in what is otherwise a personal claim'[9], there being no question of the beneficiaries obtaining any priority prejudicial to D2's creditors in the event of D2's insolvency.

Causal link between the breach of trust or fiduciary duty and the defendant's receipt

In *Brown v Bennett*[10] Morritt LJ held that the defendant's receipt of misapplied trust property 'must be the direct consequence of the alleged breach of trust or fiduciary duty of which the recipient is said to have notice', and he amplified this finding as follows[11]:

'The matter, I think, can be tested in this way. Let us assume a mansion house vested in trustees. The trustees fail to perform their fiduciary duties and allow it to fall into appalling disrepair. They are then replaced by other trustees who decide

---

8 The same analysis could also be adopted in the event that the courts were to recognise that D2 was strictly liable to the beneficiaries in an action for unjust enrichment, and indeed, might also be adopted in the context of claims for dishonest assistance, as suggested by the facts of *Agip (Africa) Ltd v Jackson* [1991] Ch 547 esp at 561.

9 S Fennell, 'Misdirected Funds: Problems of Uncertainty and Inconsistency', (1994) 57 MLR 38 at 45.

10 [1999] 1 BCLC 649 at 655.

11 [1999] 1 BCLC 649 at 655. This principle does not apply in the case where a defendant receives and deals with an unlawful dividend for his own benefit, where the case is not pleaded on the basis that the defendant has dishonestly received and dealt with the property with knowledge that the directors breached their fiduciary duty to the company when they authorised the dividend, but is pleaded on the different basis that the defendant owes the company a restitutionary obligation in the law of unjust enrichment, based on the fact that the company lacked the capacity to pay him the unlawful dividend: *Allied Carpets Group plc v Nethercott* [2001] BCC 81.

that the matter has gone too far and decide to sell the property. They sell the property to a next-door neighbour, who for the previous 40 years has watched the mansion house falling into disrepair. The sale by the new trustees to the neighbour is entirely proper, at a proper price. The neighbour unquestionably has notice of the previous breaches of duty, because he watched them happen, but the breaches of duty did not give rise to any receipt by the neighbour; the neighbour was not in any way responsible for them and he paid the full value for what he received from the new trustees when he bought. I can see no reason why in those circumstances there should be any [knowing receipt] liability imposed upon the neighbour merely because he watched the house fall into disrepair before he was enabled to buy it.'

Applying this principle to the facts of *Brown v Bennett*, Morritt LJ concluded that even if the defendant had purchased the assets of an insolvent company in the knowledge that the company had been forced into insolvency as a consequence of the directors' breaches of fiduciary duty, it could not be said that there was a direct causal link between the defendant's acquisition of the corporate assets and the directors' breaches of duty, and it followed from this that the defendant could not be liable[12].

Beneficial receipt

Under the present law, a defendant cannot be liable for receiving and dealing with misapplied trust property for his own benefit, if he has acted in a ministerial capacity – ie if he has received property as agent for a principal to whom he owes an immediate duty to account for the property (or an equivalent sum), and who is himself immediately liable to the claimant on the defendant's receipt from the claimant[13]. In these circumstances, however, the defendant can be liable for dishonest assistance if he has dealt with the property in accordance with his principal's instructions, knowing that he is thereby facilitating a breach of trust, and knowing that his actions would be regarded as dishonest by right-thinking people[14]. The reason for this is that liability for dishonest assistance is a wrong-based liability that does not turn on the question whether the defendant has derived a benefit from his actions.

If the courts were to hold that dishonestly receiving and dealing with misapplied trust property for one's own benefit is an equitable wrong analogous to the wrong of dishonest dealing by agents described in Article 100(2), then consistently with what has been said about dishonest assistants, it would not be open to a defendant to rely on the fact that he has acted in a ministerial capacity in his defence to an action based on this wrong. However, if the courts also hold that those who receive misapplied trust property and deal with it for their own benefit are strictly liable to make restitution to the beneficiaries on the ground of unjust enrichment, then defendants could

---

12 [1999] 1 BCLC 649 at 654–657, affirming the trial judge's analysis to the same effect, reported at [1998] 2 BCLC 97 at 104.

13 *Barnes v Addy* (1874) 9 Ch App 244 at 254–255; *Adams v Bank of New South Wales* [1984] 1 NSWLR 285 at 290–292; *Westpac Banking Corp v Savin* [1985] 2 NZLR 41 at 69; *Agip (Africa) Ltd v Jackson* [1990] Ch 265 at 291–292; *Cukurooa Celik Enduustrisi AS v Hill Taylor Dickinson (a firm)* (1 June 1996, unreported); *Trustor AB v Smallbone (No 2)* [2001] 3 All ER 987 at 994; *Twinsectra Ltd v Yardley* [2002] 2 AC 164 at 194.

14 See eg *British North American Elevator Co v Bank of British North America* [1919] AC 658, but note that this case predates the discussion of the mental element required for liability as a dishonest assistant in *Royal Brunei Airline Sdn Bhd v Tan* [1995] 2 AC 378 and *Twinsectra Ltd v Yardley* [2002] 2 AC 164.

rely on the defence of ministerial receipt in reply to an action of this sort, just as they can currently rely on the defence in reply to other claims in unjust enrichment[15].

The question has arisen in a series of cases concerned with the liability of banks who have received and dealt with misapplied trust property, whether they should properly be sued on the basis that they have received and dealt with the property for their own benefit, or on the basis that they have acted ministerially, with the result that they can only be sued for dishonest assistance in a breach of trust[16]. To answer this question it is necessary to distinguish the situation where the misapplied trust property has been deposited with the bank by the account-holder from the situation where the property has been deposited with the bank by a third party.

In the first situation, the bank always receives the money beneficially, and never receives it ministerially: there is simply a loan of money from the account-holder to the bank, or if the account is overdrawn, a repayment of the debt owed to the bank by the account-holder. Hence, the bank is potentially liable to claims that are predicated on the basis that it has received and dealt with misapplied trust property for its own benefit, where a trustee or fiduciary himself deposits trust money into his personal account[17]. It is submitted that cases to the contrary, which suggest that in this situation a bank can only be liable as a dishonest assistant, are incorrect in principle[18].

In the second situation, where cash is deposited with a bank by a person other than the account holder, or the bank's own account with a central clearing bank is credited as result of instructions from such a person, the bank will almost always take the proceeds of the transaction ministerially as agent for the account-holder[19] – and it follows that the bank cannot be sued on the basis that it has received and dealt with the property for its own benefit, although it can be liable for dishonest assistance. It has been hard for the courts and academic commentators to accept this proposition, although cases can be marshalled in its support. One reason for their reluctance may be that they have not always clearly understood that a bank which receives a third-party deposit on its customer's behalf does not receive 'beneficially' simply because it takes good title to the money and thereafter uses the money as its own[20]: 'beneficial receipt' as distinguished from 'ministerial receipt' of

---

15 *National Westminster Bank Ltd v Barclays Bank Ltd* [1975] QB 654; *Chase Manhattan Bank NA v Israel-British Bank (London) Ltd* [1981] Ch 105; *ANZ Banking Group Ltd v Westpac Banking Corpn* (1988) 164 CLR 662; *Portman Building Society v Hamlyn Taylor Neck (a firm)* [1998] 4 All ER 202 at 207.

16 The following discussion draws on the arguments contained in J P Moore, 'Restitution from Banks', unpublished DPhil dissertation, University of Oxford, 2000.

17 As in eg *Director, Real Estate and Business Brokers v NRS Mississauga Inc* (2000) 194 DLR (4th) 527.

18 For example, *Polly Peck International plc v Nadir (No 2)* [1993] BCLC 187.

19 The only exception to this rule arises where the bank has some prior right of its own to be paid by the third party, pursuant to an arrangement previously entered by the third party and the bank: *Continental Caoutchouc and Gutta Percha Co v Kleinwort Sons & Co* (1904) 90 LT 474 at 476 per Collins MR. In *Standard Bank London Ltd v Canara Bank* [2002] EWHC 1032 (Comm) at para 99, Moore-Bick J considered that Collins MR's observations on this point were irreconcilable with *Barclays Bank Ltd v W J Simms, Son & Cooke (Southern) Ltd* [1980] QB 677 at 695, and *Lloyds Bank plc v Independent Insurance Co Ltd* [2000] QB 110. With respect, though, these two lines of authority are not irreconcilable because they are not concerned with the same issue.

20 Cf R Cranston, *Principles of Banking Law* (1997) 207-8; M Bryan, 'Recovering Misdirected Money from Banks: Ministerial Receipt at Law and in Equity' in F D Rose (ed) *Restitution and*

money entails not merely that a defendant takes good title to the money, but also that the defendant should not have to account for an equivalent sum to a principal who is himself legally liable to the claimant from the moment of the defendant's receipt. A second, related reason may be that it is not immediately obvious what happens when a bank receives a third-party deposit on a customer's behalf, particularly where the account is overdrawn. Properly understood, though, such transactions always work in the same way, regardless of the state of the account between the bank and the customer: first, the bank receives the deposit ministerially, as agent for its customer; then, in a separate transaction, the bank either borrows the money from its customer and credits the amount in its books as a debt which it owes to the customer, or where his account is overdrawn, applies the amount on his behalf in reduction of the debt which he owes to the bank.

Authority for this analysis, at least where the customer's account is in credit, can be found in *Agip (Africa) Ltd v Jackson*[1], where Millett J (as he then was) stated that:

'The essential feature of [claims in knowing receipt] ... is that the recipient must have received the property for his own use and benefit. This is why neither the paying nor the collecting bank can normally be brought within it.'

It can also be found in a recent Scottish case, *Compagnie Commerciale Andre SA v Artibell Shipping Co Ltd* where Lord Macfadyen held that[2]:

'There is, no doubt, a sense in which money paid to a bank to the credit of the account of one of its customers becomes, on receipt, the bank's money – as Lord Mackay said in *Royal Bank of Scotland v Skinner*[3] it is "simply consumed by the banker." But in that simple situation, the bank is not thereby enriched, because it grants an immediate obligation of corresponding amount to its customer. Receipt by the bank in that way would not ... afford the necessary foundation for an argument that in the event of the money becoming repayable by the customer to the payer, the bank had been unjustly enriched.'

There are also earlier cases which support the proposition that the same analysis applies where misdirected money is credited to an overdrawn account by a third party. In *Continental Caoutchouc and Gutta Percha Co v Kleinwort Sons & Co*[4], Collins MR considered that a bank can rely on the defence of ministerial receipt where it has not received money in its own right pursuant to some prior agreement between the bank and the third party, but has instead received the money purely in its capacity as the customer's agent, and has then credited the money to the customer's overdrawn account, as in these circumstances the bank will have 'constructively sent [the money on] and received it back, and [will have] done nothing incompatible with [its] position as a conduit-pipe or intermediary'. In *British North American Elevator Co v Bank of British North America*[5], the Privy Council held a bank liable as an accessory to a breach of trust, but not as a beneficial recipient of trust property, where the bank had 'knowingly [become a party] to a mis-

Banking Law (1998) 161, 181–187; L D Smith 'Unjust Enrichment, Property, and the Structure of Trusts' (2000) 116 LQR 412 at 433; E P Ellinger, E Lomnicka, and R J A Hooley, *Modern Banking Law* (3rd edn, 2002) 239–242.

1 [1990] Ch 265, 291; affd [1991] Ch 547.
2 2001 SC 563 at 661–662.
3 1931 SLT 382 at 384.
4 (1904) 90 LT 474 at 476.
5 [1919] AC 658.

application of what were trust funds'[6] paid into an overdrawn account by a person other than the bank's customer. Finally, in *Bank of New South Wales v Vale Corpn (Management) Ltd*[7], the corporate manager of a unit trust wrongfully deposited money it had received as subscriptions for units into the overdrawn account of companies belonging to the same corporate group, and the New South Wales Court of Appeal considered that 'it was not the [defendant] bank, but rather it was the [corporate group] which was the recipient of almost the entirety of the moneys paid out of [the manager's] account.'

Against this line of authority are a number of decisions and dicta, which include Millett J's further statement in the *Agip* case that[8]:

> 'if the collecting bank uses the money to reduce or discharge the company's overdraft ... it receives the money for its own benefit.'

Lord Millett (as he has since become) shifted his position after the *Agip* case, writing extra-judicially that a bank can only be said to have received third-party deposits beneficially where there has been 'some conscious appropriation of the sum paid into the account in reduction of the over-draft'[9]. Against this, however, it must be said that when a bank receives a payment from a third party who designates the relevant account at the time of his payment, the bank has no choice which account to credit with the money, and so is not in a position to make a 'conscious appropriation' of the third party's deposit.

Knowledge of the breach of trust

In common with the cases on liability for assisting in a breach of trust which were decided prior to *Royal Airlines Sdn Bhd v Tan*[10], the cases on personal liability where misapplied trust property has been received and dealt with by a defendant for his own benefit have often adopted the classification of knowledge approved by Peter Gibson J in *Baden, Delvaux v Société Générale pour Favoriser le Développement du Commerce et de l'Industrie en France SA*[11], namely: (i) actual knowledge; (ii) wilfully shutting one's eyes to the obvious; (iii) wilfully and recklessly failing to make such inquiries as an honest and reasonable man would make; (iv) knowledge of circumstances which would indicate the facts to an honest and reasonable man; (v) knowledge of circumstances which would put an honest and reasonable man on inquiry. It should be noted, however, that there is no clear alignment between dishonesty and types (i)–(iii) on the one hand, and negligence and types (iv)–(v) on the other hand, with the result that it can be difficult to interpret decisions which are expressed in the language of *Baden, Delvaux* into the language of dis-honesty and negligence. It should also be noted that the cases are divided on the question whether liability can be incurred only by those who fall within

6 [1919] AC 658 at 663.
7 (21 October 1981, unreported), NSWCA.
8 [1990] Ch 265 at 292; affd [1991] Ch 547. See too *Foxton v Manchester and Liverpool District Banking Co* (1881) 44 LT 406; *Coleman v Bucks and Oxon Union Bank* [1897] 2 Ch 243; *Citadel General Assurance Co v Lloyds Bank Canada* [1997] 3 SCR 805; *Peppiatt v Nichol* (21 August 1998, unreported), Ontario Ct (Gen Div) at paras 316–346.
9 Sir P Millett (now Lord Millett) 'Tracing the Proceeds of Fraud' (1991) 107 LQR 70, 83, n 46, noted without deciding the issue by the NZCA in *Westpac Banking Corpn v M M Kembla New Zealand Ltd* [2001] 2 NZLR 298 at 316–317.
10 [1995] 2 AC 378.
11 [1993] 1 WLR 509n at 577.

the scope of categories (i)–(iii)[12].

Authorities expressly requiring dishonesty are: *Dubai Aluminium Co Ltd v Salaam* [1999] 1 Lloyd's Rep 415 at 453 (not considered by CA on appeal); *Bank of America v Arnell* [1999] Lloyd's Rep Bank 399 at 406–407 per Aikens J, citing *Twinsectra Ltd v Yardley* [1999] Lloyd's Rep Bank 438 at 463–466, where however Potter LJ seems to have been concerned solely with the question whether the defendant had been dishonest for the purposes of a claim in dishonest assistance; *Bank of Credit and Commerce International (Overseas) Ltd v Akindele* [1999] BCC 669, overruled on this point in the CA: [2001] Ch 437 at 448. or whether liability can also be incurred by those who fall within the scope of categories (iv) and (v)[13].

Having said this, however, it is clear that a person who receives trust or fiduciary property for his own benefit in circumstances where he has actual, 'Nelsonian' or 'naughty' knowledge of a misapplication by the trustee or fiduciary will be liable, being clearly at fault, while those who receive misapplied property without such knowledge will escape liability[14]. 'Nelsonian' knowledge (after Admiral Nelson putting his telescope to his blind eye to avoid knowledge of flag signals ordering him to withdraw at the Battle of Copenhagen) covers the deliberate shutting of eyes to what would otherwise be obvious[15]. A defendant has 'naughty' knowledge where he deliberately or recklessly fails to make the inquiries that an honest, reasonable man would make in circumstances where the defendant's suspicions were aroused[16]. Moreover, if the circumstances were such that the suspicions of an honest, reasonable man would have been aroused then the court will be slow to accept the defendant's protestations that his suspicions were not aroused and so will be ready to infer that his suspicions were aroused[17]. Essentially it is a matter of fact – a jury question[18] – whether or not the defendant exhibited dishonesty by virtue of having actual, Nelsonian, or naughty knowledge of the misapplication, bearing in mind that where he 'knows of circumstances which may on the one hand make the payment a misapplication but which may on the other hand be consistent with perfect propriety ... such a case might be determined on its particular facts by the principle that a party to a commercial agreement should not be fixed with notice simply because in a

12 *Re Montagu's Settlement Trusts* [1987] Ch 264; *Lipkin Gorman v Karpnale Ltd* [1987] 1 WLR 987 at 1005; *Barclays Bank plc v Quincecare Ltd* [1992] 4 All ER 363 at 375; *Eagle Trust plc v SBC Securities Ltd* [1992] 4 All ER 488 at 509; *Cowan de Groot Properties Ltd v Eagle Trust plc* [1992] 4 All ER 700 at 759; *Polly Peck International plc v Nadir (No 2)* [1992] 4 All ER 769 at 777; *Jonathan v Tilley* (1988) 12 Tru LI 36.

13 *Selangor United Rubber Estates Ltd v Cradock (No 3)* [1968] 1 WLR 1555; *Belmont Finance Corpn v Williams Furniture Ltd (No 2)* [1980] 1 All ER 393 at 405; *International Sales and Agencies Ltd v Marcus* [1982] 3 All ER 551 at 558; *Baden, Delvaux v Société Générale pour Favoriser le Développement du Commerce et de l'Industrie en France SA* [1993] 1 WLR 509n at 582; *Houghton v Fayers* [2000] 1 BCLC 511.

14 *Allen v Rea Bros Trustees Ltd* (2002) 4 ITELR 627 at 645, CA.

15 *Baden, Delvaux v Société Générale pour Favoriser le Développement du Commerce et de l'Industrie en France SA* [1993] 1 WLR 509n at 576. See too *The Star Sea* [2001] 2 WLR 170 at 207 per Lord Scott: 'an imputation of blind-eye knowledge requires an amalgam of suspicion that certain facts may exist and a decision to refrain from taking any step to confirm their existence'.

16 As pointed out in *Assets Co Ltd v Mere Roihi* [1905] AC 176 at 201: 'If it can be shown that his suspicions were aroused and that he abstained from making inquiries for fear of learning the truth ... fraud may be ascribed to him.'

17 *Eagle Trust plc v SBC Securities Ltd* [1992] 4 All ER 488 at 509; *El Ajou v Dollar Land Holdings plc* [1993] 3 All ER 717 at 739.

18 *Agip (Africa) Ltd v Jackson* [1990] Ch 265 at 293.

loose sense he has been put on inquiry'[19].

A defendant will not be liable if he knows that it would constitute a breach of trust if he were to receive trust property from the trustees, but he genuinely forgets this before he receives and deals with the property for his own benefit[20]. If a defendant knows at the time of receiving the property that it is misapplied trust property, then his conscience will be affected and he will hold the property on constructive trust for the beneficiaries from that time onwards, with the result that he will be liable by way of surcharging and falsifying his accounts to compensate the beneficiaries and/or to disgorge his gains to them, in the event that he deals with the property for his own benefit[1]. If a defendant receives misapplied trust property innocently, however, and only subsequently acquires knowledge of its improper provenance, then he will only be personally liable to the beneficiaries in respect of those dealings with the property that have taken place after he acquired knowledge[2]. On the basis that the defendant holds the property on constructive trust for the beneficiaries from the time that his conscience is affected with knowledge that the property is theirs, he will be strictly liable to compensate them by way of falsification of his accounts even in the exceptional case where the property is stolen or destroyed by an act of God after he knows that it should be returned to the beneficiaries.

Future development of the law

An attempt was recently made to cut through the terminological problems engendered by the *Baden, Delvaux* classification of knowledge by Nourse LJ in *BCCI (Overseas) Ltd v Akindele*[3], where he held that dishonesty will suffice, but is not required, to make a defendant liable where he has received and dealt with misapplied trust property for his own benefit[4], and that as a general rule a defendant will be liable whenever his 'state of knowledge [is] … such as to make it unconscionable for him to retain the benefit of the receipt'[5]. With respect to Nourse LJ, however, unconscionability is an uncertain concept, reference to which seems unlikely to bring clarity to this area of the law. Indeed, unconscionability was expressly rejected by Lord Nicholls in the *Royal Brunei* case as the test for assistance liability for precisely this reason[6].

It is submitted that the courts would do better to develop the law in this area by holding that dishonestly receiving and dealing with misapplied trust property for one's own benefit is a fault-based equitable wrong analogous to the wrong of dishonest dealing with trust property by agents described in Article 100(2). This could be achieved by reinterpreting the cases requiring fault for liability in this area as having been concerned with equitable

---

19 *Criterion Properties plc v Stratford UK Properties LLC* [2002] EWHC 496 (Ch), [2002] 2 BCLC 151 at 173.
20 *Re Montagu's Settlement Trusts* [1987] Ch 264 at 285.
1 *Rolled Steel Products (Holdings) Ltd v British Steel Corpn* [1986] Ch 246 at 303–304; *Westdeutsche Landesbank Girozentrale v Islington London Borough Council* [1996] AC 669 at 707.
2 *Re Diplock* [1948] Ch 465 at 477; *Allen v Rea Bros Trustees Ltd* (2002) 4 ITELR 627 at 642–643 and 645–646, CA.
3 [2001] Ch 437.
4 [2001] Ch 437 at 448, followed in *Criterion Properties plc v Stratford UK Properties LLC* [2002] EWHC 496 (Ch), [2002] 2 BCLC 151 at 171.
5 [2001] Ch 437 at 455.
6 [1995] 2 AC 378 at 392. Cf *Marshall Futures Ltd v Marshall* [1992] 1 NZLR 316 at 325; *Criterion Properties plc v Stratford UK Properties LLC* [2002] EWHC 496 (Ch), [2002] 2 BCLC 151 at 171.

wrongdoing. At the same time, the courts should also recognise that a strict liability claim in unjust enrichment will also lie against the recipients of mis-applied trust property. These twin developments have been advocated extra-judicially by Lord Nicholls[7], who has also indicated in obiter dicta that he favours a 'radical reappraisal' of the tort of conversion along the same lines[8].

Judicial observations suggesting that the courts are poised to develop the law relating to beneficial receipt and dealing with misapplied trust property in this way include[9]: Lord Nicholls' statement in *Royal Brunei Airlines Sdn Bhd v Tan* that 'recipient liability is restitution-based'[10]; the Court of Appeal's statement in *Grupo Torras SA v Al-Sabah (No 5)* that liability for knowing receipt is 'a receipt-based liability which may on examination prove to be either a vindication of persistent property rights or a personal restitutionary claim based on unjust enrichment by subtraction'[11]; and Lord Millett's statement in *Twinsectra Ltd v Yardley* that[12]:

> 'Liability for 'knowing receipt' is receipt-based. It does not depend on fault. The cause of action is restitutionary and is available only where the defendant received or applied the money in breach of trust for his own use and benefit ... There is no basis for requiring actual knowledge of the breach of trust, let alone dishonesty, as a condition of liability. Constructive notice is sufficient, and may not even be necessary. There is powerful academic support for the proposition that the liability of the recipient is the same as in other cases of restitution, that is to say strict but subject to a change of position defence.'

A dissenting note was struck by Nourse LJ in *Bank of Credit and Commerce International (Overseas) Ltd v Akindele*[13], who remarked of claims against those who receive and deal with misapplied trust property for their own benefit that 'it may be possible to sympathise with a tendency to subsume a further part of our law of restitution under the principles of unjust enrichment', but who begged 'leave to doubt whether strict liability coupled with a change of position defence would be preferable to fault-based liability in many com-mercial transactions.' In the same case, Nourse LJ also considered that to develop the law in the manner advocated here, it would be necessary for a claimant to take his case to the House of Lords[14]. However, if the existing authorities requiring fault for liability were construed to mean that fault is required for a wrong-based liability, then arguably they would not contradict

---

7 In his article 'Knowing Receipt: The Need for a New Landmark', in W R Cornish et al (eds) *Restitution: Past, Present and Future* (1998) at p 231. See too P Birks, 'Receipt', in P Birks and A Pretto (eds), *Breach of Trust* (2002) at p 213; but for a different view, see L D Smith, 'Unjust Enrichment, Property, and the Structure of Trusts' (2000) 116 LQR 412.

8 *Kuwait Airlines Corpn v Iraqi Airways Co (No 3)* [2002] 3 All ER 209 at 230.

9 See too *Powell v Thompson* [1991] 1 NZLR 597 at 607; *Equiticorp Industries Group Ltd v R* [1996] 3 NZLR 586 at 604 (Smellie J); *Kooratang Nominees Pty Ltd v Australia and New Zealand Banking Group Ltd* [1998] 3 VR 16 at 99 ff. A different model has been pursued in Canada, where knowing receipt has been held to be a fault-based claim in unjust enrichment, contrary to the general position that liability in unjust enrichment is strict: see *Gold v Rosenberg* [1997] 3 SCR 767 and *Citadel General Assurance Co v Lloyds Bank Canada* [1997] 3 SCR 805, criticised in P Birks, 'The Role of Fault in the Law of Unjust Enrichment', in W Swadling and G Jones (eds), *The Search for Principle* (1999) 235, at 235–238 and 268–271; M Bryan, 'The Receipt-Based Constructive Trust: A Case Study of Personal and Proprietary Restitution in the Supreme Court' (1999) 37 Alberta LR 73, at 90–93.

10 [1995] 2 AC 378 at 382.

11 [2001] Lloyd's Rep Bank 36 at 62.

12 [2002] 2 AC 164 at 194.

13 [2001] Ch 437 at 456.

14 [2001] Ch 437 at 456.

the proposition that a separate, strict liability claim in unjust enrichment can also lie.

In addition to the dicta which have already been cited, there are three further sources of authority upon which a claimant might draw to support the introduction of a strict liability claim in unjust enrichment against the recipients of misapplied trust property. First, it was held by the House of Lords in *Ministry of Health v Simpson*[15] that the recipients of funds improperly distributed in the administration of a deceased person's estate are strictly liable to repay the persons properly entitled to the estate, and it is submitted that there is no compelling reason of principle why this situation should be treated differently from the situation where trust assets are misdirected. Secondly, it was held by the House of Lords in *Lipkin Gorman v Karpnale Ltd*[16] that a common law action for money had and received would lie where a claimant's property was wrongfully taken from him by a third party and transferred without his knowledge to the defendant, and again it is submitted that there is no compelling reason of principle why this situation should be treated differently from the situation where trust assets are misdirected. Thirdly, it has been held that where trust assets are misappropriated by a trustee and used to pay off a security charged on property belonging to an innocent third party, the beneficiaries are entitled to be subrogated to the extinguished rights which were formerly possessed by the charge-holder, and to be treated, by a legal fiction, as though these rights were not extinguished, but were instead assigned to the beneficiaries in order that they might enforce them against the innocent third party for their own benefit[17].

The English courts have now recognised that subrogation is a remedy awarded to reverse unjust enrichment[18], and it is submitted that if the beneficiaries are entitled to acquire proprietary rights against innocent third parties via subrogation on the ground of unjust enrichment, then *a fortiori* they ought also to be entitled to a direct personal claim in unjust enrichment against innocent third parties who are enriched at the beneficiaries' expense.

In the event that the recipients of misapplied trust property were made strictly liable to make restitution to the beneficiaries on the ground of unjust enrichment, the question arises whether any room would then be left in practice for a wrong-based knowing receipt action, where proof of fault was required: ie would circumstances ever arise in which a claimant might wish to bring a wrong-based claim? One answer to this question is that a defendant who received trust property ministerially would have a good defence to the unjust enrichment claim, but would not have a defence against the wrong-based claim[19]. Another is that a claimant might suffer a loss that is greater than the benefit received by the defendant, with the result that the claimant

---

15 [1951] AC 251.

16 [1991] 2 AC 548.

17 *McCullough v Marsden* (1919) 45 DLR 645 at 646–647, Albert CA; subsequent proceedings: *McCullough v Elliott* (1922) 62 DLR 257; *Boscawen v Bajwa* [1996] 1 WLR 328 might also be viewed as a relevant authority, if it is correct to say that the claimant's entitlement to subrogation in the case derived from the fact that the money used to pay off the charge to which it was subrogated had been impressed with a *Quistclose* trust in its favour.

18 *Banque Financière de la Cité v Parc (Battersea) Ltd* [1999] 1 AC 221 at 228 per Lord Steyn and at 234 per Lord Hoffmann (also emphasising at 236 the fictional nature of treating the claimant as though the creditor's extinguished rights have been 'kept alive' and transferred to him); *Birmingham Midshires Mortgage Services Ltd v Sabherwal* (1999) 80 P & CR 256 at 264 per Robert Walker LJ.

19 See p 970, ante.

would be better off seeking a compensatory rather than a restitutionary remedy. Extra-judicially, Lord Nicholls has argued that in such a case, the claimant should be entitled to recover compensation from the defendant, provided that the defendant has acted dishonestly[20]. One example of a situation where such an award might be appropriate would be where a defendant receives half of a claimant's 60% company shareholding, where the shares received by the defendant are worth less to him (as a minority holding) than they are to the claimant (as the difference between a minority and a majority holding). Another example is provided by the facts of a recent Canadian case, *Treaty Group Inc v Simpson*[1], where the claimant company successfully pursued an action for 'knowing receipt' and was awarded 'aggravated damages' over and above the amount of money which the defendant had received at its expense, to compensate the claimant for the loss of profits which it had sustained when its employees' time and energy had been diverted from their usual duties into the task of unravelling the wrongdoing fiduciary's fraud.

Change of position defence

In the event that the courts hold that a claim in unjust enrichment lies against the recipients of misapplied trust property, it seems likely that recipients who are sued on this basis will often attempt to raise a change of position defence. It therefore seems apposite to give a brief account here of the circumstances in which this defence is available.

In practice, the defence of change of position is most often relied upon by defendants who have incurred extraordinary expenditure in reliance on their receipt of the benefit which forms the subject-matter of the claim: ie because they have received the benefit, they have been led to spend their money on something which they would not otherwise have bought. However, the defence is available to a wider class of defendants than this, and there is no need to show that the change in a defendant's position came about because he consciously incurred expenditure in reliance on his receipt of the benefit, although there must be a causal link 'at least on a "but-for" test' between the receipt of the benefit and the change in the defendant's position[2]. Thus, a defendant who is paid £5,000 and then immediately loses it when his wallet is stolen can raise the defence even though it cannot be said that he changed his position in reliance on his receipt. A defendant who changes his position in anticipation of a benefit which is subsequently paid to him can also raise the defence[3]. In the event that a defendant changes his position by purchasing an asset which remains in his possession at the time when the claim is

---

20 Lord Nicholls, 'Knowing Receipt: The Need for a New Landmark', in W R Cornish et al (eds) *Restitution: Past, Present and Future* (1998) 231 at 244: 'in the case of dishonest recipients, liability is not confined to the value of the property received'.

1 (2001) 103 ACWS (3d) 1072 at paras 29–31.

2 *Derby v Scottish Equitable plc* [2001] EWCA Civ 369, [2001] 3 All ER 818 at 827. Quaere whether even this was made out on the facts of *Philip Collins Ltd v Davies* [2000] 3 All ER 808, where at 829 Jonathan Parker J was 'unable to find that any particular item of expenditure was directly referable to the overpayments of royalties' received by the defendant musician, but at 830 proceeded to hold nonetheless that in a 'general' way, the defendant's outgoings were larger than they would have been, had he not been overpaid, because he had pursued a general life strategy of spending all his income whenever he got it. The judge allowed defence to half the claim, adopting a 'broad approach' which rode roughshod over the rules of evidence.

3 *Dextra Bank and Trust Co Ltd v Bank of Jamaica* [2002] 1 All ER (Comm) 193, PC.

made, he cannot rely on the defence to the extent that he remains enriched by his possession of the asset[4].

In *Lipkin Gorman v Karpnale Ltd*[5], Lord Goff held that the defence is available only to those who change their position in good faith, a formulation which clearly excludes defendants who have been consciously dishonest, but which may also exclude those who have failed 'to act in a commercially acceptable way' and those who have engaged in 'sharp practice of a kind that falls short of outright dishonesty'[6]. On the other hand, 'mere negligence on the part of the recipient is not sufficient to deprive him of the defence of change of position'[7].

PARAGRAPH 5

Where one of the beneficiaries has joined in the breach his beneficial interest is liable to make good the loss

As stated in the fifth paragraph of the present Article, the equitable interest of one of several beneficiaries, who has made himself liable by joining in a breach of trust, may be stopped at the instance of his co-beneficiaries, until the whole loss to the estate has been made good. This right *of the beneficiaries* must not, however, be confused with the limited right *of the trustee* (treated of in Article 99, ante) to impound the interest of a beneficiary who has requested, instigated, or consented in writing to a breach of trust, by way of indemnifying the trustee himself. The two rights are essentially different, and it is apprehended that beneficiaries might have the right referred to in paragraph 5 of the present Article in cases where the trustee (who as particeps criminis) might not be allowed to impound the interest of the instigating beneficiary. It must also be understood that the rule laid down in paragraph 5 of the present Article applies a fortiori to the case of a beneficiary who is also a trustee.

It should be noted that a trustee will not be ordered to pay a debt to the trust fund if (or to the extent that) it can be recouped simply by withholding from him the property to which he would otherwise be entitled as beneficiary[8].

Retainer of income to make good breach instigated by tenant for life

A trustee, in breach of trust, lent the trust fund to AB, the tenant for life. The trustee afterwards concurred in a creditor's deed, by which AB's life interest

---

4 *Lipkin Gorman v Karpnale Ltd* [1991] 2 AC 548 at 560 per Lord Templeman, whose view is to be preferred to the contrary conclusion which was apparently reached by the Newfoundland CA in *RBC Dominion Securities Inc v Dawson* (1994) 111 DLR (4th) 230.

5 [1991] 2 AC 548 at 580.

6 *Niru Battery Manufacturing Co v Milestone Trading Ltd* [2002] EWHC 1425 (Comm) at para 135.

7 *Niru Battery Manufacturing Co v Milestone Trading Ltd* [2002] EWHC 1425 (Comm) at para 125 per Moore-Bick J, relying on *Dextra Bank and Trust Co Ltd v Bank of Jamaica* [2002] 1 All ER (Comm) 193, where at paras 42–45 the Privy Council declined to hold that the relative fault of the claimant and the defendant can affect the availability of the defence, and also held that 'if fault is to be taken into account at all, it would surely be unjust to take into account the fault of one party (the defendant) but to ignore fault on the part of the other (the plaintiff).'

8 *Re VGM Holdings Ltd* [1942] Ch 235, [1942] 1 All ER 224; *Selangor United Rubber Estates Ltd v Cradock (No 4)* [1969] 3 All ER 965, [1969] 1 WLR 1773.

was to be applied in payment of his debts, and the trustee received there-under a debt due to him from AB. Before the other creditors had been paid, the trustee retained the life income to make good the breach of trust. It was held that the court would not restrain the trustee from making good the breach of trust out of the life income; for although the trustee, being a creditor and party to the deed, had, qua himself, no right to retain the life interest, yet, as representing the beneficiaries, he was justified in so doing[9].

Rule applies to derivative as well as to original shares

The rule applies not only to shares taken directly under the settlement creating the trust, but also to shares purchased from or otherwise derived through or under immediate beneficiaries. Thus, where a Mrs D, who was trustee and life tenant under a will, took assignments from two of the bene-ficiaries entitled in remainder, and committed divers breaches of trust which only came to light on her death, it was held that the two shares which she had purchased were liable to make good the loss to the estate. Moreover, this right of the beneficiaries was held to take priority over the rights of persons to whom Mrs D had mortgaged the shares in question[10]. The fact that the mortgagees were bona fide mortgagees for value without notice was imma-terial, for the equitable interest in question was a chose in action, and pur-chasers of choses in action take subject to all equities. Indeed, so far has this been carried, that such purchasers have been held to take subject to breaches of trust committed *after* the purchase[11].

But not to independent trust created by same instrument

The rule, however, has no application to beneficial interests under inde-pendent trusts even although created by the same settlor and by the same instrument. Thus where a person is beneficially interested in (or even a trustee of) settled residuary estate and is liable for a breach of trust com-mitted in relation thereto, his beneficial interest under a trust of specific property created by the same will cannot be impounded[12].

Retainer of beneficiary's interest to make good a debt due from him to the trust estate, even where statute barred

The rule now under consideration is not confined to cases of breach of trust, but is equally applicable where a beneficiary is indebted to the trust estate. By a separation deed, after reciting that the husband and wife had agreed to live apart, the husband assigned certain leaseholds to trustees in trust to pay the rents to the wife for life[13], and then to sell and hold the proceeds (in the

---

9 *Fuller v Knight* (1843) 6 Beav 205; and see also *Carson v Sloane* (1884) 13 LR Ir 139; *Bolton v Curre* [1895] 1 Ch 544.

10 *Doering v Doering* (1889) 42 Ch D 203 and cases there cited; and see also *Re Akerman* [1891] 3 Ch 212; *Re Dacre* [1915] 2 Ch 480; on appeal [1916] 1 Ch 344; *Re Melton* [1918] 1 Ch 37; and *Re Jewell's Settlement* [1919] 2 Ch 161.

11 Per Hall V-C in *Hooper v Smart* (1875) 1 Ch D 90 at 98; and see also *Morris v Livie* (1842) 1 Y & C Ch Cas 380; *Irby v Irby* (1858) 25 Beav 632; *Barnett v Sheffield* (1852) 1 De GM & G 371; *Cole v Muddle* (1852) 10 Hare 186; and *Re Pain* [1919] 1 Ch 38; *Re Knapman* (1881) 18 Ch D 300 at 307, CA.

12 *Re Towndrow* [1911] 1 Ch 662.

13 Since this was long before 1926 the leaseholds did not become settled land.

events which happened) in trust for himself; and he covenanted to make up the wife's income to £300 a year. The husband paid nothing under the covenant, and he was subsequently adjudicated a bankrupt. The trustees proved for arrears due down to the date of the bankruptcy, but there were further arrears due to them since that date. On the death of the wife, the husband's assignee in bankruptcy claimed the leaseholds. It was held, however, that the trustees were entitled to retain them until the arrears were satisfied, and it seems that the right of trustees to retain trust property as against a beneficiary who owes money to them as trustees under the instrument creating the trust, exists in favour of trustees of a voluntary settlement which has been so completed as to be enforceable by the court[14]. The rule applies even where the debt is statute barred[15], provided that it was a debt for which, but for the statute[16], the debtor could have been sued[17]. Trustees cannot, however, retain the share of a beneficiary as against *future instalments* of a debt repayable by instalments[18].

Acceptance of a composition from defaulting trustee-beneficiary

Where a defaulting trustee who is also a beneficiary in remainder makes a composition which is accepted by the new trustees they cannot afterwards claim to retain his beneficial interest to make good the balance of the loss[19].

Where plaintiff is also the residuary legatee of person who has benefited by breach

A somewhat curious complication arises where money has, in breach of trust, been paid to a person whose estate subsequently devolves on or is bequeathed to the plaintiff. Thus, where a trustee had wrongfully paid part of the capital of the trust fund to the plaintiff's father under whose intestacy the plaintiff was entitled to and received two-thirds of his estate, it was held that the father's assets in the hands of the plaintiff were primarily liable to make good two-thirds of the trust fund in exoneration of the trustee[20].

How far beneficiary who has been innocently overpaid is liable to refund

Where a trustee has made any over-payment to a beneficiary in error, whether of fact or law[1], he can, on behalf of the other beneficiaries, and where the trust property is still in his hands on behalf of himself if he also be a beneficiary[2], recoup the trust out of the overpaid beneficiary's interest or

---

14 *Re Weston* [1900] 2 Ch 164; *Re Akerman* [1891] 3 Ch 212; and see and consider analogous right of executors, *Re Taylor* [1894] 1 Ch 671.
15 *Re Akerman* [1891] 3 Ch 212; *Re Wheeler* [1904] 2 Ch 66.
16 Now the Limitation Act 1980.
17 See *Re Wheeler* [1904] 2 Ch 66.
18 *Re Abrahams* [1908] 2 Ch 69.
19 *Re Sewell* [1909] 1 Ch 806.
20 *Orrett v Corser* (1855) 21 Beav 52.
1 *Re Musgrave* [1916] 2 Ch 417; *Re Wooldridge* [1920] WN 78.
2 *Re Reading* [1916] WN 262, in which the contrary decision of Warrington J in *Re Horne* [1905] 1 Ch 76 (criticised by Goff & Jones, *Law of Restitution* (5th edn, 1998) at p 224) was said not to be of general application.

capital or income which subsequently becomes due to such beneficiary[3]: this is part of the equitable accounting process in the administration of the trust, the trustee's set-off being a defence for him[4]. On the other hand, the court will not, as a rule, order the over-paid beneficiary personally to refund to the trustee who has been disallowed the item in his accounts[5]. However, it may be that a *co-beneficiary* could compel repayment of the excess or so much thereof as could not be recovered from the trustee as the party responsible for the over-payment[6], but the onus would lie upon him of proving that what the other beneficiary had received was an over-payment, having regard to the value of the estate at the date of the payment, and did not arise merely by reason of *subsequent* depreciation[7]. This, of course, presupposes that payment at all, at the date in question, was proper, for otherwise, if the date for payment to the knowledge of the payee had not arisen, the payment would itself have been a breach of trust to which the payee would have been privy.

Where personal representatives had acted upon a wrong view of the effect of a will, and had distributed the estate amongst persons who had no title at all but were mere strangers to the estate, the House of Lords held that the recipients were personally liable, at the suit of the true beneficiaries or of creditors, to refund the sums paid to them, so far as such sums could not be recovered from the personal representatives, but without interest[8]. Such strict liability, subject to the defence of change of position, should extend to wrongful recipients of trust property, whether a mistake of fact or law is involved, so as to prevent the unjust enrichment of such recipients[9].

No recouping of excess income derived from improper investment

It appears to be settled that, where a beneficiary for life has received a high rate of interest from a security on which the trustees ought not to have invested, and which subsequently turns out to be insufficient, he will not be liable to account for any part of the income received[10] unless he was either one of the trustees[11], or with full knowledge, a consenting party to the investment[12]. Per contra he will not get any arrears of income on realisation of the security without bringing into hotchpot all income received by him

---

3 *Livesey v Livesey* (1827) 3 Russ 287; *Dibbs v Goren* (1849) 11 Beav 483; *IVS Enterprises Ltd v Chelsea Cloisters Management Ltd* (1999) 13 Tru LR 111, and discussed by P Matthews [1994] Rest LR 44. *Re Musgrave* [1916] 2 Ch 417 (but there is no such right where the income arises under a covenant, and not a trust: *Re Hatch* [1919] 1 Ch 351).

4 He has a lien for this purpose: *Dibbs v Goren* (1849) 11 Beav 483; *Williams v Allen (No 2)* (1863) 32 Beav 650.

5 *Downes v Bullock* (1858) 25 Beav 54; *Bate v Hooper* (1855) 5 De GM & G 338; but cf *Hood v Clapham* (1854) 19 Beav 90, where it was allowed; and consider *Allcard v Walker* [1896] 2 Ch 369 at 384, as to the converse case, where funds have been erroneously paid to the trustees.

6 *Harris v Harris (No 2)* (1861) 29 Beav 110; *Baynard v Woolley* (1855) 20 Beav 583; *Re Robinson* [1911] 1 Ch 502 at 508; *Ministry of Health v Simpson* [1951] AC 251 at 274.

7 *Re Winslow* (1890) 45 Ch D 249; *Fenwick v Clarke* (1862) 4 De GF & J 240; *Peterson v Peterson* (1866) LR 3 Eq 111; and *Hilliard v Fulford* (1876) 4 Ch D 389.

8 *Minister of Health v Simpson* [1951] AC 251, [1950] 2 All ER 1137.

9 See p 977 above. The rule that an action in unjust enrichment will not lie to recover money paid under a mistake of law was abolished in *Kleinwort Benson Ltd v Lincoln City Council* [1999] 2 AC 349.

10 See *Re Bird* [1901] 1 Ch 916, and comments thereon of Warrington KC arguendo in *Re Alston* [1901] 2 Ch 584 at 587; *Re Horne* [1905] 1 Ch 76.

11 See *Re Sharp* [1906] 1 Ch 793 at 796.

12 See *Griffiths v Porter* (1858) 25 Beav 236.

during its continuance[13]; but this will not be so where the investment was not improperly made (eg where it was made by the testator himself)[14].

ARTICLE 101

Tracing and following trust property and its proceeds into the hands of third parties

(1) If trust property or its traceable product is found in the hands of any person in circumstances inconsistent with the trust, he will hold it as constructive trustee[15] subject to the interests of beneficiaries under the trust except to the extent that he proves[16] that the defence of change of position is available to him, or that he or some person through whom he claims[17] has bona fide acquired the property for valuable consideration and without receiving notice, before the transaction was completed[18], that the acquisition was a breach of trust, and:

(a) has acquired the legal (as distinguished from a mere equitable) title[19]; or

(b) having acquired a mere equitable title has been induced to acquire it for value by the fraud or negligence of the persons having the legal title[20]; or

(c) the property, being a chose in action[1], consists of a negotiable instrument[2], or an instrument which was intended by the parties thereto to be transferable free from all equities attaching to it[3].

(2) A person who purchases property with notice of an equitable

---

13 *Griffiths v Porter* (1858) 25 Beav 236.

14 *Re Coaks* [1911] 1 Ch 171; and see Article 53, ante.

15 *Peffer v Rigg* [1977] 1 WLR 285 at 294; *Baden v Societe Generate* [1992] 4 All ER 161 at 231; *Re Montagu's Settlement Trusts* [1987] Ch 264 at 270, 276, 285 [1992] 4 All ER 308 at 318, 322, 329; *Polly Peck International plc v Nadir (No 2)* [1992] 4 All ER 769 at 781 per Scott LJ; *Boscawen v Bajwa* [1996] 1 WLR 328 at 335, per Millett LJ; *Bauhgesellschaft Berlin AG v Makris* (22 January 1998, unreported), QBD (Comm Ct).

16 The defendant prima facie, cannot claim a better title than the trustee-transferor to him, so to defend wholly or pro tanto the prior equitable interest which burdens his title it is up to him to establish a defence: *Re Nisbett & Pott's Contract* [1905] 1 Ch 391 at 398; *Barclays Bank plc v Boulter* [1999] 4 All ER 513 at 518, per Lord Hoffman.

17 *Harrison v Forth* (1695) Prec Ch 51; *Mertins v Joliffe* (1756) Amb 311; *M'Queen v Farquhar* (1805) 11 Ves 467.

18 *Bassett v Nosworthy* (1673) Cas temp Finch 102, 2 White & Tud LC 163; *Boursot v Savage* (1866) LR 2 Eq 134; *Mackreth v Symmons* (1808) 15 Ves 329, 2 White & Tud LC 946; *Pilcher v Rawlins* (1872) 7 Ch App 259; *London and Canadian Loan and Agency Co v Duggan* [1893] AC 506; and as to the time at which the notice is effectual, *Lady Bodmin v Vandenbendy* (1683) 1 Vern 179; *Jones v Thomas* (1734) 3 P Wms 243; *A-G v Gower* (1736) 2 Eq Cas Abr 685, pl 11; *More v Mayhow* (1663) 1 Cas in Ch 34. Registered land requires separate consideration: see p 1003, post.

19 See per Lord Westbury in *Phillips v Phillips* (1861) 4 De GF & J 208; *Rimmer v Webster* [1902] 2 Ch 163.

20 See *Walker v Linom* [1907] 2 Ch 104.

1 *Turton v Benson* (1719) 1 P Wms 496; *Ord v White* (1840) 3 Beav 357; *Mangles v Dixon* (1852) 3 HL Cas 702; *Doering v Doering* (1889) 42 Ch D 203.

2 *Anon* (1697) 1 Com 43.

3 *Re Blakely Ordnance Co* (1867) 3 Ch App 154; *Re General Estates Co* (1868) 3 Ch App 758; *Crouch v Credit Foncier of England* (1873) LR 8 QB 374.

interest affecting that property will hold such property subject thereto unless it has been validly discharged[4].

PARAGRAPH 1

Relative rights of legal and equitable claimants

The rule enunciated in this paragraph is derived from well-known property principles namely:

(1) where the equities are equal the law prevails so a bona fide purchaser for value of a legal interest without notice of an equitable interest prevails over the holder of the equitable interest; and

(2) as between mere equitable claimants qui prior in tempore, potior in jure est.

In fact, where one of two innocent parties must suffer, then as equity is not called upon to interfere on behalf of either of them, the common law must take its course; and the one who has the legal estate, or its equivalent, will take priority over the one who has a mere equitable claim, notwithstanding that the title of the legal claimant may have accrued after that of the equitable one. The rule is very strikingly and completely illustrated by the case of *Cave v Cave*[5] where a trustee, who was a solicitor, fraudulently misappropriated the trust fund, and with it bought an estate which was conveyed to his brother. The brother then mortgaged the property, by legal, and afterwards by equitable, mortgages, the solicitor-trustee acting on all such occasions as the solicitor both for mortgagor *and mortgagees*. The parties beneficially entitled under the trust claimed to follow their trust money into the property which had been bought with it, on the ground that, as the solicitor of the mortgagees had notice of the breach of trust, that notice must be imputed to the mortgagees themselves.

It was held, however, that, as the solicitor was a party to the fraud, notice of the equity of the beneficiaries could not be imputed constructively to the clients, the mortgagees, for the conduct of the agent raised a conclusive presumption that he would not communicate to the client the facts in controversy. Consequently their equities and the equity of the beneficiaries were equal, whence it followed, on the maxim 'where the equities are equal the law prevails', that the legal mortgagee, having the legal estate, took priority over the beneficiaries, but that the latter took priority over the equitable mortgagees because their equity was first in point of date[6].

A recent instructive case is *Kleinwort Benson v Vaughan*[7] where V stole £248,000 from his employer to buy a house in the name of himself and his wife with the further assistance of a £70,000 mortgage loan from the employer, which sold the mortgage to N. Ultimately, the employer, B, discovered what had happened and traced its money into the house, so the

---

4 *Jared v Clements* [1903] 1 Ch 428 (vendor, who had failed to disclose an equitable mortgage, subsequently produced a forged discharge which the purchaser relied upon in completing the purchase, having discovered and raised requisitions on the equitable mortgage, but the purchaser was bound by the mortgage); *Boursot v Savage* (1866) LR 2 Eq 134.

5 (1880) 15 Ch D 639; and see also *Powell v London and Provincial Bank* [1893] 2 Ch 555, CA; and *Capell v Winter* [1907] 2 Ch 376.

6 See also *Pilcher v Rawlins* (1872) 7 Ch App 259.

7 [1994] NPC 31.

court charged the house with repayment of the money and B was enabled to sell the house but only after paying N off so as to be able to confer an unincumbered title on the purchaser. Having paid off N, the employer claimed to recoup from Mr and Mrs V the money paid to discharge their mortgage. This claim was rejected. After all, N was a bona fide purchaser of a legal mortgage without notice of the employer's equitable interest, so that qua mortgagee N could have sold the house and taken the moneys due to it, thereby preventing from arising any question of the employer having any claim against Mr and Mrs V in respect of such moneys by subrogation or otherwise. The fact that it was the employer chargee, rather than N, which exercised the power of sale could not change matters: the employer's right extended only to the equity of redemption subject to N's charge and they could not enlarge such rights by voluntarily paying off N's charge to enable them to sell a title unencumbered by such charge rather than encumbered thereby.

Notice of doubtful equity

To deprive a person who has acquired a legal right to property for valuable consideration the notice of a superior equity must be notice of facts which would clearly show the existence of such equity, at all events, to a lawyer. Thus, a bona fide purchaser for value is not bound by notice of a very doubtful equity, for instance, where the construction of a trust is ambiguous or equivocal[8].

Thus, in *Carl Zeiss Stiftung v Herbert Smith & Co (No 2)*[9] a firm of solicitors received money in payment of their costs from a company for which they acted. These costs were incurred in an action in which another organisation or foundation claimed all the assets of their client company and alleged that their client company held all its assets upon trust for the other foundation; but these claims were unresolved when the payment was received and they involved complicated questions of fact and of law, both English and German. The other foundation then brought a subsidiary action against the solicitors to recover the money paid to them on the ground that they had received it with knowledge of the facts averred in the main action and thus with notice that the money belonged to the foundation.

The Court of Appeal held, however, that such notice was merely notice of a doubtful equity. When they received the money, the solicitors did not know whether the claim was well founded or not and the mere knowledge of its existence was not enough to make them constructive trustees for the foundation.

Purchasing from two sets of trustees who are mortgagees under a contributory mortgage

It has been held that where two sets of trustees have joined in advancing money on a contributory mortgage (on the face of which their fiduciary characters appeared), and they sell under their power of sale, the purchaser

---

8 *Hardy v Reeves* (1800) 5 Ves 426; *Cordwell v Mackrill* (1766) Amb 515; *Warrick v Warrick and Kniveton* (1745) 3 Atk 291; but see and consider per Lord St Leonards in *Thompson v Simpson* (1841) 1 Dr & War 459.
9 [1969] 2 Ch 276, CA; cp *United Mizrahi Bank v Doherty* [1988] 1 WLR 435.

is not bound to see that each set of trustees gets their due proportion of the purchase-money on the ground, apparently, that the purchase-money is not the debt, but only a security therefore[10].

Trust money paid in to trustee's private overdrawn account

Where a trustee has overdrawn his banking account, his bankers have a first and paramount legal lien on all moneys paid in by him, unless they have notice, not only that they are trust moneys[11], but also that payment to them constitutes a breach of trust[12].

Costs paid by defaulting trustee to his solicitor

On similar grounds it has been held that the solicitor of a trustee is not debarred from accepting payments out of the estate in respect of costs properly incurred, unless he had knowledge that, at the time when he accepted them, the trustee had been guilty of such a breach of trust as would preclude him from resorting to the trust estate for payment of costs[13]. Where, however, a solicitor receives money with knowledge of a breach of trust, a summary order may be made upon him to pay into court, without the necessity of an action[14].

What constitutes notice

The subject of notice is now governed by s 199 of the Law of Property Act 1925 which is in the following words:

> (1) A purchaser shall not be prejudicially affected by notice of—
> > (i) any instrument or matter capable of registration under the provisions of the Land Charges Act 1925, or any enactment which it replaces, which is void or not enforceable as against him under that Act or enactment, by reason of the non-registration thereof[15];
> > (ii) any other instrument or matter or any fact or thing unless—
> > > (a) it is within his own knowledge, or would have come to his knowledge

---

10 *Re Parker and Beech's Contract* (1887) 56 LJ Ch 358, sed quaere. Now see ss 107, 111, 113 of the Law of Property Act 1925 so that a purchaser may assume the mortgagees are entitled on a joint account and may jointly give a valid receipt.

11 *Thomson v Clydesdale Bank* [1893] AC 282, HL (considered in *Selangor United Rubber Estates Ltd v Cradock (a bankrupt) (No 3)* [1968] 2 All ER 1073, [1968] 1 WLR 1555). As to notice, see *Texas Co v Bombay Banking Co* (1919) LR 46 Ind App 250.

12 *Coleman v Bucks and Oxon Union Bank* [1897] 2 Ch 243; *Union Bank of Australia Ltd v Murray-Aynsley* [1898] AC 693, PC; *Re Spencer* (1881) 51 LJ Ch 271; but cf *Mutton v Peat* [1900] 2 Ch 79.

13 *Re Blundell* (1888) 40 Ch D 370.

14 *Re Carroll* [1902] 2 Ch 175.

15 In connection with the sale of land, it is necessary to consider also the provisions of ss 24 and 25 of the Law of Property Act 1969, which came into force on 1 January 1970. Briefly, s 24 provides that where under a contract for the sale of unregistered land, any question arises as to whether the purchaser had notice, at the time of entering into it, of a registered land charge, that question is to be determined by reference to his actual knowledge and without regard to the provisions of s 198 of the Law of Property Act 1925 (whereby registration is deemed to constitute actual notice). Section 25 is concerned with cases in which the purchaser completes his purchase in ignorance of a registered land charge which he has failed to discover because it is registered against the name of someone who does not figure in the title to the property (ie, generally because the title commences too late to include him), and provides for compensation to be paid to such a purchaser.

> if such inquiries and inspections had been made as ought reasonably to have been made by him[16], or
> (b) in the same transaction with respect to which a question of notice to the purchaser arises, it has come to the knowledge of his counsel, as such, or of his solicitor or other agent, as such, or would have come to the knowledge of his solicitor or other agent, as such, if such inquiries and inspections had been made as ought reasonably to have been made by the solicitor or other agent.
>
> (2) Paragraph (ii) of the last subsection shall not exempt a purchaser from any liability under, or any obligation to perform or observe, any covenant, condition, provision, or restriction contained in any instrument under which his title is derived, mediately or immediately; and such liability or obligation may be enforced in the same manner and to the same extent as if that paragraph had not been enacted.
> (3) A purchaser shall not by reason of anything in this section be affected by notice in any case where he would not have been so affected if this section had not been enacted.
> (4) This section applies to purchases made either before or after the commencement of this Act.

It will be perceived that sub-s (1)(ii)(a) relates to actual or constructive notice of the party affected personally, and that sub-s (1)(ii)(b) relates to actual or constructive notice of his agents which is imputed to him.

The protection afforded by the legal estate to a purchaser of land is further extended by statute, so that in many cases he is able to purchase free from equitable interests even though he has notice of them. The provisions having this effect are contained in s 2 of the Law of Property Act 1925 which, as amended by the Law of Property (Amendment) Act 1926 and the Trusts of Land and Appointment of Trustees Act 1996 is in the following words:

> (1) A conveyance to a purchaser of a legal estate in land shall overreach[17] any equitable interest or power affecting that estate, whether or not he has notice thereof, if—
> (i) the conveyance is made under the powers conferred by the Settled Land Act, 1925, or any additional powers conferred by a settlement, and the equitable interest or power is capable of being overreached thereby, and the statutory requirements respecting the payment of capital money arising under the settlement are complied with;
> (ii) the conveyance is made by trustees of land and the equitable interest or power is at the date of the conveyance capable of being overreached by such trustees under for provisions of subsection (2) of this section or independently of that subsection, and the requirements of section 27 of this Act respecting the payment of capital money arising on such a conveyance;
> (iii) the conveyance is made by a mortgagee or personal representative in the exercise of his paramount powers, and the equitable interest or power is capable of being overreached by such conveyance, and any capital money arising from the transaction is paid to the mortgagee or personal representative;
> (iv) the conveyance is made under an order of the court and the equitable interest or power is bound by such order, and any capital money arising

---

16 Nowadays, a purchaser is under a duty to inquire of a wife in occupation whether or not she claims any equitable interest: *Kingsnorth Trust Ltd v Tizard* [1986] 2 All ER 54, [1986] 1 WLR 783.

17 Overreaching occurs whether or not the mortgagor receives any capital money from the mortgagee at the time of the mortgage: *State Bank of India v Sood* [1997] Ch 276, CA.

from the transaction is paid into, or in, accordance with the order of, the court.

(2) [Where the legal estate affected is subject to a trust of land, then if at the date of a conveyance made after the commencement of this Act by the trustees, trustees (whether original or substituted) are either—

    (a)   two or more individuals approved or appointed by the court or the successors in office of the individuals so approved or appointed; or

    (b)   a trust corporation;

[any equitable interest or power having priority to the trust] shall, not-withstanding any stipulation to the contrary, be overreached by the conveyance, and shall, according to its priority, take effect as if created or arising by means of a primary trust affecting the proceeds of sale and the income of the land until sale.

(3) The following equitable interests and powers are excepted from the operation of subsection (2) of this section, namely—

    (i)   Any equitable interest protected by a deposit of documents relating to the legal estate affected;

    (ii) The benefit of any covenant or agreement restrictive of the user of land;

    (iii) Any easement, liberty, or privilege over or affecting land and being merely an equitable interest (in this Act referred to as an 'equitable easement');

    (iv) The benefit of any contract (in this Act referred to as an 'estate contract') to convey or create a legal estate, including a contract conferring either expressly or by statutory implication a valid option to purchase, a right of pre-emption, or any other like right;

    (v) Any equitable interest protected by registration under the Land Charges Act 1925 or 1972 other than—

        (a)   an annuity within the meaning of Part II of that Act;

        (b)   a limited owner's charge or a general equitable charge within the meaning of that Act.

(4) Subject to the protection afforded by this section to the purchaser of a legal estate, nothing contained in this section shall deprive a person entitled to an equitable charge of any of his rights or remedies for enforcing the same.

(5) So far as regards the following interests, created before the commencement of this Act (which accordingly are not within the provisions of the Land Charges Act 1925 or 1972), namely—

    (a)   the benefit of any covenant or agreement restrictive of the user of the land;

    (b)   any equitable easement;

    (c)   the interest under a puisne mortgage within the meaning of the Land Charges Act 1925 or 1972, unless and until acquired under a transfer made after the commencement of this Act;

    (d)   the benefit of an estate contract, unless and until the same is acquired under a conveyance made after the commencement of this Act;

a purchaser of a legal estate shall only take subject thereto if he has notice thereof, and the same are not overreached under the provisions contained or in the manner referred to in this section.

By s 3, however, although a purchaser is free from liability, the person having the power of sale has to give effect to all equitable interests and powers which have been overreached by the sale. Save as above, the old rules as to notice (whether actual or constructive) still remain in force.

Actual notice

With regard to actual notice, knowledge is absolutely necessary except where registration under the Land Charges Act 1925 or 1972 is deemed to give persons actual notice[18]. Mere gossip or report is not sufficient. It does not seem that the notice must be given by a party interested or his agent.

The statutory definition of actual notice (therein differing from the definition of imputed notice) does not state that the instrument, fact, or thing must have come to the party's knowledge in the *same* transaction, nor have been notified by a party interested. Indeed, it would seem that actual notice is entirely a matter of evidence; and if the court comes to the conclusion that a party had in fact, at the date of the transaction, such knowledge as would operate on the mind of any rational man, or man of business, and make him act with reference to the knowledge he has so acquired, then he will be taken to have had actual notice. Whether he acquired his knowledge before or at the time of the transaction, and whether he acquired it from a party interested or not, appears to be immaterial[19].

Constructive notice

A purchaser has constructive notice of matters that would have come to his knowledge if such inquiries and inspections had been made as *ought*[20] reasonably to have been made by him. Where the purchase of land is concerned there are elaborate inquiries and inspections that have to be made but a wise purchaser employs a solicitor or licensed conveyancer to make these so that any actual or constructive notice obtained by such person will be imputed to the purchaser[1]. In the purchase of property other than land the purchaser usually acts for himself since matters are normally straightforward, there being no duty to make investigations as to title in the absence of suspicious circumstances, since the courts are most reluctant to import a duty of inquiry as to title which would restrict the flow of commerce[2].

While Megarry V-C has emphasised[3] the differences between the artificialities of the cold calculus of constructive *notice* and the realities of *knowledge*, it now seems that in the commercial context (not involving conveyancing procedures) a purchaser will not have 'constructive notice' unless suspicious circumstances existed but he deliberately or recklessly failed to make the inquiries an honest reasonable man would have made so as to have 'naughty knowledge' of the relevant matter[4].

---

18 Law of Property Act 1925, s 198.
19 *Lloyd v Banks* (1868) 3 Ch App 488; and see also *London and Canadian Loan and Agency Co Ltd v Duggan* [1893] AC 506, PC; and *Redman v Rymer* (1889) 60 LT 385; and see also on the subject of actual (and forgotten) knowledge and the distinction between notice and knowledge *Re Montagu's Settlements* [1987] Ch 264.
20 What *ought* to have been done in all the circumstances and thus the nature and extent of the *duty* to make reasonable inquiries will vary according to the circumstances: *Carl Zeiss Stiftung v Herbert Smith & Co (a firm) (No 2)* [1969] 2 Ch 276 at 297; *Polly Peck International plc v Nadir (No 2)* [1992] 4 All ER 769 at 782; *Eagle Trust Securities plc v SBC Securities Ltd* [1992] 4 All ER 488 at 497–498; *Criterion Properties plc v Stratford UK Properties LLC* [2002] 2 BCLC 151 at 173. A donee does not have to look a gift horse in the mouth and is under no duty of inquiry unless the circumstances are very suspicious: *Re Diplock* [1948] Ch 465 at 478–479, *Re Montagu's Settlements* [1987] Ch 264. A volunteer must return trust property or its product in his possession irrespective of notice.
1 Constructive notice is thus considered when discussing agents at p 990, post.
2 *Baden Delvaux and Lecuit v Société Générale* [1992] 4 All ER 161; *Joseph v Lyons* (1884) 15 QBD 280 CA; *Manchester Trust v Furness* [1895] 2 QB 539, CA; *Feuer Leather Corpn v Frank Johnstone & Sons* [1981] Com LR 251, *Eagle Trust plc v SBC Securities Ltd* [1992] 4 All ER 488 at 507–508.
3 *Re Montagu's Settlement Trusts* [1987] Ch 264.
4 *Polly Peck International plc v Nadir (No 2)* [1992] 4 All ER 769, CA.

Imputed notice

With regard to imputed notice, on the other hand, it is quite clear that a man is not liable for notice acquired by his counsel, solicitor, or agent, unless it has come to the latter's knowledge in the very transaction with respect to which the question of notice arises. The fact that a solicitor has been in the habit of acting for a particular person cannot reasonably constitute that solicitor the agent of the client to bind him by receiving notices or information; for apart from the burden which it would impose on the memory of a solicitor, it may be that the client may have ceased to regard him as his solicitor[5]. On similar grounds Parliament has enacted that:

'A trustee or personal representative acting for the purposes of more than one trust or estate shall not, in the absence of fraud, be affected by notice of any instrument, matter, fact or thing in relation to any particular trust or estate if he has obtained notice thereof merely by reason of his acting or having acted for the purposes of another trust or estate.'[6]

It has also been held in *Cave v Cave*[7] that constructive notice of an equity through counsel, solicitor, or agent is not imputed to the client, where the counsel, solicitor, or agent is party to a fraud which would be exposed if he had communicated the notice to his client. This case must, however, be carefully distinguished from the earlier cases of *Boursot v Savage*[8] and *Bradley v Riches*[9], which seem at first sight in direct conflict with it. The point in *Boursot v Savage* was that where a client has *notice of the existence of a trust* and intends to get the equitable interests of beneficiaries *from them*, the fact that he gets the legal estate from a trustee who happens to be his solicitor does not protect him if the solicitor forges the signatures of the beneficiaries; for he had notice of the equitable interests, and the fact that he was the innocent victim of a forgery does not give him an equal equity with the beneficiaries. In *Bradley v Riches* the point decided was that the presumption that a solicitor has communicated to his client facts which he ought to have made known is not rebutted by proof that it was to the solicitor's *interest* to conceal the facts. There the fact omitted to be communicated was the existence of a valid mortgage, whereas in *Cave v Cave* the fact omitted to be communicated was the prior commission of a fraud by the solicitor himself[10].

Constructive notice of agent imputed to principal

The imputed notice mentioned in s 199(1) of the Law of Property Act 1925[11] extends to notice of:

an instrument, fact, or thing which has come to the party's knowledge, or to the knowledge of his counsel, solicitor or agent as such, or would have come to the

---

5 *Saffron Walden Second Benefit Building Society v Rayner* (1880) 14 Ch D 406, CA.
6 Trustee Act 1925, s 28.
7 (1880) 15 Ch D 639, discussed p 984, ante, also see *Selangor United Rubber Estates Ltd v Cradock (No 3)* [1968] 2 All ER 1073, [1968] 1 WLR 1555.
8 (1866) LR 2 Eq 134.
9 (1878) 9 Ch D 189.
10 And see also and distinguish *Lloyds Bank v Bullock* [1896] 2 Ch 192; *Halifax Mortgage Services Ltd v Stepsky* [1996] Ch 207.
11 See p 986, ante, and note 17 on that page. And see *Newman v Real Estate Debenture Corpn Ltd and Flower Decorations Ltd* [1940] 1 All ER 131.

knowledge of his solicitor or other agent (not his counsel) as such, if such inquiries or inspections had been made as ought reasonably to have been made by them.

Thus in *Patman v Harland*[12] it was held that a lessee had imputed constructive notice of those matters he would have discovered if he had stipulated for full investigation of title even though under an open contract he was deprived by statute of his right to investigate the superior title: he could have contracted out of the statute and by not doing so he was in the same position as if he had agreed to accept a short title not going back for the full period over which title should be investigated. This has been reversed by Law of Property Act 1925, s 44(5), though a lessee may still find himself bound by a land charge registered against the name of a superior owner whom he could not have discovered[13].

It must also be borne in mind that notice of the existence of a deed affecting the title, or which *necessarily* affects it, is notice of its contents if it can be got at:

'Of course there may be cases where the deed cannot be got at, or for some other reason, where, with the exercise of all the prudence in the world, you cannot see it, and then there may be no constructive notice affecting the title. ... There is a class of cases, of which I think *Jones v Smith*[14] is the most notorious, where the purchaser was told of a deed which might or might not affect the title, and was told at the same time that it did not affect the title [and in such cases there is no constructive notice[15]]. Supposing you are buying land of a married man as in *Jones v Smith*, and you are told at the same time that there is a marriage settlement, but the deed does not affect the land in question, you have no constructive notice of its contents, because although you know there is a settlement you are told it does not affect the land. If every marriage settlement necessarily affected all a man's land then you would have constructive notice, but as a settlement may not relate to his land at all, or only to some other portions of it, the mere fact of your having heard of a settlement does not give you constructive notice of its contents, if you are told at the same time that it does not affect the land.'[16]

In addition to documents, constructive notice may be imputed to a purchaser from the state, appearance or occupation[17] of property. Thus the existence of a sea-wall bounding property has been held to give constructive notice of a liability to keep it in repair[18]. So notice of a tenancy is notice of its terms though there is no duty to inquire of the tenant whether the terms of his tenancy accurately reflect his agreement with his landlord, so that there is no constructive notice of any right of the tenant to rectify the tenancy for mistake[19]. Generally, where a person purchases property where a visible state

---

12 (1881) 17 Ch D 353.
13 *White v Bijou Mansions Ltd* [1937] Ch 610, [1937] 3 All ER 269, CA, revealing that Law of Property Act 1925, s 198, prevails over s 44(5). No compensation under Law of Property Act 1969, s 25 is available: see s 25(9), (10).
14 (1841) 1 Hare 43.
15 A fortiori where he has no notice of the existence of any settlement.
16 Per Jessel MR in *Patman v Harland* (1881) 17 Ch D 353.
17 See *Hunt v Luck* [1902] 1 Ch 428; *Kingsnorth Trust Ltd v Tizard* [1986] 2 All ER 54, [1986] 1 WLR 783.
18 *Morland v Cook* (1868) LR 6 Eq 252.
19 *Smith v Jones* [1954] 2 All ER 823, [1954] 1 WLR 1089 though such mere equity of an actual occupier of registered land will be an overriding interest within Land Registration Act 1925, s 70(1)(g): *Blacklocks v JB Developments (Godalming) Ltd* [1982] Ch 183, [1981] 3 All ER 392; *Collings v Lee* [2001] 2 All ER 332; all doubts being resolved by the Land Registration Act 2002, s 116.

of things exists, which could not legally exist, or is very unlikely to exist without the property being subject to some burden, he is taken to have notice of the nature and extent of the burden[20].

Imputing knowledge to a company

In *El Ajou v Dollar Land Holdings plc*[1] the Court of Appeal emphasised that an individual's knowledge can be imputed to a company either if the individual was its directing mind and will in relation to the act or omission in point or was its agent in the relevant transaction. These are separate alternatives though it is easy to confuse them.

For the first ground it suffices that the individual had de facto control and management of the relevant arrangements even if he had ceased to have such when some of the arrangements put in train by him were actually carried into effect. Different persons may for different purposes be 'identified' with the company for the purpose of imputing knowledge, or a particular state of mind to the company, a point which was subsequently elaborated by Lord Hoffman, in the Privy Council decision, *Meridian Global Funds Management Asia Ltd v Securities Commission*[2]. In *London Underground Ltd v NURMTW*[3], Robert Walker LJ considered the 'essential point' of *Meridian* to be that:

> 'in determining the mental state of an artificial person (when some ... rule requires that rather fictional exercise to be carried out) it may be necessary to look, not only at the body's formal constitution, but also at the way it actually organises its activities, and at the scope and purpose of the ... rule.'

For the second ground the knowledge of its agent will be imputed to a company where the company is under a duty to investigate or to make disclosure and employs the agent to discharge such duty (so long as the agent is not committing a fraud against his principal) or where the agent has actual or ostensible authority to receive communications on behalf of the principal. It does not suffice that the agent had private knowledge of facts into which his principal had no duty to inquire, even if he was under a duty to inform his principal of such facts, so long as he did not actually so inform his principal.

In the particular circumstances the Court of Appeal applying the above principles of law held that F's knowledge could be imputed to the defendant company on the first ground but not the second.

Absence of notice will not protect a volunteer

If an alienee of trust property is a volunteer, then the estate will remain burdened with the trust, whether he had notice of the trust or not[4] as a volunteer has no equity as against a true owner. Where, therefore, the trust property can be followed into the hands of a volunteer, and no question of mixing arises, an order for restoration will be made against him. Indeed, a volunteer will be personally liable to repay the beneficiaries if after acquiring knowledge of the trust he dissipated the trust property so that no proprietary

---

20 *Allen v Seckham* (1879) 11 Ch D 790, and note 17, above.
1 [1994] 2 All ER 685.
2 [1995] 2 AC 500.
3 [2001] ICR 647 at 662.
4 *Mansell v Mansell* (1732) 2 P Wms 678; *Re Strachan* (1876) 4 Ch D 123, CA; *Spurgeon v Collier* (1758) 1 Eden 55; *Banque Belge Pour l'Etranger v Hambrouck* [1921] 1 KB 321.

tracing claim lies against him, as should also be the case even if he had no knowledge of the trust at the time of dissipation[5], though then the defence of change of position may be available to such innocent volunteer.

Tracing, following, and claiming

In *Foskett v McKeown*[6], Lord Millett distinguished 'tracing', 'following', and 'claiming':

> '[Tracing and following] are both exercises in locating assets which are or may be taken to represent an asset belonging to the plaintiffs and to which they assert ownership. The processes of following and tracing are, however, distinct. Following is the process of following the same asset as it moves from hand to hand. Tracing is the process of identifying a new asset as the substitute for the old. Where one asset is exchanged for another, a claimant can elect whether to follow the original asset into the hands of the new owner or to trace its value into the new asset in the hands of the same owner. ... Tracing is also distinct from claiming. It identifies the traceable proceeds of the claimant's property. It enables the claimant to substitute the traceable proceeds for the original asset as the subject matter of his claim. But it does not affect or establish his claim. That will depend on a number of factors including the nature of his interest in the original asset. He will normally be able to maintain the same claim to the substituted asset as he could have maintained to the original asset. ... But his claim may also be exposed to potential defences as a result of intervening transactions.'

It follows that where a trustee has misdirected trust assets to a third party who still has them in the form in which he received them it will be unnecessary for the beneficiaries to 'trace' the value inherent in their property into some other asset, and they need merely 'follow' their property into the third party's hands, before asserting a proprietary claim to the property. However, it will be necessary for the beneficiaries to 'trace' and 'follow', before they can assert a claim to assets in the hands of a third party, in the event that the trustee has mixed trust assets with other property, or substituted trust assets for other property, before transferring the traceable proceeds of the trust property to the third party; and the same can also be said of the situation where the third party mixes the trust assets or their traceable proceeds with other property, or substitutes trust assets or their traceable proceeds after receiving them.

Trust funds mixed with volunteer's own moneys: *Re Diplock* approach

Where trust funds are wrongfully mixed with the moneys of an innocent volunteer then, provided means of identification or disentanglement exist, the volunteer and the beneficiary will each be entitled to a pari passu charge on the mixed fund for his own money, and this is so whether the mixing was done by the trustee[7] or by the volunteer himself[8]. If the mixing has occurred through trust moneys being paid into the volunteer's current account at the

---

5 See p 975 ante.
6 [2001] 1 AC 102 at 129–130, adopting the terminology suggested in L D Smith *The Law of Tracing* (1997). See too *Boscawen v Bajwa* [1996] 1 WLR 328 at 334.
7 *Sinclair v Brougham* [1914] AC 398, HL.
8 *Re Diplock* [1948] Ch 465, [1948] 2 All ER 318, CA; affd sub nom *Ministry of Health v Simpson* [1951] AC 251, [1950] 2 All ER 1137, where only the in personam claim was considered.

bank the rule in *Clayton's Case*[9] has traditionally been applied, the money first paid in being deemed to be that first drawn out, but the rule will not be applied where stocks are bought out of a mixed fund consisting of trust moneys and the volunteer's own moneys and then sold piecemeal. In such case each sum of stock sold will be treated as containing an aliquot proportion of that bought with the trust money[10]. For reasons which have already been discussed, it is submitted that the courts should now hold that the rule in *Clayton's* case is no longer applicable in this situation, and that the *Re Diplock* rateable proportion approach should be used instead[11].

Where, however, trust moneys are spent by an innocent volunteer on the improvement or alteration of some asset of its own, such as land and buildings, the Court of Appeal has held the moneys 'cannot be traced in any true sense,' so, the volunteer will hold the resulting 'mixed asset' free from any trust and the beneficiaries will be confined to their personal remedy[12]. This finding was recently reaffirmed by Lord Browne-Wilkinson in *Foskett v McKeown*[13], on the basis that:

'cases where the money of one person has been expended on improving or maintaining the physical property of another raise special problems [because the] property left at the end of the day is incapable of being physically divided into its separate constituent assets, ie the land and the money spent on it.'

Modern approach for innocent volunteers

Where trust property is wrongly transferred gratuitously to D, D must take the property subject to the trust. If such property be money, or if he sells such property so converting it into money, and he then mixes the money with his own money in a deposit account which he draws upon to purchase assets various questions arise. If D had actual, Nelsonian or naughty knowledge[14] that he had received trust property then any asset so purchased must belong to the trust until D has reinstated the trust fund, D (like a wrongdoing trustee[15]) not being able until then to prove that he used his own money. Otherwise, at most the asset will belong to the trust and D pro rata according to the proportion that the trust money in the mixed account bore to D's own

---

9 *Devaynes v Noble, Clayton's Case* (1816) 1 Mer 529 at 572, applied in *Re Diplock* [1948] Ch 465.

10 *Re Diplock* [1948] Ch 465, [1948] 2 All ER 318, CA.

11 See p 894 ante.

12 *Re Diplock* [1948] Ch 465, [1948] 2 All ER 318, CA. A volunteer who knowingly so spent trust moneys will not as a constructive trustee be able to complain if the trust claims a charge or a proportionate share in respect of the improved property. See p 885, ante.

13 [2001] 1 AC 102 at 109.

14 'Nelsonian' and 'naughty' knowledge represent the knowledge that D is deemed to have from wilfully shutting his eyes to the obvious, or from wilfully or recklessly failing to make the enquiries an honest and reasonable man would make in the suspicious circumstances: see p 974, ante. Strictly, an innocent volunteer means one without actual constructive or imputed notice (as assumed in *Re Diplock* [1948] Ch 465) but in line with the liberal approaches in *Re Tilley's Will Trusts* [1967] Ch 1179; *Westdeutsche Landesbank v Islington LBC* [1996] AC 669 and *Re Montagu's Settlements* [1987] Ch 264 it is submitted that, nowadays, the state of knowledge of D's conscience has more relevance and, in any event, a donee is almost inevitably only going to have constructive notice of matters of which he has naughty knowledge, a donee not normally having any duty to make inquiries.

15 See p 885, ante.

money when the asset was purchased[16]. However, if D can prove that he could have bought the asset without the assistance of the trust money and would have done so if he had known that the trust money was trust money, then he has not unjustly enriched himself at the expense of the trust, so that the asset should not be held on a constructive trust for D and the trust beneficiaries in proportionate shares. Instead, the asset should belong to D subject only to a lien for the trust money[17], as Ungoed-Thomas J would have held in *Re Tilley's Will Trusts*[18] if he had been dealing with an innocent donee, whose position is a fortiori that of the innocent trustee, Mrs Tilley. However, as the majority of the House of Lords recently made clear in *Foskett v McKeown*[19], this argument is not open to the innocent donee of an asset purchased with trust money by a fraudulent trustee who could have used his own money to buy the asset, since the argument would not be open to the trustee himself and the donee can be in no better position than the fraudster from whom he received the gift.

The position ought not to be different where no mixing has occurred because D has innocently received X Ltd shares which he sold and replaced with Y Ltd shares which he sold and replaced with Z Ltd shares. Instead of a 'money input' of his there has been an 'expertise input'. If D can prove that he could have bought the Y Ltd and Z Ltd shares without the assistance of the proceeds of sale of the X Ltd shares and would have done so if he had known that the X Ltd shares were trust property, then he has not unjustly enriched himself at the expense of the trust, so that the Z Ltd shares should not be held on constructive trust for the trust beneficiaries. D should own the shares subject to a lien for the value of the X Ltd shares at the time he received them[20].

What, however, if D's investments produced a loss, the Z Ltd shares being worth less than the value of the X Ltd shares when received by D? Clearly the trust must be able to fall back upon a lien over the Z Ltd shares to secure the value of the X Ltd shares[1]. Will the position be any different if the loss flowed from a mixing of assets[2] as where D innocently spent his £10,000 and the trust's £10,000 on a £20,000 car which has halved in value? Can the trust claim a lien over the car, so entitling it to the car to the exclusion of D, who thereby loses all his £10,000?

New potential in defence of change of position

D can argue that he changed his position in reliance upon the belief that he had £20,000 available to purchase a car: if he had known only half of the £20,000 was available he would only have bought a £10,000 car so as only to

---

16 *Re Diplock* [1948] Ch 465 at 524, 539, 546, 554 but in the context of the plaintiff only claiming a charge which was held not to rank in priority over the volunteer without notice but pari passu with such innocent volunteer's claim, each being regarded as having proprietary interests of the same priority.

17 See *Scott on Trusts* (4th edn) Vol V, pp 588–589; DJ Hayton (1990) 106 LQR 87 at 100.

18 [1967] Ch 1179, discussed p 888, ante.

19 See especially [2001] 1 AC 102 at 127 and 131, per Lord Millett; for the minority's finding to the contrary, see Lord Steyn's speech at 112–113.

20 See *Scott on Trusts* (4th edn) Vol V, pp 588–589.

1 *Scott on Trusts* (4th edn) Vol V, pp 588–589; *Re Diplock* [1948] Ch 465.

2 It is here assumed that the mixing and withdrawals do not relate to a current account where *Re Diplock* [1948] Ch 465 applied *Clayton's* case: on the justifiability of this see pp 891–894, ante.

lose half its value, namely £5,000. This change of position makes it inequitable for the trust to have a lien over the car[3] for more than £5,000, so that the trust and D should rateably bear the loss.

This result is already achieved by *Re Diplock* treating the trust and D as each having equitable proprietary interests of the same priority, so that assets purchased out of their mixed moneys are owned equally (or technically subject to two equal priority liens for £10,000 each) when it comes to allocation of losses. This approach will probably continue where it achieves a rough and ready measure of justice so avoiding complications. However, strictly speaking there ought to be scope for D to argue that the depreciation on a £10,000 car is less than that on the £20,000 car, so that if he had purchased a £10,000 car it would now be worth £6,000, so that his change of position defence should entitle him to have a lien for £6,000 on the car and the trust only to a lien for £4,000.

The availability of the defence of change of position[4] enables one to see that in *Re Diplock* the Court of Appeal should have found that the plaintiff's moneys could have been traced into altered or improved real property to enable a charge to have been imposed thereon, but that the defence of change of position should have been available at least to the extent that the defendant charities in the case should have been given time to go back to the charge-holders whose securities they had paid off with the claimants' money, and take out new loans from the lenders on terms as favourable as those which the defendants had originally enjoyed[5].

In *Lipkin Gorman v Karpnale Ltd*[6], Lord Goff stated that the defence of change of position is:

'available to a person whose position has so changed that it would be inequitable in all the circumstances to require him to make restitution, or to make restitution in full.'

Lord Goff also recognised that change of position would help the development of 'a more consistent approach to tracing claims', and there seems scope for change of position to replace the peculiar tracing rules applicable to innocent volunteers, as appears from the example discussed four paragraphs above. Rather than a pro rata rule for the trust's money mixed with D's money or, in the case of a current account, a first in first out *Clayton's Case* approach, should the court not consider simply whether the position of the innocent volunteer, D, has so changed that it would be inequitable in all the circumstances to require him to make restitution or restitution in full, especially when the justification for both the change of position defence and the tracing rules is a combination of the prevention of unjust enrichment and the avoidance of hardship to innocent persons?

Take the case where D is wrongly paid £1,200 from a trust fund of which P is a beneficiary and pays this into his deposit account containing £600. Then, D takes a holiday costing £1,200 which he would not have taken but for receiving £1,200. According to traditional case law the £600 remaining in D's account should be charged pro rata in favour of P and D and so be shared

---

3 See car example of Lord Templeman in *Lipkin Gorman v Karpnale Ltd* [1991] 2 AC 548 at 559–560.
4 For existing case law see pp 978–979, ante; for possible ramifications see P Birks (ed) *Pressing Problems in the Law: Laundering and Tracing* (OUP, 1995) Ch 6 (RC Nolan).
5 As Millett LJ held in *Boscawen v Bajwa* [1996] 1 WLR 328.
6 [1991] 2 AC 548 at 580.

£400 for P and £200 for D; while if the account had been a current account D would have been taken to have spent all his £600 first so that the £600 remaining would belong to P though if P's £1,200 had been paid in before D's £600 then the £600 remaining would belong to D. The impact of the change of position defence is that the remaining £600 should belong to D because D has a complete defence to the claim for £1,200.

Essentially the position is that P's claim is a restitutionary power to vest himself with a proprietary interest in traced assets by way of a lien or charge over such assets as security for the value of his claim which abates to the extent that the defence of change of position is established. He only has power to claim a lien or charge to the value of such abated claim. Thus, in the above example P can establish no lien, so there is no need to consider tracing a fund over which a lien could be imposed. However, if D's holiday only cost £1,100 then there should be a lien for £100 over anything remaining in the account or purchased with money from the account.

Where change of position is not directed at proving that the defendant is not in fact enriched but is directed at proving that the enduring enrichment of the defendant is just, D must surely have a defence to P's claim for a proportionate share of an appreciated asset if D can prove that he would anyhow have bought the asset with his own money alone if he had known that the money derived from P was such and therefore should not be taken to have detrimentally changed his position, having accidentally and unknowingly used P's money, for this would be unjustly to enrich P at D's expense. It thus suffices to allow P a lien over D's asset for P's money (and interest) until D reimburses P for the use of P's money.

No need to sue trustee personally before making proprietary claim

The strict personal claim available to unpaid creditors, legatees or next of kin against recipients of a deceased's estate can only be made after the personal claim against the blundering personal representatives has been exhausted. Thus in *Re Diplock*[7] where such a personal claim was brought as well as a proprietary claim and £15,000 was recovered from the personal representatives, it followed that the money had to be credited rateably to all the defendant innocent volunteers 'prima facie and subject to discussion.' However, where beneficiaries are bringing a proprietary tracing claim to recover their property or its traceable product there can be no possible ground for restricting exercise of such proprietary right until personal claims against the trustee have been exhausted. Significantly, Oliver J in *Re J Leslie Engineers Co Ltd*[8] having mentioned the need to exhaust personal claims against the wrongdoing fiduciary before proceeding with a personal claim against third parties did not mention such prior need when going on to deal with a proprietary tracing claim.

Fosket v McKeown now makes it clear that[9], 'the transmission of a claimant's

---

7 [1948] Ch 465 at 556. Writing extra-judicially, Lord Nicholls considered that this was an unfair rule and that in the event that a strict liability claim in *Re Diplock* was extended to all recipients of misapplied trust funds, 'the opportunity should be taken to decide that this form of relief is no longer subject to the pre-condition that a plaintiff must first exhaust his remedies against the trustees': 'Knowing Receipt: The Need for a New Landmark' in WR Cornish et al (eds) *Restitution: Past, Present and Future* (1998) at pp 231 and 241.

8 [1976] 2 All ER 85 at 91–92.

9 [2001] 1 AC 102 at 127, per Lord Millett.

property rights from one asset to its traceable proceeds is part of our laws of property': the claim is[10] an 'assertion of' an 'equitable proprietary interest in identified property'. Thus one can assert one's proprietary rights without first taking advantage of any personal claims as was held in *Hagan v Waterhouse*[11].

Can defendant plead equitable jus tertii?

In *El Ajou v Dollar Land Holdings plc*[12] the defendant was found to have been in knowing receipt of £2.325 million, representing the traceable proceeds of fraud, so as not to be a bona fide purchaser without notice. The plaintiff was the most significant of the 1,986 victims and had brought a personal money claim for the whole £2.325 million, while the defendant argued that the plaintiff could only claim 24% or 40% or 70%.

Millett J and the Court of Appeal found that 6.673 million dollars of the plaintiff were within 9.547 million dollars of victims traceable via Panama into assets whose proceeds of sale amounted to £2.325 million. The fraudulent boiler-room operation was run from Amsterdam via Dutch companies and a Mr Apeldoorn had been appointed by the Dutch courts to look after the interests of the victims without the need for any powers of attorney from them (though to assist with Swiss proceedings 1,590 victims had given powers of attorney to Mr Apeldoorn). Apeldoorn and the plaintiff entered into a sharing agreement in 1988 providing for the plaintiff's compensation in the English action and his costs to be divided in shares of 70:30 between the plaintiff and Apeldoorn.

Walker J pointed out[13] that the tracing of the plaintiff's money had not been on a pro rata basis with that of the other victims as in *Barlow Clowes International Ltd v Vaughan*[14] but on a more stringent basis, which would entitle the plaintiff to an equitable charge over the £2.325 million to cover his net losses in excess of 5 million dollars. He concluded that there was nothing inequitable in permitting the plaintiff to claim the whole £2.325 million when no other claimant was seeking to assert a charge ranking rateably with the plaintiff's charge and there was no realistic possibility of such a claim being made in the future. He stated:

> 'There is not any rigid rule to be applied as to whether a defendant can ever plead a sort of equitable jus tertii in this type of case. It must depend on the circumstances.'

He indicated that the court would not be inclined to look with favour upon a defendant 'who has no claim to retain the traceable money subject to the equitable charges'.

Tracing through non-trust jurisdictions

A wrongdoer cannot exploit transactions occurring in foreign non-trust

---

10 [2001] 1 AC 102 at 108 and 'It is a case of hard-nosed property rights' at 109, per Lord Browne-Wilkinson.
11 (1991) 34 NSWLR 308 at 369–370, affd on appeal.
12 [1993] 3 All ER 717 reversed by CA imputing knowledge of its director to the defendant company [1994] 2 All ER 685 and remitting the case to the High Court for assessment of compensation.
13 *El Ajou v Dollar Land Holdings plc (No 2)* [1995] 2 All ER 213.
14 [1992] 4 All ER 22, CA.

jurisdictions to thwart the tracing processes of the English forum to determine the amount for which he is personally liable[15], nor should he thereby thwart a proprietary claim to the traced English assets that establish the amount of that personal liability. However, it would seem that an innocent defendant (an innocent volunteer) who acquired title under a foreign *lex situs* should have a good defence if subsequently sued in England over the relevant asset brought into England when he had acquired an unimpeachable title under the *lex situs*[16].

Transfer of fund into court equivalent to alienation for value

Some transfers, apparently voluntary, have been held to be equivalent to alienations for value. Thus, in *Thorndike v Hunt*[17] a trustee of two different settlements having applied to his own use funds subject to one of the settlements, replaced them by funds which, under a power of attorney from his co-trustee under the other, he transferred into the names of himself and his co-trustee in the former. In a suit in respect of breaches of trust of the former settlement, the trustees of it transferred the fund thus replaced into court.

It was held by the Court of Appeal that the transfer into court was equivalent to an alienation for value without notice, and that the beneficiaries under the other settlement could not follow the trust fund. The transfer was to satisfy an existing debt and so was for value and the legal title was in the Accountant General on trust for beneficiaries under the former settlement.

So incumbrancers on a fund in court which has been transferred to a separate account before the incumbrances were created, are not postponed to prior equitable claims of other beneficiaries under the same settlement, subsequently discovered[18]. This is because, when a fund is carried over to a separate account in an action for administering the trust, it is released from the general questions in the action, and becomes ear-marked as subject only to the questions arising upon the particular matter referred to in the heading of the account[19]. All other questions are in fact treated as res judicata. The fund has been awarded by the court to the parties falling under the heading of the separate account, and it is too late for others to try to upset the court's award. It is, in fact, equivalent to a transfer of the legal estate or interest.

Purchaser with notice from purchaser without

A purchaser with notice (or a donee) from a purchaser without notice is safe. If he were not, an innocent purchaser for value would be prejudiced, being incapable of ever alienating the property which he had acquired without breach of duty and without loss, and such a restraint on alienation would necessarily create that stagnation against which the law has always set its

---

15 *El Ajou v Dollar Land Holdings plc* [1993] 3 All ER 717 at 736–737, accepted on appeal [1994] 2 All ER 685.
16 Cf *Winkworth v Christie Manson & Woods Ltd* [1980] Ch 496.
17 (1859) 3 De G & J 563; and see *Case v James* (1861) 3 De GF & J 256; *Re Bankhead's Trusts* (1856) 2 K & J 560; and *Dawson v Prince* (1857) 2 De G & J 41; but cf *Cloutte v Storey* [1911] 1 Ch 18.
18 *Re Eyton* (1890) 45 Ch D 458.
19 Per Lord Langdale MR in *Re Jervoise* (1848) 12 Beav 209.

face[20]. However, if a trustee disposes of trust property to a purchaser without notice and later re-acquires the property he will again hold it subject to the trusts[1].

Where purchaser has only acquired equitable interest

The preceding examples all refer to cases in which the third party has acquired the legal title to property the subject of a trust, in which case the validity of his title depends entirely on the absence of notice. Where, however, the third party has only acquired an equitable interest, the question of notice is, as a rule, immaterial, for he does not have the legal estate, and therefore his equity, being no stronger than that of the beneficiaries, the maxim 'qui prior in tempore, potior in jure est' applies[2].

Where equities are equal and no legal estate in either claimant

Thus, where a trustee, holding a mortgage[3] or a lease[4], deposits the deed with another to secure an advance to himself, the lender as equitable mortgagee will have no equity against the beneficiaries however bona fide he may have acted, and however free he may have been of notice of the trustee's fraud.

On the same principle, where a trustee has wrongfully spent trust funds in the purchase of property, which he has afterwards contracted to sell to a third party without notice, then, if the legal estate has not been conveyed to the third party, the beneficiaries will have priority over him[5]. For they have a right to trace the trust fund into the property into which it has been converted, and to take it or to have a charge upon it, at their election; and as their right was prior in time to that of the third party, and as he does not have the legal estate, the maxim above referred to applies[6].

When protection of legal estate may be lost against later equitable interest

One line of authorities lays down the principle that either direct fraud, or negligence so gross as to amount to evidence of fraud, must be proved against a legal owner, to estop him from claiming the protection afforded by

---

20 See *Brandlyn v Ord* (1738) 1 Atk 571; *Lowther v Carlton* (1741) 2 Atk 242; *Peacock v Burt* (1834) 4 LJ Ch 33; but the doctrine is not to be extended (*West London Commercial Bank v Reliance Permanent Building Society* (1885) 29 Ch D 954, CA).

1 *Re Stapleford Colliery Co* (1880) 14 Ch D 432 at 445; *Gordon v Holland* (1913) 82 LJPC 81.

2 But the beneficiaries will be postponed where their title is based on a document misleading in form and the third parties acted wholly innocently and were misled by the settlor through whom the beneficiaries claim (*Re King's Settlement* [1931] 2 Ch 294). As between competing equitable interests the first in time prevails unless the person having the first equitable interest (or someone claiming under him) is estopped from claiming such priority through having misled the second person by his fraud or negligent conduct: *Abigail v Lapin* [1934] AC 491, PC; *Freeguard v Royal Bank of Scotland* (1998) 79 P & CR 81.

3 *Newton v Newton* (1868) 4 Ch App 143; and *Joyce v De Moleyns* (1845) 2 Jo & Lat 374.

4 *Re Morgan* (1881) 18 Ch D 93. After the Law of Property (Miscellaneous Provisions) Act 1989 the equitable mortgage needs to be in signed writing: *United Bank of Kuwait plc v Sahib* [1997] Ch 107, CA.

5 *Frith v Cartland* (1865) 2 Hem & M 417.

6 And see, as to deposit of share certificates with blank transfers forming part of a trust estate, *Powell v London and Provincial Bank* [1893] 2 Ch 555, CA.

the legal estate[7]. Another line of authorities supplements this by asserting that where the relation between the legal owner and custodian of the deeds and other persons claiming beneficially is that of trustee and beneficiary or solicitor and client, then the beneficiary or client does not lose priority by reason of the improper or negligent acts of the trustee or solicitor, unless of course the beneficiary or client has notice of, and is privy to, the impropriety or negligence[8]. Thus, the equitable interests of a beneficiary under a trust where the legal estate is vested in trustees will prevail over subsequent equitable interests, whether or not involving fraud or negligence on the trustees' part, unless the beneficiary's involvement precludes the beneficiary from asserting priority in time or the overreaching provisions of the 1925 legislation protect the subsequent equitable owner. Exceptionally, in *Walker v Linom*[9], Parker J, after elaborately reviewing all the authorities, came to the conclusion that where trustees of a marriage settlement (to whom the legal fee simple in lands had been conveyed) negligently failed to obtain from the settlor-husband the deed by which he had purchased the property, and thus enabled him to pose as the owner and mortgage it, their negligence was such that their legal estate must be postponed to the subsequent equitable estate of the mortgagee and a purchaser from him, *and that the beneficiaries were in no better position than the trustees*. The position would have been different if the trustees had obtained all the relevant title deeds, but the trustees and the beneficiaries had to take the unprotected title conferred upon them by the settlor subject to any risks inherent in such title.

Choses in action are assigned subject to all equities

Choses in action are generally taken subject to all equities affecting them, because at law they were originally not transferable; and although by statute they are now transferable, it is directed that they should be transferred subject to all equities. Thus, in *Turton v Benson*[10] a mother agreed to give her son, on his marriage, as a portion a sum equal to that with which his intended father-in-law should endow the intended wife. The son, in order to induce the mother to give him a larger portion, entered into a collusive arrangement with the father-in-law, whereby, in consideration of the latter nominally endowing his daughter with £3,000, the son gave him a bond to repay him £1,000, part of it. This bond, being made upon a fraudulent consideration, was void in the hands of the father-in-law, and it was held that, being a chose in action, he could not confer a better title upon his assignee.

Negotiable instruments

Negotiable instruments are, however, an exception to the rule as to choses in

---

7 *Evans v Bicknell* (1801) 6 Ves 174; *Hewitt v Loosemore* (1851) 9 Hare 449; *Ratcliffe v Barnard* (1871) 6 Ch App 652, CA; *Northern Counties of England Fire Insurance Co v Whipp* (1884) 26 Ch D 482, CA; *Re Greer* [1907] 1 IR 57; and see doubt expressed by HL in *Taylor v Russell* [1892] AC 244 at 262; *Re Castell & Brown Ltd* [1898] 1 Ch 315; *Re Valletort Sanitary Steam Laundry Co Ltd* [1903] 2 Ch 654.

8 Per Stirling LJ in *Taylor v London and County Banking Co* [1901] 2 Ch 231 at 261; and see *Oliver v Hinton* [1899] 2 Ch 264; *Capell v Winter* [1907] 2 Ch 376; *Cave v Cave* (1880) 15 Ch D 639, *Newton v Newton* (1868) 4 Ch App 143.

9 [1907] 2 Ch 104. No point was taken over the preparedness of the mortgagee to lend money on the strength of only one recent title deed.

10 (1718) 1 P Wms 496.

action passing subject to all prior equities, for the *common law*, with regard to them, adopted the custom of merchants, and recognised that such instruments were transferable. Consequently, the transferee of a negotiable instrument has a legal, as well as an equitable, interest; and where the equities are equal he is protected against prior equities by his legal title[11]. Of course, however, the transferee will be postponed where he has notice[12] of prior equities.

Bona fide purchasers from trustees cannot get legal estate from them after notice

The bona fide purchaser of an equitable interest, without notice of an express trust, cannot defend his position by subsequently, and after notice, getting in an outstanding legal estate *from the trustee*, for by so doing he would be guilty of taking part in a new breach of trust[13]. If, however, he can perfect his legal title without being a party to a new breach of trust (as, for instance, by registering a transfer of shares which have been actually transferred before notice, or by getting in the legal estate from a third party), he may legitimately do so[14].

Dealings with equitable interests under trusts

Priority depends upon the order in which notice in writing of the mortgage or other dealing is received by the trustees of land or the Settled Land Act trustees or, otherwise, the estate owner of land or legal owner of other property, unless the trust instrument or the trustees have nominated a trust corporation to receive notices instead, when notice should be given to such corporation[15]. If for any reason a valid notice cannot be served (eg because there are no trustees) a purchaser (eg a mortgagee) can protect himself by having a memorandum indorsed on the trust instrument[16]. On the application of any person interested in the equitable interest the trustees or legal title holder must produce any notices served on them or their predecessors[17].

Exceptionally, a mortgagee who had actual or constructive notice of a prior mortgage when he lent his money cannot gain priority by giving notice first[18]. However, if he had no notice of a prior mortgage when he lent his money he will not be prevented from claiming priority under a notice given by him to the trustees after learning of the prior mortgage[19].

---

11 *London Joint Stock Bank v Simmons* [1892] AC 201, HL.
12 See *Earl of Sheffield v London Joint Stock Bank* (1888) 13 App Cas 333, HL.
13 *Saunders v Dehew* (1692) 2 Vern 271; *Collier v McBean* (1865) 34 Beav 426; affd 1 Ch App 81; *Sharples v Adams* (1863) 32 Beav 213; *Carter v Carter* (1857) 3 K & J 617; *McCarthy & Stone Ltd v Julian Hodge & Co Ltd* [1971] 1 WLR 1547 at 1556.
14 *Dodds v Hills* (1865) 2 Hem & M 424.
15 Law of Property Act 1925, ss 137, 138; *Dearle v Hall* (1823) 3 Russ 1, *Re Dallas* [1904] 2 Ch 385; Ward. See J De Lacy 'The Rule of Dearle v Hall Re-stated' [1999] Conv 311.
16 Law of Property Act 1925, s 137(4), (5), (6).
17 Law of Property Act 1925, s 137(8), (9) emasculating *Low v Bouverie* [1891] 3 Ch 82.
18 *Re Holmes* (1885) 29 Ch D 786.
19 *Mutual Life Assurance Society v Langley* (1886) 32 Ch D 460. If the second assignee be a volunteer he cannot gain priority over the earlier assignee by giving notice: he can take no more than the assignor could give: *Justice v Wynne* (1860) 12 I Ch R 289; *Fraser v Imperial Bank of Canada* (1912) 10 DLR 232.

It is advisable to give notice to all trustees[20] so that it remains effective indefinitely even though they all die or retire without communicating the notice to their successors. Of course, the written notices should be preserved with the trust documents but if they are not and new trustees, without notice of the incumbrance, distribute the trust fund to other incumbrancers or the beneficiaries they will not be personally liable[1].

Registered land

Where trust property is registered land and it is transferred to a purchaser such purchaser will take the property subject only to interests protected by entry on the register and to overriding interests[2], though if the purchaser is party to some fraud then an equitable in personam remedy may lie against him[3]. The doctrine of notice has no application to overriding interests[4] such as the proprietary rights of persons in actual occupation save where inquiry is made of such persons and the rights are not disclosed. A purchaser will thus be absolutely bound by the proprietary rights of such persons irrespective of questions of notice. A wife will be treated as herself in actual occupation if the husband appears as sole registered proprietor though her presence is explicable qua wife of the actual occupier[5]. An interest under a Settled Land Act settlement cannot be an overriding interest[6] though it has been held[7] that rights under a trust of land can be overriding interests if supported by actual occupation and not duly overreached by payment of purchase moneys to two trustees or a trust corporation[8].

---

20 Notice to one of several trustees was not effective against incumbrancers who lent money after the death or retirement of that trustee unless he had communicated the notice to one or more of the continuing trustees: *Timson v Ramsbottom* (1837) 2 Heen 35.

1 *Hallows v Lloyd* (1888) 39 Ch D 686.

2 Land Registration Act 1925, ss 20(1), 23(1) and Land Registration Act 2002, ss 29 and 30, minor interests being those interests that are not registered and do not rank as overriding interests. Payment of capital moneys to trustees in accordance with the entry of a restriction will overreach the beneficiaries' interests: *City of London Building Society v Flegg* [1988] AC 54, [1987] 3 All ER 435, HL.

3 *Lyus v Prowsa Developments Ltd* [1982] 2 All ER 953; *Ashburn Anstalt v Arnold* [1989] Ch 1, and Article 100.

4 *Williams and Glyn's Bank Ltd v Boland* [1981] AC 487, [1980] 2 All ER 408, HL; *Blacklocks v JB Developments (Godalming) Ltd* [1982] Ch 183, [1981] 3 All ER 392; *Kling v Keston Properties Ltd* (1983) 49 P & CR 212.

5 *Williams and Glyn's Bank v Boland* [1981] AC 487, [1980] 2 All ER 408, HL. Minors are not capable of being in actual occupation in their own right unless aged 16 years and co-habiting in emancipated fashion: *Hypo-Mortgage Services Ltd v Robinson* [1997] 2 FLR 71, CA.

6 Land Registration Act 1925, s 86(2). Under the Land Registration Act 2002, s 33(a) it can only be protected by a restriction and not a notice.

7 *Williams and Glyn's Bank v Boland* [1981] AC 487, [1980] 2 All ER 408, HL.

8 *City of London Building Society v Flegg* [1988] AC 54, [1987] 2 WLR 1266.

Conflict of Laws and The Hague Trusts Convention

CHAPTER 23

Conflict of Laws and The Hague Trusts Convention

The conflict of laws rules for England and Wales, Northern Ireland and Scotland are set out in the Hague Convention on the Law Applicable to Trusts and on their Recognition, as implemented and extended by the Recognition of Trusts Act 1987, except that preliminary issues concerning the creation or launching of a trust are outside the scope of such Convention and Act which are now set out.

ARTICLE 102

The Hague Convention on the Law Applicable to Trusts and on their Recognition, implemented by the Recognition of Trusts Act 1987

The Hague Convention

CHAPTER ONE—SCOPE

Article 1
This Convention specifies the law applicable to trusts and governs their recognition.

Article 2
For the purposes of this Convention, the term 'trust' refers to the legal relationships created—inter vivos or on death—by a person, the settlor, when assets have been placed under the control of a trustee for the benefit of a beneficiary or for a specified purpose.
A trust has the following characteristics—
a   the assets constitute a separate fund and are not a part of the trustee's own estate;
b   title to the trust assets stands in the name of the trustee or in the name of another person on behalf of the trustee;
c   the trustee has the power and the duty, in respect of which he is accountable, to manage, employ or dispose of the assets in accordance with the terms of the trust and the special duties imposed upon him by law.
The reservation by the settlor of certain rights and powers and the fact that the trustee may himself have rights as a beneficiary, are not necessarily inconsistent with the existence of a trust.

Article 3
The Convention applies only to trusts created voluntarily and evidenced in writing.

Article 4
The Convention does not apply to preliminary issues relating to the validity of wills or of other acts by virtue of which assets are transferred to the trustee.

Article 5
The Convention does not apply to the extent that the law specified by Chapter II does not provide for trusts or the category of trusts involved.

CHAPTER II—APPLICABLE LAW

Article 6
A trust shall be governed by the law chosen by the settlor. The choice must be express or be implied in the terms of the instrument creating or the writing evidencing the trust, interpreted, if necessary, in the light of the circumstances of the case.

Where the law chosen under the previous paragraph does not provide for trusts or the category of trust involved, the choice shall not be effective and the law specified in Article 7 shall apply.

Article 7
Where no applicable law has been chosen, a trust shall be governed by the law with which it is most closely connected.

In ascertaining the law with which a trust is most closely connected reference shall be made in particular to—
a   the place of administration of the trust designated by the settlor;
b   the situs of the assets of the trust;
c   the place of residence or business of the trustee;
d   the objects of the trust and the places where they are to be fulfilled.

Article 8
The law specified by Article 6 or 7 shall govern the validity of the trust, its construction, its effects, and the administration of the trust.

In particular that law shall govern—
a   the appointment, resignation and removal of trustees; the capacity to act as a trustee, and the devolution of the office of trustee;
b   the rights and duties of trustees among themselves;
c   the right of trustees to delegate in whole or in part the discharge of their duties or the exercise of their powers;
d   the power of trustees to administer or to dispose of trust assets, to create security interests in the trust assets, or to acquire new assets;
e   the powers of investment of trustees;
f   restrictions upon the duration of the trust, and upon the power to accumulate the income of the trust.
g   the relationships between the trustees and the beneficiaries including the personal liability of the trustees to the beneficiaries;
h   the variation or termination of the trust;
i   the distribution of the trust assets;
j   the duty of trustees to account for their administration.

Article 9
In applying this Chapter a severable aspect of the trust, particularly matters of administration, may be governed by a different law.

Article 10
The law applicable to the validity of the trust shall determine whether that law or the law governing a severable aspect of the trust may be replaced by another law.

CHAPTER III—RECOGNITION

Article 11
A trust created in accordance with the law specified by the preceding Chapter shall be recognised as a trust. Such recognition shall imply, as a minimum, that the trust property constitutes a separate fund, that the trustee may sue and be sued in his

capacity as trustee, and that he may appear or act in this capacity before a notary or any person acting in an official capacity.

In so far as the law applicable to a trust requires or provides, such recognition shall imply, in particular—

a   that personal creditors of the trustee shall have no recourse against the trust assets;

b   that the trust assets shall not form part of the trustee's estate upon his insolvency or bankruptcy;

c   that the trust assets shall not form part of the matrimonial property of the trustee or his spouse nor part of the trustee's estate upon his death;

d   that the trust assets may be recovered when the trustee, in breach of trust, has mingled trust assets with his own property or has alienated trust assets. However, the rights and obligations of any third party holder of the assets shall remain subject to the law determined by the choice of law rules of the forum.

Article 12

Where the trustee desires to register assets, movable or immovable, or documents of title to them, he shall be entitled, in so far as this is not prohibited by or inconsistent with the law of the State where registration is sought, to do so in his capacity as trustee or in such other way that the existence of the trust is disclosed.

Article 13

No State shall be bound to recognise a trust the significant elements of which, except for the choice of the applicable law, the place of administration and the habitual residence of the trustee, are more closely connected with States which do not have the institution of the trust or the category of trust involved.

Article 14

The Convention shall not prevent the application of rules of law more favourable to the recognition of trusts.

CHAPTER IV—GENERAL CLAUSES

Article 15

The Convention does not prevent the application of provisions of the law designated by the conflicts rules of the forum, in so far as those provisions cannot be derogated from by voluntary act, relating in particular to the following matters—

a   the protection of minors and incapable parties;

b   the personal and proprietary effects of marriage;

c   succession rights, testate and intestate, especially the indefeasible shares of spouses and relatives;

d   the transfer of title to property and security interests in property;

e   the protection of creditors in matters of insolvency;

f   the protection, in other respects, of third parties acting in good faith.

If recognition of a trust is prevented by application of the preceding paragraph, the court shall try to give effect to the objects of the trust by other means.

Article 16

The Convention does not prevent the application of those provisions of the laws of the forum which must be applied even to international situations, irrespective of rules of conflict of laws.

If another State has a sufficiently close connection with a case then, in exceptional circumstances, effect may also be given to rules of that State which have the same character as mentioned in the preceding paragraph.

Any Contracting State may, by way of reservation, declare that it will not apply the second paragraph of this article.

Article 17

In the Convention the word 'law' means the rules of law in force in a State other than its rules of conflict of laws.

Article 18
The provisions of the Convention may be disregarded when their application would be manifestly incompatible with public policy (*ordre public*).

Article 19
Nothing in the Convention shall prejudice the powers of States in fiscal matters.

Article 20
Any Contracting State may, at any time, declare that the provisions of the Convention will be extended to trusts declared by judicial decisions.

This declaration shall be notified to the Ministry of Foreign Affairs of the Kingdom of the Netherlands and will come into effect on the day when this notification is received.

Article 31 is applicable to the withdrawal of this declaration in the same way as it applies to a denunciation of the Convention.

Article 21
Any Contracting State may reserve the right to apply the provisions of Chapter III only to trusts the validity of which is governed by the law of a Contracting State.

Article 22
The Convention applies to trusts regardless of the date on which they were created.

However, a Contracting State may reserve the right not to apply the Convention to trusts created before the date on which, in relation to that State, the Convention enters into force.

Article 23
For the purpose of identifying the law applicable under the Convention, where a State comprises several territorial units each of which has its own rules of law in respect of trusts, any reference to the law of that State is to be construed as referring to the law in force in the territorial unit in question.

Article 24
A State within which different territorial units have their own rules of law in respect of trusts is not bound to apply the Convention to conflicts solely between the laws of such units.

Recognition of Trusts Act 1987

1 (1) The provisions of the Convention set out in the Schedule hereto [Articles 1–12,14–18 and 22 above set out] shall have the force of law[1] in the United Kingdom.

(2) Those provisions shall, so far as practicable, have effect not only in relation to the trusts described in Articles 2 and 3 of the Convention but also in relation to any other trusts of property arising under the law of any part of the United Kingdom or by virtue of a judicial decision whether in the United Kingdom or elsewhere.

(3) In accordance with Articles 15 and 16 such provisions of the law as are there mentioned shall, to the extent there specified, apply to the exclusion of the other provisions of the Convention.

(4) In Article 17 the reference to a State includes a reference to any country or territory (whether or not a party to the Convention and whether or not forming part of the United Kingdom) which has its own system of law.

(5) Article 22 shall not be construed as affecting the law to be applied

1 As from 1 August 1987 by SI 1987/1177.

in relation to anything done or omitted before the coming into force of this Act.

THE CONFLICT OF LAWS

The conflict of laws is concerned with situations where a matter has connections with the legal systems of more than one State (with some States like the UK and the USA having many legal systems within them). Such a conflict might arise if eg a settlor domiciled in England and Wales creates a trust of property located in Scotland and Ontario, to be held on trust by Ontarian trustees for New York and Saskatchewan beneficiaries. It might also arise if a settlor domiciled in England and Wales wishes to create a trust which is in all respects purely domestic to England and Wales, save that he chooses the law of another legal system, eg New South Wales, to govern the trust.

Essentially, three key questions arise: in what circumstances will an English court be prepared to hear and decide transnational litigation (being the technical question whether it will exercise jurisdiction over the case); which legal system will it apply to resolve the dispute on the merits (the choice of law question); and in which circumstances will an English court recognise and enforce a judgment delivered overseas?

Discussion in this chapter will focus on the choice of law rules applicable to international trusts. These rules are mostly contained in the Hague Convention on the Law Applicable to Trusts and on their Recognition. Brief discussion will follow on the law concerning the English courts' jurisdiction relating to transnational trusts litigation[2] and the recognition and enforcement of foreign judgments.

THE HAGUE TRUSTS CONVENTION – BASIC CONCEPTS

Background

The Hague Trusts Convention was adopted at the Fifteenth Session of the Hague Conference on Private International Law in 1984[3]. It has now been

---

2 Most of the rules of jurisdiction are not trusts specific and it is accordingly not intended to cover them in detail here. Discussion will be confined to the trusts specific bases of jurisdiction.

3 See the *Proceedings of the Fifteenth Session of the Hague Conference on Private International Law (1984), Book II – Trusts – Applicable Law and Recognition* (hereafter 'The Proceedings'). For detailed discussion of the Convention, see J Harris *The Hague Trusts Convention* (2002) Hart Publishing, Oxford. See also F Albisinni and R Gambino (1993) 2 J Int P 73; L Collins (ed) *Dicey and Morris, The Conflict of Laws* (13th edn 2000) Sweet and Maxwell, London, Chapter 29; A Dyer (1999) 32 Van J Trans Law; E Gaillard and D Trautman (1987) 35 Am J Comp Law 307; D Hayton (1987) 36 ICLQ 260; D Hayton (1994) 1 J Int P 23; D Hayton in J Glasson (ed) *International Trust Laws*, Jordans, looseleaf, Bristol, Chapter C3; H Kötz in D Hayton (ed) *Modern International Developments in Trust Law* (1999) Kluwer, The Hague, Chapter 3; M Lupoi (1995) 1(3) Trusts and Trustees 15; M Lupoi *Trusts: a Comparative Study* (1997) Giuffrè, Milan, translated by S Dix, (2001) Cambridge University Press, Cambridge, Chapter 6; J Mowbray, L Tucker, N Le Poidevin and E Simpson *Lewin on Trusts* (17th edn, 2000) Sweet and Maxwell, London, Chapter 11; P North and J Fawcett *Cheshire and North's Private International Law* (13th edn, 1999) Butterworths, London, Chapter 35; J Schoenblum, (1994) 3 J Int Corp P 5. A bibliography to the Hague Trusts Convention is provided by the Hague Conference and is updated regularly. It can be found at www.hcch.net/e/conventions/bibl30e.html.

ratified by[4], and has entered into force in, Australia[5], Canada[6], Hong Kong[7], Italy[8], Malta[9], the Netherlands[10] and the United Kingdom[11]. It has also been signed, though not ratified by Cyprus[12], France[13], Luxembourg[14] and the United States[15].

In the United Kingdom, the Recognition of Trusts Act 1987 gives effect to the Convention. It appears as a Schedule to s 1 of the 1987 Act[16]. Section 1(1) of the Act states that 'the provisions of the Convention ... shall have the force of law in the United Kingdom'. Upon ratification by three States, the United Kingdom, Australia and Italy, the Convention came into force on 1 January 1992.

It is beyond doubt that the Convention is the dominant source of choice of law rules in England for trusts. The United Kingdom extended the ambit of the Convention, so that now only a small minority of international trusts fall outside its scope. For those trusts which do fall outside the Convention's scope, the common law choice of law rules will apply. However, these differ little from the Convention in any event. Accordingly, discussion will focus on the Convention. The common law rules will be referred to only in those few areas where they are significantly different from the Convention position.

The Explanatory Report on the Convention by Professor von Overbeck[17] details the evolution of the Convention and provides detailed commentary

---

4 For a list of States which have signed and/or ratified the Convention and the date of entry into force of the Convention into those countries, see www.hcch.net/e/stat30e.html.

5 See the Trusts (Hague Convention) Act 1991. It entered into force on 1 January 1992.

6 It entered into force on 1 January 1993 in Alberta, British Columbia, New Brunswick, Newfoundland and Prince Edward Island. The Convention currently applies to the States of Alberta, British Columbia, Manitoba (entry into force in Manitoba: 1 July 1994), New Brunswick, Newfoundland and Prince Edward Island and Saskatchewan (entry into force in Saskatchewan: 1 September 1994).

7 The United Kingdom had extended the application of the Convention to Hong Kong with effect from 1 January 1992. The Government of the People's Republic of China determined that the Convention would continue to apply to the Hong Kong Special Administrative Region with effect from 1 July 1997. Details of the correspondence can be found on the Hague Conference website at: www.hcch.net/e/status/stat30e.html.

8 It entered into force on 1 January 1992. The Italian ratification instrument (Law 364 of 16 October 1989) can be found in M Lupoi *Trust Laws of the World* (1996), ETI, Rome, 26.

9 It entered into force on 1 March 1996.

10 It entered into force on 1 February 1996.

11 This includes Bermuda, British Antarctic Territories, the British Virgin Islands, the Falkland Islands, Gibraltar, Guernsey (the UK extended the operation of the Convention to Guernsey on 28 April 1993), the Isle of Man, Jersey (the UK Recognition of Trusts Act 1987 was not extended to Jersey, but Jersey became a party to the Convention on 1 March 1992, having brought its Trusts (Jersey) Law 1984 into line with the Convention by the Trusts (Amendment No 2) (Jersey) Law 1991), Montserrat, St Helena and Dependencies, South Georgia, the South Sandwich Islands and the Turks and Caicos Islands (entry into force in Turks and Caicos: 1 July 1993). See also Recognition of Trusts Act 1987, s 2. The United Kingdom signed the Convention on 10 January 1986 and ratified it on 17 November 1989. It entered into force in the United Kingdom and in the territories to which it was initially extended on 1 January 1992.

12 Signed on 11 March 1998.

13 Signed on 26 November 1991.

14 Signed on 1 July 1985. Legislation has recently been tabled to implement the Convention: see D Hayton 'Private Client Business' [2001] 361, 369–370.

15 Signed on 13 June 1988.

16 Not all provisions of the Convention eg Article 13, are scheduled to the Act.

17 The Official Report by Professor A von Overbeck, (hereafter 'the von Overbeck Report'), starts at p 370 of The Proceedings, note 3 above.

on each Article of the Convention. The courts of Contracting States may, of course, refer to this and may find it persuasive in resolving ambiguities[18].

The effect of the Convention in non-trust States

The Convention does not introduce the trust into the domestic law of States which do not have the trust concept. It requires those States to recognise trusts falling within the Convention's scope for private international law purposes only[19]. Of course, it is quite possible that this will act as a catalyst for such States to develop their own domestic trust concept of a segregated ring-fenced fund immune from the claims of the owner creditors and heirs[20]; but there is absolutely no obligation on them to do so.

The open-ended nature of the Convention

The Convention is not reciprocal in nature. For matters within its scope there is no territorial limit and it applies even if the law applicable to the trust is that of a non-Contracting State. However, a Contracting State may enter a reservation[1] so that it only applies the Convention to trusts governed by the law of a Contracting State. The United Kingdom has made no such reservation[2].

The time factor

Article 22 provides that, 'the Convention applies to trusts regardless of the date on which they were created' but permits Contracting States to reserve the right not to apply the Convention to trusts created before the date on which the Convention enters into force in that Contracting State[3]. By the Recognition of Trusts Act 1987, s 1(5), out of an abundance of caution in case (which it did not believe) the Convention rules differed from the common law rules on which there was a paucity of authority, the United Kingdom therefore provided that, 'Article 22 shall not be construed as affecting the law to be applied in relation to anything done or omitted before the coming into force of this Act', so that breaches of trust committed before such date (but not after) are to be judged according to the common law rules applicable before that date (1 August 1987)[4].

---

18 See also *Tod v Barton* [2002] EWHC 264 (Ch), (2002) 4 ITELR 715, para 30 of Lawrence Collins J.

19 But they must recognise it *qua* trust, rather than translating it into an analogous institution in their domestic legal systems, so the domestic law must recognise that the trustee's trust property is immune from claims of the trustee's own creditors and heirs: von Overbeck Report, para 108.

20 See L Thevenoz *Trusts in Switzerland (Ratification of The Hague Convention on Trusts and Codification of Fiduciary Transfers)* (2001) Schulthess, Zurich.

1 Pursuant to Article 21.

2 Article 21 is omitted from the schedule to the Recognition of Trusts Act 1987.

3 See also the decision of the Supreme Court of New South Wales in *Saliba v Falzon* [1998] NSWSC 302.

4 See SI 1987/1177.Thus, Lawrence Collins J applied a number of provisions of the Hague Trusts Convention to a trust created in 1975 in *Chellaram v Chellaram (No 2)* [2002] EWHC 632 (Ch), [2002] WTLR 675, paras 147, 160–162, 166–167. However, the alleged breaches of trust occurred before 1987, so that the common law rules would apply and prevail if leading to a different result as he indicated at para 164, but he doubted there was any significant difference between them: para 166.

The two main functions of the Convention: choice of law rules and the recognition of trusts

The Convention serves two key functions: it harmonises the choice of law rules applicable in Contracting States and then expressly provides for the recognition of trusts falling within its scope. The former function helps bring clarity to an area previously governed by common law rules which were never highly developed or clear. As to the recognition of trusts, it is important to understand what we mean. The word 'recognition' does not have anything to do with recognition of foreign trust judgments. The Hague Convention does not affect the rules on recognition of foreign judgments. Recognition and enforcement of foreign judgments must be and are still governed by the 'general' rules on recognition of foreign judgments of the State addressed[5]. The Hague Convention's 'recognition' rules are to be understood as simply giving guidance to Contracting non-trust States faced with a trust governed by the law of Trustopia as to what effect they must give that trust in their legal system, rather than leave it to their judges and notaries to work out for themselves the logical implications flowing from application of the Trustopian applicable law ascertained by applying the Convention's choice of law rules.

Exclusion of fiscal matters

Article 19 states that 'nothing in the Convention shall prejudice the powers of States in fiscal matters'. Although this is not scheduled to the Recognition of Trusts Act 1987, it goes without saying that a Convention on the private international law of trusts will not affect the taxation of trusts in the United Kingdom. Non-trust States will need to develop rules for the taxation of foreign trusts[6].

TYPES OF TRUSTS FALLING WITHIN THE CONVENTION

What is a 'trust' for Convention purposes?

The Convention seeks to lay down the key characteristics of a trust. This is not intended as an exhaustive statement of its characteristics, still less a definition. The Convention is not limited to the common law trust and is also intended to cover civil law institutions which exhibit certain core characteristics of the trust[7]. Structurally similar institutions to the common law trust, such as exist in States such as Argentina, Egypt, Ethiopia, Israel, Japan, Liechtenstein, Louisiana, Panama, Peru, Quebec and Venezuela may very well be 'trusts' for the purposes of the Convention.

The first paragraph of Article 2 explains that a trust is a relationship created *inter vivos* or on death by which a settlor places assets under the control of a trustee for a beneficiary. However, it also makes clear that purpose trusts shall be included within the Convention's scheme. Whilst some provision for purpose trusts was necessary to cover Scots purpose trusts, which may be valid

---

5 See p 1060 post.
6 See F Sonneveldt in F Sonneveldt and H van Mens (eds) *The Trust-Bridge or Abyss between Common and Civil Law Jurisdictions?* (1992) Kluwer, Deventer, Chapter 1, p 17.
7 So the institution must not have legal personality enabling it to own property.

even if non-charitable, and a limited number of anomalous testamentary purpose trusts permitted by English and many American States' laws, the unrestricted scope of this provision means that the Convention can apply to non-charitable purpose trusts, even though such trusts are usually invalid in English domestic law[8].

Article 2 does not refer to the fiduciary nature of trusteeship since civil law lawyers argued the word 'fiduciary' as adjective or noun could not meaningfully be translated into their legal language. Although, to an English or other trust lawyer, fiduciary duties inevitably are implicit in the fact that the trustee holds assets received from another person for the benefit of another, this is not expressed as an essential characteristic of a Convention 'trust'.

Where a settlor declares himself as trustee, so switching particular assets from his private property to fiduciary property, it is doubtful whether it can be said that 'assets have been placed under the control of a trustee' within the meaning of Article 2. This might suggest that declarations of trust are excluded from the Convention[9]. However, there seems to be no reason why a declaration by the settlor of himself as trustee should be excluded; provided that the trust is validly created[10], its applicable law and its entitlement to recognition should be identical to that of a trust created by transfer of assets to a trustee. Accordingly, it is suggested that trusts created by the declarations of the settlor of himself as trustee do fall within the Convention, at least once they have been effectively 'launched'[11].

Article 2(2)(a) emphasises that trust assets constitute a separate fund which is not part of the trustee's own private estate. It is not necessary that the concept of equitable ownership be known in a legal system for it to have a 'trust' within the meaning of the Convention[12]. Accordingly, the trusts of India, Scotland, South Africa, Liechtenstein, Quebec and Japan fall within the Convention.

Sub-paragraph (b) of Article 2(2) is designed to make clear that title to the trust assets need not necessarily be held by the trustee, provided that it is held 'in the name of another person to hold on behalf of the trustee', as where legal title to shares is vested in a custodian (although the equitable title therein is vested in the trustee). The danger is that the sub-paragraph appears at first sight to be broad enough to cover some forms of agency or mandate (although there is no provision in the Convention dealing with its relationship to the earlier Hague Convention on Agency) eg the transfer by an owner to an agent of control (but not ownership) of assets for the benefit of the owner and others[13]. This risk is exacerbated by Article 2(1) referring only to assets being placed under the 'control' of the trustee. The word 'ownership' is not used. Indeed, it has been suggested that if this makes

---

8 See the discussion of public policy and of the recognition of trusts below.

9 See the United Kingdom delegate's remarks: *Actes et Documents* 237), and M Lupoi *Trusts: a Comparative Study*, 335. See also M Lupoi in *The Reform of Property Law* (1997) Ashgate, Aldershot, 222, 228.

10 Which is a preliminary matter falling outside the scope of the Convention, discussed below.

11 M Lupoi also argues that, 'On balance, the arguments in favour of extending the Convention to include self-declared trusts seem to me to be convincing': *Trusts: a Comparative Study*, 335.

12 For example, ring-fenced funds immune from the claims of the owner's creditors and heirs. See D Hayton (ed) *Modern International Developments in Trust Law*, Chapter 2, p 23 and D Hayton (ed) *Extending the Boundaries of Trusts and Similar Ring-Fenced Funds* (2002) Kluwer Law International, pp 1–133.

13 See also D Hayton, S Kortmann & R Verhagen *Principles of European Trusts Law* (1999) Kluwer Law International, pp 39–40 and D Hayton (2000) 8 J Int Corp P 159, 167.

Article 2 cover agency-management as well as ownership-management, then 'non-trust' States within the meaning of the Convention are extremely rare, or even non-existent[14], in which case there is no scope for the application of Article 13 applicable only where significant elements are more closely connected with non-trust States. Thus, the Convention should be construed as concerned with ownership management and not agency management, so covering situations where the trustee owns what laymen regard as trust assets directly or indirectly via a nominee (eg in the case of shares), so that the assets do not form part of his own private estate[15]. Accordingly, agency and mandate should fall outside the scope of the Convention.

Sub-paragraph (c) of Article 2(2) of the Convention makes clear that a trustee is subject to any obligations specified in the trust instrument, and also to duties imposed on him by law. It does not say to whom he is accountable, although under orthodox English trust law there is accountability to the beneficiaries (or the Attorney-General or the Charity Commission for charitable purpose trusts) and not the settlor once he has dropped out of the picture, having completed his gift to the trustee. There seems no good reason, however, why a foreign trust, like an American charitable trust or a Chinese or Liechtenstein trust, should not be covered by the Convention merely because the trustee is accountable to the settlor[16]. This, though, runs the serious risk that the trust will be viewed as nothing but a sham unless, in addition, the trustee is also accountable to the beneficiaries. A non-charitable purpose trust which specifies an 'enforcer' to uphold the terms of the trust, such as is permitted in a number of offshore States, should fall within Article 2.

The final paragraph of Article 2 indicates that a trustee may himself be a beneficiary, although not the sole beneficiary. Equally, the settlor may be a beneficiary of the trust. The 'reservation by the settlor of certain rights and powers'[17] is also permitted. The Convention does not say which rights they are. To the extent that the assets remain effectively under the control of the settlor, the trust should be treated as a sham trust, not for the designated beneficiaries but for the settlor alone.

What types of trust are governed by the Hague Convention?

Evidenced in writing

Article 3 states that the Convention applies only to 'trusts created voluntarily and evidenced in writing'. A trust created orally may fall within the Convention, if it is subsequently evidenced in writing as under s 53(1)(b) of the Law of Property Act 1925 and as envisaged by Article 5(6) of the Brussels Convention on Jurisdiction and Enforcement of Judgments which was the inspiration for Article 3 of the Trusts Convention (as von Overbeck points

---

14 M Lupoi (1995) 1(3) Trusts and Trustees 15. He describes Italy as a trust State under the terms of Article 2 and argues that the shapeless trust can be found 'from Ecuador to Russia to the Philippines.'

15 D Hayton (2000) 11 KCLJ 48, 53.

16 M Lupoi asks 'How could an "institution" be "analogous" to the Anglo-Saxon trust if the trustee were to be accountable to the "settlor"?' (1995) 1(3) Trusts and Trustees 15, 16, but so long as there is also accountability to other enforcers there are sufficient obligations to persons other than the settlor for there to be a proper trust within Article 2.

17 See the extensive powers permitted by some offshore jurisdictions discussed by D W M Waters in D Hayton *Extending the Boundaries of Trusts and Similar Ring-Fenced Funds*, pp 243–290.

out in paragraph 52 of his Report). It appears that a trust can be sufficiently 'evidenced in writing' even if it has not been signed by the settlor. Indeed, it seems that the trustee could put the terms of an orally declared trust in writing and that this would suffice to bring it within the Convention's ambit. That said, 'evidenced in writing' must mean sufficiently evidenced to represent the will of the settlor. Whilst it cannot be said that the written evidence of the trust *must* be signed by any particular party, there must be sufficient evidence that the settlor intended to create the trust. This may require more than the mere existence of a written document stating that fact. In practice, it is safest for the written instrument to be signed by the settlor.

A trust which satisfies the formality requirements continues to fall within the Convention, even if affected by a later court decision replacing a trustee or varying the trust[18].

Where a party transfers additional assets to be held on the terms of a pre-existing trust which was created and evidenced in writing, it is not certain whether the transfer has also to be evidenced in writing at some stage eg in the trust accounts. To err on the side of caution, it is wise for the transfer of additional assets also to be evidenced in writing: the best evidence will be that provided by the settlor at the time of the transfer.

Voluntary trusts

It appears that the trust must reflect the will of the settlor (even if he did not expressly declare and constitute that trust). Trusts voluntarily created as a means of discharging an obligation imposed by law, eg to discharge a maintenance obligation, are not, however, excluded[19]. Moreover, once there is an expressly created voluntary trust evidenced in writing, subsequent actions of the court will not lead to the trust's exclusion, eg where the court intervenes to appoint a trustee[20] or to vary trusts pursuant to powers under the Matrimonial Causes Act 1973 or the Variation of Trusts Act 1958, or to use the *cy-près* doctrine in the case of charitable purpose trusts.

Resulting trusts

It appears that automatic resulting trusts fall within the Convention[1]. The trust in question need not itself be expressly constituted, it seems, providing that a trust arises from the express declaration of trust. It is sensible that the law which determines that an express trust fails should determine whether that failure gives rise to a resulting trust[2].

The position with regard to presumed resulting trusts[3], such as that which might arise where a jointly purchased property is registered in the name of one party only, is much less clear. Suppose S and T jointly purchase a property in England, which is conveyed into T's sole name. T then sells the

---

18 Von Overbeck, para 50, p 380.

19 Von Overbeck, para 49, p 380.

20 Von Overbeck, para 50, p 380.

1 Von Overbeck, para 51, pp 380–381.

2 R Stevens, 'Resulting Trusts in the Conflict of Laws' in P Birks and F Rose (eds) *Restitution and Equity, Volume 1: Resulting Trusts and Equitable Compensation* (2000) Mansfield Press, London, pp 147, 157.

3 The questions whether the Recognition of Trusts Act 1987 extends to presumed resulting trusts was left open by Peter Gibson LJ in *Lightning v Lightning Electrical Contractors Ltd* (23 April 1998, unreported).

property and reinvests the proceeds of sale in property situated in Civilopia (a Contracting State to The Hague Convention). An English court holds that a presumption of a resulting trust arises. If a Civilopian court was faced with a claim by S to be recognised as a beneficiary under this presumed resulting trust, should Civilopia recognise the trust under the Convention? It might be argued that the trust was created 'voluntarily', in the sense that it is presumed to reflect the settlor's intention in contributing to the purchase price. The difficulty is that the resulting trust does not appear itself to be 'evidenced in writing'[4]. But if the phrase 'evidenced in writing' imposes a requirement only of sufficiency of evidence of the trust, then the trust might still fall within the Convention. True, a Civilopian court would naturally not relish investigating oral evidence of an alleged presumed resulting trust. However, if an English court has already declared that T held the property and proceeds of sale on a presumed trust, it could be said that the English court's declaration is *itself* the necessary written element evidencing a voluntarily created trust, so that its recognition in Civilopia should fall within the Convention[5].

Constructive trusts

It is clear that the personal remedy imposed upon a third party to an (express) trust making him liable to account as a 'constructive trustee' for losses or gains made as if he were an express trustee cannot be within Article 3, since 'The Convention ... is [concerned] with trusts of specific property'[6].

It is far from certain precisely when a constructive trust of property will fall within the Convention. Some forms of constructive trust will clearly fall outside the scope of Article 3, since they are in no sense created voluntarily. This would include the trust imposed where a trustee renews a lease for himself personally, or purchases for himself the freehold reversion to a lease held by him as trustee, or obtains for himself assets which he should have acquired for the trust.

Other types of constructive trust will clearly fall within the scope of Article 3. One such example is where duly executed written mutual wills are made[7]. There will be written documentation which reflects the voluntary intention of the parties to be contractually bound by the mutual wills and, if necessary, to have them enforced by a constructive trust, which should suffice to bring the trust within the Convention.

Similarly, where a written contract is made which is specifically enforceable, this may give rise to a constructive trust from the time of conclusion of the contract[8]. It may be said that the parties voluntarily contract, that they know that a constructive trust will arise and that there is written evidence of the agreement which generates that trust. The written contract creates a voluntary obligation and the parties willingly submit themselves to a legal framework; if that framework decrees that a constructive trust arises, then the trust may be said to arise voluntarily.

---

4 And Article 3 states that the trust in issue must be both created voluntarily and evidenced in writing.
5 D Hayton (1987) 36 ICLQ 260 at 264;cf *Webb v Webb* C-294/92 [1994] QB 696, [1994] ECR I-1717.
6 D Hayton (1987) 36 ICLQ 260 at 264.
7 M Lupoi *Trusts: a Comparative Study*, 342–343.
8 In English domestic law, the constructive trust arises as soon as a specifically enforceable contract of sale is concluded: see Art 36.

Indeed, a secret testamentary trust (especially if half-secret) should also fall within the Convention where a testator leaves property by will to T, but only because T had agreed with him to hold the property after his death for X, and there is sufficient written evidence provided by him or T to X or, perhaps, a written court decision, to establish that T holds the property on constructive trust for X.

Where the assets of an expressly created trust change during the lifetime of the trust, any substituted assets in the trustee's hands now representing the trust fund fall within the Convention's scope, whether or not (as often happens) the trust instrument defines the Trust Fund as 'the property in the Schedule hereto and any further property accepted by the Trustee and the property from time to time representing the same', because this is the inevitable corollary to the original holding of particular property as trust property. The trust concept, with the ring-fenced protection of trust property, would be illusory, having very little protective practical significance, if recognition of an expressly created trust overseas depended on the trust assets remaining the same as when the trust initially came into effect[9].

It also appears that claims to recover trust assets of an express trust (evidenced in writing) wrongfully dissipated to a third party who is alleged to hold the assets on constructive trust should be included within the Convention. The ability to recover trusts assets from a third party is pivotal to the common law trust[10] and the constructive trust should remain within the Convention[11]. In effect, the constructive trust in this scenario is treated as a core incident of the express trust initially created under the Convention[12] and is vital to the vindication of such trust. However, it should be noted that a beneficiary may not be able to claim trust assets from a third party if that party has acquired good title to them[13], as will normally be the case if the *lex situs* of the transfer to such party were that of a civil law jurisdiction.

A difficult case arises where persons voluntarily intend to create a trust of their home which cannot take effect as an express trust because of a failure to comply with the requisite statutory formalities (under s 53(1)(b) of the Law of Property Act 1925), but the court intervenes to vindicate the unenforceable express trust by imposing a constructive trust, so as to prevent the sole homeowner from fraudulently retaining the property wholly for himself after the detrimental reliance of his cohabitee[14]. It can be said that this reflects the settlor's intentions (whether subjective or as objectively reasonably perceived by the misled cohabitee) and that the court order evidences the pre-existing trust. However, it may be argued that the constructive trust effectively acts as a *substitute* for an express trust and this constructive trust is not a trust *itself* created voluntarily[15].

At this stage, an important point of principle arises. If evidence that a trust was created voluntarily can be supplied by a court decree that the trust exists, the scope of Article 3 is very wide, so only trusts imposed regardless of the

---

9 See also D Hayton in J Glasson (ed) *International Trust Laws*, Chapter C3, p 7.
10 Although Article 2 extends beyond the common law trust: see above.
11 D Hayton (1987) 36 ICLQ, 260 at 266.
12 But not all agree. M Koppenol-Laforce, *Het Haagse Trustverdrag* (1997) Kluwer, Deventer, p 266 argues that this constructive trust is only included where a State has enacted provisions pursuant to Article 20 extending the scope of the Convention.
13 See the discussion of the following and tracing of trust assets below.
14 D Hayton (1987) 36 ICLQ 260, 264; see also P Matthews (1995) 1 Trusts and Trustees 7.
15 See J Harris *The Hague Trusts Convention*, 128–134.

intention of the parties should be excluded from Article 3. This would mean that the constructive trust imposed in the case of testamentary secret trusts and family home constructive trusts are both within the Convention. On the other hand, it can be argued that Article 3 requires the instant trust *itself* to have been both created voluntarily and evidenced in writing. The constructive trusts considered here are imposed to *reflect* the perceived intentions of the parties, but they are not themselves created voluntarily by a settlor: they are created by the court, albeit as a result of the settlor's action which is the *causa sine qua non*. However, it may well be that, in order to give as wide a berth as possible to the Convention and provide justifiable protection to vulnerable persons, a court will hold that as long as the trust in some sense reflects a voluntary undertaking of the parties and is sufficiently evidenced in some writing, it should fall within the Convention[16].

Statutory trusts

Statutory trusts, such as those which arise upon a person's intestacy or the co-purchase of land[17], and which are automatically triggered by certain scenarios, are probably excluded from the Convention. Although the settlor has voluntarily chosen not to make a will or to be a co-purchaser, the statutory trust is imposed without his consent: he may very well be ignorant that a trust would arise. It is suggested that such a statutory trust lacks the necessary element of consensus and must be regarded as falling outside the Convention.

Extended scope of the Convention in the United Kingdom

Article 20(1) allows a State to extend the ambit of the Convention. Those States which are comfortable with applying the Convention's rules to trusts declared[18] by judicial decision are free to do so; indeed, a sovereign State is free to extend the Convention within its own boundaries as it wishes, eg to cover any trusts arising under its own or a foreign law that would not otherwise fall within the Convention. In the United Kingdom[19], s 1(2) of the Recognition of Trusts Act 1987 states that:

> 'Those provisions [of the Convention] shall, so far as applicable, have effect not only in relation to the trusts described in Articles 2 and 3 of the Convention but also in relation to any other trusts of property arising under the law of any part of the United Kingdom or by virtue of a judicial decision whether in the United Kingdom or elsewhere.'

For the UK this makes academic much of the above debate about which trusts should fall within Article 3 of the Convention. In so far as the Con-

---

16 But see J Harris *The Hague Trusts Convention*, 128–34, preferring a more literal and narrower construction of the Convention's scope; and see Recognition of Trusts Act 1987, s 1(2), p 1010, ante. The applicability of LPA 1925, s 55(d) may be crucial: see p 423 ante.

17 Administration of Estates Act 1925, s 33; Trusts of Land and Appointment of Trustees Act 1996.

18 Contrast the French 'créés'. The English version suggests that Convention may be extended to trust whose existence is affirmed by the court; the French version tends to suggest that the trust must be *imposed* by the court.

19 In Canada, 'All the provinces that have implemented the Convention have extended it to trusts created by virtue of judicial decision, including constructive trusts and resulting trusts': J-G Castel *Canadian Conflict of Laws* (4th edn, 1997) Butterworths, Toronto and Vancouver, p 545.

vention has been extended to cover resulting and constructive trusts, one would normally focus upon the objective 'applicable law ... the law with which it is most closely connected'[20], so it is very curious that the Hague Convention's choice of law rules receive almost no discussion in the few English cases where the existence of a constructive trust in a transnational context has been at issue[1]. However, where the constructive trust inevitably applies to the property from time to time representing the original trust property held under an express trust, the law governing the latter must govern the former, just as the law governing property held on a resulting trust upon failure of all or part of an express trust must be the same as the law governing the express trust. In the case of presumed resulting trusts of property the *lex situs* should be the key factor.

Trusts arising under the law of a part of the United Kingdom

The Convention applies to 'any other trusts of property arising under the law of any part of the United Kingdom'[2]. This creates something of a paradox since until one knows what choice of law rules to apply to the trust, one cannot know if it is governed by the law of a part of the United Kingdom; but one cannot know which choice of law rules to apply until one knows whether the Convention applies or not. Accordingly, the extension must apply if it *appears* that the law of a part of the United Kingdom is *putatively* applicable.

Statutory trusts such as those arising on intestacy or the co-purchase of land clearly are 'trusts arising under the law of any part of the UK'.

As Lord Browne-Wilkinson points out in *Westdeutsche Landesbank v Islington London Borough Council*[3],'Under an institutional constructive trust the trust arises by operation of law as from the date of the circumstances which give rise to it: the function of the court is merely to declare that such trust has arisen in the past', so that institutional constructive trusts of property – and resulting trusts – which are declared to have arisen under the law of any part of the UK are covered by s 1(2) of the 1987 Act to the extent not already covered by Article 3 of the Convention.

---

20 J-G Castel *Canadian Conflict of Laws* (4th edn, 1997) Butterworths, Toronto and Vancouver, p 551; save, of course, in the rare case where an express or implied choice of law can be found (an example might be a purported express trust which contained a choice of law clause for English law, where the trust failed for want of formalities, but where equity stepped in to impose a trust to prevent a statute being used as a cloak for fraud).

1 For example, *El Ajou v Dollar Land Holdings plc* [1993] 3 All ER 717 (reversed on different grounds: [1994] 2 All ER 685); *Arab Monetary Fund v Hashim (No 9)* (1994) Times, 11 October; *Trustor AB v Smallbone* (9 May 2000, unreported), CA; *Kuwait Oil Tanker v Al Bader* [2000] 2 All ER (Comm) 271 (and see G Virgo (2000) 8 RLR 122); *Grupo Torras v Al-Sabah (No 5)* [2001] Lloyd's Rep Bank 36 (noted by J Garton (2001) 15 Trust Law International 93). In *Arab Monetary Fund v Hashim (No 9)*, Chadwick J remarked that '[I]n cases involving a foreign element in which an English court is asked to treat a defendant as a constructive trustee of assets which he has acquired through misuses of his powers, the relevant questions are: (i) what is the proper law which governs the relationship between the defendant and the person for whose benefit those powers have been conferred; (ii) what, under that law, are the duties to which the defendant is subject in relation to those powers; (iii) is the nature of those duties such that they would be regarded by an English court as fiduciary duties; and (iv) if so, is it unconscionable for the defendant to retain those assets.'

2 This also means that the Convention rules will apply to disputes solely between the application of English and Scottish law.

3 [1996] AC 669 at 716.

Trusts 'arising' by judicial decision in any legal system

It is easy to see that 'statutory jurisdiction trusts'[4] are covered by this provision. Hence, if an English or foreign court were to create a new trust of property pursuant to a divorce jurisdiction or a Mental Health Act jurisdiction or a statutory jurisdiction for damages for personal injuries of infants, such a trust would fall within the Act.

The question then needing to be answered is whether constructive or resulting trusts of property not arising under the law of a part of the UK but under some foreign law are trusts 'arising by virtue of a judicial decision' within s 1(2). It has already been seen that, traditionally, in England constructive and resulting trusts of property are retrospectively confirmed or declared by the court as old trusts that arose earlier as a result of the law's view of the voluntary actions of relevant parties, rather than being new trusts arising by virtue of a judicial decision. Thus, if the foreign law responsible for the existence of a constructive or resulting trust of property operates on the same basis as English law, then s 1(2) and the Convention will be inapplicable[5]. It will then only be in respect of remedial constructive trusts (not yet part of English law)[6] that are first created and imposed by a court order that the Convention will apply.

This strict literal approach[7] has the curious effect that trusts arising by virtue of a discretionary judicial decision are included within the Act, while the well-known institutional constructive and resulting trusts arising other than under the law of a part of the UK are excluded. Because it is odd so to discriminate against foreign constructive or resulting trusts and Article 20, that underlies the enactment of s 1(2), refers to trusts 'declared' by judicial decision, it may well be that a broad purposive approach should be taken to treat s 1(2) as a broad sweeping-up provision, so as to treat 'arising ... by virtue of a judicial decision' as covering 'declared or created': then foreign (as well as UK) constructive and resulting trusts will be covered.

PRELIMINARY MATTERS EXCLUDED FROM THE CONVENTION

The 'rocket' and the 'rocket launcher'

The Convention is applicable only to matters which concern the validity of the trust itself. However, for a trust to be brought into existence, it must be validly declared and constituted. When contained in a written instrument, that written instrument must itself be valid, both as to form and substance. When involving the transfer of property into the hands of the trustee, the property must have been validly transferred. When the type of trust in question can be created only by certain types of person, then the settlor must have the capacity to create the trust. Article 4 states that these preliminary

---

4 These are 'trusts created pursuant to a court order made under a statutory jurisdiction and dealing with unique factual circumstances...': D Hayton (1987) 36 ICLQ 260, 266.

5 As assumed by *Dicey & Morris* at p 1096 suggesting, therefore, use of the proper law of the obligation to make restitution. See also R Stevens in F Rose (ed) *Restitution and The Conflict of Laws* (1995) Mansfield Press, Oxford, Chapter 5, pp 216–218 and P Matthews (1995) 1 Trusts and Trustees 7.

6 *Re Polly Peck International (in administration) (No 2)* [1998] 3 All ER 812, CA; *Westdeutsche Landesbank v Islington London Borough Council* [1996] AC 669 at 716.

7 Favoured by J Harris *The Hague Trust Convention*, pp 145–147.

matters are outside the scope of the Convention. 'The image employed was that of the launcher and the rocket; it will always be necessary to have a "launcher", for example a will, a gift or another act with legal effects, which then launches the "rocket", the trust. The preliminary act with legal effects, the "launcher", does not fall under the Convention's coverage.'[8]

The choice of law rules applicable to many of these 'rocket launching' matters are themselves highly uncertain. Moreover, it is difficult in some cases to determine precisely where the distinction between 'rocket-launcher' and 'rocket' should be drawn.

It is contended that the essential distinction to be drawn is between those rules which are applicable to *any* disposition of property and those which specifically affect the ability to create a trust of property. The former should be seen as 'rocket launching' preliminary matters outside the scope of the Convention; the latter as 'rocket' matters within the Convention's scope[9].

It is possible to say that certain issues are clearly part of the rocket-launching process and outside the Convention. These include the transfer of property to trustees, the validity of a will as to form and substance and the capacity of the settlor to create the trust. But it is not possible to say that other, more specific legal rules, such as rules on forced heirship or rules against perpetuities, are or are not outside the Convention. In so far as they relate to the right to transfer property at all, they are outside; in so far as they relate to the creation of the trust structure, they are inside.

It is now necessary to look at some of the most important preliminary issues that might arise[10].

Capacity to create a trust

Capacity rules define a particular class of persons who by a given law cannot enter into a transaction into which other people generally may enter.

The settlor

The capacity of a settlor to transfer assets to the trustee is an issue which appears to fall outside the Hague Convention[11]. There is very little cogent authority on the choice of law rule governing the settlor's capacity to create a trust[12]. There is some support for application of the law of the settlor's domicile[13]. However, these cases are almost all largely concerned with matrimonial capacity or marriage settlements.

It is important to appreciate that there are in fact two distinct aspects to the capacity to create a trust: the capacity of the settlor to alienate property *at all*

---

8 Von Overbeck Report, para 53 at p 381.

9 This view appears to be supported by the decision in *Tod v Barton*, [2002] EWHC 264 (Ch), (2002) 4 ITELR 715, judgment of Lawrence Collins J.

10 For more detailed coverage, see J Harris, 'Launching the Rocket: Capacity and the Creation of *Inter Vivos* Transnational Trusts', in J Glasson (ed) *International Trust Laws*, Chapter C2; and J Harris *The Hague Trusts Convention*, Part 1.

11 'In the end the Commission did not expressly exclude general capacity, although a consensus emerged that this was not to be governed by the Convention, while the specific capacity to become a trustee was to be so governed': von Overbeck Report, para 59 at p 382.

12 At least outside the context of marriage settlements.

13 See *Sottomayor v De Barros* (1877) 3 PD 1, 5; *Re Cooke's Trusts* (1887) 56 LJ Ch 637, 639; *Cooper v Cooper* (1888) 13 App Cas 88, 99–100. See also *Viditz v O'Hagan* [1900] 2 Ch 87 (a case relied upon by the authors of *Lewin on Trusts* (17th edn), p 303). See also *Re Bankes* [1902] 2 Ch 333.

and the capacity of the settlor to create the trust structure with that property. The first question arises because a settlor who seeks to transfer property to a trustee is disposing of his property no less than an owner who simply gives away or sells his property to another person absolutely. Since the alienation by the settlor ultimately affects title to property and since it is important that any decision on capacity be enforceable in the courts of the place where the property is located, it is suggested that the law of the place where the property is situated (*lex situs*) should apply to this first question[14], at least where the trust is to be created *inter vivos*[15].

There is then a second question as to whether the settlor, who has capacity to alienate property according to the *lex situs,* has capacity to create the trust structure with that property. Here, it is suggested that there is a much stronger case for settlor autonomy. The restrictions upon a settlor seem legitimately targeted at the question whether he may dispose of property at all, not whether he may dispose thereof on trust[16]. Moreover, use of any other law on this second question might lead to a trust failing because the law in question does not know the trust concept at all.

How should this test apply if the settlor simply declares himself trustee of his property? Arguably, he has not alienated his legal title, so the first question above does not apply. The settlor has merely created the trust structure with the property, which, on the view advocated here, would be a second question issue, to be resolved by the chosen law. However, if the first step of asking whether the settlor has capacity to alienate his property is not taken where declarations of trust are concerned, the effect might be the equitable alienation of property of which the settlor may not dispose *at all* according to the *lex situs.* Rather, it is suggested that, in the case of the declaration of trust, one should ask (i) does the settlor have power to alienate *any* interest in his property by the *lex situs*; (ii) if so, does he have power to create a trust according to the proper law of the trust?

In summary, the following choice of law is suggested as appropriate to determine the capacity of a settlor to create an *inter vivos* trust:

(1) The capacity of a settlor to dispose of any property right *inter vivos* is governed by the *lex situs* at the time of the purported transfer[17].

(2) The capacity of any settlor to create a trust of any property of which he may, according to rule (1), dispose is governed by the proper law of the trust[18].

The capacity of the trustee

Article 8(2)(a) of the Convention states that the capacity of the intended trustee is governed by the law applicable to the trust[19]. However, it is suggested that this deals only with the specific issue of his capacity to act as

---

14 But see *Black v Black's Trustees* 1950 SLT (Notes) 32, where the *lex situs* was applied only in respect of immovable trust property and not in respect of movable property.

15 In the case of testamentary trusts of movable property, it is suggested that the *lex successionis,* the law of the deceased's domicile at death should be applied, as this is consistent with the law applied to the essential validity of testamentary transfers of movables.

16 A view supported by P Nygh *Conflict of Laws in Australia* (6th edn, 1995) Butterworths, Australia, p 518.

17 For testamentary trusts of movables, the law of the deceased's last domicile should apply.

18 Which will normally be the law chosen by the settlor to govern the trust.

19 See also von Overbeck, para 59, p 382.

trustee. The intended trustee must also have 'general' capacity to receive property at all[20].

Accordingly, the following choice of law rule is suggested:

(1) The capacity of a 'trustee'[1] to receive any property right *inter vivos*[2] is governed by the *lex situs* at the time of the purported transfer.
(2) The capacity of a 'trustee' to act as trustee of any property which he may, according to rule (1), receive is governed by the proper law of the trust.

The capacity of the beneficiary

A putative beneficiary likewise requires capacity to receive property at all[3], and specifically to receive a benefit under a trust. Where a beneficiary lacks capacity in English domestic law, he will not normally be able to give a good receipt for trust capital and/or income and alternative arrangements will need to be made.

It might appear that a beneficiary's capacity is a trusts specific issue, and should be subjected to the law governing the trust. However, since the governing law of the trust might allow the beneficiary to terminate the trust and claim the property absolutely, the *lex situs* is likely also to have a legitimate interest in the matter. It is submitted that the 'general' capacity of a beneficiary to receive any form of benefit under the trust should be determined by the *lex situs*. It is then suggested that the 'specific' question whether a person in principle entitled to take a benefit may do so in the capacity of a beneficiary under a trust (including the question of whether he is presently entitled to take a beneficial interest in possession under the trust) should be seen as a trusts specific matter for the law applicable to the trust.

Accordingly, the following choice of law rule is suggested:

(1) The capacity of a person to receive property at all *inter vivos*[4] is determined by the *lex situs* at the time of the purported transfer of property to the trustee.
(2) The capacity of a person who may, according to rule (1), receive property, to assert a beneficial interest under a trust, including the question of whether he is presently entitled to that benefit, is governed by the proper law of the trust.

The vesting of property in the trustee

'Article 4 is intended to exclude from the Convention's scope of application both the substantive validity and the formal validity of the transfers which are preliminary to the creation of the trust.'[5] The question whether property has

---

20 An example of a 'general' property rule regulating capacity in England is the Trusts of Land and Appointment of Trustees Act 1996, s 1(1), Sch 1, which provides that a purported transfer of land to a minor is ineffective to pass legal title, but operates as a declaration that the land is to be held in trust for the minor.
1 Ie a putative trustee.
2 In the case of a testamentary disposition of movables, the law of the deceased's last domicile would apply.
3 We are concerned here with restrictions which the law imposes on the receipt of a benefit by a person or class of persons, not with further restrictions which the trust instrument might expressly impose on a minor as to when he may become entitled to an interest in possession.
4 In the case of a testamentary disposition of movables, the law of the deceased's last domicile would be applicable to this matter.
5 Von Overbeck Report, para 55, p 382.

successfully been vested in the trustees is thus excluded from the Convention. This must be governed by the general choice of laws rules for the transfer of property, which will be set out below.

Technically, one could argue that two questions arise as to the passing of property: (i) the transfer of legal title to the trustee; (ii) the transfer of equitable title to the beneficiary. However, civil law systems know nothing of equitable title and, once legal title has validly been transferred to B, the 'rocket-launching' process is concluded. It follows that the sole question with which the *lex situs* should concern itself is whether legal title to an interest may be alienated. It should not be a reason to invalidate the rocket-launching process that the *situs* does not know the trust concept. The particular interest which the beneficiary acquires under the trust should be seen as an aspect of the relationship between trustee and beneficiary[6], and governed by the applicable law of the trust, as determined by the rules of The Hague Trusts Convention.

Where the settlor declares himself trustee of property, matters are less certain. Although there will be no transfer of legal title, there will still be the passing of *a* right from the would-be settlor, namely the right to the beneficial interest in the property. It is suggested the question whether *any* property right has passed from the settlor should be governed by the *lex situs*, so as not to evade the application of that law to property transfers[7]; but the question whether the beneficiary has received a ring-fenced beneficial should be determined by the proper law of the trust[8].

Classification of property

For conflict of laws purposes, the distinction drawn in English domestic law between real and personal property is not used. Rather, a distinction is made between movable and immovable property. Within the former category, the law distinguishes between tangible and intangible property. It is the law of the *situs* of the property which decides whether that property is movable or immovable[9]. Where the *situs* is England, English law treats mortgages[10] and leases of land[11] as immovable property. The same is true for land subject to a trust for sale[12], at least prior to sale[13].

In order to understand what we mean when we say that the transfer of legal title to the trustee should be governed by the *lex situs*, it is necessary to look at the various types of property in turn.

---

6 Which Article 8(2)(g) states to be within the Convention's scope: see p 1042, post.

7 But note that the authors of *Lewin on Trusts* (17th edn), p 288 disagree and take the view that as there is no transfer of legal title, there is no preliminary issue to be decided about any transfer.

8 The *lex situs* should not apply its domestic property concepts. If it did, a trust could fail simply because the *lex situs* does not know the concept of a trust.

9 *Re Berchtold* [1923] 1 Ch 192; *Philipson-Stow v IRC* [1961] AC 727.

10 *Re Hoyles* [1911] 1 Ch 179.

11 *Freke v Carbery* (1873) LR 16 Eq 461; *Pepin v Bruyère* [1902] 1 Ch 24.

12 *Re Berchtold* [1923] 1 Ch 192.

13 Interests in the proceeds of sale of land are not treated as immovable: *Re Piercy* [1895] 1 Ch 83.

Immovable property

The *lex situs* applies to the essential validity[14] and formalities[15] necessary for a transfer of immovable property[16]. This is justified by the fact that the courts of the *situs* have exclusive control over land located within the jurisdiction. This makes it futile to decide a dispute other than the way that a judge in the courts of the *situs* would decide it, since any English order would otherwise probably be ineffective.

The doctrine of *renvoi* will also be applied here[17]. *Renvoi* essentially entails the English court seeking to decide a case using the substantive law that a judge in the courts of the *situs* would use. In other words, the whole of the law of the *situs* will apply, including its rules of private international law. If the law of the *situs* has its own choice of law rules which lead to the application of a different law, then an English court must apply the choice of law rule of the *situs*.

The doctrine of *renvoi* can lead to something of a logical paradox. Suppose that an English court has to determine title to land located in Utopia purportedly transferred by one English domiciliary to another. English choice of law rules point to the law of the *situs*, Utopian law. Suppose that on the facts a Utopian judge would apply the law of England to resolve the dispute[18]. Application of *renvoi* leads back to English law. But we know already that English choice of law rules refer to *Utopian* law. So which law should an English court apply? The answer is that it depends if Utopia *itself* has a doctrine of *renvoi*. If not, an English court should apply English law, since when Utopian law stated that English law should apply, it meant simply the *domestic* law of England, ignoring its choice of law rules. This is known as single *renvoi*[19]. However, if Utopia *itself* has a doctrine of *renvoi* (or, to put it another way, when Utopian law stated that English law should apply, it meant all of English law, including its choice of law rules), the matter is sent back to Utopian law and it is that law which an English court should apply. This is known as double *renvoi*[20].

Succession to immovables is also governed by the *lex situs*[1]. The doctrine of *renvoi* is also applicable to succession to immovables[2].

---

14 *Nelson v Bridport* (1846) 8 Beav 547.

15 *Adams v Clutterbuck* (1883) 10 QBD 403.

16 However, a contract to transfer an interest in land need not satisfy the formal requirements of the *lex situs* – *Re Smith, Lawrence v Kitson* [1916] 2 Ch 206. Article 9(2) of the Rome Convention states that a contract is formally valid if it satisfies the formal requirements of either the applicable law of the contract or the law of the place where either party was at the time of conclusion of the contract. Article 9(6) states that in the case of contracts for the sale of land, these formality rules still apply but are subject to 'the mandatory requirements of form of the law of the country where the property is situated if by that law those requirements are imposed irrespective of the country where the contract is concluded and irrespective of the law governing the contract.'

17 On which, see *Dicey and Morris*, Chapter 4; *Cheshire and North*, Chapter 5.

18 This might be because it applies the law of the domicile, where buyer and seller are domiciled in the same State.

19 See *Re Duke of Wellington* [1947] Ch 506.

20 See *Re Annesley* [1926] Ch 692.

1 *Nelson v Bridport* (1846) 8 Beav 547; *Freke v Carbery* (1873) LR 16 Eq 461; *Duncan v Lawson* (1889) 41 Ch D 394; *Re Ross* [1930] 1 Ch 377.

2 *Re Ross* [1930] 1 Ch 377; *Re Duke of Wellington* [1947] Ch 506. The exception is formal validity, where the application of *renvoi* is excluded by Wills Act 1963, s 6(1).

Tangible movable property

Individual[3] transfers of tangible movable property *inter vivos* are governed by the *lex situs*. This means the law of the place where the property was located at the time of the last purported transfer of that property[4]. There are a few exceptions to this rule, such as (a) where goods are in transit, with a casual or unknown presence[5]; (b) where the application of the *lex situs* is contrary to English public policy; (c) where an English statute prescribes the mandatory application of English law.

There is some support for the application of this doctrine in relation to *inter vivos* transfers of tangible movable property in *Winkworth v Christie*, where Slade J stated that he 'supposes' it would be open to a claimant to plead *renvoi*[6]. Application of the doctrine is also supported by *Dicey and Morris*[7]. The main reason for application of the *lex situs* is to decide a dispute as it would be decided by a judge in the courts of the *situs* for reasons of enforceability. For this reason, application of the doctrine of *renvoi* should be supported, since it means that an English court will apply the same law as a judge would in the courts of that State.

By contrast, transfers of tangible movable property on death are governed by the law of the deceased's domicile at the time of death[8]. It appears that the doctrine of *renvoi* is applicable[9]. Some writers argue that *renvoi* should not be applied to testamentary transfers of movables[10]. There is something to be said for this view, since a testator might expect that, in so far as the law of his domicile at death determines succession to his property, the domestic law of that State would apply. However, even here, *renvoi* has much to commend it, as it promotes unity of outcome. Without it, an English court might apply a different law from that which the courts of the testator's domicile would apply. This might mean that English courts take a different view as to who succeeds to property from the courts of the State of the deceased's domicile. It also provides an incentive for a claimant to forum-shop[11]. On balance, it is suggested that the doctrine of *renvoi* should be preserved in this area.

Intangible movable property

Although it might seem curious to ascribe a *situs* to intangible property, the law does exactly that. Shares have their *situs* in the country where they may be dealt with between shareholder and company. So, if shares are only transferable by entry on the register, they are situated in the country where the

---

3 Special rules apply to general assignments on bankruptcy, which are normally governed by the law of the domicile of the bankrupt: *Dicey and Morris*, Chapter 31.
4 *Cammell v Sewell* 3 (1858) H & N 617; *Winkworth v Christie* [1980] Ch 496.
5 *Winkworth v Christie* [1980] Ch 496 at 501. For the applicable law in such a case, see *Cheshire and North*, 951–2. It is likely that the law with which the transaction is objectively most closely connected will apply.
6 *Winkworth v Christie* [1980] Ch 496 at 514.
7 *Dicey and Morris* at 966.
8 *Re Groos* [1915] 1 Ch 572; *Re Annesley* [1926] Ch 692; *Re Ross* [1930] 1 Ch 377.
9 *Re Annesley* [1926] Ch 692; *Re Ross* [1930] 1 Ch 377; *Re O'Keefe* [1940] Ch 124. The exception is formal validity, where the application of *renvoi* is excluded by Wills Act 1963, s 6(1).
10 *Lewin on Trusts* (17th edn) at p 284. The authors contend that, since the relevant authorities are at first instance, the Court of Appeal should restrict the application of *renvoi* to immovables.
11 Ie to choose a State to sue in where he thinks he will get the most favourable outcome on the merits.

register is kept[12]. If the company has a register in two countries, and the transfer may be registered in either, the *situs* is the place where in the ordinary course of business the transfer would be registered[13].

A beneficial interest under a trust is located where the trustees of the original trust might be sued to enforce the terms of the trust. This will apply if the claimant has at present only a right to enforce the trust[14]. An interest in an as yet unadministered estate is located in the place where the estate ought naturally to be administered[15]. However, if the claimant asserts equitable ownership of property held subject to a trust, that equitable title is located where the property which is subject to the trust is itself located[16].

Transfers of a debt due under a contract[17] give rise to certain problems. A debt is generally regarded as having its *situs* where the debtor resides[18], because that is where it generally needs to be enforced. If he has more than one residence, it is where the creditor stipulates for the debt to be paid[19] and in the absence of such a stipulation, where it is payable in the normal course of business[20].

Where a purported assignment of a debt[1] occurs, questions relating to the assignability of the debt and to the relationship between that debtor and assignee are to be governed by the law governing the right which is to be assigned[2]. Whether a debt which *can* be assigned actually *has* been assigned is a matter for the law applicable to the contract of assignment[3].

Conclusion on transfers of property

The following choice of law rule is suggested to determine the essential validity of purported transfers of property on trust:

(1) The question whether any proprietary interest has been transferred *inter vivos*[4] from a would-be settlor to a would-be trustee is determined by the *lex situs* at the time of transfer[5].

---

12 See eg *Brassard v Smith* [1925] AC 371; *Erie Beach Co v A-G for Ontario* [1930] AC 161; *R v Williams* [1942] AC 541; *Macmillan Inc v Bishopsgate Trust plc (No 3)* [1996] 1 WLR 387.

13 *Treasurer of Ontario v Blonde* [1947] AC 24; *Standard Chartered Bank Ltd v IRC* [1978] 3 All ER 644.

14 *Re Smyth* [1898] 1 Ch 89; *A-G v Johnson* [1907] 2 KB 885; *Favorke v Steinkopff* [1922] 1 Ch 174; *Re Cigala's Settlement Trusts* (1878) 7 Ch D 351. See *Dicey and Morris*, p 934.

15 *Lord Sudeley v A-G* [1897] AC 11; *Dr Barnado's Homes National Incorporated Association v Comr for Special Purposes of the Income Tax Acts* [1921] 2 AC 1; *Comr of Stamp Duties (Queensland) v Livingstone* [1965] AC 694.

16 *Re Berchtold* [1923] 1 Ch 192; *Philipson-Stow v IRC* [1961] AC 727.

17 Or any contractual right.

18 *New York Life Insurance Co v Public Trustee* [1924] 2 Ch 101.

19 *Kwok Chi Leung Karl v Estate Duty Comrs* [1988] 1 WLR 1035.

20 *Power Curber International Ltd v National Bank of Kuwait SAK* [1981] 3 All ER 607.

1 Or a contractual right.

2 Ie the law applicable to the contract which created the debt. For matters within the scope of the Rome Convention, this is stated in Article 12(2). Article 1(2)(g), Rome Convention excludes from the scope of the Convention the constitution of trusts. However, it appears that the same approach is taken at common law: *Trendtex v Crédit Suisse* [1980] QB 629.

3 See Article 12(1), Rome Convention; *Trendtex v Crédit Suisse* [1980] QB 629.

4 For testamentary transfers of movables, the law of the deceased's domicile at death should apply.

5 However, in the case of debts, the assignability of the debt will be determined by the law under which the debt arose; and the question whether the debt has been assigned to the trustee will be determined by the law governing the assignment itself.

(2) Whether such disposition is effective to transfer equitable title to the would-be beneficiary[6] is determined by the proper law of the trust.

Perpetuity

It is suggested that the English rules both against perpetuities and accumulations should be treated as 'rocket' matters and applicable when (but only when) English law is the law governing the trust[7]. This is because, in practice, they are predominantly focused upon the validity of trusts which are necessary where property is to be tied up for a period of time. After all, '... the problems of future interests, apart from questions of construction and of tax liability, essentially resolve themselves into the question of the application of the perpetuity rule to equitable interests under trusts.'[8] Moreover, the fact that the trust contravenes the rule against accumulations or the rule against remoteness of vesting does not prevent the trust from being launched: it only means the accumulations cannot continue beyond the applicable accumulation period and the trust itself cannot continue beyond the statutory 'wait and see' period of statutory lives in being plus twenty-one years.

Forced heirship

The classification of forced heirship claims is complex where, say, the deceased's three children are entitled to three quarters of his estate, extending to include property given away to individuals or to a trustee in an unlimited or prescribed period before death. The key question is whether a claim affects the trust structure itself or the transfer of title to the trustee. In so far as it affects only the ability to create the trust structure (because it does not impeach the alienation of legal title to the trustee) it falls within the Trusts Convention, and the mandatory rules of the law applicable to succession may be applied pursuant to Article 15(1)(c)[9]. Only if the alleged forced heirship rule impugns the transfer of title to the trustee, as in the case of a testamentary gift to a trustee where the *lex successionis* has forced heirship rules, should it be regarded as affecting the initial transfer and thus fall outside the Convention (but the general rule for *inter vivos* gifts is that the deceased was free while alive to transfer his property[10], so the transferee is only liable to pay compensation to the heirs to the extent necessary to make up the value of three quarters of the aggregate of the deceased's actual estate at death plus the value of the earlier valid gifts).

In the case of a vitiated testamentary transfer, since forced heirship rules are most naturally to be classified as rules of succession[11], the law governing

---

6 And the nature and extent of that equitable interest.

7 This view is supported by the decision of the Supreme Court of New South Wales in *Saliba v Falzon* [1998] NSWSC 302, where a testamentary disposition infringed the rule against accumulations of English law, but not New South Wales law and where the court felt bound to consider the law applicable to the trust to determine whether the accumulation period was infringed.

8 E Burn *Cheshire and Burn's Real Property* (16th edn, 2000) Butterworths, London, p 309. See also *Re Fitzgerald* [1904] 1 Ch 573.

9 See the discussion of mandatory rules and Article 15(1)(c) of the Convention below.

10 See D Hayton (ed) *European Succession Laws* (2nd edn, 2002) Jordan Publishing, para 1–67.

11 See A Duckworth in J Glasson (ed) *International Trust Laws*, Chapter B1, p 32, who considers other possible classifications, but concludes that the succession classification is the most likely.

succession to the deceased's estate[12] should determine whether, and to what extent, a testamentary disposition should be restricted by forced heirship rules[13]. However, it should be noted that where assets have already validly been disposed of on *inter vivos* trust, then in the English (or a similar common law) forum there is no question of that trust being affected by forced heirship rules of the law applicable to succession. That law should only be applied to assets which the law of the forum regards as forming part of the deceased's estate at death, rather than having been taken out of such estate by an earlier transfer, unimpeachable according to the applicable *lex situs*[14].

DETERMINING THE GOVERNING LAW OF A TRUST UNDER THE HAGUE CONVENTION

Express choice of law

Article 6 provides that the settlor may choose the law to govern a trust. This reflects the common law approach to express trusts[15]. However, it does not matter under the Convention that the chosen law has no objective connection with the trust. This appears to be a departure from the common law position, where it was thought that the settlor must choose a law with some objective connection to the trust[16]. However, Article 13[17] affords a State or its judicial officers the option to refuse to recognise a trust which has (save for its chosen law, the place of administration and the habitual residence of the trustee) its other significant connections with a non-trust State. Nor is there a requirement that a trust be objectively connected to more than one State; it is possible to choose the law of trusts State A to govern a trust objectively connected entirely to State B.

It should be noted that the settlor is free to choose the governing law, even in respect of trusts of land located overseas. This is something of a departure from the English common law, where it was necessary for a trust of land located overseas to be valid by the law of the *situs* of the land[18]. Such an

---

12 And not just the mandatory rules of the law of succession.

13 A view supported by *Re Annesley* [1926] Ch 692. See also E Scoles, P Hay, P Borchers and S Symeonides *The Conflict of Laws* (3rd edn), pp 1018-1021; *Bullen v Wisconsin* 240 US 625, 36 Sup Ct 473 (1916); *In Re Estate of Clark* 21 NY 2d 478, 288 NYS 2d 993 (1968); contrast *In Re Estate of Renard* 56 NY 2d 973, 453 NYS 3d 625 (considered by M Lupoi *Trusts: a Comparative Study*, 152).

14 See further the discussion of mandatory rules and Article 15(1)(c) below, p 1047.

15 See eg *Re Hernando* (1884) 27 Ch D 284; *Re Fitzgerald* [1904] 1 Ch 573; *Iveagh v IRC* [1954] Ch 365; *Trustees Executors and Agency Co. Ltd v Margottini* [1960] VR 417. M Lupoi *Trusts: a Comparative Study*, 349 points out that even the Cour d'appel of Paris, (10 January 1970, [1971] Revue Critique de Droit International Privé 518) accepted the freedom to choose the applicable law of a trust created by a Frenchman over securities situated in the United States.

16 In the Australian case of *Augustus v Permanent Trustee Company (Canberra) Ltd* (1971) 124 CLR 245 Walsh J expressed the view that the general choice of law principles applicable to contracts at common law should extend to trusts. In contract, it was required at common law that a choice be '*bona fide* and legal': per Lord Wright in *Vita Foods Products Inc v Unus Shipping Co Ltd* [1939] AC 277 at 290.

17 This Article was deliberately omitted from the Recognition of Trusts Act 1987: see p 1055 post.

18 *Re Piercy* [1895] 1 Ch 83. But once the land was sold, the law of the *situs* of the land no longer applied and the law chosen by the settlor to govern the trust alone applied. See also *Re Berchtold* [1923] 1 Ch 192. See further *Webb v Webb* C-294/92 [1994] ECR I–1717, where the ECJ held that a claim to assert a beneficial interest in land did not have as its object 'right *in rem* in immovable property' for the purposes of [what was then] Article 16(1) of the Brussels Convention (now Article 22(1) of the Brussels I Regulation, considered in the discussion of jurisdiction p 1057 post).

approach was justified by the fact that the courts of the *situs* of land have exclusive control thereof, so that there was little point in an English court deciding a dispute differently from the way that a judge in the *situs* would, as any English order might prove unenforceable overseas. The Hague Convention, however, places a higher currency on settlor autonomy and the convenient efficiency of one law governing all trust assets through the trust period.

The choice must be that of an individual legal system. Article 23 provides that 'where a State comprises several territorial units each of which has its own rules of law in respect of trusts, any reference to the law of that State is to be construed as referring to the law in force in the territorial unit.'[19] The intent of this infelicitously drafted Article is that, whilst it would be possible to choose the law of Ontario to govern a trust, a choice of Canadian law to govern a trust would be treated as meaningless and ignored[20]. Thus, in the absence of a choice of a valid law, the governing law will be determined under Article 7.

The settlor must choose the law of a trust State to govern a trust. Article 6(2) states that where a law has been chosen to govern a trust and that law, 'does not provide for trusts or the category of trust involved[1], the choice shall not be effective and the law ... [applicable in the absence of choice] ... shall apply.' If application of Article 7 points to the law of closest connection being that of a non-trust State, the Convention's rules[2] shall not be applicable. However, von Overbeck comments that, in searching for the law of closest connection in this context, 'one would think that ... the judge will have a tendency to conclude that a trust is most closely connected with a State which has this institution'[3].

A difficult question might arise if a settlor creates a trust by vesting assets in the trustee and then subsequently another person transfers assets to the trustee to be held under the same settlement[4]. What if the original settlor chooses the law of Utopia to govern the trust but the subsequent transferor-settlor of assets to the trust[5] chooses the law of Ruritania? It is suggested that the latter choice would be ineffective. Where a person transfers assets to be held on the terms of a pre-existing trust, he has no choice but to submit to the law already governing that trust[6]. Of course, the subsequent disposition must still be 'launched' by the rules which determine the transfer of assets to a trustee[7].

---

19 This Article is not scheduled to the Recognition of Trusts Act 1987.
20 See von Overbeck Report para 176 and also D Hayton (1987) 36 ICLQ 260, 269.
 1 So that a choice of English law to govern a non-charitable purpose trust would fail, unless the English courts replace the beneficiary principle with the enforcer principle: p 114, ante.
 2 Including, paradoxically, Article 7.
 3 Von Overbeck Report, para 61, p 383. See also Report of the Special Commission, Preliminary Document No 9 of 9 March 1984, No 50.
 4 D Hayton (1987) 36 ICLQ 260 at 270 gives the examples of a unit trust and of the establishment of a pension fund, friendly society or unincorporated association.
 5 See *Galmerrow Securities Ltd v National Westminster Bank plc* [2002] WTLR 125 at p 140, 147, Harman J in a unit trust case p 1029, ante.
 6 It would seem that a trustee of an English trust cannot accept an addition of property except subject to English law, unless the trust instrument expressly authorises the trustee to accept added property as a sub-trust thereof subject to another trust law so far as not invalidated by English trust law.
 7 On which, see p 1029, ante.

Implied choice of law

If the settlor has not made a valid express choice of law, one should then look to see if he impliedly made a choice. The factors to which regard should be had in ascertaining whether the settlor impliedly made a choice of law are ones which reveal something of the settlor's subjective intentions; accordingly, those factual matters showing where the centre of gravity of the trust lies are not relevant at this stage.

An implied choice must be determined from the 'terms of the instrument creating the trust or the writing evidencing the trust, interpreted, if necessary, in the light of the circumstances of the case'. The court should begin by confining itself to the trust instrument as the first point of reference in the search for an implied choice[8], but if the position is then ambiguous it will become necessary to look at the circumstances of the case to reveal the settlor's intentions. Thus, in the trust instrument the use of terms resonant of a particular legal system, or the reference to powers contained in a specified Statute of a particular system or to purposes charitable under the law of a specified system, or the specification of a place of administration or a choice of court clause for resolution of disputes, should normally determine the issue without the need to refer to extrinsic circumstances which, in any event, will not be relevant if not indicative of the settlor's intentions.

If helpful, common law case law can still be referred to by English courts in deciding whether a choice can be implied, but an implied intention may not be inferred only from the circumstances of the case in the absence of assistance from the trust instrument or other written evidence thereof[9]. The common law cases reveal a number of interesting points[10]. In the case of testamentary trusts, it appears that the deceased's last domicile is normally a most influential circumstance in ascertaining the settlor's intentions. However, it is far from determinative[11]. In the case of *inter vivos* trusts, the insertion of a jurisdiction clause will be a powerful indicator of the settlor's intention[12]. Furthermore, if the trust is created by virtue of, or pursuant to, a judicial settlement[13], the inference that the law of the forum was intended to govern will be strong[14]. Use of terminology resonant of a particular legal system, or of a form known in only one system, will be a strong indicator of the settlor's intentions, although it has not proved to be anything like determinative[15]. The place of administration will frequently be given great prominence[16]. However, since under The Hague Convention the principal focus is on the trust instrument itself, this factor should be treated as espe-

---

8 Von Overbeck Report, para 69, p 385.

9 Von Overbeck Report, para 69, p 385.

10 See further J Harris *The Hague Trusts Convention*, pp 198–211. However, most of the common law cases do not distinguish between an implied choice of law and the applicable law in the absence of choice.

11 See, in particular, *A-G v Campbell* (1872) LR 5 HL 524; *Saliba v Falzon* [1998] NSWSC 302; *Tod v Barton* (2002) 4 ITELR 715, Lawrence Collins J.

12 As in *A-G v Jewish Colonization Association* [1901] 1 KB 123.

13 Since, in the United Kingdom, the Hague Convention has been extended to apply to such trusts by s 1(2) of the Recognition of Trusts Act 1987.

14 As in *Revenue Comrs v Pelly* [1940] IR 122.

15 *Peillon v Brooking* (1858) 25 Beav 218; *Re Lord Cable* [1977] 1 WLR 7; *Lindsay v Miller* [1949] VLR 13; *Revenue Comrs v Pelly* [1940] IR 122; *Iveagh v IRC* [1954] Ch 364.

16 As in *Chellaram v Chellaram* [1985] Ch 409, *Lindsay v Miller* [1949] VLR 13. However, it was accorded far less prominence in *Chellaram v Chellaram (No 2)* [2002] EWHC 632 (Ch), [2002] 3 All ER 17.

cially important only where the place of administration is expressly specified therein. Little inference can normally be drawn from the domicile or residence of the original trustees[17]. However, there are two obvious exceptions to this principle. First, where all the original trustees are domiciled or resident in one State, and their identity was stipulated in the trust instrument, this may itself lead to an irresistible inference as to where the settlor intended the trust to be administered[18]. That place of administration itself becomes a key factor in the search for an implied intention. Secondly, where the trustee is a company established specifically to hold the trust assets, the inference is that the law of the place of incorporation of the trust company will govern[19].

The *situs* of the assets may prove to be an important factor where the bulk of the trust property is immovable. However, where movable property is concerned, the *situs* appears to be a relevant, but not especially important factor and may tell a court little about the settlor's intentions[20]. Personal connecting factors relating to the settlor or a primary beneficiary are unlikely to be given much weight in the case of *inter vivos* trusts, save in the case of a family settlement where all parties to the trust are domiciled or resident in one State[1]. The place where a deed was prepared and executed does not normally reveal very much about the settlor's intentions[2], but it may[3]. The policy underlying the trust might tell the court something of the settlor's intentions but should only prove relevant where that policy is readily apparent[4].

It is not clear if a court may assume that the settlor intended to choose a law by which the trust is valid. Presumably, the settlor's purpose can be considered as one of the 'circumstances of the case' relevant to shedding light on the construction of the written trust document. However, such a purpose cannot itself be conclusive as to the intended applicable law, since Article 6 requires that the choice derives from the written instrument itself (or the written evidence thereof), interpreted, if necessary, by reference to the surrounding factors[5].

It appears that the settlor's intention should be ascertained as of the time of creation of the trust. Subsequent factors should only prove relevant in so far as they shed light on the settlor's intentions at the time of creation of the trust[6].

---

17 *Revenue Comrs v Pelly* [1940] IR 122; *Iveagh v IRC* [1954] Ch 364.
18 *Chellaram v Chellaram* [1985] Ch 409.
19 As in *A-G v Jewish Colonization Association* [1901] 1 KB 123.
20 *A-G v Campbell* (1872) LR 5 HL 524; *Lindsay v Miller* [1949] VLR 13; *Iveagh v IRC* [1954] Ch 364.
 1 As in *Iveagh v IRC* [1954] Ch 364.
 2 *Duke of Marlborough v AG* [1945] Ch 78; *Harris Investment Ltd v Smith* [1934] 1 DLR 748; *Lindsay v Miller* [1949] VLR 13; *Iveagh v IRC* [1954] Ch 364.
 3 *Chellaram v Chellaram (No 2)* [2002] WTLR 675, Lawrence Collins J at para 167 re Art 7.
 4 This is suggested by the comments of von Overbeck, para 67, p 384.
 5 *Augustus v Permanent Trustee Co (Canberra) Ltd* (1971) 124 CLR 25. This appears to accord with the policy of the Convention, whereby a choice of a non-trust State is disregarded altogether and the law of closest connection is used (Article 6(2)).
 6 As for sham trusts: *Midland Bank v Wyatt* [1995] 1 FLR 697.See also *Dicey and Morris*, 1216 and P Nygh *Autonomy in International Contracts* (1999) Clarendon Press, Oxford, p 112, for a similar view in relation to contracts.

Applicable law in the absence of choice

If the settlor has neither expressly nor impliedly chosen a law or has made an invalid choice of a non-trust State, the governing law of a trust must be objectively determined under Article 7. In trust-States the courts take into account a bewildering array of different factors with different weights attached to those factors in the circumstances of particular cases, where the nature of the trust is of much significance eg *inter vivos* or testamentary or a charitable trust or a marriage settlement or a fixed interest trust or a very broad discretionary trust. However non-trust States required simple guidance, preferably with a hierarchy or cascade of only the four most significant factors. The Convention therefore specifies 'in particular' (and so without prejudice to taking account of other factors) four factors which are to be regarded as of especial importance in ascertaining the law of closest connection for all trusts, albeit being of significance primarily for *inter vivos* trusts: the place of administration of the trust designated by the settlor; the *situs* of the trust assets; the residence or place of business of the trustees; and the place of performance of the purposes of the trust. As the von Overbeck Report states this enables non-trust judges and notaries to regard these factors as 'an implicit hierarchy which would satisfy the needs of practice. But the text will also allow the judges of the common law countries to take into account, as they have the habit of doing, all factors at the same time.'[7]

In practice, the potential for a Civilopian judge to reach a different result from a Trustopian judge, eg in the case of a testamentary trust (where the testator's Trustopian domicile is a most significant factor, though not determinative) is very limited[8]. Normally, it will be left to the Trustopian courts to determine matters affecting the trustee-beneficiary obligation and the Civilopian court will accept such determination, it normally being concerned only with the rights of third parties dealing in Civilopia with the trust property. In the exceptionally rare case where the Civilopian court has to work out for itself the governing law of the trust, then the Trustopian expert will be able to produce clear evidence as to which one or two factors (not limited to the four specified) are the key ones for determining the governing law-and which the court is free to take into account under the flexible wording of Article 7.

It should be noted that where the place of administration is designated by the settlor, this will be a very strong indicator of an implied choice of law pursuant to Article 6; in which case, the cases where Article 7(2)(a) may be relied upon to establish the law of closest connection will indeed be rare. As to the *situs* of the assets, since the character of the Convention is to treat the trust rather more as a matter of the law of obligations than the law of property, its role may not be especially significant. That said, one might expect the role of the *situs* to be stronger where the trust property consists wholly or principally of immovables. The difficulties which might arise in enforcing an order relating to the trust property itself in the State where the property is located mean that an English court should be slow to decide a dispute differently from the way that a judge in the court of the *situs* would decide it, unless the court can exercise *in personam* jurisdiction over the

---

7 Von Overbeck Report, para 77 at p 387. In *Chellaram v Chellaram (No 2)* [2002] EWHC 632 (Ch) [2002] WTLR 675, Lawrence Collins J stated at para 166, 'I doubt if there is any significant difference between Article 7 and the likely approach at common law'.

8 Fear of this led Ontario to refuse to implement the Convention.

defendant landowner to compel him to do as it orders[9]. The third factor mentioned, namely the place of residence or business of the trustee, is one whose importance in the common law cases varied from almost irrelevance[10] to near decisiveness. Where the original trustees are domiciled or habitually resident in different States, this factor is likely to be of very little relevance; on the other hand, if the trustees are domiciled or habitually resident in the same State, or the settlor sets up a trust company in a certain State, the factor may well be of considerable importance[11]. The final factor mentioned in Article 7 is the objects of the trust and their place of fulfilment. It is submitted that, under Article 7, a great deal of importance should not ordinarily be attached to a trust's 'objects' or purposes. Article 7 is about determining the law of closest connection objectively. The objects of the trust do not tell the court much about this, unless it is possible to infer from them something objective about the trust, such as where the assets should be invested, or the trust administered[12].

It should be noted that the domicile of a testator-settlor and the residence of the beneficiaries and the settlor are omitted from the list of factors mentioned in Article 7. However, as explained above, the list of Article 7 factors is not closed[13], so these factors can still be considered, though in *Tod v Barton*[14] Lawrence Collins J, in taking account of the law of Texas, the law of the testator's domicile, for Article 7 purposes, did not find it to be the governing law of the testamentary trust.

A court is likely to be reluctant to find that a trust is most closely connected with the law of a non-trust State, since this will take the trust outside the Convention altogether. However, in principle at least, the law of closest connection is to be determined entirely objectively and such a consideration ought not to be relevant.

A related question is whether, in ascertaining the law of closest connection, any relevance should be attached to the fact that by X law the trust is valid, whereas by Y law, it is not[15]. Although not mentioned in the non-exhaustive list in Article 7, some commentators appears to suggest validity is a relevant

---

9 *Webb v Webb* C-294/92 [1994] QB 696; *Chellaram v Chellaram* [1985] Ch 409.

10 The trustees' residence was discounted in *Harris Investments Ltd v Smith* [1934] 1 DLR 748 and *Jewish National Fund Inc v Royal Trust Co* (1965) 53 DLR (2d) 577. Little importance was attached to it in *Chellaram v Chellaram (No 2)* [2002] EWHC 632 (Ch), [2002] WTLR 675. In *Re Carapiet's Trusts* [2002] WTLR 989, however, the settlor had removed assets from India to England and settled them on a professional trustee based in England, with a discretion concerning investment of the assets in English property, so Jacobs J held the settlor wanted the assets controlled from England (para 12), demonstrating that the law of closest connection under Article 7 was English law.

11 *A-G v Jewish Colonization Association* [1901] 1 KB 123.

12 In *Chellaram v Chellaram* [1985] Ch 409, Scott J took the view that the trust before him was created, in part, to escape Indian tax and exchange control regulation and that the trust was to be administered in England. However, in *Chellaram v Chellaram (No 2)* [2002] EWHC 632 (Ch), [2002] WTLR 675 at para 167, Lawrence Collins J still found that the law of closest connection to the trust at the time of its creation was Indian law.

13 In *Chellaram v Chellaram (No 2)* [2002] EWHC 632 (Ch), [2002] WTLR 675, Collins J found that the four factors listed in Article 7 did not clearly reveal a law of closest connection. Rather, he determined the law of closest connection by reference to factors not mentioned in Article 7, such as the place of drafting and the origin of the family for whose benefit the trust was created. Also see *Re Carapiet's Trusts* [2002] WTLR 989.

14 (2002) 4 ITELR 715 at para 36.

15 Compare *National Shawmut Bank v Cumming* 325 Mass 457 (1950), summarised in M Rosenberg, P Hay and R Weintraub *Cases and Materials: Conflict of Laws* (10th edn), p 803.

matter[16]. Moreover, it could be said that one of the 'objects of the trust' is to create a valid trust in the first place. However, the better view is that no such presumption of validity exists. It is true that a settlor would probably not have chosen a law by which the trust was invalid. However, where there is no choice of law, the law of closest connection is a purely objective concept. A law of closest connection remains the law of closest connection regardless of whether it leads to the validity or invalidity of the trust.

Article 7 does not say at what time the law of closest connection should be ascertained. Nevertheless, it is submitted that, in principle, the law of closest connection to an *inter vivos* trust should be determined as of the time when the trust was created[17], since if a trust is to be validly created, it must be subject to a particular legal system from the moment of commencement[18]. This accords with the common law approach[19].

Exclusion of renvoi

Article 17 excludes the application of the doctrine of *renvoi*[20]. In other words, once the governing law of the trust has been determined, its domestic law is applied, without regard to any choice of law rules of the State identified. Suppose that a settlor chooses Utopian law to govern a trust. As a matter of Utopian private international law, the settlor may not choose the applicable law and a trust is governed by the law with which it has its closest connection. It may be that a Utopian judge would actually apply Ruritanian domestic law to the trust. Under the Convention, this fact is ignored and Utopian domestic law applied.

Splitting the applicable law; the distinction between validity and administration of trusts

The Convention permits the use of *dépeçage*, so that separate aspects of the trust may be subjected to different laws. This separation may be especially

---

16 A von Overbeck at www.isdc.ch/e/vO97.asp. See also P Nygh *Conflict of Laws in Australia* (6th edn), p 516, considering *Augustus v Permanent Trustee Co (Canberra) Ltd* (1971) 124 CLR 245. The same view is expressed by A Oakley *Parker and Mellows, The Modern Law of Trusts* (7th edn), p 757.

17 In the case of testamentary trusts, this rule would be unsatisfactory, however, since the trust will not come into existence until the testator's death, and not at the time of creation of the will. In the intervening period, the testator's domicile may change, as may that of the trustees or beneficiaries. Accordingly, it is suggested that the Article 7 factors should, in the case of testamentary trusts, be determined as of the date of creation of a will. This view is supported by the decision in *Jewish National Fund Inc v Royal Trust Co* (1965) 53 DLR (2d) 577, where the Supreme Court of Canada refused to consider supervening changes in the determining the law of closest connection. But cf M O'Sullivan (1993) 2 J Int Corp P 65 at 69.

18 This is also the view of *Cheshire and North*, 1037 and of P Nygh *Conflict of Laws in Australia* (6th edn), p 517. *Dicey and Morris* state (at 1090), perhaps a touch too firmly, that it is 'clear' that the law should be ascertained as at the point of creation.

19 At common law, subsequent changes clearly did not affect the law of closest connection (at least where it was not alleged that the applicable law had been changed): see *Duke of Marlborough v A-G* [1945] Ch 78; *Iveagh v IRC* [1954] Ch 364; *Devos v Devos* (1970) 10 DLR (3d) 603; *Chellaram v Chellaram* [1985] Ch 409. A similar position prevailed at common law in contract (see *Amin Rasheed Shipping Corpn v Kuwait Insurance Co* [1984] AC 50, discussed in *Dicey and Morris*, 1215–1216), but it now appears that, under the Rome Convention, supervening factors may be considered: Giuliano and Lagarde Report, OJ 1980 C282/4, p 20.

20 On which see the discussion of the preliminary issue of the vesting of property in the trustee p 1025, ante.

appropriate in relation to matters of administration[1]. Hence the settlor might provide, for example, that the validity of the trust be governed by English law, whereas its administration be governed by New South Wales law. However, the scope of Article 9 is wider than this and any severable[2] aspect of the trust might be subjected to a different law from that which governed the rest of the trust. Furthermore, although the splitting of the trust will usually be effected by express choice of the settlor, it may in an appropriate case be achieved under Article 7 in the absence of choice, if a particular aspect of the trust (eg Manitoban land where no perpetuity rules are applicable under Manitoban law, though they are under the law of the jurisdiction objectively applicable to the rest of the trust) is objectively more closely connected with a law other than that which governs the rest of the trust[3].

Of course, distinguishing matters of validity from matters of administration can be very difficult in practice[4]. It might be said that the difference between validity and administration is essentially one between matters which affect the substantive rights and interests of the beneficiaries and matters which simply go to the obligations of the trustees to take due care of the trust property and manage and invest it properly[5]. Certain issues will on any view be treated as matters of administration. These would include the trustees' powers of investment, right to remuneration, the appointment and removal of trustees, the power of the courts to confer additional powers on the trustees, the trustees' powers of delegation, of acquisition and disposal of trust assets and of paying debts and expenses and settling claims. The distinction between what constitutes capital and income is also most naturally to be seen as a matter of administration[6]. Powers of maintenance and advancement, on the other hand, have such a potentially significant impact on the nature and extent of the beneficiaries' interests that they may better be seen as matters affecting validity[7].

However, it is important to appreciate that the words 'administration' and

---

1 The settlor may choose the law of any trust State to govern administration, but it is envisaged that the place of administration may provide the most appropriate law: von Overbeck Report, para 91, pp 389–390. For the common law position, see A Wallace, (1987) 36 ICLQ 454 at 473–482.

2 The meaning of the word 'severable' is not wholly clear. P Matthews *Trusts: Migration and Change of Proper Law* (1997) Key Haven, London, p 60 argues that '..."severable" must mean *either* a qualitative difference in the type of exercise being done, eg construction of the substantive provisions as opposed to matters of administration, or a physical division of the trust into two or more parts, each having separate assets and being governed by separate substantive provisions, for example like separate appointments constituting separate trusts for capital gains tax purposes.'

3 Von Overbeck Report, paras 93–94, pp 390–391.

4 *Chellaram v Chellaram* [1985] Ch 409; (compare *Re Hewitt's Settlement* [1915] 1 Ch 228). See also the more recent Ontarian decision in *Branco v Veira* (1995) ETR (2d) 49.

5 But see the critical views of Scott J in *Chellaram v Chellaram* [1985] Ch 409 at 432: 'The rights and duties of trustees, for example, may be regarded as matters of administration but they also concern the effect of the settlement. The rights of the trustees are enjoyed as against the beneficiaries; the duties of the trustees are owed to the beneficiaries'; Scott J's words were approved by the South Australian Full Court in *Re Estate of Webb* (1992) 57 SASR 193. In *Chellaram v Chellaram (No 2)* [2002] EWHC 632 (Ch), [2002] WTLR 675, Lawrence Collins J was happier with the distinction

6 But, of course, the *nature and extent* of the interests of the beneficiaries in the capital and income is a matter of validity.

7 So that the powers contained in ss 31 and 32 of the Trustee Act 1925 would apply when English law governed the validity of a trust, even if the administration of the trust was governed by a different law but would not apply in the converse scenario.

'validity' are not terms of art and do not have an autonomous meaning. Essentially the issue in question is one of construction. If a settlor states eg that he wishes New South Wales law to govern the administration of the trust, a court should determine what *he* meant by the word 'administration'. Accordingly, whichever law governs the construction of the trust should determine what is meant respectively by 'validity' and 'administration'[8]. Where the settlor does not specify a law to govern construction and only subjects the administration of the trust to a separate law, it may be assumed that construction is to be subjected to the same law as that which governs validity.

Changing the governing law

Article 10 states that the law applicable to the validity of a trust shall decide if that law or the law governing a severable aspect thereof (eg administration) may be replaced by another law. So, if it is purported to change from the law of England to the law of Ontario, English law will decide if the change is permissible. A right to replace the governing law with another can be expressly contained in the trust instrument[9], but it is doubtful whether it can be implied into the trust instrument, even though judges normally allow what could be expressly contained in an instrument to be capable of being necessarily implied therein[10]. An example of where such implication might be drawn is where the trust instrument authorises the trustees to retire in favour of foreign trustees in another trust State and to transfer the assets to those new trustees: can one not necessarily infer that at least the law governing administration was then intended by the settlor to change to the law of the new State of administration?

Where there was no initial choice of law, what happens if it is argued that the law of closest connection has changed[11] ? If, for example, the trust assets are vested in the hands of new trustees who are resident in a different State, it may be that the law of closest connection changes. It seems then that the relevant question is whether, according to the law of closest connection at the time of the trust's creation, the applicable law may be changed in this manner.

---

8 Compare *Lindsay v Miller* [1949] VLR 13.

9 In English domestic law, the right to change the governing law may be expressly contained in the trust instrument or an application may be made to change the governing law under the Variation of Trusts Act 1958. See *Richard v Mackay* (4 March 1987, unreported), Ch D, (transcript in (1997) 11 Trust Law International 22); *Chellaram v Chellaram (No 2)* [2002] EWHC 632 (Ch), [2002] WTLR 675 at para 146.

10 In *Duke of Marlborough v A-G* [1945] Ch 78, the Court of Appeal took the view that, in the absence of an express provision in the trust instrument, the applicable law could be changed only with the concurrence of all the beneficiaries, and that this would result in a new settlement being created. However, it is difficult to see why an implied power to change the governing law of an existing settlement should not be permitted, providing it is clear that the settlor did intend this. That is a question of degree of evidence, not of substance. See also P Nygh *Conflict of Laws in Australia* (6th edn), p 517 who tentatively supports implied change, citing the case of *Duyvewaardt v Barber* (1992) 43 RFL (Can) (3rd) 139 in support. J-G Castel *Canadian Conflict of Laws* (4th edn), p 540 suggests that a change can be effected at common law only by an express power reserved to the settlor, by agreement between all the beneficiaries or by court order. See also *Chellaram v Chellaram (No 2)* [2002] EWHC 632 (Ch), [2002] WTLR 675 at para 146.

11 Such 'objective' change of law is also covered by Article 10: von Overbeck Report, para 99, p 392.

Where the governing law has been purportedly replaced by another governing law pursuant to an express power in that behalf, does this amount to the creation of a new trust altogether, like a re-settlement[12]? The Supreme Court of Delaware believed so in *Wilmington Trust Co v Mutual Life Insurance Co of New York*[13]. On the other hand, it might be said that such a power is like a power of appointment that permits the creation of a sub-trust within the umbrella of the original or head trust, so that a change from English to Suntopian law is only permitted because the English 'birth' law so decrees and the English trust should be treated as a continuing subsisting head trust when the applicable law is changed to Suntopian law, so that any provisions of Suntopian law (eg as to perpetuities and accumulations or to trusts always being revocable or being revocable in limited circumstances) which go beyond provisions of English law are inoperative – which, if overlooked, would invalidate the exercise of the power on *Re Hastings-Bass* principles[14]. If a replacement of the applicable law involves the creation of a new trust, there may be very unattractive capital gains tax implications for the trust[15], as well as very unattractive income tax implications eg if such change could possibly enable the settlor or his spouse to benefit in any way[16]. The safest advice is to insert powers to change the governing law only when considered essential, perhaps restricting the power to one to change the law governing administration only. When used, such clauses need very careful drafting and consideration of the possible taxation implications, eg such powers being expressed to be exercisable only to the extent no possible benefit is conferred on the settlor or his spouse[17].

SCOPE OF THE GOVERNING LAW OF THE TRUST

General matters

The list of factors to be determined by the applicable law is not intended to be exhaustive[18]. Indeed, it is meant in part to assist non-trust States to understand the nature of the issues involved in dealing with trusts.

Under Article 8(1) the applicable law not only governs the validity and effects of a trust, as one might expect, but also governs the construction and the administration of the trust. At common law[19] the law governing validity normally governs construction; indeed, validity often hinges on a question of construction. However, it is possible under Article 9 for a settlor expressly to choose another law to govern construction eg under a trust governed by

---

12 P Matthews *Trusts: Migration and Change of Proper Law*, 67.
13 26 Del Ch 397; P Matthews *Trusts: Migration and Change of Proper Law*, 68.
14 Discussed p 694 ante.
15 Taxation of Chargeable Gains Act 1992, s 71; *Hart v Briscoe* [1979] Ch 1; *Bond v Pickford* [1983] STC 517.
16 Income and Corporation Taxes Act 1988, s 660A(2), *IRC v Botnar* [1999] STC 711, CA.
17 P Matthews *Trusts: Migration and Change of Proper Law*, 80–81. As he points out (at 73–74) a preferable strategy may be to appoint assets of an English trust to an existing foreign trust having the same beneficiaries: indeed, the trust instrument might specify a particular foreign trust to which assets may be appointed, allowing the assets to be moved from their existing location in times of economic or political difficulty (a 'pilot' trust).
18 Von Overbeck Report, para 81, pp 387–388.
19 *Re Pilkington's Will Trusts* [1937] Ch 574; *Trustees Executors and Agency Co Ltd v Margottini* [1960] VR 417; *Philipson-Stow v IRC* [1961] AC 727; *Re Levick's Will Trusts* [1963] 1 WLR 311; *Perpetual Executors and Trustees Association of Australia Ltd v Roberts* [1970] VR 732.

English law the settlor could provide that a specified clause defining the terms used, like 'Beneficiaries', in the Trust Deed, shall be determined under Bahamian law at the date of the Trust Deed (thereby excluding non-marital issue).The law applicable to the administration of a trust may be less straightforward. It may be that the settlor will have selected a law to govern the administration of the trust which differs from that which governs the trust as a whole[20]. The 'effects' of the trust are also governed by the applicable law. This rather general term does not reveal much[1]. Presumably, the effects are primarily those stated in Article 8 (and also in Article 11).

Specific matters subject to the governing law of the trust

Article 8(2) lays down a list of matters which are to be subjected to the governing law of the trust.

Article 8(2)(a) covers 'the appointment, resignation and removal of trustees'. This is an important departure from the English common law position under which the English court may make *in personam* orders according to English law where trustees of a trust governed by a foreign law are properly brought before the court. Provided that the relevant court has jurisdiction to remove and replace trustees of a foreign settlement, it should now use the applicable law to determine whether to do so[2]. The other important matter covered by Article 8(2)(a) is the capacity to act as a trustee. It was argued (p 1024, above) that it is only the trustee's capacity to act *qua* trustee which is covered by Article 8(2)(a). The questions whether he has 'general' capacity to receive a property interest *at all* (as opposed to whether he can act as trustee of that interest) is not a trusts specific matter and ought to be governed by general property principles, which would tend to point to the *lex situs*[3].

Article 8(2)(b) subjects the rights and duties of the trustees among themselves to the applicable law. Despite this, it should be noted that where a trustee has been sued for breach of trust and then brings a contribution claim against the others, the Civil Liability (Contribution) Act 1978 applies in an English court regardless of the applicable law of the trust and to the exclusion of that applicable law[4].

Article 8(2)(c) provides that the trustee's right to delegate is determined by the applicable law. However, whilst this provision deals with the right to delegate, it does not deal with the consequences of such delegation. It is suggested that whilst the applicable law of the trust should determine if and

---

20 Pursuant to Article 9.
 1 If anything.
 2 Where English law governs the trust, it appears that a court will not appoint a trustee resident overseas to an existing trust (of which the trustees are presently English residents) unless the trust has subsequently acquired a very strong connection with an overseas State, such as where the beneficiaries have become resident there: *Re Liddiard* (1880) 14 Ch D 310; *Re Whitehead's Trusts* [1971] 1 WLR 833; see also *In the Estate of Ardagh* [1914] 1 IR 5. However, English court's now take a more relaxed view when a trustee with an express power of appointment chooses to appoint foreign trustees and will not intervene unless no reasonable trustee could have made such a choice: *Richard v Mackay* (1987) 11 Tru LI 23, Ch D and *Re Beatty's Will Trust (No 2)* (1991) 11 Tru LI 77, Ch D.
 3 In the case of *inter vivos* transfers. In the case of testamentary transfers of movables, it would point to the law of the deceased's last domicile. See the discussion of the capacity of the trustee, p 1025 ante.
 4 *Arab Monetary Fund v Hashim (No 9)* (1994) Times, 11 October; A Briggs, [1995] LMCLQ 437. See also *The Kapetan Georgis* [1988] 1 Lloyd's Rep 352 at 357–359; *Petroleo Brasiliero SA v Mellitus Shipping Inc* [2001] EWCA Civ 418, [2001] 2 Lloyd's Rep 203.

when a trustee might be liable for the acts of a properly appointed delegate, the nature and terms of the relationship formed between the trustee and the delegate is a matter for whatever law governs the relationship between them[5].

Article 8(2)(d) deals with the administration of the trust and the trustee's power to deal with and acquire trust property. In the absence of *dépeçage*, it is important to note that the vast body of law that is administration of trusts is subjected to the law applicable to the trust. Whilst this might seem not in the least surprising, there is English common law authority which applies certain English statutory provisions concerning trustees' powers to trusts governed by a foreign law, where the trustee is appointed in an English court[6]. It has been held that where a grant of administration is made in England, s 33(1) of the Administration of Estates Act 1925 (which grants statutory powers to the trustee to postpone sale) applies irrespective of the law applicable to the trust[7]. The same is true of the maintenance and advancement powers contained in ss 31 and 32, Trustee Act 1925[8]. *Dicey and Morris* suggest that such common law authorities 'appear not to be affected by [the Recognition of Trust Act 1987's] provisions.'[9] However, they are powers which arise pursuant to a valid trust. It follows that their application should be governed by the Hague Convention and it is suggested that such statutory provisions should not be applied to a trust governed by a foreign law[10].

The other matter mentioned in Article 8(2)(d) is the trustees' power to create security interests in trust property. Although the governing law of the trust decides whether a security interest in trust property can be created, or trust property disposed of, the title acquired by the transferee is a property law question and is a matter for the *lex situs* as recognised by Article 15(1)(d).

Article 8(2)(e) deals with the investment powers of the trustees. The power of investment is one of the most essential aspects of the proper administration of the trust. It follows that English legislative provisions on investment should only be applied if English law governs the trust. Such rules should not be treated as mandatory rules of English law, since even in a domestic context they can be derogated from if the settlor lays down different investment rules in the trust instrument.

Restrictions upon the duration of the trust, and upon the power to accumulate the income of the trust are covered by Article 8(2)(f). In England, s 164 of the Law of Property Act 1925, the Perpetuities and Accumulations Act 1964 and the rule against inalienability (also known as the rule against purpose trusts of excessive duration) should, accordingly, be applied only where English law is the governing law of the trust[11].

Article 8(2)(g) states that the 'relationships between the trustees and the beneficiaries, including the personal liability of the trustees to the bene-

---

5 Of course, there may very well be a contract between the trustee and the delegate; in which case, the governing law of the contract will determine the relationship between them. See also *Dicey and Morris*, 1526
6 Or, more precisely, where the trustee is appointed according to English law in an English court. See *Re Wilks* [1935] Ch 645; *Re Kehr* [1952] Ch 26; *Re Ker's Settlement Trusts* [1963] Ch 553; *Chellaram v Chellaram* [1985] Ch 409.
7 *Re Wilks* [1935] Ch 645.
8 *Re Kehr* [1952] Ch 26. See also *Dicey and Morris*, 1094.
9 *Dicey and Morris*, 1094.
10 There seems no pressing policy reason to treat them as overriding mandatory rules of the forum.
11 Even if the property is located overseas. See also the discussion of perpetuities when considering preliminary issues, p 1030 above.

ficiaries', are subject to the governing law of the trust. It seems this law will also determine the fiduciary duties owed by the trustee to the beneficiary under the Convention. The question of whether a fiduciary relationship arises in a transnational context appears not to be the subject of an orthodox choice of law rule at all, at least where there is no other 'specific relationship' between claimant and defendant[12], so that the Federal Court of Australia in *Paramasivam v Flynn*[13], treated the law of the forum as the governing law for 'general' breaches of fiduciary duty. However, in the context of the trustee/beneficiary relationship, it is submitted that the law governing the trust should determine the trustee's fiduciary duties. Article 8(2)(g) is not expressly confined to the personal liability of the trustee to the beneficiary *qua trustee*. Furthermore, that provision only 'includes' personal liability as one aspect of 'the relationships between the trustees and the beneficiaries'. Moreover, the court in *Paramasivam v Flynn* expressly excluded from its ruling fiduciary duties arising from agreement, suggesting that they might better be governed by the law applicable to the specific relationship from which they arise. Although the fiduciary relationship is not trusts specific, in so far as the rights and obligations arise because of the existence of a valid trust, it only makes sense for the law governing the trust also to regulate that relationship.

Article 8(2)(g) does not deal with the liability of the trustees to third parties. Von Overbeck makes clear that this is quite deliberate[14]. If a trustee harms a third party's interest eg by breaking a contract with him or wrongfully misappropriating his property and mixing it with the trust fund, there is no reason why the third party's personal or proprietary right of recovery should in any way be affected by a trust to which he was not party. Of course, the Convention also does not deal with the personal liability of a third party who receives trust property and then dishonestly or innocently deals with it inconsistently with the trust, or who dishonestly assists in a breach of trust[15].

Article 8(2)(h) deals with the variation and termination of trusts. The variation of trusts raises particularly complex questions in England[16]. The matter is complicated by statutory provisions of English law which purport to confer 'jurisdiction' on an English court to vary a settlement[17]. It is not clear

---

12 *Paramasivam v Flynn* (1998–99) 160 ALR 203. See also *El Ajou v Dollar Land Holdings plc* [1993] 3 All ER 717 (reversed on different grounds: [1994] 2 All ER 685); *Arab Monetary Fund v Hashim (No 9)* (1994) Times, 11 October; *Trustor AB v Smallbone* (9 May 2000, unreported), CA; *Kuwait Oil Tanker v Al Bader* [2000] 2 All ER (Comm) 271 (and see G Virgo (2000) 8 RLR 122); *Grupo Torras v Al-Sabah (No 5)*[2001] Lloyd's Rep Bank 36 (J Garton (2001) 15 Trust Law International 93).

13 (1998–99) 160 ALR 203.

14 Von Overbeck Report, para 87, p 389.

15 Claims for dishonest assistance in a breach of fiduciary duty have been treated for the purposes of Article 5(3) of the Brussels Convention as matters relating to tort: see *Casio Computer Co Ltd v Sayo* [2001] EWCA Civ 661, [2001] IL Pr 694; *Dexter v Harley* (2001) Times, 2 April, Ch D (both cases are discussed by T Yeo (2001) 117 LQR 560). The same approach might be taken for choice of law purposes. The same cases also assumed that claims based on dishonest dealings with fiduciary property received for one's own benefit could be classified for Brussels Convention purposes as matters relating to tort. However, in the case of such personal liability and particularly for innocent dealings, the claim might be classified as one in unjust enrichment for choice of law purposes (see *Dicey and Morris*, Chapter 34, Rule 200).

16 The subject is examined in detail in J Harris *The Hague Trusts Convention*, 256–270.

17 This is not a reference to *in personam* jurisdiction of the court over the defendant, which must, of course, still be established (and is considered below). The 'jurisdiction' here is rather the conferral of competence to vary a trust on an English court which already has *in personam* jurisdiction.

what happens where that 'jurisdiction' is lacking. Furthermore, pre-Convention case-law suggests that the English statutory variation provisions[18] may be applied to trusts governed by foreign law.

It is clear from s 24(1)(c) of the Matrimonial Causes Act 1973[19] that an English court has the power to vary a trust governed by English law when it has jurisdiction over divorce, nullity or legal separation proceedings involving the same parties[20]. Section 17 of the Matrimonial and Family Proceedings Act 1984 confers a similar power on the court in respect of foreign decrees. In both cases, the decision to vary is at the court's discretion. Section 24 further provides a basis of competence to vary a trust governed by foreign law. However, whether a court with competence should actually vary a foreign trust raises a question governed by the applicable law of the trust. Article 8(2)(h) of the Trusts Convention makes clear that if a foreign law governs the trust, then it is that foreign law's substantive provisions on variation of trusts which should be applied, not those of English law[1]. It must follow that it is to the applicable law of the trust that an English court should first look when deciding whether to vary the trust.

A similar approach should be taken to the Variation of Trusts Act 1958, s 1. In *Re Paget's Settlement*[2], Cross J suggested that an English court would be empowered to vary a foreign settlement. However, it might choose in its discretion not to do so. 'Obviously, however, where there are substantial foreign elements in the case, the court must consider carefully whether it is proper for it to exercise the jurisdiction.'[3] However, there was no suggestion in *Re Paget's Settlement* that the power to vary should be exercised in accordance with the applicable law of the trust. Instead, an English statute was applied to a foreign settlement. Such an approach would now appear incompatible with Article 8(2)(h)[4].

That said, there must be limits to the English court's willingness to exercise its jurisdiction to vary a trust governed by a foreign law. In particular, if an English court were to vary a trust governed by foreign law and with no objective connection to England, this would risk incurring the displeasure of foreign courts and might render any variation order unenforceable overseas[5]. It is submitted that the test which the English court should apply is to ask

---

18 On the Variation of Trusts Act 1958, see *Re Ker's Settlement Trusts* [1963] Ch 553; *Re Paget's Settlement* [1965] 1 WLR 1046. On the Matrimonial Causes Act 1973, see *Nunneley v Nunneley and Marrian* (1890) 15 PD 186.

19 Family Law Act 1996, s 15, was intended to introduce certain changes in this area, including allowing ancillary orders to be made prior to a divorce or legal separation. It is not presently in force. See also Sch 2 to the 1996 Act.

20 It may also adjust the interests of the parties, or extinguish the interest of one party: s 24(1)(d). See also *Cammell v Cammell* [1965] P 467; *Tallack v Tallack* [1927] P 211.

1 Subject to the application of mandatory rules and public policy (on which, see Articles 15(1)(b), 16 and 18, at pp 1046–1052, post).

2 [1965] 1 WLR 1046.

3 [1965] 1 WLR 1046 at 1050.

4 Unless it could be said to be a mandatory statutory rule of English law applicable under Article 16. However, there seems no principled reason why an English court should insist on applying English rules on variation to a foreign trust. See further J Harris *The Hague Trusts Convention*, 264-9.

5 See *Goff v Goff* [1934] P 107 at 114 and *Re Rabaiotti 1989 Settlement* [2000] WTLR 953, [2000] 2 ITELR 763 commented upon in (2000) 4 Jersey Law Review 317; D Benest (2000) 6 Trusts and Trustees 6; D Benest (2001) 7 Trusts and Trustees 16; C Davies (2000) 6 Trusts and Trustees 33. Also see *E v E* [1990] 2 FLR 233 at 242 and *T v T* [1996[2 FLR 357 at 363 not referring to the Convention.

whether, (assuming that it has *in personam* jurisdiction over the defendant) it is a natural forum in which to grant the particular variation order sought. In deciding this, it should attach considerable weight to the law governing the trust and to the strength of objective connection of the trust to England. However, against this, it must weigh three main factors: (i) that the philosophy of Article 8(2)(h) makes clear that the mere fact that a foreign law governs the trust is nothing like a conclusive reason for the forum not to exercise the jurisdiction to vary in accordance with such law; (ii) that England may well be the natural forum on the basis that it is more appropriate eg for divorce proceedings and a variation order of what in English law rank as ante-nuptial or post-nuptial settlements, to be dealt with by the same court; and (iii) an English court should be reluctant to refuse to vary a trust if it appears that no other court overseas would be competent, or willing, to vary the trust.

In divorce proceedings, where final resolution of matters is a fundamental goal and where the court may invoke Articles 15(1)(b),16 and 18 to buttress its Matrimonial Causes Act, the English court should be prepared to exercise its MCA jurisdiction, but probably subject to acceptance by the court in the jurisdiction of the applicable law before final resolution of the divorce issues. However, this will be pointless if the policy of the foreign applicable law eg The Bahamas[6] is specifically to protect the settled property from rights conferred by foreign law upon any person by reason of a personal relationship to the settlor, such as marriage. Otherwise, even if the State whose law governs the trust happens to have no legislation conferring equivalent powers on its own courts, it may well be that such courts will not object to the impact of the overriding powers of the English court, treating interests under such trust as from the outset subject to such foreign overriding process where key persons involved as settlor or trustee or beneficiaries thereunder have legitimately been subjected to the jurisdiction of the English court.

As to the termination of a trust, Article 8(2)(h) will cover the rights of both trustee (under an express power) and beneficiary (under the English *Saunders v Vautier*[7] principle, which only applies in one USA State) to terminate the trust. Where the right to terminate is exercised, the vesting of the property in the beneficiary ought to be determined by the applicable law of the trust[8].

Article 8(2)(i) deals with the distribution of trust assets. This provision will cover the decision of a trustee of a discretionary trust as to whom should benefit from the trust and in what proportions. Presumably, it also covers the interpretation of the trust deed, in order to determine who are the permissible beneficiaries under the trust.

Finally, the core duty of the trustee to produce accounts for falsification or surcharge in respect of breaches of trust is subject to the trust's governing law under Article 8(2)(j). This will extend to the duties to inform adult beneficiaries they be such, to keep and produce accounts for inspection and verification and to produce trust documents for inspection which may, perhaps, extend to letters of wishes.

---

6 Trusts (Choice of Governing Law) Act 1989, s 8(b).
7 (1841) 4 Beav 115.
8 Although this involves a transfer of legal title to the beneficiary, the *lex situs* should not be applied. That law need only be applied to 'launch' a trust in the first place. Here, the question is one of termination of a trust.

LIMITS ON THE SCOPE OF THE GOVERNING LAW OF THE TRUST

For matters within the scope of the Convention, the role of the law applicable to the trust or a severable aspect is not unlimited. The provisions of Articles 15, 16 and 18 respectively preserve the application of domestic mandatory rules in areas related to the law of trusts, the international mandatory rules of the forum and the public policy of the forum.

Mandatory rules and public policy distinguished

Mandatory rules are *positive* rules of law of a legal system which a State insists upon applying, even where a different law is applicable to the cause of action. They are superimposed onto the governing law. Mandatory rules are ones from which the settlor is not free to derogate. They contrast with use of public policy, which is a negative process. A court invokes its public policy where giving effect to the governing law would be unacceptable on the facts. It is a *negative* process leading to the disapplication of the governing law in whole or in part.

Mandatory rules of the law applicable to related areas of law

Article 15 preserves the application of domestic mandatory rules in areas related to trusts law. In case of conflict, the law applicable to the trust must[9] give way, but only in so far as the rules in a related area are mandatory. Article 15 is concerned not with the mandatory rules of the forum in related areas, but with the mandatory rules of the State whose law is designated by the forum's choice of law rules as applicable to those areas.

Article 15 provides a non-exhaustive list of areas of law related to the trust.

Article 15(1)(a) deals with rules for the protection of minors and incapable parties. This will often manifest itself in rules on capacity. Its scope of application may be rather narrow, since the capacity of a settlor to create a trust is in any event a preliminary issue excluded from the Convention[10]; and it appears that the capacity of a beneficiary to receive a benefit is also excluded[11]. The capacity to act as a trustee is, however, within the Convention[12]. A State might for example designate a personal connecting factor, or the *lex situs,* to determine the capacity of a party to hold and manage property. The mandatory rules of that State will be superimposed over the trust[13].

---

9 Although Article 15 (based on a French text then translated into English) states that it 'shall not prevent' the application of mandatory rules, s 1(3) of the Recognition of Trusts Act 1987 makes it clear that the provisions of Articles 15 and 16 positively '*shall* to the extent there specified, apply to the exclusion of other provisions of the Convention' (emphasis added).

10 See the discussion of the settlor's capacity in relation to the preliminary issues considered above.

11 See Article 8(2)(a), above.

12 Article 8(2)(a). More accurately, the specific capacity to act as a trustee is included; the 'general' capacity to receive property at all is excluded.

13 But a State should be slow to reach this conclusion. It is our contention that 'general' rules of property law should be applied only to the 'rocket-launching' matter of vesting legal title in the trustee and not to the 'rocket' matter of the creation of the trust structure with that property. Accordingly, mandatory rules should be applied under Article 15(1)(a) only where the restriction on the trustee's capacity relates specifically to his competence to hold and manage *trust* property.

Article 15(1)(b) concerns the effects of marriage on the trust[14], especially marital regimes having a form of community of property and the effects to be given to an ante-nuptial contract. Community of property is a common phenomenon in a number of States[15]. Where there is no contract, an English court will apply the law of the matrimonial domicile[16] to determine the effects of marriage on title to movable property[17]. Where there is a marriage contract, its effect is to be governed by the proper law of the contract[18]. The parties may expressly or impliedly agree on this law[19]; in the absence of choice, the law of the matrimonial domicile will govern[20].

Article 15(1)(c) applies to succession rights, testate and intestate, especially the indefeasible shares of spouses and relatives. It may apply, in particular, to preserve forced heirship rights under the law applicable to succession. However, the scope of Article 15(1)(c) is much narrower than might first appear because Article 4 will operate to prevent a testamentary trust from getting off the ground to the extent it purports to cover that part of the deceased's estate reserved for the heirs[1].

The most serious concern regarding forced heirship from an English or common lawyer's viewpoint (but not that of a civil law lawyer) is the fear that even an *inter vivos* trust might fall prey to 'claw-back' claims of the law applicable to succession, although it is more appropriate to regard these as 'add-back' claims, being personal, not proprietary claims.

Take S, who transfers English assets worth £24million to English resident trustees of a trust governed by English law and then dies a few years later with a £12million estate. Under his Civilopian *lex situs* S had power to make valid gifts of his property, but the value of them has to be added back to the value of his estate at death in order to calculate his three children's reserved three quarter shares of the notional £36million estate. To obtain their £27million the three children take the whole £12 million in S's actual estate and have a personal claim to recover £15 million from the donee-trustees of the £24 million gift (or, perhaps, from beneficiaries who had actually received part thereof).

However, it is almost certain that an English court will not permit a validly created *inter vivos* trust subsequently to be impugned by foreign forced heirship rules[2], just as it would not permit the operation of S's *inter vivos* joint account of money or other investments to be frustrated by any heir's claim against the surviving joint tenant even if S's *lex successionis* considered the joint account arrangement to be a testamentary one[3]. Characterisation of an

---

14 See generally *Dicey and Morris*, Chapter 28; *Cheshire and North*, Chapter 34.
15 See the brief survey in *Dicey and Morris*, 1067–1068. They divide the various systems of community of property into three categories: full community (giving the examples of the Netherlands and South Africa), community of gains (Spain) and community of chattels and gains.
16 *Dicey and Morris*, Rule 148 at p 1066. The rule is expressly limited to movable property. On immovables, see *Re De Nicols (No 2)* [1900] 2 Ch 410.
17 Where the spouses have different domiciles at the time of marriage, historically the husband's domicile prevails. However, such a rule has very little to commend it today and *Dicey and Morris* (at 1069) prefer to apply the 'law of the country with which the parties and the marriage have the closest connection...'.
18 *Dicey and Morris*, Rule 149 at pp 1073–1074.
19 For example, *Re Hernando* (1884) 27 Ch D 284; *Re Hewitt's Settlement* [1915] 1 Ch 228.
20 *Duke of Marlborough v A-G* [1945] Ch 78; *Dicey and Morris*, Rule 149 at pp 1073–1074.
1 A Duckworth, in J Glasson (ed) *International Trust Laws*, Chapter B1, p 24.
2 *Lewin on Trusts* (17th edn, 2000), para 11–59; P Matthews (2001) 5 Chase Journal 15; D Hayton (ed) *European Succession Laws* (2nd edn, 2002), paras 1–67 to 1–69.
3 *Sanchez v Sanchez* 547 So 2d 945 (1989); *Hutchinson v Ross* 211 Ne 2d 637.

issue as testamentary or *inter vivos* is a matter for the English forum. The English court will surely characterise a transfer by a live settlor to trustees (or into a joint account) as the case of an *inter vivos* transfer which is a preliminary issue outside the Trusts Convention, although, if within it, its paramount effect would be recognised under Article 15(1)(d). The only relevant question then is whether, at the time when the settlor purported to create an *inter vivos* trust, he could, and did, validly alienate his property to the trustee according to the *lex situs*. If the transfer is valid by the *lex situs* (and the trust itself is valid by its applicable law), it has validly come into effect and cannot later be impugned on the testator's death by forced heirship rules under the law happening to be the law applicable to succession because it so happened that the settlor died many years later domiciled in a forced heirship jurisdiction and left an actual estate inadequate to cover the amount of the reserved shares. It can also be argued that it would hardly be consistent with English public policy (protected by Article 18) to require trustees to have to wait upon such uncertainties for many years (adding-back rules in States like France and Italy being without limit of time) and so not exercise their distributive powers as to the value of the property received from the settlor, not having any protection such as that provided by s 13 of the Inheritance (Provision for Family and Dependants) Act 1975.

An English court should only apply the law applicable to succession to assets which are part of the deceased's estate at death. Thus, in *Pouey v Hordern*[4] property, appointed by will by a French-domiciled testatrix pursuant to a special power of appointment in her 1880 *inter vivos* settlement, was not subject to her children's forced heirship claims because there was 'no disposition of property belonging to the testatrix'. Assets which have been validly disposed of on *inter vivos* trusts are not part of the deceased's estate and so the law applicable to succession should not be applied to them. However, a judge in a civil law jurisdiction, faced with an English trust of some assets located in his jurisdiction or with some beneficiaries resident therein, is likely to consider that these issues are succession issues from his forum's viewpoint, and so enforce forced heirs' rights against such assets or beneficiaries[5].

Article 15(1)(d) preserves the application of mandatory rules concerning transfer of title to property and security interests in property. The term 'transfer of title to property' is intended to emphasise that not every property issue falls within the sub-paragraph[6]. Article 15(1)(d) cannot be concerned, as one might first think, with the transfer of property to the trustee, since this is a 'rocket-launching' matter within Article 4 and so is outside the scope of the Convention. For common law trusts, it might be applied to questions of transfer of equitable title to the beneficiary[7]. Questions such as whether equitable title has vested in the beneficiary and at what stage, whether the

---

4 [1900] 1 Ch 492 at 494.
5 D Hayton in J Glasson (ed) *International Trust Laws*, Chapter C3, p 14. See *Holzberg v Sasson* (1986) 75 Revue Critique de Droit International Privé 685 and *Caron v Odell* (1986) 75 Revue Critique de Droit International Privé 66.
6 Compare the German proposal in Working Document No 44 (discussed by von Overbeck, para 143, p 402) to refer simply to 'property'; see also A von Overbeck at www.isdc.ch/e/vO97.asp.
7 D Hayton (1996) 5 J Int Trust & Corp P 127 at 128. One exception might be where a settlor declares himself trustee of his property, in order to defraud his personal creditors. Hayton notes that, in English law, the creditors will be able to claim the trust assets under the Insolvency Act 1986: (1987) 36 ICLQ 260 at 275.

beneficiary's interest in the property transferred is in possession, vested, contingent or determinable and perhaps whether a beneficiary absolutely entitled can terminate the trust and call for the trust property to be transferred to him might be covered by paragraph (d). It should apply to the circumstances in which a good title to trust property may be passed to a third party.

Article 15(1)(e) covers the protection of creditors in matters of insolvency. It is not necessary that a creditor should have acted in good faith[8]. Article 15(1)(e) should be taken to concern the protection of creditors upon the beneficiary's insolvency, not the trustee's insolvency. The protective trust might be viewed as a means of frustrating the claims of a creditor and may be vulnerable to the mandatory rules of the designated foreign law[9].

Article 15(1)(f) preserves the application of mandatory rules for the protection of third parties acting *bona fide*. It is not limited to purchasers and might extend to other third party recipients of trust property[10].

Article 15(2) states that where a mandatory rule is applied under Article 15(1), 'the court shall try to give effect to the objects of the trust by other means'. There is no obligation to do so. However, it might allow a non-trust State which cannot recognise the trust *qua* trust to give some effect to it by 'translating' it into the nearest domestic law analogue[11].

International mandatory rules of the forum

Article 16 preserves the application of the forum's international mandatory rules (a nebulous flexible concept for common law States) and not the domestic mandatory rules of the jurisdiction designated by application of the forum's choice of law rules. These are those rules which the settlor may not derogate from and which are intended to be applied *irrespective* of the law governing the trust[12]. This will allow a State to apply its own international mandatory rules in any areas that might affect particular trusts so as to override such trust's terms so far as necessary eg so as to prevent export of heritage objects to a beneficiary or, perhaps, requiring exercise of its statutory variation of trust rules to produce a final resolution of a divorce of spouses whose affairs involve international ante-nuptial or post-nuptial trusts[13].

---

8 Von Overbeck, para 145 at p 403; Working Document No 58.

9 Or, indeed, be seen as contrary to the public policy of a State asked to recognise a protective trust governed by English law under Article 18.

10 A third party who has dissipated the trust property may be personally liable as discussed at pp 967–978 ante: but this personal claim is not covered by the Convention in any event and it may be that it is subject to the choice of law rules governing claims in unjust enrichment. See eg *Chase Manhattan Bank NA v Israel-British Bank (London) Ltd* [1981] Ch 105; *El Ajou v Dollar Land Holdings plc* [1993] 3 All ER 717 (reversed on different grounds: [1994] 2 All ER 685); *Arab Monetary Fund v Hashim (No 9)* (1994) Times, 11 October; *Trustor AB v Smallbone* (9 May 2000, unreported), CA; *Kuwait Oil Tanker v Al Bader* [2000] 2 All ER (Comm) 271; *Grupo Torras v Al-Sabah (No 5)*[2001] Lloyd's Rep Bank 36.

11 On which, see D Hayton in J Glasson (ed) *International Trust Laws*, Chapter C3 at pp 18–23.

12 The wording used to describe these mandatory rules is much more emphatic than in Article 15. Article 16 speaks of rules which must be applied 'even to international situations, irrespective of rules of conflict of laws'. See also von Overbeck, para 149 at pp 404–405.

13 'Among the laws which fall in this category, mention may be made of those which are intended to protect the cultural heritage of a country, public health, certain vital economic interests, the protection of employees or of the weaker party to another contract. The French delegation asked that in the Report currency exchange regulations be mentioned in this connection.': von Overbeck, para 149 at pp 403–404.

Article 16(2) permits the application 'in exceptional circumstances' of the international mandatory rules of a State of close connection with the case, whose law is neither the law of the forum nor the applicable law. However, for some States the extra uncertainties engendered by this provision represented a step too far. Article 16(3) thus offers Contracting States the option to enter a reservation as to the application of Article 16(2)[14]. The Recognition of Trusts Act 1987 simply omits Article 16(2)[15], so that only the international mandatory rules of the forum may be applied[16]. Despite that, an English court is hardly likely to require a trustee to act in a manner which is illegal in the place where it is to be effected[17].

Public policy

Article 18 states that 'the provisions of the Convention may be disregarded when their application would be manifestly contrary to public policy'. The provision encompasses the choice of law rules and the recognition of trusts. It may be applied to any[18] or all provisions of the Convention.

However, it is likely that Article 18 will be interpreted restrictively[19], in order not to undermine the other provisions of the Convention. The word 'manifestly' indicates a strong threshold. In particular, the fact that a technique necessitated by the trust is unfamiliar in a given State is not in itself grounds to invoke public policy[20]. Thus one would expect Article 18 to be confined to rules which are discriminatory, oppressive, infringe human rights or are impossible to give effect to[1] or contravene the irreducible core content

---

14 The procedural mechanism for making a reservation is dealt with in Article 26.

15 Nor does the provision apply in Alberta: s 1(4) of the International Convention Implementation Act 1990.

16 The United Kingdom has done exactly the same in the contract sphere. Article 7(1), Rome Convention allows a State to apply the international mandatory rules of 'another country with which the situation has a close connection'. Article 22(1)(a) allowed Contracting States to enter a reservation on the application of this provision. The United Kingdom did so in s 2(2) of the Contracts (Applicable Law) Act 1990, which states that Article 7(1) 'shall not have the force of law in the United Kingdom.' However, it should be noted that Australia has not entered this reservation, even though Australian courts appear to give very little effect to the mandatory rules of third States at common law: see P Nygh *Conflict of Laws in Australia* (6th edn), at pp 307–308, 519–520.

17 'Since a Court of Equity will do nothing in vain and will not require a person to do an act that is illegal where it is to be done, so that sufficient protection exists, there seems no need for a common law country to adopt this paragraph [ie Article 16(2)] of worryingly wide ambit'. (D Hayton, in J Glasson (ed) *International Trust Laws*, Chapter C3 at p 15).

18 Although Article 18 strictly refers to disapplication of 'the provisions of the Convention' and not to 'any one or more of the Convention provisions', it would be extraordinary if the public policy provision could only be applied to the Convention on an all or nothing basis.

19 M Koppenol-Laforce *Het Haagse Trustverdrag*, 270 remarks of Articles 16 and 18: 'From experiences with similar articles it follows that such articles are hardly ever applied. I see no reason why this should be different in trust-cases. Article 15 is the real danger to recognition of the trust.' This author would agree only in part. The unique problems created by the recognition of the trust in States which do not know the institution in their domestic law provides a real prospect that Article 18 may be used more widely than corresponding provisions of other Convention as a route of last resort to prevent recognition of a trust.

20 Thus in *Re Fitzgerald* [1904] 1 Ch 573, CA the non-assignability of a life interest under a Scots trust (which would have been assignable if the trust had been English) was recognised, so that a mortgage of it by the English domiciled life tenant to his English creditors was invalid.

1 *Oppenheim v Cattermole* [1976] AC 249; see also *Kuwait Airways Corpn v Iraqi Airways Co (No 3)* [2002] UKHL 19, [2002] 3 All ER 209: On the use of public policy in the conflict of laws, see *Dicey and Morris*, Chapter 2; *Cheshire and North* at pp 123–132. Typical cases where public policy is invoked (largely taken from contract law) include where the applicable law is fundamen-

of ownership rights, but, otherwise, it is better to utilise Articles 15 or 16 or rules that apply to preliminary issues which fall outside the Convention by virtue of Article 4 thereof. However, if particular English property is held on valid foreign trusts preventing that very property from being alienated in any way for a period exceeding that permitted by the Perpetuities and Accumulations Act 1964, then it would seem that English public policy would not permit such infringement of a very fundamental English property right attached to ownership[2]. On the other hand, if the trust property is freely alienable, but the interests of the beneficiaries in the changing investments representing the trust fund from time to time may arise outside the English perpetuity period laid down in the Perpetuities and Accumulations Act, then there seems no adequate reason to allow Article 18 to be invoked to trump Article 8(2)(f)[3].

Article 18 says only that the applicable law *may* be disregarded. It imposes no obligation. However, it is difficult to imagine a State whose own public policy is manifestly infringed not invoking its public policy.

Article 18 does not state that only the forum's public policy may be applied. However, it is extremely unlikely that an English court would apply anything other than its own public policy. It would indeed be very curious if a third State's public policy were applied by an English court, when the international mandatory rules of such a State may not be[4].

One question of particular practical importance is the effect to be given to non-charitable purpose trusts in England and whether their recognition should be refused on public policy grounds. In particular, should STAR trusts be enforced in England[5]? These trusts, originating from the Cayman

tally contrary to basic principles of human liberty (eg *Forbes v Cochrane* (1824) 2 B & C 448), English standards of justice (eg *Royal Boskalis Westminster NV v Mountain* [1999] QB 674) or English morality (eg *Lemenda Trading Co Ltd v African Middle East Petroleum Ltd* [1988] QB 448; though it may also be necessary in this 'weaker' category that the place of performance take the same view as to the morality of the agreement). Public policy may also be invoked where the United Kingdom's interests are adversely affected by the applicable law (eg *Dynamit Actein-Gesellschaft v Rio Tinto Co Ltd* [1918] AC 260) or where good relations with a friendly foreign State may be adversely affected (eg *Foster v Driscoll* [1929] 1 KB 470).

2 (1917) 33 LQR 11 (E Jenks); Megarry & Wade *The Law of Real Property* (6th edn) at para 3–071.
3 See *Lewin on Trusts* (17th edn) at para 11–34. It may be tempting to invoke Art 18 where an English settlor transfers English assets, particularly land, to English trustees for descendants of his grandfather, John Bull, for ever under a trust governed by a law (like Manitoban law) validating such trust, so as not to allow settlors to undermine and 'cock a snook' at English trust law, but once Manitoban or other foreign settlors under a favourable foreign trust law can do this for English investments that are comprised in their trust funds the pass is sold, even dramatically different treatment under a foreign trust law not being a reason to refuse to recognise it: *Re Fitzgerald* [1904] 1 Ch 573, CA. No line should be drawn between trust laws that permit 80 years or 125 years or 150 years or unlimited periods, so for Article 13 purposes, trusts with unlimited lives should not be regarded as a separate 'category of trust' from trusts with limited lives. In any event English law permits an extensive 'wait & see' period which could last for 100–125 years before the English court would need to consider the issue, by which time it will surely have a very relaxed attitude to perpetual trusts.
4 But see J Schoenblum in E McKendrick (ed) *Commercial Aspects of Trusts and Fiduciary Obligations*, Chapter 11 at pp 238–239, who points out that *Dicey and Morris* at one stage asserted that the strong public policy of the law with which the trust had its closest connection would also be applied at common law.
5 See the Special Trusts (Alternative Regime) Law 1997. See A Duckworth, *STAR Trusts*; A Duckworth, in J Glasson (ed) *International Trust Laws*, Chapter A7 at pp 28–36; G Thomas in J Glasson (ed) *International Trust Laws*, Chapter B4, pp 36-45. See also D Hayton (1998) 4 Amicus Curiae 13; D Hayton (1998) 8 Offshore Taxation Review 43; P Matthews (1997) 11 Trust Law International 67; A Duckworth (1998) 12 Trust Law International 16; P Matthews (1998) 12 Trust Law International 98; A Duckworth (1999) 13 Trust Law International 158.

Islands, allow a settlor to create a trust for beneficiaries or for purposes, or for both. Such purposes may be charitable or non-charitable. The beneficiaries do not ordinarily have a right in the trust property itself unless and until it is transferred to them. The trusts are enforced by appointed enforcers. The beneficiary has no right to enforce the trust unless also appointed as an enforcer of the trust. Although the matter is far from clear, it is submitted that, in general, such trusts should be recognised in England. Provided that the trust has an appointed enforcer, there is someone who can compel the trustee to fulfil his duties; and though an English court might dislike the tying up of capital for non-charitable purposes, it is by no means impossible to give effect to the trust[6]. English courts should be very slow to use public policy simply because a trust governed by a foreign law shows different characteristics to the English domestic trust[7], when the Convention asks contracting non-trust States to go much further and to recognise an institution not known in its legal system[8].

Exceptionally, if the STAR trust is for beneficiaries (eg a discretionary trust for the descendants of X for ever), the irreducible core content of the trust obligation[9] requires that a beneficiary (as opposed to an object of a power of appointment) must have rights to make the trustee account for its trusteeship. If some beneficiaries are not expressly appointed as enforcers there is the problem that, as stated by Millett LJ in *Armitage v Nurse*[10], 'There is an irreducible core of obligations owed by the trustees to the beneficiaries and enforceable by them which is fundamental to the concept of a trust. If the beneficiaries have no rights enforceable against the trustees there are no trusts' for the beneficiaries, only a resulting trust for the settlor, with the 'beneficiaries' being characterised by the English forum as mere objects of a power of appointment to whom the trustee is authorised to distribute trust assets till the settlor (beneficially entitled under a resulting trust) countermands his gratuitous mandate[11].

Where there is a true trust for non-charitable purposes so that the beneficial interest is exhausted (the income actually being spent an achieving some purpose eg the furthering of the purposes of the Jersey Conservative Party or of the Manx legal profession) the trust should be upheld by the English court as where it is alleged that there is a resulting trust of English assets so that they are available to creditors or heirs of the settlor. However, if the purpose of the trust is the inward or self-serving purpose to hold a particular shareholding or a collection of paintings or a ship[12] or to develop the value of the trust fund, so that the terms of the trust amount to an investment or holding clause and do not dispose of the settlor's underlying beneficial interest, then there should simply be a resulting trust for the settlor.

---

6 D Hayton (2001) 117 LQR 96, 100.

7 For example, *Re Fitzgerald* [1904] 1 Ch 573, CA.

8 A point made by A Duckworth (1999) 13 Trust Law International 158, 162.

9 See D Hayton 'The Irreducible Core Content of Trusteeship', Chapter 3 in A J Oakley (ed) *Trends in Contemporary Trust Law* (1996) Oxford and D Hayton 'The Obligation Characteristic of The Trust' (2001) 117 LQR 97.

10 [1998] Ch 241 at 253.

11 As he can: *Vandervell v IRC* [1967] 2 AC 291 at 317 per Lord Upjohn.

12 If the specific asset was to be wholly inalienable for longer than the permitted English perpetuity period, then this should contravene English public policy.

RECOGNITION OF TRUSTS

The requirements of recognition

A trust demonstrating the characteristics described in Article 2, meeting the requirement of Article 3[13] and governed by the law of a trust State is entitled to recognition under Article 11. The word 'recognition' has nothing to do with the effects to be given to foreign judgments in trust matters. A Contracting State to the Hague Convention will not be compelled to recognise an English trust judgment unless the English court is jurisdictionally competent in the eyes of the State of recognition. Likewise, a non-contracting, non-trust State will be compelled to recognise an English judgment if its criteria for the recognition of foreign judgments are met.

Article 11 simply explains certain key consequences of giving effect to a trust under its applicable law determined by the earlier Articles, primarily for the benefit of non-trust States. It is intended to lay down minimum requirements of recognition. A State which wishes to apply more favourable rules for the recognition of trusts is free to do so[14]. Article 11(2) lays down a uniform rule and states that the trust assets are separate from the personal assets of the trustee. The trustee's capacity to sue and be sued is also covered by Article 11(2). It makes clear that this extends beyond lawsuits and covers any relevant appearances before an authority or public notary[15].

Article 11(3) spells out more detailed consequence of recognition. However, these consequences are not required as a matter of uniform law and only apply in so far as the law governing the trust so provides. The trust assets are not available to satisfy claims brought against the trustee by his personal creditors, or upon the trustee's bankruptcy or insolvency, nor do they form part of his matrimonial property or estate[16]. Whilst these seem uncontroversial, it should be noted that Article 11 is subject to the mandatory rule provisions of Articles 15 and 16[17], which throws some doubt on the question whether the trust assets *must* be treated as a separate fund from the trustee's personal wealth. What happens if the requirement in Article 11 that the trust property constitutes a separate fund from the trustee's personal assets itself infringes the mandatory rules of property law of the forum, or the law designated by the forum to apply to property matters[18]? Could a trust still function without the separate fund element, or would it be stripped of any meaning or function[19]? As pointed out in the von Overbeck Report at paragraph 108, the separate fund requirement 'is an essential element of a trust, without which its recognition would have no meaning'.

It should therefore be the case that Article 15 preserves the application of

---

13 Unless the Contracting State has extended the operation of the Convention pursuant to Article 20 beyond such trusts, as the United Kingdom has done in s 1(2) of the Recognition of Trusts Act 1987.

14 Article 14. Of course, Contracting States might choose to extend the operation of the Convention's rules, so that recognition of a broader range of trusts would automatically follow. This is what the United Kingdom has done in s 1(2) of the Recognition of Trusts Act 1987.

15 See also K Lipstein in K Lipstein (ed) *International Encyclopaedia of Comparative Law*, Chapter 23 at p 27.

16 On these provisions, see von Overbeck, para 112 at pp 394–395.

17 Von Overbeck, para 105 at pp 393–394.

18 Article 15(1)(d) preserves the mandatory rules of the law applicable to transfers of title to property and security interests in property; Article 16 preserves the mandatory rules of the law of the forum.

19 D Hayton (1996) 5 J Int Corp P 127at 128.

mandatory rules in relation to matters of transfer of property and security interests in property in so far as they affect the beneficiary's interest under the trust. They should not normally be applied to affect the nature of the trustee's interest[20]. It follows that Article 15 does not detract from the separate status of the trust assets from the trustee's personal wealth and that this separation of the trust assets is required by the Convention[1]. This view is also supported by the Dutch ratification of the Convention. Although Dutch law did not permit separation of personal and fiduciary patrimony[2], the legislation implementing the Hague Convention[3] provides that Dutch laws on transfer of property, security interests and creditor protection shall not prevent the recognition of a trust otherwise satisfying the Hague Convention's requirements[4].

Following and tracing trust assets

Article 11(3)(d) deals with the tracing of assets or their value and the recovery of them in providing 'that the trust assets may be recovered when the trustee, in breach of trust, has mingled trust assets with his own property or has alienated trust assets'. The provision covers both recovery of the trust assets, which should cover assets from time to time representing the trust fund itself, and the mixing of trust assets with the trustee's own property. However, Article 11(3)(d) is not as far reaching as it may first appear. It mentions expressly the mixing of trust assets with the trustee's own property; it does not expressly deal with the mixing of the trust assets with a third party's assets (when, although the *lex situs* may not have equitable tracing rules, it may have less-refined proprietary subrogation principles dealing with, for example, property substituted for marital regime property or commercial partnership property). More fundamentally, where the property or its value is to be recovered from a third party holder of the assets, the final sentence of Article 11(3)(d) provides that the third party's 'rights and obligations shall remain subject to the law determined by the choice of law rules of the forum', which will be of crucial significance where that law is the *lex situs* of a civil law or Muslim jurisdiction not knowing of equitable proprietary interests or tracing processes.

However, it is suggested that such final sentence should only be invoked in England where the issue concerns acquisition by the third party and whether under the *lex situs* he takes an unimpeachable title[5]. It would not be relevant to the question whether the trust assets or their value could be traced into the third party's hands, which is determined under the first sentence of Article 11(3)(d) by the law applicable to the trust[6].

---

20 Unless, of course, the trustee is also a beneficiary of the fund.
 1 For the likely interpretation of Article 15(1)(d) and (e) were Switzerland to ratify the Convention, see A von Overbeck (1996) 4 Trusts and Trustees 6, 9.
 2 Article 84, s (3) of Book 3, Dutch Civil Code.
 3 Article 4, Wet Conflichtenrecht Trusts 1995.
 4 See also M Koppenol-Laforce *Het Haagse Trustverdrag*, 271. See also D Hayton (1996) 5 J Int Corp P 127.
 5 Which should be a matter for the *lex situs:* see *Macmillan Inc v Bishopsgate Investment Trust plc (No 3)* [1996] 1 WLR 387.
 6 There seems no good reason for the rules on *identification* of property to be subject to different laws, depending upon whether a third party is involved. However, the question whether identifiable property may be *claimed* from a third party depends on whether that third party took good title to it; and that is a property law question. Further see J Harris 'Tracing and the Conflict of Laws' in *British Yearbook of International Law 2003*.

Accordingly, there should be a two-stage process to determine the ability to recover trust assets or their value from the hands of a third party under the Convention:
(1) The law governing the trust determines whether the assets or their value can be followed or traced into the hands of the third party. If they may not be, then they cannot be recovered from the third party;
(2) If they can, the *lex situs* shall determine whether a third party recipient has taken free of the claims of the beneficiaries under the trust. If he has, the assets or their value cannot be recovered from him; if he has not, then their value can be recovered or even the assets themselves, depending on whether the *lex situs* recognises the beneficiaries as not merely having a personal claim but an *in personam ad rem* claim or, even an *in rem* proprietary claim.

Right to refuse recognition to trusts objectively connected to non-trust States

Article 13 is concerned with cases where the settlor has selected the law of a trust State to govern the trust, or has designated that the trust be administered in such a State, or has chosen trustees who are habitually resident in that State, but where the other significant elements point objectively to the law of one or more non-trust States[7]. This provision allows a court to refuse to recognise a trust otherwise qualifying for recognition under Article 11[8]. It reinforces the fact that the trust is not introduced by the Convention into non-trust States' domestic legal systems. It also applies if the State of closest connection knows the concept of the trust in its domestic legal system, but does not provide for the category of trust in question.

Article 13 was considered to recreate uncertainty and to have no useful application in the United Kingdom and is omitted from the schedule to the Recognition of Trusts Act 1987. However, the non-enactment of Article 13 may have considerable ramifications. The broad scope of Article 2 of the Convention means that an English court might be faced with a number of institutions qualifying for recognition under Article 11 and that it will be compelled to recognise them. Such institutions would include non-charitable purpose trusts, so that '... pure purpose trusts, variant types of trusts, and so on, can now be formed by Englishmen under the law of, say, Belize or Cyprus, even if all the elements of the trust are connected with England.'[9] The Recognition of Trusts Act 1987 appears to have the effect of authorising an English settlor in an otherwise wholly domestic context to create a trust[10] unknown or unauthorised in English domestic trust law, by the simple expedient of choosing a foreign law to govern it. Moreover, it was argued

---

7 Article 13 refers only to 'States' in the plural, but it would be extraordinary if it did not apply when all objective elements pointed to a single non-trust State: see von Overbeck, para 122 at p 397.
8 Rather than relying on wholesale use of mandatory rules and pubic policy to prevent recognition, Article 13 was adopted in Italy (see A Paton and R Grosso (1994) 43 ICLQ, 654 at 655), but not Malta and is not recommended for Switzerland in L Thevenoz *Trusts in Switzerland*, Schulthess, Zurich. The Cayman Isles have not implemented the Convention, fearing that this will encourage the invocation of Art 13 against its trusts, but Civilopian judges under existing Civilopian laws have plenty of power to refuse to recognise Cayman trusts that are Civilopian except for choosing Cayman law, and, perhaps a Cayman trustee, too.
9 M Lupoi in P Jackson and D Wilde (eds) *The Reform of Property Law*, 222 at 225; see also M Lupoi *Trusts: a Comparative Study*, 362.
10 Ie a 'trust' as that term is understood in Article 2.

above that non-charitable trusts should not be denied recognition on public policy grounds[11]. If a person is identified by the settlor as responsible for enforcing a non-charitable purpose trust[12], to whom the trustee owes obligations, it is not obvious why recognition of the trust should not be permitted in English law: after all, the core accounting obligation of the trustee to someone able to enforce it is present[13].

REGISTRATION OF TRUSTS

Article 12 is primarily concerned with the need to reflect on the public registers of non-trust States the existence of a trust if the trust property is to be protected against the insolvency of the otherwise apparent beneficial owner. It also applies to private registers having a public function, such as a shareholders' register[14]. Where a trust is entitled to recognition, the trustee may ask for the trust to appear on the register, or, if this cannot be done, for it otherwise to be reflected on it[15]. He will need to produce any relevant documentation and comply with the requisite formalities of the place of purported registration[16]. In Italy it has been held that the Land Registrar, if requested, must register the existence of the trust, even where it is the registered proprietor who is declaring foreign trusts over his property[17]. Article 12 states that registration may be refused to the extent that it is prohibited by or inconsistent within the law of the State addressed. Clearly, registration will be prohibited if the trust is not entitled to recognition under Article 11[18]. Since in England the crucially important doctrine of over-reaching is available, details of a trust of English land or of shares in English companies cannot be inserted on the registers of land or shares[19].

JURISDICTION AND THE ENFORCEMENT OF FOREIGN JUDGMENTS IN TRANSNATIONAL TRUSTS LITIGATION

Synopsis

The law which determines the jurisdiction of English courts in transnational litigation is a complex and detailed subject. A brief consideration of the most important rules in this area is given here[20].

---

11 See the discussion at pp 1050–1052, ante of public policy in considering limits on the scope of the governing law of the trust.

12 The concept of an 'enforcer' of the trust is well known in offshore jurisdictions.

13 Although it was suggested at p 1051, ante that public policy might be invoked in respect of trust assets located in England if those specific assets were intended to be wholly inalienable for longer than the permitted English perpetuity period.

14 Von Overbeck Report, para 121 at p 396.

15 Von Overbeck Report, para 119 at p 396.

16 Von Overbeck Report, para 119 at p 396.

17 *Daniele Muritano v Agencia del Territorio, Ufficio Provinciale di Pisa* Tribunale di Pisa (22 December 2001), reported in *Trusts e attivita fiduciarie* (April 2002) at p 241.

18 On the problems which might be experienced in civil law States from registration of the trust, see A Dyer and H van Loon *Report on Trusts and Analogous Institutions*, para 177 at p 91.

19 See s 360 of the Companies Act 1985, which precludes registration of a trust on the share register of an English company; and Land Registration Act 1925, s 74.

20 For more detail, see J Harris 'Jurisdiction and the Enforcement of Foreign Judgments' in J Glasson (ed) *International Trusts Laws*, Chapter C1.

In England, two principal sets of jurisdictional rules exist: the harmonised rules contained in the relevant European Regulation (and Conventions) and the common law. The European harmonised rules are now the first point of reference. The application of the common law rules is residual. Moreover, the European harmonised rules do not apply only to disputes between domiciliaries of Member States. In civil or commercial matters[1], the European rules will apply if the defendant is domiciled in a Member State and even, in some cases, when neither party is domiciled in Europe.

Jurisdiction under the European regime

The Regulation on Jurisdiction and the Recognition and Enforcement of Judgments in Civil and Commercial Matters ('the Brussels Regulation')[2] provides a set of uniform jurisdictional rules for European Member States. It entered into force on 1 March 2002[3].

The Regulation applies to civil or commercial matters[4]. It excludes such matters as the status or legal capacity of natural persons, matrimonial property rights, wills and succession, bankruptcy and insolvency and arbitration. While not free from doubt, once the law concerning wills and succession has fully applied (so becoming *functus officio*) so that the relevant property has become vested in the trustee on trusts which give rise to litigation, say 20 years later, the Regulation should apply to this 20-year-old trust in the same way it would apply to a 20 years old *inter vivos* trust, there being no sensible reason to treat them differently. Where applicable, the Regulation lays down a general rule in Article 2, to the effect that the defendant is entitled to be sued in the courts of his domicile[5]. Exceptions to this rule are to be construed narrowly[6].

The most powerful exception to the defendant domicile principle is contained in Article 22(1), which provides that jurisdiction shall vest in the

---

1 Falling within Article 1 of the Regulation on Jurisdiction and the Recognition and Enforcement of Judgments in Civil and Commercial Matters (the Brussels Regulation) or the Lugano Convention on Jurisdiction and the Enforcement of Judgments in Civil and Commercial Matters 1988 (the Lugano Convention), as amended.

2 Regulation (EC) No 44/2001 of 22 December 2000: OJ 2001 L 12/1.

3 Save in the case of jurisdictional disputes between Denmark and one or more other European Member States. As the Brussels Regulation does not apply to Denmark, an English court must continue to apply the Brussels Convention to such jurisdictional disputes. There exists also a parallel Convention to the Brussels Convention, concluded at Lugano on 16 April 1988 (the Lugano Convention) (see Sch 3C of the Civil Jurisdiction and Judgments Act 1982 (CJJA), inserted by Sch 1 of the CJJA 1991. The Lugano Convention applies between European Union Member States and certain European Union non-Member States. Today, the Lugano Convention must still be applied in an English court to jurisdictional disputes between Member States and Iceland, Norway, Poland and Switzerland. There are also separate provisions, closely modelled on the European regime, for Anglo-Scottish conflicts contained in the CJJA 1982 and in Sch 4 to the Act (as modified by the Civil Jurisdiction and Judgments (Amendment) Order 2001).

4 Article 1.

5 There is a European autonomous definition of domicile for corporate defendants, contained in Article 60(1), Brussels Regulation. There is no such definition of domicile for individual defendants. In order to determine whether an individual defendant is domiciled in the United Kingdom (and, if so, in which part of the United Kingdom), a court should apply s 41(2) of the CJJA 1982 (reproduced in Sch 1, para 9 of the Civil Jurisdiction and Judgments Order 2001).

6 See, eg, *Reichert v Dresdner Bank* 115/88 [1990] ECR I-27; *Kalfelis v Bankhaus Schröeder* 189/87 [1988] ECR 5565; *Marinari v Lloyds Bank plc* C-364/93 [1995] ECR I-2719.

following courts regardless of the domicile of the defendant: 'in proceedings which have as their object rights *in rem* in immovable property or tenancies of immovable property, the court of the Member State in which the property is situated.' However, the ECJ held in *Webb v Webb*[7] that where a party asserts a beneficial interest under a trust of land, the right asserted is to be treated for Regulation purposes as *in personam*, so that this provision does not apply.

The other key exception to the defendant domicile rule in the trusts context is where a valid choice of court clause is inserted in a trust instrument[8]. A choice of court clause contained in a trust deed for a Member State will be binding and confer exclusive[9] jurisdiction on the chosen State 'in any proceedings brought against a settlor, trustee or beneficiary, if relations between these persons or their rights or obligations under the trust are involved'[10]. However, it is not absolutely clear whether Article 23(4) applies to litigation between trustee and beneficiary, since neither party will ordinarily have executed the trust instrument. Although it has been suggested that an exclusive jurisdiction clause for another Member State would not prevent a beneficiary of a trust governed by English law from suing in England[11], it is submitted that this view is incorrect. The interest received by a beneficiary will be subject to any terms or conditions of the trust instrument, which includes the jurisdiction clause. Put differently, with the 'benefit' of the interest under the trust goes the 'burden' of the jurisdiction clause. Moreover, Article 23(4) is a trusts specific provision. As such, it is intended to extend the effect of jurisdiction clauses in the trust context beyond the scope of expressly consenting parties[12]. Accordingly, a jurisdiction clause must also bind the beneficiaries of a trust.

Where neither of the above exceptions apply and jurisdiction is available against the defendant on the basis of his domicile[13], there are also rules contained in Article 5 and 6 which provide the claimant with further fora in which he can sue. However, although the claimant has a choice, he may only commence proceedings in one State of jurisdictional competence[14].

The most important of these additional bases of competence in the trusts context is Article 5(6), which allows a defendant domiciled in a Member State also to be sued 'as settlor, trustee or beneficiary[15] of a trust created by the operation of a statute, or by a written instrument, or created orally and evidenced in writing, in the courts of the Member State in which the trust is domiciled'[16]. This provision applies to the internal relationship between the

---

7 C-294/92 [1994] ECR I-1717. The instant claim was to be declared beneficial owner under a presumed resulting trust.

8 Special rules apply if the clause is caught by the rules protecting consumers, employees or insured parties under the Regulation.

9 Unless the clause states to the contrary.

10 Article 23(4) of the Brussels Regulation.

11 A Oakley *Parker and Mellows: Modern Law of Trusts* (7th edn) at p 749.

12 *Explanatory Report on the Brussels Convention, as amended by the United Kingdom, Irish and Danish Accession Convention*, by Prof Dr P Schlosser ('Schlosser Report') [1979] OJ C 59 p 71 at para 178.

13 Note that Articles 5 and 6 do not apply if one of the exceptions to the defendant domicile rule discussed above is applicable.

14 See Articles 27 and 28. The court 'first seised' of a dispute alone has jurisdiction (see Article 30).

15 The defendant must be a trustee or beneficiary at the time at which proceedings are instituted: *Chellaram v Chellaram (No 2)* [2002] EWHC 632 (Ch), [2002] 3 All ER 17.

16 It appears that constructive trusts fall outside the scope of this provision: *Chellaram v Chellaram (No 2)* [2002] EWHC 632 (Ch), [2002] 3 All ER 17.

parties: 'as between the trustees themselves, between persons claiming the status of trustees and, above all, between trustees on the one hand and the beneficiaries of a trust on the other'[17].

The place where a trust is domiciled is left to Member States to determine[18]. In the United Kingdom, s 45(3) of the Civil Jurisdiction and Judgments Act 1982[19] states that 'A trust is domiciled in a part of the United Kingdom if and only if the system of law of that part[20] is the system of law with which the trust has its closest and most real connection'[1].

Jurisdiction at common law

At common law, an English court has jurisdiction as of right over a defendant who can be served with a claim form whilst he is within the jurisdiction[2]. A company registered in England may be served at its registered office[3]. If the company is incorporated abroad but has a branch in England, it must file with the registrar of companies the name and address of those persons resident in Britain who are authorised to accept service on its behalf[4]. The court will also have jurisdiction as of right if a defendant submits to proceedings in England (though not if he merely contests the court's jurisdiction)[5].

If the court has jurisdiction as of right, the defendant may seek a stay of proceedings. He must show that, objectively, the natural forum for the litigation is in an overseas State. Even then, he will denied a stay if the claimant can show that it would be (subjectively) unjust for him to be denied the right to sue in England[6]. However, special rules apply if the proceedings were brought in England in breach of a foreign exclusive jurisdiction clause. Then, the defendant would have to show strong reasons why the stay should not be granted[7].

---

17 Schlosser Report, para 111.

18 Article 60(3) states that 'in order to determine whether a trust is domiciled in the Member State whose courts are seised of the matter, the court shall apply its rules of private international law'.

19 The provision in now reproduced in Sch 1, para 12 of the Civil Jurisdiction and Judgments Order 2001. See also s 7(2).

20 If different laws are applicable under the trust to questions of validity and administration, the relevant law for the purposes of s 45(3)of the CJJA 1982 is the law governing validity: *Chellaram v Chellaram (No 2)* [2002] EWHC 632 (Ch), [2002] WTLR 675.

 1 Lawrence Collins J stated in *Chellaram v Chellaram (No 2)* [2002] EWHC 632 (Ch), [2002] WTLR 675. that if the settlor had chosen law X to govern a trust, this fact could be used to negate a claim that law Y was the law of closest connection. This must be on the basis that while s 45(3) of the CJJA 1982 lays down an apparently objective test to determine the domicile of a trust, the law giving birth to the trust is the expressly chosen law and as the *sine qua non* of the trust is the closest and most real connection. This will make it simple and certain to determine where most trusts are domiciled, but it does not appear that the point was fully argued.

 2 *Maharanee of Baroda v Wildenstein* [1972] 2 QB 283. But note that even if an English court has *in personam* jurisdiction, it will not hear a case which is solely concerned with legal title to land situated overseas: *British South Africa Co v Companhia de Mocambique* [1893] AC 602.

 3 Companies Act 1985, s 725.

 4 Companies Act 1985, s 690A(2).

 5 *Williams and Glyn's Bank plc v Astro Dinamico Cia Naviera SA* [1984] 1 All ER 760.

 6 These principles were laid down by the House of Lords in *Spiliada Maritime Corpn v Cansulex Ltd* [1987] AC 460.

 7 See eg *The Elefthria* [1970] P 94; *The El Amria* [1981] 2 Lloyd's Rep 119; *The Pioneer Container* [1994] 2 AC 324; *Bouygues Offshore SA v Caspian Shipping Co* [1998] Lloyd's Rep 461. For an example of a stay case concerning an exclusive jurisdiction clause contained in a trust instrument, see the Royal Court of Jersey's decision in *EMM Capricorn Trustees Ltd v Compass Trustees Ltd* (2002) 4 ITELR 34.

If the defendant is outside the jurisdiction and does not submit to proceedings in England, the claimant must ask the court for permission to serve the defendant with a claim form outside the jurisdiction. In order to do so, he must show, *inter alia*, a good arguable case that his claim falls within one of the provisions of the Civil Procedure Rules (CPR), r 6.20[8]. He must also show that the natural forum for the litigation is England[9] and must assert in his application that he believes that he has a reasonable prospect of success on the merits[10].

Several of the provisions of CPR, r 6.20 are specifically concerned with trusts[11]. They are as follows[12]:

(11) a claim is made for any remedy which might be obtained in proceedings to execute the trusts of a written instrument where–
   (a) the trusts ought to be executed according to English law[13]; and
   (b) the person on whom the claim form is to be served is a trustee of the trusts;

(12) a claim is made for any remedy which might be obtained in proceedings for the administration of the estate of a person who died domiciled within the jurisdiction;

(13) a claim is made in probate proceedings which includes a claim for the rectification of a will;

(14) a claim is made for a remedy against the defendant as constructive trustee where the defendant's alleged liability arises out of acts committed within the jurisdiction[14];

(15) a claim is made for restitution where the defendant's alleged liability arises out of acts committed within the jurisdiction.

Recognition and enforcement of foreign judgments under the European regime

A judgment given in a Member State of the European Union in a civil or commercial matter[15] will normally be enforced in other Member States

---

8 *Seaconsar (Far East) Ltd v Bank Markazi Jomhouri Iran* [1994] 1 AC 438. However, the good arguable case test applies only to factual matters. Where satisfaction of a head of CPR, r 6.20 depends on a matter of law or construction, the court must authoritatively decide that issue, rather than applying the good arguable case test. So, in the case of CPR, r 6.20(11), the court must decide at the jurisdiction stage whether the trust is governed by English law. See *Chellaram v Chellaram (No 2)* [2002] EWHC 632 (Ch), [2002] WTLR 675.

9 *Spiliada Maritime Corp v Cansulex Ltd* [1987] AC 460; *Seaconsar (Far East) Ltd v Bank Markazi Jomhouri Iran* [1994] 1 AC 438. For a recent example of the application of the natural forum test to trusts litigation, see *Chellaram v Chellaram (No 2)* [2002] EWHC 632 (Ch), [2002] WTLR 675.

10 CPR, r 6.21(1)(b).

11 Specifically, CPR, r 6.20(11)–(15).

12 Note also that CPR, r 6.20(10) might be used in respect of trusts of land. It applies where 'the whole subject-matter of a claim relates to property located within the jurisdiction.'

13 If different laws govern the validity and the administration of a trust, it would suffice that either is governed by English law: *Chellaram v Chellaram (No 2)* [2002] EWHC 632 (Ch), [2002] 3 All ER 17. It should be noted that the applicable law should be ascertained at the time at which permission to serve out is sought, not at the time when the cause of action allegedly accrued: *Chellaram v Chellaram (No 2)* [2002] EWHC 632 (Ch), [2002] 3 All ER 17.

14 In *ISC Technologies v Guerin* [1992] 2 Lloyd's Rep 430, Hoffmann J remarked *obiter* that it would suffice that some of the acts inducing liability occurred in England, even if other acts occurred overseas.

15 Ie a judgment falling within the subject matter of Article 1 of the Brussels or Lugano scheme.

without any special procedure being required[16]. The defendant might apply to have registration set aside if: recognition is manifestly contrary to the State of recognition's public policy; the judgment was a default one and the defendant was not duly served in sufficient time and in such a way as to enable him to arrange his defence; the judgment is irreconcilable with a judgment of the courts of the State of recognition; or the judgment is irreconcilable with an earlier judgment delivered in another Member State, or in a non-Member State, if that earlier judgment also meets the conditions for recognition in the State addressed[17].

Enforcement of foreign judgments under the statutory schemes and at common law

Where a judgment was not given in a Member State of the European Union[18], its recognition will be governed by the Administration of Justice Act 1920, the Foreign Judgments (Reciprocal Enforcement) Act 1933 or the common law. The statutory schemes apply on a reciprocal basis to money judgments delivered in superior courts of certain States[19]; if there is no such arrangement, the common law applies[20].

Whichever of these three scheme applies, the substantive[1] rules on recognition are very similar. The judgment will be recognised if and only if the defendant was resident (or, in the case of the common law, it seems, present)[2] in the foreign State at the time that proceedings were instituted[3], or the defendant submitted to proceedings there[4]. Even then, the defendant may resist recognition if he can show that the judgment was procured by the judgment creditor's fraud, was in breach of natural justice, infringed English public policy, violated a choice of court clause[5] or was inconsistent with another judgment[6]. A judgment will not be enforced[7] unless final, conclusive

---

16 Article 41 of the Brussels Regulation. However, Article 35(1) states that a judgment should not be recognised if the foreign State which gave judgment did so in violation of the exclusive jurisdiction provisions of Article 22 or the insurance or consumer contract provisions.

17 These defences are contained in Article 34.

18 Or falls outside the scope of Article 1 of the Brussels or Lugano scheme.

19 In countries to which an Order in Council has been made extending its provisions.

20 But note that there are different and much more liberal rules for the enforcement of a judgment from one part of the United Kingdom in another part: The CJJA 1982 provides for the free recognition and enforcement of a judgment of the courts of one part of the United Kingdom in any other part: see, in particular, ss 18 and 19; Schs 6 and 7.

1 The procedure differs. A scheme of registration is used under the statutes. At common law, the claimant must commence proceedings to have the judgment enforced.

2 *Adams v Cape Industries* [1990] Ch 433.

3 For a corporate defendant, it was decided in *Adams v Cape Industries* [1990] Ch 433 that there must be a fixed place of business maintained at the company's own expense from which it has carried out its own business in the overseas jurisdiction. It will suffice that its business is transacted at that place through representatives of the company carrying out the corporation's business (*Littauer Glove Corpn v FW Millington* (1928) 44 TLR 746).

4 Appearance by the defendant solely to contest the court's jurisdiction, or to seek a stay, does not constitute submission: s 33 of the CJJA 1982.

5 CJJA 1982, s 32(1).

6 Under the statutory schemes, recognition may also be resisted pending an appeal in the State of origin.

7 A judgment needs to be recognised and enforced where a person asks the English court to give effect to a remedy granted in a foreign court eg an award of damages. Recognition alone will suffice where no remedy is sought eg where the judgment relates to status, or is used as a defence to further proceedings against a defendant in England.

and for a fixed sum of money, and it must not order the payment of penal damages to the State[8], or the payment of multiple damages[9].

---

8 If it does and it is possible to identify which part of the damages is compensatory and which penal, the judgment may be enforced solely in respect of the compensatory part: *Raulin v Fischer* [1911] KB 93.

9 Protection of Trading Interests Act 1980, s 5.

Index

All references are to page number.

Absolute gift with superadded direction
power to extinguish trust, and, 731–732
Abuse of statutory provisions
prevention of fraudulent conduct, and,
410–411
Acceptance of trust
acquiescence, by, 451
acts of ownership, by, 451
conduct, by, 452
express agreement, by, 451
generally, 451
long silence, by, 452–453
taking out probate, by, 451–452
Acceptance of (additional) trust property
conflict between fiduciary duty and self-
interest, and, 485–486
generally, 485
money-laundering, and
generally, 487–490
suspicious transaction reports, 490
onerous responsibilities, and, 486
vitiation of transfer to trustees, and, 486–
487
worthless responsibilities, and, 486
Accounting for profits
election, 874–875
generally, 873–874
Accounts and records, trustee's duties as to
accountability to beneficiaries, 672–673
confidentiality of deliberations, 680
costs of action, 677–678
disclosure under CPR, 678–679
expensive information, 687
generally, 671–672
inaccurate accounts, 678
inspection of documents, 677
investment information, 678
letters of wishes, 680–685
modification of duties and rights, 675–677
notice to beneficiaries, 673–674
notices of incumbrances, 685
other trust documents, 678–679
private companies, as to, 686
privilege against self-incrimination, 685

Accounts, taking of
allowing funds to remain in trustee's
business, 879
'but for' causation test, 855–859
compensatory award, 867
contributory negligence, 865–867
examples, 861–865
falsification, 11, 38, 851, 853, 857
generally, 853–854
improper retention of authorised
investment, 872
improper sale of authorised investment,
872–873
loss of interest, 867–869
mixing funds with trustee's own funds,
869
rate of interest, 870–871
replacement without regard to fiscal
liabilities, 859–861
restorative liability, 855
retention of unauthorised investment, 872
surcharge, 11, 38, 852, 853, 857
use of funds in trustee's own business, 870
Accrued shares
resulting trusts, and, 375
Accumulations of income, excessive
exclusion from rules, 205–208
introduction, 203–205
purpose of purchasing land, 208–209
termination of accumulations, 205
Acquiescence
acceptance of trust, and, 451
Acquiescence by settlor
undue influence, and, 285–286
Acquiescence of beneficiaries
bar, as, 934–935
claimant party to breach, 932
generally, 931–932
knowledge, and, 935–936
minors, and, 935
over period, 933–934
reversioner, by, 934
Act jointly with other trustees, duty to
trustee's duties, and, 644–648

Acting honestly and reasonably, protection of trustees
discretion of court, 919–920
generally, 913
profit for trustees, 920
reasonable conduct, 918–919
reasonableness, 914–917
unreasonable conduct, 917–918
Acting in good faith
trustee's powers, and, 691
Acting upon expert's advice
trustee's duties, and, 497
Acting without remuneration
basis of rule, 651
exceptions
agreement of beneficiaries, 658–659
authorisation by settlement, 652–653
custodian trustees, 658
order of court, 655–658
Public Trustee, 658
rule in *Cradock v Piper*, 653
statutory authorisation, 653–655
generally, 651
Active trusts
definition, 58
example, 58–59
sham trusts, and, 59–63
Acts of ownership
acceptance of trust, and, 451
Actuary's advice
trustee's duties, and, 495–496
Additions to trust property
persons in fiduciary position, and, 385–386
Administration of deceased's estate
trusts, and, 17–20
Administration of trust
and see under individual headings
acceptance of part of trust, 453
acceptance of trust
acquiescence, by, 451
acts of ownership, by, 451
conduct, by, 452
express, 451
generally, 451
long silence, by, 452–453
taking out probate, by, 451–452
adverse possession of trust land
beneficiary, by, 459
generally, 458–459
stranger, by, 459–460
appointment of judicial trustees
discretion of court, 788
generally, 785–787
purpose of statutory provisions, 787–788
Rules, 788
appointment of new trustees
effect if invalid, 775
express power, under, 752–755
generally, 751–752

Administration of trust – *continued*
appointment of new trustees – *continued*
mental health jurisdiction, under, 769
new trusts created under limited powers, for, 803–809
order of court, by, 763–769
powers, 770
removal of trustee, and, 750
retirement of trustee, and, 744
selection of trustees, 770–774
statutory power, under, 755–763
appointment of trustees for sale of land, 775
bankruptcy of trustee, 460–462
beneficiaries' powers
extinguishments of trust, 729–736
partial interest in special trust, with, 737–739
death of trustee
co-trustee, 741–742
generally, 740–741
sole trustee, 742–743
surviving trustee, 742–743
direction of court, under, 846–848
disclaimer of part of trust, 453
disclaimer of trust
costs, 450
effect, 450
generally, 449
methods, 449–450
prior consent to undertake trust, and, 449
estate taken by trustee
assent, 454–456
equitable estate, 454
generally, 454
legal estate, 454
incidents of trustee's estate
collective enfranchisement, 457–458
commencing actions, 456
commonhold ownership, 458
custody of deeds, 457
enfranchisement and extension of lease, 457
generally, 456
liability for rates and taxes, 456
liability to business creditors, 457
management of block of flats, 458
planning rights, 457
proof in bankruptcy, 456
insolvency of trustee, 460–462
permissible number of trustees, 447–448
Public Trustee
appointment, 794–796
custodian trustee, as, 796–800
establishment and functions, 789–793
special rules, 801—802
removal of trustee
appointment of new trustee, on, 750
directions of beneficiaries, 749–750

Administration of trust – *continued*
removal of trustee – *continued*
generally, 743–744
illustration, 747
mental disorder, by reason of, 750
order of court, by, 750
qualifying requirements, 748–749
retirement of trustee
appointment of new trustee, on, 744
consent of beneficiaries, by, 746–747
discharge, and, 744–746
generally, 743–744
order of court, by, 747
release from liability, and, 747
statutory power, under, 746
Settled Land Act settlements, 463–465
trustee's duties
acceptance of trust property, as to, 485–493
accounts and records, as to, 671–687
act jointly, to, 644–648
delegation, as to, 631–644
gratuitous acts, and, 652–659
handling of property, as to, 623–631
impartiality between beneficiaries, of, 529–548
investment of funds, as to, 597–622
jus tertii, and, 648–650
loss to trust, and, 659–671
obey directions of settlement, to, 493–529
payment of outgoings, as to, 563–575
profiting from trust property, and, 659–671
property pending conversion, as to, 552–563
reasonable care and skill, of, 575–597
sale of improper property, as to, 548–551
trafficking in trust property, and, 659–671
trustee's powers
administration, 707–708
advancement, 717–726
general principles, 688–703
investment of funds, 597–622
maintenance to infants, 709–717
management of land, 703–705
receipts, 705–706
reversionary interests, 706–707
suspension of, 726–728
trustee's rights
administration of trust under direction of court, 846–848
directions of court as to specific questions, 832–845
discharge on completion of trusteeship, 827–828
official audit of trust, 831–832
pay funds into court, 829–830
reimbursement and indemnity, 810–826

Administration of trust – *continued*
trusts of land
assistance of court, 479–482
consents, 474–475
consultation with interest in possession beneficiary, 475–476
conversion under trusts for sale, 471
generally, 465–469
occupation by interest in possession beneficiary, 476–478
partition by trustees, 472–473
prior to 1997, 463–465
purchaser protection, 483
relevant property, 469
transfer to absolutely entitled beneficiary, 473–474
trustee's powers, 471–472
trusts for sale, 470–471
use of two deeds, 469–470
vesting of trust property in new trustees
court made vesting orders, 779–784
generally, 776
implied vesting declarations, 776–779
Administration of trust, workability of
generally, 91–93
initial unworkability, 98–99
powers, 93–98
supervening unworkability, 98–99
Administration, powers of
generally, 707–708
Administrative powers
fixed trusts, and, 65–66
Advancement, powers of
application of power, 718
cash brought into account, 719
consent of person with prior interest, 724–726
ensuring purpose effected, 721–722
exhaustion of exercise of power, 719
generally, 717–718
property brought into account, 719
purpose, 719–721
rule against perpetuities, 724
settlement, by way of, 722–724
tax considerations, 726
Advancement, presumption of
augmentation of settled property, 364
generally, 361–362
mother and child, 364–365
persons in loco parentis, 366–367
rebuttal, 362
surrounding circumstances, 362–364
wife's money invested in name of husband, 365–366
Adverse possession of trust land
beneficiary, by, 459
generally, 458–459
stranger, by, 459–460
Adverse title, assisting or setting up
trustee's duties, and, 648–650

Advertisements
transfer of property to beneficiaries, and, 627–628

Agency
trusts, and, 7–9

Agents, default of
reasonable care and skill, and, 590

Agents, insolvent
prevention of fraudulent conduct, and, 437

Agreements to create trusts
generally, 139
joint wills, 140
marriage articles, 139–140
mutual wills, 140

Alienation, restraint on
legality of objects in trusts, and, 214–215

Alienations for value
property traced into hands of third parties, and, 999

Aliens
appointment of new trustees, and, 774
incapacity of beneficiaries, and, 273

Aliquot share
partial interest in special trust, and, 738–739

Allow maintenance to infants, power to
class gifts, 716–717
contrary intention, 715
generally, 709–711
gifts carrying intermediate income, 712–713
legacies carrying interest, 713–714
portions charged on land, 714
residuary gift to infant, 714
statutory provision, 711–712
vested interests converted into contingent interests, 715–716

Alteration of prescribed rules of devolution
introduction, 209
protective trusts, 214
settlements against bankruptcy law, 209–214

Alterations
repairs, and, 573

Amendment, power of
power, 498–499

Animals, maintenance of
language sufficient to create trusts, and, 122

Annual charges
current expenses, and, 568

Annuities
discretionary distributive powers, and, 532–533
generally, 532–533
tax-free sums, 533–535

Application of property
language sufficient to create trusts, and, 82–83

Appointment of judicial trustees
discretion of court, 788
generally, 785–787
purpose of statutory provisions, 787–788
Rules, 788

Appointment of new trustees
beneficiary's wishes, against, 767–768
breach of trust, on, 766–767
death of trustee, on, 759
defeating trustee's rights, and, 767
effect if invalid, 775
express power, under
fiduciary nature of power, 754–755
generally, 752–754
mentally ill person, on behalf of, 755
minor, by, 755
personal nature of power, 754
expression by trustee to be discharged, on, 760
generally, 751–752
incapacity of trustee, on, 761
mental health jurisdiction, under, 769
new trusts created under general powers, for
donee under inter vivos instrument, by, 804
generally, 803
personal representatives under testamentary instrument, by, 804
new trusts created under special powers, for
delegation of discretions, 808–809
discretion as to manner and form of appointment, 805–806
donee, by, 804–805
generally, 803
mere power of selection, 805
powers in the wider form, 806–808
order of court, by
applicants, 768–769
bankrupt as trustee, where, 766
breach of trust, on, 766–767
costs, 769
criminal as trustee, where, 766
criteria for application, 764–765
donees cannot agree, where, 765
doubtful cases, in, 765
friction, in cases of, 765–766
generally, 763–764
minor is trustee or donee of express power, where, 764–765
no donee of power, where, 764
no original trustees, where, 764
practice, 768–769
summary procedure, 768
powers, 770
refusal of trustee to act, on, 761
removal of trustee, and, 750
residence of trustee abroad, on, 759
retirement of trustee, and, 744

Appointment of new trustees – *continued*
 selection of new trustees
  aliens, 774
  beneficiaries' bankers, 772
  corporation sole, 774
  donee of power, 771
  generally, 770–774
  life interest, person entitled to, 771
  near relations, 772
  persons out of jurisdiction, 772–774
  remainderman, 771
  solicitor to the trust, 771–772
  trust company, 774
 severance of trusts, and, 762
 statutory power, under
  appointor, 761
  donees of express power differ over
    appointment, 762–763
  exercisability of power, 759–761
  generally, 755–758
  increase in number of trustees, 761–762
  inviolability of the power, 759
  reduction in number of trustees, 761–
    762
  severance of trusts, 762
 unfitness of trustee, on, 761
 vacancy, on, 760–761
Appointment of Public Trustee
 court, by, 795
 generally, 794
 will or codicil, by, 794–795
Appropriation
 answer particular shares, to, 543–544
 cash value, at, 544–545
 generally, 542–543
 proportion of trust fund, at, 544–545
 statutory power, 545–546
**Approval of court to modification to
  directions of settlement**
 introduction, 522
 pre-1926 jurisdiction, 522–525
 Settled Land Act 1925, under
  extended powers, 528–529
  particular transactions, 527
 Trustee Act 1925, under
  extended powers, 528–529
  particular transactions, 525–527
 Variation of Trusts Act 1958, under
  arrangements for which approval be
    given, 508–519
  effect of approval, 519–520
  generally, 499–501
  jurisdiction of court, 520–522
  persons on whose behalf approval be
    given, 501–508
  statutory provision, 501
Arrears of interest
 capital charges, and, 567–568
Arrears of rent
 reasonable care and skill, and, 579

Articles of marriage
 agreements to create trusts, and, 139–140
 executory trusts, and, 67
Assent
 estate taken by trustee, and, 454–456
Asset management function
 investment of funds, and, 621–622
Asset segregation
 commercial purpose trusts, and, 42–44
Assignment, deed of
 transfer of property to beneficiaries, and,
  629–630
Assignments for value of future property
 prevention of fraudulent conduct, and,
  437–438
Assistance of court
 trusts of land, and, 479–482
**Attempts to alter prescribed rules of
  devolution**
 introduction, 209
 protective trusts, 214
 settlements against bankruptcy law, 209–
  214
Audit of trust
 trustee's rights, and, 831–832
Audit of trust accounts
 payment of outgoings, and, and, 574–575
Augmentation of capital
 bonuses, 535–538
 capital profits dividends, 538
 demergers, 539
 director's fee, 542
 enhanced scrip dividends, 539–540
 generally, 535
 profit on investment realisation, 540
 profit on reconstruction of company, 542
 stocks 'cum dividend', 540–542
 unit trusts, 542
Augmentation of settled property
 presumption of advancement, and, 364
Available assets of settlor
 sham trusts, and, 62–63

Bailment
 trusts, and, 16–17
Bank accounts
 tracing, and, 900–901
Bankruptcy
 appointment of new trustees, and, 766
 property capable of being subject of trust,
  and, 185–186
Bankruptcy following voluntary arrangement
 resulting trusts, and, 340–341
Bankruptcy of settlor
 criminal offences, 291
 dispositions in two to five year period, 290
 generally, 287–289
 persons without notice of relevant
  circumstances, 291
 statutory provision, 289–290

Bankruptcy of trustee
administration of trust, and, 460–462
appointment of new trustees, and, 766
Bare trusts
definition, 57
example, 58
***Beddoe* application**
costs, and, 845
indemnity for trustees, and, 816
Beneficiary
adverse possession, and, 459
definition, 3
Beneficiaries' bankers
appointment of new trustees, and, 772
Beneficiaries, incapacity of
aliens, 273
introduction, 272
minors, 273
persons of unsound mind, 273
settlors, 273
trustees, 273
Beneficiaries, liability of
and see under individual headings
involvement in breach of trust, for
dealing by agents, 952–956
dishonest assistance, 956–967
generally, 950–951
impounding equitable interests in trust, 979–983
intermeddling strangers, 951–952
misapplied trust property, 967–979
Beneficiaries, powers of
extinguish trust, to
absolute gift with superadded direction, 731–732
basic principles, 734–735
generally, 729–730
illustrations, 730–731
indefeasible absolute beneficial; entitlement, 732–734
legacies to purchase annuities, 732
modification of trusts, 735–736
possible future beneficiaries, 735
partial interest in special trust, with aliquot share, 738–739
claim for possession, 739
equitable interests, 738
generally, 737
inalienability of interests, 738
protective trusts, 738
restraint on alienation, 738
Beneficiaries, uncertainty as to
discretionary trusts, under, 85–91
fixed trust, under, 84
generally, 82–83
Beneficiary principle
drafting points, 117–118
enforcer clause, and, 114–116
introduction, 110–111
loan purpose trusts, and, 116–117

Beneficiary principle – *continued*
purpose trusts, and, 111–114
Beneficiary's wishes
appointment of new trustees, and, 767–768
Bills of lading
transfer of property to trust, and, 152
Binding upon donor
constitution of trust, and, 165–166
Bona vacantia
resulting trusts, and, 337–338
Bonuses
augmentation of capital, and, 535–538
Breach of trust
appointment of new trustees, and, 766–767
definition, 5–6
Breach of trust, consequences of
and see under individual headings
liability of beneficiaries
involvement in breach, for, 950–983
liability of third parties
involvement in breach, for, 950–983
property traced into their hands, for, 983–1003
liability of trustees
criminal proceedings, and, 907–912
interim applications to safeguard trust property, 903–906
joint and several, 877–878
measure of, 851–877
set-off, and, 878–879
tracing claims, 880–903
protection of trustees
acted reasonably and honestly, 913–920
concurrence of beneficiaries, 931–937
co-trustee's acts, against, 938–940
indemnity by instigator of breach, 940–949
limitation of actions by beneficiaries, 920–931
release by beneficiaries, 931–937
waiver by beneficiaries, 931–937
'But for' causation test
taking of accounts, and, 855–859

Calls on shares
capital charges, and, 568
indemnity for trustees, and, 813
Capacity to create trust
beneficiary, 1025
introduction, 1023
settlor, 1023–1024
trustee, 1024–1025
Capital charges
arrears of interest, 567–568
calls on shares, 568
generally, 565
local government charges, 566–567
losses, 571
purchase of annuities, 566

Capital gains tax
powers of advancement, and, 726
Capital growth
discretionary distributive powers, and,
531–532
Capital profits dividends
augmentation of capital, and, 538
Care and skill, duty of
arrears of rent, 579
collective investment scheme trustees,
and, 577–578
controlling interests in private companies,
586–588
default of agents, nominees or custodians,
590
depreciatory conditions of sale, 581
errors of judgment, 584–585
'gazumping', 582
generally, 575–576
grant of leases, 583
improvident lettings, 583
improvident purchases, 583
improvident sales, 581
insurance against risks, 588–589
inventory of chattels, 586
life policies, 580
mortgage-assisted purchases, 583–584
neglect of fund investment, 586
neglect of trust securities, 585–586
options, 583
ousting jurisdiction of court
deliberate breach of duty, 594–595
dishonest breach of duty, 593–594
generally, 590–591
non-excludable duties, 593
particular property, 591–593
statutory prohibitions, 595–596
undue influence, 596–597
pension schemes trustees, and, 577–578
proof in bankruptcy, 580
realisation of debts, 578–579
realisation of unauthorised investments,
579
relevant time for judging conduct, 590
renewal of tenancies, 581–582
repair liability, 589
retired trustee, liability of, 589–590
sale of contiguous properties, 580–581
theft of trust property, 585
Trustee Act 2000, under, 576–590
Carrying on business, liabilities of
indemnity for trustees, and, 814
Causation
mixing of trust property with other
property, and, 888–890
Certainty of powers of appointment, 85
Certainty of trusts
beneficiaries, 84–89
language, 75–76, 133–136
property, 78–81

Cestuis que trust
and see BENEFICIARY
generally, 3
Change of position
misapplied trust property, and, 978–979
property traced into hands of third
parties, and, 995–997
Change of status
undue influence, and, 286
Charges
trusts, and, 34–36
Charges on goods supplied on credit
introduction, 12
Quistclose trusts, 12–14
reservation of title clauses, 14–16
Twinsectra trusts, 12–14
Charitable funds, contributions to
resulting trusts, and, 341–342
Charitable trusts
introduction, 71
Public Trustee, and, 791
rule against inalienability, and, 203
Chattels
transfer of property to trust, and, 151
'Chinese Walls'
constructive trusts, and, 405–406
Choice of investments
discretionary distributive powers, and, 531
Choses in action
property capable of being subject of trust,
and, 183
property traced into hands of third
parties, and, 1001
transfer of property to trust, and, 151–152
Claim for possession
partial interest in special trust, and, 739
Class gifts
maintenance to infants, and, 716–717
Class or to survivors, gift to
resulting trusts, and, 374–375
Club trustees
indemnity for trustees, and, 823
Clubs, dissolution of
resulting trusts, and, 338–240
Codicils
precatory words, and, 136
Collective enfranchisement
incidents of trustee's estate, and, 457–458
Collective investment schemes
commercial purpose trusts, and, 45–46
reasonable care and skill of trustees, and,
577–578
Commencing actions
incidents of trustee's estate, and, 456
Commercial purposes, trusts for
asset segregation, 42–44
collective investment schemes, 45–46
conclusion, 48
employee trusts, 47
generally, 39

Commercial purposes, trusts for – *continued*
 miscellaneous uses, 47–48
 pension funds, 46–47
 security, 39–42
 trading trusts, 44–45
 unit trusts, 45–46
Commercial transactions
 persons in fiduciary position, and, 400–401
Common intention constructive trusts
 date of valuation of interest, 425
 detrimental reliance
  express common intention, 419–420
  inferred common intention, 420–421
 equitable estoppel, and, 425–427
 financial relief, and, 427
 express agreement
  detrimental reliance, 419–420
  generally, 414–415
 generally, 412–414
 inferred agreement
  detrimental reliance, 420–421
  generally, 415–419
 legal title in both names, 421–422
 size of share, 422–425
Commonhold ownership
 incidents of trustee's estate, and, 458
Compensatory awards
 taking of accounts, and, 867
Completely constituted trusts
 executed trusts, and, 67–68
Compliance with formal requirements
 contracts to create trusts, 234–235
 contracts to dispose of existing equitable interests, 235–236
 dealings with equitable interests
  databases of interests, 245
  examples, 239–245
  introduction, 238
  nature of dealings, 238–239
  registers of interests, 245
  s 53(1)(c) dispositions, 245–247
 declarations of trusts, 236–238
 equitable proprietary estoppel
  detrimental reliance, 250–252
  historical background, 249–250
  introduction, 248–249
  purchasers' viewpoint, 253–254
 generally, 232–234
 instrument of fraud, statute not to be used as
  inter vivos trusts, 254–256
  introduction, 254
  secret trusts, 258–267
  testamentary trusts, 257
 introduction, 72
 secret trusts
  beneficiary predeceasing testator, 263–264
  floating trusts, 266–267

Compliance with formal requirements – *continued*
 secret trusts – *continued*
  fully secret trusts, 260–261
  gifts to several intended trustees without communication, 262–263
  half-secret trusts, 261–262
  introduction, 258–259
  operation independent of will, 264–266
  parol evidence, and, 259–260
 testamentary trusts, 247–248
Concurrence of beneficiaries
 claimant party to breach, 932
 generally, 931–932
Conditional gifts
 trusts, and, 34–36
Conditional words
 expectation, of, 138
 explanatory of motive, of, 138
 introduction, 136–137
 illustrations, 137–138
Conditions precedent
 investment of funds, and, 602–603
 language sufficient to create trust, and, 99–100
Conditions subsequent
 generally, 100–101
 parentage, as to, 102–103
 profession or office, as to, 102
 religion, as to, 102–103
 residence, as to, 101–102
Conduct
 acceptance of trust, and, 452
Conduct of sales
 management of land, and, 704–705
Confidentiality of deliberations
 accounts and records, and, 680
Conflict of laws
 background, 1011–1013
 basic concepts
  determination of governing law, 1031–1040
  enforcement of foreign judgments, 1056–1062
  excluded preliminary matters, 1022–1031
  generally, 1011–1014
  limits on scope of governing law, 1046–1052
  recognition of trusts, 1053–1056
  registration of trusts, 1056
  relevant trusts, 1014–1022
  scope of governing law, 1040–1045
 capacity to create trust
  beneficiary, 1025
  introduction, 1023
  settlor, 1023–1024
  trustee, 1024–1025
 changing the governing law, 1039–1040
 dépeçage, and, 1037–1039

Conflict of laws – *continued*
determination of governing law
applicable law in absence of choice,
1035–1037
dépeçage, 1037–1039
express choice of law, 1031–1032
implied choice of law, 1033–1034
renvoi, 1037
effect in non-trust states, 1013
enforcement of foreign judgments
common law jurisdiction, 1059–1060
European jurisdiction, 1057–1059
generally, 1060–1062
synopsis, 1056–1057
excluded preliminary matters
capacity to create to trust, 1023–1025
forced heirship, 1030–1031
introduction, 1022–1023
perpetuity, 1030
vesting of property in trustee, 1025–
1030
exclusion of fiscal matters, 1014
functions, 1014
Hague Trusts Convention
applicable law, 1008
general clauses, 1009–1010
recognition, 1008–1009
scope, 1007–1008
introduction, 1007
limits on scope of governing law
domestic mandatory laws, 1046–1049
international mandatory rules, 1049–
1050
introduction, 1046
mandatory rules, 1046
public policy, 1050–1052
meaning of 'trust', 1014–1016
nature of a trust, and, 6–7
recognition of trusts
following trust assets, 1054–1055
requirements, 1053–1054
right to refuse, 1055–1056
tracing trust assets, 1054–1055
registration of trusts, 1056
relevant trusts
constructive trusts, 1018–1020
evidence in writing, and, 1016–1017
extension of scope in UK, 1020–1021
judicial decisions, and, 1022
resulting trusts, 1017–1018
statutory trusts, 1020
voluntary trusts, 1017
renvoi, and, 1037
scope of governing law
general matters, 1040–1041
limits, 1046–1056
specific matters, 1041–1045
territorial extent, 1013
vesting of property in trustee
classification of property, 1026

Conflict of laws – *continued*
vesting of property in trustee – *continued*
conclusion, 1029–1030
immovable property, 1027
intangible movable property, 1028–1029
introduction, 1025–1026
tangible movable property, 1028
Consent of person with prior interest
powers of advancement, and, 724–726
Consent to marriage
legality of objects in trusts, and, 221
Consents
trusts of land, and, 474–475
Consequences of breach of trust
and see under individual headings
liability of beneficiaries
involvement in breach, for, 950–983
liability of third parties
involvement in breach, for, 950–983
property traced into their hands, for,
983–1003
liability of trustees
criminal proceedings, and, 907–912
interim applications to safeguard trust
property, 903–906
joint and several, 877–878
measure of, 851–877
set-off, and, 878–879
tracing claims, 880–903
protection of trustees
acted reasonably and honestly, 913–920
concurrence of beneficiaries, 931–937
co-trustee's acts, against, 938–940
indemnity by instigator of breach, 940–
949
limitation of actions by beneficiaries,
920–931
release by beneficiaries, 931–937
waiver by beneficiaries, 931–937
Constitution of express trusts
binding upon donor, 165–166
conveyance to minor, 157
declaration of self as trustee, 145–148
declaration of trust
introduction, 144
present irrevocable declaration, 149
settlor as trustee, 145–148
enforceability of trust
contracts, 170–172
generally, 166–168
introduction, 144–145
third party rights, 168–169
trustee's action at common law, 179–182
voluntary covenants, 172–179
volunteers' action at common law, 169
equitable proprietary estoppel, 157
exceptional cases
conveyance to minor, 157
equitable proprietary estoppel, 157
rule in *Strong v Bird*, 157–163

Constitution of express trusts – *continued*
exceptional cases – *continued*
settlor does everything necessary to
effect transfer, 154–157
generally, 144–145
introduction, 71–72
rule in *Strong v Bird*
erroneous perfection of gift by
administrators, 161
forgiveness of debts, 159–161
generally, 157–159
intent to make immediate gift, 161–163
lifetime acquisition of legal title, 163–
164
mistaken perfection of gift by executors,
164
transfer of property
generally, 149–154
introduction, 144
Constructive trusts
analysis, 322
'Chinese Walls', and, 405–406
common intention constructive trusts
date of valuation of interest, 425
detrimental reliance, 419–421
equitable estoppel, and, 425–427
express agreement, 414–415
financial relief, and, 427
generally, 412–414
inferred agreement, 415–419
legal title in both names, 421–422
size of share, 422–425
contractual ouster of financial obligations,
and, 403–404
defences to claims
'Chinese Walls', 405–406
contractual ouster of financial
obligations, 403–404
due authorisation, 401–402
information barriers, 405–406
mere use of knowledge or opportunity,
402–403
definition, 55–57
doctrine of conversion
effect, 439
operation, 439–440
due authorisation, and, 401–402
equitable estoppel, and, 425–427
fiduciary position, of products owned by
persons in
additions to trust property, 385–386
commercial transactions, 400–401
directors obtaining profits, 390–393
employee inventions, 399–400
executors de son tort, 382
generally, 379
lessee purchasing reversion expectant
on lease, 383–385
profits by agents, 393–398
profits by partners, 398

Constructive trusts – *continued*
fiduciary position, of products owned by
persons in – *continued*
profits by tippees, 398–399
profits by trustee from property or
position, 386–388
profits by trustee's parent company, 388
proprietary and personal liability, 381
renewal of lease by partial owner, 385
tenant for life of leaseholds renewing to
himself, 383
tenant for life of mortgaged property
purchasing mortgagee's interest, 385
tenant for life receiving money for
settled land, 386
tracing, 379–381
trustees de son tort, 381–382
trustees obtaining commission, 389–390
trustees obtaining directorship fees,
388–389
trustees taking renewal of lease himself,
382–382
financial relief, and, 427
fraudulent conduct, to prevent
abuse of statutory provisions, 410–411
assignments for value of future
property, 437–438
common intention constructive trusts,
412–427
criminal may not benefit from crime,
434–435
donor does all obliged to do to transfer
legal title, 433–434
generally, 409–410
mutual wills, 427–432
receipts by insolvent agents, 437
rescission of voidable transfers, 435–436
secret trusts, 433
use of property principles, 411–412
generally, 322–323
information barriers, and, 405–406
institutional trusts of property, 324–327
measure of trustee's liability for breach of
trust, and, 871
ouster of financial obligations, and, 403–
404
personal accountability, 323–324
remedial trusts of property, 324–327
specifically enforceable contract, under
doctrine of conversion, 439–441
generally, 438
purchaser's position, 442–444
vendor's trusteeship, 441–442
strangers to trust, products owned by
generally, 406–407
priorities, 407–408
traceable products, of
persons in fiduciary position, owned by,
379–406
strangers to trust, owned by, 406–408

Constructive trusts – *continued*
unconscionable conduct, to prevent
abuse of statutory provisions, 410–411
assignments for value of future
property, 437–438
common intention constructive trusts,
412–427
criminal may not benefit from crime,
434–435
donor does all obliged to do to transfer
legal title, 433–434
generally, 409–410
mutual wills, 427–432
receipts by insolvent agents, 437
rescission of voidable transfers, 435–436
secret trusts, 433
use of property principles, 411–412
**Consultation with interest in possession
beneficiary**
trusts of land, and, 475–476
Contiguous properties, sale of
reasonable care and skill, and, 580–581
Contract
enforceability of trust, and, 170–172
trusts, and, 9–11
Contracts to create trusts
formal requirements, and, 234–235
generally, 139
joint wills, 140
marriage articles, 139–140
mutual wills, 140
**Contracts to dispose of existing equitable
interests**
formal requirements, and, 235–236
Contractual licence
purchaser's undertaking, and, 327–328
Contractual ouster of financial obligations
constructive trusts, and, 403–404
Contrary intention
maintenance to infants, and, 715
Contrary to public policy
legality of objects in trusts, and, 218–219
Contribution between trustees
joint and several liability for breach of
trust, and, 878
Contributions to charitable funds
resulting trusts, and, 341–342
Contributory negligence
taking of accounts, and, 865–867
Control of trust property
trustee's duties, and, 493
Controlling interests in private companies
reasonable care and skill, and, 586–588
Conversion directed
resulting trusts, and, 371–372
Conversion, doctrine of
effect, 439
operation, 439–440
Conversion of trust property into other form
money produced by chattels, 883

Conversion of trust property into other form
– *continued*
money produced by misuse of position,
883
sale of wrongfully acquired property, 883–
884
stock bought with money, 882–883
wrongful sale by vendor, 883
Conversion under trusts for sale
trusts of land, and, 471
Conveyance to minor
constitution of express trusts, and, 157
Copies of deeds
trustee's rights, and, 828
Copyright
transfer of property to trust, and, 152
Corporate bodies
custodian trustee, and, 797–799
Corporation sole
appointment of new trustees, and, 774
Corporations
incapacity of settlors, and, 270–271
Corpus, charges against
arrears of interest, 567–568
calls on shares, 568
generally, 565
local government charges, 566–567
losses, 571
purchase of annuities, 566
Costs
accounts and records, and, 677–678
appointment of new trustees, and, 769
directions of court as to specific questions,
and
appeal, on, 842–843
Beddoe applications, 845
court's jurisdiction, 840
established principles, 840–841
hostile litigation, 841
nature of disputes, 841–842
prospective orders, 843–844
rule of court, 840
disclaimer of trust, and, 450
Costs paid to solicitor
property traced into hands of third
parties, and, 986
Co-trustee, death of
generally, 741–742
Co-trustees, protection against
generally, 938–940
Counsel's advice, reliance on
indemnity for trustees, and, 816–817
transfer of property to beneficiaries, and,
626–627
Court vesting orders
vesting of trust in new trustees, and, 779–
784
**Covenants to settle property in marriage
settlement**
after-acquired property, 310–313

Covenants to settle property in marriage settlement – *continued*
binding on wife, 305–306
definite interests in property, 314–315
excluded property, 306–310
property exceeding certain value, 315–317
property to which presently entitled, 310
Cradock v Piper, **rule in**
remuneration of trustees, and, 653
Creditors' deeds, inferences relating to
illusory trusts, and, 141–142
Criminal may not benefit from crime
generally, 434–435
statutory relief, 435
Criminal proceedings
compensation, 912
generally, 907
other offences, 911
theft
actus reus, 907–910
generally, 907
mens rea, 910–911
Criminals
appointment of new trustees, and, 766
Crown, rights of
resulting trusts, and, 377–378
'Cum dividend' stocks
augmentation of capital, and, 540–542
Current expenses
annual charges, 568
insurance premiums, 568–570
losses on trust business, 570
redemption of rentcharge, 570
Custodian trustee
advantages, 797
corporate bodies, 797–799
duties, rights and liabilities, 799–800
generally, 796
profits from trusts, 799
remuneration, 658
Custodians, default of
reasonable care and skill, and, 590
Custodians, holdings by
appointment of custodian, 619–621
exclusions, 621
generally, 619
nature of duty, 621
restrictions, 621
Custody of deeds
incidents of trustee's estate, and, 457

Damages for voluntary carers' services
illusory trusts, and, 143
Damages recovered by third parties
indemnity for trustees, and, 813
Dealing by agents
dishonesty, 954–955
generally, 952–953
lawful receipt of trust property, 953–954
pleading issues, 955–956

Dealings with equitable interests
databases of interests, 245
examples, 239–245
introduction, 238
nature of dealings, 238–239
registers of interests, 245
s 53(1)(c) dispositions, 245–247
Death of trustee
appointment of new trustees, and, 759
co-trustee, 741–742
generally, 740–741
sole trustee
execution of trusts by personal
representatives, 742
generally, 742
surviving trustee
execution of trusts by personal
representatives, 742
generally, 742
Debts paid
tracing, and, 901–903
Deceptive statements, publication of
dishonest breach of trust, and, 911
Declaration of self as trustee
constitution of trust, and, 145–148
Declaration of trust
formal requirements, and, 236–238
introduction, 144
present irrevocable declaration, 149
settlor as trustee, 145–148
Declared trusts
and see EXPRESS TRUSTS
analysis, 71–72
Deed of assignment
transfer of property to beneficiaries, and,
629–630
Deeds, custody of
incidents of trustee's estate, and, 457
Default of agents, nominees or custodians
reasonable care and skill, and, 590
Defeating trustee's rights
appointment of new trustees, and, 767
Definitions
active trusts, 58–59
bare trusts, 57–58
beneficiary, 3
breach of trust, 5–6
constructive trusts, 55–57
discretionary, 63–66
equitable estate, 48–53
executed trusts, 66–68
executory trusts, 66–68
express trusts, 53–54
fixed trusts, 63–66
implied trusts, 53–54
legal estates, 48–50
resulting trusts, 54–55
settlor, 4
sham trusts, 59–63
simple trusts, 57–58

Definitions – *continued*
special trusts, 58–59
trust, 3–7
trustee, 3
Delegation by trustee
asset management functions
generally, 638
investment of funds, and, 621–622
background to rule, 634
beneficiary, to
generally, 641–642
land, 639–640
distributive functions, and, 628–630
duration, 640
eligible delegates, 636
generally, 631–634
investment of funds, and, 621–622
statutory rule
exceptions, 635–641
generally, 634–635
temporary period, for, 642–644
terms, 637–638
transfer of property to beneficiaries, and,
628–630
Demergers
augmentation of capital, and, 539
Dépeçage
conflict of laws, and, 1037–1039
Depreciation reserves
discretionary distributive powers, and, 535
Depreciatory conditions of sale
reasonable care and skill, and, 581
Derivative title
transfer of property to beneficiaries, and,
628–630
Detrimental reliance
equitable proprietary estoppel, and, 250–
252
prevention of fraudulent conduct, and
express common intention, 419–420
inferred common intention, 420–421
Direct claims on estate
indemnity for trustees, and, 825–826
**Direction of court, administration of trust
under**
trustee's rights, and, 846–848
Directions of court as to specific questions
case management, 838–839
commencement of proceedings, 836–837
costs
appeal, on, 842–843
Beddoe applications, 845
court's jurisdiction, 840
established principles, 840–841
hostile litigation, 841
nature of disputes, 841–842
prospective orders, 843–844
rule of court, 840
evidence, 837–838
generally, 832–835

Directions of court as to specific questions –
continued
hearings, 838–839
jurisdiction of court, 835–836
jus tertii, and, 648–650
parties, 836
Direction to employ and pay named persons
illusory trusts, and, 142–143
Direction to pay costs
illusory trusts, and, 142
Director's fee
augmentation of capital, and, 542
Directors obtaining profits
persons in fiduciary position, and, 390–
393
Disallowance of unreasonable expenses
indemnity for trustees, and, 817
Discharge on completion of trusteeship
trustee's rights, and, 827–828
Disclaimer of trust
costs, 450
effect, 450
generally, 449
methods, 449–450
prior consent to undertake trust, and, 449
Disclosure under CPR
accounts and records, and, 678–679
Discretion
appointment of judicial trustees, and, 788
payment of outgoings, and, and, 564–565
Discretionary distributive powers
annuities, 532–533
capital growth as if income, 531–532
choice of investments, 531
depreciation reserves, 535
generally, 530–531
Discretionary trusts
administrative powers, 65–66
benevolent purposes, for, 105–106
generally, 63–64
illustrations, 64–65
tax treatment, 64
uncertainty as to beneficiaries, and, 85–91
Dishonest breach of trust
compensation, and, 912
generally, 907
other offences, and, 911
theft, and
actus reus, 907–910
generally, 907
mens rea, 910–911
Dishonest assistance
assistance by defendant, 958–959
breach of trust or duty, 957–958
causal link between breach and loss/gain,
958
dishonest state of mind, 959–965
existence of trust or fiduciary relationship,
957
generally, 956

Dishonest assistance – *continued*
  vicarious liability of defendant's partners,
    965–966
Dishonest dealing by agents
  dishonesty, 954–955
  generally, 952–953
  lawful receipt of trust property, 953–954
  pleading issues, 955–956
Disposition to trustees
  resulting trusts, and, 332
Dispositive powers
  fixed trusts, and, 65–66
Dissolution of clubs
  resulting trusts, and, 338–240
Divesting gifts
  resulting trusts, and, 375–376
Doctrine of conversion
  effect, 439
  operation, 439–440
Donatio mortis causa
  prevention of fraudulent conduct, and,
    433–434
  transfer of property to trust, and, 150
Donee of power
  appointment of new trustees, and, 771
Donees cannot agree
  appointment of new trustees, and, 765
Doubtful cases
  appointment of new trustees, and, 765
Due authorisation
  constructive trusts, and, 401–402
Due care, exercise of
  trustee's powers, and, 699–700
Duration of trust
  language sufficient to create trust, and,
    83–84

Employ named persons, direction to
  illusory trusts, and, 142–143
Employee inventions
  persons in fiduciary position, and, 399–
    400
Employee trusts
  commercial purpose trusts, and, 47
Enforceability of trust
  contracts, 170–172
  generally, 166–168
  introduction, 144–145
  third party rights, 168–169
  trustee's action at common law, 179–182
  voluntary covenants, 172–179
  volunteers' action at common law, 169
Enforcement of foreign judgments
  common law jurisdiction, 1059–1060
  European jurisdiction, 1057–1059
  generally, 1060–1062
  synopsis, 1056–1057
Enforcer principle
  language sufficient to create trust, and,
    114–116

Enfranchisement of lease
  incidents of trustee's estate, and, 457
English movables, testamentary trusts of
  legality of objects in trusts, and, 231–232
Enhanced scrip dividends
  augmentation of capital, and, 539–540
Equitable charges
  language sufficient to create trust, and, 77
Equitable choses in action
  transfer of property to trust, and, 151–152
Equitable estate or interest
  definition, 48–50
  estate taken by trustee, and, 454
  mere equities, and, 50
  minor interests, and, 50–51
  overriding interests, and, 50–51
  property capable of being subject of trust,
    and, 183
  rights in rem and in personam, 51–53
  transfer of property to trust, and, 151
Equitable estoppel
  constructive trusts, and, 425–427
Equitable interests
  partial interest in special trust, and, 738
  property traced into hands of third
    parties, and, 1000–1001
**Equitable interests not wholly disposed of,
    trusts where**
  admissibility of evidence, 342–343
  bankruptcy following voluntary
    arrangement, 340–341
  bona vacantia, 337–338
  broad propositions, 330–332
  contributions to charitable funds, 341–342
  disposition to trustees, 332
  dissolution of clubs, 338–240
  donee intended to take beneficially, 334–
    336
  failure of express trust, 332–333
  failure of life interest, 333–334
  generally, 329–330
  Quistclose trusts, 342
  residue after satisfaction of express trust,
    334
  uncertainty of express trust, 332–333
  voluntary contributions to assist distressed
    individuals, 336
Equitable lease
  transfer of property to trust, and, 151
Equitable proprietary estoppel
  constitution of express trusts, and, 157
  detrimental reliance, 250–252
  historical background, 249–250
  introduction, 248–249
  purchasers' viewpoint, 253–254
Erection of monuments and graves
  language sufficient to create trust, and,
    119–121
Errors of judgment,
  reasonable care and skill, and 584–585

Estate contract
transfer of property to trust, and, 151
Estate taken by trustee
assent, 454–456
equitable estate, 454
generally, 454
legal estate, 454
Excessive accumulations of income
exclusion from rules, 205–208
introduction, 203–205
purpose of purchasing land, 208–209
termination of accumulations, 205
Executed trusts
completely constituted trusts, and, 67–68
generally, 66
significance, 66–67
tax treatment, 66–67
wills, and, 67
Executors *de son tort*
persons in fiduciary position, and, 382
Executors of deceased trustee
measure of trustee's liability for breach of
trust, and, 873
Executory trusts
generally, 66
interim pension trusts, and, 67
interpretation of
covenants to settle property, and, 305–
317
general rules, 299–302
introduction, 72
marriage articles, and, 302–305
marriage settlements, and, 305–310
wills, and, 302–305
marriage articles, and, 67
significance, 66–67
tax treatment, 66–67
wills, and, 67
Exemption clauses
deliberate breaches, 594
dishonest breaches, 594
excluding duties, 591
exempting liability, 593
generally, 576
statutory prohibitions, 595
Expectancies
property capable of being subject of trust,
and, 184–185
Expectation, words of
express trusts, and, 138
Expensive information
accounts and records, and, 687
Explanatory of motive, words
express trusts, and, 138
Express common intention
detrimental reliance, 419–420
generally, 414–415
Express declaration
language sufficient to create trust, and,
75–76

Express trusts
and see under individual headings
administration of trust, workability of
generally, 91–93
initial unworkability, 98–99
powers, 93–98
supervening unworkability, 98–99
agreements to create trusts
generally, 139
joint wills, 140
marriage articles, 139–140
mutual wills, 140
analysis, 71–72
animals, maintenance of, 122
application of property, 82–83
beneficiaries, uncertainty as to
discretionary trusts, under, 85–91
fixed trust, under, 84
generally, 82–83
beneficiary principle
drafting points, 117–118
enforcer clause, and, 114–116
introduction, 110–111
loan purpose trusts, and, 116–117
purpose trusts, and, 111–114
binding upon donor, 165–166
compliance with formal requirements
contracts to create trusts, 234–235
contracts to dispose of existing
equitable interests, 235–236
dealings with equitable interests, 238–
247
declarations of trusts, 236–238
equitable proprietary estoppel, 248–254
generally, 232–234
introduction, 72
secret trusts, 254–267
testamentary trusts, 247–248
conditional words
expectation, of, 138
explanatory of motive, of, 138
introduction, 136–137
illustrations, 137–138
conditions precedent, 99–100
conditions subsequent
generally, 100–101
parentage, as to, 102–103
profession or office, as to, 102
religion, as to, 102–103
residence, as to, 101–102
constitution of trust
binding upon donor, 165–166
declaration of trust, 145–148
enforceability, 166–182
exceptional cases, 154–165
generally, 144–145
introduction, 71–72
transfer of property, 149–154
declaration of self as trustee, 145–148

Express trusts – *continued*
  declaration of trust
    introduction, 144
    present irrevocable declaration, 149
    settlor as trustee, 145–148
  definition, 53–54
  discretionary trusts for benevolent
      purposes, 105–106
  duration of trust, as to, 83–84
  enforceability of trust
    contracts, 170–172
    generally, 166–168
    introduction, 144–145
    third party rights, 168–169
    trustee's action at common law, 179–182
    voluntary covenants, 172–179
    volunteers' action at common law, 169
  enforcer principle, 114–116
  equitable charges, and, 77
  erection of monuments and graves, 119–
      121
  essential elements
    complete constitution of trust, 144–182
    compliance with formal requirements,
        232–267
    introduction, 71–72
    language sufficient to create trust, 73–143
    legality of object of trust, 189–232
    property capable of being subject of
        trust, 182–189
  exceptional cases
    erection and maintenance of
        monuments and graves, 119–121
    introduction, 118–119
    maintenance of animals, 122
    management of inanimate objects, 123
    saying of masses, 122–123
    unincorporated associations, 123–129
  expectation, words of, 138
  explanatory of motive, words, 138
  express declaration, 75–76
  floating trusts, 81–82
  graves, erection and maintenance of, 119–
      121
  illusory trusts
    damages claims for voluntary carers'
        services, 143
    direction to employ and pay named
        persons, 142–143
    direction to pay costs, 142
    funds confined to state officials for
        distribution, 143
    inferences relating to creditors' deeds,
        141–142
    introduction, 140–141
  inanimate objects, management of, 123
  intent to create trust, 75
  interpretation of executory trusts
    covenants to settle property, and, 305–
        317

Express trusts – *continued*
  interpretation of executory trusts –
      continued
    general rules, 299–302
    introduction, 72
    marriage articles, and, 302–305
    marriage settlements, and, 305–310
    wills, and, 302–305
  language sufficient to create trust
    agreements to create trusts, 139–140
    conditional words, 136–138
    generally, 73–75
    illusory trusts, 140–143
    introduction, 71
    powers in the nature of trusts, 130–133
    precatory words, 133–136
    technical language unnecessary, 75–129
  latent flaws
    ad hoc legislative provisions, 297–298
    bankruptcy of settlor, 287–291
    failure of consideration, 273–275
    fraud, 281
    ignorance or mistake, 275–281
    incapacity of beneficiaries, 272–273
    incapacity of settlors, 268–272
    intention to defeat claims for
        inheritance provision, 295–297
    intention to defeat claims of future
        purchasers, 72
    intention to defeat dependants, 295–
        297
    intention to prejudice creditors, 291–
        295
    introduction, 72
    undue influence, 281–287
  legality of object of trust
    attempts to alter prescribed rules of
        devolution, 209–214
    effect of illegal trust on other trusts,
        224–231
    excessive accumulations of income,
        203–209
    generally, 189–190
    infringement of Human Rights Act,
        219–223
    introduction, 72
    ousting jurisdiction of courts, 215–217
    promotion of immorality, 217–219
    restraint on alienation, 214–215
    statutorily illegal trusts, 223–224
    testamentary trusts of English movables,
        231–232
    tying up of property for unlawful
        period, 191–203
  loan purpose trusts, and, 116–117
  masses, saying of, 122–123
  monuments, erection and maintenance
      of, 119–121
  names and arms clauses, 103–104

Express trusts – *continued*
powers in the nature of trusts
apparent intention to benefit, 131–132
gifts over in default of appointment, 130–131
introduction, 130
release of powers, 132–133
precatory words
authorities for modern rule, 134
codicil, in, 136
contrasting modern and former rules, 133–134
illustrations of modern rule, 135–136
introduction, 133
property capable of being subject of trust
choses in action, 183
effect of bankruptcy, 185–186
equitable interests, 183
expectancies, 184–185
foreign immovables, 187–189
future property, 184–185
generally, 182–183
introduction, 72
property inalienable by reason of public policy, 186
property inalienable by statute, 187
reversionary interests, 184
purpose trusts, and, 111–114
release of powers, 132–133
saying of masses, 122–123
separate trust property, 76–77
statutory validation, 107–110
suspended trusts, 81–82
technical language unnecessary
administratively workable, 91–99
beneficiary principle, 110–118
equitable charges, and, 77
exceptional cases, 118–123
express declaration, 75–76
floating trusts, 81–82
intent to create trust, 75
separate trust property, 76–77
suspended trusts, 81–82
uncertainty, 77–110
unincorporated associations, 123–129
want of trustee, 77
transfer of property
generally, 149–154
introduction, 144
uncertainty as to objects
administration of trusts, as to, 91–99
application of property, as to, 82–83
beneficiaries, as to, 82–83
beneficiaries under discretionary trusts, as to, 85–91
beneficiaries under fixed trust, as to, 84
conditions precedent, 99–100
conditions subsequent, 100–103
discretionary trusts for benevolent purposes, 105–106

Express trusts – *continued*
uncertainty as to objects – *continued*
duration of trust, as to, 83–84
generally, 77
illustrations, 78–81
names and arms clauses, 103–104
statutory validation, 107–110
unincorporated associations, 123–129
want of trustee, 77
Expression by trustee to be discharged
appointment of new trustees, and, 760
Extension of lease
incidents of trustee's estate, and, 457
Extinguish trust, power to
absolute gift with superadded direction, 731–732
basic principles, 734–735
generally, 729–730
illustrations, 730–731
indefeasible absolute beneficial; entitlement, 732–734
legacies to purchase annuities, 732
modification of trusts, 735–736
possible future beneficiaries, 735

Failure of consideration
generally, 274–275
introduction, 273
Failure of express trust
resulting trusts, and, 332–333
Failure of life interest
resulting trusts, and, 333–334
Failure of trusts
admissibility of evidence, 342–343
bankruptcy following voluntary arrangement, 340–341
bona vacantia, 337–338
broad propositions, 330–332
contributions to charitable funds, 341–342
disposition to trustees, 332
dissolution of clubs, 338–240
donee intended to take beneficially, 334–336
failure of express trust, 332–333
failure of life interest, 333–334
generally, 329–330
Quistclose trusts, 342
residue after satisfaction of express trust, 334
uncertainty of express trust, 332–333
voluntary contributions to assist distressed individuals, 336
Fair dealing rule
limitation of actions by beneficiaries, and, 927–928
profiting from trust property, and, 670–671
False accounting
dishonest breach of trust, and, 911

False statements, publication of
dishonest breach of trust, and, 911
Falsification of accounts
and see TAKING OF ACCOUNTS
Family provision, intention to defeat claims for
generally, 297
introduction, 295–296
Fees
Public Trustee, and, 792–793
Fencing of unfenced land
repairs, and, 573–574
Fettering exercise of discretions
trustee's powers, and, 690–691
Fiduciary duty
acceptance of trust property, and, 485–486
Fiduciary position, trusts for products owned by persons in
additions to trust property, 385–386
commercial transactions, 400–401
directors obtaining profits, 390–393
employee inventions, 399–400
executors de son tort, 382
generally, 379
lessee purchasing reversion expectant on lease, 383–385
profits by agents, 393–398
profits by partners, 398
profits by tippees, 398–399
profits by trustee from property or position, 386–388
profits by trustee's parent company, 388
proprietary and personal liability, 381
renewal of lease by partial owner, 385
tenant for life of leaseholds renewing to himself, 383
tenant for life of mortgaged property purchasing mortgagee's interest, 385
tenant for life receiving money for settled land, 386
tracing, 379–381
trustees de son tort, 381–382
trustees obtaining commission, 389–390
trustees obtaining directorship fees, 388–389
trustees taking renewal of lease himself, 382–382
Fiduciary powers
personal powers, and, 29–34, 97
Fiduciary relationship
debt, and, 25
generally, 20–24
Financial relief claims
constructive trusts, and, 427
Financial relief claims, intention to defeat
generally, 296
introduction, 295–296
Fixed trusts
administrative powers, 65–66
generally, 63–64

Fixed trusts – *continued*
illustrations, 64–65
tax treatment, 64
uncertainty as to beneficiaries, and, 84
Floating trusts
language sufficient to create trust, and, 81–82
secret trusts, and, 266–267
Foreign immovables
property capable of being subject of trust, and, 187–189
Foreigners
incapacity of settlors, and, 270
Forged document
transfer of property to beneficiaries, and, 624–625
Formal requirements, compliance with
contracts to create trusts, 234–235
contracts to dispose of existing equitable interests, 235–236
dealings with equitable interests
databases of interests, 245
examples, 239–245
introduction, 238
nature of dealings, 238–239
registers of interests, 245
s 53(1)(c) dispositions, 245–247
declarations of trusts, 236–238
equitable proprietary estoppel
detrimental reliance, 250–252
historical background, 249–250
introduction, 248–249
purchasers' viewpoint, 253–254
generally, 232–234
instrument of fraud. statute not to be used as
inter vivos trusts, 254–256
introduction, 254
secret trusts, 258–267
testamentary trusts, 257
introduction, 72
secret trusts
beneficiary predeceasing testator, 263–264
floating trusts, 266–267
fully secret trusts, 260–261
gifts to several intended trustees without communication, 262–263
half-secret trusts, 261–262
introduction, 258–259
operation independent of will, 264–266
parol evidence, and, 259–260
testamentary trusts, 247–248
Fraud, cancellation for
generally, 281
introduction, 275–276
Fraudulent conduct, trusts for prevention of
abuse of statutory provisions, 410–411
assignments for value of future property, 437–438

Fraudulent conduct, trusts for prevention of
  – continued
  common intention constructive trusts
    date of valuation of interest, 425
    detrimental reliance, 419–421
    equitable estoppel, and, 425–427
    financial relief, and, 427
    express agreement, 414–415
    generally, 412–414
    inferred agreement, 415–419
    legal title in both names, 421–422
    size of share, 422–425
  criminal may not benefit from crime
    generally, 434–435
    statutory relief, 435
  detrimental reliance
    express common intention, 419–420
    inferred common intention, 420–421
  donor does all obliged to do to transfer
      legal title, 433–434
  express common intention
    detrimental reliance, 419–420
    generally, 414–415
  generally, 409–410
  inferred common intention
    detrimental reliance, 420–421
    generally, 415–419
  mutual wills
    binding agreement for survivor to carry
        out agreed arrangement, 428–430
    generally, 427–428
    property subject to trust, 431–431
    secret truss, and, 432
    trust effecting arrangement, 430–431
  receipts by insolvent agents, 437
  rescission of voidable transfers, 435–436
  secret trusts
    generally, 433
    mutual wills, and, 432
  use of property principles, 411–412
Fraud on power
  transfer of property to beneficiaries, and,
      631
Freehold or leasehold land
  investment of funds, and 607–609
Friction, cases of
  appointment of new trustees, and, 765–
      766
FSMA regulation
  incapacity of settlors, and, 271–272
Fully secret trusts
  secret trusts, and, 260–261
Fund investment
  custodian holdings
    appointment of custodian, 619–621
    exclusions, 621
    generally, 619
    nature of duty, 621
    restrictions, 621

Fund investment *– continued*
  delegation of asset management function,
      621–622
  duties
    generally, 597–599
    nature, 613–618
  express powers, 611–612
  general power
    ambit, 601–602
    conditions precedent, 602–603
    exclusions, 604
    generally, 599–601
    loans secured on land, 605
    mortgages, 606
    proper advice, and, 604–605
    restrictions, 604
    securities in company, 606–607
  generally, 597–599
  nominee holdings
    appointment of custodian, 619–621
    exclusions, 621
    generally, 619
    nature of duty, 621
    restrictions, 621
  occupational pension schemes, and, 600–
      601
  Settled Land Act settlements, 610–611
  specific powers
    freehold or leasehold land, 607–609
    investment property, 609–610
Fund investment, neglect of
  reasonable care and skill, and, 586
**Funds confined to state officials for
    distribution**
  illusory trusts, and, 143
Future beneficiaries
  power to extinguish trust, and, 735
Future illegitimate children
  legality of objects in trusts, and, 217–218
Future property
  property capable of being subject of trust,
      and, 184–185
Future property, assignments for value of
  prevention of fraudulent conduct, and,
      437–438
**Future purchasers, intention to defeat claims
    of**
  generally, 72

'Gazumping'
  reasonable care and skill, and, 582
Gifts carrying intermediate income
  maintenance to infants, and, 712–713
Gifts of property
  resulting trusts, and, 367–368
Governing law
  and see HAGUE TRUSTS CONVENTION
  determination, 1031–1040
  limits on scope, 1046–1052
  scope, 1040–1045

Governmental obligation
trusts, and, 7
Grant of leases
reasonable care and skill, and, 583
Graves, erection and maintenance of,
language sufficient to create trust, and,
119–121

Hague Trusts Convention
background, 1011–1013
basic concepts
determination of governing law, 1031–
1040
enforcement of foreign judgments,
1056–1062
excluded preliminary matters, 1022–
1031
generally, 1011–1014
limits on scope of governing law, 1046–
1052
recognition of trusts, 1053–1056
registration of trusts, 1056
relevant trusts, 1014–1022
scope of governing law, 1040–1045
capacity to create trust
beneficiary, 1025
introduction, 1023
settlor, 1023–1024
trustee, 1024–1025
changing the governing law, 1039–1040
dépeçage, and, 1037–1039
determination of governing law
applicable law in absence of choice,
1035–1037
dépeçage, 1037–1039
express choice of law, 1031–1032
implied choice of law, 1033–1034
renvoi, 1037
effect in non-trust states, 1013
enforcement of foreign judgments
common law jurisdiction, 1059–1060
European jurisdiction, 1057–1059
generally, 1060–1062
synopsis, 1056–1057
excluded preliminary matters
capacity to create to trust, 1023–1025
forced heirship, 1030–1031
introduction, 1022–1023
perpetuity, 1030
vesting of property in trustee, 1025–1030
exclusion of fiscal matters, 1014
functions, 1014
introduction, 1007
limits on scope of governing law
domestic mandatory laws, 1046–1049
international mandatory rules, 1049–
1050
introduction, 1046
mandatory rules, 1046
public policy, 1050–1052

Hague Trusts Convention – *continued*
meaning of 'trust', 1014–1016
nature of a trust, and, 6–7
recognition of trusts
following trust assets, 1054–1055
requirements, 1053–1054
right to refuse, 1055–1056
tracing trust assets, 1054–1055
registration of trusts, 1056
relevant trusts
constructive trusts, 1018–1020
evidence in writing, and, 1016–1017
extension of scope in UK, 1020–1021
judicial decisions, and, 1022
resulting trusts, 1017–1018
statutory trusts, 1020
voluntary trusts, 1017
renvoi, and, 1037
scope of governing law
general matters, 1040–1041
limits, 1046–1056
specific matters, 1041–1045
territorial extent, 1013
text
applicable law, 1008
general clauses, 1009–1010
recognition, 1008–1009
scope, 1007–1008
vesting of property in trustee
classification of property, 1026
conclusion, 1029–1030
immovable property, 1027
intangible movable property, 1028–1029
introduction, 1025–1026
tangible movable property, 1028
Half-secret trusts
secret trusts, and, 261–262
Holding title to trust property
indemnity for trustees, and, 813–814
Hotchpot provision
impartiality of trustee, and, 546–548
***Howe v Lord Dartmouth*, rule in**
expressed contrary intention, and, 550–551
generally, 548–549
impact of Trustee Act 2000, 549–550
impliedly negatived intention, and, 551–
552
implied trust for sale, and, 550
Human Rights Act, infringement of
legality of objects in trusts, and, 219–220

Ignorance, cancellation for
generally, 276–277
introduction, 275–276
negligence of legal advisers, 280–281
rectification
marriage settlements, of, 279–280
pension trusts, of, 279–280
unilateral transaction, of, 277–279
wills, of, 280

Illegal trusts, resulting trusts arising from
claims through transferor, 348–349
conveyance to qualify for game licence, 344
fraudulent conveyance, 345–346
generally, 343–344
presumption of advancement, 347–348
reliance after carrying out illegal purpose, 348
settlement for illegal consideration, 344–345
spouses' fraudulent designs, 346–347

Illegality by statute
legality of objects in trusts, and, 223–224

Illegitimate children
legality of objects in trusts, and, 217–218
transfer of property to beneficiaries, and, 626

Illusory trusts
damages claims for voluntary carers' services, 143
direction to employ and pay named persons, 142–143
direction to pay costs, 142
funds confined to state officials for distribution, 143
inferences relating to creditors' deeds, 141–142
introduction, 140–141

Immorality, promotion of
future illegitimate children, 217–218
separation of spouses, 218

Impartiality between beneficiaries, duty of
annuities
generally, 532–533
tax-free sums, 533–535
appropriation
answer particular shares, to, 543–544
cash value, at, 544–545
generally, 542–543
proportion of trust fund, at, 544–545
statutory power, 545–546
augmentation of capital
bonuses, 535–538
capital profits dividends, 538
demergers, 539
director's fee, 542
enhanced scrip dividends, 539–540
generally, 535
profit on investment realisation, 540
profit on reconstruction of company, 542
stocks 'cum dividend', 540–542
unit trusts, 542
discretionary distributive powers
annuities, 532–533
capital growth as if income, 531–532
choice of investments, 531
depreciation reserves, 535
generally, 530–531

Impartiality between beneficiaries, duty of –
continued
generally, 529–530
hotchpot provision, 546–548
threats against beneficiary's interest, 532

Implied trusts
and see CONSTRUCTIVE TRUSTS
and see RESULTING TRUSTS
analysis, 321–322
definition, 53–54

Implied vesting declarations
vesting of property in new trustees, and, 776–779

Impossible condition
legality of objects in trusts, and, 230–231

Impounding equitable interests in trust
involvement in breach of trust, and, 979–983

Improper retention of authorised investment
taking of accounts, and, 872

Improper sale of authorised investment
taking of accounts, and, 872–873

Improvident lettings
reasonable care and skill, and, 583

Improvident purchases
reasonable care and skill, and, 583

Improvident sales
reasonable care and skill, and, 581

Inaccurate accounts
accounts and records, and, 678

Inalienability of interests
partial interest in special trust, and, 738

Inalienability, rule against
generally, 202–203
introduction, 191–192

Inalienable by reason of public policy, property
property capable of being subject of trust, and, 186

Inalienable by statute, property
property capable of being subject of trust, and, 187

Inanimate objects, management of
language sufficient to create trust, and, 123

Incapacity
appointment of new trustees, and, 761
beneficiaries, of
aliens, 273
introduction, 272
minors, 273
persons of unsound mind, 273
settlors, 273
trustees, 273
settlors, of
corporations, 270–271
foreigners, 270
FSMA regulation, and, 271–272
introduction, 268
minors, 268–269
persons of unsound mind, 269–270

Incapacity of trustee
appointment of new trustees, and, 761
Incidental costs of administration
payment of outgoings, and, 574–575
Incidents of trustee's estate
collective enfranchisement, 457–458
commencing actions, 456
commonhold ownership, 458
custody of deeds, 457
enfranchisement and extension of lease, 457
generally, 456
liability for rates and taxes, 456
liability to business creditors, 457
management of block of flats, 458
planning rights, 457
proof in bankruptcy, 456
Income, charges against
annual charges, 568
insurance premiums, 568–570
losses on trust business, 570
redemption of rentcharge, 570
Incompletely constituted trusts
executed trusts, and, 67–68
Indefeasible absolute beneficial entitlement
power to extinguish trust, and, 732–734
Indemnity by instigator of breach
commission at instigation or request of beneficiaries, 947–949
contribution between trustees, 941–944
generally, 940–941
less guilty co-trustees, 945–947
new appointees, and, 947
trustee-beneficiaries, and, 944–945
Indemnity for expenses
basis of taxed costs in litigation, 815
beneficiary, from
club trustees, and, 823
generally, 821–822
limits, 822–823
calls on shares, 813
carrying on business, 814
damages recovered by third parties, 813
direct claims on estate, 825–826
disallowance of unreasonable expenses, 817
generally, 810–811
holding title to trust property, 813–814
insolvent trustee, 826
interest, 818
lien, and
continues to bind successor trustees, 820
expenses, 818
express preservation, 820
legal costs where settlement void, 818–819
mixed funds, 819
refusal to transfer property, 819–820
nature, 812–813

Indemnity for expenses – *continued*
new trustees, from, 820–821
payment from taxed income, 818
prospective *Beddoe* application, 816
reimbursement of costs incurred, 815
reliance on counsel's advice, 816–817
set-off, and, 823–824
solicitors' costs, 814
subrogation claims, and, 824–825
third party litigation expenses, 815
unnecessary costs, 817–818
voluntary subscriptions, 817
Independent advice
undue influence, and, 285
Inferences relating to creditors' deeds
illusory trusts, and, 141–142
Inferred common intention
detrimental reliance, 420–421
generally, 415–419
Information barriers
constructive trusts, and, 405–406
Infringement of Human Rights Act
legality of objects in trusts, and, 219–220
Inheritance provision, intention to defeat claims for
generally, 297
introduction, 295–296
Inheritance tax
discretionary trusts, and, 64
executed trusts, and, 66–67
executory trusts, and, 66–67
fixed trusts, and, 64
Injunctions to safeguard trust property
principles, 904
property in danger, 904–905
restraint of improper sale, 905–906
Inquiries as to trust property
acts of predecessors, 491–492
generally, 490–491
losses, 492
notices of incumbrances, 492–493
Insolvency of trustee
administration of trust, and, 460–462
Insolvent agents, receipts by
prevention of fraudulent conduct, and, 437
Insolvent trustee
indemnity for trustees, and, 826
Inspection of documents
accounts and records, and, 6777
Institutional trusts of property
constructive trusts, and, 324–327
Instrument of fraud. statute not to be used as
inter vivos trusts, 254–256
introduction, 254
secret trusts
beneficiary predeceasing testator, 263–264
floating trusts, 266–267

Instrument of fraud. statute not to be used as – *continued*
  secret trusts – *continued*
    fully secret trusts, 260–261
    gifts to several intended trustees without communication, 262–263
    half-secret trusts, 261–262
    introduction, 258–259
    operation independent of will, 264–266
    parol evidence, and, 259–260
    testamentary trusts, 257
Insurance against risks
  reasonable care and skill, and, 588–589
Insurance premiums
  current expenses, and, 568–570
Insurance proceeds
  mixing of trust property with other property, and, 890
Intent to create trust
  language sufficient to create trust, and, 75
Intention to defeat claims for inheritance provision
  generally, 297
  introduction, 295–296
Intention to defeat claims of future purchasers
  generally, 72
Intention to defeat financial relief claims
  generally, 296
  introduction, 295–296
Intention to prejudice creditors
  flexible orders, 293
  generally, 291–292
  insolvency cases, 292
  onus of proof, 293
  other cases, 292
  purpose, 294–295
  without limit of time, 293–294
Inter vivos **gifts**
  transfer of property to trust, and, 150
Inter vivos **trusts**
  statute not to be used as instrument of fraud, and, 254–256
Interest
  indemnity for trustees, and, 818
Interest, loss of
  taking of accounts, and, 867–869
Interference with parental duty
  legality of objects in trusts, and, 222–223
Interim applications to safeguard trust property
  generally, 903
  injunctions
    principles, 904
    property in danger, 904–905
    restraint of improper sale, 905–906
  payments into court, 906
Interim pension trusts
  executory trusts, and, 67

Intermeddling strangers
  involvement in breach of trust, and, 951–952
Interpretation of executory trusts
  covenants to settle property in marriage settlement, and
    after-acquired property, 310–313
    binding on wife, 305–306
    definite interests in property, 314–315
    excluded property, 306–310
    property exceeding certain value, 315–317
    property to which presently entitled, 310
  executory will trusts, and, 303–304
  general rules, 299–302
  introduction, 72
  marriage articles, and, 302–305
  wills, and, 302–305
Interpretation of wills
  precatory words, and, 136
Inventory of chattels
  reasonable care and skill, and, 586
Investigation
  transfer of property to beneficiaries, and, 630–631
Investment in particular securities
  duty to obey directions of settlement, and, 496
Investment information
  accounts and records, and, 678
Investment of funds
  custodian holdings
    appointment of custodian, 619–621
    exclusions, 621
    generally, 619
    nature of duty, 621
    restrictions, 621
  delegation of asset management function, 621–622
  duties
    generally, 597–599
    nature, 613–618
  express powers, 611–612
  general power
    ambit, 601–602
    conditions precedent, 602–603
    exclusions, 604
    generally, 599–601
    loans secured on land, 605
    mortgages, 606
    proper advice, and, 604–605
    restrictions, 604
    securities in company, 606–607
  generally, 597–599
  nominee holdings
    appointment of custodian, 619–621
    exclusions, 621
    generally, 619
    nature of duty, 621
    restrictions, 621

Investment of funds – *continued*
occupational pension schemes, and, 600–
601
Settled Land Act settlements, 610–611
specific powers
freehold or leasehold land, 607–609
investment property, 609–610
Investment property
investment of funds, and, 609–610
Involvement in breach of trust, liability for
dealing by agents
dishonesty, 954–955
generally, 952–953
lawful receipt of trust property, 953–954
pleading issues, 955–956
dishonest assistance
assistance by defendant, 958–959
breach of trust or duty, 957–958
causal link between breach and loss/
gain, 958
dishonest state of mind, 959–965
existence of trust or fiduciary
relationship, 957
generally, 956
vicarious liability of defendant's
partners, 965–966
generally, 950–951
impounding equitable interests in trust,
979–983
intermeddling strangers, 951–952
misapplied trust property
causal link between breach and receipt,
969–970
change of position, and, 978–979
dealing with receipt to defendant's
benefit, 970–973
future developments of law, 975–978
generally, 967
knowledge of breach, 973–975
misapplication of property, 968
property held on trust or duty, 968
receipt of property or proceeds, 968–969
money laundering, and, 966–967
strangers, 951–952
trustees *de son tort*, 951–952

**Joint and several liability of trustee's for
breach of trust**
contribution between trustees, 878
equal liability of parties to breach, 877
generally, 877
Joint wills
agreements to create trusts, and, 140
Judicial trustees, appointment of
discretion of court, 788
generally, 785–787
Public Trustee, and, 789
purpose of statutory provisions, 787–788
Rules, 788

Jurisdiction of court
directions of court as to specific questions,
and, 835–836
Jus tertii
property traced into hands of third
parties, and, 998
trustee's duties, and, 648–650

Knowledge
acquiescence of beneficiaries, and, 935–
936
actual, 973, 994
imputed, 992
misapplied trust property, and, 973–975
naughty, 974–975, 994
Nelsonian, 974–975, 994

Laches
limitation of actions by beneficiaries, and,
929–930
Language sufficient to create trust
administration of trust, workability of
generally, 91–93
initial unworkability, 98–99
powers, 93–98
supervening unworkability, 98–99
agreements to create trusts
generally, 139
joint wills, 140
marriage articles, 139–140
mutual wills, 140
analysis, 71–72
animals, maintenance of, 122
application of property, 82–83
beneficiaries, uncertainty as to
discretionary trusts, under, 85–91
fixed trust, under, 84
generally, 82–83
beneficiary principle
drafting points, 117–118
enforcer clause, and, 114–116
introduction, 110–111
loan purpose trusts, and, 116–117
purpose trusts, and, 111–114
conditional words
expectation, of, 138
explanatory of motive, of, 138
introduction, 136–137
illustrations, 137–138
conditions precedent, 99–100
conditions subsequent
generally, 100–101
parentage, as to, 102–103
profession or office, as to, 102
religion, as to, 102–103
residence, as to, 101–102
definition, 53–54
discretionary trusts for benevolent
purposes, 105–106
duration of trust, as to, 83–84

Language sufficient to create trust –
continued
enforcer principle, 114–116
equitable charges, and, 77
erection of monuments and graves, 119–121
exceptional cases
  erection and maintenance of monuments and graves, 119–121
  introduction, 118–119
  maintenance of animals, 122
  management of inanimate objects, 123
  saying of masses, 122–123
  unincorporated associations, 123–129
expectation, words of, 138
explanatory of motive, words, 138
express declaration, 75–76
floating trusts, 81–82
generally, 73–75
graves, erection and maintenance of, 119–121
illusory trusts
  damages claims for voluntary carers' services, 143
  direction to employ and pay named persons, 142–143
  direction to pay costs, 142
  funds confined to state officials for distribution, 143
  inferences relating to creditors' deeds, 141–142
  introduction, 140–141
inanimate objects, management of, 123
intent to create trust, 75
introduction, 71
loan purpose trusts, and, 116–117
masses, saying of, 122–123
monuments, erection and maintenance of, 119–121
names and arms clauses, 103–104
powers in the nature of trusts
  apparent intention to benefit, 131–132
  gifts over in default of appointment, 130–131
  introduction, 130
  release of powers, 132–133
precatory words
  authorities for modern rule, 134
  codicil, in, 136
  contrasting modern and former rules, 133–134
  illustrations of modern rule, 135–136
  introduction, 133
purpose trusts, and, 111–114
release of powers, 132–133
saying of masses, 122–123
separate trust property, 76–77
statutory validation, 107–110
suspended trusts, 81–82

Language sufficient to create trust –
continued
technical language unnecessary
  administratively workable, 91–99
  beneficiary principle, 110–118
  equitable charges, and, 77
  exceptional cases, 118–123
  express declaration, 75–76
  floating trusts, 81–82
  intent to create trust, 75
  separate trust property, 76–77
  suspended trusts, 81–82
  uncertainty, 77–110
  unincorporated associations, 123–129
  want of trustee, 77
uncertainty as to objects
  administration of trusts, as to, 91–99
  application of property, as to, 82–83
  beneficiaries, as to, 82–83
  beneficiaries under discretionary trusts, as to, 85–91
  beneficiaries under fixed trust, as to, 84
  conditions precedent, 99–100
  conditions subsequent, 100–103
  discretionary trusts for benevolent purposes, 105–106
  duration of trust, as to, 83–84
  generally, 77
  illustrations, 78–81
  names and arms clauses, 103–104
  statutory validation, 107–110
unincorporated associations, 123–129
want of trustee, 77
***Lassence v Tierney*, rule in**
resulting trusts, and, 372–374
Last surviving trustee, death of
execution of trusts by personal representatives, 742
generally, 742
Latent matters, validity in relation to
ad hoc legislative provisions, 297–298
bankruptcy of settlor
  criminal offences, 291
  dispositions in two to five year period, 290
  generally, 287–289
  persons without notice of relevant circumstances, 291
  statutory provision, 289–290
failure of consideration
  generally, 274–275
  introduction, 273
fraud
  generally, 281
  introduction, 275–276
ignorance or mistake, cancellation for
  generally, 276–277
  introduction, 275–276
  negligence of legal advisers, 280–281

Latent matters, validity in relation to –
  continued
  ignorance or mistake, cancellation for –
    continued
    rectification of marriage settlements,
      279–280
    rectification of pension trusts, 279–280
    rectification of unilateral transaction,
      277–279
    rectification of wills, 280
  incapacity of beneficiaries
    aliens, 273
    introduction, 272
    minors, 273
    persons of unsound mind, 273
    settlors, 273
    trustees, 273
  incapacity of settlors
    corporations, 270–271
    foreigners, 270
    FSMA regulation, and, 271–272
    introduction, 268
    minors, 268–269
    persons of unsound mind, 269–270
  intention to defeat claims for inheritance
      provision
    generally, 297
    introduction, 295–296
  intention to defeat claims of future
      purchasers, 72
  intention to defeat financial relief claims
    generally, 296
    introduction, 295–296
  intention to prejudice creditors
    flexible orders, 293
    generally, 291–292
    insolvency cases, 292
    onus of proof, 293
    other cases, 292
    purpose, 294–295
    without limit of time, 293–294
  introduction, 72
  transactions at an undervalue
    criminal offences, 291
    dispositions in two to five year period, 290
    generally, 287–289
    persons without notice of relevant
      circumstances, 291
    statutory provision, 289–290
  undue influence
    acquiescence by settlor, 285–286
    awareness of trustees, 284–285
    change of status, 286
    generally, 281–282
    independence of advice, 285
    introduction, 275–276
    parents, by, 283–284
    solicitor, by, 283
    third parties, and, 287
    wills, and, 282–283

Latent matters, validity in relation to –
  continued
  unfair preferences
    criminal offences, 291
    dispositions in two to five year period,
      290
    generally, 287–289
    persons without notice of relevant
      circumstances, 291
    statutory provision, 289–290
Leasehold land
  investment of funds, and 607–609
Legacies carrying interest
  maintenance to infants, and, 713–714
Legacies to purchase annuities
  power to extinguish trust, and, 732
Legal choses in action
  transfer of property to trust, and, 152
Legal estate or interest
  definition, 48–50
  estate taken by trustee, and, 454
Legality of object of trust
  attempts to alter prescribed rules of
      devolution
    introduction, 209
    protective trusts, 214
    settlements against bankruptcy law,
      209–214
  consent to marriage requirement, 221
  contrary to public policy, 218–219
  effect of illegal trust on other trusts, 224–
      231
  excessive accumulations of income
    exclusion from rules, 205–208
    introduction, 203–205
    purpose of purchasing land, 208–209
    termination of accumulations, 205
  future illegitimate children, 217–218
  generally, 189–190
  gifts until marriage, 221
  illegal by statute, 223–224
  impossible condition, 230–231
  infringement of Human Rights Act, 219–
      220
  interference with parental duty, 222–223
  introduction, 72
  ousting jurisdiction of courts
    generally, 215–216
    preventing beneficiaries applying to
      courts, 216–217
  promotion of immorality
    future illegitimate children, 217–218
    separation of spouses, 218
  protective trusts, 214
  restraint of marriage
    generally, 220
    second marriages, and, 220–221
    ulterior motive, and, 220
  restraint on alienation, 214–215

Legality of object of trust – *continued*
rule against inalienability
generally, 202–203
introduction, 191–192
rule against remoteness
exceptions, 201–202
illegal trusts, and, 225–228
introduction, 191–192
possible events, 192–194
reform, 202
statutory changes to law, 195–197
trust for sale, 200–201
validity of powers, 198
validity of trusts created under powers of
appointment, 198–200
vesting in interest, 197–198
'wait and see' principle, 195–197
separation of parent and child, 221–222
separation of spouses, 218
settlements against bankruptcy law, 209–214
statutorily illegal trusts, 223–224
testamentary trusts of English movables,
231–232
tying up of property for unlawful period
introduction, 191–192
rule against inalienability, 202–203
rule against remoteness, 192–202
'wait and see' principle, 195–197
Legitimated children
transfer of property to beneficiaries, and,
626
**Lessee purchasing reversion expectant on
lease**
persons in fiduciary position, and, 383–385
Letters of wishes
accounts and records, and, 680–685
sham trusts, and, 61–62
**Liability for debts incurred in running
business**
incidents of trustee's estate, and, 457
Liability for rates and taxes
incidents of trustee's estate, and, 456
Liability of beneficiaries
and see under individual headings
involvement in breach, for
dealing by agents, 952–956
dishonest assistance, 956–967
generally, 950–951
impounding equitable interests in trust,
979–983
intermeddling strangers, 951–952
misapplied trust property, 967–979
Liability of third parties
and see under individual headings
involvement in breach, for
dealing by agents, 952–956
dishonest assistance, 956–967
generally, 950–951

Liability of third parties – *continued*
involvement in breach, for – *continued*
impounding equitable interests in trust,
979–983
intermeddling strangers, 951–952
misapplied trust property, 967–979
property traced into their hands, for
alienations for value, and, 999
change of position, and, 995–997
choses in action, 1001
claiming, 993
cost paid to solicitor, 986
equitable interests, and, 1000–1001
generally, 983–984
jus tertii, and, 998
mortgages under contributory
mortgage, 985–986
negotiable instruments, 1001–1002
non-trust jurisdictions, 998–999
notice, and, 986–993
notice of doubtful equity, 985
overdrawn account, 986
relative rights, 984–985
trust funds mixed with volunteer's own
moneys, 993–994
Liability of trustees for breach of trust
and see under individual headings
criminal proceedings, and
compensation, 912
generally, 907
other offences, 911
theft, 907–911
following, and, 881–882
interim applications to safeguard trust
property
generally, 903
injunctions, 904–906
payments into court, 906
joint and several
contribution between trustees, 878
equal liability of parties to breach, 877
generally, 877
measure of
accounting for profits, 873–875
generally, 851–853
loss to beneficiary only, 875–877
taking of accounts, 853–873
set-off, and, 878–879
tracing claims
conversion of trust property into other
form, 882–884
fiduciary relationship as to property,
894–899
generally, 880–881
identifiable, traceable property, 899–903
introduction, 881–882
mixing of trust property with other
property, 884–891
mixing of trust property with property
of another trust, 891–894

Lien on trust property
continues to bind successor trustees, 820
expenses, 818
express preservation, 820
legal costs where settlement void, 818–819
mixed funds, 819
refusal to transfer property, 819–820
Life assurance policies
transfer of property to trust, and, 152
Life interest, person entitled to
appointment of new trustees, and, 771
Life policies
reasonable care and skill, and, 580
Limitation of actions by beneficiaries
actions for account, 928
excess over proper share, 925
extension of period, 930–931
fair dealing rule, and, 927–928
generally, 920–922
laches, and, 929–930
long-stop period, 928
perpetual liability. 923–925
self dealing rule, and, 927–928
six years period, 925–928
statutory provision, 922
war-time extensions, 929
Loan purpose trusts
language sufficient to create trust, and,
116–117
Loans secured on land
investment of funds, and, 605
Local government charges
capital charges, and, 566–567
Loco parentis, **persons in**
presumption of advancement, and, 366–
367
Long silence
acceptance of trust, and, 452–453
Loss of interest
taking of accounts, and, 867–869
Losses
capital charges, and, 571
Losses on trust business
current expenses, and, 570

Maintenance to infants, powers to allow
class gifts, 716–717
contrary intention, 715
generally, 709–711
gifts carrying intermediate income, 712–
713
legacies carrying interest, 713–714
portions charged on land, 714
residuary gift to infant, 714
statutory provision, 711–712
vested interests converted into contingent
interests, 715–716
Mala fides, nvestigation of
transfer of property to beneficiaries, and,
630–631

Management of block of flats
incidents of trustee's estate, and, 458
Management of land
conduct of sales, 704–705
extent of powers, 703–704
generally, 703
raising capital money, 704
Marriage articles
agreements to create trusts, and, 139–140
executory trusts, and, 67
Marriage, gifts until
legality of objects in trusts, and, 221
Marriage, restraint of
generally, 220
second marriages, and, 220–221
ulterior motive, and, 220
**Marriage settlement, covenants to settle
property in**
after-acquired property, 310–313
binding on wife, 305–306
definite interests in property, 314–315
excluded property, 306–310
property exceeding certain value, 315–317
property to which presently entitled, 310
Marriage settlements
rectification, and, 279–280
resulting trusts, and, 370–371
Masses, saying of
language sufficient to create trust, and,
122–123
Matrimonial relief claims, intention to defeat
generally, 296
introduction, 295–296
**Measure of trustee's liability for breach of
trust**
accounting for profits
election, 874–875
generally, 873–874
accounts, taking of
allowing funds to remain in trustee's
business, 879
'but for' causation test, 855–859
compensatory award, 867
contributory negligence, 865–867
examples, 861–865
generally, 853–854
improper retention of authorised
investment, 872
improper sale of authorised investment,
872–873
loss of interest, 867–869
mixing funds with trustee's own funds,
869
rate of interest, 870–871
replacement without regard to fiscal
liabilities, 859–861
restorative liability, 855
retention of unauthorised investment, 872
use of funds in trustee's own business,
870

Measure of trustee's liability for breach of trust – *continued*
constructive trustee, and, 871
executors of deceased trustee, and, 873
generally, 851–853
loss to beneficiary only, 875–877
Mental health jurisdiction
appointment of new trustees, and, 769
Mentally ill person
appointment of new trustees, and, 755
Mere equities
equitable estate, and, 50
Minor interests
equitable estate, and, 50–51
Minor is trustee or donee of express power
appointment of new trustees, and, 764–765
Minors
acquiescence of beneficiaries, and, 935
appointment of new trustees, and, 755
incapacity of beneficiaries, and, 273
incapacity of settlors, and, 268–269
Misapplied trust property
causal link between breach and receipt, 969–970
change of position, and, 978–979
dealing with receipt to defendant's benefit, 970–973
future developments of law, 975–978
generally, 967
knowledge of breach, 973–975
misapplication of property, 968
property held on trust or duty, 968
receipt of property or proceeds, 968–969
Misleading statements, publication of
dishonest breach of trust, and, 911
Mistake, cancellation for
generally, 276–277
introduction, 275–276
negligence of legal advisers, 280–281
rectification
marriage settlements, of, 279–280
pension trusts, of, 279–280
unilateral transaction, of, 277–279
wills, of, 280
Mixing funds with trustee's own funds
taking of accounts, and, 869
Mixing of trust property with other property
causation, and, 888–890
introduction, 884–891
mixing with trustee's property, 885–887
mortgage-assisted purchase, 891
tracing into property insurance proceeds, 890
Mixing of trust property with property of another trust
generally, 891–89
Money-laundering
generally, 487–490
involvement in breach of trust, and, 966–967

Money-laundering – *continued*
suspicious transaction reports, 490
Monuments, erection and maintenance of
language sufficient to create trust, and, 119–121
Mortgage-assisted purchase
mixing of trust property with other property, and, 891
reasonable care and skill, and, 583–584
Mortgages
investment of funds, and, 606
property traced into hands of third parties, and, 985–986
Mutual wills
agreements to create trusts, and, 140
binding agreement for survivor to carry out agreed arrangement, 428–430
generally, 427–428
property subject to trust, 431–431
secret trusts, and, 432
trust effecting arrangement, 430–431

Names and arms clauses
language sufficient to create trust, and, 103–104
Near relations
appointment of new trustees, and, 772
Neglect of fund investment
reasonable care and skill, and, 586
Neglect of trust securities
reasonable care and skill, and, 585–586
Negligence of legal advisers
mistake or ignorance, and, 280–281
Negotiable instruments
property traced into hands of third parties, and, 1001–1002
New trustees
and see under individual headings
appointment
effect if invalid, 775
express power, under, 752–755
generally, 751–752
mental health jurisdiction, under, 769
new trusts created under limited powers, by, 803–809
order of court, by, 763–769
powers, 770
removal of trustee, and, 750
retirement of trustee, and, 744
selection of trustees, 770–774
statutory power, under, 755–763
selection
aliens, 774
beneficiaries' bankers, 772
corporation sole, 774
donee of power, 771
generally, 770–774
life interest, person entitled to, 771
near relations, 772
persons out of jurisdiction, 772–774

New trustees – *continued*
selection – *continued*
remainderman, 771
solicitor to the trust, 771–772
trust company, 774
vesting of trust property
court made vesting orders, 779–784
generally, 776
implied vesting declarations, 776–779
No donee of power
appointment of new trustees, and, 764
No original trustees
appointment of new trustees, and, 764
Nominees, default of
reasonable care and skill, and, 590
Nominees, holdings by
appointment of custodian, 619–621
exclusions, 621
generally, 619
nature of duty, 621
restrictions, 621
Non-trust jurisdictions
property traced into hands of third
parties, and, 998–999
Notice, doctrine of
actual, 986
constructive, 986–987, 989
imputed, 986–987, 990
Notice of doubtful equity
property traced into hands of third
parties, and, 985
Notice to beneficiaries
accounts and records, and, 673–674
Notices of incumbrances
accounts and records, and, 685
inquiries as to trust property, and, 492–493
transfer of property to beneficiaries, and,
629
Number of trustees
administration of trust, and, 447–448

**Obey directions of settlement, trustee's duty
to**
acting upon expert's advice, 497
actuary's advice, 495–496
approval of court, with
introduction, 522
pre-1926 jurisdiction, 522–525
Settled Land Act 1925, 527
Trustee Act 1925, 525–527
Variation of Trusts Act 1958, 499–522
approval of court under SLA 1925, with
extended powers, 528–529
particular transactions, 527
approval of court under TA 1925, with
extended powers, 528–529
particular transactions, 525–527
approval by court under VTA 1958, with
arrangements for which approval be
given, 508–519

**Obey directions of settlement, trustee's duty
to** – *continued*
approval by court under VTA 1958, with –
continued
effect of approval, 519–520
generally, 499–501
jurisdiction of court, 520–522
persons on whose behalf approval be
given, 501–508
statutory provision, 501
conditions imposed on powers, 496–497
effect of failure to obtain approval, 529
exceptions to duty
generally, 493–494
modification of duty by beneficiaries,
497–499
power of amendment in trust
instrument, 498–499
sanction by court, 499–520
failure to deal with property, 496
generally, 493–494
investment in particular securities, 496
nature of duty, 494–495
payment to beneficiaries, 496
Obligations
trusts, and, 36
Obtaining pecuniary advantage by deception
dishonest breach of trust, and, 911
Obtaining property by deception
dishonest breach of trust, and, 911
**Occupation by interest in possession
beneficiary**
trusts of land, and, 476–478
Occupational pension schemes
investment of funds, and, 600–601
Official audit of trust
trustee's rights, and, 831–832
Options
reasonable care and skill, and, 583
Ouster of financial obligations
constructive trusts, and, 403–404
Ousting jurisdiction of courts
generally, 215–216
preventing beneficiaries applying to
courts, 216–217
reasonable care and skill, and
deliberate breach of duty, 594–595
dishonest breach of duty, 593–594
generally, 590–591
non-excludable duties, 593
particular property, 591–593
statutory prohibitions, 595–596
undue influence, 596–597
Overdrawn accounts
property traced into hands of third
parties, and, 986
Overriding interests
equitable estate, and, 50–51
Ownership-management
nature of a trust, and, 5–7

Parent and child, separation of
legality of objects in trusts, and, 221–222
Parentage
conditions subsequent, and, 102–103
Parental duty, interference with
legality of objects in trusts, and, 222–223
Parental influence
undue influence, and, 283–284
Parol evidence
secret trusts, and, 259–260
Partial interest in special trust, powers as to
aliquot share, 738–739
claim for possession, 739
equitable interests, 738
generally, 737
inalienability of interests, 738
protective trusts, 738
restraint on alienation, 738
Partition by trustees
trusts of land, and, 472–473
Patents
transfer of property to trust, and, 152
Pay named persons, direction to
illusory trusts, and, 142–143
Payment from taxed income
indemnity for trustees, and, 818
Payment of fund into court
safeguarding trust property, and, 906
suspension of trustee's powers, and, 728
trustee's rights, and, 829–830
Payment of outgoings
audit of trust accounts, and, 574–575
capital charges
arrears of interest, 567–568
calls on shares, 568
generally, 565
local government charges, 566–567
losses, 571
purchase of annuities, 566
current expenses
annual charges, 568
insurance premiums, 568–570
losses on trust business, 570
redemption of rentcharge, 570
discretion, 564–565
generally, 563–564
incidental costs of administration, 574–
575
repairs
alterations, 573
fencing of unfenced land, 573–574
generally, 571–573
statutory discretion, 564–565
Pension funds
commercial purpose trusts, and, 46–47
Pension schemes trustees
reasonable care and skill, and, 577–578
Pension trusts
rectification, and, 279–280

Perpetuities
and see REMOTENESS, RULE AGAINST
generally, 191–182
Person of unsound mind
incapacity of beneficiaries, and, 273
incapacity of settlors, and, 269–270
Personal accountability
resulting trusts, and, 323–324
Personal obligations
trusts, and, 34–36
Personal powers
fiduciary powers, and, 29–34, 90, 97
Personam, **rights in**
equitable estate, and, 51–53
Persons in *loco parentis*
presumption of advancement, and, 366–
367
Persons out of jurisdiction
appointment of new trustees, and, 772–
774
Planning rights
incidents of trustee's estate, and, 457
Portions charged on land
maintenance to infants, and, 714
Possible future beneficiaries
power to extinguish trust, and, 735
Power of attorney
transfer of property to beneficiaries, and,
628
Power to compromise
claims, 707–708
Powers
trusts, and, 25–28
Powers in the nature of trusts
apparent intention to benefit, 131–132
gifts over in default of appointment, 130–
131
introduction, 130
release of powers, 132–133
Powers of appointment
certainty, 85
general, 200, 804
re-settlement, 804–808
special, 205
sub-settlement, 804–808
Precatory words
authorities for modern rule, 134
codicil, in, 136
contrasting modern and former rules,
133–134
illustrations of modern rule, 135–136
introduction, 133
Preferences
criminal offences, 291
dispositions in two to five year period, 290
generally, 287–289
persons without notice of relevant
circumstances, 291
statutory provision, 289–290

Prejudice creditors, intention to
flexible orders, 293
generally, 291–292
insolvency cases, 292
onus of proof, 293
other cases, 292
purpose, 294–295
without limit of time, 293–294
Present irrevocable declaration
declaration of trust, and, 149
Presumption of advancement
augmentation of settled property, 364
generally, 361–362
mother and child, 364–365
persons in loco parentis, 366–367
rebuttal, 362
surrounding circumstances, 362–364
wife's money invested in name of
husband, 365–366
Principles of European Trust Law
nature of a trust, and, 7
Prior consent to undertake trust
disclaimer of trust, and, 449
Private companies, controlling interests in
accounts and records, and, 686
reasonable care and skill, and, 586–588
Privilege against self-incrimination
accounts and records, and, 685
Probate, taking out
acceptance of trust, and, 451–452
Profession or office
conditions subsequent, and, 102
Profit on investment realisation
augmentation of capital, and, 540
Profit on reconstruction of company
augmentation of capital, and, 542
Profiting in trust property
constructive trusts of profits, 660–661
fair-dealing rule, 670–671
generally, 659–660
self-dealing rule
beneficiaries' remedies, 670
exceptional circumstances, 662–669
generally, 661–662
Profits
agents, by, 393–398
partners, by, 398
tippees, by, 398–399
trustee from property or position, by, 386–
388
trustee's parent company, by, 388
Promotion of immorality
future illegitimate children, 217–218
separation of spouses, 218
Proof in bankruptcy
incidents of trustee's estate, and, 456
reasonable care and skill, and, 580
Proper advice
investment of funds, and, 604–605

Properly informed decisions, make
trustee's powers, and, 694–699
Property capable of being subject of trust
choses in action, 183
effect of bankruptcy, 185–186
equitable interests, 183
expectancies, 184–185
foreign immovables, 187–189
future property, 184–185
generally, 182–183
introduction, 72
property inalienable by reason of public
policy, 186
property inalienable by statute, 187
reversionary interests, 184
Property insurance proceeds
mixing of trust property with other
property, and, 890
Property pending conversion
entitlement to income, 553–563
generally, 552–553
Property traced into hands of third parties
alienations for value, and, 999
change of position, and, 995–997
choses in action, 1001
claiming, 993
cost paid to solicitor, 986
equitable interests, and, 1000–1001
generally, 983–984
jus tertii, and, 998
mortgages under contributory mortgage,
985–986
negotiable instruments, 1001–1002
non-trust jurisdictions, 998–999
notice, and, 986–993
notice of doubtful equity, 985
overdrawn account, 986
relative rights, 984–985
trust funds mixed with volunteer's own
moneys, 993–994
Proprietary and personal liability
persons in fiduciary position, and, 381
Prospective *Beddoe* application
indemnity for trustees, and, 816
**Protection of trustees in case of breach of
trust**
acquiescence of beneficiaries
bar, as, 934–935
claimant party to breach, 932
generally, 931–932
knowledge, and, 935–936
minors, and, 935
over period, 933–934
reversioner, by, 934
acted reasonably and honestly, where
generally, 913
discretion of court, 919–920
profit for trustees, 920
reasonable conduct, 918–919
reasonableness, 914–917

Protection of trustees in case of breach of trust – *continued*
acted reasonably and honestly, where – *continued*
  unreasonable conduct, 917–918
concurrence of beneficiaries
  claimant party to breach, 932
  generally, 931–932
co-trustee's acts, against, 938–940
indemnity by instigator of breach
  commission at instigation or request of beneficiaries, 947–949
  contribution between trustees, 941–944
  generally, 940–941
  less guilty co-trustees, 945–947
  new appointees, and, 947
  trustee-beneficiaries, and, 944–945
limitation of actions by beneficiaries
  actions for account, 928
  excess over proper share, 925
  extension of period, 930–931
  fair dealing rule, and, 927–928
  generally, 920–922
  laches, and, 929–930
  long-stop period, 928
  perpetual liability. 923–925
  self dealing rule, and, 927–928
  six years period, 925–928
  statutory provision, 922
  war-time extensions, 929
release of beneficiaries
  claimant party to breach, 932
  generally, 931–932
  inferred from breach, 933
  knowledge, and, 935–936
  minors, and, 935
  recently-attained majority, 937
  recitation of breach in deed, 936–937
waiver by beneficiaries, 931–932
Protective trusts
legality of objects in trusts, and, 214
partial interest in special trust, and, 738
Protectors
trusts, and, 29–34
Public obligation
trusts, and, 7
Public policy, contrary to
legality of objects in trusts, and, 218–219
Public Trustee
appointment
  court, by, 795
  generally, 794
  will or codicil, by, 794–795
charitable trusts, 791
custodian trustee, as
  advantages, 797
  corporate bodies, 797–799
  duties, rights and liabilities, 799–800
  generally, 796
  profits from trusts, 799

Public Trustee – *continued*
establishment, 791
fees, 792–793
generally, 789–791
judicial trustee, as, 789
religious purpose trusts, 791
remuneration, 658
sole trustee, as, 795
special rules, 801—802
state guarantee, 792
Publication of false, etc, statements
dishonest breach of trust, and, 911
Purchase made in another's name, trusts where
advancement, presumption of
  augmentation of settled property, 364
  generally, 361–362
  mother and child, 364–365
  persons in loco parentis, 366–367
  rebuttal, 362
  surrounding circumstances, 362–364
  wife's money invested in name of husband, 365–366
contrast with constructive trusts, 353–355
declaration of trust, 353
equitable accounting, 355–357
evidence of intention to benefit, 358
generally, 349–350
joint bank accounts, 359–361
loans, 357–358
purchase money contributed by two persons, 350–353
purchase money provided by one person, 353
Purchase of annuities
capital charges, and, 566
Purchaser, protection of
trusts of land, and, 483
Purchaser's undertaking
contractual licences, and, 327–328
Purpose trusts
language sufficient to create trust, and, 111–114

Quistclose **trusts**
charges, and, 12–14
resulting trusts, and, 342

Raising capital money
management of land, and, 704
Rates, liability for
incidents of trustee's estate, and, 456
Realisation of debts
reasonable care and skill, and, 578–579
Realisation of unauthorised investments
reasonable care and skill, and, 579
Reasonable care and skill
arrears of rent, 579
collective investment scheme trustees, and, 577–578

Reasonable care and skill – *continued*
controlling interests in private companies, 586–588
default of agents, nominees or custodians, 590
depreciatory conditions of sale, 581
errors of judgment, 584–585
'gazumping', 582
generally, 575–576
grant of leases, 583
improvident lettings, 583
improvident purchases, 583
improvident sales, 581
insurance against risks, 588–589
inventory of chattels, 586
life policies, 580
mortgage-assisted purchases, 583–584
neglect of fund investment, 586
neglect of trust securities, 585–586
options, 583
ousting jurisdiction of court
deliberate breach of duty, 594–595
dishonest breach of duty, 593–594
generally, 590–591
non-excludable duties, 593
particular property, 591–593
statutory prohibitions, 595–596
undue influence, 596–597
pension schemes trustees, and, 577–578
proof in bankruptcy, 580
realisation of debts, 578–579
realisation of unauthorised investments, 579
relevant time for judging conduct, 590
renewal of tenancies, 581–582
repair liability, 589
retired trustee, liability of, 589–590
sale of contiguous properties, 580–581
theft of trust property, 585
Trustee Act 2000, under, 576–590
Reasonableness and honesty of trustee
discretion of court, 919–920
generally, 913
profit for trustees, 920
reasonable conduct, 918–919
reasonableness, 914–917
unreasonable conduct, 917–918
limitation of actions by beneficiaries
Receipts by insolvent agents
prevention of fraudulent conduct, and, 437
Receipts, powers to give
generally, 705–706
Recognition of trusts
following trust assets, 1054–1055
requirements, 1053–1054
right to refuse, 1055–1056
tracing trust assets, 1054–1055
Recognition of Trusts Act 1987
generally, 1010–1011

Redemption of rentcharge
current expenses, and, 570
Refusal of trustee to act
appointment of new trustees, and, 761
Registered land, estate in
transfer of property to trust, and, 150–151
Registration of trusts
conflict of laws, and, 1056
Reimbursement for expenses, indemnity for
basis of taxed costs in litigation, 815
beneficiary, from
club trustees, and, 823
generally, 821–822
limits, 822–823
calls on shares, 813
carrying on business, 814
damages recovered by third parties, 813
direct claims on estate, 825–826
disallowance of unreasonable expenses, 817
generally, 810–811
holding title to trust property, 813–814
insolvent trustee, 826
interest, 818
lien, and
continues to bind successor trustees, 820
expenses, 818
express preservation, 820
legal costs where settlement void, 818–819
mixed funds, 819
refusal to transfer property, 819–820
nature, 812–813
new trustees, from, 820–821
payment from taxed income, 818
prospective *Beddoe* application, 816
reimbursement of costs incurred, 815
reliance on counsel's advice, 816–817
set-off, and, 823–824
solicitors' costs, 814
subrogation claims, and, 824–825
third party litigation expenses, 815
unnecessary costs, 817–818
voluntary subscriptions, 817
Reimbursement of costs incurred
indemnity for trustees, and, 815
Release by deed
trustee's rights, and, 827
Release of beneficiaries
claimant party to breach, 932
generally, 931–932
inferred from breach, 933
knowledge, and, 935–936
minors, and, 935
recently-attained majority, 937
recitation of breach in deed, 936–937
Release of powers
language sufficient to create trust, and, 132–133

Reliance on counsel's advice
indemnity for trustees, and, 816–817
transfer of property to beneficiaries, and, 626–627

Religion
conditions subsequent, and, 102–103

Religious purpose trusts
Public Trustee, and , 791

Rem, **rights in**
equitable estate, and, 51–53

Remainder, gifts in
resulting trusts, and, 375–376

Remainderman
appointment of new trustees, and, 771

Remedial trusts of property
constructive trusts, and, 324–327

Remoteness, rule against
exceptions, 201–202
illegal trusts, and, 225–228
introduction, 191–192
possible events, 192–194
reform, 202
resulting trusts, and, 376
statutory changes to law, 195–197
trust for sale, 200–201
validity of powers, 198
validity of trusts created under powers of appointment, 198–200
vesting in interest, 197–198
'wait and see' principle, 195–197

Removal of trustee
appointment of new trustee, on, 750
directions of beneficiaries, 749–750
generally, 743–744
illustration, 747
mental disorder, by reason of, 750
order of court, by, 750
qualifying requirements, 748–749

Remuneration of trustees
agreement of beneficiaries, 658–659
authorisation by settlement, 652–653
basis of rule, 651
custodian trustees, 658
generally, 651
order of court, 655–658
Public Trustee, 658
rule in *Cradock v Piper*, 653
statutory authorisation, 653–655

Renewal of lease by partial owner
persons in fiduciary position, and, 385

Renewal of tenancies
reasonable care and skill, and, 581–582

Rentcharge, redemption of
current expenses, and, 570

Renvoi
conflict of laws, and, 1037

Repair liability
reasonable care and skill, and, 589

Repairs
alterations, 573

Repairs – *continued*
fencing of unfenced land, 573–574
generally, 571–573

Replacement without regard to fiscal liabilities
taking of accounts, and, 859–861

Rescission of voidable transfers
prevention of fraudulent conduct, and, 435–436

Reservation of title clauses
trusts, and, 14–16

Residence
conditions subsequent, and, 101–102

Residence of trustee abroad
appointment of new trustees, and, 759

Residuary gift to infant
maintenance to infants, and, 714

Restorative liability
taking of accounts, and, 855

Restraint of marriage
generally, 220
second marriages, and, 220–221
ulterior motive, and, 220

Restraint on alienation
legality of objects in trusts, and, 214–215
partial interest in special trust, and, 738

Resulting trusts
analysis, 321–322
beneficiary of
accrued shares, 375
conversion directed, 371–372
divesting gifts, 375–376
generally, 369–370
gift to class or to survivors, 374–375
historical background, 370
Lassence v Tierney, rule in, 372–374
marriage settlements, 370–371
no conversion directed, 371
remainder, gifts in, 375–376
surplus moneys, 370
Crown, rights of, 377–378
definition, 54–55
equitable interests not wholly disposed of, where
admissibility of evidence, 342–343
bankruptcy following voluntary arrangement, 340–341
bona vacantia, 337–338
broad propositions, 330–332
contributions to charitable funds, 341–342
disposition to trustees, 332
dissolution of clubs, 338–240
donee intended to take beneficially, 334–336
failure of express trust, 332–333
failure of life interest, 333–334
generally, 329–330
Quistclose trusts, 342

Resulting trusts – *continued*
  equitable interests not wholly disposed of,
      where – *continued*
    residue after satisfaction of express
        trust, 334
    uncertainty of express trust, 332–333
    voluntary contributions to assist
        distressed individuals, 336
  failure of trusts, on
    admissibility of evidence, 342–343
    bankruptcy following voluntary
        arrangement, 340–341
    bona vacantia, 337–338
    broad propositions, 330–332
    contributions to charitable funds, 341–
        342
    disposition to trustees, 332
    dissolution of clubs, 338–240
    donee intended to take beneficially,
        334–336
    failure of express trust, 332–333
    failure of life interest, 333–334
    generally, 329–330
    Quistclose trusts, 342
    residue after satisfaction of express
        trust, 334
    uncertainty of express trust, 332–333
    voluntary contributions to assist
        distressed individuals, 336
  generally, 322–323
  gifts of property, and, 367–368
  illegal express trusts, arising from
    claims through transferor, 348–349
    conveyance to qualify for game licence,
        344
    fraudulent conveyance, 345–346
    generally, 343–344
    presumption of advancement, 347–348
    reliance after carrying out illegal
        purpose, 348
    settlement for illegal consideration,
        344–345
    spouses' fraudulent designs, 346–347
  personal accountability, 323–324
  presumption of advancement, and
    augmentation of settled property, 364
    generally, 361–362
    mother and child, 364–365
    persons in loco parentis, 366–367
    rebuttal, 362
    surrounding circumstances, 362–364
    wife's money invested in name of
        husband, 365–366
  purchase made in another's name, where
    advancement, presumption of, 361–366
    contrast with constructive trusts, 353–
        355
    declaration of trust, 353
    equitable accounting, 355–357
    evidence of intention to benefit, 358

Resulting trusts – *continued*
  purchase made in another's name, where
      – *continued*
    generally, 349–350
    joint bank accounts, 359–361
    loans, 357–358
    purchase money contributed by two
        persons, 350–353
    purchase money provided by one
        person, 353
    remoteness, and, 376
    rule against accumulations, and, 349
    rule against perpetuities, and, 349
    voluntary transfers of property, and
      generally, 350
      gifts of property, 367–368
    way in which property held, 376–377
Retention of unauthorised investment
  taking of accounts, and, 872
Retired trustee, liability of
  reasonable care and skill, and, 589–590
Retirement of trustee
  appointment of new trustee, on, 744
  consent of beneficiaries, by, 746–747
  discharge, and, 744–746
  generally, 743–744
  order of court, by, 747
  release from liability, and, 747
  statutory power, under, 746
Reversionary interests
  property capable of being subject of trust,
      and, 184
  trustee's powers, and, 706–707
Reversioner
  acquiescence of beneficiaries, and, 934
Review of discretions
  trustee's powers, and, 689–690
Right to manage (RTM)
  incidents of trustee's estate, and, 458
Rights *in rem* **and** *in personam*
  equitable estate, and, 51–53
Rule against accumulations
  resulting trusts, and, 349
Rule against inalienability
  generally, 202–203
  introduction, 191–192
Rule against perpetuities
  powers of advancement, and, 724
  resulting trusts, and, 349
Rule against remoteness
  exceptions, 201–202
  illegal trusts, and, 225–228
  introduction, 191–192
  possible events, 192–194
  reform, 202
  statutory changes to law, 195–197
  trust for sale, 200–201
  validity of powers, 198
  validity of trusts created under powers of
      appointment, 198–200

Rule against remoteness – *continued*
vesting in interest, 197–198
'wait and see' principle, 195–197
Rule in *Cradock v Piper*
remuneration of trustees, and, 653
Rule in *Howe v Lord Dartmouth*
expressed contrary intention, and, 550–551
generally, 548–549
impact of Trustee Act 2000, 549–550
impliedly negatived intention, and, 551–552
implied trust for sale, and, 550
Rule in *Strong v Bird*
erroneous perfection of gift by administrators, 161
forgiveness of debts, 159–161
generally, 157–159
intent to make immediate gift, 161–163
lifetime acquisition of legal title, 163–164
mistaken perfection of gift by executors, 164

Sale of contiguous properties
reasonable care and skill, and, 580–581
Sale of improper property
generally, 548
rule in *Howe v Lord Dartmouth*, 548–552
Saying of masses
language sufficient to create trust, and, 122–123
Second marriages
legality of objects in trusts, and, 220–221
Secret trusts
beneficiary predeceasing testator, 263–264
floating trusts, 266–267
fully secret trusts, 260–261
gifts to several intended trustees without communication, 262–263
half-secret trusts, 261–262
introduction, 258–259
mutual wills, and, 432
operation independent of will, 264–266
parol evidence, and, 259–260
prevention of fraudulent conduct, and, 433
Securities in company
investment of funds, and, 606–607
Selection of new trustees
aliens, 774
beneficiaries' bankers, 772
corporation sole, 774
donee of power, 771
generally, 770–774
life interest, person entitled to, 771
near relations, 772
persons out of jurisdiction, 772–774
remainderman, 771
solicitor to the trust, 771–772
trust company, 774

Self-dealing rule
beneficiaries' remedies, 670
exceptional circumstances, 662–669
generally, 661–662
limitation of actions by beneficiaries, and, 927–928
Self-incrimination, privilege against
accounts and records, and, 685
Self interest
acceptance of trust property, and, 485–486
Separate trust property
language sufficient to create trust, and, 76–77
Separation of parent and child
legality of objects in trusts, and, 221–222
Separation of spouses
legality of objects in trusts, and, 218
Set-off
indemnity for trustees, and, 823–824
trustee's liability for breach of trust, and, 878–879
Settle property in marriage settlement, covenants to
after-acquired property, 310–313
binding on wife, 305–306
definite interests in property, 314–315
excluded property, 306–310
property exceeding certain value, 315–317
property to which presently entitled, 310
Settled Land Act settlements
investment of funds, and, 610–611
trusts of land, and, 463–465
Settlements against bankruptcy law
legality of objects in trusts, and, 209–214
Settlor
beneficiary, as, 273
definition, 4
Settlors, bankruptcy of
criminal offences, 291
dispositions in two to five year period, 290
generally, 287–289
persons without notice of relevant circumstances, 291
statutory provision, 289–290
Settlors, incapacity of
corporations, 270–271
foreigners, 270
FSMA regulation, and, 271–272
introduction, 268
minors, 268–269
persons of unsound mind, 269–270
Severance of trusts
appointment of new trustees, and, 762
Sham trusts
available assets of settlor, and, 62–63
generally, 59–61
letters of wishes, 61–62
Shares, calls on
capital charges, and, 568
indemnity for trustees, and, 813

Shares in companies
transfer of property to trust, and, 151
Simple trusts
definition, 57
example, 58
Societies, dissolution of
resulting trusts, and, 338–240
Sole trustee
Public Trustee, and, 795
Sole trustee, death of
execution of trusts by personal
representatives, 742
generally, 742
Solicitor to the trust
appointment of new trustees, and, 771–
772
Solicitors
undue influence, and, 283
Solicitors' costs
indemnity for trustees, and, 814
Solicitors' master insurance policy
trusts, and, 7
Special trusts
definition, 58
example, 58–59
sham trusts, and, 59–63
Specific questions, directions of court as to
case management, 838–839
commencement of proceedings, 836–837
costs
appeal, on, 842–843
Beddoe applications, 845
court's jurisdiction, 840
established principles, 840–841
hostile litigation, 841
nature of disputes, 841–842
prospective orders, 843–844
rule of court, 840
evidence, 837–838
generally, 832–835
hearings, 838–839
jurisdiction of court, 835–836
parties, 836
**Specifically enforceable contract, trusts
under**
doctrine of conversion, 439–441
generally, 438
purchaser's position, 442–444
vendor's trusteeship, 441–442
State guarantee
Public Trustee, and, 792
**State officials for distribution, funds
confined to**
illusory trusts, and, 143
Statute not to be used as instrument of fraud
inter vivos trusts, 254–256
introduction, 254
secret trusts
beneficiary predeceasing testator, 263–
264

Statute not to be used as instrument of fraud
– *continued*
secret trusts – *continued*
floating trusts, 266–267
fully secret trusts, 260–261
gifts to several intended trustees without
communication, 262–263
half-secret trusts, 261–262
introduction, 258–259
operation independent of will, 264–266
parol evidence, and, 259–260
testamentary trusts, 257
Statutory validation
language sufficient to create trust, and,
107–110
Stock bought with money
conversion of trust property into other
form, and, 882–883
Stocks 'cum dividend'
augmentation of capital, and, 540–542
Strangers
adverse possession, and, 459–460
involvement in breach of trust, and, 951–
952
Strangers to trust, trusts for products owned by
generally, 406–407
priorities, 407–408
Strong v Bird, **rule in**
erroneous perfection of gift by
administrators, 161
forgiveness of debts, 159–161
generally, 157–159
intent to make immediate gift, 161–163
lifetime acquisition of legal title, 163–164
mistaken perfection of gift by executors, 164
Subrogation claims
indemnity for trustees, and, 824–825
unjust enrichment, 977
Suppression of documents
dishonest breach of trust, and, 911
Surplus moneys
resulting trusts, and, 370
Surviving trustee, death of
execution of trusts by personal
representatives, 742
generally, 742
Suspended trusts
language sufficient to create trust, and,
81–82
Suspension of trustee's powers
after judgment, 726–727
before judgment, 727
generally, 726
payment of fund into court, after, 728
Suspicious transaction reports
money-laundering, and, 490

Taking of accounts
allowing funds to remain in trustee's
business, 879

Taking of accounts – *continued*
'but for' causation test, 855–859
compensatory award, 867
contributory negligence, 865–867
examples, 861–865
falsification, 11, 38, 851, 853, 857
generally, 853–854
improper retention of authorised
investment, 872
improper sale of authorised investment,
872–873
loss of interest, 867–869
mixing funds with trustee's own funds, 869
rate of interest, 870–871
replacement without regard to fiscal
liabilities, 859–861
restorative liability, 855
retention of unauthorised investment, 872
surcharge, 11, 38, 852, 853, 857
use of funds in trustee's own business, 870
Taking out probate
acceptance of trust, and, 451–452
Tax considerations
powers of advancement, and, 726
Tax treatment
discretionary trusts, and, 64
executed trusts, and, 66–67
executory trusts, and, 66–67
fixed trusts, and, 64
Taxed costs in litigation
indemnity for trustees, and, 815
Taxed income, payment from
indemnity for trustees, and, 818
Taxes, liability for rates
incidents of trustee's estate, and, 456
Technical language unnecessary
administration of trust, workability of
generally, 91–93
initial unworkability, 98–99
powers, 93–98
supervening unworkability, 98–99
analysis, 71–72
animals, maintenance of, 122
application of property, 82–83
beneficiaries, uncertainty as to
discretionary trusts, under, 85–91
fixed trust, under, 84
generally, 82–83
beneficiary principle
drafting points, 117–118
enforcer clause, and, 114–116
introduction, 110–111
loan purpose trusts, and, 116–117
purpose trusts, and, 111–114
conditions precedent, 99–100
conditions subsequent
generally, 100–101
parentage, as to, 102–103
profession or office, as to, 102
religion, as to, 102–103

Technical language unnecessary – *continued*
conditions subsequent – *continued*
residence, as to, 101–102
discretionary trusts for benevolent
purposes, 105–106
duration of trust, as to, 83–84
enforcer principle, 114–116
equitable charges, and, 77
erection of monuments and graves, 119–
121
exceptional cases
erection and maintenance of
monuments and graves, 119–121
introduction, 118–119
maintenance of animals, 122
management of inanimate objects, 123
saying of masses, 122–123
unincorporated associations, 123–129
express declaration, 75–76
floating trusts, 81–82
graves, erection and maintenance of, 119–
121
inanimate objects, management of, 123
intent to create trust, 75
loan purpose trusts, and, 116–117
masses, saying of, 122–123
monuments, erection and maintenance
of, 119–121
names and arms clauses, 103–104
purpose trusts, and, 111–114
saying of masses, 122–123
separate trust property, 76–77
statutory validation, 107–110
suspended trusts, 81–82
uncertainty as to objects
administration of trusts, as to, 91–99
application of property, as to, 82–83
beneficiaries, as to, 82–83
beneficiaries under discretionary trusts,
as to, 85–91
beneficiaries under fixed trust, as to, 84
conditions precedent, 99–100
conditions subsequent, 100–103
discretionary trusts for benevolent
purposes, 105–106
duration of trust, as to, 83–84
generally, 77
illustrations, 78–81
names and arms clauses, 103–104
statutory validation, 107–110
unincorporated associations, 123–129
want of trustee, 77
Tenants for life
leaseholds renewing to himself, of, 383
mortgaged property purchasing
mortgagee's interest, of, 385
receiving money for settled land, 386
Testamentary trusts
formal requirements, and, 247–248
legality of objects in trusts, and, 231–232

1102   *Index*

Testamentary trusts – *continued*
  statute not to be used as instrument of
    fraud, and, 257
Theft of trust property
  actus reus, 907–910
  generally, 907
  mens rea, 910–911
  reasonable care and skill, and, 585
Third party litigation expenses
  indemnity for trustees, and, 815
Third party rights
  enforceability of trust, and 168–169
  undue influence, and, 287
Threats against beneficiary's interest
  discretionary distributive powers, and, 532
Total failure of consideration
  generally, 274–275
  introduction, 273
Traceable products, trusts of
  fiduciary position, owned by persons in
    additions to trust property, 385–386
    commercial transactions, 400–401
    directors obtaining profits, 390–393
    employee inventions, 399–400
    executors de son tort, 382
    generally, 379
    lessee purchasing reversion expectant
      on lease, 383–385
    profits by agents, 393–398
    profits by partners, 398
    profits by tippees, 398–399
    profits by trustee from property or
      position, 386–388
    profits by trustee's parent company, 388
    proprietary and personal liability, 381
    renewal of lease by partial owner, 385
    tenant for life of leaseholds renewing to
      himself, 383
    tenant for life of mortgaged property
      purchasing mortgagee's interest, 385
    tenant for life receiving money for
      settled land, 386
    tracing, 379–381
    trustees de son tort, 381–382
    trustees obtaining commission, 389–390
    trustees obtaining directorship fees,
      388–389
    trustees taking renewal of lease himself,
      382–382
  strangers to trust, owned by
    generally, 406–407
    priorities, 407–408
Tracing
  conversion of trust property into other
    form
    money produced by chattels, 883
    money produced by misuse of position,
      883
    sale of wrongfully acquired property,
      883–884

Tracing – *continued*
  conversion of trust property into other
    form – *continued*
    stock bought with money, 882–883
    wrongful sale by vendor, 883
  fiduciary relationship as to property, 894–
    899
  generally, 880–881
  hands of third parties, into
    alienations for value, and, 999
    change of position, and, 995–997
    choses in action, 1001
    claiming, 993
    cost paid to solicitor, 986
    equitable interests, and, 1000–1001
    generally, 983–984
    jus tertii, and, 998
    mortgages under contributory
      mortgage, 985–986
    negotiable instruments, 1001–1002
    non-trust jurisdictions, 998–999
    notice, and, 986–993
    notice of doubtful equity, 985
    overdrawn account, 986
    relative rights, 984–985
    trust funds mixed with volunteer's own
      moneys, 993–994
  identifiable, traceable property
    bank accounts, 900–901
    debts paid, 901–903
    generally, 899–900
  introduction, 881–882
  mixing of trust property with other
    property
    causation, and, 888–890
    introduction, 884–891
    mixing with trustee's property, 885–887
    mortgage-assisted purchase, 891
    tracing into property insurance
      proceeds, 890
  mixing of trust property with property of
    another trust, 891–894
  persons in fiduciary position, and, 379–381
  procedure, 897–899
  rules, 895–897
Trading trusts
  commercial purpose trusts, and, 44–45
Trafficking in trust property
  constructive trusts of profits, 660–661
  fair-dealing rule, 670–671
  generally, 659–660
  self-dealing rule
    beneficiaries' remedies, 670
    exceptional circumstances, 662–669
    generally, 661–662
Transactions at an undervalue
  criminal offences, 291
  dispositions in two to five year period, 290
  generally, 287–289

Transactions at an undervalue – *continued*
  persons without notice of relevant
    circumstances, 291
  statutory provision, 289–290
Transfer of property
  generally, 149–154
  introduction, 144
**Transfer property to beneficiaries, etc., duty
  to**
  derivative title, 628–630
  generally, 623–628
  investigation of title, 630–631
Transfer to absolutely entitled beneficiary
  trusts of land, and, 473–474
Trust
  administration of deceased's estate, and,
    17–20
  agency, and, 7–9
  bailment, and, 16–17
  charges, and, 34–36
  charges on goods supplied on credit
    introduction, 12
    Quistclose trusts, 12–14
    reservation of title clauses, 14–16
    Twinsectra trusts, 12–14
  commercial purposes, for
    asset segregation, 42–44
    collective investment schemes, 45–46
    conclusion, 48
    employee trusts, 47
    generally, 39
    miscellaneous uses, 47–48
    pension funds, 46–47
    security, 39–42
    trading trusts, 44–45
    unit trusts, 45–46
  conditional gifts, and, 34–36
  contract, and, 9–11
  definition, 3–7
  fiduciary relationship, and
    debt, 25
    generally, 20–24
    personal powers, 29–34
  governmental obligation, and, 7
  personal obligations, and, 34–36
  personal powers, and, 29–34
  powers, and, 25–28
  protectors, and, 29–34
  public obligation, and, 7
  reservation of title clauses, and, 14–16
  summary, 36–38
Trust company
  appointment of new trustees, and, 774
Trust securities, neglect of
  reasonable care and skill, and, 585–586
Trustee
  definition, 3
Trustees
  death
    co-trustee, 741–742

Trustees – *continued*
  death – *continued*
    generally, 740–741
    sole trustee, 742–743
    surviving trustee, 742–743
  fiduciary position, and
    obtaining commission, 389–390
    obtaining directorship fees, 388–389
    taking renewal of lease himself, 382–382
  incapacity of beneficiaries, and, 273
  removal
    appointment of new trustee, on, 750
    directions of beneficiaries, 749–750
    generally, 743–744
    illustration, 747
    mental disorder, by reason of, 750
    order of court, by, 750
    qualifying requirements, 748–749
  retirement
    appointment of new trustee, on, 744
    consent of beneficiaries, by, 746–747
    discharge, and, 744–746
    generally, 743–744
    order of court, by, 747
    release from liability, and, 747
    statutory power, under, 746
Trustees *de son tort*
  involvement in breach of trust, and, 951–
    952
  persons in fiduciary position, and, 381–
    382
Trustees for sale of land
  appointment, 77
Trustee's action at common law
  enforceability of trust, and, 179–182
Trustee's duties
  and see under individual headings
  acceptance of (additional) trust property,
    as to
    conflict between fiduciary duty and self-
      interest, 485–486
    generally, 485
    money-laundering, 487–490
    onerous responsibilities, 486
    vitiation of transfer to trustees, 486–487
    worthless responsibilities, 486
  accounts and records, as to
    accountability to beneficiaries, 672–673
    confidentiality of deliberations, 680
    costs of action, 677–678
    disclosure under CPR, 678–679
    expensive information, 687
    generally, 671–672
    inaccurate accounts, 678
    inspection of documents, 677
    investment information, 678
    letters of wishes, 680–685
    modification of duties and rights, 675–
      677
    notice to beneficiaries, 673–674

Trustee's duties – *continued*
    accounts and records, as to – *continued*
        notices of incumbrances, 685
        other trust documents, 678–679
        private companies, as to, 686
        privilege against self-incrimination, 685
    act jointly, to, 644–648
    acting upon expert's advice, and, 497
    acting without remuneration, and
        basis of rule, 652
        exceptions, 653–659
        generally, 652
    actuary's advice, and, 495–496
    control of trust property, as to, 493
    delegation, as to
        background to rule, 634
        beneficiary, to, 641–642
        exceptions to rule, 635–641
        generally, 631–634
        statutory rule, 634–635
        temporary period, for, 642–644
    impartiality between beneficiaries, of
        appropriation, 542–546
        augmentation of capital, 535–542
        exercise of powers, 530–535
        generally, 529–530
        hotchpot provision, 546–548
    inquiries as to trust property, as to
        acts of predecessors, 491–492
        generally, 490–491
        losses, 492
        notices of incumbrances, 492–493
    investment of funds, as to
        generally, 597–599
        nature of duty, 613–618
    jus tertii, and, 648–650
    money-laundering, and
        generally, 487–490
        suspicious transaction reports, 490
    obey directions of settlement, to
        acting upon expert's advice, 497
        actuary's advice, 495–496
        conditions imposed on powers,
            496–497
        exceptions to duty, 497–522
        failure to deal with property, 496
        generally, 493–494
        investment in particular securities, 496
        nature of duty, 494–495
        payment to beneficiaries, 496
    payment of outgoings, as to
        capital charges, 565–568
        current expenses, 568–571
        generally, 563–564
        incidental costs of administration, 574–
            575
        repairs, 571–574
        statutory discretion, 564–565
    profiting from trust property, and
        constructive trusts of profits, 660–661

Trustee's duties – *continued*
    profiting from trust property, and –
        continued
        fair-dealing rule, 670–671
        generally, 659–660
        self-dealing rule, 661–670
    property pending conversion, as to
        entitlement to income, 553–563
        generally, 552–553
    reasonable care and skill, of
        generally, 575–576
        ousting jurisdiction of court, 590–597
        relevant time for judging conduct,
            590
        Trustee Act 2000, under, 576–590
    sale of improper property, as to
        generally, 548
        rule in *Howe v Lord Dartmouth*, 548–552
    trafficking in trust property, and
        constructive trusts of profits, 660–661
        fair-dealing rule, 670–671
        generally, 659–660
        self-dealing rule, 661–670
    transfer of property to beneficiaries, etc.,
        as to
        derivative title, 628–630
        generally, 623–628
        investigation of title, 630–631

Trustee's liability for breach of trust
    and see under individual headings
    criminal proceedings, and
        compensation, 912
        generally, 907
        other offences, 911
        theft, 907–911
    following, and, 881–882
    interim applications to safeguard trust
        property
        generally, 903
        injunctions, 904–906
        payments into court, 906
    joint and several
        contribution between trustees, 878
        equal liability of parties to breach, 877
        generally, 877
    measure of
        accounting for profits, 873–875
        generally, 851–853
        loss to beneficiary only, 875–877
        taking of accounts, 853–873
    set-off, and, 878–879
    tracing claims
        conversion of trust property into other
            form, 882–884
        fiduciary relationship as to property,
            894–899
        generally, 880–881
        identifiable, traceable property, 899–
            903
        introduction, 881–882

Trustee's liability for breach of trust –
continued
tracing claims – *continued*
mixing of trust property with other
property, 884–891
mixing of trust property with property
of another trust, 891–894
Trustee's powers
and see under individual headings
administration, 707–708
advancement
application of power, 718
cash brought into account, 719
consent of person with prior interest,
724–726
ensuring purpose effected, 721–722
exhaustion of exercise of power, 719
generally, 717–718
property brought into account, 719
purpose, 719–721
rule against perpetuities, 724
settlement, by way of, 722–724
tax considerations, 726
general principles
act in good faith, 691
avoid breaking duty of undivided
loyalty, 701
avoid fettering exercise of discretions,
690–691
exercise due care, 699–700
exercise of discretions for purposes
intended, 691–693
generally, 688–689
keep discretions under review, 689–690
make properly informed decisions, 694–
699
summary, 701–703
investment of funds, as to
custodian holdings, 619–621
delegation of asset management
function, 621–622
express powers, 611–612
general power, 599–607
generally, 597–599
nominee holdings, 619–621
specific powers, 607–611
maintenance to infants
class gifts, 716–717
contrary intention, 715
generally, 709–711
gifts carrying intermediate income, 712–
713
legacies carrying interest, 713–714
portions charged on land, 714
residuary gift to infant, 714
statutory provision, 711–712
vested interests converted into
contingent interests, 715–716
management of land
conduct of sales, 704–705

Trustee's powers – *continued*
management of land – *continued*
extent of powers, 703–704
generally, 703
raising capital money, 704
receipts, 705–706
reversionary interests, 706–707
suspension of
after judgment, 726–727
before judgment, 727
generally, 726
payment of fund into court, after, 728
trusts of land, and, 471–472
Trustee's rights
and see under individual headings
administration of trust under direction of
court, 846–848
copies of deeds, and, 828
directions of court as to specific questions,
to
costs, 840–845
generally, 832–835
jurisdiction of court, 835–836
procedure, 836–839
discharge on completion of trusteeship,
to, 827–828
indemnity for expenses, to
basis of taxed costs in litigation, 815
calls on shares, 813
carrying on business, 814
damages recovered by third parties, 813
direct claims on estate, 825–826
disallowance of unreasonable expenses,
817
generally, 810–811
holding title to trust property, 813–814
insolvent trustee, 826
interest, 818
nature, 812–813
payment from taxed income, 818
prospective *Beddoe* application, 816
reimbursement of costs incurred, 815
reliance on counsel's advice, 816–817
set-off, and, 823–824
solicitors' costs, 814
subrogation claims, and, 824–825
third party litigation expenses, 815
unnecessary costs, 817–818
voluntary subscriptions, 817
indemnity from beneficiary, to
club trustees, and, 823
generally, 821–822
limits, 822–823
indemnity from new trustees, to, 820–821
lien on trust property, to
continues to bind successor trustees, 820
expenses, 818
express preservation, 820
legal costs where settlement void, 818–
819

Trustee's rights – *continued*
  lien on trust property, to – *continued*
    mixed funds, 819
    refusal to transfer property, 819–820
  official audit of trust, 831–832
  pay funds into court, 829–830
  reimbursement, to
    basis of taxed costs in litigation, 815
    calls on shares, 813
    carrying on business, 814
    damages recovered by third parties, 813
    direct claims on estate, 825–826
    disallowance of unreasonable expenses,
      817
    generally, 810–811
    holding title to trust property, 813–814
    insolvent trustee, 826
    interest, 818
    nature, 812–813
    payment from taxed income, 818
    prospective *Beddoe* application, 816
    reimbursement of costs incurred, 815
    reliance on counsel's advice, 816–817
    set-off, and, 823–824
    solicitors' costs, 814
    subrogation claims, and, 824–825
    third party litigation expenses, 815
    unnecessary costs, 817–818
    voluntary subscriptions, 817
  release by deed, and, 827
Trusts for sale
  trusts of land, and, 470–471
Trusts of land
  assistance of court, 479–482
  consents, 474–475
  consultation with interest in possession
    beneficiary, 475–476
  conversion under trusts for sale, 471
  generally, 465–469
  occupation by interest in possession
    beneficiary, 476–478
  partition by trustees, 472–473
  prior to 1997, 463–465
  purchaser protection, 483
  relevant property, 469
  transfer to absolutely entitled beneficiary,
    473–474
  trustee's powers, 471–472
  trusts for sale, 470–471
  use of two deeds, 469–470
Twinsectra **trusts**
  charges, and, 12–14
Tying up of property for unlawful period
  introduction, 191–192
  rule against inalienability
    generally, 202–203
    introduction, 191–192
  rule against remoteness
    exceptions, 201–202
    illegal trusts, and, 225–228

Tying up of property for unlawful period –
  continued
  rule against remoteness – *continued*
    introduction, 191–192
    possible events, 192–194
    reform, 202
    statutory changes to law, 195–197
    trust for sale, 200–201
    validity of powers, 198
    validity of trusts created under powers of
      appointment, 198–200
    vesting in interest, 197–198
    'wait and see' principle, 195–197

Uncertainty of express trust
  resolution, 89–91
  resulting trusts, and, 332–333
**Unconscionable conduct, trusts for
  prevention of**
  abuse of statutory provisions, 410–411
  assignments for value of future property,
    437–438
  common intention constructive trusts
    date of valuation of interest, 425
    detrimental reliance, 419–421
    equitable estoppel, and, 425–427
    express agreement, 414–415
    financial relief, and, 427
    generally, 412–414
    inferred agreement, 415–419
    legal title in both names, 421–422
    size of share, 422–425
  criminal may not benefit from crime
    generally, 434–435
    statutory relief, 435
  detrimental reliance
    express common intention, 419–420
    inferred common intention, 420–421
  donor does all obliged to do to transfer
    legal title, 433–434
  express common intention
    detrimental reliance, 419–420
    generally, 414–415
  generally, 409–410
  inferred common intention
    detrimental reliance, 420–421
    generally, 415–419
  mutual wills
    binding agreement for survivor to carry
      out agreed arrangement, 428–430
    generally, 427–428
    property subject to trust, 431–431
    secret truss, and, 432
    trust effecting arrangement, 430–431
  receipts by insolvent agents, 437
  rescission of voidable transfers, 435–436
  secret trusts
    generally, 433
    mutual wills, and, 432
  use of property principles, 411–412

Undervalue, transactions at an
criminal offences, 291
dispositions in two to five year period, 290
generally, 287–289
persons without notice of relevant
 circumstances, 291
statutory provision, 289–290
Undivided loyalty, duty of
trustee's powers, and, 701
Undue influence
acquiescence by settlor, 285–286
awareness of trustees, 284–285
change of status, 286
generally, 281–282
independence of advice, 285
introduction, 275–276
parents, by, 283–284
solicitor, by, 283
third parties, and, 287
wills, and, 282–283
Unfair preferences
criminal offences, 291
dispositions in two to five year period, 290
generally, 287–289
persons without notice of relevant
 circumstances, 291
statutory provision, 289–290
Unfenced land, fencing of
repairs, and, 573–574
Unfitness of trustee
appointment of new trustees, and, 761
Unilateral transaction
rectification, and, 277–279
Unincorporated associations
language sufficient to create trust, and,
 123–129
Unit trusts
augmentation of capital, and, 542
commercial purpose trusts, and, 45–46
Unnecessary costs
indemnity for trustees, and, 817–818
Unreasonable expenses
indemnity for trustees, and, 817
Unregistered land, estate in
transfer of property to trust, and, 150
Use of funds in trustee's own business
taking of accounts, and, 870
Use of property principles
prevention of fraudulent conduct, and,
 411–412

Vacancy for trustee
appointment of new trustees, and, 760–761
Variation of trusts, 501–522
**Vested interests converted into contingent
interests**
maintenance to infants, and, 715–716
Vesting of property in trustee
classification of property, 1026
conclusion, 1029–1030

Vesting of property in trustee – *continued*
immovable property, 1027
intangible movable property, 1028–1029
introduction, 1025–1026
tangible movable property, 1028
Vesting of trust property in new trustees
court made vesting orders, 779–784
generally, 776
implied vesting declarations, 776–779
Vicarious liability
dishonest assistance, and, 965–966
Vinculum juris
trusts, and, 36
Vitiation of transfer to trustees
acceptance of trust property, and, 486–487
Voidable transfers, rescission of
prevention of fraudulent conduct, and,
 435–436
Voluntary arrangements
resulting trusts, and, 340–341
Voluntary carers' services, damages for
illusory trusts, and, 143
**Voluntary contributions to assist distressed
individuals**
resulting trusts, and, 336
Voluntary covenants
enforceability of trust, and, 172–179
Voluntary subscriptions
indemnity for trustees, and, 817
Voluntary transfers of property
generally, 350
gifts of property, 367–368
Volunteers' action at common law
enforceability of trust, and, 169
**Volunteer's own moneys, trust funds mixed
with**
property traced into hands of third
 parties, and, 993–994

'Wait and see' principle
rule against remoteness, and, 195–197
Want of trustee
language sufficient to create trust, and, 77
War-time
limitation of actions by beneficiaries, and, 929
Will trusts
executory trusts, and, 67
Wills
executed trusts, and, 67
executory trusts, and
 generally, 67
 interpretation, 302–305
rectification, and, 280
undue influence, and, 282–283
Wrongful sale by vendor
conversion of trust property into other
 form, and, 883
Wrongfully acquired property, sale of
conversion of trust property into other
 form, and, 883–884